Summer 2016 Volume 26, Number 1

Municipal
YELLOW BOOK

who's who in
the leading city and
county governments
and local authorities

LEADERSHIP DIRECTORIES, INC.

www.leadershipdirectories.com
info@leadershipdirectories.com

New York Office
1407 Broadway Suite 318
New York, NY 10018
(212) 627-4140
Fax (212) 645-0931

Washington, DC Office
1667 K Street, NW, Suite 801
Washington, DC 20006
(202) 347-7757
Fax (202) 628-3430

Congressional
YELLOW BOOK
who's who in congress, including committees and key staff

Federal
YELLOW BOOK
who's who in federal departments and agencies

State
YELLOW BOOK
who's who in the executive and legislative branches of the 50 state governments

Municipal
YELLOW BOOK
who's who in the leading city and county governments and local authorities

Federal Regional
YELLOW BOOK
who's who in the federal government's departments, agencies, diplomatic missions, military installations and service academies outside of Washington, DC

Judicial
YELLOW BOOK
who's who in federal and state courts

Corporate
YELLOW BOOK
who's who at the leading U.S. companies

Financial
YELLOW BOOK
who's who at the leading U.S. financial institutions

News Media
YELLOW BOOK
who's who among reporters, writers, editors and producers in the leading national news media

Associations
YELLOW BOOK
who's who at the leading U.S. trade and professional associations

Law Firms
YELLOW BOOK
who's who in the management of the leading U.S. law firms

Government Affairs
YELLOW BOOK
who's who in government affairs

Foreign Representatives
YELLOW BOOK
who's who in the U.S. offices of foreign corporations, foreign nations, the foreign press and intergovernmental organizations

Nonprofit Sector
YELLOW BOOK
who's who in the management of the leading foundations, universities, museums, and other nonprofit organizations

The Leadership Library®
who's who in the leadership of the United States

Leadership Directories, Inc.
MUNICIPAL YELLOW BOOK

Summer 2016, Volume 26, Number 1

ISBN: 978-0-87289-489-1

Printed in the United States of America.

The *Municipal Yellow Book* (ISSN 1054-4062) is published semiannually by Leadership Directories, Inc., 1407 Broadway, Suite 318, New York, NY 10018. Annual subscription: $485. Additional subscriptions delivered to the same individual and address: $364. For air mail postage: Canada and Mexico add $75 per subscription. Outside North America add $100 per subscription.

POSTMASTER: Send address changes to *Municipal Yellow Book*, Leadership Directories, Inc., 1407 Broadway, Suite 318, New York, NY 10018.

For additional information, including details about other Leadership Directories, Inc. publications, please call (212) 627-4140.

Municipal
YELLOW BOOK

Summer 2016

Table of Contents

Municipal HIGHLIGHTS

By Brian Combs
Senior Content Manager, *Municipal Yellow Book*

May 24, 2016

The *Municipal Yellow Book* is a semiannual directory of more than 33,000 elected and administrative officials in the leading city and county governments and local authorities. The Summer 2016 edition contains senior personnel and organizational changes that have taken place between December 2015 and May 2016. This edition features 310 cities, 153 counties, and 71 authorities.

The Leadership® Content Commitment

Leadership Directories provides high quality, accurate and up to date information on the key leaders in government, business, legal, media and nonprofit organizations in the United States. Every item of information on more than 750,000 people and 150,000 organizations has been verified at the source.

Municipal Yellow Book Online

Leadership® State-Muni Premium is the online version of the *Municipal Yellow Book*. It is available as an annual subscription and includes daily updates and additional content not available in the print directory, plus searching, list-building, and exporting capabilities. For more information, please contact us at (212) 627-4140.

New Mayors

Appointments and elections held since the last edition of the *Municipal Yellow Book* have resulted in 31 new Mayors for cities listed in the directory. The following is a list of the newly elected Mayors:

City	New Mayor	Former Mayor
Bellevue, WA	John Stokes	Claudia Balducci
Burbank, CA	Jess Talamantes	Robert Frutos
Cambridge, MA	E. Denise Simmons	David P. Maher
Columbia, MO	Brian Treece	Robert McDavid
Concord, CA	Laura Hoffmeister	Tim Grayson
Corona, CA	Jason Scott	Eugene Montanez
Daly City, CA	Gonzalo Torres	Raymond A. Buenaventura
Downey, CA	Alex Saab	Luis H. Marquez
Fullerton, CA	Jennifer Fitzgerald	Greg Sebourn
Gainesville, FL	Lauren Poe	Ed Braddy
Glendale, CA	Paula Devine	Ara James Najarian
Hampton, VA	Donnie R. Tuck	George E. Wallace
Houston, TX	Sylvester Turner	Annise Parker
Huntington Beach, CA	Jim Katapodis	Jill Hardy
Juneau, AK	Ken Koelsch	Greg Fisk
Killeen, TX	Jose L. Segarra	Scott Cosper
Lowell, MA	Edward J. Kennedy, Jr.	Rodney Elliott
Lubbock, TX	Daniel M. Pope	Glen Robertson

(continued on next page)

New Mayors—continued

City	New Mayor	Former Mayor
Modesto, CA	Ted Brandvold	Garrad Marsh
Moreno Valley, CA	Yxstian Gutierrez	Jesse L. Molina
Norfolk, VA	Kenneth Alexander	Paul D. Fraim
Norman, OK	Lynne Miller	Cindy S. Rosenthal
Norwalk, CA	Michael Mendez	Leonard Shryock
Roanoke, VA	Sherman P. Lea	David A. Bowers
Santa Clara, CA	Lisa M. Gillmor	Jamie Matthews
Santa Clarita, CA	Bob Kellar	Marsha McLean
Sunnyvale, CA	Glenn Hendricks	James Griffith
Thousand Oaks, CA	Joel Price	Al Adam
Ventura, CA	Erik Nasarenko	Cheryl Heitmann
Waco, TX	Kyle Deaver	Malcolm Duncan, Jr.
West Covina, CA	James Toma	Frederick Sykes

No Mayor at Press Time

Lynchburg, VA—The City Council will choose a new Mayor on July 1, 2016.

New County Executives

Appointments and elections held since the last edition of the *Municipal Yellow Book* have resulted in 50 new County Executives/Chairmen of the County Board for the counties listed in the directory. The following is a list of the new county chief executives:

County	New Executive	Former Executive
Arapahoe, CO	Nancy A. Doty	Nancy N. Sharpe
Arlington, VA	Libby Garvey	Mary Hughes Hynes
Bernalillo, NM	Art De La Cruz	Maggie Hart Stebbins
Burlington, NJ	Bruce D. Garganio	Mary Ann O'Brien
Cass, ND	Mary Scherling	Chad Peterson
Clark, WA	Marc Boldt	David Madore
Contra Costa, CA	Candace Andersen	John Gioia
Dakota, MN	Nancy Schouweiler	Thomas A. Egan
El Paso, CO	Amy Lathen	Dennis Hisey
Franklin, OH	John O'Grady	Marilyn Brown
Fresno, CA	Buddy Mendes	Deborah A. Poochigian
Guilford, NC	Jeff Phillips	Hank Henning
Hamilton, OH	Chris R. Monzel	Greg Hartmann
Jackson, MS	Melton Harris, Jr.	Barry Cumbest
Jackson, MO	Frank White, Jr.	Michael D. Sanders
Jefferson, CO	Libby Szabo	Casey P. Tighe
Kent, MI	Jim Saalfeld	Dan Koorndyk
Kern, CA	Mick K. Gleason	David Couch
Lake, IN	Gerry Scheub	Roosevelt Allen, Jr.
Laramie, WY	Keith Holmes	Amber Ash

New County Executives—continued

County	New Executive	Former Executive
Los Angeles, CA	Hilda Solis	Michael D. Antonovich
Merced, CA	Hubert Walsh	John Pedrozo
Monmouth, NJ	Thomas A. Arnone	Gary J. Rich
Monterey, CA	Jane Parker	Simon Salinas
Montgomery, OH	Judy Dodge	Deborah A. Lieberman
Niagara, NY	William Keith McNall	William L. Ross
Ocean, NJ	John Kelly	John C. Bartlett, Jr.
Orange, CA	Lisa Bartlett	Todd Spitzer
Passaic, NJ	Theodore O. Best, Jr.	Hector C. Lora
Pinellas, FL	Charles Justice	John Morroni
Polk, FL	John Hall	George Lindsey
Polk, IA	Thomas Hockensmith	Angela Connolly
Ramsey, MN	Victoria Reinhardt	James McDonough
Riverside, CA	John J. Benoit	Marion Ashley
Sacramento, CA	Roberta MacGlashan	Phillip R. Serna
San Diego, CA	Ron Roberts	Bill Horn
San Joaquin, CA	Moses Zapien	Kathy Miller
San Mateo, CA	Warren Slocum	Carole Groom
Santa Barbara, CA	Peter Adam	Janet Wolf
Sedgwick, KS	Jim Howell	Richard Ranzau
Sonoma, CA	Efren Carrillo	Susan Gorin
Spokane, WA	Shelly O'Quinn	Todd Mielke
Stanislaus, CA	Dick Monteith	Terry Withrow
Stark, OH	Janet Weir Creighton	Thomas M. Bernabei
Tulare, CA	Mike Ennis	J. Steven Worthley
Tulsa, OK	Karen Keith	John M. Smaligo, Jr.
Union, NJ	Bruce Bergen	Mohamed Jalloh
Ventura, CA	Linda Parks	Kathy I. Long
Washoe, NV	Katrina Jung	Marsha Berkbigler
York, PA	Susan Byrnes	M. Steve Chronister

New Heads of Local Authorities

Since the last edition of the *Municipal Yellow Book*, there are 26 new Chairmen for the authorities listed in the directory. The following is a list of the new Chairmen:

Authority	New Chairman	Former Chairman
Alameda County Water District	Judy Huang	Martin Koller
Central Contra Costa Sanitary District	Tad Pilecki	Michael R. McGill
Corpus Christi Regional Transportation Authority	Curtis Rock	Vangie Chapa
Dallas Area Rapid Transit Authority	Faye Wilkins	Robert Strauss

(continued on next page)

New Heads of Local Authorities—continued

Authority	New Chairman	Former Chairman
Dallas/Fort Worth International Airport	David Samuel Coats	Lillie M. Biggins
Eugene Water and Electric Board	John M. Simpson	Steve Mital
Massachusetts Bay Transportation Authority	Stephanie Pollack	Ruth Bonsignore
Metropolitan Nashville Airport Authority	Robert Joslin	Juli H. Mosley
Metropolitan Utilities District	Jack Frost	Thomas Dowd
Milwaukee Metro Sewerage District	John Hermes	Benjamin Gramling
Nebraska Public Power District	Ken Kunze	Edward J. Schrock
Omaha Public Power District	Michael Mines	Anne McGuire
Orange County Transportation Authority	Lori Donchak	Jeffrey Lalloway
Port of Brownsville	John Wood	Louis Raphael Cowen
Port of New Orleans	William T. Bergeron	Scott Cooper
Port of Oakland	Earl S. Hamlin	Alan S. Yee
Port of Stockton	R. Jay Allen	Gary Christopherson
Port of Tacoma	Constance Bacon	Don Johnson
Sacramento Municipal Utility District	Nancy Bui-Thompson	Rob Kerth
San Diego Regional Economic Development Corporation	James Zortman	Vincent Mudd
San Diego Unified Port District	Marshall Merrifield	L. Daniel Malcolm
Snohomish County Public Utility District	Tanya Olson	Kathleen Vaughn
South Carolina State Ports Authority	Patrick McKinney	Bill Stern
Toledo-Lucas County Port Authority	James Tuschman	Nadeem Salem
Washington Metropolitan Area Transit Authority	Jack Evans	Mortimer Downey III
Wayne County Airports Authority	Suzanne Hall	Michael Jackson

As always, the editors of the *Municipal Yellow Book* extend our sincere thanks to the hundreds of contacts who help us maintain the high quality of the information in our products by consistently taking time out of their busy schedules to provide accurate and timely updates. We welcome your comments and invite you to call us at (212) 627-4140 or send an email to info@leadershipdirectories.com.

User's Guide

The *Municipal Yellow Book* is designed to give you direct access to more than 33,000 leaders in city and county governments and local authorities. The book is divided into three sections: Cities and Towns, Counties, and Authorities. Each entry lists the chief elected officials and their staff first, followed by other elected officials and departments in alphabetical order by office name. Each office is structured to show the hierarchy by office and job titles. Listings include:

1 Official name of the municipality, followed by the main address. In some cases, there is a brief note stating that city and county governments are combined.

2 General information, such as the county or county seat and whether elections are partisan or nonpartisan (consisting of ballots free from political party designations and affiliations).

3 Photographs of the chief elected official, when available.

4 Office name, with mailing address, general information telephone number, fax number, TTY number and e-mail address, when available.

5 Names and job titles of personnel listed hierarchically by job title, as well as a direct-dial phone number, fax number and e-mail address, when available. The expiration date for a term of office is included for elected officials. When an individual's address is different from the main bold heading, it will be included directly under that person's name.

6 Educational background, including school name, year graduated, and degree(s), when available.

7 Special coded symbols identify elected and appointed officials.

Saint Paul, MN

1 **City of Saint Paul, Minnesota**

City Hall, 15 West Kellogg Boulevard, Room 160, St. Paul, MN 55102
Tel: (651) 266-8989 (Information) Internet: http://www.stpaul.gov/

2 **County:** Ramsey **Election Type:** Nonpartisan **Charter:** 1900
Population: 300,851 (2015) **Employees:** 2,923 **Fiscal Year:** 2016
Budget: $548,277,000

3 **Christopher B. "Chris" Coleman**
Mayor
Began Service: January 2006
Term Expires: December 31, 2017
Education: Minnesota BA, 1987 JD

4 **Office of the Mayor**

City Hall, 15 West Kellogg Boulevard, Room 390, St. Paul, MN 55102
Tel: (651) 266-8510 Fax: (651) 266-8521
Internet: https://www.stpaul.gov/departments/mayors-office

Employees: 16 **Fiscal Year:** 2016 **Budget:** $2,371,000

★ Mayor **Christopher B. "Chris" Coleman** . . . . . (651) 266-8510
E-mail: chris.coleman@ci.stpaul.mn.us
5 Assistant to the Mayor/Scheduler **Chris Rider** . . . . . (651) 266-8535
E-mail: chris.rider@ci.stpaul.mn.us
Deputy Mayor **Kristin Beckmann** . . . . . (651) 266-8569
E-mail: kristin.beckmann@ci.stpaul.mn.us
Education: Minnesota MPA
Policy Director **Nancy Homans** . . . . . (651) 266-8568
■ Chief of Staff **Dana Bailey** . . . . . (651) 266-8878
Education: Minnesota St (Mankato) 2000 BS
6 Communications Director **Tonya Tennessen** . . . . . (651) 266-8518
E-mail: tonya.tennessen@ci.stpaul.mn.us
Education: Wisconsin BA
Press Secretary **Ashley Aram** . . . . . (651) 266-8571
Arts and Culture Policy Associate **Joe Spencer** . . . . . (651) 266-8524
Education Policy Analyst **Peter Grafstrom** . . . . . (651) 266-8516
Director of Outreach **Matt Freeman** . . . . . (651) 266-8531
Governmental Relations **Katie Knutson** . . . . . (651) 266-8519
E-mail: katie.knutson@ci.stpaul.mn.us
Events, Marketing and Communications Coordinator
Liz Xiong . . . . . (651) 266-8527
E-mail: liz.xiong@ci.stpaul.mn.us
Deputy Policy Director for Environment **Anne Hunt** . . . . . (651) 266-8520
Policy Associate **Ana Vang** . . . . . (651) 266-8536
E-mail: ana.vang@ci.stpaul.mn.us
Communications Associate, Constituent Services
Fedha Abera . . . . . (651) 266-8512
E-mail: fedha.abera@ci.stpaul.mn.us
Volunteers in Service to America (VISTA) Manager
Morgan Weis . . . . . (651) 266-8582
E-mail: morgan.weis@ci.stpaul.mn.us
Office Manager **Jean Karpe** . . . . . (651) 266-8526

Office of the City Council

City Hall, 15 West Kellogg Boulevard, Room 310, St. Paul, MN 55102
Tel: (651) 266-8560 Fax: (651) 266-8574

Employees: 28 **Fiscal Year:** 2016 **Budget:** $3,152,000

★ Council President **Russ Stark** (Ward 4) . . . . . (651) 266-8640
Term Expires: December 31, 2019
E-mail: ward4@ci.stpaul.mn.us
★ Council Member **Dai Thao** (Ward 1) . . . . . (651) 266-8610
Term Expires: December 31, 2019
E-mail: ward1@ci.stpaul.mn.us

Office of the City Council *continued*

★ Council Member **Rebecca Noecker** (Ward 2) . . . . . (651) 266-8620
Term Expires: December 31, 2019
★ Council Member **Chris Tolbert** (Ward 3) . . . . . (651) 266-8630
Term Expires: December 31, 2019
E-mail: ward3@ci.stpaul.mn.us
★ Council Member **Amy Brendmoen** (Ward 5) . . . . . (651) 266-8650
Term Expires: December 31, 2019
E-mail: ward5@ci.stpaul.mn.us
★ Council Member **Dan Bostrom** (Ward 6) . . . . . (651) 266-8660
Term Expires: December 31, 2019
E-mail: ward6@ci.stpaul.mn.us
★ Council Member **Jane Prince** (Ward 7) . . . . . (651) 266-8670
Term Expires: December 31, 2019
○ City Council Operations Director **Trudy Moloney** . . . . . (651) 266-8575
E-mail: trudy.moloney@ci.stpaul.mn.us

Office of the City Attorney

City Hall, 15 West Kellogg Boulevard, Room 400,
St. Paul, MN 55102-1635
Fax: (651) 298-5619

Employees: 66 **Fiscal Year:** 2016 **Budget:** $9,299,000

■ City Attorney **Samuel "Sammy" Clark** . . . . . (651) 266-8710
Deputy City Attorney, Civil Division
Jerry Hendrickson . . . . . (651) 266-8710
Deputy City Attorney, Criminal Division **Laura Pietan** . . . . . (651) 266-8740

Office of the City Clerk

City Hall, 15 West Kellogg Boulevard, Room 310,
St. Paul, MN 55102-1635
Fax: (651) 266-8574 E-mail: cityclerk@ci.stpaul.mn.us
Internet: https://www.stpaul.gov/departments/city-clerk

○ City Clerk **Shari Moore** . . . . . (651) 266-8686
E-mail: shari.moore@ci.stpaul.mn.us
Education: Mankato State SeB

Emergency Management Department

357 Grove Street, 5th Floor, St. Paul, MN 55101
Fax: (651) 266-5493

Employees: 8 **Fiscal Year:** 2016 **Budget:** $1,392,000

■ Emergency Management Director **Rick Larkin** . . . . . (651) 266-5494
E-mail: rick.larkin@ci.stpaul.mn.us
Emergency Coordinator **Terrance Sieben** . . . . . (651) 266-5495
E-mail: terry.sieben@ci.stpaul.mn.us

Office of Financial Services [OFS]

City Hall, 15 West Kellogg Boulevard, Room 700, St. Paul, MN 55102
Tel: (651) 266-8800 Fax: (651) 266-8541

Employees: 46 **Fiscal Year:** 2016 **Budget:** $14,816,000

■ Director **Todd Hurley** . . . . . (651) 266-8800
E-mail: Contact-OFS@ci.stpaul.mn.us

Contract and Analysis Services

Director **Jessica Kingston** Room 280 . . . . . (651) 266-8900
E-mail: jessica.kingston@ci.stpaul.mn.us

Saint Paul Fire Department

645 Randolph Avenue, St. Paul, MN 55102
Fax: (651) 228-6255
Internet: https://www.stpaul.gov/departments/fire-paramedics

Employees: 479 **Fiscal Year:** 2016 **Budget:** $65,649,000

Fire Chief **Tim Butler** . . . . . (651) 222-0477
E-mail: tim.butler@ci.stpaul.mn.us
Assistant Fire Chief **Butch Inks** . . . . . (651) 228-6212
Assistant Fire Chief **Matt Simpson** . . . . . (651) 228-6270
E-mail: matt.simpson@ci.stpaul.mn.us
Building and Maintenance Supervisor **Dave Hiveley** . . . . . (651) 771-7840
E-mail: dave.hiveley@ci.stpaul.mn.us

(continued on next page)

7 ★ Elected Official ▲ Appointed by Legislature ▼ Appointed by Governor ► Appointed by Board or Commission ● Appointed by Judge
■ Appointed by Mayor ○ Appointed by Freeholders ▽ Appointed by Supervisor ◇ Appointed by County Executive ○ Appointed by Council

Summer 2016 © Leadership Directories, Inc. Municipal Yellow Book

Indexes

Geographical Index

Cities, counties, and authorities are listed alphabetically by state.

Name Index

Alphabetical listing of every individual listed in the *Municipal Yellow Book*.

Organization Index

Alphabetical listing of all cities, counties, and authorities featured in the *Municipal Yellow Book*.

Selection Criteria

The selection of the top cities and counties was based on 2010 Census Bureau data. To represent counties on the Census list that do not have a county government, we profiled the government of the largest city in that county, and listed it in the Cities section. The criteria for the authorities was based on a combination of revenue and subscriber interest.

Cities and Towns

City of Abilene, Texas

555 Walnut, Abilene, TX 79601
P.O. Box 60, Abilene, TX 79604
Internet: www.abilenetx.com

County: Taylor **Election Type:** Nonpartisan **Population:** 121,721 (2015) **Employees:** 1,203 **Fiscal Year:** 2016 **Budget:** $187,274,000

Norm Archibald
Mayor

Began Service: 2004
Term Expires: May 2017
Education: Texas A&M BS, MEd; Abilene Christian 1975 MS; Texas Tech EdD
Career: Council Member, Office of the Mayor and City Council, City of Abilene, Texas; Vice President, Hendrick Hospital, Abilene, Texas

Office of the Mayor and City Council

P.O. Box 60, Abilene, TX 79604
Employees: 18 **Fiscal Year:** 2016 **Budget:** $118,000

★ Mayor **Norm Archibald** .... (325) 676-6206
E-mail: norm.archibald@abilenetx.com

★ Council Member **Shane Price** (Place 1) .... (325) 676-6205
Term Expires: May 2018 Fax: (325) 670-2209
E-mail: shane.price@abilenetx.com

★ Council Member **Bruce Kreitler** (Place 2) .... (325) 676-6205
Term Expires: May 2018 Fax: (325) 672-1086
E-mail: bruce.kreitler@abilenetx.com

★ Council Member **Anthony Williams** (Place 3) .... (325) 676-6205
Term Expires: May 1, 2017 Fax: (325) 674-6883
E-mail: anthony.williams@abilenetx.com
Education: McMurry 1993 BS

★ Council Member **Jay Hardaway** (Place 4) .... (325) 676-6205
Term Expires: May 1, 2017
E-mail: jay.hardaway@abilenetx.com

★ Council Member **Kyle McAlister** (Place 5) .... (325) 676-6205
Term Expires: May 2019
E-mail: kyle.mcalister@abilenetx.com

★ Council Member **Steve Savage** (Place 6) .... (325) 201-4100
Term Expires: May 15, 2019
E-mail: steve.savage@abilenetx.com

Office of the City Attorney

P.O. Box 60, Abilene, TX 79604
Fax: (325) 676-6439
Fiscal Year: 2016 **Budget:** $843,000

■ City Attorney (Interim) **Stanley Smith** .... (325) 676-6256
E-mail: stanley.smith@abilenetx.com Fax: (325) 676-6439

Office of the City Secretary

P.O. Box 60, Abilene, TX 79604
Fax: (325) 676-6229
Fiscal Year: 2016 **Budget:** $240,000

■ City Secretary **Danette Dunlap** .... (325) 676-6202
E-mail: danette.dunlap@abilenetx.com Fax: (325) 676-6229

Office of the City Manager

P.O. Box 60, Abilene, TX 79604
Fiscal Year: 2016 **Budget:** $742,000

■ City Manager **Robert Hanna** .... (325) 676-6206
Fax: (325) 676-6229

Office of the City Manager *continued*

Assistant City Manager **James Childers** .... (325) 676-6386
E-mail: james.childers@abilenetx.com
Education: Midwestern State 2001 BA; North Texas 2003 MPA

Assistant City Manager **Mindy Patterson** .... (325) 676-6386
E-mail: mindy.patterson@abilenetx.com

Office of the Internal Auditor

P.O. Box 60, Abilene, TX 79604
Internal Auditor **Karen Thompson** .... (325) 676-6495

Abilene Civic Center

1100 N. Sixth St., Abilene, TX 79601
Fax: (325) 676-6343
Fiscal Year: 2016 **Budget:** $1,296,000
Manager **Molly Moser** .... (325) 676-6211 ext. 054

Abilene Regional Airport

P.O. Box 60, Abilene, TX 79604
Employees: 20 **Fiscal Year:** 2016 **Budget:** $2,654,000
Director **Don Green** .... (325) 676-6368

Administrative Services

P.O. Box 60, Abilene, TX 79604
Employees: 32 **Fiscal Year:** 2016 **Budget:** $3,192,000

Director **Ronnie Kidd** .... (325) 676-6469
E-mail: ronnie.kidd@abilenetx.com
Education: Hardin-Simmons 1981 BBA

Human Resources Manager **Patti Watson** .... (325) 676-6259
E-mail: patti.watson@abilenetx.com

Community Services Department

P.O. Box 60, Abilene, TX 79604
Employees: 160 **Fiscal Year:** 2016 **Budget:** $381,000
Director (Interim) **Lesli Andrews** .... (325) 676-6221

Abilene Zoo

2070 Zoo Lane, Nelson Park, Abilene, TX 79602
P.O. Box 60, Abilene, TX 79604
Fax: (325) 676-6084
Fiscal Year: 2016 **Budget:** $2,726,000
Director **Bill Gersonde** .... (325) 676-6085 ext. 6590

Library

P.O. Box 60, Abilene, TX 79604
Fiscal Year: 2016 **Budget:** $2,795,000
Librarian **Lori Grumet** .... (325) 676-6328
E-mail: lori.grumet@abilenetx.com

Parks Services Division

P.O. Box 60, Abilene, TX 79604
Fiscal Year: 2016 **Budget:** $2,729,000
Superintendent **Richard Rodgers** .... (325) 676-6216

Public Health Department

P.O. Box 60, Abilene, TX 79604
Fax: (325) 690-6707
Director **Derrick Neal** .... (325) 692-5600

Recreation and Senior Citizens Division

P.O. Box 60, Abilene, TX 79604
Fiscal Year: 2016 **Budget:** $1,897,000
Recreation and Senior Citizens Administrator
Jeff White .... (325) 734-5306
E-mail: jeff.white@abilenetx.com

★ Elected Official ▲ Appointed by Legislature ▼ Appointed by Governor ► Appointed by Board or Commission ● Appointed by Judge
■ Appointed by Mayor △ Appointed by Freeholders ▽ Appointed by Supervisor ▷ Appointed by County Executive ○ Appointed by Council

Economic Development Department
P.O. Box 60, Abilene, TX 79604
Fax: (325) 676-6377

Chief Executive Officer **Kent Sharp** .... (325) 676-6390

Finance Department
P.O. Box 60, Abilene, TX 79604

Employees: 76 **Fiscal Year:** 2016 **Budget:** $10,352,000

Director **Mike Rains** .... (325) 676-6324

Purchasing Department
P.O. Box 60, Abilene, TX 79604

Purchasing Agent **Pascual Mirelez** .... (325) 676-6226
E-mail: pascual.mirelez@abilenetx.com

Fire Department
P.O. Box 60, Abilene, TX 79604

Employees: 181 **Fiscal Year:** 2016 **Budget:** $18,872,000

Fire Chief **Ken Dozier** .... (325) 676-6676
E-mail: ken.dozier@abilenetx.com

Planning and Development Services
P.O. Box 60, Abilene, TX 79604

Employees: 31 **Fiscal Year:** 2016 **Budget:** $2,261,000

Director **Dana L. Schoening** .... (325) 676-6490

Animal Services Division
P.O. Box 60, Abilene, TX 79604

Program Manager **Aaron Vannoy** .... (325) 437-4585

Building Inspection Division
P.O. Box 60, Abilene, TX 79604

Building Official **David Sartor** .... (325) 676-6272

Police Department
P.O. Box 60, Abilene, TX 79604
Internet: http://www.abilenepolice.com

Employees: 265 **Fiscal Year:** 2016 **Budget:** $26,872,000

Police Chief **Stan Standridge** .... (325) 676-6601
Fax: (325) 676-6242

Public Works Department
P.O. Box 60, Abilene, TX 79604

Employees: 74 **Fiscal Year:** 2016 **Budget:** $7,002,000

Director **Michael Rice** .... (325) 676-6284
Fax: (325) 734-3300
Assistant Director **(Vacant)** .... (325) 676-6284
City Engineer **(Vacant)** .... (325) 676-6315
Fax: (325) 734-3300
Stormwater Utility Administrator **Srini Valavala** .... (325) 676-6280
Fax: (325) 734-3300
Inspection Services Manager **George Votaw** .... (325) 676-6077
Fax: (325) 676-6242

Water Utilities Department
P.O. Box 60, Abilene, TX 79604

Director (Interim) **Rodney Taylor** .... (325) 676-6416
Wastewater Treatment Supervisor **Mickey Chaney** .... (325) 676-6416
Water Distribution/Sewage Collection Supervisor
Jerry Garcia .... (325) 676-6416
Water Treatment Supervisor **Richard Williams** .... (325) 676-6416

Abilene Independent School District
241 Pine Street, Abilene, TX 79601
Fax: (325) 794-1325 Internet: www.abileneisd.org
Internet: http://www.abileneisd.org/Page/11154

Superintendent of Schools **David Young** ....(325) 677-1444 ext. 2613
★ President **Dr. Danny Wheat** (Place 5) .... (325) 677-1444
Term Expires: May 31, 2018
E-mail: danny.wheat@abileneisd.org
★ Vice President **Randy Piersall** (Place 2) .... (325) 677-1444
Term Expires: May 31, 2020
E-mail: randy.piersall@abileneisd.org
★ Secretary **Cindy Parker Earles** (Place 4) .... (325) 677-1444
Term Expires: May 31, 2018
E-mail: cindy.earles@abileneisd.org
★ Assistant Secretary **Daryl Zeller** (Place 3) .... (325) 677-1444
Term Expires: May 31, 2020
E-mail: daryl.zeller@abileneisd.org
★ Trustee **Jeff Arrington** (Place 1) .... (325) 677-1444
Term Expires: May 31, 2020
E-mail: jeff.arrington@abileneisd.org
★ Trustee **Stan Lambert** (Place 6) .... (325) 677-1444
Term Expires: May 31, 2018
E-mail: stan.lambert@abileneisd.org
★ Trustee **Angie Wiley** (Place 7) .... (325) 677-1444
Term Expires: May 31, 2020
E-mail: angie.wiley@abileneisd.org

City of Akron, Ohio

Municipal Building, 166 South High Street, Akron, OH 44308
Tel: (330) 375-2311 (Information) Internet: www.akronohio.gov

County: Summit **Election Type:** Partisan **Population:** 197,542 (2015)

Office of the Mayor
Municipal Building, 166 South High Street, Akron, OH 44308
Tel: (330) 375-2345 Fax: (330) 375-2468

★ Mayor **Daniel M. Horrigan** (D) .... (330) 375-2345
Began Service: January 1, 2016
Term Expires: December 31, 2019
E-mail: Mayor@AkronOhio.gov
Executive Secretary **Laurie L. Hoffman** Room 200 ..... (330) 375-2345
E-mail: hoffmla@ci.akron.oh.us
■ Chief of Staff **James Hardy** Room 200 .... (330) 375-2345
E-mail: JHardy@AkronOhio.gov
■ Economic Development Deputy Mayor
Samuel DeShazior Room 202 .... (330) 375-2133
E-mail: sdeshazior@akronohio.gov
Education: Clark Atlanta BA; Akron 1993 MURP
■ Assistant to the Mayor for Education, Health and Family
Terry Albanese (D) Room 200 .... (330) 375-2345
E-mail: TAlbanese@AkronOhio.gov
■ Deputy Mayor for Public Safety **Charles Brown**
Room 200 .... (330) 375-2345
E-mail: CBrown@AkronOhio.gov
■ Deputy Mayor for Labor Relations **Randy D. Briggs**
CitiCenter Building, Room 202 .... (330) 375-2280
E-mail: RBriggs@akronohio.gov
Education: Akron 1983 JD
Assistant to the Mayor for Community Relations
Billy Soule .... (330) 375-2660
E-mail: BSoule@AkronOhio.gov
Chief Information Officer **Phillip J. Montgomery** (D) ... (330) 375-2137
E-mail: PMontgomery@AkronOhio.gov
Date of Birth: December 17, 1981
Education: DeVry U BBA; Ohio Dominican U MBA
Deputy Mayor for Intergovernmental Affairs and Senior
Advisor to the Mayor **Marco S. Sommerville** (D) ..... (330) 375-2345
E-mail: MSommerville@AkronOhio.gov

★ Elected Official ▲ Appointed by Legislature ▼ Appointed by Governor ▶ Appointed by Board or Commission ● Appointed by Judge
■ Appointed by Mayor △ Appointed by Freeholders ▽ Appointed by Supervisor ▷ Appointed by County Executive ○ Appointed by Council

Office of the Mayor *continued*

Director of Communications **Christine R. Curry** .... (330) 375-2345
E-mail: CCurry@AkronOhio.gov

Finance Department

Municipal Building, 166 South High Street, Room 502, Akron, OH 44308
Fax: (330) 375-2291

■ Director **Diane L. Miller-Dawson** .... (330) 375-2316
E-mail: DMiller-Dawson@akronohio.gov
Education: Akron 1981 BS, 1994 MBA

■ Deputy Director **Steve Fricker** .... (330) 375-2316
E-mail: sfricker@akronohio.gov

Assistant Treasurer **Sherill Bryson** .... (330) 375-2330
161 South High Street, Room 200, Akron, OH 44308

Accounting Manager **Kimberly Guseman** Room 505 .... (330) 375-2620
E-mail: kguseman@akronohio.gov

Information Technology Manager **William Fatica**
Room 901 .... (330) 375-2560
E-mail: WFatica@akronohio.gov
Education: Akron 1991 BS

Purchasing Division Manager **Jerry Roberts** Room 501 .. (330) 375-2060
E-mail: JRoberts@akronohio.gov

Tax Division

One Cascade Plaza, Akron, OH 44308
E-mail: incometax@akronohio.gov

Commissioner **Art Preiksa** .... (330) 375-2498
E-mail: apreiksa@akronohio.gov

Fire Department

CitiCenter Building, 146 South High Street, Room 1011,
Akron, OH 44308
Fax: (330) 375-2146

Fire Chief **Edward Hiltbrand** .... (330) 375-2410
E-mail: ehiltbrand@akronohio.gov

Deputy Chief/Operations **Richard Vober** .... (330) 375-2411

Deputy Chief/Administration **Charles Twigg** .... (330) 375-2411

District Chief for Communications **Brad Carr** .... (330) 375-2341

Human Resources Department

CitiCenter Building, 146 South High Street, Suite 100, Akron, OH 44308
Fax: (330) 375-2299 E-mail: csc@akronohio.gov

▶ Director and Secretary to the Civil Service Commission
Donald Rice .... (330) 375-2780
E-mail: DRice@AkronOhio.gov

Assistant Director **(Vacant)** .... (330) 375-2780

Executive Assistant **Nicole Elton** .... (330) 375-2780
E-mail: nelton@akronohio.gov

Classification and Compensation **(Vacant)** .... (330) 375-2067
E-mail: classification@akronohio.gov

Personnel Officer **Stacey Doty** .... (330) 375-2720
E-mail: sdoty@akronohio.gov

Personnel Records Supervisor **Michele Simon** .... (330) 375-2710
E-mail: msimon@akronohio.gov

Training and Equal Employment Opportunity Officer
Myra Snipes .... (330) 375-2704
E-mail: msnipes@akronohio.gov Fax: (330) 375-2299

Law Department

Ocasek Building, 161 South High Street, Suite 202, Akron, OH 44308
Fax: (330) 375-2041 E-mail: law@akronohio.gov

■ Director **Eve Belfance** (D) .... (330) 375-2030
E-mail: EBelfance@AkronOhio.gov
Date of Birth: 1962
Education: Yale 1984 BA; Case Western 1990 JD

Criminal Division

217 South High Street, Akron, OH 44308
Fax: (330) 375-2281

■ Chief City Prosecutor **Gertrude Wilms** Room 203 ...... (330) 375-2730
E-mail: gwilms@akronohio.gov
Education: Ohio State 1994 BA; Akron 2001 JD, 2001 MPA

Neighborhood Assistance Department

166 South High Street, Akron, OH 44308
Tel: (330) 375-2324

Director of Neighborhood Assistance **John W. Valle** ..... (330) 375-2324
E-mail: JValle@AkronOhio.gov

Recreation Bureau

220 South Balch Street, Akron, OH 44302
Fax: (330) 375-2818 E-mail: recreation@akronohio.gov

Manager (Interim) **Brittany Schmoekel** .... (330) 375-2850

Housing and Community Services Division

166 South High Street, Room 100, Akron, OH 44308

Housing Rehabilitation Administrator **Thomas Tatum** .... (330) 375-2050
E-mail: ttatum@akronohio.gov

Housing Rehabilitation Manager **Dwayne Gregor** .... (330) 375-2050

311 Contact Center

Building 2, 1420 Triplett Boulevard, Akron, OH 44306
Fax: (330) 375-2899

Manager **Sheryl Maslanka** .... (330) 375-2311

Planning and Urban Development Department

Municipal Building, 166 South High Street, Akron, OH 44308
Fax: (330) 375-2387

Director **Jason Segedy** .... (330) 375-2770
E-mail: JSegedy@AkronOhio.gov

Deputy Director **(Vacant)** .... (330) 375-2770

Akron Metropolitan Area Transportation Study Division [AMATS]

CitiCenter Building, 146 South High Street, Room 806, Akron, OH 44308

Director (Interim) **Curtis Baker** .... (330) 375-2436

Comprehensive Planning

Comprehensive Planning Administrator **Helen Tomic** ..... (330) 375-2090
161 South High Street, Suite 201, Akron, OH 44308
E-mail: htomic@akronohio.gov

Strategic Initiatives Division

166 South High Street, Room 403, Akron, OH 44308

Manager **Helen Tomic** .... (330) 375-2084
E-mail: htomic@akronohio.gov

Zoning Division

Zoning Manager **Michael Antenucci** Room 405 .... (330) 375-2350

Police Department

217 South High Street, Akron, OH 44308
Tel: (330) 375-2181 Fax: (330) 375-2135 E-mail: police@akronohio.gov

■ Police Chief **James Nice** .... (330) 375-2244
E-mail: jnice@akronohio.gov
Education: Akron BA; East Texas State MA; Dallas MBA

Investigative Deputy Police Chief
Major Kenneth Ball II .... (330) 375-2490

Services Deputy Police Chief **Capt. Melissa Schnee** .... (330) 375-2470

Uniform Deputy Police Chief **Major Paul Calvaruso** .... (330) 375-2900

Communications Department

1240 Triplett Boulevard, Akron, OH 44306

Communications Manager **Malcolm Valentine** .... (330) 375-2670
E-mail: MValentine@akronohio.gov

(continued on next page)

★ Elected Official ▲ Appointed by Legislature ▼ Appointed by Governor ▶ Appointed by Board or Commission ● Appointed by Judge
■ Appointed by Mayor △ Appointed by Freeholders ▽ Appointed by Supervisor ▷ Appointed by County Executive ○ Appointed by Council

Communications Department *continued*

Communications Supervisor **John Heffernan** . . . . (330) 375-2685
E-mail: jheffernan@akronohio.gov

Radio Communications Supervisor **Kevin Hamilton** . . . . . (330) 375-2661
E-mail: khamilton@akronohio.gov

Public Service Department

Municipal Building, 166 South High Street, Akron, OH 44308
Fax: (330) 375-2100

■ Director **John Moore** Room 201 . . . . (330) 375-2270
E-mail: JMoore@AkronOhio.gov
Education: Akron 1984 BA

Deputy Service Director **Chris Ludle** . . . . (330) 375-2270
E-mail: CLudle@Akronohio.gov

Building Maintenance Division

CitiCenter Building, 146 South High Street, Akron, OH 44308
Fax: (330) 375-2091

Facilities Maintenance Manager **Gary Arman** . . . . (330) 375-2724
E-mail: armanga@ci.akron.oh.us

Engineering Bureau

Fax: (330) 375-2288 E-mail: akronengineering@akronohio.gov

City Engineer **James Hewitt** . . . . (330) 375-2355
E-mail: jhewitt@akronohio.gov

Traffic Engineering Division

1420 Triplett Boulevard, Akron, OH 44306
Fax: (330) 375-2307

Traffic Engineer **Dave Gasper** . . . . (330) 375-2851
E-mail: gaspeda@ci.akron.oh.us

Plans and Permits Division

1030 East Tallmadge Avenue, Akron, OH 44310
E-mail: plans&permits@akronohio.gov

Manager **(Vacant)** . . . . (330) 375-2010

Public Works Bureau

1436 Triplett Boulevard, Akron, OH 44306
Fax: (330) 375-2822 E-mail: publicworks@akronohio.gov

Manager **Jim Hall** . . . . (330) 375-2834

Airport Division Superintendent **(Vacant)** . . . . (330) 733-3950
1800 Triplett Blvd., Akron, OH 44308

Highway Maintenance Division Superintendent
(Vacant) . . . . (330) 375-2311
Fax: (330) 375-2815

Parks Maintenance Division Superintendent
John Nutter . . . . (330) 375-2841

Sanitation and Recycling Superintendent **Robert Harris** . . . (330) 375-2801

Street Cleaning Division Superintendent **Kevin Miller** . . . . (330) 375-2886

Engineering Services **(Vacant)** . . . . (330) 375-2831

Sewer Bureau

2460 Akron Peninsula Rd., Akron, OH 44313

Water Reclamation Facility Manager **Brian Gresser** . . . . . . (330) 928-1164
Fax: (330) 928-2285

Water Supply Bureau

1570 Ravenna Road, Kent, OH 44240
Fax: (330) 375-2072

Water Supply Division Manager **Jeff Bronowski** . . . . (330) 678-0077
Fax: (330) 678-0927

Office of the City Council

Municipal Building, 166 South High Street, 3rd Floor, Room 301, Akron, OH 44308
Fax: (330) 375-2298

★ President **Marilyn Keith** (D-Ward 8) . . . . (330) 375-2256
Term Expires: December 31, 2019
E-mail: ward8@akronohio.gov

Office of the City Council *continued*

★ President Pro Tem **Donnie Kammer** (D-Ward 7) . . . . (330) 375-2256
Term Expires: December 31, 2019
E-mail: ward7@akronohio.gov

★ Vice President **Margo Sommerville** (D-Ward 3) . . . . (330) 375-2256
Term Expires: December 31, 2019
E-mail: ward3@akronohio.gov

★ Council Member **Rich Swirsky** (D-Ward 1) . . . . (330) 375-2256
Term Expires: December 31, 2019
E-mail: Ward1@akronohio.gov

★ Council Member **Bruce Kilby** (D-Ward 2) . . . . (330) 375-2256
Term Expires: December 31, 2019

★ Council Member **Russell C. Neal, Jr.** (D-Ward 4) . . . . (330) 375-2256
Term Expires: December 31, 2019
E-mail: ward4@akronohio.gov

★ Council Member **Tara Mosley-Samples** (D-Ward 5) . . . . . (330) 375-2256
Term Expires: December 31, 2019
E-mail: Ward5@akronohio.gov

★ Council Member **Robert Hoch** (D-Ward 6) . . . . (330) 375-2256
Term Expires: December 31, 2019
E-mail: ward6@akronohio.gov

★ Council Member **Mike Freeman** (D-Ward 9) . . . . (330) 375-2256
Term Expires: December 31, 2019
E-mail: ward9@akronohio.gov

★ Council Member **Zack Milkovich** (D-Ward 10) . . . . (330) 375-2256
Term Expires: December 31, 2019

★ Council Member **Jeff Fusco** (D-At-Large) . . . . (330) 375-2256
Term Expires: December 31, 2019

★ Council Member **Linda Omobien** (D-At-Large) . . . . (330) 375-2256
Term Expires: December 31, 2019
E-mail: atlarge2@akronohio.gov

★ Council Member **Veronica R. Sims** (D-At-Large) . . . . (330) 375-2256
Term Expires: December 31, 2019

○ Clerk of Council **Bob Keith** (D) . . . . (330) 375-2256
E-mail: bkeith@akronohio.gov

Deputy Clerk **Connie Genevish** . . . . (330) 375-2256
E-mail: cgenevish@akronohio.gov

Akron Public Schools

70 North Broadway, Akron, OH 44308
Tel: (330) 761-1661 Fax: (330) 761-3225
Internet: www.akronschools.com/

Superintendent of Schools **David W. James** . . . . (330) 761-2921

City of Albany, New York

City Hall, Albany, NY 12207

County: Albany **Election Type:** Partisan **Population:** 98,469 (2015)
Fiscal Year: 2016 **Budget:** $180,607,000

Office of the Mayor

City Hall, Albany, NY 12207
Fax: (518) 434-5013

Employees: 8 **Fiscal Year:** 2016 **Budget:** $667,000

★ Mayor **Katherine M. "Kathy" Sheehan** (D) . . . . (518) 434-5100
Began Service: January 1, 2014
Term Expires: December 31, 2017

Chief of Staff **Matt Peter** . . . . (518) 434-5100
Education: SUNY (Albany) MS

Senior Policy Advisor **Shalyn M. Morrison Ranellone** . . (518) 434-5100
Education: SUNY (Cortland); Albany Law JD

Scheduling Assistant **Martha Mahoney** . . . . (518) 434-5100

Communications Director **Dennis Gaffney** . . . . (518) 434-5076

■ Budget Director **(Vacant)** . . . . (518) 434-5078

★ Elected Official ▲ Appointed by Legislature ▼ Appointed by Governor ► Appointed by Board or Commission ● Appointed by Judge
■ Appointed by Mayor △ Appointed by Freeholders ▽ Appointed by Supervisor ▷ Appointed by County Executive ○ Appointed by Council

Office of the Common Council

City Hall, Albany, NY 12207
Fax: (518) 434-5081

Employees: 20 **Fiscal Year:** 2016 **Budget:** $650,000

★Council President **Carolyn McLaughlin** (D) .... (518) 434-5087
Term Expires: December 31, 2017
E-mail: onlybelv@aol.com

★President Pro Tempore **Richard Conti** (D-Ward 6) .... (518) 434-5087
Term Expires: December 31, 2017
E-mail: rc6thward@aol.com

★Council Member **Darcey L. Applyrs** (D-Ward 1) .... (518) 434-5087
Term Expires: December 31, 2017
E-mail: dorceyapplyrs@gmail.com

★Council Member **Vivian D. Kornegay** (D-Ward 2) .... (518) 434-5087
Term Expires: December 31, 2017
E-mail: vdk1960@gmail.com

★Council Member **Ronald Bailey** (D-Ward 3) .... (518) 434-5087
Term Expires: December 31, 2017
E-mail: ronald.bailey47@yahoo.com

★Council Member **Kelly Kimbrough** (D-Ward 4) .... (518) 434-5087
Term Expires: December 31, 2017
E-mail: kellykimbrough4@gmail.com

★Council Member **Mark Robinson** (D-Ward 5) .... (518) 434-5087
Term Expires: December 31, 2017
E-mail: 5thwardalbany@gmail.com

★Council Member **Catherine M. Fahey** (D-Ward 7) ...... (518) 434-5087
Term Expires: December 31, 2017
E-mail: cathyfahey7@yahoo.com

★Council Member **Jack Flynn** (D-Ward 8) .... (518) 434-5087
Term Expires: December 31, 2017
E-mail: jackflynn8thward@gmail.com

★Council Member **Judy Doesschate** (D-Ward 9) .... (518) 434-5087
Term Expires: December 31, 2017
E-mail: judydoesschate@nycap.rr.com

★Council Member **Leah Golby** (D-Ward 10) .... (518) 434-5087
Term Expires: December 31, 2017
E-mail: leah.golby@gmail.com

★Council Member **Judd W. Krasher** (D-Ward 11) .... (518) 434-5087
Term Expires: December 31, 2017
E-mail: councilmankrasher@outlook.com

★Council Member **Michael O'Brien** (D-Ward 12) .... (518) 434-5087
Term Expires: December 31, 2017
E-mail: twelfward@aol.com

★Council Member/Majority Leader
Daniel Herring (D-Ward 13) .... (518) 434-5087
Term Expires: December 31, 2017
E-mail: danherring47@hotmail.com

★Council Member **Joseph Igoe** (D-Ward 14) .... (518) 434-5087
Term Expires: December 31, 2017
E-mail: jigoe19932@aol.com

★Council Member **Frank Commisso, Jr.** (D-Ward 15) .... (518) 434-5087
Term Expires: December 31, 2017
E-mail: commissofrank@gmail.com

Office of the City Clerk

City Hall, Room 202, Albany, NY 12207
Fax: (518) 434-5081

Employees: 6 **Fiscal Year:** 2016 **Budget:** $317,000

○City Clerk **Nala Woodard** .... (518) 434-5090
E-mail: cityclerk@ci.albany.ny.us

Deputy City Clerk **Gerald Campbell** .... (518) 434-5090
E-mail: gcampbell@albanyny.gov

Board of Contract and Supply

City Hall, Albany, NY 12207

★Mayor **Katherine M. "Kathy" Sheehan** (D) .... (518) 434-5092
Term Expires: December 31, 2017

City Treasurer **Darius Shahinfar** (D) .... (518) 434-5023
Secretary/City Clerk **Nala Woodard** .... (518) 434-5090
General Services Commissioner **Daniel Mirabile** .... (518) 434-5092
Corporation Counsel **John Reilly** .... (518) 434-5092

Board of Contract and Supply *continued*

City Engineer **Randy Milano** .... (518) 427-7481

Vital Statistics

City Hall, Room 254M, Albany, NY 12207

Employees: 5 **Fiscal Year:** 2016 **Budget:** $263,000

■Registrar **Denise Kelley** .... (518) 434-5045
E-mail: kelleyd@ci.albany.ny.us

Office of the City Auditor

City Hall, Albany, NY 12207

Employees: 4 **Fiscal Year:** 2016 **Budget:** $428,000

Chief City Auditor **Leif C. Engstrom** .... (518) 434-5023
Term Expires: December 31, 2017

Office of the Treasurer

City Hall, 24 Eagle Street, Albany, NY 12207
Fax: (518) 434-5041

Employees: 18 **Fiscal Year:** 2016 **Budget:**

★Treasurer **Darius Shahinfar** (D) .... (518) 434-5036
Term Expires: December 31, 2017
E-mail: dshahinfar@albanyny.gov

Administrative Services

Employees: 12 **Fiscal Year:** 2016 **Budget:** $1,007,000

Albany Municipal Civil Service Commission

City Hall, Room 301, Albany, NY 12207

Commissioner **Erin Apostol** .... (518) 434-5049
Commissioner **Thomas McNaughton** .... (518) 434-5049
Commissioner **Andrew Phelan** .... (518) 434-5049

Equal Opportunity and Fair Housing

City Hall, Room 301, Albany, NY 12207

Equal Employment Opportunity/Affirmative Action/
Human Rights Coordinator **Kory Hogan** .... (518) 434-5296

Minority and Women Business Enterprise/Fair Housing
Coordinator **Kory Hogan** .... (518) 434-5284

Personnel Division

City Hall, Albany, NY 12207

Human Resources Director/ADA Coordinator
Miriam Dixon .... (518) 434-5284

Purchasing Office

City Hall, Albany, NY 12207

Director **Ann DiLillo** .... (518) 434-5135
E-mail: adilillo@albanyny.gov

Albany Public Library

161 Washington Avenue, Albany, NY 12210
Fax: (518) 449-3386 Internet: www.albanypubliclibrary.org

Library Director **Scott Jarzombek** .... (518) 427-4300 ext. 379
E-mail: jarzombeks@albanypubliclibrary.org

Assessment Department

City Hall, Albany, NY 12207

Employees: 6 **Fiscal Year:** 2016 **Budget:** $635,000

■Commissioner **Keith McDonald** .... (518) 434-5155
E-mail: kmcdonald@albanyny.gov

★Elected Official ▲Appointed by Legislature ▼Appointed by Governor ▶Appointed by Board or Commission ●Appointed by Judge
■Appointed by Mayor △Appointed by Freeholders ▽Appointed by Supervisor ▷Appointed by County Executive ○Appointed by Council

Department of Buildings and Regulatory Compliance

City Hall, 24 Eagle Street, 3rd Floor, Albany, NY 12207
Tel: (518) 434-5165 (Buildings) Tel: (518) 434-5995 (Codes)

Employees: 22 **Fiscal Year:** 2016 **Budget:** $1,448,000

■ Director **Robert McGee** .... (518) 434-5165
E-mail: rmcgee@albanyny.gov
Chief Inspector **Carlo Figliomeni** .... (518) 434-5165

Department of Planning and Community Development

200 Henry Johnson Boulevard, Albany, NY 12210

Employees: 15 **Fiscal Year:** 2016 **Budget:** $128,000

■ Commissioner **Bradley Glass** .... (518) 434-5240

Community Development Agency

200 Henry Johnson Boulevard, Albany, NY 12210

■ Director **Faye Andrews** .... (518) 434-5240
E-mail: andrewsf@ci.albany.ny.us

Planning Division

21 Lodge Street, Albany, NY 12207

■ Director **Christopher P. Spencer** .... (518) 434-5262
E-mail: cspencer@albanyny.gov

Fire, Emergency and Building Services Department

26 Broad Street, Albany, NY 12202

Employees: 270 **Fiscal Year:** 2016 **Budget:** $32,123,000

■ Chief of Department **Warren W. Abriel, Jr.** .... (518) 447-7879
E-mail: wabriel@albanyny.gov

General Services Department

One Conners Blvd., Albany, NY 12204
Fax: (518) 427-7499

Employees: 20 **Fiscal Year:** 2016 **Budget:** $1,440,000

■ Commissioner **Daniel Mirabile** .... (518) 434-2489
E-mail: dmirabile@albanyny.gov
Fleet Maintenance Supervisor **Jeff Hunt** .... (518) 445-0726

Engineering Division

One Conners Blvd., Albany, NY 12204

■ City Engineer **Randy Milano** .... (518) 427-7481
E-mail: milanor@ci.albany.ny.us

Special Events Office

City Hall, Room 402, Albany, NY 12207
Internet: http://www.albanyevents.org

Director **(Vacant)** .... (518) 434-2032

Housing Authority

200 S. Pearl St., Albany, NY 12202
Fax: (518) 641-7547 Internet: http://www.albanyhousing.org

■ Director **Steven Longo** .... (518) 641-7500
E-mail: info@albanyhousing.org

Law Department

City Hall, Albany, NY 12207
Fax: (518) 434-5070

Employees: 12 **Fiscal Year:** 2016 **Budget:** $1,534,000

■ Corporation Counsel **John Reilly** .... (518) 434-5050

Information Technology Unit

City Hall, Albany, NY 12207

Employees: 9 **Fiscal Year:** 2016 **Budget:** $1,083,000

Chief Information Technology Officer **Mark Dorry** .... (518) 434-5016
E-mail: mdorry@albanyny.gov
Webmaster **Sarah Kampf** .... (518) 434-5103
E-mail: skampf@albanyny.gov

Police Department

Public Safety Bldg., 165 Henry Johnson Blvd., Albany, NY 12210

Employees: 465 **Fiscal Year:** 2016 **Budget:** $53,641,000

■ Chief of Police **Brendan Cox** .... (518) 462-8015
Deputy Chief of Police, Professional Standards
Michael Hicks .... (518) 462-8012
Deputy Chief of Police **Robert Sears** .... (518) 462-8012
Traffic Engineer **Bill Trudeau** .... (518) 458-5610
E-mail: wtrudeau@albany-ny.org

Animal Control

165 Henry Johnson Boulevard, Albany, NY 12210

Supervisor **David Hayes** .... (518) 462-7107

Recreation , Youth and Workforce Services Department

175 Central Ave., Albany, NY 12206

Employees: 14 **Fiscal Year:** 2016 **Budget:** $1,000,000

■ Commissioner **Jonathan Jones** .... (518) 434-5699
E-mail: jjones@albanyny.gov

Water Department

35 Erie Blvd., Albany, NY 12204

■ Commissioner **Joseph E. Coffey, Jr.** .... (518) 434-5300

Albany City School District

Academy Park, Albany, NY 12207
Fax: (518) 475-6014 Internet: www.albanyschools.org/

Superintendent **Marguerite Vanden Wyngaard** .... (518) 475-6010

City of Albuquerque, New Mexico

City/County Government Center, One Civic Plaza, NW, Albuquerque, NM 87102
P.O. Box 1293, Albuquerque, NM 87103
Tel: (505) 768-2000 (Information) Internet: www.cabq.gov

County: Bernalillo **Election Type:** Nonpartisan **Population:** 559,121 (2015) **Employees:** 5,788 **Fiscal Year:** 2016 **Budget:** $915,327,000

Office of the Mayor

City/County Government Center, One Civic Plaza, NW, 11th Floor, Albuquerque, NM 87102
P.O. Box 1293, Albuquerque, NM 87103
Fax: (505) 768-3019 Internet: www.cabq.gov/mayor/

Employees: 6 **Fiscal Year:** 2016 **Budget:** $993,000

★ Mayor **Richard J. Berry** .... (505) 768-3000
Began Service: December 1, 2009
Term Expires: November 30, 2017
E-mail: mayorberry@cabq.gov
Education: New Mexico 1986 BS
■ Deputy Chief of Staff **Nina Martinez** .... (505) 768-3000
E-mail: dwoodward@cabq.gov

★ Elected Official ▲ Appointed by Legislature ▼ Appointed by Governor ▶ Appointed by Board or Commission ● Appointed by Judge
■ Appointed by Mayor △ Appointed by Freeholders ▽ Appointed by Supervisor ▷ Appointed by County Executive ○ Appointed by Council

Office of the Mayor *continued*

■ Constituent Services Director **Alan B. Armijo** . . . . (505) 768-3000
Education: JFK School Govt; New Mexico BA
■ Director of Communications **Rhiannon Schroeder** . . . . . . (505) 768-3000
E-mail: rschroeder@cabq.gov
Scheduler to the Mayor **Angela Aragon** . . . . (505) 768-3000
E-mail: scheduler@cabq.gov

Office of the Chief Administrative Officer

City/County Government Center, One Civic Plaza, NW, 11th Floor, Albuquerque, NM 87102
P.O. Box 1293, Albuquerque, NM 87103
Fax: (505) 768-3019 Tel: (505) 768-3000

Employees: 14 **Fiscal Year:** 2016 **Budget:** $1,598,000

■ Chief Administrative Officer **Robert J. "Rob" Perry** . . . . . (505) 768-3000
E-mail: rjperry@cabq.gov
Assistant to the Chief Administrative Officer
Giselle Alvarez . . . . (505) 768-3058
E-mail: galvarez@cabq.gov
Deputy Chief Administrative Officer **Gilbert Montaño** . . . (505) 768-3000
E-mail: gamontano@cabq.gov
Chief Operations Officer **Michael Riordan** . . . . (505) 768-3000

Office of the City Attorney/Legal Department

City/County Bldg., One Civic Plaza, NW, 4th Floor, Room 4072, Albuquerque, NM 87102
P.O. Box 2248, Albuquerque, NM 87103
Fax: (505) 768-4525 Internet: www.cabq.gov/legal/

Employees: 58 **Fiscal Year:** 2016 **Budget:** $5,670,000

City Attorney **Jessica M. Hernandez** . . . . (505) 768-4500
E-mail: jmhernandez@cabq.gov
Education: New Mexico 1999 BA, 2002 JD
Fiscal Officer **(Vacant)** . . . . (505) 768-4500

Office of Diversity and Human Rights

One Civic Plaza, NW, Albuquerque, NM 87102

Director **Gabriel "Gabe" Campos** . . . . (505) 758-4589

Economic Development Department

One Civic Plaza, NW, Room 11015, Albuquerque, NM 87102
P.O. Box 1293, Albuquerque, NM 87103
Fax: (505) 768-3280 Internet: http://www.cabq.gov/economicdevelopment

Employees: 9 **Fiscal Year:** 2016 **Budget:** $4,469,000

■ Director **Gary Oppedahl** . . . . (505) 768-3270
E-mail: garyo@cabq.gov

Finance and Administrative Services Department

City/County Government Center, One Civic Plaza, NW, Albuquerque, NM 87102
P.O. Box 1293, Albuquerque, NM 87103
Fax: (505) 768-3581

Employees: 208 **Fiscal Year:** 2016 **Budget:** $63,223,000

■ Director **Lou Hoffman** . . . . (505) 768-2000
E-mail: lhoffman@cabq.gov
Assistant to the Director **Olivia Padilla-Jackson** . . . . (505) 768-3364
E-mail: opadilla-jackson@cabq.gov
City Treasurer **Cilia Aglialoro** . . . . (505) 768-3309
Assistant Accounting Officer **Jesse Muniz** . . . . (505) 768-3373
E-mail: jmuniz@cabq.gov
Materials Management Officer
Ramona "Mona" Martinez . . . . (505) 768-3342
E-mail: ramonam@cabq.gov
Assistant Purchasing Officer **Viola Cunningham** . . . . (505) 768-3340
E-mail: vcunningham@cabq.gov

Finance and Administrative Services Department *continued*

Risk Manager **Peter Ennen** . . . . (505) 768-3209
E-mail: pennen@cabq.gov
Senior Administrative Assistant **Rebbekka Sanouvong** . . (505) 768-3066
Citizen Services Division Manager **Ester Tenenbaum** . . . . (505) 924-3741
E-mail: etenenbaum@cabq.gov
Assistant to the Citizens Services Division **Betty Dinelli** . . (505) 924-3212
E-mail: bdinelli@cabq.gov
Fleet Management **(Vacant)** . . . . (505) 857-8087

Office of Management and Budget

One Civic Plaza, NW, 11th Floor, Albuquerque, NM 87102
Fax: (505) 768-3301 Internet: www.cabq.gov/budget/

Budget Officer **Gerald Romero** . . . . (505) 768-2953
E-mail: gromero@cabq.gov

Fire Department

11500 Sunset Gardens, SW, Albuquerque, NM 87121
Fax: (505) 768-9340 Internet: www.cabq.gov/fire/

Employees: 702 **Fiscal Year:** 2016 **Budget:** $77,267,000

■ Fire Chief **David Downey** . . . . (505) 768-9322
E-mail: ddowney@cabq.gov
Deputy Fire Chief **Curtis Green** . . . . (505) 768-9307
E-mail: cgreen@cabq.gov
Deputy Fire Chief **Gil Santistevan** . . . . (505) 768-9328
E-mail: gsaint@cabq.gov
Deputy Fire Chief **Karl Isselhard** . . . . (505) 768-9305
E-mail: kisselhard@cabq.gov
Deputy Fire Chief **Victor Padilla, Jr.** . . . . (505) 768-9301
E-mail: victorpadilla@cabq.gov
Fire Marshal **Scott Esposito** . . . . (505) 764-6304
E-mail: sesposito@cabq.gov

Human Resources Department

400 Marquette NW, 7th Floor, Suite 703, Albuquerque, NM 87103
Tel: (505) 768-3700 Fax: (505) 768-3777 TTY: (505) 768-3730
E-mail: humanresources@cabq.gov

Employees: 34 **Fiscal Year:** 2016 **Budget:** $64,820,000

Director **Mary Scott** . . . . (505) 768-3700
E-mail: mscott@cabq.gov

Police Department

400 Roma St., NW, Albuquerque, NM 87102
Fax: (505) 768-2331 Internet: www.cabq.gov/police/
E-mail: pdweb@cabq.gov

Employees: 1,463 **Fiscal Year:** 2016 **Budget:** $166,143,000

■ Police Chief **Gorden E. Eden, Jr.** . . . . (505) 768-2200
E-mail: geden7@cabq.gov
Education: U Phoenix
Assistant Chief **Robert Huntsman** . . . . (505) 768-2200
Deputy Chief, Support Services **Will Roseman** . . . . (505) 768-2200
Deputy Chief, Investigations **Eric Garcia** . . . . (505) 768-2200
Public Information Officer **(Vacant)** . . . . (505) 768-2200

Office of Emergency Management

11510 Sunset Gardens, SW, Albuquerque, NM 87121
Fax: (505) 831-7906
Internet: www.cabq.gov/police/emergency-management-office

Director **Roger Ebner** . . . . (505) 833-7381
E-mail: rebner@cabq.gov
Emergency Operations Center Officer **Gary Jones** . . . . (505) 831-7917
E-mail: gjones@cabq.gov
Emergency Management Planning Officer
Frederick Hogan . . . . (505) 833-7248
E-mail: fhogan@cabq.gov
Senior Administrative Assistant **Liz Saavedra** . . . . (505) 833-7327
E-mail: Lsaavedra@cabq.gov

★ Elected Official ▲ Appointed by Legislature ▼ Appointed by Governor ► Appointed by Board or Commission ● Appointed by Judge
■ Appointed by Mayor △ Appointed by Freeholders ▽ Appointed by Supervisor ▷ Appointed by County Executive ○ Appointed by Council

Chief of Staff/Deputy Chief Administrative Officer

One Civic Plaza, NW, 11th Floor, Albuquerque, NM 87102

■ Chief of Staff/Deputy Chief Administrative Officer
Gilbert Montaño .... (505) 768-3000
E-mail: gamontano@cabq.gov

Technology and Innovation Department

One Civic Plaza, NW, 2nd Floor, Albuquerque, NM 87102

Employees: 87 **Fiscal Year:** 2016 **Budget:** $17,792,000

Chief Information Officer **Peter Ambs** .... (505) 768-2930
E-mail: pambs@cabq.gov

Chief Operations Officer

One Civic Plaza, NW, Albuquerque, NM 87102

Family and Community Services Department

City/County Government Center, One Civic Plaza, NW, Room 504, Albuquerque, NM 87102-2167
P.O. Box 1293, Albuquerque, NM 87103-1293
Fax: (505) 768-3204 Internet: www.cabq.gov/family/

Employees: 285 **Fiscal Year:** 2016 **Budget:** $67,841,000

■ Director **Douglas H. Chaplin** .... (505) 768-2860
E-mail: dchaplin@cabq.gov
Deputy Director **Danny K. Placencio** .... (505) 768-2860
Community Development Block Grants Division Manager **Valerie Bargas** .... (505) 768-3068
E-mail: vbargas@cabq.gov

Childcare and Development Programs

Child Development Division Manager
Anita Fernandez .... (505) 767-6500
Fax: (505) 767-6525
Community Recreation and Education Initiatives Manager **Jess Martinez** .... (505) 767-5800
Fax: (505) 767-5844

Operations, Fiscal and Grants

Fax: (505) 768-3204

Fiscal Officer **Anna Marie Lujan** .... (505) 768-2909

Animal Welfare Department

8920 Lomas Boulevard, NE, Albuquerque, NM 87112
Fax: (505) 764-1145 Internet: www.cabq.gov/pets/

Employees: 139 **Fiscal Year:** 2016 **Budget:** $11,103,000

Deputy Director **Paul R. Caster** .... (505) 768-1975

Aviation Department

P.O. Box 9948, Albuquerque, NM 87119
Fax: (505) 842-4278 Internet: www.cabq.gov/airport/

Employees: 280 **Fiscal Year:** 2016 **Budget:** $67,410,000

■ Aviation Director **Jim Hinde** .... (505) 244-7700
E-mail: jhinde@cabq.gov
Finance/Administration Associate Director **Pam White** ... (505) 244-7700
E-mail: pwhite@cabq.gov
Operations Associate Director **(Vacant)** .... (505) 244-7700
Planning and Development Associate Director
Jack Scherer .... (505) 244-7700
Public Information Officer **Daniel Jiron** .... (505) 244-7780
E-mail: djiron@cabq.gov Fax: (505) 842-4278
Human Resource Manager **Lisa Zamora** .... (505) 244-7700
E-mail: lzamora@cabq.gov Fax: (505) 842-4278

Cultural Services Department

City/County Government Center, One Civic Plaza, NW, Suite 605, Albuquerque, NM 87102
P.O. Box 1293, Albuquerque, NM 87103
Fax: (505) 768-2846 Internet: www.cabq.gov/crs/

Employees: 333 **Fiscal Year:** 2016 **Budget:** $39,035,000

Director **Dana Feldman** .... (505) 768-3553
Deputy Director **Dave Matthews** .... (505) 768-3528
Media Services Manager **Diego Lucero** .... (505) 768-3556
Events and Operations Supervisor **Bree Ortiz** .... (505) 768-3556
E-mail: bortiz@cabq.gov
Events and Operations Supervisor **Eric Werner** .... (505) 768-3556
E-mail: ewerner@cabq.gov

Albuquerque-Bernalillo County Library System

501 Copper Street, NW, Albuquerque, NM 87102

Director **Dean Smith** .... (505) 768-5195
E-mail: dpsmith@cabq.gov

Environmental Health Department

City/County Government Center, One Civic Plaza, NW, 3rd Floor, Room 3023, Albuquerque, NM 87102
P.O. Box 1293, Albuquerque, NM 87103
Fax: (505) 768-2617 Internet: www.cabq.gov/envhealth/

Employees: 75 **Fiscal Year:** 2016 **Budget:** $7,899,000

■ Director **Mary Lou Leonard** .... (505) 768-2631
E-mail: mleonard@cabq.gov
Deputy Director **Dr. Mark DiMenna** .... (505) 768-2620
Deputy Director **Danny Nevarez** .... (505) 768-2706
Air Quality Division Manager **Isreal Tavarez** .... (505) 768-1965
Air Quality Official **Fabian Macias** .... (505) 768-1969
11850 Sunset Gardens SW, Albuquerque, NM 87121
Urban Biology Division Manager **Paul Smith** .... (505) 452-5301
3600 Los Picaros Row, S.E., Albuquerque, NM 87105
Consumer Health Protection Division Manager
Lorie Stoller .... (505) 768-2718
Environmental Services Division Manager **Bart Faris** ..... (505) 768-2658
Vehicle Pollution Management Division Manager
Fabian Macias .... (505) 764-1110
1500 Broadway, N.E., Albuquerque, NM 87102

Department of Municipal Development

City/County Government Center, One Civic Plaza, NW, 7th Floor, Albuquerque, NM 87102
Tel: (505) 768-3830 Fax: (505) 768-2310
Internet: www.cabq.gov/municipaldev/

Employees: 462 **Fiscal Year:** 2016 **Budget:** $52,349,000

Director (Acting) **Melissa Lozoya** .... (505) 768-3830
E-mail: mlozoya@cabq.gov
Executive Assistant **Jeanne Taylor** .... (505) 768-2685
Deputy Director **Melissa Lozoya** .... (505) 857-8053
Deputy Director **Greg Smith** .... (505) 857-8053
Construction Coordination **Bryan Wolfe** .... (505) 924-3625
E-mail: bwolfe@cabq.gov
Traffic Engineering **John Kolessar** .... (505) 857-8621
E-mail: jkolessar@cabq.gov

Parks and Recreation Department

Building A, 1801 Fourth Street, Northwest, Albuquerque, NM 87102
Fax: (505) 768-5305

Employees: 268 **Fiscal Year:** 2016 **Budget:** $33,295,000

■ Director **Barbara Taylor** .... (505) 768-5395
E-mail: bbaca@cabq.gov
Golf Management Division Superintendent **David Salas** .. (505) 768-5347
Open Space Division Head **Matthew Schmader** .... (505) 452-5214
P.O. Box 1293, Albuquerque, NM 87103
Recreation Division Manager **Alex Kiska** .... (505) 768-5324

★ Elected Official ▲ Appointed by Legislature ▼ Appointed by Governor ► Appointed by Board or Commission ● Appointed by Judge
■ Appointed by Mayor △ Appointed by Freeholders ▽ Appointed by Supervisor ▷ Appointed by County Executive ○ Appointed by Council

Planning Department

P.O. Box 1293, Albuquerque, NM 87103
Fax: (505) 924-3339 Internet: www.cabq.gov/planning/

Employees: 163 **Fiscal Year:** 2016 **Budget:** $14,913,000

■ Director **Suzanne Lubar** .... (505) 924-3860
E-mail: slubar@cabq.gov
Associate Director (Acting) **Brennon Williams** .... (505) 924-3454
City Engineer **Shahab Biazar** .... (505) 924-3999
E-mail: sbiazar@cabq.gov
Chief Building Official **Land Clark** .... (505) 924-3313
Public Information Officer **Melissa Perez** .... (505) 924-3349
E-mail: mperez@cabq.gov

Senior Affairs Department

714 7th St., SW, Albuquerque, NM 87102
Fax: (505) 764-6455 E-mail: seniorinformation@cabq.gov
Internet: www.cabq.gov/seniors/index.html

Employees: 115 **Fiscal Year:** 2016 **Budget:** $14,654,000

Director **Jorja Armijo-Brasher** .... (505) 764-6431
Executive Assistant **Charlotte Garcia** .... (505) 764-6469
E-mail: charlottegarcia@cabq.gov
Associate Director **Anthony R. Romero** .... (505) 764-6406
Fiscal Manager **Karen Lopez** .... (505) 764-6446
Recreation Division Manager, Senior Centers/Sports and Fitness Centers **Rhonda Methvin** .... (505) 764-6450

Solid Waste Management Department

4600 Edith Blvd., NE, Albuquerque, NM 87107
Fax: (505) 761-8187 Internet: www.cabq.gov/SolidWaste/

Employees: 457 **Fiscal Year:** 2016 **Budget:** $65,667,000

■ Director **John W. Soladay** .... (505) 761-8100
E-mail: JSoladay@cabq.gov
Associate Director (Acting) **James Mora** .... (505) 761-8100
Deputy Director **Jill Holbert** .... (505) 761-8100
Education: Michigan 1987 BS
Clean City Division Superintendent **Marco Holloway** .... (505) 761-8100
Commercial Collection Division Superintendent **James Mora** .... (505) 761-8100
Disposal Division Superintendent **(Vacant)** .... (505) 761-8100
Residential Collection Division Superintendent **Joseph Pafoya** .... (505) 761-8100
Vehicle Maintenance Division Superintendent **Martin Vargas** .... (505) 761-8100

Transit Department [ABQRide]

100 First Street, SW, Albuquerque, NM 87102
Fax: (505) 724-3111 Internet: www.cabq.gov/transit

Employees: 569 **Fiscal Year:** 2016 **Budget:** $44,193,000

■ Director **Bruce Rizzieri** .... (505) 724-3181
E-mail: brizzieri@cabq.gov

Office of the City Council

City/County Government Center, One Civic Plaza, NW, 9th Floor, Albuquerque, NM 87102
P.O. Box 1293, Albuquerque, NM 87103
Fax: (505) 768-3227 Internet: www.cabq.gov/council/

Employees: 26 **Fiscal Year:** 2016 **Budget:** $3,545,000

★ Council President **Dan Lewis** (District 5) .... (505) 768-3189
Term Expires: November 30, 2017
E-mail: danlewis@cabq.gov
Education: Grand Canyon BA; Southwestern Baptist MA
Policy Analyst **Rachel Miller** .... (505) 768-3189
★ Council Vice President **Klarissa J. Pena** (District 3) .... (505) 768-3186
Term Expires: November 30, 2017
E-mail: kpena@cabq.gov
Policy Analyst **Nancy Montaño** .... (505) 768-3127

Office of the City Council *continued*

★ Council Member **Ken Sanchez** (District 1) .... (505) 768-3183
Term Expires: November 30, 2017
E-mail: kensanchez@cabq.gov
Policy Analyst **Elaine Romero** .... (505) 768-3183
★ Council Member **Isaac Benton** (District 2) .... (505) 768-3186
Term Expires: November 30, 2019
E-mail: ibenton@cabq.gov
Policy Analyst **Diane Dolan** .... (505) 768-3186
★ Council Member **Brad D. Winter** (District 4) .... (505) 768-3101
Term Expires: November 30, 2019
E-mail: bwinter@cabq.gov
Education: Oklahoma BA; New Mexico DEd
Policy Analyst **Rebekka Burt** .... (505) 768-3101
★ Council Member **Patrick "Pat" Davis** (District 6) .... (505) 768-3152
Term Expires: November 30, 2019
Education: Berry 2000 BS; New Mexico State 2009 MS
Policy Analyst **Sean Foran** .... (505) 768-3152
★ Council Member **Diane G. Gibson** (District 7) .... (505) 768-3136
Term Expires: November 30, 2017
E-mail: dgibson@cabq.gov
Policy Analyst **Chris Sylvan** .... (505) 768-3136
★ Council Member **Trudy Jones** (District 8) .... (505) 768-3106
Term Expires: November 30, 2019
E-mail: trudyjones@cabq.gov
Policy Analyst **Aziza Chavez** .... (505) 768-3106
★ Council Member **Don Harris** (District 9) .... (505) 768-3123
Term Expires: November 30, 2017
E-mail: dharris@cabq.gov
Policy Analyst **Dawn Marie Emillio** .... (505) 768-3123
Council Services Director **Jon Zaman** .... (505) 768-3100
E-mail: jzaman@cabq.gov
Clerk of the Council **Crystal L. Ortega** .... (505) 768-3100
E-mail: cortega@cabq.gov

Office of the City Clerk

Plaza del Sol, 600 2nd NW, 7th Floor, Albuquerque, NM 87102
Fax: (505) 924-3660 E-mail: cityclerk@cabq.gov
Internet: www.cabq.gov/clerk

Employees: 17 **Fiscal Year:** 2016 **Budget:** $2,218,000

City Clerk **Natalie Y. Howard** .... (505) 924-3651
E-mail: nhoward@cabq.gov

Internal Audit

Employees: 7 **Fiscal Year:** 2016 **Budget:** $808,000

○ Director **Debra D. Yoshimura** .... (505) 768-3150
E-mail: DYoshimura@cabq.gov
Education: New Mexico Tech BS; Corpus Christi State MBA

Albuquerque/Bernalillo County Water Utility Authority [ABCWUA]

City/County Government Center, Rm. 5027, One Civic Plaza, NW, Albuquerque, NM 87102
P.O. Box 1293, Albuquerque, NM 87103-1293
Fax: (505) 289-3065 Internet: www.abcwua.org/

▶ Executive Director **Mark S. Sanchez** .... (505) 289-3000

Albuquerque Public Schools

6400 Upton Boulevard, NE, Albuquerque, NM 87110
Fax: (505) 872-8855 Internet: www.aps.edu/

Superintendent (Acting) **Raquel Reedy** .... (505) 880-3713

★ Elected Official ▲ Appointed by Legislature ▼ Appointed by Governor ▶ Appointed by Board or Commission ● Appointed by Judge
■ Appointed by Mayor △ Appointed by Freeholders ▽ Appointed by Supervisor ▷ Appointed by County Executive ○ Appointed by Council

CITIES AND TOWNS

Albuquerque Convention Center

401 2nd Street, NW, Albuquerque, NM 87102
Tel: (505) 768-4575 Fax: (505) 768-3239
E-mail: info@albuquerquecc.com Internet: www.albuquerquecc.com

■ General Manager **Jose Garcia** .... (505) 768-4575
E-mail: jgarcia@cabq.gov

City of Alexandria, Virginia

City Hall, 301 King St., Alexandria, VA 22314-3211
P.O. Box 178, Alexandria, VA 22313
Tel: (703) 746-4357 (Information)

County: None **Election Type:** Partisan **Year Founded:** 1749
Year Incorporated: 1779 **Charter:** 1950 **Population:** 153,511 (2015)
Employees: 2,542 **Fiscal Year:** 2016 **Budget:** $912,698,000

Office of the Mayor and City Council

City Hall, 301 King St., Alexandria, VA 22314
P.O. Box 178, Alexandria, VA 22313
Tel: (703) 746-4500 Fax: (703) 838-6433
Internet: http://alexandriava.gov/Council

Employees: 19 **Fiscal Year:** 2016 **Budget:** $524,000

★ Mayor **Allison Silberberg** (D-At-Large) .... (703) 746-4500
Began Service: January 4, 2016
Term Expires: December 31, 2018

★ Vice Mayor **Justin Wilson** (D-At-Large) .... (703) 746-4500
Term Expires: December 31, 2018
E-mail: justin.wilson@alexandriava.gov
Education: VCU 2001 BS

★ Council Member **Willie F. Bailey, Sr.** (D-At-Large) ...... (703) 746-4500
Term Expires: December 31, 2018

★ Council Member **John Taylor Chapman** (D-At-Large) ... (703) 746-4500
Term Expires: December 31, 2018
E-mail: john.taylor.chapman@alexandriava.gov

★ Council Member **Timothy Bertil Lovain** (D-At-Large) ... (703) 746-4500
Term Expires: December 31, 2018
E-mail: timothy.lovain@alexandriava.gov
Date of Birth: October 5, 1948
Education: Chicago 1970 BA; Princeton 1978 MA; U Washington 1983 JD

★ Council Member **Redella S. "Del" Pepper** (D-At-Large) .... (703) 746-4500
Term Expires: December 31, 2018
E-mail: del.pepper@alexandriava.gov
Education: Grinnell BA
Administrative Aide **Shelli Gilliam** .... (703) 746-4500
E-mail: shelli.gilliam@alexandriava.gov

★ Council Member **Paul C. Smedberg** (D-At-Large) ...... (703) 746-4500
Term Expires: December 31, 2018
E-mail: paul.smedberg@alexandriava.gov
Education: Allegheny 1983 BA, 1983 BS
Administrative Aide **Nancy Perkins** .... (703) 746-4500
E-mail: nancy.perkins@alexandriava.gov
Administrative Aide **Nancy Lacey** .... (703) 746-4500

City Clerk **Jackie Henderson** .... (703) 746-4550
E-mail: jackie.henderson@alexandriava.gov

Deputy City Clerk **Gloria Sitton** .... (703) 746-4550
E-mail: gloria.sitton@alexandriava.gov

○ City Attorney **James L. Banks, Jr.** .... (703) 746-3750
E-mail: james.banks@alexandriava.gov Fax: (703) 838-4810
Education: Gettysburg 1980 BA; Virginia 1987 JD
Supervisory Administrative Assistant **Robin Wilson** .... (703) 746-3750
E-mail: robin.wilson@alexandriava.gov

Office of the Commonwealth's Attorney

Courthouse, 520 King St., Suite 301, Alexandria, VA 22314
Fax: (703) 746-4466 Internet: http://alexandriava.gov/commattorney/

Employees: 27 **Fiscal Year:** 2016 **Budget:** $3,208,000

★ Commonwealth's Attorney **Bryan Porter** (D) .... (703) 746-4100
Term Expires: December 31, 2017
E-mail: bryan.porter@alexandriava.gov

Chief Deputy Commonwealth's Attorney **Molly Sullivan** .... (703) 746-4100
E-mail: molly.sullivan@alexandriava.gov

Office Administrator **Donald Harrison-Wright** .... (703) 746-4100
E-mail: donald.harrison-wright@alexandriava.gov

Office of the Registrar of Voters

132 N. Royal St., Suite 100, Alexandria, VA 22314
Fax: (703) 838-6449 Internet: http://alexandriava.gov/Elections

Employees: 6 **Fiscal Year:** 2016 **Budget:** $1,332,000

Registrar **Anna Leider** .... (703) 746-4050
Deputy Registrar **Angela Maniglia Turner** .... (703) 746-4050
Elections Administrator **Eric Spicer** .... (703) 746-4050

Alexandria Sheriff's Office

2003 Mill Rd., Alexandria, VA 22314
Tel: (703) 838-4114 Fax: (703) 746-5033
Internet: http://alexandriava.gov/sheriff/

Employees: 210 **Fiscal Year:** 2016 **Budget:** $31,496,000

★ Sheriff **Dana Lawhorne** (D) .... (703) 746-4114
Term Expires: December 31, 2017
E-mail: dana.lawhorne@alexandriava.gov

Judicial and Special Operations Undersheriff **Tim Gleeson** .... (703) 746-5006
E-mail: tim.gleeson@alexandriava.gov

Detention Center Bureau Chief Deputy **Wendy Webb** .... (703) 746-5010

Administrative and Support Services Bureau, Chief Deputy **Wendy Webb** .... (703) 746-5010
E-mail: wendy.webb@alexandriava.gov

Captain of Day Shift **Capt. Shelbert Williams** .... (703) 746-5038
E-mail: shelbert.williams@alexandriava.gov

Human Resources and Training Section Director **George Baldwin** .... (703) 746-5011
E-mail: george.baldwin@alexandriava.gov

Captain of Administrative Services **Robyn Nicholes** ..... (703) 746-5120
E-mail: robyn.nichols@alexandriava.gov

Captain of Judicial and Special Operations **Mike Eller** .... (703) 746-5088
E-mail: mike.eller@alexandriava.gov

Captain of Night Shift **Mavis Thomas** .... (703) 746-5047
E-mail: mavis.thomas@alexandriava.gov

Chief Financial Officer **Cindy Caltlett** .... (703) 746-5149
E-mail: cindy.catlett@alexandriava.gov

Information and Technology Director **Cdr. Michele McCarty** .... (703) 746-5158
E-mail: michele.mccarty@alexandriava.gov

Public Defender

132 North Royal Street, Suite 200, Alexandria, VA 22314
Fax: (703) 838-6483

Public Defender **Melinda Douglas** .... (703) 746-4477

Office of the City Manager

301 King St., Room 3500, Alexandria, VA 22314
Fax: (703) 838-6343 Internet: http://alexandriava.gov/Manager

Employees: 14 **Fiscal Year:** 2016 **Budget:** $2,363,000

○ City Manager **Mark B. Jinks** .... (703) 746-4300
E-mail: mark.jinks@alexandriava.gov
Education: Penn State BA, MPA

Assistant to the City Manager (Acting) **Sermaine McLean** .... (703) 746-4300
E-mail: sermaine.mclean@alexandriava.gov

★ Elected Official ▲ Appointed by Legislature ▼ Appointed by Governor ▶ Appointed by Board or Commission ● Appointed by Judge
■ Appointed by Mayor △ Appointed by Freeholders ▽ Appointed by Supervisor ▷ Appointed by County Executive ○ Appointed by Council

Office of the City Manager *continued*

Special Assistant to the City Manager **Noraine Buttar** . . (703) 746-4300
Education: George Washington BA, MA
Deputy City Manager **Emily A. Baker** . . . . (703) 746-4300
E-mail: emily.baker@alexandriava.gov
Education: Virginia Tech BSCE; UC Berkeley MSCE
Deputy City Manager **Debra R. Collins** . . . . (703) 746-4300
E-mail: debra.collins@alexandriava.gov
Deputy City Manager **Laura B. Triggs** . . . . (703) 746-4300
E-mail: laura.triggs@alexandriava.gov
Education: Southwestern BBA

Office of Communications and Public Information

301 King Street, Room 3230, Alexandria, VA 22314

Employees: 7 **Fiscal Year:** 2016 **Budget:** $1,271,000

Director of Communications **Craig T. Fifer** . . . . (703) 746-3965
E-mail: craig.fifer@alexandriava.gov
Education: Virginia Tech BA; George Mason MPA
Communications Officer **Andrea Blackford** . . . . (703) 746-3959
E-mail: andrea.blackford@alexandriava.gov
Communications Officer **Melissa Riddy** . . . . (703) 746-3961
E-mail: melissa.riddy@alexandriava.gov

Department of Community and Human Services

720 North St. Asaph Street, 2nd Floor, Alexandria, VA 22314
Fax: (703) 838-5070 E-mail: acsb@alexandria.gov

Employees: 574 **Fiscal Year:** 2016 **Budget:** $88,971,000

Director **Katherine A. "Kate" Garvey** . . . . (703) 746-3400
Executive Deputy Director/Director of Social Services
Suzanne Chis . . . . (703) 746-3400
Deputy Director for Adult Services **Carol Layer** . . . . (703) 746-3500
Director for Community Support **Connie Juntunen** . . . . . (703) 746-3500
Deputy Director for Children and Family
Deborah Warren . . . . (703) 746-3400
Emergency Services Team Leader **Gabriel Duer** . . . . (703) 746-3400
E-mail: gabriel.duer@alexandriava.gov
Reimbursement Director **LaKeisha Flores** . . . . (703) 746-3400
Research and Evaluation Director **Jennifer Kane** . . . . (703) 746-3400
Human Resources Manager **Jeff Bollen** . . . . (703) 746-5665
2525 Mount Vernon Avenue, Alexandria, VA 22301
E-mail: jeff.bollen@alexandriava.gov
Fiscal Officer III **Raphael Obenwa** . . . . (703) 746-3677

Commission for Women

421 King Street, Suite 400, Alexandria, VA 22314
Fax: (703) 838-4976

Director **(Vacant)** . . . . (703) 746-3120

Mental Health Center

720 N. St. Asaph St., 2nd Floor, Alexandria, VA 22314
Fax: (703) 838-5062

Clinical and Emergency Services Director
Elizabeth "Liz" Wixson . . . . (703) 746-3400
Emergency Services Team Leader **Bill Rooney** . . . . (703) 746-3400

Behavioral Health Services

720 North St., 4th Floor, Alexandria, VA 22314
Tel: (703) 838-5060 (Case Management Program)
Tel: (703) 370-5138 (Vocational Program) Fax: (703) 838-5070

Case Management Recovery Team Leader **(Vacant)** . . . . . . (703) 746-3400

Substance Abuse Services

2355 Mill Rd., Alexandria, VA 22314
Fax: (703) 746-3584

Director **Susan Tatum** . . . . (703) 746-3600
Detox Services Team Leader **Jennifer Miller** . . . . (703) 746-3600

Department of Emergency Communications

3600 Wheeler Avenue, Alexandria, VA 22304
Tel: (703) 746-1888 Fax: (703) 746-1889

Employees: 55 **Fiscal Year:** 2016 **Budget:** $7,162,000

Director **Renee Gordon** . . . . (703) 746-1888

Finance Department

City Hall, 301 King Street, Room 1600, Alexandria, VA 22314
Tel: (703) 746-3900 Fax: (703) 838-4987
Internet: http://alexandriava.gov/finance/default.aspx

Employees: 107 **Fiscal Year:** 2016 **Budget:** $14,170,000

Director of Finance **Kendel Taylor** . . . . (703) 746-3900 ext. 7
Comptroller **(Vacant)** . . . . (703) 746-4312
100 North Pitt Street, Suite 305, Alexandria, VA 22314
Assistant Director of Finance/Revenue **Michael Stewart**
Room 1700 . . . . (703) 746-3900
E-mail: michael.stewart@alexandriava.gov
Assistant Director of Finance/Treasury **David Clark**
Room 1510 . . . . (703) 746-3871
Retirement Administrator (Acting) **Kadira Coley**
Room 1400 . . . . (703) 746-3879
Purchasing Agent (Acting) **Michael Hauer** . . . . (703) 746-4294
100 North Pitt Street, Suite 301, Alexandria, VA 22314
E-mail: michael.hauer@alexandriava.gov

Fire Department

900 Second St., Alexandria, VA 22314
Tel: (703) 746-5200 Fax: (703) 838-5093
Internet: http://alexandriava.gov/fire/

Employees: 276 **Fiscal Year:** 2016 **Budget:** $47,110,000

Fire Chief **Robert C. Dubé** . . . . (703) 746-5200
E-mail: robert.dube@alexandriava.gov
Administrative Assistant **Cameron Hall** . . . . (703) 746-5241
E-mail: cameron.hall@alexandriava.gov
Assistant Fire Chief **Rudolph "Rudy" Thomas** . . . . (703) 746-5200
E-mail: rudolph.thomas@alexandriava.gov
Safety Officer **Jeffrey Merryman** . . . . (703) 746-5273
E-mail: jeff.merryman@alexandriava.gov
Deputy Fire Chief of Emergency Management and
Homeland Security **Corey Smedley** . . . . (703) 746-5200

Administrative Services

Tel: (703) 746-5200

Fire Personnel Commander **Amanda Jackson** . . . . (703) 746-5239
E-mail: amanda.jackson@alexandriava.gov
Administrative Division Chief **Matt Bosse** . . . . (703) 746-5262
E-mail: matt.bosse@alexandriava.gov
IT Coordinator **James Burke** . . . . (703) 746-5255
E-mail: james.burke@alexandriava.gov

Office of Building and Fire Code Administration

City Hall, 301 King St., Room 4200, Alexandria, VA 22314
Fax: (703) 838-3880

Director **Gregg Fields** . . . . (703) 746-4200
Deputy Director **(Vacant)** . . . . (703) 746-4183
Chief Fire Marshal **Russell Furr** . . . . (703) 746-4247

Training Division

1108 Jefferson Street, Alexandria, VA 22314
Fax: (703) 519-5946

Training Officer Battalion Chief **Tony Washington** . . . . . . (703) 746-4650
E-mail: tony.washington@alexandriava.gov
Training Captain **Jason Wehmeyer** . . . . (703) 746-4650
E-mail: jason.wehmeyer@alexandriava.gov
EMS Supervisor **Kelsea Bonkoski** . . . . (703) 746-4650
E-mail: kelsea.bonkoski@alexandriava.gov

Department of General Services
110 North Royal Street, Suite 300, Alexandria, VA 22314
Fax: (703) 519-3332

Employees: 69 **Fiscal Year:** 2016 **Budget:** $14,218,000

Director **Jeremy McPike** (D) . . . . (703) 746-4770
E-mail: jeremy.mcpike@alexandriava.gov
Deputy Director **Alfred Coleman** . . . . (703) 746-4770
E-mail: alfred.coleman@alexandriava.gov
Deputy Director of Facilities Construction and Planning **(Vacant)** . . . . (703) 746-4770 ext. 241
100 North Pitt Street, Room 307, Alexandria, VA 22314
Fleet Services Division Chief **Darrell Reynolds** . . . . (703) 519-5989
3550 Wheeler Ave., Alexandria, VA 22314
Fiscal Officer **Cole Fazenbaker** . . . . (703) 746-4770 ext. 248
Administration Division Chief **(Vacant)** . . . . (703) 746-4770

Office of Historic Alexandria
220 North Washington Street, Alexandria, VA 22314
Fax: (703) 838-6451 Internet: www.historicalexandria.org

Employees: 26 **Fiscal Year:** 2016 **Budget:** $3,686,000

Director **J. Lance Mallamo** . . . . (703) 746-4554
Education: SUNY (Stony Brook) BA; Hunter MUP

Archaeology
105 North Union Street, Suite 327, Alexandria, VA 22314
Fax: (703) 838-6491

City Archaeologist **Francine Bromberg** . . . . (703) 746-4399

Office of Housing
421 King Street, Suite 200, Alexandria, VA 22314
Tel: (703) 746-4990 Fax: (703) 706-3940
Internet: http://alexandriava.gov/housing/default.aspx

Employees: 15 **Fiscal Year:** 2016 **Budget:** $3,478,000

Director **Helen McIlvaine** . . . . (703) 746-4990
Education: Maryland BA; Rutgers JD
Deputy Director **(Vacant)** . . . . (703) 746-4990
Fiscal Officer **(Vacant)** . . . . (703) 746-4990
Administrative Division Chief **Eric Keeler** . . . . (703) 746-4990
E-mail: eric.keeler@alexandriava.gov
Landlord/Tenant Relations Division Chief **Melodie Seau** . . . . (703) 746-4990
Program Implementation Division Chief **Shane Cochran** . . . . (703) 746-4990
Client Intake Services **Juanita Norwood** . . . . (703) 746-4990

Human Resources Department
City Hall, 301 King St., Room 2510, Alexandria, VA 22314
Fax: (703) 838-3850 Internet: http://alexandriava.gov/HR

Employees: 25 **Fiscal Year:** 2016 **Budget:** $3,653,000

Director (Acting) **Steven J. "Steve" Mason, Jr.** . . . . (703) 746-3772
E-mail: steve.mason@alexandriava.gov
Benefits Division Chief **Penny Prue** . . . . (703) 746-3786
E-mail: penny.prue@alexandriava.gov
Total Compensation Assistant Director **Ryan Touhill** . . . . . (703) 746-3796
E-mail: ryan.touhill@alexandriava.gov
Employee Relations and Training Assistant Director **(Vacant)** . . . . (703) 746-3772

Human Rights Office
421 King Street, Suite 400, Alexandria, VA 22314
Fax: (703) 838-4976 Internet: http://alexandriava.gov/humanrights/

Employees: 6 **Fiscal Year:** 2016 **Budget:** $763,000

Director **Jean Kelleher Niebauer** . . . . (703) 746-3140

Information Technology Services
123 North Pitt Street, Suite 250, Alexandria, VA 22314
Tel: (703) 746-3001 Fax: (703) 519-3301
Internet: http://alexandriava.gov/Technology

Employees: 58 **Fiscal Year:** 2016 **Budget:** $10,173,000

Director and Chief Information Officer (Acting) **Laura B. Triggs** . . . . (703) 746-3001
E-mail: laura.triggs@alexandriava.gov
Education: Southwestern BBA
Deputy Director **(Vacant)** . . . . (703) 746-3001
Operations Division Chief **(Vacant)** . . . . (703) 746-3001
Database Management Division Chief **Curtis Ney** . . . . (703) 746-3001
E-mail: curtis.ney@alexandriava.gov
Network Management Division Chief **Kevin O'Shaughnessy** . . . . (703) 746-3001
Information Technology Project Management Division Chief **Marco Gorni** . . . . (703) 746-3001
E-mail: marco.gorni@alexandriava.gov
GIS Division Chief **Steven Chozick** . . . . (703) 746-3822

Library Department
5005 Duke St., Alexandria, VA 22304
Fax: (703) 746-1738 Internet: www.alexandria.lib.va.us/

Employees: 72 **Fiscal Year:** 2016 **Budget:** $7,220,000

Director **Rose T. Dawson** . . . . (703) 746-1701
E-mail: rdawson@alexandria.lib.va.us
Deputy Director **Renee DiPilato** . . . . (703) 746-1724
E-mail: rdipilato@alexandria.lib.va.us
Administrative Services Division Chief **Linda Wesson** . . . (703) 746-1701
E-mail: lwesson@alexandria.lib.va.us
Talking Book Service **Kym Robertson** . . . . (703) 746-1760
E-mail: krobertson@alexandria.lib.va.us
Communications Officer **Anton Murray** . . . . (703) 746-1770
E-mail: amurray@alexandria.lib.va.us
Information Technology Services Manager **(Vacant)** . . . . . . (703) 746-1780

Office of Management and Budget [OMB]
City Hall, 301 King St., Suite 3630, Alexandria, VA 22314
Fax: (703) 706-3991

Employees: 11 **Fiscal Year:** 2016 **Budget:** $1,297,000

Director **Morgan E. Routt** . . . . (703) 746-3737

Department of Planning and Zoning
City Hall, 301 King St., Room 2100, Alexandria, VA 22314
Tel: (703) 746-4666 Fax: (703) 838-6393
Internet: http://alexandriava.gov/Planning

Employees: 45 **Fiscal Year:** 2016 **Budget:** $5,677,000

Director **Karl W. Moritz** . . . . (703) 746-4666
Deputy Director, Urban Design **Jeffrey Farner** . . . . (703) 746-3803
Deputy Director, Strategic and Long Range Planning **(Vacant)** . . . . (703) 746-3802
Deputy Director, Land Use and Administration **(Vacant)** . . (703) 746-4646
Development Division Chief **Robert Kerns** . . . . (703) 746-3811
Land Use Services Division Chief **Alex Dambach** . . . . (703) 746-3829
Neighborhood Planning & Community Development Division Chief **Carrie Beach** . . . . (703) 746-3853
E-mail: carrie.beach@alexandriava.gov
Historic Preservation **Al Cox** . . . . (703) 746-3830

Department of Project Implementation
301 King Street, Alexandria, VA 22314

Director **Mitchell C. Bernstein** . . . . (703) 746-4500

Police Department

3600 Wheeler Avenue, Alexandria, VA 22304
Tel: (703) 838-4444 Fax: (703) 746-1945
Internet: http://alexandriava.gov/police/

Employees: 418 **Fiscal Year:** 2016 **Budget:** $60,854,000

Police Chief **Earl L. Cook** .... (703) 746-4700
Education: Duke BA
Investigations Bureau Deputy Chief
Capt. David Huchler .... (703) 746-6163
Administrative Services Bureau Deputy Chief **(Vacant)** ... (703) 746-1964
Patrol Operations Bureau Deputy Chief
Capt. Eddie Reyes .... (703) 746-1987
Fiscal/Fleet Management Division Chief
Brenda D'Sylva .... (703) 746-6224
Internal Investigations **Sgt Linda Erwin** .... (703) 746-6767
Technology, Data and Analysis Division Chief
Philip Antonucci .... (703) 746-6698
E-mail: philip.antonucci@alexandriava.gov
Operations Support Bureau Deputy Chief
Capt. Dianne Gittins .... (703) 746-6772
E-mail: diane.gittins@alexandriava.gov
Sector I Commander **Don Hayes** .... (703) 746-6800
Sector II Commander **(Vacant)** .... (703) 746-6800
Sector III Commander **Shahram Fard** .... (703) 746-6800

Real Estate Assessments

City Hall, 301 King St., Room 2600, Alexandria, VA 22314
Tel: (703) 746-4646 Fax: (703) 706-3979
Internet: http://alexandriava.gov/realestate/

Director **W. Bryan Page** .... (703) 746-4575
E-mail: bryan.page@alexandriava.gov
Deputy Director **(Vacant)** .... (703) 746-4646

Recreation, Parks and Cultural Activities

1108 Jefferson St., Alexandria, VA 22314-3999
Tel: (703) 746-5500 Fax: (703) 684-6826
Internet: http://alexandriava.gov/Recreation

Employees: 154 **Fiscal Year:** 2016 **Budget:** $22,344,000

Director **James B. Spengler** .... (703) 746-5500
Education: Virginia BA, MA; Texas (Arlington) MBA
Deputy Director, Recreation Services **William Chesley** ... (703) 746-5500
Deputy Director, Office of the Arts **Diane Ruttiero** ...... (703) 746-5500
Deputy Director, Park Operations **Dinesh Tiwari** .... (703) 746-5500
Public Relations, Special Events and Waterfront Division
Chief **Jack Browand** .... (703) 746-5504
E-mail: jack.browand@alexandriava.gov
Park Planning and Capital Projects Division Chief
Ron Kawaga .... (703) 746-5500

Transportation and Environmental Services Department

City Hall, 301 King St., Suite 4100, Alexandria, VA 22314
Tel: (703) 746-4025 Fax: (703) 519-3356
Internet: http://alexandriava.gov/tes/

Employees: 209 **Fiscal Year:** 2016 **Budget:** $39,245,000

Director **Yon Lambert** Room 4100 .... (703) 746-4025
Administration Division Chief (Acting)
Megan Cummings .... (703) 746-4025
Permits Supervisor **Wayne Lightfoot** .... (703) 746-4035
Infrastructure Right of Way/Transportation/Engineering
Section (Acting) **Lisa Jaatinen** .... (703) 746-4065
E-mail: lisa.jaatinen@alexandriava.gov
Resource Recovery & Waste Management Deputy
Director **Alton Weaver** .... (703) 746-4357
2900 Business Center Drive, Alexandria, VA 22314
Infrastructure/Environmental Quality **William Skrabak**
Room 3000 .... (703) 746-4065
Public Works Services Deputy Director **Jeffrey Duval** .... (703) 746-4357
2900 Business Center Drive, Alexandria, VA 22314

Alexandria City Public Schools

1340 Braddock Place, Alexandria, VA 22314
Fax: (703) 619-8091 Internet: www.acps.k12.va.us/

★ Chairman **Karen Graf** (District A) .... (703) 619-8019
Term Expires: December 31, 2018
E-mail: karen.graf@acps.k12.va.us
★ Vice Chairman **Christopher J. Lewis** (District C) .... (703) 619-8019
Term Expires: December 31, 2018
E-mail: christopher.lewis@acps.k12.va.us
★ Board Member **Cindy Anderson** (District B) .... (703) 619-8019
Term Expires: December 31, 2018
★ Board Member **Ronnie Campbell** (District C) .... (703) 619-8019
Term Expires: December 31, 2018
E-mail: ronnie.campbell@acps.k12.va.us
★ Board Member
William E. "Bill" Campbell (District A) .... (703) 619-8019
Term Expires: December 31, 2018
E-mail: bill.campbell@acps.k12.va.us
★ Board Member
Dr. Henry E. "Hal" Cardwell (District A) .... (703) 619-8019
Term Expires: December 31, 2018
★ Board Member **Ramee A. Gentry** (District C) .... (703) 619-8019
Term Expires: December 31, 2018
★ Board Member **Margaret Lorber** (District B) .... (703) 619-8019
Term Expires: December 31, 2018
★ Board Member **Veronica Nolan** (District B) .... (703) 619-8019
Term Expires: December 31, 2018
Clerk of the Board **Jennifer Abbruzzese** .... (703) 619-8314

Office of the Superintendent

1340 Braddock Place, Alexandria, VA 22314
Tel: (703) 619-8001

Superintendent **Alvin Crawley** .... (703) 619-8001
Fax: (703) 619-8091
Chief Student Services Officer **Julie Crawford** .... (703) 619-8034
Fax: (703) 824-6741
Executive Director of Specialized Instruction
Theresa A. Werner .... (703) 619-8023
Chief Academic Officer **Terri Mozingo** .... (703) 619-8020
Chief Operations Officer **Clarence E. Stukes** .... (703) 619-8097
E-mail: clarence.stukes@acps.k12.va.us
Chief of Staff **Tammy Ignacio** .... (703) 619-8001

City of Allentown, Pennsylvania

City Hall, 435 Hamilton St., Allentown, PA 18101
Internet: www.allentownpa.gov

County: Lehigh **Election Type:** Nonpartisan **Year Incorporated:** 1867
Population: 120,207 (2015)

Office of the Mayor

City Hall, 435 Hamilton St., Allentown, PA 18101
Fax: (610) 437-8730

★ Mayor **Edwin "Ed" Pawlowski** .... (610) 437-7546
Term Expires: January 1, 2018
Education: Moody Bible BA; Illinois MUP
Communications Manager **Mike Moore** .... (610) 437-7653
Special Assistant **Ismael Arcelay** .... (610) 437-7743

Office of the City Solicitor

City Hall, 435 Hamilton St., Allentown, PA 18101
Fax: (610) 437-8781

■ City Solicitor **Susan Ellis Wild** .... (610) 437-7545
E-mail: susan.wild@allentownpa.gov
Education: George Washington JD

★ Elected Official ▲ Appointed by Legislature ▼ Appointed by Governor ▶ Appointed by Board or Commission ● Appointed by Judge
■ Appointed by Mayor △ Appointed by Freeholders ▽ Appointed by Supervisor ▷ Appointed by County Executive ○ Appointed by Council

Office of the Managing Director

435 Hamilton Street, Allentown, PA 18101

■ Managing Director **(Vacant)** . . . . (610) 437-7781

Community and Economic Development Department

City Hall, 435 Hamilton Street, Allentown, PA 18101

■ Director **(Vacant)** . . . . (610) 437-7610
Operations Manager **(Vacant)** . . . . (610) 437-5981

Building Standards and Safety Bureau

City Hall, 435 Hamilton St., Allentown, PA 18101

Director **Carmen Dragotta** . . . . (610) 437-7690

Health Bureau

City Hall, 435 Hamilton St., Allentown, PA 18101

Director **Vicky Kistler** . . . . (610) 437-7760

Bureau of Planning and Zoning

City Hall, 435 Hamilton St., Allentown, PA 18101

■ Director **Shannon Calluori** . . . . (610) 437-7611
E-mail: Shannon.Calluori@allentownpa.gov

Finance Department

City Hall, 435 Hamilton St., Allentown, PA 18101

■ Director **Brent Hartzell** . . . . (610) 437-7500
E-mail: Brent.Hartzell@allentownpa.gov
Deputy Finance Director **Deb Bowman** . . . . (610) 437-7500

Fire Department

Public Safety Building, 425 Hamilton St., Allentown, PA 18101
Fax: (610) 437-7766

Fire Chief **Lee T. Laubach, Jr.** . . . . (610) 437-7765
E-mail: Lee.Laubach@allentownpa.gov

Human Resources Department

City Hall, 435 Hamilton St., Allentown, PA 18101
Fax: (610) 437-7675

■ Human Resources Deputy Director **John Marchetto** . . . . . (610) 437-7523
E-mail: john.marchetto@allentownpa.gov

Parks and Recreation Department

3000 Parkway Boulevard, Allentown, PA 18104
Fax: (610) 437-7796

■ Director **Lindsay Taylor** . . . . (610) 437-7628

Police Department

Public Safety Building, 425 Hamilton St., Allentown, PA 18101
Fax: (610) 437-8721

■ Police Chief **Keith Morris** . . . . (610) 437-7777
E-mail: keith.morris@allentownpa.gov
Assistant Police Chief, Operations **Glen Dorney** . . . . (610) 437-7755
E-mail: glen.dorney@allentownpa.gov
Assistant Police Chief, Support Services **Gail Struss** . . . . . (610) 439-5915

Public Works Department

City Hall, 435 Hamilton St., Allentown, PA 18101

Director of Public Works (Interim) **Craig Messinger** . . . . . (610) 437-7587

Building Maintenance Bureau

1825 Grammes Road, Allentown, PA 18103
Tel: (610) 437-7650

Facilities Manager **Don Hoegg** . . . . (610) 437-7650
E-mail: don.hoegg@allentownpa.gov

Recycling and Solid Waste Bureau

1400 Martin Luther King Jr. Drive, Allentown, PA 18102
Tel: (610) 437-8729

Manager **Ann Saurman** . . . . (610) 437-8729
Education: Penn State 1983 BS

Streets Department

1825 Grammes Road, Allentown, PA 18103
Tel: (610) 437-7638 Fax: (610) 437-8719

Streets Superintendent **Mark Shahda** . . . . (610) 437-7638
E-mail: mark.shahda@allentownpa.gov

Traffic Planning and Control Bureau

610 South 10th Street, 3rd Floor, Allentown, PA 18101
Tel: (610) 437-7735 Fax: (610) 437-7614

Traffic Control Superintendent **Nelson Varughese** . . . . (610) 437-7735

Water Resources Bureau

City Hall, 435 Hamilton St., Allentown, PA 18101
Fax: (610) 437-8744

Director **Jason Gruber** . . . . (610) 437-7646

Office of the City Council

435 Hamilton Street, Allentown, PA 18101

★ President **Ray O'Connell** . . . . (484) 866-0988
Term Expires: January 1, 2018
E-mail: ray.oconnell@allentownpa.gov
★ Vice President **Daryl L. Hendricks** . . . . (610) 437-7556
Term Expires: January 1, 2018
E-mail: daryl.hendricks@allentownpa.gov
★ Council Member **Candida Affa** . . . . (610) 437-7539
Term Expires: January 1, 2020
★ Council Member **Julio A. Guridy** . . . . (610) 906-7955
Term Expires: January 1, 2018
E-mail: julio.guridy@allentownpa.gov
★ Council Member **Roger J. MacLean** . . . . (610) 437-7539
Term Expires: January 1, 2020
★ Council Member **David McGuire** . . . . (610) 437-7556
Term Expires: January 1, 2020
★ Council Member **Cynthia Mota** . . . . (484) 951-3093
Term Expires: January 1, 2018
E-mail: cynthia.mota@allentownpa.gov
Education: East Stroudsburg BA; Pacific Oaks MA

Office of the City Clerk

City Hall, 435 Hamilton St., Allentown, PA 18101
Fax: (610) 437-8781

■ City Clerk **Michael Hanlon** . . . . (610) 437-7539
E-mail: michael.hanlon@allentownpa.gov

Office of the Controller

City Hall, 435 Hamilton St., Allentown, PA 18101

★ Controller **Jeff Glazier** . . . . (610) 437-7527
Term Expires: January 1, 2018
E-mail: jeff.glazier@allentownpa.gov

Allentown School District

P.O. Box 328, Allentown, PA 18105
Internet: www.allentownsd.org/

Superintendent of Schools **C. Russell Mayo** . . . . (484) 765-4230
Education: Old Dominion BS; Virginia EdD
★ President **David F. Zimmerman** . . . . (484) 765-4266
Term Expires: December 9, 2017
E-mail: zimmermand@allentownsd.org
★ Vice President **Ce-Ce Gerlach** . . . . (484) 765-4266
Term Expires: December 7, 2019
E-mail: gerlachc@allentownsd.org

★ Elected Official ▲ Appointed by Legislature ▼ Appointed by Governor ▶ Appointed by Board or Commission ● Appointed by Judge
■ Appointed by Mayor △ Appointed by Freeholders ▽ Appointed by Supervisor ▷ Appointed by County Executive ○ Appointed by Council

Allentown School District *continued*

★Member **Ellen B. Bishop** . . . . . (484) 765-4266
Term Expires: December 9, 2017
E-mail: bishope@allentownsd.org

★Member **Debra H. Lamb** . . . . . (484) 765-4266
Term Expires: December 9, 2017
E-mail: lambd@allentownsd.org

★Member **Elizabeth Martinez** . . . . . (484) 765-4266
Term Expires: December 7, 2019
E-mail: martineze@allentownsd.org

★Member **Audrey Mathison** . . . . . (484) 765-4266
Term Expires: December 7, 2019

★Member **Robert E. Smith, Jr.** . . . . . (484) 765-4266
Term Expires: December 7, 2019
E-mail: robertsmith.board@allentownsd.org

★Member **Charles Thiel** . . . . . (484) 765-4266
Term Expires: December 7, 2019

★Member **Mike Welsh** . . . . . (484) 765-4266
Term Expires: December 9, 2017

Secretary to the Board **Janet Morillo** . . . . . (484) 765-4266
E-mail: morilloj@allentownsd.org

City of Amarillo, Texas

City Hall, 509 E. Seventh Ave., Amarillo, TX 79101-2539
P.O. Box 1971, Amarillo, TX 79105
Tel: (806) 378-3000 (Information) Internet: www.amarillo.gov

County: Potter; Randall **Election Type:** Nonpartisan **Year Founded:** 1887 **Year Incorporated:** 1889 **Charter:** 1913
Population: 198,645 (2015)

Office of the Mayor and City Council

City Hall, 509 East 7th Avenue, Room 303, Amarillo, TX 79101
Fax: (806) 378-9394

★Mayor **Paul Harpole** . . . . . (806) 378-3010
Began Service: May 24, 2011
Term Expires: May 19, 2017
E-mail: mayor@amarillo.gov

★Council Member **Elisha Demerson** (Place 1) . . . . . (806) 353-2360
Term Expires: May 19, 2017
E-mail: Place1@amarillo.gov

★Council Member **Brian Eades** (Place 2) . . . . . (806) 355-6330
Term Expires: May 19, 2017
E-mail: place2@amarillo.gov

★Council Member **Randy Burkett** (Place 3) . . . . . (806) 358-9226
Term Expires: May 19, 2017
E-mail: Place3@amarillo.gov

★Council Member **Mark Nair** (Place 4) . . . . . (806) 290-1662
Term Expires: May 19, 2017
E-mail: Place4@amarillo.gov

Office of the City Manager

City Hall, 509 E. 7th Ave., Room 303, Amarillo, TX 79101
Tel: (806) 378-3014

○City Manager **Terry Lee Childers** . . . . . (806) 378-3011

Deputy City Manager **(Vacant)** . . . . . (806) 378-4222

Assistant City Manager for Development Services
Bob Cowell . . . . . (806) 378-4222
Education: Saint Louis U BS; Tennessee MUP

Assistant City Manager for Financial Services
Michelle C. Bonner . . . . . (806) 378-4209
E-mail: michelle.bonner@amarillo.gov

Office of the City Secretary

City Hall, 509 E. 7th Ave., Room 303, Amarillo, TX 79101

City Secretary **Frances Hibbs** . . . . . (806) 378-3014
E-mail: frances.hibbs@amarillo.gov

Rick Husband Amarillo International Airport

10801 Airport Boulevard, Amarillo, TX 79111-1211
Fax: (806) 335-1672

Director of Aviation **Sara A. Freese** . . . . . (806) 335-1671
Education: Central Missouri State BSAv, MS; Upper Iowa MBA

Deputy Director of Aviation **(Vacant)** . . . . . (806) 335-1671

Operations Manager **Tyler Hurst** . . . . . (806) 335-1671
E-mail: tyler.hurst@amarillo.gov

Operations Manager **Thomas Oscarsson** . . . . . (806) 335-1671
E-mail: thomas.oscarsson@amarillo.gov

Airport Police Commander **Greg Daniel** . . . . . (806) 335-4403
E-mail: greg.daniel@amarillo.gov

Administrative Technician **Kiley Navarrete** . . . . . (806) 335-1671

Community Services Division

Animal Management and Welfare

3501 S. Osage St., Amarillo, TX 79103
Fax: (806) 342-1565

Director **Richard Havens** . . . . . (806) 378-3070

Assistant Director **Christie Fisher** . . . . . (806) 378-6034

Environmental Health

821 S. Johnson St., Amarillo, TX 79101
Fax: (806) 378-9353

Director **Shaun May** . . . . . (806) 378-9472

Food Establishments and Complaints **Cora Bethel** . . . . . (806) 378-9472

Sanitarian IV **David Moody** . . . . . (806) 378-9472

Onsite Sewer Inspections Division Director **John Gates** . . (806) 378-9472

Public Health

1000 Martin Road, Amarillo, TX 79107
Fax: (806) 351-7275

Public Health Authority **Dr. Roger Smalligan** . . . . . (806) 351-7225

Director **Casie Stoughton** . . . . . (806) 351-7262

Assistant Director **(Vacant)** . . . . . (806) 351-7304

Transit System

800 E. 23rd Ave., Amarillo, TX 79103
Fax: (806) 378-6846

Manager **Judy Phelps** . . . . . (806) 378-6842

Fixed Route Operations Supervisor **Brett Lawler** . . . . . (806) 378-6860
E-mail: brett.lawler@amarillo.gov

Spec-Trans Operations Supervisor **Alan Terry** . . . . . (806) 378-6843
E-mail: alan.terry@amarillo.gov

Women's, Infant's, and Children's Nutrition Department [WIC]

411 S. Austin St., Amarillo, TX 79106
Fax: (806) 342-1577

Director **Margaret Payton** . . . . . (806) 371-1121

Office of Emergency Management

808 South Buchanan, Amarillo, TX 79101
Fax: (806) 378-9366 E-mail: amarillo.dem@amarillo.gov
Internet: http://oem.amarillo.gov/

Emergency Management Coordinator **Kevin Starbuck** . . . . (806) 378-3077
E-mail: kevin.starbuck@amarillo.gov

Assistant Emergency Management Coordinator
Chip Orton . . . . . (806) 378-9315
E-mail: chip.orton@amarillo.gov

Technical Hazards Coordinator **Brad Britten** . . . . . (806) 378-9377
E-mail: brad.britten@amarillo.gov

Administrative Assistant **Alice Ely** . . . . . (806) 378-3004
E-mail: alice.ely@amarillo.gov

★Elected Official ▲Appointed by Legislature ▼Appointed by Governor ▶Appointed by Board or Commission ●Appointed by Judge
■Appointed by Mayor △Appointed by Freeholders ▽Appointed by Supervisor ▷Appointed by County Executive ○Appointed by Council

Facilities Administration
823 S. Johnson St., Amarillo, TX 79101
Fax: (806) 378-9353

Facilities Manager **Jerry Danforth** .... (806) 378-4298
E-mail: jerry.danforth@amarillo.gov

Finance Division
City Hall, 509 E. 7th Ave., Room 303, Amarillo, TX 79101
Fax: (806) 378-3018

Assistant City Manager, Finance **Michelle C. Bonner** .... (806) 378-4209
E-mail: michelle.bonner@amarillo.gov
Director **Laura Storrs** .... (806) 378-6207
City Auditor **Valerie Kuhnert** .... (806) 378-3015
Internal Auditor **Yume Tao** .... (806) 378-4217
Secretary **Andrea McDonald** .... (806) 378-6213
E-mail: andrea.mcdonald@amarillo.gov

Purchasing
Purchasing Agent **Trent Davis** .... (806) 378-3570
E-mail: trent.davis@amarillo.gov
Assistant Purchasing Agent **Trae Kepley** .... (806) 378-3029
E-mail: trae.kepley@amarillo.gov
Senior Buyer **Lupe Quinonez** .... (806) 378-4214
E-mail: lupe.quinonez@amarillo.gov
Contract Buyer **Mickey Brown** .... (806) 378-6241
E-mail: mickey.brown@amarillo.gov

Utility Billing Office
Fax: (806) 378-3026

Manager **Jennifer Gonzalez** .... (806) 378-4241
Assistant Manager **(Vacant)** .... (806) 378-4271
Secretary **Shawna Hammonds** .... (806) 378-6251
E-mail: shawna.hammonds@amarillo.gov

Vital Statistics
Deputy Registrar **(Vacant)** .... (806) 378-9344

Information Technology
P.O. Box 1971, Amarillo, TX 79105
Fax: (806) 378-4278

Director **(Vacant)** .... (806) 378-3071
Manager **Tanya Champion** .... (806) 378-6216
E-mail: tanya.champion@amarillo.gov
Assistant Manager **Robert Rasmussen** .... (806) 378-6217
E-mail: robert.rasmussen@amarillo.gov

Fire Department
310 S. Van Buren St., Amarillo, TX 79101
Fax: (806) 378-3515 Internet: http://fire.amarillo.gov/
E-mail: afdinfo@amarillofire.com

Fire Chief **Jeff Greenlee** .... (806) 378-9360
E-mail: jeff.greenlee@amarillo.gov
Deputy Chief **Marc Lusk** .... (806) 378-9360
E-mail: marc.lusk@amarillo.gov
Deputy Chief **Sam Baucom** .... (806) 378-9360
E-mail: sam.baucom@amarillo.gov
Fire Marshal **(Vacant)** .... (806) 378-4238

Legal Department
City Hall, 509 S.E. 7th Ave., Room 303, Amarillo, TX 79101
Fax: (806) 378-5262 Internet: www.amarillo.gov/?page_id=140

City Attorney **(Vacant)** .... (806) 378-4208
Deputy City Attorney **Claud Drinnen** .... (806) 378-4208
E-mail: claud.drinnen@amarillo.gov
Assistant City Attorney **Bryan McWilliams** .... (806) 378-4208
E-mail: bryan.mcwilliams@amarillo.gov
Police Legal Advisor **(Vacant)** .... (806) 378-6067
Legal Assistant **Staci Gaffney** .... (806) 378-4208
E-mail: staci.gaffney@amarillo.gov

Prosecutor's Offices
201 SE 4th Ave., Amarillo, TX 79101

Assistant City Attorney **Pamela Denholm** .... (806) 378-3016
E-mail: pamela.denholm@amarillo.gov
Assistant City Attorney **Kerry Tilley** .... (806) 378-3016
E-mail: kerry.tilley@amarillo.gov
Assistant City Attorney **Sherryl L. Sanders** .... (806) 378-3016

Parks and Recreation Division
City Hall, 509 E. 7th Ave., Amarillo, TX 79101
P.O. Box 1971, Amarillo, TX 79105-1971
Fax: (806) 378-3021 E-mail: parks@amarillo.gov
Internet: www.amarilloparks.org

Director **Rod Tweet** .... (806) 378-4290
Assistant Director **Pat Westbrook** .... (806) 378-3037
Parks Superintendent **Clint Stoddard** .... (806) 378-6822
Athletic Supervisor **Andy Tarkington** .... (806) 378-6015
Recreation Supervisor **(Vacant)** .... (806) 378-9399
Office Manager **Sherylene Morris** .... (806) 378-9397

Golf Division
Comanche Trail Golf Course Professional
George Priolo .... (806) 378-4281
4200 S. Grand, Amarillo, TX 79103
Ross Rogers Golf Course Professional **Sherwin Cox** ..... (806) 378-3086
722 Northwest 24th Street, Amarillo, TX 79107

Police Department
200 SE 3rd Ave., Amarillo, TX 79101
Tel: (806) 378-9452 Internet: http://police.amarillo.gov/

Police Chief **Robert Taylor** .... (806) 378-3055
Assistant Chief of Police **Martin Birkenfeld** .... (806) 378-4252
Assistant Chief of Police **Col. Ken Funtek** .... (806) 378-4254
Detective Division Commander **Tam Boatler** .... (806) 378-4260
Support Services Division Commander
CAPT Brad Lancaster .... (806) 378-4269
Uniform Division Commander **(Vacant)** .... (806) 378-4255
Training and Personnel Director **Jim Burgess** .... (806) 378-6170
E-mail: jim.burgess@amarillo.gov
Computer Operations **(Vacant)** .... (806) 378-4212
Internal Affairs **Marvin Hill** .... (806) 378-4200

Crime Prevention/Public Information Office
Crime Prevention Coordinator **Brent Barbee** .... (806) 378-6147
Crime Prevention Coordinator **Cpl Jerry Neufeld** .... (806) 378-6148
Crime Stoppers Coordinator **Cpl Sean Slover** .... (806) 378-6100
Victim Assistance **Susy Valencia** .... (806) 378-6107

Public Services Division
City Hall, 509 East 7th Avenue, Amarillo, TX 79101

Assistant City Manager **(Vacant)** .... (806) 378-4222

Amarillo Civic Center Complex
Amarillo Civic Center Complex, 401 South Buchanan Street, Amarillo, TX 79101
P.O. Box 1971, Amarillo, TX 79105-1971
Tel: (806) 378-4297 Fax: (806) 378-4234
Internet: http://www.amarillociviccenter.com

General Manager **Sherman Bass** .... (806) 378-4247
Education: West Texas A&M

Amarillo Public Library
413 SE 4th Street, Amarillo, TX 79101-1523
P.O. Box 2171, Amarillo, TX 79189-2171
Tel: (806) 378-3054 TTY: (806) 378-9328 Fax: (806) 378-9327
Internet: www.amarillolibrary.org/

Library Director **Amanda Barrera** .... (806) 378-3050
E-mail: amanda.barrera@amarillolibrary.org
Assistant Director **Cindi Wynia** .... (806) 378-9330
E-mail: cindi.wynia@amarillolibrary.org

★ Elected Official ▲ Appointed by Legislature ▼ Appointed by Governor ▶ Appointed by Board or Commission ● Appointed by Judge
■ Appointed by Mayor △ Appointed by Freeholders ▽ Appointed by Supervisor ▷ Appointed by County Executive ○ Appointed by Council

Amarillo Public Library *continued*

Technical Services Coordinator **Melody Boren** .... (806) 378-9331
E-mail: melody.boren@amarillolibrary.org
Youth Coordinator **(Vacant)** .... (806) 378-3089

Building Safety
Tel: (806) 378-3041 Fax: (806) 378-3085

Building Official **Scott McDonald** .... (806) 378-3045
509 S.E. 7th Avenue, Room 105, Amarillo, TX 79101
Deputy Building Official **Randy Schuster** .... (806) 378-6258
509 S.E. 7th Avenue, Room 105, Amarillo, TX 79101
Deputy Building Official **Kevin Robinson** .... (806) 378-6258
509 S.E. 7th Avenue, Amarillo, TX 79101

Community Development
Fax: (806) 378-9389

Community Development Administrator **James Allen** .... (806) 378-3023
509 S.E. 7th Avenue, Room 104, Amarillo, TX 79101
E-mail: james.allen@amarillo.gov
Homeless Program Coordinator **Kathryn Foster** .... (806) 378-3005
509 S.E. 7th Avenue, Room 104, Amarillo, TX 79101
Rehabilitation Inspector II **Duane Bilderback** .... (806) 378-4206
509 S.E. 7th Avenue, Room 104, Amarillo, TX 79101
E-mail: duane.bilderback@amarillo.gov

Housing Assistance
Administrator **(Vacant)** .... (806) 378-4203
509 S.E. 7th Avenue, Room 104, Amarillo, TX 79101
Housing Assistant **Charissa Dowling** .... (806) 378-6282
509 S.E. 7th Avenue, Room 104, Amarillo, TX 79101
Housing Inspector **Billy Forbes** .... (806) 378-4204
509 S.E. 7th Avenue, Room 104, Amarillo, TX 79101
Housing Technician **Derrick White** .... (806) 378-4204
509 S.E. 7th Avenue, Room 104, Amarillo, TX 79101
Supportive Housing Coordinator **Umeka Johnson** ...... (806) 378-6281
509 S.E. 7th Avenue, Room 104, Amarillo, TX 79101

Human Resources Department
City Hall, 509 E. 7th Ave., Room 207, Amarillo, TX 79105
Fax: (806) 378-9478 Internet: http://www.amarillo.gov/?page_id=3137

Director **Clifton Beck** .... (806) 378-3090
E-mail: clifton.beck@amarillo.gov
Assistant Director **(Vacant)** .... (806) 378-6066

Risk Management
Risk Management Director **Jim Smith** .... (806) 378-3091
E-mail: jim.smith@amarillo.gov
Claims Administrator **Maria Gibbs** .... (806) 378-9310
E-mail: maria.gibbs@amarillo.gov
Safety Coordinator **Charles Sanchez** .... (806) 378-9315

Planning
509 S.E. 7th Avenue, Room 206, Amarillo, TX 79101
Fax: (806) 378-9388

Director **Kelley Shaw** .... (806) 378-3020
Senior Planner **Cris Valverde** .... (806) 378-6289

Public Works Division
City Hall, 509 E. 7th Ave., Room 210, Amarillo, TX 79101-2539
P.O. Box 1971, Amarillo, TX 79105-1971

Director (Interim) **Van E. Hagan** .... (806) 378-9337
Assistant Director **Van E. Hagan** .... (806) 378-3024

Utilities Division
City Hall, 509 E. 7th Ave., Room 101, Amarillo, TX 79105-1971
Fax: (806) 378-3027 Internet: www.amarillo.gov/?page_id=210

Director (Interim) **Floyd Hartman** .... (806) 378-4266
Assistant Director of Utilities, Operations and Maintenance **Floyd Hartman** .... (806) 378-9086
E-mail: floyd.hartman@amarillo.gov

Utilities Division *continued*

Assistant Director of Utilities, Projects and Environmental Programs **(Vacant)** .... (806) 378-9085
Chief Utilities Engineer **Jonathan Gresham** .... (806) 378-4265
E-mail: jonathan.gresham@amarillo.gov
Civil Engineer **Marco Bravo** .... (806) 378-4265
Civil Engineer **Melissa Guynes** .... (806) 378-3035
Civil Engineer **(Vacant)** .... (806) 378-9493
Resource Administrator **Sysavath Sysombath** .... (806) 378-9475
E-mail: sysavath.sysombath@amarillo.gov
Senior Projects Coordinator **David Mullins** .... (806) 378-9306

City of Anaheim, California

City Hall, 200 South Anaheim Boulevard, Anaheim, CA 92805
Tel: (714) 765-5100 (Information) Tel: (714) 765-4311 (Information)
Internet: http://www.anaheim.net

County: Orange **Election Type:** Nonpartisan **Year Founded:** 1857
Year Incorporated: 1857 **Population:** 350,742 (2015)

Office of the Mayor and City Council
City Hall, 200 South Anaheim Boulevard, Suite 733, Anaheim, CA 92805

★ Mayor **Thomas "Tom" Tait** .... (714) 765-5247
Began Service: December 7, 2010
Term Expires: December 2018
E-mail: ttait@anaheim.net
Education: Wyoming BS; Vanderbilt MBA, 1985 JD
★ Mayor Pro Tem **Lucille Kring** .... (714) 765-5247
Term Expires: December 2016
Education: Western State U San Diego JD
★ Council Member **Jordan Brandman** .... (714) 765-5247
Term Expires: December 2016
E-mail: jbrandman@anaheim.net
★ Council Member **Kristine L. "Kris" Murray** .... (714) 765-5247
Term Expires: December 2018
Education: Cal State (Long Beach) BA
★ Council Member **James Vanderbilt** .... (714) 765-5247
Term Expires: December 2018
Public Information Specialist **Erin Wahlen** .... (714) 765-5247

Office of the City Attorney
City Hall, 200 S. Anaheim Blvd., Suite 356, Anaheim, CA 92805
Fax: (714) 765-5123

○ City Attorney **Michael Houston** .... (714) 765-5169
E-mail: mhouston@anaheim.net
Education: Chapman BA; Vanderbilt JD
Senior Assistant City Attorney **Kristin Pelletier** .... (714) 765-5169
E-mail: kpelletier@anaheim.net

Office of the City Clerk
City Hall, 200 South Anaheim Boulevard, Suite 217, Anaheim, CA 92805

○ City Clerk **Linda Andal** .... (714) 765-5166
E-mail: landal@anaheim.net
Deputy City Clerk **Theresa Bass** .... (714) 765-5166
E-mail: tbass@anaheim.net

Office of the City Treasurer
Anaheim West Tower, 201 South Anaheim Boulevard, Suite 901, Anaheim, CA 92805
Tel: (714) 765-5117 Fax: (714) 765-5232

○ City Treasurer **Henry W. Stern** .... (714) 765-5117
E-mail: hstern@anaheim.net

★ Elected Official ▲ Appointed by Legislature ▼ Appointed by Governor ► Appointed by Board or Commission ● Appointed by Judge
■ Appointed by Mayor △ Appointed by Freeholders ▽ Appointed by Supervisor ▷ Appointed by County Executive ○ Appointed by Council

Office of the City Manager

City Hall, 200 South Anaheim Boulevard, Suite 733, Anaheim, CA 92805
Tel: (714) 765-5162 Fax: (714) 765-5164

○City Manager **Paul Emery** .... (714) 765-5165
Assistant City Manager (Interim) **Kristine Ridge** .... (714) 765-5094
Assistant City Manager **(Vacant)** .... (714) 765-4590
Deputy City Manager **Greg Garcia** .... (714) 765-5094
Audit Manager **Joe Romines** .... (714) 765-5056
External Affairs Manager **(Vacant)** .... (714) 765-5092

Anaheim City School District

1001 South East St., Anaheim, CA 92805-5749
Internet: http://www.acsd.us/

Superintendent **Dr. Linda Wagner** .... (714) 517-7500
★Board President **Bob Gardner** .... (714) 517-7500
Term Expires: December 11, 2016
E-mail: bgardner340@gmail.com
★Board Member **Jeff Cole** .... (714) 517-7500
Term Expires: December 31, 2018
E-mail: mbiconsulting@msn.com
★Board Member **Jackie Filbeck** .... (714) 517-7500
Term Expires: December 31, 2016
E-mail: tld1@pacbell.net
★Board Member **David Robert Heywood** .... (714) 517-7500
Term Expires: December 31, 2018
E-mail: dheywood@acsd.us
★Board Member **Ryan Ruelas** .... (714) 517-7500
Term Expires: December 31, 2018
E-mail: rruelas@acsd.us

Community Development Department

Anaheim West Tower, 201 South Anaheim Boulevard, 10th Floor, Anaheim, CA 92805

Community Development Director **John Woodhead** .... (714) 765-4332
E-mail: jwoodhead@anaheim.net
Deputy Community Development Director
Brad Hobson .... (714) 765-4319
E-mail: bhobson@anaheim.net
Community Development Manager **(Vacant)** .... (714) 765-4337
Community Investment Manager **David Gottlieb** .... (714) 765-4306
E-mail: dgottlieb@anaheim.net

Community Services Department

City Hall, 200 South Anaheim Boulevard, Suite 433, Anaheim, CA 92805

Director **Terry Lowe** .... (714) 765-5160
E-mail: tlowe@anaheim.net
Community Services Superintendent **Joe Perez** .... (714) 765-5244
E-mail: jperez@anaheim.net
Parks Manager **Larry Pasco** .... (714) 765-5155
Golf Operations Superintendent **Michael Lautenbach** .... (714) 221-2729
E-mail: mlautenbach@anaheim.net
Community Services Manager **Sjany Larson-Cash** .... (714) 765-5167
E-mail: slarson@anaheim.net

Anaheim Public Library

500 West Broadway, Anaheim, CA 92805
Tel: (714) 765-1880

City Librarian **Audrey Lujan** .... (714) 765-1810
E-mail: alujan@anaheim.net
Library Administration/Operations Manager (Acting)
Karen Gerth .... (714) 765-1728
E-mail: kgerth@anaheim.net

Convention, Sports and Entertainment

800 West Katella Avenue, Anaheim, CA 92802

Executive Director **Tom Morton** .... (714) 765-8920
Convention Center Manager **David Meek** .... (714) 765-8951

Finance

City Hall, 200 S. Anaheim Blvd., Suite 643, Anaheim, CA 92805

Director **Debbie Moreno** .... (714) 765-5195
Administrative Services Manager **Jean Ibalio** .... (714) 765-5195
E-mail: jibalio@anaheim.net
Risk Manager **David Nunley** .... (714) 765-4380
E-mail: dnunley@anaheim.net

Fire Department

Anaheim West Tower, 201 South Anaheim Boulevard, 3rd Floor, Anaheim, CA 92805

Fire Chief **Randy Bruegman** .... (714) 765-4032
E-mail: rbruegman@anaheim.net
Fire Marshal **Jeff Lutz** .... (714) 765-4042
E-mail: jlutz@anaheim.net
Deputy Chief **Rusty Coffelt** .... (714) 765-4014
E-mail: rcoffelt@anaheim.net

Human Resources and Labor Relations

Anaheim West Tower, 201 South Anaheim Boulevard, 5th Floor, Anaheim, CA 92805
Tel: (714) 765-5111

Director (Interim) **Chris Chase** .... (714) 765-5390
E-mail: CCHase@anaheim.net
Deputy Human Resources Director **(Vacant)** .... (714) 765-5210
Senior Personnel Analyst **Ed Cruz** .... (714) 765-5243

Planning Department

City Hall, 200 S. Anaheim Blvd., Suite 162, Anaheim, CA 92805
Tel: (714) 765-5139

Director **David Belmer** .... (714) 765-5010
Planning Services Manager **Jonathan Borrego** .... (714) 765-5016
Technology Development Manager **Lorri Gonzalez** .... (714) 765-5231
E-mail: lgonzalez@anaheim.net
Community Preservation Manager **Sandra Sagert** .... (714) 765-4413
Revenue and Licensing Supervisor **Sylvia Frias** .... (714) 765-5194

Police Department

425 S. Harbor Blvd., Anaheim, CA 92805

Police Chief **Raul Quezada** .... (714) 765-1986
Deputy Police Chief **Dan Cahill** .... (714) 765-1600
Deputy Police Chief **Julian Harvey** .... (714) 765-1600
Public Safety Public Information Officer **Eric Trapp** .... (714) 765-1521
E-mail: etrapp@anaheim.net

Public Utilities

Anaheim West Tower, 201 South Anaheim Boulevard, Suite 1101, Anaheim, CA 92805
Tel: (714) 765-5173 Fax: (714) 765-4138
Internet: www.anaheim.net/section.asp?id=54

General Manager **Dukku Lee** .... (714) 765-5173
Public Information Officer **Ruth Ruiz** .... (714) 765-5060

Public Works

City Hall, 200 S. Anaheim Blvd., Suite 276, Anaheim, CA 92805

Director **Natalie Meeks** .... (714) 765-5176
Financial and Administrative Services Manager
Edina Goode .... (714) 765-5176

Maintenance Department

955 S. Melrose Ave., Anaheim, CA 92805

Fleet and Facilities Services Manager **Julie Lyons** .... (714) 765-6800
Streets and Sanitation Manager **Ayumi Takayasu** .... (714) 765-6860

Field Services

Operations Manager **Dan DeBassio** .... (714) 765-6845

★Elected Official ▲Appointed by Legislature ▼Appointed by Governor ▶Appointed by Board or Commission ●Appointed by Judge
■Appointed by Mayor △Appointed by Freeholders ▽Appointed by Supervisor ▷Appointed by County Executive ○Appointed by Council

Design Services Division
City Engineer (Interim) **Rudy Emami** .... (714) 765-5148
E-mail: remami@anaheim.net

Development Services
Development Services Manager **Ed Fernandez** .... (714) 765-5176

Traffic and Transportation Services
200 South Anaheim Boulevard, Suite 276, Anaheim, CA 92805
Fax: (714) 765-5225

Traffic and Transportation Manager **Jamie Lai** .... (714) 765-5049
Principal Traffic Engineer **John Thai** .... (714) 765-5066
E-mail: jthai@anaheim.net

Municipality of Anchorage, Alaska
632 West 6th Street, Anchorage, AK 99501
P.O. Box 196650, Anchorage, AK 99519-6650
Tel: (907) 343-7100 (Information) Internet: www.muni.org

County: Anchorage **Election Type:** Nonpartisan **Year Incorporated:** 1920 **Population:** 298,695 (2015)

Office of the Mayor
P.O. Box 196650, Anchorage, AK 99519-6650
Tel: (907) 343-7100 Fax: (907) 343-7180

★ Mayor **Ethan A. Berkowitz** .... (907) 343-7101
Began Service: July 1, 2015
Term Expires: June 30, 2018
Education: Harvard 1983 AB; Cambridge 1986 MPH; Hastings 1990 JD
Executive Assistant **Sharon Lane** .... (907) 343-7100
Chief of Staff **Susanne Fleek-Green** .... (907) 343-7100
Deputy Chief of Staff **Ona Brause** .... (907) 343-7100
Communications Director **Myer Hutchinson** .... (907) 343-7100
Special Assistant/Press Assistant **Nora Morse** .... (907) 343-7100
Special Assistant **Amy Coffman** .... (907) 343-7100

Office of the Municipal Attorney
Tel: (907) 343-4545 Fax: (907) 343-4550

■ Municipal Attorney **William Falsey** .... (907) 343-4545
Education: Yale 2005 JD
■ Deputy Attorney **Deitra Ennis** .... (907) 343-4545
E-mail: ennisd@muni.org
■ Municipal Prosecutor **Seneca Theno** .... (907) 343-4250
E-mail: thenos@muni.org

Office of Management and Budget
P.O. Box 196650, Anchorage, AK 99519
Tel: (907) 343-4496 Fax: (907) 343-6998
Internet: www.muni.org/departments/budget/

■ Director **Lance Wilber** .... (907) 343-4281
Deputy Director **Marilyn Banzhaf** .... (907) 343-4281
E-mail: banzhafm@muni.org

Office of the Municipal Manager
P.O. Box 196650, Anchorage, AK 99519-6650
Fax: (907) 343-7140

■ Municipal Manager **Michael K. Abbott** .... (907) 343-7110
E-mail: abbottmk@muni.org
■ Executive Assistant **Joy P. Maglaqui** .... (907) 343-7120
E-mail: maglaquijp@muni.org

Airport, Merrill Field
P.O. Box 19665, Anchorage, AK 99519-6650
Fax: (907) 276-8421

■ Manager **Paul Bowers** .... (907) 343-6301
E-mail: bowerspd@muni.org
■ Assistant Airport Manager **Alex B. Jumao-As** .... (907) 343-6311
E-mail: jumaoasb@muni.org

Emergency Management
P.O. Box 196650, Anchorage, AK 99519-6650
1305 E Street, Anchorage, AK 99501
Fax: (907) 343-1441 E-mail: wwoem@muni.org
Internet: www.muni.org/departments/oem/

Office of Emergency Management Director
Kevin P. Spillers .... (907) 343-1401
E-mail: spillersk@muni.org

Employee Relations Department
632 West 6th Avenue, Suite 610, Anchorage, AK 99501
Tel: (907) 343-4425 Fax: (907) 343-4450
Internet: www.muni.org/departments/employee_relations/

■ Director **Karen L. Turner** .... (907) 343-4399
E-mail: useranb@muni.org
■ Labor Director **Candace Sherwood** .... (907) 343-4571
E-mail: sherwoodcm@muni.org
Employment Classification and Records Management
Director **Karen Norsworthy** .... (907) 343-4512
E-mail: norsworthykh@muni.org
■ Director of Benefits **Juna Penney** .... (907) 343-4514
E-mail: pennyjm@muni.org

Equal Opportunity Office
632 West 6th Street, Suite 620, Anchorage, AK 99501

■ Equal Opportunity Director **Heather MacAlpine** .... (907) 343-4897
Fax: (907) 343-4454

Fire Department
100 E. 4th Ave., Anchorage, AK 99501
Tel: (907) 267-4936 Fax: (907) 267-4977
Internet: www.muni.org/departments/fire/

■ Fire Chief **Denis C. LeBlanc** .... (907) 267-4936
E-mail: leblancd@muni.org Fax: (907) 267-4977
Division Chief, Administration **(Vacant)** .... (907) 267-4936
Division Chief, Operations **James Vignola** .... (907) 267-5091
E-mail: vignolajf@muni.org
Division Chief, Public Affairs **(Vacant)** .... (907) 267-4993
Fax: (907) 267-4977

Health and Human Services Department
825 L Street, Anchorage, AK 99501
Tel: (907) 343-6718 Fax: (907) 343-6740
Internet: www.muni.org/departments/health/

■ Director **Melinda Freemon** .... (907) 343-6460
E-mail: freemonm@muni.org Fax: (907) 249-7553
■ Deputy Director/Environmental Services Manager
Steve Morris .... (907) 343-6976
E-mail: morriss@muni.org Fax: (907) 249-7960
■ Medical Officer **Bruce Chandler** .... (907) 343-6723
E-mail: chandlerbp@muni.org
■ Cemetery Director **Robert Jones** .... (907) 343-6814
E-mail: jonesrg@muni.org Fax: (907) 343-6826
■ Public Health Initiatives and Partnerships Manager
Steven P. Ashman .... (907) 343-6147
E-mail: ashmansp@muni.org
■ Direct Services Manager **Natasha Pineda** .... (907) 343-6718

★ Elected Official ▲ Appointed by Legislature ▼ Appointed by Governor ▶ Appointed by Board or Commission ● Appointed by Judge
■ Appointed by Mayor △ Appointed by Freeholders ▽ Appointed by Supervisor ▷ Appointed by County Executive ○ Appointed by Council

Municipal Light and Power [ML&P]

1200 East 1st Avenue, Anchorage, AK 99501
Tel: (907) 279-7671 Fax: (907) 263-5828 Internet: www.mlandp.com

■ General Manager **Mark Johnston** .... (907) 263-5202
E-mail: johnstonma@muni.org Fax: (907) 263-5204
Chief Engineer **Gary Agron** .... (907) 263-5408
Fax: (907) 263-5321
Customer Service Manager **Beverly A. Jones** .... (907) 263-5316
Fax: (907) 263-5821
Chief Financial Officer **Mollie Morrison** .... (907) 263-5205
Fax: (907) 263-5888
Generation Manager **Eugene Ori** .... (907) 263-5339
Fax: (907) 263-5441
Operations Light and Power Superintendent
Timothy Prior .... (907) 263-5883
Fax: (907) 263-5472
Regulatory Affairs Manager **Mark Johnston** .... (907) 263-5825
Fax: (907) 263-5876
Systems/Communications Manager **Terrance Pearson** .... (907) 263-5220
E-mail: pearsonts@muni.org Fax: (907) 263-5890
Public Relations Manager **Julie Harris** .... (907) 263-5423

Police Department

4501 Elmore Road, Anchorage, AK 99507
Tel: (907) 786-8500 Fax: (907) 786-8510
Internet: www.muni.org/departments/police/

■ Police Chief **Christopher Tolley** .... (907) 786-8595
E-mail: ctolley@muni.org
Administrative Deputy Police Chief **Garry Gilliam** .... (907) 786-8647

Port of Anchorage

2000 Anchorage Port Road, Anchorage, AK 99501
Tel: (907) 343-6200 Fax: (907) 277-5636
Internet: www.portofanchorage.org/

■ Director **Stephen Ribuffo** .... (907) 343-6201
E-mail: ribuffos@muni.org
Education: Golden Gate 1987 MBA; Air Force Inst Tech 1988 MS
Deputy Port Director **Sharen Walsh** .... (907) 343-6203
E-mail: walshsa@muni.org
Engineer **Todd Cowles** .... (907) 343-6209
E-mail: cowlestc@muni.org
Director of External Affairs **Jim Jager** .... (907) 538-3277
Director of Operations/Maintenance/Security
Stuart Greydanus .... (907) 343-6202
E-mail: greydanussb@muni.org

Public Transportation Department

3600 Dr. Martin Luther King, Jr. Avenue, Anchorage, AK 99507
Tel: (907) 343-8402 Fax: (907) 343-4042
Internet: www.muni.org/departments/transit/

■ Director, Public Transportation **Jody Karcz-Banks** .... (907) 343-8484
E-mail: karcz-banksjm@muni.org
Operations and Maintenance Superintendent
Abul Hassan .... (907) 343-8294
E-mail: hassana@muni.org
Public Transportation Customer Service Manager
Will Brown .... (907) 343-4536
Communications Manager **Michelle Felix** .... (907) 343-8491
E-mail: felixmd@muni.org
Planning Manager **Christine Sondej** .... (907) 343-8490

Public Works Department

4700 Elmore Road, Anchorage, AK 99507

Director **Ron Thompson** .... (907) 343-8191
Deputy Director **Maury Robinson** .... (907) 343-8191
Street Maintenance Manager **Paul Vanlandingham** .... (907) 343-8277

Maintenance and Operations Department

3640 East Tudor Road, Anchorage, AK 99507
Tel: (907) 343-8340 Fax: (907) 343-8350

Deputy Director **Alan Czajkowski** .... (907) 343-8340

Project Management and Engineering

P.O. Box 196650, Anchorage, AK 99519-6650
Fax: (907) 343-8088

Director (Interim) **Jerry Hansen** .... (907) 343-8135
Deputy Director **Jerry Hansen** .... (907) 343-8135

Traffic Division

4700 Elmore Road, Anchorage, AK 99507
Tel: (907) 343-8406 Fax: (907) 343-8488

Municipal Traffic Engineer **Stephanie Mormilo** .... (907) 343-8406
E-mail: mormilosl@muni.org

Risk Management Department

632 West 6th Street, Anchorage, AK 99501
Tel: (907) 343-2529

Risk Manager **Connie J. Ernst** .... (907) 343-2529

Safety Department

632 West 6th Street, Suite 860, Anchorage, AK 99501
Tel: (907) 343-2521

Municipal Safety Manager **Anneliese Roberts** .... (907) 343-2521

Solid Waste Services

1111 E. 56th Ave., Anchorage, AK 99518
Tel: (907) 343-6262 Fax: (907) 561-1357
Internet: www.muni.org/departments/sws/

■ Director **Paul Alcantar** .... (907) 343-6262
E-mail: AlcantarPF@muni.org

Transportation Inspection Department

4501 Elmore Road, Anchorage, AK 99507
Tel: (907) 786-8525

Transportation Inspector **Eric Musser** .... (907) 786-8525

Water and Wastewater Utility

3000 Arctic Blvd., Anchorage, AK 99503
Tel: (907) 564-2700 Fax: (907) 562-3421 Internet: www.awwu.biz
E-mail: awwucustserv@awwu.biz

■ General Manager **J. Brett Jokela** .... (907) 786-5506
E-mail: brett.jokela@awwu.biz
Customer Service Director **Jayne Fritts** .... (907) 564-2727
Fax: (907) 562-0702
Engineering Director **Kurt Vause** .... (907) 564-2779
E-mail: kurt.vause@awwu.biz Fax: (907) 562-0824
Finance Director **Glenda Gibson** .... (907) 786-5623
Operations and Maintenance Director **Mark Spafford** .... (907) 550-5901
E-mail: mark.spafford@awwu.biz Fax: (907) 344-7325
Treatment Director **David A. Persinger** .... (907) 564-2799
Fax: (907) 786-5681

Office of the Chief Fiscal Officer

P.O. Box 196650, Anchorage, AK 99519-6650
Tel: (907) 343-6610 Fax: (907) 343-6616
Internet: www.muni.org/departments/finance/

■ Chief Fiscal Officer **Robert E. Harris** .... (907) 343-6610

Central Payroll

632 West 6th Street, Suite 710, Anchorage, AK 99501
Tel: (907) 343-6805 Fax: (907) 343-4400

Payroll Director **Cindy Becker** .... (907) 343-6805

★ Elected Official ▲ Appointed by Legislature ▼ Appointed by Governor ► Appointed by Board or Commission ● Appointed by Judge
■ Appointed by Mayor △ Appointed by Freeholders ▽ Appointed by Supervisor ▷ Appointed by County Executive ○ Appointed by Council

Controller Division
632 West 6th Street, Suite 710, Anchorage, AK 99501
Tel: (907) 343-6805

■ Controller **Thomas A. Fink** .... (907) 343-6926
E-mail: finkt@muni.org
Education: Bradley 1950 BS; Illinois 1952 JD

Information Technology Department
632 West 6th Avenue, Suite 430, Anchorage, AK 99501
Fax: (907) 343-6810 Internet: www.muni.org/departments/it/

Information Technology Director **Zal Parakh** .... (907) 343-6900
E-mail: ParakhZK@ci.anchorage.ak.us
Deputy Director **Gail Turner** .... (907) 343-6887
E-mail: turnerag@muni.org
Technology Services Manager **John Roberts** .... (907) 343-6903
E-mail: robertsjc@muni.org
Accounting Clerk **Edith Burden** .... (907) 343-6919
E-mail: burdene@muni.org

Property Appraisal Division
632 West 6th Street, Suite 300, Anchorage, AK 99501
Tel: (907) 343-6770

■ Assessor/Property Appraisal Division Manager
Bryant Robbins .... (907) 343-6770
E-mail: robbinsb@muni.org

Public Finance and Investments Division
632 West 6th Street, Suite 810, Anchorage, AK 99501
Tel: (907) 343-6610

Director **Ross Risvold** .... (907) 343-6610

Purchasing Department
P.O. Box 196650, Anchorage, AK 99519-6650
Fax: (907) 343-4595 E-mail: wwpur@muni.org

■ Purchasing Officer **Ron Hadden** .... (907) 343-4590
E-mail: wwpur@muni.org
Deputy Purchasing Officer **Dave Cloninger** .... (907) 343-4692
E-mail: cloningerd@muni.org

Treasury Division
632 West 6th Street, Suite 330, Anchorage, AK 99501
Tel: (907) 343-6663

■ Treasurer **Dan Moore** .... (907) 343-4092
E-mail: mooreda@muni.org

Community Development Department
4700 Elmore Road, Anchorage, AK 99507
Fax: (907) 343-8200
Internet: www.muni.org/departments/ocpd/pages/default.aspx

Director **(Vacant)** .... (907) 343-8301

Real Estate Department
P.O. Box 196650, Anchorage, AK 99519-6650
Tel: (907) 343-4334 Fax: (907) 343-4526
E-mail: wwmmhlb@ci.anchorage.ak.us

■ Director **Tammy Oswald** .... (907) 343-7533
E-mail: oswaldtr@muni.org

Anchorage Public Library
3600 Denali Street, Anchorage, AK 99503
Tel: (907) 343-2975

■ Director of Municipal Libraries **Mary Jo Torgeson** .... (907) 343-2975
E-mail: torgesonm@muni.org Fax: (907) 343-2817

Parks and Recreation Department
P.O. Box 196650, Anchorage, AK 99519-6650
Fax: (907) 343-6523

■ Director **John Rodda** .... (907) 343-4562
E-mail: roddajh@muni.org

Planning Department
P.O. Box 196650, Anchorage, AK 99519-6650
Tel: (907) 343-7909 Fax: (907) 343-7927

Director **Hal Hart** .... (907) 343-7909
Long Range Planning Manager **Carol Wong** .... (907) 343-7920
Current Planning Manager **Erika Mcconnell** .... (907) 343-7917
Chief of Inspections (Acting) **Gary Hile** .... (907) 343-8390
Lead Electrical Inspection Chief **Victor Fosburg** .... (907) 343-8330
Engineering Services Manager **Ross Noffsinger** .... (907) 343-8330
E-mail: noffsingerr@muni.org

Assembly
P.O. Box 196650, Anchorage, AK 99519-6650
Tel: (907) 343-4311 Fax: (907) 343-4313 E-mail: wwmas@muni.org
Internet: www.muni.org/departments/assembly/

★ Assembly Chair **Elvi Gray-Jackson** (District 4) .... (907) 343-4118
Term Expires: April 2017
E-mail: gray-jacksone@muni.org
★ Assembly Vice Chair **Dick Traini** (District 4) .... (907) 561-4526
Term Expires: April 2019
E-mail: trainid@muni.org
Education: Alaska BA, MPA
★ Assembly Member **Patrick Flynn** (District 1) .... (907) 278-8462
Term Expires: April 2017
E-mail: flynnpp@muni.org
★ Assembly Member **Amy Demboski** (District 2) .... (907) 688-2671
Term Expires: April 2019
E-mail: demboskia@muni.org
★ Assembly Member **Bill Starr** (District 2) .... (907) 694-5060
Term Expires: April 2017
E-mail: starrwe@muni.org
★ Assembly Member **Eric Croft** (District 3) .... (907) 343-4311
Term Expires: April 2019
Education: Stanford 1987 BS; Hastings 1992 JD
★ Assembly Member **Tim Steele** (District 3) .... (907) 277-7663
Term Expires: April 2017
E-mail: steelet@muni.org
★ Assembly Member **Forrest Dunbar** (District 5) .... (907) 343-4311
Term Expires: April 2019
★ Assembly Member **Pete Petersen** (District 5) .... (907) 240-1049
Term Expires: April 2017
E-mail: petersenp@muni.org
Education: Northern Iowa 1973 BA
★ Assembly Member **Bill Evans** (District 6) .... (907) 343-4311
Term Expires: April 2017
E-mail: evansb@muni.org
★ Assembly Member **John Weddleton** (District 6) .... (907) 343-4311
Term Expires: April 2019
▲ Municipal Clerk **Barbara A. Jones** .... (907) 343-4311
E-mail: jonesbar@muni.org
▲ Ombudsman **Darrel W. Hess** .... (907) 343-4461
E-mail: hessdw@muni.org

Internal Audit Department
632 West 6th Street, Suite 600, Anchorage, AK 99501
Tel: (907) 343-4438

Internal Audit Director (Acting) **Michael Chadwick** .... (907) 343-4438

★ Elected Official ▲ Appointed by Legislature ▼ Appointed by Governor ► Appointed by Board or Commission ● Appointed by Judge
■ Appointed by Mayor △ Appointed by Freeholders ▽ Appointed by Supervisor ▷ Appointed by County Executive ○ Appointed by Council

Anchorage School District

5530 East Northern Lights Road, Anchorage, AK 99504-3135
Tel: (907) 742-4000 Internet: www.asdk12.org

▶ Superintendent **Ed Graff** .... (907) 742-4312
E-mail: graff_ed@asdk12.org
Executive Assistant **Janet Hayes** .... (907) 742-4312
E-mail: hayes_janet@asdk12.org

City of Ann Arbor, Michigan

Larcom City Hall, 301 East Huron Street, Ann Arbor, MI 48104
Tel: (734) 794-6000 (Customer Service) Internet: www.a2gov.org

County: Washtenaw **Election Type:** Partisan **Year Founded:** 1824
Year Incorporated: 1851 **Charter:** 1956 **Population:** 117,070 (2015)

Office of the Mayor and City Council

Larcom City Hall, 301 East Huron Street, 3rd Floor,
Ann Arbor, MI 48104
Fax: (734) 994-8296 Tel: (734) 794-6161

★ Mayor **Christopher Taylor** (D)........................ (734) 794-6161
Began Service: November 10, 2014
Term Expires: November 2016
E-mail: CTaylor@a2gov.org
Assistant to the Mayor **Christine Schopieray** .... (734) 794-6161
★ Mayor Pro-Tem **John Eaton** (D-Ward 4)............... (734) 794-6161
Term Expires: November 2017
E-mail: JEaton@a2gov.org
★ Council Member **Sabra Briere** (D-Ward 1)............. (734) 794-6161
Term Expires: November 2017
E-mail: sbriere@a2gov.org
★ Council Member **Sumi Kailasapathy** (D-Ward 1) .... (734) 794-6161
Term Expires: November 10, 2016
E-mail: skailasapathy@a2gov.org
★ Council Member **Jane Lumm** (I-Ward 2)............... (734) 677-4010
Term Expires: November 2017
E-mail: jlumm@a2gov.org
★ Council Member **Kirk Westphal** (D-Ward 2) .... (734) 794-6161
Term Expires: November 2016
E-mail: KWestphal@a2gov.org
★ Council Member **Julie Grand** (D-Ward 3) .... (734) 794-6161
Term Expires: November 2016
E-mail: JGrand@a2gov.org
★ Council Member **Zachary Ackerman** (D-Ward 3) .... (734) 794-6161
Term Expires: November 2017
E-mail: ZAckerman@a2gov.org
★ Council Member **Graydon Krapohl** (D-Ward 4)......... (734) 794-6161
Term Expires: November 2016
E-mail: GKrapohl@a2gov.org
★ Council Member **Chip Smith** (D-Ward 5).............. (734) 794-6161
Term Expires: November 2017
E-mail: ChSmith@a2gov.org
★ Council Member **Chuck Warpehoski** (D-Ward 5) .... (734) 794-6161
Term Expires: November 2016
E-mail: cwarpehoski@a2gov.org

Office of the City Administrator

Larcom City Hall, 301 East Huron Street, 3rd Floor,
Ann Arbor, MI 48104
Fax: (734) 994-8297

○ City Administrator (Interim) **Tom Crawford** .... (734) 794-6110
E-mail: tcrawford@a2gov.org
Communications Director **Lisa Wondrash** .... (734) 794-6152
E-mail: lwondrash@a2gov.org

Human Resources Services

Larcom City Hall, 301 East Huron Street, 6th Floor,
Ann Arbor, MI 48104
Fax: (734) 994-5961

Human Resources Services Director **Robyn Wilkerson** ... (734) 794-6120
E-mail: rwilkerson@a2gov.org

Office of the City Attorney

Larcom City Hall, 301 East Huron Street, 3rd Floor,
Ann Arbor, MI 48104
Fax: (734) 994-4954

○ City Attorney **Stephen K. Postema** .... (734) 794-6170 ext. 3
E-mail: spostema@a2gov.org

Downtown Development Authority

150 South Fifth, Suite 301, Ann Arbor, MI 48104
Fax: (734) 997-1491

Executive Director **Susan Pollay** .... (734) 994-6697
E-mail: spollay@a2dda.org

Housing Commission

727 Miller Avenue, Ann Arbor, MI 48103
Fax: (734) 994-0781

■ President **Ronald C. Woods** .... (734) 794-6721
Note: Will continue to serve until reappointed or replaced
Term Expires: April 30, 2016
E-mail: ronald.woods@emich.edu
Education: Wittenberg 1969 BA; Michigan 1971 MA, 1974 JD
■ Commissioner **Timothy L. "Tim" Colenback** .... (734) 794-6721
Term Expires: April 30, 2018
■ Commissioner **Daniel Lee** .... (734) 794-6721
Term Expires: May 6, 2019
■ Commissioner **Audrey Wojtkowiak** .... (734) 794-6721
Term Expires: May 1, 2017
■ Commissioner **Gwenyth Hayes** .... (734) 794-6721
Term Expires: May 4, 2020
Executive Director **Jennifer Hall** .... (734) 794-6720

Community Services Administration

Larcom City Hall, 301 East Huron Street, 1st Floor,
Ann Arbor, MI 48104

Community Services Administrator
Derek Delacourt .... (734) 794-6000 ext. 43902
E-mail: ddelacourt@a2gov.org

City Clerk Services Unit

Larcom City Hall, 301 East Huron Street, 2nd Floor,
Ann Arbor, MI 48104
Fax: (734) 994-8296

City Clerk **Jacqueline Beaudry** .... (734) 794-6140
E-mail: jbeaudry@a2gov.org

Planning Services Unit

Larcom City Hall, 301 East Huron Street, 1st Floor,
Ann Arbor, MI 48104
Fax: (734) 994-8460

Planning Manager (Interim) **Ben Carlisle** .... (734) 794-6000

Parks and Recreation Customer Service Office

Larcom City Hall, 301 East Huron Street, 1st Floor,
Ann Arbor, MI 48104
Fax: (734) 994-8460

Manager **Colin Smith** .... (734) 794-6000 ext. 42500

★ Elected Official ▲ Appointed by Legislature ▼ Appointed by Governor ▶ Appointed by Board or Commission ● Appointed by Judge
■ Appointed by Mayor △ Appointed by Freeholders ▽ Appointed by Supervisor ▷ Appointed by County Executive ○ Appointed by Council

Financial Services Area

Larcom City Hall, 301 East Huron Street, 5th Floor, Ann Arbor, MI 48104

Chief Financial Officer (Acting)
Matt Horning .... (734) 794-6000 ext. 45444

Assessor Services Unit

Larcom City Hall, 301 East Huron Street, 5th Floor, Ann Arbor, MI 48104
Fax: (734) 997-1437

Assessor **David Petrak** .... (734) 794-6530
E-mail: dpetrak@a2gov.org

Financial/Budget Planning Unit

Larcom City Hall, 301 East Huron Street, 5th Floor, Ann Arbor, MI 48104
Fax: (734) 994-2777

Manager **Karen Lancaster** .... (734) 794-6500 ext. 45209
E-mail: klancaster@a2gov.org

Information Technology Unit

Justice Center, 301 East Huron Street, 1st Floor, Ann Arbor, MI 48104
Fax: (734) 994-3031

Manager **Thomas "Tom" Shewchuk** .... (734) 794-6550 ext. 45510
E-mail: tshewchuk@a2gov.org

Retirement Services Unit

532 South Maple, Ann Arbor, MI 48103
Fax: (734) 994-9205

Executive Director **Nancy Walker** .... (734) 794-6710
Pension Analyst **Daniel Gustafson** .... (734) 794-6710

Treasury Services Unit

Larcom City Hall, 301 East Huron Street, 5th Floor, Ann Arbor, MI 48104
Fax: (734) 997-1271

Treasurer **Matt Horning** .... (734) 944-2833

Public Services Administration

Larcom City Hall, 301 East Huron Street, 6th Floor, Ann Arbor, MI 48104
Fax: (734) 994-1816

Area Administrator **Craig Hupy** .... (734) 794-6310 ext. 43777

Customer Services/Call Center

301 East Huron Street, 1st Floor, Ann Arbor, MI 48104
Fax: (734) 794-6320

Supervisor **Jean Pearson** .... (734) 794-6310 ext. 43202

Field Operations Services Unit

4251 Stone School, Ann Arbor, MI 48108
Fax: (734) 794-6374

Manager **Molly Maciejewski** .... (734) 794-6000 ext. 43958

Fleet and Facilities Maintenance Services Unit

4251 Stone School, Ann Arbor, MI 48108
Fax: (734) 971-0079

Manager **Matt Kulhanek** .... (734) 972-9112
E-mail: mjkulhanek@a2gov.org

Project Management Unit

Larcom City Hall, 301 East Huron Street, 4th Floor, Ann Arbor, MI 48104
Fax: (734) 994-1744

City Engineer **Nick Hutchinson** .... (734) 794-6410 ext. 43633
E-mail: nhutchinson@a2gov.org

Systems Planning Unit

Larcom City Hall, 301 East Huron Street, 4th Floor, Ann Arbor, MI 48104
Fax: (734) 996-3064

Manager **Cresson Slotten** .... (734) 794-6430 ext. 43700
E-mail: cslotten@a2gov.org

Wastewater Treatment Services Unit

49 South Dixboro, Ann Arbor, MI 48105
Fax: (734) 971-9704

Manager **Earl Kenzie** .... (734) 794-6450

Water Treatment Services Unit

919 Sunset, Ann Arbor, MI 48103
Fax: (734) 994-0151

Manager **Brian Steglitz** .... (734) 794-6426

Safety Services Area

Police Department

Justice Center, 301 East Huron Street, 2nd Floor, Ann Arbor, MI 48104

Police Chief **Jim Baird** .... (734) 794-6921
Support Services Deputy Chief **Greg Bazick** .... (734) 794-6920

Office of Emergency Management

111 North Fifth Avenue, Ann Arbor, MI 48104

Director of Emergency Management **Rick Norman** ...... (734) 794-6980
E-mail: rnorman@a2gov.org

Fire Department

111 North Fifth Avenue, Ann Arbor, MI 48104
Fax: (734) 994-8814

Fire Chief **Larry Collins** .... (734) 794-6978
E-mail: lcollins@a2gov.org
Education: Franklin U

Assistant Chief **Ellen Taylor** .... (734) 794-6961
E-mail: etaylor@a2gov.org

City of Annapolis, Maryland

160 Duke of Gloucester Street, Annapolis, MD 21401
Internet: http://www.annapolis.gov

County: Anne Arundel **Election Type:** Partisan **Year Founded:** 1649
Year Incorporated: 1708 **Population:** 39,474 (2015)

Office of the Mayor

160 Duke of Gloucester St., Room 105, Annapolis, MD 21401
Fax: (410) 216-9284

★ Mayor **Mike Pantelides** (R) .... (410) 263-7997
Began Service: December 2, 2013
Term Expires: December 2, 2017
E-mail: mayor@annapolis.gov

■ Executive Assistant **Michele Cross** .... (410) 260-7997
E-mail: MCross@annapolis.gov

■ Ombudsman **Robert Agee** .... (410) 263-7997
Education: Western Maryland BA

(continued on next page)

★ Elected Official ▲ Appointed by Legislature ▼ Appointed by Governor ► Appointed by Board or Commission ● Appointed by Judge
■ Appointed by Mayor △ Appointed by Freeholders ▽ Appointed by Supervisor ▷ Appointed by County Executive ○ Appointed by Council

Office of the Mayor *continued*

- ■Community Relations Specialist **Jacalyn Bierman** . . . . (410) 263-7997
- ■Community Relations Specialist **Tara Hargadon** . . . . (410) 263-7997
  E-mail: thargadon@annapolis.gov
- ■Boards and Commissions Coordinator **Jacalyn Bierman** . . (410) 263-7997
- ■Small/Minority Business Enterprise Coordinator
  Consuella Caudill . . . . (410) 263-7939
  E-mail: CMCaudill@annapolis.gov

Public Information Office
160 Duke of Gloucester St., Annapolis, MD 21401
Fax: (410) 216-9284 E-mail: info@annapolis.gov

- ■Public Information Officer **Rhonda Wardlaw** . . . .(410) 263-7997
  E-mail: rwardlaw@annapolis.gov

Office of the City Attorney
160 Duke of Gloucester Street, Annapolis, MD 21401
Fax: (410) 268-3916

- ■City Attorney **Michael G. Leahy** . . . .(410) 263-7954
  E-mail: mgleahy@annapolis.gov

Office of the City Clerk
160 Duke of Gloucester Street, Annapolis, MD 21401
Fax: (410) 280-1853

City Clerk **Regina Watkins-Eldridge** . . . . (410) 263-7942
E-mail: rceldridge@annapolis.gov

Office of the City Manager
160 Duke of Gloucester St., Annapolis, MD 21401
Fax: (410) 216-9284

- ■City Manager **Thomas C. Andrews** . . . . (410) 263-7997
  E-mail: TCAndrews@annapolis.gov

Finance Department
160 Duke of Gloucester St., Annapolis, MD 21401
Fax: (410) 263-7529

- ■Director **Bruce T. Miller** . . . . (410) 263-7952
  E-mail: finance@annapolis.gov
  Education: Baltimore BA

Central Purchasing Office
145 Gorman Street, 2nd Floor, Annapolis, MD 21401
Fax: (410) 263-8120 E-mail: centserv@annapolis.gov

Procurement Officer **Brian D. Snyder** . . . . (410) 263-7997
E-mail: bids@annapolis.gov

Fire Department
1790 Forest Dr., Annapolis, MD 21401
Fax: (410) 268-1846

- ■Fire Chief **David L. Stokes, Jr.** . . . . (410) 263-7975
  E-mail: afdinfo@annapolis.gov

Emergency Management Department
199 Taylor Avenue, Annapolis, MD 21401

Director **Kevin J. Simmons** . . . .(410) 216-9167
E-mail: kjsimmons@annapolis.gov

Human Resources Department
145 Gorman Street, 2nd Floor, Annapolis, MD 21401
Fax: (410) 295-7999 E-mail: personnel@annapolis.gov

- ■Director (Acting) **Patricia L. Hopkins** . . . . (410) 263-7998
  E-mail: plhopkins@annapolis.gov

Department of Neighborhood and Environmental Programs
160 Duke of Gloucester Street, Annapolis, MD 21401

Director **Maria Broadbent** . . . . (410) 263-7946

Planning and Zoning Department
145 Gorman Street, 3rd Floor, Annapolis, MD 21401
Fax: (410) 263-1129 E-mail: planzone@annapolis.gov

- ■Director **C. Peter "Pete" Gutwald** . . . . (410) 263-7961
  E-mail: pgutwald@annapolis.gov

Police Department
199 Taylor Ave., Annapolis, MD 21401
Fax: (410) 268-9472

- ■Chief of Police **Michael J. Pristoop** . . . . (410) 268-9000
  E-mail: police@annapolis.gov

Public Works Department
145 Gorman Street, 2nd Floor, Annapolis, MD 21401
Fax: (410) 263-3322 E-mail: pubworks@annapolis.gov

- ■Director **David A. Jarrell** . . . . (410) 263-7949
  E-mail: pubworks@annapolis.gov
  Education: Ohio State BSCE; Purdue MSCE

Public Works Services Superintendent
Robert D. Couchenour, Sr. . . . . (410) 263-7967
935 Spa Road, Annapolis, MD 21401 Fax: (410) 263-7969

Utilities Superintendent **J. Michael Bunker** . . . . (410) 263-7970
935 Spa Road, Annapolis, MD 21401 Fax: (410) 263-7969

Water Plant Superintendent **James FitzGerald** . . . . (410) 224-2140
Fax: (410) 224-4627

Recreation and Parks Department
273 Hilltop Lane, Annapolis, MD 21403
Fax: (410) 626-9731 E-mail: recpark@annapolis.gov

- ■Director **Michael Morris** . . . . (410) 263-7958
  E-mail: mamorris@annapolis.gov
  Education: Old Dominion MEd

Transportation Department
308 Chinquapin Round Rd., Annapolis, MD 21401
Fax: (410) 263-4508

- ■Director **J. Rick Gordon** . . . . (410) 263-7964
  E-mail: transit@annapolis.gov

Office of the City Council
160 Duke of Gloucester St., Annapolis, MD 21401

- ★Alderman **Joe Budge** (D-Ward 1) . . . . (410) 260-3401
  Term Expires: December 3, 2017
  E-mail: aldbudge@annapolis.gov
- ★Alderman **Frederick M. Paone** (R-Ward 2) . . . . (410) 263-7942
  Term Expires: December 3, 2017
  E-mail: aldpaone@annapolis.gov
- ★Alderman **Rhonda Pindell Charles** (D-Ward 3) . . . . (410) 263-6857
  Term Expires: December 3, 2017
  E-mail: aldpindellcharles@annapolis.gov
- ★Alderman **Sheila M. Finlayson** (D-Ward 4) . . . . (443) 626-0071
  Term Expires: December 3, 2017
  E-mail: aldfinlayson@annapolis.gov
- ★Alderman **Jared S. Littmann** (D-Ward 5) . . . . (410) 268-3939
  Term Expires: December 3, 2017
  E-mail: jared@annapolisward5.com
  Education: Washington U (MO) BS; Maryland Law JD
- ★Alderman **Kenneth A. Kirby** (D-Ward 6) . . . . (410) 263-7997
  Term Expires: December 3, 2017
  E-mail: aldkirby@annapolis.gov
- ★Alderman **Ian M. Pfeiffer** (D-Ward 7) . . . . (410) 263-7997
  Term Expires: December 3, 2017
  E-mail: aldpfeiffer@annapolis.gov
  Education: Sonoma State 1995 BA; Rutgers 2005 MPA
- ★Alderman **Ross Arnett III** (D-Ward 8) . . . . (443) 745-2901
  Term Expires: December 3, 2017
  E-mail: aldarnett@annapolis.gov

★Elected Official ▲Appointed by Legislature ▼Appointed by Governor ▶Appointed by Board or Commission ●Appointed by Judge
■Appointed by Mayor △Appointed by Freeholders ▽Appointed by Supervisor ▷Appointed by County Executive ○Appointed by Council

City of Antioch, California

P.O. Box 5007, Antioch, CA 94531-5007
Internet: www.ci.antioch.ca.us

County: Contra Costa **Election Type:** Nonpartisan **Year Incorporated:** 1872 **Population:** 110,542 (2015)

Office of the Mayor and City Council

P.O. Box 5007, Antioch, CA 94531-5007
Internet: www.ci.antioch.ca.us/CityGov/CityCouncil.htm

★Mayor **Wade Harper** .... (925) 437-4300
Began Service: December 4, 2012
Term Expires: December 2016
E-mail: wharper@ci.antioch.ca.us

★Mayor Pro Tem **Lori Ogorchock** .... (925) 628-7764
Term Expires: December 2018
E-mail: logochock@ci.antioch.ca.us

★Council Member **Mary Helen Rocha** .... (925) 207-7220
Term Expires: December 2016
E-mail: mrocha@ci.antioch.ca.us

★Council Member **Tony Tiscareno** .... (925) 234-3639
Term Expires: December 2018
E-mail: ttiscareno@ci.antioch.ca.us

★Council Member **Monica Wilson** .... (925) 628-0749
Term Expires: December 2016
E-mail: mwilson@ci.antioch.ca.us

Administration Department

P.O. Box 5007, Antioch, CA 94531-5007
Tel: (925) 779-7000 Fax: (925) 779-7003
Internet: www.ci.antioch.ca.us/CityGov/Administration/

City Manager **Steven Duran** .... (925) 779-7011
E-mail: sduran@ci.antioch.ca.us

○City Attorney **(Vacant)** .... (925) 779-7015
Fax: (925) 779-7003

City Clerk **Arne Simonsen** .... (925) 779-7009
E-mail: asimonsen@ci.antioch.ca.us

Deputy City Clerk **Christina Garcia** .... (925) 779-7009
E-mail: cgarcia@ci.antioch.ca.us

Treasurer **Donna Conley** .... (925) 779-7005

Capital Improvements Division

P.O. Box 5007, Antioch, CA 94531-5007
Fax: (925) 779-7062
Internet: www.ci.antioch.ca.us/CityGov/CapitalImp/CIP/

Director **Ron Bernal** .... (925) 779-6950
E-mail: rbernal@ci.antioch.ca.us

Community Development Department

P.O. Box 5007, Antioch, CA 94531-5007
Fax: (925) 779-7034 Internet: www.ci.antioch.ca.us/CityGov/CommDev/

Director **Forrest Ebbs** .... (925) 779-7038
E-mail: febbs@ci.antioch.ca.us

Building Division

P.O. Box 5007, Antioch, CA 94531-5007
Internet: www.ci.antioch.ca.us/CityGov/CommDev/BldgDiv.htm#

Director **Forrest Ebbs** .... (925) 779-7065

Planning Division

P.O. Box 5007, Antioch, CA 94531-5007

Director **Forrest Ebbs** .... (925) 779-7038

Economic Development Department [EDD]

P.O. Box 5007, Antioch, CA 94531-5007
Internet: www.ci.antioch.ca.us/CityGov/Finance/EconDev/

Economic Development Manager **Lizeht Zepeda** .... (925) 779-6168
E-mail: lzepeda@ci.antioch.ca.us

Finance Department

P.O. Box 5007, Antioch, CA 94531-5007
Fax: (925) 779-7054 Internet: www.ci.antioch.ca.us/CityGov/Finance/

Finance Director **Dawn Merchant** .... (925) 779-7055
Assistant Finance Director **Jo Castro** .... (925) 779-7055

Purchasing Division

P.O. Box 5007, Antioch, CA 94531-5007
Fax: (925) 779-6817
Internet: www.ci.antioch.ca.us/CityGov/Finance/Purchasing/

Purchasing Clerk **Jo Castro** .... (925) 779-6134
E-mail: jcastro@ci.antioch.ca.us

Human Resources Department

P.O. Box 5007, Antioch, CA 94531-5007
Fax: (925) 779-7002
Internet: www.ci.antioch.ca.us/CityGov/Human-Resources/

Director **Michelle Fitzer** .... (925) 779-7020
E-mail: mfitzer@ci.antioch.ca.us

Information Systems Department

P.O. Box 5007, Antioch, CA 94531-5007
Internet: www.ci.antioch.ca.us/CityGov/Information-Systems/

Director **Alan Barton** .... (925) 779-6103

Recreation Department

P.O. Box 5007, Antioch, CA 94531-5007
Internet: www.ci.antioch.ca.us/LeisureSvcs/

Director **Nancy Kaiser** .... (925) 776-3050

Police Department

P.O. Box 5007, Antioch, CA 94531-5007
Internet: www.ci.antioch.ca.us/CityGov/Police/

Chief of Police **Allan Cantando** .... (925) 779-6902

Public Works Department

P.O. Box 5007, Antioch, CA 94531-5007
Fax: (925) 779-6897 Internet: www.ci.antioch.ca.us/CityGov/PublicWorks/

Director **Ron Bernal** .... (925) 779-6820
Operations Deputy Director **Mike Bechtholdt** .... (925) 779-6953
E-mail: mbechtholdt@ci.antioch.ca.us
Sewer Collections Superintendent **Brandon Chalk** .... (925) 779-6962
Water Distribution Superintendent **Adam Molinar** .... (925) 779-6952
Treatment Plant **Duane Anderson** .... (925) 779-7027

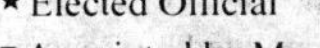
★Elected Official ▲Appointed by Legislature ▼Appointed by Governor ▶Appointed by Board or Commission ●Appointed by Judge
■Appointed by Mayor △Appointed by Freeholders ▽Appointed by Supervisor ▷Appointed by County Executive ○Appointed by Council

City of Arlington, Texas

101 West Abram Street, Arlington, TX 76010
P.O. Box 90231, Arlington, TX 76004-0231
Tel: (817) 275-3271 (Information) Internet: www.arlington-tx.gov

County: Tarrant **Election Type:** Nonpartisan **Year Founded:** 1875
Year Incorporated: 1884 **Charter:** 1920 **Population:** 388,125 (2015)

Office of the Mayor and City Council

P.O. Box 90231, Arlington, TX 76004-0231
Fax: (817) 459-6120

★Mayor **Jeff Williams** .... (817) 459-6121
Began Service: May 26, 2015
Term Expires: May 26, 2017
Assistant to the Mayor **Angie Summers** .... (817) 459-6121
E-mail: angie.summers@arlingtontx.gov
★Mayor Pro Tem **Sheri Capehart** (District 2) .... (817) 459-6141
Term Expires: May 31, 2018
E-mail: sheri.capehart@arlingtontx.gov
★Deputy Mayor Pro Tem **Lana Wolff** (District 5) .... (817) 459-6141
Term Expires: May 31, 2017
E-mail: lana.wolff@arlingtontx.gov
★Council Member **Charlie Parker** (District 1) .... (817) 459-6141
Term Expires: May 31, 2018
E-mail: charlie.parker@arlingtontx.gov
★Council Member **Robert Rivera** (District 3) .... (817) 459-6143
Term Expires: May 31, 2017
E-mail: robert.rivera@arlingtontx.gov
Education: Texas (Arlington) BA
★Council Member **Kathryn Wilemon** (District 4) .... (817) 459-6141
Term Expires: May 31, 2017
E-mail: kathryn.wilemon@arlingtontx.gov
★Council Member **Victoria Farrar-Myers** (At-Large) .... (817) 459-6143
Term Expires: May 31, 2018
★Council Member **Michael Glaspie** (At-Large) .... (817) 459-6143
Term Expires: May 31, 2017
E-mail: michael.glaspie@arlingtontx.gov
★Council Member **Robert Shepard** (At-Large) .... (817) 459-6141
Term Expires: May 31, 2018
E-mail: robert.shepard@arlingtontx.gov
Director of Management Resources
Jennifer Wichmann .... (817) 459-6408
E-mail: jennifer.wichmann@arlingtontx.gov Fax: (817) 459-6410

Office of the City Attorney

101 South Mesquite Street, Suite 300, MS 63-0300, Arlington, TX 76010
P.O. Box 90231, Arlington, TX 76004-0231
Fax: (817) 459-6897

○City Attorney **Teris Solis** .... (817) 459-6878
E-mail: teris.solis@arlingtontx.gov
Assistant City Attorney, Municipal Law **David Barber** .... (817) 459-6878
Citizen Services Assistant City Attorney
Ursula Monroe Patterson .... (817) 459-6878
E-mail: ursula.patterson@arlingtontx.gov
Discipline Assistant City Attorney **(Vacant)** .... (817) 459-6878
Collections (Acting) **Ursula Monroe Patterson** .... (817) 459-6878
Land Use **Ken Bennett** .... (817) 459-6878
Chief Prosecutor **David Johnson** .... (817) 459-6878
Prosecutor **Matt Dixon** .... (817) 459-6878
Prosecutor **Sam Hawk** .... (817) 459-6878
Prosecutor **Ava Mathis** .... (817) 459-6878
Prosecutor **Steven Meyer** .... (817) 459-6878
Litigation/Employment Assistant City Attorney **(Vacant)** .... (817) 459-6878
Employment **Pamela Johnson** .... (817) 459-6878
E-mail: pamela.hutson@arlingtontx.gov
Litigation **Robert Fugate** .... (817) 459-6878
E-mail: robert.fugate@arlingtontx.gov
Litigation **Elisabeth Kaylor** .... (817) 459-6878
Police Legal Advisor **Tiffany Bull** .... (817) 459-5329
Assistant Police Legal Advisor **Sarah Martin** .... (817) 459-6878

Office of the City Attorney *continued*

Contracts **Eddie Martin** .... (817) 459-6878
Contracts **Christina Weber** .... (817) 459-6878
Economic Development **Molly Shortall** .... (817) 457-6878

Office of the City Auditor

101 West Abram Street, Third Floor, Arlington, TX 76010
Fax: (817) 459-6180 Internet: www.arlingtontx.gov/cityauditor/index.html

City Auditor **Lori Brooks** .... (817) 459-6243
Assistant City Auditor **Susan Edwards** .... (817) 459-6243

Office of the City Manager

P.O. Box 90231, Arlington, TX 76004-3231
Tel: (817) 459-6100 Fax: (817) 459-6116

○City Manager **Trey Yelverton** .... (817) 459-6101
E-mail: trey.yelverton@arlingtontx.gov
Administrative Services Coordinator **Donna King** .... (817) 459-6101
E-mail: donna.king@arlingtontx.gov
Deputy City Manager **Dr. Theron Bowman** .... (817) 459-6105
E-mail: theron.bowman@arlingtontx.gov
Education: Texas (Arlington) 1997 PhD
Deputy City Manager **James "Jim" Parajon** .... (817) 459-6103
E-mail: jim.parajon@arlingtontx.gov
Deputy City Manager **Gilbert Perales** .... (817) 459-6111
E-mail: gilbert.perales@arlingtontx.gov

Office of the City Secretary

MS 01-0360, P.O. Box 90231, Arlington, TX 76004-3231
Tel: (817) 459-6186 Fax: (817) 459-6189

City Secretary **Mary Supino** .... (817) 459-6188
E-mail: mary.supino@arlingtontx.gov

Arlington Housing Authority [AHA]

501 West Sanford Street, Suite 20, Mail Stop 28-0100,
Arlington, TX 76011
P.O. Box 90231, Arlington, TX 76004-3231
Fax: (682) 367-1020

Executive Director **David Zappasodi** .... (817) 276-6790

Arlington Municipal Airport

5000 South Collins Street, Arlington, TX 76018
Fax: (817) 466-8653

Airport Manager **Karen Vanwinkle** .... (817) 459-5559

Arlington Public Library

101 E. Abram St., Arlington, TX 76010
Tel: (817) 459-6900 Fax: (817) 459-6936
Internet: www.arlingtonlibrary.org/

Director **(Vacant)** .... (817) 459-6916

Bob Duncan Center

2800 S. Center St., Arlington, TX 76014
Fax: (817) 465-6663

Facility Administrator **Michael Debrecht** .... (817) 465-6661 ext. 8283
E-mail: michael.debrecht@arlingtontx.gov

Community Development and Planning Department

P.O. Box 90231, Arlington, TX 76004-3231
Tel: (817) 459-6502 Fax: (817) 459-6669

Director (Interim) **James "Jim" Parajon** .... (817) 459-6666
E-mail: jim.parajon@arlingtontx.gov

★Elected Official ▲Appointed by Legislature ▼Appointed by Governor ▶Appointed by Board or Commission ●Appointed by Judge
■Appointed by Mayor △Appointed by Freeholders ▽Appointed by Supervisor ▷Appointed by County Executive ○Appointed by Council

Environmental Services Department

P.O. Box 90231, Arlington, TX 76004-0231
Fax: (817) 459-6585

Recycling Coordinator **Lorrie Anderle** . . . . (817) 459-6778

Finance Department

101 South Mesquite Street, #800, Arlington, TX 76010
P.O. Box 90231, Arlington, TX 76004-3231
Tel: (817) 459-6300 Fax: (817) 459-6315
E-mail: finance@arlingtontx.gov

Director of Finance/Chief Financial Officer
Michael Finley . . . . (817) 459-6345
E-mail: mike.finley@arlingtontx.gov
Education: Texas A&M 1989 BA, 1993 MPA

Office of Communication

P.O. Box 90231, Arlington, TX 76004-3231

Marketing and Communications Manager **Jay Warren** . . . . (817) 459-6412
E-mail: jay.warren@arlingtontx.gov

Purchasing Division

101 South Mesquite, 8th Floor, Arlington, TX 76010
Fax: (817) 459-6334 E-mail: purch@arlingtontx.gov

Purchasing Manager **Debra K. Carrejo** . . . . (817) 459-6305
E-mail: debra.carrejo@arlingtontx.gov

Fire Department

P.O. Box 90231, Arlington, TX 76004-3231
Fax: (817) 459-5507 Internet: http://www.arlington-tx.gov/fire/

Fire Chief **Don Crowson** . . . . (817) 459-5505
E-mail: don.crowson@arlingtontx.gov
Fire Rescue Assistant Chief **Bill McQuatters** . . . . (817) 459-5500
E-mail: bill.mcquatters@arlingtontx.gov
Fire Administration Assistant Chief **Jim Self** . . . . (817) 459-5500
E-mail: jim.self@arlingtontx.gov
Fire Rescue Support Assistant Chief **David Stapp** . . . . (817) 459-5500
E-mail: david.stapp@arlingtontx.gov
Emergency Operations Administrator **Irish Hancock** . . . . (817) 459-6942
E-mail: irish.hancock@arlingtontx.gov

Human Resources Department

101 South Mesquite Street, Suite 790, Arlington, TX 76004
P.O. Box 90231, Arlington, TX 76004
Tel: (817) 459-6869 Fax: (817) 459-6870
E-mail: careers@ci.arlington.tx.us

Director **Kari Zika** . . . . (817) 459-6869
E-mail: kari.zika@arlingtontx.gov

Information Technology Department

101 South Mesquite Street, 5th Floor, Arlington, TX 76010
Tel: (817) 459-6700 Fax: (817) 459-6702

Information Technology Director **Dennis John** . . . . (817) 459-6700
E-mail: dennis.john@arlingtontx.gov

Parks and Recreation Department

717 W. Main St., Arlington, TX 76013
P.O. Box 90231, Arlington, TX 76004-3231
Fax: (817) 459-5495 E-mail: parksdepartment@arlingtontx.gov
Internet: www.naturallyfun.org

Director **Lemuel Randolph** . . . . (817) 459-5474

Police Department

620 W. Division St., Arlington, TX 76011
Tel: (817) 459-5600 Fax: (817) 459-5722
E-mail: policeadmin@arlingtontx.gov

Police Chief **Will Johnson** . . . . (817) 459-5717
Assistant Chief, Field Operations **Kevin F. Colbye** . . . . (817) 459-5621
Assistant Chief, Support Operations **Jaime Ayala** . . . . (817) 459-5718

Police Department *continued*

Deputy Chief **Os Flores** . . . . (817) 459-5713
Deputy Chief **Jeff Matthews** . . . . (817) 459-6042
Deputy Chief **David McGinty** . . . . (817) 459-5583
Deputy Chief **Jeff Petty** . . . . (817) 459-5616

Department of Public Works and Transportation

P.O. Box 90231, Arlington, TX 76004-3231
Tel: (817) 459-6550 Fax: (817) 459-6585
E-mail: publicworks@arlingtontx.gov
Internet: www.arlingtontx.gov/publicworks/

Director **Keith Melton** . . . . (817) 459-6354
Education: Texas (Arlington) 1983 BSCE
Assistant Director for Engineering and Construction
David Wynn . . . . (817) 459-6560
E-mail: David.Wynn@arlingtontx.gov
Assistant Director for Operations **Mindy Carmichael** . . . . (817) 459-6553
E-mail: mindy.carmichael@arlingtontx.gov
Education: Texas BSCE
Assistant Director for Support Services **Nora Coronado** . . (817) 459-6564
Special Projects Manager **Keith Brooks** . . . . (817) 459-6534
Traffic Operations Manager **(Vacant)** . . . . (817) 459-5401
Street Superintendent **Bill Bateman** . . . . (817) 459-5435
Administrative Manager **Juanita Bridges** . . . . (817) 459-6578
E-mail: juanita.bridges@arlingtontx.gov
Education: Texas Wesleyan U 1991 BBA, 1998 MBA
Construction Manager **Alf Bumgardner** . . . . (817) 459-6558
E-mail: alf.bumgardner@arlingtontx.gov
Engineering Operations Manager **Keith Brooks** . . . . (817) 459-6552
E-mail: keith.brooks@arlingtontx.gov
Fleet Manager **Tom Jelley** . . . . (817) 459-5451

Water Utilities

101 West Abram Street, 2nd Floor, Arlington, TX 76010
P.O. Box 90231, Arlington, TX 76004-0231
Fax: (817) 459-6626 Internet: www.arlingtontx.gov/water/index.html

Director **Walter "Buzz" Pishkur** . . . . (817) 459-6603
Assistant Director, Water Utilities Operations
Darryl Westbrook . . . . (817) 459-6601
E-mail: darryl.westbrook@arlingtontx.gov
Assistant Director, Water Utilities Engineering
Brad Franklin . . . . (817) 459-6632
E-mail: brad.franklin@arlingtontx.gov
Assistant Director/Treatment **Craig M. Cummings** . . . . (817) 457-7550
Information Services Manager **Bob Lemus** . . . . (817) 457-6604
E-mail: robert.lemus@arlingtontx.gov

Arlington Independent School District [AISD]

1203 W. Pioneer Prkwy., Arlington, TX 76013
Tel: (682) 867-4611 Fax: (817) 459-7286 E-mail: pio@aisd.net
Internet: http://www.aisd.net

Superintendent of Schools **Dr. Marcelo Cavazos** . . . . (682) 867-7344
Chief Academic Officer **Dr. Steven Wurtz** . . . . (682) 867-7300
Chief Financial Officer **Cindy Powell** . . . . (682) 867-7243
Assistant Superintendent/Technology **Chad Branum** . . . . (682) 867-7314
E-mail: cbranum@aisd.net
★ President **Jamie Sullins** (Place 5) . . . . (817) 692-1799
Term Expires: May 1, 2019
E-mail: JamieSullins.AISD@gmail.com
★ Vice President **Dr. Aaron D. Reich** (Place 3) . . . . (817) 277-5498
Term Expires: May 1, 2018
E-mail: areich.aisd@tx.rr.com
★ Secretary **John Hibbs** (Place 4) . . . . (817) 478-3049
Term Expires: May 1, 2019
E-mail: hibbsaisd@gmail.com
★ Board Member **Bowie Hogg** (Place 6) . . . . (817) 565-2636
Term Expires: May 1, 2017 Fax: (817) 459-7299
E-mail: bowie@bowiehogg.com

(continued on next page)

★ Elected Official ▲ Appointed by Legislature ▼ Appointed by Governor ► Appointed by Board or Commission ● Appointed by Judge
■ Appointed by Mayor △ Appointed by Freeholders ▽ Appointed by Supervisor ▷ Appointed by County Executive ○ Appointed by Council

Arlington Independent School District *continued*

★ Board Member **Kristen Hudson** (Place 2) .... (682) 793-6423
Term Expires: May 2018 Fax: (817) 459-7299
E-mail: kristenhudsonAISD@gmail.com

★ Board Member **Kecia Mays** (Place 7) .... (972) 814-3098
Term Expires: May 2017
E-mail: keciaforarlington@gmail.com

★ Board Member **Polly Walton** (Place 1) .... (817) 261-1729
Term Expires: May 2018 Fax: (817) 459-7299
E-mail: pollywalton.aisd@gmail.com

City of Arvada, Colorado

P.O. Box 8101, Arvada, CO 80001-8101
Internet: www.arvada.org

County: Adams and Jefferson **Election Type:** Nonpartisan
Year Incorporated: 1904 **Population:** 115,368 (2015)

Office of the Mayor and City Council

P.O. Box 8101, Arvada, CO 80001-8101

★ Mayor **Marc Williams** .... (720) 898-7500
Began Service: November 7, 2011
Term Expires: November 2019
E-mail: mwilliams@arvada.org

★ Mayor Pro Tem **Bob Fifer** (At-Large) .... (720) 898-7500
Term Expires: November 2019
E-mail: bfifer@arvada.org

★ Council Member **Nancy Ford** (District 1) .... (303) 810-0571
Term Expires: November 2019
E-mail: nford@arvada.org

★ Council Member **Mark McGoff** (District 2) .... (720) 898-7500
Term Expires: November 2019
E-mail: mmcgoff@arvada.org

★ Council Member **John Marriott** (District 3) .... (720) 898-7500
Term Expires: November 4, 2017
E-mail: jmarriott@arvada.org

★ Council Member **David Jones** (District 4) .... (720) 898-7500
Term Expires: November 2019
E-mail: djones@arvada.org

★ Council Member **Don Allard** (At-Large) .... (720) 898-7500
Term Expires: November 4, 2017
E-mail: dallard@arvada.org

Office of the City Attorney

P.O. Box 8101, Arvada, CO 80001-8101

City Attorney **Chris Daly** .... (720) 898-7180
E-mail: chris-d@arvada.org

Office of the City Manager

P.O. Box 8101, Arvada, CO 80001-8101

City Manager **Mark Deven** .... (720) 898-7510
E-mail: mdeven@arvada.org
City Clerk **Kristen Rush** .... (720) 898-7550

Deputy City Manager Ray

8001 Ralston Road, Arvada, CO 80002
Tel: (720) 898-7500

Deputy City Manager **Bill Ray** .... (720) 898-7500

Information Technology

8001 Ralston Road, Arvada, CO 80002
Fax: (720) 898-7841

Director **Ron Czarnecki** .... (720) 898-7870
E-mail: ron-c@arvada.org

Parks, Golf and Hospitality Services Department

8101 Ralston Road, Arvada, CO 80002
Fax: (720) 898-7401

Director **Gordon Reusink** .... (720) 898-7400

Police Department

P.O. Box 8101, Arvada, CO 80001-8101
Tel: (720) 898-6900

Chief of Police **Don Wick** .... (720) 898-6665
Deputy Chief **Lynn Johnson** .... (720) 898-6650

Utilities Department

8001 Ralston Road, Arvada, CO 80002
Tel: (720) 898-7760

Director of Utilities **James Sullivan** .... (720) 898-7760

Deputy City Manager Gillis

8001 Ralston Road, Arvada, CO 80002
Tel: (720) 898-7500

Deputy City Manager **Lori Gillis** .... (720) 898-7500

Public Works and Utilities Department

P.O. Box 8101, Arvada, CO 80001-8101

Director **Bob Manwaring** .... (720) 898-7600

Community Development Department

P.O. Box 8101, Arvada, CO 80001-8101

Director **Rita McConnell** .... (720) 898-7435
E-mail: rmcconnell@arvada.org
Code Enforcement Manager **Greg Carr** .... (720) 898-7465
Housing and Revitalization Manager
Edward G. "Ed" Talbot .... (720) 898-7494
E-mail: etalbot@arvada.org

Arvada Housing Authority

8001 Ralston Road, Arvada, CO 80002
Tel: (720) 898-7494

Executive Director **Edward G. "Ed" Talbot** .... (720) 898-7494

Economic Development Department

P.O. Box 8101, Arvada, CO 80001-8101

Director **Ryan Stachelski** .... (720) 898-7010
E-mail: rstachelski@arvada.org

Finance Department

8001 Ralston Road, Arvada, CO 80002

Director **Bryan Archer** .... (720) 898-7120
Purchasing Manager **Pete Toth** .... (720) 898-7099
E-mail: ptoth@arvada.org
Risk Manager **Sharon Habegger** .... (720) 898-7590
E-mail: shabegger@arvada.org

Human Resources Department

P.O. Box 8101, Arvada, CO 80001-8101
Tel: (720) 898-7555

Director **Linda Haley** .... (720) 898-7555
E-mail: lhaley@arvada.org

Arvada Fire Protection District

7903 Allison Way, Arvada, CO 80005
E-mail: arvada.fire@arvadafire.com Internet: http://www.arvadafire.com

Fire Chief **Jon Greer** .... (303) 424-3012
E-mail: jon.greer@arvadafire.com

★ Elected Official ▲ Appointed by Legislature ▼ Appointed by Governor ► Appointed by Board or Commission ● Appointed by Judge
■ Appointed by Mayor △ Appointed by Freeholders ▽ Appointed by Supervisor ▷ Appointed by County Executive ○ Appointed by Council

Unified Government of Athens-Clarke County, Georgia

301 College Avenue, Athens, GA 30601
P.O. Box 1868, Athens, GA 30603
Internet: www.athensclarkecounty.com

County: Clarke **Election Type:** Nonpartisan **Population:** 122,604 (2015)

Form of Municipal Government: City and county governments are combined.

Office of the Mayor and Commissioners

301 College Ave., Athens, GA 30601-2770
P.O. Box 1868, Athens, GA 30603-1868
Fax: (706) 613-3029

★ Mayor **Nancy Denson** .... (706) 613-3010
Began Service: January 4, 2011
Term Expires: January 2019
E-mail: nancy.denson@athensclarkecounty.com
Education: Georgia BBA

★ Commissioner **Sharyn Dickerson** (District 1) .... (706) 613-2416
Term Expires: January 2, 2019
E-mail: sharyn.dickerson@athensclarkecounty.com

★ Commissioner **Harry Sims** (District 2) .... (706) 546-1683
Term Expires: January 3, 2017
E-mail: harry.sims@athensclarkecounty.com
Education: Georgia BS

★ Commissioner **Melissa Link** (District 3) .... (706) 372-3382
Term Expires: January 2, 2019
E-mail: melissa.link@athensclarkecounty.com

★ Commissioner **Allison Wright** (District 4) .... (706) 549-3518
Term Expires: January 3, 2017
E-mail: allison.wright@athensclarkecounty.com

★ Commissioner **Jared Bailey** (District 5) .... (706) 338-9019
Term Expires: January 2019
E-mail: jared.bailey@athensclarkecounty.com

★ Commissioner **Jerry Nesmith** (District 6) .... (706) 248-3547
Term Expires: January 3, 2017
E-mail: jerry.nesmith@athensclarkecounty.com

★ Commissioner **Diane F. Bell** (District 7) .... (706) 548-0314
Term Expires: January 2, 2019
E-mail: diane.bell@athensclarkecounty.com

★ Commissioner **Andy Herod** (District 8) .... (706) 543-0281
Term Expires: January 3, 2017
E-mail: andy.herod@athensclarkecounty.com

★ Commissioner **Kelly Girtz** (District 9) .... (706) 369-9457
Term Expires: January 2, 2019
E-mail: kelly.girtz@athensclarkecounty.com

★ Commissioner **Mike Hamby** (District 10) .... (706) 338-3970
Term Expires: January 3, 2017
E-mail: mike.hamby@athensclarkecounty.com

Clerk of Commission **Gloria Jean Spratlin** .... (706) 613-3031
E-mail: jean.spratlin@athensclarkecounty.com

Office of the Manager

301 College Avenue, Room 303, Athens, GA 30601
P.O. Box 1868, Athens, GA 30603-1868
Fax: (706) 613-3029

■ Manager **Blaine Williams** .... (706) 613-3020
E-mail: blaine.williams@athensclarkecounty.com

Assistant Manager **Robert Hiss** .... (706) 613-3020
E-mail: robert.hiss@athensclarkecounty.com

Assistant Manager **(Vacant)** .... (706) 613-3020

Executive Assistant **Cynthia Lambright** .... (706) 613-3020
E-mail: cynthia.lambright@athensclarkecounty.com

Office of the Attorney

P.O. Box 1868, Athens, GA 30603-1868
Fax: (706) 613-3037

■ Attorney **William C. Berryman, Jr.** .... (706) 613-3035
E-mail: bill.berryman@athensclarkecounty.com

Operational Analysis Office

P.O. Box 1868, Athens, GA 30603-1868
Fax: (706) 613-3029

■ Internal Auditor **Stephanie Maddox** .... (706) 613-3013
E-mail: stephanie.maddox@athensclarkecounty.com

Airport

P.O. Box 1868, Athens, GA 30603-1868
Fax: (706) 613-3425 E-mail: airport@athensclarkecounty.com

Director **Tim Beggerly** .... (706) 613-3420

Building Inspection Department

P.O. Box 1868, Athens, GA 30603-1868
Fax: (706) 613-3527

Chief Building Official **Doug Hansford** .... (706) 613-3520

Central Services Department

P.O. Box 1868, Athens, GA 30603-1868
Fax: (706) 613-3533

Director **David Fluck** .... (706) 613-3530
E-mail: david.fluck@athensclarkecounty.com

Computer Information Services

P.O. Box 1868, Athens, GA 30603-1868
Fax: (706) 425-4069 E-mail: cis@athensclarkecounty.com

Director **Steve Davis** .... (706) 613-3075
E-mail: steve.davis@athensclarkecounty.com

Coroner

3195 Atlanta Highway, Athens, GA 30601

★ Coroner **Sonny Wilson** .... (706) 613-3999
Term Expires: December 31, 2016
E-mail: coroner@athensclarkecounty.com

Correctional Institute

P.O. Box 1868, Athens, GA 30603-1868
Fax: (706) 613-3404

Warden **Ray Covington** .... (706) 613-3400

District Attorney

P.O. Box 1868, Athens, GA 30603-1868
Fax: (706) 613-3247

★ District Attorney **Ken Mauldin** .... (706) 613-3240
Term Expires: December 31, 2016
E-mail: ken.mauldin@athensclarkecounty.com

Economic Development Department

246 West Hancock Avenue, Athens, GA 30601
Fax: (706) 765-2510

Administrator **Ryan Moore** .... (706) 613-3233
E-mail: ryan.moore@athensclarkecounty.com

Board of Elections

P.O. Box 1868, Athens, GA 30603-1868
Fax: (706) 613-3840

Superintendent **Gail Schrader** .... (706) 613-3150

★ Elected Official ▲ Appointed by Legislature ▼ Appointed by Governor ► Appointed by Board or Commission ● Appointed by Judge
■ Appointed by Mayor △ Appointed by Freeholders ▽ Appointed by Supervisor ▷ Appointed by County Executive ○ Appointed by Council

Finance Department
P.O. Box 1868, Athens, GA 30603-1868
Fax: (706) 613-3043

Director **David Boyd** .... (706) 613-3040
Assistant Director of Finance **Chris Caldwell** .... (706) 613-3683
Accounting Administrator **Eric Griffin** .... (706) 613-3062
E-mail: eric.griffin@athensclarkecounty.com
Financial Services Administrator **Chuck Moore** .... (706) 613-3052
Budget Administrator **Tim Taylor** .... (706) 613-3061
E-mail: tim.taylor@athensclarkecounty.com
Purchasing Administrator **Julie Ann Donohue** .... (706) 613-3066
E-mail: julie.donahue@athensclarkecounty.com

Fire and Emergency Services
700 College Ave., Athens, GA 30601-2638
Fax: (706) 613-3372

Fire Chief **Jeffrey Scarbrough** .... (706) 613-3360
E-mail: jeffrey.scarbrough@athensclarkecounty.com

Housing and Community Development Department
P.O. Box 1868, Athens, GA 30603-1868
Fax: (706) 613-3158

Director **Rob Trevena** .... (706) 613-3155
E-mail: rob.trevena@athensclarkecounty.com
Community Development Administrator
Joanne Selgin .... (706) 613-3155 ext. 1204
E-mail: joanne.selgin@athensclarkecounty.com

Human Resources Department
P.O. Box 1868, Athens, GA 30603-1868
Fax: (706) 613-3118 E-mail: jobs@athensclarkecounty.com

Director **Lisa Ward** .... (706) 613-3090
E-mail: lisa.ward@athensclarkecounty.com

Leisure Services Department
P.O. Box 1868, Athens, GA 30603-1868
Fax: (706) 613-3805

Director **Pam Reidy** .... (706) 613-3800
Education: Central Michigan BA; Florida State MA

Organizational Development
P.O. Box 1868, Athens, GA 30603-1868
Fax: (706) 613-3113

Administrator **Catherine Bennett** .... (706) 613-3110
E-mail: catherine.bennett@athensclarkecounty.com

Planning Department
P.O. Box 1868, Athens, GA 30603-1868
Fax: (706) 613-3844

Director **Brad Griffin** .... (706) 613-3515

Police Department
3035 Lexington Rd., Athens, GA 30605-2444
Fax: (706) 613-3861 E-mail: central@accpd.org

Chief of Police **R. Scott Freeman** .... (706) 613-3888 ext. 244

Public Information Office
P.O. Box 1868, Athens, GA 30603-1868
Fax: (706) 613-3026 E-mail: info@athensclarkecounty.com

Public Information Officer **Jeff Montgomery** .... (706) 613-3795
E-mail: jeff.montgomery@athensclarkecounty.com
Public Information Media Analyst **Jason Harwell** .... (706) 613-3795
E-mail: jason.harwell@athensclarkecounty.com Fax: (706) 613-3026

Public Utilities Department
P.O. Box 1868, Athens, GA 30603-1868
Fax: (706) 613-3476

Director **Gary Duck** .... (706) 613-3470

Sheriff's Office
P.O. Box 1868, Athens, GA 30603-1868
Fax: (706) 613-3255

★ Sheriff **Ira Edwards** .... (706) 613-3250
Term Expires: December 31, 2016
E-mail: sheriff@athensclarkecounty.com

Solicitor General
P.O. Box 1868, Athens, GA 30603-1868
Fax: (706) 613-3229

★ Solicitor General **C. R. Chisolm, Jr.** .... (706) 613-3215
Term Expires: December 31, 2018
E-mail: solicitor@athensclarkecounty.com

Solid Waste Department
P.O. Box 1868, Athens, GA 30603-1868
Fax: (706) 613-3504
Internet: http://www.athensclarkecounty.com/178/Solid-Waste
E-mail: recycle@acc-recycle.org

Director **Suki Janssen** .... (706) 613-3501 ext. 305

Tax Assessors' Office
P.O. Box 1868, Athens, GA 30603-1868
Fax: (706) 613-3146

Chief Tax Appraiser **Kirk Dunagan** .... (706) 613-3140
E-mail: kirk.dunagan@athensclarkecounty.com

Tax Commissioner
P.O. Box 1868, Athens, GA 30603-1868
Fax: (706) 613-3129

★ Tax Commissioner **Mitch Schrader** .... (706) 613-3120
Term Expires: December 31, 2016
E-mail: mitch.schrader@athensclarkecounty.com

Transit Department
P.O. Box 1868, Athens, GA 30603-1868
Fax: (706) 613-3433
Internet: http://www.athensclarkecounty.com/199/Transit

Director **Knox "Butch" McDuffie** .... (706) 613-3437

Transportation and Public Works Department
P.O. Box 1868, Athens, GA 30603-1868
Fax: (706) 613-3444

Director **David Clark** .... (706) 613-3440

Fleet Management Division
225 Newton Bridge Road, Athens, GA 30607

Fleet Management Superintendent **Steve Hinsch** .... (706) 613-3447

Clarke County School District
240 Mitchell Bridge Road, Athens, GA 30606
Fax: (706) 208-9124 Internet: www.clarke.k12.ga.us

Superintendent **Philip Lanoue** .... (706) 546-7721 ext. 18230
Education: Vermont BA, MEd; Mercer PhD
★ Board President **Charles Worthy** (District 6) .... (706) 546-7721
Term Expires: December 31, 2016
E-mail: worthyc@clarke.k12.ga.us
★ Vice President **Sarah Ellis** (District 5) .... (706) 546-7721
Term Expires: December 31, 2018
E-mail: elliss@clarke.k12.ga.us

★ Elected Official ▲ Appointed by Legislature ▼ Appointed by Governor ▶ Appointed by Board or Commission ● Appointed by Judge
■ Appointed by Mayor △ Appointed by Freeholders ▽ Appointed by Supervisor ▷ Appointed by County Executive ○ Appointed by Council

Clarke County School District *continued*

★Board Member **Gregory Davis** (District 1) .... (706) 546-7721
Term Expires: December 31, 2018

★Board Member **Vernon Payne** (District 2) .... (706) 546-7721
Term Expires: December 31, 2016
E-mail: paynev@clarke.k12.ga.us

★Board Member **Linda E. Davis** (District 3) .... (706) 546-7721
Term Expires: December 31, 2018
E-mail: davisl@clarke.k12.ga.us

★Board Member **Carl Parks** (District 4) .... (706) 546-7721
Term Expires: December 31, 2016

★Board Member **Carol S. Williams** (District 7) .... (706) 546-7721
Term Expires: December 31, 2018
E-mail: williamscar@clarke.k12.ga.us
Education: Abraham Baldwin AS; Georgia BA

★Board Member **David Knox Huff** (District 8) .... (706) 546-7721
Term Expires: December 31, 2016
E-mail: huffd@clarke.k12.ga.us

★Board Member **Ovita Thornton** (District 9) .... (706) 546-7721
Term Expires: December 31, 2018
E-mail: thorntono@clarke.k12.ga.us

City of Atlanta, Georgia

City Hall, 55 Trinity Ave., SW, Atlanta, GA 30335
Tel: (404) 330-6000 (Information) Internet: www.atlantaga.gov

County: Fulton **Election Type:** Nonpartisan **Year Founded:** 1837
Charter: 1985 **Population:** 463,878 (2015) **Employees:** 9,053
Fiscal Year: 2016 **Budget:** $1,313,830,000

Office of the Mayor

City Hall, 55 Trinity Avenue, SW, Suite 2400, Atlanta, GA 30303
Fax: (404) 658-7372

Employees: 316 **Fiscal Year:** 2016 **Budget:** $35,509,000

★Mayor **M. Kasim Reed** .... (404) 330-6100
Began Service: January 4, 2010
Term Expires: December 31, 2017
E-mail: ATLMedia@atlantaga.gov
Education: Howard U BA, JD

■Chief of Staff **Candace Byrd** .... (404) 330-6100
E-mail: cbyrd@atlantaga.gov
Education: Howard U 1994 JD

■Chief Service Officer **Michelle Maziar** .... (404) 330-6100
E-mail: mmaziar@atlantaga.gov

■Senior Advisor **Melissa Mullinax** .... (404) 330-6100
E-mail: mjmullinax@atlantaga.gov

Atlanta Workforce Development Agency

818 Pollard Blvd., Atlanta, GA 30315

■Director **Michael Sterling** .... (404) 546-3000
Executive Assistant **Phillis D. Bryant** .... (404) 546-3026
E-mail: pbryant@atlantaga.gov
Director of Operations **Tammy Lipsey** .... (404) 546-3002
E-mail: tlipsey@atlantaga.gov
Deputy Director of Operations **Lillie Madali** .... (404) 546-3050
E-mail: lmadali@atlantaga.gov
Director of Finance **Karen B. Simmons** .... (404) 546-3056
E-mail: ksimmons@atlantaga.gov
Deputy Director of Finance **Pamela Ferrell** .... (404) 546-3042
E-mail: pferrell@atlantaga.gov
Director of Performance Management **Phillip Olaleye** .... (404) 546-3087
Business Relationship Manager **Amit Khanduri** .... (404) 546-3050
E-mail: akhanduri@atlantaga.gov
Director of Communications **Jennifer Ogunsola** .... (404) 546-3035
E-mail: jogunsola@atlantaga.gov

Office of Communications

Tel: (404) 330-6004 Fax: (404) 658-6893

■Communications Director **Anne Torres** .... (404) 330-6423
E-mail: amtorres@atlantaga.gov
Education: Fashion Inst Tech BA
Deputy Director of Communications **Jenna Garland** ..... (404) 330-6612
E-mail: jgarland@atlantaga.gov
e-Communications Manager **Tkeban Jahannes** .... (404) 330-6868
E-mail: tjahannes@atlantaga.gov
City Chanel 26 Station Manager **Michael Carswell** ...... (404) 330-6086
E-mail: mcarswell@atlantaga.gov

Office of Constituent Services

Fax: (404) 658-7088

■Director **Andrea Boone** .... (404) 330-6023
E-mail: aboone@atlantaga.gov
Office of Human Services Manager **Brenda Cornelius** ... (404) 546-3069
Fax: (404) 658-7877

Office of Contract Compliance

City Hall, 55 Trinity Avenue, Southwest, Suite 1700, Atlanta, GA 30303
Fax: (404) 658-7359

■Director **Larry Scott** .... (404) 330-6010
E-mail: lscott@atlantaga.gov

Mayor's Office of Cultural Affairs

Harris Tower, 233 Peachtree Street, NE, Suite 1700, Atlanta, GA 30303
Tel: (404) 546-6788

Executive Director **Camille Russell Love** .... (404) 546-6788
Management Analyst **Morgan Garriss** .... (404) 546-6823

Office of Enterprise Assets Management [OEAM]

City Hall Tower, 68 Mitchell Street, SW, Suite 1225, Atlanta, GA 30335
Fax: (404) 658-7787

Director **Billy Warren** .... (404) 330-6225
E-mail: bmwarren@atlantaga.gov

Office of Film and Entertainment

55 Trinity Avenue SW, Suite 4350, Atlanta, GA 30303

■Director **Christopher Hicks** .... (404) 330-6006
E-mail: atlfilm@atlantaga.gov
Production Manager **Cardellia Hunter** .... (404) 330-6207
Special Project Manager **Tiphanie Watson** .... (404) 330-6186
E-mail: twatson@atlantaga.gov
Digital Entertainment Officer **Patty Miranda** .... (404) 330-6067

Office of Intergovernmental Affairs

55 Trinity Avenue, Atlanta, GA 30303

Intergovernmental Affairs Manager
Megan S. Middleton .... (404) 330-6361
Legislative Analyst **Gabrielle A. Sanders** .... (404) 330-6504

Office of International Affairs

City Hall, 55 Trinity Avenue, Southwest, Atlanta, GA 30303

Director **Claire Angelle** .... (404) 614-8307
E-mail: ccangelle@atlantaga.gov
International Project Manager **Bettina Gardner** .... (404) 614-8299
E-mail: bgardner@atlantaga.gov
Chief of Protocol **Vanessa Ibarra** .... (404) 614-8331
E-mail: vibarra@atlantaga.gov

Mayor's Office of Special Events

City Hall, 55 Trinity Avenue, SW, Atlanta, GA 30303
Tel: (404) 330-6741

Director of Special Events **Ebony Barley** .... (404) 330-6741
E-mail: ebarley@atlantaga.gov
Special Events Manager **Andre Stalling** .... (404) 330-6350
E-mail: ajstalling@atlantaga.gov
Special Events Coordinator **(Vacant)** .... (404) 330-6765

★Elected Official ▲Appointed by Legislature ▼Appointed by Governor ▶Appointed by Board or Commission ●Appointed by Judge
■Appointed by Mayor △Appointed by Freeholders ▽Appointed by Supervisor ▷Appointed by County Executive ○Appointed by Council

Office of Sustainability
55 Trinity Avenue, SW, Suite 2400, Atlanta, GA 30303

Director of Sustainability **Stephanie Stuckey Benfield** . . (404) 865-8717
Education: Georgia 1989 BA, 1992 JD

Finance Department
City Hall Tower, 68 Mitchell Street, SW, Suite 11100, Atlanta, GA 30335
Tel: (404) 330-6430 Fax: (404) 546-2062

Employees: 153 **Fiscal Year:** 2016 **Budget:** $14,052,000

■ Chief Financial Officer **J. Anthony "Jim" Beard** . . . . (404) 330-6453
E-mail: jbeard@atlantaga.gov

Treasury, Debt and Investment Chief (Interim)
Paul Kwaw Suite 1300 . . . . (404) 330-6769

Deputy Chief Financial Officer **John Gaffney** . . . . (404) 330-6084

Budget Chief **Youlanda Carr** . . . . (404) 330-6949
City Hall Tower, 68 Mitchell Street, SW,
Suite 1300, Atlanta, GA 30303
E-mail: ycarr@atlantaga.gov

Budget Administration Director **Shawn A. Gabriel**
Suite 10100 . . . . (404) 865-8442
E-mail: sagabriel@atlantaga.gov

Controller **Madhavi Rajdev** . . . . (404) 865-8453

Revenue Director **Felicia Daniel** City Hall South . . . . (404) 330-6270
E-mail: fdaniel@atlantaga.gov

Director of Grant Services **Lee Hannah** Suite 8100 . . . . . . (404) 330-6632
Fax: (404) 546-8900

Law Department
City Hall Tower, 68 Mitchell Street, SW, Suite 4100,
Atlanta, GA 30303-3520
Tel: (404) 546-4100 Fax: (404) 546-9379
E-mail: lawdepartment@atlantaga.gov

Employees: 85 **Fiscal Year:** 2016 **Budget:** $6,322,000

■ City Attorney **Cathy Hampton** . . . . (404) 546-4100
E-mail: cathyhampton@atlantaga.gov

Deputy City Attorney, Aviation **Kimberly Patrick** . . . . (404) 546-4162

Deputy City Attorney, Compliance **Jeffrey B. Norman** . . . (404) 546-4161

Deputy City Attorney, Litigation and Employment
Laura Burton . . . . (404) 546-4123

Deputy City Attorney, Watershed Management
Roger Bhandari . . . . (404) 546-4117

Deputy City Attorney, Finance **Marc Goncher** . . . . (404) 546-4139

Deputy City Attorney, Infrastructure **Karen Thomas** . . . . . (404) 546-4179

Office of the Chief Operating Officer
55 Trinity Avenue, Atlanta, GA 30303

■ Chief Operating Officer **Daniel L. "Dan" Gordon** . . . . (404) 330-6809
E-mail: dgordon@atlantaga.gov

Deputy Chief Operating Officer **William M. Johnson** . . . . (404) 330-6809
Education: Mississippi BS; Missouri MScE

Deputy Chief Operating Officer **Kristin Wilson** . . . . (404) 330-6809
E-mail: kwilson@atlantaga.gov
Education: Dartmouth BS; Stanford MBA

Department of Aviation
Hartsfield -Jackson Atlanta International Airport,
6000 North Terminal Parkway, Suite 4000, Atlanta, GA 30320
P.O. Box 20509, Atlanta, GA 30320-2509
Tel: (404) 530-6600 Fax: (404) 209-2942
Internet: www.atlanta-airport.com

Employees: 648 **Fiscal Year:** 2016 **Budget:** $194,842,000

■ General Manager (Interim) **Roosevelt Council, Jr.** . . . . (404) 530-6600
E-mail: miguel.southwell@atlanta-airport.com

Aviation Senior Deputy General Manager
Michael L. Smith . . . . (404) 530-6600

Assistant General Manager, Operations, Maintenance
and Transportation **Paul Meyer** . . . . (404) 530-6600
E-mail: paul.meyer@atlanta-airport.com

Department of Aviation *continued*

Assistant General Manager, Public Safety and Security
Richard L. Duncan . . . . (404) 530-6600
E-mail: richard.duncan@atlanta-airport.com

Assistant General Manager, Planning and Development
Franklin Rucker . . . . (404) 530-6600

Chief Financial Officer/Deputy Aviation General
Manager **Roosevelt Council, Jr.** . . . . (404) 530-6600

Director of Aviation Information Systems
Sharon Jones . . . . (404) 209-4080 ext. 258

Director of Human Resources **Jim Beam** . . . . (404) 530-6600
E-mail: jbeam@atlantaga.gov

Director, Marketing and Stakeholder Engagement
Myrna White . . . . (404) 209-1700
E-mail: mwhite@atlantaga.gov

Department of Corrections
254 Peachtree St., SW, Atlanta, GA 30303
Tel: (404) 865-8001 Fax: (404) 658-6064
Internet: www.atlantaga.gov/index.aspx?page=185

Employees: 346 **Fiscal Year:** 2016 **Budget:** $32,891,000

Chief **Patrick Labat** . . . . (404) 865-8063

Assistant Chief **Diane Jones** . . . . (404) 865-8059

Director of Nursing **Kathy Brawner** . . . . (404) 865-8057

Atlanta Fire Rescue Department
226 Peachtree Street, SW, Atlanta, GA 30303
Fax: (404) 546-7245

Employees: 1,129 **Fiscal Year:** 2016 **Budget:** $82,295,000

■ Fire Chief **Joel G. Baker** . . . . (404) 546-7000
E-mail: jgbaker@atlantaga.gov

First Deputy Chief **Randall B. Slaughter** . . . . (404) 546-7000
E-mail: rbslaughter@atlantaga.gov

Office of Field Operations Deputy Chief
Roderick M. Smith . . . . (404) 546-7000
E-mail: rmsmith@atlantaga.gov

Office Technical Services Deputy Chief **Chad Jones** . . . . . (404) 546-7000

Operations Deputy Chief **Randall B. Slaughter** . . . . (404) 546-7000 ext. 4

Office of Support Services Deputy Chief
Michael D. Simmons . . . . (404) 546-7000 ext. 3
E-mail: mdsimmons@atlantaga.gov

Office of Airport Services Deputy Chief **Kevin L. Ware** . . (404) 546-7000

Atlanta-Fulton County Emergency Management Agency [AFCEMA]
Public Safety Building, 130 Peachtree Street SW, Suite G-157,
Atlanta, GA 30303
Tel: (404) 730-5600 Fax: (404) 730-5625 Internet: www.afcema.com

Director **Matthew "Matt" Kallmyer** . . . . (404) 730-5600
E-mail: matthew.kallmyer@fultoncountyga.gov

Deputy Director **Pansy Ricks** . . . . (404) 730-5600
E-mail: pansy.ricks@fultoncountyga.gov

Operations Officer **Donnie Reece** . . . . (404) 730-5600
E-mail: donnie.reece@fultoncountyga.gov

Administrative Services Manager **Wanda Floyd** . . . . (404) 730-5600
E-mail: wanda.floyd@fultoncountyga.gov
Education: Georgia State MPA

Department of Human Resources [DHR]
City Hall Tower, 68 Mitchell St., SW, Suite 2150, Atlanta, GA 30303
Tel: (404) 330-6360
Tel: (404) 330-6456 (Employment Services 24 Hour Information Hot-line)
Tel: (404) 330-6375 (Business Support)
Tel: (404) 330-6377 (Public Safety Promotional Testing)
Fax: (404) 658-6892
Fax: (404) 331-8920 (Employment Verification Request)

Employees: 134 **Fiscal Year:** 2016 **Budget:** $5,742,000

■ Commissioner **Yvonne Cowser Yancy** . . . . (404) 330-6408
E-mail: yyancy@atlantaga.gov

★ Elected Official ▲ Appointed by Legislature ▼ Appointed by Governor ► Appointed by Board or Commission ● Appointed by Judge
■ Appointed by Mayor △ Appointed by Freeholders ▽ Appointed by Supervisor ▷ Appointed by County Executive ○ Appointed by Council

Department of Human Resources *continued*

Deputy Commissioner **Angela Addison** . . . . (404) 330-6853
E-mail: aaddison@atlantaga.gov
Deputy Commissioner **Catherine LeMay** . . . . (404) 330-6652
E-mail: clemay@atlantaga.gov
Benefits Director **Louis Amis** . . . . (404) 330-6930
Data and Records Director **Elaine Gooden** . . . . (404) 330-6375
E-mail: epgooden@atlantaga.gov
Labor Relations **Lydia Jamison** . . . . (404) 330-6460
E-mail: ljamison@atlantaga.gov
Employee Development Manager **Valencia White** . . . . (404) 330-6743
E-mail: vwhite@atlantaga.gov
Psychological Services Chief **Dr. Adriene Bradford** . . . . . (404) 546-3074
818 Pollard Boulevard, Atlanta, GA 30315
E-mail: acbradford@atlantaga.gov
Talent Acquisition **Patricia Simon** . . . . (404) 330-6837
E-mail: psimon@atlantaga.gov

Department of Information Technology [IT]

55 Trinity Avenue SW, Suite G700, Atlanta, GA 30303
Fax: (404) 546-2129

Employees: 157 **Fiscal Year:** 2016 **Budget:** $31,511,000

Chief Information Officer **Samir Saini** . . . . (404) 330-6110
E-mail: ssaini@atlantaga.gov
Chief Technology Officer **Jason Watkins** . . . . (404) 330-6110
E-mail: jwatkins@atlantaga.gov
Chief of Staff **Daphne Rackley** . . . . (404) 546-1164
E-mail: drackley@atlantaga.gov
End User Support Manager **Melvin Tanks** . . . . (404) 330-6110
E-mail: mtanks@atlantaga.gov
Telecom Manager **Tameka Neely-Dudley** . . . . (404) 546-7822
Chief Security Officer **Taiye Lambo** . . . . (404) 330-6110

Department of Parks, Recreation and Cultural Affairs

Harris Towers, 233 Peachtree Street, NE, Suite 1600, Atlanta, GA 30303
Tel: (404) 546-6788

Employees: 393 **Fiscal Year:** 2016 **Budget:** $34,627,000

Commissioner **Amy Phuong** . . . . (404) 546-6788
Education: Georgia Tech 2005 BS
Civic Center Director **(Vacant)** . . . . (404) 523-6275
Fax: (404) 525-4634
Parks Director **Doug Voss** . . . . (404) 546-6742
Fax: (404) 546-9440
Office of Recreation Executive Director (Interim)
LaChandra Butler-Burks . . . . (404) 546-7662
Parks Design Director **Alvin Dodson** . . . . (404) 546-7843
Fax: (404) 546-9355

Department of Planning and Community Development

City Hall, 55 Trinity Ave., Suite 1450, Atlanta, GA 30303
Tel: (404) 330-6070 Fax: (404) 546-8654

Employees: 272 **Fiscal Year:** 2016 **Budget:** $3,844,000

■ Commissioner **Tim Keane** . . . . (404) 330-6037
E-mail: tkeane@atlantaga.gov
Assistant to the Commissioner **Cora Kilpatrick** . . . . (404) 330-6037
E-mail: ckilpatrick@atlantaga.gov
Deputy Commissioner **Terri Lee** . . . . (404) 330-6070
55 Trinity Avenue, SW, Suite 1450, Atlanta, GA 30335
E-mail: telee@atlantaga.gov
Office of Housing Director **Michelle Lewis** . . . . (404) 330-6390
Fax: (404) 658-6950
Planning Office Director **Charletta Wilson Jacks** . . . . (404) 330-6145
Office of Buildings Director (Interim) **Michael Nagy** . . . . (404) 330-6152
55 Trinity Avenue, Southwest, Suite 3900, Atlanta, GA 30303

Urban Design Commission, Atlanta

City Hall, 55 Trinity Avenue SW, Suite 3400, Atlanta, GA 30303
Fax: (404) 658-6734

Executive Director **Doug Young** . . . . (404) 330-6702

Police Department

226 Peachtree Street, SW, 5th Floor, Atlanta, GA 30303
Fax: (404) 653-7975 Internet: www.atlantapd.org/

Employees: 2,548 **Fiscal Year:** 2016 **Budget:** $174,588,000

■ Police Chief **George N. Turner** . . . . (404) 546-6900
Chief of Staff **Vincent "Vince" Moore** . . . . (404) 546-6839
Assistant Chief **Shawn Jones** . . . . (404) 546-4236
Deputy Chief/Support Services Division
Major Erika Shields . . . . (404) 546-7290
Deputy Chief/Field Operations Division
Joseph Spillane . . . . (404) 546-4224
Taxicabs and Vehicles for Hire Bureau Manager
(Vacant) . . . . (404) 658-7600
818 Washington St., Atlanta, GA 30312
Public Affairs Director **Elizabeth Espy** . . . . (404) 546-2531
E-mail: enespy@atlantaga.gov

Department of Procurement

55 Trinity Avenue, Suite 1790, Atlanta, GA 30303
Tel: (404) 330-6204 Fax: (404) 658-7705

Employees: 41 **Fiscal Year:** 2016 **Budget:** $920,000

Chief Procurement Officer **Adam L. Smith** . . . . (404) 330-6204
E-mail: asmith@atlantaga.gov
Deputy Chief Procurement Officer **Keith O. Brooks** . . . . . (404) 330-6204
E-mail: kbrooks@atlantaga.gov
Deputy Chief Procurement Officer **David Chapman** . . . . . (404) 330-6204
E-mail: dchapman@atlantaga.gov
Deputy Chief Procurement Officer **Girard Geeter** . . . . (404) 330-6204
E-mail: ggeeter@atlantaga.gov

Department of Public Works

55 Trinity Avenue, SW, Suite 4700, Atlanta, GA 30303
Tel: (404) 330-6240 Fax: (404) 658-7552
E-mail: publicworks@atlantaga.gov

Employees: 921 **Fiscal Year:** 2016 **Budget:** $33,983,000

Commissioner **Richard Mendoza** . . . . (404) 330-6240
Executive Assistant to the Commissioner
Kim King-Forde . . . . (404) 330-6340
Deputy Commissioner **Larry King** . . . . (404) 330-6240
Program Management Officer **Gayla Dodson** . . . . (404) 330-6236
Transportation Deputy Commissioner **(Vacant)** . . . . (404) 330-6240
Program Management Officer (Operations)
Cotena Alexander . . . . (404) 330-6501
E-mail: calexander@atlantaga.gov
Public Relations Director **Valerie Winrow** . . . . (404) 330-6240
E-mail: vwinrow@atlantaga.gov

Office of Fleet Services

23 Claire Drive, Southeast, Atlanta, GA 30315

Director **Dale Fambrough** . . . . (404) 622-7681

Department of Watershed Management

55 Trinity Ave., SW, Suite 5400, Atlanta, GA 30303
Tel: (404) 658-6500 Fax: (404) 658-7194

Employees: 1,553 **Fiscal Year:** 2016 **Budget:** $155,221,000

Commissioner (Interim) **William M. Johnson** . . . . (404) 330-6081
Education: Mississippi BS; Missouri MScE

Office of Communications

55 Trinity Avenue, Suite 5400, Atlanta, GA 30303
Fax: (404) 658-6637

Director of Communications and Community Relations
Lillian Govus . . . . (404) 546-3218
E-mail: lgovus@atlantaga.gov

★ Elected Official ▲ Appointed by Legislature ▼ Appointed by Governor ▶ Appointed by Board or Commission ● Appointed by Judge
■ Appointed by Mayor △ Appointed by Freeholders ▽ Appointed by Supervisor ▷ Appointed by County Executive ○ Appointed by Council

Office of Linear Infrastructure Operations
55 Trinity Avenue, Suite 5400, Atlanta, GA 30303
Fax: (404) 658-6637

Deputy Commissioner (Interim) **Terrell Gibbs** .... (404) 624-0753
E-mail: tgibbs@atlantaga.gov

Office of Engineering Services
55 Trinity Avenue, Suite 5400, Atlanta, GA 30303
Fax: (404) 658-6637

Deputy Commissioner **Rob Bocarro** .... (404) 658-6500
E-mail: rbocarro@AtlantaGa.Gov

Office of Financial Administration
55 Trinity Avenue SW, Suite 5400, Atlanta, GA 30303
Fax: (404) 658-6637

Deputy Commissioner (Interim) **Mohamed Balla** .... (404) 658-6500
E-mail: mballa@atlantaga.gov

Office of Water Treatment and Reclamation
55 Trinity Avenue, Southwest, Atlanta, GA 30303

Deputy Commissioner (Interim) **Richard Parker** .... (404) 546-1432

Office of Watershed Protection
55 Trinity Avenue, Suite 5400, Atlanta, GA 30303
Fax: (404) 658-6637

Deputy Commissioner (Interim) **Jay Ash** .... (404) 546-1351

City Auditor's Office

55 Trinity Avenue, Southwest, Suite 12100, Atlanta, GA 30303

Employees: 16 **Fiscal Year:** 2016 **Budget:** $1,768,000

City Auditor **Leslie Ward** .... (404) 330-6452 ext. 1
Deputy City Auditor **Amanda Noble** .... (404) 330-6452 ext. 2

Office of the City Council

City Hall, 55 Trinity Ave., SW, Atlanta, GA 30303
Fax: (404) 658-6454
Internet: http://citycouncil.atlantaga.gov/CONTACTS.HTM

Employees: 49 **Fiscal Year:** 2016 **Budget:** $12,051,000

★President **Ceasar C. Mitchell** .... (404) 330-6030
Term Expires: December 31, 2017
E-mail: ccmitchell@atlantaga.gov
Education: Morehouse Col 1991 BA; Georgia 1995 JD

★Council Member **Carla Smith** (District 1)............. (404) 330-6030
Term Expires: December 31, 2017
E-mail: csmith@atlantaga.gov

★Council Member **Kwanza Hall** (District 2) .... (404) 330-6030
Term Expires: December 31, 2017
E-mail: khall@atlantaga.gov

★Council Member **Ivory Lee Young, Jr.** (District 3) ...... (404) 330-6030
Term Expires: December 31, 2017
E-mail: ilyoung@atlantaga.gov

★Council Member **Cleta Winslow** (District 4)........... (404) 330-6030
Term Expires: December 31, 2017
E-mail: cwinslow@atlantaga.gov

★Council Member
Natalyn Mosby Archibong (District 5)............... (404) 330-6030
Term Expires: December 31, 2017
E-mail: narchibong@atlantaga.gov

★Council Member **Alex Wan** (District 6)................ (404) 330-6030
Term Expires: December 31, 2017
E-mail: awan@atlantaga.gov

★Council Member **Howard Shook** (District 7)........... (404) 330-6030
Term Expires: December 31, 2017
E-mail: hshook@atlantaga.gov

★Council Member **Yolanda Adrean** (District 8) .... (404) 330-6030
Term Expires: December 31, 2017
E-mail: yadrean@atlantaga.gov

★Council Member **Felicia A. Moore** (District 9).......... (404) 330-6030
Term Expires: December 31, 2017
E-mail: fmoore@atlantaga.gov

Office of the City Council *continued*

★Council Member **Clarence T. Martin, Jr.** (District 10).... (404) 330-6030
Term Expires: December 31, 2017
E-mail: cmartin@atlantaga.gov

★Council Member **Kiesha Lance Bottoms** (District 11) ... (404) 330-6030
Term Expires: December 31, 2017
E-mail: kbottoms@atlantaga.gov

★Council Member **Joyce Sheperd** (District 12) .... (404) 330-6030
Term Expires: December 31, 2017
E-mail: jmsheperd@atlantaga.gov

★Council Member
Michael Julian Bond (At-Large, Post 1) .... (404) 330-6030
Term Expires: December 31, 2017
E-mail: mbond@atlantaga.gov

★Council Member **Mary Norwood** (At-Large, Post 2)..... (404) 330-6030
Term Expires: December 31, 2017
E-mail: mnorwood@atlantaga.gov

★Council Member **Andre Dickens** (At-Large, Post 3) ..... (404) 330-6030
Term Expires: December 31, 2017
E-mail: adickens@atlantaga.gov

Communications Director **Dexter Chambers** .... (404) 330-6309
E-mail: dchambers@atlantaga.gov

○Municipal Clerk **Rhonda Johnson** .... (404) 330-6032
E-mail: rjohnson@atlantaga.gov

Office of the Public Defender

150 Garnett Street, SW, Atlanta, GA 30303
Fax: (404) 658-6848

Employees: 38 **Fiscal Year:** 2016 **Budget:** $3,490,000

Director (Interim) **Rosalie M. Joy** .... (404) 658-6838

Office of the City Solicitor

150 Garnett Street, 3rd Floor, Atlanta, GA 30303
Fax: (404) 658-7956

Employees: 76 **Fiscal Year:** 2016 **Budget:** $6,483,000

City Solicitor **Raines Carter** .... (404) 658-6618
E-mail: rfcarter@atlantaga.gov

Invest Atlanta

86 Pryor Street, SW, Suite 300, Atlanta, GA 30303-3131
Fax: (404) 880-9333

■President and Chief Executive Officer
Eloisa Klementich .... (404) 614-8314
E-mail: eklementich@investatlanta.com
Education: Pitzer 1992 BA; Monterrey Tech (Mexico) 1995 MBA; UCLA 2001 MURP; LaVerne 2010 PhD

Executive Assistant **(Vacant)** .... (404) 588-5477

■Executive Vice President and Chief Operating Officer
Ernestine Garey .... (404) 880-4100
E-mail: egarey@investatlanta.com

Atlanta Public Schools

130 Trinity Avenue, SW, Atlanta, GA 30303
Tel: (404) 802-3500 Fax: (404) 802-1803
Internet: www.atlantapublicschools.us

Superintendent of Schools **Dr. Meria Joel Carstarphen** .. (404) 802-2820
Education: Tulane BA; Auburn EdD; Harvard EdD

Deputy Superintendent of Instruction **David Jernigan** .... (404) 802-2724
Chief Academic Officer **Olivine Roberts** .... (404) 802-2790

Board of Education
Tel: (404) 802-2200 Fax: (404) 802-1204

★Chair **Courtney English** (At-Large, Seat 7) .... (404) 802-2200
Term Expires: December 31, 2017
E-mail: cenglish@atlanta.k12.ga.us

★Elected Official ▲Appointed by Legislature ▼Appointed by Governor ▶Appointed by Board or Commission ●Appointed by Judge
■Appointed by Mayor △Appointed by Freeholders ▽Appointed by Supervisor ▷Appointed by County Executive ○Appointed by Council

Board of Education *continued*

★Vice Chair **Nancy Meister** (District 4) .... (404) 802-2200
Term Expires: December 31, 2017
E-mail: nmeister@atlanta.k12.ga.us

★Board Member **Leslie Grant** (District 1) .... (404) 802-2200
Term Expires: December 31, 2017

★Board Member **Byron D. Amos** (District 2) .... (404) 802-2200
Term Expires: December 31, 2017

★Board Member **Matt Westmoreland** (District 3) .... (404) 802-2200
Term Expires: December 31, 2017

★Board Member **Steven Lee** (District 5) .... (404) 802-2200
Term Expires: December 31, 2016

★Board Member **Eshé Collins** (District 6) .... (404) 802-2200
Term Expires: December 31, 2016

★Board Member
Cynthia Briscoe Brown (At-Large, Seat 8) .... (404) 802-2200
Term Expires: December 31, 2016

★Board Member **Jason Esteves** (At-Large, Seat 9) .... (404) 802-2200
Term Expires: December 31, 2016

Consolidated Government of Augusta-Richmond County, Georgia

530 Greene Street, Suite 806, Augusta, GA 30901
Internet: www.augustaga.gov

County: Richmond **Election Type:** Nonpartisan **Population:** 197,182 (2015)

Form of Municipal Government: City and county governments are combined.

Office of the Mayor and Commission

530 Greene Street, Room 806, Augusta, GA 30901
Fax: (706) 821-1835

★Mayor **Hardie Davis, Jr.** .... (706) 821-1831
Began Service: January 1, 2015
Term Expires: December 31, 2018
Education: Georgia Tech 1992 BEE
Chief of Staff **Lynthia Owens** .... (706) 821-1831

★Mayor Pro Tem **Grady Smith** (District 10) .... (706) 821-1820
Term Expires: December 31, 2018
E-mail: cgradysmith@augustaga.gov
Education: Augusta 1975 BS

★Commissioner **William "Bill" Fennoy** (District 1) .... (706) 821-1820
Term Expires: December 31, 2016
E-mail: fennoy@augustaga.gov

★Commissioner **Dennis Williams** (District 2) .... (706) 821-1820
Term Expires: December 31, 2018

★Commissioner **Mary Davis** (District 3) .... (706) 821-1820
Term Expires: December 31, 2016
E-mail: mfdavis@augustaga.gov

★Commissioner **Sammy Sias** (District 4)
Term Expires: December 31, 2018

★Commissioner **William "Bill" Lockett** (District 5) .... (706) 821-1820
Term Expires: December 31, 2016
E-mail: wlockett@augustaga.gov

★Commissioner **Ben Hasan** (District 6) .... (706) 821-1820
Term Expires: December 31, 2018

★Commissioner **Sean Frantom** (District 7) .... (706) 564-1663
Term Expires: December 31, 2016

★Commissioner **Wayne Guilfoyle** (District 8) .... (706) 821-1820
Term Expires: December 31, 2018
E-mail: cwayneguilfoyle@augustaga.gov

★Commissioner **Marion F. Williams** (District 9) .... (706) 821-1820
Term Expires: December 31, 2016
E-mail: mfwilliams@augustaga.gov

Office of the Mayor and Commission *continued*

Clerk of the Commission **Lena Bonner** .... (706) 821-1820
E-mail: lbonner@augustaga.gov Fax: (706) 821-1838

Office of the Coroner

912 Eighth Street, Augusta, GA 30901

★Coroner **Mark Bowen** .... (706) 821-2382
Term Expires: December 31, 2016
E-mail: mbowen@augustaga.gov

Office of the District Attorney

735 James Brown Boulevard, Suite 2400, Augusta, GA 30901

District Attorney **Ashley Wright** .... (706) 821-1135
E-mail: awright@augustaga.gov

Administrator's Office

530 Greene St., Room 801, Augusta, GA 30901
Fax: (706) 821-2819

▶Administrator **Janice Allen Jackson** .... (706) 821-2400
E-mail: administrator@augustaga.gov
Education: William & Mary BA; Duke MA

Augusta 311

530 Greene Street, Room 902, Augusta, GA 30901
Fax: (706) 826-4780

Manager **Kelly Walker** .... (706) 821-2300
E-mail: walker@augustaga.gov

Augusta 911 Center

911 Fourth St., Augusta, GA 30901
Tel: (706) 821-1242 (Administration) Fax: (706) 821-1213

▶Assistant Director **Cathy Plaster** .... (706) 821-1209
E-mail: cplaster@augustaga.gov

Animal Services Department

4164 Mack Ln., Augusta, GA 30906
Fax: (706) 798-8978

▶Director **Sharon Broady** .... (706) 790-6836
E-mail: sbroady@augustaga.gov

Augusta-Richmond County Public Library

902 Greene St., Augusta, GA 30901

Director (Interim) **Marshell Fashion** .... (706) 821-2600
E-mail: fashionm@arcpls.org

Board of Elections and Registration

530 Greene St., Room 104, Augusta, GA 30911
Fax: (706) 821-2814

Executive Director **Lynn M. Bailey** .... (706) 821-2340

Emergency Management Department

911 Fourth St., Augusta, GA 30901
Fax: (706) 821-1246

Director **Chief Christopher James** .... (706) 821-1155
E-mail: cjames@augustaga.gov

Engineering

530 Greene Street, Room 701, Augusta, GA 30901
Fax: (706) 821-1708

▶Director **Abie Ladson** .... (706) 821-1706
E-mail: aladson@augustaga.gov
Assistant Director **Hameed Malik** .... (706) 821-1706
E-mail: hmalik@augustaga.gov

(continued on next page)

★Elected Official ▲Appointed by Legislature ▼Appointed by Governor ▶Appointed by Board or Commission ●Appointed by Judge
■Appointed by Mayor △Appointed by Freeholders ▽Appointed by Supervisor ▷Appointed by County Executive ○Appointed by Council

Engineering *continued*

Traffic Engineer **Steven J. Cassell** .... (706) 821-1850
507 Telfair Street, Augusta, GA 30901 Fax: (706) 821-1724

Environmental Services Department

4330 Deans Bridge Road, Blythe, GA 30805-9779
Fax: (706) 592-1658

Director **Mark Johnson** .... (706) 592-3200

Finance Department

530 Greene St., Room 207, Augusta, GA 30901
Fax: (706) 821-2520

▶ Finance Director **Donna Williams** .... (706) 821-2429
E-mail: dwilliams@augustaga.gov

Fleet Management

1568 Broad St., Augusta, GA 30904
Fax: (706) 821-2893

Fleet Manager **Ron Crowden** .... (706) 821-2892

Fire Department

3117 Deans Bridge Road, Augusta, GA 30906
Tel: (706) 821-2909 (Administration) Fax: (706) 821-2907

▶ Fire Chief **Chief Christopher James** .... (706) 821-2909
E-mail: cjames@augustaga.gov

Housing and Economic Development Department

925 Laney Walker Boulevard, 2nd Floor, Augusta, GA 30901
Fax: (706) 821-1784

▶ Director **Hawthorne E. Welcher, Jr.** .... (706) 821-1797

Human Resources

530 Greene Street, Room 400A, Augusta, GA 30901
Fax: (706) 821-2867

▶ Director **Michael J. Loeser** .... (706) 821-2303
E-mail: mloeser@augustaga.gov

Compensation and Benefits Manager **Michelle A. Elam** .. (706) 849-5917
E-mail: melam@augustaga.gov

Information Technology Department

530 Greene Street, Augusta, GA 30901
Fax: (706) 821-2530

▶ Director **Tameka Allen** .... (706) 821-2522
E-mail: allen@augustaga.gov

Geographic Information Systems Manager
Michele Pearman .... (706) 821-2864
E-mail: mpearman@augustaga.gov

Web Administrator **(Vacant)** .... (706) 821-2522
Fax: (706) 821-2530

Law Department

Building 3000, 535 Telfair Street, Augusta, GA 30901
Fax: (706) 842-5556

▶ General Counsel **Andrew MacKenzie** .... (706) 842-5550
E-mail: amackenzie@augustaga.gov

Planning and Development

535 Telfair Street, Suite 300, Augusta, GA 30901
Fax: (706) 821-1806

Director **Melanie Wilson** .... (706) 821-1796
Deputy Director **Paul DeCamp** .... (706) 821-1796
Deputy Director **Robert Sherman** .... (706) 821-1796

Procurement Department

530 Greene Street, Room 605, Augusta, GA 30901
Fax: (706) 821-2811

▶ Director **Geri Sams** .... (706) 821-2422
E-mail: gsams@augustaga.gov

Recreation, Parks and Facilities Department

2027 Lumpkin Rd., Augusta, GA 30906

▶ Director **Ron Houck** .... (706) 796-5025
E-mail: rhouck@augustaga.gov

Facilities Maintenance Division

501 Greene St., Augusta, GA 30901
Fax: (706) 821-2484

Deputy Director **Lonnie Wimberly** .... (706) 821-1948
E-mail: lwimberly@augustaga.gov

Trees and Landscape Division

1559 Eagles Way, Augusta, GA 30904
Fax: (706) 821-1672

Assistant Director **Sam Smith** .... (706) 796-5025

Richmond County Correctional Institution [RCCI]

2314 Tobacco Rd., Augusta, GA 30906
Fax: (706) 798-8110

▶ Warden **Evan Joseph** .... (706) 771-2921
E-mail: ejoseph@augustaga.gov

Richmond County Extension Service

602 Greene St., Augusta, GA 30901

Coordinator **Sid Mullis** .... (706) 821-2349

Richmond County Marshal's Department

530 Greene Street, Room 704, Augusta, GA 30901
Fax: (706) 821-2557

Marshal **M. Steve Smith** .... (706) 821-2368
E-mail: ssmith@augustaga.gov

Richmond County Sheriff's Office

Law Enforcement Center, 401 Walton Way, Augusta, GA 30901
Tel: (706) 821-1000 Fax: (706) 821-1064

★ Sheriff **Richard Roundtree** .... (706) 821-1000
Term Expires: December 31, 2016
E-mail: rroundtree@augustaga.gov

Risk Management

530 Greene Street, Room 217, Augusta, GA 30901
Fax: (706) 821-2502

Manager **Sandy Wright** .... (706) 821-2301
E-mail: swright@augustaga.gov

Tax Assessor

530 Greene Street, Room 102, Augusta, GA 30901
Fax: (706) 821-2325

Chief Assessor **Alveno Ross** .... (706) 821-2310
E-mail: aross@augustaga.gov

Tax Commission

530 Greene Street, Room 117, Augusta, GA 30901
Fax: (706) 821-2419

★ Commissioner **Steven Kendrick** .... (706) 821-2391
Term Expires: December 31, 2016
E-mail: skendrick2@augustaga.gov

★ Elected Official ▲ Appointed by Legislature ▼ Appointed by Governor ▶ Appointed by Board or Commission ● Appointed by Judge
■ Appointed by Mayor △ Appointed by Freeholders ▽ Appointed by Supervisor ▷ Appointed by County Executive ○ Appointed by Council

Utilities Department
360 Bay Street, Suite 180, Augusta, GA 30901
Fax: (706) 312-4123

▶ Director **Tom Wiedmeier** .... (706) 312-4154
E-mail: twiedmeier@augustaga.gov

City of Augusta, Maine
City Hall, 16 Cony St., Augusta, ME 04330
Fax: (207) 626-2304 (City Hall) Internet: www.augustamaine.gov

County: Kennebec **Election Type:** Nonpartisan **Population:** 18,471 (2015)

Office of the Mayor and City Council
City Hall, 16 Cony St., Augusta, ME 04330-5298
Fax: (207) 620-8174 E-mail: council@augustamaine.gov
Internet: http://www.augustamaine.gov

★ Mayor **David M. Rollins** .... (207) 626-2300
Began Service: November 6, 2014
Term Expires: December 31, 2018
E-mail: mark.obrien@augustamaine.gov
Assistant to the Mayor **Loretta Lathe** .... (207) 626-2300
E-mail: loretta.lathe@augustamaine.gov

★ Council Member **Linda J. Conti** (Ward 1) .... (207) 626-2300
Term Expires: December 31, 2017

★ Council Member **Darek M. Grant** (Ward 2) .... (207) 626-2300
Term Expires: December 31, 2018
E-mail: darek.grant@augustamaine.gov

★ Council Member **Patrick E. Paradis** (Ward 3) .... (207) 626-2300
Term Expires: December 31, 2016
E-mail: patrick.paradis@augustamaine.gov

★ Council Member **Anna D. Blodgett** (Ward 4) .... (207) 626-2300
Term Expires: December 31, 2017
E-mail: anna.blodgett@augustamaine.gov

★ Council Member **Marci Alexander** (At-Large) .... (207) 626-2300
Term Expires: December 31, 2018

★ Council Member **Jeff Bilodeau** (At-Large) .... (207) 626-2300
Term Expires: December 31, 2017
E-mail: jeffrey.bilodeau@augustamaine.gov

★ Council Member **Dale McCormick** (At-Large) .... (207) 626-2300
Term Expires: December 31, 2016
E-mail: dale.mccormick@augustamaine.gov
Education: Iowa 1970 BA

★ Council Member **Cecil E. Munson** (At-Large) .... (207) 626-2300
Term Expires: December 31, 2016
E-mail: cecil.munson@augustamaine.gov

Augusta Airport
75 Airport Rd., Augusta, ME 04330
Tel: (207) 626-2306 (Flights and Services) Fax: (207) 626-2309
E-mail: airport_info@augustaairport.org

Airport Manager **John Guimond** .... (207) 626-2307

Community Services Department
City Hall, 16 Cony St., Augusta, ME 04330

Director **Leif Dahlin** .... (207) 626-2305

Augusta Civic Center
76 Community Dr., Augusta, ME 04330
Tel: (207) 626-2400 (Schedule and Ticket Information)
E-mail: info@augustaciviccenter.org
Internet: http://www.augustaciviccenter.org

Director **Dana Colwill** .... (207) 626-2405

Bureau of Health and Welfare
Director **Leif Dahlin** .... (207) 626-2325

Lithgow Public Library
45 Winthrop Street, Augusta, ME 04330

Director **Elizabeth Pohl** .... (207) 626-2415
E-mail: betsy.pohl@augustamaine.gov

Old Fort Western
Fax: (207) 626-2304 E-mail: oldfort@oldfortwestern.org
Internet: http://www.oldfortwestern.org

Director **Linda Novak** .... (207) 626-2385

Bureau of Parks, Cemeteries and Trees
Director **James Goulet** .... (207) 626-2352
Bicentennial Park Manager **James Goulet** .... (207) 620-7010

Bureau of Recreation and Child Care
Recreation Director **Bruce Chase** .... (207) 626-2350
Child Care Director **Karen Hatch** .... (207) 626-2350

Development Services
Director **Matthew Nazar** .... (207) 626-2336
E-mail: matt.nazar@augustamaine.gov
Deputy Director **Keith Luke** .... (207) 626-2366
E-mail: keith.luke@augustamaine.gov

Engineering Bureau
City Hall, 16 Cony St., Augusta, ME 04330

City Engineer **Lionel Cayer** .... (207) 626-2365
E-mail: lionel.cayer@augustamaine.gov

Facilities and Maintenance
Manager **Robert LaBreck** .... (207) 626-2365
E-mail: bob.labreck@augustamaine.gov

Bureau of Codes
Director **Matthew Nazar** .... (207) 626-2366

Executive Department
City Hall, 16 Cony St., Augusta, ME 04330
Fax: (207) 620-8174

○ City Manager **William R. Bridgeo** .... (207) 626-2300
E-mail: bill.bridgeo@augustamaine.gov
Education: St Michael's 1972 BA; Hartford 1979 MPA

Bureau of Assessors
Tax Assessor **Lisa Morin** .... (207) 626-2320
E-mail: lisa.morin@augustamaine.gov

City Clerk's Office
City Hall, 16 Cony St., Augusta, ME 04330
Tel: (207) 626-2360 (Board of Voter Registration)

City Clerk **Barbara Wardwell** .... (207) 626-2310
E-mail: barbara.wardwell@augustamaine.gov

Finance and Administration Department
City Hall, 16 Cony St., Augusta, ME 04330

Director **Raphael E. St. Pierre** .... (207) 626-2300

Bureau of Audit
City Auditor **Tracy Roy** .... (207) 626-2340

Human Resources Bureau
City Center, 16 Cony St., Augusta, ME 04330
Fax: (207) 620-8174

Director **Kristina Gould** .... (207) 626-2353
E-mail: kristina.gould@augustamaine.gov

Bureau of Information Systems
Director **Fred Kahl** .... (207) 626-2345
E-mail: fred.kahl@augustamaine.gov
Assistant Technology Administrator **Michael Schriver** .... (207) 626-2345
E-mail: mike.schriver@augustamaine.gov Fax: (207) 626-2304

★ Elected Official ▲ Appointed by Legislature ▼ Appointed by Governor ▶ Appointed by Board or Commission ● Appointed by Judge
■ Appointed by Mayor △ Appointed by Freeholders ▽ Appointed by Supervisor ▷ Appointed by County Executive ○ Appointed by Council

CITIES AND TOWNS

Bureau of Treasury and Tax Collection
Treasurer/Tax Collector **Barbara Wardwell** .... (207) 626-2316

Fire Department
3 Grove Street, Augusta, ME 04330
Fire Chief **Roger Audette** .... (207) 626-2421
E-mail: roger.audette@augustamaine.gov

Police Department
33 Union St., Augusta, ME 04330
Chief of Police **Robert C. Gregoire** ....(207) 626-2370

Public Works Department
Director **Lesley Jones** .... (207) 626-2435

Bureau of Solid Waste
Director **Lesley Jones** .... (207) 626-2435

City of Aurora, Colorado

15151 East Alameda Parkway, Aurora, CO 80012
Tel: (303) 739-7000 (Information) Internet: www.auroragov.org

County: Adams and Arapahoe; Douglas **Election Type:** Nonpartisan
Population: 359,407 (2015)

Office of the Mayor and City Council

15151 East Alameda Parkway, Suite 5800, Aurora, CO 80012
Tel: (303) 739-7015 Fax: (303) 739-7594
E-mail: citycouncil@auroragov.org

★Mayor **Steve Hogan** .... (303) 739-7015
Began Service: November 14, 2011
Term Expires: November 2019
E-mail: shogan@auroragov.org
Assistant **Chanell Reed** .... (303) 739-7015
E-mail: creed@auroragov.org
★Mayor Pro Tem **Renie Peterson** (Ward 2) .... (303) 739-7506
Term Expires: November 2017
E-mail: rrpeters@auroragov.org
★Council Member **Sally Mounier** (Ward 1) .... (303) 739-7502
Term Expires: November 2017
E-mail: smounier@auroragov.org
★Council Member **Marsha Berzins** (Ward 3) .... (303) 739-7508
Term Expires: November 2017
E-mail: mberzins@auroragov.org
★Council Member **Charlie Richardson** (Ward 4) .... (303) 739-7015
Term Expires: November 2019
★Council Member **Bob Roth** (Ward 5) .... (303) 739-7510
Term Expires: November 2019
E-mail: broth@auroragov.org
★Council Member **Francoise Michelle Bergan** (Ward 6) .. (303) 739-7015
Term Expires: November 2019
★Council Member **Barbara Cleland** (At-Large) .... (303) 739-7524
Term Expires: November 2017
E-mail: bcleland@auroragov.org
★Council Member **Angela Lawson** (At-Large) ....(303) 739-7015
Term Expires: November 2019
Education: UC Berkeley BA; Colorado (Denver) MPA, MS; Georgetown MPP
★Council Member **Bob LeGare** (At-Large) .... (303) 739-7015
Term Expires: November 2019
E-mail: blegare@auroragov.org
★Council Member **Brad Pierce** (At-Large) .... (303) 739-7514
Term Expires: November 2017

Office of the City Attorney
15151 E. Alameda Pkwy., Aurora, CO 80012
○City Attorney **Michael Hyman** .... (303) 739-7030
E-mail: mhyman@auroragov.org

Office of the City Manager

15151 E. Alameda Pkwy., Aurora, CO 80012
Tel: (303) 739-7010 Fax: (303) 739-7123
E-mail: citymanager@auroragov.org

○City Manager **George "Skip" Noe** .... (303) 739-7010
E-mail: citymanager@auroragov.org
Administrative Services Deputy City Manager
Michelle Wolfe .... (303) 739-7010
E-mail: mwolfe@auroragov.org
Operations Deputy City Manager **Nancy Freed** .... (303) 739-7010
Education: Goucher BA; Denver MPA

Office of the City Clerk
15151 E. Alameda Pkwy., Aurora, CO 80012
E-mail: cityclerk@auroragov.org
City Clerk **Janice Napper** .... (303) 739-7094
E-mail: jnapper@auroragov.org

Office of Development Assistance
15151 East Alameda Parkway, Fifth Floor, Aurora, CO 80012
Fax: (303) 739-7503 E-mail: oda@auroragov.org
Manager **Vinessa Irvin** .... (303) 739-7345
E-mail: oda@auroragov.org

Fire Department
15151 East Alameda Parkway, Suite 4100, Aurora, CO 80014
Fax: (303) 326-8986 E-mail: fire@auroragov.org
Fire Chief **Mike Garcia** .... (303) 326-8999
E-mail: mgarcia@auroragov.org

Police Department
15001 E. Alameda Pkwy., Aurora, CO 80012
E-mail: police@auroragov.org
Chief **Nicholas "Nick" Metz** .... (303) 739-6000

Administration Deputy City Manager
15151 E. Alameda Pkwy., Aurora, CO 80012
Administration Deputy City Manager **Michelle Wolfe** .... (303) 739-7010
E-mail: mwolfe@auroragov.org

Finance Department
15151 E. Alameda Pkwy., Aurora, CO 80012
E-mail: finance@auroragov.org
Director **Jason Batchelor** .... (303) 739-7055

Internal Services and Human Resources Department
15151 E. Alamada Pkwy., Aurora, CO 80012
E-mail: humanresources@auroragov.org
Director of Internal Services **Dan Quillen** .... (303) 739-7225
E-mail: humanresources@auroragov.org
Human Resources Division Director **Noel Mink** .... (303) 739-7229
E-mail: humanresources@auroragov.org
Risk Management Division Director
Renee Pettinato-Mosley .... (303) 739-7003
Purchasing Services Division Director **Bryn Fillinger** .... (303) 739-7100
E-mail: internalservicesdept@auroragov.org
Fleet Maintenance Division Director **Mark Hinterreiter** . . . (303) 326-8046

Information Technology
15151 E. Alameda Pkwy., Aurora, CO 80012
Director **(Vacant)** .... (303) 739-7369

★Elected Official ▲Appointed by Legislature ▼Appointed by Governor ▶Appointed by Board or Commission ●Appointed by Judge
■Appointed by Mayor △Appointed by Freeholders ▽Appointed by Supervisor ▷Appointed by County Executive ○Appointed by Council

Operations Deputy City Manager
15151 E. Alameda Pkwy., Aurora, CO 80012

Operations Deputy City Manager **Nancy Freed** .... (303) 739-7010
Education: Goucher BA; Denver MPA

Communications Department
15151 East Alameda Parkway, Aurora, CO 80012
Tel: (303) 739-7046

Director **Kim Stuart** .... (303) 739-7046
E-mail: communications@auroragov.org

Library and Cultural Services
14949 E. Alameda Pkwy., Aurora, CO 80012
Tel: (303) 739-6640 Fax: (303) 739-6586 E-mail: library@auroragov.org
Internet: http://auroralibrary.org

Director **Patti Bateman** .... (303) 739-6580
E-mail: pbateman@auroragov.org

Neighborhood Services
15151 E. Alameda Pkwy., Aurora, CO 80012
E-mail: neighborhood@auroragov.org

Director (Interim) **Ron Moore** .... (303) 739-7280
E-mail: neighborhood@auroragov.org

Parks, Recreation and Open Space Department
15151 E. Alameda Pkwy., Aurora, CO 80012
E-mail: parks@aurorgov.org

Director **Tom Barrett** .... (303) 739-7168

Planning and Development Services Department
15151 East Alameda Parkway, 2nd Floor, Aurora, CO 80012
E-mail: planning@auroragov.org Fax: (303) 739-7268

Director **Robert Watkins** .... (303) 739-7541
E-mail: rwatkins@auroragov.org
FasTracks Team Manager **John Fernandez** .... (303) 739-7269
E-mail: jfernand@auroragov.org
Planning Division Manager **Jim Sayre** .... (303) 739-7185
E-mail: jsayre@auroragov.org
Development Services Manager
Andrea Solat Amonick .... (303) 739-7129
E-mail: aamonick@auroragov.org

Public Works Department
15151 E. Alameda Pkwy., Aurora, CO 80012

Director **Dave Chambers** .... (303) 739-7300

Water Department
15151 East Alameda Parkway, Aurora, CO 80012
E-mail: utilities@auroragov.org

Director **Marshall Brown** .... (303) 739-7370

Aurora Public Schools
15701 East 1st Avenue, Suite 206, Aurora, CO 80011
Tel: (303) 344-8060 Internet: www.aps.k12.co.us

Superintendent **Demetri E. "Rico" Munn** .... (303) 365-7800
15701 East First Avenue, Aurora, CO 80011 Fax: (303) 326-1280
Education: Midland Lutheran 1993 BA; Denver 1996 JD

★ President **Amber Drevon** .... (303) 344-8060
Term Expires: November 2017
E-mail: adrevon@aps.k12.co.us

★ Vice President **Dan Jorgensen** .... (303) 345-8981
Term Expires: November 2019
E-mail: ddjorgensen@aps.k12.co.us

★ Secretary **Eric Nelson** .... (303) 344-8060
Term Expires: November 2017
E-mail: ENelson@aps.k12.co.us

★ Treasurer **Barbara Yamrick** .... (303) 344-8060
Term Expires: November 2017
E-mail: byamrick@aps.k12.co.us

Aurora Public Schools *continued*

★ Director **Monica Colbert** .... (303) 344-8060
Term Expires: November 2019

★ Director **Julie Marie Shepherd** .... (303) 365-7800
Term Expires: November 2017
E-mail: jshepherd@aps.k12.co.us

★ Director **Cathy Wildman** .... (303) 745-0594
Term Expires: November 2019
E-mail: cwildman@aps.k12.co.us

City of Aurora, Illinois
City Hall, 44 E. Downer Place, Aurora, IL 60507
Internet: http://www.aurora-il.org

County: DuPage; Kane; Kendall; Will **Election Type:** Nonpartisan
Year Founded: 1857 **Population:** 200,661 (2015)

Office of the Mayor and City Council
City Hall, 44 E. Downer Place, Aurora, IL 60507
Fax: (630) 256-3019

★ Mayor **Thomas J. Weisner** .... (630) 256-3010
Term Expires: April 25, 2017
E-mail: mayorsoffice@aurora-il.org
Chief Management Officer **Carie Anne Ergo** .... (630) 256-3010
Assistant Chief of Staff **Rick Guzman** .... (630) 256-3010
E-mail: rguzman@aurora-il.org
Assistant Chief of Staff **Alex Voigt** .... (630) 256-3010
E-mail: avoigt@aurora-il.org

★ Alderman **Kristina "Tina" Bohman** (Ward 1) .... (630) 256-3020
Term Expires: April 22, 2019
E-mail: tbohman@aurora-il.org

★ Alderman **Juany Garza** (Ward 2) .... (630) 256-3020
Term Expires: April 25, 2017
E-mail: jgarza@aurora-il.org

★ Alderman **Theodoros "Ted" Mesiacos** (Ward 3) .... (630) 256-3020
Term Expires: April 2019
E-mail: aldermanmesiacos@comcast.net

★ Alderman **William Donnell** (Ward 4) .... (630) 256-3020
Term Expires: April 25, 2017
E-mail: wmdonnellald4@gmail.com

★ Alderman **Carl Franco** (Ward 5) .... (630) 256-3020
Term Expires: May 5, 2019
E-mail: cfranco@aurora-il.or

★ Alderman **Michael Saville** (Ward 6) .... (630) 256-3020
Term Expires: April 22, 2019
E-mail: msaville@aurora-il.org
Education: Illinois (Chicago) BA

★ Alderman **Scheketa Hart-Burns** (Ward 7) .... (630) 256-3020
Term Expires: April 25, 2017
E-mail: shart-burns@aurora-il.org

★ Alderman **Richard B. "Rick" Mervine** (Ward 8) .... (630) 256-3020
Term Expires: April 22, 2019
E-mail: aldermanmervine@gmail.com

★ Alderman **Edward J. Bugg** (Ward 9) .... (630) 256-3020
Term Expires: April 22, 2017
E-mail: AldermanBugg@gmail.com

★ Alderman **Lynne Johnson** (Ward 10) .... (630) 256-3020
Term Expires: April 22, 2017
E-mail: AldermanLJohnson@aol.com

★ Alderman **Richard C. Irvin** (At-Large) .... (630) 256-3020
Term Expires: April 22, 2019
E-mail: rirvin@aurora-il.org

★ Alderman **Robert J. O'Connor** (At-Large) .... (630) 256-3020
Term Expires: April 25, 2017
E-mail: roconnor@aurora-il.org
Education: Illinois BA; Notre Dame JD

★ Elected Official ▲ Appointed by Legislature ▼ Appointed by Governor ▶ Appointed by Board or Commission ● Appointed by Judge
■ Appointed by Mayor △ Appointed by Freeholders ▽ Appointed by Supervisor ▷ Appointed by County Executive ○ Appointed by Council

Office of the City Clerk
City Hall, 44 E. Downer Place, Aurora, IL 60507
Fax: (630) 256-3079

City Clerk **Wendy McCambridge** . . . . (630) 256-3070
E-mail: wmccambridge@aurora-il.org Fax: (630) 256-3079
Education: Marquette BA; Chicago MPP

Community Services
5 South Broadway, Aurora, IL 60505
Fax: (630) 256-3409

Director **Daniel Barreiro** . . . . (630) 256-3401
E-mail: dbarreiro@aurora-il.org

Community Relations Division
5 East Downer Place, Aurora, IL 60505

Director **Clayton Muhammad** . . . . (630) 256-3360
E-mail: cmuhammad@aurora-il.org

Customer Service Division
3770 McCoy Drive, Aurora, IL 60504

Director **Cecilia Soto** . . . . (630) 256-4636

Neighborhood Redevelopment Division
5 South Broadway, Aurora, IL 60505
Fax: (630) 256-3329

Director (Interim) **Chuck Nelson** . . . . (630) 256-3321
E-mail: cnelson@aurora-il.org

Youth and Senior Services Division
5 South Broadway, Aurora, IL 60505

Director **Ken Maurice** . . . . (630) 256-3402

Corporation Counsel
5 East Downer Place, Aurora, IL 60505

Corporation Counsel **Alayne M. Weingartz** . . . . (630) 256-3060

Development Services Department
1 South Broadway, Aurora, IL 60505
Fax: (630) 256-3169

Director **Bill Wiet** . . . . (630) 256-3100
E-mail: bwiet@aurora-il.org

Aurora Municipal Airport
Veterans Memorial Parkway, 43W636 US 30, Sugar Grove, IL 60554
Fax: (630) 466-1166 Internet: http://www.auroraairport.com

Airport Director (Interim) **Elizabeth "Beth" Penesis** . . . . (630) 256-3120

Building and Permits Division
65 Water Street, Aurora, IL 60507
Fax: (630) 256-3139

Director **John Curley** . . . . (630) 256-3130

Economic Development Commission
43 West Galena Boulevard, Aurora, IL 60506
Fax: (630) 256-3169

Director **David Hulseberg** . . . . (630) 256-3160

Planning and Zoning Division
1 South Broadway, Aurora, IL 60505

Director **Stephane Phifer** . . . . (630) 256-3081
E-mail: sphifer@aurora-il.org

Finance Department
City Hall, 44 East Downer Place, Aurora, IL 60507
Fax: (630) 256-3509

Chief Financial Officer **Brian W. Caputo** . . . . (630) 256-3500
Education: West Point BS; DePaul MS; Northern Illinois MPA, 2015 PhD

Accounting Division
City Hall, 44 East Downer Place, Aurora, IL 60507

Assistant Director of Finance **Linda Read** . . . . (630) 256-3510
E-mail: lread@aurora-il.org

Budgeting Division
City Hall, 44 East Downer Place, Aurora, IL 60507

Director **Stacey Hamling** . . . . (630) 256-3540
E-mail: shamling@aurora-il.org

Purchasing Division
City Hall, 44 East Downer Place, Aurora, IL 60507

Director **Esther Phillips** . . . . (630) 256-3550
E-mail: ephillips@aurora-il.org

Revenue and Collections Division
City Hall, 44 East Downer Place, Aurora, IL 60507
Fax: (630) 256-3569

Director **Charles Koch** . . . . (630) 256-3560
E-mail: ckoch@aurora-il.org

Water Billing Division
City Hall, 44 East Downer Place, Aurora, IL 60507
Fax: (630) 256-3609 E-mail: btorres@aurora-il.org

Director **Beatrice Torres** . . . . (630) 256-3600

Fire Department
75 N. Broadway, Aurora, IL 60505
Fax: (630) 256-4009

■ Fire Chief **Gary Krienitz** . . . . (630) 256-4000
E-mail: fire@aurora-il.org

Human Resources Division
City Hall, 44 E. Downer Place, Aurora, IL 60507
Fax: (630) 265-3439

Director **Alisia Lewis** . . . . (630) 256-3430
E-mail: alewis@aurora-il.org

Information Technology Division
City Hall, 44 East Downer Place, Aurora, IL 60507

Chief Technology Officer **Ted Beck** . . . . (630) 256-3471
E-mail: tbeck@aurora-il.org

Library
101 South River Street, Aurora, IL 60506
Internet: http://www.aurora.lib.il.us Fax: (630) 859-1909

Director **Daisy Porter-Reynolds** . . . . (630) 264-4106
E-mail: Daisy@aurorapubliclibrary.org

Neighborhood Standards Department
1 South Broadway, Aurora, IL 60505
Fax: (630) 256-3779

Director of Neighborhood Standards **Chuck Nelson** . . . . . (630) 256-3490
E-mail: cnelson@aurora-il.org

Animal Control Division
606 South River Street, Aurora, IL 60505
Fax: (630) 256-3779

Director **Rick Smith** . . . . (630) 256-3630

Maintenance Services Division
720 North Broadway, Aurora, IL 60505

Superintendent **Joseph Hopp** . . . . (630) 256-3650
E-mail: jhopp@aurora-il.org

Parks and Recreation Division
901 Moses Drive, Aurora, IL 60505

Director **Dan Anderson** . . . . (630) 256-3730

★ Elected Official ▲ Appointed by Legislature ▼ Appointed by Governor ► Appointed by Board or Commission ● Appointed by Judge
■ Appointed by Mayor △ Appointed by Freeholders ▽ Appointed by Supervisor ▷ Appointed by County Executive ○ Appointed by Council

Parks and Recreation Division *continued*

Philips Park Zoo Manager **(Vacant)** .... (630) 256-3860

Property Standards Division

1 South Broadway, Aurora, IL 60505
Fax: (630) 256-3779

Director **Kelvin Beene** .... (630) 256-3770

Police Department

1200 East Indian Trail, Aurora, IL 60506
Fax: (630) 896-1187 E-mail: info@apd.aurora.il.us
Internet: http://www.aurora-il.org/apd

■ Police Chief **Kristen Ziman** .... (630) 256-5008
E-mail: zimank@apd.aurora.il.us

Emergency Management Division

1200 East Indian Trail, Aurora, IL 60505

Emergency Management Coordinator **Joseph Jones** ..... (630) 256-5800

Public Works Department

City Hall, 44 East Downer Place, Aurora, IL 60507
Fax: (630) 256-3209

Director **Ken Schroth** .... (630) 256-3200
Assistant City Engineer **Steve Andras** .... (630) 256-3200
E-mail: sandras@aurora-il.org

Streets Division

720 North Broadway, Aurora, IL 60505
Fax: (630) 256-3689

Superintendent **Timothy Forbes** .... (630) 256-3680

Water and Sewer Maintenance Division

649 South River Street, Aurora, IL 60506
Fax: (630) 256-3719

Director **Eric Shoney** .... (630) 256-3710

City of Austin, Texas

301 West Second Street, Austin, TX 78701
P.O. Box 1088, Austin, TX 78767-1088
Tel: (512) 974-2000 (Information) TTY: (512) 974-2249
Internet: www.austintexas.gov

County: Hays; Travis; Williamson **Election Type:** Nonpartisan
Population: 931,830 (2015)

Office of the Mayor and City Council

301 West Second Street, Suite 2009, Austin, TX 78701

★ Mayor **Stephen "Steve" Adler** .... (512) 978-2100
Began Service: January 6, 2015 Fax: (512) 978-2120
Term Expires: January 2019
Education: Princeton 1978 BA; Texas 1982 JD
Chief of Staff **John-Michael V. Cortez** .... (512) 978-2130
Executive Assistant **Barbara Shack** .... (512) 978-2100
E-mail: barbara.shack@austintexas.gov

★ Mayor Pro Tem **Kathie Tovo** (District 9) .... (512) 974-2109
Term Expires: January 6, 2019 Fax: (512) 974-2119
E-mail: kathie.tovo@austintexas.gov

★ Council Member **Ora Houston** (District 1) .... (512) 978-2140
Term Expires: January 2019

★ Council Member **Delia Garza** (District 2) .... (512) 978-2102
Term Expires: January 2017 Fax: (512) 978-2112

★ Council Member **Sabino "Pio" Renteria** (District 3) .... (512) 978-2103
Term Expires: January 2019 Fax: (512) 978-2113

★ Council Member **Gregorio Casar** (District 4) .... (512) 978-2104
Term Expires: January 2017 Fax: (512) 978-2114

Office of the Mayor and City Council *continued*

★ Council Member **Ann Kitchen** (District 5) .... (512) 978-2105
Term Expires: January 2019 Fax: (512) 978-2115

★ Council Member **Don Zimmerman** (District 6) .... (512) 978-2106
Term Expires: January 2017 Fax: (512) 978-2116

★ Council Member **Leslie Pool** (District 7) .... (512) 978-2107
Term Expires: January 2017 Fax: (512) 978-2117

★ Council Member **Ellen Troxclair** (District 8) .... (512) 978-2108
Term Expires: January 2019 Fax: (512) 978-2118

★ Council Member **Sheri Gallo** (District 10) .... (512) 978-2110
Term Expires: January 2017 Fax: (512) 978-2121

Office of the City Clerk

301 West Second Street, Suite 1120, Austin, TX 78701
Internet: http://www.austintexas.gov/department/city-clerk

○ City Clerk **Jannette Goodall** .... (512) 974-2211
E-mail: jannette.goodall@austintexas.gov

City Auditor

301 West Second Street, Suite 2130, Austin, TX 78701
Fax: (512) 974-2078

○ City Auditor **Corrie Stokes** .... (512) 974-2468
E-mail: corrie.stokes@austintexas.gov
Deputy City Auditor **(Vacant)** .... (512) 974-2468

Office of the City Manager

301 West Second Street, 3rd Floor, Austin, TX 78701
Fax: (512) 974-2833
Internet: www.austintexas.gov/department/city-manager

○ City Manager **Marc Ott** .... (512) 974-2200
E-mail: marc.ott@austintexas.gov
Education: Oakland U 1979 BA, 1981 MPA

Assistant City Manager (Interim) **Mark Washington** ..... (512) 974-2200
E-mail: mark.washington@austintexas.gov
Education: Tarleton State 1993 BABA; Southwestern Baptist MA; Amberton U MBA

Chief Sustainability Officer **Lucia Athens** .... (512) 974-2200

Integrity Office

301 West Second Street, Austin, TX 78701

Integrity Officer **Sabine Romero** .... (512) 974-2180

Austin Energy

721 Barton Springs Rd., Austin, TX 78704
Tel: (512) 322-6514 Internet: www.austinenergy.com

General Manager (Interim) **Mark Dombroski** .... (512) 322-6002

Finance and Administrative Services

301 West Second Street, Austin, TX 78701
Fax: (512) 974-3344
Internet: www.austintexas.gov/department/financial-services

Vice President of Finance **Elaine Hart** .... (512) 974-2589
Education: Texas (Arlington) BABA

Deputy Chief Financial Officer **Greg Canally** .... (512) 974-2609

Deputy Chief Financial Officer, Budget **Ed Van Eenoo** ... (512) 974-2638
E-mail: ed.vaneenoo@austintexas.gov
Education: Virginia Tech MS

Building Services Officer **Eric Stockton** .... (512) 974-7948
411 Chicon Street, Austin, TX 78701 Fax: (512) 974-3961
E-mail: eric.stockton@austintexas.gov

Controller **Diana Thomas** .... (512) 974-2600
124 West 8th Street, Suite 140, Austin, TX 78701
E-mail: diana.thomas@austintexas.gov

Fleet Services Officer **Gerry Calk** .... (512) 974-1540
1190 Hargrove Street, Austin, TX 78701

Purchasing Officer **Urcha Crespo** .... (512) 974-2050
124 West 8th Street, Austin, TX 78701
E-mail: byron.johnson@austintexas.gov

(continued on next page)

★ Elected Official ▲ Appointed by Legislature ▼ Appointed by Governor ► Appointed by Board or Commission ● Appointed by Judge
■ Appointed by Mayor △ Appointed by Freeholders ▽ Appointed by Supervisor ▷ Appointed by County Executive ○ Appointed by Council

Finance and Administrative Services *continued*

Communications and Technology Management\Chief Information Officer **Stephen Elkins** . . . . . (512) 974-1644
625 E. 10th St., Suite 900, Austin, TX 78701
E-mail: stephen.elkins@austintexas.gov

Telecommunications Officer **Rondella Hawkins** . . . . . (512) 974-2999
124 West Eighth Street, Austin, TX 78701
E-mail: rondella.hawkins@austintexas.gov

Treasurer **Art Alfaro** . . . . . (512) 974-7882
700 Lavaca St., Suite 1510, Austin, TX 78701

Law Department

301 West Second Street, 4th Fl, Austin, TX 78701
Fax: (512) 974-2894 Internet: www.austintexas.gov/department/law

City Attorney (Interim) **Ann Morgan** . . . . . (512) 974-2177
E-mail: ann.morgan@austintexas.gov

Office of the Police Monitor

Building 1, 1520 Rutherford Lane, Suite 2.200A, Austin, TX 78767
Internet: www.austintexas.gov/department/police-monitor

Deputy Police Monitor **Margo L. Frasier** . . . . . (512) 974-9007
E-mail: margo.frasier@austintexas.gov

Chief of Staff

301 West Second Street, Austin, TX 78701
Fax: (512) 974-2833

Chief of Staff (Interim) **Ray Baray** . . . . . (512) 974-2435
Executive Assistant **Robin Otto** . . . . . (512) 974-7744
E-mail: robin.otto@austintexas.gov
Executive Secretary **Mary Lou Rodriguez** . . . . . (512) 974-6339
E-mail: marylou.rodriguez@austintexas.gov

Agenda Office

Agenda Manager **Leander Davilla** . . . . . (512) 974-2306
E-mail: leander.davila@austintexas.gov

Communications and Public Information Office

301 West Second Street, 3rd FL, Austin, TX 78701
Tel: (512) 974-2220 Fax: (512) 974-2405
Internet: www.austintexas.gov/department/communications

Director of Communications and Public Information **Douglas Matthews** . . . . . (512) 974-2231
E-mail: douglas.matthews@austintexas.gov
Education: Central Florida BA
Deputy Director **David Matustik** . . . . . (512) 974-2406
E-mail: david.matustik@austintexas.gov
Web Content Administrator **(Vacant)** . . . . . (512) 974-2980

Government Relations

301 West Second Street, 3rd FL, Austin, TX 78701

Government Relations Officer **(Vacant)** . . . . . (512) 974-2285

Human Resources Department

505 Barton Springs Road, Suite 600, Austin, TX 78704
Tel: (512) 974-3211 Fax: (512) 974-3214
Internet: www.austintexas.gov/department/human-resources

Human Resources Director (Interim) **Joya Hayes** . . . . . (512) 974-3215
E-mail: joya.hayes@austintexas.gov
Assistant Director **Joya Hayes** . . . . . (512) 974-3211
E-mail: joya.hayes@austintexas.gov
Assistant Director **Karen Sharp** . . . . . (512) 974-1402
E-mail: karen.sharp@austintexas.gov
Assistant Director **Tommy Tucker** . . . . . (512) 974-3220
E-mail: tommy.tucker@austintexas.gov
Assistant Director **Judy Wallace** . . . . . (512) 974-1356
E-mail: carla.scales@austintexas.gov

Neighborhood Housing and Community Development Office

1000 East 11th Street, Austin, TX 78702
Fax: (512) 974-3112 Internet: www.austintexas.gov/department/housing

Director **Betsy Spencer** . . . . . (512) 974-3182
E-mail: betsy.spencer@austintexas.gov
Assistant Director **Rebecca Giello** . . . . . (512) 974-3045
E-mail: rebecca.giello@austintexas.gov
Human Resources Coordinator **Chris Jones** . . . . . (512) 974-3182
Housing Development Manager **David Potter** . . . . . (512) 974-3192
E-mail: david.potter@austintexas.gov
Neighborhood Liaison **Ateja Dukes** . . . . . (512) 974-3192
E-mail: ateja.dukes@austintexas.gov

Office of the Deputy City Manager

301 West Second Street, 3rd FL, Austin, TX 78701

Deputy City Manager **(Vacant)** . . . . . (512) 974-2307

Office of Homeland Security and Emergency Management [HESM]

P.O. Box 1088, Austin, TX 78767-1088
Fax: (512) 974-0499

Director **Otis J. Latin, Sr.** . . . . . (512) 974-0461
E-mail: otis.latin@austintexas.gov

Emergency Medical Services Department

15 Waller St., 2nd Floor, Austin, TX 78701
Tel: (512) 972-7200 Internet: http://www.ci.austin.tx.us/ems

Director **Ernesto Rodriguez** . . . . . (512) 972-7203

Fire Department

4201 Ed Bluestein Boulevard, Austin, TX 78721
Internet: www.austintexas.gov/department/fire

Fire Chief **Rhoda Mae Kerr** . . . . . (512) 974-0131
Education: William Paterson U BA; Florida International MPA

Police Department

715 E. Eighth St., Austin, TX 78701
Tel: (512) 974-5000 Fax: (512) 974-6611
Internet: www.austintexas.gov/department/police

Chief of Police **Art Acevedo** . . . . . (512) 974-4278
Chief of Staff **Brian Manley** . . . . . (512) 974-5030
Assistant Chief **Jason Dusterhoft** . . . . . (512) 974-5030
Assistant Chief **Troy Gay** . . . . . (512) 974-5030
Assistant Chief **Pat Ockletree** . . . . . (512) 974-5030
Assistant Chief **Jessica Robledo** . . . . . (512) 974-5030

Office of the Assistant City Manager

301 West Second Street, #3026, Austin, TX 78701
Fax: (512) 974-2833

Assistant City Manager **(Vacant)** . . . . . (512) 974-2410
Executive Assistant **Kathleen Nowell** . . . . . (512) 974-2611
E-mail: kathleen.nowell@austintexas.gov

Austin Convention Center Department

500 E. Cesar Chavez St., Austin, TX 78701
Fax: (512) 404-4416 Internet: http://www.austinconventioncenter.com

Director **Mark Tester** . . . . . (512) 404-4040

Austin Water Utility

625 E. 10th St., Suite 800, Austin, TX 78701
Tel: (512) 972-0101 Internet: www.austintexas.gov/department/water

Director **Greg Meszaros** . . . . . (512) 972-0108
Assistant Director **Ruth Jane Burazer** . . . . . (512) 972-0133
Assistant Director, Engineering/Field Operations **George Calhoun** . . . . . (512) 972-0256
E-mail: george.calhoun@austintexas.gov

★ Elected Official ▲ Appointed by Legislature ▼ Appointed by Governor ► Appointed by Board or Commission ● Appointed by Judge
■ Appointed by Mayor △ Appointed by Freeholders ▽ Appointed by Supervisor ▷ Appointed by County Executive ○ Appointed by Council

Contract Management Department [CLMD]
105 West Riverside Drive, Suite 200, Austin, TX 78704
Fax: (512) 469-1719
Internet: www.austintexas.gov/department/contract-management

Director **Rosie Truelove** .... (512) 974-3064
E-mail: rosie.truelove@austintexas.gov

Small and Minority Business Resources
4100 Ed Bluestein Boulevard, Austin, TX 78721
Tel: (512) 974-7600 Fax: (512) 974-7601

Director **Veronica Lara** .... (512) 974-2156
E-mail: veronica.lara@austintexas.gov

Office of the Assistant City Manager
301 West 2nd Street, Austin, TX 78701
Fax: (512) 974-2833

Assistant City Manager **Bert Lumbreras** .... (512) 974-2200
E-mail: bert.lumbreras@austintexas.gov
Executive Secretary **Laura Polio** .... (512) 974-7717
E-mail: laura.polio@austintexas.gov

Health and Human Services Department
Building E, 7201 Levander Loop, Austin, TX 78744
P.O. Box 1088, Austin, TX 78767-1088
Tel: (512) 972-5400 Fax: (512) 972-5016
Internet: www.austintexas.gov/department/health

Director **Shannon Jones III** .... (512) 972-5416
Deputy Director **Stephanie Hayden** .... (512) 972-5400
Animal Services Officer **Tawny Hammond** .... (512) 978-0507
Health Authority **Dr. Philip Huang** .... (512) 972-5408

Library Department
John Henry Faulk Library, 800 Guadalupe, Austin, TX 78701
Tel: (512) 974-7400 Internet: http://library.austintexas.gov/

Director **Brenda Branch** .... (512) 974-7444
E-mail: brenda.branch@austintexas.gov

Parks and Recreation Department
200 S. Lamar Blvd., Austin, TX 78704
Tel: (512) 974-6700 Fax: (512) 974-6703

Director **Sara L. Hensley** .... (512) 974-6783
Education: Arkansas 1979 BS, 1981 MSEd

Office of the Assistant City Manager
301 West Second Street, Austin, TX 78701
P.O. Box 1088, Austin, TX 78767
Fax: (512) 974-2833

Assistant City Manager **Sue Edwards** .... (512) 974-7820
E-mail: sue.edwards@austintexas.gov
Executive Assistant **Marie Sandoval** .... (512) 974-3298
E-mail: marie.sandoval@austintexas.gov

Economic Development Department
301 West Second Street, Austin, TX 78701
Tel: (512) 974-7819 Fax: (512) 974-7825
Internet: www.austintexas.gov/department/economic-growth

Director **Kevin Johns** .... (512) 974-7802
E-mail: kevin.johns@austintexas.gov
Deputy Director **Rodney Gonzales** .... (512) 974-2313
E-mail: rodney.gonzales@austintexas.gov
Assistant Director **Sylnovia Holt-Rabb** .... (512) 974-3131
E-mail: sylnovia.holt-rabb@austintexas.gov
Redevelopment Manager **Fred Evins** .... (512) 974-7131
E-mail: fred.evins@austintexas.gov
Mueller Project Manager **Pam Hefner** .... (512) 974-3511
E-mail: pam.hefner@austintexas.gov
Economic Development Manager **Margaret Shaw** .... (512) 974-6497
E-mail: margaret.shaw@austintexas.gov
International Program Manager **Ben Ramirez** .... (512) 974-6416
E-mail: ben.ramirez@austintexas.gov

Economic Development Department *continued*

Cultural Arts Division Manager **Megan Crigger** .... (512) 974-9312
E-mail: megan.crigger@austintexas.gov
Small Business Development Manager **Vicky Valdez** .... (512) 974-7620
E-mail: vicky.valdez@austintexas.gov

Planning and Development Review Department
505 Barton Springs Rd., 5th Floor, Austin, TX 78704
Internet: www.austintexas.gov/department/planning

Director **Greg Guernsey** .... (512) 974-2387

Watershed Protection Department
One Texas Center, 505 Barton Springs Road, 12th Floor, Austin, TX 78704
Tel: (512) 974-2501 Fax: (512) 974-3343

Director **Victoria J. Li** .... (512) 974-9195
Deputy Director **Joe Pantalion** .... (512) 974-2652

Office of the Assistant City Manager
301 West Second Street, Austin, TX 78701

Assistant City Manager **Robert D. Goode** .... (512) 974-7717
E-mail: robert.goode@austintexas.gov

Aviation Department
3600 Presidential Boulevard, Suite 411, Austin, TX 78719
Fax: (512) 530-7686
Internet: www.austintexas.gov/department/austin-airport

Executive Director **Jim Smith** .... (512) 530-7518

Code Compliance Department
301 West Second Street, Austin, TX 78701
Fax: (512) 974-9049
Internet: www.austintexas.gov/department/code-compliance

Director **Carl Smart** .... (512) 974-1970

Austin Resource Recovery Department
PO Box 1088, Austin, TX 78767
1520 Rutherford Lane, Austin, TX 78754
Tel: (512) 494-9400

Director **Robert Gedert** .... (512) 974-1926
Assistant Director **Tammie Williamson** .... (512) 974-1997

Public Works Department
505 Barton Springs Rd., 13th Floor, Austin, TX 78704
Tel: (512) 974-7065 Fax: (512) 974-7084

Director **Howard Lazarus** .... (512) 974-7190

Transportation Department
301 West Second Street, Austin, TX 78701
Internet: www.austintexas.gov/department/transportation
Internet: http://twitter.com/austinmobility

Director **Robert Spillar** .... (512) 974-2488

Austin Independent School District
1111 W. Sixth St., Austin, TX 78703
Tel: (512) 414-1700 Fax: (512) 414-1486 E-mail: trustees@austinisd.org
Internet: www.austinisd.org

Superintendent **Dr. Paul Cruz** .... (512) 414-2412
★ President **Kendall Pace** (At-Large, Position 9) .... (512) 414-2413
Term Expires: November 6, 2018
★ Vice President **Paul M. Saldana** (District 6) .... (512) 414-2413
Term Expires: November 2018
★ Secretary **Julie Cowan** (District 4) .... (512) 414-2413
Term Expires: November 2018
★ Trustee **Edmund T. Gordon** (District 1) .... (512) 414-2413
Term Expires: November 2018
★ Trustee **Jayme Mathias** (District 2) .... (512) 414-2413
Term Expires: November 2016
E-mail: trustees@austinisd.org

(continued on next page)

★ Elected Official ▲ Appointed by Legislature ▼ Appointed by Governor ► Appointed by Board or Commission ● Appointed by Judge
■ Appointed by Mayor △ Appointed by Freeholders ▽ Appointed by Supervisor ▷ Appointed by County Executive ○ Appointed by Council

Austin Independent School District *continued*

★Trustee **Ann Teich** (District 3) . . . . (512) 414-2413
Term Expires: November 2016
E-mail: trustees@austinisd.org

★Trustee **Amber Elenz** (District 5) . . . . (512) 414-2413
Term Expires: November 2016
E-mail: trustees@austinisd.org

★Trustee **Yasmin Wagner** (District 7) . . . . (512) 414-2413
Term Expires: November 2016
E-mail: trustees@austinisd.org

★Trustee **Gina Hinojosa** (At-Large, Position 8) . . . . (512) 414-2413
Term Expires: November 2016
E-mail: trustees@austinisd.org
Executive Assistant to the Board **Elaine Hopkins** . . . . . . (512) 414-2413
E-mail: elaine.hopkins@austinisd.org

Town of Babylon, New York

Town Hall, 200 E. Sunrise Hwy., Lindenhurst, NY 11757
Tel: (631) 957-3072 (Information) Internet: www.townofbabylon.com

County: Suffolk **Election Type:** Partisan **Population:** 213,776 (2015)

Office of the Town Supervisor and Town Council

Town Hall, 200 E. Sunrise Hwy., Lindenhurst, NY 11757
Fax: (631) 957-7440 E-mail: info@townofbabylon.com

★Town Supervisor **Richard Schaffer** . . . . (631) 957-3072
Began Service: January 2012
Term Expires: December 31, 2017
Chief of Staff **Ronald Kluesener** . . . . (631) 957-3072

★Council Member **Thomas Donnelly** (D) . . . . (631) 957-3081
Term Expires: December 31, 2019

★Council Member **Jacqueline A. Gordon** (D) . . . . (631) 957-3125
Term Expires: December 31, 2019

★Council Member **Lindsay P. Henry** (I) . . . . (631) 957-4482
Term Expires: December 31, 2017

★Council Member **Antonio Martinez** (D) . . . . (631) 957-4472
Term Expires: December 31, 2017

○Communications Director **Kevin Bonner** . . . . (631) 957-7487
E-mail: kbonner@townofbabylon.com

Office of the Comptroller

Town Hall, 200 E. Sunrise Hwy., Lindenhurst, NY 11757

○Town Comptroller **Victoria Marotta** . . . . (631) 957-7438
E-mail: vmarotta@townofbabylon.com

Office of the Receiver of Taxes

Town Hall, 200 E. Sunrise Hwy., Lindenhurst, NY 11757

★Receiver of Taxes **Corinne DiSomma** . . . . (631) 957-3082
Term Expires: December 31, 2019
E-mail: cdisomma@townofbabylon.com

Office of the Town Assessor

Town Hall, 200 E. Sunrise Hwy., Lindenhurst, NY 11757

○Town Assessor **Joan Ball** . . . . (631) 957-3020
E-mail: jball@townofbabylon.com

Office of the Town Attorney

Town Hall, 200 E. Sunrise Hwy., Lindenhurst, NY 11757

○Town Attorney **Joseph Wilson** . . . . (631) 957-3029
E-mail: jwilson@townofbabylon.com

Office of the Town Clerk

Town Hall, 200 E. Sunrise Hwy., Lindenhurst, NY 11757

★Town Clerk **Carol Quirk** (D) . . . . (631) 957-4291
Term Expires: December 31, 2017 Fax: (631) 957-7490
E-mail: cquirk@townofbabylon.com

Babylon School District

50 Railroad Ave., Babylon, NY 11702

Superintendent of Schools **Linda Rozzi** . . . . (631) 893-7925
Assistant Superintendent for Curriculum and Instruction **Daniel D'Amico** . . . . (631) 893-7924

★President **Ann Donaldson** . . . . (631) 893-7900
Term Expires: June 30, 2018
E-mail: adonaldson@babylonufsd.org

★Vice President **Dominick Montalto** . . . . (631) 893-7900
Term Expires: June 30, 2017
E-mail: dmontalto@babylonufsd.org

★Board Member **Elizabeth Altbacker** . . . . (631) 893-7900
Term Expires: June 30, 2016
E-mail: ealtbacker@babylonufsd.org

★Board Member **Dominic Bencivenga** . . . . (631) 893-7900
Term Expires: June 30, 2016
E-mail: dbencivenga@babylonufsd.org

★Board Member **Carol Dell'Erba** . . . . (631) 893-7900
Term Expires: June 30, 2016

★Board Member **Linda Jurs** . . . . (631) 893-7900
Term Expires: June 30, 2016
E-mail: ljurs@babylonufsd.org

★Board Member **Tricia Pané** . . . . (631) 893-7900
Term Expires: June 30, 2017
E-mail: tpane@babylonufsd.org

Environmental Control Department

Babylon Town Annex, 281 Phelps Lane, North Babylon, NY 11704

Commissioner **Victoria Russell** . . . . (631) 422-7695
Animal Rescue Center Director **Chris Elton** . . . . (631) 643-9270
51 Lamar St., Babylon, NY 11704

Fire Prevention/Emergency Preparedness

999 North Indiana Ave., Lindenhurst, NY 11757

Fire Chief/Fire Marshal **Patrick Farrell** . . . . (631) 422-7600
E-mail: pfarrell@townofbabylon.com

General Services and Purchasing Department

Town Hall, 200 E. Sunrise Hwy., Lindenhurst, NY 11757

○Commissioner/Data Processing/Purchasing Director **Theresa Sabatino** . . . . (631) 957-3025
E-mail: tsabatino@townofbabylon.com

Handicapped Services

Babylon Town Annex, 281 Phelps Lane, Room 4, North Babylon, NY 11704

○Director **Claire Mckeon** . . . . (631) 893-1053
E-mail: cmckeon@townofbabylon.com

Human Services Department

1 Commerce Boulevard, Amityville, NY 11701

○Commissioner **Madeline Bayton** . . . . (631) 464-4340
E-mail: mbayton@townofbabylon.com

Parks, Recreation and Cultural Affairs Department

151 Phelps Lane, North Babylon, NY 11703

○Commissioner **Frank Bachety** . . . . (631) 893-2100
E-mail: fbachety@townofbabylon.com

Planning and Development Department
Town Hall, 200 E. Sunrise Hwy., Lindenhurst, NY 11757

○ Commissioner **Ann Marie Jones** .... (631) 957-7414
E-mail: ajones@townofbabylon.com

Public Works Department
Town Hall, 200 E. Sunrise Hwy., Lindenhurst, NY 11757

Commissioner **Tom Stay** .... (631) 957-3167
Electrical Service Supervisor **David Proulx** .... (631) 957-3177

Youth Bureau
Babylon Town Annex, 281 Phelps Lane, North Babylon, NY 11704

○ Director **Claire Mckeon** .... (631) 422-7660
E-mail: cmckeon@townofbabylon.com

City of Bakersfield, California
1600 Truxtun Avenue, Bakersfield, CA 93301
Tel: (661) 326-3000 (Information) Internet: www.bakersfieldcity.us

County: Kern **Election Type:** Nonpartisan **Population:** 373,640 (2015)

Harvey L. Hall
Mayor

Began Service: 2001
Term Expires: January 2017
Career: President and Founder, Hall Medical Equipment Supply; Trustee, Kern Community College District (1996-2000)

Office of the Mayor and City Council
1600 Truxtun Avenue, Bakersfield, CA 93301
Tel: (661) 326-3770 Fax: (661) 323-3780
E-mail: city_council@bakersfieldcity.us

★ Mayor **Harvey L. Hall** .... (661) 326-3770
E-mail: mayor@bakersfieldcity.us Fax: (661) 852-2035
Administrative Assistant **Keitha Turner** .... (661) 326-3770
E-mail: kturner@bakersfieldcity.us Fax: (661) 852-2035
★ Vice Mayor **Harold Hanson** (Ward 5) .... (661) 326-3767
Term Expires: November 2016
E-mail: city_council@bakersfieldcity.us
Education: Windsor BS
★ Council Member **P. "Willie" Rivera** (Ward 1) .... (661) 326-3767
Term Expires: November 2018
★ Council Member **Terry Maxwell** (Ward 2) .... (661) 326-3767
Term Expires: November 2016
★ Council Member **Kenton A. Weir, Jr.** (Ward 3) .... (661) 326-3767
Term Expires: November 2018
E-mail: city_council@bakersfieldcity.us
★ Council Member **Bob Smith** (Ward 4) .... (661) 326-3767
Term Expires: November 2018
E-mail: city_council@bakersfieldcity.us
★ Council Member **Jacquie Sullivan** (Ward 6) .... (661) 326-3767
Term Expires: November 2016
E-mail: city_council@bakersfieldcity.us
★ Council Member **Chris Parlier** (Ward 7) .... (661) 326-3767
Term Expires: November 2018

Office of the City Manager
1600 Truxtun Avenue, 5th Floor, Bakersfield, CA 93301
Fax: (661) 324-1850

○ City Manager **Alan Tandy** .... (661) 326-3751
E-mail: admmgr@bakersfieldcity.us
Education: Oregon 1971 BA; Iowa 1972 MA
City Clerk **Roberta Gafford** .... (661) 326-3767
E-mail: city_clerk@bakersfieldcity.us Fax: (661) 323-3780
Assistant City Clerk **Julie Drimakis** .... (661) 326-3767
E-mail: jdrimakis@bakersfieldcity.us Fax: (661) 323-3780
Human Resources Director **Christi Tenter** .... (661) 326-3770
E-mail: AdmHrs@bakersfieldcity.us
Information Technology Director **Dave Hecht** .... (661) 326-3016
E-mail: dhecht@bakersfieldcity.us

Office of the City Attorney
1600 Truxtun Avenue, 4th Floor, Bakersfield, CA 93301
Fax: (661) 852-2020

○ City Attorney **Virginia "Ginny" Gennaro** .... (661) 326-3721
E-mail: vgennaro@bakersfieldcity.us

Bakersfield City School District
1300 Baker Street, Bakersfield, CA 93305
Tel: (661) 631-4600 Fax: (661) 326-1485 E-mail: contactus@bcsd.com
Internet: http://www.bcsd.com

Superintendent **Dr. Robert J. Arias** .... (661) 631-4610
Assistant Superintendent, Academic Improvement and Accountability **Dr. Aida Molina** .... (661) 631-4743
Education: Cal State (Sacramento) 1991 BA, 1998 MEd
Assistant Superintendent of Human Resources **Dr. Diane Cox** .... (661) 631-4856
E-mail: dcox@bakersfieldcity.us
Chief Business Officer **Steve McClain** .... (661) 631-4675
★ President **Dr. Fred L. Haynes** .... (661) 631-4610
Term Expires: November 1, 2016
★ President Pro Tem **Lillian Tafoya** .... (661) 631-4610
Term Expires: November 1, 2016
★ Clerk **Andrae Gonzales** .... (661) 631-4610
Term Expires: November 1, 2018
★ Board Member **Pamela Baugher** .... (661) 631-4610
Term Expires: November 1, 2018
★ Board Member **Dr. Raymond J. Gonzales** .... (661) 631-4610
Term Expires: November 1, 2016

Community Development Department [EDCD]
1715 Chester Avenue, Bakersfield, CA 93301
Tel: (661) 326-3765 Fax: (661) 852-2138
E-mail: edcd@bakersfieldcity.us

Economic Development Director **Douglas McIsaac** .... (661) 326-3765
E-mail: edcd@bakersfieldcity.us
Education: Cal State (Fresno) BS; Cal State (Long Beach) MPA

Planning Division
1715 Chester Ave., Bakersfield, CA 93301
Fax: (661) 852-2136 E-mail: devpln@ci.bakersfield.ca.us

Planning Director **Jacquelyn R. Kitchen** .... (661) 326-3733

Building Division
1715 Chester Avenue, Bakersfield, CA 93301
Fax: (661) 325-0266 E-mail: devbld@bakersfieldcity.us

Director **Phil Burns** .... (661) 326-3720

Financial Services
1501 Truxtun Ave., Bakersfield, CA 93301
Tel: (661) 326-3742 Fax: (661) 852-2041
E-mail: finance@ci.bakersfield.ca.us

Director **Nelson K. Smith** .... (661) 326-3030
Education: Cal Poly San Luis Obispo 1982 BS; Cal State (Bakersfield) 2003 MBA Fax: (661) 326-3760

(continued on next page)

★ Elected Official ▲ Appointed by Legislature ▼ Appointed by Governor ► Appointed by Board or Commission ● Appointed by Judge
■ Appointed by Mayor △ Appointed by Freeholders ▽ Appointed by Supervisor ▷ Appointed by County Executive ○ Appointed by Council

Financial Services *continued*

Assistant Director **Sandra Jimenez** .... (661) 326-3031
Fax: (661) 326-3760

City Treasurer **Tessa Andrews** .... (661) 326-3761
Fax: (661) 852-2041

Purchasing Officer **Kim Berrigan** .... (661) 326-3744
E-mail: AdmPur@BakersfieldCity.us Fax: (661) 852-2100

Real Property Manager **Don Anderson** .... (661) 326-3061
Education: St Ambrose 1980 Fax: (661) 326-3760

Fire Department

2101 H St., Bakersfield, CA 93301
Tel: (661) 326-3911 Fax: (661) 852-2170
E-mail: fire@ci.bakersfield.ca.us

Fire Chief **Douglas R. Greener** .... (661) 326-3911
E-mail: dgreener@bakersfieldcity.us

Special Services Deputy Fire Chief-Operations
Ross Kelly .... (661) 326-3911
E-mail: rkelly@bakersfieldcity.us

Operations Deputy Fire Chief **Tyler Hartley** .... (661) 326-3911
E-mail: thartley@bakersfieldcity.us

Training Chief **Trever Martinusen** .... (661) 399-4697
5642 Victor St., Bakersfield, CA 93308
E-mail: tmartinu@bakersfieldfire.us

Fire Marshal **Howard Wines III** .... (661) 326-3911
E-mail: hwines@bakersfieldcity.us

Police Department

1601 Truxtun Ave., Bakersfield, CA 93301
P.O. Box 59, Bakersfield, CA 93302-0059
Tel: (661) 327-7111 Fax: (661) 852-2152
Fax: (661) 852-2158 (Records Fax)

Police Chief **Greg Williamson** .... (661) 326-3880
Assistant Chief of Police **Lyle Martin** .... (661) 326-3827
Operations-West Side **Rene Chow** .... (661) 852-7851
Homeland Security Detective **Shane Shaff** .... (661) 323-9665
E-mail: sshaff@bakersfieldpd.us
Homeland Security **Lt. Joe Mullins** .... (661) 326-3153
E-mail: jmullins@bakersfieldpd.us
Operations - East Side **Capt. Brian Clayton** .... (661) 326-3824
E-mail: bclayton@bakersfieldpd.us
Operations-West Side **Joe Bianco** .... (661) 326-3954
E-mail: jbianco@bakersfieldpd.us
Support Services Captain **Capt. Scott McDonald** .... (661) 326-3849
Public Information **Sgt Gary Carruesco** .... (661) 326-3803
E-mail: Gcarrues@bakersfieldpd.us
Planning, Research and Training **Lt. Mike Hale** .... (661) 326-3845
E-mail: mhale@bakersfieldpd.us

Public Works

1501 Truxtun Avenue, Bakersfield, CA 93301
Fax: (661) 852-2120

Director **Nick Fidler** .... (661) 326-3724
Assistant Director **Ted Wright** .... (661) 326-3575
Public Works Operations Manager **Stuart Patteson** .... (661) 326-3781

Engineering Division

Civil Engineer IV (Capital Improvement Program)
Navdip Grewal .... (661) 326-3724
E-mail: ngrewal@bakersfieldcity.us
Civil Engineer IV (Engineering Subdivision)
Marian Shaw .... (661) 326-3724
E-mail: mshaw@bakersfieldcity.us
Thomas Roads Improvement Program Manager
Kristina Budak .... (661) 326-3700
E-mail: kbudak@bakersfieldcity.us
Thomas Roads Improvement Program Manager
Luis Topete .... (661) 326-3700
E-mail: ltopete@bakersfieldcity.us
Traffic Engineer **Ryan Starbuck** .... (661) 326-3995
E-mail: PW_TRF@bakersfieldcity.us

Engineering Division *continued*

Construction Superintendent **Rob Voyles** .... (661) 326-3049
E-mail: PW_Con@bakersfieldcity.us

Equipment Division

4101 Truxtun Avenue, Bakersfield, CA 93309

Fleet Superintendent **Michael Vogel** .... (661) 326-3795

General Services Division

4101 Truxtun Ave., Bakersfield, CA 93309

Superintendent **Sean Cacal** .... (661) 326-3781

Solid Waste Division

4101 Truxtun Avenue, Bakersfield, CA 93309

Director **Kevin P. Barnes** .... (661) 326-3114
Superintendent **Sal Moretti** .... (661) 326-3136

Streets Division

4101 Truxtun Avenue, Bakersfield, CA 93309

Superintendent **Mike Conner** .... (661) 326-3111

Wastewater Division

8101 Ashe Road, Bakersfield, CA 93313
Fax: (661) 852-2125

Manager **Zachary Meyer** .... (661) 326-3249

Recreation and Parks

1600 Truxtun Avenue, Bakersfield, CA 93301
Tel: (661) 326-3866 Fax: (661) 852-2140
E-mail: compks@bakersfieldcity.us

Director **Dianne L. Hoover** .... (661) 326-3866
Assistant Director **Darin Budak** .... (661) 326-3866

Water Resources Department

1000 Buena Vista Rd., Bakersfield, CA 93311
Fax: (661) 852-2127 E-mail: water@bakersfieldcity.us

Manager **Art R. Chianello** .... (661) 326-3715

City of Baltimore, Maryland

City Hall, 100 North Holliday Street, Baltimore, MD 21202
Tel: (410) 396-3100 (Information) Internet: www.baltimorecity.gov/

County: None **Election Type:** Partisan **Year Founded:** 1729
Year Incorporated: 1797 **Charter:** 1964 **Population:** 621,849 (2015)

Office of the Mayor

City Hall, 100 North Holliday Street, Room 250, Baltimore, MD 21202
Tel: (410) 396-3835 Fax: (410) 576-9425

★ Mayor **Stephanie C. Rawlings-Blake** (D) .... (410) 396-3835
Began Service: February 4, 2010
Term Expires: December 1, 2016
E-mail: mayor@baltimorecity.gov
Date of Birth: March 17, 1970
Education: Oberlin 1992 BA; Maryland 1995 JD
Secretary to the Mayor **Angelica Parthemos** .... (410) 396-3882
E-mail: angelica.parthemos@baltimorecity.gov
Chief of Staff **Kaliope Parthemos** .... (410) 396-4876
Education: Maryland Baltimore County BA; Maryland Law JD
Deputy Chief of Staff **Kimberly Morton** .... (410) 396-4876
Deputy Mayor, Economic and Neighborhood
Development **Colin Tarbert** .... (410) 396-7987
E-mail: colin.tarbert@baltimorecity.gov
Education: Maryland BS, MArch
Deputy Mayor, Health, Human Services, Education and
Youth **Dawn Kirstaetter** .... (410) 396-3835

Office of the Mayor *continued*

Deputy Mayor, Office of Intergovernmental Relations
Andrew Smullian . . . . (410) 396-7208
E-mail: andrew.smullian@baltimorecity.gov

■ Deputy Mayor, Operations **Khalil A. Zaied** . . . . . . (410) 396-6802
Education: Maryland BSME

Chief of Public Affairs **(Vacant)** . . . . . . (410) 545-3406

Director of Strategic Planning and Policy **(Vacant)** . . . . (410) 396-3835

Legislative Reference Director **Avery Aisenstark** . . . . (410) 396-4733

Scheduling Director **Ashley Day** . . . . . . (410) 396-1800
E-mail: ashley.day@baltimorecity.gov

Special Assistant to the Mayor **Lindsey C. Hill** (I) . . . . (410) 396-1800
E-mail: lindsey.hill@baltimorecity.gov
Date of Birth: December 2, 1986
Education: Morgan State 2008 BS

Chief Service Officer **Vu Dang** . . . . . . (410) 576-9425
Education: Harvard; Houston

Director of Administration **Kathe Hammond** . . . . . (410) 396-1661
E-mail: Kathe.Hammond@baltimorecity.gov

Baltimore Office of Promotion and the Arts [BOPA]

10 East Baltimore Street, 10th Floor, Baltimore, MD 21202
Fax: (410) 385-0361 Internet: www.promotionandarts.org

■ Executive Director **William B. Gilmore** . . . . . . (410) 752-8632

Mayor's Office on Public Safety [MOCJ]

City Hall, 100 North Holliday Street, Baltimore, MD 21202

■ Director **Neal M. Janey** . . . . . . (410) 545-3355
E-mail: Neal.Janey2@baltimorecity.gov

Mayor's Commission on Disabilities

201 East Baltimore Street, Suite 300, Baltimore, MD 21202
Tel: (443) 984-1617 Tel: (410) 396-4930 (City TTY)
Fax: (410) 396-9838 (TTY 711)

■ Executive Director **Nollie P. Wood, Jr.** . . . . . . (443) 984-3170
E-mail: nollie.wood@baltimorecity.gov

Mayor's Office of Economic and Neighborhood Development

City Hall, 100 North Holliday Street, Baltimore, MD 21202

Deputy Chief, Economic and Neighborhood
Development **Colin Tarbert** . . . . . . (410) 396-7987
E-mail: colin.tarbert@baltimorecity.gov
Education: Maryland BS, MArch

Mayor's Office of Employment Development [MOED]

417 East Fayette Street, Suite 468, Baltimore, MD 21202
Fax: (410) 752-6625 Internet: www.oedworks.com

Director **Jason Perkins-Cohen** . . . . . . (410) 396-1910
E-mail: jperkins-cohen@oedworks.com

Assistant Director of Workforce **Mary Sloat** . . . . . (410) 396-1910
E-mail: msloat@oedworks.com

Assistant Director, Youth Services **Ernest Dorsey** . . . . (410) 396-6722
E-mail: edorsey@oedworks.com

Communications Director **Brice Freeman** . . . . . (410) 396-9928
E-mail: bfreeman@oedworks.com

Executive Liaison for Public Policy **Richard Chambers** . . (410) 396-1910
E-mail: rchambers@oedworks.com

Finance Manager **Abeyomi Adeyinka** . . . . . . (410) 396-1910
E-mail: aadeyinka@oedworks.com

Assistant Director/Comptroller **Malcolm Leggett** . . . . (410) 396-1910
E-mail: mleggett@oedworks.com

Facilities Manager **Charles Loskarn** . . . . . . (410) 396-1910
E-mail: closkarn@oedworks.com

Information Technology Director **Kevin McLamb** . . . . (410) 396-1910
E-mail: kmclamb@oedworks.com

Director of Human Resources **Valarie McNeese** . . . . (410) 396-1910
E-mail: vmcneese@oedworks.com

Director of Performance and Planning **Patricia Morfe** . . . (410) 396-1910
E-mail: pmorfe@oedworks.com

Mayor's Office of Employment Development *continued*

Workforce Operations Director **Craig Lewis** . . . . . (410) 396-1910
E-mail: clewis@oedworks.com

Welfare to Work Director **Adrianne McAuley** . . . . . (410) 396-1910
E-mail: amcauley@oedworks.com

Mayor's Office of Emergency Management

1201 East Cold Spring Lane, Baltimore, MD 21239
Internet: http://emergency.baltimorecity.gov/

Director **Robert Michael Maloney** . . . . . . (410) 396-6188

Mayor's Office of Human Services

4 South Frederick Street, 3rd Floor, Baltimore, MD 21202
Tel: (410) 396-3757 Fax: (410) 396-1590

■ Director **Jacquelyn Duval-Harvey** . . . . . . (410) 396-7370
Education: Hofstra BA; Penn State 1997 PhD

Mayor's Office of Information Technology [MOIT]

401 E. Fayette St., Baltimore, MD 21202
Tel: (410) 396-3902 Fax: (410) 837-0546

Chief Technology Officer **Jerome Mullen** . . . . . (410) 396-6648
E-mail: jerome.mullen@baltimorecity.gov

Mayor's Office of Immigrant and Multicultural Affairs

City Hall, Suite 250, Baltimore, MD 21202

Director **Catalina Rodriguez-Lima** . . . . . . (410) 396-3835

Mayor's Office of Minority and Women-Owned Business Development [MWBD]

City Hall, 100 North Holliday Street, Baltimore, MD 21202
Fax: (410) 576-9425

Director **Christine Bivens** . . . . . . (410) 396-3818
E-mail: christine.bivens@baltimorecity.gov

Mayor's Office of Neighborhoods [MON]

Director **Gussener "Guss" Augustus** . . . . . (443) 984-1081
E-mail: gussener.augustus@baltimorecity.gov

Deputy Director **Alexandra Smith** . . . . . . (410) 396-4735
E-mail: alexandra.smith@baltimorecity.gov

Director, Office of Constituent Services
Daphney Williams . . . . . . (410) 396-4735
E-mail: daphney.williams@baltimorecity.gov

Office of Civil Rights and Wage Enforcement

7 East Redwood Street, 9th Floor, Baltimore, MD 21202
Fax: (410) 244-0176

Director **Kisha A. Brown** . . . . . . (410) 396-3141
E-mail: kisha.brown@baltimorecity.gov

Office Manager **Michelle Masters** . . . . . . (410) 396-3141

Office of the Inspector General [OIG]

100 North Holliday Street, Suite 640, Baltimore, MD 21202
Tel: (800) 417-0430 (Toll Free) Fax: (410) 837-1033

■ Inspector General **Robert H. Pearre, Jr.** . . . . . (443) 984-3690
E-mail: robert.pearre@baltimorecity.gov

Office of the Labor Commissioner [OLC]

417 East Fayette St., Suite 1405, Baltimore, MD 21202
Tel: (410) 361-9200 (Information)

■ Labor Commissioner **Deborah Moore-Carter** . . . . . (410) 396-4365
E-mail: deborah.moore-carter@baltimorecity.gov

Sheriff's Office
Clarence Mitchell Jr. Courthouse, 100 North Calvert Street, Room 104, Baltimore, MD 21202
Tel: (410) 396-1155 (Information)
Tel: (410) 396-5069 (Security Division)
Tel: (410) 396-7412 (District Court Division) Fax: (410) 396-3545

★Sheriff **John W. Anderson** (D) ....(443) 984-1793
Term Expires: January 11, 2019
E-mail: john.anderson@baltimorecity.gov
Secretary to the Sheriff **Victoria Gibson** ....(443) 984-1793
E-mail: victoria.gibson@baltimorecity.gov
Chief Deputy **Henry Martin** ....(443) 984-1793
E-mail: henry.martin@baltimorecity.gov

Department of Finance
City Hall, 100 North Holliday Street, Room 454, Baltimore, MD 21202
Fax: (410) 962-1490 E-mail: deptoffinance@baltimorecity.gov

■Director **Henry J. Raymond** ....(410) 396-4940
E-mail: henry.raymond@baltimorecity.gov
Education: North Carolina A&T BA; Baltimore MPA; Bowie State MA
Deputy Director **Steve Kraus** ....(410) 396-4676

Bureau of Accounting and Payroll
401 E. Fayette St., Baltimore, MD 21202
Tel: (410) 396-3745 Fax: (410) 396-3770

Bureau Chief (Acting) **Sandra Stecker** ....(410) 396-3745
E-mail: sandra.stecker@baltimorecity.gov
Deputy Chief **Sandra Stecker** ....(410) 396-3740
E-mail: sandra.stecker@baltimorecity.gov
Payroll Division Manager **John Bennett** ....(410) 396-3760

Bureau of Budget and Management Research
Tel: (410) 396-5944 Fax: (410) 396-4236

■Budget Director **Andrew W. Kleine** ....(410) 396-4941
E-mail: andrew.kleine@baltimorecity.gov
Education: Washington U (MO) BA; Michigan MPP
Deputy Budget Director **Robert Cenname** ....(410) 396-4948
E-mail: robert.cenname@baltimorecity.gov
Public Policy Analyst Supervisor **William Voorhees** ....(410) 396-4961

Bureau of Purchases
231 E. Baltimore St., Baltimore, MD 21202
Fax: (410) 396-1822

Purchasing Agent **Timothy Krus** ....(410) 396-5700
E-mail: timothy.krus@baltimorecity.gov

Bureau of Revenue Collections
200 Holiday Street, Room 7, Baltimore, MD 21202
E-mail: baltimorecitycollections@baltimorecity.gov

Chief **Janice Simmons** ....(410) 396-3961

Bureau of Treasury Management
200 Holiday Street, Baltimore, MD 21202
Tel: (410) 396-4751 Fax: (410) 396-5876

Bureau Chief **Jennell Rogers** ....(410) 396-3386
Treasury Manager **(Vacant)** ....(410) 396-1918

Office of Risk Management
401 East Fayette Street, Baltimore, MD 21202
Tel: (410) 396-5115 Fax: (410) 396-1071

Risk Manager **Doug Kerr** ....(410) 396-9588
E-mail: doug.kerr@baltimorecity.gov
Risk and Finance Manager **Charmane McDaniel** ....(410) 396-9589
E-mail: charmane.mcdaniel@baltimorecity.gov
Claims and Systems Manager **(Vacant)** ....(410) 396-1984
Risk Management Officer **Douglas S. Kerr** ....(410) 396-5115
E-mail: douglas.kerr@baltimorecity.gov

Fire Department
Department Headquarters, 401 East Fayette Street, Baltimore, MD 21202
Fax: (410) 625-2699

■Fire Chief **Dr. Niles Ford** ....(410) 396-3083
E-mail: niles.ford@baltimorecity.gov
Education: Athens State BA; Faulkner MS; Capella U PhD
Fire Marshal **Shawn Belton** ....(410) 396-7546
E-mail: shawn.belton@baltimorecity.gov
Public Information Officer **Samuel Johnson** ....(410) 396-3083
E-mail: samuel.johnson@baltimorecity.gov
Assistant Fire Chief **Jeffrey Segal** ....(410) 396-3083
E-mail: jeffrey.segal@baltimorecity.gov

Department of General Services [DGS]
Abel Wolman Municipal Building, Room 800, Baltimore, MD 21202
Tel: (410) 396-3704 Fax: (410) 385-2417

■Director **Steve Sharkey** ....(410) 396-3704
E-mail: steve.sharkey@baltimorecity.gov
Education: McDaniel BA; Maryland Baltimore County MPP
Design and Construction Division Chief
Bambi Stevens ....(410) 396-4600
E-mail: bambi.stevens@baltimorecity.gov
Facilities Maintenance Division Chief **Steve Stricklin** ....(410) 396-3702
E-mail: Stephen.Stricklin@baltimorecity.gov
Fleet Management Executive **Robert Gibson** ....(410) 396-1010
The George L. Winfield Fleet Maintenance Facility,
3800 East Biddle Street, Baltimore, MD 21213

Health Department
1001 East Fayette Street, Baltimore, MD 21202
Tel: (410) 396-4398 Fax: (410) 396-1617
Internet: www.baltimorehealth.org

■Commissioner of Health **Dr. Leana S. Wen** ....(410) 396-4387
E-mail: health.commissioner@baltimorecity.gov
Education: Cal State (Los Angeles) BS; Washington U (MO) MD
Deputy Commissioner of Youth and Families
Olivia Farrow ....(410) 396-4398
Adult, School and Community Health Division Assistant
Commissioner **Francine J. Childs** ....(410) 396-4522
Maternal and Child Health Division Assistant
Commissioner **Rebecca Dineen** ....(410) 396-4452
Deputy Commissioner for Population Health and
Disease Prevention **Dawn O'Neill** ....(410) 396-4438
Acute Communicable Diseases Director
Mary Grace White ....(410) 396-4438

Bureau of Animal Control
301 Stockholm St., Baltimore, MD 21230

Director **Sharon Miller** ....(410) 396-4688

Department of Human Resources
201 East Baltimore Street, Suite 300, Baltimore, MD 21202
Fax: (410) 396-1523 E-mail: deptofpersonnel@baltimorecity.gov

■Director and Chief Human Capital Officer
Mary H. Talley ....(410) 396-3851
E-mail: deptofpersonnel@baltimorecity.gov

Law Department
City Hall, 100 North Holliday Street, Room 101, Baltimore, MD 21202-3427
E-mail: law-dept@baltimorecity.gov

■City Solicitor **George A. Nilson** ....(410) 396-8393
E-mail: george.nilson@baltimorecity.gov
Education: Yale 1963 BA, 1967 MURS, 1967 LLB
■Deputy City Solicitor **David Ralph** ....(410) 396-3659
E-mail: david.ralph@baltimorecity.gov
Education: Fordham BA; Maryland Law 1992 JD

★Elected Official ▲Appointed by Legislature ▼Appointed by Governor ►Appointed by Board or Commission ●Appointed by Judge
■Appointed by Mayor △Appointed by Freeholders ▽Appointed by Supervisor ▷Appointed by County Executive ○Appointed by Council

Planning Department
417 East Fayette Street, 8th Floor, Baltimore, MD 21202
Tel: (410) 396-7526 Fax: (410) 244-7358
E-mail: deptofplanning@baltimorecity.gov

Director **Thomas J. "Tom" Stosur** . . . . . (410) 396-4327
Education: Boston Col 1984 AB; Cornell 1987 MCR
Comprehensive Planning Division Chief
Sara Paranilam . . . . . (410) 396-5935
Historical and Architectural Preservation Division Chief
Eric Holcomb . . . . . (443) 984-2728
Education: St Mary's Col (MD) BA; Boston U MA
Land Use and Urban Design Division Chief
Wolde Ararsa . . . . . (410) 396-4488
Research Strategic Planning Division Chief
Jessica Varsa . . . . . (410) 396-6812
Office of Sustainability, Division Chief
Beth Strommen . . . . . (410) 396-8360
Assistant Director **Laurie Feinberg** . . . . . (410) 396-1275
Assistant Director **Theo Ngongang** . . . . . (410) 396-8337

Police Department
242 West 29th Street, Baltimore, MD 21211-2908
Tel: (410) 396-2525 Fax: (410) 396-2023
E-mail: questions@baltimorepolice.org Internet: www.baltimorepolice.org/

■ Police Commissioner **Kevin F. Davis** . . . . . (410) 396-2020
E-mail: kevin.davis@baltimorepolice.org
Deputy Commissioner, Operations **Dean Palmere** . . . . . (410) 396-2363
E-mail: dean.palmere@baltimorepolice.org
Deputy Commissioner, Administration **Darryl DeSousa** . . (410) 396-2525
Deputy Commissioner for Professional Standards
Rodney Hill . . . . . (410) 637-8866
Patrol Division **Melissa Hyatt** . . . . . (410) 396-2363
Media Relations Section Deputy Director **T.J. Smith** . . . . . (410) 396-2012
Legal Affairs Section, Chief Legal Counsel
Glenn T. Marrow . . . . . (410) 396-2495

Department of Public Works [DPW]
Abel Wolman Municipal Building, Room 600, Baltimore, MD 21202
Tel: (410) 396-3310 Fax: (410) 396-3314

■ Director **Rudolph S. Chow** . . . . . (410) 396-3310
E-mail: rudy.chow@baltimorecity.gov
Special Assistant to the Director **Cathy Stump** . . . . . (410) 396-3310
E-mail: cathy.stump@baltimorecity.gov
Deputy Director **S. Dale Thompson** . . . . . (410) 396-3310
Contract Administration **Tonorah Houston-Burgee** . . . . . (410) 396-4041
Communications Center **Bernard Gilliam** . . . . . (410) 545-3651
601 East Fayette Street, 4th Floor, Baltimore, MD 21202
E-mail: bernard.gilliam@baltimorecity.gov
Compliance Office/EEO **Monica Wilson** . . . . . (410) 396-4707
Fiscal (Operating Capital) **Parvathy Murali** . . . . . (410) 396-3313
Legislation **Marcia Collins** . . . . . (410) 396-1960
Communications and Community Affairs
Jeffrey Raymond . . . . . (410) 545-6541
E-mail: jeffrey.raymond@baltimorecity.gov
Human Resources Division **Pamela Beckham** . . . . . (410) 396-3330
E-mail: pamela.beckham@baltimorecity.gov

Bureau of Solid Waste
Abel Wolman Municipal Building, Room 1000, Baltimore, MD 21202
Tel: (410) 396-5134 Fax: (410) 545-6117

Bureau Head **Valentina I. Ukwuoma** . . . . . (410) 396-5134
Environmental Services Division Chief **John Chalmers** . . (410) 396-8450
Special Services Division Superintendent
Michael Lucas . . . . . (410) 396-1300
Recycling Coordinator **Robert Murrow** . . . . . (410) 396-4511
Property Management Division Chief **Tonya Simmons** . . . (410) 396-1023
E-mail: tonya.simmons@baltimorecity.gov

Bureau of Water and Wastewater
Abel Wolman Municipal Building, Room 300, Baltimore, MD 21202
Tel: (410) 396-3500 Fax: (410) 539-0955

Bureau Head (Acting) **Kumasi Vines** . . . . . (410) 396-3500
Construction Management Chief **Samuel Atolaiye** . . . . . (410) 396-1886
Environmental Services Chief **James Price** . . . . . (410) 396-0539
Ashburton Filtration, 3001 Druid Park Drive, Baltimore, MD 21215
Water and Wastewater Engineering Division Chief
Art Shapiro . . . . . (410) 396-3437
E-mail: art.shapiro@baltimorecity.gov
Maintenance Division Chief **Anthony Galloway** . . . . . (410) 396-7870
2331 N. Fulton Ave., Baltimore, MD 21217
Customer Support and Services Division Chief
Maria DeChellis . . . . . (410) 396-5890

Department of Recreation and Parks [BCRP]
Druid Hill Park, 3001 East Drive, Baltimore, MD 21217
Tel: (410) 396-7900 Fax: (410) 889-3856
E-mail: bcrpgeninfo1@baltimorecity.gov

■ Director **Ernest W. Burkeen, Jr.** . . . . . (410) 396-6132
E-mail: ernest.burkeen@baltimorecity.gov Fax: (410) 889-3856
Education: Michigan 1975 BA, 1976 MA
Executive Assistant to the Director
Valerie Scott-Oliver . . . . . (410) 396-6690
E-mail: valerie.scott-oliver@baltimorecity.gov Fax: (410) 889-3856
Special Assistant to the Director **Rebecca Ebaugh** . . . . . (410) 396-6134
E-mail: rebecca.ebaugh@baltimorecity.gov Fax: (410) 889-3856
Chief of Parks **Tom Jeannetta** . . . . . (410) 396-7946
Fax: (410) 396-7945
Chief of Recreation **Robert Wall** . . . . . (410) 396-7010
Fax: (410) 396-7038
Budget and Administrative Services, Chief of
Administration **Kenn King** . . . . . (410) 396-7604
E-mail: kenn.king@baltimorecity.gov Fax: (410) 889-7941
Director of Human Resources **Yvonne Carter** . . . . . (410) 396-6131
E-mail: yvonne.carter@baltimorecity.gov Fax: (410) 889-3856
Information Technology Director **Jerilyn Saunders** . . . . . (410) 396-6697
E-mail: jerilyn.saunders@baltimorecity.gov Fax: (410) 889-3856
Chief of Capital Development and Planning
Gennady Schwartz . . . . . (410) 396-7948
Fax: (410) 396-0928

Department of Transportation [DOT]
417 East Fayette Street, Room 527, Baltimore, MD 21202
Tel: (410) 396-6802 Fax: (410) 547-1036
E-mail: transportation@baltimorecity.gov

■ Director (Acting) **Frank Murphy** . . . . . (410) 396-6802
E-mail: frank.murphy@baltimorecity.gov
Deputy Director of Administration **Lindsay Wines** . . . . . (410) 396-6802
E-mail: lindsay.wines@baltimorecity.gov
Senior Advisor **Frank Murphy** . . . . . (410) 396-6802
E-mail: frank.murphy@baltimorecity.gov
Transit and Marine Services Division Chief **(Vacant)** . . . . . (410) 984-3696
Planning Division Chief **Valorie LaCour** . . . . . (443) 984-4095
Safety Division Chief **Yolanda Cason** . . . . . (410) 545-6942
620 Fallsway, Baltimore, MD 21202
E-mail: yolanda.cason@baltimorecity.gov
Traffic Division Chief **(Vacant)** . . . . . (443) 984-2150
Transportation, Engineering and Construction Division
Chief **Bimal Devkota** . . . . . (410) 396-6930
E-mail: bimal.devkota@baltimorecity.gov
Operations Bureau Chief **Richard Hooper** . . . . . (410) 396-6802
520 Fallsway, Baltimore, MD 21202
E-mail: richard.hooper@baltimorecity.gov

Office of Aging and CARE Services [CARE]
10 North Calvert Street, Suite 300, Baltimore, MD 21202
Fax: (410) 385-0381 E-mail: care@baltimorecity.gov

Executive Director **Arnold Eppel** . . . . . (410) 396-4489

★ Elected Official ▲ Appointed by Legislature ▼ Appointed by Governor ▶ Appointed by Board or Commission ● Appointed by Judge
■ Appointed by Mayor △ Appointed by Freeholders ▽ Appointed by Supervisor ▷ Appointed by County Executive ○ Appointed by Council

Baltimore Convention Center

1 West Pratt Street, Baltimore, MD 21201
Tel: (410) 649-7000 Fax: (410) 649-7008 Internet: www.bccenter.org

■ Executive Director **Peggy Daidakis** .... (410) 649-7111
E-mail: pdaidakis@bccenter.org
Deputy Director **Claire Copsey** .... (410) 649-7121

Baltimore Workforce Investment Board

417 East Fayette Street, Suite 468, Baltimore, MD 21202
Tel: (410) 396-1910 Fax: (410) 752-6625
Internet: www.baltoworkforce.com

■ Chairman **Andrew Bertamini** .... (410) 396-1910
Administrative Support **Jon Smeton** .... (410) 396-1910
E-mail: jsmeton@oedworks.com

Board of Municipal and Zoning Appeals

417 East Fayette Street, Suite 1432, Baltimore, MD 21202
Fax: (410) 625-8422

Executive Director **David Tanner** .... (410) 396-4301

Enoch Pratt Free Library

400 Cathedral Street, Baltimore, MD 21201
Tel: (410) 396-5430 Fax: (410) 396-1441 Internet: www.prattlibrary.org

Administration

Chief Executive Officer **Carla Diane Hayden** .... (410) 396-5395
Note: President Barack Obama has announced his intention to nominate Carla Hayden as Librarian of Congress.
E-mail: chayden@prattlibrary.org
Date of Birth: August 10, 1952
Education: Roosevelt 1973 BA; Chicago 1977 MA, 1987 PhD
Director, Administrative Services **Gordon E. Krabbe** .... (410) 545-3108
E-mail: gkrabbe@prattlibrary.org Fax: (410) 361-9610
Director, Institutional Development and Advancement
Cindi Monahan .... (410) 396-5314
Fax: (410) 396-8134
Building Operations Manager **John Richardson** .... (410) 396-7554
E-mail: jrichard@prattlibrary.org Fax: (410) 361-1911
Chief, Human Resources **John F. Kinsella** .... (410) 396-5355
E-mail: jkinsell@prattlibrary.org Fax: (410) 396-5044
Chief, Information Access **Wendy Allen** .... (410) 396-5358
E-mail: wallen@prattlibrary.org Fax: (410) 396-3526
Chief, Neighborhood Services **Eunice Anderson** .... (410) 545-7132
E-mail: eanderso@prattlibrary.org Fax: (410) 545-6946
Coordinator, Programs and Publications
Judith Cooper .... (410) 396-5494
E-mail: jcooper@prattlibrary.org Fax: (410) 837-0582
Chief, State Library Resource Center **Wesley Wilson** .... (410) 396-5429
Fax: (410) 837-0582
Children's Services Coordinator
Jessica Hoptay-Brown .... (410) 545-0701
E-mail: jhoptay@prattlibrary.org Fax: (410) 396-6946
Coordinator, School and Student Services **Deb Taylor** .... (410) 396-5356
E-mail: dtaylor@prattlibrary.org Fax: (410) 396-1095
Chief of Planning, Programs and Partnerships
Ellen Riordan .... (410) 396-5204
E-mail: eriordan@prattlibrary.org
Web Manager **Xiaoyu Zhou** .... (410) 396-5430
E-mail: xzhou@prattlibrary.org

Housing Authority of Baltimore City

417 E. Fayette St., Baltimore, MD 21202
P.O. Box 1917, Baltimore, MD 21202
Tel: (410) 396-3232 Fax: (410) 545-7771 E-mail: info@habc.org
Internet: http://www.baltimorehousing.org

■ Housing Commissioner **Paul T. Graziano** .... (410) 396-3232
E-mail: paul.graziano@habc.org
Education: MIT BS, MCP
Chief of Staff **Kimberly Washington** .... (410) 396-3232
Deputy Commissioner HCD, Permits and Code Enforcement Office **Michael Braverman** .... (443) 984-1806

Deputy Commissioner, Land Resources **Julia Day** .... (410) 396-3232
Deputy Commissioner, Community Services and Ombudsman **Reginald Scriber** .... (410) 396-1977
E-mail: reggie.scriber@baltimorecity.gov
Associate Executive Director, FHEO Enforcement
Amy Wilkinson .... (410) 396-8437
Deputy Executive Director **Anthony Scott** .... (410) 396-5844
Assistant Commissioner, Research and Compliance
Stephen Janes .... (410) 396-4051
General Counsel **Jan Goslee** .... (410) 396-3887
Chief Communications Officer **Tania Baker** .... (410) 396-4709
E-mail: tania.baker@habc.org
Chief Financial Officer **Rainbow Lin** .... (410) 396-8303
Chief Information Officer **Jimmy L. Thomas** .... (410) 361-9669
E-mail: jimmy.thomas@habc.org
Director of Human Resources **Paula Walton** .... (410) 396-6823
E-mail: paula.walton@habc.org

Office of the City Council

City Hall, 100 North Holliday Street, Baltimore, MD 21202
Internet: http://www.baltimorecitycouncil.com

★ President **Bernard C. "Jack" Young** (D) .... (410) 396-4804
Term Expires: December 9, 2016 Fax: (410) 539-0647
E-mail: councilpresident@baltimorecity.gov
Administrative Assistant **Mary Demory** .... (410) 545-7487
E-mail: mary.demory@baltimorecity.gov
Scheduler **Zoe Michal** .... (410) 545-7487
E-mail: Zoe.Michal@baltimorecity.gov
★ Vice President **Edward L. Reisinger** (D-District 10) ..... (410) 396-4822
Term Expires: December 9, 2016 Fax: (410) 545-7353
E-mail: edward.reisinger@baltimorecity.gov
★ Council Member **James Kraft** (D-District 1) .... (410) 396-4821
Term Expires: December 9, 2016 Fax: (410) 361-9908
E-mail: james.kraft@baltimorecity.gov
★ Council Member **Brandon M. Scott** (D-District 2) ...... (410) 396-4808
Term Expires: December 9, 2016 Fax: (410) 396-4414
E-mail: brandon.scott@baltimorecity.gov
★ Council Member **Robert W. Curran** (D-District 3) .... (410) 396-4812
Term Expires: December 9, 2016 Fax: (410) 396-8621
E-mail: robert.curran@baltimorecity.gov
★ Council Member **William "Bill" Henry** (D-District 4) .... (410) 396-4830
Term Expires: December 9, 2016 Fax: (410) 659-1792
E-mail: bill.henry@baltimorecity.gov
★ Council Member
Rochelle "Rikki" Spector (D-District 5) .... (410) 396-4819
Term Expires: December 9, 2016 Fax: (410) 396-6800
E-mail: rikki.spector@baltimorecity.gov
★ Council Member
Sharon Green Middleton (D-District 6) .... (410) 396-4832
Term Expires: December 9, 2016 Fax: (410) 396-6800
E-mail: sharon.middleton@baltimorecity.gov
Education: Morgan State BA
★ Council Member **Nick Mosby** (D-District 7) .... (410) 396-4810
Term Expires: December 9, 2016 Fax: (410) 347-0537
E-mail: nick.mosby@baltimorecity.gov
★ Council Member **Helen L. Holton** (D-District 8) .... (410) 396-4818
Term Expires: December 9, 2016 Fax: (410) 396-4828
E-mail: helen.holton@baltimorecity.gov
Education: Baltimore 1982 BS; Johns Hopkins 1995 MBA
★ Council Member
William A. "Pete" Welch (D-District 9) .... (410) 396-4815
Term Expires: December 9, 2016 Fax: (410) 545-3857
E-mail: william.welch@baltimorecity.gov
★ Council Member **Eric Costello** (D-District 11) .... (410) 396-4816
Term Expires: December 9, 2016 Fax: (410) 545-7464
E-mail: eric.costello@baltimorecity.gov
○ Council Member **Carl Stokes** (D-District 12) .... (410) 396-4811
Term Expires: December 9, 2016 Fax: (410) 396-1594
E-mail: carl.stokes@baltimorecity.gov

★ Elected Official ▲ Appointed by Legislature ▼ Appointed by Governor ▶ Appointed by Board or Commission ● Appointed by Judge
■ Appointed by Mayor △ Appointed by Freeholders ▽ Appointed by Supervisor ▷ Appointed by County Executive ○ Appointed by Council

Office of the City Council *continued*

★Council Member **Warren Branch** (D-District 13) . . . . (410) 396-4829
Term Expires: December 9, 2016 Fax: (410) 347-0534
E-mail: warren.branch@baltimorecity.gov

★Council Member **Mary Pat Clarke** (D-District 14) . . . . (410) 396-4814
Term Expires: December 9, 2016 Fax: (410) 545-7585
E-mail: marypat.clarke@baltimorecity.gov

Director of Communications and Media Relations
Lester Davis . . . . (410) 396-4804
E-mail: lester.davis@baltimorecity.gov

Office of the Comptroller

City Hall, 100 North Holliday Street, Room 204, Baltimore, MD 21202
Fax: (410) 685-4416 Internet: www.comptroller.baltimorecity.gov/

★Comptroller **Joan M. Pratt** (D) . . . . (410) 396-4755
Term Expires: December 31, 2016
E-mail: joan.pratt@baltimorecity.gov

Deputy Comptroller **Bernice H. Taylor** . . . . (410) 396-4755

City Auditor **Robert L. McCarty, Jr.** . . . . (410) 396-4783

Communication Services Director **Simon Etta** . . . . (410) 396-4926
E-mail: simon.etta@baltimorecity.gov

Municipal Post Office Supervisor **Perin Tinsley** . . . . (410) 545-3007

Department of Real Estate

City Hall, 100 North Holliday Street, Room 304, Baltimore, MD 21202
Fax: (410) 528-1437

Real Estate Officer **Walter J. Horton** . . . . (410) 396-4768

Office of the State's Attorney for Baltimore City

120 East Baltimore Street, 9th Floor, Baltimore, MD 21202
Internet: www.stattorney.org/ E-mail: mail@stattorney.org

★State's Attorney **Marilyn J. Mosby** . . . . (443) 984-6000
Term Expires: January 3, 2019
E-mail: mail@stattorney.org
Education: Tuskegee 2002 BA; Boston Col 2005 JD

Chief Deputy State's Attorney **Michael Schatzow** . . . . . . (443) 984-6000
Education: Case Western 1970 AB; Chicago 1973 JD; Georgetown 1978 LLM

Chief of External Affairs **Tammy Brown** . . . . (443) 984-6000
Education: American U BA; Baltimore JD

Chief of Administration **Steward D. Beckham** (D) . . . . . . (443) 984-6000
Education: Howard Col BBA; Baltimore JD

Deputy State's Attorney for Criminal Justice
Janice Bledsoe . . . . (443) 984-6000
Education: Loyola U (Maryland) BA; Baltimore JD

Deputy State's Attorney of Operations **Patricia DeMaio** . . (443) 984-6000
Education: Morgan State BS; Temple JD

Deputy State's Attorney of Major Crimes
Antonio Gioia . . . . (443) 984-6000
Education: Baltimore BS, JD

Chief of Staff **Caron Brace** . . . . (443) 984-6000
Education: Coppin State U BA; Baltimore MPA, JD

Baltimore City Public Schools

200 E. North Ave., Baltimore, MD 21202
Tel: (443) 984-2000 Fax: (410) 396-8898
Internet: www.baltimorecityschools.org/

Chief Executive Officer (Interim) **Tammy Turner** . . . . (410) 396-8803
Note: Until June 30, 2016

Chief Executive Officer **Dr. Sonja Brookins Santelises** . . (410) 396-8803
Note: Effective July 1, 2016
Education: Brown U 1989 AB; Harvard 1999 EdM

Chief of Staff **Naomi Gubernick** . . . . (410) 396-8805
Fax: (410) 396-8898

Special Assistant **Jennie Wu** . . . . (410) 396-8803
E-mail: jwu@bcps.k12.md.us Fax: (410) 396-8898

Baltimore City Public Schools *continued*

Chief Academic Officer **Linda Chen** . . . . (410) 396-8810
Fax: (410) 396-9663

Chief Financial Officer **Donald Kennedy** . . . . (410) 396-8745
E-mail: dkennedy@kcw-et.com Fax: (410) 396-7589

Chief Operating Officer **J. Keith Scroggins** . . . . (410) 396-8721
E-mail: kscroggins@bcps.k12.md.us Fax: (410) 396-8614

Manager of Public Information **Edie House-Foster** . . . . . . (410) 545-7296
E-mail: EHouse@bcps.k12.md.us Fax: (410) 396-8474

Chief Information Technology Officer **Ken Thompson** . . . (410) 396-8501
E-mail: kthompson@bcps.k12.md.us Fax: (410) 396-5804

Chief Achievement and Accountability Officer
Theresa Jones . . . . (410) 396-8969
Fax: (410) 396-5632

General Counsel **Tammy Turner** . . . . (410) 396-2981
Fax: (410) 396-2955

Chief School Supports Officer **Karl E. Perry** . . . . (443) 984-2000

Human Capital Officer (Interim) **Deborah T. Sullivan** . . . . (410) 396-8880
E-mail: dsullivan@bcps.k12.md.us Fax: (410) 545-0897

Legislative Liaison **Dawana Sterrette** . . . . (410) 396-8709
E-mail: dsterrette@bcps.k12.md.us Fax: (410) 545-3613

Procurement Director **Jeff Parker** . . . . (410) 396-8757
E-mail: jparker@bcps.k12.md.us Fax: (410) 396-8816

Enrollment Choice and Transfer Coordinator
Lara Ohanian . . . . (410) 396-8602
Fax: (410) 396-5668

School Board Executive
Alvaro Joseph Bellido de Luna . . . . (410) 396-8709
Fax: (410) 545-3613

School Police Chief **Marshall T. "Toby" Goodwin** (D) . . (410) 396-8588
Note: On administrative leave
Education: Sojourner-Douglass 1989 AB; Coppin State Col 1991 MS

Board of School Commissioners

Chair **Marnell A. Cooper** . . . . (410) 396-8709
Education: Maryland BA; Francis King Carey Law JD

Vice Chair **Tina Marie Hike-Hubbard** . . . . (410) 396-8709
Education: Northwest Missouri State BS

Board Member **Lisa Akchin** . . . . (410) 396-8709
Education: Tennessee 1978 BA

Board Member **Muriel Berkeley** . . . . (410) 396-8709

Board Member **Cheryl A. Casciani** . . . . (410) 396-8709

Board Member **Linda Chinnia** . . . . (410) 396-8709

Board Member **Andrew B. Frank** . . . . (410) 396-8709

Board Member **Martha James-Hassan** . . . . (410) 396-8709

Board Member **Peter Kannam** . . . . (410) 396-8709

★Elected Official ▲Appointed by Legislature ▼Appointed by Governor ▶Appointed by Board or Commission ●Appointed by Judge
■Appointed by Mayor △Appointed by Freeholders ▽Appointed by Supervisor ▷Appointed by County Executive ○Appointed by Council

City of Baton Rouge and East Baton Rouge Parish, Louisiana

222 St. Louis Street, Baton Rouge, LA 70802
P.O. Box 1471, Baton Rouge, LA 70821
Tel: (225) 389-3000 (Information) Internet: www.brgov.com

County: East Baton Rouge Parish **Election Type:** Partisan
Year Founded: 1810 **Year Incorporated:** 1817 **Charter:** 1949
Population: 228,590 (2015) **Employees:** 4,476 **Fiscal Year:** 2016
Budget: $880,425,000

Form of Municipal Government: City and parish governments are combined.

Melvin L. "Kip" Holden (D)
Mayor/President

Began Service: 2005
Term Expires: January 1, 2017
Education: LSU 1974 BA:
Southern U (New Orleans) 1982 MA, 1985 JD

Office of the Mayor/President and the Metropolitan Council

222 St. Louis St., Baton Rouge, LA 70802
P.O. Box 1471, Baton Rouge, LA 70821
Tel: (225) 389-5100 Fax: (225) 389-5203

Employees: 12 **Fiscal Year:** 2016 **Budget:** $1,460,000

★Mayor/President **Melvin L. "Kip" Holden** (D) .... (225) 389-3100
E-mail: mayor@brgov.com
Executive Assistant to the Mayor **Susan Boudreaux** ... (225) 389-5102
E-mail: sboudreaux@brgov.com

★Council Member **J.E. "Trae" Welch** (D-District 1) .... (225) 389-5170
Term Expires: January 1, 2017
E-mail: council-dist1@brgov.com

★Council Member **Chauna Banks-Daniel** (D-District 2) ... (225) 389-4699
Term Expires: January 1, 2017 Fax: (225) 774-8340
E-mail: council-dist2@brgov.com

★Council Member **Chandler Loupe** (R-District 3) .... (225) 389-5162
Term Expires: January 1, 2017
E-mail: council-dist3@brgov.com

★Council Member **M. Scott Wilson** (R-District 4) .... (225) 389-5166
Term Expires: January 1, 2017

★Council Member **Erika L. Green** (D-District 5) .... (225) 389-5171
Term Expires: January 1, 2017
E-mail: council-dist5@brgov.com

★Council Member **Donna Collins-Lewis** (D-District 6) .... (225) 389-5165
Term Expires: January 1, 2017
E-mail: council-dist6@brgov.com

★Council Member **LaMont Cole** (D-District 7) .... (225) 389-4691
Term Expires: January 1, 2017
E-mail: council-dist7@brgov.com

★Council Member **Buddy Amaroso** (R-District 8) .... (225) 272-9088
Term Expires: January 1, 2017 Fax: (225) 272-9782

★Council Member **Joel Boé** (R-District 9) .... (225) 389-4688
Term Expires: January 1, 2017
E-mail: council-dist9@brgov.com

★Council Member **Tara Wicker** (D-District 10) .... (225) 389-5140
Term Expires: January 1, 2017
E-mail: council-dist10@brgov.com

★Council Member **Ryan Heck** (R-District 11) .... (225) 389-5169
Term Expires: January 1, 2017
E-mail: council-dist11@brgov.com

★Council Member **John Delgado** (R-District 12) .... (225) 389-4697
Term Expires: January 1, 2017
E-mail: council-dist12@brgov.com

Chief Administrative Officer

222 St. Louis Street, 3rd Floor, Baton Rouge, LA 70802

■Chief Administrative Officer **William Daniel** .... (225) 389-5103
E-mail: wdaniel@brgov.com

■Assistant Chief Administrative Officer **Gail Grover** ...... (225) 389-5350
E-mail: ggrover@brgov.com

■Assistant Chief Administrative Officer **John J. Price** ..... (225) 389-5161
E-mail: jprice@brgov.com

Office of the Council Administrator/Treasurer

222 St. Louis St., Baton Rouge, LA 70802
P.O. Box 1471, Baton Rouge, LA 70821
Tel: (225) 389-3123 Fax: (225) 389-3127

Employees: 15 **Fiscal Year:** 2016 **Budget:** $2,086,000

Council Administrator/Treasurer **Casey Cashio** .... (225) 389-3123
E-mail: ccashio@brgov.com
Assistant Council Administrator **Dorothy Cobbs** .... (225) 389-3123
E-mail: dcobbs@brgov.com
Council Budget Officer **Joseph R. Toups** .... (225) 389-3051
E-mail: jtoups@brgov.com Fax: (225) 389-5450
Mailroom Supervisor **Marla Smith** .... (225) 389-3290
E-mail: msmith@brgov.com

Office of the Assessor

222 St. Louis Street, Room 126, Baton Rouge, LA 70802
Tel: (225) 389-3920 (Main Office)
Tel: (225) 389-3901 (East Baton Rouge Office) Internet: www.ebrpa.org/

★Assessor **Brian Wilson** (R) .... (225) 389-3920
Term Expires: January 1, 2017
E-mail: bwilson@ebrpa.org
Chief Deputy Assessor **Kerry Hicks** .... (225) 389-3920 ext. 333
E-mail: khicks@ebrpa.org

Office of the City Constable

233 St. Louis Street, Room B46, Baton Rouge, LA 70802
P.O. Box 1471, Baton Rouge, LA 70821
Tel: (225) 389-3004 Fax: (225) 389-3029
Internet: http://brgov.com/dept/constable/

Employees: 40 **Fiscal Year:** 2016 **Budget:** $2,940,000

★City Constable **Reginald R. Brown, Sr.** (D) .... (225) 389-3004
Term Expires: December 31, 2018
E-mail: rbrown@brgov.com
Education: Southern U A&M BA
Chief Deputy Constable **Laurance "Larry" Navarre** ..... (225) 389-3004

Office of the Coroner

4030 TB Herndon Avenue, Baton Rouge, LA 70807
Fax: (225) 389-3447 E-mail: coroner@brgov.com

Fiscal Year: 2016 **Budget:** $2,788,000

★Coroner **William "Beau" Clark** .... (225) 389-3047
Term Expires: March 28, 2020
E-mail: wclarkmd@brgov.com
Chief of Investigations **Shane Evans** .... (225) 389-3047
Chief of Operations **Treva Parolli-Barnes** .... (225) 389-3047
Administrative Coordinator **Stephanie Price** .... (225) 389-3047

Office of the District Attorney

222 St. Louis Street, Suite 550, Baton Rouge, LA 70802
Tel: (225) 389-3400 Fax: (225) 389-5482 Internet: www.ebrda.org/

Fiscal Year: 2016 **Budget:** $5,411,000

★District Attorney **Hillar C. Moore III** (D) .... (225) 389-3400
Term Expires: January 1, 2019
E-mail: hillar.moore@ebrda.org
Executive Secretary **Linda Southall** .... (225) 389-3400
E-mail: lsouthall@ebrda.org
First Assistant District Attorney **Tracey Ewing-Barbera** .. (225) 389-3400
Chief of Administration **Mark Dumaine** .... (225) 389-3400
E-mail: mdumaine@ebrda.org

★Elected Official ▲Appointed by Legislature ▼Appointed by Governor ►Appointed by Board or Commission ●Appointed by Judge
■Appointed by Mayor △Appointed by Freeholders ▽Appointed by Supervisor ▷Appointed by County Executive ○Appointed by Council

Office of the District Attorney *continued*

Chief of Litigation **Dana Cummings** . . . . (225) 389-3400
Chief of Special Prosecutions and Services
Stephen Pugh . . . . (225) 389-3400
Executive Secretary **Karen Wright** . . . . (225) 389-3400
E-mail: kwright@ebrda.org

Office of the Parish Attorney

222 St. Louis Street, Baton Rouge, LA 70802
P.O. Box 1471, Baton Rouge, LA 70821
Fax: (225) 389-5554 E-mail: pa@brgov.com
Internet: http://brgov.com/dept/parishattorney/

Employees: 95 **Fiscal Year:** 2016 **Budget:** $7,460,000

○ Parish Attorney **Lea Anne Batson** . . . . (225) 389-3114
E-mail: pa@brgov.com
First Assistant Parish Attorney **Tedrick Knightshead** . . . . (225) 389-3114
City Prosecutor **Anderson Dotson** . . . . (225) 389-3119
Alcohol Beverage Control Board /Gaming Director
Chris Cranford . . . . (225) 389-3364
Bingo Enforcement Division Assistant Director
Chris Cranford . . . . (225) 389-5490
Litigation Division Director **(Vacant)** . . . . (225) 389-8730
Risk Management Division Director **Eugene Booth** . . . . (225) 389-8389
E-mail: gbooth@brgov.com
Collections Division Director **Randy Ligh** . . . . (225) 389-3114
Administration Division Director **Dawn Guillot** . . . . (225) 389-3114

Office of the Registrar of Voters

222 St Louis Street, Room 201, Baton Rouge, LA 70802
Fax: (225) 389-5340

Fiscal Year: 2016 **Budget:** $855,000

○ Registrar **Steve Raborn** . . . . (225) 389-3940
Chief Deputy Registrar **Sharon Bankston** . . . . (225) 389-3940
Confidential Assistant **Shamel Johnson** . . . . (225) 389-3940

Office of the Sheriff

8900 Jimmy Wedell Drive, Baton Rouge, LA 70807
P.O. Box 3277, Baton Rouge, LA 70821
Fax: (225) 389-5032 Internet: http://www.ebrso.org

Fiscal Year: 2016 **Budget:** $9,296,000

★ Sheriff **Sid Gautreaux** (D) . . . . (225) 389-5055
Term Expires: July 1, 2016
E-mail: sgautreaux@ebrso.org
Civil Chief Deputy **Skip Rhorer, Jr.** . . . . (225) 389-4929
E-mail: srhorer@ebrso.org
Education: LSU 1976 BS, 1978 MS
Criminal Chief Deputy **Lawrence McLeary** . . . . (225) 389-3274
E-mail: lmcleary@brgov.com
Chief of Operations **(Vacant)** . . . . (225) 389-5259
Fax: (225) 389-3259

Parish Prison

2867 Brigadier Gen. Issac Smith Blvd., Baton Rouge, LA 70807
P.O. Box 3277, Baton Rouge, LA 70821
Warden **Dennis Grimes** . . . . (225) 358-4002

Baton Rouge Metropolitan Airport

9430 Jackie Cochran Drive, Suite 300, Baton Rouge, LA 70807
Tel: (225) 355-0333 Fax: (225) 355-2334 Internet: www.flybtr.com/

○ Director **Anthony J. Marino** . . . . (225) 355-0333
E-mail: amarino@brgov.com
Assistant Director **Ralph Hennessy** . . . . (225) 355-0333
Executive Assistant **Jo Ann Cobb** . . . . (225) 355-0333
E-mail: jcobb@brgov.com
Airport Safety and Operations Manager **Mike Edwards** . . (225) 355-0333
E-mail: medwards@brgov.com
Airport Business Manager **Cary Morgan** . . . . (225) 355-0333
E-mail: cmorgan@brgov.com

Baton Rouge Metropolitan Airport *continued*

Information Technology Manager **Greg Pierson** . . . . (225) 355-0333
E-mail: gpierson@brgov.com
Airport Marketing Manager **Jim Caldwell** . . . . (225) 355-0333
Administrative and Development Manager
Joshua Anderson . . . . (225) 355-0333
E-mail: janderson@brgov.com
Airport Police Chief **Anthony Williams** . . . . (225) 358-4221
E-mail: awilliams@brgov.com Fax: (225) 358-4230
Airport Police/Training **Michael Wallis** . . . . (225) 358-4221
E-mail: mwallis@brgov.com Fax: (225) 355-7964
Airport Legal Counsel **Michael J. Taffaro** . . . . (225) 355-0333
Legal Secretary **Kim Nolan** . . . . (225) 355-0333

Animal Control and Rescue Center

2680 Progress Rd., Baton Rouge, LA 70807
Fax: (225) 774-7876 E-mail: acc@brgov.com

Employees: 22 **Fiscal Year:** 2016 **Budget:** $1,659,000

○ Director **Hilton Cole** . . . . (225) 774-7700 ext. 101
E-mail: hcole@brgov.com

Baton Rouge Area Alcohol and Drug Center [BRAADC]

1819 Florida Blvd., Baton Rouge, LA 70802
Fax: (225) 389-5334
Executive Director **Lisa Bailey** . . . . (225) 389-3325

East Baton Rouge Parish Communications District

3773 Harding Boulevard, Baton Rouge, LA 70807
Fax: (225) 389-2194

Employees: 53 **Fiscal Year:** 2016 **Budget:** $5,674,000

○ District Director **Matt Hobson** . . . . (225) 389-2911
E-mail: mhobson@brgov.com
Chief of Operations **Stacy Simmons** . . . . (225) 389-2911
E-mail: ssimmons@brgov.com

Downtown Development District

247 Florida Street, Baton Rouge, LA 70801
Fax: (225) 389-5523 E-mail: ddd1@brgov.com
Executive Director **Davis Rhorer** . . . . (225) 389-5520
E-mail: drhorer@brgov.com
Assistant Director **Gabe Vicknair** . . . . (225) 389-5520
E-mail: gvicknair@brgov.com
Development Project Director **Whitney Cooper** . . . . (225) 389-5520
E-mail: wcooper@brgov.com
Development Project Director **Casey Tate** . . . . (225) 389-5520
E-mail: ctate@brgov.com

East Baton Rouge Parish Library

7711 Goodwood Blvd., Baton Rouge, LA 70806
Tel: (225) 231-3750 Fax: (225) 231-3759
Director **Spencer Watts** . . . . (225) 231-3700
E-mail: spencerwatts@brgov.com
Assistant Director for Administration **Mary Stein** . . . . (225) 231-3710
E-mail: mstein@ebrpl.com
Assistant Director for Branch Services
Patricia Husband . . . . (225) 231-3780
E-mail: phusband@ebrpl.com
Business Manager **Rhonda Pinsonat** . . . . (225) 231-3705
E-mail: rpinsonat@brgov.com
Deputy Library Director **(Vacant)** . . . . (225) 231-3700

East Baton Rouge Parish School System

1050 South Foster Drive, Baton Rouge, LA 70806
Tel: (225) 922-5400 Fax: (225) 922-5600 Internet: www.ebrschools.org
Superintendent of Schools **Warren Drake** . . . . (225) 922-5400

★ Elected Official ▲ Appointed by Legislature ▼ Appointed by Governor ► Appointed by Board or Commission ● Appointed by Judge
■ Appointed by Mayor △ Appointed by Freeholders ▽ Appointed by Supervisor ▷ Appointed by County Executive ○ Appointed by Council

Department of Emergency Medical Services

P.O. Box 1471, Baton Rouge, LA 70821
3801 Harding Boulevard, Baton Rouge, LA 70807
Tel: (225) 389-5155 Fax: (225) 389-5235 E-mail: emsinfo@brgov.com
Internet: http://brgov.com/dept/ems/

Employees: 169 **Fiscal Year:** 2016 **Budget:** $23,763,000

EMS Administrator **Chad Guillot** .... (225) 389-5155 ext. 7301
Communications Manager **Matt Hobson** .... (225) 389-2911
E-mail: mhobson@brgov.com
Public Education Manager **Mike Chustz** .... (225) 389-5155 ext. 7365
E-mail: mchustz@brgov.com
Training Director **Arthur J. Lewis II** .... (225) 389-5155 ext. 7341
E-mail: alewis@brgov.com

Finance Department

222 St. Louis Street, Room 439, Baton Rouge, LA 70802
P.O. Box 1471, Baton Rouge, LA 70821
Fax: (225) 389-5673 E-mail: finance@brgov.com
Internet: www.brgov.com/dept/finance

Employees: 121 **Fiscal Year:** 2016 **Budget:** $9,740,000

Director **Marsha Hanlon** .... (225) 389-3061 ext. 314
Education: Southeastern Louisiana 1981 BS
Assistant Director **Linda Hunt** .... (225) 389-3061 ext. 304
Financial Projects Coordinator
Debbie McClure .... (225) 389-3061 ext. 302
Education: LSU 1986 BS
Assistant Financial Projects Coordinator
Nan Drew-Butler .... (225) 389-3067 ext. 301

Fire Department

8011 Merle Gustafson Dr., Baton Rouge, LA 70807
Tel: (225) 354-1400 Fax: (225) 354-1427
E-mail: brfdinfo@ci.baton-rouge.la.us Internet: http://brgov.com/dept/fire/

Employees: 610 **Fiscal Year:** 2016 **Budget:** $49,317,000

■ Fire Chief **Ed Smith** .... (225) 354-1401
E-mail: esmith@brgov.com Fax: (225) 354-1427
Administrative Assistant **Charles Major** .... (225) 354-1406
E-mail: cmajor@brgov.com Fax: (225) 354-1427
Arson Division Chief **Rob Stewart** .... (225) 354-1736
E-mail: rstewart@brgov.com Fax: (225) 354-1420
Communications Division Chief **Beth Miller** .... (225) 389-2063
E-mail: bmiller@brgov.com Fax: (225) 389-5137
Fire Prevention Division Chief **David Sevier** .... (225) 354-1431
E-mail: dsevier@brgov.com Fax: (225) 354-1423
Hazardous Materials Division Chief **Richard Sullivan** .... (225) 354-1421
E-mail: rsullivan@brgov.com Fax: (225) 354-1423
Operations Division Chief **Den Estess** .... (225) 354-1403
E-mail: destess@brgov.com Fax: (225) 354-1427
Safety Division Chief **Otis Autrey** .... (225) 354-1407
E-mail: oautrey@brgov.com Fax: (225) 354-1413
Special Services Division Chief **Michael Williams** ...... (225) 354-1412
E-mail: mwilliams@brgov.com Fax: (225) 354-1413
Training Division Chief **Scotty Shelton** .... (225) 354-1430
E-mail: sshelton@brgov.com
Public Information Officer **Mark Miles** .... (225) 354-1449
E-mail: mmiles@brgov.com Fax: (225) 354-1413
Public Information Officer **Curt Monte** .... (225) 354-1410
E-mail: cmonte@brgov.com Fax: (225) 254-1413

Division of Human Development and Services

4523 Plank Road, Baton Rouge, LA 70805
Tel: (225) 358-4583 Fax: (225) 356-7868
Internet: http://brgov.com/dept/dhds/

Employees: 8 **Fiscal Year:** 2016 **Budget:** $744,000

■ Director **Paula Merrick-Roddy** .... (225) 358-4583
E-mail: proddy@brgov.com
Assistant Director **(Vacant)** .... (225) 358-4512
Senior Administrative Specialist **Diane Matthews** .... (225) 358-4590
E-mail: dmatthews@brgov.com

Division of Human Development and Services *continued*

Executive Assistant **Debra D. Selvage** .... (225) 358-4519
E-mail: dselvage@brgov.com

Human Resources Department

1755 Florida St., Suite 200, Baton Rouge, LA 70802
P.O. Box 1471, Baton Rouge, LA 70821
Tel: (225) 389-3141 Fax: (225) 389-3118 E-mail: hr@brgov.com
Internet: http://brgov.com/dept/hr/

Employees: 38 **Fiscal Year:** 2016 **Budget:** $3,232,000

■ Director (Interim) **Brian Bernard** .... (225) 389-3129
E-mail: bbernard@brgov.com
Assistant Director **(Vacant)** .... (225) 389-5307
Employee Relations **Micheline Millender** .... (225) 389-8727
E-mail: mmillender@brgov.com
Payroll and Benefits **(Vacant)** .... (225) 389-3134
Recruitment and Examination Manager **David West** ..... (225) 389-3132
E-mail: dwest@brgov.com

Information Services Department

P.O. Box 1471, Baton Rouge, LA 70821
Fax: (225) 389-7745 E-mail: is@brgov.com
Internet: http://brgov.com/dept/IS/

Employees: 56 **Fiscal Year:** 2016 **Budget:** $5,807,000

■ Director **Eric Romero** .... (225) 389-3070
E-mail: is@brgov.com

Mayor's Office of Homeland Security and Emergency Preparedness [MOHSEP]

3773 Harding Boulevard, Baton Rouge, LA 70807
P.O. Box 1471, Baton Rouge, LA 70821
Tel: (225) 389-2100 Fax: (225) 389-2114 E-mail: oep@brgov.com
Internet: http://brgov.com/dept/oep/

Employees: 7 **Fiscal Year:** 2016 **Budget:** $771,000

■ Director **JoAnne H. Moreau** .... (225) 389-2100
E-mail: jmoreau@brgov.com
Assistant Director **Tuesday Mills** .... (225) 389-2100
E-mail: tmills@brgov.com
Chief of Operations **Jonathan Adams** .... (225) 389-2100
E-mail: kjones@brgov.com

Mosquito Abatement and Rodent Control

2829 Lt. Gen. Ben Davis Jr. Ave., Baton Rouge, LA 70807
Fax: (225) 356-9864 E-mail: marc@brgov.com
Internet: http://brgov.com/dept/ebrmarc/

Employees: 37 **Fiscal Year:** 2016 **Budget:** $5,509,000

○ Director **Dr. Todd Walker** .... (225) 356-3297
E-mail: twalker@brgov.com
Assistant Director **Randy Vaeth** .... (225) 356-3297
Administrative Assistant **Audrey Harrell** .... (225) 356-3297
E-mail: aharrell@brgov.com

Planning Commission Office

1100 Laurel Street, Suite 104, Baton Rouge, LA 70802
Tel: (225) 389-3144 Fax: (225) 389-5342 E-mail: planning@brgov.com

Employees: 24 **Fiscal Year:** 2016 **Budget:** $1,479,000

Director **Frank M. Duke** .... (225) 389-3144
Assistant Planning Director **Ryan Holcomb** .... (225) 389-3144
Executive Assistant **Annette Chambliss** .... (225) 389-3144
E-mail: achambliss@brgov.com
Comprehensive Plan Information **Lael Holton** .... (225) 389-3144
Current Planning **Glenn Hanna** .... (225) 389-3144
Project Coordinator **Gilles Morin** .... (225) 389-3144
Geographic Information System Coordinator
Justin Priola .... (225) 389-3144
E-mail: jpriola@brgov.com

★ Elected Official ▲ Appointed by Legislature ▼ Appointed by Governor ▶ Appointed by Board or Commission ● Appointed by Judge
■ Appointed by Mayor △ Appointed by Freeholders ▽ Appointed by Supervisor ▷ Appointed by County Executive ○ Appointed by Council

Police Department
9000 Airline Highway, Baton Rouge, LA 70815
P.O. Box 2406, Baton Rouge, LA 70821
Tel: (225) 389-3800 Fax: (225) 389-7630 E-mail: brpdinfo@brgov.com
Internet: http://brgov.com/dept/brpd/

Employees: 881 **Fiscal Year:** 2016 **Budget:** $88,560,000

■ Police Chief **Carl Robert Dabadie, Jr.** . . . . (225) 389-3802
E-mail: cdabadie@brgov.com
Deputy Chief of Staff **Sgt David Hamilton** . . . . (225) 389-3802
Commander of Administrative Services
Capt. Lynn Ferguson . . . . (225) 389-3802
Media Relations **Lt. Jonathan Dunnam** . . . . (225) 389-3948
E-mail: jdunnam@brgov.com

Public Information Office
222 St. Louis St., Baton Rouge, LA 70802
P.O. Box 1471, Baton Rouge, LA 70821
Fax: (225) 389-5450 E-mail: brinfo@brgov.com
Internet: http://brgov.com/dept/pubinfo/

Employees: 3 **Fiscal Year:** 2016 **Budget:** $415,000

○ Public Information Officer **Dennis McCain** . . . . . (225) 389-3121 ext. 213
E-mail: dmccain@brgov.com
Public Relations Coordinator **Sharon Phillips** . . . (225) 389-3121 ext. 211
E-mail: sphillips@brgov.com

Public Works Department
222 Saint Louis Street, 8th Floor, Baton Rouge, LA 70802
Fax: (225) 389-5391 Internet: http://www.brgov.com/dept/dpw/

■ Assistant Chief Administrative Officer (Interim)
Carey Chauvin . . . . (225) 389-3158
Workforce Development and Safety, Health and
Training Assistant Director **Monica Sprull** . . . . (225) 389-4640
E-mail: msprull@brgov.com
Director of Maintenance **Chris Burnett** . . . . (225) 389-3158
E-mail: cburnett@brgov.com
Recycling Director **Susan Hamilton** . . . . (225) 389-5194
Environmental Services Financial Manager
Mark LeBlanc . . . . (225) 389-3170 ext. 365

Purchasing Department
City Hall, 222 Saint Louis Street, Room 826, Baton Rouge, LA 70802
P.O. Box 1471, Baton Rouge, LA 70821-1471
Fax: (225) 389-4841 Internet: http://brgov.com/dept/purchase/
E-mail: purchasinginfo@brgov.com

Employees: 13 **Fiscal Year:** 2016 **Budget:** $968,000

■ Director **Patti J. Wallace** . . . . (225) 389-3259 ext. 304
E-mail: pwallace@brgov.com
Inventory Manager **Jerrel Jones** . . . . (225) 389-3259 ext. 321

Baton Rouge River Center
275 S. River Rd., Baton Rouge, LA 70802
Fax: (225) 389-4954

General Manager **Michael Day** . . . . (225) 389-3030
Assistant General Manager **(Vacant)** . . . . (225) 389-3030
Finance Director **Carla Mazique** . . . . (225) 389-3030
Marketing Coordinator **(Vacant)** . . . . (225) 389-3030
Operations Manager **Curtis Appleby** . . . . (225) 389-3030

City of Beaumont, Texas
City Hall, 801 Main Street, Beaumont, TX 77701
P.O. Box 3827, Beaumont, TX 77704-3827

County: Jefferson **Election Type:** Nonpartisan **Population:** 118,129 (2015)

Office of the Mayor and City Council
City Hall, 801 Main St., Suite 300, Beaumont, TX 77701

★ Mayor **Becky Ames** . . . . (409) 880-3736
Began Service: 2007
Term Expires: May 2017
E-mail: bames@ci.beaumont.tx.us
Career: Council Member, Office of the Mayor and City Council, City of Beaumont, Texas
★ Council Member **Claude F. Guidroz** (Ward 1) . . . . (409) 880-3770
Term Expires: May 2017
★ Council Member **Mike Getz** (Ward 2) . . . . (409) 880-3770
Term Expires: May 2017
E-mail: mdgetz@ci.beaumont.tx.us
★ Council Member **Audwin M. Samuel** (Ward 3) . . . . (409) 880-3770
Term Expires: May 2017
E-mail: asamuel@ci.beaumont.tx.us
Education: Lamar BS; Texas Southern JD
★ Council Member **Robin Mouton** (Ward 4) . . . . (409) 880-3770
Term Expires: May 2017
★ Council Member **W. L. Pate, Jr.** (At-Large) . . . . (409) 880-3770
Term Expires: May 2017
E-mail: wlpate@ci.beaumont.tx.us
★ Council Member
Gethrel "Get" Williams-Wright (At-Large) . . . . (409) 880-3770
Term Expires: May 2017
E-mail: gwilliams-wright@ci.beaumont.tx.us

Office of the City Attorney
City Hall, 801 Main St., Suite 325, Beaumont, TX 77701
Fax: (409) 880-3121

○ City Attorney **Tyrone Cooper** . . . . (409) 880-3715
E-mail: tcooper@ci.beaumont.tx.us

Office of the City Clerk
City Hall, 801 Main Street, Suite 125, Beaumont, TX 77701
Fax: (409) 880-3740

○ City Clerk **Tina Broussard** . . . . (409) 880-3745
E-mail: tbroussard@ci.beaumont.tx.us

Office of the City Manager
City Hall, 801 Main St., Suite 300, Beaumont, TX 77701
Fax: (409) 880-3112

○ City Manager **Kyle Hayes** . . . . (409) 880-3770
E-mail: khayes@ci.beaumont.tx.us
Education: Texas 1991 BA; Trinity U 1994 MS

Convention and Visitors' Bureau
50 South Willow Street, Beaumont, TX 77701
Tel: (409) 880-3749 Fax: (409) 880-3750

Director **Dean Conwell** . . . . (409) 880-3749

Event Facilities
701 Main Street, Beaumont, TX 77701
Fax: (409) 838-3715

Director **Lenny Caballero** . . . . (409) 838-3435 ext. 4205
E-mail: lcaballero@beaumonttexas.gov

★ Elected Official ▲ Appointed by Legislature ▼ Appointed by Governor ▶ Appointed by Board or Commission ● Appointed by Judge
■ Appointed by Mayor △ Appointed by Freeholders ▽ Appointed by Supervisor ▷ Appointed by County Executive ○ Appointed by Council

CITIES AND TOWNS

Finance
City Hall, 801 Main St., Suite 320, Beaumont, TX 77701
Fax: (409) 880-3132

Chief Finance Officer **Laura Clark** .... (409) 880-3789
Controller **Todd Simoneaux** .... (409) 880-3789
E-mail: tsimoneaux@ci.beaumont.tx.us

Fire and Rescue Services
400 Walnut, Beaumont, TX 77701
Fax: (409) 880-3934

Fire Chief/Director **Anne Huff** .... (409) 880-3916
E-mail: ahuff@ci.beaumont.tx.us

Human Resources
City Hall, 801 Main St., Suite 135, Beaumont, TX 77701
Fax: (409) 880-3108

Human Resources Director **Lillie Babino** .... (409) 880-3777
E-mail: lbabino@ci.beaumont.tx.us

Information Technology
801 Main Street, Suite 320, Beaumont, TX 77701
Tel: (409) 880-3752 Fax: (409) 880-3712

Director **Bart Bartkowiak** .... (409) 880-3752
E-mail: bbartkowiak@ci.beaumont.tx.us

Parks and Recreation
801 Main St., Beaumont, TX 77701
Fax: (409) 880-3747

Director **Ryan Slott** .... (409) 838-3613
2930 Gulf Street, Beaumont, TX 77703
E-mail: rslott@ci.beaumont.tx.us
Recreation Superintendent **Stacey Lewis** .... (409) 838-3613
2930 Gulf Street, Beaumont, TX 77703 Fax: (409) 838-4206
Recreation Superintendent **Jimmy Neale** .... (409) 838-3613
2930 Gulf Street, Beaumont, TX 77703 Fax: (409) 838-4206

Police
255 College St., Beaumont, TX 77701
Fax: (409) 880-3844 Internet: www.beaumontpd.com/

Police Chief **James P. Singletary** .... (409) 880-3801

Public Health Department
3040 College Street, Beaumont, TX 77701
Fax: (409) 832-4270

Director **Sherry Ulmer** .... (409) 832-4000

Public Works
City Hall, 801 Main St., Suite 210, Beaumont, TX 77701
Tel: (409) 880-3725 Fax: (409) 880-3732

Director **Joe Majdalani** .... (409) 880-3725
Beaumont Municipal Transit System Manager
Bill Munson .... (409) 835-7895
550 Milam St., Beaumont, TX 77701 Fax: (409) 832-3609
Building Official **Boyd Meier** .... (409) 880-3762
Fax: (409) 880-3110
Building Services Superintendent **Keith Folsom** .... (409) 880-3792
1848 Pine, Beaumont, TX 77703 Fax: (409) 833-9332
E-mail: kfolsom@ci.beaumont.tx.us
Community Development Block Grants Manager
Johnny Beatty Room 225 .... (409) 880-3763
Fax: (409) 880-3129
City Engineer **Zheng Z. Tan** .... (409) 880-3725
Community Development Director **Chris Boone** .... (409) 880-3725
801 Main Street, Fax: (409) 880-3732
Room 210, Beaumont, TX 77701
E-mail: cboone@ci.beaumont.tx.us
Environmental Specialist (Hazardous Waste)
Yolanda Duriso .... (409) 880-3725

Public Works *continued*

Fleet Management Superintendent **(Vacant)** .... (409) 842-5885
4955 Lafin Rd., Beaumont, TX 77705 Fax: (409) 842-0851
Planning Manager **(Vacant)** Room 205 .... (409) 880-3764
Fax: (409) 880-3133
Streets and Drainage Supervisor **Thomas Gill** .... (409) 838-5016
Fax: (409) 838-6153
Transportation Specialist **Joe Flores** .... (409) 838-6527
Transportation Manager **Mark Horelica** .... (409) 880-3725

Garbage Collection and Disposal
4955 Lafin Rd., Beaumont, TX 77705
Fax: (409) 842-1722

Operations Manager **Bengy Williams** .... (409) 842-1483
E-mail: bwilliams@ci.beaumont.tx.us
Landfill Superintendent **Felecia Thibodeaux** .... (409) 842-5686

Water Utilities
1350 Langham Road, Beaumont, TX 77707
Tel: (409) 866-0026 Fax: (409) 861-4836

Director **Hani Tohme** .... (409) 866-0026

Beaumont Independent School District
Administration Bldg., 3395 Harrison Ave., Beaumont, TX 77706
Internet: www.bmtisd.com Internet: www.facebook.com/bmtisd

Superintendent of Schools **John W. Frossard** .... (409) 617-5132
Fax: (409) 617-5184
Chief of Operations **Robert Calvert** .... (409) 617-5004
E-mail: rcalvert@beaumont.k12.tx.us Fax: (409) 617-5197
Human Resources Director **Katie Adams** .... (409) 617-5099
E-mail: kadams@beaumont.k12.tx.us

School Board
Note: The Board of Managers was appointed by the Texas Education Agency.

▶ President **Dr. James M. "Jimmy" Simmons** .... (409) 617-5000
Education: Memphis State BS; Houston MM; McNeese State
▶ Vice President **Joseph "Joe" Domino** .... (409) 617-5000
Education: Lamar
▶ Secretary **Robert Turner** .... (409) 617-5000
▶ Board Member **A. B. Bernard** .... (409) 617-5000
▶ Board Member **Lenny Caballero** .... (409) 617-5000
▶ Board Member **Jack Carroll** .... (409) 617-5000
▶ Board Member **Vernice Monroe** .... (409) 617-5000

City of Bellevue, Washington
450 110th Avenue, Northeast, Bellevue, WA 98004
P.O. Box 90012, Bellevue, WA 98009-9012
Internet: www.bellevuewa.gov

County: King **Election Type:** Nonpartisan **Year Incorporated:** 1953
Population: 139,820 (2015)

Office of the Mayor and City Council
P.O. Box 90012, Bellevue, WA 98009-9012
Fax: (425) 452-7919

★ Mayor **John Stokes** .... (425) 452-7810
Began Service: January 3, 2012
Term Expires: December 31, 2019
★ Deputy Mayor **John L. Chelminiak** .... (425) 452-7810
Term Expires: December 31, 2019
E-mail: jchelminiak@bellevuewa.gov
Education: Washington State BA

★ Elected Official ▲ Appointed by Legislature ▼ Appointed by Governor ▶ Appointed by Board or Commission ● Appointed by Judge
■ Appointed by Mayor △ Appointed by Freeholders ▽ Appointed by Supervisor ▷ Appointed by County Executive ○ Appointed by Council

Office of the Mayor and City Council *continued*

★Council Member **Conrad Lee** .... (425) 452-7810
Term Expires: December 31, 2017
Education: Michigan 1962 BS; U Washington 1980 MBA

★Council Member **Jennifer Robertson** .... (425) 452-7810
Term Expires: December 31, 2019
E-mail: jrobertson@bellevuewa.gov

★Council Member **Lynne Robinson** .... (425) 452-7810
Term Expires: December 31, 2017

★Council Member **Vandana Slatter** .... (425) 452-7810
Term Expires: December 31, 2019

★Council Member **Kevin Wallace** .... (425) 452-7810
Term Expires: December 31, 2017
E-mail: k.wallace@bellevuewa.gov

Office of the City Manager

P.O. Box 90012, Bellevue, WA 98009-9012
Fax: (425) 452-5241

○City Manager **Brad Miyake** .... (425) 452-4096
E-mail: bmiyake@bellevuewa.gov
Executive Assistant **Nancy Krodani-Lee** .... (425) 452-4096

Deputy City Manager **Mary Kate Berens** .... (425) 452-4616
E-mail: mkberens@bellevuewa.gov
Education: U Washington BS, JD

Intergovernmental Relations Director **Joyce Nichols** .... (425) 452-4225
E-mail: jnichols@bellevuewa.gov

Strategic Communications Advisor (Acting)
Brad Harwood .... (425) 452-6837
E-mail: bharwood@bellevuewa.gov

Land Surveying Division

P.O. Box 90012, Bellevue, WA 98009-9012

Survey Manager **Lynn Call** .... (425) 452-6460
E-mail: lcall@bellevuewa.gov

Office of the City Attorney

P.O. Box 90012, Bellevue, WA 98009-9012
Fax: (425) 452-7256

City Attorney **Lori Riordan** .... (425) 452-6829
E-mail: lriordan@bellevuewa.gov

Office of the City Clerk

P.O. Box 90012, Bellevue, WA 98009-9012
Fax: (425) 452-2734

City Clerk/Assistant City Manager (Interim)
Kyle Stannert .... (425) 452-2733
E-mail: kstannert@bellevuewa.gov

Finance Department

P.O. Box 90012, Bellevue, WA 98009-9012
Fax: (425) 452-6163

Director **Jan Hawn** .... (425) 452-6846

Fire Department

P.O. Box 90012, Bellevue, WA 98009-9012
Fax: (425) 452-5287

Fire Chief **Mark Risen** .... (425) 452-6892
E-mail: mrisen@bellevuewa.gov

Human Resources Department

P.O. Box 90012, Bellevue, WA 98009-9012
Fax: (425) 452-4071

Director **Kerry Sievers** .... (425) 452-6838
E-mail: ksievers@bellevuewa.gov

Information Technology Department

P.O. Box 90012, Bellevue, WA 98009-9012
Fax: (425) 452-7882

Chief Information Officer **Toni Cramer** .... (425) 452-2972
E-mail: tcramer@bellevuewa.gov

Parks and Community Services Department

P.O. Box 90012, Bellevue, WA 98009-9012
Fax: (425) 452-7259

Director **Patrick Foran** .... (425) 452-6881
E-mail: pforan@bellevuewa.gov

Facilities Manager **Frank Pinney** .... (425) 452-6049
E-mail: fpinney@bellevuewa.gov Fax: (425) 452-6163

Planning and Community Development Department

P.O. Box 90012, Bellevue, WA 98009-9012
Fax: (425) 452-5225

Director **Chris Salomone** .... (425) 452-6800
E-mail: csalomone@bellevuewa.gov

Planning Director **Dan Stroh** .... (425) 452-5255
E-mail: dstroh@bellevuewa.gov

Comprehensive Planning Manager **Paul Inghram** .... (425) 452-4070
E-mail: pinghram@bellevuewa.gov
Education: U Washington 1993 BA; Seattle MBA

Police Department

P.O. Box 90012, Bellevue, WA 98009-9012
Fax: (425) 452-6110

Police Chief **Steve Mylett** .... (425) 452-6952
Deputy Police Chief, Operations **Jim Jolliffe** .... (425) 452-6952
Deputy Police Chief **(Vacant)** .... (425) 452-6952
Public Information Officer **Seth Tyler** .... (425) 452-6952
E-mail: styler@bellevuewa.gov

Probation

P.O. Box 90012, Bellevue, WA 98009-9012

Manager **Tandra Schwamberg** .... (425) 452-6956

Purchasing

P.O. Box 90012, Bellevue, WA 98009-9012

Manager **Jamie Robinson** .... (425) 452-6894
E-mail: jrobinson@bellevuewa.gov

Risk Management

P.O. Box 90012, Bellevue, WA 98009-9012

Manager **Peter Bourgeault** .... (425) 452-2746
E-mail: pbourgeault@ci.bellevue.wa.us

Transportation Department

P.O. Box 90012, Bellevue, WA 98009-9012
Fax: (425) 452-2052

Director **Dave Berg** .... (425) 452-4338
Advisor, Transportation Policy **Kimberly Becklund** .... (425) 452-4491

Utilities Department

P.O. Box 90012, Bellevue, WA 98009-9012
Fax: (425) 452-5214 Internet: www.ci.bellevue.wa.us/utilities.htm

Director **Nav Otal** .... (425) 452-4497
Education: British Columbia BS

★Elected Official ▲Appointed by Legislature ▼Appointed by Governor ▶Appointed by Board or Commission ●Appointed by Judge
■Appointed by Mayor △Appointed by Freeholders ▽Appointed by Supervisor ▷Appointed by County Executive ○Appointed by Council

Bellevue School District

12111 NE First St., Bellevue, WA 98005
P.O. Box 90010, Bellevue, WA 98009-9010
E-mail: pubinfo@bsd405.org Internet: http://www.bsd405.org

Superintendent **Dr. Tim Mills** .... (425) 456-4172
★President **Steve McConnell** (District 1) .... (425) 456-4000
Term Expires: December 31, 2019
★Vice President **Christine Chew** (District 4) .... (425) 456-4000
Term Expires: December 31, 2019
E-mail: chewc@bsd405.org
★Member **Carolyn Watson** (District 2) .... (425) 456-4000
Term Expires: December 31, 2019
★Member **Chris Marks** (District 3) .... (425) 456-4000
Term Expires: December 31, 2017
E-mail: marksc@bsd405.org
★Member **My-Linh Thai** (District 5) .... (425) 456-4000
Term Expires: December 31, 2017

City of Berkeley, California

City Hall, 2180 Milvia Street, Berkeley, CA 94704-1122
Internet: www.cityofberkeley.info

County: Alameda **Election Type:** Nonpartisan **Year Incorporated:** 1878
Charter: 1909 **Population:** 120,972 (2015)

Tom Bates
Mayor

Began Service: 2002
Term Expires: November 30, 2016
Date of Birth: February 9, 1938
Education: UC Berkeley 1961 BA
Career: Supervisor, Board of Supervisors, County of Alameda, California (1972-1976); State Representative (D-CA, District 14), California State Assembly (1976-1996)

Office of the Mayor

City Hall, 2180 Milvia Street, Berkeley, CA 94704-1122
Tel: (510) 981-7190 (TTY)

★Mayor **Tom Bates** .... (510) 981-7100
E-mail: mayor@cityofberkeley.info Fax: (510) 981-7199
■Chief of Staff **Calvin Fong** .... (510) 981-7102
E-mail: cfong@cityofberkeley.info
■Senior Aide **Gregory Magofña** .... (510) 981-7190
E-mail: gmagofna@cityofberkeley.info
■Director of Communications **Charles Burress** .... (510) 981-7100
E-mail: cburress@cityofberkeley.info
■Legislative Aide **(Vacant)** .... (510) 981-7100

Office of the City Council

City Hall, 2180 Milvia Street, 5th Floor, Berkeley, CA 94704-1122

★Council Member **Linda Maio** (District 1) .... (510) 981-7110
Term Expires: November 30, 2018 Fax: (510) 981-7111
E-mail: lmaio@cityofberkeley.info
Legislative Assistant **Nicole Drake** .... (510) 981-7110
E-mail: ndrake@cityofberkeley.info
★Council Member **Darryl Moore** (District 2) .... (510) 981-7120
Term Expires: November 30, 2016 Fax: (510) 981-7122
E-mail: dmoore@cityofberkeley.info
Aide **Ryan Lau** .... (510) 981-7126
E-mail: rlau@cityofberkeley.info
★Council Member **Max Anderson** (District 3) .... (510) 981-7130
Term Expires: November 30, 2016 Fax: (510) 981-7133
E-mail: manderson@cityofberkeley.info

Office of the City Council *continued*

Aide **Charlene Washington** .... (510) 981-7131
E-mail: cwashington@cityofberkeley.info
★Council Member **Jesse Arreguin** (District 4) .... (510) 981-7140
Term Expires: November 30, 2018 Fax: (510) 981-7144
E-mail: jarreguin@cityofberkeley.info
Chief of Staff **Anthony Sanchez** .... (510) 981-7140
★Council Member **Laurie Capitelli** (District 5) .... (510) 981-7150
Term Expires: November 30, 2016 Fax: (510) 981-7155
E-mail: lcapitelli@ci.berkeley.ca.us
Legislative Assistant **Jill Martinucci** .... (510) 981-7151
★Council Member **Susan Wengraf** (District 6) .... (510) 981-7160
Term Expires: November 30, 2016 Fax: (510) 981-7166
E-mail: swengraf@cityofberkeley.info
Aide **Anna Avellar** .... (510) 981-7162
E-mail: aavellar@cityofberkeley.info
★Council Member **Kriss Worthington** (District 7) .... (510) 981-7170
Term Expires: November 30, 2018 Fax: (510) 981-7177
E-mail: kworthington@cityofberkeley.info
Legislative Assistant **Alejandro Soto-Vigil** .... (510) 981-7171
★Council Member **Lori Droste** (District 8) .... (510) 981-7180
Term Expires: November 30, 2018 Fax: (510) 981-7188
E-mail: ldroste@CityofBerkeley.info

Office of the Auditor

City Hall, 2180 Milvia Street, Berkeley, CA 94704-1122
Tel: (510) 981-6750 (Information) Tel: (510) 981-6770 (Payroll)
Fax: (510) 981-6760

★Auditor **Ann-Marie Hogan** .... (510) 981-6750
Term Expires: November 30, 2018 Fax: (510) 981-6760
E-mail: auditor@cityofberkeley.info

Office of the City Manager

City Hall, 2180 Milvia Street, Berkeley, CA 94704-1122
Tel: (510) 981-7000 Tel: (510) 981-2489 (City Center Information)
Tel: (510) 981-6903 (TTY) Fax: (510) 981-7099

○City Manager (Interim) **Dee Williams-Ridley** .... (510) 981-7004
E-mail: manager@cityofberkeley.info
Secretary **Yvette Gan** .... (510) 981-7004
E-mail: ygan@ci.berkeley.ca.us
Deputy City Manager (Interim) **Gilbert Dong** .... (510) 981-7000
Chief Resilience Officer **Tim Burroughs** .... (510) 981-7000
E-mail: tburroughs@ci.berkeley.ca.us

Office of the City Attorney

2180 Milvia Street, Berkeley, CA 94704-1122
Tel: (510) 981-6950 Fax: (510) 981-6960

City Attorney **Zach Cowan** .... (510) 981-6950
E-mail: attorney@cityofberkeley.info
Education: San Francisco State U 1976 BA; Hastings 1980 JD

Office of the City Clerk

2180 Milvia Street, Berkeley, CA 94704-1122
Tel: (510) 981-6900 TTY: (510) 981-6903 Fax: (510) 981-6901

City Clerk **Mark Numainville** .... (510) 981-6900
E-mail: clerk@cityofberkeley.info
Deputy City Clerk **Rose Thompson** .... (510) 981-6900
E-mail: rthompson@ci.berkeley.ca.us

Berkeley Public Library

2090 Kittredge Street, Berkeley, CA 94704-1427
Tel: (510) 981-6100 TTY: (510) 981-6903 Fax: (510) 981-6111

Director **Jeff Scott** .... (510) 981-6195
E-mail: jscott@ci.berkeley.ca.us

★Elected Official ▲Appointed by Legislature ▼Appointed by Governor ▶Appointed by Board or Commission ●Appointed by Judge
■Appointed by Mayor △Appointed by Freeholders ▽Appointed by Supervisor ▷Appointed by County Executive ○Appointed by Council

City Planning and Development Department

2120 Milvia Street, Berkeley, CA 94704-1113
Tel: (510) 981-7400 Tel: (510) 981-7474 (TTY Permit Service Center)
Fax: (510) 981-7470

Director **(Vacant)** . . . . (510) 981-7400
E-mail: planning@cityofberkeley.info

Economic Development Office

2180 Milvia Street, Berkeley, CA 94704-1113
Tel: (510) 981-7530 Fax: (510) 981-7099 Tel: (510) 981-6903 (TDD)
E-mail: ecodev@ci.berkeley.ca.us

Manager **Michael Caplan** . . . . (510) 981-2490
E-mail: mcaplan@cityofberkeley.info

Finance Department

2180 Milvia St., Berkeley, CA 94704
Tel: (510) 981-7300 (Administration)
Tel: (510) 981-7200 (Customer Service)
Tel: (510) 981-7250 (TTY Customer Service)
Fax: (510) 981-7390 (Administration)
Fax: (510) 981-7210 (Customer Service)

Director **(Vacant)** . . . . (510) 981-7300

Department of Fire and Emergency Services

2100 Martin Luther King, Jr. Way, Berkeley, CA 94704-1109
Tel: (510) 981-3473 Tel: (510) 981-6903 (TDD)
Tel: (510) 981-5900 (Communication Center (non-emergency))
Tel: (510) 981-5585 (Fire Prevention) Fax: (510) 981-5579

Fire Chief **Gilbert Dong** . . . . (510) 981-5500
E-mail: fire@cityofberkeley.info
Deputy Chief **Avery Webb** . . . . (510) 981-5501
E-mail: awebb@cityofberkeley.info

Department of Health, Housing and Community Services

2180 Milvia Street, 2nd Floor, Berkeley, CA 94704-1122
Tel: (510) 981-5100 Tel: (510) 981-6903 (TDD) Fax: (510) 981-5112

Director **Jane Micallef** . . . . (510) 981-5100
Education: Michigan BA; Boalt Hall 1989 JD
Deputy Director **Kelly Wallace** . . . . (510) 981-5100

Public Health Division

1947 Center Street, Second Floor, Berkeley, CA 94704
Fax: (510) 981-5395

Public Health Officer **Janet Berreman** . . . . (510) 981-5300

Housing Authority

1901 Fairview Street, Berkeley, CA 94703-2718
Tel: (510) 981-5470 Tel: (510) 981-5495 (TDD) Fax: (510) 981-5480

Manager **Tia Ingram** . . . . (510) 981-5470

Human Resources Department

2180 Milvia Street, Berkeley, CA 94704-1122
Tel: (510) 981-6800 Fax: (510) 981-6860 TTY: (510) 981-6830

Director **David Abel** . . . . (510) 981-6807
E-mail: DAbel@cityofberkeley.info
Occupational Health and Safety Officer
Terry Gunderson . . . . (510) 981-6825
Training Officer **Liz Schiff** . . . . (510) 981-6823
E-mail: lschiff@cityofberkeley.info

Information Technology Department

2180 Milvia Street, 4th Floor, Berkeley, CA 94704-1122
Tel: (510) 981-6500 Fax: (510) 981-6560
E-mail: helpdesk@cityofberkeley.info

Director **Donna Lasala** . . . . (510) 981-6500
E-mail: dlasala@cityofberkeley.info

Parks, Recreation and Waterfront Department

2180 Milvia Street, Berkeley, CA 94704-1122
Tel: (510) 981-6700 Tel: (510) 981-6903 (TTY) Fax: (510) 981-6710

Director **Scott Ferris** . . . . (510) 981-6700

Police Department

2100 Martin Luther King, Jr. Way, Berkeley, CA 94704-1109
Tel: (510) 981-5900 Tel: (510) 981-5799 (TDD) Fax: (510) 981-5744

Chief of Police **Michael K. Meehan** . . . . (510) 981-5700

Public Works Department

2180 Milvia Street, Berkeley, CA 94704-1122
Tel: (510) 981-6300 TTY: (510) 981-6345 Fax: (510) 981-6320
E-mail: pwadmin@cityofberkeley.info

Director **Andrew Clough** . . . . (510) 981-6300
Deputy Director **Phillip L. Harrington** . . . . (510) 981-6300

Rent Stabilization Board

2125 Milvia Street, Berkeley, CA 94704-1112
Fax: (510) 981-4940

Executive Director **Jay Kelekian** . . . . (510) 981-7368

Berkeley Unified School District

2134 Martin Luther King, Jr. Way, Berkeley, CA 94704-1180
Internet: www.berkeley.net/

Superintendent **Dr. Donald Evans** . . . . (510) 644-6206

Board of Education

2134 Martin Luther King, Jr. Way, Berkeley, CA 94704-1180
Tel: (510) 644-6550 Fax: (510) 540-5358

★ President **Judy Appel** . . . . (510) 644-6550
Term Expires: December 31, 2016
E-mail: judyappel@berkeley.net
★ Vice President **Beatriz Leyva-Cutler** . . . . (510) 644-6550
Term Expires: December 31, 2016
E-mail: BeatrizLeyvaCutler@berkeley.net
★ Clerk **Karen Hemphill** . . . . (510) 644-6550
Term Expires: December 31, 2018
E-mail: karenhemphill@comcast.net
★ Director **Ty Alper** . . . . (510) 644-6550
Term Expires: December 31, 2018
E-mail: tyalper@berkeley.net
★ Director **Josh Daniels** . . . . (510) 644-6550
Term Expires: December 31, 2018
E-mail: JoshDaniels@berkeley.net
Secretary to the Board **Deborah Turner** . . . . (510) 644-6550

City of Billings, Montana

210 N. 27th, Billings, MT 59101
P.O. Box 1178, Billings, MT 59103
Tel: (406) 657-8433 (Information) Internet: http://ci.billings.mt.us

County: Yellowstone **Election Type:** Nonpartisan **Population:** 110,263 (2015)

Office of the Mayor and City Council

P.O. Box 1178, Billings, MT 59103
Fax: (406) 657-8390

★ Mayor **Tom Hanel** . . . . (406) 657-8296
Began Service: January 1, 2010
Term Expires: December 31, 2017
E-mail: hanelt@ci.billings.mt.us

(continued on next page)

★ Elected Official ▲ Appointed by Legislature ▼ Appointed by Governor ▶ Appointed by Board or Commission ● Appointed by Judge
■ Appointed by Mayor △ Appointed by Freeholders ▽ Appointed by Supervisor ▷ Appointed by County Executive ○ Appointed by Council

Office of the Mayor and City Council *continued*

Executive Secretary **Wynnette Maddox** . . . . (406) 657-8433
E-mail: maddoxw@ci.billings.mt.us

★Council Member **Brent R. Cromley** (Ward 1) . . . . (406) 252-3512
Term Expires: December 31, 2019
E-mail: cromleyb@ci.billings.mt.us

★Council Member **Mike Yakawich** (Ward 1) . . . . (406) 254-2445
Term Expires: December 31, 2017

★Council Member **Larry Brewster** (Ward 2) . . . . (406) 657-8296
Term Expires: December 31, 2019

★Council Member **Angela Cimmino** (Ward 2) . . . . (406) 698-9763
Term Expires: December 31, 2017
E-mail: cimminoa@ci.billings.mt.us

★Council Member **Chris Friedel** (Ward 3) . . . . (406) 657-8296
Term Expires: December 31, 2019

★Council Member **Richard McFadden** (Ward 3) . . . . (406) 545-9481
Term Expires: December 31, 2017
E-mail: mcfaddenr@ci.billings.mt.us

★Council Member **Ryan Sullivan** (Ward 4) . . . . (406) 657-8296
Term Expires: December 31, 2019

★Council Member **Alvin Swanson** (Ward 4) . . . . (406) 671-5917
Term Expires: December 31, 2017

★Council Member **Shaun Brown** (Ward 5) . . . . (406) 698-2328
Term Expires: December 31, 2017

★Council Member **Richard "Dick" Clark** (Ward 5) . . . . (406) 657-8296
Term Expires: December 31, 2019
Date of Birth: February 27, 1940

Office of the City Administrator

P.O. Box 1178, Billings, MT 59103
Fax: (406) 657-8390

City Administrator **Christina Volek** . . . . (406) 657-8430
E-mail: volekc@ci.billings.mt.us

Assistant City Administrator **Bruce McCandless** . . . . (406) 657-8222
E-mail: mccandlessb@ci.billings.mt.us

Information Technology Division

P.O. Box 1178, Billings, MT 59103
Fax: (406) 657-3064

Chief Information Officer **David Watterson** . . . . (406) 657-8330
E-mail: wattersond@ci.billings.mt.us

Office of the City Attorney

P.O. Box 1178, Billings, MT 59103
Internet: http://ci.billings.mt.us/index.aspx?nid=102 Fax: (406) 657-3067

City Attorney **Brent Brooks** . . . . (406) 657-8202
E-mail: brooksb@ci.billings.mt.us

Office of the City Clerk

P.O. Box 1178, Billings, MT 59103
Fax: (406) 657-8390

City Clerk **Billie Guenther** . . . . (406) 657-8210
E-mail: guentherb@ci.billings.mt.us

Deputy City Clerk **Toni Keehner** . . . . (406) 657-8210
E-mail: keehnert@ci.billings.mt.us

Administrative Services Department

P.O. Box 1178, Billings, MT 59103
Fax: (406) 657-8390

Director **Bruce McCandless** . . . . (406) 657-8222
E-mail: mccandlessb@ci.billings.mt.us

Purchasing Division **Liz Kampa-Weatherwax** . . . . (406) 657-8216
E-mail: kampal@ci.billings.mt.us

Fleet Services Superintendent **Larry Deschene** . . . . (406) 657-8229

Billings Municipal Airport

1901 Terminal Circle, Room 216, Billings, MT 59105
Internet: http://www.flybillings.com

Director of Aviation and Transit **Kevin Ploehn** . . . . (406) 657-8495

Billings Public Library

510 North Broadway, Billings, MT 59101
Tel: (406) 657-8258 Internet: http://ci.billings.mt.us/index.aspx?nid=258

Director **William Cochran** . . . . (406) 657-8292
E-mail: cochranb@ci.billings.mt.us

Fire Department

P.O. Box 1178, Billings, MT 59103
Fax: (406) 657-8456 Internet: http://ci.billings.mt.us/index.aspx?nid=110

Fire Chief **Paul A. Dextras** . . . . (406) 657-8421
E-mail: dextrasp@ci.billings.mt.us

Human Resources

P.O. Box 1178, Billings, MT 59103
Fax: (406) 657-8390 Internet: http://ci.billings.mt.us/index.aspx?NID=108

Human Resources Manager **Karla Stanton** . . . . (406) 657-8204
E-mail: stantonk@ci.billings.mt.us

Parks, Recreation and Public Lands Department

P.O. Box 1178, Billings, MT 59103

Director **Michael Whitaker** . . . . (406) 657-8369

Planning and Community Services Department

P.O. Box 1178, Billings, MT 59103
Fax: (406) 657-8327

Planning Director **Candi Millar** . . . . (406) 657-8249

Building Division

P.O. Box 1178, Billings, MT 59103
Fax: (406) 657-8252

Building Official **Brian Anderson** . . . . (406) 657-8273

Community Development Department

P.O. Box 1178, Billings, MT 59103
Fax: (406) 657-8252

Community Development Manager **Brenda Beckett** . . . . . (406) 657-8286
E-mail: beckettb@ci.billings.mt.us

Police Department

P.O. Box 1178, Billings, MT 59103

Chief of Police **Richard St. John** . . . . (406) 657-8462

Public Works Department

P.O. Box 1178, Billings, MT 59103
Fax: (406) 237-6291 Internet: http://ci.billings.mt.us/index.aspx?nid=66

Director **David Mumford** . . . . (406) 657-8232

Engineering Division

P.O. Box 1178, Billings, MT 59103
Fax: (406) 657-8252

City Engineer **Debi Meling** . . . . (406) 657-3097
E-mail: melingd@ci.billings.mt.us

Solid Waste Division

P.O. Box 1178, Billings, MT 59103
Fax: (406) 247-8626

Director **Vester Wilson** . . . . (406) 657-8260

Street-Traffic Division

P.O. Box 1178, Billings, MT 59103

Superintendent **Bill Kemp** . . . . (406) 657-8354

★Elected Official ▲Appointed by Legislature ▼Appointed by Governor ►Appointed by Board or Commission ●Appointed by Judge
■Appointed by Mayor △Appointed by Freeholders ▽Appointed by Supervisor ▷Appointed by County Executive ○Appointed by Council

Street-Traffic Division *continued*

Traffic Engineer **Terry Smith** . . . . (406) 657-8234
E-mail: smitht@ci.billings.mt.us

Transportation Department
P.O. Box 1178, Billings, MT 59103

Metropolitan Transit Superintendent **Ron Wenger** . . . . (406) 657-8221

Utilities Division
P.O. Box 1178, Billings, MT 59103
Fax: (406) 657-8319

Deputy Director **Vern Heisler** . . . . (406) 657-8236

City of Birmingham, Alabama
City Hall, 710 North 20th Street, Birmingham, AL 35203
Tel: (205) 254-2000 (Information)

County: Jefferson **Election Type:** Nonpartisan **Population:** 212,461 (2015) **Employees:** 4,831 **Fiscal Year:** 2016 **Budget:** $411,425,000

Office of the Mayor
City Hall, 710 N. 20th St., Birmingham, AL 35203
Fax: (205) 254-2926

Employees: 92 **Fiscal Year:** 2016 **Budget:** $9,814,000

★ Mayor **William A. Bell, Sr.** . . . . (205) 254-2277
Began Service: January 26, 2010
Term Expires: November 24, 2017
E-mail: william.bell@birminghamal.gov

■ Chief of Staff **(Vacant)** . . . . (205) 254-2285

■ Chief of Operations **Jarvis Patton** . . . . (205) 254-2320
E-mail: jarvis.patton@birminghamal.gov

■ Public Information Officer **April Odom** . . . . (205) 254-2823
E-mail: april.odom@birminghamal.gov
Education: Alabama Birmingham BA

Executive Administrative Assistant **Charles Long** . . . . (205) 254-2609
E-mail: charles.long@birminghamal.gov

Chief Administrative Analyst **Terry Burney** . . . . (205) 254-2388
E-mail: terry.burney@birminghamal.gov

Mayor's Office of Economic Development
710 North 20th Street, Birmingham, AL 35203
Tel: (205) 254-2799

Director of Economic Development **Lisa Cooper** . . . . (205) 254-2799
E-mail: lisa.cooper@birminghamal.gov

Office of the City Attorney
City Hall, 710 N. 20th St., 6th Floor, Birmingham, AL 35203
Fax: (205) 254-2502

Employees: 43 **Fiscal Year:** 2017 **Budget:** $7,123,000

■ City Attorney **(Vacant)** . . . . (205) 254-2369

■ Chief Assistant City Attorney **Frederic L. Fullerton II** . . . . (205) 254-2369
E-mail: frederic.fullerton@birminghamal.gov

■ Chief Assistant City Attorney **James C. Stanley** . . . . (205) 254-2369
E-mail: james.stanley@birminghamal.gov

Office of the City Clerk
City Hall, 710 N. 20th St., 3rd Floor, Birmingham, AL 35203
Fax: (205) 254-2115

Employees: 12 **Fiscal Year:** 2016 **Budget:** $1,285,000

■ City Clerk **Lee Frazier** . . . . (205) 254-2290
E-mail: lee.frazier@birminghamal.gov

■ Deputy City Clerk **(Vacant)** . . . . (205) 254-2290

Albert Boutwell Auditorium
1930 Eighth Ave. North, Birmingham, AL 35203
Fax: (205) 254-2929

Employees: 32 **Fiscal Year:** 2016 **Budget:** $1,433,000

Director **Kevin Arrington** . . . . (205) 254-2820

Community Development Department
City Hall, 710 N. 20th St., Room 1000, Birmingham, AL 35203
Fax: (205) 254-2282

Employees: 63 **Fiscal Year:** 2016 **Budget:** $800,000

■ Director **John Colon** . . . . (205) 254-2309
E-mail: john.colon@birminghamal.gov

Equipment Management
515 Sixth Ave. South, Birmingham, AL 35205
Fax: (205) 254-6578

Employees: 63 **Fiscal Year:** 2016 **Budget:** $16,778,000

Director **George R. "Bob" Rainey** . . . . (205) 254-6301
E-mail: bob.rainey@birminghamal.gov

Deputy Manager **Cedric Roberts** . . . . (205) 254-6301
E-mail: cedric.roberts@birminghamal.gov

Finance Department
City Hall, 710 N. 20th St., Room 205, Birmingham, AL 35203
Fax: (205) 254-2937

Employees: 126 **Fiscal Year:** 2016 **Budget:** $11,888,000

■ Director **J. Thomas Barnett, Jr.** . . . . (205) 254-2205
E-mail: tom.barnett@birminghamal.gov

Deputy Director **Barbara McGrue** . . . . (205) 254-2205

Deputy Director **Betty Griss** . . . . (205) 254-2205

Fire Department
1808 Seventh Ave. North, Birmingham, AL 35203
Fax: (205) 254-2440

Employees: 729 **Fiscal Year:** 2016 **Budget:** $59,418,000

■ Fire Chief **Charles Gordon** . . . . (205) 254-2052
E-mail: charles.gordon@birminghamal.gov

Human Resources Department
City Hall, 710 N. 20th St., 8th Floor, Birmingham, AL 35203
Fax: (205) 254-2415

Employees: 36 **Fiscal Year:** 2016 **Budget:** $6,196,000

■ Director **Peggy Washington Polk** . . . . (205) 254-2829
E-mail: peggy.polk@birminghamal.gov

Information Management Services
IMS Building, 712 North 19th Street, Birmingham, AL 35203
Fax: (205) 254-2010

Employees: 61 **Fiscal Year:** 2016 **Budget:** $14,865,000

■ Director **Srikanth "Sri" Karra** . . . . (205) 254-2672
E-mail: skarra@birminghamal.gov

Parks and Recreation Department
400 Graymont Ave. West, Birmingham, AL 35204
Fax: (205) 254-2515

Employees: 301 **Fiscal Year:** 2016 **Budget:** $13,669,000

Director **Kevin Moore** . . . . (205) 254-2391

Planning, Engineering and Permits Department
City Hall, 710 N. 20th St., Room 220, Birmingham, AL 35203
Fax: (205) 254-2407

Employees: 167 **Fiscal Year:** 2016 **Budget:** $13,316,000

■ Director **Andre Bittas** . . . . (205) 254-2336 ext. 2424
E-mail: andre.bittas@birminghamal.gov

★ Elected Official ▲ Appointed by Legislature ▼ Appointed by Governor ▶ Appointed by Board or Commission ● Appointed by Judge
■ Appointed by Mayor △ Appointed by Freeholders ▽ Appointed by Supervisor ▷ Appointed by County Executive ○ Appointed by Council

Police Department
1710 1st Avenue North, Birmingham, AL 35203
Fax: (205) 254-1703

Employees: 1,232 **Fiscal Year:** 2016 **Budget:** $92,974,000

Chief of Police **MG A.C. Roper, Jr.** .... (205) 254-1709
Deputy Chief **Henry Irby III** .... (205) 254-1700
Deputy Chief **Jamal McCaskey** .... (205) 254-1700
Deputy Chief **W. Ray Tubbs** .... (205) 254-1700
Deputy Chief **Irene Williams** .... (205) 254-1700

Public Works Department
501 Sixth Ave. South, Birmingham, AL 35205
Fax: (205) 254-6550

Employees: 1,186 **Fiscal Year:** 2016 **Budget:** $46,536,000

■ Director **Stephen Francher** .... (205) 254-6316
E-mail: Stephen.Fancher@birminghamal.gov
Assistant Director **Allistar Hickman** .... (205) 254-6316
Assistant Director **Herman Wilhite** .... (205) 254-6316
Assistant Director **(Vacant)** .... (205) 254-6316

Traffic Engineering Department
City Hall, 710 N. 20th St., Room 900, Birmingham, AL 35203
Fax: (205) 254-7789

Employees: 72 **Fiscal Year:** 2016 **Budget:** $10,465,000

■ Director **Greg Dawkins** .... (205) 254-2450
E-mail: greg.dawkins@birminghamal.gov
Assistant Traffic Engineer **Cedric Rutledge** .... (205) 254-2450
E-mail: cedric.rutledge@birminghamal.gov

Office of the City Council
City Hall, 710 N. 20th St., Birmingham, AL 35203
Fax: (205) 254-2603

Employees: 47 **Fiscal Year:** 2016 **Budget:** $3,603,000

★ Council President **Johnathan F. Austin** (District 5) ...... (205) 254-2678
Term Expires: November 2017
E-mail: johnathan.austin@birminghamal.gov
★ Council Member **Lashunda Scales** (District 1) .... (205) 254-2294
Term Expires: November 2017
E-mail: lashunda.scales@birminghamal.gov
★ Council Member **Kimberly "Kim" Rafferty** (District 2) .. (205) 254-2294
Term Expires: November 2017
E-mail: kimberly.rafferty@birminghamal.gov
★ Council Member **Valerie A. Abbott** (District 3) .... (205) 254-2294
Term Expires: November 2017
E-mail: valerie.abbott@birminghamal.gov
★ Council Member **William Parker** (District 4) .... (205) 254-2294
Term Expires: November 2017
E-mail: william.parker@birminghamal.gov
★ Council Member **Sheila Tyson** (District 6) .... (205) 254-2294
Term Expires: November 2017
E-mail: sheila.tyson@birminghamal.gov
★ Council Member **Jay Roberson** (District 7) .... (205) 254-2294
Term Expires: November 2017
E-mail: jay.roberson@birminghamal.gov
★ Council Member **Steven W. Hoyt** (District 8) .... (205) 254-2294
Term Expires: November 2017
E-mail: steven.hoyt@birminghamal.gov
★ Council Member **Marcus Lundy** (District 9) .... (205) 254-2294
Term Expires: October 22, 2017
E-mail: marcus.lundy@birminghamal.gov
○ Council Administrator **Cheryl Kidd** .... (205) 254-2294
E-mail: cheryl.kidd@birminghamal.gov
Deputy Council Administrator **Chaz Mitchell** .... (205) 254-2294
E-mail: chaz.mitchell@birminghamal.gov
Public Information Officer **Brittany Sharp** .... (205) 254-2036
E-mail: brittany.sharp@birminghamal.gov

Birmingham Airport Authority
5900 Messer Airport Highway, Birmingham, AL 35212
Fax: (205) 599-0538 Internet: www.flybirmingham.com
E-mail: info@flybirmingham.com

President and Chief Executive Officer
Alfonso "Al" Denson .... (205) 595-0533

Library
2100 Park Place, Birmingham, AL 35203
Fax: (205) 226-3743 Internet: http://www.bplonline.org

Employees: 303 **Fiscal Year:** 2016 **Budget:** $15,494

Director **Angela Fisher Hall** .... (205) 226-3600
E-mail: bpldirector@bham.lib.al.us

Museum of Art
2000 Rev. Abraham Woods, Jr. Boulevard, Birmingham, AL 35203
Fax: (205) 254-2714 E-mail: museum@artsbma.org
Internet: http://www.artsbma.org

Employees: 40 **Fiscal Year:** 2016 **Budget:** $3,593,000

Director **Gail Andrews** .... (205) 254-2565 ext. 2855

Parking Authority
1732 5th Avenue North, Birmingham, AL 35203
Fax: (205) 321-7050 Internet: www.bhamparking.com/

Director **Lynn Thomas** .... (205) 321-7040
Executive Assistant **Wanda Knight** .... (205) 321-7038
E-mail: wanda@bhamparking.com

Birmingham City Schools
2015 Park Place, Birmingham, AL 35203
Fax: (205) 231-4761

Superintendent of Schools **Kelley Castlin-Gacutan** ...... (205) 231-4600
Education: Tennessee State BS; Brenau U MEd;
Nova Southeastern DEd
★ President **Wardine T. Alexander** (District 7) .... (205) 231-4600
Term Expires: November 1, 2017
E-mail: alxnchrg@aol.com
★ Vice President **Lyord Watson** (District 2) .... (205) 231-4600
Term Expires: November 1, 2017
★ Member **Sherman Collins, Jr.** (District 1) .... (205) 231-4600
Term Expires: November 1, 2017
★ Member **Brian Giattina** (District 3) .... (205) 231-4600
Term Expires: November 1, 2017
E-mail: bgiattina@bhm.k12.al.us
★ Member **Daagye Hendricks** (District 4) .... (205) 231-4600
Term Expires: November 1, 2017
★ Member **Randall Woodfin** (District 5) .... (205) 231-4600
Term Expires: November 1, 2017
★ Member **Cheri Gardner** (District 6) .... (205) 231-4600
Term Expires: November 1, 2017
★ Member **April M. Williams** (District 8) .... (205) 231-4600
Term Expires: November 1, 2017
E-mail: AprilMyersWilliams@email.com
★ Member **Sandra Brown** (District 9) .... (205) 231-4600
Term Expires: November 1, 2017

★ Elected Official ▲ Appointed by Legislature ▼ Appointed by Governor ► Appointed by Board or Commission ● Appointed by Judge
■ Appointed by Mayor △ Appointed by Freeholders ▽ Appointed by Supervisor ▷ Appointed by County Executive ○ Appointed by Council

City of Bismarck, North Dakota

221 N. Fifth St., Bismarck, ND 58501
P.O. Box 5503, Bismarck, ND 58506-5503
Internet: http://www.bismarcknd.gov/

County: Burleigh **Election Type:** Nonpartisan **Year Incorporated:** 1873
Charter: 1986 **Population:** 71,167 (2015)

Office of the Mayor and City Commission

221 N. Fifth St., Bismarck, ND 58501
Fax: (701) 222-6470

★Mayor and Commission President **Michael Seminary** .... (701) 355-1300
Began Service: July 1, 2014
Term Expires: June 22, 2018
E-mail: mseminary@nd.gov

★Commissioner **Josh Askvig** .... (701) 355-1300
Term Expires: June 22, 2018
E-mail: jaskvig@bismarcknd.gov

★Commissioner **Parrell D. Grossman** .... (701) 355-1300
Term Expires: June 24, 2016
Education: Minot State 1978 BS; North Dakota 1989 JD

★Commissioner **Nancy Guy** .... (701) 355-1300
Term Expires: June 22, 2018
E-mail: nguy@bismarcknd.gov

★Commissioner **Steve Marquardt** .... (701) 355-1300
Term Expires: June 24, 2016
E-mail: smarquardt@bismarcknd.gov

Office of the City Attorney

Fax: (701) 221-3572

►City Attorney **Charlie Whitman** .... (701) 355-1340
E-mail: cwhitman@bismarcknd.gov

Library

515 N. Fifth St., Bismarck, ND 58501

Director **Christine Kujawa** .... (701) 355-1480
E-mail: ckujawa@cldn.info

Administration and Management Department

221 N. Fifth St., Bismarck, ND 58501
P.O. Box 5503, Bismarck, ND 58506-5503
Fax: (701) 222-6470

►City Administrator **Keith J. Hunke** .... (701) 355-1300
E-mail: khunke@bismarcknd.gov
Assistant City Administrator **(Vacant)** .... (701) 355-1300

Airport

P.O. Box 991, Bismarck, ND 58502
Fax: (701) 221-6886

Manager **Greg Haug** .... (701) 355-1800

Bismarck Event Center

601 East Sweet Avenue, Bismarck, ND 58501
Fax: (701) 222-6599 Internet: http://bismarckeventcenter.com/

Manager **Charlie Jeske** .... (701) 355-1370
Career: Executive Director, Alerus Center

City/County Communications Center

P.O. Box 5503, Bismarck, ND 58506-5503
Fax: (701) 221-6804

Communications Director **Mike Dannenfelzer** .... (701) 222-6727
E-mail: mdannenfelzer@bismarcknd.gov

Community Development Department

221 North Fifth Street, Bismarck, ND 58501
Fax: (701) 222-6450

City Planner **Carl Hokenstad** .... (701) 355-1840

Building Inspections

P.O. Box 5503, Bismarck, ND 58502-5503
Tel: (701) 355-1465 Fax: (701) 258-2073
Internet: http://www.bismarcknd.gov/index.aspx?nid=111

Director **Brady Blaskowski** .... (701) 355-1465

Bismarck-Burleigh Public Health [BBPH]

P.O. Box 5503, Bismarck, ND 58506-5503
Tel: (701) 355-1540 Fax: (701) 221-6883

Director **Renae Moch** .... (701) 355-1540

Engineering Department

221 North Fifth Street, Bismarck, ND 58501
Fax: (701) 222-6593

City Engineer **Mel Bullinger** .... (701) 355-1505
E-mail: mbullinger@bismarcknd.gov

Finance Department

221 North 5th Street, Bismarck, ND 58501
Fax: (701) 222-6606

Director of Finance **Sheila Hillman** .... (701) 355-1600

Fire Department

1020 East Central Avenue, Bismarck, ND 58501
Fax: (701) 222-6524

Fire Chief **Joel Boespflug** .... (701) 355-1400
E-mail: jboespflug@bismarcknd.gov

Human Resources Department

P.O. Box 5503, Bismarck, ND 58506
Fax: (701) 222-6470

Director **Robert McConnell** .... (701) 355-1330

Police Department

700 South Ninth Street, Bismarck, ND 58504
Fax: (701) 221-7284

Chief of Police **Dan Donlin** .... (701) 223-1212

Public Works

601 South 26th Street, Bismarck, ND 58504
Fax: (701) 221-6840

Service Operations Director **Jeff Heintz** .... (701) 355-1700
E-mail: jheintz@bismarcknd.gov
Utilities Operations Director **Michelle Klose** .... (701) 355-1700
E-mail: mklose@bismarcknd.gov

★Elected Official ▲Appointed by Legislature ▼Appointed by Governor ►Appointed by Board or Commission ●Appointed by Judge
■Appointed by Mayor △Appointed by Freeholders ▽Appointed by Supervisor ▷Appointed by County Executive ○Appointed by Council

City of Boise, Idaho

City Hall, 150 N. Capitol Blvd., Boise, ID 83702
P.O. Box 500, Boise, ID 83701-0500
Tel: (208) 384-4422 Internet: www.cityofboise.org

County: Ada **Election Type:** Nonpartisan **Population:** 218,281 (2015)

David H. Bieter
Mayor

Term Expires: January 1, 2020
Education: Col St Thomas BA; Idaho JD
Career: State Representative, House of Representatives, Idaho Legislature

Office of the Mayor and City Council

City Hall, 150 N. Capitol Blvd., Boise, ID 83702
Fax: (208) 384-4420 E-mail: citycouncil@cityofboise.org

★Mayor **David H. Bieter** .... (208) 384-4422
E-mail: mayor@cityofboise.org
Administrative Assistant to the Mayor **Tracy Hall** .... (208) 384-4422
E-mail: thall@cityofboise.org
★Mayor Pro Tem **Lauren McClean** .... (208) 384-4410
Term Expires: January 5, 2018
★Council President **Elaine Clegg** .... (208) 384-4410
Term Expires: January 1, 2020
★Council Member **Maryanne Jordan** .... (208) 384-4410
Term Expires: January 5, 2018
★Council Member **Scott Ludwig** .... (208) 384-4410
Term Expires: January 1, 2020
★Council Member **Ben Quintana** .... (208) 384-4410
Term Expires: January 1, 2018
★Council Member **T.J. Thomson** .... (208) 384-4410
Term Expires: January 5, 2018
Administrative Assistant to the Council
Amanda Brown .... (208) 384-4410

Accounting Office

City Hall, 150 N. Capitol Blvd., Boise, ID 83702

Controller **Jim McMahon** .... (208) 384-3798
E-mail: jmcmahon@cityofboise.org

Budget Office

City Hall, 150 N. Capitol Blvd., Boise, ID 83702
Fax: (208) 384-3995

Budget Manager **Brent Davis** .... (208) 395-7820
E-mail: bdavis@cityofboise.org

Human Resources Department

601 W. Idaho St., Boise, ID 83702
Fax: (208) 384-3868 E-mail: hr@cityofboise.org

■Director **Shawn Miller** .... (208) 972-8090
E-mail: HR@cityofboise.org
Risk Management Officer **Corey Pence** .... (208) 384-3788
E-mail: cpence@cityofboise.org Fax: (208) 388-4743

Office of Internal Audit

City Hall, 150 N. Capitol Blvd., Boise, ID 83702

Director **Steven Rehn** .... (208) 384-4410

Technology Department

City Hall, 150 N. Capitol Blvd., Boise, ID 83702
Tel: (208) 384-3755 Fax: (208) 433-5661

Chief Information Officer **Garry Beaty** .... (208) 384-3755
E-mail: gbeaty@cityofboise.org

Technology Department *continued*

Webmaster **Janson Lytle** .... (208) 384-3791
E-mail: jlytle@cityofboise.org

Treasury Office

City Hall, 150 N. Capitol Blvd., Boise, ID 83702

■Treasurer **Richard Downen** .... (208) 384-3783
E-mail: rdownen@cityofboise.org Fax: (208) 388-4743

City Attorney's Office

City Hall, 150 N. Capitol Blvd., Boise, ID 83702
Fax: (208) 384-4454

■City Attorney **Robert Luce** .... (208) 384-3870
E-mail: rluce@cityofboise.org

Aviation and Public Transportation

3201 Airport Way, Boise, ID 83705
Fax: (208) 343-9667

■Director/Airport Manager **Rebecca Hupp** .... (208) 383-3110
E-mail: RHupp@cityofboise.org

Finance and Administration Department

City Hall, 150 North Capitol Boulevard, Boise, ID 83702
Internet: http://dfa.cityofboise.org/contact-us/

■Director **Lynda Lowry** .... (208) 384-3722
E-mail: llowry@cityofboise.org

City Print and Mail Services

City Hall, 150 N. Capitol Blvd., Boise, ID 83702

Supervisor **Sylvia Marmon** .... (208) 384-3748
E-mail: smarmon@cityofboise.org

Office of the City Clerk

City Hall, 150 N. Capitol Blvd., Boise, ID 83702
Fax: (208) 384-3711

■Administrative Services Manager **Craig Croner** .... (208) 384-3710
E-mail: cityclerk@cityofboise.org
■Deputy City Clerk **Jamie Heinzerling** .... (208) 384-3710
E-mail: city_clerk@cityofboise.org

Parking Services

City Hall, 150 N. Capitol Blvd., Boise, ID 83702

Supervisor **Craig Croner** .... (208) 384-3770

Purchasing

City Hall, 150 N. Capitol Blvd., Boise, ID 83702
Fax: (208) 384-3995 E-mail: boisepurchasing@cityofboise.org

■Senior Purchasing Specialist **Colin Millar** .... (208) 384-3775
E-mail: cmillar@cityofboise.org

Fire Department

333 North Sailfish Place, Boise, ID 83704
Fax: (208) 570-6586

■Fire Chief **Dennis L. Doan** .... (208) 570-6500
E-mail: ddoan@cityofboise.org

Parks and Recreation Department

1104 Royal Blvd., Boise, ID 83706
Fax: (208) 384-4127

■Director **Doug Holloway** .... (208) 608-7600
E-mail: bpr@cityofboise.org

Zoo Boise

355 Julia Davis Drive, Boise, ID 83702
Tel: (208) 364-4260 Internet: www.zooboise.org

Director **Steve Burns** .... (208) 384-4125 ext. 203

★Elected Official ▲Appointed by Legislature ▼Appointed by Governor ▶Appointed by Board or Commission ●Appointed by Judge
■Appointed by Mayor △Appointed by Freeholders ▽Appointed by Supervisor ▷Appointed by County Executive ○Appointed by Council

Planning and Development Services
City Hall, 150 N. Capitol Blvd., Boise, ID 83702
Fax: (208) 384-3753

■ Director **Derick O'Neill** .... (208) 384-3853
E-mail: doneill@cityofboise.org

Economic Development Division
City Hall, 150 N. Capitol Blvd., Boise, ID 83702
Fax: (208) 384-4420

Manager **Nicolas Miller** .... (208) 384-4421

Housing and Community Development Division
150 North Capitol Boulevard, Boise, ID 83702
Tel: (208) 570-6830 Fax: (208) 384-4195

Manager **AnaMarie Guiles** .... (208) 570-6839

Zoning Code Enforcement Division
City Hall, 150 N. Capitol Blvd., Boise, ID 83702
Fax: (208) 384-3753

Senior Department Specialist **Pam Harmon** .... (208) 384-3845

Police Department
333 North Sailfish Place, Boise, ID 83704
Fax: (208) 570-6199

■ Police Chief **William L. "Bill" Bones** .... (208) 570-6190
E-mail: wbones@cityofboise.org

Boise Public Library
P.O. Box 500, Boise, ID 83701
Fax: (208) 384-4025

■ Library Director **Kevin Booe** .... (208) 384-4238
E-mail: askalibrarian@cityofboise.org

Public Works Department
City Hall, 150 N. Capitol Blvd., Boise, ID 83702
Fax: (208) 433-5650

■ Director **Neal Oldemeyer** .... (208) 384-3900

Engineering Division
City Hall, 150 N. Capitol Blvd., Boise, ID 38702
Fax: (208) 384-3905

City Engineer **John Tensen** .... (208) 384-3900
E-mail: jtensen@cityofboise.org

Environmental Division
City Hall, 150 N. Capitol Blvd., Boise, ID 83702
Fax: (208) 433-5650

Environmental Manager **Steve Burgos** .... (208) 384-3901
Water Quality Manager **Robbin Finch** .... (208) 384-3901
520 West Idaho Street, Boise, ID 83702
Solid Waste Program Manager **Catherine Chertudi** .... (208) 384-3901
Groundwater Program Coordinator **Elizabeth Cody** .... (208) 384-3982
Hazardous Materials Program Coordinator
Angela Deckers .... (208) 384-3983
Pretreatment Program Coordinator **Walt Baumgartner** .... (208) 384-3991
520 West Idaho Street, Boise, ID 83702
Stormwater Program Coordinator **Amy Hughes** .... (208) 388-4703

Government Buildings Division
City Hall, 150 N. Capitol Blvd., Boise, ID 83702

Building Facilities Manager **Scott Canning** .... (208) 384-4255
E-mail: scanning@cityofboise.org Fax: (208) 384-4492

City of Boston, Massachusetts
Boston City Hall, One City Hall Square, Boston, MA 02201-2006
Tel: (617) 635-4000 (Information) Internet: www.cityofboston.gov

County: Suffolk **Election Type:** Partisan **Year Founded:** 1630
Year Incorporated: 1822 **Population:** 667,137 (2015)

Form of Municipal Government: City and county governments are combined.

Martin J. "Marty" Walsh (D)
Mayor
Began Service: January 6, 2014
Term Expires: December 31, 2017

Office of the Mayor
Boston City Hall, One City Hall Plaza, Boston, MA 02201
Tel: (617) 635-4500 Fax: (617) 635-4090
Internet: www.cityofboston.gov/mayor
Internet: http://www.cityofboston.gov/mayor/

★ Mayor **Martin J. "Marty" Walsh** (D) .... (617) 635-4500
Chief of Staff **Daniel Arrigg Koh** .... (617) 635-4500
Assistant to the Chief of Staff **Olivia Nelson** .... (617) 635-4500
Chief Communications Officer **Laura Oggeri** .... (617) 635-4461
Press Secretary **Bonnie McGilpin** .... (617) 635-4461
Education: Northeastern
Press Assistant **Gabrielle Farrell** .... (617) 635-4461
Chief of Civic Engagement **Jerome Smith** .... (617) 635-4500
E-mail: jerome.smith@boston.gov
Education: Connecticut 1999 BA
Chief of Operations **Patrick Brophy** .... (617) 635-4500
Chief of Policy **Joyce Linehan** .... (617) 635-4500
Education: UMass (Boston) BA, MA
Chief of Streets **Chris Osgood** .... (617) 635-4500

Law Department
Fax: (617) 635-3199 Internet: www.cityofboston.gov/law

■ Corporation Counsel
Eugene L. "Gene" O'Flaherty (D) Room 615 .... (617) 635-4017
E-mail: gene.oflaherty@mahouse.gov
Education: Suffolk BS; UMass (Amherst) JD
First Assistant Corporation Counsel **Henry Luthin**
Room 615 .... (617) 635-4024

Mayor's Office of Arts and Culture
One City Hall Plaza, Boston, MA 02201

■ Chief of Arts and Culture **Julie Burros** .... (617) 635-3911
E-mail: julie.burros@boston.gov

Mayor's Office of Diversity
City Hall, One City Hall Plaza, Boston, MA 02201

■ Chief Diversity Officer **Danielson Tavares** .... (617) 635-4500

Mayor's Office of Economic Development
Boston City Hall, One City Hall Square, Boston, MA 02201-2006

■ Chief of Economic Development **John Barros** .... (617) 635-4500
■ Director of Growth Strategies **Shaun Blugh** .... (617) 635-4500
■ Director of Business Strategy **Lauren Jones** .... (617) 635-4500
Education: Providence 2005 BA

★ Elected Official ▲ Appointed by Legislature ▼ Appointed by Governor ► Appointed by Board or Commission ● Appointed by Judge
■ Appointed by Mayor △ Appointed by Freeholders ▽ Appointed by Supervisor ▷ Appointed by County Executive ○ Appointed by Council

CITIES AND TOWNS

Mayor's Office of Emergency Management
One City Hall Square, Room 204, Boston, MA 02201-2015
Fax: (617) 635-2974 Internet: www.cityofboston.gov/oem

■ Director **Rene Fielding** .... (617) 635-1400
E-mail: oem@boston.gov

Mayor's Office of Jobs and Community Services
43 Hawkins Steet, Boston, MA 02114
Tel: (617) 918-5252

Director (Interim) **Trinh T. Nguyen** .... (617) 918-5252
E-mail: trinh.nguyen@cityofboston.gov

Mayor's Office of New Bostonians
One City Hall Square, Room 803, Boston, MA 02201-2030
Tel: (617) 635-2980 Fax: (617) 635-4540
E-mail: NewBostonians@boston.gov

Director (Interim) **Alejandra St. Guillen** .... (617) 635-2980
Education: Wesleyan U BA; CCNY MEd

Office of Administration and Finance
Boston City Hall, One City Hall Plaza, Room 608, Boston, MA 02201
E-mail: A&F@boston.gov
Internet: www.cityofboston.gov/administrationfinance

■ Collector, Treasurer, Chief Financial Officer
David Sweeney .... (617) 635-2840
E-mail: a&f@boston.gov Fax: (617) 635-3334
Education: Providence 2005 BA

Chief of Staff **Gail Hackett** .... (617) 635-2840

Office of Budget Management
Boston City Hall, One City Hall Square, Room 813,
Boston, MA 02201-2037
Tel: (617) 635-3870 Fax: (617) 635-3152 E-mail: budget@boston.gov
Internet: www.cityofboston.gov/budget

■ Budget Director **Katie Hammer** .... (617) 635-3870
One City Hall Plaza, Fax: (617) 635-3152
Room 813, Boston, MA 02201
E-mail: budget@boston.gov
Education: Washington U (MO) BA; Princeton MPA

Office of Human Resources
Boston City Hall, One City Hall Square, Room 612,
Boston, MA 02201-2006
Tel: (617) 635-3370 Fax: (617) 635-2950 E-mail: ohr@boston.gov
Internet: www.cityofboston.gov/ohr/

Director of Human Resources **Vivian Leonard** .... (617) 635-4698
One City Hall Plaza, Room 612, Boston, MA 02201
E-mail: ohr@boston.gov

Retirement Board Executive Officer **Timothy Smyth** .... (617) 635-4305
General Counsel, Retirement Board **Susan D'Amato** ... (617) 635-2415
General Counsel, Retirement Board **Padraic Lydon** .... (617) 635-2415

Director of Health Benefits and Insurance **Tina Wells** .... (617) 635-4570
One City Hall Plaza, Room 807, Boston, MA 02201

Office of Labor Relations
Boston City Hall, One City Hall Square, Room 624,
Boston, MA 02201-2020
Fax: (617) 635-3690 E-mail: laborrelations@boston.gov
Internet: www.cityofboston.gov/labor/

Director **Alexis Tkachuk** .... (617) 635-4525

Assessing Department
Boston City Hall, One City Hall Square, Room 301,
Boston, MA 02201-2006
Internet: www.cityofboston.gov/assessing/

Assessing Commissioner **Ronald W. Rakow** .... (617) 635-4264
One City Hall Plaza, Fax: (617) 635-3101
Room 301, Boston, MA 02201
E-mail: ronald.rakow@cityofboston.gov

Auditing Department
Boston City Hall, One City Hall Square, Room M-4,
Boston, MA 02201-2001
Tel: (617) 635-4671 Fax: (617) 635-4339
E-mail: cityauditor@boston.gov Internet: www.cityofboston.gov/auditing

City Auditor **Sally D. Glora** .... (617) 635-4671
One City Hall Plaza, Fax: (617) 635-4339
Room M-4, Boston, MA 02201

Purchasing Department
Boston City Hall, One City Hall Square, Boston, MA 02201-2006
Internet: www.cityofboston.gov/purchasing/

Purchasing Agent (Interim) **Kevin Coyne** .... (617) 635-4564
One City Hall Plaza, Fax: (617) 635-2777
Room 808, Boston, MA 02201
E-mail: purchasing@cityofboston.gov

Treasury Department
Boston City Hall, One City Hall Square, Room M-33,
Boston, MA 02201-2004
Tel: (617) 635-4131 E-mail: treasury@boston.gov
Internet: www.cityofboston.gov/treasury

Treasury Division 1st Assistant Collector-Treasurer
Vivian M. Leo .... (617) 635-4140
One City Hall Plaza, Fax: (617) 635-4142
Room M-5, Boston, MA 02201
E-mail: treasury@boston.gov

Treasury Division 2nd Assistant Collector-Treasurer
Richard DePiano .... (617) 635-4140
One City Hall Plaza, Fax: (617) 635-4142
Room M-5, Boston, MA 02201
E-mail: treasury@boston.gov

Collecting Division 2nd Assistant Collector-Treasurer
Celia Barton .... (617) 635-4494
One City Hall Plaza, Fax: (617) 635-4702
Room M-5, Boston, MA 02201
E-mail: treasury@boston.gov

Boston Public Library [BPL]
700 Boylston Street, Boston, MA 02116
Tel: (617) 536-5400 Fax: (617) 236-4306 E-mail: info@bpl.org
Internet: www.bpl.org

Administration
President (Interim) **David Leonard** .... (617) 859-2034
Note: Until Summer 2016
E-mail: dleonard@bpl.org

President **Jill Bourne**
Note: Effective Summer 2016, pending contract negotiations.
Education: NYU BA; U Washington MSLIS

Chief of Communications **Melina Schuler** .... (617) 859-2273
E-mail: mschuler@bpl.org

Chief Financial Officer **Ellen Donaghey** .... (617) 859-2345

Director, Administration and Technology [Interim Director, Administration and Finance] **David Leonard** .. (617) 859-2034
E-mail: dleonard@bpl.org

Registry of Vital Records
One City Hall Plaza, Room 213, Boston, MA 02201
Internet: www.cityofboston.gov/registry/ Fax: (617) 635-3775

City Register **Patricia A. McMahon** .... (617) 635-4175

Office of Human Services
Boston City Hall, One City Hall Plaza, 5th Floor, Boston, MA 02201
Tel: (617) 635-1845 Fax: (617) 635-4540
Internet: www.cityofboston.gov/humanservices/
E-mail: HumanServices@boston.gov

■ Chief of Health and Human Services
Felix G. Arroyo (D) .... (617) 635-1845
E-mail: felix.arroyo@boston.gov

★ Elected Official ▲ Appointed by Legislature ▼ Appointed by Governor ▶ Appointed by Board or Commission ● Appointed by Judge
■ Appointed by Mayor △ Appointed by Freeholders ▽ Appointed by Supervisor ▷ Appointed by County Executive ○ Appointed by Council

Office of Fair Housing and Equity [FHE]
Boston City Hall, Room 966, Boston, MA 02201
Tel: (617) 635-2500 Fax: (617) 635-3290
Internet: http://www.cityofboston.gov/fairhousing/
E-mail: fairhousing@boston.gov

■ Executive Director **Janine Anzalota** . . . . (617) 635-2500
E-mail: janine.anzalota@boston.gov

Veterans' Services Department
43 Hawkins Steet, 3rd Floor, Boston, MA 02114
Tel: (617) 635-3026 Fax: (617) 635-3957 E-mail: veterans@boston.gov
Internet: www.cityofboston.gov/veterans

■ Commissioner **Giselle Sterling** . . . . (617) 635-3037
E-mail: giselle.sterling@boston.gov
Education: UMass (Lowell) BA
Chief of Staff **(Vacant)** . . . . (617) 635-3713
Senior Administrative Analyst, Human Resources/
Administration **Bella Giambeuso** . . . . (617) 635-3030
E-mail: bella.giambeuso@boston.gov
Executive Secretary **Stephanie Siragusa** . . . . (617) 635-4726
E-mail: stephanie.siragusa@boston.gov

Office of Women's Advancement
Boston City Hall, One City Hall Square, Room 806,
Boston, MA 02201-2006
E-mail: bostonwomen@boston.gov

■ Executive Director **Megan Costello** . . . . (617) 635-3138
E-mail: bostonwomen@boston.gov

Commission on Affairs of the Elderly
One City Hall Square, Room 271, Boston, MA 02201-2006
Fax: (617) 635-3213 E-mail: elderly@boston.gov
Internet: www.cityofboston.gov/elderly/

Commissioner **Emily Shea** . . . . (617) 635-4366
Education: Boston U MPH

Emergency Shelter Commission
860 Harrison Avenue, Boston, MA 02118
Fax: (617) 534-2719 E-mail: eshelter@boston.gov

Director **Jim Greene** . . . . (617) 534-2710
Room 716, Boston, MA 02201

Boston Centers for Youth and Families
1483 Tremont Street, Boston, MA 02120
Fax: (617) 635-4524 Internet: www.cityofboston.gov/bcyf

■ Executive Director **William Morales** . . . . (617) 635-4920
E-mail: bcyf@boston.gov
Deputy Commissioner of Programming
Christopher Byner . . . . (617) 635-4920
Deputy Commissioner of Operations and Finance
Michael Sulprizio . . . . (617) 635-4920

Boston Public Schools
Bruce C. Bolling Building, 2300 Washington Street, 5th Floor,
Roxbury, MA 02119
Tel: (617) 635-9000 Internet: www.bostonpublicschools.org

Superintendent **Tommy Chang** . . . . (617) 635-9050
Fax: (617) 635-9059
■ School Committee Chairperson **Michael D. O'Neill** . . . . . . (617) 635-9014
Term Expires: January 2, 2017 Fax: (617) 635-9689
E-mail: moneill2@bostonpublicschools.org
Education: Boston Col BS; Babson MBA
■ School Committee Vice Chairman
Dr. Hardin L. K. Coleman . . . . (617) 635-9014
Term Expires: January 1, 2018 Fax: (617) 635-9689
E-mail: hcoleman2@bostonpublicschools.org
Education: Williams 1975 BA; Vermont 1980 MEd; Stanford 1992 PhD
■ School Committee Member **Michael Loconto** . . . . (617) 635-9014
Term Expires: January 1, 2018 Fax: (617) 635-9689
E-mail: mloconto@bostonpublicschools.org

Boston Public Schools *continued*

■ School Committee Member **Alexandra Oliver-Davila** . . . . (617) 635-9014
Term Expires: January 2020
■ School Committee Member **Jeri Robinson** . . . . (617) 635-9014
Term Expires: January 5, 2019
Education: Wheelock BS, MSEd
■ School Committee Member **Regina Robinson** . . . . (617) 635-9014
Term Expires: January 2019 Fax: (617) 635-9689
■ School Committee Member **Miren Uriarte** . . . . (617) 635-9014
Term Expires: January 4, 2020 Fax: (617) 635-9689
Executive Secretary to School Committee
Elizabeth Sullivan . . . . (617) 635-9014
E-mail: esullivan3@bostonpublicschools.org Fax: (617) 635-9689
Director of Communications **Richard Weir** . . . . (617) 635-9265
Fax: (617) 635-9568

Boston Redevelopment Authority [BRA]
Boston City Hall, One City Hall Square, 9th Floor,
Boston, MA 02201-2015
Fax: (617) 248-1937

Director **Brian Paul Golden** (D) . . . . (617) 918-4326
E-mail: brian.golden@boston.gov
Chief of Staff **Heather Campisano** . . . . (617) 918-4404
Director of Planning **Sara Myerson** . . . . (617) 918-4471
Director of Research **Alvaro Lima** . . . . (617) 918-4428
E-mail: alvaro.lima@boston.gov
Director of Administration and Finance **Chris Giuliani** . . . (617) 918-4313
E-mail: chris.giuliani1@boston.gov
Director of Real Estate **Edward O'Donnell** . . . . (617) 635-4300
General Counsel **Renee LeFevre** . . . . (617) 918-4277
Senior Advisor for Regulatory Reforms
Bryan Glascock . . . . (617) 918-4404
Director of Communications **Nick Martin** . . . . (617) 918-4404
E-mail: nick.martin@boston.gov
Startup Manager **Rory Cuddyer** . . . . (617) 722-4300

Board of Directors
Chairman **Timothy Burke** . . . . (617) 918-4336
Vice Chair **Priscilla Rojas** . . . . (617) 918-4336
Board Member **Carol Downs** . . . . (617) 918-4336
Board Member **Theodore C. Landsmark** . . . . (617) 918-4336
Board Member **Michael P. Monahan** . . . . (617) 918-4336

Boston Residents Jobs Policy Office
43 Hawkins Street, 1st Floor, Boston, MA 02114
Tel: (617) 918-5460 Fax: (617) 918-5474 E-mail: brjp@boston.gov
Internet: www.cityofboston.gov/brjp

Director **Keith Williams** . . . . (617) 635-4084

Small and Local Business Enterprise Office
One City Hall Plaza, Room 717, Boston, MA 02201
Fax: (617) 635-3235 Internet: www.cityofboston.gov/slbe
E-mail: SLBE@boston.gov

Director **Keith Williams** . . . . (617) 635-4084
E-mail: keith.williams@boston.gov

Environment, Energy and Open Space
Boston City Hall, One City Hall Plaza, Room 603, Boston, MA 02201
Internet: www.cityofboston.gov/environmentalandenergy/

Chief **Austin Blackmon** . . . . (617) 635-3425

Inspectional Services Department
1010 Massachusetts Ave., Boston, MA 02118
Tel: (617) 635-5300 Fax: (617) 635-5660
Internet: www.cityofboston.gov/isd/

Commissioner **William Christopher** . . . . (617) 635-5300
Chief of Staff **Indira Alvarez** . . . . (617) 961-3311
Assistant Commissioner, Environmental Services
Leo Boucher . . . . (617) 961-3327
Assistant Commissioner, Health **John Meaney** . . . . (617) 961-3212

(continued on next page)

★ Elected Official ▲ Appointed by Legislature ▼ Appointed by Governor ▶ Appointed by Board or Commission ● Appointed by Judge
■ Appointed by Mayor △ Appointed by Freeholders ▽ Appointed by Supervisor ▷ Appointed by County Executive ○ Appointed by Council

Inspectional Services Department *continued*

Assistant Commissioner/Inspector of Buildings
Gary Moccia . . . . (617) 961-3272
Director, Plans and Zoning **Susan Rice** . . . . (617) 961-3287
Director, Zoning Board of Appeals **Derric Small** . . . . (617) 635-5300

Weights and Measures
Assistant Commissioner **Elaine Vieira** . . . . (617) 635-5300

Ground Water Trust
229 Berkeley Street, Suite 410, Boston, MA 02116
Tel: (617) 859-8439

Executive Director **(Vacant)** . . . . (617) 859-8439

Environment Department
Boston City Hall, One City Hall Plaza, Room 805,
Boston, MA 02201-2031
Fax: (617) 635-3435 Internet: www.cityofboston.gov/environment

■ Commissioner **Carl Spector** . . . . (617) 635-3850
E-mail: environment@boston.gov

Boston Landmarks Commission [BLC]
Boston City Hall, One City Hall Square, Room 805, Boston, MA 02201
Fax: (617) 635-3435 Internet: www.cityofboston.gov/landmarks

Executive Director **Rosanne Foley** . . . . (617) 635-3850

Fire Department
115 Southampton St., Boston, MA 02118-2713
Fax: (617) 343-2104 E-mail: publicinfo.bfd@boston.gov
Internet: www.cityofboston.gov/fire/

■ Fire Commissioner/Chief **Joseph Finn** . . . . (617) 343-3610
E-mail: joseph.finn@cityofboston.gov Fax: (617) 343-2104
District Chief **Paul Burke** . . . . (617) 343-3610
E-mail: pburke@cityofboston.gov
Chief of Operations **Gerard T. Fontana** . . . . (617) 343-2105
E-mail: gfontana@cityofboston.gov Fax: (617) 343-2198
Chief of Operations (Field Services) **John F. Hasson** . . . . (617) 343-2105
E-mail: jhasson@cityofboston.gov Fax: (617) 343-2198
Deputy Commissioner of Administration and Finance
(Vacant) . . . . (617) 343-3003
Fax: (617) 343-2104
Deputy Commissioner, Labor Relations, Human
Resources and Legal Affairs **Connie Wong** . . . . (617) 343-2251
E-mail: karen.glasgow.bfd@boston.gov Fax: (617) 343-2104
Public Information Officer **Steve MacDonald** . . . . (617) 343-3415
E-mail: steve.macdonald.bfd@boston.gov Fax: (617) 343-3515

Department of Innovation and Technology [DoIT]
Boston City Hall, One City Hall Plaza, Room 703,
Boston, MA 02201-2021
Fax: (617) 263-3035 E-mail: doit@boston.gov
Internet: www.cityofboston.gov/DoIT/

■ Chief Information Officer **Jascha Franklin-Hodge** . . . . . . (617) 635-4783
One City Hall Plaza, Boston, MA 02201
E-mail: jascha.franklin-hodge@cityofboston.gov
■ Chief Digital Officer **Lauren Lockwood** . . . . (617) 635-4783
One City Hall Plaza, Boston, MA 02201
E-mail: llockwood@cityofboston.gov
Education: Vassar BA; Harvard 2014 MBA

Office of Cable Communications
43 Hawkins Steet, Boston, MA 02114
Tel: (617) 635-3112 Fax: (617) 635-4475 E-mail: cable@boston.gov
Internet: www.cityofboston.gov/cable

Director **Michael Lynch** . . . . (617) 635-3112
43 Hawkins St., Boston, MA 02114

Department of Neighborhood Development [DND]
26 Court St., 11th Floor, Boston, MA 02108
Fax: (617) 635-0407 Internet: www.cityofboston.gov/dnd/

■ Director **Sheila A. Dillon** . . . . (617) 635-4352
E-mail: neighborhooddevelopment.dnd@boston.gov
Administration and Finance Deputy Director
Noah Stockman . . . . (617) 635-0251
E-mail: noah.stockman@boston.gov
Neighborhood Housing Deputy Director
Teresa Gallagher . . . . (617) 635-0325
E-mail: teresa.gallagher@boston.gov
Policy, Development and Research Deputy Director
Robert Gehret . . . . (617) 635-0242
E-mail: robert.hehret@boston.gov
Real Estate Management and Sales Deputy Director
Donald Wright . . . . (617) 635-0398
General Counsel **James McDonough** . . . . (617) 635-0205
Director of Public Relations **Lisa Mansdorf Pollack** . . . . . (617) 635-4352
E-mail: lmansdorf@cityofboston.gov
Deputy Director of Public Relations **Kerry O'Brien** . . . . (617) 635-0334
E-mail: kerry.obrien@boston.gov

Office of Business Development [OBD]
26 Court Street, 9th Floor, Boston, MA 02108
Tel: (617) 635-0355 Fax: (617) 635-0282
Internet: www.cityofboston.gov/dnd/obd/

Office of the Business Development Deputy Director
Rafael Carbonell . . . . (617) 635-0615
E-mail: rafael.carbonell@boston.gov

Police Department
One Schroeder Plaza, Boston, MA 02120-2014
Tel: (617) 343-4200 Fax: (617) 343-5003
E-mail: mediarelations.bpd@boston.gov
Internet: www.cityofboston.gov/police/

■ Commissioner **William "Bill" Evans** . . . . (617) 343-4500
E-mail: bill.evans@cityofboston.gov Fax: (617) 343-5003
Chief of Staff/Superintendent **Kevin Buckley** . . . . (617) 343-4500
■ Superintendent in Chief **William Gross** . . . . (617) 343-4500
E-mail: wgross@cityofboston.gov Fax: (617) 343-5003
Administrative Hearings Deputy Superintendent
Colm Lydon . . . . (617) 343-5043
Fax: (617) 343-5894
Bureau of Administration and Technology Chief
Edward Callahan . . . . (617) 343-4577
E-mail: ecallahan@cityofboston.gov Fax: (617) 343-4480
Field Services Bureau Superintendent
Bernard O'Rourke . . . . (617) 343-4500
Investigative Services Bureau Superintendent
Gregory Long . . . . (617) 343-4498
Fax: (617) 343-4727
Bureau of Professional Development **Lisa Holmes** . . . . (617) 343-4256
Fax: (617) 343-5129
Family Justice Center **Capt. Mark Hayes** . . . . (617) 343-4350
Fax: (617) 343-5129
Professional Standards Bureau Superintendent
Frank Mancini . . . . (617) 343-4955
Director of Labor Relations Deputy Superintendent
Steven Whitman . . . . (617) 343-4544
Operation Division Deputy Superintendent **Michael Cox** . . (617) 343-4200
Director of Media Relations **Lt. Michael McCarthy** . . . . . (617) 343-4520
Fax: (617) 343-4481
Special Events Coordinator **Sgt Beth Donovna** . . . . (617) 343-4300
E-mail: bdonovna@cityofboston.gov Fax: (617) 343-5400

Boston Public Health Commission
1010 Massachusetts Avenue, 6th Floor, Boston, MA 02118
Tel: (617) 534-5395 Fax: (617) 534-5358 Internet: www.bphc.org

■ Chair **Dr. Paula A. Johnson** . . . . (617) 534-5855
Education: Harvard 1985 MD, 1985 MPH
■ Board Member **Joseph Betancourt** . . . . (617) 534-5855

Boston Public Health Commission *continued*

■ Board Member **Harold D. Cox** . . . . . . (617) 534-5855
E-mail: david.mulligan@boston.gov
Education: North Texas State BA; Texas MSSW

■ Board Member **Manny Lopes** . . . . . . (617) 534-5855

■ Board Member **Dr. Myechia Minter-Jordan** . . . . . . (617) 534-5855
Education: Brown U MD; W.P. Carey Business MBA

■ Board Member **Kathleen E. "Kate" Walsh** . . . . . . (617) 534-5855
E-mail: elaine.ullian@boston.gov
Education: Yale 1977 BA, 1979 MPH

■ Board Member **Celia Wcislo** . . . . . . (617) 534-5855
E-mail: celia.wcislo@boston.gov
Education: UMass (Boston) BS

Executive Director **Monica Valdes Lupi** . . . . . . (617) 534-5264
Education: Bryn Mawr 1994 AB; Penn State 1997 JD; Boston U 1998 MPH

Medical Director **Huy Nguyen** . . . . . . (617) 534-5264

Child, Adolescent and Family Health Bureau Director **Deborah Allen** . . . . . . (617) 534-5757

Community Health Education Center Director **Margaret Hogerty** . . . . . . (617) 534-2396

Community Initiatives Bureau Deputy Director **Gerry Thomas** . . . . . . (617) 534-2390

Homeless Services Bureau Director **Beth Grand** . . . . . . (617) 534-6110

Deputy Director **Rita Nieves** . . . . . . (617) 534-5264

Infectious Disease Bureau Director **Anita Barry** . . . . . . (617) 534-5611

Media Relations Manager **(Vacant)** . . . . . . (617) 534-5264

Research and Evaluation Director **Dr. Snehal Shah** . . . . . . (617) 534-2397

Boston Emergency Medical Services

785 Albany Street, Boston, MA 02118
Fax: (617) 343-1191 Internet: www.bostonems.org

■ Chief **James W. Hooley** . . . . . . (617) 343-2367
E-mail: hooley@bostonems.org

Emergency Medical Services (EMS) Medical Director **Sophia Dyer** . . . . . . (617) 343-1125
Education: Massachusetts Pharmacy BS; Boston U MD

Property and Construction Management Department

One City Hall Plaza, Room 811, Boston, MA 02201
Fax: (617) 635-3250
Internet: http://www.cityofboston.gov/propertymanagement/

■ Chief of Public Property **John Hanlon** . . . . . . (617) 635-4100

Mayor's Office of Tourism, Sports and Entertainment

Fax: (617) 635-4447 Internet: http://www.cityofboston.gov/arts

■ Director **Kenneth "Ken" Brissette** . . . . . . (617) 635-3911
Note: On administrative leave
One City Hall Plaza, Room 802, Boston, MA 02201
E-mail: kenneth.brissette@boston.gov

Animal Control

1010 Massachusetts Avenue, Boston, MA 02118
Internet: www.cityofboston.gov/animals Fax: (617) 635-5348

Director **(Vacant)** . . . . . . (617) 635-5348

Enforcement Supervision **Patrick Conroy** . . . . . . (617) 635-5348

Consumer Affairs and Licensing Department

One City Hall Plaza, Room 817, Boston, MA 02201
Internet: www.cityofboston.gov/consumeraffairs/

Director **Patricia Malone** . . . . . . (617) 635-3834

Elections Department

One City Hall Plaza, Room 241, Boston, MA 02201
Tel: (617) 635-3767 Fax: (617) 635-4483
Internet: www.cityofboston.gov/elections/

■ Commissioner **Shawn Burke** . . . . . . (617) 635-4637
E-mail: shawn.burke@boston.gov

■ Chairman **Dion Irish** . . . . . . (617) 635-4634
E-mail: election@boston.gov

Elections Department *continued*

■ Commissioner **Kyron Owens** . . . . . . (617) 635-3833
E-mail: kyron.owens@boston.gov

■ Commissioner **Ellen Rooney** . . . . . . (617) 635-4637
E-mail: ellen.rooney@boston.gov
Education: Wisconsin

Personnel Officer **Lynne Onishuk** . . . . . . (617) 635-4643
E-mail: lynne.onishuk@boston.gov

Parks and Recreation Department

1010 Massachusetts Ave., 3rd Floor, Boston, MA 02118
Tel: (617) 635-7275 Fax: (617) 635-3173

Commissioner **Christopher Cooke** . . . . . . (617) 635-4505

Secretary to the Commissioner **Lucy Porro** . . . . . . (617) 635-4505
E-mail: lucy.porro@boston.gov

Deputy Commissioner **(Vacant)** . . . . . . (617) 635-4505

Property Management Department

One City Hall Plaza, Room 811, Boston, MA 02201
Internet: www.cityofboston.gov/propertymanagement/

Deputy Commissioner **Joseph Callahan** . . . . . . (617) 635-4484
E-mail: joseph.callahan@boston.gov

Administration and Finance Division Director **Michael Kearney** . . . . . . (617) 635-4560
E-mail: michael.kearney@boston.gov

Superintendent of Maintenance **Jim Hughes** . . . . . . (617) 635-4133
E-mail: jim.hughes@boston.gov

Public Works Department

One City Hall Square, Room 714, Boston, MA 02201-2006
Fax: (617) 635-7499 E-mail: publicworks@boston.gov
Internet: www.cityofboston.gov/publicworks/

■ Commissioner **Michael Dennehy** . . . . . . (617) 635-4900
One City Hall Plaza, Room 714, Boston, MA 02201
E-mail: publicworks@boston.gov

Deputy Commissioner **Michael Brohel** . . . . . . (617) 635-4900

Director of Central Fleet Maintenance **(Vacant)** . . . . . . (617) 635-7555
400 Frontage Rd., Boston, MA 02118

Code Enforcement Director **Michael Macken** . . . . . . (617) 635-4896
1010 Massachusetts Avenue, Boston, MA 02118

Boston Transportation Department [BTD]

One City Hall Square, Room 721, Boston, MA 02201-2006
Fax: (617) 635-4295 Internet: www.cityofboston.gov/transportation/
E-mail: BTD@boston.gov Tel: (617) 635-4680

■ Commissioner **Gina Fiandaca** . . . . . . (617) 635-3669
One City Hall Plaza, Room 721, Boston, MA 02201
E-mail: gina.fiandaca@boston.gov
Education: Suffolk BSBA; Boston U MBA

Enforcement Division Director **Gregory Rooney** . . . . . . (617) 635-4680
200 Frontage Rd., Boston, MA 02118

Operations Division Director **Stephen Passacantilli** . . . . . . (617) 635-2753
112 Southampton St., Boston, MA 02118

Office of the City Council

Boston City Hall, One City Hall Square, Boston, MA 02201
Tel: (617) 635-3040 Fax: (617) 635-4203
E-mail: city.council@boston.gov
Internet: www.cityofboston.gov/citycouncil

★ Council President **Michelle Wu** (At-Large) . . . . . . (617) 635-3040
Term Expires: December 31, 2017
E-mail: mwu@cityofboston.gov

★ Council Member **Salvatore La Mattina** (D-District 1) . . . (617) 635-3200
Term Expires: December 31, 2017
E-mail: salvatore.lamattina@boston.gov

★ Council Member **Bill Linehan** (D-District 2) . . . . . . (617) 635-3203
Term Expires: December 31, 2017
E-mail: bill.linehan@boston.gov

(continued on next page)

★ Elected Official ▲ Appointed by Legislature ▼ Appointed by Governor ▶ Appointed by Board or Commission ● Appointed by Judge
■ Appointed by Mayor △ Appointed by Freeholders ▽ Appointed by Supervisor ▷ Appointed by County Executive ○ Appointed by Council

Office of the City Council *continued*

★Council Member **Frank Baker** (District 3) .... (617) 635-3455
Term Expires: December 31, 2017 Fax: (617) 635-3734
E-mail: frank.baker@boston.gov

★Council Member **Andrea Joy Campbell** (D-District 4) . . . (617) 635-3040
Term Expires: December 31, 2017

★Council Member **Timothy P. McCarthy** (District 5) ...... (617) 635-4210
Term Expires: December 31, 2017
E-mail: tmccarthy@cityofboston.gov

★Council Member **Matt O'Malley** (D-District 6) .... (617) 635-4220
Term Expires: December 31, 2017
E-mail: momalley@cityofboston.gov

★Council Member **Tito Jackson** (D-District 7) .... (617) 635-3510
Term Expires: December 31, 2017
E-mail: tito.jackson@boston.gov
Education: New Hampshire 1997 BA

★Council Member **Josh Zakim** (District 8) .... (617) 635-4225
Term Expires: December 31, 2017
E-mail: jzakim@cityofboston.gov

★Council Member **Mark S. Ciommo** (D-District 9) .... (617) 635-3113
Term Expires: December 31, 2017
E-mail: mark.ciommo@boston.gov

★Council Member **Michael Flaherty** (At-Large) .... (617) 635-3040
Term Expires: December 31, 2017
E-mail: mflaherty@cityofboston.gov

★Council Member **Annissa E. George** (D-At-Large) ...... (617) 635-3040
Term Expires: December 31, 2017

★Council Member **Ayanna Pressley** (D-At-Large) .... (617) 635-3040
Term Expires: December 31, 2017
E-mail: apressley@cityofboston.gov

Office of the City Clerk

Fax: (617) 635-4658 Fax: (617) 364-8679 (Archives Division)
Internet: www.cityofboston.gov/cityclerk/

City Clerk **Maureen E. Feeney** .... (617) 635-4601
One City Hall Square, Room 601, Boston, MA 02201
E-mail: maureen.e.feeney@boston.gov

Assistant City Clerk **Alex Geourntas** .... (617) 635-4600
One City Hall Square, Room 601, Boston, MA 02201
E-mail: alex.geourntas@boston.gov

■City Registrar **Patricia A. McMahon** .... (617) 635-4175
One City Hall Square, Room 213, Boston, MA 02201
E-mail: patty.mcmahon@boston.gov

Boston Housing Authority [BHA]

52 Chauncy St., 11th Floor, Boston, MA 02111-2375
Tel: (617) 988-4130 TTY: (800) 545-1833 Fax: (617) 988-4133
Internet: www.bostonhousing.org

■Administrator **William "Bill" McGonagle** .... (617) 988-4124
E-mail: bill.mcgonagle@cityofboston.gov

Director of Communications and Public Affairs
Lydia Agro .... (617) 988-4109
E-mail: lydia_agro@bostonhousing.org

Boston Water and Sewer Commission

980 Harrison Avenue, Boston, MA 02119
Internet: www.bwsc.org

Chair **Michael J. Woodall** .... (617) 989-7000
Commissioner **Muhammad Ali-Salaam** .... (617) 989-7000
Commissioner **Cathleen Douglas Stone** .... (617) 989-7000
Executive Director and Chief Financial Officer
Henry Vitale .... (617) 989-7000
Chief Operations Officer **Joseph Crossen** .... (617) 989-7900
Chief Engineer **John P. Sullivan, Jr.** .... (617) 989-7000

City of Boulder, Colorado

1777 Broadway Street, Boulder, CO 80302
P.O. Box 791, Boulder, CO 80306-0791
Tel: (303) 441-3388 (Information) Internet: www.bouldercolorado.gov

County: Boulder **Election Type:** Nonpartisan **Population:** 107,349 (2015)

Office of the Mayor and City Council

1777 Broadway St., Boulder, CO 80302
P.O. Box 791, Boulder, CO 80306-0791
Fax: (303) 441-4478 E-mail: council@bouldercolorado.gov

★Mayor **Suzanne R. "Zan" Jones** .... (303) 441-3002
Began Service: November 15, 2011
Term Expires: November 20, 2019
E-mail: joness@bouldercolorado.gov
Education: Cornell 1986 BS; Michigan MS

★Mayor Pro Tem **Mary Young** .... (303) 441-3002
Term Expires: November 20, 2017
E-mail: youngm@bouldercolorado.gov

★Council Member **Matthew Appelbaum** .... (303) 441-3002
Term Expires: November 20, 2017
E-mail: appelbaumm@bouldercolorado.gov
Education: Wisconsin

★Council Member **Aaron Brockett** .... (303) 441-3002
Term Expires: November 2019

★Council Member **Jan Burton** .... (303) 441-3002
Term Expires: November 2017

★Council Member **Lisa Morzel** .... (303) 441-3002
Term Expires: November 20, 2019
E-mail: morzell@bouldercolorado.gov

★Council Member **Andrew Shoemaker** .... (303) 441-3002
Term Expires: November 20, 2017
E-mail: shoemakera@bouldercolorado.gov

★Council Member **Sam Weaver** .... (303) 441-3002
Term Expires: November 20, 2017
E-mail: weavers@bouldercolorado.gov

★Council Member **Bob Yates** .... (303) 441-3002
Term Expires: November 2019

Office of the City Attorney

1777 Broadway St., Boulder, CO 80302
P.O. Box 791, Boulder, CO 80306-0791

City Attorney **Thomas Carr** .... (303) 441-3020
E-mail: carrt@bouldercolorado.gov

Office of the City Manager

1777 Broadway St., Boulder, CO 80302
P.O. Box 791, Boulder, CO 80306-0791
Fax: (303) 441-4478 Tel: (303) 441-3090

City Manager **Jane S. Brautigam** .... (303) 441-3090
E-mail: brautigamj@bouldercolorado.gov
Education: Allegheny BA; Pennsylvania 1976 JD

Assistant City Manager **Mary Ann Weideman** .... (303) 441-3006

Office of the City Clerk/Support Services

1777 Broadway St., Boulder, CO 80302
P.O. Box 791, Boulder, CO 80306-0791
Fax: (303) 441-4478

City Clerk **Lynnette Beck** .... (720) 441-4222
Director of Support Services **Alisa Lewis** .... (720) 564-2175

Boulder Municipal Airport

3300 Airport Rd., Box K, Boulder, CO 80301
Fax: (303) 440-1490 E-mail: BMA@bouldercolorado.gov

Manager **Tim Head** .... (303) 441-3108

★Elected Official ▲Appointed by Legislature ▼Appointed by Governor ▶Appointed by Board or Commission ●Appointed by Judge
■Appointed by Mayor △Appointed by Freeholders ▽Appointed by Supervisor ▷Appointed by County Executive ○Appointed by Council

Communication Department
1777 Broadway Street, Boulder, CO 80302
Tel: (303) 441-4959

Communication Director **Patrick von Keyserling** .... (303) 441-4959
E-mail: vonkeyserlingp@bouldercolorado.gov
Deputy Director of Communications **Sarah Huntley** ..... (303) 441-3155
E-mail: huntleys@bouldercolorado.gov
Communications Manager **Jim Winchester** .... (303) 441-4247
E-mail: winchesterj@bouldercolorado.gov

Planning, Housing and Sustainability Department
1739 Broadway St., Boulder, CO 80302
P.O. Box 791, Boulder, CO 80306-0791

Executive Director **David Driskell** .... (303) 441-3425
E-mail: driskelld@bouldercolorado.gov
Education: Stanford 1986 AB; MIT 1991 MCR
Deputy Director **Susan Richstone** .... (303) 441-1880
E-mail: richstones@bouldercolorado.gov
Chief Resilience Officer **Gregory Guibert** .... (303) 441-1990
E-mail: guibertg@bouldercolorado.gov

Downtown/University Hill Management Division and Parking Services
1500 Pearl St., Ste. 302, Boulder, CO 80302

Director **Molly Winter** .... (303) 413-7317
E-mail: winterm@cityofboston.gov

Emergency Management
3280 Airport Road, Boulder, CO 80301
Internet: http://www.boulderoem.com/ Fax: (303) 441-3884

Director **Mike Chard** .... (303) 441-3390

Finance Department
1777 Broadway St., Boulder, CO 80302
P.O. Box 791, Boulder, CO 80306-0791
Fax: (303) 447-4381 Internet: www.bouldercolorado.gov/finance

Chief Financial Officer **Robert W. "Bob" Eichem** ...... (303) 441-2040
Budget Officer **Peggy Bunzli** .... (303) 441-1848
E-mail: bunzlip@bouldercolorado.gov

Fire and Rescue Department
1805 33rd St., Boulder, CO 80301

Fire Chief **Michael Calderazzo** .... (303) 441-3350

Human Services Department
1101 Arapahoe Ave., Boulder, CO 80302
P.O. Box 791, Boulder, CO 80306-0791
Fax: (303) 441-4368

Director **Karen Rahn** ....(303) 441-3161
Housing Manager **Jeff Yegian** .... (303) 441-4363
Deputy Director, Senior Services Manager
Betty Kilsdonk ....(303) 441-4365
Planning Manager **Wendy Schwartz** ....(303) 441-1818
Community Relations Manager **Carmen Atilano** .... (303) 441-3141
E-mail: atilanoc@bouldercolorado.gov

Human Resources Department
1101 Arapahoe Avenue, Boulder, CO 80302
P.O. Box 791, Boulder, CO 80306-0791
Fax: (303) 441-3049

Director **Joyce Lira** .... (303) 441-3070

Information Technology
1101 Arapahoe Ave., Boulder, CO 80302
P.O. Box 791, Boulder, CO 80306-0791
Fax: (303) 441-4013

Director **Don Ingle** .... (303) 441-4183
E-mail: ingled@bouldercolorado.gov

Boulder Public Library
1001 Arapahoe Avenue, Boulder, CO 80302
E-mail: feedback@boulder.lib.co.us

Director **David Farnan** .... (303) 441-3104
E-mail: farnand@boulderlibrary.org

Open Space and Mountain Parks Department
66 S. Cherryvale Rd., Boulder, CO 80302

Director **Tracy Winfree** ....(303) 441-3200

Parks and Recreation Department
3198 Broadway St., Boulder, CO 80304
Internet: www.bouldercolorado.gov/parks_recreation

Director **Yvette Bowden** .... (303) 413-7242
Parks and Planning Manager **Jeff Haley** .... (303) 413-7233

Police Department
1805 33rd St., Boulder, CO 80301

Chief of Police **Greg Testa** ....(303) 441-3310

Public Works Department
1739 Broadway St., Boulder, CO 80302
P.O. Box 791, Boulder, CO 80306-0791

Executive Director of Public Works **Maureen Rait** ....(303) 441-3227
Transportation Division Director **(Vacant)** ....(303) 441-4164
Utilities Division Director **Jeff Arthur** ....(303) 441-3209

City of Bridgeport, Connecticut

City Hall, 45 Lyon Terrace, Bridgeport, CT 06604
Internet: www.bridgeportct.gov

County: Fairfield **Election Type:** Partisan **Year Incorporated:** 1836
Population: 147,629 (2015)

Office of the Mayor
Margaret E. Morton Government Center, 999 Broad Street, Bridgeport, CT 06604
Tel: (203) 576-7201 Fax: (203) 576-3913

★ Mayor **Joseph P. "Joe" Ganim** (D) .... (203) 576-7201
Began Service: December 1, 2015
Term Expires: November 30, 2019
E-mail: mayor@bridgeportct.gov
Education: Connecticut 1981 BA; Bridgeport 1985 JD
■ Chief of Staff/Government Affairs **Daniel Roach** .... (203) 576-7201
■ Senior Advisor, Governmental Accountability
Edward Adams .... (203) 576-7201
■ Senior Advisor, Community Outreach and Diversity
Charles L. "Charlie" Stallworth (D) ....(203) 576-7201
■ Advisor **Tom Gaudett** ....(203) 576-7201
■ Communications Director **Av Harris** ....(203) 257-1049
E-mail: av.harris@bridgeportct.gov

★ Elected Official ▲ Appointed by Legislature ▼ Appointed by Governor ▶ Appointed by Board or Commission ● Appointed by Judge
■ Appointed by Mayor △ Appointed by Freeholders ▽ Appointed by Supervisor ▷ Appointed by County Executive ○ Appointed by Council

Office of the Chief Administrative Officer

Margaret E. Morton Government Center, 999 Broad Street,
Bridgeport, CT 06604
Fax: (203) 332-5652

■ Chief Administrative Officer **John Gomes** . . . . (203) 576-3964
E-mail: john.gomes@bridgeportct.gov
Deputy Chief Administrative Officer **Gina Malheiro** . . . . . (203) 337-2341

Office of the City Attorney

Margaret E. Morton Government Center, 999 Broad Street,
Bridgeport, CT 06604
Fax: (203) 576-8252

City Attorney **R. Christopher Meyer** . . . . (203) 576-7647
E-mail: rchristopher.meyer@bridgeportct.gov
Deputy City Attorney **John Bohannon** . . . . (203) 576-7647

Office of the Comptroller

999 Broad Street, First Floor, Bridgeport, CT 06604
Fax: (203) 576-7067

Comptroller **(Vacant)** . . . . (203) 576-7256

Department on Aging

Eisenhower Senior Center, 263 Golden Hill Street, Bridgeport, CT 06604
Fax: (203) 576-7521

Director **Rosemarie Hoyt** . . . . (203) 576-7989

Archives and Records

City Hall, 45 Lyon Terrace, Room 13, Bridgeport, CT 06604
Fax: (203) 576-8193

Director **Patricia Ulatowski** . . . . (203) 576-8192

Civil Service Commission

City Hall, 45 Lyon Terrace, Room 106, Bridgeport, CT 06604
Fax: (203) 576-7102

Personnel Director **David Dunn** . . . . (203) 576-7103
E-mail: david.dunn@bridgeportct.gov

Office of Emergency Management and Homeland Security

581 North Washington Avenue, Bridgeport, CT 06604
Fax: (203) 579-3881 Internet: www.bridgeportct.gov/EmergencyMgmt/

Director **Scott Appleby** . . . . (203) 579-3822
E-mail: scott.appleby@bridgeportct.gov

Finance Department

999 Broad Street, Bridgeport, CT 06604
Fax: (203) 576-7067

■ Finance Director **Kenneth A. "Ken" Flatto** . . . . (203) 576-7251
E-mail: kenneth.flatto@bridgeportct.gov
Education: Cornell MBA

Fire Department

30 Congress St., Bridgeport, CT 06604
Fax: (203) 333-4940

Fire Chief **Brian Rooney** . . . . (203) 337-2070
E-mail: brian.rooney@bridgeportct.gov

Health and Social Services Department

999 Broad Street, Bridgeport, CT 06604
Fax: (203) 576-8311

Director of Health (Acting) **Albertina Baptista** . . . . (203) 576-7680

Human Services Department

999 Broad Street, Bridgeport, CT 06604
Fax: (203) 576-8311

Social Services Director (Acting) **Albertina Baptista** . . . . . (203) 576-7471
752 East Main Street, Bridgeport, CT 06608

Central Grants and Community Development Department

Margaret E. Morton Government Center, 999 Broad Street,
Bridgeport, CT 06604
Fax: (203) 332-5657

Director **Christina B. Smith** . . . . (203) 332-5665
E-mail: christinab.smith@bridgeportct.gov

Human Resources Department

City Hall, 45 Lyon Terrace, Room 106, Bridgeport, CT 06604
Fax: (203) 332-5618 Internet: www.bridgeportct.gov/HR/

Human Resources Manager **Jodie Paul-Arndt** . . . . (203) 576-8474
E-mail: Jodie.Paul-Arndt@bridgeportct.gov
Benefits Manager **Richard Weiner** . . . . (203) 576-7007

Information Technology Services

City Hall, 45 Lyon Terrace, Room 6, Bridgeport, CT 06604
Fax: (203) 576-8330

Director **Adam Heller** . . . . (203) 576-8188
E-mail: adam.heller@bridgeportct.gov

Klein Memorial Auditorium

910 Fairfield Ave., Bridgeport, CT 06605
Internet: www.theklein.org/

Executive Director **Laurence A. Caso** . . . . (800) 424-0160 ext. 5

Parks and Recreation Department

7 Trumbull Rd., Trumbull, CT 06611
Tel: (203) 576-7233 Fax: (203) 576-7235

Director **Charles Carroll** . . . . (203) 576-7233
Recreation Superintendent **Luann Conine** . . . . (203) 576-8080

Office of Persons with Disabilities

752 East Main Street, 2nd Floor, Bridgeport, CT 06608
Fax: (203) 332-5643

Special Projects Manager **Dennis C. Scinto** . . . . (203) 576-7452

Office of Planning and Economic Development [OPED]

Margaret E. Morton Government Center, 999 Broad Street,
Bridgeport, CT 06604
Fax: (203) 332-5611

■ Director **David M. Kooris** (D) . . . . (203) 576-7221
E-mail: david.kooris@bridgeportct.gov

Police Department

300 Congress Street, Bridgeport, CT 06604
Fax: (203) 576-8130

Police Chief **Armando J. "AJ" Perez** . . . . (203) 581-5100

Office of Policy and Management

Margaret E. Morton Government Center, 999 Broad Street,
Bridgeport, CT 06604
Fax: (203) 332-5589

Director **Nestor Nkwo** . . . . (203) 576-7967
E-mail: nestor.nkwo@bridgeportct.gov

★ Elected Official ▲ Appointed by Legislature ▼ Appointed by Governor ► Appointed by Board or Commission ● Appointed by Judge
■ Appointed by Mayor △ Appointed by Freeholders ▽ Appointed by Supervisor ▷ Appointed by County Executive ○ Appointed by Council

Public Facilities Administration
Margaret E. Morton Government Center, 999 Broad Street, Bridgeport, CT 06604
Fax: (203) 576-3957

■ Director **John Ricci** .... (203) 576-7130
E-mail: john.ricci@bridgeportct.gov

Airport, Sikorsky Memorial [KBDR]
1000 Great Meadow Rd., Stratford, CT 06615
Fax: (203) 576-8166 Internet: www.sikorskymemorialairport.com/

Airport Manager (Interim) **Steve Ferguson** .... (203) 576-8163
Superintendent of Operations **Stephen "Steve" Ford** .... (203) 576-8163
E-mail: stephen.ford@bridgeportct.gov

Building Department
City Hall, 45 Lyon Terrace, Room 220, Bridgeport, CT 06604
Fax: (203) 576-7138

Building Official (Acting) **Bruce A. Nelson** .... (203) 576-7225

Purchasing Department
City Hall, 45 Lyon Terrace, Room 324, Bridgeport, CT 06604
Fax: (203) 576-8421

Director (Acting) **Bernd Tardy** .... (203) 576-7161
E-mail: bernd.tardy@bridgeportct.gov

Tax Department
City Hall, 45 Lyon Terrace, Room 105, Bridgeport, CT 06604
Fax: (203) 332-5521

Assessor **Elaine T. Carvalho** .... (203) 576-7241
Tax Collector **Veronica Jones** .... (203) 576-7271
E-mail: veronica.jones@bridgeportct.gov Fax: (203) 332-5628

Treasury Department
City Hall, 45 Lyon Terrace, Room 110, Bridgeport, CT 06604
Fax: (203) 576-7609

Treasurer **Teri Coward** .... (203) 576-7287

Veterans' Affairs
263 Golden Hill Street, Bridgeport, CT 06604
Fax: (203) 332-5643

Director **Milta Feliciano** (D) .... (203) 576-8348

Office of Vital Records
999 Broad Street, Bridgeport, CT 06604
Fax: (203) 332-5633

Assistant Registrar **Patricia Ulatowski** .... (203) 576-8192

Zoning Department
City Hall, 45 Lyon Terrace, Room 210, Bridgeport, CT 06604
Tel: (203) 576-7217 Fax: (203) 576-7213

Zoning Administrator **Dennis Buckley** .... (203) 576-7217
Zoning Enforcement Officer **Neil H. Bonney** .... (203) 576-7217

Bridgeport Public Library
925 Broad St., Bridgeport, CT 06604
Fax: (203) 333-0253 Internet: http://bportlibrary.org/

City Librarian **Scott Hughes** .... (203) 576-7777
E-mail: shughes@bridgeportpubliclibrary.org
History Center Head **Mary Witkowski** .... (203) 576-7417

Office of the Town Clerk
City Hall, 45 Lyon Terrace, Room 122, Bridgeport, CT 06604
Fax: (203) 330-2811

★ Town Clerk **Charles D. "Don" Clemons, Jr.** (D) .... (203) 576-7278
Term Expires: November 30, 2019
E-mail: Charles.ClemonsJr@bridgeportct.gov
Education: Florida A&M

Office of the Registrar of Voters
Margaret E. Morton Government Center, 999 Broad Street, Bridgeport, CT 06604
Fax: (203) 332-5629

★ Democratic Registrar **Santa Ayala** (D) .... (203) 576-7281
Term Expires: January 6, 2017
E-mail: sandi.ayala@bridgeportct.gov
★ Republican Registrar **Linda Grace** (R) .... (203) 576-7281
Term Expires: January 6, 2017
E-mail: linda.grace@bridgeportct.gov

Office of the City Clerk
City Hall, 45 Lyon Terrace, Room 204, Bridgeport, CT 06604
Fax: (203) 332-5608

★ City Clerk **Lydia N. Martinez** (D) .... (203) 576-7081
Term Expires: November 30, 2019

Bridgeport Public Schools
City Hall, 45 Lyon Terrace, Room 203, Bridgeport, CT 06604
Fax: (203) 337-0150 Internet: www.bridgeportedu.com/

Superintendent (Interim) **Frances Rabinowitz** .... (203) 275-1000 ext. 15

Office of the City Council
Margaret E. Morton Government Center, 999 Broad Street, Bridgeport, CT 06604
Fax: (203) 332-3013

★ Council President
Thomas C. McCarthy (D-District 133) .... (203) 332-3006
Term Expires: November 30, 2017
E-mail: tom.mccarthy@bridgeportct.gov
★ Council Member
Kathryn M. Bukovsky (D-District 130) .... (203) 332-3006
Term Expires: November 30, 2017
★ Council Member **Scott Burns** (D-District 130) .... (203) 332-3006
Term Expires: November 30, 2017
★ Council Member **Jack O. Banta** (D-District 131) .... (203) 332-3006
Term Expires: November 30, 2017
E-mail: jack.banta@bridgeportct.gov
★ Council Member **Denese Taylor-Moye** (D-District 131) .. (203) 332-3006
Term Expires: November 30, 2017
E-mail: denese.taylor-moye@bridgeportct.gov
★ Council Member **M. Evette Brantley** (D-District 132) ... (203) 332-3006
Term Expires: November 30, 2017
★ Council Member **John W. Olson** (D-District 132) .... (203) 332-3006
Term Expires: November 30, 2017
★ Council Member **Jeanette Herron** (D-District 133) ...... (203) 332-3006
Term Expires: November 30, 2017
★ Council Member **Michelle Lyons** (D-District 134) .... (203) 332-3006
Term Expires: November 30, 2017
E-mail: michelle.lyons@bridgeportct.gov
★ Council Member
AmyMarie Vizzo-Paniccia (D-District 134) .... (203) 332-3006
Term Expires: November 30, 2017
E-mail: amymarie.vizzo-paniccia@bridgeportct.gov
★ Council Member **Mary McBride-Lee** (D-District 135) .... (203) 332-3006
Term Expires: November 30, 2017
E-mail: mary.mcbride-lee@bridgeportct.gov

(continued on next page)

★ Elected Official ▲ Appointed by Legislature ▼ Appointed by Governor ► Appointed by Board or Commission ● Appointed by Judge
■ Appointed by Mayor △ Appointed by Freeholders ▽ Appointed by Supervisor ▷ Appointed by County Executive ○ Appointed by Council

Office of the City Council *continued*

★Council Member **Richard Salter** (D-District 135) .... (203) 332-3006
Term Expires: November 30, 2017
E-mail: richard.salter@bridgeportct.gov

★Council Member **Jose R. Casco** (D-District 136) .... (203) 332-3006
Term Expires: November 30, 2017
E-mail: Jose.Casco@bridgeportct.gov

★Council Member **Alfredo Castillo** (D-District 136) ...... (203) 332-3006
Term Expires: November 30, 2017
E-mail: Alfredo.Castillo@bridgeportct.gov

★Council Member **Milta Feliciano** (D-District 137) .... (203) 332-3006
Term Expires: November 30, 2017
E-mail: milta.feliciano@bridgeportct.gov

★Council Member **Aidee Nieves** (D-District 137) .... (203) 332-3006
Term Expires: November 30, 2017
E-mail: Aidee.Nieves@bridgeportct.gov

★Council Member **Nessah J. Smith** (D-District 138) ..... (203) 332-3006
Term Expires: November 30, 2017

★Council Member
Anthony Robert Paoletto (D-District 138) .... (203) 332-3006
Term Expires: November 30, 2017

★Council Member **James Holloway** (D-District 139) ..... (203) 332-3006
Term Expires: November 30, 2017
E-mail: james.holloway@bridgeportct.gov

★Council Member **Eneida Martinez** (D-District 139) ...... (203) 332-3006
Term Expires: November 30, 2017
E-mail: Eneida.Martinez@bridgeportct.gov

Town of Brookhaven, New York

One Indpendence Hill, Farmingville, NY 11738
Internet: www.brookhaven.org

County: Suffolk **Election Type:** Nonpartisan **Population:** 489,278 (2015)

Office of the Town Supervisor

One Indpendence Hill, Farmingville, NY 11738
Fax: (631) 451-6677

★Town Supervisor **Edward P. Romaine** .... (631) 451-9100
Began Service: November 26, 2012
Term Expires: December 31, 2017
Education: Adelphi 1968 BA; Long Island 1973 MA

Personnel Director **Catherine R. Diamante** .... (631) 451-6633
Fax: (631) 451-6958

Public Information Division

One Indpendence Hill, Farmingville, NY 11738
Fax: (631) 451-6258

Communications Director **Jack Krieger** .... (631) 451-6260
E-mail: jkrieger@brookhaven.org

Office of the Superintendent of Highways

1140 Old Town Road, Coram, NY 11727
Fax: (631) 732-2584

★Superintendent of Highways
Daniel P. "Dan" Losquadro .... (631) 451-9200
Term Expires: December 31, 2017
E-mail: dlosquadro@brookhaven.org

Receiver of Taxes

One Indpendence Hill, Suite 110, Farmingville, NY 11738
Fax: (631) 451-9009

★Receiver of Taxes **Louis J. Marcoccia** .... (631) 451-9009
Term Expires: December 31, 2017
E-mail: lmarcoccia@brookhaven.org

Economic Development Division

One Indpendence Hill, Farmingville, NY 11738
Fax: (631) 451-6925

Director **Lisa Mulligan** .... (631) 451-6563
E-mail: lmulligan@brookhaven.org

Finance Department

One Indpendence Hill, Farmingville, NY 11738
Fax: (631) 451-6692

Commissioner of Finance **Tamara Wright** .... (631) 451-6680
Deputy Commissioner **Kathryn Scott** .... (631) 451-6680
Principal Accountant **(Vacant)** .... (631) 451-6680

Department of General Services

One Indpendence Hill, Farmingville, NY 11738
Tel: (631) 451-6331

Commissioner/Fleet Manager **Martin W. Haley** .... (631) 451-6331

Housing and Human Services

One Indpendence Hill, Farmingville, NY 11738
Fax: (631) 451-6597

Commissioner **Diana Weir** .... (631) 451-6600
E-mail: dweir@brookhaven.org

Deputy Commissioner **Leah Jefferson** .... (631) 451-6600
E-mail: ljefferson@brookhaven.org

Law Department

One Indpendence Hill, Farmingville, NY 11738
Fax: (631) 698-4489

Town Attorney **Annette Eaderesto** .... (631) 451-6500
E-mail: aeaderesto@brookhaven.org

Chief Deputy Town Attorney **Kevin R. Johnston** .... (631) 451-6500
Deputy Town Attorney **David J. Moran** .... (631) 451-6500

Parks, Recreation, Sports and Cultural Resources

1130 Old Town Road, Coram, NY 11727
Fax: (631) 451-6980

Commissioner **Edward Morris** .... (631) 451-6100
Deputy Commissioner of Parks **Robert Maag** .... (631) 451-6100
Superintendent of Recreation **Kurt F. Leuffen** .... (631) 451-6100

Planning, Environment and Land Management Department

One Indpendence Hill, Farmingville, NY 11738
Fax: (631) 451-6419

Commissioner **Tullio Bertoli** .... (631) 451-6400

Building Division

One Indpendence Hill, Farmingville, NY 11738

Commissioner **Tullio Bertoli** .... (631) 451-6400
Chief Building Inspector **Arthur Gerhauser** .... (631) 451-6400

Public Safety Department

One Indpendence Hill, Farmingville, NY 11738
Fax: (631) 451-6908

Commissioner **Peter O'Leary** .... (631) 451-6291
E-mail: poleary@brookhaven.org

Deputy Commissioner **(Vacant)** .... (631) 451-6291

Division of Fire Prevention

One Indpendence Hill, Farmingville, NY 11738
Tel: (631) 451-6262 Fax: (631) 451-6283

Chief Fire Marshal **Christopher J. Mehrman** .... (631) 451-6274
E-mail: cmehrman@brookhaven.org

★Elected Official ▲Appointed by Legislature ▼Appointed by Governor ▶Appointed by Board or Commission ●Appointed by Judge
■Appointed by Mayor △Appointed by Freeholders ▽Appointed by Supervisor ▷Appointed by County Executive ○Appointed by Council

Waste Management Department
One Indpendence Hill, Farmingville, NY 11738
Fax: (631) 451-6391

Chief Deputy Commissioner **Matthew Minor** .... (631) 451-6222
Deputy Commissioner **(Vacant)** .... (631) 451-6222

Office of the Town Council
One Indpendence Hill, Farmingville, NY 11738
Fax: (631) 451-6447

★Deputy Supervisor **Daniel J. Panico** (District 6) .... (631) 451-6502
Term Expires: December 31, 2017
★Councilwoman **Valerie M. Cartright** (District 1) .... (631) 451-6963
Term Expires: December 31, 2017
★Councilwoman **Jane Bonner** (District 2)...............(631) 451-6964
Term Expires: December 31, 2017
★Councilman **Kevin J. La Valle** (District 3) .... (631) 451-6647
Term Expires: December 31, 2017
★Councilman **Michael Loguercio** (District 4)............(631) 451-6968
Term Expires: December 31, 2019
★Councilman **Neil Foley** (District 5) .... (631) 451-6645
Term Expires: December 31, 2017
E-mail: CouncilmanFoley@brookhaven.org

Office of the Town Clerk
One Indpendence Hill, Farmingville, NY 11738
Fax: (631) 451-9264

★Town Clerk **Donna Lent**............................(631) 451-9101
Term Expires: December 31, 2017
E-mail: dlent@brookhaven.org

City of Brownsville, Texas
P.O. Box 911, Brownsville, TX 78522-0911
1001 East Elizabeth Street, Brownsville, TX 78520
Internet: www.cob.us

County: Cameron **Election Type:** Nonpartisan **Year Incorporated:** 1853
Population: 183,887 (2015)

Office of the Mayor and Commission
P.O. Box 911, Brownsville, TX 78522-0911
Tel: (956) 548-6005

★Mayor **Antonio "Tony" Martinez**....................(956) 548-6007
Began Service: May 2011
Term Expires: May 2019
E-mail: mayormartinez@cob.us
★City Commissioner **Ricardo Longoria, Jr.** (District 1)....(956) 459-5606
Term Expires: May 2019
E-mail: ricardo@cob.us
★City Commissioner **Jessica Tetreau-Kalifa** (District 2)... (956) 459-4444
Term Expires: May 2019
E-mail: jtetreau@cob.us
★City Commissioner **Deborah Portillo** (District 3)........(956) 525-3507
Term Expires: May 2017
E-mail: deborah.portillo@cob.us
★City Commissioner **John Villarreal** (District 4) .... (956) 459-8945
Term Expires: May 2017
E-mail: john.villarreal@cob.us
Education: Texas (Brownsville) 2005 BBA, 2008 MBA
★City Commissioner
César De León (At-Large, Position A)...............(956) 346-6237
Term Expires: May 2019
E-mail: cesar.deleon@cob.us
★City Commissioner
Rose M. Gowen (At-Large, Position B)..............(956) 548-6005
Term Expires: May 2017 Fax: (956) 504-9199
E-mail: rose.gowen@cob.us

Office of the City Manager
1001 East Elizabeth Street, Brownsville, TX 78520
P.O. Box 911, Brownsville, TX 78522-0911
Fax: (956) 546-4021

City Manager **Charlie Cabler**........................(956) 548-6005
E-mail: charlie@cob.us
Deputy City Manager/Chief Financial Officer
Pete Gonzalez..................................(956) 548-6020
E-mail: peteg@cob.us

Office of the City Secretary
P.O. Box 911, Brownsville, TX 78522-0911
1034 East Levee, Brownsville, TX 78522
Fax: (956) 546-2130

City Secretary **Michael L. Lopez**....................(956) 548-6001
E-mail: michael.lopez@cob.us
Assistant City Secretary **Griselda Rosas**...............(956) 548-6001
E-mail: griselda@cob.us

Public Information Services
2600 Central Blvd., Brownsville, TX 78520
Fax: (956) 548-0684 Internet: http://www.brownsville.lib.tx.us

Department Director **Jerry Hedgecock**................(956) 548-1055
E-mail: jerry@cob.us
Director of Library Services **Juan Guerra** ..... (956) 548-1055 ext. 2125
E-mail: juan@cob.us
Southmost Branch Library Manager
Corinna Galvan..........................(956) 548-1055 ext. 2127
4320 Southmost Road, Brownsville, TX 78520 Fax: (956) 544-4336
E-mail: cory@cob.us
Central Branch Library Manager
Brenda Trevino.........................(956) 548-1055 ext. 2121
4320 Southmost Road, Brownsville, TX 78520 Fax: (956) 544-4336
E-mail: brenda.trevino@cob.us

Brownsville Public Utilities Board
1425 Robinhood Drive, Brownsville, TX 78523
P.O. Box 3270, Brownsville, TX 78523-3270
Tel: (956) 983-6100 Fax: (956) 574-6100
Internet: www.brownsville-pub.com

Chairman **Nurith Galonsky**.........................(956) 983-6100
General Manager and Chief Executive Officer
John S. Bruciak..................................(956) 983-6277
Chief Operations Officer **Fernando Saenz**.............(956) 983-6266
Communications and Administrative Services Director
Lucila Cano Hernandez..........................(956) 983-6437
E-mail: lhernandez@brownsville-pub.com
Customer and Information Services Director
Eddy E. Hernandez...............................(956) 983-6130
Environmental Services Director **Albert Gomez, Jr.**.....(956) 983-6251
Director of Electrical Systems
James "Jimmy" McCann..........................(956) 983-6204
Water and Wastewater Planning Operations Director
Marie C. Leal....................................(956) 983-6275

Brownsville/South Padre Island International Airport
700 S. Minnesota Ave., Brownsville, TX 78521
E-mail: info@flybrownsville.com Fax: (956) 542-4374

Director (Interim) **Sesha Vorrey**.....................(956) 542-4373

Emergency Medical Services [EMS]
12th Street and Market Square, Brownsville, TX 78520

Assistant Fire Chief **Sam Ortega**.....................(956) 548-6077
E-mail: sam@cob.us

★Elected Official ▲Appointed by Legislature ▼Appointed by Governor ▶Appointed by Board or Commission ●Appointed by Judge
■Appointed by Mayor △Appointed by Freeholders ▽Appointed by Supervisor ▷Appointed by County Executive ○Appointed by Council

Finance Department
P.O. Box 911, 1001 East Elizabeth Street, Brownsville, TX 78522-0911
Fax: (956) 548-6086 Internet: http://finance.cob.us/
Director **Lupe Granado III** .... (956) 548-6015

Fire Department
12th and Market Square, Brownsville, TX 78520
P.O. Box 911, Brownsville, TX 78522-0911
Fax: (956) 546-8539
Fire Chief (Interim) **Joseph Horn** .... (956) 546-3195
E-mail: jhorn@cob.us

Human Resources
P.O. Box 911, 1001 East Elizabeth Street, Brownsville, TX 78522-0911
Fax: (956) 546-2429
Director **Oscar Salinas** .... (956) 548-6109
E-mail: oscar.salinas@cob.us

Parks and Recreation Department
1207 South Central Avenue, Brownsville, TX 78520
P.O. Box 911, Brownsville, TX 78522-0911
Fax: (956) 982-1049
Director **Damaris McGlone** .... (956) 542-2064

Permitting Department
1034 East Levee, Brownsville, TX 78522
P.O. Box 911, Brownsville, TX 78522-0911
Fax: (956) 550-8802
Director of Operations **Evaristo Gamez** .... (956) 550-8345

Planning and Zoning Department
P.O. Box 911, Brownsville, TX 78522-0911
Fax: (956) 548-6144
Director of Operations for Planning **Constanza Miner** ... (956) 548-6150
E-mail: constanza.miner@cob.us

Police Department
P.O. Box 911, Brownsville, TX 78522-0911
Fax: (956) 548-7000 (General Information) Fax: (956) 548-7009
Police Chief **Orlando Rodriguez** .... (956) 548-7050
Fax: (956) 548-7058

Public Health Department
1034 East Levee, Brownsville, TX 78522
P.O. Box 911, Brownsville, TX 78522-0911
Fax: (956) 546-4355
Health Director **Art Rodriguez** .... (956) 542-3437

Public Works Department
P.O. Box 911, Brownsville, TX 78522-0911
Fax: (956) 838-6307
Director **Santana Torres** .... (956) 838-6253
Landfill Supervisor **Jose Roberto Maldonado** .... (956) 831-3641

Purchasing and Contracts Department
P.O. Box 911, Brownsville, TX 78522-0911
Fax: (956) 546-2711
Director **Roberto C. Luna** .... (956) 548-6087
E-mail: roberto@cob.us

Office of the City Attorney
City Hall, 1001 East Elizabeth Street, Brownsville, TX 78520
P.O. Box 911, Brownsville, TX 78520
Fax: (956) 546-4291 Internet: http://cityattorney.cob.us
City Attorney **Mark Sossi** .... (956) 548-6011
E-mail: mark.sossi@cob.us
Assistant City Attorney **Allison Bastiam** .... (956) 548-6011

City of Buffalo, New York

City Hall, 65 Niagara Square, Buffalo, NY 14202
Tel: (716) 851-4200 (Information) Internet: www.city-buffalo.com

County: Erie **Election Type:** Partisan **Year Founded:** 1790
Year Incorporated: 1832 **Population:** 258,071 (2015)

Byron W. Brown (D)
Mayor

Term Expires: December 31, 2017
Education: SUNY (Buffalo) 1983 BA
Career: Intergovernmental Affairs Assistant Minority Leader, New York State Senate; State Senator (D-NY, District 60), New York State Senate (2001-2005)

Office of the Mayor
201 City Hall, 65 Niagara Square, Buffalo, NY 14202
Fax: (716) 851-4360 E-mail: mayordept@city-buffalo.com
Internet: www.ci.buffalo.ny.us/home/leadership/mayor

★ Mayor **Byron W. Brown** (D) .... (716) 851-4841
E-mail: mayor@city-buffalo.com
Executive Assistant/Scheduling Secretary
Bernadette Taylor .... (716) 851-4841
Deputy Mayor/Chief of Staff **Elizabeth Betsey Ball** .... (716) 851-4841
Deputy Mayor **(Vacant)** .... (716) 851-4851
Director of Communications **Mike DeGeorge** .... (716) 851-5841
E-mail: mdegeorge@city-buffalo.com
Deputy Director of Communications **Lorey Schultz** .... (716) 851-4841
E-mail: lschultz@city-buffalo.com
Chief Diversity Officer **Crystal J. Rodriguez** .... (716) 851-4841

Office of the Common Council
1408 City Hall, 65 Niagara Square, 13th Floor, Buffalo, NY 14202
Tel: (716) 851-4138 Fax: (716) 851-4869
E-mail: council@ci.buffalo.ny.us
Internet: www.ci.buffalo.ny.us/Home/Leadership/CommonCouncil

★ Council President **Darius G. Pridgen** (D-Ellicott) 1315 City Hall, Room 1408 .... (716) 851-4980
Term Expires: December 31, 2019
E-mail: dpridgen@city-buffalo.com

★ President Pro Tem **David A. Rivera** (D-Niagara) .... (716) 851-5125
Term Expires: December 31, 2019
E-mail: darivera@city-buffalo.com

★ Council Member **Joel Feroleto** (D-Delaware) .... (716) 851-5155
Term Expires: December 31, 2019
Capitol Building, Room 1405, Buffalo, NY 14202
E-mail: jferoleto@city-buffalo.com

★ Council Member **Richard A. Fontana** (D-Lovejoy) 1315 City Hall, Room 1414 .... (716) 851-5151
Term Expires: December 31, 2019
E-mail: rfontana@city-buffalo.com

★ Council Member **David A. Franczyk** (D-Fillmore) .... (716) 851-4138
Term Expires: December 31, 2019 Fax: (716) 851-4869
E-mail: dfranczyk@city-buffalo.com

★ Elected Official ▲ Appointed by Legislature ▼ Appointed by Governor ► Appointed by Board or Commission ● Appointed by Judge
■ Appointed by Mayor △ Appointed by Freeholders ▽ Appointed by Supervisor ▷ Appointed by County Executive ○ Appointed by Council

Office of the Common Council *continued*

★Council Member **Joseph Golombek, Jr.** (D-North)
1315 City Hall, Room 1502 .... (716) 851-5116
Term Expires: December 31, 2019
E-mail: jgolombek@city-buffalo.com

○Council Member **Christopher Scanlon** (D-South) 1315
City Hall, Room 1401 .... (716) 851-5169
Term Expires: December 31, 2019
E-mail: cscanlon@city-buffalo.com

★Council Member **Ulysees O. Wingo** (D-Masten) 1315
City Hall, Room 1316-A .... (716) 851-5145
Term Expires: December 31, 2019

★Council Member **Rasheed N.C. Wyatt** (D-University)
1315 City Hall, Room 1508 .... (716) 851-5165
Term Expires: December 31, 2019
E-mail: rwyatt@city-buffalo.com

Office of the City Clerk

1308 City Hall, 65 Niagara Square, Buffalo, NY 14202
Tel: (716) 851-5431 Fax: (716) 851-4845

○City Clerk **Gerald Chwalinski** .... (716) 851-5431
E-mail: gchwalinski@city-buffalo.com

Records Management Officer/Registrar
Gerald Chwalinski .... (716) 874-6401
85 River Rock Drive, Suite 301, Buffalo, NY 14207

Vital Statistics

1302 City Hall, 65 Niagara Square, Buffalo, NY 14202

Deputy City Clerk of Vital Statistics **Milly Castro** .... (716) 851-5442

Office of the Comptroller

1225 City Hall, 65 Niagara Square, Buffalo, NY 14202
Fax: (716) 851-4031

★Comptroller **Mark J.F. Schroeder** (D) .... (716) 851-5255
Term Expires: December 31, 2019
E-mail: markjfschroeder@city-buffalo.com
Education: Empire Col BA

Deputy Comptroller **Anne Forti-Sciarrino** .... (716) 851-5276
Education: Canisius MBA Fax: (716) 851-4358

City Accountant **William Ferguson** .... (716) 851-5258
E-mail: wferguson@city-buffalo.com

City Auditor **Kevin Kaufman** .... (716) 851-5265
Fax: (716) 854-4358

Cash and Debt Office

Cash and Debt Officer **Gregg Szymanski** ...... (716) 851-5264 ext. 286
Fax: (716) 851-4633

Office of Strategic Planning

920 City Hall, 65 Niagara Square, Buffalo, NY 14202-3376
Tel: (716) 851-2872 Fax: (716) 851-4388
E-mail: strategicplanning@city-buffalo.com

■Executive Director **Brendan R. Mehaffy** .... (716) 851-5275
E-mail: bmehaffy@city-buffalo.com

Director of Real Estate **Christie Nelson** .... (716) 851-5275

Director of Housing **Yvonne McCray** .... (716) 851-5416

Comprehensive Planning and Programming **Keith Lucas** .. (716) 851-4901

Director of Planning **Nadine Marrero** .... (716) 851-5029

Planning and Data Analysis **Eric Birner** .... (716) 851-5073

Administration, Finance, Policy and Urban Affairs Department

203 City Hall, 65 Niagara Square, Buffalo, NY 14202
Fax: (716) 851-5710

■Commissioner of Administration, Finance, Policy and Urban Affairs **Donna J. Estrich** .... (716) 851-5922
E-mail: destrich@city-buffalo.com

Treasury and Collections Director **Michael A. Seaman** .. (716) 851-5716
E-mail: mseaman@city-buffalo.com

Division of Purchase

65 Niagara Square, Room 1901, Buffalo, NY 14202
Tel: (716) 851-5222 Fax: (716) 851-5231

■Director **William L. Sunderlin** .... (716) 851-5222
E-mail: wsunderlin@city-buffalo.com

Assistant Director **(Vacant)** .... (716) 851-5222
Fax: (716) 851-5231

Assessment and Taxation Department

101 City Hall, 65 Niagara Square, Buffalo, NY 14202-3385
Fax: (716) 851-5730

■Commissioner **Martin F. Kennedy** .... (716) 851-5739
E-mail: mkennedy@city-buffalo.com

Community Services and Recreational Programming

1701 City Hall, 65 Niagara Square, Buffalo, NY 14202
Internet: www.ci.buffalo.ny.us/Home/City_Departments/CSRP

Deputy Commissioner **Otis T. Barker, Sr.** ...... (716) 851-4001 ext. 4165
E-mail: obarker@city-buffalo.com

Division of Senior Citizens

City Hall, 65 Niagara Square, Room 8A, Buffalo, NY 14202-3317
Fax: (716) 851-5030 Internet: https://www.ci.buffalo.ny.us/Home/Seniors

Director **Douglas Ruffin** .... (716) 851-4115

Fire Department

195 Court Steet, Buffalo, NY 14202-2692
Fax: (716) 851-4364

○Commissioner **Garnell W. Whitfield, Jr.** .... (716) 851-5333 ext. 355
E-mail: gwhitfield@bfdny.org

Deputy Commissioner **(Vacant)** .... (716) 851-5333 ext. 351

Deputy Commissioner **(Vacant)** .... (716) 851-5333 ext. 352

Battalion Chief of Health and Safety **(Vacant)** ... (716) 851-5333 ext. 317

Fire Prevention Bureau

321 City Hall, 65 Niagara Square, Buffalo, NY 14202
Fax: (716) 851-4680

Battalion Chief **Mark Morganti** .... (716) 851-5333 ext. 750
E-mail: mmorganti@ci.buffalo.ny.us

Fire Training Bureau

3359 Broadway, Cheektowaga, NY 14225
Fax: (716) 681-1013

Battalion Chief **Thomas J. Meldrum** .... (716) 681-1011
E-mail: tjmeldrum@bfdny.org

Office of Homeland Security/Emergency Management

195 Court Steet, Buffalo, NY 14202-2692
Fax: (716) 851-5341
Internet: www.ci.buffalo.ny.us/Home/City_Departments/EMS

■Director of Homeland Security/Emergency Management **Garnell W. Whitfield, Jr.** .... (716) 851-5333 ext. 355
E-mail: gwhitfield@bfdny.org

Human Resources Department

1007 City Hall, 65 Niagara Square, Buffalo, NY 14202

Commissioner **Gladys Herndon-Hill** .... (716) 851-5900
E-mail: gherndon-hill@citybuffalo.com

Compensation and Benefits Division Director
Antoinette Palmer .... (716) 851-9677
E-mail: apalmer@city-buffalo.com

Employment and Training Center Director
Demone A. Smith (D) .... (716) 851-5900
E-mail: dsmith@city-buffalo.com

★Elected Official ▲Appointed by Legislature ▼Appointed by Governor ▶Appointed by Board or Commission ●Appointed by Judge
■Appointed by Mayor △Appointed by Freeholders ▽Appointed by Supervisor ▷Appointed by County Executive ○Appointed by Council

Law Department

1100 City Hall, 65 Niagara Square, Buffalo, NY 14202
Tel: (716) 851-4343 Fax: (716) 851-4105
E-mail: lawdept@city-buffalo.com

■ Corporation Counsel **Timothy A. Ball** . . . . . (716) 851-4334
E-mail: tball@city-buffalo.com

Parking Department

City Hall, 65 Niagara Square, Room 111, Buffalo, NY 14202

Commissioner **Kevin J. Helfer** . . . . . (716) 851-5182

Permit and Inspection Services Department

City Hall, 65 Niagara Square, Room 920, Buffalo, NY 14202

Commissioner **James Comerford** . . . . . (716) 851-4972

Police Department

74 Franklin St., Buffalo, NY 14202
Tel: (716) 851-4444 Fax: (716) 851-4081
E-mail: bpdmis@acsu.buffalo.edu Internet: www.bpdny.org/

■ Commissioner **Daniel Derenda** . . . . . (716) 851-4571
E-mail: dderenda@bpdny.org Fax: (716) 851-4081

Inspector of Administration and Communications/Chief of Staff **Joseph F. Strano** . . . . . (716) 851-4624
Fax: (716) 851-6523

First Deputy Police Commissioner **Byron C. Lockwood** . . . . . (716) 851-4040
Fax: (716) 851-5288

Deputy Commissioner **Kimberly Beaty** . . . . . (716) 851-4526
Fax: (716) 851-5179

Public Works, Parks, and Streets Department

City Hall, 65 Niagara Square, Room 502, Buffalo, NY 14202-3305
Tel: (716) 851-5636 Fax: (716) 851-4201

■ Commissioner **Steven J. Stepniak** . . . . . (716) 851-5636
E-mail: sstepniak@city-buffalo.com

Deputy Commissioner for Parks, Recreation and Forestry **Andrew Rabb** . . . . . (716) 851-5636

City Engineer **Michael J. Finn** . . . . . (716) 851-5631
E-mail: mfinn@city-buffalo.com

Traffic Engineer **Eric Schmarder** Room 512 . . . . . (716) 851-5366
E-mail: eschmarder@citybuffalo.com

Buildings Planning and Design **Rishawn T. Sonubi** . . . . . (716) 851-5850
65 Niagara Square, Room 616, Buffalo, NY 14202-3306 Fax: (716) 851-4080

Street Cleaning and Snow Removal Director **Henry Jackson** . . . . . (716) 851-5661

Street Sanitation Director **Paul Sullivan** . . . . . (716) 851-5987
65 Niagara Square, Room 502, Buffalo, NY 14202

Street Sanitation Department

City Hall, 65 Niagara Square, Room 502, Buffalo, NY 14202
Fax: (716) 851-5358

Director of Refuse and Recycling **Paul Sullivan** . . . . . (716) 851-5987

Buffalo Public Schools

City Hall, 65 Niagara Square, Room 801, Buffalo, NY 14202
Fax: (716) 851-3937 Internet: www.buffaloschools.org

Superintendent **Dr. Kriner Cash** . . . . . (716) 816-3575

Chief Academic Officer **Anne Botticelli** Room 701 . . . . . (716) 816-7101

Chief Financial Officer (Interim) **Geofrey Pritchard** Room 708 . . . . . (716) 816-3676

Chief Operations Officer **Kevin Eberle** Room 708 . . . . . (716) 816-3030
E-mail: keberle@buffaloschools.org

Executive Director of Plant Services **Joseph P. Giusiana** Room 403 . . . . . (716) 816-3560
E-mail: jgiusiana@buffaloschools.org

Executive Director, Human Resources (Interim) **Brian Lorentz** . . . . . (716) 816-3579

Buffalo Public Schools *continued*

Media/Community Relations **Elena Cala** Room 712 . . . . . (716) 816-3600
E-mail: ecala@buffaloschools.org

Communications Director **(Vacant)** . . . . . (716) 816-3007

Chief Technology Officer **Sanjay Gilani** . . . . . (716) 816-3611
E-mail: sgilani@buffaloschools.org

Labor Relations Executive **Nate Kuzma** Room 725 . . . . . (716) 816-3742

Staff Development Director **(Vacant)** . . . . . (716) 816-3048

Security Officer (Acting) **Lori Conroy** . . . . . (716) 816-3707

Buffalo Police Chief of School Safety and Security **Kevin Brinkworth** . . . . . (716) 816-3660

City of Burbank, California

City Hall, 275 E. Olive Ave., Burbank, CA 91502
P.O. Box 6459, Burbank, CA 91510
Tel: (818) 238-5850 (Information)

County: Los Angeles **Election Type:** Nonpartisan **Year Incorporated:** 1911 **Charter:** 1927 **Population:** 105,319 (2015)

Office of the Mayor and City Council

City Hall, 275 E. Olive Ave., Burbank, CA 91502
Fax: (818) 238-5757

★ Mayor **Jess Talamantes** . . . . . (818) 238-5751
Began Service: May 2009
Term Expires: April 30, 2017
E-mail: jtalamantes@burbankca.gov

★ Vice Mayor **Will Rogers** . . . . . (818) 238-5751
Term Expires: April 30, 2019
E-mail: wrogers@burbankca.gov

★ Council Member **Robert "Bob" Frutos** . . . . . (818) 238-5751
Term Expires: April 30, 2017
E-mail: bfrutos@burbankca.gov

★ Council Member **Emily Gabel-Luddy** . . . . . (818) 238-5751
Term Expires: April 30, 2019
E-mail: egabel-luddy@burbankca.gov

★ Council Member **Dr. David Gordon** . . . . . (818) 238-5751
Term Expires: April 30, 2017
E-mail: dgordon@burbankca.gov

Office of the City Attorney

P.O. Box 6459, Burbank, CA 91510
Fax: (818) 238-5724

○ City Attorney **Amy Albano** . . . . . (818) 238-5700
E-mail: aalbano@burbankca.gov

Office of the City Clerk

P.O. Box 6459, Burbank, CA 91510
Fax: (818) 238-5853 E-mail: cityclerk@burbankca.gov

★ City Clerk **Zizette Mullins** . . . . . (818) 238-5851
Term Expires: May 1, 2017
E-mail: zmullins@burbankca.gov

Office of the City Treasurer

P.O. Box 6459, Burbank, CA 91510
Fax: (818) 238-5885

★ City Treasurer **Debbie Kukta** . . . . . (818) 238-5880
Term Expires: May 1, 2017
E-mail: dkukta@burbankca.gov

Office of the City Manager

P.O. Box 6459, Burbank, CA 91510
Fax: (818) 238-5804

○ City Manager (Interim) **Ronald E. "Ron" Davis** . . . . . (818) 238-5800
E-mail: rdavis@burbankca.gov
Education: Eastern Washington 1981 BA

★ Elected Official ▲ Appointed by Legislature ▼ Appointed by Governor ▶ Appointed by Board or Commission ● Appointed by Judge
■ Appointed by Mayor △ Appointed by Freeholders ▽ Appointed by Supervisor ▷ Appointed by County Executive ○ Appointed by Council

Office of the City Manager *continued*

Assistant City Manager **Justin Hess** . . . . (818) 238-5810

Burbank Water and Power [BWP]

164 West Magnolia, Burbank, CA 91502
Fax: (818) 238-3560 Internet: www.burbankwaterandpower.com

General Manager (Acting) **Jorge Somoano** . . . . (818) 238-3550
Assistant General Manager, Customer Service and Marketing **Joanne Fletcher** . . . . (818) 238-3550
Assistant General Manager, Electrical Distribution (Acting) **Cesar Ancheta** . . . . (818) 238-3550
Chief Financial Officer **Bob Liu** . . . . (818) 238-3550
Assistant General Manager, Power **Fred Fletcher** . . . . (818) 238-3550
Assistant General Manager, Water **Bill Mace** . . . . (818) 238-3550

Community Development Department

150 North Third Street, Burbank, CA 91502

Director **Patrick Prescott** . . . . (818) 238-5250
E-mail: pprescott@burbankca.gov

Financial Services Department

301 E. Olive Ave., Burbank, CA 91502
Fax: (818) 238-5482

Director **Cindy Giraldo** . . . . (818) 238-5500

Fire Department

311 East Orange Grove Avenue, Burbank, CA 91502
Fax: (818) 238-3483 E-mail: burbankfire@burbankca.gov

Fire Chief **Tom Lenahan** . . . . (818) 238-3480
E-mail: tlenahan@burbankca.gov

Information Technology Department

275 East Olive Avenue, Burbank, CA 91502
Fax: (818) 238-5104

Director **(Vacant)** . . . . (818) 238-5091

Library Services Department

110 N. Glenoaks Blvd., Burbank, CA 91502
Fax: (818) 238-5553 Internet: http://www.burbank.lib.ca.us

Director **Elizabeth Goldman** . . . . (818) 238-5551
E-mail: egoldman@burbankca.gov

Management Services Department

301 East Olive Avenue, Burbank, CA 91502
Fax: (818) 230-5025

Management Services Director **Betsy Dolan** . . . . (818) 238-5026
E-mail: edolan@burbankca.gov

Park, Recreation and Community Services Department

150 North Third Street, Burbank, CA 91502
Fax: (818) 238-5321

Director **Judie Wilke** . . . . (818) 238-5310
E-mail: jwilke@burbankca.gov

Police Department

200 N. Third St., Burbank, CA 91502
Fax: (818) 238-3209

Chief of Police **Scott LaChasse** . . . . (818) 238-3200

Public Information Office

275 East Olive Avenue, Burbank, CA 91502

Public Information Officer **Drew Sugars** . . . . (818) 238-5840
E-mail: dsugars@burbankca.gov

Public Works Department

150 North Third Street, Burbank, CA 91502
Fax: (818) 238-3918 Tel: (818) 238-3915

Director **Bonnie Teaford** . . . . (818) 238-3915
E-mail: bteaford@burbankca.gov

Public Works Department *continued*

Assistant Public Works Director, Street and Sanitation Division **John Molinar** . . . . (818) 238-3915
124 South Lake Street, Burbank, CA 91502
Assistant Public Works Director, Traffic Engineer **Ken Johnson** . . . . (818) 238-3915
E-mail: kjohnson@burbankca.gov
Senior Engineer, Engineering/Environmental Services Division **(Vacant)** . . . . (818) 238-3915

Building and Fire Code Appeals Board

P.O. Box 6459, Burbank, CA 91510

Chairman **(Vacant)** . . . . (818) 238-5220

Civil Service Board

P.O. Box 6459, Burbank, CA 91510

○ Chairman **Matt Doyle** . . . . (818) 238-5026
Fax: (818) 238-5104

Greater Los Angeles County Vector Control District

12545 Florence Avenue, Santa Fe Springs, CA 90670
Internet: http://www.glacvcd.org

Manager **Dr. Jeff D. Wassem** . . . . (562) 944-9656

Landlord/Tenant Commission

P.O. Box 6459, Burbank, CA 91510

○ Chairman **Judy Smith** . . . . (818) 238-5160

Parks, Recreation and Community Services Board

P.O. Box 6459, Burbank, CA 91510

○ Chairperson **Michael "Mickey" DePalo** . . . . (818) 238-5300

Planning Board

P.O. Box 6459, Burbank, CA 91510

○ Chairman **(Vacant)** . . . . (818) 238-5250

City of Burlington, Vermont

City Hall, 149 Church St., Burlington, VT 05401
Tel: (802) 865-7000 (Information) Tel: (802) 865-7136 (Elections)
Internet: www.burlingtonvt.gov/

County: Chittenden **Election Type:** Partisan **Year Founded:** 1763
Year Incorporated: 1864 **Charter:** 1949 **Population:** 42,452 (2015)

Office of the Mayor and City Council

City Hall, 149 Church Street, Room 34, Burlington, VT 05401
Fax: (802) 865-7270

Note: Party affiliation P refers to the Progressive Coalition

★ Mayor **Miro Weinberger** (D) . . . . (802) 865-7272
Began Service: April 2, 2012
Term Expires: April 2018
E-mail: mayor@burlingtonvt.gov
Chief of Staff **Brian Lowe** . . . . (802) 865-7275
Project Coordinator/Communications **Jennifer Kaulius** . . (802) 865-7275
★ Council President **Dr. Jane E. Knodell** (P-Central) . . . . . . (802) 865-7136
Term Expires: April 2017
E-mail: jknodell@burlingtonvt.gov
Education: Stanford 1976 AB, 1984 PhD
★ Council Member **Sharon Foley Bushor** (I-Ward 1) . . . . . . (802) 865-7136
Term Expires: April 2018
E-mail: sbushor@burlingtonvt.gov

(continued on next page)

★ Elected Official ▲ Appointed by Legislature ▼ Appointed by Governor ▶ Appointed by Board or Commission ● Appointed by Judge
■ Appointed by Mayor △ Appointed by Freeholders ▽ Appointed by Supervisor ▷ Appointed by County Executive ○ Appointed by Council

CITIES AND TOWNS

Office of the Mayor and City Council *continued*

★Council Member **Max Tracy** (P-Ward 2) . . . . (802) 865-7136
Term Expires: April 2018
E-mail: mtracy@burlingtonvt.gov
★Council Member **Sara Giannoni** (P-Ward 3) . . . . (802) 865-7136
Term Expires: April 2018
E-mail: sgiannoni@burlingtonvt.gov
★Council Member **Kurt Wright** (R-Ward 4) . . . . (802) 865-7136
Term Expires: April 1, 2018
E-mail: kwright@burlingtonvt.gov
★Council Member **William "Chip" Mason** (D-Ward 5) . . . . (802) 865-7136
Term Expires: April 2018
E-mail: cmason@burlingtonvt.gov
★Council Member **Karen Paul** (I-Ward 6) . . . . (802) 865-7136
Term Expires: April 2018
E-mail: kpaul@burlingtonvt.gov
★Council Member **Tom Ayres** (D-Ward 7) . . . . (802) 865-7136
Term Expires: April 2018
E-mail: tayres@burlingtonvt.gov
★Council Member **Adam S. Roof** (I-Ward 8) . . . . (802) 865-7136
Term Expires: April 2018
E-mail: aroof@burlingtonvt.gov
★Council Member **Selene Colburn** (P-East) . . . . (802) 865-7136
Term Expires: April 2018
E-mail: scolburn@burlingtonvt.gov
★Council Member **David Hartnett** (D-North) . . . . (802) 865-7136
Term Expires: April 2017
E-mail: dhartnett@burlingtonvt.gov
★Council Member **Joan Shannon** (D-South) . . . . (802) 865-7136
Term Expires: April 2017
E-mail: jshannon@burlingtonvt.gov
Council Administrative Secretary **Lori Olberg** . . . . (802) 865-7136
E-mail: lolberg@burlingtonvt.gov

Office of the Assessor

City Hall, 149 Church Street, Room 17, Burlington, VT 05401

■Assessor **John Vickery** . . . . (802) 865-7114
E-mail: jvickery@burlingtonvt.gov

Office of the City Attorney

City Hall, 149 Church St., Burlington, VT 05401

■City Attorney **Eileen Blackwood** . . . . (802) 865-7121
E-mail: eblackwood@burlingtonvt.gov

Office of the Clerk/Treasurer

City Hall, 149 Church St., Burlington, VT 05401

■Chief Administrative Officer **Robert "Bob" Rusten** (D) . . (802) 865-7012
E-mail: brusten@burlingtonvt.gov

Burlington City Arts

135 Church Street, Burlington, VT 05401

Executive Director **Doreen Kraft** . . . . (802) 865-7156

Burlington Electric Department [BED]

585 Pine St., Burlington, VT 05401-4891
Fax: (802) 865-7400 Internet: www.burlingtonelectric.com

■General Manager **Neale F. Lunderville** . . . . (802) 865-7415
E-mail: nlunderville@burlingtonelectric.com
Education: American U BA

Burlington Housing Authority

65 Main Street, Burlington, VT 05401

■Executive Director **Paul Dettman** . . . . (802) 864-0538 ext. 210
E-mail: pdettman@burlingtonhousing.org

Burlington International Airport

Burlington Internat'l. Airport, Airport Dr., Box 1,
South Burlington, VT 05403
Fax: (802) 863-7947

■Director of Aviation **Gene Richards** . . . . (802) 863-2874
E-mail: grichards@btv.aero

Burlington Telecom

200 Church Street, Burlington, VT 05401
Fax: (802) 652-4220

General Manager **Stephen Barraclough** . . . . (802) 540-0007
E-mail: sbarraclough@burlingtontelecom.com

Cemetery Department

455 North Avenue, Burlington, VT 05401

○Cemetery Assistant **Jeff Shedd** . . . . (802) 863-2075
E-mail: jshedd@burlingtonvt.gov

Church Street Marketplace

2 Church Street, Burlington, VT 05401

○Executive Director **Ronald Redmond** . . . . (802) 863-1648 ext. 4
E-mail: rredmond@burlingtonvt.gov

Code Enforcement Department

645 Pine Street, Burlington, VT 05401
Fax: (802) 652-4221

■Director **William Ward** . . . . (802) 863-0442
E-mail: wward@burlingtonvt.gov

Community and Economic Development Office

City Hall, 149 Church Street, Room 32, Burlington, VT 05401
Fax: (802) 865-7024

■Director **Peter Owens** . . . . (802) 865-7144
E-mail: peter@burlingtonvt.gov

Fire Department

136 S. Winooski Ave., Burlington, VT 05401
Tel: (802) 864-4554 Fax: (802) 864-5945
Internet: http://www.burlingtonvt.gov/Fire

■Fire Chief **Steven Locke** . . . . (802) 864-4553
E-mail: slocke@burlingtonvt.gov

Fletcher Free Library

235 College St., Burlington, VT 05401
Fax: (802) 865-7227

■Director **Rubi Simon** . . . . (802) 863-3403
Reference Librarian **Robert Coleburn** . . . . (802) 863-3403
E-mail: rcoleburn@burlingtonvt.gov
Reference Librarian **Robert Resnik** . . . . (802) 863-3403
E-mail: rresnik@burlingtonvt.gov

Human Resources Department

200 Church Street, Suite 102, Burlington, VT 05401

■Director **Susan Leonard** . . . . (802) 865-7145
E-mail: sleonard@burlingtonvt.gov

Parks, Recreation and Waterfront Department

645 Pine Street, Suite B, Burlington, VT 05401

■Director **Jesse Bridges** . . . . (802) 864-0123
E-mail: jbridges@burlingtonvt.gov

Planning and Zoning Department

149 Church Street, Burlington, VT 05401

○Director **David E. White** . . . . (802) 865-7194
E-mail: DEWhite@burlingtonvt.gov

★Elected Official ▲Appointed by Legislature ▼Appointed by Governor ►Appointed by Board or Commission ●Appointed by Judge
■Appointed by Mayor △Appointed by Freeholders ▽Appointed by Supervisor ▷Appointed by County Executive ○Appointed by Council

Police Department
One North Ave., Burlington, VT 05401

■ Police Chief **Brandon del Pozo** .... (802) 540-2107
E-mail: bdelpozo@bpdvt.org

Public Works Department
645 Pine Street, Burlington, VT 05401
P.O. Box 849, Burlington, VT 05402-0849
Fax: (802) 863-0466 Internet: http://www.burlingtonvt.gov/DPW

■ Director **Chapin Spencer** .... (802) 863-9094
Education: Trinity Col (CT) 1993 BA
Technical Services Assistant Director/City Engineer
Norman J. Baldwin .... (802) 865-5826
E-mail: nbaldwin@burlingtonvt.gov

Retirement Board
200 Church Street, Suite 102, Burlington, VT 05401

■ Retirement Administrator **Stephanie Hanker** .... (802) 865-7097
E-mail: shanker@burlingtonvt.gov

Burlington School District
150 Colchester Ave., Burlington, VT 05401
Fax: (802) 864-8501 Internet: www.bsdvt.org

Superintendent **Yaw Obeng** .... (802) 865-5332
Administrative Assistant **Maryann Kalman** .... (802) 864-8474
E-mail: mkalman@bsdvt.org

★ School Commissioner **Mark Porter** (Ward I) .... (802) 862-5332
Term Expires: April 2018

★ School Commissioner **Kat Kleman** (Ward II) .... (802) 658-5332
Term Expires: April 2018

★ School Commissioner **Liz Curry** (Ward III) .... (802) 658-5332
Term Expires: April 1, 2018

★ School Commissioner **Anne Judson** (Ward IV) .... (802) 865-5332
Term Expires: April 2018

★ School Commissioner
Susanmarie Harrington (Ward V) .... (802) 865-5332
Term Expires: April 2018

★ School Commissioner **Stephanie Seguino** (Ward VI) .... (802) 865-5332
Term Expires: April 2018

★ School Commissioner **David Kirk** (Ward VII) .... (802) 865-5332
Term Expires: April 2018

★ School Commissioner
Lauren Berrizbeitia (District VIII) .... (802) 865-5332
Term Expires: April 2018

★ School Commissioner **Mark Barlow** (North) .... (802) 865-5332
Term Expires: April 2017

★ School Commissioner **Brian Cina** (Central) .... (802) 865-5332
Term Expires: April 2017

★ School Commissioner **Kyle Dodson** (East) .... (802) 865-5332
Term Expires: April 2017

★ School Commissioner **Miriam Stoll** (South) .... (802) 865-5332
Term Expires: April 1, 2017

City of Cambridge, Massachusetts
795 Massachusetts Avenue, Cambridge, MA 02139
Tel: (617) 349-4000 (Information) TTY: (617) 492-0235
Internet: www.cambridgema.gov

County: Middlesex **Election Type:** Nonpartisan **Year Founded:** 1630
Year Incorporated: 1846 **Charter:** 1945 **Population:** 110,402 (2015)

Office of the Mayor and City Council
795 Massachusetts Ave., Cambridge, MA 02139
Tel: (617) 349-4321 Fax: (617) 349-4287

★ Mayor **E. Denise Simmons** .... (617) 349-4321
Began Service: 2002
Term Expires: December 31, 2017
E-mail: dsimmons@cambridgema.gov
Education: UMass (Boston) BA

★ Vice Mayor **Marc McGovern** .... (617) 349-4321
Term Expires: December 31, 2017
E-mail: mmcgovern@cambridgema.gov
Education: UMass (Boston) BA; Simmons MSW

★ Council Member **Dennis Carlone** .... (617) 349-4321
Term Expires: December 31, 2017
E-mail: dcarlone@cambridgema.gov

★ Council Member **Leland Cheung** .... (617) 349-4280
Term Expires: December 31, 2017
E-mail: lcheung@cambridgema.gov
Education: Stanford BS; Harvard 2011 MPA, 2011 MBA

★ Council Member **Jan Devereux** .... (617) 349-4321
Term Expires: December 31, 2017
E-mail: jdevereux@cambridgema.gov

★ Council Member **Craig Kelley** .... (617) 349-4280
Term Expires: December 31, 2017
E-mail: ckelley@cambridgema.gov

★ Council Member **David P. Maher** .... (617) 349-4321
Term Expires: December 31, 2017
E-mail: dmaher@cambridgema.gov
Education: Suffolk BS

★ Council Member **Nadeem A. Mazen** .... (617) 349-4321
Term Expires: December 31, 2017
E-mail: nmazen@cambridgema.gov

★ Council Member **Timothy J. Toomey, Jr.** .... (617) 349-4280
Term Expires: December 31, 2017
E-mail: ttoomey@cambridgema.gov
Education: Suffolk BS

Office of the Auditor
795 Massachusetts Ave., Cambridge, MA 02139

○ City Auditor **James Monagle** .... (617) 349-4240
E-mail: jmonagle@cambridgema.gov

Office of the City Clerk
795 Massachusetts Ave., Cambridge, MA 02139
Tel: (617) 349-4280 Fax: (617) 349-4269

○ City Clerk **Donna Lopez** .... (617) 349-4260
E-mail: dlopez@cambridgema.gov
Deputy City Clerk **Paula Crane** .... (617) 349-4280
E-mail: pcrane@cambridgema.gov

Office of the City Manager
795 Massachusetts Ave., Cambridge, MA 02139
Fax: (617) 349-4307

○ City Manager **Richard C. Rossi** .... (617) 349-4300
Education: Salem State Col BS; Northeastern MPA
Assistant to the City Manager **Taja Jennings** .... (617) 349-4302
E-mail: tjennings@cambridgema.gov

(continued on next page)

★ Elected Official ▲ Appointed by Legislature ▼ Appointed by Governor ▶ Appointed by Board or Commission ● Appointed by Judge
■ Appointed by Mayor △ Appointed by Freeholders ▽ Appointed by Supervisor ▷ Appointed by County Executive ○ Appointed by Council

Office of the City Manager *continued*

Deputy City Manager **Lisa Peterson** . . . . (617) 349-4300
E-mail: lpeterson@cambridgema.gov
Director of Communications and Community Relations
Lee Gianetti . . . . (617) 349-3317
E-mail: lgianetti@cambridgema.gov
Public Information Officer **Ini Tomeu** . . . . (617) 349-4339
E-mail: itomeu@cambridgema.gov

Office of the City Solicitor
795 Massachusetts Ave., Cambridge, MA 02139

City Solicitor **Nancy Glowa** . . . . (617) 349-4121
E-mail: nglowa@cambridgema.gov

Office of Affirmative Action
795 Massachusetts Ave., Cambridge, MA 02139

Director **Duane Brown** . . . . (617) 349-4331

Animal Commission
344 Broadway, Cambridge, MA 02139

Executive Director **Mark McCabe** . . . . (617) 349-4376

Arts Council
344 Broadway, Cambridge, MA 02139

Executive Director **Jason Weeks** . . . . (617) 349-4383

Assessing Department
795 Massachusetts Ave., Cambridge, MA 02139

Director **Bob Reardon** . . . . (617) 349-4343
E-mail: rreardon@cambridgema.gov

Budget Department
795 Massachusetts Ave., Cambridge, MA 02139

Director **Jeana Franconi** . . . . (617) 349-4270
E-mail: jfranconi@cambridgema.gov

Cambridge Electrical Department
250 Fresh Pond Parkway, Cambridge, MA 02138

City Electrician **Steve Lenkauskas** . . . . (617) 349-4925

Cambridge Housing Authority
675 Massachusetts Avenue, Cambridge, MA 02139

Executive Director **Gregory Russ** . . . . (617) 520-6229

Cambridge Public Schools
16 Felton Street, Cambridge, MA 02138
Tel: (617) 349-6400 Fax: (617) 349-6624 Internet: http://www3.cpsd.us/

School Superintendent **Dr. Jeffrey M. Young** . . . . (617) 349-6494
Chairman **David P. Maher** . . . . (617) 349-4321
Education: Suffolk BS
Committee Member **Fran Cronin** . . . . (617) 349-6620
Committee Member **Alfred Fantini** . . . . (617) 349-6620
Education: Bentley Col BA; Cambridge 1999 MA
Committee Member **Richard Harding, Jr.** . . . . (617) 349-6620
Education: Fitchburg State BA
Committee Member **Kathleen Kelly** . . . . (617) 349-6620
Committee Member **Patricia Nolan** . . . . (617) 349-6620
Committee Member **Mervan F. Osborne** . . . . (617) 349-6620

Community Development Department
344 Broadway, Cambridge, MA 02139
Fax: (617) 349-4669

Assistant City Manager for Community Development
(Acting) **Iram Farooq** . . . . (617) 349-4600
E-mail: cddat344@cambridgema.gov

Conservation Commission
344 Broadway, Cambridge, MA 02139
Fax: (617) 349-4669

Director **Jennifer Letourneau** . . . . (617) 349-4680

Election Commission
51 Inman St., Cambridge, MA 02139

Director **Tanya Ford** . . . . (617) 349-4361

Finance Department
795 Massachusetts Ave., Cambridge, MA 02139
Tel: (617) 349-4220 E-mail: treasurer@cambridgema.gov

Fiscal Affairs Assistant City Manager/Treasurer
Louis DePasquale . . . . (617) 349-4220
E-mail: ldepasquale@cambridgema.gov

Historical Commission
831 Massachusetts Avenue, Cambridge, MA 02139
Fax: (617) 349-3116 E-mail: histcomm@cambridgema.gov

Executive Director **Charles Sullivan** . . . . (617) 349-4683
Assistant Director **Kathleen Rawlins** . . . . (617) 349-4683
E-mail: krawlins@cambridgema.gov

Human Rights Commission
51 Inman Street, Cambridge, MA 02139

Executive Director **Nancy Schlacter** . . . . (617) 349-4396

Human Service Programs Department
51 Inman St., Cambridge, MA 02139

Assistant City Manager for Human Services
Ellen Semonoff . . . . (617) 349-6200
E-mail: esemonoff@cambridgema.gov
Education: Brandeis BA; Harvard 1975 JD

Information Technology Systems
831 Massachusetts Avenue, Cambridge, MA 02139
Fax: (617) 349-6165

Chief Information Officer **Mary Hart** . . . . (617) 349-4140
E-mail: mhart@cambridgema.gov
Web Administrator **Carol Cheung** . . . . (617) 349-4076
E-mail: ccheung@cambridgema.gov

Inspectional Services Department
831 Massachusetts Ave., Cambridge, MA 02139
Fax: (617) 349-6132

Commissioner **Ranjit Singanayagam** . . . . (617) 349-6100

Library
449 Broadway, Cambridge, MA 02138
Internet: www.cambridgema.gov/cpl Fax: (617) 349-4028

Director **Susan Flannery** . . . . (617) 349-4040
E-mail: sflannery@cambridgema.gov

License Commission
831 Massachusetts Ave., Cambridge, MA 02139-3068
Fax: (617) 349-6148 E-mail: license@cambridgema.gov

Executive Director **Elizabeth Y. Lint** . . . . (617) 349-6140

Peace Commission
51 Inman Street, Cambridge, MA 02139

Executive Director **Brian Corr** . . . . (617) 349-4766
E-mail: bcorr@cambridgema.gov

★ Elected Official ▲ Appointed by Legislature ▼ Appointed by Governor ▶ Appointed by Board or Commission ● Appointed by Judge
■ Appointed by Mayor △ Appointed by Freeholders ▽ Appointed by Supervisor ▷ Appointed by County Executive ○ Appointed by Council

Personnel Department
795 Massachusetts Ave., Cambridge, MA 02139
Fax: (617) 349-4312

Director **Sheila Keady Rawson** ....(617) 349-4332
E-mail: skeady@cambridgema.gov

Persons With Disabilities Commission
51 Inman St., 2nd Floor, Cambridge, MA 02139
TTY: (617) 492-0235

Executive Director **Michael Muehe** ....(617) 349-4692

Emergency Communications Department [ECC]
795 Massachusetts Ave., Cambridge, MA 02139

Emergency Communications Director
Christina Giacobbe ....(617) 349-3300
125 6th Street, Cambridge, MA 02142
E-mail: cgiacobbe@cambridge911.org
Education: Northeastern 1995 BS

Fire Department
491 Broadway, Cambridge, MA 02138
Fax: (617) 349-4912

Fire Chief **Gerald Reardon** ....(617) 349-4900
E-mail: greardon@cambridgefire.org

Emergency Management
491 Broadway, Cambridge, MA 02138

Deputy Chief **Gerard Mahoney** ....(617) 349-4970
E-mail: gmahoney@cambridgefire.org

Police Department
125 Sixth Street, Cambridge, MA 02142
Fax: (617) 349-3320

Commissioner **Robert C. Haas** ....(617) 349-3378
Education: William Paterson U; Rutgers
Director of Communications and Media Relations
Jeremy Warnick ....(617) 349-3237

Public Works Department
147 Hampshire St., Cambridge, MA 02139
Tel: (617) 349-4800 Fax: (617) 349-4868 TTY: (617) 349-4805
Internet: www.cambridgema.gov/TheWorks/

Commissioner **Owen O'Riordan** ....(617) 349-4807

Purchasing Department
795 Massachusetts Ave., Cambridge, MA 02139
Fax: (617) 349-4008 E-mail: purchasing@cambridgema.gov

Director **Amy Witts** ....(617) 349-4310
E-mail: awitts@cambridgema.gov

Retirement Department
255 Bent St., 3rd Floor, Cambridge, MA 02141
Fax: (617) 868-3477

Executive Director **Ellen Philbin** ....(617) 868-3401

Traffic, Parking and Transportation Department
344 Broadway, Cambridge, MA 02139
Fax: (617) 349-4747

Director **Joseph Barr** ....(617) 349-4700

Veterans' Services Department
51 Inman St., 2nd FL, Cambridge, MA 02139
Fax: (617) 349-4097

Director **Stephen A. Vesce** ....(617) 349-4760

Water Department
250 Fresh Pond Pkwy., Cambridge, MA 02138
Fax: (617) 349-4796

Director **Sam Corda** ....(617) 349-4770
Assistant Director for Operations **Mark Gallagher** ....(617) 349-4770
E-mail: mgallagher@cambridgema.gov

Administration Division
Director of Administration **Fred Centanni** ....(617) 349-6887
E-mail: fcentanni@cambridgema.gov

Distribution and Engineering Operations
Director of Distribution and Engineering Operations
Mark Gallagher ....(617) 349-7754
E-mail: mgallagher@cambridgema.gov

Distribution and Transmission Division
Supervisor **Bill Connell** ....(617) 349-4770

Engineering and Program Development Division
Manager **Steve Lush** ....(617) 349-4770
E-mail: slush@cambridgema.gov
Facilities Manager **Mike Bonacci** ....(617) 349-4770
E-mail: mbonacci@cambridgema.gov

Water Board
President **Ann Roosevelt** ....(617) 349-4770

Water Operations Division
Director of Water Operations
Timothy W.D. MacDonald ....(617) 349-4773
Maintenance Manager **Allan Cheung** ....(617) 349-4770
E-mail: acheung@cambridgema.gov
Laboratory Manager **Edward Dowling** ....(617) 349-4770
Production Manager **Jim Rita** ....(617) 349-4770
Water Quality Supervisor **Krystyna McInally** ....(617) 349-4770
Water Quality Supervisor **Richard Langerholm** ....(617) 349-4770

Watershed Management Division
Manager **(Vacant)** ....(617) 349-4770
Reservoir Systems Manager **Vincent Falcione** ....(617) 349-4770

Weights and Measures Department
831 Massachusetts Ave., Cambridge, MA 02139

Sealer of Weights and Measures **James P. Cassidy, Jr.** ....(617) 349-6133

Women's Commission
51 Inman Street, Cambridge, MA 02139
Fax: (617) 349-4766

Executive Director **Kimberly Sansoucy** ....(617) 349-4697
Program Coordinator **Emily Shield** ....(617) 349-4697

City of Cape Coral, Florida

P.O. Box 150027, Cape Coral, FL 33915-0027
Internet: www.capecoral.net

County: Lee **Election Type:** Nonpartisan **Year Incorporated:** 1970
Population: 175,229 (2015)

Office of the Mayor and City Council
P.O. Box 150027, Cape Coral, FL 33915-0027
Fax: (239) 574-0429 E-mail: council@capecoral.net

★Mayor **Marni L. Sawicki** ....(239) 574-0436
Began Service: November 18, 2013
Term Expires: November 7, 2017
E-mail: msawicki@capecoral.net

(continued on next page)

★Elected Official ▲Appointed by Legislature ▼Appointed by Governor ▶Appointed by Board or Commission ●Appointed by Judge
■Appointed by Mayor △Appointed by Freeholders ▽Appointed by Supervisor ▷Appointed by County Executive ○Appointed by Council

Office of the Mayor and City Council *continued*

★ Council Member **James Burch** (District 1) . . . . . (239) 574-0437
Term Expires: November 7, 2017
E-mail: jburch@capecoral.net
Education: VCU BA

★ Council Member **John Carioscia, Sr.** (District 2) . . . . . (239) 242-3288
Term Expires: November 2019
E-mail: jcariosc@capecoral.net

★ Council Member **Marilyn Stout** (District 3) . . . . . (239) 242-3288
Term Expires: November 2019
E-mail: mstout@capecoral.net

★ Council Member **Richard Leon** (District 4) . . . . . (239) 242-3288
Term Expires: November 7, 2017
E-mail: rleon@capecoral.net

★ Council Member **Rana Erbrick** (District 5) . . . . . (239) 574-0437
Term Expires: November 5, 2019
E-mail: rerbrick@capecoral.net

★ Council Member **Rick Williams** (District 6) . . . . . (239) 574-0437
Term Expires: November 7, 2017
E-mail: rwilliam@capecoral.net

★ Council Member **Jessica Cosden** (District 7) . . . . . (239) 574-0437
Term Expires: November 5, 2019
E-mail: jcosden@capecoral.net

Office of the City Auditor

P.O. Box 150027, Cape Coral, FL 33915-0027
Tel: (239) 574-0401

City Auditor **Margaret Krym** . . . . . (239) 242-3383

Office of the City Attorney

P.O. Box 150027, Cape Coral, FL 33915-0027
Fax: (239) 574-0404

City Attorney **Dolores D. Menendez** . . . . . (239) 574-0408
E-mail: dmenendez@capecoral.net
Education: Stetson 1979 JD

Office of the City Clerk

P.O. Box 150027, Cape Coral, FL 33915-0027
Fax: (239) 574-5344 E-mail: ctyclk@capecoral.net

City Clerk **Rebecca van Deutekom** . . . . . (239) 574-0417
E-mail: rvandeutekom@capecoral.net

Office of the City Manager

P.O. Box 150027, Cape Coral, FL 33915-0027
Tel: (239) 574-0447

City Manager **John Szerlag** . . . . . (239) 574-0451
E-mail: jszerlag@capecoral.net
Education: Ferris State BS; Detroit MA

Assistant City Manager **Michael Ilczyszyn** . . . . . (239) 574-0451
E-mail: milczysz@capecoral.net

Community Development Department

P.O. Box 150027, Cape Coral, FL 33915-0027
Fax: (239) 574-0594 E-mail: comdev@capecoral.net

Director **Vince Cautero** . . . . . (239) 574-0600
E-mail: vcautero@capecoral.net

Building Official **Paul Dickson** . . . . . (239) 574-0598

Economic Development Office

P.O. Box 150027, Cape Coral, FL 33915-0027
Fax: (239) 547-0452

Economic Development Manager **Dana Brunett** . . . . . (239) 574-0444
E-mail: dbrunett@capecoral.net
Education: SUNY (Fredonia) BA

Financial Services Department

P.O. Box 150027, Cape Coral, FL 33915-0027
Fax: (239) 574-0734

Director **Victoria L. Bateman** . . . . . (239) 574-0491
Education: Towson U BS

Customer and Field Services Manager **Bill Boyd** . . . . . (239) 574-7722

Fire Department

P.O. Box 150027, Cape Coral, FL 33915-0027
Fax: (239) 242-3309 E-mail: ccfire@capecoral.net

Fire Chief **Donald Cochran** . . . . . (239) 242-3601
E-mail: dcochran@capecoral.net

Human Resources Department

P.O. Box 150027, Cape Coral, FL 33915-0027
Fax: (239) 574-0453

Human Resources Director **Lisa Sonego** . . . . . (239) 574-0530
E-mail: lsonego@capecoral.net

Information Technology Services Department

P.O. Box 150027, Cape Coral, FL 33915-0027
Fax: (239) 574-0454 E-mail: its@capecoral.net

Director **Michelle Hoffmann** . . . . . (239) 574-0455
E-mail: mhoffmann@capecoral.net

Parks and Recreation Department

P.O. Box 150027, Cape Coral, FL 33915-0027
Fax: (239) 573-3130 E-mail: ccpks@capecoral.net

Director **Steve Pohlman** . . . . . (239) 573-3128

Parks Superintendent **Kerry Runyon** . . . . . (239) 573-3128

Recreation and Facilities Superintendent **Keith Locklin** . . . (239) 573-3128
E-mail: klocklin@capecoral.net

Special Facilities and Athletics Superintendent
Arthur Avellino . . . . . (239) 573-3128
E-mail: aavellino@capecoral.net Fax: (239) 573-3129

Police Department

1100 Cultural Park Boulevard, Cape Coral, FL 33990
P.O. Box 150027, Cape Coral, FL 33915
Fax: (239) 574-0641 E-mail: ccpol@capecoral.net

Chief of Police **Bart Connelly** . . . . . (239) 574-0699

Deputy Chief of Police **David Newlan** . . . . . (239) 574-0685

Public Works Department

P.O. Box 150027, Cape Coral, FL 33915-0027

Director **Steve Neff** . . . . . (239) 574-0706
Education: Purdue BSCE

Utilities Department

P.O. Box 150027, Cape Coral, FL 33915
Fax: (239) 574-0731

Director **Jeff Pearson** . . . . . (239) 574-0710

★ Elected Official ▲ Appointed by Legislature ▼ Appointed by Governor ▶ Appointed by Board or Commission ● Appointed by Judge
■ Appointed by Mayor △ Appointed by Freeholders ▽ Appointed by Supervisor ▷ Appointed by County Executive ○ Appointed by Council

City of Carrollton, Texas

City Hall, 1945 East Jackson Road, Carrollton, TX 75006
Internet: www.cityofcarrollton.com/

County: Collin; Dallas; Denton **Election Type:** Nonpartisan
Year Incorporated: 1913 **Population:** 133,168 (2015)

Office of the Mayor and City Council

City Hall, 1945 E. Jackson Rd., Carrollton, TX 75006
Fax: (972) 466-3252

★ Mayor **Matthew H. Marchant** . . . . (972) 466-3001
Began Service: May 23, 2011
Term Expires: May 2017
E-mail: matthew.marchant@cityofcarrollton.com
Education: Southern Nazarene 1998 BS; Texas 2000 JD

★ Mayor Pro Tem **Anthony Wilder** (Place 2, At-Large) . . . . (972) 466-3001
Term Expires: May 2017
E-mail: anthony.wilder@cityofcarrollton.com

★ Deputy Mayor Pro Tem
Doug Hrbacek (Place 3, Southwest) . . . . (972) 466-3001
Term Expires: May 2017

★ Council Member **James Lawrence** (Place 1, Northeast) . . (972) 466-3001
Term Expires: May 2018

★ Council Member **Bob Garza** (Place 4, At-Large) . . . . (972) 466-3001
Term Expires: May 2017
E-mail: bob.garza@cityofcarrollton.com

★ Council Member **Glen Blanscet** (Place 5, Northwest) . . . . (972) 466-3001
Term Expires: May 19, 2018

★ Council Member **Steve Babick** (Place 6, At-Large) . . . . . . (972) 466-3257
Term Expires: May 2017
E-mail: steve.babick@cityofcarrollton.com

★ Council Member **John Sutter** (Place 7, Southeast) . . . . . . (972) 466-3001
Term Expires: May 19, 2018

Office of the City Manager

1945 E. Jackson Rd., Carrollton, TX 75006
Fax: (972) 466-3252

City Manager **Leonard Martin** . . . . (972) 466-3006
Administrative Services Director **Ashley D. Mitchell** . . . (972) 466-3021
E-mail: ashley.mitchell@cityofcarrollton.com

Assistant City Manager for Culture and Leisure and Support Services **Erin Rinehart** . . . . (972) 466-3001
E-mail: erin.rinehart@cityofcarrollton.com

Assistant City Manager for Public Safety and Development Services **Marc Guy** . . . . (972) 466-3001
E-mail: marc.guy@cityofcarrollton.com

Office of the City Attorney

1945 E. Jackson Rd., Carrollton, TX 75006
Fax: (972) 466-3252

City Attorney **Meredith A. Ladd** . . . . (972) 466-3025
E-mail: meredith.ladd@cityofcarrollton.com
Education: Texas Wesleyan U BA; Texas A&M JD

Office of the City Secretary

1945 E. Jackson Rd., Carrollton, TX 75006
Fax: (972) 466-3252

City Secretary/Administrative Services Manager
Laurie Garber . . . . (972) 466-3005
E-mail: laurie.garber@cityofcarrollton.com

Development Services

1945 East Jackson Road, Carrollton, TX 75006
Fax: (972) 466-3193

Director **Ravi Shah** . . . . (972) 466-3040
E-mail: ravi.shah@cityofcarrollton.com
Education: Texas (Arlington)

Planning Department

1945 East Jackson Road, Carrollton, TX 75006
Tel: (972) 466-3040

Development Manager **Krystle F. Nelinson** . . . . (972) 466-3040

Economic Development Department

1945 East Jackson Road, Carrollton, TX 75006
Fax: (972) 466-4882

Director **Tom Latchem** . . . . (972) 466-3299
E-mail: Thomas.Latchem@cityofcarrollton.com

Engineering Department

1945 East Jackson Road, Carrollton, TX 75006
Fax: (972) 466-3193

Director **Cesar Molina** . . . . (972) 466-3200
E-mail: cesar.molina@cityofcarrollton.com

Environmental Services Department

1945 E. Jackson Rd., Carrollton, TX 75006

Director **Scott Hudson** . . . . (972) 466-5727

Animal Services

2247 Sandy Lake Road, Carrollton, TX 75007
Fax: (972) 466-4873

Manager **Carl Shooter** . . . . (972) 466-3420

Finance Department

1945 E. Jackson Rd., Carrollton, TX 75006
Fax: (972) 466-3535

Assistant City Manager/Chief Financial Officer
Robert B. "Bob" Scott . . . . (972) 466-3110
E-mail: bob.scott@cityofcarrollton.com

Controller **Pamela Hodges** . . . . (972) 466-3113
Fax: (972) 466-3175

Purchasing Manager **Vince Priolo** . . . . (972) 466-3133
E-mail: vince.priolo@cityofcarrollton.com Fax: (972) 466-3175

Fire Department

1945 E. Jackson Rd., Carrollton, TX 75006
Fax: (972) 466-4886

Fire Chief **John G. Murphy** . . . . (972) 466-3070
E-mail: john.murphy@cityofcarrollton.com
Education: Abilene Christian 1979 BBA

Assistant Chief **Gregg Salmi** . . . . (972) 466-3070
E-mail: gregg.salmi@cityofcarrollton.com

Information Technology Department

1945 East Jackson Road, Carrollton, TX 75006
Fax: (972) 466-3175

Information Technology Manager **Lon Fairless** . . . . (972) 466-3178
E-mail: lon.fairless@cityofcarrollton.com

Marketing Services

City Hall, 1945 East Jackson Road, 2nd Floor, Carrollton, TX 75006
Fax: (972) 466-3175

Marketing Director **Kelli Lewis** . . . . (972) 466-4816

Parks and Recreation

4220 North Josey Lane, Carrollton, TX 75010
Fax: (972) 466-4722

Director **Scott Whitaker** . . . . (972) 466-3080

Police Department

2025 East Jackson Rd., Carrollton, TX 75006
Fax: (972) 466-3522

Police Chief **Rex Redden** . . . . (972) 466-3287

★ Elected Official ▲ Appointed by Legislature ▼ Appointed by Governor ▶ Appointed by Board or Commission ● Appointed by Judge
■ Appointed by Mayor △ Appointed by Freeholders ▽ Appointed by Supervisor ▷ Appointed by County Executive ○ Appointed by Council

Carrollton Public Library
4220 North Josey Lane, Carrollton, TX 75010
Fax: (972) 466-4722

City Librarian **Sue Haas** .... (972) 466-3362
E-mail: sue.haas@cityofcarrollton.com

Public Works Department
1945 E. Jackson Rd., Carrollton, TX 75006

Director **Robert Kopp** .... (972) 466-4291
Water and Wastewater Manager **Brian Little** .... (972) 466-3200

Workforce Services Department
1945 E. Jackson Rd., Carrollton, TX 75006
Fax: (972) 466-4789

Director **Chrystal Davis** .... (972) 466-3090
E-mail: chrystal.davis@cityofcarrollton.com

Carson City, Nevada

City Hall, 201 N. Carson St., Carson City, NV 89701-4289
Internet: www.carson.org

County: None **Election Type:** Nonpartisan **Population:** 54,521 (2015)

Office of the Mayor and Board of Supervisors
City Hall, 201 North Carson Street, Suite 2, Carson City, NV 89701

★ Mayor **Robert L. Crowell** .... (775) 887-2100
Began Service: January 1, 2009
Term Expires: January 2, 2017
E-mail: bcrowell@carson.org
Education: Stanford 1967 AB; Hastings 1973 JD
Career: President, Board of School Trustees, City of Carson City, Nevada (2005); Partner, Crowell, Susich, Tackes & Griffin, Ltd.

★ Supervisor **Karen Abowd** (Ward 1) .... (775) 887-2100
Term Expires: January 5, 2019
E-mail: kabowd@carson.org
Education: Nevada (Reno) BS

★ Supervisor **Brad Bonkowski** (Ward 2) .... (775) 887-2100
Term Expires: January 2, 2017
E-mail: bbonkowski@carson.org

★ Supervisor **Lori Bagwell** (Ward 3) .... (775) 887-2100
Term Expires: January 5, 2019

★ Supervisor **Jim Shirk** (Ward 4) .... (775) 887-2100
Term Expires: January 2, 2017
E-mail: jshirk@carson.org

Office of the Assessor
City Hall, 201 North Carson Street, Suite 6, Carson City, NV 89701-4289
Fax: (775) 887-2139 E-mail: assr@carson.org

★ Assessor **Dave Dawley** .... (775) 887-2130
Term Expires: January 1, 2019
E-mail: ddawley@carson.org

Office of the District Attorney
885 E. Musser St., Suite 2030, Carson City, NV 89701-3795

★ District Attorney **Jason Woodbury** .... (775) 887-2072
Term Expires: January 5, 2019
E-mail: jwoodbury@carson.org

Office of the Sheriff/Coroner
911 East Musser Street, Carson City, NV 89701
Fax: (775) 887-2026

★ Sheriff **Kenneth T. Furlong** .... (775) 887-2500
Term Expires: January 1, 2019
E-mail: kfurlong@carson.org

Office of the Treasurer
City Hall, 201 North Carson Street, Suite 5, Carson City, NV 89701-4289
Fax: (775) 887-2102

★ Treasurer **Gayle T. Robertson** .... (775) 887-2092
Term Expires: January 1, 2019
E-mail: treasurer@carson.org

Office of the City Manager
City Hall, 201 North Carson Street, Suite 2, Carson City, NV 89701-4289
Fax: (775) 887-2286 E-mail: cceo@carson.org

City Manager **Nick Marano** .... (775) 887-2100
E-mail: nmarano@carson.org
Deputy City Manager **(Vacant)** .... (775) 887-2100

Carson City Public Library
900 N. Roop St., Carson City, NV 89701-3101
Fax: (775) 887-2273 E-mail: cclb@carson.org

Director **Sena Loyd** .... (775) 887-2244
E-mail: sloyd@carson.org

Cooperative Extension
2621 Northgate Ln., Suite 15, Carson City, NV 89706-1619

Extension Educator **(Vacant)** .... (775) 887-2252

Finance Department
City Hall, 201 North Carson Street, Suite 3, Carson City, NV 89701-5218
Fax: (775) 887-2107

Chief Financial Officer **Nancy Paulson** .... (775) 887-2133

Purchasing and Contracts Division
201 North Carson Street, Suite 11, Carson City, NV 89701-4289
Fax: (775) 887-2107 E-mail: purchasing@carson.org

Coordinator **Laura Tadman** .... (775) 283-7137
E-mail: ltadman@carson.org

Fire Department
777 S. Stewart St., Carson City, NV 89701-5218
Fax: (775) 887-2210 E-mail: ccfd@carson.org

Fire Chief/Emergency Manager
Robert Schreihans .... (775) 887-2210 ext. 4
E-mail: rschreihansi@carson.org

Emergency Management Division
777 S. Stewart St., Carson City, NV 89701-5218

Deputy Emergency Manager **Stacey Belt** .... (775) 887-2210 ext. 4
E-mail: sbelt@carson.org

Health and Human Services Department
900 East Long Street, Carson City, NV 89706
E-mail: cchealth@carson.org Internet: http://gethealthycarsoncity.org/

Health Director **Nicki Aaker** .... (775) 887-2190

Human Resource Department
City Hall, 201 North Carson Street, Suite 4, Carson City, NV 89701-4289
Fax: (775) 887-2067 E-mail: cchr@carson.org

Director **Melanie Bruketta** .... (775) 887-2103
E-mail: mbruketta@carson.org

Information Technology Department
City Hall, 201 North Carson Street, Suite 7, Carson City, NV 89701-4289
Fax: (775) 887-2288

Chief Information Officer **Eric Von Schimmelmann** .... (775) 887-2160

★ Elected Official ▲ Appointed by Legislature ▼ Appointed by Governor ▶ Appointed by Board or Commission ● Appointed by Judge
■ Appointed by Mayor △ Appointed by Freeholders ▽ Appointed by Supervisor ▷ Appointed by County Executive ○ Appointed by Council

Juvenile Detention/Probation Department

1545 E. Fifth St., Carson City, NV 89701-5023
Fax: (775) 887-2036

Chief Juvenile Probation Officer **Ben Bianchi** . . . . (775) 887-2033

Parks and Recreation Department

Bldg. #9, 3303 Butti Way, Carson City, NV 89701-3488
Fax: (775) 887-2145 E-mail: ccpr@carson.org

Director **Roger Moellendorf** . . . . (775) 887-2262

Public Works Department

3505 Butti Way, Carson City, NV 89701-3488

Public Works Director **Darren Schulz** . . . . (775) 887-2355
Operations Chief **Curtis Horton** . . . . (775) 283-7378
E-mail: chorton@carson.org
Water Operations Manager **Rit Palmer** . . . . (775) 283-7393
E-mail: rpalmer@carson.org

Building and Safety Division

108 East Proctor Street, Carson City, NV 89701-4240
Fax: (775) 887-2202

Chief Building Official **Shawn Keating** . . . . (775) 887-2310

Business License Division

108 East Proctor Street, Carson City, NV 89701-4240
Fax: (775) 887-2202

Manager **Lena Reseck** . . . . (775) 887-2310 ext. 7059

Development Engineering Division

3505 Butti Way, Suite 54, Carson City, NV 89701-3498

Engineering Manager **Daniel Rotter** . . . . (775) 283-7084
E-mail: drotter@carson.org

Planning and Community Development Division

108 East Proctor Street, Carson City, NV 89701-4240
Fax: (775) 887-2278 E-mail: plandept@carson.org

Director **Lee Plemel** . . . . (775) 887-2180

Streets Division

Building 7, 3505 Butti Way, Carson City, NV 89701-3488

Transportation Manager **Patrick Pittenger** . . . . (775) 283-7396

Town of Cary, North Carolina

Town Hall, 316 North Academy Street, Cary, NC 27513
Internet: www.townofcary.org

County: Chatham; Wake **Election Type:** Nonpartisan
Population: 159,769 (2015)

Office of the Mayor and Town Council

Town Hall, 316 North Academy Street, Cary, NC 27513

★ Mayor **Harold Weinbrecht, Jr.** . . . . (919) 469-4011
Began Service: December 1999 Fax: (919) 460-4910
Term Expires: December 2019
E-mail: harold.weinbrecht@townofcary.org
Date of Birth: June 2, 1956
Education: North Carolina State BS
★ Mayor Pro Tem **Ed Yerha** (At-Large) . . . . (919) 469-4011
Term Expires: December 2017
E-mail: ed.yerha@townofcary.org
★ Council Member **Jennifer Robinson** (District A) . . . . (919) 469-4011
Term Expires: December 2017 Fax: (919) 460-4910
E-mail: jennifer.robinson@townofcary.org
Date of Birth: February 14, 1970
Education: Virginia BA

Office of the Mayor and Town Council *continued*

★ Council Member **Don Frantz** (District B) . . . . (919) 612-6870
Term Expires: December 2019 Fax: (919) 481-0733
E-mail: don.frantz@townofcary.org
Date of Birth: May 18, 1971
★ Council Member **Jack Smith** (District C) . . . . (919) 460-4910
Term Expires: December 2017 Fax: (919) 854-0766
E-mail: jack.smith@townofcary.org
Education: Oklahoma BS
★ Council Member **Ken George** (District D) . . . . (919) 469-4011
Term Expires: December 2019
E-mail: ken.george@townofcary.org
★ Council Member **Lori Bush** (At-Large) . . . . (919) 469-4011
Term Expires: December 2019
E-mail: lori.bush@townofcary.org

Office of the Town Manager

Town Hall, 316 North Academy Street, Cary, NC 27513
Fax: (919) 460-4910

Town Manager (Interim) **Michael "Mike" Bajorek** . . . . . . (919) 469-4007
E-mail: mike.bajorek@townofcary.org
Deputy Town Manager **Michael "Mike" Bajorek** . . . . (919) 469-4007
E-mail: mike.bajorek@townofcary.org
Assistant Town Manager **Tim Bailey** . . . . (919) 469-4007
E-mail: tim.bailey@townofcary.org
Assistant Town Manager **Russ Overton** . . . . (919) 469-4007
E-mail: russ.overton@townofcary.org
Budget Director **Karl Knapp** . . . . (919) 462-3911
E-mail: karl.knapp@townofcary.org
Public Information Officer **Susan Moran** . . . . (919) 469-4951
E-mail: susan.moran@townofcary.org Fax: (919) 460-4910
Downtown Manager **Ted Boyd** . . . . (919) 469-5007
E-mail: ted.boyd@townofcary.org

Office of the Town Clerk

316 North Academy Street, Cary, NC 27513
Fax: (919) 460-4910

Town Clerk **Virginia Johnson** . . . . (919) 460-4941
E-mail: Virginia.johnson@townofcary.org
Deputy Town Clerk **Karen Gray** . . . . (919) 469-4011
E-mail: karen.gray@townofcary.org

Finance Department

Town Hall, 316 North Academy Street, First Floor, Cary, NC 27513
Tel: (919) 469-4380 Fax: (919) 469-4306

Finance Director **Karen Mills** . . . . (919) 469-4110
Controller **Michelle Price** . . . . (919) 469-4048
Deputy Treasurer **Mary Beth Huber** . . . . (919) 462-3957
Accounting Operations Manager **Susan Morey** . . . . (919) 469-4312
E-mail: susan.morey@townofcary.org
Procurement and Risk Services Manager **Cheryl Perry** . . . (919) 469-4077
E-mail: cheryl.perry@townofcary.org

Fire Department

100 North Academy Street, Cary, NC 27513
Fax: (919) 460-4911

Fire Chief **Allan Cain** . . . . (919) 469-4058
E-mail: allan.cain@townofcary.org
Assistant Fire Chief, Logistics **David Ranes** . . . . (919) 319-4578
E-mail: david.ranes@townofcary.org
Assistant Fire Chief, Operations **Mike Cooper** . . . . (919) 469-4378
E-mail: mike.cooper@townofcary.org
Assistant Fire Chief, Training and Safety **Ed Moore** . . . . . (919) 462-3825
E-mail: ed.moore@townofcary.org

★ Elected Official ▲ Appointed by Legislature ▼ Appointed by Governor ► Appointed by Board or Commission ● Appointed by Judge
■ Appointed by Mayor △ Appointed by Freeholders ▽ Appointed by Supervisor ▷ Appointed by County Executive ○ Appointed by Council

Human Resources Department
Town Hall, 316 North Academy Street, Cary, NC 27513
Tel: (919) 469-4070 Fax: (919) 319-4567

Director **Renee Poole** .... (919) 469-4373
E-mail: renee.poole@townofcary.org
Employee Benefits Manager **Laura Turk** .... (919) 481-5195
E-mail: laura.turk@townofcary.org
Employee Relations Manager **Karen Spurlin** .... (919) 469-4075
E-mail: karen.spurlin@townofcary.org
Employee Safety Coordinator **Gail O'Connell** .... (919) 460-4975
E-mail: gail.oconnell@townofcary.org

Inspections and Permits Department
Town Hall, 316 North Academy Street, Cary, NC 27513
Tel: (919) 469-4043 Fax: (919) 462-3840

Director **Scot Berry** .... (919) 469-4046
Chief Code Enforcement Official **Doug Beninate** .... (919) 469-4345

Parks, Recreation and Cultural Resources Department
City Hall, 316 North Academy Street, Cary, NC 27513
Fax: (919) 469-4344

Director **Doug McRainey** .... (919) 469-4061
Athletics Program Manager **William Davis** .... (919) 469-4062
Cultural Arts Manager **Lyman Collins** .... (919) 469-4061
Recreation Programs Manager **Dwayne Jones** .... (919) 469-4061
Marketing Specialist **Jennifer Warner** .... (919) 469-4061

Planning Department
Town Hall, 316 North Academy Street, 3rd Floor, Cary, NC 27513
Tel: (919) 469-4082 Fax: (919) 388-1103

Director **Jeff Ulma** .... (919) 319-4580
GIS Planning Supervisor **Bill Moore** .... (919) 462-3883
Regulations and Compliance Principal Planner
Rob Wilson .... (919) 462-3885

Police Department
Town Hall, 316 North Academy Street, Cary, NC 27513
Fax: (919) 460-4904

Chief of Police **Tony Godwin** .... (919) 469-4023

Public Works and Utilities Department
400 James Jackson Avenue, Cary, NC 27513
Fax: (919) 469-4304

Public Works Director **Scott Hecht** .... (919) 469-4090
Utilities Director **Jamie Revels** .... (919) 469-4090

Technology Services Department
120 Wilkinson Avenue, Cary, NC 27513
Fax: (919) 319-4597

Chief Information Officer **Nicole Raimundo** .... (919) 462-3925
E-mail: nicole.raimundo@townofcary.org

Transportation and Facilities Department
Town Hall, 316 North Academy Street, Cary, NC 27513
Fax: (919) 469-4030

Director **Lori Cove** .... (919) 462-3937
E-mail: lori.cove@townofcary.org
Civil Design Technical Services Supervisor
Paul Middleton .... (919) 460-4931
E-mail: paul.middleton@townofcary.org
Real Estate Manager **Donna Lunsford** .... (919) 469-4039
E-mail: donna.lunsford@townofcary.org
Traffic and Transportation Engineering Manager
Jerry J. Jensen .... (919) 469-4035
E-mail: Jerry.jensen@townofcary.org
Sustainability Manager **Emily Barrett** .... (919) 469-5125

Water Resources
316 North Academy Street, Cary, NC 27513
Fax: (919) 460-4935

Director of Water Resources **Stephen J. Brown** .... (919) 462-3830
Stormwater Engineering Manager **Billy Lee** .... (919) 462-3932
E-mail: billy.lee@townofcary.org
Utility Engineering Manager **Glen Harrell** .... (919) 460-4933
E-mail: glen.harrell@townofcary.org
Infrastructure Field Services Manager **David Johnson** .... (919) 462-3832
E-mail: david.johnson@townofcary.org

City of Cedar Rapids, Iowa
101 First Street, SE, Cedar Rapids, IA 52401
Tel: (319) 286-5555 (Information) Internet: www.cedar-rapids.org

County: Linn **Election Type:** Nonpartisan **Year Incorporated:** 1848
Charter: 1908 **Population:** 130,405 (2015)

Office of the Mayor and City Council
101 First Street, SE, Cedar Rapids, IA 52401

★ Mayor **Ron Corbett** .... (319) 286-5051
Began Service: January 1, 2010
Term Expires: December 31, 2017
E-mail: ron.corbett@cedar-rapids.org
★ Council Member **Kris Gulick** (District 1) .... (319) 286-5051
Term Expires: December 31, 2017
E-mail: kris.gulick@cedar-rapids.org
Education: Northern Iowa 1980 BS; Iowa 1982 MA; Coe 1986 BS
★ Council Member **Scott Overland** (District 2) .... (319) 286-5051
Term Expires: December 31, 2019
E-mail: s.overland@cedar-rapids.org
★ Council Member **Pat Shey** (District 3) .... (319) 286-5051
Term Expires: December 31, 2017
E-mail: pat.shey@cedar-rapids.org
★ Council Member **Scott Olson** (District 4) .... (319) 286-5051
Term Expires: December 31, 2019
E-mail: scott.olson@cedar-rapids.org
★ Council Member **Justin Shields** (District 5) .... (319) 286-5051
Term Expires: December 31, 2017
E-mail: justin.shields@cedar-rapids.org
★ Council Member **Ann Poe** (At-Large) .... (319) 286-5051
Term Expires: December 31, 2019
E-mail: ann.poe@cedar-rapids.org
★ Council Member **Ralph Russell** (At-Large) .... (319) 286-5051
Term Expires: December 31, 2017
★ Council Member **Susie Weinacht** (At-Large) .... (319) 286-5051
Term Expires: December 31, 2019

Office of the City Manager
101 First Street, SE, Cedar Rapids, IA 52401

City Manager **Jeff Pomeranz** .... (319) 286-5080
E-mail: citymanager@cedar-rapids.org
Assistant City Manager **Sandi Fowler** .... (319) 286-5080
E-mail: s.fowler@cedar-rapids.org
Communications Division Manager **Maria Johnson** .... (319) 286-5080

Office of the Assessor
1211 6th Street, SW, Cedar Rapids, IA 52404

○ Assessor **Beth Weeks** .... (319) 286-5888

Office of the City Clerk
101 First Street, SE, Cedar Rapids, IA 52401
Fax: (319) 286-5130

○ City Clerk **Amy Stevenson** .... (319) 286-5060
E-mail: a.stevenson@cedar-rapids.org

★ Elected Official ▲ Appointed by Legislature ▼ Appointed by Governor ► Appointed by Board or Commission ● Appointed by Judge
■ Appointed by Mayor △ Appointed by Freeholders ▽ Appointed by Supervisor ▷ Appointed by County Executive ○ Appointed by Council

Office of the City Attorney
101 First Street, SE, Cedar Rapids, IA 52401

○ City Attorney **James Flitz** .... (319) 286-5025
E-mail: jamesf@cedar-rapids.org

Community Development and Planning Department
101 First Street, SE, Cedar Rapids, IA 52401
Fax: (319) 286-5130 E-mail: communitydevelopment@cedar-rapids.org

Community Development Director **Jennifer Pratt** .... (319) 268-5047
E-mail: j.pratt@cedar-rapids.org
Assistant Director **Bill Micheel** .... (319) 268-5045
E-mail: w.micheel@cedar-rapids.org

Building Services Department
500 15th Avenue, SW, Cedar Rapids, IA 52404

Building Official **Kevin Ciabatti** .... (319) 286-5831

Development Services Department
101 First Street, SE, Cedar Rapids, IA 52401

Executive Administrator **Sandi Fowler** .... (319) 286-5077
E-mail: s.fowler@cedar-rapids.org
Development Services Manager **Joe Mailander** .... (319) 286-5822

Eastern Iowa Airport
2515 Wright Brothers Blvd., SW, Cedar Rapids, IA 52404

Director **Martin Lenss** .... (319) 362-3131

Finance Department
101 First Street, SE, Cedar Rapids, IA 52401

Finance Director **Casey Drew** .... (319) 286-5006
E-mail: c.drew@cedar-rapids.org

Fire Department
713 1st Avenue, SE, Cedar Rapids, IA 52403

Fire Chief **Mark English** .... (319) 286-5201
E-mail: m.english@cedar-rapids.org

Human Resources Department
101 First Street, SE, Cedar Rapids, IA 52401
Fax: (888) 611-7101

Director **Conni Huber** .... (319) 286-5000
E-mail: c.huber@cedar-rapids.org

Information Technology Department
500 15th Avenue, SW, Cedar Rapids, IA 52404

Chief Information Officer **Nic Roberts** .... (319) 286-5500
E-mail: n.roberts@cedar-rapids.org

Parks and Recreation
4900 Council Street, NE, Cedar Rapids, IA 52402

Parks and Recreation Director **Sven Leff** .... (319) 286-5731

Police Department
505 1st St., SW, Cedar Rapids, IA 52404

Chief of Police **Wayne Jerman** .... (319) 286-5375
Deputy Chief of Police **Tom Jonker** .... (319) 286-5375

Cedar Rapids Public Library
425 4th Avenue, SE, Suite 330, Cedar Rapids, IA 52401
Internet: www.crlibrary.org

Director **Dara Schmidt** .... (319) 398-5123
E-mail: schmidtd@crlibrary.org

Public Works Department
500 15th Avenue, SW, Cedar Rapids, IA 52404

Public Works Director/City Engineer **Jen L. Winter** .... (319) 286-5803
E-mail: j.winter@cedar-rapids.org

Solid Waste and Recycling Services Department
500 15th Avenue, SW, Cedar Rapids, IA 52404

Manager **Mark Jones** .... (319) 286-5897

Utilities Division
1111 Shaver Rd., NE, Cedar Rapids, IA 52404

Utilities Director **Steve Hershner** .... (319) 286-5900
E-mail: s.hershner@cedar-rapids.org

City of Centennial, Colorado

13133 East Arapahoe Road, Centennial, CO 80112
Tel: (303) 325-8000 Fax: (720) 488-0933
Internet: http://www.centennialco.gov/

County: Arapahoe **Year Incorporated:** 2001 **Charter:** June 10, 2008
Population: 109,741 (2015)

Office of the Mayor and City Council
13133 East Arapahoe Road, Centennial, CO 80112

★ Mayor **Cathy Noon** (At-Large) .... (303) 754-3350
Term Expires: January 2018
E-mail: cnoon@centennialco.gov
Education: Maryland Baltimore County; Colorado (Denver)
★ Mayor Pro Tem **Kenneth L. "Ken" Lucas** (District 3) .... (303) 754-3367
Term Expires: January 2020
E-mail: klucas@centennialco.gov
★ Council Member **Candace Moon** (District 1) .... (303) 754-3324
Term Expires: January 1, 2020
E-mail: cmoon@CentennialCO.gov
★ Council Member **Kathy Turley** (District 1) .... (303) 754-3352
Term Expires: January 2018
E-mail: kturley@centennialco.gov
★ Council Member **Carrie Penaloza** (District 2) .... (303) 754-3324
Term Expires: January 2020
E-mail: cpenaloza@CentennialCO.gov
★ Council Member **Doris Truhlar** (District 2) .... (720) 934-4645
Term Expires: January 6, 2018
E-mail: dtruhlar@centennialco.gov
★ Council Member **Mark Gotto** (District 3) .... (303) 754-3405
Term Expires: January 2018
E-mail: mgotto@centennialco.gov
★ Council Member **Stephanie Piko** (District 4) .... (303) 754-3374
Term Expires: January 1, 2020
E-mail: spiko@centennialco.gov
★ Council Member **Charles "CJ" Whelan** (District 4) .... (303) 754-3343
Term Expires: January 2018
E-mail: cwhelan@centennialco.gov

Office of the City Manager
13133 East Arapahoe Road, Centennial, CO 80112

○ City Manager **John Danielson** .... (303) 754-3375
E-mail: jdanielson@centennialco.gov
Innovation Team Manager **Scott Blumenreich** .... (303) 754-3375

Office of Code Enforcement
13133 East Arapahoe Road, Centennial, CO 80112

Code Enforcement Officer **Tamara Gregory** .... (303) 754-3320

★ Elected Official ▲ Appointed by Legislature ▼ Appointed by Governor ► Appointed by Board or Commission ● Appointed by Judge
■ Appointed by Mayor △ Appointed by Freeholders ▽ Appointed by Supervisor ▷ Appointed by County Executive ○ Appointed by Council

Office of Communications
13133 East Arapahoe Road, Centennial, CO 80112

Communications Director **Sheri Chadwick** ....(303) 754-3443
E-mail: schadwick@centennialco.gov

Office of Economic Development
13133 East Arapahoe Road, Centennial, CO 80112
Fax: (720) 488-0933

Manager **Neil Marciniak** ....(303) 754-3351
E-mail: nmarciniak@CentennialCO.gov

Office of Support Services
13133 East Arapahoe Road, Centennial, CO 80112
Tel: (303) 325-8000

Deputy City Manager **Wayne Reed** ....(303) 325-8000
E-mail: wreed@centennialco.gov
Information Technology Manager **Carla Coburn** ....(303) 325-8000
E-mail: ccoburn@centennialco.gov

Community Development
13133 East Arapahoe Road, Centennial, CO 80112

Director of Community Development **Andy Firestine** ....(303) 754-3336
E-mail: afirestine@centennialco.gov

Finance Department
13133 East Arapahoe Road, Centennial, CO 80112

Director **Dawn Priday** ....(303) 325-8000

Human Resources Department
13133 East Arapahoe Road, Centennial, CO 80112
Tel: (303) 325-8000 E-mail: resumes@centennialco.gov

Director **Paula Gibson** ....(303) 325-8000
E-mail: pgibson@centennialco.gov Fax: (303) 648-4111

Public Works Department
13133 East Arapahoe Road, Centennial, CO 80112
Tel: (303) 325-8000

Director **Craig Faessler** ....(303) 325-8000

Office of the City Clerk
13133 East Arapahoe Road, Centennial, CO 80112
Tel: (303) 754-3324

City Clerk **Barbara Setterlind** ....(303) 754-3324
E-mail: bsetterlind@centennialco.gov
Deputy City Clerk **Ebony Brewington** ....(303) 754-3324
E-mail: ebrewington@centennialco.gov
Licensing and Records Clerk **Sandra Maxwell** ....(303) 754-3324
E-mail: smaxwell@centennialco.gov

City of Chandler, Arizona

P.O. Box 4008, Chandler, AZ 85244
Internet: www.chandleraz.gov

County: Maricopa **Election Type:** Nonpartisan **Year Incorporated:** 1920 **Population:** 260,828 (2015)

Office of the Mayor and City Council
175 South Arizona Avenue, 5th Floor, Chandler, AZ 85225
P.O. Box 4008, Chandler, AZ 85244
Fax: (480) 782-2233 E-mail: mayor&council@chandleraz.gov

★ Mayor **Jay Tibshraeny** ....(480) 782-2200
Began Service: January 13, 2011
Term Expires: January 2019
Education: Arizona State BS
Career: Mayor, City of Chandler, Arizona (1994-2002); Majority Whip, Arizona Senate (2006)
★ Vice Mayor **Jack Sellers** ....(480) 782-2200
Term Expires: January 2017
★ Council Member **Nora Ellen** ....(480) 782-2200
Term Expires: January 2017
★ Council Member **Kevin Hartke** ....(480) 782-2200
Term Expires: January 2019
★ Council Member **Rick Heumann** ....(480) 782-2200
Term Expires: January 2017
★ Council Member **Rene Lopez** ....(480) 782-2200
Term Expires: January 2019
★ Council Member **Terry Roe** ....(480) 782-2200
Term Expires: January 2019

Office of the City Attorney
175 South Arizona Avenue, 2nd Floor, Chandler, AZ 85225
Fax: (480) 782-4652

○ City Attorney **Kay Bigelow** ....(480) 782-4640
E-mail: kay.bigelow@chandleraz.gov

Office of the City Clerk
175 South Arizona Avenue, 1st Floor, Chandler, AZ 85225
Fax: (480) 782-2185

○ City Clerk **Marla Paddock** ....(480) 782-2182
E-mail: marla.paddock@chandleraz.gov

Office of the City Magistrate
200 E. Chicago St., Chandler, AZ 85225
Fax: (480) 782-4752

○ Presiding City Magistrate **Michael Traynor** ....(480) 782-4740
E-mail: michael.traynor@chandleraz.gov

Office of the City Manager
175 South Arizona Avenue, 5th Floor, Chandler, AZ 85225
Fax: (480) 782-2209

City Manager **Marsha Reed** ....(480) 782-2210
E-mail: marsha.reed@chandleraz.gov
Education: Texas Tech 1988 BSCE, 2000 MPA
Assistant City Manager **Nachie Marquez** ....(480) 782-2210
E-mail: nachie.marquez@chandleraz.gov
Assistant City Manager **(Vacant)** ....(480) 782-2210
Intergovernmental Affairs Coordinator **Ryan Peters** ......(480) 782-2210

Airport Administration
Chandler Municipal Airport, 2380 S. Stinson Way, Chandler, AZ 85249
Fax: (480) 782-3541

Airport Administrator **Chris Andres** ....(480) 782-3540

★ Elected Official ▲ Appointed by Legislature ▼ Appointed by Governor ▶ Appointed by Board or Commission ● Appointed by Judge
■ Appointed by Mayor △ Appointed by Freeholders ▽ Appointed by Supervisor ▷ Appointed by County Executive ○ Appointed by Council

Chandler Public Library
22 S. Delaware St., Chandler, AZ 85225

Cultural Affairs Director **Brenda Brown** .... (480) 782-2817
E-mail: brenda.brown@chandleraz.gov

Communications and Public Affairs Department
175 South Arizona Avenue, 5th Floor, Chandler, AZ 85225
Fax: (480) 782-2209

Director **Matthew Burdick** .... (480) 782-2232
E-mail: matthew.burdick@chandleraz.gov
Chief Information Officer **Steven Philbrick** .... (480) 782-2441
E-mail: steven.philbrick@chandleraz.gov Fax: (480) 782-2440

Community and Neighborhood Services
175 South Arizona Avenue, 4th Floor, Chandler, AZ 85225
Fax: (480) 782-2713

Director (Acting) **Leah Powell** .... (480) 782-2660
E-mail: leah.powell@chandleraz.gov

Recreation Division
125 E. Commonwealth Ave., Chandler, AZ 85225
Fax: (480) 782-2713

Director (Acting) **Barbara Young** .... (480) 782-2727

Chandler Fire, Health and Medical Department
151 East Boston Street, Chandler, AZ 85225
Fax: (480) 782-2125

Fire Chief (Interim) **Tom Dwiggins** .... (480) 782-2120
E-mail: tom.dwiggins@chandleraz.gov
Fire Marshal **Marcina Sunderhaus** .... (480) 782-2135
E-mail: marcina.sunderhaus@chandleraz.gov

Human Resources Department
175 South Arizona Avenue, 2nd Floor, Chandler, AZ 85225

Director **Deborah Stapleton** .... (480) 782-2351
E-mail: deborah.stapleton@chandleraz.gov
Organizational Development Coordinator
Beth Chepelsky .... (480) 782-2351

Management Services Department
175 South Arizona Avenue, 3rd Floor, Chandler, AZ 85225
Fax: (480) 782-2253

Director **Dawn Lang** .... (480) 782-2250

Purchasing Division
175 South Arizona Avenue, 3rd Floor, Chandler, AZ 85225

Purchasing Manager **Christina Pryor** .... (480) 782-2400
E-mail: christina.pryor@chandleraz.gov
Purchasing and Material Supervisor **Jose Tapia** .... (480) 782-2416
E-mail: jose.tapia@chandleraz.gov

Municipal Utilities
975 East Armstrong Way, Chandler, AZ 85248

Director (Acting) **Gregg Capps** .... (480) 782-3800

Transportation and Development Department
215 East Buffalo Street, Suite 104, Chandler, AZ 85225
Fax: (480) 782-3010

Director **R.J. Zeder** .... (480) 782-3019
E-mail: rj.zeder@chandleraz.gov

Police Department
250 E. Chicago St., Chandler, AZ 85225
Fax: (480) 782-4110

Chief of Police **Sean Duggan** .... (480) 782-4101

Public Works Administration
215 E. Buffalo St., Chandler, AZ 85225
Fax: (480) 782-3415

Director **R.J. Zeder** .... (480) 782-3401

City of Charleston, South Carolina

City Hall, 80 Broad St., Charleston, SC 29401
P.O. Box 652, Charleston, SC 29402
Tel: (843) 577-6970 (Information) Internet: www.charleston-sc.gov

County: Charleston **Election Type:** Nonpartisan **Population:** 130,113 (2015)

Office of the Mayor
P.O. Box 652, Charleston, SC 29402
Fax: (843) 720-3827

★ Mayor **John Tecklenburg** .... (843) 577-6970
Began Service: January 11, 2016
Term Expires: January 2020

Children, Youth and Families, Mayor's Office of
50 Broad Street, Charleston, SC 29401
Fax: (843) 965-4192

Executive Director **Mindy Sturm** .... (843) 965-4190

City Council
P.O. Box 304, Charleston, SC 29402
Fax: (843) 720-3959

★ Council Member **F. Gary White, Jr.** (District 1) .... (843) 364-1876
Term Expires: January 2020
E-mail: whiteg@charleston-sc.gov
★ Council Member **Rodney Williams** (District 2) .... (843) 822-8024
Term Expires: January 2018
★ Council Member **James Lewis, Jr.** (District 3) .... (843) 219-8018
Term Expires: January 2020
★ Council Member **Robert M. Mitchell** (District 4) .... (843) 853-2057
Term Expires: January 2018
E-mail: mitchellro@charleston-sc.gov
★ Council Member **Marvin Wagner** (District 5) .... (843) 723-7458
Term Expires: January 2020
E-mail: wagnerm@charleston-sc.gov
★ Council Member **William Dudley Gregorie** (District 6) .. (843) 720-1232
Term Expires: January 1, 2018
E-mail: gregoriewd@charleston-sc.gov
Education: Benedict BS; Howard U MA
★ Council Member **Perry K. Waring** (District 7) .... (843) 763-5388
Term Expires: January 2020
E-mail: waringp@charleston-sc.gov
Education: South Carolina 1977 BS
★ Council Member
Michael S. "Mike" Seekings (District 8) .... (843) 364-8583
Term Expires: January 2018
E-mail: seekingsm@charleston-sc.gov
★ Council Member **Peter Shahid** (District 9) .... (843) 724-3727
Term Expires: January 2020
★ Council Member **Dean C. Riegel** (District 10) .... (843) 708-0245
Term Expires: January 1, 2018 Fax: (843) 747-7150
E-mail: riegeld@charleston-sc.gov
Education: Ohio State 1972 BS; Central Michigan 1976 MA
★ Council Member **Bill Moody** (District 11) .... (843) 364-5292
Term Expires: January 2020
E-mail: moodyw@charleston-sc.gov
Education: Citadel 1965 BS

(continued on next page)

★ Elected Official ▲ Appointed by Legislature ▼ Appointed by Governor ▶ Appointed by Board or Commission ● Appointed by Judge
■ Appointed by Mayor △ Appointed by Freeholders ▽ Appointed by Supervisor ▷ Appointed by County Executive ○ Appointed by Council

City Council *continued*

★Council Member **Kathleen Wilson** (District 12) .... (843) 795-7507
Term Expires: January 2018
E-mail: aquaharp@bellsouth.net
Clerk of Council **Vanessa Turner-Maybank** .... (843) 724-3727
E-mail: maybankv@charleston-sc.gov

Legal Department
P.O. Box 304, Charleston, SC 29402
Corporation Counsel **Frances Cantwell** .... (843) 724-3730

Budget, Finance and Revenue Collections Department
116 Meeting Street, Charleston, SC 29401
Fax: (843) 579-7529
Chief Financial Officer **Stephen A. Bedard** .... (843) 579-7529

Cultural Affairs Office
180 Meeting Street, Suite 200, Charleston, SC 29401
Fax: (843) 720-3967
Director **Scott Watson** .... (843) 724-7305

Fire Department
46 1/2 Wentworth Street, Charleston, SC 29401
Tel: (843) 720-1981 Fax: (843) 720-3991
■Fire Chief **Karen E. Brack** .... (843) 720-1981
E-mail: kbrack@charleston-sc.gov
Deputy Fire Chief (Acting) **William F. Finley** .... (843) 720-1981
E-mail: wfinley@charleston-sc.gov

Housing and Community Development Department
145 King Street, Suite 400, Charleston, SC 29401
Director **Geona S. Johnson** .... (843) 724-3766
E-mail: housing&cd@charleston-sc.gov

Human Resources and Organizational Development Department
75 Calhoun Street, Suite 3600, Charleston, SC 29401
Fax: (843) 724-7358
Director **Kay Cross** .... (843) 724-7388
E-mail: crossk@charleston-sc.gov

Parks Department
823 Meeting Street, Charleston, SC 29403
Fax: (843) 724-7300
Director **Jerry Ebeling** .... (843) 724-7324

Planning, Preservation and Sustainability
75 Calhoun Street, Charleston, SC 29401
Fax: (843) 724-3772
Director **Jacob Lindsey** .... (843) 958-6473

Police Department
180 Lockwood Boulevard, Charleston, SC 29403
Chief of Police **Gregory Mullen** .... (843) 720-2401

Public Information Office
50 Broad Street, Charleston, SC 29401
Fax: (843) 724-3734
Media Relations and Public Information Director
Jack O'Toole .... (843) 518-3288
E-mail: otoolej@charleston-sc.gov

Public Service Department
75 Calhoun Street, Charleston, SC 29401
Fax: (843) 973-7261
Director **Laura S. Cabiness** .... (843) 724-3754
Deputy Director of Operations **Michael R. Metzler** ...... (843) 958-6492
2150 Milford Street, Charleston, SC 29405
E-mail: metzlerm@charleston-sc.gov

Engineering-Technical Services Division
Fax: (843) 724-7198
Deputy Director of Technical Services
Thomas F. O'Brien .... (843) 724-3761
E-mail: tobrien@charleston-sc.gov

Environmental Services Division
2150 Milford Street, Charleston, SC 29405
Superintendent **Sam Price** .... (843) 724-7365
Fax: (843) 805-3231

Charleston Water System
103 St. Philip Street, Charleston, SC 29403
P.O. Box B, Charleston, SC 29402
Tel: (843) 727-6800 Fax: (843) 727-7121
Internet: www.charlestonwater.com
Chairman **Thomas B. Pritchard** .... (843) 727-6856
Vice Chairman **David E. Rivers** .... (843) 727-6856
Commissioner **William E. Koopman, Jr.** .... (843) 727-6856
Ex Officio Commissioner **John Tecklenburg** .... (843) 727-6856
Ex Officio Commissioner **Perry K. Waring** .... (843) 727-6856
Education: South Carolina 1977 BS
Chief Executive Officer **Kin Hill** .... (843) 727-6856
Chief Administrative Officer **Dorothy Harrison** .... (843) 727-6856
Chief Financial Officer **Wesley Ropp** .... (843) 727-6856
Chief Operating Officer **Andy Fairey** .... (843) 727-6856
Capital Projects Officer **Mark Cline** .... (843) 727-6856

Recreation Department
823 Meeting Street, Charleston, SC 29403
Fax: (843) 720-3943
Director **Laurie Yarbrough** .... (843) 724-7470

Office of Tourism Management
32 Ann Street, Charleston, SC 29403
Fax: (843) 579-7673
Director **Vanessa Turner-Maybank** .... (843) 724-7395

Traffic and Transportation Department
180 Lockwood Drive, Charleston, SC 29403
Director **Hernan Peña, Jr.** .... (843) 724-7368

City of Charleston, West Virginia

City Hall, 501 Virginia St. East, Charleston, WV 25301
P.O. Box 2749, Charleston, WV 25330
Tel: (304) 348-8000 (Information) Internet: www.cityofcharleston.org

County: Kanawha **Election Type:** Partisan **Population:** 49,736 (2015)

Office of the Mayor and City Council
501 Virginia St. East, Charleston, WV 25301
Fax: (304) 348-8034 Tel: (304) 348-8179

★Mayor **Danny Jones** (R) .... (304) 348-8174
Began Service: 2003
Term Expires: June 16, 2019

★Elected Official ▲Appointed by Legislature ▼Appointed by Governor ▶Appointed by Board or Commission ●Appointed by Judge
■Appointed by Mayor △Appointed by Freeholders ▽Appointed by Supervisor ▷Appointed by County Executive ○Appointed by Council

Office of the Mayor and City Council *continued*

Senior Assistant to the Mayor **Rod Blackstone** . . . . (304) 348-8174
E-mail: rod.blackstone@cityofcharleston.org
Date of Birth: August 4, 1963
Education: Syracuse 1985 ABJ

Administrative Executive Assistant **Beverly Page** . . . . . . (304) 348-8174
E-mail: beverly.page@cityofcharleston.org

★Council Member **Bernard Slater** (D-Ward 1) . . . . (304) 348-8179
Term Expires: June 15, 2019
E-mail: brutusjr@gmail.com

★Council Member **Bobby Haas** (D-Ward 2) . . . . (304) 345-2236
Term Expires: June 16, 2019
E-mail: bobbyhaas1586@yahoo.com

★Council Member
Charles "Chuck" Overstreet (D-Ward 3) . . . . (304) 348-8179
Term Expires: June 16, 2019
E-mail: covers6053@aol.com

★Council Member **Rev. James Ealy** (D-Ward 4) . . . . (304) 343-5240
Term Expires: June 2019
E-mail: jamesealy@hotmail.com

★Council Member **Jeanine Faegre** (D-Ward 5) . . . . (304) 348-8179
Term Expires: June 16, 2019
E-mail: jfaegre@hotmail.com

★Council Member **Edward Talkington** (D-Ward 6) . . . . (304) 545-5162
Term Expires: June 2019
E-mail: ed.talkington@cityofcharleston.org

★Council Member
Arthur J. "Archie" Chestnut (D-Ward 7) . . . . (304) 741-0781
Term Expires: June 16, 2019
E-mail: archiechestnut@frontier.com

★Council Member **Cubert Smith** (I-Ward 8) . . . . (304) 344-1958
Term Expires: June 16, 2019
E-mail: cuberts@yahoo.com

★Council Member **Mary Beth Hoover** (D-Ward 9) . . . . (304) 543-4082
Term Expires: June 16, 2019
E-mail: hoovermb74@hotmail.com

★Council Member **Keeley Steele** (D-Ward 10) . . . . (304) 348-8179
Term Expires: June 16, 2019
E-mail: keeleysteele@gmail.com

★Council Member **Shannon Snodgrass** (D-Ward 11) . . . . . (304) 545-2032
Term Expires: June 16, 2019
E-mail: snodgrassshannon@aol.com

★Council Member **Susie Kortz Salisbury** (R-Ward 12) . . . . (304) 744-4038
Term Expires: June 16, 2019
E-mail: ssalisbury@charlestonareaalliance.org

★Council Member **Brent Burton** (R-Ward 13) . . . . (304) 541-0991
Term Expires: June 16, 2019
E-mail: brent@ciswv.com

★Council Member **Courtney C. Persinger** (R-Ward 14) . . . (304) 545-1856
Term Expires: June 16, 2019
E-mail: courtney.c.persinger@gmail.com

★Council Member **Samuel A. Minardi** (D-Ward 15) . . . . . . (304) 342-4685
Term Expires: June 16, 2019
E-mail: sam.minardi@gmail.com

★Council Member
Robert "Bobby" Reishman (R-Ward 16) . . . . (304) 346-4643
Term Expires: June 16, 2019
E-mail: robert@reishman.com

★Council Member **John H. Miller, Jr.** (R-Ward 17) . . . . (304) 346-4643
Term Expires: June 16, 2019
E-mail: jhmiller@yahoo.com

★Council Member **Rick Burka** (R-Ward 18) . . . . (304) 925-3548
Term Expires: June 16, 2019
E-mail: rburka@frontier.com

★Council Member **Jack E. Harrison** (D-Ward 19) . . . . (304) 345-1177
Term Expires: June 16, 2019
E-mail: jeh@goodwingoodwin.com
Education: West Virginia 1970 BSJ, 1971 MPA

★Council Member **Michael Clowser** (D-Ward 20) . . . . (304) 345-0066
Term Expires: June 16, 2019
E-mail: mclowser@cawv.org

★Council Member **Becky Ceperley** (D-At-Large) . . . . (304) 348-8179
Term Expires: June 16, 2019
E-mail: ceperleyb@gmail.com

Office of the Mayor and City Council *continued*

★Council Member **Mary Jean Davis** (D-At-Large) . . . . (304) 342-8303
Term Expires: June 16, 2019

★Council Member **Karan Ireland** (D-At-Large) . . . . (304) 348-8179
Term Expires: June 16, 2019

★Council Member **Tom Lane** (R-At-Large) . . . . (304) 720-1499
Term Expires: June 16, 2019
E-mail: tlane@bowlesrice.com

★Council Member **Andy Richardson** (D-At-Large) . . . . (304) 348-8179
Term Expires: June 16, 2019

★Council Member **Jerry L. Ware** (D-At-Large) . . . . (304) 345-6319
Term Expires: June 16, 2019
E-mail: wareatlarge@suddenlink.net

Office of the City Manager

City Hall, 501 Virginia St. East, Charleston, WV 25301
E-mail: citymanager@cityofcharleston.org Fax: (304) 348-8157

City Manager **Dave Molgaard** . . . . (304) 348-8014
E-mail: david.molgaard@cityofcharleston.org

Building Department

City Hall, 501 Virginia St. East, Charleston, WV 25301

Commissioner **Tony Harmon** . . . . (304) 348-6833

Charleston Civic Center

200 Civic Center Dr., Charleston, WV 25301

General Manager **John Robertson** . . . . (304) 345-1500

Economic and Community Development Department

City Hall, 501 Virginia St. East, Charleston, WV 25301

Director **Brian King** . . . . (304) 348-8035
E-mail: brian.king@cityofcharleston.org

Engineering Department

City Hall, 501 Virginia Street East, Charleston, WV 25301
E-mail: engineer2@cityofcharleston.org

City Engineer **Chris Knox** . . . . (304) 348-8106
E-mail: chris.knox@cityofcharleston.org

Finance Department

City Hall, 501 Virginia St. East, Charleston, WV 25301

Director **Joe Estep** . . . . (304) 348-8028

Fire and Emergency Services Department

City Hall, 501 Virginia St. East, Charleston, WV 25301
Fax: (304) 348-6476 Internet: http://www.charlestonfire.com

Chief **Scott Shaffer** . . . . (304) 348-8137

Housing Authority

PO Box 86, Charleston, WV 25321-0086

Executive Director **Mark Taylor** . . . . (304) 348-6451 ext. 322

Human Resources Department

City Hall, 501 Virginia St. East, Charleston, WV 25301
Fax: (304) 348-8055

Director **Charles Thompson** . . . . (304) 348-8015
E-mail: charles.thompson@cityofcharleston.org

Information Systems

City Hall, 501 Virginia St. East, Charleston, WV 25301

Manager **Peter Gallo** . . . . (304) 348-8048
E-mail: peter.gallo@cityofcharleston.org

★ Elected Official ▲ Appointed by Legislature ▼ Appointed by Governor ▶ Appointed by Board or Commission ● Appointed by Judge
■ Appointed by Mayor △ Appointed by Freeholders ▽ Appointed by Supervisor ▷ Appointed by County Executive ○ Appointed by Council

Parks and Recreation Department

City Hall, 501 Virginia St. East, Charleston, WV 25301
Tel: (304) 348-6860 E-mail: parks-recreation@cityofcharleston.org

Director **John Chamock** (R) .... (304) 348-6860

Planning Department

City Hall, 501 Virginia St. East, Charleston, WV 25301

Director **Dan Vriendt** .... (304) 348-8021

Police Department

City Hall, 501 Virginia St. East, Charleston, WV 25301
Internet: http://www.charlestonwvpolice.org

Chief of Police **Brent Webster** .... (304) 348-6460

Public Works Department

City Hall, 501 Virginia St. East, Charleston, WV 25301
E-mail: publicworks@cityofcharleston.org

Director **Gary Taylor** .... (304) 348-6850
Refuse Director **John Shannon** .... (304) 348-6831
Sanitary Board General Manager **Larry L. Roller** (R) ..... (304) 348-1084
208 26th Street, Charleston, WV 25312
Sanitary Board Operations Manager **(Vacant)** .... (304) 348-1084
208 26th Street, Charleston, WV 25312
Equipment Maintenance Supervisor **Linda Walker** .... (304) 348-6456

Purchasing Department

City Hall, 501 Virginia St. East, Charleston, WV 25301

Director **Dave Molgaard** .... (304) 348-8014
E-mail: david.molgaard@cityofcharleston.org

Streets Department

City Hall, 501 Virginia St. East, Charleston, WV 25301

Commissioner **Gary Taylor** .... (304) 348-6850
Beautification Director **Travis Bostic** .... (304) 348-6458
Parking System Director **George Jarrett** .... (304) 348-0739
Traffic Engineer **Michael Schrader** .... (304) 348-6872
E-mail: michael.schrader@cityofcharleston.org

Office of the City Attorney

City Hall, 501 Virginia St. East, Charleston, WV 25301

City Attorney **Paul Ellis** .... (304) 348-8032
E-mail: cityattorney@cityofcharleston.org
Assistant City Attorney **Mandy Carter** .... (304) 348-8032

Office of the City Clerk

City Hall, 501 Virginia St. East, Charleston, WV 25301

○ City Clerk **J.B. Akers** .... (304) 348-8179

Office of the City Collector

City Hall, 501 Virginia St. East, Charleston, WV 25301

City Collector **Tonya C. Cotton** .... (304) 348-8024
E-mail: citycollector@cityofcharleston.org

Office of the City Treasurer

City Hall, 501 Virginia St. East, Charleston, WV 25301

★ City Treasurer **Vic Grigoraci** (D) .... (304) 348-8029
Term Expires: June 16, 2019

City of Charlotte, North Carolina

Charlotte-Mecklenburg Government Center, 600 East Fourth Street, Charlotte, NC 28202
Tel: (704) 336-7600 (Information) Internet: www.charmeck.org

County: Mecklenburg **Election Type:** Partisan **Population:** 827,097 (2015)

Office of the Mayor and City Council

Charlotte-Mecklenburg Government Center, 600 E. Fourth St., Charlotte, NC 28202-2244
Tel: (704) 336-2241

★ Mayor **Jennifer W. Roberts** (D) .... (704) 336-3131
Began Service: December 7, 2015
Term Expires: December 2017
E-mail: mayor@charlottenc.gov
Education: North Carolina 1982 BA; Toronto 1986 MA; Johns Hopkins 1988 MA
Press Secretary **Ashley Simmons** .... (704) 336-3438
E-mail: asimmons@charlottenc.gov Fax: (704) 336-3097
Education: North Carolina 2008 BA; North Carolina Pembroke 2013 MPA

★ Mayor Pro Tem **Vi Alexander Lyles** (At-Large) .... (704) 336-3431
Term Expires: December 6, 2017
E-mail: vlyles@charlottenc.gov

★ Council Member **Patsy B. Kinsey** (D-District 1) .... (704) 336-3432
Term Expires: December 6, 2017
E-mail: pkinsey@charlottenc.gov

★ Council Member **Alvin Austin** (D-District 2) .... (704) 336-3185
Term Expires: December 6, 2017
E-mail: aaustin@charlottenc.gov

★ Council Member **LaWana Mayfield** (D-District 3) .... (704) 336-3435
Term Expires: December 6, 2017
E-mail: lmayfield@charlottenc.gov

★ Council Member **Greg Phipps** (D-District 4) .... (704) 336-3436
Term Expires: December 6, 2017
E-mail: gaphipps@charlottenc.gov

★ Council Member **John Autry** (D-District 5) .... (704) 336-2777
Term Expires: December 6, 2017
E-mail: jautry@charlottenc.gov

★ Council Member **Kenny Smith** (R-District 6) .... (704) 336-3433
Term Expires: December 6, 2017
E-mail: krsmith@charlottenc.gov

★ Council Member **Edmund "Ed" Driggs** (R-District 7) ... (704) 432-7077
Term Expires: December 6, 2017
E-mail: edriggs@charlottenc.gov
Education: Princeton BA

★ Council Member **Julie Eiselt** (D-At-Large) .... (704) 336-2241
Term Expires: December 2017

★ Council Member **Claire Fallon** (D-At-Large) .... (704) 336-6105
Term Expires: December 6, 2017
E-mail: cfallon@charlottenc.gov

★ Council Member **James E. Mitchell, Jr.** (D-At-Large) ... (704) 336-2241
Term Expires: December 2019
Education: North Carolina Central BABA

Office of the City Manager

Charlotte-Mecklenburg Government Center, 600 E. Fourth St., Charlotte, NC 28202-2853
Tel: (704) 336-2241 Fax: (704) 336-6644

○ City Manager **Ron Carlee** .... (704) 336-2241
Note: Until June 30, 2016
Education: Montevallo 1975 BA; Alabama 1979 MA; George Mason 1995 PhD

Intergovernmental Relations Manager **Dana Fenton** ...... (704) 336-2009
E-mail: dfenton@charlottenc.gov

★ Elected Official ▲ Appointed by Legislature ▼ Appointed by Governor ▶ Appointed by Board or Commission ● Appointed by Judge
■ Appointed by Mayor △ Appointed by Freeholders ▽ Appointed by Supervisor ▷ Appointed by County Executive ○ Appointed by Council

Office of the City Manager *continued*

Deputy City Manager **Ron Kimble** .... (704) 336-4169
E-mail: rkimble@charlottenc.gov
Assistant City Manager **Debra Campbell** .... (704) 336-3656
Assistant City Manager **Ann Wall** .... (704) 336-3187
Assistant City Manager **Hyong Yi** .... (704) 336-3187
Corporate Communications and Marketing Director
Sandy D'Elosua .... (704) 336-2643
E-mail: sdelosua@charlottenc.gov
Charmeck 311 Director **Janice Quintana** .... (704) 432-4001
E-mail: jquintana@charlottenc.gov
Education: New Mexico BA
Community Relations Executive Director
Willie Ratchford .... (704) 336-2424
E-mail: wratchford@charlottenc.gov

Aviation/Charlotte Douglas International Airport

C-D International Airport, P.O. Box 19066, Charlotte, NC 28219
Fax: (704) 359-4030 Internet: http://charlottedouglasintlairport.com/

Director (Interim) **Brent Cagle** .... (704) 359-4000
Education: Baylor BA; Texas Tech MPA

Charlotte Area Transit System [CATS]

600 East Fourth Street, Charlotte, NC 28202
Fax: (704) 432-1285

Transit Executive Director **John M. Lewis, Jr.** .... (704) 336-7902
Deputy Director for Development **John M. Muth** .... (704) 336-7902
Assistant Director and Chief Financial Officer
Dymphna "Dee" Pereira .... (704) 336-7902
Assistant Director and Director of Marketing and
Communications **Olaf Kinard** .... (704) 336-2275
E-mail: kkinard@ci.charlotte.nc.us
Chief Operations Planning Officer, Assistant Director of
Public Transit **Larry Kopf** .... (704) 336-7902
E-mail: lkopf@ci.charlotte.nc.us
General Manager, Rail Operations **Allen Smith** .... (704) 336-7902
General Manager, Safety and Security
Laverne McElveen .... (704) 336-7902
E-mail: lmcelveen@ci.charlotte.nc.us

Engineering and Property Management

Charlotte-Mecklenburg Government Center, 600 E. Fourth St.,
Charlotte, NC 28202-2844
Fax: (704) 336-6586

City Engineer **Jeb Blackwell** .... (704) 336-3603
E-mail: jblackwell@ci.charlotte.nc.us

Fire Department

228 East Ninth Street, Charlotte, NC 28202
Tel: (704) 336-4174 Fax: (704) 336-4170

Fire Chief **Jon Hannan** .... (704) 336-2791
E-mail: jhannan@charlottenc.gov

Emergency Management Office

228 East 9th Street, Charlotte, NC 28202
Fax: (704) 336-4204

Director **Rich Granger** .... (704) 336-2412
E-mail: rgranger@charlottenc.gov

Human Resources Department

200 East Trade Street, Suite 200, Charlotte, NC 28202
Fax: (704) 336-6588

Director **Cheryl Brown** .... (704) 336-5902
E-mail: cbrown@charlottenc.gov
Education: North Carolina BA; North Carolina Charlotte MPA

Innovation and Technology Department

600 East Fourth Street, Charlotte, NC 28202

Chief Information Officer **Jeff Stovall** .... (704) 336-2460
E-mail: jstovall@charlottenc.gov
Education: MIT BSME; Virginia MBA
Corporate Strategic Technology Planner
Twyla McDermott .... (704) 336-8066
E-mail: tmcdermott@charlottenc.gov

Management and Financial Services

600 East Fourth Street, Charlotte, NC 28202

Chief Financial Officer **Randy Harrington** .... (704) 336-3992
Assistant to the Director **Maria Cantor** .... (704) 336-3992
E-mail: mcantor@charlottenc.gov

Office of Strategy and Budget

Charlotte-Mecklenburg Government Center, 600 E. Fourth St.,
Charlotte, NC 28202-2842

Director **Kim Eagle** .... (704) 336-2306

Finance Department

Charlotte-Mecklenburg Government Center, 600 E. Fourth St.,
Charlotte, NC 28202-2847

Financial Controller **Robert Campbell** .... (704) 336-5885

Fleet Management

600 East Fourth Street, Charlotte, NC 28202

Fleet Manager **Chris Trull** .... (704) 336-7153

Administrative Management Department

Charlotte-Mecklenburg Government Center, 600 East Fourth Street,
9th Floor, Charlotte, NC 28202
Fax: (704) 336-2258

Director **Maria Dennis** .... (704) 432-3539
E-mail: mdennis@charlottenc.gov
Procurement Manager **Kay Elmore** .... (704) 336-2524
E-mail: kelmore@charlottenc.gov

Neighborhood and Business Services

600 E. Trade St., Charlotte, NC 28202
Fax: (704) 336-2904

Director **Patrick Mumford** (R) .... (704) 336-3380
E-mail: pmumford@charlottenc.gov
Deputy Director **Pamela Wideman** .... (704) 336-3380

Economic Development Division

600 East Fourth Street, Charlotte, NC 28202

Director, Economic Development **Kevin Dick** .... (704) 336-3380
E-mail: kevin.dick@durhamnc.gov

Planning Department

Charlotte-Mecklenburg Government Center, 600 E. Fourth St.,
Charlotte, NC 28202-2853
Fax: (704) 336-5123
Internet: www.charmeck.org/Departments/Planning/Home.htm

Director (Interim) **Ed McKinney** .... (704) 336-8307

Charlotte-Mecklenburg Police Department

601 East Trade Street, Charlotte, NC 28202-2889
Tel: (704) 336-2352
Internet: www.charmeck.org/Departments/CMPD/home.htm

Police Chief **Kerr Putney** .... (704) 336-2337

Solid Waste Services

1105 Otts Street, Suite 208, Charlotte, NC 28205

Director **Victoria O. Johnson** .... (704) 336-2218

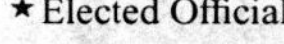

★ Elected Official ▲ Appointed by Legislature ▼ Appointed by Governor ▶ Appointed by Board or Commission ● Appointed by Judge
■ Appointed by Mayor △ Appointed by Freeholders ▽ Appointed by Supervisor ▷ Appointed by County Executive ○ Appointed by Council

Department of Transportation [CDOT]
Charlotte-Mecklenburg Government Center, 600 E. Fourth St., Charlotte, NC 28202-2858
Fax: (704) 336-4400

Director **Danny Pleasant** .... (704) 336-3879
Deputy Director **Liz Babson** .... (704) 336-3916
Assistant Director **Phil Reiger** .... (704) 336-4896

Charlotte Water
422 Westmont Drive, Charlotte, NC 28217
Fax: (704) 393-2219

Director **Barry Gullet** .... (704) 399-2221
Deputy Director **Barry Shearin** .... (704) 391-5137
Chief of Operations **Jackie Jarrell** .... (704) 336-4460
 4222 Westmont Drive, Charlotte, NC 28217
 E-mail: jjarrell@charlottenc.gov
 Education: North Carolina Charlotte BS
Field Operations Division Superintendent **Angela Lee** .... (704) 391-5190
 5730 General Commerce Dr., Charlotte, NC 28213
Water Treatment Division Superintendent **John Huber** ... (704) 399-2426
Engineering Division Chief Engineer **Carl Wilson** .... (704) 432-5097

Office of the City Attorney
Charlotte-Mecklenburg Government Center, 600 E. Fourth St., Charlotte, NC 28202-2841
Tel: (704) 336-2254

○ City Attorney **Robert E. Hagemann** .... (704) 336-2651
 E-mail: rhagemann@charlottenc.gov
 Education: Northwestern BA; North Carolina 1986 JD
Senior Deputy City Attorney **Carolyn Johnson** .... (704) 336-2254
 Education: North Carolina BA; Washington and Lee JD
Deputy City Attorney **Hope Root** .... (704) 336-2254

Office of the City Clerk
Charlotte-Mecklenburg Government Center, 600 E. Fourth St., Charlotte, NC 28202-2857
Tel: (704) 336-2248 Fax: (704) 336-7588

○ City Clerk **Stephanie C. Kelly** .... (704) 336-4515
 E-mail: sckelly@charlottenc.gov
Deputy City Clerk **Emily A. Kunze** .... (704) 336-4516
 E-mail: ekunze@charlottenc.gov

Charlotte Housing Authority
400 East Boulevard, Charlotte, NC 28203
Fax: (704) 336-5237 Internet: http://www.cha-nc.org

President and Chief Executive Officer
 A. Fulton Meachem, Jr. .... (704) 336-5183

City of Chattanooga, Tennessee
City Hall, 101 East 11th Street, Chattanooga, TN 37402
Tel: (423) 425-7800 (Information) Internet: www.chattanooga.gov

County: Hamilton **Election Type:** Nonpartisan **Year Incorporated:** 1839 **Population:** 176,588 (2015)

Office of the Mayor
City Hall, 101 East 11th Street, Chattanooga, TN 37402
Tel: (423) 643-7800 Fax: (423) 757-0005

★ Mayor **Andy Berke** .... (423) 643-7800
 Began Service: April 15, 2013
 Term Expires: April 2017
 E-mail: mayor@chattanooga.gov
 Education: Stanford 1990 BS; Chicago 1994 JD
Chief of Staff **Stacy Richardson** .... (423) 643-7800
 Deputy Chief of Staff **Justin Wilkins** .... (423) 643-7800
Chief Information Officer **Brent Messer** .... (423) 643-6345
 E-mail: CIO@chattanooga.gov
Chief Operating Officer **Maura B. Sullivan** .... (423) 643-7800

Air Pollution Control Bureau
6125 Preservation Drive, Chattanooga, TN 37416
Fax: (423) 643-5972

Director **Robert H. Colby** .... (423) 643-5970

Office of the City Attorney
100 East 11th Street, Suite 200, Chattanooga, TN 37402
Fax: (423) 643-8255

○ City Attorney **Wadrick A. "Wade" Hinton** .... (423) 643-8250
 E-mail: hinton_w@chattanooga.com
 Education: Emory 1996 BA; U Memphis 1999 JD

Economic and Community Development
100 East 11th Street, Suite 200, Chattanooga, TN 37402

Manager **Sandra Gober** .... (423) 643-7300
 E-mail: gober_sandra@chattanooga.gov

Fire Department
910 Wisdom St., Chattanooga, TN 37406
Fax: (423) 643-5610

■ Fire Chief **Chris Adams** .... (423) 643-5601
Executive Deputy/Operations Chief **Randy Jacks** .... (423) 643-5600
Administration Deputy Fire Chief **Seth Miller** .... (423) 643-5600
Fire Marshal **William Matlock** .... (423) 643-5648

Finance and Administration Department
City Hall, 101 East Eleventh Street, Chattanooga, TN 37402
Fax: (423) 757-0681

■ Administrator and City Finance Officer
 Daisy W. Madison .... (423) 643-7360
 E-mail: madison_d@chattanooga.gov

Fleet Management Division
3102 Elmendorf Circle, Chattanooga, TN 37406
Fax: (423) 643-5560

Fleet Manager **Brian S. Kiesche** .... (423) 697-1492

Purchasing
101 East 11th Street, Suite G13, Chattanooga, TN 37402
Fax: (423) 643-7244

Deputy Purchasing Agent **David Carmody** .... (423) 643-7230

★ Elected Official ▲ Appointed by Legislature ▼ Appointed by Governor ▶ Appointed by Board or Commission ● Appointed by Judge
■ Appointed by Mayor △ Appointed by Freeholders ▽ Appointed by Supervisor ▷ Appointed by County Executive ○ Appointed by Council

Treasurer
City Hall, 101 East Eleventh Street, 1st Floor, Chattanooga, TN 37402
■ Treasurer **Barry Teague** .... (423) 757-5560
E-mail: teague_b@mail.chattanooga.gov

General Services Department
100 East 11th Street, Chattanooga, TN 37402
Fax: (423) 757-5079

Director of General Services **Cary Bohannon** .... (423) 643-7505
E-mail: bohannon_c@chattanooga.gov

Chattanooga Housing Authority
P.O. Box 1486, Chattanooga, TN 37401
Tel: (423) 752-4893 Fax: (423) 752-4462 E-mail: ed@chahousing.org
Internet: www.chahousing.org/

Executive Director **Elizabeth McCright** .... (423) 668-2374

Chattanooga Public Library
1001 Broad St., Chattanooga, TN 37402
E-mail: library@lib.chattanooga.gov

Director **Corinne Hill** .... (423) 757-5310
E-mail: chill@lib.chattanooga.gov
Executive Assistant **Karen Brown** .... (423) 757-5029
E-mail: kbrown@lib.chattanooga.gov
Assistant Director, Public Services **Eva Johnston** .... (423) 757-5310
E-mail: ejohnston@lib.chattanooga.gov
Fiscal Analyst **Natalie Phillips** .... (423) 757-5310
E-mail: nphillips@lib.chattanooga.gov
Personnel Officer **James Cooper** .... (423) 757-5310
E-mail: jcooper@lib.chattanooga.gov
Children's and Young Adult Services Coordinator **Lee Hope** .... (423) 757-5310
E-mail: lhope@lib.chattanooga.gov

Office of Economic and Community Development
City Hall, 101 East Eleventh Street, Suite 200, Chattanooga, TN 37402
Fax: (423) 643-7342 E-mail: neighborhoodsvcs@mail.chattanooga.gov

■ Administrator **Donna Williams** .... (423) 643-7300
E-mail: williams_donna@chattanooga.gov
Deputy Administrator **Nick Wilson** .... (423) 643-7340
E-mail: sammons_a@mail.chattanooga.gov
Codes and Neighborhood Relations Manager **Donna Casteel** .... (423) 425-3731
Director, Outdoor Chattanooga **Philip Grymes** .... (423) 643-6888
200 River Street, Chattanooga, TN 37405

Human Resources Department
City Hall Annex, 101 East 11th Street, Suite 201, Chattanooga, TN 37402
Tel: (423) 643-7200 Fax: (423) 757-5456

■ Director **Todd Dockery** .... (423) 643-7200
E-mail: dockery_t@chattanooga.com
Deputy Human Resources Director **Tina Camba** .... (423) 643-7200
Development and Training Coordinator **Tyna Hector** .... (423) 643-7200
Benefits and Risk Manager **Madeline Green** .... (423) 643-7220
E-mail: green_m@mail.chattanooga.gov
Executive Assistant **Emily Sewell** .... (423) 643-7200
E-mail: sewell_e@chattanooga.gov

Police Department
3410 Amnicola Hwy., Chattanooga, TN 37406-1708
Fax: (423) 643-5138
Internet: www.chattanooga.gov/74_PoliceDepartment.htm

■ Chief of Police **Fred Fletcher** .... (423) 643-5111
E-mail: fletcher_fred@chattanooga.gov
Public Information Officer **Timothy McFarland** .... (423) 643-5165
E-mail: mcfarland_t@chattanooga.gov
Chief Training Officer **Lt. Jerri A. Sutton** .... (423) 643-5228
E-mail: sutton_j@mail.chattanooga.gov Fax: (423) 643-5065

Public Works Department
Development Resource Center, 1250 Market St., Chattanooga, TN 37402
Fax: (423) 757-0586

■ Administrator **(Vacant)** .... (423) 643-6000
Deputy Administrator **Justin Holland** .... (423) 757-5110
City-Wide Services Division Director **Jim Templeton** .... (423) 757-5182
Engineering/Storm Water Management Division City Engineer **William C. "Bill" Payne** .... (423) 757-5117
Waste Resources Division Director **(Vacant)** .... (423) 757-5026
Parks Director **Keith Montgomery** .... (423) 643-6000

Youth and Family Development Department
501 West 12th Street, Chattanooga, TN 37402
Fax: (423) 757-5294

■ Administrator **Lurone "Coach" Jennings, Sr.** .... (423) 643-6400
E-mail: jennings_le@chattanooga.com
Director, Recreation Division, Recreation Centers and Programs **Greta Hayes** .... (423) 643-6064

Office of the City Council
1000 Lindsay St., Chattanooga, TN 37402
Tel: (423) 643-7170 Fax: (423) 643-7199

★ Chairwoman **Carol B. Berz** (District 6) .... (423) 643-7181
Term Expires: April 2017
E-mail: cberz@chattanooga.gov
★ Vice Chair **Moses Freeman** (District 8) .... (423) 643-7182
Term Expires: April 2017
E-mail: mfreeman@chattanooga.gov
★ Council Member **Chip Henderson** (District 1) .... (423) 643-7186
Term Expires: April 2017
E-mail: cchenderson@chattanooga.gov
★ Council Member **Jerry Mitchell** (District 2) .... (423) 643-7187
Term Expires: April 2017
E-mail: jmitchell@chattanooga.gov
★ Council Member **Ken Smith** (District 3) .... (423) 643-7188
Term Expires: April 2017
E-mail: kensmith@chattanooga.gov
★ Council Member **Larry Grohn** (District 4) .... (423) 643-7184
Term Expires: April 2017
E-mail: lgrohn@chattanooga.gov
★ Council Member **Russell Gilbert** (District 5) .... (423) 643-7183
Term Expires: April 2017
E-mail: rgilbert@chattanooga.gov
★ Council Member **Chris Anderson** (District 7) .... (423) 643-7180
Term Expires: April 2017
E-mail: canderson@chattanooga.gov
★ Council Member **Yusuf Hakeem** (District 9) .... (423) 643-7185
Term Expires: April 2017
E-mail: yhakeem@chattanooga.gov
○ Clerk to City Council **Nicole Gwyn** .... (423) 643-7173
E-mail: nsgwyn@chattanooga.gov
○ Management Analyst **Thomas Tansil** .... (423) 643-7174
E-mail: tatansil@chattanooga.gov

★ Elected Official ▲ Appointed by Legislature ▼ Appointed by Governor ▶ Appointed by Board or Commission ● Appointed by Judge
■ Appointed by Mayor △ Appointed by Freeholders ▽ Appointed by Supervisor ▷ Appointed by County Executive ○ Appointed by Council

City of Chesapeake, Virginia

City Hall, 306 Cedar Rd., Chesapeake, VA 23322
Tel: (757) 382-6345 (Information) Internet: www.cityofchesapeake.net/

County: None **Election Type:** Nonpartisan **Population:** 235,429 (2015)

Office of the Mayor and City Council

City Hall, 306 Cedar Rd., Chesapeake, VA 23322
Tel: (757) 382-6151 E-mail: council@cityofchesapeake.net

★Mayor **Alan P. Krasnoff** .... (757) 382-6151
Began Service: July 2, 2008 Fax: (757) 547-9268
Term Expires: June 30, 2018
E-mail: akrasnoff@cityofchesapeake.net
Education: Queens Col (NY) BA; National U DC; Norfolk State MA

★Vice Mayor **Dr. John M. deTriquet** .... (757) 382-6151
Term Expires: June 30, 2018 Fax: (757) 484-0014
E-mail: johndetriquet@aol.com
Education: St Vincent Col; Temple MD

★Council Member **Lonnie E. Craig** .... (757) 382-6151
Term Expires: June 30, 2018 Fax: (757) 382-6678
E-mail: lcraig@cityofchesapeake.net

★Council Member **Roland J. Davis, Jr.** .... (757) 382-6947
Term Expires: June 30, 2018 Fax: (757) 410-9409

★Council Member **Robert Ike** .... (757) 382-6151
Term Expires: June 30, 2018 Fax: (757) 299-8410
E-mail: rike@cityofchesapeake.net

★Council Member **Suzy H. Kelly** .... (757) 382-6949
Term Expires: June 30, 2018 Fax: (757) 523-0903
E-mail: suzy@jokell.com
Education: Loyola U (New Orleans) BS; Old Dominion

★Council Member **S. Z. "Debbie" Ritter** .... (757) 382-6948
Term Expires: June 30, 2018 Fax: (757) 482-6356
E-mail: dritter@cityofchesapeake.net

★Council Member **Dr. Ella Porter Ward** .... (757) 382-6950
Term Expires: June 30, 2018 Fax: (757) 488-4713
E-mail: eward@cityofchesapeake.net
Education: Norfolk State 1969 BA, 1978 MA;
Old Dominion 1993 MS; Virginia Tech 1999 CAS, 2000 EdD

★Council Member **Dr. Richard W. "Rick" West** .... (757) 463-1915
Term Expires: June 30, 2018 Fax: (757) 390-3598
E-mail: rwest@cityofchesapeake.net
Education: Old Dominion 1974; Virginia 1979 MEd

Office of the City Attorney

City Hall, 306 Cedar Rd., Chesapeake, VA 23322
Tel: (757) 382-6586 Fax: (757) 382-8749

○City Attorney **Jan L. Proctor** .... (757) 382-6586
E-mail: cityattorney@cityofchesapeake.net

Office of the City Clerk

City Hall, 306 Cedar Rd., Chesapeake, VA 23322
Tel: (757) 382-6151 Fax: (757) 382-6678

○City Clerk (Acting) **Beverly L. Pender** .... (757) 382-6151
E-mail: bpender@cityofchesapeake.net
Chief Deputy City Clerk **Beverly L. Pender** .... (757) 382-6151
E-mail: bpender@cityofchesapeake.net
Deputy City Clerk **Debra A. Hanbury** .... (757) 382-6151
E-mail: dhanbury@cityofchesapeake.net
Deputy City Clerk **Mitzie Wright** .... (757) 382-6151
E-mail: mwright@cityofchesapeake.net

Office of the Real Estate Assessor

City Hall, 306 Cedar Rd., Chesapeake, VA 23322
Tel: (757) 382-6235 Fax: (757) 382-6844

○Real Estate Assessor **David B. Sanford** .... (757) 382-6235
E-mail: assessor@cityofchesapeake.net

Office of the Registrar

411 Cedar Rd., Chesapeake, VA 23322
Tel: (757) 277-9797 Fax: (757) 547-5402

Registrar **Mary Lynn A. Pinkerman** .... (757) 277-9797

Audit Services Department

City Hall, 5th Fl., 306 Cedar Rd., Chesapeake, VA 23322
Tel: (757) 382-8511 Fax: (757) 382-8860

○City Auditor **Jay Poole** .... (757) 382-8511
E-mail: jpoole@cityofchesapeake.net

Office of the City Manager

City Hall, 306 Cedar Rd., Chesapeake, VA 23322
Tel: (757) 382-6166 Fax: (757) 382-6507

○City Manager **James Baker** .... (757) 382-6988
E-mail: citymanager@cityofchesapeake.net
Assistant to City Manager **Anna D'Antonio** .... (757) 382-6323
Assistant to City Manager **Mary Ann Saunders** .... (757) 382-6323

Budget Department

City Hall, 5th Floor, 306 Cedar Rd., Chesapeake, VA 23322
Tel: (757) 382-6158 Fax: (757) 382-8936

Budget Director **Steve Jenkins** .... (757) 382-6158

Economic Development

676 Independence Parkway, Suite 200, Chesapeake, VA 23320-5117
Tel: (757) 382-8040 Fax: (757) 382-8050

Director **Steven Wright** .... (757) 382-8040
E-mail: scwright@chesapeakeva.biz
Assistant Director **Ben White** .... (757) 382-8040
E-mail: bwhite@chesapeakeva.biz

Finance Department

City Hall, 306 Cedar Rd., Chesapeake, VA 23322
Tel: (757) 382-6156 Fax: (757) 382-8102

Director **Nancy Tracy** .... (757) 382-6931

Fire Department/EMS

304 Albemarle Drive, Chesapeake, VA 23322
Tel: (757) 382-6297 Fax: (757) 382-8313

Fire Chief **Edmund E. Elliott** .... (757) 382-6297
E-mail: eelliott@cityofchesapeake.net

Human Resources Department

City Hall, 4th Floor, 306 Cedar Rd., Chesapeake, VA 23322
Tel: (757) 382-6492 Fax: (757) 382-8501
E-mail: selection@cityofchesapeake.net

Director **Donna L. Mears** .... (757) 382-6055
E-mail: dmears@cityofchesapeake.net
Assistant Director **Allison Myers** .... (757) 382-6583
E-mail: amyers@cityofchesapeake.net Fax: (757) 382-8501

Information Technology Department

300 Shea Dr., Chesapeake, VA 23320
Tel: (757) 382-6391 Fax: (757) 382-8255

Chief Information Officer **Peter R. Wallace** .... (757) 382-6659
E-mail: pwallace@cityofchesapeake.net

Police Department

304 Albemarle Dr., Chesapeake, VA 23322
Tel: (757) 382-6161 Fax: (757) 382-6821
E-mail: cpdofficeofthechief@cityofchesapeake.net

Chief of Police **Kelvin L. Wright** .... (757) 382-6404

★Elected Official ▲Appointed by Legislature ▼Appointed by Governor ►Appointed by Board or Commission ●Appointed by Judge
■Appointed by Mayor △Appointed by Freeholders ▽Appointed by Supervisor ▷Appointed by County Executive ○Appointed by Council

Public Communications Department
City Hall, 306 Cedar Rd., Chesapeake, VA 23322
Tel: (757) 382-6241 Fax: (757) 382-8538

Director **Mark S. Cox** .... (757) 382-6241
E-mail: mcox@cityofchesapeake.net

Deputy City Manager
City Hall, 306 Cedar Road, Chesapeake, VA 23322

Deputy City Manager **Dr. Wanda Barnard-Bailey** .... (757) 382-6013
Education: Norfolk State PhD

Chesapeake Public Libraries
298 Cedar Rd., Chesapeake, VA 23322-5512
Tel: (757) 410-7100 Fax: (757) 410-7112
Internet: http://www.chesapeake.lib.va.us

Director **Victoria Strickland-Cordial** .... (757) 410-7104

Human Services Department
100 Outlaw Street, Chesapeake, VA 23320
Tel: (757) 382-2000 Fax: (757) 543-1644

Director **S. Michelle Cowling** .... (757) 382-2050

Parks and Recreation Department
1224 Progressive Drive, Suite 200, Chesapeake, VA 23322
Tel: (757) 382-6411 Fax: (757) 382-8418
E-mail: prgeneral@cityofchesapeake.net

Director **Michael D. Barber** .... (757) 382-6636

Deputy City Manager
City Hall, 306 Cedar Rd., Chesapeake, VA 23328
Fax: (757) 382-6507

Deputy City Manager **CAPT Robert N. "Bob" Geis** ..... (757) 382-6166
Note: Effective July 1, 2016
Education: UC San Diego 1986 BA

Agriculture Department/Virginia Cooperative Extension
310 Shea Dr., Chesapeake, VA 23322
Tel: (757) 382-6348 Fax: (757) 382-6665

Unit Coordinator **Watson Lawrence** .... (757) 382-6349

Department of Development and Permits
City Hall, 2nd Floor, 306 Cedar Road, Chesapeake, VA 23322
Tel: (757) 382-6018 Fax: (757) 382-8448

Director **Jay Tate** .... (757) 382-6018
E-mail: jtate@cityofchesapeake.net

Community Programs Administrator **Mary Riley** .... (757) 382-6456
City Hall, 306 Cedar Rd., 5th Floor, Chesapeake, VA 23322
E-mail: mriley@cityofchesapeake.net

Youth Services Coordinator **Mary Riley** .... (757) 382-6191
City Hall, 306 Cedar Rd., 5th Floor, Chesapeake, VA 23322
E-mail: mriley@cityofchesapeake.net

Planning Department
City Hall, 306 Cedar Road, Chesapeake, VA 23322
Tel: (757) 382-6176 Fax: (757) 382-8356
E-mail: planning@cityofchesapeake.net

Director **Jaleh Shea** .... (757) 382-6176

Public Utilities
City Hall, 2nd Floor, 306 Cedar Rd., Chesapeake, VA 23322
Tel: (757) 382-6352 Fax: (757) 382-8352
E-mail: water@cityofchesapeake.net

Director **David Jurgens** .... (757) 382-6368

Public Works Department
City Hall, 306 Cedar Rd., Chesapeake, VA 23322
Tel: (757) 382-6101 Fax: (757) 382-6310

Director **Eric Martin** .... (757) 382-6226
Education: Washington State BCE; Old Dominion 1990 MEM

Public Works Department *continued*

Assistant Director **Earl Sorey** .... (757) 382-6513
E-mail: easorey@cityofchesapeake.net

Chesapeake Expressway Administrator **Gary Walton** ..... (757) 382-6101

Operations Administrator **Ted Garty** .... (757) 382-3305

Stormwater Administrator **Richard Broad** .... (757) 382-3221

Waste Management Division Administrator
David Thompson .... (757) 382-3439

Facilities Maintenance Division
431 Albemarle Dr., Chesapeake, VA 23322
Fax: (757) 382-8855

Administrator **Tim Winslow** .... (757) 382-8951

Office of the Commissioner of Revenue
City Hall, 306 Cedar Rd., Chesapeake, VA 23322
Tel: (757) 382-6455 Fax: (757) 382-8369

★ Commissioner **Ray A. Conner** .... (757) 382-6455
Term Expires: January 1, 2018
E-mail: comrev@cityofchesapeake.net

Office of the Commonwealth's Attorney
Circuit Court Bldg., 307 Albemarle Drive, Suite 200A,
Chesapeake, VA 23322
Tel: (757) 382-3200 Fax: (757) 382-3227

★ Commonwealth's Attorney **Nancy G. Parr** .... (757) 382-3200
Term Expires: November 2017
E-mail: nparr@cityofchesapeake.net

Office of the Sheriff
401 Albemarle Dr., Chesapeake, VA 23322
P.O. Box 15125, Chesapeake, VA 23328
Fax: (757) 382-8392

★ Sheriff **James J. O'Sullivan** .... (757) 382-6837
Term Expires: January 1, 2018
E-mail: josullivan@cityofchesapeake.net

Office of the Treasurer
City Hall, 306 Cedar Rd., Chesapeake, VA 23322
P.O. Box 16495, Chesapeake, VA 23328
Tel: (757) 382-6764 Fax: (757) 382-8145

★ Treasurer **Barbara O. Carraway** .... (757) 382-6281
Term Expires: January 1, 2018
E-mail: bcarrawa@cityofchesapeake.net

Chesapeake Public Schools
312 Cedar Road, Chesapeake, VA 23322
P.O. Box 15204, Chesapeake, VA 23328
Fax: (757) 547-0196 Internet: www.cpschools.com

Superintendent of Schools **Dr. James T. "Jim" Roberts** .. (757) 547-0165
Education: Old Dominion BS, MS, PhD

Chesapeake Conference Center
900 Greenbrier Circle, Chesapeake, VA 23320
Tel: (757) 382-2500 Fax: (757) 382-2525

Executive Director **Troy E. Thorn** .... (757) 382-2500

Operations Manager **Devontae L. Johnson** .... (757) 382-2500

★ Elected Official ▲ Appointed by Legislature ▼ Appointed by Governor ▶ Appointed by Board or Commission ● Appointed by Judge
■ Appointed by Mayor △ Appointed by Freeholders ▽ Appointed by Supervisor ▷ Appointed by County Executive ○ Appointed by Council

City of Cheyenne, Wyoming

2101 O'Neil Ave., Cheyenne, WY 82001
Tel: (307) 637-6200 (Information) Internet: www.cheyennecity.org

County: Laramie **Election Type:** Nonpartisan **Population:** 63,335 (2015)

Office of the Mayor and City Council

2101 O'Neil Ave., Cheyenne, WY 82001
Fax: (307) 637-6454 E-mail: mayor@cheyennecity.org
E-mail: citycouncil@cheyennecity.org

★ Mayor **Richard L. "Rick" Kaysen** .... (307) 637-6300
Began Service: January 5, 2009 Fax: (307) 637-6378
Term Expires: January 3, 2017
Date of Birth: October 28, 1946
Education: Western State Col BA
Executive Secretary to the Mayor **Virginia Riley** .... (307) 637-6300
E-mail: vriley@cheyennecity.org Fax: (307) 637-6378

★ Council Member **Scott D. Roybal** (Ward I) .... (307) 637-6357
Term Expires: January 5, 2019 Fax: (307) 637-6454

★ Council Member **Jeff White** (Ward I) .... (307) 637-6357
Term Expires: January 3, 2017 Fax: (307) 637-6454
E-mail: jwhite@cheyennecity.org

★ Council Member **Annette Williams** (Ward I) .... (307) 637-6357
Term Expires: January 3, 2017 Fax: (307) 637-6454
E-mail: awilliams@cheyennecity.org

★ Council Member **Bryan M. Cook** (Ward II) .... (307) 637-6357
Term Expires: January 3, 2017 Fax: (307) 637-6454
E-mail: bcook@cheyennecity.org

★ Council Member **Dr. Mark Rinne** (Ward II) .... (307) 637-6357
Term Expires: January 5, 2019
E-mail: mrinne@cheyennecity.org

★ Council Member **Dicky Shanor** (Ward II) .... (307) 637-6357
Term Expires: January 3, 2017 Fax: (307) 637-6454
E-mail: dshanor@cheyennecity.org

★ Council Member **Jim Brown** (Ward III) .... (307) 637-6357
Term Expires: January 3, 2017
E-mail: jbrown@cheyennecity.org

★ Council Member **Richard Johnson** (Ward III) .... (307) 637-6357
Term Expires: January 5, 2019 Fax: (307) 637-6454

★ Council Member **Mike Luna** (Ward III) .... (307) 637-6357
Term Expires: January 3, 2017 Fax: (307) 637-6454
E-mail: mluna@cheyennecity.org

Office of the City Clerk

2101 O'Neil Ave., Cheyenne, WY 82001
E-mail: cityclerk@cheyennecity.org

■ City Clerk **Carol Intlekofer** .... (307) 637-6335
E-mail: cintlekofer@cheyennecity.org Fax: (307) 638-4340

Risk Management

2101 O'Neil Ave., Cheyenne, WY 82001

Risk Manager **Bill Tennant** .... (307) 637-6333
E-mail: btennant@cheyennecity.org

Office of the City Attorney

2101 O'Neil Ave., Cheyenne, WY 82001
E-mail: attorney@cheyennecity.org

■ City Attorney **Daniel E. White** .... (307) 637-6306
E-mail: dwhite@cheyennecity.org Fax: (307) 637-6373

Office of the Treasurer

2101 O'Neil Ave., Cheyenne, WY 82001
Fax: (855) 484-6955

■ Treasurer **Lois A. Huff** .... (307) 637-6336
E-mail: lhuff@cheyennecity.org

Purchasing Division

2101 O'Neil Ave., Cheyenne, WY 82001
Tel: (307) 637-6345 Fax: (855) 491-1859

Manager **Sara Vasquez** .... (307) 637-6345
E-mail: svasquez@cheyennecity.org

Engineering Department

2101 O'Neil Avenue, Room 206, Cheyenne, WY 82001
Tel: (307) 638-4315 Fax: (307) 637-6256

■ City Engineer **John Hall** .... (307) 638-4314
Fax: (307) 637-6454

Assistant City Engineer **Nathan Beauheim** .... (307) 638-4334
E-mail: nbeauheim@cheyennecity.org

Fire Department

2101 O'Neil Ave., Cheyenne, WY 82001
E-mail: mconnour@cheyennecity.org

■ Fire Chief **James Martin** .... (307) 637-6311
E-mail: jmartin@cheyennecity.org Fax: (307) 637-6454

Human Resources Department

2101 O'Neil Ave., Cheyenne, WY 82001

Director **Rich Wiederspahn** .... (307) 637-6343
E-mail: rwiederspahn@cheyennecity.org Fax: (307) 637-6342

Cheyenne Municipal Airport

P.O. Box 2210, Cheyenne, WY 82003
Fax: (307) 632-1206 E-mail: info@cheyenneairport.com
Internet: www.cheyenneairport.com

Director of Aviation **Tim Barth** .... (307) 634-7071
Fax: (307) 632-1206

Parks and Recreation Department

2101 O'Neil Avenue, Cheyenne, WY 82001

■ Director **Rick L. Parish** .... (307) 638-4356
E-mail: rparish@cheyennecity.org Fax: (307) 638-4355

Planning and Development

2101 O'Neil Ave., Cheyenne, WY 82001

■ Planning Services Director (Acting)
Brandon Cammarata .... (307) 637-6206
E-mail: bcammarata@cheyennecity.org Fax: (307) 637-6308

Development Office

2101 O'Neil Ave., Cheyenne, WY 82001
Fax: (307) 637-6366

Development Director **Brandon Cammarata** .... (307) 637-6282
E-mail: bcammarata@cheyennecity.org

Police Department

2020 Capitol, Cheyenne, WY 82001

■ Chief of Police **Brian N. Kozak** .... (307) 637-6521
E-mail: bkozak@cheyennepd.org Fax: (307) 637-6558
Education: U Phoenix BA, MEd

Board of Public Utilities

2416 Snyder Avenue, Cheyenne, WY 82001
Internet: www.cheyennebopu.org

President **Joe Bonds** .... (307) 637-6469
Secretary **Brad Oberg** .... (307) 637-6469
Member **Mary B. Guthrie** .... (307) 637-6469
Member **James Murphy** .... (307) 637-6469
Member **Matthew Pope** .... (307) 637-6469
Director **Tim Wilson** .... (307) 637-6469
Fax: (307) 637-7672
Administration Manager **Randy Hays** .... (307) 637-6471
Engineering/Water Resource Manager **Brad Brooks** ...... (307) 637-6471

★ Elected Official ▲ Appointed by Legislature ▼ Appointed by Governor ▶ Appointed by Board or Commission ● Appointed by Judge
■ Appointed by Mayor △ Appointed by Freeholders ▽ Appointed by Supervisor ▷ Appointed by County Executive ○ Appointed by Council

Board of Public Utilities *continued*

Operations/Maintenance Manager **Frank Strong** . . . . (307) 637-6471
Water Reclamation Manager **Jim Hughes** . . . . (307) 637-6469
Water Treatment Manager **Clint Bassett** . . . . (307) 637-6469

Public Works Department

2101 O'Neil Avenue, Room 210, Cheyenne, WY 82001
Fax: (307) 637-6256

■ Public Works Director **Vicki Nemecek** . . . . (307) 637-6279
E-mail: vnemecek@cheyennecity.org Fax: (307) 637-6256

Concrete/Storm Sewer Maintenance

Fax: (307) 637-6256

Director **Craig Lavoy** . . . . (307) 637-6288

Facilities Maintenance Division

Director **Mike Wright** . . . . (307) 637-6262
E-mail: mwright@cheyennecity.org

Fleet Maintenance Division

2731 Happy Jack Road, Cheyenne, WY 82001
Fax: (307) 637-6450

Director **Dennis Bell** . . . . (307) 637-6445

Sanitation Division

220 North College Drive, Cheyenne, WY 82001
Fax: (307) 637-6443

Director **Dennis Pino** . . . . (307) 637-6440

Street and Alley Division

Fax: (307) 637-6232

Director **Bill Obermeier** . . . . (307) 637-6263

Traffic Division

Director **Dennis Fanning** . . . . (307) 637-6263
Traffic Engineer **(Vacant)** . . . . (307) 637-6263

City of Chicago, Illinois

City Hall, 121 North LaSalle Street, Chicago, IL 60602
Tel: (312) 744-5000 (Information) TTY: (312) 744-8599
Internet: www.cityofchicago.org

County: Cook **Election Type:** Nonpartisan **Population:** 2,720,546 (2015) **Employees:** 34,328 **Fiscal Year:** 2016 **Budget:** $7,840,000,000

Rahm I. Emanuel
Mayor

Began Service: May 16, 2011
Term Expires: May 2019
Date of Birth: November 29, 1959
Education: Sarah Lawrence 1981 BA; Northwestern 1985 MA
Career: U.S. Representative (D-IL, District 5), Office of Representative Rahm Emanuel, United States House of Representatives (2003-2008); Assistant to the President and Chief of Staff, Executive Office of the President, Barack Obama Administration (2009-2010)

Office of the Mayor

City Hall, 121 North LaSalle Street, Room 507, Chicago, IL 60602
Tel: (312) 744-3300 TTY: (312) 744-2966 Fax: (312) 744-2324

Employees: 80 **Fiscal Year:** 2016 **Budget:** $9,520,000

★ Mayor **Rahm I. Emanuel** . . . . (312) 744-3300
E-mail: mayorsoffice@cityofchicago.org

Office of the Mayor *continued*

Executive Secretary **Veronica Castro** . . . . (312) 744-3300
E-mail: veronica.castro@cityofchicago.org
Executive Secretary **Jasmine Magana** . . . . (312) 744-3300
E-mail: jasmine.magana@cityofchicago.org
Deputy Mayor **Steven Koch** . . . . (312) 744-3300
E-mail: steven.koch@cityofchicago.org
Education: Hampshire 1974 BA; Chicago MBA, JD
Deputy Mayor and Chief Neighborhood Development Officer **Andrea L. Zopp** . . . . (312) 744-3300
Education: Harvard 1978 AB, 1981 JD
■ Chief of Staff **Eileen Mitchell** . . . . (312) 744-3300
Education: Loyola U (Chicago) BA
■ Deputy Chief of Staff **Ken Bennett** . . . . (312) 744-3300
E-mail: ken.bennett@cityofchicago.org
Chief Operating Officer **Joe Deal** . . . . (312) 744-3300
Deputy Chief of Staff for Education **(Vacant)** . . . . (312) 744-3300
■ Senior Advisor **Michael "Mike" Rendina** . . . . (312) 744-9500
E-mail: michael.rendina@cityofchicago.org
■ Director, Office of Legislative Counsel and Government Affairs **Anna Valencia** . . . . (312) 744-9500
First Deputy Director, Office of Legislative Counsel and Government Affairs **Victoria Watkins** . . . . (312) 744-9500
E-mail: victoria.watkins@cityofchicago.org
■ Washington Intergovernmental Affairs Director **Melissa Green** . . . . (202) 783-0911
1301 Pennsylvania Avenue, NW, 4th Floor, Washington, DC 20004
E-mail: mgreen@cityofchicago.org
Director of Communications **Kelley Quinn** . . . . (312) 744-3334
E-mail: kelley.quinn@cityofchicago.org
Press Secretary **(Vacant)** . . . . (312) 744-3334
Senior Advisor to the Mayor **(Vacant)** . . . . (312) 744-3300
Chief of Strategic Planning **Clo Ewing** . . . . (312) 744-3300
Policy Chief **Michael Negron** . . . . (312) 744-3300
Senior Policy Advisor, Public Safety **Tony U. Iweagwu** . . (312) 744-3300
■ Chief Financial Officer **Carole L. Brown** . . . . (312) 742-6608
Education: Harvard 1986 BA; Kellogg 1989 MA
■ Chief Data Officer **John Lim** . . . . (312) 744-3300
E-mail: john.lim@cityofchicago.org
■ Digital Director **Alexis Neisser** . . . . (312) 744-3334
E-mail: alexis.neisser@cityofchicago.org
Director of Scheduling and Advance **Abby Hall** . . . . (312) 744-3300
■ Chief Resilience Officer **Aaron Koch** . . . . (312) 744-3300

Mayor's Office for People with Disabilities

TTY: (312) 744-7833

Employees: 29 **Fiscal Year:** 2016 **Budget:** $5,525,000

■ Commissioner **Karen Tamley** Room 1104 . . . . (312) 744-7209
E-mail: ktamley@cityofchicago.org
Education: UC Berkeley BA

Mayor's Office of Public Engagement

City Hall, 121 North LaSalle Street, Chicago, IL 60602

Deputy Chief of Staff and Director **Ken Bennett** . . . . (312) 744-3300
E-mail: ken.bennett@cityofchicago.org

Office of Budget and Management [OBM]

City Hall, 121 North LaSalle Street, Room 604, Chicago, IL 60602
Tel: (312) 744-6670 TTY: (312) 744-6819 Fax: (312) 744-3618
Internet: http://www.cityofchicago.org/budget/

Employees: 45 **Fiscal Year:** 2016 **Budget:** $16,817,000

■ Budget Director **Alexandra Holt** . . . . (312) 744-3323
E-mail: budget@cityofchicago.org
Education: Texas 1989 BA; Chicago 1992 MPP, 2007 JD

Office of Compliance

333 South State Street, Suite 540, Chicago, IL 60604
Tel: (312) 744-4900 Fax: (312) 744-9687
Internet: www.cityofchicago.org/city/en/depts/comp.html

Deputy Procurement Officer **Monica Jimenez** . . . . (312) 744-0845
E-mail: mjiminez@cityofchicago.org

★ Elected Official ▲ Appointed by Legislature ▼ Appointed by Governor ► Appointed by Board or Commission ● Appointed by Judge
■ Appointed by Mayor △ Appointed by Freeholders ▽ Appointed by Supervisor ▷ Appointed by County Executive ○ Appointed by Council

Office of Emergency Management and Communications [OEMC]

1411 West Madison Street, Chicago, IL 60607-1809
Tel: (312) 746-9400 Fax: (312) 746-9555

Employees: 1,845 **Fiscal Year:** 2016 **Budget:** $229,840,000

■ Executive Director **COL Alicia Tate-Nadeau** .... (312) 746-9400
Public Affairs Director **Melissa Stratton** .... (312) 746-9454
E-mail: melissa.straton@cityofchicago.org
■ 311 City Services Director **Audrey Mathis** .... (312) 746-9760
E-mail: audrey.mathis@cityofchicago.org

Office of Inspector General [OIG]

P.O. Box 2996, Chicago, IL 60654-2996
740 North Sedgwick Avenue, Suite 200, Chicago, IL 60654
TTY: (773) 478-2066 Fax: (773) 478-3949
Internet: www.chicagoinspectorgeneral.org

Employees: 64 **Fiscal Year:** 2016 **Budget:** $6,010,000

■ Inspector General **Joseph M. "Joe" Ferguson** .... (773) 478-7799
E-mail: reportcorruption@chicagoinspectorgeneral.org
General Counsel **Brian Dunn** .... (773) 478-7799
Education: Northwestern 2003 JD
Deputy Inspector General **William Marback** .... (773) 478-7799
Chief of Staff **Karen Randolph** .... (773) 478-7799

Department of Administrative Hearings

740 North Sedgwick Avenue, Chicago, IL 60654

Employees: 42 **Fiscal Year:** 2016 **Budget:** $8,188,000

■ Director/Chief Administrative Law Officer
Patricia "Pat" Jackowiak .... (312) 742-8200
E-mail: patricia.jackowiak@cityofchicago.org
Deputy Director **Steven N. Sheely** .... (312) 742-8200
E-mail: steven.sheely@cityofchicago.org

Buildings Hearings Division

Division Chief **Michele McSwain** .... (312) 742-8254

Environmental Safety and Consumer Affairs Division

Division Chief **Deborah Gogola** .... (312) 742-8252

Municipal Hearings Division

Division Chief **Thaddeus Wilkins** .... (312) 742-8475
Education: John Marshall LLM; Oklahoma City JD

Vehicle Hearings Division

Division Chief **Anthony Rizzo** .... (312) 742-8255

Chicago Department of Aviation [CDA]

O'Hare International Airport, P.O. Box 66142, Chicago, IL 60666
Tel: (773) 686-2200 TTY: (773) 601-8333 Fax: (773) 686-3424

Employees: 202 **Fiscal Year:** 2016 **Budget:** $154,515,000

■ Commissioner **Ginger Evans** .... (773) 686-8060
E-mail: Ginger.Evans@cityofchicago.org
Education: Colorado State BCE, MCE
First Deputy Commissioner **Susan Warner-Dooley** ...... (773) 686-7091
Chief Operating Officer **Jonathan Leach** .... (773) 462-7311
E-mail: jonathan.leach@cityofchicago.org
Chief Safety and Security Officer **Richard Edgeworth** ... (773) 686-2397
E-mail: REdgeworth@cityofchicago.org
Deputy Commissioner for Air Services Development
Susan L. Kurland .... (773) 686-2200
Education: Brandeis; Boston U JD
General Counsel **Jessica Sampson** .... (773) 686-3587

Chicago Midway Airport

5700 S. Cicero Ave., Chicago, IL 60638
Tel: (773) 838-0600 TTY: (773) 582-9152

Managing Deputy Commissioner **Erin O'Donnell** .... (773) 838-0608
Staff Assistant **Rose Thompson** .... (773) 838-0610
E-mail: rthompson@cityofchicago.org

O'Hare International Airport

10510 West Zemke Road, Chicago, IL 60666
Tel: (773) 686-2200

■ First Deputy Commissioner **Susan Warner-Dooley** ...... (773) 686-7091
E-mail: michael.boland@cityofchicago.org

Department of Buildings

120 North Racine, Chicago, IL 60607
Tel: (312) 743-9021 Fax: (312) 743-9123
Internet: www.cityofchicago.org/city/en/depts/bldgs.html

Employees: 287 **Fiscal Year:** 2016 **Budget:** $38,424,000

■ Commissioner **Judy Frydland** .... (312) 743-9021
E-mail: judy.frydland@cityofchicago.org
Education: Chicago-Kent JD
Managing Deputy Commissioner **Marlene Hopkins** ..... (312) 743-9021
First Deputy Commissioner **Matthew Beaudet** .... (312) 744-6585

Business Affairs and Consumer Protection Department [BACP]

Daley Center, 50 West Washington Street, Room 208, Chicago, IL 60602
Tel: (312) 922-3100 (Maxwell Street Market)
Tel: (312) 742-4453 (Citizen Complaint Investigation)
Fax: (312) 742-8700
Internet: http://www.cityofchicago.org/consumerservices/

Employees: 193 **Fiscal Year:** 2016 **Budget:** $19,519,000

■ Commissioner **Maria Guerra Lapacek** .... (312) 744-6060
E-mail: mguerra@cityofchicago.org

Business Licenses and Permit Operations

Deputy Commissioner **Joy Adelizzi** .... (312) 746-4390
Assistant Commissioner **(Vacant)** .... (312) 744-5485

Cable and Telecommunications Administration

121 North LaSalle Street, Suite 805, Chicago, IL 60602
TTY: (312) 744-2941 Fax: (312) 744-5440

Deputy Commissioner **James "Jim" McVane** .... (312) 744-5428

Enforcement Division

33 North LaSalle Street, Chicago, IL 60602

Deputy Commissioner **(Vacant)** .... (312) 743-1433

Local Liquor Control Division

Commissioner **Gregg Steadman** .... (312) 744-5443

Protections and Investigations Division

50 West Washington Street, Room 208, Chicago, IL 60602
Tel: (312) 744-4006 Fax: (312) 744-9089

Deputy Commissioner **Barbara Gressel** .... (312) 744-5287

Public Vehicle Licensing Division

Ogden Building, 2350 West Ogden, 1st Floor, Chicago, IL 60608
Tel: (312) 746-4200 Fax: (312) 746-9406

Public Vehicle Licensing Deputy Commissioner
Rupal Bapat .... (312) 746-8656
Taxicab Chauffeur Licensing Assistant Commissioner
Michael Evans .... (312) 742-0531

Small Business Center

Chief Small Business Officer **Roxanne Nava** .... (312) 744-6060

★ Elected Official ▲ Appointed by Legislature ▼ Appointed by Governor ▶ Appointed by Board or Commission ● Appointed by Judge
■ Appointed by Mayor △ Appointed by Freeholders ▽ Appointed by Supervisor ▷ Appointed by County Executive ○ Appointed by Council

Department of Cultural Affairs and Special Events [DCASE]

Chicago Cultural Center, 78 East Washington Street, Chicago, IL 60602
Tel: (312) 744-3316 Fax: (312) 744-8523
E-mail: dcase@cityofchicago.org
Internet: http://www.cityofchicago.org/dcase

Employees: 77 **Fiscal Year:** 2016 **Budget:** $32,606,000

■ Commissioner **Michelle T. Boone** .... (312) 744-8923
E-mail: michelle.boone@cityofchicago.org
Education: Indiana BA, MA
Assistant to the Commissioner **Sue Vopicka** .... (312) 744-8923
E-mail: svopicka@cityofchicago.org
■ Chief of Staff **David McDermott** .... (312) 744-8933
E-mail: David.McDermott@cityofchicago.org
Cultural Planning and Operations Deputy Commissioner **Matthew Nielson** .... (312) 744-1373
E-mail: mnielson@cityofchicago.org
Finance and Administration Deputy Commissioner **Kenya Merritt** .... (312) 742-7389
E-mail: kenya.merritt@cityofchicago.org
Arts and Creative Industries Deputy Commissioner **Tracie Hall** .... (312) 744-2390
Strategic Initiatives and Partnerships Deputy Director **(Vacant)** .... (312) 744-0567
Director of Public Affairs **Jamey Lundblad** .... (312) 744-2493
E-mail: jamey.lundblad@cityofchicago.org
Director of Special Events **David Kennedy** .... (312) 744-0293

Department of Family and Support Services

1615 West Chicago Avenue, Chicago, IL 60622
Tel: (312) 743-0300 Fax: (312) 743-0400
Internet: www.cityofchicago.org/city/en/depts/fss.html

Employees: 403 **Fiscal Year:** 2016 **Budget:** $348,060,000

■ Commissioner **Lisa Morrison Butler** .... (312) 743-0100
E-mail: lisa.butler@cityofchicago.org
Education: Indiana BS
■ First Deputy Commissioner **Jennifer A. Welch** .... (312) 743-0300
E-mail: jennifer.welch@cityofchicago.org
Managing Deputy Commissioner **David Wells** .... (312) 746-8545
Deputy Commissioner **Joel Mitchell** .... (312) 746-9954
Children Services Deputy Commissioner **(Vacant)** .... (312) 743-0300
Youth Services Deputy Commissioner **(Vacant)** .... (312) 743-0300
Finance Deputy Commissioner **Jonathan Ernst** .... (312) 746-4349
Grants Director **Brandie Knazze** .... (312) 743-0300
Management Information Systems Division Director **John Mikols** .... (312) 746-8774
E-mail: jonathan.lam@cityofchicago.org
Monitoring and Reporting Division Director **Consuella Richardson** .... (312) 746-8340
Public Affairs Office/Communication Director **Cristina Villarreal** .... (312) 746-8585
E-mail: cristina.villarreal@cityofchicago.org
Deputy Commissioner **Alexandra Lyons Cooney** .... (312) 743-0300
Deputy Commissioner **Yolanda Curry** .... (312) 743-0300
Human Resources and Administration Managing Deputy Commissioner **Monica Rafac** .... (312) 743-0300
E-mail: monica.rafac@cityofchicago.org

Department of Finance

121 North LaSalle Street, Chicago, IL 60602
Tel: (312) 744-2204 E-mail: finance@cityofchicago.org
Internet: http://www.cityofchicago.org/finance/

Employees: 33 **Fiscal Year:** 2016 **Budget:** $2,981,000

■ City Comptroller (Acting) **Erin Keane** .... (312) 744-2204
Assistant to the Director **Roxanne Garza** .... (312) 742-0602
E-mail: roxanne.garza@cityofchicago.org
Intergovernmental Affairs and Public Information **Molly Poppe** .... (312) 744-1030
Financial Systems and Support **Ian Webster** .... (312) 744-4204

Accounting and Financial Reporting

Tel: (312) 744-3013

Deputy Comptroller **Maru Mendoza** .... (312) 744-9325
E-mail: maru.mendoza@cityofchicago.org
Deputy Comptroller **Rolando Deluna** .... (312) 744-8629
E-mail: rdeluna@cityofchicago.org

Financial Strategy and Operations

Tel: (312) 744-5990

Financial Policy Deputy Comptroller **Kelly Flannery** ..... (312) 744-7106
Cash Management and Disbursements Deputy Comptroller **(Vacant)** .... (312) 744-9399
Benefits Manager **Nancy Currier** .... (312) 744-6725
333 South State Street, Room 400, Chicago, IL 60604
Risk Manager **Susan Schmitz** .... (312) 747-7830
333 South State Street, Chicago, IL 60604
E-mail: susan.schmitz@cityofchicago.org
Payroll Systems and Operations Deputy Comptroller **John Arvetis** .... (312) 745-3280

Revenue Services and Operations

121 North LaSalle Street, Room 107A, Chicago, IL 60602

Tax Policy and Administration Deputy Director **(Vacant)** .. (312) 747-0659
333 South State Street, Suite 300, Chicago, IL 60604
Accounts Receivable Deputy Director **Joel Flores** .... (312) 744-5886
E-mail: joel.flores@cityofchicago.org

Fire Department [CFD]

3510 South Michigan Avenue, Chicago, IL 60653
Tel: (312) 745-4200 Internet: www.cityofchicago.org/fire/

Employees: 5,173 **Fiscal Year:** 2016 **Budget:** $621,291,000

■ Fire Commissioner **José A. Santiago** .... (312) 745-4200
E-mail: jose.santiago@cityofchicago.org
Education: Southern Illinois BS
Executive Assistant to the Fire Commissioner **Joshua Dennis** .... (312) 745-4200
E-mail: joshua.dennis@cityofchicago.org
First Deputy Fire Commissioner **(Vacant)** .... (312) 745-4190
Administrative Services Deputy Commissioner **Adrianne Bryant** .... (312) 745-4207
E-mail: abryant@cityofchicago.org
Employee Relations Bureau Deputy Fire Commissioner **Anthony Vasquez** .... (312) 745-3759
E-mail: avasquez@cityofchicago.org
Fire Prevention Bureau Deputy Fire Commissioner **Richard Ford** .... (312) 744-4723
E-mail: richard.ford@cityofchicago.org
Operation Bureau Deputy Fire Commissioner **(Vacant)** ... (312) 745-4210
Support Services Bureau Deputy Fire Commissioner **Michael Callahan** .... (312) 745-4199
E-mail: michael.callahan@cityofchicago.org
Finance and Fiscal Management Director **Steven Swanson** .... (312) 745-4198

Department of Fleet and Facility Management [DFL]

1685 North Throop Street, Chicago, IL 60642
Tel: (312) 744-3901 Fax: (312) 744-5244
E-mail: fleet@cityofchicago.org
Internet: www.cityofchicago.org/city/en/depts/dgs.html

Employees: 618 **Fiscal Year:** 2016 **Budget:** $100,943,000

■ Commissioner **David J. Reynolds** .... (312) 744-3901
E-mail: dreynolds@cityofchicago.org

Architecture, Engineering, Construction and Trades

Fax: (312) 744-8843

City Architect **Thomas Vukovich** .... (312) 744-2708

★ Elected Official ▲ Appointed by Legislature ▼ Appointed by Governor ▶ Appointed by Board or Commission ● Appointed by Judge
■ Appointed by Mayor △ Appointed by Freeholders ▽ Appointed by Supervisor ▷ Appointed by County Executive ○ Appointed by Council

Bureau of Graphic Services
City Hall, 121 N. LaSalle St., Room 3M-19, Chicago, IL 60602
Tel: (312) 744-8679 Fax: (312) 744-3448
Internet: http://www.cityofchicago.org/graphicsrepro/

Bureau Chief **Patricia Cornelio** .... (312) 744-5792
Creative Director **Alberto Ferrari** .... (312) 744-9591
E-mail: aferrari@cityofchicago.org
Print Coordinator **Joe Maul** .... (312) 744-4984
E-mail: jmaul@cityofchicago.org
Photography Supervisor **Walter Mitchell** .... (312) 744-4958

Finance and Administration
30 North LaSalle Street, Suite 300, Chicago, IL 60602-2586
Fax: (312) 744-6097

Deputy Commissioner **Carmen Rocha** .... (312) 744-0262

Facilities Management
Fax: (312) 742-9811

Assistant Commissioner **Julie Bedore** .... (312) 744-7594
E-mail: jbedore@cityofchicago.org

Trades and Engineering
1685 North Throop Street, Chicago, IL 60622-1516
Fax: (312) 744-6692

Director of Operations **(Vacant)** .... (312) 744-9800
Assistant Commissioner **(Vacant)** .... (312) 744-9800

Department of Human Resources
City Hall, 121 North LaSalle Street, Room 1100, Chicago, IL 60602-1252
E-mail: humanresources@cityofchicago.org
Internet: http://www.cityofchicago.org/humanresources

Employees: 77 **Fiscal Year:** 2016 **Budget:** $6,601,000

■ Commissioner **Soo Choi** .... (312) 744-1937
E-mail: schoi@cityofchicago.org
Education: Duke BA; Chicago MA; Cornell 2001 JD
First Deputy Commissioner **Chris Owen** .... (312) 744-9233
Employment Services Deputy Commissioner **Christina Batorski** .... (312) 744-9133
E-mail: christina.batorski@cityofchicago.org
Information Services Deputy Commissioner **Alix Meza** .... (312) 744-9715
E-mail: alix.meza@cityofchicago.org

Department of Innovation and Technology [DoIT]
Richard J. Daley Center, 50 West Washington Street, Suite 2700, Chicago, IL 60602
Tel: (312) 744-5844 Fax: (312) 744-8600
Internet: www.cityofchicago.org/city/en/depts/doit.html

Employees: 118 **Fiscal Year:** 2016 **Budget:** $28,466,000

■ Commissioner and Chief Information Officer **Brenna Berman** .... (312) 744-9363
E-mail: brenna.berman@cityofchicago.org
Executive Assistant **Laticia Latham** .... (312) 744-0240
E-mail: laticia.latham@cityofchicago.org
Chief Technology Officer and First Deputy Commissioner **(Vacant)** .... (312) 744-0245
Managing Deputy Chief Information Officer **(Vacant)** .... (312) 744-9408
Assistant Chief Information Officer, Network Integration **Francisco Rico** .... (312) 744-7985
E-mail: frico@cityofchicago.org

Department of Law
City Hall, 121 North LaSalle Street, Room 600, Chicago, IL 60602
Tel: (312) 744-0200 TTY: (312) 744-2963 Fax: (312) 744-5185
Internet: www.cityofchicago.org/law

Employees: 436 **Fiscal Year:** 2016 **Budget:** $36,893,000

■ Corporation Counsel **Stephen R. Patton** .... (312) 744-0220
E-mail: stephen.patton@cityofchicago.org
Education: Indiana BA; Georgetown 1978 JD
First Assistant Corporation Counsel **Jane E. Notz** .... (312) 744-3993

Department of Law *continued*

Chief Labor Negotiator **Joseph P. Martinico** .... (312) 744-5395
Administrative Deputy Corporation Counsel **James L. Dunn** .... (312) 744-1558
Appeals Deputy Corporation Counsel **Benna Ruth Solomon** .... (312) 744-7764
Education: Georgia 1979 JD
Building and License Enforcement Deputy Corporation Counsel **Kimberly Roberts** .... (312) 744-5004
Collections, Ownership and Administrative Litigation Deputy Corporation Counsel **Natalie L. Frank** .... (312) 744-8713
Commercial and Policy Litigation Deputy Corporation Counsel **Mardell Nereim** .... (312) 744-6975
Employment Litigation Deputy Corporation Counsel **David Seery** .... (312) 744-2825
Federal Civil Rights Litigation Deputy Corporation Counsel **Liza Franklin** .... (312) 742-0170
Federal Civil Rights Litigation Deputy Corporation Counsel **Matthew A. Hurd** .... (312) 742-0234
Federal Civil Rights Litigation Deputy Corporation Counsel **Tom Platt** .... (312) 742-0170
Finance Deputy Corporation Counsel **James McDonald** .... (312) 744-1574
Labor Deputy Corporation Counsel **Judy Dever** .... (312) 744-2101
Legal Counsel Chief Assistant Corporation Counsel **Jeffrey Levine** .... (312) 744-7787
Real Estate Deputy Corporation Counsel **Richard A. Wendy** .... (312) 744-6934
Aviation, Environmental, Regulatory and Contracts Deputy Corporation Counsel **Diane Pezanoski** .... (312) 744-6996
Education: Northwestern 1985 JD
Revenue Litigation Deputy Corporation Counsel **Weston Hanscom** .... (312) 744-9077
Torts Deputy Corporation Counsel **Mary E. Ruether** .... (312) 744-9072
Chief Law Librarian **Scott Burgh** .... (312) 744-7632
E-mail: scott.burgh@cityofchicago.org
Legal Information, Investigations and Prosecutions City Prosecutor **Lynda Peters** .... (312) 744-2816

Department of Planning and Development
City Hall, 121 North LaSalle Street, Room 1000, Chicago, IL 60602
Tel: (312) 744-4190 TTY: (312) 744-2578 Fax: (312) 744-2271

Employees: 231 **Fiscal Year:** 2016 **Budget:** $141,215,000

■ Commissioner **David L. Reifman** .... (312) 744-9476
Education: Illinois BA, MA; Northwestern JD
Senior Assistant to the Commissioner **Lynette Wilson** .... (312) 744-9362
E-mail: lwilson@cityofchicago.org
First Deputy Commissioner **(Vacant)** .... (312) 744-6452
Assistant to the Deputy Commissioner **(Vacant)** .... (312) 744-9445
Assistant to the Deputy Commissioner for Housing **Patricia Sulewski** .... (312) 744-6926
Administration Division Deputy Commissioner **Peter Murawski** .... (312) 744-6228
33 North LaSalle, Room 1000, Chicago, IL 60602
E-mail: pmurawski@cityofchicago.org
Home Ownership Center Project Assistant Commissioner **Irma Morales** .... (312) 744-0885
E-mail: irma.morales@cityofchicago.org
Construction Administration Deputy Commissioner **(Vacant)** .... (312) 742-0493
Managing Deputy Commissioner for Economic Development **Aarti Kotak** .... (312) 744-0421
Business Development Deputy Commissioner **Mary Bonome** .... (312) 744-9413
E-mail: mary.bonome@cityofchicago.org
Preservation Deputy Commissioner **(Vacant)** .... (312) 744-4190
Real Estate Assistant Commissioner **Robert Wolf** .... (312) 744-9463
E-mail: rwolf@cityofchicago.org
Workforce Solutions Assistant Commissioner **Will Edwards** .... (312) 744-9471
E-mail: wedwards@cityofchicago.org
Legislative Affairs Deputy Commissioner **Brad McConnell** .... (312) 744-9143
Education: Notre Dame 1994 BBA; Georgetown 2006 MPP

★ Elected Official ▲ Appointed by Legislature ▼ Appointed by Governor ► Appointed by Board or Commission ● Appointed by Judge
■ Appointed by Mayor △ Appointed by Freeholders ▽ Appointed by Supervisor ▷ Appointed by County Executive ○ Appointed by Council

Department of Planning and Development *continued*

Managing Director, Housing **Lawrence Grisham**
Room 1003 .... (312) 744-9475
Deputy Commissioner/Communications Director
Peter Strazzabosco .... (312) 744-9267
E-mail: peter.strazzabosco@cityofchicago.org
Delegate Agencies **Leona Barth** .... (312) 744-0891

Land Use Planning and Policy Division

City Hall, 121 N. La Salle St., Room 905, Chicago, IL 60602
Tel: (312) 744-5777 TTY: (312) 744-2950 Fax: (312) 744-6552
Internet: http://www.cityofchicago.org/zoning/

■ Zoning Administrator **Patricia "Patti" Scudiero** .... (312) 744-5765
E-mail: patti.scudiero@cityofchicago.org
Assistant Zoning Administrator **Steven Valenziano** ..... (312) 744-5777
Director of Administration **(Vacant)** .... (312) 744-7946
Code Enforcement Director **(Vacant)** .... (312) 744-3888
Administrative Assistant **Mary Reblin** .... (312) 744-5765
E-mail: mreblin@cityofchicago.org

Police Department [CPD]

3510 South Michigan Avenue, Chicago, IL 60653
Tel: (312) 745-6100 Tel: (312) 745-6110 (News Affairs)
E-mail: police@cityofchicago.org
Internet: www.cityofchicago.org/communitypolicing/

Employees: 13,793 **Fiscal Year:** 2016 **Budget:** $1,452,492,000

■ Superintendent **Eddie T. Johnson** .... (312) 745-6100
Fax: (312) 745-6963
First Deputy Superintendent **John Escalante** .... (312) 745-6200
Chief, Bureau of Administration **Eugene Williams** ...... (312) 745-6800
E-mail: eugene.williams@chicagopolice.org
Deputy Chief, Bureau of Administration **Marvin Shear** .. (312) 745-5600
Chief of Patrol **(Vacant)** .... (312) 745-5600

Department of Procurement Services

City Hall, 121 North LaSalle Street, Room 403, Chicago, IL 60602
TTY: (312) 744-2949 Fax: (312) 744-0010
Internet: http://www.cityofchicago.org/procurement

Employees: 91 **Fiscal Year:** 2016 **Budget:** $7,859,000

■ Chief Procurement Officer **Jamie Rhee** .... (312) 744-9750
E-mail: jamie.rhee@cityofchicago.org
First Deputy Procurement Officer **Richard Butler** .... (312) 744-4500
E-mail: richard.butler@cityofchicago.org
Deputy Procurement Officer, Compliance Unit
Monica Jimenez .... (312) 744-0845
E-mail: monica.jimenez@cityofchicago.org
Managing Deputy Procurement Officer and General
Counsel **James McIsaac** .... (312) 742-5080
E-mail: james.mcisaac@cityofchicago.org

Department of Public Health [CDPH]

DePaul Center, 333 South State Street, Room 200,
Chicago, IL 60604-3973
Tel: (312) 747-9884 Internet: http://www.cityofchicago.org/health/

Employees: 614 **Fiscal Year:** 2016 **Budget:** $149,204,000

■ Commissioner **Dr. Julie Morita** .... (312) 747-9870
E-mail: julie.morita@cityofchicago.org
Staff Assistant **Maria Gallegos** .... (312) 747-9872
E-mail: maria.gallegos@cityofchicago.org
Managing Deputy Commissioner **Jaime Dircksen** .... (312) 747-9435
Deputy Commissioner **Tiosha Gross** .... (312) 747-8841
Deputy Commissioner **Brian Richardson** .... (312) 747-9805
Deputy Commissioner **Tonya Tucker** .... (312) 747-1199
First Deputy Commissioner **(Vacant)** .... (312) 747-9878
Director of Human Resources **(Vacant)** .... (312) 747-9766
Manager of Finance **(Vacant)** .... (312) 747-8826

Department of Streets and Sanitation

City Hall, 121 N. LaSalle St., Chicago, IL 60602
Tel: (312) 744-4611 TTY: (312) 744-2971
Fax: (312) 744-5317 E-mail: streetsandsan@cityofchicago.org
Internet: http://www.cityofchicago.org/streetsandsan/

Employees: 2,205 **Fiscal Year:** 2016 **Budget:** $256,127,000

■ Commissioner **Charles L. Williams** .... (312) 744-4611
E-mail: cwilliams@cityofchicago.org Fax: (312) 744-4737
First Deputy Commissioner **(Vacant)** .... (312) 744-4611
121 North LaSalle Street, Fax: (312) 744-5317
Room 701, Chicago, IL 60602
Managing Deputy Commissioner, Street Operations
Dominic Salerno Room 704 .... (312) 744-8098
E-mail: dsalerno@cityofchicago.org
Deputy Commissioner of Forestry **Malcolm Whiteside** ... (312) 746-5224
2352 South Ashland Avenue, Fax: (312) 747-7682
Third Floor, Chicago, IL 60608
Deputy Commissioner of Sanitation **John Tully**
Room 704 .... (312) 744-4611
Fax: (312) 744-1017
Deputy Commissioner, Bureau of Street Operations
John Tully .... (312) 744-5036
121 North LaSalle Street, Fax: (312) 744-1017
Room 704, Chicago, IL 60602
E-mail: jtully@cityofchicago.org
Deputy Commissioner, Bureau of Traffic Services
Steve Sorfleet .... (312) 746-6955
120 North Racine, Chicago, IL 60607 Fax: (312) 746-9645
Public Information Officer **Anne Sheahan** Room 700 .... (312) 744-6430
E-mail: anne.sheahan@cityofchicago.org Fax: (312) 744-5317

Chicago Department of Transportation [CDOT]

30 North LaSalle Street, Suite 1100, Chicago, IL 60602-2570
Tel: (312) 744-3600 Fax: (312) 744-1200
E-mail: CDOTnews@cityofchicago.org
Internet: www.cityofchicago.org/transportation/

Employees: 1,274 **Fiscal Year:** 2016 **Budget:** $256,127,000

■ Commissioner **Rebekah Scheinfeld** .... (312) 744-3600
E-mail: rebekah.scheinfeld@cityofchicago.org
First Deputy Commissioner **Randy Conner** .... (312) 744-3501
Managing Deputy Commissioner **Kevin O'Malley** .... (312) 744-7335
Managing Deputy Commissioner **(Vacant)** Suite 600 ..... (312) 744-5649
Fax: (312) 744-4399
Engineering Division Deputy Commissioner
Dan Burke Room 400 .... (312) 744-3520
E-mail: dan.burke@cityofchicago.org Fax: (312) 744-6438
Infrastructure Managing Division Deputy
Commissioner **William Cheaks** .... (312) 743-1419
1501 West Pershing Road, Chicago, IL 60609 Fax: (312) 747-8309
Project Development Division Deputy Commissioner
Luann Hamilton Room 500 .... (312) 744-1987
Fax: (312) 747-6525
Signs and Markings Bureau Deputy Commissioner
Mark Maloney .... (312) 747-2210
3458 S. Lawndale Ave., Chicago, IL 60623 Fax: (312) 743-1394
Public Information Officer **Peter Scales** .... (312) 744-0707
E-mail: pete.scales@cityofchicago.org Fax: (312) 744-1200

Department of Water Management

Jardine Water Purification Plant, 1000 East Ohio Street,
Chicago, IL 60611
Tel: (312) 744-7001 TTY: (312) 744-2967 Fax: (312) 744-9631
Internet: www.cityofchicago.org/water/

Employees: 1,983 **Fiscal Year:** 2016 **Budget:** $307,856,000

■ Commissioner (Interim) **Barrett Murphy** .... (312) 744-7001
E-mail: bmurphy@cityofchicago.org
Assistant to the Commissioner **Sonia Avila** .... (312) 744-7001
E-mail: savila@cityofchicago.org
Assistant to the Commissioner **Jessica Billows** .... (312) 744-7002
E-mail: jbillows@cityofchicago.org
First Deputy Commissioner **Julie Hernandez-Tomlin** .... (312) 744-7001

★ Elected Official ▲ Appointed by Legislature ▼ Appointed by Governor ▶ Appointed by Board or Commission ● Appointed by Judge
■ Appointed by Mayor △ Appointed by Freeholders ▽ Appointed by Supervisor ▷ Appointed by County Executive ○ Appointed by Council

Meter Services
DePaul Center, 333 South State Street, Room 410, Chicago, IL 60604
TTY: (312) 747-7956

Managing Deputy Commissioner **Marisol Santiago** ..... (312) 747-7956
Assistant to the Commissioner **MaryEllyn Scalise** ..... (312) 747-7388
Water Meter Division Assistant Commissioner
Matthew Quinn .... (312) 745-8715
1424 West Pershing Road, Chicago, IL 60609

Bureau of Administrative Support
333 South State Street, Room 410, Chicago, IL 60604
Fax: (312) 742-0297

Managing Deputy Commissioner **(Vacant)** .... (312) 747-7089
Deputy Commissioner **(Vacant)** .... (312) 747-8039

Bureau of Operations and Water Distribution
Jardine Water Purification Plant, 1000 East Ohio Street, Level 51, Chicago, IL 60611

Managing Deputy Commissioner **William Bresnahan** .... (312) 744-7010

Bureau of Water Supply
1000 East Ohio Street, Level 38, Chicago, IL 60611

Deputy Commissioner **Alan Stark** .... (312) 744-3702
Engineer of Water Pumping **Mark O'Malley** .... (312) 744-3700
E-mail: momalley@cityofchicago.org

Engineering Services
1000 East Ohio Street, Level 51, Chicago, IL 60611

Deputy Commissioner **Burt Rezko** .... (312) 741-0741
E-mail: brezko@cityofchicago.org

Board of Election Commissioners
69 West Washington, Suite 600, Chicago, IL 60602
Fax: (312) 269-3278 E-mail: cboe@chicagoelections.net

Employees: 118 **Fiscal Year:** 2016 **Budget:** $14,769,000

Chairman **Marisel A. Hernandez** .... (312) 269-7900
Secretary **William J. Kresse** .... (312) 269-7900
Commissioner **Jonathan T. Swain** .... (312) 269-7900
Executive Director **Lance Gough** .... (312) 269-7900
Assistant Executive Director **Kelly Bateman** .... (312) 269-3285
Communications Director **James "Jim" Allen** .... (312) 269-7857
E-mail: jallen@cityofchicago.org

Board of Ethics
740 North Sedgwick St., Suite 500, Chicago, IL 60654
Fax: (312) 744-2793 Internet: http://www.cityofchicago.org/Ethics/

Employees: 9 **Fiscal Year:** 2016 **Budget:** $857,000

■ Chair **Stephen W. Beard** .... (312) 744-9660
Term Expires: 2016
Education: Illinois BA; Indiana JD
■ Board Member **Zaid Abdul-Aleem** .... (312) 744-9660
Term Expires: 2018
Education: Duke BA, MA
■ Board Member **Russ S. Carlson** .... (312) 744-9660
Term Expires: 2017
■ Board Member **Mary Trout Carr** .... (312) 744-9660
Term Expires: 2019
■ Board Member **Fran R. Grossman** .... (312) 744-9660
Term Expires: 2016
■ Board Member **Dr. Daisy S. Lezama** .... (312) 744-9660
Term Expires: 2018
■ Board Member **(Vacant)** .... (312) 744-9660
■ Executive Director **Steven I. Berlin** .... (312) 744-9660
E-mail: sberlin@cityofchicago.org

Chicago Housing Authority [CHA]
60 East Van Buren Street, Chicago, IL 60605
Tel: (312) 742-8500 E-mail: geninquiries@thecha.org
Internet: www.thecha.org

■ Chief Executive Officer **Eugene Jones, Jr.** .... (312) 742-8500
E-mail: ejones@thecha.org
Education: Albuquerque BA; New Mexico Highlands MBA

Board of Commissioners
■ Chairman of the Board **John T. Hooker** .... (312) 913-7278
E-mail: jhooker@thecha.org
Education: Chicago State
■ Commissioner **Matthew Brewer** .... (312) 742-8500
Education: Stanford BA; Harvard MBA; Yale JD
■ Commissioner **Craig Chico** .... (312) 742-8500
■ Commissioner **Mark Cozzi** .... (312) 742-8500
E-mail: mcozzi@thecha.org
■ Commissioner **Dr. Mildred C. Harris** .... (312) 742-8500
E-mail: mharris@thecha.org
■ Commissioner **Harriet Johnson** .... (312) 742-8500
■ Commissioner **John G. Markowski** .... (312) 742-8500
■ Commissioner **M. Bridget Reidy** .... (312) 742-8500
■ Commissioner **Francine Washington** .... (312) 742-8500

Chicago Public Library [CPL]
400 South State Street, Chicago, IL 60605-1203
Tel: (312) 747-4999 Fax: (312) 747-4968
Internet: www.chicagopubliclibrary.org

Year Founded: 1873 **Employees:** 954 **Fiscal Year:** 2016
Budget: $75,789,000

Administration
Commissioner **Brian Bannon** .... (312) 747-4090
E-mail: bbannon@chipublib.org Fax: (312) 747-4968
Education: Pacific Lutheran; U Washington 1999 MLIS
Executive Secretary **Desiree Kettler** .... (312) 747-4098
E-mail: dkettler@chipublib.org
First Deputy Commissioner **Andrea Sáenz** .... (312) 747-4018
E-mail: asaenz@chipublib.org Fax: (312) 747-4076
Deputy Commissioner, Administration and Finance
Baronica Roberson .... (312) 747-4030
E-mail: broberson@chipublib.org Fax: (312) 747-4078
Assistant Commissioner, Central Library **(Vacant)** .... (312) 747-4070
Fax: (312) 747-4077
Assistant Commissioner, Neighborhood Services
Andrea Telli .... (312) 747-4212
E-mail: atelli@chipublib.org

Chicago Public Schools [CPS]
42 West Madison Street, 3rd Floor, Chicago, IL 60602
Fax: (773) 553-1601 Internet: www.cps.edu

■ Chief Executive Officer **Forrest Claypool** .... (773) 553-1500
Education: Southern Illinois BS; Illinois (Chicago) 1981 JD Fax: (773) 553-1502
Senior Advisor **Denise Little** .... (773) 553-1500
Fax: (773) 553-1502
Chief of Staff **Doug Kucia** .... (773) 553-1000
Education: DePaul; Arizona State MA
Chief Education Officer **Janice K. Jackson** .... (773) 553-1300
Chief Administrative Officer **(Vacant)** .... (773) 553-1000
Chief Communications Officer **(Vacant)** .... (773) 553-1620
Chief Family and Community Engagement Officer
(Vacant) .... (773) 553-3223
Chief Financial Officer **(Vacant)** .... (773) 553-2710
Chief Information Officer **(Vacant)** .... (773) 553-1000
Fax: (773) 553-1301
Chief Leadership Development Officer **(Vacant)** .... (773) 553-1000
Chief of Media Relations **Hayley K. Meadvin** .... (773) 553-1620
E-mail: hkmeadvin@cps.edu
Education: Tulane BA; Penn State JD
Chief Officer for Public Policy **Arnaldo "Arnie" Rivera** .. (773) 553-1000

★ Elected Official ▲ Appointed by Legislature ▼ Appointed by Governor ▶ Appointed by Board or Commission ● Appointed by Judge
■ Appointed by Mayor △ Appointed by Freeholders ▽ Appointed by Supervisor ▷ Appointed by County Executive ○ Appointed by Council

Chicago Public Schools *continued*

Chief Procurement Officer **Sébastien De Longeaux** ..... (773) 553-2280
E-mail: sdelongeaux@cps.edu
Chief Talent Officer **(Vacant)** ..... (773) 553-4748
Chief Teaching and Learning Officer **Annette Gurley** ..... (773) 553-2517
General Counsel **(Vacant)** ..... (773) 553-1752

Chicago Board of Education

1 North Dearborn Street, Suite 950, Chicago, IL 60602
Fax: (773) 553-1601 Internet: http://www.cpsboe.org/

■ President **Frank M. Clark, Jr.** ..... (773) 553-1600
Term Expires: June 30, 2017
Education: DePaul BBA, 1976 JD
■ Vice President **Jaime Guzman** ..... (773) 553-1600
Term Expires: June 30, 2017
■ Member **Mark F. Furlong** ..... (773) 553-1600
Term Expires: June 30, 2019
Education: Southern Illinois 1981 BS
■ Member **Rev. Michael Garazini** ..... (773) 553-1600
Term Expires: June 30, 2019
■ Member **Dr. Mahalia Hines** ..... (773) 553-1600
Term Expires: June 30, 2017
■ Member **Dominique Jordan Turner** ..... (773) 553-1600
Term Expires: June 30, 2019
■ Member **Gail Ward** ..... (773) 553-1600
Term Expires: June 30, 2019
Secretary to the Board **Estela G. Beltran** ..... (773) 553-1600

Commission on Animal Care and Control [ACC]

2741 South Western Ave., Chicago, IL 60608
Fax: (312) 747-1409

Employees: 73 **Fiscal Year:** 2016 **Budget:** $5,703,000

■ Executive Director **Susan Russell** ..... (312) 747-1408
Deputy Director **Ivan J. Capifali** ..... (312) 747-1386
Fax: (312) 747-1409

Chicago Commission on Human Relations [CCHR]

740 North Sedgwick Street, Chicago, IL 60654-8488
Tel: (312) 744-4111 Fax: (312) 744-1081

Employees: 20 **Fiscal Year:** 2016 **Budget:** $2,313,000

■ Chairman and Commissioner **Mona Noriega** ..... (312) 744-4100
E-mail: mona.noriega@cityofchicago.org

License Appeal Commission

50 West Washington Street, Concourse Level 21, Chicago, IL 60602
Fax: (312) 742-0759 Internet: www.cityofchicago.org/lac

Employees: 1 **Fiscal Year:** 2016 **Budget:** $176,000

Chairman **Dennis M. Fleming** ..... (312) 744-4095

Public Building Commission

Richard J. Daley Center, Rm. 200, 50 West Washington Street, Chicago, IL 60602
Fax: (312) 744-8005 E-mail: pbc@pbcchicago.com
Internet: http://pbcchicago.com/

■ Executive Director **Felicia S. Davis** ..... (312) 744-3090
E-mail: fdavis@cityofchicago.org Fax: (312) 742-8005
Education: Howard U BA

Office of the City Council

City Hall, 121 North LaSalle Street, Room 201, Chicago, IL 60602
Tel: (312) 744-6800 Fax: (312) 744-6824

Employees: 235 **Fiscal Year:** 2016 **Budget:** $27,415,000

Note: Council Members run and are elected on a non-partisan basis.

★ President Pro Tem **Margaret Laurino** (Ward 39) ..... (312) 744-7242
Term Expires: May 2019
E-mail: ward39@cityofchicago.org
Education: Northeastern Illinois BA, MA
★ Vice Mayor **Brendan Reilly** (Ward 42) ..... (312) 744-3062
Term Expires: May 2019
E-mail: office@ward42chicago.com
Education: Hobart 1994 BA
★ Alderman **Proco "Joe" Moreno III** (Ward 1) ..... (312) 744-3063
Term Expires: May 2019
E-mail: ward01@cityofchicago.org
★ Alderman **Brian Hopkins** (Ward 2) ..... (312) 744-6836
Term Expires: May 2019
E-mail: ward02@cityofchicago.org
★ Alderman **Pat Dowell** (Ward 3) ..... (312) 744-8734
Term Expires: May 2019
E-mail: ward03@cityofchicago.org
Education: Rochester BA; Chicago MSSA
★ Alderman **Sophia King** (Ward 4) ..... (312) 744-2690
Term Expires: May 2019
E-mail: ward04@cityofchicago.org
Education: Illinois BS; Northwestern MA
★ Alderman **Leslie A. Hairston** (Ward 5) ..... (312) 744-6832
Term Expires: May 2019
E-mail: leslie.hairston@cityofchicago.org
Education: Wisconsin BA; Loyola U (Chicago) JD
★ Alderman **Roderick T. Sawyer** (Ward 6) ..... (312) 744-6868
Term Expires: May 2019
E-mail: ward06@cityofchicago.org
Date of Birth: April 12, 1963
Education: DePaul 1985 BS; Chicago-Kent 1990 JD
★ Alderman **Gregory I. Mitchell** (Ward 7) ..... (312) 744-6833
Term Expires: May 2019
E-mail: ward07@cityofchicago.org
★ Alderman **Michelle A. Harris** (Ward 8) ..... (312) 744-3075
Term Expires: May 2019
E-mail: ward08@cityofchicago.org
★ Alderman **Anthony A. Beale** (Ward 9) ..... (312) 744-6838
Term Expires: May 2019
E-mail: ward09@cityofchicago.org
★ Alderman **Susan Sadlowski Garza** (Ward 10) ..... (312) 744-3078
Term Expires: May 2019
E-mail: ward10@cityofchicago.org
★ Alderman **Patrick Daley Thompson** (Ward 11) ..... (312) 744-6663
Term Expires: May 2019
E-mail: ward11@cityofchicago.org
★ Alderman **George A. Cárdenas** (Ward 12) ..... (312) 744-3068
Term Expires: May 2019
E-mail: ward12@cityofchicago.org
Education: Northeastern Illinois BS, MA
★ Alderman **Marty Quinn** (Ward 13) ..... (312) 744-3058
Term Expires: May 2019
E-mail: ward13@cityofchicago.org
★ Alderman **Edward M. Burke** (Ward 14) ..... (312) 744-3380
Term Expires: May 2019
E-mail: ward14@cityofchicago.org
Education: DePaul 1965 BA, 1968 JD
★ Alderman **Raymond A. Lopez** (Ward 15) ..... (312) 744-4321
Term Expires: May 2019
E-mail: ward15@cityofchicago.org
★ Alderman **Toni L. Foulkes** (Ward 16) ..... (312) 744-6850
Term Expires: May 2019
E-mail: ward16@cityofchicago.org
★ Alderman **David H. Moore** (Ward 17) ..... (312) 744-3435
Term Expires: May 2019
E-mail: ward17@cityofchicago.org

(continued on next page)

★ Elected Official ▲ Appointed by Legislature ▼ Appointed by Governor ▶ Appointed by Board or Commission ● Appointed by Judge
■ Appointed by Mayor △ Appointed by Freeholders ▽ Appointed by Supervisor ▷ Appointed by County Executive ○ Appointed by Council

Office of the City Council *continued*

★Alderman **Derrick G. Curtis** (Ward 18) . . . . (312) 744-6856
Term Expires: May 2019
E-mail: ward18@cityofchicago.org

★Alderman **Matthew J. O'Shea** (Ward 19) . . . . (312) 744-3072
Term Expires: May 2019
E-mail: ward19@cityofchicago.org

★Alderman **Willie B. Cochran** (Ward 20) . . . . (312) 744-6840
Term Expires: May 2019
E-mail: ward20@cityofchicago.org
Education: Eastern Illinois 1975 BA; Illinois Tech 1988 MPA

★Alderman **Howard B. Brookins, Jr.** (Ward 21) . . . . (312) 744-4810
Term Expires: May 2019
E-mail: ward21@cityofchicago.org
Education: Southern Illinois BA; Northern Illinois MA

★Alderman **Ricardo Muñoz** (Ward 22) . . . . (312) 744-9491
Term Expires: May 2019
E-mail: ward22@cityofchicago.org
Education: Northern Illinois 1987 BA

★Alderman **Michael R. Zalewski** (Ward 23) . . . . (312) 744-6828
Term Expires: May 2019
E-mail: michael.zalewski@cityofchicago.org

★Alderman **Michael Scott, Jr.** (Ward 24) . . . . (312) 744-6839
Term Expires: May 2019
E-mail: ward24@cityofchicago.org

★Alderman **Daniel S. Solis** (Ward 25) . . . . (312) 744-6845
Term Expires: May 2019
E-mail: ward25@cityofchicago.org

★Alderman **Roberto Maldonado** (Ward 26) . . . . (312) 744-6853
Term Expires: May 2019
E-mail: ward26@cityofchicago.org
Education: Puerto Rico BA, MA

★Alderman **Walter Burnett, Jr.** (Ward 27) . . . . (312) 744-6124
Term Expires: May 2019
E-mail: ward27@cityofchicago.org
Education: Northeastern Illinois 1998 BA

★Alderman **Jason Ervin** (Ward 28) . . . . (312) 744-3066
Term Expires: May 2019
E-mail: ward28@cityofchicago.org

★Alderman **Christopher Taliaferro** (Ward 29) . . . . (312) 744-8805
Term Expires: May 2019
E-mail: ward29@cityofchicago.org

★Alderman **Ariel E. Reboyras** (Ward 30) . . . . (312) 744-3304
Term Expires: May 2019
E-mail: ward30@cityofchicago.org
Education: Illinois (Chicago) BA

★Alderman **Milagros "Milly" Santiago** (Ward 31) . . . . (312) 744-6102
Term Expires: May 2019
E-mail: ward31@cityofchicago.org

★Alderman **Scott Waguespack** (Ward 32) . . . . (312) 744-6567
Term Expires: May 2019
E-mail: ward32@cityofchicago.org
Education: Colorado State BA; Chicago-Kent 2000 JD

★Alderman **Deborah Mell** (Ward 33) . . . . (312) 744-3373
Term Expires: May 2019
E-mail: ward33@cityofchicago.org
Education: Cornell Col BA

★Alderman **Carrie M. Austin** (Ward 34) . . . . (312) 744-6820
Term Expires: May 2019
E-mail: ward34@cityofchicago.org

★Alderman **Carlos Ramirez-Rosa** (Ward 35) . . . . (312) 744-6835
Term Expires: May 2019
E-mail: ward35@cityofchicago.org

★Alderman **Gilbert Villegas** (Ward 36) . . . . (312) 744-4324
Term Expires: May 2019
E-mail: ward36@cityofchicago.org

★Alderman **Emma M. Mitts** (Ward 37) . . . . (312) 744-3180
Term Expires: May 2019
E-mail: ward37@cityofchicago.org

★Alderman **Nicholas Sposato** (Ward 38) . . . . (312) 744-6857
Term Expires: May 2019
E-mail: ward38@cityofchicago.org

Office of the City Council *continued*

★Alderman **Patrick J. O'Connor** (Ward 40) . . . . (312) 744-6858
Term Expires: May 2019
E-mail: ward40@cityofchicago.org

★Alderman **Anthony V. Napolitano** (Ward 41) . . . . (312) 744-3942
Term Expires: May 2019
E-mail: ward41@cityofchicago.org

★Alderman **Michele Smith** (Ward 43) . . . . (312) 744-5685
Term Expires: May 2019
E-mail: ward43@cityofchicago.org
Education: SUNY (Buffalo) 1976 BA; Chicago 1979 JD

★Alderman **Thomas M. Tunney** (Ward 44) . . . . (312) 744-3073
Term Expires: May 2019
E-mail: ward44@cityofchicago.org
Education: Illinois BA; Cornell 1979 MPS

★Alderman **John Arena** (Ward 45) . . . . (312) 744-6841
Term Expires: May 2019
E-mail: ward45@cityofchicago.org

★Alderman **James Cappleman** (Ward 46) . . . . (312) 744-6831
Term Expires: May 2019
E-mail: ward46@cityofchicago.org

★Alderman **Ameya Pawar** (Ward 47) . . . . (312) 744-0446
Term Expires: May 2019
E-mail: ward47@cityofchicago.org

★Alderman **Harry Osterman** (Ward 48) . . . . (312) 744-6834
Term Expires: May 2019
E-mail: ward48@cityofchicago.org

★Alderman **Joseph A. Moore** (Ward 49) . . . . (312) 744-3067
Term Expires: May 2019
E-mail: ward49@cityofchicago.org
Education: Knox (IL) 1980 BA; DePaul 1984 JD

★Alderman **Debra Silverstein** (Ward 50) . . . . (312) 744-6855
Term Expires: May 2019
E-mail: ward50@cityofchicago.org

Office of the City Clerk

City Hall, 121 North LaSalle Street, Room 107, Chicago, IL 60602-1295
TTY: (312) 744-2939 Tel: (312) 744-6861 Fax: (312) 744-1711
Internet: http://www.chicityclerk.com/

Employees: 96 **Fiscal Year:** 2016 **Budget:** $10,046,000

★City Clerk **Susana A. Mendoza** . . . . (312) 744-8590
Term Expires: May 2019
E-mail: susana.mendoza@cityofchicago.org
Education: Northeast Missouri State BA
Executive Secretary **Amanda Prentice** . . . . (312) 744-8590
E-mail: amanda.prentice@cityofchicago.org

Deputy City Clerk **Carina Sanchez** . . . . (312) 744-8590
E-mail: carina.sanchez@cityofchicago.org

Press Secretary **Patrick Corcoran** . . . . (312) 744-2507

Program Director **Halyna Shuruk** . . . . (312) 744-6865
E-mail: halyna.schuruk@cityofchicago.org

Director of Collection Processing **Gery Halper** . . . . (312) 744-6625
E-mail: gery.halper@cityofchicago.org

Business License Administration Manager
Phyllis Powell . . . . (312) 744-1341

Managing Editor (City Council) **Peter Polacek** . . . . (312) 744-6870

Office of the City Treasurer

City Hall, 121 North LaSalle Street, Room 106, Chicago, IL 60602
Tel: (312) 744-3356 TTY: (312) 744-6920 Fax: (312) 742-0981
Internet: www.chicagocitytreasurer.com

Employees: 33 **Fiscal Year:** 2016 **Budget:** $4,192,000

★City Treasurer **Kurt Summers** . . . . (312) 744-3356
Term Expires: May 2019
E-mail: kurt.summers@cityofchicago.org
Education: Washington U (MO) 2000; Harvard 2005 MBA

Chief Operating Officer and Deputy Treasurer
Kristi Lafleur . . . . (312) 742-1852
E-mail: kristi.lafleur@cityofchicago.org

★Elected Official ▲Appointed by Legislature ▼Appointed by Governor ►Appointed by Board or Commission ●Appointed by Judge
■Appointed by Mayor △Appointed by Freeholders ▽Appointed by Supervisor ▷Appointed by County Executive ○Appointed by Council

Office of the City Treasurer *continued*

General Counsel and Deputy Chief Operating Officer
Drew Beres . . . . (312) 744-7957
Director of Communications **Katie Hickey** . . . . (312) 744-2432
E-mail: lilia.chacon@cityofchicago.org

City of Chula Vista, California

City Hall, 276 Fourth Avenue, Chula Vista, CA 91910
Tel: (619) 691-5031 (Information) Fax: (619) 409-5884
Internet: www.chulavistaca.gov

County: San Diego **Election Type:** Nonpartisan **Population:** 265,757 (2015)

Office of the Mayor and City Council

276 Fourth Avenue, Chula Vista, CA 91910
Fax: (619) 476-5379

★ Mayor **Mary Casillas Salas** . . . . (619) 691-5044
Began Service: December 2014
Term Expires: December 2018
E-mail: msalas@chulavistaca.gov

★ Council Member **Patricia Aguilar** . . . . (619) 691-5044
Term Expires: December 2018
E-mail: paguilar@chulavistaca.gov

★ Council Member **Pamela Bensoussan** . . . . (619) 691-5044
Term Expires: December 2016
E-mail: pbensoussan@chulavistaca.gov

★ Council Member **John McCann** . . . . (619) 691-5044
Term Expires: December 2018
E-mail: jmccann@chulavistaca.gov

★ Council Member **Steve Miesen** . . . . (619) 691-5044
Term Expires: December 2016
E-mail: smiesen@chulavistaca.gov

Office of the City Clerk

276 Fourth Avenue, Chula Vista, CA 91910
Fax: (619) 585-5774

○ City Clerk **Donna Norris** . . . . (619) 691-3006
E-mail: cityclerk@chulavistaca.gov

Assistant City Clerk **Kerry Bigelow** . . . . (619) 407-3590
E-mail: kbigelow@chulavistaca.gov

Office of the City Manager

276 4th Avenue, Chula Vista, CA 91910
Fax: (619) 409-5884

○ City Manager **Gary Halbert** . . . . (619) 691-5031
E-mail: ghalbert@chulavistaca.gov
Education: UC San Diego BS; San Diego State MPA

Deputy City Manager **Kelley Bacon** . . . . (619) 691-5144
E-mail: kbacon@chulavistaca.gov

Deputy City Manager **Maria Kachadoorian** . . . . (619) 691-5028
E-mail: mkachadoorian@chulavistaca.gov
Education: San Diego State BS, MPA

Marketing and Communications Manager
Anne Steinberger . . . . (619) 691-5296
E-mail: asteinberger@chulavistaca.gov

Development Services Department

276 4th Avenue, Chula Vista, CA 91910
Fax: (619) 409-5861 (Planning Administration Fax)
Fax: (619) 585-5681 (Building Fax)
Fax: (619) 409-5859 (Environmental Fax)

Director **Kelly Broughton** . . . . (619) 691-5233
Education: Penn State BA

Development Planning Manager **Mary Ladiana** . . . . (619) 409-5432
E-mail: mladiana@chulavistaca.gov

Finance Department

276 4th Avenue, Chula Vista, CA 91910
Fax: (619) 409-5814

Finance Director **David Bilby** . . . . (619) 691-5250

Fire Department

447 F Street, Chula Vista, CA 91910
Fax: (619) 691-5057

Fire Chief **Jim Geering** . . . . (619) 409-5854
E-mail: jgeering@chulavistaca.gov

Deputy Fire Chief **Jeff Peter** . . . . (619) 409-5847
E-mail: jpeter@chulavistaca.gov

Fire Division Chief **Justin Gipson** . . . . (619) 409-5841
E-mail: jgipson@chulavistaca.gov

Human Resources Department

276 4th Avenue, Chula Vista, CA 91910
Fax: (619) 691-5199

Director **Courtney Chase** . . . . (619) 409-5927
E-mail: cchase@chulavistaca.gov

Risk Manager **Teri Enos** . . . . (619) 691-4050
E-mail: tenos@chulavistaca.gov

Information Technology Services

276 Fourth Avenue, Chula Vista, CA 91910
Fax: (619) 476-5399

Director **Edward Chew** . . . . (619) 691-5013
E-mail: echew@chulavistaca.gov

Library Department

365 F Street, Chula Vista, CA 91910
Fax: (619) 427-4246

Director **Betty Waznis** . . . . (619) 691-5170
E-mail: bwaznis@chulavistaca.gov

Principal Librarian **Stephanie Loney** . . . . (619) 691-5288
E-mail: sloney@chulavistaca.gov

Police Department

315 Fourth Avenue, Chula Vista, CA 91910
Fax: (619) 691-5281

Police Chief **David Bejarano** . . . . (619) 691-5150

Public Works Department

1800 Maxwell Road, Chula Vista, CA 91911
Tel: (619) 397-6000
Fax: (619) 397-6250 (Administration/Engineering Fax)
Fax: (619) 397-6259 (Operations Fax)

Director of Public Works Operations **Richard Hopkins** . . . (619) 409-5873

Engineering Division

276 4th Avenue, Chula Vista, CA 91910
Fax: (619) 691-5171

Director of Public Works Operations **Richard Hopkins** . . . (619) 409-5873
E-mail: rahopkins@chulavistaca.gov

Assistant Director of Public Works **Iracsema Quilantan** . . (619) 397-6066
E-mail: iquilantan@chulavistaca.gov

Principal Civil Engineer **Tom Adler** . . . . (619) 409-6066
E-mail: tadler@chulavistaca.gov

Recreation Department

276 4th Avenue, Chula Vista, CA 91910
Fax: (619) 585-5618

Director **Kristi McClure Huckaby** . . . . (619) 409-5979

★ Elected Official ▲ Appointed by Legislature ▼ Appointed by Governor ▶ Appointed by Board or Commission ● Appointed by Judge
■ Appointed by Mayor △ Appointed by Freeholders ▽ Appointed by Supervisor ▷ Appointed by County Executive ○ Appointed by Council

Redevelopment and Housing Authority
276 Fourth Avenue, Chula Vista, CA 91910
Fax: (619) 585-5698

Development Services Director **Kelly Broughton** .... (619) 691-5233
E-mail: kbroughton@chulavistaca.gov
Education: Penn State BA

Office of the City Attorney
276 4th Avenue, Chula Vista, CA 91910
Fax: (619) 409-5823

★City Attorney **Glen Googins** .... (619) 691-5039
Term Expires: December 2018
E-mail: ggoogins@chulavistaca.gov

City of Cincinnati, Ohio
City Hall, 801 Plum St., Cincinnati, OH 45202
Tel: (513) 352-3000 (Information) Internet: www.cincinnati-oh.gov

County: Hamilton **Election Type:** Nonpartisan **Year Founded:** 1788
Year Incorporated: 1819 **Population:** 298,550 (2015)

Office of the Mayor
City Hall, 801 Plum Street, Room 150, Cincinnati, OH 45202-1979
Fax: (513) 352-5201

★Mayor **John J. Cranley** .... (513) 352-3250
Began Service: December 1, 2013
Term Expires: December 1, 2017
Education: John Carroll BA; Harvard 1999 JD, MTh

Office of the City Manager
City Hall, 801 Plum St., Cincinnati, OH 45202
Tel: (513) 352-3243 Fax: (513) 352-6284
Internet: www.cincinnati-oh.gov/cmgr/pages/-3046-/

■City Manager **Harry E. Black** .... (513) 352-3742
Date of Birth: 1963 Fax: (513) 352-6284
Education: Virginia State 1985 BPA; Virginia 1987 MPA
Assistant City Manager **Sheila Hill-Christian** .... (513) 352-3475
Education: VCU BBA; Averett U MBA Fax: (513) 352-2458

Citizen Complaint Authority
Two Centennial Plaza, 805 Central Ave., Cincinnati, OH 45202
Fax: (513) 352-3158

Director **Kim Neal** .... (513) 352-1600
E-mail: kim.neal@cincinnati-oh.gov
Chief Investigator **Pamela King** .... (513) 352-3150
E-mail: pam.king@cincinnati-oh.gov

Office of Performance and Data Analytics
City Hall, 801 Plum Street, Cincinnati, OH 45202

Director **Chad Kenney, Jr.** .... (513) 352-5368
E-mail: chad.kenney@cincinnati-oh.gov

Buildings and Inspections Department
3300 Central Parkway, Cincinnati, OH 45225
Tel: (513) 352-3260 Fax: (513) 352-1504
Internet: http://www.cincinnati-oh.gov/buildings

Director **Arthur "Art" Dahlberg** .... (513) 352-3271
Education: Kansas State BSCE
Zoning Administrator **Matthew Shad** .... (513) 352-3430

Cincinnati Board of Health
3101 Burnet Avenue, Cincinnati, OH 45229-3098

Health Department
3101 Burnet Avenue, Cincinnati, OH 45229-3098
Tel: (513) 357-7200 Fax: (513) 357-7290
Internet: www.cincinnati-oh.gov/health/pages/-5092-/

Commissioner **Dr. Noble Maseru** .... (513) 357-7280
Education: Wayne State U BS; Emory MPH; Atlanta PhD
Medical Director **Dr. O'dell M. Owens** .... (513) 357-7366
Education: Antioch Col BA; Yale 1976 MD

Cincinnati Parks
950 Eden Park Dr., Cincinnati, OH 45202
Tel: (513) 352-4080 TTY: (513) 352-3380 Fax: (513) 352-4096
Internet: www.cincinnatiparks.com

Director **Willie F. Carden, Jr.** .... (513) 352-4079

Department of Enterprise Technology Solutions [ETS]
805 Central Avenue, Suite 300, Cincinnati, OH 45202
Tel: (513) 352-6400 Fax: (513) 352-6430 E-mail: ets@cincinnati-oh.gov

Chief Information Officer **Jayson Dunn** .... (513) 352-4261
E-mail: jayson.dunn@cincinnati-oh.gov Fax: (513) 352-6430
Assistant Deputy **Jack Johnson** .... (513) 352-5350
E-mail: jack.johnson@cincinnati-oh.gov
CAGIS (Cincinnati Area Geographic Information Systems) Administrator **Raj Chundur** .... (513) 352-1644
E-mail: raj.chundur@cincinnati-oh.gov
Enterprise Technology Solutions Business Analytics Manager **Sean Ware** .... (513) 352-4282
E-mail: sean.ware@cincinnati-oh.gov
Citco - City County Information Technology Services **Richard Walker** .... (513) 352-4279
E-mail: richard.walker@cincinnati-oh.gov
CLEAR (Cincinnati/Hamilton County Law Enforcement Systems)/HAMCO Manager **Peggy O'Neill** .... (513) 352-4774
E-mail: peggy.oneill@cincinnati-oh.gov

Finance Department
City Hall, 801 Plum Street, Room 250, Cincinnati, OH 45202
Tel: (513) 352-3731 Fax: (513) 352-2370

Director **Reginald Zeno** .... (513) 352-3731
Assistant Finance Director (Interim) **Karen Alder** .... (513) 352-2570
Tax Commissioner **Ted Nussman** .... (513) 352-3838
805 Central Ave., Cincinnati, OH 45202
E-mail: ted.nussman@cincinnati-oh.gov
Treasurer **Nicole Lee** .... (513) 352-4781
Deputy Treasurer **William Feldman** .... (513) 352-6980
Supervising Management Analyst **Nicole Lee** .... (513) 352-3224
Audits and Accounts Finance Manager **Mark Ashworth** .. (513) 352-3221
Finance Manager/Purchasing Agent **Patrick Duhaney** .... (513) 352-3211
E-mail: Patrick.Duhaney@cincinnati-oh.gov
Retirement System Executive Director **Paula Tilsley** ..... (513) 352-3227
Risk Manager **Deborah Allison** .... (513) 352-3337
E-mail: deborah.allison@cincinnati-oh.gov

Office of Budget and Evaluation
Fax: (513) 352-3233

Director **Christopher Bigham** .... (513) 352-3232
E-mail: chris.bigham@cincinnati-oh.gov

Fire Department
430 Central Ave., Cincinnati, OH 45202
Fax: (513) 352-1548

Fire Chief **Richard A. Braun** .... (513) 352-6220
E-mail: richard.braun@cincinnati-oh.gov
Fire Prevention Assistant Chief **Robert "Bob" Kuhn** .... (513) 564-1742
E-mail: robert.kuhn@cincinnati-oh.gov

★Elected Official ▲Appointed by Legislature ▼Appointed by Governor ▶Appointed by Board or Commission ●Appointed by Judge
■Appointed by Mayor △Appointed by Freeholders ▽Appointed by Supervisor ▷Appointed by County Executive ○Appointed by Council

Human Resources Department

Two Centennial Plaza, 805 Central Ave., Suite 200, Cincinnati, OH 45202
Tel: (513) 352-2400 Fax: (513) 352-5223
Internet: http://www.cincinnati-oh.gov/hr/

Director **Georgetta Kelly** . . . . . (513) 352-2436
E-mail: georgetta.kelly@cincinnati-oh.gov
Assistant Human Resources Director **Nancy Olind** . . . . . (513) 352-2400
E-mail: nancy.olind@cincinnati-oh.gov
Shared Services Division Manager **Lisa Berning** . . . . . (513) 352-2417
E-mail: lisa.berning@cincinnati-oh.gov

Law Department

City Hall, 801 Plum Street, Room 214, Cincinnati, OH 45202
Tel: (513) 352-3334 Fax: (513) 352-1515
Internet: www.cincinnati-oh.gov/law

City Solicitor **Paula Boggs Muething** . . . . . (513) 352-3320
E-mail: paula.boggsmuething@cincinnati-oh.gov
Education: Kentucky BA, BS; Cincinnati JD
Deputy City Solicitor **Luke Blocher** . . . . . (513) 352-4893
Deputy City Solicitor **Terrance Nestor** . . . . . (513) 352-3327
Economic and Community Development Division Chief Counsel **Patricia Braxton** . . . . . (513) 352-3613
Chief Counsel, General Counsel **Roshani Hardin** . . . . . (513) 352-1570
Real Estate Manager **Thomas Klumb** . . . . . (513) 352-1571
Chief Counsel, Litigation/Labor and Employment **Peter Stackpole** . . . . . (513) 352-3350
Chief Counsel, Metropolitan Sewer District **Diana Christy** . . . . . (513) 244-5123
Chief Counsel, Prosecution **Natali Harris** . . . . . (513) 352-4702
Chief Counsel, Quality of Life/Affirmative Action **Jessica Powell** . . . . . (513) 352-3945
Chief Counsel, Transportation and Major Transportation **Andrew Garth** . . . . . (513) 352-3345

Office of Administrative Hearings

805 Central Avenue, Suite 110, Cincinnati, OH 45202
Fax: (513) 352-4895

Hearing Examiner **Thomas Beridon** . . . . . (513) 352-3618

Department of City Planning

801 Plum Street, Cincinnati, OH 45202
Tel: (513) 352-4845

Planning Director **Charles Graves III** . . . . . (513) 352-4851
Supervising City Planner **Katherine Keough-Jurs** . . . . . (513) 352-4859

Public Services Department

1115 Bates Avenue, Cincinnati, OH 45225
Tel: (513) 352-5480 Fax: (513) 352-1639
Internet: www.cincinnati-oh.gov/public-services/

Director **Maraskeshia S. Smith** . . . . . (513) 352-5480
Education: Kentucky BA; Eastern Kentucky MBA

Facility Management

1408 Queen City Avenue, Cincinnati, OH 45214

Deputy Director **Joel Koopman** . . . . . (513) 352-6391
E-mail: joel.koopman@cincinnati-oh.gov
Assistant Facilities Maintenance Manager **Daniel "Dan" Helm** . . . . . (513) 352-6391
E-mail: dan.helm@cincinnati-oh.gov
Assistant Facilities Maintenance Manager **Jeff Linneman** . . . . . (513) 352-6391
E-mail: jeff.linneman@cincinnati-oh.gov

Fleet Services Division

1106 Bates Avenue, Cincinnati, OH 45225

Manager **David Cavanaugh** . . . . . (513) 352-5457

Neighborhood Operations Division

3320 Millcreek Rd., Cincinnati, OH 45223
Fax: (513) 352-3698

Superintendent **Jude Johnson** . . . . . (513) 357-2680

Traffic and Road Operations

3300 Colerain Avenue, Cincinnati, OH 45225
Fax: (513) 591-6069

Superintendent **Jarrod Bolden** . . . . . (513) 591-6050

Police Department

310 Ezzard Charles Dr., Cincinnati, OH 45214
Fax: (513) 352-2949 E-mail: cpd.webmaster@cincinnati-oh.gov

Police Chief **Lt. Col. Eliot Isaac** . . . . . (513) 352-3536
Executive Assistant Chief **David J. Bailey** . . . . . (513) 765-1212
Assistant Police Chief **Michael K. John** . . . . . (513) 765-1212
Assistant Police Chief **Paul Neudigate** . . . . . (513) 765-1212
Assistant Police Chief **Teresa Theetge** . . . . . (513) 765-1212

Department of Trade and Development

Two Centennial Plaza, 805 Central Ave., Suite 700, Cincinnati, OH 45202
Fax: (513) 352-6113 E-mail: communitydevelopment@cincinnati-oh.gov

Director **Oscar Bedolla** . . . . . (513) 352-6146
E-mail: oscar.bedolla@cincinnati-oh.gov

Parking Facilities

300 West 6th Street, Cincinnati, OH 45202
Fax: (513) 352-5311

Superintendent **Robert Schroer** . . . . . (513) 352-1902 ext. 1

Transportation and Engineering Department [CDOTE]

City Hall, 801 Plum St., Room 450, Cincinnati, OH 45202
Fax: (513) 352-6246 Internet: www.cincinnati-oh.gov/dote/

Director **Michael Moore** . . . . . (513) 352-3303
E-mail: michael.moore@cincinnati-oh.gov Fax: (513) 352-6246
Engineering Division, City Engineer **Don Gindling** . . . . . (513) 352-1518
E-mail: don.gindling@cincinnati-oh.gov Fax: (513) 352-1581
Transportation Planning and Urban Design, City Architect (Acting) **Matthew Andrews** . . . . . (513) 352-3284
Fax: (513) 352-5336
City Traffic Engineer **Dennis Lechlak** . . . . . (513) 352-6229
E-mail: dennis.lechlak@cincinnati-oh.gov
Education: Toledo BSCE, MSCE

Aviation Division

262 Wilmer Ave., Cincinnati, OH 45226
Fax: (513) 871-6801

Airport Manager **Fred Anderton** . . . . . (513) 352-6340

Greater Cincinnati Water Works [GCWW]

4747 Spring Grove Avenue, Cincinnati, OH 45232
Tel: (513) 591-7700 (Customer Service)
Fax: (513) 591-6519 E-mail: info@gcww.cincinnati-oh.gov
Internet: http://www.cincinnati-oh.gov/water/

Director **Cathy Bailey** . . . . . (513) 591-7977
Deputy Director **Verna Arnette** . . . . . (513) 244-5535
Deputy Director **(Vacant)** . . . . . (513) 244-5182
Chief Engineer (Interim) **Russ Weber** . . . . . (513) 557-5187
E-mail: russ.weber@gcww.cincinnati-oh.gov
Chief Financial Officer **(Vacant)** . . . . . (513) 244-1305
Commercial Services Division Superintendent **Gary Wiest** . . . . . (513) 591-6575
Distribution Division Superintendent (Interim) **Jason Fleming** . . . . . (513) 591-7908
Supply Division Superintendent **Jeffrey Pieper** . . . . . (513) 624-5804
5651 Kellogg Avenue, Cincinnati, OH 45230

(continued on next page)

★ Elected Official ▲ Appointed by Legislature ▼ Appointed by Governor ► Appointed by Board or Commission ● Appointed by Judge
■ Appointed by Mayor △ Appointed by Freeholders ▽ Appointed by Supervisor ▷ Appointed by County Executive ○ Appointed by Council

Greater Cincinnati Water Works *continued*

Water Quality Management Division Superintendent
Jeff Swertfeger .... (513) 624-5608
5651 Kellogg Avenue, Cincinnati, OH 45230
Information Technology Division Superintendent
Bryan May .... (513) 591-7791
E-mail: bryan.may@gcww.cincinnati-oh.gov

Metropolitan Sewer District

1600 Gest St., Cincinnati, OH 45204
Tel: (513) 352-4900 Internet: www.msdgc.org/

Executive Director **Gérald R. Checco** .... (513) 244-5121
Fax: (513) 244-1399
Deputy Director **Mary Lynn Lodor** .... (513) 244-5121
Industrial Waste Superintendent **Jennifer Richmond** ..... (513) 244-7000
Fax: (513) 557-7050
Information Technology **Don Sander** .... (513) 557-7151
Fax: (513) 244-1399
Stormwater Management, Sewers Chief Engineer
Michael L. Pittinger .... (513) 244-1380
Fax: (513) 557-7169
Wastewater Administration Superintendent **(Vacant)** ...... (513) 244-1308
Fax: (513) 244-1384
Wastewater Collection Superintendent
Michael L. Pittinger .... (513) 352-4201
225 W. Galbraith Rd., Cincinnati, OH 45215 Fax: (513) 352-4913
Project and Business Development Sewers Chief
Engineer **Pat Arnette** .... (513) 244-5187
Fax: (513) 244-7193
Wastewater Treatment Superintendent
Vanessa Smedley .... (513) 244-5502
Fax: (513) 557-5950

Office of the City Council

City Hall, 801 Plum Street, Cincinnati, OH 45202
Tel: (513) 352-3246 Fax: (513) 352-2578

★ Vice Mayor **David Mann** Room 349 .... (513) 352-4611
Term Expires: December 1, 2017
E-mail: david.mann@cincinnati-oh.gov
★ President Pro Tem **Yvette Simpson** Room 346B .... (513) 352-5260
Term Expires: December 1, 2017
E-mail: yvette.simpson@cincinnati-oh.gov
★ Council Member **Kevin Flynn** Room 348 .... (513) 352-4550
Term Expires: December 1, 2017
E-mail: kevin.flynn@cincinnati-oh.gov
★ Council Member **Amy Murray** Room 346A .... (513) 352-3640
Term Expires: December 1, 2017
E-mail: amy.murray@cincinnati-oh.gov
★ Council Member **Chris Seelbach** Room 350 .... (513) 352-5210
Term Expires: December 1, 2017
E-mail: chris.seelbach@cincinnati-oh.gov
★ Council Member **Paul G. "P.G." Sittenfeld** Room 354 ... (513) 352-5270
Term Expires: December 1, 2017
E-mail: paul.sittenfeld@cincinnati-oh.gov
Education: Princeton; Occidental
★ Council Member **Christopher Smitherman**
Room 346B .... (513) 352-3464
Term Expires: December 1, 2017
E-mail: christopher.smitherman@cincinnati-oh.gov
★ Council Member **Charlie Winburn** Room 351 .... (513) 352-5304
Term Expires: December 1, 2017 Fax: (513) 352-4657
E-mail: charlie.winburn@cincinnati-oh.gov
★ Council Member **Wendell Young** Room 351 .... (513) 352-3466
Term Expires: December 1, 2017
E-mail: wendell.young@cincinnati-oh.gov
Clerk of the Council **Melissa Autry** Room 308 .... (513) 352-3246
E-mail: clerkofcouncil@cincinnati-oh.gov Fax: (513) 352-2578
Chief Deputy Clerk **Brenda Williams** Room 308 .... (513) 352-3247
E-mail: brenda.williams@cincinnati-oh.gov

Cincinnati Human Relations Commission [CHRC]

Fax: (513) 352-2496
Director **Dr. Ericka King-Betts** .... (513) 352-3237

Cincinnati Recreation Commission [CRC]

805 Central Ave., Suite 800, Cincinnati, OH 45202-1979
Tel: (513) 352-4000 Fax: (513) 352-1634 E-mail: info@cincyrec.org
Director **Daniel Betts** .... (513) 352-4961
Superintendent of Recreation **Steve Gerth** .... (513) 352-4043

Cincinnati Public Schools

2651 Burnet Ave., Cincinnati, OH 45219
P.O. Box 5381, Cincinnati, OH 45201-5381
Fax: (513) 363-0035 Internet: www.cps-k12.org

Superintendent **Mary Ronan** .... (513) 363-0070
Chief Officer for Public Affairs **Janet Walsh** .... (513) 363-0023
Fax: (513) 363-0025
★ President **Ericka Copeland-Dansby** .... (513) 363-0040
Term Expires: December 31, 2017
★ Vice President **Melanie Bates** .... (513) 363-0040
Term Expires: December 31, 2017
E-mail: batesme@cps-k12.org
★ Member **Eve Bolton** .... (513) 363-0040
Term Expires: December 31, 2019
E-mail: boltone@cps-k12.org
★ Member **Elissa Hoffman** .... (513) 363-0040
Term Expires: December 31, 2017
★ Member **Carolyn L. Jones** .... (513) 363-0040
Term Expires: December 31, 2019
★ Member **Daniel Minera** .... (513) 363-0040
Term Expires: December 31, 2017
★ Member **A. Chris Nelms** .... (513) 363-0040
Term Expires: December 31, 2019
E-mail: nelmsch@cps-k12.org

City of Clarksville, Tennessee

One Public Square, Clarksville, TN 37040
Internet: www.cityofclarksville.com

County: Montgomery **Election Type:** Nonpartisan **Year Incorporated:** 1819 **Population:** 149,176 (2015)

Office of the Mayor

One Public Square, Clarksville, TN 37040
Fax: (931) 552-7479

★ Mayor **Kim McMillan** .... (931) 645-7444
Began Service: January 3, 2011
Term Expires: December 31, 2018
E-mail: mayormcmillan@cityofclarksville.com
Chief of Staff **Charlie Gentry** .... (931) 648-6173
City Information Director **Jennifer Rawls** .... (931) 648-6128
E-mail: jennifer.rawls@cityofclarksville.com
Constituent Services Director **Dora McCary** .... (931) 553-2463
E-mail: dora.mccary@cityofclarksville.com

Office of the City Attorney

One Public Square, Clarksville, TN 37040
Fax: (931) 221-0122

○ City Attorney **Lance Baker** .... (931) 553-2475
E-mail: lance.baker@cityofclarksville.com

★ Elected Official ▲ Appointed by Legislature ▼ Appointed by Governor ▶ Appointed by Board or Commission ● Appointed by Judge
■ Appointed by Mayor △ Appointed by Freeholders ▽ Appointed by Supervisor ▷ Appointed by County Executive ○ Appointed by Council

Office of the City Clerk
One Public Square, Clarksville, TN 37040
Fax: (931) 221-0122

○ City Clerk **Sylvia Skinner** .... (931) 648-6121
E-mail: sylvia.skinner@cityofclarksville.com

Office of the City Engineer
2215 Madison St., Clarksville, TN 37043
Fax: (931) 648-5983

○ City Engineer **Brian Goodwin** .... (931) 645-7418
E-mail: brian.goodwin@cityofclarksville.com

Buildings and Codes Department
100 South Spring St., Clarksville, TN 37040
Fax: (931) 645-7430

Director **Mike Baker** .... (931) 645-7426

Finance and Revenue Department
One Public Square, Suite 300, Clarksville, TN 37040
Fax: (931) 553-2471

○ Commissioner **Laurie Matta** .... (931) 645-7437
E-mail: laurie.matta@cityofclarksville.com

Housing and Community Development
One Public Square, Suite 201, Clarksville, TN 37040
Fax: (931) 503-3092

Director **Keith D. Lampkin** .... (931) 648-6133
E-mail: keith.lampkin@cityofclarksville.com

Fire Department
802 Main St., Clarksville, TN 37040
Internet: http://www.clarksvillefirerescue.org/

Fire Chief **Michael E. Roberts** .... (931) 645-7456
E-mail: mike.roberts@cityofclarksville.com

Gas and Water Department
2215 Madison St., Clarksville, TN 37043
Internet: http://www.clarksvillegw.com/

General Manager **Pat Hickey** .... (931) 645-7400
Chief Financial Officer **(Vacant)** .... (931) 645-7400
Billing and Metering Manager **Eddie Glenn** .... (931) 645-7400
Gas Distribution Manager **Ralph Tate** .... (931) 221-0748
Gas Manager **Michael Young** .... (931) 645-7422
Purchasing Manager (Interim) **Camille Thomas** .... (931) 553-2477
E-mail: camile.thomas@cityofclarksville.com
Water and Wastewater Construction and Collections Manager **Chris Lambert** .... (931) 553-2424
Wastewater Plant Superintendent **Tommy Williams** .... (931) 645-7495
Seven Quarry Road, Clarksville, TN 37040
Water Plant Superintendent **Kenny Vaughan** .... (931) 553-2440
Pumping Station Road, Clarksville, TN 37040
Gas Construction Supervisor **Randall Lewis** .... (931) 645-7470
2015 Ft. Campbell Boulevard, Clarksville, TN 37040
Safety and Security Administrator **Gary Busch** .... (931) 645-7400
E-mail: gary.busch@cityofclarksville.com
Water and Wastewater Construction Supervisor **Shane Davenport** .... (931) 645-7471
Wastewater Collection Supervisor **Mike Crawford** .... (931) 553-2424

Human Resources Department
One Public Square, Suite 200, Clarksville, TN 37040
Tel: (931) 645-7451 Fax: (931) 648-2341

Human Resources Director **William "Will" Wyatt** .... (931) 648-6125 ext. 6204
E-mail: will.wyatt@cityofclarksville.com

Information Technology
One Public Square, Clarksville, TN 37040
Fax: (931) 648-6115

Director **Amie Wilson** .... (931) 645-4593
E-mail: amie.wilson@cityofclarksville.com

Parks and Recreation Department
102 Public Square, Clarksville, TN 37040
Fax: (931) 553-2432
Internet: http://www.cityofclarksville.com/parks%26rec/

Director **Mark Tummons** .... (931) 645-7476

Street Department
199 10th St., Clarksville, TN 37043
Fax: (931) 645-7464 Internet: http://www.cityofclarksville.com/street/

Director **David Shepard** .... (931) 645-7464
Assistant Director **(Vacant)** .... (931) 645-7464
Operations Manager **Scott Bibb** .... (931) 645-7464
E-mail: scott.bibb@cityofclarksville.com
Senior Engineer **Jack Frazier** .... (931) 645-7464
E-mail: jack.frazier@cityofclarksville.com
GIS Technician **Jackie Overholser** .... (931) 645-7464

Clarksville Transit System
430 Bollin Lane, Clarksville, TN 37040
Fax: (931) 553-2401

Director **Arthur Bing** .... (931) 645-7414

Office of the City Council
One Public Square, Clarksville, TN 37040

★ Mayor Pro Tem **James Lewis** (Ward 3) .... (931) 648-8603
Term Expires: December 31, 2016
E-mail: james.lewis@cityofclarksville.com

★ Council Member **Richard Garrett** (Ward 1) .... (931) 648-6121
Term Expires: December 31, 2018
E-mail: richard.garrett@cityofclarksville.com

★ Council Member **Deanna McLaughlin** (Ward 2) .... (931) 645-0315
Term Expires: December 31, 2018
E-mail: deanna.mclaughlin@cityofclarksville.com

★ Council Member **Wallace Redd** (Ward 4) .... (931) 216-5640
Term Expires: December 31, 2016
E-mail: wallace.redd@cityofclarksville.com

★ Council Member **Valerie Guzman** (Ward 5) .... (931) 648-6121
Term Expires: December 31, 2016
E-mail: valerie.guzman@cityofclarksville.com

★ Council Member **Wanda Smith** (Ward 6) .... (931) 648-6121
Term Expires: December 31, 2018
E-mail: wanda.smith@cityofclarksville.com

★ Council Member **Geno Grubbs** (Ward 7) .... (931) 320-0774
Term Expires: December 31, 2018
E-mail: geno.grubbs@cityofclarksville.com

★ Council Member **David Allen** (Ward 8) .... (931) 648-4574
Term Expires: December 31, 2016
E-mail: david.allen@cityofclarksville.com

★ Council Member **Joel Wallace** (Ward 9) .... (931) 647-5439
Term Expires: December 31, 2016
E-mail: joel.wallace@cityofclarksville.com
Education: U Memphis 1999 AB, 2005 JD

★ Council Member **Mike Alexander** (Ward 10) .... (931) 648-6121
Term Expires: December 31, 2018
E-mail: mike.alexander@cityofclarksville.com

★ Council Member **Bill Powers** (Ward 11) .... (931) 648-6121
Term Expires: December 31, 2018
E-mail: bill.powers@cityofclarksville.com

★ Council Member **Jeff Burkhart** (Ward 12) .... (931) 206-6949
Term Expires: December 31, 2016
E-mail: jeff.burkhart@cityofclarksville.com

★ Elected Official ▲ Appointed by Legislature ▼ Appointed by Governor ▶ Appointed by Board or Commission ● Appointed by Judge
■ Appointed by Mayor △ Appointed by Freeholders ▽ Appointed by Supervisor ▷ Appointed by County Executive ○ Appointed by Council

Office of the City Judge
One Public Square, Clarksville, TN 37040

★City Judge **Charles W. Smith** .... (931) 647-2323
Term Expires: December 31, 2016

City of Clearwater, Florida
112 S. Osceola, Clearwater, FL 34616
P.O. Box 4748, Clearwater, FL 33758-4748
Internet: www.myclearwater.com

County: Pinellas **Election Type:** Nonpartisan **Population:** 113,003 (2015)

Office of the Mayor and City Commission
P.O. Box 4748, Clearwater, FL 33758-4748
Fax: (727) 562-4052

★Mayor **George N. Cretekos** (Seat 1) .... (727) 562-4050
Began Service: January 13, 2012
Term Expires: March 2020
E-mail: george.cretekos@myclearwater.com
Education: Davidson 1969 AB; Pittsburgh 1970 MPA

★Vice Mayor **Doreen Caudell** (Seat 2) .... (727) 562-4050
Term Expires: March 2020
E-mail: Doreen.Hock-DiPolito@myclearwater.com

★Council Member **Dr. Bob Cundiff** (Seat 3) .... (727) 562-4050
Term Expires: March 2020
E-mail: bob.cundiff@myclearwater.com

★Council Member **Bill Jonson** (Seat 4) .... (727) 562-4050
Term Expires: March 9, 2018
E-mail: Bill.Jonson@myClearwater.com

★Council Member **Hoyt Hamilton** (Seat 5) .... (727) 562-4050
Term Expires: April 2018
E-mail: hoyt.hamilton@myclearwater.com

Office of the City Attorney
P.O. Box 4748, Clearwater, FL 33758-4748

City Attorney **Pam Akin** .... (727) 562-4010
E-mail: Pam.Akin@myclearwater.com

Office of the City Clerk
P.O. Box 4748, Clearwater, FL 33758-4748
Fax: (727) 562-4086

City Clerk **Rosemarie Call** .... (727) 562-4091
E-mail: rosemarie.call@myclearwater.com

Office of the City Manager
P.O. Box 4748, Clearwater, FL 33758-4748
Fax: (727) 562-4052

City Manager **Bill Horne** .... (727) 562-4043
E-mail: William.Horne@myclearwater.com

Assistant City Manager **Jill Silverboard** .... (727) 562-4043
E-mail: jill.silverboard@myclearwater.com

Budget Department
P.O. Box 4748, Clearwater, FL 33758-4748

Director **Kayleen Kastel** .... (727) 562-4542
E-mail: kayleen.kastel@myclearwater.com

Clearwater Customer Service
P.O. Box 4748, Clearwater, FL 33758-4748

Director of Customer Service **Cynthia Boyd** .... (727) 562-4556

Economic Development Department
P.O. Box 4748, Clearwater, FL 33758-4748
Fax: (727) 562-4075

Director **Geraldine "Geri" Lopez** .... (727) 562-4220
E-mail: geraldine.lopez@myclearwater.com

Engineering Department
100 South Myrtle Avenue, Room 220, Clearwater, FL 33756
Fax: (727) 562-4755
Internet: www.clearwater-fl.com/gov/depts/pwa/engin/

Engineering Director **Michael Quillen** .... (727) 562-4743
E-mail: michael.quillen@myclearwater.com

Clearwater Parking System
100 South Myrtle Avenue, Clearwater, FL 33756

Parking Manager **Charles "Eric" Wilson** .... (727) 562-4704

Finance Department
P.O. Box 4748, Clearwater, FL 33758-4748
Fax: (727) 562-4535

Administrator **Jay Ravins** .... (727) 562-4530

Purchasing Manager **Alyce Benge** .... (727) 562-4630
E-mail: alyce.benge@myclearwater.com

Fire Department
P.O. Box 4748, Clearwater, FL 33758-4748
Fax: (727) 562-4328

Fire Chief **Robert Weiss** .... (727) 562-4334
E-mail: robert.weiss@myclearwater.com

Clearwater Gas System
400 North Myrtle Avenue, Clearwater, FL 33755
Fax: (727) 562-4902

Managing Director
Charles S. "Chuck" Warrington, Jr. .... (727) 562-4901

Human Resources Department
Municipal Services Bldg., 1st Fl., 100 South Myrtle Avenue, Clearwater, FL 33756
P.O. Box 4748, Clearwater, FL 33758-4748
Fax: (727) 562-4877

Director **Joe Roseto** .... (727) 562-4870
E-mail: joseph.roseto@myclearwater.com

Information Technology
P.O. Box 4748, Clearwater, FL 33758-4748
Fax: (727) 562-4696

Director **Dan Mayer** .... (727) 562-4662
E-mail: Dan.Mayer@myclearwater.com

Web Master **Derek Ferguson** .... (727) 562-4667

Internal Audit
P.O. Box 4748, Clearwater, FL 33758-4748

Director **Dorcas "Yvonne" Taylor** .... (727) 562-4550

Library
P.O. Box 4748, Clearwater, FL 33758-4748
Fax: (727) 562-4977

Librarian/Director **Barbara Pickell** .... (727) 562-4971
E-mail: barbara.pickell@myclearwater.com

Marina
P.O. Box 4748, Clearwater, FL 33758-4748

Harbormaster **William "Bill" Morris** .... (727) 462-6954
E-mail: william.morris@myclearwater.com

Parks and Recreation Department
P.O. Box 4748, Clearwater, FL 33758-4748
E-mail: parksrec@myclearwater.com Fax: (727) 562-4825
Director **Kevin Dunbar** .... (727) 562-4800

Planning and Development Services
P.O. Box 4748, Clearwater, FL 33758-4748
Fax: (727) 562-4576
Planning Director **Michael Delk** .... (727) 562-4567
E-mail: michael.delk@myclearwater.com

Police Department
P.O. Box 4748, Clearwater, FL 33758-4748
Fax: (727) 562-4221
Chief of Police **Daniel Slaughter** .... (727) 562-4343

Public Communications Department
P.O. Box 4748, Clearwater, FL 33758-4748
Fax: (727) 562-4696
Director **Joelle Castelli** .... (727) 562-4284
E-mail: joelle.castelli@myclearwater.com
Education: Florida BA

Public Utilities Department
P.O. Box 4748, Clearwater, FL 33758-4748
Fax: (727) 562-4691
Director (Interim) **David Porter** .... (727) 562-4960

Solid Waste Department
P.O. Box 4748, Clearwater, FL 33758-4748
Fax: (727) 562-4939
Director **Earl Gloster** .... (727) 562-4930

City of Cleveland, Ohio
City Hall, 601 Lakeside Avenue, NE, Cleveland, OH 44114
Tel: (216) 664-2000 (Information) Internet: www.city.cleveland.oh.us

County: Cuyahoga **Election Type:** Partisan **Year Founded:** 1796
Year Incorporated: 1836 **Population:** 388,072 (2015)

Frank G. Jackson (D)
Mayor
Began Service: 2006
Term Expires: December 31, 2017
Education: Cleveland State BA, MA, JD
Career: Council Member, Office of the City Council, City of Cleveland, Ohio (1990-2002); Council President, Office of the City Council, City of Cleveland, Ohio (2002-2006)

Office of the Mayor
City Hall, 601 Lakeside Avenue, Room 202, Cleveland, OH 44114
Tel: (216) 664-3990 Fax: (216) 420-8766
★ Mayor **Frank G. Jackson** (D) .... (216) 664-3990
Executive Assistant **Martin L. Flask** .... (216) 664-3990
Executive Assistant **Sheryl Nechvatal** .... (216) 664-3990
Chief of Staff **Ken Silliman** .... (216) 664-3990
Chief of Education **Monyka Price** .... (216) 664-2220
Chief of Government and International Affairs
Valarie J. McCall (D) .... (216) 664-3990
Education: Cleveland State BA, MPA
Chief Operating Officer **Darnell Brown** .... (216) 664-3990

Office of the Mayor *continued*
Chief of Public Affairs **Natoya J. Walker Minor** .... (216) 664-2220
Chief of Regional Development **Edward W. Rybka** ...... (216) 664-3990
Education: John Carroll BA; Cleveland-Marshall JD
Chief of Sustainability **Jenita McGowan** .... (216) 664-2405
Media Relations Director **Dan Williams** .... (216) 664-2223
Communications Manager **Beth Zietlow-DeJesus** .... (216) 664-2220

Mayor's Action Center
Mayor's Action Center Manager **Jacqueline Sutton** ..... (216) 664-2900
E-mail: jsutton@city.cleveland.oh.us

Aging Department
75 Erieview Plaza, 2nd Floor, Cleveland, OH 44114
■ Director **Jane E. Fumich** .... (216) 664-2833
E-mail: jfumich@city.cleveland.oh.us

Building and Housing Department
601 Lakeside Avenue, NE, Room 510, Cleveland, OH 44114
Fax: (216) 664-3590
Director of Building and Housing
Ronald J. H. O'Leary .... (216) 420-7625
Code Enforcement Commissioner **Thomas Vanover** ..... (216) 420-8416
Chief Building Official **Thomas Vanover** .... (216) 420-8416

City Planning Commission
City Hall, 601 Lakeside Avenue, NE, Room 501, Cleveland, OH 44114
Tel: (216) 664-2210 Fax: (216) 664-3281
Internet: http://planning.city.cleveland.oh.us
■ Director of City Planning **Freddy L. Collier, Jr.** .... (216) 664-2210
E-mail: fcollier@city.cleveland.oh.us
Assistant Director of City Planning
Christopher Garland .... (216) 664-3817
Education: Wayne State U MURP; Purdue BA

Civil Service Commission
City Hall, 601 Lakeside Avenue, Room 119, Cleveland, OH 44114
Fax: (216) 664-3879
■ Civil Service Commission - Secretary **Lucille Ambroz** ... (216) 664-2470

Cleveland Public Library [CPL]
325 Superior Avenue, NE, Cleveland, OH 44144-1271
Tel: (216) 623-2800 Fax: (216) 623-7017 E-mail: info@cpl.org
Internet: www.cpl.org

Administration
Director **Felton Thomas, Jr.** .... (216) 623-2827
E-mail: felton.thomas@cpl.org
Education: Hawaii MLS
Chief Knowledge Officer
Timothy R. "Tim" Diamond .... (216) 623-2832
E-mail: Tim.Diamond@cpl.org
Deputy Director and Chief Operations Officer
Cynthia "Cindy" Lombardo .... (216) 623-2878
E-mail: cindy.lombardo@cpl.org
Education: Kent State MLS, MPA; Ohio State PhD
Director of Property Management **Myron Scruggs** ...... (216) 623-2845
E-mail: myron.scruggs@cpl.org
Chief Financial Officer **Carrie Krenicky** .... (216) 623-2844
Director of Human Resources **Madeline Corchado** ...... (216) 623-2892
E-mail: madeline.corchado@cpl.org
Director of Public Services **John Skrtic** .... (216) 623-2878
E-mail: john.skrtic@cpl.org
Director of Marketing and Communications
Cathy Poilpre .... (216) 623-2955
E-mail: cathy.poilpre@cpl.org
Director of Technical Services **Patricia E. Lowrey** ...... (216) 623-2817
E-mail: Patricia.Lowrey@cpl.org

★ Elected Official ▲ Appointed by Legislature ▼ Appointed by Governor ▶ Appointed by Board or Commission ● Appointed by Judge
■ Appointed by Mayor △ Appointed by Freeholders ▽ Appointed by Supervisor ▷ Appointed by County Executive ○ Appointed by Council

Community Development Department

City Hall, 601 Lakeside Avenue, NE, Room 320, Cleveland, OH 44114
Tel: (216) 664-4000 Fax: (216) 664-4006

■ Director **Daryl Rush** .... (216) 664-4000
E-mail: drush@city.cleveland.oh.us
Education: Cincinnati BA; Howard U JD
Executive Assistant **(Vacant)** .... (216) 664-2351
Assistant Director **Michael Cosgrove** .... (216) 420-7634
E-mail: mcosgrove@city.cleveland.oh.us
■ Administrative Services Commissioner (Acting)
Joy Anderson .... (216) 664-2055
E-mail: janderson2@city.cleveland.oh.us
Real Estate Commissioner **(Vacant)** .... (216) 664-4061
■ Neighborhood Services Commissioner
Louise V. Jackson .... (216) 664-4074
E-mail: ljackson@city.cleveland.oh.us

Community Relations Board

City Hall, 601 Lakeside Avenue, NE, Room 11, Cleveland, OH 44114
Fax: (216) 664-2311

■ Executive Director **Blaine A. Griffin** .... (216) 664-3290
E-mail: bgriffin@city.cleveland.oh.us

Economic Development Department

City Hall, 601 Lakeside Avenue, NE, Room 210,
Cleveland, OH 44114-1027
Fax: (216) 664-3681

Director **Tracey Nichols** .... (216) 664-3611
E-mail: tnichols2@city.cleveland.oh.us
Assistant Director **David Ebersole** .... (216) 664-2204
E-mail: debersole@city.cleveland.oh.us
Fiscal Manager **Dan Rehor** .... (216) 664-3610

Finance Department

City Hall, 601 Lakeside Avenue, NE, Room 104, Cleveland, OH 44114
Fax: (216) 664-2535

■ Director **Sharon Dumas** .... (216) 664-2536
E-mail: sdumas@city.cleveland.oh.us
Treasurer **James Hartley** .... (216) 644-2536
Education: Franklin U 1990 BS Fax: (216) 664-2535
Accounts Commissioner **Lonya Moss-Walker**
Room 19 .... (216) 664-2640
Fax: (216) 664-3417
Assessments/Licenses Commissioner
Dedrick Stephens Room 122 .... (216) 664-2260
E-mail: dstephens@city.cleveland.oh.us Fax: (216) 664-4592
Information Technology Services Commissioner
Douglas Divish .... (216) 664-2941
205 St. Clair, Cleveland, OH 44113 Fax: (216) 664-3789
E-mail: ddivish@city.cleveland.oh.us
Printing/Reproduction Commissioner **Michael Hewett** ... (216) 664-3015
1735 Lakeside Ave., Cleveland, OH 44114 Fax: (216) 664-4016
E-mail: mhewett@city.cleveland.oh.us
Purchasing/Supplies Commissioner
Tiffany White-Johnson Room 128 .... (216) 664-2620
E-mail: twhite@city.cleveland.oh.us Fax: (216) 664-2177
Taxation Administrator **Nassim Lynch** .... (216) 664-2070
205 St. Clair, Cleveland, OH 44113 Fax: (216) 664-8299
E-mail: nlynch@city.cleveland.oh.us
Tax Administrator **(Vacant)** Room 116 .... (216) 664-2240
Fax: (216) 664-2247
Controller **James Gentile** Room 18 .... (216) 664-3881
E-mail: jgentile@city.cleveland.oh.us Fax: (216) 664-4168
Budget Administrator **Greg Cordek** .... (216) 664-6360
E-mail: gcordek@city.cleveland.oh.us Fax: (216) 664-2535
Capital Budget Manager **Tina Magistro** .... (216) 664-3647
E-mail: tmagistro@city.cleveland.oh.us Fax: (216) 664-2535
Internal Audit Manager (Interim) **Natasha Brandt**
Room 24 .... (216) 664-4157
Fax: (216) 664-2316

Finance Department *continued*

Risk Manager **Eduardo A. Romero** Room 28 .... (216) 664-3698
E-mail: eromero@city.cleveland.oh.us Fax: (216) 664-4253
Sinking Fund Assistant Secretary **Betsy Hruby** .... (216) 664-3663
Fax: (216) 664-2535

Human Resources

City Hall, 601 Lakeside Avenue, NE, Room 121,
Cleveland, OH 44114-1015
Fax: (216) 664-3489

■ Director (Interim) **Nycole D. West** .... (216) 664-2493
E-mail: nwest@city.cleveland.oh.us
EEO Manager **Gina L. Routen** .... (216) 664-2135
Employee Records **Michelle Parker** .... (216) 664-2113
E-mail: mparker@city.cleveland.oh.us
Employee Relations/Benefits Manager **Robert Masseria** .. (216) 664-2600
E-mail: HR-Benefits@city.cleveland.oh.us
Labor Relations Manager **(Vacant)** .... (216) 664-2458
Secretary of Civil Service **Lucille Ambroz** .... (216) 664-2470
E-mail: lambroz@city.cleveland.oh.us

Department of Law

City Hall, 601 Lakeside Avenue, NE, Room 106,
Cleveland, OH 44114-1077
Tel: (216) 664-2800 Fax: (216) 664-2663
E-mail: lawdepartment@city.cleveland.oh.us

■ Director of Law **Barbara A. Langhenry** .... (216) 664-2893
E-mail: blanghenry@city.cleveland.oh.us
Chief Counsel **Gary S. Singletary** .... (216) 664-2737
Chief Corporate Counsel **Richard F. Horvath** .... (216) 664-2808
Chief Trial Counsel **Thomas J. Kaiser** .... (216) 664-2852
Chief Assistant Prosecutor (Interim)
Kimberly G. Barnett-Mills .... (216) 664-4807
First Assistant Prosecutor **(Vacant)** .... (216) 664-2800
Chief Assistant Director of Law, Code Enforcement
Michele R. Comer .... (216) 664-3572
Chief Assistant Director of Law, Operations and
Sustainability **Harold A. Madorsky** .... (216) 664-2819
Chief Assistant Director of Law, Legislation, Finance
and Contracts **Ronda G. Curtis** .... (216) 664-4506
Chief Assistant Director of Law, Litigation
Joseph F. Scott .... (216) 664-3727
Chief Assistant Director of Law, Public Safety
William M. Menzalora .... (216) 664-4285
Chief Assistant Director of Law, Real Estate and
Development **Richard Bertovich** .... (216) 664-3312

Mayor's Office of Capital Projects

City Hall, 601 Lakeside Avenue, NE, Room 113,
Cleveland, OH 44114-1015
Fax: (216) 664-2198

■ Director **Matthew Spronz** .... (216) 664-2231
E-mail: mspronz@city.cleveland.oh.us

Division of Architecture and Site Development

City Hall, 601 Lakeside Ave., NE, Room 517, Cleveland, OH 44114

Chief Architect **Christopher Diehl** .... (216) 664-3577
Fax: (216) 664-4220

Engineering and Construction Division

601 Lakeside Avenue, NE, Room 518, Cleveland, OH 44114

Administration Bureau Manager **Richard Switalski** ...... (216) 664-2381
E-mail: rswitalski@city.cleveland.oh.us Fax: (216) 664-2289

Real Estate Division

City Hall, 601 Lakeside Avenue, NE, Room 518, Cleveland, OH 44114

Commissioner **James DeRosa** .... (216) 664-4052

★ Elected Official ▲ Appointed by Legislature ▼ Appointed by Governor ► Appointed by Board or Commission ● Appointed by Judge
■ Appointed by Mayor △ Appointed by Freeholders ▽ Appointed by Supervisor ▷ Appointed by County Executive ○ Appointed by Council

Department of Port Control

Cleveland Hopkins International Airport, 5300 Riverside Dr., Cleveland, OH 44135-3193
P.O. Box 81009, Cleveland, OH 44181-0009
Tel: (216) 265-6030 (Information) Fax: (216) 265-6021

■ Director (Interim) **Fred Szabo** .... (216) 265-6022
E-mail: fszabo@clevelandairport.com Fax: (216) 265-6096
Chief of Staff **(Vacant)** .... (216) 265-3364
Fax: (216) 265-6096
Chief of Administration and Performance Management
(Vacant) .... (216) 265-6110
Fax: (216) 265-6069
Chief of Business Development and Management
Pat Singleton .... (216) 265-6121
Fax: (216) 265-6021
Chief of Finance **Christine Gilmartin** .... (216) 265-2683
Fax: (216) 265-6069
Chief of Information Technology **Matt Crowley** .... (216) 265-2710
E-mail: mcrowley@clevelandairport.com
Chief of Marketing and Air Service Development
Todd Payne .... (216) 265-6790
Fax: (216) 265-6096
Chief of Planning and Engineering **Renato Camacho** .... (216) 265-6793
E-mail: rcamacho@clevelandairport.com Fax: (216) 265-6185

Burke Lakefront Airport

1501 N. Marginal Rd., Cleveland, OH 44114
Fax: (216) 781-5738 Internet: http://www.clevelandairport.com/burke

Commissioner **Khalid Bahhur** .... (216) 664-5030
Fax: (216) 781-5438

Cleveland Hopkins International Airport

5300 Riverside Dr., Cleveland, OH 44135-3193
P.O. Box 81009, Cleveland, OH 44181-0009
Fax: (216) 265-6021 Internet: http://www.clevelandairport.com

Commissioner **Fred Szabo** .... (216) 265-6100
Fax: (216) 265-6021

Department of Public Health [CDPH]

75 Erieview Plaza, Cleveland, OH 44114
Fax: (216) 664-2197 Internet: www.clevelandhealth.org

■ Director (Interim) **Natoya J. Walker Minor** .... (216) 664-6790

Department of Public Safety

City Hall, 601 Lakeside Avenue, NE, Room 230, Cleveland, OH 44114-1015
Fax: (216) 664-3734

■ Director **Michael McGrath** .... (216) 664-3736
E-mail: mmcgrath@city.cleveland.oh.us
Assistant Director **Edward Eckart** .... (216) 664-2560
E-mail: eeckart@city.cleveland.oh.us
Assistant Director **Tim Hennessy** .... (216) 664-2205
E-mail: thennessy@city.cleveland.oh.us
Assistant Director **Laura Palinkas** .... (216) 664-4131
E-mail: lpalinkas@city.cleveland.oh.us
Assistant Director **Barry A. Withers** .... (216) 664-2227
E-mail: bwithers@city.cleveland.oh.us
Office of Professional Standards **Damon Scott** .... (216) 664-4618
E-mail: dscott@city.cleveland.oh.us
Animal Control Officer **Edward Jamison** .... (216) 664-3069
2690 West 7th Street, Cleveland, OH 44114

Emergency Medical Service

1701 Lakeside Avenue, Cleveland, OH 44114

■ Commissioner **Nicole Carlton** .... (216) 664-2001
E-mail: ncarlton@city.cleveland.oh.us

Fire Division

1645 Superior, Cleveland, OH 44114
Fax: (216) 664-6816

Fire Chief **Angelo Calvillo** .... (216) 664-6397

Police Division

Justice Center, 1300 Ontario St., Cleveland, OH 44114
Fax: (216) 623-5584

■ Chief of Police **Calvin Williams** .... (216) 623-5005
E-mail: cwilliams3@city.cleveland.oh.us

Department of Public Utilities

1201 Lakeside Ave., Cleveland, OH 44114

■ Director **Robert L. Davis** .... (216) 664-2444 ext. 5604
Fax: (216) 664-3454

Office of Radio Communications

Administrative Manager **Brad Handke** .... (216) 664-3259
Fax: (216) 664-3996

Cleveland Public Power

Commissioner **Ivan Henderson** .... (216) 664-3922
1300 Lakeside Ave., Cleveland, OH 44114 Fax: (216) 420-7514

Division of Fiscal Control

Chief Financial Officer **Frank Badalamenti** .... (216) 664-2444
Fax: (216) 664-4452

Division of Water

Commissioner **Alex Margevicius** .... (216) 664-2444 ext. 5500
Fax: (216) 664-3330
Administration Assistant Commissioner **(Vacant)** .... (216) 664-2444
Customer Account Services Assistant Commissioner
Sharonda Denson .... (216) 664-2444
Distribution Maintenance Assistant
Commissioner **Payton Hall** .... (216) 664-2444 ext. 3000
Engineering Assistant Commissioner **Alex Margevicius** .. (216) 664-2444
Tel: (216) 664-3990 5500
Plant Operations Assistant Commissioner **(Vacant)** .... (216) 664-2444
GIS Project Manager **(Vacant)** .... (216) 664-2444 ext. 4615
Fax: (216) 420-8752
Information Technology Assistant Commissioner
Isaac Khoury .... (216) 664-2444

Division of Water Pollution Control

12302 Kirby Avenue, Cleveland, OH 44108
Fax: (216) 664-3477

Commissioner **Rachid Zoghaib** .... (216) 664-2750
Deputy Commissioner **Ramona Lowery** .... (216) 664-2750

Department of Public Works

500 Lakeside Ave., Cleveland, OH 44114-1099
Fax: (216) 664-4086 (Director's Office)

Director **Michael E. Cox** .... (216) 664-2485
Fax: (216) 664-4086
Assistant Director **(Vacant)** .... (216) 664-2485
Fax: (216) 664-4086
Assistant Director **Kim Johnson** .... (216) 664-2485
Fax: (216) 664-4086
Park Maintenance and Properties Commissioner
Richard Silva .... (216) 664-3550
1230 East Sixth Street, 4th Floor, Cleveland, OH 44114-1099 Fax: (216) 664-4087
Parking Facilities Commissioner
Antionette Thompson .... (216) 664-2711
E-mail: athompson@city.cleveland.oh.us Fax: (216) 664-4005
Property Management Commissioner **Thomas Nagel** .... (216) 664-3459
Building 2, 4150 East 49th Street, Cleveland, OH 44105-3206 Fax: (216) 664-4077
E-mail: tnagel@city.cleveland.oh.us
Recreation Commissioner **Samuel Gisstennar** .... (216) 664-3987
601 Lakeside Avenue, Room 8, Cleveland, OH 44114-1090 Fax: (216) 664-4675
Special Events Manager **(Vacant)** .... (216) 664-2012
Fax: (216) 420-8122
Urban Forestry Manager **Jennifer Braman** .... (216) 664-3104
750 E. 88th St., Cleveland, OH 44108-4100 Fax: (216) 664-3233

(continued on next page)

★ Elected Official ▲ Appointed by Legislature ▼ Appointed by Governor ► Appointed by Board or Commission ● Appointed by Judge
■ Appointed by Mayor △ Appointed by Freeholders ▽ Appointed by Supervisor ▷ Appointed by County Executive ○ Appointed by Council

Department of Public Works *continued*

Greenhouse Manager **Perrin Verzi** . . . . (216) 664-2512
750 East 88th Street, Cleveland, OH 44108-4100

Cleveland Public Auditorium and Conference Center

500 Lakeside Avenue, Cleveland, OH 44114-1099

Commissioner **Susie Claytor** . . . . (216) 348-2275
Fax: (216) 348-2218

Motor Vehicle Maintenance Division

Harvard Yards, 4150 East 49th Street, Cleveland, OH 44105-3206

Commissioner (Interim) **Jeffrey Brown** . . . . (216) 420-8100
Fax: (216) 420-8129

Assistant Commissioner **Jeffrey Brown** . . . . (216) 420-8100

Streets Division

601 Lakeside Avenue, NE, Room 25, Cleveland, OH 44114

Commissioner (Interim) **Randell T. Scott** . . . . (216) 664-2150
Fax: (216) 664-2167

Traffic Engineering Division

Harvard Yards, 4150 East 49th Street, Cleveland, OH 44105-3206

Commissioner **Robert Mavec** . . . . (216) 664-3194
City Hall, 601 Lakeside Ave., NE, Fax: (216) 664-3167
Room 518, Cleveland, OH 44114
E-mail: rmavec@city.cleveland.oh.us

Waste Collection Division

Carr Center, 5600 Carnegie Avenue, Cleveland, OH 44103
Fax: (216) 664-2655

Commissioner **(Vacant)** . . . . (216) 664-2156

Office of the City Council/City Clerk

City Hall, 601 Lakeside Avenue, NE, Room 220, Cleveland, OH 44114
Tel: (216) 664-2840 Fax: (216) 664-3837
E-mail: webmaster@clevelandcitycouncil.org
Internet: www.clevelandcitycouncil.org

★Council President **Kevin J. Kelley** (D-Ward 13) . . . . (216) 664-2943
Term Expires: December 31, 2017
E-mail: council13@clevelandcitycouncil.org

★Majority Leader **Phyllis Cleveland** (D-Ward 5) . . . . (216) 664-2309
Term Expires: December 31, 2017

★Council Member **CPT Terrell H. Pruitt** (D-Ward 1) . . . . . . (216) 664-4944
Term Expires: December 31, 2017
Education: Cleveland State BA

★Council Member **Zachary "Zack" Reed** (D-Ward 2) . . . . . (216) 664-4945
Term Expires: December 31, 2017
E-mail: council2@clevelandcitycouncil.org

★Council Member **Kerry McCormack** (D-Ward 3) . . . . (216) 664-2691
Term Expires: December 31, 2017
E-mail: council3@clevelandcitycouncil.org

★Council Member **Kenneth L. Johnson** (D-Ward 4) . . . . . . (216) 664-4941
Term Expires: December 31, 2017

★Council Member **Mamie J. Mitchell** (D-Ward 6) . . . . (216) 664-4234
Term Expires: December 31, 2017
E-mail: council6@clevelandcitycouncil.org
Education: Cleveland State BBA, MBA; Cleveland-Marshall JD

★Council Member **T.J. Dow** (D-Ward 7) . . . . (216) 664-2908
Term Expires: December 31, 2017

★Council Member **Michael D. Polensek** (D-Ward 8) . . . . . . (216) 664-4236
Term Expires: December 31, 2017
E-mail: mpolensek@clevelandcitycouncil.org

★Council Member **Kevin Conwell** (D-Ward 9) . . . . (216) 664-4252
Term Expires: December 31, 2017
E-mail: council9@clevelandcitycouncil.org

★Council Member **Jeff Johnson** (D-Ward 10) . . . . (216) 664-4743
Term Expires: December 31, 2017
E-mail: jjohnson@clevelandcitycouncil.org

★Council Member **Dona Brady** (D-Ward 11) . . . . (216) 664-3708
Term Expires: December 31, 2017
E-mail: dbrady@clevelandcitycouncil.org

Office of the City Council/City Clerk *continued*

★Council Member **Anthony Brancatelli** (D-Ward 12) . . . . . (216) 664-4233
Term Expires: December 31, 2017

★Council Member **Brian J. Cummins** (D-Ward 14) . . . . (216) 664-4238
Term Expires: December 31, 2017

★Council Member **Matthew "Matt" Zone** (D-Ward 15) . . . (216) 664-4235
Term Expires: December 31, 2017
E-mail: mzone@clevelandcitycouncil.org

★Council Member **Brian Kazy** (D-Ward 16) . . . . (216) 664-2942
Term Expires: December 31, 2017

★Council Member **Martin J. Keane** (D-Ward 17) . . . . (216) 664-4239
Term Expires: December 31, 2017
E-mail: mkeane@clevelandcitycouncil.org
Education: Ohio State BA; Cleveland-Marshall JD

○City Clerk/Clerk of Council **Patricia J. Britt** (D) . . . . (216) 664-4551
E-mail: pbritt@clevelandcitycouncil.org Fax: (216) 664-3837

Deputy Clerk **Allan Dreyer** . . . . (216) 664-4198
E-mail: adreyer@clevelandcitycouncil.org

Chief of Communications **Joan Mazzolini** . . . . (216) 664-4466

Director of Media Relations **Michael O'Malley** . . . . (216) 664-6137

Chief Legislative Secretary **Charlene Berry** . . . . (216) 664-2981
E-mail: cberry@clevelandcitycouncil.org

Chief City Archivist **Martin Hauserman** . . . . (216) 664-3054

Research and Policy Analysis Manager **John James** . . . . . (216) 644-3179

Cleveland Metropolitan School District

1111 Superior Avenue East, Cleveland, OH 44114
Tel: (216) 574-8000 Fax: (216) 436-5144
Internet: http://clevelandmetroschools.org/

Chief Executive Officer **Eric S. Gordon** . . . . (216) 574-8500

■Chair **Denise Link** . . . . (216) 574-8585
Term Expires: June 30, 2019

■Vice Chair **Louise P. Dempsey** . . . . (216) 574-8585
Term Expires: June 30, 2019
Education: McGill (Canada) BA; Cleveland-Marshall JD

■School Board Member **Anne E. Bingham** . . . . (216) 574-8585
Term Expires: June 30, 2017

■School Board Member **Robert M. Heard, Sr.** . . . . (216) 574-8585
Term Expires: June 30, 2017
Education: Cleveland State BS

■School Board Member **Willetta A. Milam** . . . . (216) 574-8585
Term Expires: June 30, 2017
Education: Pittsburgh BA; Antioch Law JD

■School Board Member **Shaletha Mitchell** . . . . (216) 574-8585
Term Expires: June 30, 2019

■School Board Member **Justin L. Monday** . . . . (216) 574-8585
Term Expires: June 30, 2019

■School Board Member **Stephanie Morales** . . . . (216) 574-8585
Term Expires: June 30, 2019

■School Board Member **Lisa Thomas** . . . . (216) 574-8585
Term Expires: June 30, 2017

Ex Officio Board Member **Dr. Ronald M. Berkman** . . . . . (216) 574-8585
Education: Princeton 1977 PhD

Ex Officio Board Member **Alex Johnson** . . . . (216) 574-8585
Education: Winston-Salem State; Lehman Col; Penn State 1978 DEd

★Elected Official ▲Appointed by Legislature ▼Appointed by Governor ▶Appointed by Board or Commission ●Appointed by Judge
■Appointed by Mayor △Appointed by Freeholders ▽Appointed by Supervisor ▷Appointed by County Executive ○Appointed by Council

City of Colorado Springs, Colorado

City Administration Bldg., 30 S. Nevada Ave.,
Colorado Springs, CO 80903
Tel: (719) 385-5900 (Information) Internet: https://coloradosprings.gov/

County: El Paso **Election Type:** Nonpartisan **Year Founded:** 1859
Year Incorporated: 1872 **Population:** 456,568 (2015)

Office of the Mayor

30 South Nevada Avenue, Suite 601, Colorado Springs, CO 80903
Fax: (719) 385-5488

★Mayor **John W. Suthers** .... (719) 385-5900
Began Service: June 2, 2015
Term Expires: June 2019
E-mail: mayorsoffice@springsgov.com
Date of Birth: October 18, 1951
Education: Notre Dame 1974 BA; Colorado 1977 JD
Chief of Staff **Jeff Greene** .... (719) 385-5900
Chief Communications Officer **Jamie Fabos** .... (719) 385-5900

Office of the City Attorney

City Administration Bldg., 30 South Nevada Avenue, Suite 501,
Colorado Springs, CO 80903
Fax: (719) 385-5535 E-mail: cityatty@springsgov.com

■City Attorney **Wynetta Massey** .... (719) 385-5909
E-mail: wmassey@springsgov.com
Deputy City Attorney **Tom Florczak** .... (719) 385-5909
Legislative Counsel **David Andrews** .... (719) 385-5909
Legal Administrator **Kandi Anthony** .... (719) 385-5909
Division Chief **Michael Curran** .... (719) 385-5925
Division Chief **Richard Griffith** .... (719) 385-5909
Division Chief **Britt Haley** .... (719) 385-5909
Division Chief **Tracey Lessig** .... (719) 385-5909
Division Chief **Shane White** .... (719) 385-5909

Office of the Auditor

107 North Nevada Avenue, Suite 200, Colorado Springs, CO 80903
Fax: (719) 385-5699

○Auditor **Denny Nester** .... (719) 385-5991
E-mail: dnester@springsgov.com
Education: Purdue 1983 MBA
Assistant Auditor **Jacqueline Rowland** .... (719) 385-5694

Office of the City Clerk

City Administration Bldg., 30 S. Nevada Ave., Suite 101,
Colorado Springs, CO 80903
Fax: (719) 385-5114 E-mail: cityclerk@springsgov.com

○City Clerk **Sarah B. Johnson** .... (719) 385-5103
E-mail: sbjohnson@springsgov.com

Colorado Springs Airport

P.O. Box 1575, Colorado Springs, CO 80901

Aviation Director **Dan Gallagher** .... (719) 550-1910
Assistant Director of Aviation, Operations and
Maintenance **John McGinley** .... (719) 550-1905
Assistant Director of Aviation, Planning and
Development **(Vacant)** .... (719) 550-1904
Parking Administrator **Greg Wamke** .... (719) 385-5682

Finance Department

City Administration Bldg., 30 South Nevada Avenue,
Colorado Springs, CO 80903
Fax: (719) 385-5280

Chief Financial Officer **Kara L. Skinner** .... (719) 385-5859

Finance Department *continued*

Procurement Services Manager **(Vacant)** .... (719) 385-5910
Risk and Safety Supervisor **Victoria McColm** .... (719) 385-5669
E-mail: vmccolm@springsgov.com
Public Communications Division Manager **(Vacant)** .... (719) 385-5254

Fire Department

375 Printers Parkway, Colorado Springs, CO 80910
Fax: (719) 385-7388

Fire Chief **Christopher Riley** .... (719) 385-5950
Fire Marshal **Brett Lacey** .... (719) 385-7355
E-mail: blacey@springsgov.com
Deputy Chief of Operations **Steve Dubay** .... (719) 385-7207
E-mail: sdubay@springsgov.com
Deputy Chief of Support Services **Ted Collas** .... (719) 385-7203
E-mail: tcollas@springsgov.com

Human Resources

City Administration Bldg., 30 South Nevada Avenue, Suite 701,
Colorado Springs, CO 80903

Human Resource Director **Michael Sullivan** .... (719) 385-5117
E-mail: msullivan@springsgov.com

Information Technology Department

30 South Nevada Avenue, Colorado Springs, CO 80903

Chief Information Officer **Carl Nehls** .... (719) 385-2489
E-mail: cnehls@springsgov.com

Planning and Development Department

30 South Nevada, Suite 105, Colorado Springs, CO 80903
Fax: (719) 385-5167

Land use Review Manager **Peter Wysocki** .... (719) 385-5905

Parks, Recreation and Cultural Services

1401 Recreation Way, Colorado Springs, CO 80905
Fax: (719) 385-6599 E-mail: spark@springsgov.com

Director of Parks, Recreation and Cultural Services
Karen Palus .... (719) 385-6501
Education: South Florida 1989 BS; Central Florida 2000 MPA
Assistant to the Director **Julie Lafitte** .... (719) 385-6502
E-mail: jlafitte@spingsgov.com
Recreation and Administration Manager **Kim King** .... (719) 385-6509
Park Operations and Planning Manager **Kurt Schroeder** .... (719) 385-6555

Pioneers Museum

215 South Tejon Street, Colorado Springs, CO 80903
Fax: (719) 385-5645 E-mail: cosmuseum@springsgov.com

Director **Matthew Mayberry** .... (719) 385-5990

Police Department

705 S. Nevada Ave., Colorado Springs, CO 80903
Fax: (719) 578-6169

Police Chief **Peter Carey** .... (719) 444-7401
Education: St Joseph's U BA; Colorado (Colo Springs) MPA
Police Deputy Chief **Vincent Niski** .... (719) 444-7404
Police Deputy Chief **Mark Smith** .... (719) 444-7401

Public Works Department

30 South Nevada Avenue, Suite 401, Colorado Springs, CO 80903
Fax: (719) 385-5497

■Public Works Director/City Engineer **Travis Easton** .... (719) 385-5457
E-mail: teaston@springsgov.com
Transportation Manager **Kathleen Krager** .... (719) 385-7628
Fleet Manager **Ryan Trujillo** .... (719) 385-6602

★Elected Official ▲Appointed by Legislature ▼Appointed by Governor ▶Appointed by Board or Commission ●Appointed by Judge
■Appointed by Mayor △Appointed by Freeholders ▽Appointed by Supervisor ▷Appointed by County Executive ○Appointed by Council

Streets Division
688 Geiger Court, Colorado Springs, CO 80915
Fax: (719) 385-6834

Manager **Corey Farkas** . . . . . (719) 385-5934

Pike's Peak, America's Mountain
P.O. Box 1575, Colorado Springs, CO 80901
Fax: (719) 684-0942

Pikes Peak America's Mountain Division Manager
Jack Glavan . . . . . (719) 385-7714

Colorado Springs Utilities
121 South Tejon Street, Fifth Floor, Colorado Springs, CO 80903
Tel: (719) 668-4800 Fax: (719) 668-4288 Internet: http://www.csu.org

Chief Executive Officer **Jerry Forte** . . . . . (719) 668-4800
Chief Customer and Corporate Services Officer
Carl Cruz . . . . . (719) 448-4800
Chief Planning and Finance Officer **Bill Cherrier** . . . . . (719) 448-4800
Chief Strategy and External Affairs Officer
Sherri Newell Winkinson . . . . . (719) 448-4800
E-mail: snewell@csu.org

Office of the City Council
City Hall, 107 North Nevada Avenue, Suite 300,
Colorado Springs, CO 80903
P.O. Box 1575, Colorado Springs, CO 80901
Tel: (719) 385-5986 Fax: (719) 385-5495

★ President **Merv Bennett** (At-Large) . . . . . (719) 385-5469
Term Expires: April 14, 2019
E-mail: mbennett@springsgov.com
★ President Pro Tem **Jill Gaebler** (District 5) . . . . . (719) 385-5483
Term Expires: April 2017
E-mail: jgaebler@springsgov.com
★ Council Member **Don Knight** (District 1) . . . . . (719) 385-5487
Term Expires: April 2017
E-mail: dknight@springsgov.com
★ Council Member **Larry Bagley** (District 2) . . . . . (719) 385-5493
Term Expires: April 14, 2019
E-mail: lbagley@spingsgov.com
★ Council Member **Keith C. King** (District 3) . . . . . (719) 385-5470
Term Expires: April 2017
E-mail: kcking@springsgov.com
★ Council Member **Helen Collins** (District 4) . . . . . (719) 385-5492
Term Expires: April 2017
E-mail: hcollins@springsgov.com
★ Council Member **Andy Pico** (District 6) . . . . . (719) 385-5491
Term Expires: April 2017
E-mail: apico@springsgov.com
★ Council Member **Bill Murray** (At-Large) . . . . . (719) 385-5485
Term Expires: April 2019
E-mail: bmurray@springsgov.com
★ Council Member **Tom Strand** (At-Large) . . . . . (719) 385-5486
Term Expires: April 2019
E-mail: tstrand@springsgov.com

Colorado Springs School District 11
Administration Building, 1115 N. El Paso St.,
Colorado Springs, CO 80903
Internet: www.d11.org/

Superintendent of Schools **Dr. Nicholas Gledich** . . . . . (719) 520-2001
★ School Board President **LuAnn Long** . . . . . (719) 520-2004
Term Expires: December 2017
★ Vice President **Martin Herrera** . . . . . (719) 520-2004
Term Expires: December 2019
★ School Board Treasurer **Nora Brown** . . . . . (719) 520-2004
Term Expires: December 2019
★ School Board Member **Jim Mason** . . . . . (719) 520-2004
Term Expires: December 2017

Colorado Springs School District 11 *continued*

★ School Board Member **Linda Mojer** . . . . . (719) 520-2004
Term Expires: December 2017
★ School Board Member **Elaine Naleski** . . . . . (719) 520-2004
Term Expires: December 2019
★ School Board Member **Bob Null** . . . . . (719) 520-2004
Term Expires: December 2019

City of Columbia, Missouri
701 East Broadway, Columbia, MO 65201
P.O. Box 6015, Columbia, MO 65205
Tel: (573) 874-7111

County: Boone **Election Type:** Nonpartisan **Year Incorporated:** 1826
Population: 119,108 (2015)

Office of the Mayor and City Council
P.O. Box 6015, Columbia, MO 65205
Fax: (573) 442-8828

★ Mayor **Brian Treece** . . . . . (573) 874-7222
Began Service: April 2016
Term Expires: April 2019
E-mail: mayor@CoMo.gov
★ Mayor Pro Tem **Laura Nauser** (Ward 5) . . . . . (573) 874-7222
Term Expires: April 2017
E-mail: ward5@gocolumbiamo.com
★ Councilman **Clyde Ruffin** (Ward 1) . . . . . (573) 874-7222
Term Expires: April 2017
E-mail: ward1@gocolumbiamo.com
★ Councilman **Michael Trapp** (Ward 2) . . . . . (573) 874-7222
Term Expires: April 2018
E-mail: ward2@gocolumbiamo.com
★ Councilman **Karl Skala** (Ward 3) . . . . . (573) 874-7222
Term Expires: April 2019
E-mail: ward3@gocolumbiamo.com
★ Councilman **Ian Thomas** (Ward 4) . . . . . (573) 874-7222
Term Expires: April 2019
E-mail: ward4@gocolumbiamo.com
★ Councilwoman **Betsy Peters** (Ward 6) . . . . . (573) 874-7222
Term Expires: April 2018
E-mail: ward6@gocolumbiamo.com

Office of the City Clerk
P.O. Box 6015, Columbia, MO 65205

City Clerk **Sheela Amin** . . . . . (573) 874-7208
E-mail: skamin@gocolumbiamo.com

Office of the City Manager
P.O. Box 6015, Columbia, MO 65205
Fax: (573) 442-8828

○ City Manager **Mike Matthes** . . . . . (573) 874-6338
E-mail: mematthe@gocolumbiamo.com

Office of Cultural Affairs [OCA]
P.O. Box 6015, Columbia, MO 65205
Fax: (573) 443-3986

Manager **JJ Musgrove** . . . . . (573) 874-7512

Office of Sustainability
701 East Broadway, 2nd Floor, Columbia, MO 65201

Sustainability Manager **Barbara Buffaloe** . . . . . (573) 817-5025
E-mail: babuffal@gocolumbiamo.com

★ Elected Official ▲ Appointed by Legislature ▼ Appointed by Governor ▶ Appointed by Board or Commission ● Appointed by Judge
■ Appointed by Mayor △ Appointed by Freeholders ▽ Appointed by Supervisor ▷ Appointed by County Executive ○ Appointed by Council

Community Development Department
P.O. Box 6015, Columbia, MO 65205
Fax: (573) 874-7546
Director **Tim Teddy** .... (573) 874-7239
E-mail: planning@gocolumbiamo.com

Office of Neighborhood Services
P.O. Box 6015, Columbia, MO 65205
Director **Leigh Britt** .... (573) 874-7504
E-mail: lcnutter@gocolumbiamo.com

Finance Department
P.O. Box 6015, Columbia, MO 65205
Finance Director **John Blattel** .... (573) 874-7457
Assistant Finance Director **Lynn Cannon** .... (573) 874-7333
Finance Project Manager **Ron Barrett** .... (573) 874-7371
Budget Officer **Laura Peveler** .... (573) 874-7541
E-mail: lauras@gocolumbiamo.com
Treasurer **Bette Wordelman** .... (573) 874-7369
Purchasing Agent **Cale Turner** .... (573) 874-7375
E-mail: dcturner@gocolumbiamo.com
Business Services Manager **Janice Finley** .... (573) 874-7747
Utility Accounts Supervisor **(Vacant)** .... (573) 874-7458
Risk Manager **Sarah Perry** .... (573) 874-7377
E-mail: sarah@gocolumbiamo.com

Fire Department
201 Orr Street, Columbia, MO 65201
Fax: (573) 874-7446 E-mail: fire@gocolumbiamo.com
Fire Chief **Randy E. White** .... (573) 874-7391
E-mail: rew@gocolumbiamo.com

Human Resources Department
P.O. Box 6015, Columbia, MO 65205
Fax: (573) 874-7736 Internet: http://www.como.gov/hr/
Director **Margrace F. Buckler** .... (573) 874-7235
E-mail: mfb@gocolumbiamo.com

Information Technologies Department
P.O. Box 6015, Columbia, MO 65205
Chief Information Officer **Jim Chapdelaine** .... (573) 874-7500
E-mail: cityit@gocolumbiamo.com

Law Department
P.O. Box 6015, Columbia, MO 65205
City Counselor **Nancy Thompson** .... (573) 874-7227
701 East Broadway, Columbia, MO 65201 Fax: (573) 424-8828
E-mail: njthomps@gocolumbiamo.com
City Prosecutor **Stephen Richey** .... (573) 874-7229
600 East Broadway, Columbia, MO 65201 Fax: (573) 874-7533

Parks and Recreation Department
1 South 7th Street, Columbia, MO 65201
Director **Mike B. Griggs** .... (573) 874-7463

Police Department
600 East Walnut, Columbia, MO 65201-4491
Fax: (573) 874-3142
Chief of Police **Kenneth M. Burton** .... (573) 874-7404

Community Relations Department
P.O. Box 6015, Columbia, MO 65205
Internet: http://www.como.gov/Public_Comm/index.php
Community Relations Director **Steven Sapp** .... (573) 875-1231
Public Communications Specialist **Sara Humm** .... (573) 874-7240
E-mail: SEHUMM@GoColumbiaMo.com

Department of Public Health and Human Services
P.O. Box 6015, Columbia, MO 65205
Fax: (573) 874-7756
Director **Stephanie Browning** .... (573) 874-7345

Public Works Department
P.O. Box 6015, Columbia, MO 65205
Fax: (573) 874-7132
Director **David A. "Dave" Nichols** .... (573) 874-7645

Columbia Convention and Visitors Bureau
300 South Providence Road, Columbia, MO 65203
Fax: (573) 443-3986 Internet: www.visitcolumbiamo.com/
Director **Amy Schneider** .... (573) 875-1231 ext. 5578

Columbia Water and Light
P.O. Box 6015, Columbia, MO 65205
Fax: (573) 443-6875
Director of Utilities **Tad Johnsen** .... (573) 874-7325

City of Columbia, South Carolina

1737 Main St., Columbia, SC 29201
P.O. Box 147, Columbia, SC 29217
Tel: (803) 545-3000 (Information) Internet: www.columbiasc.net/

County: Richland **Election Type:** Nonpartisan **Year Founded:** 1786
Population: 133,803 (2015)

Office of the Mayor and City Council

P.O. Box 147, Columbia, SC 29217
Fax: (803) 733-8633
★ Mayor **Stephen K. "Steve" Benjamin** .... (803) 545-3075
Began Service: July 1, 2010
Term Expires: December 31, 2017
★ Council Member **Sam Davis** (District 1) .... (803) 545-3061
Term Expires: December 31, 2017
E-mail: sdavis@columbiasc.net
★ Council Member **Ed McDowell** (District 2) .... (803) 545-3061
Term Expires: December 31, 2019
E-mail: ehmcdowell@columbiasc.net
★ Council Member **Moe Baddourah** (District 3) .... (803) 545-4424
Term Expires: December 31, 2019
E-mail: mobaddourah@columbiasc.net
★ Council Member **Leona K. Plaugh** (District 4) .... (803) 782-1947
Term Expires: December 31, 2017
E-mail: lkplaugh@columbiasc.net
★ Council Member **Tameika Isaac Devine** (At-Large) .... (803) 254-8868
Term Expires: December 31, 2017
E-mail: tidevine@columbiasc.net
★ Council Member **Howard Duvall** (At-Large) .... (803) 544-4401
Term Expires: December 31, 2019
E-mail: heduvall@columbiasc.net

Office of the City Clerk

P.O. Box 147, Columbia, SC 29217
Fax: (803) 255-8936
City Clerk **Erika Moore** .... (803) 545-3045
E-mail: edmoore@columbiasc.net

★ Elected Official ▲ Appointed by Legislature ▼ Appointed by Governor ▶ Appointed by Board or Commission ● Appointed by Judge
■ Appointed by Mayor △ Appointed by Freeholders ▽ Appointed by Supervisor ▷ Appointed by County Executive ○ Appointed by Council

Office of the City Manager

P.O. Box 147, Columbia, SC 29217

City Manager **Teresa Wilson** .... (803) 545-3011
E-mail: tbwilson@columbiasc.net

Senior Assistant City Manager **S. Allison Baker** .... (803) 545-3030
E-mail: abaker@columbiasc.net

Assistant City Manager **Melissa Smith Gentry** .... (803) 545-3037
E-mail: msgentry@columbiasc.net

Assistant City Manager **Jeff Palen** .... (803) 545-4308
E-mail: jmpalen@columbiasc.net

Office of the City Attorney

P.O. Box 147, Columbia, SC 29217

City Attorney **Teresa A. Knox** .... (803) 737-4242
E-mail: taknox@columbiasc.net

Community Development Department

P.O. Box 147, Columbia, SC 29217

Director **Deborah Livingston** .... (803) 545-3373
E-mail: djlivingston@columbiasc.net

Economic Development Department

P.O. Box 147, Columbia, SC 29217
E-mail: development@columbiasc.net

Director **Ryan Coleman** .... (803) 734-2700
E-mail: rtcoleman@columbiasc.net

Finance Department

P.O. Box 147, Columbia, SC 29217

Director **Janice Alonso** .... (803) 545-3409
Purchasing Agent **Sandra A. Wright** .... (803) 545-3475
E-mail: sawright@columbiasc.net Fax: (803) 733-8408

Fire Department

P.O. Box 147, Columbia, SC 29217
Internet: http://www.columbiasc.net/fire

Fire Chief **Aubrey Jenkins** .... (803) 545-3700
E-mail: cfdajenkins@columbiasc.net

Inspections Department

P.O. Box 147, Columbia, SC 29217

Building Official **Jerry Thompson** .... (803) 545-3420
Chief Code Enforcement Officer **David Hatcher** .... (803) 545-3430

Parks and Recreation

P.O. Box 147, Columbia, SC 29217
Fax: (803) 343-8744 Internet: http://www.columbiasc.net/city/parks.htm

Director (Acting) **Randy Davis** .... (803) 545-3100

Personnel Department

P.O. Box 147, Columbia, SC 29217

Director **Pam Benjamin** .... (803) 545-3005
E-mail: prbenjamin@columbiasc.net

Planning and Development Services Department

1136 Washington Street, 1st Floor, Columbia, SC 29201

Director **Krista Hampton** .... (803) 545-3222

Police Department

P.O. Box 147, Columbia, SC 29217
Internet: http://www.columbiasc.net/city/police.htm

Chief of Police **Skip Holbrook** .... (803) 545-3500

Public Relations Department

P.O. Box 147, Columbia, SC 29217
Fax: (803) 343-8719

Director **Leshia Utsey** .... (803) 545-3020
E-mail: lutsey@columbiasc.net

Public Works Department

P.O. Box 147, Columbia, SC 29217
Fax: (803) 733-8648 E-mail: projadmn@columbiasc.net
Internet: http://www.columbiasc.net/city/city1a3.htm

Director **Robert A. Anderson** .... (803) 545-3830

Solid Waste Division

Superintendent **John Hooks** .... (803) 545-3800
Assistant Superintendent **Emmanuel Lawson** .... (803) 545-3800

Street Division

Superintendent **Robert Sweatt** .... (803) 545-3790
Assistant Street Supervisor **Destin Goins** .... (803) 545-3790

Traffic Engineering Division

City Traffic Engineer **David Brewer** .... (803) 545-3850
E-mail: ddbrewer@columbiasc.net
Assistant City Traffic Engineer **Ron Armstead** .... (803) 545-3850
E-mail: rearmstead@columbiasc.net

Utilities and Engineering Department

P.O. Box 147, Columbia, SC 29217
Internet: www.columbiasc.net/Engineering

Director **Joey Jaco** .... (803) 545-3300

Zoning Department

1136 Washington Street, Columbia, SC 29201

Director of Development Services **Krista Hampton** ...... (803) 545-3333

City of Columbus, Georgia

Government Center, 100 10th St., Columbus, GA 31901
P.O. Box 1340, Columbus, GA 31902-1340
Internet: www.columbusga.org

County: Muscogee **Election Type:** Nonpartisan **Population:** 200,579 (2015)

Form of Municipal Government: City and county governments are combined.

Office of the Mayor and City Council

Government Center, 100 10th St., Columbus, GA 31901
P.O. Box 1340, Columbus, GA 31902-1340
Fax: (706) 653-4970 Internet: www.columbusga.org/mayor/

★Mayor **Teresa Tomlinson** .... (706) 653-4712
Began Service: January 3, 2011 Fax: (706) 653-4970
Term Expires: January 4, 2019
E-mail: ttomlinson@columbusga.org
Date of Birth: February 19, 1965
Education: Sweet Briar 1987 BA; Emory 1991 JD
Executive Assistant **Judy Tucker** .... (706) 653-4712
E-mail: jtucker@columbusga.org

★Mayor Pro Tem **Evelyn Turner Pugh** (District 4) .... (706) 682-1642
Term Expires: January 5, 2017
E-mail: epugh@columbusga.org

★Councilor **Jerry "Pops" Barnes** (District 1) .... (706) 442-0249
Term Expires: January 5, 2019
E-mail: jbarnes@columbusga.org

★Councilor **Glenn Davis** (District 2) .... (706) 323-1005
Term Expires: January 7, 2017
E-mail: glenndavis@columbusga.org

★Elected Official ▲Appointed by Legislature ▼Appointed by Governor ▶Appointed by Board or Commission ●Appointed by Judge
■Appointed by Mayor △Appointed by Freeholders ▽Appointed by Supervisor ▷Appointed by County Executive ○Appointed by Council

Office of the Mayor and City Council *continued*

★Councilor **Bruce Huff** (District 3) .... (706) 322-8713
Term Expires: January 5, 2019
E-mail: bhuff@columbusga.org

★Councilor **Mike Baker** (District 5) .... (706) 568-3186
Term Expires: January 5, 2019
E-mail: mbaker@columbusga.org

★Councilor **R. Gary Allen** (District 6) .... (706) 323-3431
Term Expires: January 7, 2017
E-mail: gallen@columbusga.org

★Councilor **Evelyn "Mimi" Woodson** (District 7) .... (706) 689-7009
Term Expires: January 5, 2019
E-mail: mwoodson@columbusga.org

★Councilor **Thomas Bryant "Tom" Buck III** (District 8) .. (706) 324-3385
Term Expires: January 7, 2017
E-mail: tbuck@columbusga.org
Education: Emory BA, LLB

★Councilor **Judy Thomas** (At-Large, Post 9) .... (706) 327-4926
Term Expires: January 5, 2019
E-mail: jthomas@columbusga.org

★Councilor
Berry "Skip" Henderson (At-Large, Post 10) .... (706) 321-9024
Term Expires: January 7, 2017
E-mail: skiphenderson@columbusga.org

○Clerk of Council **Tiny B. Washington** .... (706) 653-4013
E-mail: twashington@columbusga.org

Office of the City Attorney

Government Center, 100 10th Street, 6th Floor, Columbus, GA 31901
P.O. Box 1340, Columbus, GA 31902-1340
Fax: (706) 653-4023

○City Attorney **Clifton C. Fay** .... (706) 653-4025
E-mail: cfay@columbusga.org
Assistant City Attorney **Lucy T. Sheftall** .... (706) 653-4025

Office of the Coroner

510 10th Street, Columbus, GA 31902
P.O. Box 1866, Columbus, GA 31902-1866
Fax: (706) 653-3264 Internet: www.columbusga.org/Coroner/

★Coroner **Buddy Bryan** .... (706) 225-3260
Term Expires: November 2016
E-mail: bbryan@columbusga.org
Deputy Coroner **Charles Newton** .... (706) 225-3260
Deputy Coroner **Freeman Worley** .... (706) 225-3260
Administrative Assistant **Malika Hampton** .... (706) 225-3260
E-mail: mhampton@columbusga.org

Muscogee County Marshal

Government Center, 100 10th St., Columbus, GA 31901
P.O. Box 1340, Columbus, GA 31902-1340
Fax: (706) 653-4382 Internet: www.columbusga.org/Marshal/

★Marshal **Greg Countryman** .... (706) 653-4385
Term Expires: January 3, 2017
E-mail: gcountryman@columbusga.org

Muscogee County Sheriff's Office

Government Center, 100 10th Street, 4th Floor, Columbus, GA 31901
P.O. Box 1338, Columbus, GA 31902-1338
Fax: (706) 653-4234 E-mail: muscosheriff@columbusga.org
Internet: www.columbusga.org/Sheriff/

★Sheriff **John Darr** .... (706) 653-4225
Term Expires: December 31, 2016
E-mail: jdarr@columbusga.org
Education: Columbus State AA
Chief Deputy **John Fitzpatrick** .... (706) 653-4225
Administration **Major Larry Mitchell** .... (706) 653-4225
Operations Bureau **Major Mike Massey** .... (706) 653-4225
Training Division **Lt. Shawn Riley** .... (706) 653-4220
E-mail: sriley@columbusga.org

Muscogee County Sheriff's Office *continued*

Jail Commander **Dane Collins** .... (706) 653-4258
E-mail: dcollins@columbusga.org

Office of the City Manager

Government Center, 100 Tenth Street, 6th Floor, Columbus, GA 31902
P.O. Box 1340, Columbus, GA 31902-1340
Fax: (706) 653-4032 Internet: www.columbusga.org/citymanager/

○City Manager **Isaiah Hugley** .... (706) 653-4029
E-mail: ihugley@columbusga.org
Education: Talladega BA; Mississippi State MPA
Deputy City Manager (Current Operations)
Lisa Goodwin .... (706) 653-4029
E-mail: lgoodwin@columbusga.org
Education: Tuskegee BS; Troy U MA
Deputy City Manager (Planning and Development)
Pamela Hodge .... (706) 653-4029
E-mail: phodge@columbusga.org
Education: Wichita State 1998 BS

Office of the Tax Assessor

City Service Center, 3111 Citizens Way, Columbus, GA 31906
Fax: (706) 225-3800 Internet: www.columbusga.org/TaxAssessors/

Chief Appraiser **Betty J. Middleton** .... (706) 653-4398
E-mail: bmiddleton@columbusga.org

Office of the Tax Commissioner

3111 Citizens Way, Columbus, GA 31906
Fax: (706) 225-3773 Internet: www.columbusga.org/TaxCommissioner/

Tax Commissioner **Lula L. Huff** .... (706) 653-4211
E-mail: lhuff@columbusga.org
Chief Deputy Tax Commissioner
Darrell A. "Tony" Floyd .... (706) 653-4211
E-mail: tfloyd@columbusga.org

Columbus Airport

3250 West Britt David Road, Columbus, GA 31909-5399
Fax: (706) 324-1016 Internet: www.flycolumbusga.com

Director **Richard Howell** .... (706) 324-2449 ext. 1410

Columbus Water Works [CWW]

1421 Veterans Parkway, Columbus, GA 31902
P.O. Box 1600, Columbus, GA 31902-1600
Fax: (706) 327-3845 Internet: www.cwwga.org

President **Steve Davis** .... (706) 649-3430
Senior Vice President, Water Resources Operations
John Peebles .... (706) 649-3458
E-mail: jpeebles@cwwga.org

311 Citizens Service Center

Government Center, 100 10th St., Columbus, GA 31902

Assistant to City Manager/311 Citizens Service Center
Manager **Teasha Johnson** .... (706) 653-4000
E-mail: teashajohnson@columbusga.org Fax: (706) 653-4673

Community Reinvestment Department

420 10th Street, 2nd Floor, Columbus, GA 31901
P.O. Box 1340, Columbus, GA 31902-1340
Fax: (706) 653-4486
Internet: www.columbusga.org/CommunityReinvestment/

Manager **Laura Johnson** .... (706) 225-4613

★Elected Official ▲Appointed by Legislature ▼Appointed by Governor ▶Appointed by Board or Commission ●Appointed by Judge
■Appointed by Mayor △Appointed by Freeholders ▽Appointed by Supervisor ▷Appointed by County Executive ○Appointed by Council

Cooperative Extension Department
Government Center, Annex Bldg., 420 10th St., Columbus, GA 31901-1340
Fax: (706) 653-4203
Internet: www.columbusga.org/Cooperative_Extension/

Director **Rhea Bentley** .... (706) 653-4200

Elections and Registration Office
3111 Citizens Way, Columbus, GA 31906
Tel: (706) 653-4392 Fax: (706) 225-4394
Internet: www.columbusga.org/elections/

Executive Director **Nancy Boren** .... (706) 653-4392

Engineering Department
Annex Building, 420 10th Street, 2nd Floor, Columbus, GA 31901
P.O. Box 1340, Columbus, GA 31902-1340
Tel: (706) 653-4441 Fax: (706) 653-4439
Internet: www.columbusga.org/engineering2/

○ Director **Donna Newman** .... (706) 225-3945
E-mail: dnewman@columbusga.org
Education: Auburn 1984 BCE

Traffic Engineer **Walter "Doc" Dorsey** .... (706) 653-4135

Finance Department
Government Center, 100 10th St., Columbus, GA 31901
P.O. Box 1340, Columbus, GA 31902-1340
Tel: (706) 653-4087 Fax: (706) 653-4670
Internet: www.columbusga.org/finance/

Finance Director (Interim) **Pamela Hodge** .... (706) 653-4087
Education: Wichita State 1998 BS

Accounting Division Manager **Jody Davis** .... (706) 653-4087
E-mail: jldavis@columbusga.org

Purchasing Manager **Andrea McCorvey** .... (706) 653-4087
E-mail: amccorvey@columbusga.org Fax: (706) 653-4109

Assistant Finance Director **Angelica Alexander** .... (706) 653-4086

Department of Fire and Emergency Medical Services
510 10th Street, Columbus, GA 31901
Fax: (706) 653-3504
Internet: www.columbusga.org/fire/commprograms.htm

○ Fire Chief **Jeff Meyer** .... (706) 225-4204
E-mail: jmeyer@columbusga.org

Assistant Chief **Robert Futrell** .... (706) 225-4213
E-mail: rfutrell@columbusga.org

Administrative Services Deputy Chief **Mike Higgins** .... (706) 225-4226
E-mail: mhiggins@columbusga.org

Emergency Management Deputy Director **Riley Land** .... (706) 225-4072
E-mail: rland@columbusga.org Fax: (706) 653-3271

Operations Deputy Chief **Thomas Streeter, Sr.** .... (706) 225-4248
E-mail: tstreeter@columbusga.org

Division Chief **CAPT Marie Harrell** .... (706) 225-4215
E-mail: mharrell@columbusga.org

EMS Coordinator **Dan Woods** .... (706) 225-4224

Fire Prevention Division Chief/Fire Marshal **Ricky Shores** .... (706) 225-4212
E-mail: rshores@columbusga.org

Training Division Chief **Tim Smith** .... (706) 653-3543
E-mail: tsmith@columbusga.org Fax: (706) 653-3546

Training/Fire Prevention Deputy Chief **Greg Lang** .... (706) 225-4218
E-mail: glang@columbusga.org

Human Resources Department
P.O. Box 1340, Columbus, GA 31902-1340
Fax: (706) 653-4066 Internet: www.columbusga.org/hr/

Human Resources Director **Reather Hollowell** .... (706) 653-4059
E-mail: rhollowell@columbusga.org

Human Resources Department *continued*

Assistant Director of Human Resources and Affirmative Action **Iris B. Jessie** .... (706) 653-4059
E-mail: ijessie@columbusga.org

Department of Information Technology
Government Center, 100 10th St., Columbus, GA 31901-2718
P.O. Box 1340, Columbus, GA 31902-1340
Fax: (706) 225-4053 Internet: www.columbusga.org/it/

Director **Forrest Toelle** .... (706) 653-4045
E-mail: ftoelle@columbusga.org

Inspections and Codes Division
420 10th Street, Columbus, GA 31901-1340
P.O. Box 1340, Columbus, GA 31902-1340
Fax: (706) 653-4123 Internet: www.columbusga.org/inscode/

Director (Interim) **Pamela Hodge** .... (706) 653-4126
Education: Wichita State 1998 BS

Assistant Director **Fred Cobb** .... (706) 225-3899

Job Training Division
420 10th Street, Columbus, GA 31901
Fax: (706) 653-4533 Internet: www.columbusga.org/WIA/

Director **Howard Pendleton** .... (706) 653-4529

Metra Transit System
814 Linwood Blvd., Columbus, GA 31902
P.O. Box 1340, Columbus, GA 31902-1340
Fax: (706) 653-4420 E-mail: metrainfo@columbusga.org

Transportation Director **Saundra Hunter** .... (706) 653-4410

Parks and Recreation Department
3111 Citizens Way, Columbus, GA 31906
Fax: (706) 255-4514 Internet: www.columbusga.org/parks/

Director **Dr. James D. Worsley** .... (706) 225-4658

Assistant Director **Holli Browder** .... (706) 225-4658

Police Department
510 10th St., Columbus, GA 31902
P.O. Box 1866, Columbus, GA 31902-1866
Fax: (706) 653-3114 Internet: www.columbusga.org/police/

Police Chief **Richard T. "Ricky" Boren** .... (706) 653-3100

Public Works
Building E, 602 11th Avenue, Columbus, GA 31901
Fax: (706) 653-4576

Director **Patricia C. Biegler** .... (706) 225-4676
Education: South Florida BS; USC MS

Deputy Director, Operations **Ron Smith** .... (706) 225-4665
E-mail: rsmith@columbusga.org

Cemeteries Division
1000 Victory Drive, Columbus, GA 31901
Fax: (706) 653-4576

Cemetery Chief **Darrell Meadows** .... (706) 653-4579
E-mail: dmeadows@columbusga.org

Community Services
Fax: (706) 653-4576

Community Service Coordinator **Al Lyons** .... (706) 225-4949
E-mail: alyons@columbusga.org

Facilities Maintenance Division
Division Chief **Bruce Gilbreath** .... (706) 653-4079
E-mail: bgilbreath@columbusga.org

★ Elected Official ▲ Appointed by Legislature ▼ Appointed by Governor ▶ Appointed by Board or Commission ● Appointed by Judge
■ Appointed by Mayor △ Appointed by Freeholders ▽ Appointed by Supervisor ▷ Appointed by County Executive ○ Appointed by Council

Fleet Maintenance
Fax: (706) 653-4172

Deputy Director of Budget and Logistics **Harvey Milner** . . (706) 225-4955
E-mail: hmilner@columbusga.org

Special Enforcement Animal Control Division
4910 Milgen Road, Columbus, GA 31907

Special Enforcement Chief **Drale Short** . . . . (706) 653-4512

Street Maintenance Division
Division Chief **Michelle Brown-Mang** . . . . (706) 317-2318

Urban Forestry and Beautification Division
Division Chief **Scott Jones** . . . . (706) 225-4762
Assistant Manager, Forestry **Marvin Coverson** . . . . (706) 225-4764
Assistant Manager, Beautification **Michael Jordan** . . . . . . (706) 225-4948

Waste Management Division
Sanitation Chief **Les T. Moore** . . . . (706) 225-4681
Assistant Sanitation Chief **James Mang** . . . . (706) 225-4680
Recycle Center Manager **Carl Nunley** . . . . (706) 225-4505

Columbus Georgia Convention and Trade Center
P.O. Box 1340, Columbus, GA 31902-1340
Fax: (706) 327-0162 Internet: www.conventiontradecenter.com/

Executive Director **David Bevans** . . . . (706) 327-4522
Fax: (706) 327-0162

City of Columbus, Ohio
City Hall, 90 West Broad Street, Columbus, OH 43215
Tel: (614) 645-7671 (Information) Internet: www.cityofcolumbus.org

County: Franklin **Year Founded:** 1812 **Year Incorporated:** 1834
Population: 850,106 (2015)

Office of the Mayor
City Hall, 90 West Broad Street, Room 247, Columbus, OH 43215
Fax: (614) 645-7811 Internet: http://mayor.columbus.gov/

★ Mayor **Andrew J. Ginther** . . . . (614) 645-7671
Began Service: January 1, 2016
Term Expires: December 31, 2019
E-mail: aginther@columbus.gov
Chief of Staff **Greg J. Davies** . . . . (614) 645-7671
Deputy Chief of Staff **Kenneth Paul** . . . . (614) 645-7671

City Treasurer
City Hall, 90 W. Broad St., 1st Fl., Columbus, OH 43215
Fax: (614) 645-3874 Internet: http://treasurer.columbus.gov/

○ City Treasurer **Deborah Klie** . . . . (614) 645-7737
E-mail: dklie@columbus.gov

Civil Service Commission
Beacon Building, 50 West Gay Street, 6th Floor, Room 600, Columbus, OH 43215-9038
Tel: (614) 645-8300 Tel: (614) 645-6200 (TDD) Fax: (614) 645-8379
Internet: https://csc.columbus.gov/webapp/

Commission President **Grady L. Pettigrew** . . . . (614) 645-7605
Term Expires: February 1, 2018
Education: Ohio State 1965 BA, 1971 JD
Commissioner **Delena Edwards** . . . . (614) 645-7605
Note: Will continue to serve until reappointed or replaced.
Term Expires: January 31, 2014
Education: Ohio 1981 BA; Iowa 1985 JD
Commissioner **(Vacant)** . . . . (614) 645-7605
Term Expires: January 31, 2016

Civil Service Commission *continued*

Executive Director **Amy DeLong** . . . . (614) 645-7605
E-mail: adelong@columbus.gov
Education: Capital U BA, JD

Community Relations Commission
1111 East Broad Street, Columbus, OH 43205
Tel: (614) 645-1993 Fax: (614) 645-1862
Internet: http://crc.columbus.gov/

Chairman **Mary Howard** . . . . (614) 645-1993

Staff
■ Executive Director **Derek Anderson** . . . . (614) 645-1993
Education Coordinator **Neal Semel** . . . . (614) 645-1972
E-mail: nasemel@columbus.gov
Community Relations Coordinator **Gale Gray** . . . . (614) 645-1993
E-mail: gagray@columbus.gov
New American Outreach Coordinator **Abdikhayr H. Soofe** . . . . (614) 645-1952
E-mail: ahsoofe@columbus.gov
New American Initiative Coordinator **Guadalupe Velasquez** . . . . (614) 645-1995
E-mail: gvelasquez@columbus.gov
Equal Opportunity Officer **Nelson Hewitt** . . . . (614) 645-1977

Department of Development
50 W. Gay St., 3rd Fl., Columbus, OH 43215-9040
Tel: (614) 645-7795 Fax: (614) 645-6675
Internet: http://development.columbus.gov/

■ Director **Steven R. "Steve" Schoeny** . . . . (614) 645-8595
E-mail: srschoney@columbus.gov
Education: Ohio 1993 BA; Maryland 1995 MPM
Assistant Director **Mike Schadek** . . . . (614) 645-7795

Code Enforcement Division
757 Carolyn Avenue, Columbus, OH 43224

Administrator **Dana Rose** . . . . (614) 645-7897

Economic Development Division
150 South Front Street, #220, Columbus, OH 43215
Tel: (614) 645-8172 Internet: http://edps.td.ci.columbus.oh.us/

Administrator **Mark Lundine** . . . . (614) 645-6679
E-mail: malundine@columbus.gov

Housing Services Division
50 West Gay Street, Columbus, OH 43215
Tel: (614) 645-7795 Fax: (614) 645-6675
Internet: http://hcs.td.ci.columbus.oh.us/

Administrator **Rita Parise** . . . . (614) 645-6115

Land Redevelopment Office
109 North Front Street, Columbus, OH 43215-9023
Tel: (614) 645-5263 Fax: (614) 645-3092

Administrator **John Turner** . . . . (614) 645-5885

Planning Division
109 North Front Street, Columbus, OH 43215-9023
Tel: (614) 645-8664 Fax: (614) 645-1483

Administrator **Kevin Wheeler** . . . . (614) 645-6057

Equal Business Opportunity Office
1393 East Broad Street, Columbus, OH 43215
Fax: (614) 645-6669 E-mail: eboco@columbus.gov

■ Chief Diversity Officer **Stephen Francis** . . . . (614) 645-4764

★ Elected Official ▲ Appointed by Legislature ▼ Appointed by Governor ▶ Appointed by Board or Commission ● Appointed by Judge
■ Appointed by Mayor △ Appointed by Freeholders ▽ Appointed by Supervisor ▷ Appointed by County Executive ○ Appointed by Council

Department of Finance and Management
City Hall, 90 W. Broad St., 4th Floor, Columbus, OH 43215
Fax: (614) 645-7139 Internet: http://finance.columbus.gov/

■ Director **Joe A. Lombardi** .... (614) 645-8200
E-mail: jalombardi@columbus.gov
Deputy Director **Brian Clark** .... (614) 645-8200
Deputy Director **Giangardella Dan** .... (614) 645-8200
Deputy Director **Kathy A. Owens** .... (614) 645-8200
E-mail: kaowens@columbus.gov
Energy Manager **Willie Overmann** .... (614) 645-8200
E-mail: wsovermann@columbus.gov

Construction Management Office
Construction Management Administrator
Barry N. Bryant .... (614) 645-8339
E-mail: bnbryant@columbus.gov

Facilities Management Division
Facilities Administrator **Johnny Scales** .... (614) 645-7181
E-mail: jbscales@columbus.gov

Financial Management Division
Financial Management Administrator **Adam Robins** .... (614) 645-8200
Budget Management Officer **Aileen N. Heiser** .... (614) 645-8200
E-mail: anheiser@columbus.gov
Debt Management Coordinator **Rob Newman** .... (614) 645-8200
Grants Management Coordinator **Phillip Carter** .... (614) 645-8200
E-mail: pdcarter@columbus.gov
Purchasing Manager **Sean S. Fouts** .... (614) 645-8315
E-mail: sfouts@columbus.gov

Fleet Management Division
4211 Groves Road, Columbus, OH 43232
Fax: (614) 645-7347 Internet: http://pubserv.ci.columbus.oh.us/fleet.htm

Administrator **Kelly W. Reagan** .... (614) 645-8281

Real Estate Management Office
Real Estate Management Office Administrator
Ann Kelly .... (614) 645-5189

Human Resources Department
77 North Front Street, 1st Floor, Suite 101, Columbus, OH 43215
Fax: (614) 645-5940

■ Director **Nichole Brandon** .... (614) 645-7206
E-mail: nmbrandon@columbus.gov
Deputy Director **(Vacant)** .... (614) 645-7206
Labor Relations Manager **(Vacant)** .... (614) 645-7206
Risk Manager **Teresa "Midge" Slemmer** .... (614) 645-8065
E-mail: tslemmer@columbus.gov
Training Manager **Drema Kirkling** .... (614) 645-7206
E-mail: kpkirkling@columbus.gov
Equal Employment Opportunity Office
Shannon Freeman .... (614) 645-8871
E-mail: sdfreeman@columbus.gov

Public Safety Department
Beacon Bldg., 50 West Gay Street, 2nd Floor, Columbus, OH 43215-9035
Fax: (614) 645-8268

■ Director **George Speaks** .... (614) 645-8210
E-mail: gespeaks@columbus.gov
Assistant Director **Robert Stewart** .... (614) 645-8210
E-mail: rstewart@columbus.gov

Division of Fire
3675 Parsons Ave., Columbus, OH 43207-4054
Internet: http://fire.columbus.gov/

Fire Chief **Kevin O'Connor** .... (614) 645-7533
E-mail: koconnor@columbus.gov Fax: (614) 645-4203
Assistant Chief **David Walton** .... (614) 645-6017
E-mail: dwalton@columbus.gov Fax: (614) 645-3040
Emergency Services Bureau Assistant Chief **(Vacant)** .... (614) 645-4128
Fax: (614) 645-3040

Division of Fire *continued*

Assistant Chief, Fire Prevention Bureau
David Whiting .... (614) 645-7641
E-mail: dwhiting@columbus.gov Fax: (614) 645-0110
Assistant Chief, Fire Support Services Bureau **(Vacant)** .... (614) 645-6385
3839 Parsons Ave., Columbus, OH 43207-4054 Fax: (614) 645-3214
Fire Training Assistant Chief **David Whiting** .... (614) 645-6360
Fax: (614) 645-4245

License Section
750 Piedmont Road, Columbus, OH 43224
Fax: (614) 645-8912

Manager **Thom Ibinson** .... (614) 645-6009

Police Division
120 Marconi Blvd., Columbus, OH 43215-0009
Fax: (614) 645-4551 Internet: www.columbuspolice.org

Chief of Police **Cdr. Kim Jacobs** .... (614) 645-4600
Administrative Subdivision Deputy Chief
Timothy Becker .... (614) 645-4580
Investigative Subdivision Deputy Chief **Richard Bash** .... (614) 645-4770
Patrol South Subdivision Deputy Chief **Ken Kuebler** .... (614) 645-4770
Patrol North Subdivision Deputy Chief
Thomas Quinlan .... (614) 645-4770
Homeland Security Subdivision Deputy Chief
Michael Woods .... (614) 645-4770
E-mail: mwoods@columbuspolice.org
Police Academy Superintendent **Robert Meader** .... (614) 645-4611
2609 McKinley Ave., Columbus, OH 43204 Fax: (614) 645-4516

Support Services Division
220 Greenlawn Ave., Columbus, OH 43223
Internet: http://www.publicsafety.ci.columbus.oh.us/commf.html

Administrator **Ramona P. Patts** .... (614) 645-7710
E-mail: rpatts@columbus.gov Fax: (614) 645-4819

Weights and Measures
750 Piedmont Road, Columbus, OH 43224

Sealer of Weights and Measures **Thomas B. Maynard** .... (614) 645-7397
Fax: (614) 645-3994

Public Service Department
50 West Gay Street, 2nd Floor, Columbus, OH 43215-9035
Tel: (614) 645-8290 Fax: (614) 645-7805
Internet: http://publicservice.columbus.gov/

■ Director **Jennifer L. Gallagher** .... (614) 645-8290
E-mail: jlgallagher@columbus.gov
Education: Ohio State BSCE, MSCE
Deputy Director **(Vacant)** .... (614) 645-8290

Public Utilities Department
910 Dublin Road, 4th Floor, Columbus, OH 43215
Fax: (614) 645-8019 Internet: http://utilities.columbus.gov

■ Director **(Vacant)** .... (614) 645-6141
Administration Deputy Director **Mark E. Kouns** .... (614) 645-6141
E-mail: mekouns@columbus.gov

Power and Water Division
910 Dublin Road, 3rd Floor, Columbus, OH 43215

Water Administrator **Rick Westerfield** .... (614) 645-8371

Sewerage and Drainage Division
1250 Fairwood Avenue, Columbus, OH 43206
Fax: (614) 645-3801

Administrator **Dax Blake** .... (614) 645-7175

★ Elected Official ▲ Appointed by Legislature ▼ Appointed by Governor ▶ Appointed by Board or Commission ● Appointed by Judge
■ Appointed by Mayor △ Appointed by Freeholders ▽ Appointed by Supervisor ▷ Appointed by County Executive ○ Appointed by Council

Recreation and Parks Department

1111 East Broad Street, Suite 200, Columbus, OH 43205
Fax: (614) 645-5801

▶ Director **Tony Collins** .... (614) 645-5932
E-mail: tacollins@columbus.gov
Assistant Director **Steve Aumiller** .... (614) 645-3329
Fax: (614) 645-5801
Assistant Director **Terri S. Leist** .... (614) 645-5420
Recreation Administrator **Marilyn Taylor** .... (614) 645-0702

Golf Division

1111 East Broad Street, Suite 100, Columbus, OH 43223
Administrator **Terri S. Leist** .... (614) 645-3375
Fax: (614) 645-5767

Technology Department

The Jerry Hammond Center, 1111 East Broad Street, Suite 300, Columbus, OH 43205
Fax: (614) 645-2400 Internet: http://dot.columbus.gov
Chief Information Officer/ Director of Technology
Gary R. Cavin .... (614) 645-2550
E-mail: grcavin@columbus.gov

Columbus Metropolitan Library

96 South Grant Avenue, Columbus, OH 43215
Tel: (614) 645-2275 Internet: www.columbuslibrary.org

Administration

Chief Executive Officer **Patrick "Pat" Losinski** .... (614) 849-1005
E-mail: plosinski@columbuslibrary.org
Education: Wisconsin (Stevens Point) BS; Wisconsin MLS
Chief Customer Experience Officer **Alison Circle** .... (614) 849-1044
E-mail: acircle@columbuslibrary.org
Chief Finance Officer **Paula Miller** .... (614) 849-1037
Chief Operating Officer **Nate Oliver** .... (614) 479-3029
E-mail: noliver@columbuslibrary.org

Columbus Zoo and Aquarium

4850 West Powell Road, Powell, OH 43065
P.O. Box 400, Powell, OH 43065
Fax: (614) 645-3465 Internet: http://www.columbuszoo.org
President and Chief Executive Officer **Tom Stalf** .... (614) 645-3400
Senior Vice President of Animal Care and Conservation
Lewis Greene .... (614) 645-3400
Director Emeritus **Jack Hanna** .... (614) 645-3400

Office of the City Council

City Hall, 90 West Broad Street, 2nd Floor, Columbus, OH 43215-9015
Tel: (614) 645-7380 Fax: (614) 645-6164
Internet: http://www.columbuscitycouncil.org

★ Council President **Zachary M. Klein** .... (614) 645-8558
Term Expires: December 31, 2019
E-mail: zklein@columbus.gov
Education: Ohio State 2001 BA; Capital U 2004 JD
★ President Pro Tem **Priscilla Tyson** .... (614) 645-2933
Term Expires: December 31, 2017
E-mail: prtyson@columbus.gov
Education: Franklin U BSBA
★ Council Member **Elizabeth "Liz" Brown** .... (614) 645-7380
Term Expires: December 31, 2019
★ Council Member **Mitchell J. Brown** .... (614) 645-8529
Term Expires: December 31, 2017
E-mail: mbrown@columbus.gov
★ Council Member **Shannon G. Hardin** .... (614) 645-7380
Term Expires: December 31, 2017
E-mail: sghardin@columbus.gov
★ Council Member **Jaiza N. Page** .... (614) 645-8521
Term Expires: December 31, 2019
E-mail: jnpage@columbus.gov

Office of the City Council *continued*

★ Council Member **Michael Stinziano, Jr.** .... (614) 645-7380
Term Expires: December 31, 2019
Education: Richmond 2002 BA; George Washington 2004 MPA; Ohio State 2007 JD

Council Staff

City Hall, 90 W. Broad St., Columbus, OH 43215-9015
Director of the Legislative Office **Michael Kasler** .... (614) 645-5590
E-mail: mlkasler@columbus.gov
Director of Community Engagement **Gretchen James** .... (614) 645-5346
E-mail: gdjames@columbus.gov
Legislative Advisor **John Oswalt** .... (614) 645-1701
E-mail: JDOswalt@columbus.gov
Communications Director **Lee Cole** .... (614) 645-5530
E-mail: lacole@columbus.gov

City Clerk

City Hall, 90 W. Broad St., Room 218, Columbus, OH 43215-9015
City Clerk **Andrea Blevins** .... (614) 645-7431
E-mail: anblevins@columbus.gov

Office of the City Attorney

77 North Front Street, Room 200, Columbus, OH 43215
Fax: (614) 645-6949 Internet: www.columbuscityattorney.org/

★ City Attorney **Richard C. Pfeiffer, Jr.** .... (614) 645-6904
Term Expires: December 31, 2017
E-mail: rcpfeiffer@columbus.gov
Education: Oberlin 1966 BA; Ohio State 1972 JD
Chief of Staff **Bill Hedrick** .... (614) 645-8874
Education: Purdue 1987 BA; Indiana 1989 MLS; Purdue 1991 MA; Ohio State 1996 JD
Chief Prosecutor **Lara Baker** .... (614) 645-8081
Education: Miami U (OH) 1991 BA; Ohio State 1994 JD
Chief Counsel **Joshua Cox** .... (614) 645-0816
Claims Division Chief Attorney **Nancy Weidman** .... (614) 645-6908
E-mail: nlweidman@columbus.gov
Education: Miami U (OH) 1980 BA; Capital U 1988 JD
Labor and Employment Division Chief Attorney
Pamela Gordon .... (614) 645-6943
Education: Ohio State 1982 BS, 1985 JD
Litigation Division Chief Attorney **Tim Mangan** .... (614) 645-6964
Education: Xavier (OH) 1971 BSBA; Ohio State 1976 MSW; Capital U 1982 JD
Police Legal Advisor Attorney **Jeffrey Furbee** .... (614) 645-4523
Education: Wittenberg 1988 BA; Capital U 1993 JD
Real Estate Division Chief Attorney **David E. Peterson** .... (614) 645-7913
E-mail: depeterson@columbus.gov
Education: Ohio State 1992 BS; Capital U 1997 JD

Office of the City Auditor

City Hall, 90 W. Broad St., Room 109, Columbus, OH 43215-9046
Fax: (614) 645-8444 E-mail: cityauditor@columbus.gov

★ City Auditor **Hugh J. Dorrian** .... (614) 645-7615
Term Expires: December 31, 2017
E-mail: hjdorrian@columbus.gov
Education: Ohio State BA

★ Elected Official ▲ Appointed by Legislature ▼ Appointed by Governor ▶ Appointed by Board or Commission ● Appointed by Judge
■ Appointed by Mayor △ Appointed by Freeholders ▽ Appointed by Supervisor ▷ Appointed by County Executive ○ Appointed by Council

City of Concord, California

1950 Parkside Dr., Concord, CA 94519-2578
Internet: www.cityofconcord.org

County: Contra Costa **Election Type:** Nonpartisan **Year Incorporated:** February 9, 1905 **Population:** 128,667 (2015)

Office of the Mayor and City Council

1950 Parkside Drive, Concord, CA 94519
Fax: (925) 798-0636 E-mail: citycouncil@cityofconcord.org
E-mail: cityinfo@cityofconcord.org

★ Mayor **Laura Hoffmeister** .... (925) 671-3158
Began Service: 1997
Term Expires: December 7, 2018
E-mail: citycouncil@cityofconcord.org
Education: UC Davis BS

★ Vice Mayor **Ron Leone** .... (925) 671-3158
Term Expires: December 7, 2018
E-mail: citycouncil@cityofconcord.org

★ Council Member **Edi E. Birsan** .... (925) 671-3158
Term Expires: December 7, 2016
E-mail: edi.birsan@cityofconcord.org

★ Council Member **Tim Grayson** .... (925) 671-3158
Term Expires: December 7, 2018
E-mail: citycouncil@cityofconcord.org

★ Council Member **Daniel C. Helix** .... (925) 671-3158
Term Expires: December 7, 2016
E-mail: citycouncil@cityofconcord.org
Education: UC Berkeley BA; San Francisco State U MA

Office of the City Clerk

1950 Parkside Dr., Concord, CA 94519
Fax: (925) 671-3375

○ City Clerk **Joelle Fockler** .... (925) 671-3495
E-mail: joelle.fockler@cityofconcord.org

Office of the City Treasurer

1950 Parkside Dr., Concord, CA 94519
Fax: (925) 671-3198

★ City Treasurer **Tim McGallian** .... (925) 671-3183
Term Expires: November 2018
E-mail: finance@cityofconcord.org

Office of the City Manager

1950 Parkside Dr., Concord, CA 94519
Fax: (925) 798-0636

City Manager **Valerie Barone** .... (925) 671-3150
E-mail: valerie.barone@cityofconcord.org
Education: Humboldt State BS; Cal State (Sacramento) MBA

Deputy City Manager **Jovan Grogan** .... (925) 671-3150

Office of the City Attorney

1950 Parkside Dr., Concord, CA 94519
Fax: (925) 671-3469

City Attorney **(Vacant)** .... (925) 671-3160

Community and Economic Development

1950 Parkside Dr., Concord, CA 94519
Fax: (925) 671-3381

Director **Victoria Walker** .... (925) 671-3434
E-mail: victoria.walker@cityofconcord.org Fax: (925) 798-0636

Finance Department

1950 Parkside Dr., Concord, CA 94519
Fax: (925) 671-3353

Director **Karan Reid** .... (925) 671-3192

Human Resources

2974 Salvio St., Concord, CA 94519
Fax: (925) 671-3496

Director (Interim) **Elia Bamberger** .... (925) 671-3310
E-mail: hrdept@cityofconcord.org

Information Technology Department

1950 Parkside Dr., Concord, CA 94519
Fax: (925) 671-3198

Director **Jeff Lewis** .... (925) 671-3189
E-mail: jeff.lewis@cityofconcord.org

Police Department

1950 Parkside Dr., Concord, CA 94519
Fax: (925) 691-6640
Internet: http://www.cityofconcord.org/page.asp?pid=1026

Chief of Police **Guy A. Swanger** .... (925) 671-3194

Public Works and Engineering Department

1957 Parkside Dr., Concord, CA 94519
Fax: (925) 798-9692

Director **Justin Ezell** .... (925) 671-3231
Education: U San Francisco BS

Chief Engineer **Robert Ovadia** .... (925) 671-3470
E-mail: robert.ovadia@cityofconcord.org

Mt. Diablo Unified School District

1936 Carlotta Dr., Concord, CA 94519
Internet: www.mdusd.org

School Superintendent **Nellie Meyer** .... (925) 682-8000 ext. 4000

★ President **Cheryl J. Hansen** .... (925) 682-8000
Term Expires: December 2018
E-mail: hansenc@mdusd.org

★ Vice President **Debra Mason** .... (925) 682-8000
Term Expires: December 2018

★ Board Member **Brian T. Lawrence** .... (925) 682-8000
Term Expires: December 2016
E-mail: lawrenceb@mdusd.org

★ Board Member **Linda K. Mayo** .... (925) 682-8000
Term Expires: December 2018
E-mail: mayol@mdusd.org

★ Board Member **Barbara Oaks** .... (925) 682-8000
Term Expires: December 2016
E-mail: oaksb@mdusd.org

★ Elected Official ▲ Appointed by Legislature ▼ Appointed by Governor ► Appointed by Board or Commission ● Appointed by Judge
■ Appointed by Mayor △ Appointed by Freeholders ▽ Appointed by Supervisor ▷ Appointed by County Executive ○ Appointed by Council

City of Concord, New Hampshire

41 Green St., Concord, NH 03301
Internet: www.concordnh.gov/

County: Merrimack **Election Type:** Nonpartisan **Charter:** 1992
Population: 42,620 (2015)

Office of the Mayor and City Council

41 Green St., Concord, NH 03301
Tel: (603) 225-8500 (Information) Fax: (603) 225-8592

★Mayor **James P. "Jim" Bouley** .... (603) 230-3671
Began Service: 2008
Term Expires: December 31, 2017
E-mail: jpbouley@comcast.net
Date of Birth: 1966
Education: New Hampshire 1988 BA
Career: Councilor, Office of the Mayor and City Council, City of Concord, New Hampshire (1997-2007); Mayor Pro Tem, Office of the Mayor and City Council, City of Concord, New Hampshire (2002-2007)

★Councilor **Brent Todd** (Ward 1) .... (603) 225-8500
Term Expires: December 31, 2017
E-mail: brenttoddconcord@gmail.com

★Councilor **Allan Herschlag** (Ward 2) .... (603) 225-8500
Term Expires: December 31, 2017
E-mail: aherschlag@concordnh.gov

★Councilor **Jennifer Kretovic** (Ward 3) .... (603) 225-8500
Term Expires: December 31, 2017

★Councilor **Byron Champlin** (Ward 4) .... (603) 225-8500
Term Expires: December 31, 2017
E-mail: chamby@comcast.net

★Councilor **Robert Werner** (Ward 5) .... (603) 225-8500
Term Expires: December 31, 2017
E-mail: rwerner@concordnh.gov

★Councilor **Linda B. Kenison** (Ward 6) .... (603) 225-8500
Term Expires: December 31, 2017

★Councilor **Keith Nyhan** (Ward 7) .... (603) 225-8500
Term Expires: December 31, 2017
E-mail: knyhan@concordnh.gov

★Councilor **Gail Matson** (Ward 8) .... (603) 225-8500
Term Expires: December 31, 2017
E-mail: gmatson@concordnh.gov

★Councilor **Candace C. W. Bouchard** (Ward 9) .... (603) 225-8500
Term Expires: December 31, 2017
E-mail: cwbouchard@concordnh.gov

★Councilor **Dan St. Hilaire** (Ward 10) .... (603) 225-8500
Term Expires: December 31, 2017
E-mail: dsthilaire@concordnh.gov

★Councilor **Mark Coen** (At-Large) .... (603) 225-8500
Term Expires: December 31, 2019
E-mail: mcoen@concordnh.gov

★Councilor **Fred B. Keach** (At-Large) .... (603) 225-8500
Term Expires: December 31, 2017
E-mail: fkeach@concordnh.gov

★Councilor **Amanda Grady Sexton** (At-Large) .... (603) 225-8500
Term Expires: December 31, 2017
E-mail: agradysexton@concordnh.gov
Education: Simmons 2001 BA

★Councilor **Stephen J. "Steve" Shurtleff** (At-Large) ..... (603) 225-8500
Term Expires: December 31, 2019
E-mail: ssurtleff@concordnh.gov

City Clerk **Janice Bonenfant** .... (603) 225-8500
E-mail: jbonenfant@concordnh.gov Fax: (603) 225-8592

Office of the City Manager

41 Green St., Concord, NH 03301
Fax: (603) 225-8558

○City Manager **Thomas J. Aspell** .... (603) 225-8570
E-mail: citymanager@concordnh.gov

Assessing

41 Green St., Concord, NH 03301
Fax: (603) 225-8534 E-mail: assessing@concordnh.gov

Director **Kathryn Temchack** .... (603) 225-8550
E-mail: ktemchack@concordnh.gov

Community Development Department

41 Green St., Concord, NH 03301
E-mail: communitydevelopment@concordnh.gov

Deputy City Manager, Development **Carlos Baia** .... (603) 225-8595
E-mail: cbaia@concordnh.gov
Education: Brandeis 1994 BA; UMass (Amherst) 1996 AM; Florida 1999 MA

City Engineer **Edward Roberge** .... (603) 225-8520
E-mail: eroberge@concordnh.gov

City Planner **Nancy Larson** .... (603) 225-8515

Code Administrator **Michael Santa** .... (603) 225-8580
E-mail: msanta@concordnh.gov

Concord Public Library

45 Green St., Concord, NH 03301
Fax: (603) 230-3693 E-mail: library@concordnh.gov

Library Director **Andrew "Todd" Fabian** .... (603) 225-8670
E-mail: tfabian@concordnh.gov

Finance Department

41 Green Street, Concord, NH 03301
Fax: (603) 230-3684 E-mail: finance@concordnh.gov

Deputy City Manager- Finance **Brian LeBrun** .... (603) 225-8560
E-mail: blebrun@concordnh.gov

Purchasing Manager **Douglas Ross** .... (603) 225-8530
E-mail: dross@concordnh.gov

Treasurer/Tax Collector **Michael Jache** .... (603) 225-8540

Deputy Treasurer/Tax Collector **Esaundra Gaudette** ..... (603) 225-8540
E-mail: egaudette@concordnh.gov

Fire Department

24 Horseshoe Pond Ln., Concord, NH 03301
Fax: (603) 225-5833 E-mail: fire@concordnh.gov

Fire Chief **Dan Andrus** .... (603) 225-8650
E-mail: dandrus@concordnh.gov

Deputy Fire Chief **Sean Toomey** .... (603) 225-8651
E-mail: stoomey@concordnh.gov

General Services Department

311 North State Street, Concord, NH 03301
Fax: (603) 224-6729

Director **Earle "Chip" Chesley** .... (603) 228-2737
E-mail: generalservices@concordnh.gov

Human Resources Department

41 Green St., Concord, NH 03301
Fax: (603) 230-3726

Human Resources and Labor Relations Director
Jennifer Johnston .... (603) 225-8535
E-mail: jjohnston@concordnh.gov

Human Services Department

28 Commercial Street, Concord, NH 03301
Fax: (603) 227-0763

Director **Jacqueline Whatmough** .... (603) 225-8575

★Elected Official ▲Appointed by Legislature ▼Appointed by Governor ▶Appointed by Board or Commission ●Appointed by Judge
■Appointed by Mayor △Appointed by Freeholders ▽Appointed by Supervisor ▷Appointed by County Executive ○Appointed by Council

Legal Services Department
41 Green St., Concord, NH 03301
Fax: (603) 225-8558 E-mail: legal@concordnh.gov

City Solicitor **James W. Kennedy** .... (603) 225-8505
E-mail: jkennedy@concordnh.gov

Police Department
35 Green St., Concord, NH 03301
Fax: (603) 225-8519 E-mail: police@concordnh.gov

Chief of Police **Brad C. Osgood** .... (603) 225-8600

Recreation Department
14 Canterbury Road, Concord, NH 03301
Fax: (603) 225-8589 E-mail: recreation@concordnh.gov

Parks and Recreation Director **David Gill** .... (603) 225-8690

City of Coral Springs, Florida
9551 W. Sample Rd., Coral Springs, FL 33065
Internet: www.coralsprings.org

County: Broward **Election Type:** Nonpartisan **Year Incorporated:** 1963
Population: 129,485 (2015)

Office of the Mayor and City Commission
9551 West Sample Road, Coral Springs, FL 33065

★ Mayor **Walter G. "Skip" Campbell, Jr.** .... (954) 344-5906
Began Service: November 2014
Term Expires: November 2016
E-mail: wcampbell@coralsprings.org
Education: Florida 1970 BA, 1973 JD

★ Vice Mayor **Dan Daley** .... (954) 344-5906
Term Expires: November 2018
E-mail: ddaley@coralsprings.org

★ Commissioner **Joy Carter** .... (954) 344-5906
Term Expires: November 2016
E-mail: jcarter@coralsprings.org

★ Commissioner **Lou Cimaglia** .... (954) 344-5906
Term Expires: November 2018
E-mail: LCimaglia@coralsprings.org

★ Commissioner **Larry Vignola** .... (954) 344-5906
Term Expires: November 2016
E-mail: lvignola@coralsprings.org

Office of the City Manager
9551 W. Sample Rd., Coral Springs, FL 33065
Fax: (954) 344-1043

▶ City Manager **Erdal Dönmez** .... (954) 344-1004
E-mail: edonmez@coralsprings.org

Deputy City Manager **Jennifer Bramley** .... (954) 344-5906
E-mail: jbramley@coralsprings.org
Education: Florida Atlantic BA

Deputy City Manager **Susan Grant** .... (954) 344-5906
E-mail: sgrant@coralsprings.org
Education: Florida 1990 BS

Office of the City Attorney
9551 W. Sample Rd., Coral Springs, FL 33065
Fax: (954) 344-5930

▶ City Attorney **John J. Hearn** .... (954) 344-5977
E-mail: jhearn@coralsprings.org

Deputy City Attorney **Sherry Whitacre** .... (954) 344-5977
E-mail: swhitacre@coralsprings.org
Education: Nova JD

Office of the City Clerk
9551 West Sample Road, Coral Springs, FL 33065
Fax: (954) 344-1016

City Clerk **Debbra Dore Thomas** .... (954) 344-1065
E-mail: dthomas@coralsprings.org

Community Development Department
9551 W. Sample Rd., Coral Springs, FL 33065
Fax: (954) 344-5948

Director of Development Services
Susan Hess Krisman .... (954) 344-1041
E-mail: skrisman@coralsprings.org

Assistant Director of Development Services
James Hickey .... (954) 344-1158
E-mail: jhickey@coralsprings.org

Zoning Review Officer **Julie Krolak** .... (954) 344-1061

Communications and Marketing Department
9551 W. Sample Rd., Coral Springs, FL 33065
Fax: (954) 344-1198

Director of Communications and Marketing
Liz Kolodney .... (954) 344-5920
E-mail: LKolodney@coralsprings.org

Financial Services Department
9551 W. Sample Rd., Coral Springs, FL 33065
Fax: (954) 344-1198 E-mail: cn@ci.coral-springs.fl.us

Director of Financial Services **Melissa Pinto Heller** ..... (954) 344-1088

City Controller **Kim Moskowitz** .... (954) 344-1086
E-mail: kmoskowitz@coralsprings.org

Purchasing Administrator **Angelo Salomone** .... (954) 344-1100
E-mail: asalomone@coralsprings.org

Risk Coordinator **(Vacant)** .... (954) 344-5917

Fire Department
9551 W. Sample Rd., Coral Springs, FL 33065
Fax: (954) 344-5933 E-mail: csfd@coralsprings.org

Fire Chief **Frank Babinec** .... (954) 344-5934
E-mail: fbabinec@coralsprings.org

Fire Marshal **Larry Archacki** .... (954) 346-1397
E-mail: lra@coralsprings.org

Human Resources Department
9551 W. Sample Rd., Coral Springs, FL 33065
Fax: (954) 344-1151

Director **Dale Pazdra** .... (954) 344-5912
E-mail: dpazdra@coralsprings.org
Education: Elmhurst 1990 BS; Barry 2010 MPA

Community Relations Manager **Joyce Campos** .... (954) 344-1005
E-mail: jcampos@coralsprings.org

Information Technology Department
9551 W. Sample Rd., Coral Springs, FL 33065
Fax: (954) 344-5947

Director **Curlie O. Matthews** .... (954) 344-1002
E-mail: cmatthews@coralsprings.org
Education: Southern Methodist BA; Cal Lutheran U MBA; USC MPA

GIS/Data Administrator **Ronald Bartholf** .... (954) 344-1081
E-mail: rbartholf@coralsprings.org

Parks and Recreation Department
1300 Coral Springs Dr., Coral Springs, FL 33065
Fax: (954) 345-2111

Director **Rick Engle** .... (954) 345-2200

Police Department

2801 Coral Springs Dr., Coral Springs, FL 33065
Fax: (954) 346-1210

Chief of Police **Tony Pustizzi** .... (954) 346-1201
Assistant to Chief **Luanne Smith-Horton** .... (954) 346-1378
E-mail: lsmith-horton@coralsprings.org

Public Works Department

9551 W. Sample Rd., Coral Springs, FL 33065
Fax: (954) 344-5959

Director **Rich Michaud** .... (954) 344-1165
Chief Building Official **(Vacant)** .... (954) 344-1023
Fleet Services Superintendent **Steve Harbin** .... (954) 345-2215
4181 NW 121st Avenue, Coral Springs, FL 33065-7625
Streets Superintendent **Glen Gordon** .... (954) 345-2210
Utilities Operations Manager **Juan Robby** .... (954) 345-2161
E-mail: jrobby@coralsprings.org

City of Corona, California

City Hall, 400 South Vicentia Avenue, Corona, CA 92882
Internet: www.discovercorona.org

County: Riverside **Election Type:** Nonpartisan **Year Incorporated:** July 13, 1896 **Population:** 164,226 (2015)

Office of the Mayor and City Council

City Hall, 400 South Vicentia Avenue, Corona, CA 92882
E-mail: council@ci.corona.ca.us

★Mayor **Jason Scott** .... (951) 736-2371
Began Service: November 2008
Term Expires: December 4, 2016
E-mail: jscott@ci.corona.ca.us
★Vice Mayor **Dick Haley** .... (951) 736-2371
Term Expires: December 4, 2016
E-mail: DHaley@ci.corona.ca.us
★Council Member **Randy Fox** .... (951) 736-2371
Term Expires: November 30, 2018
★Council Member **Eugene Montanez** .... (951) 736-2371
Term Expires: November 30, 2018
E-mail: emontanez@ci.corona.ca.us
★Council Member **Karen S. Spiegel** .... (951) 736-2371
Term Expires: November 30, 2018
E-mail: kspiegel@ci.corona.ca.us

Office of the City Manager

City Hall, 400 South Vicentia Avenue, Corona, CA 92882
Fax: (951) 736-2493

City Manager **Darrell Talbert** .... (951) 279-3670
E-mail: Darrell.Talbert@ci.corona.ca.us
Assistant City Manager **Mike Abel** .... (951) 736-2294
Assistant City Manager **Kerry Eden** .... (951) 736-2294
E-mail: Kerry.Eden@ci.corona.ca.us

Office of the City Clerk

City Hall, 400 South Vicentia Avenue, Corona, CA 92882
Fax: (951) 736-2399

City Clerk **Lisa Mobley** .... (951) 736-2201
E-mail: lisa.mobley@ci.corona.ca.us

Community Development Department

City Hall, 400 South Vicentia Avenue, Corona, CA 92882
Fax: (951) 279-3550

Director **Joanne Coletta** .... (951) 736-2262
Planning Manager, Advance Planning **Terri Manuel** ...... (951) 736-2262

Building Division

City Hall, 400 South Vicentia Avenue, Corona, CA 92882
Fax: (951) 739-4893

Building Official **(Vacant)** .... (951) 736-2250

Finance Department

City Hall, 400 South Vicentia Avenue, Corona, CA 92882
Fax: (951) 817-5770

Director **Kerry Eden** .... (951) 279-3500
Human Resources Manager **Edelia Carney** .... (951) 279-3501
E-mail: edelia.carney@ci.corona.ca.us

Office of the City Treasurer

City Hall, 400 South Vicentia Avenue, Corona, CA 92882

City Treasurer **Aaron Hake** .... (951) 279-3500

Fire Department

City Hall, 400 South Vicentia Avenue, Corona, CA 92882
Fax: (951) 736-2497

Fire Chief **David Duffy** .... (951) 736-2220
E-mail: David.Duffy@ci.corona.ca.us

Information Technology Department

City Hall, 400 South Vicentia Avenue, Corona, CA 92882
Fax: (951) 736-2493

Information Technology Director **(Vacant)** .... (951) 279-3513

Library and Recreation Services Department

City Hall, 400 South Vicentia Avenue, Corona, CA 92882
Fax: (951) 279-3683

Director **David Montgomery-Scott** .... (951) 739-4985
E-mail: Abigail.Schellberg@ci.corona.ca.us

Police Department

730 Corporation Yard Way, Corona, CA 92880
Fax: (951) 739-4899

Police Chief **Mike Abel** .... (951) 736-2330

Public Works Department

City Hall, 400 South Vicentia Avenue, Corona, CA 92882
Fax: (951) 736-2496

Director **Nelson Nelson** .... (951) 736-2266

Water and Power Department

City Hall, 400 South Vicentia Avenue, Corona, CA 92882
Fax: (951) 736-2231

DPW General Manager **Jonathan Daly** .... (951) 736-2440
E-mail: jonathan.daly@ci.corona.ca.us

★Elected Official ▲Appointed by Legislature ▼Appointed by Governor ▶Appointed by Board or Commission ●Appointed by Judge
■Appointed by Mayor △Appointed by Freeholders ▽Appointed by Supervisor ▷Appointed by County Executive ○Appointed by Council

City of Corpus Christi, Texas

City Hall, 1201 Leopard St., Corpus Christi, TX 78401
Tel: (361) 826-3000 (Information) Internet: www.cctexas.com

County: Nueces **Election Type:** Nonpartisan **Year Founded:** 1839
Year Incorporated: 1852 **Population:** 324,074 (2015)

Office of the Mayor and City Council

City Hall, 1201 Leopard St., Corpus Christi, TX 78401
P.O. Box 9277, Corpus Christi, TX 78469-9277
Fax: (361) 826-3103

★ Mayor **Nelda Martinez** .... (361) 826-3100
Began Service: November 2012
Term Expires: November 2016
E-mail: neldam@cctexas.com
Education: Wright State 1978 BSN, 1982 MS; Ohio State 1992 PhD
Chief of Staff **Elizabeth Hardin** .... (361) 826-3100
Executive Assistant **(Vacant)** .... (361) 826-3100

★ Council Member **Carolyn Vaughn** (District 1) .... (361) 826-3105
Term Expires: November 2016
E-mail: carolyn.vaughn@cctexas.com

★ Council Member **Brian Rosas** (District 2) .... (361) 826-3105
Term Expires: November 2016
E-mail: brian.rosas@cctexas.com

★ Council Member **Lucy Rubio** (District 3) .... (361) 826-3105
Term Expires: November 2016
E-mail: lucy.rubio@cctexas.com

★ Council Member **Colleen McIntyre** (District 4) .... (361) 826-3105
Term Expires: November 2016
E-mail: colleen.mcintyre@cctexas.com

★ Council Member **Rudy Garza, Jr.** (District 5) .... (361) 826-3105
Term Expires: November 2016
E-mail: rudy.garza@cctexas.com

★ Council Member **Michael Hunter** (At-Large) .... (361) 826-3105
Term Expires: November 2016

★ Council Member **Chad McGill** (At-Large) .... (361) 826-3105
Term Expires: November 2016
E-mail: chad.magill@cctexas.com

★ Council Member **Mark Scott** (At-Large) .... (361) 826-3105
Term Expires: November 2016
E-mail: markscott338@gmail.com

Office of the City Secretary

City Hall, 1st Fl., 1201 Leopard St., Corpus Christi, TX 78401

○ City Secretary **Rebecca Huerta** .... (361) 826-3105
E-mail: rebeccah@cctexas.com
Assistant City Secretary **Paul Pierce** .... (361) 826-3105
E-mail: paulp@cctexas.com

Office of the City Manager

City Hall, 1201 Leopard St., Corpus Christi, TX 78401
Tel: (361) 826-3220 Fax: (361) 826-3839

City Manager **Ronald L. "Ron" Olson** .... (361) 826-3220
E-mail: rono@cctexas.com
Assistant to the City Manager **Martha Quiroz** .... (361) 826-3220
E-mail: marthaq@cctexas.com
Deputy City Manager **Margie C. Rose** .... (361) 826-3230
E-mail: margier@cctexas.com
Assistant City Manager for Safety, Health and Neighborhoods **(Vacant)** .... (361) 826-3232
Assistant City Manager for Public Works and Utilities **Gustavo "Gus" Gonzalez** .... (361) 826-3235
E-mail: gustavogo@cctexas.com

Office of the City Attorney

City Hall, 5th Fl., 1201 Leopard St., Corpus Christi, TX 78401
Fax: (361) 826-3239

○ City Attorney **Miles Risley** .... (361) 826-3360
E-mail: milesr@cctexas.com

Business Support Services

1201 Leopard Street, 5th Floor, Corpus Christi, TX 78401

Assistant City Manager for General Government and Operations Support **(Vacant)** .... (361) 823-3082

Aviation Department (Corpus Christi International Airport)

1000 International Dr., Corpus Christi, TX 78406
Fax: (361) 289-0251

Director **Fred Segundo** .... (361) 289-0171

Financial Services

City Hall, 1201 Leopard Street, 4th Floor, Corpus Christi, TX 78401
Fax: (361) 826-3601

Director **Constance Sanchez** .... (361) 826-3227

General Services

Building 3B, 5352 Ayers Street, Corpus Christi, TX 78415
Fax: (361) 826-1905

Director **Jim Davis** .... (361) 826-1909
E-mail: jimd@cctexas.com
Fleet Maintenance Director **Jim Davis** .... (361) 826-1909

Health Department

1702 Horne Rd., Corpus Christi, TX 78401
Tel: (361) 851-7200 Fax: (361) 851-7295

Director **Annette Rodriguez** .... (361) 851-7205

Public Libraries

805 Comanche, Corpus Christi, TX 78401
Fax: (361) 826-7046 Internet: http://www.cclibraries.com/

Director (Interim) **Laura Garcia** .... (361) 826-7070
E-mail: lauraga@cctexas.com

Museum of Science and History

1900 N. Chaparral, Corpus Christi, TX 78401
Fax: (361) 884-7392

Director **Carol Rehtmeyer** .... (361) 826-4660

Convention Facilities

101 North Shoreline Boulevard, Suite 430, Corpus Christi, TX 78401
Fax: (361) 883-0788

Chief Executive Officer **Paulette Kluge** .... (361) 881-1888
Communications Director **Ashley Higson** .... (361) 881-1818
E-mail: ahigson@visitcorpuschristitx.org

Communications Department

City Hall, 1201 Leopard St., Corpus Christi, TX 78401
Fax: (361) 826-3208

Director **Kim Womack** .... (361) 826-3210
E-mail: kimw@cctexas.com

Fire Department

2406 Leopard, Suite 300, Corpus Christi, TX 78401
Internet: www.cctexas.com/government/fire/

Fire Chief **Robert Rocha** .... (361) 826-3932
E-mail: rrocha@cctexas.com

Housing and Community Development Department

City Hall, 2nd Fl., 1201 Leopard St., Corpus Christi, TX 78401
Fax: (361) 826-3005

Director **Rudy Bentancourt** .... (361) 826-3044
E-mail: rudyb@cctexas.com

Human Relations Division

City Hall, 1201 Leopard St., 1st Floor, Corpus Christi, TX 78401
Fax: (361) 826-3192

Human Relations Administrator **Sylvia V. Wilson** .... (361) 826-3196

★ Elected Official ▲ Appointed by Legislature ▼ Appointed by Governor ► Appointed by Board or Commission ● Appointed by Judge
■ Appointed by Mayor △ Appointed by Freeholders ▽ Appointed by Supervisor ▷ Appointed by County Executive ○ Appointed by Council

Human Resources Department
City Hall, 2nd Fl., 1201 Leopard St., Corpus Christi, TX 78401
Tel: (361) 826-3300 Fax: (361) 826-3322

Director **Yasmine Chapman** .... (361) 826-3315
E-mail: yasminec@cctexas.com

Management and Budget Department
City Hall, 5th Fl., 1201 Leopard St., Corpus Christi, TX 78401

Assistant Director **Eddie Houlihan** .... (361) 826-3235
E-mail: eddieho@cctexas.com

Municipal Information Services
City Hall, 1201 Leopard Street, 4th Floor, Corpus Christi, TX 78401
Fax: (361) 826-3741

Chief Information Officer/Director **Belinda Mercado** .... (361) 826-3740
E-mail: BMercado@cctexas.com

Park and Recreation Department
City Hall, 1201 Leopard Street, Third Floor, Corpus Christi, TX 78401
Fax: (361) 826-3864

Director **E. Jay Ellington** .... (361) 826-3464

Police Department
321 John Sartain, Corpus Christi, TX 78401
P.O. Box 9016, Corpus Christi, TX 78469
Fax: (361) 886-2607 Internet: http://cctexas.com/government/ccpd/index

Chief of Police **Mike Markle** .... (361) 886-2604

Public Works Department
City Hall, 1201 Leopard St., Corpus Christi, TX 78401
Fax: (361) 880-3230

Executive Director **Valerie H. Gray** .... (361) 826-3500

Capital Programs
City Hall, 3rd Fl., 1201 Leopard St., Corpus Christi, TX 78401

Director **J.H. Edmonds** .... (361) 826-3500

Street Operations
2525 Hygeia St., Corpus Christi, TX 78415
Fax: (361) 857-1971

Director **Valerie H. Gray** .... (361) 857-1881
Assistant Director, Streets **Andy Leal** .... (361) 857-1940
Assistant Director, Planning **Edgar Leonard** .... (361) 826-1870

Utilities Department
2726 Holly Road, Corpus Christi, TX 78415

Executive Director **Mark Van Vleck** .... (361) 826-1874
Assistant Director, Maintenance of Lines **Bill Mahaffey** .. (361) 857-1881

Gas Department
4225 South Port Avenue, Corpus Christi, TX 78415
Fax: (361) 853-3200

Director **Debbie Marroquin** .... (361) 885-6924
Assistant Director, Maintenance and Lines **(Vacant)** ...... (361) 885-6907
Petroleum Superintendent **Jesse Cantu** .... (361) 885-6941

City of Costa Mesa, California

Civic Center, 77 Fair Drive, Costa Mesa, CA 92626
P.O. Box 1200, Costa Mesa, CA 92628-1200
Internet: http://www.costamesaca.gov/

County: Orange **Election Type:** Nonpartisan **Year Incorporated:** 1953
Population: 113,204 (2015)

Office of the Mayor and City Council

Civic Center, 77 Fair Dr., Costa Mesa, CA 92626
P.O. Box 1200, Costa Mesa, CA 92628-1200
Fax: (714) 754-5330 E-mail: cmcouncil@costamesaca.gov

★ Mayor **Stephen M. Mensinger** .... (714) 754-5285
Began Service: 2011
Term Expires: December 2016
E-mail: stephen.mensinger@costamesaca.gov

★ Mayor Pro Tem **James M. Righeimer** .... (949) 274-9909
Term Expires: December 2018
E-mail: jim.righeimer@costamesaca.gov

★ Council Member **Katrina Foley** .... (714) 754-5285
Term Expires: December 2018
E-mail: katrina.foley@costamesaca.gov

★ Council Member **Sandra "Sandy" Genis** .... (714) 754-5284
Term Expires: December 2016
E-mail: sandra.genis@costamesaca.gov

★ Council Member **Gary Monahan** .... (714) 754-5284
Term Expires: December 2016
E-mail: gary.monahan@costamesaca.gov

Office of the City Attorney

Civic Center, 77 Fair Dr., Costa Mesa, CA 92626
P.O. Box 1200, Costa Mesa, CA 92628-1200

City Attorney **Thomas P. Duarte** .... (714) 754-5399
E-mail: tpd@jones-mayer.com

Parks and Recreation Commission

Civic Center, 77 Fair Dr., Costa Mesa, CA 92626
P.O. Box 1200, Costa Mesa, CA 92628-1200

Chairman **Brett Eckles** .... (714) 754-5009
Vice Chairman **Robert Graham** .... (714) 754-5009
Commissioner **Byron de Arakal** .... (714) 754-5009
Commissioner **Donald Harper** .... (714) 754-5009
Commissioner **Kim Pederson** .... (714) 754-5009
Commission Secretary **Sanjuana Pacheco** .... (714) 754-5300
E-mail: sanjuana.pacheco@costamesaca.gov

Planning Commission

Civic Center, 77 Fair Dr., Costa Mesa, CA 92626
P.O. Box 1200, Costa Mesa, CA 92628-1200
E-mail: planningcommission@costamesaca.gov

Chair **Robert L. Dickson** .... (714) 754-5088
Vice Chair **Jeff Mathews** .... (714) 754-5088
Commissioner **Stephan Andranian** .... (714) 754-5088
Commissioner **Colin McCarthy** .... (714) 754-5088
Commissioner **Tim Sesler** .... (714) 754-5088
Commission Secretary **Claire Flynn** .... (714) 754-5088
E-mail: claire.flynn@costamesaca.gov

Chief Executive's Office

Civic Center, 77 Fair Dr., Costa Mesa, CA 92626
P.O. Box 1200, Costa Mesa, CA 92628-1200

Chief Executive Officer **Thomas Hatch** .... (714) 754-5328
E-mail: tom.hatch@costamesaca.gov
Assistant Chief Executive Officer **Rick Francis** .... (714) 754-5099
E-mail: rick.francis@costamesaca.gov

(continued on next page)

Chief Executive's Office *continued*

Assistant Chief Executive Officer **Tony Dodero** .... (714) 754-5288
E-mail: tony.dodero@costamesaca.gov
Public Affairs Manager **Dane Bora** .... (714) 754-5098
E-mail: dane.bora@costamesaca.gov

Office of the City Clerk
Fax: (714) 754-4942

City Clerk **Brenda Green** .... (714) 754-5221
E-mail: Brenda.Green@costamesaca.gov
Deputy City Clerk **Michael Dunn** .... (714) 754-5327
E-mail: michael.dunn@costamesaca.gov
Deputy City Clerk **Jessica Mejia** .... (714) 754-5213
E-mail: jessica.mejia@costamesaca.gov

Housing and Community Development Division
E-mail: HCD@costamesaca.gov

Principal Planner/Zoning Administrator
Willa Bouwens-Killeen .... (714) 754-5153
E-mail: willa.bouwens-killeen@costamesaca.gov

Risk Management Division
Administrator **Ryan Thomas** .... (714) 754-5104
E-mail: ryan.thomas@costamesaca.gov

Development Services Department
Civic Center, 77 Fair Dr., Costa Mesa, CA 92626
P.O. Box 1200, Costa Mesa, CA 92628-1200

Economic and Development Services Director/Deputy Chief Executive Officer **Gary Armstrong** .... (714) 754-5270
E-mail: gary.armstrong@costamesaca.gov

Building Safety Division
Building Official **Khanh Nguyen** .... (714) 754-5604

Planning Division
Economic and Development Services Director
Gary Armstrong .... (714) 754-5278
E-mail: gary.armstrong@costamesaca.gov
Assistant Development Services Director **Claire Flynn** .... (714) 754-5278

Finance Department
Civic Center, 77 Fair Dr., Costa Mesa, CA 92626
P.O. Box 1200, Costa Mesa, CA 92628-1200

Director (Interim) **Steve Dunivent** .... (714) 754-5243
E-mail: steve.dunivent@costamesaca.gov

Fire Department
P.O. Box 1200, Costa Mesa, CA 92628-1200

Fire Chief **Dan Stefano** .... (714) 754-5106
E-mail: firedepartment@costamesaca.gov

Human Resources Department
Manager **Lance Nakamoto** .... (714) 754-5172
E-mail: Lance.Nakamoto@costamesaca.gov

Information Technology Department
77 Fair Drive, Costa Mesa, CA 92626

Director **Steve Ely** .... (714) 754-4891
E-mail: steve.ely@costamesaca.gov

Police Department
P.O. Box 1200, Costa Mesa, CA 92628-1200

Police Chief **Robert "Rob" Sharpnack** .... (714) 754-5117
Education: Vanguard U (California) BABA

Public Services Department
Civic Center, 77 Fair Dr., Costa Mesa, CA 92626
P.O. Box 1200, Costa Mesa, CA 92628-1200

Director **Ernesto Munoz** .... (714) 754-5343
Note: Until June 10, 2016

Engineering Division
City Engineer **(Vacant)** .... (714) 754-5378

Maintenance Services Division
Manager **Bruce Hartley** .... (714) 754-5164
E-mail: bruce.hartley@costamesaca.gov

Recreation Division
Manager **Justin Martin** .... (714) 754-5065

Transportation Services Division
Manager **Raja Sethuraman** .... (714) 754-5032

City of Cranston, Rhode Island

869 Park Avenue, Cranston, RI 02910
TTY: (401) 785-2036 Internet: www.cranstonri.com

County: Providence **Election Type:** Partisan **Population:** 81,073 (2015)

Office of the Mayor
869 Park Ave., Cranston, RI 02910

★ Mayor **Allan W. Fung** (R) .... (401) 461-1000
Began Service: January 7, 2008 Fax: (401) 780-3180
Term Expires: January 2017
E-mail: afung@cranstonri.org
Date of Birth: February 25, 1970
Education: Suffolk 1995 JD
■ Constituent Affairs Director **(Vacant)** .... (401) 780-3123

Office of the City Solicitor
869 Park Ave., Cranston, RI 02910

■ City Solicitor **Christopher Rawson** .... (401) 461-1000 ext. 3133
E-mail: crawson@cranstonri.org

Administration Department
869 Park Ave., Cranston, RI 02910

Director **Robert J. Coupe** .... (401) 780-3167
Information Technology Director **William Aguiar** .... (401) 461-1000
E-mail: waguiar@cranstonri.org
Purchasing Agent **Mark Marchesi** .... (401) 461-1000
E-mail: mmarchesi@cranstonri.org

Community Development
1090 Cranston St., Cranston, RI 02920
Fax: (401) 943-3966

Director (Acting) **Stephanie Susi** .... (401) 461-1000 ext. 7226
E-mail: ssusi@cranstonri.org

Comprehensive Community Action Program
311 Doric Avenue, Cranston, RI 02910

Director **Joanne McGunagle** .... (401) 461-1000

Finance Department
869 Park Ave., Cranston, RI 02910

Director **Robert Strom** .... (401) 461-1000 ext. 3248

★ Elected Official ▲ Appointed by Legislature ▼ Appointed by Governor ► Appointed by Board or Commission ● Appointed by Judge
■ Appointed by Mayor △ Appointed by Freeholders ▽ Appointed by Supervisor ▷ Appointed by County Executive ○ Appointed by Council

Assessment Division
869 Park Ave., Cranston, RI 02910
Fax: (401) 780-3361

Tax Assessor **Salvatore Saccoccio** .... (401) 461-1000 ext. 3188
E-mail: ssaccoccio@cranstonri.org

Office of the City Controller
869 Park Ave., Cranston, RI 02910

City Controller **Michael Igoe** .... (401) 461-1000
E-mail: migoe@cranstonri.org

Office of the Treasurer
869 Park Ave., Cranston, RI 02910

Treasurer **David Capuano** .... (401) 780-3247

Fire Department
301 Pontiac Ave., Cranston, RI 02910
Tel: (401) 461-5000 (Information) Fax: (401) 467-1560
Internet: http://www.cranstonfire.net

Fire Chief **William McKenna** .... (401) 461-4161
E-mail: wmckenna@cranstonri.org

Library
140 Sockanoset Crossroad, Cranston, RI 02920
Fax: (401) 946-5079 Internet: http://cranstonlibrary.org/

Director **Edward Garcia** .... (401) 943-9080
E-mail: central@cranstonlibrary.org

Parks and Recreation Department
1090 Cranston Street, Cranston, RI 02920

Director **Anthony J. Liberatore** .... (401) 461-1000 ext. 6170

Personnel Department
869 Park Ave., Cranston, RI 02910

Director (Acting) **Robert Strom** .... (401) 780-3207

Planning Department
869 Park Avenue, Cranston, RI 02910
Fax: (401) 780-3363

Director **Peter Lapolla** .... (401) 780-3136

Police Department
5 Garfield Avenue, Cranston, RI 02920
Fax: (401) 477-5113 Internet: www.cranstonpolice.com

■ Chief of Police **Lt. Col. Michael Winquist** .... (401) 942-2211
E-mail: mwinquist@cranstonri.org
Education: Roger Williams 1993; Anna Maria 1998

Public Works Department
869 Park Ave., Cranston, RI 02910

Director **Kenneth Mason** .... (401) 461-1000 ext. 3175
City Engineer **Nicholas Capezza** .... (401) 461-1000 ext. 3175
E-mail: ncapezza@cranstonri.org
Traffic Engineer **Stephen Mulcahy** .... (401) 461-1000 ext. 3175
E-mail: smulcahy@cranstonri.org
Highways Superintendent **John Corso** .... (401) 461-1000 ext. 3301

Department of Senior Services
1070 Cranston Street, Cranston, RI 02920
Tel: (401) 780-6000 Fax: (401) 946-5909

Executive Director **(Vacant)** .... (401) 780-6000

Housing Authority
50 Birch St., Cranston, RI 02920

Executive Director **Elaine Wolohoojian** .... (401) 944-7210

Office of the City Council
869 Park Ave., Cranston, RI 02910

★ President **John E. Lanni, Jr.** (D-At-Large) .... (401) 946-7373
Term Expires: January 2017
E-mail: John.Lanni@Yahoo.com

★ Vice President
Richard D. Santamaria, Jr. (D-At-Large) .... (401) 569-0007
Term Expires: January 2017
E-mail: ritatj10@yahoo.com

★ Councilman **Steven Stycos** (D-Ward 1) .... (401) 461-2618
Term Expires: January 2017
E-mail: steven@stycos.com

★ Councilman **Donald Botts, Jr.** (R-Ward 2) .... (401) 461-1000
Term Expires: January 2017
E-mail: dbotts@cranstonri.org

★ Councilman **Paul H. Archetto** (D-Ward 3) .... (401) 461-1000
Term Expires: January 2017
E-mail: parchetto@ccri.edu

★ Councilman **Mario Aceto** (D-Ward 4) .... (401) 461-1000
Term Expires: January 2017
E-mail: maceto@cranstonri.org

★ Councilman
Christopher G. "Chris" Paplauskas (R-Ward 5) ...... (401) 996-9196
Term Expires: January 2017
E-mail: ChrisPaplauskas@gmail.com

★ Councilman **Michael Favicchio** (R-Ward 6) .... (401) 946-7108
Term Expires: January 2017
E-mail: mfavicchio@cranstonri.org

★ Councilman **Michael J. Farina** (R-At-Large) .... (401) 461-1000
Term Expires: January 2017
E-mail: mfarina@cranstonri.org

Internal Audit
869 Park Ave., Cranston, RI 02910

Internal Auditor **Judy Aubin** .... (401) 461-1000 ext. 3233

Office of the City Clerk
869 Park Ave., Cranston, RI 02910
Fax: (401) 780-3165

○ City Clerk **Maria Medeiros Wall** .... (401) 461-1000 ext. 3198
E-mail: mmedeiros@cranstonri.org

Cranston Public Schools
845 Park Ave., Cranston, RI 02910
Internet: http://www.cps.k12.ri.us Fax: (401) 270-8703

Superintendent of Schools **Judith Lundsten** .... (401) 270-8170

★ Elected Official ▲ Appointed by Legislature ▼ Appointed by Governor ▶ Appointed by Board or Commission ● Appointed by Judge
■ Appointed by Mayor △ Appointed by Freeholders ▽ Appointed by Supervisor ▷ Appointed by County Executive ○ Appointed by Council

CITIES AND TOWNS

City of Dallas, Texas

City Hall, 1500 Marilla St., Dallas, TX 75201
Internet: www.dallascityhall.com

County: Dallas **Election Type:** Nonpartisan **Year Founded:** 1841
Year Incorporated: 1871 **Population:** 1,300,092 (2015)

Office of the Mayor and City Council

City Hall, 1500 Marilla Street, Dallas, TX 75201-6300
Tel: (214) 670-3301 Fax: (214) 670-0646

★Mayor **Michael S. "Mike" Rawlings** .... (214) 670-3301
Began Service: June 27, 2011
Term Expires: June 22, 2019
E-mail: mike.rawlings@dallascityhall.com
Education: Boston Col 1976 BA
Chief of Policy and Communications **Scott Goldstein** .. (214) 670-7977
E-mail: scott.goldstein@dallascityhall.com
Chief of Community Relations **Vana Hammond** ...... (214) 670-7894
Community Relations Coordinator **Brenda Allen** .... (214) 671-5419

★Mayor Pro Tem **Monica R. Alonzo** (District 6) .... (214) 670-4199
Term Expires: June 22, 2017 Fax: (214) 670-5117
E-mail: monica.alonzo@dallascityhall.com

★Deputy Mayor Pro Tem **Erik Wilson** (District 8) .... (214) 670-4066
Term Expires: June 22, 2017 Fax: (214) 670-5117

★Council Member **Scott Griggs** (District 1) .... (214) 670-0776
Term Expires: June 22, 2017 Fax: (214) 670-5117
E-mail: scott.griggs@dallascityhall.com
Education: Texas A&M BA; Texas 2001 JD

★Council Member **Adam Medrano** (District 2) .... (214) 670-4048
Term Expires: June 22, 2017 Fax: (214) 670-1816
E-mail: adam.medrano@dallascityhall.com

★Council Member **Casey Thomas** (District 3) .... (214) 670-0777
Term Expires: June 2017 Fax: (214) 670-5117

★Council Member **Carolyn King Arnold** (District 4) ...... (214) 670-0781
Term Expires: June 2017 Fax: (214) 670-5117

★Council Member **Rickey D. Callahan** (District 5) .... (214) 670-4052
Term Expires: June 22, 2017 Fax: (214) 670-5117
E-mail: rick.callahan@dallascityhall.com

★Council Member **Tiffinni A. Young** (District 7) .... (214) 670-4689
Term Expires: June 22, 2017 Fax: (214) 670-1819

★Council Member **Mark Clayton** (District 9) .... (214) 670-4069
Term Expires: June 22, 2017 Fax: (214) 670-1813

★Council Member **B. Adam McGough** (District 10) ...... (214) 670-4068
Term Expires: June 22, 2017 Fax: (214) 670-1843

★Council Member **Lee M. Kleinman** (District 11) .... (214) 670-7817
Term Expires: June 22, 2017 Fax: (214) 670-5117
E-mail: lee.kleinman@dallascityhall.com

★Council Member **Sandy Greyson** (District 12) .... (214) 670-4067
Term Expires: June 22, 2017 Fax: (214) 670-5650
E-mail: sandy.greyson@dallascityhall.com

★Council Member **Jennifer S. Gates** (District 13) .... (214) 670-3816
Term Expires: June 22, 2017 Fax: (214) 670-5117
E-mail: jennifer.gates@dallascityhall.com

★Council Member **Philip T. Kingston** (District 14) .... (214) 670-5415
Term Expires: June 22, 2017 Fax: (214) 670-5117
E-mail: philip.kingston@dallascityhall.com

Office of the City Attorney

City Hall, 1500 Marilla St., Room 7D North, Dallas, TX 75201
Tel: (214) 670-3519 Fax: (214) 670-0622

■City Attorney **(Vacant)** .... (214) 670-3491
First Assistant City Attorney
Christopher D. "Chris" Bowers .... (214) 670-3519
E-mail: chris.bowers@dallascityhall.com
Date of Birth: October 31, 1963
Education: Texas A&M 1986 BS; Cornell 1989 JD
Contracts/Transactions and Advisory Administrative
Assistant City Attorney **Ileana Fernandez** .... (214) 670-3519

Office of the City Attorney *continued*

Dallas-Fort Worth International Airport Administrative
Assistant City Attorney **Elaine Flud Rodriguez** .... (972) 973-5480
E-mail: erodriguez@dfwairport.com
Education: Loyola U (New Orleans) 1978 BA; Tulane 1982 JD
Zoning and Related Litigation Assistant City Attorney
Tammy L. Palomino .... (214) 670-3519
E-mail: tammy.palomino@dallascityhall.com
Executive Secretary **Dedrea Kearney** .... (214) 670-3491
E-mail: dedrea.kearney@dallascityhall.com

Office of the City Auditor

City Hall, 1500 Marilla St., Room 2F North, Dallas, TX 75201-6390
Fax: (214) 670-0854

○City Auditor **Craig Kinton** .... (214) 670-3223
E-mail: craig.kinton@dallascityhall.com

Office of the City Secretary

City Hall, 1500 Marilla St., Room 5D South, Dallas, TX 75201-6350
Fax: (214) 670-5029

○City Secretary **Rosa A. Rios** .... (214) 670-3738
E-mail: rosa.rios2@dallascityhall.com
Assistant City Secretary **Bilierae Johnson** .... (214) 670-5654
E-mail: bilierae.johnson@dallascityhall.com
Records Management Officer **Lois Dillard** .... (214) 670-3738
Elections Manager **Brylon Franklin** .... (214) 670-5657

Office of the City Manager

City Hall, 1500 Marilla St., Room 4E North, Dallas, TX 75201
Fax: (214) 670-3946

○City Manager **A. C. Gonzalez** .... (214) 670-3314
E-mail: ac.gonzalez@dallascityhall.com
Assistant to the City Manager (Interim)
Nikki Christmas .... (214) 670-1858
E-mail: nikki.christmas@dallascityhall.com
Assistant to the City Manager **Harim Logan** .... (214) 670-4549
E-mail: harim.logan@dallascityhall.com
First Assistant City Manager **Ryan Evans** .... (214) 670-1875
E-mail: ryan.evans@dallascityhall.com
Assistant City Manager **Eric Campbell** .... (214) 670-3255
E-mail: eric.campbell@dallascityhall.com
Assistant City Manager **Mark L. McDaniel** .... (214) 670-3256
E-mail: mark.mcdaniel@dallascityhall.com
Education: North Texas BA, MPA
Assistant City Manager **Jill A. Jordan** .... (214) 670-5299
E-mail: jill.jordan@dallascityhall.com
Assistant City Manager **Joey Zapata** .... (214) 670-3009
E-mail: joey.zapata@dallascityhall.com
Chief of Neighborhood Plus **Alan E. Sims** .... (214) 670-1611

Office of Cultural Affairs [OCA]

1925 Elm Street, Suite 500, Dallas, TX 75201
Fax: (214) 670-1404 Internet: www.dallasculture.org

Director (Interim) **David Fisher** .... (214) 670-3687
Assistant Director **David Fisher** .... (214) 670-3687
Business Operations Manager **Clifton Gillespie** .... (214) 670-3996
E-mail: clifton.gillespie@dallascityhall.com
Facilities Manager **(Vacant)** .... (214) 670-4428

Office of Economic Development

City Hall, 1500 Marilla St., Room 5C South, Dallas, TX 75201
Tel: (214) 670-1685 Fax: (214) 670-0158
Internet: www.dallas-ecodev.org/

Director **F. Karl Zavitkovsky** .... (214) 670-1685
E-mail: karl.zavitkovsky@dallascityhall.com
Education: Georgetown 1965 MSFS
Assistant Director **Hammond Perot** .... (214) 670-1685
E-mail: hammond.perot@dallascityhall.com

★Elected Official ▲Appointed by Legislature ▼Appointed by Governor ►Appointed by Board or Commission ●Appointed by Judge
■Appointed by Mayor △Appointed by Freeholders ▽Appointed by Supervisor ▷Appointed by County Executive ○Appointed by Council

Office of Emergency Management
1500 Marilla Street, L2AN, Dallas, TX 75201
Fax: (214) 670-4677 E-mail: oem@dallascityhall.com

Director **Rocky Vaz** . . . . . (214) 670-4275
E-mail: oem@dallascityhall.com

Office of Environmental Quality
1500 Marilla Street, Room L2F South, Dallas, TX 75201
Fax: (214) 670-0134

Managing Director (Interim) **William Madison** . . . . . (214) 670-1200

Fair Housing Office
1500 Marilla Street, Room 1B North, Dallas, TX 75201
Fax: (214) 670-0665

Assistant Director **Beverly Davis** . . . . . (214) 670-5677

Public Information Office [PIO]
City Hall, 1500 Marilla St., Room 4E South, Dallas, TX 75201-6300
Fax: (214) 670-0160

Public Information Officer **Sana Syed** . . . . . (214) 670-3322
E-mail: sana.syed@dallascityhall.com
Managing Director **Shawn P. Williams** . . . . . (214) 670-9508
E-mail: shawn.williams@dallascityhall.com

Office of Financial Services
City Hall, 1500 Marilla St., 4FN, Dallas, TX 75201
Tel: (214) 670-3659 Fax: (214) 659-7008

Chief Financial Officer **Jeanne Chipperfield** . . . . . (214) 670-5631
Director **Jack Ireland** . . . . . (214) 670-3659
E-mail: jack.ireland@dallascityhall.com
City-Wide Capital and Operating Budgets Assistant Director **Jing Xiao** . . . . . (214) 670-3660
E-mail: jing.xiao@dallascityhall.com
Manager, Utility Management **Nikolaus "Nick" Fehrenbach** . . . . . (214) 670-5173
Education: Southern Methodist 1985 BA; Tarleton State 1990 MBA
Grant Administration Assistant Director **Chan Williams** . . (214) 670-5544
E-mail: chan.williams@dallascityhall.com
Coordinator (Interim) **Juanita Delgado-Cruz** . . . . . (214) 670-3641
Secretary **Juanita Delgado-Cruz** . . . . . (214) 670-3659
E-mail: juanita.delgadocruz@dallascityhall.com

Office of the City Controller
1500 Marilla Street, Room 2BS, Dallas, TX 75201
Fax: (214) 670-3543

City Controller **Edward Scott** . . . . . (214) 670-3856
Assistant City Controller **Lance Sehorn** . . . . . (214) 670-3547
Assistant Director **(Vacant)** . . . . . (214) 670-3536

Communication and Information Services Department
City Hall, 1500 Marilla St., Room 4D South, Dallas, TX 75201
Fax: (214) 670-4448

Chief Information Officer\Director **William Finch** . . . . . (214) 670-3918
E-mail: william.finch@dallascityhall.com
Assistant Director, Business Management Services **Sheila Robinson** . . . . . (214) 671-9200
E-mail: sheila.robinson@dallascityhall.com
Assistant Director, Business Technology Services **Justine Tran** . . . . . (214) 670-1890
E-mail: justine.tran@dallascityhall.com
Assistant Director, IT Planning, Standards and Compliance **Tony Aguilar** . . . . . (214) 670-0783
E-mail: tony.aguilar@dallascityhall.com
Assistant Director, Technology Infrastructure Services **Chester Helt** . . . . . (214) 671-8927
E-mail: chester.helt@dallascityhall.com
Chief Technology Architect **Girish Ramachandran** . . . . . (214) 671-8052

Business Development and Procurement Services
1500 Marilla Street, Room 3F North, Dallas, TX 75201

Director **Mike Frosch** . . . . . (214) 670-3326
E-mail: mike.frosch@dallascityhall.com

Aviation Department
8008 Herb Kelleher Way, Dallas, TX 75235
Tel: (214) 670-5683 Fax: (214) 670-6051

Director **Mark Duebner** . . . . . (214) 670-6077
Operations Assistant Director **Terry Lee Mitchell** . . . . . (214) 670-6086
E-mail: Terry.Mitchell@dallascityhall.com
Capital Improvements Assistant Director **Lana Furra** . . . . . (214) 670-6149
E-mail: lana.furra@dallascityhall.com
Airport Facilities Manager **Barry Strzala** . . . . . (214) 670-0080
Airport Operations Manager **Cliff York** . . . . . (214) 670-6157
E-mail: clifford.york@dallascityhall.com
Business and Finance Manager **(Vacant)** . . . . . (214) 670-6140
Dallas Executive Airport Manager **Darrell Phillips** . . . . . (214) 670-7612
Fax: (214) 670-6791
Dallas Heliport Manager **(Vacant)** . . . . . (214) 670-6086
Fax: (214) 670-0736
Environmental Manager **Sana Drissi** . . . . . (214) 670-6654
Contract Compliance Manager **Robert Miville** . . . . . (214) 670-6087
Property Manager **Dawn Blair** . . . . . (214) 670-6153
Airport Engineer **(Vacant)** . . . . . (214) 670-6144
Assistant Director, Administration and Finance **Lynetta Kidd** . . . . . (214) 670-6084
Manager, Customer Relations **Sheneice M. Hughes** . . . . . (214) 670-0548

Civil Service Department
City Hall, 1500 Marilla St., Room 1C-South, Dallas, TX 75201-6300
Fax: (214) 670-5521

Director **Patricia Marsolais** . . . . . (214) 670-3748
E-mail: p.marsolais@dallascityhall.com
Assistant Director **Michelle Hanchard** . . . . . (214) 670-3752
E-mail: michelle.hanchard@dallascityhall.com

Department of Code Compliance
3112 Canton Street, Suite 102, Room A, Dallas, TX 75226
Fax: (214) 670-3652

Director **Kris Sweckard** . . . . . (214) 670-3118
Assistant Director, Administration **Janette Weedon** . . . . . (214) 671-9415
E-mail: janette.weedon@dallascityhall.com
Assistant Director, Nuisance Abatement **Tom Varghese** . . (214) 671-9116
Assistant Director **Ben Collins** . . . . . (214) 670-5708

Convention and Event Services Department
650 S. Griffin St., Dallas, TX 75202
Tel: (214) 939-2750 Fax: (214) 939-2795
Internet: http://www.dallasconventioncenter.com

■ Executive Director **Ron King** . . . . . (214) 939-2950
E-mail: ron.king@dallasconventioncenter.com
Executive Assistant (Interim) **Brenda DeLeon** . . . . . (214) 939-2750
E-mail: brenda.deleon@dallascityhall.com
Director of Finance **Juanita Ortiz** . . . . . (214) 939-2794
Assistant Director of Sales, Marketing and Event Excellence **John Johnson** . . . . . (214) 939-2972
Facilities Manager **Bonnie Zitek** . . . . . (214) 939-2864
E-mail: bonnie.zitek@dallasconventioncenter.com

Equipment and Building Services Department
3202 Canton Street, Dallas, TX 75226
Fax: (214) 670-5149

Director **Errick Thompson** . . . . . (214) 670-0196
E-mail: errick.thompson@dallascityhall.com
Facility Management Assistant Director **James Davis** . . . . (214) 671-9440
E-mail: james.davis2@dallascityhall.com
Fleet Management Assistant Director **Cheritta L. Johnson** . . . . . (214) 670-1892

(continued on next page)

★ Elected Official ▲ Appointed by Legislature ▼ Appointed by Governor ▶ Appointed by Board or Commission ● Appointed by Judge
■ Appointed by Mayor △ Appointed by Freeholders ▽ Appointed by Supervisor ▷ Appointed by County Executive ○ Appointed by Council

Equipment and Building Services Department *continued*

Assistant Director **Melissa De La Cruz** . . . . (214) 671-0195
E-mail: melissa.delacruz@dallascityhall.com

Dallas Fire-Rescue Department

City Hall, 1500 Marilla St., Room 7A South, Dallas, TX 75201
Fax: (214) 670-4564 Internet: http://www.dallasfirerescue.com

Fire Chief **Tommy Tine** . . . . (214) 670-4610
E-mail: tommy.tine@dallascityhall.com
Fire Marshall **Ted Padgett** . . . . (214) 670-7951
E-mail: ted.padgett@dallascityhall.com
Assistant Chief, Emergency Response Bureau
Fernando Gray . . . . (214) 670-4611
E-mail: fernando.gray@dallascityhall.com
Executive Assistant Chief, Emergency Response/
Homeland Security **Tommy Tine** . . . . (214) 670-5084
E-mail: tommy.tine@dallascityhall.com
Assistant Chief, Technology and Personnel
Daniel Salazar . . . . (214) 670-1475
E-mail: daniel.salazar@dallascityhall.com
Assistant Chief, Training and Support **Harold Holland** . . . (214) 670-4562
E-mail: harold.holland@dallascityhall.com
Public Information Officer **Jason Evans** . . . . (214) 670-7949
E-mail: jason.evans@dallascityhall.com

Housing/Community Services Department

City Hall, 1500 Marilla St., Room 6D North, Dallas, TX 75201-6320
Fax: (214) 670-0156

Director (Interim) **Bernadette Mitchell** . . . . (214) 670-4028
Assistant Director **Bernadette Mitchell** . . . . (214) 670-3619
E-mail: bernadette.mitchell@dallascityhall.com
Assistant Director **Karen D. Rayzer** . . . . (214) 670-4648
E-mail: karen.rayzer@dallascityhall.com
Assistant Director **(Vacant)** . . . . (214) 670-3633
Housing Transformation Czar **C. Donald Babers** . . . . (214) 670-4028
Education: Texas (Arlington) 1969 BA

Human Resources Department

City Hall, 1500 Marilla St., Room 6A North, Dallas, TX 75201-6390
Fax: (214) 670-3764

Director **Molly Carroll** . . . . (214) 670-3562
E-mail: molly.carroll@dallascityhall.com

Performance Management

Assistant Director **Yasmin Barnes** . . . . (214) 670-5417
E-mail: yasmin.barnes@dallascityhall.com

Risk Management

Director **Zeronda Smith** . . . . (214) 671-9015
E-mail: zeronda.smith@dallascityhall.com

Park and Recreation Department

City Hall, 1500 Marilla Street, 6FN, Dallas, TX 75201
Tel: (214) 670-4100 Fax: (214) 670-3205
Internet: http://www.dallasparks.org/

Director **Willis Winters** . . . . (214) 670-4074
Education: Texas 1980 BARCH
Administration and Business Services Deputy Director
John Jenkins . . . . (214) 670-4073
8007 E.NW Highway, Dallas, TX 75238 Fax: (214) 670-8856
E-mail: john.jenkins@dallascityhall.com
Fair Park and Community Services Assistant Director
Daniel Huerta . . . . (214) 670-8463
E-mail: daniel.huerta@dallascityhall.com
Planning, Facility and Environmental Services Assistant
Director **Louise Elam** . . . . (214) 670-4074
E-mail: louise.elam@dallascityhall.com
Recreation Services Assistant Director **Crystal Ross** . . . . . (214) 670-8958
3012 South Hampton, Dallas, TX 75224 Fax: (214) 670-6892
Human Resources Manager **(Vacant)** . . . . (214) 670-4287

Park and Recreation Department *continued*

Marketing/Public Information Manager
Andrea Hawkins . . . . (214) 670-4678
E-mail: andrea.hawkins@dallascityhall.com
Park Board Office Manager **Dawna Ray** . . . . (214) 670-4078
Fax: (214) 670-3205
Park Maintenance Services Assistant Director
Oscar Carmona . . . . (214) 670-8871
3012 South Hampton, Dallas, TX 75224

Police Department

Jack Evans Headquarters, 1400 South Lamar Street, 6th Floor,
Dallas, TX 75215
Tel: (214) 671-3901 Fax: (214) 670-8685 Internet: www.dallaspolice.net

Police Chief **David O. Brown** . . . . (214) 671-3901
First Executive Assistant Chief **(Vacant)** . . . . (214) 671-3927
Executive Assistant Chief **David Pughes** . . . . (214) 671-3901
Executive Assistant Chief **Cynthia Villarreal** . . . . (214) 671-3924
Assistant Chief\Chief of Staff **Brigitte Gassaway** . . . . (214) 671-3921
Assistant Chief **Randall Blankenbaker** . . . . (214) 671-3922
Assistant Chief **Tammie Hughes** . . . . (214) 671-3922
Assistant Chief **Patricia Paulhill** . . . . (214) 671-3922

Public Works Department

320 East Jefferson, Room 101, Dallas, TX 75203
Tel: (214) 948-4650 Fax: (214) 948-4653

Director **Rick Galceran** . . . . (214) 948-4650
Administration Assistant Director **Kenneth Odu** . . . . (214) 948-4185
E-mail: kenneth.odu@dallascityhall.com
Construction, Survey and Engineering Services
Assistant Director **Tim Starr** . . . . (214) 948-4226
320 East Jefferson Boulevard, Fax: (214) 948-4680
Room 307, Dallas, TX 75203
E-mail: timothy.starr@dallascityhall.com
Facilities Architecture and Engineering Services
Assistant Director **Zaida Basora** . . . . (214) 948-5360
320 East Jefferson Boulevard, Fax: (214) 948-4653
Room 321, Dallas, TX 75203
E-mail: zaida.basora@dallascityhall.com
Interagency Transportation Construction Administrator
Mark Rauscher . . . . (214) 670-7748
1500 Marilla Street, L1BS, Dallas, TX 75201

Sanitation Services Department

3112 Canton Street, Suite 200, Dallas, TX 75226
Fax: (214) 670-3670

Director **Kelly High** . . . . (214) 670-3555
Assistant Director **Liza Bustamante** . . . . (214) 670-3555

Department of Street Services

2710 Municipal Street, Dallas, TX 75215
Fax: (214) 670-8207

Director **Dennis Ware** . . . . (214) 670-4491
Assistant Director **Jerry Ortega** . . . . (214) 670-4491
Assistant Director **(Vacant)** . . . . (214) 670-4491
Assistant Director, Transportation **Aurobindo Majundar** . . (214) 670-4491

Water Utilities Department

City Hall, 1500 Marilla St., Room 4A North, Dallas, TX 75201
Tel: (214) 651-1441 (Customer Service)

Director **Jody Puckett** . . . . (214) 670-3146
Fax: (214) 670-3154
Executive Assistant **Beto Hernandez** . . . . (214) 670-3188
Fax: (214) 670-3154

★ Elected Official ▲ Appointed by Legislature ▼ Appointed by Governor ▶ Appointed by Board or Commission ● Appointed by Judge
■ Appointed by Mayor △ Appointed by Freeholders ▽ Appointed by Supervisor ▷ Appointed by County Executive ○ Appointed by Council

Dallas Public Library

J. Erik Jonsson Central Library, 1515 Young Street, Dallas, TX 75201-5499
Tel: (214) 670-1400 Fax: (214) 670-7839 Internet: www.dallaslibrary.org

Year Founded: 1901

Administration

Library Director **Jo Giudice** .... (214) 670-7803
E-mail: director@dallaslibrary.org
Assistant Director, Customer Experience **Kjerstine Nielsen** .... (214) 670-7809
E-mail: kjerstine.nielsen@dallascityhall.com
Assistant Director, Technical Services **Zulema Garcia** .... (214) 670-7809
E-mail: zulema.garcia@dallascityhall.com
Assistant Director, Operations **(Vacant)** .... (214) 670-7809
Administrator, Central Library **Val Armstrong** .... (214) 670-7809
E-mail: val.armstrong@dallascityhall.com
Administrator, Adult Programming **Ronnie Jessie** .... (214) 670-7809
E-mail: ronnie.jessie@dallascityhall.com
Business Manager **Clinton Lawrence** .... (214) 670-7809
E-mail: clinton.lawrence@dallascityhall.com

Intergovernmental Services

1500 Marilla Street, Room 4BN, Dallas, TX 75201
Fax: (214) 670-5798

Director **Brett Wilkinson** .... (214) 670-5047
E-mail: brett.wilkinson@dallascityhall.com
Intergovernmental Services Executive Officer **(Vacant)** ... (214) 670-5363
Intergovernmental Affairs Manager **Anna Lamberti Holmes** .... (214) 670-5099
E-mail: anna.holmes@dallascityhall.com

Sustainable Development and Construction

City Hall, 1500 Marilla St., Room 5D North, Dallas, TX 75201
Fax: (214) 670-5755

Director **David Cossum** .... (214) 670-4127
Fax: (214) 670-5755
Real Estate Division Assistant Director **Ashley Eubanks** .... (214) 670-4209
Fax: (214) 670-4210
Building Inspection Division, Building Official **Larry Holmes** .... (214) 948-4330
320 East Jefferson Boulevard, Dallas, TX 75203 Fax: (214) 948-4511
Strategic Planning Division Assistant Director **Peer Chacko** .... (214) 670-3972
Fax: (214) 670-0728

Dallas Independent School District [DISD]

3700 Ross Avenue, Box 2, Dallas, TX 75204
Tel: (972) 925-3720 Internet: http://www.dallasisd.org

Board of Trustees

3700 Ross Avenue, Box 1, Dallas, TX 75204

★President **Bernadette Nutall** (District 9) .... (972) 925-3720
Term Expires: May 2018
★First Vice President **Miguel Solis** (District 8) .... (972) 925-3720
Term Expires: May 2017
★Second Vice President **Dr. Lew Blackburn** (District 5) ... (972) 925-3720
Term Expires: May 2019
E-mail: lblackburn@dallasisd.org
Education: East Texas State BS; Texas A&M (Commerce) MA; Texas PhD
★Trustee **Dr. Edwin S. Flores** (District 1) .... (972) 925-3720
Term Expires: May 28, 2018
★Trustee **(Vacant)** (District 2) .... (972) 925-3720
Note: A runoff election between Dustin Marshall amd Mita Havlick is scheduled for June 18, 2016.
Term Expires: May 2017

Board of Trustees *continued*

★Trustee **Daniel J. Micciche** (District 3) .... (972) 925-3720
Term Expires: May 2018
E-mail: danmicciche@dallasisd.org
Education: SUNY (Stony Brook) 1978 BA; Chicago 1981 JD
★Trustee **Jaime Resendez** (District 4) .... (972) 925-3720
Term Expires: May 2019
★Trustee **Joyce Foreman** (District 6) .... (972) 925-3720
Term Expires: May 2017
E-mail: joyceforeman@dallasisd.org
★Trustee **Audrey Pinkerton** (District 7) .... (972) 925-3720
Term Expires: May 2019

Superintendent of Schools

3700 Ross Avenue, Box 2, Dallas, TX 75204
Fax: (972) 925-3201

Superintendent of Schools **Dr. Michael Hinojosa** .... (972) 925-3200
Education: Texas Tech 1979; North Texas 1983; Texas 2001 EdD
Administrative Assistant **Andrea Rodriguez** .... (972) 925-3220
E-mail: arodriguez@dallasisd.org
Chief of Staff **Dr. Cynthia Wilson** .... (972) 925-3220
Education: Houston BA, MA; South Carolina State DEd
Deputy Superintendent **Ann Smisko** .... (972) 925-3617
Chief Communications Officer **Toni Cordova** .... (972) 925-3902
Chief of Finance **James Terry** .... (972) 925-3655
Chief of Human Capital Management **Karry Chapman** ... (972) 925-4288
E-mail: kchapman@dallasisd.org
Chief Internal Auditor **Michael Singleton** .... (972) 925-3656
Chief of Operations **Wanda Paul** .... (972) 925-5109
E-mail: wpaul@dallasisd.org
Chief of School Leadership **Stephanie Elizalde** .... (972) 925-4662
Chief of Technology **Bob Moore** .... (972) 925-3613
E-mail: bmoore@dallasisd.org
Chief of Transformation and Innovation **Mike Koprowski** .... (972) 925-3720
E-mail: mkiprowski@dallasisd.org
Senior Executive for Intergovernmental Affairs and Community Relations **Paula Blackmon** .... (972) 925-3294
E-mail: pblackmon@dallasisd.org
Education: Texas Tech

Daly City, California

City Hall, 333 90th St., Daly City, CA 94015-1895
Internet: www.dalycity.org

County: San Mateo **Year Incorporated:** 1911 **Population:** 106,562 (2015)

Office of the Mayor and City Council

City Hall, 333 90th St., Daly City, CA 94015
Fax: (650) 991-5759

★Mayor **Gonzalo "Sal" Torres** .... (650) 991-8008
Began Service: 1996
Term Expires: November 4, 2016
★Vice Mayor **David J. Canepa** .... (650) 991-8008
Term Expires: November 4, 2016
★Council Member **Raymond A. Buenaventura** .... (650) 991-8008
Term Expires: November 8, 2018
★Council Member **Judith Christensen** .... (650) 991-8008
Term Expires: December 2018
★Council Member **Michael P. Guingona** .... (650) 991-8008
Term Expires: November 4, 2018

Office of the City Attorney

City Hall, 333 90th St., Daly City, CA 94015

City Attorney **Rose L. Zimmerman** .... (650) 991-8122
E-mail: rzimmerman@dalycity.org

★Elected Official ▲Appointed by Legislature ▼Appointed by Governor ▶Appointed by Board or Commission ●Appointed by Judge
■Appointed by Mayor △Appointed by Freeholders ▽Appointed by Supervisor ▷Appointed by County Executive ○Appointed by Council

Office of the City Clerk
City Hall, 333 90th St., Daly City, CA 94015
Fax: (650) 991-8091

★City Clerk **K. Annette Hipona** .... (650) 991-8078
Term Expires: November 4, 2016
E-mail: ahipona@dalycity.org

Office of the City Treasurer
City Hall, 333 90th St., Daly City, CA 94015

★City Treasurer **Daneca Halvorson** .... (650) 991-8047
Term Expires: November 4, 2016
E-mail: dhalvorson@dalycity.org

Office of the City Manager
City Hall, 333 90th St., Daly City, CA 94015

City Manager **Patricia E. Martel** .... (650) 991-8127
E-mail: pmartel@dalycity.org
Education: USC BS, MPA

Assistant City Manager **Julie Thuy Underwood** .... (650) 991-8127
E-mail: junderwood@dalycity.org
Education: George Mason BA; Virginia Tech MPA

Community Service Center
350 90th St., Daly City, CA 94015

Community Services Center Coordinator **Pat Bohm** ...... (650) 991-8007

Department of Library and Recreation Services
40 Wembly Dr., Daly City, CA 94015

Director **Joseph Curran** .... (650) 991-8025
E-mail: jcurran@dalycity.org

Economic and Community Development Department
City Hall, 333 90th St., Daly City, CA 94015
Tel: (650) 991-8034

Director (Acting) **Tatum Mothershead** .... (650) 991-8034
E-mail: tmothershead@dalycity.org

Chief Building Supervisor **Val Mandapat** .... (650) 991-8034

Finance and Administrative Services Department
City Hall, 333 90th St., Daly City, CA 94015

Director **Lawrence Chiu** .... (650) 991-8048

Fire Department
10 Wembly Dr., Daly City, CA 94015

Fire Chief **Ron Myers** .... (650) 991-8138
E-mail: rmyers@dalycity.org

Human Resources Department
295 89th Street, Suite 105, Daly City, CA 94015
Fax: (650) 991-8228

Director **Shawnna Maltbie** .... (650) 991-8248
E-mail: smaltbie@dalycity.org

Imagination Station
Child Development Center, 280 92nd St., Daly City, CA 94015

Director **Raeli Aguirre** .... (650) 746-8356

Police Department
City Hall, 333 90th St., Daly City, CA 94015

Chief of Police **Manuel Martinez, Jr.** .... (650) 991-8142
Education: Lincoln Law 2004 JD; St Mary's Col (CA) 1999 BA

Public Works Department
City Hall, 333 90th St., Daly City, CA 94015

Director **John Fuller** .... (650) 991-8038

Water and Wastewater Resources Department
153 Lake Merced Blvd., Daly City, CA 94015

Director **Patrick Sweetland** .... (650) 991-8200

City of Davenport, Iowa
226 West 4th Street, Davenport, IA 52801

County: Scott **Election Type:** Nonpartisan **Year Incorporated:** 1839
Population: 102,582 (2015)

Office of the Mayor and City Council
226 West 4th Street, Davenport, IA 52801
Fax: (563) 328-6728

★Mayor **Frank Klipsch** .... (563) 326-7701
Began Service: January 2016
Term Expires: January 2018
E-mail: fklipsch@ci.davenport.ia.us

★Alderman **Rick Dunn** (Ward 1) .... (563) 888-2070
Term Expires: January 2018

★Alderman **Maria Dickmann** (Ward 2) .... (563) 888-2070
Term Expires: January 2018
E-mail: mdickmann@ci.davenport.ia.us

★Alderman **Bill Boom** (Ward 3) .... (563) 888-2070
Term Expires: January 2018
E-mail: bboom@ci.davenport.ia.us

★Alderman **Ray Ambrose** (Ward 4) .... (563) 888-2070
Term Expires: January 2018
E-mail: rambose@ci.davenport.ia.us

★Alderman **Rita Rawson** (Ward 5) .... (563) 888-2070
Term Expires: January 2018
E-mail: rrawson@ci.davenport.ia.us

★Alderman **Jeff Justin** (Ward 6) .... (563) 888-2070
Term Expires: January 2018
E-mail: jjustin@ci.davenport.ia.us

★Alderman **Mike Matson** (Ward 7) .... (563) 888-2070
Term Expires: January 2018
E-mail: mmatson@ci.davenport.ia.us

★Alderman **Kerri Tompkins** (Ward 8) .... (563) 888-2070
Term Expires: January 2018
E-mail: ktompkins@ci.davenport.ia.us

★Alderman **Jason Gordon** (At-Large) .... (563) 888-2070
Term Expires: January 2018
E-mail: jgordon@ci.davenport.ia.us

★Alderman **Kyle Gripp** (At-Large) .... (563) 888-2070
Term Expires: January 2018
E-mail: kgripp@ci.davenport.ia.us

Office of the City Administrator
226 West 4th Street, Davenport, IA 52801
Fax: (563) 326-7736

■City Administrator **Corri Spiegel** .... (563) 326-6139
E-mail: cspiegel@ci.davenport.ia.us

Communications Director **Jennifer Nahra** .... (563) 326-7763
E-mail: jen@ci.davenport.ia.us

Office of the City Clerk
226 West 4th Street, Room 301, Davenport, IA 52801
Fax: (563) 326-7736

Deputy City Clerk **Jackie Holecek** .... (563) 326-6163
E-mail: jet@ci.davenport.ia.us

★Elected Official ▲Appointed by Legislature ▼Appointed by Governor ►Appointed by Board or Commission ●Appointed by Judge
■Appointed by Mayor △Appointed by Freeholders ▽Appointed by Supervisor ▷Appointed by County Executive ○Appointed by Council

Civil Rights Commission
226 West 4th Street, Room 106, Davenport, IA 52801
Fax: (563) 326-7956

Director **Latrice Lacey** . . . . (563) 326-7888

Office of the City Assessor
600 West 4th Street, Davenport, IA 52801-1030

City Assessor **Nick Van Camp** . . . . (563) 326-8659
E-mail: ncamp@ci.davenport.ia.us

Community Planning and Economic Development Department
226 West 4th Street, Davenport, IA 52801
Fax: (563) 326-7748

Director **Bruce Berger** . . . . (563) 328-6706
E-mail: beb@ci.davenport.ia.us

Neighborhood Services Specialist **Roy DeWitt** . . . . (563) 888-3440
E-mail: rdewitt@ci.davenport.ia.us Fax: (563) 328-6714

Finance Department
226 West 4th Street, Room 201, Davenport, IA 52801
Fax: (563) 888-2079

Finance Director **Brandon Wright** . . . . (563) 326-7789

Accounting Division
226 West 4th Street, Room 203, Davenport, IA 52801
Fax: (563) 328-6742

Assistant Finance Director **Linda S. Folland** . . . . (563) 328-6789
E-mail: lsf@ci.davenport.ia.us

Revenue Division
226 West 4th Street, Room 102, Davenport, IA 52801
Fax: (563) 326-7722

Revenue Manager **Jim Odean** . . . . (563) 326-7737

Purchasing Division
226 West 4th Street, Davenport, IA 52801
Fax: (563) 888-2079

Purchasing Manager **Kristy Keller** . . . . (563) 888-2156
E-mail: kkeller@ci.davenport.ia.us

Risk Management Division
226 West 4th Street, Room 201, Davenport, IA 52801
Fax: (563) 888-2079

Risk Manager **Jim Forsyth** . . . . (563) 888-2156
E-mail: jforsyth@ci.davenport.ia.us

Fire Department
331 Scott Street, Davenport, IA 52801-1132
Fax: (563) 328-7232

Fire Chief **Lynn Washburn-Livingston** . . . . (563) 326-7906 ext. 1
E-mail: lwashburn@ci.davenport.ia.us

Fire Marshal **Mike Hayman** . . . . (563) 326-7906
E-mail: f513@ci.davenport.ia.us

Human Resources Department
226 West 4th Street, Davenport, IA 52801
Fax: (563) 328-6773

Director **Dawn Sherman** . . . . (563) 326-7719
E-mail: dsherman@ci.davenport.ia.us

Information Technology Department
226 West 4th Street, Davenport, IA 52801

Chief Information Officer **Rob Henry** . . . . (563) 326-7791
E-mail: rhenry@ci.davenport.ia.us

Legal Department
226 West 4th Street, Room 303, Davenport, IA 52801
Fax: (563) 328-6767

Corporation Counsel **Tom D. Warner** . . . . (563) 326-7735

Parks and Recreation Department
1757 West 12th Street, Davenport, IA 52804
Fax: (563) 326-7815

Director **Scott Hock** . . . . (563) 326-7812

Police Department
416 North Harrison Street, Davenport, IA 52801
Tel: (563) 326-7979

Chief of Police **Don Schaeffer** . . . . (563) 326-7778

Davenport Public Library
321 Main Street, Davenport, IA 52801
Fax: (563) 326-7809

Director **Amy Groskopf** . . . . (563) 326-7843
E-mail: agroskopf@davenportlibrary.com

Public Works Department
1200 East 46th Street, Davenport, IA 52807
Tel: (563) 326-7923 Fax: (563) 327-5182

Director **Michael Clarke** . . . . (563) 326-7734

Davenport Municipal Airport
1200 East 46th Street, Davenport, IA 52807

Airport Manager **Thomas Vesalga** . . . . (563) 326-7783

Building Inspections Division
1200 East 46th Street, Davenport, IA 52807
Fax: (563) 327-5182

Building Inspection Manager **Mike G. McGee** . . . . (563) 326-7745

Citibus Transit
300 West River Drive, Davenport, IA 52801

Transit Manager **Kurt Scheible** . . . . (563) 888-2151

Davenport Compost Facility
2707 Railroad Avenue, Davenport, IA 52802
Fax: (563) 328-7227

Director **Marcia Mount** . . . . (563) 328-7225

Engineering Division
1200 East 46th Street, Davenport, IA 52807
Fax: (563) 327-5182

City Engineer **Brian Schadt** . . . . (563) 326-7729
E-mail: bschadt@ci.davenport.ia.us

Facilities Maintenance Division
1200 East 46th Street, Davenport, IA 52807
Fax: (563) 327-5182

Facilities Manager **Andy E. Dibbern** . . . . (563) 326-7810
E-mail: aed@ci.davenport.ia.us

Fleet Management Division
1200 East 46th Street, Davenport, IA 52807
Fax: (563) 326-7945

Vehicle Service Superintendent **Jon K. Meeks** . . . . (563) 326-7920

Forestry Division
1200 East 46th Street, Davenport, IA 52807
Fax: (563) 327-5182

City Arborist **Chris Johnson** . . . . (563) 326-7923

★ Elected Official ▲ Appointed by Legislature ▼ Appointed by Governor ▶ Appointed by Board or Commission ● Appointed by Judge
■ Appointed by Mayor △ Appointed by Freeholders ▽ Appointed by Supervisor ▷ Appointed by County Executive ○ Appointed by Council

Natural Resources Division
1200 East 46th Street, Davenport, IA 52807
Fax: (563) 327-5182

Director **Brian Stineman** .... (563) 326-7923

Solid Waste Division
1200 East 46th Street, Davenport, IA 52807
Fax: (563) 327-5182

Solid Waste Superintendent **Todd M. Jones** .... (563) 326-7732

Wastewater Treatment Plant
1200 East 46th Street, Davenport, IA 52807
Fax: (563) 326-7858

Director **Dan Miers** .... (563) 326-7877

Davenport Community School District

1606 Brady Street, Davenport, IA 52803
Fax: (563) 336-5080

Superintendent **Dr. Arthur Tate** .... (563) 336-5083

City of Dayton, Ohio

City Hall, 101 W. Third St., Dayton, OH 45402
P.O. Box 22, Dayton, OH 45401-0022
Tel: (937) 333-3333 (Information) Fax: (937) 333-4269
Internet: www.daytonohio.gov

County: Montgomery **Election Type:** Nonpartisan **Year Founded:** 1796
Year Incorporated: 1805 **Population:** 140,599 (2015)

Office of the Mayor and City Commission

City Hall, 101 W. Third St., Dayton, OH 45402
P.O. Box 22, Dayton, OH 45401-0022
Fax: (937) 333-4297 E-mail: cityhall@daytonohio.gov
Internet: http://www.daytonohio.gov

★ Mayor **Nan Whaley** .... (937) 333-3636
Began Service: January 6, 2014
Term Expires: January 2018

★ Commissioner **Matt Joseph** .... (937) 333-3636
Term Expires: January 1, 2020

★ Commissioner **Jeffrey J. Mims, Jr.** .... (937) 333-3636
Term Expires: January 2018

★ Commissioner **Chris Shaw** .... (937) 333-3636
Term Expires: January 1, 2020

★ Commissioner **Joey Williams** .... (937) 333-3636
Term Expires: January 7, 2018

▶ Clerk **Rashella Lavender** .... (937) 333-3636

Executive Assistant to the Commission **Kery Gray** .... (937) 333-3636
E-mail: kery.gray@daytonohio.gov

Office of the City Manager

City Hall, 101 W. Third St., Dayton, OH 45402
P.O. Box 22, Dayton, OH 45401-0022
Fax: (937) 333-4298 E-mail: cityhall@daytonohio.gov

▶ City Manager **Shelley Dickstein** .... (937) 333-3600
E-mail: shelley.dickstein@cityofdayton.org

Deputy City Manager **Tammi Clements** .... (937) 333-3600
E-mail: tammi.clements@daytonohio.gov

Deputy City Manager **Joe Parlette** .... (937) 333-3600
E-mail: joe.parlette@cityofdayton.org

Aviation Department

Dayton International Airport, Terminal Bldg., Vandalia, OH 45377
Tel: (937) 454-8200 Fax: (937) 454-8284

Director **Terrence G. "Terry" Slaybaugh** .... (937) 454-8212

Deputy Director **Gilbert Turner** .... (937) 454-8202

Administrative and Finance Manager **Joe Homan** .... (937) 454-8211
E-mail: jhoman@flydayton.com

Aircraft Rescue and Firefighting Manager **Bruce Bales** .... (937) 264-3529
E-mail: bruce.bales@cityofdayton.org

Airport Police Chief **Michael Etter** .... (937) 454-8328

Operations and Facilities Manager **Don Faley** .... (937) 264-3530
E-mail: dfaley@flydayton.com

Communications Systems Coordinator **Pam Hixon** .... (937) 264-3594

Airport Planning, Design and Construction Manager **Liz Zelinski** .... (937) 264-3584

Department of Building Services

371 West Second Street, Dayton, OH 45402
Fax: (937) 333-4284

Chief Building Official **Scott Adams** .... (937) 333-3911

Housing Inspection Manager **Kevin Powell** .... (937) 333-3945

Central Services Department

City Hall, 101 W. Third St., Dayton, OH 45402

Director **Peter Hager** .... (937) 333-4200
E-mail: pete.hager@daytonohio.gov
Education: Wright State MS

Facilities Management Manager **Romona Carver** .... (937) 333-4010
E-mail: romona.carver@daytonohio.gov

Purchasing Agent (Acting) **Peter Hager** .... (937) 333-4030
E-mail: pete.hager@daytonohio.gov
Education: Wright State MS

Information Technology Services
130 W. Second St., Suite 320, Dayton, OH 45402

Division Manager **Desa Foster** .... (937) 333-6349
E-mail: desa.foster@daytonohio.gov

City Wide Development Corporation

Eight N. Main St., Dayton, OH 45402-1916

Executive Director **Steven J. Budd** .... (937) 226-0457
Education: Dayton BA, MPA

Civil Service Board

371 West Second Street, Dayton, OH 45402
Fax: (937) 333-2125

Secretary and Chief Examiner **Maurice Evans** .... (937) 333-2300
E-mail: cs@daytonohio.gov

Office of Economic Development

City Hall, 101 W. Third St., Dayton, OH 45402
P.O. Box 22, Dayton, OH 45401-0022
Fax: (937) 333-3827

Director of Economic Development **Ford P. Weber III** .... (937) 333-3623
Education: Toledo BA, JD

Assistant City Manager **(Vacant)** .... (937) 333-3634

Small Business Advocate **Jeffrey Bankston** .... (937) 333-3689
E-mail: jeffrey.bankston@daytonohio.gov

Finance Department

City Hall, 101 W. Third St., Dayton, OH 45402
P.O. Box 22, Dayton, OH 45401-0022
Fax: (937) 333-4280

Director **C. LaShea Smith** .... (937) 333-3578

Financial Services Supervisor **Valerie Henderson** .... (937) 333-3552

Deputy Director **Bejoy John** .... (937) 333-3510

Revenue Manager **(Vacant)** .... (937) 333-3560

★ Elected Official ▲ Appointed by Legislature ▼ Appointed by Governor ▶ Appointed by Board or Commission ● Appointed by Judge
■ Appointed by Mayor △ Appointed by Freeholders ▽ Appointed by Supervisor ▷ Appointed by County Executive ○ Appointed by Council

Fire Department
300 N. Main St., Dayton, OH 45402
Fax: (937) 333-4561

Director and Chief **Jeffrey L. Payne** . . . . (937) 333-4506
E-mail: jeffrey.payne@cityofdayton.org
Assistant Chief **Michael Caudill** . . . . (937) 333-4500
E-mail: michael.caudill@cityofdayton.org
Assistant Chief **Paul Sheehan** . . . . (937) 333-4502
E-mail: paul.sheehan@cityofdayton.org

Human Relations Council
130 W. Second St., Suite 730, Dayton, OH 45402
Fax: (937) 222-4589

Executive Director **Catherine Crosby** . . . . (937) 333-1400
Assistant Director **(Vacant)** . . . . (937) 333-1395

Human Resources
City Hall, 101 W. Third St., Dayton, OH 45402
P.O. Box 22, Dayton, OH 45401-0022
Fax: (937) 333-4293

Director **Kenneth R. Couch** . . . . (937) 333-4067
E-mail: kenneth.couch@daytonohio.gov
Deputy Director **Brent McKenzie** . . . . (937) 333-4062
E-mail: brent.mckenzie@daytonohio.gov

Law Office
City Hall, 101 W. Third St., Dayton, OH 45402
P.O. Box 22, Dayton, OH 45401-0022
Tel: (937) 333-4100 Fax: (937) 333-3628

Director **Barbara Doseck** . . . . (937) 333-4100
Deputy Director **Lynn Donaldson** . . . . (937) 333-4100
Chief Prosecutor **Stephanie Cook** . . . . (937) 333-4400

Office of Management and Budget
City Hall, 101 W. Third St., Dayton, OH 45402
P.O. Box 22, Dayton, OH 45401-0022
Fax: (937) 333-4282

Director **Barbara LaBrier** . . . . (937) 333-3750
E-mail: barbara.labrier@daytonohio.gov

Department of Planning and Community Development
City Hall, 101 W. Third St., Dayton, OH 45402
P.O. Box 22, Dayton, OH 45401-0022

Director **Aaron Sorrell** . . . . (937) 333-3670
E-mail: aaron.sorrell@daytonohio.gov
Planning Manager **Brian Inderrieden** . . . . (937) 333-3670
E-mail: brian.inderrieden@daytonohio.gov
Community Development Manager **Amy Riegel** . . . . (937) 333-3670
E-mail: amy.riegel@daytonohio.gov

Police Department
335 W. Third St., Dayton, OH 45402
Fax: (937) 333-1321

Director and Chief of Police **Richard S. Biehl** . . . . (937) 333-1082
Deputy Director (Acting) **Major Brian Johns** . . . . (937) 333-1082
Office of the Chief **Mark Ecton** . . . . (937) 333-1330
E-mail: mark.ecton@daytonohio.gov
Division of Investigations and Administrative Support
Major Christopher Williams . . . . (937) 333-1110
E-mail: christopher.williams@cityofdayton.org

Public Affairs
City Hall, 101 W. Third St., Dayton, OH 45402
P.O. Box 22, Dayton, OH 45401-0022
Fax: (937) 333-4269

Director **Toni Bankston** . . . . (937) 333-3616
E-mail: toni.bankston@daytonohio.gov

Public Works Department
City Hall, 101 W. Third St., Dayton, OH 45402
P.O. Box 22, Dayton, OH 45401-0022
Fax: (937) 333-4261

Director **Fred Stovall** . . . . (937) 333-4070
Assistant Director/City Engineer **Steve Finke** . . . . (937) 333-3839
E-mail: steve.finke@daytonohio.gov
Fleet Management Manager **Matt Newton** . . . . (937) 333-4850
1010 Ottawa St., Dayton, OH 45402
Street Maintenance Manager **Fred Stovall** . . . . (937) 333-4809
1071 E. Monument Ave., Dayton, OH 45402
Waste Collection Manager **Tom Ritchie, Jr.** . . . . (937) 333-4825
1010 Ottawa St., Dayton, OH 45402

Recreation and Youth Services Department
City Hall, 101 W. Third St., Dayton, OH 45402
Fax: (937) 333-6019

Director (Interim) **Robin Williams** . . . . (937) 333-8400
Convention Center Manager **Michael Cashman** . . . . (937) 333-4700
Recreation Administration Manager **Robin Williams** . . . . . (937) 333-8400
E-mail: robin.williams@cityofdayton.org
Golf Manager **Kelly Pressel** . . . . (937) 333-3378

Water Department
320 W. Monument Ave., Dayton, OH 45402
E-mail: waterweb@daytonohio.gov Fax: (937) 333-2833

Director (Acting) **Michael Powell** . . . . (937) 333-3735
Deputy Director (Acting) **Aaron Zonnin** . . . . (937) 333-3735
2800 Guthrie Rd., Dayton, OH 45418
Administration Manager **Pete Hannah** . . . . (937) 333-3728
E-mail: pete.hannah@daytonohio.gov
Environmental Manager **Michele Simmons** . . . . (937) 333-3796
Fax: (937) 333-2833
Wastewater Treatment Manager **Jason Tincu** . . . . (937) 333-1834
2800 Guthrie Rd., Dayton, OH 45418 Fax: (937) 333-5277
Water/Utility and Field Operations Manager
David Shade . . . . (937) 333-4904
Water Supply and Treatment Manager **Phil Van Atta** . . . . . (937) 333-6030
3210 Chuck Wagner Lane, Dayton, OH 45414 Fax: (937) 333-6025
Water Engineer Manager **Scott Holmes** . . . . (937) 333-3737
3210 Chuck Wagner Lane, Dayton, OH 45414

City of Denton, Texas

215 East McKinney Street, Denton, TX 76201
Tel: (940) 349-8307 Internet: www.cityofdenton.com/

County: Denton **Election Type:** Nonpartisan **Population:** 131,044 (2015)

Office of the Mayor and City Council
215 East McKinney Street, Denton, TX 76201

★ Mayor **Chris Watts** . . . . (940) 349-7717
Began Service: May 20, 2014
Term Expires: May 2018
Education: North Texas 1983 BS, 1992 MA; Texas Wesleyan U 2000 JD
★ Mayor Pro Tem **Kevin Roden** (District 1) . . . . (940) 349-7717
Term Expires: May 19, 2017
E-mail: kevin.roden@cityofdenton.com
Education: North Texas 1998 BA; Dallas 2007 MA

(continued on next page)

★ Elected Official ▲ Appointed by Legislature ▼ Appointed by Governor ▶ Appointed by Board or Commission ● Appointed by Judge
■ Appointed by Mayor △ Appointed by Freeholders ▽ Appointed by Supervisor ▷ Appointed by County Executive ○ Appointed by Council

Office of the Mayor and City Council *continued*

★Council Member **Keely Briggs** (District 2) . . . . (940) 349-7717
Term Expires: May 19, 2017
★Council Member **Kathleen Wazny** (District 3) . . . . (940) 349-7717
Term Expires: May 19, 2017 Fax: (940) 349-8596
★Council Member **Joey Hawkins** (District 4) . . . . (940) 349-7717
Term Expires: May 2017
★Council Member **Dalton Gregory** (At-Large) . . . . (940) 349-7717
Term Expires: May 2018
E-mail: dalton.gregory@cityofdenton.com
Education: Texas 1974 BS; Sam Houston State 1981 MEd
★Council Member **Sara Bagheri** (At-Large) . . . . (940) 349-7717
Term Expires: May 2018

Office of the City Attorney

215 East McKinney Street, Denton, TX 76201
Fax: (940) 382-7923

City Attorney **Anita Burgess** . . . . (940) 349-8333
E-mail: anita.burgess@cityofdenton.com

Office of the City Auditor

215 East McKinney Street, Denton, TX 76201
Fax: (940) 349-7923

City Auditor **(Vacant)** . . . . (940) 349-8996

Office of the City Manager

215 East McKinney Street, Denton, TX 76201
Fax: (940) 349-8596

City Manager **George C. Campbell** . . . . (940) 349-8307
E-mail: george.campbell@cityofdenton.com
Education: Texas Tech 1969 BA; Texas (Arlington) 1989 MA
Assistant to the City Manager **Jessica Rogers** . . . . (940) 349-8302
E-mail: Jessica.Rogers@cityofdenton.com
Assistant City Manager **John Cabrales** . . . . (940) 349-8509
E-mail: john.cabrales@cityofdenton.com
Assistant City Manager **Jon Fortune** . . . . (940) 349-8535
E-mail: jon.fortune@cityofdenton.com
Assistant City Manager **Bryan Langley** . . . . (940) 349-8224
E-mail: bryan.langley@cityofdenton.com
Assistant City Manager **Howard Martin** . . . . (940) 349-8232
E-mail: howard.martin@cityofdenton.com
Public Information and Intergovernmental Relations
Officer **Lindsey Baker** . . . . (940) 349-8234
E-mail: lindsey.baker@cityofdenton.com

Office of the City Secretary

215 East McKinney Street, Denton, TX 76201
Fax: (940) 349-8596

City Secretary **Jennifer Walters** . . . . (940) 349-8309
E-mail: jennifer.walters@cityofdenton.com
Assistant City Secretary **Jane Richardson** . . . . (940) 349-8304
E-mail: jane.richardson@cityofdenton.com

Denton Airport

5000 Airport Road, Denton, TX 76207

Director of Aviation **Quentin Hix** . . . . (940) 349-7744
Airport Operations Manager **Dave Schaumburg** . . . . (940) 349-7738

Economic Development Department

215 East McKinney Street, Denton, TX 76201

Director **Aimee Bissett** . . . . (940) 349-7774
E-mail: aimee.bissett@cityofdenton.com

Facilities Management Department

869 South Woodrow, Denton, TX 76205

Facilities Manager **Dean Hartley** . . . . (940) 349-7200
E-mail: dean.heatley@cityofdenton.com

Finance Department

215 East McKinney Street, Denton, TX 76201
Tel: (940) 349-8566

Assistant City Manager and Chief Financial Officer
Bryan Langley . . . . (940) 349-8224
Director of Finance **Chuck Springer** . . . . (940) 349-8260
Assistant Finance Director **Tony Puente** . . . . (940) 349-7283
E-mail: antonio.puente@cityofdenton.com
Budget Manager **Nancy Towle** . . . . (940) 349-7709
E-mail: nancy.towle@cityofdenton.com
Controller **Harvey Jarvis** . . . . (940) 349-8174
Purchasing Agent **Elton Brock** . . . . (940) 349-7100
901-B Texas Street, Denton, TX 76209
E-mail: elton.brock@cityofdenton.com

Fire Department

332 East Hickory, Denton, TX 76201

Fire Chief **Robin F. Paulsgrove** . . . . (940) 349-8840
E-mail: DentonFire@cityofdenton.com
Education: Western Illinois 1991 BA

Fleet Services Department

869 South Woodrow, Denton, TX 76205

Fleet Services Superintendent **Terry Kader** . . . . (940) 349-8429

Human Resources Department

601 East Hickory, Suite A, Denton, TX 76205
Fax: (940) 349-8384

Human Resources Director **Carla Romine-Haggmark** . . . . (940) 349-8344
E-mail: hr@cityofdenton.com
Risk Manager **Scott Payne** . . . . (940) 349-7836
E-mail: scott.payne@cityofdenton.com

Parks and Recreation Department

601 East Hickory, 2nd Floor, Denton, TX 76205
Fax: (940) 349-8384

Director **Emerson Vorel** . . . . (940) 349-7275

Department of Development Services

221 North Elm Street, Denton, TX 76201

Director **Aimee Bissett** . . . . (940) 349-8378
E-mail: aimee.bissett@cityofdenton.com
Deputy Director **Munal Mauladad** . . . . (940) 349-8541
E-mail: Munal.Mauladad@cityofdenton.com

Building Inspection Department

221 North Elm Street, Denton, TX 76201
Fax: (940) 349-7208

Building Official **Rodney Patterson** . . . . (940) 349-8360

Code Enforcement Division

601 East Hickory, Suite B, Denton, TX 76205

Manager **Lancine Bentley** . . . . (940) 349-7489

Community Development Division

601 East Hickory, Suite B, Denton, TX 76205

Coordinator **Luisa Rodriguez-Garcia** . . . . (940) 349-7238
E-mail: luisa.garcia@cityofdenton.com

Police Department

601 East Hickory, Denton, TX 76205

Chief of Police **Lee Howell** . . . . (940) 349-7923
Administrative Assistant **Susan Miller** . . . . (940) 349-7923
E-mail: susan.miller@cityofdenton.com

★Elected Official ▲Appointed by Legislature ▼Appointed by Governor ▶Appointed by Board or Commission ●Appointed by Judge
■Appointed by Mayor △Appointed by Freeholders ▽Appointed by Supervisor ▷Appointed by County Executive ○Appointed by Council

Denton Public Library
802 Oakland Street, Denton, TX 76201

Director of Libraries **Terri Gibbs** .... (940) 349-8750
E-mail: Terri.Gibbs@cityofdenton.com

Technology Services Department
601 East Hickory, Suite A, Denton, TX 76205

Director of Technology Services **Melissa Kraft** .... (940) 349-7823
E-mail: Melissa.Kraft@cityofdenton.com
Education: Troy U BS

Solid Waste Department
601 East Hickory, Suite F, Denton, TX 76205
Fax: (940) 349-7211

Manager **Vance Kemler** .... (940) 349-8700

Water Utilities Department
601 East Hickory, Denton, TX 76205

Manager **(Vacant)** .... (940) 349-8200

Denton Municipal Electric
601 East Hickory, Denton, TX 76205

General Manager **Phil Williams** .... (940) 349-8487

Denton Independent School District
1307 North Locust, Denton, TX 76201

Superintendent **Jamie Wilson** .... (940) 369-0030
Education: North Texas BA, MA, DEd

City and County of Denver, Colorado

City and County Building, 1437 Bannock Street, Denver, CO 80202
Tel: (720) 865-9000 (Information) TTY: (720) 865-9010
Internet: www.denvergov.org

County: Denver **Election Type:** Nonpartisan **Year Founded:** 1858 **Year Incorporated:** 1861 **Population:** 682,545 (2015) **Employees:** 10,985 **Fiscal Year:** 2016 **Budget:** $1,830,000,000

Note: City and County governments are combined

Office of the Mayor
City and County Bldg., 1437 Bannock St., Room 350, Denver, CO 80202
Tel: (720) 865-9000 Fax: (720) 865-8787

Employees: 14 **Fiscal Year:** 2016 **Budget:** $1,619,000

★ Mayor **Michael B. Hancock** .... (720) 913-1311
Began Service: July 18, 2011
Term Expires: July 2019
Scheduler/Executive Assistant **Rosalind Alston** .... (720) 865-9011
■ Chief of Staff **Janice Sinden** .... (720) 865-9102
Deputy Chief of Staff **Evan F. Dreyer** .... (720) 865-9015
Deputy Chief of Staff **Penny May** .... (720) 865-9015
Executive Director of Marijuana Policy **Ashley Kilroy** .. (720) 865-9022
■ Director of Sustainability Development
Jerome Tinianow .... (720) 865-9072
Deputy Director of Community Affairs **Michael Sapp** ... (720) 865-9024
Office Director **LaTonya Lacy** .... (720) 865-9025
Boards and Commissions Director **Anthony Aragon** ..... (720) 865-9032
Senior Advisor for Community Communications
Rowena Alegria .... (720) 865-9016
Education: Metro State Col Denver BA
Communications Manager **Michael Strott** .... (720) 865-9031
Director of Communications **Amber Miller** .... (720) 865-9095

Office of the Mayor *continued*

Senior Advisor for Policy and Legislation **Skye Stuart** ... (720) 865-9058
Director of Regional Affairs **Anthony E. Graves** .... (720) 865-9015
Education: DePauw BA; Denver MBA

Arts and Venues Denver
Fax: (720) 865-4315 Internet: www.denvergov.org/doca/

■ Executive Director **Kent Rice** .... (720) 865-4202
■ Deputy Director **Ginger White Brunetti** .... (720) 865-4314

Office of Economic Development [OED]
Wellington E. Webb Municipal Building, 201 West Colfax Avenue, 2nd Floor, Department 208, Denver, CO 80202
Tel: (720) 913-1999 Fax: (720) 913-1802

Employees: 39 **Fiscal Year:** 2016 **Budget:** $4,739,000

■ Director **Paul E. Washington** .... (720) 913-1612
E-mail: paul.washington@denvergov.org
■ Economic Development Deputy Director
John R. Lucero .... (720) 865-2953
■ Director of Small Business Opportunity **Chris Martinez** .. (720) 913-1612
E-mail: chris.martinez@denvergov.org
Chief Operating Officer **Amy Mueller Edinger** .... (720) 865-2953

Development Services
201 West Colfax Avenue, Department 203, Denver, CO 80202
Tel: (720) 865-2982 Fax: (720) 865-3020
E-mail: developmentservices@denvergov.org

■ Director **Steve Ferris** .... (720) 865-2913
E-mail: steve.ferris@denvergov.org
Education: Marquette BSCE; Cornell MA; Denver MBA

Office of Children's Affairs
201 West Colfax Avenue, Room 1101, Denver, CO 80202-5322
Fax: (720) 913-0928

Employees: 11 **Fiscal Year:** 2016 **Budget:** $2,601,000

Executive Director **Erin Brown** .... (720) 913-0900

Office of Employee Assistance
City and County Building, 1437 Bannock Street, 5th Floor, Denver, CO 80202
Fax: (720) 913-3205

Director **Christopher Weimer** .... (720) 913-3203
E-mail: christopher.weimer@denverda.org

Office of the Independent Monitor
201 West Colfax, Department 1201, Denver, CO 80202
Fax: (720) 913-3305

Independent Monitor **Nicholas Mitchell** .... (720) 913-3306

Office of the City Attorney
City and County Building, 1437 Bannock Street, Room 353, Denver, CO 80202-5375
Fax: (720) 865-8796

Employees: 211 **Fiscal Year:** 2016 **Budget:** $28,864,000

■ City Attorney (Interim) **Cristal DeHerrera** .... (720) 865-8600
Note: Effective June 1, 2016
Education: Boalt Hall 2006 JD
Deputy City Attorney **Cristal DeHerrera** .... (720) 865-8600
Education: Boalt Hall 2006 JD
Director of Administration **Nicole Holmlund** .... (720) 865-8750
Fax: (720) 913-3183
Airport Legal Services **Xavier DuRán** .... (303) 342-2540
Airport Office Building, 8500 Pena Boulevard, Room 9810, Denver, CO 80249-6340 Fax: (303) 342-2552
Human Services **Katie Smith** .... (720) 944-2978
1200 Federal Blvd., Denver, CO 80204 Fax: (720) 944-2979
Litigation Section Manager **Robert D. Nespor** .... (720) 913-3100
201 West Colfax Avenue, Denver, CO 80202 Fax: (720) 913-3190

(continued on next page)

★ Elected Official ▲ Appointed by Legislature ▼ Appointed by Governor ▶ Appointed by Board or Commission ● Appointed by Judge
■ Appointed by Mayor △ Appointed by Freeholders ▽ Appointed by Supervisor ▷ Appointed by County Executive ○ Appointed by Council

Office of the City Attorney *continued*

Litigation Section **Karla Pierce** . . . . . . (720) 913-3100
201 West Colfax Avenue, Fax: (720) 913-3190
Department 1108, Denver, CO 80202
Litigation Section **Wendy Shea** . . . . . . (720) 913-3100
201 West Colfax Avenue, Denver, CO 80202 Fax: (720) 913-3190
Municipal Operations **T. Shaun Sullivan** . . . . . . (720) 913-3261
201 West Colfax Avenue, Fax: (720) 913-3180
Department 1207, Denver, CO 80202-5332
Prosecution and Code Enforcement Section
Chad Sublet . . . . . . (720) 913-8067
201 West Colfax Avenue, Fax: (720) 913-8010
Department 1207, Denver, CO 80202-5332

Department of Aviation

Denver International Airport, 8500 Pena Boulevard,
Denver, CO 80249-6340
Fax: (303) 342-2215

■ Chief Executive Officer **Kim Day** . . . . . . (303) 342-2206 ext. 2206
E-mail: kim.day@flydenver.com
Education: Cornell 1977 BA

Denver International Airport

8500 Pena Boulevard, Denver, CO 80249-6340
Tel: (303) 342-2000 Fax: (303) 342-2215 Internet: www.flydenver.com

■ Chief Executive Officer **Kim Day** . . . . . . (303) 342-2206
E-mail: kim.day@flydenver.com
Education: Cornell 1977 BA
Chief of Staff **Eric Hiraga** . . . . . . (303) 342-2241
Chief Financial Officer/Executive Vice President of
Finance **Gisela Shanahan** . . . . . . (303) 342-2000
Education: Maryland BS; Nebraska MBA
Chief Operating Officer and Executive Vice President
Ken Greene . . . . . . (303) 342-2254
E-mail: ken.greene@flydenver.com
Chief Revenue Officer and Executive Vice President
Bhavesh A. Patel . . . . . . (303) 342-2497
Maintenance Senior Vice President **Dave LaPorte** . . . . . . (303) 342-2269
E-mail: dave.laporte@flydenver.com
Operations Senior Vice President **(Vacant)** . . . . . . (303) 342-4005
Technologies Senior Vice President **Robert Kastelitz** . . . . (303) 342-2020
E-mail: robert.kastelitz@flydenver.com
Global Communications Senior Vice President
Stacey Stegman . . . . . . (303) 342-2276
Fax: (303) 342-2266
Commercial Senior Vice President **(Vacant)** . . . . . . (303) 342-2000

Community Planning and Development [CPD]

Wellington E. Webb Municipal Office Bldg., 201 West Colfax Avenue,
Department 205, 2nd Floor, Denver, CO 80202
Fax: (720) 865-3050 Internet: www.denvergov.org/cpd

Employees: 214 **Fiscal Year:** 2016 **Budget:** $14,295,000

■ Executive Director **Brad Buchanan** . . . . . . (720) 865-2714
E-mail: brad.buchanan@denvergov.org
Deputy Director **Evelyn Baker** . . . . . . (720) 865-2714
E-mail: evelyn.baker@denvergov.org
Deputy Director **(Vacant)** . . . . . . (720) 865-2714
Deputy Director **Jill Jennings Golich** . . . . . . (720) 865-2714
E-mail: jill.jenningsgolich@denvergov.org
Marketing, Public and Employee Relations Coordinator
Andrea Bums . . . . . . (720) 865-2969
E-mail: andrea.burns@denvergov.org

Department of Environmental Health

200 West 14th Avenue, Denver, CO 80204
Fax: (720) 865-5530 Internet: www.denvergov.org/deh

Employees: 170 **Fiscal Year:** 2016 **Budget:** $49,774,000

■ Executive Director **Bob McDonald** . . . . . . (720) 865-5365
E-mail: bob.mcdonald@denvergov.org

Department of Excise and Licenses

201 West Colfax Avenue, Room 206, Denver, CO 80202-5322
Fax: (720) 865-2882

Employees: 22 **Fiscal Year:** 2016 **Budget:** $3,231,000

■ Director **Stacie Loucks** . . . . . . (720) 865-2740
E-mail: stacie.loucks@denvergov.org
Education: Lewis & Clark BA

Finance Department

201 West Colfax Avenue, Department 1010, Denver, CO 80202
Tel: (720) 913-5500 Fax: (720) 913-4103
Internet: www.denvergov.org/finance

Employees: 391 **Fiscal Year:** 2016 **Budget:** $74,908,000

■ Chief Financial Officer/Deputy Mayor **Brendan Hanlon** . . (720) 913-5500
Deputy Chief Financial Officer **Gretchen Hollrah** . . . . . . (720) 913-5500

Assessor's Office

201 West Colfax Avenue, Department 406, Denver, CO 80202
Fax: (720) 913-4101 E-mail: assessor@denvergov.org

Assessor **Keith Erffmeyer** . . . . . . (720) 913-4035
E-mail: keith.erffmeyer@denvergov.org
Deputy Assessor/Chief Appraiser **(Vacant)** . . . . . . (720) 913-4038

Budget and Management Office

201 West Colfax Avenue, Department 1010, Denver, CO 80202
Tel: (720) 913-5500 Fax: (720) 913-5599
Internet: www.denvergov.org/budget

Budget Director (Acting) **Stephanie Adams** . . . . . . (720) 913-5500
E-mail: Stephanie.Adams@denvergov.org

Controller's Office

201 West Colfax Avenue, Department 1109, Denver, CO 80202

City Controller **Beth Machann** . . . . . . (720) 913-5500

Motor Vehicle Division

4685 Peoria Street, Suite 101, Denver, CO 80239
Fax: (303) 376-2209

Director **Anthony "Tony" Frazzini** . . . . . . (303) 376-2200
Deputy Director **P.J. Taylor** . . . . . . (303) 376-2200

Real Estate Division

201 West Colfax Avenue, Department 904, Denver, CO 80202
Fax: (720) 865-7585

Director **Jeffrey J. Steinberg** . . . . . . (303) 865-7505

Risk Management Office

201 West Colfax Avenue, Department 1105, Denver, CO 80202

Director of Risk Management **Ray Sibley** . . . . . . (720) 913-3330
E-mail: raymond.sibley@denvergov.org

Treasury Division

201 West Colfax Avenue, Department 1009, Denver, CO 80202

Treasurer **Steve Ellington** . . . . . . (720) 913-9384

Department of General Services

Wellington E. Webb Municipal Office Building, 201 West Colfax Avenue,
Department 1110, Denver, CO 80202
Fax: (720) 865-7175 Internet: www.denvergov.org/General_Services

Employees: 143 **Fiscal Year:** 2016 **Budget:** $51,218,000

■ Manager **(Vacant)** . . . . . . (720) 865-7104
Senior Human Resources Specialist **Anne Carter** . . . . . . (720) 913-0757
E-mail: anne.carter@denvergov.org

Purchasing Division

Fax: (720) 913-8121

Director of Purchasing **John Utterback** . . . . . . (720) 913-8121
E-mail: john.utterback@denvergov.org

★ Elected Official ▲ Appointed by Legislature ▼ Appointed by Governor ▶ Appointed by Board or Commission ● Appointed by Judge
■ Appointed by Mayor △ Appointed by Freeholders ▽ Appointed by Supervisor ▷ Appointed by County Executive ○ Appointed by Council

Department of Human Services [DDHS]
1200 Federal Boulevard, Denver, CO 80204-3221
Fax: (720) 944-3019 Internet: www.denvergov.org/HumanServices

■ Manager **Donald J. "Don" Mares** .... (720) 944-3666
Education: Stanford 1979 BA; Pennsylvania 1982 JD
■ Chief Operating Officer **Jay Morein** .... (720) 944-3666
Deputy Manager **Andrea Albo** .... (720) 944-3666
Deputy Manager **Mitch McKee** .... (720) 944-3666
Deputy Manager **Jeff Holliday** .... (720) 944-3666

Parks and Recreation Department
Wellington E. Webb Municipal Office Building, 201 West Colfax Avenue, Department 601, Denver, CO 80202
Tel: (720) 913-0739 Fax: (720) 913-0784

Employees: 990 **Fiscal Year:** 2016 **Budget:** $106,536,000

■ Executive Director **Allegra "Happy" Haynes** .... (720) 913-0739
E-mail: allegra.haynes@denvergov.org
Education: Barnard 1975 BA; Colorado (Denver) MPP
Director of Marketing and Communications
Yolanda Quesada .... (720) 913-0633
E-mail: yolanda.quesada@denvergov.org
■ Deputy Manager of Parks **Scott Gilmore** .... (720) 913-0739
E-mail: scott.gilmore@denvergov.org
■ Deputy Manager of Recreation **John Martinez** .... (720) 913-0739
E-mail: john.martinez@denvergov.org

Public Health Department
605 Bannock Street, Denver, CO 80204
Fax: (303) 602-3676 Internet: http://denverhealth.org/

Employees: 37 **Fiscal Year:** 2016 **Budget:** $3,331,000

Director **Dr. William Berman** .... (303) 602-3683
Associate Director **Judith Shlay** .... (303) 602-3700
Director of Public Health Informatics
Arthur "Art" Davidson .... (303) 436-4000

Public Works Department
201 West Colfax Avenue, Department 608, Denver, CO 80202
Fax: (720) 865-8795 Internet: http://denvergov.org/publicworks

Employees: 849 **Fiscal Year:** 2016 **Budget:** $117,151,000

■ Executive Director of Public Works **Jose Cornejo** .... (720) 865-8630
City Engineer/Deputy Director **Lesley Thomas** .... (720) 865-8630
Chief Operating Officer/Deputy Director
George Delaney .... (720) 865-8630

Department of Safety
1331 Cherokee Street, Room 302, Denver, CO 80204
Fax: (720) 913-7028 Internet: www.denvergov.org/safety

Employees: 442 **Fiscal Year:** 2016 **Budget:** $4,511,000

■ Executive Director **Stephanie Y. O'Malley** .... (720) 913-6020
E-mail: stephanie.omalley@denvergov.org
Deputy Director **Christopher Lujan** .... (720) 913-6020
E-mail: christopher.lujan@denvergov.org
Deputy Director **Jess Vigil** .... (720) 913-6020
E-mail: jess.vigil@denvergov.org
Deputy Director **Laura Wachter** .... (720) 913-6020
E-mail: laura.wachter@ci.denver.co.us

Fire Department
745 West Colfax Avenue, Denver, CO 80204
Tel: (720) 913-3473 Internet: http://www.denvergov.org/dfd

Employees: 1,027 **Fiscal Year:** 2016 **Budget:** $128,032,000

■ Fire Chief **Eric Tade** .... (720) 913-3491
Fax: (720) 913-3597
Deputy Chief **Todd A. Bower** .... (720) 913-3445
E-mail: todd.bower@denvergov.org
Administration Division Chief **Desmond Fulton** .... (720) 913-3413
E-mail: desmond.fulton@denvergov.org Fax: (720) 913-3599

Fire Department *continued*

Denver International Airport/Division Chief
Angela R. Cook .... (303) 342-4345
Denver International Airport, Fax: (303) 342-4261
8525 Newcastle Street, Denver, CO 80249
E-mail: angela.cook@flydenver.com
Fire Prevention Division Chief **Joseph L. Gonzales** ..... (720) 913-3414
E-mail: joseph.gonzales@denvergov.org Fax: (720) 913-3587
Operations Division Chief **Charlie Drennan** .... (720) 913-3421
E-mail: charles.drennan@denvergov.org Fax: (720) 913-3595
Safety and Training Division Chief **Scott E. Heiss** ...... (720) 865-3952
Rocky Mountain Fire Academy, Fax: (720) 865-4176
5440 Roslyn Street, Denver, CO 80216
E-mail: scott.heiss@denvergov.org
Technical Services Division Chief **Steve Ellis** .... (720) 913-3446
Fax: (720) 915-3400

Police Department
Fax: (720) 913-7018 Internet: www.denvergov.org/police

Employees: 1,783 **Fiscal Year:** 2016 **Budget:** $211,875,000

■ Police Chief **Robert C. White** .... (720) 913-6527
E-mail: robert.white@denvergov.org
Administration Deputy Chief **Matt Murray** .... (720) 913-6016
E-mail: matthew.murray@denvergov.org
Operations Deputy Chief **David Quinones** .... (720) 913-6017
Chief of Staff **(Vacant)** .... (720) 913-6527

Denver Sheriff Department
201 West Colfax Avenue, Denver, CO 80202

Employees: 1,016 **Fiscal Year:** 2016 **Budget:** $131,959,000

■ Sheriff **Patrick Firman** .... (720) 337-0780
E-mail: patrick.firman@denvergov.org
Chief of Operations **Paul Oliva** .... (720) 337-0780
Chief of Administration **Connie Coyle** .... (720) 337-0780

Technology Services Department
201 West Colfax Avenue, Department 301, Denver, CO 80202
Tel: (720) 913-1311 Fax: (720) 913-5237 E-mail: 311@denvergov.org

Employees: 289 **Fiscal Year:** 2016 **Budget:** $55,942,000

Chief Information Officer **Scott Cardenas** .... (720) 913-1311
E-mail: scott.cardenas@denvergov.org
Deputy Chief Information Officer **Chris Binnicker** .... (720) 913-1311
E-mail: chris.binnicker@denvergov.org

Denver Public Library [DPL]
10 West 14 Avenue Parkway, Denver, CO 80204
Tel: (720) 865-1363 Internet: www.denverlibrary.org

Employees: 551 **Fiscal Year:** 2016 **Budget:** $43,191,000

Administration
City Librarian **Michelle Jeske** .... (720) 865-2105
E-mail: mjeske@denverlibrary.org
Executive Assistant **Rebecca Czarnecki** .... (720) 865-2100
E-mail: rczarnecki@denverlibrary.org
Education: Guilford Col 2005
Director, Administrative Services **Letty Icolari** .... (720) 865-2070
E-mail: licolari@denverlibrary.org
Director, Collections, Technology and Innovation
Zeth Lietzau .... (720) 865-2005
E-mail: zlietzau@denverlibrary.org
Director, Community Relations and Friends Foundation
Diane Lapierre .... (720) 865-2048
E-mail: dlapierr@denverlibrary.org
Director, Finance and Business Processes **Ron Miller** ..... (720) 865-2020
Director, Neighborhood Services **Susan Kotarba** .... (720) 865-2009
E-mail: skotarba@denverlibrary.org
Manager, Information Technology **Matt Hamilton** .... (720) 865-1363
E-mail: mhamilton@denverlibrary.org

★ Elected Official ▲ Appointed by Legislature ▼ Appointed by Governor ▶ Appointed by Board or Commission ● Appointed by Judge
■ Appointed by Mayor △ Appointed by Freeholders ▽ Appointed by Supervisor ▷ Appointed by County Executive ○ Appointed by Council

Denver Water

1600 West 12th Avenue, Denver, CO 80204-3412
Internet: www.denverwater.org

■ President **Penfield W. "Pen" Tate III** .... (303) 628-6500
Term Expires: July 10, 2017
E-mail: dbwc@denverwater.org
Education: Colorado State BA; Antioch Law JD

■ First Vice President **John R. Lucero** .... (303) 628-6500
Term Expires: July 10, 2021
E-mail: dbwc@denverwater.org

Vice President **H. Gregory Austin** .... (303) 628-6500
Term Expires: July 10, 2019

■ Vice President **Thomas A. "Tom" Gougeon** .... (303) 628-6500
Term Expires: July 10, 2017
E-mail: dbwc@denverwater.org
Education: Denver BS; Harvard 1980 MA

■ Vice President **Paula Herzmark** .... (303) 628-6500
Term Expires: July 10, 2019
E-mail: dbwc@denverwater.org
Education: Texas (El Paso) BA; Texas MPA

Chief Executive Officer/Manager
James S. "Jim" Lochhead .... (303) 628-6500
Education: Colorado 1974 BA, 1978 JD

Deputy Manager of Organizational Improvement
Brian B. Good .... (303) 628-6000

General Counsel **Patricia L. Wells** .... (303) 628-6000

Engineering Director **Robert J. Mahoney** .... (303) 628-6000
E-mail: robert.mahoney@denverwater.org

Finance Director **Angela Bricmont** .... (303) 628-6000

Human Resources Director **Gail Cagle** .... (303) 628-6000
E-mail: gail.cagle@denverwater.org

Information Technology Director **Chris Dermody** .... (303) 628-6000
E-mail: chris.dermody@denverwater.org

Operations and Maintenance Director
Thomas J. Roode .... (303) 628-6000
E-mail: tom.roode@denverwater.org

Planning Director **Mike King** .... (303) 628-6000
Education: Colorado 1989 BS; Denver 1992 JD; Colorado (Denver) 1998 MPA

Public Affairs Director **Sally C. Covington** .... (303) 628-6000
E-mail: sally.covington@denverwater.org

Customer Relations Director **Julie Anderson** .... (303) 628-6000

Intergovernmental Affairs Coordinator **Chris Piper** .... (303) 628-6000
E-mail: chris.piper@denverwater.org
Education: Colorado State 1995 BSCE

Mayor's Office of Emergency Management and Homeland Security [OEMHS]

City County Building, 1437 Bannock Street, Room 3, Denver, CO 80202
Tel: (720) 865-7600 Fax: (720) 865-7691
Internet: www.denvergov.org/oem

■ Director **Matt Buehler** .... (720) 865-7603
E-mail: matt.buehler@denvergov.org

Agency for Human Rights and Community Relations [HRCR]

201 West Colfax Avenue, Department 1102, Denver, CO 80202-5322
Tel: (720) 913-8450 TTY: (720) 913-8484 Fax: (720) 913-8470
Internet: www.denvergov.org/Home/tabid/430784/

Employees: 13 **Fiscal Year:** 2016 **Budget:** $1,914,000

Executive Director **Derek Okubo** .... (720) 913-8454
E-mail: derek.okubo@denvergov.org
Education: Northern Colorado 1982 BA

Agency for Human Rights and Community Partnerships
Deputy Director **Jamie Torres** .... (720) 913-8471
E-mail: jamie.torres@ci.denver.co.us

■ Office on Aging Director **Amanda Gregg** .... (720) 913-8477
E-mail: loretta.martinez@denverda.org

Denver Office of Disability Rights Director
Aisha Rousseau .... (720) 913-8485

Agency for Human Rights and Community Relations *continued*

Denver Anti-Discrimination Office Director
Darius Smith .... (720) 913-8459

Office on Women and Families Director
Kimberly Desmond .... (720) 913-8465

Board of Ethics

201 West Colfax Avenue, Department 703, Denver, CO 80202

○ Chair **Brian J. Spano** .... (720) 865-8412
Term Expires: April 30, 2017
Education: Michigan 1984 BA; Illinois 1987 JD

■ Vice Chair **Sylvia Smith** .... (720) 865-8412
Term Expires: June 24, 2017

■ Board Member **Andrew Armatas** .... (720) 865-8412
Term Expires: April 30, 2017

■ Board Member **Roy V. Wood** .... (720) 865-8412
Term Expires: April 20, 2019
Education: Denver BA, MA, PhD

○ Board Member **(Vacant)** .... (720) 865-8412
Term Expires: April 30, 2019

Executive Director **Michael Henry** .... (720) 865-8412

Office of the City Council

City and County Building, 1437 Bannock Street, Room 451, Denver, CO 80202
Tel: (720) 337-2000 E-mail: dencc@denvergov.org
Internet: www.denvergov.org/citycouncil

Employees: 44 **Fiscal Year:** 2016 **Budget:** $4,691,000

★ President **Christopher Herndon** (District 8) .... (720) 337-8888
Term Expires: July 15, 2019
E-mail: Christopher.Herndon@denvergov.org

★ President Pro Tem **Paul D. López** (District 3) .... (720) 337-3333
Term Expires: July 15, 2019 Fax: (720) 337-3337
E-mail: paul.lopez@denvergov.org

★ Council Member **Rafael Espinoza** (District 1) .... (720) 337-7701
Term Expires: July 15, 2019
E-mail: rafael.espinoza@denvergov.org

★ Council Member **Kevin Flynn** (District 2) .... (720) 337-2222
Term Expires: July 15, 2019
E-mail: kevin.flynn@denvergov.org

★ Council Member **Kendra Black** (District 4) .... (720) 337-4444
Term Expires: July 15, 2019
E-mail: kendra.black@denvergov.org

★ Council Member **Mary Beth Susman** (District 5) .... (720) 337-5555
Term Expires: July 15, 2019 Fax: (720) 337-5559
E-mail: marybeth.susman@denvergov.org

★ Council Member **Paul Kashmann** (District 6) .... (720) 337-6666
Term Expires: July 15, 2019 Fax: (720) 337-6661
E-mail: paul.kashmann@denvergov.org

★ Council Member **Jolon Clark** (District 7) .... (720) 337-7777
Term Expires: July 15, 2019 Fax: (720) 865-9540
E-mail: jolon.clark@denvergov.org

★ Council Member **Albus Brooks** (District 9) .... (720) 337-7709
Term Expires: July 15, 2019 Fax: (720) 337-9994
E-mail: albus.brooks@denvergov.org

★ Council Member **Wayne New** (District 10) .... (720) 337-7710
Term Expires: July 15, 2019 Fax: (720) 337-7717
E-mail: wayne.new@denvergov.org

★ Council Member **Stacie Gilmore** (District 11) .... (720) 337-7711
Term Expires: July 15, 2019
E-mail: stacie.gilmore@denvergov.org

★ Council Member **Robin Kniech** (At-Large) .... (720) 337-7712
Term Expires: July 15, 2019 Fax: (720) 337-7725
E-mail: robin.kniech@denvergov.org

★ Council Member
Deborah "Debbie" Ortega (At-Large) .... (720) 337-7713
Term Expires: July 15, 2019 Fax: (720) 337-7729
E-mail: deborah.ortega@denvergov.org

Staff Director **Janna B. Young** .... (720) 337-2001
E-mail: janna.young@denvergov.org

★ Elected Official ▲ Appointed by Legislature ▼ Appointed by Governor ► Appointed by Board or Commission ● Appointed by Judge
■ Appointed by Mayor △ Appointed by Freeholders ▽ Appointed by Supervisor ▷ Appointed by County Executive ○ Appointed by Council

Office of the City Council *continued*

Council Secretary **Kelly Velez** ....(720) 337-2002
E-mail: kelly.velez@denvergov.org

Civil Service Commission

201 West Colfax Avenue, 2nd Floor, Denver, CO 80202-5322
Fax: (720) 913-3373 Internet: www.denvergov.org/civilservice

Executive Director **Earl Peterson** ....(720) 913-3370
E-mail: earl.peterson@ci.denver.co.us
Education: SUNY (Geneseo) BS

Office of the Auditor

201 West Colfax Avenue, Department 705, Denver, CO 80202
Tel: (720) 913-5000 Fax: (720) 913-5253 E-mail: auditor@denvergov.org
Internet: www.denvergov.org/auditor

Employees: 52 **Fiscal Year:** 2016 **Budget:** $6,848,000

★ Auditor **Timothy O'Brien** ....(720) 913-5010
Term Expires: July 21, 2019
E-mail: auditor@denvergov.org

Agency Human Resources Director **Tammy Phillips** .....(720) 913-5006
E-mail: tammy.phillips@denvergov.org

Director of Audit Services **Kip Memmott** ....(720) 913-5027

Office of the Clerk and Recorder

201 West Colfax, Department 101, Denver, CO 80202
E-mail: clerkandrecorder@denvergov.org
Internet: www.denverclerkandrecorder.org

Employees: 30 **Fiscal Year:** 2016 **Budget:** $2,860,000

★ Clerk and Recorder **Debra Johnson** ....(720) 913-1311
Term Expires: July 2019
E-mail: clerkandrecorder@denvergov.org

Elections Division

200 West 14th Avenue, Denver, CO 80204
Tel: (720) 913-8683 TTY: (720) 913-8657 Fax: (720) 913-8600
Internet: www.denvervotes.org

Director **Amber McReynolds** ....(720) 913-8683

Denver District Attorney's Office

201 West Colfax Avenue, Department 801, Denver, CO 80202
Fax: (720) 913-9035 E-mail: info@denverda.org
Internet: www.denverda.org/

Employees: 192 **Fiscal Year:** 2016 **Budget:** $22,737,000

★ District Attorney **Mitchell R. Morrissey** ....(720) 913-9000
Term Expires: January 1, 2017
E-mail: mrm@denverda.org
Education: Colorado BA; Denver JD

Senior Chief Deputy District Attorney
James D. Jackson ....(720) 913-9000
E-mail: JDJ@DenverDA.org

Senior Chief Deputy District Attorney **S. Lamar Sims** ...(720) 913-9021

Chief Deputy District Attorney **Victoria A. Sharp** ....(720) 913-9000

Legal Administrator **Liza C. Willis** ....(720) 913-9021

Denver Board of Education

Emily Griffith Campus, 1860 Lincoln Street, Room 703B,
Denver, CO 80203
Fax: (720) 423-3216 E-mail: board@dpsk12.org
Internet: http://board.dpsk12.org/

★ President **Anne Rowe** (District 1) ....(720) 423-3210
Term Expires: November 30, 2019

★ Vice President **Barbara O'Brien** (At-Large) ....(720) 423-3210
Term Expires: November 30, 2017
Education: UCLA 1972 BA; Columbia 1981 PhD

Denver Board of Education *continued*

★ Secretary **Allegra "Happy" Haynes** (At-Large).........(720) 423-3210
Term Expires: November 30, 2019
Education: Barnard 1975 BA; Colorado (Denver) MPP

★ Treasurer **Mike Johnson** (District 3)...................(720) 423-3210
Term Expires: November 30, 2017

★ Board of Education Member **Lisa Flores** (District 5).....(720) 423-3210
Term Expires: November 30, 2019

★ Board of Education Member
Rosemary E. Rodriguez (District 2)...............(720) 423-3210
Term Expires: November 30, 2017

★ Board of Education Member
MiDian Homes (District 4).......................(720) 423-3210
Term Expires: November 30, 2017

Denver Public Schools

900 Grant Street, Suite 701, Denver, CO 80203-2907
Tel: (720) 423-3300 E-mail: email@dpsk12.org
Internet: www.facebook.com/DenverPublicSchools

► Superintendent of Schools **Tom Boasberg** ....(720) 423-3301
Note: On leave
E-mail: superintendent@dpsk12.org
Education: Yale 1986 BA; Stanford 1994 JD

► Superintendent of Schools (Acting) **Susana Cordova** ....(720) 423-3301
E-mail: susana_cordova@dpsk12.org

Safety and Security Director **Michael Eaton**..............(720) 423-3476
E-mail: michael_eaton@dpsk12.org

Chief Operating Officer **David Suppes** ....(720) 423-3222
E-mail: david_suppes@dpsk12.org

Chief Academic Officer **Susana Cordova** ....(720) 423-3414

Regional Transportation District [RTD]

1600 Blake Street, Denver, CO 80202

General Manager **David A. Genova**...................(303) 299-2673

City of Des Moines, Iowa

City Hall, 400 Robert D. Ray Drive, Des Moines, IA 50309
Tel: (515) 283-4500 (Information) Fax: (515) 237-1815
Internet: www.dmgov.org

County: Polk **Election Type:** Nonpartisan **Population:** 210,330 (2015)

Office of the Mayor and City Council

400 Robert D. Ray Drive, Des Moines, IA 50309
Fax: (515) 237-1645

★ Mayor **T.M. Franklin "Frank" Cownie**...............(515) 283-4944
Began Service: January 2002
Term Expires: January 1, 2020
E-mail: fcownie@dmgov.org

Administrative Assistant **Monica McCroskey** ....(515) 283-4944
E-mail: mjmccroskey@dmgov.org

★ Council Member **Bill Gray** (Ward 1) ....(515) 283-4944
Term Expires: January 1, 2018
E-mail: wsgray@dmgov.org

★ Council Member **Linda Westergaard** (Ward 2).........(515) 237-1624
Term Expires: January 1, 2020
E-mail: LindaW@dmgov.org

★ Council Member **Christine Hensley** (Ward 3) ....(515) 237-1625
Term Expires: January 1, 2018
E-mail: CLHensley@dmgov.org

★ Council Member **Joe Gatto** (Ward 4) ....(515) 237-1626
Term Expires: January 1, 2020
E-mail: jpgatto@dmgov.org

★ Council Member **Chris Coleman** (At-Large)............(515) 237-1622
Term Expires: January 1, 2020
E-mail: ccoleman@dmgov.org

(continued on next page)

★ Elected Official ▲ Appointed by Legislature ▼ Appointed by Governor ► Appointed by Board or Commission ● Appointed by Judge
■ Appointed by Mayor △ Appointed by Freeholders ▽ Appointed by Supervisor ▷ Appointed by County Executive ○ Appointed by Council

Office of the Mayor and City Council *continued*

★ Council Member **Skip Moore** (At-Large) . . . . (515) 237-1621
Term Expires: January 1, 2018
E-mail: lfmoore@dmgov.org

Office of the City Clerk

400 Robert D. Ray Drive, Des Moines, IA 50309
Fax: (515) 237-1645

○ City Clerk **Diane Rauh** . . . . (515) 283-4209
E-mail: dirauh@dmgov.org
Chief Deputy Clerk **Laura Baumgartner** . . . . (515) 283-4209
E-mail: llbaumgartner@dmgov.org

Legal Department

400 Robert D. Ray Drive, Des Moines, IA 50309
Fax: (515) 237-1643

○ City Attorney **Jeff Lester** . . . . (515) 283-4130
E-mail: jlester@dmgov.org
Infrastructure Deputy City Attorney
Kathleen Vanderpool . . . . (515) 283-4130
E-mail: kavanderpool@dmgov.org
Intergovernmental Deputy City Attorney
Lawrence McDowell . . . . (515) 283-4130
E-mail: lrmcdowell@dmgov.org
Litigations Deputy City Attorney **Carol Moser** . . . . (515) 237-1561
E-mail: cjmoser@dmgov.org Fax: (515) 237-1748

Office of the City Manager

400 Robert D. Ray Drive, Des Moines, IA 50309
Fax: (515) 237-1300 E-mail: citymanager@dmgov.org

○ City Manager **Scott Sanders** . . . . (515) 283-4141
E-mail: citymanager@dmgov.org
Education: Iowa State BS, MRP

Office of Economic Development

400 Robert D. Ray Drive, Des Moines, IA 50309
Tel: (515) 283-4004 Fax: (515) 237-1667 Internet: http://www.dmoed.org
E-mail: oed@dmgov.org

Economic Development Coordinator **Carrie Kruse** . . . . (515) 283-4012
E-mail: cakruse@dmgov.org
Economic Development Project Manager **Ryan Moffatt** . . (515) 238-4013
E-mail: rlmoffatt@dmgov.org
Economic Development Coordinator **Terry Vorbrich** . . . . . (515) 237-1375
E-mail: tnvorbrich@dmgov.org

Aviation Department

5800 Fleur Dr., Des Moines, IA 50321
Fax: (515) 256-5025 E-mail: dsmairport@dsmairport.com
Internet: http://www.dsmairport.com/

Director **Kevin Foley** . . . . (515) 256-5100
Director of Engineering **Bryan Belt** . . . . (515) 256-5100
E-mail: bbelt@dmgov.org
Director of Finance **Brian Mulcahy** . . . . (515) 256-5100
Deputy Director of Operations **A.J. Graff** . . . . (515) 256-5100
E-mail: ajgraff@dmgov.org
Airport Contract Manager **Steve Dawson** . . . . (515) 256-5100
Airport Facilities Superintendent **Alan Whitlatch** . . . . (515) 256-5100
E-mail: awwhitlatch@dsmairport.com

Civil and Human Rights Commission

602 Robert D. Ray Drive, Des Moines, IA 50309
Tel: (515) 283-4284 Fax: (515) 237-1408

Director **Joshua Barr** . . . . (515) 237-1457

Community Development Department

602 Robert D. Ray Drive, Des Moines, IA 50309
Fax: (515) 283-4270

Director **Phil Delafield** . . . . (515) 283-4182
E-mail: pmdelafield@dmgov.org
Chief Building Inspector **Cody Christensen** . . . . (515) 283-4200

Engineering Department

400 Robert D. Ray Drive, Des Moines, IA 50309
Tel: (515) 283-4920 Fax: (515) 283-4112

City Engineer **Pamela S. Cooksey** . . . . (515) 283-4920
E-mail: pcooksey@dmgov.org

Finance Department

400 Robert D. Ray Drive, Des Moines, IA 50309
Tel: (515) 283-4921 Fax: (515) 237-1670

Director **Dan Ritter** . . . . (515) 283-4854
Procurement Administrator **Mike Valen** . . . . (515) 283-4228
E-mail: mlvalen@dmgov.org Fax: (515) 237-1668

Fire Department

900 Mulberry St., Des Moines, IA 50309
Tel: (515) 283-4237 Fax: (515) 283-4907

Fire Chief **John TeKippe** . . . . (515) 283-4237
E-mail: jftekippe@dmgov.org

Housing Services Department

100 East Euclid, Suite 101, Des Moines, IA 50313
Tel: (515) 323-8950 Fax: (515) 242-2844

Director (Acting) **Jackie Lloyd** . . . . (515) 323-8981

Human Resources

400 Robert D. Ray Drive, Des Moines, IA 50309
Tel: (515) 283-4213 Fax: (515) 237-1680

Director **James Wells** . . . . (515) 283-4213
E-mail: jrwells@dmgov.org

Information Technology Department

602 Robert D. Ray Drive, Des Moines, IA 50309
Tel: (515) 283-4060 Fax: (515) 237-1775

Chief Information Officer **John Newman** . . . . (515) 283-4700
E-mail: jrnewman@dmgov.org
Webmaster **Jasmin Zulic** . . . . (515) 283-4739
E-mail: jzulic@dmgov.org

Park and Recreation Department

1551 East Martin Luther King Jr. Parkway, Des Moines, IA 50317
Fax: (515) 237-1407

Director **Ben Page** . . . . (515) 237-1386

Police Department

25 E. First St., Des Moines, IA 50309
Tel: (515) 283-4800 Fax: (515) 237-1665

Police Chief **Dana Wingert** . . . . (515) 283-4800

Public Information Office

400 Robert D. Ray Drive, Des Moines, IA 50309
Fax: (515) 237-1815

Communications Specialist (Acting) **Shekinah Young** . . . . (515) 283-4057
E-mail: SMYoung@dmgov.org

Public Library
1000 Grand Avenue, Des Moines, IA 50309
Tel: (515) 283-4152 Fax: (515) 237-1654 E-mail: reference@dmpl.org
Internet: www.dmpl.org

Director **Greg Heid** ....(515) 283-4288
E-mail: GGHeid@dmgov.org

Public Works Department
216 SE Fifth St., Des Moines, IA 50309
Fax: (515) 237-1655

Director **Jonathan Gano** ....(515) 237-1425
Education: West Point BSCE; Missouri Science and Tech MSE

Des Moines Public Schools
2323 Grand Avenue, Des Moines, IA 50312
Tel: (515) 242-7911 Internet: www.dmschools.org/

Superintendent of Schools **Thomas Ahart** ....(515) 242-7766
Fax: (515) 242-7679
Chief Financial Officer **Thomas Harper** ....(515) 242-7745
Fax: (515) 242-8295

School Board
Fax: (515) 242-7679 Internet: www.dmschools.org/board/

★Chair **Rob X. Barron** ....(515) 242-7713
Term Expires: September 2017
E-mail: rxbarron@gmail.com
★Vice Chair **Teree Caldwell-Johnson** ....(515) 242-7713
Term Expires: September 2017
E-mail: teree.caldwell-johnson@dmschools.org
Education: Spelman 1978 BA; Kansas MPA
★Member **Heather Anderson** ....(515) 242-7713
Term Expires: September 2019
E-mail: heather.anderson@dmschools.org
★Member **Connie Boesen** ....(515) 242-7713
Term Expires: September 2017
E-mail: connie.boesen@dmschools.org
★Member **Cindy Elsbernd** ....(515) 242-7713
Term Expires: September 2019
E-mail: cindy.elsbernd@dmschools.org
★Member **Dionna Langford** ....(515) 242-7713
Term Expires: September 2017
★Member **Natasha Newcomb** ....(515) 242-7713
Term Expires: September 2019

City of Detroit, Michigan
Coleman A. Young Municipal Center, 2 Woodward Ave.,
Detroit, MI 48226
Tel: (313) 224-3400 (Information) Internet: www.detroitmi.gov

County: Wayne **Election Type:** Nonpartisan **Population:** 677,116 (2015)

Office of the Mayor
Coleman A. Young Municipal Center, 2 Woodward Ave., Suite 1126,
Detroit, MI 48226
Tel: (313) 224-3400 Fax: (313) 224-4433

★Mayor **Michael E. "Mike" Duggan** ....(313) 224-3400
Began Service: January 1, 2014
Term Expires: December 31, 2017
Education: Michigan JD
Chief of Staff **Alexis Wiley** ....(313) 224-4451
Deputy Chief of Staff **David P. Massaron** ....(313) 224-3400
Deputy Mayor **Isaiah "Ike" McKinnon** ....(313) 224-3400

Office of the Mayor *continued*

Deputy Mayor for Economic Policy, Planning and Strategy **Carol O'Cleireacain** ....(313) 224-3153
E-mail: caroloc@detroitmi.gov
Education: Michigan 1968 BA, 1970 MA;
London School Econ (UK) 1977 PhD
Chief Talent Officer **Bryan Barnhill** ....(313) 224-3400
Group Executive, Department of Neighborhoods
Charles Beckham ....(313) 224-3400
Group Executive for Jobs and Economic Growth
F. Thomas Lewand ....(313) 224-3400
E-mail: lewandt@detroitmi.gov
Education: Detroit 1968 BA; Wayne State U 1970 JD
Group Executive for Operations **Dave Manardo** ....(313) 224-3400
Education: Wayne State Col BSME, MSCE; Detroit MBA
Director of Government Affairs **Lisa Howze** ....(313) 224-3400
Director of Communications **John M. Roach** ....(313) 224-3400
Deputy Communications Director **Dan Austin** ....(313) 224-3400
Executive Assistant and Director of Lean Process Management **Aimee Cowher** ....(313) 224-3400
Director of Youth Services **Shawn Blanchard** ....(313) 224-3400

Airport Department
Coleman A. Young International Airport, 11499 Conner Avenue,
Detroit, MI 48213-1283

Director **Jason Watt** ....(313) 628-2141
Operations Manager **Gregory Williams** ....(313) 628-2145
E-mail: williamsg@detroitmi.gov

Budget Department
Coleman A. Young Municipal Center, Two Woodward Avenue,
Room 1106, Detroit, MI 48226
Tel: (313) 224-6260 Fax: (313) 224-2827

■Chief Financial Officer **Tanya Stoudemire** ....(313) 628-0972
E-mail: scalesp@detroitmi.gov
■Deputy Director **Tina Tolliver** ....(313) 224-3381

Buildings, Safety Engineering and Environmental Department [BSEE]
Coleman A. Young Municipal Center, Two Woodward Avenue, Suite 401,
Detroit, MI 48226
Tel: (313) 224-2733 (Information) Fax: (313) 224-1467

■Director (Interim) **David Bell** ....(313) 224-3252
E-mail: belld@detroitmi.gov
■Deputy Director **(Vacant)** ....(313) 224-3258
Executive Secretary III **Lillian Ortiz** ....(313) 224-3258
E-mail: ortizl@detroitmi.gov
General Manager **Andrew Anyanwu** ....(313) 224-3254
E-mail: anyanwua@detroitmi.gov
General Manager **Raymond Scott** ....(313) 471-5108
General Manager **James Foster** ....(313) 224-7311
Executive Secretary II **Yvette Willis** ....(313) 224-3252
E-mail: willisy@detroitmi.gov

Finance Department
Coleman A. Young Municipal Center, Two Woodward Avenue, Suite 1200,
Detroit, MI 48226-3440
Fax: (313) 224-4466

■Chief Financial Officer **John W. Hill, Jr.** ....(313) 224-3400
E-mail: hillj@detroitmi.gov
Education: Maryland BSAcc
Finance Director **John Naglick** ....(313) 224-3419
Executive Secretary **(Vacant)** ....(313) 224-3491
■Deputy Director **Michael Jamison** ....(313) 224-3821
E-mail: jamisonm@detroitmi.gov

Accounts Division
■Accounting Manager **Eric Higgs** Room 801 ....(313) 224-6957
E-mail: higgse@detroitmi.gov

★Elected Official ▲Appointed by Legislature ▼Appointed by Governor ►Appointed by Board or Commission ●Appointed by Judge
■Appointed by Mayor △Appointed by Freeholders ▽Appointed by Supervisor ▷Appointed by County Executive ○Appointed by Council

Assessors Division
Tel: (313) 224-3011 Fax: (313) 224-9400

■ Chief Assessor **Gary L. Evanko** Room 804 .... (313) 224-3011
E-mail: evankog@detroitmi.gov

■ Assessor **Alvin Horhn** Room 804 .... (313) 224-3010
E-mail: horhna@detroitmi.gov

Debt Management
Manager II **Donita Crumpler** Room 1210 .... (313) 224-3310
E-mail: crumplerd@detroitmi.gov Fax: (313) 224-5506

Pension Division
One Detroit Center, 500 Woodward Avenue, Suite 3000, Detroit, MI 48226
Tel: (313) 224-3362 Fax: (313) 224-9194

Manager II **Cynthia Thomas** .... (313) 224-3362
Two Woodward Avenue, Room 908, Detroit, MI 48226
E-mail: thomasc@detroitmi.gov

Income Tax Division
Tel: (313) 224-3315

Manager **(Vacant)** Room 1212 .... (313) 224-3315

Purchasing Division
Tel: (313) 224-4600 Fax: (313) 224-4374

Chief Procurement Officer **Boysie Jackson** Room 1008 .. (313) 224-4619
E-mail: jacksonb@detroitmi.gov

Risk Management
Tel: (313) 224-2282 Fax: (313) 224-4247

Executive Manager **Donald Settles** Room 611 .... (313) 224-2282
E-mail: settlesd@detroitmi.gov

Treasury Division
Tel: (313) 224-3540 Fax: (313) 224-3541

■ Treasurer (Interim) **John Naglick** Room 1010 .... (313) 224-4153
E-mail: naglickj@detroitmi.gov

Fire Department
1301 Third Street, Detroit, MI 48226
Tel: (313) 596-2900 Fax: (313) 596-2888

■ Executive Fire Commissioner **Eric Jones** .... (313) 596-2901
E-mail: jonese@detroitmi.gov

Deputy Fire Commissioner **John Berlin** .... (313) 596-2903
E-mail: berlinj@detroitmi.gov

Chief of Fire Operations **John King** .... (313) 596-2921
E-mail: kingj@detroitmi.gov

Fire Marshal **Robin Eagan** .... (313) 237-2656
E-mail: eaganr@detroitmi.gov

EMS Superintendent **Sean Larkins** .... (313) 596-5188
E-mail: larkinss@detroitmi.gov

Community Relations Coordinator **Chief Dale Bradley** ... (313) 596-2959
E-mail: communityrelations@detroitmi.gov

General Services Department
18100 Meyers Road, Detroit, MI 48235

Director **Bradley Dick** .... (313) 628-0900
E-mail: dickb@detroitmi.gov

Department of Health and Wellness Promotion
1600 West Lafayette, Suite 200, Detroit, MI 48216
Tel: (313) 876-4000 Fax: (313) 876-0906

■ Director and Public Health Officer **Dr. Abdul El-Sayed** ... (313) 876-4300
Fax: (313) 876-0906

■ Deputy Director **Leseliey Welch** .... (313) 876-4228
Fax: (313) 876-0906

Head Accountant **Joseph Mutebi** .... (313) 876-4347
E-mail: mutebij@detroitmi.gov Fax: (313) 876-0309

Human Resources Department
Coleman A. Young Municipal Center, Two Woodward Avenue, Suites 314 & 316, Detroit, MI 48226
Tel: (313) 224-3700 Tel: (313) 224-3723 (Job Information Hotline)
Tel: (800) 367-5690 (Employment Verification) Fax: (313) 224-5609

■ Director **Denise Starr** 316 Coleman A. Young Municipal Center .... (313) 224-3710
E-mail: starrd@detroitmi.gov

Deputy Director/Chief Employee Services Officer **Ursula Holland** 316 Coleman A. Young Municipal Center .... (313) 224-3710
E-mail: hollandu@detroitmi.gov

Labor Relations Division/Benefits Division
Fax: (313) 224-0738

■ Director/Chief Labor Relations Officer **Michael A. Hall** 322 Coleman A. Young Municipal Center .... (313) 224-2395
E-mail: mahall@detroitmi.gov

Deputy Director **Valerie A. Colbert-Osamuede** 322 Coleman A. Yong Municipal Center .... (313) 224-2395

Human Rights Department
Coleman A. Young Municipal Center, Two Woodward Avenue, Room 1240, Detroit, MI 48226
Tel: (313) 224-4950 Tel: (313) 224-4950 (Information Complaints)
Fax: (313) 224-3434 TTY: (313) 224-4960

■ Director **Portia L. Roberson** .... (313) 224-9507
E-mail: robersonp@detroitmi.gov

Business Specialist **Tashawna Parker** .... (313) 224-9505
E-mail: parkert@detroitmi.gov

Department of International and Immigrant Affairs
Two Woodward Avenue, Detroit, MI 48226

■ Director of Immigrant Affairs **Fayrouz Saad** .... (313) 224-3400
Education: Michigan BA; JFK School Govt MPA

Department of Innovation and Technology
Coleman A. Young Municipal Center, Two Woodward Avenue, Room 1212, Detroit, MI 48226
Tel: (313) 224-2900 Fax: (313) 224-2158

Chief Information Officer **Beth Niblock** .... (313) 224-3400

■ Director **Charles Dodd** .... (313) 224-2900
E-mail: cdodd@detroitmi.gov

Communications and Creative Services Division [CCSD]
Coleman A. Young Municipal Center, Two Woodward Avenue, Suite 526, Detroit, MI 48226
Tel: (313) 224-3757

Supervising Publicist **Rose Love** .... (313) 224-3757
E-mail: lover@detroitmi.gov

Law Department
1650 First National Bldg., 660 Woodward Ave., Detroit, MI 48226
Tel: (313) 224-4550 Fax: (313) 224-5505

■ Corporation Counsel **Melvin Butch Hollowell** .... (313) 237-3018
E-mail: hollowellm@detroitmi.gov

Deputy Corporation Counsel **Charles N. Raimi** .... (313) 224-4550

Municipal Parking Department [MPD]
1600 West Lafayette, Detroit, MI 48216
Tel: (313) 221-2500 Fax: (313) 224-5505

■ Director **Norman L. White** .... (313) 221-2516

■ Deputy Director **Keith Hutchings** .... (313) 221-2516

★ Elected Official ▲ Appointed by Legislature ▼ Appointed by Governor ► Appointed by Board or Commission ● Appointed by Judge
■ Appointed by Mayor △ Appointed by Freeholders ▽ Appointed by Supervisor ▷ Appointed by County Executive ○ Appointed by Council

Planning and Development Department

65 Cadillac Square, Room 2300, Detroit, MI 48226
Tel: (313) 224-6380 Fax: (313) 224-1629

■ Planning and Development Director **Maurice Cox** (313) 224-1421
Executive Secretary III **Karen Beaver** (313) 224-4509
E-mail: beaverk@detroitmi.gov

Housing Services Division

65 Cadillac Square, Suite 1900, Detroit, MI 48226

Manager **Arthur Jemison** (313) 224-6525
Fax: (313) 224-9149

Neighborhood Support Services Division

65 Cadillac Square, Suite 1400, Detroit, MI 48226
Fax: (313) 224-2321

Executive Manager **Chidi Nyeche** (313) 224-9974
E-mail: cnyeche@detroitmi.gov

Planning Division

65 Cadillac Square, Suite 1300, Detroit, MI 48226
Tel: (313) 224-1339 Fax: (313) 224-1310

Director **Maurice Cox** (313) 224-1421

Police Department [DPD]

1300 Beaubien, Detroit, MI 48226
1301 Third Street, Detroit, MI 48226
Tel: (313) 596-1800

■ Chief of Police **James E. Craig** (313) 596-1800
E-mail: craigj@detroitmi.gov Fax: (313) 596-6818
Office of Public Information **Sgt Michael Woody** (313) 596-2200
Director of Police Personnel **Gail A. Oxendine**
Suite 659 (313) 596-2730
E-mail: oxendineg@detroitmi.gov Fax: (313) 596-2686
First Assistant Chief **Lt. Lashinda T. Stair** (313) 596-1803
Education: Wayne State U BA Fax: (313) 596-6818
Assistant Chief **James White** (313) 596-2750

Detroit Police Athletic League [PAL]

111 W. Willis, Detroit, MI 48201
Tel: (313) 833-1600 Fax: (313) 833-1616 Internet: www.detroitpal.org

Chief Executive Officer **Tim Richey** (313) 833-1600

Public Lighting Authority of Detroit

65 Cadillac Square, Suite 3100, Detroit, MI 48226

Chief Executive Officer **Nicolette Carlone** (313) 324-8290

Department of Public Works

Coleman A. Young Municipal Center, Two Woodward Avenue, Room 802, Detroit, MI 48226
Fax: (313) 224-1464

■ Director **Ron Brundidge** (313) 224-3901
Executive Secretary **Pam Parker** (313) 224-3901
■ Deputy Director **Jose Abraham** (313) 224-3901

City Engineering Division

Coleman A. Young Municipal Center, Two Woodward Avenue, Suite 601, Detroit, MI 48226-3462
Fax: (313) 224-3471

■ City Engineer **Richard Doherty** (313) 224-3955
E-mail: dohertyri@detroitmi.gov
Head Engineer **Jessy Jacob** (313) 224-3953
E-mail: jacobj@detroitmi.gov
Administrative Assistant **Adrienne D. Smith** (313) 224-3950
E-mail: adrienns1@detroitmi.gov
Field Engineer **Amir Masood** (313) 224-3925
E-mail: masooda@detroitmi.gov
Permit Center **Michael Twyman** (313) 224-3935
Streets Engineering Bureau **Gregory Mayhew** (313) 224-3964
E-mail: mayhewg@detroitmi.gov

City Engineering Division *continued*

Maps and Records Bureau **Keith McCrary** (313) 224-3970

Recreation Department

18100 Meyers Road, Detroit, MI 48235
Tel: (313) 224-1100 Fax: (313) 224-1734

■ Director **Alicia C. Bradford** (313) 224-1123
E-mail: bradforda@detroitmi.gov Fax: (313) 224-1860
Administration Support Supervisor **Jescelia Reddick** (313) 224-1159
E-mail: reddickj@detroitmi.gov Fax: (313) 224-3544
Northwest District Manager/Aquatics **Mike Williams** (313) 628-0942

Butzel Family Center

7737 Kercheval Avenue, Detroit, MI 48214
Fax: (313) 628-1121

Executive Director **Cecilia Walker** (313) 628-2103
Deputy Director, Detroit Recreation Department
(Vacant) (313) 628-2100

Detroit Department of Transportation [DDOT]

1301 E. Warren Ave., Detroit, MI 48207
Tel: (313) 933-1300 Fax: (313) 833-5523

■ Director **Dan Dirks** (313) 833-7670
E-mail: dandirks@detroitmi.gov
Executive Secretary III **Jamie Ringo** (313) 833-7670
E-mail: ringoj@detroitmi.gov
Deputy Director **Paul Toliver** (313) 833-7671
General Manager of Vehicle Maintenance **Larry Luckett** (313) 833-7676
General Manager of Administration **(Vacant)** (313) 833-7365
General Manager of Operations **Kim Jones** (313) 833-6432
Marketing Manager **SuVon Treece** (313) 833-7292
Human Resources Manager II **(Vacant)** (313) 833-7202
Inventory Control and Warehousing Manager
Duane Yuille (313) 833-9776
Management Information Systems Manager
Michelle McNutt (313) 833-4700
Purchasing/Contract Manager **Don Bryant** (313) 833-7715
Quality Assurance/Research Manager **(Vacant)** (313) 833-9711
Scheduling Manager **Neil Greenberg** (313) 833-7634
Security Administrator **Sidney Bogan** (313) 833-1477
Plant Maintenance and Construction Manager
Warren Emerson (313) 833-3000
E-mail: emersonw@detroitmi.gov

Water and Sewerage Department

Water Board Bldg., 735 Randolph St., Detroit, MI 48226
Tel: (313) 224-4800 Fax: (313) 224-6067

■ Director **Gary Brown** (313) 224-4701
Executive Assistant **Renee Baker** (313) 224-4702
E-mail: rbaker@dwsd.org
■ Deputy Director/Chief Customer Service Officer
Darryl A. Latimer (313) 224-4784
■ Deputy Director/Chief Engineer **Palencia Mobley** (313) 224-4800
Executive Assistant **Mellyn Pierce** (313) 224-4785
Wastewater Director **(Vacant)** (313) 297-4300
Fax: (313) 297-0110
Field Services Director **Keyonna Jackson** (313) 267-1215
Fax: (313) 267-6284
Public Affairs Officer **Linda Clark** (313) 237-7302
Fax: (313) 964-9370
Financial Services Chief Financial Officer
Marcus Hudson (313) 964-9220
Fax: (313) 964-9270
Director, Information Technology **Dan Rainey** (313) 964-9390
E-mail: rainey@dwsd.org Fax: (313) 224-6067
Industrial Waste Control **Stephen Kuplicki** (313) 297-5804
Fax: (313) 297-5805
Chief Operating Officer **Robert Presnell** (313) 926-8135
Fax: (313) 926-8120
Chief Planning Officer **(Vacant)** (313) 224-4800

★ Elected Official ▲ Appointed by Legislature ▼ Appointed by Governor ▶ Appointed by Board or Commission ● Appointed by Judge
■ Appointed by Mayor △ Appointed by Freeholders ▽ Appointed by Supervisor ▷ Appointed by County Executive ○ Appointed by Council

Detroit Building Authority [DBA]
1301 Third Street, Suite 328, Detroit, MI 48226
Fax: (313) 224-4998

■ Director **Dave Manardo** .... (313) 224-7242
Education: Wayne State Col BSME, MSCE; Detroit MBA

Detroit Historical Society
Detroit Historical Museum, 5401 Woodward Ave., Detroit, MI 48202
Tel: (313) 833-7935 Fax: (313) 833-5342
Internet: www.detroithistorical.org

Executive Director and Chief Executive Officer
Robert "Bob" Bury .... (313) 833-5767
Managing Director **Kate Baker** .... (313) 833-1627
E-mail: kateb@detroithistorical.org
Education: Smith BA
Executive Secretary **Rita Taub** .... (313) 833-1800
E-mail: ritat@detroithistorical.org
Director of Marketing and Sales **Robert "Bob" Sadler** ... (313) 833-7937
E-mail: bobsadler@detroithistorical.org

Dossin Great Lakes Museum
100 Strand Dr., Belle Isle, Detroit, MI 48207
Tel: (313) 821-2661

Curator **Joel Stone** .... (313) 297-8366
Curator of Collections **Adam Lovell** .... (313) 297-8391

Historic Fort Wayne
6325 W. Jefferson, Detroit, MI 48209
Fax: (313) 297-8361

Curator of Collections **Adam Lovell** .... (313) 297-8391

Detroit-Wayne Joint Building Authority
Coleman A. Young Municipal Center, Two Woodward Avenue, Suite 1316, Detroit, MI 48226
Fax: (313) 309-2400

Executive Director **Gregory McDuffee** .... (313) 309-2300
E-mail: gregory_mcduffee@dwjba.com
Assistant General Manager **(Vacant)** .... (313) 309-2300

Office of the City Council
Coleman A. Young Municipal Center, Two Woodward Avenue, Suite 1340, Detroit, MI 48226
Tel: (313) 224-3443

★ President **Brenda Jones** Room 1340 .... (313) 224-1245
Term Expires: December 31, 2017 Fax: (313) 224-4095
E-mail: bjones_mb@detroitmi.gov
★ President Pro Tem **George Cushingberry, Jr.** .... (313) 224-4535
Term Expires: December 31, 2017 Fax: (313) 224-1524
E-mail: cushingberryg@detroitmi.gov
★ Council Member **Janeé L. Ayers** .... (313) 224-4248
Term Expires: December 31, 2017 Fax: (313) 224-1524
★ Council Member **Scott Benson** .... (313) 224-1198
Term Expires: December 31, 2017 Fax: (313) 224-1684
E-mail: BensonS@detroitmi.gov
★ Council Member **Raquel Castañeda-López** .... (313) 224-2450
Term Expires: December 31, 2017 Fax: (313) 224-1189
E-mail: councilmemberraquel@detroitmi.gov
★ Council Member **Gabe Leland** .... (313) 224-2151
Term Expires: December 31, 2017 Fax: (313) 224-2155
E-mail: LelandG@detroitmi.gov
★ Council Member **Mary Sheffield** .... (313) 224-4505
Term Expires: December 31, 2017 Fax: (313) 224-0367
E-mail: CouncilMemberSheffield@detroitmi.gov
★ Council Member **Andre L. Spivey** .... (313) 224-4841
Term Expires: December 31, 2017 Fax: (313) 224-0369
E-mail: councilmanspivey@detroitmi.gov
★ Council Member **James Tate** .... (313) 224-1027
Term Expires: December 31, 2017 Fax: (313) 224-0372
E-mail: councilmembertate@detroitmi.gov

Office of the Auditor General
Coleman A. Young Municipal Center, Two Woodward Avenue, Room 216, Detroit, MI 48226
Tel: (313) 224-3101 Fax: (313) 224-4091

○ Auditor General **Mark W. Lockridge** .... (313) 224-3101
E-mail: markl@detroitmi.gov
Executive Secretary **Cheryl McRoy** .... (313) 224-3101
E-mail: mcroyc@detroitmi.gov
Deputy Auditor General **Jeffrey Vedua** .... (313) 224-3101

Office of the Ombudsman
Coleman A. Young Municipal Center, Two Woodward Avenue, Room 114, Detroit, MI 48226
Fax: (313) 224-1911

○ Ombudsman **Bruce Simpson** .... (313) 224-6000

Board of Zoning Appeals
Coleman A. Young Municipal Center, Two Woodward Avenue, Room 212, Detroit, MI 48226
Fax: (313) 224-4597

Director **James Ribbron** .... (313) 224-3595
Appeals Specialist **Lyall Hoggatt** .... (313) 224-3595
Zoning Inspector **April Purofoy** .... (313) 224-3595
Executive Secretary **Thomina Davidson** .... (313) 224-3595
E-mail: davidsont@detroitmi.gov

Office of the City Clerk
Coleman A. Young Municipal Center, Two Woodward Avenue, Room 200, Detroit, MI 48226
Tel: (313) 224-3261 Fax: (313) 224-1466

★ City Clerk **Janice Marie Winfrey** .... (313) 224-3261
Term Expires: December 31, 2017
E-mail: winfreyj@detroitmi.gov
Deputy City Clerk **Vivian A. Hudson** .... (313) 224-3261
E-mail: hudsonv@detroitmi.gov
Senior City Council Committee Clerk **Louise Jones** ..... (313) 224-1583
E-mail: jonesl@detroitmi.gov
Senior City Council Committee Clerk **Deonte Agee** ..... (313) 224-1993
E-mail: ageed@detroitmi.gov
Executive Secretary II **Angela Jones** .... (313) 224-3264
E-mail: jonesan@detroitmi.gov
Executive Secretary II **Fallon Walker** .... (313) 224-1990
E-mail: walkerf@detroitmi.gov

Department of Elections
2978 West Grand Boulevard, Detroit, MI 48202-3069
Tel: (313) 876-0190 Tel: (313) 876-0212 (Information Absentee Ballots)
Fax: (313) 876-0053

Director **Daniel A. Baxter** .... (313) 876-0222
Deputy Director **Gina Avery-Walker** .... (313) 876-0221
Executive Secretary **Melissa King** .... (313) 876-9799
E-mail: kingm@detroitmi.gov
Elections Specialist **Alicia Brown** .... (313) 876-0847
Information Technology Manager **Ray Meredith** .... (313) 876-0543

Detroit Public Schools
3011 West Grand Boulevard, Suite 485, Detroit, MI 48202
Fax: (313) 873-7439 Internet: http://www.detroitk12.org

▼ Transition Manager **Steven W. Rhodes** .... (313) 870-3772
Date of Birth: 1948 Fax: (313) 870-3726
Education: Purdue 1970 BS; Michigan 1973 JD
Superintendent **Alycia Meriweather** .... (313) 873-7922
Senior Executive Director, Strategic Support
Lamont Satchel .... (313) 873-7922
Deputy Superintendent of Finance and Operations
Marios Demetriou .... (313) 873-4057
E-mail: marios.demetriou@detroitk12.org Fax: (313) 873-4476

★ Elected Official ▲ Appointed by Legislature ▼ Appointed by Governor ► Appointed by Board or Commission ● Appointed by Judge
■ Appointed by Mayor △ Appointed by Freeholders ▽ Appointed by Supervisor ▷ Appointed by County Executive ○ Appointed by Council

Detroit Public Schools *continued*

Communications Executive Director
Michelle A. Zdrodowski . . . . . (313) 873-3494
E-mail: michelle.zdrodowski@detroitk12.org Fax: (313) 873-6269

Detroit Public Library [DPL]

Main Library, 5201 Woodward Avenue, Detroit, MI 48202
Tel: (313) 481-1339 Fax: (313) 833-3310 Fax: (313) 833-2327
Internet: www.detroitpubliclibrary.org

Year Founded: 1865

Administration

Executive Director **Jo Anne Mondowney** . . . . . (313) 481-1302
E-mail: jmondowney@detroitpubliclibrary.org
Education: Hampton BS; Clark Atlanta MLS
Director, Business and Financial Operations
Antonio Brown . . . . . (313) 481-1315
Director, Human Resources **Trinee Moore** . . . . . (313) 481-1329
E-mail: tmoore@detroitpubliclibrary.org
Assistant Director, Technical Services and Main Library Branch **J. Randolph Call** . . . . . (313) 833-1000
Director for Public Services (Interim) **Margaret Bruni** . . . (313) 481-1308
E-mail: mbruni@detroitpubliclibrary.org
Assistant Director, Facilities **Cledos Powell** . . . . . (313) 481-1882
E-mail: cpowell@detroitpubliclibrary.org
Assistant Director, Marketing **A. J. Funchess** . . . . . (313) 481-1338
Manager, Security (Acting) **Talisha Williams** . . . . . (313) 481-1372
Special Assistant to the Executive Director
Alma Simmons . . . . . (313) 481-1348
E-mail: asimmons@detroitpubliclibrary.org

District of Columbia

Tel: (202) 737-4404 (State Information or call 311) Internet: www.dc.gov

County: None **Election Type:** Partisan **Population:** 672,228 (2015); Rank 49

Muriel Bowser (D)
Mayor

Began Service: January 2, 2015
Term Expires: January 2, 2019
Date of Birth: April 2, 1972
Education: Chatham BA; American U MPP

Office of the Mayor

1350 Pennsylvania Avenue, NW, Washington, DC 20004
Tel: (202) 727-6300 Fax: (202) 727-0505 E-mail: eom@dc.gov
Internet: www.mayor.dc.gov

★ Mayor **Muriel Bowser** (D) . . . . . (202) 727-6300
Chief of Staff **John Falcicchio** . . . . . (202) 727-6300
Deputy Chief of Staff **Lindsey Parker** . . . . . (202) 727-6300
Education: Yale
Senior Advisor **Beverly L. Perry** . . . . . (202) 727-6300
Education: George Washington; Georgetown 1981 JD
General Counsel **Elizabeth "Betsy" Cavendish** . . . . . (202) 727-6300
Education: Yale 1982, 1988
Deputy General Counsel **Rob Hawkins** . . . . . (202) 727-6300
Education: Virginia Tech 2002 BA; Pittsburgh 2007 JD
Director of Scheduling **Jason Fink** . . . . . (202) 727-6300

Office of the Attorney General

441 Fourth Street NW, Washington, DC 20001
Tel: (202) 727-3400 Fax: (202) 347-8922 E-mail: dc.oag@dc.gov
Internet: www.oag.dc.gov

Employees: 785 **Fiscal Year:** 2015 **Budget:** $85,738,000

★ Attorney General **Karl A. Racine** (D) . . . . . (202) 727-3400
Term Expires: January 2, 2019
E-mail: karl.racine@dc.gov
Education: Pennsylvania 1985 BA; Virginia 1989 JD
Chief of Staff **Kim M. Whatley** . . . . . (202) 727-3400
Chief Information Officer (Acting) **Kim M. Whatley** . . . . . (202) 727-3400
E-mail: kim.whatley@dc.gov
Communications Director **Robert Marus** . . . . . (202) 724-5646
E-mail: robert.marus@dc.gov
Public Affairs Specialist **Andrew Phifer** . . . . . (202) 741-7652
Senior Counsel **Stephanie Litos** . . . . . (202) 727-3400
Senior Counsel **Elizabeth W. Wilkins** . . . . . (202) 727-3400
Education: Yale BA, 2013 JD

Office of the Inspector General

717 14th Street NW, 5th Floor, Washington, DC 20005
Tel: (202) 727-2540 Fax: (202) 727-9903 Internet: www.oig.dc.gov

Employees: 112

Inspector General **Daniel W. Lucas** . . . . . (202) 727-2540
Education: Col Charleston 1994 BSBA; Oklahoma 2004
Principal Deputy Inspector General **Marie Hart** . . . . . (202) 727-2540
Deputy Inspector General for Business Management
Jaime Yarussi . . . . . (202) 727-2540
Deputy Inspector General for Operations
Matt Wilcoxson . . . . . (202) 727-2540
Deputy Inspector General for Quality Management
Slemo Warigon . . . . . (202) 727-2540
Deputy Inspector General for Risk Assessment and Future Planning **James Duginske** . . . . . (202) 727-2540
General Counsel **Karen E. Branson** . . . . . (202) 727-2540
Assistant Inspector General for Medicaid Fraud
Brentton Wolfingbarger . . . . . (202) 727-2245
Fax: (202) 727-5937

Office of the Secretary of the District of Columbia

1350 Pennsylvania Avenue, NW, Room 419, Washington, DC 20004
Tel: (202) 727-6306 Fax: (202) 727-3582 E-mail: secretary@dc.gov

■ Secretary **Lauren C. Vaughan** . . . . . (202) 727-6306
E-mail: lauren.vaughan@dc.gov
Education: Hampton; George Washington
Deputy Secretary **Joy Holland** . . . . . (202) 727-6306
Executive Assistant **Arlethia Denise Thompson** . . . . . (202) 727-6306
E-mail: arlethia.thompson@dc.gov
Date of Birth: January 22, 1975
Special Assistant **(Vacant)** . . . . . (202) 727-6306

Executive Office of Communications

1350 Pennsylvania Avenue, NW, Washington, DC 20004
Tel: (202) 727-5011 Fax: (202) 727-9561

Senior Communications Officer **LaToya Foster** . . . . . (202) 727-9691
E-mail: latoya.foster@dc.gov

Mayor's Office of Community Affairs [MOCA]

1350 Pennsylvania Avenue NW, Suite 332, Washington, DC 20004
Tel: (202) 442-8150

Director **Charon P.W. Hines** . . . . . (202) 442-8150
E-mail: charon.hines@dc.gov
Education: Mary Baldwin

DC Youth Advisory Council [DCYAC]

Tel: (202) 727-7966 E-mail: dcyac@dc.gov

■ Executive Director **Dionne Burkett-Lewis** . . . . . (202) 727-7966
E-mail: dionne.burkett@dc.gov

★ Elected Official ▲ Appointed by Legislature ▼ Appointed by Governor ► Appointed by Board or Commission ● Appointed by Judge
■ Appointed by Mayor △ Appointed by Freeholders ▽ Appointed by Supervisor ▷ Appointed by County Executive ○ Appointed by Council

Mayors Office on Volunteerism [Serve DC]

Frank D. Reeves Municipal Center, 2000 14th Street NW, Suite 101, Washington, DC 20009
Tel: (202) 727-7925 TTY: (202) 727-8421

Chief Service Officer/Executive Director **Delano Hunter** . . . . . (202) 727-7925
Education: Delaware State BS

Deputy Director of Grants and Finance **Sareeta Spriggs** . . . . . (202) 727-7925
Education: Norfolk State BS; Strayer U MBA

Office on African Affairs [OAA]

Franklin D. Reeves Center of Municipal Affairs, 2000 14th Street, NW, Suite 400, Washington, DC 20009
Tel: (202) 727-5634 Fax: (202) 727-2357

■ Director **Mamadou Samba** . . . . . (202) 727-5634
E-mail: mamadou.samba@dc.gov
Education: South Carolina; Kennesaw State U MPA

Office of Lesbian, Gay, Bisexual, Transgender and Questioning Affairs [LGBTQ]

John A. Wilson Building, 1350 Pennsylvania Avenue, NW, Suite 211, Washington, DC 20001
Tel: (202) 727-9493 TTY: (202) 727-9493 Fax: (202) 727-5931
E-mail: lgbtq@dc.gov

■ Director **Sheila Alexander-Reid** . . . . . (202) 442-5143
E-mail: sheila.alexander-reid@dc.gov

Deputy Director **Terrance Laney** . . . . . (202) 442-8150

Office of Religious Affairs

1350 Pennsylvania Avenue, NW, Suite 332, Washington, DC 20004
Tel: (202) 698-4722 E-mail: onecongregationonefamily@dc.gov

Director **Donald L. Isaac, Sr.** . . . . . (202) 442-8150
E-mail: donald.isaac@dc.gov
Education: UDC BS; Southeastern U MPA

Office on Returning Citizen Affairs [ORCA]

2100 Martin Luther King Jr. Avenue SE, Suite 100, Washington, DC 20020
Tel: (202) 715-7670 Fax: (202) 715-7672 E-mail: orca@dc.gov

■ Director **Charles Thornton** . . . . . (202) 715-7670
E-mail: charles.thornton@dc.gov

Office on Women's Policy and Initiatives

1350 Pennsylvania Avenue, NW, Suite 327, Washington, DC 20004
Tel: (202) 724-7690 Fax: (202) 727-2357 E-mail: women@dc.gov

Director **Kimberly A. Bassett** (D) . . . . . (202) 724-7690
Education: North Carolina Central BA; North Carolina A&T MA

Mayor's Office of Community Relations and Services [MOCRS]

1350 Pennsylvania Avenue, NW, Suite 332, Washington, DC 20004
Tel: (202) 442-8150 Fax: (202) 727-5931 E-mail: mocrs@dc.gov

Mayor's Correspondence Unit Director **Jim Slattery** . . . . . (202) 545-3119

Executive Assistant **Jeanne Loeher** . . . . . (202) 727-3000
E-mail: jeanne.loeher@dc.gov

Director **Gregory Jackson, Jr.** . . . . . (202) 442-8150
E-mail: gregoryn.jackson@dc.gov
Education: Virginia BA

Mayor's Office of Federal and Regional Affairs

1350 Pennsylvania Avenue, NW, Washington, DC 20004

Senior Associate Director **Arlen E. Herrell** . . . . . (202) 727-6300

Mayor's Office on Latino Affairs [OLA]

Reeves Center, 2000 - 14th Street, NW, 2nd Floor, Washington, DC 20009
Tel: (202) 671-2825 Fax: (202) 673-4557 Internet: http://ola.dc.gov

■ Executive Director **Jackie Reyes** . . . . . (202) 671-1896
E-mail: jackie.reyes@dc.gov

Mayor's Office on Latino Affairs *continued*

Deputy Director **Julio Güity-Guevara** . . . . . (202) 478-1396

Community Outreach Specialist **Olimpia Lopez** . . . . . (202) 673-4557
E-mail: olimpia.lopez@dc.gov

Grants Management Specialist **Eduardo Perdomo** . . . . . (202) 340-7761

Mayor's Office of Legal Counsel [MOLC]

Director **Mark H. Tuohey III** . . . . . (202) 727-6300
E-mail: mark.tuohey@dc.gov
Education: St Bonaventure 1968 BA; Fordham 1973 JD

Mayor's Office of Veterans Affairs [OVA]

441 Fourth Street, NW, Suite 870 North, Washington, DC 20001
Tel: (202) 724-5454 Fax: (202) 724-7117 E-mail: ova@dc.gov
Internet: www.ova.dc.gov

■ Director **Tammi Lambert** . . . . . (202) 724-5454
E-mail: tammi.lambert@dc.gov

Deputy Director **Wanda Smith Battle** . . . . . (202) 724-5454

Office of Policy and Legislative Affairs

1350 Pennsylvania Avenue, NW, Room 511, Washington, DC 20001
Tel: (202) 727-6979 Fax: (202) 727-3765

■ Director **Maia Hunt Estes** . . . . . (202) 727-6979
E-mail: maia.hunt.estes@dc.gov
Education: Spelman BA; Georgetown JD

Deputy Director **(Vacant)** . . . . . (202) 727-6979

Office of the City Administrator [OCA]

John A. Wilson Building, 1350 Pennsylvania Avenue, NW, Suite 513, Washington, DC 20004
Tel: (202) 478-9200 Fax: (202) 535-1224

Employees: 41 **Fiscal Year:** 2015 **Budget:** $5,027,000

■ City Administrator **Rashad M. Young** . . . . . (202) 478-9200
E-mail: oca.eom@dc.gov
Date of Birth: 1976
Education: Dayton 1998 BS, 2002 MBA

Special Assistant to the City Administrator **Sean M. Garrick** . . . . . (202) 478-9200
E-mail: sean.garrick@dc.gov

Deputy City Administrator **Kevin Donahue** . . . . . (202) 478-9200
E-mail: kevin.donahue.eom@dc.gov
Education: Georgetown 1994 BA; Harvard 1999 MPP

Director of Agency Operations **(Vacant)** . . . . . (202) 478-9200

General Counsel and Senior Policy Advisor **Barry Kreiswirth** . . . . . (202) 478-9200

Metropolitan Police Department [MPDC]

300 Indiana Avenue, NW, Washington, DC 20001
Tel: (202) 727-8599 Fax: (202) 727-9524 TTY: (202) 671-2864
E-mail: mail.chief-of-police@dc.gov

Employees: 4,581 **Fiscal Year:** 2015 **Budget:** $525,631,000

■ Chief of Police **Cathy L. Lanier** . . . . . (202) 727-4218
E-mail: cathy.lanier@dc.gov
Education: Johns Hopkins BA, MA; Naval Postgrad MA

Assistant Chief **(Vacant)** . . . . . (202) 727-4218

Homeland Security Bureau Assistant Chief **Lamar Greene** . . . . . (202) 727-4218
E-mail: lamar.greene@dc.gov

Internal Affairs Bureau Assistant Chief **Kimberly Chisley-Missouri** . . . . . (202) 576-6600
801 Shepherd Street, NW, Washington, DC 20011-5822

Patrol Services and School Security Bureau Assistant Chief **Diane Groomes** . . . . . (202) 727-4218

Investigative Services Bureau Assistant Chief **Peter Newsham** . . . . . (202) 727-4295

★ Elected Official ▲ Appointed by Legislature ▼ Appointed by Governor ► Appointed by Board or Commission ● Appointed by Judge
■ Appointed by Mayor △ Appointed by Freeholders ▽ Appointed by Supervisor ▷ Appointed by County Executive ○ Appointed by Council

Department of Motor Vehicles [DMV]
95 M Street, SW, Suite 300, Washington, DC 20024
Tel: (202) 737-4404 Fax: (202) 727-1010 E-mail: dmv@dc.gov

Employees: 263 **Fiscal Year:** 2015 **Budget:** $38,215,000

■ Director **Lucinda M. Babers** . . . . (202) 727-2200
E-mail: lucinda.babers@dc.gov
Education: Georgia Tech BIE; Johns Hopkins MS

Public Affairs Specialist **Vanessa E. Newton** . . . . . . (202) 729-7020
Fax: (202) 729-7180

Office of the Chief Medical Examiner [OCME]
401 E Street SW, 6th Floor, Washington, DC 20024
Tel: (202) 698-9000 Fax: (202) 698-9101 E-mail: ocme@dc.gov

Chief Medical Examiner **Dr. Roger A. Mitchell, Jr.** . . . . . . (202) 698-9001
Education: Howard U 1996 BS; U Medicine/Dentistry NJ 2003 MD
Executive Assistant to the Chief Medical Examiner
Viola Hiers . . . . (202) 698-9000
E-mail: viola.hiers@dc.gov

Deputy Chief **Dr. Jan M. Gorniak** . . . . (202) 698-9000

Office of Human Rights [OHR]
One Judiciary Square, 441 Fourth Street, NW, Suite 570N, Washington, DC 20001
Tel: (202) 727-4559 TTY: (202) 724-2050 Fax: (202) 727-9589

■ Director **Mónica Palacio** . . . . (202) 727-4559
Education: Fordham 1990 BA; Georgetown 1993 JD

Office of Labor Relations and Collective Bargaining [OLRCB]
441 4th Street NW, Suite 820N, Washington, DC 20001
Tel: (202) 724-4953 Fax: (202) 727-6887 E-mail: olrcb.eom@dc.gov

■ Director **Lionel Sims** . . . . (202) 724-4953
E-mail: lionel.sims@dc.gov
Education: Wayne State U BS; Detroit Mercy JD

Office of Planning [OP]
1100 4th Street SW, Suite E650, Washington, DC 20024
Tel: (202) 442-7600 Fax: (202) 442-7638 E-mail: op@dc.gov

■ Director **Eric D. Shaw** . . . . (202) 442-7600
E-mail: eric.shaw@dc.gov

Deputy Director for Development Review and Historic Preservation **Jennifer Steingasser** . . . . (202) 442-8808
Education: Texas BS; Virginia MS

Deputy Director for Planning, Engagement and Design
Tanya Stern . . . . (202) 442-7635

Office of Public-Private Partnerships [OP3]
Tel: (202) 478-9200

Director **Seth Miller Gabriel** . . . . (202) 478-9200
Education: Washington Col; George Washington

Deputy Director **Judah Gluckman** . . . . (202) 478-9200
Education: Chicago; Washington College of Law JD

Office of Administrative Hearings [OAH]
441 Fourth Street, NW, Suite 450N, Washington, DC 20001-2714
Tel: (202) 442-9094 E-mail: oah@dc.gov Internet: www.oah.dc.gov

Employees: 77 **Fiscal Year:** 2015 **Budget:** $9,561,000

Chief Administrative Law Judge **Eugene A. Adams** . . . . . (202) 442-9099
Education: Wesleyan U; Connecticut JD

Principal Administrative Law Judge **John P. Dean** . . . . (202) 727-8284

Principal Administrative Law Judge **Paul B. Handy** . . . . . . (202) 727-8282

Principal Administrative Law Judge
Samuel McClendon . . . . (202) 727-3821
E-mail: samuel.mcclendon@dc.gov

Principal Administrative Law Judge **Erika L. Pierson** . . . . (202) 478-1465
E-mail: erika.pierson@dc.gov
Education: Grinnell; Northern Illinois JD

Principal Administrative Law Judge **Robert Sharkey** . . . . . (202) 442-9092
E-mail: robert.sharkey@dc.gov

Office of Administrative Hearings *continued*

Principal Administrative Law Judge
Arabella Wattles Teal . . . . (202) 478-1414
E-mail: arabella.teal@dc.gov
Education: Harvard BA; Georgetown JD

Principal Administrative Law Judge **Wanda R. Tucker** . . . (202) 478-1413
E-mail: wanda.tucker@dc.gov

Principal Administrative Law Judge **Ann C. Yahner** . . . . . . (202) 442-8168
Education: Wellesley; Harvard JD

Council of the District of Columbia
John A. Wilson Building, 1350 Pennsylvania Avenue, NW, Washington, DC 20004
Tel: (202) 724-8000 TTY: (202) 347-5181 Fax: (202) 347-3070
Internet: www.dccouncil.us

★ Chairman of the Council
Phil Mendelson (D-At-Large) . . . . (202) 724-8032
Term Expires: January 2, 2019 Fax: (202) 724-8099
E-mail: pmendelson@dccouncil.us
Education: American U 1981 BA

★ Council Member **Yvette M. Alexander** (D-Ward 7) . . . . . (202) 724-8068
Term Expires: January 2, 2017 Fax: (202) 741-0911
E-mail: yalexander@dccouncil.us

★ Council Member **Charles Allen** (D-Ward 6) . . . . (202) 724-8072
Term Expires: January 2, 2019
E-mail: callen@dccouncil.us

★ Council Member **Anita Bonds** (D-At-Large) . . . . (202) 724-8064
Term Expires: January 2, 2019 Fax: (202) 724-8086
E-mail: abonds@dccouncil.us

★ Council Member **Mary M. Cheh** (D-Ward 3) . . . . (202) 724-8062
Term Expires: January 2, 2019 Fax: (202) 724-8118
E-mail: mcheh@dccouncil.us
Education: Douglass BA; Rutgers JD; Harvard 1977 LLM

★ Council Member **Jack Evans** (D-Ward 2) . . . . (202) 724-8058
Term Expires: January 2, 2017 Fax: (202) 724-8023
E-mail: jevans@dccouncil.us
Education: Wharton 1975 BA; Pittsburgh 1978 JD

★ Council Member **David Grosso** (I-At-Large) . . . . (202) 724-8105
Term Expires: January 2, 2017 Fax: (202) 724-8071
E-mail: dgrosso@dccouncil.us
Education: Earlham 1997 BP

★ Council Member **LaRuby May** (D-Ward 8) . . . . (202) 724-8045
Term Expires: January 2, 2017 Fax: (202) 724-8055
E-mail: lmay@dccouncil.us
Education: Eckerd BA; George Washington MA

★ Council Member **Kenyan McDuffie** (D-Ward 5) . . . . (202) 724-8028
Term Expires: January 2, 2019 Fax: (202) 724-8076
E-mail: kmcduffie@dccouncil.us
Education: Howard U BS; Maryland JD

★ Council Member **Brianne Nadeau** (D-Ward 1) . . . . (202) 724-8181
Term Expires: January 2, 2019 Fax: (202) 724-8109
E-mail: bnadeau@dccouncil.us

★ Council Member **Vincent B. Orange, Sr.** (D-At-Large) . . . (202) 724-8174
Term Expires: January 2, 2017 Fax: (202) 727-8210
E-mail: vorange@dccouncil.us
Education: U Pacific 1979 BS, 1980 BA; Howard U 1983 JD; Georgetown 1988 MLT

★ Council Member **Elissa Silverman** (I-At-Large) . . . . (202) 724-7772
Term Expires: January 2, 2019 Fax: (202) 724-8087
E-mail: esilverman@dccouncil.us

★ Council Member **Brandon T. Todd** (D-Ward 4) . . . . (202) 724-8052
Term Expires: January 2, 2017 Fax: (202) 741-0908
E-mail: btodd@dccouncil.us
Education: Bowie State BS

Secretary to the Council **Nyasha Smith** . . . . (202) 724-8080
E-mail: nsmith@dccouncil.us

Assistant Secretary **Jamaine Taylor** . . . . (202) 724-8080

General Counsel **Ellen Efros** . . . . (202) 724-8026
Fax: (202) 724-8129

Budget Director **Jennifer Budoff** . . . . (202) 724-5689
E-mail: jbudoff@dccouncil.us Fax: (202) 724-7819

(continued on next page)

★ Elected Official ▲ Appointed by Legislature ▼ Appointed by Governor ► Appointed by Board or Commission ● Appointed by Judge
■ Appointed by Mayor △ Appointed by Freeholders ▽ Appointed by Supervisor ▷ Appointed by County Executive ○ Appointed by Council

Council of the District of Columbia *continued*

Chief Information Officer **Chris Warren** . . . . (202) 724-8018
E-mail: cwarren@dccouncil.us

Office of the Chief Financial Officer [OCFO]

John A. Wilson Building, 1350 Pennsylvania Avenue, NW, Suite 203, Washington, DC 20004
Tel: (202) 727-2476 Fax: (202) 727-1643 E-mail: ocfo@dc.gov
Internet: cfo.dc.gov

Employees: 957 **Fiscal Year:** 2015 **Budget:** $136,336,000

■ Chief Financial Officer **Jeffrey S. DeWitt** . . . . (202) 727-2476
Term Expires: June 2017
Education: Eastern Illinois BS; Southern Illinois MS

Deputy Chief Financial Officer and Chief of Staff
Angell Jacobs . . . . (202) 727-2476

Continuous Improvement Officer **Baraka Ondiek** . . . . (202) 727-2476

Chief Information Officer (Interim) **Richard Weil** . . . . (202) 727-8775

Chief Risk Officer **Marshelle Richardson** . . . . (202) 727-2476
E-mail: marshelle.richardson@dc.gov

Public Affairs Officer **David Umansky** . . . . (202) 727-6391
E-mail: david.umansky@dc.gov

Primary and Secondary Education Cluster

1200 First Street, NE, 11th Floor, Washington, DC 20002
Tel: (202) 442-6078 Fax: (202) 442-5807

Associate Chief Financial Officer **Deloras A. Shepherd** . . (202) 442-6078

Office of Budget and Planning [OBP]

1350 Pennsylvania Avenue, NW, Suite 229, Washington, DC 20004
Tel: (202) 727-1239 Fax: (202) 724-5222

Deputy Chief Financial Officer **Gordon McDonald** . . . . . . (202) 727-6343
Education: Howard U BABA, MBA

Associate Deputy Chief Financial Officer
Jim Spaulding . . . . (202) 727-1782

Director for Budget Administration **Eric M. Cannady** . . . . (202) 727-1072

Director for Capital Improvements Program **David Clark** . . (202) 727-2055

Director for Financial Planning, Analysis, and Management Services **Leticia Stephenson** . . . . (202) 727-1036
E-mail: leticia.stephenson@dc.gov

Office of Finance and Treasury [OFT]

1101 Fourth Street SW, Eigth Floor, Washington, DC 20005
Fax: (202) 727-6049

Treasurer **Jeffrey Barnette** . . . . (202) 727-6055

Associate Treasurer for Asset Management **John Henry** . . (202) 727-6288
E-mail: john.henry@dc.gov
Education: Virginia State BA; Howard U MBA

Associate Treasurer for Banking and Operations
Clarice Wood . . . . (202) 727-0760

Associate Treasurer for Debt and Grants Management
Carmen Pigler . . . . (202) 727-6055
Education: Columbia MBA

Office of Financial Operations and Systems [OFOS]

1100 4th Street SW, Suite E800, Washington, DC 20024
Fax: (202) 442-8201

Deputy Chief Financial Officer **Bill Slack** . . . . (202) 442-8200

Deputy Comptroller **Diji Omisore** . . . . (202) 727-2476
Education: Towson U

Office of Revenue Analysis

1101 Fourth Street SW, Suite 770W, Washington, DC 20005
Tel: (202) 727-7775 E-mail: ora@dc.gov

Deputy Chief Financial Officer and Chief Economist
Fitzroy Lee . . . . (202) 727-7775
Education: U West Indies (Jamaica) BS; Georgia State PhD

Economic Affairs Director **Farhad Niami** . . . . (202) 727-7775
Education: Oregon State PhD

Fiscal and Legislative Analysis Director **Yesim Yilmaz** . . . (202) 727-7775
Education: Boğaziçi U (Turkey) BA; George Mason PhD

Revenue Estimation Director **Steven Giachetti** . . . . (202) 727-7775

Office of the Deputy Mayor for Education [DME]

1350 Pennsylvania Avenue, NW, Suite 307, Washington, DC 20004
Tel: (202) 727-3636 Fax: (202) 727-8198 E-mail: dme@dc.gov

■ Deputy Mayor **Jennifer C. Niles** . . . . (202) 727-0953
E-mail: jennifer.niles@dc.gov

Chief of Staff **Margie Yeager** . . . . (202) 727-0953

Executive Assistant **Tara Lynch** . . . . (202) 727-3636
E-mail: tara.lynch@dc.gov

Data Analyst **Cecilia Kaltz** . . . . (202) 727-3636

Office of the State Superintendent of Education [OSSE]

810 First Street, NE, 9th Floor, Washington, DC 20002
Tel: (202) 727-6436 Fax: (202) 727-2019 Internet: http://osse.dc.gov

Employees: 360 **Fiscal Year:** 2015 **Budget:** $406,901,000

■ State Superintendent **Hanseul Kang** . . . . (202) 727-6436
E-mail: hanseul.kang@dc.gov
Education: Georgetown; Harvard JD

Executive Assistant **Maisha Hayes** . . . . (202) 727-3471
E-mail: maisha.hayes@dc.gov

Chief of Staff **Shana Young** . . . . (202) 727-6436

Deputy Chief of Staff **Jessie Harteis** . . . . (202) 344-9805
E-mail: jessie.harteis@dc.gov

Special Assistant for Policy **Bridget Kelly** . . . . (202) 322-1727

Chief Operating Officer (Acting) **Gregory Ellis** . . . . (202) 727-6436

Assistant Superintendent of Health and Wellness
Donna Anthony . . . . (202) 727-6436

Agency Fiscal Officer **Paris Saunders** . . . . (202) 727-6436

Director of Communications **Patience Peabody** . . . . (202) 654-6120
E-mail: patience.peabody@dc.gov

Director of Student Transportation **Gretchen Brumley** . . . (202) 724-5675

Director of Talent and Human Resources **Pete Siu** . . . . (202) 727-6436
E-mail: pete.siu@dc.gov

General Counsel (Interim) **Sarah Jane Forman** . . . . (202) 727-6436

State Board of Education

441 Fourth Street, NW, Suite 723 North, Washington, DC 20001
Tel: (202) 741-0888 Fax: (202) 741-0879 Internet: http://sboe.dc.gov

★ President **Jack N. Jacobson** (D-Ward 2) . . . . (202) 741-0888
Term Expires: January 2, 2017
E-mail: jack.jacobson@dc.gov
Education: Augustana (IL) 2000 BA

★ Vice President **Karen Williams** (D-Ward 7) . . . . (202) 741-0888
Term Expires: January 2, 2017
E-mail: karen.williams5@dc.gov
Education: George Washington BE

★ Board Member **D. Kamili Anderson** (D-Ward 4) . . . . (202) 257-3380
Term Expires: January 2, 2017
E-mail: kamili.anderson@dc.gov

★ Board Member **Tierra Jolly** (Ward 8) . . . . (202) 812-1464
Term Expires: January 2, 2017
E-mail: tierra.jolly@dc.gov

★ Board Member **Mark Jones** (Ward 5) . . . . (202) 302-7294
Term Expires: January 2, 2019
E-mail: mark.jones@dc.gov

★ Elected Official ▲ Appointed by Legislature ▼ Appointed by Governor ▶ Appointed by Board or Commission ● Appointed by Judge
■ Appointed by Mayor △ Appointed by Freeholders ▽ Appointed by Supervisor ▷ Appointed by County Executive ○ Appointed by Council

State Board of Education *continued*

★Board Member **Mary Lord** (D-At-Large) . . . . . (202) 257-3226
Term Expires: January 2, 2017
E-mail: mary.lord@dc.gov
Education: Harvard

★Board Member **Laura Wilson Phelan** (Ward 1) . . . . . (202) 276-5859
Term Expires: January 2, 2019
E-mail: laura.wilson.phelan@dc.gov

★Board Member **Ruth Wattenberg** (Ward 3) . . . . . (202) 431-5379
Term Expires: January 2, 2019
E-mail: ruth.wattenberg@dc.gov

★Board Member **Joe Weedon** (Ward 6) . . . . . (202) 431-5369
Term Expires: January 2, 2019
E-mail: joe.weedon@dc.gov

Executive Director **John-Paul C. Hayworth** . . . . . (202) 741-0888
Education: Baylor 2001 AB; Connecticut 2003 AM

DC Public School System [DCPS]

1200 First Street, NE, Washington, DC 20002
Tel: (202) 442-5885 Fax: (202) 442-5026

Chancellor **Kaya K. Henderson** . . . . . (202) 535-1581
Education: Georgetown 1992

Senior Adviser **Kenneth S. Slaughter** . . . . . (202) 442-5885
Education: Georgetown 1976 JD

Chief Operating Officer **Nathaniel Savio Beers** . . . . . (202) 442-5885
Education: Rochester; George Washington MD; JFK School Govt MPA

Chief of Staff **Peter Weber** . . . . . (202) 442-5885

General Counsel **D. Scott Barash** . . . . . (202) 442-5000
Education: Yale 1985 BA; Chicago 1988 JD

Chief Financial Officer **Deloras A. Shepherd** . . . . . (202) 442-5300

Chief of College and Career **Emily Durso** . . . . . (202) 442-5885
Education: Georgetown; Catholic U

Chief of Innovation and Research
Dr. Robert W. Simmons III . . . . . (202) 442-5885
Education: Western Michigan; Lawrence Tech MS

Chief of Schools **John Davis** . . . . . (202) 442-5618
E-mail: john.davis@dc.gov

Chief of Talent and Culture **Crystal Jefferson** . . . . . (202) 442-5417

Chief of Teaching and Learning **Brian Pick** . . . . . (202) 442-5611
Education: Princeton Fax: (202) 442-5081

Deputy Chief of Educational Technology and Library Programs **David Rose** . . . . . (202) 442-5885
E-mail: david.rose@dc.gov

Family and Public Engagement Chief
Josephine Bias Robinson (R) . . . . . (202) 719-6613
E-mail: josephine.robinson@dc.gov Fax: (202) 442-5418
Education: Georgetown 1991 BSFS

Family and Public Engagement Deputy Chief
Sarah Parker . . . . . (202) 442-5308

Budget Director **Donald Sink** . . . . . (202) 442-5300
E-mail: donald.sink@dc.gov

Chief of Communications **Ernestine Walls Benedict** . . . . . (202) 442-8854
E-mail: ernestine.benedict@dc.gov
Education: Temple

Department of Parks and Recreation [DPR]

1250 U Street NW, 2nd Floor, Washington, DC 20010
1480 Girard Street, NW, 4th Floor, Washington, DC 20009
Tel: (202) 673-7647 Fax: (202) 673-2087 Internet: www.dpr.dc.gov

Employees: 570 **Fiscal Year:** 2015 **Budget:** $42,223,000

■Director **Keith A. Anderson** . . . . . (202) 671-2321
E-mail: keith.anderson@dc.gov
Education: Hampton

Chief Operations Officer **(Vacant)** . . . . . (202) 316-4236

Chief of Staff **Jason Yuckenberg** . . . . . (202) 273-2195

Office of the Deputy Mayor for Greater Economic Opportunity

Deputy Mayor **Courtney Snowden** . . . . . (202) 737-4404
Education: Beloit 2000 BA

Office on African American Affairs

Director **Rahman Branch** . . . . . (202) 442-8150

Department of Employment Services [DOES]

4058 Minnesota Avenue NE, Suite 5000, Washington, DC 20019
Tel: (202) 671-1900 TTY: (202) 673-6994 Fax: (202) 673-6976
Internet: www.does.dc.gov

Employees: 580 **Fiscal Year:** 2015 **Budget:** $113,796,000

■Director **Deborah A. Carroll** . . . . . (202) 671-1900
E-mail: does@dc.gov
Education: Temple BS, JD

Chief of Staff **Rámon Pérez-Goizueta** . . . . . (202) 671-1673

Operations Deputy Director **Jerome Johnson** . . . . . (202) 671-1900
E-mail: jerome.johnson@dc.gov

General Counsel **Tonya Saap** . . . . . (202) 671-1500

Department of Small and Local Business Development [DSLBD]

One Judiciary Square, 441 Fourth Street, NW, Suite 850N, Washington, DC 20001
Tel: (202) 727-3900 Fax: (202) 724-3786 E-mail: dslbd@dc.gov

Employees: 37 **Fiscal Year:** 2015 **Budget:** $9,501,000

Director **Ana Recio Harvey** . . . . . (202) 727-3900
E-mail: ana.harvey@dc.gov
Education: Houston

Administrative Officer to the Director
Gabrielle Richards . . . . . (202) 727-3900
E-mail: gabrielle.richards@dc.gov

Office of the Deputy Mayor for Health and Human Services

1350 Pennsylvania Avenue, NW, Suite 223, Washington, DC 20004
Tel: (202) 727-7973 Fax: (202) 442-5066

■Deputy Mayor **Brenda Donald** . . . . . (202) 727-6300
E-mail: brenda.donald@dc.gov
Education: George Washington BA; Arkansas (Little Rock) MPA

Chief of Staff **Rachel Joseph** . . . . . (202) 727-7973

Senior Policy Advisor **Jenna Cevasco** . . . . . (202) 727-7973

Child and Family Services Agency [CFSA]

400 Sixth Street, SW, 5th Floor, Washington, DC 20024
Tel: (202) 442-6100 Fax: (202) 727-7700 Fax: (202) 727-6505
E-mail: cfsa@dc.gov

Employees: 793 **Fiscal Year:** 2015 **Budget:** $230,672,000

■Director **Raymond C. Davidson** . . . . . (202) 442-6175
E-mail: raymond.davidson@dc.gov
Education: George Washington MBA

Executive Assistant **Verrita Kelly** . . . . . (202) 442-6175
E-mail: verrita.kelly@dc.gov

Staff Assistant **Amber Tate** . . . . . (202) 442-6175
E-mail: amber.tate@dc.gov

Department on Disability Services [DDS]

1125 - 15 Street, NW, Washington, DC 20005
Tel: (202) 730-1700 Fax: (202) 730-1843

Employees: 430 **Fiscal Year:** 2015 **Budget:** $156,255,000

■Director (Interim) **Andrew Reese** . . . . . (202) 730-1700
E-mail: andrew.reese@dc.gov

Deputy Director of Administration **Deborah Bonsack** . . . . . (202) 730-1715
E-mail: deborah.bonsack@dc.gov

★Elected Official ▲Appointed by Legislature ▼Appointed by Governor ▶Appointed by Board or Commission ●Appointed by Judge
■Appointed by Mayor △Appointed by Freeholders ▽Appointed by Supervisor ▷Appointed by County Executive ○Appointed by Council

Department of Health [DOH]

899 North Capitol Street, NE, Washington, DC 20002
Tel: (202) 442-5955 Tel: (202) 442-9303 (Vital Records)
Fax: (202) 442-4795

Employees: 599 **Fiscal Year:** 2015 **Budget:** $266,124,000

■ Director **Dr. LaQuandra S. Nesbitt** .... (202) 442-5955
E-mail: laquandra.nesbitt@dc.gov
Education: Michigan BS; Wayne State U MD; Harvard MPH
Executive Assistant **Monique Johnson** .... (202) 442-5955
E-mail: monique.johnson@dc.gov
General Counsel **Phillip Husband** .... (202) 442-5970
Date of Birth: September 25, 1962 Fax: (202) 442-4797
Deputy General Counsel **(Vacant)** .... (202) 442-5977
Director of Communications
Marcus Anthony Williams (D) .... (202) 724-7481
E-mail: marcus.williams@dc.gov
Date of Birth: May 28, 1984
Education: Penn State 2007 BA; Georgetown 2010 MPS
Labor Management Liaison **Earl Murphy** .... (202) 442-9189

Department of Health Care Finance [DHCF]

441 Fourth Street, NW, Suite 900S, Washington, DC 20001
Tel: (202) 442-5988 Fax: (202) 442-4790

Employees: 217 **Fiscal Year:** 2015 **Budget:** $2,764,826,000

■ Director **Wayne M. Turnage** .... (202) 442-5988
E-mail: wayne.turnage@dc.gov
Education: North Carolina A&T 1980 BS; Ohio State 1982 MPA
Chief of Staff **Melisa Byrd** .... (202) 478-5809
Chief Operating Officer **Kenneth Evans** .... (202) 442-8436
Deputy Director of Finance **Sumita Chaudhuri** .... (202) 478-5925
Health Care Policy and Research Administration
Director **Alice M. Weiss** (D) .... (202) 442-9107
Education: Haverford 1991 AB; Northeastern 1997 JD
Chief Information Officer **David Sidransky** .... (202) 478-1375
Health Care Ombudsman **Maude Holt** .... (202) 299-2114

Department of Human Services [DHS]

64 New York Avenue, NE, 6th Floor, Washington, DC 20002
P.O. Box 54047, Washington, DC 20032
Tel: (202) 671-4200 TTY: (202) 671-4495 Fax: (202) 671-4326

Employees: 1,215 **Fiscal Year:** 2015 **Budget:** $397,845,000

■ Director **Laura Green Zeilinger** .... (202) 671-4200
E-mail: laura.zeilinger@dc.gov
Education: Sarah Lawrence 1995 BA;
Washington College of Law 2005 JD
Chief Operating Officer **Sharon Kershbaum** .... (202) 671-4200
Education: Pennsylvania 1992 BA; Wharton 1998 MBA
Senior Advisor for Policy and Program Support
Sakina Thompson .... (202) 671-4451
Family Services Administrator (Acting)
Kristi Greenwalt .... (202) 698-4171
E-mail: kristi.greenwalt@dc.gov
General Counsel **Monica J. Brown** .... (202) 671-4346

Department of Youth Rehabilitation Services [DYRS]

450 H Street NW, Washington, DC 20001
Tel: (202) 299-5362 Fax: (202) 299-5608 E-mail: dyrs@dc.gov

Employees: 558 **Fiscal Year:** 2015 **Budget:** $96,002,000

■ Director **Clinton Lacey** .... (202) 299-5362
E-mail: clinton.lacey@dc.gov
Education: CCNY BA
Senior Deputy Director **Linda Harllee Harper** .... (202) 299-5362
Deputy Director for Secure Programs **Willie Fullilove** .... (202) 299-5362
Deputy Director for Youth and Family Services
Garine Dalce .... (202) 299-5362
Chief of Staff **(Vacant)** .... (202) 299-5362
Chief Administrative Officer **Hugo Tovar** .... (202) 299-5362
E-mail: hugo.tovar@dc.gov

Department of Youth Rehabilitation Services *continued*

Freedom of Information Act (FOIA) Officer **(Vacant)** .... (202) 299-5362
1000 Mount Olivet Road, NE, Washington, DC 20002
General Counsel (Acting) **Lindsey Appiah** .... (202) 299-5362
Human Resources Director **Timothy Howell** .... (202) 299-5362

Office on Aging [DCOA]

500 K Street NE, Washington, DC 20002
Tel: (202) 727-6603 Fax: (202) 724-4979 E-mail: dcoa@dc.gov
Internet: www.dcoa.dc.gov

■ Executive Director (Acting) **Laura Newland** .... (202) 724-4382
E-mail: laura.newland@dc.gov
Education: Kalamazoo BA; Georgetown JD
Resource Allocation Officer **Eden Teklebrhane** .... (202) 727-8372
Aging and Disability Division Manager and Executive
Team Lead **Sara Tribe** .... (202) 535-1444
Education: Colgate Darden 2001; Boston U 2007
Budget Analyst **Berthell Epes** .... (202) 724-5622
E-mail: berthell.epes@dc.gov
Communications Director **Darrell Jackson, Jr.** .... (202) 727-5622
E-mail: darrell.jacksonjr@dc.gov
Community Relations Officer **Krystal Branton** .... (202) 727-8370
E-mail: krystal.branton@dc.gov
Customer and Information Services Specialist
Darlene Nowlin .... (202) 727-8364
E-mail: darlene.nowlin@dc.gov
Employment Specialist **Maria Anderson** .... (202) 727-0374

Office of Disability Rights

441 4th Street NW, Suite 729 North, Washington, DC 20001
Tel: (202) 724-5055

Director **Alexis P. Taylor** .... (202) 727-8005
Education: Georgetown BSNE, JD; DePaul LLM
Attorney Advisor **Jessica Hunt** .... (202) 727-0287

Office of the Deputy Mayor for Planning and Economic Development [DMPED]

John A. Wilson Building, 1350 Pennsylvania Avenue, NW, Suite 317, Washington, DC 20004
Tel: (202) 727-6365 Fax: (202) 727-6703 E-mail: dmped.eom@dc.gov

Employees: 80 **Fiscal Year:** 2015 **Budget:** $34,469,000

■ Deputy Mayor **Brian T. Kenner** .... (202) 727-6365
E-mail: brian.kenner@dc.gov
Education: Iowa; Harvard MPP
Chief of Staff **Andrew Trueblood** .... (202) 727-6365
Senior Advisor for Housing **(Vacant)** .... (202) 727-6365
Executive Director of the Workforce Investment Council
Odie Donald II .... (202) 727-6365
Education: Georgia State BA, MBA

Department of Consumer and Regulatory Affairs [DCRA]

1100 4th Street SW, Washington, DC 20024
Tel: (202) 442-4000 Fax: (202) 442-9445 Internet: http://dcra.dc.gov

Employees: 268

Director **Melinda M. Bolling** .... (202) 442-4000
Education: Georgia Tech; Columbus Law JD
Chief Building Official **Jatinder Singh Khokhar** .... (202) 442-8937
Education: Punjab U (India) BSEE
Staff Assistant **Kandice Taylor** .... (202) 442-8947
E-mail: kandice.taylor@dc.gov
Support Service Deputy Director **Gilbert Davidson** ...... (202) 442-8943
E-mail: gilbert.davidson@dc.gov

★ Elected Official ▲ Appointed by Legislature ▼ Appointed by Governor ► Appointed by Board or Commission ● Appointed by Judge
■ Appointed by Mayor △ Appointed by Freeholders ▽ Appointed by Supervisor ▷ Appointed by County Executive ○ Appointed by Council

Department of Energy and the Environment [DOEE]

1200 First Street, NE, 5th Floor, Washington, DC 20002
Tel: (202) 535-2600 Fax: (202) 535-2881 E-mail: doee@dc.gov

Employees: 249

■ Director **Tommy Wells** (D) .... (202) 478-1417
E-mail: tommy.wells@dc.gov
Education: Alabama 1979 BA; Minnesota 1983 MA; Columbus Law 1991 JD
Chief of Staff **Adrianna Hochberg** .... (202) 478-1417
Administrative Services Deputy Director **Michelle Dee** ... (202) 481-3839
Energy Administration Deputy Director **Teresa Lawrence** .... (202) 299-3339
Environmental Services Deputy Director **Richard Jackson** .... (202) 673-6710
Energy Affordability Program Chief **Teresa Lawrence** ... (202) 442-4177
Natural Resources Deputy Director **Hamid Karimi** .... (202) 535-2600
Youth Conservation Program Coordinator **Johnnie Philson** .... (202) 673-6700
Policy and Sustainable Solutions Chief (Interim) **William Updike** .... (202) 671-3307

Department of Housing and Community Development [DHCD]

Anacostia Gateway Government Center,
1800 Martin Luther King Jr. Avenue, SE, Washington, DC 20020
Tel: (202) 442-7200 Fax: (202) 442-7078 Internet: www.dhcd.dc.gov

Employees: 152 **Fiscal Year:** 2015 **Budget:** $128,707,000

■ Director **Polly Donaldson** .... (202) 442-7200
E-mail: polly.donaldson@dc.gov
Chief of Staff **Allison Ladd** .... (202) 442-7230
Chief Administrative Officer **(Vacant)** .... (202) 442-7200
Chief Program Officer **Vonda J. Orders** .... (202) 442-7200
E-mail: vonda.orders@dc.gov
Education: Maryland 1996 BA, 2002 JD
Administrative Services Support Manager **Laverne E. Law** .... (202) 442-7170
E-mail: laverne.law@dc.gov
Agency Fiscal Officer **Douglas A. Kemp** .... (202) 442-7200
E-mail: douglas.kemp@dc.gov
Education: Adrian BA
Director of Communications and Community Outreach **(Vacant)** .... (202) 442-7253
General Counsel **(Vacant)** .... (202) 442-7220

Department of Insurance, Securities and Banking [DISB]

810 First Street, NE, Suite 701, Washington, DC 20002
Tel: (202) 727-8000 Fax: (202) 535-1207 E-mail: disb@dc.gov

Employees: 138 **Fiscal Year:** 2015 **Budget:** $18,531,000

■ Commissioner **Stephen C. Taylor** .... (202) 442-7760
Education: Fordham 1989 BS; Georgetown 1992 JD, 1996 LLM
Deputy Commissioner (Acting) **Dana Sheppard** .... (202) 442-7820
Education: Texas 1991 JD; Georgetown 2004 LLM
Banking Associate Commissioner **Christopher Weaver** .. (202) 442-7774
Chief of Administration and Policy **Katrice Purdie** ...... (202) 442-7773
E-mail: katrice.purdie@dc.gov
Enforcement and Consumer Protection Division Associate Commissioner (Acting) **Greg Marsillo** ...... (202) 442-7109
Insurance Bureau Associate Commissioner **Philip Barlow** .... (202) 442-7823
Education: Georgia State 1993 BBA
Risk Finance Bureau Associate Commissioner **Dana Sheppard** .... (202) 442-7820
E-mail: dana.sheppard@dc.gov
Education: Texas 1991 JD; Georgetown 2004 LLM
Securities Bureau Associate Commissioner **Theodore A. Miles** .... (202) 442-7800
Education: Harvard 1959 BA; Howard U 1963 LLB

District Department of Transportation [DDOT]

55 M Street SE, Suite 400, Washington, DC 20003
Tel: (202) 673-6813 TTY: (202) 673-6813 Fax: (202) 671-0127
Internet: www.ddot.dc.gov

Employees: 544 **Fiscal Year:** 2015 **Budget:** $91,506,000

■ Director **Leif A. Dormsjo** .... (202) 671-4097
E-mail: leif.dormsjo@dc.gov
Deputy Director **Greer Johnson Gillis** .... (202) 671-4691
Education: Georgia Tech BSCE, MSCE
Chief of Staff **Adrea Turner** .... (202) 673-6813
Education: Col Charleston BS, MPA
Deputy Chief of Staff **(Vacant)** .... (202) 673-6813
General Counsel **Frank Seales, Jr.** .... (202) 673-6813
Education: Tennessee State BS; Indiana JD
Associate Director of Administrative Services **(Vacant)** ... (202) 673-6813
Associate Director of Policy, Planning and Sustainability Administration **Sam D. Zimbabwe** .... (202) 673-6813
Associate Director of Public Space Regulation Administration **Matthew Marcou** .... (202) 359-6497
2217 14th Street, NW, Washington, DC 20009
Associate Director of Transportation Operations Administration **Suzette Robinson** .... (202) 671-1366
Associate Director of Urban Forestry **(Vacant)** .... (202) 671-1490
2217 14th Street, NW, Washington, DC 20009
Chief Administrative Officer **Dorinda R. Floyd** .... (202) 673-6813
Chief Engineer **(Vacant)** .... (202) 673-6813
Chief Information Officer **José Colón** .... (202) 741-8913
Chief Operations Officer **(Vacant)** .... (202) 673-6813
Chief Performance Officer **John P. Thomas** .... (202) 673-6813
Public Information Officer **Terry Owens** .... (202) 671-5124
E-mail: terry.owens@dc.gov
Education: Michigan State

Office of the Deputy Mayor for Public Safety and Justice

Tel: (202) 724-7173

Employees: 21 **Fiscal Year:** 2015 **Budget:** $26,302,000

Deputy Mayor **Kevin Donahue** .... (202) 724-7173
E-mail: kevin.donahue.eom@dc.gov
Education: Georgetown 1994 BA; Harvard 1999 MPP

Corrections Information Council

2901 14th Street NW, Washington, DC 20009
Tel: (202) 478-9211 E-mail: dc.cic@dc.gov Internet: www.cic.dc.gov

Board Chair **Phylisa Carter** .... (202) 478-9211
Board Member **Katherine A. Huffman** .... (202) 478-9211
Education: Emory; Yale JD
Director **Michelle Bonner** .... (202) 478-9211
Education: Johns Hopkins; London School Econ (UK) MS; Stanford JD

Fire and Emergency Medical Services Department [FEMS]

1923 Vermont Avenue, NW, Suite 201 South, Washington, DC 20001
Tel: (202) 673-3320 Fax: (202) 462-0807

Employees: 2,028

■ Chief **Gregory M. Dean** .... (202) 673-3320
E-mail: gregory.dean@dc.gov
Education: U Phoenix BA
Assistant Chief of Emergency Medical Services **Edward R. Mills III** .... (202) 673-3320
E-mail: edward.mills@dc.gov
Assistant Fire Chief of Services **David Foust** .... (202) 673-3320
E-mail: david.foust@dc.gov
Chief Communications Officer **Doug Buchanan** .... (202) 673-3320
Education: Temple BAJ
Public Information Officer **Tim Wilson** .... (202) 673-3331
E-mail: tim.wilson@dc.gov

★ Elected Official ▲ Appointed by Legislature ▼ Appointed by Governor ▶ Appointed by Board or Commission ● Appointed by Judge
■ Appointed by Mayor △ Appointed by Freeholders ▽ Appointed by Supervisor ▷ Appointed by County Executive ○ Appointed by Council

Homeland Security and Emergency Management Agency [HSEMA]

2720 Martin Luther King Jr. Avenue, SE, Washington, DC 20032
Tel: (202) 727-6161 TTY: (202) 730-0488 Fax: (202) 715-7288
E-mail: ema@dc.gov

Employees: 87 **Fiscal Year:** 2015 **Budget:** $74,994,000

■ Director **Christopher T. Geldart** .... (202) 727-6161
E-mail: christopher.geldart@dc.gov
Education: Maryland BA
Chief of Staff **Brian Baker** .... (202) 727-6161
E-mail: brian.baker@dc.gov

Office of the Chief Technology Officer [OCTO]

200 I Street SE, 5th Floor, Washington, DC 20003
Tel: (202) 727-2277 TTY: (202) 727-8673 Fax: (202) 727-6857
E-mail: octo@dc.gov

Employees: 283 **Fiscal Year:** 2015 **Budget:** $101,770,000

■ Chief Technology Officer **Archana Vemulapalli** .... (202) 727-2277
Education: Madras (India); Pennsylvania; Georgetown
Chief Data Officer **Dervel Reed** .... (202) 727-2277
E-mail: dervel.reed@dc.gov
Chief of Staff (Interim) **Carol Washington** .... (202) 727-2277
E-mail: carol.washington@dc.gov
Communications Director **Michael Rupert** .... (202) 724-5178
E-mail: michael.rupert@dc.gov

Office of Contracting and Procurement [OCP]

One Judiciary Square, 441 Fourth Street, NW, Suite 700 South, Washington, DC 20001
Tel: (202) 727-0252 Fax: (202) 727-3229 E-mail: ocp@dc.gov
Internet: www.ocp.dc.gov

■ Chief Procurement Officer **George A. Schutter** .... (202) 724-4242
E-mail: george.schutter@dc.gov
Education: Illinois Tech BSAcc; Naval Postgrad MS
Executive Assistant **Kimberly Diggs** .... (202) 724-5262
E-mail: kimberly.diggs@dc.gov
Chief of Staff **Gina Toppin** .... (202) 724-4089
E-mail: gina.toppin@dc.gov
Assistant Director for Procurement **Sheila Mobley** ...... (202) 724-4388
E-mail: sheila.mobley@dc.gov
Chief Learning Officer **Michael "Mike" Wooten** .... (202) 727-5557
Human Resources Officer **(Vacant)** .... (202) 724-4365
Business Operations Manager **(Vacant)** .... (202) 724-8759

Office of Unified Communications [OUC]

2720 Martin Luther King Jr. Avenue, SE, Washington, DC 20032
Tel: (202) 730-0524 Fax: (202) 730-0504 E-mail: director.ouc@dc.gov
Internet: www.ouc.dc.gov

■ Director **Karima Holmes** .... (202) 730-0503
E-mail: karima.holmes@dc.gov
Education: Augusta State BA

Department of Corrections [DOC]

Reese Building, 20009 14th Street NW, 7th Floor, Washington, DC 20001
Tel: (202) 673-7316 Fax: (202) 332-1470 Internet: http://doc.dc.gov

Employees: 863

■ Director **Thomas N. Faust** (D) .... (202) 673-7316
E-mail: thomas.faust@dc.gov
Education: Virginia Tech 1976 BS; George Mason 1989 MPA
Executive Assistant **Sallie Thomas** .... (202) 671-2314
E-mail: sallie.thomas@dc.gov
Warden **William J. Smith** .... (202) 673-7316
General Counsel **Maria Amato** .... (202) 671-2042
Government and Public Affairs Coordinator **Sylvia Lane** .. (202) 671-2137
E-mail: sylvia.lane@dc.gov

Department of General Services [DGS]

2000 14th Street, NW, 8th Floor, Washington, DC 20009
Tel: (202) 727-2800 Fax: (202) 727-9877

Employees: 651 **Fiscal Year:** 2015 **Budget:** $423,275,000

■ Director **RADM Christopher E. Weaver** .... (202) 727-2800
Education: Naval Acad 1971 BS; George Washington 1993 MPA
Chief of Staff **Latrina Owens** .... (202) 727-4400
E-mail: latrina.owens@dc.gov
Chief Financial Officer **Massimo Marchiori** .... (202) 727-2800

Department of Human Resources [DCHR]

One Judiciary Square, 441 Fourth Street, NW, Suite 330S, Washington, DC 20001
Tel: (202) 442-9700 Fax: (202) 727-6827 Internet: www.dchr.dc.gov

Employees: 133 **Fiscal Year:** 2015 **Budget:** $15,973,000

■ Director **Ventris Cassandra Gibson** (D) .... (202) 442-9700
Education: Maryland University Col
Deputy Director **(Vacant)** .... (202) 442-9700
Associate Director for Policy and Compliance
Justin Zimmerman .... (202) 442-9700
Administrative Officer **Laverne Harvey** .... (202) 442-9641
E-mail: laverne.harvey-johnson@dc.gov
Benefits and Retirement Group Associate Director
Candice Ahwah-Gonzalez .... (202) 442-9611
Learning and Development Associate Director (Interim)
Nicole Cook .... (202) 442-9654
E-mail: nicole.cook@dc.gov

Department of Public Works [DPW]

2000 14th Street, NW, 6th Floor, Washington, DC 20009
Tel: (202) 673-6833 TTY: (202) 673-6833 Fax: (202) 671-0642
E-mail: dpw@dc.gov

Employees: 1,417 **Fiscal Year:** 2015 **Budget:** $155,141,000

■ Director (Interim) **Christopher Shorter** .... (202) 673-6812
Special Assistant **Viola McIver** .... (202) 673-6812
E-mail: viola.mciver@dc.gov
Deputy Director **Karla Kirby** .... (202) 673-6833
Chief Financial Officer **Perry Fitzpatrick** .... (202) 671-2300
Fax: (202) 671-0626
Chief Information Officer **(Vacant)** .... (202) 671-0096
Fax: (202) 671-0637
Fleet Management Administrator **Edward Hamilton** ..... (202) 576-6799
E-mail: edward.hamilton@dc.gov Fax: (202) 576-7715
Parking Enforcement Management Administrator
Teri Adams .... (202) 541-6083
E-mail: teri.doke@dc.gov Fax: (202) 541-6113
Education: Hampton; Howard U JD
Solid Waste Management Administrator
Jeffrey H. Powell .... (202) 645-7044
E-mail: jeffrey.powell@dc.gov Fax: (202) 645-6040
Education: Virginia State; Howard U MBA
Freedom of Information Act (FOIA) Officer
Christine Davis .... (202) 673-2030
Fax: (202) 673-4555
Public Information Officer **Linda Grant** .... (202) 671-2375
E-mail: linda.grant@dc.gov

Office of the District of Columbia Auditor [ODCA]

717 14th Street NW, Washington, DC 20005
Tel: (202) 727-3600 TTY: (202) 855-1000 Fax: (202) 724-8814
E-mail: odca@dc.gov Internet: www.dcauditor.org

Auditor **Kathleen "Kathy" Patterson** (D) .... (202) 727-3600
Education: Northwestern 1970 BS; Georgetown 1990 MA
Deputy Auditor **Lawrence Perry** .... (202) 727-3600
Chief of Staff **Stacie Pittell** .... (202) 727-3600
General Counsel **Amy Bellanca** .... (202) 727-3600

★ Elected Official ▲ Appointed by Legislature ▼ Appointed by Governor ▶ Appointed by Board or Commission ● Appointed by Judge
■ Appointed by Mayor △ Appointed by Freeholders ▽ Appointed by Supervisor ▷ Appointed by County Executive ○ Appointed by Council

Office of Zoning [DCOZ]

441 4th Street NW, Suite 200 South, Washington, DC 20001
Tel: (202) 727-6311 Fax: (202) 727-6072 E-mail: dcoz@dc.gov

Director **Sara Bardin** .... (202) 727-5372
Education: Dayton BFA

DC Housing Finance Agency [DCHFA]

815 Florida Avenue, NW, Washington, DC 20001
Tel: (202) 777-1600 Fax: (202) 986-6736 Internet: www.dchfa.org

Board of Directors

Chair **Buwa Binitie** .... (202) 777-1600
Term Expires: 2017
Education: NYU BS; Johns Hopkins MS
Vice Chair **Stephen M. Green** .... (202) 777-1600
Term Expires: 2016
Member **Bryan "Scottie" Irving** .... (202) 777-1600
Term Expires: 2017
Education: Central State BS
Member **Stanley Jackson** .... (202) 777-1600
Term Expires: 2016
Education: Fayetteville State BS; Howard U MBA

Office of the Executive Director

Executive Director and CEO (Interim) **Todd A. Lee** .... (202) 777-1601
Deputy Executive Director **Fran D. Makle** .... (202) 777-1636
Associate Executive Director **W. David Watts** .... (202) 777-1600
Public Relations Manager **Yolanda McCutchen** .... (202) 777-1600
E-mail: yolanda.mccutchen@dc.gov
Executive Assistant **Karen Harris** .... (202) 777-1600

District of Columbia Water and Sewer Authority [DC Water]

5000 Overlook Ave., SW, Washington, DC 20032
Tel: (202) 787-2000 Fax: (202) 787-2333 E-mail: info@dcwater.com

Chairman **Matthew Brown** .... (202) 787-2330
Affiliation: Director, Office of Budget and Finance, Office of the City Administrator, District of Columbia
Education: Texas Wesleyan U BA; George Washington MPA
Principal Member **Ellen O. Boardman** .... (202) 787-2330
Principal Member **Rachna Butani** .... (202) 787-2330
Principal Member **Elisabeth "Lisa" Feldt** .... (202) 787-2330
Education: Union Col (NY) 1980 BSCE; George Washington 1984 BSCE
Principal Member **Timothy L. Firestine** .... (202) 787-2330
Principal Member **Bradley W. Frome** .... (202) 787-2330
Principal Member **Nicholas A. Majett** .... (202) 787-2330
Education: Howard U BS, 1985 JD
Principal Member **Obiora Menkiti** .... (202) 787-2330
Principal Member **James Patteson** .... (202) 787-2330
Principal Member **(Vacant)** .... (202) 787-2330
Principal Member **(Vacant)** .... (202) 787-2330
Secretary to the Board **Linda R. Manley** .... (202) 787-2330
E-mail: lmanley@dcwater.com

Management

Chief Executive Officer and General Manager
George S. Hawkins .... (202) 787-2609
Education: Princeton 1983 AB; Harvard 1987 JD
Chief of Staff **Mustaafa Dozier** .... (202) 787-2025
Chief Engineer **Leonard R. Benson** .... (202) 787-2609
E-mail: leonard.benson@dcwater.com
Chief Operating Officer **Biju George** .... (202) 787-2000
Engineering and Technical Services Director
Liliana Maldonado .... (202) 787-2358
Chief Marketing Officer **Alan R. Heymann** .... (202) 787-2000

Public Service Commission of the District of Columbia [PSC]

1333 H Street, NW, Second Floor West Tower, Washington, DC 20005
Tel: (202) 626-5100 Fax: (202) 626-9174 TTY: (202) 628-2428
Internet: www.dcpsc.org

Chairperson **Betty Ann Kane** .... (202) 626-5125
Education: Middlebury BA; Yale 1964 MA
Executive Assistant **Wendy Newkirk** .... (202) 626-5119
E-mail: wnewkirk@psc.dc.gov
Commissioner **Joanne Doddy Fort** .... (202) 626-5115
Education: Bryn Mawr BA
Executive Assistant **Mable Spears** .... (202) 626-5118
E-mail: mspears@psc.dc.gov
Executive Assistant **LaWanda Hale** .... (202) 626-9207
E-mail: lhale@psc.dc.gov

Board of Elections [BOEE]

One Judiciary Square, 441 Fourth Street, NW, Suite 250 North, Washington, DC 20001-2745
Tel: (202) 727-2525 TTY: (202) 639-8916 Fax: (202) 347-2648
Internet: www.dcboee.org

Chairman **David Michael Bennett** .... (202) 727-2525
Education: Duke 1977 BA; George Washington JD
Member **Michael "Mike" Gill** .... (202) 727-2525
Education: Dayton BA; Johns Hopkins MA; Columbus Law JD
Member **Dionna Maria Lewis** .... (202) 727-2525
Member-Designate **Andrew T. "Chip" Richardson** .... (202) 727-2525
Note: Andrew Richardson's nomination must be confirmed by the City Council.
Education: Purdue BA; William & Mary 1995 JD
Executive Director (Acting) **Terri Stroud** .... (202) 727-2525
Education: North Carolina; Georgetown JD

Campaign Finance Office [OCF]

Reeves Municipal Building, 2000 - 14th Street, NW, Suite 420, Washington, DC 20009
Fax: (202) 671-0658 Internet: www.ocf.dc.gov

Director **Cecily E. Collier-Montgomery** .... (202) 671-0550
Education: Howard U 1972 BA
Administrative Officer **Nadine Journiette** .... (202) 671-0547
E-mail: nadine.journiette@dc.gov
Chief Technology Officer **(Vacant)** .... (202) 671-0547

District of Columbia Public Library [DCPL]

901 G Street, NW, Washington, DC 20001-4531
Tel: (202) 727-1101 Fax: (202) 727-1129 TTY: (202) 727-2145
Internet: www.dclibrary.org

Administration

Executive Director **Richard Reyes-Gavilan** .... (202) 727-1101
E-mail: richard.reyes-gavilan@dc.gov
Education: SUNY (Albany); Texas MLIS
Martin Luther King, Jr. Memorial Library Associate Director **Kimberly Zablud** .... (202) 727-1222
E-mail: kimberly.zablud@dc.gov
Education: Carleton 2002 BA; Rutgers 2006 MLIS
Human Resources Director **Barbara L. Kirven** .... (202) 727-1131
E-mail: barbara.kirven@dc.gov
Education: Howard U
Marketing and Communications Director **Joi Mecks** .... (202) 727-1186
E-mail: joilette.mecks@dc.gov
Strategic Planning Director **Judi Greenberg** .... (202) 727-4919
E-mail: judi.greenberg@dc.gov
Information Technology and Systems Head
Odunlami Aromire .... (202) 727-5725
E-mail: odunlami.aromire@dc.gov
Workforce Training and Development Manager **(Vacant)** .. (202) 727-1101

★ Elected Official ▲ Appointed by Legislature ▼ Appointed by Governor ▶ Appointed by Board or Commission ● Appointed by Judge
■ Appointed by Mayor △ Appointed by Freeholders ▽ Appointed by Supervisor ▷ Appointed by County Executive ○ Appointed by Council

City of Dover, Delaware

City Hall, 15 E. Loockerman St., Dover, DE 19901
P.O. Box 475, Dover, DE 19903-0475
Internet: www.cityofdover.com

County: Kent **Election Type:** Nonpartisan **Population:** 37,522 (2015)

Office of the Mayor

P.O. Box 475, Dover, DE 19903-0475
Fax: (302) 736-7002

★ Mayor **Robin R. Christiansen** . . . . (302) 736-7005
Began Service: June 25, 2014
Term Expires: April 18, 2019
E-mail: rchristiansen@dover.de.us

Office of the City Council

P.O. Box 475, Dover, DE 19903-0475
Fax: (302) 736-7177

★ Council President **Timothy A. Slavin** (At-Large) . . . . (302) 736-7006
Term Expires: May 13, 2017
E-mail: timslavin1@gmail.com

★ Council Member **James Hosfelt, Jr.** (District 1) . . . . (302) 736-7006
Term Expires: May 18, 2019
E-mail: hosdover@msn.com

★ Council Member **James L. Hutchison** (District 1) . . . . (302) 736-7006
Term Expires: May 2017
E-mail: jlhutch9595@yahoo.com

★ Council Member **William F. Hare** (District 2) . . . . (302) 736-7006
Term Expires: May 2017
E-mail: billh2323@comcast.net

★ Council Member **Brian E. Lewis** (District 2) . . . . (302) 736-7006
Term Expires: May 18, 2019
E-mail: belewis1966@hotmail.com

★ Council Member **Scott W. Cole** (District 3) . . . . (302) 736-7006
Term Expires: May 18, 2019
E-mail: scott.cole@dsea.org

★ Council Member **Fred Neil** (District 3) . . . . (302) 678-3288
Term Expires: May 2017
E-mail: fredneilbooks@comcast.net

★ Council Member **David L. Anderson** (District 4) . . . . (302) 736-7006
Term Expires: May 2017
E-mail: davidlevianderson@gmail.com

★ Council Member **Roy Sudler, Jr.** (District 4) . . . . (302) 736-7006
Term Expires: May 18, 2019
E-mail: roysudlerjr@comcast.net

Office of the Assessor

P.O. Box 475, Dover, DE 19903-0475
Tel: (302) 736-7022 Fax: (302) 736-4450
E-mail: taxassessor@cityofdover.com

○ City Tax Assessor **Cheryl Bundek** . . . . (302) 376-7022
E-mail: cbundek@dover.de.us

Office of the City Clerk

P.O. Box 475, Dover, DE 19903-0475
Fax: (302) 736-5068

○ City Clerk **Traci A. McDowell** . . . . (302) 736-7008
E-mail: tmcdowell@dover.de.us

Office of the City Manager

P.O. Box 475, Dover, DE 19903-0475
Fax: (302) 736-7002

○ City Manager **Scott Koenig** . . . . (302) 736-7005
E-mail: skoenig@dover.de.us

Office of the Solicitor

P.O. Box 475, Dover, DE 19903-0475
Fax: (302) 674-1830

○ City Solicitor **Nicholas H. Rodriguez** . . . . (302) 674-0140
E-mail: nrodriguez@schmittrod.com

○ Deputy Solicitor **William W. Pepper, Sr.** . . . . (302) 674-0140

Customer Service Department

P.O. Box 7100, Dover, DE 19903-7100
Fax: (302) 736-7193 E-mail: adminservices@cityofdover.com

Director **Kathy Divver** . . . . (302) 736-7058
E-mail: kdivver@dover.de.us

Electric Department

860 Buttner Pl., Dover, DE 19904
Tel: (302) 736-7070 Fax: (302) 736-7081
E-mail: electric@cityofdover.com

Generation Manager **Harry A. Maloney III** . . . . (302) 736-7088

Finance Department

P.O. Box 475, Dover, DE 19903-0475
Fax: (302) 736-7177 E-mail: finance@cityofdover.com

○ Controller and Treasurer **Donna S. Mitchell** . . . . (302) 736-7018
E-mail: dmitchell@dover.de.us

Fire Department

103 S. Governors Ave., Dover, DE 19904
Tel: (302) 736-7168 Fax: (302) 736-7166 E-mail: fire@cityofdover.com

Fire Chief **Carleton Carey, Jr.** . . . . (302) 736-7167
E-mail: mhall@dover.de.us

Human Resources Department

P.O. Box 475, Dover, DE 19903-0475
Tel: (302) 736-7073 Fax: (302) 736-7093 E-mail: hr@cityofdover.com

Director **Kim Hawkins** . . . . (302) 736-7073
E-mail: khawkins@dover.de.us

Information Technology Department

P.O. Box 475, Dover, DE 19903-0475
Fax: (302) 672-1847 E-mail: it@cityofdover.com

Director **Andrew Siegel** . . . . (302) 736-5071
E-mail: asiegel@dover.de.us

Library

P.O. Box 475, Dover, DE 19903-0475

Director **Margery Cyr** . . . . (302) 736-7030
E-mail: margery.cyr@lib.de.us

Parks and Recreation Department

P.O. Box 475, Dover, DE 19903-0475
Tel: (302) 736-7050 Fax: (302) 736-7154 E-mail: parks@cityofdover.com

Director **Ann Marie Townshend** . . . . (302) 736-7050

Planning and Inspections Department

P.O. Box 475, Dover, DE 19903-0475
Fax: (302) 736-4217 E-mail: planning@cityofdover.com

Director **Ann Marie Townshend** . . . . (302) 736-7010

Police Department

400 S. Queen St., Dover, DE 19904
Tel: (302) 736-7111 Fax: (302) 736-7157
Internet: http://www.doverpolice.org

■ Chief of Police **Paul M. Bernat** . . . . (302) 736-7100
E-mail: Paul.Bernat@cj.state.de.us

★ Elected Official ▲ Appointed by Legislature ▼ Appointed by Governor ▶ Appointed by Board or Commission ● Appointed by Judge
■ Appointed by Mayor △ Appointed by Freeholders ▽ Appointed by Supervisor ▷ Appointed by County Executive ○ Appointed by Council

Public Works Department
P.O. Box 475, Dover, DE 19903-0475
Tel: (302) 736-7025 Fax: (302) 736-7177
E-mail: publicworks@cityofdover.com

Director **Sharon Duca** .... (302) 736-7025

City of Downey, California

11111 Brookshire Ave., Downey, CA 90241
Tel: (562) 904-7246 Internet: www.downeyca.org

County: Los Angeles **Election Type:** Nonpartisan **Population:** 114,219 (2015)

Office of the Mayor and City Council
11111 Brookshire Ave., Downey, CA 90241

★ Mayor **Alex Saab** (District 5) .... (562) 904-7274
Began Service: December 11, 2012
Term Expires: December 1, 2016
E-mail: asaab@downeyca.org

★ Mayor Pro Tem **Fernando Vasquez** (District 4) .... (562) 904-7274
Term Expires: December 1, 2018
E-mail: fvasquez@downeyca.org

★ Council Member **Luis H. Marquez** (District 1) .... (562) 904-7274
Term Expires: December 1, 2016
E-mail: lmarquez@downeyca.org

★ Council Member **Sean Ashton** (District 2) .... (562) 904-7274
Term Expires: December 1, 2018
E-mail: sashton@downeyca.org

★ Council Member **Roger C. Brossmer** (District 3) .... (562) 904-7274
Term Expires: December 1, 2016
E-mail: rbrossmer@downeyca.org

City Administration Department
11111 Brookshire Ave., Downey, CA 90241

City Manager **Gilbert Livas** .... (562) 904-7284
Assistant to the City Manager **Shannon DeLong** ...... (562) 904-7286
E-mail: sdelong@downeyca.org

Assistant City Manager **John Oskoui** .... (562) 904-7282
E-mail: joskoui@downeyca.org

Office of the City Attorney
11111 Brookshire Avenue, Downey, CA 90241
Tel: (562) 904-7288 Fax: (562) 923-6388

City Attorney **Yvette M. Abich Garcia** .... (562) 904-7288
E-mail: ygarcia@downeyca.org
Education: Loyola Marymount BA; Loyola Law JD

Office of the City Clerk
11111 Brookshire Ave., Downey, CA 90241

City Clerk **Adria Jimenez** .... (562) 904-7280
E-mail: ajimenez@downeyca.org

Community Development
11111 Brookshire Avenue, Downey, CA 90241
Fax: (562) 622-4816

Director **Aldo Schindler** .... (562) 904-7168
E-mail: aschindler@downeyca.org
Education: San Diego State BA; Cal State (Long Beach) MPA

Building and Safety Division
11111 Brookshire Avenue, Downey, CA 90241
Fax: (562) 622-4816

Building Official **Rik Hobbie** .... (562) 904-7142

Planning Division
11111 Brookshire Avenue, Downey, CA 90241

City Planner **William Davis** .... (562) 904-7154

Finance Department
11111 Brookshire Avenue, Downey, CA 90241
Tel: (562) 904-7265 Fax: (562) 904-7270

Finance and Technology Director **Anil H. Gandhy** .... (562) 904-7265
E-mail: agandhy@downeyca.org

Downey City Library
11121 Brookshire Ave., Downey, CA 90241-7015
Fax: (562) 923-3763

Senior Librarian **Dan Martin** .... (562) 904-7360
E-mail: dmartin@downeyca.org

Downey Unified School District
11627 Brookshire Ave., Downey, CA 90241
Internet: www.dusd.net Tel: (562) 469-6500

Superintendent **Dr. John A. Garcia, Jr.** .... (562) 469-6500

★ Board Member **Tod M. Corrin** .... (562) 469-6500
Term Expires: November 2019
E-mail: tcorrin@dusd.net

★ Board Member **William A. Gutierrez** .... (562) 469-6500
Term Expires: November 2019
E-mail: wgutierrez@dusd.net
Education: U Redlands 1980 BA

★ Board Member **Donald E. LaPlante** .... (562) 469-6500
Term Expires: November 2019
E-mail: dlaplante@dusd.net
Date of Birth: January 27, 1955
Education: USC 1967 BA; Point Loma 2003 MA

★ Board Member **D. Mark Morris** .... (562) 469-6500
Term Expires: November 2019
E-mail: mmorris@dusd.net

★ Board Member **Barbara Samperi** .... (562) 469-6500
Term Expires: November 2017
E-mail: bsamperi@dusd.net

★ Board Member **Martha E. Sodetani** .... (562) 469-6500
Term Expires: November 2017
E-mail: msodetani@dusd.net

★ Board Member **Nancy Swenson** .... (562) 469-6500
Term Expires: November 2017
E-mail: nswenson@dusd.net

Fire Department
11111 Brookshire Avenue, Downey, CA 90241

Fire Chief **Mark Gillaspie** .... (562) 904-7345
E-mail: mgillaspie@downeyca.org

Parks and Recreation Department
7850 Quill Drive, Downey, CA 90242

Parks and Recreation Director **Arlene Salazar** .... (562) 904-7238

Police Department
10911 South Brookshire Ave., Downey, CA 90241

Chief of Police **Carl Charles** .... (562) 861-0771

Public Works Department
City Hall, 11111 Brookshire Ave., Downey, CA 90241-7016
P.O Box 7016, Downey, CA 90241
Fax: (562) 904-7296

Director **Mohammad Mostahkami** .... (562) 904-7102

★ Elected Official ▲ Appointed by Legislature ▼ Appointed by Governor ▶ Appointed by Board or Commission ● Appointed by Judge
■ Appointed by Mayor △ Appointed by Freeholders ▽ Appointed by Supervisor ▷ Appointed by County Executive ○ Appointed by Council

City of Durham, North Carolina

101 City Hall Plaza, Durham, NC 27701-3329
Tel: (919) 560-1200 (Information) Internet: www.durhamnc.gov

County: Durham **Election Type:** Nonpartisan **Population:** 257,636 (2015)

William V. "Bill" Bell
Mayor

Began Service: 2001
Term Expires: December 2, 2017
Education: Howard U 1961 BSEE; NYU 1968 MSEE
Career: Senior Engineer, International Business Machines Corporation (1986-1996); Member, Board of Commissioners, County of Durham, North Carolina (1996-2000)

Office of the Mayor and City Council

101 City Hall Plaza, Durham, NC 27701-3329
Fax: (919) 560-4801 E-mail: citycouncil@durhamnc.gov

★Mayor **William V. "Bill" Bell** .... (919) 560-4333
E-mail: bill.bell@durhamnc.gov
★Mayor Pro Tempore **Cora Cole-McFadden** (Ward 1) ..... (919) 560-4396
Term Expires: December 2, 2017
E-mail: cora.cole-mcfadden@durhamnc.gov
★Council Member **Eddie Davis** (Ward 2) .... (919) 560-4396
Term Expires: December 2, 2017
E-mail: eddie.davis@durhamnc.gov
★Council Member **Don Moffitt** (Ward 3) .... (919) 560-4396
Term Expires: December 2, 2017
E-mail: don.moffitt@durhamnc.gov
★Council Member **Jillian Jonson** (At-Large) .... (919) 560-4396
Term Expires: December 3, 2019
★Council Member **Charlie Reece** (At-Large) .... (919) 560-4396
Term Expires: December 3, 2019
★Council Member **Steve Schewel** (At-Large) .... (919) 560-4396
Term Expires: December 3, 2019
E-mail: steve.schewel@durhamnc.gov

Office of the City Attorney

101 City Hall Plaza, Durham, NC 27701-3329
Fax: (919) 560-4660

○City Attorney **Patrick Baker** .... (919) 560-4158
E-mail: patrick.baker@durhamnc.gov

Office of the City Clerk

101 City Hall Plaza, Durham, NC 27701-3329
Fax: (919) 560-4835

○City Clerk **D. Ann Gray** .... (919) 560-4166
E-mail: ann.gray@durhamnc.gov

Office of the City Manager

101 City Hall Plaza, Durham, NC 27701-3329
Fax: (919) 560-4949

○City Manager **Thomas J. Bonfield** .... (919) 560-4222
E-mail: tom.bonfield@durhamnc.gov
Deputy City Manager **Keith Chadwell** .... (919) 560-4222
E-mail: keith.chadwell@durhamnc.gov
Deputy City Manager **Wanda Page** .... (919) 560-4222
E-mail: wanda.page@durhamnc.gov
Deputy City Manager **William "Bo" Ferguson** .... (919) 560-4222
E-mail: bo.ferguson@durhamnc.gov

Audit Service

101 City Hall Plaza, Durham, NC 27701-3329
Fax: (919) 560-1007

Director **Germaine Brewington** .... (919) 560-4213

Budget and Management Services

101 City Hall Plaza, Durham, NC 27701-3329
Fax: (919) 560-4687

Director **Bertha Johnson** .... (919) 560-4111
E-mail: bertha.johnson@durhamnc.gov

Community Development Department

401 Lakewood Ave., Durham, NC 27701-3329
Fax: (919) 560-4090

Director **Reginald Johnson** .... (919) 560-4570
E-mail: reginald.johnson@durhamnc.gov Fax: (919) 560-4090

Office of Economic and Workforce Development [OEWD]

101 City Hall Plaza, Durham, NC 27701-3329
Fax: (919) 560-4965

Director **(Vacant)** .... (919) 560-4965
Fax: (919) 560-4986

Emergency Communications

505 W. Chapel Hill St., Durham, NC 27701-3329
Fax: (919) 560-4713

Manager **James Soukup** .... (919) 560-4500
E-mail: james.soukup@durhamnc.gov

Equal Opportunity/Equity Assurance

211 Rigsbee Ave., Durham, NC 27701-3329
Fax: (919) 560-4513

Director **Deborah Giles** .... (919) 560-4180

Finance Department

101 City Hall Plaza, Durham, NC 27701-3329
Fax: (919) 560-1091

Director **David Boyd** .... (919) 560-4455
Deputy Finance Director **Keith R. Herrmann** .... (919) 560-4455
Education: Yale 1988 MBA Fax: (919) 687-0896
Treasury Manager **Chad Cowan** .... (919) 560-4511
Fax: (919) 560-1091
Business Services Manager **Monte Evans** .... (919) 560-4700
Fax: (919) 560-4842
Financial Operations Manager **Sue Sandhoff** .... (919) 560-4455
E-mail: sue.sandhoff@durhamnc.gov
Risk Management Manager **Glenn LeGrande** .... (919) 354-2740
E-mail: glenn.legrande@durhamnc.gov Fax: (919) 560-1151
Senior Safety Officer **Michael Anderson** .... (919) 560-4381
Fax: (919) 560-4632

Fire Department

2008 E. Club Blvd., Durham, NC 27701-3329
Fax: (919) 560-4256

Fire Chief **Daniel Curia** .... (919) 560-4242
E-mail: daniel.curia@durhamnc.gov

Fire Marshall

2422 Broad St., Durham, NC 27704
Fax: (919) 560-0670

Director/Fire Marshal **Eddie Reid** .... (919) 560-4233
E-mail: eddie.reid@durhamnc.gov Fax: (919) 560-1094

★Elected Official ▲Appointed by Legislature ▼Appointed by Governor ▶Appointed by Board or Commission ●Appointed by Judge
■Appointed by Mayor △Appointed by Freeholders ▽Appointed by Supervisor ▷Appointed by County Executive ○Appointed by Council

General Services
2011 Fay St., Durham, NC 27704
Fax: (919) 560-4970

Director **Steven W. Hicks** .... (919) 560-4197
E-mail: steven.hicks@durhamnc.gov

Fleet Management
1900 Camden Ave., Durham, NC 27701

Assistant Director **Joe Clark** .... (919) 560-4101
Fax: (919) 560-4631

Human Resources Department
101 City Hall Plaza, Durham, NC 27701-3329
Tel: (919) 560-4214 Fax: (919) 560-4969

Director **Regina Youngblood** .... (919) 560-4214
E-mail: regina.youngblood@durhamnc.gov Fax: (919) 560-4969

City/County Inspection
101 City Hall Plaza, Durham, NC 27701-3329
Fax: (919) 560-4484

Director **William E. "Gene" Bradham** .... (919) 560-4144

Neighborhood Improvement Services
401 Lakewood Ave., Durham, NC 27701-3329
Fax: (919) 560-4090

Director **Constance Stancil** .... (919) 560-1647
E-mail: constance.stancil@durhamnc.gov

Parks and Recreation Department
400 Cleveland Street, Durham, NC 27701
Fax: (919) 560-4021

Director **Rhonda B. Parker** .... (919) 560-4355
Programs Assistant Director **Joy Guy** .... (919) 560-4355

Planning, City/County
101 City Hall Plaza, Ground Floor, Durham, NC 27701
Fax: (919) 560-4641

Planning Director **Steven L. Medlin** .... (919) 560-4137

Police Department
505 W. Chapel Hill St., 5th Floor, Durham, NC 27701
Fax: (919) 560-4971 Internet: http://www.durhampolice.com

Police Chief (Interim) **Larry C. Smith** .... (919) 560-4322

Public Affairs
101 City Hall Plaza, Durham, NC 27701-3329
Fax: (919) 560-4949

Manager **Beverly B. Thompson** .... (919) 560-4123
E-mail: beverly.thompson@durhamnc.gov

Public Works Department
101 City Hall Plaza, Durham, NC 27701-3329
Fax: (919) 560-4316

Director **Marvin Williams** .... (919) 560-4326
Stormwater Services Manager **Ed Venable** .... (919) 560-4326
Transportation Director **Mark Ahrendsen** .... (919) 560-4366
Fax: (919) 560-4561

Department of Solid Waste Management
1833 Camden Ave., Durham, NC 27704
Fax: (919) 560-4647

Director **Donald Long** .... (919) 560-4186
Fax: (919) 560-4647
Assistant Director for Solid Waste Management Operations **Wayne Fenton** .... (919) 560-4186
E-mail: wayne.fenton@durhamnc.gov

Technology Solutions Department
101 City Hall Plaza, Durham, NC 27701-3329
Fax: (919) 560-4808

Director **Kerry Goode** .... (919) 560-4122
E-mail: kerry.goode@durhamnc.gov Fax: (919) 560-4699
GIS Development Administrator **Marcus Bryant** .... (919) 560-4122
E-mail: marcus.bryant@durhamnc.gov Fax: (919) 560-4699
Web Manager **John Stinson** .... (919) 560-4122
E-mail: john.stinson@durhamnc.gov Fax: (919) 560-4699

Water Management
1600 Mist Lake Dr., Durham, NC 27701-3329
Fax: (919) 560-4479

Director **Don Greeley** .... (919) 560-4381
Customer and Billing Services Manager **Maurice Chambers** .... (919) 560-4412
Fax: (919) 560-1107

City of El Monte, California

City Hall, 11333 Valley Blvd., El Monte, CA 91731-3293
Internet: www.elmonteca.gov

County: Los Angeles **Election Type:** Nonpartisan **Year Incorporated:** 1912 **Population:** 116,732 (2015)

Office of the Mayor and City Council
City Hall East, 11333 Valley Blvd., El Monte, CA 91731-3293
Fax: (626) 453-3612 E-mail: citycouncil@elmonteca.gov

★ Mayor **Andre Quintero** .... (626) 580-2001
Began Service: December 1, 2009
Term Expires: November 30, 2017
E-mail: citycouncil@elmonteca.gov
★ Mayor Pro Tem **Victoria "Vicky" Martinez** .... (626) 580-2001
Term Expires: November 30, 2019
E-mail: citycouncil@elmonteca.gov
★ Councilman **Juventino "J" Gomez** .... (626) 580-2001
Term Expires: November 30, 2017
E-mail: citycouncil@elmonteca.gov
★ Councilwoman **Norma Macias** .... (626) 580-2001
Term Expires: November 30, 2017
E-mail: citycouncil@elmonteca.gov
★ Councilman **Jerry Velasco** .... (626) 580-2001
Term Expires: November 30, 2019

Office of the City Manager
City Hall East, 11333 Valley Blvd., El Monte, CA 91731-3293
Fax: (626) 453-3612

City Manager **Jesus Gomez** .... (626) 580-2001
E-mail: jgomez@elmonteca.gov
Assistant City Manager **Alex Hamilton** .... (626) 580-2001

Office of the City Attorney
City Hall East, 11333 Valley Blvd., El Monte, CA 91731-3293
Fax: (626) 580-2290

City Attorney **Rick R. Olivarez** .... (626) 580-2010
E-mail: rolivarez@ogplaw.com
Senior Deputy City Attorney **David F. Gondek** .... (626) 580-2010
E-mail: dgondek@elmonteca.gov
Deputy City Attorney **Richard Padilla** .... (626) 580-2010
E-mail: rpadilla@elmonteca.gov

★ Elected Official ▲ Appointed by Legislature ▼ Appointed by Governor ▶ Appointed by Board or Commission ● Appointed by Judge
■ Appointed by Mayor △ Appointed by Freeholders ▽ Appointed by Supervisor ▷ Appointed by County Executive ○ Appointed by Council

Office of the City Clerk
City Hall East, 11333 Valley Blvd., El Monte, CA 91731
Fax: (626) 580-2274

★City Clerk **Jonathan Hawes** .... (626) 580-2016
Term Expires: November 30, 2017
E-mail: jhawes@elmonteca.gov
Chief Deputy City Clerk **M. Helen Mireles** .... (626) 580-2016
E-mail: hmireles@elmonteca.gov

Economic Development Department
City Hall West, 11333 Valley Blvd., El Monte, CA 91731
Fax: (626) 258-8659

Economic Development Director **Minh Thai** .... (626) 580-2093
E-mail: redevelopment@elmonteca.gov

Building Division
City Hall West, 11333 Valley Blvd., El Monte, CA 91731
Fax: (626) 258-8659

Chief Building Official **James Guerra** .... (626) 580-2050

Environmental Services Division
Fax: (626) 454-3143

Management Analyst **Susan Contreras** .... (626) 580-2058

Housing Division
City Hall West, 11333 Valley Blvd, El Monte, CA 91731
Fax: (626) 258-8629

Housing Programs Coordinator **Fernando Lopez** .... (626) 580-2070

Planning Division
City Hall West, 11333 Valley Blvd., El Monte, CA 91731
Fax: (626) 258-8659

Planning Services Manager **Jason Mikaelian** .... (626) 258-8626
Fax: (626) 258-8628

Finance Department
City Hall East, 11333 Valley Blvd., El Monte, CA 91731
Fax: (626) 443-2304

Finance Director **Ernestine Jones** .... (626) 580-2023

Information Technology Division
City Hall East, 11333 Valley Blvd., El Monte, CA 91731
Fax: (626) 443-2304

Information Technology Manager **Ahn Tran** .... (626) 580-2185
E-mail: atran@elmontepd.org

License and Treasury Division
City Hall East, 11333 Valley Blvd., El Monte, CA 91731
Fax: (626) 443-2102

★City Treasurer **(Vacant)** .... (626) 580-2031
Term Expires: November 30, 2017

Human Resources Department
City Hall East, 11333 Valley Blvd., El Monte, CA 91731
Fax: (626) 350-6197

Human Resources Director **Deborah Scott-Leistra** ...... (626) 580-2040
E-mail: humanresources@elmonteca.gov

Parks, Recreation, and Transportation Department
Community Center, 3150 Tyler Ave., El Monte, CA 91730
Fax: (626) 580-2237

Deputy City Manager for Community Services
Alexandra Lopez .... (626) 580-2200
E-mail: alopez@elmonteca.gov Fax: (626) 258-8668
Senior Services Manager **Marian Last** .... (626) 580-2200
E-mail: seniorservices@elmonteca.gov Fax: (626) 444-5056
Education: Cal State (Long Beach) MA

Parks, Recreation, and Transportation Department *continued*

Transportation Services Manager **Gwynn Stevens** ...... (626) 580-2217
3629 Cypress Ave., El Monte, CA 91731
Tel: (626) 580-2238

Police Department
Main Building, 11333 Valley Blvd., El Monte, CA 91731
Fax: (626) 444-2206

Chief of Police **David Reynoso** .... (626) 580-2110
Fax: (626) 580-2196
Communications Manager **Shannon Nurre** .... (626) 580-2168
Fax: (626) 580-2196

Public Works Department
3527 Santa Anita Ave., El Monte, CA 91731
Fax: (626) 580-2253 E-mail: publicworksmaintenance@elmonteca.gov

Director **Elaine Jeng** .... (626) 580-2250
Water Systems Supervisor **Victor Jimenez** .... (626) 580-2024
Fax: (626) 580-2253
Public Works Maintenance Division Superintendent
Michael Rodriguez .... (626) 580-2251
E-mail: pwmaintenance@elmonteca.gov

City of El Paso, Texas

300 North Campbell, El Paso, TX 79901
Tel: (915) 212-0000 (Information) Internet: www.elpasotexas.gov

County: El Paso **Election Type:** Nonpartisan **Population:** 681,124 (2015)

Office of the Mayor and City Council
City Hall, Two Civic Center Plaza, 10th Floor, El Paso, TX 79901-1153

★Mayor **Oscar Leeser** .... (915) 212-0021
Began Service: June 24, 2013
Term Expires: June 22, 2017
★Council Member **Peter Svarzbein** (District 1) .... (915) 212-0001
Term Expires: June 2019 Fax: (915) 212-0011
★Council Member **(Vacant)** (District 2) .... (915) 212-0002
Term Expires: June 22, 2017 Fax: (915) 212-0012
E-mail: district2@elpasotexas.gov
★Council Member **Emma Acosta** (District 3) .... (915) 212-0003
Term Expires: June 22, 2017 Fax: (915) 212-0013
E-mail: district3@elpasotexas.gov
★Council Member **Carl L. Robinson** (District 4) .... (915) 212-0004
Term Expires: June 22, 2017 Fax: (915) 212-0014
E-mail: district4@elpasotexas.gov
★Council Member **Mike Noe** (District 5) .... (915) 212-0005
Term Expires: June 13, 2019 Fax: (915) 212-0015
E-mail: district5@elpasotexas.gov
★Council Member **Claudia Ordaz** (District 6) .... (915) 212-0006
Term Expires: June 13, 2019 Fax: (915) 212-0015
E-mail: district6@elpasotexas.gov
★Council Member **Lilly Limon** (District 7) .... (915) 212-0007
Term Expires: June 22, 2017 Fax: (915) 212-0017
E-mail: district7@elpasotexas.gov
★Council Member **Cortney Niland** (District 8) .... (915) 212-0008
Term Expires: June 13, 2019 Fax: (915) 212-0018
E-mail: district8@elpasotexas.gov

Office of the City Manager
300 North Campbell, El Paso, TX 79901
Fax: (915) 212-0024 Internet: http://home.elpasotexas.gov/city-manager/

City Manager **Tommy Gonzalez** .... (915) 212-0023
E-mail: citymanager@elpasotexas.gov
Education: Eastern New Mexico BS; Texas Tech MPA

★Elected Official ▲Appointed by Legislature ▼Appointed by Governor ►Appointed by Board or Commission ●Appointed by Judge
■Appointed by Mayor △Appointed by Freeholders ▽Appointed by Supervisor ▷Appointed by County Executive ○Appointed by Council

Office of the City Manager *continued*

Public Information and Marketing Corporate Manager
Juliet Lozano . . . . . (915) 212-0031
Fax: (915) 212-0032
Assistant to the City Manager **Laura Cruz-Acosta** . . . . . (915) 212-0023
Assistant to the City Manager **Aeon James Downey** . . . . (915) 212-0023

Deputy City Manager for Health and Safety

300 North Cambpell, El Paso, TX 79901
Fax: (915) 212-0024

Deputy City Manager for Health and Safety **(Vacant)** . . . . (915) 212-1069

Office of the Municipal Clerk

City Hall, Two Civic Center Plaza, 2nd Floor, El Paso, TX 79901-1153
Fax: (915) 212-0050 E-mail: cityclerk@elpasotexas.gov
Internet: http://www.elpasotexas.gov/muni_clerk/

City Clerk **Richarda Duffy Momsen** . . . . . (915) 212-0049
E-mail: ClerksOffice@elpasotexas.gov
Assistant Municipal Clerk **(Vacant)** . . . . . (915) 212-0049

Municipal Court

300 North Campbell, El Paso, TX 79901
Tel: (915) 546-2901 Fax: (915) 546-2939

Municipal Court Clerk **Richarda Duffy Momsen** . . . . . (915) 546-2955
Assistant Municipal Court Clerk **Lelila Worrell** . . . . . (915) 546-2955

Department of Community and Human Development [DCHD]

801 Texas, El Paso, TX 79901
Fax: (915) 541-4846 Internet: http://www.elpasotexas.gov/commdev/

Director **Verónica Soto** . . . . . (915) 212-0138
E-mail: sotov@elpasotexas.gov
Housing Program Manager **Patricia A. White** . . . . . (915) 212-0139

Environmental Services and Code Enforcement Department

7968 San Paulo Drive, El Paso, TX 79907
Fax: (915) 212-6100
Internet: www.elpasotexas.gov/environmental_services/

Director **Ellen A. Smyth** . . . . . (915) 212-6048

Fire Department

8600 Montana, El Paso, TX 79925
Internet: http://home.elpasotexas.gov/fire-department/

Fire Chief **Samuel Peña** . . . . . (915) 485-5610
E-mail: epfd@elpasotexas.gov
Assistant Fire Chief **Mario D'Agostino** . . . . . (915) 485-5608
E-mail: dagostinomm@elpasotexas.gov
Assistant Fire Chief **Calvin Shanks** . . . . . (915) 485-5632
E-mail: shankscd@elpasotexas.gov
Emergency Management Coordinator
Avelardo Talavera . . . . . (915) 838-3260

Police Department

911 N. Raynor, El Paso, TX 79903
Internet: http://www.elpasotexas.gov/police/

Police Chief **Gregory Allen** . . . . . (915) 564-7308

Department of Public Health

5115 El Paso Drive, El Paso, TX 79905-2818
Tel: (915) 212-0200 Fax: (915) 212-0167
Internet: https://www.elpasotexas.gov/public-health

Director **Robert Resendes** . . . . . (915) 212-6502
Administrative Assistant **Perla Ramos** . . . . . (915) 212-0200
E-mail: ramosgp1@elpasotexas.gov
Deputy Director **Angela Mora** . . . . . (915) 212-0200
Epidemiology Program Manager **Fernando Gonzalez** . . . . (915) 212-0200
WIC (Women, Infants, and Children) Manager
Bertha Amaya . . . . . (915) 212-0200
Health Education and Training **Sue E. Beatty** . . . . . (915) 212-0200
E-mail: sue.e.beatty@elpasotexas.gov

Chief Financial Officer

300 North Cambpell, 2nd Floor, El Paso, TX 79901
Fax: (915) 212-0025

Chief Financial Officer **Mark D. Sutter** . . . . . (915) 212-1069
Comptroller **Pat Degman** . . . . . (915) 212-0040
Assistant to the Chief Financial Officer **Fred Lopez** . . . . . (915) 212-1145

Office of the Tax Assessor/Collector

City Hall, Two Civic Center Plaza, First Floor, El Paso, TX 79901-1196
P.O. Box 2992, El Paso, TX 79999-2992
Fax: (915) 212-0107

Tax Assessor/Collector **Maria O. Pasillas** . . . . . (915) 212-0106
E-mail: pasillasm@elpasotexas.gov

Engineering and Construction Management Department

City Hall, Two Civic Center Plaza, 4th Floor, El Paso, TX 79901-1153
Fax: (915) 212-0066

Director of Engineering **Irene Ramirez** . . . . . (915) 212-0065
E-mail: engineeringhelpdesk@elpasotexas.gov
Assistant City Engineer **John K. Glendon** . . . . . (915) 212-0065
E-mail: clerksoffice@elpasotexas.gov
Engineering Program Manager **Javier Reyes** . . . . . (915) 212-0065
E-mail: reyesj@elpasotexas.gov

Facilities and Fleet Management Department

1059 Lafayette, El Paso, TX 79907
Fax: (915) 621-6818
Internet: http://home.elpasotexas.gov/general-services/

Deputy Director **(Vacant)** . . . . . (915) 621-6821
Sustainability Office Director **Lauren Baldwin** . . . . . (915) 212-1621
Building 3, 1059 Lafayette Drive, El Paso, TX 79907

Purchasing Division

300 North Campbell, El Paso, TX 79901
Fax: (915) 212-0043

Purchasing Manager **Bruce Collins** . . . . . (915) 212-0041
E-mail: purmail@elpasotexas.gov

Streets and Maintenance Department

7968 San Paulo Drive, El Paso, TX 79907
Fax: (915) 212-0119 Internet: http://www.elpasotexas.gov/streets

Director **Ted Marquez** . . . . . (915) 212-0118

El Paso Water Utilities

1154 Hawkins Blvd., El Paso, TX 79925
P.O. Box 511, El Paso, TX 79961-0001
Fax: (915) 594-5666 Internet: http://www.epwu.org

President and Chief Executive Officer **John E. Balliew** . . . (915) 594-5501
Vice President, Operations and Technical Services
Alan Shubert . . . . . (915) 594-5644
E-mail: ashubert@epwu.org
Vice President, Strategic, Financial and Management Services **Marcela Navarrete** . . . . . (915) 594-5614
Chief Financial Officer **Arturo Duran** . . . . . (915) 594-5549
Chief Operations Officer **Fernie Rico** . . . . . (915) 594-5502
E-mail: frico@epwu.org
Chief Technical Officer **Gilbert Trejo** . . . . . (915) 594-5597
E-mail: gtejo@epwu.org
General Counsel **Lupe Cuellar** . . . . . (915) 594-5636
Assistant General Counsel **Lowell M. Stokes** . . . . . (915) 594-5507
Government Affairs Manager **Hector Gonzalez** . . . . . (915) 594-5661
E-mail: hegonzalez@epwu.org
Human Resources Manager **Ana Sanchez** . . . . . (915) 594-5519
E-mail: asanchez@epwu.org
Marketing and Communications Manager
Christina Montoya . . . . . (915) 594-5596
E-mail: cmontoya@epwu.org

★ Elected Official ▲ Appointed by Legislature ▼ Appointed by Governor ▶ Appointed by Board or Commission ● Appointed by Judge
■ Appointed by Mayor △ Appointed by Freeholders ▽ Appointed by Supervisor ▷ Appointed by County Executive ○ Appointed by Council

Public Service Board
1154 Hawkins Blvd., El Paso, TX 79925
P.O. Box 511, El Paso, TX 79961-0001

○ Chair **Henry Gallardo** .... (915) 594-5501
E-mail: hgallardo@epwu.org
○ Vice Chair **Christopher Antcliff** .... (915) 594-5501
E-mail: cantcliff@epwu.org
○ Secretary-Treasurer **Terri Garcia** .... (915) 594-5501
E-mail: tgarcia@epwu.org
○ Member **Oscar Leeser** .... (915) 541-4145
E-mail: oleeser@epwu.org
○ Member **Kristina D. Mena** .... (915) 594-5501
○ Member **Bradley Roe** .... (915) 594-5501
○ Member **Dr. Richard T. Schoephoerster** .... (915) 594-5501
E-mail: rschoephoerster@epwu.org
Education: Iowa 1985 BS, 1986 MSME, 1989 PhD

Chief Performance Officer
300 North Campbell, El Paso, TX 79901

Chief Performance Officer **Nancy Bartlett** .... (915) 212-0024
E-mail: bartlettn@elpasotexas.gov
Strategic Planning Coordinator **Cheryl Feldman** .... (915) 212-0023

Office of Management and Budget
Wells Fargo Plaza, 221 North Kansas, 16th Floor, El Paso, TX 79901
Fax: (915) 212-0037

Director **Robert Cortinas** .... (915) 212-1092
E-mail: cortinasr@elpasotexas.gov

Human Resources Department
300 North Campbell, El Paso, TX 79901
Fax: (915) 212-0046 E-mail: cityhr@elpasotx.gov
Internet: http://www.elpasotexas.gov/personnel/

Human Resources Director **Linda Ball-Thomas** .... (915) 212-0045
E-mail: CityHR@elpasotexas.gov

Information Technology Department [DoITS]
218 North Campbell Street, El Paso, TX 79901
Fax: (915) 212-0073

Director **Enrique Martinez, Jr.** .... (915) 212-0072
E-mail: it@elpasotexas.gov
Project Manager **Araceli Guerra** .... (915) 212-0072
E-mail: guerraa@elpasotexas.gov

Quality of Life Managing Director
City Hall, Two Civic Center Plaza, El Paso, TX 79901-1153
Fax: (915) 541-4576

Quality of Life Managing Director **Bryan Crowe** .... (915) 212-0000

Convention and Visitors Bureau
One Civic Center Plaza, El Paso, TX 79901
Internet: http://www.elpasocvb.com/

Director **Bryan Crowe** .... (915) 534-0601
Fax: (915) 534-0687
Director of Finance **Cori Navado** .... (915) 534-0602
Fax: (915) 534-0680

El Paso Public Library
501 N. Oregon St., El Paso, TX 79901
Fax: (915) 543-5410 Internet: www.elpasotexas.gov/library/

Library Director **Dionne Mack-Harvin** .... (915) 543-5401
E-mail: mack-harvind@elpasotexas.gov
Education: SUNY (Brockport) 1994 BS; SUNY (Albany) 1995 MA, 1996 MLIS

Museums and Cultural Affairs Department [MCAD]
400 West San Antonio Avenue, Suite A, El Paso, TX 79901
Fax: (915) 541-4902 Internet: www.elpasotexas.gov/mcad/

Director **Tracey Jerome** .... (915) 212-0110
Fax: (915) 212-0111

Museums and Cultural Affairs Department *continued*

Art Museum Director **Michael Tomor** .... (915) 532-1707
One Arts Festival Plaza, El Paso, TX 79901 Fax: (915) 532-1010
History Museum Director **Julia Bussinger** .... (915) 351-3588
510 North Santa Fe Street, El Paso, TX 79901 Fax: (915) 351-4345
Archaeology Museum Director **Julia Bussinger** .... (915) 755-4332
4301 Transmountain Road, El Paso, TX 79924 Fax: (915) 759-6824

Parks and Recreation Department
801 Texas Avenue, 2nd Floor, El Paso, TX 79901
Fax: (915) 212-0093 Internet: http://home.elpasotexas.gov/parks/

Director **Tracy Novak** .... (915) 212-0092
Aquatics Manager **Wright Stanton III** .... (915) 212-0092
Fax: (915) 533-5640
Park Operations Manager **Richard Garcia** .... (915) 212-0092
Zoo Director **Steve Marshall** .... (915) 521-1854
4001 East Paisano, El Paso, TX 79905 Fax: (915) 521-1857

Economic Development Department
801 Texas Avenue, El Paso, TX 79901
Tel: (915) 212-0094

Director **Cary S. Westin** .... (915) 212-0094
E-mail: westinc@elpasotexas.gov

El Paso International Airport
6701 Convair Rd., El Paso, TX 79925
Fax: (915) 779-5452 E-mail: airportpublicrelations@elpasotexas.gov
Internet: http://www.elpasointernationalairport.com/

Aviation Director **Monica Lombraña** .... (915) 780-4700

Planning and Inspections Department
801Texas Avenue, El Paso, TX 79901
Fax: (915) 212-0083
Internet: http://home.elpasotexas.gov/city-development/

Director of Planning **Larry Nichols** .... (915) 212-0083
Fax: (915) 212-0086

Mass Transit Department/Sun Metro
10151 Montana, El Paso, TX 79925
Fax: (915) 212-3302 Internet: http://www.sunmetro.net/

Director **Jay Banasiak** .... (915) 212-3333

Office of the City Attorney
300 North Campbell, El Paso, TX 79901
Internet: http://home.elpasotexas.gov/city-attorney/

○ City Attorney **Sylvia B. Firth** .... (915) 212-0033
E-mail: cityattorney@elpasotexas.gov
Deputy City Attorney **Theresa Cullen** .... (915) 212-1102
Deputy City Attorney **Laura Gordon** .... (915) 212-1101
Education: Texas Tech 1983 JD

★ Elected Official ▲ Appointed by Legislature ▼ Appointed by Governor ► Appointed by Board or Commission ● Appointed by Judge
■ Appointed by Mayor △ Appointed by Freeholders ▽ Appointed by Supervisor ▷ Appointed by County Executive ○ Appointed by Council

City of Elgin, Illinois

150 Dexter Court, Elgin, IL 60120-5570
Tel: (847) 931-6100 Internet: www.cityofelgin.org

County: Kane; Cook **Election Type:** Nonpartisan **Year Incorporated:** 1854 **Population:** 112,111 (2015)

Office of the Mayor and City Council

150 Dexter Court, Elgin, IL 60120-5555
Tel: (847) 931-5595 Fax: (847) 931-5610

★Mayor **David Kaptain** .... (847) 931-5598
Began Service: April 27, 2011
Term Expires: April 27, 2019
E-mail: mayor@cityofelgin.org
Education: Bradley BS

★Council Member **Richard Dunne** .... (847) 931-5590
Term Expires: April 27, 2017
E-mail: rdunne@cityofelgin.org

★Council Member **Terry L. Gavin** .... (847) 931-5590
Term Expires: April 27, 2017
E-mail: gavin_t@cityofelgin.org

★Council Member **Rosamaria Martinez** .... (847) 931-5590
Term Expires: April 27, 2019

★Council Member **Tish Powell** .... (847) 931-5590
Term Expires: April 27, 2019
E-mail: powell_t@cityofelgin.org

★Council Member **John Prigge** .... (847) 931-5590
Term Expires: April 27, 2017
E-mail: prigge_j@cityofelgin.org

★Council Member **Carol Rauschenberger** .... (847) 931-5590
Term Expires: April 27, 2017
E-mail: rauschenberger_c@cityofelgin.org

★Council Member **Toby Shaw** .... (847) 931-5590
Term Expires: April 27, 2019
E-mail: shaw_t@cityofelgin.org

★Council Member **F. John Steffen** .... (847) 931-5590
Term Expires: April 27, 2019
E-mail: steffen_j@cityofelgin.org
Education: Illinois BA; John Marshall JD

Office of the City Manager

150 Dexter Court, Elgin, IL 60120-5570
Tel: (847) 931-5590 Fax: (847) 931-5610

○City Manager **Sean R. Stegall** .... (847) 931-5590
E-mail: roder_n@cityofelgin.org
Education: Western Illinois BA; Northern Illinois MPA

Assistant City Manager **Richard G. Kozal** .... (847) 931-6633
E-mail: kozal_r@cityofelgin.org
Education: Lake Forest Col BA; Loyola U (Chicago) JD

Communications Director **Kristine Rogowski** .... (847) 931-6091
E-mail: rogowski_k@cityofelgin.org

311 Citizen Services Director **Colby Basham** .... (847) 931-5978
E-mail: basham_c@cityofelgin.org

Office of the City Clerk

150 Dexter Court, Elgin, IL 60120-5570
Fax: (847) 931-6027

City Clerk **Kim Dewis** .... (847) 931-5660
E-mail: dewis_k@cityofelgin.org

Deputy City Clerk **Jennifer Quinton** .... (847) 931-5666
E-mail: quinton_j@cityofelgin.org

Community Development Department

150 Dexter Court, Elgin, IL 60120-5570
Fax: (847) 931-6790

Director **Marc Mylott** .... (847) 931-5914
E-mail: mylott_m@cityofelgin.org

Community Development Department *continued*

Administrative Assistant **Crystal McGuire** .... (847) 931-5939
E-mail: mcguire_c@cityofelgin.org

Code Administration and Development Services Division

150 Dexter Court, Elgin, IL 60120-5570
Fax: (847) 931-6790

Code Enforcement Manager **Vincent Cuchetto** .... (847) 931-5629
Public Health Coordinator **Brad Bohner** .... (847) 931-5934

Planning and Neighborhood Services Division

150 Dexter Court, Elgin, IL 60120-5570

Senior Planner **Sarosh Saher** .... (847) 931-5943
Historic Preservation and Grants Planner
Christen Sundquist .... (847) 931-6004

Finance Department

150 Dexter Court, Elgin, IL 60120-5570
Fax: (847) 931-5622

Chief Financial Officer **Debra Nawrocki** .... (847) 931-5624

Fire Administration

550 Summit Street, Elgin, IL 60120
Tel: (847) 931-6175 Fax: (847) 931-6179

Fire Chief **John Fahy** .... (847) 931-6180
E-mail: fahy_j@cityofelgin.org

Assistant Fire Chief **David Schmidt** .... (847) 931-6175
E-mail: schmidt_d@cityofelgin.org

Assistant Fire Chief **Bryan McMahon** .... (847) 931-6181

Human Resources Department

150 Dexter Court, Elgin, IL 60120-5570
Tel: (847) 931-6076 Fax: (847) 931-5906

Human Resources Director **Gail Cohen** .... (847) 931-5607
E-mail: cohen_g@cityofelgin.org

Information Technology Services

150 Dexter Court, Elgin, IL 60120-5570
Tel: (847) 931-5641 Fax: (847) 931-6109

Manager **Jeff Massey** .... (847) 931-5642
E-mail: massey_j@cityofelgin.org

Legal Department

150 Dexter Court, Elgin, IL 60120-5570
Tel: (847) 931-5655 Fax: (847) 931-5665

Corporation Counsel **William Cogley** .... (847) 931-5659
Assistant Corporation Counsel **Christopher Beck** .... (847) 931-5657
Assistant Corporation Counsel **Michael Gehrman** .... (847) 931-5658

Parks and Recreation Department

100 Symphony Way, Elgin, IL 60120
Tel: (847) 931-6123 Fax: (847) 531-7020

Director **Randy Reopelle** .... (847) 931-6127

Police Department

151 Douglas Avenue, Elgin, IL 60120-5570
Tel: (847) 289-2740 Fax: (847) 289-2750

Police Chief **Jeff Swoboda** .... (847) 289-2760
Police Deputy Chief **Bill Wolf** .... (847) 289-2762

Public Works Department

1900 Holmes Road, Elgin, IL 60123
Tel: (847) 697-3160 Fax: (847) 931-5983
E-mail: elginpw@cityofelgin.org

Superintendent of Parks **Greg Rokos** .... (847) 931-5966

★Elected Official ▲Appointed by Legislature ▼Appointed by Governor ▶Appointed by Board or Commission ●Appointed by Judge
■Appointed by Mayor △Appointed by Freeholders ▽Appointed by Supervisor ▷Appointed by County Executive ○Appointed by Council

Building Maintenance Department
1900 Holmes Road, Elgin, IL 60123

Building Maintenance Superintendent **Richard "Rich" Hoke** . . . . (847) 931-5650
E-mail: hoke_r@cityofelgin.org

Engineering Division
1900 Holmes Road, Elgin, IL 60123
Tel: (847) 931-5955 Fax: (847) 931-5965

City Engineer **Joe Evers** . . . . (847) 931-5958
E-mail: evers_j@cityofelgin.org

Purchasing Department
150 Dexter Court, Elgin, IL 60120-5570
Fax: (847) 931-5689

Purchasing Officer **Daina DeNye** . . . . (847) 931-5604
E-mail: denye_d@cityofelgin.org

Water Department
375 West River Road, Elgin, IL 60120
Tel: (847) 931-6150

Water Director **Kyla Jacobsen** . . . . (847) 931-6160

City of Elizabeth, New Jersey
City Hall, 50 Winfield Scott Plaza, Elizabeth, NJ 07201
Internet: www.elizabethnj.org

County: Union **Election Type:** Partisan **Year Founded:** 1664
Year Incorporated: 1855 **Charter:** 1961 **Population:** 129,007 (2015)

J. Christian Bollwage (D)
Mayor

Began Service: 1993
Term Expires: December 31, 2016
Career: Sales, Marketing, and Public Relations Representative, A & J Trading Corporation; Traffic Coordinator, Kerr Steamship Inc.

Office of the Mayor
City Hall, 50 Winfield Scott Plaza, Elizabeth, NJ 07201

★ Mayor **J. Christian Bollwage** (D) . . . . (908) 820-4170
E-mail: cbollwage@njslom.org

Department of Administration
City Hall, 50 Winfield Scott Plaza, Elizabeth, NJ 07201

■ Business Administrator **Bridget S. Zellner** . . . . (908) 820-4280
E-mail: bzellner@elizabethnj.org
Assistant Business Administrator **Marie Krupinski** . . . . (908) 820-4277
E-mail: mkrupinski@elizabethnj.org
Personnel Officer **Anita Pritchard** . . . . (908) 820-4284
E-mail: apritchard@elizabethnj.org
Employee Benefits **(Vacant)** . . . . (908) 820-4281
Purchasing Agent **Jill McDonough** . . . . (908) 820-4174
E-mail: jmcdonough@elizabethnj.org

Department of Finance
City Hall, 50 Winfield Scott Plaza, Elizabeth, NJ 07201

Accounts and Controls Comptroller/Chief Financial Officer **Anthony Zengaro** . . . . (908) 820-4097
E-mail: AZengaro@ElizabethNJ.org

Department of Finance *continued*

City Assessor **Enrico Emma** . . . . (908) 820-4140
E-mail: eemma@elizabethnj.org
Revenue Tax Collector and Treasurer **Paul Lesniak** . . . . (908) 820-4111
E-mail: plesniak@elizabethnj.org

Elizabeth Public Library
11 S. Broad St., Elizabeth, NJ 07201

Director **Mary Faith Chmiel** . . . . (908) 354-6060 ext. 7253

Fire Department
316 Irvington Ave., Elizabeth, NJ 07201

■ Director **Onofrio Vitullo** . . . . (908) 820-2805
E-mail: ovitullo@elizabethnj.org
Fire Chief **Thomas McNamarra** . . . . (908) 820-2806
E-mail: tmcnamarra@ucnj.org

Department of Health and Human Services
City Hall, 50 Winfield Scott Plaza, Elizabeth, NJ 07201
Fax: (908) 820-4290

■ Director **Krishna H. Garlic** . . . . (908) 820-4049
E-mail: kgarlic@elizabethnj.org
Health Officer **Mark Colicchio** . . . . (908) 820-4060
Chief Housing Inspector **Hassan Abdur-Rahman** . . . . (908) 820-4059
Housing Division Relocation **Rev. Joe Adair** . . . . (908) 820-4215
Weights and Measures Bureau Superintendent **(Vacant)** . . . . (908) 820-4113

Department of Law
City Hall, 50 Winfield Scott Plaza, Elizabeth, NJ 07201
Fax: (908) 352-8658

■ City Attorney **William R. Holzapfel** . . . . (908) 820-4009
E-mail: wholzapfel@elizabethnj.org
First Assistant **Raymond T. Bolanowski** . . . . (908) 820-4009
Second Assistant **Rocco Di Paola** . . . . (908) 820-4009
Special Counsel **Jorge Estrada** . . . . (908) 820-4009
Special Counsel **Robert J. Lenahan, Jr.** . . . . (908) 820-4009

Police Department
One Police Plaza, Elizabeth, NJ 07201
Fax: (908) 558-2097

■ Director **James M. Cosgrove** . . . . (908) 558-2020
E-mail: jcosgrove@ucnj.org
Chief of Police **Patrick Shannon** . . . . (908) 558-2020
Emergency Medical Services **Richard Biedrzycki** . . . . (908) 558-2020

Planning and Community Development
City Hall, 50 Winfield Scott Plaza, Elizabeth, NJ 07201
Fax: (908) 820-3776

■ Director **Eduardo J. Rodriguez** . . . . (908) 820-4160
Elizabeth Home Improvement **Susan Ucci** . . . . (908) 352-8450
E-mail: succi@elizabethnj.org
Home Improvement Program Housing Coordinator **Jumilah S. Abdul-Baatin** . . . . (908) 352-8450
E-mail: jabdul-baatin@elizabethnj.org
Public Information Officer **Kelly Vence** . . . . (908) 820-4124
E-mail: kvence@elizabethnj.org
Planning and Zoning Board **Marta Rivera** . . . . (908) 820-4023
Construction Official **Raywant Sarran** . . . . (908) 820-4091
Housing Division Code Enforcement **Edward Kirk** . . . . (908) 820-4068
Licensing Division Chief Inspector **Clara Goodridge** . . . . (908) 820-4179

Department of Public Works
City Hall, 50 Winfield Scott Plaza, Elizabeth, NJ 07201
Fax: (908) 820-4011

■ Director **John F. Papetti, Jr.** . . . . (908) 820-4101
E-mail: jpapetti@elizabethnj.org

★ Elected Official ▲ Appointed by Legislature ▼ Appointed by Governor ▶ Appointed by Board or Commission ● Appointed by Judge
■ Appointed by Mayor △ Appointed by Freeholders ▽ Appointed by Supervisor ▷ Appointed by County Executive ○ Appointed by Council

Department of Public Works *continued*

Engineering and Administration Engineer
Daniel J. Loomis . . . . (908) 820-4269
E-mail: dloomis@elizabethnj.org
Maintenance and Construction Superintendent
Carlos Carvalho . . . . (908) 820-4173
E-mail: ccarvalho@elizabethnj.org
Recycling Coordinator **Pasquale A. Vella** . . . . . . (908) 820-4154
Public Buildings, Markets, and Docks Superintendent
Anthony Bottitta . . . . (908) 820-4105
E-mail: abottitta@elizabethnj.org

Recreation Department

City Hall, 50 Winfield Scott Plaza, Elizabeth, NJ 07201
Fax: (908) 820-4224

■ Director **Paul M. Addessa** . . . . (908) 820-4226
E-mail: paddessa@elizabethnj.org
Assistant Superintendent **Joseph Sullivan** . . . . . . (908) 820-4223

Office of the City Council

City Hall, 50 Winfield Scott Plaza, Elizabeth, NJ 07201
Fax: (908) 820-4021

★ Council President **Nelson Gonzalez** (D-Ward 2) . . . . (908) 820-4130
Term Expires: December 31, 2018
E-mail: ngonzalez@elizabethnj.org
★ Council Member **Carlos Torres** (D-Ward 1) . . . . . (908) 820-4130
Term Expires: December 31, 2018
E-mail: councilmantorres@gmail.com
★ Council Member **Kevin Kiniery** (D-Ward 3) . . . . . (908) 820-4130
Term Expires: December 31, 2018
★ Council Member **Carlos Cedeno** (D-Ward 4) . . . . . (908) 820-4130
Term Expires: December 31, 2018
E-mail: councilmancedeno@gmail.com
★ Council Member **William Gallman, Jr.** (D-Ward 5) . . . . (908) 820-4130
Term Expires: December 31, 2018
E-mail: cwgallman@yahoo.com
★ Council Member **Frank O. Mazza** (D-Ward 6) . . . . . (908) 820-4130
Term Expires: December 31, 2018
E-mail: francomazza2004@yahoo.com
★ Council Member **Frank J. Cuesta** (D-At-Large) . . . . (908) 820-4130
Term Expires: December 31, 2016
E-mail: elzorro@optonline.net
★ Council Member **Manny Grova, Jr.** (D-At-Large) . . . . (908) 820-4130
Term Expires: December 31, 2016
E-mail: mgrova@msgld.com
★ Council Member
Patricia Perkins-Auguste (D-At-Large) . . . . . (908) 820-4130
Term Expires: December 31, 2016
E-mail: ppauguste@yahoo.com
○ Municipal Clerk **Yolanda M. Roberts** . . . . . . (908) 820-4131
E-mail: yroberts@elizabethnj.org
Deputy Clerk **Mary C. Murphy** . . . . (908) 820-4133

City of Elk Grove, California

8400 Laguna Palms Way, Elk Grove, CA 95758
Internet: www.eklgrovecity.org

County: Sacramento **Election Type:** Nonpartisan **Year Incorporated:** 2000 **Population:** 166,913 (2015)

Office of the Mayor and City Council

8400 Laguna Palms Way, Elk Grove, CA 95758
Fax: (916) 627-4400

★ Mayor **Gary Davis** . . . . (916) 478-2201
Began Service: December 8, 2012
Term Expires: December 14, 2016
E-mail: gdavis@elkgrovecity.org

Office of the Mayor and City Council *continued*

★ Vice Mayor **Steve Ly** (District 4) . . . . (916) 478-2201
Term Expires: December 12, 2018
E-mail: stevely@elkgrovecity.org
★ Council Member **Darren Suen** (District 1) . . . . . (916) 478-2201
Term Expires: December 14, 2016
E-mail: dsuen@elkgrovecity.org
★ Council Member **Patrick Hume** (District 2) . . . . . (916) 478-2201
Term Expires: December 2018
E-mail: phume@elkgrovecity.org
★ Council Member **Steven M. Detrick** (District 3) . . . . (916) 478-2201
Term Expires: December 14, 2016
E-mail: sdetrick@elkgrovecity.org

Office of the City Attorney

8400 Laguna Palms Way, Elk Grove, CA 95758
Fax: (916) 691-2001

City Attorney **Jonathan P. Hobbs** . . . . (916) 478-3615
Education: Washington State 1993 BA; McGeorge 1996 JD
Assistant City Attorney **Jennifer Alves** . . . . . . (916) 478-3615
Assistant City Attorney **Suzanne Kennedy** . . . . . (916) 478-3615
Executive Administrative Assistant **Sherrie Peritore** . . . . (916) 478-3615
E-mail: speritore@elkgrovecity.org

Office of the City Clerk

8400 Laguna Palms Way, Elk Grove, CA 95758
Fax: (916) 627-4400

City Clerk **Jason Lindgren** . . . . (916) 478-2286
E-mail: jlindgren@elkgrovecity.org
Assistant City Clerk **Brenda Haggard** . . . . (916) 627-3453
E-mail: bhaggard@elkgrovecity.org

Office of the City Manager

8401 Laguna Palms Way, Elk Grove, CA 95758

City Manager **Laura S. Gill** . . . . (916) 478-2201
E-mail: lgill@elkgrovecity.org
Executive Administrative Assistant **Carrie Baierlein** . . . . (916) 478-2201
E-mail: cbaierlein@elkgrovecity.org
Deputy City Manager **Kara Reddig** . . . . (916) 478-2249
E-mail: kreddig@elkgrovecity.org
Public Affairs Manager **Kristyn Nelson** . . . . . . (916) 478-3632
E-mail: knelson@elkgrovecity.org

Development Services

8400 Laguna Palms Way, Elk Grove, CA 95758
Fax: (916) 691-3168

Assistant City Manager **Jason Behrmann** . . . . . . (916) 478-3656
E-mail: jbehrmann@elkgrovecity.org
Economic Development Director **Darrell Doan** . . . . . (916) 478-3690
E-mail: ddoan@elkgrovecity.org
Economic Development Coordinator **Rachael Brown** . . . . (916) 478-3686
E-mail: rbrown@elkgrovecity.org

Building Safety and Inspection

8400 Laguna Palms Way, Elk Grove, CA 95758
Fax: (916) 691-4757

Assistant Development Services Director **Shane Diller** . . . (916) 478-2248

Code Enforcement

10250 Iron Rock Way, Elk Grove, CA 95624
Fax: (916) 686-2692

Code Enforcement Manager **Shane Diller** . . . . . . (916) 687-3023
Code Enforcement Supervisor **(Vacant)** . . . . (916) 687-3072

Planning

8400 Laguna Palms Way, Elk Grove, CA 95758
Fax: (916) 691-3175

Planning Director **Darren Wilson** . . . . (916) 627-3446

(continued on next page)

★ Elected Official ▲ Appointed by Legislature ▼ Appointed by Governor ▶ Appointed by Board or Commission ● Appointed by Judge
■ Appointed by Mayor △ Appointed by Freeholders ▽ Appointed by Supervisor ▷ Appointed by County Executive ○ Appointed by Council

Planning *continued*

Planning Manager **Jessica Jordan** .... (916) 627-3335

Public Works

8400 Laguna Palms Way, Elk Grove, CA 95758
Fax: (916) 691-3173

Public Works Director/City Engineer
Robert "Bob" Murdoch .... (916) 478-2287
Traffic Engineer **Farhad Iranitalab** .... (916) 478-2253
E-mail: firanitalab@elkgrovecity.org
Capital Improvements Manager **Rick Carter** .... (916) 478-2232
E-mail: rcarter@elkgrovecity.org

Integrated Waste

8400 Laguna Palms Way, Elk Grove, CA 95758

Program Manager (Interim) **Heather Neff** .... (916) 478-3686

Transit Services

8401 Laguna Palms Way, Elk Grove, CA 95758
Fax: (916) 714-4635

Transit Manager **Jean Foletta** .... (916) 678-3030

Finance Department

8400 Laguna Palms Way, Elk Grove, CA 95758

Finance Director **Bradley Koehn** .... (916) 627-3221
Purchasing Manager **Joe Simone** .... (916) 478-3606
E-mail: jsimone@elkgrovecity.org

Facilities and Fleet

8400 Laguna Palms Way, Elk Grove, CA 95758
Fax: (916) 691-0415

Manager **Doug Scott** .... (916) 627-3443
E-mail: dscott@elkgrovecity.org

Human Resources

8400 Laguna Palms Way, Elk Grove, CA 95758

Human Resources Manager **Jacqui Langenberg** .... (916) 478-3686
E-mail: jlangenberg@elkgrovecity.org

Police Department

8400 Laguna Palms Way, Elk Grove, CA 95758

Chief of Police **Robert M. Lehner** .... (916) 627-3300
Education: Arizona MBA

Animal Services

10250 Iron Rock Way, Elk Grove, CA 95624

Animal Services Supervisor **Maureen McCann** .... (916) 687-3072

City of Erie, Pennsylvania

Municipal Building, 626 State Street, Erie, PA 16501-1128
Internet: www.erie.pa.us

County: Erie **Election Type:** Partisan **Year Founded:** 1795
Population: 99,475 (2015)

Office of the Mayor

Municipal Building, 626 State Street, Room 500, Erie, PA 16501-1128
Fax: (814) 870-1208

★ Mayor **Joseph Sinnott** (D) .... (814) 870-1204
Term Expires: December 31, 2017
E-mail: jsinnott@erie.pa.us
Education: Gannon 1988 BS; Case Western 1999 JD
Assistant to the Mayor **Jill Beck** .... (814) 870-1206
E-mail: jbeck@erie.pa.us Fax: (814) 870-1208

Office of the Controller

Municipal Building, 626 State Street, Room 302, Erie, PA 16501-1128
Fax: (814) 870-1413

★ Controller **Teresa Stankiewicz** (D) .... (814) 870-1339
Term Expires: December 31, 2017
E-mail: tstankiewicz@erie.pa.us
Deputy Chief Controller **Lucy Brabender** .... (814) 870-1339
E-mail: lbrabender@erie.pa.us

Office of the City Solicitor

626 State Street, Room 505, Erie, PA 16501-1128
Fax: (814) 455-9438

City Solicitor **Greg Karle** .... (814) 870-1230
E-mail: gkarle@erie.pa.us
City Solicitor **Gerry Villella** .... (814) 870-1230

Office of the City Treasurer

Municipal Building, 626 State Street, Room 105, Erie, PA 16501-1128
Fax: (814) 870-1288

★ Treasurer **Susan DiVecchio** (D) .... (814) 870-1211
Term Expires: December 31, 2019
E-mail: sdivecchio@erie.pa.us
Deputy Treasurer **Ed Williams** .... (814) 870-1219

Economic and Community Development Department

Municipal Building, 626 State Street, Room 404, Erie, PA 16501-1128
Fax: (814) 870-1443

Director **Kim Green** .... (814) 870-1270
E-mail: kgreen@erie.pa.us
Assistant Director **(Vacant)** .... (814) 870-1270

Finance Department

Municipal Building, 626 State Street, Room 309, Erie, PA 16501-1128
Fax: (814) 870-1386

Director **Paul Lichtenwalter** .... (814) 870-1306
E-mail: plichtenwalter@erie.pa.us
Purchasing Director **Sid Goldstein** .... (814) 870-1281
E-mail: sgoldstein@erie.pa.us

Fire Department

626 State Street, Room 509, Erie, PA 16501-1128
Fax: (814) 454-5372

Fire Chief **Tony Pol** .... (814) 870-1400
E-mail: apol@erie.pa.us
Chief Fire Inspector **Guy Santone** .... (814) 870-1402
311 Marsh Street, Erie, PA 16501
E-mail: gsantone@erie.pa.us
Assistant Fire Chief **Joe Walko** .... (814) 870-1596
E-mail: jwalko@erie.pa.us

Human Resources Department

Municipal Building, 626 State Street, Room 300, Erie, PA 16501-1128
Fax: (814) 870-1386

Director **Connie Cook** .... (814) 870-1244
E-mail: ccook@erie.pa.us

Office of Information Technology

626 State Street, Room 305, Erie, PA 16501-1128
Fax: (814) 870-1468

Chief Information Officer **Brian King** .... (814) 870-1423
E-mail: bking@erie.pa.us

Police Department

Municipal Building, 626 State Street, Room 111, Erie, PA 16501-1128
Tel: (814) 870-1125 Fax: (814) 870-1174

Police Chief **Randy Bowers** .... (814) 870-1113

★ Elected Official ▲ Appointed by Legislature ▼ Appointed by Governor ▶ Appointed by Board or Commission ● Appointed by Judge
■ Appointed by Mayor △ Appointed by Freeholders ▽ Appointed by Supervisor ▷ Appointed by County Executive ○ Appointed by Council

Department of Public Works, Property and Parks
Municipal Building, 626 State Street, Room 504, Erie, PA 16501-1128
Fax: (814) 870-1567

Director **Doug Mitchell** .... (814) 870-1450
Assistant Director **Dave Mulvihill** .... (814) 870-1450

Sewer Department
68 Port Access Road, Erie, PA 16507
Fax: (814) 454-4737

Bureau Chief **Rob Munro** .... (814) 870-1364
Assistant Bureau Chief **Basil Ronzitti** .... (814) 870-1360
Lab Supervisor **Paula Trapp** .... (814) 870-1360
Maintenance Superintendent **Howard Buzzell** .... (814) 870-1360
E-mail: hbuzzell@erie.pa.us
Industrial Pretreatment Coordinator **Tim Huemmrich** .... (814) 870-1360

Office of the City Council and City Clerk
Municipal Building, 626 State Street, Room 104, Erie, PA 16501-1128
Tel: (814) 870-1291 Fax: (814) 870-1296

★Council President **Robert E. "Bob" Merski** (D) .... (814) 870-1291
Term Expires: December 31, 2019
E-mail: bmerski@erie.pa.us
★Council Member **Sonya Arrington** (D) .... (814) 870-1291
Term Expires: December 31, 2019
★Council Member **David Brennan** (D) .... (814) 870-1291
Term Expires: December 31, 2017
E-mail: dbrennan@erie.pa.us
★Council Member **Curtis Jones, Jr.** (D) .... (814) 870-1291
Term Expires: December 31, 2017
E-mail: curtis.jones75@yahoo.com
★Council Member **Casimir Kwitowski** (D) .... (814) 870-1291
Term Expires: December 31, 2017
E-mail: ckwitowski@erie.pa.us
★Council Member **Jim Winarski** (D) .... (814) 870-1291
Term Expires: December 31, 2017
E-mail: jimwski@gmail.com
★Council Member **Melvin Witherspoon** (D) .... (814) 870-1291
Term Expires: December 31, 2019
E-mail: mwitherspoon@erie.pa.us
Education: Gannon 1968
City Clerk **Rose Robie** .... (814) 870-1291
E-mail: rrobie@erie.pa.us

Erie City School District
142 West 21st Street, Erie, PA 16502
Fax: (814) 874-6010

Superintendent **Jay Badams** .... (814) 874-6001

City of Escondido, California

City Hall, 201 North Broadway, Escondido, CA 92025
Internet: www.escondido.org

County: San Diego **Election Type:** Nonpartisan **Year Incorporated:** 1888 **Population:** 151,451 (2015)

Office of the Mayor and City Council
City Hall, 201 N. Broadway, Escondido, CA 92025
Fax: (760) 839-4578

★Mayor **Sam Abed** .... (760) 839-4638
Began Service: December 1, 2010
Term Expires: December 2018
E-mail: sabed@escondido.org

Office of the Mayor and City Council *continued*

★Deputy Mayor **Michael Morasco** .... (760) 839-4638
Term Expires: December 2016
E-mail: mmorasco@escondido.org
★Council Member **Olga Diaz** .... (760) 839-4638
Term Expires: December 2016
E-mail: odiaz@escondido.org
Education: Santa Clara U BS
★Council Member **Ed Gallo** .... (760) 839-4638
Term Expires: December 2018
E-mail: egallo@escondido.org
★Council Member **John Masson** .... (760) 839-4638
Term Expires: December 2018
E-mail: jmasson@escondido.org

Office of the City Manager
City Hall, 201 North Broadway, 2nd Floor, Escondido, CA 92025
Fax: (760) 839-4578

City Manager **Graham Mitchell** .... (760) 839-4631
Education: BYU BA; USC MPA
Assistant City Manager **Jay Petrek** .... (760) 839-4631
E-mail: jpetrek@escondido.org
Director of Economic Development and Community Relations **Joyce Masterson** .... (760) 839-4621
E-mail: jmasterson@escondido.org Fax: (760) 739-7003
Education: Brooklyn 1976 BA

Office of the City Attorney
City Hall, 201 N. Broadway, Escondido, CA 92025
Fax: (760) 741-7541

City Attorney **Jeffrey R. Epp** .... (760) 839-4608
E-mail: jepp@escondido.org
Education: Wyoming 1981 BA, 1984 JD

Office of the City Clerk
City Hall, 201 N. Broadway, Escondido, CA 92025
Fax: (760) 735-5782

City Clerk **Diane Halverson** .... (760) 839-4617
E-mail: dhalverson@escondido.org
Education: Pacific Union BA; San Diego State MA
Assistant City Clerk **Eva Heter** .... (760) 839-4617
E-mail: eheter@escondido.org
Executive Office Coordinator **Jen Klein** .... (760) 839-4617

Office of the City Treasurer
City Hall, 201 N. Broadway, Escondido, CA 92025
Fax: (760) 746-0612

★City Treasurer **Kenneth Hugins** .... (760) 839-4619
Term Expires: December 2016
E-mail: khugins@escondido.org

Community Development
City Hall, 201 N. Broadway, Escondido, CA 92025
Fax: (760) 839-4313

Director **Bill Martin** .... (760) 839-4671

Community Services
City Hall, 201 N. Broadway, Escondido, CA 92025
Fax: (760) 739-7015

Director **Loretta McKinney** .... (760) 839-4691
E-mail: lmckinney@escondido.org
Assistant Community Services Director **Danielle Lopez** .... (760) 432-0635
210 Park Ave., Escondido, CA 92025 Fax: (760) 739-0675
E-mail: dlopez@escondido.org

★Elected Official ▲Appointed by Legislature ▼Appointed by Governor ▶Appointed by Board or Commission ●Appointed by Judge
■Appointed by Mayor △Appointed by Freeholders ▽Appointed by Supervisor ▷Appointed by County Executive ○Appointed by Council

Housing Division
City Hall, 201 North Broadway, First Floor, Escondido, CA 92025
Fax: (760) 741-0619

Management Analyst **Karen Youel** .... (760) 839-4841

Escondido Public Library
239 South Kalmia Street, Escondido, CA 92025
Fax: (760) 741-4255

Principal Librarian **Loretta McKinney** .... (760) 839-4684
E-mail: lmckinney@escondido.org

Finance Department
City Hall, 201 N. Broadway, Escondido, CA 92025
Fax: (760) 746-0612

Director **Sheryl Bennett** .... (760) 839-4676
Fax: (760) 746-0612

Fire Department
City Hall, 201 N. Broadway, Escondido, CA 92025
Fax: (760) 739-7060

Fire Chief **Russell Knowles** .... (760) 839-5400
Note: Effective June 5, 2016

Human Resources
City Hall, 201 N. Broadway, Escondido, CA 92025
Fax: (760) 739-7055

Director **Sheryl Bennett** .... (760) 839-6360
E-mail: sbennett@escondido.org Fax: (760) 739-7055

Information Systems Department
City Hall, 201 North Broadway, 2nd Floor, Escondido, CA 92025
Fax: (760) 739-7094

Director of Information Systems **Mark Becker** .... (760) 839-4821
E-mail: mbecker@escondido.org

Police Department
1163 North Centre City Parkway, Escondido, CA 92026
Tel: (760) 839-4791 (Information) Fax: (760) 839-4919

Chief of Police **Craig Carter** .... (760) 839-4722
Education: Bellevue U BS

Public Works Department
City Hall, 201 N. Broadway, Escondido, CA 92025
Fax: (760) 839-4597

Public Works Director/City Engineer **Ed Domingue** ..... (760) 839-4813
E-mail: edomingue@escondido.org

Assistant Director of Public Works/Engineering
Julie Procopio .... (760) 839-4573
E-mail: jprocopio@escondido.org

Deputy Director of Public Works, Maintenance
Rich O'Donnell .... (760) 839-4668
E-mail: rodonnell@escondido.org

Geographic Information Systems Manager
Daniel Hildebrand .... (760) 839-4033
E-mail: dhildebrand@escondido.org

Maintenance and Operations Division
475 North Spruce Street, Escondido, CA 92025
Fax: (760) 739-7040

Deputy Director **Rich O'Donnell** .... (760) 839-4668
E-mail: rodonnell@escondido.org

Building Maintenance Superintendent **Ira C. Morgan II** ... (760) 839-4895
E-mail: imorgan@escondido.org Fax: (760) 739-7089

Fleet Superintendent **Raul Juarez** .... (760) 839-4883
Fax: (760) 739-7045

Recycling and Waste Reduction Coordinator
Laura Robinson .... (760) 839-6212

Streets and Parks Superintendent **Dan Young** .... (760) 839-4668
E-mail: dyoung@escondido.org Fax: (760) 739-7040

Utilities Department
City Hall, 201 North Broadway, First Floor, Escondido, CA 92025
Fax: (760) 432-9512 Internet: www.escondido.org/utilities.aspx

Director **Chris McKinney** .... (760) 839-4657
Education: MIT BS, MSEE

City of Eugene, Oregon

125 East 8th Avenue, Eugene, OR 97401-2793
Tel: (541) 682-5010 Internet: www.eugene-or.gov

County: Lane **Election Type:** Nonpartisan **Year Incorporated:** 1862
Population: 163,460 (2015)

Office of the Mayor and City Council
125 East 8th Avenue, Eugene, OR 97401-2793
Fax: (541) 682-5414

★ Mayor **Kitty Piercy** .... (541) 682-5010
Term Expires: January 2, 2017
E-mail: kitty.piercy@ci.eugene.or.us

★ Council Member **George R. Brown** (Ward 1) .... (541) 682-8341
Term Expires: January 2, 2017
E-mail: george.r.brown@ci.eugene.or.us

★ Council Member **Betty L. Taylor** (Ward 2) .... (541) 338-9947
Term Expires: January 2, 2017
E-mail: betty.l.taylor@ci.eugene.or.us
Education: Illinois State BS; Illinois MA; Oregon 1986 PhD

★ Council Member **Alan Zelenka** (Ward 3) .... (541) 682-8343
Term Expires: January 5, 2019
E-mail: alan.zelenka@ci.eugene.or.us

★ Council Member **George A. Poling** (Ward 4) .... (541) 517-3110
Term Expires: January 5, 2019
E-mail: george.a.poling@ci.eugene.or.us

★ Council Member **Mike Clark** (Ward 5) .... (541) 682-8345
Term Expires: January 5, 2019
E-mail: mike.clark@ci.eugene.or.us

★ Council Member **Greg A. Evans** (Ward 6) .... (541) 682-8346
Term Expires: January 5, 2019
E-mail: greg.a.evans@ci.eugene.or.us

★ Council Member **Claire M. Syrett** (Ward 7) .... (541) 862-8347
Term Expires: January 2, 2017
E-mail: claire.m.syrett@ci.eugene.or.us

★ Council Member **Chris E. Pryor** (Ward 8) .... (541) 682-8348
Term Expires: January 2, 2017
E-mail: chris.e.pryor@ci.eugene.or.us

Intergovernmental Relations
125 East 8th Avenue, Eugene, OR 97401-2793
Fax: (541) 682-5414

Manager **Lisa A. Gardner** .... (541) 682-5010
E-mail: lisa.a.gardner@ci.eugene.or.us
Date of Birth: 1967
Education: Bowdoin 1989 AB; Oregon 1995 MCP

City Manager's Office
125 East 8th Avenue, Eugene, OR 97401-2793
TTY: (541) 682-5010 Fax: (541) 682-5414

City Manager **Jon R. Ruiz** .... (541) 682-5336
E-mail: jon.r.ruiz@ci.eugene.or.us
Education: Colorado State BA; Colorado 1988 MBA

Assistant City Manager **Sarah J. Medary** .... (541) 682-8817
E-mail: sarah.j.medary@ci.eugene.or.us

City Attorney's Office
125 East 8th Avenue, Eugene, OR 97401-2793

City Attorney **Glenn Klein** .... (541) 682-8447
E-mail: glenn.klein@ci.eugene.or.us

★ Elected Official ▲ Appointed by Legislature ▼ Appointed by Governor ► Appointed by Board or Commission ● Appointed by Judge
■ Appointed by Mayor △ Appointed by Freeholders ▽ Appointed by Supervisor ▷ Appointed by County Executive ○ Appointed by Council

Central Services Department
100 West 10th Avenue, 4th Floor, Eugene, OR 97401

Executive Director **Kristie A. Hammitt** .... (541) 682-5524
E-mail: kristie.a.hammitt@ci.eugene.or.us

Finance
100 West 10th Avenue, Suite 400, Eugene, OR 97401

Manager **Sue L. Cutsogeorge** .... (541) 682-5589

Fire and Emergency Medical Services Department
1705 W. 2nd Ave., Eugene, OR 97402

Fire Chief **Randy Groves** .... (541) 682-7115
E-mail: randy.b.groves@ci.eugene.or.us

Human Resources and Risk Services
940 Willamette Street, Suite 200, Eugene, OR 97401

Manager **Alana M. Holmes** .... (541) 682-5765
E-mail: alana.m.holmes@ci.eugene.or.us

Library, Recreation and Cultural Services
100 West 10th Avenue, Suite 321, Eugene, OR 97401

Executive Director **Renee Grube** .... (541) 682-6065
E-mail: renee.l.grube@ci.eugene.or.us

Planning and Development Department
99 West 10th Street, Suite 240, Eugene, OR 97401
Fax: (541) 682-5414

Executive Director **Sarah J. Medary** .... (541) 682-8817
Building Official **Stuart G. Ramsing** .... (541) 682-6801
Planning Director **Robin Hostick** .... (541) 682-5507
E-mail: robin.a.hostick@ci.eugene.or.us

Police Department
300 Country Club Road, Eugene, OR 97401

Police Chief **Peter M. Kerns** .... (541) 682-5102

Public Works Department
101 East Broadway, Suite 400, Eugene, OR 97401
Fax: (541) 682-6826

Executive Director **Kurt A. Corey** .... (541) 682-5258
Administration Division Manager **Robert Tintle** .... (541) 682-8476
Airport Director **Timothy Doll** .... (541) 682-8352
28855 Lockheed Drive, Eugene, OR 97402 Fax: (541) 682-6838
Engineering Division Manager **Mark A. Schoening** ..... (541) 682-5243
90 East Broadway, Suite 400, Eugene, OR 97401
E-mail: mark.a.schoening@ci.eugene.or.us
Maintenance Division Manager **Jeff Lankston** .... (541) 682-4800
1820 Roosevelt Boulevard, Eugene, OR 97402 Fax: (541) 682-4882
E-mail: jeff.lankston@ci.eugene.or.us
Parks and Open Space Division Manager
Craig Carnagey .... (541) 682-4800
1820 Roosevelt Boulevard, Eugene, OR 97402 Fax: (541) 682-4882
Wastewater Division Manager **Michele Cahill** .... (541) 682-8600
410 River Avenue, Eugene, OR 97404 Fax: (541) 682-8601
Urban Forester **Mark Snyder** .... (541) 682-4800
1820 Roosevelt Boulevard, Eugene, OR 97402

City of Evansville, Indiana
One NW Martin Luther King, Jr. Boulevard, Evansville, IN 47708
TTY: (812) 436-5483 Fax: (812) 436-4966
Internet: www.evansville.in.gov

County: Vanderburgh **Election Type:** Partisan **Population:** 119,943 (2015)

Office of the Mayor
One NW Martin Luther King, Jr. Boulevard, Room 302, Evansville, IN 47708
Fax: (812) 436-4966

★ Mayor **Lloyd Winnecke** (D) .... (812) 436-4962
Began Service: January 1, 2012
Term Expires: December 31, 2019
E-mail: mayor@evansville.in.gov
Executive Assistant/Scheduler **Marianne Hill** .... (812) 436-4969
E-mail: mecox@evansville.in.gov
Chief of Staff **Steve Schaefer** .... (812) 436-4962
Communications Director **Ella Johnson-Watson** .... (812) 436-4965

Office of the City Council
One NW Martin Luther King, Jr. Boulevard, Room 314, Evansville, IN 47708

★ Council President **Missy Mosby** (D-Ward 2) .... (812) 401-9400
Term Expires: December 31, 2019
E-mail: mmosby@evansville.in.gov
★ Council Vice President **Jonathan Weaver** (D-At-Large) .. (812) 586-0562
Term Expires: December 31, 2019
E-mail: jweaver@evansville.in.gov
★ Council Member **Dan McGinn** (R-Ward 1) .... (812) 479-6336
Term Expires: December 31, 2019
E-mail: danmcginn@wowway.com
★ Council Member **Anna Hargis** (R-Ward 3) .... (812) 436-4992
Term Expires: December 31, 2019
E-mail: ahargis@evansville.in.gov
★ Council Member **Connie Robinson** (D-Ward 4) .... (812) 423-3869
Term Expires: December 31, 2019
E-mail: connie@hmrdistribution.com
★ Council Member **Justin Elpers** (R-Ward 5) .... (812) 436-4992
Term Expires: December 31, 2019
E-mail: jelpers@evansville.in.gov
★ Council Member **Jim Brinkmeyer** (D-Ward 6) .... (812) 436-4992
Term Expires: December 31, 2019
E-mail: jbrinkmeyer@evansville.in.gov
★ Council Member **H. Dan Adams** (D-At-Large) .... (812) 425-4220
Term Expires: December 31, 2019
E-mail: drhda501@aol.com
★ Council Member **Michelle Mercer** (R-At-Large) .... (812) 436-4992
Term Expires: December 31, 2019
E-mail: mmercer@evansville.in.gov

Office of the City Clerk
One NW Martin Luther King, Jr. Boulevard, Room 314, Evansville, IN 47708
Fax: (812) 436-4999

★ City Clerk **Laura Windhorst** .... (812) 436-4992
Term Expires: December 31, 2019
E-mail: lwindhorst@evansville.in.gov
Deputy City Clerk **Ashten Stenftenagel** .... (812) 436-4992
E-mail: astenftenagel@evansvillegov.org

Parking Meter Department
Office Manager/Traffic Clerk **Shelly Wilson** .... (812) 436-4994

★ Elected Official ▲ Appointed by Legislature ▼ Appointed by Governor ▶ Appointed by Board or Commission ● Appointed by Judge
■ Appointed by Mayor △ Appointed by Freeholders ▽ Appointed by Supervisor ▷ Appointed by County Executive ○ Appointed by Council

Office of the Controller/Finance Department

One NW Martin Luther King, Jr. Boulevard, Room 300,
Evansville, IN 47708-1833
Fax: (812) 436-4926 Internet: www.evansvillegov.org/index.aspx?page=45

Controller **Russell G. Lloyd, Jr.** (R) .... (812) 436-4919
E-mail: rlloyd@evansvillegov.org
Date of Birth: 1957
Education: Indiana 1979 BS; Evansville 1985 MBA
Deputy Controller **Janet Coudret** .... (812) 436-4919
Finance Officer **Julie Probus** .... (812) 436-4919
Office Manager **Jean Carlson** .... (812) 436-4919
License Clerk/Receptionist **Phyllis Sanders** .... (812) 436-4919
E-mail: psanders@evansvillegov.org
Internal Auditor **Tamara Masden** .... (812) 436-4919

Administrative Services Department

203 Civic Center Complex, One NW Martin Luther King, Jr. Boulevard,
Evansville, IN 47708-1833
Tel: (812) 436-4934 Fax: (812) 436-4942
Internet: www.evansvillegov.org/Index.aspx?page=43

■ Executive Director **George Fithian** .... (812) 436-4935
E-mail: gfithian@evansvillegov.org

Evansville Vanderburgh Airport Authority/ Evansville Regional Airport

7801 Bussing Dr., Evansville, IN 47725-6799
Tel: (812) 421-4401 Fax: (812) 421-4412 Internet: www.evvairport.com

Executive Director **Douglas P. Joest** .... (812) 421-4401

Area Plan Commission

One NW Martin Luther King. Jr. Boulevard, Room 312,
Evansville, IN 47708-1833
Tel: (812) 435-5226 Fax: (812) 435-5237
Internet: www.evansvilleapc.com

Executive Director **Ron London** .... (812) 435-5882
Assistant Director/Planner **Blaine Oliver** .... (812) 435-5881
Planner **John Ansbro** .... (812) 435-5060
Department Administrator **Ryan Key** .... (812) 435-5979
E-mail: rkey@evansvilleapc.com

Zoning

Administrator **Janet Greenwell** .... (812) 435-5978
Enforcement Officer **Karen Pickett** .... (812) 435-5887
Enforcement Officer **Donna Holderfield** .... (812) 435-5977
Investigator **Joel Wiegand** .... (812) 435-5883
Chief Draftsman **Brenda Hill** .... (812) 435-5886
CAD/GIS **Jim McReynolds** .... (812) 435-5236
E-mail: jmcreynolds@evansvilleapc.com
Bookkeeper/Office Manager **Karen Yokel** .... (812) 435-5226
Senior Secretary **April Spraggs** .... (812) 435-5226
E-mail: amspraggs@evansvilleapc.com

Evansville-Vanderburgh County Building Authority

One NW Martin Luther King, Jr. Boulevard, Room 317,
Evansville, IN 47708
Fax: (812) 435-5994

General Manager **W. David Rector** .... (812) 435-5801
Engineer/Maintenance Supervisor **Ralph Kissinger** ...... (812) 435-5805

Building Commission

One NW Martin Luther King, Jr. Boulevard, Room 310,
Evansville, IN 47708
Tel: (812) 436-7867 Fax: (812) 436-7869
Internet: www.evansvillegov.org/Index.aspx?page=44

■ Building Commissioner **Ronald Beane** .... (812) 436-7884
E-mail: rbeane@evansvillegov.org
License Clerk **Cathy Evenson** .... (812) 436-7880

Building Commission *continued*

Secretary **Sheryl Lemmer** .... (812) 436-7867
E-mail: slemmer@evansvillegov.org

Computer Services Department

One NW Martin Luther King, Jr. Boulevard, Room 205,
Evansville, IN 47708
Fax: (812) 435-2529

Chief Information Officer **Mark Uhrin** .... (812) 436-7859
E-mail: muhrin@evansville.in.gov
Network Administrator **Ryan Connor** .... (812) 435-5097
E-mail: rconnor@evansvillegov.org
GIS Specialist **(Vacant)** .... (812) 435-5071

Fire Department

550 SE 8th. St., Evansville, IN 47713-1786
Fax: (812) 435-6248 Internet: www.evansvillegov.org/Index.aspx?page=53

Fire Chief **Mike Connelly** .... (812) 435-6235
E-mail: cconnelly@evansvillefiredepartment.com
Executive Secretary **Cathleen Tamez** .... (812) 435-6235
E-mail: ctamez@evansvillegov.org
Assistant Fire Chief **Paul Anslinger** .... (812) 435-6235
E-mail: panslinger@evansvillegov.org
Chief of Health and Safety **Daniel Grimm** .... (812) 435-6235
Chief of Operations **Charles "Chuck" Hertzberger** ..... (812) 435-6235
E-mail: chertzberger@evansvillegov.org
Training Chief **Ken Zuber** .... (812) 435-6235
E-mail: kzuber@evansvillefiredepartment.com
Special Teams Chief **Ken Zuber** .... (812) 435-6235
E-mail: kzuber@evansvillefiredepartment.com
Bookkeeper **Kelly Frankenberger** .... (812) 435-6235
Communication Specialist **Ryan Hobbs** .... (812) 435-6235
Fire Marshal **Greg Main** .... (812) 435-6235

Evansville Housing Authority [EHA]

402 Court Street, Suite B, Evansville, IN 47708
Tel: (812) 428-8500 Fax: (812) 428-8560
Internet: www.evansvillehousing.org

► Executive Director **Rick Moore** .... (812) 428-8500
E-mail: rick.moore@evansvillehousing.org Fax: (812) 428-8560
Executive Assistant **Allison Gauer** .... (812) 428-8500
E-mail: allison.gauer@evansvillehousing.org Fax: (812) 428-8560
Finance Director **Eric Kremer** .... (812) 428-8500
Fax: (812) 428-8514
Housing Choice Voucher Program Director
Marques Terry .... (812) 428-8548
411 S. E. 8th Street, Evansville, IN 47713 Fax: (812) 428-8538
Caldwell Homes **Tequeda Sheriff** .... (812) 428-8527
736 Cross Street, Evansville, IN 47713 Fax: (812) 428-8535
Fulton Square **Carlotta Iafrate** .... (812) 428-8516
1328 Dresden St., Evansville, IN 47710 Fax: (812) 428-8536
George Buckner Towers **Ruby McGlown** .... (812) 428-8521
717 Cherry St., Evansville, IN 47713 Fax: (812) 436-4756
John Cable Complex **Tequeda Sheriff** .... (812) 402-5993
1111 Cherry Street, Evansville, IN 47713
White Oak Manor **Myra Bates** .... (812) 428-8532
509 N. St. Joseph Ave., Evansville, IN 47712 Fax: (812) 436-4753
William G. Schnute Apartments **Myra Bates** .... (812) 428-8531
1030 W. Franklin St., Evansville, IN 47710 Fax: (812) 436-4752
Director of Operations **Tim Martin** .... (812) 428-8500
E-mail: tim.martin@evansvillehousing.org Fax: (812) 428-8565
Scattered Sites **Tequeda Sheriff** .... (812) 402-5993
Fax: (812) 402-7895
John F. Kennedy Tower **Ruby McGlown** .... (812) 428-8520
315 SE Martin L. King Jr. Boulevard, Fax: (812) 436-4762
Evansville, IN 47713

★ Elected Official ▲ Appointed by Legislature ▼ Appointed by Governor ► Appointed by Board or Commission ● Appointed by Judge
■ Appointed by Mayor △ Appointed by Freeholders ▽ Appointed by Supervisor ▷ Appointed by County Executive ○ Appointed by Council

Human Relations Commission
Civic Center, One NW Martin Luther King, Jr. Boulevard, Room 209, Evansville, IN 47708
Fax: (812) 436-4929 Internet: www.evansvillegov.org/Index.aspx?page=55

■ Director **Diane Clements-Boyd** . . . . . (812) 436-4927
E-mail: dclements-boyd@evansvillegov.org
Secretary/Office Manager **Bonnie Fox** . . . . . (812) 436-4927
E-mail: bfox@evansvillegov.org

Law Department
P.O. Box 1065, Evansville, IN 47706
Fax: (812) 402-7977

■ Corporation Counsel **Ted C. Ziemer, Jr.** . . . . . (812) 424-7575
E-mail: tziemer@evansvillegov.org

Evansville-Vanderburgh Levee Authority
1300 Waterworks Rd., Evansville, IN 47713
Tel: (812) 435-6137 Fax: (812) 435-6218

■ Superintendent **Jay Perry** . . . . . (812) 435-6137
E-mail: jperry@evansvillegov.org
Secretary **Joni Evans** . . . . . (812) 435-6137
E-mail: jevans@evansvillegov.org

Department of Metropolitan Development [DMD]
One NW Martin Luther King, Jr. Boulevard, Room 306, Evansville, IN 47708-1869
Fax: (812) 436-7809 Internet: www.evansvillegov.org/Index.aspx?page=47

■ Executive Director **Kelley Coures** . . . . . (812) 436-7806
E-mail: kcoures@evansvillegov.org
Historic Preservation Officer **Dennis Au** . . . . . (812) 436-7823
Community Development Coordinator **Josh Calhoun** . . . . (812) 436-7823
E-mail: jtcalhoun@evansville.in.gov

Department of Parks and Recreation
100 E. Walnut St., Evansville, IN 47713-1999
Fax: (812) 435-6142 Internet: www.evansvillegov.org/Index.aspx?page=48

■ Executive Director **Brian Holtz** . . . . . (812) 435-6141
E-mail: bholtz@evansvillegov.org
Secretary **Sheila Whitaker** . . . . . (812) 435-6141
E-mail: swhitaker@evansvillegov.org
Deputy Director **(Vacant)** . . . . . (812) 435-6141
Fendrich Golf Course Superintendent **Mark Peters** . . . . . (812) 435-6071
1900 Diamond Ave., Evansville, IN 47711
Helfrich Golf Course Superintendent **Elmer P. Roby, Jr.** . . (812) 435-6076
1550 Mesker Park Dr., Evansville, IN 47720
McDonald/Wesselman Par 3 Golf Course Superintendent
Bill Lampkins . . . . . (812) 475-2577
2905 E. Morgan Ave., Evansville, IN 47711
Recreation Superintendent **Robin S. Hayes** . . . . . (812) 435-6161
Finance Officer **Barbara Kuebler** . . . . . (812) 435-6163
Sports Director **Lisa Wube** . . . . . (812) 435-6162
Assistant Sports Director **Suzie Dillman** . . . . . (812) 435-2534
Revenue Account Clerk **Angela Blair** . . . . . (812) 435-2533

Old National Events Plaza
715 Locust Street, Evansville, IN 47708
Fax: (812) 435-5500

General Manager **Darren Stearns** . . . . . (812) 435-5770 ext. 201

Mesker Park Zoo
2421 Bement Avenue, Evansville, IN 47720
TTY: (812) 426-4925 Fax: (812) 435-6140

Director **Amos Morris** . . . . . (812) 435-6143 ext. 401

Police Department
15 NW Martin Luther King, Jr. Boulevard, Evansville, IN 47708-1816
Fax: (812) 435-6175 Internet: http://www.evansvillepolice.com

Police Chief **Billy Bolin** . . . . . (812) 436-7896

Department of Transportation and Services
One NW Martin Luther King, Jr. Boulevard, Room 321, Evansville, IN 47708
Fax: (812) 436-4981 Internet: www.evansvillegov.org/Index.aspx?page=49

■ Director **Todd M. Robertson** . . . . . (812) 436-4988
E-mail: trobertson@evansvillegov.org
Office Manager **Robin Morris** . . . . . (812) 436-4988
Assistant to the Director **Kerry Kamp** . . . . . (812) 436-4988
E-mail: kkamp@evansvillegov.org

Animal Care and Control
815 Uhlhorn St., Evansville, IN 47710
Tel: (812) 436-4905 (TDD) Fax: (812) 435-6273

Superintendent **Alisa Webster** . . . . . (812) 435-6015

City Engineer's Office
■ City Engineer **Brent Schmitt** . . . . . (812) 436-4990
E-mail: baschmitt@evansvillegov.org
Education: Evansville BSCE
Assistant City Engineer **Chris Weil** . . . . . (812) 436-4990
E-mail: cweil@evansvillegov.org

Metropolitan Evansville Transit System [METS]
601 John Street, Evansville, IN 47713
Tel: (812) 435-6166 Fax: (812) 435-6159

General Manager **(Vacant)** . . . . . (812) 435-6166
Operation Superintendent **Rick Wilson** . . . . . (812) 435-6166
Maintenance/Mechanic Supervisor **Jonathan Siebeking** . . (812) 435-6166
Mobility Manager **Charles Farmer** . . . . . (812) 435-6166

Oak Hill Cemetery
1400 East Virginia Street, Evansville, IN 47711

Superintendent **Chris Cooke** . . . . . (812) 435-6045

Street Maintenance Department
1304 Waterworks Road, Evansville, IN 47713

Superintendent (Interim) **Greg Bryant** . . . . . (812) 435-6000

Traffic Engineering
Tel: (812) 435-6000

Foreman **Jim Cruse** . . . . . (812) 435-6003
E-mail: jcruse@evansville.in.gov

Urban Forestry
1000 Oak Hill Road, Evansville, IN 47711

Arborist **Shawn Dickerson** . . . . . (812) 475-1426

Water and Sewer Utility
One NW Martin Luther King, Jr. Boulevard, Room 104, Evansville, IN 47740-0001
Tel: (812) 436-7846 Tel: (812) 436-7864 (TDD) Fax: (812) 436-7863
Internet: www.evansvillegov.org/Index.aspx?page=60

Director **Allen Mounts** . . . . . (812) 436-4560
Wastewater Superintendent **Harry H. Lawson** . . . . . (812) 428-0548
Fax: (812) 428-6941
Water Superintendent **Pat Keepes** . . . . . (812) 421-2120 ext. 2204
Fax: (812) 421-2116
Water Production Manager **Rick Glover** . . . . . (812) 426-6567 ext. 11
Fax: (812) 423-1277

Weights and Measures Department
2901 East Morgan, Evansville, IN 47711
Fax: (812) 435-5077 E-mail: vcwm@evansville.net

Director **Loretta Townsend** . . . . . (812) 435-5745

★ Elected Official ▲ Appointed by Legislature ▼ Appointed by Governor ▶ Appointed by Board or Commission ● Appointed by Judge
■ Appointed by Mayor △ Appointed by Freeholders ▽ Appointed by Supervisor ▷ Appointed by County Executive ○ Appointed by Council

Willard Library
21 First Avenue, Evansville, IN 47710-1294
Tel: (812) 425-4309 Fax: (812) 421-9742
Internet: http://www.willard.lib.in.us

Director **Greg Hager** . . . . . (812) 425-4309
E-mail: ghager@willard.lib.in.us
Archivist **Pat Sides** . . . . . (812) 425-4309
E-mail: psides@willard.lib.in.us
Adult Services Librarian **Arrika Dedmond** . . . . . (812) 425-4309
Children's Librarian **Rhonda Mort** . . . . . (812) 425-4309
E-mail: rmort@willard.lib.in.us
Special Collections Librarian **Lyn Martin** . . . . . (812) 425-4309
E-mail: lmartin@willard.lib.in.us
Technical Services Librarian **John Scheer** . . . . . (812) 425-4309
E-mail: jscheer@willard.lib.in.us
Business Manager **Emily Phillips** . . . . . (812) 425-4309
E-mail: ephillips@willard.lib.in.us

City of Everett, Washington

2930 Wetmore Avenue, Everett, WA 98201
Tel: (425) 257-8700

County: Snohomish **Year Incorporated:** 1893 **Population:** 108,010 (2015)

Office of the Mayor
2930 Wetmore Avenue, Suite 10-A, Everett, WA 98201
Tel: (425) 257-7115 Fax: (425) 257-8729

★ Mayor **Ray Stephanson** . . . . . (425) 257-7115
Term Expires: December 31, 2017
Public Information Director **Meghan Pembroke** . . . . . (425) 257-8687
E-mail: mpembroke@everettwa.gov Fax: (425) 257-8729

Office of the City Clerk
2930 Wetmore Avenue, Suite 1-A, Everett, WA 98201
Tel: (425) 257-8610 Fax: (425) 257-8741

City Clerk **Sharon Fuller** . . . . . (425) 257-8610
E-mail: sfuller@everettwa.gov

Office of Governmental Affairs
2930 Wetmore Avenue, Suite 10-A, Everett, WA 98201
Tel: (425) 257-7104 Fax: (425) 257-8729

Director **Patrick J. McClain** . . . . . (425) 257-7104
E-mail: pmcclain@everettwa.gov

Animal Services Department
333 Smith Island Road, Everett, WA 98201
Tel: (425) 257-6000 Fax: (425) 257-6018

Director **Shannon Johnson** . . . . . (425) 257-6000

Arts and Culture Department
2930 Wetmore Avenue, Everett, WA 98201
Tel: (425) 257-7101 Fax: (425) 257-8729

Manager **Carol Thomas** . . . . . (425) 257-7101

Facilities and Property Management Department
3101 Cedar Street, Everett, WA 98201
Tel: (425) 257-8848 Fax: (425) 257-8916

Director **Mike Palacios** . . . . . (425) 257-8848
E-mail: mpalacios@everettwa.gov

Finance Department
2930 Wetmore Avenue, Suite 10-B, Everett, WA 98201
Tel: (425) 257-7091 Fax: (425) 257-8607

Chief Financial Officer **Debra Bryant** . . . . . (425) 257-7091

Budget Division
2930 Wetmore Avenue, Everett, WA 98201
Tel: (425) 257-7091

Budget Manager **Rae Ann Weighter** . . . . . (425) 257-7091
E-mail: rweighter@everettwa.gov

Office of the Treasurer
2930 Wetmore Avenue, Suite 10-B, Everett, WA 98201
Tel: (425) 257-8612 Fax: (425) 257-8607

Treasurer **Susy Haugen** . . . . . (425) 257-8612
E-mail: shaugen@everettwa.gov

Purchasing Division
3200 Cedar Street, Everett, WA 98201
Tel: (425) 257-8840 Fax: (425) 257-8864
E-mail: purchasing@everettwa.gov

Manager **Clark Langstraat** . . . . . (425) 257-8840
E-mail: clangstraat@everettwa.gov

Fire Department
2930 Wetmore Avenue, Suite 7-A, Everett, WA 98201
Tel: (425) 257-8100 Fax: (425) 257-8139 E-mail: fire@everettwa.gov

Fire Chief **Murray Gordon** . . . . . (425) 257-8100
E-mail: mgordon@everettwa.gov

Human Resources Department
2930 Wetmore Avenue, 5th Floor, Everett, WA 98201
Tel: (425) 257-8767 Fax: (425) 257-8754
E-mail: employment-hr@everettwa.gov

Director **Sharon DeHaan** . . . . . (425) 257-8767
E-mail: sdehaan@everettwa.gov

Information Technology Department
2930 Wetmore Avenue, Suite 6-A, Everett, WA 98201
Fax: (425) 257-8620 E-mail: it@everettwa.gov

Information Technology Director **Steven Hellyer** . . . . . (425) 257-8686
E-mail: shellyer@everettwa.gov
Manager of Information Technology and Telecommunications **Jeanette Postma** . . . . . (425) 257-7701
E-mail: jpostma@everettwa.gov

Legal Department
2930 Wetmore Avenue, Suite 10-C, Everett, WA 98201
Tel: (425) 257-7000 Fax: (425) 257-8693
E-mail: cwiersma@everettwa.gov

City Attorney **James D. Iles** . . . . . (425) 257-7000
E-mail: jiles@everettwa.gov

Parks and Recreation Department
802 East Mukilteo Boulevard, Everett, WA 98203
Tel: (425) 257-8300 Fax: (425) 257-8384 E-mail: parks@everettwa.gov

Director **Paul Kaftanski** . . . . . (425) 257-8300

Planning and Community Development Department
2930 Wetmore Avenue, Suite 8-A, Everett, WA 98201
Tel: (425) 257-8731 Fax: (425) 257-8742
E-mail: planning@everettwa.gov

Director **Allan Giffen** . . . . . (425) 257-8731
E-mail: agiffen@everettwa.gov

★ Elected Official ▲ Appointed by Legislature ▼ Appointed by Governor ▶ Appointed by Board or Commission ● Appointed by Judge
■ Appointed by Mayor △ Appointed by Freeholders ▽ Appointed by Supervisor ▷ Appointed by County Executive ○ Appointed by Council

Police Department
3002 Wetmore Avenue, Everett, WA 98201
Tel: (425) 257-8400 Fax: (425) 257-6500 E-mail: police@everettwa.gov

Police Chief **Dan Templeman** .... (425) 257-8400

Public Works Department
3200 Cedar Street, Everett, WA 98201
Tel: (425) 257-8800 Fax: (425) 257-8882
E-mail: everettpw@everettwa.gov

Director **Dave Davis** .... (425) 257-8800

Design and Project Management Division
3200 Cedar Street, Everett, WA 98201
Tel: (425) 257-8810 Fax: (425) 257-8856

City Engineer **Ryan L. Sass** .... (425) 257-8810
E-mail: rsass@everettwa.gov

Public Services Division
3200 Cedar Street, Everett, WA 98201
Tel: (425) 257-8810 Fax: (425) 257-8857
E-mail: everetteps@everettwa.gov

Building Official **Tony Lee** .... (425) 257-8810
E-mail: tlee@everettwa.gov

Real Property Management Division
3200 Cedar Street, Everett, WA 98201
Tel: (425) 257-8938 Fax: (425) 257-8856

Manager **Mike Palacios** .... (425) 257-8938
E-mail: mpalacios@everettwa.gov

Support Services Division
3200 Cedar Street, Everett, WA 98201
Tel: (425) 257-8922 Fax: (425) 257-8856

Engineering Services Manager **Richard Tarry** .... (425) 257-8922
E-mail: rtarry@everettwa.gov

Transportation Engineering Division
3200 Cedar Street, Everett, WA 98201
Tel: (425) 257-8810 Fax: (425) 257-8857

Traffic Engineer **Tim Miller** .... (425) 257-8977
E-mail: tmiller@everettwa.gov

Transportation Services
3225 Cedar Street, Everett, WA 98201
Tel: (425) 257-7777 Fax: (425) 257-8945 E-mail: etmail@everettwa.gov
Internet: http://www.everetttransit.org/

Director **Tom Hingson** .... (425) 257-7777

Office of the City Council
2930 Wetmore Avenue, Suite 9A, Everett, WA 98201
Tel: (425) 257-8703 Fax: (425) 257-8691

★ President **Scott Murphy** (Position 3) .... (425) 257-8703
Term Expires: December 31, 2017
E-mail: scmurphy@everettwa.gov

★ Council Member **Paul Roberts** (Position 1) .... (425) 257-8703
Term Expires: December 31, 2017
E-mail: proberts@everettwa.gov

★ Council Member **Jeff Moore** (Position 2) .... (425) 257-8703
Term Expires: December 31, 2017
E-mail: jmoore@everettwa.gov

★ Council Member **Cassie Franklin** (Position 4) .... (425) 257-8703
Term Expires: December 31, 2019

★ Council Member **Scott Bader** (Position 5) .... (425) 257-8703
Term Expires: December 31, 2019
E-mail: sbader@everettwa.gov

★ Council Member **Brenda Stonecipher** (Position 6) ...... (425) 257-8786
Term Expires: December 31, 2019
E-mail: bstonecipher@everettwa.gov

Office of the City Council *continued*

★ Council Member **Judy Touhy** (Position 7) .... (425) 257-8703
Term Expires: December 31, 2019
E-mail: jtouhy@everettwa.gov

City of Fairfield, California
1000 Webster Street, Fairfield, CA 94533
Tel: (707) 428-7400 Fax: (707) 428-7798 Internet: www.fairfield.ca.gov

County: Solano **Election Type:** Nonpartisan **Year Incorporated:** 1903
Population: 112,970 (2015)

Office of the Mayor and City Council
1000 Webster Street, Fairfield, CA 94533
Fax: (707) 428-7798
Internet: www.fairfield.ca.gov/gov/city_council/default.asp

★ Mayor **Harry T. Price** .... (707) 429-6298
Began Service: December 2005
Term Expires: December 2018
Education: Lock Haven BA; Western Washington 1970 BS

★ Vice Mayor **Chuck Timm** .... (707) 429-6298
Term Expires: December 2018

★ Council Member **Pamela Bertani** .... (707) 429-6298
Term Expires: December 2016

★ Council Member **Catherine Moy** .... (707) 429-6298
Term Expires: December 2018
Education: Cal State (Hayward) BA

★ Council Member **Rick Vaccaro** .... (707) 429-6298
Term Expires: December 2016
Education: Cal State (Sacramento) BA; Chapman MEd

Deputy City Clerk/Manager to Mayor and Council
Eva Hoff .... (707) 428-7402
E-mail: ehoff@fairfield.ca.gov

Office of the City Attorney
1000 Webster Street, Fairfield, CA 94533
Fax: (707) 428-7631
Internet: www.fairfield.ca.gov/gov/attorney/default.asp

○ City Attorney **Greg Stepanicich** .... (707) 428-7402
E-mail: gstepanicich@fairfield.ca.gov
Education: UC Riverside AB; Hastings JD

Office of the City Clerk
1000 Webster Street, Fairfield, CA 94533
Fax: (707) 428-7798
Internet: www.fairfield.ca.gov/gov/city_clerk/default.asp

★ City Clerk **Karen L. Rees** .... (707) 428-7394
Term Expires: December 2016
E-mail: klrees@fairfield.ca.gov

Office of the City Treasurer
1000 Webster Street, Fairfield, CA 94533
Fax: (707) 428-7597 Internet: www.fairfield.ca.gov/gov/treasurer.asp

★ City Treasurer **Oscar Reyes, Jr.** .... (707) 428-7497
Term Expires: December 2016
E-mail: oreyes@fairfield.ca.gov

Office of the City Manager
1000 Webster Street, Fairfield, CA 94533
Tel: (707) 428-7400 Fax: (707) 428-7798

○ City Manager **David White** .... (707) 428-7400
E-mail: dwhite@fairfield.ca.gov
Education: MIT MCP; UCLA BA

(continued on next page)

★ Elected Official ▲ Appointed by Legislature ▼ Appointed by Governor ► Appointed by Board or Commission ● Appointed by Judge
■ Appointed by Mayor △ Appointed by Freeholders ▽ Appointed by Supervisor ▷ Appointed by County Executive ○ Appointed by Council

Office of the City Manager *continued*

Executive Assistant to the City Manager **Alicia Henry** . . . . (707) 428-7401
E-mail: ahenry@fairfield.ca.gov

Administration Division
1000 Webster Street, Fairfield, CA 94533

Assistant City Manager **Laura Snideman** . . . . (707) 428-7398
E-mail: lsnideman@fairfield.ca.gov

Communications Division
1000 Webster Street, Fairfield, CA 94533

Communications Manager/Public Information Officer
Gale Spears . . . . (707) 428-7611
E-mail: gspears@fairfield.ca.gov

Employee Relations Division
1000 Webster Street, Fairfield, CA 94533
Tel: (707) 428-7394 Fax: (707) 428-7631
Internet: www.fairfield.ca.gov/gov/depts/hr/default.asp

Employee Relations Manager **Steve Janice** . . . . (707) 428-7758
E-mail: sjanice@fairfield.ca.gov

Information Technology Division
1000 Webster Street, Fairfield, CA 94533
Internet: www.fairfield.ca.gov/gov/depts/finance/it.asp

Chief Information Officer **Steve Garrison** . . . . (707) 428-7530
E-mail: sgarrison@fairfield.ca.gov

Payroll/Purchasing Division
1000 Webster Street, Fairfield, CA 94533

Financial Services Manager **Wade Brown** . . . . (707) 428-7596
E-mail: wbrown@fairfield.ca.gov

Finance Department
1000 Webster Street, Fairfield, CA 94533
Tel: (707) 428-7496 Fax: (707) 428-7597

Director of Finance **Fred Marsh** . . . . (707) 428-7498

Accounting/Accounts Payable Division
1000 Webster Street, Fairfield, CA 94533

Accounting Manager **Michael Less** . . . . (707) 428-7569
E-mail: mless@fairfield.ca.gov

Revenue Division
1000 Webster Street, Fairfield, CA 94533
Internet: www.fairfield.ca.gov/gov/depts/finance/revenue.asp

Accounts Receivable **Kim Bothwell** . . . . (707) 428-7596

Community Development Department
1000 Webster Street, Fairfield, CA 94533
Fax: (707) 428-7621
Internet: www.fairfield.ca.gov/gov/depts/cd/default.asp

Director **Karl Dumas** . . . . (707) 428-7454
E-mail: kdumas@fairfield.ca.gov

Building and Fire Safety Division
1000 Webster Street, 2nd Floor, Fairfield, CA 94533
Tel: (707) 428-7451 Fax: (707) 428-7324

Building Official **David Doyle** . . . . (707) 428-7444

Planning Division
1000 Webster Street, Fairfield, CA 94533
Tel: (707) 428-7461 Fax: (707) 428-7621
E-mail: planning@ci.fairfield.ca.us

Principal Planner **Joseph Lucchio** . . . . (707) 428-7647

Community Resources Department
1000 Webster Street, Fairfield, CA 94533
Tel: (707) 428-7465 Fax: (707) 428-7627
Internet: www.fairfield.ca.gov/gov/depts/cr/default.asp

Director **Ann Mottola** . . . . (707) 428-7465
E-mail: amottola@fairfield.ca.gov

Assistant Director **(Vacant)** . . . . (707) 428-7420

Adult Activity Programs
1000 Webster Street, Fairfield, CA 94533

Community Resources Manager **Marna Rollins** . . . . (707) 428-7741

Affordable Housing Division
1000 Webster Street, Fairfield, CA 94533

Housing Division Manager **Nicole Holloway** . . . . (707) 428-7387

Aquatics, Sports and Facilities Division
1000 Webster Street, Fairfield, CA 94533

Community Resources Manager **Ron Collins** . . . . (707) 428-7676

Youth Activities Division
1000 Webster Street, Fairfield, CA 94533

Manager **Tom Work** . . . . (707) 428-7660

Fire Department
1200 Kentucky Street, Fairfield, CA 94533
Tel: (707) 428-7375 Fax: (707) 399-0860
Internet: www.fairfield.ca.gov/gov/depts/fire/default.asp

Fire Chief **Tony Velasquez** . . . . (707) 436-7226
E-mail: tvelasquez@fairfield.ca.gov

Police Department
1000 Webster Street, Fairfield, CA 94533
Tel: (707) 428-7362 Fax: (707) 428-7576
Internet: www.fairfield.ca.gov/gov/depts/police/default.asp

Chief of Police **Joseph "Joe" Allio** . . . . (707) 428-7374
Education: Union Inst BS

Public Works Department
1000 Webster Street, Fairfield, CA 94533
Tel: (707) 428-7458 Fax: (707) 428-7607
Internet: www.fairfield.ca.gov/gov/depts/pw/default.asp

Director **George Hicks** . . . . (707) 428-7491

Engineering Division
1000 Webster Street, Fairfield, CA 94533
Fax: (707) 428-7607
Internet: www.fairfield.ca.gov/gov/depts/pw/eng/default.asp

City Engineer **George Hicks** . . . . (707) 428-7494

Operations Division
420 Gregory Street, Fairfield, CA 94533
Fax: (707) 428-7638
Internet: www.fairfield.ca.gov/gov/depts/pw/ops/default.asp

Superintendent **Pat Giles** . . . . (707) 428-7410
E-mail: pgiles@fairfield.ca.gov

Building Maintenance Manager **Michael Allen** . . . . (707) 428-7563
E-mail: mallen@fairfield.ca.gov

Transportation Division
1000 Webster Street, Fairfield, CA 94533
Fax: (707) 426-3298 E-mail: transit@fairfield.ca.gov

Transportation Manager **Nathan Atherstone** . . . . (707) 434-3804

Water Division
1000 Webster Street, Fairfield, CA 94533

Assistant Director **Felix Riesenberg** . . . . (707) 428-7680

★ Elected Official ▲ Appointed by Legislature ▼ Appointed by Governor ▶ Appointed by Board or Commission ● Appointed by Judge
■ Appointed by Mayor △ Appointed by Freeholders ▽ Appointed by Supervisor ▷ Appointed by County Executive ○ Appointed by Council

City of Fayetteville, North Carolina

433 Hay St., Fayetteville, NC 28301-5537
Internet: www.cityoffayetteville.org/

County: Cumberland **Election Type:** Nonpartisan **Year Incorporated:** 1893 **Population:** 201,963 (2015)

Office of the Mayor and City Council

433 Hay St., Fayetteville, NC 28301-5537
Fax: (910) 433-1948

★ Mayor **Nat Robertson** . . . . (910) 433-1992
Began Service: December 2, 2013 Fax: (910) 433-1948
Term Expires: December 8, 2017
E-mail: mayor@ci.fay.nc.us

★ Mayor Pro Tem **Mitch Colvin** (District 3) . . . . (910) 433-1329
Term Expires: December 8, 2017
E-mail: Mitch.Colvin@ci.fay.nc.us

★ Council Member **Kathy Keefe Jensen** (District 1) . . . . (910) 433-1992
Term Expires: December 8, 2017
E-mail: KJensen@ci.fay.nc.us

★ Council Member **Kirk deViere** (District 2) . . . . (910) 920-0525
Term Expires: December 8, 2017
E-mail: KDeViere@ci.fay.nc.us

★ Council Member **Chalmers "Chet" McDougald** (District 4) . . . . (910) 433-1992
Term Expires: December 8, 2017
E-mail: Chalmers.McDougald@ci.fay.nc.us

★ Council Member **Bobby Hurst** (District 5) . . . . (910) 481-0900
Term Expires: December 8, 2017
E-mail: bobbyhurst@aol.com

★ Council Member **Bill Crisp** (District 6) . . . . (910) 864-1669
Term Expires: December 8, 2017
E-mail: wjlcrisp@aol.com

★ Council Member **Larry O. Wright, Sr.** (District 7) . . . . (910) 433-1329
Term Expires: December 8, 2017
E-mail: Larry.Wright@ci.fay.nc.us

★ Council Member **Ted Mohn** (District 8) . . . . (910) 495-3634
Term Expires: December 8, 2017
E-mail: TMohn@ci.fay.nc.us

★ Council Member **Jim Arp** (District 9) . . . . (910) 433-1992
Term Expires: December 8, 2017
E-mail: jarp@ci.fay.nc.us

Office of the City Manager

433 Hay St., Fayetteville, NC 28301
Fax: (910) 433-1948

City Manager **Ted Voorhees** . . . . (910) 433-1990
E-mail: tvoorhees@ci.fay.nc.us

Deputy City Manager **Kristoff T. Bauer** . . . . (910) 433-1993
E-mail: kbauer@ci.fay.nc.us
Education: U Washington 1989 BA, 1989 BABA, 1992 MBA, 1993 JD

Deputy City Manager **Rochelle Small-Toney** . . . . (910) 433-1979
E-mail: RSmall-Toney@ci.fay.nc.us

Assistant City Manager **Jay Reinstein** . . . . (910) 433-1994
E-mail: jayreinstein@ci.fay.nc.us

City Clerk **Pamela Megill** . . . . (910) 433-1989
E-mail: pmegill@ci.fay.nc.us

Corporate Communications Director **COL Kevin Arata** . . . (910) 433-1451
E-mail: karata@ci.fay.nc.us

Office of the City Attorney

433 Hay St., Fayetteville, NC 28301
Fax: (910) 433-1980

City Attorney **Karen M. McDonald** . . . . (910) 433-1985
E-mail: kmcdonald@ci.fayetteville.nc.us

Assistant City Attorney **Jeff Bradford** . . . . (910) 433-1985

Assistant City Attorney **Lisa Harper** . . . . (910) 433-1985

Assistant City Attorney **(Vacant)** . . . . (910) 433-1985

Office of the City Attorney *continued*

Assistant City Attorney/Police Department **Michael Parker** . . . . (910) 433-1985

Airport

400 Airport Road, Suite 1, Fayetteville, NC 28306
Fax: (910) 433-1765

Director **Bradley S. Whited** . . . . (910) 433-1160

Community Development Department

433 Hay Street, 3rd Floor, Fayetteville, NC 28301
Fax: (910) 433-1592

Director **Victor D. Sharpe** . . . . (910) 433-1601
E-mail: vsharpe@ci.fay.nc.us

Development Services

433 Hay Street, 1st Floor, Fayetteville, NC 28301
P.O Box 1846, Fayetteville, NC 28302-1846
Fax: (910) 433-1588

Chief Development Officer **Scott Shuford** . . . . (910) 433-1701
E-mail: sshuford@ci.fay.nc.us

Development Advocate **Marsha Bryant** . . . . (910) 433-1701
E-mail: mbryant@ci.fay.nc.us

Economic and Business Development Department

433 Hay Street, Fayetteville, NC 28301

Director (Acting) **Rochelle Small-Toney** . . . . (910) 433-1264
E-mail: RSmall-Toney@ci.fay.nc.us

Economic Development Manager **Susan J. Monroe** . . . . . (910) 433-1321
E-mail: smonroe@ci.fay.nc.us

Engineering and Infrastructure Department

433 Hay St., Fayetteville, NC 28301

Director **Rob Stone** . . . . (910) 433-1691
E-mail: RStone@ci.fay.nc.us

Environmental Services Department

455 Grove St., Fayetteville, NC 28301
Fax: (910) 433-1516

Solid Waste Director **Jerry Dietzen** . . . . (910) 433-1984

Fayetteville Area System Transit [FAST]

455 Grove St., Fayetteville, NC 28301
Fax: (910) 433-1064

Director **Randall "Randy" Hume** . . . . (910) 433-1743
Education: Missouri 1974 BSBA

Finance Department

433 Hay Street, 2nd Floor, Fayetteville, NC 28301
Tel: (910) 433-1675 Fax: (910) 433-1680

Chief Financial Officer **Lisa Smith** . . . . (910) 433-1682

Fire/Emergency Management Department

433 Hay St., Fayetteville, NC 28301
Fax: (910) 433-1757

Fire Chief **Benjamin Major** . . . . (910) 433-1725
E-mail: bmajor@ci.fay.nc.us
Education: North Carolina Pembroke BBA

Human Relations Department

433 Hay Street, 3rd Floor, Fayetteville, NC 28301
Fax: (910) 433-1535

Deputy Director **Erica Hoggard** . . . . (910) 433-1583

★ Elected Official ▲ Appointed by Legislature ▼ Appointed by Governor ▶ Appointed by Board or Commission ● Appointed by Judge
■ Appointed by Mayor △ Appointed by Freeholders ▽ Appointed by Supervisor ▷ Appointed by County Executive ○ Appointed by Council

CITIES AND TOWNS

Human Resource Development Department

433 Hay Street, 1st Floor, Fayetteville, NC 28301
Tel: (910) 433-1636 (Jobline) Fax: (910) 433-1055

Director **Barbara Hill** . . . . . . (910) 433-1643
E-mail: bhill@ci.fay.nc.us
Safety Officer **Greg Schaefer** . . . . . . (910) 433-1635
E-mail: gschaefer@ci.fay.nc.us

Information Technology Department

433 Hay St., Fayetteville, NC 28301
Fax: (910) 433-1082

Chief Information Officer **Dwayne Campbell** . . . . . . (910) 433-1991
E-mail: dwcampbell@ci.fay.nc.us
Education: North Carolina Greensboro BS; Pfeiffer U MBA

Police Department

467 Hay St., Fayetteville, NC 28301
Tel: (910) 433-1529 (Non-emergency) Fax: (910) 433-1895

Chief of Police **Harold Medlock** . . . . . . (910) 433-1819

Public Works Commission

P.O. Box 1089, Fayetteville, NC 28302
Tel: (910) 483-1401 Tel: (910) 483-1382 (Customer Service)
Internet: www.faypwc.com

○ Chairman **Michael G. "Mike" Lallier** . . . . . . (910) 223-4001
○ Vice Chairman **Lynne Greene** . . . . . . (910) 223-4001
○ Secretary **Wade R. Fowler, Jr.** . . . . . . (910) 223-4001
○ Treasurer **Darsweil Rogers** . . . . . . (910) 223-4001
▶ General Manager and Chief Executive Officer
Steven K. Blanchard . . . . . . (910) 223-4001

Administrative Division

Facilities and Maintenance Director **Charles Johnson** . . . . (910) 223-4361
Information Systems Director **James Koenig** . . . . (910) 223-4321
Chief Corporate Services Officer **Susan Fritzen** . . . . (910) 223-4004
Warehouse Manager **Chris McKinney** . . . . (910) 223-4351
Fleet Management Manager **Tony Eakins** . . . . (910) 223-4298

Electric Systems Division

Tel: (910) 223-4516

Electric Systems Chief Operations Officer
David W. Trego . . . . . . (910) 223-4012
E-mail: electricalengr@faypwc.com
Education: Penn State 1980, 1993 MBA
Electric Operations Manager **Marcus Tunstall** . . . . (910) 223-4502
Electric Engineer Manager **Richard Andersen** . . . . (910) 223-4517
Director, Generation, Power Supply and Compliance
Reginald Wallace . . . . . . (910) 223-4813
Power Contracts and Trading Manager **Keith Lynch** . . . . (910) 223-4516
Electric Support Services Manager **Joel Valley** . . . . (910) 223-4549

Finance Division

Tel: (910) 223-4006

Chief Financial Officer **Dwight Miller** . . . . (910) 223-4005
Controller **Brenda Brown** . . . . (910) 223-4101
Customer Service Director **Bevan Grice** . . . . (910) 223-4131
Financial Planning and Capital Projects Director
Rhonda Haskins . . . . . . (910) 223-4102
Risk Manager **Ike Copeland** . . . . (910) 223-4116
Purchasing Manager **Gloria Wrench** . . . . (910) 223-4337

Management Division

Human Resources Officer **Bobby Russell** . . . . (910) 223-4122

Water Resources Division

Tel: (910) 223-4730

Water Resources Chief Operations Officer **Mick Noland** . . (910) 223-4733
Water Resources Operations Manager **Rick Davis** . . . . (910) 223-4718
Engineering Manager **Joe Glass** . . . . (910) 223-4740
Environmental Program Manager **Chad Ham** . . . . (910) 223-4702

Water Resources Division *continued*

Wastewater Treatment Facilities Manager **Chuck Baxley** . . (910) 223-4701
Water Treatment Facilities Manager **Chris Smith** . . . . (910) 223-4708

Fayetteville-Cumberland Parks, Recreation and Building Maintenance Department

121 Lamon Street, Fayetteville, NC 28301
Fax: (910) 433-1762

Director of Parks, Recreation, and Building Maintenance
Michael Gibson . . . . . . (910) 433-1547

City of Flint, Michigan

City Hall, 1101 South Saginaw Street, Flint, MI 48502-1420
Tel: (810) 766-7413 (Information) Internet: www.cityofflint.com

County: Genesee **Election Type:** Nonpartisan **Population:** 98,310 (2015)

Office of the Mayor

City Hall, 1101 S. Saginaw St., Flint, MI 48502-1420
Fax: (810) 766-7218

★ Mayor **Dr. Karen Williams Weaver** . . . . . . (810) 766-7346
Began Service: November 9, 2015
Term Expires: November 2019
E-mail: mayor@cityofflint.com
Education: Michigan State PhD

Office of the City Administrator

1101 South Saginaw Street, Flint, MI 48502-1420
Fax: (810) 766-7218

■ City Administrator **(Vacant)** . . . . . . (810) 766-7346

Office of the City Attorney

City Hall, 1101 S. Saginaw St., Flint, MI 48502-1420

■ City Attorney **Stacy Erwin Oakes** . . . . . . (810) 766-7146

Office of the City Clerk

City Hall, 1101 S. Saginaw St., Flint, MI 48502-1420

City Clerk **Inez Brown** . . . . . . (810) 766-7414
E-mail: ibrown@cityofflint.com

Budget and Finance

City Hall, 1101 S. Saginaw St., Flint, MI 48502-1420
Fax: (810) 766-7351

■ Finance Director **Jody Lundquist** . . . . . . (810) 766-7041
E-mail: jlundquist@cityofflint.com

Office of the Assessor

City Hall, 1101 S. Saginaw St., Flint, MI 48502-1420
Fax: (810) 341-5081 E-mail: assess@cityofflint.com

Assessor **William Fowler** . . . . . . (810) 766-7255
E-mail: wfowler@cityofflint.com

Office of the Treasurer

City Hall, 1101 S. Saginaw St., Flint, MI 48502-1420
Tel: (810) 766-7015 Fax: (810) 238-8481

■ Treasurer (Interim) **Doug Bingaman** . . . . . . (810) 766-7015
E-mail: dbingaman@cityofflint.com

★ Elected Official ▲ Appointed by Legislature ▼ Appointed by Governor ▶ Appointed by Board or Commission ● Appointed by Judge
■ Appointed by Mayor △ Appointed by Freeholders ▽ Appointed by Supervisor ▷ Appointed by County Executive ○ Appointed by Council

Purchasing Department
City Hall, 1101 S. Saginaw St., Flint, MI 48502-1420
Tel: (810) 766-7340 Fax: (810) 766-7240

Director of Purchasing **Derrick F. Jones** . . . . (810) 766-7340
E-mail: djones@cityofflint.com

Economic Development Corporation
City Hall, 1101 South Saginaw Street, Room N102, Flint, MI 48502-1420
Fax: (810) 766-7351

Director **Tracy Atkinson** . . . . (810) 766-7436
E-mail: tatkinson@cityofflint.com

Fire Department
310 E. Fifth Ave., Flint, MI 48502-1420
Fax: (810) 762-7340

■ Fire Chief **Raymond Barton** . . . . (810) 762-7336

Human Relations Office
City Hall, 1101 S. Saginaw St., Flint, MI 48502-1420
Fax: (810) 234-8460

■ Director **(Vacant)** . . . . (810) 766-7430

Human Resources Department and Benefits Administration
City Hall, 1101 S. Saginaw St., Flint, MI 48502-1420

■ Director **(Vacant)** . . . . (810) 766-7280

Information Services
1101 South Saginaw Street, Flint, MI 48502-1420
Fax: (810) 766-7467

Help Desk Manager **Jeff Keen** . . . . (810) 766-7155

Parks and Recreation Department
City Hall, 1101 S. Saginaw St., Flint, MI 48502-1420
Fax: (810) 766-7468 E-mail: dpr@cityofflint.com

■ Director of Planning and Development **Brian Larkin** . . . . . (810) 766-7426
E-mail: blarkin@cityofflint.com

Police Department
210 E. Fifth Ave., Flint, MI 48502-1420

■ Chief of Police **Timothy Johnson** . . . . (810) 237-6800

Department of Public Works
City Hall, 1101 S. Saginaw St., Flint, MI 48502-1420
Fax: (810) 766-7249 E-mail: dpw@cityofflint.com

Public Works Director **Howard Croft** . . . . (810) 766-7135 ext. 2606
Transportation Director **Kay Muhammed** . . . . (810) 766-7165
Traffic Engineering **Rod McGaha** . . . . (810) 766-7135 ext. 2622

Utilities Department
Utilities Administrator **Michael Glasgow** . . . . (810) 787-6537
Water Distribution and Sewer Maintenance
Supervisor **Robert Bincsik** . . . . (810) 766-7202 ext. 3413
3310 East Court Street, Flint, MI 48502 Fax: (810) 742-6283
Water Plant Supervisor **JoLisa McDay** . . . . (810) 787-6537
Water Pollution Control Supervisor
Robert Case . . . . (810) 766-7210 ext. 3621
G-4652 Beecher Road, Flint, MI 48432 Fax: (810) 230-3154

Office of the City Council
City Hall, 1101 S. Saginaw St., Flint, MI 48502-1420
Fax: (810) 766-7032

★ Council President **Kerry Nelson** (Ward 3) . . . . . (810) 766-7418 ext. 3159
Term Expires: November 2017
E-mail: knelson@cityofflint.com

Office of the City Council *continued*

★ Council Vice President **Vicki Van Buren** (Ward 8) . . . . (810) 766-7413
Term Expires: November 2017
E-mail: vburen@cityofflint.com

★ Council Member **Eric Mays** (Ward 1) . . . . (810) 922-4860
Term Expires: November 2017
E-mail: emays@cityofflint.com

★ Council Member **Jacqueline Poplar** (Ward 2) . . (810) 766-7418 ext. 3162
Term Expires: November 2017
E-mail: jpoplar@cityofflint.com

★ Council Member **Kate Fields** (Ward 4) . . . . (810) 766-7418
Term Expires: November 2017

★ Council Member **Wantwaz Davis** (Ward 5) . . . . (810) 766-7413
Term Expires: November 2017
E-mail: wdavis@cityofflint.com

★ Council Member **Herbert Winfrey** (Ward 6) . . . (810) 766-7418 ext. 3165
Term Expires: November 2017
E-mail: hwinfrey@cityofflint.com

★ Council Member **Monica Galloway** (Ward 7) . . . . (810) 766-7413
Term Expires: November 2017
E-mail: mgalloway@cityofflint.com

★ Council Member **Scott Kincaid** (Ward 9) . . . . . . (810) 766-7418 ext. 3158
Term Expires: November 2017
E-mail: skincaid@cityofflint.com

Office of the Ombudsman
801 S. Saginaw St., Flint, MI 48502-1420
Fax: (810) 766-7262

Deputy Ombudsman **(Vacant)** . . . . (810) 766-7335

City of Fontana, California
City Hall, 8353 Sierra Ave., Fontana, CA 92335-3528
Internet: www.fontana.org

County: San Bernardino **Election Type:** Nonpartisan **Year Incorporated:** 1952 **Population:** 207,460 (2015)

Office of the Mayor and City Council
City Hall, 8353 Sierra Ave., Fontana, CA 92335-3528
Fax: (909) 350-6613

★ Mayor **Acquanetta Warren** . . . . (909) 350-7601
Began Service: December 2010
Term Expires: November 2018
E-mail: awarren@fontana.org

★ Mayor Pro Tem **Michael Tahan** . . . . (909) 350-7605
Term Expires: November 2018
E-mail: mtahan@fontana.org

★ Council Member **John B. Roberts** . . . . (909) 350-7605
Term Expires: November 2018
E-mail: jroberts@fontana.org

★ Council Member **Lydia Salazar-Wibert** . . . . (909) 350-7605
Term Expires: November 2016
E-mail: lwibert@fontana.org

★ Council Member **Jesus "Jesse" Sandoval** . . . . (909) 350-7605
Term Expires: November 2016
E-mail: jsandoval@fontana.org

★ City Treasurer **Janet Koehler-Brooks** . . . . (909) 350-7605
Term Expires: November 2018
E-mail: jkoehlerbrooks@fontana.org

Office of the City Manager
City Hall, 8353 Sierra Ave., Fontana, CA 92335-3528

■ City Manager **Kenneth R. Hunt** . . . . (909) 350-7653
E-mail: khunt@fontana.org Fax: (909) 350-6613

★ Elected Official ▲ Appointed by Legislature ▼ Appointed by Governor ► Appointed by Board or Commission ● Appointed by Judge
■ Appointed by Mayor △ Appointed by Freeholders ▽ Appointed by Supervisor ▷ Appointed by County Executive ○ Appointed by Council

Office of the City Clerk
City Hall, 8353 Sierra Ave., Fontana, CA 92335-3528
Fax: (909) 350-6613

★City Clerk **Tonia Lewis** .... (909) 350-7655
Term Expires: November 2018
E-mail: tlewis@fontana.org

Deputy City Clerk **Cecilia Lopez-Henderson** .... (909) 350-7602
E-mail: clerks@fontana.org

Community Development Department
City Hall, 8353 Sierra Ave., Fontana, CA 92335-3528
Fax: (909) 350-7676

Director of Community Development **James R. Troyer** ... (909) 350-6718
E-mail: jtroyer@fontana.org

Building and Safety Division
Fax: (909) 350-7676

Building Official **Gil Estrada** .... (909) 350-7645

Planning Division
Fax: (909) 350-7676

Planning Manager **Zai AbuBakar** .... (909) 350-7625

Traffic Engineering Division
Fax: (909) 350-6618

Traffic Engineer **(Vacant)** .... (909) 350-7610

Public Works Department
16489 Orange Way, Fontana, CA 92355-3528

Director **Chuck Hays** .... (909) 350-6685
Fax: (909) 350-6755

Community Services Department
16860 Valencia Avenue, Fontana, CA 92335
Fax: (909) 349-6911

Director **Garth Nelson** .... (909) 349-6900
E-mail: gnelson@fontana.org Fax: (909) 349-6911

Parks and Landscape Division
Manager **Dan West** .... (909) 350-6518
Supervisor **Eric Garwick** .... (909) 350-6536

Public Works Division
Manager **Dan Chadwick** .... (909) 350-6798

Utilities and Streets Division
Supervisor **Todd Heagstedt** .... (909) 350-6764

Housing and Business Development Department\Deputy City Manager
City Hall, 8353 Sierra Ave., Fontana, CA 92335-3528
Fax: (909) 350-6616

Manager\Deputy City Manager **David Edgar** .... (909) 350-6739
E-mail: dedgar@fontana.org

Economic Development
8353 Sierra Ave., Fontana, CA 92335-3528
Fax: (909) 350-6616 Internet: www.fontanabusiness.org/

Economic Development Manager **Elisa Grey** .... (909) 350-6741
E-mail: egrey@fontana.org

Housing Authority
8353 Sierra Ave., Fontana, CA 92335-3528
Fax: (909) 350-6616
Internet: www.fontanabusiness.org/housing/index.html

Housing Manager **Brent Mickey** .... (909) 350-6657
E-mail: bmickey@fontana.org

Police Department
17005 Upland Ave., Fontana, CA 92335-3528

Police Chief **Rod Jones** .... (909) 350-7702
Fax: (909) 356-7111

Information Technology Department
City Hall, 8353 Sierra Ave., Fontana, CA 92335-3528
Fax: (909) 350-6506

Director **Dennis Vlasich** .... (909) 350-6676
E-mail: dvlasich@fontana.org

Fontana Unified School District
9680 Citrus Ave., Fontana, CA 92335
P.O. Box 5090, Fontana, CA 92334
Internet: www.fusd.net

►Superintendent of Schools **Dr. Leslie Boozer** .. (909) 357-7600 ext. 29109
E-mail: leslie.boozer@fusd.net

★President **Lorena Corona** .... (909) 357-5000
Term Expires: December 31, 2016
E-mail: lorena.corona@fusd.net

★Vice President **Mary Sandoval** .... (909) 357-5000
Term Expires: December 31, 2018
E-mail: Mary.Sandoval@fusd.net

★School Board Member **Jessie Armendarez** .... (909) 357-5000
Term Expires: December 31, 2018
E-mail: Jesse.Armendarez@fusd.net

★School Board Member **BarBara Chavez** .... (909) 357-5000
Term Expires: December 31, 2016
E-mail: chavez.barbara@fusd.net

★School Board Member **Matthew Slowik** .... (909) 357-5000
Term Expires: December 31, 2018
E-mail: Matt.Slowik@fusd.net

City of Fort Collins, Colorado
City Hall, 300 LaPorte Ave., Fort Collins, CO 80521
P.O. Box 580, Fort Collins, CO 80522-0580
Tel: (970) 221-6700 (Information) Internet: www.fcgov.com

County: Larimer **Election Type:** Nonpartisan **Population:** 161,175 (2015)

Office of the Mayor and City Council
P.O. Box 580, Fort Collins, CO 80522-0580
Fax: (970) 224-6107

★Mayor **Wade Troxell** .... (970) 416-2154
Began Service: April 2015
Term Expires: April 2017
E-mail: wtroxell@fcgov.com

★Council Member **Bob Overbeck** (District 1) .... (970) 221-6878
Term Expires: April 9, 2017
E-mail: boverbeck@fcgov.com

★Council Member **Ray Martinez** (District 2) .... (970) 221-6878
Term Expires: April 2019
E-mail: rmartinez@fcgov.com

★Council Member **Gino Campana** (District 3) .... (970) 221-6878
Term Expires: April 9, 2017
E-mail: gcampana@fcgov.com

★Council Member **Kristin Stephens** (District 4) .... (970) 221-6878
Term Expires: April 5, 2019
E-mail: kstephens@fcgov.com

★Council Member **Ross Cunniff** (District 5) .... (970) 221-6878
Term Expires: April 9, 2017
E-mail: rcunniff@fcgov.com

★Council Member **Gerry Horak** (District 6) .... (970) 221-6878
Term Expires: April 5, 2019
E-mail: ghorak@fcgov.com

★Elected Official ▲Appointed by Legislature ▼Appointed by Governor ►Appointed by Board or Commission ●Appointed by Judge
■Appointed by Mayor △Appointed by Freeholders ▽Appointed by Supervisor ▷Appointed by County Executive ○Appointed by Council

Office of the City Manager
P.O. Box 580, Fort Collins, CO 80522-0580
Tel: (970) 221-6505 Fax: (970) 224-6107

City Manager **Darin Atteberry** . . . . (970) 221-6684
E-mail: datteberry@fcgov.com
Deputy City Manager **Jeff Mihelich** . . . . (970) 221-6684
E-mail: jmihelich@fcgov.com
Deputy City Manager **Wendy Williams** . . . . (970) 416-2899
E-mail: wwilliams@fcgov.com
Assistant City Manager, Employee and Communication Services **Kelly DiMartino** . . . . (970) 416-2028
E-mail: kdimartino@fcgov.com
Education: Hastings Col 1997 BA

Communications and Public Involvement
Fax: (970) 224-6107

Director **Amanda King** . . . . (970) 416-2045
E-mail: aking@fcgov.com

Council Policy
Policy and Project Manager **Dan Weinheimer** . . . . (970) 416-2253
E-mail: dweinheimer@fcgov.com
Policy and Project Manager **Ginny Sawyer** . . . . (970) 224-6094

Neighborhood Services
Neighborhood Services Manager **Delynn Coldiron** . . . . . . (970) 221-6676
E-mail: decoldiron@fcgov.com

Cultural Services
Director of Cultural Services **Jill Stilwell** . . . . (970) 416-2935

Office of the City Clerk
P.O. Box 580, Fort Collins, CO 80522-0580
Fax: (970) 221-6295

City Clerk **Wanda Winkelmann** . . . . (970) 221-6515
E-mail: wwinkelmann@fcgov.com
Chief Deputy City Clerk **Rita Knoll** . . . . (970) 221-6515
E-mail: rknoll@fcgov.com

Office of the City Attorney
P.O. Box 580, Fort Collins, CO 80522-0580
Tel: (970) 221-6520 Fax: (970) 221-6327

○ City Attorney **Carrie Daggett** . . . . (970) 221-6520
E-mail: cdaggett@fcgov.com

Economic Health Department
P.O. Box 580, Fort Collins, CO 80522-0580

Economic Health Director **Josh Birks** . . . . (970) 221-6324
E-mail: jbirks@fcgov.com

Finance Department
P.O. Box 580, Fort Collins, CO 80522-0580

Chief Financial Officer **Michael N. "Mike" Beckstead** . . . (970) 221-6788

Budget, Accounting, Sales Tax and Treasury
Controller/Assistant Financial Officer **John Voss** . . . . (970) 221-6772
E-mail: jvoss@fcgov.com
Budget and Performance Management Manager **Lawrence Pollack** . . . . (970) 416-2439
E-mail: lpollack@fcgov.com

Fort Collins Utilities
P.O. Box 580, Fort Collins, CO 80522-0580
Fax: (970) 221-6619 E-mail: utilities@fcgov.com
Internet: www.fcgov.com/utilities/

Executive Director **Kevin Gertig** . . . . (970) 416-2232

Planning, Development and Transportation
P.O. Box 580, Fort Collins, CO 80522-0580
Fax: (970) 416-2081

Director **Laurie Kadrich** . . . . (970) 221-6287
E-mail: lkadrich@fcgov.com

Community Development and Neighborhood Services
Director (Interim) **Tom Leeson** . . . . (970) 221-6287
E-mail: tleeson@fcgov.com

Natural Areas Department
215 North Mason Street, Fort Collins, CO 80524
Fax: (970) 224-6177

Director **John Stokes** . . . . (970) 221-6263
Environmental Services Director **Lucinda Smith** . . . . (970) 224-6085
Natural Areas Manager **Mark Sears** . . . . (970) 416-2096
Senior Environmental Planner **Susie Gordon** . . . . (970) 221-6265

Transportation Services
P.O. Box 580, Fort Collins, CO 80522-0580
Fax: (970) 221-6608

Deputy Director **Mark Jackson** . . . . (970) 416-2029
Transport/Dial-a-Ride General Manager **Kurt Ravenschlag** . . . . (970) 221-6386
Parking Services Manager **Craig Dubin** . . . . (970) 224-9196
E-mail: cdubin@fcgov.com
Streets Superintendent **Larry Schneider** . . . . (970) 221-6755

Police Services
P.O. Box 580, Fort Collins, CO 80522-0580
2221 South Timberline Road, Fort Collins, CO 80525
Fax: (970) 224-6088

Chief of Police **John Hutto** . . . . (970) 221-6550
Projects and Public Information Manager **Catherine Kimble** . . . . (970) 221-6628
E-mail: kkimble@fcgov.com

Poudre Fire Authority
102 Remington Street, Fort Collins, CO 80524
Tel: (970) 416-2892 Fax: (970) 416-2809
Internet: http://www.poudre-fire.org

Fire Chief **Tom Demint** . . . . (970) 416-2870
E-mail: tdemint@poudre-fire.org

Social Sustainability Department
P.O. Box 580, Fort Collins, CO 80522-0580

Director of Social Sustainability **Beth Sowder** . . . . (970) 221-6752
Chief Sustainability Officer **Jackie Kozak Thiel** . . . . (970) 416-2332

Poudre River Public Library District
301 East Olive Street, Fort Collins, CO 80524

Executive Director **Holly C. Carroll** . . . . (970) 221-6740
E-mail: hcarroll@poudrelibraries.org
Education: Wooster BA; Kent State MLS; Cleveland State MPA

★ Elected Official ▲ Appointed by Legislature ▼ Appointed by Governor ▶ Appointed by Board or Commission ● Appointed by Judge
■ Appointed by Mayor △ Appointed by Freeholders ▽ Appointed by Supervisor ▷ Appointed by County Executive ○ Appointed by Council

City of Fort Lauderdale, Florida

City Hall, 100 North Andrews Avenue, Fort Lauderdale, FL 33301
Tel: (954) 828-5000 (Information) Internet: www.fortlauderdale.gov

County: Broward **Election Type:** Nonpartisan **Year Incorporated:** 1911
Population: 178,590 (2015)

Office of the Mayor and City Commission

City Hall, 100 North Andrews Avenue, Fort Lauderdale, FL 33301
Fax: (954) 828-5667

★ Mayor **John P. "Jack" Seiler** .... (954) 828-5003
Began Service: March 17, 2009
Term Expires: March 20, 2018
E-mail: jack.seiler@fortlauderdale.gov
Date of Birth: May 27, 1963
Education: Notre Dame 1985 BBA; Miami 1988 JD
Career: State Representative (D-FL, District 92), Florida House of Representatives (2001-2008)

★ Vice Mayor **Robert L. McKinzie** (District 3) .... (954) 828-5004
Term Expires: March 20, 2018
E-mail: rmckinzie@fortlauderdale.gov

★ Commissioner **Bruce Roberts** (District 1) .... (954) 828-5004
Term Expires: March 20, 2018
E-mail: broberts@fortlauderdale.gov

★ Commissioner **Dean J. Trantalis** (District 2) .... (954) 828-5004
Term Expires: March 20, 2018
E-mail: dtrantalis@fortlauderdale.gov

★ Commissioner **Romney C. Rogers** (District 4) .... (954) 828-5004
Term Expires: March 20, 2018
E-mail: rrogers@fortlauderdale.gov

Office of the City Attorney

City Hall, 100 N. Andrews Ave., Fort Lauderdale, FL 33301
Fax: (954) 828-5915

▶ City Attorney **Cynthia A. Everett** .... (954) 828-5037
E-mail: ceverett@fortlauderdale.gov

Office of the City Clerk

City Hall, 100 N. Andrews Ave., 7th Floor, Fort Lauderdale, FL 33301
Fax: (954) 828-5017

▶ City Clerk **Jeffrey A. Modarelli** .... (954) 828-5006
E-mail: jmodarelli@fortlauderdale.gov

Office of the City Manager

City Hall, 100 N. Andrews Ave., Fort Lauderdale, FL 33301
Fax: (954) 828-5021

▶ City Manager **Lee Feldman** .... (954) 828-5013
E-mail: lfeldman@fortlauderdale.gov
Assistant to the City Manager **Hal Barnes** .... (954) 828-5013
E-mail: hbarnes@fortlauderdale.gov

Assistant City Manager **Stanley D. Hawthorne** .... (954) 828-6802
E-mail: shawthorne@fortlauderdale.gov

Assistant City Manager **Christopher J. Lagerbloom** .... (954) 828-5013
E-mail: clagerbloom@fortlauderdale.gov

Public Affairs Manager **Chaz Adams** .... (954) 828-4737
E-mail: chaza@fortlauderdale.gov

Assistant to the City Manager, Budget and Grants
Laura Reece .... (954) 828-5392
E-mail: lreece@fortlauderdale.gov

Finance Department

City Hall, 100 N. Andrews Ave., Fort Lauderdale, FL 33301
Fax: (954) 828-5168

Director **Kirk W. Buffington** .... (954) 828-6572
Education: Florida State 1979 BSA; Webster 1996 MBA

Assistant Director of Finance **Linda Logan-Short** .... (954) 828-5933
E-mail: llogan-short@fortlauderdale.gov

Fire-Rescue Department

528 NW 2nd Street, Fort Lauderdale, FL 33311
Fax: (954) 828-6843

Fire Chief **Robert F. Hoecherl** .... (954) 828-6821
E-mail: rhoecherl@fortlauderdale.gov

Human Resources Department

City Hall, 100 N. Andrews Ave., Fort Lauderdale, FL 33301
Fax: (954) 828-5315

Director **Averill Dorsett** .... (954) 828-5307
E-mail: adorsett@fortlauderdale.gov

Parks and Recreation Department

1350 W. Broward Blvd., Fort Lauderdale, FL 33312
Fax: (954) 828-5650

Director **Phil Thornburg** .... (954) 828-5348

Sustainable Development Department

700 NW 19th Avenue, Fort Lauderdale, FL 33311

Director **Jenni Morejon** .... (954) 828-5266

Community Redevelopment Agency [CRA]

914 NW Sixth Street, Suite 200, Fort Lauderdale, FL 33311
Fax: (954) 828-4500

Director **(Vacant)** .... (954) 828-4514

Police Department

1300 W. Broward Blvd., Fort Lauderdale, FL 33312
Fax: (954) 828-6676

Chief **Frank Adderley** .... (954) 828-5591

Public Works Department

100 North Andrews Avenue, Fort Lauderdale, FL 33301
Fax: (954) 828-7881

Director **Paul Berg** .... (954) 828-5240

City of Fort Wayne, Indiana

Citizens Square, 200 East Berry Street, Fort Wayne, IN 46802
Tel: (260) 427-1111 (Information) Internet: www.cityoffortwayne.org

County: Allen **Election Type:** Partisan **Year Founded:** 1827
Year Incorporated: 1873 **Population:** 260,326 (2015)

Office of the Mayor

Citizens Square, 200 East Berry, 4th Floor, Fort Wayne, IN 46802
Fax: (260) 427-1115 E-mail: mayor@ci.ft-wayne.in.us

★ Mayor **Tom Henry** (D) .... (260) 427-1111
Began Service: 2008
Term Expires: December 31, 2019
E-mail: mayor@ci.ft-wayne.in.us
Education: U St Francis 1974 BA, MBA

■ Deputy Mayor **Karl Bandemer** .... (260) 427-1111
E-mail: karl.bandemer@cityoffortwayne.org

■ Executive Assistant **Leslie Lanier-Torres** .... (260) 427-1111
E-mail: leslie.lanier-torres@cityoffortwayne.org

★ Elected Official ▲ Appointed by Legislature ▼ Appointed by Governor ▶ Appointed by Board or Commission ● Appointed by Judge
■ Appointed by Mayor △ Appointed by Freeholders ▽ Appointed by Supervisor ▷ Appointed by County Executive ○ Appointed by Council

Office of the Mayor *continued*

■ Community Liaison **Palermo Galindo** . . . . (260) 427-1122
■ Director of Public Information **John Perlich** . . . . . . (260) 427-1120
E-mail: john.perlich@cityoffortwayne.org
■ Business and Legislative Liaison **Stephanie Crandall** . . . . (260) 427-2625
E-mail: stephanie.crandall@cityoffortwayne.org
■ Hispanic and Immigrant Liaison **Palermo Galindo** . . . . . . (260) 427-6214
E-mail: palermo.galindo@cityoffortwayne.org

Office of the City Controller

Citizens Square, 200 East Berry Street, Suite 470, Fort Wayne, IN 46802
Fax: (260) 427-1446

■ City Controller **Len Poehler** . . . . (260) 427-1106
One Main St., Room 930, Fort Wayne, IN 46802
E-mail: len.poehler@cityoffortwayne.org
Education: Indiana BA

City Utilities/Operations Department

200 East Berry Street, Suite 270, Fort Wayne, IN 46802
Fax: (260) 427-2540 Internet: www.cityoffortwayne.org/utilities/

Director **Kumar Menon** . . . . (260) 427-1381
Education: Madras (India) BSEc, MEcon
Chief Financial Officer **Justin Brugger** . . . . (260) 427-1381
Education: Indiana BA, MPM

Human Resources

200 East Berry Street, Suite 370, Fort Wayne, IN 46802
Fax: (260) 427-1177 E-mail: cofwhr@cityoffortwayne.org
Internet: www.cityoffortwayne.org/human-resources.html

Director **Carolyn Ovitt** . . . . (260) 427-1180
E-mail: carolyn.ovitt@cityoffortwayne.org Fax: (260) 427-1177

Purchasing Department

200 East Berry Street, Suite 490, Fort Wayne, IN 46802
Fax: (260) 427-1393 Internet: www.cityoffortwayne.org/purchasing.html

Director **Steven Gillette** . . . . (260) 427-1101
E-mail: steve.gillette@cityoffortwayne.org

Risk Management Department

200 East Berry Street, Suite 470, Fort Wayne, IN 46802
Fax: (260) 427-6947

Director **Nancy McAfee** . . . . (260) 427-1164

Community Development Division

Citizens Square, 200 East Berry Street, Suite 320, Fort Wayne, IN 46802
Fax: (260) 427-1132 Internet: http://www.fwcommunitydevelopment.org/

■ Division Director **Greg Leatherman** . . . . (260) 427-1127
E-mail: greg.leatherman@cityoffortwayne.org
Education: Treveca Nazarene U BA; Indiana MA

Office of Housing and Neighborhood Services

Fax: (260) 427-1447

Deputy Director **Heather Presley-Cowen** . . . . (260) 427-1127
E-mail: heather.presley@ci.ft-wayne.in.us

Planning and Policy Department

Deputy Director **Pam Holocher** . . . . (260) 427-1127

Redevelopment Commission

Fax: (260) 427-1375

Commission President **Christopher Guerin** . . . . (260) 427-1127
E-mail: christopher.guerin@cityoffortwayne.org
Redevelopment Director **Nancy Townsend** . . . . (260) 427-1127

Parks and Recreation Department

705 E. State Blvd., Fort Wayne, IN 46805
Fax: (260) 427-6020 Internet: www.fortwayneparks.org

■ Executive Director **Alvin R. Moll, Jr.** . . . . (260) 427-6001
E-mail: al.moll@cityoffortwayne.org
Leisure Services/Deputy Director **Chuck Reddinger** . . . . . (260) 427-6009

Parks and Recreation Department *continued*

Asset Management Deputy Director **Steve McDaniel** . . . . (260) 427-6407
E-mail: steve.mcdaniel@cityoffortwayne.org
Zoo Superintendent **Jim Anderson** . . . . (260) 427-6805
Education: Purdue 1979 BS; Indiana 1992 MPA
Finance and Support Services Deputy Director
Garry Morr . . . . (260) 427-6060
E-mail: garry.morr@cityoffortwayne.org
Education: Indiana 1980 BS

Department of Public Safety

One East Main Street, Fort Wayne, IN 46802
Tel: (260) 427-1222

Director of Public Safety **Russell P. "Rusty" York** . . . . . . (260) 427-1222
E-mail: rusty.york@ci.ft-wayne.in.us

Animal Control Department

3020 Hillegas Rd., Fort Wayne, IN 46808
Fax: (260) 427-5514

■ Director **Amy-Jo Sites** . . . . (260) 427-1244

Fort Wayne 911 Communications Center

One East Main Street, Fort Wayne, IN 46802
Tel: (260) 427-1213 Fax: (260) 427-1366

Director **William Bassett** . . . . (260) 427-1213

Fire Department

307 Murray St., Fort Wayne, IN 46803
Fax: (260) 427-1277 Internet: http://fortwaynefiredepartment.org/

■ Fire Chief **Eric Lahey** . . . . (260) 427-1478
E-mail: eric.lahey@ci.ft-wayne.in.us
Fire Marshall **Paul Veldman** . . . . (260) 427-1478
Deputy Fire Chief **Adam O'Connor** . . . . (260) 427-1478
E-mail: mark.nelson@ci.ft-wayne.in.us

Neighborhood Code Enforcement Department

Citizens Square, 200 East Berry Street, Suite 320, Fort Wayne, IN 46802
Fax: (260) 427-1409

Director **Cindy Joyner** . . . . (260) 427-1323
E-mail: cindy.joyner@cityoffortwayne.org

Police Department [FWPD]

Police Operations Center, 1320 East Creighton Street,
Fort Wayne, IN 46803
Internet: http://www.fwpd.org Tel: (260) 427-1222

■ Police Chief **Gary Hamilton** . . . . (260) 427-1230
E-mail: gary.hamilton@ci.ft-wayne.in.us

Public Works Division

Citens Square, 200 East Berry Street, Suite 210, Fort Wayne, IN 46802
Fax: (260) 427-1269 Internet: www.cityoffortwayne.org/publicworks/

Director **Bob Kennedy** . . . . (260) 427-6971
City Engineer **Shan Gunawardena** . . . . (260) 427-6169
E-mail: shan.gunawardena@cityoffortwayne.org

Vendor Compliance Department

200 East Berry Street, Suite 490, Fort Wayne, IN 46802
Fax: (260) 427-6938

Compliance Supervisor **Kelly Lundberg** . . . . (260) 427-2445

Solid Waste Department

Fax: (260) 427-1454

Manager **Matthew Gratz** 2nd Floor . . . . (260) 427-2474

Traffic Engineering Department

Assistant Traffic Engineer **Kyle Winling** . . . . (260) 427-1172
E-mail: kyle.winling@cityoffortwayne.org Fax: (260) 427-1269

★ Elected Official ▲ Appointed by Legislature ▼ Appointed by Governor ▶ Appointed by Board or Commission ● Appointed by Judge
■ Appointed by Mayor △ Appointed by Freeholders ▽ Appointed by Supervisor ▷ Appointed by County Executive ○ Appointed by Council

Transportation Engineering Services
Manager **Mario Trevino** . . . . (260) 427-1172
E-mail: mario.trevino@cityoffortwayne.org

Fort Wayne Housing Authority [FWHA]
7315 Hanna Street, Fort Wayne, IN 46816
Internet: www.fwha.org/

Executive Director **Maynard Scales** . . . . (260) 267-9300 ext. 7100

Office of the City Council
Citizens Square, 200 East Berry Street, Suite 110, Fort Wayne, IN 46802
Fax: (260) 427-1371 Internet: www.cityoffortwayne.org/city-council.html

★Council Member **Paul Ensley** (R-District 1) . . . . (260) 427-1221
Term Expires: December 31, 2019

★Council Member **Russell Jehl** (R-District 2) . . . . (260) 427-1221
Term Expires: December 31, 2019
E-mail: russell.jehl@cityoffortwayne.org

★Council Member **Thomas F. Didier** (R-District 3) . . . . (260) 427-1221
Term Expires: December 31, 2019
E-mail: thomas.didier@cityoffortwayne.org

★Council Member **Jason Arp** (R-District 4) . . . . (260) 427-1221
Term Expires: December 31, 2019

★Council Member **Geoff Paddock** (D-District 5) . . . . (260) 427-1221
Term Expires: December 31, 2019
E-mail: geoffreypaddock@aol.com

★Council Member **Glynn A. Hines** (D-District 6) . . . . (260) 427-1221
Term Expires: December 31, 2019
E-mail: glynnhines@aol.com
Education: St Francis Col (IN) BA

★Council Member **Michael Barranda** (R-At-Large) . . . . (260) 427-1221
Term Expires: December 31, 2019

★Council Member **John N. Crawford** (R-At-Large) . . . . (260) 433-0295
Term Expires: December 31, 2019
E-mail: jncrawfordmd@gmail.com
Education: LSU Medical Center MD

★Council Member
Thomas "Tom" Freistroffer (R-At-Large) . . . . (260) 427-1221
Term Expires: December 31, 2019

Council Administrator **Molly McCray** . . . . (260) 427-1445
E-mail: molly.mccray@cityoffortwayne.org

Office of the City Clerk
Citizens Square, 200 East Berry Street, Suite 110, Fort Wayne, IN 46802
Fax: (260) 427-1371 Internet: www.cityoffortwayne.org/city-clerk.html

★City Clerk **Lana R. Keesling** (R) . . . . (260) 427-1221
Term Expires: December 31, 2019
Chief Deputy Clerk **Sarah Rogers** . . . . (260) 427-1221
E-mail: sarah.rogers@cityoffortwayne.org
Deputy Clerk **Stacey Reed** . . . . (260) 427-1221

City of Fort Worth, Texas
Municipal Bldg., 1000 Throckmorton St., Fort Worth, TX 76102
Tel: (817) 392-8900 (Information) Internet: http://fortworthtexas.gov/

County: Tarrant **Election Type:** Nonpartisan **Year Founded:** 1849
Year Incorporated: 1873 **Population:** 833,319 (2015)

Office of the Mayor and City Council
City Hall, 1000 Throckmorton Street, 3rd Floor, Fort Worth, TX 76102
Tel: (817) 392-6118 Fax: (817) 392-2409

★Mayor **Betsy Price** (At-Large) . . . . (817) 392-6118
Began Service: July 11, 2011 Fax: (817) 392-2409
Term Expires: May 1, 2017
E-mail: betsy.price@fortworthtexas.gov
Education: Texas (Arlington) 1972 BS

Office of the Mayor and City Council *continued*

Chief of Staff **Mattie J. Parker** . . . . (817) 392-6217
Fax: (817) 392-2409
Aide **Alex Skelpsa** . . . . (817) 392-6214
Fax: (817) 392-2409
Mayor's Scheduler **Beth Ellis** . . . . (817) 392-6064
Fax: (817) 392-2409

★Mayor Pro Tem **Sal Espino** (District 2) . . . . (817) 392-8802
Term Expires: May 1, 2017 Fax: (817) 392-6187
E-mail: district2@fortworthtexas.gov
Education: Texas Christian BS; Southern Methodist JD
Aide **Pilar Candia** . . . . (817) 392-8802
E-mail: pilar.candia@fortworthtexas.gov Fax: (817) 392-6187

★Council Member
W.B. "Zim" Zimmerman (District 3) . . . . (817) 392-8803
Term Expires: May 1, 2017 Fax: (817) 392-6187
E-mail: district3@fortworthtexas.gov
Aide **Sandi Breaux** . . . . (817) 392-8803
E-mail: sandra.breaux@fortworthtexas.gov Fax: (817) 392-6187

★Council Member **Cary Moon** (District 4) . . . . (817) 392-8804
Term Expires: May 1, 2017 Fax: (817) 392-6187
Aide **Alicia Ortiz** . . . . (817) 392-8804
E-mail: alicia.ortiz@fortworthtexas.gov Fax: (817) 392-6187

★Council Member **Gyna Bivens** (District 5) . . . . (817) 392-8805
Term Expires: May 1, 2017 Fax: (817) 392-6187
Aide **Cynthia Triche** . . . . (817) 392-8804
E-mail: cynthia.triche@fortworthtexas.gov Fax: (817) 392-6187

★Council Member **Jungus Jordan** (District 6) . . . . (817) 392-8806
Term Expires: May 1, 2017 Fax: (817) 392-6187
E-mail: district6@fortworthtexas.gov
Aide **Jamie Wilson** . . . . (817) 392-8806
E-mail: jamie.phillips@fortworthtexas.gov Fax: (817) 392-6187

★Council Member **Dennis Shingleton** (District 7) . . . . (817) 392-8807
Term Expires: May 1, 2017 Fax: (817) 392-6187
E-mail: district7@fortworthtexas.gov
Aide **Sami Roop** . . . . (817) 392-8807
E-mail: sami.roop@fortworthtexas.gov Fax: (817) 392-6187

★Council Member **Kelly Allen Gray** (District 8) . . . . (817) 392-8808
Term Expires: May 1, 2017 Fax: (817) 392-6187
E-mail: district8@fortworthtexas.gov
Education: Texas A&M (Commerce)
Aide **Maribeth Ashley** . . . . (817) 392-8808
E-mail: maribeth.ashley@fortworthtexas.gov Fax: (817) 392-6187

★Council Member **Ann Zadeh** (District 9) . . . . (817) 392-8809
Term Expires: May 1, 2017 Fax: (817) 392-6187
E-mail: district9@fortworthtexas.gov
Aide **Katherine Smith** . . . . (817) 392-8809
E-mail: katherine.smith@fortworthtexas.gov Fax: (817) 392-6187

City Attorney's Office
Municipal Bldg., 1000 Throckmorton Street, 3rd Floor,
Fort Worth, TX 76102
Tel: (817) 392-7600 Fax: (817) 392-8359
Internet: http://fortworthtexas.gov/cityattorney/

○City Attorney **Sarah Fullenwider** . . . . (817) 392-7600
E-mail: sarah.fullenwider@fortworthtexas.gov
Administrative Services Coordinator **Tracey McVay** . . . . (817) 392-7600
E-mail: tracey.mcvay@fortworthtexas.gov

City Secretary's Office
Municipal Bldg., 1000 Throckmorton Street, 3rd Floor,
Fort Worth, TX 76102
Tel: (817) 392-6150 Fax: (817) 392-6196
E-mail: citysecretarywebmail@fortworthtexas.gov
Internet: http://fortworthtexas.gov/citysecretary/

City Secretary **Mary J. Kayser** . . . . (817) 392-6161
E-mail: mary.kayser@fortworthtexas.gov
Assistant to the City Secretary **Allison Tidwell** . . . . (817) 392-6152
E-mail: allison.tidwell@fortworthtexas.gov
Assistant City Secretary **Ronald Gonzales** . . . . (817) 392-6164
E-mail: ronald.gonzales@fortworthtexas.gov

★Elected Official ▲Appointed by Legislature ▼Appointed by Governor ▶Appointed by Board or Commission ●Appointed by Judge
■Appointed by Mayor △Appointed by Freeholders ▽Appointed by Supervisor ▷Appointed by County Executive ○Appointed by Council

Internal Audit Department
1000 Throckmorton Street, 3rd Floor, Fort Worth, TX 76102
Tel: (817) 392-6158 Fax: (817) 392-6133

○ City Auditor **Patrice Randle** .... (817) 392-6132
E-mail: patrice.randle@fortworthtexas.gov Fax: (817) 392-6133
Education: Sam Houston State BS
Assistant City Auditor **Terry Holderman** .... (817) 392-6141
Administrative Assistant **Joanna Ramirez** .... (817) 392-6158
E-mail: joanna.ramirez@fortworthgov.org Fax: (817) 392-6133

Office of the City Manager
Municipal Bldg., 1000 Throckmorton St., Fort Worth, TX 76102-6311
Tel: (817) 392-6111 Fax: (817) 392-6134
Internet: http://fortworthtexas.gov/citymanager/

○ City Manager **David Cooke** .... (817) 392-6116
Executive Secretary **Linda Hirrlinger** .... (817) 392-6116
Assistant City Manager **Susan Alanis** .... (817) 392-2689
E-mail: susan.alanis@fortworthtexas.gov
Assistant City Manager **Jesus "Jay" Chapa** .... (817) 392-7504
E-mail: jesus.chapa@fortworthtexas.gov
Assistant City Manager **Fernando Costa** .... (817) 392-7504
E-mail: fernando.costa@fortworthtexas.gov
Assistant City Manager **Valerie Washington** .... (817) 392-7504
E-mail: Valerie.Washington@fortworthtexas.gov

Cable Communication Office
Fax: (817) 871-6190

Cable Service Manager **Jack McGee** .... (817) 392-6169

Aviation Department/Fort Worth Meacham International Airport
Fort Worth Meacham International Airport, 4201 North Main Street, Suite 200, Fort Worth, TX 76106-2749
Tel: (817) 392-5400 Fax: (817) 392-5413
Internet: http://fortworthtexas.gov/aviation/

Aviation Director **Bill Welstead** .... (817) 392-5402
Meacham International Airport Manager **Jeff Kloska** .... (817) 392-5400

Alliance Airport
222 Alliance Blvd., Fort Worth, TX 76177-4300
Fax: (817) 890-1099

Alliance Air Services President **Tom Harris** .... (817) 890-1000

Fort Worth Spinks Airport
13451 Wing Way, Suite 109, Fort Worth, TX 76028
Fax: (817) 447-8334

Manager **Aaron Barth** .... (817) 392-5400

Code Compliance Department
818 Missouri Avenue, Fort Worth, TX 76104
Fax: (817) 392-2249 E-mail: codecares@fortworthtexas.gov
Internet: http://fortworthtexas.gov/codecompliance/

Director **Brandon Bennett** .... (817) 392-6322

Animal Care and Control Division
4900 Martin St., Fort Worth, TX 76119
Fax: (817) 561-3741 Internet: http://fortworthtexas.gov/animals/

Superintendent **Sandra Shelby** .... (817) 392-3743
Administrative Secretary **(Vacant)** .... (817) 392-3742

Consumer Health Division
818 Missouri Avenue, Fort Worth, TX 76104
Fax: (817) 392-3713 Internet: http://fortworthtexas.gov/health/

Superintendent **Elmer Depaula** .... (817) 392-3713
Senior Administrative Assistant **Wendy Cooper** .... (817) 392-3713
E-mail: wendy.cooper@fortworthtexas.gov

Financial Management Services
Municipal Bldg., 1000 Throckmorton Street, 3rd Floor, Fort Worth, TX 76102
Tel: (817) 392-8185 Fax: (817) 392-8502
Internet: http://fortworthtexas.gov/finance/

Chief Financial Officer **Aaron J. Bovos** .... (817) 392-8517
Assistant Finance Director **Trey Imes** .... (817) 392-2438
Assistant Finance Director and FSA **(Vacant)** .... (817) 392-8325
Budget Director **T. Alvin Hanson** .... (817) 392-7934

Budget and Research Division
Tel: (817) 392-8500 Fax: (817) 392-8502
Internet: www.fortworttexas.gov/budget

Budget Manager **Alan Shuror** .... (817) 392-8505
E-mail: alan.shuror@fortworthtexas.gov

Financial Systems Administration
Fax: (817) 392-1254

Financial Systems Manager **Steven Nesbit** .... (817) 392-2673

Purchasing
Tel: (817) 392-8360 Fax: (817) 392-8440

Purchasing Manager **Jack Dale** .... (817) 392-8357
E-mail: jack.dale@fortworthtexas.gov
Purchasing Supervisor **Carlos Marmojelos** .... (817) 392-7648
E-mail: carlos.marmojelos@fortworthgov.org
Purchasing Supervisor-Contracts **Marilyn Jackson** .... (817) 392-2059
E-mail: marilyn.jackson@fortworthtexas.gov

Risk Management
Tel: (817) 392-7402 Fax: (817) 392-5874

Risk Manager **Joey Page** .... (817) 392-7761
E-mail: joey.page@fortworthgov.org

Treasury Division
Tel: (817) 392-8519 Fax: (817) 392-2438

City Treasurer **John Butkus** .... (817) 392-2435
Assistant City Treasurer **Jenny Kerzman** .... (817) 392-6030

Fire Department
505 West Felix Street, Fort Worth, TX 76115
Tel: (817) 392-6800 Fax: (817) 392-6859

Fire Chief **Rudy Jackson** .... (817) 392-6801
E-mail: rudy.jackson@fortworthtexas.gov
Education: Dallas Baptist BBA, MBA
Administrative Assistant **Brenda Josselet** .... (817) 392-6888
E-mail: brenda.josselet@fortworthtexas.gov
Executive Assistant Chief **David Coble** .... (817) 392-6849
E-mail: david.coble@fortworthtexas.gov Fax: (817) 392-8436
Operations Assistant Chief **Tim Hatch** .... (817) 392-6858
Fax: (817) 871-8591
Assistant Director, Administrative Services
Scott Hanlan .... (817) 392-6803
E-mail: scott.hanlan@fortworthtexas.gov Fax: (817) 392-6859
Educational/Support Services Assistant Chief
Pat Vasquez .... (817) 392-6173
E-mail: pat.vasquez@fortworthgov.org Fax: (817) 392-6180
Emergency Management Coordinator **Juan Ortiz** .... (817) 392-6810
E-mail: juan.ortiz@fortworthtexas.gov
Fire Marshal/Battalion Chief **Bobby Tatum** .... (817) 392-6808
E-mail: bobby.tatum@fortworthtexas.gov
Battalion Chief **Richard Harrison** .... (817) 392-6800
Fax: (817) 392-6859

Housing and Economic Development
1000 Throckmorton St., Fort Worth, TX 76102
Tel: (817) 392-7540 Fax: (817) 392-7328

Director (Acting) **Robert Sturns** .... (817) 871-6025
Senior Administrative Assistant **Bette Chapman** .... (817) 392-6125
E-mail: bette.chapman@fortworthtexas.gov

★ Elected Official ▲ Appointed by Legislature ▼ Appointed by Governor ▶ Appointed by Board or Commission ● Appointed by Judge
■ Appointed by Mayor △ Appointed by Freeholders ▽ Appointed by Supervisor ▷ Appointed by County Executive ○ Appointed by Council

CITIES AND TOWNS

Minority/Women Business Enterprise Office [MWBE]
Fax: (817) 212-2681

Assistant Business Development Manager
Robert Sturns (817) 212-2674

Human Resources Department
City Hall, 1000 Throckmorton St., Fort Worth, TX 76102
Tel: (817) 392-8554 Fax: (817) 392-8869
Internet: http://fortworthtexas.gov/hr/

Director **Brian R. Dickerson** (817) 392-7783
E-mail: brian.dickerson@fortworthgov.org
Education: Friends BA; Nebraska (Omaha) MBA
Assistant Director **Margaret Wise** (817) 392-8058
E-mail: margaret.wise@fortworthgov.org
Human Resources Analyst **Monique Schomp** (817) 392-8554
E-mail: monique.schomp@fortworthgov.org

Information Technology Solutions
Chief Information Officer **Kevin Gunn** (817) 392-8781
E-mail: kevin.gunn@fortworthgov.org
Education: Texas A&I BS; Tarleton State MBA
Administrative Assistant **Neaita Wortham** (817) 392-8450
E-mail: neaita.wortham@fortworthtexas.gov

Park and Recreation Department
4200 South Freeway, Suite 2200, Fort Worth, TX 76115-1499
Fax: (817) 392-5724

Director **Richard Zavala** (817) 392-5704
E-mail: richard.zavala@fortworthtexas.gov
Executive Secretary **Adriana Maldonado** (817) 392-5704
Assistant Director **Sandra Youngblood** (817) 392-5755
E-mail: sandra.youngblood@fortworthtexas.gov
Fiscal Services **Christine Taylor** (817) 392-5725
Employee Relations **Lisa Totton** (817) 392-5751
E-mail: lisa.totton@fortworthtexas.gov
Volunteer Coordinator/Public Information Officer
Whitney Ellis (817) 392-5778

Planning and Development Department
City Hall, 1000 Throckmorton St., Lower Level, Fort Worth, TX 76102
Tel: (817) 392-7820

Director **Randle Harwood** (817) 392-6101
E-mail: randle.harwood@fortworthtexas.gov
Administrative Assistant **Maria Medina** (817) 392-5884
E-mail: maria.medina@fortworthtexas.gov Fax: (817) 392-7430
Administrative Services Manager **Jullianna Barron** (817) 392-8318
E-mail: jullianna.barron@fortworthtexas.gov
Transportation Utility and Planning Administrator
David Schroeder (817) 392-7918
Development Facilitation Manager **Julie Westerman** (817) 392-2239
E-mail: julie.westerman@fortworthtexas.gov
Senior Administrative Assistant **Irma Saenz** (817) 392-2731
E-mail: irma.saenz@fortworthtexas.gov Fax: (817) 392-2320

Police Department
505 West Felix Street, Fort Worth, TX 76102
Tel: (817) 392-4200 Fax: (817) 392-4216
Internet: www.fortworthpd.com/

Police Chief **Joel F. Fitzgerald, Sr.** (817) 392-4210
Senior Administrative Assistant **Tami Wadlington** (817) 392-4213
E-mail: tami.wadlington@fortworthtexas.gov
Finance/Personnel Bureau Assistant Chief
Abdul Pridgen (817) 392-4230
E-mail: abdul.pridgen@fortworthtexas.gov
Administrative Support Assistant Director
Shallah Graham (817) 392-4229
Special Investigation **David McElroy** (817) 392-4182
Operational Command Deputy Chief **Vance Keyes** (817) 392-4247
E-mail: vance.keyes@fortworthtexas.gov
Patrol Assistant Chief **Kenneth Dean** (817) 392-4130

Police Department *continued*

North Command Deputy Chief
Capt. Sharon Renee Kamper (817) 392-3901
South Command Deputy Chief **Ty Hadsell** (817) 392-4644
Support Assistant Chief **Edwin Kraus** (817) 392-4140
Investigative and Support Command Deputy Chief
Arthur Barclay (817) 392-4120
Tactical Command Deputy Chief **Charles E. Ramirez** (817) 392-3403
Chaplain **Dean Nichols** (817) 923-1921 ext. 7330

Property Management Department
4100 Columbus Trail, Fort Worth, TX 76133-7578
Tel: (817) 392-5100 Fax: (817) 392-5119

Director **Steve Cooke** (817) 392-5100
E-mail: steve.cook@fortworthgov.org

Public Events Department
Fort Worth Convention Center, 1201 Houston Street,
Fort Worth, TX 76102
Fax: (817) 392-2756

Director **Kirk Slaughter** (817) 392-2501
Assistant Director **Feleshia Cochran** (817) 392-2529
Convention Sales Director **Charles Mayer** (817) 392-2735
Sales Manager **Blake Moorman** (817) 392-2692

Will Rogers Memorial Center
3401 W. Lancaster Ave., Fort Worth, TX 76107-3078
Fax: (817) 392-8170

Assistant Director **Kevin Kemp** (817) 392-5982
Manager **Chris Harmon** (817) 392-5988
Director of Sales **David Reeves** (817) 392-8160

Transportation and Public Works Department
Municipal Bldg., 1000 Throckmorton Street, 2nd Floor,
Fort Worth, TX 76102
Tel: (817) 392-7801 Internet: http://fortworthtexas.gov/tpw/

Director **Douglas W. Wiersig** (817) 392-7801
Education: Nevada (Reno) BSCE; Texas MSCE; Tennessee PhD
Senior Administrative Assistant **Judy Burns** (817) 392-6311
E-mail: judy.burns@fortworthgov.org
Assistant Director **Alonzo Linan** (817) 392-7861

Water Department
1000 Throckmorton St., Fort Worth, TX 76102
Tel: (817) 392-8240 Fax: (817) 392-8195

Director **John Carman** (817) 392-8246

Business Services
Assistant Director **Kara Shuror** (817) 392-8819
Senior Administrative Services Manager **Janet Hale** (817) 392-8438
E-mail: janet.hale@fortworthtexas.gov
Water Customer Relations Manager **Fran Peterson** (817) 392-8260
Senior Management Analyst **Noreen Mitchell** (817) 392-8198
Customer Service Manager **Shannon Swayzer** (817) 392-2718
Field Operations Superintendent **David Cook** (817) 871-8051
Field Operations Superintendent **Rick Davis** (817) 454-3719
Water Conservation Manager **Micah Reed** (817) 392-8211
Public Education Program Coordinator **Mary Gugliuzza** (817) 392-8253

Fort Worth Library
500 W. 3rd St., Fort Worth, TX 76102
Tel: (817) 392-7706 Fax: (817) 392-7734
Internet: http://fortworthtexas.gov/Library/

Director **Gleniece Robinson** (817) 392-7706
E-mail: gleneice.robinson@fortworthtexas.gov
Assistant Director **Sheila Scullock** (817) 392-7705
E-mail: sheila.scullock@fortworthtexas.gov

★ Elected Official ▲ Appointed by Legislature ▼ Appointed by Governor ► Appointed by Board or Commission ● Appointed by Judge
■ Appointed by Mayor △ Appointed by Freeholders ▽ Appointed by Supervisor ▷ Appointed by County Executive ○ Appointed by Council

Fort Worth Library *continued*

Assistant Director for Public Services **Chris Dennis** . . . . . (817) 392-7712
E-mail: chris.dennis@fortworthtexas.gov
Acquisitions Manager **Kathryn King** . . . . . (817) 392-7718
E-mail: kathryn.king@fortworthgov.org
Collections Administrator **Deborah Duke** . . . . . (817) 392-7725
E-mail: deborah.duke@fortworthtexas.gov
Facilities Administrator **Ken Hopkins** . . . . . (817) 392-7797
E-mail: ken.hopkins@fortworthgov.org
Administrative Assistant **Lee Niata Johnson** . . . . . (817) 392-7709
E-mail: lee.johnson@fortworthtexas.gov

Fort Worth Independent School District

100 North Univesity Drive, Fort Worth, TX 76107
Fax: (817) 814-1905 Internet: http://www.fwisd.org

Superintendent **Dr. Kent P. Scribner** . . . . . (817) 814-1900
Education: Carleton BA; Temple MEd; Arizona State PhD

City of Frankfort, Kentucky

315 West Second, Frankfort, KY 40601
P.O. Box 697, Frankfort, KY 40602-0697
Fax: (502) 875-8502 (City Hall Fax) Internet: www.frankfort.ky.gov

County: Franklin **Election Type:** Nonpartisan **Population:** 27,830 (2015)

Office of the Mayor and City Commission

P.O. Box 697, Frankfort, KY 40602-0697

★ Mayor **William I. May, Jr.** . . . . . (502) 875-8500
Began Service: January 2, 2013
Term Expires: December 31, 2016
E-mail: william.may59@gmail.com
Date of Birth: March 19, 1959
Education: Kentucky State 1986 BS
★ Commissioner **Lynn Bowers** . . . . . (502) 875-8500
Term Expires: December 31, 2016
E-mail: lbowers@frankfort.ky.gov
Education: Transylvania BA; Spalding MA; Kentucky MSW; Kentucky State MPA; Kentucky PhD
★ Commissioner **Tommy Haynes** . . . . . (502) 875-8500
Term Expires: December 31, 2016
E-mail: thaynes@frankfort.ky.gov
★ Commissioner **Robert Roach** . . . . . (502) 875-8500
Term Expires: December 31, 2016
E-mail: clefford@aol.com
★ Commissioner **John Sower** . . . . . (502) 875-8500
Term Expires: December 31, 2016
E-mail: jsower@frankfort.ky.gov

Office of the City Manager

P.O. Box 697, Frankfort, KY 40602-0697

City Manager **Tim Zisoff** . . . . . (502) 875-8500
E-mail: tzisoff@frankfort.ky.gov
Human Resources Director **Kathy Fields** . . . . . (502) 875-8500
E-mail: kfields@frankfort.ky.gov
Fleet Maintenance Supervisor **Mike Chapman** . . . . . (502) 875-8558

Office of the City Attorney

P.O. Box 697, Frankfort, KY 40602-0697

▶ City Attorney **Robert C. Moore** . . . . . (502) 227-2271
E-mail: rmoore@hazelcox.com

Office of the City Clerk

P.O. Box 697, Frankfort, KY 40602-0697

▶ City Clerk **Chermie Maxwell** . . . . . (502) 875-8500
E-mail: cmaxwell@frankfort.ky.gov

E911 Dispatch Center

P.O. Box 697, Frankfort, KY 40602-0697
Fax: (502) 875-4426

Director **Deron Rambo** . . . . . (502) 875-8582
E-mail: drambo@frankfort.ky.gov

Finance Department

P.O. Box 697, Frankfort, KY 40602-0697

▶ Director **Steve Dawson** . . . . . (502) 875-8500
E-mail: sdawson@frankfort.ky.gov

Fire Department

P.O. Box 697, Frankfort, KY 40602-0697
Fax: (502) 875-8533

Fire Chief **Eddie Slone** . . . . . (502) 875-8511
E-mail: eslone@frankfort.ky.gov

Information Technology Department

308 West Second Street, Frankfort, KY 40601
Tel: (502) 875-8500

Information Technology Manager **Bobby Ripy** . . . . . (502) 875-8500

Parks and Recreation Department

P.O. Box 697, Frankfort, KY 40602-0697
E-mail: parksrec@mis.net

▶ Director **Jim Parrish** . . . . . (502) 875-8575
E-mail: jparrish@frankfort.ky.gov

Planning and Building Codes Department

P.O. Box 697, Frankfort, KY 40602-0697

▶ Director **Gary A. Muller** . . . . . (502) 875-8500
E-mail: gmuller@frankfort.ky.gov

Police Department

P.O. Box 697, Frankfort, KY 40602-0697
Fax: (502) 223-7193

▶ Police Chief **Jeff Abrams** . . . . . (502) 875-8523
E-mail: jabrams@frankfort.ky.gov

Public Works Department

P.O. Box 697, Frankfort, KY 40602-0697
Fax: (502) 875-8502

▶ Director **Tom Bradley** . . . . . (502) 875-8500
E-mail: tbradley@frankfort.ky.gov

Purchasing and Risk Management Department

315 West Second, Frankfort, KY 40601

Purchasing Agent **Angela Disponette** . . . . . (502) 352-2101
E-mail: adisponette@frankfort.ky.gov

Sewer Department

1200 Kentucky Avenue, Frankfort, KY 40601
Fax: (502) 223-7857

Director **William R. Scalf, Jr.** . . . . . (502) 875-2448

★ Elected Official ▲ Appointed by Legislature ▼ Appointed by Governor ▶ Appointed by Board or Commission ● Appointed by Judge
■ Appointed by Mayor △ Appointed by Freeholders ▽ Appointed by Supervisor ▷ Appointed by County Executive ○ Appointed by Council

City of Fremont, California

3300 Capitol Ave., Fremont, CA 94538
P.O. Box 5006, Fremont, CA 94537-5006
Tel: (510) 284-4000 (Information) Fax: (510) 284-4001
Internet: www.fremont.gov

County: Alameda **Election Type:** Nonpartisan **Year Incorporated:** 1956
Population: 232,206 (2015)

Office of the Mayor and City Council

3300 Capitol Ave., Fremont, CA 94538
P.O. Box 5006, Fremont, CA 94537-5006
Tel: (510) 284-4000 Fax: (510) 284-4001
Internet: http://www.fremont.gov/598/Mayor

★ Mayor **Bill Harrison** .... (510) 284-4011
Began Service: December 5, 2006 Fax: (510) 284-4001
Term Expires: December 2016
E-mail: bharrison@fremont.gov

★ Vice Mayor **Lily Mei** .... (510) 284-4082
Term Expires: December 2018 Fax: (510) 284-4001
E-mail: lmei@fremont.gov

★ Council Member **Vinnie Bacon** .... (510) 284-4084
Term Expires: December 2016 Fax: (510) 284-4001
E-mail: vbacon@fremont.gov

★ Council Member **Suzanne Lee Chan** .... (510) 284-4081
Term Expires: December 2016 Fax: (510) 284-4001
E-mail: schan@fremont.gov
Education: Illinois BS; Cal State (Los Angeles) MS

★ Council Member **Rick Jones** .... (510) 284-4083
Term Expires: December 2018 Fax: (510) 284-4001
E-mail: councilmemberjones@fremont.gov

Office of the City Manager

3300 Capitol Ave., Fremont, CA 94538
P.O. Box 5006, Fremont, CA 94537-5006
Tel: (510) 284-4000 Fax: (510) 284-4001

○ City Manager **Fred Diaz** .... (510) 284-4000
E-mail: fdiaz@fremont.gov
Education: Cal State (Fullerton) BA, MPA

Assistant City Manager **Jessica von Borck** .... (510) 284-4000
E-mail: jvborck@fremont.gov

Deputy City Manager **Karena McGee Shackelford** .... (510) 284-4000
E-mail: kshackelford@fremont.gov
Education: San José State BS

Deputy City Manager **Brian Stott** .... (510) 284-4000
E-mail: bstott@fremont.gov

Office of the City Attorney

3300 Capitol Ave., Fremont, CA 94538
P.O. Box 5006, Fremont, CA 94537-5006
Tel: (510) 284-4030 Fax: (510) 284-4031
E-mail: cityattorneysoffice@fremont.gov

○ City Attorney **Harvey Levine** .... (510) 284-4030
E-mail: hlevine@fremont.gov
Education: UCLA BA; Hastings JD

Assistant City Attorney **Debra Margolis** .... (510) 284-4030

Office of the City Clerk

3300 Capitol Ave., Fremont, CA 94538
P.O. Box 5006, Fremont, CA 94537-5006
Tel: (510) 284-4060 Fax: (510) 284-4061 E-mail: cclerk@fremont.gov
Internet: http://www.fremont.gov/72/City-Clerk

City Clerk **Susan Gauthier** .... (510) 284-4060
E-mail: cclerk@fremont.gov

Community Development Department

39550 Liberty Street, Fremont, CA 94538
Tel: (510) 494-4440 Fax: (510) 494-4402
Internet: http://www.fremont.gov/514/Community-Development

Community Development Director **Jeff Schwob** .... (510) 494-4527
E-mail: jschwob@fremont.gov Fax: (510) 494-4402
Education: Oregon BArch

Building and Safety Division

39550 Liberty Street, Fremont, CA 94538
Tel: (510) 494-4460 Fax: (510) 494-4820 E-mail: bldinfo@fremont.gov
Internet: http://www.fremont.gov/303/Building-Safety

Building Official **David Chung** .... (510) 494-4470
Fax: (510) 494-4398

Planning Division

39550 Liberty Street, Fremont, CA 94538
Tel: (510) 494-4440 Fax: (510) 494-4457
E-mail: planninginfo@fremont.gov

Planning Manager **Kristie Wheeler** .... (510) 494-4440

Community Services Department

3300 Capitol Ave., Fremont, CA 94538
P.O. Box 5006, Fremont, CA 94537-5006
Tel: (510) 494-4300 Fax: (510) 494-4753
Internet: http://www.fremont.gov/1234/Community-Services

Director **Annabell Holland** .... (510) 494-4329
Education: San Francisco State U BA; U Phoenix MA

Environmental Services Division

39550 Liberty Street, Fremont, CA 94538
Tel: (510) 494-4570 Fax: (510) 494-4571
Internet: http://www.fremont.gov/133/Environmental-Services
E-mail: environment@fremont.gov

Environmental Services Manager **Kathy Cote** .... (510) 494-4570

Office of Economic Development

3300 Capitol Ave., Fremont, CA 94538
P.O. Box 5006, Fremont, CA 94537-5006
Tel: (510) 284-4020 Fax: (510) 284-4001 E-mail: econdev@fremont.gov
Internet: http://www.fremont.gov/524/Economic-Development

Economic Development Director **Kelly Kline** .... (510) 284-4024
E-mail: kkline@fremont.gov

Finance Department

3300 Capitol Avenue, Fremont, CA 94538
P.O. Box 5006, Fremont, CA 94537-5006
Tel: (510) 494-4610 Fax: (510) 494-4611 E-mail: finance@fremont.gov
Internet: http://www.fremont.gov/526/Finance

Finance Director **David Persselin** .... (510) 494-4610

Fire Department

Administration, 3300 Capitol Avenue, Fremont, CA 94538
P.O. Box 5006, Fremont, CA 94537-5006
Tel: (510) 494-4200 Fax: (510) 494-4250
E-mail: fremontfire@fremont.gov
Internet: http://www.fremont.gov/96/Fire-Department

Fire Chief **Geoff LaTendresse** .... (510) 494-4224
E-mail: glatendresse@fremont.gov Fax: (510) 494-4250

Human Resources Department

3300 Capitol Avenue, Fremont, CA 94538
P.O. Box 5006, Fremont, CA 94537-5006
Tel: (510) 494-4660 Fax: (510) 494-4659 E-mail: jobs@fremont.gov
Internet: http://www.fremont.gov/412/Human-Resources

Deputy City Manager/Human Resources Director
Brian Stott .... (510) 494-4660
E-mail: bstott@fremont.gov

★ Elected Official ▲ Appointed by Legislature ▼ Appointed by Governor ▶ Appointed by Board or Commission ● Appointed by Judge
■ Appointed by Mayor △ Appointed by Freeholders ▽ Appointed by Supervisor ▷ Appointed by County Executive ○ Appointed by Council

Risk Management Division

3300 Capitol Ave., Fremont, CA 94538
P.O. Box 5006, Fremont, CA 94537-5006
Tel: (510) 284-4050 Fax: (510) 284-4051
E-mail: riskmanagement@fremont.gov

Risk Manager **Steven Schwarz** .... (510) 284-4050
E-mail: sschwarz@fremont.gov

Human Services Department

3300 Capitol Ave., Fremont, CA 94538
P.O. Box 5006, Fremont, CA 94537-5006
Tel: (510) 574-2050 Fax: (510) 574-2054
E-mail: humanservicesinfo@fremont.gov
Internet: http://www.fremont.gov/216/Human-Services

Human Services Director **Suzanne Shenfil** .... (510) 574-2050
Education: U San Francisco; UC Berkeley MSW

Information Technology Services Department

3300 Capitol Avenue, Fremont, CA 94538
P.O. Box 5006, Fremont, CA 94537-5006
Tel: (510) 494-4800 Fax: (510) 494-4821 E-mail: helpdesk@fremont.gov

Director **Marilyn Crane** .... (510) 494-4800
E-mail: mcrane@fremont.gov

Police Department

2000 Stevenson Blvd., Fremont, CA 94538
Tel: (510) 790-6800 Fax: (510) 790-6801
Internet: www.fremontpolice.org

Chief of Police **Richard Lucero** .... (510) 790-6811
Fax: (510) 790-6801

Public Works Department

39550 Liberty Street, Fremont, CA 94538
P.O. Box 5006, Fremont, CA 94537-5006
Fax: (510) 494-4751 Internet: http://www.fremont.gov/601/Public-Works

Director **Norm Hughes** .... (510) 494-4748
Education: San José State BSCE

Engineering Division

39550 Liberty Street, Fremont, CA 94538
P.O. Box 5006, Fremont, CA 94537-5006
Tel: (510) 494-4700 Fax: (510) 494-4721
E-mail: engineering@fremont.gov
Internet: http://www.fremont.gov/230/Engineering

City Engineer **Hans F. Larsen** .... (510) 494-4748

City of Fresno, California

City Hall, 2600 Fresno St., Fresno, CA 93721
Tel: (559) 621-2489 (Information) Internet: www.fresno.gov

County: Fresno **Election Type:** Nonpartisan **Year Incorporated:** 1885
Population: 520,052 (2015)

Office of the Mayor and City Council

City Hall, 2600 Fresno St., Fresno, CA 93721-3600
Fax: (559) 621-7990

★ Mayor **Ashley Swearengin** .... (559) 621-8000
Began Service: January 6, 2009
Term Expires: January 5, 2017
E-mail: mayor@fresno.gov
Education: Cal State (Fresno) BA

■ Chief of Staff **Georgeanne White** .... (559) 621-8000
E-mail: georgeanne.white@fresno.gov
Education: Cal State (Fresno) BABA

Office of the Mayor and City Council *continued*

■ Deputy Chief of Staff **Kelli Furtado** .... (559) 621-8000
E-mail: kelli.furtado@fresno.gov

■ Special Assistant to the Mayor **Cheryl Burns** .... (559) 621-8000
E-mail: cheryl.burns@fresno.gov
Education: Cal State (Fresno) BA

■ Administrative Assistant **(Vacant)** .... (559) 621-8000

■ Government Affairs Manager **Danielle Bergstrom** ..... (559) 621-7910
E-mail: danielle.bergstrom@fresno.gov

★ Council President **Paul "Cap" Caprioglio** (District 4) .... (559) 621-8000
Term Expires: January 5, 2017

★ Council Member **Esmeralda Soria** (District 1) .... (559) 621-8000
Term Expires: January 5, 2019

★ Council Member **Steve Brandau** (District 2) .... (559) 621-8000
Term Expires: January 5, 2017

★ Council Member **Oliver Baines** (District 3) .... (559) 621-8000
Term Expires: January 2019
E-mail: district3@fresno.gov

★ Council Member **Sal Quintero** (District 5) .... (559) 621-8000
Term Expires: January 5, 2019
E-mail: district5@fresno.gov

★ Council Member **Lee Brand** (District 6) .... (559) 621-8000
Term Expires: January 5, 2017
E-mail: district6@fresno.gov

★ Council Member **Clint Olivier** (District 7) .... (559) 621-8000
Term Expires: January 2019
E-mail: district7@fresno.gov

Office of the City Manager

City Hall, 2600 Fresno St., Fresno, CA 93721-3601
Fax: (559) 621-7776 E-mail: citymanager@fresno.gov

■ City Manager **Bruce Rudd** .... (559) 621-7780
E-mail: bruce.rudd@fresno.gov

Assistant City Manager **Renena Smith** .... (559) 621-7770
E-mail: renena.smith@fresno.gov

Deputy City Manager **Wilma Quan-Schecter** .... (559) 621-7784

City Communications Department

City Hall, 2600 Fresno St., Fresno, CA 93721
Fax: (559) 621-7776

Director of Communications and Public Affairs
Mark Standriff .... (559) 621-7777
E-mail: mark.standriff@fresno.gov

Office of the City Attorney

City Hall, 2600 Fresno St., Fresno, CA 93721-3602
Fax: (559) 488-1084

City Attorney **Doug Sloan** .... (559) 621-7500
E-mail: doug.sloan@fresno.gov

Office of the City Clerk

City Hall, 2600 Fresno St., Fresno, CA 93721-3603
Fax: (559) 488-1005 E-mail: clerk@fresno.gov

City Clerk **Yvonne Spence** .... (559) 621-7650
E-mail: clerk@fresno.gov

Assistant City Clerk **Todd Stermer** .... (559) 621-7650
E-mail: todd.stermer@fresno.gov

Airports Department

4995 East Clinton Way, Fresno, CA 93727-1504
Fax: (559) 498-5549

Director of Aviation **Kevin Meikle** .... (559) 621-4523

Development and Resource Management Department

City Hall, 2600 Fresno Street, Room 2156-02, Fresno, CA 93721-3608
Fax: (559) 457-1504

Director **Jennifer K. Clark** .... (559) 621-8003

(continued on next page)

★ Elected Official ▲ Appointed by Legislature ▼ Appointed by Governor ▶ Appointed by Board or Commission ● Appointed by Judge
■ Appointed by Mayor △ Appointed by Freeholders ▽ Appointed by Supervisor ▷ Appointed by County Executive ○ Appointed by Council

Development and Resource Management Department *continued*

Assistant Director **(Vacant)** .... (559) 621-8003
Economic Development Manager **Larry Westerlund** .... (559) 621-8355
E-mail: larry.westerlund@fresno.gov
Neighborhood Revitalization Manager
Elaine Robles-McGraw .... (559) 621-8360
E-mail: elaine.robles-mcgraw@fresno.gov
Local Business Initiatives Manager **Amy Fuentes** .... (559) 621-8362
E-mail: amy.fuentes@fresno.gov
Urban Planning Specialist **Wilma Quan-Schecter** .... (559) 621-8371
Incentive Zone Manager **Kelly Trevino** .... (559) 621-8350
E-mail: kelly.trevino@fresno.gov

Finance Department

City Hall, 2600 Fresno Street, Room 2156, Fresno, CA 93721
Fax: (559) 488-4636

Controller/Finance Director **Michael "Mike" Lima** .... (559) 621-7006
Education: Cal State (Fresno) BSBA, MBA
Assistant City Controller **Karen Bradley** .... (559) 621-7048
Purchasing Manager **Gary Watahira** .... (559) 621-1153
E-mail: gary.watahira@fresno.gov
Education: Cal State (Fresno) BSBA

Fire Department

911 H Street, Fresno, CA 93721
Fax: (559) 498-4261 E-mail: firedept@fresno.gov

Fire Chief **Kerri Donis** .... (559) 621-4199
E-mail: kerri.donis@fresno.gov

Fresno Convention and Entertainment Center

848 M Street, 2nd Floor, Fresno, CA 93721
Fax: (559) 445-8110

General Manager-SMG **Bill Overfelt** .... (559) 445-8100
Sales Manager **Natalie Ortega** .... (559) 445-8172

Information Services Department

2600 Fresno St., Room 1059, Fresno, CA 93721-3608
Fax: (559) 488-1021

Assistant Chief Information Officer **Byron Horn** .... (559) 621-7100
E-mail: byron.horn@fresno.gov

Parks, After School, Recreation and Community Services Department

2326 Fresno St., Room 101, Fresno, CA 93721-1824
Fax: (559) 498-1588 E-mail: parks.department@fresno.gov

Director **Manuel Mollinedo** .... (559) 621-7784
Education: Cal State (Los Angeles) BS, MS
Assistant Director **(Vacant)** .... (559) 621-2900
Administrative Manager **Karen Norris** .... (559) 621-2900
E-mail: karen.norris@fresno.gov

Personnel Services Department

City Hall, 2600 Fresno St., Room 1030, Fresno, CA 93721-3614
Fax: (559) 498-4775

Personnel Director **Jeffrey T. "Jeff" Cardell** .... (559) 621-6950
E-mail: jeff.cardell@fresno.gov
Labor Relations Manager **Kenneth G. Phillips** .... (559) 621-6950

Police Department

Police Headquarters, 2323 Mariposa St., Fresno, CA 93721
Fax: (559) 498-5168

Police Chief **Jerry Dyer** .... (559) 621-2000

Department of Public Utilities

City Hall, 2600 Fresno St., Room 3065, Fresno, CA 93721-3624
Fax: (559) 498-1304

Director **Thomas Esqueda** .... (559) 621-8650

Department of Public Utilities *continued*

Assistant Director **Robert Anderson** .... (559) 621-8610

Public Works Department

City Hall, 2600 Fresno St., Fresno, CA 93721-3623
Fax: (559) 488-1045 E-mail: publicworks@fresno.gov

Director **Scott Mozier** .... (559) 621-8650
Facilities Manager **Kelly S. Riddle** .... (559) 621-1487
E-mail: kelly.riddle@fresno.gov

Department of Transportation

2223 G Street, Fresno, CA 93706-1600
Fax: (559) 488-1065

Director of Transportation **Brian Marshall** .... (559) 621-1439
Operations Manager **Dean Huss** .... (559) 621-1431
E-mail: dean.huss@fresno.gov
Assistant Director **Ken A. Nerland** .... (559) 621-1393
Fleet Management Manager **Jim Schaad** .... (559) 621-1101

City of Frisco, Texas

George A. Purefoy Municipal Center, 6101 Frisco Square Boulevard, Frisco, TX 75034
Tel: (972) 292-5000 Internet: www.friscotexas.gov

County: Collin; Denton **Election Type:** Nonpartisan **Year Founded:** 1902 **Population:** 154,407 (2015)

Office of the Mayor and City Council

George A. Purefoy Municipal Center, 6101 Frisco Square Boulevard, Frisco, TX 75034
Tel: (972) 292-5050 Internet: http://www.friscotexas.gov/585/City-Council

★ Mayor **Maher Maso** .... (972) 292-5050
Began Service: 2000
Term Expires: May 2017
E-mail: mmaso@friscotexas.gov
Education: Texas (Arlington) 2008 MBA
★ Deputy Mayor Pro Tem **Will Sowell** (Place 3) .... (972) 292-5053
Term Expires: May 2018
E-mail: wsowell@friscotexas.gov
★ Council Member **Bob Allen** (Place 1) .... (972) 292-5051
Term Expires: May 2018
E-mail: ballen@friscotexas.gov
★ Council Member **(Vacant)** (Place 2)
Note: A runoff election between Shona Huffman and Terri Green is scheduled for June 18, 2016.
Term Expires: May 2019
★ Council Member **(Vacant)** (Place 4) .... (972) 292-5054
Note: A runoff election between Cindy Asche and Bill Woodard is scheduled for June 18, 2016.
Term Expires: May 2019
★ Council Member **Tim Nelson** (Place 5) .... (972) 292-5055
Term Expires: May 2017
E-mail: tnelson@friscotexas.gov
★ Council Member **Scott Johnson** (Place 6) .... (972) 292-5056
Term Expires: May 2017
E-mail: sjohnson@friscotexas.gov
Education: Auburn 1993

Office of the City Secretary

George A. Purefoy Municipal Center, 6101 Frisco Square Boulevard, Frisco, TX 75034
Tel: (972) 292-5020 Fax: (972) 292-5028
Internet: http://www.friscotexas.gov/606/City-Secretary

○ City Secretary **Jenny Page** .... (972) 292-5020
E-mail: jpage@friscotexas.gov

Office of the City Manager

George A. Purefoy Municipal Center, 6101 Frisco Square Boulevard, Frisco, TX 75034
Tel: (972) 292-5105

○ City Manager **George Purefoy** .... (972) 292-5105
E-mail: gpurefoy@friscotexas.gov
Education: East Texas State MPA

Deputy City Manager **Henry J. Hill III** .... (972) 292-5109
E-mail: hhill@friscotexas.gov

Assistant City Manager **Ron Patterson** .... (972) 292-5102
E-mail: rpatterson@friscotexas.gov

Assistant City Manager **Nell Lange** .... (972) 292-5110
E-mail: nlange@friscotexas.gov

Special Assistant to the City Manager **Mack Borchardt** .. (972) 292-5127
E-mail: mborchardt@friscotexas.gov

Department of Communications and Media Relations

George A. Purefoy Municipal Center, 6101 Frisco Square Boulevard, Frisco, TX 75034
Tel: (972) 292-5080

Director **Dana Baird** .... (972) 292-5080
E-mail: dbaird@friscotexas.gov

Department of Development Services

George A. Purefoy Municipal Center, 6101 Frisco Square Boulevard, 3rd Floor, Frisco, TX 75034
Tel: (972) 292-5300 Fax: (972) 292-5388

Director **John Lettelleir** .... (972) 292-5310
E-mail: jlettelleir@friscotexas.gov

Senior Administrative Assistant **Lori Cross** .... (972) 292-5314
E-mail: lcross@friscotexas.gov

Frisco Economic Development Corporation

6801 Gaylord Parkway, Suite 400, Frisco, TX 75034-1507
Tel: (972) 292-5160 Fax: (972) 292-5166

President **James L. Gandy** .... (972) 292-5150
E-mail: jgandy@friscoedc.com

Department of Engineering Services

George A. Purefoy Municipal Center, 6101 Frisco Square Boulevard, 3rd Floor, Frisco, TX 75034
Tel: (972) 292-5400 Fax: (972) 292-5016

Director **Paul Knippel** .... (972) 292-5400
E-mail: pknippel@friscotexas.gov
Education: Texas A&M 1989 BS; Lamar 1992 MEng

Department of Environmental Services

6616 Walnut Street, Frisco, TX 75034
Tel: (972) 292-5900 Fax: (972) 731-4946
E-mail: environmentalservices@friscotexas.gov

Manager **Jeremy Starritt** .... (972) 292-5910

Department of Financial Services

George A. Purefoy Municipal Center, 6101 Frisco Square Boulevard, 4th Floor, Frisco, TX 75034
Tel: (972) 292-5500 Fax: (972) 292-5583

Director **Anita Cothran** .... (972) 292-5510

Fire Department

8601 Gary Burns Drive, Frisco, TX 75034
Tel: (972) 292-6300 Fax: (972) 292-6319

Fire Chief **Mark Piland** .... (972) 292-6310
E-mail: mpiland@friscofire.com

Department of Health and Food Safety

George A. Purefoy Municipal Center, 6101 Frisco Square Boulevard, 3rd Floor West, Frisco, TX 75034
Tel: (972) 292-5304 Fax: (972) 292-5313 E-mail: health@friscotexas.gov
Internet: http://www.friscotexas.gov/173/Health-Food-Safety

Environmental Health Supervisor **Julie Stallcup** .... (972) 292-5304

Department of Human Resources and Employment

George A. Purefoy Municipal Center, 6101 Frisco Square Boulevard, 4th Floor, Frisco, TX 75034
Fax: (972) 292-5229 E-mail: employment@friscotexas.gov

Director **Lauren Safranek** .... (972) 292-5210
E-mail: lsafranek@friscotexas.gov

Frisco Public Library

George A. Purefoy Municipal Center, 6101 Frisco Square Boulevard, Suite 3000, Frisco, TX 75034
Tel: (972) 292-5669 Fax: (972) 292-5699
E-mail: askus@friscolibrary.com

Director **Shelley Holley** .... (972) 292-5669
E-mail: sholley@friscotexas.gov

Department of Parks and Recreation

6726 Walnut Street, Frisco, TX 75034
Tel: (972) 292-6500 E-mail: friscofun@friscotexas.gov

Director **Rick Wieland** .... (972) 292-6510

Office Manager **Jonette Lingenfelder** .... (972) 292-6511
E-mail: jlingenfelder@friscotexas.gov

Police Department

7200 Stonybrook Parkway, Frisco, TX 75034
Tel: (972) 292-6010 Internet: http://www.friscotexas.gov/239/Police

Chief of Police **John Bruce** .... (972) 292-6103

Department of Public Works

11300 Research Road, Frisco, TX 75034
Tel: (972) 292-5800 Fax: (972) 292-5891
E-mail: publicworks@friscotexas.gov
Internet: http://www.friscotexas.gov/154/Public-Works

Director **Gary Hartwell** .... (972) 292-5800
E-mail: ghartwell@friscotexas.gov
Education: Texas (Arlington) 1974 BSCE, 1979 MS

Purchasing Department

George A. Purefoy Municipal Center, 6101 Frisco Square Boulevard, 1st Floor, Frisco, TX 75034
Tel: (972) 292-5541 Fax: (972) 292-5586

Manager **Daniel Ford** .... (972) 292-5545
E-mail: dford@friscotexas.gov

Utility Billing Division

City Hall, 6101 Frisco Square Boulevard, First Floor, Frisco, TX 75034
Tel: (972) 292-5575 Fax: (972) 292-5585
Internet: http://www.friscotexas.gov/133/Utility-Billing

Manager **April Spann** .... (972) 292-5115

Frisco Convention and Visitors Bureau

6801 Gaylord Parkway, Suite 401, Frisco, TX 75034
Tel: (877) 463-7472 Fax: (972) 292-5251

Executive Director **Marla Roe** .... (972) 292-5252

★ Elected Official ▲ Appointed by Legislature ▼ Appointed by Governor ▶ Appointed by Board or Commission ● Appointed by Judge
■ Appointed by Mayor △ Appointed by Freeholders ▽ Appointed by Supervisor ▷ Appointed by County Executive ○ Appointed by Council

City of Fullerton, California

303 W. Commonwealth, Fullerton, CA 92832
Internet: www.cityoffullerton.com

County: Orange **Election Type:** Nonpartisan **Year Founded:** 1887
Year Incorporated: 1904 **Population:** 140,847 (2015)

Office of the Mayor and City Council

303 West Commonwealth, Fullerton, CA 92832
Fax: (714) 738-6758 E-mail: council@ci.fullerton.ca.us

★Mayor **Jennifer Fitzgerald** .... (714) 738-6311
Began Service: December 4, 2012
Term Expires: December 7, 2016
E-mail: jenniferf@cityoffullerton.com

★Mayor Pro Tem **Jan M. Flory** .... (714) 738-6311
Term Expires: December 7, 2016
E-mail: janf@cityoffullerton.com

★Council Member **Doug Chaffee** .... (714) 738-6311
Term Expires: December 5, 2018
E-mail: dougc@cityoffullerton.com

★Council Member **Greg Sebourn** .... (714) 738-6311
Term Expires: December 5, 2018
E-mail: gregs@cityoffullerton.com

★Council Member **Bruce Whitaker** .... (714) 738-6311
Term Expires: December 7, 2016
E-mail: bwwhitaker@live.com

Office of the City Clerk

303 W. Commonwealth, Fullerton, CA 92832
Fax: (714) 525-8071

City Clerk/Clerk Services Manager **Lucinda Williams** ... (714) 738-6350
E-mail: lucindaw@cityoffullerton.com

Fullerton Public Library

353 W. Commonwealth, Fullerton, CA 92832
Fax: (714) 447-3280

Library Director **Maureen Gebelein** .... (714) 738-6380
E-mail: Maureeng@ci.fullerton.ca.us

Office of the City Manager

303 W. Commonwealth, Fullerton, CA 92832
Fax: (714) 738-6758

City Manager **Joe Felz** .... (714) 738-6310
E-mail: citymanager@cityoffullerton.com

Public Information Coordinator **Erin Haselton** .... (714) 738-6317
Note: Until May 31, 2016
E-mail: erinh@cityoffullerton.com

Administrative Services

303 W. Commonwealth, Fullerton, CA 92832
Fax: (714) 738-3168

Director **Julia James** .... (714) 738-6521
E-mail: juliaj@cityoffullerton.com

City Treasurer/Revenue and Utility Services Manager
Julia James .... (714) 738-6573
Fax: (714) 525-8071

Information Technology Manager **Helen Hall** .... (714) 738-5309
E-mail: helenh@cityoffullerton.com Fax: (714) 738-3365

Purchasing Manager **Margot Cronce** .... (714) 738-6533
E-mail: margotc@cityoffullerton.com Fax: (714) 738-3168

Community Development Services

303 W. Commonwealth, Fullerton, CA 92832
Fax: (714) 738-3110

Director **Karen Haluza** .... (714) 738-6554
E-mail: KarenH@cityoffullerton.com

Fire Department

312 E. Commonwealth, Fullerton, CA 92832
Fax: (714) 738-5355

Fire Chief **Wolfgang Knabe** .... (714) 738-3116
E-mail: WKnabe@fullertonfire.org

Human Resources

303 W. Commonwealth, Fullerton, CA 92832
Fax: (714) 738-3113

Director **Gretchen Beatty** .... (714) 738-6888
E-mail: gretchenb@cityoffullerton.com

Parks & Recreation

303 W. Commonwealth, Fullerton, CA 92832
Fax: (714) 738-6599

Director **Hugo Curiel** .... (714) 738-6575

Police Department

237 W. Commonwealth, Fullerton, CA 92832
Fax: (714) 738-0961

Chief of Police **Daniel R. Hughes** .... (714) 738-6827

Public Works Department

303 W. Commonwealth, Fullerton, CA 92832
Fax: (714) 738-3115

Director **Don Hoppe** .... (714) 738-6845
E-mail: dhoppe@cityoffullerton.com

Airport Administration

4011 W. Commonwealth, Fullerton, CA 92832
Fax: (714) 738-3112

Manager **Brendan O'Reilly** .... (714) 738-6323

Building and Facilities Maintenance Division

Superintendent **Bob St. Paul** .... (714) 738-6897
E-mail: maintenance@cityoffullerton.com

Building and Facilities Supervisor **Dana Huffman** .... (714) 738-6897
E-mail: danah@cityoffullerton.com

Equipment Maintenance Division

Superintendent **Bob St. Paul** .... (714) 738-6306

Landscape Maintenance Division

Superintendent **Dennis Quinlivan** .... (714) 738-6306

Landscape Maintenance Supervisor **Phil Kisor** .... (714) 738-5345
E-mail: philk@cityoffullerton.com

Street Maintenance Division

Superintendent **Daniel Diaz** .... (714) 738-6306

Street Maintenance Supervisor **Ty Richter** .... (714) 738-5344

Water System Maintenance Division

Superintendent **(Vacant)** .... (714) 738-6306

Sanitary Sewer Supervisor **Bill Roseberry** .... (714) 738-6373

Water Production and Storage Supervisor **Kevin Coe** .... (714) 738-6374

Water Transmission and Distribution Supervisor
Ken Stewart .... (714) 738-6372

★Elected Official ▲Appointed by Legislature ▼Appointed by Governor ►Appointed by Board or Commission ●Appointed by Judge
■Appointed by Mayor △Appointed by Freeholders ▽Appointed by Supervisor ▷Appointed by County Executive ○Appointed by Council

City of Gainesville, Florida

City Hall, 200 E. University Ave., Gainesville, FL 32601
P.O. Box 490, Gainesville, FL 32627
Internet: www.cityofgainesville.org

County: Alachua **Election Type:** Nonpartisan **Population:** 130,128 (2015)

Office of the Mayor and City Commission

City Hall, 200 E. University Ave., Gainesville, FL 32601
Fax: (352) 334-2036

★ Mayor **Lauren Poe** (At-Large) . . . . . . (352) 334-5015
Began Service: May 5, 2016
Term Expires: May 2019

★ Commissioner **Charles Goston** (District 1) . . . . . . (352) 334-5015
Term Expires: May 2018

★ Commissioner **Todd Chase** (District 2) . . . . . . (352) 334-5015
Term Expires: May 2017
E-mail: chasetn@cityofgainesville.org

★ Commissioner **Craig Carter** (District 3) . . . . . . (352) 334-5015
Term Expires: May 2017
E-mail: carterce@gainesville.org

★ Commissioner **Adrian Hayes-Santos** (District 4) . . . . . . (352) 334-5015
Term Expires: May 2019

★ Commissioner **Harvey Budd** (At-Large) . . . . . . (352) 334-5015
Term Expires: May 2018

★ Commissioner **Helen Warren** (At-Large) . . . . . . (352) 334-5015
Term Expires: May 2017

▶ Clerk of the Commission **Kurt Lannon** . . . . . . (352) 334-5015
E-mail: lannonkm@cityofgainesville.org

Deputy Clerk of the Commission **(Vacant)** . . . . . . (352) 334-5015

Office of the City Attorney

200 E. University Ave., Gainesville, FL 32601
Fax: (352) 334-2229

▶ City Attorney **Nicolle M. Shalley** . . . . . . (352) 334-5011
E-mail: shalleynm@cityofgainesville.org

Office of the City Auditor

City Hall, 2nd Fl., 200 E. University Ave., Gainesville, FL 32601
Fax: (352) 334-2096 E-mail: auditors@ci.gainesville.fl.us

▶ City Auditor **Carlos Holt** . . . . . . (352) 334-5020
E-mail: auditors@cityofgainesville.org

Office of Equal Opportunity

P.O. Box 490, Gainesville, FL 32627

▶ Director **Torey L. Alston** . . . . . . (352) 334-5051
E-mail: alstontl@cityofgainesville.org
Education: Florida A&M MBA

Office of the City Manager

City Hall, 200 East University Avenue, 4th Floor, Gainesville, FL 32601
Fax: (352) 334-3119

▶ City Manager (Interim) **Anthony Lyons** . . . . . . (352) 334-5010
E-mail: citymgr@cityofgainesville.org

Assistant City Manager **Paul Folkers** . . . . . . (352) 334-5010
E-mail: folkerspe@cityofgainesville.org

Assistant City Manager **Frederick Murry** . . . . . . (352) 334-5010
E-mail: murryfj@cityofgainesville.org

Gainesville Regional Airport

3880 NE 39th, Gainesville, FL 32609
Fax: (352) 374-8368 Internet: http://www.flygainesville.com

Chief Executive Officer **Alan Penska** . . . . . . (352) 373-0249 ext. 111

Planning and Development Services Department

Bldg. B, 306 NE Sixth Avenue, Gainesville, FL 32601
Fax: (352) 334-2648 E-mail: commdev@ci.gainesville.fl.us

Director **(Vacant)** . . . . . . (352) 334-5022

Building Inspection Department

P.O. Box 490, Gainesville, FL 32602-0490
Fax: (352) 334-2207 E-mail: bldg@cityofgainesville.org

Director **John Freeland** . . . . . . (352) 334-5050

Economic Development Department

P.O. Box 490, Gainesville, FL 32602
Fax: (352) 334-2648

Director **Erik Bredfeldt** . . . . . . (352) 334-5012
E-mail: bredfeldea@cityofgainesville.org

Budget and Finance Department

City Hall, 3rd Fl., 200 E. University Ave., Gainesville, FL 32601
Fax: (352) 334-2271 E-mail: finance@ci.gainesville.fl.us

Director **Mark Benton** . . . . . . (352) 334-5054

Assistant Finance Director **April Shuping** . . . . . . (352) 334-5054

Purchasing Director **Aleta Cozart** . . . . . . (352) 334-5021
E-mail: cozarta@cityofgainesville.org Fax: (352) 334-3163

Fire-Rescue Department

1025 NE 13th Street, Gainesville, FL 32601
Fax: (352) 334-2529 Internet: http://www.gfr.org

Fire Chief **Jeff Lane** . . . . . . (352) 334-5078

Human Resources Department

222 E. University Ave., Gainesville, FL 32601
Fax: (352) 334-2291 E-mail: hr@ci.gainesville.fl.us

Director **Cheryl McBride** . . . . . . (352) 334-5077
E-mail: mcbridecf@cityofgainesville.org

Information Systems Department

301 SE Fourth Ave., Gainesville, FL 32601
Fax: (352) 334-3183

Department Head **(Vacant)** . . . . . . (352) 334-3400 ext. 1312

Library

401 E. University Ave., Gainesville, FL 32601

Director **Shaney Livingston** . . . . . . (352) 334-3910
E-mail: slivingston@aclib.us

Police Department

721 NW Sixth St., Gainesville, FL 32601
Tel: (352) 334-2400 Fax: (352) 334-2058
E-mail: gpd@ci.gainesville.fl.us Internet: http://www.gainesvillepd.org

Chief of Police **Tony Jones** . . . . . . (352) 334-2411

Public Works Department

Bldg. B, 306 NE Sixth Ave., Gainesville, FL 32601
Fax: (352) 334-2271 E-mail: pubwrk@ci.gainesville.fl.us

Director **Teresa Scott** . . . . . . (352) 334-5070

Solid Waste Division

405 NW 39th Avenue, Gainesville, FL 32609

Solid Waste Manager **Steve Joplin** . . . . . . (352) 334-2010

Recreation and Parks Department

Station 24, P.O. Box 490, Gainesville, FL 32602

Director **Steve Phillips** . . . . . . (352) 334-5067

★ Elected Official ▲ Appointed by Legislature ▼ Appointed by Governor ▶ Appointed by Board or Commission ● Appointed by Judge
■ Appointed by Mayor △ Appointed by Freeholders ▽ Appointed by Supervisor ▷ Appointed by County Executive ○ Appointed by Council

Division of Cultural Affairs
Bldg. A, 302 NE Sixth Ave., Gainesville, FL 32601
Fax: (352) 334-2314 E-mail: cultural@ci.gainesville.fl.us

Director **Russell Etling** .... (352) 334-5067

Regional Transit System
P.O. Box 490, Gainesville, FL 32627
Tel: (352) 334-2600 Fax: (352) 334-2607 E-mail: rts@ci.gainesville.fl.us

Director **Jesus M. Gomez** .... (352) 334-2600

Gainesville Regional Utilities [GRU]
301 SE Fourth Ave., Gainesville, FL 32601
P.O. Box 147117, Gainesville, FL 32614-7117
Internet: http://www.gru.com

►General Manager **Edward Bielarski** .... (352) 334-3400
Chief Customer Officer **Bill J. Shepherd** .... (352) 393-1035
Energy Delivery Assistant General Manager (Acting)
Gary Baysinger .... (352) 334-1513
Advisor to the General Manager **David E. Beaulieu** ..... (352) 334-1513
Energy Supply Officer (Acting) **Dino De Leo** .... (352) 334-1789
Water/ Wastewater Officer (Acting)
Anthony Cunningham .... (352) 393-1612
Advisor to the General Manager **David M. Richardson** ... (352) 334-1312
Chief Information Officer **Walter Banks** .... (352) 334-3400
Utilities Attorney **Shayla L. McNeill** .... (352) 393-1016
Community Relations Director **S. Yvette Carter** .... (352) 393-1297
Chief Business Services Officer **Lewis Walton** .... (352) 393-1039
Chief Financial Officer **Justin Locke** .... (352) 334-1312

City of Garden Grove, California

11222 Acacia Pkwy., Garden Grove, CA 92840
P.O. Box 3070, Garden Grove, CA 92842
Tel: (714) 741-5000 (Information) Internet: www.ci.garden-grove.ca.us

County: Orange **Election Type:** Nonpartisan **Year Founded:** 1874
Year Incorporated: 1956 **Population:** 175,393 (2015)

Office of the Mayor and City Council
P.O. Box 3070, Garden Grove, CA 92842
Fax: (714) 741-5044

★Mayor **Bao Nguyen** .... (714) 741-5104
Began Service: December 9, 2014
Term Expires: December 2018
E-mail: baon@garden-grove.org
★Mayor Pro Tem **Steve Jones** .... (714) 741-5104
Term Expires: December 2016
E-mail: stevej@garden-grove.org
★Council Member **Kris C. Beard** .... (714) 741-5104
Term Expires: December 2018
E-mail: kbeard@garden-grove.org
★Council Member **Phat Bui** .... (714) 741-5104
Term Expires: December 2018
E-mail: phatb@garden-grove.org
★Council Member **Christopher Phan** .... (714) 741-5104
Term Expires: December 2016
E-mail: chrisp@garden-grove.org

Office of the City Attorney
P.O. Box 3070, Garden Grove, CA 92842

○City Attorney (Acting) **Omar Sandoval** .... (714) 741-5368

Office of the City Manager
P.O. Box 3070, Garden Grove, CA 92842
Fax: (714) 741-5044

○City Manager **Scott C. Stiles** .... (714) 741-5100
E-mail: sstiles@ci.garden-grove.ca.us
Deputy City Manager **Maria Stipe** .... (714) 741-5100
E-mail: marias@ci.garden-grove.ca.us

Office of the City Clerk
P.O. Box 3070, Garden Grove, CA 92842
Tel: (714) 741-5040

City Clerk **Kathy Bailor** .... (714) 741-5035
E-mail: kathyb@ci.garden-grove.ca.us

Community Development Department
P.O. Box 3070, Garden Grove, CA 92842

Director **Lisa Kim** .... (714) 741-5121

Community Services Department
P.O. Box 3070, Garden Grove, CA 92842

Director **Kim Huy** .... (714) 741-5200
E-mail: kihuy@ci.garden-grove.ca.us

Finance Department
P.O. Box 3070, Garden Grove, CA 92842

Finance Director **Kingsley C. Okereke** .... (714) 741-5060
E-mail: kingsley@ci.garden-grove.ca.us
Education: John F Kennedy BS, MBA

Fire Department
P.O. Box 3070, Garden Grove, CA 92842

Fire Chief **Tom Schultz** .... (714) 741-5600
E-mail: toms@ci.garden-grove.ca.us

Human Resources Department
P.O. Box 3070, Garden Grove, CA 92842
Fax: (714) 741-5030

Director **Laura Stover** .... (714) 741-5008
E-mail: lauras@ci.garden-grove.ca.us

Information Technology Department
P.O. Box 3070, Garden Grove, CA 92842

Director **Charles Kalil** .... (714) 741-5095
E-mail: charlesk@ci.garden-grove.ca.us

Police Department
P.O. Box 3070, Garden Grove, CA 92842

Police Chief **Todd Elgin** .... (714) 741-5901

Public Works Department
P.O. Box 3070, Garden Grove, CA 92842

Director **Bill Murray** .... (714) 741-5375
City Engineer **Dan Candelaria** .... (714) 741-5184
E-mail: danc@ci.garden-grove.ca.us

★Elected Official ▲Appointed by Legislature ▼Appointed by Governor ►Appointed by Board or Commission ●Appointed by Judge
■Appointed by Mayor △Appointed by Freeholders ▽Appointed by Supervisor ▷Appointed by County Executive ○Appointed by Council

City of Garland, Texas

200 N. 5th, Garland, TX 75040
P.O. Box 469002, Garland, TX 75046-9002
Tel: (972) 205-2000 (Information) Fax: (972) 205-2504
Internet: https://www.garlandtx.gov/

County: Dallas **Election Type:** Nonpartisan **Population:** 236,897 (2015)

Office of the Mayor and City Council

P.O. Box 469002, Garland, TX 75046-9002
Tel: (972) 205-2400 Fax: (972) 205-2504

★Mayor **Douglas Athas** .... (972) 205-2400
Began Service: May 21, 2013
Term Expires: May 2017

★Mayor Pro Tem **B.J. Williams** (District 4) .... (972) 205-2465
Term Expires: May 10, 2018
E-mail: council4@garlandtx.gov

★Deputy Mayor Pro Tem **Lori Dodson** (District 6) .... (972) 205-2465
Term Expires: May 10, 2017
E-mail: council6@garlandtx.gov

★Council Member **David Gibbons** (District 1) .... (214) 205-2465
Term Expires: May 2018
E-mail: council1@garlandtx.gov

★Council Member **Anita Goebel** (District 2) .... (972) 205-2465
Term Expires: May 10, 2018
E-mail: council2@garlandtx.gov

★Council Member **Stephen W. Stanley** (District 3) .... (214) 205-2465
Term Expires: May 2017

★Council Member **Richard Aubin** (District 5) .... (972) 205-2465
Term Expires: May 2018

★Council Member **Scott LeMay** (District 7) .... (972) 205-2465
Term Expires: May 2017

★Council Member **Jim Cahill** (District 8) .... (972) 205-2465
Term Expires: May 10, 2017
E-mail: council8@garlandtx.gov

Office of the City Manager

P.O. Box 469002, Garland, TX 75046-9002
Tel: (972) 205-2465 Fax: (972) 205-2504

○City Manager **Bryan Bradford** .... (972) 205-2465
E-mail: admin@garlandtx.gov

Deputy City Manager **Martin Glenn** .... (972) 205-2465
E-mail: mglenn@garlandtx.gov

Assistant City Manager **John Baker** .... (972) 205-2465
E-mail: bbaker@garlandtx.gov

Public and Media Relations Director **Dorothy White** .... (972) 205-2879
E-mail: dwhite@garlandtx.gov

Office of the City Secretary

P.O. Box 469002, Garland, TX 75046-9002
E-mail: citysec@garlandtx.gov

○City Secretary **René Dowl** .... (972) 205-2404
E-mail: rdowl@garlandtx.gov

Budget and Research Department

P.O. Box 469002, Garland, TX 75046-9002

Director of Budget **Ron Young** .... (972) 205-2735
E-mail: ryoung@garlandtx.gov

Building Inspection Department

P.O. Box 469002, Garland, TX 75046-9002
E-mail: bldginsp@garlandtx.gov Fax: (972) 205-2839

Building Official **Jim Olk** .... (972) 205-2304
Building Code Official **Mike Gaiter** .... (972) 205-2304

Code Compliance Department

P.O. Box 469002, Garland, TX 75046-9002

Director **Steve Killeen** .... (972) 485-6408

Economic Development Department

P.O. Box 469002, Garland, TX 75046-9002
Tel: (972) 205-2445

Economic Development Director **David Gwin** .... (972) 205-2445
E-mail: dgwin@garlandtx.gov
Education: Oklahoma State BA, MS

Emergency Management Office

P.O. Box 469002, Garland, TX 75046
Fax: (972) 781-7222 E-mail: oem@garlandtx.gov

Coordinator **Molly Gilmore Rivas** .... (972) 781-7274
E-mail: mrivas@garlandtx.gov

Engineering Department

P.O. Box 469002, Garland, TX 75046-9002
E-mail: engineer@garlandtx.gov

Director **Michael Polocek** .... (972) 205-2170

Environmental Waste Services

P.O. Box 469002, Garland, TX 75046-9002
Fax: (972) 205-3703 E-mail: swr@garlandtx.gov

Managing Director **Lonnie Banks** .... (972) 205-3424

Facilities Management Department

P.O. Box 469002, Garland, TX 75046-9002
Fax: (972) 205-3055

Manager **Ginny Holliday** .... (972) 205-3085
E-mail: gholliday@garlandtx.gov

Financial Services Department

P.O. Box 469002, Garland, TX 75046-9002
E-mail: finance@garlandtx.gov

Managing Director **David Schuler** .... (972) 205-2355

Tax Department

P.O. Box 462010, Garland, TX 75046-9002
Fax: (972) 205-3834 E-mail: tax@garlandtx.gov

Tax Assessor/Collector **Corey Worsham** .... (972) 205-2410
E-mail: cworsham@garlandtx.gov

Fire Department

P.O. Box 469002, Garland, TX 75046-9002
E-mail: fire@garlandtx.gov

Fire Chief **Raymond Knight** .... (972) 781-7100
E-mail: rknight@garlandtx.gov

Assistant Fire Chief **Carl Coan** .... (972) 781-7102
E-mail: ccoan@garlandtx.gov

Assistant Fire Chief **Eric Lovett** .... (972) 781-7104
E-mail: elovett@garlandtx.gov

Assistant Fire Chief **Kelly Miller** .... (972) 781-7105
E-mail: kmiller@garlandtx.gov

Fleet Services Department

P.O. Box 469002, Garland, TX 75046-9002
Fax: (972) 205-3533

Director **Terry Anglin** .... (972) 205-2484

Health Department

P.O. Box 469002, Garland, TX 75046-9002
E-mail: health@garlandtx.gov

Managing Director **Richard Briley** .... (972) 205-3460

Animal Services Division
P.O. Box 469002, Garland, TX 75046-9002
Animal Services Manager **Uriel Villalpando** .... (972) 205-3570

Housing/Neighborhood Services Office
P.O. Box 469002, Garland, TX 75046-9002
E-mail: neighbor@garlandtx.gov
Director of Housing Department **Steve Fitch** .... (972) 205-3391

Human Resources Department
P.O. Box 469002, Garland, TX 75046-9002
E-mail: humanres@garlandtx.gov Fax: (972) 205-2706
Senior Managing Director **Priscilla Wilson** .... (972) 205-2475

Information Technology Services Department
P.O. Box 469002, Garland, TX 75046-9002
Chief Information Officer **Steve Niekamp** .... (972) 781-7200
E-mail: sniekamp@garlandtx.gov

Nicholson Memorial Library System
P.O. Box 469002, Garland, TX 75046-9002
E-mail: library@garlandtx.gov
Director **Claire Bausch** .... (972) 205-2543
E-mail: cbausch@garlandtx.gov

Parks and Recreation Department
P.O. Box 469002, Garland, TX 75046-9002
Fax: (972) 205-2751 E-mail: parks@garlandtx.gov
Managing Director **Jermel Stevenson** .... (972) 205-2758
Parks Superintendent **Barry Swisher** .... (972) 205-3587

Planning and Community Department
P.O. Box 469002, Garland, TX 75046-9002
Fax: (972) 205-2474 E-mail: planner@garlandtx.gov
Director **Will Guerin** .... (972) 205-2445
Senior Managing Director **Neil Montgomery** .... (972) 205-2445

Police Department
P.O. Box 469002, Garland, TX 75046-9002
E-mail: police@garlandtx.gov
Police Chief **Mitch Bates** .... (972) 205-2011
Assistant Police Chief **Jeff Bryan** .... (972) 485-4846
Assistant Police Chief **Gary Gregory** .... (972) 205-1679
Assistant Police Chief **Larry Ray** .... (972) 205-1616
Assistant Police Chief **Charles Rene** .... (972) 205-2086

Purchasing Department
P.O. Box 469002, Garland, TX 75046-9002
Fax: (972) 205-2495 E-mail: purchase@garlandtx.gov
Purchasing Director **Gary Holcomb** .... (972) 205-2425
E-mail: gholcomb@garlandtx.gov

Street Department
P.O. Box 469002, Garland, TX 75046-9002
Director **Steve Oliver** .... (972) 205-3558

Transportation Department
P.O. Box 469002, Garland, TX 75046-9002
E-mail: transport@garlandtx.gov
Director **Paul Luedtke** .... (972) 205-2430

Water Utilities
P.O. Box 469002, Garland, TX 75046-9002
E-mail: waterrecs@garlandtx.gov
Managing Director **Wes Kucera** .... (972) 205-3200
Wastewater Collection Manager **Brent Erickson** .... (972) 205-3227
E-mail: bericks@garlandtx.gov
Water/Wastewater Administrator **Robert Ashcraft** .... (972) 205-3209

Garland Power and Light
P.O. Box 469002, Garland, TX 75046-9002
Tel: (972) 205-2650 E-mail: info@garlandpower-light.org
Managing Director **Jeff Janke** .... (972) 205-2651
Chief Operations Officer **Tom Hancock** .... (972) 205-2217
Customer Services Managing Director **Kevin Slay** .... (972) 205-2671

Office of the City Auditor
P.O. Box 469002, Garland, TX 75046-9002
○ City Auditor **Jedson M. Johnson** .... (972) 205-2245
E-mail: jjohnson@garlandtx.gov

Office of the City Attorney
P.O. Box 469002, Garland, TX 75046-9002
E-mail: attorney@garlandtx.gov
○ City Attorney **Brad Neighbor** .... (972) 205-2380
E-mail: bneighbor@garlandtx.gov

Town of Gilbert, Arizona

Municipal Center, 50 East Civic Center Drive, Gilbert, AZ 85296
Tel: (480) 503-6000 Internet: www.gilbertaz.gov

County: Maricopa **Election Type:** Nonpartisan **Year Incorporated:** July 1920 **Population:** 247,542 (2015)

Office of the Mayor and Town Council
Municipal Center, 50 East Civic Center Drive, Gilbert, AZ 85296
Fax: (480) 497-4943

★ Mayor **John Lewis** .... (480) 503-6860
Note: Resigning Summer 2016
Began Service: June 16, 2009
Term Expires: December 31, 2016
E-mail: mayor@gilbertaz.gov

★ Vice Mayor **Jared Taylor** .... (480) 503-6764
Term Expires: December 31, 2016
E-mail: jared.taylor@gilbertaz.gov

★ Council Member **Eddie Cook** .... (480) 503-6764
Term Expires: December 31, 2018
E-mail: eddie.cook@gilbertaz.gov

★ Council Member **Jenn Daniels** .... (480) 503-6764
Term Expires: December 31, 2016
E-mail: jenn.daniels@gilbertaz.gov

★ Council Member **Victor Petersen** .... (480) 503-6764
Term Expires: December 31, 2018
E-mail: victor.petersen@gilbertaz.gov

★ Council Member **Brigette Peterson** .... (480) 503-6764
Term Expires: December 31, 2018
E-mail: brigette.peterson@gilbertaz.gov

★ Council Member **Jordan Ray** .... (480) 503-6764
Term Expires: December 31, 2018
E-mail: jordan.ray@gilbertaz.gov

★ Elected Official ▲ Appointed by Legislature ▼ Appointed by Governor ▶ Appointed by Board or Commission ● Appointed by Judge
■ Appointed by Mayor △ Appointed by Freeholders ▽ Appointed by Supervisor ▷ Appointed by County Executive ○ Appointed by Council

Planning and Zoning Commission
90 East Civic Center Drive, Gilbert, AZ 85296
E-mail: planning@gilbertaz.gov

Chair **Joshua Oehler** .... (480) 503-6743
Vice Chair **Kristopher Sippel** .... (480) 503-6743
Board Member **David Blaser** .... (480) 503-6743
Board Member **Carl Bloomfield** .... (480) 503-6743
Board Member **David Cavenee** .... (480) 503-6743
Board Member **Brent Mutti** .... (480) 503-6743
Board Member **Jennifer Wittman** .... (480) 503-6743
Board Member **Brett Young** .... (480) 503-6743

Office of the Town Attorney
50 East Civic Center Drive, Gilbert, AZ 85296

Town Attorney **L. Michael Hamblin** .... (480) 503-6871
E-mail: michael.hamblin@gilbertaz.gov

Office of the Town Clerk
Municipal Center, 50 East Civic Center Drive, Gilbert, AZ 85296
Tel: (480) 503-6871 E-mail: clerk@gilbertaz.gov

Town Clerk **Cathy Templeton** .... (480) 503-6861
E-mail: cathy.templeton@gilbertaz.gov
Deputy Town Clerk **Lisa Maxwell** .... (480) 503-6867
E-mail: lisa.maxwell@gilbertaz.gov

Office of the Prosecutor
55 East Civic Center Drive, Suite 205, Gilbert, AZ 85296
Fax: (480) 635-7910

Prosecutor **Lynn Arouh** .... (480) 635-7900

Office of the Town Manager
Municipal Center, 50 East Civic Center Drive, Gilbert, AZ 85296

Town Manager **Patrick Banger** .... (480) 503-6864
E-mail: patrick.banger@gilbertaz.gov
Education: Missouri State U BS; Webster MA

Communications Department
50 East Civic Center Drive, Gilbert, AZ 85296

Chief Digital Officer **Dana Berchman** .... (480) 503-6765
E-mail: dana.berchman@gilbertaz.gov
Education: Arizona State BA; American U MA

Economic Development Department
90 East Civic Center Drive, Gilbert, AZ 85296
Tel: (480) 503-6010 Fax: (480) 503-6170 E-mail: econdev@gilbertaz.gov

Director **Dan Henderson** .... (480) 503-6891
E-mail: dan.henderson@gilbertaz.gov
Management Support Coordinator **Kelly Patton** .... (480) 503-6873
E-mail: kelly.patton@gilbertaz.gov
Management Support Analyst **John Zupon** .... (480) 503-6762
E-mail: john.zupon@gilbertaz.gov

Human Resources Department
50 East Civic Center Drive, Gilbert, AZ 85296
Tel: (480) 503-6859 Fax: (480) 503-6712

Human Resources Director **Carrie Bosley** .... (480) 503-6859
E-mail: HR@gilbertaz.gov

Office of Information Technology
Director **Mark Kramer** .... (480) 503-6898
E-mail: mark.kramer@gilbertaz.gov
Systems Administrator **Chad Hurlburt** .... (480) 503-6786
E-mail: chad.hurlburt@gilbertaz.gov

Office of Management and Budget
50 East Civic Center Drive, Gilbert, AZ 85296
Tel: (480) 503-6871

Budget Director **Kelly Pfost** .... (480) 503-6828
E-mail: kelly.pfost@gilbertaz.gov

Deputy Town Manager
Municipal Center, 50 East Civic Center Drive, Gilbert, AZ 85296

Deputy Town Manager **(Vacant)** .... (480) 503-6000

Development Services Department
90 East Civic Center Drive, Gilbert, AZ 85296
E-mail: code@gilbertaz.gov

Director of Development Services **Kyle Mieras** .... (480) 503-6705
Code Compliance Administrator **Lorrie DeOrio** .... (480) 503-6834

Finance and Management Services Department
50 East Civic Center Drive, Gilbert, AZ 85296

Finance Director **Cindi Mattheisen** .... (480) 503-6856

Fire and Rescue Department
85 East Civic Center Drive, Gilbert, AZ 85296

Fire Chief **Jim Jobusch** .... (480) 503-6300
E-mail: jim.jobusch@gilbertaz.gov

Parks and Recreation Department
90 East Civic Center Drive, Gilbert, AZ 85296
Tel: (480) 503-6200

Recreation Director **Rod Buchanan** .... (480) 503-6284

Police Department
75 East Civic Center Drive, Gilbert, AZ 85296

Chief of Police **Tim Dorn** .... (480) 503-6500

Public Works Department
525 N. Lindsay Rd., Gilbert, AZ 85234
Tel: (480) 503-6842

Director **Kenneth Morgan** .... (480) 503-6842
Environmental Services Manager
Steven Pietrzykowski .... (480) 503-6426
Wastewater Manager **Mark Horn** .... (480) 503-6420
Facilities Maintenance Manager **(Vacant)** .... (480) 503-6424
Water Resource Manager **Hakon Johanson** .... (480) 503-6840

City of Glendale, Arizona

5850 West Glendale Avenue, Glendale, AZ 85301
Tel: (623) 930-2960 (Information) Internet: www.glendaleaz.com

County: Maricopa **Election Type:** Nonpartisan **Year Incorporated:** 1910 **Population:** 240,126 (2015)

Office of the Mayor and City Council
5850 W. Glendale Ave., Glendale, AZ 85301
Fax: (623) 937-2764

★ Mayor **Jerry P. Weiers** .... (623) 930-2260
Began Service: January 15, 2013
Term Expires: December 2016
★ Vice Mayor **Ian Hugh** .... (623) 930-2249
Term Expires: December 2016 Fax: (623) 931-8526
★ Council Member **Jamie Aldama** .... (623) 930-2249
Term Expires: December 2018 Fax: (623) 931-8526
★ Council Member **Sam Chavira** .... (623) 930-2249
Term Expires: December 2016 Fax: (623) 931-8526
★ Council Member **Ray Malnar** .... (623) 930-2249
Term Expires: December 2016 Fax: (623) 931-8526
E-mail: rmalnar@glendaleaz.com

(continued on next page)

★ Elected Official ▲ Appointed by Legislature ▼ Appointed by Governor ▶ Appointed by Board or Commission ● Appointed by Judge
■ Appointed by Mayor △ Appointed by Freeholders ▽ Appointed by Supervisor ▷ Appointed by County Executive ○ Appointed by Council

Office of the Mayor and City Council *continued*

★Council Member **Lauren Tolmachoff** . . . . (623) 930-2249
Term Expires: December 2018 Fax: (623) 931-8526

★Council Member **Bart Turner** . . . . (623) 930-2249
Term Expires: December 2018 Fax: (623) 931-8526

Office of the City Attorney

5850 W. Glendale Ave., Glendale, AZ 85301

City Attorney **Michael Bailey** . . . . (623) 930-2930
E-mail: mbailey@glendaleaz.com
Education: Chapman JD; American Public MPA

Office of the City Clerk

5850 W. Glendale Ave., Glendale, AZ 85301

○City Clerk **Pam Hanna** . . . . (623) 930-2252 ext. 1
E-mail: phanna@glendaleaz.com Fax: (623) 915-2391

Office of the City Manager

5850 W. Glendale Ave., Glendale, AZ 85301

○City Manager **Kevin Phelps** . . . . (623) 930-2870

Assistant City Manager **Jennifer Campbell** . . . . (623) 930-2870
Fax: (623) 847-1399

Assistant City Manager **Tom Duensing** . . . . (623) 930-2870
Fax: (623) 847-1399

Economic Development Director **Brian Friedman** . . . . (623) 930-2984
E-mail: bfriedman@glendaleaz.com Fax: (623) 931-5730

Human Resources Director **Jim Brown** . . . . (623) 930-2270
E-mail: jwbrown@glendaleaz.com Fax: (623) 915-2697

Intergovernmental Program Director **Brent Stoddard** . . . . (623) 930-2078
E-mail: bstoddard@glendaleaz.com Fax: (623) 930-2194

Airport, Glendale Municipal

6801 N. Glen Harbor Blvd., Glendale, AZ 85307
Fax: (623) 872-1278

Airport Administrator **Walter Fix** . . . . (623) 930-2188

Communications Department

5850 West Glendale Avenue, Glendale, AZ 85301
Tel: (623) 930-3077

Public Information Officer and Communications Manager **Sue Breding** . . . . (623) 930-2964
E-mail: Sbreding@glendaleaz.com

Public Information Officer **Kim Larson** . . . . (623) 930-2989
E-mail: klarson@glendaleaz.com

Finance and Technology Department

5850 W. Glendale Ave., Glendale, AZ 85301

Finance Director **(Vacant)** . . . . (623) 930-2480
Fax: (623) 915-2827

Purchasing and Materials Control Manager
Jackie Behrens . . . . (623) 930-2865
6829 North 58th Drive, Fax: (623) 915-2694
Suite 202, Glendale, AZ 85301-3222
E-mail: jbehrens@glendaleaz.com

Fire Department

6829 North 58th Drive, Glendale, AZ 85301

Fire Chief **Terry Garrison** . . . . (623) 930-4400

Information Technology Department

6830 North 57th Drive, Glendale, AZ 85301

Chief Information Technology Officer **Charles Murphy** . . . (623) 930-2880
E-mail: cmurphy@glendaleaz.com Fax: (623) 939-8113

Parks, Recreation and Library Services

5850 W. Glendale Ave., Glendale, AZ 85301
Fax: (623) 931-9651

Director **Erik Strunk** . . . . (623) 930-2820
Fax: (623) 931-9651

Glendale Public Library

5959 W. Brown St., Glendale, AZ 85302

Director **Cheryl Kennedy** . . . . (623) 930-3562
E-mail: ckennedy@glendaleaz.com Fax: (623) 842-2161

Police Department

6835 N. 57th Dr., Glendale, AZ 85301
E-mail: policemail@ci.glendale.az.us

Chief of Police **Debora Black** . . . . (623) 930-3229
Fax: (623) 931-2103

Public Works

5850 W. Glendale Ave., Glendale, AZ 85301

Executive Director **Jack Friedline** . . . . (623) 930-2600
Education: SUNY (Buffalo) BS; Arizona State MPA Fax: (623) 915-3124

City Engineer **David Beard** . . . . (623) 930-3630
E-mail: dbeard@glendaleaz.com Fax: (623) 915-2861

Water Services

6210 West Myrtle, Suite 112, Glendale, AZ 85302
Fax: (623) 915-3094

Executive Director **Craig Johnson** . . . . (623) 930-2700
Fax: (623) 915-3094

City of Glendale, California

City Hall, 613 E. Broadway, Glendale, CA 91206-3402
Tel: (818) 548-4000 (Information)

County: Los Angeles **Election Type:** Nonpartisan **Population:** 201,020 (2015)

Office of the Mayor and City Council

City Hall, 613 East Broadway, Suite 200, Glendale, CA 91206
Fax: (818) 547-6740

★Mayor **Paula Devine** . . . . (818) 548-4844
Began Service: June 2014
Term Expires: April 2019
E-mail: pdevine@glendaleca.gov
Secretary to the Mayor and Council
Hourik Hayrapetian . . . . (818) 548-4844
E-mail: jjahyrpetian@glendaleca.gov

★Council Member **Laura Friedman** . . . . (818) 548-4844
Term Expires: April 2017
E-mail: lfriedman@glendaleca.gov

★Council Member **Vartan Gharpetian** . . . . (818) 548-4844
Term Expires: April 27, 2019
E-mail: vgharpetian@glendaleca.gov

★Council Member **Ara James Najarian** . . . . (818) 548-4844
Term Expires: April 2017
E-mail: anajarian@glendaleca.gov
Education: Occidental 1982 BA; USC 1985 JD

★Council Member **Zareh Sinanyan** . . . . (818) 548-4844
Term Expires: April 2017
E-mail: zsinanyan@glendaleca.gov

★Elected Official ▲Appointed by Legislature ▼Appointed by Governor ▶Appointed by Board or Commission ●Appointed by Judge
■Appointed by Mayor △Appointed by Freeholders ▽Appointed by Supervisor ▷Appointed by County Executive ○Appointed by Council

Office of the City Attorney

City Hall, 613 East Broadway, Suite 220, Glendale, CA 91206-4394
Fax: (818) 547-3402 E-mail: coglegal@glendaleca.gov

○ City Attorney **Michael J. Garcia** .... (818) 548-2080
E-mail: mgarcia@glendaleca.gov
Chief Assistant City Attorney **Ann Maurer** .... (818) 548-2080
Chief Assistant City Attorney **Gillian Van Muyden** ...... (818) 548-2080
E-mail: gvanmuyden@glendaleca.gov
Senior Assistant City Attorney **Christine Godinez** .... (818) 548-2080
E-mail: cgodinez@glendaleca.gov
Senior Assistant City Attorney **Michael Grant** .... (818) 548-2080
E-mail: mgrant@glendaleca.gov
Assistant City Attorney **Dorine Martirosian** .... (818) 548-2080
Assistant City Attorney **Yvette Neukian** .... (818) 548-3700
Assistant City Attorney **Miah Yun** .... (818) 548-2080
Senior Assistant City Attorney **Lucy Varpetian** .... (818) 548-2080
E-mail: lvarpetian@glendaleca.gov
Deputy City Attorney **Andrew Rawcliffe** .... (818) 548-2080
General Counsel - Police **Carmen Merino** .... (818) 548-2080

Office of the City Manager

City Hall, 613 East Broadway, Suite 200, Glendale, CA 91206-4391
Fax: (818) 547-6740

○ City Manager **Scott Ochoa** .... (818) 548-4844
E-mail: sochoa@glendaleca.gov
Secretary **Gloria Melendez** .... (818) 548-4844
E-mail: gmelendez@glendaleca.gov
Assistant City Manager **Yasmin Beers** .... (818) 548-4844
E-mail: ybeers@glendaleca.gov
Deputy City Manager **John Takhtalian** .... (818) 548-4844
E-mail: jtakhtalian@glendaleca.gov

Community Development Department

633 East Broadway, Room 301, Glendale, CA 91206
Fax: (818) 548-3724

Director **Philip S. Lanzafame** .... (818) 548-2140
E-mail: PLanzafame@GlendaleCA.GOV
Education: San Diego State BA; Cal State (Northridge) MPA
Deputy Director **Tim Foy** .... (818) 548-2144
E-mail: tfoy@glendaleca.gov
Deputy Director of Housing **Peter Zovak** .... (818) 548-2060
E-mail: pzovak@glendaleca.gov

Planning Division

633 East Broadway, Suite 103, Glendale, CA 91206
Fax: (818) 240-0392

Director **(Vacant)** .... (818) 548-2140

Building and Safety Division

633 East Broadway, Room 101, Glendale, CA 91206-4390
Fax: (818) 548-3215

Building Official **Jan Edwards** .... (818) 548-3212

Community Services and Parks Department

City of Glendale, 613 East Broadway, Room 120, Glendale, CA 91206
Fax: (818) 548-3789

Director **Jess Duran** .... (818) 548-2000
E-mail: jduran@glendaleca.gov
Workforce Development Administrator (Acting)
Judith Velasco .... (818) 548-2053
E-mail: jvelasco@glendaleca.gov

Finance Department

141 N. Glendale Ave., Suite 346, Glendale, CA 91206
Fax: (818) 956-3286

Director **Robert "Bob" Elliot** .... (818) 548-2085
E-mail: belliot@glendaleca.gov

Purchasing Department

141 N. Glendale Ave., Room 346, Glendale, CA 91206-4499
E-mail: purchasing@glendaleca.gov Fax: (818) 956-3286

Purchasing Manager **Afshin Bokaei** .... (818) 548-2102
E-mail: abokaei@glendaleca.gov

Fire Department

421 Oak St., Glendale, CA 91204-1298
Fax: (818) 547-1031 E-mail: fireoncall@glendaleca.gov

Fire Chief **Greg Fish** .... (818) 548-4814
E-mail: gfish@glendaleca.gov

Glendale Water and Power [GWP]

141 N. Glendale Ave., 4th Level, Glendale, CA 91206-4496
Fax: (818) 552-2852

General Manager **Stephen M. "Steve" Zurn** .... (818) 548-2107
Education: UCLA BA; Cal State (Long Beach) MPA
Chief Assistant General Manager **Ramon Abueg** .... (818) 548-3297

Water and Power Commission

President **Terry Chan** .... (818) 548-2107
Commissioner **Hrand Avanessian** .... (818) 548-2107
Commissioner **Manuel Camargo** .... (818) 548-2107
Commissioner **Matthew Hale** .... (818) 548-2107
Commissioner **Sarojini Lall** .... (818) 548-2107

Human Resources

City Hall, 613 East Broadway, Room 100, Glendale, CA 91206-4392
Fax: (818) 243-8428

Director **Matt Doyle** .... (818) 548-2110 ext. 2154
E-mail: mdoyle@glendaleca.gov

Information Services Department

141 N. Glendale Ave., Suite 314, Glendale, CA 91206
Fax: (818) 543-3247

Chief Information Officer **Brian Ganley** .... (818) 548-4095
E-mail: bganley@glendaleca.gov
Education: USC BS; Cal State (Northridge) MPA

Glendale Library, Arts and Culture

222 E. Harvard St., Glendale, CA 91205
Fax: (818) 548-7225

Director **Cindy Cleary** .... (818) 548-2030
E-mail: ccleary@glendaleca.gov

Police Department

131 N. Isabel St., Glendale, CA 91206-4382
Tel: (818) 548-4840 (Information) Tel: (818) 548-3135 (Record Bureau)
Fax: (818) 507-0967

Police Chief **Robert Castro** .... (818) 548-3140

Public Works Department

633 East Broadway, Room 209, Glendale, CA 91206-4385
Fax: (818) 546-2207

Director **Roubik Golanian** .... (818) 548-3900

Engineering Division

633 E. Broadway, Ste. 205, Glendale, CA 91206-4388
Fax: (818) 242-7087

City Engineer (Acting) **Roubik Golanian** .... (818) 548-3945
E-mail: rgolanian@glendaleca.gov

Integrated Waste Management Division

548 W. Chevy Chase Dr., Glendale, CA 91204-1814
Fax: (818) 507-6128

Deputy Director **Dan Hardgrove** .... (818) 548-3916

(continued on next page)

★ Elected Official ▲ Appointed by Legislature ▼ Appointed by Governor ► Appointed by Board or Commission ● Appointed by Judge
■ Appointed by Mayor △ Appointed by Freeholders ▽ Appointed by Supervisor ▷ Appointed by County Executive ○ Appointed by Council

Integrated Waste Management Division *continued*

Recycling Coordinator **Regina Wheeler** . . . . (818) 548-3916
Fax: (818) 507-6128

Maintenance Services Division

541 W. Chevy Chase Dr., Glendale, CA 91204-1813
Fax: (818) 547-0637

Deputy Public Works Director **Dan Hardgrove** . . . . (818) 548-3950
E-mail: dhardgrove@glendaleca.gov
Wastewater Superintendent **John Hicks** . . . . (818) 548-3950

Fleet Services Division

541 West Chevy Chase Drive, Glendale, CA 91204
Fax: (818) 409-7001

Fleet Manager **Karl Vogeley** . . . . (818) 548-3952

Office of the City Clerk

City Hall, 613 East Broadway, Suite 110, Glendale, CA 91206-4393
Tel: (818) 548-2090 Fax: (818) 241-5386

★City Clerk **Ardashes "Ardy" Kassakhian** . . . . (818) 548-2094
Term Expires: April 11, 2017
E-mail: akassakhian@glendaleca.gov

Office of the City Treasurer

141 N. Glendale Ave., Room 438, Glendale, CA 91206-4495
Fax: (818) 246-5133

★City Treasurer **Rafi Manoukian** . . . . (818) 548-2066
Term Expires: April 2017
E-mail: rmanoukian@glendaleca.gov
Education: Cal State (Northridge) 1984 BA; Cal State (Dominguez) 2004 MBA
Assistant City Treasurer **Guia Murray** . . . . (818) 548-2066

City of Grand Prairie, Texas

City Hall, 317 W. College St., Grand Prairie, TX 75050
Internet: www.gptx.org

County: Dallas; Ellis; Tarrant **Election Type:** Nonpartisan
Year Incorporated: 1909 **Population:** 187,809 (2015)

Office of the Mayor and City Council

City Hall, 317 W. College St., Grand Prairie, TX 75050
Fax: (972) 237-8317

★Mayor **Ron Jensen** . . . . (972) 237-8062
Began Service: May 21, 2013
Term Expires: May 2019
E-mail: pmarcum@gptx.org
Education: Texas (Arlington) 1973 BS
★Mayor Pro Tem **Jim Swafford** (District 2) . . . . (972) 237-8022
Term Expires: May 4, 2019
Education: Texas (Arlington) BA; Southern Methodist MA
★Deputy Mayor Pro Tem **Jorja Clemson** (District 1) . . . . . . (972) 237-8022
Term Expires: May 2017
★Council Member **Lila Thorn** (District 3) . . . . (972) 237-8022
Term Expires: May 3, 2017
★Council Member **Richard Fregoe** (District 4) . . . . (972) 237-8022
Term Expires: May 4, 2019
Education: Florida State BS
★Council Member **Tony Shotwell** (District 5) . . . . (972) 237-8022
Term Expires: May 13, 2018
★Council Member **Jeff Wooldridge** (District 6) . . . . (972) 237-8022
Term Expires: May 13, 2018
★Council Member **Jeff Copeland** (At-Large) . . . . (972) 237-8022
Term Expires: May 3, 2017
★Council Member **Greg Giessner** (At-Large) . . . . (972) 237-8022
Term Expires: May 13, 2018

Office of the City Manager

City Hall, 317 W. College St., Grand Prairie, TX 75050
Fax: (972) 237-8088

City Manager **Tom Hart** . . . . (972) 237-8012
Education: North Texas BS

Office of the City Secretary

City Hall, 317 W. College St., Grand Prairie, TX 75050
Fax: (972) 237-8030

City Secretary **Cathy DiMaggio** . . . . (972) 237-8035
E-mail: cdimaggio@gptx.org
Education: Michigan BA

Animal Services Division

1225 W. Freeway, Grand Prairie, TX 75051
Fax: (972) 237-8579

Manager **Danielle Tate** . . . . (972) 237-8575

Budget and Research Department

200 W. Main St., Grand Prairie, TX 75050
Fax: (972) 237-8273

Director **Kathleen Mercer** . . . . (972) 237-8239
E-mail: kmercer@gptx.org
Education: North Texas MPA

Building Inspection Division

206 W. Church, Grand Prairie, TX 75050
Fax: (972) 237-8234

Building Inspector **Rob Ard** . . . . (972) 237-8230
Education: DeVry Inst BS

Code Enforcement Division

201 NW 2nd Street, Room 150, Grand Prairie, TX 75050
Fax: (972) 237-8187

Manager **Steve Collins** . . . . (972) 237-8296

Communications and Marketing Department

City Hall, 317 W. College St., Grand Prairie, TX 75050
Fax: (972) 237-8317

Director **Amy Sprinkles** . . . . (972) 237-8140
E-mail: asprinkles@gptx.org
Education: Arizona State BS, MBA

Community Development Division

201 NW 2nd Street, Room 150, Grand Prairie, TX 75050
Fax: (972) 237-8459

Manager **Bill Hills** . . . . (972) 237-8166

Economic Development Department

City Hall, 317 W. College St., Grand Prairie, TX 75050
Fax: (972) 237-8288

Director **Bob O'Neal** . . . . (972) 237-8160
E-mail: boneal@gptx.org
Education: Austin State BA; North Texas BS

Environmental Services Department

201 NW 2nd Street, Room 100, Grand Prairie, TX 75050
Fax: (972) 237-8228

Director **Jim Cummings** . . . . (972) 237-8055
Education: Tulane BS; Ohio State BS

★Elected Official ▲Appointed by Legislature ▼Appointed by Governor ►Appointed by Board or Commission ●Appointed by Judge
■Appointed by Mayor △Appointed by Freeholders ▽Appointed by Supervisor ▷Appointed by County Executive ○Appointed by Council

Finance Department
City Hall, 317 W. College St., Grand Prairie, TX 75050
Fax: (972) 237-8080

Chief Financial Officer **Diana Ortiz** .... (972) 237-8067
Education: Texas A&I BS; Corpus Christi State MBA

Accounting Department
City Hall, 317 W. College St., Grand Prairie, TX 75050
Fax: (972) 237-8080

Controller **Cheryl Estes** .... (972) 237-8099
E-mail: cestes@gptx.org

Fire Department
1525 Arkansas Lane, Room 200, Grand Prairie, TX 75052
Fax: (972) 237-8309

Fire Chief **Robert Fite** .... (972) 237-8300
E-mail: rfite@gptx.org

Housing and Neighborhood Services Department
205 W. Church, Grand Prairie, TX 75050
Fax: (972) 237-8318

Director **William Hills** .... (972) 237-8176
E-mail: bhills@gptx.org

Human Resources Department
318 W. Main St., Grand Prairie, TX 75050
Fax: (972) 237-8286

Director **Lisa Norris** .... (972) 237-8192
E-mail: lnorris@gptx.org
Education: Baylor BS

Information Technology Department
City Hall, 317 W. College St., Grand Prairie, TX 75050
Fax: (972) 237-8161

Director **Bob O'Neal** .... (972) 237-8382
Education: Austin State BA; North Texas BS

Legal Services Department
City Hall, 317 W. College St., Grand Prairie, TX 75050
Fax: (972) 237-8030

City Attorney **Don Postell** .... (972) 237-8026
E-mail: dpostell@gptx.org
Education: St Mary's U (TX) BA; Texas JD

Library
901 Conover Dr., Grand Prairie, TX 75051
Fax: (972) 237-5750

Director **Amy Sprinkles** .... (972) 237-5700
E-mail: asprinkles@gptx.org
Education: Arizona State BS, MBA

Municipal Airport
3116 S. Great Southwest Pkwy., Grand Prairie, TX 75052
Fax: (972) 336-0414

Airport Director **Randy Byers** .... (972) 237-7591

Parks and Recreation Department
326 W. Main St., Grand Prairie, TX 75050
Fax: (972) 237-8267

Director **Rick Herold** .... (972) 237-8100
Education: North Texas BS, MS

Planning and Development Department
206 W. Church, Grand Prairie, TX 75050
Fax: (972) 237-8234

Director **Bill Crolley** .... (972) 237-8255
E-mail: bcrolley@gptx.org
Education: Southwest Texas State BA; Texas (Arlington) MCR

Police Department
1525 West Arkansas Lane, Grand Prairie, TX 75052
Fax: (972) 237-8714

Police Chief **Steve Dye** .... (972) 237-8710

Public Works Department
206 W. Church St., Grand Prairie, TX 75050

Director **Ron McCuller** .... (972) 237-8154
Education: North Texas BA, MA Fax: (972) 237-8116
City Engineer **Romin Khavari** .... (972) 237-8141
Education: Texas A&M BS Fax: (972) 237-8116
Solid Waste Division Manager **Patricia Redfearn** .... (972) 237-4550
Fax: (972) 237-8147
Street Services Manager **(Vacant)** .... (972) 237-8525
Fax: (972) 237-8533

Purchasing Division
318 W. Main St., Grand Prairie, TX 75050
Fax: (972) 237-8265

Manager **Robert Myers** .... (972) 237-8271
E-mail: rmyers@gptx.org

Transportation Services Department
206 W. Church St., Grand Prairie, TX 75050
Fax: (972) 237-8116

Director **Walter Shumac** .... (972) 237-8139

Water Bills
City Hall, 317 W. College St., Grand Prairie, TX 75050
Fax: (972) 237-8206

Manager **Doug Cuny** .... (972) 237-8200
Education: Texas BA

Water Utilities Division
620 Small Hill, Grand Prairie, TX 75050
Fax: (972) 237-8412

Manager **Jim Siddall** .... (972) 237-8413

City of Grand Rapids, Michigan

300 Monroe Ave. NW, Grand Rapids, MI 49503
Tel: (616) 456-3000 (Information) Internet: www.grcity.us

County: Kent **Election Type:** Nonpartisan **Year Founded:** 1826 **Year Incorporated:** 1850 **Population:** 195,097 (2015) **Employees:** 1,485 **Fiscal Year:** 2016 **Budget:** $461,978,000

Office of the Mayor and City Commission

300 Monroe Ave., NW, Grand Rapids, MI 49503
Tel: (616) 456-3168 Fax: (616) 456-3111 E-mail: cogrexec@grcity.us

Employees: 13 **Fiscal Year:** 2016 **Budget:** $12,944,000

★ Mayor **Rosalynn Bliss** .... (616) 456-3168
Began Service: January 1, 2016
Term Expires: December 31, 2019
E-mail: mayor@grcity.us

(continued on next page)

★ Elected Official ▲ Appointed by Legislature ▼ Appointed by Governor ► Appointed by Board or Commission ● Appointed by Judge
■ Appointed by Mayor △ Appointed by Freeholders ▽ Appointed by Supervisor ▷ Appointed by County Executive ○ Appointed by Council

CITIES AND TOWNS

Office of the Mayor and City Commission *continued*

Assistant to the Mayor **Amy Snow** .... (616) 456-3168
★ Commissioner **Jon O'Connor** (Ward 1) .... (616) 456-3035
Term Expires: December 31, 2019
★ Commissioner **Dave Shaffer** (Ward 1) .... (616) 456-3035
Term Expires: December 31, 2017
★ Commissioner **Ruth Kelly** (Ward 2) .... (616) 456-3035
Term Expires: December 31, 2019
★ Commissioner **(Vacant)** (Ward 2) .... (616) 456-3035
Term Expires: December 31, 2017
★ Commissioner **Dave Allen** (Ward 3) .... (616) 456-3035
Term Expires: December 31, 2019
★ Commissioner **Senita Lenear** (Ward 3) .... (616) 456-3035
Term Expires: December 31, 2017
E-mail: slenear@grcity.us

Office of the City Attorney

300 Monroe Ave., NW, Grand Rapids, MI 49503
Fax: (616) 456-4569

Employees: 17 **Fiscal Year:** 2016 **Budget:** $2,476,000

▶ City Attorney **Catherine M. Mish** .... (616) 456-3181
E-mail: cmish@grcity.us
Education: Wayne State U 1999 JD

Office of the City Clerk

300 Monroe Ave., NW, Grand Rapids, MI 49503
Tel: (616) 456-3010 Fax: (616) 456-4607

Employees: 9 **Fiscal Year:** 2016 **Budget:** $2,128,000

▶ City Clerk **Darlene O'Neal** .... (616) 456-3010
E-mail: doneal@grcity.us
Deputy City Clerk **Stephanie McMillen** .... (616) 456-3014

Office of the Comptroller

300 Monroe Ave., NW, Grand Rapids, MI 49503
Tel: (616) 456-3189 Fax: (616) 456-3454

Employees: 17 **Fiscal Year:** 2016 **Budget:** $2,562,000

★ Comptroller **Sara Vander Werff** .... (616) 456-3193
Term Expires: December 31, 2017
E-mail: swerff@grcity.us
Deputy Comptroller **Ruth Lueders** .... (616) 456-3194

Office of the Treasurer

300 Monroe Avenue, 2nd Floor, Grand Rapids, MI 49503
Tel: (616) 456-3020 Fax: (616) 456-3413

Employees: 18 **Fiscal Year:** 2016 **Budget:** $2,878,000

▶ Treasurer **John Globensky** .... (616) 456-3020
E-mail: jglobensky@grcity.us
Deputy Treasurer **Fred Raabe** .... (616) 456-3023

Office of the City Manager

300 Monroe Ave., NW, Grand Rapids, MI 49503
Tel: (616) 456-3166 Fax: (616) 456-3111

Employees: 17 **Fiscal Year:** 2016 **Budget:** $2,354,000

▶ City Manager **Greg Sundstrom** .... (616) 456-3165
E-mail: gsundstr@grcity.us
Assistant to the City Manager **Tom Almonte** .... (616) 456-3165
E-mail: talmonte@grcity.us
Deputy City Manager **Eric DeLong** .... (616) 456-3166
E-mail: edelong@grcity.us
Chief Financial Officer/Deputy City Manager
Scott Buhrer .... (616) 456-3951

Assessor Department

300 Monroe Ave., NW, Grand Rapids, MI 49503
Tel: (616) 456-3081 Fax: (616) 456-4608

Assessor **Scott Engerson** .... (616) 456-3081
E-mail: sengerso@grcity.us
Deputy Assessor **Paula Grivinf-Jaftifer** .... (616) 456-3155
E-mail: pgrivinf-jaftifer@grcity.us

Community Development Office

300 Monroe Ave., NW, Grand Rapids, MI 49503
Tel: (616) 456-3677 Fax: (616) 456-4619

Employees: 39 **Fiscal Year:** 2016 **Budget:** $10,903,000

Managing Director **Connie Bohatch** .... (616) 456-3677
E-mail: cbohatch@grcity.us
Administrative Services Officer **Mary Thornton** .... (616) 456-3675
E-mail: mthornton@grcity.us
Our Communities Children Director **Lynn Heemstra** .... (616) 456-4353
E-mail: lheemstra@grcity.us

Diversity and Inclusion Office

300 Monroe Ave., NW, Grand Rapids, MI 49503
Tel: (616) 456-3027 TTY: (616) 456-3210 Fax: (616) 456-3199

Manager **Patti Caudill** .... (616) 456-3027

Engineering Department

300 Monroe Ave., NW, Grand Rapids, MI 49503
Tel: (616) 456-3060 Fax: (616) 456-3828

Employees: 34 **Fiscal Year:** 2016 **Budget:** $6,924,000

City Engineer **Mark deClercq** .... (616) 456-3063
E-mail: mdeclercq@grcity.us
Assistant City Engineer **Jeff McCaul** .... (616) 456-3075
E-mail: jmccaul@grcity.us

Environmental Services Department

1300 Market St., SW, Grand Rapids, MI 49503
Tel: (616) 456-3625 Fax: (616) 456-3700

Environmental Services Manager **Michael Lunn** .... (616) 456-3625

Fire Department

38 LaGrave, SE, Grand Rapids, MI 49503
Fax: (616) 456-3898

Employees: 199 **Fiscal Year:** 2016 **Budget:** $27,663,000

Fire Chief **Laura Knapp** .... (616) 456-3900
E-mail: lknapp@grcity.us
Deputy Fire Chief **Kevin Sehlmeyer** .... (616) 456-3721
E-mail: ksehlmeyer@grcity.us

Devos Place/Van Andel Arena

130 W. Fulton, Grand Rapids, MI 49503
Tel: (616) 742-6600 Fax: (616) 742-6197

General Manager **Richard MacKeigan** .... (616) 742-6190

Human Resources Department

300 Monroe Ave., NW, Grand Rapids, MI 49503
Tel: (616) 456-3176 Fax: (616) 456-3728

Employees: 20 **Fiscal Year:** 2016 **Budget:** $31,643,000

Managing Director of Administrative Services
Mari Beth Jelks .... (616) 456-3176
E-mail: jobs@grcity.us

Income Tax Department

300 Monroe Ave., NW, Grand Rapids, MI 49503
Tel: (616) 456-3415 Fax: (616) 456-4540

Income Tax Administrator **John Schaut** .... (616) 456-3823
E-mail: jschaut@grcity.us

★ Elected Official ▲ Appointed by Legislature ▼ Appointed by Governor ▶ Appointed by Board or Commission ● Appointed by Judge
■ Appointed by Mayor △ Appointed by Freeholders ▽ Appointed by Supervisor ▷ Appointed by County Executive ○ Appointed by Council

Income Tax Department *continued*

Income Tax Examiner **Bill Butts** . . . . . (616) 456-3822
E-mail: bbutts@grcity.us

Information Technology Department
300 Monroe, NW, Grand Rapids, MI 49503
Tel: (616) 456-3069 Fax: (616) 456-3448

Employees: 4 **Fiscal Year:** 2016 **Budget:**

Director of Technology and Change Management
Paul Klimas . . . . . (616) 456-3069
E-mail: pklimas@grcity.us

Grand Rapids Public Library
111 Library Street, NE, Grand Rapids, MI 49503
Tel: (616) 988-5400

Employees: 150 **Fiscal Year:** 2016 **Budget:** $11,074,000

Director **Marcia Warner** . . . . . (616) 988-5400
E-mail: mwarner@grpl.org
Assistant Director **Marla Ehlers** . . . . . (616) 988-5702
E-mail: mehlers@grcity.us

Facilities and Fleet Management
333 Market St., SW, Grand Rapids, MI 49503
Tel: (616) 456-3223 Fax: (616) 456-4156

Employees: 46 **Fiscal Year:** 2016 **Budget:** $24,531,000

Director **Gary Reimer** . . . . . (616) 456-3223
E-mail: greimer@grcity.us

Parks Recreation and Forestry Department
201 Market Avenue, SW, Grand Rapids, MI 49503

Employees: 31 **Fiscal Year:** 2016 **Budget:** $10,730,000

Director **David Marquardt** . . . . . (616) 456-3696

Planning Department
1120 Monroe Avenue, NW, Grand Rapids, MI 49503
Tel: (616) 456-3031 Fax: (616) 456-4568

Director **Suzanne Schulz** . . . . . (616) 456-4100
DDA Director **Kristopher Larson** . . . . . (616) 456-3034

Police Department
One Monroe Center, Grand Rapids, MI 49503
Tel: (616) 456-3400 Fax: (616) 456-3490

Employees: 377 **Fiscal Year:** 2016 **Budget:** $57,187,000

Police Chief **David Rahinsky** . . . . . (616) 456-3364

Public Housing Department
1420 Fuller Street, SE, Grand Rapids, MI 49507
Tel: (616) 235-2600 Fax: (616) 235-2660

Director **Carlos A. Sanchez** . . . . . (616) 235-2600

Public Services Department
1120 Monroe, NW, Grand Rapids, MI 49503
Tel: (616) 456-3053 Fax: (616) 456-3453

Employees: 73 **Fiscal Year:** 2016 **Budget:** $52,916,000

Public Services Director **James Hurt** . . . . . (616) 456-3232

Purchasing Office
300 Monroe NW, Room 720, Grand Rapids, MI 49503
Tel: (616) 456-3173 Fax: (616) 456-3339

Purchasing Agent **Amie Merren** . . . . . (616) 456-3952
E-mail: amerren@grcity.us

Recycling and Refuse
201 Market Avenue, SW, Grand Rapids, MI 49503
Tel: (616) 456-3232 Fax: (616) 456-4561

Director **James Hurt** . . . . . (616) 456-3232

Traffic Safety Department
509 Wealthy Street, SW, Grand Rapids, MI 49503
Tel: (616) 456-3066 Fax: (616) 456-3665

Traffic System Engineer **Christopher Zull** . . . . . (616) 456-3066
E-mail: czull@grcity.us

Water Department
1900 Oak Industrial Drive, NE, Grand Rapids, MI 49505
Tel: (616) 456-4550 Fax: (616) 456-3138

Water System Manager **Joellen Thompson** . . . . . (616) 456-4680

City of Green Bay, Wisconsin

City Hall, 100 N. Jefferson St., Green Bay, WI 54301
Internet: http://greenbaywi.gov/

County: Brown **Election Type:** Nonpartisan **Year Incorporated:** 1854
Population: 105,207 (2015)

James J. "Jim" Schmitt
Mayor

Began Service: 2003
Term Expires: April 1, 2019
Date of Birth: 1958
Education: St Norbert 1980 BBS
Career: Little Rapids Corporation; Founder, Famis Manufacturing, Inc. (1993-2003)

Office of the Mayor
City Hall, 100 N. Jefferson St., Green Bay, WI 54301
Fax: (920) 448-3081

★ Mayor **James J. "Jim" Schmitt** . . . . . (920) 448-3005
E-mail: jimsc@greenbaywi.gov
Chief of Staff **Andy Rosendahl** . . . . . (920) 448-3006

Office of the City Assessor
City Hall, 100 N. Jefferson St., Green Bay, WI 54301

■ City Assessor **Russ Schwandt** . . . . . (920) 448-3070
E-mail: russsc@greenbaywi.gov

Law Department
City Hall, 100 N. Jefferson St., Green Bay, WI 54301
Fax: (920) 448-3081

■ City Attorney (Interim)
Anthony S. "Tony" Wachewicz III . . . . . (920) 448-3080
E-mail: TonyWa@greenbaywi.gov
Assistant City Attorney **Kristen Bohnert** . . . . . (920) 448-3080
Assistant City Attorney **Joanne Bungert** . . . . . (920) 448-3080
Assistant City Attorney **Joseph Faulds** . . . . . (920) 448-3080

Office of the City Clerk/Treasurer
City Hall, 100 N. Jefferson St., Green Bay, WI 54301
Fax: (920) 448-3016

■ City Clerk **Kris Teske** . . . . . (920) 448-3010
E-mail: kriste@greenbaywi.gov

★ Elected Official ▲ Appointed by Legislature ▼ Appointed by Governor ▶ Appointed by Board or Commission ● Appointed by Judge
■ Appointed by Mayor △ Appointed by Freeholders ▽ Appointed by Supervisor ▷ Appointed by County Executive ○ Appointed by Council

Human Resources Department
100 N. Jefferson St., Green Bay, WI 54301
Fax: (920) 448-3128

Director **Lynn Boland** . . . . . (920) 448-3356
E-mail: lynnbo@greenbaywi.gov

Economic Development Department
City Hall, 100 North Jefferson Street, Room 200, Green Bay, WI 54301
Fax: (920) 448-3081

Director **Kevin J. Vonck** . . . . . (920) 448-3397
E-mail: kevinvo@greenbaywi.gov

Finance Department
City Hall, 100 N. Jefferson St., Green Bay, WI 54301
Fax: (920) 448-3022

■ Director **Dawn Foeller** . . . . . (920) 448-3020
E-mail: dawnfo@greenbaywi.gov

Purchasing Department
City Hall, 100 North Jefferson Street, Room 101, Green Bay, WI 54301
Fax: (920) 448-3050

Purchasing Agent **Rick Jensen** . . . . . (920) 448-3047
E-mail: jensenri@greenbaywi.gov

Risk Management Department
City Hall, 100 N. Jefferson St., Green Bay, WI 54301
Fax: (920) 448-3128

Benefit Analyst **Jean Adams** . . . . . (920) 448-3023
E-mail: jeanad@greenbaywi.gov
Safety Manager **Coleen Hinz** . . . . . (920) 448-3125
E-mail: coleenhi@greenbaywi.gov

Fire Department
501 S. Washington St., Green Bay, WI 54301
Fax: (920) 448-3281

Fire Chief **David W. Litton** . . . . . (920) 448-3280
E-mail: davidli@greenbaywi.gov

Information Technology Services Department
100 N. Jefferson St., Green Bay, WI 54301

■ Director **Mike Hronek** . . . . . (920) 448-3033
E-mail: mikehr@greenbaywi.gov
Programmer/Analyst **Matt Sorenson** . . . . . (920) 448-3033

Parks, Recreation and Forestry Department
City Hall, 100 N. Jefferson St., Green Bay, WI 54301
Fax: (920) 448-3393

■ Director **Dawne Kramer** . . . . . (920) 448-3365
E-mail: kramerda@greenbaywi.gov

Planning and Development Division
100 North Jefferson Street, Room 608, Green Bay, WI 54301
Fax: (920) 448-3426

Planning Director **Kim Flom** . . . . . (920) 448-3400

Police Department
307 S. Adams St., Green Bay, WI 54301
Fax: (920) 448-3256

Chief of Police **Andrew Smith** . . . . . (920) 448-3200

Public Works Department
City Hall, 100 N. Jefferson St., Green Bay, WI 54301
Fax: (920) 448-3102

■ Director **Steve Grenier** . . . . . (920) 448-3100
E-mail: stevengr@greenbaywi.gov

Transit Department
318 S. Washington St., Green Bay, WI 54301
Fax: (920) 448-3461

Director **Patty Kiewiz** . . . . . (920) 448-3450

Water Department
631 S. Adams St., Green Bay, WI 54301
Fax: (920) 448-3486

General Manager **Nancy Quirk** . . . . . (920) 448-3480

Office of the Common Council
City Hall, 100 N. Jefferson St., Green Bay, WI 54301
Tel: (920) 448-3010 Fax: (920) 448-3016
Internet: http://greenbaywi.gov/agencies/common-council-3/

★ President **Thomas De Wane** (District 2) . . . . . (920) 465-7803
Term Expires: April 1, 2018
E-mail: district2@greenbaywi.gov
★ Vice President **Mark Steuer** (District 10) . . . . . (920) 494-4494
Term Expires: April 1, 2018
E-mail: district10@greenbaywi.gov
★ Alderman **Barbara Dorff** (District 1) . . . . . (920) 469-0969
Term Expires: April 1, 2018
E-mail: district1@greenbaywi.gov
★ Alderman **Andy Nicholson** (District 3) . . . . . (920) 465-3564
Term Expires: April 1, 2018
E-mail: district3@greenbaywi.gov
★ Alderman **Bill Galvin** (District 4) . . . . . (920) 639-4640
Term Expires: April 1, 2018
E-mail: district4@greenbaywi.gov
★ Alderman **David Nennig** (District 5) . . . . . (920) 437-2318
Term Expires: April 1, 2018
E-mail: district5@greenbaywi.gov
★ Alderman **Joe Moore** (District 6) . . . . . (920) 445-0145
Term Expires: April 1, 2018
E-mail: district6@greenbaywi.gov
★ Alderman **Randy Scannell** (District 7) . . . . . (920) 609-9820
Term Expires: April 1, 2018
E-mail: district7@greenbaywi.gov
★ Alderman **Christopher Werry** (District 8) . . . . . (920) 490-9282
Term Expires: April 1, 2018
E-mail: district8@greenbaywi.gov
★ Alderman **Guy Zima** (District 9) . . . . . (920) 499-3614
Term Expires: April 1, 2018
E-mail: district9@greenbaywi.gov
★ Alderman **John A. Vander Leest** (District 11) . . . . . (920) 499-0996
Term Expires: April 1, 2018
E-mail: district11@greenbaywi.gov
★ Alderman **Thomas Sladek** (District 12) . . . . . (920) 499-7701
Term Expires: April 1, 2018
E-mail: district12@greenbaywi.gov

★ Elected Official ▲ Appointed by Legislature ▼ Appointed by Governor ► Appointed by Board or Commission ● Appointed by Judge
■ Appointed by Mayor △ Appointed by Freeholders ▽ Appointed by Supervisor ▷ Appointed by County Executive ○ Appointed by Council

City of Greensboro, North Carolina

300 West Washington Street, Greensboro, NC 27402
P.O. Box 3136, Greensboro, NC 27402-3136
Tel: (336) 373-2489 (Information) Internet: www.greensboro-nc.gov

County: Guilford **Election Type:** Nonpartisan **Year Founded:** 1749
Year Incorporated: 1807 **Charter:** 1808 **Population:** 285,342 (2015)

Office of the Mayor and City Council

P.O. Box 3136, Greensboro, NC 27402-3136
Fax: (336) 574-4003

★ Mayor **Nancy Vaughan** .... (336) 373-2396
Began Service: December 3, 2013 Fax: (336) 574-4003
Term Expires: December 1, 2017
E-mail: nancy.vaughan@greensboro-nc.gov

★ Mayor Pro Tem **Yvonne J. Johnson** (At-Large) .... (336) 373-2396
Term Expires: December 1, 2017
E-mail: yvonne.johnson@greensboro-nc.gov

★ Council Member **Sharon Hightower** (District 1) .... (336) 373-2396
Term Expires: December 3, 2017 Fax: (336) 574-4003
E-mail: sharon.hightower@greensboro-nc.gov

★ Council Member **Jamal T. Fox** (District 2) .... (336) 373-2396
Term Expires: December 3, 2017
E-mail: jamal.fox@greensboro-nc.gov

★ Council Member **Justin Outling** (District 3) .... (336) 373-2396
Term Expires: December 3, 2017

★ Council Member **Nancy Hoffmann** (District 4) .... (336) 373-2396
Term Expires: December 3, 2017
E-mail: nancy.hoffmann@greensboro-nc.gov

★ Council Member **Tony Wilkins** (District 5) .... (336) 373-2396
Term Expires: December 3, 2017
E-mail: tony.wilkins@greensboro-nc.gov

★ Council Member **Marikay Abuzuaiter** (At-Large) .... (336) 373-2396
Term Expires: December 3, 2017
E-mail: marikay.abuzuaiter@greensboro-nc.gov

★ Council Member **Michael Barber** (At-Large) .... (336) 373-2396
Term Expires: December 3, 2017
E-mail: mike.barber@greensboro-nc.gov

Office of the City Attorney

P.O. Box 3136, Greensboro, NC 27402-3136
Fax: (336) 373-2078

City Attorney **Tom Carruthers** .... (336) 373-2320
E-mail: thomas.carruthers@greensboro-nc.gov

Office of the City Clerk

P.O. Box 3136, Greensboro, NC 27402-3136
Fax: (336) 574-4003

City Clerk **Betsey Richardson** .... (336) 373-2697
E-mail: betsey.richardson@greensboro-nc.gov

Deputy City Clerk **Angela Lord** .... (336) 373-2397
E-mail: angela.lord@greensboro-nc.gov

Office of the City Manager

P.O. Box 3136, Greensboro, NC 27402-3136
Fax: (336) 373-2117

○ City Manager **Jim Westmoreland** .... (336) 373-2002
E-mail: jim.westmoreland@greensboro-nc.gov

Assistant City Manager **David A. Parrish** .... (336) 373-2002
E-mail: david.parrish@greensboro-nc.gov
Education: North Carolina Greensboro BS; North Carolina MPA

Assistant City Manager **Chris Wilson** .... (336) 373-2002
E-mail: christian.wilson@greensboro-nc.gov

Assistant City Manager **(Vacant)** .... (336) 373-2002

Assistant City Manager **(Vacant)** .... (336) 373-2002

Office of the City Manager *continued*

Small Business Coordinator **Reggie Delahanty** .... (336) 373-4624
Education: Wake Forest BA; Georgia Tech MA

Economic Development and Business Support Manager
Kathi Dubel .... (336) 373-4579
E-mail: kathi.dubel@greensboro-nc.gov

Budget and Evaluation

P.O. Box 3136, Greensboro, NC 27402-3136
Internet: www.greensboro-nc.gov/Departments/Budget

Director **Larry Davis** .... (336) 373-2291
E-mail: larry.davis@greensboro-nc.gov

Community Relations

P.O. Box3136, Greensboro, NC 27402
Fax: (336) 373-4656

Director **Donna Gray** .... (336) 373-4583
E-mail: donna.gray@greensboro-nc.gov

Communications and Marketing Department

P.O. Box 3136, Greensboro, NC 27402-3136
Fax: (336) 373-2117

Communications and Marketing Manager **(Vacant)** .... (336) 373-2105

Emergency Management

P.O. Box 3136, Greensboro, NC 27402-3136
Fax: (336) 373-2557 Internet: www.greensboroready.com

Coordinator **Jim Robinson** .... (336) 574-4082
E-mail: jim.robinson@greensboro-nc.gov

Engineering and Inspections

P.O. Box 3136, Greensboro, NC 27402-3136
Fax: (336) 373-2338
Internet: www.greensboro-nc.gov/departments/engineering

Director **Kenney McDowell** .... (336) 373-4578
E-mail: kenney.mcdowell@greensboro-nc.gov

Engineering Division

P.O. Box 3136, Greensboro, NC 27402-3136
Fax: (336) 373-2338

City Engineer **Ted Partrick** .... (336) 373-2302
E-mail: ted.partrick@greensboro-nc.gov

Facilities Construction Division

P.O. Box 3136, Greensboro, NC 27402-3136

Division Manager **Butch Shumate** .... (336) 412-5794
E-mail: butch.shumate@greensboro-nc.gov

Field Operations Department

P.O. Box 3136, Greensboro, NC 27402-3136
Internet: www.greensboro-nc.gov/Departments/fieldops/

Director **Dale Wyrick** .... (336) 373-2783
E-mail: dale.wyrick@greensboro-nc.gov

Solid Waste Division Manager **Sheldon D. Smith** .... (336) 373-4379

Financial and Administrative Services

P.O. Box 3136, Greensboro, NC 27402-3136
Fax: (336) 373-2138
Internet: www.greensboro-nc.gov/departments/finance1

Director **Rick Lusk** .... (336) 373-2077

Collections Division

P.O. Box 3136, Greensboro, NC 27402-3136
Fax: (336) 373-4393

Collections Manager **Teresa Childress** .... (336) 433-7276
E-mail: teresa.childress@greensboro-nc.gov

★ Elected Official ▲ Appointed by Legislature ▼ Appointed by Governor ▶ Appointed by Board or Commission ● Appointed by Judge
■ Appointed by Mayor △ Appointed by Freeholders ▽ Appointed by Supervisor ▷ Appointed by County Executive ○ Appointed by Council

Purchasing Division
P.O. Box 3136, Greensboro, NC 27401-3136
Fax: (336) 373-2544

Purchasing Director **Dale Dillon** . . . . . (336) 373-2300
E-mail: dale.dillon@greensboro-nc.gov

Fire Department
P.O. Box 3136, Greensboro, NC 27402-3136
Tel: (336) 373-2356
Internet: www.greensboro-nc.gov/departments/fire/default.htm

Fire Chief **Bobby Nugent** . . . . . (336) 574-4088
E-mail: bobby.nugent@greensboro-nc.gov
Deputy Chief **Clarence Hunter** . . . . . (336) 373-2357
E-mail: clarence.hunter@greensboro-nc.gov
Deputy Chief/Business Services **(Vacant)** . . . . . (336) 373-2187

Greensboro Coliseum Complex
P.O. Box 3136, Greensboro, NC 27402-3136
Internet: www.greensborocoliseum.com/

Managing Director **Matt Brown** . . . . . (336) 373-7406

Greensboro Housing Authority
450 North Church Street, Greensboro, NC 27401
Tel: (336) 275-8501 Fax: (336) 378-1307 Internet: www.gha-nc.org/

President and Chief Executive Officer
Tina Akers Brown . . . . . (336) 303-3116
Chief Operating Officer **James Cox** . . . . . (336) 303-3004
Chief Financial Officer **Nancy Thomas** . . . . . (336) 275-8501
Fax: (336) 271-3319

Historical Museum
P.O. Box 3136, Greensboro, NC 27402-3136
Fax: (336) 373-2204 Internet: www.greensborohistory.org

Director **Carol Hart** . . . . . (336) 373-2306

Human Relations
P.O. Box 3136, Greensboro, NC 27402-3136
Internet: www.greensboro-nc.gov/departments/relations/default.htm

Director **Dr. Love Crossling** . . . . . (336) 373-2038
E-mail: love.crossling@greensboro-nc.gov

Human Resources
P.O. Box 3136, Greensboro, NC 27402-3136
Fax: (336) 373-2511

Director **Connie Hammond** . . . . . (336) 373-4629
E-mail: connie.hammond@greensboro-nc.gov

Information Technology Department
P.O. Box 3136, Greensboro, NC 27402-3136

Director **Jane Nickles** . . . . . (336) 373-2490
E-mail: jane.nickles@greensboro-nc.gov
Geographic Information Services Manager
Steve Averett . . . . . (336) 373-2057
E-mail: steve.averett@greensboro-nc.gov

Libraries
P.O. Box 3136, Greensboro, NC 27402-3136
Fax: (336) 333-6781 Internet: www.greensborolibrary.org

Director **Brigitte Blanton** . . . . . (336) 373-2699
E-mail: brigitte.blanton@greensboro-nc.gov
Education: North Carolina BA; North Carolina Greensboro MLS

Minority/Women's Business Program [MWBE]
P.O. Box 3136, Greensboro, NC 27402-3136
Internet: www.greensboro-nc.gov/departments/executive/mwbe

Coordinator **Gwen Carter** . . . . . (336) 373-2674

Neighborhood Development Department
P.O. Box 3136, Greensboro, NC 27402-3136
Tel: (336) 373-2349

Director **Barbara Harris** . . . . . (336) 373-2509
E-mail: barbara.harris@greensboro-nc.gov

Parks and Recreation
P.O. Box 3136, Greensboro, NC 27402-3136
Internet: www.greensboro-nc.gov/departments/parks

Director **Wade Walcutt** . . . . . (336) 373-2964

Planning Department
P.O. Box 3136, Greensboro, NC 27402-3136
Internet: www.greensboro-nc.gov/departments/hcd/default.htm

Director **Sue Schwartz** . . . . . (336) 373-2149
E-mail: sue.schwartz@greensboro-nc.gov
Education: Pittsburgh BS; North Carolina Charlotte MA

Police Department
P.O. Box 3136, Greensboro, NC 27402-3136

Police Chief **Wayne Scott** . . . . . (336) 373-2450
Deputy Police Chief **Brian Cheek** . . . . . (336) 373-2450
Deputy Police Chief **James Hinson** . . . . . (336) 373-2450
Deputy Police Chief **Joe Smith** . . . . . (336) 373-2450
Deputy Police Chief **(Vacant)** . . . . . (336) 373-2450

Transportation
P.O. Box 3136, Greensboro, NC 27402-3136
Internet: www.greensboro-nc.gov/departments/GDOT/

Director **Adam Fischer** . . . . . (336) 373-4368

Water Resources Department
P.O. Box 3136, Greensboro, NC 27402-3136
Internet: www.greensboro-nc.gov/departments/water/

Director **Steven Drew** . . . . . (336) 373-2055
Education: North Carolina Greensboro BA
Manager **(Vacant)** . . . . . (336) 373-4578

Stormwater Management Division
P.O. Box 3136, Greensboro, NC 27402
Fax: (336) 412-6305
Internet: www.greensboro-nc.gov/Departments/Water/stormwater/

Operations Management Supervisor **David Phlegar** . . . . . (336) 373-2707
E-mail: david.phlegar@greensboro-nc.gov
Planning and Engineering Supervisor
Michael "Mike" Borchers . . . . . (336) 373-2494
E-mail: michael.borchers@greensboro-nc.gov
Water Quality Supervisor **Barry Parsons** . . . . . (336) 373-7643

Water Reclamation Division
Supervisor **Lori Cooper** . . . . . (336) 373-4502
Fax: (336) 373-7720
North Buffalo Water Reclamation Facility
Superintendent **Ed Osborne** . . . . . (336) 433-7224
2199 White Street, Greensboro, NC 27405 Fax: (336) 373-7585
Industrial Waste and Laboratory Services Supervisor
Martie Groome . . . . . (336) 433-7229

★ Elected Official ▲ Appointed by Legislature ▼ Appointed by Governor ► Appointed by Board or Commission ● Appointed by Judge
■ Appointed by Mayor △ Appointed by Freeholders ▽ Appointed by Supervisor ▷ Appointed by County Executive ○ Appointed by Council

City of Gresham, Oregon

1333 NW Eastman Parkway, Gresham, OR 97030
Tel: (503) 661-3000 Internet: http://greshamoregon.gov/

County: Multnomah **Election Type:** Nonpartisan **Year Incorporated:** 1905 **Population:** 110,553 (2015)

Office of the Mayor and City Council

1333 NW Eastman Parkway, Gresham, OR 97030
Tel: (503) 618-2871

★ Mayor **Shane Bemis** .... (503) 618-2584
Began Service: January 2, 2007
Term Expires: December 31, 2018
E-mail: mayorbemis@greshamoregon.gov

★ Council President **Mario Palmero** (Position 4) .... (503) 618-2871
Term Expires: December 31, 2018
E-mail: mario.palmero@greshamoregon.gov

★ Councilor **Jerry Hinton** (Position 1) .... (503) 618-2871
Term Expires: December 31, 2016
E-mail: jerry.hinton@greshamoregon.gov

★ Councilor **Kirk French** (Position 2) .... (503) 618-2254
Term Expires: December 31, 2018
E-mail: kirk.french@greshamoregon.gov

★ Councilor **Karylinn Echols** (Position 3) .... (503) 618-2426
Term Expires: December 31, 2016
E-mail: karylinn.echols@greshamoregon.gov

★ Councilor **David Widmark** (Position 5) .... (503) 618-2871
Term Expires: December 31, 2016
E-mail: david.widmark@greshamoregon.gov

★ Councilor **Lori Stegmann** (Position 6) .... (503) 618-2871
Term Expires: December 31, 2018
E-mail: lori.stegmann@greshamoregon.gov

Office of the City Manager

1333 NW Eastman Parkway, 3rd Floor, Gresham, OR 97030
Fax: (503) 618-3301

○ City Manager **Erik Kvarsten** .... (503) 618-2871
E-mail: Teresa.Hall@GreshamOregon.gov
Education: Oregon BA

Assistant City Manager **Rachael Fuller** .... (503) 618-2255
E-mail: rachael.fuller@greshamoregon.gov

Public Affairs Director **Elizabeth Coffey** .... (503) 618-2247
E-mail: Elizabeth.Coffey@GreshamOregon.gov

City Attorney's Office

1333 NW Eastman Parkway, 3rd Floor, Gresham, OR 97030
Fax: (503) 667-3031

City Attorney **David R. Ris** .... (503) 661-3000
E-mail: caomail@greshamoregon.gov

Community Development Services

1333 NW Eastman Parkway, Gresham, OR 97030
Fax: (503) 618-2333

Director **Eric Schmidt** .... (503) 618-2860
E-mail: alexandra.walker@greshamoregon.gov

Building Division

1333 NW Eastman Parkway, 2nd Floor, Gresham, OR 97030
Fax: (503) 492-4291

Assistant Building Official **Mark Krenz** .... (503) 618-2172

Code Compliance Division

1333 NW Eastman Parkway, 1st Floor, Gresham, OR 97030
Fax: (503) 618-2309

Senior Code Officer **Rita Humphrey** .... (503) 618-2463

Economic Development Services

1333 NW Eastman Parkway, Gresham, OR 97030
Fax: (503) 618-2640

Director **Shannon Stadey** .... (503) 618-2640
E-mail: Shannon.Stadey@GreshamOregon.gov

Environmental Services

1333 NW Eastman Parkway, 2nd Floor, Gresham, OR 97030
Fax: (503) 661-5927

Director **Steve Fancher** .... (503) 618-2583
Education: Alabama Birmingham BS, MBA

Recycling and Solid Waste Division

1333 NW Eastman Parkway, 2nd Floor, Gresham, OR 97030
Fax: (503) 661-5927

Manager **(Vacant)** .... (503) 618-2525

Transportation and Streets Division

1333 NW Eastman Parkway, 2nd Floor, Gresham, OR 97030
Fax: (503) 661-5927

Manager **Chris Strong** .... (503) 618-2563

Water Division

1333 NW Eastman Parkway, 2nd Floor, Gresham, OR 97030
Fax: (503) 661-5927

Manager **Brian Stahl** .... (503) 618-2525

Wastewater Services Division

1333 NW Eastman Parkway, 2nd Floor, Gresham, OR 97030
Fax: (503) 661-5927

Director **Brian Stahl** .... (503) 618-2525

Watershed Management Division

1333 NW Eastman Parkway, 2nd Floor, Gresham, OR 97030
Fax: (503) 661-5927

Manager **Brian Stahl** .... (503) 618-2525

Finance and Management Services

1333 NW Eastman Parkway, 3rd Floor, Gresham, OR 97030
Fax: (503) 661-6073

Finance Director **Bernard Seeger** .... (503) 618-2445

Fire Department

1333 NW Eastman Parkway, Gresham, OR 97030
Fax: (503) 666-8330

Fire Chief **Greg Matthews** .... (503) 618-2355
E-mail: gfes@greshamoregon.gov

Human Resources

1333 NW Eastman Parkway, 3rd Floor, Gresham, OR 97030
Fax: (503) 665-4553

Director **Karen Pearson** .... (503) 618-2308
E-mail: Karen.Pearson@GreshamOregon.gov

Information Technology Department

1333 NW Eastman Parkway, 3rd, Gresham, OR 97030
Fax: (503) 661-6073

Director **Patrick Hartley** .... (503) 618-2520
E-mail: pat.hartley@greshamoregon.gov

Police Department

1333 NW Eastman Parkway, Gresham, OR 97030
Fax: (503) 618-2750

Chief of Police **Craig Junginger** .... (503) 618-2318

★ Elected Official ▲ Appointed by Legislature ▼ Appointed by Governor ► Appointed by Board or Commission ● Appointed by Judge
■ Appointed by Mayor △ Appointed by Freeholders ▽ Appointed by Supervisor ▷ Appointed by County Executive ○ Appointed by Council

Urban Design and Planning Services
1333 NW Eastman Parkway, 2nd Floor, Gresham, OR 97030
Fax: (503) 618-2333

Urban Design Manager **David Berniker** .... (503) 618-2235
Comprehensive Planning Director **David Berniker** .... (503) 618-2235

City of Hampton, Virginia
22 Lincoln St., Hampton, VA 23669
Tel: (757) 727-8311 (Information) Internet: http://www.hampton.gov

County: None **Election Type:** Nonpartisan **Population:** 136,454 (2015)

Office of the Mayor and City Council
22 Lincoln St., Hampton, VA 23669
Fax: (757) 728-3037 E-mail: council@hampton.gov

★Mayor-Elect **Donnie R. Tuck** .... (757) 826-9078
Began Service: July 1, 2016
Term Expires: June 30, 2020
E-mail: dtuck@hampton.gov
Education: Duke 1976 BA; Old Dominion 1993 MPA

★Vice Mayor **Linda D. Curtis** .... (757) 727-6315
Term Expires: June 30, 2020
E-mail: lcurtis@hampton.gov

★Council Member-Elect **Jimmy Gray** .... (757) 727-6315
Term Expires: June 30, 2018

★Council Member **W.H. "Billy" Hobbs** .... (757) 727-6315
Term Expires: June 30, 2020
E-mail: bhobbs@hampton.gov

★Council Member **Will J. Moffett** .... (757) 727-6315
Term Expires: June 30, 2018
E-mail: wmoffett@hampton.gov

★Council Member **Teresa Vanasse Schmidt** .... (757) 727-6315
Term Expires: June 30, 2018
E-mail: tvschmidt@hampton.gov

★Council Member **Chris Snead** .... (757) 727-6315
Term Expires: June 30, 2020
E-mail: csnead@hampton.gov

Office of the City Attorney
22 Lincoln St., Hampton, VA 23669
Fax: (757) 727-6788

○City Attorney **Vanessa T. Valldejuli** .... (757) 727-6127
E-mail: vvalldejuli@hampton.gov

Office of the Commissioner of Revenue
One Franklin Street, Suite 101, Hampton, VA 23669
Fax: (757) 727-6330

★Commissioner of Revenue **Ross A. Mugler** .... (757) 727-6183
Term Expires: January 1, 2018
E-mail: rmugler@hampton.gov
Education: Old Dominion BS

Office of the Commonwealth's Attorney
236 N. King St., Hampton, VA 23669
Fax: (757) 727-6802

★Commonwealth's Attorney **Anton Bell** .... (757) 727-6442
Term Expires: January 1, 2018
E-mail: abell@hampton.gov

Deputy Commonwealth's Attorney **John Hough** .... (757) 727-6442

Office of the Sheriff
1928 W. Pembroke Ave., Hampton, VA 23661
Fax: (757) 926-2537 Internet: http://www.hampton.va.us/sheriff/

★Sheriff **B. J. Roberts** .... (757) 926-2540
Term Expires: January 1, 2018
E-mail: broberts@hampton.gov
Education: Hampton BS

Office of the Treasurer
One Franklin Street, Suite 100, Hampton, VA 23669
Fax: (757) 727-6796

★Treasurer **Bob Williams** .... (757) 727-6374
Term Expires: January 1, 2018
E-mail: treasurer@hampton.gov
Education: St Leo Col 1995 BS; Troy State 1998 MPA

Office of the City Manager
22 Lincoln St., Hampton, VA 23669
Fax: (757) 728-3037

○City Manager **Mary B. Bunting** .... (757) 727-6392
E-mail: mbunting@hampton.gov

Senior Executive Assistant **Donna L. Hodges** .... (757) 727-6392
E-mail: dlhodges@hampton.gov

Assistant City Manager **Steve Bond** .... (757) 727-6884
E-mail: sbond@hampton.gov

Assistant City Manager **Laura Fitzpatrick** .... (757) 727-6884
E-mail: lafitzpatrick@hampton.gov

Assistant City Manager **James A. Peterson** .... (757) 727-6884
E-mail: ppeterson@hampton.gov

Office of the City Assessor
One Franklin Street, Suite 602, Hampton, VA 23669
Fax: (757) 728-3510

City Assessor **Brian E. Gordineer** .... (757) 727-8311
E-mail: bgordineer@hampton.gov

Office of the Registrar
Court House, 101 King's Way, Hampton, VA 23669
Fax: (757) 727-6084

Registrar **Tara Morgan** .... (757) 727-6218

Citizen's Unity Commission
22 Lincoln St., Hampton, VA 23669
Fax: (757) 727-1381 E-mail: unity@hampton.gov

Director **Michelle Jones** .... (757) 728-3279
E-mail: mjones@hampton.gov

Community Development Department
22 Lincoln Street, 5th Floor, Hampton, VA 23669
Fax: (757) 728-2449

Director **Terry P. O'Neill** .... (757) 727-6140
E-mail: toneill@hampton.gov

Deputy Director **Steve Shapiro** .... (757) 727-6246
E-mail: sshapiro@hampton.gov

Zoning Administrator **Jeff Conkle** .... (757) 728-5229
E-mail: jconkle@hampton.gov

Convention and Visitor Bureau
1919 Commerce Dr., Suite 290, Hampton, VA 23666
Fax: (757) 727-1310 E-mail: hct@hampton.gov
Internet: http://www.hamptoncvb.com

Director **Mary Fugere** .... (757) 728-5327
Fax: (757) 727-1310

Hampton Coliseum Director **Joe Tsao** .... (757) 838-5650
1000 Coliseum Dr., Hampton, VA 23666 Fax: (757) 838-2595

★Elected Official ▲Appointed by Legislature ▼Appointed by Governor ▶Appointed by Board or Commission ●Appointed by Judge
■Appointed by Mayor △Appointed by Freeholders ▽Appointed by Supervisor ▷Appointed by County Executive ○Appointed by Council

Economic Development Department
One Franklin Street, Suite 600, Hampton, VA 23669
Fax: (757) 727-6895

Director **Leonard Sledge** .... (757) 727-6237
E-mail: business@hampton.gov

Finance Department
22 Lincoln St., Hampton, VA 23669

Director **Karl Daughtry** .... (757) 727-6230
Procurement Manager **Lavina "Lin" Whitley** .... (757) 727-2200
E-mail: lavinia.whitley@hampton.gov Fax: (757) 727-2206

Fire Department
22 Lincoln St., Hampton, VA 23669
Fax: (757) 727-6094

Fire Chief **David E. Layman** .... (757) 727-6580
E-mail: dlayman@hampton.gov
Emergency Management Director **Hui-Shan Walker** ..... (757) 727-6414
E-mail: hwalker@hampton.gov

Fleet Services
413 North Armistead Avenue, Hampton, VA 23669
Fax: (757) 727-1981

Fleet Manager **Rick Russ** .... (757) 726-2960

Human Resources Department
22 Lincoln St., Hampton, VA 23669
Fax: (757) 727-6449 E-mail: hrdept@hampton.gov

Director **Nicole Clark** .... (757) 727-6407
E-mail: hrdept@hampton.gov

Information Technology Department
22 Lincoln St., Hampton, VA 23669
Fax: (757) 727-6631

Director **Leslie Fuentes** .... (757) 727-6350
E-mail: lfuentes@hampton.gov

Library, Hampton Public
4207 Victoria Blvd., Hampton, VA 23669
Fax: (757) 727-1152

Director **Valerie Gardner** .... (757) 727-1154
E-mail: vgardner@hampton.gov

Parks and Recreation Department
22 Lincoln St., Hampton, VA 23669
Fax: (757) 726-6980

Director **Jim Wilson** .... (757) 727-6347
Arts Commissioner **(Vacant)** .... (757) 722-2787

Police Department
40 Lincoln St., Hampton, VA 23669
Fax: (757) 727-6774

Police Chief **Terry L. Sult** .... (757) 727-6510
Education: Gardner-Webb BS; Pfeiffer U MBA

Public Works Department
22 Lincoln St., Hampton, VA 23669
Fax: (757) 727-6123

Director **Lynn Allsbrook** .... (757) 727-6346

Redevelopment and Housing Authority
22 Lincoln St., Hampton, VA 23669
Fax: (757) 727-6368 Internet: http://hrha.org/

Executive Director **Ronald Jackson** .... (757) 727-6493
E-mail: rjackson@hampton.gov
Education: Cincinnati BABA; Old Dominion MPA

Risk Management Department
22 Lincoln St., Hampton, VA 23669
Fax: (757) 727-1470

Director **Joe Sanders** .... (757) 727-6617
E-mail: jsanders@hampton.gov

Social Services Department
4320 LaSalle Ave., Hampton, VA 23669
P.O. Box 9347, Hampton, VA 23669
Fax: (757) 727-1835

Director **Wanda Rogers** .... (757) 727-1821

Hampton City Schools
One Franklin St., Hampton, VA 23666
Fax: (757) 727-2003

Superintendent of Schools **Dr. Jeffery O. Smith** .... (757) 727-2030

City of Harrisburg, Pennsylvania
10 North Second Street, Harrisburg, PA 17101-1680
Internet: www.harrisburgpa.gov

County: Dauphin **Election Type:** Partisan **Population:** 49,081 (2015)

Office of the Mayor and City Council
10 North Second Street, Suite 305, Harrisburg, PA 17101-1680

★Mayor **Eric Papenfuse** (D) .... (717) 255-3040
Began Service: January 6, 2014
Term Expires: January 2018
E-mail: epapenfuse@cityofhbg.com
Education: Yale BA, MA
Senior Advisor to the Mayor **Karl Singleton** .... (717) 255-3040
Communications Director **Joyce Davis** .... (717) 255-3040
★Council President **Wanda Williams** (D) .... (717) 255-3060
Term Expires: January 7, 2018
E-mail: wwilliams@cityofhbg.com
★Council Member **Ben Allatt** (D) .... (717) 255-3060
Term Expires: January 2018
E-mail: ballatt@cityofhbg.com
★Council Member **Jeffrey Baltimore** (D) .... (717) 255-3060
Term Expires: January 2020
E-mail: jbaltimore@cityofhbg.com
★Council Member **Shamaine Daniels** (D) .... (717) 255-3060
Term Expires: January 2018
E-mail: sdaniels@cityofhbg.com
★Council Member **Destini Y. Hodges** .... (717) 255-3060
Term Expires: January 2018
★Council Member **Cornelius Johnson** .... (717) 255-3060
Term Expires: January 2020
★Council Member **Westburn Majors** .... (717) 255-3060
Term Expires: January 2020

Office of the Business Administrator
10 North Second Street, Harrisburg, PA 17101-1680
Tel: (717) 255-3004

■Chief of Staff/Business Administrator **(Vacant)** .... (717) 255-3004
Deputy Chief of Staff/Business Administrator **(Vacant)** ... (717) 255-3004
■Director of Human Resources **Joni Willingham** .... (717) 255-6475
E-mail: jwillingham@cityofhbg.com

★Elected Official ▲Appointed by Legislature ▼Appointed by Governor ▶Appointed by Board or Commission ●Appointed by Judge
■Appointed by Mayor △Appointed by Freeholders ▽Appointed by Supervisor ▷Appointed by County Executive ○Appointed by Council

Office of the City Clerk
10 North Second Street, Harrisburg, PA 17101-1680
Fax: (717) 255-3081

City Clerk **Kirk Petroski** . . . . . (717) 255-3060
E-mail: kpetroski@cityofhbg.com

Office of the Controller
10 North Second Street, Harrisburg, PA 17101-1680

★ Controller **Charles DeBrunner** (D) . . . . . (717) 255-3070
Term Expires: January 2018
E-mail: cdebrunner@cityofhbg.com
Education: Susquehanna; Penn State MPA

Office of the Solicitor
10 North Second Street, Harrisburg, PA 17101-1680

■ Solicitor **Neil Grover** . . . . . (717) 255-3065
E-mail: ngrover@cityofhbg.com
Deputy City Solicitor **Doug Walmer** . . . . . (717) 255-3065
Assistant City Solicitor **Rebecca Kunkel** . . . . . (717) 255-3065

Office of the Treasurer
10 North Second Street, Harrisburg, PA 17101-1680

★ Treasurer **Tyrell Spradley** . . . . . (717) 255-3046
Term Expires: January 5, 2020
E-mail: tspradley@cityofhbg.com

Arts, Culture and Tourism Department
10 North Second Street, Suite 405, Harrisburg, PA 17101-1680

Director **(Vacant)** . . . . . (717) 255-3020

Building and Housing Development Department
10 North Second Street, Harrisburg, PA 17101-1680

Director **Roy Christ** . . . . . (717) 255-6480
Deputy Director **Dave Patton** . . . . . (717) 255-6553

Office of Financial Management
10 North Second Street, Harrisburg, PA 17101-1680

■ Director of Financial Management **Bruce Weber** . . . . . (717) 255-6474
E-mail: bweber@cityofhbg.com

Fire Department
123 Walnut St., Harrisburg, PA 17101-1693

■ Fire Chief (Acting) **Brian Enterline** . . . . . (717) 255-6465
E-mail: benterline@cityofhbg.com

Harrisburg School District
Building #2, 2101 North Front Street, Harrisburg, PA 17110-1081
Tel: (717) 703-4000

Superintendent **Dr. Sybil Knight-Burney** . . . . . (717) 703-4022
Chief Recovery Officer **Dr. Audrey Utley** . . . . . (717) 703-4000
Note: Appointed by the Pennsylvania Secretary of Education

Police Department
123 Walnut St., Harrisburg, PA 17101-1693

■ Police Chief **Thomas Carter** . . . . . (717) 255-3103
E-mail: tcarter@cityofhbg.com

Public Works Department
1690 S. 19th St., Harrisburg, PA 17104-3204

■ Director (Acting) **Aaron Johnson** . . . . . (717) 236-4802
E-mail: ajohnson@cityofhbg.com
Bureau of Water Director **Raly Bey** . . . . . (717) 238-8725
Harrisburg Authority Executive Director
Shannon G. Williams . . . . . (717) 525-7677
212 Locust Street, Fax: (717) 525-7688
Suite 302, Harrisburg, PA 17101

Town and City of Hartford, Connecticut
City Hall, 550 Main St., Hartford, CT 06103
Tel: (860) 757-9563 (Information) Internet: www.hartford.gov

County: Hartford **Election Type:** Partisan **Year Incorporated:** 1784
Population: 124,006 (2015)

Office of the Mayor
550 Main Street, Hartford, CT 06103
Fax: (860) 722-6606 Internet: www.hartford.gov/mayors-office

★ Mayor **Luke A. Bronin** . . . . . (860) 757-9500
Began Service: January 4, 2016
Term Expires: December 31, 2019
Education: Yale 1997 BA; Oxford (UK) MA; Yale JD
■ Executive Assistant **Mubera Becirovic** . . . . . (860) 757-9500
■ Chief of Staff **Thea Montanez** . . . . . (860) 757-9500
Education: Syracuse
■ Director of Communications and New Media
Brett Broesder . . . . . (860) 757-9731
E-mail: brett.broesder@hartford.gov
Education: Rhode Island Col BA
Director of Community Engagement **Janice Castle** . . . . . (860) 757-9563
Director of Intergovernmental Affairs **DeVaughn Ward** . . . (860) 757-9563

Office of the Town and City Clerk
City Hall, 550 Main St., Room 105, Hartford, CT 06103
Fax: (860) 722-8041

○ Town and City Clerk **John V. Bazzano** (D) . . . . . (860) 757-9755
E-mail: bazzj001@hartford.gov

Office of the Corporation Counsel
City Hall, 550 Main St., Hartford, CT 06103
Fax: (860) 722-8114 Internet: http://www.hartford.gov/corporation-counsel

■ Corporation Counsel **Howard G. Rifkin** . . . . . (860) 757-9700
E-mail: howard.rifkin@hartford.gov

Development Services Department
250 Constitution Plaza, 4th Floor, Hartford, CT 06103
Fax: (860) 722-6630

Director **Thomas E. Deller** . . . . . (860) 757-9040
E-mail: tdeller@hartford.gov
Economic Development Division Director
Stephen Cole . . . . . (860) 757-9077
E-mail: wibenjamin@hartford.gov
Housing Director **Brian Matthews** . . . . . (860) 757-9005
Fax: (860) 722-6444
Licenses and Inspections Division Director **Daniel Loos** . . (860) 757-9235
260 Constitution Plaza, 1st Floor, Hartford, CT 06103
Planning Division Director **(Vacant)** . . . . . (860) 757-9054

Families, Children, Youth and Recreation Department
City Hall, 550 Main Street, Hartford, CT 06103
Tel: (860) 757-4881 Fax: (860) 722-6001

Executive Director **Dr. Jose F. Colon-Rivas** . . . . . (860) 757-4885
Education: Puerto Rico BA; Inter American MA; Penn State PhD
Assistant Director **Troy C. Stewart** . . . . . (860) 757-4885

Finance Department
City Hall, 550 Main St., Hartford, CT 06103
Fax: (860) 722-6024 ext. 79606

Director (Acting) **Leigh Ann Ralls** . . . . . (860) 757-9665

★ Elected Official ▲ Appointed by Legislature ▼ Appointed by Governor ▶ Appointed by Board or Commission ● Appointed by Judge
■ Appointed by Mayor △ Appointed by Freeholders ▽ Appointed by Supervisor ▷ Appointed by County Executive ○ Appointed by Council

Assessment Division
City Hall, 550 Main Street, Room 108, Hartford, CT 06103
Tel: (860) 757-9640 Fax: (860) 722-6142

Assessor **John S. Philip** . . . . (860) 757-9645
E-mail: philj002@hartford.gov

Fire Department
275 Pearl St., Hartford, CT 06103
Tel: (860) 757-4500 Fax: (860) 722-8205 Internet: www.hartford.gov/fire

Fire Chief **Reginald D. Freeman** . . . . (860) 757-4500
Fire Prevention Chief/Fire Marshal **Roger Martin** . . . . (860) 757-4530
E-mail: martr002@hartford.gov Fax: (860) 722-8249
Assistant Chief, Emergency Services **Darren Hudson** . . . . (860) 757-4500
Assistant Chief, Support Services **Frank Costello** . . . . (860) 757-4500
Executive Assistant **Janice Rodriguez** . . . . (860) 757-4500
E-mail: jrodriguez@hartford.gov

Department of Health and Human Services
131 Coventry Street, Hartford, CT 06112
Fax: (860) 722-6851 Internet: http://www.hartford.gov/hhs

Director **Dr. Gary Rhule** . . . . (860) 757-4744
Education: Rochester 1988 MD

Department of Human Resources
City Hall, 550 Main St., Hartford, CT 06103
Tel: (860) 757-9800 Fax: (860) 722-8042

Human Resources and Labor Relations Director
Henry Burgos . . . . (860) 757-9800
E-mail: henry.burgos@hartford.gov
Assistant Human Resources Director **Debra Carabillo** . . . . (860) 757-9817
E-mail: colld002@hartford.gov

Management, Budget and Grants Department
City Hall, 550 Main Street, Hartford, CT 06103
Fax: (860) 722-6158

Management and Budget Director **Melissa McCaw** . . . . . . (860) 757-9554
E-mail: melissa.mccaw@hartford.gov

Police Department
253 High Street, Hartford, CT 06103
Tel: (860) 757-4000 Fax: (860) 722-8270
Internet: www.hartford.gov/Police/

■ Chief of Police **James C. Rovella** . . . . (860) 757-4010
E-mail: policechief@hartford.gov
Assistant Police Chief **(Vacant)** . . . . (860) 757-4010
Deputy Chief of Police **Neville Brooks** . . . . (860) 757-4307
Deputy Chief of Police **Joseph Buyak** . . . . (860) 757-4010
Deputy Chief of Police **Brian Foley** . . . . (860) 757-4000
Deputy Chief of Police **Robert E. Ford** . . . . (860) 757-4000
Deputy Chief of Police **William Long III** . . . . (860) 757-4000
Deputy Chief of Police **Dustin Rendock** . . . . (860) 757-4000

Hartford Public Library
500 Main St., Hartford, CT 06103-3075
Tel: (860) 695-6300 Fax: (860) 722-6900 Internet: http://www.hplct.org

Chief Executive Officer (Interim) **Mary Tzambazakis** . . . . (860) 695-6312
E-mail: mtzambazakis@hplct.org
Senior Executive Assistant **Andrea Figueroa** . . . . (860) 695-6348
E-mail: afigueroa@hplct.org

Department of Public Works
50 Jennings Road, 2nd Floor, Hartford, CT 06120
Fax: (860) 722-6215

Director **Keith Chapman** . . . . (860) 757-9900
E-mail: kchapman@hartford.gov

Court of Common Council
City Hall, 550 Main St., 2nd Floor, Room 208, Hartford, CT 06103
Fax: (860) 722-6591

★ Council President **Thomas "T.J." Clarke** (D) . . . . (860) 757-9560
Term Expires: December 31, 2019
★ Council Member **Wildaliz Bermudez** . . . . (860) 757-9560
Term Expires: December 31, 2019
E-mail: wildaliz.bermudez@hartford.gov
★ Council Member **Julio Concepción** (D) . . . . (860) 757-9560
Term Expires: December 31, 2019
★ Council Member **Larry Deutsch** . . . . (860) 757-9577
Term Expires: December 31, 2019
E-mail: deutl001@hartford.gov
★ Council Member **John Gale** (D) . . . . (860) 757-9560
Term Expires: December 31, 2019
★ Council Member **Cynthia Jennings** . . . . (860) 757-9572
Term Expires: December 31, 2019
E-mail: jennc002@hartford.gov
★ Council Member **James Sanchez** (D) . . . . (860) 757-9560
Term Expires: December 31, 2019
★ Council Member **Gwendolyn H. Thames** (D) . . . . (860) 757-9560
Term Expires: December 31, 2019
★ Council Member **Rosenzina Joyce "rJo" Winch** (D) . . . . (860) 757-9560
Term Expires: December 31, 2019

Office of the City Treasurer
550 Main Street, Hartford, CT 06103
Fax: (860) 722-6126 Internet: http://www.hartford.gov/treasurer

★ City Treasurer **Adam Morgan Cloud** . . . . (860) 757-9110
Term Expires: December 31, 2019
E-mail: acloud@hartford.gov

Office of the Registrars of Voters
City Hall, 550 Main St., Hartford, CT 06103
Fax: (860) 722-6331

★ Democratic Registrar of Voters **Olga Iris Vázquez** . . . . . . (860) 757-9839
Term Expires: January 2017
★ Republican Registrar of Voters **Sheila N. Hall** . . . . (860) 757-9832
Term Expires: January 2017
E-mail: halls002@hartford.com
★ Working Families Registrar of Voters **Shari Williams** . . . . (860) 757-9849
Term Expires: January 2017

Hartford Public Schools
960 Main Street, 8th Floor, Hartford, CT 06103
Fax: (860) 722-8502 Internet: http://www.hartfordschools.org

Superintendent **Beth Schiavino-Narvaez** . . . . (860) 695-8401
Chief Financial Officer **Paula Altieri** . . . . (860) 695-8419
Chief Academic Officer **Kathleen England** . . . . (860) 695-8833
Chief of Staff **Dr. Gislaine Ngounou** . . . . (860) 695-8425
Director of Communications and Marketing
Pedro Zayas . . . . (860) 695-8862
E-mail: pedro.zayas@hartfordschools.org
Chief Labor and Legal Services Officer
Jill Cutler Hodgman . . . . (860) 695-8412
E-mail: jcutler-hodgeman@hartfordschools.org

★ Elected Official ▲ Appointed by Legislature ▼ Appointed by Governor ▶ Appointed by Board or Commission ● Appointed by Judge
■ Appointed by Mayor △ Appointed by Freeholders ▽ Appointed by Supervisor ▷ Appointed by County Executive ○ Appointed by Council

City of Hayward, California

City Hall, 777 B Street, Hayward, CA 94541
Internet: www.hayward-ca.gov

County: Alameda **Election Type:** Nonpartisan **Charter:** 1956
Population: 158,289 (2015)

Mayor and City Council

City Hall, 777 B Street, Hayward, CA 94541
Fax: (510) 583-3601

★Mayor **Barbara Halliday** .... (510) 583-4340
Began Service: July 2014
Term Expires: July 2018
E-mail: Barbara.Halliday@hayward-ca.gov

★Mayor Pro Tem **Al Mendall** .... (510) 583-4353
Term Expires: July 2016
E-mail: al.mendall@hayward-ca.gov

★Council Member **Greg Jones** .... (510) 583-4355
Term Expires: July 2016
E-mail: greg.jones@hayward-ca.gov

★Council Member **Sara Lamnin** .... (510) 583-4358
Term Expires: July 2018
E-mail: Sara.Lamnin@hayward-ca.gov

★Council Member **Elisa Márquez** .... (510) 583-4357
Term Expires: July 2016
E-mail: Elisa.Marquez@hayward-ca.gov

★Council Member **Marvin Peixoto** .... (510) 583-4356
Term Expires: July 2018
E-mail: marvin.peixoto@hayward-ca.gov

★Council Member **Francisco Zermeño** .... (510) 583-4352
Term Expires: July 2016
E-mail: francisco.zermeno@hayward-ca.gov

Office of the City Manager

City Hall, 777 B St., Hayward, CA 94541
Fax: (510) 583-3601

○City Manager **Fran David** .... (510) 583-4302
E-mail: fran.david@hayward-ca.gov
Education: Cal State (East Bay) BS; Golden Gate MBA

Assistant City Manager **Kelly McAdoo** .... (510) 583-4305
E-mail: kelly.mcadoo@hayward-ca.gov

Office of the City Attorney

City Hall, 777 B St., Hayward, CA 94541
Fax: (510) 583-3660

○City Attorney **Michael Lawson** .... (510) 583-4455
E-mail: michael.lawson@hayward-ca.gov Fax: (510) 583-3660
Education: Cal State (Hayward) BA; UC Davis JD

Office of the City Clerk

City Hall, 777 B St., Hayward, CA 94541
Fax: (510) 583-3636

○City Clerk **Miriam Lens** .... (510) 583-4401
E-mail: miriam.lens@hayward-ca.gov

Development Services

City Hall, 777 B Street, Hayward, CA 94541
Fax: (510) 583-3650

Director **David Rizk** .... (510) 583-4004
E-mail: david.rizk@hayward-ca.gov

Finance

City Hall, 777 B St., Hayward, CA 94541
Fax: (510) 583-3600

Director **Tracy Vesely** .... (510) 583-4010

Fire

City Hall, 777 B St., Hayward, CA 94541
Fax: (510) 583-3640

Fire Chief **Garrett Contreras** .... (510) 583-4945
E-mail: garrett.contreras@hayward-ca.gov

Human Resources

City Hall, 777 B St., Hayward, CA 94541
Fax: (510) 583-3655

Director **Nina Morris-Collins** .... (510) 583-4544
E-mail: Nina.Collins@hayward-ca.gov

Library and Community Services

835 C St., Hayward, CA 94541
Fax: (510) 733-6669

Director **Sean Reinhart** .... (510) 881-7956
E-mail: sean.reinhart@hayward-ca.gov

Maintenance Services

24505 Soto Road, Hayward, CA 94544
Fax: (510) 538-7080

Director of Maintenance Services **Todd Rullman** .... (510) 881-7746

Facilities Division

24499 Soto Road, Hayward, CA 94544
Fax: (510) 583-3600

Facilities and Building Manager **Allen Koscinski** .... (510) 583-8556
E-mail: Allen.Koscinski@hayward-ca.gov

Street Maintenance Division

16 Barnes Court, Hayward, CA 94544
Fax: (510) 537-0436

Street Maintenance Manager **Rodney Affonso** .... (510) 881-7747
E-mail: rodney.affonso@hayward-ca.gov

Police

300 W. Winton Ave., Hayward, CA 94544
Fax: (510) 293-7183 Internet: http://www.haywardpd.org

Police Chief **Diane Urban** .... (510) 293-7056
Education: Cal State (East Bay) BS; Boston U MA

Public Works

City Hall, 777 B St., Hayward, CA 94541
Fax: (510) 583-3610

Director **Morad Fakhrai** .... (510) 583-4740

Engineering and Transportation Division

Fax: (510) 583-3620

Assistant City Engineer **Yaw Owusu** .... (510) 583-4762
E-mail: yaw.owusu@hayward-ca.gov

Senior Transportation Engineer **Abhishek Parikh** .... (510) 583-4791

Hayward Executive Airport

20301 Skywest Drive, Hayward, CA 94541
Fax: (510) 783-4556

Airport Manager **Doug McNeely** .... (510) 293-5460

Administrative Analyst II **Noemi Dostal** .... (510) 293-5461

Utilities and Environmental Services

City Hall, 777 B Street, Hayward, CA 94541

Director **Alex Ameri** .... (510) 583-4710

Administration Division

Solid Waste Manager **Vera Dahle-Lacaze** .... (510) 583-4700

Management Analyst II **Corinne Ferreyra** .... (510) 583-4713
E-mail: corinne.ferreyra@hayward-ca.gov

★Elected Official ▲Appointed by Legislature ▼Appointed by Governor ▶Appointed by Board or Commission ●Appointed by Judge
■Appointed by Mayor △Appointed by Freeholders ▽Appointed by Supervisor ▷Appointed by County Executive ○Appointed by Council

Administration Division *continued*

Senior Utility Service Representative **Alicia Sargiotto** . . . . (510) 583-4727
E-mail: alicia.sargiotto@hayward-ca.gov

Utilities Division
Fax: (510) 881-7903

Utilities Operations and Maintenance Manager
Bert Weiss . . . . (510) 881-7901
24505 Soto Road, Hayward, CA 94544
E-mail: bert.weiss@hayward-ca.gov
Water Pollution Control Facility Manager **Ray Busch** . . . . (510) 881-5212

Information Technology
City Hall, 777 B Street, Hayward, CA 94541

Director **Adam Kostrzak** . . . . (510) 583-4857
E-mail: adam.kostrzak@hayward-ca.gov

City of Helena, Montana

316 N. Park Ave., Helena, MT 59623
Internet: www.helenamt.gov/

County: Lewis and Clark **Election Type:** Nonpartisan
Population: 30,581 (2015)

Office of the Mayor and City Commission
316 N. Park Ave., Room 321, Helena, MT 59623
Fax: (406) 447-8434

★ Mayor **James E. Smith** . . . . (406) 447-8410
Began Service: January 2002
Term Expires: December 31, 2017
E-mail: jsmith@helenamt.gov
Education: Carroll Col (MT) 1970 BA; Montana State 1992 MPA
Career: Commissioner, Commissioner's Board, City of Helena, Montana (2000-2001)

★ Commissioner **Dan Ellison** . . . . (406) 447-8410
Term Expires: December 31, 2017
E-mail: DEllison@helenamt.gov

★ Commissioner **Robert Farris-Olsen** . . . . (406) 447-8410
Term Expires: December 31, 2019

★ Commissioner **Andres Haladay** . . . . (406) 447-8410
Term Expires: December 31, 2017
E-mail: ahaladay@helenamt.gov
Education: Montana 2010 JD

★ Commissioner **Ed Noonan** . . . . (406) 447-8410
Term Expires: December 31, 2019

City Clerk **Debbie Havens** . . . . (406) 447-8410
E-mail: dhavens@helenamt.gov
Deputy City Clerk **Robyn Brown** . . . . (406) 447-8409

Office of the City Manager
316 N. Park Ave., Room 331, Helena, MT 59623

▶ City Manager **Ron Alles** . . . . (406) 447-8401
E-mail: ralles@helenamt.gov

Office of the City Attorney
316 North Park Avenue, Room 203, Helena, MT 59623

City Attorney **Thomas Jodoin** . . . . (406) 457-8595

Administrative Services
316 N. Park Ave., Room 311, Helena, MT 59623

Director **Glenn Jorgenson** . . . . (406) 447-8406
E-mail: gjorgenson@helenamt.gov

Community Development
316 N. Park Ave., Room 440, Helena, MT 59623
Fax: (460) 447-8460

Director **Sharon Haugen** . . . . (406) 447-8445
E-mail: shaugen@helenamt.gov

Building Division
316 N. Park Ave., Room 435, Helena, MT 59623

Chief Building Official **John Pallister** . . . . (406) 447-8438

Community Facilities Department
340 Neill Avenue, Helena, MT 59601

Director **Gery Carpenter** . . . . (406) 447-8484
E-mail: gcarpenter@helenamt.gov

Civic Center
340 Neill Avenue, Helena, MT 59601

Manager **Diane Stavnes** . . . . (406) 447-8482

Fire Department
300 Neil Avenue, Helena, MT 59601

Fire Chief **Mark Emert** . . . . (406) 447-8470

Human Resource Division
316 N. Park Ave., Room 148, Helena, MT 59623

Human Resource Director **James Sehr** . . . . (406) 447-8405
E-mail: jsehr@helenamt.com

Parks, Recreation and Open Lands
316 N. Park Ave., Room 428, Helena, MT 59623

Parks and Recreation Director **Amy Teegarden** . . . . (406) 447-8462

Police Department
221 Breckenridge, Helena, MT 59601

Chief of Police **Troy McGee** . . . . (406) 447-8476

Public Works Department
316 N. Park Ave., Room 421, Helena, MT 59623

Director **Randall Camp** . . . . (406) 447-8428
Assistant Director **Phil Hauck** . . . . (406) 447-8427

Engineering Division
316 N. Park Ave., Room 417, Helena, MT 59623

City Engineer **Ryan Leland** . . . . (406) 447-8433
E-mail: rleland@helenamt.gov

Fleet Maintenance Division
3001 E. Lyndale, Helena, MT 59601

Superintendent **Ben Sautter** . . . . (406) 447-1565

Solid Waste Division
1975 N. Benton, Helena, MT 59601

Solid Waste Supervisor **Pete Anderson** . . . . (406) 447-8087
Recycling Supervisor **Kim Carley** . . . . (406) 447-8084
316 North Park Avenue, Helena, MT 59623

Street and Traffic Division
3001 E. Lyndale, Helena, MT 59601

Superintendent **Ben Sautter** . . . . (406) 447-1566
Street Supervisor **Harlan Erskine** . . . . (406) 447-1566

Wastewater Treatment Division
2108 Custer Avenue, East, Helena, MT 59602

Water/Wastewater Treatment Superintendent
Donald Clark . . . . (406) 457-8556
Administrative Coordinator **Lynora Rogstad** . . . . (406) 457-8555
E-mail: lrogstad@helenamt.gov

★ Elected Official ▲ Appointed by Legislature ▼ Appointed by Governor ▶ Appointed by Board or Commission ● Appointed by Judge
■ Appointed by Mayor △ Appointed by Freeholders ▽ Appointed by Supervisor ▷ Appointed by County Executive ○ Appointed by Council

Utility Maintenance Division
Fax: (406) 447-1552

Superintendent **Kevin Hart** . . . . (406) 457-8576
Sewer Maintenance Supervisor **Bill Horner** . . . . (406) 457-8576
Water Maintenance Supervisor **(Vacant)** . . . . (406) 457-8574

Town of Hempstead, New York

Town Hall Plaza, One Washington St., Hempstead, NY 11550
Tel: (516) 489-5000 (Information) Internet: www.toh.li

County: Nassau **Election Type:** Partisan **Year Founded:** 1644
Population: 771,018 (2015)

Office of the Town Supervisor and Council Members
Town Hall Plaza, One Washington St., Hempstead, NY 11550

★Town Supervisor **Anthony J. Santino** (R) . . . . (516) 812-3260
Began Service: January 1, 2016
Term Expires: December 31, 2017
E-mail: asantino@tohmail.org
Chief of Staff **Stephen D'Esposito** . . . . (516) 489-5000 ext. 3256

★Council Member
Dorothy L. Goosby (D-District 1) . . . . (516) 489-5000 ext. 4304
Term Expires: December 31, 2017
E-mail: dgoosby@tohmail.org

★Council Member
Edward A. Ambrosino (R-District 2) . . . . (516) 489-5000 ext. 3179
Term Expires: December 31, 2019
E-mail: eambrosino@tohmail.org
Education: NYU 1989 JD

★Council Member **Bruce A. Blakeman** (R-District 3) . . . . (516) 812-3523
Term Expires: December 31, 2019
E-mail: bblakeman@tohmail.org
Education: Arizona State; Cal Western JD

★Council Member **Anthony P. D'Esposito** (R-District 4) . . (516) 812-3242
Term Expires: December 31, 2017
E-mail: adesposito@tohmail.org
Education: Hofstra 2004 BA

★Council Member **Erin King Sweeney** (R-District 5) . . . . (516) 812-3285
Term Expires: December 31, 2019
E-mail: ekingsweeney@tohmail.org

★Council Member **Gary Hudes** (R-District 6) . . . (516) 489-5000 ext. 3180
Term Expires: December 31, 2017
E-mail: ghudes@tohmail.org

►Communications Director **Mike Deery** . . . . (516) 812-3310
E-mail: mdeery@tohmail.org Fax: (516) 481-3183

Office of the Receiver of Taxes
200 N. Franklin St., Hempstead, NY 11550
Fax: (516) 292-9050

★Receiver of Taxes **Donald X. Clavin, Jr.** (R) . . . . (516) 538-1500
Term Expires: December 31, 2019
E-mail: dclavin@tohmail.org
Education: Canisius BA; Hofstra JD

Office of the Town Attorney
Town Hall Plaza, One Washington St., Hempstead, NY 11550

►Town Attorney **Joseph J. Ra** . . . . (516) 489-5000 ext. 3188
E-mail: jra@tohmail.org
►Chief Deputy Town Attorney **Charles Kovit** . . . . (516) 489-5000 ext. 3205

Office of the Town Clerk
Town Hall Plaza, One Washington St., Hempstead, NY 11550
Fax: (516) 481-9124

★Town Clerk **Nasrin G. Ahmad** . . . . (516) 489-5000 ext. 3046
Term Expires: December 31, 2017
E-mail: nahmad@tohmail.org

Office of the Town Comptroller
350 Front St., Hempstead, NY 11550
Fax: (516) 292-7335

►Town Comptroller **Kevin Conroy** . . . . (516) 489-5000 ext. 3169
E-mail: kconroy@tohmail.org

Building Department
Town Hall Plaza, One Washington St., Hempstead, NY 11550
Fax: (516) 483-1573

Commissioner **John E. Rottkamp** . . . . (516) 812-3050

Conservation and Waterways Department
P.O. Box 180, Point Lookout, NY 11569

Commissioner (Acting) **Steve Esposito** . . . . (516) 431-9200

Department of General Services
350 Front St., Hempstead, NY 11550-4037
Fax: (516) 489-0794

►Commissioner **Gerald C. Marino** . . . . (516) 489-5000
E-mail: gmarino@tohmail.org
1st Deputy Commissioner **Thomas O. Dauscher** . . . . (516) 489-5000
E-mail: tdauscher@tohmail.org
2nd Deputy Commissioner **(Vacant)** . . . . (516) 489-5000
3rd Deputy Commissioner **(Vacant)** . . . . (516) 489-5000
Animal Shelter Division Director **Mike Pastore** . . . . (516) 785-5220
3320 Beltagh Avenue, Wantagh, NY 11793
Cemeteries Division Director **(Vacant)** . . . . (516) 483-6500
650 Nassau Rd., Uniondale, NY 11553
Reproduction Division Director **Jim Piedimonte** . . . . (516) 489-5000
E-mail: jpiedimonte@tohmail.org
Traffic Control Director **(Vacant)** . . . . (516) 378-2260
1580 Merrick Rd., Merrick, NY 11566

Highway Department
350 Front St., Hempstead, NY 11550
Fax: (516) 481-0339 Internet: http://toh.li/content/cs/highway.html

►Commissioner **Thomas Toscano** . . . . (516) 489-5000 ext. 3475
E-mail: thomtos@tohmail.org

Human Resources Department
350 Front St., Hempstead, NY 11550-4037
Fax: (516) 489-5750

►Director **William F. Sammon, Jr.** . . . . (516) 489-5000 ext. 3405
E-mail: wsammon@tohmail.org

Information and Technology Department
Town Hall Plaza, One Washington St., Hempstead, NY 11550
Fax: (516) 489-1571

►Commissioner **Arthur Primm** . . . . (516) 489-5000 ext. 3212
E-mail: aprimm@tohmail.org

Department of Occupational Resources [DOOR]
50 Clinton Street, Suite 400, Hempstead, NY 11550
Fax: (516) 485-5009 E-mail: info@hempsteadworks.com
Internet: http://www.toh.li/occupational-resources

▽Commissioner **Ana-Maria Hurtado** . . . . (516) 485-5000 ext. 1105
E-mail: amh@hempsteadworks.com
▽First Deputy Commissioner **Gregory Becker** . . . (516) 485-5000 ext. 1104
E-mail: gbecker@hempsteadworks.com

Department of Parks and Recreation
200 North Franklin Street, Second Floor, Hempstead, NY 11550
Fax: (516) 292-0527 Internet: http://www.toh.li/content/rc/parksrec.html

►Commissioner **Michael J. Zappolo** . . . . (516) 292-9000 ext. 7201
E-mail: michzap@tohmail.org

★Elected Official ▲Appointed by Legislature ▼Appointed by Governor ►Appointed by Board or Commission ●Appointed by Judge
■Appointed by Mayor △Appointed by Freeholders ▽Appointed by Supervisor ▷Appointed by County Executive ○Appointed by Council

Department of Planning and Economic Development
200 N. Franklin St., Hempstead, NY 11550
Fax: (516) 719-7966

Commissioner **George Bakich** . . . . (516) 538-7100 ext. 349
E-mail: gbakich@tohmail.org

Public Safety Department
200 North Franklin Street, Hempstead, NY 11550
Fax: (516) 485-4547 Internet: http://toh.li/public-safety-department

Commissioner **Thomas De Maria** . . . . (516) 538-1900
Deputy Commissioner **Patrick J. Bentivegna** . . . . (516) 538-1900
E-mail: pbentivegna@tohmail.org

Purchasing Department
350 Front St., Hempstead, NY 11550
Fax: (516) 483-6353

▶ Director **Gary Parisi** . . . . (516) 489-5000 ext. 4500
E-mail: gparisi@tohmail.org

Department of Sanitation
1600 Merrick Rd., Merrick, NY 11566
Internet: http://www.toh.li/sanitation-department

▶ Commissioner **(Vacant)** . . . . (516) 378-4210
E-mail: sanitation@tohmail.org

Department of Senior Enrichment
200 N. Franklin St., Hempstead, NY 11550
Fax: (516) 485-0420 Internet: http://www.toh.li/senior-enrichment

▶ Commissioner **Johanna Scarlata** . . . . (516) 485-8100
E-mail: jscarlata@tohmail.org

Water Department
1995 Prospect Ave., East Meadow, NY 11554
Fax: (516) 794-1355

▶ Commissioner **John L. Reinhardt III** . . . . (516) 794-8300
E-mail: jreinhardt@tohmail.org
▶ Deputy Commissioner **Donald O'Connell** . . . . (516) 794-8300

Board of Appeals
Town Hall Plaza, One Washington St., Hempstead, NY 11550
Fax: (516) 483-0432

▶ Chairman **David P. Weiss** . . . . (516) 812-3005
▶ Secretary to Board **Richard Regina** . . . . (516) 812-3005
E-mail: rregina@tohmail.org

Civil Service Commission
Town Hall, 350 Front St., Hempstead, NY 11550
Fax: (516) 481-8010

▶ Executive Director **Robert Schmidt** . . . . (516) 489-5000 ext. 3390
E-mail: rschmidt@tohmail.org

Housing Authority
760 Jerusalem Avenue, Uniondale, NY 11553-2929
Fax: (516) 485-6123 Internet: http://toh.li/content/tr/housing.html

▶ Executive Director **Ronnie W. Lawrence** . . . . (516) 485-9666
Deputy Executive Director **Ralph J. Serzo** . . . . (516) 485-9666

Industrial Development Agency
350 Front St., Hempstead, NY 11550-4037
Fax: (516) 489-3179

▶ Executive Director **Frederick J. Parola, Jr.** . . . . . (516) 489-5000 ext. 4200
E-mail: fparola@tohmail.org

Tourism Office
Town Hall Plaza, One Washington St., Hempstead, NY 11550

▶ Director **Diane Conlon** . . . . (516) 489-5000 ext. 3601
E-mail: dconlon@tohmail.org

Town/Village Aircraft Safety and Noise Abatement Committee [TVASNAC]
1 Washington Street, Hempstead, NY 11550

Director **Kevin Denning** . . . . (516) 489-5000 ext. 3253
Town Hall Plaza, 1 Washington St., Hempstead, NY 11550-4923

Urban Renewal
200 N. Franklin St., Hempstead, NY 11550
Fax: (516) 538-5046

Director **Eric S. Rosenblum** . . . . (516) 292-0808
E-mail: ericros@tohmail.org

City of Henderson, Nevada

P.O. Box 95050, Henderson, NV 89009-5050
Internet: www.cityofhenderson.com

County: Clark **Election Type:** Nonpartisan **Year Incorporated:** 1953
Population: 285,667 (2015)

Office of the Mayor and City Council
P.O. Box 95050, Henderson, NV 89009-5050
Fax: (702) 267-2081

★ Mayor **Andy A. Hafen** . . . . (702) 267-2085
Began Service: June 16, 2009
Term Expires: June 16, 2017
Education: UNLV 1976 BS
Executive Assistant **Diana Saviano** . . . . (702) 267-2406
E-mail: diana.saviano@cityofhenderson.com
★ Councilwoman **Gerri Schroder** (Ward I) . . . . (702) 267-2085
Term Expires: June 16, 2019
E-mail: gerri.schroder@cityofhenderson.com
★ Councilwoman **Debra March** (Ward II) . . . . (702) 267-2085
Term Expires: June 16, 2019
★ Councilman **John Marz** (Ward III) . . . . (702) 267-2085
Term Expires: June 16, 2017
E-mail: john.marz@cityofhenderson.com
★ Councilman **Sam Bateman** (Ward IV) . . . . (702) 267-2085
Term Expires: June 16, 2019
E-mail: sam.bateman@cityofhenderson.com

Office of the City Attorney
P.O. Box 95050, Henderson, NV 89009-5050

○ City Attorney **Josh M. Reid** . . . . (702) 267-1200
E-mail: josh.reid@cityofhenderson.com
Education: BYU 1995 BS; Yale 1997 MS; Arizona 2000 JD

Office of the City Clerk
P.O. Box 95050, Henderson, NV 89009-5050
Fax: (702) 267-1401

○ City Clerk **Sabrina Mercadante** . . . . (702) 267-1400
E-mail: sabrina.mercadante@cityofhenderson.com

Office of the City Manager
P.O. Box 95050, Henderson, NV 89009-5050
Fax: (702) 267-2081

○ City Manager **Robert Murnane** . . . . (702) 267-2080
E-mail: Robert.Murnane@cityofhenderson.com
Assistant City Manager **Gregory W. Blackburn** . . . . (702) 267-2063
E-mail: Greg.Blackburn@cityofhenderson.com
Education: U Phoenix BA, MBA

(continued on next page)

★ Elected Official ▲ Appointed by Legislature ▼ Appointed by Governor ▶ Appointed by Board or Commission ● Appointed by Judge
■ Appointed by Mayor △ Appointed by Freeholders ▽ Appointed by Supervisor ▷ Appointed by County Executive ○ Appointed by Council

Office of the City Manager *continued*

Assistant City Manager **Bristol Ellington** .... (702) 267-2062
E-mail: bristol.ellington@cityofhenderson.com

Information Technology Department

P.O. Box 95050, Henderson, NV 89009-5050
Fax: (702) 267-4301

Chief Information Officer **Laura Fucci** .... (702) 267-4300
E-mail: laura.fucci@cityofhenderson.com

Alternative Sentencing

243 South Water Street, MS 601, Henderson, NV 89015
Fax: (702) 267-1351

Chief Marshal **Ian Massey** .... (702) 267-1350

Animal Control

Animal Control Facility, 300 East Galleria, Henderson, NV 89011
Fax: (702) 267-4971

Animal Control Administrator **Kathryn Baker** .... (702) 267-4970

Community Development and Services Department

P.O. Box 95050, Henderson, NV 89009-5050
Fax: (702) 267-1501

Director **Stephanie Garcia-Vause** .... (702) 267-1500
E-mail: stephanie.garcia-vause@cityofhenderson.com

Economic Development and Tourism Department

P.O. Box 95050, Henderson, NV 89009-5050
Fax: (702) 267-1651

Economic Development and Tourism Manager
Barbra Coffee .... (702) 267-1654
E-mail: barbra.coffee@cityofhenderson.com

Finance Department

P.O. Box 95050, Henderson, NV 89009-5050
Fax: (702) 267-1702

Chief Financial Officer **Richard A. Derrick** .... (702) 267-1708
Education: UNLV BA, MPA

Fire Department

P.O. Box 95050, Henderson, NV 89009-5050
Fax: (702) 267-2223

Fire Chief **Matthew Morris** .... (702) 267-2222

Building and Fire Safety

P.O. Box 95050, Henderson, NV 89009-5050
Fax: (702) 267-3604

Division Manager **Mohammad Jadid** .... (702) 267-3694
E-mail: mohammad.jadid@cityofhenderson.com

Human Resources Department

P.O. Box 95050, Henderson, NV 89009-5050
Fax: (702) 267-1903

Director **Jennifer Fennema** .... (702) 267-1911
E-mail: jennifer.fennema@cityofhenderson.com

Neighborhood Services Division

240 Water Street, Henderson, NV 89015
Fax: (702) 267-2001

Neighborhood Relations Manager **Barbara A. Geach** .... (702) 267-2000

Police Department

P.O. Box 95050, Henderson, NV 89009-5050
Fax: (702) 267-5000

Chief of Police **Patrick Moers** .... (702) 267-4501
Education: Nevada State BA

Public Information Office

P.O. Box 95050, Henderson, NV 89009-5050
Fax: (702) 267-2091

Director **Bud Cranor** .... (702) 267-2053
E-mail: bud.cranor@cityofhenderson.com
Education: BYU 1995 BA

Public Works, Parks and Recreation Department

P.O. Box 95050, Henderson, NV 89009-5050
Fax: (702) 267-3001

Director **Robert C. Herr** .... (702) 267-3030
Assistant Public Works Director **(Vacant)** .... (702) 267-3038
City Traffic Engineer **John Penuelas** .... (702) 267-3080
E-mail: john.penuelas@cityofhenderson.com
Quality Control Manager **Thomas Davy** .... (702) 267-3104
E-mail: thomas.davy@cityofhenderson.com

Utility Services Division

City Hall, 240 Water Street, Henderson, NV 89015
P.O. Box 95050, Henderson, NV 89009-5050
Fax: (702) 267-2501

Director **Priscilla Howell** .... (702) 267-2507

City of Hialeah, Florida

501 Palm Ave., Hialeah, FL 33010
Tel: (305) 883-5800 (Information) Internet: www.hialeahfl.gov

County: Miami-Dade **Election Type:** Nonpartisan **Year Incorporated:** 1925 **Population:** 237,069 (2015)

Office of the Mayor

501 Palm Ave., Hialeah, FL 33010-4789
Fax: (305) 883-5992

★ Mayor **Carlos Hernandez** .... (305) 883-5800
Began Service: May 23, 2011
Term Expires: November 16, 2017
E-mail: mayorchernandez@hialeahfl.gov
Education: St Thomas (Cuba)

Office of the City Attorney

501 Palm Ave., Hialeah, FL 33010
Fax: (305) 883-5896

■ City Attorney **Lorena Bravo** .... (305) 883-5926
E-mail: lbravo@hialeahfl.gov
Assistant City Attorney **Owen Kohler** .... (305) 863-2960
E-mail: okohler@hialeahfl.gov
Assistant City Attorney **Daylen Docampo Perez** .... (305) 883-5923
E-mail: ddocampo@hialeahfl.gov

Office of the City Clerk

501 Palm Ave., Room 310, Hialeah, FL 33010
Fax: (305) 883-5814

■ City Clerk **Marbelys Fatjo** .... (305) 883-5820
E-mail: cityclerk@hialeahfl.gov
Deputy City Clerk **Carmen Hernandez** .... (305) 883-5824
E-mail: cbhernandez@hialeahfl.gov

Finance Department

501 Palm Ave., Hialeah, FL 33010
Tel: (305) 883-5856 Fax: (305) 883-5961

■ Finance Director **Javier Collazo** .... (305) 883-5856
Director of Budget Services **Ines Beecher** .... (305) 883-5931
E-mail: ibeecher@hialeahfl.gov
Director of Grants and Human Services
Annette Quintero .... (305) 883-5839

★ Elected Official ▲ Appointed by Legislature ▼ Appointed by Governor ▶ Appointed by Board or Commission ● Appointed by Judge
■ Appointed by Mayor △ Appointed by Freeholders ▽ Appointed by Supervisor ▷ Appointed by County Executive ○ Appointed by Council

Fire Department
86 E. Sixth St., Hialeah, FL 33010
Fax: (305) 883-5991

■ Fire Chief **Miguel Anchia** .... (305) 883-6909
E-mail: manchia@hialeahfl.gov
Fire Marshal (Acting) **Gerry Caldas** .... (305) 883-6914
E-mail: gcaldas@hialeahfl.gov

John F. Kennedy Library
190 W. 49th St., Hialeah, FL 33012
Fax: (305) 824-5744

Director (Acting) **Grisel Torralbas** .... (305) 821-2700 ext. 221
E-mail: gtorralbas@hialeahfl.gov

Human Resources
501 Palm Ave., Hialeah, FL 33010
Fax: (305) 883-8061

■ Director **Gelien Perez** .... (305) 883-8053
E-mail: geperez@hialeahfl.gov

Information Systems
501 Palm Ave., Hialeah, FL 33010
Fax: (305) 883-5829

■ Chief Information Officer **Ricky Suarez** .... (305) 883-8051
E-mail: rsuarez@hialeahfl.gov

Planning and Development
501 Palm Ave., Hialeah, FL 33010
Fax: (305) 883-5949

Building Official **Alexis Riveron** .... (305) 883-5830
Principal Planner **Debora Storch** .... (305) 492-2012

Construction and Maintenance
900 East 56th Street, Hialeah, FL 33013
Fax: (305) 687-2642

■ Director **Vicente Rodriguez** .... (305) 687-2660
E-mail: vrodriguez@hialeahfl.gov

Police Department
5555 E. Eighth Ave., Hialeah, FL 33013
Fax: (305) 953-5330

■ Police Chief **Sergio Velazquez** .... (305) 953-5300
E-mail: svelazquez@hialeahfl.gov

Recreation and Community Services
5601 E. Eighth Ave., Hialeah, FL 33013
Tel: (305) 687-2650 Fax: (305) 687-2632

■ Director (Acting) **Joseph Dziedzic** .... (305) 687-2641
E-mail: jdziedzic@hialeahfl.gov

Solid Waste
900 East 56th Street, Hialeah, FL 33013
Fax: (305) 687-2628

■ Director **Armando Vidal** .... (305) 687-2625
E-mail: avidal@hialeahfl.gov

Streets Department
Building 4, 5601 East 8th Avenue, Hialeah, FL 33013
Fax: (305) 687-2632

Superintendent **Jorge Hernandez** .... (305) 687-2656

Water and Sewers Department
3700 W. Fourth Ave., Hialeah, FL 33012
Fax: (305) 827-0811

■ Director **Armando Vidal** .... (305) 556-3800 ext. 2512
E-mail: avidal@hialeahfl.gov

Office of the City Council
501 Palm Ave., Hialeah, FL 33010-4789
Tel: (305) 883-5820 Fax: (305) 883-5814

★ President **Luis Gonzalez** .... (305) 883-5922
Term Expires: November 13, 2017
E-mail: luisgonzalez@hialeahfl.gov
★ Vice President **Katharine Cue-Fuente** .... (305) 883-8064
Term Expires: November 13, 2017
E-mail: kcuefuente@hialeahfl.gov
★ Council Member **Jose Caragol** .... (305) 883-8002
Term Expires: November 2019
E-mail: jcaragolsr@hialeahfl.gov
★ Council Member **Vivian Casals-Munoz** .... (305) 883-5954
Term Expires: November 16, 2019
E-mail: vivian.hialeah@gmail.com
★ Council Member **Isis Garcia-Martinez** .... (305) 883-5966
Term Expires: November 2019
E-mail: isisgmartinez67@gmail.com
★ Council Member **Paul B. Hernandez** .... (305) 883-8035
Term Expires: November 13, 2017
E-mail: pbhernandez@hialeahfl.gov
★ Council Member **Lourdes Lozano** .... (305) 883-8003
Term Expires: November 2019
E-mail: llozano@hialeahfl.gov

City of High Point, North Carolina

211 South Hamilton Street, High Point, NC 27260
P.O. Box 230, High Point, NC 27261
Internet: www.highpointnc.gov

County: Guilford **Election Type:** Nonpartisan **Population:** 110,268 (2015)

Office of the Mayor and City Council
211 South Hamilton Street, High Point, NC 27260-5321
P.O. Box 230, High Point, NC 27261
Fax: (336) 883-3052

★ Mayor **Bill Bencini** .... (336) 883-3293
Began Service: December 8, 2014
Term Expires: December 4, 2017
Executive Assistant **Cindy Smith** .... (336) 883-3293
E-mail: cindy.smith@highpointnc.gov
★ Council Member **Jeff Golden** (Ward 1) .... (336) 883-3536
Term Expires: December 4, 2017
★ Council Member **Chris Williams** (Ward 2) .... (336) 883-0881
Term Expires: December 9, 2017
★ Council Member **Alyce Hill** (Ward 3) .... (336) 883-3536
Term Expires: December 4, 2017
★ Council Member **Jay W. Wagner** (Ward 4) .... (336) 883-3536
Term Expires: December 4, 2017
★ Council Member **James Davis** (Ward 5) .... (336) 883-3536
Term Expires: December 4, 2017
★ Council Member **Jason Ewing** (Ward 6) .... (336) 883-3536
Term Expires: December 4, 2017
★ Council Member **Latimer B. Alexander IV** (At-Large) ... (336) 883-3293
Term Expires: December 2017
E-mail: latimer.alexander@highpointnc.gov
★ Council Member **Cynthia "Cindy" Davis** (At-Large) .... (336) 883-3536
Term Expires: December 4, 2017

★ Elected Official ▲ Appointed by Legislature ▼ Appointed by Governor ▶ Appointed by Board or Commission ● Appointed by Judge
■ Appointed by Mayor △ Appointed by Freeholders ▽ Appointed by Supervisor ▷ Appointed by County Executive ○ Appointed by Council

Office of the City Clerk
P.O. Box 230, High Point, NC 27261
Fax: (336) 822-7067

○ City Clerk **Lisa B. Vierling** .... (336) 883-3536
E-mail: lisa.vierling@highpointnc.gov

Office of the City Manager
P.O. Box 230, High Point, NC 27261
Fax: (336) 883-3052

○ City Manager **Greg Demko** .... (336) 883-8556
E-mail: greg.demko@highpointnc.gov
Deputy City Manager **Randy E. McCaslin** .... (336) 883-3291
E-mail: randy.mccaslin@highpointnc.gov
Assistant City Manager **Randy Hemann** .... (336) 883-3052
E-mail: randy.hemann@highpointnc.gov
Director of Public Information **Jeron Hollis** .... (336) 883-8507
E-mail: jeron.hollis@highpointnc.gov
Webmaster **Nina McNeilly** .... (336) 883-3113
E-mail: nina.mcneilly@highpointnc.gov

Office of the City Attorney
P.O. Box 230, High Point, NC 27261
Fax: (336) 883-3052

○ City Attorney **JoAnne Carlyle** .... (336) 883-3301
E-mail: joanne.carlyle@highpointnc.gov

Economic Development Department
P.O. Box 230, High Point, NC 27261
Fax: (336) 883-3057

Director **Loren Hill** .... (336) 883-3116
E-mail: loren.hill@highpointnc.gov

Community Development Department
P.O. Box 230, High Point, NC 27261
Fax: (336) 883-3676

Director **Michael McNair** .... (336) 883-3676
E-mail: michael.mcnair@highpointnc.gov

Customer Service Department
P.O. Box 230, High Point, NC 27261
Fax: (336) 883-3068

Director **Robert Martin** .... (336) 883-3178

Electric Utilities Department
P.O. Box 230, High Point, NC 27261
Fax: (336) 883-3478 Internet: www.high-point.net/electric/

Director **Garey Edwards** .... (336) 883-3172
Fax: (336) 883-3478

Engineering Services Department
Director **Keith Pugh** .... (336) 883-3197
E-mail: keith.pugh@highpointnc.gov

Finance Department
P.O. Box 230, High Point, NC 27261
Fax: (336) 883-8572

Director **Jeffrey Moore** .... (336) 883-3238

Fire Department
P.O. Box 230, High Point, NC 27261
Fax: (336) 883-3550

Fire Chief **Thomas Reid** .... (336) 883-3358
E-mail: thomas.reid@highpointnc.gov

Emergency Management Division
P.O. Box 230, High Point, NC 27261

Emergency Manager **Glenn Clapp** .... (336) 883-3543
E-mail: glenn.clapp@highpointnc.gov

Fleet Services Department
Fax: (336) 883-6699

Fleet Director **Gary Smith** .... (336) 883-3598

Housing Authority
500 East Russell Street, High Point, NC 27260

Chief Executive Officer **Angela G. McGill** .... (336) 887-2661
E-mail: amcgill@hpha.net

Human Relations Department
P.O. Box 230, High Point, NC 27261
Fax: (336) 822-4777

Director (Interim) **Jeron Hollis** .... (336) 883-3124
E-mail: jeron.hollis@highpointnc.gov

Human Resources Department
P.O. Box 230, High Point, NC 27261
Fax: (336) 883-8581

Director **Angela C. Kirkwood** .... (336) 883-3258
E-mail: angela.kirkwood@highpointnc.gov

Information Technology Services
P.O. Box 230, High Point, NC 27261
Fax: (336) 883-3419

Director of Communications **Steve Lingerfelt** .... (336) 883-3286
E-mail: steve.lingerfelt@highpointnc.gov

Library
P.O. Box 230, High Point, NC 27261
Fax: (336) 883-3636

Director **Mary Sizemore** .... (336) 883-3631
E-mail: mary.sizemore@highpointnc.gov

Parks and Recreation Department
P.O. Box 230, High Point, NC 27261

Director **Lee Tillery** .... (336) 883-3473

Planning and Development Department
P.O. Box 230, High Point, NC 27261

Director **Lee Burnette** .... (336) 883-3328
E-mail: lee.burnette@highpointnc.gov

Police Department
1009 Leonard Ave., High Point, NC 27260
Fax: (336) 887-7972

Chief of Police **Kenneth J. Shultz** .... (336) 887-7970

Public Services Department
211 South Hamilton Street, Suite 206, High Point, NC 27260-5321
P.O. Box 230, High Point, NC 27261

Director **Terry Houk** .... (336) 883-3215
Fax: (336) 883-1675

Transportation Department
P.O. Box 230, High Point, NC 27261

Director **Mark McDonald** .... (336) 883-3225
Fax: (336) 883-8568

★ Elected Official ▲ Appointed by Legislature ▼ Appointed by Governor ► Appointed by Board or Commission ● Appointed by Judge
■ Appointed by Mayor △ Appointed by Freeholders ▽ Appointed by Supervisor ▷ Appointed by County Executive ○ Appointed by Council

City of Hollywood, Florida

2600 Hollywood Blvd., Hollywood, FL 33022
P.O. Box 229045, Hollywood, FL 33022-9045
Tel: (954) 921-3211 (Information) Internet: www.hollywoodfl.org/

County: Broward **Election Type:** Nonpartisan **Population:** 149,728 (2015)

Office of the Mayor and City Commission

P.O. Box 229045, Hollywood, FL 33022-9045
Fax: (954) 921-3386

★ Mayor **Peter Bober** .... (954) 921-3321
Began Service: 2008
Term Expires: November 20, 2016
E-mail: pbober@hollywoodfl.org
Education: Texas 1994 BA; Pennsylvania 1997 JD

★ Vice Mayor **Kevin Biederman** (District 5) .... (954) 921-3321
Term Expires: November 20, 2018
E-mail: kbiederman@hollywoodfl.org

★ Commissioner **Patricia Asseff** (District 1) .... (954) 921-3321
Term Expires: November 20, 2018
E-mail: passeff@hollywoodfl.org

★ Commissioner **Peter D. Hernandez** (District 2) .... (954) 921-3321
Term Expires: November 20, 2016
E-mail: phernandez@hollywoodfl.org

★ Commissioner **Traci Lynn Callari** (District 3) .... (954) 921-3321
Term Expires: November 20, 2018
E-mail: tcallari@hollywoodfl.org

★ Commissioner **Richard S. "Dick" Blattner** (District 4) .... (954) 921-3321
Term Expires: November 20, 2016
E-mail: rblattner@hollywoodfl.org

★ Commissioner **Linda Sherwood** (District 6) .... (954) 921-3321
Term Expires: November 20, 2016
E-mail: lsherwood@hollywoodfl.org

Office of the City Attorney

P.O. Box 229045, Hollywood, FL 33022-9045
Fax: (954) 921-3081

► City Attorney **Jeffrey P. Sheffel** .... (954) 921-3435
E-mail: jsheffel@hollywoodfl.org

Office of the City Manager

P.O. Box 229045, Hollywood, FL 33022-9045
Fax: (954) 921-3314

► City Manager **Wazir A. Ishmael** .... (954) 921-3201
E-mail: wishmeal@hollywoodfl.org

Assistant City Manager for Finance and Administration
George Keller .... (954) 921-3211
E-mail: gkeller@hollywoodfl.org

Assistant City Manager for Sustainable Development
Gus Zambrano .... (954) 921-3211
E-mail: gzambrano@hollywoodfl.org

Assistant City Manager for Public Safety **Mel Standley** .. (954) 921-3211
E-mail: mstandley@hollywoodfl.org

Chief Civic Affairs Officer **Lorie Mertens-Black** .... (954) 921-3211
E-mail: lmblack@hollywoodfl.org

Chief Development Officer **Shiv Snowaldass** .... (954) 921-3211
E-mail: snowaldass@hollywoodfl.org

Office of the City Clerk

P.O. Box 229045, Hollywood, FL 33022-9045
Fax: (954) 921-3233

City Clerk **Patricia A. Cerny** .... (954) 921-3211
E-mail: pcerny@hollywoodfl.org

Office of Labor Relations

P.O. Box 229045, Hollywood, FL 33022-9045

Director **Raquel Elejabarrieta** .... (954) 921-3519

Building Department

P.O. Box 229045, Hollywood, FL 33022-9045
Tel: (954) 921-3335

Chief Building Official **Phil Sauer** .... (954) 921-3300
Fax: (954) 921-3037

Department of Financial Services

P.O. Box 229045, Hollywood, FL 33022-9045
Fax: (954) 921-3064

Director (Interim) **Mirtha Dziedzic** .... (954) 921-3231

Purchasing Agent **Joel Wasserman** .... (954) 921-3210
E-mail: jwasserman@hollywoodfl.org

Department of Fire Rescue and Beach Safety

P.O. Box 229045, Hollywood, FL 33022-9045
Fax: (954) 967-4253

Fire Chief **Eric Busenbarrick** .... (954) 967-4248
E-mail: ebusenbarrick@hollywoodfl.org

Department of Community and Economic Development

P.O. Box 229045, Hollywood, FL 33022-9045

Director **(Vacant)** .... (954) 921-3271

Office of Human Resources

P.O. Box 229045, Hollywood, FL 33022-9045
Fax: (954) 921-3487

Director **Tammie Hechler** .... (954) 921-3216
E-mail: thechler@hollywoodfl.org

Department of Information Technology

P.O. Box 229045, Hollywood, FL 33022-9045
Tel: (954) 921-3488

Director of Information Technology
Raheem Seecharan .... (954) 921-3479
E-mail: rseecharan@hollywoodfl.org

Office of Parking

Director **(Vacant)** .... (954) 921-3599

Parks, Recreation and Cultural Arts Department

1405 South 28th Avenue, Hollywood, FL 33022
Fax: (954) 921-3572

Director **Chuck Ellis** .... (954) 921-3460

Assistant Director **David Vasquez** .... (954) 921-3404

Department of Planning

P.O. Box 229045, Hollywood, FL 33022-9045
Fax: (954) 921-3347

Director **Jaye Epstein** .... (954) 921-3471

Police Department

P.O. Box 229045, Hollywood, FL 33022-9045
Fax: (954) 967-4300 E-mail: police@hollywoodfl.org

Chief of Police **Tomas Sanchez** .... (954) 967-4300

Office of Public Affairs and Marketing

Director **Raelin Storey** .... (954) 921-3098

★ Elected Official ▲ Appointed by Legislature ▼ Appointed by Governor ► Appointed by Board or Commission ● Appointed by Judge
■ Appointed by Mayor △ Appointed by Freeholders ▽ Appointed by Supervisor ▷ Appointed by County Executive ○ Appointed by Council

Department of Public Utilities
P.O. Box 229045, Hollywood, FL 33022-9045

Director **Steve Joseph** .... (954) 967-4455
Fax: (954) 921-3304
Deputy Director, Finance **Mark Moore** .... (954) 921-4526
Deputy Director, Operations **Francois Domond** .... (954) 921-3522
E-mail: fdomond@hollywoodfl.org
Wastewater Treatment Manager **Coy Mathis** .... (954) 921-3288
Fax: (954) 921-3258
Water Treatment Manager **Taylor "Bud" Calhoun** .... (954) 967-4230
Fax: (954) 967-4232
Assistant Director, Engineering and Construction
Jidendra Patel .... (954) 921-3930
E-mail: jpatel@hollywoodfl.org

Public Works Department
Director **Sylvia Glazer** .... (954) 967-4526
Building and Grounds Operations Manager
Greg Gibson .... (954) 967-4563
E-mail: ggibson@hollywoodfl.org
City Engineer/Assistant Director of Public Works
Jonathan Vogt .... (954) 921-3254
E-mail: jvogt@hollywoodfl.org
Environmental Services Supervisor, Sanitation and Recycling **Charles Lassiter** .... (954) 967-4320
Fleet Management Coordinator **Joel Wall** .... (954) 967-4555

City and County of Honolulu, Hawaii
City Hall, 530 S. King St., Honolulu, HI 96813-3014
Tel: (808) 768-4385 (Information) Internet: www.honolulu.gov

County: Honolulu **Election Type:** Nonpartisan **Population:** 352,769 (2015)

Form of Municipal Government: City and county governments are combined.

Office of the Mayor
City Hall, 530 S. King St., Room 300, Honolulu, HI 96813
Fax: (808) 768-5552

★ Mayor **Kirk Caldwell** .... (808) 768-4141
Began Service: January 2, 2013
Term Expires: January 2, 2017
E-mail: mayor@honolulu.gov
Date of Birth: August 4, 1952
Education: Tufts 1975 BA; Fletcher Law & Diplomacy 1978 MALD; Hawaii 1984 JD
Chief of Staff **Raynard C. Soon** .... (808) 768-5225
Education: Hawaii 1971 BA; Harvard 1976 MA

Managing Director
530 S. King St., Room 306, Honolulu, HI 96813
Fax: (808) 768-4242

Managing Director **Roy Amemiya** .... (808) 768-6634
E-mail: ramemiya@honolulu.gov
Education: Purdue BA; Hawaii MBA
Deputy Director **Georgette T. Deemer** .... (808) 768-6634
E-mail: gdeemer@honolulu.gov
■ Agriculture Liaison **(Vacant)** .... (808) 768-6634
Information Officer **Andrew Pereira** .... (808) 768-6634
E-mail: andrew.peveira@honolulu.gov

Culture and the Arts Office
550 South King Street, 2nd Floor, Honolulu, HI 96813
Fax: (808) 768-6622 E-mail: moca-info@honolulu.gov

■ Executive Director **Misty M. Kelai** .... (808) 768-6622

Department of Emergency Management
Municipal Bldg., 650 S. King St., Basement, Honolulu, HI 96813
Fax: (808) 524-3439 E-mail: dem@honolulu.gov

Director **Melvin N. Kaku** .... (808) 723-8960
E-mail: mkaku@honolulu.gov
Deputy Director **Peter Hirai** .... (808) 723-8960
E-mail: phirai@honolulu.gov

Economic Development Office
530 S. King St., Room 306, Honolulu, HI 96813
Fax: (808) 768-4242

■ Executive Director **Nicole A. Velasco** .... (808) 768-5764
E-mail: nvelasco@honolulu.gov
Education: Princeton BA

Honolulu Film Office
530 S. King St., Suite 306, Honolulu, HI 96813
Tel: (808) 768-6100 Fax: (808) 768-6102
E-mail: info@filmhonolulu.com

Film Commissioner **Walea L. Constantinau** .... (808) 768-6100

Neighborhood Commission Office
530 S.King St., Room 306, Honolulu, HI 96813
Fax: (808) 768-3711

■ Executive Secretary **Shawn Hamamoto** .... (808) 768-3710
E-mail: shamamotol@honolulu.gov

Royal Hawaiian Band
2805 Monsarrat Ave., Honolulu, HI 96815
Fax: (808) 924-2841

■ Bandmaster **Clarke L.K. Bright** .... (808) 922-5331
E-mail: cbright@honolulu.gov

Office of the City Council
City Hall, 530 S. King St., 2nd Floor, Honolulu, HI 96813
Tel: (808) 768-5010 Fax: (808) 768-5011

★ Chairman **Ernest Y. Martin** (District II) .... (808) 768-5002
Term Expires: January 2, 2019
E-mail: emartin@honolulu.gov
★ Vice Chairman **J. Ikaika Anderson** (District III) .... (808) 768-5003
Term Expires: January 2, 2017
E-mail: ianderson@honolulu.gov
★ Council Member **Kymberly Marcos Pine** (District I) .... (808) 768-5001
Term Expires: January 2, 2017
E-mail: kmpine@honolulu.gov
★ Council Member **Trevor Ozawa** (District IV) .... (808) 768-5004
Term Expires: January 2, 2019
E-mail: tozawa@honolulu.gov
★ Council Member **Ann H. Kobayashi** (District V) .... (808) 768-5005
Term Expires: January 2, 2017
E-mail: akobayashi@honolulu.gov
★ Council Member **Carol Fukunaga** (District VI) .... (808) 768-5006
Term Expires: January 2, 2019
E-mail: cafukunaga@honolulu.gov
Education: Hawaii BA, 1976 JD
★ Council Member **Joey Manahan** (District VII) .... (808) 768-5007
Term Expires: January 2, 2017
E-mail: jmanahan@honolulu.gov
Education: Hawaii BComm
★ Council Member **Brandon Elefante** (District VIII) .... (808) 768-5008
Term Expires: January 1, 2019
E-mail: belefante@honolulu.gov
★ Council Member **Ron Menor** (District IX) .... (808) 768-5009
Term Expires: January 2, 2017
E-mail: rmenor@honolulu.gov
Education: UCLA 1977 BA; Georgetown 1980 JD

★ Elected Official ▲ Appointed by Legislature ▼ Appointed by Governor ▶ Appointed by Board or Commission ● Appointed by Judge
■ Appointed by Mayor △ Appointed by Freeholders ▽ Appointed by Supervisor ▷ Appointed by County Executive ○ Appointed by Council

Office of the City Auditor
1001 Kamokila Boulevard, Suite 216, Kapolei, HI 96707
Fax: (808) 768-3135

City Auditor **Edwin S.W. Young** .... (808) 768-3134

Office of the City Clerk
City Hall, 530 S. King St., Room 100, Honolulu, HI 96813
Fax: (808) 768-3835 E-mail: clerks@honolulu.gov

○ City Clerk **Glen Takahashi** .... (808) 768-3810
E-mail: clerks@honolulu.gov

Office of Council Services
City Hall, 530 S. King St., 2nd Fl., Honolulu, HI 96813
Fax: (808) 527-5581 E-mail: ocs@honolulu.gov

○ Director **Charmaine T. Doran** .... (808) 768-3809

Budget and Fiscal Services Department
City Hall, 530 S. King St., Room 208, Honolulu, HI 96813
Fax: (808) 768-3179

■ Director **Nelson H. Koyanagi, Jr.** .... (808) 768-3901
E-mail: bfsmail@honolulu.gov
Deputy Director **Gary T. Kurokawa** .... (808) 768-3901

Department of Community Services
715 S. King St., Room 311, Honolulu, HI 96813
Fax: (808) 768-7792

■ Director **Gary Nakata** .... (808) 768-7762
E-mail: gnakata@honolulu.gov
Deputy Director **Barbara Yamashita** .... (808) 768-7762
E-mail: b.yamashita@honolulu.gov
Education: Hawaii MSW

Office of Strategic Development
530 South King Street, 3rd Floor, Honolulu, HI 96813

Strategic Development Officer **Sandra S. Pfund** .... (808) 768-4291
E-mail: spfund@honolulu.gov
Asset Management Administrator
Elizabeth A. "Libby" Char .... (808) 768-4141
E-mail: csadayasu@honolulu.gov

Corporation Counsel Department
City Hall, 530 S. King St., Room 110, Honolulu, HI 96813
Fax: (808) 768-5105 E-mail: cor@honolulu.gov

■ Corporation Counsel **Donna Y.L. Leong** .... (808) 768-5100
E-mail: cor@honolulu.gov
Education: Stanford 1976 AB; U Washington 1979 JD
First Deputy Corporation Counsel **Paul S. Aoki** .... (808) 768-5100

Customer Services Department
550 South King Street, Honolulu, HI 96813
Fax: (808) 768-3750 E-mail: csd@honolulu.gov

■ Director **Sheri T. Kajiwara** .... (808) 768-3391
E-mail: csd@honolulu.gov
Licensing Administrator, Division of Motor Vehicles
and Licensing **Galen Onouye** .... (808) 532-7730
P.O. Box 30320, Honolulu, HI 96820 Fax: (808) 532-7722

Design and Construction Department
Municipal Building, 650 South King Street, 11th Floor,
Honolulu, HI 96813
Fax: (808) 768-4567

■ Director **Robert J. Kroning** .... (808) 768-8480
E-mail: rkroning@honolulu.gov
Deputy Director **Mark K. Yonamine** .... (808) 768-8480

Enterprise Services Department
777 Ward Avenue, Honolulu, HI 96814
Fax: (808) 768-5433 E-mail: aud@honolulu.gov

■ Director **Guy Kaulukukui** .... (808) 768-5400
E-mail: guy.kaulukukui@honolulu.gov
Education: Hawaii BA; Hawaii Pacific MBA; Kansas PhD
Deputy Director **Tracy S. Kubota** .... (808) 768-5400

Environmental Services Department
1000 Uluohia Street, Suite 308, Kapolei, HI 96707
Fax: (808) 768-3487 E-mail: env@honolulu.gov

Director **Lori M.K. Kahikina** .... (808) 768-3486
Deputy Director **Timothy A. "Tim" Houghton** .... (808) 768-3486
Education: San Francisco State U BA; USC MS

Facility Maintenance Department
1000 Uluohia Street, Suite 215, Kapolei, HI 96707
Fax: (808) 768-3381

Director **Ross S. Sasamura** .... (808) 768-3343
E-mail: rsasamura@honolulu.gov
Deputy Director **Eduardo P. Manglallan** .... (808) 768-3343
E-mail: emanglallan@honolulu.gov

Automotive Equipment Service Division
99-999 Iwaena Street, Aiea, HI 96701
Tel: (808) 768-3343 Fax: (808) 768-3381

Division Chief **Robert Primiano** .... (808) 768-3501
Assistant Chief **Clyde Omija** .... (808) 768-3502

Fire Department, Honolulu
636 South Street, Honolulu, HI 96813-5007
Fax: (808) 723-7111

○ Fire Chief **Manuel Neves** .... (808) 723-7139
E-mail: mneves@honolulu.gov
Education: Hawaii BBA, MPA
Deputy Chief **Lionel Camara, Jr.** .... (808) 723-7139
E-mail: lcamara1@honolulu.gov

Honolulu Emergency Services Department
3375 Koapaka St., Suite H450, Honolulu, HI 96819-1869
Fax: (808) 723-7800 E-mail: esd@honolulu.gov

■ Director **Mark K. Rigg** .... (808) 723-7800
E-mail: mrigg@honolulu.gov
Deputy Director **Ian T.T. Santee** .... (808) 723-7811

Human Resources Department
650 S. King St., 10th Floor, Honolulu, HI 96813
Fax: (808) 768-5563

■ Director **Carolee C. Kubo** .... (808) 768-8500
E-mail: ckubo1@honolulu.gov
■ Assistant Director **Noel T. Ono** .... (808) 768-8500
E-mail: nono@honolulu.gov

Information Technology Department
Municipal Bldg., 650 South King Street, 5th Floor, Honolulu, HI 96813
Fax: (808) 768-7807

■ Director and Chief Information Officer **Mark D. Wong** ... (808) 768-7684
E-mail: dit@honolulu.gov
Education: Yale BS
Deputy Director **Keith G.H. Ho** .... (808) 768-7621
E-mail: dit@honolulu.gov

Department of the Medical Examiner
835 Iwilei Rd., Honolulu, HI 96817
Fax: (808) 768-3099

■ Medical Examiner **Dr. Christopher Happy** .... (808) 768-3090
E-mail: chappy@honolulu.gov
Education: Saint Louis U MD

(continued on next page)

★ Elected Official ▲ Appointed by Legislature ▼ Appointed by Governor ▶ Appointed by Board or Commission ● Appointed by Judge
■ Appointed by Mayor △ Appointed by Freeholders ▽ Appointed by Supervisor ▷ Appointed by County Executive ○ Appointed by Council

Department of the Medical Examiner *continued*

Deputy Medical Examiner **Dr. Rachel Lange** . . . . (808) 768-3090

Parks and Recreation Department

1000 Uluohia Street, Suite 309, Kapolei, HI 96707
Fax: (808) 768-3053 E-mail: parks@honolulu.gov

■ Director **Michele Nekota** . . . . (808) 768-3003
E-mail: mnekota@honolulu.gov
Education: BYU BA; U Phoenix MBA
Deputy Director **Jeanne C. Ishikawa** . . . . (808) 768-3002

Planning and Permitting Department

Municipal Bldg., 650 South King Street, 7th Floor, Honolulu, HI 96813
Fax: (808) 768-6743 E-mail: info@honoluludpp.org

■ Director **George I. Atta** . . . . (808) 768-8000
E-mail: gatta@honolulu.gov
■ Deputy Director **Arthur D. Challacombe** . . . . (808) 768-8001
E-mail: achallacombe@honolulu.gov

Police Department

801 S. Beretania St., Honolulu, HI 96813
Tel: (808) 529-3111 Fax: (808) 723-3946 E-mail: hpd@honolulupd.org

▶ Police Chief **Louis M. Kealoha** . . . . (808) 723-3848
E-mail: lkealoha@honolulu.gov
Deputy Chief **David Kayihiro** . . . . (808) 723-3848
Deputy Chief **Marie McCauley** . . . . (808) 723-3848

Department of the Prosecuting Attorney

1060 Richards Street, Honolulu, HI 96813
Fax: (808) 768-7515 E-mail: prosecutor@honolulu.gov

★ Prosecuting Attorney **Keith Kaneshiro** . . . . (808) 768-7400
Term Expires: January 2, 2017
E-mail: kkaneshiro@honolulu.gov
First Deputy (Acting) **Armina Ching** . . . . (808) 768-7400

Transportation Services Department

650 South King Street, 3rd Floor, Honolulu, HI 96813
Fax: (808) 768-4730

■ Director **Michael D. "Mike" Formby** . . . . (808) 768-8303
E-mail: mformby@honolulu.gov
Education: Texas A&M 1980 BS; South Texas 1983 JD
Deputy Director **Mark N. Garrity** . . . . (808) 768-8304

Board of Water Supply

630 S. Beretania St., Honolulu, HI 96813
Fax: (808) 550-9114 E-mail: contactus@hbws.org

○ Manager and Chief Engineer **Ernest Y.W. Lau** . . . . (808) 748-5000
Deputy Manager **Ellen Kitamura** . . . . (808) 748-5000

City of Houston, Texas

City Hall, 901 Bagby St., Houston, TX 77002
P.O. Box 1562, Houston, TX 77251-1562
Internet: www.houstontx.gov

County: Harris **Election Type:** Nonpartisan **Year Founded:** 1836
Year Incorporated: 1837 **Population:** 2,296,224 (2015)

Office of the Mayor

City Hall, 901 Bagby Street, 3rd Floor, Houston, TX 77002
P.O. Box 1562, Houston, TX 77251-1562
TTY: (713) 247-1940 Fax: (713) 247-2484
Internet: http://www.houstontx.gov/mayor/index.html

★ Mayor **Sylvester Turner** . . . . (832) 393-1000
Began Service: January 4, 2016
Term Expires: December 31, 2017
E-mail: sylvester.turner@houstontx.gov
Internet: https://twitter.com/sylvesterturner
Education: Houston 1977 BA; Harvard 1980 JD
Communications Director **Janice Evans** . . . . (832) 393-0800
E-mail: janice.evans@houstontx.gov
Press Secretary **Darian Ward** . . . . (832) 393-0804
E-mail: darian.ward@houstontx.gov
Director of Education **Juliet K. Stipeche** . . . . (832) 393-0800

Office of Business Opportunity [OBO]

611 Walker Street, 7th Floor, Houston, TX 77002
Fax: (713) 837-9055 Internet: www.houstontx.gov/obo

Director **Carlecia D. Wright** . . . . (713) 837-9000
Education: Columbia Col Chicago 1999 BA; NYU 2003 MPA

Mayor's Citizens' Assistance Office [MCAO]

900 Bagby Street, Houston, TX 77002
Fax: (832) 393-0952 Internet: www.houstontx.gov/cao/

Director **Katye Tipton** . . . . (832) 393-1038
E-mail: ktipton@houstontx.gov
Assistant Director **Landon Taylor** . . . . (832) 393-1038
Division Manager **(Vacant)** . . . . (832) 393-0955
Administrative Assistant to Division Manager
Melissa Mayorga . . . . (832) 393-0955
E-mail: mmayorga@houstontx.gov
Administrative Assistant to the Director
Nikki Maddox . . . . (832) 393-1038
E-mail: nikki.maddox@houstontx.gov
Acres Homes Liaison Office **Anita Ivery** . . . . (832) 393-4117
6719 W. Montgomery, Houston, TX 77091
E-mail: anita.ivery@houstontx.gov
Eastside Liaison **Maria Bolanos** . . . . (713) 560-1149
7037 Capitol, Houston, TX 77011
E-mail: maria.bolanos@houstontx.gov
Fifth Ward Liaison Office **Amy Tran** . . . . (713) 560-1101
4014 Market Street, Houston, TX 77004
E-mail: amy.tran@houstontx.gov
Heights Liaison Office **Jack Valenski** . . . . (713) 560-1245
170 Heights Blvd., Houston, TX 77007
E-mail: jack.valinski@houstontx.gov
Kashmere Liaison Office **Kelli Bradford** . . . . (832) 393-5493
901 Bagby Street, Houston, TX 77002
E-mail: kelli.bradford@houstontx.gov
Kingwood Liaison Office **Melissa Mayorga** . . . . (713) 515-3848
E-mail: mmayorga@houstontx.gov
Southwest Liaison Office **Veronica Hernandez** . . . . (713) 560-1153
6400 Highstar, Houston, TX 77081
E-mail: veronica.hernandez@houstontx.gov
Sunnyside/South Park Liaison **Angela Solis** . . . . (713) 560-1152
4605 Wilmington, Houston, TX 77051
E-mail: angela.solis@houstontx.gov
Third Ward Liaison Office **Carl Davis** . . . . (713) 320-7606
3611 Ennis, Houston, TX 77004
E-mail: carl.davis@houstontx.gov

★ Elected Official ▲ Appointed by Legislature ▼ Appointed by Governor ▶ Appointed by Board or Commission ● Appointed by Judge
■ Appointed by Mayor △ Appointed by Freeholders ▽ Appointed by Supervisor ▷ Appointed by County Executive ○ Appointed by Council

Mayor's Citizens' Assistance Office *continued*

South Central Liaison and Office Manager
Rhonda Sauter . . . . (832) 393-1143
900 Bagby, Public Level, Houston, TX 77096
E-mail: rsauter@houstontx.gov

Mayor's Crime Victims Assistance

Fax: (713) 247-1340

■ Director **Andy Kahan** . . . . (713) 308-9063
E-mail: andy.kahan@houstontx.tov

Mayor's Office of Sustainability

■ Director **(Vacant)** . . . . (832) 393-0849

Mayor's Office for People with Disabilities

170 Heights, Houston, TX 77007

■ Executive Director **Stan Looper** . . . . (713) 803-1075
E-mail: stan.looper@houstontx.tov

Mayor's Office for Public Safety and Homeland Security

■ Director **Dennis Joseph Storemski** . . . . (832) 393-0880
E-mail: dennis.storemski@houstontx.tov

Houston Emergency Center

Director **(Vacant)** . . . . (713) 884-3611

Office of the City Secretary

P.O. Box 1562, Houston, TX 77251-1562
Tel: (832) 393-1100 Fax: (832) 393-1109
E-mail: citysecretary@houstontx.gov Internet: www.houstontx.gov/citysec/

■ City Secretary **Anna Russell** . . . . (832) 393-1100
E-mail: anna.russell@houstontx.tov

Office of Emergency Management

5320 North Sheperd Drive, Houston, TX 77091
Tel: (713) 884-4500 Internet: http://www.houstonoem.org

Emergency Management Coordinator
John R. "Rick" Flanagan . . . . (713) 884-4500
E-mail: rick.flanagan@houstontx.gov

Deputy Emergency Management Coordinator, Planning
Sharon Nalls . . . . (713) 884-4500
E-mail: sharon.nalls@houstontx.gov

Assistant Deputy Emergency Management Coordinator, Operations **Christopher Perkins** . . . . (713) 884-4500
E-mail: christopher.perkins@houstontx.gov

Administration and Regulatory Affairs Department

P.O. Box 1562, Houston, TX 77251-1562
Fax: (832) 395-9505 E-mail: aracontactus@houstontx.gov
Internet: www.houstontx.gov/ara/

Director **Tina Paez** . . . . (832) 837-9630
E-mail: tina.paez@houstontx.gov

Finance Department

P.O. Box 1562, Houston, TX 77251-1562
Internet: www.houstontx.gov/finance

Director **Kelly Dowe** . . . . (832) 393-9034

Deputy Director, Financial Planning and Analysis
Tantri Emo . . . . (832) 393-9076
E-mail: tantri.emo@houstontx.gov

Deputy Director, Financial Reporting and Operations
Arif Rasheed . . . . (832) 393-9013
E-mail: arif.rasheed@houstontx.gov

Deputy Assistant Director, Performance Improvement
Jesse Bounds . . . . (832) 393-9120
E-mail: jesse.bounds@houstontx.gov

Assistant Director, Treasury and Capital Management
Jennifer Olenick . . . . (832) 393-9112

City Council Administration Division

P.O. Box 4997, Houston, TX 77210
Internet: www.houstontx.gov/ara/council.html

Division Manager **Vernita Jones** . . . . (832) 393-0791
E-mail: vernita.jones@houstontx.gov

Strategic Procurement Division

P.O. Box 4997, Houston, TX 77210
Internet: http://purchasing.houstontx.gov/index.shtml

Chief Procurement Officer **John Gillespie** . . . . (832) 393-9126
E-mail: john.gillespie@houstontx.gov

Deputy Director **Calvin Wells** . . . . (832) 393-8700
E-mail: calvin.wells@houstontx.gov

Fire Department

600 Jefferson Street, 7th Floor, Houston, TX 77002
Tel: (832) 394-6700 E-mail: hfdpubinfo@houstontx.gov

Fire Chief (Interim) **Rodney West** . . . . (832) 394-6702
E-mail: rodney.west@houstontx.gov

Administrative Specialist **Denise Estrada** . . . . (832) 394-6702
E-mail: denise.estrada@houstontx.tov

Emergency Response Executive Assistant Chief
Richard Mann . . . . (832) 394-8700
E-mail: richard.mann@houstontx.tov

Prevention Division Executive Assistant Chief
Jerry Ford . . . . (832) 394-6900
E-mail: jerry.ford@houstontx.tov

Planning and Homeland Security Assistant Chief
Cynthia Vargas . . . . (832) 394-6748
E-mail: cynthia.vargas@houstontx.tov

Staff Services Command Executive Assistant Chief
Michelle McLeod . . . . (832) 394-6734
E-mail: michelle.mcleod@houstontx.gov

Support Command Executive Assistant Chief
Rodney West . . . . (832) 394-6745
E-mail: rodney.west@houstontx.gov

Finance and Administration Deputy Director
Neil DePascal . . . . (832) 394-8700
E-mail: neil.depascal@houstontx.tov

Communications Specialist **Alicia Whitehead** . . . . (713) 495-7906
500 Jefferson, 16th Floor, Houston, TX 77002 Fax: (713) 646-5321
E-mail: alicia.whitehead@houstontx.tov

Fleet Management Department

City Hall Annex, 900 Bagby, Public Level, Houston, TX 77096
Tel: (832) 393-6910

Director **Victor Ayres** . . . . (832) 393-6910
Fleet Maintenance Manager **Dan Tralor** . . . . (832) 393-6910
Asset Manager **WeiYao Chang** . . . . (832) 393-6910

General Services Department [GSD]

P.O. Box 61189, Houston, TX 77208-1189
Internet: www.houstontx.gov/generalservices/

■ Director **Scott Minnix** . . . . (832) 393-8019
E-mail: scott.minnix@houstontx.gov

Assistant Director/City Engineer **Humberto Bautista** . . . . (832) 393-8027
E-mail: humberto.bautista@houstontx.gov
Education: Texas (El Paso) 1977 MS

Public Information Officer **Jacquelyn Nisby** . . . . (832) 393-8023
E-mail: jacquelyn.nisby@houstontx.gov

Department of Health and Human Services [HDHHS]

8000 North Stadium Drive, Houston, TX 77054
Tel: (832) 393-5169 Fax: (832) 393-5259 TTY: (713) 794-9969
Internet: www.houstontx.gov/health/

■ Director **Stephen L. Williams** . . . . (832) 393-5169
E-mail: stephen.williams@houstontx.gov

(continued on next page)

★ Elected Official ▲ Appointed by Legislature ▼ Appointed by Governor ▶ Appointed by Board or Commission ● Appointed by Judge
■ Appointed by Mayor △ Appointed by Freeholders ▽ Appointed by Supervisor ▷ Appointed by County Executive ○ Appointed by Council

Department of Health and Human Services *continued*

Assistant Director, Division of Aging, Chronic Disease and Injury Prevention **Faith E. Foreman** . . . . (832) 393-5042
Education: Texas Southern 1992 BA; Texas 1994 MS, 2000 PhD
Chief of Public Affairs **Kathy Barton** . . . . (832) 393-5045
E-mail: kathy.barton@houstontx.gov
Administrative Services Assistant Director **Benjamin Hernandez** . . . . (832) 393-5005
E-mail: benjamin.hernandez@houstontx.gov
Senior Staff Analyst **Barbara Sudhoff-McGill** . . . . (832) 393-5037

Housing and Community Development Department [HCDD]

601 Sawyer, 4th Floor, Houston, TX 77007
Tel: (832) 394-6200 Internet: www.houstontx.gov/housing/

■ Director **Neal Rackleff** . . . . (832) 394-6200
E-mail: housingdirector@houstontx.gov
Commercial Assistant Director **Eta Paransky** . . . . (832) 394-6200
E-mail: eta.paransky@houstontx.gov
Chief Financial Officer/Assistant Director **Steven Rawlinson** . . . . (832) 394-6200
Planning and Grants Management Assistant Director **Brenda Scott** . . . . (832) 394-6279
Public Information Officer **Marc Eichenbaum** . . . . (832) 393-0959
E-mail: marc.eichenbaum@houstontx.gov

Houston First Corporation

P.O. Box 61469, Houston, TX 77208
Tel: (713) 853-8000 Internet: www.houstonfirst.com/

■ President **Dawn R. Ullrich** . . . . (713) 853-8083
E-mail: dawnr.ullrich@houstonfirst.com
Education: Wisconsin (Eau Claire) BA; Houston JD

Human Resources Department

611 Walker Street, 4th Floor, Houston, TX 77002
Fax: (713) 393-7208 Internet: www.houstontx.gov/hr/

■ Director (Interim) **Jane Cheeks** . . . . (832) 393-6043
E-mail: jane.cheeks@houstontx.gov
Deputy Director **Ramiro Cano** . . . . (832) 393-6060
E-mail: ramiro.cano@houstontx.gov
Deputy Director **Robert D. Thomas** . . . . (832) 393-6058
E-mail: robert.thomas@houstontx.gov

Houston Information Technology Services [HITS]

611 Walker, 8th Floor, Houston, TX 77002
Fax: (832) 393-0075 Internet: http://www.houstontx.gov/hits/

■ Director (Interim) **Tina Carkhuff** . . . . (832) 393-0082
E-mail: tina.carkhuff@houstontx.gov
Deputy Director, Project Management Office **Daniel Adeyemo** . . . . (832) 393-0028
E-mail: daniel.adeyemo@houstontx.gov Fax: (713) 837-9945
Deputy Director, Radio Communication Services **Tom Sorley** . . . . (832) 393-0300
E-mail: tom.sorley@houstontx.gov
Deputy Director, Infrastructure Services **Tina Carkhuff** . . . (832) 393-0300
E-mail: tina.carkhuff@houstontx.gov Fax: (832) 395-0009
Deputy Director, Application Services **Reenie Askew** . . . . (832) 393-0291
E-mail: reenie.askew@houstontx.gov

Legal Department

City Hall Annex, 900 Bagby St., 4th Floor, Houston, TX 77002-2527
P.O. Box 368, Houston, TX 77001-0368
Fax: (832) 393-6259 Internet: www.houstontx.gov/legal

■ City Attorney **Ronald C. Lewis** . . . . (832) 393-6491
First Assistant City Attorney **Tom P. Allen** . . . . (832) 393-6491
First Assistant City Attorney **Harlan D. Heilman** . . . . (832) 393-6491
First Assistant City Attorney **Deidra Penny** . . . . (832) 393-6491

Parks and Recreation Department [HPARD]

2999 S. Wayside Dr., Houston, TX 77023
P.O. Box 1562, Houston, TX 77251-1562
Tel: (832) 395-7000 Internet: www.houstontx.gov/parks/

■ Director **Joe Turner** . . . . (832) 395-7050
E-mail: joe.turner@houstontx.gov
Executive Assistant **Erika Madison** . . . . (832) 395-7061
E-mail: erika.madison@houstontx.gov
Houston Parks Board Executive Director (Interim) **Mike Nichols** . . . . (713) 942-8500
Fax: (713) 942-7664
Facilities Development and Maintenance Deputy Director **Mark Ross** . . . . (832) 395-7040
E-mail: mark.ross@houstontx.gov
Greenspace Management Deputy Director **Abel Gonzales** . . . . (832) 395-7031
Management and Finance Deputy Director **Cheryl Johnson** . . . . (832) 395-7064
Park Administration Assistant Director **Rick Dewees** . . . . (832) 395-7591
Communications Manager **Estella Espinosa** . . . . (832) 395-7022
E-mail: estella.espinosa@houstontx.gov
Recreation and Wellness Division Deputy Director **Kenneth Allen** . . . . (832) 395-7291
Recreation and Wellness Division Deputy Director **Debra Lathan** . . . . (832) 395-7294
Lake Houston Park Manager **Eric Spurgeon** . . . . (281) 354-6881
Urban Park Rangers Division Manager **Harold Norris** . . . . (832) 395-7002

Planning and Development Department

611 Walker Street, 6th Floor, Houston, TX 77002
P.O. Box 1562, Houston, TX 77251-1562
Fax: (832) 837-7703 Internet: http://www.houstontx.gov/planning

■ Director **Patrick Walsh** . . . . (832) 393-6600
E-mail: patrick.walsh@houstontx.tov
Deputy Director **Margaret Wallace Brown** . . . . (832) 393-6600
E-mail: mbrown@houstontx.gov
Management Services Deputy Assistant Director **Roger Hamilton** . . . . (832) 393-6600
Chief of Public Affairs **Suzy Hartgrove** . . . . (832) 393-6600
Development Services Division Assistant Director **Mike Kramer** . . . . (832) 393-6600
Neighborhood Services Manager **Nicole Smothers** . . . . . . (832) 393-6600
E-mail: nsmothers@houstontx.gov
Community Sustainability Director **Nicole Smothers** . . . . (832) 393-6600
Historic Preservation Officer **Diana Ducroz** . . . . (832) 393-6600

Police Department

1200 Travis St., Houston, TX 77002
Tel: (713) 308-1600 Fax: (713) 308-1601
Internet: www.houstonpolice.org

Chief of Police (Interim) **Martha Montalvo** . . . . (713) 308-1600
Field Operations/Executive Assistant Chief **M. A. Dirden** . . . . (713) 308-1600
Investigative Operations/ Executive Assistant Chief **T. N. Oettmeier** . . . . (713) 308-1540
Strategic Operations/Executive Assistant Chief **George T. Buenik** . . . . (713) 308-1850

Public Works and Engineering Department

611 Walker, Houston, TX 77002

■ Director **Dale Rudick** . . . . (832) 395-2500
E-mail: dale.rudick@houstontx.gov Fax: (832) 395-2480
Chief of Staff **Howard Hillard** . . . . (832) 395-2511
Fax: (832) 395-2480
City Engineer **Tim Lincoln** . . . . (832) 394-9140
Engineering and Construction Division Deputy Director (Interim) **Carol Ellinger Haddock** . . . . (832) 395-2202
E-mail: carol.haddock@houstontx.gov Fax: (832) 395-2083
Planning Development Services Deputy Director **Mark Loethen** . . . . (832) 395-2511

★ Elected Official ▲ Appointed by Legislature ▼ Appointed by Governor ▶ Appointed by Board or Commission ● Appointed by Judge
■ Appointed by Mayor △ Appointed by Freeholders ▽ Appointed by Supervisor ▷ Appointed by County Executive ○ Appointed by Council

Public Works and Engineering Department *continued*

Resource Management Division Deputy Director
Susan Bandy .... (832) 395-2469
E-mail: susan.bandy@houstontx.gov Fax: (832) 395-2477

Street and Drainage Division Deputy Director
Eric Dargan .... (713) 837-7502

Traffic Operations Division Deputy Director
Jeffrey Weatherford .... (832) 395-2460

Media Relations **Alvin Wright** .... (832) 395-2455
Fax: (832) 395-2479

Public Utilities Division

Deputy Director **Jun Chang** .... (832) 395-2465
Fax: (832) 395-2483

Solid Waste Management Department [SWMD]

P.O. Box 1562, Houston, TX 77251-1562

Director **Harry J. Hayes** .... (832) 393-1078
Education: Texas Southern 1988 BA

North Operations Division Deputy Director **(Vacant)** .... (713) 837-9107
Fax: (713) 837-9222

South Operations Division Deputy Director
Anthony Bowie .... (713) 837-9136
E-mail: anthony.bowie@houstontx.tov

Support Services Deputy Director **Randy Tims** .... (832) 393-0443
E-mail: randy.tims@houstontx.tov

Maintenance Division Assistant Director **Ralph Stevens** .. (832) 393-6960

Human Resources Manager **Carolyn Wright** .... (832) 393-0449
E-mail: carolyn.wright@houstontx.tov

North East Operations Deputy Assistant Director
Kimberly Lamott Jones .... (832) 393-9690
E-mail: kimberly.jones@houstontx.tov

Public Information Officer **Irma Reyes** .... (832) 393-0475
E-mail: irma.reyes@houstontx.tov

Houston Airport System

16930 J.F. Kennedy Blvd., Houston, TX 77032
P.O. Box 60106, Houston, TX 77205-0106
Tel: (281) 233-3000 Fax: (281) 233-1874 TTY: (281) 230-2855
Internet: http://www.fly2houston.com

■ Director **Mario C. Diaz** .... (281) 233-1816
E-mail: mario.diaz@houstontx.gov
Education: Rutgers (Newark) BA; Rutgers MBA

Deputy Director, External Affairs **Saba Abashawl** .... (281) 233-1829

Chief Commercial Officer **Ian Wadsworth** .... (281) 233-1892

Chief Development Officer **Jeffrey Brown** .... (281) 233-1999

Chief Technology Officer **Lisa Kent** .... (281) 233-1971
E-mail: lisa.kent@houstontx.gov

Chief Operating Officer **Balram "B" Bheodari** .... (281) 233-3000

Houston Public Library

500 McKinney, Houston, TX 77002-2534
Tel: (832) 393-1313 TTY: (832) 393-1539
Internet: www.houstonlibrary.org

Year Founded: 1904

Administration

Director **Rhea Brown Lawson** .... (832) 393-1300
E-mail: library.director@houstontx.gov
Education: Morgan State BA; Maryland 1981 MLS; Wisconsin PhD

Deputy Director, Library Administration
Roosevelt Weeks .... (832) 393-1327
E-mail: roosevelt.weeks@houstontx.gov

Deputy Director, Customer Experience
Michele Gorman .... (832) 393-1329
E-mail: michele.gorman@houstontx.gov

Assistant Director, Communications **(Vacant)** .... (832) 393-1333

Assistant Director, Planning and Facilities
John Middleton .... (832) 393-1681
E-mail: john.middleton@houstontx.gov

Assistant Director, Digital Strategies **Ricardo Peralez** .... (832) 393-1400

Administration *continued*

Chief Financial Officer **Hope Obika Waobikeze** .... (832) 393-1348
Date of Birth: April 27, 1970
Education: Texas Southern 1991 BBA; Houston Baptist 1997 BBA; Our Lady of Lake 2000 MBA

Chief, Technical Services **(Vacant)** .... (832) 393-1484

Division Manager, Human Resources
Ophelia Cespedes .... (832) 393-1343
E-mail: ophelia.cespedes@houstontx.gov

Manager, Houston Metropolitan Research Center
Laney McAdow .... (832) 393-1662
E-mail: laney.mcadow@houstontx.gov

Volunteer Services Manager **(Vacant)** .... (832) 393-1481

Coordinator, Materials Selection **(Vacant)** .... (832) 393-1479

Webmaster **George Eggleston** .... (832) 393-1415
E-mail: george.eggleston@houstontx.gov

Office of the City Council

City Hall Annex, 900 Bagby St., 1st Floor, Houston, TX 77002
P.O. Box 1562, Houston, TX 77251-1562
Tel: (832) 393-0791 Internet: http://www.houstontx.gov/council/

★ Mayor Pro Tem **Ellen Cohen** (District C) .... (832) 393-3004
Term Expires: December 31, 2017 Fax: (832) 393-3239
E-mail: districtc@houstontx.gov
Education: Northwood BBA

★ Council Member **Brenda Stardig** (District A) .... (832) 393-3010
Term Expires: December 31, 2017 Fax: (832) 393-9500
E-mail: districta@houstontx.gov

★ Council Member **Jerry Davis** (District B) .... (832) 393-3009
Term Expires: December 31, 2017 Fax: (832) 393-3291
E-mail: districtb@houstontx.gov

★ Council Member **Dwight Boykins** (District D) .... (832) 393-3001
Term Expires: December 31, 2017 Fax: (832) 393-3201
E-mail: districtd@houstontx.gov

★ Council Member **Dave Martin** (District E) .... (832) 393-3008
Term Expires: December 31, 2017 Fax: (832) 393-3279
E-mail: districte@houstontx.gov

★ Council Member **Steve Le** (District F) .... (832) 393-0791
Term Expires: December 31, 2017 Fax: (832) 393-3212
E-mail: districtf@houstontx.gov

★ Council Member **Greg Travis** (District G) .... (832) 393-3007
Term Expires: December 31, 2017

★ Council Member **Karla Cisneros** (District H) .... (832) 393-3003
Term Expires: December 31, 2017

★ Council Member **Robert Gallegos** (District I) .... (832) 393-3011
Term Expires: December 31, 2017 Fax: (832) 393-3313
E-mail: districti@houstontx.gov

★ Council Member **Mike Laster** (District J) .... (832) 393-0791
Term Expires: December 31, 2017 Fax: (832) 393-0783
E-mail: districtj@houstontx.gov

★ Council Member **Larry Green** (District K) .... (832) 393-0791
Term Expires: December 31, 2017 Fax: (832) 393-0783
E-mail: districtk@houstontx.gov

★ Council Member **Mike Knox** (At-Large, Position 1) .... (832) 393-3014
Term Expires: December 31, 2017

★ Council Member
David Robinson (At-Large, Position 2) .... (832) 393-3013
Term Expires: December 31, 2017 Fax: (832) 393-3336
E-mail: atlarge2@houstontx.gov

★ Council Member
Michael Kubosh (At-Large, Position 3) .... (832) 393-3005
Term Expires: December 31, 2017 Fax: (832) 393-3251
E-mail: atlarge3@houstontx.gov

★ Council Member
Amanda Edwards (At-Large, Position 4) .... (832) 393-3012
Term Expires: December 31, 2017

★ Council Member **Jack Christie** (At-Large, Position 5) .... (832) 393-3006
Term Expires: December 31, 2017 Fax: (832) 393-3261
E-mail: atlarge5@houstontx.gov

★ Elected Official ▲ Appointed by Legislature ▼ Appointed by Governor ► Appointed by Board or Commission ● Appointed by Judge
■ Appointed by Mayor △ Appointed by Freeholders ▽ Appointed by Supervisor ▷ Appointed by County Executive ○ Appointed by Council

Office of the City Controller

P.O. Box 1562, Houston, TX 77251-1562
Fax: (832) 393-3416 E-mail: controllers@houstontx.gov
Internet: www.houstontx.gov/controller/

★City Controller **Chris Brown** .... (832) 393-3402
Term Expires: December 31, 2019
Deputy Director, Administrative Division **Alex Obregon** .. (832) 393-3403
Deputy Controller, Operation and Technical Services
Shannan Nobles .... (832) 393-3456
E-mail: shannan.nobles@houstontx.gov
Deputy Controller, Treasury **Charisse Moseley** .... (832) 393-3529
City Auditor **Courtney Smith** .... (832) 393-3464
Director, Communications and Governmental Affairs
Roger Widmeyer .... (832) 393-3407
E-mail: roger.widmeyer@houstontx.gov
Scheduler/Executive Assistant to City Controller
Jackie Pope .... (832) 393-3402
E-mail: jpope@houstontx.gov

Houston Independent School District [HISD]

4400 West 18th Street, Houston, TX 77092
Fax: (713) 556-6015 Internet: www.houstonisd.org

Superintendent (Interim) **Kenneth Huewitt** .... (713) 556-6300
Chief of Staff **Jason Spencer** .... (713) 556-6300
Chief Academic Officer **Dr. Andrew Houlihan** .... (713) 556-6900
Fax: (713) 556-6015
Chief Operating Officer **(Vacant)** .... (713) 556-6150
Fax: (713) 556-6015
Deputy Superintendent/Chief Financial Officer
Kenneth Huewitt .... (713) 556-6600
Fax: (713) 556-6015
Legal Services/General Counsel
Elneita Hutchins-Taylor .... (713) 556-7245
Fax: (713) 556-7269
Chief Human Resources Officer **Gloria Cavazos** .... (713) 556-7353
E-mail: gcavazos@houstonisd.org Fax: (713) 556-6015
Chief Communications Officer **Helen Spencer** .... (713) 556-6380
E-mail: hspencer@houstonisd.org
Press Secretary **Holly Huffman** .... (713) 556-6393
Assistant Superintendent for Research and
Accountability **Carla Stevens** .... (713) 556-6700
Chief Elementary School Officer **Karla Loria** .... (713) 556-7100
Chief Elementary School Officer **Samuel Sarabia** .... (713) 556-7100
Chief High School Officer **Jason Bernal** .... (713) 556-7143
Chief Middle School Officer **Michael A. Cardona** .... (713) 556-7102
Chief School Officer, Elementary Transformation
Dr. Grenita Lathan .... (713) 556-7100
Internal Audit **Richard Patton** .... (713) 556-6325
Fax: (713) 556-6374
Chief Information Technology Officer **Lenny Schad** .... (713) 556-6200
E-mail: lschad@houstonisd.org Fax: (713) 556-6194
Chief Student Support Officer **Mark Smith** .... (713) 556-6300

Board of Education

Fax: (713) 556-6115

President **Manuel Rodríguez, Jr.** (District III) .... (713) 556-6121
First Vice President **Wanda Adams** (District IX) .... (713) 556-6121
Second Vice President **Diana Dávila** (District VIII) .... (713) 556-6121
Secretary **Jolanda Jones** (District IV) .... (713) 556-6121
Trustee **Anna Eastman** (District I) .... (713) 556-6121
Trustee **Rhonda Skillern-Jones** (District II) .... (713) 556-6121
Trustee **Michael L. Lunceford** (District V) .... (713) 556-6121
Education: Texas A&M (Commerce) BBA; Southern Methodist MPA
Trustee **Greg Meyers** (District VI) .... (713) 556-6121
Trustee **Harvin C. Moore** (District VII) .... (713) 556-6121

City of Huntington Beach, California

City Hall, 2000 Main St., Huntington Beach, CA 92648
Tel: (714) 536-5227 (City Clerk Information)
Tel: (714) 536-5511 (Information) Internet: www.huntingtonbeachca.gov

County: Orange **Election Type:** Nonpartisan **Population:** 201,899 (2015)

Office of the Mayor and City Council

City Hall, 2000 Main St., Huntington Beach, CA 92648
Fax: (714) 536-5233

★Mayor **Jim Katapodis** .... (714) 536-5553
Began Service: December 4, 2012
Term Expires: December 1, 2016
E-mail: jim.katapodis@surfcity-hb.org
★Mayor Pro Tem **Dave Sullivan** .... (714) 536-5553
Term Expires: December 1, 2016
E-mail: dave.sullivan@surfcity-hb.org
★Council Member **Barbara Delgleize** .... (714) 536-5553
Term Expires: December 2018
E-mail: barbara.delgleize@surfcity-hb.org
★Council Member **Jill Hardy** .... (714) 536-5553
Term Expires: December 1, 2016
E-mail: jill.hardy@surfcity-hb.org
Education: UC Santa Barbara 1992 BA;
Cal State (Long Beach) 2002 MA
★Council Member **William "Billy" O'Connell** .... (714) 536-5553
Term Expires: December 2018
E-mail: billy.oconnell@surfcity-hb.org
★Council Member **Erik Peterson** .... (714) 536-5553
Term Expires: December 2018
E-mail: erik.peterson@surfcity-hb.org
★Council Member **Mike Posey** .... (714) 536-5553
Term Expires: December 2018
E-mail: mike.posey@surfcity-hb.org
City Council Secretary **Cathy Fikes** .... (714) 536-5553
E-mail: cfikes@surfcity-hb.org

Office of the City Attorney

City Hall, 2000 Main St., Huntington Beach, CA 92648-2702
Fax: (714) 374-1590

★City Attorney **Michael E. Gates** .... (714) 536-5555
Term Expires: December 2018
E-mail: michael.gates@surfcity-hb.org
Senior Deputy City Attorney **Neal Moore** .... (714) 536-5555
Senior Deputy City Attorney **John Fujii** .... (714) 536-5555
Deputy City Attorney III **Daniel K. Ohl** .... (714) 536-5555
Chief Assistant City Attorney **Michael Vigliotta** .... (714) 536-5555
Assistant City Attorney **Scott Field** .... (714) 536-5555

Office of the City Clerk/Passport Facility

City Hall, 2nd Fl., 2000 Main St., Huntington Beach, CA 92648
Fax: (714) 374-1557

★City Clerk **Joan L. Flynn** .... (714) 536-5227
Term Expires: November 9, 2016
E-mail: jflynn@surfcity-hb.org

Office of the City Treasurer

City Hall, 2000 Main St., Huntington Beach, CA 92648-2702
Tel: (714) 536-5200 Fax: (714) 374-1603

★City Treasurer **Alisa Cutchen** .... (714) 536-5200
Term Expires: November 7, 2016
E-mail: acutchen@huntingtonbeachca.gov
Deputy City Treasurer **Joyce M. Zacks** .... (714) 536-5990
E-mail: jzacks@surfcity-hb.org
Administrative Assistant **Linda Wine** .... (714) 536-5445
E-mail: linda.wine@surfcity-hb.org

★Elected Official ▲Appointed by Legislature ▼Appointed by Governor ▶Appointed by Board or Commission ●Appointed by Judge
■Appointed by Mayor △Appointed by Freeholders ▽Appointed by Supervisor ▷Appointed by County Executive ○Appointed by Council

Office of the City Manager
City Hall, 2000 Main Street, 4th Floor, Huntington Beach, CA 92648
Tel: (714) 536-5202 Fax: (714) 536-5233

City Manager **Fred Wilson** .... (714) 536-5575
Executive Assistant **Johanna Dombo** .... (714) 536-5575
E-mail: jstephenson@surfcity-hb.org
Assistant City Manager **Ken Domer** .... (714) 536-5358
Director of Communications/Public Information Officer
Julie Toledo .... (714) 536-5577
E-mail: jtoledo@surfcity-hb.org
Finance Manager **Lori Ann Farrell** .... (714) 536-5228

Accounting and Records
Fax: (714) 374-1571

Principal Accountant **Dahle Bulosan** .... (714) 536-5907
E-mail: dbulosan@surfcity-hb.org

Budget and Research
Budget Manager **Carol Molina-Espinoza** .... (714) 374-1526
E-mail: carol.molina-espinoza@surfcity-hb.org

Central Services
Tel: (714) 536-5221

Buyer **Marilyn Goldstein** .... (714) 374-1569
E-mail: mgoldstein@surfcity-hb.org
Buyer **Sharon Griffith** .... (714) 960-8876
E-mail: sgriffith@huntingtonbeachca.gov

Information Services
Tel: (714) 960-8893

Director **(Vacant)** .... (714) 536-5514

Human Resources Department
Human Resources Director **Michele Warren** .... (714) 536-5586
E-mail: Michele.Warren@surfcity-hb.org
Personnel Assistant **Jenny Jackson** .... (714) 374-1562
E-mail: jjackson@surfcity-hb.org

Risk Management Office
Tel: (714) 536-5252 Fax: (714) 374-1597

Risk Manager **Patti Williams** .... (714) 536-5589
E-mail: pwilliams@surfcity-hb.org
Administrative Secretary **Teresa De Coite** .... (714) 536-5252
E-mail: tdecoite@surfcity-hb.org

Office of Business Development
Tel: (714) 536-5542

Deputy Director **Kellee Fritzal** .... (714) 374-1519
E-mail: kfritzal@surfcity-hb.org

Housing Office
Administrative Analyst **Denise Bazant** .... (714) 536-5470
E-mail: denise.bazant@surfcity-hb.org

Real Estate Services
Real Estate Services Manager **Duran Villegas** .... (714) 536-5544

Community Services Department
City Hall, 2000 Main Street, Huntington Beach, CA 92648
Tel: (714) 536-5486 Fax: (714) 374-1654

Director **Janeen Laudenback** .... (714) 536-5495
E-mail: jlaudenback@surfcity-hb.org
Administrative Assistant **Carrie Gonzales** .... (714) 536-5292
E-mail: kgonzales@surfcity-hb.org

Fire Department
City Hall, 2000 Main St., Huntington Beach, CA 92648
Tel: (714) 536-5411 Fax: (714) 374-1551
E-mail: fire.department@surfcity-hb.org

Fire Chief (Interim) **Eric G. Engberg** .... (714) 536-5402
E-mail: eengberg@surfcity-hb.org

Fire Department *continued*

Administrative Assistant **Lorene Ernst** .... (714) 536-5402
E-mail: lernst@surfcity-hb.org
Administrative Analyst Senior **Kevin Justen** .... (714) 536-5235
E-mail: kjusten@surfcity-hb.org

Department of Community Development
City Hall, 2000 Main St., Huntington Beach, CA 92648
Tel: (714) 536-5241 (Building Info & Questions) Fax: (714) 374-1647

Director **Scott Hess** .... (714) 536-5276
Administrative Assistant **Kimberly De Coite** .... (714) 536-5276
E-mail: kdecoite@surfcity-hb.org

Building Division
Inspection Manager **Mark Carnahan** .... (714) 374-1792
Permit Supervisor **Michele Diaz** .... (714) 375-5149

Planning Division
City Hall, 2000 Main St., Huntington Beach, CA 92648
Tel: (714) 536-5271 Fax: (714) 374-1540

Planning Manager **Jane James** .... (714) 536-5438
Planning Manager **(Vacant)** .... (714) 536-5550

Police Department
City Hall, 2000 Main St., Huntington Beach, CA 92648
Tel: (714) 960-8811 Fax: (714) 536-2895

Police Chief **Robert Handy** .... (714) 536-5902
Education: Arizona BSPA; Arizona State MPA
Administrative Assistant **Ingrid Ono** .... (714) 536-5903
E-mail: iono@hbpd.org
Administrative Operations Division Captain
David Bunetta .... (714) 960-8811
Investigation Division Captain **Bill Stuart** .... (714) 960-8811
Uniform Division Captain **Capt. Russell Reinhart** .... (714) 960-8811
Training **Greg Davis** .... (714) 960-8811
E-mail: gdavis@hbpd.org

Public Library System
7111 Talbert Ave., Huntington Beach, CA 92648-1296
Tel: (714) 842-4481 Fax: (714) 375-5146 Internet: www.hbpl.org
E-mail: library@hbpl.org

Director **Stephanie Beverage** .... (714) 960-8836
E-mail: stephanie.beverage@surfcity-hb.org
Administrative Assistant **Michelle Roesner** .... (714) 960-8836
E-mail: michelle.roesner@surfcity-hb.org
Youth Services **Barbara Richardson** .... (714) 374-5338
E-mail: brichardson@surfcity-hb.org
Literacy Coordinator **Diane Moseley** .... (714) 375-5102
E-mail: diane.moseley@surfcity-hb.org
Media Services Coordinator/Circulation
Richard Crosthwaite .... (714) 375-5108
E-mail: rcrosthwaite@huntingtonbeachca.gov
Meeting Room Facilities Coordinator **Reneé Brown** .... (714) 375-8425
Principal Librarian **Mary Wilson** .... (714) 374-5335
E-mail: wilsonm@hbpl.org
Public and Information Services **Lia Bushong** .... (714) 374-1669
E-mail: lia.bushong@surfcity-hb.org
Volunteer Services Coordinator **Monica Miltko** .... (714) 375-5114
E-mail: mmiltko@huntingtonbeachca.gov

Public Works Department
City Hall, 2000 Main St., Huntington Beach, CA 92648
Tel: (714) 536-5431 Fax: (714) 374-1573

Public Works Director **Travis Hopkins** .... (714) 536-5437
Administrative Assistant **Kristy Wapner** .... (714) 536-5437
E-mail: risty.wapner@surfcity-hb.org
Deputy Director **(Vacant)** .... (714) 536-5431
Project Manager **Ken Dills** .... (714) 375-5055

★ Elected Official ▲ Appointed by Legislature ▼ Appointed by Governor ► Appointed by Board or Commission ● Appointed by Judge
■ Appointed by Mayor △ Appointed by Freeholders ▽ Appointed by Supervisor ▷ Appointed by County Executive ○ Appointed by Council

Engineering Division
Tel: (714) 536-5431

City Engineer **Tom Herbel** .... (714) 375-5077
E-mail: tom.herbel@surfcity-hb.org
Contract Administrator **Dave Verone** .... (714) 375-8471
Construction Manager **Joe Dale** .... (714) 536-5915
E-mail: jdale@surfcity-hb.org
Principal Civil Engineer **M. Todd Broussard** .... (714) 536-5247
E-mail: tbroussard@surfcity-hb.org
Principal Civil Engineer **Debbie De Bow** .... (714) 536-5528
E-mail: ddebow@surfcity-hb.org
Principal Civil Engineer **Terri Elliott** .... (714) 375-8494
E-mail: telliott@surfcity-hb.org
Principal Civil Engineer **Duncan Lee** .... (714) 375-5118
E-mail: dlee@surfcity-hb.org

General Services Division
General Services Manager **Jerry Thompson** .... (714) 960-8845
Customer Service Representative **Doris Powell** .... (714) 536-5522
Fleet Operations Supervisor **Robert LaRoche** .... (714) 375-5050

Maintenance Division
Corporate Yard, 17371 Gothard St., Huntington Beach, CA 92647
Tel: (714) 960-8861 Fax: (714) 375-5099

Operations Manager **Denny Bacon** .... (714) 960-8861
E-mail: dbacon@surfcity-hb.org
Department Analyst **Debra Jubinsky** .... (714) 374-5321
Street Supervisor **Derek Livermore** .... (714) 374-1732
E-mail: dlivermore@huntingtonbeachca.gov

Transportation Division
Transportation Manager **Bob Stachelski** .... (714) 536-5523
Principal Civil Engineer **Bill Janusz** .... (714) 374-1628
E-mail: wjanusz@surfcity-hb.org

Utilities Division
19001 Huntington St., Huntington Beach, CA 92648
Tel: (714) 536-5921 Fax: (714) 847-1067

Utilities Manager **Brian Ragland** .... (714) 536-5503
E-mail: brian.ragland@surfcity-hb.org
Distribution Water Supervisor **Rudy Ocampo** .... (714) 536-5453
Sewer Service Maintenance **Dorien McElroy** .... (714) 375-5040
E-mail: dorien.mcelroy@surfcity-hb.org

Town of Huntington, New York

100 Main Street, Huntington, NY 11743
Tel: (631) 351-3014 (Information) Internet: www.huntingtonny.gov/

County: Suffolk **Election Type:** Partisan **Population:** 204,398 (2015)

Office of the Town Supervisor
100 Main St., Huntington, NY 11743
Fax: (631) 424-7856

★ Town Supervisor **Frank P. Petrone** (D) .... (631) 351-3030
Began Service: 1993 Fax: (631) 424-7856
Term Expires: December 31, 2017
E-mail: fpetrone@huntingtonny.gov
Date of Birth: 1944
Education: SUNY (Albany) 1967 BS; Denver 1970 MA; Long Island 1982 MPA
Public Information Officer **A.J. Carter** .... (631) 351-3349
E-mail: ajcarter@huntingtonny.gov Fax: (631) 424-7856

Office of the Assessor
100 Main St., Huntington, NY 11743
Fax: (631) 425-0128

○ Assessor **Roger Ramme** .... (631) 351-3226
E-mail: assessor@huntingtonny.gov

Office of the Comptroller
100 Main St., Huntington, NY 11743
Fax: (631) 351-2898

○ Comptroller **Peggy Karayianakis** .... (631) 351-3310
E-mail: auditandcontrol@huntingtonny.gov
○ Deputy Comptroller **Peter Leodis** .... (631) 351-3262
E-mail: pleodis@huntingtonny.gov

Office of the Town Attorney
100 Main St., Huntington, NY 11743
Fax: (631) 351-3032

○ Town Attorney **Cindy Elan-Mangano** .... (631) 351-3042
E-mail: townattorney@huntingtonny.gov

Community Development Department
100 Main St., Huntington, NY 11743
Fax: (631) 351-2889

○ Director **Joan Cergol** .... (631) 351-2881
E-mail: community_dev@huntingtonny.gov

Department of Engineering Services
100 Main St., Huntington, NY 11743
Fax: (631) 351-3212

○ Director **Joseph F. Cline** .... (631) 351-3151
E-mail: jcline@huntingtonny.gov

Environmental Waste Management Department
100 Main St., Huntington, NY 11743
Fax: (631) 351-3330

○ Director (Interim) **Matthew Laux** .... (631) 351-3186

General Services Department
100 Main St., Huntington, NY 11743
Fax: (631) 351-3337

○ Director **Mark Tyree** .... (631) 351-3050
E-mail: genservices@huntingtonny.gov

Heckscher Museum
Two Prime Ave., Huntington, NY 11743
Tel: (631) 351-3250 Fax: (631) 423-2145 E-mail: info@heckscher.org
Internet: www.heckscher.org

○ Executive Director **Dr. Michael W. Schantz** .... (631) 351-3005
E-mail: mschantz@huntingtonny.gov

Office of the Historian
100 Main St., Huntington, NY 11743
Fax: (631) 351-3245

▽ Historian **Robert C. Hughes** .... (631) 351-3244
E-mail: rhughes@huntingtonny.gov

Human Services Department
100 Main St., Huntington, NY 11743
Fax: (631) 425-0746

○ Director **Jillian Guthman-Abadom** .... (631) 351-3058
E-mail: jguthman-abadom@huntingtonny.gov
Director, Senior Citizens Division **Holli Dunayer** .... (631) 351-3253
Village Green Center, Fax: (631) 351-3221
423 Park Avenue, Huntington, NY 11743

Information Technology Department
100 Main Street, Room 311, Huntington, NY 11743
Tel: (631) 351-3161

Director **Bill Crowley** .... (631) 351-3161

Maritime Services Department
100 Main Street, Room 300, Huntington, NY 11743
Fax: (631) 351-3373

○ Director **Edward Carr** .... (631) 351-3192
E-mail: ecarr@huntingtonny.gov

Parks and Recreation Department
100 Main St., Huntington, NY 11743
Fax: (631) 351-3100

○ Director **Don McKay** .... (631) 351-3309
E-mail: dmckay@huntingtonny.gov

Personnel Department
100 Main St., Huntington, NY 11743
Fax: (631) 351-3279

Personnel Officer [Civil Service] **Lisa Baisley** .... (631) 351-3026
E-mail: lbaisley@huntingtonny.gov

Planning and Environment Department
100 Main St., Huntington, NY 11743
Fax: (631) 351-3257

○ Director **Anthony Aloisio** .... (631) 351-3196
E-mail: Planning@HuntingtonNY.gov

Public Safety Department
100 Main St., Huntington, NY 11743
Fax: (631) 351-3169

Director **Joseph Rose** .... (631) 351-3167
E-mail: public_safety@huntingtonny.gov

Animal Control Department
106 Deposit Road, East Northport, NY 11731

Shelter Supervisor **Gerald Mosca** .... (631) 754-8722

Purchasing Department
100 Main St., Huntington, NY 11743
Fax: (631) 351-2833

Director **Lori Finger** .... (631) 351-3177
E-mail: lfinger@huntingtonny.gov

Transportation and Traffic Safety Department
100 Main Street, 109, Huntington, NY 11743
Tel: (631) 351-3053 Fax: (631) 351-3066

Director **Stephen McCloin** .... (631) 351-3053

Youth Bureau
423 Park Avenue, Huntington, NY 11743
Fax: (516) 271-1360

Director **Maria E. Georgiou** .... (631) 351-3061

Office of the Town Council
100 Main Street, Huntington, NY 11743

Deputy Supervisor **Patricia DelCol** .... (631) 351-3301
E-mail: pdelcol@huntingtonny.gov Fax: (631) 424-7856

★ Council Member **Susan A. Berland** (D) .... (631) 351-3173
Term Expires: December 31, 2019
E-mail: sberland@huntingtonny.gov

★ Council Member **Eugene Cook** (I) .... (631) 351-3174
Term Expires: December 31, 2019
E-mail: ecook@huntingtonny.gov

★ Council Member **Mark Cuthbertson** (D) .... (631) 351-3172
Term Expires: December 31, 2017
E-mail: mcuthbertson@huntingtonny.gov

★ Council Member **Tracy Edwards** (D) .... (631) 351-3175
Term Expires: December 31, 2017
E-mail: tedwards@huntingtonny.gov

Office of the Town Clerk
100 Main St., Huntington, NY 11743
Tel: (631) 351-3206 Fax: (631) 351-3205

★ Town Clerk and Registrar of Vital Statistics
Jo-Ann Raia (R) .... (631) 351-3216
Term Expires: December 31, 2019
E-mail: jraia@huntingtonny.gov

Archivist **Antonia Mattheou** .... (631) 351-3035
E-mail: amattheou@huntingtonny.gov

Office of the Receiver of Taxes
100 Main St., Huntington, NY 11743
Fax: (631) 351-2874

★ Receiver of Taxes **Ester Bivona** (D) .... (631) 351-3217
Term Expires: December 31, 2019
E-mail: ebivona@huntingtonny.gov

Highway Office
30 Rofay Dr., Huntington, NY 11743
Fax: (631) 499-3512

★ Superintendent **Peter Gunther** (R) .... (631) 351-3076
Term Expires: December 31, 2017
E-mail: pgunther@huntingtonny.gov

City of Huntsville, Alabama

308 Fountain Circle, Huntsville, AL 35801
P.O. Box 308, Huntsville, AL 35804-0308
Internet: www.huntsvilleal.gov

County: Madison **Election Type:** Nonpartisan **Population:** 190,582 (2015)

Office of the Mayor
P.O. Box 308, Huntsville, AL 35804
Fax: (256) 427-5257

★ Mayor **Tommy Battle** .... (256) 427-5000
Began Service: November 3, 2008
Term Expires: November 2016
E-mail: tommy.battle@huntsvilleal.gov
Date of Birth: 1956
Education: Alabama

City Administrator **John S. Hamilton** .... (256) 427-5009
E-mail: john.hamilton@huntsvilleal.gov

Operation Green Team Director **Joy McKee** .... (256) 427-5048

Director of Communications **Kelly Cooper Schrimsher** .. (256) 425-5006
E-mail: kelly.schrimsher@huntsvilleal.gov

Multicultural Affairs Officer **Kenneth Anderson** .... (256) 425-5000
E-mail: kenny.anderson@huntsvilleal.gov

Office of the City Council
P.O. Box 308, Huntsville, AL 35804
Fax: (256) 427-5024

★ President **Will F. Culver** (District 5) .... (256) 427-5011
Term Expires: November 2016
E-mail: will.culver@huntsvilleal.gov

★ Council Member **Richard Showers, Sr.** (District 1) ...... (256) 427-5011
Term Expires: November 2016
E-mail: richard.showers@huntsvilleal.gov
Education: Alabama A&M BS, MS

★ Council Member **Mark Russell** (District 2) .... (256) 427-5011
Term Expires: November 2018
E-mail: mark.russell@huntsvilleal.gov
Education: Alabama Huntsville BS

(continued on next page)

★ Elected Official ▲ Appointed by Legislature ▼ Appointed by Governor ▶ Appointed by Board or Commission ● Appointed by Judge
■ Appointed by Mayor △ Appointed by Freeholders ▽ Appointed by Supervisor ▷ Appointed by County Executive ○ Appointed by Council

Office of the City Council *continued*

★Council Member **Jennie Robinson** (District 3) . . . . (256) 427-5011
Term Expires: November 2018
E-mail: jennie.robinson@huntsvilleal.gov

★Council Member **Bill Kling, Jr.** (District 4) . . . . (256) 427-5011
Term Expires: November 2018
E-mail: bill.kling@huntsvilleal.gov
Education: Alabama BS; Alabama A&M MS

Office of the City Attorney

P.O. Box 308, Huntsville, AL 35804

■City Attorney **Trey Riley** . . . . (256) 427-5026
E-mail: Trey.Riley@huntsvilleal.gov

Office of the City Clerk/Treasurer

P.O. Box 308, Huntsville, AL 35804
Fax: (256) 427-5095

■City Clerk/Treasurer **Kenneth Benion** . . . . (256) 427-5088
E-mail: kenneth.benion@huntsvilleal.gov

Animal Services Department

P.O. Box 308, Huntsville, AL 35804

■Manager **Karen Sheppard** . . . . (256) 883-3630
E-mail: karen.sheppard@huntsvilleal.gov

Cemetery Department

P.O. Box 308, Huntsville, AL 35804

■Manager **Joy McKee** . . . . (256) 427-5730
E-mail: joy.mckee@huntsvilleal.gov

Community Development Department

P.O. Box 308, Huntsville, AL 35804

■Director **Michelle Jordan** . . . . (256) 427-5400
E-mail: michelle.jordan@huntsvilleal.gov

Emergency Management Department

P.O. Box 308, Huntsville, AL 35804
Fax: (256) 427-5140

■Director **Jeff Birdwell** . . . . (256) 427-5123
E-mail: jeff.birdwell@huntsvilleal.gov

Engineering Department

P.O. Box 308, Huntsville, AL 35804

■Director **Kathy Martin** . . . . (256) 427-5300
E-mail: kathy.martin@huntsvilleal.gov

Finance Department

P.O. Box 308, Huntsville, AL 35804

■Director **Peggy Sargent** . . . . (256) 427-5080

Fire Department

P.O. Box 308, Huntsville, AL 35804

■Fire Chief **Howard McFarlen** . . . . (256) 427-7401
E-mail: howard.mcfarlen@huntsvilleal.gov

Fleet Management Department

P.O. Box 308, Huntsville, AL 35804

■Manager (Acting) **Mike Blankenship** . . . . (256) 883-3937
E-mail: mike.blankenship@huntsvilleal.gov

General Services Department

P.O. Box 308, Huntsville, AL 35804

■Director **Jeff Easter** . . . . (256) 427-5660
E-mail: jeff.easter@huntsvilleal.gov

Human Resources Department

P.O. Box 308, Huntsville, AL 35804
Tel: (256) 427-5240 Fax: (256) 427-5245

■Director **Byron Thomas** . . . . (256) 427-5240
E-mail: byron.thomas@huntsvilleal.gov

Information Technology Services

300 Madison St., Huntsville, AL 35801
P.O. Box 308, Huntsville, AL 35804
Tel: (256) 427-6700 Fax: (256) 427-6755

■Manager **Bill Steiner** . . . . (256) 427-6700
E-mail: bill.steiner@huntsvilleal.gov

Inspection Department

P.O. Box 308, Huntsville, AL 35804

■Manager **Randy Cunningham** . . . . (256) 427-5336
E-mail: randy.cunningham@huntsvilleal.gov

Natural Resources and Environmental Management Department

P.O. Box 308, Huntsville, AL 35804
Fax: (256) 427-5751

■Manager **Danny Shea** . . . . (256) 427-5750
E-mail: danny.shea@huntsvilleal.gov

Parking and Public Transit

P.O. Box 308, Huntsville, AL 35804

■Director **Tommy Brown** . . . . (256) 427-6800
E-mail: tommy.brown@huntsvilleal.gov

Police Department

P.O. Box 308, Huntsville, AL 35804

■Chief of Police **Mark McMurray** . . . . (256) 427-7009
E-mail: mark.mcmurray@huntsvilleal.gov
Services Bureau Deputy Chief **Corey Harris** . . . . (256) 564-5265
Operations Bureau Deputy Chief **Kirk Giles** . . . . (256) 427-7186
E-mail: kirk.giles@huntsvilleal.gov

Public Works Services Department

P.O. Box 308, Huntsville, AL 35804
Tel: (256) 883-3944 Fax: (256) 883-3954

■Director **Chris McNeese** . . . . (256) 883-3944
E-mail: chris.mcneese@huntsvilleal.gov

Sanitation Division

Manager **ReDonald Scott** . . . . (256) 883-3964

Street and Drainage Maintenance Division

Manager **Jackie Burgreen** . . . . (256) 883-3956

Parks and Recreation Department

P.O. Box 308, Huntsville, AL 35804

■Director **Steve Ivey** . . . . (256) 564-8026
E-mail: steve.ivey@huntsvilleal.gov
Metro Kiwanis SportsPlex Manager **Jay Cloys** . . . . (256) 427-5790

Traffic Engineering and Operations Department

P.O. Box 308, Huntsville, AL 35804

Director **L. Dan Sanders** . . . . (256) 427-6850
E-mail: dan.sanders@huntsvilleal.gov
Director of Long Range Planning **Dennis Madsen** . . . . (256) 427-5100

Urban Development

P.O. Box 308, Huntsville, AL 35804

■Director **Shane Davis** . . . . (256) 427-5300
E-mail: shane.davis@huntsvilleal.gov

★Elected Official ▲Appointed by Legislature ▼Appointed by Governor ►Appointed by Board or Commission ●Appointed by Judge
■Appointed by Mayor △Appointed by Freeholders ▽Appointed by Supervisor ▷Appointed by County Executive ○Appointed by Council

Water Pollution Control Department
P.O. Box 308, Huntsville, AL 35804

Director **Shane Cook** . . . . (256) 883-3719

City of Independence, Missouri
111 East Maple Avenue, Independence, MO 64050
P.O. Box 1019, Independence, MO 64051
Tel: (816) 325-7000 (Information) Internet: www.independencemo.org

County: Jackson **Election Type:** Nonpartisan **Year Incorporated:** 1849
Population: 117,255 (2015)

Office of the Mayor and City Council
111 East Maple Avenue, Independence, MO 64050
Fax: (816) 325-7012 Internet: www.ci.independence.mo.us/citycouncil/

★Mayor **Eileen Weir** . . . . (816) 325-7027
Began Service: April 2014
Term Expires: April 15, 2018
E-mail: eweir@indepmo.org
Secretary **Sheila Saxton** . . . . (816) 325-7022
E-mail: ssaxton@indepmo.org

★Council Member **John Perkins** (District 1) . . . . . . (816) 325-7022
Term Expires: April 17, 2020
E-mail: JPerkins@indepmo.org

★Council Member **Curt Dougherty** (District 2) . . . . . . (816) 325-7022
Term Expires: April 17, 2020
E-mail: cdougherty@indepmo.org

★Council Member **Scott Roberson** (District 3) . . . . . . (816) 325-7022
Term Expires: April 17, 2020
E-mail: sroberson@indepmo.org

★Council Member **Tom Van Camp** (District 4) . . . . . . (816) 305-3092
Term Expires: April 17, 2020
E-mail: TVanCamp@indepmo.org

★Council Member **Karen DeLuccie** (At-Large) . . . . . . (816) 325-7022
Term Expires: April 15, 2018
E-mail: kdeluccie@indepmo.org

★Council Member **Christopher Whiting** (At-Large) . . . . . . (816) 325-7022
Term Expires: April 15, 2018
E-mail: cwhiting@indepmo.org

○Management Analyst **(Vacant)** . . . . (816) 325-7025

Office of the City Clerk
111 East Maple Avenue, Independence, MO 64050
Tel: (816) 325-7010

○City Clerk **Sarah Carnes-Lemp** . . . . (816) 325-7015
E-mail: scarnes-lemp@indepmo.org
Secretary **Becky Behrens** . . . . (816) 325-7010
E-mail: rbehrens@indepmo.org

Records Center/Assistant City Clerk **Sheri Thacker** . . . . . . (816) 325-7017
E-mail: sthacker@indepmo.org

Office of the City Manager
111 East Maple Avenue, Independence, MO 64050
Fax: (816) 325-7024

○City Manager **John Pinch** . . . . (816) 325-7019
E-mail: jpinch@indepmo.org
Secretary **Emily Brazeal** . . . . (816) 325-7019
E-mail: ebrazeal@indepmo.org

Deputy City Manager **Larry Kaufman** . . . . (816) 325-7172
E-mail: lkaufman@indepmo.org

Assistant City Manager **Zachary Walker** . . . . (816) 325-7019
E-mail: ZWalker@indepmo.org

Public Information Officer **Craig Brenner** . . . . (816) 325-7086
E-mail: cbrenner@indepmo.org

Law Department
111 East Maple Avenue, Independence, MO 64050
Fax: (816) 325-7219

City Counselor **Dayla Bishop Schwartz** . . . . (816) 325-7220
Secretary **Donna Williams** . . . . (816) 325-7220
E-mail: dmwilliams@indepmo.org

Deputy City Counselor **Collin Dietiker** . . . . (816) 325-7218
Assistant City Counselor **Jeff Deane** . . . . (816) 325-7983

Community Development
111 East Maple Avenue, Independence, MO 64050
Fax: (816) 325-7400

Director **Tom Scannell** . . . . (816) 325-7830
E-mail: tscannell@indepmo.org
Education: Iowa State BA; Wisconsin MURP

Assistant Director of Planning **Charlie Dissell** . . . . (816) 325-7830
Senior Planner **Stuart Borders** . . . . (816) 325-7421
Building Inspections Manager **(Vacant)** . . . . (816) 325-7403
Tourism Department **Eric Urfer** . . . . (816) 325-6234
E-mail: eurfer@indepmo.org

Finance Department
111 East Maple, Independence, MO 64050
Fax: (816) 325-7075

Director **Brian Watson** . . . . (816) 325-7080
Education: Emporia State BS; Park U MBA
Secretary **Ruth Henneberg** . . . . (816) 325-7080
E-mail: rhenneberg@indepmo.org

Controller **(Vacant)** . . . . (816) 325-7065
Budget Manager **Theresa Danielsen** . . . . (816) 325-7789
E-mail: tdanielsen@indepmo.org

Purchasing Agent **Russell Pankey** . . . . (816) 325-7091
E-mail: RPankey@indepmo.org

Fire Department
950 N. Spring St., Independence, MO 64050
Fax: (816) 325-7130

Fire Chief **John Greene** . . . . (816) 325-7124
E-mail: jgreene@indepmo.org
Secretary **Patty Keever** . . . . (816) 325-7124
E-mail: pkeever@indepmo.org

Emergency Preparedness Coordinator **Dante Gliniecki** . . . . (816) 325-7133
E-mail: dgliniecki@indepmo.org

Health Department
515 South Liberty, Independence, MO 64050
Fax: (816) 325-7074

Director **Andrew Warlen** . . . . (816) 325-7986
Secretary **Darlene Dieckmann** . . . . (816) 325-7986
E-mail: ddieckmann@indepmo.org

Assistant Health Director **Michael Jackson** . . . . (816) 325-7008
Public Health Manager, Disease Prevention
Alicia Nelson . . . . (816) 325-7006

Human Resources Department
111 East Maple Avenue, Independence, MO 64050
Fax: (816) 325-7393 E-mail: hronline@indepmo.org

Director **Debra Craig** . . . . (816) 325-7385
E-mail: dcraig@indepmo.org

Parks and Recreation Department
201 N. Dodgion, Independence, MO 64050
Tel: (816) 325-7843

Director **Eric Urfer** . . . . (816) 325-6234

★Elected Official ▲Appointed by Legislature ▼Appointed by Governor ▶Appointed by Board or Commission ●Appointed by Judge
■Appointed by Mayor △Appointed by Freeholders ▽Appointed by Supervisor ▷Appointed by County Executive ○Appointed by Council

Police Department
223 N. Memorial Dr., Independence, MO 64050
Fax: (816) 325-7316

Chief of Police **Tom Dailey** .... (816) 325-7271
Secretary **Shari Rector** .... (816) 325-7271
E-mail: srector@indepmo.org
Public Information Officer **John Syme** .... (816) 325-7643
E-mail: jsyme@indepmo.org

Power and Light Department
21500 E. Truman Rd., Independence, MO 64056
P.O. Box 1019, Independence, MO 64051
Fax: (816) 325-7470

Director **Leon Daggett** .... (816) 325-7437

Mid-Continent Public Library
15616 East 24 Highway, Independence, MO 64050
Tel: (816) 836-5200 Fax: (816) 521-7253 E-mail: info@mcpl.lib.mo.us
Internet: www.mcpl.lib.mo.us

Year Founded: 1892

Administration
Director **Steven V. Potter** .... (816) 836-5200
E-mail: spotter@mymcpl.org

Public Works Department
111 East Maple Avenue, Independence, MO 64050

Director **Tim Gramling** .... (816) 325-7606
Education: Missouri (Rolla) BSCE

Technology Services Department
223 N. Memorial Dr., Independence, MO 64050
Tel: (816) 325-7000

Director **Mark Baumann** .... (816) 325-7032
E-mail: mbaumann@indepmo.org
Education: Pittsburg State BBA

Water Department
11610 East Truman Road, Independence, MO 64050
Tel: (816) 325-7700

Director **Dan Montgomery** .... (816) 325-7693

Water Pollution Control Department
9600 Norledge Street, Independence, MO 64053
Tel: (816) 325-7711

Director **Dick Champion** .... (816) 325-7711

City of Indianapolis and Marion County, Indiana
City-County Bldg., 200 E. Washington St., Indianapolis, IN 46204
Tel: (317) 327-4348 (Information) Internet: www.indy.gov

County: Marion **Election Type:** Partisan **Year Founded:** 1820
Population: 853,173 (2015)

Form of Municipal Government: City and county governments are combined.

Office of the Mayor
2501 City-County Bldg., 200 E. Washington St., Indianapolis, IN 46204
Tel: (317) 327-3601 Fax: (317) 327-3980
Internet: www.indy.gov/eGov/Mayor/Pages/home.aspx

★ Mayor **Joseph H. "Joe" Hogsett** (D) .... (317) 327-3601
Began Service: January 1, 2016
Term Expires: December 31, 2019
Education: Indiana 1978 AB, 1981 JD; Butler 1987 MA; Christian Sem 1999 MTS; Indiana 2007 MA
Executive Assistant/Scheduler **Julie Marvel** .... (317) 327-3601
E-mail: julie.marvel@indy.gov

■ Chief of Staff **Thomas Cook** .... (317) 327-3601
E-mail: thomas.cook@indy.gov

■ Deputy Mayor for Economic Development **Angela Smith-Jones** .... (317) 327-3601
E-mail: angela.smithjones@indy.gov
Education: Miami U (OH) 1989 BS; DePaul 1995 JD

■ Deputy Mayor for Community Development **Jeff Bennett** .... (317) 327-3601
E-mail: jeff.bennett@indy.gov

■ Deputy Mayor for Neighborhoods **David Hampton** .... (317) 327-3601
E-mail: david.hampton@indy.gov

■ Communications Director **Taylor Schaffer** .... (317) 327-3601
E-mail: taylor.schaffer@indy.gov

Mayor's Action Center
2160 City-County Bldg., 200 E. Washington St., Indianapolis, IN 46204

■ Administrator **Amanda Ortman** .... (317) 327-4622
E-mail: aortman@mchd.com

Office of the Controller
2222 City-County Bldg., 200 E. Washington St., Indianapolis, IN 46204-3389
Fax: (317) 327-3953

■ Controller **Fady Qaddoura** .... (317) 327-4310
E-mail: fady.Qaddoura@indy.gov

Purchasing Division
1522 City-County Bldg., 200 E. Washington St., Indianapolis, IN 46204
Fax: (317) 327-4493

Administrator **(Vacant)** .... (317) 327-4900
Deputy Administrator **David Condon** .... (317) 327-4892

Human Resources Division
1541 City-County Building, 200 East Washington Street, Indianapolis, IN 46204-3307
Fax: (317) 327-4435

Director **Daniel L. Hackler** .... (317) 327-5211
E-mail: daniel.hackler@indy.gov
Education: Trenton State 1977 BSBA; Thomas Col (ME) 1982 MSM
Training Manager **Liz Miller** .... (317) 327-5101
Fax: (317) 327-4435

Office of the Corporation Counsel [OCC]

1601 City-County Bldg., 200 E. Washington St.,
Indianapolis, IN 46204-3372
Fax: (317) 327-3968 Tel: (317) 327-4055 Internet: www.indy.gov/occ

■ Corporation Counsel **Anne Mullin O'Connor** .... (317) 327-4055
Education: Miami U (OH) BA; Indiana JD

Office of Minority and Women Business Development

1260 City-County Building, 200 East Washington Street,
Indianapolis, IN 46204-3307
Fax: (317) 327-4482

■ Director **Maxine Russell** .... (317) 327-5262
Senior Manager **Ralplh Adams** .... (317) 327-5262

Code Enforcement Department

1200 Madison Avenue, Suite 100, Indianapolis, IN 46225
Fax: (317) 327-8973 Internet: www.indy.gov/dce

Director **Jason Larrison** .... (317) 327-2588
E-mail: jason.larrison@indy.gov

Indianapolis-Marion County Public Library [IMCPL]

2450 North Meridian Street, Indianapolis, IN 46208
P.O. Box 211, Indianapolis, IN 46206-0211
Tel: (317) 275-4100 Internet: www.imcpl.org

Year Founded: 1873

Administration

Chief Executive Officer
M. Jacqueline "Jackie" Nytes (D) .... (317) 275-4001
E-mail: jnytes@imcpl.org
Chief Financial Officer **Rebecca R. Dixon** .... (317) 275-4850
Deputy Director, Public Services **(Vacant)** .... (317) 275-4012
Director, Central Library **Michael Williams** .... (317) 275-4808
E-mail: mwilliams@imcpl.org
Director, Collection Management **Deborah N. Lambert** .. (317) 275-4721
E-mail: dlambert@imcpl.org
Director, Human Resources Services **Katherine Lerg** .... (317) 275-4806
E-mail: klerg@imcpl.org
Director, Information Technology **Debra Champ** .... (317) 275-4910
E-mail: dchamp@imcpl.org
Director, Project Development **Christine Cairo** .... (317) 275-4080
Manager, Facilities and Management **Sharon Smith** ..... (317) 275-4821
E-mail: ssmith@imcpl.org
Webmaster **Brian Dunten** .... (317) 275-4914
E-mail: bdunten@imcpl.org Fax: (317) 269-1820

Information Services Agency [ISA]

City-County Bldg., 200 E. Washington St., Suite 1942,
Indianapolis, IN 46204
Tel: (317) 327-3100 Fax: (317) 327-3756

Chief Information Officer (Interim) **Ken Clark** .... (317) 327-2989
E-mail: beth.howen@indy.gov

Marion County Board of Voters Registration

W131 City-County Bldg., 200 E. Washington St., Suite W131,
Indianapolis, IN 46204-3355
Fax: (317) 327-5042 Internet: http://www.indy.gov/eGov/County/Voter/

Democratic Director **LaDonna Freeman** .... (317) 327-5050
Republican Director **Cindy Mowery** .... (317) 327-5051

Marion County Coroner's Office

521 West McCarty Street, Indianapolis, IN 46225
Tel: (317) 327-4744 Fax: (317) 327-4563

★ Coroner **Frank P. Lloyd, Jr.** (D) .... (317) 327-4744
Term Expires: December 31, 2016
E-mail: flloyd@mchd.com
Education: DePauw BS; Indiana MD

Marion County Prosecutor's Office

251 East Ohio Street, Suite 160, Indianapolis, IN 46204
Fax: (317) 327-5325
Internet: www.indy.gov/eGov/County/Pros/Pages/home.aspx

★ County Prosecutor **Terry Curry** .... (317) 327-3522
Term Expires: December 31, 2018
E-mail: mcpo@indy.gov

Marion County Public Defender Agency

151 North Delaware Street, Suite 200, Indianapolis, IN 46204
Fax: (317) 327-3932
Internet: www.indy.gov/eGov/County/PubDef/Pages/home.aspx

Chief Public Defender **Robert J. Hill** .... (317) 327-6874

Marion County Sheriff's Department

40 South Alabama Street, Indianapolis, IN 46204
Fax: (317) 327-1315
Internet: www.indy.gov/egov/county/mcsd/Pages/home.aspx

Sheriff **John R. Layton** .... (317) 327-1310

Department of Metropolitan Development [DMD]

City-County Building, 200 East Washington Street, Suite 2042,
Indianapolis, IN 46204
Tel: (317) 327-5355
Internet: www.indy.gov/eGov/City/DMD/Pages/home.aspx

Director **Emily Mack** .... (317) 327-5355
200 East Washington Street, Room 2042, Indianapolis, IN 46204-3328
E-mail: emily.mack@indy.gov
Deputy Director of Operations **Peggy Frazier** .... (317) 327-5815
200 East Washington Street, Room 2042, Indianapolis, IN 46204-3328
E-mail: peggy.frazier@indy.gov
Public Information Officer **John Bartholomew** .... (317) 327-6709
200 East Washington Street, Room 2042, Indianapolis, IN 46204-3328
E-mail: john.bartholomew@indy.gov
Economic Development Administrator **Jennifer Fults** .... (317) 327-5899
200 East Washington Street, Room 2042, Indianapolis, IN 46204-3328
E-mail: jennifer.fults@indy.gov
Historic Preservation Division Administrator
David L. Baker .... (317) 327-4409
200 East Washington Street, Room 1821, Indianapolis, IN 46204-3328
Education: Texas BA; Rhode Island MA
Planning Division Administrator **Keith Holdsworth** ..... (317) 327-5114
200 East Washington Street, Room 1821, Indianapolis, IN 46204-3328
Chief Financial Officer **Cindy Snyder** Room 2042 .... (317) 327-3934

Parks and Recreation Department

2301 City-County Bldg., 200 East Washington Street, Suite 2301,
Indianapolis, IN 46204
Tel: (317) 327-7050 Fax: (317) 327-7033

■ Director **Linda Broadfoot** .... (317) 327-7148
E-mail: linda.broadfoot@indy.gov
Chief Financial Officer **Angie Clark** .... (317) 327-7018
Senior Project Manager **Julee Jacob** .... (317) 327-7015
Superintendent of Operations **Elaine Dillahunt** .... (317) 327-7145
E-mail: elaine.dillahunt@indy.gov

★ Elected Official ▲ Appointed by Legislature ▼ Appointed by Governor ► Appointed by Board or Commission ● Appointed by Judge
■ Appointed by Mayor △ Appointed by Freeholders ▽ Appointed by Supervisor ▷ Appointed by County Executive ○ Appointed by Council

Public Safety Department
50 N. Alabama St., Indianapolis, IN 46204
Tel: (317) 327-5090 Fax: (317) 327-3446
Internet: www.indy.gov/eGov/City/DPS/Pages/home.aspx

■ Director **(Vacant)** Room E220 .... (317) 327-5090

Animal Care and Control Division
2600 S. Harding St., Indianapolis, IN 46221
Fax: (317) 327-1390
Internet: www.indy.gov/eGov/City/DPS/ACCD/Pages/home.aspx

Administrator **(Vacant)** .... (317) 327-1391

Emergency Management Agency
47 S. State St., Indianapolis, IN 46201-3876
Fax: (317) 327-7508

Director **Gary S. Coons** .... (317) 327-7500
E-mail: gcoons@mchd.com

Fire Department
555 N. New Jersey, Indianapolis, IN 46204
Fax: (317) 327-6090
Internet: www.indy.gov/eGov/City/DPS/IFD/Pages/home.aspx

Fire Chief **Ernest Malone** .... (317) 327-6091
50 North Alabama, E208, Indianapolis, IN 46204
E-mail: emalone@mchd.com
Assistant Fire Chief **Tim Baughman** .... (317) 327-6091
EMS Division Chief **Dr. Charles Miramonti** .... (317) 327-8660
E-mail: cmiramonti@mchd.com
Emergency Operations Assistant Chief **Kenny Bacon** .... (317) 327-6054
E-mail: kbacon@mchd.com
Deputy Chief, Homeland Security **Michael Bates** .... (317) 327-6087
Public Information Officer **Rita Reith** .... (317) 327-6086
E-mail: rreith@mchd.com

Indianapolis Metropolitan Police Department
50 North Alabama Street, Indianapolis, IN 46204
Tel: (317) 327-3811 (Non-Emergency Dispatch) Fax: (317) 327-3289
Internet: www.indy.gov/eGov/IMPD/Pages/home.aspx

■ Chief of Police **Troy Riggs** .... (317) 327-3282
E-mail: triggs@mchd.com
Education: Louisville BA; Sullivan U EMBA
Police Complaints Executive Director **Laura White** .... (317) 327-3440

Public Works Department
2460 City-County Bldg., 200 E. Washington St., Indianapolis, IN 46204
Tel: (317) 327-4000 Fax: (317) 327-4954

■ Director **Andy Lutz** .... (317) 327-7837
E-mail: andy.lutz@indy.gov
Chief of Staff **Jeremiah Shirk** .... (317) 327-5225
Deputy Director, Communications **Stephanie Sample** ... (317) 327-5591
Administrator (Acting) **Alan Bacon** .... (317) 327-2904
E-mail: alan.bacon@indy.gov
Chief Financial Officer **Janice Mitchell** .... (317) 327-3060
Public Information Officer **Scott Manning** .... (317) 517-0072
E-mail: scott.manning@indy.gov

Customer Service
1375 West 16th Street, Indianapolis, IN 46202

Assistant Administrator **Steve Pruitt** .... (317) 327-2484

Engineering Division
1200 Madison Avenue, Suite 200, Indianapolis, IN 46225

Deputy Director of Engineering **Melody Park** .... (317) 327-8729

Fleet Services
1651 West 30th Street, Indianapolis, IN 46225
Fax: (317) 327-2755

Administrator **(Vacant)** .... (317) 327-4148

Solid Waste Management
2700 S. Belmont, Indianapolis, IN 46221
Fax: (317) 327-2958

Administrator **Marlon Wright** .... (317) 327-2372

Office of Sustainability
200 East Washington Street, Indianapolis, IN 46204-3307

Director **Melody Park** .... (317) 327-7686
Project Manager **Jeff Meek** .... (317) 327-4932
Project Manager **David Hirschle** .... (317) 327-4141
Compliance Manager **Matt Mosier** .... (317) 327-4141

Office of the City - County Council
241 City-County Building, 200 East Washington Street,
Indianapolis, IN 46204
Tel: (317) 327-4242 Fax: (317) 327-4230
Internet: www.indy.gov/eGov/Council/

★ Council President **Maggie Lewis** (D-District 10) .... (317) 327-4242
Term Expires: December 31, 2019
E-mail: maggie.lewis@indy.gov
★ Vice President **Zach Adamson** (D-District 17) .... (317) 683-9224
Term Expires: December 31, 2019
E-mail: adamsonforindy@aol.com
★ Council Member **Leroy Robinson** (D-District 1) .... (317) 329-0923
Term Expires: December 31, 2019
E-mail: leroy.robinson@indy.gov
★ Council Member **Colleen Fanning** (R-District 2) .... (317) 935-4776
Term Expires: December 31, 2019
E-mail: fanningINDY@gmail.com
★ Council Member **Christine Scales** (R-District 3) .... (317) 578-8901
Term Expires: December 31, 2019
E-mail: cscales_2000@yahoo.com
★ Council Member **Michael J. McQuillen** (R-District 4) ... (317) 374-1481
Term Expires: December 31, 2019
E-mail: mike@mikemcquillen.com
★ Council Member **Jeff Coats** (R-District 5) .... (317) 590-1478
Term Expires: December 31, 2019
E-mail: jefferycoats@sbcglobal.net
★ Council Member
Janice Shattuck McHenry (R-District 6) .... (317) 298-5285
Term Expires: December 31, 2019
E-mail: jfmchenry@iquest.net
★ Council Member
Joseph "Joe" Simpson (D-District 7) .... (317) 710-3612
Term Expires: December 31, 2019
E-mail: jesimp7754@sbcglobal.net
★ Council Member **Monroe Gray, Jr.** (D-District 8) .... (317) 327-4242
Term Expires: December 31, 2019
E-mail: monroe.gray@indy.gov
★ Council Member
William C. "Duke" Oliver (D-District 9) .... (317) 201-6770
Term Expires: December 31, 2019
E-mail: william.oliver@indy.gov
★ Council Member **Vop Osili** (D-District 11) .... (317) 332-0877
Term Expires: December 31, 2019
E-mail: voposili@gmail.com
★ Council Member **Blake Johnson** (D-District 12) .... (317) 721-3487
Term Expires: December 31, 2019
E-mail: blake.johnson@indy.gov
Education: Eckerd; Marian Col (IN)
★ Council Member **Stephen Clay** (D-District 13) .... (317) 921-6779
Term Expires: December 31, 2019
E-mail: stephen.clay@indy.gov
★ Council Member **La Keisha Jackson** (D-District 14) .... (317) 354-9283
Term Expires: December 31, 2019
E-mail: lakeisha.jackson@indy.gov
★ Council Member **Marilyn Pfisterer** (R-District 15) .... (317) 244-7156
Term Expires: December 31, 2019
E-mail: cpfist1061@aol.com
★ Council Member **Jeff Miller** (R-District 16) .... (317) 490-5588
Term Expires: December 31, 2019
E-mail: miller4council@gmail.com

★ Elected Official ▲ Appointed by Legislature ▼ Appointed by Governor ▶ Appointed by Board or Commission ● Appointed by Judge
■ Appointed by Mayor △ Appointed by Freeholders ▽ Appointed by Supervisor ▷ Appointed by County Executive © Appointed by Council

Office of the City - County Council *continued*

★Council Member **Susie Cordi** (R-District 18) . . . . (317) 935-4776
Term Expires: December 31, 2019
E-mail: scordi@comcast.net

★Council Member **David Ray** (D-District 19) . . . . (317) 442-1574
Term Expires: December 31, 2019
E-mail: david.ray@indy.gov

★Council Member **Jason Holliday** (R-District 20) . . . . (317) 517-8118
Term Expires: December 31, 2019
E-mail: jasonhollidayccc20@gmail.com

★Council Member **Frank Mascari** (D-District 21) . . . . (317) 788-0520
Term Expires: December 31, 2019
E-mail: frank.mascari@indy.gov

★Council Member **Jared Evans** (D-District 22) . . . . (317) 442-1574
Term Expires: December 31, 2019
E-mail: jaredevans79@gmail.com

★Council Member **Scott A. Kreider** (R-District 23) . . . . (317) 327-4242
Term Expires: December 31, 2019
E-mail: scott.kreider@indy.gov

★Council Member **Jack Sandlin** (R-District 24) . . . . (317) 714-3266
Term Expires: December 31, 2019
E-mail: jack.sandlin@att.net

★Council Member **Aaron Freeman** (R-District 25) . . . . (317) 327-4242
Term Expires: December 31, 2019
E-mail: aaronfreemanlaw@gmail.com

○Clerk of the Council **NaTrina DeBow** . . . . (317) 327-4243
E-mail: natrina.debow@indy.gov

○General Counsel **Fred R. Biesecker** . . . . (317) 327-4242
E-mail: fred.biesecker@indy.gov
Education: IU-Purdue U Indianapolis 1976 BA; Yale 1979 JD

○Chief Financial Officer **Bart Brown** . . . . (317) 327-4242
E-mail: bart.brown@indy.gov

○Administrative Assistant **Leslie Williams** . . . . (317) 327-4245
E-mail: leslie.williams@indy.gov

Indianapolis Housing Agency

1919 North Meridian Street, Indianapolis, IN 46202
Tel: (317) 261-7200 Internet: www.indyhousing.org/

Indianapolis Housing Agency Director **Bud Myers** . . . . . . (317) 261-7331

Indianapolis Public Schools

JMF Center for Education Services, 120 East Walnut Street, Indianapolis, IN 46204
Fax: (317) 226-4936 Internet: www.myips.org

Superintendent **Dr. Lewis D. Ferebee** . . . . (317) 226-4000

City of Inglewood, California

City Hall, One Manchester Blvd., Inglewood, CA 90301
Internet: http://www.cityofinglewood.org

County: Los Angeles **Election Type:** Nonpartisan **Year Incorporated:** 1908 **Population:** 111,666 (2015)

Office of the Mayor

City Hall, One Manchester Blvd., Inglewood, CA 90301
P.O. Box 6500, Inglewood, CA 90312
Fax: (310) 412-8788

★Mayor **James T. Butts, Jr.** . . . . (310) 412-5300
Began Service: February 1, 2011
Term Expires: April 2017
E-mail: mayor@cityofinglewood.org

Senior Assistant to the Mayor **Melanie McDade** . . . . (310) 412-5300

City Attorney

City Hall, One Manchester Blvd., Inglewood, CA 90301
Fax: (310) 412-8865

City Attorney **Ken Campos** . . . . (310) 412-5372
E-mail: kcampos@cityofinglewood.org

Police Department

One West Manchester Boulevard, Inglewood, CA 90301
Fax: (310) 412-9798

Police Chief **Mark Fronterotta** . . . . (310) 412-5200

Office of the City Manager

City Hall, One West Manchester Blvd., 9th Floor, Inglewood, CA 90301
Fax: (310) 412-8788

City Manager **Artie Fields** . . . . (310) 412-5301
E-mail: afields@cityofinglewood.org
Education: USC BA, MPA

Executive Assistant to the City Manager **Tunisia Johnson** . . . . (310) 412-5301
E-mail: tjohnson@cityofinglewood.org

Assistant City Manager

City Hall, One Manchester Boulevard, Inglewood, CA 90301

Assistant City Manager II **David Esparza** . . . . (310) 412-5301
E-mail: dlesparza@cityofinglewood.org

Finance Department

City Hall, One Manchester Blvd., Inglewood, CA 90301
Fax: (310) 330-5785

Chief Financial Officer **David Esparza** . . . . (310) 412-5257

Public Works Department

City Hall, One Manchester Blvd., Inglewood, CA 90301
Fax: (310) 412-5552

Director **Louis Atwell** . . . . (310) 412-5333

Principal Engineer, Water Resources **Barmbshwar Rai** . . . (310) 412-5333
E-mail: brai@cityofinglewood.org

Assistant City Manager

Assistant City Manager **Michael Falkow** . . . . (310) 412-5301
E-mail: mfalkow@cityofinglewood.org

Human Resources Department

City Hall, One Manchester Blvd., Inglewood, CA 90301
Fax: (310) 330-5777

Director **Jose Cortes** . . . . (310) 412-5460
E-mail: jcortes@cityofinglewood.org

Parks, Recreation and Library Services

City Hall, One Manchester Blvd., Inglewood, CA 90301
Fax: (310) 330-5750

Director **Sabrina Barnes** . . . . (310) 412-8750
E-mail: sbarnes@cityofinglewood.org

Economic and Community Development Department

City Hall, One Manchester Blvd., Inglewood, CA 90301
Fax: (310) 412-5680

Manager **Christopher E. Jackson, Sr.** . . . . (310) 412-5230
E-mail: cejackson@cityofinglewood.org

Information Technology and Communication Services

City Hall, One Manchester Blvd., Inglewood, CA 90301
Fax: (310) 412-5591

Information Technology Director **Matthew Chambers** . . . (310) 412-5446
E-mail: mchambers@cityofinglewood.org
Education: Cal State (Dominguez) BS

(continued on next page)

★Elected Official ▲Appointed by Legislature ▼Appointed by Governor ▶Appointed by Board or Commission ●Appointed by Judge
■Appointed by Mayor △Appointed by Freeholders ▽Appointed by Supervisor ▷Appointed by County Executive ○Appointed by Council

CITIES AND TOWNS

Information Technology and Communication Services *continued*

Webmaster **Josh Howe** .... (310) 412-5446
E-mail: jhowe@cityofinglewood.org
Enterprise Services Manager **Charles Kindred** .... (310) 412-4270
E-mail: ckindred@cityofinglewood.org

City Treasurer

City Hall, One Manchester Blvd., Inglewood, CA 90301
Fax: (310) 330-5764

★Treasurer **Wanda M. Brown** .... (310) 412-5642
Term Expires: April 1, 2019
E-mail: wbrown@cityofinglewood.org
Education: Cal State (Long Beach) 1969 BS; UCLA 1973 MBA

City Clerk

City Hall, One Manchester Blvd., Inglewood, CA 90301
Fax: (310) 412-5533

★City Clerk **Yvonne Horton** .... (310) 412-5280
Term Expires: April 22, 2019
E-mail: yhorton@cityofinglewood.org
Deputy City Clerk **Aisha Thompson** .... (310) 412-5280
E-mail: athompson@cityofinglewood.org

Office of the City Council

City Hall, One Manchester Boulevard, 9th Floor, Inglewood, CA 90301
Fax: (310) 412-8788

★Council Member **George Dotson** (District 1) .... (310) 412-8602
Term Expires: April 22, 2017
E-mail: gdotson@cityofinglewood.org
★Council Member **Alex Padilla** (District 2) .... (310) 412-8601
Term Expires: April 22, 2017
E-mail: apadilla@cityofinglewood.org
★Council Member **Eloy Morales, Jr.** (District 3) .... (310) 412-8603
Term Expires: April 22, 2019
E-mail: emorales@cityofinglewood.org
★Council Member **Ralph Franklin** (District 4) .... (310) 412-8605
Term Expires: April 22, 2019
E-mail: rfranklin@cityofinglewood.org

Inglewood Unified School District

401 South Englewood Avenue, Inglewood, CA 90301
Tel: (310) 419-2700 Fax: (310) 680-5144 Internet: http://iusd.net/

▼State Trustee **Dr. Vincent C. Matthews** .... (310) 419-2705
E-mail: vmatthews@inglewood.k12.ca.us
Education: San Francisco State U BA, MA, EdD

City of Irvine, California

One Civic Center Plaza, Irvine, CA 92606-5208
Internet: www.cityofirvine.org/

County: Orange **Election Type:** Nonpartisan **Year Incorporated:** 1971
Population: 256,927 (2015)

Office of the Mayor and City Council

One Civic Center Plaza, Irvine, CA 92606-5208
Tel: (949) 724-6233

★Mayor **Steven S. Choi** .... (949) 724-6233
Began Service: December 11, 2012
Term Expires: December 2016
E-mail: schoi@cityofirvine.org

Office of the Mayor and City Council *continued*

★Mayor Pro Tem **Jeffrey Lalloway** .... (949) 724-6233
Term Expires: December 2018
E-mail: jeffreylalloway@cityofirvine.org
Education: Rutgers 1986 BA; Villanova 1989 JD
★Council Member **Beth Krom** .... (949) 724-6233
Term Expires: December 2016
E-mail: bethkrom@cityofirvine.org
Education: Texas BS
★Council Member **Lynn Schott** .... (949) 724-6233
Term Expires: December 2018
E-mail: lschott@cityofirvine.org
★Council Member **Christina L. Shea** .... (949) 724-6233
Term Expires: December 2016
E-mail: christinashea@cityofirvine.org
Council Services Manager **Pamela Baird** .... (949) 724-6241
E-mail: pbaird@cityofirvine.org

Office of the City Attorney

One Civic Center Plaza, Irvine, CA 92606-5208

City Attorney **Todd Liftin** .... (949) 724-6242
E-mail: tliftin@cityofirvine.org

Office of the City Clerk

One Civic Center Plaza, Irvine, CA 92606-5208
Fax: (949) 724-6188 E-mail: clerk@cityofirvine.org

City Clerk **Molly McLaughlin** .... (949) 724-6205
E-mail: mollymclaughlin@cityofirvine.org
Assistant City Clerk **Carl Petersen** .... (949) 724-6205
E-mail: cpetersen@cityofirvine.org
Municipal Records Administrator **Debbie Tracy** .... (949) 724-6281

Office of the City Manager

One Civic Center Plaza, Irvine, CA 92606-5208
E-mail: cm@irvine.org

City Manager **Sean Joyce** .... (949) 724-6246
E-mail: sjoyce@cityofirvine.org
Assistant to the City Manager **Michelle Grettenberg** .... (949) 724-6252
E-mail: mgrettenberg@cityofirvine.org
Assistant City Manager **Sharon Landers** .... (949) 724-6250
E-mail: slanders@cityofirvine.org
Director of Public Affairs and Communications
Craig Reem .... (949) 724-6077
E-mail: creem@cityofirvine.org
Multicultural Affairs Coordinator **Emma Evans** .... (949) 724-6340

Administrative Services

One Civic Center Plaza, Irvine, CA 92606-5208

Director **Grace Leung** .... (949) 724-6255
E-mail: as@cityofirvine.org
Purchasing Agent **Tracy Hamilton** .... (949) 724-6181
E-mail: thamilton@cityofirvine.org

Community Development Department

One Civic Center Plaza, Irvine, CA 92606-5208
Fax: (949) 724-6440 E-mail: cd@cityofirvine.org

Director of Community Development **Susan Emery** .... (949) 724-6451
E-mail: semery@cityofirvine.org
Education: Cal State (Long Beach) BA; Cal State (Fullerton) MPA
Chief Building Official **Joseph Kirkpatrick** .... (949) 724-6320
E-mail: jkirkpatrick@cityofirvine.org
Code Enforcement Supervisor **Louis Kirk** .... (949) 724-6430
Deputy Director **Tim Gehrich** .... (949) 724-6363
E-mail: tgehrich@cityofirvine.org
Manager of Housing **Mark Asturias** .... (949) 724-7448

★Elected Official ▲Appointed by Legislature ▼Appointed by Governor ▶Appointed by Board or Commission ●Appointed by Judge
■Appointed by Mayor △Appointed by Freeholders ▽Appointed by Supervisor ▷Appointed by County Executive ○Appointed by Council

Community Services Department
One Civic Center Plaza, Irvine, CA 92606-5208
E-mail: cs@cityofirvine.org

Director of Community Services **Laurie Hoffman** . . . . (949) 724-6692
E-mail: lhoffman@cityofirvine.org
Community Services Superintendent (Athletics)
Ed Crofts . . . . (949) 724-6660
E-mail: ecrofts@cityofirvine.org
Community Services Manager **Bonnie Hagan** . . . . (949) 724-6694
E-mail: bhagan@cityofirvine.org
Community Services Manager
Corinne Schneider-Jones . . . . (949) 724-6685
E-mail: cschneider-jones@cityofirvine.org
Facility Maintenance Superintendent **Dale Schuck** . . . . (949) 724-6618

Police Department
One Civic Center Plaza, Irvine, CA 92606-5208
E-mail: ps@cityofirvine.org

Chief of Police **Michael Hamel** . . . . (949) 724-7101

Public Works Department
One Civic Ceter Plaza, Irvine, CA 92623
E-mail: pw@cityofirvine.org

Director **Manuel Gomez** . . . . (949) 724-7509
Deputy Director **Shohreh Dupuis** . . . . (949) 724-7526

City of Irving, Texas
City Hall, 825 W. Irving Blvd., Irving, TX 75060
P.O. Box 152288, Irving, TX 75015-2288
Tel: (972) 721-2600 (Information) Internet: www.cityofirving.org

County: Dallas **Election Type:** Nonpartisan **Population:** 236,607 (2015)

Office of the Mayor and City Council
City Hall, 825 W. Irving Blvd., Irving, TX 75060
P.O. Box 152288, Irving, TX 75015-2288
Fax: (972) 721-2384 E-mail: ccouncil@cityofirving.org

★Mayor **Beth Van Duyne** . . . . (972) 721-2410
Began Service: July 7, 2011
Term Expires: May 2017
E-mail: mayor@cityofirving.org
★Mayor Pro Tem **Dennis Lee Webb** (Place 3) . . . . (972) 849-9421
Term Expires: May 2017
E-mail: denniswebb@cityofirving.org
★Council Member **John Carter Danish** (Place 1) . . . . (972) 721-2410
Term Expires: May 2019
E-mail: jcdanish@cityofirving.org
★Council Member **Allan E. Meagher** (Place 2) . . . . (972) 721-2410
Term Expires: May 2019
E-mail: ameagher@cityofirving.org
★Council Member **Phil Riddle** (Place 4) . . . . (972) 721-2410
Term Expires: May 2018
E-mail: priddle@cityofirving.org
★Council Member **Oscar Ward** (Place 5) . . . . (972) 721-2410
Term Expires: May 2017
E-mail: oward@cityofirving.org
★Council Member **Brad M. LaMorgese** (Place 6) . . . . (972) 721-2410
Term Expires: May 2018
E-mail: blamorgese@cityofirving.org
★Council Member **Kyle Taylor** (Place 7) . . . . (972) 721-2410
Term Expires: May 2019
E-mail: ktaylor@cityofirving.org
★Council Member **David Palmer** (Place 8) . . . . (972) 721-2110
Term Expires: May 2018
E-mail: dpalmer@cityofirving.org

Office of the City Attorney
P.O. Box 152288, Irving, TX 75015-2288
Fax: (972) 721-2750

○City Attorney **Charles Anderson** . . . . (972) 721-2541
E-mail: canderson@cityofirving.org

Office of the City Secretary
P.O. Box 152288, Irving, TX 75015-2288
Fax: (972) 721-2384

○City Secretary **Shanae Jennings** . . . . (972) 721-2605
E-mail: sjennings@cityofirving.org

Office of the City Manager
P.O. Box 152288, Irving, TX 75015-2288
Fax: (972) 721-2420

○City Manager **Christopher Hillman** . . . . (972) 721-2521
E-mail: chillman@cityofirving.org
Deputy City Manager **Michael E. Morrison** . . . . (972) 721-8029
E-mail: mmorrison@cityofirving.org
Education: Florida 1976 BA; North Carolina 1978 MA
Assistant City Manager **Max Duplant** . . . . (972) 721-4615
E-mail: mduplant@cityofirving.org

Building Inspections Department
P.O. Box 152288, Irving, TX 75015-2288
Fax: (972) 721-2481

Director of Inspections **Gary Miller** . . . . (972) 721-2371

Capital Improvement Program Department
P.O. Box 152288, Irving, TX 75015-2288
Fax: (972) 721-2658

Director **Casey Tate** . . . . (972) 721-2611
E-mail: ctate@cityofirving.org

Engineering Department
P.O. Box 152288, Irving, TX 75015-2288

City Engineer **Wayne Lee** . . . . (972) 721-2611
E-mail: wlee@cityofirving.org

Code Enforcement Department
P.O. Box 152288, Irving, TX 75015-2288
Fax: (972) 721-3634

Director of Code Enforcement **Teresa Adrian** . . . . (972) 721-4829

Economic Development Department
P.O. Box 152288, Irving, TX 75015-2288

Economic Development Director **Scott Connell** . . . . (972) 721-2398
E-mail: sconnell@cityofirving.org

Financial Services Department
P.O. Box 152288, Irving, TX 75015-2288
Fax: (972) 721-2733

Chief Financial Officer **Jeff Litchfield** . . . . (972) 721-2401
E-mail: jlitchfield@cityofirving.org

Fire Department
P.O. Box 152288, Irving, TX 75015-2288
Fax: (972) 721-2795

Fire Chief **Victor Conley** . . . . (972) 721-2514
E-mail: vconley@cityofirving.org

★Elected Official ▲Appointed by Legislature ▼Appointed by Governor ►Appointed by Board or Commission ●Appointed by Judge
■Appointed by Mayor △Appointed by Freeholders ▽Appointed by Supervisor ▷Appointed by County Executive ○Appointed by Council

Information Technology Department
P.O. Box 152288, Irving, TX 75015-2288
Fax: (972) 721-2560

Information Technology Director **Leisha Meine-Bailey** . . . (972) 721-2290
E-mail: lmeinebailey@cityofirving.org

Parks and Libraries Department
P.O. Box 152288, Irving, TX 75015-2288
Fax: (972) 721-2658

Director of Parks **Ray Cerda** . . . . (972) 721-2501
Library Director **Christine Dobson** . . . . (972) 721-2606
E-mail: cdobson@cityofirving.org

Human Resources/Performance Office
P.O. Box 152288, Irving, TX 75015-2288
Fax: (972) 721-2420

Director **Ike Obi** . . . . (972) 721-2709
E-mail: iobi@cityofirving.org

Police Department
305 N. O'Connor Rd., Irving, TX 75060
P.O. Box 152288, Irving, TX 75015-2288
Internet: http://www.irvingpd.com

Chief of Police **Larry Boyd** . . . . (972) 721-2650
Education: LeTourneau 1993 BS; Texas (Arlington) 1998 MPA

Public Works Department
P.O. Box 152288, Irving, TX 75015-2288

Assistant City Manager **Ramiro Lopez** . . . . (972) 721-8078
E-mail: rlopez@cityofirving.org

Solid Waste Services Department
P.O. Box 152288, Irving, TX 75015-2288
Fax: (972) 721-3639

Director **Brenda Haney** . . . . (972) 721-8059

Traffic and Transportation Department
P.O. Box 152288, Irving, TX 75015-2288

Director **Dan Vedral** . . . . (972) 721-2464

Water Utilities Department
P.O. Box 152288, Irving, TX 75015-2288

Director **Todd Reck** . . . . (972) 721-2281

Town of Islip, New York

Town Hall, 655 Main St., Islip, NY 11751
Tel: (631) 224-5691 (Information) Internet: www.townofislip-ny.gov

County: Suffolk **Election Type:** Partisan **Population:** 336,113 (2015)

Office of the Town Supervisor and Town Council
Town Hall, 655 Main St., Islip, NY 11751

★Town Supervisor **Angie M. Carpenter** (R) . . . . (631) 224-5500
Began Service: May 2013
Term Expires: December 31, 2019
Chief of Staff **Tracey Kurt** . . . . (631) 224-5500
★Council Member **Trish Bergen Weichbrodt** (R) . . . . (631) 224-5502
Term Expires: December 31, 2017
★Council Member **John Cochrane, Jr.** (R) . . . . (631) 224-5500
Term Expires: December 31, 2019

Office of the Town Supervisor and Town Council *continued*

★Council Member **Steve J. Flotteron** (R) . . . . (631) 224-5565
Term Expires: December 31, 2017
E-mail: sflotteron@townofislip-ny.gov
★Council Member **Mary Kate Mullen** (R) . . . . (631) 224-5500
Term Expires: December 31, 2019
▽Public Information Director **Patricia Kaloski** . . . . (631) 224-5485
E-mail: publicinfo@townofislip-ny.gov Fax: (631) 224-5487

Office of the Assessor
40 Nassau Ave., Islip, NY 11751
Fax: (631) 224-5572

○Assessor **Anne M. Danziger** . . . . (631) 224-5585
E-mail: assessorsoffice@townofislip-ny.gov

Office of the Comptroller
Town Hall, 655 Main St., Islip, NY 11751
Fax: (631) 224-5701

○Comptroller **Joseph Ludwig** . . . . (631) 595-3840
E-mail: comptrollersoffice@townofislip-ny.gov

Office of the Receiver of Taxes
40 Nassau Ave., Islip, NY 11751
Fax: (631) 224-5543

★Receiver of Taxes **Alexis Weik** (R) . . . . (631) 224-5580
Term Expires: December 31, 2019
E-mail: aweik@townofislip-ny.gov

Office of the Town Attorney
Town Hall, 655 Main St., Islip, NY 11751
Fax: (631) 224-5573

○Town Attorney **Mea Knapp** . . . . (631) 224-5550
E-mail: townattorney@townofislip-ny.gov

Office of the Town Clerk
Town Hall, 655 Main St., Islip, NY 11751
Fax: (631) 224-5574

★Town Clerk **Olga Hopkins-Murray** (R) . . . . (631) 224-5490
Term Expires: December 31, 2019
E-mail: omurray@townofislip-ny.gov

Animal Shelter
210 S. Denver Ave., Bay Shore, NY 11706
Fax: (631) 224-5787

Director **Joanne Daly** . . . . (631) 224-5660

Community Development Agency
15 Shore Lane, Bay Shore, NY 11706
Fax: (631) 665-0036

Executive Director **(Vacant)** . . . . (631) 665-1185

Economic Development Office
40 Nassau Ave., Islip, NY 11751
Fax: (631) 224-5532

Director **William G. Mannix** . . . . (631) 224-5512
E-mail: ecodev@townofislip-ny.gov
Education: SUNY (Brockport)

Engineering Office
401 Main St., Islip, NY 11751
Fax: (631) 224-5465

○Town Engineer **Richard Zapolski** . . . . (631) 224-5366
E-mail: rzapolski@townofislip-ny.gov

★Elected Official ▲Appointed by Legislature ▼Appointed by Governor ▶Appointed by Board or Commission ●Appointed by Judge
■Appointed by Mayor △Appointed by Freeholders ▽Appointed by Supervisor ▷Appointed by County Executive ○Appointed by Council

Environmental Control Office
401 Main St., Islip, NY 11751
Fax: (631) 224-5651

○ Commissioner **James H. Heil** . . . . . (631) 595-3630
E-mail: commissioner-dec@townofislip-ny.gov

Foreign Trade Zone Authority
One Trade Zone Dr., Ronkonkoma, NY 11779
Fax: (631) 588-6712

Director **(Vacant)** . . . . . (631) 588-5757

Human Services Office
401 Main St., Islip, NY 11751
Fax: (631) 224-5316

○ Commissioner **Arthur Abbate** . . . . . (631) 224-5310
E-mail: commissioner-hs@townofislip-ny.gov
Senior Citizens Services Director **Patricia Lozier** . . . . . (631) 224-5340
Youth Services Executive Director **Ann Mendes** . . . . . (631) 224-5320

Parks, Recreation and Cultural Affairs Department
Brookwood Hall, 50 Irish Lane, East Islip, NY 11730

○ Commissioner **Tom Owens** . . . . . (631) 224-5411
E-mail: commissioner-rec@townofislip-ny.gov Fax: (631) 224-5440
Art Museum Executive Director **Lynda A. Moran** . . . . . (631) 224-5402
Fax: (631) 224-5417
Nature Center Director **Alison Tewes** . . . . . (631) 224-5436
Sports and Aquatics Director **(Vacant)** . . . . . (631) 224-5404

Personnel Department
Town Hall, 655 Main St., Islip, NY 11751
Fax: (631) 224-5771

○ Director **Arthur Abbate** . . . . . (631) 224-5520

Planning and Development
Town Hall, 655 Main St., Islip, NY 11751
Fax: (631) 224-5444

○ Commissioner **Richard Zapolski** . . . . . (631) 224-5450
E-mail: commissioner-pd@townofislip-ny.gov

Public Safety Enforcement
28 Nassau Avenue, Islip, NY 11751
Fax: (631) 224-5756

Commissioner **John Carney** . . . . . (631) 224-5548
E-mail: commissioner-ps@townofislip-ny.gov

Fire Prevention
One Manitton Ct., Islip, NY 11751

Chief Fire Marshal **Michael Catalano** . . . . . (631) 224-5477
E-mail: mcatalano@townofislip-ny.gov

Public Works Office
401 Main St., Islip, NY 11751
Fax: (631) 224-5243

○ Commissioner **Tom Owens** . . . . . (631) 224-5600
E-mail: commissioner-dpw@townofislip-ny.gov

City of Jackson, Mississippi
City Hall, 219 South President Street, Jackson, MS 39201
P.O. Box 17, Jackson, MS 39205
Tel: (601) 960-1084 (Information) Fax: (601) 960-2193
Internet: www.jacksonms.gov

County: Hinds **Election Type:** Partisan **Year Founded:** 1821
Year Incorporated: 1833 **Population:** 170,674 (2015)

Office of the Mayor
City Hall, 219 South President Street, Jackson, MS 39205
P.O. Box 17, Jackson, MS 39205-0017
Tel: (601) 960-1084 Fax: (601) 960-2504

★ Mayor **Tony Yarber** (D) . . . . . (601) 960-1084
Began Service: April 2014
Term Expires: July 1, 2017
■ Executive Assistant to the Mayor **Charity F. Clark** . . . . . (601) 960-1084
Education: Jackson State U
■ Office Coordinator **(Vacant)** . . . . . (601) 960-1084
■ Chief of Staff **Jackie Anderson Woods** . . . . . (601) 960-1084
■ Communications Director **Sheila Byrd** . . . . . (601) 960-1084
E-mail: press@city.jackson.ms.us
■ Director of Policy **(Vacant)** . . . . . (601) 960-2173

Mayor's Action Line
Fax: (601) 960-2194

Manager **Andy Boone** . . . . . (601) 960-1111
E-mail: aboone@jacksonms.gov

Housing Authority
2747 Livingston Rd., Jackson, MS 39213
P.O. Box 11327, Jackson, MS 39283-1327
Fax: (601) 982-4733

Executive Director (Interim) **Allison Cox** . . . . . (601) 362-0885 ext. 114

Jackson Convention and Visitors Bureau
111 East Capitol Street, Suite 102, Jackson, MS 39201
P.O. Box 1450, Jackson, MS 39215-1450
Fax: (601) 960-1827 Internet: www.visitjackson.com

President and Chief Executive Officer
Wanda Collier-Wilson . . . . . (601) 960-1891
Executive Vice President **Rickey L. Thigpen** . . . . . (601) 960-1891
Finance and Administration Vice President
Jennifer Chance . . . . . (601) 960-1891
Marketing Vice President **Jonathan Pettus** . . . . . (601) 960-1891
Sales Vice President **Shun Hatten** . . . . . (601) 960-1891

Office of the City Attorney
455 East Capitol St., Jackson, MS 39201
P.O. Box 2779, Jackson, MS 39207
Fax: (601) 960-1756

■ City Attorney **Monica D. Joiner** . . . . . (601) 960-1799
E-mail: Mjoiner@city.jackson.ms.us

Office of the Chief Administrative Officer
200 South President Street, Jackson, MS 39201
Tel: (601) 960-2314 Tel: (601) 960-2210

Chief Administrative Officer **Gus McCoy** . . . . . (601) 960-2314
Deputy Chief Administrative Officer
Marshand K. Crisler (D) . . . . . (601) 960-2314
Education: Jackson State U BS, MPPA
Deputy Chief Administrative Officer **(Vacant)** . . . . . (601) 960-2314

★ Elected Official ▲ Appointed by Legislature ▼ Appointed by Governor ► Appointed by Board or Commission ● Appointed by Judge
■ Appointed by Mayor △ Appointed by Freeholders ▽ Appointed by Supervisor ▷ Appointed by County Executive ○ Appointed by Council

Administration Department
200 S. President St., Jackson, MS 39201
Fax: (601) 960-1049
Internet: www.jacksonms.gov/government/administration/

■ Director **Lee A. Unger** .... (601) 960-1005
E-mail: lunger@jacksonms.gov
Executive Office Coordinator **Montana Triplett** .... (601) 960-1005
E-mail: mtriplett@jacksonms.gov
Deputy Director of Administration **Rick Hill** .... (601) 960-1097
E-mail: rhill@jacksonms.gov
Deputy Director (Acting) **Frederick Wilson** .... (601) 960-1246
E-mail: fwilson@city.jackson.ms.us

Finance
200 South President Street, Jackson, MS 39201
Fax: (601) 960-1049

Finance Manager **Diane Pope** .... (601) 960-2040
Treasurer **Felicia Young** .... (601) 960-2005
Budget Manager **LaaWandaa Jones Horton** .... (601) 960-1010
E-mail: lhorton@jacksonms.gov
Assistant Budget Manager **Phillip Causey** .... (601) 960-1450
E-mail: pcausey@city.jackson.ms.us

Information Systems
353 South Congress Street, Jackson, MS 39201
Tel: (601) 960-1246 Fax: (601) 960-1254

Deputy Director **Frederick Wilson** .... (601) 960-1395
E-mail: fwilson@city.jackson.ms.us
Network Manager **Oliver Hines** .... (601) 960-1693
E-mail: ohines@city.jackson.ms.us
Database Manager **Rick Blakeney** .... (601) 960-2387
E-mail: rblakeney@city.jackson.ms.us

Publications Office
300 North State Street, Jackson, MS 39201-1799
Fax: (601) 960-1437

Manager **Sheila Williams-Sheriff** .... (601) 960-1065
E-mail: swsheriff@city.jackson.ms.us

Purchasing
200 S. President St., Jackson, MS 39201
Fax: (601) 960-1049

Manager **Hellene Greer** .... (601) 960-1533
E-mail: hgreer@jacksonms.gov
Purchasing Supervisor **Janet Allison** .... (601) 960-1022
E-mail: jallison@city.jackson.ms.us

Records Management
2525 Robinson Rd., Jackson, MS 39209
Fax: (601) 960-2496

Manager **Ruby Garvins** .... (601) 960-2331

Telecommunications
2320 Riverside Dr., Jackson, MS 39202
Tel: (601) 960-1696 Fax: (601) 960-1698

Manager **George Brown** .... (601) 960-1696
E-mail: gbrown@jacksonms.gov

Fire Department
555 S. West St., Jackson, MS 39201
Tel: (601) 960-1392 Fax: (601) 960-2198
Internet: http://www.jacksonms.gov/government/fire/

■ Fire Chief **Willie G. Owens** .... (601) 960-1392
E-mail: wowens@jacksonms.gov

Human and Cultural Services Department
1000 Metrocenter, Suite 101, Jackson, MS 39209-7503
Fax: (601) 960-1572

■ Director **Dr. Adrian Dorsey-Kidd** .... (601) 960-0764
E-mail: adorsey-kidd@city.jackson.ms.us

Human and Cultural Services Department *continued*

Deputy Director, Cultural Services **Michael Raff** .... (601) 960-0764
Deputy Director, Human Services **Louis Armstrong** ..... (601) 960-0764
Executive Office Coordinator **Gloria Fields-Anderson** ... (601) 960-0383
E-mail: gfanderson@city.jackson.ms.us
Homeless Program Coordinator **Cathy Funches** .... (601) 960-2178
Fresh Start Program Coordinator **Wanda Smith** .... (601) 960-0326

Jackson/Hinds Library System
300 North State Street, Jackson, MS 39201-1705
Fax: (601) 968-5817 Internet: www.jhlibrary.com

Executive Director **Patty Furr** .... (601) 968-5825
E-mail: pfurr@jhlibrary.com
Assistant Director for Finance (Interim) **Justin Carter** .... (601) 968-5825
Assistant Director for Human Resources
Brenette Nichols .... (601) 968-5825
E-mail: bnichols@jhlibrary.com
Assistant Director for Public Service **(Vacant)** .... (601) 968-5807
Assistant Director for Technical Services **Miao Jin** ...... (601) 968-5828
E-mail: mjin@city.jackson.ms.us
Executive Secretary **Ellen McLean** .... (601) 968-5825
E-mail: emclean@jhlibrary.com

Parks and Recreation Department
1000 Metrocenter, Suite 104, Jackson, MS 39209-7503
Tel: (601) 960-0471

Director **Allen Jones** .... (601) 960-0471
Deputy Director **(Vacant)** .... (601) 960-0471
Executive Office Coordinator **D. Patrice Bernard** .... (601) 960-0471
E-mail: pbernard@jacksonms.gov
Programs Recreational Manager **Lisa Wilson** .... (601) 960-0635
Park Maintenance Manager **Stanley Smith** .... (601) 960-1848
Fax: (601) 960-1983

Personnel Management
711 West Capitol Street, Jackson, MS 39003
P.O. Box 17, Jackson, MS 39205-0017
Tel: (601) 960-1053 Fax: (601) 960-1187

■ Director (Interim) **Denise McKay** .... (601) 960-1746
E-mail: dmckay@city.jackson.ms.us
■ Assistant Director **Toya Martin** .... (601) 960-1746
E-mail: tmartin@city.jackson.ms.us
Human Resource Officer II **Debra Ellis** .... (601) 960-1327
E-mail: dellis@city.jackson.ms.us

Department of Planning and Development
200 S. President St., Jackson, MS 39201
Fax: (601) 960-2208
Internet: http://www.jacksonms.gov/government/planning/

■ Director **Bennie Hopkins** .... (601) 960-1993
E-mail: bhopkins@city.jackson.ms.us

City Planning Office
Deputy Director **Carl Allen** .... (601) 960-2071
Zoning Administrator **Ester L. Ainsworth** .... (601) 960-2071
Land Use/Neighborhood Planning Manager **Biqi Zhao** .... (601) 960-2001
Education: Louisville 2004 MURP
Transportation Manager **(Vacant)** .... (601) 960-1887

Code Services Office
Fax: (601) 960-1287

Deputy Director **Kenneth Taylor** .... (601) 960-1159
Building Permits (Administration) Manager **(Vacant)** ..... (601) 960-1159
Building Permits (Inspections) Manager **John McGee** .... (601) 960-1990
Sign and License Manager **Terry Coleman** .... (601) 960-1154

★ Elected Official ▲ Appointed by Legislature ▼ Appointed by Governor ▶ Appointed by Board or Commission ● Appointed by Judge
■ Appointed by Mayor △ Appointed by Freeholders ▽ Appointed by Supervisor ▷ Appointed by County Executive ○ Appointed by Council

Economic Development Office
218 S. President St., Jackson, MS 39201
Fax: (601) 960-2403

Deputy Director **Michael Davis** .... (601) 960-1055
E-mail: mdavis@jacksonms.gov
Equal Business Opportunity Division Manager
Pamela Confer .... (601) 960-1638

Housing and Community Development Office
Deputy Director **Ivory Williams** .... (601) 960-2155
E-mail: iwilliams@jacksonms.gov
Development Assistance Manager **Leo Stevens** .... (601) 960-2155
E-mail: lstevens@jacksonms.gov
Neighborhood Enhancement Manager
Bertha Barrett-Frazier .... (601) 960-1438
E-mail: bgfrazier@city.jackson.ms.us

Police Department
327 East Pascagoula Street, Jackson, MS 39205
Tel: (601) 960-1234 Fax: (601) 960-1368
Internet: http://www.jacksonms.gov/government/police/

■ Police Chief **Rebecca Coleman** .... (601) 960-1217
E-mail: rcoleman@jacksonpd.org
Assistant Police Chief **Lee Vance** .... (601) 960-1926
Deputy Chief of Administration **Lindsey Horton** .... (601) 960-1950
E-mail: lindseyh@city.jackson.ms.us
Deputy Chief of Investigations **Brent Winstead** .... (601) 960-1512
Deputy Chief of Patrol Operations **Eric Wall** .... (601) 960-1808
Deputy Chief of Training and Standards **William Parker** .. (601) 960-1234
E-mail: wparker@city.jackson.ms.us
Executive Office Coordinator **(Vacant)** .... (601) 960-1217

Public Safety Communications Center
355 Tombigbee St., Jackson, MS 39201

Division Manager **Veria Wright** .... (601) 960-1234

Public Works Department
200 S. President St., Jackson, MS 39205
Fax: (601) 960-1174

■ Director **Kishia L. Powell** .... (601) 960-2091
Deputy Director of Administration **Andrada S. Butler** ... (601) 960-2419
E-mail: abutler@city.jackson.ms.us

Office of the City Council
219 South President Street, Jackson, MS 39205
P.O. Box 17, Jackson, MS 39205
Tel: (601) 960-1033 Fax: (601) 960-1032

★ Council President **Melvin V. Priester, Jr.** (D-Ward 2) .... (601) 960-1033
Term Expires: July 1, 2017
E-mail: mpriester@jacksonms.gov
★ Council Member **Ashby Foote** (D-Ward 1) .... (601) 960-1033
Term Expires: July 6, 2017
E-mail: afoote@city.jackson.ms.us
★ Council Member **Kenneth I. Stokes** (D-Ward 3) .... (601) 960-1090
Term Expires: July 1, 2017
E-mail: kstokes@city.jackson.ms.us
★ Council Member **De'Keither Stamps** (D-Ward 4) .... (601) 960-1033
Term Expires: July 1, 2017
E-mail: dstamps@jacksonms.gov
★ Council Member **Charles H. Tillman** (D-Ward 5) .... (601) 960-1092
Term Expires: July 1, 2017
E-mail: tillmanc@jacksonms.gov
★ Council Member **Tyrone Hendrix** (D-Ward 6) .... (601) 960-1089
Term Expires: July 1, 2017
E-mail: thendrix@city.jackson.ms.us
★ Council Member
Margaret Carroll Barrett-Simone (D-Ward 7) .... (601) 960-1063
Term Expires: July 1, 2017
E-mail: mbarrett@jacksonms.gov

Office of the City Clerk
219 South President Street, Jackson, MS 39205
P.O. Box 17, Jackson, MS 39205
Tel: (601) 960-1035 Fax: (601) 960-1032

○ City Clerk **Brenda Pree** .... (601) 960-1036
E-mail: bpree@jacksonms.gov

Greater Jackson Arts Council
201 East Pascagoula Street, Jackson, MS 39201
P.O. Box 17, Jackson, MS 39205
Fax: (601) 960-1596 E-mail: info@jacksonartscouncil.org
Internet: http://greaterjacksonartscouncil.com/

Executive Director **Janet Scott** .... (601) 960-1557 ext. 226

Jackson Municipal Airport Authority
Terminal Bldg., 3rd Fl., 100 International Dr., Jackson, MS 39208
P.O. Box 98109, Jackson, MS 39298-8109
Fax: (601) 664-3598 Internet: http://www.jmaa.com

Chief Executive Officer **Carl D. Newman** ...... (601) 939-5631 ext. 500
Education: Arizona BS; Embry-Riddle MS
Executive Assistant **Cynthia D. Crotchett** .... (601) 664-3504
E-mail: ccrotchett@jmaa.com

City of Jacksonville, Florida
City Hall at St. James, 117 West Duval Street, Suite 400,
Jacksonville, FL 32202
Tel: (904) 630-1776 (Information) Internet: www.coj.net

County: Duval **Election Type:** Partisan **Population:** 868,031 (2015)
Employees: 7,110 **Fiscal Year:** 2016 **Budget:** $1,151,186,000

Form of Municipal Government: City and county governments are combined.

Office of the Mayor
City Hall at St. James, 117 West Duval Street, Suite 400,
Jacksonville, FL 32202
Fax: (904) 630-2391 Internet: www.coj.net/Mayor

Employees: 32 **Fiscal Year:** 2016 **Budget:** $4,475,000

★ Mayor **Lenny Curry** .... (904) 630-1776
Began Service: July 1, 2015
Term Expires: June 30, 2019
E-mail: MayorLennyCurry@coj.net
Education: Florida
Executive Assistant to the Mayor **Jessica Laird** .... (904) 630-1776
Chief of Staff **Kerri Stewart** .... (904) 630-1776
Education: North Florida BA
Director of Intergovernmental Affairs
Allison Korman Shelton .... (904) 630-1776
Director of Public Affairs **Marsha Oliver** .... (904) 630-1776
Director of Community Affairs **Charles E. Moreland** .... (904) 630-1776
Director of Policy **Robin Lumb** (R) .... (904) 630-1776

Office of the General Counsel
City Hall at St. James, 117 West Duval Street, Suite 480,
Jacksonville, FL 32202
Tel: (904) 630-1700 Fax: (904) 630-1731
Internet: http://www.coj.net/ogc.aspx

Employees: 63 **Fiscal Year:** 2016 **Budget:** $3,359,000

■ General Counsel **Jason R. Gabriel** .... (904) 630-1724
E-mail: jgabriel@coj.net
Education: Florida 1998 BA, 2001 JD
Executive Assistant **Paula Shoup** .... (904) 630-1836
Managing Deputy **Peggy Sidman** .... (904) 630-4647

(continued on next page)

★ Elected Official ▲ Appointed by Legislature ▼ Appointed by Governor ► Appointed by Board or Commission ● Appointed by Judge
■ Appointed by Mayor △ Appointed by Freeholders ▽ Appointed by Supervisor ▷ Appointed by County Executive ○ Appointed by Council

CITIES AND TOWNS

Office of the General Counsel *continued*

Deputy General Counsel **Sean B. Granat** (904) 630-1859
Education: Florida 1994 BS, 1997 JD
Deputy General Counsel **Jason R. Teal** (904) 630-1087
Deputy General Counsel, General Litigation Department
Jon R. Phillips (904) 630-1609
Education: Tulane 1975 BA; Florida 1978 JD
Deputy General Counsel, Government Operations
Lawsikia Hodges (904) 630-1276

Office of the Chief Administrative Officer

117 West Duval Street, Suite 400, Jacksonville, FL 32202
Fax: (904) 630-2391

■ Chief Administrative Officer **Sam Mousa** (904) 630-1776
Deputy Chief Administrator **Kandi Begue** (904) 630-1776

Duval County Health Department [DCHD]

900 University Boulevard North, Jacksonville, FL 32211
Tel: (904) 253-1000 Internet: http://www.dchd.net

Director **Dr. Kelli T. Wells** (904) 253-1010 ext. 4
Fax: (904) 253-2254
Assistant Director **(Vacant)** (904) 253-2676
900 University Boulevard, North, Jacksonville, FL 32211-9203 Fax: (904) 253-2254
Assistant Director **(Vacant)** (904) 253-1006
Fax: (904) 253-2254
Disease Control Assistant Director **Dr. Max Wilson** (904) 253-2590
900 University Boulevard, North, Jacksonville, FL 32211-9203 Fax: (904) 253-2744
Nutrition and Chronic Disease Division Director
J. Spencer Greenwood (904) 253-2291
900 University Boulevard, North, Jacksonville, FL 32211-9203 Fax: (904) 745-3099
Environmental Health Administrator **Scott Turner** (904) 253-2422
900 University Boulevard, North, Jacksonville, FL 32211-9203 Fax: (904) 253-2480
Medical Director **Pauline Rolle** (904) 253-1735
Maternal and Child Health Division Director
Karen Tozzi (904) 253-1021
Fax: (904) 253-1935

Employee Services Department

117 West Duval Street, Suite 100, Jacksonville, FL 32202
Tel: (904) 630-1287 Fax: (904) 630-1431

Employees: 50 **Fiscal Year:** 2016 **Budget:** $98,941,000

Director **Kelli O'Leary** (904) 630-1287
E-mail: koleary@coj.net

Office of Ethics, Compliance and Oversight

117 West Duval Street, Room 450, Jacksonville, FL 32202
Internet: www.coj.net/Departments/Ethics+Office/

Employees: 1 **Fiscal Year:** 2016 **Budget:** $228,000

■ Ethics Officer **Carla Miller** (904) 630-1476
E-mail: carlam@coj.net

Finance Department

City Hall at St. James, 117 W. Duval St., Jacksonville, FL 32202
Fax: (904) 630-3615 Internet: www.coj.net/Departments/Finance.aspx

Employees: 94 **Fiscal Year:** 2016 **Budget:** $67,029,000

■ Chief Financial Officer
Michael B. "Mike" Weinstein (R) Suite 300 (904) 630-7660
E-mail: mweinstein@coj.net
Date of Birth: February 6, 1949
Education: Hartwick BA; Cal State (Long Beach) MS; Florida State; Florida JD

Accounting Division

Fax: (904) 630-1890

■ City Comptroller **Kevin Stork** Room 375 (904) 630-2955

Budget Division

■ Budget Officer **Angela Moyer** Room 325 (904) 630-1301
E-mail: amoyer@coj.net Fax: (904) 630-2904

Equal Business Opportunity Office

214 North Hogan Street, Jacksonville, FL 32202
Fax: (904) 255-8842

Jacksonville Business Assistance Administrator
Mario Rubio (904) 255-8840

Risk Management Division

117 West Duval Street, Suite 335, Jacksonville, FL 32202
Fax: (904) 630-2913

■ General Manager **Twane Duckworth** (904) 630-7521
E-mail: twaned@coj.net
Employee Safety Officer **Bruce Tyson** (904) 630-7332
E-mail: btyson@coj.net

Treasury Division

■ Treasurer **Joey Greive** Room 300 (904) 630-1640
E-mail: pgreive@coj.net Fax: (904) 630-3615
Senior Investment Analyst **Randall E. Barnes**
Room 300 (904) 630-1640
Pension Administrator **Raymond Ferngren** Room 302 (904) 255-7280
Fax: (904) 588-0524

Fire and Rescue Department

515 N. Julia St., Jacksonville, FL 32202-4218
Fax: (904) 630-0521
Internet: www.coj.net/Departments/Fire+and+Rescue/

Employees: 1,304 **Fiscal Year:** 2016 **Budget:** $210,344,000

Director/Fire Chief **Kurtis R. Wilson** (904) 630-7873
Fax: (904) 630-4660
Director of Emergency Management
Steven C. Woodard (904) 630-0606
E-mail: swoodard@coj.net Fax: (904) 630-0600
Fire Operations Chief **Keith Powers** (904) 630-7871
E-mail: kpowers@coj.net Fax: (904) 630-0478
Fire Prevention/Fire Marshal **Kevin Jones** (904) 630-0459
Fax: (904) 630-4203
Rescue Division Chief **David Castleman** (904) 630-8044
Fax: (904) 630-0478
Human Resources Manager **Archie B Cullen, Jr.** (904) 630-2076
E-mail: acullen@coj.net Fax: (904) 630-4202
Public Information Officer **Thomas A. Francis** (904) 630-0329
E-mail: tfrancis@coj.net Fax: (904) 630-0478
Training Chief **Gail Loput** (904) 630-1776
Fax: (904) 630-0478

Housing and Community Development Department

214 North Hogan Street, 3rd Floor, Jacksonville, FL 32202
Internet: www.coj.net/Departments/Housing+and+Neighborhoods/default.htm Fax: (904) 255-8285

Chief (Acting) **Diana Seydlorsky** (904) 255-8200

Intra-Governmental Services

214 North Hogan Street, Jacksonville, FL 32202
Fax: (904) 255-8688

Employees: 313 **Fiscal Year:** 2016 **Budget:** $97,242,000

Director **Craig "C.J." Thompson** (904) 630-1776

★ Elected Official ▲ Appointed by Legislature ▼ Appointed by Governor ► Appointed by Board or Commission ● Appointed by Judge
■ Appointed by Mayor △ Appointed by Freeholders ▽ Appointed by Supervisor ▷ Appointed by County Executive ○ Appointed by Council

Information Technologies Division
214 North Hogan Street, 9th Floor, Jacksonville, FL 32202
Tel: (904) 255-8010 Fax: (904) 232-6932

■ Division Chief and Chief Information Officer
Ken Lathrop . . . . . (904) 255-8010
E-mail: lathrop@coj.net
Finance Manager **John Proctor** . . . . . (904) 255-8104
Technology Infrastructure Manager **Robert Gray** . . . . . (904) 255-8004
Security Manager **Craig Galley** . . . . . (904) 255-8061
E-mail: cgalley@coj.net

Fleet Management Division
2581 Commonwealth Ave., Jacksonville, FL 32254-2013

Chief **(Vacant)** . . . . . (904) 255-7437
Administrator **Cris Tongol** . . . . . (904) 387-8880
E-mail: ctongol@coj.net

Procurement Division
214 North Hogan Street, Suite 800, Jacksonville, FL 32202
Fax: (904) 255-8838

Chief of Procurement **Gregory E. Pease** . . . . . (904) 255-8801
E-mail: gpease@coj.net

City Link
214 North Hogan Street, Jacksonville, FL 32202
Fax: (904) 630-1294

Administrative Management Improvement Officer
Monica Cichowlas . . . . . (904) 630-7670
E-mail: monicac@coj.net

Military Affairs, Veterans and Disabled Service Division
117 West Duval Street, Room 175, Jacksonville, FL 32202
E-mail: vetsvcs@coj.net

Employees: 14 **Fiscal Year:** 2016 **Budget:** $1,095,000

■ Manager **CDR William S. "Bill" Spann** . . . . . (904) 630-3680
Senior Veterans Services Officer **Rafael Santiago** . . . . . (904) 630-3680
Disabled Services **Beth Meyer** . . . . . (904) 630-4940

Parks and Recreation Department
City Hall at St. James, 117 West Duval Street, Suite 210,
Jacksonville, FL 32202
Fax: (904) 630-3639

Employees: 279 **Fiscal Year:** 2016 **Budget:** $52,110,000

■ Director **Daryl Joseph** . . . . . (904) 255-7903
E-mail: djoseph@coj.net
Recreation and Community Programming Division
Sherry Wilson . . . . . (904) 255-7917
Fax: (904) 255-7940
Marketing and Community Relations Manager **(Vacant)** . . . (904) 255-7902
Security Division Officer **Laurie McEwen** . . . . . (904) 255-7905
Waterfront Management Division Chief **Tera Meeks** . . . . . (904) 255-7912

Senior Services Division
Fax: (904) 630-3452 E-mail: adultsvcs@coj.net

■ Chief **Gloria Crawford** . . . . . (904) 630-3450
E-mail: gcrawford@coj.net Fax: (904) 630-3639
Foster Grandparent Program Manager **Richard Green** . . . . (904) 630-5450
150 E. First St., Jacksonville, FL 32206
E-mail: rgreen@coj.net
Retired and Senior Volunteer Program Manager
Yvette Jefferson . . . . . (904) 630-0998
150 E. First St., Jacksonville, FL 32206
Independent Living Program Manager **Latonja Osborne** . . (904) 630-0966
1093 W. 6th St., Jacksonville, FL 32209

Office of Special Events
117 West Duval Street, Suite 280, Jacksonville, FL 32202
Fax: (904) 630-3693

Director (Acting) **Sarah Horn Ausherman** . . . . . (904) 630-3690

Senior Services Division *continued*

Mayor's Special Events for Senior Citizens Coordinator
Mary Ferrell Suite 220 . . . . . (904) 630-3450

Behavioral and Human Services Division
1809 Art Museum Drive, Suite 100, Jacksonville, FL 32207
Fax: (904) 858-2800
Internet: www.coj.net/Community+Services/Mental+Health+and+Welfare/

Chief **Johnetta Moore** . . . . . (904) 630-0844
Emergency Social Services Program Manager
Martha Hemphill . . . . . (904) 630-3520
Social Services Supervisor **Rebecca Jerido** . . . . . (904) 630-6300
Social Services Supervisor **Johnetta Moore** . . . . . (904) 630-4720
Ryan White Program Manager **Dee Kelley** . . . . . (904) 630-3957

Duval County Extension Service
1010 North McDuff Avenue, Jacksonville, FL 32254-2081
Fax: (904) 387-8902 E-mail: duval@gnv.ifas.ufl.edu

Director **Mike Sweat** . . . . . (904) 255-7450

Extension Agriculture Program Area
Urban Horticulture Agent **Terry B. DelValle** . . . . . (904) 255-7450
Production Agriculture Agent **(Vacant)** . . . . . (904) 255-7450
Commercial Horticulture Agent **Erin Harlow** . . . . . (904) 255-7450
Urban Forestry Agent **Larry Figart** . . . . . (904) 255-7450

Extension Family and Consumer Science Program Area
Child Development and Family Living Extension Agent
Stephanie Toelle . . . . . (904) 255-7450
EFNEP-Adult Extension Agent **Natasha Parks** . . . . . (904) 255-7450
Family Resource Management Extension Agent
Melanie Thomas . . . . . (904) 255-7450

Extension 4-H Youth Development Program Area
Agriculture Extension 4-H Agent **Andy Toelle** . . . . . (904) 255-7450
4-H Youth Development Agent **Stacie Amolsch** . . . . . (904) 255-7450
Extension Traditional 4H Agent **(Vacant)** . . . . . (904) 255-7450

City Canning Center
2525 Commonwealth Ave., Jacksonville, FL 32254-2083

Coordinator **Jeannie Crosby** . . . . . (904) 255-7450

Planning and Development Department
214 North Hogan Street, 3rd Floor, Jacksonville, FL 32202
Fax: (904) 255-7886

Employees: 168 **Fiscal Year:** 2016 **Budget:** $17,560,000

■ Director **William B. "Bill" Killingsworth** . . . . . (904) 255-7800
E-mail: billk@coj.net
Chief, Community Planning **Kristen Reed** . . . . . (904) 255-7837
E-mail: kreed@coj.net
Chief of Current Planning **Folks Huxford** . . . . . (904) 255-7817
E-mail: fhuxford@coj.net

Building Inspections Division
Ed Ball Building, 214 North Hogan Street, 2nd Floor,
Jacksonville, FL 32202
Fax: (904) 255-8553

■ Chief, Building Inspection **Tom Goldsbury** . . . . . (904) 255-8505
E-mail: TomG@coj.net

Development Services
Ed Ball Building, 214 North Hogan Street, Room 2100,
Jacksonville, FL 32202
Fax: (904) 255-8311

Chief **Mike Sands** . . . . . (904) 255-8575
E-mail: msands@coj.net

★ Elected Official ▲ Appointed by Legislature ▼ Appointed by Governor ▶ Appointed by Board or Commission ● Appointed by Judge
■ Appointed by Mayor △ Appointed by Freeholders ▽ Appointed by Supervisor ▷ Appointed by County Executive ○ Appointed by Council

Public Works Department
Ed Ball Building, 214 North Hogan Street, 10th Floor, Jacksonville, FL 32202
Fax: (904) 255-8929 Internet: www.coj.net/Departments/Public+Works/

Employees: 520 **Fiscal Year:** 2016 **Budget:** $248,159,000

■ Director **John Pappas** .... (904) 255-8786
Education: Florida 1985 BSCE
Operations Director **William Joyce** .... (904) 255-8786

Engineering and Construction Management Division
Fax: (904) 255-8926

■ Chief/City Engineer **Tom Fallin** .... (904) 255-8762
E-mail: joyce@coj.net

Public Buildings Division
930 Liberty St., Jacksonville, FL 32206
Fax: (904) 630-3568

■ Chief **Luis Flores** .... (904) 630-3525
E-mail: lflores@coj.net

Real Estate Division
Fax: (904) 255-8948

■ Chief **Stephanie Burch** .... (904) 255-8700
220 East Bay Street, Room 1208, Jacksonville, FL 32202-3493

Right of Way and Grounds Maintenance
609 St. Johns Bluff Road, Jacksonville, FL 32206
Fax: (904) 998-5387

■ Chief **S. D. Long** .... (904) 472-2900
E-mail: slong@coj.net

Solid Waste Division
1031 Superior Street, Jacksonville, FL 32254
Fax: (904) 387-8905

■ Division Chief (Interim) **Will Williams** .... (904) 255-7245

Traffic Engineering Division
1007 Superior St., Jacksonville, FL 32254
Fax: (904) 387-8894

■ Chief **Nelson Caparas** .... (904) 387-8762
Traffic Operations Superintendent **(Vacant)** .... (904) 387-8969

Neighborhoods Department
214 North Hogan Street, 5th Floor, Jacksonville, FL 32202
Tel: (904) 255-7200

Employees: 206 **Fiscal Year:** 2016 **Budget:** $20,330,000

Director (Interim) **Kimberly Scott** .... (904) 255-7245

Animal Care and Protective Services Division
2020 Forest Street, Jacksonville, FL 32202

Division Chief **(Vacant)** .... (904) 630-2489

Environmental Quality Division
407 North Laura Street, Jacksonville, FL 32202

Division Chief **Melissa Long** .... (904) 255-7100
Administrative Assistant **Sandra K. Assidy** .... (904) 255-7100
E-mail: assidy@coj.net

Mosquito Control Division
1321 Eastport Rd., Jacksonville, FL 32218-2297
Fax: (904) 751-5925

■ Division Chief **John Shellhorn** .... (904) 696-4374

Municipal Code Compliance Division
407 North Laura Street, Suite 200, Jacksonville, FL 32202
Fax: (904) 588-0510

Division Chief (Interim) **Bryan Mosier** .... (904) 255-7000

Office of Economic Development
One West Adams Street, Suite 200, Jacksonville, FL 32202
Fax: (904) 630-2919

Executive Director **Kirk Wendland** .... (904) 630-7063
Deputy Executive Director **Paul Crawford** .... (904) 630-7063
E-mail: paulc@coj.net
Business Recruitment and Retention Coordinator **Joe Whitaker** .... (904) 630-1624
E-mail: josephw@coj.net
Redevelopment Manager **Karen Nasrallah** .... (904) 630-2272
E-mail: karenn@coj.net

Public Parking Office
231 East Forsyth Street, Room 450, Jacksonville, FL 32202
Fax: (904) 630-2471

■ Division Chief **Robert Carle** .... (904) 630-1399
E-mail: rcarle@coj.net

Jacksonville Housing Finance Authority [JHA]
1300 Broad St., Jacksonville, FL 32202-3938
Fax: (904) 630-3888

President and Chief Executive Officer **Fred McKinnies** .... (904) 630-3825
Vice President, Housing Assistance **Larry Gonzalez** .... (904) 665-3038
Vice President, Resident Services **Rhonda Lattimore** .... (904) 366-6091
Fax: (904) 366-6079
Chief Financial Officer **Maxine Person** .... (904) 665-3037
Human Resources Director **Bernadette Brown** .... (904) 630-3868
E-mail: bbrown@jaxha.org

Jacksonville Public Library [JPL]
303 North Laura Street, Jacksonville, FL 32202-3374
Tel: (904) 630-2665 Fax: (904) 630-1343 Internet: www.jpl.coj.net

Employees: 296 **Fiscal Year:** 2016 **Budget:** $33,319,000

Administration
Director **Barbara A. B. Gubbin** .... (904) 630-1994
E-mail: libdir@coj.net
Deputy Library Director **Jennifer Giltrop** .... (904) 630-1636
Deputy Director, Administration and Finance **Mark Merritt** .... (904) 630-1171
E-mail: mmerritt@coj.net

Jacksonville Transportation Authority [JTA]
P.O. Drawer O, Jacksonville, FL 32203
Internet: www.jtafla.com

Chief Executive Officer **Nathaniel P. Ford, Sr.** .... (904) 630-3181
Education: Mercer Fax: (904) 630-3166
Chief of Staff **(Vacant)** .... (904) 630-3181
Fax: (904) 630-3166
Vice President, Compliance and Risk **Cleveland Ferguson** .... (904) 630-3181
E-mail: cferguson@jtafla.com Fax: (904) 630-3166
Vice President, External Affairs **Jacquie Gibbs** .... (904) 630-3181
E-mail: jgibbs@jtafla.com Fax: (904) 630-3166
Vice President, Finance and Administration/Chief Financial Officer **(Vacant)** .... (904) 630-3181
Fax: (904) 630-3166
Vice President, Long Range Planning **Brad Thoburn** .... (904) 630-3181
Fax: (904) 630-3166
Vice President, Transit Operations **Ellisa "Lisa" Darnall** .... (904) 630-3181
E-mail: elisa.darnall@jtafla.com Fax: (904) 630-3166

JEA
21 W. Church St., Jacksonville, FL 32202
Tel: (904) 665-6000 Fax: (904) 665-4238 Internet: www.jea.com

Managing Director/Chief Executive Officer **Paul McElroy** .... (904) 665-7220
Chief Financial Officer **Melissa Dykes** .... (904) 665-7054

★ Elected Official ▲ Appointed by Legislature ▼ Appointed by Governor ▶ Appointed by Board or Commission ● Appointed by Judge
■ Appointed by Mayor △ Appointed by Freeholders ▽ Appointed by Supervisor ▷ Appointed by County Executive ○ Appointed by Council

JEA *continued*

Chief Human Resources Officer **Angelia Hiers** .... (904) 665-4747
E-mail: hierar@jea.com
Chief Information Officer **Paul J. Cosgrave** .... (904) 665-7217
Education: Rensselaer Poly BS, MS
Chief Public Affairs Officer
Michael R. "Mike" Hightower .... (904) 665-7313
Chief Customer Officer **Monica Whiting** .... (904) 665-8609
Vice President/General Manager, Electric Systems
Mike Brost .... (904) 665-7547
Chief Compliance Officer **Ted E. Hobson** .... (904) 665-7126
Vice President and General Manager, Water/Wastewater
Systems **Brian Roche** .... (904) 665-6580
Director, Government Affairs **Nancy Kilgo** .... (904) 665-6439
E-mail: kilgna@jea.com

Office of Sports and Entertainment

1 West Adams Street, Suite 200, Jacksonville, FL 32202
Fax: (904) 630-3606

Employees: 18 **Fiscal Year:** 2016 **Budget:** $41,376,000

■ Sports and Entertainment Director **Dave Herrell** .... (904) 630-3600
E-mail: dherrell@coj.net
Education: Missouri BA
Manager of Business Development and Communications
Joel Lamp .... (904) 630-3600
E-mail: jlamp@coj.net
Film and Television Office Manager **Todd Roobin** .... (904) 630-2522
E-mail: troobin@coj.net

Office of the City Council

City Hall at St. James, 117 West Duval Street, Suite 425,
Jacksonville, FL 32202-3700
Tel: (904) 630-1377 Fax: (904) 630-2906
Internet: www.coj.net/city-council.aspx

Employees: 79 **Fiscal Year:** 2016 **Budget:** $16,127,000

★ President **Lori N. Boyer** (R-District 5) .... (904) 630-1382
Term Expires: June 30, 2019
E-mail: lboyer@coj.net
★ Vice President **John R. Crescimbeni** (D-At-Large 2) .... (904) 630-1381
Term Expires: June 30, 2019
E-mail: jrc@coj.net
★ Council Member **Joyce Morgan** (D-District 1) .... (904) 630-1389
Term Expires: June 30, 2019
E-mail: joycemorgan@coj.net
★ Council Member **Al Ferraro** (R-District 2) .... (904) 630-1392
Term Expires: June 30, 2019
E-mail: ferraro@coj.net
★ Council Member **CAPT Aaron Bowman** (R-District 3) ... (904) 630-1386
Term Expires: June 30, 2019
E-mail: abowman@coj.net
★ Council Member **Scott Wilson** (R-District 4) .... (904) 630-1394
Term Expires: June 30, 2019
E-mail: swilson@coj.net
★ Council Member **Matt Schellenberg** (R-District 6) ...... (904) 630-1388
Term Expires: June 30, 2019
E-mail: matts@coj.net
★ Council Member
Reginald "Reggie" Gaffney (R-District 7) .... (904) 630-1384
Term Expires: June 30, 2019
E-mail: rgaffney@coj.net
★ Council Member **Katrina Brown** (D-District 8) .... (904) 630-1385
Term Expires: June 30, 2019
E-mail: kbrown@coj.net
★ Council Member **Garrett Dennis** (D-District 9) .... (904) 630-1395
Term Expires: June 30, 2019
E-mail: garrettd@coj.net
★ Council Member **Reggie Brown** (D-District 10) .... (904) 630-1684
Term Expires: June 30, 2019
E-mail: rbrown@coj.net

Office of the City Council *continued*

★ Council Member **Danny Becton** (R-District 11) .... (904) 630-1383
Term Expires: June 30, 2019
E-mail: dbecton@coj.net
★ Council Member **Doyle Carter** (R-District 12) .... (904) 630-1380
Term Expires: June 30, 2019
E-mail: doylec@coj.net
★ Council Member **William Gulliford** (R-District 13) ...... (904) 630-1397
Term Expires: June 30, 2019
E-mail: Gulliford@coj.net
★ Council Member **Jim Love** (R-District 14) .... (904) 630-1390
Term Expires: June 30, 2019
E-mail: jimlove@coj.net
★ Council Member **Anna Lopez Brosche** (R-At-Large 1) .. (904) 630-1393
Term Expires: June 30, 2019
E-mail: abrosche@coj.net
★ Council Member **Tommy Hazouri** (D-At-Large 3) .... (904) 630-1396
Term Expires: June 30, 2019
E-mail: thazouri@coj.net
Council Member **Greg Anderson** (R-At-Large 4) .... (904) 630-1398
Term Expires: June 30, 2019
E-mail: ganderson@coj.net
★ Council Member **Samuel C. Newby** (R-At-Large 5) ..... (904) 630-1387
Term Expires: June 30, 2019
E-mail: snewby@coj.net
Director and Council Secretary **Cheryl L. Brown** .... (904) 630-1452
E-mail: clbrown@coj.net
○ Administrative Services Chief **Kristi Sikes** .... (904) 630-1401
E-mail: kcsikes@coj.net
○ Research Division Chief **Jeff Clements** .... (904) 630-1405
E-mail: jeffc@coj.net
○ Legislative Services Chief **Dana Farris** .... (904) 630-1404
E-mail: dmfarris@coj.net
○ Tourist Development Council Executive Director
Annette Hastings .... (904) 630-7625
E-mail: annetteh@coj.net
○ Council Auditor **Kirk Sherman** .... (904) 630-1625
E-mail: ksherman@coj.net

Office of the Medical Examiner

2100 Jefferson St., Jacksonville, FL 32206-3534
Fax: (904) 630-0964

Employees: 27 **Fiscal Year:** 2016 **Budget:** $3,920,000

▼ Chief Medical Examiner **Dr. Valerie Rao** .... (904) 255-4000
E-mail: vrao@coj.net
Associate Medical Examiner **Dr. Robert Buchsbaum** .... (904) 255-4000
Associate Medical Examiner **Dr. Peter Gillespie** .... (904) 255-4000
Associate Medical Examiner **Dr. Aurelian Nicolaescu** ... (904) 255-4000
Associate Medical Examiner **(Vacant)** .... (904) 255-4000

Office of the Property Appraiser

Yates Bldg., 231 East Forsyth Street, Suite 270, Jacksonville, FL 32202
Tel: (904) 630-2011 Fax: (904) 630-2922 E-mail: paadmin@coj.net
Internet: www.coj.net/pa

Employees: 120 **Fiscal Year:** 2016 **Budget:** $10,207,000

★ Property Appraiser **Jerry Holland** (R) .... (904) 630-2014
Term Expires: June 30, 2019
Date of Birth: 1961
Education: North Florida 1983 BA, 1997 MA
Administrative Assistant **Yadira Botero** .... (904) 630-2014
E-mail: ybotero@coj.net
Finance Officer **Kathleen Tyson** .... (904) 630-2014
Chief Administrative Officer **Kay Ehas** .... (904) 630-2014
E-mail: kehas@coj.net
Chief Appraiser **Keith Hicks** .... (904) 630-2014
E-mail: kdhicks@coj.net
Chief of Land Records **Curt Crossley** .... (904) 630-7524
E-mail: ccrossley@coj.net
Chief of Customer Service **Dana Clark** .... (904) 630-2020

(continued on next page)

★ Elected Official ▲ Appointed by Legislature ▼ Appointed by Governor ► Appointed by Board or Commission ● Appointed by Judge
■ Appointed by Mayor △ Appointed by Freeholders ▽ Appointed by Supervisor ▷ Appointed by County Executive ○ Appointed by Council

Office of the Property Appraiser *continued*

Community Relations Manager **Sheri Treadwell** .... (904) 630-2014
E-mail: streadwell@coj.net
Information Services Director **Teresa Pulley** .... (904) 630-3432
E-mail: tpulley@coj.net

Office of the Sheriff

Police Bldg., 501 E. Bay St., Room 304, Jacksonville, FL 32202
Fax: (904) 630-1772
Internet: www.coj.net/departments/sheriffs-office.aspx

Employees: 3,102 **Fiscal Year:** 2016 **Budget:** $404,854,000

★Sheriff **Michael Williams** .... (904) 630-2120
Term Expires: June 30, 2019
Senior Public Relations and Public Affairs Executive
Lauri-Ellen Smith .... (904) 630-2538
E-mail: lesmith@jaxsheriff.org
Undersheriff **P.L. Ivey** .... (904) 630-2120
E-mail: pivey@jtafla.com
Administrative Secretary **Terry Monroe** .... (904) 630-2229
E-mail: terrym@coj.net
Legal Advisor **Vanessa Moore** .... (904) 630-2120
Corrections Department Director **M.D. Bruno** .... (904) 630-2120
Director of Investigations and Homeland Security
Tom "T.R." Hackney .... (904) 630-5847
E-mail: taraw@coj.net
Patrol and Enforcement **R.L. Walden** .... (904) 630-2120
Personnel and Professional Standards Director
M.E. Cook .... (904) 630-2120
Police Services Director **T.R. Davis** .... (904) 630-2120

Duval County Clerk of Courts

Duval County Courthouse, 501 West Adams Street, Room 103,
Jacksonville, FL 32202
Internet: www.duvalclerk.com

Employees: 32 **Fiscal Year:** 2016 **Budget:**

Clerk of the Circuit and County Courts
Ronnie Fussell (R) .... (904) 255-2000

Duval County Public Schools

1701 Prudential Dr., Jacksonville, FL 32207-8182
Fax: (904) 390-2586 Internet: www.duvalschools.org
Superintendent **Nikolai Vitti** .... (904) 390-2115

Duval County Tax Collector

231 E. Forsyth St., Jacksonville, FL 32202
Tel: (904) 630-1916 (Tax Collector "One Call" Center)
E-mail: taxcollector@coj.net

★Tax Collector **Michael L. Corrigan** (R) .... (904) 630-1916
Term Expires: June 30, 2019
E-mail: taxcollector@coj.net
Chief Administrative Officer **Sherry Hall** .... (904) 630-1916
E-mail: sherryh@coj.net

Supervisor of Elections

105 East Monroe Street, Jacksonville, FL 32202
Fax: (904) 630-2920 Internet: www.duvalelections.com

Employees: 33 **Fiscal Year:** 2016 **Budget:** $6,907,000

★Supervisor of Elections **Mike Hogan** (R) .... (904) 630-1414
Term Expires: June 30, 2019
Date of Birth: September 30, 1949
Education: South Florida 1972 BA
Chief Elections Assistant **Robert Phillips** .... (904) 630-8018

Supervisor of Elections *continued*

Deputy Supervisor and Director of Education
Tracie Davis .... (904) 630-8026

Downtown Investment Authority

City Hall, 117 West Duval Street, Jacksonville, FL 32202
Tel: (904) 630-3492

Chief Executive Officer **Aundra Wallace** .... (904) 630-3487
E-mail: awallace@coj.net

Jefferson City, Missouri

John G. Christy Municipal Bldg., 320 E. McCarty St.,
Jefferson City, MO 65101
Internet: www.jeffcitymo.org

County: Cole **Election Type:** Nonpartisan **Year Incorporated:** 1825
Population: 43,169 (2015)

Office of the Mayor and City Council

John G. Christy Municipal Bldg., 320 E. McCarty St.,
Jefferson City, MO 65101
Fax: (573) 634-6329

★Mayor **Carrie Tergin** .... (573) 634-6303
Began Service: April 20, 2015
Term Expires: April 2017
★Council Member **Jim Branch** (Ward 1) .... (573) 634-6311
Term Expires: April 2017
E-mail: jbranch@jeffcitymo.org
★Council Member **Rick Prather** (Ward 1) .... (573) 634-6311
Term Expires: April 2018
E-mail: rprather@jeffcitymo.org
★Council Member **J. Rick Mihalevich** (Ward 2) .... (573) 634-6311
Term Expires: April 16, 2018
E-mail: rmihalevich@jeffcitymo.org
★Council Member **Laura A. Ward** (Ward 2) .... (573) 634-6311
Term Expires: April 2017
E-mail: lward@jeffcitymo.org
★Council Member **Ken Hussey** (Ward 3) .... (573) 634-6311
Term Expires: April 2017
E-mail: khussey@jeffcitymo.org
★Council Member **Erin L. Wiseman** (Ward 3) .... (573) 634-6311
Term Expires: April 2018
E-mail: ewiseman@jeffcitymo.org
★Council Member **Glen Costales** (Ward 4) .... (573) 634-6311
Term Expires: April 16, 2018
E-mail: gcostales@jeffcitymo.org
★Council Member **Carlos M. Graham** (Ward 4) .... (573) 634-6311
Term Expires: April 2017
E-mail: cgraham@jeffcitymo.org
★Council Member **Larry Henry** (Ward 5) .... (573) 634-2482
Term Expires: April 16, 2018
E-mail: lhenry@jeffcitymo.org
★Council Member **Mark Charles Schreiber** (Ward 5) ...... (573) 634-6311
Term Expires: April 2017

Office of the City Clerk

John G. Christy Municipal Bldg., 320 E. McCarty St.,
Jefferson City, MO 65101
Fax: (573) 634-6329

○City Clerk **Phyllis Powell** .... (573) 634-6311
E-mail: ppowell@jeffcitymo.org

★Elected Official ▲Appointed by Legislature ▼Appointed by Governor ►Appointed by Board or Commission ●Appointed by Judge
■Appointed by Mayor △Appointed by Freeholders ▽Appointed by Supervisor ▷Appointed by County Executive ○Appointed by Council

Office of the City Prosecutor
John G. Christy Municipal Bldg., 320 E. McCarty St.,
Jefferson City, MO 65101
Fax: (573) 634-6458

★City Prosecutor **Brian K. Stumpe** .... (573) 634-6316
Term Expires: April 2017
E-mail: bstumpe@jeffcitymo.org
Education: Notre Dame JD

Office of the City Administrator
John G. Christy Municipal Bldg., 320 E. McCarty St.,
Jefferson City, MO 65101
Fax: (573) 634-6329

○City Administrator **Steve Crowell** .... (573) 634-6306
E-mail: scrowell@jeffcitymo.org
Communications Manager **(Vacant)** .... (573) 634-6377

Finance/Information Technology Department
John G. Christy Municipal Bldg., 320 E. McCarty St.,
Jefferson City, MO 65101
Fax: (573) 634-6329

Director/Information Technology Manager **(Vacant)** ...... (573) 634-6320

Fire Department
305 East Miller Street, Jefferson City, MO 65101
Fax: (573) 634-6402

Fire Chief **Matthew Schofield** .... (573) 634-6401

Human Resources Department
John G. Christy Municipal Bldg., 320 E. McCarty St.,
Jefferson City, MO 65101
Fax: (573) 634-6329

Director **Gail Strope** .... (573) 634-6309
E-mail: gstrope@jeffcitymo.org

Law Department
P.O. Box 1029, Jefferson City, MO 65102-1029
Fax: (573) 634-6504

City Counselor **Drew Hilpert** .... (573) 634-6313
E-mail: dhilpert@jeffcitymo.org

Parks and Recreation Department
John G. Christy Municipal Bldg., 320 E. McCarty St.,
Jefferson City, MO 65101
Fax: (573) 634-6489 E-mail: jcparks@jeffcitymo.org

Director **Bill Lockwood** .... (573) 634-6593

Planning and Protective Services Department
John G. Christy Municipal Bldg., 320 E. McCarty St.,
Jefferson City, MO 65101
Fax: (573) 634-6562

Director **Janice McMillan** .... (573) 634-6521
E-mail: jmcmillan@jeffcitymo.org
Director of Environmental Health **David Grellner** .... (573) 634-6410

Police Department
John G. Christy Municipal Bldg., 320 E. McCarty St.,
Jefferson City, MO 65101

Chief of Police **Roger Schroeder** .... (573) 634-6334
Director of Animal Protection and Control
Karen Jennings .... (573) 634-6410

Public Works Department
John G. Christy Municipal Building, 320 E. McCarty St.,
Jefferson City, MO 65101
Fax: (573) 634-6562

Director **Matt J. Morasch** .... (573) 634-6410

Wastewater Maintenance Division
2320 Hyde Park Road, Jefferson City, MO 65101
Fax: (573) 634-6323

Director for Wastewater Services **Eric Seaman** .... (573) 634-6455

Jersey City, New Jersey
City Hall, 280 Grove St., Jersey City, NJ 07302
Tel: (201) 547-5000 (Information) Fax: (201) 547-4288
Internet: www.cityofjerseycity.com

County: Hudson **Election Type:** Nonpartisan **Year Founded:** 1630
Population: 264,290 (2015)

Office of the Mayor
City Hall, 280 Grove Street, Room 223, Jersey City, NJ 07302
Fax: (201) 547-4288

★Mayor **Steven M. Fulop** .... (201) 547-5500
Began Service: July 1, 2013
Term Expires: June 30, 2017
E-mail: sfulop@jcnj.org
Chief of Staff **Mark Albiez** .... (201) 547-5200
Deputy Mayor **Vivian Brady-Phillips** .... (201) 547-5200
E-mail: vbrady-phillips@jcnj.org
Deputy Mayor **Marcos Vigil** .... (201) 547-5200
E-mail: mvigil@jcnj.org
Communications Director **(Vacant)** .... (201) 547-5200 ext. 4836
Press Secretary **Jennifer Morrill** .... (201) 547-5200 ext. 4836
E-mail: jenniferm@jcnj.org

Resident Response Center
Director **Althea Bernheim** .... (201) 547-4900
E-mail: abernheim@jcnj.org

Administration Department
City Hall, 280 Grove St., Jersey City, NJ 07302
Fax: (201) 547-4833

■Business Administrator **Robert Kakoleski** Room 108 .... (201) 547-5147
E-mail: rjkakoleski@jcnj.org
Information Technology Director **Allan Guglielmi** .... (201) 547-4440
Purchasing Agent **Peter Folgado** .... (201) 547-5155
E-mail: peterf@jcnj.org
■Chief Financial Officer **Donna Mauer** .... (201) 547-5252
E-mail: dmauer@jcnj.org
Tax Assessor **Eduardo Toloza** .... (201) 547-4797
E-mail: etoloza@jcnj.org
Tax Collector **Maureen Cosgrove** .... (201) 547-5120
E-mail: mcosgrove@jcnj.org
Treasurer **Peter O'Reilly** .... (201) 547-4985
Payroll **Maximo Inciong** .... (201) 547-5024
Pension **Alice T. Purcell** .... (201) 547-5143

Management and Budget Division
Director **Donna Mauer** .... (201) 547-4642
E-mail: dmauer@jcnj.org

Economic Opportunity Division
121-125 Newark Ave., Jersey City, NJ 07302
Fax: (201) 860-0007

Director (Acting) **Judi Sass** .... (201) 547-5611
E-mail: jsass@jcnj.org

(continued on next page)

★Elected Official ▲Appointed by Legislature ▼Appointed by Governor ►Appointed by Board or Commission ●Appointed by Judge
■Appointed by Mayor △Appointed by Freeholders ▽Appointed by Supervisor ▷Appointed by County Executive ○Appointed by Council

Economic Opportunity Division *continued*

Affirmative Action Director **Mark Bunbury** . . . . (201) 547-5732
City Hall, 280 Grove Street, Room 103, Jersey City, NJ 07302

Engineering Division

575 Grove Street, Route 440, Jersey City, NJ 07305

Municipal Engineer **Joe Cunha** . . . . (201) 547-4413
E-mail: jcunha@jcnj.org

Department of Human Resources

Fax: (201) 547-5022

Director **Nancy Ramos** Room 103 . . . . (201) 547-5217
E-mail: nramos@jcnj.org

Health and Human Services

201 Cornelision Avenue, Room 314, Jersey City, NJ 07302
Tel: (201) 547-6800 Fax: (201) 547-6816

■ Director **Stacey Lea Flanagan** . . . . (201) 547-6808
E-mail: sflanagan@jcnj.org
Health Officer **Vera Smith** . . . . (201) 547-5545

Housing, Economic Development, and Commerce Department

30 Montgomery St., Jersey City, NJ 07302
Fax: (201) 547-6566

■ Director **Anthony Cruz** . . . . (201) 547-5070
E-mail: acruz@jcnj.org
Commerce **Maynard Woodson** . . . . (201) 547-5139
E-mail: mwoodson@jcnj.org
Construction Code Official **Raymond Meyer** . . . . (201) 547-5055
City Planning **Robert Cotter** . . . . (201) 547-5010
Economic Development **Jose Arango** . . . . (201) 547-6567
E-mail: jarango@jcnj.org
Housing Code Enforcement **Ed Coleman** . . . . (201) 547-4824
E-mail: ecoleman@jcnj.org
Zoning **Nick Taylor** . . . . (201) 547-6564

Division of Parking Enforcement

1 Journal Square Plaza, Jersey City, NJ 07307
Fax: (201) 653-7617

Chief Executive Officer **Mary Paretti** . . . . (201) 653-6969

Law Department

City Hall, 280 Grove Street, Room 301, Jersey City, NJ 07302
Fax: (201) 547-5230

○ Corporation Counsel **Jeremy Farrell** . . . . (201) 547-5229
E-mail: jfarrell@jcnj.org
Prosecutor **Alan Pearlman** . . . . (201) 547-5229

Library, Jersey City Public

472 Jersey Ave., Jersey City, NJ 07302
Tel: (201) 547-4500

Director **Priscilla Gardner** . . . . (201) 547-4788
E-mail: pgardner@jclibrary.org
Personnel Technician **Lynese Jackson** . . . . (201) 547-4509
E-mail: ljackson@jcnj.org

Department of Public Safety

1 Journal Square Plaza, 4th Floor, Jersey City, NJ 07307

■ Director of Public Safety **James Shea** . . . . (201) 547-5000
E-mail: jshea@jcnj.org

Division of Police

1 Journal Square Plaza, 4th Floor, Jersey City, NJ 07307

■ Chief of Police **Philip Zacche** . . . . (201) 547-5301
E-mail: pzacche@njjcps.org

Division of Fire and Emergency Services

465 Marin Boulevard, Jersey City, NJ 07302
Fax: (201) 547-4398

Fire Chief **Darren Rivers** . . . . (201) 547-4247
E-mail: drivers@njjcps.org

Office of Emergency Management and Homeland Security

465 Marin Boulevard, Jersey City, NJ 07302
Tel: (201) 547-5566 Fax: (201) 547-5999

Director **Sgt W. Greg Kierce** . . . . (201) 547-5566
E-mail: wkierce@njjcps.org

Department of Public Works

Municipal Services Complex, 15 Linden Avenue East, Suite 200, Jersey City, NJ 07305
Tel: (201) 547-4402 Fax: (201) 547-4803

■ Director **Mark Redfield** . . . . (201) 547-4402
E-mail: mredfield@jcnj.org
Assistant Director **John McGrath** . . . . (201) 547-4903

Department of Recreation

Caven Point Complex, One Chapel Ave., Jersey City, NJ 07305
Fax: (201) 547-4586

■ Director **Kevin Williamson** . . . . (201) 547-5269

Office of the Municipal Council

City Hall, 280 Grove Street, Room 201, Jersey City, NJ 07302
Tel: (201) 547-5204

★ Council President **Rolando Lavarro** (At-Large) . . . . (201) 547-5134
Term Expires: June 30, 2017
E-mail: rlavarro@jcnj.org
★ Council Member **Frank Gajewski** (Ward A) . . . . (201) 547-5098
Term Expires: June 30, 2017
E-mail: fgajewski@jcnj.org
★ Council Member **(Vacant)** (Ward B) . . . . (201) 547-5092
Term Expires: June 30, 2017
★ Council Member **Richard Boggiano** (Ward C) . . . . (201) 547-5159
Term Expires: June 30, 2017
E-mail: rboggiano@jcnj.org
★ Council Member **Michael Yun** (Ward D) . . . . (201) 547-5485
Term Expires: June 30, 2017
E-mail: myun@jcnj.org
★ Council Member **Candice Osborne** (Ward E) . . . . (201) 547-5315
Term Expires: June 30, 2017
E-mail: cosborne@jcnj.org
★ Council Member **Diane Coleman** (Ward F) . . . . (201) 547-5338
Term Expires: June 30, 2017
E-mail: dcoleman@jcnj.org
★ Council Member **Daniel Rivera** (At-Large) . . . . (201) 547-4634
Term Expires: June 30, 2017
E-mail: drivera@jcnj.org
★ Council Member **Joyce Watterman** (At-Large) . . . . (201) 547-5268
Term Expires: June 30, 2017
E-mail: jwatterman@jcnj.org
Council Secretary **Margaret DeVico** . . . . (201) 547-5053

Office of the City Clerk

City Hall, 280 Grove St., Room 118, Jersey City, NJ 07302
Fax: (201) 547-5461

○ City Clerk **Robert Byrne** . . . . (201) 547-5150
E-mail: rbyrne@jcnj.org

★ Elected Official ▲ Appointed by Legislature ▼ Appointed by Governor ▶ Appointed by Board or Commission ● Appointed by Judge
■ Appointed by Mayor △ Appointed by Freeholders ▽ Appointed by Supervisor ▷ Appointed by County Executive ○ Appointed by Council

City of Joliet, Illinois

City Hall, 150 W. Jefferson St., Joliet, IL 60432
Tel: (815) 724-4000 (Information) Internet: www.cityofjoliet.info

County: Will **Election Type:** Nonpartisan **Population:** 147,861 (2015)

Office of the Mayor and City Council

City Hall, 150 W. Jefferson St., Joliet, IL 60432
Fax: (815) 724-3715

★Mayor **Bob O'Dekirk** (At-Large) .... (815) 724-3700
Began Service: May 4, 2015
Term Expires: May 2019
E-mail: ROdekirk@jolietcity.org

★Council Member **Larry Hug** (District 1) .... (815) 325-0875
Term Expires: May 1, 2019
E-mail: Lhug@jolietcity.org

★Council Member **Pat Mudron** (District 2) .... (815) 724-3741
Term Expires: May 2019
E-mail: pmudron@jolietcity.org

★Council Member **John E. Gerl** (District 3) .... (815) 724-3718
Term Expires: May 2019
E-mail: jgerl@jolietcity.org

★Council Member **Bettye J. Gavin** (District 4) .... (815) 724-3745
Term Expires: May 2019
E-mail: bgavin@jolietcity.org

★Council Member **Terry Morris** (District 5) .... (815) 724-3742
Term Expires: May 2019
E-mail: tmorris@jolietcity.org

★Council Member **Jim McFarland** (At-Large) .... (815) 714-8787
Term Expires: May 1, 2017
E-mail: jmcfarland@jolietcity.org

★Council Member **Jan Quillman** (At-Large) .... (815) 724-3718
Term Expires: May 1, 2017
E-mail: janquillman@att.net

★Council Member **Michael Turk** (At-Large) .... (815) 724-3718
Term Expires: May 1, 2017
E-mail: miket@sowic.org

Office of the City Manager

City Hall, 150 W. Jefferson St., Joliet, IL 60432

○City Manager **Jim Hock** .... (815) 724-3720
E-mail: jhock@jolietcity.org

Office of the City Clerk

150 W. Jefferson St., Joliet, IL 60432
Fax: (815) 724-3785

City Clerk **Christa Desiderio** .... (815) 724-3780
E-mail: cdesiderio@jolietcity.org

Administrative/Human Services Department

City Hall, 150 W. Jefferson St., Joliet, IL 60432

Director **Ken Mihelich** .... (815) 724-4020
E-mail: kmihelich@jolietcity.org

Community and Economic Development Department

City Hall, 150 W. Jefferson St., Joliet, IL 60432
Fax: (815) 724-4056

Director **James M. Haller** .... (815) 724-4040
E-mail: jhaller@jolietcity.org

Fire Department

101 E. Clinton St., Joliet, IL 60432

Fire Chief **Joe Formhals** .... (815) 724-3500
E-mail: jformhals@jolietcity.org

Finance Department

City Hall, 150 W. Jefferson St., Joliet, IL 60432

Director **James "Jim" Ghedotte** .... (815) 724-3900
E-mail: jghedotte@jolietcity.org

Legal Department

City Hall, 150 W. Jefferson St., Joliet, IL 60432
Fax: (815) 724-3801

Corporation Counsel **Martin J. "Marty" Shanahan, Jr.** .. (815) 724-3800
Education: U St Francis BA; John Marshall JD

Police Department

150 W. Washington St., Joliet, IL 60432

Chief of Police **Brian Benton** .... (815) 724-3201

Public Works and Utilities Department

City Hall, 150 W. Jefferson St., Joliet, IL 60432

Director of Public Works **Jim Trizna** .... (815) 724-4200
Director of Public Utilities **James Eggen** .... (815) 724-4230
Administrator **Greg Ruddy** .... (815) 724-4210
E-mail: gruddy@jolietcity.org

City and Borough of Juneau, Alaska

155 South Seward Street, Juneau, AK 99801
Internet: www.juneau.org
Internet: http://www.juneau.org/news/currenthot.php

County: Juneau **Election Type:** Nonpartisan **Population:** 32,756 (2015)

Office of the Mayor and Assembly

155 S. Seward St., Juneau, AK 99801
Fax: (907) 586-5385 E-mail: borough_assembly@juneau.org

★Mayor **Ken Koelsch** .... (907) 586-5240
Began Service: March 2016
Term Expires: October 2018
Executive Assistant **Susan Phillips** .... (907) 586-5240
E-mail: susan.phillips@juneau.org

★Deputy Mayor **Jesse Kiehl** (District 1) .... (907) 586-5278
Term Expires: October 2017

★Assembly Member **Loren Jones** (District 1) .... (907) 586-5278
Term Expires: October 2018

★Assembly Member **Barbara Sheinberg** (District 1) ...... (907) 586-5278
Term Expires: October 2016

★Assembly Member **Jamie Lynn Bursell** (District 2) ..... (907) 586-5278
Term Expires: October 2016

★Assembly Member **Jerry Nankervis** (District 2) .... (907) 586-5278
Term Expires: October 2018

★Assembly Member **Debbie White** (District 2) .... (907) 586-5278
Term Expires: October 2017

★Assembly Member **Maria Gladziszewski** (At-Large) ..... (907) 586-5278
Term Expires: October 2017

★Assembly Member **Kate Troll** (At-Large) .... (907) 586-5278
Term Expires: October 2016

Office of the City Attorney

155 South Seward Street, Juneau, AK 99801
Fax: (907) 586-1147 Internet: www.cbjlaw.com

City Attorney **Amy Mead** .... (907) 586-5242
E-mail: amy.mead@juneau.org
Deputy City Attorney **Jane Sebens** .... (907) 586-5242
E-mail: jane.sebens@juneau.org

★Elected Official ▲Appointed by Legislature ▼Appointed by Governor ►Appointed by Board or Commission ●Appointed by Judge
■Appointed by Mayor △Appointed by Freeholders ▽Appointed by Supervisor ▷Appointed by County Executive ○Appointed by Council

Office of the City Manager

155 S. Seward St., Juneau, AK 99801
Fax: (907) 586-5385

○ City Manager **Kim Kiefer** .... (907) 586-5240
E-mail: kim.kiefer@juneau.org
Deputy City Manager **Mila Cosgrove** .... (907) 586-5240
E-mail: mila.cosgrove@juneau.org

Human Resources and Risk Management Division

155 South Seward Street, Juneau, AK 99801
Human Resources and Risk Management Director
Dallas Hargrave .... (907) 586-5250
E-mail: dallas.hargrave@juneau.org Fax: (907) 586-5392
Education: Pacific Lutheran Sem BA; Alaska Southeast MPA; Denver JD
Risk Management Officer **Jennifer Mannix** .... (907) 586-0323
E-mail: jennifer.mannix@juneau.org Fax: (907) 586-5347

Office of the City Clerk

155 S. Seward St., Juneau, AK 99801
Fax: (907) 586-4552 E-mail: city.clerk@juneau.org

City Clerk **Laurie J. Sica** .... (907) 586-5278
E-mail: laurie.sica@juneau.org
Deputy Clerk **Beth McEwen** .... (907) 586-5278
E-mail: beth.mcewen@juneau.org

Community Development Department

155 S. Seward St., Juneau, AK 99801
Fax: (907) 586-3365

Director **Rob Steedle** .... (907) 586-0757
E-mail: Rob.Steedle@juneau.org
Building Official **Charlie Ford** .... (907) 586-0767
Chief Building Inspector IV **Guy Gleason** .... (907) 586-0707
Planning Manager **Beth McKibben** .... (907) 586-0465
Senior Planner **Laura Boyce** .... (907) 586-0753
Senior Planner **Teri Camery** .... (907) 586-0755

Engineering Department

155 S. Seward St., Juneau, AK 99801
Tel: (907) 586-0800 Fax: (907) 463-2606

Director **Rorie Watt** .... (907) 586-0800
E-mail: rorie.watt@juneau.org

Finance Department

155 S. Seward St., Juneau, AK 99801
Tel: (907) 586-5215 Fax: (907) 586-0358

Director **Bob Bartholomew** .... (907) 586-5215
Education: San Diego State BS
Assessor **Robin Potter** .... (907) 586-5220
E-mail: robin.potter@juneau.org Fax: (907) 586-5367
Controller **Mary Norcross** .... (907) 586-5216
E-mail: mary.norcross@juneau.org
Purchasing Officer **Renee Loree** .... (907) 586-5258
E-mail: renee.loree@juneau.org
Sales Tax Administrator **Clinton Singletary** .... (907) 586-5265
E-mail: clinton.singletary@juneau.org
Treasurer **Cheryl Crawford** .... (907) 586-5218

Fire Department

155 S. Seward St., Juneau, AK 99801
Tel: (907) 586-5322 Fax: (907) 586-8323

Fire Chief **Rich Etheridge** .... (907) 586-0251
E-mail: rich.etheridge@juneau.org

Harbor Department

155 S. Seward St., Juneau, AK 99801
Tel: (907) 586-0292 Fax: (907) 586-0295

Port Director **Carl Uchytil** .... (907) 586-0292

Juneau School District

10014 Crazy Horse Dr., Juneau, AK 99801
Fax: (907) 523-1708

Superintendent **Mark Miller** .... (907) 523-1701

Parks and Recreation Department

155 S. Seward St., Juneau, AK 99801
Fax: (907) 586-5677

Director **Kirk Duncan** .... (907) 586-5226

Police Department

6255 Alaway Avenue, Juneau, AK 99801
Tel: (907) 586-0600 Fax: (907) 586-4030

Chief of Police **Bryce Johnson** .... (907) 586-0600

Public Works Department

5433 Shaune Drive, Juneau, AK 99801
Tel: (907) 586-5254 Fax: (907) 780-4637

Director **Rorie Watt** .... (907) 586-5254

Capital Transit

Superintendent **Ed Foster** .... (907) 789-6903
Fax: (907) 789-2132

Streets Division

Superintendent **Ed Foster** .... (907) 586-5256

Wastewater Utility Division

Superintendent **Samantha Stoughtenger** .... (907) 586-0393

Water Utility Division

Fax: (907) 780-4637

Superintendent **David Crabtree** .... (907) 780-6888

Unified Government of Wyandotte County and Kansas City, Kansas

Municipal Office Building, 701 North Seventh Street, 9th Floor, Kansas City, KS 66101
Tel: (913) 573-5000 (Information) Internet: www.wycokck.org

County: Wyandotte **Election Type:** Nonpartisan **Population:** 151,306 (2015)

Office of the Mayor and Chief Executive Officer

Municipal Office Bldg., 701 N. Seventh St., Kansas City, KS 66101
Fax: (913) 573-5020

★ Mayor and Chief Executive Officer **Mark R. Holland** .... (913) 573-5010
Began Service: April 2013
Term Expires: April 1, 2017
E-mail: mholland@wycokck.org

Office of the County Administrator

Municipal Office Bldg., 701 N. Seventh St., Kansas City, KS 66101
Fax: (913) 573-5540

○ County Administrator **Douglas G. "Doug" Bach** .... (913) 573-5030
E-mail: dbach@wycokck.org
Education: Fort Hays State 1988 BA; Kansas State 1990 MPA
Assistant County Administrator
Joseph M. "Joe" Connor .... (913) 573-5030
E-mail: jconnor@wycokck.org
Education: Emporia State BA

★ Elected Official ▲ Appointed by Legislature ▼ Appointed by Governor ▶ Appointed by Board or Commission ● Appointed by Judge
■ Appointed by Mayor △ Appointed by Freeholders ▽ Appointed by Supervisor ▷ Appointed by County Executive ○ Appointed by Council

Office of the County Administrator *continued*

Assistant County Administrator **Gordon Criswell** . . . . (913) 573-5030
E-mail: gcriswell@wycokck.org
Public Relations Director **Mike Taylor** . . . . (913) 573-5565
E-mail: mtaylor@wycokck.org
Assistant County Administrator **Melissa Mundt** . . . . (913) 573-5030

Unified Clerk

Municipal Office Bldg., 701 N. Seventh St., Suite 323,
Kansas City, KS 66101
Fax: (913) 573-5299
Internet: www.wycokck.org/dept.aspx?id=350&menu_id=554

Unified Government County Clerk **Bridgette Cobbins** . . . (913) 573-5260
E-mail: bcobbins@wycokck.org
Deputy County Clerk **Carol Godsil** . . . . (913) 573-5263
E-mail: cgodsil@wycokck.org

Coroner Department

40 South 18th Street, Kansas City, KS 66102
Fax: (913) 299-4931

Coroner **Alan Hancock** . . . . (913) 299-1474

Legal Department

Municipal Office Building, 701 North Seventh Street, Suite 961,
Kansas City, KS 66101
Fax: (913) 573-5243

Chief Counsel **Kenneth J. Moore** . . . . (913) 573-5060

Economic Development Department

Municipal Office Bldg., 701 N. Seventh St., Room 421,
Kansas City, KS 66101
Fax: (913) 573-5745

Director of Economic Development **George Brajkovic** . . . (913) 573-5730
E-mail: gbrajkovic@wycokck.org
Economic Development Analyst **Charles Brockman** . . . . . (913) 573-5733
E-mail: cbrockman@kckps.org

Emergency Management Department

Municipal Office Building, 701 North Seventh Street, Room B20,
Kansas City, KS 66101
Fax: (913) 573-6363

Director **Matt May** . . . . (913) 573-6300
E-mail: mmay@wycokck.org

Department of Finance

Municipal Office Bldg., 701 N. Seventh St., Suite 330,
Kansas City, KS 66101
Fax: (913) 573-5003

Chief Financial Officer **Kathleen VonAchen** . . . . (913) 573-5186
Budget Manager **Reginald Lindsey** . . . . (913) 573-5271
E-mail: rlindsey@wycokck.org
Research Manager **Mike Grimm** . . . . (913) 573-5157
E-mail: mgrimm@wycokck.org
Treasury Director **Debbie Pack** . . . . (913) 573-2821

Fire Department

815 N. Sixth St., Kansas City, KS 66101
Fax: (913) 342-9610 Internet: www.wycokck.org/DefaultFire.aspx

Fire Chief **John Paul Jones** . . . . (913) 573-5550
E-mail: jjones@kckps.org

Human Resources Department

Municipal Office Building, 701 N. Seventh Street, Suite 646,
Kansas City, KS 66101
Fax: (913) 573-5006

Director **J. Renee Ramirez** . . . . (913) 573-5660
E-mail: jobs@wycokck.org

Neighborhood Resource Center [NRC]

4601 State Avenue, Kansas City, KS 66102
Fax: (913) 573-8731
Internet: www.wycokck.org/dept.aspx?id=866&menu_id=1014

Director **Greg Talkin** . . . . (913) 573-8600
Chief Building Inspector **Anthony Hutchingson** . . . . (913) 573-8620
Fax: (913) 573-8622
License Administrator **Phillip Henderson** . . . . (913) 573-8780
Fax: (913) 573-8622
Code Enforcement Division Director **Wayne Wilson** . . . . . (913) 573-8601
Fax: (913) 573-8731
Demolition and Abatement Program Coordinator
Erin Downing . . . . (913) 573-8647
Livable Neighborhoods Executive Director
Andrea Generaux . . . . (913) 573-8737
E-mail: ageneraux@wycokck.org Fax: (913) 573-8731
Operation Brightside Program Coordinator **Kirk Suther** . . . (913) 573-8735
E-mail: ksuther@wycokck.org Fax: (913) 573-8714
Rental Licensing Program Coordinator **Debbie Graber** . . . (913) 573-8649
E-mail: dgraber@wycokck.org Fax: (913) 573-8731

Parks and Recreation Department

5033 State Avenue, Kansas City, KS 66102
Fax: (913) 573-8328 Internet: www.wycokck.org/parks/

Director **Jeremy Rogers** . . . . (913) 573-8327

Police Department

700 Minnesota Avenue, Kansas City, KS 66101
Fax: (913) 573-6016 Internet: www.kckpd.org

Chief of Police **Terry R. Zeigler** . . . . (913) 573-6010
Education: MidAmerica Nazarene 1998 BA; Kansas 2009 MPA

Public Health Department

619 Ann Ave., Kansas City, KS 66101
Fax: (913) 321-7932

Director **Terry Brecheisen** . . . . (913) 573-8855

Public Library

625 Minnesota Avenue, Kansas City, KS 66101
Fax: (913) 279-2032

Director of Libraries **Carol Levers** . . . . (913) 551-3280
E-mail: clevers@kckpl.org

Public Works Department

Municipal Office Building, 701 North Seventh Street, Room 712,
Kansas City, KS 66101
Fax: (913) 573-5435

Director (Interim) **Mike Tobin** . . . . (913) 573-5400
Fax: (913) 573-5435
Water Pollution Control Director **Trent Foglesong** . . . . (913) 573-1300
Fax: (913) 573-1351
Public Works Deputy Director **Mike Tobin** . . . . (913) 573-5400
Fax: (913) 573-5435
County Engineer **(Vacant)** . . . . (913) 573-5700
Fax: (913) 573-5727
Traffic Engineering Manager **Lideana Laboy** . . . . (913) 573-5770
E-mail: llaboy@wycokck.org Fax: (913) 573-5727
Fleet Administrator **Merle McCullough** . . . . (913) 573-8371

★ Elected Official ▲ Appointed by Legislature ▼ Appointed by Governor ▶ Appointed by Board or Commission ● Appointed by Judge
■ Appointed by Mayor △ Appointed by Freeholders ▽ Appointed by Supervisor ▷ Appointed by County Executive ○ Appointed by Council

CITIES AND TOWNS

Buildings and Logistics Division
Municipal Office Bldg., 701 N. Seventh St., Room 532,
Kansas City, KS 66101
Fax: (913) 573-5340

Director **Donald P. Jones, Jr.** .... (913) 573-5330
E-mail: djones@wycokck.org

Transit Department
Fleet Maintenance Complex, 5033 State Ave., Kansas City, KS 66102
Fax: (913) 573-8315

Transit Manager (Interim) **Justus Welker** .... (913) 573-8351
Operations General Superintendent **Irvin Jackson** .... (913) 573-8309
E-mail: ijackson@wycokck.org
Program Coordinator **Rhoda Bell** .... (913) 573-8313

Urban Planning and Land Use Department
City Hall, 701 North Seventh Street, Room 423, Kansas City, KS 66101
Tel: (913) 573-5750 Fax: (913) 573-5796
E-mail: planninginfo@wycokck.org Internet: www.wycokck.org/planning

Director of Planning **Rob Richardson** ....(913) 573-5750 ext. 8

Board of Commissioners
Municipal Office Bldg., 701 N. Seventh St., Room 979,
Kansas City, KS 66101
Fax: (913) 573-5050

★Commissioner **Gayle E. Townsend** (District 1) .... (913) 573-5040
Term Expires: April 1, 2017
E-mail: gtownsend@wycokck.org
★Commissioner **Brian McKiernan** (District 2)............(913) 573-5040
Term Expires: April 1, 2019
E-mail: bmckiernan@wycokck.org
★Commissioner **Ann Brandau-Murguia** (District 3) ...... (913) 573-5040
Term Expires: April 1, 2019
E-mail: amurguia@wycokck.org
Education: Ottawa U 1993 BA; Baker U 1997 MBA
★Commissioner **Harold Johnson** (District 4) .... (913) 573-5040
Term Expires: April 2019
★Commissioner **Mike T. Kane** (District 5)...............(913) 573-5040
Term Expires: April 1, 2017
E-mail: mkane@wycokck.org
★Commissioner **Angela Markley** (District 6) .... (913) 573-5040
Term Expires: April 1, 2019
E-mail: amarkley@wycokck.org
★Commissioner **Jim Walters** (District 7)................(913) 573-5040
Term Expires: April 1, 2017
E-mail: jwalters@wycokck.org
★Commissioner **Jane Philbrook** (District 8) .... (913) 573-5040
Term Expires: April 1, 2017
E-mail: jphilbrook@wycokck.org
★Commissioner **Melissa Brune Bynum** (At-Large 1) ..... (913) 573-5040
Term Expires: April 2019
★Commissioner **Harold T. "Hal" Walker** (At-Large 2).....(913) 573-5040
Term Expires: April 1, 2017
E-mail: hwalker@wycokck.org

Office of the District Attorney
Criminal Justice Complex, 701 North Seventh Street, Suite 10,
Kansas City, KS 66101
Fax: (913) 573-2948

★District Attorney **Jerome Gorman** .... (913) 573-2851
Term Expires: December 31, 2016
E-mail: jgorman@kckps.org

Office of the Register of Deeds
701 North Seventh Street, Suite 100, Kansas City, KS 66101
Fax: (913) 573-2977

★Register of Deeds **Nancy W. Burns** .... (913) 573-2841
Term Expires: April 1, 2019
E-mail: nburns@wycokck.org

Office of the Sheriff
701 North Seventh Street, Kansas City, KS 66101

★Wyandotte County Sheriff **Don Ash** .... (913) 573-2865
Term Expires: April 1, 2017 Fax: (913) 573-2972
E-mail: dash@wycokck.org

Kansas City, Kansas Public Schools
2010 North 59th Street, Kansas City, KS 66104
Fax: (913) 279-2085 Internet: www.kckps.org

Superintendent of Schools **Dr. Cynthia Lane** .... (913) 551-3200

Kansas City, Missouri
City Hall, 414 E. 12th St., Kansas City, MO 64106
Internet: www.kcmo.gov

County: Jackson **Election Type:** Nonpartisan **Year Founded:** 1838
Year Incorporated: 1850 **Population:** 475,378 (2015)
Employees: 6,813 **Fiscal Year:** 2016 **Budget:** $1,531,821,000

Office of the Mayor
City Hall, 414 East 12th Street, 29th Floor, Kansas City, MO 64106
Fax: (816) 513-3518

Employees: 18 **Fiscal Year:** 2016 **Budget:** $1,803,000

★Mayor **Sylvester "Sly" James, Jr.** .... (816) 513-3500
Began Service: May 2, 2011
Term Expires: August 1, 2019
E-mail: mayor@kcmo.org
Chief of Staff **Joni Wickham** .... (816) 513-3500
Senior Advisor for Community Affairs **(Vacant)** .... (816) 513-3500
Director of Council and Community Relations
Jim Giles .... (816) 513-3500
E-mail: jim.giles@kcmo.org
Senior Advisor for Operations **(Vacant)**............... (816) 513-3500
Chief Innovation Officer **(Vacant)** .... (816) 513-3500
Education Advisor **Julie Holland**....................... (816) 513-3500
Director of Policy **McClain Bryant** .... (816) 513-3500

Office of the City Auditor
City Hall, 414 East 12th Street, 21st Floor, Kansas City, MO 64106
Tel: (816) 513-3300 Fax: (816) 513-3305

Employees: 12 **Fiscal Year:** 2016 **Budget:** $1,338,000

○City Auditor **Douglas Jones** .... (816) 513-3303
E-mail: douglas.jones@kcmo.org
Audit Manager **Mary Jo Emanuele** .... (816) 513-3304
Audit Manager **Nancy Hunt**............................ (816) 513-3309
Audit Manager **Suzanne Polys** .... (816) 513-3308

Office of the City Clerk
City Hall, 414 East 12th Street, 25th Floor, Kansas City, MO 64106
Fax: (816) 513-3353 E-mail: clerk@kcmo.org

Employees: 6 **Fiscal Year:** 2016 **Budget:** $484,000

○City Clerk **Marilyn Sanders** .... (816) 513-6402
E-mail: marilyn.sanders@kcmo.org

★Elected Official ▲Appointed by Legislature ▼Appointed by Governor ▶Appointed by Board or Commission ●Appointed by Judge
■Appointed by Mayor △Appointed by Freeholders ▽Appointed by Supervisor ▷Appointed by County Executive ○Appointed by Council

Office of the City Manager

City Hall, 414 East 12th Street, 29th Floor, Kansas City, MO 64106
Fax: (816) 513-1363 E-mail: manager@kcmo.org

Employees: 91 **Fiscal Year:** 2016 **Budget:** $12,027,000

○City Manager **Troy Schulte** .... (816) 513-1408
E-mail: troy_schulte@kcmo.org
Assistant City Manager for Infrastructure
Sherri McIntyre .... (816) 513-1369
E-mail: sherri.mcintyre@kcmo.org
Education: Iowa BSCE; Missouri MSCE
Assistant City Manager **Kimiko C. Gilmore** .... (816) 513-1376
E-mail: kimiko.gilmore@kcmo.org
Education: Missouri (Kansas City) 1989 AB; Troy State 2001 MPA
Assistant City Manager **Earnest J. Rouse** .... (816) 513-1408
E-mail: earnest.rouse@kcmo.org
Assistant City Manager **Richard Usher** .... (816) 513-1376
E-mail: richard.usher@kcmo.org
Assistant City Manager **John A. Wood** .... (816) 513-1369
E-mail: john.a.wood@kcmo.org
City Council Liaison **Sammy Panettiere** .... (816) 513-1408
E-mail: sammy.panettiere@kcmo.org
Director of Citywide Marketing **(Vacant)** .... (816) 513-1371
Security Manager **David Severenuk** .... (816) 513-1409

City Communications Office

414 East Twelfth Street, Suite 2101, Kansas City, MO 64106
Tel: (816) 513-1349 Fax: (816) 513-1351

Communications Director **Chris Hernandez** .... (816) 513-1349
E-mail: chris.hernandez@kcmo.org
Press Secretary **Michael Grimaldi** .... (816) 513-6582
E-mail: michael.grimaldi@kcmo.org

Office of Environmental Quality

City Hall, 414 East 12th Street, 24th Floor, Kansas City, MO 64106

Chief Environmental Officer **Dennis Murphey** .... (816) 513-3459
Environmental Compliance Manager **Andy Savastino** .... (816) 513-3460

Aviation Department

Kansas City International Airport, 601 Brasilia Avenue,
Kansas City, MO 64153-2054
P.O. Box 20047, Kansas City, MO 64153-2054
Tel: (816) 243-3000 Fax: (816) 585-7602

Employees: 501 **Fiscal Year:** 2016 **Budget:** $165,835,000

Director of Aviation **Mark Van Loh** .... (816) 243-3100
Deputy Director **Ian A. Redhead** .... (816) 243-3100
E-mail: ian_redhead@kcmo.org
Education: Embry-Riddle 1986 AS, 1987 BS
Manager of Operations **Bob Johnson** .... (816) 243-5248
E-mail: bob.johnson@kcmo.org
Chief of Airport Police **Steve Newman** .... (816) 243-2249
Manager of Operations, Downtown Airport
Michael Roper .... (816) 513-0800
Chalres B. Wheeler Downtown Airport, Fax: (816) 513-0790
300 Richards Road, Kansas City, MO 64116
E-mail: michael.roper@kcmo.org

City Planning and Development Department

City Hall,, 414 East 12th Street, 15th Floor, Kansas City, MO 64106
Fax: (816) 513-2838 E-mail: planning@kcmo.org
Internet: http://kcmo.gov/planning/

Employees: 136 **Fiscal Year:** 2016 **Budget:** $13,538,000

Director **Jeffrey Williams** .... (816) 513-1500
E-mail: planning@kcmo.org
Executive Assistant **Lisa Wheeler** .... (816) 513-1500
E-mail: lisa.wheeler@kcmo.org

Office of Economic Development

City Hall, 414 East Twelfth Street, Kansas City, MO 64106

Director of Economic Development **Kerrie Tyndall** ...... (816) 513-6539

Convention and Entertainment Facilities

301 W. 13th St., Suite 100, Kansas City, MO 64105
Fax: (816) 513-5001 Tel: (800) 821-7060 (Toll Free)
Internet: http://www.kcconvention.com

Employees: 94 **Fiscal Year:** 2016 **Budget:** $29,865,000

Director **Oscar McGaskey, Jr.** .... (816) 513-5051
Deputy Director **Michael C. Young** .... (816) 513-5253
E-mail: Michael.C.Young@kcmo.org
Senior Sales Manager **Gemma Zook** .... (816) 513-5019

Finance Department

City Hall, 3rd Fl., 414 E. 12th St., Kansas City, MO 64106
Fax: (816) 513-1174 E-mail: finance@kcmo.org

Employees: 95 **Fiscal Year:** 2016 **Budget:** $15,898,000

Director of Finance **Randall J. Landes** .... (816) 513-1173
Deputy Director of Finance **Tammy Queen** .... (816) 513-1019
City Controller **Eric Clevenger** .... (816) 513-1187
Commissioner of Revenue **Mari Ruck** .... (816) 513-1089
E-mail: mari.ruck@kcmo.org
City Treasurer **Douglas Buehler** .... (816) 513-1024

Office of Management and Budget

City Hall, 414 East Twelfth Street, 13th Floor, Kansas City, MO 64106
Fax: (816) 513-1324

Budget Officer **Scott Huizenga** .... (816) 513-1326
E-mail: scott.huizenga@kcmo.org
Education: North Dakota BA; Kansas MPA

Fire Department

Fire Headquarters, Century Towers, 635 Woodland Avenue, Suite 2100,
Kansas City, MO 64106
Fax: (816) 784-9230 E-mail: kcfd@kcmo.org
Internet: http://kcmo.gov/fire/

Employees: 1,301 **Fiscal Year:** 2016 **Budget:** $155,300,000

Fire Chief **Paul Berardi** .... (816) 513-4600
E-mail: paul.berardi@kcmo.org
Education: Baker U BS; Missouri (Kansas City) MPA
Executive Assistant **Michelle Hardiman** .... (816) 513-4600
E-mail: michelle.hardiman@kcmo.org

General Services Department

City Hall, 414 East 12th Street, First Floor, Kansas City, MO 64106

Employees: 11 **Fiscal Year:** 2016 **Budget:** $1,261,000

Fleet Administrator **Sam Swearingen** .... (816) 513-4808

Health Department

2400 Troost, Suite 4000, Kansas City, MO 64108
Fax: (816) 513-6293 E-mail: health@kcmo.org
Internet: http://kcmo.gov/health/

Employees: 187 **Fiscal Year:** 2016 **Budget:** $22,925,000

Director **Rex D. Archer** .... (816) 513-6247
Deputy Director **Tracie McClendon-Cole** .... (816) 513-6247

Human Relations Department

City Hall, 414 East 12th Street, 4th Floor, Kansas City, MO 64106
Fax: (816) 513-1805 E-mail: humanrelations@kcmo.org

Employees: 13 **Fiscal Year:** 2016 **Budget:** $1,737,000

Director **Phillip Yelder** .... (816) 513-1801

Human Resources Department

City Hall, 414 East 12th Street, 12th Floor, Kansas City, MO 64106
Fax: (816) 513-2639 E-mail: jobs@kcmo.org

Employees: 35 **Fiscal Year:** 2016 **Budget:** $3,789,000

Director **Gary O'Bannon** .... (816) 513-1947
E-mail: gary_obannon@kcmo.org

★Elected Official ▲Appointed by Legislature ▼Appointed by Governor ►Appointed by Board or Commission ●Appointed by Judge
■Appointed by Mayor △Appointed by Freeholders ▽Appointed by Supervisor ▷Appointed by County Executive ○Appointed by Council

CITIES AND TOWNS

Information Technology Division
1111 Locust, 3rd Floor, Kansas City, MO 64106
Fax: (816) 513-3620 E-mail: infotech@kcmo.org

Employees: 48 **Fiscal Year:** 2016 **Budget:** $8,731,000

Chief Information Officer **Mary J. Miller** .... (816) 513-0811
E-mail: infotech@kcmo.org

Law Department
City Hall, 28th Fl., 414 E. 12th St., Kansas City, MO 64106
Fax: (816) 513-3133 E-mail: law@kcmo.org

Employees: 48 **Fiscal Year:** 2016 **Budget:** $5,542,000

City Attorney **William Geary** .... (816) 513-3118
E-mail: bill.geary@kcmo.org
Education: Central Missouri State BS; Missouri (Kansas City) JD, LLM

Neighborhoods and Housing Services Department
City Hall, 414 East 12th Street, Suite 402, Kansas City, MO 64106
Fax: (816) 513-3201 E-mail: ncs@kcmo.org

Employees: 8 **Fiscal Year:** 2016 **Budget:** $1,544,000

Director/Assistant City Manager **John A. Wood** .... (816) 513-3200
E-mail: john.a.wood@kcmo.org

Parks and Recreation Department
4600 East 63rd Street, Kansas City, MO 64130
Tel: (816) 513-7500 Fax: (816) 513-7719 E-mail: parks@kcmo.org
Internet: http://kcparks.org/

Employees: 364 **Fiscal Year:** 2016 **Budget:** $65,867,000

Director **Mark McHenry** .... (816) 513-7503
Deputy Director **Terry Rynard** .... (816) 513-7505

Police Department
1125 Locust, Kansas City, MO 64106-2687
Tel: (816) 234-5000 Fax: (816) 234-5013
Internet: http://kcmo.gov/police/

Employees: 1,978 **Fiscal Year:** 2016 **Budget:** $242,526,000

Police Chief **Darryl Forte** .... (816) 234-5010

Public Works Department
City Hall, 20th Fl., 414 E. 12th St., Kansas City, MO 64106-2748
Tel: (816) 513-9970 E-mail: pubworks@kcmo.org

Employees: 273 **Fiscal Year:** 2016 **Budget:** $119,017,000

Director of Public Works **Sherri McIntyre** .... (816) 513-2628
Education: Iowa BSCE; Missouri MSCE
Assistant to the Director **Marvin Davis** .... (816) 513-2613
E-mail: marvin_davis@kcmo.org
Assistant Director **Ralph Davis** .... (816) 513-9988

Engineering Services Division
City Engineer **Jeff Martin** .... (816) 513-2585
E-mail: jeff_martin@kcmo.org

Solid Waste Division
Assistant Director **Michael Shaw** .... (816) 513-6993
City Hall, 414 East Twelfth Street, 23rd Floor, Kansas City, MO 64106 Fax: (816) 513-1418

Water Services Department
4800 East 63rd Street, Kansas City, MO 64130
Fax: (816) 513-0185 E-mail: water@kcmo.org

Employees: 1,019 **Fiscal Year:** 2016 **Budget:** $363,490,000

Director **Terry Leeds** .... (816) 513-0238
Assistant Director **John Thigpen** .... (816) 513-0854
Business Operations Manager **Kathy Whalen** .... (816) 513-0238

Office of the City Council
City Hall, 414 East Twelfth Street, 24th Floor, Kansas City, MO 64106
Fax: (816) 513-1612 E-mail: council@kcmo.org

Employees: 12 **Fiscal Year:** 2016 **Budget:** $1,325,000

★ Council Member **Heather Hall** (District 1) .... (816) 513-1368
Term Expires: August 1, 2019
★ Council Member **Dan Fowler** (District 2) .... (816) 513-1368
Term Expires: August 1, 2019
★ Council Member **Jermaine Reed** (District 3) .... (816) 513-1368
Term Expires: August 1, 2019
E-mail: jermaine.reed@kcmo.org
★ Council Member **Jolie Justus** (District 4) .... (816) 513-1368
Term Expires: August 1, 2019
Education: Southwest Missouri State 1994 BS; Missouri (Kansas City) 1998 JD
★ Council Member **Alissia Canady** (District 5) .... (816) 513-1368
Term Expires: August 1, 2019
★ Council Member **Kevin McManus** (District 6) .... (816) 513-1368
Term Expires: August 1, 2019
★ Council Member **Scott Wagner** (At-Large, District 1) ... (816) 513-1368
Term Expires: August 1, 2019
E-mail: scott.wagner@kcmo.org
★ Council Member **Teresa Loar** (At-Large, District 2) ...... (816) 513-1368
Term Expires: August 1, 2019
Education: Park BA
★ Council Member **Quinton Lucas** (At-Large, District 3) ... (816) 513-1368
Term Expires: August 1, 2019
Education: Cornell 2009 JD
★ Council Member **Katheryn J. Shields** (At-Large, District 4) .... (816) 513-1368
Term Expires: August 1, 2019
Education: Missouri (Kansas City) 1968 BA, 1971 MA, 1978 JD
★ Council Member **Lee Barnes, Jr.** (At-Large, District 5) ... (816) 513-1368
Term Expires: August 1, 2019
★ Council Member **Scott Taylor** (At-Large, District 6) ..... (816) 513-1368
Term Expires: August 1, 2019
E-mail: scott.taylor@kcmo.org

Election Board
30 West Pershing Road, Suite 2800, Kansas City, MO 64108
Tel: (816) 842-4820 Fax: (816) 472-4960 Internet: http://www.kceb.org/

Democrat Director **A. Shelley McThomas** .... (816) 842-4820
Republican Director **Shawn Kieffer** .... (816) 842-4820

Kansas City Public Library
14 West 10th Street, Kansas City, MO 64105
Tel: (816) 701-3400 Fax: (816) 701-3401 Internet: www.kclibrary.org

Year Founded: 1873

Administration
Executive Director **R. Crosby Kemper III** .... (816) 701-3501
E-mail: crosbyk@kclibrary.org
Deputy Director of Administration/Chief Financial Officer **Debbie Siragusa** .... (816) 701-3515
E-mail: debbiesiragusa@kclibrary.org
Deputy Director of Library Services **Joel Jones** .... (816) 701-3504
E-mail: joeljones@kclibrary.org
Deputy Director, Strategic Initiatives **Cheptoo Kositany-Buckner** .... (816) 701-3508
E-mail: cheptookositany@kclibrary.org

Board of Police Commissioners
1125 Locust, Kansas City, MO 64106-2687

▼ President **Michael Rader** .... (816) 234-5000
▼ Vice President **Leland Shurin** .... (816) 234-5000
▼ Commissioner **Alvin L. Brooks** .... (816) 234-5000
Education: Missouri (Kansas City) BA, MA

★ Elected Official ▲ Appointed by Legislature ▼ Appointed by Governor ► Appointed by Board or Commission ● Appointed by Judge
■ Appointed by Mayor △ Appointed by Freeholders ▽ Appointed by Supervisor ▷ Appointed by County Executive ○ Appointed by Council

Board of Police Commissioners *continued*

▼Commissioner **Angela Wasson-Hunt** . . . . (816) 234-5000
▼Commissioner **Sylvester "Sly" James, Jr.** . . . . (816) 234-5000

City of Killeen, Texas

City Hall, 101 North College Street, Killeen, TX 76541
Tel: (254) 501-7600 Internet: www.killeentexas.gov

County: Bell **Election Type:** Nonpartisan **Population:** 140,806 (2015)

Office of the Mayor and City Council

City Hall, 101 North College Street, Killeen, TX 76541
Tel: (254) 501-7600

★Mayor **Jose L. Segarra** . . . . (254) 501-7717
Began Service: May 2016
Term Expires: May 2018
E-mail: jsegarra@killeentexas.gov

★Council Member **Shirley Fleming** (District 1) . . . . (254) 392-2719
Term Expires: May 2017
E-mail: sfleming@killeentexas.gov

★Council Member **(Vacant)** (District 2) . . . . (254) 251-7153
Term Expires: May 2017

★Council Member **Jim Kilpatrick** (District 3) . . . . (254) 526-2710
Term Expires: May 2017
E-mail: jkilpatrick@killeentexas.gov

★Council Member **Brockley Moore** (District 4) . . . . (254) 247-8183
Term Expires: May 2017
E-mail: bmoore@killeentexas.gov

★Council Member **Gregory Johnson** (At-Large) . . . . (254) 634-5090
Term Expires: May 2018
E-mail: gjohnson@killeentexas.gov

★Council Member **Jonathan Okray** (At-Large) . . . . (254) 368-8966
Term Expires: May 2018
E-mail: jokray@killeentexas.gov

★Council Member **Juan Rivera** (At-Large) . . . . (254) 251-7149
Term Expires: May 2018
E-mail: jrrivera@killeentexas.gov

Office of the City Secretary

City Hall, 101 North College Street, 3rd Floor, Killeen, TX 76541

City Secretary **Dianna Barker** . . . . (254) 501-7717
E-mail: dbarker@killeentexas.gov

Office of the City Manager

City Hall, 101 North College Street, Killeen, TX 76541

○City Manager **Glenn Morrison** . . . . (254) 501-7700
E-mail: gmorrison@killeentexas.gov
Education: Texas A&M BA

Assistant City Manager, Internal Services **Ann Farris** . . . . .(254) 616-3230
E-mail: afarris@killeentexas.gov

Office of the City Attorney

City Hall, 101 North College Street, 3rd Floor, Killeen, TX 76541

City Attorney **Kathryn H. Davis** . . . . (254) 501-7710
E-mail: kdavis@killeentexas.gov

Building Inspections Division

100 East Avenue C, Killeen, TX 76541

Building Official **Earl Abbott** . . . . (254) 501-7608

Civic and Conference Center

3601 South W.S. Young Drive, Killeen, TX 76541

Director **Connie Kuehl** . . . . (254) 501-3888

Community Development Department

Building E, 802 North 2nd Street, Killeen, TX 76541
Fax: (254) 501-6524

Executive Director **Leslie Hinkle** . . . . (254) 501-7847
E-mail: lhinkle@killeentexas.gov

Community Services Department

1700 East Stan Schlueter Loop, Killeen, TX 76542
Fax: (254) 501-6388

Executive Director **Brett Williams** . . . . (254) 501-6390

Office of Emergency Management and Homeland Security

P.O. Box 1329, Killeen, TX 76540-1329

Coordinator **Chad Berg** . . . . (254) 501-7706
E-mail: cberg@killeentexas.gov

Finance Department

City Hall, 101 North College Street, Killeen, TX 76541

Executive Director of Finance **Jonathan Locke** . . . . (254) 501-7730
Accounting Manager **(Vacant)** . . . . (254) 501-7745

Support Services Department

City Hall, 101 North College Street, Killeen, TX 76541

Executive Director **Stuart G. McLennan III** . . . . (254) 501-7639
E-mail: smclennan@killeentexas.gov Fax: (254) 501-6308
Fleet Manager **Frank Tydlacka** . . . . (254) 501-7789

Fire Department

201 North 28th Street, Killeen, TX 76541

Fire Chief **Jerry "J. D." Gardner** . . . . (254) 501-7667
E-mail: jgardner@killeentexas.gov
Deputy Fire Chief **Leon Adamski** . . . . (254) 501-7672
E-mail: ladamski@killeentexas.gov
Deputy Fire Chief **Brian Brank** . . . . (254) 501-7671
E-mail: bbrank@killeentexas.gov
Deputy Fire Chief **Kenneth Hawthorne** . . . . (254) 501-7673
E-mail: khawthorne@killeentexas.gov
Deputy Fire Chief **Cody Simmons** . . . . (254) 501-7662
E-mail: csimmons@killeentexas.gov
Fire Marshal **James Chism** . . . . (254) 501-6584
3800 Westcliff Road, Killeen, TX 76542 Fax: (254) 501-6582
E-mail: jchism@killeentexas.gov

Human Resources Department

City Hall, 101 North College Street, Killeen, TX 76541

Executive Director **Eva Bark** . . . . (254) 501-7836
E-mail: ebark@killeentexas.gov

Information Technology Services Department

218-B East Avenue D, Killeen, TX 76541

Executive Director **Thomas Moore** . . . . (254) 501-7892
E-mail: tmoore@killeentexas.gov

Killeen-Fort Hood Regional Airport

8101 South Clear Creek Road, Box C, Killeen, TX 76549

Executive Director of Aviation
Matthew Van Valkenburgh . . . . (254) 501-8700

Killeen City Cemetery

2408 East Rancier Avenue, Killeen, TX 76543

Cemetery Superintendent **Robin Dehart** . . . . (254) 200-7947

★Elected Official ▲Appointed by Legislature ▼Appointed by Governor ▶Appointed by Board or Commission ●Appointed by Judge
■Appointed by Mayor △Appointed by Freeholders ▽Appointed by Supervisor ▷Appointed by County Executive ○Appointed by Council

Killeen City Library System
205 East Church Avenue, Killeen, TX 76541

Director of Library Services **Deanna Frazee** .... (254) 501-8990
E-mail: library@killeentexas.gov

Planning and Development Services Department
200 East Avenue D, 2nd Floor, Killeen, TX 76541

Executive Director **Dr. Ray Shanaa** .... (254) 501-7630
E-mail: rshanaa@killeentexas.gov

Police Department
3304 Community Boulevard, Killeen, TX 76541

Chief of Police **Dennis Baldwin** .... (254) 501-8800
Assistant Chief of Police **Larry Longwell** .... (254) 501-8800
Assistant Chief of Police **Capt. Margaret Young** .... (254) 501-8800

Animal Control
3118 Commerce, Killeen, TX 76543

Animal Control Manager **Edward Tucker** .... (254) 526-4455

Public Information Department
City Hall, 101 North College Street, Killeen, TX 76541

Executive Director **Hilary Shine** .... (254) 501-7751
E-mail: hshine@killeentexas.gov

Public Works Department
200 East Avenue D, Killeen, TX 76541

Executive Director **Scott Osburn** .... (254) 501-7620

Engineering Division
200 East Avenue D, Killeen, TX 76541
Fax: (254) 501-7628

City Engineer **John P. Nett** .... (254) 501-7621
E-mail: jnett@killeentexas.gov

Environmental Services Division
200 East Avenue D, Killeen, TX 76541

Director of Environmental Services **Kristina Ramirez** .... (254) 501-7627
E-mail: kramirez@killeentexas.gov

Solid Waste Division
2003 Little Nolan Road, Killeen, TX 76542

Director of Solid Waste **Michael Cleghorn** .... (254) 501-7785
Recycle Center Manager **Peter DiLillo** .... (254) 554-7572
111 East Avenue F, Killeen, TX 76541

Street Services Division
3201-A South W.S. Young Drive, Killeen, TX 76541

Director **John Koester** .... (254) 616-3153

Transportation Division
3201-A South W.S. Young Drive, Level 1, Killeen, TX 76541

Director of Transportation Services **(Vacant)** .... (254) 616-3180

Water and Sewer Division
1901 Botanical Drive, Killeen, TX 76542

Director of Utility Services **Steve Kana** .... (254) 634-7130
Director of Water and Sewer Services **Robert White** ..... (254) 634-7130

Senior Centers
1700 B East Stan Schlueter Loop, Killeen, TX 76542
Fax: (254) 501-6389

Senior Centers Manager **Debbie Edwards** .... (254) 501-6399

City of Knoxville, Tennessee
City County Building, 400 Main Street, Knoxville, TN 37902
P.O. Box 1631, Knoxville, TN 37901
Tel: (865) 215-2000 (Information) Internet: http://www.knoxvilletn.gov/

County: Knox **Election Type:** Nonpartisan **Year Incorporated:** 1815
Population: 185,291 (2015)

Office of the Mayor
City County Building, 400 Main Street, Room 691, Knoxville, TN 37902
P.O. Box 1631, Knoxville, TN 37901
Fax: (865) 215-2085

★ Mayor **Madeline Rogero** .... (865) 215-2040
Began Service: December 17, 2011
Term Expires: December 31, 2019
E-mail: mayor@knoxvilletn.gov
■ Community Relations Director **(Vacant)** .... (865) 215-2048
Fax: (865) 215-2085

Office of the City Recorder
City County Building, 400 Main Street, Room 460, Knoxville, TN 37902
Fax: (865) 215-4269

○ City Recorder **Will Johnson** .... (865) 215-2075
E-mail: wjohnson@knoxvilletn.gov

Civil Service Department
City County Bldg., 400 Main St., Room 569, Knoxville, TN 37902
Fax: (865) 215-4270

Director **Vicki Hatfield** .... (865) 215-2106
E-mail: vhatfield@knoxvilletn.gov

Fire Department
900 Hill Avenue, Suite 430, Knoxville, TN 37915
Fax: (865) 595-4482

■ Fire Chief **Stan Sharp** .... (865) 595-4480
E-mail: ssharp@knoxvilletn.gov
Education: Tennessee BA, MA

Knoxville's Community Development Corporation [KCDC]
901 Broadway NE, Knoxville, TN 37917
P.O. Box 3550, Knoxville, TN 37927-3550
Fax: (865) 403-1117 Internet: www.kcdc.org

■ Chairman **Daniel P. "Dan" Murphy** .... (865) 403-1100
■ Vice Chairman **Jacqueline Arthur** .... (865) 403-1100
Treasurer **Phyllis Patrick** .... (865) 403-1100
■ Commissioner **Bruce Anderson** .... (865) 403-1100
■ Commissioner **John Turner** .... (865) 403-1100
■ Commissioner **John T. Winemiller** .... (865) 403-1100
Education: Tennessee 2000 JD
■ Commissioner **(Vacant)** .... (865) 403-1100
Chief Executive Officer **Art Cate** .... (865) 403-1100
E-mail: acate@kcdc.org
Chief Operating Officer/Executive Director **(Vacant)** ..... (865) 403-1100
Senior Vice President, Housing **Sean Gilbert** .... (865) 403-1100
Vice President and Chief Financial Officer **Tracee Pross** .. (865) 403-1100
E-mail: tpross@kcdc.org
Human Resources Director **Denise Campbell** .... (865) 403-1100
E-mail: dcampbell@kcdc.org
Strategic Planning and Development Director
Joyce Floyd .... (865) 403-1100

★ Elected Official ▲ Appointed by Legislature ▼ Appointed by Governor ▶ Appointed by Board or Commission ● Appointed by Judge
■ Appointed by Mayor △ Appointed by Freeholders ▽ Appointed by Supervisor ▷ Appointed by County Executive ○ Appointed by Council

Knoxville Emergency Management Agency [KEMA]
605 Bernard Avenue, Knoxville, TN 37921
Fax: (865) 215-1177

Director **Alan Lawson** .... (865) 215-1166
E-mail: alawson@knoxvilletn.gov Fax: (865) 215-1177
Emergency Communications District Director
Bob Coker .... (865) 215-1100
Fax: (865) 215-1134

Law Department
City County Building, 400 Main Street, Room 699, Knoxville, TN 37902
P.O. Box 1631, Knoxville, TN 37901
Fax: (865) 215-2643

■ Director **Charles Swanson** .... (865) 215-2050
E-mail: cswanson@knoxvilletn.gov

Metropolitan Planning Commission
City County Building, 400 Main Street, Suite 403, Knoxville, TN 37902
Tel: (865) 215-2500 Fax: (865) 215-2068
Internet: http://www.knoxmpc.org

Executive Director (Interim) **Jeff Welch** .... (865) 215-2500

Parks and Recreation Department
400 Main Street, Room 303, Knoxville, TN 37902
Tel: (865) 215-4311

Director **Joe Walsh** .... (865) 215-4311
Deputy Director **Aaron Browning** .... (865) 215-4311

Police Department
800 Howard Baker Jr. Avenue, Knoxville, TN 37915
Fax: (865) 971-1412

■ Chief of Police **David Rausch** .... (865) 215-7229
E-mail: chiefofpolice@knoxvilletn.gov
Deputy Chief **Nate Allen** .... (865) 215-7298
Education: North Carolina BABA
Deputy Chief **Cindy Gass** .... (865) 215-7339
Deputy Chief **Gary Holliday** .... (865) 215-7223
Deputy Chief **Monty Houk** .... (865) 215-7298

Chief Operating Officer
City County Building, 400 Main Street, Room 467, Knoxville, TN 37902
P.O. Box 1631, Knoxville, TN 37901
Fax: (865) 215-2420

■ Deputy to the Mayor Chief Operating Officer
Christi Branscom .... (865) 215-2806
E-mail: cbranscom@knoxvilletn.gov
Education: Tennessee BS; U Memphis JD
Fleet Services Director **Keith Shields** .... (865) 215-2529
Fax: (865) 215-2514
Purchasing Agent **Boyce Evans** .... (865) 215-2070
E-mail: bevans@knoxvilletn.gov
Information Systems Director **Janet Wright** .... (865) 215-2524
E-mail: jwright@knoxvilletn.gov
Education: Tennessee BS, MS

Engineering Department
City County Building, 400 Main Street, Room 480, Knoxville, TN 37902
Fax: (865) 215-2631

■ Director of Engineering **James R. Hagerman** .... (865) 215-2148
E-mail: jhagerman@knoxvilletn.gov
Building Inspections Director **Peter M. Ahrens** .... (865) 215-3938
Fax: (865) 215-6109
Traffic Engineer **Jeff Branham** .... (865) 215-2148
E-mail: jbranham@knoxvilletn.gov
Public Service Director **David Brace** .... (865) 215-2060
Fax: (865) 215-2420

Finance Department
City County Bldg., 400 Main St., Room 681, Knoxville, TN 37902
Fax: (865) 215-2277

Finance Director **Jim York** .... (865) 215-2013

Chief Policy Officer
City County Building, 400 Main Street, Room 655, Knoxville, TN 37902
Fax: (865) 215-3035

■ Deputy to the Mayor and Chief Policy Officer
William Lyons .... (865) 215-2029
E-mail: wlyons@knoxvilletn.gov
Education: Rhodes 1970 BA; Oklahoma 1974 PhD
Director of Redevelopment **Bob Whetsel** .... (865) 215-2543
E-mail: bwhetsel@knoxvilletn.gov
Education: Emory & Henry 1974 BA

Community Development Department
City County Building, 400 Main Street, Room 532, Knoxville, TN 37902
Fax: (865) 215-2962

Director **Becky Wade** .... (865) 215-2865
E-mail: bwade@knoxvilletn.gov

South Waterfront Development
City County Building, 400 Main Street, Knoxville, TN 37902
Fax: (865) 215-2631

Deputy Director **Dawn Michelle Foster** .... (865) 215-3764
E-mail: dfoster@knoxvilletn.gov Fax: (865) 215-2527
Education: Western Kentucky 1985 BA; Tennessee 1999 MURP

Department of Communications
400 Main Street, Room 691, Knoxville, TN 37902
Fax: (865) 215-2085

Communications Director **Jesse Fox Mayshark** .... (865) 215-3710
E-mail: jmayshark@knoxvilletn.gov
Communications Manager **Eric Vreeland** .... (865) 215-3710
E-mail: evreeland@knoxvilletn.gov
Webmaster **Traci McDonell** .... (865) 215-2177
E-mail: tmcdonell@knoxvilletn.gov

Office of Special Events
City County Building, 400 Main Street, Room 578, Knoxville, TN 37902
Fax: (865) 215-4298

Director **Judith Foltz** .... (865) 215-4248
E-mail: jfoltz@knoxvilletn.gov

Office of the City Council
City County Bldg., 400 Main St., Knoxville, TN 37902
Fax: (865) 215-4269

★ Vice Mayor **Duane Grieve** (District 2) .... (865) 215-2075
Term Expires: December 31, 2017
E-mail: dgrieve@knoxvilletn.gov
★ Council Member **Nick Pavlis** (District 1) .... (865) 215-2075
Term Expires: December 31, 2017
E-mail: npavlis@comcast.net
★ Council Member **Brenda Palmer** (District 3) .... (865) 215-2075
Term Expires: December 31, 2017
E-mail: bpalmer@knoxvilletn.gov
★ Council Member **Nick Della Volpe** (District 4) .... (865) 215-2075
Term Expires: December 31, 2017
E-mail: ndellavolpe@knoxvilletn.gov
★ Council Member **Mark Campen** (District 5) .... (865) 215-2075
Term Expires: December 31, 2017
E-mail: mcampen@knoxvilletn.gov
★ Council Member **Daniel Brown** (District 6) .... (865) 215-2075
Term Expires: December 31, 2017
E-mail: dbrown@knoxvilletn.gov
Education: Tennessee State BA
★ Council Member **Finbarr Saunders** (At-Large) .... (865) 215-2075
Term Expires: December 31, 2019
E-mail: fsaunders@knoxvilletn.gov

(continued on next page)

★ Elected Official ▲ Appointed by Legislature ▼ Appointed by Governor ▶ Appointed by Board or Commission ● Appointed by Judge
■ Appointed by Mayor △ Appointed by Freeholders ▽ Appointed by Supervisor ▷ Appointed by County Executive ○ Appointed by Council

Office of the City Council *continued*

★Council Member **Marshall Stair** (At-Large) . . . . (865) 215-2075
Term Expires: December 31, 2019
E-mail: marshallstair@knoxvilletn.gov

★Council Member **George Wallace** (At-Large) . . . . (865) 215-2075
Term Expires: December 31, 2019
E-mail: gwallace@knoxvilletn.gov

○City Council Attorney **Robert B. Frost, Jr.** . . . . (865) 546-3653

Metropolitan Knoxville Airport Authority

P.O. Box 15600, Knoxville, TN 37901
Fax: (865) 342-3050 Internet: www.tys.org/

President **William F. Marrison** . . . . (865) 342-3001

Lafayette Consolidated Government, Louisiana

City/Parish Government Building, 705 West University Avenue, Lafayette, LA 70506
P.O. Box 4017C, Lafayette, LA 70502
Internet: www.lafayettela.gov

County: Lafayette Parish **Election Type:** Partisan **Population:** 127,657 (2015)

Form of Municipal Government: City and parish governments are combined.

Office of the City-Parish President

705 West University Avenue, Lafayette, LA 70506
P.O. Box 4017C, Lafayette, LA 70502
Fax: (337) 291-8399

★Mayor-President **Joel C. Robideaux** (R) . . . . (337) 291-8300
Began Service: January 4, 2016
Term Expires: January 1, 2020
Education: Southwestern Louisiana BS; LSU MS
Executive Secretary **Becky Perret** . . . . (337) 291-8300
E-mail: bperret@lafayettela.gov
Assistant to President **Cydra Wingerter** . . . . (337) 291-8307
E-mail: cwingerter@lafayettela.gov

Office of the Chief Administrative Officer

Chief Administrative Officer **Dee Stanley** . . . . (337) 291-8311
Education: LSU 1981 BA Fax: (337) 291-8309
Chief Development Officer **Carlee Alm-LaBar** . . . . (337) 291-8307

Office of the City-Parish Council

705 West University Avenue, Lafayette, LA 70506
P.O. Box 4017C, Lafayette, LA 70502
Tel: (337) 291-8800 Fax: (337) 291-8822

★Council Member **Kevin Naquin** (District 1) . . . . (337) 291-8801
Term Expires: January 1, 2020

★Council Member **Jay Castille** (District 2) . . . . (337) 291-8802
Term Expires: January 1, 2020
E-mail: jaycastille@lafayettela.gov

★Council Member **Patrick "Pat" Lewis** (District 3) . . . . (337) 291-8800
Term Expires: January 1, 2020

★Council Member **Kenneth P. Boudreaux** (District 4) . . . . . (337) 291-8804
Term Expires: January 1, 2020
Date of Birth: July 30, 1968
Education: Southwestern Louisiana

★Council Member **Jared Bellard** (District 5) . . . . (337) 291-8805
Term Expires: January 1, 2020
E-mail: jaredbellard@lafayettela.gov
Education: Southwestern Louisiana 1996

Office of the City-Parish Council *continued*

★Council Member **Bruce Conque** (District 6) . . . . (337) 291-8800
Term Expires: January 1, 2020

★Council Member **Nanette Cook** (R-District 7) . . . . (337) 291-8810
Term Expires: January 1, 2020

★Council Member
Elizabeth Webb "Liz" Herbert (District 8) . . . . (337) 291-8800
Term Expires: January 1, 2020

★Council Member **William G. Theriot** (District 9) . . . . (337) 291-8809
Term Expires: January 1, 2020
E-mail: williamtheriot@lafayettela.gov
Education: Southwestern Louisiana 1986 BSBA

○Clerk of the Council **Veronica Williams** . . . . (337) 291-8810
E-mail: vwilliams@lafayettela.gov

Office of the City-Parish Attorney

P.O. Box 4017C, Lafayette, LA 70502

City/Parish Attorney **Michael D. Hebert** . . . . (337) 291-8015
E-mail: mhebert@lafayettela.gov Fax: (337) 232-7273

Community Development Department

705 West University Avenue, Lafayette, LA 70506
P.O. Box 4017C, Lafayette, LA 70502

Director **Patricia Leyendecker** . . . . (337) 291-8402
Fax: (337) 291-8434

Emergency Operations & Security

705 W. University Ave., Lafayette, LA 70506

Emergency Operations and Security Coordinator
Bobby Cormier . . . . (337) 291-8358
E-mail: bcormier@LafayetteLA.gov Fax: (337) 291-8399

Office of Finance and Management

705 W. University Ave., Lafayette, LA 70506
P.O. Box 4017C, Lafayette, LA 70502

Chief Financial Officer **Lorrie Toups** . . . . (337) 291-8202
Fax: (337) 291-8310
Controller **Melinda Felps** . . . . (337) 291-8201
Fax: (337) 291-8310
Executive Secretary **Emily Beard** . . . . (337) 291-8201
E-mail: ebeard@lafayettela.gov Fax: (337) 291-8310
Account Manager **Tammie Andrus** . . . . (337) 291-8205
E-mail: tandrus@lafayettela.gov Fax: (337) 291-8060
Budget Manager **Kerney Simoneaux** . . . . (337) 291-8246
E-mail: ksimoneaux@lafayettela.gov Fax: (337) 291-8060
Purchasing and Property Manager **Thomasina Oliver** . . . . (337) 291-8259
E-mail: toliver@lafayettela.gov Fax: (337) 291-8269

Fire Department

300 E. Vermilion, Lafayette, LA 70501
P.O. Box 4017C, Lafayette, LA 70502
Tel: (337) 291-8701

Fire Chief **Robert P. Benoit** . . . . (337) 291-8703
E-mail: rpbenoit@lafayettela.gov Fax: (337) 291-8787

Lafayette Public Library

301 W. Congress St., Lafayette, LA 70501

Director **Sona Dombourian** . . . . (337) 261-5775
E-mail: sdombour@state.lib.la.us Fax: (337) 261-5782

Parks and Recreation Department

500 Girard Park Dr., Lafayette, LA 70503
P.O. Box 4017C, Lafayette, LA 70502

Director **Gerald Boudreaux** (D) . . . . (337) 291-8361
Fax: (337) 291-8389

★Elected Official ▲Appointed by Legislature ▼Appointed by Governor ►Appointed by Board or Commission ●Appointed by Judge
■Appointed by Mayor △Appointed by Freeholders ▽Appointed by Supervisor ▷Appointed by County Executive ○Appointed by Council

Planning, Zoning and Codes Department
Building B, 220 West Willow, Lafayette, LA 70501
P.O. Box 4017C, Lafayette, LA 70502

Director **Eleanor Bouy** .... (337) 291-8013
Fax: (337) 291-8003

Police Department
900 E. University, Lafayette, LA 70503
P.O. Box 4017C, Lafayette, LA 70502

■ Chief of Police (Interim) **Reginald "Reggie" Thomas** ... (337) 291-8654
E-mail: rthomas@lafayettela.gov Fax: (337) 291-5665

Public Works Department
1515 E. University Ave., Lafayette, LA 70501
P.O. Box 4017C, Lafayette, LA 70502

Director **Kevin Blanchard** .... (337) 291-8502
Fax: (337) 291-8592

Lafayette Utilities System
1314 Walker Road, Lafayette, LA 70506
P.O. Box 4017C, Lafayette, LA 70502
Tel: (337) 291-8280 Fax: (337) 291-8082 Internet: www.lus.org

Director **Terry J. Huval** .... (337) 291-5804
Fax: (337) 291-8318

Lafayette Housing Authority
115 Katie Drive, Lafayette, LA 70501
Tel: (337) 233-1327 Fax: (337) 593-9942 E-mail: info@thelha.com

Executive Director **Katie Anderson** .... (337) 233-1327

Lafayette Parish Public School System
113 Chaplin Dr., Lafayette, LA 70508
P.O. Drawer 2158, Lafayette, LA 70502-2158
Tel: (337) 236-6800 Fax: (337) 233-0977
Internet: http://www.lpssonline.com

Superintendent **Dr. Donald W Aguillard** .... (337) 236-6826

City of Lakewood, Colorado
480 S. Allison Parkway, Lakewood, CO 80226
Tel: (303) 987-7000 (Information) Internet: www.lakewood.org

County: Jefferson **Election Type:** Nonpartisan **Population:** 152,597 (2015)

Office of the Mayor and City Council
480 S. Allison Parkway, Lakewood, CO 80226-3127
Tel: (303) 987-7050 Fax: (303) 987-7063

★ Mayor **Adam A. Paul** .... (303) 987-7040
Began Service: November 23, 2015
Term Expires: November 2019
E-mail: apaul@lakewood.org

★ Council Member **Charley Able** (Ward 1) .... (303) 233-7275
Term Expires: November 2019

★ Council Member **Ramey Johnson** (Ward 1) .... (303) 987-7050
Term Expires: November 2017
E-mail: rjohnson@lakewood.org

★ Council Member **Scott Koop** (Ward 2) .... (303) 987-7050
Term Expires: November 2017
E-mail: skoop@lakewood.org

★ Council Member **Sharon Vincent** (Ward 2) .... (303) 987-7050
Term Expires: November 2019

★ Council Member **Shakti** (Ward 3) .... (303) 987-7050
Term Expires: November 2017
E-mail: shakti@lakewood.org

Office of the Mayor and City Council *continued*

★ Council Member **Pete Roybal** (Ward 3) .... (303) 987-7050
Term Expires: November 2019
E-mail: proybal@lakewood.org

★ Council Member **Barbara Franks** (Ward 4) .... (303) 987-7050
Term Expires: November 2019

★ Council Member **David Wiechman** (Ward 4) .... (303) 987-7050
Term Expires: November 2017
E-mail: dwiechman@lakewood.org
Date of Birth: May 1, 1955
Education: Illinois 1979 BSE

★ Council Member **Dana Gutwein** (Ward 5) .... (303) 987-7050
Term Expires: November 2019

★ Council Member **Karen Harrison** (Ward 5) .... (303) 987-7050
Term Expires: November 12, 2017
E-mail: kharrison@lakewood.org

Office of the City Attorney
480 S. Allison Parkway, Lakewood, CO 80226-3127
Fax: (303) 716-3762

City Attorney **Timothy Cox** .... (303) 987-7450
E-mail: tcox@lakewood.org

Office of the City Clerk
480 S. Allison Parkway, Lakewood, CO 80226-3127
Fax: (303) 987-7088

City Clerk **Margy Greer** .... (303) 987-7080
E-mail: margre@lakewood.org

Office of the City Manager
480 S. Allison Parkway, Lakewood, CO 80226-3127
TTY: (303) 987-7057 Fax: (303) 987-7063

○ City Manager **Kathy Hodgson** .... (303) 987-7050
E-mail: kathod@lakewood.org

Deputy City Manager **Nanette Neelan** .... (303) 987-7050
E-mail: nannee@lakewood.org

Community Resources Department
480 S. Allison Parkway, Lakewood, CO 80226-3127
Fax: (303) 987-7821 E-mail: crinfo@lakewood.org

Director **Kit Newland** .... (303) 987-7800
E-mail: kitnew@lakewood.org
Education: VCU 1980

Employee Relations Department
480 S. Allison Parkway, Lakewood, CO 80226-3127
Fax: (303) 987-7711

Director **Jeff Dolan** .... (303) 987-7701
E-mail: jefdol@lakewood.org

Finance Department
480 South Allison Parkway, Lakewood, CO 80226-3127
Fax: (303) 987-7662

Director **Larry Dorr** .... (303) 987-7601

Office of the Treasurer
480 South Allison Parkway, Lakewood, CO 80226

Treasurer **Larry Dorr** .... (303) 987-7601

Information Technology Department
445 S. Allison Pkwy., Lakewood, CO 80226-3127
Fax: (303) 987-7546

Chief Information Officer **Mark Pray** .... (303) 987-7676
E-mail: mpray@lakewood.org

★ Elected Official ▲ Appointed by Legislature ▼ Appointed by Governor ▶ Appointed by Board or Commission ● Appointed by Judge
■ Appointed by Mayor △ Appointed by Freeholders ▽ Appointed by Supervisor ▷ Appointed by County Executive ○ Appointed by Council

Planning Department
480 South Allison Parkway, Lakewood, CO 80226-3127
Fax: (303) 987-7990

Director **Travis Parker** .... (303) 987-7500

Police Department
445 S. Allison Parkway, Lakewood, CO 80226-3107
Fax: (303) 987-7296

Police Chief **Kevin Paletta** .... (303) 987-7102

Public Works Department
480 S. Allison Parkway, Lakewood, CO 80226-3127
Fax: (303) 987-7910

Director **Jay Hutchison** .... (303) 987-7900

City of Lancaster, California
44933 Fern Ave., Lancaster, CA 93534
Internet: www.cityoflancasterca.org

County: Los Angeles **Election Type:** Nonpartisan **Year Incorporated:** 1977 **Population:** 161,103 (2015)

Office of the Mayor and City Council
44933 Fern Ave., Lancaster, CA 93534
Fax: (661) 723-6141

★Mayor **R. Rex Parris** .... (661) 723-6019
Began Service: 2008
Term Expires: April 2020
E-mail: rrparris@cityoflancasterca.org

★Vice Mayor **Marvin "Marv" Crist** .... (661) 723-6019
Term Expires: April 2018
E-mail: mcrist@cityoflancasterca.org

★Council Member **Raj Malhi** .... (661) 723-6019
Term Expires: April 2018

★Council Member **Ken Mann** .... (661) 723-6019
Term Expires: April 2020
E-mail: kmann@cityoflancasterca.org

★Council Member **Angela Underwood-Jacobs** .... (661) 723-6019
Term Expires: April 2020

Administrative Services Department
44933 Fern Ave., Lancaster, CA 93534
Fax: (661) 723-6141

City Manager **Mark V. Bozigian** .... (661) 723-6133
E-mail: mbozigian@cityoflancasterca.org

Deputy City Manager **Jason Caudle** .... (661) 723-6010
E-mail: jcaudle@cityoflancasterca.org

Assistant to the City Manager **(Vacant)** .... (661) 723-6008

Communications Manager **Joseph Cabral** .... (661) 723-6053
E-mail: jcabral@cityoflancasterca.org Fax: (661) 723-5843

Office of the City Clerk
44933 Fern Ave., Lancaster, CA 93534

City Clerk **Britt Avrit** .... (661) 723-6020
E-mail: bavrit@cityoflancasterca.org Fax: (661) 723-5847

Economic Development
44933 Fern Ave., Lancaster, CA 93534
Fax: (661) 723-6128

Economic Development Director **Vern Lawson** .... (661) 723-6128
E-mail: vlawson@cityoflancasterca.org

Economic Development *continued*

Housing/Neighborhood Revitalization Director
Elizabeth Brubaker .... (661) 723-6193
E-mail: ebrubaker@cityoflancasterca.org

Finance Department
44933 Fern Ave., Lancaster, CA 93534
Fax: (661) 723-6180

Director **Barbara Boswell** .... (661) 723-6033

Purchasing Agent **Cathy DeFalco** .... (661) 723-6023
E-mail: cdefalco@cityoflancasterca.org

Human Resources Department
44933 Fern Ave., Lancaster, CA 93534
Fax: (661) 723-6187

Director **(Vacant)** .... (661) 723-6050

Parks, Recreation and Arts Department
44933 Fern Ave., Lancaster, CA 93534
Fax: (661) 723-5913

Director **Ronda Perez** .... (661) 723-6077

Planning Department
44933 Fern Ave., Lancaster, CA 93534

Director **Brian Ludicke** .... (661) 723-6100
E-mail: bludicke@cityoflancasterca.org Fax: (661) 723-5926

Public Works Department
44933 Fern Ave., Lancaster, CA 93534
Fax: (661) 723-6182

Director (Interim) **Carlyle Workman** .... (661) 723-6046

Development Engineering Manager **(Vacant)** .... (661) 723-6150

Utility Services Manager **Carlyle Workman** .... (661) 945-6863
E-mail: cworkman@cityoflancasterca.org

Maintenance Services Manager **Richard Long** .... (661) 723-6225
Fax: (661) 723-6222

City of Lansing, Michigan
City Hall, 124 W. Michigan Ave., Lansing, MI 48933
Internet: www.lansingmi.gov

County: Ingham **Election Type:** Nonpartisan **Population:** 115,056 (2015)

Virgil "Virg" Bernero
Mayor

Began Service: January 1, 2006
Term Expires: December 31, 2017
Date of Birth: March 31, 1964
Education: Adrian 1986 BA
Career: Commissioner, Board of Commissioners, County of Ingham, Michigan (1991-1999); Chief Legislative Aide, State Senator Jim Berryman (D-SD, Adrian), Michigan Senate, Michigan Legislature, State of Michigan; State Senate (D-MI, District 23), Michigan Senate

Office of the Mayor
City Hall, 124 West Michigan Avenue, 9th Floor,
Lansing, MI 48933-1694
TTY: (517) 483-4479 Fax: (517) 483-6066

★Mayor **Virgil "Virg" Bernero** .... (517) 483-4141
E-mail: lansing.mayor@lansingmi.gov

★Elected Official ▲Appointed by Legislature ▼Appointed by Governor ►Appointed by Board or Commission ●Appointed by Judge
■Appointed by Mayor △Appointed by Freeholders ▽Appointed by Supervisor ▷Appointed by County Executive ○Appointed by Council

Office of the Mayor *continued*

■ Chief of Staff **Randy Hannan** ....(517) 483-4141
E-mail: randy.hannan@lansingmi.gov

Office of the City Council

City Hall, 10th Fl., 124 W. Michigan Ave., Lansing, MI 48933
Tel: (517) 483-4177 Fax: (517) 483-7630
Internet: http://www.lansingmi.gov/City_Council

★ President **Judi Brown Clarke** (At-Large) ....(517) 483-4180
Term Expires: December 31, 2017
★ Vice President **Tina Houghton** (Ward 2) ....(517) 483-4184
Term Expires: December 31, 2017
★ Council Member **Jody Washington** (Ward 1) ....(517) 483-4181
Term Expires: December 31, 2019
E-mail: jwashington@lansingmi.gov
★ Council Member **Adam Hussain** (Ward 3) ....(517) 483-4177
Term Expires: December 31, 2019
★ Council Member **Jessica Yorko** (Ward 4) ....(517) 483-4190
Term Expires: December 31, 2017
★ Council Member **Kathie Dunbar** (At-Large)............(517) 483-4171
Term Expires: December 31, 2017
E-mail: kdunbar@lansingmi.gov
★ Council Member **Patricia A. Spitzley** (At-Large)........(517) 483-4177
Term Expires: December 31, 2019
Education: Central Michigan 1988 BS; Michigan State 2006 JD
★ Council Member **Carol Wood** (At-Large)...............(517) 483-4188
Term Expires: December 31, 2019
E-mail: cwood@lansingmi.gov
Administrative Assistant **(Vacant)** ....(517) 483-4177
○ Internal Auditor **Jim DeLine** ....(517) 483-4159
E-mail: jdeline@lansingmi.gov
Office Manager **Sherrie Boak** ....(517) 483-7683

Office of the City Attorney

City Hall, 5th Fl., 124 W. Michigan Ave., Lansing, MI 48933
Fax: (517) 483-4081 E-mail: cityatty@lansingmi.gov

■ City Attorney **Janene McIntyre** ....(517) 483-4320
E-mail: cityatty@lansingmi.gov

Office of the City Clerk

City Hall, 124 West Michigan Avenue, 9th Floor,
Lansing, MI 48933-1695
Tel: (517) 483-4131 Fax: (517) 377-0068
Internet: www.lansingmi.gov/clerk/

★ City Clerk **Chris Swope**............................(517) 483-4131
Term Expires: December 31, 2017
E-mail: city.clerk@lansingmi.gov

Finance Department

City Hall, 124 West Michigan Avenue, 8th Floor, Lansing, MI 48933
Fax: (517) 483-4524 Internet: www.lansingmi.gov/finance/

■ Director **Angela Bennett** ....(517) 483-4511
E-mail: abennett@lansingmi.gov
Accounting Manager **Randy Endsley** ....(517) 483-4515 ext. 4
E-mail: rendsley@lansingmi.gov
■ Assessor **William Fowler** ....(517) 483-4020
E-mail: wfowler@lansingmi.gov
Treasurer **Antonia Kraus** ....(517) 483-4112
Education: Michigan State 1986 BA; Central Michigan 1987 MA
Purchasing Agent **Stephanie Robinson** ....(517) 483-4128
E-mail: srobinson@lansingmi.gov

Property Management Division

621 East Hazel Street, Lansing, MI 48912
Fax: (517) 483-4834
Internet: http://www.lansingmi.gov/Property_Management1

Property Manager **Marty Riel**.......................(517) 483-4079
E-mail: marty.riel@lansingmi.gov

Fire Department

120 E. Shiawassee St., Lansing, MI 48933
Fax: (517) 483-4488

■ Fire Chief **Randy Taliffaro** ....(517) 483-4200
Assistant Fire Chief **Michael Hamel** ....(517) 483-4200
E-mail: mhamel@lansingmi.gov
Assistant Fire Chief **Marc Tyler** ....(517) 483-4200
E-mail: mtyler@lansingmi.gov
Fire Marshal **Marshaun Blake**.......................(517) 483-4200
316 North Capitol Avenue, Suite C-1, Lansing, MI 48933
E-mail: mblake@lansingmi.gov

Housing Commission

310 Seymour Avenue, Lansing, MI 48933
Fax: (517) 487-6977 Internet: http://www.lanshc.org/

Director **Patricia Baines-Lake** ....(517) 372-7996

Human Relations and Community Services Department

City Hall, 124 West Michigan Avenue, 4th Floor, Lansing, MI 48933
Tel: (517) 483-4477 TTY: (517) 483-4479 Fax: (517) 377-0078
Internet: www.lansingmi.gov/hrcs/

■ Director **Dr. Joan Jackson-Johnson** ....(517) 483-4477
E-mail: jjjohnso@lansingmi.gov

Human Resources Department

City Hall, 124 West Michigan Avenue, 8th Floor, Lansing, MI 48933
Fax: (517) 483-6064 E-mail: recruiter@lansingmi.gov

■ Director **Mary P. Riley**.............................(517) 483-4010
E-mail: mriley@lansingmi.gov

Parks and Recreation Department

200 North Foster Street, 2nd Floor, Lansing, MI 48912
Tel: (517) 483-4276 Fax: (517) 377-0180
Internet: www.lansingmi.gov/parks/ E-mail: parks@lansingmi.gov

■ Director **Brett Kaschinske** ....(517) 483-4042
E-mail: brett.kaschinske@lansingmi.gov

Planning and Neighborhood Development Office

316 North Capitol Avenue, Lansing, MI 48933
Tel: (517) 483-4060 Fax: (517) 483-6036
Internet: www.lansingmi.gov/pnd/

Director **Bob Johnson** Room D-1....................(517) 483-4060
E-mail: robert.johnson@lansingmi.gov
Building Official **Jim Bennett**......................(517) 483-4375
316 N. Capitol Ave., Room C-1, Lansing, MI 48933
Development Manager **(Vacant)** Room D-2............(517) 483-4050
Assistant Planning Manager **William "Bill" Rieske**
Room D-1 ....(517) 483-4091
Parking Services Manager **Traci Shell** ....(517) 483-6621
316 North Grand Avenue, Lansing, MI 48933-1238
E-mail: tshell@lansingmi.gov

Police Department

120 W. Michigan Ave., Lansing, MI 48933
Tel: (517) 483-4600 Fax: (517) 377-0162
Internet: www.lansingmi.gov/police/

■ Chief of Police **Mike Yankowski** ....(517) 483-4600
E-mail: myankowski@lansingmi.gov

Public Service Department

City Hall, 7th Fl., 124 W. Michigan Ave., Lansing, MI 48933
Tel: (517) 483-4455 Fax: (517) 483-6082
Internet: http://www.lansingmi.gov/pubserv/

■ Director **Chad Gamble**.............................(517) 483-4146
E-mail: cgamble@lansingmi.gov Fax: (517) 483-6082

(continued on next page)

★ Elected Official ▲ Appointed by Legislature ▼ Appointed by Governor ► Appointed by Board or Commission ● Appointed by Judge
■ Appointed by Mayor △ Appointed by Freeholders ▽ Appointed by Supervisor ▷ Appointed by County Executive ○ Appointed by Council

Public Service Department *continued*

City Engineer **Dean Johnson** . . . . (517) 483-4458
E-mail: djohnson@lansingmi.gov Fax: (517) 483-6082
Education: Michigan 1983 BS

Operations and Maintenance Superintendent
Victor Rose . . . . (517) 483-4161
Fax: (517) 483-4483

Wastewater Treatment Plant Superintendent
Sid Scrimger . . . . (517) 483-4404
Fax: (517) 483-4536

Recycling Coordinator **Lori Miller** . . . . (517) 483-4599

City of Laredo, Texas

P.O. Box 579, Laredo, TX 78042-0579
Tel: (956) 791-7300 (Information) Internet: www.cityoflaredo.com

County: Webb **Election Type:** Nonpartisan **Year Founded:** 1755
Population: 255,473 (2015)

Office of the Mayor and City Council

1110 Houston Street, Laredo, TX 78040
P.O. Box 579, Laredo, TX 78042-0579
Fax: (956) 791-7491

★ Mayor **Pete Saenz, Jr.** . . . . (956) 791-7400
Began Service: November 12, 2014
Term Expires: November 2018
Executive Secretary to the Mayor **Clarissa Rangel** . . . . (956) 791-7304
E-mail: crangel@ci.laredo.tx.us

★ Mayor Pro Tem **Juan Narvaez** (District 4) . . . . (956) 791-7389
Term Expires: November 2, 2016

★ Council Member **Rudy Gonzalez, Jr.** (District 1) . . . . (956) 791-7389
Term Expires: November 2018

★ Council Member **Vidal Rodriguez** (District 2) . . . . (956) 791-7389
Term Expires: November 2, 2018

★ Council Member
Alejandro "Alex" Perez, Jr. (District 3) . . . . (956) 791-7389
Term Expires: November 2018
E-mail: alexperezjrdistrict3@gmail.com

★ Council Member **Roque Vela, Jr.** (District 5) . . . . (956) 791-7389
Term Expires: November 2, 2016 Fax: (956) 791-7314

★ Council Member **Charlie San Miguel** (District 6) . . . . (956) 791-7389
Term Expires: November 2, 2016 Fax: (956) 791-7314

★ Council Member **George Altgelt** (District 7) . . . . (956) 645-2231
Term Expires: November 2, 2016 Fax: (956) 791-7314

★ Council Member **Roberto Balli** (District 8) . . . . (956) 791-7389
Term Expires: November 2018 Fax: (956) 791-7314

Office of the City Secretary

1110 Houston Street, Laredo, TX 78040
Fax: (956) 791-7491 E-mail: citysec@ci.laredo.tx.us

City Secretary (Acting) **Doanh T. "Zone" Nguyen** . . . . (956) 791-7308

Office of the City Manager

1110 Houston Street, Laredo, TX 78040
Fax: (956) 791-7498

City Manager **Jesus Olivares** . . . . (956) 791-7302
Deputy City Manager **Cynthia Collazo** . . . . (956) 791-7302
Assistant City Manager **Horacio De Leon, Jr.** . . . . (956) 791-7466
Assistant City Manager **Robert A. Eads** . . . . (956) 791-7466
Public Information Officer **Xochitl Mora Garcia** . . . . (956) 791-7461
E-mail: lmora@ci.laredo.tx.us

Office of the City Attorney

1110 Houston Street, Laredo, TX 78040
Fax: (956) 791-7494

City Attorney **Raul Casso** . . . . (956) 791-7319
E-mail: rcasso@ci.laredo.tx.us

Budget Department

1110 Houston Street, Laredo, TX 78040

Manager **Martin Aleman** . . . . (956) 791-7439
E-mail: maleman@cityoflaredo.com Fax: (956) 791-7383

Building Development Services Department

1120 San Bernardo St., Laredo, TX 78042
Fax: (956) 795-2998

Director **Ramon E. Chavez** . . . . (956) 794-1625
Building Official **(Vacant)** . . . . (956) 794-1628

Community Development Department

1301 Farragut St., Laredo, TX 78040
Fax: (956) 795-2689

Director (Acting) **Arturo Garcia** . . . . (956) 795-2675
E-mail: agarcia@ci.laredo.tx.us

Convention and Visitors Bureau

501 San Agustin Ave., Laredo, TX 78040
Fax: (956) 795-2185

Director **Blasita Lopez** . . . . (956) 795-2200

Engineering Department

1110 Houston Street, Laredo, TX 78040
P.O. Box 579, Laredo, TX 78042-0579
Fax: (956) 791-7496 E-mail: engineer@ci.laredo.tx.us

City Engineer **Rogelio Rivera** . . . . (956) 791-7346
E-mail: rrivera@ci.laredo.tx.us
Assistant City Engineer **Gabriel Martinez, Jr.** . . . . (956) 791-7346
E-mail: gmartinez@ci.laredo.tx.us
City Hall Maintenance **Rene Ramos** . . . . (956) 791-7355
E-mail: rramos0@ci.laredo.tx.us

Environmental Services

619 Reynolds, Laredo, TX 78040
Fax: (956) 727-7944

Director (Acting) **John Porter** . . . . (956) 794-1650

Hazardous Materials Division Environmental Specialist
Fernando Sotelo . . . . (956) 794-1650

Stormwater Division Environmental Specialist
Gerardo Cantu . . . . (956) 794-1650

Finance Department

1110 Houston Street, Laredo, TX 78040
Fax: (956) 791-7477

Director **Rosario Camarillo-Cabello** . . . . (956) 791-7425
Fax: (956) 791-7477

Fire Department

One Guadalupe St., Laredo, TX 78040
Fax: (956) 795-2914

Fire Chief/Emergency Coordinator, Homeland Security
Steve Landin . . . . (956) 795-2150
E-mail: slandin@ci.laredo.tx.us

Health Department

2600 Cedar Avenue, Laredo, TX 78040
Fax: (956) 726-2632

Director **Dr. Héctor F. Gonzalez** . . . . (956) 795-4905

★ Elected Official ▲ Appointed by Legislature ▼ Appointed by Governor ► Appointed by Board or Commission ● Appointed by Judge
■ Appointed by Mayor △ Appointed by Freeholders ▽ Appointed by Supervisor ▷ Appointed by County Executive ○ Appointed by Council

Human Resources Department
1110 Houston Street, Laredo, TX 78040
Fax: (956) 795-3073

Director **Monica Flores** .... (956) 791-7474
E-mail: mflores@ci.laredo.tx.us

Information Services and Telecommunications Department
1102 Bob Bullock Loop 20, Laredo, TX 78040
Fax: (956) 727-6509

Director **Heberto "Beto" Ramirez** .... (956) 727-6500
E-mail: hramirez@ci.laredo.tx.us

Communications and Support Services Division (311)
912 Matamoros Street, Laredo, TX 78040
Fax: (956) 791-1789

Customer Service Coordinator **Linda Evelyn Tays** .... (956) 721-2481

Laredo Bridge System
World Trade Bridge, 1601 FM 1472, Laredo, TX 78044
Fax: (956) 729-2061

Bridge Manager **Mario Maldonado** .... (956) 791-2200

Laredo International Airport
5210 Bob Bullock Loop, Laredo, TX 78041
E-mail: airport@ci.laredo.tx.us

Manager **Jose Luis Flores** .... (956) 795-2000
Fax: (956) 795-2572
Marketing Manager **Timothy Franciscus-Timm** .... (956) 795-2000

Laredo Public Library
1120 E. Calton Rd., Laredo, TX 78041
Fax: (956) 795-2403

Librarian/Director **Maria G. Soliz** .... (956) 795-2400
E-mail: mgsoliz@laredolibrary.org

Laredo Transit System (El Metro)
1301 Farragut Street, 3rd Floor, Laredo, TX 78040

General Manager (Acting)
Claudia San Miguel .... (956) 795-2280 ext. 234
Fax: (956) 795-2258

Assistant General Manager, Operations
Rosa E. Soto .... (956) 795-2250 ext. 106
E-mail: rsoto@ci.laredo.tx.us
Maintenance Manager **Juan R. Vaquera** .... (956) 795-2250 ext. 112

Parks and Leisure Services Department
2201 Piedra China, Laredo, TX 78040
Fax: (956) 795-2353

Director **Osbaldo Guzman** .... (956) 795-2350

Planning and Zoning Department
1120 San Bernardo St., Laredo, TX 78042
Fax: (956) 794-1624

Director **Nathan R. Bratton** .... (956) 794-1613

Police Department
4712 Maher, Laredo, TX 78041
Tel: (956) 795-2800

Police Chief **Raymond E. Garner** .... (956) 795-2899
911 Communications Manager **Patricia Trevino** .... (956) 795-2809
Fax: (956) 795-2874

Public Works Department
5512 Thomas Avenue, Laredo, TX 78043
Tel: (956) 795-2500 Fax: (956) 795-2507

Manager **John Orfila, Jr.** .... (956) 795-2500
Creeks and Right-of-way Maintenance **Calixto Flores** .... (956) 795-2500
Construction Superintendent **Adan Cedillo** .... (956) 795-2500
Building Rehabilitation Supervisor **Juan Jose Medina** .... (956) 795-2500
E-mail: jmedina@ci.laredo.tx.us
Fleet General Manager **Jack Dunn** .... (956) 727-6455
1102 Bob Bullock Loop 20, Laredo, TX 78040
Street Cleaning and Maintenance **Fernando Liendo** .... (956) 795-2500
Street Construction Supervisor **Jaime Cantu** .... (956) 795-2500
Street Construction Supervisor **Federico Guerrero** .... (956) 795-2500
Street Construction Supervisor **Alfredo Liendo** .... (956) 795-2500
Street Construction Supervisor **Ruben Rizo** .... (956) 795-2500
Street Construction Supervisor **Antonio Saenz** .... (956) 795-2500

Solid Waste Division
6912 Highway 359, Laredo, TX 78040
Fax: (956) 796-1105

Manager **Stephen Geiss** .... (956) 795-2510

Tax Department
1102 Bob Bullock Loop 20, Laredo, TX 78040
Fax: (956) 791-7492

Tax Assessor/Collector **Elizabeth Martinez** .... (956) 791-7401
E-mail: emartinez@ci.laredo.tx.us

Traffic Department
5512 Thomas Avenue, Laredo, TX 78043
Fax: (956) 795-2127

Manager **Roberto Murillo** .... (956) 795-2550
Sign and Signal Superintendent **(Vacant)** .... (956) 795-2550
Traffic Engineer **Robert F. Pena** .... (956) 795-2550
E-mail: rpena@ci.laredo.tx.us

Utilities Department
P.O. Box 2950, Laredo, TX 78042-0579
Fax: (956) 721-2001 Internet: www.ci.laredo.tx.us/Utilities05/

Director (Interim) **Riazul Mia** .... (956) 721-2000
Customer Service Superintendent
Margarita Ayala .... (956) 721-2000 ext. 3025
Distribution Superintendent **Santos Segura** .... (956) 721-2000
Water Plant Superintendent **Tony Moreno** .... (956) 795-2620
Wastewater Treatment Superintendent **Jose Chavarria** .... (956) 795-2720

City of Las Vegas, Nevada

City Hall, 495 South Main Street, Las Vegas, NV 89101
Tel: (702) 229-6011 (Information) TTY: (702) 386-9108
Internet: www.ci.las-vegas.nv.us

County: Clark **Election Type:** Nonpartisan **Year Incorporated:** 1911
Population: 623,747 (2015)

Office of the Mayor and City Council
City Hall, 495 South Main Street, Las Vegas, NV 89101
Tel: (702) 229-6405 Fax: (702) 382-8558

★ Mayor **Carolyn Goodman** .... (702) 229-6241
Began Service: July 6, 2011
Term Expires: July 2019
E-mail: cgoodman@lasvegasnevada.gov
Executive Assistant to the Mayor **Cheryl Russo** .... (702) 229-6241
E-mail: crusso@lasvegasnevada.gov
Special Assistant **Lora Kalkman** .... (702) 229-6241
E-mail: lkalkman@lasvegasnevada.gov

(continued on next page)

★ Elected Official ▲ Appointed by Legislature ▼ Appointed by Governor ▶ Appointed by Board or Commission ● Appointed by Judge
■ Appointed by Mayor △ Appointed by Freeholders ▽ Appointed by Supervisor ▷ Appointed by County Executive ○ Appointed by Council

Office of the Mayor and City Council *continued*

★Mayor Pro Tem **Steve Ross** (Ward 6) . . . . (702) 229-6405
Term Expires: July 2017
E-mail: sross@lasvegasnevada.gov
Special Assistant **Jana Buner** . . . . (702) 229-6405
E-mail: jbuner@lasvegasnevada.gov
★Council Member **Lois Tarkanian** (Ward 1) . . . . (702) 229-6405
Term Expires: July 2019
E-mail: ltarkanian@lasvegasnevada.gov
Special Assistant **Kimberly Reid** . . . . (702) 229-6405
E-mail: kreid@lasvegasnevada.gov
★Council Member **Robert "Bob" Beers** (Ward 2) . . . . (702) 229-6405
Term Expires: July 2017
E-mail: rbeers@lasvegasnevada.gov
Date of Birth: 1959
Education: UNLV 1987 BS
Special Assistant **Vicky Skilbred** . . . . (702) 229-6405
★Council Member **Bob Coffin** (Ward 3) . . . . (702) 229-6405
Term Expires: July 2019
E-mail: bcoffin@lasvegasnevada.gov
Education: UNLV BS
Special Assistant **Susan Finucan** . . . . (702) 229-6405
E-mail: sfinucan@lasvegasnevada.gov
★Council Member **Stavros S. Anthony** (Ward 4) . . . . (702) 229-6405
Term Expires: July 2017
E-mail: santhony@lasvegasnevada.gov
Education: Wayne State U 1980 BS; UNLV 1987 MA, 1999 PhD
Special Assistant **Rebecca Skouson** . . . . (702) 229-6405
E-mail: rskouson@lasvegasnevada.gov
★Council Member **Ricki Y. Barlow** (Ward 5) . . . . (702) 229-6405
Term Expires: July 2019
E-mail: rbarlow@lasvegasnevada.gov
Special Assistant **Tanya Jackson-Renter** . . . . (702) 229-6405
E-mail: trenter@lasvegasnevada.gov

Office of the City Attorney

495 South Main Street, 6th Floor, Las Vegas, NV 89101
Tel: (702) 229-6629 Fax: (702) 386-1749

○City Attorney **Bradford R. Jerbic** . . . . (702) 229-6590
E-mail: bjerbic@lasvegasnevada.gov
Intergovernmental Relations/Chief Deputy City Attorney
Val Steed . . . . (702) 229-6629
E-mail: vsteed@lasvegasnevada.gov
Chief Deputy City Attorney **Philip R. Byrnes** . . . . (702) 229-6629
Human Resources/Chief Deputy City Attorney
Morgan Davis . . . . (702) 229-6629
E-mail: mdavis@lasvegasnevada.gov
Transactions/Zoning Chief Assistant City Attorney
Teri Ponticello . . . . (702) 229-6629
E-mail: tponticello@lasvegasnevada.gov
Assistant City Attorney (Civil) **Bryan K. Scott** . . . . (702) 229-6629
E-mail: bscott@lasvegasnevada.gov
Assistant City Attorney (Criminal) **Edward Poleski** . . . . . . (702) 229-6201
E-mail: epoleski@lasvegasnevada.gov
Executive Assistant (Criminal) **Lupe Gonzalez** . . . . (702) 229-6201
E-mail: lgonzalez@lasvegasnevada.gov
Victim Witness Advocate **Marisol Ciotti** . . . . (702) 229-2525
Victim Witness Advocate **Dawn Cox** . . . . (702) 229-2525
Victim Witness Advocate **Suzette Landholm** . . . . (702) 229-2525

Office of the City Auditor

City Hall, 495 South Main Street, Las Vegas, NV 89101
Fax: (702) 386-9252

City Auditor **Radford Snelding** . . . . (702) 229-2472

Office of the City Manager

City Hall, 495 South Main Street, Las Vegas, NV 89101
Fax: (702) 388-1807 E-mail: contactcmo@lasvegasnevada.gov

○City Manager **Elizabeth N. "Betsy" Fretwell** . . . . (702) 229-6501
E-mail: efretwell@lasvegasnevada.gov
Education: Georgia BA

Office of the City Manager *continued*

Deputy City Manager **Scott D. Adams** . . . . (702) 229-6501
E-mail: sadams@lasvegasnevada.gov
Deputy City Manager **Orlando L. Sanchez** . . . . (702) 229-6501
E-mail: osanchez@lasvegasnevada.gov
Education: New Mexico State BA
Chief Internal Services Officer **Mark R. Vincent** . . . . (702) 229-6321
400 Stewart Avenue, Las Vegas, NV 89101 Fax: (702) 383-0769
E-mail: mvincent@lasvegasnevada.gov
Education: UNLV 1978 BSBA

Office of Communications

City Hall, 495 South Main Street, Las Vegas, NV 89101
Fax: (702) 384-7197

Communications Director **David Riggleman** . . . . (702) 229-6501
E-mail: driggleman@lasvegasnevada.gov
Communications Manager **Diana Paul** . . . . (702) 229-6501
E-mail: dpaul@lasvegasnevada.gov

Administrative Services Department

City Hall, 495 South Main Street, 7th Floor, Las Vegas, NV 89101
Fax: (702) 388-1807
Internet: www.lasvegasnevada.gov/Government/admin.htm

Director **Ted Olivas** . . . . (702) 229-6501
E-mail: tolivas@lasvegasnevada.gov

Office of the City Clerk

Fax: (702) 382-4803
Internet: www.lasvegasnevada.gov/Government/clerk.htm

City Clerk **LuAnn D. Holmes** . . . . (702) 229-6313
E-mail: ldholmes@lasvegasnevada.gov
Chief Deputy City Clerk **Stacey Campbell** . . . . (702) 229-6078
E-mail: slcampbell@lasvegasnevada.gov
Enterprise Records Officer **Scott Widney** . . . . (702) 229-6311
E-mail: swidney@lasvegasnevada.gov

Building and Safety Department

731 South Fourth Street, Las Vegas, NV 89101

Director **Chris Knight** . . . . (702) 229-6251
Education: Eastern Washington BA
Construction Manager, Land Development and Offsite
Inspection and Testing **Michael Cunningham** . . . . (702) 229-6484

Office of Community Services

495 South Main Street, Las Vegas, NV 89101
Tel: (702) 229-2330 Fax: (702) 598-3898

Director **Stephen K. Harsin** . . . . (702) 229-2330
E-mail: sharsin@lasvegasnevada.gov
Deputy Director **Lisa Morris Hibbler** . . . . (702) 229-2330
E-mail: lmorris@lasvegasnevada.gov
Manager **Kathi Thomas-Gibson** . . . . (702) 229-1836
Supervisor **Marty Toledo** . . . . (702) 229-6364
Supervisor **Joyce Barrow** . . . . (702) 229-3312

Office of Cultural Affairs

495 South Main Street, Las Vegas, NV 89101
Fax: (702) 383-1129 Internet: www.artslasvegas.org/

Manager **Nancy Deaner** . . . . (702) 229-6511

Detention and Enforcement

3300 Stewart Ave., Las Vegas, NV 89101
Tel: (702) 229-6617 Tel: (702) 229-6444 (Inmate Information)
Fax: (702) 386-7070

Chief **Michele Freeman** . . . . (702) 229-6444
Education: UNLV BS, MPA
Deputy Chief **Michael Brown** . . . . (702) 229-6444
Deputy Chief **Timothy Shattler** . . . . (702) 229-6444
Animal Control Director **Scott Barney** . . . . (702) 229-6444

★Elected Official ▲Appointed by Legislature ▼Appointed by Governor ►Appointed by Board or Commission ●Appointed by Judge
■Appointed by Mayor △Appointed by Freeholders ▽Appointed by Supervisor ▷Appointed by County Executive ○Appointed by Council

Economic and Urban Development Department

495 South Main Street, Las Vegas, NV 89101
Fax: (702) 385-3128 E-mail: obd@lasvegasnevada.gov
Internet: www.lasvegasnevada.gov/eud

Director **Bill Arent** .... (702) 229-6551
E-mail: barent@lasvegasnevada.gov
Education: Pennsylvania 1993 BA; UNLV 2001 MPA
Economic Development Manager **Romeo Betea** .... (702) 229-6551
E-mail: rbetea@lasvegasnevada.gov
Parking Enforcement Supervisor **Brandy Stanley** .... (702) 229-6444
E-mail: bstanley@lasvegasnevada.gov
Parking Enforcement Supervisor **(Vacant)** .... (702) 229-6444

Department of Finance

495 South Main Street, 4th Floor, Las Vegas, NV 89101
Fax: (702) 383-0769

Director **Venetta F. Appleyard** .... (702) 229-6823
Accounting Operations Division Manager
Kathleen M. Fauerbach .... (702) 229-6321
E-mail: kfauerbach@lasvegasnevada.gov Fax: (702) 382-6441
Purchasing Contracts Manager **Yolanda C. Jones** .... (702) 229-6021
E-mail: yjones@lasvegasnevada.gov Fax: (702) 384-9964

Las Vegas Fire and Rescue

500 N. Casino Center Blvd., Las Vegas, NV 89101
Tel: (702) 383-2888 Fax: (702) 464-5736
Internet: www.lasvegasnevada.gov/government/fire.htm

Fire Chief **William "Willie" McDonald** .... (702) 229-0323
E-mail: wmcdonald@lasvegasnevada.gov
Education: Cal State (Fresno) BA; Cal State (Hayward) MBA
Administrative Secretary **Amy Cornelison** .... (702) 229-0323
E-mail: acornelison@lasvegasnevada.gov
Fire Marshal/Deputy Chief **Robert Nolan** .... (702) 229-0436
E-mail: rnolan@lasvegasnevada.gov
Operations Deputy Fire Chief **Thomas Miramontes** ..... (702) 229-4184
E-mail: tmiramontes@lasvegasnevada.gov
Support Services Deputy Fire Chief **Eddie Vigil** .... (702) 229-0322
E-mail: evigil@lasvegasnevada.gov
Training Assistant Chief **(Vacant)** .... (702) 229-0735
Fire Alarm Supervisor **Louis Amell** .... (702) 229-0237
E-mail: lamell@lasvegasnevada.gov
Public Education Officer **Timothy Szymanski** .... (702) 229-0331
E-mail: tszymanski@lasvegasnevada.gov Fax: (702) 229-0152

Human Resources Department

City Hall, 495 South Main Street, 2nd Floor, Las Vegas, NV 89101
Tel: (702) 229-6315 Fax: (702) 385-1259
Internet: www.lasvegasnevada.gov/Government/hr.htm

Director **Dan Tarwater** .... (702) 229-6315
E-mail: dtarwater@lasvegasnevada.gov

Information Technologies Department

495 South Main Street, 5th Floor, Las Vegas, NV 89101
Fax: (702) 385-9369

Chief Information Officer/Director (Acting)
Steven "Steve" Martin .... (702) 229-6291

Operations and Maintenance

333 North Rancho Drive, Las Vegas, NV 89106
Tel: (702) 229-1030 Fax: (702) 382-0848

Director (Acting) **Daphnee Legarza** .... (702) 229-1030
Management Analyst **Janet DiAmbrosio-Smith** .... (702) 229-2211

Facilities Management Division

3104 E. Bonanza Road, Las Vegas, NV 89101
Fax: (702) 382-0619

Deputy Director **Steven R. Ford** .... (702) 229-6220
E-mail: sford@lasvegasnevada.gov
Management Analyst II **(Vacant)** .... (702) 229-2499

Operations and Maintenance *continued*

Facilities Project Manager **Marshall Hutchinson** .... (702) 229-6094
E-mail: mhutchinson@lasvegasnevada.gov

Fleet and Transportation Services Division

2950 Ronemus Dr., Las Vegas, NV 89128

Manager **Tracee Scott** .... (702) 229-6971

Streets and Sanitation Division

2875 Ronemus Drive, Las Vegas, NV 89128
Tel: (702) 229-6227 Fax: (702) 256-7817

Deputy Director **Jerry Walker** .... (702) 229-6227

Parks and Recreation Department

2875 Ronemus Drive, Las Vegas, NV 89128
Tel: (702) 229-6571 Fax: (702) 229-6144

Manager **Timothy Hacker** .... (702) 229-6988
Education: Iowa State BA; Southern Illinois MPA
Business Specialist II **Lynnae Gillespie** .... (702) 229-2257
E-mail: lgillespie@lasvegasnevada.gov

Department of Planning

333 North Rancho Drive, Las Vegas, NV 89106
Tel: (702) 229-6301 Fax: (702) 474-7463

○ Director **Tom Perrigo** .... (702) 229-6353
E-mail: tperrigo@lasvegasnevada.gov

Public Works Department

333 North Rancho Drive, 9th Floor, Las Vegas, NV 89106
Tel: (702) 229-6276 Fax: (702) 382-0848

Director **David Bowers** .... (702) 229-6276
Senior Management Analyst **Erin Keller** .... (702) 229-6909
Management Analyst II **(Vacant)** .... (702) 229-1611
Administrative Officer **Ebony Folk** .... (702) 229-6737
E-mail: efolk@lasvegasnevada.gov
Business Specialist **Kristina Hayes** .... (702) 229-5289
E-mail: khayes@lasvegasnevada.gov

City Engineer Division

333 North Rancho Drive, 8th Floor, Las Vegas, NV 89106
Tel: (702) 229-6272 Fax: (702) 382-3232

City Engineer **Allen Pavelka** .... (702) 229-5926
E-mail: apavelka@lasvegasnevada.gov
City Surveyor **Alan Reikki** .... (702) 229-6217
E-mail: areikki@lasvegasnevada.gov
Roadway Planning **Greg McDermott** .... (702) 229-2143
E-mail: gmcdermott@lasvegasnevada.gov
Engineering Program Manager **Kristina L. Swallow** ..... (702) 229-6272
Construction Manager-Capital Improvement Projects
(Vacant) .... (702) 229-6735
Environmental Planning Officer **Sherri McMahan** .... (702) 229-2338
E-mail: smcmahan@lasvegasnevada.gov
Engineering Project Manager **Tim Parks** .... (702) 229-2178
E-mail: tparks@lasvegasnevada.gov

Environmental Division

Water Pollution Control Facility, 6005 E. Vegas Valley Dr.,
Las Vegas, NV 89142
Tel: (702) 229-6200 Fax: (702) 641-9738

Environmental Manager **David Mendenhall** .... (702) 229-6200
Operations and Maintenance Manager **Brian Oswalt** ..... (702) 229-6495
E-mail: boswalt@lasvegasnevada.gov
Laboratory Superintendent **Daniel Fischer** .... (702) 229-2440
Water Pollution Control Facility Safety Officer
Woody Smith .... (702) 229-7222

Traffic Engineering Division

333 North Rancho Drive, 8th Floor, Las Vegas, NV 89106
Tel: (702) 229-6327

City Traffic Engineer **Joanna Wadsworth** .... (702) 229-2214
E-mail: jwadsworth@lasvegasnevada.gov

(continued on next page)

★ Elected Official ▲ Appointed by Legislature ▼ Appointed by Governor ► Appointed by Board or Commission ● Appointed by Judge
■ Appointed by Mayor △ Appointed by Freeholders ▽ Appointed by Supervisor ▷ Appointed by County Executive ○ Appointed by Council

Public Works Department *continued*

Transportation Manager/Deputy Director
Michael Janssen . . . . . . (702) 229-6327
E-mail: mjanssen@lasvegasnevada.gov

Traffic Engineering/Maintenance

3001 Ronemus Drive, Las Vegas, NV 89128
Tel: (702) 229-6331

Assistant Traffic Manager **Niel T. Rohleder** . . . . . . (702) 229-6015
Engineering Project Manager **Tom Kruse** . . . . . . (702) 229-6327
333 North Rancho Drive, 8th Floor, Las Vegas, NV 89106
Right-of-Way **Nancy Peace-Almanzan** . . . . . . (702) 229-6343
E-mail: nalmanzan@lasvegasnevada.gov

Las Vegas Convention and Visitors Authority [LVCVA]

3150 Paradise Road, Las Vegas, NV 89109
Internet: www.lvcva.com/

President and Chief Executive Officer
Rossi Ralenkotter . . . . . . (702) 892-0711
Senior Vice President, Marketing **Cathy Tull** . . . . . . (702) 892-0711
Fax: (702) 892-7685
Vice President, Sales **Chris Meyer** . . . . . . (702) 892-2855
Vice President of Public Affairs **(Vacant)** . . . . . . (702) 892-2984

City of Lewisville, Texas

151 West Church Street, Lewisville, TX 75057
Tel: (972) 219-3400 Fax: (972) 219-3410
Internet: www.cityoflewisville.com/

County: Denton **Election Type:** Nonpartisan **Charter:** 1925
Population: 104,039 (2015)

Office of the Mayor and City Council

151 West Church Street, Lewisville, TX 75057
Fax: (972) 219-3410

★ Mayor **Rudy Durham** . . . . . . (972) 219-3404
Began Service: May 2015
Term Expires: May 2018
E-mail: rdurham@cityoflewisville.com
Education: North Texas BA
★ Mayor Pro Tem **TJ Gilmore** . . . . . . (972) 219-3404
Term Expires: May 2017
E-mail: tgilmore@cityoflewisville.com
★ Deputy Mayor Pro Tem **Leroy Vaughn** . . . . . . (972) 219-3404
Term Expires: May 2017
★ Councilman **Brent Daniels** . . . . . . (972) 219-3404
Term Expires: May 2019
E-mail: bdaniels@cityoflewisville.com
★ Councilman **Neil Ferguson** . . . . . . (972) 219-3404
Term Expires: May 2018
★ Councilman **Brandon Jones** . . . . . . (972) 219-3404
Term Expires: May 2019

Office of the City Attorney

151 West Church Street, Lewisville, TX 75057

City Attorney **Lizbeth Plaster** . . . . . . (972) 219-5058
E-mail: lplaster@cityoflewisville.com

Office of the City Secretary

151 West Church Street, Lewisville, TX 75057

City Secretary **Julie Heinze** . . . . . . (972) 219-3411
E-mail: jheinze@cityoflewisville.com

Office of the City Manager

151 West Church Street, Lewisville, TX 75057

City Manager **Donna Barron** . . . . . . (972) 219-3405
E-mail: donna.barron@cityoflewisville.com
Assistant City Manager **Steven Bacchus** . . . . . . (972) 219-3406
E-mail: sbacchus@cityoflewisville.com
Assistant City Manager **Eric Ferris** . . . . . . (972) 219-3405
E-mail: eferris@cityoflewisville.com
Assistant City Manager **Melinda Galler** . . . . . . (972) 219-3405
E-mail: mgaller@cityoflewisville.com

Community Development Department

151 West Church Street, Lewisville, TX 75057

Director **Eric Ferris** . . . . . . (972) 219-3460
E-mail: eferris@cityoflewisville.com

Engineering Division

151 West Church Street, Lewisville, TX 75057

Lead City Engineer **David Salmon** . . . . . . (972) 219-3490
E-mail: dsalmon@cityoflewisville.com

Building Inspection Division

151 West Church Street, Lewisville, TX 75057

Building Official **Cleve Joiner** . . . . . . (972) 219-3471

Fire Prevention Division

151 West Church Street, Lewisville, TX 75057

Fire Marshal **Tim Ippolito** . . . . . . (972) 219-3466

Health and Code Enforcement Division

151 West Church Street, Lewisville, TX 75057

Manager **Sherry Harper** . . . . . . (972) 219-3481

Community Relations and Tourism Department

151 West Church Street, Lewisville, TX 75057
Fax: (972) 219-3410

Director **James Kunke** . . . . . . (972) 219-3726
E-mail: jkunke@cityoflewisville.com

Economic Development and Planning Department

151 West Church Street, Lewisville, TX 75057
Internet: www.ecodevlewisville.com/

Economic Development Director **Nika Reinecke** . . . . . . (972) 219-3750
E-mail: nreinecke@cityoflewisville.com

Finance Department

151 West Church Street, Lewisville, TX 75057

Finance Director **Brenda Martin** . . . . . . (972) 219-3775

Purchasing Division

151 West Church Street, Lewisville, TX 75057

Purchasing Manager **Todd White** . . . . . . (972) 219-3764
E-mail: awhite@cityoflewisville.com

Fire Department

188 North Valley Parkway, Lewisville, TX 75067

Fire Chief **Timothy Tittle** . . . . . . (972) 219-3589
E-mail: ttittle@cityoflewisville.com

Human Resources Department

151 West Church Street, Lewisville, TX 75057
Fax: (972) 219-5005

Human Resources Director/Assistant City Manager
Melinda Galler . . . . . . (972) 219-3452

★ Elected Official ▲ Appointed by Legislature ▼ Appointed by Governor ► Appointed by Board or Commission ● Appointed by Judge
■ Appointed by Mayor △ Appointed by Freeholders ▽ Appointed by Supervisor ▷ Appointed by County Executive ○ Appointed by Council

Information Technology Services [ITS]
151 West Church Street, Lewisville, TX 75057

Director **Chris Lee** ....(972) 219-5047

Parks and Leisure Services Department
151 West Church Street, Lewisville, TX 75057

Director **Bob Monaghan** ....(972) 219-3552

Police Department
184 North Valley Parkway, Lewisville, TX 75067

Chief of Police **Russell Kerbow** ....(972) 219-3667
Education: North Texas BA

Public Services Department
1100-D North Kealy Avenue, Lewisville, TX 75057

Director of Public Services **Keith Marvin** ....(972) 219-3531

Public Works Division
1100-D North Kealy Avenue, Lewisville, TX 75057
Fax: (972) 219-3508

Public Works Manager **(Vacant)** ....(972) 219-3525

Utilities Division
1100-D North Kealy Avenue, Lewisville, TX 75057

Utilities Manager **Karen Emadiazar** ....(972) 219-5078

Lexington-Fayette Urban County Government, Kentucky

Lexington-Fayette Government Center, 200 East Main Street, Lexington, KY 40507
Tel: (859) 425-2255 (Information) Internet: www.lexingtonky.gov

County: None **Election Type:** Nonpartisan **Year Founded:** 1775
Year Incorporated: 1832 **Charter:** 1972 **Population:** 314,488 (2015)

Office of the Mayor
Lexington-Fayette Government Center, 200 E. Main St., Lexington, KY 40507
Fax: (859) 258-3194

★Mayor **Jim Gray** ....(859) 258-3100
Began Service: January 1, 2011
Term Expires: December 31, 2018
E-mail: mayor@lexingtonky.gov
Executive Assistant to the Mayor **Maureen Watson** ....(859) 258-3100
Chief of Staff (Acting) **Geoff Reed** ....(859) 258-3100
Education: Kentucky BA, MPA
Chief Development Officer **Kevin Atkins** ....(859) 258-3100
E-mail: katkins@lexingtonky.gov
Education: Austin Peay State BS
Senior Advisor **Chris Corcoran** ....(859) 258-3100
Education: Harvard 2007 AB
Chief Innovation Officer **Scott Shapiro** ....(859) 258-3100
E-mail: sshapiro@lexingtonky.gov
Education: JFK School Govt 2011 MPA
Program Specialist **Hilary Angelucci** ....(859) 258-3100
E-mail: hangelucci@lexingtonky.gov
Education: Kentucky BS
Deputy Chief of Staff **(Vacant)** ....(859) 258-3100
Communications Director **Susan Straub** ....(859) 258-3100
E-mail: sstraub@lexingtonky.gov
Education: Kentucky BA

Office of the Chief Administrative Officer
Lexington-Fayette Government Center, 200 East Main Street, Lexington, KY 40507

■Chief Administrative Officer **Sally Hamilton** ....(859) 258-3133
E-mail: shamilton2@lexingtonky.gov
Executive Assistant **Shauntae Hall** ....(859) 258-3133
E-mail: shall@lexingtonky.gov
Education: Kentucky BA
Deputy Chief Administrative Officer **Glenn Brown** ......(859) 258-3121
E-mail: gbrown3@lexingtonky.gov
Advisor to the Chief Administrative Officer **(Vacant)** .....(859) 258-3133
Government Communications Director **(Vacant)** ....(859) 258-3008
■Chief Information Officer **Aldona Valicenti** ....(859) 258-3730
Education: Wayne State U MS
Computer Services Director **Mike Nugent** ....(859) 258-3730
Fax: (859) 258-3399
GIS Division Manager **Philip Stiefel** ....(859) 258-3730
Senior Advisor to the Chief Administrative Officer **(Vacant)** ....(859) 258-3133
Executive Assistant to the Chief Administrative Officer **(Vacant)** ....(859) 258-3133

Budgeting Division
Government Center, 200 East Main Street, 10th Floor, Lexington, KY 40507

Director **Melissa Lueker** ....(859) 258-3060
E-mail: mlueker@lexingtonky.gov

Department of Environmental Quality and Public Works
Government Center, 200 East Main Street, 9th Floor, Lexington, KY 40507
Internet: www.lexingtonky.gov/index.aspx?page=1131

Commissioner **Dowell Hoskins-Squier** ....(859) 258-3400
Education: Vanderbilt 2003 BA
Executive Assistant **Sandra Burke** ....(859) 258-3401
E-mail: commeqpwea@lexingtonky.gov

Environmental Services Division
200 East Main Street, Lexington, KY 40507

Director **Susan Plueger** ....(859) 425-2800
Education: Indiana BS

Streets and Roads Division
1555 Old Frankfort Pike, Lexington, KY 40504
Fax: (859) 253-1014

Director **Albert Miller** ....(859) 258-3451

Traffic Engineering Division
101 East Vine Street, Suite 300, Lexington, KY 40507
Fax: (859) 425-2054

Director **Jeff Neal** ....(859) 258-3830
E-mail: jneal@lexingtonky.gov
Deputy Director **Jim Woods** ....(859) 258-3830
E-mail: jimw@lexingtonky.gov

Waste Management Division
675 Byrd Thurman Dr., Lexington, KY 40510

Director **Tracey Thurman** ....(859) 258-3473
Education: Belmont U BA
Deputy Director **John Howard** ....(859) 425-2856

Water Quality Division
301 Lisle Industrial Avenue, Lexington, KY 40511
Tel: (859) 425-2400

Director **Charles Martin** ....(859) 425-2455

★Elected Official ▲Appointed by Legislature ▼Appointed by Governor ►Appointed by Board or Commission ●Appointed by Judge
■Appointed by Mayor △Appointed by Freeholders ▽Appointed by Supervisor ▷Appointed by County Executive ○Appointed by Council

Finance and Administration Department
Lexington-Fayette Government Center, 200 E. Main St., Lexington, KY 40507
Tel: (859) 258-3300 Fax: (859) 258-3385
Internet: www.lexingtonky.gov/index.aspx?page=160

■ Commissioner **William T. "Bill" O'Mara** .... (859) 258-3300
E-mail: billo@lexingtonky.gov
Financial Management Administrator **Chad Hancock** .... (859) 258-3300
Administrative Officer Senior **Wes Holbrook** .... (859) 258-3300
Education: Kentucky BA
Finance and Investment Analyst **Stephen Mulligan** ...... (859) 258-3300
E-mail: smulligan@lexingtonky.gov

Accounting Division
200 East Main Street, 3rd Floor, Lexington, KY 40507
Fax: (859) 258-3385

Director **Phyllis Cooper** .... (859) 258-3310
E-mail: pcooper@lexingtonky.gov

Central Purchasing Division
200 East Main Street, Room 338, Lexington, KY 40507

Director **Todd Slatin** .... (859) 258-3320
E-mail: tslatin@lexingtonky.gov

Grants and Special Programs
Government Center, 200 E. Main St., 6th Floor, Lexington, KY 40507
Tel: (859) 258-3070 Fax: (859) 258-3081

Director **Irene Gooding** .... (859) 258-3070
E-mail: ireneg@lexingtonky.gov
Grants Manager **Theresa Reynolds** .... (859) 258-3070
E-mail: teresar2@lexingtonky.gov

Human Resources Division
Government Center, 200 E. Main St., 8th Floor, Lexington, KY 40507
Fax: (859) 258-3059

Director **John Maxwell** .... (859) 258-3030
E-mail: jmaxwell2@lexingtonky.gov
Benefits Section Manager **Mary Lyle** .... (859) 258-3043
Employment Section Manager **Paula Williams** .... (859) 258-3055
Training Section Manager **Jeremy Hobbs** .... (859) 258-3048
E-mail: jhobbs@lexingtonky.gov

Risk Management Division
Government Center, 200 E. Main St., 9th Floor, Lexington, KY 40507
Tel: (859) 258-3094 Fax: (859) 425-2476

Director **Patrick Johnston** .... (859) 258-3290
E-mail: patrickj@lexingtonky.gov
Industrial Hygiene/Loss Control Specialist
Kelly Survant .... (859) 425-2481
E-mail: ksurvant@lexingtonky.gov
Safety and Loss Control Section Manager
Michael Skidmore .... (859) 425-2478
E-mail: mskidmor@lexingtonky.gov

Division of Revenue
200 East Main Street, Lexington, KY 40507

Director **Russell Cook** .... (859) 258-3340
E-mail: rcook@lexingtonky.gov

General Services Department
Lexington-Fayette Government Center, 200 E. Main St., Lexington, KY 40507
Fax: (859) 258-3909 Internet: www.lexingtonky.gov/index.aspx?page=155

■ Commissioner **Geoff Reed** .... (859) 258-3900
E-mail: greed@lexingtonky.gov
Education: Kentucky BA, MPA

Facilities and Fleet Management Division
1555 Old Frankfort Pike, Lexington, KY 40504
Fax: (859) 258-3925

Director **Jamshid Baradaran** .... (859) 258-3920
E-mail: jbaradaran@lexingtonky.gov
Education: Kentucky BA; Cincinnati MA
Deputy Director **Ben Turpin** .... (859) 258-3920
E-mail: bturpin@lexingtonky.gov
Design and Construction Operations Manager
Mark Arnold .... (859) 258-3920
E-mail: marnold@lexingtonky.gov
Fleet Director **Mark Caton** .... (859) 258-3910

Parks and Recreation Division
469 Parkway Drive, Lexington, KY 40504
Tel: (859) 288-2900 Fax: (859) 254-0142

Director **Monica Conrad** .... (859) 288-2900
Deputy Director, Parks **Chris Cooperrider** .... (859) 288-2980
Deputy Director of Enterprise **Brian Rogers** .... (859) 288-2929
Maintenance Superintendent **Edmond Chaney** .... (859) 288-2937
Planning and Design Superintendent
Michelle Kosieniak .... (859) 288-2979

Lexington-Fayette County Health Department
650 Newtown Pike, Lexington, KY 40508
Fax: (859) 288-2359 Internet: www.lexingtonhealthdepartment.org/

Commissioner **Dr. Kraig Eckman Humbaugh** .... (859) 288-2486
Note: Effective June 2016 Fax: (859) 288-2359
Education: Yale 1989 MD
Public Health Officer **Roanya Rice** .... (859) 288-2490
Communicable Disease Manager **Jessica Cobb** .... (859) 889-4299
Fax: (859) 231-9459
Public Health Clinical Services Manager **(Vacant)** .... (859) 288-2316
Fax: (859) 252-0292
Public Health Nursing Manager **Lois A. Davis** .... (859) 288-2323
Fax: (859) 288-2319

Department of Planning
101 East Vine Street, #700, Lexington, KY 40507
Fax: (859) 258-3163

Director **Christopher D. "Chris" King** .... (859) 258-3262

Building Inspection Division
101 East Vine Street, 2nd Floor, Lexington, KY 40507
Fax: (859) 258-3780

Director **Dewey Crowe** .... (859) 258-3770

Code Enforcement
101 East Vine Street, 1st Floor, Lexington, KY 40507
Fax: (859) 425-2274

Director **Ken Armstrong** .... (859) 425-2255

Engineering Division
101 East Vine Street, 4th Floor, Lexington, KY 40507

Chief Engineer **Doug Burton** .... (859) 258-3410
E-mail: dburton@lexingtonky.gov

Historic Preservation Division
Government Center, 200 E. Main St., Lexington, KY 40507
Tel: (859) 258-3265 Fax: (859) 258-3394

Director **Bettie Kerr** .... (859) 258-3265

Law Department
Lexington-Fayette Government Center, 200 E. Main St., Lexington, KY 40507
Fax: (859) 258-3538 Internet: www.lexingtonky.gov/index.aspx?page=310

■ Commissioner **Janet M. Graham** .... (859) 258-3500
E-mail: jgraham@lexingtonky.gov
Education: Kentucky JD

★ Elected Official ▲ Appointed by Legislature ▼ Appointed by Governor ► Appointed by Board or Commission ● Appointed by Judge
■ Appointed by Mayor △ Appointed by Freeholders ▽ Appointed by Supervisor ▷ Appointed by County Executive ○ Appointed by Council

Law Department *continued*

Managing Attorney **David J. Barberie** . . . . (859) 258-3500
Managing Attorney **Glenda H. George** . . . . (859) 258-3500
Managing Attorney **Michael Keith Horn** . . . . (859) 258-3500

Public Safety Department

200 E. Main St., Lexington, KY 40507
Tel: (859) 258-3280 Fax: (859) 258-3103
Internet: www.lexingtonky.gov/index.aspx?page=30

■ Commissioner **Ronnie Bastin** . . . . (859) 258-3280
E-mail: rbastin@lexingtonky.gov

Community Corrections Division

600 Old Frankfort Circle, Lexington, KY 40507
Fax: (859) 425-2605 Internet: www.lexingtonky.gov/index.aspx?page=176

Director **(Vacant)** . . . . (859) 425-2700

Division of Enhanced 911

200 East Main Street, Suite 313, Lexington, KY 40507
Internet: www.lexingtonky.gov/index.aspx?page=1399

Director **Robert Stack** . . . . (859) 425-2552
E-mail: rstack@lexingtonky.gov Fax: (859) 258-3103

Environmental and Emergency Management Division

115 Cisco Road, Lexington, KY 40504
Fax: (859) 252-8689

Director **Pat Dugger** . . . . (859) 258-3784
E-mail: patd@lexingtonky.gov

Fire and Emergency Services Division

219 E. Third St., Lexington, KY 40507
Fax: (859) 281-6136 Internet: www.lexingtonky.gov/index.aspx?page=31
Internet: http://www.lexingtonky.gov/index.aspx?page=32

■ Fire Chief **Kristin Chilton** . . . . (859) 231-5600

Division of Police

150 E. Main St., Lexington, KY 40507
Fax: (859) 258-3574 Internet: www.lexingtonky.gov/index.aspx?page=67

Police Chief **Mark G. Barnard** . . . . (859) 258-3600
Assistant Police Chief **(Vacant)** . . . . (859) 258-3600

Department of Social Services

Lexington-Fayette Urban-County Government Center,
200 East Main Street, Room 328, Lexington, KY 40507
Tel: (859) 258-3804 Fax: (859) 258-3406

■ Commissioner **Chris Ford** . . . . (859) 258-3819
E-mail: cford2@lexingtonky.gov

Adult and Tenant Services Division

Central Kentucky Job Center Building, 1055 Industry Road,
Lexington, KY 40505
Fax: (859) 425-2055 Internet: www.lexingtonky.gov/index.aspx?page=314

Director **Connie Godfrey** . . . . (859) 258-3810

Division of Family Services

1135 Red Mile Place, Lexington, KY 40504
Tel: (859) 288-4040 Fax: (859) 288-4061
Internet: www.lexingtonky.gov/index.aspx?page=316

Director **Joanna Rodes** . . . . (859) 288-4040

Youth Services Division

1177 Red Mile Place, Lexington, KY 40504
Tel: (859) 246-4370 Fax: (859) 231-1213
Internet: www.lexingtonky.gov/index.aspx?page=317

Director **Stephanie Hong** . . . . (859) 246-4393

Lexington-Fayette Urban County Council

Lexington-Fayette Government Center, 200 E. Main St.,
Lexington, KY 40507
Tel: (859) 258-3200 Fax: (859) 258-3838
Internet: www.lexingtonky.gov/index.aspx?page=325

★ Vice Mayor **Steve Kay** (At-Large) . . . . (859) 258-3219
Term Expires: December 31, 2018
E-mail: skay@lexingtonky.gov
★ Council Member **James Brown** (District 1) . . . . (859) 258-3216
Term Expires: December 31, 2016
E-mail: jbrown2@lexingtonky.gov
★ Council Member **Shevawn Akers** (District 2) . . . . (859) 258-3217
Term Expires: December 31, 2016
E-mail: sakers@lexingtonky.gov
★ Council Member **Jake Gibbs** (District 3) . . . . (859) 258-3222
Term Expires: December 31, 2016
E-mail: jgibbs@lexingtonky.gov
★ Council Member **Susan Lamb** (District 4) . . . . (859) 258-3223
Term Expires: December 31, 2016
E-mail: slamb@lexingtonky.gov
★ Council Member **William "Bill" Farmer, Jr.** (District 5) . . (859) 258-3213
Term Expires: December 31, 2016
E-mail: bfarmer@lexingtonky.gov
Education: Kentucky BBA
★ Council Member **Angela Evans** (District 6) . . . . (859) 258-3212
Term Expires: December 31, 2016
E-mail: aevans@lexingtonky.gov
★ Council Member **Jennifer Scutchfield** (District 7) . . . . . . (859) 258-3214
Term Expires: December 31, 2016
E-mail: jscutchfield@lexingtonky.gov
★ Council Member **Fred V. Brown** (District 8) . . . . (859) 258-3220
Term Expires: December 31, 2016
E-mail: fbrown@lexingtonky.gov
Education: Kentucky BS
★ Council Member **Jennifer Mossotti** (District 9) . . . . (859) 258-3215
Term Expires: December 31, 2016
E-mail: jmossotti@lexingtonky.gov
Education: Eastern Kentucky BA
★ Council Member **Amanda Mays Bledsoe** (District 10) . . . (859) 258-3224
Term Expires: December 31, 2016
E-mail: abledsoe@lexingtonky.gov
★ Council Member **Peggy Henson** (District 11) . . . . (859) 258-3218
Term Expires: December 31, 2016
E-mail: phenson@lexingtonky.gov
★ Council Member **Russ Hensley** (District 12) . . . . (859) 258-3221
Term Expires: December 31, 2016
E-mail: rhensley@lexingtonky.gov
★ Council Member **Richard Moloney** (At-Large) . . . . (859) 258-3211
Term Expires: December 31, 2018
E-mail: rmoloney@lexingtonky.gov
★ Council Member **Kevin O. Stinnett** (At-Large) . . . . (859) 258-3225
Term Expires: December 31, 2018
E-mail: kstinnett@lexingtonky.gov
Council Administrator **Stacey Maynard** . . . . (859) 258-3200
E-mail: smaynard@lexingtonky.gov
Council Clerk **Martha Allen** . . . . (859) 258-3240
Fax: (859) 258-3393

Office of the Coroner

247 E. Second St., Lexington, KY 40507-2103

★ Coroner **Gary W. Ginn** . . . . (859) 455-5700
Term Expires: December 31, 2018
E-mail: gginn@lexingtonky.gov
Assistant Coroner **Claire Dixon-Conder** . . . . (859) 455-5700
Chief Deputy **(Vacant)** . . . . (859) 455-5700
Deputy **Albert Beatty** . . . . (859) 455-5700
Deputy **John Cox** . . . . (859) 455-5700
Deputy **Michael Durbin** . . . . (859) 455-5700
Deputy **John McCarty** . . . . (859) 455-5700

(continued on next page)

★ Elected Official ▲ Appointed by Legislature ▼ Appointed by Governor ▶ Appointed by Board or Commission ● Appointed by Judge
■ Appointed by Mayor △ Appointed by Freeholders ▽ Appointed by Supervisor ▷ Appointed by County Executive ○ Appointed by Council

Office of the Coroner *continued*

Deputy **Shea Willis** .... (859) 455-5700

Office of the County Clerk

162 E. Main St., Lexington, KY 40507
Fax: (859) 231-9619 Internet: www.fayettecountyclerk.com/

★County Clerk **Donald W. "Don" Blevins, Jr.** .... (859) 253-3344
Term Expires: December 31, 2018
E-mail: info@fayettecountyclerk.com
Education: Kentucky 1959 BS

Office of the County Attorney

201 East Main Street, Suite 600, Lexington, KY 40507
Fax: (859) 253-2487 Internet: www.fayettecountyattorney.com/

★County Attorney **Larry S. Roberts** .... (859) 254-4941
Term Expires: December 31, 2018
E-mail: larrys.roberts@fayettecountyattorney.com
Education: Kentucky 1966 BA, 1969 JD

Office of the Fayette County Sheriff

150 North Limestone, Suite 265, Lexington, KY 40507
Tel: (859) 252-1771 Fax: (859) 259-0973
Internet: www.fayettesheriff.com/

★Sheriff **Kathy H. Witt** .... (859) 252-1771
Term Expires: December 31, 2018 Fax: (859) 259-0972
E-mail: fayettesheriff@fayettesheriff.com

Fayette County Public Schools

701 East Main Street, Lexington, KY 40502
Fax: (859) 381-4303 Internet: www.fcps.net/

Superintendent **Emmanuel "Manny" Caulk** .... (859) 381-4104

City of Lincoln, Nebraska

County-City Bldg., 555 S. 10th St., Lincoln, NE 68508
Tel: (402) 441-7171 (Information) Internet: www.lincoln.ne.gov

County: Lancaster **Election Type:** Nonpartisan **Year Founded:** 1867
Year Incorporated: 1869 **Population:** 277,348 (2015)
Employees: 1,953 **Fiscal Year:** 2016 **Budget:** $306,336,000

Office of the Mayor

County-City Building, 555 South 10th Street, Suite 208,
Lincoln, NE 68508
Tel: (402) 441-7511 Fax: (402) 441-7120
Internet: http://lincoln.ne.gov/city/mayor/

Employees: 14 **Fiscal Year:** 2016 **Budget:** $796,000

★Mayor **Chris Beutler** .... (402) 441-7511
Began Service: 2007
Term Expires: May 2019
E-mail: mayor@lincoln.ne.gov
Date of Birth: 1942
Education: Yale 1966 BA; Nebraska 1973 JD
Career: Member, Reference Committee, Select Committees, Nebraska Unicameral Legislature; State Senator, State Senator Chris Beutler (I-NE, District 28), Nebraska Unicameral Legislature (1982-2006)

Chief of Staff **Rick Hoppe** .... (402) 441-6036
Deputy Chief of Staff **(Vacant)** .... (402) 441-8044
Aide to the Mayor **Millie Burton** .... (402) 441-7511
Aide to the Mayor **Denise Pearce** .... (402) 441-8044
Scheduler **Jamie Phillips** .... (402) 441-6897

Office of the Mayor *continued*

Ombudsman **Linda K. Quenzer** .... (402) 441-7511
E-mail: lquenzer@lincoln.ne.gov

Aging Partners

1005 O Street, Lincoln, NE 68508
Tel: (402) 441-7070 Fax: (402) 441-7160
E-mail: agingpartners@lincoln.ne.gov
Internet: http://lincoln.ne.gov/city/mayor/aging/

■Director **Randy Jones** .... (402) 441-7070
E-mail: agingpartners@lincoln.ne.gov Fax: (402) 441-7160
Area Programs and Nutrition **Denise Boyd** .... (402) 441-6160
Fax: (402) 441-6154

Citizen Information Center

555 S. 10th St., Suite 208, Lincoln, NE 68508
Fax: (402) 441-7120 E-mail: cic@lincoln.ne.gov

Manager **Diane Gonzolas** .... (402) 441-7831
E-mail: dgonzolas@lincoln.ne.gov
Education: Kansas State 1980 BS
Government Access Television Studio Coordinator
Jamie Wenz .... (402) 441-6688
E-mail: jwenz@lincoln.ne.gov
Graphic Design Supervisor **(Vacant)** .... (402) 441-7317

Human Rights Commission/Affirmative Action Office

555 South 10th Street, Suite 340, Lincoln, NE 68508
Tel: (402) 441-7624 Fax: (402) 441-6937

■Director **Kimberley Taylor-Riley** .... (402) 441-8691
E-mail: ktaylor-riley@lincoln.ne.gov

Office of the City Attorney/Law Department

County-City Building, 555 South 10th Street, Suite 300,
Lincoln, NE 68508
Fax: (402) 441-8812 E-mail: attorney@lincoln.ne.gov

Employees: 32 **Fiscal Year:** 2016 **Budget:** $3,113,000

■City Attorney **Jeff Kirkpatrick** .... (402) 441-7281
E-mail: jkirkpatrick@lincoln.ne.gov
Chief Prosecutor **John C. McQuinn II** .... (402) 441-7281

Lincoln Airport Authority

P.O. Box 80407, Lincoln, NE 68501
Fax: (402) 458-2490 Internet: www.lincolnairport.com

Executive Director **David S. Haring** .... (402) 458-2400
Deputy Director of Administration **April McDaniel** .... (402) 458-2400
E-mail: amcdaniel@lincolnairport.com
Deputy Director of Engineering **Jon Large** .... (402) 458-2400
E-mail: jlarge@lincolnairport.com
Education: Nebraska BS
Deputy Director of Operations **Bob McNally** .... (402) 458-2400
E-mail: rmcnally@lincolnairport.com
Education: North Dakota BA

Building and Safety Department

City-County Building, 555 South 10th Street, Room 203,
Lincoln, NE 68508-3995
Fax: (402) 441-8214 E-mail: bldgsafe@lincoln.ne.gov
Internet: http://lincoln.ne.gov/city/build/index.htm

■Director (Interim) **Chad Blahak** .... (402) 441-7049
E-mail: cblahak@lincoln.ne.gov

Lincoln Electric System

1040 O St., Lincoln, NE 68508-3635
P.O. Box 80869, Lincoln, NE 68501-0869
Tel: (402) 475-4211 Fax: (402) 475-9759 Internet: www.les.com

Administrator and Chief Executive Officer
Kevin G. Wailes .... (402) 475-4211

★Elected Official ▲Appointed by Legislature ▼Appointed by Governor ▶Appointed by Board or Commission ●Appointed by Judge
■Appointed by Mayor △Appointed by Freeholders ▽Appointed by Supervisor ▷Appointed by County Executive ○Appointed by Council

Finance Department

City-County Bldg., 555 S. 10th St., Room 103, Lincoln, NE 68508
Fax: (402) 441-8325 E-mail: finance@lincoln.ne.gov

Employees: 30 **Fiscal Year:** 2016 **Budget:** $2,458,000

■ Director **Steve Hubka** .... (402) 441-7411
E-mail: shubka@lincoln.ne.gov
Payroll Administrator **Madalyn Popken** .... (402) 441-7430
E-mail: mpopken@lincoln.ne.gov
Purchasing Agent **Robert Walla** .... (402) 441-7416
E-mail: rwalla@lincoln.ne.gov

Office of the City Controller

City Controller **Peggy Tharnish** .... (402) 441-7421

Office of the Budget Officer

Budget Analyst **Jan Bolin** .... (402) 441-8306
E-mail: jbolin@lincoln.ne.gov

Office of the City Clerk

City Clerk **Teresa Meier** .... (402) 441-7436
E-mail: tmeier@lincoln.ne.gov
Deputy City Clerk **Sony Phan** .... (402) 441-7437
E-mail: sphan@lincoln.ne.gov

Office of the City Treasurer

City Treasurer **Melinda Jones** .... (402) 441-7458
Assistant City Treasurer **Joel Wittrock** .... (402) 441-8310

Emergency Communications

Hall of Justice, 575 S. 10th St., Lincoln, NE 68508
Fax: (402) 476-0528

911 Communications Director **Julie Righter Dove** .... (402) 441-7252
E-mail: jrighter@lincoln.ne.gov

Information Services

233 South 10th Street, Suite 200, Lincoln, NE 68508-2250
Fax: (402) 441-6189

Chief Information Officer **Steven L. Henderson** .... (402) 441-7823
E-mail: shenderson@lincoln.ne.gov
Microcomputer/Network Support Coordinator
Craig Gifford .... (402) 441-7582
E-mail: cgifford@lincoln.ne.gov
Systems Coordinator **James Anderson** .... (402) 441-7268
E-mail: janderson@lincoln.ne.gov

Lincoln Fire and Rescue

1801 Q St., Lincoln, NE 68508
Fax: (402) 441-7098 E-mail: fire@lincoln.ne.gov

Employees: 264 **Fiscal Year:** 2016 **Budget:** $26,136,000

■ Fire Chief **Tim Linke** .... (402) 441-8350
E-mail: tlinke@lincoln.ne.gov

Lincoln-Lancaster County Health Department [LLCHD]

3140 N Street, Lincoln, NE 68510-1514
Tel: (402) 441-8000 Fax: (402) 441-6229 E-mail: health@lincoln.ne.gov
Internet: www.lincoln.ne.gov/city/health

Employees: 84 **Fiscal Year:** 2016 **Budget:** $10,902,000

■ Director **Judith A. Halstead** .... (402) 441-8001
E-mail: jhalstead@lincoln.ne.gov
Assistant Director **(Vacant)** .... (402) 441-8042
Dental Division Manager **Gwendy Meginnis** .... (402) 441-8014
Environmental Public Health Division Manager
Scott Holmes .... (402) 441-8019
Health Promotion and Outreach Division Manager
Charlotte Burke .... (402) 441-8045
Community Health Services Division Manager
Andrea Haberman .... (402) 441-8054
Animal Control Program Manager **Steve Beal** .... (402) 441-7900
Information and Fiscal Manager **Kathy Cook** .... (402) 441-8092
E-mail: kcook@lincoln.ne.gov

Lincoln-Lancaster County Health Department *continued*

System Specialist III **Trudy Franssen** .... (402) 441-8097
E-mail: tfranssen@lincoln.ne.gov
Date of Birth: November 28, 1956

Human Resources Department

City-County Bldg., 555 S. 10th St., Lincoln, NE 68508
Tel: (402) 441-7597 Fax: (402) 441-8748
Internet: http://www.lincoln.ne.gov/city/person/

Employees: 21 **Fiscal Year:** 2016 **Budget:** $1,090,000

■ Director **Doug McDaniel** .... (402) 441-7888
E-mail: dmcdaniel@lincoln.ne.gov
Personnel Coordinator **Kari Foote** .... (402) 441-7880
E-mail: pkant@lincoln.ne.gov Fax: (402) 441-8748
Risk Manager **William C. Kostner** .... (402) 441-6009
E-mail: bkostner@lincoln.ne.gov Fax: (402) 441-6800

Lincoln City Libraries

136 S. 14th St., Lincoln, NE 68508-1899
Tel: (402) 441-8500 TTY: (402) 441-8589 Fax: (402) 441-8586
E-mail: library@lincolnlibraries.org Internet: www.lincolnlibraries.org/

Employees: 104 **Fiscal Year:** 2016 **Budget:** $8,714,000

▶ Director **Pat Leach** .... (402) 441-8510
E-mail: p.leach@lincolnlibraries.org
Assistant Director **Julee Hector** .... (402) 441-8511
E-mail: j.hector@lincolnlibraries.org

Parks and Recreation Department

2740 A St., Lincoln, NE 68502
Tel: (402) 441-7847 Fax: (402) 441-8706 E-mail: parks@lincoln.ne.gov
Internet: http://lincoln.ne.gov/city/parks/

Employees: 240 **Fiscal Year:** 2016 **Budget:** $13,339,000

Director **Lynn Johnson** .... (402) 441-7847

Planning Department

County-City Building, 555 S. 10th St., Room 213, Lincoln, NE 68508
Fax: (402) 441-6377 E-mail: plan@lincoln.ne.gov
Internet: http://lincoln.ne.gov/city/plan/

Employees: 20 **Fiscal Year:** 2016 **Budget:** $1,754,000

■ Director of Planning **David R. Cary** .... (402) 441-7491
E-mail: dcary@lincoln.ne.gov
Historic Preservation **Edward Zimmer** .... (402) 441-6360
Administrative Officer **Geri Rorabaugh** .... (402) 441-6365
E-mail: grorabaugh@lincoln.ne.gov

Police Department

575 South 10th Street, Lincoln, NE 68508-2293
Tel: (402) 441-6000 Fax: (402) 441-8492 E-mail: lpd@cjis.lincoln.ne.gov
Internet: http://lincoln.ne.gov/city/police/

Employees: 466 **Fiscal Year:** 2016 **Budget:** $44,946,000

■ Chief of Police (Interim) **Brian Jackson** .... (402) 441-7238
E-mail: bjackson@lincoln.ne.gov
Assistant Chief **Brian Jackson** .... (402) 441-7201
Information Systems Manager **Clair Lindquist** .... (402) 441-7707
E-mail: lpd172@cjis.lincoln.ne.gov Fax: (402) 441-7010

Public Works and Utilities

City-County Bldg., 555 S. 10th St., Lincoln, NE 68508
Tel: (402) 441-7548 Fax: (402) 441-7590
E-mail: pubworks@lincoln.ne.gov
Internet: http://lincoln.ne.gov/city/pworks/

Employees: 38 **Fiscal Year:** 2016 **Budget:** $4,071,000

■ Director (Interim) **Thomas S. Shafer** .... (402) 441-7566
E-mail: tshafer@lincoln.ne.gov
Public Works and Utilities Business Manager (Acting)
Cynthia Roth .... (402) 441-7539

★ Elected Official ▲ Appointed by Legislature ▼ Appointed by Governor ▶ Appointed by Board or Commission ● Appointed by Judge
■ Appointed by Mayor △ Appointed by Freeholders ▽ Appointed by Supervisor ▷ Appointed by County Executive ○ Appointed by Council

Urban Development Department

555 South 10th Street, Suite 205, Lincoln, NE 68508
Tel: (402) 441-7606 Fax: (402) 441-8711
E-mail: urbandev@lincoln.ne.gov Internet: http://lincoln.ne.gov/city/urban/

Employees: 10 **Fiscal Year:** 2016 **Budget:** $850,000

Director **David M. Landis** .... (402) 441-7126
E-mail: dlandis@lincoln.ne.gov
Date of Birth: June 10, 1948
Education: Nebraska 1970 BA, 1971 JD, 1995 MCRP; Nebraska (Omaha) 1984 MPA

Assistant Director **Dallas McGee** .... (402) 441-7857
E-mail: dmcgee@lincoln.ne.gov

Community Development Manager **Wynn Hjermstad** .... (402) 441-8211
E-mail: whjermstad@lincoln.ne.gov

Real Estate and Relocation/Property Management Manager **Steve Werthmann** .... (402) 441-8621
E-mail: swerthmann@lincoln.ne.gov

Workforce Development Manager **Vicki Leech** .... (402) 441-7121
1010 O Street, Lincoln, NE 68508 Fax: (402) 441-6038
E-mail: vleech@lincoln.ne.gov

Office of the City Council

County-City Bldg., 555 S. 10th St., Room 111, Lincoln, NE 68508
Fax: (402) 441-6533 E-mail: council@lincoln.ne.gov
Internet: http://lincoln.ne.gov/city/council/

Employees: 8 **Fiscal Year:** 2016 **Budget:** $248,000

★ Chair **Trent Fellers** (At-Large) .... (402) 441-7515
Term Expires: May 2017
E-mail: tfellers@lincoln.ne.gov

★ Vice Chair **Leirion Gaylor Baird** (At-Large) .... (402) 441-7515
Term Expires: May 2017
E-mail: lgaylorbaird@lincoln.ne.gov

★ Council Member **Cynthia Lamm** (District 1) .... (402) 441-7515
Term Expires: May 2019
Education: Nebraska JD

★ Council Member **Jon Camp** (District 2) .... (402) 441-7515
Term Expires: May 2019
E-mail: jcamp@lincoln.ne.gov
Education: Nebraska BS, JD

★ Council Member **Jane Raybould** (District 3) .... (402) 441-7515
Term Expires: May 2019
Education: Creighton; Georgetown

★ Council Member **Carl Eskridge** (District 4) .... (402) 441-7515
Term Expires: May 2019
E-mail: ceskridge@lincoln.ne.gov
Education: St Andrews 1975 BA; Nebraska 1996 JD

★ Council Member **Roy A. Christensen** (At-Large) .... (402) 441-7515
Term Expires: May 2017
E-mail: rchristensen@lincoln.ne.gov

Clerk **Mary Meyer** .... (402) 441-7515
E-mail: mmeyer@lincoln.ne.gov

City of Little Rock, Arkansas

City Hall, 500 West Markham, Little Rock, AR 72201
Tel: (501) 371-4510 (Information) Internet: www.littlerock.org

County: Pulaski **Election Type:** Nonpartisan **Population:** 197,992 (2015)

Office of the Mayor and Board of Directors

City Hall, 500 West Markham, Suite 203, Little Rock, AR 72201
Tel: (501) 371-4510 Fax: (501) 371-4498 E-mail: board@littlerock.org

★ Mayor **Mark Stodola** .... (501) 371-4510
Began Service: 2007
Term Expires: December 31, 2018
E-mail: mayor@littlerock.org
Education: Iowa BA; Arkansas JD
Career: City Attorney, Office of the City Attorney, City of Little Rock, Arkansas (1985-1990); Prosecuting Attorney, Sixth District, State of Arkansas (1990-1996)
Administrative Assistant **Starla Frazier** .... (501) 371-4791
E-mail: sfrazier@littlerock.org

★ Board Member **Erma Hendrix** (Ward 1) .... (501) 371-4510
Term Expires: December 31, 2018
E-mail: ehendrix@littlerock.org

★ Board Member **Ken Richardson** (Ward 2) .... (501) 371-4510
Term Expires: December 31, 2018
E-mail: krichardson@littlerock.org

★ Board Member **Kathy Webb** (Ward 3) .... (501) 371-4510
Term Expires: December 31, 2018
E-mail: kwebb@littlerock.org

★ Board Member **Brad Cazort** (Ward 4) Room 203 .... (501) 371-4510
Term Expires: December 31, 2016
E-mail: bcazort@littlerock.org
Education: Arkansas (Little Rock) 1985 BA, 1988 JD

★ Board Member **Lance Hines** (Ward 5) .... (501) 371-4510
Term Expires: December 31, 2018
E-mail: lhines@littlerock.org

★ Board Member **Doris Wright** (Ward 6) .... (501) 371-4510
Term Expires: December 31, 2018
E-mail: board@littlerock.org

★ Board Member **B. J. "Brenda" Wyrick** (Ward 7) .... (501) 371-4510
Term Expires: December 31, 2018
E-mail: bwyrick@littlerock.org

★ Board Member **Joan Adcock** (At-Large) .... (501) 371-4510
Term Expires: December 31, 2016
E-mail: jadcock@littlerock.org

★ Board Member **Gene Fortson** (At-Large) .... (501) 371-4510
Term Expires: December 31, 2016
E-mail: gfortson@littlerock.org

★ Board Member **Dean Kumpuris** (At-Large) .... (501) 371-4510
Term Expires: December 31, 2016
E-mail: dkumpuris@littlerock.org
Education: Washington and Lee BA; Emory MD

Office of the City Attorney

City Hall, 500 W. Markham, Suite 310, Little Rock, AR 72201
Fax: (501) 371-4675

▶ City Attorney **Thomas M. Carpenter** Room 300 .... (501) 371-4527
E-mail: tcarpenter@littlerock.org

Office of the City Clerk

City Hall, 500 West Markham, Room 200, Little Rock, AR 72201
Fax: (501) 371-4857

City Clerk **Susan Langley** .... (501) 371-6803
E-mail: slangley@littlerock.org

Assistant City Clerk **Toya Robinson** .... (501) 244-5494
E-mail: tarobinson@littlerock.org

★ Elected Official ▲ Appointed by Legislature ▼ Appointed by Governor ▶ Appointed by Board or Commission ● Appointed by Judge
■ Appointed by Mayor △ Appointed by Freeholders ▽ Appointed by Supervisor ▷ Appointed by County Executive ○ Appointed by Council

Office of the City Manager
City Hall, 500 W. Markham, Little Rock, AR 72201
Tel: (501) 371-4510 Fax: (501) 371-4498

▶ City Manager **Bruce T. Moore** Room 203 .... (501) 371-4510
E-mail: bmoore@littlerock.org
Education: Henderson State 1989 BS; Arkansas State 1994 MA
Assistant City Manager **James Jones** .... (501) 371-4788
E-mail: jejones@littlerock.org

Ambulance Authority
P.O. Box 2452, Little Rock, AR 72203-2452
Tel: (501) 301-1400

Executive Director **Jon Swanson** .... (501) 301-1400

Arts and Culture Commission
City Hall, 500 W. Markham, Room 203, Little Rock, AR 72201
Fax: (501) 371-4498

Assistant **Scott Carter** .... (501) 918-5262

Bill and Hillary Clinton National Airport
One Airport Dr., Little Rock, AR 72202-4489
Fax: (501) 372-0612

Executive Director/Airport Manager **Ronald Mathieu** .... (501) 372-3439

Finance Department
City Hall, 500 W. Markham, Suite 208, Little Rock, AR 72201
Tel: (501) 371-4806 Fax: (501) 244-5446
Internet: www.littlerock.org/citydepartments/finance/

Finance Director and Treasurer **Sara Lenehan** .... (501) 371-4806

Fire Department
624 South Chester, Little Rock, AR 72201
Tel: (501) 918-3700 Fax: (501) 918-3734
Internet: www.littlerock.org/citydepartments/fire/

Fire Chief **Gregory Summers** .... (501) 918-3700
E-mail: gsummers@littlerock.org

Housing and Neighborhood Programs
500 West Markham, Suite 120, Little Rock, AR 72201
Tel: (501) 371-4849

Director **Andre Bernard** .... (501) 371-4849

Animal Services Division
4500 Kramer Street, Little Rock, AR 72204
Fax: (501) 376-7856

Manager **Tracy Roark** .... (501) 376-3067

Neighborhood Programs Division
City Hall, 500 West Markham, #120W, Little Rock, AR 72201

Code Enforcement Manager **Edward J. Garland** .... (501) 371-4748

Human Resources Department
City Hall, 500 West Markham, Suite 130W, Little Rock, AR 72201
Fax: (501) 371-4496 E-mail: HR-Employment@littlerock.state.ar.us

Director **Stacey Witherell** .... (501) 371-4590
E-mail: switherell@littlerock.org

Information Technology Department
718 W. Markham, Little Rock, AR 72201
Fax: (501) 371-4616

Director **Randy Foshee** .... (501) 371-4745
E-mail: rfoshee@littlerock.org

Central Arkansas Library System
100 Rock St., Little Rock, AR 72201
Fax: (501) 375-7451 Internet: www.cals.org

Library Director **Nate Coulter** .... (501) 918-3051

Little Rock Convention and Visitors Bureau
P.O. Box 3232, Little Rock, AR 72203
Internet: www.littlerock.com

Chief Executive Officer **Gretchen Hall** .... (501) 376-4781

Little Rock School District
810 West Markham, Little Rock, AR 72201
Internet: www.lrsd.org/

School Superintendent **Michael Poore** .... (501) 447-1000
Note: Effective July 1, 2016. Appointed by Arkansas Department of Education.

Metropolitan Housing Alliance
100 South Arch, Little Rock, AR 72201
Tel: (501) 340-4821 Fax: (501) 340-4845 Internet: www.mhapha.org

Executive Director and Director of Finance
Rodney L. Forte .... (501) 340-4821

The Museum of Discovery
500 President Clinton Avenue, Little Rock, AR 72201
Internet: http://museumofdiscovery.org/

Executive Director **Kelley Bass** .... (501) 396-7050

Parks and Recreation Department
City Hall, 500 West Markham, Room 108, Little Rock, AR 72201
Fax: (501) 371-6832

Director **Truman Tolefree** .... (501) 371-4770

Planning and Development Department
723 W. Markham, Little Rock, AR 72201
Fax: (501) 399-3435

Director **Tony Bozynski** .... (501) 371-4790
E-mail: tbozynski@littlerock.org
Adjustment Board Contact **Monte Moore** .... (501) 371-4790
E-mail: mmoore@littlerock.org
Building Code Appeals Board Contact **Charles Givens** ... (501) 371-4828
Fax: (501) 371-6863
Little Rock Planning Commission Contact **Dana Carney** .. (501) 371-4790
Historic District Commission Contact **Brian Minyard** .... (501) 371-4790

Police Department
700 W. Markham, Little Rock, AR 72201
Tel: (501) 371-4605 Fax: (501) 399-3469
Internet: http://www.littlerock.org/citydepartments/police

Chief of Police **Kenton Buckner** .... (501) 371-4621
Assistant Police Chief **Wayne Bewley** .... (501) 371-4621
Assistant Police Chief **Haywood Finks** .... (501) 371-4621
Assistant Police Chief **Alice Fulk** .... (501) 371-4621
Communications Center Manager **Laura Martin** .... (501) 371-4540

Port Authority
10600 Industrial Harbor Drive, Little Rock, AR 72206
Fax: (501) 490-1800 Internet: http://lrport.dina.org
E-mail: lrport@dina.org

Executive Director **Bryan Day** .... (501) 490-1468

Public Works Department
701 W. Markham, Little Rock, AR 72201
Fax: (501) 371-4843

Director **Jon Honeywell** .... (501) 371-4475

★ Elected Official ▲ Appointed by Legislature ▼ Appointed by Governor ▶ Appointed by Board or Commission ● Appointed by Judge
■ Appointed by Mayor △ Appointed by Freeholders ▽ Appointed by Supervisor ▷ Appointed by County Executive ○ Appointed by Council

City of Long Beach, California

333 West Ocean Boulevard, Long Beach, CA 90802
Tel: (562) 570-6555 (Information) Internet: www.longbeach.gov

County: Los Angeles **Election Type:** Nonpartisan **Year Incorporated:** 1897 **Population:** 474,140 (2015)

Office of the Mayor and City Council

Civic Center Plaza, 333 West Ocean Boulevard, 14th Floor, Long Beach, CA 90802
Tel: (562) 570-6801 TTY: (562) 570-6629 Fax: (562) 570-6538

★Mayor **Dr. Robert Garcia** . . . . . (562) 570-6801
Began Service: July 15, 2014
Term Expires: July 17, 2018
E-mail: mayor@longbeach.gov
Chief of Staff **Mark Taylor** . . . . . (562) 570-6801
Legislative Deputy **Devin Cotter** . . . . . (562) 570-5229
★Council Member **Lena Gonzazlez** (District 1) . . . . . (562) 570-6919
Term Expires: July 17, 2018 Fax: (562) 570-6590
E-mail: district1@longbeach.gov
★Council Member **Suja Lowenthal** (District 2) . . . . . (562) 570-6684
Term Expires: July 12, 2016 Fax: (562) 570-6882
E-mail: district2@longbeach.gov
Education: UCLA; Cal State (Los Angeles) MBA; USC PhD
★Council Member **Suzie Price** (District 3) . . . . . (562) 570-6300
Term Expires: July 17, 2018 Fax: (562) 570-6186
E-mail: district3@longbeach.gov
★Council Member **Daryl Supernaw** (District 4) . . . . . (562) 570-6918
Term Expires: July 12, 2016 Fax: (562) 570-5235
★Council Member **Stacy Mungo** (District 5) . . . . . (562) 570-5555
Term Expires: July 17, 2018 Fax: (562) 570-6857
E-mail: district5@longbeach.gov
★Council Member **Dee Andrews** (District 6) . . . . . (562) 570-6816
Term Expires: July 12, 2016 Fax: (562) 570-7135
E-mail: dee.andrews@longbeach.gov
★Council Member **Roberto Uranga** (District 7) . . . . . (562) 570-7777
Term Expires: July 17, 2018 Fax: (562) 570-6954
E-mail: district7@longbeach.gov
★Council Member **Al Austin** (District 8) . . . . . (562) 570-6685
Term Expires: July 12, 2016 Fax: (562) 570-5982
E-mail: district8@longbeach.gov
★Council Member **Rex Richardson** (District 9) . . . . . (562) 570-6137
Term Expires: July 17, 2018 Fax: (562) 570-6659
E-mail: district9@longbeach.gov

Office of the City Manager

Civic Center Plaza, 333 West Ocean Boulevard, 13th Floor, Long Beach, CA 90802
Fax: (562) 570-6583

○City Manager **Patrick H. "Pat" West** . . . . . (562) 570-6916
E-mail: citymanager@longbeach.gov
Education: UC Irvine BA; Cal State (Los Angeles) MA; Cal State (Dominguez) MBA
Assistant City Manager **Tom Modica** . . . . . (562) 570-5091
E-mail: tom.modica@longbeach.gov
Deputy City Manager **Arturo Sanchez** . . . . . (562) 570-5028
E-mail: arturo.sanchez@longbeach.gov
Education: UC Berkeley 1996 BA; New Col California 1999 JD
Public Affairs Specialist, Media Relations
Edward Kamlan . . . . . (562) 570-6814
E-mail: edward.kamlan@longbeach.gov

Office of the City Clerk

Civic Center Plaza, 333 W. Ocean Blvd., Long Beach, CA 90802
Tel: (562) 570-6101 Fax: (562) 570-6789
E-mail: cityclerk@longbeach.gov

City Clerk **Maria de la Luz Garcia** . . . . . (562) 570-6101
E-mail: cityclerk@longbeach.gov

Civil Service

Civic Center Plaza, 333 West Ocean Boulevard, 7th Floor, Long Beach, CA 90802
Tel: (562) 570-6202 Fax: (562) 570-5293
E-mail: civilservice@longbeach.gov

Executive Director **Kandice Taylor-Sherwood** . . . . . (562) 570-6163
E-mail: kandice.taylor-sherwood@longbeach.gov
Deputy Director of Employment Services **(Vacant)** . . . . . (562) 570-7057

Department of Disaster Preparedness and Emergency Communications

2990 Redondo Avenue, Long Beach, CA 90806
Tel: (562) 570-9250 Fax: (562) 570-9254

Director **Reginald "Reggie" Harrison** . . . . . (562) 570-9460
E-mail: reginald.harrison@longbeach.gov

Development Services [LBDS]

Civic Center Plaza, 333 West Ocean Boulevard, 4th Floor, Long Beach, CA 90802

Director **Amy J. Bodek** . . . . . (562) 570-6428
E-mail: amy.bodek@longbeach.gov
Education: Cornell BS; NYU 1992 MUP
Housing Development Officer **Patrick Ure** . . . . . (562) 570-6026
E-mail: patrick.ure@longbeach.gov
Deputy Director of Development (Acting)
Rob Zur Schmiede . . . . . (562) 570-6369
E-mail: robert.zurschmiede@longbeach.gov
Communications Specialist **Jacqueline Gilmore** . . . . . (562) 570-3827
E-mail: jacque.gilmore@longbeach.gov
Superintendent of Building and Safety **David Khorram** . . . (562) 570-7713
Planning Bureau Manager **Linda Tatum** . . . . . (562) 570-6261
Administrative and Financial Services Bureau Manager
Lisa Fall . . . . . (562) 570-6853
E-mail: lisa.fall@longbeach.gov

Financial Management Department

Civic Center Plaza, 333 West Ocean Boulevard, 6th Floor, Long Beach, CA 90802

Director **John Gross** . . . . . (562) 570-6237
Education: Carnegie Mellon BSME, MUPP
Budget Management Bureau Manager **Lea Eriksen** . . . . . (562) 570-6425
E-mail: lea.eriksen@longbeach.gov
Fleet Services Bureau **Dan Berlenbach** . . . . . (562) 570-5400

Fire Department

3205 Lakewood Boulevard, Long Beach, CA 90808
Tel: (562) 570-2500 Fax: (562) 570-2506

Fire Chief **Mike DuRee** . . . . . (562) 570-2500
E-mail: mike.duree@longbeach.gov
Deputy Chief of Support Services **David Segura** . . . . . (562) 570-2501
E-mail: david.segura@longbeach.gov
Deputy Chief, Operations Bureau **Mike Sarjeant** . . . . . (562) 570-2530
E-mail: mike.sarjeant@longbeach.gov

Harbor Department (Port of Long Beach)

4801 Airport Plaza Drive, Long Beach, CA 90815
Tel: (562) 283-7000 E-mail: info@polb.com Internet: www.polb.com

Chief Executive Officer **Jon W. Slangerup** . . . . . (562) 283-7080
Managing Director of Commercial Operations/Chief Commercial Officer **Dr. Noel Hacegaba** . . . . . (562) 283-7071
E-mail: noel.hacegaba@polb.com
Managing Director, Finance and Administration
Steven Rubin . . . . . (562) 283-7055
E-mail: steve.rubin@polb.com
Supply Chain Optimization, Senior Executive Lead
Michael Christensen . . . . . (562) 283-7095
Administrative Officer to the Board **Shana Ortiz** . . . . . (562) 283-7070
Director of Communications **Noelia Rodriguez** . . . . . (562) 283-7000

★Elected Official ▲Appointed by Legislature ▼Appointed by Governor ▶Appointed by Board or Commission ●Appointed by Judge
■Appointed by Mayor △Appointed by Freeholders ▽Appointed by Supervisor ▷Appointed by County Executive ○Appointed by Council

Health and Human Services Department
2525 Grand Avenue, Long Beach, CA 90815
Tel: (562) 570-4000 Fax: (562) 570-4049
Internet: www.longbeach.gov/health

Director **Kelly Colopy** .... (562) 570-4016
Education: Smith BA; Duke MPP
Manager, Housing Authority of the City of Long Beach
Darnisa Tyler .... (562) 570-6011

Human Resources Department
Civic Center Plaza, 333 West Ocean Boulevard, 13th Floor, Long Beach, CA 90802
Fax: (562) 570-6107

Director **Alejandrina "Alex" Basquez** .... (562) 570-6621
E-mail: alex.basquez@longbeach.gov
Personnel Operations Manager **Cynthia Stafford** .... (562) 570-5045
E-mail: cynthia.stafford@longbeach.gov
Workforce Investment Network Executive Director
Nick Schultz .... (562) 570-3701
E-mail: nick.schultz@longbeach.gov

Long Beach Airport
4100 East Donald Douglas Drive, 2nd Floor, Long Beach, CA 90808
Tel: (562) 570-2600 Fax: (562) 570-2601 E-mail: lgbarpt@longbeach.gov
Internet: www.lgb.org/

Airport Director **(Vacant)** .... (562) 570-2619

Long Beach Gas and Oil [LBGO]
2400 East Spring Street, Long Beach, CA 90806
Tel: (562) 570-2000 Fax: (562) 570-2050

Director (Acting) **Edward Farrell** .... (562) 570-2001 ext. 82001

Long Beach Public Library
101 Pacific Ave., Long Beach, CA 90822-1097
Fax: (562) 570-7408 E-mail: lbpl_comments@lbpl.org
Internet: http://www.lbpl.org

Director **Glenda Williams** .... (562) 570-7500
E-mail: glenda.williams@lbpl.org

Parks, Recreation and Marine Department
2760 Studebaker, Long Beach, CA 90815
Tel: (562) 570-3100 Fax: (562) 570-3109
Internet: www.longbeach.gov/park

Director **Marie Knight** .... (562) 570-3170
Business Operations Manager **(Vacant)** .... (562) 570-3200

Police Department
400 West Broadway, Long Beach, CA 90802
Tel: (562) 570-7260 Fax: (562) 570-7114

Police Chief **Robert G. Luna** .... (562) 570-7301
Education: Cal State (Long Beach) BS, MPPA

Public Works Department
Civic Center Plaza, 333 West Ocean Boulevard, 9th Floor, Long Beach, CA 90802
Fax: (562) 570-6012

Director **(Vacant)** .... (562) 570-2700

Technology and Innovation Department
Civic Center Plaza, 333 West Ocean Boulevard, 12th Floor, Long Beach, CA 90802

Director of Technology and Innovation
Bryan M. Sastokas .... (562) 570-6455
Education: Cambridge MS

Water Department
1800 East Wardlow Road, Long Beach, CA 90807
Tel: (562) 570-2300 Fax: (652) 570-2306
Internet: http://www.lbwater.org

General Manager **Christopher J. Garner** .... (562) 570-2300
Education: Loyola Marymount BS, MSBA

Office of the City Attorney
Civic Center Plaza, 333 West Ocean Boulevard, 11th Floor, Long Beach, CA 90802

★ City Attorney **Charles Parkin** .... (562) 570-2200
Term Expires: July 17, 2018
E-mail: cityattorney@longbeach.gov
Assistant City Attorney **Michael Mais** .... (562) 570-2230
E-mail: michael.mais@longbeach.gov

Office of the City Auditor
Civic Center Plaza, 333 West Ocean Boulevard, 8th Floor, Long Beach, CA 90802
Fax: (562) 570-6167 E-mail: auditor@longbeach.gov

★ City Auditor **Laura Doud** .... (562) 570-6751
Term Expires: July 17, 2018
E-mail: auditor@longbeach.gov
Special Assistant to the City Auditor
Olivia Silver Maiser .... (562) 570-6434

Office of the City Prosecutor
333 West Ocean Boulevard, 2nd Floor, Long Beach, CA 90802
E-mail: prosecutor@longbeach.gov

★ City Prosecutor **Doug Haubert** .... (562) 570-5600
Term Expires: July 17, 2018
E-mail: prosecutor@longbeach.gov
Assistant City Prosecutor **Randall C. Fudge** .... (562) 570-5608

Long Beach Unified School District [LBUSD]
1515 Hughes Way, Long Beach, CA 90810
Fax: (562) 997-8280 Internet: www.lbschools.net

Superintendent **Christopher J. Steinhauser** .... (562) 997-8242
Education: Cal State (Long Beach) BA, MA
School Board President **Felton Williams** .... (562) 997-8240
School Board Vice President **Jon Meyer** .... (562) 997-8240
School Board Member **Diana Craighead** .... (562) 997-8240
School Board Member **Megan Kerr** .... (562) 997-8240
School Board Member **John McGinnis** .... (562) 997-8240

★ Elected Official ▲ Appointed by Legislature ▼ Appointed by Governor ► Appointed by Board or Commission ● Appointed by Judge
■ Appointed by Mayor △ Appointed by Freeholders ▽ Appointed by Supervisor ▷ Appointed by County Executive ○ Appointed by Council

City of Los Angeles, California

City Hall, 200 N. Spring St., Los Angeles, CA 90012
Tel: (213) 485-2121 (Information) Internet: http://www.lacity.org

County: Los Angeles **Election Type:** Nonpartisan **Year Founded:** 1781
Year Incorporated: 1850 **Population:** 3,971,883 (2015)

Office of the Mayor

City Hall, 200 N. Spring St., Room 303, Los Angeles, CA 90012
Internet: http://mayor.lacity.org/index.htm

★Mayor **Eric Garcetti** .... (213) 978-0600
Began Service: July 1, 2013 Fax: (213) 978-0650
Term Expires: July 1, 2017
E-mail: mayor.garcetti@lacity.org
Education: Columbia 1992 BA, 1995 MA; London School Econ (UK) PhD
Executive Assistant **(Vacant)** .... (213) 922-9747
Office Manager **Sally Castro** .... (213) 978-0610
E-mail: sally.castro@lacity.org
Director of Scheduling **Lidia Manzanares** .... (213) 922-9747
■Chief of Staff **Ana Guerrero** .... (213) 978-0600
E-mail: ana.guerrero@lacity.org
■Deputy Chief of Staff **Rick Jacobs** .... (213) 978-0600
E-mail: rick.jacobs@lacity.org
■Deputy Mayor for Budget and Innovation **Matt Szabo** ... (213) 922-9772
Education: Notre Dame BA
■Chief Data Officer **Lilian Coral** .... (213) 922-9772
■Deputy Mayor, City Services **Barbara Romero** .... (213) 978-0724
E-mail: barbara.romero@lacity.org
■Deputy Mayor of Economic Development **Kelli J. Bernard** .... (213) 978-1626
E-mail: kelli.bernard@lacity.org
■Deputy Mayor, Homeland Security and Public Safety **Jeff Gorell** .... (213) 978-0600
Education: UC Davis 1992 BA; McGeorge 1998 JD
■Legislative Deputy Director **Cecilia Cabello** .... (213) 922-9788
E-mail: cecilia.cabello@lacity.org
■Communications Director **Naomi Seligman** .... (213) 978-0741
E-mail: naomi.seligman@lacity.org
Communications Associate Director **Vicki Curry** .... (213) 978-0741
E-mail: vicki.curry@lacity.org
■Director of External Affairs **Heather M. Repenning** ..... (213) 922-9788
E-mail: heather.repenning@lacity.org
■Press Secretary **Connie Llanos** .... (213) 978-0741
■Press Secretary **Carl Marziali** .... (213) 978-0741
■Constituent Services Deputy Director **Henry Casas** ...... (213) 922-9788
E-mail: henry.casas@lacity.org
■Director of Transportation Services **Borja Leon** .... (213) 978-0648
E-mail: borja.leon@lacity.org
Education: UC Davis BSCE
■Performance Management Director **Bob Stone** .... (213) 978-3132
E-mail: bob.stone@lacity.org
■Gang Reduction and Youth Development Director **(Vacant)** .... (213) 978-0600
■Legal Counsel to the Mayor **Rich Llewellyn** .... (213) 978-0600
E-mail: richard.llewellyn@lacity.org
■Deputy Counsel to the Mayor **Manav Kumar** .... (213) 978-0600
E-mail: manav.kumar@lacity.org
■Chief of Immigrant Affairs **Linda Lopez** .... (213) 978-0733
E-mail: linda.lopez@lacity.org
■Chief Sustainability Officer **Matt Petersen** .... (213) 922-9778
E-mail: matt.petersen@lacity.org
Education: Cal State (Chico) BA; USC MPA
■Chief Technology Officer **Peter Marx** .... (213) 922-9778
E-mail: peter.marx@lacity.org
■Chief Advisor on Motion Picture and Television Production **Kenneth Ziffren** .... (213) 485-2121
Date of Birth: June 24, 1940
Education: Northwestern 1962 BA; UCLA 1965 JD

Office of the City Administrative Officer

City Hall East, 200 N. Main St., Room 1500, Los Angeles, CA 90012-4137
Fax: (213) 473-7540 Internet: http://cao.lacity.org/

■City Administrative Officer **Miguel A. Santana** .... (213) 473-7534
E-mail: miguel.santana@lacity.org
Systems Support **Jody A. Yoxsimer** .... (213) 473-7577
E-mail: jody.yoxsimer@lacity.org

Employee Relations, Proprietary Analysis, Risk Management Division

200 North Main Street, Suite 1500, Los Angeles, CA 90012

Assistant City Administrative Officer **(Vacant)** .... (213) 473-7522
Employee Relations Division (Acting) **Maritta H. Aspen** .... (213) 978-7641
E-mail: maritta.aspen@lacity.org
Risk Management **Victor T. Parker** .... (213) 978-7655
E-mail: victor.parker@lacity.org
Citywide Services Chief **Mary Therese Sauer** .... (213) 473-7556

Economic Development, Municipal Facilities, Physical Plant, Public Safety and Office Support Division

200 North Main Street, Suite 1500, Los Angeles, CA 90012

Assistant City Administrative Officer and Executive Officer **Patricia Huber** .... (213) 978-0605
E-mail: patty.huber@lacity.org
Municipal Facilities **Maria R. Cardenas** .... (213) 473-7543
E-mail: maria.cardenas@lacity.org
Physical Plant Director **David H. Hirano** .... (213) 978-7621
E-mail: david.hirano@lacity.org
Public Safety **Edward F. Roes** .... (213) 978-7623
Economic Development **Aurora C. Abracia** .... (213) 473-7566
E-mail: aurora.abracia@lacity.org
Office Administration and Accounting Services **Sylvia J. Romero** .... (213) 473-7591
E-mail: sylvia.romero@lacity.org

Finance, Debt, Systems Support/Technology Projects, Special Studies Division

200 North Main Street, Suite 1500, Los Angeles, CA 90012

Assistant City Administrative Officer **Ben Ceja** .... (213) 473-7688
E-mail: ben.ceja@lacity.org
Debt Management **Natalie R. Brill** .... (213) 473-7526
Revenue Projections **Melissa Krance** .... (213) 473-7582
Budget **Jacob Wexler** .... (213) 473-7523
E-mail: jacob.wexler@lacity.org

Office of the City Clerk

City Hall, 200 N. Spring St., Room 360, Los Angeles, CA 90012
Tel: (213) 978-1020 Fax: (213) 978-1027

■City Clerk **Holly L. Wolcott** .... (213) 978-1020
E-mail: holly.wolcott@lacity.org Fax: (213) 978-1027
Administrative Services Division Manager **John R. Chavez** .... (213) 978-1101
E-mail: john.chavez@lacity.org Fax: (213) 978-1107
Council and Public Services Division Manager **Shannon Hoppes** .... (213) 978-1079
E-mail: shannon.hoppes@lacity.org Fax: (213) 978-1040
Election Division Manager **Jinny Pak** .... (213) 978-0444
E-mail: jinny.pak@lacity.org Fax: (213) 978-0376
Records Management Officer **Todd Gaydowski** .... (213) 473-8449
Fax: (213) 473-8450
Systems Division Manager **Richard Truong** .... (213) 978-0351
E-mail: richard.truong@lacity.org Fax: (213) 978-0343

Department of Aging [LADOA]

200 North Spring Street, Room 279, Los Angeles, CA 90012
Tel: (213) 482-7252 Tel: (800) 510-2020 TTY: (800) 735-2929
Fax: (213) 482-7256 E-mail: ageinfo@lacity.org
Internet: http://aging.lacity.org/

■General Manager **Laura Trejo** .... (213) 202-5645
E-mail: laura.trejo@lacity.org

★Elected Official ▲Appointed by Legislature ▼Appointed by Governor ►Appointed by Board or Commission ●Appointed by Judge
■Appointed by Mayor △Appointed by Freeholders ▽Appointed by Supervisor ▷Appointed by County Executive ○Appointed by Council

Department of Aging *continued*

Assistant General Manager **James Don** . . . . (213) 202-5612
Deputy Director **Marco A. Perez** . . . . (213) 202-5637
Support Services Division Administration
Dale Osborne . . . . (213) 202-5636
E-mail: dale.osborne@lacity.org
Program Management Division **C. Jacob Wood** . . . . (213) 202-5646
Direct Services Division **Anat Louis** . . . . (213) 202-5613
Council on Aging **Charles Shivers** . . . . (213) 202-5611
Title 5 Division **Mariella Freire** . . . . (213) 482-7252

Department of Animal Services

221 North Figuera street, 6th Floor, Suite 600, Los Angeles, CA 90012
Tel: (213) 482-9558 Fax: (213) 482-9511
Internet: http://www.laanimalservices.com

■ General Manager **Brenda F. Barnette** . . . . (213) 482-9558
E-mail: brenda.barnette@lacity.org
Education: Virginia Tech BS
Assistant General Manager **Dana Brown** . . . . (213) 482-9558
Assistant General Manager, Administration **(Vacant)** . . . . . (213) 482-9558
Accounting Services Chief Accountant **Lilia Liclican** . . . . . (213) 482-9526
E-mail: lilia.liclican@lacity.org
System Management Division Senior Systems Analyst II
Dara Ball . . . . (213) 482-9509
E-mail: dara.ball@lacity.org

Veterinary Services Division

Chief Veterinarian **Dr. Jeremy Prupas** . . . . (213) 482-9598

Building and Safety Department [LADBS]

201 North Figueroa Street, Suite 1000, Los Angeles, CA 90012
Internet: http://www.ladbs.org/ Fax: (213) 482-6850

■ Superintendent and General Manager **Raymond Chan** . . . (213) 482-6800
E-mail: raymond.chan@lacity.org
Executive Officer **Frank Bush** . . . . (213) 482-6800

Code Enforcement Bureau

3550 Wilshire Boulevard, 18th Floor, Los Angeles, CA 90010
Fax: (213) 252-3911

Chief **Lincoln Lee** . . . . (213) 252-3904
Tel: (213) 485-2121
Assistant Chief **David Lara** . . . . (213) 252-3310

Inspection Bureau

Fax: (213) 482-0303

Chief **Larry Galstian** . . . . (213) 252-3904
221 North Figueroa Street, Room 400, Los Angeles, CA 90012
Commercial Inspection Assistant Bureau Chief
David Lara Room 400 . . . . (213) 252-3310
Chief of Residential Inspections **Michael Tharpe** . . . . (213) 482-0338
221 North Figueroa Street, Room 400, Los Angeles, CA 90012
Building Inspection Section Chief **Todd Borzi**
Room 400 . . . . (213) 482-0342
Electrical Inspection Section Chief (Acting)
David MacLean Room 400 . . . . (213) 482-0341
Elevator/Pressure Vessel Inspection Section Chief
Peter Callas . . . . (213) 202-9831
221 North Figueroa Street, Room 400, Los Angeles, CA 90012
Heating/Ventilation and Refrigeration (HVAC)
and Plumbing/Heating Inspection Section Chief
Bradley Neighbors . . . . (213) 482-6787
221 North Figueroa Street, Room 830, Los Angeles, CA 90012
Training and Emergency Management Division Chief
Luke Zamperini . . . . (213) 482-6788
221 North Figueroa Street, Room 400, Los Angeles, CA 90012
E-mail: luke.zamperini@lacity.org

Permit and Engineering Bureau

Fax: (213) 482-0017

Chief **Ifa Kashefi** Room 1030 . . . . (213) 482-0440
E-mail: ifa.kashefi@lacity.org

Permit and Engineering Bureau *continued*

Assistant Chief, Casework **Ken Gill** Room 1030 . . . . (213) 482-0440
E-mail: ken.gill@lacity.org
Counter Services Supervisor **David Chang** . . . . (213) 482-0092
E-mail: david.chang@lacity.org
Electrical Plan Check **Behzad Eghtesady** . . . . (213) 482-7309
E-mail: behzad.eghtesady@lacity.org
Mechanical Plan Check Assistant Chief **Osama Younan** . . (213) 482-7407
E-mail: osama.younan@lacity.org
Metro Structural Plan Check Assistant Chief
Colin Kumabe Room 880 . . . . (213) 482-0447
E-mail: colin.kumabe@lacity.org
South Los Angeles Office Manager **Wesley Farrell** . . . . . . (213) 789-2782
8475 South Vermont Avenue, 2nd Floor, Los Angeles, CA 90044
E-mail: wesley.farrell@lacity.org
West Los Angeles Office Manager **Shahen Akelyan** . . . . . (310) 575-8122
1828 Sawtelle Boulevard, 2nd Floor, Los Angeles, CA 90025
E-mail: shahen.akelyan@lacity.org
Van Nuys District Office Manager **Sia Poursabahian** . . . . (818) 374-4302
6262 Van Nuys Boulevard, 2nd Floor, Van Nuys, CA 91401
E-mail: sia.poursabahian@lacity.org
San Pedro District Counter Services **Felix Figueroa** . . . . . . (310) 732-4578
638 South Beacon Street, 2nd Floor, San Pedro, CA 90731

Resource Management Bureau

Fax: (213) 482-6753

Chief **Steve Ongele** Room 960 . . . . (213) 482-6703
Education: Southeastern U BA; UDC MBA
Customer Call Center **Chauntel Martin** . . . . (213) 482-6549
Administrative Services Division Chief **(Vacant)** . . . . (213) 482-6755
Financial Services Section Chief **(Vacant)** . . . . (213) 482-6816
Management Information Systems/Applications Division
Chief **Giovani Dacumos** Room 600 . . . . (213) 482-6712
E-mail: giovani.dacumos@lacity.org

City Ethics Commission

200 North Spring Street, Room 2410, Los Angeles, CA 90012
Tel: (213) 978-1960 Fax: (213) 978-1988 Internet: http://ethics.lacity.org/

President **Jessica A. Levinson** . . . . (213) 978-1960
Education: Loyola Law 2005 JD
Vice President **Serena Oberstein** . . . . (213) 978-1960
Commissioner **Ana Dahan** . . . . (213) 978-1960
Commissioner **Nathan J. Hochman** . . . . (213) 978-1960
Education: Brown U 1985 BA; Stanford 1988 JD
Commissioner **Melinda Murray** . . . . (213) 978-1960
Executive Director **Heather Holt** . . . . (213) 978-1960

Economic and Workforce Development Department

1200 West 7th Street, 6th Floor, Los Angeles, CA 90017
Tel: (213) 744-7300 Fax: (213) 744-9061

General Manager **Jan Perry** . . . . (213) 744-7300
E-mail: jan.perry@lacity.org
Education: USC 1977 BA, 1981 MPA
Assistant General Manager, Economic Development
(Interim) **Samuel Hughes** . . . . (213) 744-9723
E-mail: samuel.hughes@lacity.org
Assistant General Manager, Operations **Robert Sainz** . . . . (213) 744-7396
E-mail: robert.sainz@lacity.org
Computer Systems Division Director **(Vacant)** . . . . (213) 744-7244
Financial Management Division Director
Catherine Bondoc . . . . (213) 744-7294
Human Resource Division Departmental Personnel
Officer **Tonja Bellard** . . . . (213) 744-7279
E-mail: tonja.bellard@lacity.org
Youth Services Division Director **Lisa Salazar** . . . . (213) 744-7191
Economic Development Division Director **(Vacant)** . . . . . . (213) 744-7111
Workforce Development Division Director
Jaime Pacheco-Orozco . . . . (213) 744-7124
E-mail: jaime.pacheco-orozco@lacity.org

★ Elected Official ▲ Appointed by Legislature ▼ Appointed by Governor ▶ Appointed by Board or Commission ● Appointed by Judge
■ Appointed by Mayor △ Appointed by Freeholders ▽ Appointed by Supervisor ▷ Appointed by County Executive ○ Appointed by Council

Department of Convention and Tourism Development

Los Angeles Convention Center, 1201 S. Figueroa St., Los Angeles, CA 90015
Fax: (213) 765-4266 Internet: http://www.lacclink.com

■ Executive Director **Robert "Bud" Ovrom** .... (213) 741-1151
Assistant General Manager and Chief Operating Officer **Thomas Fields** .... (213) 741-1151
Assistant General Manager **Diana Mangioglu** .... (213) 741-1151
Senior Vice President and General Manager **Brad Gessner** .... (213) 765-4430
Vice President, Operations **Greg Rosicky** .... (213) 765-4630
E-mail: grosicky@lacclink.com
Vice President, Sales and Marketing **Ellen Schwartz** .... (213) 765-4660
Vice President, Security and Guest Services **Ruben Lechuga** .... (213) 765-4460
Vice President, Event Services **Carisa Norton** .... (213) 765-4640
Parking Manager **Abraham Reyes** .... (213) 741-1151 ext. 5850

Department of Cultural Affairs

221 North Figueroa Street, Suite 1400, Los Angeles, CA 90012
Tel: (213) 202-5500 Fax: (213) 202-5517
Internet: http://www.culturela.org

■ General Manager **Danielle Brazell** .... (213) 202-5509
E-mail: danielle.brazell@lacity.org
Assistant General Manager **Daniel Tarica** .... (213) 202-5533
Administrative Services Director **Alma Gibson** .... (213) 202-5530
E-mail: alma.gibson@lacity.org
Community Arts Director **Leslie A. Thomas** .... (323) 644-6295
Cultural Facilities Director/Special Projects **(Vacant)** .... (213) 202-5524
Cultural Grant Program Director **Joe Smoke** .... (213) 202-5548
E-mail: joe.smoke@lacity.org
Marketing and Development Director **Will Caperton y Montoya** .... (213) 202-5538
Fax: (213) 202-5511
Public Art Director **Felicia Filer** .... (213) 202-5547

Department on Disability

221 North Figueroa Street, Suite 100, Los Angeles, CA 90012
Fax: (213) 202-2715 Internet: http://disability.lacity.org/

■ Executive Director **Stephen David Simon** .... (213) 202-2764
Education: UCLA BA, JD

Emergency Management Department

City Hall, 200 N. Spring St., Room 1533, Los Angeles, CA 90012
Fax: (213) 978-0517 Internet: http://emergency.lacity.org/

General Manager (Interim) **Aram Sahakian** .... (213) 978-2222
Assistant General Manager **Anna Burton** .... (213) 978-2222
E-mail: anna.burton@lacity.org
Executive Administrative Assistant **Cecilia Law** .... (213) 978-2222
E-mail: cecilia.law@lacity.org
Administrative Services Division Chief **Bruce Aoki** .... (213) 978-2222
E-mail: bruce.aoki@lacity.org

Employee Relations Board

City Hall East, 200 North Main Street, Room 1100, Los Angeles, CA 90012-4124
Tel: (213) 473-9700 Fax: (213) 473-7751 Internet: http://erb.lacity.org/

■ Chairman **R. Douglas Collins** .... (213) 473-9700
■ Vice Chairman **Christopher Ruiz Cameron** .... (213) 473-9700
■ Board Member **Rhonda Hilyer** .... (213) 473-9700
■ Board Member **Rosalinda Lugo** .... (213) 473-9700
■ Board Member **Anthony Miller** .... (213) 473-9700
Executive Director **Robert R. Bergeson** .... (213) 473-9700
E-mail: robert.bergeson@lacity.org
Commission Executive Assistant **Guadalupe N. Rodarte** .... (213) 473-9700
E-mail: guadalupe.rodarte@lacity.org

Office of Finance

City Hall, 200 North Spring Street, Room 220, Los Angeles, CA 90012
Tel: (844) 663-4411 Fax: (213) 978-1780
Internet: http://finance.lacity.org/

■ General Manager **Claire Bartels** .... (844) 663-4411
Note: Pending City Council approval
E-mail: claire.bartels@lacity.org
Assistant Director **Ed Cabrera** .... (213) 978-1516
Assistant Director **Saul Romo** .... (213) 978-1757
Revenue Manager **Wai Yee Lau** .... (213) 978-1781
E-mail: wai.y.lau@lacity.org
Tax and Permit Division Chief **Robert Lee** .... (213) 978-1501
E-mail: robert.lee@lacity.org
Director of Systems **Carl Sampson** .... (213) 928-9092
E-mail: carl.sampson@lacity.org
Chief Investment Officer **Thomas Juarez** .... (213) 978-4039

Fire Department

City Hall East, 200 North Main Street, Room 1800, Los Angeles, CA 90012
Tel: (213) 978-3800 Fax: (213) 978-3815 Internet: www.lafd.org

■ Fire Chief **Ralph Terrazas** .... (213) 978-3800
E-mail: lafdfirechief@lacity.org
Chief of Staff **Graham Everett** .... (213) 978-3840
E-mail: graham.everett@lacity.org
Fire Prevention and Public Safety Bureau/Fire Marshal Deputy Chief **John Vidovich** .... (213) 978-3570
E-mail: john.vidovich@lacity.org
Training and Support Bureau/Deputy Chief **Richard Rideout** .... (213) 978-3550
E-mail: richard.rideout@lacity.org
Administrative Operations Chief Deputy **Fred Mathis** .... (213) 978-3855
E-mail: fred.mathis@lacity.org
Emergency Operations Chief Deputy **Mario D. Rueda** .... (213) 978-6300
Public Information Officer **Daniel Curry** .... (213) 978-6300
E-mail: daniel.curry@lacity.org

Los Angeles Fire and Police Pensions [LAFPP]

701 East 3rd Street, Suite 200, Los Angeles, CA 90013
Tel: (213) 279-3000 Fax: (213) 628-7716 E-mail: pensions@lafpp.com
Internet: http://www.lafpp.com

▶ General Manager **Raymond P. Ciranna** .... (213) 279-3015
E-mail: pensions@lafpp.com
Chief Investment Officer **Tom Lopez** .... (213) 279-3021
E-mail: tom.lopez@lafpp.com
Executive Officer **William Raggio** .... (213) 279-3035
Pensions Division Assistant Manager **Joseph Salazar** .... (213) 279-3095

General Services Department

City Hall South, 111 East First Street, Room 701, Los Angeles, CA 90012
Tel: (213) 928-9555 Fax: (213) 928-9515 Internet: http://gsd.lacity.org/

■ General Manager and City Purchasing Agent **Tony M. Royster** .... (213) 928-9555
E-mail: tony.royster@lacity.org
Executive Administrative Assistant III **(Vacant)** .... (213) 928-9555
Assistant General Manager, Administration and Building Support Services **Valerie Melloff** Room 712 .... (213) 928-9586
E-mail: valerie.melloff@lacity.org
Assistant General Manager, Fleet and Fuel Management **Angela Sherick-Bright** Room 702 .... (213) 928-9575
E-mail: angela.sherick@lacity.org
Assistant General Manager, Property Management **David A. Paschal** .... (213) 928-9566
E-mail: david.paschal@lacity.org
Assistant General Manager, Supply Services **Deborah J. Ramos** .... (213) 928-9559
E-mail: deborah.ramos@lacity.org
Building Maintenance Director **India Griffin** .... (213) 978-7222
E-mail: india.griffin@lacity.org
Finance and Special Services Director **Victor Yee** .... (213) 928-9588

★ Elected Official ▲ Appointed by Legislature ▼ Appointed by Governor ▶ Appointed by Board or Commission ● Appointed by Judge
■ Appointed by Mayor △ Appointed by Freeholders ▽ Appointed by Supervisor ▷ Appointed by County Executive ○ Appointed by Council

General Services Department *continued*

Fleet Services Director **Richard Coulson** . . . . . (323) 526-9200
Fuel Services and Environmental Compliance Director
Rene Villa-Agustin . . . . . (213) 978-3795
Personnel Director **Dan Yoshimura** . . . . . (213) 922-8577
E-mail: dan.yoshimura@lacity.org
Publishing Services Director **Gerald St. Onge** . . . . . (213) 473-8401
Standards Testing Director **Ray Solomon** . . . . . (213) 847-0928
E-mail: ray.solomon@lacity.org
Supply Chain Services Director (Acting)
Melissa Yusilon . . . . . (213) 928-9557
Supplier and Customer Relations Director
John Trevgoda . . . . . (213) 928-9504
Supply Management System Support Manager
Renee Mustafa . . . . . (213) 473-7840
E-mail: renee.mustafa@lacity.org
Special Services Manager **Eric Robles** . . . . . (213) 928-9572
Management Information Services Director
Michael Sakamoto . . . . . (213) 922-8598
E-mail: michael.sakamoto@lacity.org
Custodial Services Director **Loretta Quenon** . . . . . (213) 978-8755
E-mail: loretta.quenon@lacity.org
Facilities Services Director **Melody McCormick** . . . . . (213) 978-8770
E-mail: melody.mccormick@lacity.org
Mail Services Manager **Aram Salmasi** . . . . . (213) 978-0287
E-mail: aram.salmasi@lacity.org
Parking Manager **Benjamin Setiarto** . . . . . (213) 978-0728
Construction Forces Director **Kelly Cooper** . . . . . (213) 978-2600
E-mail: kelly.cooper@lacity.org
Departmental Chief Accountant III **Ivy Yan** . . . . . (213) 928-9597
E-mail: ivy.yan@lacity.org
Chief Sustainability Officer **Lisa Gabriel** . . . . . (213) 928-9585

Harbor Department/Port of Los Angeles

425 South Palos Verdes Street, San Pedro, CA 90731
P.O. Box 151, San Pedro, CA 90733-0151
Tel: (310) 732-7678 Fax: (310) 831-6936 Internet: www.portofla.org/

■ Executive Director **Gene Seroka** . . . . . (310) 732-3456
Education: New Orleans BS, MBA
Executive Secretary **Eileen Tankersley** . . . . . (310) 732-3456
E-mail: etankersley@portla.org
Deputy Executive Director, Marketing and Customer Relations **Michael DiBernardo** . . . . . (310) 732-3440
E-mail: mdibernardo@portla.org
Deputy Executive Director of External Relations
(Vacant) . . . . . (310) 732-0350
Deputy Executive Director of Port Development
(Vacant) . . . . . (310) 732-3440
General Counsel **Janna Sidley** . . . . . (310) 732-3750
E-mail: jsidley@portla.org Fax: (310) 372-3750
Chief Financial Officer **Marla Bleavins** . . . . . (310) 732-7703
Chief Harbor Engineer **David Walsh** . . . . . (310) 732-3877
E-mail: dwalsh@portla.org Fax: (310) 519-0178
Construction Director/Chief Harbor Engineer
Shaun Shahrestani . . . . . (310) 732-3670
E-mail: sshahrestani@portla.org
Senior Director, Government Affairs **David Libatique** . . . . (310) 732-3905
E-mail: dlibatique@portla.org
Education: UC Berkeley BA; Harvard MPP
Construction and Maintenance Director **(Vacant)** . . . . . (310) 732-3555
500 Pier A Street, Fax: (310) 834-8248
Berth 161, Wilmington, CA 90744
Environmental Management Director
Christopher Cannon . . . . . (310) 732-3497
Education: Dartmouth BA; Boalt Hall JD Fax: (310) 547-4643
Homeland Security Director **George Cummings** . . . . . (310) 732-3474
E-mail: gcummings@portla.org
Chief Information Officer **Lance Kaneshiro** . . . . . (310) 732-7742
E-mail: lkaneshiro@portla.org Fax: (310) 519-7501
Director of Business and Trade Development
Eric Caris . . . . . (310) 732-3162
Fax: (310) 831-4896

Harbor Department/Port of Los Angeles *continued*

Human Resources Director **Tish Lorenzana** . . . . . (310) 732-3484
E-mail: tlorenzana@portla.org Fax: (310) 521-8344
Planning and Economic Development Director **(Vacant)** . . (310) 732-3850
Real Estate Director **Jack Hedge** . . . . . (310) 732-3860
Education: Texas A&M Fax: (310) 732-1725
Chief Wharfinger **Diane Boskovich** . . . . . (310) 732-3810
Risk Manager **Kathy Merkovsky** . . . . . (310) 732-3971
E-mail: kmerkovsky@portla.org Fax: (310) 833-8230
Contracts and Purchasing Director **Tricia Carey** . . . . . (310) 732-7656
500 Pier A Street, Fax: (310) 513-6234
Berth 161, Wilmington, CA 90744
E-mail: tcarey@portla.org
Director of Media Relations **Phillip Sanfield** . . . . . (310) 732-3568
E-mail: psanfield@portla.org
Director of Community Relations
Theresa Adams-Lopez . . . . . (310) 732-3507
E-mail: tadams-lopez@portla.org
Chief of Public Safety and Emergency Management
(Interim) **Tom Gazsi** . . . . . (310) 732-3515
Education: USC 1979 BA
Deputy Police Chief **(Vacant)** . . . . . (310) 732-3515
Director of Goods Movement **Kerry Cartwright** . . . . . (310) 732-7700

Housing Authority of the City of Los Angeles

2600 Wilshire Boulevard, 3rd Floor, Los Angeles, CA 90057-3400
Fax: (213) 383-9719 Internet: www.hacla.org/

Board of Commissioners

■ Chair **Ben Besley** . . . . . (213) 252-1826
■ Vice Chair **Erica L. Jacquez** . . . . . (213) 252-1826
■ Commissioner **Maria "Lou" Calanche** . . . . . (213) 252-1826
■ Commissioner **Kimberly Freeman** . . . . . (213) 252-1826
■ Commissioner **Lucelia Hooper** . . . . . (213) 252-1826
■ Commissioner **Paul C. Hudson** . . . . . (213) 252-1826
■ Commissioner **Daria Nunez** . . . . . (213) 252-1826
Executive Assistant to the Commission **Tiffany Prescott** . . (213) 252-1826

Administration

Fax: (213) 383-8249

▶ President and Chief Executive Officer **Douglas Guthrie** . . (213) 252-1810
E-mail: douglas.guthrie@lacity.org
Senior Executive Assistant **Mariela Osorio** . . . . . (213) 252-1810
Chief Operating Officer **Ken Simmons** . . . . . (213) 252-1818
Chief Financial Officer **Marlene Garza** . . . . . (213) 252-6190
Asset Management Director **Tina Booth** . . . . . (213) 252-8844
Legal Services Director **Howard Baum** . . . . . (213) 252-1268
Housing Services Director (Interim) **Martin Peery** . . . . . (213) 252-1820
Human Resources Director **Caroline Chung** . . . . . (213) 252-5327
Policy and Planning Director **John King** . . . . . (213) 252-5464
Section 8 Director **Carlos VanNatter** . . . . . (213) 252-2570
Intergovernmental and Community Relations Director
Eric Brown . . . . . (213) 252-1871
Development Services Director **Jenny Scanlin** . . . . . (213) 252-2680

Los Angeles Housing and Community Investment Department [HCIDLA]

Garland Center, 1200 West 7th Street, 9th Floor, Los Angeles, CA 90017
Fax: (213) 808-8616

General Manager **Rushmore D. Cervantes** . . . . . (213) 808-8808
E-mail: rushmore.cervantes@lacity.org
Executive Administrative Assistant **Mary Arredondo** . . . (213) 808-8808
E-mail: mary.arredondo@lacity.org
Assistant General Manager **Luz Santiago** . . . . . (213) 808-8899
Fax: (213) 808-8999
Housing Development Assistant General Manager
Helmi Hisserich . . . . . (213) 808-8662
E-mail: helmi.hisserich@lacity.org Fax: (213) 808-8610
Regulatory Compliance and Code Enforcement General Manager **Roberto Aldape** . . . . . (213) 808-8826
Fax: (213) 808-8818

(continued on next page)

★ Elected Official ▲ Appointed by Legislature ▼ Appointed by Governor ▶ Appointed by Board or Commission ● Appointed by Judge
■ Appointed by Mayor △ Appointed by Freeholders ▽ Appointed by Supervisor ▷ Appointed by County Executive ○ Appointed by Council

Los Angeles Housing and Community Investment Department *continued*

Executive Officer **Laura K. Guglielmo** . . . . . . (213) 808-8405
Fax: (213) 808-8999

Human Relations Commission

City Hall, 200 North Spring Street, Room 2111,
Los Angeles, CA 90012-3255
Fax: (213) 978-1668 E-mail: hrcinfo@lacity.org
Internet: http://hrc.lacity.org/

■ President **Nirinjan Singh-Khalsa** . . . . . . (213) 978-1664
■ Commissioner **Leni Isaacs Boorstin** . . . . . . (213) 978-1664
■ Commissioner **Daniel Campos** . . . . . . (213) 978-1664
■ Commissioner **Melany Dela Cruz-Viesca** . . . . . . (213) 978-1664
■ Commissioner **Evelina Fernández** . . . . . . (213) 978-1664
■ Commissioner **James Herr** . . . . . . (213) 978-1664
■ Commissioner **Courtney Morgan-Greene** . . . . . . (213) 978-1664
■ Commissioner **Gaspar Rivera-Salgado** . . . . . . (213) 978-1664
■ Commissioner **Mark Rothman** . . . . . . (213) 978-1664
■ Commissioner **Rosa Russell** . . . . . . (213) 978-1664
■ Commissioner **Irene Tovar** . . . . . . (213) 978-1664
■ Executive Director **Patricia M. Villaseñor** . . . . . . (213) 978-1664

Information Technology Agency [ITA]

City Hall East, 200 North Main Street, Room 1400,
Los Angeles, CA 90012
Tel: (213) 978-3311 Fax: (213) 978-3311
Internet: http://ita.lacity.org/index.htm

■ General Manager **Ted Ross** . . . . . . (213) 978-3311
E-mail: ted.ross@lacity.org Fax: (213) 978-3310
Assistant General Manager **Joyce Edson** 14th Floor . . . . . . (213) 978-3311
E-mail: joyce.edson@lacity.org Fax: (213) 978-3310
Payroll and Revenue Applications Division Manager **Sylvia Bergstrom** 13th Floor . . . . . . (213) 978-1695
E-mail: sylvia.bergstrom@lacity.org Fax: (213) 922-7718
Applications and Database Development Manager **Jackie Johnson** 13th Floor . . . . . . (213) 922-7742
Fax: (213) 922-7716
Financial Management Systems Manager **Jose Alvarez** . . . (213) 978-0896
E-mail: jose.alvarez@lacity.org

Business and Administration Services

City Hall East, 200 North Main Street, Room 1400,
Los Angeles, CA 90012
Fax: (213) 978-3310

Executive Officer **(Vacant)** . . . . . . (213) 978-3311
Fax: (213) 978-3310
Finance and Administrative Services Chief Management Analyst **Laura Ito** . . . . . . (213) 978-3322
E-mail: laura.ito@lacity.org
Budget and Contracts Senior Management Analyst II **Tita Zara** . . . . . . (213) 978-3346
E-mail: tita.zara@lacity.org Fax: (213) 978-3310
Personnel Director **Ruben B. Vasquez, Jr.** . . . . . . (213) 978-3390
E-mail: ruben.vasquez@lacity.org Fax: (213) 978-0513
TDD: (213) 485-1781
Applications and Webservers Manager **(Vacant)** . . . . . . (213) 978-3381
Chief Management Analyst **Agnes Lung-Tam** 10th Floor . . . . . . (213) 978-3064
E-mail: agnes.lung-tam@lacity.org
311 Director **Donna Arrechea** . . . . . . (213) 473-3228
E-mail: donna.arrechea@lacity.org

Communications Services Division

Director of Communications Services **Omotayo Ige** 14th Floor . . . . . . (213) 978-1515
E-mail: omotayo.ige@lacity.org Fax: (213) 485-8719

Infrastructure and Communications Bureau

Fax: (213) 978-2966

Assistant General Manager **Russell Kaurloto** . . . . . . (213) 978-3311

Infrastructure and Communications Bureau *continued*

Enterprise Systems and Operations Services **Sung Kim** . . . (213) 978-6333
E-mail: sung.kim@lacity.org
Enterprise Services Management **Nee Truong** . . . . . . (213) 978-6783
E-mail: nee.truong@lacity.org
Director of Communications Services **Anne Wu** . . . . . . (213) 978-0088
E-mail: anne.wu@lacity.org Fax: (213) 485-1597
Network Operations Support Manager **Bill Lau** Room P-4 . . . . . . (213) 978-6708
E-mail: bill.lau@lacity.org
Communications Engineer **Ramil Lopez** . . . . . . (213) 978-4034
E-mail: ramil.lopez@lacity.org
Field Services Section Manager **Bob Aune** . . . . . . (213) 473-0671
555 Ramirez Street, Fax: (213) 473-2575
Space 140, Los Angeles, CA 90012
E-mail: bob.aune@lacity.org
Voice Radio and Transmission Engineering Section Manager **Ken Chan** . . . . . . (213) 978-0872
E-mail: ken.chan@lacity.org Fax: (213) 978-0868
Manager, Public Safety Applications **Judy Chu** 14th Floor . . . . . . (213) 473-7088
E-mail: judy.chu@lacity.org

Los Angeles City Employees' Retirement System [LACERS]

202 West First Street, Suite 500, Mail Stop 175,
Los Angeles, CA 90012-4401
Tel: (800) 779-8328 Fax: (213) 473-7296
E-mail: lacers.services@lacity.org Internet: www.lacers.org

■ General Manager **Thomas Moutes** . . . . . . (213) 473-7280
E-mail: tom.moutes@lacers.org Fax: (213) 473-7296
Education: Cal State (Northridge) BSBA, MPA
Executive Administrative Assistant **Bella Cabulong** . . . . (213) 473-7280
E-mail: bella.cabulong@lacers.org Fax: (213) 473-7296
Assistant General Manager **Li Hsi** . . . . . . (213) 473-7280
Fax: (213) 473-7296
Assistant General Manager **Lita Payne** . . . . . . (213) 473-7280
Fax: (213) 473-7296
Fiscal Management **Mikyong Jang** . . . . . . (213) 473-7227
Fax: (213) 687-4174
Retirement Services **Karen Freire** . . . . . . (213) 473-7171
Fax: (213) 687-4174
Training Coordinator **Ruth Perry** . . . . . . (213) 473-7166
E-mail: ruth.perry@lacers.org Fax: (213) 687-4174
Commission Executive Assistant **Tanzi Cole** . . . . . . (213) 473-7169
E-mail: tanzi.cole@lacers.org Fax: (213) 473-7296
Administrative Services **Dale Wong Nguyen** . . . . . . (213) 473-7258
E-mail: dale.wong.nguyen@lacers.org Fax: (213) 473-7296
Health and Communications **Alex Rabrenovich** . . . . . . (213) 473-7161
E-mail: alex.rabrenovich@lacers.org Fax: (213) 687-4174
Chief Investment Officer **Rodney June** . . . . . . (213) 473-7124
Education: Cal State (Long Beach) BS; Auburn MBA

Los Angeles Memorial Coliseum Commission

500 West Temple Street, Room 383, Los Angeles, CA 90012
Tel: (213) 765-6711

President **Mark Ridley-Thomas** . . . . . . (213) 747-7111
Date of Birth: November 6, 1954
Education: Immaculate Heart; USC 1989 PhD
Vice President **William Chadwick** . . . . . . (213) 747-7111
Commissioner **Curren D. Price, Jr.** . . . . . . (213) 747-7111
Education: Stanford 1972 BA; Santa Clara U 1976 JD
Ex-Officio Commissioner **Reginald Byron Jones-Sawyer, Sr.** . . . . . . (213) 473-7008
Education: USC BA
Ex-Officio Commissioner **Ricardo Lara** . . . . . . (213) 747-7111
Education: San Diego State 1999 BAGS
Executive Director **Robert Osborne** . . . . . . (213) 765-6314 ext. 317
Fax: (213) 748-5828

★ Elected Official ▲ Appointed by Legislature ▼ Appointed by Governor ▶ Appointed by Board or Commission ● Appointed by Judge
■ Appointed by Mayor △ Appointed by Freeholders ▽ Appointed by Supervisor ▷ Appointed by County Executive ○ Appointed by Council

Los Angeles Public Library

630 West Fifth Street, Los Angeles, CA 90071
Tel: (213) 228-7000 Fax: (213) 228-7519 E-mail: liadmin@lapl.org
Internet: www.lapl.org

Administration

■ City Librarian **John F. Szabo** . . . . . . (213) 228-7515
Education: Alabama 1990 BComm; Michigan MLIS
Director, Branch Library Services **Cheryl Collins** . . . . . . (213) 228-7570
E-mail: ccollins@lapl.org Fax: (213) 228-7039
Director, Central Library Services **Eva Mitnick** . . . . . . (213) 228-7470
Fax: (213) 228-7429
Director, Human Resources
Michael "Mike" Bolokowicz . . . . . . (213) 228-7431
E-mail: mbolokowicz@lapl.org
Director, Information Technology **Susan Browman** . . . . . . (213) 228-7564
Fax: (213) 228-7519
Director, Public Relations and Marketing
Peter V. Persic . . . . . . (213) 228-7555
E-mail: pubinfo@lapl.org Fax: (213) 228-7569
Business Manager **Madeline Rackley** . . . . . . (213) 228-7465
Fax: (213) 228-7449
Assistant General Manager, Libraries **Kristina Morita** . . . . (213) 228-7461
E-mail: kmorita@lapl.org Fax: (213) 228-7519
Education: UCLA BA; USC MLS
Chief of Security **David Aguirre** . . . . . . (213) 228-7171
Fax: (213) 228-7199

Los Angeles World Airports

P.O. Box 92216, Los Angeles, CA 90009
Tel: (424) 646-6250 Fax: (424) 646-9220 Internet: www.lawa.org

■ Executive Director **Deborah Flint** . . . . . . (424) 646-6250
Education: San José State BS
Chief Operating Officer **Stephen "Steve" Martin** . . . . . . (424) 646-5040
Education: Lowell BA; Northeastern MA
Administration Deputy General Manager
Samson Mengistu . . . . . . (424) 646-6251
E-mail: smengistu@lawa.org Fax: (424) 646-9205
Deputy General Manager and Comptroller **Wei Chi** . . . . . (424) 646-9118
Education: Columbia BS; Wharton MBA Fax: (424) 646-9201
Airports Development Group Deputy General Manager
Roger A. Johnson . . . . . . (424) 646-7553
E-mail: rogerjohnson@lawa.org
Operations and Emergency Management Deputy
General Manager **Jacqueline Yaft** . . . . . . (424) 646-5060
E-mail: jyaft@lawa.org Fax: (424) 646-9205
Commercial Development Deputy Executive Director
Debbie Bowers . . . . . . (424) 646-7142
Education: South Alabama BS; Fax: (424) 646-9204
Florida Atlantic MBA; Chicago-Kent JD
Facilities Engineering Deputy General Manager
David Shuter . . . . . . (424) 646-5111
E-mail: dshuter@lawa.org
Chief of Airport Engineering II **Jeffrey Smith** . . . . . . (424) 646-5701
E-mail: jsmith@lawa.org Fax: (424) 646-9345
Maintenance Services Director **Ralph Morones** . . . . . . (424) 646-7900
E-mail: rmorones@lawa.org Fax: (310) 215-5399
Chief Information Officer **Dominic Nessi** . . . . . . (424) 646-5001
E-mail: dnessi@lawa.org Fax: (424) 646-9217
Chief Technology Officer **Nathan Look** . . . . . . (424) 646-5326
E-mail: nlook@lawa.org
Law Enforcement and Homeland Security Deputy
Executive Director **Patrick Gannon** . . . . . . (424) 646-5045
Fax: (424) 646-9202
Rideshare Program Manager **Devon Deming** . . . . . . (424) 646-7665
Fax: (424) 646-9261
Government Affairs Director **Mark Adams** . . . . . . (424) 646-5030
Fax: (424) 646-9222
Airport Parking Manager I **Elias Constantinides** . . . . . . (424) 646-6457
Fax: (424) 646-9256
Real Estate Deputy General Manager **(Vacant)** . . . . . . (424) 646-7239
Risk Manager II **Jim McGuirk** . . . . . . (424) 646-5489
E-mail: jmcguirk@lawa.org Fax: (424) 646-9264

Los Angeles World Airports *continued*

Airport Environmental Manager **Robert Freeman** . . . . . . (424) 646-6474
Fax: (424) 646-6197
Personnel Director **Paula Adams** . . . . . . (424) 646-5900
E-mail: padams@lawa.org Fax: (310) 646-7698
General Counsel **Raymond Ilgunas** . . . . . . (424) 646-5010
Fax: (310) 646-9617
Managing Director of Media and Public Relations
Mary E. Grady . . . . . . (424) 646-5267
E-mail: mgrady@lawa.org
Public Relations Director **Nancy Suey Castles** . . . . . . (424) 646-5260
E-mail: ncastles@lawa.org Fax: (424) 646-9207
Operations Director, Los Angeles International Airport
(Vacant) . . . . . . (424) 646-9108

Los Angeles Zoo and Botanical Gardens

5333 Zoo Drive, Los Angeles, CA 90027-1498
Fax: (323) 662-9786 Internet: http://www.lazoo.org

General Manager/Director **John R. Lewis** . . . . . . (323) 644-4202
Executive Assistant **Denise Tamura** . . . . . . (323) 644-4202
E-mail: denise.tamura@lacity.org
Deputy Director **Denise M. Verret** . . . . . . (323) 644-4200
Director of Administration and Operations **Mei Kwan** . . . . (323) 644-4200
E-mail: mei.kwan@lacity.org
Human Resources Division **Mae Huey** . . . . . . (323) 644-4200
E-mail: mae.huey@lacity.org
General Curator **Beth Schaefer** . . . . . . (323) 644-4200
Chief Veterinarian **Lisa Naples** . . . . . . (323) 644-6018
Director of Marketing and Public Relations **(Vacant)** . . . . . (323) 644-4273
Director of Education **Kirsten Perez** . . . . . . (323) 644-4200
Planning and Development Division **Darryl Pon** . . . . . . (323) 644-4200

Department of Neighborhood Empowerment [DONE]

200 North Spring Street, Suite 2005, Los Angeles, CA 90012-2601
Fax: (213) 978-1751 Internet: www.empowerla.org

■ Board President **Leonard "Len" Shaffer** . . . . . . (213) 978-1551
E-mail: leonard.shaffer@lacity.org
■ Vice President **Joy Atkinson** . . . . . . (213) 978-1551
■ Commissioner **Lydia Grant** . . . . . . (213) 978-1551
E-mail: lydia.grant@lacity.org
■ Commissioner **Josh LaFarga** . . . . . . (213) 978-1551
E-mail: Commission@Empowerla.org
■ Commissioner **Eli Lipmen** . . . . . . (213) 978-1551
■ Commissioner **Karen Mack** . . . . . . (213) 978-1551
E-mail: karen.mack@lacity.org
■ Commissioner **Olivia Rubio** . . . . . . (213) 978-1551
E-mail: olivia.rubio@lacity.org
General Manager **Grayce Liu** . . . . . . (213) 978-1551
E-mail: grayce.liu@lacity.org
Education: UC Santa Cruz BA; Loyola Law JD
Executive Administrative Assistant **(Vacant)** . . . . . . (213) 978-1551

Personnel Department

700 East Temple Street, Los Angeles, CA 90012
Tel: (213) 473-3470 Internet: http://per.lacity.org/

■ General Manager **Wendy G. Macy** Room 305 . . . . . . (213) 473-3470
E-mail: wendy.macy@lacity.org Fax: (213) 473-9347
Education: Harvard 1989 AB, 1992 JD
Assistant General Manager **Gregory T. Dion** Room 320 . . (213) 473-3470
E-mail: gregory.dion@lacity.org
Assistant General Manager **Phyllis Lynes** Room 305 . . . . . (213) 473-3470
Assistant General Manager **Gloria Sosa** . . . . . . (213) 473-3470
Equal Employment Office Manager **Raelynn Napper**
Room 380 . . . . . . (213) 473-0182
E-mail: raelynn.napper@lacity.org
Employee Benefits Division Chief **Steven Montagna** . . . . (213) 978-1621
E-mail: steven.montagna@lacity.org
Section Division **Tina Lee Rodriguez** Room 320 . . . . . . (213) 473-9163
E-mail: tina.lee.rodriguez@lacity.org

(continued on next page)

★ Elected Official ▲ Appointed by Legislature ▼ Appointed by Governor ▶ Appointed by Board or Commission ● Appointed by Judge
■ Appointed by Mayor △ Appointed by Freeholders ▽ Appointed by Supervisor ▷ Appointed by County Executive ○ Appointed by Council

Personnel Department *continued*

Administrative Services Division Chief **Susan Nakafuji** . . (213) 473-9120
E-mail: susan.nakafuji@lacity.org
Medical Services Division Director **Joanne O'Brien** . . . . . (213) 473-7037
423 East Temple Street, Los Angeles, CA 90012
Public Safety Bureau Chief **John Dunlop** . . . . (213) 473-9483
E-mail: john.dunlop@lacity.org
Classification Division Chief **Raul Lemus** . . . . (213) 473-9159
E-mail: raul.lemus@lacity.org
Workers' Compensation Division Chief
David Noltemeyer Room 210 . . . . (213) 473-3400
E-mail: david.noltemeyer@lacity.org

Department of City Planning

City Hall, 200 North Spring Street, Room 525,
Los Angeles, CA 90012-2601
Fax: (213) 978-1275 Internet: http://cityplanning.lacity.org/Index.htm

■ Director-Designate **Vince Bertoni** . . . . (213) 978-1271
E-mail: vince.bertoni@lacity.org
Education: San Diego State 1988 BA
Deputy Director **(Vacant)** . . . . (213) 978-1272
Deputy Director, Community Planning **Lisa Webber** . . . . . (213) 978-1274
Deputy Director, Citywide Planning **Jan Zatorski** . . . . (213) 978-1273

Board of Police Commissioners

100 West First Street, Room 134, Los Angeles, CA 90012
Fax: (213) 485-8861

■ President **Matthew Johnson** . . . . (213) 236-1400
■ Vice President **Steven L. "Steve" Soboroff** . . . . (213) 236-1400
Education: Arizona
■ Commissioner **Sandra Figueora-Villa** . . . . (213) 236-1400
■ Commissioner **Kathleen Kim** . . . . (213) 236-1400
■ Commissioner **Robert M. Saltzman** . . . . (213) 236-1400
Education: Dartmouth BA; Harvard 1979 JD
Executive Director **Richard M. Tefank** . . . . (213) 236-1400
Inspector General **Alex Bustamante** . . . . (213) 202-5866
201 North Figueroa Street, Fax: (213) 482-1247
Room 610, Los Angeles, CA 90012

Los Angeles Police Department [LAPD]

100 West First Street, Los Angeles, CA 90012
Tel: (213) 485-3202 Internet: www.lapdonline.org

■ Chief of Police **Charles "Charlie" Beck** . . . . (213) 486-0150
150 North Los Angeles Street, Room 619, Los Angeles, CA 90012
E-mail: Charlie.Beck@lapd.lacity.org
Deputy Chief/Professional Standards Bureau
Commanding Officer **Debra J. McCarthy** . . . . (213) 486-0150
304 South Broadway, Fax: (213) 473-6324
Room 200, Los Angeles, CA 90013
Deputy Chief/Training **Bill Murphy** . . . . (213) 486-0150
304 South Broadway, Los Angeles, CA 90013
E-mail: murphyw@lapd.lacity.org
Chief of Staff/First Assistant Chief **Sean Malinowski** . . . . (213) 486-0150
150 North Los Angeles Street, Fax: (213) 485-3129
Room 613, Los Angeles, CA 90012
Office of Operations/Assistant Chief **Earl C. Paysinger** . . . (213) 486-0150
150 North Los Angeles Street, Fax: (213) 847-3589
Room 604, Los Angeles, CA 90012
E-mail: paysinge@lapd.lacity.org
Information and Technology Bureau/Chief Information
Officer **Maggie Goodrich** . . . . (213) 847-3836
250 East First Street, Fax: (213) 485-0889
Room 1500, Los Angeles, CA 90012
Counter-Terrorism and Special Operations Bureau
Deputy Chief **Michael P. Downing** . . . . (213) 485-3211
150 North Los Angeles Street, Fax: (213) 473-6720
Room 630, Los Angeles, CA 90012
E-mail: downingm@lapd.lacity.org
Ombuds Officer **Gregory Doyle** . . . . (213) 202-5488
221 North Figuera street, Fax: (213) 202-5414
Room 550, Los Angeles, CA 90012

Los Angeles Police Department *continued*

Personnel Group Commanding Officer **Gloria Grube** . . . . . (213) 485-8890
150 North Los Angeles Street, Fax: (213) 847-8674
Room 534, Los Angeles, CA 90012
E-mail: grubeg@lapd.lacity.org

Operations

Chief of Detectives **Kirk J. Albanese** . . . . (213) 486-7000
251 East 6th Street, Room 163, Los Angeles, CA 90014
Operations-Central Bureau Commanding Officer/
Deputy Chief **Jose Perez** . . . . (213) 485-3101
251 East 6th Street, Fax: (213) 485-1865
Room 163, Los Angeles, CA 90014
E-mail: perezj@lapd.lacity.org
Operations-Valley Bureau Commanding Officer/Deputy
Chief **Robert Green** . . . . (213) 485-4251
7600 South Broadway, Fax: (213) 847-0183
Room 117, Los Angeles, CA 90003
E-mail: greenr@lapd.lacity.org
Assistant Chief **Jorge Villegas** . . . . (818) 838-9465
11121 North Sepulveda Boulevard, Fax: (818) 838-9460
Room 276, Mission Hills, CA 91345
E-mail: villegasj@lapd.lacity.org
Deputy Chief, Personnel and Training Bureau **(Vacant)** . . . (213) 473-0277
4849 West Venice Boulevard, Fax: (213) 473-0285
Room 213, Los Angeles, CA 90019

Board of Public Works

City Hall, 200 North Spring Street, Room 361,
Los Angeles, CA 90012-3239
Tel: (213) 978-0262 Tel: (213) 978-0333 (Public Affairs Office)
Fax: (213) 978-0278 Internet: http://bpw.lacity.org/

■ President **Kevin James** . . . . (213) 978-0249
E-mail: kevin.james@lacity.org
■ Vice President **Monica Rodriguez** . . . . (213) 978-0252
E-mail: monica.rodriguez@lacity.org
■ President Pro Tem **Heather M. Repenning** . . . . (213) 978-0255
E-mail: heather.repenning@lacity.org
■ Commissioner **Mike Davis** . . . . (213) 978-0254
E-mail: mike.davis@lacity.org
Education: North Carolina Charlotte BA; Cal State (Northridge) MPA;
Cal State (Dominguez) 1996 MA
■ Commissioner **Joel F. Jacinto** . . . . (213) 978-0248
E-mail: joel.jacinto@lacity.org
Executive Officer **Fernando Campos** . . . . (213) 978-0250
Assistant Executive Officer **Teri Schmidt** . . . . (213) 978-0256
Office of Community Beautification Director **Paul Racs** . . (213) 978-0229

Bureau of Engineering

1149 South Broadway, 7th Floor, Los Angeles, CA 90015
Tel: (213) 485-4935 Fax: (213) 485-4923

City Engineer **Gary Lee Moore** . . . . (213) 485-4935
E-mail: gary.lee.moore@lacity.org
Education: UCLA BS
Chief Deputy City Engineer **Deborah Weintraub** . . . . (213) 485-5499
E-mail: deborah.weintraub@lacity.org
Deputy City Engineer **Ted Allen** . . . . (213) 485-4915
Deputy City Engineer **Kenneth R. Redd** . . . . (213) 485-4906
Deputy City Engineer **(Vacant)** . . . . (213) 485-4920
Administration Division Head **Robert Kadomatsu** . . . . . . (213) 485-4944
E-mail: robert.kadomatsu@lacity.org
Architectural Division Head **Mahmood Karimzadeh** . . . . (213) 485-4282
E-mail: mahmood.karimzadeh@lacity.org

Bureau of Sanitation

1149 South Broadway, 9th Floor, Los Angeles, CA 90015
Tel: (213) 485-2210

Director **Enrique Zaldivar** . . . . (213) 485-2210
Chief Operating Officer **Traci Minamide** . . . . (213) 485-2210
E-mail: traci.minamide@lacity.org
Assistant Director **Adel H. Hagekhalil** . . . . (213) 485-2210
E-mail: adel.hagekhalil@lacity.org
Assistant Director **Alex Helou** . . . . (213) 485-2210

★ Elected Official ▲ Appointed by Legislature ▼ Appointed by Governor ▶ Appointed by Board or Commission ● Appointed by Judge
■ Appointed by Mayor △ Appointed by Freeholders ▽ Appointed by Supervisor ▷ Appointed by County Executive ○ Appointed by Council

Bureau of Sanitation *continued*

Assistant Director **(Vacant)** . . . . (213) 485-2210

Bureau of Street Lighting
1149 South Broadway, 2nd Floor, Los Angeles, CA 90015
Tel: (213) 847-1891 Fax: (213) 847-1860

Director **Ed Ebrahimian** . . . . (213) 847-2020
Assistant Director **Norma Isahakian** . . . . (213) 847-6402
Senior Engineering Manager **Michael Cates** . . . . (213) 847-1473
E-mail: mike.cates@lacity.org
Senior Engineering Manager **Kerney Marine** . . . . (213) 847-1484
E-mail: kerney.marine@lacity.org
Administrative Services Division Manager
Carleen Marquez . . . . (213) 847-1327
E-mail: carleen.marquez@lacity.org
Field Operations Division Superintendent
Chris Mosman . . . . (323) 913-4742
E-mail: chris.mosman@lacity.org

Department of Recreation and Parks
221 North Figueroa Street, 7th Floor, Los Angeles, CA 90012
Tel: (213) 202-2700 Internet: www.laparks.org

General Manager **Mike Shull** . . . . (213) 202-2633
Secretary **Monika Leisring** . . . . (213) 202-2633
E-mail: monika.leisring@lacity.org
Assistant General Manager, Partnership Branch
Vicki Israel . . . . (213) 202-2633
Assistant General Manager, Planning, Construction and Maintenance **Ramon Barajas** . . . . (213) 202-2681
E-mail: ramon.barajas@lacity.org
Assistant General Manager, Operations Branch
Kevin Regan . . . . (213) 202-2633
E-mail: kevin.regan@lacity.org
Director of Budget, Accounting and Administrative Resources **Noel Williams** . . . . (213) 202-4380
E-mail: noel.williams@lacity.org
Director of Grants Administration **Isophine Atkinson** . . . . (213) 202-4376
E-mail: isophine.atkinson@lacity.org
Personnel Director **Harold Fujita** . . . . (213) 202-3222
E-mail: harold.fujita@lacity.org
Public Information Director **Rose Watson** . . . . (213) 202-2700
E-mail: rose.watson@lacity.org
Metro Region Superintendent **Sophia Pina-Cortez** . . . . . . (213) 485-8744
3900 W. Chevy Chase Dr., Los Angeles, CA 90039
Pacific Region Superintendent **Carl Cooper** . . . . (310) 548-7644
1670 Palos Verdes Dr. North, Harbor City, CA 90710
Valley Region Superintendent **Charles Singer** . . . . (818) 756-9404
6335 Woodley Ave., Van Nuys, CA 91406

Department of Transportation [LADOT]
100 South Main Street, 10th Floor, Los Angeles, CA 90012
Tel: (213) 972-8470 Fax: (213) 972-8410
Internet: http://www.ladottransit.com/

■ General Manager **Seleta J. Reynolds** . . . . (213) 972-8480
E-mail: seleta.reynolds@lacity.org
Education: Brown U BA
Chief of Staff **Bridget Smith** . . . . (213) 972-8480
Education: UC Berkeley BS
Transportation Technology Strategist Fellow
Ashley Z. Hand . . . . (213) 972-8480
Education: McGill (Canada) BA; Pratt Inst MArch

Administration
Accounting Bureau Chief Accountant **Sue Chen** . . . . (213) 972-8440
E-mail: sue.chen@lacity.org
Senior Management Analyst **Will Halverson** . . . . (213) 972-8420
E-mail: william.halverson@lacity.org
Information Services Bureau Director of Systems
Michael Shimokochi . . . . (213) 972-8402
E-mail: michael.shimokochi@lacity.org
Human Resources Director **Shelly Del Rosario** . . . . (213) 972-5999
E-mail: shelly.delrosario@lacity.org

Office of Parking Management and Regulations
Executive Officer **Ken Husting** . . . . (213) 972-8422
Parking Operations Support and Adjudication
Robert Andalon . . . . (213) 972-5099
Parking Enforcement and Traffic Control Executive Officer **Greg Savelli** . . . . (213) 972-5090
E-mail: greg.savelli@lacity.org

Operations and Administration
Executive Officer, Finance and Operations
Selwyn Hollins . . . . (213) 972-8424
E-mail: selwyn.hollins@lacity.org
Education: Cal State (Long Beach) BSBA; USC MA
Field Operations Bureau **Scott Morrill** . . . . (213) 972-8436
E-mail: scott.morrill@lacity.org
District Operations, East **Roy Kim** . . . . (213) 972-8432
District Operations, West **Brian Gallagher** . . . . (213) 972-8424
E-mail: brian.gallagher@lacity.org
Transportation Design **Verej Janoyan** . . . . (213) 972-8428

Office of the City Council
City Hall, 200 N. Spring St., Room 395, Los Angeles, CA 90012

★ Council President **Herb J. Wesson, Jr.** (District 10) . . . . . (213) 473-7010
Term Expires: June 30, 2019 Fax: (213) 485-9829
E-mail: councilmember.wesson@lacity.org
Date of Birth: November 11, 1951
Education: Lincoln U (PA) 1999 BA
★ Councilmember **Gilbert A. "Gil" Cedillo** (District 1) . . . . (213) 473-7462
Term Expires: June 30, 2017 Fax: (213) 485-8907
E-mail: councilmember.cedillo@lacity.org
Date of Birth: March 25, 1954
Education: UCLA 1977 BA; People's Col (UK) JD
★ Councilmember **Paul Krekorian** (District 2) . . . . (213) 473-7002
Term Expires: June 30, 2019 Fax: (213) 978-3092
E-mail: councilmember.krekorian@lacity.org
★ Councilmember
Robert J. "Bob" Blumenfield (District 3) . . . . (213) 473-7003
Term Expires: June 30, 2017 Fax: (213) 473-7567
E-mail: councilmember.blumenfield@lacity.org
Date of Birth: September 13, 1967
Education: Duke 1989 BA; UCLA 2002 MBA
★ Councilmember **David Ryu** (District 4) . . . . (213) 473-7004
Term Expires: June 30, 2019 Fax: (213) 473-2311
E-mail: david.ryu@lacity.org
★ Councilmember **Paul Koretz** (District 5) . . . . (213) 473-7005
Term Expires: June 30, 2017 Fax: (213) 978-2250
E-mail: paul.koretz@lacity.org
Education: UCLA 1979 BA
★ Councilmember **Nury Martinez** (District 6) . . . . (213) 473-7006
Term Expires: June 30, 2019 Fax: (213) 473-7999
E-mail: nury.martinez@lacity.org
★ Councilmember **Felipe Fuentes** (District 7) . . . . (213) 473-7007
Term Expires: June 30, 2017 Fax: (213) 847-0707
E-mail: councilmember.fuentes@lacity.org
Education: UCLA BA
★ Councilmember
Marqueece Harris-Dawson (District 8) . . . . (213) 473-7008
Term Expires: June 30, 2019 Fax: (213) 485-7683
E-mail: councilmember.harris-dawson@lacity.org
★ Councilmember **Curren D. Price, Jr.** (District 9) . . . . (213) 473-7009
Term Expires: June 30, 2017 Fax: (213) 473-5946
E-mail: councilmember.price@lacity.org
Education: Stanford 1972 BA; Santa Clara U 1976 JD
★ Councilmember **Mike Bonin** (District 11) . . . . (213) 473-7011
Term Expires: June 30, 2017 Fax: (213) 473-6926
E-mail: mike.bonin@lacity.org
★ Councilmember **Mitchell Englander** (District 12) . . . . (213) 473-7012
Term Expires: June 30, 2019 Fax: (213) 473-6925
E-mail: councilmember.englander@lacity.org
★ Councilmember **Mitch O'Farrell** (District 13) . . . . (213) 473-7013
Term Expires: June 30, 2017 Fax: (213) 473-7734
E-mail: councilmember.ofarrell@lacity.org

(continued on next page)

★ Elected Official ▲ Appointed by Legislature ▼ Appointed by Governor ► Appointed by Board or Commission ● Appointed by Judge
■ Appointed by Mayor △ Appointed by Freeholders ▽ Appointed by Supervisor ▷ Appointed by County Executive ○ Appointed by Council

Office of the City Council *continued*

★Councilmember **José L. Huizar** (District 14) . . . . (213) 473-7014
Term Expires: June 30, 2019 Fax: (213) 847-0680
E-mail: jose.huizar@lacity.org
Education: UC Berkeley BA; Princeton 1994 MPAUP

★Councilmember **Joe Buscaino** (District 15) . . . . (213) 473-7015
Term Expires: June 30, 2017 Fax: (213) 626-5431

Executive Officer **(Vacant)** . . . . (213) 978-1023
Fax: (213) 978-1027

Office of the Chief Legislative Analyst

City Hall, 200 N. Spring St., Room 255, Los Angeles, CA 90012
Fax: (213) 485-8983

○Chief Legislative Analyst **Sharon M. Tso** . . . . (213) 473-5713
E-mail: sharon.tso@lacity.org

Executive Officer **Karen Kalfayan** . . . . (213) 978-1759
E-mail: karen.kalfayan@lacity.org
Education: Occidental BA; Claremont Grad MBA

Executive Assistant **Donna J. Currens** . . . . (213) 473-5708
E-mail: donna.currens@lacity.org

Los Angeles Unified School District [LAUSD]

333 South Beaudry Avenue, 24th Floor, Los Angeles, CA 90017
Tel: (213) 241-7002 Fax: (213) 241-8443 Internet: http://www.lausd.net

▶Superintendent of Schools **Michelle King** . . . . (213) 241-7000
E-mail: superintendent@lausd.net

★President **Steve Zimmer** (District 4) . . . . (213) 241-6387
Term Expires: June 30, 2017
E-mail: szimmer@lausd.net
Administrative Assistant **Celia Lopez** . . . . (213) 241-6094
E-mail: celia.lopez@lausd.net

★Vice President **Dr. George McKenna** (District 1) . . . . (213) 241-6382
Term Expires: December 30, 2020
Administrative Assistant **Veronica Aguilar** . . . . (213) 241-6079
E-mail: veronica.aguilar@lausd.net

★Board Member **Mónica Garciá** (District 2) . . . . (213) 241-6180
Term Expires: June 30, 2017
E-mail: monica.garcia@lausd.net
Executive Office Manager **Sonia Reza** . . . . (213) 241-6180

★Board Member **Scott Mark Schmerelson** (District 3) . . . . (213) 241-8333
Term Expires: December 30, 2020
Chief of Staff **Arlene Irlando** . . . . (213) 241-8333

★Board Member **Ref Rodriguez** (District 5) . . . . (213) 241-5555
Term Expires: June 30, 2019
Chief of Staff **Aixle Aman** . . . . (213) 241-5646

★Board Member **Monica Ratliff** (District 6) . . . . (213) 241-6388
Term Expires: June 30, 2017
Director of Administration **Rosemary Duff** . . . . (213) 241-6096
E-mail: rosemary.duff@lausd.net

★Board Member **Richard Vladovic** (District 7) . . . . (213) 241-6385
Term Expires: December 31, 2020
E-mail: richard.vladovic@lausd.net
Deputy Chief of Staff **Nancy Ceballos** . . . . (213) 241-6385
E-mail: nancy.ceballos@lausd.net

Executive Officer of the Board **Jefferson Crain** . . . . (213) 241-7002
E-mail: jefferson.crain@lausd.net
Administrative Assistant **Juanita "Janet" Saavedra** . . . (213) 241-7002
E-mail: janet.saavedra@lausd.net

Chief of School Police **Steven K. Zipperman** . . . . (213) 202-4508

Office of the Controller

City Hall East, 200 N. Main St., Room 300, Los Angeles, CA 90012
Fax: (213) 978-7211 Internet: http://controller.lacity.org/

★Controller **Ron Galperin** . . . . (213) 978-7200
Term Expires: June 30, 2017
E-mail: controller.galperin@lacity.org

Chief Deputy Controller **(Vacant)** . . . . (213) 978-7200
Principal Deputy Controller **Vijay Singhal** . . . . (213) 978-7208

Office of the Controller *continued*

Accounting/Compliance Audit Division Chief
Accountant **(Vacant)** . . . . (213) 978-7376
Auditing Division Director **Farid Saffar** . . . . (213) 978-7392
Systems Division Director **Linh Vo** . . . . (213) 978-7293
Chief Management Analyst **JoVonne Lavender** . . . . (213) 978-7257
E-mail: jovonne.lavender@lacity.org
Director of Financial Reporting **Todd Bouey** . . . . (213) 978-7300

Office of the City Attorney

City Hall East, 200 North Main Street, 8th Floor,
Los Angeles, CA 90012-4131
Fax: (213) 978-8312 Internet: http://www.lacityattorney.org/

★City Attorney **Mike Feuer** . . . . (213) 978-8100
Term Expires: June 30, 2017
E-mail: mike.feuer@lacity.org
Chief of Staff **Leela A. Kapur** . . . . (213) 978-8100

Chief Deputy City Attorney **Jim Clark** . . . . (213) 978-8100

Metropolitan Government of Louisville and Jefferson County, Kentucky

County Courthouse, 527 W. Jefferson St., Louisville, KY 40202
Fax: (502) 574-4303 Tel: (502) 574-3131 (Information)
Internet: www.louisvilleky.gov Internet: http://www.louisvilleky.gov/News/

County: Jefferson **Election Type:** Partisan **Year Founded:** 1778
Year Incorporated: 1828 **Population:** 615,366 (2015)

Form of Municipal Government: City and county governments are combined.

Office of the Mayor

County Courthouse, 527 W. Jefferson St., Suite 400, Louisville, KY 40202
Fax: (502) 574-5354 Internet: www.louisvilleky.gov/Mayor/

★Mayor **Greg Fischer** (D) . . . . (502) 574-2003
Began Service: January 3, 2011
Term Expires: January 1, 2019
E-mail: mayor@louisvilleky.gov
Date of Birth: January 14, 1958
Education: Vanderbilt 1980 BA

■Chief of Staff **Ellen M. Hesen** . . . . (502) 574-2010
E-mail: ellen.hesen@louisvilleky.gov
■Deputy Chief of Staff **Katie Allison Dailinger** . . . . (502) 574-1905
E-mail: katie.dailinger@louisvilleky.gov
Education: Oberlin

■Chief of Public Services **Doug Hamilton** . . . . (502) 574-8142
E-mail: doug.hamilton@louisvilleky.gov

■General Counsel **Kellie Watson** . . . . (502) 574-2019
E-mail: kellie.watson@louisvilleky.gov

■Communications Director **Chris Poynter** . . . . (502) 574-2003
E-mail: chris.poynter@louisvilleky.gov

■Chief of Civic Innovation **Ted Smith** . . . . (502) 574-5305
E-mail: ted.smith@louisvilleky.gov
Education: Allegheny BS; Miami U (OH) MA, PhD

■Boards and Commissions **Nicole Yates** . . . . (502) 574-2022
E-mail: nicole.yates@louisvilleky.gov

■Chief, Office of Performance and Technology
Theresa Reno-Weber . . . . (502) 574-2003
E-mail: theresa.reno-weber@louisvilleky.gov
Education: JFK School Govt MPP

■Chief of Community Building **Col. Yvette Gentry** . . . . . . (502) 574-3131
E-mail: yvette.gentry@louisvilleky.gov

Office of the County Attorney
600 W. Jefferson St., Louisville, KY 40202
Fax: (502) 574-5366

★County Attorney **Mike O'Connell** (D) . . . . (502) 574-6336
Term Expires: December 2018
E-mail: mike.oconnell@louisvilleky.gov
First Assistant County Attorney **Julie Lott Hardesty** . . . . (502) 574-6336
E-mail: julie.hardesty@louisvilleky.gov
Civil Division Director **E. Patrick "Pat" Mulvihill** (D) . . . (502) 574-6333
Criminal Division Director **Susan Ely** . . . . (502) 574-6336
E-mail: susan.ely@louisvilleky.gov

Office of Internal Audit
609 W. Jefferson St., Louisville, KY 40202
Fax: (502) 574-3599

■Internal Auditor **Ingram Quick** . . . . (502) 574-3291
E-mail: ingram.quick@louisvilleky.gov
Education: Tennessee State BS
Assistant Director (Acting) **May Porter** . . . . (502) 574-3291

Codes and Regulations Department
444 South 5th Street, Louisville, KY 40202
Fax: (502) 574-5245

■Director **Robert Kirchdorfer** . . . . (502) 574-2508
E-mail: robert.kirchdorfer@louisvilleky.gov
Assistant Director **Donald Robinson** . . . . (502) 574-3216

Planning and Design Services
444 South 5th Street, Suite 900, Louisville, KY 40202
Fax: (502) 574-8129

Director **Emily Liu** . . . . (502) 574-6678

Office for Globalization
444 South First Street, Louisville, KY 40202
Fax: (502) 574-4201

Director **Suhas Kulkarni** . . . . (502) 574-8138

Department of Community Services and Revitalization
745 W. Main St., 3rd Floor, Louisville, KY 40202-2633
TTY: (502) 574-3749

Director **Katina Whitlock** . . . . (502) 574-5972
E-mail: katina.whitlock@louisvilleky.gov

Office of Management and Budget
611 West Jefferson Street, Louisville, KY 40202
Fax: (502) 574-4384

■Chief Financial Officer **Daniel Frockt** . . . . (502) 574-6095
E-mail: daniel.frockt@louisvilleky.gov
Finance Director **Monica L. Harmon** . . . . (502) 574-6095
Budget Director **Aaron Jackson** . . . . (502) 574-6095
E-mail: aaron.jackson@louisvilleky.gov
Administrator of Finance Operations **Angela Dunn** . . . . (502) 574-3822

Fleet Services Division
444 South 5th Street, Louisville, KY 40202

Department Director **Cathy Duncan** . . . . (502) 574-3211
Fleet Administrator **Matt Maskey** . . . . (502) 574-3180

Louisville/Jefferson County Revenue Commission
101 South 8th Street, Suite 100, Louisville, KY 40202-2687
Fax: (502) 574-4818

Secretary-Treasurer **Kim Johnson** . . . . (502) 574-4860
E-mail: kim.johnson@louisvilleky.gov

Human Resources Department
517 Court Place, Suite 501, Louisville, KY 40202-3305
Fax: (502) 574-8126

Director **Sherri Toohey-Taylor** . . . . (502) 574-3045
E-mail: sherri.toohey-taylor@louisvilleky.gov
Civil Service Board Director **Steve Wilkins** . . . . (502) 574-3611
E-mail: steve.wilkins@louisvilleky.gov

Information Technology Department
410 South 5th Street, Louisville, KY 40202

Director **Jason Ballard** . . . . (502) 574-4347
E-mail: jason.ballard@louisvilleky.gov

Louisville Forward
444 South 5th Street, Louisville, KY 40202

Chief **Mary Ellen Wiederwohl** . . . . (502) 574-4140
E-mail: mary.wiederwohl@louisvilleky.gov
Education: Louisville
■Director of Economic Development **Jeff Mosley** . . . . (502) 574-4140
E-mail: jeff.mosley@louisvilleky.gov

Develop Louisville
600 West Main Street, 3rd Floor, Louisville, KY 40202-2344
Fax: (502) 574-1342

■Director **Deborah A. Bilitski** . . . . (502) 574-2824
Education: Pittsburgh BA; Louisville 1995 JD
■Deputy Director **(Vacant)** . . . . (502) 574-4140
Executive Administrator of Community Development **Theresa Zawacki** . . . . (502) 574-4140
E-mail: theresa.zawacki@louisvilleky.gov
Parking Authority of River City (PARC) Assistant Director **Tiffany R. Smith** . . . . (502) 574-3817
Fax: (502) 574-4143
Transportation Planning Deputy Director **Patti Clare** . . . . (502) 574-4140
■Director of Sustainability **Maria Koetter** . . . . (502) 574-6250
E-mail: maria.koetter@louisvilleky.gov
Education: Western Kentucky 1989 BS

Louisville and Jefferson County Community Action Agency
810 Barrett Avenue, Louisville, KY 40204-2197
Fax: (502) 574-5548

Director **Katina Whitlock** . . . . (502) 574-6128
E-mail: katina.whitlock@louisvilleky.gov

Louisville Metro Police
633 W. Jefferson St., Louisville, KY 40202-2786
Fax: (502) 574-2450 Internet: www.louisvilleky.gov/MetroPolice/

■Chief of Police **Steven "Steve" Conrad** . . . . (502) 574-7660
E-mail: steven.conrad@louisvilleky.gov
Education: Louisville BS, MS
Chief of Staff, Deputy Chief **Col. Ozzy Gibson** . . . . (502) 574-7660
Administrative Bureau Assistant Chief **Lt. Col. Michael Sullivan** . . . . (502) 574-7660
E-mail: michael.sullivan@louisvilleky.gov
Patrol Services Deputy Chief **Kim Kraeszig** . . . . (502) 574-7660
Support Bureau Assistant Chief **Lt. Col. Gregory Burns** . . (502) 574-7660
Policy Attorney **William Dennis Sims** . . . . (502) 574-7660

Metro Parks and Recreation
1297 Trevilian Way, Louisville, KY 40213
Fax: (502) 456-3269 Internet: www.louisvilleky.gov/MetroParks/

Director **Seve Ghose** . . . . (502) 456-8130
Assistant Director **Marty Storch** . . . . (502) 456-8100

★Elected Official ▲Appointed by Legislature ▼Appointed by Governor ▶Appointed by Board or Commission ●Appointed by Judge
■Appointed by Mayor △Appointed by Freeholders ▽Appointed by Supervisor ▷Appointed by County Executive ○Appointed by Council

Public Health and Wellness
400 E. Gray St., Louisville, KY 40202
Tel: (502) 574-6520 Fax: (502) 574-6588
Internet: www.louisvilleky.gov/Health/

Director **Sarah Moyer** . . . . (502) 574-8058
Deputy Director **Ryan Irvine** . . . . (502) 574-6520
Education: Louisville BS
Deputy Director **Matt Rhodes** . . . . (502) 574-6520
Education: Cumberland Col BS
Chief of Staff **Tammy Anderson** . . . . (502) 574-6520
Director of Nursing **Heather Beeber** . . . . (502) 574-6520

Public Protection Department
Animal Services
P.O. Box 16346, Louisville, KY 40256
Fax: (502) 363-9742

Director **Justin Scally** . . . . (502) 361-1318
Assistant Director **Donald Robinson** . . . . (502) 361-1318

Corrections Department
400 S. Sixth St., Louisville, KY 40202
Fax: (502) 574-2184 E-mail: jccd@louisvilleky.gov

Director **Mark E. Bolton** . . . . (502) 574-2188
Deputy Director **Eric Troutman** . . . . (502) 574-2167
Chief of Staff **Dwayne Clark** . . . . (502) 574-2167

Criminal Justice Commission
514 W. Liberty St., Suite 106, Louisville, KY 40202
Fax: (502) 574-5299

Executive Director **Kim M. Allen** . . . . (502) 574-5088

Emergency Management Agency
410 South 5th Street, Louisville, KY 40202
Fax: (502) 574-2693

■ Executive Director **Deborah "Debbie" Fox** . . . . (502) 574-3900
E-mail: deborah.fox@louisvilleky.gov
Deputy Director **Diane Bagby** . . . . (502) 572-3451
E-mail: diane.bagby@louisvilleky.gov
Plans and Operations Coordinator **Tim Osburn** . . . . (502) 574-3900
E-mail: tim.osburn@louisvilleky.gov
Resource/Mitigation Coordinator **Jim McKinney** . . . (502) 574-3900 ext. 2
E-mail: jim.mckinney@louisvilleky.gov
Technological Hazards/RMP Coordinator
Jim Bottom . . . . (502) 572-3459 ext. 3
E-mail: jim.bottom@louisvilleky.gov

Emergency Medical Services
514 West Liberty Street, 4th Floor, Louisville, KY 40202
Fax: (502) 574-4372

Director **Lee Dennison** . . . . (502) 574-8142

Louisville Fire and Rescue
1135 W. Jefferson St., Louisville, KY 40203-1997
Fax: (502) 574-2929

■ Fire Chief **Gregory Frederick** . . . . (502) 574-3701
E-mail: gregory.frederick@louisvilleky.gov
Assistant Chief **Douglas Recktenwald** . . . . (502) 574-3701
E-mail: douglas.recktenwald@louisvilleky.gov

Public Works Department
444 South 5th Street, Louisville, KY 40202
Fax: (502) 574-5924

■ Director **Vanessa Burns** . . . . (502) 574-5904
City Engineer **Dan O'Dea** . . . . (502) 574-6785
E-mail: dan.odea@louisvilleky.gov
Streets and Roads **Jeff Brown** . . . . (502) 574-6785

Solid Waste Management and Services
600 Meriwether Ave., Louisville, KY 40217-1146
Fax: (502) 574-4155

■ Director **Vanessa Burns** . . . . (502) 574-3571
E-mail: vanessa.burns@louisvilleky.gov
Assistant Director **Keith Hackett** . . . . (502) 574-3571

Louisville and Jefferson County Kentuckiana Works
410 West Chestnut Street, Suite 200, Louisville, KY 40202
Fax: (502) 574-4288 Internet: www.kentuckianaworks.org/

Executive Director **Michael Gritton** . . . . (502) 574-2500

Louisville Metro Housing Authority
420 South 8th Street, Louisville, KY 40203
Fax: (502) 569-3459

Executive Director **Tim Barry** . . . . (502) 569-3400

Louisville Zoo
1100 Trevilan Way, Louisville, KY 40213
P.O. Box 37250, Louisville, KY 40233
Internet: http://www.louisvillezoo.org

■ Director **John Walczak** . . . . (502) 459-2181
E-mail: john.walczak@louisvilleky.gov

Louisville Free Public Library
301 York Street, Louisville, KY 40203-2257
Tel: (502) 574-1760 TTY: (502) 574-1621 Fax: (502) 574-1693
Internet: www.lfpl.org/

■ Director **James L "Jim" Blanton** . . . . (502) 574-1760
Assistant Director **(Vacant)** . . . . (502) 574-1760
Executive Administrator **Belinda S. Catman** . . . . (502) 574-1760
E-mail: belinda.catman@louisvilleky.gov

Transit Authority of River City [TARC]
1000 W. Broadway, Louisville, KY 40203
Fax: (502) 213-3244 Internet: www.ridetarc.org/

Executive Director **J. Barry Barker** . . . . (502) 561-5100
Assistant Executive Director **Alyce French-Johnson** . . . . (502) 561-5104

Office of the Metropolitan Council
601 West Jefferson Street, Louisville, KY 40202
Tel: (502) 574-1100 Fax: (502) 574-1199

★ President **David W. Tandy** (D-District 4) . . . . (502) 574-1104
Term Expires: January 2017
E-mail: david.tandy@louisvilleky.gov
★ President Pro Tem **David James** (D-District 6) . . . . (502) 574-1106
Term Expires: January 2017
E-mail: david.james@louisvilleky.gov
★ Council Member **Jessica Green** (D-District 1) . . . . (502) 574-1101
Term Expires: January 1, 2019
E-mail: jessica.green@louisvilleky.gov
★ Council Member **Barbara Shanklin** (D-District 2) . . . . (502) 574-1102
Term Expires: January 2017
E-mail: barbara.shanklin@louisvilleky.gov
★ Council Member **Mary Woolridge** (D-District 3) . . . . (502) 574-1103
Term Expires: January 1, 2019
E-mail: mary.woolridge@louisvilleky.gov
★ Council Member **Cheri Bryant Hamilton** (D-District 5) . . (502) 574-1105
Term Expires: January 1, 2019
E-mail: cheri.hamilton@louisvilleky.gov
★ Council Member **Angela Leet** (R-District 7) . . . . (502) 574-1107
Term Expires: January 1, 2019
E-mail: angela.leet@louisvilleky.gov
★ Council Member **Tom Owen** (D-District 8) . . . . (502) 574-1108
Term Expires: January 2017
E-mail: tom.owen@louisvilleky.gov

★ Elected Official ▲ Appointed by Legislature ▼ Appointed by Governor ► Appointed by Board or Commission ● Appointed by Judge
■ Appointed by Mayor △ Appointed by Freeholders ▽ Appointed by Supervisor ▷ Appointed by County Executive ○ Appointed by Council

Office of the Metropolitan Council *continued*

★Council Member **Bill Hollander** (D-District 9) . . . . (502) 574-1109
Term Expires: January 1, 2019
E-mail: bill.hollander@louisvilleky.gov

★Council Member
E. Patrick "Pat" Mulvihill (D-District 10) . . . . (502) 574-1110
Term Expires: January 2017
E-mail: steve.magre@louisvilleky.gov

★Council Member **Kevin Kramer** (R-District 11) . . . . (502) 574-1111
Term Expires: January 1, 2019
E-mail: kevin.kramer@louisvilleky.gov

★Council Member **Rick Blackwell** (D-District 12) . . . . (502) 574-1112
Term Expires: January 2017
E-mail: rick.blackwell@louisvilleky.gov

★Council Member **Vicki Aubrey Welch** (D-District 13) . . . . (502) 574-1113
Term Expires: January 1, 2019
E-mail: vicki.welch@louisvilleky.gov

★Council Member **Cindi Fowler** (D-District 14) . . . . (502) 574-1114
Term Expires: January 2017
E-mail: cindi.fowler@louisvilleky.gov

★Council Member **Marianne Butler** (D-District 15) . . . . (502) 574-1115
Term Expires: January 1, 2019
E-mail: marianne.butler@louisvilleky.gov

★Council Member **Kelly Downard** (R-District 16) . . . . (502) 574-1116
Term Expires: January 2017
E-mail: kelly.downard@louisvilleky.gov

★Council Member **Glen Stuckel** (R-District 17) . . . . (502) 574-1117
Term Expires: January 1, 2019
E-mail: glen.stuckel@louisvilleky.gov

★Council Member **Marilyn Parker** (R-District 18) . . . . (502) 574-1118
Term Expires: January 2017
E-mail: marilyn.parker@louisvilleky.gov

★Council Member **Julie Carmen Denton** (R-District 19) . . (502) 574-1119
Term Expires: January 1, 2019
E-mail: julie.denton@louisvilleky.gov

★Council Member **Stuart Benson** (R-District 20) . . . . (502) 574-1120
Term Expires: January 2017
E-mail: stuart.benson@louisvilleky.gov

★Council Member **Dan Johnson** (D-District 21) . . . . (502) 574-1121
Term Expires: January 1, 2019
E-mail: dan.johnson@louisvilleky.gov

★Council Member **Robin Engel** (R-District 22) . . . . (502) 574-1122
Term Expires: January 2017
E-mail: robin.engel@louisvilleky.gov

★Council Member **James Peden** (R-District 23) . . . . (502) 574-1123
Term Expires: January 1, 2019
E-mail: james.peden@louisvilleky.gov

★Council Member **Madonna Flood** (D-District 24) . . . . (502) 574-1124
Term Expires: January 2017
E-mail: madonna.flood@louisvilleky.gov

★Council Member **David Yates** (D-District 25) . . . . (502) 574-1125
Term Expires: January 1, 2019
E-mail: david.yates@louisvilleky.gov

★Council Member **Brent T. Ackerson** (D-District 26) . . . . . (502) 574-1126
Term Expires: January 2017
E-mail: brent.ackerson@louisvilleky.gov

Office of the Commonwealth's Attorney

514 W. Liberty St., Louisville, KY 40202
Fax: (502) 595-3381

★Commonwealth's Attorney **Thomas B. Wine** . . . . (502) 595-2340
Term Expires: December 31, 2018
E-mail: tbwine@louisvilleprosecutor.com
Education: Louisville 1977, 1980 JD

First Assistant **Mark L. Miller** . . . . (502) 595-2340
E-mail: mmiller@louisvilleprosecutor.com

Office of the Coroner

Urban County Government Center, 810 Barret Ave., 7th Floor, Louisville, KY 40204
Tel: (502) 574-6262 Fax: (502) 574-5355
Internet: www.louisvilleky.gov/Coroner/

Coroner **Dr. Barbara Weakley-Jones** (D) . . . . (502) 377-2992
Term Expires: January 6, 2019
Education: Stephens AA; Louisville BS, MD

Chief Deputy Coroner **Jo-Ann Farmer** . . . . (502) 693-9735
Education: Kentucky BS

Office of the County Clerk

County Courthouse, 527 W. Jefferson St., Suite 105, Louisville, KY 40202
Tel: (502) 574-5700 Fax: (502) 574-5566

★County Clerk **Barbara "Bobbie" Holsclaw** (R) . . . . (502) 574-5680
Term Expires: January 31, 2019
E-mail: barbara.holsclaw@louisvilleky.gov

Elections Center

Urban County Government Center, 810 Barret Avenue, Suite 103, Louisville, KY 40204
Fax: (502) 574-5044

Co-Director **Luke Ash** . . . . (502) 574-6100

Co-Director **James Young** . . . . (502) 574-6100

Office of the Sheriff

Fiscal Court Bldg., 531 Court Place, Suite 600, Louisville, KY 40202-3394
Fax: (502) 574-6909 Internet: www.jcsoky.org/

★Sheriff **Col. John E. Aubrey** (D) . . . . (502) 574-5400
Term Expires: January 6, 2019
E-mail: john.aubrey@louisvilleky.gov

Commander of Community Services and Training
Lt. Col. Carl Yates . . . . (502) 574-5400
E-mail: carl.yates@louisvilleky.gov

Jefferson County Public Schools

Van Hoose Education Center, 3332 Newburg Rd., Louisville, KY 40218
Fax: (502) 485-3640

Superintendent of Schools **Donna Hargens** . . . . (502) 485-3251
Fax: (502) 485-3991

Chief Communications Officer **Allison Martin** . . . . (502) 485-3357
E-mail: allison.martin@jefferson.kyschools.us Fax: (502) 485-3629

City of Lowell, Massachusetts

City Hall, 375 Merrimack St., Lowell, MA 01852
Tel: (978) 970-4000 (Information) Fax: (978) 970-4007
Internet: www.lowellma.gov

County: Middlesex **Election Type:** Nonpartisan **Population:** 110,699 (2015)

Office of the Mayor and City Council

City Hall, 375 Merrimack St., Lowell, MA 01852

★Mayor **Edward J. Kennedy** . . . . (978) 674-4040
Began Service: January 1, 2016
Term Expires: December 31, 2017
E-mail: ekennedy@lowell.k12.ma.us

★Councilor **Corey A. Belanger** . . . . (978) 674-4040
Term Expires: December 31, 2017
E-mail: cbelanger@lowell.k12.ma.us

(continued on next page)

★ Elected Official ▲ Appointed by Legislature ▼ Appointed by Governor ▶ Appointed by Board or Commission ● Appointed by Judge
■ Appointed by Mayor △ Appointed by Freeholders ▽ Appointed by Supervisor ▷ Appointed by County Executive ○ Appointed by Council

Office of the Mayor and City Council *continued*

★Councilor **Rodney Elliott** . . . . . (978) 674-4040
Term Expires: December 31, 2017
E-mail: relliott@lowellma.gov

★Councilor **John J. Leahy** . . . . . (978) 674-4040
Term Expires: December 31, 2017
E-mail: jleahy@lowell.k12.ma.us

★Councilor **Jim Leary** . . . . . (978) 674-4040
Term Expires: December 31, 2017

★Councilor **Rita Mercier** . . . . . (978) 674-4040
Term Expires: December 31, 2017
E-mail: rmercier@lowellma.gov

★Councilor **James L. Milanazzo** . . . . . (978) 674-4040
Term Expires: December 31, 2017
E-mail: jmilanazzo@lowell.k12.ma.us

★Councilor **Daniel P. Rourke** . . . . . (978) 674-4040
Term Expires: December 31, 2017
E-mail: drourke@lowell.k12.ma.us

★Councilor **William "Bill" Samaras** . . . . . (978) 674-4040
Term Expires: December 31, 2017

Office of the City Clerk
City Hall, 375 Merrimack St., Lowell, MA 01852
Fax: (978) 970-4162

○City Clerk **Michael Q. Geary** . . . . . (978) 674-4161
E-mail: mgeary@ci.lowell.ma.us

Office of the City Manager
City Hall, 375 Merrimack St., Lowell, MA 01852

○City Manager **Kevin Murphy** . . . . . (978) 674-1000
E-mail: citymanager@lowellma.gov
Education: Suffolk 1983 JD

Assistant City Manager **Mike McGovern** . . . . . (978) 674-1002
E-mail: mmcgovern@lowellma.gov

Office of the Assessor
City Hall, 375 Merrimack St., Lowell, MA 01852

Assessor **Susan A. LeMay** . . . . . (978) 674-4200
E-mail: slemay@lowellma.gov
Date of Birth: February 2, 1955

Office of the Treasurer/Tax Collector
City Hall, 375 Merrimack St., Lowell, MA 01852

City Treasurer **Cheryl Robertson** . . . . . (978) 674-4222
E-mail: crobertson@ci.lowell.ma.us

Finance Department
City Hall, 375 Merrimack St., Lowell, MA 01852

Chief Financial Officer **Conor Baldwin** . . . . . (978) 674-4000

Fire Department
50 Arcand Dr., Lowell, MA 01852

Fire Chief **(Vacant)** . . . . . (978) 459-5553

Health Department
341 Pine Street, Lowell, MA 01854
Tel: (978) 970-4010 Fax: (978) 970-4011
Internet: www.lowellma.gov/depts/health

Director **Kerran Vigroux** . . . . . (978) 674-4010

Lowell Housing Authority
City Hall, 375 Merrimack St., Lowell, MA 01852

Housing Authority Director **Gary Wallace** . . . . . (978) 674-3500

Library
401 Merrimack St., Lowell, MA 01852

Director **Victoria Woodley** . . . . . (978) 674-4120
E-mail: vwoodley@lowellma.gov

Human Relations Department
City Hall, 375 Merrimack St., Lowell, MA 01852

Human Resources Manager **Mary Callery** . . . . . (978) 674-4105
E-mail: mcallery@ci.lowell.ma.us

Department of Planning and Development
City Hall, 375 Merrimack St., Lowell, MA 01852

Assistant City Manager/Director **Diane Tradd** . . . . . (978) 674-1401
E-mail: dtradd@lowellma.gov

Police Department
City Hall, 375 Merrimack St., Lowell, MA 01852

Chief of Police **William Taylor** . . . . . (978) 937-3224

Lowell Public Schools
43 Highland Street, Lowell, MA 01852

Superintendent of Schools **Dr. Salah Khelfaoui** . . . . . (978) 674-4324

Public Works Department
1361 Middlesex Street, Lowell, MA 01852
Fax: (978) 970-4071

Commissioner **Ralph Snow** . . . . . (978) 674-4111

Purchasing Department
City Hall, 375 Merrimack St., Lowell, MA 01852

Chief Procurement Officer **P. Michael Vaughn** . . . . . (978) 674-4110
E-mail: pmvaughn@lowellma.gov

City of Lubbock, Texas
1625 13th St., Lubbock, TX 79401
P.O. Box 2000, Lubbock, TX 79457
Tel: (806) 775-3000 (Information) Internet: www.ci.lubbock.tx.us

County: Lubbock **Election Type:** Nonpartisan **Population:** 249,042 (2015)

Office of the Mayor and City Council
1625 13th Street, Lubbock, TX 79401
P.O. Box 2000, Lubbock, TX 79457
Fax: (806) 775-3335

★Mayor **Daniel M. "Dan" Pope** . . . . . (806) 775-2010
Began Service: May 17, 2016
Term Expires: May 2018
E-mail: dpope@mylubbock.us

★Council Member **(Vacant)** (District 1) . . . . . (806) 775-2050
Note: A runoff election between Juan Chadis and Frank Gutierrez is scheduled for June 25, 2016.
Term Expires: May 13, 2018

★Council Member **(Vacant)** (District 2) . . . . . (806) 775-2050
Note: A runoff election between Sheila Patterson Harris and Jared B. Hall is scheduled for June 25, 2016.
Term Expires: May 2020

★Council Member **Jeff Griffith** (District 3) . . . . . (806) 775-2050
Term Expires: May 31, 2018
E-mail: JGriffith@mylubbock.us

★Council Member **Steve Massengale** (District 4) . . . . . (806) 775-2050
Term Expires: May 2020
E-mail: smassengale@mylubbock.us

★Elected Official ▲Appointed by Legislature ▼Appointed by Governor ▶Appointed by Board or Commission ●Appointed by Judge
■Appointed by Mayor △Appointed by Freeholders ▽Appointed by Supervisor ▷Appointed by County Executive ○Appointed by Council

Office of the Mayor and City Council *continued*

★Council Member **Karen Gibson** (District 5) . . . . (806) 775-2050
Term Expires: May 31, 2018
E-mail: kgibson@mylubbock.us
★Council Member **Latrelle Joy** (District 6) . . . . (806) 775-2050
Term Expires: May 2020
E-mail: ljoy@mylubbock.us
City Council Chief of Staff **Bob Goodwin** . . . . (806) 775-2052

Office of the City Attorney

1625 13th St., Room 205, Lubbock, TX 79401
P.O. Box 2000, Lubbock, TX 79457
Tel: (806) 775-2210 (Law Library) Fax: (806) 775-3307

○City Attorney **Chad Weaver** . . . . (806) 775-2222
E-mail: cweaver@mylubbock.us
First Deputy City Attorney **Mitchell Satterwhite** . . . . (806) 775-2222
Deputy City Attorney, Litigation **Jeff Hartsell** . . . . (806) 775-2222

Office of the City Secretary

1625 13th St., Room 206, Lubbock, TX 79401
P.O. Box 2000, Lubbock, TX 79457
Fax: (806) 775-3983

○City Secretary **Rebecca Garza** . . . . (806) 775-2061
E-mail: bgarza@mylubbock.us
Education: Texas Tech BBA, MPA

Office of the City Manager

1625 13th St., Room 201, Lubbock, TX 79401
P.O. Box 2000, Lubbock, TX 79457
Tel: (806) 775-2003 Fax: (806) 775-3924

City Manager **James W. Loomis** . . . . (806) 775-2016
E-mail: jloomis@mylubbock.us
Executive Assistant **Celia Webb** . . . . (806) 775-2003
E-mail: cwebb@mylubbock.us
Education: Texas Tech BBA
Internal Auditor **Ramesh Ganesh** . . . . (806) 775-2135
Deputy City Manager **Quincy White** . . . . (806) 775-2015
E-mail: qwhite@mylubbock.us

Animal Services

3323 SE Loop 289, Lubbock, TX 79404
P.O. Box 2000, Lubbock, TX 79457
Tel: (806) 775-2057 Fax: (806) 775-2717

Director **George Torres** . . . . (806) 775-2057

Building Inspection Department

1625 13th St., Room 106, Lubbock, TX 79401
P.O. Box 2000, Lubbock, TX 79457
Tel: (806) 775-2087 Fax: (806) 775-2089

Chief Building Official **Steven O'Neal** . . . . (806) 775-2080
Assistant Building Official **Aubrey Long** . . . . (806) 775-2081

Citibus

801 Texas Avenue, Lubbock, TX 79401
P.O. Box 2000, Lubbock, TX 79457
Tel: (806) 712-2000 Fax: (806) 712-2012
Internet: http://www.citibus.com

General Manager **Maurice Pearl** . . . . (806) 712-2000 ext. 230
Chief Financial Officer and Assistant General Manager **Michael Mangum** . . . . (806) 712-2000 ext. 228
Chief Information Officer **(Vacant)** . . . . (806) 712-2000 ext. 224
Fax: (806) 712-2012
Human Resource Director **Chris Mandrell** . . . . . . (806) 712-2000 ext. 223
E-mail: cmandrell@citibus.com
Sales and Marketing Coordinator **Val Cochran** . . . (806) 712-2000 ext. 248
City Access Supervisor **Christopher Quigley** . . . (806) 712-2000 ext. 252

Citibus *continued*

Director of Operations **Serena Stevenson** . . . . . . (806) 712-2000 ext. 242
E-mail: sstevenson@citibus.com

Community Development

1611 10th Street, 2nd Floor, Lubbock, TX 79401
P.O. Box 2000, Lubbock, TX 79457-2000
Fax: (806) 775-3917

Community Development Director **Karen Murfee** . . . . (806) 775-2288
E-mail: kmurfee@mylubbock.us

Facilities Management

P.O. Box 2000, Lubbock, TX 79457
Fax: (806) 775-3267

Director of Facilities **Wesley Everett** . . . . (806) 775-3078
E-mail: weverett@mylubbock.us
Assistant Director/Building and Energy Administrator **George Lisenbe** . . . . (806) 775-2200
E-mail: glisenbe@mylubbock.us
Education: Texas Tech 1982 BSME
Asbestos Coordinator **Tommy J. Carpenter** . . . . (806) 775-3078
E-mail: tcarpenter@mylubbock.us
Facilities Maintenance Supervisor **Sid Beach** . . . . (806) 775-2276
E-mail: sbeach@mylubbock.us

Finance Department

1625 13th St., Room 201, Lubbock, TX 79401
Tel: (806) 775-2985 Fax: (806) 775-2051

Director of Fiscal Policy **Cheryl Brock** . . . . (806) 775-2019

Human Resources Department

1625 13th St., Room 104, Lubbock, TX 79401
P.O. Box 2000, Lubbock, TX 79457
Fax: (806) 775-3316

Director **Leisa Hutcheson** . . . . (806) 775-2303
E-mail: lhutcheson@mylubbock.us

Purchasing Department

1625 13th St., Room 204, Lubbock, TX 79401-3830
P.O. Box 2000, Lubbock, TX 79457
Fax: (806) 775-2164

Director of Purchasing **Marta Alvarez** . . . . (806) 775-2572
E-mail: malvarez@mylubbock.us

Fire Department

1515 E. Ursuline, Lubbock, TX 79403
Tel: (806) 775-2632

Fire Chief **Lance Phelps** . . . . (806) 775-2630
E-mail: lphelps@mylubbock.us
Operations Deputy Fire Chief **Shaun Fogerson** . . . . (806) 775-2633
E-mail: sfogerson@mylubbock.us
Support Services Deputy Fire Chief **Rob Keinast** . . . . (806) 775-2631
E-mail: rkeinast@mylubbock.us
Fire Marshal **Garrett Nelson** . . . . (806) 775-2644
E-mail: gnelson@mylubbock.us
Fire Training Battalion Chief **Nick Wilson** . . . . (806) 775-2649
E-mail: nwilson@mylubbock.us

Emergency Management and Homeland Security

P.O. Box 2000, Lubbock, TX 79457
Fax: (806) 775-3510

Coordinator **Jay Parchman** . . . . (806) 775-3463
E-mail: jparchman@mylubbock.us

Fleet Services

206 Municipal Dr., Lubbock, TX 79403
P.O. Box 2000, Lubbock, TX 79457

Manager **Leslie Cox** . . . . (806) 775-2175
Support and Acquisition Coordinator **(Vacant)** . . . . (806) 775-2177

Health Department
806 18th Street, Lubbock, TX 79411
P.O. Box 2548, Lubbock, TX 79408
Tel: (806) 775-2902 Fax: (806) 775-3209

Public Health Director **Katherine Wells** . . . . (806) 775-2899
Laboratory Services Manager **Kim Swacina** . . . . (806) 775-2946
Prevention Services Manager **Beckie Brawley** . . . . (806) 775-2939
Education: Texas Tech 1988 BSN
Surveillance Manager **Beckie Brawley** . . . . (806) 775-2941
Education: Texas Tech 1988 BSN

Information Technology
916 Texas Avenue, Room 104, Lubbock, TX 79401
P.O. Box 2000, Lubbock, TX 79457
Tel: (806) 775-3000 Fax: (806) 775-3033

Director **Mark Yearwood** . . . . (806) 775-2355
E-mail: myearwood@ci.lubbock.tx.us

Library
1306 Ninth St., Lubbock, TX 79401

Director **Jane Clausen** . . . . (806) 775-2824
E-mail: jclausen@mylubbock.us

Lubbock Memorial Civic Center
1501 Mac Davis Lane, Lubbock, TX 79401
Fax: (806) 775-3240

Director **Freddy Chavez** . . . . (806) 775-2236
Assistant Director **Lisa Thomason** . . . . (806) 775-2237

Lubbock Preston Smith International Airport
5401 North Martin Luther King Boulevard, Lubbock, TX 79403
Tel: (806) 775-2044 Fax: (806) 775-3133

Director **Kelly A. Campbell** . . . . (806) 775-3126
Safety and Operations Deputy Director
Steve Nicholson . . . . (806) 775-2036
E-mail: snicholson@mylubbock.us
Business Finance Deputy Director **(Vacant)** . . . . (806) 775-3131

Parks and Recreation Department
1611 10th Street, Lubbock, TX 79401
Fax: (806) 775-2686

Director **Bridget Faulkenberry** . . . . (806) 775-2671
Management Assistant **Pam Casarez** . . . . (806) 775-2669
E-mail: pcasarez@mylubbock.us
Administrative Assistant **Patricia Thomas** . . . . (806) 775-2687
E-mail: patthomas@mylubbock.us

Planning and GIS Department
1625 13th St., Room 107, Lubbock, TX 79401
P.O. Box 2000, Lubbock, TX 79457
Tel: (806) 775-2102 Fax: (806) 775-2100

Director **Andrew "Drew" Paxton** . . . . (806) 775-2103

Police Department
916 Texas Ave., Lubbock, TX 79401
P.O. Box 2000, Lubbock, TX 79457
Tel: (806) 775-2790 Fax: (806) 775-2781

Chief of Police **Greg Stevens** . . . . (806) 775-2750
Management Assistant **Elisa Sanchez** . . . . (806) 775-2755
E-mail: esanchez@mylubbock.us
Administration Assistant Chief **Jon Caspell** . . . . (806) 775-2749
Investigations Assistant Chief **Jerry Brewer** . . . . (806) 775-2759
Patrol Assistant Chief **Neal Barron** . . . . (806) 775-2960
Training Division Captain **Joshua Crouch** . . . . (806) 775-2752

Public Information Office
1625 13th St., Lubbock, TX 79401
P.O. Box 2000, Lubbock, TX 79457
Fax: (806) 775-3252

Public Information Manager **(Vacant)** . . . . (806) 775-3268
Public Information Specialist, Audio/Video
Mike Robles . . . . (806) 775-3312
E-mail: mrobles@mylubbock.us
Public Information Specialist **Majo Miselem** . . . . (806) 775-2279
E-mail: mmiselem@mylubbock.us

Department of Public Works
1625 13th Street, Lubbock, TX 79401

Director **L. Wood Franklin** . . . . (806) 775-2343
E-mail: wfranklin@mylubbock.us

Engineering Department
1625 13th St., Room 107, Lubbock, TX 79401
P.O. Box 2000, Lubbock, TX 79457-2000
Fax: (806) 775-3074

City Engineer **Mike Keenum** . . . . (806) 775-2393
E-mail: mkeenum@mylubbock.us
Right-of-Way Agent **Dave Booher** . . . . (806) 775-2352
Water Utilities Engineering Manager **John Turpin** . . . . (806) 775-2342
E-mail: jturpin@mylubbock.us Fax: (806) 775-3344
Municipal Planning Organization Director **David Jones** . . (806) 775-1671
916 Main Street, Suite 706, Lubbock, TX 79401
E-mail: djones@mylubbock.us

Street Department
502 North Interstate 27, Lubbock, TX 79457
P.O. Box 2000, Lubbock, TX 79457
Fax: (806) 775-2744

Street Superintendent **(Vacant)** . . . . (806) 775-2600
Paved Streets Supervisor **Timothy Merritt** . . . . (806) 775-2597
Pipeline Maintenance Supervisor **Brian Bearden** . . . . (806) 775-2628

Traffic Engineering
915 Avenue J, Room 212, Lubbock, TX 79457
P.O. Box 2000, Lubbock, TX 79457
Tel: (806) 775-2132 Fax: (806) 775-2152

City Traffic Engineer **Sharmon Owens** . . . . (806) 775-2130
E-mail: sowens@mylubbock.us
Traffic Engineering Capital Projects Manager
David Bragg . . . . (806) 775-2135
E-mail: dbragg@mylubbock.us

Water Utilities
P.O. Box 2000, Lubbock, TX 79457
Fax: (806) 775-3027

Director of Water Utilities **Aubrey Spear** . . . . (806) 775-2585
Wastewater Superintendent **Mary Gonzales** . . . . (806) 775-3227
Water Treatment Superintendent **Bruce Blalack** . . . . (806) 775-2613
Land Application Supervisor **Mary Gonzales** . . . . (806) 767-3157
Industrial Waste and Pretreatment Coordinator
Craig Henderson . . . . (806) 775-3229
Wildlife Biologist **Diane Selby** . . . . (806) 775-2602

Solid Waste Department
208 Municipal Drive, Lubbock, TX 79403
P.O. Box 2000, Lubbock, TX 79457
Fax: (806) 775-3013

Manager of Collections **Penny Morin** . . . . (806) 775-2481
Manager of Disposal **Catrennia Williamson** . . . . (806) 757-2151
Customer Service Supervisor **Raquel Padilla** . . . . (806) 775-3149
Keep Lubbock Beautiful Liaison **Raquel Padilla** . . . . (806) 775-3149

Lubbock Power and Light

P.O. Box 2000, Lubbock, TX 79457
Internet: www.lpandl.com/

Director of Electric Utilities **David McCalla** . . . . (806) 775-2500
Distribution Superintendent **Steve Comey** . . . . (806) 775-2509
Customer Service Manager **Dana Box** . . . . (806) 775-2524
Fax: (806) 775-3112
Chief Operating Officer **Blair McGinnis** . . . . (806) 775-2509

City of Lynchburg, Virginia

City Hall, 900 Church Street, Lynchburg, VA 24504
Tel: (434) 856-2489 (Information) Internet: www.lynchburgva.gov

County: None **Election Type:** Nonpartisan **Population:** 79,812 (2015)

Office of the Mayor and City Council

City Hall, 900 Church St., Lynchburg, VA 24504

Note: The City Council will choose a new Mayor on July 1, 2016.

★ Council Member-Elect
MaryJane Tousignant Dolan (Ward I) . . . . (434) 455-3995
Term Expires: June 30, 2020

★ Council Member-Elect **Sterling Wilder** (Ward II) . . . . (434) 455-3995
Term Expires: June 30, 2020

★ Council Member **Jeff S. Helgeson** (Ward III) . . . . (434) 455-3995
Term Expires: June 30, 2020
E-mail: jeff.helgeson@lynchburgva.gov

★ Council Member **Turner Perrow** (Ward IV) . . . . (434) 455-3995
Term Expires: June 30, 2020

★ Council Member **Joan Foster** (At-Large) . . . . (434) 455-3995
Term Expires: June 30, 2018
E-mail: joan.foster@lynchburgva.gov
Education: Lynchburg BA, MEd

★ Council Member
John Randolph "Randy" Nelson (At-Large) . . . . (434) 455-3995
Term Expires: June 30, 2018

★ Council Member **Treney Tweedy** (At-Large) . . . . (434) 455-3995
Term Expires: June 30, 2018

○ Clerk of Council **Valeria P. Chambers** . . . . (434) 455-3995
E-mail: valeria.chambers@lynchburgva.gov

Office of the City Attorney

City Hall, 900 Church St., Lynchburg, VA 24504

○ City Attorney **Walter C. Erwin** . . . . (434) 455-3973
E-mail: walter.erwin@lynchburgva.gov
Risk Management Director **Blake E. Isley III** . . . . (434) 455-3811
E-mail: blake.isley@lynchburgva.gov

Clerk of Council

City Hall, 900 Church St., Lynchburg, VA 24504
Fax: (434) 847-1536

○ Clerk of the Council **Valeria P. Chambers** . . . . (434) 455-3995
E-mail: valeria.chambers@lynchburgva.gov
○ Deputy Clerk of Council **Kyna Thomas** . . . . (434) 455-3985
E-mail: kyna.thomas@lynchburgva.gov

Office of the City Manager

City Hall, 900 Church St., Lynchburg, VA 24504
E-mail: city.manager@lynchburgva.gov

○ City Manager **L. Kimball Payne III** . . . . (434) 455-3990
E-mail: kpayne@lynchburgva.gov
Deputy City Manager **Bonnie Svrcek** . . . . (434) 455-3990
E-mail: bonnie.svrcek@lynchburgva.gov

Assessment and Real Estate

City Hall, 900 Church St., Lynchburg, VA 24504
Fax: (434) 847-1452

City Assessor **Gregory H. Daniels** . . . . (434) 455-3821
E-mail: greg.daniels@lynchburgva.gov

Aviation Department

Lynchburg Regional Airport, 4308 Wards Road, Suite 100, Lynchburg, VA 24502
Fax: (434) 239-9027

Airport Director **Mark F. Courtney** . . . . (434) 582-1150 ext. 6089

Budget Office

City Hall, 900 Church St., Lynchburg, VA 24504

Director **Donna Witt** . . . . (434) 455-3968
E-mail: donna.witt@lynchburgva.gov

Community Development Department

City Hall, 900 Church St., Lynchburg, VA 24504
Fax: (434) 845-7630

Director **Kent White** . . . . (434) 455-3902
E-mail: kent.white@lynchburgva.gov

Communications and Marketing

City Hall, 900 Church St., Lynchburg, VA 24504

Director **JoAnn B. Martin** . . . . (434) 455-3801
E-mail: joann.martin@lynchburgva.gov Fax: (434) 847-2083

Economic Development Department

City Hall, 900 Church Street, Lynchburg, VA 24504
Fax: (434) 847-2067

Director **Marjette Upshur** . . . . (434) 455-4493
E-mail: marjette.upshur@lynchburgva.gov

Department of Emergency Services

3621 Candlers Mountain Road, Lynchburg, VA 24504

Director of Emergency Services **Melissa Foster** . . . . (434) 847-1602
E-mail: melissa.foster@lynchburgva.gov

Financial Services

City Hall, 900 Church St., Lynchburg, VA 24504

Director **Donna Witt** . . . . (434) 455-3968

Fire Department

800 Madison St., Lynchburg, VA 24504

Fire Chief **Steven B. Ferguson** . . . . (434) 455-6346
E-mail: steven.ferguson@lynchburgva.gov

Human Resources

City Hall, 900 Church St., Lynchburg, VA 24504
Fax: (434) 845-4304

Director **Margaret Schmitt** . . . . (434) 455-4208
E-mail: margaret.schmitt@lynchburgva.gov
Education: Hampton BS; Troy State MPA

Human Services Department

99 Ninth Street, Lynchburg, VA 24504

Director **Tamara Rosser** . . . . (434) 455-5794

Information Technology Department

3550 Young Place, Lynchburg, VA 24501

Director **Michael Goetz** . . . . (434) 455-6002
E-mail: mike.goetz@lynchburgva.gov

★ Elected Official ▲ Appointed by Legislature ▼ Appointed by Governor ▶ Appointed by Board or Commission ● Appointed by Judge
■ Appointed by Mayor △ Appointed by Freeholders ▽ Appointed by Supervisor ▷ Appointed by County Executive ○ Appointed by Council

Library Department
Lynchburg Public Library, 2315 Memorial Avenue, Lynchburg, VA 24501
Director (Interim) **Marilyn Martin** .... (434) 455-6301
E-mail: marilyn.martin@lynchburgva.gov

Lynchburg Visitor Information Center
216 12th Street, Lynchburg, VA 24504
Tel: (800) 732-5821 Internet: www.discoverlynchburg.org
Manager **Alison Chadbourne** .... (434) 485-7290

Parks and Recreation Department
301 Grove St., Lynchburg, VA 24501
Fax: (434) 528-2794
Director **Jennifer Jones** .... (434) 455-5868

Police Department
905 Court St., Lynchburg, VA 24504
Internet: http://www.lynchburgpolice.org
Chief of Police **Raul Diaz** .... (434) 455-6045

Tourism Department
901 Church Steet, Lynchburg, VA 24504
Director **Sergei Troubetzkoy** .... (434) 485-7297

Public Works Department
1700 Memorial Ave., Lynchburg, VA 24501
E-mail: public.works@lynchburgva.gov
Director **Gaynelle Hart** .... (434) 455-4406

Department of Water Resources
900 Church Street, Lynchburg, VA 24504
Director **Timothy Mitchell** .... (434) 455-4252

Office of the Commissioner of Revenue
City Hall, 900 Church St., Lynchburg, VA 24504
★Commissioner of Revenue **Mitchell W. Nuckles** .... (434) 455-3871
Term Expires: December 31, 2017
E-mail: mitchell.nuckles@lynchburgva.gov

Office of the Commonwealth's Attorney
901 Church Steet, Lynchburg, VA 24504
E-mail: prosecutor@ocalynchburg.com
★Commonwealth's Attorney **Michael R. Doucette** .... (434) 455-3760
Term Expires: December 31, 2017
E-mail: mdoucette@ocalynchburg.com

Office of the Sheriff
907 Clay Street, Lynchburg, VA 24504
★Sheriff **Ronald Gillispie** .... (434) 847-1301
Term Expires: December 31, 2017
E-mail: ronald.gillispie@lynchburgva.gov

Office of the Treasurer
City Hall, 900 Church St., Lynchburg, VA 24504
★Treasurer **Robert Bailey** .... (434) 455-4245
Term Expires: December 31, 2017

City of Lynn, Massachusetts
City Hall, City Hall Square, Lynn, MA 01901
Internet: www.ci.lynn.ma.us

County: Essex **Election Type:** Nonpartisan **Year Incorporated:** 1850
Population: 92,457 (2015)

Office of the Mayor
City Hall, City Hall Square, Room 306, Lynn, MA 01901
Tel: (781) 598-4000 Fax: (781) 599-8875
★Mayor **Judith Flanagan Kennedy** .... (781) 598-4000
Began Service: January 4, 2010
Term Expires: January 7, 2018
■Chief of Staff **Jamie Cerulli** .... (781) 598-4000
E-mail: jcerulli@ci.lynn.ma.us
■Mayoral Aide **Mary Fountain** .... (781) 598-4000
E-mail: mchalmers@ci.lynn.ma.us
■Mayoral Aide **(Vacant)** .... (781) 598-4000

Office of the City Council
City Hall, City Hall Square, Lynn, MA 01901
Tel: (781) 586-6740
★President **Daniel F. "Dan" Cahill** (At-Large) .... (781) 586-6740
Term Expires: January 1, 2020
E-mail: DanielFCahill@gmail.com
Education: Northeastern BS; Suffolk MS, JD
★Councilor **Wayne A. Lozzi** (Ward 1) .... (781) 586-6740
Term Expires: January 1, 2020
E-mail: wayne.lozzi@lynnma.gov
★Councilor **William R. Trahant, Jr.** (Ward 2) .... (781) 586-6740
Term Expires: January 1, 2020
E-mail: william.trahant@lynnma.gov
★Councilor **Darren P. Cyr** (Ward 3) .... (781) 586-6740
Term Expires: January 1, 2020
E-mail: darren.cyr@lynnma.gov
★Councilor **Richard C. Colucci** (Ward 4) .... (781) 586-6740
Term Expires: January 1, 2020
E-mail: richard.colucci@lynnma.gov
★Councilor **Dianna Chakoutis** (Ward 5) .... (781) 586-6740
Term Expires: January 1, 2020
E-mail: dianna.chakoutis@lynnma.gov
★Councilor **Peter L. Capano** (Ward 6) .... (781) 586-6740
Term Expires: January 1, 2020
E-mail: peter.capano@lynnma.gov
★Councilor **John "Jay" Walsh, Jr.** (Ward 7) .... (781) 586-6740
Term Expires: January 1, 2020
E-mail: John.Walsh@lynnma.gov
★Councilor **Gorden "Buzzy" Barton** (At-Large) .... (781) 586-6740
Term Expires: January 1, 2020
E-mail: buzzy.barton@lynnma.gov
★Councilor **Brian LaPierre** (At-Large) .... (781) 586-6740
Term Expires: January 1, 2020
E-mail: Brian.LaPierre@lynnma.gov
★Councilor **Hong L. Net** (At-Large) .... (781) 586-6740
Term Expires: January 1, 2020
E-mail: hong.net@lynnma.gov

Office of the City Clerk and Elections
City Hall, City Hall Square, Room 201, Lynn, MA 01901
Fax: (781) 477-7032
○City Clerk and Elections Chief
Mary F. Audley .... (781) 598-4000 ext. 6726
E-mail: maudley@lynnma.gov

Office of the Comptroller
City Hall, City Hall Square, Room 312, Lynn, MA 01901
○Comptroller **Stephen Spencer** .... (781) 598-4000
E-mail: sspencer@lynnma.gov

★Elected Official ▲Appointed by Legislature ▼Appointed by Governor ▶Appointed by Board or Commission ●Appointed by Judge
■Appointed by Mayor △Appointed by Freeholders ▽Appointed by Supervisor ▷Appointed by County Executive ○Appointed by Council

Office of Economic Development and Industrial Corporation
City Hall, City Hall Square, Room 311, Lynn, MA 01901
Fax: (781) 477-7026

Executive Director **James M. Cowdell** .... (781) 598-4000 ext. 6930
E-mail: jcowdell@broadviewnet.net

Office of the Tax Collector
City Hall, City Hall Square, Room 204, Lynn, MA 01901

○ Collector **Frederick B. Cronin, Jr.** .... (781) 598-4000 ext. 6746
E-mail: fcronin@ci.lynn.ma.us

Office of the Treasurer
City Hall, City Hall Square, Room 206, Lynn, MA 01901
Fax: (781) 477-7076

■ Treasurer **Richard J. Fortucci** .... (781) 598-4000 ext. 6904
E-mail: rfortucci@ci.lynn.ma.us
Assistant City Treasurer **Lynne E. Quinn** ...... (781) 589-4000 ext. 6904

Assessors' Department
City Hall, City Hall Square, Room 202, Lynn, MA 01901
Fax: (781) 477-7160

Director of Assessing and Chief Financial Officer **Peter Caron** .... (781) 598-4000 ext. 6702
E-mail: pcaron@ci.lynn.ma.us
Assessor **Michael Fisher** .... (781) 598-4000 ext. 6702
E-mail: mfisher@lynnma.gov
Assessor **Christopher Gaeta** .... (781) 598-4000 ext. 6702
E-mail: cgaeta@lynnma.gov

Election Commission
City Hall, City Hall Square, Lynn, MA 01901
Fax: (781) 477-7032

Elections Chief **Mary F. Audley** .... (781) 598-4000 ext. 6805

Fire Department
725 Western Ave., Lynn, MA 01905
Fax: (781) 596-1480

Fire Chief **James McDonald** .... (781) 593-1234 ext. 10
E-mail: jmcdonald@lynnma.gov
Deputy Fire Chief **William Murray** .... (781) 593-1234 ext. 11
E-mail: wmurray@lynnma.gov

Health Department
City Hall, City Hall Square, Lynn, MA 01901

Health Director **Mary Ann O'Connor** .... (781) 598-4000

Inspectional Services
City Hall, City Hall Square, Lynn, MA 01901

■ Chief **Michael J. Donovan** .... (781) 598-4000
E-mail: mdonovan@lynnma.gov
Health Division Head **Mary Ann O'Connor** .... (781) 598-4000
Facilities Director **Lloyd "Butch" Barnes** .... (781) 598-4000
E-mail: lbarnes@lynnma.gov

Information Technology Department
City Hall, City Hall Square, Room 100, Lynn, MA 01901

Director **Peter Efstratios** .... (781) 598-4000
E-mail: pefstrat@ci.lynn.ma.us

Legal Department
City Hall, City Hall Square, Room 406, Lynn, MA 01901
Fax: (781) 477-7043

○ City Solicitor **Michael Barry** .... (781) 598-4000 ext. 6843
E-mail: mbarry@lynnma.gov

Legal Department *continued*

Assistant Solicitor **George Markopoulos** ...... (781) 598-4000 ext. 6843
E-mail: gmarkopoulos@lynnma.gov
Assistant Solicitor **Richard Vitali** .... (781) 598-4000 ext. 6843
E-mail: rvitali@lynnma.gov

Library
5 North Common Street, Lynn, MA 01902
Fax: (781) 592-5050

Chief Librarian **Theresa Hurley** .... (781) 595-0567
E-mail: thurley@lynnma.gov

Parking Department
City Hall, City Hall Square, Room 102, Lynn, MA 01901

Director **L. Jay Fenton** .... (781) 598-4000
Executive Assistant **(Vacant)** .... (781) 586-6873

Personnel and Human Resources
City Hall, City Hall Square, Room 412, Lynn, MA 01901

■ Director **Joseph P. Driscoll** .... (781) 598-4000
E-mail: jdriscoll@lynnma.gov

Police Department
300 Washington Street, Lynn, MA 01902
Fax: (781) 477-7069

■ Chief of Police **Kevin F. Coppinger** .... (781) 595-2000
E-mail: kcoppinger@lynnpolice.org
Confidential Assistant **Elizabeth Polonsky** .... (781) 595-2000
Deputy Chief of Police **Leonard E. Desmarais** .... (781) 595-2000
Deputy Chief of Police **Michael A. Mageary** .... (781) 595-2000

Public Works Department
250 Commercial Street, Lynn, MA 01901
Tel: (781) 477-7099 Fax: (781) 477-7074

■ Commissioner **Andrew J. Hall** .... (781) 268-8000
E-mail: ahall@lynnma.gov
Associate Commissioner **Lisa J. Nerich** .... (781) 268-8000

Purchasing Department
City Hall, City Hall Square, Room 205, Lynn, MA 01901
Fax: (781) 477-7027

■ Director **Charles White** .... (781) 598-4000 ext. 6893
E-mail: cwhite@ci.lynn.ma.us

Veterans Affairs Office
City Hall, City Hall Square, Room 307, Lynn, MA 01901
Tel: (781) 477-7144

■ Director **Michael F. Sweeney** .... (781) 586-6917
E-mail: msweeney@lynnma.gov

Water and Sewer Commission
400 Parkland Ave., Lynn, MA 01905
Fax: (781) 595-1420 Internet: www.lynnwaterserver.org

Director of Management Operations **Daniel F. O'Neill** .... (781) 596-2400 ext. 223
E-mail: doneill@lynnwatersewer.org

★ Elected Official ▲ Appointed by Legislature ▼ Appointed by Governor ▶ Appointed by Board or Commission ● Appointed by Judge
■ Appointed by Mayor △ Appointed by Freeholders ▽ Appointed by Supervisor ▷ Appointed by County Executive ○ Appointed by Council

City of Madison, Wisconsin

City-County Bldg., 210 Martin Luther King, Jr. Blvd.,
Madison, WI 53703-3342
Tel: (608) 266-4611 (Information) Internet: www.cityofmadison.com

County: Dane **Election Type:** Nonpartisan **Year Founded:** 1832
Year Incorporated: 1856 **Population:** 248,951 (2015)

Office of the Mayor

City-County Bldg., 210 Martin Luther King, Jr. Blvd., Room 403,
Madison, WI 53703
Fax: (608) 267-8671 Internet: www.cityofmadison.com/mayor/

★ Mayor **Paul R. Soglin** .... (608) 266-4611
Began Service: April 19, 2011
Term Expires: April 19, 2019
E-mail: mayor@cityofmadison.com
Executive Assistant to the Mayor **Monica Sundal** ...... (608) 266-4611

Deputy Mayor for Administration and Finance
Enis T. Ragland .... (608) 266-4611
E-mail: eragland@cityofmadison.com

Deputy Mayor for Planning and Transportation
Anne Monks .... (608) 266-4611
E-mail: amonks@cityofmadison.com

Deputy Mayor for Public Safety, Civil Rights and Community Services **Gloria Reyes** .... (608) 266-4611
E-mail: greyes@cityofmadison.com

Deputy Mayor for Public Works and Communication
Katie Crawley .... (608) 266-4611
E-mail: kcrawley@cityofmadison.com

Government Relations Officer/Legislative Analyst
Nicholas Zavos .... (608) 266-4611
E-mail: nzavos@cityofmadison.com

Office of the City Assessor

City-County Building, 210 Martin Luther King, Jr. Boulevard,
Madison, WI 53703
Fax: (608) 266-4257 E-mail: assessor@cityofmadison.com
Internet: www.cityofmadison.com/assessor/

City Assessor **Mark Hanson** .... (608) 266-4531
210 Martin Luther King, Jr. Boulevard,
Room 101, Madison, WI 53703-3342
E-mail: mhanson@cityofmadison.com

Assistant Assessor **(Vacant)** .... (608) 266-4531
210 Martin Luther King, Jr. Boulevard,
Room 101, Madison, WI 53703-3342

Assessment Services Supervisor **Sally Sweeney** .... (608) 266-4531
210 Martin Luther King, Jr. Boulevard,
Room 101, Madison, WI 53703-3342
E-mail: ssweeney@cityofmadison.com

Assistant Assessor, Residential **JoAnn Terasa** .... (608) 266-4531
210 Martin Luther King, Jr. Boulevard,
Room 101, Madison, WI 53703-3342
E-mail: jterasa@cityofmadison.com

Office of the City Attorney

City-County Bldg., 210 Martin Luther King, Jr. Blvd., Room 401,
Madison, WI 53703-3345
Tel: (608) 266-4511 Fax: (608) 267-8715
E-mail: attorney@cityofmadison.com
Internet: www.cityofmadison.com/attorney

City Attorney **Michael May** .... (608) 266-4511
E-mail: mmay@cityofmadison.com

Office of the City Clerk

210 Martin Luther King, Jr. Blvd., Room 103, Madison, WI 53703-3342
Tel: (608) 266-4601 Fax: (608) 266-4666
E-mail: clerk@cityofmadison.com
Internet: www.cityofmadison.com/clerk/

■ City Clerk **Maribeth Witzel-Behl** .... (608) 266-4601
E-mail: clerk@cityofmadison.com

Office of the City Treasurer

City-County Building, 210 Martin Luther King, Jr. Boulevard,
Madison, WI 53703
Tel: (608) 266-4771 Fax: (608) 266-4128
E-mail: treasurer@cityofmadison.com
Internet: www.cityofmadison.com/Treasurer/

■ City Treasurer **David M. Gawenda** .... (608) 266-4771
210 Martin Luther King, Jr. Boulevard,
Room 107, Madison, WI 53703-3342
E-mail: dgawenda@cityofmadison.com

Department of Civil Rights [DCR]

City-County Building, 210 Martin Luther King, Jr. Boulevard, Room 523,
Madison, WI 53703
Tel: (608) 266-4910 Tel: (866) 704-2314 (TTY/Textnet)
Fax: (608) 266-6514 E-mail: dcr@cityofmadison.com
Internet: www.cityofmadison.com/dcr/

Director (Interim) **Gloria Reyes** .... (608) 266-5916
Equal Opportunities Division Manager **(Vacant)** .... (608) 267-4915
Affirmative Action Division Manager **Norman D. Davis** .. (608) 267-8759
Disability Rights Specialist **Jason Glozier** .... (608) 267-4900

Finance Department

City-County Bldg., 210 Martin Luther King, Jr. Blvd., Room 406,
Madison, WI 53703-3345
Tel: (608) 266-4671 Fax: (608) 267-8705
Internet: www.cityofmadison.com/finance/

Finance Director **David Schmiedicke** .... (608) 267-8710
Budget and Program Evaluation Manager **Larua Larsen** .. (608) 267-4913
E-mail: llarsen@cityofmadison.com

Accounting Services

Accounting Services Manager **Patricia A. McDermott** ... (608) 266-4478
E-mail: pmcdermott@cityofmadison.com

Risk Management Office

Risk Manager **Eric Veum** .... (608) 266-5965
E-mail: eveum@cityofmadison.com

Fire Department

30 West Mifflin Street, Madison, WI 53703
Tel: (608) 266-4420 Fax: (608) 267-1153
E-mail: fire@cityofmadison.com Internet: www.cityofmadison.com/fire/

Fire Chief **Steven A. Davis** .... (608) 266-6564
E-mail: sdavis@cityofmadison.com

Assistant Chief of Administration **Laura Laurenzi** .... (608) 267-8674
E-mail: llaurenzi@cityofmadison.com

Assistant Chief of Operations **Lance Langer** .... (608) 266-4789
E-mail: llanger@cityofmadison.com

Assistant Chief of Personnel **Michael Popovich** .... (608) 266-5946
E-mail: mpopovich@cityofmadison.com

Assistant Chief of Support Services
Clayton Christenson .... (608) 266-5956

Fire Marshal **Edwin Ruckriegel** .... (608) 266-4457
E-mail: eruckriegel@cityofmadison.com Fax: (608) 267-1153

Administrative Services Manager **(Vacant)** .... (608) 266-5957
Fax: (608) 267-1153

Administrative Assistant **Velma Avalos** .... (608) 266-9215
E-mail: vavalos@cityofmadison.com

★ Elected Official ▲ Appointed by Legislature ▼ Appointed by Governor ► Appointed by Board or Commission ● Appointed by Judge
■ Appointed by Mayor △ Appointed by Freeholders ▽ Appointed by Supervisor ▷ Appointed by County Executive ○ Appointed by Council

Human Resources Department

City-County Bldg., 210 Martin Luther King, Jr. Blvd., Room 501, Madison, WI 53703
Tel: (608) 266-4615 Tel: (866) 704-2340 (TTY/Textnet)
Fax: (608) 267-1115 Internet: www.cityofmadison.com/hr/

■ Human Resources Director **Brad Wirtz** . . . . . (608) 266-4001
E-mail: bwirtz@cityofmadison.com
Employee and Labor Relations Manager **Greg Leifer** . . . . . (608) 266-4615
Human Resources Services Manager **Michael Lipski** . . . . . (608) 266-4615
E-mail: mlipski@cityofmadison.com
Employee Assistance Program Coordinator
Tresa Martinez . . . . . (608) 266-6561
Madison Municipal Bldg., 215 Martin Luther King, Jr. Blvd. Madison, WI 53709
E-mail: tmartinez@cityofmadison.com
Organizational Development and Training Coordinator
Karl Van Lith . . . . . (608) 266-9037
Madison Municipal Bldg, 215 Martin Luther King, Jr. Blvd., Madison, WI 53709
E-mail: kvanlith@cityofmadison.com

Information Technology Department

City-County Bldg., 210 Martin Luther King, Jr. Blvd., Room 500, Madison, WI 53703
Tel: (608) 266-4193 Fax: (608) 261-9289 E-mail: is@cityofmadison.com

■ Director **Paul Kronenberger** . . . . . (608) 266-4454
Data Center Manager **Richard Beadles** . . . . . (608) 261-9649
E-mail: rbeadles@cityofmadison.com
Systems and Programming Manager **David Faust** . . . . . (608) 267-4909
E-mail: dfaust@cityofmadison.com

Madison City Channel

Madison Municipal Bldg., 215 Martin Luther King, Jr. Blvd., Room 210, Madison, WI 53710
Tel: (608) 266-6501 Internet: www.cityofmadison.com/citychannel/

Manager **Boyce Johnson** . . . . . (608) 266-6393
E-mail: bjohnson@cityofmadison.com

Planning and Community and Economic Development Department

Madison Municipal Bldg., 215 Martin Luther King, Jr. Blvd., Room LL-100, Madison, WI 53703
Tel: (608) 266-4635 Fax: (608) 267-8739
E-mail: planning@cityofmadison.com
Internet: www.cityofmadison.com/planning/

Director **Natalie Erdman** . . . . . (608) 266-4635
E-mail: nerdman@cityofmadison.com

Police Department

211 S. Carroll St., Madison, WI 53703-3303
Tel: (608) 266-4022 Fax: (608) 266-4855
Internet: www.madisonpolice.com

Chief of Police **Michael C. Koval** . . . . . (608) 266-4022

Madison Public Library

201 W. Mifflin St., Madison, WI 53703
Tel: (608) 266-6300 TTY: (608) 266-6314 Fax: (608) 266-4338
Internet: www.madisonpubliclibrary.org/

Director **Greg Mickells** . . . . . (608) 266-6363
E-mail: gmickells@madisonpubliclibrary.org

Public Works Department

City-County Bldg., 210 Martin Luther King, Jr. Blvd., Room 115, Madison, WI 53703
Fax: (608) 264-9275 E-mail: publicworks@cityofmadison.com
Internet: www.cityofmadison.com/business/pw/

Director **William Vanden Brook** . . . . . (608) 246-4546
200 N. First St., Madison, WI 53704

Public Works Department *continued*

Sanitary and Storm Sewer Principal Engineer
Greg Fries . . . . . (608) 267-1199

Engineering Division

210 Martin Luther King, Jr. Blvd., Room 215, Madison, WI 53703-3342
Tel: (608) 266-4751 Fax: (608) 264-9275
Internet: http://www.cityofmadison.com/engineering/

City Engineer **Robert F. Phillips** . . . . . (608) 266-4090
E-mail: rphillips@cityofmadison.com
Construction Principal Engineer **John Fahrney** . . . . . (608) 266-9091
1602 Emil Street, Madison, WI 53703
E-mail: jfahrney@cityofmadison.com
Sewer Maintenance Operations Supervisor
Kathleen M. Cryan . . . . . (608) 266-4819
E-mail: kcryan@cityofmadison.com

Fleet Services

210 Martin Luther King, Jr. Blvd., Madison, WI 53703-3342

Fleet Service Superintendent **William Vanden Brook** . . . . (608) 246-4546
200 N. First St., Madison, WI 53704

Parks Division

210 Martin Luther King, Jr. Boulevard, Suite 104, Madison, WI 53703
Tel: (608) 266-4711 Fax: (608) 267-1162

Parks Superintendent **Eric Knepp** . . . . . (608) 266-4711

Madison Water Utility

119 East Olin Avenue, Madison, WI 53713
Tel: (608) 266-4651 Fax: (608) 266-4644
Internet: www.cityofmadison.com/water/

Water Utility General Manager **Tom Heikkinen** . . . . . (608) 266-4651
Principal Engineer **Alan Larson** . . . . . (608) 266-4653
E-mail: alarson@madisonwater.org
Accounting/Financial Manager **Michael Krentz** . . . . . (608) 266-4656
E-mail: mkrentz@madisonwater.org

Metro Transit

Tel: (608) 266-4904 Fax: (608) 267-8778

Transit General Manager **Chuck Kamp** . . . . . (608) 266-4904
1245 East Washington Avenue, Madison, WI 53703
Transit Service Manager **Ann Gullickson** . . . . . (608) 266-4904
1101 E. Washington Ave., Madison, WI 53703

Streets Division

210 Martin Luther King, Jr. Blvd., Madison, WI 53703-3342

Streets and Sidewalks Principal Engineer
Christina M. Bachmann . . . . . (608) 266-4095
E-mail: cbachmann@cityofmadison.com

Traffic Engineer Division

215 Martin Luther King, Jr. Blvd, Suite 100, Madison, WI 53709
Tel: (608) 266-4761 Fax: (608) 267-1158

City Traffic Engineer **David C. Dryer** . . . . . (608) 266-4761
215 Martin Luther King Boulevard, Room 100, Madison, WI 53703-2986
E-mail: ddryer@cityofmadison.com

Senior Center

330 West Mifflin Street, Madison, WI 53703
Tel: (608) 266-6581 Fax: (608) 267-8684
E-mail: seniorcenter@cityofmadison.com

Director **Christine K. Beatty** . . . . . (608) 267-8652

Overture Center for the Arts

201 State St., Madison, WI 53703
Fax: (608) 258-4971 Internet: www.overturecenter.org

■ Director **Ted DeDee** . . . . . (608) 258-4177
E-mail: tdedee@cityofmadison.com

★ Elected Official ▲ Appointed by Legislature ▼ Appointed by Governor ▶ Appointed by Board or Commission ● Appointed by Judge
■ Appointed by Mayor △ Appointed by Freeholders ▽ Appointed by Supervisor ▷ Appointed by County Executive ○ Appointed by Council

Office of the Common Council

City-County Bldg., 210 Martin Luther King, Jr. Blvd., Room 417, Madison, WI 53703
Tel: (608) 266-4071 Fax: (608) 267-8669
Internet: www.cityofmadison.com/council/

★President **Michael Verveer** (District 4) . . . . (608) 266-4071
Term Expires: April 18, 2017
E-mail: district4@cityofmadison.com

★President Pro Tem **Marsha Rummel** (District 6) . . . . (608) 266-4071
Term Expires: April 18, 2017
E-mail: district6@cityofmadison.com

★Council Member
Barbara Harrington-McKinney (District 1) . . . . (608) 266-4071
Term Expires: April 18, 2017
E-mail: district1@cityofmadison.com

★Council Member **Ledell Zellers** (District 2) . . . . (608) 266-4071
Term Expires: April 18, 2017
E-mail: district2@cityofmadison.com

★Council Member **Amanda Hall** (District 3) . . . . (608) 266-4071
Term Expires: April 18, 2017

★Council Member **Shiva Bidar-Sielaff** (District 5) . . . . (608) 266-4071
Term Expires: April 18, 2017
E-mail: district5@cityofmadison.com

★Council Member **Steve King** (District 7) . . . . (608) 266-4071
Term Expires: April 18, 2017
E-mail: district7@cityofmadison.com

★Council Member **Zachary Wood** (District 8) . . . . (608) 266-4071
Term Expires: April 18, 2017

★Council Member **Paul Skidmore** (District 9) . . . . (608) 266-4071
Term Expires: April 18, 2017
E-mail: district9@cityofmadison.com

★Council Member **Maurice Cheeks** (District 10) . . . . (608) 266-4071
Term Expires: April 18, 2017
E-mail: district10@cityofmadison.com

★Council Member **Tim Gruber** (District 11) . . . . (608) 266-4071
Term Expires: April 4, 2017
E-mail: district11@cityofmadison.com

★Council Member **Larry Palm** (District 12) . . . . (608) 266-4071
Term Expires: April 18, 2017
E-mail: district12@cityofmadison.com

★Council Member **Sara Eskrich** (District 13) . . . . (608) 266-4071
Term Expires: April 18, 2017

★Council Member **Sheri Carter** (District 14) . . . . (608) 266-4071
Term Expires: April 18, 2017

★Council Member **David Ahrens** (District 15) . . . . (608) 266-4071
Term Expires: April 18, 2017
E-mail: district15@cityofmadison.com

★Council Member **Denise DeMarb** (District 16) . . . . (608) 266-4071
Term Expires: April 18, 2017
E-mail: district16@cityofmadison.com

★Council Member **Samba Baldeh** (District 17) . . . . (608) 266-4071
Term Expires: April 18, 2017

★Council Member **Rebecca Kemble** (District 18) . . . . (608) 266-4071
Term Expires: April 18, 2017

★Council Member **Mark Clear** (District 19) . . . . (608) 266-4071
Term Expires: April 18, 2017
E-mail: district19@cityofmadison.com

★Council Member
Matthew J. "Matt" Phair (District 20) . . . . (608) 266-4071
Term Expires: April 18, 2017
E-mail: district20@cityofmadison.com

Administrative Assistant **Lisa Veldran** . . . . (608) 266-4071
E-mail: lveldran@cityofmadison.com

Madison Metropolitan School District [MMSD]

545 W. Dayton St., Madison, WI 53703
Tel: (608) 663-1879 Fax: (608) 204-0341
Internet: www.madison.k12.wi.us

Superintendent of Schools **Jennifer Cheatham** . . . . (608) 663-1607
Chief of Staff **Kelly Ruppel** . . . . (608) 663-1879

Madison Metropolitan School District *continued*

Assistant Superintendent, Business Services
Michael Barry . . . . (608) 663-1658
E-mail: mbarry@cityofmadison.com

Chief of School Operations **Mike Hertting** . . . . (608) 663-1879
E-mail: mhertting@madison.k12.wi.us

Chief of Schools, Secondary **Alex Fralin** . . . . (608) 663-1635

Assistant Superintendent for Teaching and Learning
Lisa Kvistad . . . . (608) 663-5216
E-mail: lkvistad@madison.k12.wi.us Fax: (608) 442-3471

Coordinator of Security **Luis Yudice** . . . . (608) 663-1904
Fax: (608) 204-0341

Chief Information Officer **Andrew Statz** . . . . (608) 663-1879
Fax: (608) 204-0341

Government and Media Relations Director
Rachel Strauch-Nelson . . . . (608) 663-1903
E-mail: rmstrauchnel@madison.k12.wi.us
Education: Wisconsin BA

City of Manchester, New Hampshire

City Hall, One City Hall Plaza, Manchester, NH 03101
Tel: (603) 624-6455 (Information) Internet: www.manchesternh.gov

County: Hillsborough **Election Type:** Nonpartisan **Year Incorporated:** 1846 **Population:** 110,229 (2015)

Office of the Mayor and Board of Aldermen

City Hall, One City Hall Plaza, Manchester, NH 03101
Fax: (603) 624-6481

★Mayor **Theodore L. "Ted" Gatsas** . . . . (603) 624-6500
Began Service: January 1, 2010
Term Expires: January 2, 2018
E-mail: mayor@manchesternh.gov
Education: New Hampshire BA

Chief of Staff **Samantha Piatt** . . . . (603) 624-6500
Fax: (603) 624-6576

Special Assistant to the Mayor **Carrie Perry** . . . . (603) 624-6500
E-mail: cperry@manchesternh.gov Fax: (603) 624-6576

Constituent Services Representative **Vicki Ferraro** . . . . . . (603) 624-6500
Fax: (603) 624-6576

★Alderman **Kevin J. Cavanaugh** (Ward 1) . . . . (603) 624-6455
Term Expires: January 2, 2018

★Alderman **Ron Ludwig** (Ward 2) . . . . (603) 623-7724
Term Expires: January 2, 2018
E-mail: rludwig@manchesternh.gov

★Alderman **Patrick T. Long** (Ward 3) . . . . (603) 668-1037
Term Expires: January 2, 2018
E-mail: plong@manchesternh.gov

★Alderman **Christopher J. Herbert** (Ward 4) . . . . (603) 624-6455
Term Expires: January 2, 2018

★Alderman **Anthony "Tony" Sapienza** (Ward 5) . . . . (603) 622-6463
Term Expires: January 2, 2018

★Alderman **Nick Pappas** (Ward 6) . . . . (603) 624-6455
Term Expires: January 2, 2018

★Alderman **William P. Shea** (Ward 7) . . . . (603) 622-8079
Term Expires: January 2, 2018

★Alderman **Thomas Katsiantonis** (Ward 8) . . . . (603) 624-6500
Term Expires: January 2, 2018
E-mail: thomaskatsiantonis@gmail.com

★Alderman **Barbara E. Shaw** (Ward 9) . . . . (603) 626-4681
Term Expires: January 2, 2018
E-mail: bshaw@manchesternh.gov
Date of Birth: March 7, 1942

★Alderman **Bill Barry** (Ward 10) . . . . (603) 669-0494
Term Expires: January 2, 2018

★Elected Official ▲Appointed by Legislature ▼Appointed by Governor ▶Appointed by Board or Commission ●Appointed by Judge
■Appointed by Mayor △Appointed by Freeholders ▽Appointed by Supervisor ▷Appointed by County Executive ○Appointed by Council

Office of the Mayor and Board of Aldermen *continued*

★ Alderman **Normand Gamache** (Ward 11) . . . . (603) 669-5817
Term Expires: January 2, 2018
E-mail: ngamache@manchesternh.gov

★ Alderman **Keith D. Hirschmann** (Ward 12) . . . . (603) 657-0975
Term Expires: January 2, 2018

★ Alderman **Joseph "Kelly" Levasseur** (At-Large) . . . . (603) 624-6500
Term Expires: January 2, 2018
E-mail: jrwaa2@aol.com

★ Alderman **Daniel P. O'Neil** (At-Large) . . . . (603) 668-9814
Term Expires: January 2, 2018
E-mail: doneil@manchesternh.gov

Office of the City Clerk

City Hall, One City Hall Plaza, Manchester, NH 03101
Fax: (603) 624-6481

▶ City Clerk **Matthew Normand** . . . . (603) 624-6455
E-mail: cityclerk@manchesternh.gov

Office of the City Solicitor

City Hall, One City Hall Plaza, Manchester, NH 03101
Fax: (603) 624-6528

▶ City Solicitor **Thomas R. Clark** . . . . (603) 624-6523
E-mail: solicitor@manchesternh.gov

Office of the Risk Manager

City Hall, One City Hall Plaza, Manchester, NH 03101
Fax: (603) 624-6528

▶ Risk Manager **(Vacant)** . . . . (603) 624-6503

Manchester Economic Development Office

One City Hall Plaza, Manchester, NH 03101
Tel: (603) 624-6505 Fax: (603) 624-6308

Economic Development Director **William Craig** . . . . (603) 624-6505
E-mail: wcraig@manchesternh.gov
Education: Suffolk JD

Finance Department

City Hall, One City Hall Plaza, Manchester, NH 03101
Fax: (603) 624-6549
Internet: http://www.manchesternh.gov/Departments/Finance

▶ Finance Officer **William E. Sanders** . . . . (603) 624-6460
E-mail: finance@manchesternh.gov

Fire Department

100 Merrimack St., Manchester, NH 03103
Fax: (603) 669-7707

Fire Chief **James A. Burkush** . . . . (603) 669-2256
E-mail: fire@manchesternh.gov
Date of Birth: November 26, 1958
Education: Granite State 2006 SB

Health Department

Carol M. Rines Center, 1528 Elm St., Manchester, NH 03104
Fax: (603) 628-6004

Health Officer **Timothy M. Soucy** . . . . (603) 624-6466
Education: Vermont BS; Boston U MPH

Human Resources Department

City Hall, One City Hall Plaza, Manchester, NH 03101
Fax: (603) 628-6065

Director **Jane Gile** . . . . (603) 624-6543
E-mail: humanresources@manchesternh.gov

Information Systems Department

100 Merrimack St., Manchester, NH 03103
Fax: (603) 624-6320

▶ Director **Jennie Angell** . . . . (603) 624-6577
E-mail: info@manchesternh.gov

Web Master **Kevin LaFramboise** . . . . (603) 624-6577
E-mail: klaframboise@manchesternh.gov

Manchester Boston Regional Airport

One Airport Way, Manchester, NH 03103
Fax: (603) 628-6038 Internet: http://www.flymanchester.com

Director **Mark P. Brewer** . . . . (603) 624-6539 ext. 301

Assistant Airport Director
Stephen J. Adams, Jr. . . . . (603) 624-6539 ext. 306

Parks, Recreation and Cemetery Department

625 Mammoth Rd., Manchester, NH 03104
Fax: (603) 624-6569

▶ Director **Don Pinard** . . . . (603) 624-6565 ext. 301
E-mail: parks@manchesternh.gov

Planning and Community Development Department

City Hall, One City Hall Plaza, Manchester, NH 03101
Fax: (603) 624-6529

Director **Leon LaFreniere** . . . . (603) 624-6450
E-mail: planning@manchesternh.gov

Police Department

405 Valley Street, Manchester, NH 03103
Fax: (603) 628-6137 E-mail: manchesterpd@grolen.com

Chief of Police **Nick Willard** . . . . (603) 668-8711

Manchester Public Library

405 Pine St., Manchester, NH 03104
Fax: (603) 624-6559

Librarian **Denise van Zanten** . . . . (603) 624-6550
E-mail: dvanzant@manchesternh.gov

Public Works Department

475 Valley Street, Manchester, NH 03103
Fax: (603) 624-6487

Public Works Director **Kevin Sheppard** . . . . (603) 624-6444

Environmental Protection Division

300 Winston Street, Manchester, NH 03103
Fax: (603) 628-6234

Chief Sanitary Engineer **Fred McNeill** . . . . (603) 624-6341

Wastewater Treatment Plant Superintendent
Rick Cantu . . . . (603) 624-6526
Fax: (603) 628-6086

Facilities Division

Fax: (603) 624-6487

Chief Facilities Manager **Kevin O'Maley** . . . . (603) 624-6555
E-mail: komaley@manchesternh.gov

Highway Division

475 Valley Street, Manchester, NH 03103
Fax: (603) 624-6487

Director **Kevin Sheppard** . . . . (603) 624-6444

Tax Collection Department

City Hall, One City Hall Plaza, Manchester, NH 03101
Fax: (603) 628-6162

▶ Collector of Taxes (Acting) **Brenda Masewic Adams** . . . (603) 624-6575
E-mail: taxcollector@manchesternh.gov

★ Elected Official ▲ Appointed by Legislature ▼ Appointed by Governor ▶ Appointed by Board or Commission ● Appointed by Judge
■ Appointed by Mayor △ Appointed by Freeholders ▽ Appointed by Supervisor ▷ Appointed by County Executive ○ Appointed by Council

Water Works Department
281 Lincoln St., Manchester, NH 03103
Fax: (603) 628-6020

Director and Chief Engineer **Philip Croasdale** .... (603) 624-6494
E-mail: waterworks@manchesternh.gov
Assistant Director **Robert Beaurivage** .... (603) 624-6494
Water Distribution Administrator **Guy Chabot** .... (603) 624-6494
Water Supply Administrator **(Vacant)** .... (603) 624-6494
Water Financial Administrator **Guy Beloin** .... (603) 624-6494

Welfare Department
Rines Center, 1528 Elm St., Manchester, NH 03104
Fax: (603) 624-6423

★ Commissioner **Paul R. R. Martineau** .... (603) 624-6484
Term Expires: January 2, 2018
E-mail: pmartine@manchesternh.gov

Youth Services Department
Rines Center, 1528 Elm St., Manchester, NH 03104
Fax: (603) 628-6285 E-mail: oys@oys.mv.com

Executive Director **Jonathan Donovan** .... (603) 624-6470

School District
286 Commerical Street, Manchester, NH 03101
Fax: (603) 644-0357

Superintendent **Debra Livingston** .... (603) 624-6300

City of McAllen, Texas
City Hall, 1300 W. Houston St., McAllen, TX 78501
Internet: www.mcallen.net

County: Hidalgo **Election Type:** Nonpartisan **Year Incorporated:** 1911
Population: 140,269 (2015)

Office of the Mayor and City Commission
P.O. Box 220, McAllen, TX 78505-0220
Fax: (956) 681-1010

★ Mayor **James "Jim" Darling** .... (956) 681-1003
Began Service: May 28, 2013
Term Expires: May 1, 2017
E-mail: jdarling@mcallen.net
★ Mayor Pro Tem **Aida Ramirez** (District 4) .... (956) 681-1003
Term Expires: May 1, 2019
E-mail: aidaramirez@mcallen.net
★ Commissioner **Richard F. Cortez** (District 1) .... (956) 681-1003
Term Expires: May 1, 2017
★ Commissioner **Trey Pebley** (District 2) .... (956) 681-1003
Term Expires: May 1, 2017
E-mail: pebley@gmail.com
★ Commissioner **Hilda Escochea-Salinas** (District 3) .... (956) 681-1003
Term Expires: May 1, 2017
E-mail: hsalinas3@aol.com
★ Commissioner **John J. Ingram** (District 5) .... (956) 681-1003
Term Expires: May 1, 2019
E-mail: ingramlaw2000@aol.com
★ Commissioner **Veronica Whitacre** (District 6) .... (956) 681-1003
Term Expires: May 1, 2019

Office of the City Manager
City Hall, 1300 Houston Ave., McAllen, TX 78501
P.O. Box 220, McAllen, TX 78505-0220
Fax: (956) 681-1010

○ City Manager **Roel "Roy" Rodriguez** .... (956) 681-1001
E-mail: roel_rodriguez@mcallen.net
Assistant City Manager **Jeff Johnston** .... (956) 681-1001
E-mail: jjohnston@mcallen.net
Assistant City Manager **Michelle Rivera Leftwich** .... (956) 681-1001
E-mail: mleftwich@mcallen.net
Assistant City Manager **Joe Vera** .... (956) 681-1001
E-mail: jvera@mcallen.net
City Commission Liaison **Elma S. Vela** .... (956) 681-1003
E-mail: evela@mcallen.net

Office of the City Attorney
City Hall, 1300 Houston Ave., McAllen, TX 78501
P.O. Box 220, McAllen, TX 78505-0220
Fax: (956) 681-1099

○ City Attorney **Kevin Pagan** .... (956) 681-1090
E-mail: kpagan@mcallen.net

Office of the City Secretary
City Hall, 1300 Houston Ave., McAllen, TX 78501
P.O. Box 220, McAllen, TX 78505-0220
Fax: (956) 681-1029

○ City Secretary (Interim) **Perla Lara** .... (956) 681-1020
E-mail: plara@mcallen.net

Development Corporation
City Hall, 1300 Houston Ave., McAllen, TX 78501
P.O. Box 220, McAllen, TX 78505-0220
Fax: (956) 681-1010

Executive Director **Roel "Roy" Rodriguez** .... (956) 681-1001
E-mail: roel_rodriguez@mcallen.net

Finance Department
City Hall, 1300 Houston Ave., McAllen, TX 78501
P.O. Box 220, McAllen, TX 78501
Fax: (956) 681-1084

Director (Interim) **Susan Lozano** .... (956) 681-1060

Fire Department
201 North 21st Street, McAllen, TX 78501
Fax: (956) 681-2519

○ Chief **Rafael Balderas** .... (956) 681-2500
E-mail: rbalderas@mcallen.net

Library
4001 North 23rd Street, McAllen, TX 78504
Fax: (956) 681-3009

Library Director **Kathleen Horan** .... (956) 681-3000
E-mail: khoran@mcallen.net

McAllen-Miller International Airport
2500 S. Bicentennial, McAllen, TX 78503
Fax: (956) 681-1509

Director **Elizabeth Suarez** .... (956) 681-1500

Parks and Recreation Department
1000 S. Ware Rd., McAllen, TX 78501
P.O. Box 220, McAllen, TX 78505
Fax: (956) 681-3300

Director **Mike Hernandez** .... (956) 681-3333

★ Elected Official ▲ Appointed by Legislature ▼ Appointed by Governor ▶ Appointed by Board or Commission ● Appointed by Judge
■ Appointed by Mayor △ Appointed by Freeholders ▽ Appointed by Supervisor ▷ Appointed by County Executive ○ Appointed by Council

Human Resources Department
City Hall, 1300 Houston Ave., McAllen, TX 78501
Fax: (956) 681-1054

Director **Juan Gonzalez** . . . . (956) 681-1045
E-mail: juan_gonzalez@mcallen.net

Police Department
1601 North Bicentennial Boulevard, McAllen, TX 78501
Fax: (956) 681-2045

○ Police Chief **Victor Rodriguez** . . . . (956) 681-2040
E-mail: vrodriguez@mcallenpd.net

Public Works Department
4201 North Bentsen Road, McAllen, TX 78504
Fax: (956) 681-4035

Director **Carlos Sanchez** . . . . (956) 681-4000

Purchasing Department
City Hall, 1300 Houston Ave., McAllen, TX 78501
P.O. Box 220, McAllen, TX 78505
Fax: (956) 681-1138

Director **Gerardo Noriega** . . . . (956) 681-1130
E-mail: gnoriega@mcallen.net

Tax Office
311 N. 15th, McAllen, TX 78501
P.O. Box 220, McAllen, TX 78505
Fax: (956) 681-1349

Tax Collector **Rebecca Grimes** . . . . (956) 681-1330
E-mail: rgrimes@mcallen.net

City of McKinney, Texas
222 North Tennessee Street, McKinney, TX 75069
Internet: www.mckinneytexas.org
Internet: http://www.mckinneytexas.org/index.aspx?NID=207

County: Collin **Election Type:** Nonpartisan **Year Incorporated:** 1848
Population: 162,898 (2015)

Office of the Mayor and City Council
222 North Tennessee Street, McKinney, TX 75069
Fax: (972) 547-2607
Internet: www.mckinneytexas.org/Index.aspx?NID=138

★ Mayor **Brian Loughmiller** . . . . (972) 547-7507
Began Service: May 2009
Term Expires: May 2017
E-mail: bloughmiller@mckinneytexas.org

★ Mayor Pro Tem **Travis Ussery** (District 3) . . . . (972) 542-0342
Term Expires: May 2017
E-mail: tussery@mckinneytexas.org

★ Council Member **Don Day** (District 1) . . . . (972) 547-7501
Term Expires: May 2017
E-mail: dday@mckinneytexas.org

★ Council Member **Rainey Rogers** (District 2) . . . . (972) 547-7507
Term Expires: May 2019
E-mail: rrogers@mckinneytexas.org

★ Council Member **Chuck Branch** (District 4) . . . . (972) 547-7507
Term Expires: May 2019
E-mail: cbranch@mckinneytexas.org

★ Council Member **Randy Pogue** (At-Large) . . . . (972) 562-9004
Term Expires: May 2017
E-mail: rpogue@mckinneytexas.org

★ Council Member **Tracy Rath** (At-Large) . . . . (972) 547-7507
Term Expires: May 2019
E-mail: trath@mckinneytexas.org

Office of the City Manager
222 North Tennessee Street, McKinney, TX 75069
Fax: (972) 547-2607
Internet: www.mckinneytexas.org/Index.aspx?NID=141

City Manager (Interim)
Thomas H. "Tom" Muehlenbeck . . . . (972) 547-7501
E-mail: cm@mckinneytexas.org
Education: Lamar 1964 BS; Kansas 1966 MPA

Deputy City Manager **Jose Madrigal** . . . . (972) 547-7510
E-mail: jmadrigal@mckinneytexas.org
Education: Texas Tech BA, MPA

Director of Strategic Services **Chandler Merritt** . . . . (972) 547-7616
E-mail: cmerritt@mckinneytexas.org

Assistant City Manager **Barry Shelton** . . . . (972) 547-7527
E-mail: bshelton@mckinneytexas.org
Education: BYU BA

Office of the City Secretary
222 North Tennessee Street, McKinney, TX 75069
Fax: (972) 547-7617
Internet: http://www.mckinneytexas.org/Index.aspx?NID=140

City Secretary **Sandy Hart** . . . . (972) 547-7505
E-mail: shart@mckinneytexas.org

Assistant City Secretary **Denise Vice** . . . . (972) 547-7504
E-mail: dvice@mckinneytexas.org

Records Management Specialist **Pam Yentzer** . . . . (972) 547-7588

Records Management Specialist **Sarah Hoyle** . . . . (972) 547-7588

Communications and Marketing Department
222 North Tennessee Street, McKinney, TX 75069
Fax: (972) 547-2607
Internet: www.mckinneytexas.org/Index.aspx?NID=154

Director **CoCo Good** . . . . (972) 547-7508
E-mail: cgood@mckinneytexas.org

Communications and Media Manager **Denise Lessard** . . . (972) 547-7556
E-mail: dlessard@mckinneytexas.org

Development Services Department
222 North Tennessee Street, McKinney, TX 75069
Fax: (972) 547-2604
Internet: www.mckinneytexas.org/Index.aspx?NID=156

Executive Director **Michael Quint** . . . . (972) 547-7402
E-mail: mquint@mckinneytexas.org

Facilities Construction Manager **Patricia Jackson** . . . . (972) 547-7439
E-mail: pjackson@mckinneytexas.org

Building Inspections/Permits Department
222 North Tennessee Street, McKinney, TX 75069
Fax: (972) 547-2605
Internet: www.mckinneytexas.org/index.aspx?NID=243

Chief Building Official **Rick Herzberger** . . . . (972) 547-7453

Assistant Chief Building Official **Jason Smith** . . . . (972) 547-2664

Code Enforcement Division
314 South Chestnut Street, McKinney, TX 75069
Fax: (972) 547-2606

Code Compliance Supervisor **Mike Morrisey** . . . . (972) 547-7397

Environmental Health Manager **Lori Dees** . . . . (972) 547-7441

Engineering Department
222 North Tennessee Street, McKinney, TX 75069
Fax: (972) 547-2604
Internet: www.mckinneytexas.org/index.aspx?NID=244

Director of Engineering **Mark Hines** . . . . (972) 547-7421
E-mail: mhines@mckinneytexas.org

Assistant Director of Engineering **Michael Hebert** . . . . (972) 547-7424
E-mail: mhebert@mckinneytexas.org

★ Elected Official ▲ Appointed by Legislature ▼ Appointed by Governor ▶ Appointed by Board or Commission ● Appointed by Judge
■ Appointed by Mayor △ Appointed by Freeholders ▽ Appointed by Supervisor ▷ Appointed by County Executive ○ Appointed by Council

Planning Department
222 North Tennessee Street, McKinney, TX 75069
Fax: (972) 547-2604
Internet: www.mckinneytexas.org/index.aspx?NID=245

Director of Planning **Brian Lockley** .... (972) 547-7378
Education: Cal Poly (Pomona) BS; Texas (Arlington) MPA
Planning Manager **Jennifer Arnold** .... (972) 547-7415
Planning Manager **Matt Robinson** .... (972) 547-2632

Financial Services Department
222 North Tennessee Street, McKinney, TX 75069
Fax: (972) 547-2611
Internet: www.mckinneytexas.org/Index.aspx?NID=152

Chief Financial Officer (Acting) **Mark Holloway** .... (972) 547-7536
Executive Assistant **Amy Sallaway** .... (972) 547-2084
E-mail: asallaway@mckinneytexas.org
Senior Financial Services Manager **Trudy Mathis** .... (972) 547-7528
E-mail: tmathis@mckinneytexas.org
Investment and Treasury Manager **Kelvin Bryant** .... (972) 547-7512
E-mail: kbryant@mckinneytexas.org

Fire Department
2200 Taylor-Burk Drive, McKinney, TX 75071
Fax: (972) 547-2858
Internet: www.mckinneytexas.org/Index.aspx?NID=157

Fire Chief **Danny Kistner** .... (972) 547-2864
E-mail: dkistner@mckinneytexas.org
Education: Oklahoma State MS
Assistant Fire Chief **Chris Lowry** .... (972) 547-2851
E-mail: clowry@mckinneytexas.org
Assistant Fire Chief **Tim Mock** .... (972) 547-2851
E-mail: tmock@mckinneytexas.org

Housing and Community Development Department
314 South Chestnut Street, Suite 101, McKinney, TX 75069
Fax: (972) 547-2681

Manager **Janay Tieken** .... (972) 547-7578
E-mail: jtieken@mckinneytexas.org
Affordable Housing Administrator **Cristel Todd** .... (972) 547-7519
E-mail: ctodd@mckinneytexas.org
Community Development Block Grant Administrator
Shirletta Best .... (972) 547-7577
E-mail: sbest@mckinneytexas.org

Human Resources Department
314 South Chestnut Street, McKinney, TX 75069
Fax: (972) 547-2608
Internet: http://www.mckinneytexas.org/Index.aspx?NID=161

Director (Interim) **Barry Robinson** .... (972) 547-7562
E-mail: brobinson@mckinneytexas.org

Information Technology Department
222 North Tennessee Street, McKinney, TX 75069
Fax: (972) 547-2600

Chief Information Officer (Interim) **Jose Madrigal** ...... (972) 547-7502
E-mail: jmadrigal@mckinneytexas.org
Education: Texas Tech BA, MPA

McKinney Main Street/McKinney Performing Arts Center
314 South Chestnut Street, McKinney, TX 75069
Fax: (972) 547-2622
Internet: http://www.mckinneytexas.org/Index.aspx?NID=115

Director **Amy Rosenthal** .... (972) 547-2652
E-mail: arosenthal@mckinneytexas.org

McKinney National Airport
1500 East Industrial Boulevard, Suite 201, McKinney, TX 75069
Fax: (972) 542-6686 Internet: http://www.flytki.com/

Executive Director **Kenneth F. Wiegand** .... (972) 562-4053
Operations Manager **Eric Pratt** .... (972) 562-4096
E-mail: epratt@mckinneytexas.org
Management Specialist **Cindy Rowe** .... (972) 562-4214
E-mail: crowe@mckinneytexas.org

McKinney Public Library
101 East Hunt Street, McKinney, TX 75069
Tel: (972) 547-7323 Fax: (972) 542-0868
Internet: http://www.mckinneytexas.org/Index.aspx?NID=116

Library Director **Spencer Smith** .... (972) 547-7302
E-mail: ssmith3@mckinneytexas.org

Parks, Recreation and Open Space Department
1611 North Stonebridge Drive, McKinney, TX 75071
Tel: (972) 547-7330 Fax: (972) 547-7487
Internet: www.mckinneytexas.org/Index.aspx?NID=114

Director **Rhoda Savage** .... (972) 547-7481

Police Department
2200 Taylor-Burk Drive, McKinney, TX 75071
Tel: (972) 547-2700 Fax: (972) 548-2190
Internet: http://www.mckinneytexas.org/Index.aspx?NID=166

Chief of Police **Greg Conley** .... (972) 547-1050
Education: Texas (Arlington) MA; Baptist Bible BA
Assistant Chief of Police, Field Operations
Joe Ellenburg .... (972) 547-1050
Assistant Chief of Police, Support Services
Randy Roland .... (972) 547-2713

Public Works Department
1550 South College Street, McKinney, TX 75069
Fax: (972) 547-2612
Internet: http://www.mckinneytexas.org/Index.aspx?NID=167

Director (Interim) **Chandler Merritt** .... (972) 547-7616
Assistant Director of Public Works **Paul Sparkman** ...... (972) 547-7350
Facility Maintenance Superintendent **Brian Caraway** ..... (972) 547-7390
E-mail: bcaraway@mckinneytexas.org
Water/Wastewater Superintendent **Morgan Dadgostar** .... (972) 547-7361
Environmental Services Manager **Eric Hopes** .... (972) 547-7385

Purchasing Department
1550-D South College Street, McKinney, TX 75069
Fax: (972) 547-7585
Internet: http://www.mckinneytexas.org/Index.aspx?NID=168

Purchasing Manager **Lisa Littrell** .... (972) 547-7583
1550 South College Street, McKinney, TX 75069
E-mail: llittrell@mckinneytexas.org

★ Elected Official ▲ Appointed by Legislature ▼ Appointed by Governor ► Appointed by Board or Commission ● Appointed by Judge
■ Appointed by Mayor △ Appointed by Freeholders ▽ Appointed by Supervisor ▷ Appointed by County Executive ○ Appointed by Council

City of Memphis, Tennessee

125 N. Main St., Memphis, TN 38103
Tel: (901) 576-6500 (Information) Internet: www.memphistn.gov

County: Shelby **Election Type:** Nonpartisan **Year Founded:** 1819
Year Incorporated: 1826 **Population:** 655,770 (2015)

Office of the Mayor

125 North Main Street, 7th Floor, Memphis, TN 38103
Fax: (901) 576-6012

★Mayor **Jim Strickland** .... (901) 576-6000
Began Service: January 1, 2016
Term Expires: December 31, 2019
E-mail: mayor@memphistn.gov
Chief of Staff **(Vacant)** .... (901) 576-6007
Director of Communications **Ursula Madden** .... (901) 576-6011
E-mail: Ursula.Madden@memphistn.gov
Marketing Manager **Allison Fouchè** .... (901) 636-6881

Office of the Chief Operating Officer

125 North Main Street, Suite 308, Memphis, TN 38103
Tel: (901) 576-6586 Fax: (901) 576-6555

■Chief Operating Officer **CAPT Douglas A. McGowen** ... (901) 576-6558
Education: VMI BSCE; Naval War MA
Deputy Chief Administrative Officer **Demar Roberts** .... (901) 576-6000

Office of the City Attorney

125 North Main Street, Suite 336, Memphis, TN 38103
Fax: (901) 576-6524

■City Attorney **Bruce McMullen** .... (901) 576-6614
E-mail: cityattorney@memphistn.gov
Deputy City Attorney **Regina Morrison Newman** ...... (901) 576-6614
Senior Assistant Attorney **Felicia Cox** .... (901) 576-6614
Senior Assistant City Attorney, Housing and Community Development **Patrick Dandridge** .... (901) 576-7408
E-mail: patrick.dandridge@memphistn.gov Fax: (901) 576-7450
Assistant City Attorney **Philip Oliphant** .... (901) 576-6614
Assistant City Attorney **Zayid Saleem** .... (901) 576-6614

Office of the City Prosecutor

201 Poplar Avenue, Suite LL-10, Memphis, TN 38103
Fax: (901) 545-3470

Chief Prosecutor **Teresa Jones** .... (901) 636-3475
■Prosecutor **Lyndia C. Harris** .... (901) 636-3475
E-mail: lyndia.harris@memphistn.gov
■Prosecutor **Timothy W. Flack** .... (901) 636-3475
E-mail: timothy.flack@memphistn.gov
■Prosecutor **Tyrese Riley** .... (901) 636-3475

Claims Office

2714 Union Extended, Suite 200, Memphis, TN 38112

Claim Agent **William Larsha** .... (901) 636-6616
E-mail: william.larsha@memphistn.gov Fax: (901) 636-6605

Office of Minority and Women-Owned Business Development

125 North Main Street, Room 546, Memphis, TN 38103

Director **Joann Massey** .... (901) 636-4997
Contract Compliance Officer **Pamela Jackson-Small** .... (901) 636-4997

Intergovernmental Relations Office

125 North Main Street, Room 336, Memphis, TN 38103
Fax: (901) 636-6524

Administrator **(Vacant)** .... (901) 636-6596

Permits Office

2714 Union Extended, Suite 200, Memphis, TN 38112
Fax: (901) 323-9913

Permits/License Manager **Aubrey Howard** .... (901) 636-6711

Office of the City Engineer

125 North Main Street, Suite 644, Memphis, TN 38103
Fax: (901) 576-6960

■City Engineer **(Vacant)** .... (901) 576-6700

Division of Finance

125 North Main Street, Room 368, Memphis, TN 38103
Fax: (901) 576-6193

■Director **Brian Collins** .... (901) 576-6657
E-mail: brian.collins@memphistn.gov
Deputy Director, Administration and Financial Management **Margaret Coleman** .... (901) 576-6873
Records Management **Valerie Snipes** .... (901) 636-6223

Office of the Comptroller

125 North Main Street, Room 348, Memphis, TN 38103
Tel: (901) 576-6368 Fax: (901) 576-6191

Comptroller **Shirley Ford** .... (901) 576-6368
E-mail: shirley.ford@memphistn.gov
Deputy Comptroller **Sharon Cobbige** .... (901) 576-6651
Deputy Comptroller **Yolanda Alexander** .... (901) 576-6165

Office of the City Treasurer

125 North Main Street, Room 301, Memphis, TN 38103
Fax: (901) 576-6304

Treasurer **John Patrick Black** .... (901) 576-6306

Purchasing

125 North Main Street, Room 354, Memphis, TN 38103
Tel: (901) 576-6683 Fax: (901) 576-6191

Purchasing Agent **Eric Masye** .... (901) 636-6107
E-mail: eric.mayse@memphistn.gov

Division of Fire Services

65 S. Front St., Memphis, TN 38103
Fax: (901) 527-9516

Director **Gina Sweat** .... (901) 527-1400
E-mail: MFDInquiries@memphistn.gov
Chief of Training **Dale Lock** .... (901) 354-6781
E-mail: dale.lock@memphistn.gov Fax: (901) 357-0522

Emergency Medical Services

79 S. Flicker St., Memphis, TN 38104

Deputy Chief **Ronald Heath** .... (901) 527-1400
Deputy Chief **Daryl Patton** .... (901) 527-1400

General Services Division

125 North Main Street, Suite 568, Memphis, TN 38103-2088
Fax: (901) 576-6252

■Director **Antonio M. Adams** .... (901) 576-6326
E-mail: antonio.adams@memphistn.gov

Office of Fleet Management

671 St. Jude Place, Memphis, TN 38105
Tel: (901) 636-7502

Fleet Management Administrator **Eric Hunter** .... (901) 636-7502

Division of Housing and Community Development

701 N. Main St., Memphis, TN 38107
Fax: (901) 576-7318

■Director **Paul A. Young** .... (901) 576-7301

★Elected Official ▲Appointed by Legislature ▼Appointed by Governor ▶Appointed by Board or Commission ●Appointed by Judge
■Appointed by Mayor △Appointed by Freeholders ▽Appointed by Supervisor ▷Appointed by County Executive ○Appointed by Council

Human Resources Division
125 North Main Street, Suite 406, Memphis, TN 38103-2017
Tel: (901) 576-6571 Fax: (901) 576-6482

■ Director **Alexandria Smith** .... (901) 576-6403
E-mail: alex.smith@memphistn.gov
Deputy Director **Jill Madajczyk** .... (901) 576-6571
E-mail: jill.madajczyk@memphistn.gov
Benefits Officer **(Vacant)** .... (901) 576-6428
Compensation/Records Administration Manager
Eric Sabatini .... (901) 576-6569
Employment Manager **Deneen Lester** .... (901) 576-6509
E-mail: deneen.lester@memphistn.gov
Labor Relations/EEO Manager **Chandell Carr** .... (901) 576-6874
E-mail: chandell.carr@memphistn.gov
Office of Talent and Human Capital Executive Director
(Vacant) .... (901) 636-6014
Fax: (901) 636-6012
Testing and Selection Manager **Deneen Lester** .... (901) 576-6429
E-mail: deneen.lester@memphistn.gov

Division of Information Services
119 South Main, Suite 200, Memphis, TN 38103
Fax: (901) 385-7757

Chief Information Officer **Brent Nair** .... (901) 636-6229
E-mail: brent.nair@memphistn.gov
Deputy Chief of Information Services **Michael Jones** .... (901) 636-6229
E-mail: michael.jones@memphistn.gov
Budget and Contract Manager **Anita Drake** .... (901) 636-6245
E-mail: anita.drake@memphistn.gov
IT Services Account Manager **James Chandler** .... (901) 636-7442
E-mail: james.chandler@memphistn.gov
Applications Services Lead **Binish Gopal** .... (901) 636-2515
Data Center and Communications Services Manager
Jason Hanna .... (901) 636-6249
E-mail: jason.hanna@memphistn.gov
Desktop Support/Technology Service Desk Manager
Teresa Mason .... (901) 636-6100
GIS Enterprises Manager **Della Adams** .... (901) 636-6233
E-mail: della.adams@memphistn.gov
Project Manager **Wendy Harris** .... (901) 636-6135

Division of Parks and Neighborhoods
2599 Avery Avenue, Memphis, TN 38112
Tel: (901) 576-4200 Fax: (901) 576-4275

■ Director **Janet P. Hooks** .... (901) 576-4231
E-mail: janet.hooks@memphistn.gov

Memphis Public Library
Benjamin L. Hooks Central Library, 3030 Poplar Avenue, Memphis, TN 38111
Fax: (901) 323-7108 Internet: www.memphislibrary.org/

■ Director **Keenon McCloy** .... (901) 415-2749
E-mail: mccloyk@memphislibrary.org
Deputy Director **Chris Marszalek** .... (901) 415-2749

Police Services
Criminal Justice Center, 201 Poplar Avenue, Room 12-05, Memphis, TN 38103
Tel: (901) 636-3700 Fax: (901) 636-3749
Internet: www.memphispolice.org

■ Director (Interim) **Michael Rallings** .... (901) 636-3700
Deputy Director **Mike Ryall** .... (901) 636-3700
Special Operations Deputy Chief **Arley "Clete" Knight** .. (901) 636-3700
Uniform Patrol District I Deputy Chief **Frank Garrett** .... (901) 636-3700
Uniform Patrol District II Deputy Chief **Terry Landrum** .. (901) 636-3700
Administrative Services Deputy Chief **Rowena Adams** ... (901) 636-3700
E-mail: rowena.adams@memphistn.gov
Web Manager **Wade Kimble** .... (901) 636-3777
E-mail: wade.kimble@memphistn.gov

Public Works Division
125 North Main Street, Suite 608, Memphis, TN 38103-2091
Fax: (901) 576-7116 E-mail: publicworks@memphistn.gov

■ Director **Robert Knecht** .... (901) 636-6762
E-mail: pubworks@memphistn.gov
Environmental Engineering Administrator
Paul Patterson .... (901) 576-7125
E-mail: paul.patterson@memphistn.gov
Maintenance Deputy Director **(Vacant)** .... (901) 576-6722
Fax: (901) 576-7115
Solid Waste Management Deputy Director
Phillip Davis .... (901) 576-6851
Fax: (901) 576-6879

Office of the City Council
125 North Main Street, Suite 514, Memphis, TN 38103-2086
Tel: (901) 636-6786 Fax: (901) 576-6796
Internet: http://memphiscitycouncil.com

★ Chairman **Kemp Conrad** (District 9, Pos. 1) .... (901) 576-6786
Term Expires: December 31, 2019
E-mail: kemp.conrad@memphistn.gov
★ Vice Chairman **Edmund Ford, Jr.** (District 6) .... (901) 576-6786
Term Expires: December 31, 2019
E-mail: edmund.fordjr@memphistn.gov
Education: Tennessee State BS
★ Council Member **Bill Morrison** (District 1) .... (901) 576-6786
Term Expires: December 31, 2019
E-mail: bill.morrison@memphistn.gov
★ Council Member **Frank Colvett, Jr.** (District 2) .... (901) 576-6786
Term Expires: December 31, 2019
★ Council Member **Patrice Jordan Robinson** (District 3) .. (901) 576-6786
Term Expires: December 31, 2019
★ Council Member **Jamita E. Swearengen** (District 4) .... (901) 576-6786
Term Expires: December 31, 2019
★ Council Member **Worth Morgan** (District 5) .... (901) 576-6786
Term Expires: December 31, 2019
★ Council Member **Berlin Boyd** (District 7) .... (901) 576-6786
Term Expires: December 31, 2019
E-mail: Berlin.Boyd@memphistn.gov
Education: New Col Stamford 2000 BABA, 2003 MBA
★ Council Member **Joe Brown** (District 8, Pos. 1) .... (901) 576-6786
Term Expires: December 31, 2019
E-mail: joe.brown@memphistn.gov
★ Council Member **Janis Fullilove** (District 8, Pos. 2) ..... (901) 576-6786
Term Expires: December 31, 2019
E-mail: janis.fullilove@memphistn.gov
★ Council Member
Martavius D. Jones (District 8, Pos. 3) .... (901) 636-6786
Term Expires: December 31, 2019
E-mail: Martavius.Jones@memphistn.gov
★ Council Member
Philip C. Spinosa, Jr. (District 9, Pos. 2) .... (901) 576-6786
Term Expires: December 31, 2019
★ Council Member **Reid Hedgepeth** (District 9, Pos. 3) .... (901) 576-6786
Term Expires: December 31, 2019
E-mail: reid.hedgepeth@memphistn.gov
○ Council Administrator **Juaness Keplinger** .... (901) 576-6787
E-mail: juaness.keplinger@memphistn.gov

★ Elected Official ▲ Appointed by Legislature ▼ Appointed by Governor ▶ Appointed by Board or Commission ● Appointed by Judge
■ Appointed by Mayor △ Appointed by Freeholders ▽ Appointed by Supervisor ▷ Appointed by County Executive ○ Appointed by Council

City of Mesa, Arizona

20 East Main Street, Mesa, AZ 85201-7406
P.O. Box 1466, Mesa, AZ 85211-1466
Tel: (480) 644-2011 (Information) Internet: www.mesaaz.gov

County: Maricopa **Election Type:** Nonpartisan **Year Founded:** 1878
Year Incorporated: 1883 **Charter:** 1967 **Population:** 471,825 (2015)

Office of the Mayor and City Council

20 East Main Street, Suite 750, Mesa, AZ 85201-7406
P.O. Box 1466, Mesa, AZ 85211-1466
Tel: (480) 644-3000 Fax: (480) 644-2175

★ Mayor **John C. Giles** .... (480) 644-2388
Began Service: September 2014
Term Expires: January 2017
E-mail: mayor@Mesaaz.gov
Executive Assistant to the Mayor **Misty Wells** .... (480) 644-2388
E-mail: misty.wells@mesaaz.gov
Chief of Staff **Ian Linssen** .... (480) 644-3002

★ Vice Mayor **Dennis Kavanaugh** (District 3) .... (480) 644-3003
Term Expires: January 2017
E-mail: councilmember.kavanaugh@mesaaz.gov
Education: Saint Louis U 1975 BA; Arizona State 1978 JD

★ Council Member **Dave Richins** (District 1) .... (480) 644-4002
Term Expires: January 2017
E-mail: councilmember.richins@mesaaz.gov

★ Council Member **Alex Finter** (District 2) .... (480) 644-3772
Term Expires: January 2017

★ Council Member **Christopher "Chris" Glover** (District 4) .... (480) 644-3004
Term Expires: January 18, 2019
E-mail: councilmember.glover@mesaaz.gov

★ Council Member **David Luna** (District 5) .... (480) 644-3771
Term Expires: January 18, 2019
E-mail: councilmember.luna@mesaaz.gov

★ Council Member **Kevin Thompson** (District 6) .... (480) 644-4003
Term Expires: January 18, 2019

Office of the City Attorney

20 E. Main St., Suite 850, Mesa, AZ 85201-7406
P.O. Box 1466, Mesa, AZ 85211-1466
Tel: (480) 644-2343 Fax: (480) 644-2498

○ City Attorney **Jim Smith** .... (480) 644-2343
E-mail: jim.smith@mesaaz.gov
Deputy City Attorney-Civil Administration **MaryGrace McNear** .... (480) 644-2343
E-mail: marygrace.mcnear@mesaaz.gov
Deputy City Attorney-Civil Litigation **Alfred Smith** .... (480) 644-2343
E-mail: alfred.smith@mesaaz.gov
City Prosecutor **Jon Eliason** .... (480) 644-3199

Office of the City Auditor

20 E. Main St., Suite 820, Mesa, AZ 85201-7406
P.O. Box 1466, Mesa, AZ 85211-1466

Auditor **Jennifer Ruttman** .... (480) 644-3767

Office of the City Clerk

20 East Main Street, Suite 600, Mesa, AZ 85201-7406
P.O. Box 1466, Mesa, AZ 85211-1466
Fax: (480) 644-2821

○ City Clerk **DeeAnn Mickelsen** .... (480) 644-6987
E-mail: dee.ann.mickelsen@mesaaz.gov

Office of the City Manager

20 E. Main St., Suite 750, Mesa, AZ 85201-7406
P.O. Box 1466, Mesa, AZ 85211-1466
Tel: (480) 644-3333 Fax: (480) 644-2175

○ City Manager **Chris Brady** .... (480) 644-2066
E-mail: christopher.brady@mesaaz.gov
Education: BYU 1987 BA, 1989 MPA
Deputy City Manager **Scott J. Butler** .... (480) 644-2964
E-mail: scott.j.butler@mesaaz.gov
Deputy City Manager **Natalie Lewis** .... (480) 644-4938
E-mail: natalie.lewis@mesaaz.gov
Chief Innovation Officer **Alex Deshuk** .... (480) 644-6953
E-mail: alex.deshuk@mesaaz.gov
Public Information and Communications Director **Steven Wright** .... (480) 644-2069
E-mail: steven.wright@mesaaz.gov

Office of the Assistant City Manager

20 East Main Street, Suite 750, Mesa, AZ 85201-7406

Assistant City Manager **John Pombier** .... (480) 644-2517
E-mail: john.pombier@mesaaz.gov

Airport

Falcon Field, 4800 Falcon Drive, Mesa, AZ 85215-2506
Fax: (480) 644-2419

Director **Corinne C. Nystrom** .... (480) 644-4045

Engineering

20 East Main Street, Suite 500, Mesa, AZ 85201-7406

Director **Beth Huning** .... (480) 644-2512
E-mail: beth.huning@mesaaz.gov

Real Estate Services

20 East Main Street, Mesa, AZ 85201-7406

Real Estate Services Administrator **Kim Fallbeck** .... (480) 644-2521

Transportation

300 East 6th Street, Mesa, AZ 85201
Fax: (480) 644-3909

Transportation Director **Lenny Hulme** .... (480) 644-3125

Water and Wastewater Department

640 N. Mesa Dr., Mesa, AZ 85201-5104
P.O. Box 1466, Mesa, AZ 85211-1466

Director (Interim) **Dan Cleavenger** .... (480) 644-2947

Energy Resources Department

640 N. Mesa Dr., Mesa, AZ 85201-5104

Director of Energy Resources **Frank McRae** .... (480) 644-4444
Deputy Director, Electric **Marty Hunter** .... (480) 644-4444
Deputy Director **William Norton** .... (480) 644-2490

Office of the Assistant City Manager

20 East Main Street, Suite 750, Mesa, AZ 85201-7406

Assistant City Manager **Karolyn "Kari" Kent** .... (480) 644-4567
E-mail: karolyn.kent@mesaaz.gov
Education: Northern Arizona BS; Arizona State MPA

Arts and Cultural Affairs

1 East Main Street, Mesa, AZ 85201-7406
Fax: (480) 644-6502

Arts and Cultural Director **Cindy Ornstein** .... (480) 644-6601
Building 3, 200 South Center Street, Mesa, AZ 85201

Development and Sustainability Department

20 East Main Street, Mesa, AZ 85201-7406

Development and Sustainability Director **Christine Zielonka** .... (480) 644-3833
E-mail: christine.zielonka@mesaaz.gov

★ Elected Official ▲ Appointed by Legislature ▼ Appointed by Governor ▶ Appointed by Board or Commission ● Appointed by Judge
■ Appointed by Mayor △ Appointed by Freeholders ▽ Appointed by Supervisor ▷ Appointed by County Executive ○ Appointed by Council

Community Services
20 East Main Street, Suite 250, Mesa, AZ 85201-7406
P.O. Box 1466, Mesa, AZ 85211-1466
Fax: (480) 644-2757

Director **Ruth Giese** .... (480) 644-4546
E-mail: ruth.giese@mesaaz.gov

Library
64 East First Street, Mesa, AZ 85201-6768
Fax: (480) 644-3490

Director **Heather Wolf** .... (480) 644-2712
E-mail: heather.wolf@mesaaz.gov

Environmental Management and Sustainability
20 East Main Street, Mesa, AZ 85201-7406

Director **Scott Bouchie** .... (480) 644-4366

Office of the Chief Financial Officer
20 East Main Street, Suite 750, Mesa, AZ 85201-7406

Chief Financial Officer **Michael J. Kennington** .... (480) 644-3381

Business Services
20 East Main Street, Mesa, AZ 85201-7406
Fax: (480) 644-2655

Director **Ed Quedens** .... (480) 644-2301
E-mail: ed.quedens@mesaaz.gov

Facilities Maintenance
20 East Main Street, Mesa, AZ 85201-7406

Director **Dennis Ray** .... (480) 644-3733
E-mail: dennis.ray@mesaaz.gov

Financial Services
20 East Main Street, Suite 450, Mesa, AZ 85201-7406

Budget Director **Candace Cannistraro** .... (480) 644-4941
E-mail: candace.cannistraro@mesaaz.gov

Parks, Recreation and Commercial Facilities
Building 1, 200 South Center Street, Mesa, AZ 85210

Director **Marc Heirshberg** .... (480) 644-2667
E-mail: marc.heirshberg@mesaaz.gov

Mesa Convention Center
263 North Center Street, Mesa, AZ 85201
Fax: (480) 644-2617

Venue Manager **Dyan Dwyer Seaburg** .... (480) 644-2171

Economic Development Division
20 E. Main St., Suite 200, Mesa, AZ 85201-7406
P.O. Box 1466, Mesa, AZ 85211-1466

Economic Development Director **William Jabjiniak** ..... (480) 644-3561
E-mail: william.jabjiniak@mesaaz.gov
Education: Franklin Pierce Col BS; Southern New Hampshire MS, MBA

Fire Department
40 N. Center St., Suite 115, Mesa, AZ 85201-7300
P.O. Box 1466, Mesa, AZ 85211-1466
Tel: (480) 644-2101 Fax: (480) 644-4460

Fire Chief **Harry M. Beck** .... (480) 644-2101
E-mail: harry.beck@mesaaz.gov
Assistant Fire Chief **Jim Bloomer** .... (480) 644-5136
E-mail: jim.bloomer@mesaaz.gov
Assistant Fire Chief **Mary Cameli** .... (480) 644-2781
E-mail: mary.cameli@mesaaz.gov
Assistant Fire Chief **Mike Dunn** .... (480) 644-2631
E-mail: mike.dunn@mesaaz.gov
Assistant Fire Chief **Cori Hayes** .... (480) 644-2405
E-mail: cori.hayes@mesaaz.gov

Human Resources Department
20 East Main Street, Mesa, AZ 85201-7406
Fax: (480) 644-2380

Human Resources Director **Gary Manning** .... (480) 644-2365
E-mail: gary.manning@mesaaz.gov
Employee Benefits Administrator **Jan Ashley** .... (480) 644-2365
E-mail: janice.ashley@mesaaz.gov

Police Department
130 North Robson, Mesa, AZ 85201
P.O. Box 1466, Mesa, AZ 85211-1466
Tel: (480) 644-2324

Police Chief **John Meza** .... (480) 644-2071
Assistant Chief **Tony Filler** .... (480) 644-2571

Mesa Public Schools
63 East Main Street, Mesa, AZ 85201
Internet: http://www.mpsaz.org/

Superintendent **Michael Cowan** .... (480) 472-0200

City of Mesquite, Texas
P.O. Box 850137, Mesquite, TX 75185-0137
Internet: www.cityofmesquite.com

County: Dallas **Election Type:** Nonpartisan **Year Incorporated:** 1887
Population: 144,788 (2015)

Office of the Mayor and City Council
P.O. Box 850137, Mesquite, TX 75185-0137
Fax: (972) 216-6431

★ Mayor **Stan Pickett** .... (972) 216-6400
Began Service: May 20, 2015 Fax: (972) 216-6431
Term Expires: May 2017
★ Mayor Pro Tem **Greg Noschese** (Place 5) .... (972) 216-6293
Term Expires: May 2018
★ Council Member **Bill Porter** (Place 1) .... (972) 216-6293
Term Expires: May 2017
Education: North Texas BA, MA
★ Council Member **Jeff Casper** (Place 2) .... (972) 216-6293
Term Expires: May 2017
★ Council Member **Bruce Archer** (Place 3) .... (972) 216-6293
Term Expires: May 2018
★ Council Member **Dan Aleman** (Place 4) .... (972) 216-6293
Term Expires: May 2018
★ Council Member **Dennis Tarpley** (Place 6) .... (972) 216-6293
Term Expires: May 2017

Office of the City Manager
P.O. Box 850137, Mesquite, TX 75185-0137
Fax: (972) 216-6431

○ City Manager **Cliff Keheley** .... (972) 216-6293
E-mail: ckeheley@cityofmesquite.com
Deputy City Manager **Jerry Dittman** .... (972) 216-6293

Economic Development Division
P.O. Box 850137, Mesquite, TX 75185-0137
Fax: (972) 216-8100

Manager **Tom Palmer** .... (972) 216-6293
E-mail: tpalmer@cityofmesquite.com

★ Elected Official ▲ Appointed by Legislature ▼ Appointed by Governor ▶ Appointed by Board or Commission ● Appointed by Judge
■ Appointed by Mayor △ Appointed by Freeholders ▽ Appointed by Supervisor ▷ Appointed by County Executive ○ Appointed by Council

Office of the City Attorney
P.O. Box 850137, Mesquite, TX 75185-0137

○ City Attorney **B.J. Smith** .... (972) 216-6272
E-mail: bjsmith@cityofmesquite.com Fax: (972) 216-6442

Office of the City Secretary
P.O. Box 850137, Mesquite, TX 75185-0137
Fax: (972) 216-6469

○ City Secretary **Sonja Land** .... (972) 216-6244
E-mail: sland@cityofmesquite.com Fax: (972) 216-6469

Community Development Department
P.O. Box 850137, Mesquite, TX 75185-0137

Director **Richard Gertson** .... (972) 216-6346
E-mail: rgertson@cityofmesquite.com Fax: (972) 216-8109
Education: Texas A&M 1974 BA; Iowa 1978 JD, 1979 MA

Human Resources Department
1515 North Galloway Avenue, Mesquite, TX 75149
Tel: (972) 216-6218 Fax: (972) 216-6218

Director **Rick French** .... (972) 216-6218
E-mail: rfrench@cityofmesquite.com

Finance Department
P.O. Box 850137, Mesquite, TX 75185-0137

Finance Director **Debbie Mol** .... (972) 216-6207
Fax: (972) 216-6623

Purchasing Division
P.O. Box 850137, Mesquite, TX 75185-0137
Fax: (972) 216-6397

Manager **Le Sealey** .... (972) 216-6201
E-mail: lsealey@cityofmesquite.com

Fire Department
P.O. Box 850137, Mesquite, TX 75185-0137
Fax: (972) 216-6436

Fire Chief **Mark Kerby** .... (972) 216-6267
E-mail: mkerby@mesquitefire.org
Assistant Chief **Bob Muse** .... (972) 216-6308
E-mail: jmoore@mesquitefire.org
Assistant Chief **Larry Spurgin** .... (972) 216-6267
E-mail: lspurgin@mesquitefire.org

Mesquite Metro Airport
1130 Hudson Airport Blvd., Mesquite, TX 75181

Airport Manager **Cynthia Godfrey** .... (972) 216-4130
Fax: (972) 216-4149

Parks and Recreation Department
1515 North Galloway Avenue, Mesquite, TX 75149

Director **(Vacant)** .... (972) 216-6293
Fax: (972) 216-6431

Police Department
P.O. Box 850137, Mesquite, TX 75185-0137

Police Chief **Charles Cato** .... (972) 216-6228
Fax: (972) 216-6780

Mesquite Public Library
300 W. Grubb St., Mesquite, TX 75149

Director **Virginia Mundt** .... (972) 216-6220
E-mail: vmundt@cityofmesquite.com Fax: (972) 216-6740

Public Works Department
P.O. Box 850137, Mesquite, TX 75185-0137

Director **Tim James** .... (972) 216-6217
Fax: (972) 216-8100

Solid Waste Division
Manager **Charles Goodson** .... (972) 216-6284
Fax: (972) 216-8189

Streets Division
Manager **Mark Hodges** .... (972) 216-6928

Utilities Division
Internet: www.cityofmesquite.com/utilities/

Manager **Mike Screws** .... (972) 216-6278
Fax: (972) 329-8593

City of Miami, Florida

City Hall, 3500 Pan American Dr., Miami, FL 33133
Tel: (305) 250-5360 (Information) Internet: www.miamigov.com

County: Miami-Dade **Election Type:** Nonpartisan **Population:** 441,003 (2015)

Office of the Executive Mayor and City Commission
City Hall, 3500 Pan American Dr., Miami, FL 33133-0708
Fax: (305) 854-4001 Internet: www.miamigov.com/Mayor/

★ Mayor **Tomas Regalado** .... (305) 250-5300
Began Service: November 11, 2009 Fax: (305) 854-4001
Term Expires: November 1, 2017
E-mail: tregalado@miamigov.com
Date of Birth: May 24, 1947
Special Assistant to the Mayor **Eric Duran** .... (305) 250-5300
★ Chairman **Keon Hardemon** (District 5) .... (305) 250-5390
Term Expires: November 1, 2017
E-mail: KHardemon@miamigov.com
★ Vice Chairman **Ken Russell** (District 2) .... (305) 250-5333
Term Expires: November 2019
★ Commissioner **Wilfredo "Willy" Gort** (District 1) .... (305) 250-5430
Term Expires: November 2019 Fax: (305) 250-5456
E-mail: wgort@miamigov.com
★ Commissioner **Frank Carollo** (District 3) .... (305) 250-5380
Term Expires: November 1, 2017 Fax: (305) 250-5386
E-mail: fcarollo@miamigov.com
★ Commissioner **Francis X. Suarez** (District 4) .... (305) 250-5420
Term Expires: November 2019 Fax: (305) 856-5230
E-mail: fsuarez@miamigov.com

Office of the City Attorney
Miami Riverside Center, 444 SW 2nd Avenue, Suite 945, Miami, FL 33130-1910
Fax: (305) 416-1801 E-mail: law@miamigov.com
Internet: www.miamigov.com/cityattorney

City Attorney **Victoria Méndez** .... (305) 416-1832
E-mail: vmendez@miamigov.com
Education: Miami 1995 BA, 1999 MPA, 1999 JD
Administrative Assistant **Marta Gomez** .... (305) 416-1844
E-mail: martagomez@miamigov.com

Office of the City Clerk
City Hall, 3500 Pan American Dr., Miami, FL 33133
Fax: (305) 858-1610 Internet: www.miamigov.com/City_Clerk/

▶ City Clerk **Todd B. Hannon** .... (305) 250-5360
E-mail: clerks@miamigov.com
Assistant City Clerk **Nicole Ewan** .... (305) 250-5360
E-mail: clerks@miamigov.com

★ Elected Official ▲ Appointed by Legislature ▼ Appointed by Governor ▶ Appointed by Board or Commission ● Appointed by Judge
■ Appointed by Mayor △ Appointed by Freeholders ▽ Appointed by Supervisor ▷ Appointed by County Executive ○ Appointed by Council

CITIES AND TOWNS

Office of the City Manager
3500 Pan American Drive, Miami, FL 33133
Fax: (305) 416-1019 E-mail: citymanager@ci.miami.fl.us

City Manager **Daniel J. Alfonso** .... (305) 416-1011
E-mail: citymanager@miamigov.com
Assistant City Manager **Nzeribe "Zerry" Ihekwaba** .... (305) 416-1011
E-mail: NIhekwaba@miamigov.com
Assistant City Manager **Alberto N. Parjus** .... (305) 416-1011
E-mail: AParjus@miamigov.com
Education: Florida International 1984 BS
Assistant City Manager **Fernando Casamayor** .... (305) 416-1011
E-mail: FCasamayor@miamigov.com

Office of Auditor General
Miami Riverside Center, 444 SW 2nd Avenue, Room 711, Miami, FL 33130
Tel: (305) 416-2040 Fax: (305) 416-2046
Internet: www.miamigov.com/internal_audits/

Auditor General **Theodore Guba** .... (305) 416-2040

Finance Department
Miami Riverside Center, 444 Southwest 2nd Avenue, 6th Floor, Miami, FL 33130-1910
Fax: (305) 416-1987 Internet: www.miamigov.com/finance/

Finance Director **Jose Fernandez** .... (305) 416-1324
Assistant Director **Ericka Paschal** .... (305) 416-1327
Treasurer **Armando Blanco** .... (305) 416-1945

Building Department
Miami Riverside Center, 444 SW 2nd Avenue, 4th Floor, Miami, FL 33130
Tel: (305) 416-1100 Fax: (305) 416-2168
Internet: www.miamigov.com/building/

Building and Zoning Director **Orlando Toledo** .... (305) 416-1102
Building Official **Mariano Fernandez** .... (305) 416-1107

Civil Service Board
Miami Riverside Center, 444 SW 2nd Avenue, Suite 724, Miami, FL 33130
Fax: (305) 416-2025 E-mail: csb@ci.miami.fl.us
Internet: www.miamigov.com/Civil_Service/

Executive Secretary/Director **Tishria L. Mindingall** .... (305) 416-2020
E-mail: tmindingall@ci.miami.fl.us

Civilian Investigative Panel
970 SW 1 Street, #305, Miami, FL 33130
Fax: (305) 400-5396 Internet: www.miamigov.com/cip/

Director **Cristina Beamud** .... (305) 960-4956

Department of Community Development
Miami Riverside Center, 444 SW 2nd Ave., 2nd Floor, Miami, FL 33130
P.O. Box 330708, Miami, FL 33233-0708
Fax: (305) 416-2090
Internet: www.miamigov.com/communitydevelopment/

Director **George Mensah** .... (305) 416-1978
E-mail: gmensah@miamigov.com
Deputy Director **Alfredo Duran** .... (305) 416-1999
E-mail: aduran@miamigov.com
Assistant Director **Maria Eisenhart** .... (305) 416-1936
E-mail: meisenhart@miamigov.com
Assistant Director **Roberto Tazoe** .... (305) 416-1984
E-mail: rtazoe@miamigov.com

Miami Downtown Development Authority
Wachovia Financial Center, 200 South Biscayne Boulevard, Suite 2929, Miami, FL 33131
Fax: (305) 371-2423 Internet: www.miamidda.com
E-mail: info@miamidda.com

Executive Director **Alyce M. Robertson** .... (305) 579-6675
E-mail: robertson@miamidda.com
Education: Indiana 1977 BA, 1979 MPA

Office of Grants Administration
Miami Riverside Center, 444 SW 2nd Avenue, 5th Floor, Miami, FL 33130
Tel: (305) 416-1536 Fax: (305) 416-2151

Director **Lillian Blondet** .... (305) 416-1536
Special Projects Administrator **William Porro** .... (305) 416-2181
E-mail: wporro@miamigov.com Fax: (305) 400-5152
Environmental Program Manager **Ajani Stewart** .... (305) 961-5191

Fire-Rescue Department
1151 NW Seventh Street, 3rd Floor, Miami, FL 33136
Tel: (305) 416-5400 Fax: (305) 416-5431 E-mail: fire@ci.miami.fl.us
Internet: www.miamigov.com/Fire/

Fire Chief **Maurice L. Kemp** .... (305) 416-5401
E-mail: mkemp@ci.miami.fl.us
Education: Allen BS; Nova Southeastern MBA
Deputy Chief **Joseph Zahralban** .... (305) 416-5403
E-mail: jzahralban@ci.miami.fl.us
Deputy Chief of Operations **Edward Pidermann** .... (305) 416-5407
E-mail: epidermann@ci.miami.fl.us

Human Resources Department
Miami Riverside Center, 444 SW 2nd Ave., 7th Floor, Miami, FL 33130
P.O. Box 330708, Miami, FL 33233-0708
Fax: (305) 416-2115

Director **Amy Klose** .... (305) 416-2110
E-mail: apost@miamigov.com

Information Technology
Miami Riverside Center, 444 SW Second Avenue, 5th Floor, Miami, FL 33130
Fax: (305) 416-2151 Internet: www.miamigov.com/ITD/

Chief Information Officer **Kevin Burns** .... (305) 416-1911
E-mail: cio@miamigov.com

Office of Management and Budget
444 SW 2nd Avenue, Miami, FL 33130-1910

Director of Management and Budget **Chris Rose** .... (305) 416-1585
E-mail: crose@ci.miami.fl.us

Miami Parking Authority
40 NW 3rd Street, Miami, FL 33128
Fax: (305) 371-9451 Internet: www.miamiparking.com

Chief Executive Officer **Arthur Noriega** .... (305) 373-6789 ext. 242
Executive Assistant **Dorian Barrera** .... (305) 373-6789 ext. 226
E-mail: dbarrera@miamiparking.com
Chief Operations Officer **Alejandra C. Argudin** .. (305) 373-6789 ext. 249
E-mail: aargudin@miamiparking.com
Human Resources Director **Angela Hernandez** .. (305) 373-6789 ext. 241
E-mail: ahernandez@miamiparking.com

Parks and Recreation Department
Miami Riverside Center, 444 SW 2nd Ave., 8th Floor, Miami, FL 33130
Tel: (305) 416-1300 Fax: (305) 416-2154
Internet: www.miamigov.com/parks

Director **Kevin M. Kirwin** .... (305) 416-1320
Deputy Director **Lara de Souza** .... (305) 416-1341
Superintendent, Recreation **Zhoaming Guan** .... (305) 960-1311

★ Elected Official ▲ Appointed by Legislature ▼ Appointed by Governor ► Appointed by Board or Commission ● Appointed by Judge
■ Appointed by Mayor △ Appointed by Freeholders ▽ Appointed by Supervisor ▷ Appointed by County Executive ○ Appointed by Council

Parks and Recreation Department *continued*

Assistant Superintendent, Maintenance **(Vacant)** . . . . (305) 960-3003
Day Care Administrator **(Vacant)** . . . . (305) 759-3507
490 Northeast 61st Street, Miami, FL 33138
Persons with Disabilities Division Coordinator
Nadia Arguelles . . . . (305) 960-4962
4560 Northwest Fourth Terrace, Miami, FL 33126

Planning and Zoning Department

Miami Riverside Center, 444 SW 2nd Avenue, 3rd Floor, Miami, FL 33130
Tel: (305) 416-1400 Fax: (305) 416-2156
Internet: www.miamigov.com/planning/

Director **Francisco J. Garcia** . . . . (305) 416-1470
Assistant to the Director **Jessica Iturrey** . . . . (305) 416-1403
E-mail: JIturrey@miamigov.com
Assistant Director **Luciana L. Gonzalez** . . . . (305) 416-1404
Zoning Administrator (Acting) **Devin Cejas** . . . . (305) 416-2156

Police Department

400 NW 2nd Ave., Miami, FL 33128
Fax: (305) 372-4609 Internet: www.miami-police.org

Police Chief **Rodolfo "Rudy" Llanes** . . . . (305) 603-6100
Executive Assistant **Cdr. Armando Aguilar** . . . . (305) 603-6100
E-mail: armando.aguilar@miami-police.org
Administration Assistant Chief **Jorge Gomez** . . . . (305) 603-6120
Criminal Investigation Assistant Chief **Anita Najiy** . . . . . . (305) 603-6130
E-mail: anita.najiy@miami-police.org
Field Operations Assistant Chief **Luis E. Cabrera** . . . . (305) 603-6100
Police Information Systems Manager
Lt. Sean MacDonald . . . . (305) 603-6155
E-mail: sean.macdonald@miami-police.org
Training **Major Lazaro Farrell** . . . . (305) 603-6615

Department of Real Estate Asset Management

Miami Convention Center, 400 SE 2nd Ave., Miami, FL 33131
Fax: (305) 372-2919 Internet: www.miamigov.com/PublicFacilities/

Director **Daniel Rotenberg** . . . . (305) 416-1471
E-mail: drotenberg@ci.miami.fl.us
Assistant Director **Aldo Bustamante** . . . . (305) 416-1436
E-mail: abustamante@ci.miami.fl.us
Asset Management - Lease Manager **Mark Burns** . . . . (305) 416-1471
E-mail: mburns@ci.miami.fl.us

Dinner Key Marina

3400 Pan American Dr., Miami, FL 33133
Fax: (305) 579-6952 Internet: www.miami-marinas.com

Manager **Stephen Bogner** . . . . (305) 579-6950

James L. Knight International Center

400 SE Second Ave., 3rd Floor, Miami, FL 33131
Fax: (305) 350-7910 Internet: http://www.jlkc.com/

General Manager **Robert Murray** . . . . (305) 416-5973

Manuel Artime Community Center

900 SW 1st St., Miami, FL 33130
Tel: (305) 960-4680 Fax: (305) 960-4689
Internet: www.manuelairtimetheater.com

Manager **Junior Santana** . . . . (305) 960-4686
E-mail: ysantana@ci.miami.fl.us

Marine Stadium Marina

3501 Rickenbacker Causeway, Miami, FL 33149
Fax: (305) 365-1142 Internet: www.miami-marinas.com

Manager **Stephen Bogner** . . . . (305) 361-3316

Miamarina at Bayside

401 Biscayne Blvd., Miami, FL 33132
Fax: (305) 579-6957 Internet: www.miamimarinas.com

Manager **Stephen Bogner** . . . . (305) 579-6955

Public Works Department

Miami Riverside Center, 444 SW 2nd Avenue, 8th Floor, Miami, FL 33130
P.O. Box 330708, Miami, FL 33233-0708
Tel: (305) 416-1200 Fax: (305) 416-1278

Director **Eduardo Santamaria** . . . . (305) 416-1200
Chief Civil Engineer **Juvenal Santana** . . . . (305) 416-1218
E-mail: jsantana@ci.miami.fl.us
Chief of Maintenance **Lee Wilkins** . . . . (305) 960-2870
E-mail: lwilkins@ci.miami.fl.us

Purchasing Department

Miami Riverside Center, 444 SW 2nd Ave., 6th Floor, Miami, FL 33130
Fax: (305) 416-1925 Internet: www.miamigov.com/procurement/

Director/Chief Procurement Officer **Annie Perez** . . . . (305) 416-1910
E-mail: annieperez@miamigov.com

Risk Management Department

Miami Riverside Center, 444 SW 2nd Ave., 9th Floor, Miami, FL 33130
Fax: (305) 416-1710 Internet: www.miamigov.com/RiskManagement/

Director **Ann-Marie Sharpe** . . . . (305) 416-1381
E-mail: asharpe@miamigov.com

Solid Waste Department

1290 NW 20th St., Miami, FL 33142
Fax: (305) 960-2850 Internet: www.miamigov.com/SolidWaste/pages/

Director **Mario F. Nuñez** . . . . (305) 960-2804

City of Miami Gardens, Florida

18605 NW 27th Avenue, Miami Gardens, FL 33056
Tel: (305) 622-8000 Fax: (305) 622-8001
Internet: www.miamigardens-fl.gov

County: Miami-Dade **Election Type:** Nonpartisan **Year Incorporated:** 2003 **Population:** 113,187 (2015)

Mayor and City Council

18605 NW 27th Avenue, Miami Gardens, FL 33056

★ Mayor **Oliver G. Gilbert III** . . . . (305) 914-9170 ext. 2791
Began Service: August 30, 2012
Term Expires: August 2016
E-mail: ogilbert@miamigardens-fl.gov
Education: Florida A&M BA; Miami JD
Assistant to the Mayor **Sandra Pierre-Paul** . . . (305) 914-9170 ext. 2791
E-mail: spierrepaul@miamigardens-fl.gov
★ Vice Mayor **Felicia Robinson** (Seat 4) . . . . (305) 622-8062
Term Expires: August 2018
E-mail: frobinson@miamigardens-fl.gov
★ Councilman **Lillie Q. Odom** (Seat 1) . . . . (305) 622-8062
Term Expires: August 2016
E-mail: lOdom@miamigardens-fl.gov
★ Councilman **Lisa Davis** (Seat 2) . . . . (305) 622-8063
Term Expires: August 2018
E-mail: ldavis@miamigardens-fl.gov
★ Councilman **Rodney Harris** (Seat 3) . . . . (305) 622-8063
Term Expires: August 2016
E-mail: rharris@miamigardens-fl.gov
★ Councilman **David Williams, Jr.** (Seat 5) . . . . (305) 622-8062
Term Expires: August 2016
E-mail: dwilliamsjr@miamigardens-fl.gov

(continued on next page)

★ Elected Official ▲ Appointed by Legislature ▼ Appointed by Governor ▶ Appointed by Board or Commission ● Appointed by Judge
■ Appointed by Mayor △ Appointed by Freeholders ▽ Appointed by Supervisor ▷ Appointed by County Executive ○ Appointed by Council

Mayor and City Council *continued*

★ Councilman **Erhabor Ighodaro** (Seat 6) . . . . (305) 622-8063
Term Expires: November 2018
E-mail: eighodaro@miamigardens-fl.gov

Office of the City Attorney
18605 NW 27th Avenue, Miami Gardens, FL 33056
Tel: (305) 622-8055 Fax: (305) 622-6484

City Attorney **Sonja Dickens** . . . . (305) 622-8055 ext. 2450
E-mail: sdickens@miamigardens-fl.gov
Education: Spelman 1991 BA; Miami 1994 JD
Assistant City Attorney **Monica Barnes** . . . . (305) 622-8055 ext. 2452
Education: Howard U BA; Stetson 2003 JD
Legal Assistant **Joresha Gore-Barnes** . . . . (305) 622-8055 ext. 2451

Office of the City Clerk
18605 NW 27th Avenue, Miami Gardens, FL 33056

■ City Clerk **Ronetta Taylor** . . . . (305) 914-9129 ext. 2830
E-mail: rtaylor@miamigardens-fl.gov
Education: Barry BA
Deputy City Clerk **(Vacant)** . . . . (305) 622-8000
Administrative Assistant **Mercedia Williams** . . . . (305) 622-8000
E-mail: mwilliams@miamigardens-fl.gov
Administrative Assistant **Krista Woods** . . . . (305) 622-8000
E-mail: kwoods@miamigardens-fl.gov

Office of the City Manager
18605 NW 27th Avenue, Miami Gardens, FL 33056

○ City Manager **Cameron D. Benson** . . . . (305) 622-8000
E-mail: cbenson@miamigardens-fl.gov
Assistant City Manager **Vernita Nelson** . . . . (305) 622-8000
E-mail: vnelson@miamigardens-fl.gov

Building and Code Compliance Department
18605 NW 27th Avenue, Miami Gardens, FL 33056

Director **(Vacant)** . . . . (305) 622-8027

Building Services Division
18605 NW 27th Avenue, Miami Gardens, FL 33056
Fax: (305) 622-8557
Internet: http://www.miamigardens-fl.gov/building/index.html

Director **(Vacant)** . . . . (305) 622-8027

Code Compliance Division
18605 NW 27th Avenue, Miami Gardens, FL 33056
Internet: http://www.miamigardens-fl.gov/code/index.html

Building Official **(Vacant)** . . . . (305) 622-8000 ext. 2670

Capital Improvement Projects Department
18605 NW 27th Avenue, Miami Gardens, FL 33056
Fax: (305) 474-9871
Internet: http://www.miamigardens-fl.gov/capital/index.html

Director **(Vacant)** . . . . (305) 622-8000
Project Manager **Jimmie Allen** . . . . (305) 622-8000
E-mail: jallen@miamigardens-fl.gov
Project Manager **Anthony Smith** . . . . (305) 622-8000
E-mail: asmith@miamigardens-fl.gov

Community Development Department
18605 NW 27th Avenue, Miami Gardens, FL 33056
Internet: http://www.miamigardens-fl.gov/cd/index.html

Director/Assistant City Manager **Laurin Yoder** . . . . (305) 622-8041
E-mail: lyoder@miamigardens-fl.gov

Finance Department
18605 NW 27th Avenue, Miami Gardens, FL 33056
Internet: http://www.miamigardens-fl.gov/finance/index.html

Finance Director **Patricia Varney** . . . . (305) 622-8000
Education: Barry BA
Assistant Finance Director **Mike Quesada** . . . . (305) 622-8000
Accountant **Vanessa Castellon** . . . . (305) 622-8000
E-mail: vcastellon@miamigardens-fl.gov
Accountant **Karen Tucker** . . . . (305) 622-8000
E-mail: ktucker@miamigardens-fl.gov

General Services Department
18605 NW 27th Avenue, Miami Gardens, FL 33056

Assistant City Manager **Vernita Nelson** . . . . (305) 622-8000
E-mail: vnelson@miamigardens-fl.gov

Events and Media Division
18605 NW 27th Avenue, Miami Gardens, FL 33056

Event and Media Specialist **(Vacant)** . . . . (305) 622-8000
Public Relations Specialist **(Vacant)** . . . . (305) 622-8000

Fleet Division
18605 NW 27th Avenue, Miami Gardens, FL 33056
Fax: (305) 622-8001
Internet: http://www.miamigardens-fl.gov/fleet/index.html

Fleet Manager **David Motola** . . . . (305) 786-1276
Education: Florida Atlantic MBA

Procurement Division
18605 NW 27th Avenue, Miami Gardens, FL 33056

Procurement Director **Lindell Y. Miller** . . . . (305) 622-8000 ext. 2490
E-mail: lmiller@miamigardens-fl.gov

Human Resources Department
18605 NW 27th Avenue, Miami Gardens, FL 33056
Internet: http://www.miamigardens-fl.gov/human/index.html

Human Resources and Risk Director **Melissa Negron** . . . . (305) 914-9010
E-mail: mnegron@miamigardens-fl.gov

Information Technology Department
18605 NW 27th Avenue, Miami Gardens, FL 33056
Internet: http://www.miamigardens-fl.gov/it/index.html

Information Technology Director (Interim)
Tristan S. Lattibeaudiere . . . . (305) 622-8000
E-mail: tlattibeaudiere@miamigardens-fl.gov

Parks and Recreation Department
18605 NW 27th Avenue, Miami Gardens, FL 33056
Fax: (305) 622-6450

Director **Parvin Neloms** . . . . (305) 622-2520
Public Information Officer **Jenny Pouerie** . . . . . (305) 622-8080 ext. 2521
E-mail: jpouerie@miamigardens-fl.gov

Planning and Zoning Department
8601 NW 27th Avenue, Miami Gardens, FL 33056
Tel: (305) 622-8023 Fax: (305) 622-8857

Manager **Irma Matos** . . . . (305) 622-8000 ext. 2675

Police Department
1020 NW 163rd Drive, Miami Gardens, FL 33169
Internet: http://www.miamigardenspolice.org/

Chief of Police **Antonio G. Brooklen** . . . . (305) 474-1400

★ Elected Official ▲ Appointed by Legislature ▼ Appointed by Governor ▶ Appointed by Board or Commission ● Appointed by Judge
■ Appointed by Mayor △ Appointed by Freeholders ▽ Appointed by Supervisor ▷ Appointed by County Executive ○ Appointed by Council

Public Works Department
1050 NW 163rd Drive, Miami Gardens, FL 33169
Fax: (305) 622-8032

Director **O. Tom Ruiz** .... (786) 279-1260
Education: Nova Southeastern MPA
Administrative Analyst **Tiffany Adderley** .... (786) 279-1263
E-mail: tadderley@miamigardens-fl.gov
Keep Miami Gardens Beautiful Manager
Claudelle Joseph .... (786) 279-1268

City of Midland, Texas
City Hall, 300 North Loraine, Midland, TX 79701
Tel: (432) 685-7100 Internet: www.midlandtexas.gov

County: Midland **Election Type:** Nonpartisan **Charter:** 1940
Population: 132,950 (2015)

Office of the Mayor and City Council
City Hall, 300 North Loraine, Midland, TX 79701

★ Mayor **Jerry Morales** .... (432) 685-7204
Began Service: January 13, 2014
Term Expires: December 31, 2016
E-mail: jfmorales@midlandtexas.gov
★ Council Member **Jeff Sparks** (District 1) .... (432) 685-7204
Term Expires: December 31, 2018
E-mail: jsparks@midlandtexas.gov
Education: Texas BS
★ Council Member **John B. Love III** (District 2) .... (432) 685-7204
Term Expires: December 31, 2018
E-mail: jlove@midlandtexas.gov
★ Council Member **Sharla Hotchkiss** (District 3) .... (432) 685-7204
Term Expires: December 31, 2016
E-mail: shotchkiss@midlandtexas.gov
Education: Southwestern
★ Council Member **J. Ross Lacy** (District 4) .... (432) 685-7204
Term Expires: December 31, 2016
E-mail: jlacy@midlandtexas.gov
★ Council Member **Scott Dufford** (At-Large) .... (432) 685-7204
Term Expires: December 31, 2018
E-mail: sdufford@midlandtexas.gov
★ Council Member **Spencer Robnett** (At-Large) .... (432) 685-7204
Term Expires: December 31, 2018
E-mail: srobnett@midlandtexas.gov

Office of the City Manager
City Hall, 300 North Loraine, 3rd Floor, Midland, TX 79701
Fax: (432) 686-1600

City Manager **Courtney Sharp** .... (432) 685-7202
E-mail: csharp@midlandtexas.gov
Education: Texas A&I BA
Deputy City Manager **Tommy Hudson** .... (432) 685-7201
E-mail: thudson@midlandtexas.gov
Education: Angelo State BBA; Troy State MPA
Assistant City Manager **Robert Patrick** .... (432) 685-7205
E-mail: rwpatrick@midlandtexas.gov
Assistant City Manager **Frank Salvato** .... (432) 685-7913
E-mail: fsalvato@midlandtexas.gov

Office of the City Attorney
P.O. Box 1152, Midland, TX 79702

City Attorney **John Ohnemiller** .... (432) 685-7253
E-mail: johnemiller@midlandtexas.gov

Office of the City Auditor
P.O. Box 1152, Midland, TX 79702-1152

City Auditor **Debra M. Gotovac** .... (432) 685-7478

Office of the City Secretary
City Hall, 300 North Loraine, 3rd Floor, Midland, TX 79701

City Secretary **Amy Turner** .... (432) 685-7430
E-mail: aturner@midlandtexas.gov

Administrative Services Department
City Hall, 300 North Loraine, Midland, TX 79701

Director **Catherine Clifton** .... (432) 685-7247
E-mail: cclifton@midlandtexas.gov
Human Resources Manager **Elizabeth Balderrama** .... (432) 685-7250
E-mail: ebalderrama@midlandtexas.gov
Employee Health and Wellness Coordinator **(Vacant)** .... (432) 685-7248

Midland Animal Services
1200 North Fairgrounds, Midland, TX 79706

Director **Paul O'Neill** .... (432) 528-0950

Development Services Department
City Hall, 300 North Loraine, Midland, TX 79701

Director **Charles "Chuck" Harrington** .... (432) 685-7442

Code Administration Division
City Hall, 300 North Loraine, Midland, TX 79701
Fax: (432) 686-1609

Code Compliance Manager **Steve Thorpe** .... (432) 685-7388

Community Development Office
City Hall, 300 North Loraine, Room 410, Midland, TX 79701
Fax: (432) 686-1609

Community Development Manager **Isaac G. Garnett** .... (432) 685-7408
E-mail: igarnett@midlandtexas.gov

Engineering Services
City Hall, 300 North Loraine, Midland, TX 79701
Fax: (432) 683-1786

Director **Jose Ortiz** .... (432) 685-7288
City Engineer **Matt Carr** .... (432) 685-7415
E-mail: mcarr@midlandtexas.gov

Geographic Information Systems Division
City Hall, 300 North Loraine, Midland, TX 79701
Fax: (432) 683-1786

Manager **Ryan Farmer** .... (432) 685-7470

Planning Division
City Hall, 300 North Loraine, Midland, TX 79701
Fax: (432) 686-1609

Planning Division Manager **Jessica Carpenter** .... (432) 685-7400

Transportation Division
City Hall, 300 North Loraine, Midland, TX 79701

City Traffic Engineer **Mike Pacelli** .... (432) 685-7280
E-mail: mpacelli@midlandtexas.gov

Facilities Services Department
City Hall, 300 North Loraine, Midland, TX 79701

Manager **Mark Garcia** .... (432) 685-7371
E-mail: mgarcia@midlandtexas.gov

Purchasing Division
City Hall, 300 North Loraine, Midland, TX 79701
Tel: (432) 685-0523

Purchasing Agent **Regina Stephenson** .... (432) 685-7233
E-mail: purchasing@midlandtexas.gov

Finance and Budget Department
City Hall, 300 North Loraine, Midland, TX 79701
Manager **Pam Simecka** . . . . (432) 685-7210

Fire Department
1500 West Wall Street, Midland, TX 79701
E-mail: fireinfo@midlandtexas.gov
Fire Chief **Robert Isbell** . . . . (432) 685-7332
E-mail: risbell@midlandtexas.gov

Health and Seniors Department
3303 West Illinois, Midland, TX 79704
Fax: (432) 681-7634
Director **Sal Garcia** . . . . (432) 681-7613

Midland International Airport
P.O. Box 60305, Midland, TX 79711
Tel: (432) 560-2200
Director **Justine Ruff** . . . . (432) 560-2200 ext. 3001

Parks and Recreation Department
2300 Butternut Lane, Midland, TX 79705
Manager **Laurie Williams** . . . . (432) 685-7370
Recreation Superintendent **Joey Jolly** . . . . (432) 685-7379

Police Department
601 North Loraine, Midland, TX 79701
Fax: (432) 685-7585 E-mail: mpd@midlandtexas.gov
Chief of Police **Price Robinson** . . . . (432) 685-7103

Public Information Office
City Hall, 300 North Loraine, Midland, TX 79701
Fax: (432) 686-1600
Public Information Officer **Sara Bustilloz** . . . . . . (432) 685-7593
E-mail: sbustilloz@midlandtexas.gov

Utilities Administration Department
City Hall, 300 North Loraine, Midland, TX 79701
Director of Utilities **Laura Wilson** . . . . (432) 685-7937

City of Milwaukee, Wisconsin

City Hall, 200 East Wells Street, Milwaukee, WI 53202-3515
Tel: (414) 286-2150 (Information) TTY: (414) 286-2025
Internet: www.city.milwaukee.gov

County: Milwaukee **Election Type:** Nonpartisan **Year Incorporated:** 1846 **Population:** 600,155 (2015)

Tom Barrett
Mayor

Began Service: April 20, 2004
Term Expires: April 15, 2020
Education: Wisconsin 1976 BA, 1980 JD
Career: State Senator (D), Wisconsin State Senate (1989-1992); Representative (D-WI, District 5), United States House of Representatives (1993-2002)

Office of the Mayor
City Hall, 200 E. Wells St., Room 201, Milwaukee, WI 53202
Tel: (414) 286-2200 Fax: (414) 286-3191
Internet: http://city.milwaukee.gov/Mayor

★ Mayor **Tom Barrett** . . . . (414) 286-2200
E-mail: mayor@milwaukee.gov
Special Assistant to the Mayor **Alexis Peterson** . . . . . . (414) 286-2200
E-mail: alexis.peterson@milwaukee.gov
Chief of Staff **Patrick Curley** . . . . (414) 286-2200
Communications Director **Jodie Tabak** . . . . (414) 286-2200
E-mail: jodie.tabak@milwaukee.gov
Research and Analysis Manager **Aaron Szopinski** . . . . . . (414) 286-2200
Staff Assistant Manager **Myra Edwards** . . . . (414) 286-2200
E-mail: myra.edwards@milwaukee.gov
Staff Assistant to the Mayor **Oscar Tovar** . . . . (414) 286-2200
E-mail: oscar.tovar@milwaukee.gov
Community Outreach Liaison **Megan O'Connor** . . . . (414) 286-2200
E-mail: moconn@milwaukee.gov
Liaison Officer to the Mayor **Clifton Crump** . . . . (414) 286-2200
E-mail: ccrump@milwaukee.gov

Office of the Assessor
City Hall, 200 E. Wells St., Room 507, Milwaukee, WI 53202
Tel: (414) 286-3651 Fax: (414) 286-8447
Internet: http://city.milwaukee.gov/assessor

■ Assessment Commissioner **Steve Miner** . . . . (414) 286-3651
E-mail: sminer@milwaukee.gov
Chief Assessor **Peter Bronek** . . . . (414) 286-3178
E-mail: pbronek@milwaukee.gov

Administration and Records Division
Administrative Services Supervisor **David C. Fortney** . . . . (414) 286-3115
E-mail: dan.fortney@milwaukee.gov

Assessment Division
Manager **Gail Kern** . . . . (414) 286-3171
Manager **Scott G. Winter** . . . . (414) 286-3137

Department of Administration
City Hall, 200 E. Wells St., Milwaukee, WI 53202
Tel: (414) 286-3850 Fax: (414) 286-8547

■ Director **Sharon Robinson** Room 606 . . . . (414) 286-3828
E-mail: srobin@milwaukee.gov

Office of Environmental Sustainability
200 East Wells Street, Milwaukee, WI 53202
Environmental Sustainability Director
Erick Shambarger . . . . (414) 286-8317

Budget and Management Division
Tel: (414) 286-3741 Fax: (414) 286-5475

Budget Director **Mark Nicolini** . . . . (414) 286-5060
E-mail: mnicol@milwaukee.gov
Education: Wabash Col 1974 AB; Wisconsin 1983 MA

Office Supervisor **Crystal Ivy** Room 307 . . . . (414) 286-3449
E-mail: civy@milwaukee.gov

Community Development Block Grant Administration
Tel: (414) 286-3647 Fax: (414) 286-5003

Director **Steven L. Mahan** Room 606 . . . . (414) 286-3842
E-mail: smahan@milwaukee.gov

Associate Director **Darlene Hayes** Room 606 . . . . (414) 286-3844
E-mail: dhayes@milwaukee.gov

Grant Compliance Manager **Hettie White** Room 606 . . . . (414) 286-8146

Emerging Business Enterprise Program [EBEP]
Fax: (414) 286-8752

Manager **Nikki Purvis** Room 606 . . . . (414) 286-5553

Information and Technology Management Division
809 N. Broadway St., 4th Floor, Milwaukee, WI 53202
Fax: (414) 286-2113

■ Chief Information Officer **Nancy Olson** . . . . (414) 286-8710
E-mail: nancy.olson@milwaukee.gov

Office Supervisor **Lisa Olive** . . . . (414) 286-2336
E-mail: lolive@milwaukee.gov

Intergovernmental Relations Division
Tel: (414) 286-3747 Fax: (414) 286-8547

Director **Jennifer Gonda** Room 606 . . . . (414) 286-5562
E-mail: jennifer.gonda@milwaukee.gov

Administrative Assistant **Tobie Black** Room 606 . . . . . (414) 286-5584
E-mail: tobie.black@milwaukee.gov

Procurement Services Section
Tel: (414) 286-3501 Fax: (414) 286-5507

Director **Rhonda Kelsey** Room 601 . . . . (414) 286-3639
E-mail: rhonda.kelsey@milwaukee.gov

Procurement Administrator **Cynthia Matz** Room 601 . . . . (414) 286-3507
E-mail: cmatz@milwaukee.gov

Department of City Development [DCD]
809 N. Broadway, Milwaukee, WI 53202-3617
Tel: (414) 286-5800 Fax: (414) 286-5467
Internet: http://city.milwaukee.gov/DCD

■ Commissioner **Rocky Marcoux** . . . . (414) 286-5800
E-mail: rmarco@milwaukee.gov

Deputy Commissioner **Martha Brown** . . . . (414) 286-5810
E-mail: mbrown@milwaukee.gov

Communications Manager **Jeff Fleming** . . . . (414) 286-8580
E-mail: jeff.fleming@milwaukee.gov

City Planning Division
Tel: (414) 286-5714 Fax: (414) 286-0730

Planning Manager **Vanessa Koster** . . . . (414) 286-5716

Finance and Administration Division
Fax: (414) 286-5875

Director of Finance and Administration
David Schroeder . . . . (414) 286-5933
E-mail: dschro@milwaukee.gov

Budget and Management Reporting Manager
Lori Schmidt . . . . (414) 286-5835
E-mail: lschmi@milwaukee.gov

Contracting and Procurement Manager **Scott Stange** . . . . (414) 286-5727
E-mail: scott.stange@milwaukee.gov

General Accounting Manager **Gloria Analla** . . . . (414) 286-5837
E-mail: ganall@milwaukee.gov

Personnel Officer **Judy Allen** . . . . (414) 286-6076
E-mail: jallen@milwaukee.gov

Housing Management Division
Tel: (414) 286-5671 Fax: (414) 286-0833

Director **Antonio M. Perez** . . . . (414) 286-5671

Senior Asset Manager **Beverly Johnson** . . . . (414) 286-5825

Modernization and Development Manager
Warren Jones . . . . (414) 286-3629
5125 W. Lisbon Ave., Milwaukee, WI 53210

Central Maintenance and Support Operations Manager
Jim Wellman . . . . (414) 286-2931
5003 W. Lisbon Ave., Milwaukee, WI 53210

Community Services Manager **Ken Barbeau** . . . . (414) 286-2905
650 W. Reservoir Ave., Milwaukee, WI 53212
E-mail: kbarbe@hacm.org

Housing Intake Coordinator **Patricia Schmidtknecht** . . . . (414) 286-8264

Section 8 Housing Manager **Debra La Rosa** . . . . (414) 286-5647

Assistant Secretary of the Housing Authority
Bobbi Marsells . . . . (414) 286-2920

Neighborhood Improvement Development Corporation
Tel: (414) 286-5608 Fax: (414) 288-5447

Housing Program Director **Larry Kilmer** . . . . (414) 286-5723
E-mail: larry.kilmer@milwaukee.gov

Housing Rehabilitation Manager **Fatima Benhaddou** . . . . (414) 286-5720
E-mail: fatima.benhaddou@milwaukee.gov

Redevelopment Authority [RACM]
Tel: (414) 286-5821 Fax: (414) 286-0395

Assistant Executive Director/Secretary **Dave Misky** . . . . . . (414) 286-8682
E-mail: dmisky@milwaukee.gov

Department of Employee Relations [DER]
City Hall, Rm. 706, 200 E. Wells St., Milwaukee, WI 53202-3554
Tel: (414) 286-3751 Fax: (414) 286-0203 TTY: (414) 286-2960
E-mail: emprel@milwaukee.gov Internet: http://city.milwaukee.gov/der

■ Director **Maria Monteagudo** . . . . (414) 286-3335
200 East Wells Street, Room CH706, Milwaukee, WI 53202-3554
E-mail: mmonte@milwaukee.gov

■ Employee Benefits Director **Michael Brady**
Room CH706 . . . . (414) 286-2317
E-mail: mbrady@milwaukee.gov Fax: (414) 286-2106

Human Resources Manager **Andrea Knickerbocker**
Room CH706 . . . . (414) 286-3387
E-mail: aknick@milwaukee.gov

Human Resources Manager **Carl Nagy** Room CH706 . . . . (414) 286-8643
E-mail: cnagy@milwaukee.gov

Labor Negotiator **Deborah Ford** Room CH706 . . . . (414) 286-2108
Fax: (414) 286-2356

Employes' Retirement System [ERS]
789 North Water Street, Suite 300, Milwaukee, WI 53202
Fax: (414) 286-0880 Internet: www.cmers.com

Executive Director **Bernard J. "Jerry" Allen** . . . . (414) 286-3557

Deputy Director **Beth Conradson Cleary** . . . . (414) 286-3557
E-mail: beth.cleary@cmers.com

Chief Investment Officer **David Silber** . . . . (414) 286-3557

Fire and Police Commission
200 East Wells Street, Room 706-A, Milwaukee, WI 53202
Tel: (414) 286-5000 Fax: (414) 286-5050
Internet: www.milwaukee.gov/fpc E-mail: fpc@milwaukee.gov

■ Chair **Steven M. DeVougas** . . . . (414) 286-5000
■ Vice Chair **Michael M. O'Hear** . . . . (414) 286-5000
■ Member **Marisabel Cabrera** . . . . (414) 286-5000
■ Member **Fred Crouther** . . . . (414) 286-5000
■ Member **Kathryn Hein** . . . . (414) 286-5000
■ Member **Ann Wilson** . . . . (414) 286-5000
Executive Director **MaryNell Regan** . . . . (414) 286-5000
Community Relations Manager **(Vacant)** . . . . (414) 286-5064

★ Elected Official ▲ Appointed by Legislature ▼ Appointed by Governor ▶ Appointed by Board or Commission ● Appointed by Judge
■ Appointed by Mayor △ Appointed by Freeholders ▽ Appointed by Supervisor ▷ Appointed by County Executive ○ Appointed by Council

Fire Department [MFD]
711 West Wells Street, 3rd Floor, Milwaukee, WI 53233
Tel: (414) 286-8948 Fax: (414) 286-8996
Internet: http://city.milwaukee.gov/mfd

Fire Chief **Mark A. Rohlfing** .... (414) 286-8947
E-mail: mrohlf@milwaukee.gov
Assistant Chief, Support **Gerard M. Washington** .... (414) 286-8946
E-mail: gmwashi@milwaukee.gov
Administrative Assistant IV **Cheryl Finger** .... (414) 286-8949
E-mail: cfinger@milwaukee.gov
Assistant Chief, Operations **Daniel C. Lipski** .... (414) 286-8944
E-mail: dlipsk@milwaukee.gov
Maintenance Division Battalion Chief **John T. Litchford** .. (414) 286-8975
118 W. Virginia St., Milwaukee, WI 53204
Firefighting Deputy Chief **Brian L. Smith** .... (414) 286-8950
E-mail: blsmith@milwaukee.gov
Firefighting Deputy Chief **Aaron D. Lipski** .... (414) 286-8950
E-mail: alipsk@milwaukee.gov
Firefighting Deputy Chief **Terry W. Lintonen** .... (414) 286-8950
E-mail: tlinto@milwaukee.gov
Training Division Battalion Chief **John J. Schwengel** ... (414) 286-8971
6680 N. Teutonia Ave., Milwaukee, WI 53209
E-mail: jschwe@milwaukee.gov
Special Operations Battalion Chief **David C. Votsis** ...... (414) 286-8943
E-mail: dvotsi@milwaukee.gov
Fire Personnel Officer **Juliet Lee Battle** .... (414) 286-8942
E-mail: jbattle@milwaukee.gov
Technical Services Division Manager
Deborah K. Wilichowski .... (414) 286-8941
E-mail: dwilic@milwaukee.gov
Business Finance Manager **Yvette Rowe** .... (414) 286-5281

Police Department
Police Administration Bldg., 749 W. State St., Milwaukee, WI 53233
P.O. Box 531, Milwaukee, WI 53201-0531
Tel: (414) 933-4444 Internet: http://city.milwaukee.gov/police

Police Chief **Edward A. Flynn** .... (414) 935-7200
Education: La Salle U BA; John Jay Col MS
Central Command Assistant Chief **James Harpole** ...... (414) 935-7201
Police Academy Deputy Inspector **Terrence Gordon** ...... (414) 935-7330
E-mail: tgordo@milwaukee.gov
Strategic Management Inspector **Mary Hoerig** .... (414) 935-7565
Technical Communications Division
Capt. Andra P. Williams .... (414) 935-7470
Community Outreach and Education **Capt. Peter Pierce** .. (414) 935-7185
E-mail: ppierc@milwaukee.gov
Intelligence Division **Capt. David Salazar** .... (414) 935-7703
Narcotics Division **Jeffery Micklitz** .... (414) 221-6775
Sensitive Crimes Division **Aimee Obregon** .... (414) 935-7336

Office of Emergency Management and Homeland Security
200 East Wells Street, Room 605, Milwaukee, WI 53202
Fax: (414) 286-5050 E-mail: ohs@milwaukee.gov
Internet: www.milwaukee.gov/OfficeofHomelandSecurity.htm

Director **Steven Fronk** .... (414) 286-5062
E-mail: sfronk@milwaukee.gov

Health Department
Frank P. Zeilder Municipal Building, 841 North Broadway, 3rd Floor, Milwaukee, WI 53202-3653
Tel: (414) 286-3521 Fax: (414) 286-5990
Internet: www.milwaukee.gov/health

■ Commissioner **Bevan K. Baker** .... (414) 286-3521
E-mail: bbaker@milwaukee.gov
Health Operations Administrator **Sandra J. Rotar** .... (414) 286-3175
E-mail: srotar@milwaukee.gov
Business Operations Manager **(Vacant)** .... (414) 286-3997
Executive Assistant **Tracy Wetzel** .... (414) 286-3970
E-mail: twetzel@milwaukee.gov

Family and Community Health Services
Tel: (414) 286-3521 Fax: (414) 286-6044

Director (Interim) **Jessica Gathirimu** .... (414) 286-6269
Disease Control and Environmental Health Services
Director **Paul Biedrzycki** .... (414) 286-5787
Home Environmental Health Manager **Lisa Lien** .... (414) 286-2388

Laboratories Bureau
Fax: (414) 286-5098

Director **M. Stephen Gradus** Room 205 .... (414) 286-3526
Chief Microbiologist **Manjeet Khubbar** Room 205 ...... (414) 286-3935
Deputy Lab Director **Sanjib Bhattachayyra** Room 205 .. (414) 286-3526

Department of Neighborhood Services [DNS]
841 N. Broadway, 1st Floor, Milwaukee, WI 53202
Tel: (414) 286-3441 Fax: (414) 286-5095
Internet: www.ci.mil.wi.us/DNS

■ Commissioner **Thomas Mishefske** .... (414) 286-2543
E-mail: tmishe@milwaukee.gov
Operations Manager **(Vacant)** .... (414) 286-2548

Administration Section
Business Operations Manager **Lynne Steffen** .... (414) 286-2563
E-mail: lsteff@milwaukee.gov
Public Information and Training Coordinator
Todd N. Weiler .... (414) 286-3214
E-mail: tweile@milwaukee.gov Fax: (414) 286-5095
Network Administrator **Angela Ferrill-Browne** .... (414) 286-2127
Landlord Training Specialist **(Vacant)** .... (414) 286-8244
Property Recording Supervisor **Lakisha Bridges** .... (414) 286-3996

Building Construction Inspection Section
Construction Inspection Supervisor **Richard Paur** .... (414) 286-2512
Condemnation and Commercial Supervisor
Ronald Roberts .... (414) 286-3862
Electrical and Inspection Supervisor **Richard Paur** ...... (414) 286-2512

Code Enforcement Inspection Section
Residential Code Enforcement Supervisor **David Krey** .... (414) 286-5799

Environment/Nuisance Inspection
Environmental Supervisor **Don Schaewe** .... (414) 286-5569

Department of Public Works
841 North Broadway, Room 501, Milwaukee, WI 53202
Tel: (414) 286-3703 Fax: (414) 286-3953

■ Commissioner **Ghassan Korban** .... (414) 286-3301
E-mail: ghassan.korban@milwaukee.gov

Administrative Services Division
Administration Services Director **Dan Thomas** 11th Floor .... (414) 286-3307
E-mail: dthoma@milwaukee.gov

Bridges and Building Services
Tel: (414) 286-3402 Fax: (414) 286-5907

Facilities Director **Craig Liberto** Room 602 .... (414) 286-3408
E-mail: craig.liberto@milwaukee.gov

Fleet Services Division
Fleet Services Manager **Jeff Tews** .... (414) 286-2459

Infrastructure Services Division
Tel: (414) 286-3701 Fax: (414) 286-5994

City Engineer **Jeffrey Polenske** Room 701 .... (414) 286-2400
E-mail: jeffrey.polenske@milwaukee.gov

Operations Division
Tel: (414) 286-2489

Director of Operations **Preston D. Cole** Room 619 ...... (414) 286-2489

★ Elected Official ▲ Appointed by Legislature ▼ Appointed by Governor ▶ Appointed by Board or Commission ● Appointed by Judge
■ Appointed by Mayor △ Appointed by Freeholders ▽ Appointed by Supervisor ▷ Appointed by County Executive ○ Appointed by Council

Water Works Division

Tel: (414) 286-3710 Fax: (414) 286-8723

Superintendent **Carrie Lewis** Room 409 . . . . (414) 286-2801

Election Commission

City Hall, 200 E. Wells St., Room 501, Milwaukee, WI 53202
Fax: (414) 286-8445 Internet: http://city.milwaukee.gov/election

■ Executive Director **Neil V. Albrecht** . . . . (414) 286-6119
E-mail: neil.albrecht@milwaukee.gov

Election Services Manager **Theresa R. Gabriel** . . . . (414) 286-3962

Milwaukee Public Library [MPL]

814 W. Wisconsin Ave., Milwaukee, WI 53233
Tel: (414) 286-3000 Fax: (414) 286-2794 Internet: www.mpl.org

■ City Librarian **Paula Kiely** . . . . (414) 286-3020
E-mail: pkiely@milwaukee.gov

Deputy Director, Public Service **Joan Johnson** . . . . (414) 286-3025
E-mail: jrjohns@milwaukee.gov

Communications and Marketing Director
Christine Murphy . . . . (414) 286-3572
E-mail: cmurph@milwaukee.gov

Staff Computer Training Coordinator
Sha'Nese Burnell Jones . . . . (414) 286-3047
E-mail: smburn@milwaukee.gov Fax: (414) 286-3831

Port of Milwaukee

2323 S. Lincoln Memorial Dr., Milwaukee, WI 53207
Tel: (414) 286-3511 Fax: (414) 286-8506

Director **Paul Vornholt** . . . . (414) 286-8130
E-mail: paul.vornholt@milwaukee.gov

Board of Harbor Commissioners President **Tim Hoelter** . . (414) 286-3511

Office of the Common Council

City Hall, 200 East Wells Street, Room 205, Milwaukee, WI 53202-3570
Tel: (414) 286-2221 Fax: (414) 286-3456
Internet: http://city.milwaukee.gov/CommonCouncil

★ Council President **Michael J. Murphy** (District 10) . . . . . . (414) 286-2221
Term Expires: April 20, 2020
E-mail: mmurph@milwaukee.gov
Education: Wisconsin (Milwaukee) 1986 BS

★ Council Member **Ashanti Hamilton** (District 1) . . . . (414) 286-2221
Term Expires: April 20, 2020
E-mail: ahamil@milwaukee.gov

★ Council Member
Cavalier "Chevy" Johnson (District 2) . . . . (414) 286-2221
Term Expires: April 20, 2020
Education: Wisconsin 2009 BA

★ Council Member **Nik Kovac** (District 3) . . . . (414) 286-2221
Term Expires: April 20, 2020
E-mail: nkovac@milwaukee.gov

★ Council Member **Robert J. Bauman** (District 4) . . . . (414) 286-2221
Term Expires: April 20, 2020
E-mail: rjbauma@milwaukee.gov

★ Council Member **Jim Bohl** (District 5) . . . . (414) 286-2221
Term Expires: April 20, 2020
E-mail: jbohl@milwaukee.gov
Education: Marquette 1993 BA, 1996 MA

★ Council Member **Milele A. Coggs** (District 6) . . . . (414) 286-2221
Term Expires: April 20, 2020
E-mail: mcoggs@milwaukee.gov

★ Council Member **Khalif J. Rainey** (District 7) . . . . (414) 286-2221
Term Expires: April 20, 2020

★ Council Member **Robert G. Donovan** (District 8) . . . . (414) 286-2221
Term Expires: April 20, 2020
E-mail: rdonov@milwaukee.gov

★ Council Member **Chantia Lewis** (District 9) . . . . (414) 286-2221
Term Expires: April 20, 2020

★ Council Member **Mark A. Borkowski** (District 11) . . . . . . (414) 286-2221
Term Expires: April 20, 2020
Education: Carroll Col (WI) 1981 BS

Office of the Common Council *continued*

★ Council Member **Jose G. Perez** (District 12) . . . . (414) 286-2221
Term Expires: April 20, 2020
E-mail: jperez@milwaukee.gov

★ Council Member **Terry L. Witkowski** (District 13) . . . . (414) 286-2221
Term Expires: April 20, 2020
E-mail: twitko@milwaukee.gov

★ Council Member **Tony Zielinski** (District 14) . . . . (414) 286-2221
Term Expires: April 20, 2020
E-mail: tzieli@milwaukee.gov

★ Council Member **Russell W. Stamper II** (District 15) . . . . (414) 286-2659
Term Expires: April 20, 2020
E-mail: russell.stamperII@milwaukee.gov
Education: Alabama State 1999; Cardinal Stritch U 2004 MBA

Office of the City Clerk

City Hall, 200 East Wells Street, Room 205, Milwaukee, WI 53202
Tel: (414) 286-2221 Fax: (414) 286-3456
Internet: www.milwaukee.gov/cityclerk

○ City Clerk **Jim Owczarski** . . . . (414) 286-2221
200 East Wells Street, Room 205, Milwaukee, WI 53202-3570
E-mail: jowcza@milwaukee.gov

Deputy City Clerk/Council Records Manager
Richard Pfaff . . . . (414) 286-2998
200 East Wells Street, Room 205, Milwaukee, WI 53202-3570
E-mail: rpfaf@milwaukee.gov

Administrative Specialist **Linda Elmer** . . . . (414) 286-2236
200 East Wells Street, Room 205, Milwaukee, WI 53202-3570
E-mail: lelmer@milwaukee.gov

Management and Accounting Officer **Terry McDonald** . . . (414) 286-2366
200 East Wells Street, Fax: (414) 286-3456
Room 205, Milwaukee, WI 53202-3570
E-mail: tmcdo@milwaukee.gov

Legislative Reference Bureau [LRB]

City Hall, 200 East Wells Street, Room B-11, Milwaukee, WI 53202
Tel: (414) 286-2297 Fax: (414) 286-3004
Internet: www.milwaukee.gov/LRB

Legislative Reference Bureau Manager
Keith Broadnax . . . . (414) 286-2267
200 East Wells Street, Fax: (414) 286-3004
Room 307, Milwaukee, WI 53202-3570
E-mail: keith.broadnax@milwaukee.gov

License Division

City Hall, 200 East Wells Street, Room 105, Milwaukee, WI 53202
Tel: (414) 286-2238 Fax: (414) 286-3057
E-mail: license@milwaukee.gov Internet: www.milwaukee.gov/license

License Division Manager **Jason Schunk** . . . . (414) 286-2362
200 East Wells Street, Fax: (414) 286-3057
Room 105, Milwaukee, WI 53202-3570

Public Information Division

City Hall, 200 East Wells Street, Room 301-K, Milwaukee, WI 53202
Tel: (414) 286-3285 Fax: (414) 286-3456
Internet: www.milwaukee.gov/PublicInformation

Public Information Manager **William Arnold** . . . . (414) 286-3285
200 East Wells Street, Fax: (414) 286-3977
Room 301K, Milwaukee, WI 53202-3570
E-mail: warnol@milwaukee.gov

Office of the City Attorney

City Hall, 200 E. Wells St., Room 800, Milwaukee, WI 53202-3551
Tel: (414) 286-2601 Fax: (414) 286-8550
Internet: www.ci.mil.wi.us/CityAttorney300.htm

★ City Attorney **Grant F. Langley** . . . . (414) 286-2601
Term Expires: April 20, 2020
E-mail: glangl@milwaukee.gov
Education: Marquette 1970 JD

(continued on next page)

★ Elected Official ▲ Appointed by Legislature ▼ Appointed by Governor ▶ Appointed by Board or Commission ● Appointed by Judge
■ Appointed by Mayor △ Appointed by Freeholders ▽ Appointed by Supervisor ▷ Appointed by County Executive ○ Appointed by Council

Office of the City Attorney *continued*

Special Assistant to the City Attorney
Richard L. Withers . . . . (414) 286-2601
E-mail: rlwith@milwaukee.gov

Deputy City Attorney **Miriam R. Horwitz** . . . . . . (414) 286-2601
E-mail: mhorwi@milwaukee.gov

Deputy City Attorney **Vincent D. Moschella** . . . . . (414) 286-2601
E-mail: vmosch@milwaukee.gov

Deputy City Attorney **Adam B. Stephens** . . . . . . (414) 286-2601
E-mail: asteph@milwaukee.gov

Deputy City Attorney **(Vacant)** . . . . (414) 286-2601

Office of the City Comptroller

City Hall, 200 East Wells Street, Milwaukee, WI 53202-3567
Tel: (414) 286-3321 Fax: (414) 286-3281

★Comptroller **Martin Matson** Room 404 . . . . . . (414) 286-2301
Term Expires: April 20, 2020
E-mail: martin.matson@milwaukee.gov

Deputy Comptroller **Glenn Steinbrecher** Room 404 . . . . (414) 286-2212

Public Debt Specialist **Richard Li** Room 404 . . . . . (414) 286-2319
E-mail: rsli@milwaukee.gov

Accounts

Director and Special Deputy Comptroller
Aycha Sirvanci . . . . (414) 286-2303

General Accounting Division **Chris Wanty** Room 401 . . . (414) 286-2314
E-mail: cwanty@milwaukee.gov

Payroll Administration Division **JoAnn Nelson**
Room 404 . . . . (414) 286-2320

Revenue and Cost Division **Claudia Orugbani**
Room 401 . . . . (414) 286-2309
E-mail: corugb@milwaukee.gov

Financial Services

Director and Special Deputy Comptroller
Toni Biscobing Room 401 . . . . (414) 286-2315

Auditing Division **Stacy Mazmanian** Room 401 . . . . (414) 286-2323

Financial Advisory Division **Rocklan "Rocky" Wruck**
Room 401 . . . . (414) 286-2304

Office of the City Treasurer

City Hall, 200 E. Wells St., Room 103, Milwaukee, WI 53202-3599
Tel: (414) 286-2240 Fax: (414) 286-3186
Internet: www.milwaukee.gov/treasurer

★City Treasurer **Spencer Coggs** . . . . (414) 286-2240
Term Expires: April 18, 2020
E-mail: ctreas@milwaukee.gov
Date of Birth: August 6, 1949
Education: Milwaukee Tech 1975 AA; Wisconsin (Milwaukee) 1976 BS

Deputy City Treasurer **James F. Klajbor** . . . . . . (414) 286-2240

Administration Division

Special Assistant to the City Treasurer **Kerry Urban** . . . . (414) 286-8782
E-mail: kurban@milwaukee.gov

Business Systems Coordinator **Lee Matthias** . . . . . (414) 286-8775
E-mail: lmatth@milwaukee.gov

Customer Services Division

Tel: (414) 286-2240 Fax: (414) 286-3186

Customer Services Manager **Richard Schmidt** . . . . . (414) 286-8810
E-mail: rschmi@milwaukee.gov

Financial Services Division

Investments and Financial Services Manager
Robyn Malone . . . . (414) 286-8248
E-mail: rmalon@milwaukee.gov

Revenue Collection Division

Revenue Collection Manager **Samantha Meagher** . . . . (414) 286-3358
E-mail: smeagh@milwaukee.gov

Milwaukee Public Schools

5225 W. Vliet St., Milwaukee, WI 53208
P.O. Box 2181, Milwaukee, WI 53201-2181
Fax: (414) 475-8071 E-mail: governance@milwaukee.k12.wi.us
Internet: www.milwaukee.k12.wi.us

Superintendent of Schools **Darienne Driver** . . . . . . (414) 475-8002
Fax: (414) 475-8585

★School Board President **Mark A. Sain** (District 1) . . . . . (414) 475-8284
Term Expires: April 1, 2019
E-mail: governance@milwaukee.k12.wi.us

★School Board Vice President **Larry Miller** (District 5) . . . . (414) 475-8284
Term Expires: April 1, 2017
E-mail: governance@milwaukee.k12.wi.us

★School Board Member **Wendell Harris, Sr.** (District 2) . . . (414) 475-8284
Term Expires: April 2019

★School Board Member **Michael Bonds** (District 3) . . . . . (414) 475-8284
Term Expires: April 1, 2019
E-mail: governance@milwaukee.k12.wi.us

★School Board Member **Annie Woodward** (District 4) . . . . (414) 475-8284
Term Expires: April 1, 2017
E-mail: governance@milwaukee.k12.wi.us

★School Board Member **Tatiana Joseph** (District 6) . . . . . (414) 534-4578
Term Expires: April 1, 2017
E-mail: governance@milwaukee.k12.wi.us

★School Board Member **Claire Zautke** (District 7) . . . . . . (414) 475-8284
Term Expires: April 1, 2017
E-mail: governance@milwaukee.k12.wi.us

★School Board Member **Carol Voss** (District 8) . . . . (414) 475-8284
Term Expires: April 2019
E-mail: governance@milwaukee.k12.wi.us

★School Board Member **Terry Falk** (At-Large) . . . . (414) 475-8284
Term Expires: April 1, 2019
E-mail: governance@milwaukee.k12.wi.us

Board Clerk/Board of Governance Director
Jacqueline Mann . . . . (414) 475-8284
E-mail: governance@milwaukee.k12.wi.us

City of Minneapolis, Minnesota

City Hall, 350 South Fifth Street, Minneapolis, MN 55415
Tel: (612) 673-3000 (Information) Internet: www.minneapolismn.gov
Internet: http://www.minneapolismn.gov/news/index.htm

County: Hennepin **Election Type:** Nonpartisan **Year Founded:** 1819
Year Incorporated: 1867 **Charter:** 1920 **Population:** 410,939 (2015)

Office of the Mayor

331 City Hall, 350 S. Fifth St., Minneapolis, MN 55415-1393
Fax: (612) 673-2305 Internet: www.minneapolismn.gov/mayor/index.htm

★Mayor **Elizabeth "Betsy" Hodges** . . . . (612) 673-2100
Began Service: January 2, 2014
Term Expires: December 31, 2017
Education: Bryn Mawr 1991 AB

■Chief of Staff **John Stiles** . . . . (612) 673-3665
E-mail: john.stiles@minneapolismn.gov

■Deputy Chief of Staff **Ben Hecker** . . . . (612) 673-2283
E-mail: ben.hecker@minneapolismn.gov

■Policy Director **Peter Wagenius** . . . . (612) 673-2156
E-mail: peter.wagenius@minneapolismn.gov

Mayor's Office Associate **Tou Tou Khamsot** . . . . . (612) 673-3252

Mayor's Office Associate **Grace Goodrich** . . . . . . (612) 673-3742

Policy Aide **Nicole Archbold** . . . . (612) 673-3436

Policy Aide **Erick Garcia Luna** . . . . (612) 673-2465
E-mail: erick.garcia.luna@minneapolismn.gov

Policy Aide **Stephanie Zawistowski** . . . . . . (612) 673-2109

★Elected Official ▲Appointed by Legislature ▼Appointed by Governor ►Appointed by Board or Commission ●Appointed by Judge
■Appointed by Mayor △Appointed by Freeholders ▽Appointed by Supervisor ▷Appointed by County Executive ○Appointed by Council

Civil Rights Department
239 City Hall, 350 S. Fifth St., Minneapolis, MN 55415-1314
Tel: (612) 673-3012 Fax: (612) 673-2599
E-mail: civilrights@minneapolismn.gov

Director **Velma Korbel** .... (612) 673-3027
Education: National U BA

Communications
301M City Hall, 350 S. Fifth St., Minneapolis, MN 55415
Tel: (612) 673-2491 Fax: (612) 673-2011
E-mail: opa@minneapolismn.gov

Communications Director **David Prestwood** .... (612) 673-3825
E-mail: david.prestwood@minneapolismn.gov

Estimate and Taxation
315M City Hall, 350 S. Fifth St., Minneapolis, MN 55415-1315
Tel: (612) 673-2029 Fax: (612) 673-2888

Board Secretary **Jack A. Qvale** .... (612) 673-2029
E-mail: jack.qvale@minneapolismn.gov
Internal Auditor **William "Will" Tetsell** .... (612) 673-2056

Park and Recreation Board
2117 West River Road North, Minneapolis, MN 55415

Superintendent **Jayne Miller** .... (612) 230-6404
General Manager **Michael P. Schmidt** .... (612) 230-6408
General Manager **(Vacant)** .... (612) 230-6406
Director of Planning **Bruce Chamberlain** .... (612) 230-6409

Office of the City Council
307 City Hall, 350 S. Fifth St., Minneapolis, MN 55415-1383
Fax: (612) 673-3940 Internet: www.minneapolismn.gov/council/

★ President **Barbara Johnson** (Ward 4) .... (612) 673-2204
Term Expires: December 31, 2017
E-mail: barbara.johnson@minneapolismn.gov
★ Council Member **Kevin Reich** (Ward 1) .... (612) 673-2201
Term Expires: December 31, 2017
E-mail: kevin.reich@minneapolismn.gov
★ Council Member **Cam Gordon** (Ward 2) .... (612) 673-2202
Term Expires: December 31, 2017
E-mail: cam.gordon@minneapolismn.gov
★ Council Member **Jacob Frey** (Ward 3) .... (612) 673-2203
Term Expires: December 31, 2017
E-mail: jacob.frey@ci.minneapolis.mn.us
★ Council Member **Blong Yang** (Ward 5) .... (612) 673-2205
Term Expires: December 31, 2017
E-mail: blong.yang@ci.minneapolis.mn.us
★ Council Member **Abdi Warsame** (Ward 6) .... (612) 673-2206
Term Expires: December 31, 2017
E-mail: abdi.warsame@ci.minneapolis.mn.us
★ Council Member **Lisa R. Goodman** (Ward 7) .... (612) 673-2207
Term Expires: December 31, 2017
E-mail: lisa.goodman@minneapolismn.gov
Education: Wisconsin BA
★ Council Member **Elizabeth Glidden** (Ward 8) .... (612) 673-2208
Term Expires: December 31, 2017
E-mail: elizabeth.glidden@minneapolismn.gov
★ Council Member **Alondra Cano** (Ward 9) .... (612) 673-2209
Term Expires: December 31, 2017
E-mail: alondra.cano@ci.minneapolis.mn.us
★ Council Member **Lisa Bender** (Ward 10) .... (612) 673-2210
Term Expires: December 31, 2017
E-mail: lisa.bender@ci.minneapolis.mn.us
★ Council Member **John Quincy** (Ward 11) .... (612) 673-2211
Term Expires: December 31, 2017
E-mail: john.quincy@minneapolismn.gov
★ Council Member **Andrew Johnson** (Ward 12) .... (612) 673-2212
Term Expires: December 31, 2017
E-mail: andrew.johnson@ci.minneapolis.mn.us
★ Council Member **Linea Palmisano** (Ward 13) .... (612) 673-2213
Term Expires: December 31, 2017
E-mail: linea.palmisano@ci.minneapolis.mn.us

Office of the City Attorney
Accenture Towers, 333 S. Seventh St., Suite 300,
Minneapolis, MN 55402-2453
210 City Hall, 350 South Fifth Street, Minneapolis, MN 55415
Tel: (612) 673-2010 Fax: (612) 673-3811
Internet: www.minneapolismn.gov/attorney/index.htm

City Attorney **Susan Segal** .... (612) 673-3272
E-mail: susan.segal@minneapolismn.gov
Civil Deputy Attorney **Peter Ginder** .... (612) 673-2478
Criminal Deputy Attorney **Mary Ellen Heng** .... (612) 673-2610
Administration Manager **Colleen O'Brien** .... (612) 673-2966
E-mail: colleen.o'brien@minneapolismn.gov

Office of the City Clerk
304 City Hall, 350 S. Fifth St., Minneapolis, MN 55415-1382
Fax: (612) 673-3812 E-mail: cityclerk@minneapolismn.gov
Internet: www.minneapolismn.gov/clerk/

○ City Clerk **Casey Joe Carl** .... (612) 673-2216
E-mail: casey.carl@ci.minneapolis.mn.us
Education: Emporia State BFA
Assistant City Clerk **Grace Wachlarowicz** .... (612) 673-2073
E-mail: grace.wachlarowicz@ci.minneapolis.mn.us
Assistant City Clerk/Elections
Christian N. Rummelhoff .... (612) 673-3601

Community Planning and Economic Development [CPED]
105 Fifth Avenue South, 2nd Floor, Minneapolis, MN 55401-2534
Fax: (612) 673-5293

Executive Director **Craig Taylor** .... (612) 673-5134
E-mail: craig.taylor@ci.minneapolis.mn.us
Deputy Executive Director **Chuck Lutz** .... (612) 673-5196
E-mail: chuck.lutz@minneapolismn.gov
Housing Policy and Development Director
Andrea Brennan .... (612) 673-5115
E-mail: andrea.brennan@ci.minneapolis.mn.us Fax: (612) 675-5027

Office of the City Coordinator
301M City Hall, 350 S. Fifth St., Minneapolis, MN 55415-1376

■ City Coordinator **Spencer R. Cronk** .... (612) 673-2032
Education: Wisconsin BS

Information Technology Department
350 South 5th Street, Room 127, Minneapolis, MN 55415

Chief Information Officer **Otto Doll** .... (612) 673-2820
E-mail: otto.doll@minneapolismn.gov
Education: Virginia Tech 1975 BS

Finance and Property Services Department
City Hall, 350 S. Fifth St., Minneapolis, MN 55415
Tel: (612) 673-2079 Fax: (612) 373-2042

Finance Officer **Mark Ruff** Room 301M .... (612) 673-2079
Deputy Finance Officer **Sandra Christensen**
Room 307M .... (612) 673-2918
E-mail: sandra.christensen@minneapolismn.gov
Procurement Division Director **Gary Warnberg** .... (612) 673-2500
Tower Building, 320 2nd Avenue, South,
Suite 552, Minneapolis, MN 55401
E-mail: gary.warnberg@minneapolismn.gov
Risk Claims Management Division Director
Ellen Velasco-Thompson .... (612) 673-2023
Tower Building, 320 2nd Avenue, South,
Suite 550, Minneapolis, MN 55401
E-mail: ellen.velascothompson@minneapolismn.gov
Director of Treasury **Bruce Plante** Room 323M .... (612) 673-3008

Human Resources
100 Public Service Center, Minneapolis, MN 55415
E-mail: humanresources@minneapolismn.gov Fax: (612) 673-2533

Director **Patience Ferguson** .... (612) 673-2139
E-mail: patience.ferguson@minneapolismn.gov

★ Elected Official ▲ Appointed by Legislature ▼ Appointed by Governor ► Appointed by Board or Commission ● Appointed by Judge
■ Appointed by Mayor △ Appointed by Freeholders ▽ Appointed by Supervisor ▷ Appointed by County Executive ○ Appointed by Council

Planning Department
210 City Hall, 350 S. Fifth St., Minneapolis, MN 55415
Tel: (612) 673-2597 Fax: (612) 673-2728
E-mail: planning@minneapolismn.gov

Director **Kjersti Monson** .... (612) 673-2596

Regulatory Services
110 Public Service Center, Minneapolis, MN 55415

Director (Interim) **Noah Schuchman** .... (612) 673-2781

Assessor's Department
309 Second Ave. South, Room 100, Minneapolis, MN 55401-2234
Fax: (612) 673-3538 E-mail: assessor@minneapolismn.gov
Internet: www.minneapolismn.gov/assessor/

City Assessor **Patrick Todd** .... (612) 673-3535
E-mail: patrick.todd@minneapolismn.gov

Fire Department
230 City Hall, 350 S. Fifth St., Minneapolis, MN 55415-1387
Tel: (612) 673-2890 Fax: (612) 673-2828
Internet: www.minneapolismn.gov/fire/

Fire Chief **John Fruetel** .... (612) 673-2536
E-mail: john.fruetel@minneapolismn.gov
Assistant Fire Chief **Cheri Penn** .... (612) 673-2028
E-mail: cheri.penn@minneapolismn.gov
Staff Deputy **(Vacant)** .... (612) 673-3932
Deputy Chief of Training **Richard Christensen** .... (612) 789-9265
Fire Marshal **Brian Tyner** .... (612) 673-3270
E-mail: brian.tyner@ci.minneapolis.mn.us

Department of Health and Family Support [MDHFS]
510 Public Health Center, 250 S. Fourth St.,
Minneapolis, MN 55415-1316
E-mail: health.familysupport@minneapolismn.gov
Internet: www.minneapolismn.gov/health/

Commissioner **Gretchen Musicant** .... (612) 673-2301

Intergovernmental Relations
301M City Hall, 350 South Fifth Street, Minneapolis, MN 55415
Internet: www.minneapolismn.gov/igr/

Director **Gene Ranieri** .... (612) 673-2051
E-mail: gene.ranieri@minneapolismn.gov

Meet Minneapolis
250 Marquette Avenue South, Suite 1300, Minneapolis, MN 55401
Internet: www.minneapolis.org

President and Chief Executive Officer **Melvin Tennant** .... (612) 767-8000
Education: Rice BA
Executive Vice President **(Vacant)** .... (612) 767-8000

Neighborhood and Community Relations Department [NCR]
105 Fifth Avenue South, Room 425, Minneapolis, MN 55401
E-mail: ncr@minneapolismn.gov Internet: www.minneapolismn.gov/ncr/

Director **David Rubedor** .... (612) 673-5141
E-mail: david.rubedor@minneapolismn.gov

Police Department
130 City Hall, 350 South Fifth Street, Minneapolis, MN 55415-1389
Tel: (612) 673-2853 Fax: (612) 673-3843
E-mail: police@minneapolismn.gov
Internet: www.minneapolismn.gov/police/

Police Chief **Janeé Harteau** .... (612) 673-3559
Education: St Mary's Col (MN) BS, MS
Assistant Chief, Patrol Bureau **Kristine Arneson** .... (612) 673-2994
Investigations Bureau Deputy Chief **Bruce Folkens** .... (612) 673-5504

Police Department *continued*

Emergency Communications Director **Heather Hunt** .... (612) 673-5921

Public Works Department
City Hall, 350 S. Fifth St., Room 203, Minneapolis, MN 55415
Tel: (612) 673-2352 Fax: (612) 673-3565
E-mail: publicworks@minneapolismn.gov
Internet: www.minneapolismn.gov/publicworks/

City Engineer/Director **Steven Kotke** .... (612) 673-2443
E-mail: steven.kotke@minneapolismn.gov
Administration Director **Brett Hjelle** .... (612) 673-2365
Deputy Director **Heidi Hamilton** .... (612) 673-3316

Youth Coordinating Board
310 1/2 City Hall, 350 S. Fifth St., Minneapolis, MN 55415
Internet: http://www.ycb.org Fax: (612) 673-2346
E-mail: ycb@minneapolismn.gov

Director **Ann DeGroot** .... (612) 673-2312

Minneapolis Public Schools
1250 West Broadway, Minneapolis, MN 55411
Internet: www.mpls.k12.mn.us

Superintendent (Interim) **Michael Goar** .... (612) 668-0200
Note: Resigning June 2016
Chief Operations Officer **(Vacant)** .... (612) 668-0395
Chief Information Officer **Ibrahima Diop** .... (612) 668-0200
Executive Director of Communications **Gail Plewacki** .... (612) 668-0232
Media Relations Specialist **Dirk A. Tedmon** .... (612) 668-0230

City of Miramar, Florida

2300 Civic Center Place, Miramar, FL 33025
Tel: (954) 602-3000 Internet: www.ci.miramar.fl.us

County: Broward **Election Type:** Nonpartisan **Year Incorporated:** 1955
Population: 137,132 (2015)

Office of the Mayor and City Commission
2300 Civic Center Place, Miramar, FL 33025
Internet: http://www.ci.miramar.fl.us/media/CityOfficials/

★ Mayor **Wayne M. Messam** .... (954) 602-3151
Began Service: March 2015
Term Expires: March 2019
E-mail: wmessam@miramarfl.gov
Executive Assistant to the Mayor **Edna LaRoche** .... (954) 602-3198
E-mail: elaroche@miramarfl.gov
★ Vice Mayor **Maxwell B. Chambers** .... (954) 602-3154
Term Expires: March 2017
E-mail: mbchambers@miramarfl.gov
★ Commissioner **Winston F. Barnes** .... (954) 602-3132
Term Expires: March 2017
E-mail: wfbarnes@miramarfl.gov
★ Commissioner **Yvette Colbourne** .... (954) 602-3131
Term Expires: March 2017
E-mail: ycolbourne@miramarfl.com
★ Commissioner **Darline B. Riggs** .... (954) 602-3152
Term Expires: March 2019
E-mail: dbriggs@miramarfl.gov

CITIES AND TOWNS

Office of the City Manager
2300 Civic Center Place, Miramar, FL 33025

▶City Manager **Kathleen Woods-Richardson** .... (954) 602-3117
E-mail: kwoodsrichardson@miramarfl.gov Fax: (954) 602-3672
Executive Assistant to the Assistant City Manager
Julie Richards .... (954) 602-3117
E-mail: jrichards@miramarfl.gov Fax: (954) 602-3965
Deputy City Manager **Allyson C. Love** .... (954) 602-3120
E-mail: aclove@miramarfl.gov Fax: (954) 602-3553
Assistant City Manager for Administrative Services
Faye Munnings .... (954) 602-3116
E-mail: fmunnings@miramarfl.gov Fax: (954) 602-3456
Chief Operations Officer **J. Michael Moore** .... (954) 602-3128
E-mail: jmmoore@miramarfl.gov Fax: (954) 602-3552
Executive Assistant to the Assistant City Manager, Operational Services **Romey Connor** .... (954) 602-3122
E-mail: rconnor@miramarfl.gov Fax: (954) 602-3555
Strategic Development Officer **Hector Vazquez** .... (954) 602-3125
Fax: (954) 602-3558
Strategic Administration Officer **Shaun Gayle** .... (954) 602-3091
Fax: (954) 602-4714

Office of the City Clerk
2300 Civic Center Place, Miramar, FL 33025
Tel: (954) 602-3011 Internet: http://www.ci.miramar.fl.us/cityclerk/
E-mail: clerksoffice@miramarfl.gov

City Clerk **Denise Gibbs** .... (954) 602-3014
E-mail: dagibbs@miramarfl.gov Fax: (954) 602-3443
Deputy City Clerk **Narva Barrett-Forbes** .... (954) 602-3015
E-mail: nbarrettforbes@miramarfl.gov Fax: (954) 602-3443
Agenda Coordinator **Frederika DeJean** .... (954) 602-3018
E-mail: fdejean@miramarfl.gov Fax: (954) 602-4460

Community and Economic Development Department
2200 Civic Center Place, Miramar, FL 33025
Tel: (954) 602-3264 E-mail: comdev@miramarfl.gov

Director **Eric Silva** .... (954) 602-3274
E-mail: ebsilva@miramarfl.gov Fax: (954) 602-3539
Executive Assistant to the Director **Kameela Hack** ..... (954) 602-3248
E-mail: bkhack@miramarfl.gov Fax: (954) 602-3448

Building Division
2200 Civic Center Place, Miramar, FL 33025
Tel: (954) 602-3205 E-mail: building@miramarfl.gov
Internet: www.ci.miramar.fl.us/development/building/

Building Official **Robert O'Dell** .... (954) 602-3206
E-mail: rlodell@miramarfl.gov Fax: (954) 602-3638

Planning and Zoning Division
2200 Civic Center Place, Miramar, FL 33025
Tel: (954) 602-3264 E-mail: pandz@miramarfl.gov
Internet: www.ci.miramar.fl.us/development/planning/

Administration **Sonia Gollab-Watson** .... (954) 602-3264
Fax: (954) 602-3448
Principal Planner **Michael Alpert** .... (954) 602-3246

Construction and Facilities Management
2200 Civic Center Place, Miramar, FL 33025
Tel: (954) 602-3320 E-mail: engineer@miramarfl.gov
Internet: www.ci.miramar.fl.us/engineering/index.html

Director **Luisa M. Millan** .... (954) 602-3316
E-mail: lmmillan@miramarfl.gov Fax: (954) 602-3647
City Engineer **Bissy Vempala** .... (954) 602-3320
E-mail: bjvempala@miramarfl.gov Fax: (954) 602-3567

Cultural Affairs Department
2400 Civic Center Place, Miramar, FL 33025
Tel: (954) 602-4525

Director **Stephen Kantrowitz** .... (954) 602-4534
Deputy Director **(Vacant)** .... (954) 602-4511

Finance Department
2300 Civic Center Place, Miramar, FL 33025
Tel: (954) 602-3050 E-mail: emailfinance@miramarfl.gov
Internet: www.ci.miramar.fl.us/finance/index.html

Assistant Finance Director **Barbara Hastings** .... (954) 602-3049
Fax: (954) 602-4469
Utility Billing Manager **Paul Samuels** .... (954) 602-3045
Fax: (954) 602-3465

Fire-Rescue Department
14801 SW 27th Street, Miramar, FL 33027
Tel: (954) 602-4801 Fax: (954) 438-1290

Chief of Fire-Rescue **L. Keith Tomey** .... (954) 602-4838
E-mail: lktomey@miramarfd.org Fax: (954) 430-3754

Human Resources Department
2300 Civic Center Place, Miramar, FL 33025
Tel: (954) 602-3800 E-mail: hr-info@miramarfl.gov
Internet: www.ci.miramar.fl.us/hr/visitors/index.html

Human Resources Director **Sam Hines** .... (954) 602-3810
E-mail: swhines@miramarfl.gov Fax: (954) 602-3739

Management and Budget Department
2300 Civic Center Place, Miramar, FL 33025

Management and Budget Director **David Goldman** ...... (954) 602-3079
E-mail: dgoldman@miramarfl.gov Fax: (954) 602-3451

Parks and Recreation Department
2200 Civic Center Place, Miramar, FL 33025
Tel: (954) 602-3167 E-mail: communityserviceinfo@miramarfl.gov
Internet: www.ci.miramar.fl.us/Communityservices/index.html

Director **Terrence E. Griffin** .... (954) 602-3171
E-mail: tegriffin@miramarfl.gov Fax: (954) 602-3605
Executive Assistant to the Director **Joy-Ann Reece** .... (954) 602-3169
E-mail: jareece@miramarfl.gov Fax: (954) 602-3727

Athletics Division
7000 Miramar Parkway, Miramar, FL 33023

Operations Manager **John Kee** .... (954) 602-4780
E-mail: jckee@miramarfl.gov

Recreation Division
7000 Miramar Parkway, Miramar, FL 33023

Operations Manager **(Vacant)** .... (954) 602-3175
Fax: (954) 602-3663

Aquatics Division
6920 SW 35th Street, Miramar, FL 33023

Aquatic Coordinator **Jorge Valls** .... (954) 894-3133
Fax: (954) 602-3700

Police Department
3064 North Commerce Parkway, Miramar, FL 33025
Tel: (954) 602-4000 Internet: www.miramarpd.org/

Chief of Police (Interim) **Dexter M. Williams** .... (954) 602-4400
Assistant Chief of Police **Dexter M. Williams** .... (954) 602-4400

★ Elected Official ▲ Appointed by Legislature ▼ Appointed by Governor ▶ Appointed by Board or Commission ● Appointed by Judge
■ Appointed by Mayor △ Appointed by Freeholders ▽ Appointed by Supervisor ▷ Appointed by County Executive ○ Appointed by Council

Procurement Department
2300 Civic Center Place, Miramar, FL 33025
Tel: (954) 602-3052 E-mail: procurementdept@miramarfl.gov
Internet: www.ci.miramar.fl.us/procurement/index.html

Procurement Director **Randy Cross** .... (954) 602-3054
E-mail: rmcross@miramarfl.gov Fax: (954) 602-3483

Public Works Department
13900 Pembroke Road, Miramar, FL 33027
Tel: (954) 883-6815

Director **Tom Good** .... (954) 538-6836
Fax: (954) 602-3551

Social Services Department
6700 Miramar Parkway, Miramar, FL 33023
Tel: (954) 889-2700 E-mail: socialservicesinfo@miramarfl.gov
Internet: www.ci.miramar.fl.us/socialservices/

Director **Marva Ricketts** .... (954) 889-2741
Fax: (954) 602-3400

Utilities Department
13900 Pembroke Road, Miramar, FL 33027
Tel: (954) 602-4357 Internet: www.ci.miramar.fl.us/utilities/index.html

Director **Hong Guo** .... (954) 883-6825
Fax: (954) 602-4710

City of Mobile, Alabama
Government Plaza, 205 Government St., Mobile, AL 36644
P.O. Box 1827, Mobile, AL 36633-1827
Tel: (251) 208-7411 (Information) Internet: www.cityofmobile.org

County: Mobile **Election Type:** Nonpartisan **Year Founded:** 1702
Population: 194,288 (2015)

Office of the Mayor
Government Plaza, 205 Government St., Mobile, AL 36644
P.O. Box 1827, Mobile, AL 36633-1827
Fax: (251) 208-7548
Internet: www.cityofmobile.org/cityofficials/mayor.php

★ Mayor **William S. "Sandy" Stimpson** .... (251) 208-7395
Began Service: November 4, 2013
Term Expires: November 2017
■ Chief of Staff **Colby James Cooper** .... (251) 208-7395
E-mail: ccooper@al.com
Education: Bucknell 1999 BA
■ Executive Assistant **Marty Carrell** .... (251) 208-7395
■ Communications Director **George Talbot** .... (251) 208-7806
E-mail: gtalbot@al.com Fax: (251) 208-6206
Education: Rhodes 1994 BA
■ Senior Advisor **(Vacant)** .... (251) 208-7411

Community Affairs
P.O. Box 1827, Mobile, AL 36633-1827

Senior Director of Community Affairs **Shayla Beaco** .... (251) 208-7807
E-mail: shayla.beaco@cityofmobile.org

Community and Housing Development
205 Government Street, 5th Floor, South Tower, Mobile, AL 36644
Tel: (251) 208-6290

Senior Director **P. Nigel Roberts** .... (251) 208-6290

Financial Services Division
Government Plaza, 205 Government St., Mobile, AL 36633
P.O. Box 1827, Mobile, AL 36633-1827
Fax: (251) 208-7956

■ Executive Director **Paul Wesch** .... (251) 208-7164
E-mail: wesch@cityofmobile.org
City Comptroller **Patricia Aldrich** .... (251) 208-7407
E-mail: comptroller@cityofmobile.org
Deputy Finance Officer **Celia Sapp** .... (251) 208-7803
Payroll **John Noletto** .... (251) 208-7287
Police and Fire Pension Fund **Mary Berg** .... (251) 208-7360
Purchasing **John Paine** .... (251) 208-7434
E-mail: paine@cityofmobile.org
Revenue **Gwen Hall** .... (251) 208-7461
E-mail: mcgrew@cityofmobile.org
Treasury/Investment **Pandora Cunningham** .... (251) 208-7286

Human Resources Department
Government Plaza, 205 Government Street, 4th Floor, Mobile, AL 36644
P.O. Box 1827, Mobile, AL 36633-1827
Tel: (251) 208-7039 Fax: (251) 208-7153

Human Resources Director **Leslie Rey** .... (251) 208-7832
E-mail: leslie@cityofmobile.org

Legal Department
P.O. Box 1827, Mobile, AL 36633-1827
Fax: (251) 208-7322
Internet: www.cityofmobile.org/departments_full.php?view=19

■ City Attorney **Ricardo Woods** .... (251) 208-7416
E-mail: rwoods@cityofmobile.org
Chief Assistant City Attorney **Flo Kessler** .... (251) 208-7416
E-mail: fkessler@cityofmobile.org

Municipal Information Technology Department [MIT]
P.O. Box 1827, Mobile, AL 36633-1827
Tel: (251) 208-5007 Tel: (251) 208-7552

Municipal Information Technology Director **Sue Farni** .... (251) 208-7830
E-mail: sue@cityofmobile.org
Telecommunications Manager **Ben Durant** .... (251) 208-5825
E-mail: ben@cityofmobile.org
Network Manager **Tony Phillips** .... (251) 208-5007
E-mail: tony@cityofmobile.org

Planning and Development
P.O. Box 1827, Mobile, AL 36633-1827

Executive Director **Dianne K. Irby** .... (251) 208-7886

Real Estate/Asset Management
Director **Brad Christensen** .... (251) 208-7633
E-mail: brad.christensen@cityofmobile.org
Real Estate Office Manager **John Olszewski** .... (251) 208-7536
Mechanical Systems Superintendent **Richard Safin** ...... (251) 208-1572
E-mail: safin@cityofmobile.org
Public Buildings Superintendent **Steve Elmore** .... (251) 208-2819
E-mail: elmore@cityofmobile.org

Urban Development Department
Fax: (251) 208-7367

Director **Laura Clarke** .... (251) 208-7367

City Engineering
Director **Nick Amberger** .... (251) 208-7475
E-mail: nick.amberger@cityofmobile.org

Public Safety Department
P.O. Box 1827, Mobile, AL 36633-1827

Executive Director **RADM Richard B. Landolt** .... (251) 208-7888
E-mail: richard.landolt@cityofmobile.org
Education: Florida 1981 BA; Naval Postgrad MS

★ Elected Official ▲ Appointed by Legislature ▼ Appointed by Governor ► Appointed by Board or Commission ● Appointed by Judge
■ Appointed by Mayor △ Appointed by Freeholders ▽ Appointed by Supervisor ▷ Appointed by County Executive ○ Appointed by Council

Animal Control
855 Owens St., Mobile, AL 36604
Fax: (251) 208-2802

Animal Shelter Director **Ellen Lursen** . . . . (251) 208-2800

Fire-Rescue Department
701 St. Francis St., Mobile, AL 36602
Fax: (251) 208-5813

■ Fire Chief (Interim) **William "Billy" Pappas** . . . . (251) 208-7351
E-mail: pappas@cityofmobile.org

Police Department
2460 Government Blvd., Mobile, AL 36606
Tel: (251) 208-1700 Fax: (251) 208-1705
E-mail: mobilepd@cityofmobile.org Internet: www.mobilepd.org

■ Chief of Police **James H. Barber** . . . . (251) 208-1701
E-mail: barberj@cityofmobile.org
Assistant Chief **Lawrence Battiste** . . . . (251) 208-1706

Public Works Division
Government Plaza, 205 Government St., Mobile, AL 36633
Fax: (251) 208-7398

■ Executive Director **William "Bill" Harkins, Jr.** . . . . (251) 208-7011
E-mail: harkinsb@cityofmobile.org
Education: South Alabama BS

Municipal Garage
770 Gayle Street, Mobile, AL 36604

Manager **Gregory Beckham** . . . . (251) 208-2887

Parks and Recreation Department
48 North Sage Avenue, Mobile, AL 36607
Fax: (251) 208-1621

Director **Matthew Capps** . . . . (251) 208-1604
Park Superintendent **Dan Otto** . . . . (251) 208-1604
Fax: (251) 208-1621
Recreation Superintendent **(Vacant)** . . . . (251) 208-1655
Program Supervisor, Community Activities Program
Mellanie Johnson . . . . (251) 208-1610
E-mail: johnsonm@cityofmobile.org
Program Supervisor, Neighborhood Parks
Yolanda Broom . . . . (251) 208-1652
Program Supervisor, Special Activities **Ella Mooney** . . . . . (251) 208-1653
Athletic Coordinator **Julius Shine** . . . . (251) 208-1631
Mobile Tennis Center Superintendent **Bruce Lockette** . . . . (251) 208-5182
Operations Manager **Gloria Edwards** . . . . (251) 208-1603
E-mail: gloria.edwards@cityofmobile.org
Azalea City Golf Course Superintendent **Brian Aaron** . . . . (251) 208-5150

Public Works Administration
770 Gayle Street, Mobile, AL 36604

Superintendent **John Windley** . . . . (251) 208-2901
E-mail: windleyj@cityofmobile.org

Traffic Engineering Department
Fax: (251) 208-7398

Director **Jennifer White** . . . . (251) 208-2970
E-mail: whitej@cityofmobile.org

Office of the City Council
Government Plaza, 205 Government St., Mobile, AL 36644
P.O. Box 1827, Mobile, AL 36633-1827
Tel: (251) 208-7441 Fax: (251) 208-7482
Internet: www.cityofmobile.org/cityofficials/elected.php

★ President **Gina Gregory** (District 7) . . . . (251) 208-7441
Term Expires: November 2017
E-mail: ggregory@al.com
Education: Florida 1978 BS

Office of the City Council *continued*

★ Vice President **Fred Richardson** (District 1) . . . . (251) 208-7441
Term Expires: November 2017
E-mail: richardson@cityofmobile.org
Education: South Alabama 1974 BA
★ Council Member **Levon C. Manzie** (District 2) . . . . (251) 208-7441
Term Expires: November 5, 2017
E-mail: lmanzie@al.com
★ Council Member **C.J. Small** (District 3) . . . . (251) 208-7441
Term Expires: November 2017
E-mail: csmall@al.com
★ Council Member **John C. Williams** (District 4) . . . . (251) 208-7441
Term Expires: November 5, 2017
E-mail: john.williams@cityofmobile.org
★ Council Member **Joel T. Daves IV** (District 5) . . . . (251) 208-7441
Term Expires: November 2017
E-mail: jdaves@al.com
★ Council Member **Bess Rich** (District 6) . . . . (251) 208-7441
Term Expires: November 2017
E-mail: bess.rich@cityofmobile.org
Education: Ohio State BS

Office of the City Clerk
Government Plaza, 205 Government Street, Mobile, AL 36644
P.O. Box 1827, Mobile, AL 36633-1827
Fax: (251) 208-7576
Internet: www.cityofmobile.org/departments_full.php?view=6

○ City Clerk **Lisa C. Lambert** . . . . (251) 208-7411
E-mail: lisa.carroll@cityofmobile.org
Assistant City Clerk **Mary Ann Merchant** . . . . (251) 208-7411
E-mail: merchant@cityofmobile.org
Municipal Archives Director **Ned Harkins** . . . . (251) 208-7740
457 Church St., Mobile, AL 36602 Fax: (251) 208-7428
E-mail: edward.harkins@cityofmobile.org
Historic Development Commission Director
Cartledge Blackwell . . . . (251) 208-7281
Fax: (251) 208-7966
Neighborhood and Community Services Division
Director **Ann Rambeau** . . . . (251) 470-7731
E-mail: ann.rambeau@cityofmobile.org Fax: (251) 208-7966

Mobile Bay Convention Visitors Bureau
One South Water Street, Mobile, AL 36602
P.O. Box 204, Mobile, AL 36601-0204
Fax: (251) 208-2060 E-mail: info@mobile.org
Internet: www.mobilebay.org

Note: The MBCVB is a private, not-for-profit organization and is contracted by the city to be the marketing arm of the Mobile Bay area.

President and Chief Executive Officer **Al Hutchinson** . . . . (251) 208-2004
Education: Alabama 1982 BS
Vice President of Sales **Ron McConnell** . . . . (251) 208-2018
Vice President of Finance and Administration
Jay Garraway . . . . (251) 208-2008
E-mail: jgarraway@mobile.org
Executive Coordinator **Vanessa Washington** . . . . (251) 208-2014
E-mail: vwashington@mobile.org Fax: (251) 208-2426

Mobile Civic Center
401 Civic Center Dr., Mobile, AL 36602
Tel: (251) 208-7261 Fax: (251) 208-7551
Internet: www.mobilecivicctr.com

General Manager **Robert Brazier** . . . . (251) 208-2111
Director of Operations **Joe Delaronde** . . . . (251) 208-7937
E-mail: jdelaronde@mobilecivicctr.com
Senior Director of Finance **Sharee Self** . . . . (251) 208-7186
Marketing Manager **Cheryl Gee** . . . . (251) 208-2128
Box Office Manager **Jackie Jackson** . . . . (251) 208-7373

★ Elected Official ▲ Appointed by Legislature ▼ Appointed by Governor ► Appointed by Board or Commission ● Appointed by Judge
■ Appointed by Mayor △ Appointed by Freeholders ▽ Appointed by Supervisor ▷ Appointed by County Executive ○ Appointed by Council

Mobile Public Library
701 Government St., Mobile, AL 36602
Internet: http://www.mplonline.org

Director (Interim) **Mary Laughlin** .... (251) 208-7108
E-mail: asstdirector@mplonline.org

Mobile Museum of Art
4850 Museum Drive, Mobile, AL 36608
Fax: (251) 208-5201

Director **Deborah Velders** .... (251) 208-5200

History Museum
111 South Royal Street, Mobile, AL 36602
Fax: (251) 208-7686

Director **(Vacant)** .... (251) 208-7569

City of Modesto, California

1010 Tenth Street, Modesto, CA 95354
P.O. Box 642, Modesto, CA 95353
Tel: (209) 577-5200 (Information) Internet: www.modestogov.com

County: Stanislaus **Election Type:** Nonpartisan **Charter:** 1951
Population: 211,266 (2015)

Office of the Mayor and City Council
P.O. Box 642, Modesto, CA 95353
Fax: (209) 571-5586

★Mayor **Ted Brandvold** .... (209) 571-5597
Began Service: February 23, 2016
Term Expires: November 2019

★Vice Mayor **Bill Zoslocki** (District 4) .... (209) 571-5169
Term Expires: November 2017
E-mail: bzoslocki@modestogov.com

★Council Member **Mani Grewal** (District 1) .... (209) 577-5169
Term Expires: November 2019

★Council Member **Tony Madrigal** (District 2) .... (209) 571-5169
Term Expires: November 2017
E-mail: tmadrigal@modestogov.com

★Council Member **Kristi Ah You** (District 3) .... (209) 577-5169
Term Expires: November 2019

★Council Member **Jenny Ketcham Kenoyer** (District 5) .. (209) 571-5169
Term Expires: November 2017
E-mail: jkenoyer@modestogov.com

★Council Member **Doug Ridenour** (District 6) .... (209) 571-5169
Term Expires: November 2019

Office of the City Attorney
P.O. Box 642, Modesto, CA 95353
Fax: (209) 544-8260

○City Attorney **Adam U. Lindgren** .... (209) 577-5284
E-mail: alindgren@modestogov.com
Education: Columbia 1990 BA; Georgetown 1993 JD

Office of the City Auditor
P.O. Box 642, Modesto, CA 95353
Fax: (209) 571-5586

City Auditor **(Vacant)** .... (209) 341-2941

Office of the City Clerk
P.O. Box 642, Modesto, CA 95353
Fax: (209) 571-5152

○City Clerk **Stephanie Lopez** .... (209) 577-5396
E-mail: slopez@modestogov.com

Office of the City Manager
P.O. Box 642, Modesto, CA 95353
Fax: (209) 571-5128

○City Manager **James N. "Jim" Holgersson** .... (209) 577-5224
E-mail: jholgersson@modestogov.com

Deputy City Manager **Joe Lopez** .... (209) 577-5223
E-mail: joelopez@modestogov.com

Deputy City Manager **H. Brent Sinclair** .... (209) 577-5223
E-mail: hbsinclair@modestogov.com

Community and Economic Development
P.O. Box 642, Modesto, CA 95353
Fax: (209) 491-5798

Director **Cynthia Birdsill** .... (209) 577-5418

Finance Department
P.O. Box 642, Modesto, CA 95353
Fax: (209) 571-5880

Finance Director **Gloriette G. Genereux** .... (209) 577-5369

Fire Department
3705 Oakdale Road, Modesto, CA 95357
Fax: (209) 552-2512

Fire Chief **Sean Slamon** .... (209) 552-3858
E-mail: sslamon@modestogov.com
Education: Cal State (Long Beach) BS

Human Resources Department
P.O. Box 642, Modesto, CA 95353
Fax: (209) 571-5813

Director **Joe Lopez** .... (209) 577-5402
E-mail: joelopez@modestogov.com

Information Technology
P.O. Box 642, Modesto, CA 95353
Fax: (209) 491-4333

Chief Information Officer **John Dickey** .... (209) 577-5331

Geographic Information Systems Manager
Teri Owen-Durant .... (209) 577-5331
E-mail: tdurant@modestogov.com

Parks, Recreation and Neighborhoods Department
P.O. Box 642, Modesto, CA 95353
Fax: (209) 571-5825

Manager (Acting) **Marco Sepulveda** .... (209) 577-5346

Police Department
P.O. Box 1746, Modesto, CA 95353
Fax: (209) 523-4082

Police Chief **Galen Carroll** .... (209) 572-9500

Public Works Department
P.O. Box 642, Modesto, CA 95353
Fax: (209) 577-5477

Director **Bill Sandhu** .... (209) 341-2933
E-mail: bsandhu@modestogov.com
Education: Cal State (Sacramento) MS

Utilities Department
P.O. Box 642, Modesto, CA 95353
Fax: (209) 577-5477

Director **Larry Parliln** .... (209) 577-5213

★Elected Official ▲Appointed by Legislature ▼Appointed by Governor ►Appointed by Board or Commission ●Appointed by Judge
■Appointed by Mayor △Appointed by Freeholders ▽Appointed by Supervisor ▷Appointed by County Executive ○Appointed by Council

Modesto City Schools
426 Locust Street, Modesto, CA 95351-2699
Fax: (209) 576-4765 Internet: https://www.mcs4kids.com/district
Superintendent **Pam Able** . . . . (209) 576-4115

City of Montgomery, Alabama
103 North Perry Street, Montgomery, AL 36104
P.O. Box 1111, Montgomery, AL 36101-1111
Tel: (334) 625-2096 (Information) Internet: www.montgomeryal.gov

County: Montgomery **Election Type:** Nonpartisan **Population:** 200,602 (2015)

Todd Strange
Mayor

Began Service: March 23, 2009
Term Expires: November 10, 2019
Education: Montevallo 1966 BS

Office of the Mayor
P.O. Box 1111, Montgomery, AL 36101-1111
Fax: (334) 625-2600

★ Mayor **Todd Strange** . . . . (334) 625-2000
E-mail: mayor@montgomeryal.gov
Executive Secretary to the Mayor **Tracie Davis** . . . . (334) 625-2000
E-mail: tdavis@montgomeryal.gov
Chief of Staff **Anita L. Archie** . . . . (334) 625-2002

Office of the Chief of Staff
P.O. Box 1111, Montgomery, AL 36101-1111
Chief of Staff **Anita L. Archie** . . . . (334) 625-2002

Office of the City Clerk
P.O. Box 1111, Montgomery, AL 36101-1111
■ City Clerk **Brenda Gale Blalock** . . . . (334) 625-2096
E-mail: cityclerk@montgomeryal.gov

City Investigations Department
P.O. Box 1111, Montgomery, AL 36101-1111
Tel: (334) 625-2490 Fax: (334) 625-2420
E-mail: cityinvestigations@montgomeryal.gov
■ Director **LtGen Ronald F. Sams** . . . . (334) 625-2490
E-mail: rsams@montgomeryal.gov
Education: Michigan State 1972 BS; Chapman 1978 MA; Air Command Col 1984; Syracuse 2002

Information Technology Department
P.O. Box 1111, Montgomery, AL 36101-1111
■ Chief Information Officer **Lou Ialacci** . . . . (334) 625-2924
E-mail: lialacci@montgomeryal.gov

Personnel Department
27 Madison Avenue, Montgomery, AL 36104
Fax: (334) 625-2219
Director **Carmen Douglas** . . . . (334) 625-2675
E-mail: personnel@montgomeryal.gov

Department of Planning
25 Washington Avenue, 4th Floor, Montgomery, AL 36104
Fax: (334) 625-4431
■ Director of Planning **Robert E. Smith, Jr.** . . . . (334) 625-2218
E-mail: rsmith@montgomeryal.gov

Office of the City Attorney
P.O. Box 1111, Montgomery, AL 36101-1111
City Attorney **Kimberly Fehl** . . . . (334) 625-2091
E-mail: kfehl@montgomeryal.gov
Staff Attorney **Michael Brymer** . . . . (334) 625-2181
Staff Attorney **Stacy Reed** . . . . (334) 625-2436
Staff Attorney **Stephanie Smithee** . . . . (334) 625-2090
Senior Staff Attorney **Charles "Mickey" McInnish** . . . . . . (334) 625-2092

Department of Development
103 North Perry Street, Montgomery, AL 36104
■ Development Director **Mac McLeod** . . . . (334) 625-2737
E-mail: mmcleod@montgomeryal.gov

Finance
P.O. Box 1111, Montgomery, AL 36101-1111
■ Director **Barry Crabb** . . . . (334) 625-2025
E-mail: bcrabb@montgomeryal.gov
Deputy Director **Betty Beville** . . . . (334) 625-2428
Comptroller **Ricky Davis** . . . . (334) 625-2946

General Services Department
P.O. Box 1111, Montgomery, AL 36101-1111
Director **Steve Jones** . . . . (334) 625-5633

Parking Deck
P.O. Box 1111, Montgomery, AL 36101-1111
Supervisor **Bryan Dunn** . . . . (334) 625-2236

Fleet Management Department
P.O. Box 1111, Montgomery, AL 36101-1111
Director **Walter Lilley** . . . . (334) 625-2509
E-mail: wlilley@montgomeryal.gov

Leisure Services and Facilities Management
1010 Forest Avenue, Montgomery, AL 36106
■ Director **Scott Miller** . . . . (334) 625-4731
E-mail: smiller@montgomeryal.gov

Building Maintenance
1010 Forest Avenue, Montgomery, AL 36106
Director **Doug Jones** . . . . (334) 625-2285
E-mail: djones@montgomeryal.gov

Parks and Recreation Department
1010 Forest Avenue, Montgomery, AL 36106
■ Director **Robert Spivery** . . . . (334) 625-4731
E-mail: rspivery@montgomeryal.gov

Public Information and External Affairs
P.O. Box 1111, Montgomery, AL 36101-1111
Director **Michael Briddell** . . . . (334) 625-2005

Constituency Affairs
P.O. Box 1111, Montgomery, AL 36101-1111
Director **(Vacant)** . . . . (334) 625-2427

★ Elected Official ▲ Appointed by Legislature ▼ Appointed by Governor ► Appointed by Board or Commission ● Appointed by Judge
■ Appointed by Mayor △ Appointed by Freeholders ▽ Appointed by Supervisor ▷ Appointed by County Executive ○ Appointed by Council

Library
P.O. Box 1950, Montgomery, AL 36102-1950
Internet: http://mccpl.lib.al.us

Director **Jaunita Owes** (334) 240-4300
E-mail: jowes@mccpl.lib.al.us

Montgomery Zoo
P.O. Box Zebra, Montgomery, AL 36109

Director **Doug Goode** (334) 240-4900
Assistant Director **Marcia Woodard** (334) 240-4900

Museum of Fine Art
P.O. Box 230819, Montgomery, AL 36123-0819

■ Director **Mark Johnson** (334) 240-4341
E-mail: mjohnson@mmfa.org

Public Relations
P.O. Box 1111, Montgomery, AL 36101-1111

Administrator **(Vacant)** (334) 625-2726

Public Safety
P.O. Box 1111, Montgomery, AL 36101-1111

Director of Public Safety **Col. J. Christopher Murphy** (334) 625-4443
E-mail: jmurphy@montgomeryal.gov
Education: Auburn 1981 BS; Troy U 1997 MS

Communications
P.O. Box 1111, Montgomery, AL 36101-1111

Chief of Communications **Larry Fisher** (334) 240-4111
E-mail: lfisher@montgomeryal.gov
Chief of Staff **Melinda Chandler** (334) 240-4107
E-mail: mchandler@montgomeryal.gov

Emergency Management Agency
P.O. Box 1111, Montgomery, AL 36101-1111

Director **Calvin Brown** (334) 240-4181
E-mail: cbrown@montgomeryal.gov

Fire Department
19 Madison Avenue, Montgomery, AL 36104

■ Fire Chief **Miford Jordan** (334) 625-2930
E-mail: fire@montgomeryal.gov
Chief of Staff **J. L. Petrey** (334) 625-2930
E-mail: jpetrey@montgomeryal.gov

Police Department
P.O. Box 159, Montgomery, AL 36101-0159

■ Police Chief **Ernest Finley** (334) 625-2810
E-mail: efinley@montgomeryal.gov
Chief of Staff **John Brown** (334) 625-2810

Public Works
P.O. Box 1111, Montgomery, AL 36101-1111

Director of Public Works **Christopher W. Conway** (334) 625-2696

Engineering and Environmental Services
P.O. Box 1111, Montgomery, AL 36101-1111

City Engineer **Patrick Dunson** (334) 625-2695
E-mail: pdunson@montgomeryal.gov

Inspections Department
P.O. Box 1111, Montgomery, AL 36101-1111

Director, Chief Building Official **Jerry Russell** (334) 625-2080

Sanitation Department
P.O. Box 1111, Montgomery, AL 36101-1111

■ Director **Daniel Dickey** (334) 625-2768
E-mail: ddickey@montgomeryal.gov
Deputy Director **Diane Burke** (334) 625-2637

Street Maintenance Department
P.O. Box 1111, Montgomery, AL 36101-1111

■ Director **(Vacant)** (334) 625-2995

Traffic Engineering Department
P.O. Box 1111, Montgomery, AL 36101-1111

■ Traffic Engineer **Locke D. Bowden** (334) 625-2911
E-mail: lbowden@montgomeryal.gov

Office of the City Council
P.O. Box 1111, Montgomery, AL 36101-1111
Tel: (334) 625-2096 Fax: (334) 625-2056

★ Council President **Charles W. Jinright** (District 9) (334) 625-2097
Term Expires: November 10, 2019
E-mail: cjinright@montgomeryal.gov
★ President Pro Tem **Tracy Larkin** (District 3) (334) 819-7854
Term Expires: November 10, 2016
E-mail: tlarkin@montgomeryal.gov
★ Council Member **Richard Bollinger** (District 1) (334) 279-9093
Term Expires: November 10, 2019
E-mail: rbollinger@montgomeryal.gov
★ Council Member **Brantley W. Lyons** (District 2) (334) 625-2096
Term Expires: November 2019
★ Council Member **David Burkette** (District 4) (334) 230-9492
Term Expires: November 2019
E-mail: dburkette@montgomeryal.gov
★ Council Member **William A. Green** (District 5) (334) 625-2096
Term Expires: November 2019
★ Council Member **Fred Bell** (District 6) (334) 625-2096
Term Expires: November 2019
★ Council Member **Arch Lee** (District 7) (334) 300-4034
Term Expires: November 10, 2019
E-mail: alee@montgomeryal.gov
★ Council Member **Glen Pruitt** (District 8) (334) 300-3611
Term Expires: November 10, 2019
E-mail: gpruitt@montgomeryal.gov

City of Montpelier, Vermont

City Hall, 39 Main St., Montpelier, VT 05602
Internet: www.montpelier-vt.org

County: Washington **Election Type:** Nonpartisan **Population:** 7,592 (2015)

Office of the Mayor and City Council
City Hall, 39 Main St., Montpelier, VT 05602
Fax: (802) 223-9519

★ Mayor **John H. Hollar** (802) 223-9502
Began Service: March 2012
Term Expires: March 2018
E-mail: jhollar@montpelier-vt.org
Education: Oklahoma 1982 BA; Georgetown 1989 JD
★ Council Member **Dona Bate** (District 1) (802) 223-9502
Term Expires: March 2018
E-mail: dbate@montpelier-vt.org
★ Council Member **Tom Golonka** (District 1) (802) 223-9502
Term Expires: March 2017
E-mail: tgolonka@montpelier-vt.org
★ Council Member **Jean Olson** (District 2) (802) 223-9502
Term Expires: March 2018
★ Council Member **Anne Watson** (District 2) (802) 223-9502
Term Expires: March 2017
E-mail: awatson@montpelier-vt.org
★ Council Member **Jessica Edgerly-Walsh** (District 3) (802) 223-9502
Term Expires: March 2017
E-mail: jewalsh@montpelier-vt.org

★ Elected Official ▲ Appointed by Legislature ▼ Appointed by Governor ► Appointed by Board or Commission ● Appointed by Judge
■ Appointed by Mayor △ Appointed by Freeholders ▽ Appointed by Supervisor ▷ Appointed by County Executive ○ Appointed by Council

Office of the Mayor and City Council *continued*

★Council Member **Justin Turcotte** (District 3) . . . . (802) 223-9502
Term Expires: March 2018
E-mail: jturcotte@montpelier-vt.org

Office of the City Clerk/Treasurer

City Hall, 39 Main St., Montpelier, VT 05602
Fax: (802) 223-9523

★City Clerk/Treasurer **John Odum** . . . . (802) 223-9500
Term Expires: March 2018
E-mail: jodum@montpelier-vt.org
Deputy City Clerk **Crystal Chase** . . . . (802) 223-9500
E-mail: cchase@montpelier-vt.org

Office of the City Manager

City Hall, 39 Main St., Montpelier, VT 05602
Fax: (802) 223-9519

○City Manager **William J. Fraser** . . . . (802) 223-9502
E-mail: wfraser@montpelier-vt.org
Education: Maine 1981 BA; Harvard 1993 MPA
Assistant City Manager **Jessie Baker** . . . . (802) 262-6250
E-mail: jbaker@montpelier-vt.org

Office of the City Assessor

City Hall, 39 Main St., Montpelier, VT 05602
Fax: (802) 223-9519

City Assessor **Stephen Twombly** . . . . (802) 223-9505
E-mail: stwombly@montpelier-vt.org

Office of the City Attorney

c/o City Manager's Office, City Hall, 39 Main St., Montpelier, VT 05602

City Attorney **J. Paul Giuliani** . . . . (802) 223-9502

Finance Department

City Hall, 39 Main St., Montpelier, VT 05602
Fax: (802) 223-9529

Director **Sandra Gallup** . . . . (802) 223-9514

Fire Department

City Hall, 39 Main St., Montpelier, VT 05602
Fax: (802) 223-9518

Fire Chief/Building Inspector **Robert Gowans** . . . . (802) 229-4913
E-mail: rgowans@montpelier-vt.org

Montpelier Public School System

58 Barre St., Montpelier, VT 05602
Internet: http://mps.k12.vt.us

Superintendent of Schools **Brian Ricca** . . . . (802) 223-9796

Parks Department

39 Main St., Montpelier, VT 05602-2950

Director **Geoff Beyer** . . . . (802) 223-7335

Planning and Community Development Department

City Hall, 39 Main St., Montpelier, VT 05602
Fax: (802) 223-9524

Director **Michael Miller** . . . . (802) 223-9506
E-mail: mmiller@montpelier-vt.org

Police Department

One Pitkin Court, Montpelier, VT 05602
Fax: (802) 223-9518

Chief of Police (Interim) **Anthony Facos** . . . . (802) 223-3445

Public Works Department

City Hall, 39 Main St., Montpelier, VT 05602
Fax: (802) 223-9524

Director (Acting) **Thomas McArdle** . . . . (802) 262-6275

Recreation Department

58 Barre St., Montpelier, VT 05602
Fax: (802) 223-5645

Director **Arne McMullen** . . . . (802) 223-5141

City of Moreno Valley, California

City Hall, 14177 Frederick Street, Moreno Valley, CA 92553
P.O. Box 88005, Moreno Valley, CA 92552
Internet: www.moval.org

County: Riverside **Election Type:** Nonpartisan **Year Incorporated:** December 1984 **Population:** 204,198 (2015)

Office of the Mayor and City Council

City Hall, 14177 Frederick Street, Moreno Valley, CA 92553
Fax: (951) 413-3760

★Mayor **Yxstian Gutierrez** (District 4) . . . . (951) 413-3008
Began Service: October 2013
Term Expires: December 14, 2018
E-mail: yxstiang@moval.org
★Mayor Pro Tem **Jeffrey Giba** (District 2) . . . . (951) 413-3008
Term Expires: December 2018
E-mail: jeffg@moval.org
★Council Member **Jesse L. Molina** (District 1) . . . . (951) 413-3008
Term Expires: December 14, 2016
E-mail: jessem@moval.org
★Council Member **George Price** (District 3) . . . . (951) 413-3008
Term Expires: December 14, 2016
E-mail: georgep@moval.org
★Council Member
Delores Ladonna Jempson (District 5) . . . . (951) 413-3008
Term Expires: December 14, 2016
E-mail: ladonnaj@moval.org
Administrative Assistant **(Vacant)** . . . . (951) 413-3008
Executive Assistant to Mayor and City Council
Kathy Gross . . . . (951) 413-3006

Office of the City Attorney

P.O. Box 88005, Moreno Valley, CA 92552
Fax: (951) 413-3034

○City Attorney (Interim) **Steve Quintanila** . . . . (951) 413-3036
E-mail: cityattorney@moval.org

Office of the City Clerk

P.O. Box 88005, Moreno Valley, CA 92552
Fax: (951) 413-3009

○City Clerk **Jane Halstead** . . . . (951) 413-3001
E-mail: janeh@moval.org

Office of the City Manager

P.O. Box 88005, Moreno Valley, CA 92552
Fax: (951) 413-3750

○City Manager **Michelle Dawson** . . . . (951) 413-3036
E-mail: michelled@moval.org

★Elected Official ▲Appointed by Legislature ▼Appointed by Governor ▶Appointed by Board or Commission ●Appointed by Judge
■Appointed by Mayor △Appointed by Freeholders ▽Appointed by Supervisor ▷Appointed by County Executive ○Appointed by Council

Community and Economic Development Department
P.O. Box 88005, Moreno Valley, CA 92552
Fax: (951) 413-3478

Director **Mike Lee** . . . . (951) 413-3460
E-mail: mikel@moval.org

Financial and Management Services Department
P.O. Box 88005, Moreno Valley, CA 92552
Fax: (951) 413-3096

Chief Financial Officer **Marshall Eyerman** . . . . (951) 413-3021
E-mail: cmoffice@moval.org
Treasury Operations Division Manager
Brooke McKinney . . . . (951) 413-3060
Purchasing and Facilities Division Manager
Rix Skonberg . . . . (951) 413-3740
E-mail: rixs@moval.org Fax: (951) 413-3509
Technology Services Division Manager **Steve Hargis** . . . . (951) 413-3410
E-mail: steveh@moval.org Fax: (951) 653-5886
Animal Services Division Manager **Steve Fries** . . . . (951) 413-3790
Fax: (951) 413-3769

Fire Department
22850 Calle San Juan De Los Lagos, Moreno Valley, CA 92553
Fax: (951) 486-6790

Fire Chief **Abdul Ahmad** . . . . (951) 486-6780
E-mail: abdula@moval.org

Human Resources Department
P.O. Box 88005, Moreno Valley, CA 92552
Fax: (951) 413-3041

Administrative Services Director **Terrie Stevens** . . . . (951) 413-3045

Moreno Valley Library
25480 Alessandro Boulevard, Moreno Valley, CA 92553
Fax: (951) 413-3895

Library Services Division Manager **Ivorie Franks** . . . . (951) 413-3880
E-mail: ivorie.franks@moval-library.org

Parks and Community Services Department
Conference & Recreation Center, 14075 Frederick Street, Moreno Valley, CA 92553
Fax: (951) 413-3719

Parks and Community Services Director **(Vacant)** . . . . (951) 413-3280

Planning and Zoning Department
P.O. Box 88005, Moreno Valley, CA 92552
Fax: (951) 413-3210

Planning Official **Richard Sandzimier** . . . . (951) 413-3206

Police Department
22850 San Juan De Los Lagos, Moreno Valley, CA 92553
Fax: (951) 486-6705

Police Chief **Joel Ontiveros** . . . . (951) 486-6700

Public Works Department
P.O. Box 88005, Moreno Valley, CA 92552
Fax: (951) 413-3279

Public Works Director/City Engineer **Ahmad Ansari** . . . . (951) 413-3100

City of Murfreesboro, Tennessee

111 West Vine Street, Murfreesboro, TN 37130
Tel: (615) 893-5210 Internet: www.murfreesborotn.gov/

County: Rutherford **Election Type:** Nonpartisan **Year Incorporated:** 1817 **Population:** 126,118 (2015)

Office of the Mayor and City Council
111 West Vine Street, Murfreesboro, TN 37130

★Mayor **Shane McFarland** . . . . (615) 849-2629
Began Service: May 2014
Term Expires: August 2018
E-mail: smcfarland@murfreesborotn.gov
Education: Mid Tennessee State 1997 BA
★Vice Mayor **Doug Young** . . . . (615) 893-7721
Term Expires: August 2018
E-mail: dyoung@murfreesborotn.gov
Education: Mid Tennessee State 1971 BA
★Council Member **Madelyn Scales Harris** . . . . (615) 804-8955
Term Expires: August 2018
E-mail: mscalesharris@murfreesborotn.gov
★Council Member **Rick Lalance** . . . . (615) 962-9523
Term Expires: August 2018
E-mail: rlalance@murfreesborotn.gov
★Council Member **Bill Shacklett** . . . . (615) 893-1134
Term Expires: August 2016
E-mail: bshacklett@murfreesborotn.gov
★Council Member **Eddie Smotherman** . . . . (615) 494-9800
Term Expires: August 2016
E-mail: esmotherman@murfreesborotn.gov
★Council Member **Ron Washington** . . . . (615) 890-0097
Term Expires: August 2016
E-mail: rwashington@murfreesborotn.gov
Education: Mid Tennessee State BA

Office of the City Manager
111 West Vine Street, Murfreesboro, TN 37130
Fax: (615) 849-2679

○City Manager **Robert J. "Rob" Lyons** . . . . (615) 849-2629
E-mail: rlyons@murfreesborotn.gov
Assistant City Manager **James Crumley** . . . . (615) 849-2629
E-mail: jcrumley@murfreesborotn.gov
Assistant City Manager **Jennifer Moody** . . . . (615) 849-2629
E-mail: jmoody@murfreesborotn.gov
Purchasing Director **(Vacant)** . . . . (615) 849-2629

Building and Codes Department
111 West Vine Street, Murfreesboro, TN 37130
Fax: (615) 848-3248

Director **Robert Holtz** . . . . (615) 893-3750

Communications Department
111 West Vine Street, Murfreesboro, TN 37130
Fax: (615) 904-6510

Public Information Officer **Mike Browning** . . . . (615) 848-3245
E-mail: mbrowning@murfreesborotn.gov
Cable Television Coordinator **Alan Bozeman** . . . . (615) 848-3245

Community Development Department
211 Bridge Avenue, Murfreesboro, TN 37129-3503
Fax: (615) 217-2260

Director **John Callow** . . . . (615) 890-4660
E-mail: jcallow@murfreesborotn.gov

★Elected Official ▲Appointed by Legislature ▼Appointed by Governor ▶Appointed by Board or Commission ●Appointed by Judge
■Appointed by Mayor △Appointed by Freeholders ▽Appointed by Supervisor ▷Appointed by County Executive ○Appointed by Council

Finance and Tax Department
111 West Vine Street, Murfreesboro, TN 37130
Fax: (615) 848-3247

Finance Director/City Recorder **Melissa Wright** . . . . (615) 893-5210
E-mail: mwright@murfreesborotn.gov
Assistant Finance Director **Erin Tucker** . . . . (615) 893-5210
E-mail: etucker@murfreesborotn.gov

Fire and Rescue Department
220 NW Broad Street, Murfreesboro, TN 37130-3512
Fax: (615) 848-3201

Fire Chief **Mark A. Foulks** . . . . (615) 839-1422
E-mail: mfoulks@murfreesborotn.gov

Fleet Services Department
4753 Florence Road, Murfreesboro, TN 37129-2926
Fax: (615) 494-4591

Director **Jack Hyatt** . . . . (615) 217-3037

Human Resources Department
111 West Vine Street, Murfreesboro, TN 37130
Fax: (615) 904-6506

Director **Glen Godwin** . . . . (615) 848-2553
E-mail: ggodwin@murfreesborotn.gov

Information Technology Department [GIS]
111 West Vine Street, Murfreesboro, TN 37130
Fax: (615) 849-2606

Director **Chris Lilly** . . . . (615) 893-6441
E-mail: clilly@murfreesborotn.gov

Legal Department
111 West Vine Street, Murfreesboro, TN 37130
Fax: (615) 849-2662

City Attorney (Interim) **Craig D. Tindall** . . . . (615) 849-2616
E-mail: ctindall@murfreesborotn.gov
Tel: (615) 893-5210
Education: Arizona State 1982 BS; Southern Methodist 1991 JD
Special Counsel **Craig D. Tindall** . . . . (615) 849-2616
Education: Arizona State 1982 BS; Southern Methodist 1991 JD

Parks and Recreation Department
697 Farfield Crescent Road, Murfreesboro, TN 37128

Director **Lanny Goodwin** . . . . (615) 890-5333

Planning and Zoning Department
111 West Vine Street, Murfreesboro, TN 37130
Fax: (615) 849-2606

Planning Director **Gary Whitaker** . . . . (615) 893-6441

Police Department
302 South Church Street, Murfreesboro, TN 37130-3732
Fax: (615) 849-3260

Chief of Police **James "Karl" Durr** . . . . (615) 849-2670
Deputy Chief of Police **Michael Bowen** . . . . (615) 849-2670

Solid Waste Department
4765 Florence Road, Murfreesboro, TN 37129-2926
Fax: (615) 904-6541

Director **Joey Smith** . . . . (615) 893-3681

Street Department
620 West Main Street, Murfreesboro, TN 37129-3586
Fax: (615) 849-2606

City Engineer **Chris Griffith** . . . . (615) 893-6441
E-mail: cgriffith@murfreesborotn.gov

Transportation Department [ROVER]
4765 Florence Road, Murfreesboro, TN 37129-2926
Fax: (615) 904-6541

Director **Jim Kerr** . . . . (615) 893-6441

Urban Environmental Department
351 Overall Street, Murfreesboro, TN 37129-2798
Fax: (615) 217-3035

Director **Cynthia Holloway** . . . . (615) 895-8059

Water and Sewer Department
111 West Vine Street, Murfreesboro, TN 37130

Director **Darren Gore** . . . . (615) 890-0862

Murfreesboro Municipal Airport
1930 Memorial Boulevard, Murfreesboro, TN 37129-1502
Fax: (615) 848-3256

Airport Manager **Chad Gehrke** . . . . (615) 848-3254

Murfreesboro City Schools
2552 South Church Street, Murfreesboro, TN 37127
Internet: www.cityschools.net/

Director of Schools **Linda Gilbert** . . . . (615) 893-2313

City of Naperville, Illinois
400 South Eagle Street, Naperville, IL 60540
Internet: www.naperville.il.us

County: DuPage; Will **Election Type:** Nonpartisan **Population:** 147,100 (2015)

Office of the Mayor and City Council
400 South Eagle Street, Naperville, IL 60540

★Mayor **Steve Chirico** . . . . (630) 420-6018
Began Service: May 3, 2015
Term Expires: April 30, 2019
E-mail: mayor@naperville.il.us
Secretary **Emy Trotz** . . . . (630) 420-6018
E-mail: trotze@naperville.il.us
★Council Member **Becky Anderson** . . . . (630) 305-5300
Term Expires: April 30, 2019
E-mail: andersonb@naperville.il.us
★Council Member **Rebecca Boyd-Obarski** . . . . (630) 305-5300
Term Expires: April 30, 2019
E-mail: obarskir@naperville.il.us
★Council Member **Judith A. Brodhead** . . . . (630) 305-5335
Term Expires: April 30, 2017
E-mail: brodheadj@naperville.il.us
★Council Member **Kevin Coyne** . . . . (630) 305-5300
Term Expires: April 30, 2017
E-mail: coynek@naperville.il.us
★Council Member **Kevin Gallaher** . . . . (630) 305-5300
Term Expires: April 30, 2017
E-mail: gallaherk@naperville.il.us
★Council Member **Patricia A. Gustin** . . . . (630) 305-5300
Term Expires: April 30, 2019
E-mail: gustinp@naperville.il.us

(continued on next page)

★Elected Official ▲Appointed by Legislature ▼Appointed by Governor ▶Appointed by Board or Commission ●Appointed by Judge
■Appointed by Mayor △Appointed by Freeholders ▽Appointed by Supervisor ▷Appointed by County Executive ○Appointed by Council

Office of the Mayor and City Council *continued*

★Council Member **Paul Hinterlong** .... (630) 305-5362
Term Expires: April 30, 2019
E-mail: hinterlongp@naperville.il.us

★Council Member **John Krummen** .... (630) 305-5300
Term Expires: April 30, 2017
E-mail: krummenj@naperville.il.us

City Council Secretary **Reggie Lynch** .... (630) 548-2983
E-mail: lynchr@naperville.il.us

Office of the City Manager

400 South Eagle Street, Naperville, IL 60540
Fax: (630) 305-4466

○City Manager **Douglas Krieger** .... (630) 420-6044
E-mail: kriegerd@naperville.il.us

Deputy City Manager **Marcie Schatz** .... (630) 420-6044
E-mail: schatzm@naperville.il.us

City Clerk **Pam LaFeber** .... (630) 305-5300
E-mail: lafeberp@naperville.il.us

Web Producer **Mike Masterson** .... (630) 305-7065
E-mail: mastersonm@naperville.il.us

Communications Manager **Linda LaCloche** .... (630) 420-6707

Finance Department

400 South Eagle Street, Naperville, IL 60540

Director **Rachel Mayer** .... (630) 420-6052

Budget and Financial Reporting Manager
Lynn Lockwood .... (630) 420-6055
E-mail: lockwoodl@naperville.il.us

Chief Procurement Officer **(Vacant)** .... (630) 548-1406

Fire Department

1380 Aurora Avenue, Naperville, IL 60540
Fax: (630) 420-4094

Fire Chief **Mark Puknaitis** .... (630) 420-6142
E-mail: puknaitism@naperville.il.us

Information Technology Department

400 South Eagle Street, Naperville, IL 60540

Chief Information Officer **Pam LaFeber** .... (630) 548-2987
E-mail: lafeberp@naperville.il.us

Legal, Human Resources and Risk Management Department

400 South Eagle Street, Naperville, IL 60540

City Attorney **Jill Pelka-Wilger** .... (630) 305-3750
E-mail: pelka-wilgerj@naperville.il.us

Director of Human Resources **Jim Sheehan** .... (630) 420-4171
E-mail: sheehanj@naperville.il.us

Police Department

1350 Aurora Avenue, Naperville, IL 60540

Chief of Police **Robert W. Marshall** .... (630) 420-6666

Naperville Public Library

2035 South Naper Boulevard, Naperville, IL 60565
Internet: http://www.naperville-lib.org

Library Director **Dave Della Terza** .... (630) 961-4100 ext. 2210
E-mail: ddellaterza@naperville-lib.org

Executive Director **Julie Rothenfluh** .... (630) 961-4100 ext. 6144
E-mail: jrothenfluh@naperville-lib.org

Public Works Department

180 Fort Hill Drive, Naperville, IL 60540

Director **Dick Dublinski** .... (630) 420-6095

Department of Public Utilities

Electric Utility
400 South Eagle Street, Naperville, IL 60540

Director **Mark Curran** .... (630) 420-6131

Water and Wastewater Utility
400 South Eagle Street, Naperville, IL 60540

Director **Jim Holzapfel** .... (630) 420-6137

Transportation, Engineering and Development Business Group

400 South Eagle Street, Naperville, IL 60540

Director **Bill Novack** .... (630) 420-6100
E-mail: novackw@naperville.il.us

Development Services Team Leader **(Vacant)** .... (630) 420-6100

Engineering Team Leader **Bob Kozurek** .... (630) 420-6100
E-mail: kozurekb@naperville.il.us

Engineering Team Leader **Andy Hynes** .... (630) 420-6100
E-mail: hynesa@naperville.il.us

Transportation Team Leader **Jennifer Louden** .... (630) 420-6100

Metropolitan Government of Nashville and Davidson County, Tennessee

100 Metro Courthouse, Nashville, TN 37201
Tel: (615) 862-6000 (Information) Fax: (615) 862-6040
Internet: www.nashville.gov

County: Metropolitan Nashville-Davidson **Election Type:** Nonpartisan
Year Incorporated: 1806 **Population:** 654,610 (2015)

Form of Municipal Government: City and county governments are combined.

Office of the Mayor

100 Metro Courthouse, Nashville, TN 37201
Tel: (615) 862-6000 Fax: (615) 862-6040
Internet: http://www.nashville.gov/Mayors-Office.aspx

★Mayor **Megan Barry** .... (615) 862-6000
Began Service: September 25, 2015
Term Expires: August 31, 2019
E-mail: mayor@nashville.gov

Executive Assistant to the Mayor **Elease Waller** .... (615) 862-6000
E-mail: elease.waller@nashville.gov

■Press Secretary **Sean Braisted** .... (615) 862-6000
E-mail: sean.braisted@nashville.gov

■Communications Advisor/Speechwriter **Michael Cass** .... (615) 862-6000

■Chief Operating Officer **Richard Riebeling** .... (615) 862-6000
E-mail: richard.riebeling@nashville.gov
Education: Vanderbilt 1983 JD

■Senior Advisor **Claudia Huskey** .... (615) 862-6000
E-mail: claudia.huskey@nashville.gov

■Senior Advisor for Innovation **Nancy Shapiro** .... (615) 862-6000

■Chief of Staff **Debby Dale Mason** .... (615) 862-6000
E-mail: debby.mason@nashville.gov

■Legislative Director/State Legislature Liaison
Joseph Woodson .... (615) 862-6000

■Neighborhoods Director **Lonnell Matthews, Jr.** .... (615) 862-6000

■Director of Health Living **(Vacant)** .... (615) 862-6000

Special Assistant/Council Liaison **Martin Szeigis** .... (615) 862-6000

■Chief Services Officer **(Vacant)** .... (615) 862-6000

■Scheduler **Patrick Hamilton** .... (615) 862-6000

Council Liaison **Joseph Woodson** .... (615) 862-6000

■Director of Infrastructure **Mark Sturtevant** .... (615) 862-6000

■Transportation and Sustainability Director
Erin Hafkenschiel .... (615) 862-6000

★Elected Official ▲Appointed by Legislature ▼Appointed by Governor ▶Appointed by Board or Commission ●Appointed by Judge
■Appointed by Mayor △Appointed by Freeholders ▽Appointed by Supervisor ▷Appointed by County Executive ○Appointed by Council

Office of the Mayor *continued*

■ Transportation and Sustainability Manager
Mary Beth Ikard . . . . . (615) 862-6000
Chief Diversity Officer **Michelle Hernandez-Lane** . . . . . (615) 862-6000

Mayor's Office of Children and Youth

100 Metro Courthouse, Nashville, TN 37201
Fax: (615) 862-6040

■ Senior Advisor for Education **(Vacant)** . . . . . (615) 880-3673

Mayor's Office of Economic and Community Development

Metropolitan Courthouse, Suite 102, Nashville, TN 37201
Fax: (615) 862-6025 Internet: www.nashville.gov/ecdev/

■ Director **Matthew A. "Matt" Wiltshire** . . . . . (615) 862-6021
E-mail: matt.wiltshire@nashville.gov

Mayor's Office of Emergency Management

2060 15th Avenue South, Nashville, TN 37212
Tel: (615) 862-8530 Fax: (615) 862-8534 E-mail: oem@nashville.gov

Director **Stephen Halford** . . . . . (615) 862-5422
E-mail: stephen.halford@nashville.gov

Mayor's Office of Environment and Sustainability

100 Metro Courthouse, Nashville, TN 37201

■ Director **(Vacant)** . . . . . (615) 862-6002

Agricultural Extension Service

1417 Murfreesboro Pike, 2nd Floor, Suite 3, Nashville, TN 37219
Fax: (615) 862-5998 Internet: www.nashville.gov/aes/

Director **Michael Barry** . . . . . (615) 862-5833
Administrative Support **Carolyn Hansen** . . . . . (615) 862-4349
E-mail: chansen5@utk.edu

Metropolitan Nashville Arts Commission

800 Second Avenue South, 4th Floor, Nashville, TN 37210
P.O. Box 196300, Nashville, TN 37219-6300
Fax: (615) 862-6731 Internet: http://www.artsnashville.org
E-mail: arts@nashville.gov

Executive Director **Jennifer Cole** . . . . . (615) 862-6720

Beer Permit Board

800 2nd Avenue, North, 3rd Floor, Nashville, TN 37219
Fax: (615) 862-6754

Executive Director **Jackie Eslick** . . . . . (615) 862-6751

Codes Administration Department

Metro Office Building, 800 Second Avenue South, 3rd Floor, Nashville, TN 37210
Tel: (615) 862-6500 Fax: (615) 862-6515
E-mail: codes@metro.nashville.gov Internet: www.nashville.gov/codes/

Director **Terrence L. "Terry" Cobb** . . . . . (615) 862-6549
Education: Tennessee Tech BS
Assistant Director **Roy L. Jones** . . . . . (615) 862-6541
Education: Tennessee Tech 1972 BS; Nashville 1986 JD; Cumberland U 2002 MS
Plans Examiner Chief/Assistant Director **Wade F. Hill** . . . . (615) 862-6520
Education: Tennessee 1976 BA
Property Standards Chief/Assistant Director
William Penn, Jr. . . . . . (615) 862-6590
Administrative Assistant **Karene West** . . . . . (615) 862-6591
E-mail: karene.west@nashville.gov
Zoning Administrator **Bill Herbert** . . . . . (615) 862-6608
Building Inspection Chief **Byron Hall** . . . . . (615) 862-6550
Electrical Inspection Chief **Jeff Barnes** . . . . . (615) 862-6560
Gas/Mechanical Inspection Chief **Shannon Roberts** . . . . . (615) 862-6508
Plumbing Inspection Chief **Gary Hall** . . . . . (615) 862-6620
Zoning Examination Chief **Jon Michael** . . . . . (615) 862-6557

Codes Administration Department *continued*

Urban Forester **Stephan Kivett** . . . . . (615) 862-6488
Education: Kansas 1991 BA

Metropolitan Development and Housing Agency

701 S. Sixth St., Nashville, TN 37206
Fax: (615) 252-3677 Internet: www.nashville-mdha.org

Executive Director **James E. Harbison** . . . . . (615) 252-8410
E-mail: jharbison@nashville-mdha.org
Deputy Director **James Thiltgen** . . . . . (615) 252-8414
E-mail: jthiltge@nashville-mdha.org
Director of Communications **Jamie Berry** . . . . . (615) 252-8420
E-mail: jberry@Nashville-MDHA.org Fax: (615) 248-2170

Davidson County Election Commission

1417 Murfreesboro Pike, Nashville, TN 37217
Fax: (615) 862-8810 Internet: www.nashville.gov/vote/

Administrator of Elections **(Vacant)** . . . . . (615) 862-8800

Nashville Electric Service

1214 Church Street, Nashville, TN 37246-0002
Tel: (615) 747-3981 Fax: (615) 747-3854
Internet: http://www.nespower.com

President and Chief Executive Officer
Decosta E. Jenkins . . . . . (615) 747-3895
Vice President, Finance/Administration and Chief Financial Officer **Teresa Broyles-Aplin** . . . . . (615) 747-3895
Executive Vice President and Chief Operating Officer
Wesley Allen . . . . . (615) 747-3895
Vice President/Chief Information Officer
David Van Hooser . . . . . (615) 747-3735
E-mail: dvanhooser@nespower.com Fax: (615) 747-3390
Education: Mid Tennessee State 1984 BBA, 1992 MBA; Southwest Missouri State 2004 MSCIS
Facilities and Security Manager **Timothy S. Kinkead** . . . . (615) 747-3795
E-mail: tkinkead@nespower.com Fax: (615) 255-3256

Nashville Farmers' Market

900 Rosa L. Parks Boulevard, Nashville, TN 37208
Fax: (615) 880-2000 Internet: http://nashvillefarmersmarket.org/

Director **Tasha Kennard** . . . . . (615) 880-2001 ext. 26
Office Manager **Carolyn Sanders** . . . . . (615) 880-2001 ext. 23
Business Manager **(Vacant)** . . . . . (615) 880-2001 ext. 24
Marketing Manager **(Vacant)** . . . . . (615) 880-2001 ext. 22

Finance Department

1 Public Square, #106, Nashville, TN 37201
Tel: (615) 862-6151 Fax: (615) 862-6156
Internet: www.nashville.gov/finance

■ Director (Acting) **Talia Lomax-O'dneal** . . . . . (615) 862-6151
E-mail: talia.lomaxodneal@nashville.gov
Assistant Finance Director for Budgets **Stan Romine** . . . . (615) 862-6120
E-mail: stan.romine@nashville.gov
Deputy Director **Gene Nolan** . . . . . (615) 862-6151
Financial Operations **Kim McDoniel** . . . . . (615) 862-6114
Treasurer **Tom Eddlemon** . . . . . (615) 862-6210
Purchasing Agent **Jeff Gossage** . . . . . (615) 862-6180
E-mail: jeff.gossage@nashville.gov Fax: (615) 880-6179

Fire Department

63 Hermitage Avenue, Nashville, TN 37210
Tel: (615) 862-5421 Fax: (615) 862-5454 Internet: www.nashfire.org/

■ Chief **Rick White** . . . . . (615) 862-5424 ext. 02006
E-mail: rick.white@nashville.gov
Administration Section **Danny Yates** . . . . . (615) 862-5467
E-mail: danny.yates@nashville.gov
Operations Manager **Larry Walker** . . . . . (615) 862-4436
E-mail: larry.walker@nashville.gov

★ Elected Official ▲ Appointed by Legislature ▼ Appointed by Governor ▶ Appointed by Board or Commission ● Appointed by Judge
■ Appointed by Mayor △ Appointed by Freeholders ▽ Appointed by Supervisor ▷ Appointed by County Executive ○ Appointed by Council

General Services Department

730 Second Avenue, South, Nashville, TN 37210
Tel: (615) 862-5050 Fax: (615) 862-5035
E-mail: general.services@nashville.gov Internet: www.nashville.gov/gsa/

■ Director **Nancy Whittemore** . . . . . (615) 862-5050 ext. 8
E-mail: nancy.whittemore@nashville.gov
Administrative Services Manager **Velvet Hunter** . . . . . (615) 862-5055
E-mail: velvet.hunter@nashville.gov
Building Maintenance and Operations Division Manager **Diana Stephens** . . . . . (615) 862-8959 ext. 3
E-mail: diana.stephens@nashville.gov
Security Coordinator **Todd Best** . . . . . (615) 862-5039
Fax: (615) 862-5035
Fleet Division Manager **Stecey Wall** . . . . . (615) 862-5050

Health Department

Lentz Health Center, 2500 Charlotte Avenue, Nashville, TN 37209
Tel: (615) 340-5616 Fax: (615) 340-5665
Internet: http://health.nashville.gov/

Director **Dr. William S. Paul** . . . . . (615) 340-5616
Environmental Health Services Bureau Director **Sanmi Areola** . . . . . (615) 340-5653
Finance and Administration Bureau Director (Interim) **Jim Diamond** . . . . . (615) 340-5602
Community Health Equality Bureau Director (Interim) **Sanjana P. Stamm** . . . . . (615) 340-5655
Population Health Director **Tina Lester** . . . . . (615) 341-4375
Nursing Director **Sanjana P. Stamm** . . . . . (615) 340-5655
Cultural Competency/Training Coordinator **Michelle Birdsong** . . . . . (615) 340-2273
E-mail: michelle.birdsong@nashville.gov Fax: (615) 340-2131
Public Information Officer **Brian Todd** . . . . . (615) 340-2153
Civil Service Medical Examiner (Interim) **Dr. Deidra Parrish** . . . . . (615) 340-5616

Metropolitan Historical Commission

3000 Granny White Pike, Nashville, TN 37204
Fax: (615) 862-7974

Executive Director **Tim Walker** . . . . . (615) 862-7970

Hospital Authority

1818 Albion St., Nashville, TN 37208
Fax: (615) 341-4493

Chief Executive Officer **Joseph Webb** . . . . . (615) 341-4491
Chief Information Officer **Melanie Thomas** . . . . . (615) 341-4577
E-mail: melanie.thomas@nashvilleha.org
Administrative Director, Clinical and Support Services **Mark Brown** . . . . . (615) 341-4461
E-mail: mark.brown@nashvilleha.org
Director of Performance Excellence and Process Improvement **Cathi Phillips** . . . . . (615) 341-4451
Chief Nursing Officer **Dawn Alexander** . . . . . (615) 341-4465
Director of Human Resources **Diana Wohlfahrt** . . . . . (615) 341-4470
E-mail: diana.wohlfahrt@nashvilleha.org
Director of Marketing and Community Relations **Cathy Poole** . . . . . (615) 341-4082
E-mail: cathy.poole@nashvilleha.org

Department of Human Resources

404 James Robertson Parkway, Suite 1000, Nashville, TN 37219
Tel: (615) 862-6640 Fax: (615) 862-6659
Internet: www.nashville.gov/hr_benefits/

■ Director **Veronica Frazier** . . . . . (615) 862-6640
E-mail: veronica.frazier@nashville.gov
Education: Webster BA

Civil Service Commission/Employee Benefit Board

404 James Robertson Parkway, Suite 1000, Nashville, TN 37219
Fax: (615) 862-6654

Director **Veronica Frazier** . . . . . (615) 862-6640
E-mail: veronica.frazier@nashville.gov
Education: Webster BA

Information Technology Services Department

700 2nd Avenue, South, Nashville, TN 37210
P.O. Box 196300, Nashville, TN 37219-6300
Fax: (615) 862-6288

■ Director **Keith Durbin** . . . . . (615) 862-6220
E-mail: cio@nashville.gov
Human Resources Manager **Cyndy Maddox** . . . . . (615) 860-2573
E-mail: cyndy.maddox@nashville.gov
Assistant Director, Communications and Infrastructure Services **Margaret Keck** . . . . . (615) 860-2780
E-mail: margaret.keck@nashville.gov
Information Security Services Director **John Griffey** . . . . . (615) 860-2786
E-mail: john.griffey@nashville.gov
Assistant Director, Customer Support Services **Kelley Campbell** . . . . . (615) 862-0238
E-mail: kelley.campbell@nashville.gov
Assistant Director, Business Applications, Solutions and Support **Dawn Clark** . . . . . (615) 862-6033
E-mail: dawn.clark@nashville.gov

Legal Department

Metropolitan Courthouse, Suite 108, Nashville, TN 37201
Fax: (615) 862-6352

Director **Jon Cooper** . . . . . (615) 862-6341

Metropolitan Action Commission

800 2nd Avenue, North, Nashville, TN 37219
Fax: (615) 862-8881 Internet: www.nashville.gov/mac

■ Executive Director **Dr. Cynthia L. Croom** . . . . . (615) 862-8860
E-mail: cynthia.croom@nashville.gov
Chief Financial Officer (Interim) **Vijay Lal** . . . . (615) 862-8860 ext. 70112
E-mail: vijay.lal@nashville.gov

Metropolitan Parks and Recreation Department

511 Oman Street, Nashville, TN 37203
P.O. Box 196340, Nashville, TN 37219-6340
Tel: (615) 862-8400 Fax: (615) 862-8414
Internet: www.nashville.gov/parks

Director **Tommy Lynch** . . . . . (615) 862-8400
Finance and Administration Director **Monique Odom** . . . . (615) 862-8400
E-mail: monique.odom@nashville.gov
Greenways Director **Shain Dennison** . . . . . (615) 862-8400
Outdoor Recreation and Special Events Director **Jim Hester** . . . . . (615) 862-8400
Parks Assistant Director, Consolidated Maintenance **Rick Taylor** . . . . . (615) 862-8411
Fax: (615) 880-2262
Planning and Development Director **Tim Netsch** . . . . . (615) 862-8400
E-mail: tim.netsch@nashville.gov
Public Relations Director **Jackie Jones** . . . . . (615) 862-8400
E-mail: jackie.jones@nashville.gov
Recreation and Wellness Director **Sally Davis** . . . . . (615) 862-8400
Revenue Director **John Holmes** . . . . . (615) 862-8400

Metro Nashville/Davidson County Planning Department [MPC]

P.O. Box 196300, Nashville, TN 37219-6300
Tel: (615) 862-7150 Fax: (615) 862-7209
Internet: www.nashville.gov/mpc/

Executive Director **Doug Sloan** . . . . . (615) 862-7173
Deputy Director **Bob Leeman** . . . . . (615) 862-7183

★ Elected Official ▲ Appointed by Legislature ▼ Appointed by Governor ▶ Appointed by Board or Commission ● Appointed by Judge
■ Appointed by Mayor △ Appointed by Freeholders ▽ Appointed by Supervisor ▷ Appointed by County Executive ○ Appointed by Council

Nashville Municipal Auditorium

417 Fourth Avenue North, Nashville, TN 37201
Tel: (615) 862-6390 Fax: (615) 862-6394
Internet: www.nashvilleauditorium.com

General Manager **Bob Skoney** . . . . (615) 862-6390 ext. 223
Education: Alabama 1977 BS
Director of Sales and Marketing **Sharon Hill** . . . . (615) 862-6390 ext. 228
Education: Mid Tennessee State 1976 BS; Tennessee State 1995 MPA
Box Office Manager **Taneisha Alexander** . . . . . . (615) 862-6390 ext. 222
Fax: (615) 862-6394
Event Manager **Derrick Pentico** . . . . (615) 862-6390 ext. 226
Fax: (615) 862-6394
Building Maintenance Supervisor **Mike Taylor** . . . (615) 862-6390 ext. 232
E-mail: michael.l.taylor@nashville.gov Fax: (615) 862-6394
Finance Manager **Kristie Bailey** . . . . (615) 862-6390
E-mail: kristie.bailey@nashville.gov

Music City Center

201 5th Avenue South, Nashville, TN 33203
E-mail: conventioncenter@nashville.gov
Internet: http://www.nashvilleconventionctr.com

President and Chief Executive Officer **Charles L. Starks** . . (615) 740-1140
Executive Assistant **Beverly Bennett** . . . . (615) 401-1402
E-mail: beverly.bennett@nashvillemcc.com
Director of Finance and Administration **Heidi Runion** . . . . (615) 401-1430
E-mail: heidi.runion@nashvillemcc.com

Police Department

200 James Robertson Pkwy., Nashville, TN 37201-1202
Tel: (615) 862-7301 Internet: www.police.nashville.org

Police Chief **Steve Anderson** . . . . (615) 862-7301
Education: Nashville JD Fax: (615) 862-7787
Administrative Services Deputy Chief **Damian Huggins** . . (615) 880-1334
Investigative Services Deputy Chief **Todd Henry** . . . . (615) 862-7731
E-mail: w.todd.henry@nashville.gov
Field Operations Chief **Brian Johnson** . . . . (615) 862-7721
Public Affairs Manager **Don Aaron** . . . . (615) 862-7306
E-mail: don.aaron@nashville.gov
Strategic Development Captain **Capt. Mike Hagar** . . . . (615) 862-7790
Training Captain **Keith Stephens** . . . . (615) 862-7617
2715 Tucker Road, Nashville, TN 37218
E-mail: keith.stephens@nashville.gov

Nashville Public Library

615 Church St., Nashville, TN 37219
Tel: (615) 862-5800 Internet: www.library.nashville.org/

Director **Kenton L. Oliver** . . . . (615) 862-5800
E-mail: kent.oliver@nashville.gov

Public Works Department

750 South Fifth Street, Nashville, TN 37206
Tel: (615) 862-8700 Fax: (615) 862-8799
E-mail: public_works@nashville.org Internet: www.nashville.gov/pw/

Director (Interim) **Mark Macy** . . . . (615) 862-8700
Engineering Assistant Director **Mark Macy** . . . . (615) 862-8700
E-mail: mark.macy@nashville.gov Fax: (615) 862-5568
Finance and Administration Assistant Director
Sharon Wahlstrom . . . . (615) 862-8700
E-mail: sharon.wahlstrom@nashville.gov Fax: (615) 862-5568
Human Resources Manager **Charles Boddie** . . . . (615) 862-8710
E-mail: charles.boddie@nashville.gov
Education: Mid Tennessee State 1995 BA

Metropolitan Social Services Department

800 2nd Avenue North, Nashville, TN 37201
Fax: (615) 880-2292 E-mail: socialservices@nashville.gov
Internet: www.nashville.gov/sservices

Executive Director **Renee Pratt** . . . . (615) 862-6400

Metro Water Services

1700 Third Avenue North, Nashville, TN 37208
Fax: (615) 862-4600 Internet: www.nashville.gov/water

Director **Scott A. Potter** . . . . (615) 862-4505
Education: Vanderbilt 1986 BE
Strategic Communications **Sonia Allman** . . . . (615) 862-4494
E-mail: sonia.allman@nashville.gov
Education: Tennessee 1994 BS
Customer Services Assistant Director **Martha W. Segal** . . (615) 862-4626
Education: Old Dominion 1977 BS, 1983 MBA
Engineering Assistant Director **Cyrus Toosi** . . . . (615) 862-4906
E-mail: cyrus.toosi@nashville.gov
Operations Assistant Director **David M. Tucker** . . . . (615) 862-4584
E-mail: david.tucker@nashville.gov
Education: Tennessee State 1986 BS
Stormwater Assistant Director **Tom Palko** . . . . (615) 862-4910
Education: Tennessee 1984 BS
Systems Services Assistant Director **Hal Balthrop** . . . . (615) 862-4847
Education: Tennessee Tech 1984 BS
Administrative Services Officer **Mose Jobe** . . . . (615) 880-2729
E-mail: mose.jobe@nashville.gov
Human Resources Manager **Ivan Davis** . . . . (615) 862-4533
E-mail: ivan.davis@nashville.gov
Training Coordinator **(Vacant)** . . . . (615) 862-7240

Office of the Metropolitan Council

1 Public Square, 204 Metro Courthouse, Nashville, TN 37219
Tel: (615) 862-6780 Fax: (615) 862-6784
Internet: www.nashville.gov/council

★ Vice Mayor and President **David Briley** (At-Large) . . . . . . (615) 880-3357
Term Expires: August 31, 2019
E-mail: diane.neighbors@nashville.gov
Education: Georgetown BA; Golden Gate JD
★ Council Member **(Vacant)** (District 1) . . . . (615) 862-6780
Term Expires: September 25, 2019
★ Council Member **DeCosta Hastings** (District 2) . . . . (615) 862-6780
Term Expires: August 31, 2019
E-mail: dacosta.hastings@nashville.gov
★ Council Member **Brenda Haywood** (District 3) . . . . (615) 862-6780
Term Expires: August 31, 2019
E-mail: brenda.haywood@nashville.gov
★ Council Member **Robert Swope** (District 4) . . . . (615) 862-6780
Term Expires: August 31, 2019
E-mail: robert.swope@nashville.gov
★ Council Member **Scott Davis** (District 5) . . . . (615) 862-6780
Term Expires: August 31, 2019
E-mail: scott.davis@nashville.gov
★ Council Member **Brett Withers** (District 6) . . . . (615) 862-6780
Term Expires: August 31, 2019
E-mail: brett.withers@nashville.gov
★ Council Member **Anthony Davis** (District 7) . . . . (615) 862-6780
Term Expires: August 31, 2019
E-mail: anthony.davis@nashville.gov
★ Council Member **Nancy VanReece** (District 8) . . . . (615) 862-6780
Term Expires: August 31, 2019
E-mail: nancy.vanreece@nashville.gov
★ Council Member **Bill Pridemore, Jr.** (District 9) . . . . (615) 862-6780
Term Expires: August 31, 2019
E-mail: bill.pridemore@nashville.gov
★ Council Member **Doug "Dukie" Pardue** (District 10) . . . . (615) 862-6780
Term Expires: August 31, 2019
E-mail: doug.pardue@nashville.gov
★ Council Member **Larry Hagar** (District 11) . . . . (615) 862-6780
Term Expires: August 31, 2019
E-mail: larry.hagar@nashville.gov
★ Council Member **Steve Glover** (District 12) . . . . (615) 862-6780
Term Expires: August 31, 2019
E-mail: steve.glover@nashville.gov
★ Council Member **Holly Huezo** (District 13) . . . . (615) 862-6780
Term Expires: August 31, 2019
E-mail: holly.huezo@nashville.gov

(continued on next page)

★ Elected Official ▲ Appointed by Legislature ▼ Appointed by Governor ▶ Appointed by Board or Commission ● Appointed by Judge
■ Appointed by Mayor △ Appointed by Freeholders ▽ Appointed by Supervisor ▷ Appointed by County Executive ○ Appointed by Council

Office of the Metropolitan Council *continued*

★Council Member **Kevin Rhoten** (District 14) . . . . (615) 862-6780
Term Expires: August 31, 2019
E-mail: kevin.rhoten@nashville.gov

★Council Member **Jeff Syracuse** (District 15) . . . . (615) 862-6780
Term Expires: August 31, 2019
E-mail: jeff.syracuse@nashville.gov

★Council Member **Michael Freeman** (District 16) . . . . . . (615) 862-6780
Term Expires: September 25, 2019
E-mail: michael.freeman@nashville.gov

★Council Member **Colby Sledge** (District 17) . . . . (615) 862-6780
Term Expires: August 31, 2019
E-mail: colby.sledge@nashville.gov

★Council Member **Burkley Allen** (District 18) . . . . (615) 862-6780
Term Expires: August 31, 2019
E-mail: burkley.allen@nashville.org

★Council Member
Thomas F. "Freddie" O'Connell (District 19) . . . . (615) 862-6780
Term Expires: August 31, 2019
Education: Brown U 2000 BA, 2000 BS

★Council Member **Mary Carolyn Roberts** (District 20) . . . .(615) 862-6780
Term Expires: August 31, 2019

★Council Member **Edward Kindall** (District 21) . . . . (615) 862-6780
Term Expires: August 31, 2019
E-mail: edward.kindall@nashville.gov

★Council Member **Sheri Weiner** (District 22) . . . . (615) 862-6780
Term Expires: August 31, 2019
E-mail: sheri.weiner@nashville.gov

★Council Member **Mina Johnson** (District 23) . . . . (615) 862-6780
Term Expires: August 31, 2019
E-mail: mina.johnson@nashville.gov

★Council Member **Kathleen Murphy** (District 24) . . . . (615) 862-6780
Term Expires: August 31, 2019
E-mail: kathleen.murphy@nashville.gov

★Council Member **Russ Pulley** (District 25) . . . . (615) 862-6780
Term Expires: August 31, 2019
E-mail: russ.pulley@nashville.gov

★Council Member **Jeremy Elrod** (District 26) . . . . (615) 862-6780
Term Expires: August 31, 2019
E-mail: jeremy.elrod@nashville.gov

★Council Member
Davette Dennison Blalock (District 27) . . . . (615) 862-6780
Term Expires: August 31, 2019
E-mail: davette.blalock@nashville.gov

★Council Member **Tanaka Vercher** (District 28) . . . . (615) 862-6780
Term Expires: August 31, 2019
E-mail: tanaka.vercher@nashville.gov

★Council Member **Karen Y. Johnson** (District 29) . . . . (615) 862-6780
Term Expires: August 31, 2019
E-mail: karen.johnson@nashville.gov

★Council Member **Jason Potts** (District 30) . . . . (615) 862-6780
Term Expires: August 31, 2019
E-mail: jason.potts@nashville.gov

★Council Member **Fabian Bedne** (District 31) . . . . (615) 862-6780
Term Expires: August 31, 2019
E-mail: fabian.bedne@nashville.gov

★Council Member **Jacobia C. Dowell** (District 32) . . . . (615) 862-6780
Term Expires: August 31, 2019
E-mail: jacobia.dowell@nashville.gov

★Council Member **Samuel Coleman** (District 33) . . . . (615) 862-6780
Term Expires: August 31, 2019
E-mail: samuel.coleman@nashville.gov

★Council Member **Angie Henderson** (District 34) . . . . (615) 862-6780
Term Expires: August 31, 2019
E-mail: angie.henderson@nashville.gov

★Council Member **Dave Rosenberg** (District 35) . . . . (615) 862-6780
Term Expires: August 31, 2019
E-mail: dave.rosenberg@nashville.gov

★Council Member **John Cooper** (At-Large) . . . . (615) 862-6780
Term Expires: August 31, 2019
E-mail: john.cooper@nashville.gov

★Council Member **Erica Gilmore** (At-Large) . . . . (615) 862-6780
Term Expires: August 31, 2019
E-mail: erica.gilmore@nashville.gov

Office of the Metropolitan Council *continued*

★Council Member **Sharon Hurt** (At-Large) . . . . (615) 862-6780
Term Expires: August 31, 2019
E-mail: sharon.hurt@nashville.gov

★Council Member **Bob Mendes** (At-Large) . . . . (615) 862-6780
Term Expires: August 31, 2019
E-mail: bob.mendes@nashville.gov

★Council Member **Jim Shulman** (At-Large) . . . . (615) 862-6780
Term Expires: August 31, 2019
E-mail: jim.shulman@nashville.gov

Office of the Metropolitan Clerk

205 Metro Courthouse, Nashville, TN 37201
Fax: (615) 880-3733 E-mail: metro.clerk@nashville.gov

■Metro Clerk **Shannon Hall** . . . . (615) 862-6770
E-mail: shannon.hall@nashville.gov

Transportation Licensing Commission

1417 Murfreesboro Road, Nashville, TN 37217
P.O. Box 196300, Nashville, TN 37219-6300
Fax: (615) 862-6765

Director **Billy Fields** . . . . (615) 862-6777

Office of the Assessor of Property

700 Second Avenue, South, Suite 210, Nashville, TN 37210
Fax: (615) 862-6078

★Assessor **George L. Rooker, Jr.** . . . . (615) 862-6080
Term Expires: August 31, 2016
E-mail: george.rooker@nashville.gov

Office of the County Clerk

700 Second Avenue, South, Suite 101, Nashville, TN 37210
Tel: (615) 862-6050 (Auto Licenses and Titles)
E-mail: countyclerk@nashville.gov Internet: http://nashvilleclerk.com/

★County Clerk **Brenda P. Wynn** . . . . (615) 862-6250
Term Expires: August 31, 2018
E-mail: brenda.wynn@nashville.gov

Chief Deputy Clerk **Mike Taylor** . . . . (615) 862-6050 ext. 77108
E-mail: mike.taylor@nashville.gov

Chief Deputy Clerk **Joey Workman** . . . . (615) 862-6050 ext. 77160
E-mail: joey.workman@nashville.gov

Office of the District Attorney General

Washington Square Building, 222 Second Avenue, North, 5th Floor, Nashville, TN 37201-1649
Tel: (615) 862-5500 Fax: (615) 862-5599 Internet: www.da.nashville.gov

★District Attorney General **Glenn R. Funk** . . . . (615) 862-5500 ext. 133
Term Expires: August 31, 2018
E-mail: glen.funk@nashville.gov

Deputy District Attorney General
Tom Thurman . . . . (615) 862-5500 ext. 134
E-mail: tom.thurman@nashville.gov

Office of the Public Defender

404 James Robertson Parkway, Suite 2022, Nashville, TN 37219
Fax: (615) 862-5736 Internet: http://publicdefender.nashville.gov

★Public Defender **Dawn Deaner** . . . . (615) 862-5730
Term Expires: August 31, 2018
E-mail: dawndeaner@jis.nashville.org

Public Defender Juvenile Office

Juvenile Justice Center, 100 Woodland St., Nashville, TN 37213

Deputy Public Defender **Jerrilyn Manning** . . . . (615) 862-5740

★Elected Official ▲Appointed by Legislature ▼Appointed by Governor ►Appointed by Board or Commission ●Appointed by Judge
■Appointed by Mayor △Appointed by Freeholders ▽Appointed by Supervisor ▷Appointed by County Executive ○Appointed by Council

Office of the Register of Deeds

501 Broadway, Nashville, TN 37203
P.O. Box 196398, Nashville, TN 37219-6398
Fax: (615) 880-2039

★ Register of Deeds **Bill Garrett** .... (615) 862-6790
Term Expires: August 31, 2018
E-mail: bill.garrett@nashville.gov

Davidson County Sheriff's Office

506 Second Ave. North, Nashville, TN 37201
Fax: (615) 862-8188 E-mail: info@nashville-sheriff.net
Internet: http://www.nashville-sheriff.net

★ Sheriff **Daron Hall** .... (615) 862-8166
Term Expires: August 31, 2018
E-mail: daron.hall@nashville.gov
Assistant to the Sheriff **Jane Woodall** .... (615) 862-8166
E-mail: jwoodall@dcso.nashville.org Fax: (615) 880-3837
Chief Deputy Sheriff **John Ford** .... (615) 862-8226
E-mail: john.ford@nashville.gov
Director of Communications **Karla West** .... (615) 862-8166
Human Resources Director **Byron Grizzle** .... (615) 880-3884
E-mail: bgrizzle@dcso.nashville.org

Office of the Trustee

700 Second Avenue, South, Suite 220, Nashville, TN 37210
P.O. Box 196358, Nashville, TN 37219-6358
Fax: (615) 862-6337 Tel: (615) 862-6140 (Tax Relief/Tax Freeze)
Tel: (615) 862-6330 (Personalty Taxes)

★ Trustee **Charlie Cardwell** .... (615) 862-6330
Term Expires: August 31, 2018
E-mail: trustee@nashville.gov

Metropolitan Nashville Public Schools

2601 Bransford Avenue, Nashville, TN 37204
Tel: (615) 259-4636 Internet: www.mnps.org

Director of Schools (Interim) **Chris Henson** .... (615) 259-4636
Note: Until June 30, 2016
Director of Schools **Shawn Joseph** .... (615) 259-4636
Note: Effective July 1, 2016
Leadership and Learning Executive Officer, Elementary
Vanessa Garcia .... (615) 259-4636
Leadership and Learning Chief Academic Officer,
Middle/High School **(Vacant)** .... (615) 259-4636
Chief Financial Officer **Chris Henson** .... (615) 259-4636
Technology Information Services Executive Director
Mike Law .... (615) 259-4636
Chief Human Capital Officer **Susan Thompson** .... (615) 259-4636
E-mail: susan.thompson@mnps.org
Support Services Assistant Superintendent
Tony R. Majors .... (615) 259-4636
Chief Communications Officer **Janel Lacy** .... (615) 259-4636
E-mail: janel.lacy@mnps.org

Town and City of New Haven, Connecticut

City Hall, 165 Church St., New Haven, CT 06510
Tel: (203) 946-8200 (Information) Internet: www.cityofnewhaven.com

County: New Haven **Election Type:** Partisan **Year Incorporated:** 1784
Population: 130,322 (2015) **Employees:** 1,821 **Fiscal Year:** 2016
Budget: $652,823,000

Office of the Mayor

City Hall, 165 Church St., New Haven, CT 06510
Fax: (203) 946-7683 E-mail: nhinfo@newhavenct.gov

Employees: 12 **Fiscal Year:** 2016 **Budget:** $1,169,000

★ Mayor **Toni Nathaniel Harp** (D) .... (203) 946-7802
Began Service: January 2014
Term Expires: December 31, 2017
E-mail: mayorharp@newhavenct.gov
Education: Roosevelt BA; Yale MEVD
Chief of Staff **Tomas Reyes** .... (203) 946-7672
Deputy Chief of Staff **Patricia A. Lawlor** .... (203) 946-7802
Fax: (203) 946-2998
Public Information Officer and Director of
Communications **Laurence Grotheer** .... (203) 946-7660
Fax: (203) 946-4866
■ Legislative Liaison **Joseph "Joe" Rodriguez** (D) .... (203) 946-7671
E-mail: jrodriguez@newhavenct.gov Fax: (203) 946-5704

Office of the Chief Administrative Officer

City Hall, 165 Church St., New Haven, CT 06510

Employees: 12 **Fiscal Year:** 2016 **Budget:** $2,466,000

Chief Administrative Officer **Michael Carter** .... (203) 946-7900
E-mail: mcarter@newhavenct.gov

Office of the City Assessor

City Hall, 165 Church St., New Haven, CT 06510

Employees: 12 **Fiscal Year:** 2016 **Budget:** $783,000

■ Chief Assessor (Acting) **Alex Pullen** .... (203) 946-8057
E-mail: apullen@newhavenct.gov
Deputy Assessor **(Vacant)** .... (203) 946-8059

Engineering Department

200 Orange St., New Haven, CT 06510
Fax: (203) 946-8093

Employees: 8 **Fiscal Year:** 2016 **Budget:** $11,666,000

■ Director **Giovanni Zinn** .... (203) 946-6417
Financial Director **(Vacant)** .... (203) 946-6345
Chief Civil Engineer **Peter Lozis** .... (203) 946-8099
E-mail: plozis@newhavenct.gov
Chief Construction Engineer **Luigi DiMonaco** .... (203) 946-8103
E-mail: ldimonaco@gnhwpca.com
Senior Engineer, Records Section **(Vacant)** .... (203) 946-8097
Department Architect **(Vacant)** .... (203) 946-6798

Office of the Tax Collector

City Hall, 165 Church St., New Haven, CT 06510

Tax Collector **Maureen Villani** .... (203) 946-8054
E-mail: mvillani@newhavenct.gov

City Plan Department

City Hall, 165 Church St., New Haven, CT 06510
Fax: (203) 946-7815

Employees: 8 **Fiscal Year:** 2016 **Budget:** $1,811,000

■ Executive Director **Karyn Gilvarg** .... (203) 946-6380
E-mail: kgilvarg@newhavenct.gov
Education: Yale 1975 MAArch

★ Elected Official ▲ Appointed by Legislature ▼ Appointed by Governor ► Appointed by Board or Commission ● Appointed by Judge
■ Appointed by Mayor △ Appointed by Freeholders ▽ Appointed by Supervisor ▷ Appointed by County Executive ○ Appointed by Council

Community Services Administration
City Hall, 165 Church St., New Haven, CT 06510

Employees: 13 **Fiscal Year:** 2016 **Budget:** $5,492,000

■ Director **Martha Okafor** .... (203) 946-7907
E-mail: mokafor@newhavenct.gov
Deputy Director **Ronald Manning** .... (203) 946-7155
E-mail: rmanning@newhavenct.gov

Corporation Counsel
City Hall, 165 Church St., New Haven, CT 06510
Fax: (203) 946-7908

Employees: 18 **Fiscal Year:** 2,051 **Budget:** $1,859,000

■ Corporation Counsel (Acting) **John Rose, Jr.** .... (203) 946-7958

Economic Development Administration
City Hall, 165 Church St., New Haven, CT 06510

Employees: 10 **Fiscal Year:** 2016 **Budget:** $8,275,000

■ Economic Development Administrator
Matthew Nemerson .... (203) 946-2366
E-mail: mnemerson@newhavenct.gov

Elderly Services Department
City Hall, 165 Church St., New Haven, CT 06510

Employees: 9 **Fiscal Year:** 2016 **Budget:** $815,000

Director **Migdalia Castro** (D) .... (203) 946-7854

Emergency Management Department
200 Orange Street, New Haven, CT 06510

Deputy Director **Rick Fontana** .... (203) 946-8224
E-mail: rfontana@newhavenct.gov

Finance Department
200 Orange St., New Haven, CT 06510
Fax: (203) 946-7244

Employees: 46 **Fiscal Year:** 2016 **Budget:** $9,988,000

■ Controller **Daryl Jones** .... (203) 946-8360
E-mail: djones@newhavenct.gov
Treasurer **(Vacant)** .... (203) 946-6700

Purchasing Department
200 Orange Street, New Haven, CT 06510
Fax: (203) 946-8206

■ Purchasing Agent **Michael Fumiatti** .... (203) 946-8202
E-mail: mfumiatt@newhavenct.gov

Fire Department
952 Grand Ave., New Haven, CT 06510
P.O. Box 374, New Haven, CT 06502-0374

Employees: 366 **Fiscal Year:** 2016 **Budget:** $32,651,000

■ Fire Chief (Acting) **Ralph Black** .... (203) 946-6300
E-mail: rblack@newhavenct.gov
Assistant Fire Chief, Operations **Matt Marcarelli** .... (203) 946-6300
Fire Marshal **Robert Doyle** .... (203) 946-6300

Health Department
54 Meadow Street, New Haven, CT 06510

Employees: 68 **Fiscal Year:** 2016 **Budget:** $11,740,000

■ Director **Dr. Bryan Kennedy** .... (203) 946-6999
E-mail: bkennedy@newhavenct.gov

Housing Authority
360 Orange St., New Haven, CT 06511

■ Executive Director **Dr. Karen DuBois-Walton** .. (203) 498-8800 ext. 1001
E-mail: kdwalton@hanh-ct.org

Department of Human Resources
165 Church St., New Haven, CT 06510

Director **Stephen Librandi** .... (203) 946-6767
E-mail: slibrandi@newhavenct.gov

Parks, Recreation and Trees
720 Edgewood Ave., New Haven, CT 06515
Fax: (203) 946-8024

Employees: 58 **Fiscal Year:** 2016 **Budget:** $8,870,000

■ Director **Rebecca Bombero** .... (203) 946-6027
E-mail: rbombero@newhavenct.gov

Police Department
One Union Ave., New Haven, CT 06519
Fax: (203) 946-7294

Employees: 554 **Fiscal Year:** 2016 **Budget:** $39,349,000

■ Police Chief **Dean M. Esserman** .... (203) 946-6333
E-mail: desserman@newhavenct.gov

New Haven Public Library
133 Elm St., New Haven, CT 06510

Employees: 45 **Fiscal Year:** 2016 **Budget:** $5,577,000

City Librarian **Martha Brogan** .... (203) 946-8139
Deputy Director **Cathy DeNigris** .... (203) 946-8124
E-mail: cdenigris@nhfpl.org

Public Works Department
34 Middletown Avenue, New Haven, CT 06515
Fax: (203) 946-7357

Employees: 114 **Fiscal Year:** 2016 **Budget:** $14,489,000

Director **Jeff Pescosolido** .... (203) 946-7700

Traffic and Parking Department
200 Orange St., New Haven, CT 06510
Fax: (203) 946-8074

Employees: 34 **Fiscal Year:** 2016 **Budget:** $6,519,000

Director **Douglas Hausladen** (D) .... (203) 946-8075

Parking Authority
50 Union Avenue, 4th Floor, New Haven, CT 06519

Executive Director (Acting) **Douglas Hausladen** (D) .... (203) 946-8932
Chief Financial Officer **Brian Seholm** .... (203) 946-5553

Weights and Measures Department
54 Meadow St., New Haven, CT 06510
Fax: (203) 946-7492

■ Director/Sealer **Kristen Bayer** .... (203) 946-8369
E-mail: kbayer@newhavenct.gov
Senior Inspector **(Vacant)** .... (203) 946-8369

Office of the Board of Aldermen
City Hall, 165 Church St., New Haven, CT 06510
Fax: (203) 946-7476

Employees: 10 **Fiscal Year:** 2016 **Budget:** $961,000

★ President **Tyisha Walker** (D-Ward 23) .... (203) 946-6483
Term Expires: December 31, 2017
E-mail: ward23@newhavenct.gov
★ Alderman **Sarah Eidelson** (D-Ward 1) .... (203) 946-6483
Term Expires: December 31, 2017
E-mail: ward1@newhavenct.gov
★ Alderman **Frank E. Douglass, Sr.** (D-Ward 2) .... (203) 946-6483
Term Expires: December 31, 2017
E-mail: ward2@newhavenct.gov

★ Elected Official ▲ Appointed by Legislature ▼ Appointed by Governor ▶ Appointed by Board or Commission ● Appointed by Judge
■ Appointed by Mayor △ Appointed by Freeholders ▽ Appointed by Supervisor ▷ Appointed by County Executive ○ Appointed by Council

Office of the Board of Aldermen *continued*

★ Alderman **Latrice E. James** (D-Ward 3) . . . . (203) 901-3602
Term Expires: December 31, 2017
E-mail: ward3@newhavenct.gov

★ Alderman **Evelyn Rodriguez** (D-Ward 4) . . . . (203) 946-6483
Term Expires: December 31, 2017
E-mail: ward4@newhavenct.gov

★ Alderman **Dave Reyes, Jr.** (D-Ward 5) . . . . (203) 789-0507
Term Expires: December 31, 2017
E-mail: ward5@newhavenct.gov

★ Alderman **Delores Colon** (D-Ward 6) . . . . (203) 946-6483
Term Expires: December 31, 2017
E-mail: ward6@newhavenct.gov

★ Alderman **Alberta Witherspoon** (D-Ward 7) . . . . (203) 946-6483
Term Expires: December 31, 2017
E-mail: ward7@newhavenct.gov

★ Alderman **Aaron Greenberg** (D-Ward 8) . . . . (203) 946-6483
Term Expires: December 31, 2017
E-mail: ward8@newhavenct.gov

★ Alderman **Jessica Holmes** (D-Ward 9) . . . . (203) 946-6483
Term Expires: December 31, 2017
E-mail: ward9@newhavenct.gov

★ Alderman **Anna Festa** (D-Ward 10) . . . . (203) 946-6483
Term Expires: December 31, 2017
E-mail: ward10@newhavenct.gov

★ Alderman **Barbara Constantinople** (D-Ward 11) . . . . (203) 946-6483
Term Expires: December 31, 2017
E-mail: ward11@newhavenct.gov

★ Alderman **Gerald Antunes** (D-Ward 12) . . . . (203) 946-6483
Term Expires: December 31, 2017
E-mail: ward12@newhavenct.gov

★ Alderman **Rosa Santana** (D-Ward 13) . . . . (203) 946-6483
Term Expires: December 31, 2017
E-mail: ward13@newhavenct.gov

★ Alderman **Santiago Berrios-Bones** (D-Ward 14) . . . . (203) 782-2264
Term Expires: December 31, 2017
E-mail: ward14@newhavenct.gov

★ Alderman **Ernie G. Santiago** (D-Ward 15) . . . . (203) 407-9365
Term Expires: December 31, 2017
E-mail: ward15@newhavenct.gov

★ Alderman **Jose L. Crespo** (D-Ward 16) . . . . (203) 450-4044
Term Expires: December 31, 2017
E-mail: ward16@newhavenct.gov

★ Alderman **Alphonse Paolillo, Jr.** (D-Ward 17) . . . . (203) 946-6483
Term Expires: December 31, 2017
E-mail: ward17@newhavenct.gov

★ Alderman **Salvatore E. DeCola** (D-Ward 18) . . . . (203) 946-6483
Term Expires: December 31, 2017
E-mail: ward18@newhavenct.gov

★ Alderman **Alfreda Edwards** (D-Ward 19) . . . . (203) 946-6483
Term Expires: December 31, 2017
E-mail: ward19@newhavenct.gov

★ Alderman **Delphine Clyburn** (D-Ward 20) . . . . (203) 946-6483
Term Expires: December 31, 2017
E-mail: ward20@newhavenct.gov

★ Alderman **Brenda Foskey-Cyrus** (D-Ward 21) . . . . (203) 946-6483
Term Expires: December 31, 2017
E-mail: ward21@newhavenct.gov

★ Alderman **Jeanette Morrison** (D-Ward 22) . . . . (203) 946-6483
Term Expires: December 31, 2017
E-mail: ward22@newhavenct.gov

★ Alderman **Evette Hamilton** (D-Ward 24) . . . . (203) 946-6483
Term Expires: December 31, 2017
E-mail: ward24@newhavenct.gov

★ Alderman **Adam Marchand** (D-Ward 25) . . . . (203) 946-6483
Term Expires: December 31, 2017
E-mail: ward25@newhavenct.gov

★ Alderman **Darryl Brackeen, Jr.** (D-Ward 26) . . . . (203) 946-6483
Term Expires: December 31, 2017
E-mail: ward26@newhavenct.gov

★ Alderman **Richard Furlow** (D-Ward 27) . . . . (203) 946-6483
Term Expires: December 31, 2017
E-mail: ward27@newhavenct.gov

Office of the Board of Aldermen *continued*

★ Alderman **Jill Lila Marks** (D-Ward 28) . . . . (203) 946-6483
Term Expires: December 31, 2017
E-mail: ward28@newhavenct.gov

★ Alderman **Brian Wingate** (D-Ward 29) . . . . (203) 946-6483
Term Expires: December 31, 2017
E-mail: ward29@newhavenct.gov

★ Alderman **Carlton Staggers** (D-Ward 30) . . . . (203) 946-6483
Term Expires: December 31, 2017
E-mail: ward30@newhavenct.gov

New Haven Public Schools [NHPS]

54 Gateway Center, New Haven, CT 06510

Superintendent of Schools **Garth Harries** . . . . (203) 946-8888
Associate Superintendent of Instruction **Imma Cannelli** . . (203) 946-7871

Office of the Registrar of Voters

200 Orange St., New Haven, CT 06510
Fax: (203) 946-6561

Employees: 6 **Fiscal Year:** 2016 **Budget:** $871,000

★ Democratic Registrar **Shannel Evans** . . . . (203) 946-8034
Term Expires: December 31, 2016
E-mail: sevans@newhavenct.gov

★ Republican Registrar **Delores M. Knight** . . . . (203) 946-8033
Term Expires: December 31, 2016
E-mail: dknight@newhavenct.gov

Office of the City Clerk

200 Orange St., New Haven, CT 06510

Employees: 6 **Fiscal Year:** 2016 **Budget:** $539,000

★ City Clerk **Michael B. Smart** (D) . . . . (203) 946-8344
Term Expires: December 31, 2017
E-mail: msmart@newhavenct.gov

Deputy City Clerk **Sally J. Brown** . . . . (203) 946-8344
E-mail: sbrown@newhavenct.gov

City of New Orleans and Orleans Parish, Louisiana

City Hall, 1300 Perdido Street, New Orleans, LA 70112
Internet: www.nola.gov

County: Orleans Parish **Election Type:** Partisan **Population:** 389,617 (2015)

Form of Municipal Government: City and parish governments are combined.

Office of the Mayor

City Hall, 1300 Perdido Street, 8W03, Suite 2E04,
New Orleans, LA 70112
Tel: (504) 658-4900 Fax: (504) 658-4938

★ Mayor **Mitchell J. "Mitch" Landrieu** (D) . . . . (504) 658-4900
Began Service: May 3, 2010
Term Expires: May 2, 2018
Education: Catholic U BA; Loyola U (New Orleans) 1985 JD

■ Deputy Mayor and Chief Administrative Officer
Andrew D. "Andy" Kopplin . . . . (504) 658-4900
Education: Rice 1988 BA; Harvard 1992 MPP

■ Deputy Mayor and Chief of Staff **Brooke Smith** . . . . (504) 658-4900

■ Deputy Mayor of External Affairs **Ryan Berni** . . . . (504) 658-4900

■ Deputy Mayor of City Initiatives **Judy Reese Morse** . . . . (504) 658-4900
Education: Loyola U (New Orleans) BA; American U MPA

■ Deputy Mayor for Public Safety **(Vacant)** . . . . (504) 658-4900

(continued on next page)

★ Elected Official ▲ Appointed by Legislature ▼ Appointed by Governor ▶ Appointed by Board or Commission ● Appointed by Judge
■ Appointed by Mayor △ Appointed by Freeholders ▽ Appointed by Supervisor ▷ Appointed by County Executive ○ Appointed by Council

Office of the Mayor *continued*

Press Secretary **Bradley Neal "Brad" Howard** (D) . . . . . . (504) 658-4945
Education: Hendrix 2006 BA; American U 2008 MAC
Chief Resilience Officer **Jeff Hebert** . . . . (504) 658-4900
Director of Federal Relations
Austin Z. "Zach" Butterworth . . . . (504) 658-4967
Date of Birth: October 14, 1982
Education: LSU 2005 BA; Loyola U (New Orleans) 2009 JD

Sewerage and Water Board of New Orleans

625 St. Joseph Street, Room 233, New Orleans, LA 70165
Fax: (504) 585-2448 Internet: http://www.swbno.org/

■ Executive Director **Cedric S. Grant** . . . . (504) 585-2212
E-mail: cgrant@swbno.org
Education: Xavier (LA) 1974 BS; New Orleans 1981 MS
Deputy Director **Robert Miller** . . . . (504) 585-2212
General Superintendent **Joseph Becker** . . . . (504) 585-2365
Deputy General Superintendent **(Vacant)** . . . . (504) 585-2365

Office of the Chief Administrative Officer

City Hall, 1300 Perdido St., Room 9E06, New Orleans, LA 70112
Tel: (504) 658-8600 Tel: (504) 658-8647

■ Chief Administrative Officer
Andrew D. "Andy" Kopplin . . . . (504) 658-8900
E-mail: akopplin@nola.gov Fax: (504) 658-8647
Education: Rice 1988 BA; Harvard 1992 MPP
Confidential Assistant **Joyce E. Christopher** . . . . (504) 658-8900
E-mail: jchristopher@nola.gov
■ Chief Economist **James Husserl** . . . . (504) 658-8602
E-mail: jhusserl@nola.gov

Budget, Operations and Planning Division

Fax: (504) 658-8648

Assistant Chief Administrative Officer **Cary Grant** . . . . (504) 658-8600
E-mail: cmgrant@nola.gov
Executive Secretary **(Vacant)** . . . . (504) 658-8600
Budget Administrator **Brian Firstley** . . . . (504) 658-8600
E-mail: bfirstley@nola.gov
Fleet Administrator **(Vacant)** . . . . (504) 658-8600
3800 Alvar St., New Orleans, LA 70126

Employee and Labor Relations Division

Fax: (504) 658-8648

Assistant Chief Administrative Officer
Courtney Bagneris . . . . (504) 658-8600
Special Projects Administrator **Rene Hollins** . . . . (504) 658-8600

New Orleans Museum of Art [NOMA]

City Park, One Collins Diboll Circle, New Orleans, LA 70124
P.O. Box 19123, New Orleans, LA 70179-0123
Tel: (504) 658-4100 Fax: (504) 658-4199 E-mail: webmaster@noma.org
Internet: www.noma.org

Year Founded: 1910

Administration

The Montine McDaniel Freeman Director
Susan M. Taylor . . . . (504) 658-4156
Education: Vassar; NYU 1986 MA
Executive Assistant **Colleen Cloke** . . . . (504) 658-4100
Director, Interpretation and Audience Engagement
Allison Reid . . . . (504) 658-4159
Accountant **Nancy Oberinger** . . . . (504) 658-4119
E-mail: noberinger@noma.org

New Orleans Council on Aging

2475 Canal St., Suite 400, New Orleans, LA 70119-0067
Fax: (504) 821-1222 E-mail: administration@nocoa.org
Internet: http://nocoa.org/

Executive Director **Howard L. Rodgers III** . . . . . . (504) 821-4121 ext. 145

New Orleans Aviation Board

Louis Armstrong New Orleans International Airport,
800 - 900 Airline Dr., Kenner, LA 70062
P.O. Box 20007, New Orleans, LA 70141
Tel: (504) 303-7800 Fax: (504) 463-1049 Internet: www.flymsy.com/

Chairwoman **Cheryl Teamer** . . . . (504) 303-7800
Vice Chairperson **Doug Thornton** . . . . (504) 303-7800
Director of Aviation **Iftikhar Ahmad** . . . . (504) 303-7800
Finance Deputy Director **Raymond Anderson** . . . . (504) 303-7800
Operations Deputy Director **Walter Krygowski** . . . . (504) 303-7800
E-mail: wkrygowski@nola.gov
Planning Development Deputy Director
Walter Krygowski . . . . (504) 303-7800
Procurement Deputy Director (Acting) **Michelle Wilcut** . . (504) 303-7800
E-mail: mwilcut@nola.gov
Chief Customer Service Officer **Michelle Wilcut** . . . . (504) 303-7800
E-mail: mwilcut@nola.gov

City Civil Service Department

City Hall, 1300 Perdido Street, Room 7W03, New Orleans, LA 70112
Tel: (504) 658-3500 Fax: (504) 658-3598

Personnel Director **Lisa Hudson** . . . . (504) 658-3504
E-mail: lmhudson@nola.gov
Education: Loyola U (New Orleans) 1994 MBA
Deputy Personnel Director **Amy Trepagnier** . . . . (504) 658-3532
E-mail: abtrepagnier@nola.gov
Education: Louisiana Tech U 2000 MA

City Civil Service Commission

○ Chairman **Michelle Craig** . . . . (504) 658-3500
○ Member **Joseph S. Clark** . . . . (504) 658-3500
E-mail: jdavis@nola.gov
○ Member **Ronald P. McClain** . . . . (504) 658-3500
○ Member **Tania Tetlow** . . . . (504) 658-3500
Education: Tulane 1992 BA; Harvard 1995 JD
○ Member **Cordelia D. Tullous** . . . . (504) 658-3500

Classification and Compensation Division

Tel: (504) 658-3511

Personnel Administrator **Robert Hagmann** . . . . (504) 658-3520
E-mail: rhagmann@nola.gov
Education: New Orleans 1988 MPA
Personnel Administrator Assistant (Acting)
Samuel Stoute . . . . (504) 658-3515
E-mail: sstoute@nola.gov

Employee Growth and Development Division

Tel: (504) 658-3512

Personnel Administrator **Richard Carter** . . . . (504) 658-3520
E-mail: rcarter@nola.gov
Education: Western Kentucky 1984 MA

Management Services Division

Tel: (504) 658-3513

Personnel Administrator **Doddie Smith** . . . . (504) 658-3500
E-mail: dksmith@nola.gov
Education: Southern U (New Orleans) 1985 BS

Public and Employee Relations Division and Coordination of Substance Abuse Procedures

Tel: (504) 658-3514

Personnel Administrator **Tia Harrison** . . . . (504) 658-3543
Administrative Support Specialist **(Vacant)** . . . . (504) 658-3505

Recruitment and Selection Division

Tel: (504) 658-3516

Personnel Administrator **Shelly Stolp** . . . . (504) 658-3533
E-mail: sjstolp@nola.gov
Personnel Administrator Assistant **Anna Everette** . . . . (504) 658-3542
E-mail: aeeverette@nola.gov
Education: New Orleans 1993 MPA

★ Elected Official ▲ Appointed by Legislature ▼ Appointed by Governor ▶ Appointed by Board or Commission ● Appointed by Judge
■ Appointed by Mayor △ Appointed by Freeholders ▽ Appointed by Supervisor ▷ Appointed by County Executive ○ Appointed by Council

Test Development and Validation Division
Personnel Administrator **Richard Carter** . . . . (504) 658-3508
E-mail: rrcarter@nola.gov
Education: Western Kentucky 1984 MA

City Planning Commission
1300 Perdido Street, Room 7W03, New Orleans, LA 70112
Fax: (504) 658-7032

Chair **Kyle Wedberg** . . . . (504) 658-7033
Vice Chair **Kelly Brown** . . . . (504) 658-7033
Commissioner **Chris Allen** . . . . (504) 658-7033
Commissioner **Royce Duplessis** . . . . (504) 658-7033
Commissioner **Nolan Marshall III** . . . . (504) 658-7033
Commissioner **Craig Mitchell** . . . . (504) 658-7033
Commissioner **Alexandra Mora** . . . . (504) 658-7033
Commissioner **Robert Steeg** . . . . (504) 658-7033
Commissioner **(Vacant)** . . . . (504) 658-7033
Executive Director **Robert D. Rivers** . . . . (504) 658-7033
Assistant Director **Leslie T. Alley** . . . . (504) 658-7033
Director of Place-Based Planning **William A. Gilchrist** . . . (504) 658-7000
Education: MIT 1977 SB, 1982

Chief Financial Officer
City Hall, 1300 Perdido St., Room 3E06, New Orleans, LA 70112
Fax: (504) 658-1707

Chief Financial Officer **Norman Foster** . . . . (504) 658-1500
Deputy Director **Beverly B. Gariepy** . . . . (504) 658-1520

Accounting Bureau
Comptroller **Roy A. Guercio** . . . . (504) 658-1517
E-mail: raguerico@nola.gov
Assistant Comptroller **Kim T. DeLarge, Sr.** Room 3W03 . . (504) 658-1517
E-mail: kdelarge@nola.gov
Assistant Comptroller **Charlene S. Rollins** . . . . (504) 658-1517
E-mail: crollins@nola.gov

Purchasing Bureau
Chief Procurement Officer
Mary Kay Kleinpeter-Zamora . . . . (504) 658-1559
E-mail: mkzamora@nola.gov
Assistant Agent **Nathaniel Celestine** . . . . (504) 658-1550
E-mail: ncelestine@nola.gov

Revenue Bureau
Collector **Romy Samuel** . . . . (504) 658-1600
E-mail: rsamuel@nola.gov
Assistant Collector **Mailan Le** . . . . (504) 658-1600
E-mail: mle@nola.gov
Assistant Collector **Wendell McCall** . . . . (504) 658-1600
E-mail: wmccall@nola.gov

Treasury Bureau
Chief **Sharon B. McDonald** Room 1W37 . . . . (504) 658-1700
Assistant Chief **Julius M. Nunn** Room 1W37 . . . . (504) 658-1700

Health Department
City Hall, 1300 Perdido St., Room 8E18, New Orleans, LA 70112
Tel: (504) 658-2500 Fax: (504) 658-2520
Internet: http://www.nola.gov/health-department/

■ Director **Charlotte M. Parent** . . . . (504) 658-2527
E-mail: cparent@nola.gov
Emergency Medical Services **Dr. Jeff Elder** . . . . (504) 658-2650
Personnel Officer **Jovan Walker** . . . . (504) 658-2528
E-mail: jdbell@nola.gov

Office of Homeland Security and Emergency Preparedness
1300 Perdido Street, Room 9W03, New Orleans, LA 70112
Fax: (504) 658-8701

Director **Aaron Miller** . . . . (504) 658-8703
E-mail: almiller@nola.gov

Office of Homeland Security and Emergency Preparedness *continued*

Chief, Response and Interoperability **Collin Arnold** . . . . . . (504) 658-8729
E-mail: cmarnold@nola.gov
Chief, Planning and Preparedness **Dev Jani** . . . . (504) 658-8713
E-mail: ddjani@nola.gov

Fire Department
317 Decatur St., New Orleans, LA 70130
Fax: (504) 565-7848 Internet: ww.nola.gov/nofd

Superintendent and Fire Chief **Timothy McConnell** . . . . . (504) 658-4700
E-mail: tmcconnell@nola.gov
Deputy Superintendent of Administration
Elbert Thomas . . . . (504) 658-4700
E-mail: ethomas@nola.gov
Deputy Superintendent of Operations **Robert Eiserloh** . . . (504) 658-4700
E-mail: reiserloh@nola.gov
Deputy Superintendent of Planning **Roman Nelson** . . . . . (504) 658-4700
E-mail: rnelson@nola.gov

Mayor's Office of Criminal Justice Coordination
Fax: (504) 658-4066

Director **Charles West** . . . . (504) 658-4040

Police Department [NOPD]
715 South Broad Street, New Orleans, LA 70119
Tel: (504) 658-5757 Fax: (504) 658-5775
Internet: www.nola.gov/GOVERNMENT/NOPD/

■ Superintendent **Michael S. Harrison** . . . . (504) 658-5757
E-mail: nopdchief@nola.gov
Field Operations Bureau Deputy Superintendent
Paul Newell . . . . (504) 658-5740
Investigations and Support Bureau Deputy
Superintendent (Acting) **Rannie Mushatt** . . . . (504) 658-5300
E-mail: rmushatt@nola.gov
Management Services Bureau Deputy Chief
John Thomas . . . . (504) 658-5488
Public Integrity Division Deputy Chief
Arlinda Pierce Westbrook . . . . (504) 658-6800
Fax: (504) 658-6809
Deputy Superintendent **Timothy F. Averill** . . . . (504) 658-6800
Education: Loyola U (New Orleans) 1985 JD
Communications Director **Tyler Gamble** . . . . (504) 658-5858
E-mail: nopdpio@nola.gov

Office of Community Development
1340 Poydras Street, Suite 1000, New Orleans, LA 70112-1210
Tel: (504) 658-4200 Fax: (504) 658-6238

■ Director **Ellen M. Lee** . . . . (504) 658-4200
■ Chief Operating Officer **(Vacant)** . . . . (504) 658-4200
Neighborhood Stabilization Deputy Director
Anthony Faciane . . . . (504) 658-4219
E-mail: amfaciane@nola.gov
Director of Housing Policy and Community
Development **(Vacant)** . . . . (504) 658-4260
Code Enforcement Director **(Vacant)** . . . . (504) 658-4301
Finance and Administration Support Director
Natasha Muse . . . . (504) 658-4200
E-mail: nfmuse@nola.gov
Neighborhood Services and Facilities Director
(Vacant) . . . . (504) 658-4213
Neighborhood Development Director **(Vacant)** . . . . (504) 658-4399
Construction Director **Kerry Romain** . . . . (504) 658-4350
E-mail: kromain@nola.gov
Canal Street Development Corporation Director
Cindy Connick . . . . (504) 658-4200
E-mail: cmconnick@nola.gov
Disadvantaged Business Enterprise Office Director
(Vacant) . . . . (504) 658-4200
■ Economic Development Director **(Vacant)** . . . . (504) 658-4249
Business Retention and Expansion Manager
Ernest Gethers . . . . (504) 658-4200
E-mail: egethers@nola.gov

(continued on next page)

★ Elected Official ▲ Appointed by Legislature ▼ Appointed by Governor ▶ Appointed by Board or Commission ● Appointed by Judge
■ Appointed by Mayor △ Appointed by Freeholders ▽ Appointed by Supervisor ▷ Appointed by County Executive ○ Appointed by Council

Office of Community Development *continued*

Piazza d'Italia Corporation Director **Cindy Connick** ..... (504) 658-4200
E-mail: cmconnick@nola.gov
Rivergate Corporation Director **Cindy Connick** .... (504) 658-4207
E-mail: cmconnick@nola.gov
Environmental Affairs Director **(Vacant)** .... (504) 658-4200
New Orleans Building Corporation Director **(Vacant)** .... (504) 593-9494
Workforce Development Director **(Vacant)** .... (504) 658-4200

French Market Corporation

1008 N. Peter St., New Orleans, LA 70116
Fax: (504) 596-3419 Internet: www.frenchmarket.org

Executive Director **Jon Smith** .... (504) 522-2621
E-mail: jsmith@nola.gov
Maintenance Superintendent **Ngai Smith** .... (504) 522-2621

Historic District Landmarks Commission

1340 Poydras Street, Suite 1152, New Orleans, LA 70112
Fax: (504) 658-3802

Director **C. Elliot Perkins** .... (504) 658-7040
Deputy Director **Eleanor Burke** .... (504) 658-7041
Building Inspector II (Uptown) **Eldon S. Huner, Jr.** .... (504) 658-7040
Building Inspector (Downtown) **(Vacant)** .... (504) 658-7040
Building Plans Examiner **Bryan Block** .... (504) 658-7048
Building Plans Examiner **Kathryn Falwell** .... (504) 658-7050
Building Plans Examiner **Jessica Stevenson** .... (504) 658-7047
Architectural Historian **Lilly Haggerty** .... (504) 658-7049
Architectural Historian **Tracy St. Julien** .... (504) 658-7042

Department of Information Technology and Innovation

1300 Perdido Street, Suite 3E05, New Orleans, LA 70112
Tel: (504) 658-7800

Chief Information Officer **Lamar Gardere** .... (504) 658-7600
E-mail: lgardere@nola.gov

Department of Parks and Parkways

2829 Gentilly Blvd., New Orleans, LA 70122
Fax: (504) 658-3227 Internet: http://www.nola.gov/parks-and-parkways/

Director **Ann E. Macdonald** .... (504) 658-3200
Chief of Operations **Timothy Lavelle** .... (504) 658-3200
E-mail: tlavelle@nola.gov
Human Resources Director **Erdwin Fuentes** .... (504) 658-3200
E-mail: efuentes@nola.gov
Chief Landscape Architect **Haley Bowen** .... (504) 658-3200
Chief Urban Forester **Robert Richards** .... (504) 658-3200

New Orleans Public Library

219 Loyola Ave., New Orleans, LA 70112
Fax: (504) 596-2609 Internet: www.neworleanspubliclibrary.org

Director **Charles M. Brown** .... (504) 596-2600
E-mail: cbrown@neworleanspubliclibrary.org
Archivist **Christina Bryant** .... (504) 596-2610
E-mail: CBryant@neworleanspubliclibrary.org

Property Management Department

City Hall, 1300 Perdido St., Suite 5W08, New Orleans, LA 70112
Tel: (504) 658-3600 Fax: (504) 658-3648

■ Director **George A. Patterson** Room 5W08 .... (504) 658-3605
E-mail: gapatterson@nola.gov
■ Deputy Director **Edward F. Sens** Room 5W08 .... (504) 658-3606
E-mail: efsens@nola.gov
Director's Administrative Assistant
Adrienne Recasner .... (504) 658-3603
1300 Perdido Street, 5W08, New Orleans, LA 70112
E-mail: aarecasner@nola.gov
Operations Manager **Herman H. Hogues, Jr.**
Room 5W08 .... (504) 658-3604
E-mail: hhhogues@nola.gov

Property Management Department *continued*

Budget Coordinator **Deline Williams** Room 5W05 ...... (504) 658-3630
E-mail: dwilliams1@nola.gov
Personnel Manager **Soroya Flores** Room 5W04 .... (504) 658-3637
E-mail: sflores@nola.gov Fax: (504) 658-3642

Department of Public Works

City Hall, 1300 Perdido Street, Room 6W03, New Orleans, LA 70112
Fax: (504) 658-8007

■ Director **Lt. Col. Mark Jernigan** .... (504) 658-8000
E-mail: nphan@nola.gov
Education: Mississippi State 1991 BSCE; Missouri (Rolla) 1996 MSE
Traffic Management Principal Engineer **Allen Yrle** .... (504) 658-8040
E-mail: ayrle@nola.gov

Parking Division/Administrative Hearing Center (Parking Ticket Adjudication)

1300 Perdido Street, Room 2W89, New Orleans, LA 70112

Parking Administrator **Zepporiah Edmonds** .... (504) 658-8200
Administrative Hearing Center Administrator
Richard Boseman .... (504) 658-8250
E-mail: rboseman@nola.gov

Maintenance Division

838 S. Genois St., New Orleans, LA 70119

Maintenance Supervisor **Robert Craft** .... (504) 658-8150

New Orleans Recreation Development Commission [NORDC]

5420 Franklin Avenue, New Orleans, LA 70122
Tel: (504) 658-3052 Fax: (504) 658-3050 Internet: www.nordc.org

Chief Executive Officer **Victor N. Richard III** .... (504) 658-3052
Executive Assistant **Karla Rivera** .... (504) 658-3052
E-mail: kgrivera@nola.gov
Chief Operating Officer **Mary-jo Webster** .... (504) 658-3052
E-mail: mjwebster@nola.gov
Chief Program Officer **Shonnda Smith** .... (504) 658-3032
Recreation Centers Director **Shawn Wyatt** .... (504) 658-3052
E-mail: scwyatt@nola.gov
Director of Facilities **Jim Austin** .... (504) 658-3052
E-mail: jraustin@nola.gov
Athletics Director **Steve Martin** .... (504) 658-3052
Special Programs Director
Jahanna Cannon-Brightman .... (504) 658-3052
Management Services Director **Maya Wyche** .... (504) 658-3052

Safety and Permits Department

City Hall, 1300 Perdido Street, 7E07, New Orleans, LA 70112
Tel: (504) 658-7100 Fax: (504) 658-7208

■ Director of Safety and Permits **Jared Munster**
Room 7E07 .... (504) 658-7200
E-mail: jemunster@nola.gov
Chief Building Official **Zachary Smith** Room 7E07 ..... (504) 658-7114
Building Official **Larry Chan** Room 7E05 .... (504) 658-7100
■ Building Standards and Appeals Board
Angela Mitchell Room 7E05 .... (504) 658-7200
E-mail: amitchell@nola.gov
Management Services Supervisor
Charles Goldsborough Room 7E07 .... (504) 658-7200
E-mail: okeen@nola.gov
Assistant Chief Building Inspector **Terry Willis**
Room 7E05 .... (504) 658-7130
Chief Electrical Inspector **Charles Collins** Room 7E05 ... (504) 658-7145
Chief Mechanical Inspector **Rudy Hardouin**
Room 7E05 .... (504) 658-7153
Zoning Administrator **Edward Horan** Room 7E05 .... (504) 658-7125

★ Elected Official ▲ Appointed by Legislature ▼ Appointed by Governor ▶ Appointed by Board or Commission ● Appointed by Judge
■ Appointed by Mayor △ Appointed by Freeholders ▽ Appointed by Supervisor ▷ Appointed by County Executive ○ Appointed by Council

Department of Sanitation
1300 Perdido Street, Suite 1-W03, New Orleans, LA 70112
Fax: (504) 658-3801

Director **Cynthia M. Sylvain-Lear** .... (504) 658-3800
Deputy Director **Matt Torri** .... (504) 658-3800

Office of the City Council
City Hall, 1300 Perdido St., 2nd Floor, New Orleans, LA 70112
Internet: www.nolacitycouncil.com/

★ President **Jason Rogers Williams** (D-At-Large) .... (504) 658-1070
Term Expires: May 2018 Fax: (504) 658-1077
E-mail: jasonwilliams@nola.gov

★ Vice President **Stacy S. Head** (D-At-Large) .... (504) 658-1020
Term Expires: May 2, 2018 Fax: (504) 658-1025
E-mail: shead@nola.gov

★ Council Member **Susan G. Guidry** (D-District A) .... (504) 658-1010
Term Expires: May 2, 2018 Fax: (504) 658-1016
E-mail: sgguidry@nola.gov

★ Council Member **LaToya Cantrell** (D-District B) .... (504) 658-1020
Term Expires: May 2018 Fax: (504) 658-1025
E-mail: lcantrell@nola.gov

★ Council Member **Nadine Ramsey** (D-District C) .... (504) 658-1030
Term Expires: May 2018 Fax: (504) 658-1037
E-mail: districtc@nola.gov

★ Council Member **Jared C. Brossett** (D-District D) ...... (504) 658-1040
Term Expires: May 2, 2018 Fax: (504) 658-1048
E-mail: jcbossart@nola.gov
Education: Xavier (LA) 2004 BS

★ Council Member **James Austin Gray II** (D-District E) ... (504) 658-1050
Term Expires: May 2, 2018 Fax: (504) 658-1058
E-mail: jagray@nola.gov

Clerk of Council **Lora W. Johnson** Room 1E09 .... (504) 658-1117
Assistant Clerk of Council **Sharon Temple** Room 1E09 .. (504) 658-1085
○ Council Chief of Staff **Evelyn F. Pugh** Room 1E06 ...... (504) 658-1080
E-mail: efpugh@nola.gov

City Attorney's Office
City Hall, 1300 Perdido St., Suite 5E03, New Orleans, LA 70112-2125
Tel: (504) 658-9800 Fax: (504) 658-9868

■ City Attorney **Rebecca H. Dietz** .... (504) 658-9800
Paralegal and Executive Administrator **Sybil Lanzetta** .. (504) 658-9800
E-mail: shlanzetta@nola.gov
Chief Deputy City Attorney, Litigation
Cherrell R. Simms .... (504) 658-9800
Education: Loyola U (New Orleans) 1998 BA, 2002 JD
Chief Deputy City Attorney, Traffic and Municipal
Charlene Larche Mason .... (504) 658-8550

Office of the Assessor
City Hall, 1300 Perdido St., Room 4E01, New Orleans, LA 70112
Tel: (504) 658-1300 Fax: (504) 658-1303
Internet: http://nolaassessor.com/

Assessor **Erroll G. Williams** (D) .... (504) 658-1330
E-mail: ewilliams@nola.gov
Payroll/Human Resources Manager **Reba T. Johnson** .... (504) 658-1300
E-mail: rtjohnson@orleansassessors.com
Administrative Director **Marina M. Kahn** .... (504) 658-1300
E-mail: mkahn@nola.gov

Office of the Coroner
3001 Earhart Boulevard, New Orleans, LA 70125
Fax: (504) 658-9674

★ Coroner **Jeffrey Rouse** (D) .... (504) 658-9660
Term Expires: May 2018
E-mail: jrouse@nola.gov

Office of the District Attorney
619 South White Street, New Orleans, LA 70119

★ District Attorney **Leon A. Cannizzaro, Jr.** .... (504) 822-2414
Term Expires: January 15, 2021
E-mail: emurphy@orleansda.com
Education: New Orleans 1975 BA; Loyola U (New Orleans) 1978 JD
First Assistant District Attorney **Graymond Martin** ...... (504) 822-2414

Office of the Inspector General
525 St. Charles Avenue, New Orleans, LA 70130
Internet: www.nolaoig.org/main/ Fax: (504) 681-3230
E-mail: info@nolaoig.org

Inspector General **Edouard Quatrevaux** .... (504) 681-3200

Office of the Registrar of Voters
City Hall, 1300 Perdido St., Room 1W23, New Orleans, LA 70112-2127
Fax: (504) 658-8316

Registrar **Sandra L. Wilson** .... (504) 658-8300

Office of the Sheriff
819 South Broad Street, New Orleans, LA 70119
Fax: (504) 826-7037

★ Sheriff **Marlin N. Gusman** (D) .... (504) 826-7034
Term Expires: May 2, 2018
E-mail: mngusman@opso.us

Housing Authority of New Orleans [HANO]
4100 Touro Street, New Orleans, LA 70122
Tel: (504) 670-3300 TTY: (504) 552-4108 Fax: (504) 286-8788
Internet: www.hano.org

Executive Director **Gregg Fortner** .... (504) 670-3269
Education: Louisiana (Monroe) 1980 BA Fax: (504) 286-8788
Asset Management Director **Maggie Merrill** .... (504) 670-3390
Fax: (504) 286-1422
Senior Human Resources Generalist/Human Resources
Manager **Kelly Walker** .... (504) 670-3368
E-mail: kwalker@hano.org
General Counsel **Robert Barbor** .... (504) 670-3393
Fax: (504) 286-8786
Chief Financial Officer **Olukayode Adetayo** .... (504) 670-3282
Procurement and Contracts Director **Audrey Plessy** ...... (504) 670-3445
E-mail: aplessy@hano.org Fax: (504) 286-8224
Director of Information Technology **Allan Rivera** .... (504) 670-3415
E-mail: arivera@hano.org Fax: (504) 286-0693
Section 8 Housing Choice Voucher Program Director
Arthur N. Waller .... (504) 670-3335
Fax: (504) 286-8229

New Orleans Redevelopment Authority
1409 Oretha Castle Haley Boulevard, New Orleans, LA 70113
Fax: (504) 658-4551

■ Executive Director **Jeff Hebert** .... (504) 658-4400
E-mail: jhebert@nola.gov

★ Elected Official ▲ Appointed by Legislature ▼ Appointed by Governor ▶ Appointed by Board or Commission ● Appointed by Judge
■ Appointed by Mayor △ Appointed by Freeholders ▽ Appointed by Supervisor ▷ Appointed by County Executive ○ Appointed by Council

CITIES AND TOWNS

City of New York, New York

City Hall, New York, NY 10007
Tel: (212) 788-3000 (Information) Internet: www.nyc.gov

County: Bronx; Kings; New York; Queens; Richmond
Election Type: Partisan **Year Founded:** 1625 **Charter:** 1989
Population: 8,550,405 (2015)

Bill de Blasio (D)
Mayor

Began Service: January 1, 2014
Term Expires: December 31, 2017
Education: NYU BA; Columbia 1987 MA

Office of the Mayor

City Hall, New York, NY 10007
Fax: (212) 788-2460

★Mayor **Bill de Blasio** (D) . . . . (212) 788-3000
■Chief of Staff **Thomas Snyder** . . . . (212) 788-3000
Education: Michigan BA
Deputy Chief of Staff **Amanda Howe** . . . . (212) 788-3000
Deputy Chief of Staff **Andrea Zuniga** . . . . (212) 788-3000
First Deputy Mayor **Anthony Shorris** . . . . (212) 788-3000
E-mail: ashorris@cityhall.nyc.gov
Education: Harvard; Princeton
Chief of Staff to First Deputy Mayor
Dominic Williams . . . . (212) 788-3000
Deputy Mayor for Health and Human Services
Dr. Herminia Palacio . . . . (212) 788-3000
Education: Barnard 1983; Mount Sinai Medicine MD; UC Berkeley MPH
Deputy Mayor for Housing and Economic Development
Alicia Glen . . . . (212) 788-3000
E-mail: aglen@cityhall.nyc.gov
Deputy Mayor for Strategic Policy Initiatives
Richard R. Buery, Jr. . . . . (212) 788-3000
E-mail: rbuery@cityhall.nyc.gov
Education: Harvard BA; Yale JD
Senior Policy Advisor **Mike Nolan** . . . . (212) 788-3000
Director of Intergovernmental Affairs **Emma Wolfe** . . . . (212) 788-3000
E-mail: ewolfe@cityhall.nyc.gov
Budget Director **Dean Fuleihan** . . . . (212) 788-3000
E-mail: dfuleihan@omb.nyc.gov
Senior Advisor for Strategic Planning **Phillip Walzak** . . . . (212) 788-3000
Senior Advisor and Director of Office of Strategic Partnerships **Gabrielle Fialkoff** . . . . (212) 788-3000
Press Secretary **Karen Hinton** . . . . (212) 788-2958
Note: Resigning June 2016
Communications Director **Andrea Hagelgans** . . . . (212) 788-2958
Education: Franklin & Marshall BA; Columbia MA
■Deputy Director of Communications for Special Projects **Eric Phillips** . . . . (212) 788-2958
Education: Wisconsin BA; Northwestern
Deputy Communications Director **Marti Adams** . . . . (212) 788-2958
E-mail: madams@cityhall.nyc.gov
■Chief Speechwriter **Kate Blumm** . . . . (212) 788-3000
Education: NYU BA
■First Deputy Speechwriter **Kevin Bleyer** . . . . (212) 788-2958
Communications Advisor **Amy Spitalnick** . . . . (212) 788-2958
Communications Advisor **Erin White** . . . . (212) 788-3000
Director of Operations **Angela Banks** . . . . (212) 788-2958
E-mail: abanks@cityhall.nyc.gov
First Deputy Press Secretary **Austin Finan** . . . . (212) 788-2958
Education: Hamilton BA

Office of the Mayor *continued*

Deputy Press Secretary **Aja Worthy-Davis** . . . . (212) 788-2958
Education: Pace BA
Deputy Press Secretary for Public Safety and Criminal Justice **Monica Klein** . . . . (212) 788-2958
Assistant Press Secretary **Raul A. Contreras** . . . . (212) 788-2958
Director of Social Media and Digital Engagement
Scott Kleinberg . . . . (212) 788-2958
Director of Latino Media **Jessica Ramos** . . . . (212) 788-3000
Counsel to the Mayor **Maya Wiley** . . . . (212) 788-3000
Senior Advisor to the Mayor for Recovery, Resiliency, and Infrastructure **Bill Goldstein** . . . . (212) 788-3000
Senior Community Liaison **Pinny Ringel** . . . . (212) 788-3000
Director of Scheduling **Prisca Salazar-Rodriguez** . . . . (212) 788-3000
Chief Digital Officer **Jessica Singleton** . . . . (212) 788-3000
Deputy Director of Communications for Planning
Dan Gross . . . . (212) 788-3000
Director of Creative Communications **Rob Bennett** . . . . (212) 788-3000

Administrative Services, Facilities and Construction Management

City Hall, New York, NY 10007
Tel: (212) 788-2495

Facility Construction Management and Operations Executive Director **Catherine Drum** . . . . (212) 788-7435
E-mail: cdrum@cityhall.nyc.gov
Managing Director and Fiscal Operations Director
David Sheehan . . . . (212) 788-2463
Management Information Systems Director
Sal Giallanza . . . . (212) 788-0251
E-mail: sgiallanza@cityhall.nyc.gov
Payroll/Timekeeping Director **Carmelo Goiricelaya** . . . . (212) 788-2423
E-mail: cgoiricelaya@cityhall.nyc.gov
Human Resources Director **Bruce McDougald** . . . . (212) 788-2650
E-mail: bmcdougald@cityhall.nyc.gov
Senior Advisor for Correspondence **Jody Kaplan** . . . . (212) 788-2876
E-mail: jkaplan@cityhall.nyc.gov
Education: Maryland 1996 BA; Johns Hopkins 2001 MA

Intergovernment Affairs

Mayor's Office of Intergovernmental Affairs [MOIGA]

City Hall, New York, NY 10038
Internet: http://www.nyc.gov/html/moiga/home.html

Director **Emma Wolfe** . . . . (212) 788-2162
Chief of Staff **Regina Schwartz** . . . . (212) 341-2136
City Legislative Affairs Office Director **Jon Paul Lupo** . . . . (212) 788-2971
253 Broadway, 14th Floor, New York, NY 10007
E-mail: jlupo@cityhall.nyc.gov
■Federal Legislative Affairs Director
Maximiliano "Max" Sevillia . . . . (202) 624-5900
1301 Pennsylvania Avenue, NW, Suite 350, Washington, DC 20004 Fax: (202) 624-5926
E-mail: msevillia@cityhall.nyc.gov
Education: Florida International 1999 BA; Georgetown 2001 JD
■Senior Legislative Advisor **Georgia B. Gann** . . . . (202) 624-5912
1301 Pennsylvania Avenue, NW, Washington, DC 20004 Fax: (202) 624-5926
E-mail: ggann@cityhall.nyc.gov
■State Legislative Affairs Director **Sherif Soliman** . . . . (518) 447-5200
119 Washington Ave., Albany, NY 12210 Fax: (518) 462-5870
E-mail: ssoliman@cityhall.nyc.gov
■General Counsel **Joni Kletter** . . . . (212) 788-2162

Board of Elections

32 Broadway, 7th Floor, New York, NY 10004-1609
Internet: http://vote.nyc.ny.us/

○President **Bianka Perez** . . . . (212) 487-5300
E-mail: webmail_PerezB@boe.nyc.ny.us
○Secretary **Frederic M. Umane** . . . . (212) 487-5300
E-mail: webmail_UmaneF@boe.nyc.ny.us
○Commissioner **Jose Miguel Araujo** . . . . (212) 487-5300
E-mail: webmail_AraujoJ@boe.nyc.ny.us

★Elected Official ▲Appointed by Legislature ▼Appointed by Governor ►Appointed by Board or Commission ●Appointed by Judge
■Appointed by Mayor △Appointed by Freeholders ▽Appointed by Supervisor ▷Appointed by County Executive ○Appointed by Council

Board of Elections *continued*

○ Commissioner **John Flateau** . . . . (212) 487-5300
E-mail: webmail_JFlateau@boe.nyc.ny.us
○ Commissioner **Maria R. Guastella** . . . . (212) 487-5300
E-mail: webmail_GuastellaM@boe.nyc.ny.us
○ Commissioner **Michael Michel** . . . . (212) 487-5300
E-mail: webmail_MichelM@boe.nyc.ny.us
○ Commissioner **Michael A. Rendino** . . . . (212) 487-5300
E-mail: webmail_RendinoM@boe.nyc.ny.us
○ Commissioner **Alan Schulkin** . . . . (212) 487-5300
E-mail: webmail_SchulkinA@boe.nyc.ny.us
○ Commissioner **Simon Shamoun** . . . . (212) 487-5300
E-mail: WEBMAIL_ShamounS@boe.nyc.ny.us

Executive Office
Tel: (212) 487-5300 Tel: (866) 868-3692 (Voter Information Call Center)
Fax: (212) 487-5349

Executive Director **Michael Ryan** . . . . (212) 487-5412
Deputy Executive Director **Dawn Sandow** . . . . (212) 487-5409
Administrative Manager **Pamela Green Perkins** . . . . (212) 487-5406
Operations Manager **Georgea Kontzamanis** . . . . (212) 487-5300
E-mail: webmail_KontzamanisG@boe.nyc.ny.us
General Counsel **Steven H. Richman** . . . . (212) 487-5338
Communications and Public Affairs Director
Valerie Vazquez . . . . (212) 487-5404
E-mail: webmail_vazquezv@boe.nyc.ny.us

Mayor's Office of Media and Entertainment [MOME]
1697 Broadway, New York, NY 10019

■ Commissioner **Julie Menin** . . . . (212) 489-6710
Education: Columbia BA
Deputy Commissioner **Luis Castro** . . . . (212) 489-6710

Mayor's Office of Pensions and Investments
City Hall, New York, NY 10007

■ Director and Chief Pension Investment Advisor
John Adler . . . . (212) 788-3000
E-mail: jadler@council.nyc.gov

Mayor's Fund to Advance New York City
253 Broadway, 6th Floor, New York, NY 10007
Tel: (212) 788-7794 Fax: (212) 312-0930 E-mail: fund@cityhall.nyc.gov
Internet: http://www1.nyc.gov/site/fund/index.page

Executive Director **Darren Bloch** . . . . (212) 788-7794
Special Assistant to the Executive Director
Gloria Noel . . . . (212) 788-7794
Deputy Executive Director **Kevin Cummings** . . . . (212) 788-7794
Director of Finance and Operations **Maya Jakubowicz** . . . (212) 788-7794
Education: UC Santa Barbara BA
Director of Development **Joy Shigaki** . . . . (212) 788-7794
Director of Programs and Policy **Toya Williford** . . . . (212) 788-7794
Programs and Policy Manager **Anna Gorman** . . . . (212) 788-7794
Programs and Policy Associate **Ifran Ahmed** . . . . (212) 788-7794
Programs and Policy Associate **Sarah Batchu** . . . . (212) 788-7794
Communications Manager **Liz DeBold** . . . . (212) 788-7794
Education: NYU BA
Assistant Press Secretary **Rosemary Boeglin** . . . . (212) 788-7794

Board of Directors
■ Chairwoman **Chirlane McCray** . . . . (212) 788-3000
Chief of Staff to the First Lady **Roxanne John** . . . . (212) 788-3000
Deputy Chief of Staff to the First Lady
Jacqueline "Jackie" Bray . . . . (212) 788-3000
E-mail: jbray@cityhall.nyc.gov
■ Vice Chair **Gabrielle Fialkoff** . . . . (212) 788-7794
■ Board Member **Henry Berger** . . . . (212) 788-7794
■ Board Member **Richard R. Buery, Jr.** . . . . (212) 788-7794
Education: Harvard BA; Yale JD
■ Board Member **Maya Wiley** . . . . (212) 788-7794
■ Board Member **(Vacant)** . . . . (212) 788-7794

Mayor's Community Affairs Unit
253 Broadway, 14th Floor, New York, NY 10007
Fax: (212) 788-7754 Internet: http://www.nyc.gov/html/cau

■ Commissioner **Marco Carrión** . . . . (212) 788-7418
E-mail: mcarrion@cityhall.nyc.gov
Assistant Commissioner **(Vacant)** . . . . (212) 788-7418
Chief of Staff **Arelis Hernandez Cruz** . . . . (212) 788-7418
Assistant Commissioner, Operations **David Schmid** . . . . . . (212) 788-7418
E-mail: dschmid@cityhall.nyc.gov
Manhattan Director **Alize Beal** . . . . (212) 788-7754
E-mail: abeal@cityhall.nyc.gov
■ Senior Advisor **Sarah Sayeed** . . . . (212) 788-7418
■ Senior Community Liaison **Jonathan Soto** . . . . (212) 788-7418
Education: Fordham BA

Mayor's Office of Housing Recovery Operations [HRO]
City Hall, New York, NY 10007

■ Director **Amy Peterson** . . . . (212) 615-8329
E-mail: apeterson@cityhall.nyc.gov
Education: Bucknell 1987 BS; NYU 1996 MA

Office of Recovery and Resiliency [ORR]
City Hall, New York, NY 10007

■ Director **Daniel Zarrilli** . . . . (212) 788-3000
E-mail: dzarrilli@council.nyc.gov
Education: Lehigh BSCE; MIT MS

New York City Children's Cabinet
City Hall, New York, NY 10007

■ Executive Director **Benita Miller** . . . . (212) 788-3000

Mayor's Office of Sustainability [MOS]
253 Broadway, 7th Floor, New York, NY 10007
Fax: (212) 673-3290

■ Director **Nilda Mesa** . . . . (212) 788-9956
E-mail: nmesa@cityhall.nyc.gov

Department of Education
52 Chambers Street, New York, NY 10007
Fax: (212) 374-5588

■ Chancellor **Carmen Fariña** . . . . (212) 374-0200
E-mail: cgfarina@schools.nyc.gov
Chief of Staff **Ursulina Ramirez** . . . . (212) 374-0200
Senior Deputy Chancellor, Division of School Support
Dorita Gibson . . . . (212) 374-7858
Deputy Chancellor, English Language Learners and
Student Support **Milady Baez** . . . . (212) 374-5103
Fax: (212) 374-5588
Deputy Chancellor of Operations **Elizabeth Rose** . . . . (212) 374-0209
E-mail: erose@schools.nyc.gov
Deputy Chancellor for Specialized Instruction and
Student Support **Corrine Rello-Anselmi** . . . . (212) 374-5766
Deputy Chancellor of Strategy and Policy
Josh Wallack . . . . (212) 374-5406
Education: Yale BA; Harvard MBA Fax: (212) 374-5588
Deputy Chancellor for Teaching and Learning
Phil Weinberg . . . . (212) 374-6792
Senior Executive Director of Curriculum, Instruction
and Professional Development **Anna Commitante** . . . (212) 374-2337
E-mail: acommit@schools.nyc.gov
Chief Financial Officer **Raymond Orlando** . . . . (212) 374-1872
Chief Information Officer **Hal Friedlander** . . . . (718) 935-4500
E-mail: hfriedlander2@schools.nyc.gov
Chief Executive for Student Enrollment , Planning and
Operations **Robert Sanft** . . . . (212) 374-6702
E-mail: rsanft@schools.nyc.gov
Executive Superintendent for Family and Community
Engagement **Yolanda Torres** . . . . (212) 374-7629
E-mail: ytorres@schools.nyc.gov
Senior Advisor for Communications and External
Affairs **Maite Junco** . . . . (212) 374-3416
E-mail: mjunco@schools.nyc.gov

(continued on next page)

★ Elected Official ▲ Appointed by Legislature ▼ Appointed by Governor ▶ Appointed by Board or Commission ● Appointed by Judge
■ Appointed by Mayor △ Appointed by Freeholders ▽ Appointed by Supervisor ▷ Appointed by County Executive ○ Appointed by Council

Department of Education *continued*

Communications Director **JoAnne Wasserman** . . . . (212) 374-5141
E-mail: jwasserman7@schools.nyc.gov
Office of Intergovernmental Affairs Executive Director
Nnennaya Okezie . . . . (212) 374-4947
Office of Intergovernmental Affairs Deputy Director
Justin Brannan . . . . (212) 374-4947
State Government Relations Director **(Vacant)** . . . . (518) 449-2013
119 Washington Avenue, 1st Floor, Albany, NY 12210
Press Secretary **Devora Kaye** . . . . (212) 374-6469
E-mail: dkaye6@schools.nyc.gov
Education: Vanderbilt BA, MEd
General Counsel **(Vacant)** . . . . (212) 374-3440
The Fund for Public Schools Executive Director
(Interim) **Sarah Geisenheimer** . . . . (212) 374-7689
Office of Community Schools Executive Director
Christopher Caruso . . . . (212) 374-0326
Office of Field Support Senior Executive Director
Mariano Guzmán . . . . (212) 374-0876
Education: Manhattan Col BS, MS; Teachers Col Columbia U MA

Panel for Education Policy

Tweed Courthouse, 52 Chambers St.,, Room 314, New York, NY 10007
E-mail: panel@schools.nyc.gov

■ Chair **Vanessa Leung** . . . . (212) 374-0200
Member **Fred Baptiste** (Brooklyn) . . . . (212) 374-0200
Member **Isaac Carmignani** . . . . (212) 374-0200
■ Member **Elzora Cleveland** . . . . (212) 374-0200
Member **Deborah Dillingham** (Queens) . . . . (212) 374-0200
■ Member **Gary Linnen** . . . . (212) 374-0200
E-mail: GLinnen@schools.nyc.gov
Member **Kamillah Payne-Hanks** (Staten Island) . . . . (212) 374-0200
■ Member **Lori Podvesker** . . . . (212) 374-0200
■ Member **Benjamin "Ben" Shuldiner** . . . . (212) 374-0200
E-mail: BShuldiner@schools.nyc.gov
Education: Harvard; Baruch Col MSEd
Member **Laura Zingmond** (Manhattan) . . . . (212) 374-0200
■ Member **D. Miguelina Zorrilla-Aristy** . . . . (212) 374-0200
Member **(Vacant)** (Bronx) . . . . (212) 374-0200
Secretary **(Vacant)** . . . . (212) 374-3440

Police Department [NYPD]

One Police Plaza, New York, NY 10038
Tel: (646) 610-5000 Internet: www.nyc.gov/html/nypd/

■ Police Commissioner **William J. "Bill" Bratton** . . . . (646) 610-5410
Education: Boston State Col BS
First Deputy Commissioner **Benjamin B. Tucker** . . . . (646) 610-5420
Education: John Jay Col BS; Fordham 1981 JD
Chief of Department **James P. O'Neill** . . . . (646) 610-6710
Chief of Staff **Kevin Ward** . . . . (646) 610-5410
Deputy Commissioner of Administration
Cathleen S. Perez . . . . (646) 610-5000
Equal Employment Opportunity Deputy Commissioner
Neldra M. Zeigler . . . . (646) 610-5330
Deputy Commissioner of Intelligence and
Counterterrorism **John Jay Miller** . . . . (646) 610-5000
Director of Intelligence Analysis **Rebecca Weiner** . . . . . (646) 610-5403
E-mail: rebecca.weiner@nypd.org
Internal Affairs Deputy Commissioner **Joseph Reznick** . . (646) 610-6650
Deputy Commissioner for Legal Matters
Lawrence "Larry" Byrne . . . . (646) 610-5336
Education: Hofstra 1981 BA; NYU 1984 JD
Labor Relations Deputy Commissioner
John P. Beirne . . . . (646) 610-6100 ext. 5580
Management and Budget Deputy Commissioner
Vincent Grippo . . . . (646) 610-6670
E-mail: vincent.grippo@nypd.org
Personnel Deputy Commissioner **Michael Julian** . . . . (646) 610-6612
Public Information Deputy Commissioner
Stephen P. Davis . . . . (646) 610-6700
E-mail: stephen.davis@nypd.org Fax: (646) 610-8795

Police Department *continued*

Support Services Deputy Commissioner
Robert S. Martinez . . . . (646) 610-5763
Deputy Commissioner for Technological Development
Jessica Tisch . . . . (646) 610-6873
E-mail: jessica.tisch@nypd.org
Education: Harvard MBA
Trials Deputy Commissioner **Rosemarie Maldonaldo** . . . (646) 610-5424
Chief for Counterterrorism **James Waters** . . . . (646) 610-6169
E-mail: james.waters@nypd.org
Deputy Commissioner of Training **Tracie Keesee** . . . . (646) 610-5000
Detectives Bureau Chief **Robert Boyce** . . . . (646) 610-5430
Housing Bureau Chief **James Secreto** . . . . (646) 610-5548
Organized Crime Control Bureau Chief **Thomas Purtell** . . (646) 610-6741
Chief of Patrol **Carlos Gomez** . . . . (646) 610-5000
Chief of Transportation **Thomas Chan** . . . . (646) 610-5500
Transit Bureau Chief **Joseph Fox** . . . . (718) 694-4050
Community Affairs Bureau Chief **Joanne Jaffe** . . . . (646) 610-5323
E-mail: joanne.jaffe@nypd.org
Deputy Chief, Communications Division **Ruben Beltran** . . (646) 610-6873
E-mail: ruben.beltran@nypd.org
Inspector General **Philip Eure** . . . . (646) 610-5000

New York City Police Pension Fund

233 Broadway, 25th Floor, New York, NY 10279
Tel: (212) 693-5100

Executive Director **Kevin Holloran** . . . . (212) 693-5100

Office of the Actuary

75 Park Place, 9th Floor, New York, NY 10007
Tel: (212) 442-5775 Fax: (212) 442-5777
Internet: www.nyc.gov/html/actuary/html/home/home.shtml

■ Chief Actuary **Sherry Chan** . . . . (212) 442-5776
First Deputy Chief Actuary **Michael J. Samet** . . . . (212) 442-8098
Administration Director and Records Access Officer
Susan Flaschenberg . . . . (212) 442-5795
E-mail: sflaschenberg@actuary.nyc.gov

First Deputy Mayor

■ First Deputy Mayor **Anthony Shorris** . . . . (212) 788-2990
Education: Harvard; Princeton

Department of Buildings [DOB]

280 Broadway, 7th Floor, New York, NY 10007-1801
Fax: (212) 566-3784 TTY: (212) 566-4769
Internet: www.nyc.gov/buildings

■ Commissioner **Rick D. Chandler** . . . . (212) 393-2001
E-mail: rchandler@buildings.nyc.gov
Education: Nebraska 1984 BSCE; Columbia 1990 MSCE
Chief of Staff **Philip A. Monaco** . . . . (212) 566-4769
First Deputy Commissioner **Thomas Fariello** . . . . (212) 393-2002
Deputy Commissioner for Enforcement
Timothy E. Hogan . . . . (212) 393-2005
Education: St Anselm BS
Legal Affairs Deputy Commissioner **Alexandra Fisher** . . . (212) 393-2017
Deputy Commissioner of Strategic Policy and Planning
Archana Jayaram . . . . (212) 393-2173
E-mail: ajayaram@buildings.nyc.gov
Deputy Commissioner of Finance and Administration
Sharon Neill . . . . (212) 393-2210
E-mail: sneill@buildings.nyc.gov
Assistant Commissioner for External Affairs
Patrick Wehle . . . . (212) 393-2042
E-mail: pwehle@buildings.nyc.gov
General Counsel **Mona Sehgal** . . . . (212) 393-2017

Department of Citywide Administrative Services [DCAS]

Municipal Bldg., One Centre Street, 17th Floor, New York, NY 10007
Tel: (212) 669-7000 Fax: (212) 669-8992
Internet: http://www.nyc.gov/dcas

■ Commissioner **Lisette Camilo** . . . . (212) 386-0201

Department of Citywide Administrative Services *continued*

General Counsel **Suzanne Lynn** (212) 386-0253
E-mail: slynn@dcas.nyc.gov
Chief Citywide Diversity and Equal Employment Opportunity Officer **R. Fenimore Fisher** (212) 386-0221
E-mail: ffisher@dcas.nyc.gov
Chief Energy Management Officer **Ozgem Orneketon** (212) 386-0308
E-mail: oornektekin@ddc.nyc.gov
Asset Management Deputy Commissioner **Ricardo Elias Morales** (212) 386-0268
E-mail: rmorales@dcas.nyc.gov
Education: Amherst 1978 BA; Georgetown JD
Chief Fiscal and Management Officer **Richard Badillo** (212) 386-0212
Chief Purchasing and Reengineering Officer **Geneith Turnbull** (212) 386-0225
E-mail: gturnbull@comptroller.nyc.gov
Assistant Commissioner/ACCO **Robert Cleary** (212) 386-0400
E-mail: clearyr@ddc.nyc.gov
Assistant Commissioner, Bureau of Planning **Randal Fong** (212) 386-0618
Assistant Commissioner, Design and Construction Services **Lance Seibert** (212) 386-0240
E-mail: lseibert@dcas.nyc.gov
Assistant Commissioner, Acquisitions and Leasing **Christopher Nesterczuk** (212) 669-2620
Assistant Commissioner, Management Information Systems **Nitin Patel** (212) 386-6175
E-mail: npatel@dcas.nyc.gov
Deputy Commissioner, Intergovernmental Officer **Carmine Rivetti** (212) 386-6303
Education: Drew BA; Columbia
Associate Commissioner, Communications **Cathy Hanson** (212) 386-0238
Chief Human Capital Officer **Dawn Pinnock** (212) 386-6367
E-mail: dpinnocl@dcas.nyc.gov

Department of Correction

Bulova Corporate Center, 7520 Astoria Boulevard, East Elmhurst, NY 11370
Tel: (718) 546-0300 Fax: (718) 278-6410 Internet: www.nyc.gov/doc/

■ Commissioner of Correction **Joseph "Joe" Ponte** (718) 546-0890
E-mail: joseph.ponte@doc.nyc.gov
Executive Secretary to the Commissioner **Yvonne Newton** (718) 546-0897
E-mail: yvonne.newton@doc.nyc.gov
Chief of Staff **Jeff Thamkittikasem** (718) 546-0895
Education: Stanford 1998, 1998 MA; Columbia 2003 MPA
■ First Deputy Commissioner **Dina Simon** (718) 546-0300
E-mail: dina.simon@doc.nyc.gov
Chief of Department **Martin J. Murphy** (718) 546-1095
Deputy Warden in Command/Executive Assistant to First Deputy Commissioner **(Vacant)** (718) 546-0990
Deputy Commissioner, Adult Programming and Community Partnerships **James J. Walsh** (718) 546-0300
Deputy Commissioner, Budget Management and Planning **Frank J. Doka** (718) 546-0655
E-mail: frank.doka@doc.nyc.gov
Deputy Commissioner, Equal Employment Opportunity **Patricia Legoff** (718) 546-0865
Deputy Commissioner, Human Resources (Acting) **Claudette Wynter** (718) 546-3105
E-mail: claudette.wynter@doc.nyc.gov
Deputy Commissioner, Investigations **Michael Blake** (718) 546-0310
Deputy Commissioner, Operations **Dr. Errol Toulon, Jr.** (718) 546-0930
E-mail: errol.toulon@doc.nyc.gov
Education: Monroe Col BA; Dowling MBA, EdD
Deputy Commissioner, Program and Discharge Planning Services **Wynette Saunders-Halyard** (718) 546-0455
Deputy Commissioner, Public Information **Peter Thorne** (718) 546-0898
E-mail: peter.thorne@doc.nyc.gov
Deputy Commissioner, Quality Assurance and Integrity **Cynthia Brann** (718) 546-0300

Department of Correction *continued*

Assistant Commissioner, Environmental Health **Patricia Feeney** (718) 546-3090
Education: Union Col (NY) 1988 BS
Assistant Commissioner, Financial Management and Budget Administration **Patricia Lyons** (718) 546-0657
E-mail: patricia.lyons@doc.nyc.gov
Assistant Commissioner, Health Affairs/Forensic Services **Roderick Williams** (718) 546-8370
Assistant Commissioner, Program Administration and Discharge Planning **(Vacant)** (718) 546-0447
Executive Assistant Commissioner, Population, Analysis and Planning **(Vacant)** (718) 546-0450
General Counsel **Heidi Grossman** (718) 546-0955
Deputy General Counsel **Nadene Pinnock** (718) 546-0964
Deputy Chief of Department **(Vacant)** (718) 546-1900
Custody Management Assistant Chief **(Vacant)** (718) 546-1325
Administration Assistant Chief **(Vacant)** (718) 546-0830
Security Bureau Chief **Hazel Jennings** (718) 546-8000
1717 Hazen St., Elmhurst, NY 11367
Investigations Director **(Vacant)** (718) 546-0300
Agency Chief Contracting Assistant Commissioner **Ava B. Rice** (718) 546-0690
Press Secretary **Jack Ryan** (718) 546-0921
E-mail: jack.ryan@doc.nyc.gov
Warden/Correction Academy **Pennye L. Jones** (718) 546-0300
Executive Director, Application Investigation Unit **Dr. Larry Johnson** (718) 546-0300
E-mail: larry.johnson@doc.nyc.gov

Department of Cultural Affairs

31 Chambers Street, 2nd Floor, New York, NY 10007
Tel: (212) 513-9300 Fax: (212) 341-3812
Internet: http://www.nyc.gov/culture

■ Commissioner **Thomas "Tom" Finkelpearl** (212) 513-9319
E-mail: tfinkelpearl@dca.nyc.gov
Education: Princeton BA; Hunter MFA
Chief of Staff **Shirley Levy** (212) 513-9320
Deputy Commissioner/General Counsel **Kristin Sakoda** (212) 513-9327
Deputy Commissioner **Edwin Torres** (212) 513-9321
Capital Projects Assistant Commissioner **Andrew Burmeister** (212) 513-9333
Fax: (212) 341-3820
Cultural Institutions Assistant Commissioner **Timothy Thayer** (212) 513-9339
Program Services Assistant Commissioner **Kathleen Hughes** (212) 513-9351
Agency Chief Contracting Officer **Louise Woehrle** (212) 513-9310
E-mail: lwoehrle@culture.nyc.gov
Finance Director **Phillippa Shao** (212) 513-9315
Director of External Affairs **Ryan Max** (212) 513-9323
E-mail: rmax@culture.nyc.gov
Senior Director of Human Resources and Administration/EEO Officer **Cynthia Ingram** (212) 513-9307
E-mail: cingram@culture.nyc.gov
Executive Director of Materials for the Arts **Harriet Taub** (718) 729-2029

Department of Design and Construction [DDC]

30-30 Thomson Ave., Long Island City, NY 11101-3045
Tel: (718) 391-1000 Fax: (718) 391-1893
Internet: http://www.nyc.gov/buildnyc

■ Commissioner **Dr. Feniosky Peña-Mora** (718) 391-1580
E-mail: feniosky@ddc.nyc.gov
Education: Pedro Ureña (Dominican Republic); MIT 1991 MS, 1994 ScD
Chief of Staff **Ana Barrio** (718) 391-2300
Infrastructure Division Deputy Commissioner **Eric Macfarlane** (718) 391-2251
Fax: (718) 391-2600
Safety and Site Support Division Associate Commissioner **Mark Canu** (718) 391-1391
Fax: (718) 391-1651

(continued on next page)

★ Elected Official ▲ Appointed by Legislature ▼ Appointed by Governor ▶ Appointed by Board or Commission ● Appointed by Judge
■ Appointed by Mayor △ Appointed by Freeholders ▽ Appointed by Supervisor ▷ Appointed by County Executive ○ Appointed by Council

Department of Design and Construction *continued*

Public Building Division Deputy Commissioner **Kevin Donnelly** .... (718) 391-1280
Information Technology Services Assistant Commissioner **Raul Canabal** .... (718) 391-1668
E-mail: canabalr@ddc.nyc.gov Fax: (718) 391-1890
Public Information Director **Luis Levi** .... (718) 391-1641
Fax: (718) 391-2600
General Counsel **David Varoli** .... (718) 391-1721
Fax: (718) 391-2600
Administration Division Special Advisor **(Vacant)** .... (718) 391-2884
Fax: (718) 391-1899
Performance Metrics and Analysis **Joe Spetly** .... (718) 391-1784
Fax: (718) 391-2600
Agency Chief Contracting Officer **Charlette Hamamgian** .... (718) 391-2838
E-mail: chamamgian@ddc.nyc.gov
Engineering Audit Officer **Chris Igweatu** .... (718) 391-1097
E-mail: cigweatu@ddc.nyc.gov Fax: (718) 391-1888

Department of Environmental Protection [DEP]

59-17 Junction Boulevard, 19th Floor, Flushing, NY 11373
Fax: (718) 595-3477 Internet: http://www.nyc.gov/html/dep/home.html

■ Commissioner **Emily Lloyd** .... (718) 595-6565
E-mail: elloyd@dep.nyc.gov
Education: Wellesley BA; Pennsylvania 1970 MCP
Chief of Staff **Hannah Thonet** .... (718) 595-4516
General Counsel **(Vacant)** .... (718) 595-6711
Senior Environmental Counsel **Robin M. Levine** .... (718) 595-6586
First Deputy Commissioner **Steven W. Lawitts** .... (718) 595-6576
Deputy Commissioner for Human Resources and Administration **Zoe Ann Campbell** .... (718) 595-3411
E-mail: zcampbell@dep.nyc.gov
Deputy Commissioner for Sustainability **Angela Licata** .... (718) 595-4398
Deputy Commissioner, Bureau of Engineering Design and Construction **Vincent Sapienza** .... (718) 595-6183
Deputy Commissioner, Bureau of Police and Security **Kevin McBride** .... (718) 595-3120
Deputy Commissioner, Bureau of Wastewater Treatment **Pam Elardo** .... (718) 595-6924
Deputy Commissioner, Bureau of Water and Sewer Operations **James J. Roberts** .... (718) 595-5330
E-mail: jimr@dep.nyc.gov
Deputy Commissioner, Bureau of Water Supply **Paul V. Rush** .... (845) 340-7800
Deputy Commissioner, Bureau of Customer Services **Nancy Cianflone** .... (718) 595-6650
Associate Commissioner for Public Affairs **Eric Landau** .... (718) 595-6605
Assistant Commissioner For Budget **Joseph P. Murin** .... (718) 595-6936
E-mail: jmurin@dep.nyc.gov
Assistant Commissioner, Environmental Compliance **Michael Gilsenan** .... (718) 595-4543
Assistant Commissioner for Intergovernmental Affairs **Mario Bruno** .... (718) 595-3519
Director of Communications **Edward Timbers** .... (718) 595-4550
E-mail: etimbers@dep.nyc.gov

New York City Water Board

59-17 Junction Boulevard, 8th Floor, Flushing, NY 11373
Internet: www.nyc.gov/html/nycwaterboard/html/home/home.shtml

■ Chairman **Alfonso L. Carney, Jr.** .... (718) 595-3594
■ Member **Tawan Davis** .... (718) 595-3594
■ Member **Joseph G. Finnerty III** .... (718) 595-3594
Education: Hamilton 1982 BA; Maryland 1987 JD
■ Member **Adam Freed** .... (718) 595-3594
Education: NYU MURP
■ Member **Jonathan Goldin** .... (718) 595-3594
Education: Harvard 2000 AB, 2004 JD
■ Member **Arlene Shaw** .... (718) 595-3594
■ Member **(Vacant)** .... (718) 595-3594
► Executive Director **Mathilde O. McLean** .... (718) 595-6576
E-mail: mmclean@dep.nyc.gov

New York City Water Board *continued*

► Treasurer **Greg Ascierto** .... (718) 595-4032
E-mail: gascierto@dep.nyc.gov
► Deputy Treasurer **Greg Ascierto** .... (718) 595-3607
E-mail: gascierto@dep.nyc.gov
► Secretary **Albert Rodriguez** .... (718) 788-1160

Department of Finance

Municipal Bldg., One Centre Street, Room 500, New York, NY 10007
Tel: (212) 602-7005 Fax: (212) 669-2275

■ Commissioner **Jacques Jiha** .... (212) 602-7005
Chief of Staff **Denise Clay** .... (212) 602-7005
First Deputy Commissioner **Michael Hyman** .... (212) 602-7005
E-mail: hymanm@finance.nyc.gov
Education: CUNY 1984 MA, 1986 PhD
Deputy Commissioner for Administration and Planning **Jeffrey Shear** .... (212) 602-7005
E-mail: shearj@finance.nyc.gov
Deputy Commissioner and General Counsel **Diana H. Beinart** .... (212) 602-7005
Deputy Commissioner for Property Division **Timothy Sheares** .... (212) 291-4886
Deputy Commissioner and Sheriff **Joseph Fucito** .... (718) 610-4441
Deputy Commissioner for Treasury and Payment Services (Acting) **Jeffrey Shear** .... (212) 602-7005
E-mail: shearj@finance.nyc.gov
Assistant Commissioner for Collections **Pamela Parker-Cortijo** .... (212) 291-4433
Assistant Commissioner for Office of External Affairs **Samara Karasyk** .... (212) 602-7078
E-mail: karasyks@finance.nyc.gov
Assistant Commissioner for Employee Services **(Vacant)** .... (212) 291-4749
Assistant Commissioner for Land Records and City Register **Annette Hill** .... (212) 291-4952
Assistant Commissioner for Payment Operations **Leslie Zimmerman** .... (212) 291-4076
Education: Queens Col (NY) 1976 BA
Assistant Commissioner, Tax Policy **Karen Schlain** .... (212) 291-4041
E-mail: schlaink@finance.nyc.gov
Assistant Commissioner for Treasury **Elaine Kloss** .... (212) 291-4840
E-mail: klosse@finance.nyc.gov
Chief Financial Officer of Administration and Planning **Jacqueline James** .... (212) 602-7005
Chief Administrative Law Judge, Adjudications and Parking **Mary Gotsopoulis** .... (212) 291-4668
Department Advocate **Nancy Goodman** .... (718) 488-2173
Press Secretary **Sonia Alleyne** .... (212) 602-7005
E-mail: alleynes@finance.nyc.gov
Education: Emerson 1986 BComm
Special Advisor, Boards and Commissions **Jacqueline Gold** .... (212) 602-7005

Office of the Sheriff

30-10 Starr Avenue, Long Island City, NY 11101
Tel: (718) 610-0491 Fax: (718) 610-0486 Internet: www.nyc.gov/sheriff

■ Sheriff **Joseph Fucito** .... (718) 610-0491
E-mail: fucitoj@finance.nyc.gov

Fire Department [FDNY]

9 Metro Tech Center, Brooklyn, NY 11201-3857
Tel: (718) 999-2000 Fax: (718) 999-0033 Internet: www.nyc.gov/fdny

■ Fire Commissioner **Daniel Nigro** .... (718) 999-2004
E-mail: dnigro@cityhall.nyc.gov
First Deputy Commissioner **Robert Turner II** .... (718) 999-2070
E-mail: rturner@schools.nyc.gov
Chief of Department **James E. Leonard** .... (718) 999-2010
E-mail: jleonard@cityhall.nyc.gov

★ Elected Official ▲ Appointed by Legislature ▼ Appointed by Governor ► Appointed by Board or Commission ● Appointed by Judge
■ Appointed by Mayor △ Appointed by Freeholders ▽ Appointed by Supervisor ▷ Appointed by County Executive ○ Appointed by Council

Department of Information Technology and Telecommunications [DoITT]

255 Greenwich Street, 9th Floor, New York, NY 10007
Tel: (212) 788-6600 Fax: (212) 788-8130
Internet: http://www.nyc.gov/html/doitt/html/home/home.shtml

■ Commissioner **Anne Roest** . . . . . (212) 788-6633
E-mail: aroest@cityhall.nyc.gov
First Deputy Commissioner **Evan Hines** . . . . . (212) 788-6600
E-mail: ehines@doitt.nyc.gov
General Counsel **Charles Fraser** . . . . . (212) 788-6600
Infrastructure Management Deputy Commissioner
Michael A. Bimonte . . . . . (718) 403-8188
E-mail: mbimonte@doitt.nyc.gov
Senior Advisor/Strategic Technology Development Division Director **Steve Bezman** . . . . . (212) 788-6600
E-mail: sbezman@doitt.nyc.gov
Financial Management and Administration Deputy Commissioner **Annette Heintz** . . . . . (212) 788-6600
E-mail: aheintz@doitt.nyc.gov
Application Development Management Deputy Commissioner **Donald Sunderland** . . . . . (212) 788-6600
E-mail: dsunderland@doitt.nyc.gov
Special Council and Deputy Commissioner
Elissa Stein Cushman . . . . . (212) 788-6600
E-mail: ecushman@doitt.nyc.gov
Equal Employment Officer/Talent Management
Emily Johnson . . . . . (212) 788-6600
E-mail: ejohnson@doitt.nyc.gov
Director of External Affairs **Nicholas Sbordone** . . . . . (212) 788-6602
E-mail: nsbordone@doitt.nyc.gov

Department of Probation

33 Beaver St., 23rd Floor, New York, NY 10004
Tel: (212) 361-8969 Fax: (212) 361-8985
Internet: http://www.nyc.gov/html/prob/home.html

■ Commissioner **Ana Bermúdez** . . . . . (212) 361-8977
E-mail: abermudez@probation.nyc.gov
Administration Deputy Commissioner **Michael Forte** . . . . . (212) 361-8969
E-mail: mforte@probation.nyc.gov
Adult Operations Deputy Commissioner
Sharun Goodwin . . . . . (212) 361-8982
Juvenile Operations Deputy Commissioner
Gineen Gray . . . . . (212) 232-0468
General Counsel/Records Access Officer
Wayne S. McKenzie . . . . . (212) 232-0700
Education: CCNY 1981 BS; George Washington 1989 JD
Press and Public Relations Director **Candace Sandy** . . . . . (212) 361-8957
E-mail: csandy@probation.nyc.gov

Staten Island Juvenile Services

Tel: (718) 556-4000

Department of Records and Information Services

31 Chambers Street, Suite 305, New York, NY 10007
Tel: (212) 788-8609 Fax: (212) 788-8625 Internet: www.nyc.gov/records

■ Commissioner **Pauline Toole** . . . . . (212) 788-8607
E-mail: ptoole@records.nyc.gov
Education: Michigan BA; NYU MA
Assistant Commissioner **Kenneth R. Cobb** Room 305 . . . . . (212) 788-8604
Human Resources/Administration Director
Naomi Pacheco Room 304 . . . . . (212) 788-8622
E-mail: napacheco@records.nyc.gov Fax: (212) 788-8625
Municipal Archives Director **Terrance McCormick**
Room 105 . . . . . (212) 341-6023
Municipal Records Center Director **Pearl Boatswain**
Room 105 . . . . . (212) 788-8550
Municipal Reference and Research Center Director, Supervising Librarian **Christine Bruzzese** Room 112 . . . . . (212) 788-8595

Department of Sanitation [DSNY]

125 Worth St., 7th Floor, New York, NY 10013
Internet: www.nyc.gov/html/dsny/html/home/home.shtml

■ Commissioner **Kathryn Garcia** . . . . . (646) 885-4974
E-mail: kgarcia@schools.nyc.gov
Education: Wisconsin BA
First Deputy Commissioner for Operations
Dennis Diggins . . . . . (646) 885-4727
E-mail: ddiggins@dsny.nyc.gov
Administration and Financial Management Deputy Commissioner **Lorenzo N. Cipollina** . . . . . (646) 885-4793
E-mail: lcipollina@dsny.nyc.gov
Legal Affairs Deputy Commissioner **Robert Orlin** . . . . . (646) 885-5006
Public Affairs Deputy Commissioner **Vito A. Turso** . . . . . (646) 885-5020
E-mail: vturso@dsny.nyc.gov Fax: (212) 791-3386
Support Services Deputy Commissioner **Rocco DiRico** . . . (718) 334-8911
Agency Chief Contracting Officer/Assistant Commissioner (Acting) **Kirk Eng** . . . . . (212) 437-5053
E-mail: keng@dsny.nyc.gov
Solid Waste Management Deputy Commissioner
Jose Atkinson . . . . . (646) 885-4684
Cleaning and Collection Bureau Director
Steven Costas . . . . . (646) 885-4733
Enforcement Director **Christopher Klingler** . . . . . (718) 714-2741
Recycling and Sustainability Bureau Deputy Commissioner **Bridget Anderson** . . . . . (212) 437-4651

Department of Transportation [DOT]

55 Water Street, New York, NY 10041
Fax: (212) 839-6490 Internet: http://www.nyc.gov/html/dot

■ Commissioner **Polly Ellen Trottenberg** . . . . . (212) 839-6408
E-mail: ptrottenberg@cityhall.nyc.gov
Education: Barnard 1986 BA; Harvard 1992 MPP
Chief of Staff **Emily Gallo** . . . . . (212) 839-6408
First Deputy Commissioner **Lori Ardito** . . . . . (212) 839-6403
Bridges Deputy Commissioner **Robert "Bob" Collyer** . . . (212) 839-6300
Press Office Assistant Commissioner **Scott Gastel** . . . . . (212) 839-4850
E-mail: sgastel@dot.nyc.gov
Finance, Contracting and Program Management Deputy Commissioner **Joseph Jarrin** . . . . . (212) 839-6938
Human Resources and Facilities Management Deputy Commissioner **Marlene Hochstadt** . . . . . (212) 839-9490
E-mail: mhochstadt@dot.nyc.gov
Education: Brooklyn BA
Roadway Maintenance Deputy Commissioner
Galileo Orlando . . . . . (212) 839-9810
Sidewalks and Inspection Management Deputy Commissioner **Leon Heyward** . . . . . (212) 839-4300
Traffic Operations Deputy Commissioner
Steven Galgano . . . . . (718) 433-3350
Transportation Planning and Management Deputy Commissioner **Ryan Russo** . . . . . (212) 839-6662
Staten Island Ferry Chief Operations Officer
James C. DeSimone . . . . . (718) 876-5368
E-mail: jdesimone@dot.nyc.gov
General Counsel **Philip Damashek** . . . . . (212) 839-6503
Education: NYU 1968 BA; Columbia 1971 JD
Chief Technology Officer **Cordell Schachter** . . . . . (212) 839-8163
E-mail: cschachter@dot.nyc.gov
Education: SUNY (Buffalo) BA; NYU MS
Chief Communications Officer **Christopher Browne** . . . . . (212) 839-4853

Office of Administrative Trials and Hearings [OATH]

100 Church Street, New York, NY 10007
TTY: (212) 933-3001 Fax: (212) 933-3070

■ Commissioner/Chief Administrative Law Judge
Fidel Del Valle . . . . . (212) 933-3001
E-mail: fvalle@oath.nyc.gov
Education: Fordham BA; NYU JD
Executive Assistant **Ernestine Brunson** . . . . . (212) 933-3025
E-mail: ebrunson@oath.nyc.gov

★ Elected Official ▲ Appointed by Legislature ▼ Appointed by Governor ▶ Appointed by Board or Commission ● Appointed by Judge
■ Appointed by Mayor △ Appointed by Freeholders ▽ Appointed by Supervisor ▷ Appointed by County Executive ○ Appointed by Council

Office of Collective Bargaining
100 Gold Street, 4th Floor, New York, NY 10038
Tel: (212) 306-7160 Fax: (212) 306-7167 Internet: www.ocb-nyc.org

Chair **Susan Panepento** (212) 306-7190
Director of Representation **Karine C. Spencer** (212) 306-7176
E-mail: kspencer2@ocb.nyc.gov

Mayor's Office of Criminal Justice
One Centre Street, Room 1012, New York, NY 10007
Fax: (212) 788-6815

■ Director **Elizabeth Glazer** (212) 788-6810
E-mail: eglazer@cityhall.nyc.gov
■ Senior Advisor to the Mayor on Criminal Justice **Vincent N. Schiraldi** (212) 788-6810
E-mail: vschiraldi@probation.nyc.gov
Education: NYU MSW; SUNY (Binghamton) BA

Office of Emergency Management
165 Cadman Plaza East, Brooklyn, NY 11201
Tel: (718) 422-4600 Fax: (718) 422-4870
Internet: http://www1.nyc.gov/site/em/index.page

■ Commissioner **Joseph J. Esposito** (718) 422-4616
E-mail: esposito@cityhall.nyc.gov Fax: (718) 422-8453
Chief of Staff **Andrew D'Amora** (718) 422-4600
E-mail: adamora@oem.nyc.gov
First Deputy Commissioner **Calvin G Drayton** (718) 422-4600
E-mail: cdrayton@oem.nyc.gov
Deputy Commissioner for Agency Development and Coordination **Jacob Cooper** (718) 422-4600
E-mail: jcooper@oem.nyc.gov
Education: Alfred BA; SUNY (Binghamton) MPA
Deputy Commissioner for Finance, Policy and Communication **Stacy Rosenfeld** (718) 422-4600
E-mail: srosenfeld@oem.nyc.gov
Education: Scripps Col BA; Columbia MPA, MA
Deputy Commissioner for External Affairs **Christina Farrell** (718) 422-4600
E-mail: cfarrell@oem.nyc.gov
Education: Colgate BA; North Carolina MPA
Deputy Commissioner for Legal Affairs **Stella Guarna** (718) 422-4600
E-mail: sguarna@oem.nyc.gov
Education: CUNY BA; Cardozo JD
Deputy Commissioner for Planning and Preparedness **James Esposito** (718) 422-4600
E-mail: jesposito@oem.nyc.gov
Deputy Commissioner for Technology **Henry Jackson** (718) 422-4600
E-mail: hjackson@oem.nyc.gov
Education: Hobart BA; NYU MPA
Assistant Commissioner for Logistics **Jonathan Jenkins** (718) 422-4600
E-mail: jjenkins@oem.nyc.gov
Assistant Commissioner for Strategic Data **James McConnell** (718) 422-4600
E-mail: jmcconnell@oem.nyc.gov
Education: SUNY (Binghamton) BS
Assistant Commissioner for Training and Exercises **Anita Sher** (718) 422-4600
E-mail: asher@oem.nyc.gov

Office of Labor Relations
40 Rector Street, 4th Floor, New York, NY 10006-1705
Fax: (212) 306-7202 Internet: http://www.nyc.gov/html/olr/home.html

■ Commissioner **Robert "Bob" Linn** (212) 306-7200
E-mail: rlinn@olr.nyc.gov
Education: Haverford BA; Chicago JD
General Counsel **Mayra Bell** (212) 306-7200
First Deputy Commissioner **Renee Campion** (212) 306-7200
Deputy Commissioner **Claire Levitt** (212) 306-7200
Director, Employee Benefits Program **Georgette Gestely** (212) 306-7200
Director, Employee Assistance Program **Kevin Bulger** (212) 306-7200

Office of Operations
253 Broadway, 10th Floor, New York, NY 10013
Internet: http://www.nyc.gov/operations

■ Director **Mindy Tarlow** (212) 442-8130
E-mail: mtarlow@council.nyc.gov

Mayor's Office of Data Analytics [MODA]
City Hall, New York, NY 10007
Chief Analytics Officer **Amen Ra Mashariki** (212) 788-2816
E-mail: amashariki@council.nyc.gov
Education: Howard U MS; Morgan State
Chief of Staff **Nick O'Brien** (212) 788-2816
E-mail: nobrien@council.nyc.gov

Office for People with Disabilities [MOPD]
100 Gold Street, 2nd Floor, New York, NY 10038
TTY: (212) 788-2858 Fax: (212) 341-9843
Internet: http://www.nyc.gov/html/mopd

Commissioner **Victor Calise** (212) 788-2830

Mayor's Office of Contract Services [MOCS]
253 Broadway, 9th Floor, New York, NY 10007-2300
Fax: (212) 788-0049 Internet: http://www.nyc.gov/html/moc/home.html

■ Director **Michael Owh** (212) 788-0018
Education: UC Berkeley BA; St John's U (NY) JD

Mayor's Office of Immigrant Affairs [MOIA]
100 Gold Street, 2nd Floor, New York, NY 10038
Fax: (212) 788-9389 Internet: http://www.nyc.gov/html/imm

■ Commissioner **Nisha Agarwal** (212) 788-7654
E-mail: nagarwal@council.nyc.gov
Education: Harvard BA, JD
Deputy Commissioner **Mathilde Roman** (212) 788-7654
E-mail: mroman@council.nyc.gov

Mayor's Office of Technology and Innovation
City Hall, New York, NY 10007

■ Chief Technology Officer **Minerva Tantoco** (212) 788-3000
E-mail: mtantoco@council.nyc.gov

Mayor's Office of Veterans Affairs [MOVA]
346 Broadway, Room 818, New York, NY 10013
Fax: (212) 442-4170 E-mail: mova@cityhall.nyc.gov
Internet: http://www.nyc.gov/html/vets

■ Commissioner **BG Loree K. Sutton** (212) 442-4171
E-mail: lsutton@cityhall.nyc.gov
Education: Pacific Union BBA; Loma Linda MD

Mayor's Office of Workforce Development
City Hall, New York, NY 10007

■ Executive Director **Barbara Chang** (212) 788-0022
Education: Johns Hopkins BA; North Carolina MA
Senior Advisor for Research and Evaluation **(Vacant)** (212) 788-0022
Economic Development Advisor **Alissa Weiss** (212) 788-0022

Civilian Complaint Review Board
100 Church Street, 10th Floor, New York, NY 10007
Fax: (646) 500-6097 Internet: www.nyc.gov/html/ccrb/home.html

■ Chair (Acting) **Deborah N. Archer** (212) 912-7235
Education: Smith 1993 BA; Yale 1996 JD
Executive Director **Mina Quinto Malik** (212) 912-7262
Deputy Executive Director for Administration **Brian Connell** (212) 912-2092

Commission to Combat Police Corruption
17 Battery Place, Suite 327, New York, NY 10004
Executive Director **Marnie Blit** (212) 487-7350
E-mail: mblit@council.nyc.gov

★ Elected Official ▲ Appointed by Legislature ▼ Appointed by Governor ▶ Appointed by Board or Commission ● Appointed by Judge
■ Appointed by Mayor △ Appointed by Freeholders ▽ Appointed by Supervisor ▷ Appointed by County Executive ○ Appointed by Council

Equal Employment Practices Commission
253 Broadway, Suite 602, New York, NY 10007
Fax: (212) 615-8931

■ Chair **(Vacant)** .... (212) 615-8939
■ Commissioner **Angela Cabrera** .... (212) 615-8939
○ Commissioner **Malini Cadambi Daniel** .... (212) 615-8939
○ Commissioner **Elaine Reiss** .... (212) 615-8939
■ Commissioner **Arva R. Rice** .... (212) 615-8939
Executive Director **Charise L. Terry** .... (212) 615-8933
Deputy Director/General Counsel
Judith Garcia Quiñonez .... (212) 615-8948

Tax Commission
Municipal Building, One Centre St., Room 2400, New York, NY 10007
Fax: (212) 669-8636 Internet: www.nyc.gov/html/taxcomm

President **Ellen E. Hoffman** .... (212) 669-4401
Commissioner **Janet Alvarez** .... (212) 669-4410
Commissioner **Susan Grossman** .... (212) 669-4410
Commissioner **Richard Stabile** .... (212) 669-4410
Commissioner **Kirk P. Tzanides** .... (212) 669-4410
Commissioner **(Vacant)** .... (212) 669-4410
Commissioner **(Vacant)** .... (212) 669-4410

Commission Staff
Director of Appraisal and Hearings **Stephen Baschwitz** .. (212) 602-6257
E-mail: sbaschwitz@oata.nyc.gov
Director of Appraisal and Hearings **David Dunay** .... (212) 602-6257
E-mail: ddunay@oata.nyc.gov
Director of Appraisal and Hearings **Thomas Nichols** .... (212) 602-6257
E-mail: tnichols@oata.nyc.gov
Director of Information Technology **Iftikhar Ahmad** .... (212) 669-2954
E-mail: iahmad@oata.nyc.gov
Director of Operations **Myrna Hall** .... (212) 669-4420
E-mail: mhall@oata.nyc.gov
Special Counsel **Leonard Picker** .... (212) 669-8559
E-mail: lpicker@oata.nyc.gov

Taxi and Limousine Commission
33 Beaver Street, 22nd Floor, New York, NY 10004
Internet: www.nyc.gov/taxi

■ Commissioner/Chair **Meera Joshi** .... (212) 676-1003
E-mail: meera.joshi@tlc.nyc.gov Fax: (212) 676-1100
Education: Pennsylvania BA, JD
Executive Assistant to the Commissioner
Elaine C. Moore .... (212) 676-1007
E-mail: elaine.moore@tlc.nyc.gov Fax: (212) 676-1100
Chief Operating Officer **(Vacant)** .... (212) 676-1033
Fax: (212) 676-1038

Deputy Commissioner, General Counsel
Christopher Wilson .... (212) 676-1117
Fax: (212) 676-1102
Chief of Staff **Dawn Miller** .... (212) 676-1062
Deputy Commissioner, Licensing **Gary Weiss** .... (718) 391-5666
Fax: (718) 391-5615
Deputy Commissioner, Policy and Planning
Jeffrey Roth .... (212) 676-1035
Fax: (212) 676-1101
Deputy Commissioner, Public Affairs **Allan Fromberg** ... (212) 676-1013
E-mail: allan.fromberg@tlc.nyc.gov Fax: (212) 676-1101
Deputy Commissioner, Uniformed Service Bureau
Raymond Scanlon .... (718) 267-4515
Fax: (718) 267-4626
Chief Information Officer **Jeffrey S. Grunfeld** .... (212) 676-1050
E-mail: jeffrey.grunfeld@tlc.nyc.gov
Director of Training **Lisa Oliver** .... (212) 676-1080
E-mail: lisa.oliver@tlc.nyc.gov
Assistant Commissioner, Human Resources and EEO
Officer **Carmen Rojas** .... (212) 676-1095
E-mail: carmen.rojas@tlc.nyc.gov Fax: (212) 676-1154

The New York Public Library [NYPL]
Stephen A. Schwarzman Building, Fifth Avenue and 42nd Street,
New York, NY 10018-2788
Tel: (212) 930-0800 Tel: (917) 275-6975 Internet: www.nypl.org

Year Founded: 1895

Administration
President and Chief Executive Officer
Anthony W. Marx .... (212) 930-0800
E-mail: president@nypl.org
Date of Birth: February 28, 1959
Education: Yale 1981 BA; Princeton 1986 MPA, 1987 MA, 1990 PhD
Executive Assistant **Sarah Lugo** .... (212) 930-0698
E-mail: sarahlugo@nypl.org
Chief Operating Officer **Iris Weinshall** .... (212) 930-0580
E-mail: iweinshall@nypl.org
Education: Brooklyn 1975 BA; NYU MPA
Chief External Relations Officer **Carrie Ross Welch** .... (212) 930-0800
E-mail: carriewelch@nypl.org
Education: NYU BFA
Vice President, Office of Capital Planning and
Construction **Risa Honig** .... (212) 930-0800
Education: Washington U (MO) BArch, MArch
Vice President, Communications and Marketing
Kenneth "Ken" Weine .... (212) 592-7700
E-mail: kenweine@nypl.org
Vice President for Finance and Assistant Treasurer
Michael Dardia .... (212) 930-0800
Vice President, General Counsel and Secretary of the
Corporation **Michele Mayes** .... (212) 930-0684
E-mail: michelemayes@nypl.org
Education: Michigan 1971 BA, 1974 JD
Vice President, Deputy General Counsel and Assistant
Secretary of the Library **Jacqueline Bausch** .... (212) 930-0684
Vice President, Government and Community Affairs
George D. Mihaltses .... (212) 592-7714
E-mail: georgemihaltses@nypl.org
Education: Fordham BA; St John's U (NY) JD
Vice President, Human Resources **Louise Shea** .... (212) 592-7302
E-mail: louise_shea@nypl.org
Vice President, Information Technology and Chief
Technology Officer **Jane Aboyoun** .... (212) 621-0661
E-mail: jaboyoun@nypl.org
Chief Investment Officer **Todd M. Corbin** .... (212) 930-0800
E-mail: toddcorbin@nypl.org
Education: Colgate
Chief Library Officer **Mary Lee Kennedy** .... (212) 930-0800
E-mail: mkennedy@cityhall.nyc.gov
Education: Alberta BA; LSU MLS
Director, Foundation and Government Grants
Kathleen Donovan Reigelhaupt .... (212) 930-0738
E-mail: kathleenriegelhaupt@nypl.org
Membership and Public Affairs **Jessica Cassidy** .... (212) 930-0968
E-mail: jcassidy@nypl.org
Vice President, Public Programs **Fay Rosenfeld** .... (212) 930-0684
Chief Digital Officer **Tony Ageh** .... (212) 930-0800

The Branch Libraries Office
Vice President, Public Service **Christopher Platt** .... (917) 229-9503

The City University of New York [CUNY]
535 East 80th Street, New York, NY 10075-0767
Tel: (212) 794-5555 Fax: (212) 794-5524

Year Founded: 1847

Administration
Chancellor **James B. "J.B." Milliken** .... (212) 794-5311
Education: Nebraska 1979 BA; NYU 1983 JD Fax: (212) 794-5671
Senior University Dean and Special Counsel to the
Chancellor **Dave Fields** .... (212) 794-5313
E-mail: fields@mail.law.cuny.edu
Executive Vice Chancellor and Chief Operating Officer
Allan H. Dobrin .... (212) 794-5305
E-mail: allan.dobrin@mail.cuny.edu
Education: Queens Col (NY) BA

(continued on next page)

★ Elected Official ▲ Appointed by Legislature ▼ Appointed by Governor ▶ Appointed by Board or Commission ● Appointed by Judge
■ Appointed by Mayor △ Appointed by Freeholders ▽ Appointed by Supervisor ▷ Appointed by County Executive ○ Appointed by Council

The City University of New York *continued*

Executive Secretary **Denise Barber** . . . . . (212) 794-5306
E-mail: denise.barber@mail.cuny.edu
Executive Vice Chancellor and University Provost
Dr. Vita Carulli Rabinowitz . . . . . (646) 664-8075
Executive Secretary **Andrea Baker** . . . . . (212) 794-5415
E-mail: andrea.baker@mail.cuny.edu
Senior Vice Chancellor, Legal Affairs and General Counsel **Frederick P. Schaffer** . . . . . (212) 794-5506
Education: Harvard 1968 AB, 1973 JD Fax: (914) 794-5426
Executive Secretary **Sharon Atkins** . . . . . (646) 664-9226
E-mail: sharon.atkins@cuny.edu
Senior Vice Chancellor, University Relations and Secretary to the Board of Trustees **Jay Hershenson** . . . . (212) 794-5317
E-mail: jay.hershenson@mail.cuny.edu
Education: Queens Col (NY) BA, MA
Vice Chancellor, Budget and Finance
Matthew Sapienza . . . . . (212) 746-4275
E-mail: matthew.sapienza@mail.cuny.edu
Vice Chancellor, Facilities Planning, Construction and Management **Judith E. "Judy" Bergtraum** . . . . . (646) 664-2605
E-mail: judy.bergtraum@cuny.edu
Vice Chancellor, Human Resources Management
Gloriana B. Waters . . . . . (212) 794-5353
E-mail: gloriana.waters@mail.cuny.edu
Executive Secretary **Joy Tavss** . . . . . (212) 794-5354
E-mail: joy.tavss@mail.cuny.edu
Vice Chancellor, Labor Relations **Pamela S. Silverblatt** . . (212) 794-5568
Vice Chancellor, Research **Dr. Gillian Small** . . . . . (212) 794-5417
Note: Until July 31, 2016.
Education: U Wolverhampton (UK) BS, 1983 PhD
Vice Chancellor, Student Affairs **Dr. Frank D. Sanchez** . . (212) 794-5775
Note: Until June 30, 2016.
Education: Nebraska BA; Colorado State MS; Indiana PhD
Vice Chancellor and Chief Information Officer
Brian Cohen . . . . . (212) 541-0365
E-mail: brian.cohen@mail.cuny.edu
Senior University Dean, Academic Affairs
John Mogulescu . . . . . (212) 794-5429
Education: Brown U 1968 BA; NYU 1973 MSW
University Dean, Libraries and Information Resources
(Vacant) . . . . . (212) 794-5481
University Dean, Institutional Research and Assessment
David Crook . . . . . (212) 541-0314
University Dean, Undergraduate Studies
Dr. Lucinda Zoe . . . . . (646) 664-8055
Education: Kentucky BA, MLS; Columbia DLS
Deputy Chief Operating Officer **Ronald Spalter** . . . . . (212) 794-5609
E-mail: ronald.spalter@mail.cuny.edu
University Dean, Advancement **Carlos A. Flynn** . . . . . (212) 794-5654
University Dean, Continuing Education **Dr. Suri Duitch** . . (646) 664-8009
Note: Until August 12, 2016.
Education: Hunter MSW; CUNY PhD
Director, Admission Services **Clare Norton** . . . . . (646) 664-3620
Director, City Relations **John Kotowski** . . . . . (212) 794-5325
E-mail: john.kotowski@mail.cuny.edu
University Dean, Enrollment Management
James "Jim" Murphy . . . . . (646) 664-3502
Education: St John's U (NY); Baruch Col
University Director, Communications and Marketing
Michael Arena . . . . . (212) 794-5685
E-mail: michael.arena@mail.cuny.edu
Education: CCNY BA
University Director, Public Safety **William G. Barry** . . . . . (212) 541-0407
555 West 57th Street, Fax: (212) 541-0412
Room 1030, New York, NY 10015
Education: John Jay Col BS
Director, State Government Relations **Eileen Goldmann** . . (518) 463-2177
E-mail: eileen.goldman@mail.cuny.edu
Director, Environmental, Health, Safety and Risk Management **Howard Apsan** . . . . . (212) 794-5571
E-mail: howard.apsan@mail.cuny.edu
University Controller **(Vacant)** . . . . . (212) 397-5601

Deputy Mayor for Housing and Economic Development

City Hall, New York, NY 10007

■ Deputy Mayor for Housing and Economic Development
Alicia Glen . . . . . (212) 788-0120
Communications Advisor for Housing and Economic Development **Wiley Norvell** . . . . . (212) 788-2958
E-mail: wnorvell@cityhall.nyc.gov

Department of Parks and Recreation

The Arsenal-Central Park, 830 5th Ave., 3rd Floor, New York, NY 10065
Tel: (212) 360-1305 Tel: (888) 637-2757 (Information)
Fax: (212) 360-1345 Internet: www.nycgovparks.org/

■ Commissioner **Mitchell J. Silver** . . . . . (212) 360-1305
E-mail: msilver@health.nyc.gov
Education: Pratt Inst 1987 BARCH; Hunter MUP
First Deputy Commissioner **Liam Kavanagh** . . . . . (212) 360-1307
Chief of Staff **Margaret Nelson** . . . . . (212) 360-1395
Capital Projects Deputy Commissioner
Therese Braddick . . . . . (718) 760-6602
Management and Budget Deputy Commissioner
Robert L. Garafola . . . . . (212) 360-1302
E-mail: robert.garafola@parks.nyc.gov
Assistant Commissioner **David Stark** . . . . . (212) 360-8265
Assistant Commissioner for Communications
Sam Biederman . . . . . (212) 360-1311
E-mail: sam.biederman@parks.nyc.gov
Director of Media Relations **Crystal Howard** . . . . . (212) 360-1311
Chief of Community Outreach **Kate Spellman** . . . . . (212) 360-3475
Public Programs Assistant Commissioner **Adena Long** . . . (212) 360-3305
Planning Assistant Commissioner **Alyssa Cobb Konon** . . . (212) 360-3402
Director of Marketing **Christine Thelmo Dabrow** . . . . . (212) 360-8144
General Counsel **Alessandro G. Olivieri** . . . . . (212) 360-1314

Department of City Planning [DCP]

22 Reade St., New York, NY 10007-1216
Tel: (212) 720-3300 Internet: www.nyc.gov/html/dcp/home.html

■ Director **Carl B. Weisbrod** . . . . . (212) 720-3200
E-mail: cweisbrod@planning.nyc.gov Fax: (212) 720-3219
Education: Cornell 1965 BS; NYU 1968 JD
Chief Operating Officer **Jon Kaufman** . . . . . (212) 720-3680
E-mail: jkaufman@planning.nyc.gov Fax: (212) 720-3303
Executive Director **Purnima Kapur** . . . . . (212) 720-3500
Education: MIT MAArch; Fax: (212) 720-3219
Planning and Architecture (India) BArch
Counsel **Anita Claremont** . . . . . (212) 720-3400
Fax: (212) 720-3303
Equal Employment Opportunity **Edwin Marshall** . . . . . (212) 720-3560
Fax: (212) 720-3488
Governmental Affairs **Danielle J. Decerbo** . . . . . (212) 720-3225
E-mail: ddecerbo@planning.nyc.gov Fax: (212) 720-3219
Public Affairs **Rachaele Raynoff** . . . . . (212) 720-3471
E-mail: rraynof@planning.nyc.gov Fax: (212) 720-3219
Records Access Officer **Wendy Niles** . . . . . (212) 720-3208
Fax: (212) 720-3219

Borough Offices

Bronx Borough Office Director **Carol Samol** . . . . . (718) 220-8510
One Fordham Plaza, Fax: (718) 584-8628
5th Floor, Bronx, NY 10458-5891
Brooklyn Borough Office Director
Winston Von Engel . . . . . (718) 780-8290
16 Court Street, Fax: (718) 596-2609
7th Floor, Brooklyn, NY 11241-0139
Manhattan Borough Office Director **Edith Hsu-Chen** . . . . . (212) 720-3437
22 Reade Street, Fax: (212) 720-3488
6th Floor, New York, NY 10007-1216
Queens Borough Office Director **John Young** . . . . . (718) 286-3168
120-55 Queens Boulevard, Fax: (718) 286-3183
Room 201, Kew Gardens, NY 11424
Staten Island Borough Office Director
Leonard Garcia-Duran . . . . . (718) 556-7241
130 Stuyvesant Place, Fax: (718) 556-7305
6th Floor, Staten Island, NY 10301

★ Elected Official ▲ Appointed by Legislature ▼ Appointed by Governor ► Appointed by Board or Commission ● Appointed by Judge
■ Appointed by Mayor △ Appointed by Freeholders ▽ Appointed by Supervisor ▷ Appointed by County Executive ○ Appointed by Council

Department of City Planning *continued*

Urban Design Director **Jeff Shumaker** (212) 720-3281
Fax: (212) 720-3244

City Planning Commission

22 Reade Street, New York, NY 10007-1216
Fax: (212) 720-3219

■ Chair **Carl B. Weisbrod** (212) 720-3200
Education: Cornell 1965 BS; NYU 1968 JD
■ Vice Chairman **Kenneth J. Knuckles** (212) 720-3514
Education: Michigan BS; Howard U JD
Commissioner **Rayann Besser** (212) 720-3527
Commissioner **Irwin G. Cantor** (212) 720-3272
■ Commissioner **Alfred C. Cerullo III** (212) 720-3649
Education: St John's U (NY) BA
■ Commissioner **Cheryl Cohen Effron** (212) 720-3274
Education: Dalton (New York, NY) 1983; Brown U 1987
Commissioner **Michelle de la Uz** (212) 720-3516
Commissioner **Joseph I. Douek** (212) 720-3273
Commissioner **Richard W. Eaddy** (212) 720-3270
Education: Wesleyan U BA; Columbia 1988 MS
■ Commissioner **Hope Knight** (212) 720-3275
Commissioner **Anna Hayes Levin** (212) 720-3520
■ Commissioner **Orlando Marin** (212) 720-3271
E-mail: omarin@cityhall.nyc.gov
■ Commissioner **Larisa Ortiz** (212) 720-3512

Land Use and Environmental Review

Internet: http://www.ci.nyc.ny.us/html/dcp/html/ulpro.html

Deputy Executive Director **Jacquelyn Harris** (212) 720-3543
Fax: (212) 720-3244

Environmental Assessment and Review Director **Robert Dobruskin** (212) 720-3423
Fax: (212) 720-3495
Information Services **Anne Kelly** (212) 720-3551
E-mail: akelly@planning.nyc.gov Fax: (212) 720-3354
Land Use Review Director **James Merani** (212) 720-3362
Fax: (212) 720-3356
Technical Review Director **James Miraglia** (212) 720-3226
Fax: (212) 720-3244

Operations

Director **Maureen Brooks** (212) 720-3650
E-mail: mbrooks@cityhall.nyc.gov Fax: (212) 720-3683
Fiscal Officer **Purnell Lancaster** (212) 720-3657
Fax: (212) 720-3356
Human Resources Director **Sean Hennessy** (212) 720-3682
E-mail: shennes@planning.nyc.gov Fax: (212) 720-3683

Strategic Planning

Director **Howard S. Slatkin** (212) 720-3547
E-mail: hslatki@planning.nyc.gov Fax: (212) 720-3495
Housing, Economic, and Infrastructure Planning Director **Eric Kober** (212) 720-3322
E-mail: ekober@planning.nyc.gov Fax: (212) 720-3495
Planning Coordination Director **Sarah Goldwyn** (212) 720-3464
Fax: (212) 720-3490
Transportation Director **Jack Schmidt** (212) 442-4630
Fax: (212) 442-4724
Zoning Director **Beth Lebowitz** (212) 720-3263
Fax: (212) 720-3244

Department of Consumer Affairs [DCA]

42 Broadway, 8th Floor, New York, NY 10004-1716
Tel: (212) 436-0400 Internet: www.nyc.gov/html/dca

■ Commissioner **Lorelei Salas** (212) 436-0169
Note: Effective June 13, 2016
First Deputy Commissioner **Alba Pico** (212) 436-0173
Deputy Commissioner, External Affairs **Amit Bagga** (D) (212) 436-0179
Education: McGill (Canada)
Deputy Commissioner of Finance and Administration/Chief of Staff **Carla Van de Walle** (212) 436-0171
E-mail: cwalle@dca.nyc.gov
Education: Dalton (New York, NY) 1984

Department of Consumer Affairs *continued*

General Counsel Deputy Commissioner for Legal Affairs **Marla Tepper** (212) 436-0175
Deputy Commissioner/Executive Director, Office of Financial Empowerment **Deborah-Ellen Glickstein** (212) 436-0291
Assistant Commissioner for Agency Services/Deputy Chief of Staff **Sandra Abeles** (212) 436-0152
Executive Director **Ni Smithberg** (212) 436-0159
Assistant Commissioner for Communications and Digital Strategy **(Vacant)** (212) 436-0177

Department of Housing Preservation and Development [HPD]

100 Gold St., New York, NY 10038-1605
Tel: (212) 863-6300 Fax: (212) 863-8071
Internet: http://www.nyc.gov/hpd

■ Commissioner **Vicki L. Been** (212) 863-6100
E-mail: beenv@hpd.nyc.gov Fax: (212) 863-6302
Education: Colorado State 1978 BS; NYU 1983 JD
Chief of Staff **Leila Bozorg** (212) 863-8086
Assistant Commissioner, Administration **Joshua Cucchiaro** (212) 863-6610
E-mail: cucchiaj@hpd.nyc.gov
Press Secretary **Melissa Grace** (212) 863-5176
Internet: https://twitter.com/MelissadeTwit
Deputy Commissioner, Budget, Fiscal and Performance Analysis **Eva Trimble** (212) 863-5153
E-mail: trimblee@hpd.nyc.gov
Regulatory Compliance Officer **Baaba Halm** (212) 863-5289
Deputy Commissioner for Development **Eric Enderlin** (212) 863-6400
E-mail: enderlie@hpd.nyc.gov
Deputy Commissioner and General Counsel **Matthew Shafit** (212) 863-8686
Deputy Commissioner for Enforcement and Neighborhood Services **Vito Mustaciuolo** (212) 863-8594
Deputy Commissioner for Asset and Property Management **Ann-Marie Hendrickson** (212) 863-7301
Commissioner for Strategy, Research, and Communications **David Quart** (212) 863-6300

New York City Housing Development Corporation

110 William Street, New York, NY 10038

■ President **Gary D. Rodney** (212) 227-5500
E-mail: csanchez@nychdc.com
Chief Operating Officer, Executive Vice President and General Counsel **Tim Duvall** (212) 227-5500

Department of Small Business Services

110 William Street, 7th Floor, New York, NY 10038-3901
Tel: (212) 513-6300 Fax: (212) 618-8865
Internet: www.nyc.gov/html/sbs/html/home/home.shtml

■ Commissioner **Gregg Bishop** (212) 513-6350
E-mail: gbishop@sbs.nyc.gov
First Deputy Commissioner **Jacqueline Mallon** (212) 513-6391
Deputy Commissioner for Legal and Regulatory Affairs **Andrew Schwartz** (212) 513-6428
E-mail: aschwartz@sbs.nyc.gov
Deputy Commissioner for Business Development **(Vacant)** (212) 618-6751
Deputy Commissioner for Economic and Financial Opportunity **(Vacant)** (212) 513-6435
Deputy Commissioner for Neighborhood Development **Michael Blaise Backer** (212) 513-6300
Workforce Development Deputy Commissioner (Acting) **Jacqueline Mallon** (212) 618-8721
E-mail: jmallon@sbs.nyc.gov
Assistant Commissioner for Business Incentives **Donald Giampietro** (212) 618-8778
E-mail: dgiampietro@sbs.nyc.gov
Assistant Commissioner for Financial and Business Services **Rachel Van Tosh** (212) 513-6300
Education: Harvard BA; Pennsylvania MA

(continued on next page)

★ Elected Official ▲ Appointed by Legislature ▼ Appointed by Governor ► Appointed by Board or Commission ● Appointed by Judge
■ Appointed by Mayor △ Appointed by Freeholders ▽ Appointed by Supervisor ▷ Appointed by County Executive ○ Appointed by Council

Department of Small Business Services *continued*

Assistant Commissioner for Innovation and Strategy **(Vacant)** . . . . (212) 513-6300
Assistant Commissioner for Policy and Planning **Adira Siman** . . . . (212) 513-6300
Finance Assistant Commissioner **Shaazad Ali** . . . . (212) 618-8735
E-mail: sali@sbs.nyc.gov
Chief of Staff **Cynthia Keyser** . . . . (212) 618-6716
Director of Communications/Press Secretary **(Vacant)** . . . . (212) 618-8971
Executive Director, Emergency Response and Intergovernmental Services **Bernadette Nation** . . . . (212) 618-8706
E-mail: bnation@sbs.nyc.gov
Assistant Commissioner, Contractor Services **Helen Wilson** . . . . (212) 513-6323
E-mail: hwilson@sbs.nyc.gov
Human Resources Executive Director **Myrna Mateo** . . . . (212) 618-8932
E-mail: mmateo@sbs.nyc.gov
Assistant Commissioner, Operations **Maria Osorio** . . . . (212) 618-6320
E-mail: maosorio@sbs.nyc.gov
Bonding and Technical Assistance Director (Acting) **Jermaine Huell** . . . . (212) 618-6752
E-mail: jhuel@sbs.nyc.gov
Waterfront Permits, Facility and Property Management Director **Meenakshi Varandani** . . . . (212) 618-8822
E-mail: mvarandani@sbs.nyc.gov
Agency Chief Contracting Officer **Daryl Williams** . . . . (212) 618-8731
E-mail: dwilliams@sbs.nyc.gov
Certification Associate Director **Alfred Milton** . . . . (212) 513-6348
E-mail: amilton@sbs.nyc.gov
Executive Director of Strategic Services **(Vacant)** . . . . (212) 513-6344

Business Incentives Unit
110 William Street, 7th Floor, New York, NY 10038
Fax: (212) 618-8987

■ Assistant Commissioner **Donald Giampietro** . . . . (212) 618-8778
E-mail: dgiampietro@sbs.nyc.gov

Landmarks Preservation Commission [LPC]
One Centre Street, 9th Floor North, New York, NY 10007
Fax: (212) 669-7797 Internet: http://www.nyc.gov/landmarks

■ Chair **Meenakshi Srinivasan** . . . . (212) 669-7817
■ Commissioner **Frederick "Fred" Bland** . . . . (212) 669-7817
Date of Birth: 1945
Education: Yale
■ Commissioner **Diana D. Chapin** . . . . (212) 669-7817
■ Commissioner **Wellington Z. Chen** . . . . (212) 669-7817
■ Commissioner **Michael Devonshire** . . . . (212) 669-7817
■ Commissioner **Michael Goldblum** . . . . (212) 669-7817
■ Commissioner **John C. Gustafsson** . . . . (212) 669-7817
■ Commissioner **Adi Shamir-Baron** . . . . (212) 669-7817
■ Commissioner **Kim Lee Vauss** . . . . (212) 669-7817
■ Commissioner **(Vacant)** . . . . (212) 669-7817
■ Commissioner **(Vacant)** . . . . (212) 669-7817

Commission Staff
■ Executive Director **Sarah Carroll** . . . . (212) 669-7855
E-mail: scarroll@lpc.nyc.gov
Counsel **Mark Silberman** . . . . (212) 669-7919
Deputy Counsel **John Weiss** . . . . (212) 669-7921
Director of Preservation **Jared Knowles** . . . . (212) 669-7902
Research Director **Mary Beth Betts** . . . . (212) 669-7801

Public Design Commission
City Hall, 3rd Floor, New York, NY 10007
Fax: (212) 788-3086

■ Executive Director **Justin Moore** . . . . (212) 788-3071
Education: Columbia MArch
Director of Art and Conservation **Keri Butler** . . . . (212) 788-3071
Director of Capital Projects **Grace Han** . . . . (212) 788-3071
Manager of Archives and Special Collections **Julianna Monjeau** . . . . (212) 788-3071
Capital Projects Manager **Tom Campbell** . . . . (212) 788-3071

Board of Standards and Appeals [BSA]
240 Broadway, 29th Floor, New York, NY 10007
Tel: (212) 386-0075 Internet: www.nyc.gov/html/bsa/home.html

■ Chair **Margery Perlmutter** . . . . (212) 386-0075
■ Vice Chair **Susan M. Hinkson** . . . . (212) 386-0075
■ Commissioner **Shampa Chanda** . . . . (212) 386-0075
■ Commissioner **Eileen Montanez** . . . . (212) 386-0075
■ Commissioner **Dara Ottley-Brown** . . . . (212) 386-0075

Administration
Executive Director/Records Access Officer **Ryan Singer** . . . . (212) 386-0075
Deputy Director **Carlo Costanza** . . . . (212) 386-0068
General Counsel **David J. Schnakenberg** . . . . (212) 386-0069

New York City Economic Development Corporation [NYCEDC]
110 William St., New York, NY 10038
Tel: (888) 692-0100 (Toll Free) Tel: (212) 619-5000 (EDC Operator)
Fax: (212) 312-3913 Internet: www.nycedc.com

■ President **Maria Torres-Springer** . . . . (212) 312-3600
Executive Vice President and Chief Development Officer **Carolee Fink** . . . . (212) 312-3600
Executive Vice President and Chief of Staff **James N. Katz** . . . . (212) 312-3847
Education: Brown U BA; Harvard JD; JFK School Govt MPP
Executive Vice President and Chief Operating Officer **Euan Robertson** . . . . (212) 312-3600
Executive Vice President and General Counsel **Meredith Jones** . . . . (212) 312-3563
E-mail: mjones@nycedc.com
Executive Vice President, Real Estate Transaction Services **Charles Gans** . . . . (212) 618-5773
E-mail: cgans@nycedc.com
Executive Vice President, Real Estate Transaction Services **Jeff Nelson** . . . . (212) 312-3808
E-mail: jnelson@nycedc.com
President, Coney Island Development Corporation **Nathan Bliss** . . . . (212) 312-3845
E-mail: nbliss@nycedc.com
Senior Vice President, Administration Services **Jonathan Hurtado** . . . . (212) 312-3573
E-mail: jhurtado@nycedc.com
Senior Vice President, Development **Tom McKnight** . . . . (212) 312-3747
E-mail: tmcknight@nycedc.com
Senior Vice President, Human Resources **Carrie Weaver** . . . . (212) 312-3608
Senior Vice President, Management Information Systems **Chetan Badiani** . . . . (212) 312-3655
E-mail: cbadiani@nycedc.com
Senior Vice President, Maritime **Andrew Genn** . . . . (212) 312-3783
E-mail: agenn@nycedc.com
Senior Vice President, Marketing **Edward Hogikyan** . . . . (212) 312-3821
E-mail: ehogikyan@nycedc.com
Senior Vice President, Planning **Hardy Adasko** . . . . (212) 312-3703
Senior Vice President, Records Management **Frederic J. Grevin** . . . . (212) 312-3903
E-mail: fgrevin@nycedc.com
Senior Vice President, Strategic Planning **(Vacant)** . . . . (212) 312-3811
Vice President, Communications **Stephanie Baez** . . . . (888) 692-0100
Vice President, Contracts **Maryann Catalano** . . . . (212) 312-3536
E-mail: mcatalano@nycedc.com
Vice President, Public Affairs **Anthony Hogrebe** . . . . (212) 312-3804
E-mail: ahogrebe@nycedc.com
Managing Director, Center for Economic Transformation **Kathleen Warner** . . . . (212) 619-5000
Controller, Accounting **Spencer Hobson** . . . . (212) 312-3503
E-mail: shobson@nycedc.com

New York City Rent Guidelines Board
One Centre Street, Suite 2210, New York, NY 10007
Fax: (212) 669-7488 E-mail: ask@housingnyc.com
Internet: www.housingnyc.com

■ Chairman **Kathleen A. Roberts** . . . . (212) 669-7480
E-mail: chair@housingnyc.com

★ Elected Official ▲ Appointed by Legislature ▼ Appointed by Governor ▶ Appointed by Board or Commission ● Appointed by Judge
■ Appointed by Mayor △ Appointed by Freeholders ▽ Appointed by Supervisor ▷ Appointed by County Executive ○ Appointed by Council

New York City Rent Guidelines Board *continued*

- ■ Board Member **Harvey Epstein** .... (212) 669-7480
  Term Expires: December 31, 2016
  E-mail: board@housingnyc.com
- ■ Board Member **Steven Flax** .... (212) 669-7480
  Term Expires: December 31, 2016
  E-mail: board@housingnyc.com
- ■ Board Member **Sheila Garcia** .... (212) 669-7480
  Term Expires: December 31, 2016
- ■ Board Member **Cecilia Joza** .... (212) 669-7480
  Note: Will continue to serve until re-appointed or replaced
  Term Expires: December 31, 2014
- ■ Board Member **K. Sabeel Rahman** .... (212) 669-7480
  Term Expires: December 31, 2016
  E-mail: board@housingnyc.com
- ■ Board Member **Helen Schaub** .... (212) 669-7480
  Term Expires: December 31, 2018
  E-mail: board@housingnyc.com
- ■ Board Member **Mary Serafy** .... (212) 669-7480
  Term Expires: December 31, 2016
- ■ Board Member **J. Scott Walsh** .... (212) 669-7480
  Term Expires: December 31, 2016

Administration

- ■ Executive Director **Andrew McLaughlin** .... (212) 669-7480
  E-mail: ask@housingnyc.com
- Research Director **Brian Hoberman** .... (212) 669-7480
  E-mail: bhoberman@nycrgb.org

NYC & Company

810 Seventh Avenue, 3rd Floor, New York, NY 10019
Fax: (212) 247-6193 E-mail: info@nycvisit.com
Internet: www.nycgo.com

- ■ President and Chief Executive Officer **Fred Dixon** .... (212) 484-1200
  E-mail: fdixon@nycgo.com
- ■ Chief Marketing Officer **Abby Spatz** .... (212) 484-1200
- Chief Operating Officer and General Counsel **Bryan Grimaldi** .... (212) 484-1200
  E-mail: bgrimaldi@nycgo.com
- Chief Financial Officer **Kevin Booth** .... (212) 484-1200
- Executive Vice President, Membership and Destination Services **Kelly Curtin** .... (212) 484-1200
- Senior Vice President, Tourism and Convention Development **Jerry Cito** .... (212) 484-1200
- Senior Vice President, Global Communications **Chris Heywood** .... (212) 484-5458
  E-mail: cheywood@nycgo.com
- Chief Creative Officer **(Vacant)** .... (212) 484-1200
- Vice President, Borough Promotion and Engagement **Martin "Marty" Markowitz** (D) .... (212) 484-1200
  E-mail: mmarkowitz@nycgo.com

New York City Sports Marketing Department

810 7th Avenue, 3rd Floor, New York, NY 10019
Fax: (646) 381-9683

- Vice President **Jeff Mohl** .... (212) 484-5410
- Manager, Sports Marketing **Evan Ely** .... (212) 484-5478

New York City Loft Board

100 Gold Street, 2nd Floor, New York, NY 10038
Fax: (212) 788-7501 Internet: http://www.nyc.gov/html/loft

- Executive Director **Lanny Alexander** .... (212) 566-5663

Deputy Mayor for Health and Human Services

City Hall, New York, NY 10007

- ■ Deputy Mayor for Health and Human Services **Dr. Herminia Palacio** .... (212) 788-3000
  Education: Barnard 1983; Mount Sinai Medicine MD; UC Berkeley MPH
- Director of Children and Youth Services **Udai Tambar** .... (212) 788-3000

Board of Health

42-09 28th Street, 14th Floor, Long Island City, NY 11101-4132

- ■ Board Member **Mary Travis Bassett** .... (347) 396-6078
  Education: Harvard BA; Columbia MD; U Washington MPH
- ■ Board Member **Pamela S. Brier** .... (347) 396-6078
  Education: UC Berkeley BA; UCLA MHA
- ■ Board Member **Dr. Sixto R. Caro** .... (347) 396-6078
- ■ Board Member **Dr. Joel A. Forman** .... (347) 396-6078
- ■ Board Member **Rosa Maria Gil** .... (347) 396-6078
- ■ Board Member **Dr. Deepthiman K. Gowda** .... (347) 396-6078
- ■ Board Member **Dr. Susan Klitzman** .... (347) 396-6078
- ■ Board Member **Gail Nayowith** .... (347) 396-6078
- ■ Board Member **Ramanathan "Ram" Raju** .... (347) 396-6078
  Education: Tennessee 2000 MBA
- ■ Board Member **Karen Redlener** .... (347) 396-6078
- ■ Board Member **Dr. Lynne D. Richardson** .... (347) 396-6078

Department of Youth and Community Development [DYCD]

123 William Street, 17th Floor, New York, NY 10038
Fax: (212) 442-5998 Internet: http://www.nyc.gov/html/dycd/home.html

- ■ Commissioner **William "Bill" Chong** .... (646) 343-6710
  E-mail: bchong@dycd.nyc.gov
  - Chief of Staff **Regina Miller** .... (646) 343-6720
  - Scheduling Secretary **Sharon Robinson** .... (646) 343-6714
    E-mail: srobinson@dycd.nyc.gov
- Administration Deputy Commissioner **John Cirolia** .... (646) 343-6780
  E-mail: jcirolia@dycd.nyc.gov
- Assistant Commissioner, Planning, Research and Policy **Lisa Gulick** .... (646) 343-6710
  E-mail: lgulick@dycd.nyc.gov
- Youth Services Deputy Commissioner **Susan Haskell** .... (646) 343-6710
  E-mail: shaskell@dycd.nyc.gov
- Agency Chief Contracting Officer **Dana Cantelmi** .... (646) 343-6710
  E-mail: dcantelmi@dycd.nyc.gov
- General Counsel **Caroline Press** .... (646) 343-6710

Department of Health and Mental Hygiene

40-09 28th Street, Long Island City, NY 11101
Fax: (347) 896-8061

- ■ Commissioner **Mary Travis Bassett** .... (347) 396-4133
  E-mail: mbassett@health.nyc.gov
  Education: Harvard BA; Columbia MD; U Washington MPH
  - Senior Communications Advisor **Maibe Ponet** .... (347) 396-4133

Office of the Chief of Staff

- Chief of Staff **Emiko Otsubo** .... (347) 396-4008
  - Executive Assistant **Shavon Reid-Smith** .... (347) 396-4105
    E-mail: sreid-smith@health.nyc.gov

Office of the Chief Operating Officer

40-09 28th Street, Long Island City, NY 11101
Fax: (347) 896-8061

- Chief Operating Officer and Executive Deputy Commissioner **Dr. Oxiris Barbot** .... (347) 396-4126
  Education: Yale BA; U Medicine/Dentistry NJ MD
  - Administrator, Strategic Operations **(Vacant)** .... (347) 396-4128
- Agency Chief Contracting Officer **Judi Rich Soehren** .... (718) 546-0690

Division of Administration

- Deputy Commissioner **Julie Friesen** .... (347) 396-6509
  E-mail: jfriesen@health.nyc.gov
- Division of Informatics and Information Technology (DIIT) Deputy Commissioner/Chief Information Officer **Jian Liu** .... (347) 396-2211
  E-mail: jliu@health.nyc.gov
- Assistant Commissioner, Human Resources Bureau **Sean McFarlane** .... (347) 396-2110
  E-mail: smcfarlane@health.nyc.gov
- Equal Employment Opportunity/Chief Diversity Officer **James Hallman** .... (347) 396-6507

Office of the General Counsel of Health and Mental Hygiene

- General Counsel for Health **Thomas G. Merrill** .... (347) 396-6080

★ Elected Official ▲ Appointed by Legislature ▼ Appointed by Governor ▶ Appointed by Board or Commission ● Appointed by Judge
■ Appointed by Mayor △ Appointed by Freeholders ▽ Appointed by Supervisor ▷ Appointed by County Executive ○ Appointed by Council

Office of the Chief Medical Examiner [OCME]

520 First Avenue, New York, NY 10016
Tel: (212) 447-2030 Fax: (212) 447-2716
Internet: http://www.nyc.gov/html/ocme/html/home/home.shtml

■ Chief Medical Examiner **Dr. Barbara Sampson** . . . . (212) 447-2030
E-mail: bsampson@ocme.nyc.gov
Education: Princeton BS; Rockefeller PhD; Cornell MD
Deputy Medical Examiner **Jason Graham** . . . . (212) 447-2030

Division of Disease Control

Deputy Commissioner, Disease Control **Dr. Jay Varma** . . . (347) 396-2536
Assistant Commissioner, Acute Communicable Diseases **Marcelle Layton** . . . . (347) 396-2656
Assistant Commissioner, Bureau of HIV Prevention and Control **Dr. Demetre C. Daskalakis** . . . . (347) 396-7728
Assistant Commissioner, Immunization Program **Jane Zucker** . . . . (347) 396-2471
Assistant Commissioner, Public Health Laboratories **Jennifer Rakeman** . . . . (212) 447-2578
Assistant Commissioner, STD Control **Susan Blank** . . . . . (347) 396-7328
Assistant Commissioner, Tuberculosis Control **Dr. Joseph Burzynski** . . . . (347) 396-7511

Division of Environmental Health

Environmental Health Deputy Commissioner **Daniel Kass** . . . . (212) 788-4641
Assistant Commissioner, Environmental Disease Prevention Bureau **Nancy Clark** . . . . (212) 788-4320

Division of Epidemiology

Deputy Commissioner **Charon Gwynn** . . . . (347) 396-2946
Assistant Commissioner, Vital Statistics **Gretchen Van Wye** . . . . (646) 632-6747

Division of Family and Child Health

Deputy Commissioner **George L. Askew** . . . . (347) 396-4558
Education: Harvard 1985 BA; Case Western 1990 MD

Division of Finance and Planning

Deputy Commissioner, Financial Management **Sandy Rozza** . . . . (347) 396-6242
Assistant Commissioner, Office of the Auditor **Sarah Packman** . . . . (347) 396-6679
Assistant Commissioner, Bureau of Public Affairs **Sam Miller** . . . . (347) 396-4078
E-mail: smiller@health.nyc.gov
Education: Chicago 1989 BA; NYU 1996 MPA
Grants Director **(Vacant)** . . . . (347) 396-6038

Division of Health Care Access and Improvement

Deputy Commissioner **Dr. Sonia Angell** . . . . (347) 396-4837
Assistant Commissioner for Health Insurance and Oral Health Programs **(Vacant)** . . . . (347) 396-4628

Primary Care Information Project

Assistant Commissioner **(Vacant)** . . . . (347) 396-4008

Division of Mental Hygiene

Tel: (347) 396-7153

Executive Deputy Commissioner **Dr. Gary S. Gelkin** . . . . . (347) 396-7153
Assistant Commissioner, Children Youth and Families **Lily Tom** . . . . (347) 396-7070
Housing Services Director **Gail Wolsk** . . . . (347) 396-6933
Assistant Commissioner, Early Intervention **Dr. Marie B. Casalino** . . . . (347) 396-6974
Education: Hofstra BS; New York Medical MD; Columbia 1988 MPH
Medical Director **Myla Harrison** . . . . (347) 396-7072
Assistant Commissioner, Bureau of Mental Health (Acting) **Myla Harrison** . . . . (347) 396-7136

Department of Homeless Services

33 Beaver Street, New York, NY 10004
Fax: (212) 361-7977 Internet: www.nyc.gov/dhs

■ Commissioner **(Vacant)** . . . . (212) 361-8000
Advisor **Gilbert Taylor** . . . . (212) 361-8000
First Deputy Commissioner **Lorraine Stephens** . . . . (212) 361-7942

Department of Homeless Services *continued*

Administration Deputy Commissioner **Donald P. Brosen** . . (212) 361-8600
E-mail: dbrosen@dhs.nyc.gov
Adult Services Deputy Commissioner **Jody Rudin** . . . . (212) 361-0617
Executive Deputy Commissioner, Capacity Planning and Development **Lucille McEwen** . . . . (212) 361-0550
Family Services Deputy Commissioner **Jahmani Hylton** . . (212) 361-0626
Fiscal and Procurement Services Deputy Commissioner **Lula Urquhart** . . . . (212) 361-7946
E-mail: lurquhart@dhs.nyc.gov
Policy, Planning and Prevention Services Deputy Commissioner **Benjamin Charvat** . . . . (212) 361-7990
Communications and External Affairs Deputy Commissioner **Camille Rivera** . . . . (212) 361-7973
E-mail: camiller@dhs.nyc.gov
Press Secretary **Christopher R. Miller** . . . . (212) 361-7973
E-mail: chmiller@dhs.nyc.gov
Government and External Affairs Assistant Commissioner **Matthew Borden** . . . . (212) 607-2438
E-mail: mborden@dhs.nyc.gov
Security Deputy Commissioner **Michael Gagliardi** . . . . . . (212) 361-7918
General Counsel **Mark Neal** . . . . (212) 361-7996
Inspector General **Shelley Solomon** . . . . (212) 825-5920
Agency Medical Director **(Vacant)** . . . . (212) 361-0584
Equal Employment Opportunity Director **Athina McBean** . . . . (212) 361-7910

Department for the Aging [DFTA]

Two Lafayette Street, 7th Floor, New York, NY 10007-1392
Tel: (212) 602-4100 Fax: (212) 442-1095
Internet: http://www.nyc.gov/aging

■ Commissioner **Donna Corrado** . . . . (212) 602-4100
E-mail: dcorrado@aging.nyc.gov
Deputy Commissioner **(Vacant)** . . . . (212) 602-4100
Deputy Commissioner of External Affairs **Caryn Resnick** . . . . (212) 602-4100
Fax: (212) 442-1286
Emergency Planning and Preparedness Assistant Commissioner **Linda Whitaker** . . . . (212) 602-4100
E-mail: lwhitaker@aging.nyc.gov
Deputy Assistant Commissioner **Janice Chu** . . . . (212) 602-4100
General Counsel **Steven Foo** . . . . (212) 602-4113
Controller **John Jones** . . . . (212) 602-4100
E-mail: jjones@aging.nyc.gov
Management and Budget Assistant Commissioner **Joy Wang** . . . . (212) 602-4100
E-mail: jwang@aging.nyc.gov
Assistant Commissioner for Equal Employment Opportunity **Kim Hernandez** . . . . (212) 602-4100
Information Technology Director (Acting) **Salvador Rullan** . . . . (212) 602-4100
E-mail: srullan@aging.nyc.gov
Public Affairs Director **(Vacant)** . . . . (212) 602-4152
Fax: (212) 676-0685
Deputy Public Affairs Director **Yolanda Rodriguez** . . . . (212) 602-4153
E-mail: yrodriguez@aging.nyc.gov

Administration for Children's Services [ACS]

150 William St., 18th Floor, New York, NY 10038
Fax: (212) 341-0916 Internet: www.nyc.gov/acs

■ Commissioner **Gladys Carrión** . . . . (212) 341-0900
E-mail: gladys.carrion@acs.nyc.gov
Chief of Staff **Mary Nam** . . . . (212) 341-0900
Deputy Commissioner for Youth and Family Justice **Felipe Franco** . . . . (212) 341-0900
Education: Puerto Rico BA, MA
Chief of Staff **Michael Fanelli** . . . . (212) 341-0900
Deputy Commissioner for Communications and Community Affairs **Jill Krauss** . . . . (212) 341-0999
E-mail: jill.krauss@acs.nyc.gov
Chief of Staff **Tia Waddy** . . . . (212) 341-0999
First Deputy Commissioner **Eric Brettschneider** . . . . (212) 341-0990
Chief of Staff **Jerome White** . . . . (212) 788-9958

★ Elected Official ▲ Appointed by Legislature ▼ Appointed by Governor ► Appointed by Board or Commission ● Appointed by Judge
■ Appointed by Mayor △ Appointed by Freeholders ▽ Appointed by Supervisor ▷ Appointed by County Executive ○ Appointed by Council

Administration for Children's Services *continued*

Executive Deputy Commissioner for Child Welfare
Programs **Jacqueline McKnight** . . . . . . (212) 341-3289
Chief of Staff **Shanaz Mohammed** . . . . . . (212) 341-3289
Deputy Commissioner of Early Care and Education
Lorelei Vargas . . . . . . (212) 393-5028
Chief of Staff **Alyson Grant** . . . . . . (212) 393-5103

Health + Hospitals Corporation [HHC]

125 Worth Street, Suite 514, New York, NY 10013
Fax: (212) 788-0040

■ President and Chief Executive
Ramanathan "Ram" Raju . . . . . . (212) 788-3321
Education: Tennessee 2000 MBA Fax: (212) 788-0040
Chief of Staff **Randall L. Mark** . . . . . . (212) 788-3463
Executive Vice President and Chief Financial Officer
Plachikkat V. Anantharam . . . . . . (212) 788-3479
Executive Vice President and Corporate Chief
Operating Officer **Antonio Martin** . . . . . . (212) 788-3479
Fax: (212) 788-0040
Senior Vice President and General Counsel
Salvatore J. Russo . . . . . . (212) 788-3300
Senior Vice President, Corporate Communications and
Marketing **Ana Marengo** . . . . . . (212) 788-3386
E-mail: ana.marengo@nychhc.org Fax: (212) 788-3348
Senior Vice President, Correctional Health Services
Patricia "Patsy" Yang . . . . . . (212) 788-5400
Education: Brown U 1978 BA; Columbia 1981 MPH, 2005 DPH
Senior Vice President, Corporate Chief Medical Officer
Ross Wilson . . . . . . (212) 788-5400
Senior Assistant Vice President and Chief Corporate
Compliance Officer **Wayne McNulty** . . . . . . (212) 788-3321
Senior Assistant Vice President, Contracting
Administration and Control **Joseph Quinones** . . . . . . (212) 788-5423
Senior Assistant Vice President, Operations
Paul Albertson . . . . . . (212) 788-2256
E-mail: paul.albertson@nychhc.org
Public Affairs **Jennifer Bender** . . . . . . (212) 788-3339
E-mail: benderj1@nychhc.org
Public Affairs **Ian Michaels** . . . . . . (212) 788-3339
E-mail: Ian.Michaels@nychhc.org

Board of Directors [HHC]

■ Chair **Lilliam Barrios-Paoli** . . . . . . (212) 788-3360
Education: U Iberoamericana BA; New School PhD
■ Vice Chair **Gordon J. Campbell** . . . . . . (212) 788-3360
○ Member **Josephine Bolus** . . . . . . (718) 954-0022
Education: Brooklyn BS; Central Michigan MS
○ Member **Jo Ivey Boufford** . . . . . . (718) 499-6704 ext. 202
○ Member **Vincent Calamia** . . . . . . (718) 984-9848
○ Member **Anna Kril** . . . . . . (718) 777-5766
○ Member **Robert F. Nolan** . . . . . . (718) 880-1403
■ Member **Mark N. Page** . . . . . . (212) 788-3360
Education: Harvard 1970 AB; NYU JD
▶ Member **Ramanathan "Ram" Raju** . . . . . . (212) 788-3321
Education: Tennessee 2000 MBA
■ Member **Bernard Rosen** . . . . . . (212) 788-3360
Education: CUNY BBA, MBA
■ Member **Dr. Herminia Palacio** . . . . . . (212) 788-3359
Education: Barnard 1983; Mount Sinai Medicine MD; UC Berkeley MPH
■ Member **Emily A. Youssouf** . . . . . . (212) 306-3427
Education: New School 1977 MA
Member (ex-officio) **Dr. Gary S. Belkin** . . . . . . (347) 396-7153
Member (ex-officio) **Steven Banks** . . . . . . (212) 331-6000
Member (ex-officio) **Mary Travis Bassett** . . . . . . (347) 396-4100
Education: Harvard BA; Columbia MD; U Washington MPH
Member (ex-officio) **Barbara Lowe** . . . . . . (212) 788-3000

Human Resources Administration/Department of Social Services

180 Water St., New York, NY 10038
Tel: (212) 331-6000 Internet: http://www.nyc.gov/html/hra/home.html

■ Commissioner **Steve Banks** . . . . . . (929) 221-7315
E-mail: bankss@hra.nyc.gov Fax: (212) 331-6214
Education: Brown U 1978 BA; New York Law 1981 JD
Office of Citywide Health Insurance Access Executive
Deputy Commissioner **Marjorie A. Cadogan** . . . . . . (929) 221-7410
Education: Fordham 1985 JD
Office of Communications, Marketing and Legislative
Affairs Deputy Commissioner **David Neustadt** . . . . . . (929) 221-7336
E-mail: neustadtd@hra.nyc.gov
Education: NYU 1969 BS; Columbia 1982 MS
Office of Legal Affairs, General Counsel
Martha Calhoun . . . . . . (929) 221-7327
Planning and Performance Deputy Commissioner
Lisa Garabedian . . . . . . (929) 221-7038
E-mail: garabedianl@hra.nyc.gov Fax: (212) 331-5997
Office of Staff Resources Executive Deputy
Commissioner **Michael Laidlaw** . . . . . . (929) 221-5667
E-mail: laidlawm@hra.nyc.gov Fax: (212) 437-2184

Office to Combat Domestic Violence

100 Gold St., 2nd Fl., New York, NY 10038
Fax: (212) 788-2798

■ Commissioner **Cecile Noel** . . . . . . (212) 788-3156
Education: Columbia 1989 MSW
Director of Communications **Selvena Brooks** . . . . . . (212) 442-0490
E-mail: sbrooks@cityhall.nyc.gov

Counsel to the Mayor

City Hall, New York, NY 10007
Counsel to the Mayor **Maya Wiley** . . . . . . (212) 788-3000

Office of the Chief of Staff

City Hall, New York, NY 10007
Chief of Staff **Thomas Snyder** . . . . . . (212) 788-3000
Education: Michigan BA

Office of Special Projects and Community Events

253 Broadway, New York, NY 10007
Director **(Vacant)** . . . . . . (212) 788-2569
Deputy Director **Ellyn Canfield** . . . . . . (212) 788-2569
E-mail: ecanfield@law.nyc.gov

Mayor's Office of Appointments

253 Broadway, 10th Floor, New York, NY 10007
Fax: (212) 788-7812

■ Director **Rachel Lauter** . . . . . . (212) 341-5057
Education: Brown Col 2006 BA; Harvard 2011 JD

Mayor's Office for International Affairs

Two United Nations Plaza, 27th Floor, New York, NY 10007
Tel: (212) 319-9300

■ Commissioner **Penny Abeywardena** . . . . . . (212) 319-9300
E-mail: pabeywardena@law.nyc.gov
Chief of Staff **Jessica N. Wright** . . . . . . (212) 319-9300
Special Assistant to the Commissioner **Matt Graham** . . . . (212) 319-9300
Office Manager **Joyce Beggs** . . . . . . (212) 319-9300
Program Manager, New York Global Partners, Inc.
Travis Hardy . . . . . . (212) 319-9300
General Counsel **Marissa Jackson** . . . . . . (212) 319-9300
Education: Columbia 2010 JD
Strategic Relationships Manager **Mina Nabizada** . . . . . . (212) 319-9300
Deputy Commissioner for Operations and Partnerships
Hillary Schrenell . . . . . . (212) 319-9300
Protocol Officer **Leslie Slocum** . . . . . . (212) 319-9300
Policy Associate **Arthi Gunasekaran** . . . . . . (212) 319-9300

★ Elected Official ▲ Appointed by Legislature ▼ Appointed by Governor ▶ Appointed by Board or Commission ● Appointed by Judge
■ Appointed by Mayor △ Appointed by Freeholders ▽ Appointed by Supervisor ▷ Appointed by County Executive ○ Appointed by Council

NYC Service

253 Broadway, 8th Floor, New York, NY 10007
Fax: (212) 788-7882 Internet: www.nycservice.org

■ Chief Service Officer **Paula L. Gavin** .... (212) 788-7550
E-mail: pgavin@cityhall.nyc.gov

Office of Citywide Events Coordination and Management [CECM]

100 Gold Street, 2nd Floor, New York, NY 10038
Tel: (212) 788-7567

■ Executive Director **Michael Paul Carey** .... (212) 788-7567

Office of Management and Budget

75 Park Place, 6th Floor, New York, NY 10007
Fax: (212) 788-6300

■ Director **Dean Fuleihan** .... (212) 788-5900
E-mail: dfuleihan@omb.nyc.gov
■ Director of Public Affairs **(Vacant)** .... (212) 788-5900

Offices of the Public Administrators

Bronx County Public Administrator

851 Grand Concourse, Room 336, Bronx, NY 10451
Fax: (718) 293-7851

Public Administrator **Frank Randazzo** .... (718) 293-7660
E-mail: frandazzo@bronxpa.nyc.gov

Kings County Public Administrator

Supreme Court Building, 360 Adams Street, Room 144, Brooklyn, NY 11201
Tel: (718) 643-3032 Fax: (718) 522-4475
Internet: www.nyc.gov/html/kcpa/html/home/home.shtml

Public Administrator **Richard Buckheit** .... (718) 643-3032
E-mail: rbuckheit@kingspa.nyc.gov
Deputy Public Administrator **Aisha Glover** .... (718) 643-3032
E-mail: aaglover@kingspa.nyc.gov

New York County Public Administrator

Surrogate's Court, 31 Chambers St., Room 311, New York, NY 10007
Fax: (212) 385-0220

Public Administrator **Dahlia Damas** .... (212) 788-8430
E-mail: info@nycountypa.com
Deputy Public Administrator **Joy A. Thompson** .... (212) 788-8430
E-mail: joythompson@nycountypa.nyc.gov

Queens County Public Administrator

88-11 Sutphin Boulevard, Room 61, Jamaica, NY 11439
Fax: (718) 526-5043 E-mail: mail@queenscountypa.com
Internet: www.queenscountypa.com

Public Administrator **Lois M. Rosenblatt** .... (718) 526-5037
E-mail: mail@queenscountypa.com
Deputy Public Administrator **Susan B. Brown** .... (718) 526-5037
E-mail: mail@queenscountypa.com

Richmond County Public Administrator

130 Stuyvesant Place, 4th Floor, Suite 402, Staten Island, NY 10301
Fax: (718) 876-8377 Internet: http://nycprobate.com/20543.html

Public Administrator **Gary D. Gotlin** .... (718) 876-7228
E-mail: ggotlin@richmondpa.nyc.gov

Department of Investigation [DOI]

80 Maiden Lane, New York, NY 10038
Tel: (212) 825-5900 Fax: (212) 825-5594
Internet: http://www.nyc.gov/html/doi

■ Commissioner **Mark G. Peters** .... (212) 825-5913
E-mail: mpeters@doi.nyc.gov
Education: Brown U 1987 BA; Michigan 1990 JD
First Deputy Commissioner **Lesley Brovner** .... (212) 825-2403
E-mail: lbrovner@doi.nyc.gov Fax: (212) 825-2505

Department of Investigation *continued*

Deputy Commissioner for Agency Operations/Chief Information Officer **Ganesh Ramratan** .... (212) 825-2848
E-mail: gramratan@doi.nyc.gov
Special Commissioner of Investigation for New York City School System **Richard J. Condon** .... (212) 510-1400
Education: Pace 1965 BA; John Jay Col MA Fax: (212) 331-1550
Inspector General for NYPD **Philip Eure** .... (212) 825-5900
Fax: (212) 825-5310
General Counsel **Michael Siller** .... (212) 825-0646
Fax: (212) 825-2505
Deputy Commissioner/Chief of Investigations **Michael Carroll** .... (212) 825-3336
Fax: (212) 825-2505
Special Associate Commissioner **Susan Lambiase** ...... (212) 825-2433
Fax: (212) 825-3237
Associate Commissioner **Paul Cronin** .... (212) 825-2464
Fax: (212) 825-2506
Associate Commissioner **James Flaherty** .... (212) 825-0140
Fax: (212) 825-3343
Associate Commissioner **William Jorgenson** .... (212) 825-5619
Fax: (212) 825-2505
Assistant Commissioner, Administration **Edgardo Rivera** .... (212) 825-5899
E-mail: erivera@doi.nyc.gov Fax: (212) 825-2860
Director of Communications **Diane Struzzi** .... (212) 825-5931
E-mail: dstruzzi@doi.nyc.gov Fax: (212) 825-5594
Director of Intergovernmental Affairs **Jeri Powell** .... (212) 825-3650
Fax: (212) 825-5594
Records Access Officer **Elyse G. Hirschorn** .... (212) 825-5937
Fax: (212) 825-2504

Law Department/Office of the Corporation Counsel

100 Church Street, New York, NY 10007
Fax: (212) 356-1148 Internet: www.nyc.gov/html/law

■ Corporation Counsel **Zachary W. "Zach" Carter** .... (212) 356-0800
E-mail: zcarter@law.nyc.gov
Education: Cornell 1972 BA; NYU 1975 JD
First Assistant Corporation Counsel **Georgia Pestana** .... (212) 356-2400
E-mail: gpestana@law.nyc.gov
Executive Assistant and Chief Legal Counsel **Stephen Louis** .... (212) 356-4020
E-mail: slouis@law.nyc.gov
Executive Assistant and Chief of Appeals **Richard Dearing** .... (212) 356-2500
Executive Assistant for Commercial Law **Steven Stein Cushman** .... (212) 356-0800
Executive Assistant for Defensive Litigation **Celeste L.M. Koeleveld** .... (212) 356-2300
Note: Celeste Coeleveld has been appointed General Counsel at the New York State Department of Financial Services.
Education: Harvard 1986 BA; Columbia 1989 JD
Executive Assistant for Government Policy and Chief of Staff **Thomas Giovanni** .... (212) 356-0810
Director of Legal Recruitment **Stuart D. Smith** .... (212) 356-4070
Managing Attorney **Muriel Goode-Trufant** .... (212) 356-2200
Chief Law Librarian **Tracy Paler** .... (212) 356-2620
E-mail: tpaler@law.nyc.gov
Chief Information Officer **Jack Hupper** .... (212) 356-4090
Chief Technology Officer **Joseph Merces** .... (212) 356-2090
E-mail: jmerces@law.nyc.gov
Professional Development Director **June Witterschein** ... (212) 356-4080
E-mail: jwitters@law.nyc.gov Fax: (212) 356-0809

Office of the City Council

City Hall, New York, NY 10007
Internet: www.council.nyc.gov

★ Speaker **Melissa Mark-Viverito** (D-District 8) .... (212) 788-7210
Term Expires: December 31, 2017
E-mail: mviverito@council.nyc.gov
Date of Birth: April 1, 1969
Education: Columbia 1991 BA; Baruch Col 1995 MPA

★ Elected Official ▲ Appointed by Legislature ▼ Appointed by Governor ▶ Appointed by Board or Commission ● Appointed by Judge
■ Appointed by Mayor △ Appointed by Freeholders ▽ Appointed by Supervisor ▷ Appointed by County Executive ○ Appointed by Council

Office of the City Council *continued*

Chief of Staff **Ramon Martinez III** .... (212) 788-7155
E-mail: rmartinez@council.nyc.gov
Deputy Chief of Staff, Member Services **Joe Pressley** ... (212) 788-6899
E-mail: jpressley@council.nyc.gov
Senior Director, Member Services (Acting)
Amelia Adams .... (212) 788-7724
E-mail: aadams@council.nyc.gov
Communications Director **Eric Koch** .... (212) 788-7124
E-mail: ekoch@council.nyc.gov
Press Secretary **Robin Levine** .... (212) 788-7210
E-mail: rlevine@council.nyc.gov
Deputy Press Secretary **Pedro Julio Serrano** .... (212) 788-7210
E-mail: pserrano@council.nyc.gov
Senior Advisor **Amelia Adams** .... (212) 788-7724
Senior Advisor **Erica Gonzalez** .... (212) 788-7723
Education: Syracuse; Columbia
Senior Advisor **Joe Taranto** .... (212) 788-7725
Counsel **Kathleen Ahn** .... (212) 788-7017
Policy Director **Sasha Ahuja** .... (212) 788-9144
Legislative Assistant **Phyllis Henderson** .... (212) 788-7210

Borough of Manhattan

★Council Member **Margaret S. Chin** (D-District 1) .... (212) 587-3159
Term Expires: December 31, 2017 Fax: (212) 587-3138
E-mail: chin@council.nyc.gov
★Council Member **Rosie Mendez** (D-District 2) .... (212) 677-1077
Term Expires: December 31, 2017 Fax: (212) 677-1990
E-mail: rmendez@council.nyc.gov
Education: NYU; Rutgers (Newark)
★Council Member **Corey D. Johnson** (D-District 3) ...... (212) 564-7757
Term Expires: December 31, 2017 Fax: (212) 564-7347
E-mail: district3@council.nyc.gov
★Council Member **Daniel R. Garodnick** (D-District 4) .... (212) 818-0580
Term Expires: December 31, 2017 Fax: (212) 818-0706
E-mail: dgarodnick@council.nyc.gov
★Council Member **Ben Kallos** (D-District 5) .... (212) 860-1950
Term Expires: December 31, 2017 Fax: (212) 980-1828
E-mail: bkallos@council.nyc.gov
★Council Member **Helen K. Rosenthal** (D-District 6) ..... (212) 873-0282
Term Expires: December 31, 2017 Fax: (212) 873-0279
E-mail: hrosenthal@council.nyc.gov
★Council Member **Mark Levine** (D-District 7) .... (212) 928-6814
Term Expires: December 31, 2017 Fax: (646) 582-1408
E-mail: mlevine@council.nyc.gov
★Council Member **Melissa Mark-Viverito** (D-District 8) ... (212) 828-9800
Term Expires: December 31, 2017 Fax: (212) 722-6378
E-mail: mviverito@council.nyc.gov
Date of Birth: April 1, 1969
Education: Columbia 1991 BA; Baruch Col 1995 MPA
★Assistant Deputy Majority Leader and Council Member
Inez E. Dickens (D-District 9) .... (212) 678-4505
Term Expires: December 31, 2017 Fax: (212) 864-4379
E-mail: idickens@council.nyc.gov
★Council Member **Ydanis Rodriguez** (D-District 10) ..... (917) 521-2616
Term Expires: December 31, 2017 Fax: (917) 521-1293
E-mail: yrodriguez@council.nyc.gov

Borough of the Bronx

★Council Member **Andrew Cohen** (D-District 11) .... (718) 549-7300
Term Expires: December 31, 2017 Fax: (718) 549-9945
E-mail: acohen@council.nyc.gov
★Council Member **Andy King** (D-District 12) .... (718) 684-5509
Term Expires: December 31, 2017 Fax: (718) 684-5510
E-mail: andy.king@council.nyc.gov
★Deputy Majority Leader and Council Member
James Vacca (D-District 13) .... (718) 931-1721
Term Expires: December 31, 2017 Fax: (718) 931-1605
E-mail: jvacca@council.nyc.gov
★Council Member **Fernando Cabrera** (D-District 14) ..... (347) 590-2874
Term Expires: December 31, 2017 Fax: (347) 590-2878
E-mail: fcabrera@council.nyc.gov

Office of the City Council *continued*

★Deputy Majority Leader and Council Member
Ritchie J. Torres (D-District 15) .... (718) 842-8100
Term Expires: December 31, 2017 Fax: (347) 597-8570
E-mail: rtorres@council.nyc.gov
★Council Member **Vanessa L. Gibson** (D-District 16) ..... (718) 588-7500
Term Expires: December 31, 2017 Fax: (718) 588-7790
E-mail: vgibson@council.nyc.gov
Education: SUNY (Albany) 2001 BA; CUNY 2009 MPA
★Council Member
Rafael Salamanca, Jr. (D-District 17) .... (718) 402-6130
Term Expires: December 31, 2017 Fax: (718) 402-0539
E-mail: Salamanca@council.nyc.gov
★Council Member **Annabel Palma** (D-District 18) .... (718) 792-1140
Term Expires: December 31, 2017 Fax: (718) 931-0235
E-mail: apalma@council.nyc.gov

Borough of Queens

★Council Member **Paula A. Vallone** (D-District 19) ...... (718) 619-8611
Term Expires: December 31, 2017 Fax: (718) 631-4100
E-mail: pvallone@council.nyc.gov
★Council Member **Peter Koo** (D-District 20) .... (212) 888-8747
Term Expires: December 31, 2017 Fax: (718) 888-0331
E-mail: pkoo@council.nyc.gov
★Council Member **Julissa Ferreras** (D-District 21) .... (718) 651-1917
Term Expires: December 31, 2017 Fax: (718) 565-5937
E-mail: jferreras@council.nyc.gov
★Council Member
Costa G. Constantinides (D-District 22) .... (718) 274-4500
Term Expires: December 31, 2017
E-mail: cconstantinides@council.nyc.gov
★Council Member **Barry S. Grodenchik** (D-District 23) ... (718) 468-0137
Term Expires: December 31, 2017 Fax: (718) 468-0178
★Council Member **Rory I. Lancman** (D-District 24) ...... (718) 217-4969
Term Expires: December 31, 2017 Fax: (347) 561-6116
E-mail: rlancman@council.nyc.gov
Internet: https://twitter.com/RoryLancman
Date of Birth: March 1, 1969
Education: Queens Col (NY) 1991 BA; Columbia 1995 JD
★Council Member **Daniel Dromm** (D-District 25) .... (718) 803-6373
Term Expires: December 31, 2017 Fax: (718) 803-9832
E-mail: dromm@council.nyc.gov
★Majority Leader and Council Member
James "Jimmy" Van Bramer (D-District 26) .... (718) 383-9566
Term Expires: December 31, 2017 Fax: (718) 383-9076
E-mail: jvanbramer@council.nyc.gov
★Council Member **I. Daneek Miller** (D-District 27) .... (718) 776-3700
Term Expires: December 31, 2017 Fax: (718) 487-3580
★Council Member **Ruben Wills** (D-District 28) .... (718) 206-2068
Term Expires: December 31, 2017 Fax: (718) 206-2748
E-mail: rwills@council.nyc.gov
★Council Member **Karen Koslowitz** (D-District 29) .... (718) 544-8800
Term Expires: December 31, 2017 Fax: (718) 544-4452
E-mail: koslowitz@council.nyc.gov
★Council Member **Elizabeth S. Crowley** (D-District 30) ... (718) 366-3900
Term Expires: December 31, 2017 Fax: (718) 326-3549
E-mail: ecrowley@council.nyc.gov
Education: Fashion Inst Tech BA; Pratt Inst MA
★Council Member **Donovan Richards** (D-District 31) ..... (718) 527-4356
Term Expires: December 31, 2017 Fax: (718) 527-4402
E-mail: drichards@council.nyc.gov
★Council Member **Eric Ulrich** (R-District 32) .... (718) 738-1083
Term Expires: December 31, 2017 Fax: (718) 738-1918
E-mail: eulrich@council.nyc.gov

Borough of Brooklyn

★Council Member **Stephen T. Levin** (D-District 33) ...... (718) 875-5200
Term Expires: December 31, 2017 Fax: (718) 643-6620
E-mail: slevin@council.nyc.gov
★Council Member **Antonio Reynoso** (D-District 34) ...... (718) 963-3141
Term Expires: December 31, 2017 Fax: (347) 223-4347
E-mail: areynoso@council.nyc.gov
★Council Member **Laurie Cumbo** (D-District 35) .... (718) 260-9191
Term Expires: December 31, 2017 Fax: (718) 398-2802
E-mail: lcumbo@council.nyc.gov

(continued on next page)

★Elected Official ▲Appointed by Legislature ▼Appointed by Governor ▶Appointed by Board or Commission ●Appointed by Judge
■Appointed by Mayor △Appointed by Freeholders ▽Appointed by Supervisor ▷Appointed by County Executive ○Appointed by Council

Office of the City Council *continued*

★Council Member
Robert E. Cornegy, Jr. (D-District 36) .... (718) 919-0740
Term Expires: December 31, 2017 Fax: (718) 857-2555
E-mail: rcornegy@council.nyc.gov

★Council Member **Rafael L. Espinal, Jr.** (D-District 37) . . . (718) 642-8664
Term Expires: December 31, 2017 Fax: (718) 899-6017
E-mail: respinal@council.nyc.gov
Education: Queens Col (NY) 2007 BA

★Council Member **Carlos Menchaca** (D-District 38) ...... (718) 439-9012
Term Expires: December 31, 2017 Fax: (347) 599-0604
E-mail: cmenchaca@council.nyc.gov

★Deputy Majority Leader and Council Member
Brad S. Lander (D-District 39) .... (718) 499-1090
Term Expires: December 31, 2017 Fax: (718) 499-1997
E-mail: lander@council.nyc.gov

★Council Member **Mathieu Eugene** (D-District 40) ...... (718) 287-8762
Term Expires: December 31, 2017 Fax: (718) 287-8917
E-mail: mathieu.eugene@council.nyc.gov

★Council Member **Darlene Mealy** (D-District 41) .... (718) 953-3097
Term Expires: December 31, 2017 Fax: (718) 953-3276
E-mail: dmealy@council.nyc.gov

★Council Member **Inez Barron** (D-District 42) .... (718) 649-9495
Term Expires: December 31, 2017 Fax: (718) 649-3111
E-mail: ibarron@council.nyc.gov
Education: Hunter BA; Bank Street MS

★Deputy Majority Leader and Council Member
Vincent J. "Vinnie" Gentile (D-District 43) .... (718) 748-5200
Term Expires: December 31, 2017 Fax: (347) 587-7717
E-mail: vgentile@council.nyc.gov

★Council Member **David G. Greenfield** (D-District 44) . . . (718) 853-2704
Term Expires: December 31, 2017 Fax: (718) 853-3858
E-mail: dgreenfield@council.nyc.gov

★Deputy Majority Leader and Council Member
Jumaane D. Williams (D-District 45) .... (718) 629-2900
Term Expires: December 31, 2017 Fax: (718) 451-2136
E-mail: jwilliams@council.nyc.gov

★Council Member **Alan Maisel** (D-District 46) .... (718) 241-9330
Term Expires: December 31, 2017 Fax: (718) 531-1600
E-mail: amaisel@council.nyc.gov
Education: Long Island BA, MA

★Council Member **Mark Treyger** (D-District 47) .... (718) 373-9673
Term Expires: December 31, 2017 Fax: (718) 373-0195
E-mail: mtreyger@council.nyc.gov

★Council Member **Chaim M. Deutsch** (D-District 48) . . . (718) 368-9176
Term Expires: December 31, 2017 Fax: (718) 368-9160
E-mail: cdeutsch@council.nyc.gov

Borough of Staten Island

★Deputy Majority Leader and Council Member
Deborah L. Rose (D-District 49) .... (718) 556-7370
Term Expires: December 31, 2017 Fax: (718) 556-7389
E-mail: drose@council.nyc.gov

★Minority Leader and Council Member
Steve Matteo (R-District 50) .... (718) 980-1017
Term Expires: December 31, 2017 Fax: (718) 980-1051
E-mail: amatteo@council.nyc.gov

★Council Member **Joseph "Joe" Borelli** (R-District 51) . . . (718) 984-5151
Term Expires: December 31, 2017 Fax: (718) 984-5737
Education: Marist 2004 BA; Staten Island 2008 MA

Office of the City Clerk and Clerk of the Council

141 Worth Street, New York, NY 10013
Tel: (212) 669-8898 Fax: (212) 669-3300
Internet: www.cityclerk.nyc.gov/html/home/home.shtml

○City Clerk and Clerk of the Council
Michael McSweeney .... (212) 669-8898
E-mail: mmcsweeney@cityclerk.nyc.gov

Deputy City Clerk **Damaris B. Acosta** .... (212) 669-8898
E-mail: dacosta@cityclerk.nyc.gov

Deputy City Clerk **Alisa Fuentes** .... (212) 669-8898
E-mail: afuentes@cityclerk.nyc.gov

Counsel to the City Clerk **Patrick L. Synmoie** .... (212) 669-2610

Chief of Staff **Jose L. Gonzalez** .... (212) 669-8097

Office of the City Clerk and Clerk of the Council *continued*

Deputy Chief of Staff **Wendy Lopez** .... (212) 669-8898
E-mail: wlopez@cityclerk.nyc.gov

Director of Finance **Emmanuel Michalos** .... (212) 669-8093

Information and Technology Director **Irfan Rivera** .... (212) 669-3600
E-mail: irivera@cityclerk.nyc.gov

Borough Offices of the City Clerk

Bronx Deputy City Clerk **Shirley Saunders** .... (718) 590-5307
Supreme Court, 851 Grand Concourse,
Ground Floor, Bronx, NY 10451
E-mail: ssaunders@cityclerk.nyc.gov

Brooklyn Deputy City Clerk **Marie R. Lennon** .... (718) 802-4107
Brooklyn Municipal Building, 210 Joralemon Street,
Room 205, Brooklyn, NY 11201
E-mail: mlennon@cityclerk.nyc.gov

Queens Deputy City Clerk **Helen Sears** (DIL) .... (718) 286-2829
120-55 Queens Boulevard, Kew Gardens, NY 11424
E-mail: sears@council.nyc.gov
Education: Queens Col (NY) BA

Staten Island Deputy City Clerk **Edison Stewart** .... (718) 816-2290
Borough Hall, 10 Richmond Terrace,
3rd Floor, Room 311, Staten Island, NY 10301
E-mail: estewart@cityclerk.nyc.gov

Office of the Comptroller

Municipal Building, One Centre Street, Room 530 South,
New York, NY 10007-2341
Tel: (212) 669-3916 Fax: (212) 669-8878
Internet: www.comptroller.nyc.gov

★Comptroller **Scott M. Stringer** (D) .... (212) 669-3500
Term Expires: December 31, 2017
E-mail: sstringer@comptroller.nyc.gov
Date of Birth: April 29, 1960
Education: John Jay Col 1986 BA

Chief of Staff **Sascha Owen** .... (212) 669-3916

First Deputy Comptroller **Alaina Gilligo** .... (212) 669-2357

General Counsel **Kathryn "Kay" Diaz** .... (212) 669-3916

Deputy Comptroller for Accountancy
Michele Mark Levine .... (212) 669-2625
E-mail: mlevine@comptroller.nyc.gov

Deputy Comptroller for Audits **Marjorie Landa** .... (212) 669-2625

Director of Research and Investigations **Lisa Kutlin** .... (212) 669-2625
Education: Chicago 2000 AB; Georgetown 2005 JD

Research and Investigations Special Assistant
Sam Burness .... (212) 669-2625

Deputy Comptroller for Budget **Timothy Mulligan** ...... (212) 669-3916
E-mail: tmulligan@comptroller.nyc.gov
Education: NYU 1996 JD; Princeton MPA

Deputy Comptroller for Contracts and Procurement
Lisa M. Flores .... (212) 669-2797
E-mail: lflores@comptroller.nyc.gov

Deputy Comptroller/General Counsel **(Vacant)** .... (212) 669-2048

Deputy Comptroller for Public Affairs **Camille Joseph** . . . (212) 669-2657

Assistant Comptroller for Law and Adjustment **(Vacant)** . . (212) 669-3916

Claims and Adjudications Assistant Comptroller
James Cox .... (212) 669-2499

Deputy Comptroller of Public Finance **Carol Kostik** ..... (212) 669-8334

Corporate Governance Assistant Comptroller
Michael Garland .... (212) 669-8318
E-mail: mgarland@comptroller.nyc.gov

Director of Scheduling and Special Events
Shane Braddock .... (212) 669-2636

Director of Communications **Eric Sumberg** .... (212) 669-7461
E-mail: esumberg@comptroller.nyc.gov

Executive Director of Real Estate and ETI
Yvonne Nelson .... (212) 669-7326

Policy Director **Dave Saltonstall** .... (212) 669-3916

Chief Investment Officer **Scott C. Evans** .... (212) 669-3916
Date of Birth: May 11, 1959
Education: Tufts 1981 BA; Northwestern 1985 MBA

Chief Diversity Officer **Carra Wallace** .... (212) 669-3916
Education: Pepperdine BS; Columbia MPA

★Elected Official ▲Appointed by Legislature ▼Appointed by Governor ▶Appointed by Board or Commission ●Appointed by Judge
■Appointed by Mayor △Appointed by Freeholders ▽Appointed by Supervisor ▷Appointed by County Executive ○Appointed by Council

Office of Payroll Administration
Municipal Building, One Centre St., Room 200N, New York, NY 10007
Tel: (212) 669-8555
Internet: www.nyc.gov/html/opa/html/home/home.shtml

Executive Director **Roy Mogilanski** .... (212) 669-8555

Independent Budget Office [IBO]
110 William Street, 14th Floor, New York, NY 10038
Tel: (212) 442-0632 Fax: (212) 442-0350 E-mail: ibonews@ibo.nyc.ny.us
Internet: http://www.ibo.nyc.ny.us/

Director **Ronnie Lowenstein** .... (212) 442-0225
E-mail: ronniel@ibo.nyc.ny.us
Education: Guilford Col 1973 BA; Columbia PhD
Chief of Staff and Communications Director
Douglas Turetsky .... (212) 442-0629
E-mail: dougt@ibo.nyc.ny.us
Education: Bard BA; NYU MA
Deputy Director **Frank Posillico** .... (212) 341-6043
E-mail: frankp@ibo.nyc.ny.us
Education: Queens Col (NY) BS
Deputy Director **George Sweeting** .... (212) 341-6044
E-mail: georges@ibo.nyc.ny.us
Education: Columbia 1979 BA, 1981 MA, 1994 PhD
General Counsel **Lisa Neary** .... (212) 341-6041
E-mail: lisan@ibo.nyc.ny.us

Public Advocate for the City of New York
Municipal Building, One Centre Street, 15th Floor North,
New York, NY 10007
Tel: (212) 669-7200 TTY: (212) 669-7438
Internet: http://www.pubadvocate.nyc.gov

★ Public Advocate **Letitia "Tish" James** (DWF) .... (212) 669-4102
Term Expires: December 31, 2017
E-mail: gethelp@pubadvocate.nyc.gov
Education: CUNY BA; Howard U JD
Director of Scheduling/Advance **Wayne Collins** .... (212) 669-7173
Chief of Staff **Ibrahim Khan** .... (212) 669-7200
Deputy Chief of Staff **Laura Acosta** .... (212) 669-7200
E-mail: lacosta@pubadvocate.nyc.gov
Director of Policy **Amber Greene** .... (212) 669-7176
Deputy Director of Policy **Barbara Sherman** .... (212) 669-2412
General Counsel for Litigation **Jennifer Levy** .... (212) 669-2175
Director of Communications **Anna Brower** .... (212) 669-4301
E-mail: newsunit@pubadvocate.nyc.gov
Press Secretary **Delaney Kempner** .... (212) 669-4301
E-mail: newsunit@pubadvocate.nyc.gov
Education: Michigan
Administrator and Special Projects Director
Bianca Wheeler .... (212) 669-7081
E-mail: bwheeler@pubadvocate.nyc.gov

Office of the Special Narcotics Prosecutor [SNP]
80 Centre Street, 6th Floor, New York, NY 10013
Fax: (212) 815-0440 Internet: www.nyc.gov/html/snp/

Special Narcotics Prosecutor **Bridget B. Brennan** .... (212) 815-0400
Tel: (212) 788-3000 413
Public Information Director **Kati Cornell** .... (212) 815-0525

New York City Boroughs
Bronx Borough
Bronx Borough President
851 Grand Concourse, Bronx, NY 10451
Tel: (718) 590-3500 Fax: (718) 590-3537
Internet: http://bronxboropres.nyc.gov/

★ Borough President **Ruben Diaz, Jr.** (D) .... (718) 590-3557
Term Expires: December 31, 2017
E-mail: rdiazt@cityhall.nyc.gov

Bronx Borough President *continued*

Deputy Borough President **Aurelia Greene** (D) .... (718) 590-4036
E-mail: agreene@bronxbp.nyc.gov
Education: Rutgers 1975 BA
Chief of Staff and Senior Strategic Advisor
Paul J. Del Duca .... (718) 590-3565
E-mail: pdelduca@bronxbp.nyc.gov
Deputy Chief of Staff **Bassal Omar** .... (718) 590-6397
E-mail: bomar@bronxbp.nyc.gov
General Counsel **Raymond Sanchez** .... (718) 590-8555
Director of Administration **Erica Stack-Pabon** .... (718) 590-3545
E-mail: espabon@bronxbp.nyc.gov
Director of Borough Operations and Constituent
Services **Marisol Halpern** .... (718) 537-7113
E-mail: mhalpern@bronxbp.nyc.gov
Director of Capital Programs **James Rausse** .... (718) 590-3514
E-mail: jrausse@bronxbp.nyc.gov
Director of Community Boards Unit and Legislative
Affairs **Thomas Lucania** .... (718) 590-6005
E-mail: tlucania@bronxbp.nyc.gov
Director of Community Services **Tracy McDermott** .... (718) 590-6001
E-mail: tmcdermott@bronxbp.nyc.gov
Director of Education and Youth **Monica Major** .... (718) 590-3515
E-mail: mmajor@bronxbp.nyc.gov
Director of Fiscal and Personnel **Barbara A. Becker** .... (718) 590-5282
E-mail: bbecker@bronxbp.nyc.gov
Director of External Affairs **Dirk McCall** .... (718) 590-2509
Director of Planning and Development **Wilhelm Ronda** .... (718) 590-8087
E-mail: wronda@bronxbp.nyc.gov
Director of Communications **John DeSio** .... (718) 590-3543
Director of Policy **Victoria Reing** .... (718) 590-6815
Director of Senior Services **Larcenia Walton** .... (718) 590-6248
E-mail: lwalton@bronxbp.nyc.gov

Bronx County District Attorney
198 E. 161st St., Bronx, NY 10451
Tel: (718) 590-2000 Fax: (718) 590-2198 Internet: www.bronxda.nyc.gov

★ District Attorney **Darcel D. Clark** .... (718) 590-2000
Term Expires: December 31, 2019
Education: Boston Col 1983 BA; Howard U 1986 JD
Chief Assistant District Attorney **Odalys Alonso** .... (718) 590-2177
E-mail: alonsoo@bronxda.nyc.gov
Counsel to the District Attorney **Joseph Dawson** .... (718) 590-2175
Deputy Counsel and Policy Advisor
Julian Bond O'Connor .... (718) 590-2000

Bronx County Clerk
851 Grand Concourse, Room 118, Bronx, NY 10451
Tel: (866) 797-7214 Fax: (718) 590-8122

County Clerk **Luis M. Diaz** (D) .... (866) 797-7214
E-mail: ldiaz@cityclerk.nyc.gov

Brooklyn Borough
Brooklyn Borough President
209 Joralemon St., Brooklyn, NY 11201
Tel: (718) 802-3900 Fax: (718) 802-3522
Internet: http://www.brooklyn-usa.org

★ Borough President **Eric L. Adams** (D) .... (718) 802-3700
Term Expires: December 31, 2017
E-mail: askeric@brooklynbp.nyc.gov
Education: New York City Tech Col; Marist MPA
Chief of Staff **Sylvia Hamer** .... (718) 802-3700
Education: New Rochelle
Deputy Borough President **Diana Reyna** (DI) .... (718) 802-3700
E-mail: dreyna@brooklynbp.nyc.gov
Education: Pace BA
Senior Advisor **Ingrid P. Lewis-Martin** .... (718) 802-3700
Fax: (718) 802-3959
Administration Director **Melody Ruiz** .... (718) 802-4095
E-mail: mruiz@brooklynbp.nyc.gov Fax: (718) 802-2655
Communications Director **Stefan Ringel** .... (718) 802-3831
E-mail: sringel@brooklynbp.nyc.gov Fax: (718) 802-3778

(continued on next page)

★ Elected Official ▲ Appointed by Legislature ▼ Appointed by Governor ▶ Appointed by Board or Commission ● Appointed by Judge
■ Appointed by Mayor △ Appointed by Freeholders ▽ Appointed by Supervisor ▷ Appointed by County Executive ○ Appointed by Council

CITIES AND TOWNS

Brooklyn Borough President *continued*

Press Secretary **Patrick Rheaume** (718) 802-3700
Management Information Systems and Facilities Director **(Vacant)** (718) 802-3759
Fax: (718) 802-3979
Land Use Director **Richard Bearak** (718) 802-3890
E-mail: rbearak@brooklynbp.nyc.gov Fax: (718) 802-3920
Public Events, Special Projects and Tourism Director **(Vacant)** (718) 802-3803
Fax: (718) 802-3542
Consulting Engineer **Alvin Goodman** (718) 802-3816
E-mail: agoodman@brooklynbp.nyc.gov Fax: (718) 802-3735
Constituent Assistance Center Director **Tonya Hill** (718) 802-3863
Fax: (718) 802-3881

Kings County District Attorney

Renaissance Plaza, 350 Jay Street, Brooklyn, NY 11201-2908
Tel: (718) 250-2000 Fax: (718) 250-2210 Internet: www.brooklynda.org

★ District Attorney **Kenneth P. Thompson** (D) (718) 250-2202
Term Expires: December 31, 2017
E-mail: kthompson@law.nyc.gov
Chief of Staff **Leroy Frazer, Jr.** (718) 250-2000
Senior Executive Assistant District Attorney **Mark E. Feldman** (718) 250-2217
Education: Connecticut; Brooklyn Law
Chief Assistant District Attorney **Eric Gonzalez** (718) 250-2217
First Assistant District Attorney **Renee V. Gregory** (718) 250-3939
Counsel to the District Attorney **Maritza Mejia-Ming** (718) 250-2798
Chief of Civil Rights Bureau **Marc Fliedner** (718) 250-2000
Chief of Frauds Bureau **Felice Sontupe** (718) 250-2000
Chief of Investigations **William E. Schaeffer** (718) 250-2202
Education: Yale BA; Columbia JD; Princeton MPA
Chief, Violent Criminal Enterprises Bureau **Nicole Chavis** (718) 250-2217
Deputy Chief of Public Integrity **Emily Bradford** (718) 250-2202
Education: McGill (Canada) BA; Georgetown JD
Chief of Forensic Science Unit **Rachel Singer** (718) 250-2000

Manhattan Borough

Manhattan Borough President

Municipal Building, One Centre St., 19th Floor South, New York, NY 10007
Tel: (212) 669-8300 Tel: (212) 531-1609 (Northern Manhattan Office)
Fax: (212) 669-4900 Fax: (212) 531-4615 (Northern Manhattan Office)
Internet: http://manhattanbp.nyc.gov E-mail: info@manhattanbp.nyc.gov

Note: Also included under this jurisdiction are Franklin D. Roosevelt Island, Belmont Island, Ellis Island, Governor's Island, Liberty Island, Mill Rock Island, Randall's Island and Ward's Island.

★ Borough President **Gale A. Brewer** (D) (212) 669-8155
Term Expires: December 31, 2017
E-mail: gbrewer@manhattanbp.nyc.gov
Education: Columbia BA; Harvard 1990 MPA
Director of Arts and Culture **Maggi Peyton** (212) 669-2728
Deputy Borough President, Community and Borough Affairs **Aldrin Rafael Bonilla** (212) 669-3877
E-mail: abonilla@manhattanbp.nyc.gov
Deputy Borough President **Matthew Washington** (212) 669-8157
E-mail: mwashington@manhattanbp.nyc.gov
Chief of Staff **Jessica Mates** (212) 669-2527
E-mail: jmates@manhattanbp.nyc.gov
Director of Scheduling **Gabrielle Vallese** (212) 669-8300 ext. 2692
Director of Budget **Vladimir Martinez** (212) 669-3539
E-mail: vmartinez@manhattanbp.nyc.gov
General Counsel **Jim Caras** (212) 669-8157
Director of Human Resources and Operations **Deirdre Lyles** (212) 669-2375
E-mail: dlyles@manhattanbp.nyc.gov
Director of Policy **Shula Warren** (212) 669-8300
Communications Director **Jon Houston** (212) 669-8139
E-mail: jhouston@manhattanbp.nyc.gov Fax: (212) 669-3380
Press Secretary **Andrew Goldston** (212) 669-8300 ext. 3539
Fax: (212) 669-3380

Manhattan Borough President *continued*

Senior Advisor and Director of Digital Strategies **William Colegrove** (212) 669-8285
E-mail: wcolegrove@manhattanbp.nyc.gov
Community Affairs Director **Lucille K. Songhai** (212) 669-8300
E-mail: lsonghai@manhattanbp.nyc.gov
Constituent Services Director **Athena Moore** (212) 669-8300
E-mail: amoore@manhattanbp.nyc.gov
Director of Land Use (Acting) **Jim Caras** (212) 669-8130
E-mail: jcaras@manhattanbp.nyc.gov
Deputy Director of Land Use **Basha Gerhards** (212) 669-8300
E-mail: bgerhards@manhattanbp.nyc.gov
Northern Manhattan Office Director **Athena Moore** (212) 531-1609
163 West 125th Street, New York, NY 10027

New York County District Attorney

One Hogan Place, New York, NY 10013
Tel: (212) 335-9000 Fax: (212) 335-8999
Internet: http://www.manhattanda.org

★ District Attorney **Cyrus R. Vance, Jr.** (D) (212) 335-9000
Term Expires: December 31, 2017
E-mail: vancec@dany.nyc.gov
Education: Yale 1977 BA; Georgetown JD
Chief Assistant District Attorney **Karen Friedman Agnifilo** (212) 335-9090
E-mail: alonsod@dany.nyc.gov
General Counsel **Benjamin E. Rosenberg** (212) 335-9000
Education: Harvard 1981 BA, 1985 JD
Senior Advisor for Public Affairs and External Relations **Erin Duggan Kramer** (212) 335-9000
E-mail: ekramer@council.nyc.gov
Education: Colby BA
Chief, Tax Crimes Unit **Peirce Moser** (212) 335-9000
E-mail: pmoser@council.nyc.gov
Communications Director **Joan Vollero** (212) 335-9000
E-mail: volleroj@dany.nyc.gov

Queens Borough

Queens Borough President

120-55 Queens Blvd., Kew Gardens, NY 11424
Tel: (718) 286-3000 Fax: (718) 286-2876 E-mail: info@queensbp.org
Internet: www.queensbp.org

★ Borough President **Melinda Katz** (D) (718) 286-3000
Term Expires: December 31, 2017
E-mail: katz@queensbp.org
Deputy Borough President **Melva Miller** (718) 286-2655
E-mail: mmiller@queensbp.org
Chief of Staff **Jay Bond** (718) 286-2970
Counsel to Borough President **Elisa Velasquez** (718) 286-2881
Press Coordinator **Michael Scholl** (718) 286-2640
E-mail: MScholl@Queensbp.org
Administration and Budget Director **Richard Lee** (718) 286-2660
E-mail: rlee@queensbp.org
Cultural Affairs and Tourism Director **Nayelli Valencia** (718) 286-2669
Economic Development Director **Melva Miller** (718) 286-2655
E-mail: mmiller@queensbp.org
Education Director **Monica Gutierrez** (718) 286-2626
Health, Human and Senior Services Director **Talya Skolnik** (718) 286-2680
Housing Director **Lisa Atkins** (718) 286-2867
Immigrant Affairs Director **Susan Tanenbaum** (718) 286-2741
E-mail: stanenbaum@queensbp.org
Planning and Development Director **Irving Poy** (718) 286-2860
Consulting Engineer **(Vacant)** (718) 286-2828
Communications and Media Relations **Sharon Lee** (718) 286-2640
E-mail: slee@queensbp.org

★ Elected Official ▲ Appointed by Legislature ▼ Appointed by Governor ▶ Appointed by Board or Commission ● Appointed by Judge
■ Appointed by Mayor △ Appointed by Freeholders ▽ Appointed by Supervisor ▷ Appointed by County Executive ○ Appointed by Council

Queens County District Attorney

Queens Criminal Court Building, 125-01 Queens Boulevard, Kew Gardens, NY 11415
Tel: (718) 286-6000 Fax: (718) 286-6360
E-mail: contactqda@queensda.org Internet: www.queensda.org

★ District Attorney **Richard A. Brown** (D) .... (718) 286-6000
Term Expires: December 31, 2019
E-mail: rabrown@queensda.org
Education: Hobart 1953 BA; NYU 1956 JD

Chief Assistant District Attorney **John M. Ryan** .... (718) 286-6310
E-mail: jryan@queensda.org

Senior Executive Assistant District Attorney, Trials **James C. Quinn** .... (718) 286-6230
E-mail: jquinn@queensda.org

Executive Assistant District Attorney, Administration **Eileen M. Sullivan** .... (718) 286-6330
E-mail: esullivan@queensda.org

Executive Assistant District Attorney, Investigations **Peter A. Crusco** .... (718) 286-6600
E-mail: pcrusco@queensda.org

Executive Assistant District Attorney, Legal Affairs **Robert J. Masters** .... (718) 286-5843

Executive Assistant District Attorney, Major Crimes **Charles A. Testagrossa** .... (718) 286-7077
E-mail: ctestagrossa@queensda.org

Executive Assistant District Attorney, Special Prosecutions **Jesse J. Sligh** .... (718) 286-6400
E-mail: jjsligh@queensda.org

Counsel to the District Attorney **Lois M. Raff** .... (718) 286-6311
Education: Yale 1978 JD

Librarian **Peter Shao** .... (718) 286-5822
E-mail: pshao@queensda.org

Director of Communications **Kevin Ryan** .... (718) 286-6315
E-mail: krryan@queensda.org

Office of Immigrant Affairs Director **Carmencita N. Gutierrez** .... (718) 286-6000

Queens County Clerk

88-11 Sutphin Boulevard, 1st Floor, Jamaica, NY 11439
Tel: (718) 298-0605

County Clerk **Audrey I. Pheffer** (D) .... (718) 298-0601
E-mail: apheffer@nycourts.gov
Date of Birth: August 13, 1941
Education: Queens Col (NY) 1981 BA

Staten Island Borough

Staten Island Borough President

Borough Hall, 10 Richmond Terrace, Staten Island, NY 10301
Tel: (718) 816-2000 (Helpline) Internet: www.statenislandusa.com

★ Borough President **James S. Oddo** (R) .... (718) 816-2200
Term Expires: December 31, 2017 Fax: (718) 816-2026
E-mail: joddo@council.nyc.gov
Education: Fordham 1988 BA; New York Law 1991 JD

Executive Assistant **Chris DeCicco** .... (718) 816-2237
E-mail: cdecicco@council.nyc.gov Fax: (718) 816-2026

Deputy Borough President **Edward Burke** .... (718) 816-2231
E-mail: eburke@council.nyc.gov Fax: (718) 816-2051

Chief of Staff **Jason Razefsky** .... (718) 816-2232
E-mail: jrazefsky@statenislandusa.com Fax: (718) 816-2087

Budget Director **Robert McFeeley** .... (718) 816-2135
Fax: (718) 816-2100

Director of Constituent Services and Capital Budget **Marie Carmody-LaFrancesca** .... (718) 816-2232
E-mail: mlafrancesca@council.nyc.gov Fax: (718) 816-2087

Environment Director **(Vacant)** .... (718) 816-2057
Fax: (718) 816-3290

Help Line Director **Roland Stewart** .... (718) 816-2072
Fax: (718) 816-2152

Land Use Director **Robert Englert** .... (718) 816-2112
Fax: (718) 816-3290

Contracts and Procurement Director **Angela Shand** ...... (718) 816-2124
Fax: (718) 816-2075

Staten Island Borough President *continued*

Consulting Engineer **(Vacant)** .... (718) 816-2115
Fax: (718) 816-3290

Counsel **John Fusco** .... (718) 816-2056
Fax: (718) 816-2087

Director of Communications and External Affairs **Jennifer Sammartino** .... (718) 816-2134
Fax: (718) 816-2050

Richmond County District Attorney

130 Stuyvesant Place, Staten Island, NY 10301
Tel: (718) 876-6300 Fax: (718) 442-3584 E-mail: info@rcda.nyc.gov
Internet: http://rcda.nyc.gov/home.html

★ District Attorney **Michael E. "Mike" McMahon** (D)..... (718) 876-6300
Term Expires: December 31, 2019
Date of Birth: September 12, 1957
Education: NYU 1980 BA; Heidelberg 1982 AA; New York Law 1985 JD

Chief Assistant District Attorney **(Vacant)** .... (718) 556-7076

Communications Director **Doug Auer** .... (718) 556-7150
E-mail: douglas.auer@rcda.nyc.gov

Special Counsel to the District Attorney **Thomas Ridges** .... (718) 876-6300

Richmond County Clerk

130 Stuyvesant Place, 2nd Floor, Staten Island, NY 10301
Tel: (718) 675-7700

County Clerk **Stephen J. Fiala** .... (718) 675-7700
E-mail: stephen.fiala@rcda.nyc.gov

City of Newark, New Jersey

City Hall, 920 Broad Street, Newark, NJ 07102
Tel: (973) 733-6400 (Information)

County: Essex **Election Type:** Nonpartisan **Population:** 281,944 (2015)

Office of the Mayor

City Hall, 920 Broad Street, Room 200, Newark, NJ 07102
Tel: (973) 733-6400 Fax: (973) 733-5325

★ Mayor **Ras J. Baraka** .... (973) 733-6400
Began Service: July 1, 2014
Term Expires: June 30, 2018
Education: Howard U 1991 BA

Chief of Staff **Amiri "Middy" Baraka, Jr.** .... (973) 733-6400

Deputy Mayor **Rahaman Muhammad** .... (973) 733-3570
E-mail: muhammadr@ci.newark.nj.us Fax: (973) 424-4156

Deputy Mayor **Ugo Nwaokoro** .... (973) 733-6400

Affirmative Action Office

Manager **David Muhammad** Room B25 .... (973) 733-6394

Mayor's Office of Employment and Training/Newark One-Stop System

990 Broad Street, Newark, NJ 07103
Tel: (973) 733-8500

Director, Newark Workforce Investment Board **Amina Bey** .... (973) 733-5995

Department of Communications

920 Broad Street, Room 222, Newark, NJ 07102
Fax: (973) 733-5352

■ Communications Director **Frank Baraff** .... (973) 733-8004
E-mail: barafff@ci.newark.nj.us

■ Press Secretary **Marjorie Harris** .... (973) 733-8004

Chief of Staff **Taquan Williams** .... (973) 733-4882
E-mail: williamst@ci.newark.nj.us

Senior Press Information Officer **Brenda Jones** .... (973) 733-8004
E-mail: jonesb@ci.newark.nj.us

(continued on next page)

★ Elected Official ▲ Appointed by Legislature ▼ Appointed by Governor ▶ Appointed by Board or Commission ● Appointed by Judge
■ Appointed by Mayor △ Appointed by Freeholders ▽ Appointed by Supervisor ▷ Appointed by County Executive ○ Appointed by Council

CITIES AND TOWNS

Department of Communications *continued*

Senior Press Information Officer **David H. Lippman** . . . . . (973) 733-8004
E-mail: lippmand@ci.newark.nj.us

Administration Department

City Hall, 920 Broad St., Room 205, Newark, NJ 07102
Fax: (973) 733-3870

■ Business Administrator **John "Jack" Kelly** . . . . (973) 733-3780
■ Assistant Business Administrator **Michael E. Greene**
Room 210 . . . . (973) 733-6666
E-mail: greenem@ci.newark.nj.us
Education: Naval Acad 1993 BS; Boston U 1996 MSBA; Pace 2000 JD
Urban Enterprise Zone and Urban Initiatives Assistant
Director **(Vacant)** . . . . (973) 424-4154

Central Purchasing Division

828 Broad St., 3rd Floor, Newark, NJ 07102
Fax: (973) 733-3760

City Purchasing Director **Jerome Wakefield** . . . . (973) 733-3776
E-mail: wakefieldj@ci.newark.nj.us

Management and Budget Office

Budget Director **Darlene Tate** Room 109 . . . . (973) 733-3840
E-mail: tated@ci.newark.nj.us

Office of Information Technology

City Hall, 920 Broad Street, Room 113, Newark, NJ 07102

Chief Information Officer **Seth H. Wainer** . . . . (973) 733-3870
E-mail: wainers@ci.newark.nj.us
Education: Columbia 2006 BA

Office Services Division

Fax: (973) 733-5351

Manager **Daphne Turner** Room B1 . . . . (973) 733-6453

Personnel Division

Fax: (973) 733-4426

Human Resources Director **Kecia Daniels** Room 212 . . . . (973) 733-8008
E-mail: danielsk@ci.newark.nj.us

Department of Economic and Housing Development

City Hall, 920 Broad Street, Suite 218, Newark, NJ 07102
Tel: (973) 733-6575 Fax: (973) 733-4855

Deputy Mayor and Director **Baye Adofo-Wilson** . . . . (973) 733-6575
E-mail: adofo-wilsonb@ci.newark.nj.us
Chief of Staff/Assistant Director
Tracy Fredericks-Herrell . . . . (973) 733-6575
Director of Planning, Zoning and Sustainability
Mark Barksdale . . . . (973) 567-6020
E-mail: barksdalem@ci.newark.nj.us
Legislative Director **Larry Crump** . . . . (973) 733-6575
E-mail: crumpl@ci.newark.nj.us

Office of Boards and Commissions

Deputy Director/Zoning Officer **Ade Afolabi**
Room 112 . . . . (973) 733-6684
Fax: (973) 733-4369

Newark Planning Office

Chief Urban Designer **(Vacant)** Room 112 . . . . (973) 733-6020
E-mail: newarkplanningoffice@gmail.com

Division of Housing and Real Estate

City Hall, 920 Broad St., Room 421, Newark, NJ 07102

Director **Julio Colon** . . . . (973) 733-5979
E-mail: colonj@ci.newark.nj.us
Director of Property Management and Redevelopment
Annette Muhammad . . . . (973) 733-3914
E-mail: muhammada@ci.newark.nj.us Fax: (973) 733-8064

Engineering Department

City Hall, 920 Broad Street, Room 412, Newark, NJ 07102
Fax: (973) 733-4772

■ Director **Phillip Scott** . . . . (973) 733-8520
E-mail: scottp@ci.newark.nj.us
Supervising Engineer **Felicia Nazon** . . . . (973) 733-8520
E-mail: fnazon@ci.newark.nj.us

Motors Division

233 Wilson Ave., Newark, NJ 07105

Manager **Van Crossen** . . . . (973) 733-3714

Public Buildings

920 Broad Street, Room B31, Newark, NJ 07102

Manager **Khalif Thomas** . . . . (973) 733-8081

Traffic Signals Division

255 Central Ave., Newark, NJ 07103

Manager **Jack Nata** . . . . (973) 733-3985
E-mail: nataj@ci.newark.nj.us

Finance Department

828 Broad St., 5th Floor, Newark, NJ 07102
Fax: (973) 424-4241

■ Finance Director (Acting) **Danielle Smith** . . . . (973) 733-3930
E-mail: smithd@ci.newark.nj.us
Assistant Director **Eric Adams** . . . . (973) 733-3971
Assistant Municipal Treasurer **Paul Barton** . . . . (973) 733-3971

Office of the Comptroller

Municipal Comptroller **Victor Moneme** . . . . (973) 733-6414
E-mail: monemev@ci.newark.nj.us

Assessments Division

City Hall, 920 Broad Street, Room 101, Newark, NJ 07102

■ Tax Assessor **Romal Bullock** . . . . (973) 733-3952
E-mail: bullockr@ci.newark.nj.us
Education: Rutgers 2003 JD

Employees Retirement System

828 Broad St., 2nd Floor, Newark, NJ 07102

Secretary to the Board and Commission **(Vacant)** . . . . (973) 733-5704

Revenue Collections Division

City Hall, 920 Broad Street, Room 104, Newark, NJ 07102
Tel: (973) 733-3914

Tax Collector **Ernest Tuner** . . . . (973) 733-4799

Tax Abatements/Special Taxes Division

City Hall, 920 Broad Street, Room B26, Newark, NJ 07102

Manager **Juanita Jordan** . . . . (973) 733-3770
E-mail: jordanj@ci.newark.nj.us

Health and Community Wellness Department

110 William St., Newark, NJ 07102
Tel: (973) 733-7600

■ Director **Hanaa A. Hamdi** . . . . (973) 733-5310
E-mail: hamdih@ci.newark.nj.us Fax: (973) 733-3648
Medical Director (Interim) **Dr. Kathyann Duncan** . . . . (973) 877-6171
Assistant Director of Personal Health Services
Deborah Edwards . . . . (973) 733-3984
Chief of Staff **Vincent Caputo** Room 208 . . . . (973) 733-7538
Fax: (973) 733-3648

Environmental Health Division

Director **Mike Wilson** . . . . (973) 733-3734

Newark Homeless Health Care Project

Project Administrator **Dr. Denise Peroune** . . . . (973) 733-5488

★ Elected Official ▲ Appointed by Legislature ▼ Appointed by Governor ▶ Appointed by Board or Commission ● Appointed by Judge
■ Appointed by Mayor △ Appointed by Freeholders ▽ Appointed by Supervisor ▷ Appointed by County Executive ○ Appointed by Council

Social Services Division
10 Williams Street, Newark, NJ 07102

Social Work Services Director **Safiyyah Muhammad** . . . . (973) 733-3901

Surveillance and Prevention Division

Health Officer and Manager **Shatrughan Bastola** . . . . (973) 733-7592

Law Department

City Hall, 920 Broad Street, Room 316, Newark, NJ 07102
Tel: (973) 733-3880 Fax: (973) 733-5394

■ Corporation Counsel **Willie L. Parker** . . . . (973) 733-8935
First Assistant Corporation Counsel **Angela Foster** . . . . . . (973) 733-3880
First Assistant Corporation Counsel **Avion Benjamin** . . . . (973) 733-3880

Neighborhood and Recreational Services Department

920 Broad Street, Room 216, Newark, NJ 07102
Fax: (973) 733-4306

■ Director **Patrick Council** . . . . (973) 733-5373
E-mail: councilp@ci.newark.nj.us

Code Enforcement Division

Manager **Thomas McDonald** Room 420 . . . . (973) 733-6472

Parks and Grounds

Manager **Richard Kirkland** . . . . (973) 733-8442
62 Freelinghuysen Avenue, Newark, NJ 07112
E-mail: kirklandr@newark.nj.us

Recreation/Cultural Affairs Division
94 Williams Street, 2nd Floor, Newark, NJ 07102

Recreation Manager **Obalaji Jones** . . . . (973) 733-6454
Cultural Affairs Manager **Gwen Moten** . . . . (973) 733-5373

Sanitation Division
62 Frelinghuysen Ave., Newark, NJ 07114

Manager **Ronald Snead** . . . . (973) 733-6322

Public Safety Department

920 Broad Street, Newark, NJ 07102

■ Public Safety Director **Anthony F. Ambrose III** . . . . (973) 733-6007
Assistant Public Safety Director **Raul Malave** . . . . (973) 733-6007

Emergency Management
One Lincoln Ave., Newark, NJ 07104

Director **Dorian Herrell** . . . . (973) 733-3660

Fire Department [NFD]
1010 - 18th Avenue, Newark, NJ 07106
Tel: (973) 733-7491 Fax: (973) 733-5410

■ Director **James W. Stewart** . . . . (973) 733-7491
E-mail: stewartj@ci.newark.nj.us
Fire Chief **John G. Centanni** . . . . (973) 733-5187
E-mail: centannij@ci.newark.nj.us

Police Department
31 Green St., 4th Floor, Newark, NJ 07102
Tel: (973) 733-6007 Fax: (973) 733-6255

■ Chief of Police (Acting) **Darnell Henry** . . . . (973) 733-6007
■ Deputy Police Director **Eugene Venable** . . . . (973) 733-6007
Federal Monitor **Peter C. Harvey** . . . . (973) 733-6007
Education: Morgan State 1979 BA; Columbia 1982 JD

Alcoholic Beverage Control Board

Executive Secretary **Levi Holmes** City Hall Annex, Room 102 . . . . (973) 733-6445

Taxicab Division
City Hall Annex, Room 203 - B, Newark, NJ 07102
Fax: (973) 733-8914 Internet: http://newarkpdonline.org/taxiunit/

Manager **Sgt Fedy Pierre** . . . . (973) 733-8912

Department of Water and Sewer Utilities

City Hall, 920 Broad Street, Room B31-F, Newark, NJ 07102
Fax: (973) 733-4819

Director **Andrea Hall Adebowale** . . . . (973) 733-6303

Housing Authority

500 Broad Street, Newark, NJ 07102
Tel: (973) 273-6600 Fax: (973) 642-1242 Internet: www.newarkha.org/

Executive Director **Keith D. Kinard** . . . . (973) 273-6600

The Newark Public Library [NPL]

Five Washington Street, Newark, NJ 07102
P.O. Box 630, Newark, NJ 07101-0630
Tel: (973) 733-7784 Fax: (973) 733-5919 Internet: www.npl.org

Administration

Library Director (Interim) **Joseph J. Keenan, Jr.** . . . . (973) 733-7758
E-mail: jkeenan@npl.org

Newark Watershed

One Gateway Center, Suite 2619, Newark, NJ 07102
Fax: (973) 622-8160 E-mail: info@newarkwatershed.com

Executive Director (Interim) **Joseph M. Hartnett** . . . . (732) 382-4488

Office of the City Council

City Hall, 920 Broad Street, Room 304, Newark, NJ 07102
Tel: (973) 733-3788

★ Council President **Mildred C. Crump** (At-Large) . . . . (973) 733-8043
Term Expires: June 30, 2018 Fax: (973) 733-5481
E-mail: crumpm@ci.newark.nj.us

★ Vice President **Augusto Amador** (East Ward) . . . . (973) 733-3665
Term Expires: June 30, 2018 Fax: (973) 733-5822
E-mail: amadora@ci.newark.nj.us

★ Council Member
Gayle Chaneyfield Jenkins (Central Ward) . . . . (973) 733-3788
Term Expires: June 30, 2018

★ Council Member **Carlos Gonzalez** (At-Large) . . . . (973) 733-6425
Term Expires: June 30, 2018 Fax: (973) 733-5456
E-mail: gonzalezc@ci.newark.nj.us

★ Council Member **John Sharpe James** (South Ward) . . . . (973) 733-3788
Term Expires: June 30, 2018

★ Council Member
Joseph A. "Joe" McCallum, Jr. (West Ward) . . . . (973) 733-6427
Term Expires: June 30, 2018 Fax: (973) 733-5947

★ Council Member **Eddie Osborne** (At-Large) . . . . (973) 733-3794
Term Expires: June 30, 2018

★ Council Member **Luis A. Quintana** (At-Large) . . . . (973) 733-5880
Term Expires: June 30, 2018 Fax: (973) 733-5887
Education: Seton Hall BA

★ Council Member **Anibal Ramos, Jr.** (North Ward) . . . . (973) 733-5136
Term Expires: June 30, 2018 Fax: (973) 733-4861
E-mail: ramosa@ci.newark.nj.us

Office of the City Clerk

City Hall, 920 Broad Street, Room 306, Newark, NJ 07102
Tel: (973) 733-3669

○ City Clerk **Kenneth Louis** . . . . (973) 733-6574
E-mail: louisk@ci.newark.nj.us
○ Deputy City Clerk **Kathleen Marchetti** . . . . (973) 733-7578

★ Elected Official ▲ Appointed by Legislature ▼ Appointed by Governor ► Appointed by Board or Commission ● Appointed by Judge
■ Appointed by Mayor △ Appointed by Freeholders ▽ Appointed by Supervisor ▷ Appointed by County Executive ○ Appointed by Council

Newark Public Schools

2 Cedar Street, Room 805, Newark, NJ 07102
Fax: (973) 733-6834

▼State District Superintendent **Christopher "Chris" Cerf** . . (973) 733-7335
Education: Amherst 1977 BA; Columbia JD

City of Newport News, Virginia

City Hall, 2400 Washington Ave., Newport News, VA 23607-4301
Tel: (757) 933-2311 (Information) Internet: www.nngov.com

County: None **Election Type:** Nonpartisan **Population:** 182,385 (2015)

Office of the Mayor and City Council

City Hall, 2400 Washington Ave., Newport News, VA 23607
Fax: (757) 926-8599 E-mail: council@nngov.com

★Mayor **McKinley L. Price** (At-Large) . . . . (757) 926-8403
Began Service: July 1, 2010 Fax: (757) 926-3546
Term Expires: June 30, 2018
E-mail: council@nngov.com
Mayor's Administrative Assistant **(Vacant)** . . . . (757) 926-8403

★Council Member
Herbert H. Bateman, Jr. (Central District, B) . . . . (757) 249-7687
Term Expires: June 30, 2018
Education: Hampden-Sydney 1980 BA; Virginia 1996 MA

★Council Member
Dr. Sandra N. Cherry (South District, B) . . . . (757) 926-8618
Term Expires: June 30, 2018

★Council Member-Elect
Marcellus L. Harris III (North District, A) . . . . (757) 926-8618
Term Expires: June 30, 2020

★Council Member **Sharon P. Scott** (North District, B) . . . . (757) 926-8618
Term Expires: June 30, 2018
E-mail: spsprofessionals@msn.com

★Council Member **Tina L. Vick** (South District, A) . . . . (757) 926-8618
Term Expires: June 30, 2020
E-mail: council@nngov.com

★Council Member
Dr. Patricia P. Woodbury (Central District, A) . . . . (757) 926-8618
Term Expires: June 30, 2020

Voter Registrar

Fax: (757) 926-3653

Registrar **Vicki VanNoy Lewis** . . . . (757) 926-8683

Office of the City Attorney

City Hall, 2400 Washington Avenue, 9th Floor, Newport News, VA 23607
Fax: (757) 926-8549

○City Attorney **Collins L. Owens** . . . . (757) 926-8416
E-mail: cowens@nngov.com
Chief Deputy City Attorney **(Vacant)** . . . . (757) 926-8416

Office of the City Clerk

City Hall, 2400 Washington Ave., Newport News, VA 23607
Fax: (757) 926-8599

○City Clerk **Mabel V. Washington Jenkins** . . . . (757) 926-8634
E-mail: mwashington@nngov.com
Chief Deputy Clerk **Jennifer D. Walker** . . . . (757) 926-8634
E-mail: jwalker@nngov.com

Office of the City Treasurer

City Hall, 2400 Washington Ave., Newport News, VA 23607
Fax: (757) 926-8274

★City Treasurer **Marty G. Eubank** . . . . (757) 926-8731
Term Expires: December 31, 2017
E-mail: meubank@nngov.com

Office of the Commissioner of the Revenue

City Hall, 2400 Washington Ave., Newport News, VA 23607
12912 Jefferson Avenue, Newport News, VA 23608 (Satellite Office)
Tel: (757) 886-7671 (Satellite Office) Fax: (757) 247-2628

★Commissioner **Priscilla S. Bele** . . . . (757) 926-8752
Term Expires: December 31, 2017
E-mail: commish@nngov.com
Chief Deputy Commissioner **Dava Kauffman** . . . . (757) 926-8752
E-mail: dkauffman@nnva.gov

Office of the Commonwealth's Attorney

2501 Washington Ave., 6th Floor, Newport News, VA 23607
Fax: (757) 926-7482

★Commonwealth's Attorney **Howard E. Gwynn** . . . . (757) 926-7443
Term Expires: December 31, 2017
E-mail: hgwynn@nngov.com
Chief Deputy Commonwealth's Attorney **(Vacant)** . . . . . . (757) 926-7368

Office of the Sheriff

224 - 26th St., Newport News, VA 23607
Fax: (757) 926-8429

★Sheriff **Gabriel Morgan** . . . . (757) 926-8535
Term Expires: December 31, 2017
E-mail: sheriff@nngov.com

Office of the City Manager

City Hall, 2400 Washington Ave., Newport News, VA 23607
Fax: (757) 926-3503

○City Manager **James M. Bourey** . . . . (757) 926-8411
E-mail: jbourey@nngov.com
Assistant City Manager **Alan K. Archer** . . . . (757) 926-8411
Assistant City Manager **Cynthia D. Rohlf** . . . . (757) 926-8411
E-mail: crohlf@nngov.com
Education: Pittsburgh BA
Assistant to the City Manager for Administration
Telly Whitfield . . . . (757) 926-8411
Assistant to the City Manager for Community Relations
Cleder A. Jones . . . . (757) 926-3682

Assessor's Office

Fountain Plaza Two, 700 Town Center Dr., Suite 220,
Newport News, VA 23606
Fax: (757) 926-1940 E-mail: restate@nngov.com

City Assessor **Charles Vester** . . . . (757) 926-1926
E-mail: cvester@nngov.com
Deputy Assessor **Earl L. Wynings** . . . . (757) 926-1926
E-mail: elwynings@nngov.com

Budget and Evaluation

City Hall, 2400 Washington Ave., Newport News, VA 23607
Fax: (757) 926-6940

Director **Lisa Cipriano** . . . . (757) 926-8733
E-mail: lcipriano@nngov.com

Codes Compliance

City Hall, 2400 Washington Ave., Newport News, VA 23607
Fax: (757) 926-8311

Director **Harold L. Roach** . . . . (757) 933-2311

Development

City Hall, 2400 Washington Ave., Newport News, VA 23607
Fax: (757) 926-3504

Director **Florence Kingston** . . . . (757) 926-8428
E-mail: fkingston@nngov.com

★Elected Official ▲Appointed by Legislature ▼Appointed by Governor ▶Appointed by Board or Commission ●Appointed by Judge
■Appointed by Mayor △Appointed by Freeholders ▽Appointed by Supervisor ▷Appointed by County Executive ○Appointed by Council

Emergency Management
513 Oyster Point Rd., Newport News, VA 23602
Fax: (757) 269-2905

Deputy Coordinator **George Glazner** .... (757) 269-2901
E-mail: gglazner@nnva.gov

Engineering Department
City Hall, 2400 Washington Ave., Newport News, VA 23607
Fax: (757) 926-8300

Director **Everett Skipper** .... (757) 933-2311
E-mail: eskipper@nngov.com

Finance Department
City Hall, 2400 Washington Ave., Newport News, VA 23607
Fax: (757) 926-8894

Director **Stewart "Tom" Mitchell** .... (757) 926-8738

Fire Department
City Hall, 2400 Washington Ave., Newport News, VA 23607
Fax: (757) 926-8602

Fire Chief **R.B. Alley** .... (757) 926-8404
E-mail: rballey@nngov.com
Fire Marshal **William Rice** .... (757) 247-8873
E-mail: wrice@nngov.com

Human Resources Department
Fountain Plaza Two, 700 Town Center Dr., Suite 200,
Newport News, VA 23606
TTY: (757) 926-1841 Fax: (757) 926-1825
Fax: (757) 926-1819 (Worker's Compensation)

Director **Yvonne Manning** .... (757) 926-1800
E-mail: ymanning@nngov.com

Human Services Department
6060 Jefferson Ave., Newport News, VA 23605
Fax: (757) 926-6118

Director **Venerria Lucas-Thomas** .... (757) 926-6422
Deputy Director **Dr. Rosanne D. Walters** .... (757) 926-6645

Information Technology Department
City Hall, 2400 Washington Ave., Newport News, VA 23607
Fax: (757) 926-8433

Director **Andy Stein** .... (757) 926-8681
E-mail: astein@nngov.com

Internal Audit Department
City Hall, 2400 Washington Ave., Newport News, VA 23607
Tel: (757) 926-8521 Fax: (757) 926-7537

Director of Internal Audit **Cathy S. Matthews** .... (757) 926-8521

Juvenile Services
350 25th Street, Newport News, VA 23607
Fax: (757) 926-1685

Director **Dawn Barber** .... (757) 926-1680

Libraries and Information Services
Fountain Plaza Two, 700 Town Center Dr., Suite 300,
Newport News, VA 23606
Fax: (757) 926-1365

Director **Izabela M. Cieszynski** .... (757) 926-1350
E-mail: icieszynski@nngov.com
Education: Wisconsin (Oshkosh) BA; Wisconsin MA

Newport News Waterworks
Fountain Plaza Two, 700 Town Center Dr., Suite 500,
Newport News, VA 23606
Fax: (757) 926-1170

Director **Kofi A. Boateng** .... (757) 926-1146
Assistant Director **Scott Dewhirst** .... (757) 926-1146

Department of Parks Recreation and Tourism
Fountain Plaza Two, 700 Town Center Dr., Suite 320,
Newport News, VA 23606
Fax: (757) 926-1460

Director **Michael Poplawski** .... (757) 926-1400
Assistant Director **Michael Nealer** .... (757) 926-1400
Assistant Director of Administration **Tammy Jordan** ..... (757) 926-1400
E-mail: tjordan@nngov.com

Planning
City Hall, 2400 Washington Ave., Newport News, VA 23607
Fax: (757) 926-3639

Director **Sheila McAllister** .... (757) 926-8761
Assistant Director **Michael King** .... (757) 926-3832

Police Department
9710 Jefferson Avenue, Newport News, VA 23605
Fax: (757) 928-4607

Police Chief **Richard W. "Rick" Myers** .... (757) 928-4300

Public Works
513 Oyster Point Rd., Newport News, VA 23602
Fax: (757) 269-2725

Director **H. Reed Fowler, Jr.** .... (757) 933-2311
Education: Christopher Newport BA; Old Dominion MPA
Assistant Director **Eddie Crockett** .... (757) 269-2311
Assistant Director **Judith L. Hines** .... (757) 269-2703

Purchasing Department
City Hall, 2400 Washington Ave., Newport News, VA 23607
Fax: (757) 926-8038

Purchasing Agent **Gary Sightler** .... (757) 926-8027
E-mail: gsightler@nnva.gov
Purchasing Manager **Shari D. Colvin** .... (757) 926-8031
E-mail: scolvin@nngov.com

Vehicle and Equipment Services
525 Operations Dr., Newport News, VA 23602
Fax: (757) 269-2424

Director **Bob McElheney** .... (757) 269-2402

Newport News Public Schools
12465 Warwick Blvd., Newport News, VA 23606
Fax: (757) 599-8270 Internet: http://www.nnschools.org/

Superintendent **Dr. Ashby Kilgore** .... (757) 591-4502

★ Elected Official ▲ Appointed by Legislature ▼ Appointed by Governor ▶ Appointed by Board or Commission ● Appointed by Judge
■ Appointed by Mayor △ Appointed by Freeholders ▽ Appointed by Supervisor ▷ Appointed by County Executive ○ Appointed by Council

City of Newton, Massachusetts

1000 Commonwealth Avenue, Newton, MA 02459
Internet: www.newtonma.gov/

County: Middlesex **Election Type:** Nonpartisan **Year Founded:** 1688
Year Incorporated: 1873 **Population:** 88,817 (2015)

Office of the Mayor

1000 Commonwealth Ave., Newton, MA 02459
Fax: (617) 796-1113

★ Mayor **Setti D. Warren** .... (617) 796-1100
Began Service: January 1, 2010
Term Expires: December 31, 2017
E-mail: swarren@newtonma.gov
Education: Boston Col 1993 BA
Career: New England Regional Director, Federal Emergency Management Agency (2000-2001); National Trip Director, Kerry-Edwards 2004, Inc. (2004); Deputy State Director (D-MA), Boston Office, Office of Senator John F. Kerry, United States Senate (2004-2008)

■ Chief of Staff/Chief Financial Officer
Maureen Lemieux .... (617) 796-1100
E-mail: mlemieux@newtonma.gov

■ Chief Administrative Officer **Dori Zaleznik** .... (617) 796-1100
E-mail: dzaleznik@newtonma.gov

■ Citizen Assistance Officer **Terry Crowley** .... (617) 796-1110
E-mail: tcrowley@newtonma.gov

Office of the City Council

1000 Commonwealth Ave., Newton, MA 02459
Tel: (617) 796-1210 Fax: (617) 796-1214

★ President **Scott Lennon** (At-Large, Ward 1) .... (617) 796-1210
Term Expires: January 2, 2018
E-mail: slennon@newtonma.gov

★ Vice President **Cheryl Lappin** (Ward 8) .... (617) 796-1210
Term Expires: January 2, 2018
E-mail: clappin@newtonma.gov

★ Alderman **Alison M. Leary** (Ward 1) .... (617) 796-1210
Term Expires: January 2, 2018
E-mail: aleary@newtonma.gov

★ Alderman **Alan Ciccone, Jr.** (At-Large, Ward 1) .... (617) 796-1210
Term Expires: January 2, 2018
E-mail: acicconejr@newtonma.gov

★ Alderman **Emily Norton** (Ward 2) .... (617) 796-1210
Term Expires: January 2, 2018
E-mail: enorton@newtonma.gov

★ Alderman **Susan S. Albright** (At-Large, Ward 2) .... (617) 796-1210
Term Expires: January 2, 2018
E-mail: salbright@newtonma.gov

★ Alderman
Jacob Daniel Auchincloss (At-Large, Ward 2) .... (617) 796-1210
Term Expires: January 2, 2018

★ Alderman **Barbara Brousal-Glaser** (Ward 3) .... (857) 796-1210
Term Expires: January 2, 2018
E-mail: bglaser@newtonma.gov

★ Alderman **James R. Cote** (At-Large, Ward 3) .... (617) 796-1210
Term Expires: January 2, 2018
E-mail: jcote@newtonma.gov

★ Alderman **Ted Hess-Mahan** (At-Large, Ward 3) .... (617) 796-1210
Term Expires: January 2, 2018
E-mail: thessmahan@newtonma.gov

★ Alderman **John W. Harney** (Ward 4) .... (617) 796-1210
Term Expires: January 2, 2018
E-mail: jharney@newtonma.gov

★ Alderman **Leonard J. Gentile** (At-Large, Ward 4) .... (617) 796-1210
Term Expires: January 2, 2018
E-mail: lgentile@newtonma.gov

Office of the City Council *continued*

★ Alderman **Amy Mah Sangiolo** (At-Large, Ward 4) .... (617) 796-1210
Term Expires: January 2, 2018
E-mail: asangiolo@newtonma.gov

★ Alderman **John Rice** (Ward 5) .... (617) 796-1210
Term Expires: January 2, 2018
E-mail: jrice@newtonma.gov

★ Alderman **Deborah Crossley** (At-Large, Ward 5) .... (617) 796-1210
Term Expires: January 2, 2018
E-mail: dcrossley@newtonma.gov

★ Alderman **Brian Yates** (At-Large, Ward 5) .... (617) 796-1210
Term Expires: January 2, 2018
E-mail: byates@newtonma.gov

★ Alderman **Richard Blazar** (Ward 6) .... (617) 796-1210
Term Expires: January 2, 2018
E-mail: rblazar@newtonma.gov

★ Alderman **Victoria Danberg** (At-Large, Ward 6) .... (617) 796-1210
Term Expires: January 2, 2018
E-mail: vdanberg@newtonma.gov

★ Alderman **Greg Schwartz** (At-Large, Ward 6) .... (617) 796-1210
Term Expires: January 2, 2018
E-mail: gschwartz@newtonma.gov

★ Alderman **R. Lisle Baker** (Ward 7) .... (617) 796-1210
Term Expires: January 2, 2018
E-mail: lbaker@newtonma.gov

★ Alderman **Ruthanne Fuller** (At-Large, Ward 7) .... (617) 796-1210
Term Expires: January 2, 2018
E-mail: rfuller@newtonma.gov

★ Alderman **Marc C. Laredo** (At-Large, Ward 7) .... (617) 796-1210
Term Expires: January 2, 2018
E-mail: mlaredo@newtonma.gov

★ Alderman **David A. Kalis** (At-Large, Ward 8) .... (617) 796-1210
Term Expires: January 2, 2018
E-mail: dkalis@newtonma.gov

★ Alderman **Richard Lipof** (At-Large, Ward 8) .... (617) 796-1210
Term Expires: January 2, 2018
E-mail: rlipof@newtonma.gov

Clerk of the Board **David A. Olson** .... (617) 796-1200
E-mail: dolson@newtonma.gov Fax: (617) 796-1214
Education: Colorado MA

Office of the Assessor

1000 Commonwealth Ave., Newton, MA 02459
Fax: (617) 796-1179 Internet: www.newtonma.gov/gov/assessor/

■ Assessor **Elizabeth Dromey** .... (617) 796-1160
E-mail: dromey@newtonma.gov Fax: (617) 796-1179

Office of the City Clerk

1000 Commonwealth Ave., Newton, MA 02459
Fax: (617) 796-1214 Internet: www.newtonma.gov/gov/clerk/

► City Clerk and Clerk of the Board of Aldermen
David A. Olson .... (617) 796-1200
E-mail: dolson@newtonma.gov
Education: Colorado MA

Office of the Comptroller

1000 Commonwealth Ave., Room 108, Newton, MA 02459
Fax: (617) 796-1196

► Comptroller **David Wilkinson** .... (617) 796-1300
E-mail: dwilkinson@newtonma.gov Fax: (617) 796-1196

Office of the Treasurer-Collector

1000 Commonwealth Ave., Room 115, Newton, MA 02459
Fax: (617) 796-1343 Internet: www.newtonma.gov/gov/treasury/

■ Treasurer-Collector **James Reardon** .... (617) 796-1330
E-mail: jreardon@newtonma.gov Fax: (617) 796-1331

★ Elected Official ▲ Appointed by Legislature ▼ Appointed by Governor ► Appointed by Board or Commission ● Appointed by Judge
■ Appointed by Mayor △ Appointed by Freeholders ▽ Appointed by Supervisor ▷ Appointed by County Executive ○ Appointed by Council

Elections Department
1000 Commonwealth Ave., Newton, MA 02459
Fax: (617) 796-1359 Internet: www.newtonma.gov/gov/elections/
Fax: (617) 796-1214

▶ City Clerk **David A. Olson** .... (617) 796-1200
E-mail: dolson@newtonma.gov
Education: Colorado MA

Engineering Department
1000 Commonwealth Ave., Room 104, Newton, MA 02459
Fax: (617) 796-1051 Internet: www.newtonma.gov/gov/dpw/engineering/

■ City Engineer **Lou Taverna** .... (617) 796-1020
E-mail: ltaverna@newtonma.gov Fax: (617) 796-1051

Fire Department
1164 Centre St., Newton Center, MA 02459
Internet: www.newtonma.gov/gov/fire/

■ Fire Chief **Bruce Proia** .... (617) 796-2210
E-mail: bproia@newtonma.gov
Assistant Fire Chief **Paul Chagnon** .... (617) 796-2210
E-mail: pchagnon@newtonma.gov

Health and Human Services Department
1000 Commonwealth Avenue, Newton, MA 02459
Fax: (617) 552-7063 Internet: www.newtonma.gov/gov/health/

Director **Deborah Youngblood** .... (617) 796-1420
Fax: (617) 552-7063

Human Resources Department
1000 Commonwealth Ave., Room 218, Newton, MA 02459
Fax: (617) 796-1272 Internet: www.newtonma.gov/gov/hr/

■ Director (Interim) **Jeffrey Honig** .... (617) 796-1260
E-mail: jhonig@newtonma.gov Fax: (617) 796-1272

Information Technology Department
1000 Commonwealth Ave., Room 107, Newton, MA 02459
Fax: (617) 796-1196 Internet: www.newtonma.gov/gov/it/default.asp

■ Chief Information Officer **Joseph Mulvey** .... (617) 796-1180
E-mail: jmulvey@newtonma.gov Fax: (617) 796-1196

Inspectional Services Department (Building Code and Zoning)
1000 Commonwealth Ave., Newton, MA 02459
Fax: (617) 796-1086
Internet: www.newtonma.gov/gov/inspsvcs/default.asp

■ Commissioner **John Lojek** .... (617) 796-1060
E-mail: jlojek@newtonma.gov Fax: (617) 796-1086

Jackson Homestead-Historic Museum
527 Washington St., Newton, MA 02458

■ Director **Lisa Dady** .... (617) 796-1450
E-mail: ldady@newtonma.gov Fax: (617) 552-7228

Law Department
Newton City Hall, 1000 Commonwealth Ave., Room 208, Newton, MA 02459
Fax: (617) 796-1254
Internet: http://www.newtonma.gov/gov/legal/default.asp

■ City Solicitor **Donnalyn B. Lynch Kahn** .... (617) 796-1240
E-mail: law@newtonma.gov

Newton Free Library
330 Homer St., Newton, MA 02459
Internet: www.newtonfreelibrary.net

■ Director **Philip McNulty** .... (617) 796-1400
E-mail: pmcnulty@minlib.net Fax: (617) 965-8457

Parks and Recreation Department
Kennard Park, 246 Dudley Road, Newton, MA 02459
Fax: (617) 769-1512 E-mail: parks@newtonma.gov

■ Commissioner **Robert J. DeRubeis** .... (617) 796-1500
E-mail: rderubeis@newtonma.gov Fax: (617) 796-1512

Planning and Development Department
1000 Commonwealth Ave., Newton, MA 02459
Fax: (617) 796-1142
Internet: www.newtonma.gov/gov/planning/default.asp

Director (Interim) **James Freas** .... (617) 796-1137
E-mail: jfreas@newtonma.gov

Police Department
1321 Washington St., West Newton, MA 02465
Fax: (617) 796-3684 Internet: www.newtonpolice.com/

■ Chief of Police **David L. MacDonald** .... (617) 796-2101
E-mail: dmacdonald@newtonma.gov Fax: (617) 796-3679
Patrol Bureau Commander **Christopher Marzilli** .... (617) 796-2101
Fax: (617) 796-3679

Newton Public Schools
100 Walnut St., Newton, MA 02460
Internet: http://www.newtonpublicschools.com

Superintendent of Schools **Dr. David Fleischman** .... (617) 559-6100
Fax: (617) 559-6101

Public Works Department
1000 Commonwealth Ave., Newton, MA 02459
E-mail: dpw@newtonma.gov
Internet: www.newtonma.gov/gov/dpw/default.asp

■ Commissioner **James "Jim" McGonagle** .... (617) 796-1010
E-mail: jmcgonagle@newtonma.gov Fax: (617) 796-1050

Purchasing Department
1000 Commonwealth Ave., Room 204, Newton, MA 02459
Fax: (617) 796-1227
Internet: www.newtonma.gov/gov/purchasing/default.asp

■ Chief Procurement Officer **Nick Read** .... (617) 796-1220
E-mail: nread@newtonma.gov Fax: (617) 796-1227

Veterans' Services Department-Licensing Board
1000 Commonwealth Ave., Newton, MA 02459
Internet: www.newtonma.gov/gov/veterans/default.asp

■ Licensing Board and Veteran's Agent **(Vacant)** .... (617) 796-1090
Fax: (617) 796-1094

Weights and Measures
1000 Commonwealth Ave., Newton, MA 02459
Fax: (617) 796-1094

■ Sealer of Weights and Measures **Mitchel Baker** .... (617) 796-1099
E-mail: mbaker@newtonma.gov Fax: (617) 796-1094

★ Elected Official ▲ Appointed by Legislature ▼ Appointed by Governor ▶ Appointed by Board or Commission ● Appointed by Judge
■ Appointed by Mayor △ Appointed by Freeholders ▽ Appointed by Supervisor ▷ Appointed by County Executive ○ Appointed by Council

City of Norfolk, Virginia

City Hall, 810 Union St., Norfolk, VA 23510
Tel: (757) 664-6510 (Information) Internet: http://www.norfolk.gov

County: None **Election Type:** Nonpartisan **Population:** 246,393 (2015)

Office of the Mayor and City Council

1001 City Hall, 810 Union Street, Norfolk, VA 23510
Fax: (757) 441-2909 Internet: www.norfolk.gov/City_Hall/

★ Mayor-Elect
Kenneth Cooper "Kenny" Alexander
Began Service: July 1, 2016
Term Expires: June 30, 2020
Education: Old Dominion BS; Norwich MA
Secretary **Mary Lou Stone** . . . . (757) 664-4679

★ Vice Mayor **Angelia M. Williams Graves** (Ward 7) . . . . . (757) 664-7850
Term Expires: June 30, 2020
E-mail: angelia.williams@norfolk.gov

★ Council Member **Andrew A. Protogyrou** (Ward 1) . . . . . . (757) 664-7850
Note: Until July 1, 2016
Term Expires: June 30, 2018
E-mail: andrew.protogyrou@norfolk.gov

★ Council Member **Dr. Theresa W. Whibley** (Ward 2) . . . . . (757) 664-7850
Term Expires: June 30, 2018
E-mail: theresa.whibley@norfolk.gov

★ Council Member **Mamie B. Johnson** (Ward 3) . . . . (757) 664-7850
Term Expires: June 30, 2018

★ Council Member **Paul R. Riddick** (Ward 4) . . . . (757) 664-7850
Term Expires: June 30, 2018
E-mail: paul.riddick@norfolk.gov

★ Council Member **Thomas R. Smigiel, Jr.** (Ward 5) . . . . . . (757) 664-7850
Term Expires: June 30, 2018
E-mail: thomas.smigiel@norfolk.gov

★ Council Member-Elect **Andria McClellan** (Ward 6) . . . . . . (757) 664-7850
Term Expires: June 30, 2020

Intergovernmental Relations Director
Bryan Pennington . . . . (757) 664-4467
E-mail: bryan.pennington@norfolk.gov Fax: (757) 664-4263

Office of the City Clerk

1006 City Hall, 810 Union St., Norfolk, VA 23510
Fax: (757) 664-4290

○ City Clerk **R. Breckenridge Daughtrey** . . . . (757) 664-4289
E-mail: breck.daughtrey@norfolk.gov

Chief Deputy Clerk **Allan Bull** . . . . (757) 664-4288
E-mail: allan.bull@norfolk.gov

Records Management

City Hall, 1st Fl., East Wing, Norfolk, VA 23510

Records Administrator **Robert C. Kolstee** . . . . (757) 664-4737
Education: Maryland 1989 BS

Office of the City Attorney

810 Union Street, Suite 900, Norfolk, VA 23510
Fax: (757) 664-4201

○ City Attorney **Bernard A. Pishko** . . . . (757) 664-4529
E-mail: bernard.pishko@norfolk.gov

Office of the City Auditor

City Hall, 810 Union St., Room 806, Norfolk, VA 23510
Fax: (757) 441-2922

City Auditor **John Sanderlin** . . . . (757) 664-4044

Office of the City Real Estate Assessor

402 City Hall, 810 Union St., Norfolk, VA 23510

City Real Estate Assessor **Bill Marchand** . . . . (757) 664-4732
E-mail: real.estate@norfolk.gov

Office of the City Manager

1101 City Hall, 810 Union St., Norfolk, VA 23510
Fax: (757) 664-4239 Internet: www.norfolk.gov/CityManager/

○ City Manager **Marcus D. Jones** . . . . (757) 664-4242
E-mail: city.manager@norfolk.gov
Education: James Madison BS; VCU MPA
Deputy City Manager **Wynter Benda** . . . . (757) 664-4242
E-mail: wynter.benda@norfolk.gov

Deputy City Manager **Peter H. Chapman** . . . . (757) 664-4242
E-mail: peter.chapman@norfolk.gov

Deputy City Manager **Sabrina Joy-Hogg** . . . . (757) 664-4242
E-mail: sabrina.joy-hogg@norfolk.gov
Education: SUNY (Stony Brook) BA, MSW

Deputy City Manager **Ronald H. Williams** . . . . (757) 664-4242
E-mail: ron.williams@norfolk.gov

Chief Resilience Officer **Christine Morris** . . . . (757) 923-1133

Communications and Community Enrichment Division

302 City Hall, 810 Union Street, Norfolk, VA 23510
Fax: (757) 664-4006

Communications Director **Robert "Bob" Batcher** . . . . (757) 664-4008
E-mail: bob.batcher@norfolk.gov

Cultural Facilities, Arts and Entertainment Department

Scope Arena, Norfolk, VA 23510-2411
Fax: (757) 664-6990

Director **John S. Rhamstine** . . . . (757) 664-6953
Education: American U 1976 BA; UMass (Amherst) 1980 MS

Assistant Director **Rob Henson** . . . . (757) 664-6955

MacArthur Memorial Director **Christopher Kolakowski** . . (757) 441-2965
MacArthur Square, Norfolk, VA 23510

Accounting Supervisor **Kim Bartlett** . . . . (757) 664-6959
E-mail: kim.bartlett@norfolk.gov

Box Office Manager **Heather Mitchell** . . . . (757) 664-6965

Event Manager **(Vacant)** . . . . (757) 664-6973

Marketing Coordinator **Melissa Skinner** . . . . (757) 664-6863

Event Coordinator **Denise Christian** . . . . (757) 664-6966

Event Coordinator **Megan Mensink** . . . . (757) 664-6966

Event Coordinator **Beth Miller** . . . . (757) 664-6958

Stage Production Manager **Chris Smith** . . . . (757) 664-6956

Office Manager **Charlotte Reese** . . . . (757) 664-6951

Media Coordinator **Ma'rie Hodges** . . . . (757) 664-6966
E-mail: marie.hodges@norfolk.gov

Cultural Affairs Manager **Karen Rudd** . . . . (757) 664-6880

Development Department

500 East Main Street, 15th Floor, Suite 1500, Norfolk, VA 23510
Fax: (757) 441-2910 Internet: www.norfolkdevelopment.com/

Director **Charles E. "Chuck" Rigney, Sr.** . . . . (757) 664-4763
E-mail: chuck.rigney@norfolk.gov

Office Manager **Dawn Ryan** . . . . (757) 664-4314
E-mail: dawn.ryan@norfolk.gov

Assistant Director of Marketing **Sarah Parker** . . . . (757) 664-4338

Senior Business Development Manager **Alan Boring** . . . . . (757) 664-4317
E-mail: alan.boring@norfolk.gov

Assistant Director **Jared Chalk** . . . . (757) 664-4105
E-mail: jared.chalk@norfolk.gov

Senior Business Development/Chief Financial Officer
Leslie Osborn . . . . (757) 664-4333
E-mail: leslie.osborn@norfolk.gov

Business Development Manager **Mike Cutter** . . . . (757) 664-4329
E-mail: mike.cutter@norfolk.gov

Business Development Manager **Larry Lombardi** . . . . (757) 664-4187
E-mail: larry.lombardi@norfolk.gov
Education: Maryland 1974 BSHPhEd

Research Analyst **Janice Hurley** . . . . (757) 664-4753
E-mail: janice.hurley@norfolk.gov

Business Concierge **Chris Tillett** . . . . (757) 664-4318
E-mail: christopher.tillett@norfolk.gov

★ Elected Official ▲ Appointed by Legislature ▼ Appointed by Governor ▶ Appointed by Board or Commission ● Appointed by Judge
■ Appointed by Mayor △ Appointed by Freeholders ▽ Appointed by Supervisor ▷ Appointed by County Executive ○ Appointed by Council

Department of Finance
600 City Hall, 810 Union St., Norfolk, VA 23510
Fax: (757) 664-4110 Internet: www.norfolk.gov/fbs/

Director **Christine Garczynski** (757) 664-4346
Administrative Assistant **Sheri Eland** (757) 664-4052
E-mail: sheri.eland@norfolk.gov
Employees' Retirement System Executive Secretary **Galen Gresalfi** Room 309 (757) 664-4738
Purchasing Agent **Elizabeth Dooley** (757) 664-4787
E-mail: elizabeth.dooley@norfolk.gov Fax: (757) 664-4018

Office of Budget and Strategic Planning
1002 City Hall, 810 Union St., Norfolk, VA 23510
Fax: (757) 441-2234

Director **(Vacant)** (757) 664-4283

Department of General Services
230 East Main Street, Norfolk, VA 23510
Tel: (757) 664-4066
Internet: http://www.norfolk.gov/index.aspx?NID=1300

Director **David S. Freeman** (757) 664-4066 ext. 7
E-mail: david.freeman@norfolk.gov
Facilities Maintenance Manager **Dennis Bagley** (757) 823-4567
401 Monticello Avenue, Norfolk, VA 23510
Fleet Manager **Facundo Tassara** (757) 441-5700
401 Monticello Avenue, Norfolk, VA 23510
Parking Administrator **Bart Neu** 2nd Floor (757) 664-6229
Fax: (757) 441-2419

Human Resources Department
City Hall, East Wing, 810 Union Street, Norfolk, VA 23510-2717
Fax: (757) 664-4492 Internet: www.norfolk.gov/Human_Resources/

Director **Capri M. Stanley-Smith** (757) 664-4486
E-mail: capri.stanley@norfolk.gov

Human Services Department
741 Monticello Avenue, Norfolk, VA 23510
Tel: (757) 664-6000 Fax: (757) 664-6286
Internet: www.norfolk.gov/humanservices/

Director **Stephen K. "Steve" Hawks** (757) 664-6101
Education: Old Dominion BA; Virginia MPA
Operations Manager **Christina Francis-Talley** (757) 664-3262
E-mail: christina.francis@norfolk.gov Fax: (757) 664-6050

Information Technology Department
401 Monticello Avenue, 3rd Floor, Norfolk, VA 23510
Tel: (757) 664-4500 Fax: (757) 664-4567

Chief Information Officer **Steven H. DeBerry** (757) 664-4561
E-mail: steven.deberry@norfolk.gov
Assistant Director **(Vacant)** (757) 664-4531
Wireless Communications Manager **Jerry Burkhalter** (757) 441-5800
E-mail: jerry.burkhalter@norfolk.gov
Applications Manager **(Vacant)** (757) 664-4531
Service and Support Manager **Terri Smith** (757) 664-6895
E-mail: terri.smith@norfolk.gov
Enterprise Solutions Manager **Chip Finch** (757) 664-6888
E-mail: chip.finch@norfolk.gov
Receptionist **(Vacant)** (757) 664-4500

Libraries Department
Norfolk Public Library, 1155 Pineridge Road, Norfolk, VA 23502
Tel: (757) 664-7328 Fax: (757) 441-5863

Director of Libraries **Sonal Rastogi** (757) 441-5911
E-mail: sonal.rastogi@norfolk.gov
Information Technology Manager **Cathy Thomann** (757) 664-7328 ext. 316
E-mail: cathy.thomann@norfolk.gov
Support Services Manager **Sean Bilby** (757) 664-7328 ext. 311
E-mail: sean.bilby@norfolk.gov

Libraries Department *continued*

Public Services Manager **Susan Mercer** (757) 664-7328 ext. 308
E-mail: Susan.Mercer@norfolk.gov

Norfolk Fire-Rescue
100 Brooke Avenue, Suite 500, Norfolk, VA 23510
Fax: (757) 624-6832 Internet: www.norfolk.gov/NFR/

Fire Chief **Jeffrey F. Wise** (757) 664-6600
E-mail: firechief@norfolk.gov

Department of City Planning
508 City Hall, 810 Union St., Norfolk, VA 23510
Fax: (757) 664-4748

Director **George Homewood** (757) 664-4744
E-mail: george.homewood@norfolk.gov
Business Manager **Alice Hutton** (757) 664-4744

Building Safety Bureau
400 Granby Street, Norfolk, VA 23510-1914
Tel: (757) 664-6565 Fax: (757) 664-6899

Code Official **Richard Fortner** (757) 664-6511
Deputy Code Official **Vernell A. Woods, Jr.** (757) 664-6526

Planning Division
508 City Hall, 810 Union St., Norfolk, VA 23510

Environmental Services Bureau Manager **Edwin L. Rosenberg** (757) 664-4373
Fax: (757) 441-1569
Transportation Services Bureau Manager **Jeffrey K. Raliski** (757) 664-4752
Zoning Services Bureau Manager **Leonard M. Newcomb III** (757) 664-4752

Police Department
100 Brooke Ave., Norfolk, VA 23510-1826
Fax: (757) 664-3278

Chief of Police **Michael Goldsmith** (757) 664-3277
Education: Old Dominion 1988 BA, 1998 MA; William & Mary 2007 MBA
Administrative Services Assistant Chief **Francis Emerson** (757) 664-3277
Field Operations Assistant Chief **Larry Boone** (757) 664-3293
Assistant Chief, Police Administration and Chief of Staff **Joseph Clark** (757) 664-3277
Strategic Management **Wayne McBride** (757) 664-6504
Training **Capt. Wallace Driskell** (757) 664-6688
E-mail: wallace.driskell@norfolk.gov

Public Works Department
City Hall, 810 Union Street, 8th Floor, Norfolk, VA 23510-2717
Tel: (757) 664-4600 Fax: (757) 664-4603
Internet: http://www.norfolk.gov/publicworks/
E-mail: pworks@norfolk.gov

Director **David L. Ricks** (757) 664-4614
Assistant Director **Richard Broad** (757) 664-4600
Management Services Administrator **Janeen White** (757) 664-4611
E-mail: janeen.white@norfolk.gov
City Transportation Engineer **Rob D. Brown** (757) 664-7300
810 Union Street, 2nd Floor, Norfolk, VA 23510
E-mail: robert.brown@norfolk.gov
City Engineer **Sid Kitterman** (757) 664-4600
E-mail: sid.kitterman@norfolk.gov
Assistant City Engineer **Charles P. Joyner** (757) 664-4600
E-mail: charles.joyner@norfolk.gov
Construction Engineer **Tim McCrane** (757) 664-4600
E-mail: tim.mccrane@norfolk.gov
Design Engineer **Chris L. Chambers** (757) 664-4600
E-mail: chris.chambers@norfolk.gov

(continued on next page)

★ Elected Official ▲ Appointed by Legislature ▼ Appointed by Governor ▶ Appointed by Board or Commission ● Appointed by Judge
■ Appointed by Mayor △ Appointed by Freeholders ▽ Appointed by Supervisor ▷ Appointed by County Executive ○ Appointed by Council

Public Works Department *continued*

Structural and Waterfront Facilities Engineer
C. Wayne Webster .... (757) 664-4600
E-mail: wayne.webster@norfolk.gov

City Architect **Robert D. Meadows** .... (757) 664-4600

Storm Water Engineer **John M. White** .... (757) 823-4000
2333 McKann Ave., Norfolk, VA 23517
E-mail: john.white@norfolk.gov

Streets and Bridges Engineer (Acting) **Dave Lucas** .... (757) 823-4050
2205 McKann Avenue, Norfolk, VA 23509
E-mail: dave.lucas@norfolk.gov

Traffic Operations Superintendent
Gerald "Jerry" Riddick .... (757) 441-5818
4505 Patent Road, Norfolk, VA 23502

Waste Management Superintendent **Harvey Howard** .... (757) 664-6510
1176 Pineridge Rd., Norfolk, VA 23502 Fax: (757) 664-6510

Budget and Finance Manager **Karen Colombo** .... (757) 664-4633
E-mail: karen.colombo@norfolk.gov

City Surveyor **John Ward** .... (757) 664-4673

Clean Community Coordinator **Lisa Renee Jennings** .... (757) 441-1347

Department of Recreation, Parks and Open Space

501 Boush St., Norfolk, VA 23510
Fax: (757) 441-5423 Internet: www.norfolk.gov/rpos/

Director **Darrell Crittendon** .... (757) 441-2400

Assistant Director **Wayne Green** .... (757) 441-2400 ext. 262

Bureau Manager, Cemeteries **Armistead "Ted" Dudley** .. (757) 441-2576

Bureau Manager, Planning and Administration
(Vacant) .... (757) 441-2400 ext. 266

Bureau Manager, Recreation and Human Development
Edward Matthews .... (757) 441-2400

Parks and Urban Forestry Bureau Manager
Dean Bowles .... (757) 441-2400 ext. 245

Utilities Department

401 Monticello Avenue, Norfolk, VA 23510
P.O. Box 1080, Norfolk, VA 23501
Fax: (757) 664-6707 Internet: www.norfolk.gov/utilities/

Director **Kristen M. Lentz** .... (757) 664-6701

Assistant Director, Water Production and Utilities
Operations Manager **Eric G. Tucker** .... (757) 664-6701

Water Production Manager **Chris E. Harbin** .... (757) 441-5678
6040 Waterworks Rd., Norfolk, VA 23502

Water Quality Manager **(Vacant)** .... (757) 441-5678
6040 Waterworks Rd., Norfolk, VA 23502

Assistant Director, Accounting and Budget
Robert Carteris .... (757) 664-6701
E-mail: robert.carteris@norfolk.gov

Engineering Manager **Cherryl F. Barnett** .... (757) 664-6701
E-mail: cherryl.barnett@norfolk.gov

Reservoir Manager **David S. Rosenthal** .... (757) 441-5678

Wastewater Division Assistant Superintendent
Rodney Talley .... (757) 823-1001
1316 Ballentine Blvd, Norfolk, VA 23504

Water Distribution Division Assistant Superintendent
Sidney "Sid" Lowe, Jr. .... (757) 823-1001
1316 Ballentine Blvd., Norfolk, VA 23504

Customer Service Manager **Trinette D. Hodges** .... (757) 664-6701

Office of the City Treasurer

City Hall, 1st Fl., 810 Union St., Norfolk, VA 23510

★City Treasurer **Anthony L. Burfoot** .... (757) 664-7800
Term Expires: December 31, 2017
E-mail: anthony.burfoot@norfolk.gov

Office of the Commissioner of Revenue

City Hall, 1st Fl., 810 Union St., Norfolk, VA 23510
Tel: (757) 441-2781 Fax: (757) 441-1286

★Commissioner of Revenue **C. Evans Poston, Jr.** .... (757) 664-7890
Term Expires: December 31, 2017
E-mail: evans.poston@norfolk.gov

Office of the Commonwealth's Attorney

800 East City Hall Avenue, Suite 600, Norfolk, VA 23510-2719
Fax: (757) 664-4445 E-mail: cwainformation@norfolk.gov
Internet: www.norfolk.gov/commatty

★Commonwealth's Attorney **Gregory D. Underwood** .... (757) 664-4835
Term Expires: November 2017
E-mail: gregory.underwood@norfolk.gov
Date of Birth: June 30, 1955
Education: Fayetteville State 1980 BA; North Carolina 1987 JD

Chief Deputy Commonwealth's Attorney
Brent A. Johnson .... (757) 664-4818
E-mail: brent.johnson@norfolk.gov

Information Technology Administrator **Dmitry Rekhter** .. (757) 664-4816
E-mail: dmitry.rekhter@norfolk.gov

Office of the Sheriff

811 E. City Hall Ave., Norfolk, VA 23510
Fax: (757) 441-2531 Internet: www.norfolksheriffsoffice.com

★Sheriff **Robert J. McCabe** .... (757) 664-4700
Term Expires: December 31, 2017
E-mail: robert.mccabe@norfolk-sheriff.com

Office of Elections

P.O. Box 1531, Norfolk, VA 23501-1531
Fax: (757) 664-4685

Director of Elections and General Registrar
Stephanie Iles .... (757) 664-4353

Convention and Visitors Bureau/ VisitNorfolk

232 E. Main St., Norfolk, VA 23510
Fax: (757) 622-3663 Internet: www.visitnorfolktoday.com

President and Chief Executive Officer
Anthony J. DiFilippo .... (757) 664-6620

Vice President of Sales and Marketing **Donna Allen** .... (757) 664-6620

Director of Administration and Finance **Frank Reynolds** .. (757) 664-6620
E-mail: freynolds@visitnorfolktoday.com

Director of Convention and Visitor Services
Kristi Sinclair .... (757) 664-6620

Norfolk Public Schools

800 E. City Hall Ave., Norfolk, VA 23510
Fax: (757) 628-3820 Internet: www.nps.k12.va.us/

Superintendent **Dr. Melinda Boone** .... (757) 628-3830

Senior Director of Information Systems
Andrea Sykora .... (757) 628-3450
E-mail: andrea.sykora@norfolk.gov Fax: (757) 628-3840

Governmental Affairs Deputy Superintendent
L'Tanya Simmons .... (757) 628-3930
Fax: (757) 628-3977

★Elected Official ▲Appointed by Legislature ▼Appointed by Governor ▶Appointed by Board or Commission ●Appointed by Judge
■Appointed by Mayor △Appointed by Freeholders ▽Appointed by Supervisor ▷Appointed by County Executive ○Appointed by Council

Norfolk Redevelopment and Housing Authority

201 Granby Street, Norfolk, VA 23510-1816
P.O. Box 968, Norfolk, VA 23501-0968
Tel: (757) 623-1111 Fax: (757) 314-2105 Internet: www.nrha.us

Executive Director **John Kownack** . . . . (757) 314-1679

City of Norman, Oklahoma

201 W. Gray St., Norman, OK 73069
P.O. Box 370, Norman, OK 73070
Internet: www.ci.norman.ok.us

County: Cleveland **Election Type:** Nonpartisan **Population:** 120,284 (2015)

Office of the Mayor and City Council

201 W. Gray St., Norman, OK 73069
P.O. Box 370, Norman, OK 73070
Fax: (405) 366-5389

★ Mayor-Elect **Lynne Miller** . . . . (405) 366-5402
Began Service: July 5, 2016
Term Expires: July 2019
E-mail: mayor@normanok.gov

★ Council Member **Greg Heiple** (Ward 1) . . . . (405) 447-5535
Term Expires: July 7, 2017
E-mail: ward1@normanok.gov

★ Council Member-Elect **Aleisha Karjala** (Ward 2) . . . . (405) 366-5406
Term Expires: July 2018
E-mail: ward2@normanok.gov

★ Council Member **Robert M. Castleberry** (Ward 3) . . . . . . (405) 821-3292
Term Expires: July 7, 2017
E-mail: ward3@normanok.gov

★ Council Member-Elect **Bill Hickman** (Ward 4) . . . . (405) 366-5406
Term Expires: July 2018
E-mail: ward4@normanok.gov

★ Council Member **(Vacant)** (Ward 5) . . . . (405) 366-5406
Term Expires: July 7, 2017
E-mail: ward5@normanok.gov

★ Council Member **Jerry Lang** (Ward 6) . . . . (405) 329-0568
Note: A runoff election between Jerry Lang and Breea Clark is scheduled for June 7, 2016.
Term Expires: July 1, 2016
E-mail: ward6@normanok.gov

★ Council Member **Stephen Holman** (Ward 7) . . . . (405) 535-1491
Term Expires: July 7, 2017
E-mail: ward7@normanok.gov

★ Council Member **Kyle Allison** (Ward 8) . . . . (405) 366-5406
Term Expires: July 1, 2018
E-mail: ward8@normanok.gov

Office of the City Manager

201 W. Gray St., Norman, OK 73069
P.O. Box 370, Norman, OK 73070

○ City Manager **Steven D. Lewis** . . . . (405) 366-5402
E-mail: city.manager@normanok.gov
Education: Texas A&I BS; North Texas MPA

Administrative Assistant **Stacey D. Parker** . . . . (405) 366-5402
E-mail: stacey.parker@normanok.gov
Education: Old Dominion BA

Chief Communications Officer **Claudia Deakins** . . . . (405) 366-5402

Office of the City Attorney

201 W. Gray St., Norman, OK 73069
P.O. Box 370, Norman, OK 73070
Fax: (405) 366-5425 E-mail: cityattorney@normanok.gov
Internet: www.ci.norman.ok.us/legal/city-attorney

City Attorney **Jeff Bryant** . . . . (405) 366-5423
E-mail: jeff.bryant@normanok.gov

Office of the City Clerk

201 W. Gray St., Norman, OK 73069
P.O. Box 370, Norman, OK 73070
Fax: (405) 366-5389 E-mail: city.clerk@ci.norman.ok.us
Internet: www.ci.norman.ok.us/cityclerk/city-clerk

City Clerk **Brenda Hall** . . . . (405) 366-5406
E-mail: brenda.hall@normanok.gov

Finance Department

201-C West Gray Street, Norman, OK 73069
P.O. Box 370, Norman, OK 73070
Fax: (405) 366-5417
Internet: www.ci.norman.ok.us/finance/financial-services

Finance Director **Anthony Francisco** . . . . (405) 366-5413

Fire Department

P.O. Box 370, Norman, OK 73070
Fax: (405) 292-9785
Internet: www.ci.norman.ok.us/content/fire-department

Fire Chief **James Fullingim** . . . . (405) 292-9780
E-mail: james.fullingim@normanok.gov

Norman Housing Authority

700 North Berry Road, Norman, OK 73069
Fax: (405) 329-2542

Executive Director **Karen Canavan** . . . . (405) 329-0933 ext. 303

Norman Public Schools

131 South Flood Avenue, Norman, OK 73069

Superintendent **Dr. Joseph Siano** . . . . (405) 366-5955
Chief Financial Officer **Brenda R. Burkett** . . . . (405) 366-5801

Human Resources Department

201-C West Gray Street, Norman, OK 73069
P.O. Box 370, Norman, OK 73070
Fax: (405) 366-5488 Internet: www.ci.norman.ok.us/hr/human-resources

Director **Gala Hicks** . . . . (405) 366-5482
E-mail: gala.hicks@normanok.gov

Municipal Court Department

201-B West Gray Street, Norman, OK 73069
P.O. Box 370, Norman, OK 73070

Court Clerk **Ronda Guerrero** . . . . (405) 366-5325

Parks and Recreation Department

201-C West Gray Street, Norman, OK 73069
P.O. Box 370, Norman, OK 73070
Internet: www.ci.norman.ok.us/parks/parks-and-recreation

Director **Jud Foster** . . . . (405) 366-5472

Planning and Community Development Department

201-A West Gray Street, Norman, OK 73069
P.O. Box 370, Norman, OK 73070
Internet: www.ci.norman.ok.us/content/planning-development

Director **Susan F. Conners** . . . . (405) 366-5433
E-mail: susan.connors@normanok.gov

★ Elected Official ▲ Appointed by Legislature ▼ Appointed by Governor ► Appointed by Board or Commission ● Appointed by Judge
■ Appointed by Mayor △ Appointed by Freeholders ▽ Appointed by Supervisor ▷ Appointed by County Executive ○ Appointed by Council

Police Department
201-B West Gray Street, Norman, OK 73069
P.O. Box 370, Norman, OK 73070
Fax: (405) 366-5329
Internet: www.ci.norman.ok.us/content/police-department

Chief of Police **Keith Humphrey** .... (405) 366-5201

Public Works Department
Building A, 201-A West Gray Street, Norman, OK 73069
P.O. Box 370, Norman, OK 73070
Fax: (405) 366-5418 Internet: www.ci.norman.ok.us/content/public-works

Director **Shawn O'Leary** .... (405) 366-5453

Utilities Department
201-C West Gray Street, Norman, OK 73069
P.O. Box 370, Norman, OK 73070
Fax: (405) 366-5447 Internet: http://www.ci.norman.ok.us/content/utilities

Director **Ken Komiske** .... (405) 366-5443

City of North Las Vegas, Nevada

2250 Las Vegas Boulevard North, North Las Vegas, NV 89030
Internet: www.cityofnorthlasvegas.com

County: Clark **Year Incorporated:** 1946 **Population:** 234,807 (2015)

Office of the Mayor and City Council
2250 Las Vegas Boulevard North, North Las Vegas, NV 89030
Fax: (702) 633-1302

★Mayor **John J. Lee** (At-Large) .... (702) 633-1007
Began Service: July 1, 2013
Term Expires: June 30, 2017
E-mail: leej@cityofnorthlasvegas.com
Special Assistant to the Mayor and City Council
Amanda Dillard .... (702) 633-1007
Executive Secretary to the Mayor **Chauntelle Popp** .... (702) 633-1007

★Mayor Pro Tem **Anita Wood** (Ward 3) .... (702) 633-1010
Term Expires: June 30, 2017
E-mail: wooda@cityofnorthlasvegas.com

★Council Member **Isaac E. Barron** (Ward 1) .... (702) 633-1011
Term Expires: June 30, 2017
E-mail: barroni@cityofnorthlasvegas.com

★Council Member **Pamela Goynes-Brown** (Ward 2) ...... (702) 633-1336
Term Expires: June 30, 2019
E-mail: goynesbrownp@cityofnorthlasvegas.com

★Council Member **Richard Chericho** (Ward 4) .... (702) 633-1194
Term Expires: June 30, 2019

Office of the City Attorney
2250 Las Vegas Boulevard North, North Las Vegas, NV 89030
Fax: (702) 649-8675

○City Attorney **Sandra Douglass Moran** .... (702) 633-1021
E-mail: morgans@cityofnorthlasvegas.com
Education: UNLV 2003 JD

Legal Office Administrator **Tammy Bonner** .... (702) 633-1043

Office of the City Clerk
2250 Las Vegas Boulevard North, North Las Vegas, NV 89030
Fax: (702) 649-3846

City Clerk **Barbara A. Andolina** .... (702) 633-1030
E-mail: andolinab@cityofnorthlasvegas.com

Office of the City Manager
2250 Las Vegas Boulevard North, North Las Vegas, NV 89030

City Manager **Qiong X. Liu** .... (702) 633-1002
E-mail: liuq@cityofnorthlasvegas.com

Deputy City Manager **Ryann Patrick-Shell Juden** ...... (702) 633-1005

Director of Communications **(Vacant)** .... (702) 633-1084

Executive Assistant **Joyce Wood** .... (702) 633-1002
E-mail: woodja@cityofnorthlasvegas.com

Community Development and Compliance Department
2250 Las Vegas Boulevard North, North Las Vegas, NV 89030

Director **Gregory W. Blackburn** .... (702) 633-2948
E-mail: blackburng@cityofnorthlasvegas.com
Education: U Phoenix BA, MBA

Neighborhood and Leisure Services Department
2250 Las Vegas Boulevard North, North Las Vegas, NV 89030

Director **Cass Palmer** .... (702) 633-1171
Fax: (702) 642-9163

Executive Secretary **Jaini Christison** .... (702) 633-1171
E-mail: christisonj@cityofnorthlasvegas.com

Parks Maintenance Services Manager **John Ortega** ...... (702) 633-6274
316 East Brooks Avenue, North Las Vegas, NV 89030

Finance Department
2250 Las Vegas Boulevard North, North Las Vegas, NV 89030
Fax: (702) 649-5077

Director **Darren Adair** .... (702) 633-1462

Web Architect **Adam Cohen** .... (702) 633-1854
E-mail: cohena@cityofnorthlasvegas.com Fax: (702) 649-6027

Information Technology Division Lead **Terry Fletcher** .... (702) 633-1683

Fire Department
4040 Losee Road, North Las Vegas, NV 89030

Fire Chief **Jeff Lytle** .... (702) 633-1105
E-mail: lytlej@cityofnorthlasvegas.com

Human Resources Department
2250 Las Vegas Boulevard North, North Las Vegas, NV 89030
Fax: (702) 649-2992 Tel: (702) 633-1514 (Jobline)

Director **(Vacant)** .... (702) 633-1501

North Las Vegas Library District
2300 Civic Center Drive, North, North Las Vegas, NV 89030
Fax: (702) 649-2576

Director **Forrest Lewis** .... (702) 633-1070
E-mail: lewisf@cityofnorthlasvegas.com

Police Department
2332 Las Vegas Boulevard North, Suite 200, North Las Vegas, NV 89030
Fax: (702) 649-2655

Chief of Police **Alex Perez** .... (702) 633-9111

Public Works Department
2250 Las Vegas Boulevard North, North Las Vegas, NV 89030
Fax: (702) 649-4696

Director **Jennifer Doody** .... (702) 633-1200

Deputy Director **(Vacant)** .... (702) 633-1223

Executive Secretary **Sonya Goetz** .... (702) 633-1919
E-mail: goetzs@cityofnorthlasvegas.com

Utilities Department
2250 Las Vegas Boulevard North, North Las Vegas, NV 89030
Fax: (702) 399-0383

Director **Randall E. "Randy" DeVaul** .... (702) 633-1903

★ Elected Official ▲ Appointed by Legislature ▼ Appointed by Governor ▶ Appointed by Board or Commission ● Appointed by Judge
■ Appointed by Mayor △ Appointed by Freeholders ▽ Appointed by Supervisor ▷ Appointed by County Executive ○ Appointed by Council

City of Norwalk, California

12700 Norwalk Boulevard, Norwalk, CA 90650
Tel: (562) 929-5700 Fax: (562) 929-5773 Internet: www.norwalkca.gov/

County: Los Angeles **Year Incorporated:** 1957 **Population:** 107,140 (2015)

Office of the Mayor and City Council

12700 Norwalk Blvd., Room 3, Norwalk, CA 90650
P.O. Box 1030, Norwalk, CA 90651-1030
Tel: (562) 929-5700 Fax: (562) 929-5780

★Mayor **Michael "Mike" Mendez** .... (562) 929-5700 ext. 5305
Began Service: March 1988
Term Expires: March 2017
E-mail: mmendez@norwalkca.gov

★Vice Mayor **Cheri Kelley** .... (562) 929-5700 ext. 5305
Term Expires: March 2017
E-mail: ckelley@norwalkca.gov

★Council Member **Marcel Rodarte** .... (562) 929-5700 ext. 5305
Term Expires: March 2019
E-mail: mrodarte@norwalkca.gov

★Council Member **Leonard Shryock** .... (562) 929-5700 ext. 5305
Term Expires: March 2019
E-mail: lshryock@norwalkca.gov

★Council Member **Luigi Vernola** .... (562) 929-5700 ext. 5305
Term Expires: March 2019
E-mail: lvernola@norwalkca.gov

Office of the City Manager

12700 Norwalk Boulevard, Norwalk, CA 90650
Fax: (562) 929-5780

City Manager **Michael J. Egan** .... (562) 929-5772
E-mail: admin@norwalkca.gov

Office of the City Attorney

12700 Norwalk Boulevard, Norwalk, CA 90650

City Attorney **Roxanne Diaz** .... (562) 929-5700

Community Development Department

12700 Norwalk Boulevard, Norwalk, CA 90650

Director **Kurt H. Anderson** .... (562) 929-5744
E-mail: kanderson@norwalkca.gov

Deputy City Manager

12700 Norwalk Boulevard, Norwalk, CA 90650

Deputy City Manager **Ernie Hernandez** .... (562) 929-5721
E-mail: ehernandez@norwalkca.gov

Office of the City Clerk

12700 Norwalk Boulevard, Norwalk, CA 90650
Fax: (562) 929-5773

City Clerk **Theresa Devoy** .... (562) 929-5720
E-mail: clerk@norwalkca.gov

Finance Department

12700 Norwalk Boulevard, Norwalk, CA 90650
Fax: (562) 929-5966 E-mail: finance@norwalkca.gov

Director **Jana Stuard** .... (562) 929-5750

Human Resources Department

12700 Norwalk Boulevard, Norwalk, CA 90650
Fax: (562) 929-5782 E-mail: personnel@norwalkca.gov

Director **Ernie Hernandez** .... (562) 929-5721
E-mail: ehernandez@norwalkca.gov

Public Safety Office

12700 Norwalk Boulevard, Norwalk, CA 90650
Fax: (562) 929-5780 E-mail: publicsafety@norwalkca.gov

Director **Carlos Ramos** .... (562) 929-5732
E-mail: cramos@norwalkca.gov

Sheriff's Department

12335 Civic Center Dr., Norwalk, CA 90650

Norwalk Station Captain **Curtis Jensen** .... (562) 863-8711

Deputy City Manager

12700 Norwalk Boulevard, Norwalk, CA 90650

Deputy City Manager **Gary DiCorpo** .... (562) 929-5511
E-mail: gdicorpo@norwalkca.gov

Public Services Department

12650 Imperial Highway, Norwalk, CA 90650
Fax: (562) 929-5503

Director **Gary DiCorpo** .... (562) 929-5511

Recreation and Parks Department

12700 Norwalk Boulevard, Room 10, Norwalk, CA 90650
Tel: (562) 929-5702 E-mail: recreation@norwalkca.gov

Director **Dave Verhaaf** .... (562) 929-5702

Social Services Department

11929 Alondra Blvd., Norwalk, CA 90650
Fax: (562) 929-5515

Director **Veronica Garcia** .... (562) 929-5544

Norwalk Transit System

12650 E. Imperial Highway, Norwalk, CA 90650
Fax: (562) 929-5572 E-mail: transit@norwalkca.gov

Director **James Parker** .... (562) 929-5533

City of Oakland, California

City Hall, One Frank H. Ogawa Plaza, Oakland, CA 94612

County: Alameda **Election Type:** Nonpartisan **Population:** 419,267 (2015)

Office of the Mayor

City Hall, One Frank H. Ogawa Plaza, Suite 321, Oakland, CA 94612
Tel: (510) 238-3141 Fax: (510) 238-4731
Internet: www2.oaklandnet.com/Government/o/Mayor/

★Mayor **Libby Schaaf** .... (510) 238-3141
Began Service: January 5, 2015
Term Expires: January 1, 2019
E-mail: lschaaf@oaklandnet.com

Chief of Staff **Tomiquia Moss** .... (510) 238-3141 ext. 7168

Communications Director **Erica Terry Derryck** .. (510) 238-3141 ext. 7072
E-mail: ederryck@oaklandnet.com

Office of the City Administrator

City Hall, One Frank H. Ogawa Plaza, 3rd Floor,
Oakland, CA 94612-1932
Fax: (510) 238-2223 E-mail: citymanager@oaklandnet.com

■City Administrator **Sabrina Landreth** .... (510) 238-3301
E-mail: cityadministrator@oaklandnet.com
Education: MIT BSME; UC Berkeley 2004 MA

Deputy City Administrator **Stephanie Hom** .... (510) 238-7542
E-mail: shom@oaklandnet.com

Assistant City Administrator **Claudia Cappio** .... (510) 238-6654
E-mail: ccappio@oaklandnet.com
Education: Ohio Wesleyan BA

(continued on next page)

★Elected Official ▲Appointed by Legislature ▼Appointed by Governor ▶Appointed by Board or Commission ●Appointed by Judge
■Appointed by Mayor △Appointed by Freeholders ▽Appointed by Supervisor ▷Appointed by County Executive ○Appointed by Council

Office of the City Administrator *continued*

Assistant City Administrator **Christine Daniel** .... (510) 238-6906
E-mail: cdaniel@oaklandnet.com
Education: Mills 1986 BA; UC Davis 1989 JD
Chief Resilience Officer **Victoria Salinas** .... (510) 238-3301
E-mail: vsalinas@oaklandnet.com
Education: Georgetown 2001 BSFS; JFK School Govt 2005 MPP
Budget Director/Deputy City Administrator **Kiran Bawa** .. (510) 238-8142
E-mail: kbawa@oaklandnet.com

Office of the City Clerk

City Hall, One Frank H. Ogawa Plaza, Suite 201, Oakland, CA 94612
Fax: (510) 238-6699

○ City Clerk and Clerk of the Council
LaTonda Simmons .... (510) 238-3612
E-mail: lsimmons@oaklandnet.com

Cultural Arts and Marketing Department [CAM]

One Frank Ogawa Plaza, 9th Floor, Oakland, CA 94612
Fax: (510) 238-6341

Manager **Samee Roberts** .... (510) 238-2136 ext. 1

Finance and Management Agency

150 Frank H. Ogawa Plaza, Suite 5215, Oakland, CA 94612-2093
Tel: (510) 238-2220 Fax: (510) 238-2059

Treasurer **Katano Kasaine** .... (510) 238-2989
Accounting Division **Osborn Solitei** .... (510) 238-3916
E-mail: osolitei@oaklandnet.com
Controller **David McPherson** .... (510) 238-6650
E-mail: dmcpherson@oaklandnet.com

Fire Department

150 Frank H. Ogawa Plaza, Suite 3354, Oakland, CA 94612
Tel: (510) 238-3856 Internet: www.oaklandnet.com/fire/

■ Fire Chief **Teresa Deloach Reed** .... (510) 238-4080
E-mail: tdeloachreed@oaklandnet.com Fax: (510) 238-2284
■ Fire Marshal **Miguel Trujillo** .... (510) 238-3851
E-mail: mtrujillo@oaklandnet.com Fax: (510) 238-6739
Training Battalion Chief **Melinda Drayton** .... (510) 238-3790
E-mail: mdrayton@oaklandnet.com Fax: (510) 451-3285
Medical Services Division Manager
Stewart McGehee .... (510) 238-6957
150 Frank H. Ogawa Plaza, Fax: (510) 238-6959
Suite 3354, Oakland, CA 94612-2092

Human Resource Department

150 Frank H. Ogawa Plaza, 2nd Floor, Oakland, CA 94612
Tel: (510) 238-3112 Fax: (510) 238-2325

Director **Anil Comelo** .... (510) 238-3112
E-mail: acomelo@oaklandnet.com
Executive Assistant **Victoria Chak** .... (510) 238-3112
E-mail: vchak@oaklandnet.com
Risk and Benefits Manager **Deborah Grant** .... (510) 238-3112
E-mail: dgrant@oaklandnet.com
Recruitment and Classification Manager **Kip Walsh** ...... (510) 238-3112
E-mail: kwalsh@oaklandnet.com

Human Services Department

150 Frank H. Ogawa Plaza, Suite 4340, Oakland, CA 94612-2092
Tel: (510) 238-3121 Internet: www.oaklandhumanservices.org/

Director **Sara Bedford** .... (510) 238-3121
Education: Yale 1979 BA
Aging and Adult Services Manager **Scott Means** .... (510) 238-6137
Community Action Partnership (CAP) Program Director
Estelle Clemons .... (510) 238-3597
Multi Senior Services Program (MSSP) **Karyl Eckels** .... (510) 238-2225
Oakland Paratransit for the Elderly and Disabled
Program Director **Hakiem McGee** .... (510) 238-2311

Human Services Department *continued*

Violence Prevention/Measure Program Director
Sara Bedford .... (510) 238-6794
Education: Yale 1979 BA
Senior Companion Program/Foster Grandparent Program
Director **Andrea Turner** .... (510) 238-2987
Children and Youth Services Division Manager
Sandra Taylor .... (510) 238-7163
Community Housing Services Division Manager
Susan Shelton .... (510) 238-6186
Early Childhood and Family Services/Head Start
Division Manager **Usana Hopkins** .... (510) 238-7186
Downtown Senior Center Director **Jennifer D. King** ..... (510) 238-3284
East Oakland Senior Center Director **Leroy Slaughter** ... (510) 615-5731
West Oakland Senior Center Director **Dorothy Poston** ... (510) 238-7016
North Oakland Senior Center Director **Mary Norton** ..... (510) 597-5085

Information Technology Department

One Frank H. Ogawa Plaza, Oakland, CA 94612

Chief Information Officer (Interim) **Katano Kasaine** ..... (510) 238-2930
E-mail: KKasaine@oaklandnet.com

Oakland Parks and Recreation

250 Frank H. Ogawa Plaza, 3rd Floor, Suite 3330,
Oakland, CA 94612-2032
Tel: (510) 238-7275 Fax: (510) 238-2224
Internet: www.oaklandnet.com/Parks/

Director (Interim) **Stephanie Hom** .... (510) 238-7532

Police Department

455 7th Street, Oakland, CA 94607
Fax: (510) 238-2251 Internet: www2.oaklandnet.com/Government/o/OPD/

Police Chief **Sean C. Whent** .... (510) 238-3365
Executive Assistant **Yolanda Morris** .... (510) 238-3365
E-mail: ymorris@oaklandnet.com
Chief of Staff **Sgt Eric Milina** .... (510) 238-3131
Bureau of Field Operations I Deputy Chief
David Downing .... (510) 238-7620
Bureau of Field Operations II Deputy Chief
Oliver Cunningham .... (510) 238-7048
Bureau of Investigations Deputy Chief **John M. Lois** .... (510) 238-6093
Bureau of Services Deputy Chief **Danielle Outlaw** .... (510) 238-7048
Criminal Investigation Division **Capt. Kirk Coleman** ..... (510) 238-4486

Oakland Animal Services

1101 29th Avenue, Oakland, CA 94601
Tel: (510) 535-5602 Fax: (510) 535-5601
Internet: http://oaklandanimalservices.org/

Director **Rebecca Katz** .... (510) 535-5602

Public Ethics Commission

One Frank Ogawa Plaza, Suite 104, Oakland, CA 94612
Fax: (510) 238-3315

Executive Director **Whitney Barazoto** .... (510) 238-3593

Oakland Public Library

125 - 14th St., Oakland, CA 94612
Fax: (510) 238-2232 Internet: www.oaklandlibrary.org/

Director **Gerry Garzon** .... (510) 238-6720
E-mail: ggarzon@oaklandlibrary.org
Associate Director **Jamie Turbak** .... (510) 238-6610
E-mail: jturbak@oaklandlibrary.org
Chief Financial Officer **Gene Tom** .... (510) 238-3283

Public Works Agency

250 Frank H. Ogawa Plaza, #4314, Oakland, CA 94612
Fax: (510) 238-6428

Director **Brooke Levin** .... (510) 238-4470

★ Elected Official ▲ Appointed by Legislature ▼ Appointed by Governor ▶ Appointed by Board or Commission ● Appointed by Judge
■ Appointed by Mayor △ Appointed by Freeholders ▽ Appointed by Supervisor ▷ Appointed by County Executive ○ Appointed by Council

Public Works Agency *continued*

Executive Assistant **Kelly Pschirrer** . . . . . (510) 238-3490
E-mail: kpschirrer@oaklandnet.com
Facilities and Environment Department Assistant Director **Susan Kattchee** . . . . . (510) 615-5451
Building 2, 7101 Edgewater Drive, Oakland, CA 94621
E-mail: skattchee@oaklandnet.com
Infrastructure and Operations Department Assistant Director **Jason Mitchell** . . . . . (510) 615-5856
Building 4, 7101 Edgewater Drive, Oakland, CA 94621
E-mail: jmitchell@oaklandnet.com
Administrative Manager **Tom Morgan** . . . . . (510) 238-2908
E-mail: tmorgan@oaklandnet.com
Engineering and Construction Department Assistant Director **Michael Neary** . . . . . (510) 615-5856
7101 Edgewater Drive, Oakland, CA 94621
E-mail: mneary@oaklandnet.com

Office of Economic and Workforce Development

250 Frank H. Ogawa Plaza, Suite 3315, Oakland, CA 94612
Tel: (510) 238-3627 Fax: (510) 238-2226

Economic Development Manager **Aliza Gallo** . . . . . (510) 238-7405
E-mail: agallo@oaklandnet.com

Office of Housing and Community Development

250 Frank H. Ogawa Plaza, Suite 5313, Oakland, CA 94612
Tel: (510) 238-3015 Fax: (510) 238-3691

Director **Michele Byrd** . . . . . (510) 238-3714
E-mail: mbyrd@oaklandnet.com Fax: (510) 238-3691

Office of Neighborhood Investment

250 Frank H. Ogawa Plaza, Suite 5313, Oakland, CA 94612
Tel: (510) 238-3015 Fax: (510) 238-6455

Director **Mark Sawicki** . . . . . (510) 238-2992
E-mail: msawicki@oaklandnet.com Fax: (510) 238-6455

Office of Planning, Building and Neighborhood Preservation

250 Frank H. Ogawa Plaza, 2114, Oakland, CA 94612
Tel: (510) 238-3443 Fax: (510) 238-2263

Director **Rachel Flynn** . . . . . (510) 238-2229
E-mail: rflynn@oaklandnet.com Fax: (510) 238-4730
Deputy Planning Director **Darin Ranelletti** . . . . . (510) 238-3663
E-mail: dranelletti@oaklandnet.com Fax: (510) 238-4730

Office of the City Council

City Hall, 2nd Fl., One Frank H. Ogawa Plaza, Oakland, CA 94612-2011
Tel: (510) 238-3266 Fax: (510) 238-6129 TTY: (510) 839-6451

★Council President **Lynette Gibson McElhaney** (District 3) . . . . . (510) 238-7003
Term Expires: January 9, 2017 Fax: (510) 238-6910
E-mail: lmcelhaney@oaklandnet.com
★President Pro Tem **Larry Reid** (District 7) . . . . . (510) 238-7007
Term Expires: January 9, 2017 Fax: (510) 238-6910
E-mail: lreid@oaklandnet.com
★Council Member **Daniel Kalb** (District 1) . . . . . (510) 238-7001
Term Expires: January 9, 2017 Fax: (510) 238-6910
E-mail: dkalb@oaklandnet.com
★Council Member **Abel J. Guillén** (District 2) . . . . . (510) 238-7002
Term Expires: January 2019 Fax: (510) 238-6910
E-mail: aguillen@oaklandnet.com
★Council Member **Annie Campbell Washington** (District 4) . . . . . (510) 238-7004
Term Expires: January 2019 Fax: (510) 238-6129
E-mail: acampbell-washington@oaklandnet.com
★Council Member **Noel Gallo** (District 5) . . . . . (510) 238-7005
Term Expires: January 9, 2017 Fax: (510) 238-6129
E-mail: ngallo@oaklandnet.com

Office of the City Council *continued*

★Council Member **Desley Brooks** (District 6) . . . . . (510) 238-7006
Term Expires: January 2019 Fax: (510) 238-6129
E-mail: dbrooks@oaklandnet.com
★Council Member **Rebecca Kaplan** (At-Large) . . . . . (510) 238-7008
Term Expires: January 9, 2017 Fax: (510) 238-6910
E-mail: rkaplan@oaklandnet.com
Executive Assistant to the Council **Susan A. Sanchez** . . . (510) 238-6917
E-mail: sasanchez@oaklandnet.com Fax: (510) 238-6129

Office of the City Attorney

One Frank H. Ogawa Plaza, 6th Floor, Oakland, CA 94612-1999
Tel: (510) 238-3601 Fax: (510) 238-6500
Internet: www.oaklandcityattorney.org/

★City Attorney **Barbara J. Parker** . . . . . (510) 238-3815
Term Expires: January 2017
E-mail: bparker@oaklandcityattorney.org
Chief Assistant City Attorney **Otis McGee** . . . . . (510) 238-6520
E-mail: omcgeejr@oaklandcityattorney.org
Chief Assistant City Attorney **Doryanna Moreno** . . . . . (510) 238-3815
E-mail: dmoreno@oaklandcityattorney.org
Administrative Analyst **Marke Forte** . . . . . (510) 238-3827
E-mail: mforte@oaklandcityattorney.org
Network Administrator **Craig Strunk** . . . . . (510) 238-2165
E-mail: rcstrunk@oaklandcityattorney.org

Office of the City Auditor

City Hall, 4th Fl., One Frank H. Ogawa Plaza, Oakland, CA 94612
Fax: (510) 238-7640 Internet: www.oaklandauditor.com/

★City Auditor **Brenda Roberts** . . . . . (510) 238-3378
Term Expires: January 1, 2019
E-mail: broberts@oaklandnet.com

Oakland Unified School District [OUSD]

1025 Second Avenue, Oakland, CA 94606
Fax: (510) 879-8200

Superintendent **Antwan Wilson** . . . . . (510) 879-8200 ext. 6
Senior Executive Assistant **Julia Gordon** . . . . . (510) 879-8200
E-mail: julia.gordon@ousd.k12.ca.us
Information Technology Officer **John Krull** . . . . . (510) 879-8872
E-mail: john.krull@ousd.k12.ca.us
Chief of Communications and Public Affairs **Isaac Kos-Read** . . . . . (510) 879-4260
E-mail: isaac.kos-read@ousd.org
Education: Stanford BA

City of Oceanside, California

City Hall, 300 North Coast Highway, Oceanside, CA 92054-2885
Tel: (760) 435-4500 (Customer Care) Internet: www.ci.oceanside.ca.us

County: San Diego **Election Type:** Nonpartisan **Population:** 175,691 (2015)

Office of the Mayor and City Council

300 North Coast Highway, Oceanside, CA 92054-2885
E-mail: citycouncil@ci.oceanside.ca.us

★Mayor **Jim Wood** . . . . . (760) 435-3059
Term Expires: December 2016
E-mail: jwood@ci.oceanside.ca.us
★Deputy Mayor **Charles "Chuck" Lowery** . . . . . (760) 435-3551
Term Expires: December 2018
E-mail: clowery@ci.oceanside.ca.us
★Council Member **Jack Feller** . . . . . (760) 435-3056
Term Expires: December 2016
E-mail: jfeller@ci.oceanside.ca.us

(continued on next page)

★Elected Official ▲Appointed by Legislature ▼Appointed by Governor ▶Appointed by Board or Commission ●Appointed by Judge
■Appointed by Mayor △Appointed by Freeholders ▽Appointed by Supervisor ▷Appointed by County Executive ○Appointed by Council

CITIES AND TOWNS

Office of the Mayor and City Council *continued*

★Council Member **Jerome M. "Jerry" Kern** . . . . (760) 435-3032
Term Expires: December 2018
E-mail: jkern@ci.oceanside.ca.us

★Council Member **Esther C. Sanchez** . . . . (760) 435-3057
Term Expires: December 2016
E-mail: esanchez@ci.oceanside.ca.us
Education: Brown U 1978 BA; Hastings JD

Office of the City Manager

300 North Coast Highway, Oceanside, CA 92054-2885

○City Manager **Michelle Skaggs Lawrence** . . . . (760) 435-3065
E-mail: mlawrence@ci.oceanside.ca.us

Manager of Information Technologies
Yukari Krause-Brown . . . . (760) 435-3800
E-mail: ybrown@ci.oceanside.ca.us

Development Services Department

300 North Coast Highway, Oceanside, CA 92054-2885
Tel: (760) 435-4373 Fax: (760) 435-4374
E-mail: dscstaff@ci.oceanside.ca.us

Director **Rick Brown** . . . . (760) 435-3520
E-mail: rbrown@ci.oceanside.ca.us

City Planner **Jeff Hunt** . . . . (760) 435-3535

Engineering Division

300 North Coast Highway, Oceanside, CA 92054-2885

City Engineer **Scott Smith** . . . . (760) 435-4373
E-mail: ssmith@ci.oceanside.ca.us

Financial Services Department

300 North Coast Highway, Oceanside, CA 92054-2885

Director **Jane McPherson** . . . . (760) 435-3850
E-mail: jmcpherson@ci.oceanside.ca.us

Fire Department

300 North Coast Highway, Oceanside, CA 92054-2885
E-mail: firestaff@ci.oceanside.ca.us

Fire Chief **Darryl Hebert** . . . . (760) 435-4100
E-mail: dhebert@ci.oceanside.ca.us

Oceanside Harbor

1540 Harbor Dr. North, Oceanside, CA 92054
E-mail: harborstaff@ci.oceanside.ca.us

Manager **Paul C. Lawrence** . . . . (760) 435-4000

Human Resources Department

300 North Coast Highway, Oceanside, CA 92054-2885
Internet: https://www.ci.oceanside.ca.us/gov/hr/about.asp

Director **Patricia Nunez** . . . . (760) 435-3500
E-mail: pnunez@ci.oceanside.ca.us

Principal Human Resources Analyst
Armando Fernandez . . . . (760) 435-3501
E-mail: afernandez@ci.oceanside.ca.us Fax: (760) 435-6305

Police Department

3855 Mission Ave., Oceanside, CA 92054
Fax: (760) 435-4297 E-mail: police@ci.oceanside.ca.us
Internet: http://www.oceansidepolice.com

Police Chief **Frank McCoy** . . . . (760) 435-4900
E-mail: fmccoy@ci.oceanside.ca.us

Public Works Department

300 North Coast Highway, Oceanside, CA 92054-2885
E-mail: pvo@ci.oceanside.ca.us

Deputy Director **Hans Koger** . . . . (760) 435-5089

Water Utilities Department

300 North Coast Highway, Oceanside, CA 92054-2885
E-mail: waterstaff@ci.oceanside.ca.us
Internet: www.ci.oceanside.ca.us/gov/water/default.asp

Director **Cari Dale** . . . . (760) 435-5811

Deputy City Manager

300 North Coast Highway, Oceanside, CA 92054-2885

Deputy City Manager **Peter Weiss** . . . . (760) 435-3065

Economic and Community Development Department

300 North Coast Highway, Oceanside, CA 92054-2885
Fax: (760) 722-1057

Director **(Vacant)** . . . . (760) 435-3352

Library Department

300 North Coast Highway, Oceanside, CA 92054-2885

Library Director **Sherri Cosby** . . . . (760) 435-5609
E-mail: scosby@ci.oceanside.ca.us

Neighborhood Services Department

321 N. Nevada, Oceanside, CA 92054
Fax: (760) 435-3365

Director **Margery Pierce** . . . . (760) 435-3360

Parks and Recreation Division Manager **Eileen Turk** . . . . . (760) 435-5525

Recreation Supervisor **Terry Goodman** . . . . (760) 435-5052
300 North Coast Highway, Oceanside, CA 92054

Office of the City Attorney

300 North Coast Highway, Oceanside, CA 92054-2885

City Attorney **John Mullen** . . . . (760) 435-3969
E-mail: jmullen@ci.oceanside.ca.us

Office of the City Clerk

300 North Coast Highway, Oceanside, CA 92054-2885
Fax: (760) 967-3922

★City Clerk **Zack Beck** . . . . (760) 435-3000
Term Expires: December 2016
E-mail: zbeck@ci.oceanside.ca.us

Assistant City Clerk **Holly Trobaugh** . . . . (760) 435-3005
E-mail: htrobaugh@ci.oceanside.ca.us

Office of the City Treasurer

300 North Coast Highway, Oceanside, CA 92054-2885

★City Treasurer **Gary Ernst** . . . . (760) 435-3551
Term Expires: December 2016
E-mail: gernst@ci.oceanside.ca.us

Oceanside Unified School District

2111 Mission Avenue, Oceanside, CA 92058
Tel: (760) 966-4000 Fax: (760) 433-3191

Superintendent **Dr. Duane Coleman** . . . . (760) 966-4000

Director of Communications **Lisa Contreras** . . . . (760) 966-4010
E-mail: lisa.contreras@oside.us

City of Odessa, Texas

411 West 8th Street, Odessa, TX 79761
Tel: (432) 335-3286 E-mail: cm@odessa-tx.gov
Internet: www.odessa-tx.gov

County: Ector **Year Founded:** March 1876 **Year Incorporated:** April 18, 1927 **Population:** 118,968 (2015)

Office of the Mayor and City Council

P.O. Box 4398, Odessa, TX 79760
Tel: (432) 335-3276 Fax: (432) 335-4698
E-mail: citycouncil@odessa-tx.gov
Internet: https://www.odessa-tx.gov/index.aspx?page=44

★Mayor **David Turner** . . . . (432) 335-4104
Began Service: November 2012
Term Expires: November 2016
E-mail: dturnermayor@gmail.com
Education: Texas Tech BS

★Council Member **Amye McNeil** (District 1) . . . . (432) 335-3276
Term Expires: November 2016

★Council Member **Dewey Bryant** (District 2) . . . . (432) 335-3276
Term Expires: November 2016

★Council Member **Barbara Graff** (District 3) . . . . (432) 335-3276
Term Expires: November 2018

★Council Member **Michael Gardner** (District 4) . . . . (432) 335-3276
Term Expires: November 2018

★Council Member **Filiberto Gonzales, Jr.** (District 5) . . . . . (432) 335-3276
Term Expires: November 2018

Office of the City Manager

411 West 8th Street, 5th Floor, Odessa, TX 79761
Tel: (432) 335-3286 Fax: (432) 335-3281 E-mail: cm@odessa-tx.gov

○City Manager **Richard Morton** . . . . (432) 335-3286
E-mail: cm@odessa-tx.gov
Education: Texas A&M BS, MPA

Public Information Coordinator **Andrea Goodson** . . . . (432) 257-0537
119 West Fourth Street, Odessa, TX 79761 Fax: (432) 335-4816
E-mail: agoodson@odessa-tx.gov
Education: Texas (Permian Basin) BA

Assistant City Manager - Administrative Services
Konrad Hildebrandt . . . . (432) 335-3286
E-mail: khildebrandt@odessa-tx.gov

Deputy City Manager - Community Services
Michael Marrero . . . . (432) 335-3286
E-mail: mmarrero@odessa-tx.gov

Office of the City Secretary

411 West 8th Street, Odessa, TX 79761
Tel: (432) 335-3276 Fax: (432) 335-4160

City Secretary **Norma Grimaldo** . . . . (432) 335-3276
E-mail: cs@odessa-tx.gov
Education: Texas (Permian Basin) BBA

Billing and Collection Department

411 West 8th Street, Odessa, TX 79761
Tel: (432) 335-3204 Fax: (432) 335-3231 E-mail: bc@odessa-tx.gov

Director **Agapito Bernal** . . . . (432) 335-3204

Building Services Department

801 East Pool Road, Odessa, TX 79761
Tel: (432) 335-4840 Fax: (432) 335-4834 E-mail: bs@odessa-tx.gov

Director **Steve Davis** . . . . (432) 335-4840

Community Development Department

119 West Fourth Street, Suite 104, Odessa, TX 79761
Tel: (432) 335-4820 Fax: (432) 335-4817 E-mail: cd@odessa-tx.gov

Director **Merita Sandoval** . . . . (432) 335-4820
E-mail: msandoval@odessa-tx.gov

Equipment Services Department

801 East Pool Road, Odessa, TX 79761
Tel: (432) 335-4825 Fax: (432) 335-4848 E-mail: es@odessa-tx.gov

Director **(Vacant)** . . . . (432) 335-4825
Fleet Asset Manager **Shauna Walters** . . . . (432) 335-4825

Finance Department

411 West 8th Street, Odessa, TX 79761
Tel: (432) 335-3219 Fax: (432) 335-3298 E-mail: finance@odessa-tx.org

Director **Terri Gayhart** . . . . (432) 335-3219

Fire Department

1100 West Second Street, Odessa, TX 79761
Tel: (432) 257-0502 Fax: (432) 257-0512 E-mail: ofd@odessa-tx.gov

Fire Chief **Roger Boyd** . . . . (432) 257-0502
E-mail: ofd@odessa-tx.gov

Human Resources Department

411 West 8th Street, Odessa, TX 79761
Tel: (432) 335-3200 Fax: (432) 335-3269

Director **Bonita Hall** . . . . (432) 335-3200

Information Technology Department

119 West Fourth Street, 5th Floor, Odessa, TX 79761
Tel: (432) 335-3200

Director **Jana Walker** . . . . (432) 335-3200
E-mail: jwalker@odessa-tx.gov

Parks and Recreation Department

1100 West 42nd Street, Odessa, TX 79761
Tel: (432) 368-3548 Fax: (432) 368-3517 E-mail: parks@odessa-tx.gov

Director **Steve Patton** . . . . (432) 368-3548

Planning and Zoning Department

411 West 8th Street, Odessa, TX 79761
Tel: (432) 335-3211 Fax: (432) 335-4176 E-mail: pz@odessa-tx.gov

Director **Randy Brinlee** . . . . (432) 335-3211

Police Department

205 North Grant, Odessa, TX 79761
Tel: (432) 333-3641 E-mail: opd@odessa-tx.gov

Chief of Police **Timothy Burton** . . . . (432) 333-3641

Animal Control Division

910 West 42nd Street, Odessa, TX 79761
Tel: (432) 368-3527 Fax: (432) 368-3573

Manager **Jacqueline Adimare** . . . . (432) 368-3526

Public Works Department

411 West 8th Street, Odessa, TX 79761
Tel: (432) 335-3244 Fax: (432) 335-3225 E-mail: pw@odessa-tx.gov

Director **Thomas Kerr** . . . . (432) 335-3244

Building Inspection Division

411 West 8th Street, Odessa, TX 79761
Tel: (432) 335-3214 Fax: (432) 335-3256 E-mail: bi@odessa-tx.gov

Building Official **Ralph M. McCain** . . . . (432) 335-3214

★Elected Official ▲Appointed by Legislature ▼Appointed by Governor ▶Appointed by Board or Commission ●Appointed by Judge
■Appointed by Mayor △Appointed by Freeholders ▽Appointed by Supervisor ▷Appointed by County Executive ○Appointed by Council

Engineering Division
411 West 8th Street, Odessa, TX 79761
Tel: (432) 335-3242 Fax: (432) 335-3225
E-mail: engineering@odessa-tx.gov

City Engineer **Yervand Hmayakyan** .... (432) 335-3242
E-mail: yhmayaky@odessa-tx.gov

Solid Waste Division
1100 West 42nd Street, Odessa, TX 79761
Tel: (432) 368-3510 Fax: (432) 368-3533 E-mail: sw@odessa-tx.gov

Director **Oscar Maldonado** .... (432) 335-3204

Street Division
411 West 8th Street, Odessa, TX 79761
Tel: (432) 335-3241 Fax: (432) 335-3225 E-mail: street@odessa-tx.gov

Superintendent **Danny Garcia** .... (432) 335-3241

Traffic Engineering Division
411 West 8th Street, 4th Floor, Odessa, TX 79761
Tel: (432) 335-3239 Fax: (432) 335-3225 E-mail: traffic@odessa-tx.gov
Internet: https://www.odessa-tx.gov/index.aspx?page=76

Traffic Coordinator **Hal Feldman** .... (432) 335-3239

Utilities Department
119 West Fourth Street, 4th Floor, Odessa, TX 79761
Tel: (432) 335-4627 Fax: (432) 335-4698 E-mail: utilities@odessa-tx.gov

Director **Thomas Kerr** .... (432) 335-4627

Purchasing Department
411 West 8th Street, Odessa, TX 79761
Tel: (432) 335-3253 Fax: (432) 335-3208
E-mail: purchasing@odessa-tx.gov

Director **Phillip Urrutia** .... (432) 335-3253
E-mail: purrutia@odessa-tx.gov

Risk Management Department
308 North Lee Street, Odessa, TX 79761
Tel: (432) 335-4691 Fax: (432) 335-4696 E-mail: rm@odessa-tx.gov

Director **Darrell E. Wells** .... (432) 335-4691
E-mail: dwells@odessa-tx.gov

Legal Department
411 West 8th Street, Odessa, TX 79761
Tel: (432) 335-3228 Fax: (432) 335-3257 E-mail: legal@odessa-tx.gov

City Attorney **Larry Long** .... (432) 335-3228
E-mail: legal@odessa-tx.gov

Oklahoma City, Oklahoma

City Hall, 200 N. Walker Ave., Oklahoma City, OK 73102
Tel: (405) 297-2578 (Information) Fax: (405) 297-3124
Internet: www.okc.gov

County: Oklahoma **Election Type:** Nonpartisan **Population:** 631,346 (2015)

Mick Cornett
Mayor

Began Service: March 2, 2004
Term Expires: April 2020
Education: Oklahoma BA

Office of the Mayor
City Hall, 200 N. Walker Ave., Suite 302, Oklahoma City, OK 73102
Fax: (405) 297-3759 Internet: www.okc.gov/council/mayor/Mayor.html

★ Mayor **Mick Cornett** .... (405) 297-2424
E-mail: mayor@okc.gov
Executive Assistant **Karen Fox** .... (405) 297-2424
E-mail: karen.fox@okc.gov

Chief of Staff **Steve Hill** .... (405) 297-3073

Office of the City Council
City Hall, 200 N. Walker Ave., 3rd Floor, Oklahoma City, OK 73102
Tel: (405) 297-3884 Fax: (405) 297-3003
Internet: www.okc.gov/council/index.html

★ Council Member **James Greiner** (Ward 1) .... (405) 297-2404
Term Expires: April 2017
E-mail: ward1@okc.gov

★ Council Member **Dr. Edward "Ed" Shadid** (Ward 2) .... (405) 297-2402
Term Expires: April 2019
E-mail: ward2@okc.gov

★ Council Member **Lawrence F. McAtee, Jr.** (Ward 3) ..... (405) 297-2404
Term Expires: April 2017
E-mail: ward3@okc.gov

★ Council Member **Pete White** (Ward 4) .... (405) 297-2402
Term Expires: April 2017
E-mail: ward4@okc.gov

★ Council Member **David T. Greenwell** (Ward 5) .... (405) 297-2569
Term Expires: April 2019
Education: Oklahoma City; Oklahoma MBA

★ Council Member **Meg Salyer** (Ward 6) .... (405) 297-2402
Term Expires: April 2019
E-mail: ward6@okc.gov

★ Council Member **John Pettis, Jr.** (Ward 7) .... (405) 297-2569
Term Expires: April 2017
E-mail: ward7@okc.gov

★ Council Member **Mark K. Stonecipher** (Ward 8) .... (405) 297-2404
Term Expires: April 2019
E-mail: ward8@okc.gov
Education: Oklahoma City 1980 BS; Oklahoma 1983 JD

Council Support Team
Chief of Staff to the Council **Debi Martin** .... (405) 297-2569
E-mail: debi.martin@okc.gov

★ Elected Official ▲ Appointed by Legislature ▼ Appointed by Governor ► Appointed by Board or Commission ● Appointed by Judge
■ Appointed by Mayor △ Appointed by Freeholders ▽ Appointed by Supervisor ▷ Appointed by County Executive ○ Appointed by Council

Office of the City Manager

City Hall, 200 N. Walker Ave., Oklahoma City, OK 73102
Fax: (405) 297-2570 E-mail: citymanager@okc.gov
Internet: www.okc.gov/mgr/

○ City Manager **James D. Couch** . . . . . (405) 297-2345
E-mail: jim.couch@okc.gov
Assistant City Manager **M.T. Berry** . . . . . (405) 297-2345
E-mail: major.berry@okc.gov
Assistant City Manager **Dennis Clowers** . . . . . (405) 297-2506
Fax: (405) 297-2332
Assistant City Manager **Laura Johnson** . . . . . (405) 297-2345
Community and Government Affairs Manager
Jane Abraham . . . . . (405) 297-1501
E-mail: jane.abraham@okc.gov
Public Information Director **Kristy Yager** . . . . . (405) 297-2578
E-mail: kristy.yager@okc.gov Fax: (405) 297-3124
Special Projects Manager **Tom Anderson** . . . . . (405) 297-2345
E-mail: tom.anderson@okc.gov

Office of the City Clerk

City Hall, 200 N. Walker Ave., Oklahoma City, OK 73102
Tel: (405) 297-2391 Fax: (405) 297-3121

City Clerk **Frances Kersey** . . . . . (405) 297-2397
E-mail: cityclerk@okc.gov
Date of Birth: December 5, 1950
Education: Eastern New Mexico 1972 ScB
Assistant City Clerk **Charlotte Nelson** . . . . . (405) 297-2394
E-mail: cityclerk@okc.gov

Department of Airports

7100 Terminal Drive, Unit 937, Oklahoma City, OK 73159
Tel: (405) 316-3200 Fax: (405) 316-3311 Internet: www.flyokc.com

Director **Mark Kranenburg** . . . . . (405) 316-3260

Development Services Department

420 West Main, Suite 1050, Oklahoma City, OK 73102
Fax: (405) 297-3374 Internet: www.okc.gov/neighborhood/index.html

Director **Bob Tener** . . . . . (405) 297-2972
E-mail: bob.tener@okc.gov

Oklahoma City Animal Welfare

2811 SE 29th, Oklahoma City, OK 73129
Tel: (405) 297-3100 Fax: (405) 297-3120

Superintendent **Julie Bank** . . . . . (405) 297-3088

Finance Department

100 N. Walker Ave., Oklahoma City, OK 73102
Fax: (405) 297-2332 Internet: www.okc.gov/finance/

Finance Director **Craig Freeman** . . . . . (405) 297-2506
Purchasing Agent **Amy Simpson** . . . . . (405) 297-2741
E-mail: amy.simpson@okc.gov Fax: (405) 297-2142
Treasurer **Bob Ponkilla** . . . . . (405) 297-2965
Budget Director **Doug Dowler** . . . . . (405) 297-2701
E-mail: doug.dowler@okc.gov
Controller **Laura Papas** . . . . . (405) 297-2701
Risk Manager **Jason Smitherman** . . . . . (405) 297-3891
E-mail: jason.smitherman@okc.gov

Fire Department

820 NW 5th St., Oklahoma City, OK 73106-7425
Fax: (405) 297-3329 Internet: www.okc.gov/fire/index.html

Fire Chief **G. Keith Bryant** . . . . . (405) 297-3314
E-mail: keith.bryant@okc.gov
Fire Marshal **Kellie Sawyers** . . . . . (405) 297-3584
E-mail: kellie.sawyers@okc.gov
Deputy Chief, Support Services **Chris Goodwin** . . . . . (405) 297-3335
Deputy Chief, Operations Bureau **Richard Kelley** . . . . . (405) 297-3314
E-mail: richard.kelley@okc.gov

General Services Department

115 North Shartel Street, Oklahoma City, OK 73102
Fax: (405) 297-2078 Internet: www.okc.gov/gen_svcs/

Director **Paula Falkenstein** . . . . . (405) 297-2849
E-mail: paula.falkenstein@okc.gov

Information Technology Department

100 North Walker Avenue, 6th Floor, Oklahoma City, OK 73102
Fax: (405) 297-3021 Internet: www.okc.gov/info_tech/

Director **Schad Meldrum** . . . . . (405) 297-2303
E-mail: schad.meldrum@okc.gov

Parks and Recreation Department

420 West Main Street, Suite 210, Oklahoma City, OK 73102
Fax: (405) 297-3175 Internet: www.okc.gov/parks/

Director **Douglas R. Kupper** . . . . . (405) 297-3882
Education: Ohio State BA

Personnel Department

420 West Main Street, Suite 110, Oklahoma City, OK 73102
Fax: (405) 297-2137 Internet: www.okc.gov/personnel/

Director **Dianna L. Berry** . . . . . (405) 297-2426
E-mail: dianna.berry@okc.gov

Planning Department

420 West Main Street, 9th Floor, Oklahoma City, OK 73102-4406
Tel: (405) 297-1630 Fax: (405) 297-1631
Internet: www.okc.gov/planning/

Director **Aubrey Hammontree** . . . . . (405) 297-1630

Police Department

701 Colcord Drive, Oklahoma City, OK 73102
Tel: (405) 297-1000 Fax: (405) 235-3812 E-mail: pio.police@okc.gov
Internet: www.ocpd.com/

Police Chief **William "Bill" Citty** . . . . . (405) 297-1100
Education: Oklahoma State 1977 BS
Deputy Police Chief, Investigations Bureau
Johnny Kuhlman . . . . . (405) 297-1102
Education: Southern Nazarene 2002 BS
Deputy Police Chief, Administration Bureau
Kenneth McDonald . . . . . (405) 297-1100
E-mail: kenneth.mcdonald@okc.gov
Education: Central Oklahoma 1999 MA
Deputy Police Chief, Operations Bureau **Tom Jester** . . . . . (405) 297-1103
E-mail: tom.jester@okc.gov
Deputy Police Chief, Operations Bureau **John Scully** . . . . (405) 297-1103
E-mail: john.scully@okc.gov
Office of Professional Standards **Capt. Vance Allen** . . . . . (405) 297-1118
Office of Professional Standards
Capt. Robert Matthews . . . . . (405) 297-1118
Training Director **Major Jeff Becker** . . . . . (405) 297-1110
E-mail: bill.weaver@okc.gov
Public Information Officer **Paco Balderrama** . . . . . (405) 297-1111
911 Director **David Shupe** . . . . . (405) 297-2250
Education: Southern Nazarene 1999 BS
Assistant Public Information Officer and Technical
Writer **M-Sgt. Gary Knight** . . . . . (405) 297-1111
E-mail: pio.police@okc.gov

Public Works Department

420 West Main Street, Room 700, Oklahoma City, OK 73102-4406
Fax: (405) 297-2117 Internet: www.okc.gov/pw/index.html

Director and City Engineer **Eric J. Wenger** . . . . . (405) 297-2581
E-mail: eric.wenger@okc.gov
Traffic Engineer **Stuart Chai** . . . . . (405) 297-2003
420 West Main, Fax: (405) 297-3365
Suite 600, Oklahoma City, OK 73102
E-mail: stuart.chai@okc.gov

★ Elected Official ▲ Appointed by Legislature ▼ Appointed by Governor ▶ Appointed by Board or Commission ● Appointed by Judge
■ Appointed by Mayor △ Appointed by Freeholders ▽ Appointed by Supervisor ▷ Appointed by County Executive ○ Appointed by Council

Department of Utilities
420 West Main Street, Suite 500, Oklahoma City, OK 73102
Fax: (405) 297-3813 E-mail: water@okc.gov

Director **Marsha Slaughter** .... (405) 297-2422
Assistant Director **Bret Weingart** .... (405) 297-2422
Solid Waste Management Superintendent **James Linn** .... (405) 297-2464
Fax: (405) 755-8946

Oklahoma City-County Board of Health
2600 Northeast 63rd Street, Oklahoma City, OK 73111
Tel: (405) 425-4455 Internet: www.occhd.org/about/board-of-health

Chair **Dr. Stephen Cagle** .... (405) 425-4455
Term Expires: March 2017

Oklahoma City Zoological Park
2101 NE 50th St., Oklahoma City, OK 73111
Fax: (405) 425-0207 Internet: www.okczoo.com/

Executive Director/Chief Executive Officer
Dwight Lawson .... (405) 424-3344

Cox Convention Center and Chesapeake Energy Arena
100 West Reno, Oklahoma City, OK 73102
Cox Center, One Myriad Gardens, Oklahoma City, OK 73102
Tel: (405) 602-8500 (Cox Center)
Tel: (405) 602-8700 (The Chesapeake Energy Arena)
Fax: (405) 602-8505 E-mail: info@chesapeakearena.com
Internet: www.coxconventioncenter.com
Internet: www.chesapeakearena.co

General Manager **Gary Desjardins** .... (405) 602-8500
Director of Finance **Joe Jondahl** .... (405) 602-8500
Director of Food and Beverage **(Vacant)** .... (405) 602-8500
Fax: (405) 602-8611
Director of Marketing **Tim Linville** .... (405) 602-8500
Fax: (405) 602-5108
Communications Manager **Ryan McGhee** .... (405) 602-8500
E-mail: rmcghee@chesapeakearena.com Fax: (405) 602-5108

Office of the Municipal Counselor
City Hall, 200 North Walker Avenue, Suite 400,
Oklahoma City, OK 73102
Tel: (405) 297-2451 Fax: (405) 297-2118
Internet: www.okc.gov/counselor/index.html

○ Municipal Counselor **Kenneth Jordan** .... (405) 297-2740
Note: Appointed by Mayor and City Council
E-mail: kenneth.jordan@okc.gov
Deputy Municipal Counselor and Criminal Justice
Division Head **Cindy Richard** .... (405) 297-3671
Deputy Municipal Counselor **Wiley L. Williams** .... (405) 297-2685
Civil Litigation Division Head **Richard C. Smith** .... (405) 297-2555
Labor and Employment Law Division Head
Richard E. Mahoney .... (405) 297-2739
Land Use and Economic Development Division Head
Daniel T. Brummitt .... (405) 297-2694
E-mail: daniel.brummitt@okc.gov
Trusts, Utilities and Finance Division Head
Craig B. Keith .... (405) 297-2730

Office of the City Auditor
City Hall, 200 N. Walker Ave., Oklahoma City, OK 73102
Fax: (405) 297-2587

○ City Auditor **Jim Williamson** .... (405) 297-2297
E-mail: jim.williamson@okc.gov

Oklahoma City Public Schools
900 North Klein, Oklahoma City, OK 73106
Tel: (405) 587-0000 Internet: http://okcs.schooldesk.net

Superintendent (Acting) **Aurora Lora** .... (405) 587-0448

City of Olathe, Kansas
100 East Santa Fe Street, Olathe, KS 66061
P.O. Box 768, Olathe, KS 66051-0768
Tel: (913) 971-8600 Internet: www.olatheks.org

County: Johnson **Election Type:** Nonpartisan **Year Incorporated:** 1857
Population: 134,305 (2015)

Office of the Mayor and City Council
100 East Santa Fe Street, Olathe, KS 66061
P.O. Box 768, Olathe, KS 66051-0768

★ Mayor **Michael Copeland** .... (913) 971-8500
Began Service: April 2001
Term Expires: April 2019
E-mail: mcopeland@olatheks.org
Education: MidAmerica Nazarene 1984 BA
★ Mayor Pro Tem **Jim Randall** (Ward 2) .... (913) 424-3999
Term Expires: April 2019
E-mail: jrandall@olatheks.org
★ Council Member **Larry L. Campbell** (Ward 1) .... (913) 488-7278
Term Expires: April 2019
E-mail: lcampbell@olatheks.org
Education: Southern Nazarene BA; MidAmerica Nazarene MA
★ Council Member **R. Wesley McCoy** (Ward 3) .... (913) 971-8500
Term Expires: April 2017
E-mail: rwmccoy@olatheks.org
★ Council Member **Marge Vogt** (Ward 4) .... (913) 269-0625
Term Expires: April 2017
E-mail: mvogt@olatheks.org
★ Council Member **John Bacon** (At-Large) .... (913) 269-6305
Term Expires: April 2019
E-mail: jbacon@olatheks.org
★ Council Member
Ronald W. "Ron" Ryckman, Jr. (At-Large) .... (913) 927-5333
Term Expires: April 2017
E-mail: rryckman@olatheks.org
Education: MidAmerica Nazarene 1994 BBA

Office of the City Manager
100 East Santa Fe Street, Olathe, KS 66061
P.O. Box 768, Olathe, KS 66051-0768
Fax: (913) 971-8600

City Manager **J. Michael Wilkes** .... (913) 971-8600
E-mail: jmwilkes@olatheks.org
Assistant City Manager **Susan Sherman** .... (913) 971-8600
E-mail: ssherman@olatheks.org
Communication and Customer Services Director
Tim Danneberg .... (913) 971-8600
E-mail: tdanneberg@olatheks.org
Communication and Public Engagement Manager
Erin Vader .... (913) 971-8600
E-mail: esvader@olatheks.org

Fire Department
1225 South Hamilton Circle, Olathe, KS 66061
P.O. Box 768, Olathe, KS 66051-0768
Fax: (913) 971-7982

Fire Chief **Jeff DeGraffenreid** .... (913) 971-7900
E-mail: jgdegraffenreid@olatheks.org
Deputy Chief **Todd Hart** .... (913) 971-7900
E-mail: thart@olatheks.org

★ Elected Official ▲ Appointed by Legislature ▼ Appointed by Governor ▶ Appointed by Board or Commission ● Appointed by Judge
■ Appointed by Mayor △ Appointed by Freeholders ▽ Appointed by Supervisor ▷ Appointed by County Executive ○ Appointed by Council

Fire Department *continued*

Assistant Chief **Doug Fischer** . . . . (913) 971-7900
E-mail: dfischer@olatheks.org
Assistant Chief **Tim Richards** . . . . (913) 971-7900
E-mail: trichards@olatheks.org

Building Codes Division
Chief Building Official **Jeff DeGraffenreid** . . . . (913) 971-7900
E-mail: jdegraffenreid@olatheks.org

Information Technology Services Department
Sante Fe Building, 100 West Santa Fe Street, Olathe, KS 66061
P.O. Box 768, Olathe, KS 66051-0768

Director **Shawn Whitcomb** . . . . (913) 971-6669
Education: MidAmerica Nazarene; Baker U

Legal Department
100 East Santa Fe Street, Olathe, KS 66061
P.O. Box 768, Olathe, KS 66051-0768

City Attorney **Ron Shaver** . . . . (913) 971-8732
E-mail: rshaver@olatheks.org

Olathe Public Library
201 East Park Street, Olathe, KS 66061
Internet: http://www.olathelibrary.org

Director **Emily Baker** . . . . (913) 971-6850
E-mail: ebaker@olatheks.org

Parks and Recreation Department
200 West Santa Fe Street, Olathe, KS 66061
P.O. Box 768, Olathe, KS 66051-0768
Fax: (913) 971-6690

Director **Michael Meadors** . . . . (913) 971-8563

Police Department
501 East 56 Highway, Olathe, KS 66061
P.O. Box 768, Olathe, KS 66051-0768

Chief of Police **Steven Menke** . . . . (913) 971-7500

Public Works Department
1385 South Robinson Drive, Olathe, KS 66061
P.O. Box 768, Olathe, KS 66051-0768

Director **Mary Jaeger** . . . . (913) 971-9045

Housing Services Division
200 West Santa Fe Street, Olathe, KS 66061
P.O. Box 768, Olathe, KS 66051-0768
Tel: (913) 971-6260

Housing Manager **Kathy Rankin** . . . . (913) 971-6267
E-mail: krankin@olatheks.org

Resource Management Department
100 East Santa Fe Street, Olathe, KS 66061
P.O. Box 768, Olathe, KS 66051-0768

Director **Dianna Wright** . . . . (913) 971-8680

Office of the City Clerk
100 East Santa Fe Street, Olathe, KS 66061
P.O. Box 768, Olathe, KS 66051-0768

City Clerk **Donald T. "Tracy" Howell** . . . . (913) 971-8675
E-mail: thowell@olatheks.org

Human Resources
100 East Santa Fe Street, Olathe, KS 66061
P.O. Box 768, Olathe, KS 66051-0768
Fax: (913) 971-8715

Director **Dianna Wright** . . . . (913) 971-8680
E-mail: dswright@olatheks.org

Strategic Financial Management Division
100 East Santa Fe Street, Olathe, KS 66061
P.O. Box 768, Olathe, KS 66051-0768

Director **Alan Shorthouse** . . . . (913) 971-8718
Procurement Manager **Stephanie Creed** . . . . (913) 971-8720
E-mail: sacreed@olatheks.org Fax: (913) 971-8719

City of Olympia, Washington
City Hall, 601 4th Avenue East, Olympia, WA 98501
P.O. Box 1967, Olympia, WA 98507-1967
Internet: www.olympiawa.gov

County: Thurston **Year Incorporated:** 1859 **Population:** 50,302 (2015)

Office of the Mayor and City Council
City Hall, 601 4th Avenue East, Olympia, WA 98501
P.O. Box 1967, Olympia, WA 98507-1967
Fax: (360) 570-3791 E-mail: citycouncil@ci.olympia.wa.us

★Mayor **Cheryl L. Selby** (Position 1) . . . . (360) 753-8447
Began Service: January 1, 2016
Term Expires: December 31, 2019
E-mail: cselby@ci.olympia.wa.us
★Mayor Pro Tem **Nathaniel Jones** (Position 3) . . . . (360) 753-8447
Term Expires: December 31, 2019
E-mail: njones@ci.olympia.wa.us
★Council Member **Jessica Bateman** (Position 2) . . . . (360) 753-8447
Term Expires: December 31, 2019
★Council Member **Clark Gilman** (Position 4) . . . . (360) 753-8447
Term Expires: December 31, 2017
★Council Member **Julie Hankins** (Position 5) . . . . (360) 753-8447
Term Expires: December 31, 2017
E-mail: jhankins@ci.olympia.wa.us
★Council Member **Jeannine Roe** (Position 6) . . . . (360) 753-8447
Term Expires: December 31, 2017
E-mail: jroe@ci.olympia.wa.us
★Council Member **Jim Cooper** (Position 7) . . . . (360) 753-8447
Term Expires: December 31, 2017
E-mail: jcooper@ci.olympia.wa.us

Office of the City Manager
City Hall, 601 4th Avenue East, Olympia, WA 98501
P.O. Box 1967, Olympia, WA 98507-1967
Fax: (360) 570-3791 E-mail: cityhall@ci.olympia.wa.us

City Manager **Steven R. Hall** . . . . (360) 753-8447
E-mail: shall@ci.olympia.wa.us
Assistant City Manager **Jay Burney** . . . . (360) 753-8447
E-mail: jburney@ci.olympia.wa.us
City Attorney **Mark Barber** . . . . (360) 753-8338
E-mail: mbarber@ci.olympia.wa.us
Deputy City Attorney **Darren Neinaber** . . . . (360) 753-8338
E-mail: dnienabe@ci.olympia.wa.us
Strategic Communications Director
Kellie Purce Braseth . . . . (360) 753-8361
E-mail: kbraseth@ci.olympia.wa.us
Executive Assistant **Susan Grisham** . . . . (360) 753-8244
E-mail: sgrisham@ci.olympia.wa.us
Paralegal **Kari Pitharoulis** . . . . (360) 753-8338
Claims Manager **Connie Cobb** . . . . (360) 753-8451
E-mail: ccobb@ci.olympia.wa.us

★Elected Official ▲Appointed by Legislature ▼Appointed by Governor ►Appointed by Board or Commission ●Appointed by Judge
■Appointed by Mayor △Appointed by Freeholders ▽Appointed by Supervisor ▷Appointed by County Executive ○Appointed by Council

Administrative Services Department
601 4th Avenue East, Olympia, WA 98501
Fax: (360) 753-8165 E-mail: adminservices@ci.olympia.wa.us

Director **Jane Ragland Kirkemo** .... (360) 753-8325
E-mail: jkirkemo@ci.olympia.wa.us
City Clerk **(Vacant)** .... (360) 753-8325
Finance Manager **Dean Walz** .... (360) 753-8325
Information Services Division Manager **Shawn Ward** .... (360) 753-8325
E-mail: sward@ci.olympia.wa.us
Municipal Court Administrator **Maryam Olson** .... (360) 753-8312
Fax: (360) 753-8775
Human Resources Manager **Joe Olson** .... (360) 753-8310
E-mail: jolson@ci.olympia.wa.us

Community Planning and Development Department
P.O. Box 1967, Olympia, WA 98507-1967
Fax: (360) 753-8087 E-mail: cpdinfo@ci.olympia.wa.us

Director **Keith Stahley** .... (360) 753-8314
E-mail: kstahley@ci.olympia.wa.us
Deputy Director **Leonard Bauer** .... (360) 753-8206
E-mail: lbauer@ci.olympia.wa.us
Building Official/Permitting Services Manager
Todd Cunningham .... (360) 753-8486
Planning Services Manager **Todd Stamm** .... (360) 753-8597
Business Manager **Karen Kenneson** .... (360) 753-8277

Fire Department
100 Eastside Street, NE, Olympia, WA 98501
E-mail: fire@ci.olympia.wa.us

Fire Chief **Larry Dibble** .... (360) 753-8348
E-mail: ldibble@ci.olympia.wa.us
Fire Code Enforcement Assistant Chief **Robert Bradley** .. (360) 753-8348
E-mail: rbradley@ci.olympia.wa.us
Fire Operations Assistant Chief **Mike Buchanan** .... (360) 753-8348
E-mail: mbuchana@ci.olympia.wa.us
Fire Support Services and Administration Division
Manager **Shelley Flaherty** .... (360) 753-8348
E-mail: sflahert@ci.olympia.wa.us

Parks, Arts and Recreation Department
Olympia Center, 222 Columbia Street, NW, Olympia, WA 98501
Fax: (360) 753-8334

Director **Paul Simmons** .... (360) 753-8380
Associate Director **David Hanna** .... (360) 753-8020
Arts and Events Manager **Stephanie Johnson** .... (360) 709-2678

Police Department
601 4th Avenue East, Olympia, WA 98501
P.O. Box 1967, Olympia, WA 98507-1967
Tel: (360) 753-8300 E-mail: olympiapolice@ci.olympia.wa.us

Chief of Police **Ronnie Roberts** .... (360) 753-8147

Public Works Department
P.O. Box 1967, Olympia, WA 98507-1967
Fax: (360) 753-8330 E-mail: publicworks@ci.olympia.wa.us

Director **Rich Hoey** .... (360) 753-8495
Education: Worcester Polytech BSCE
City Engineer **Fran Eide** .... (360) 753-8422
E-mail: feide@ci.olympia.wa.us
Deputy Director **Debbie Sullivan** .... (360) 753-8482
E-mail: dsulliva@ci.olympia.wa.us
Waste Resources Director **Dan Daniels** .... (360) 753-8780
Transportation Division Director **Mark Russell** .... (360) 753-8441

City of Omaha, Nebraska

Omaha/Douglas Civic Center, 1819 Farnam Street, Omaha, NE 68183
Fax: (402) 444-6059 Internet: www.cityofomaha.org

County: Douglas **Election Type:** Nonpartisan **Population:** 443,885 (2015)

Office of the Mayor
Omaha/Douglas Civic Center, 1819 Farnam Street, Suite 300,
Omaha, NE 68183-0300
Tel: (402) 444-5555 Fax: (402) 444-6059
Internet: www.cityofomaha.org/mayor/mayors-office-home

★ Mayor **Jean Stothert** .... (402) 444-5555
Began Service: June 10, 2013
Term Expires: June 5, 2017
Executive Assistant to the Mayor **Amy Ayer** .... (402) 444-6275
E-mail: amy.ayer@cityofomaha.org
Chief of Staff **Martin "Marty" Bilek** .... (402) 444-3518
Deputy Chief of Staff, Economic Development
Cassie Paben .... (402) 444-5039
E-mail: cassie.paben@cityofomaha.org
Deputy Chief of Staff, Communications **Carrie Murphy** .. (402) 444-3520
E-mail: Carrie.Murphy@cityofomaha.org
Community Relations Director **Drey Hicks** .... (402) 444-5151
E-mail: drey.hicks@cityofomaha.org
Grants Administrator **Gail Braun** .... (402) 444-5286
Information Technology Coordinator **Bobby Wernli** ...... (402) 444-5034
E-mail: bobby.wernli@cityofomaha.org

Mayor's Hotline
TTY: (402) 444-5555

■ Hotline Associate **(Vacant)** Suite 304 .... (402) 444-4770

Keep Omaha Beautiful
Director **(Vacant)** Suite 306 .... (402) 444-7774
Secretary **Kay Replogle-McDonnell** Suite 306 .... (402) 444-7774

Mayor's Commission for Citizens with Disabilities
■ Director **Spencer Daniel, Jr.** Suite 307 .... (402) 444-5034

Office of the City Council
Omaha/Douglas Civic Center, 1819 Farnam Street, Suite LC-1,
Omaha, NE 68183
Tel: (402) 444-5520 Fax: (402) 444-5263

★ Council President **Pete Festersen** (District 1) .... (402) 444-5527
Term Expires: June 5, 2017
E-mail: pete.festersen@cityofomaha.org
Education: Connecticut Col; Nebraska (Omaha) MA
★ Vice President **Ben Gray** (District 2) .... (402) 444-5524
Term Expires: June 5, 2017
E-mail: ben.gray@cityofomaha.org
★ Council Member **Chris Jerram** (District 3) .... (402) 444-5525
Term Expires: June 5, 2017
E-mail: chris.jerram@cityofomaha.org
★ Council Member **Garry Gernandt** (District 4) .... (402) 444-5522
Term Expires: June 5, 2017
E-mail: garry.gernandt@cityofomaha.org
Education: Nebraska (Omaha) 1977 BA
★ Council Member **Rich Pahls** (District 5) .... (402) 444-5528
Term Expires: June 5, 2017
E-mail: rich.pahls@cityofomaha.org
Date of Birth: August 7, 1943
Education: Fort Hays State 1966 BA, 1967 MA; Nebraska 1979 MEd
★ Council Member **Franklin Thompson** (District 6) .... (402) 444-5523
Term Expires: June 5, 2017
E-mail: franklin.thompson@cityofomaha.org
Education: Nebraska (Omaha) 1976 BS, 1986 MS, 1992, 1996 EdD

★ Elected Official ▲ Appointed by Legislature ▼ Appointed by Governor ▶ Appointed by Board or Commission ● Appointed by Judge
■ Appointed by Mayor △ Appointed by Freeholders ▽ Appointed by Supervisor ▷ Appointed by County Executive ○ Appointed by Council

Office of the City Council *continued*

★ Council Member **Aimee S. Melton** (District 7) .... (402) 444-5526
Term Expires: June 5, 2017
E-mail: aimee.melton@cityofomaha.org
City Council Chief of Staff **Jim Dowding** .... (402) 444-5518
E-mail: james.dowding@cityofomaha.org
Council Staff Assistant **Steve Scarpello** .... (402) 444-4567
Council Staff Assistant **Liz Birkel-Leddy** .... (402) 444-5519
Council Staff Assistant **Margaret Gibson** .... (402) 444-6298
Secretary **Toni Hansen** .... (402) 444-5547
E-mail: toni.hansen@cityofomaha.org
City Lobbyist **Jack Cheloha** .... (402) 444-5521
E-mail: jack.cheloha@cityofomaha.org

Office of the City Clerk
1819 Farnam Street, Suite LC1, Omaha, NE 68183
Tel: (402) 444-5550 Fax: (402) 444-5263

City Clerk **Buster Brown** .... (402) 444-5557
E-mail: buster.brown@cityofomaha.org
Education: Nebraska BA, MA
Executive Secretary **Jenna Garcia** .... (402) 444-5553
E-mail: jenna.garcia@cityofomaha.org
Deputy City Clerk **Sandra Moses** .... (402) 444-5557
E-mail: sandra.moses@cityofomaha.org
Senior Administrative Clerk **Theresa Ellrott** .... (402) 444-5554

Facilities Management Division
Fax: (402) 444-5967

Contract Administration Manager **Mike Oestmann** ...... (402) 444-4575
1523 South 24th Street, Omaha, NE 68108
Secretary **Erin Mockler** .... (402) 444-4218
1523 South 24th Street, Omaha, NE 68108
E-mail: erin.mockler@cityofomaha.org

Vehicle Maintenance Facility Division
Building A, 2606 North 26th Street, Omaha, NE 68111
Fax: (402) 444-6339

Equipment Service Manager **Marc McCoy** .... (402) 444-6191
Vehicle Impound Lot Manager **Barb Oetter** .... (402) 444-6672
7809 F St., Omaha, NE 68183 Fax: (402) 444-4988

Finance Department
Omaha/Douglas Civic Center, 1819 Farnam St., 10th Floor, Omaha, NE 68183
Fax: (402) 546-1150

■ Director **Stephen Curtiss** .... (402) 444-5416
E-mail: stephen.curtiss@cityofomaha.org
Education: Milligan 1982 BS; Vanderbilt 1984 MBA
Executive Secretary **(Vacant)** .... (402) 444-5416
City Comptroller **Al Herink** .... (402) 444-5415
Administrative Secretary **(Vacant)** .... (402) 444-4513

Payroll Division
Payroll Manager **Deb Sander** .... (402) 444-5463

Budget and Accounting Division
Budget Manager **Andrew Brott** Room 1006 .... (402) 444-6262
E-mail: andrew.brott@cityofomaha.org
Office Manager **Virginia Lerch** Room 1006 .... (402) 444-5416

Printing Services Division
Manager **Jack Morine** .... (402) 444-5093

Purchasing Division
Tel: (402) 444-7155 Fax: (402) 444-5423

Purchasing Agent **Eric Carlson** Room 1003 .... (402) 444-5408
Buyer **Lisa Andersen** Room 1003 .... (402) 444-7156
Buyer **John Leming** Room 902 .... (402) 444-5407

Revenue Division
Manager **Donna Waller** .... (402) 444-5472
E-mail: donna.waller@cityofomaha.org

Fire Department
1516 Jackson, Omaha, NE 68102
Tel: (402) 444-5700 Fax: (402) 444-6378

Fire Chief (Interim) **Daniel Olsen** .... (402) 444-5708
E-mail: daniel.olsen@cityofomaha.org
Assistant Fire Chief "A" **Daniel Olsen** .... (402) 444-5700
E-mail: daniel.olsen@cityofomaha.org
Assistant Fire Chief "B" **Steve Ausdemore** .... (402) 444-5700
Assistant Fire Chief "C" **Shane Hunter** .... (402) 444-5700
Emergency Medical Services Bureau Battalion Chief
Lloyd Rupp .... (402) 444-5746
E-mail: lloyd.rupp@cityofomaha.org
Fire Investigation Bureau Battalion Chief **Doug Krysl** .... (402) 444-3473
Safety and Wellness Battalion Chief **Kathy Brenner** ..... (402) 444-5727
Technical Services Battalion Chief **John Stolinski** ...... (402) 444-5737
Battalion Chief-Training **Joseph Salcedo** .... (402) 444-5700
E-mail: joseph.salcedo@cityofomaha.org

Human Resources Department
Omaha/Douglas Civic Center, 1819 Farnam St., Omaha, NE 68183
Tel: (402) 444-5300 Fax: (402) 444-5314

■ Director **Mikki Frost** .... (402) 444-5307
E-mail: mikki.frost@cityofomaha.org
Executive Secretary **Janine Kirk** .... (402) 444-5327
E-mail: janine.kirk@cityofomaha.org
Benefits Manager **Stephanie Unger** .... (402) 444-5306
E-mail: stephanie.unger@cityofomaha.org
Employment Division Manager **Rebecca Nunley** .... (402) 444-5326
E-mail: rebecca.nunley@cityofomaha.org
Safety and Training Coordinator **Kimball Kinnersley** .... (402) 444-4329
E-mail: kimball.kinnersley@cityofomaha.org

Human Rights and Relations Department
Omaha/Douglas Civic Center, 1819 Farnam St., Omaha, NE 68183
Tel: (402) 444-5055 Fax: (402) 444-5058

Director **Spencer K. Danner, Jr.** .... (402) 444-5050
Compliance and Outreach Manager **Rhonda Uher** .... (402) 444-5055

Law Department
Omaha/Douglas Civic Center, 1819 Farnam St., Omaha, NE 68183
Tel: (402) 444-5115 Fax: (402) 444-5125

City Attorney **Paul D. Kratz** Room 804 .... (402) 444-5118
E-mail: paul.kratz@cityofomaha.org
Secretary **Denise Miller** Room 804 .... (402) 444-5120
E-mail: denise.miller@cityofomaha.org

Claims and Investigations Division
Fax: (402) 444-1759

Assistant City Attorney **Rosemarie Lee** Room 803 .... (402) 444-4141
E-mail: rosemarie.lee@cityofomaha.org
Legal Investigator **Larry Bakker** Room 803 .... (402) 444-5131
Claims and Investigations Secretary **(Vacant)** Room 803 .. (402) 444-4523

Prosecution Division
Two W. Hall of Justice, 1701 Farnam St., Omaha, NE 68183
Tel: (402) 444-5290 Fax: (402) 444-7730

City Prosecutor **David Smalheiser** .... (402) 444-5293
Secretary **Pam Cardenas** .... (402) 444-4516
E-mail: pam.cardenas@cityofomaha.org
Prosecutor Investigator **(Vacant)** .... (402) 444-4520

★ Elected Official ▲ Appointed by Legislature ▼ Appointed by Governor ▶ Appointed by Board or Commission ● Appointed by Judge
■ Appointed by Mayor △ Appointed by Freeholders ▽ Appointed by Supervisor ▷ Appointed by County Executive ○ Appointed by Council

Omaha Public Library (W. Dale Clark Library)
215 S. 15th St., Omaha, NE 68102-1629
Tel: (402) 444-4800 Fax: (402) 444-4504 TTY: (402) 444-3825

Executive Director **Laura Marlane** .... (402) 444-4834
E-mail: lmarlane@omahalibrary.org
Executive Secretary **Kyle Porter** .... (402) 444-4833
Assistant Director **Margeret Tarelli-Falcon** .... (402) 444-4854
E-mail: mtarelli-falcon@omahalibrary.org
Assistant Director, Community Programs and Services
(Interim) **Rachel Steiner** .... (402) 444-3470
E-mail: rsteiner@omahalibrary.org
Branch Services Senior Manager **Rachel Steiner** .... (402) 444-4800
E-mail: rsteiner@omahalibrary.org
Community Services Manager **Linda Trout** .... (402) 444-4838

Parks, Recreation and Public Property
Omaha/Douglas Civic Center, 1819 Farnam St., Omaha, NE 68183
Tel: (402) 444-5900 TTY: (402) 444-5955 Fax: (402) 444-4921

■ Director (Acting) **Brook Bench** .... (402) 444-5901
E-mail: brook.bench@cityofomaha.org
Executive Secretary **Theresa Bass** .... (402) 444-5902
Management Analyst **Amy Bell** .... (402) 444-5941
E-mail: amy.bell@cityofomaha.org

Planning Department
Omaha/Douglas Civic Center, 1819 Farnam St., 11th Floor,
Omaha, NE 68183
TTY: (402) 444-5150 Fax: (402) 444-6140

■ Planning Director **James R. "Jim" Thele** .... (402) 444-5150
E-mail: james.thele@cityofomaha.org
Executive Secretary **Debbie Hightower** .... (402) 444-5150
E-mail: debbie.hightower@cityofomaha.org

Police Department
505 South 15th Street, Omaha, NE 68102
TTY: (402) 444-5600 Fax: (402) 444-5628 (Records)

Police Chief **Todd Schmaderer** .... (402) 444-5666
Fax: (402) 444-5898
Secretary **Louise Clayton** .... (402) 444-5667
E-mail: louise.clayton@cityofomaha.org
Executive Officer, Deputy Chief **Greg Gonzalez** .... (402) 444-5644
Criminal Investigation Bureau Deputy Chief
Mary Newman .... (402) 444-5688
Police Services Bureau Deputy Chief
M. Elizabeth Davis .... (402) 444-3555
Uniform Patrol Bureau Deputy Chief **David Baker** ...... (402) 444-6009

Public Works Department
Omaha/Douglas Civic Center, 1819 Farnam St., Omaha, NE 68183
Tel: (402) 444-5220 TTY: (402) 444-5248

■ Director **Robert Stubbe** .... (402) 444-5226
E-mail: robert.stubbe@cityofomaha.org
Executive Secretary **Sylvia Hanson** .... (402) 444-5227
E-mail: sylvia.hanson@cityofomaha.org
Environmental Services Engineer **Martin Grate** .... (402) 444-5225
E-mail: martin.grate@cityofomaha.org
Transportation Services/City Engineer **Todd Pfitzer** ...... (402) 444-5228
E-mail: todd.pfitzer@cityofomaha.org

City of Ontario, California
303 East B St., Ontario, CA 91764
Tel: (909) 395-2010 (Information) Internet: http://www.ontarioca.gov/

County: San Bernardino **Election Type:** Nonpartisan
Population: 171,214 (2015)

Office of the Mayor and City Council
303 East B St., Ontario, CA 91764
Fax: (909) 395-2453 E-mail: cityhall@ci.ontario.ca.us

★ Mayor **Paul S. Leon** .... (909) 395-2011
Term Expires: December 2018
E-mail: pleon@ci.ontario.ca.us
★ Mayor Pro Tem **Debra Dorst-Porada** .... (909) 395-2011
Term Expires: December 2016
E-mail: ddorst-porada@ci.ontario.ca.us
★ Council Member **Paul Vincent Avila** .... (909) 395-2011
Term Expires: December 2016
E-mail: pvavila@ci.ontario.ca.us
★ Council Member **Jim Bowman** .... (909) 395-2011
Term Expires: December 2018
E-mail: jbowman@ci.ontario.ca.us
★ Council Member **Alan D. Wapner** .... (909) 395-2011
Term Expires: December 2018
E-mail: awapner@ci.ontario.ca.us

Office of the City Attorney
2855 East Guasti Road, Suite 400, Ontario, CA 91761

○ City Attorney **John Brown** .... (909) 989-8584
E-mail: john.brown@bbklaw.com
Education: Claremont McKenna 1971 BA; Occidental 1972 MA;
Boalt Hall 1975 JD

Office of the City Clerk
303 East B St., Ontario, CA 91764
Fax: (909) 395-2395

★ City Clerk **(Vacant)** .... (909) 395-2009
Term Expires: December 2016

Office of the City Treasurer
303 East B St., Ontario, CA 91764

★ City Treasurer **Jim Milhiser** .... (909) 395-2011
Term Expires: December 2016
E-mail: jmilhiser@ci.ontario.ca.us

Office of the City Manager
303 East B St., Ontario, CA 91764
Fax: (909) 395-2070

○ City Manager **Al C. Boling** .... (909) 395-2010
E-mail: aboling@ci.ontario.ca.us
Assistant City Manager **Jacob Green** .... (909) 395-2010
E-mail: jgreen@ci.ontario.ca.us

Administrative Services Agency
303 East B St., Ontario, CA 91764

Administrative Services/Finance Director **Grant Yee** ..... (909) 395-2015
E-mail: gyee@ci.ontario.ca.us
Fiscal Services Director **Doreen Nunes** .... (909) 395-2352
E-mail: dnunes@ci.ontario.ca.us

Community and Public Services Agency
1425 S. Bon View Ave., Ontario, CA 91761

Director **Mark Chase** .... (909) 395-2600
E-mail: mchase@ci.ontario.ca.us
Fleet Superintendent **Michael Johnson** .... (909) 395-2641

★ Elected Official ▲ Appointed by Legislature ▼ Appointed by Governor ▶ Appointed by Board or Commission ● Appointed by Judge
■ Appointed by Mayor △ Appointed by Freeholders ▽ Appointed by Supervisor ▷ Appointed by County Executive ○ Appointed by Council

Recreation and Community Services Department
1265 S. Palmetto Ave., Ontario, CA 91762

Assistant Director (Interim) **Wayne Michalak** .... (909) 395-2020
E-mail: wmichalak@ci.ontario.ca.us
Assistant Director **Julie Dorey** ....(909) 395-2020

Ontario Public Library
120 East D Street, Ontario, CA 91764

Director **Helen McAlary** ....(909) 395-2004
E-mail: hmcalary@ci.ontario.ca.us

Development Agency
303 East B St., Ontario, CA 91764

Director **Otto Kroutil** .... (909) 395-2024
E-mail: okroutil@ci.ontario.ca.us
Building Official **Kevin Shear** ....(909) 395-2023
City Engineer **Louis S. Abi-Younes** .... (909) 395-2025
E-mail: labi-younes@ci.ontario.ca.us
Planning Director **Scott Murphy** ....(909) 395-2036

Economic Development Department
303 East B St., Ontario, CA 91764

Director **John Andrews** ....(909) 395-2242
E-mail: jpandrews@ci.ontario.ca.us

Fire Department
425 East B St., Ontario, CA 91764
Fax: (909) 395-2556

Fire Chief **Floyd Clark** .... (909) 395-2002

Human Resources Department
303 East B St., Ontario, CA 91764
Tel: (909) 391-2580 (Jobline)

Director **Angela Lopez** ....(909) 395-2442
E-mail: hr@ci.ontario.ca.us

Police Department
2500 South Archibald, Ontario, CA 91761

Police Chief **Brad Kaylor** .... (909) 395-2001

City of Orange, California

City Hall, 300 E. Chapman Ave., Orange, CA 92866
Internet: www.cityoforange.org

County: Orange **Election Type:** Nonpartisan **Year Incorporated:** April 6, 1888 **Population:** 140,992 (2015)

Office of the Mayor and City Council
City Hall, 300 E. Chapman Ave., Orange, CA 92866
Fax: (714) 744-5523 E-mail: citycouncil@cityoforange.org
Internet: www.cityoforange.org/council/default.asp

★Mayor **Teresa "Tita" Smith**.........................(714) 744-2211
Began Service: December 4, 2012
Term Expires: December 2018
E-mail: tsmith@cityoforange.org
Education: UC Irvine 1970 BA; USC 1992 MA
★Mayor Pro Tem **Mark A. Murphy** .... (714) 744-2211
Term Expires: December 2016
E-mail: councilman@markamurphy.com
Education: USC BS, MBA
★Council Member **Mike Alvarez** .... (714) 744-2211
Term Expires: December 2016
E-mail: malvarez@cityoforange.org

Office of the Mayor and City Council *continued*

★Council Member **Kimberlee "Kim" Nichols** .... (714) 744-2211
Term Expires: December 2018
E-mail: citycouncil@cityoforange.org
★Council Member **Fred M. Whitaker** .... (714) 744-2211
Term Expires: December 2018
E-mail: fwhitaker@cityoforange.org

Office of the City Attorney
City Hall, 300 E. Chapman Ave., Orange, CA 92866
Fax: (714) 538-7157

City Attorney **Wayne W. Winthers** ....(714) 744-5580
E-mail: wwinthers@cityoforange.org
Senior Assistant City Attorney **Gary A. Sheatz** .... (714) 744-5580
Assistant City Attorney **Denah H. Hoard** .... (714) 744-5580

Office of the City Manager
City Hall, 300 East Chapman Avenue, Orange, CA 92866
Fax: (714) 744-5523

City Manager **Rick Otto** .... (714) 744-2222
E-mail: rotto@cityoforange.org
Deputy City Manager **Irma Hernandez** ....(714) 744-2222
E-mail: ihernandez@cityoforange.org

Community Development
City Hall, 300 E. Chapman Ave., Orange, CA 92866
Fax: (714) 744-7222

Director **William Crouch** .... (714) 744-7240
E-mail: wcrouch@cityoforange.org

Community Services
230 E. Chapman Ave., Orange, CA 92866
Fax: (714) 744-7251

Director **(Vacant)**...................................(714) 744-7264
Assistant Director **Barbara Messick** .... (714) 744-7287
E-mail: bmessick@cityoforange.org

Economic Development
230 E. Chapman Ave., Orange, CA 92866
Fax: (714) 288-2598

Director **(Vacant)**...................................(714) 288-2589

Finance
City Hall, 300 East Chapman Avenue, Orange, CA 92866
Fax: (714) 744-2275
Internet: www.cityoforange.org/depts/finance/default.asp

Director **Will Kolbow** .... (714) 744-2238

Fire Department
176 S. Grand, Orange, CA 92866

Fire Chief **Patrick Dibb**.............................(714) 288-2500
E-mail: pdibb@cityoforange.org

Human Resources Department
City Hall, 300 E. Chapman Ave., Orange, CA 92866
Fax: (714) 744-7254

Director **Steven Pham** .... (714) 744-7255
E-mail: spham@cityoforange.org

Library Services
407 East Chapman Avenue, Orange, CA 92866
Fax: (714) 771-6126

Director (Acting) **Amy Harpster** .... (714) 288-2425

Police Department
1107 N. Batavia St., Orange, CA 92867
Fax: (714) 744-7320

Police Chief **Robert Gustafson** ....(714) 744-7301

★Elected Official ▲Appointed by Legislature ▼Appointed by Governor ▶Appointed by Board or Commission ●Appointed by Judge
■Appointed by Mayor △Appointed by Freeholders ▽Appointed by Supervisor ▷Appointed by County Executive ○Appointed by Council

Public Works
City Hall, 300 E. Chapman Ave., Orange, CA 92866
Fax: (714) 744-5573

Director **Joe DeFrancesco** . . . . (714) 744-5545

Office of the City Clerk

City Hall, 300 E. Chapman Ave., Orange, CA 92866
Internet: www.cityoforange.org/depts/cityclerk/default.asp

★City Clerk **Mary E. Murphy** . . . . (714) 744-5500
Term Expires: December 2016 Fax: (714) 744-5515
E-mail: mmurphy@cityoforange.org
Chief City Clerk **Rob Zornado** . . . . (714) 744-5510
Deputy City Clerk **Pam Coleman** . . . . (714) 744-5502
Fax: (714) 744-5515

Office of the City Treasurer

City Hall, 300 East Chapman Avenue, Orange, CA 92866
Internet: www.cityoforange.org/officials/city_treasurer.asp

★City Treasurer **Richard A. Rohm** . . . . (714) 744-5500
Term Expires: December 2016

City of Orlando, Florida

City Hall, 400 South Orange Avenue, Orlando, FL 32801
P.O. Box 4990, Orlando, FL 32802-4990
Tel: (407) 246-2251 (Information) Fax: (407) 246-3613
Internet: www.cityoforlando.net

County: Orange **Election Type:** Nonpartisan **Year Incorporated:** 1875
Population: 270,934 (2015)

John "Buddy" Dyer
Mayor

Began Service: 2003
Term Expires: January 2020
Education: Brown U 1980 BSCE; Florida 1987 JD
Career: State Senator (D-FL, District 14), Florida Senate (1992-2002)

Office of the Mayor and City Commissioners

City Hall, 400 S. Orange Ave., Orlando, FL 32801
Tel: (407) 246-2221 Fax: (407) 246-2842

★Mayor **John "Buddy" Dyer** . . . . (407) 246-2221
E-mail: buddy.dyer@cityoforlando.net
Special Assistant to the Mayor **Kathy Scanlon** . . . . . . (407) 246-2221
E-mail: kathryn.scanlon@cityoforlando.net
Executive Secretary **Sharon Wilson** . . . . (407) 246-2199
E-mail: sharon.wilson@cityoforlando.net
Chief of Staff **William Frank Billingsley III** . . . . . . (407) 246-2221
Office of Communications and Neighborhood Relations Director **Michele Brennan** . . . . . . (407) 246-3845
E-mail: michele.brennan@cityoforlando.net
■Intergovernmental Relations Director **Kathleen R. Russell** . . . . (407) 246-3094
E-mail: kathleen.russell@cityoforlando.net
Education: Florida State BA
■Multicultural Affairs Director **Luis M. Martinez** . . . . . . (407) 246-4128
E-mail: luis.martinez@cityoforlando.net
★City Commissioner **Jim Gray** (District 1) . . . . (407) 246-2001
Term Expires: January 10, 2018
E-mail: jim.gray@cityoforlando.net

Office of the Mayor and City Commissioners *continued*

★City Commissioner **Antonio "Tony" Ortiz** (District 2) . . . (407) 246-2002
Term Expires: January 2020
E-mail: tony.ortiz@cityoforlando.net
★City Commissioner **Robert Stuart** (District 3) . . . . (407) 246-2003
Term Expires: January 10, 2018
E-mail: robert.stuart@cityoforlando.net
★City Commissioner **Patty Sheehan** (District 4) . . . . (407) 246-2004
Term Expires: January 2020
E-mail: patty.sheehan@cityoforlando.net
Education: Central Florida BA
★City Commissioner **Regina Hill** (District 5) . . . . (407) 246-2005
Term Expires: January 10, 2018
E-mail: regina.hill@cityoforlando.net
★City Commissioner **Samuel Ings** (District 6) . . . . (407) 246-2006
Term Expires: January 2020
E-mail: samuel.ings@cityoforlando.net
Director of Innovation **Matt Broffman** . . . . (407) 246-2221

Hispanic Office for Local Assistance [HOLA]
595 North Primrose Drive, Orlando, FL 32803

Coordinator/Hispanic Affairs Advisor **Alicia Ramirez** . . . . (407) 246-4311

Office of the City Attorney

City Hall, 400 S. Orange Ave., Orlando, FL 32801
Fax: (407) 246-2854

■City Attorney **Mayanne Downs** . . . . (407) 246-2295
E-mail: mayanne.downs@cityoforlando.net
■Deputy City Attorney **Jody M. Litchford** . . . . (407) 246-3480
E-mail: jody.litchford@cityoforlando.net
Education: Virginia JD
■City Prosecutor **Alexander Karden** . . . . (407) 246-2356
E-mail: alexander.karden@cityoforlando.net
■Chief Assistant Police Legal Advisor **Natasha W. Williams** . . . . (407) 246-2464
E-mail: natasha.williams@cityoforlando.net
Education: Florida JD

Office of the Chief Administrative Officer

City Hall, 400 S. Orange Ave., Orlando, FL 32801
Fax: (407) 246-2842

■Chief Administrative Officer **Byron Brooks** . . . . (407) 246-3091
E-mail: byron.brooks@cityoforlando.net
■Deputy Chief Administrative Officer **Deborah Girard** . . . . (407) 246-2237
E-mail: deborah.girard@cityoforlando.net
■Deputy Chief Administrative Officer **Kevin J. Edmonds** . . (407) 246-4127
E-mail: kevin.edmonds@cityoforlando.net
Education: Cincinnati 1983 BS

Office of the City Clerk

City Hall, 400 South Orange Avenue, 4th Floor, Orlando, FL 32801
Fax: (407) 246-3613

■City Clerk **Celeste Brown** . . . . (407) 246-2251
E-mail: celeste.brown@cityoforlando.net
Assistant City Clerk **Elizabeth "Beth" Davidson** . . . . . . (407) 246-2251
E-mail: elizabeth.davidson@cityoforlando.net
■Chief Information Officer **Rosa Akhtarkhavari** . . . . . . (407) 246-2124
E-mail: rosa.akhtarkhavari@cityoforlando.net Fax: (407) 246-2878
Systems Development Manager **David Gancarz** . . . . (407) 246-3062
E-mail: david.gancarz@cityoforlando.net
Client and Support Services Manager **Mark A. Crain** . . . . . (407) 246-3022
E-mail: mark.crain@cityoforlando.net
Education: Emory MA
Facilities and Fleet Management Division Manager (Acting) **David Dunn** . . . . (407) 246-3873
E-mail: david.dunn@cityoforlando.net
Human Resources Division Manager **Ana Palenzuela** . . . . (407) 246-2057
E-mail: ana.palenzuela@cityoforlando.net
Purchasing Division Manager **David Billingsley** . . . . (407) 246-2897
E-mail: david.billingsley@cityoforlando.net

★Elected Official ▲Appointed by Legislature ▼Appointed by Governor ►Appointed by Board or Commission ●Appointed by Judge
■Appointed by Mayor △Appointed by Freeholders ▽Appointed by Supervisor ▷Appointed by County Executive ○Appointed by Council

Office of the City Clerk *continued*

Minority Business Enterprise Official **Kevin Walsh** ...... (407) 246-2623
E-mail: kevin.walsh@cityoforlando.net
Education: Dartmouth 1979 AB

Records and Archives Supervisor
Ruth McLemore-Price ...... (407) 246-2762
E-mail: ruth.mclemore@cityoforlando.net

Office of Business and Financial Services

City Hall, 400 S. Orange Ave., Orlando, FL 32801
Fax: (407) 246-2707

■ Chief Financial Officer **Rebecca Sutton** ...... (407) 246-2341
E-mail: rebecca.sutton@cityoforlando.net

■ Deputy Chief Financial Officer **Brian Battles** ...... (407) 246-3469
E-mail: brian.battles@cityoforlando.net

■ Deputy Chief Financial Officer **Christopher McCullion** .. (407) 246-4274
E-mail: christopher.mccullion@cityoforlando.net

Department of Economic Development

One City Commons, 400 South Orange Avenue, Orlando, FL 32801
Fax: (407) 246-3342

Economic Development Director **Brooke Bonnett** ...... (407) 246-2719
E-mail: brooke.bonnett@cityoforlando.net

City Planning Director **Dean J. Grandin, Jr.** ...... (407) 246-2120
E-mail: dean.grandin@cityoforlando.net

Orlando Venues Director **Allen Johnson** ...... (407) 440-7070
E-mail: allen.johnson@cityoforlando.net
Education: Central Florida BA

Orlando Venues Deputy Director **(Vacant)** ...... (407) 440-7007

Permitting Division Manager **Timothy Johnson** ...... (407) 246-2075

Downtown Development Board and Community Redevelopment Agency

400 South Orange Avenue, 6th Floor, Orlando, FL 32801
Fax: (407) 246-2495

■ Executive Director **Thomas C. Chatmon, Jr.** ...... (407) 246-3361
E-mail: thomas.chatmon@cityoforlando.net

Community Redevelopment Agency Assistant Director
David Barilla ...... (407) 246-3703
E-mail: david.barilla@cityoforlando.net

Department of Families, Parks and Recreation

595 North Primrose Drive, Orlando, FL 32803
Fax: (407) 246-2875

■ Director **Lisa Early** ...... (407) 246-4319
E-mail: lisa.early@cityoforlando.net

Harry P. Leu Gardens Executive Director
Robert E. Bowden ...... (407) 246-2625
Education: Michigan MA

Parks Division Manager **John Perrone** ...... (407) 246-3856

Recreation Division Manager **Rodney Williams** ...... (407) 246-4309

Fire Department

City Hall, 400 S. Orange Ave., Orlando, FL 32801
Tel: (407) 246-2390 Fax: (407) 246-2512

■ Fire Chief **Roderick Williams** ...... (407) 246-3125

Deputy Fire Chief, Support Services Bureau
Richard E. Wales ...... (407) 246-2135
E-mail: richard.wales@cityoforlando.net

Deputy Fire Chief, Administration Services Bureau
Russell C. Nail ...... (407) 246-3992

Deputy Fire Chief, Field Operations Bureau
Keith Maddox ...... (407) 246-3838

Department of Housing and Community Development

400 South Orange Avenue, 6th Floor, Orlando, FL 32801
Fax: (407) 246-3055

■ Director **Oren Henry** ...... (407) 246-2328
E-mail: oren.henry@cityoforlando.net

Housing Director **Linda Rhinesmith** ...... (407) 246-3170

Office of Community Affairs and Human Relations

400 S. Orange Ave., Orlando, FL 32801
P.O. Box 4990, Orlando, FL 32802-4990
Tel: (407) 246-2500 Fax: (407) 246-3508

■ Chief Service Officer **Marcia Hope Goodwin** ...... (407) 246-3501
E-mail: marcia.goodwin@cityoforlando.net
Education: Howard U BA

Police Department

100 S. Hughey Ave., Orlando, FL 32801
Fax: (407) 246-2732
Internet: http://www.cityoforlando.net/police/chief-police/

■ Police Chief **John Mina** ...... (407) 246-2401
E-mail: john.mina@cityoforlando.net

Deputy Police Chief **Robert Pigman** ...... (407) 246-3835

Department of Public Works

City Hall, 400 S. Orange Ave., Orlando, FL 32801
Fax: (407) 246-2892

■ Director **Richard M. "Rick" Howard** ...... (407) 246-3222
E-mail: richard.howard@cityoforlando.net
Education: Central Florida BSE

Deputy Public Works Director/City Engineer
James "Jim" Hunt ...... (407) 246-3623
E-mail: jim.hunt@cityoforlando.net

Deputy Public Works Director/Transportation
Engineering **Charles Ramdatt** ...... (407) 246-3186
E-mail: charles.ramdatt@cityoforlando.net

Capital Improvement Infrastructure Division Manager
Tom Connery ...... (407) 246-3751

Parking Division Manager **Scott Zollars** ...... (407) 246-3859

Solid Waste Division Manager **Michael W. Carroll** ...... (407) 246-3050
Education: South Alabama BA

Streets/Stormwater Management Division Manager
Lisa Henry ...... (407) 246-3646

Wastewater Division Manager **Victor Godlewski** ...... (407) 246-3221

★ Elected Official ▲ Appointed by Legislature ▼ Appointed by Governor ▶ Appointed by Board or Commission ● Appointed by Judge
■ Appointed by Mayor △ Appointed by Freeholders ▽ Appointed by Supervisor ▷ Appointed by County Executive ○ Appointed by Council

CITIES AND TOWNS

City of Overland Park, Kansas

City Hall, 8500 Santa Fe Dr., Overland Park, KS 66212
Internet: www.opkansas.org

County: Johnson **Election Type:** Nonpartisan **Year Incorporated:** 1960
Population: 186,515 (2015)

Carl R. Gerlach
Mayor

Began Service: April 2005
Term Expires: April 4, 2017
Education: Kansas State BA
Career: Council Member, Office of the Mayor and City Council, City of Overland Park, Kansas (1995-2005); City Council President, Office of the Mayor and City Council, City of Overland Park, Kansas (2002-2003)

Office of the Mayor and City Council

City Hall, 8500 Santa Fe Dr., Overland Park, KS 66212
E-mail: city@opkansas.org

★ Mayor **Carl R. Gerlach** .... (913) 895-6104
★ Council President **Paul Lyons** (Ward 2) .... (913) 895-6105
Term Expires: April 7, 2019
E-mail: paul.lyons@opkansas.org
★ Council Member **Dave Janson** (Ward 1) .... (913) 895-6105
Term Expires: April 4, 2017
E-mail: dave.janson@opkansas.org
★ Council Member **Terry Happer Scheier** (Ward 1) .... (913) 895-6105
Term Expires: April 7, 2019
E-mail: terry.happerscheier@opkansas.org
★ Council Member **Curt Skoog** (Ward 2) .... (913) 895-6105
Term Expires: April 4, 2017
E-mail: curt.skoog@opkansas.org
★ Council Member **Jim Kite** (Ward 3) .... (913) 895-6105
Term Expires: April 4, 2017
E-mail: jim.kite@opkansas.org
★ Council Member **David White** (Ward 3) .... (913) 895-6105
Term Expires: April 7, 2019
E-mail: david.white@opkansas.org
★ Council Member **Terry Goodman** (Ward 4) .... (913) 895-6105
Term Expires: April 4, 2017
E-mail: terry.goodman@opkansas.org
Education: Missouri (Kansas City) BA
★ Council Member **Fred Spears** (Ward 4) .... (913) 895-6105
Term Expires: April 7, 2019
E-mail: fred.spears@opkansas.org
★ Council Member **John Skubal** (Ward 5) .... (913) 895-6105
Term Expires: April 7, 2019
E-mail: john.skubal@opkansas.org
★ Council Member **John Thompson** (Ward 5) .... (913) 895-6105
Term Expires: April 4, 2017
E-mail: john.thompson@opkansas.org
★ Council Member **Rick Collins** (Ward 6) .... (913) 895-6105
Term Expires: April 7, 2019
E-mail: rick.collins@opkansas.org
★ Council Member **Dan Stock** (Ward 6) .... (913) 895-6105
Term Expires: April 4, 2017
E-mail: dan.stock@opkansas.org

Office of the City Attorney

City Hall, 8500 Santa Fe Dr., Overland Park, KS 66212
Fax: (913) 895-5095

City Attorney **Mike Santos** .... (913) 895-6084
E-mail: mike.santos@opkansas.org

Office of the City Clerk

City Hall, 8500 Santa Fe Dr., Overland Park, KS 66212

City Clerk **Marian Cook** .... (913) 895-6151
E-mail: Marian.cook@opkansas.org

Office of the City Manager

City Hall, 8500 Santa Fe Dr., Overland Park, KS 66212
Fax: (913) 895-5003

○ City Manager **Bill Ebel** .... (913) 895-6102
Deputy City Manager **Kristy Stallings** .... (913) 895-6102
E-mail: kristy.stallings@opkansas.org
Assistant City Manager **Kate Gunja** .... (913) 895-6110
E-mail: kate.gunja@opkansas.org
Public Information Officer **Sean Reilly** .... (913) 895-6109
E-mail: sean.reilly@opkansas.org

Finance, Budget, and Administration Office

City Hall, 8500 Santa Fe Dr., Overland Park, KS 66212

Chief Financial Officer **Dave Scott** .... (913) 895-6154
E-mail: dave.scott@opkansas.org

Fire Department

9550 W. 95th St., Overland Park, KS 66212
Fax: (913) 888-8348 Internet: http://www.opfd.com

Fire Chief **J. Bryan Dehner** .... (913) 888-6066
E-mail: bryan.dehner@opkansas.org
Deputy Fire Chief **Mike P. Casey** .... (913) 888-6066

Human Resources Department

City Hall, 8500 Santa Fe Dr., Overland Park, KS 66212

Director **Mike Garcia** .... (913) 895-6121
E-mail: mike.garcia@opkansas.org

Parks and Recreation

11921 Hardy St., Overland Park, KS 66213

Director of Parks Services **Greg Ruether** .... (913) 327-6634
Director of Recreational Services **Tony Crosby** .... (913) 895-6351
Manager, Golf Operations **(Vacant)** .... (913) 897-3805
8500 Santa Fe Drive, Overland Park, KS 66212

Planning and Development Services

City Hall, 8500 Santa Fe Dr., Overland Park, KS 66212

Director **Jack Messer** .... (913) 895-6191
E-mail: jack.messer@opkansas.org
Codes Administrator **James T. Ryan** .... (913) 895-6251
Education: Pittsburg State BS Fax: (913) 895-5016

Police Department

12400 Foster St., Overland Park, KS 66212

Chief of Police **Frank Donchez** .... (913) 327-6937
Deputy Chief **Simon Happer** .... (913) 327-6937
Deputy Chief **Lt. Col. Mark Kessler** .... (913) 327-6834

Public Works Department

City Hall, 8500 Santa Fe Dr., Overland Park, KS 66212

Director **Tony Hofmann** .... (913) 895-6040

★ Elected Official ▲ Appointed by Legislature ▼ Appointed by Governor ► Appointed by Board or Commission ● Appointed by Judge
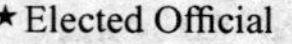
■ Appointed by Mayor △ Appointed by Freeholders ▽ Appointed by Supervisor ▷ Appointed by County Executive ○ Appointed by Council

City of Oxnard, California

City Hall, 305 W. Third St., Oxnard, CA 93030
Internet: www.ci.oxnard.ca.us

County: Ventura **Election Type:** Nonpartisan **Population:** 207,254 (2015)

Office of the Mayor and City Council

City Hall, 300 West Third Street, 4th Floor, Oxnard, CA 93030
Tel: (805) 385-7430 Fax: (805) 385-7595
E-mail: oxnardcty@ci.oxnard.ca.us

★Mayor **Timothy B. Flynn** .... (805) 385-7430
Began Service: December 4, 2012
Term Expires: December 2016
E-mail: Tim.Flynn@ci.oxnard.ca.us

★Mayor Pro Tem **Carmen Ramirez** .... (805) 385-7430
Term Expires: December 2018
E-mail: carmen4oxnard@yahoo.com

★Council Member **Bryan A. MacDonald** .... (805) 385-7430
Term Expires: December 2016
E-mail: bryan.macdonald@ci.oxnard.ca.us

★Council Member **Dorina Padilla** .... (805) 385-7430
Term Expires: December 2016
E-mail: dorina.padilla@ci.oxnard.ca.us

★Council Member **Bert Perello** .... (805) 385-7430
Term Expires: December 2018
E-mail: perellobert@gmail.com

Office of the City Attorney

City Hall, 300 West Third Street, Suite 300, Oxnard, CA 93030
Fax: (805) 385-7423

City Attorney (Interim) **Stephen Fischer** .... (805) 385-7483
E-mail: stephen.fischer@ci.oxnard.ca.us

Office of the City Clerk

City Hall, 300 West Third Street, 4th Floor, Oxnard, CA 93030
Fax: (805) 385-7806

★City Clerk **Daniel Martinez** .... (805) 385-7803
Term Expires: November 7, 2016
E-mail: daniel.martinez@ci.oxnard.ca.us

Office of the Treasurer

214 South C Street, Oxnard, CA 93030
Fax: (805) 385-7836

★Treasurer **Danielle "Dani" Navas** .... (805) 385-7810
Term Expires: November 7, 2016
E-mail: danielle.navas@ci.oxnard.ca.us

Office of the City Manager

City Hall, 300 West Third Street, Oxnard, CA 93030
Fax: (805) 385-7595

○City Manager **Greg Nyhoff** .... (805) 385-7430
E-mail: greg.nyhoff@ci.oxnard.ca.us

Assistant City Manager **Maria Hurtado** .... (805) 385-7430
Education: San José State MA

Assistant City Manager **Scott Whitney** .... (805) 385-7430

Public Information Officer (Interim) **Jason Zaragoza** .... (805) 385-7450
Fax: (805) 385-7453

Community Development Commission Successor Agency

214 South C Street, Oxnard, CA 93030
Fax: (805) 385-7408

Redevelopment Manager (Interim) **Kymberly Horner** .... (805) 385-7407
E-mail: kymberly.horner@ci.oxnard.ca.us

Development Services Department

214 South C Street, Oxnard, CA 93030
Fax: (805) 385-7833

Director (Interim) **Ashley Golden** .... (805) 385-7896

Finance Department

City Hall, 300 West Third Street, Oxnard, CA 93030
Fax: (805) 385-7466

Chief Financial Officer **(Vacant)** .... (805) 385-7475

Fire Department

360 West Second Street, Oxnard, CA 93030
Fax: (805) 385-8009

Fire Chief **Bryan Brice** .... (805) 385-7722

Fire Marshal **Sergio Martinez** .... (805) 385-7722
E-mail: sergio.martinez@ci.oxnard.ca.us

Housing Department

435 South D St., Oxnard, CA 93030
Fax: (805) 385-7969

Housing Director **Arturo Casillas** .... (805) 385-8041

Human Resources Department

City Hall, 300 West Third Street, Oxnard, CA 93030
Fax: (805) 385-8352

Director **Tabin Cosio** .... (805) 385-7596

Police Department

251 South C St., Oxnard, CA 93030
E-mail: info@oxnardpd.org Internet: http://www.oxnardpd.org

Chief of Police **Jeri L. Williams** .... (805) 385-7600
Education: Arizona State BS; Northern Arizona MA

Oxnard Public Library

251 South A St., Oxnard, CA 93030
Tel: (805) 385-7500 Fax: (805) 385-7526

Director (Interim) **Sofia Kimsey** .... (805) 385-7522
E-mail: Sofia.Kimsey@ci.oxnard.ca.us

Public Works Department

City Hall, 305 W. Third St., Oxnard, CA 93030
Fax: (805) 385-7907

Director (Interim) **Rob Roshanian** .... (805) 385-8281

Recreation and Community Services Department

555 South A Street, Suite 265, Oxnard, CA 93030
Fax: (805) 385-7939

Superintendent (Interim) **Terrel Harrison** .... (805) 385-7995

★Elected Official ▲Appointed by Legislature ▼Appointed by Governor ▶Appointed by Board or Commission ●Appointed by Judge
■Appointed by Mayor △Appointed by Freeholders ▽Appointed by Supervisor ▷Appointed by County Executive ○Appointed by Council

City of Palm Bay, Florida

120 Malabar Road, SE, Palm Bay, FL 32907
Tel: (321) 952-3400 Internet: www.palmbayflorida.org

County: Brevard **Election Type:** Nonpartisan **Year Incorporated:** January 16, 1960 **Population:** 107,888 (2015)

Office of the Mayor and City Council

120 Malabar Road, SE, Palm Bay, FL 32907
Fax: (321) 953-8971

★ Mayor **William Capote** . . . . . (321) 952-3414
Began Service: November 6, 2012
Term Expires: November 8, 2016
E-mail: mayor@palmbayflorida.org

★ Deputy Mayor **Jeff Bailey** (Seat 5) . . . . . (321) 952-3414
Term Expires: November 6, 2018
E-mail: seat5@palmbayflorida.org

★ Council Member **Harry Santiago, Jr.** (Seat 2) . . . . . (321) 952-3414
Term Expires: November 8, 2016
E-mail: seat2@palmbayflorida.org

★ Council Member **Michele Paccione** (Seat 3) . . . . . (321) 952-3414
Term Expires: November 8, 2016
E-mail: seat3@palmbayflorida.org

★ Council Member **Tres Holton** (Seat 4) . . . . . (321) 952-3414
Term Expires: November 6, 2018
E-mail: seat4@palmbayflorida.org

Office of the City Attorney

120 Malabar Road, SE, Palm Bay, FL 32907

City Attorney **Andrew Patrick Lannon** . . . . . (321) 409-7185
E-mail: legal@palmbayflorida.org
Education: Holy Cross Col 1996 BA; Columbus Law 2003 JD

Office of the City Clerk

120 Malabar Road, SE, Palm Bay, FL 32907
Fax: (321) 953-8971

City Clerk **Terese Jones** . . . . . (321) 952-3414
E-mail: terese.jones@palmbayflorida.org

Deputy City Clerk **(Vacant)** . . . . . (321) 952-3414

Office of the City Manager

120 Malabar Road, SE, Palm Bay, FL 32907
Fax: (321) 952-3412

City Manager **Gregg Lynk** . . . . . (321) 952-3411
Administrative Assistant **Christina Born** . . . . . (321) 952-3411 ext. 3208
E-mail: christina.born@palmbayflorida.org

Bayfront Community Redevelopment Agency

120 Malabar Road, SE, Palm Bay, FL 32907
Fax: (321) 952-3412

Administrator **James Marshal** . . . . . (321) 409-7187

Economic Development Department

120 Malabar Road, SE, Palm Bay, FL 32907
Fax: (321) 952-3412

Economic Development and External Affairs Director **Andy Anderson** . . . . . (321) 952-3426

Finance Department

120 Malabar Road, SE, Suite 323, Palm Bay, FL 32907
Fax: (321) 952-3412

Finance Director **Karen Barber** . . . . . (321) 952-3418

Budget Administrator **Patricia Gloade** . . . . . (321) 952-3418
E-mail: patricia.gloade@palmbayflorida.org

Accounting Division

120 Malabar Road, SE, Suite 207, Palm Bay, FL 32907
Fax: (321) 952-3401

Accounting Manager **Marcia Patacer** . . . . . (321) 952-3400 ext. 3211
E-mail: marcia.patacer@palmbayflorida.org

Purchasing and Contracts Division

120 Malabar Road, SE, Suite 200, Palm Bay, FL 32907
Fax: (321) 952-3401

Purchasing Manager **Bobbye Marsala** . . . . . (321) 952-3424
E-mail: bobbye.marsala@palmbayflorida.org

Human Resources Department

120 Malabar Road, SE, Palm Bay, FL 32907
Fax: (321) 733-3001

Human Resources Clerk **Alex Bluto** . . . . . (321) 952-3421 ext. 6326
E-mail: alex.bluto@palmbayflorida.org

Palm Bay Fire Rescue

899 Carlyle Avenue, SE, Palm Bay, FL 32909

Fire Chief **Jim Stables** . . . . . (321) 409-6366
E-mail: jim.stables@palmbayflorida.org

Police Department

130 Malabar Road, SE, Palm Bay, FL 32907
Fax: (321) 952-3404

Chief of Police **Mark Renkens** . . . . . (321) 952-3456

Deputy Chief of Police **Jim Rogers** . . . . . (321) 952-3456

Code Compliance Division

120 Malabar Road, SE, Suite 201, Palm Bay, FL 32907
Tel: (321) 952-3430 Fax: (321) 733-3086

Code Compliance Manager **Aaron Pool** . . . . . (321) 952-3430

Office of the Deputy City Manager

120 Malabar Road, SE, Palm Bay, FL 32907

Deputy City Manager **David Isnardi** . . . . . (321) 952-3411
E-mail: david.isnardi@palmbayflorida.org

Public Works Department

1050 Malabar Road, SW, Palm Bay, FL 32907

Public Works Director **(Vacant)** . . . . . (321) 953-8996

Fleet Services Division

1050 Malabar Road, SW, Palm Bay, FL 32907

Fleet Services Manager **John Cady** . . . . . (321) 953-8996

Communications and Information Technology Department

120 Malabar Road, SE, Palm Bay, FL 32907

Director **Lisa Morrell** . . . . . (321) 952-3475
E-mail: lisa.morrell@palmbayflorida.org

Public Information Officer **(Vacant)** . . . . . (321) 952-3456 ext. 4678

Growth Management Department

120 Malabar Road, SE, Palm Bay, FL 32907
Fax: (321) 409-7134

Director **David Watkins** . . . . . (321) 733-3041

Building Division

120 Malabar Road, SE, Palm Bay, FL 32907
Fax: (321) 953-8925 E-mail: building@palmbayflorida.org

Chief Building Official **Jason Mahaney** . . . . . (321) 953-8924

Parks and Recreation Department

1150 DeGroodt Road, SW, Palm Bay, FL 32908

Director **Fred Poppe** . . . . . (321) 953-8912

★ Elected Official ▲ Appointed by Legislature ▼ Appointed by Governor ► Appointed by Board or Commission ● Appointed by Judge
■ Appointed by Mayor △ Appointed by Freeholders ▽ Appointed by Supervisor ▷ Appointed by County Executive ○ Appointed by Council

Utilities Department
250 Osmosis Drive SE, Palm Bay, FL 32909
Fax: (321) 674-1852
Utilities Director **Dan Roberts** ....(321) 952-3410

City of Palmdale, California

City Hall, 38300 Sierra Hwy, Palmdale, CA 93550
Internet: www.cityofpalmdale.org

County: Los Angeles **Population:** 158,351 (2015)

James C. Ledford, Jr.
Mayor

Began Service: 1992
Term Expires: December 2016
Career: Supervisor, Lockheed Corporation

Office of the Mayor and City Council

City Hall, 38300 Sierra Hwy, Palmdale, CA 93550
Fax: (661) 267-5122

★Mayor **James C. Ledford, Jr.** ....(661) 267-5115
E-mail: jledford@cityofpalmdale.org
★Council Member **Mike Dispenza** ....(661) 267-5115
Term Expires: December 2016
E-mail: mdispenza@cityofpalmdale.org
Education: Northeast Louisiana BS
★Council Member **Steven D. Hofbauer** ....(661) 267-5115
Term Expires: December 2016
E-mail: shofbauer@cityofpalmdale.org
★Council Member **Roxana Martinez** ....(661) 267-5115
Term Expires: December 2018
E-mail: rmartinez@cityofpalmdale.org
★Council Member **Fred Thompson** ....(661) 267-5115
Term Expires: December 2018
E-mail: fthompson@cityofpalmdale.org

Office of the City Manager and Administration

City Hall, 38300 Sierra Highway, Suite A, Palmdale, CA 93550

City Manager **Jim Purtee** ....(661) 267-5115
E-mail: jpurtee@cityofpalmdale.org
Education: Cal State (Northridge) MA
Director of Administrative Services **Anne Ambrose** .....(661) 267-5107
E-mail: aambrose@cityofpalmdale.org

Finance Division
38300 Sierra Highway, Suite D, Palmdale, CA 93550
Finance Manager **Karen Johnston** ....(661) 267-5440
Fax: (661) 267-5082

Human Resources Division
823 East Avenue Q-9, Palmdale, CA 93550
Manager **Patricia Nevarez** ....(661) 267-5400
E-mail: pnevarez@cityofpalmdale.org Fax: (661) 267-5410

Office of the City Attorney

City Hall, 38300 Sierra Highway, Suite C, Palmdale, CA 93550
City Attorney **W. Matthew Ditzhazy** ....(661) 267-5108
E-mail: mditzhazy@cityofpalmdale.org Fax: (661) 267-5178

Office of the City Clerk

City Hall, 38300 Sierra Highway, Suite C, Palmdale, CA 93550
City Clerk **Rebecca Smith** ....(661) 267-5151
E-mail: rsmith@cityofpalmdale.org Fax: (661) 267-5193

Building and Safety Department

City Hall, 38250 Sierra Hwy., Palmdale, CA 93550
Building Official **Bud Davis** ....(661) 267-5353
Fax: (661) 267-5355

Communications Division

City Hall, 38300 Sierra Hwy., Suite A, Palmdale, CA 93550
Fax: (661) 267-5122
Communications Manager **John Mlynar** ....(661) 267-5115
Fax: (661) 267-5122

Community Redevelopment Agency

City Hall, 38250 Sierra Hwy., Palmdale, CA 93550

Economic Development, Marketing and Communication Department
Director **Kari Blackburn** ....(661) 267-5125
Fax: (661) 267-5155

Development Services Department

38300 Sierra Highway, Palmdale, CA 93550
Director of Development Services **Bill Padilla** ....(661) 267-5100
E-mail: bpadilla@cityofpalmdale.org

Department of Neighborhood Services

827 East Avenue Q-9, Palmdale, CA 93550
Fax: (661) 267-5554
Director **Mike Miller** ....(661) 267-5181
E-mail: mmiller@cityofpalmdale.org

Palmdale City Library

700 E. Palmdale Blvd., Palmdale, CA 93550
Internet: http://www.cityofpalmdale.org/Library
City Librarian **Thomas Vose** ....(661) 267-5600
E-mail: tvose@cityofpalmdale.org Fax: (661) 267-5606

Recreation and Culture Department

38260 10th Street East, Palmdale, CA 93550
Director **Keri Smith** ....(661) 267-5611
Fax: (661) 267-5636

Planning Division

City Hall, 38250 Sierra Hwy., Palmdale, CA 93550
Manager (Acting) **Richard Kite** ....(661) 267-5200
Fax: (661) 267-5233

Public Works Department

City Hall, 38250 Sierra Hwy., Palmdale, CA 93550
Director **Michael Mischel** ....(661) 267-5300
Fax: (661) 267-5322

Traffic Engineering Division
Assistant Director of Public Works/City Engineer
Bill Padilla ....(661) 267-5300
E-mail: bpadilla@cityofpalmdale.org Fax: (661) 267-5292

CITIES AND TOWNS

★Elected Official ▲Appointed by Legislature ▼Appointed by Governor ▶Appointed by Board or Commission ●Appointed by Judge
■Appointed by Mayor △Appointed by Freeholders ▽Appointed by Supervisor ▷Appointed by County Executive ○Appointed by Council

City of Pasadena, California

City Hall, 100 North Garfield Ave., Pasadena, CA 91109-7215
P.O. Box 7115, Pasadena, CA 91109-7215
Tel: (626) 744-7311 (Information) Internet: http://cityofpasadena.net/

County: Los Angeles **Election Type:** Nonpartisan **Year Incorporated:** 1886 **Population:** 142,250 (2015)

Office of the Mayor and City Council

City Hall, 100 North Garfield Avenue, Pasadena, CA 91109-7215
P.O. Box 7115, Pasadena, CA 91109-7215
Fax: (626) 744-3727

★Mayor **Terry Tornek** .... (626) 744-4111
Began Service: May 2015
Term Expires: May 2019
E-mail: ttornek@cityofpasadena.net
City Council District Liaison **Rhonda Stone** .... (626) 744-7147
E-mail: rstone@cityofpasadena.net
★Council Member **Tyron Hampton** (District 1) .... (626) 744-4444
Term Expires: May 2019
E-mail: district1@cityofpasadena.net
Field Representative **Cushon Bell** .... (626) 744-4444
E-mail: cbell@cityofpasadena.net
Field Representative **Cheyenne Chong** .... (626) 744-4444
E-mail: cdhong@cityofpasadena.net
★Council Member **Margaret McAustin** (District 2) .... (626) 744-4742
Term Expires: May 2019
E-mail: mmcaustin@cityofpasadena.net
Field Representative **Margo Morales** .... (626) 744-4742
E-mail: mmorales@cityofpasadena.net
★Council Member **John J. Kennedy** (District 3) .... (626) 744-4738
Term Expires: May 6, 2017
E-mail: johnjkennedy@cityofpasadena.net
Field Representative **(Vacant)** .... (626) 744-4738
★Council Member **Gene Masuda** (District 4) .... (626) 744-4740
Term Expires: May 2, 2019
E-mail: gmasuda@cityofpasadena.net
Field Representative **Noreen Sullivan** .... (626) 744-4740
E-mail: nsullivan@cityofpasadena.net
★Council Member **Victor Gordo** (District 5) .... (626) 744-4741
Term Expires: May 6, 2017
E-mail: vgordo@cityofpasadena.net
Field Representative **Vannia DeLaCuba** .... (626) 744-4741
E-mail: vdelacuba@cityofpasadena.net
★Council Member **Steve Madison** (District 6) .... (626) 744-4739
Term Expires: May 2, 2019
E-mail: smadison@cityofpasadena.net
Field Representative **Takako Suzuki** .... (626) 744-4739
E-mail: tsuzuki@cityofpasadena.net
★Council Member **Andy Wilson** (District 7) .... (626) 744-4737
Term Expires: May 6, 2017
Field Representative **Pamela Thyret** .... (626) 744-4737
E-mail: pthyret@cityofpasadena.net
Management Analyst to the Mayor and City Council
Jana Stewart .... (626) 744-4311
E-mail: janastewart@cityofpasadena.net
Administrative Assistant to the Mayor and City Council
Debra Humphrey .... (626) 744-4311
E-mail: dhumphrey@cityofpasadena.net

Office of the City Manager

P.O. Box 7115, Pasadena, CA 91109-7215
Fax: (626) 744-4784 Internet: http://cityofpasadena.net/citymanager/

○City Manager (Interim) **Steve Mermell** .... (626) 744-4333
E-mail: smermell@cityofpasadena.net
Education: Cal State (Northridge) BA, MPA
Assistant City Manager **Julie Gutierrez** .... (626) 744-6936
E-mail: jgutierrez@cityofpasadena.net
Education: Pomona BA; LaVerne MBA

Office of the City Manager *continued*

Assistant City Manager **Steve Mermell** .... (626) 744-7371
E-mail: smermell@cityofpasadena.net
Education: Cal State (Northridge) BA, MPA
Public Information Officer **William Boyer** .... (626) 744-4755

Office of the City Attorney/Prosecutor

100 North Garfield Avenue, Suite N210, Pasadena, CA 91109-7215
Fax: (626) 744-4190 Internet: www.cityofpasadena.net/cityattorney

City Attorney/City Prosecutor **Michele Beal Bagneris** ... (626) 744-4141
E-mail: mbagneris@cityofpasadena.net
Education: Stanford 1980 BA; Boalt Hall 1983 JD
Chief Assistant City Prosecutor **Wilfredo Rivera** .... (626) 744-4611
Administrative Legal Supervisor **Teresa Romero** .... (626) 744-3976
E-mail: tromero@cityofpasadena.net
Senior Administrative Analyst **Dyana Brown** .... (626) 744-4298
Fax: (626) 396-8569

Office of the City Clerk

100 North Garfield Ave., Room S228, Pasadena, CA 91109-7215
P.O. Box 7115, Pasadena, CA 91109-7215
Fax: (626) 744-3921 Internet: http://cityofpasadena.net/CityClerk/

○City Clerk **Mark Jomsky** .... (626) 744-4124
E-mail: mjomsky@cityofpasadena.net
Education: UC Irvine BA; Cal State (Long Beach) MPA
Senior Assistant City Clerk **(Vacant)** .... (626) 744-4124

Finance Department

100 North Garfield Avenue, Room S-348, Pasadena, CA 91109
Tel: (626) 744-4355 Fax: (626) 744-7093
Internet: http://cityofpasadena.net/Finance/

Director **Matt Hawkesworth** .... (626) 744-4350
Executive Assistant **Lori Eubanks** .... (626) 744-4350
E-mail: leubanks@cityofpasadena.net

Pasadena Fire Department

215 North Marengo Avenue, Suite 195, Pasadena, CA 91101-1530
Fax: (626) 585-9164 Internet: http://cityofpasadena.net/Fire/

Fire Chief **Bertral T. Washington** .... (626) 744-4655
E-mail: firechief@cityofpasadena.net
Education: Col Southern Nevada; Howard U; UNLV MPA
Executive Secretary **Peggy Galvan Palmer** .... (626) 744-4655
E-mail: ppalmer@cityofpasadena.net

Housing Department

649 North Fair Oaks, Suite 202, Pasadena, CA 91103
Fax: (626) 744-8340 Internet: http://cityofpasadena.net/housing

Director **William Huang** .... (626) 744-8300
E-mail: whuang@cityofpasadena.net

Human Resources Department

100 North Garfield Avenue, Room S 135, Pasadena, CA 91109-7215
Fax: (626) 744-7035 E-mail: humanresources@cityofpasadena.net
Internet: http://cityofpasadena.net/humanresources/

Director **Jennifer Curtis** .... (626) 744-4366
E-mail: humanresources@cityofpasadena.net
Executive Secretary **Kari Lenggiere** .... (626) 744-4368
E-mail: klenggiere@cityofpasadena.net

Human Services and Recreation Department

100 North Garfield Avenue, 2nd Floor, Pasadena, CA 91109
Fax: (626) 744-6821 Internet: http://cityofpasadena.net/HumanServices/

Director **Horace Wormely** .... (626) 744-4386
Executive Secretary **Lisette Jabola** .... (626) 744-3919
E-mail: ljabola@cityofpasadena.net

★ Elected Official ▲ Appointed by Legislature ▼ Appointed by Governor ▶ Appointed by Board or Commission ● Appointed by Judge
■ Appointed by Mayor △ Appointed by Freeholders ▽ Appointed by Supervisor ▷ Appointed by County Executive ○ Appointed by Council

The Rose Bowl and Arroyo Seco Facilities
1001 Rose Bowl Dr., Pasadena, CA 91103
Tel: (626) 577-3100 Fax: (626) 405-0992
Internet: http://www.rosebowlstadium.com
Internet: www.facebook.com/pages/Rose-Bowl/278525755719

General Manager **Darryl Dunn** .... (626) 577-3107

Department of Information Technology
100 North Garfield Avenue, Room N123, Pasadena, CA 91109
Tel: (626) 744-4220

Chief Information Officer **Phillip Leclair** .... (626) 744-4220

Planning Department
George Ellery Hale Bldg., 175 N. Garfield Ave., Pasadena, CA 91101-1704
Fax: (626) 744-7041
Internet: http://cityofpasadena.net/PlanningandDevelopment/

Director (Interim) **David Reyes** .... (626) 744-4650
E-mail: davidreyes@cityofpasadena.net
Executive Secretary **Jennifer Gorriceta** .... (626) 744-7071
E-mail: jegorriceta@cityofpasadena.net
Chief Building Official **Sarkis Nazerian** .... (626) 744-6646
Fax: (626) 396-8539
Cultural Affairs Manager **Rochelle Branch** .... (626) 744-7062
Education: Hampton BA; Columbia 1989 MFA

Police Department
207 North Garfield Avenue, Pasadena, CA 91101
Fax: (626) 744-3781 Internet: http://cityofpasadena.net/Police/

Chief of Police **Phillip L. Sanchez** .... (626) 744-4545
Education: U Redlands BA; Naval Postgrad MA
Office Support Supervisor **Beverly Bogar** .... (626) 744-4645
E-mail: bbogar@cityofpasadena.net
Deputy Chief of Police **Darryl Qualls** .... (626) 744-4533

Public Health Department
1845 North Fair Oaks Avenue, Pasadena, CA 91103
Tel: (626) 744-6005 Fax: (626) 744-6113
Internet: http://cityofpasadena.net/PublicHealth/

Director and Health Officer (Acting) **Ying-Ying Goh** ..... (626) 744-6046
Executive Secretary **Cynthia Ramos** .... (626) 744-6046
E-mail: cramos@cityofpasadena.net

Public Library
285 E. Walnut St., Pasadena, CA 91101
Tel: (626) 744-4066 Fax: (626) 585-8396
Internet: http://cityofpasadena.net/LIBRARY/

Director **Jan Sanders** .... (626) 744-4062
E-mail: jsanders@cityofpasadena.net

Public Works Department
100 North Garfield Avenue, 3rd Floor, Room N306, Pasadena, CA 91109
Fax: (626) 796-3823 Internet: http://cityofpasadena.net/PublicWorks/

Director **Ara Maloyan** .... (626) 744-4233
Executive Secretary **Yesenia Alvarado** .... (626) 744-6893
E-mail: yalvarado@cityofpasadena.net

Transportation Department
221 East Walnut Street, Suite 210, Pasadena, CA 91101
Fax: (626) 774-7478 Internet: http://cityofpasadena.net/Transportation/

Director **Frederick C. Dock** .... (626) 744-6450
Transportation Administrator **Bahman Janka** .... (626) 744-4610
Transportation Administrator **Mark Yamarone** .... (626) 744-7474

Pasadena Water and Power [PWP]
150 South Los Robles Avenue, Suite 200, Pasadena, CA 91101-2437
Tel: (626) 744-4409 Fax: (626) 744-4670
Internet: http://cityofpasadena.net/waterandpower/

General Manager (Interim) **Shari Thomas** .... (626) 744-4478
Office Support Supervisor **Susana Castro** .... (626) 744-4462
E-mail: scastro@cityofpasadena.net
Assistant General Manager **Joe Awad** .... (626) 744-4157
Fax: (626) 744-7028
Assistant General Manager **Gurcharan Bawa** .... (626) 744-7598
Fax: (626) 744-6432
Assistant General Manager **Shari Thomas** .... (626) 744-4515
E-mail: sthomas@cityofpasadena.net Fax: (626) 744-4445
Assistant General Manager **Shan Kwan** .... (626) 744-4416
Fax: (626) 744-6435

Pasadena Unified School District
351 S. Hudson Ave., Pasadena, CA 91101
Fax: (626) 795-5309 Internet: www.pusd.us

Superintendent of Schools **Brian McDonald** .... (626) 396-3619
★ Board of Education President
Elizabeth Pomeroy (Seat 5) .... (626) 396-3619
Term Expires: April 2017
E-mail: pomeroy.elizabeth@pusd.us
★ Vice President **Kim Kenne** (Seat 1) .... (626) 396-3619
Term Expires: April 2017
E-mail: kenne.kimberly@pusd.us
★ Board of Education Member
Roy Boulghourjian (Seat 2) .... (626) 720-2425
Term Expires: April 2019
★ Board of Education Member
Adrienne Ann Mullen (Seat 3) .... (626) 720-2429
Term Expires: April 2017
E-mail: mullen.adrienneann@pusd.us
★ Board of Education Member **Patrick Cahalan** (Seat 4) ... (626) 720-2440
Term Expires: April 2019
★ Board of Education Member **Larry Torres** (Seat 6) .... (626) 720-2484
Term Expires: April 2019
★ Board of Education Member **Scott Phelps** (Seat 7) ...... (626) 396-3619
Term Expires: April 2017
E-mail: phelps.scott@pusd.us

City of Pasadena, Texas
City Hall, 1211 Southmore Avenue, Pasadena, TX 77502
Internet: www.ci.pasadena.tx.us

County: Harris **Election Type:** Nonpartisan **Year Incorporated:** 1928
Population: 153,784 (2015)

Office of the Mayor
City Hall, 1211 Southmore Avenue, Pasadena, TX 77502

★ Mayor **Johnny Isbell** .... (713) 475-5501
Began Service: 2008
Term Expires: May 2017
E-mail: themayor@ci.pasadena.tx.us
Education: Houston BS
Career: Council Member, Office of the City Council, City of Pasadena, Texas (1989-1993); Mayor, City of Pasadena, Texas (1993-2001)

Office of the City Secretary
City Hall, 1211 Southmore Avenue, Pasadena, TX 77502

City Secretary **Linda Rorick** .... (713) 475-5513
E-mail: ldrorick@ci.pasadena.tx.us

★ Elected Official ▲ Appointed by Legislature ▼ Appointed by Governor ▶ Appointed by Board or Commission ● Appointed by Judge
■ Appointed by Mayor △ Appointed by Freeholders ▽ Appointed by Supervisor ▷ Appointed by County Executive ○ Appointed by Council

Budget and Finance Office
City Hall, 1211 Southmore Avenue, Pasadena, TX 77502

City Controller **Wayne Long** .... (713) 475-5530
E-mail: wflong@ci.pasadena.tx.us
Director of Financial Planning **Andy Helms** .... (713) 475-7254
E-mail: ahelms@ci.pasadena.tx.us

Community Relations
City Hall, 1211 Southmore Avenue, Pasadena, TX 77502

Director **Richard Scott** .... (713) 475-5598
E-mail: rscott@ci.pasadena.tx.us

Economic Development
1114 Davis Street, Pasadena, TX 77506

Director **Paul Davis** .... (713) 475-4827
E-mail: pdavis@ci.pasadena.tx.us

Health Department
1114 Davis Street, Pasadena, TX 77506
Fax: (713) 477-3947

Public Health Manager **Kathy Perez-Ashton** .... (713) 475-5529

Human Resources Department
1202 Southmore Avenue, Pasadena, TX 77502
Fax: (713) 475-7204

Director **Randy Perry** .... (713) 475-5523
E-mail: rperry@ci.pasadena.tx.us

Parks and Recreation Department
3111 San Augustine, Pasadena, TX 77503
Tel: (713) 475-5034 Fax: (713) 477-7210

Director **Kirby Cardenas** .... (713) 475-7291
Superintendent of Recreation **Timothy Miller** .... (713) 475-7837

Pasadena Public Library
1201 Jeff Ginn Memorial Drive, Pasadena, TX 77506

Director **Thomas Simiele** .... (713) 475-4988
E-mail: tsimiele@ci.pasadena.tx.us

Pasadena Volunteer Fire Department
1001 Shaw, Room B100, Pasadena, TX 77506

Fire Chief **Lanny Armstrong** .... (713) 475-5554
E-mail: larmstrong@ci.pasadena.tx.us

Police Department
1201 Davis, Pasadena, TX 77506

Police Chief **Michael Thaler** .... (713) 475-7256
Assistant Chief **J. Bruegger** .... (713) 475-7256
Assistant Chief **S.L. Clifton** .... (713) 475-7256
Assistant Chief **Michael P. Jackson** .... (713) 475-7256

Public Works Department
1114 Davis Street, Pasadena, TX 77506

Director of Public Works **Robin Green** .... (713) 475-7836

Office of the City Council
City Hall, 1211 Southmore Avenue, Pasadena, TX 77502

★ Council Member **Ornaldo Ybarra** (District A) .... (713) 475-7858
Term Expires: July 2017
E-mail: oybarra@ci.pasadena.tx.us
★ Council Member **Bruce Leamon** (District B) .... (713) 475-7858
Term Expires: July 2017
E-mail: bleamon@ci.pasadena.tx.us

Office of the City Council *continued*

★ Council Member **Sammy Casados** (District C) .... (713) 475-7858
Term Expires: July 1, 2017
★ Council Member **Cody Ray Wheeler** (District D) .... (713) 475-7858
Term Expires: July 2017
E-mail: cwheeler@ci.pasadena.tx.us
★ Council Member **Cary Bass** (District E) .... (713) 475-7858
Term Expires: July 1, 2017
★ Council Member **Jeff Wagner** (District F) .... (713) 475-7858
Term Expires: July 1, 2017
★ Council Member **Pat Van Houte** (District G At-Large) .... (713) 475-7858
Term Expires: July 1, 2017
★ Council Member
Darrell Morrison (District H At-Large) .... (713) 475-7858
Term Expires: July 2017
E-mail: dmorrison@ci.pasadena.tx.us
Education: Texas A&M 1983 BA

Pasadena Independent School District
Administration Bldg., 1515 Cherrybrook, Pasadena, TX 77502
Tel: (713) 740-0000 Fax: (713) 740-4040
Internet: http://www.pasadenaisd.org

Superintendent **DeeAnn Powell** .... (713) 740-0243
Fax: (713) 740-4041
★ President **Mariselle Quijano** .... (713) 740-0243
Term Expires: July 2017
★ Vice President **Vickie Morgan** .... (713) 740-0243
Term Expires: July 2019
★ Secretary **Marshall Kendrick** .... (713) 740-0243
Term Expires: July 2019
★ Trustee **Jack Bailey** .... (713) 740-0243
Term Expires: July 2017
★ Trustee **Kenny Fernandez** .... (713) 740-0243
Term Expires: July 2019
★ Trustee **Fred Roberts** .... (713) 740-0243
Term Expires: July 2017
★ Trustee **Nelda Sullivan** .... (713) 740-0243
Term Expires: July 2017

City of Paterson, New Jersey
City Hall, 155 Market St., Paterson, NJ 07505
Tel: (973) 321-1500 (Information) Internet: www.patersonnj.gov

County: Passaic **Election Type:** Nonpartisan **Population:** 147,754 (2015)

Office of the Mayor
City Hall, 155 Market Street, 2nd Floor, Paterson, NJ 07505
Fax: (973) 321-1555

★ Mayor **Jose "Joey" Torres** .... (973) 321-1600
Began Service: July 1, 2014
Term Expires: June 30, 2018
E-mail: mayortorres@patersonnj.gov

Office of the City Clerk
City Hall, 155 Market St., 3rd Floor, Paterson, NJ 07505
Tel: (973) 321-1310 Fax: (973) 321-1311

○ City Clerk **Sonia L. Gordon** .... (973) 321-1310
E-mail: sgordon@patersonnj.gov
○ Deputy City Clerk **Joan Campbell-Douglas** .... (973) 321-1310

Office of Emergency Management [OEM]
300 McBride Avenue, Paterson, NJ 07501

■ Coordinator **Rhonda Thompson** .... (973) 321-1310
E-mail: rthompson@patersonnj.gov

★ Elected Official ▲ Appointed by Legislature ▼ Appointed by Governor ► Appointed by Board or Commission ● Appointed by Judge
■ Appointed by Mayor △ Appointed by Freeholders ▽ Appointed by Supervisor ▷ Appointed by County Executive ○ Appointed by Council

Office of Emergency Management *continued*

Chief Animal Control Officer **John Decando** . . . . (973) 881-3640
Fax: (973) 720-1246

Taxi Division **Pedro Liranzo** . . . . (973) 321-1305
E-mail: pliranzo@patersonnj.gov Fax: (973) 321-1271

Business Administration Department

City Hall, 155 Market St., 2nd Floor, Paterson, NJ 07505
Tel: (973) 321-1370 Fax: (973) 321-1372

■ Director **Nellie Pou** . . . . (973) 321-1370
E-mail: npou@patersonnj.gov
Education: Kean Col; Rutgers; Virginia

Budget Officer **Russell R. Forenza** . . . . (973) 321-2372
E-mail: rforenza@patersonnj.gov
Education: Seton Hall BS, MBA

Information Technology Assistant Director
Patricia Hamlin . . . . (973) 321-1200
E-mail: phamlin@patersonnj.gov Fax: (973) 321-1201

Personnel Director **Abby Levenson** . . . . (973) 321-1323
125 Ellison Street, Fax: (973) 321-1325
3rd Floor, Paterson, NJ 07505

Purchasing Agent **Harry Cevallos** . . . . (973) 321-1340
E-mail: hcevallos@patersonnj.gov Fax: (973) 321-1341

Community Development Department

125 Ellison St., 4th Floor, Paterson, NJ 07505
Fax: (973) 321-1202

■ Director **Barbara Blake-McLennon** . . . . (973) 321-1212
E-mail: bmclennon@patersonnj.gov

Community Improvements Director **Jerry Lobozzo** . . . . . . (973) 321-1232
Fax: (973) 321-1247

Planning and Zoning Director **Michael Deutsch** . . . . (973) 321-1343
Fax: (973) 321-1345

Multicultural/Community Affairs Office Coordinator
Marcia Julian-Sotorrio . . . . (973) 321-2254
E-mail: msotorrio@patersonnj.gov

Community Relations Specialist **Nancy Grier** . . . . (973) 321-1220
E-mail: ngrier@patersonnj.gov

Paterson Museum Attendant **Robert Veronelli** . . . . (973) 321-1260
E-mail: eventspatersonmuseum@gmail.com

Housing Division

Housing Division Director **Barbara Blake-McLennon** . . . . (973) 321-1214
Fax: (973) 321-1202

Management Specialist **Joyce Gregory-Hunt** . . . . (973) 321-1212
E-mail: jhunt@patersonnj.gov

Economic Development Division

Fax: (973) 321-1356

Director **Ruben Gomez** . . . . (973) 321-1220
E-mail: rgomez@patersonnj.gov
Education: Minnesota BS; U St Thomas (MN)

Finance Department

City Hall, 155 Market Street, First Floor, Paterson, NJ 07505
Fax: (973) 321-1351

■ Director (Acting) **James Ten Hoeve** . . . . (973) 321-1350
E-mail: jtenhoeve@patersonnj.gov

Chief Tax Assessor **Richard S. Marra** . . . . (973) 321-1380
E-mail: rmarra@patersonnj.gov Fax: (973) 321-1381

Accounts and Controls Division

Accounts and Control Division Director (Acting)
James Ten Hoeve . . . . (973) 321-1304
Fax: (973) 321-1351

Revenue Collection/License Division

Revenue Collection and License Division Director
Kathleen Gibson . . . . (973) 321-1300
Fax: (973) 321-1301

Sewer Billing Division

Sewer Billing Division Director (Acting)
James Ten Hoeve . . . . (973) 321-1230
Fax: (973) 321-1231

Treasury Division

Treasury Division Director **Fabiana M. Mello** . . . . (973) 321-1390
Fax: (973) 321-1391

Fire Department

300 McBride Avenue, Paterson, NJ 07501

Fire Chief **Michael Postorino** . . . . (973) 321-1400
E-mail: mpostorino@patersonnj.gov Fax: (973) 321-1443

Department of Health and Human Services

125 Ellison Street, First Floor, Paterson, NJ 07505
Fax: (973) 321-1224

■ Director **Donna Nelson-Ivy** . . . . (973) 321-1242
E-mail: divy@patersonnj.gov Fax: (973) 321-1224

Weights and Measures Director **Luis Nieves** . . . . (973) 321-1242
Fax: (973) 321-1224

Division of Senior Services **Hilda Diaz** . . . . (973) 653-5930
165 5th Avenue, Paterson, NJ 07514 Fax: (973) 688-8782

Ryan White Program **Milagros Izquierdo** . . . . (973) 321-1234
Fax: (973) 321-1225

School Based Youth Services Program
William Smallwood . . . . (973) 321-0541
John F. Kennedy High School, Fax: (973) 720-9553
61-127 Preakness Avenue, Paterson, NJ 07522

Youth Services Bureau **LaQuan Hargrove** . . . . (973) 321-1264
60 Temple Street, Fax: (973) 595-7460
2nd Floor, Paterson, NJ 07522

Housing Authority

60 Van Houten St., Paterson, NJ 07505
Tel: (973) 345-5080 Fax: (973) 977-9085
Internet: www.patersonhousingauthority.org

Executive Director **Irma Gorham** . . . . (973) 345-5080
Fax: (973) 977-9085

Law Department

City Hall, 155 Market St., Second Floor, Paterson, NJ 07505
Fax: (973) 321-1367

■ Corporation Counsel **Domenick Stampone** . . . . (973) 321-1366
E-mail: dstampone@patersonnj.gov

First Assistant Corporation Counsel **Robert Brigliadoro** . . (973) 321-1366

Paterson Free Public Library

250 Broadway, Paterson, NJ 07501
Fax: (973) 321-1203

Director **Cindy Czesak** . . . . (973) 321-1223
E-mail: czesak@palsplus.org

Parking Authority

125 Broadway, Suite 100, Paterson, NJ 07505

Executive Director **Tony Perez** . . . . (973) 977-3999
Fax: (973) 977-8039

Police Department

111 Broadway, Paterson, NJ 07505
Fax: (973) 321-1155

■ Director of Police **Jerry Speziale, Jr.** . . . . (973) 321-1270
E-mail: jspeziale@patersonpd.com
Education: Caldwell 2008 BS; Fairleigh Dickinson 2010 MAS

Chief of Police **William G. Fraher** . . . . (973) 321-1150

Criminal Investigations Bureau Deputy Chief
Danny Nichols . . . . (973) 321-1150

Field Operations Bureau Deputy Chief **Danny Nichols** . . . (973) 321-1150

★ Elected Official ▲ Appointed by Legislature ▼ Appointed by Governor ▶ Appointed by Board or Commission ● Appointed by Judge
■ Appointed by Mayor △ Appointed by Freeholders ▽ Appointed by Supervisor ▷ Appointed by County Executive ○ Appointed by Council

Public Works Department

800 Broadway, Paterson, NJ 07514
Fax: (973) 321-1486

■ Director **Manuel Ojeda** .... (973) 321-1488
E-mail: mojeda@patersonnj.gov
City Engineering **Frederick Margron** .... (973) 321-1320
E-mail: fmargron@patersonnj.gov Fax: (973) 321-1321
Recreation Supervisor **Lucy "Cookie" Lowery** .... (973) 321-1313
Fax: (973) 321-1314
Recycling Coordinator **Diane Polifronio** .... (973) 321-1393
Fax: (973) 881-7924

Traffic Engineer Division

Fax: (973) 881-7924

Traffic Superintendent **Eddie Mowaswes** .... (973) 321-1395
Traffic Engineer **Hongchao Yu** .... (973) 321-1397
E-mail: hyu@patersonnj.gov

Recreation Division

Fax: (973) 321-1314

Recreation Coordinator **Benjie Wimberly** .... (973) 321-1313

Office of the City Council

City Hall, 155 Market St., 3rd Floor, Paterson, NJ 07505
Tel: (973) 321-1250 Fax: (973) 321-1258
Internet: http://www.patersonnj.gov/council/

★ Council President **William McKoy** (Ward 3) .... (973) 321-1210
Term Expires: June 30, 2020
E-mail: wmckoy@patersonnj.gov
★ Council Vice President
Domingo "Alex" Mendez (At-Large) .... (973) 321-1250
Term Expires: June 30, 2018
E-mail: damendez@patersonnj.gov
★ Council Member **Michael Jackson** (Ward 1) .... (973) 321-1250
Term Expires: June 30, 2020
★ Council Member-Elect **Shahin Khalique** (Ward 2) .... (973) 321-1250
Term Expires: June 30, 2020
★ Council Member **Ruby N. Cotton** (Ward 4) .... (973) 321-1250
Term Expires: June 30, 2020
E-mail: rcotton@patersonnj.gov
★ Council Member-Elect **Luis Velez** (Ward 5) .... (973) 321-1210
Term Expires: June 30, 2020
★ Council Member **Andre Sayegh** (Ward 6) .... (973) 321-1250
Term Expires: June 30, 2020
★ Council Member **Maritza Davila** (At-Large) .... (973) 321-1250
Term Expires: June 30, 2018
E-mail: mdavila@patersonnj.gov
★ Council Member **Kenneth M. Morris, Jr.** (At-Large) .... (973) 321-1250
Term Expires: June 30, 2018
E-mail: kmorris@patersonnj.gov

Paterson Public Schools

90 Delaware Avenue, Paterson, NJ 07503
Fax: (973) 321-0470 Internet: www.paterson.k12.nj.us

▼ Superintendent **Dr. Donnie W. Evans** .... (973) 321-0980
E-mail: superintendent@paterson.k12.nj.us
Education: North Carolina EdD
Chief of Staff **Jacqueline Jones** .... (973) 321-0980
Deputy Superintendent **Eileen Shafer** .... (973) 321-0980

City of Pembroke Pines, Florida

10100 Pines Blvd., Pembroke Pines, FL 33026
Tel: (954) 450-1060 (Information) Internet: www.ppines.com

County: Broward **Election Type:** Nonpartisan **Year Incorporated:** 1960
Population: 166,611 (2015)

Frank C. Ortis
Mayor

Began Service: 2004
Term Expires: March 15, 2020

Office of the Mayor and City Commission

10100 Pines Blvd., Pembroke Pines, FL 33026

★ Mayor **Frank C. Ortis** .... (954) 436-3266
E-mail: fortis@ppines.com
★ Vice Mayor **Iris A. Siple** (District 3) .... (954) 436-3266
Term Expires: March 15, 2020
E-mail: isiple@ppines.com
★ Commissioner **Carl Shechter** (District 1) .... (954) 436-3266
Term Expires: March 11, 2018
E-mail: cshechter@ppines.com
★ Commissioner **Jay Schwartz** (District 2) .... (954) 436-3266
Term Expires: March 15, 2020
E-mail: jschwartz@ppines.com
★ Commissioner **Angelo Castillo** (District 4) .... (954) 436-3266
Term Expires: March 11, 2018
E-mail: acastillo@ppines.com
Secretary **Karen Richards** .... (954) 435-6505
E-mail: krichards@ppines.com

Office of the City Manager

10100 Pines Blvd., Pembroke Pines, FL 33026

City Manager **Charles F. Dodge** .... (954) 450-1040
E-mail: cdodge@ppines.com

Office of the City Clerk

10100 Pines Blvd., Pembroke Pines, FL 33026
Fax: (954) 435-6592

City Clerk **Marlene Graham** .... (954) 435-6501
E-mail: mgraham@ppines.com

Economic Development Department

10100 Pines Blvd., Pembroke Pines, FL 33026
Fax: (954) 435-6546

Planning and Economic Development Director
Michael D. Stamm .... (954) 392-2100
E-mail: mstamm@ppines.com
Zoning Administrator **Dean Piper** .... (954) 435-6555

Building Department

10100 Pines Blvd., Pembroke Pines, FL 33026

Chief Building Official **Norman Bruhn** .... (954) 435-6502

★ Elected Official ▲ Appointed by Legislature ▼ Appointed by Governor ▶ Appointed by Board or Commission ● Appointed by Judge
■ Appointed by Mayor △ Appointed by Freeholders ▽ Appointed by Supervisor ▷ Appointed by County Executive ○ Appointed by Council

Code Compliance
18400 Johnson Street, Pembroke Pines, FL 33029
Code Compliance Administrator **Lawrence Diaco** .... (954) 431-4466

Community Services
301 NW 103 Ave., Pembroke Pines, FL 33026
Director **Jay Shechter** .... (954) 450-6888
E-mail: jshechter@ppines.com

Finance Department
10100 Pines Boulevard, 4th Floor, Pembroke Pines, FL 33026
Finance Director **Lisa Chong** .... (954) 450-1070

Fire Department
Building B, 9500 Pines Boulevard, Pembroke Pines, FL 33026
Fax: (954) 435-6713
Fire Chief **John Picarello** .... (954) 499-9600 ext. 59535
E-mail: jpicarello@ppines.com
Fire Marshal **Sandra Lluis** .... (954) 499-9600 ext. 59564
E-mail: slluis@ppines.com

Human Resources
10100 Pines Blvd., Pembroke Pines, FL 33026
Human Resources and Risk Management Director
Daniel Rotstein .... (954) 392-2090
E-mail: drotstein@ppines.com

Recreation and Cultural Arts
501 SW 172 Ave., Pembroke Pines, FL 33029
Director **Christina Sorensen** .... (954) 435-6520

Police Department
Building A, 9500 Pines Boulevard, Pembroke Pines, FL 33026
Police Chief **Dan Giustino** .... (954) 431-2466

Public Services Department
13975 Pembroke Rd., Pembroke Pines, FL 33027
Director **Shawn Denton** .... (954) 437-1116 ext. 59062
Assistant Director/Public Works **(Vacant)** .... (954) 437-1116
Assistant Director/Utilities **Skip Keibler** ...... (954) 437-1116 ext. 59603

Technology Service Department
10100 Pines Blvd., Pembroke Pines, FL 33026
Director of Technology Services **Michael Lockett** .... (954) 392-2061
E-mail: mlockett@ppines.com

City of Peoria, Arizona
8401 West Monroe Street, Peoria, AZ 85345
Internet: www.peoriaaz.gov

County: Maricopa **Year Incorporated:** 1954 **Population:** 171,237 (2015)

Office of the Mayor and City Council
8401 West Monroe Street, Peoria, AZ 85345
Fax: (623) 773-7301
★ Mayor **Cathy Carlat** (At-Large) .... (623) 773-7306
Began Service: January 6, 2015
Term Expires: January 2019
★ Council Member **Bridget Binsbacher** (Mesquite) .... (623) 773-7306
Term Expires: January 6, 2019

Office of the Mayor and City Council *continued*
★ Council Member **Jon Edwards** (Willow) .... (623) 773-7306
Term Expires: January 2017
★ Council Member **Michael Finn** (Palo Verde) .... (623) 773-7306
Term Expires: January 2019
★ Council Member **Vicki L. Hunt** (Acacia) .... (623) 773-7306
Term Expires: January 2019
Education: Grand Canyon BA; Chapman MA
★ Council Member **Carlo Leone** (Pine) .... (623) 773-7306
Term Expires: January 2019
E-mail: carlo.leone@peoriaaz.gov
Education: Mount San Antonio BA
★ Council Member **Bill Patena** (Ironwood) .... (623) 773-7306
Term Expires: January 2017

Office of the City Attorney
8401 West Monroe Street, Peoria, AZ 85345
Fax: (623) 773-7043 E-mail: cityattorney@peoriaaz.gov
City Attorney **Steve Kemp** .... (623) 773-7330
E-mail: steve.kemp@peoriaaz.gov

Office of the City Manager
8401 West Monroe Street, Peoria, AZ 85345
Fax: (623) 773-7309
City Manager **Carl Swenson** .... (623) 773-7300
E-mail: carl.swenson@peoriaaz.gov
Deputy City Manager **Julie Ayers** .... (623) 773-7572
E-mail: julie.ayers@peoriaaz.gov
Education: Arizona State 1993 BS
Deputy City Manager **Susan Daluddung** .... (623) 773-7300
E-mail: susan.daluddung@peoriaaz.gov
Education: Mankato State BA; Portland State MURP, PhD
Deputy City Manager **Jeff Tyne** .... (623) 773-7300

Office of the City Clerk
8401 West Monroe Street, Peoria, AZ 85345
Fax: (623) 773-7304
City Clerk **Rhonda Geriminsky** .... (623) 773-7340
E-mail: cityclerk@peoriaaz.gov

Community Services
9875 North 85th Avenue, Peoria, AZ 85345
Fax: (623) 773-7180 E-mail: communityservices@peoriaaz.gov
Director **John R. Sefton, Jr.** .... (623) 773-7137
E-mail: john.sefton@peoriaaz.gov

Economic Development Services
9875 North 85th Avenue, Peoria, AZ 85345
Fax: (623) 773-7519
Director **Scott Whyte** .... (623) 773-7735
E-mail: scott.whyte@peoriaaz.gov

Building Development
9875 North 85th Avenue, Peoria, AZ 85345
Fax: (623) 773-7233
Building Development Manager **Dennis Chase** .... (623) 773-8240

Engineering
9875 North 85th Avenue, Peoria, AZ 85345
Fax: (623) 773-7211 E-mail: engineeringdept@peoriaaz.gov
Director **Andrew Granger** .... (623) 773-7212
E-mail: andrew.granger@peoriaaz.gov

Finance and Budget Department
8401 West Monroe Street, Peoria, AZ 85345
Director **Brent Mattingly** .... (623) 773-7150
E-mail: brent.mattingly@peoriaaz.gov

★ Elected Official ▲ Appointed by Legislature ▼ Appointed by Governor ▶ Appointed by Board or Commission ● Appointed by Judge
■ Appointed by Mayor △ Appointed by Freeholders ▽ Appointed by Supervisor ▷ Appointed by County Executive ○ Appointed by Council

Fire Department
8351 West Cinnabar Avenue, Peoria, AZ 85345
Fax: (623) 773-7294 E-mail: firedept@peoriaaz.gov

Fire Chief **Bobby Ruiz** .... (623) 773-7279
E-mail: bobby.ruiz@peoriaaz.gov

Human Resources Department
8401 West Monroe Street, Peoria, AZ 85345
Fax: (623) 773-7623 E-mail: humanresources@peoriaaz.gov

Director **(Vacant)** .... (623) 773-7100

Planning and Community Development
9875 North 85th Avenue, Peoria, AZ 85345

Director **Chris Jacques** .... (623) 773-7209
E-mail: chris.jacques@peoriaaz.gov Fax: (623) 773-7233

Planning and Zoning
9875 North 85th Avenue, Peoria, AZ 85345
Fax: (623) 773-7256 E-mail: planning@peoriaaz.gov

Planning Manager **Chris Jacques** .... (623) 773-7200

Police Department
8351 West Cinnabar Avenue, Peoria, AZ 85345
Fax: (623) 773-7015 E-mail: policedept@peoriaaz.com

Chief of Police **Roy Minter** .... (623) 773-7096

Public Works-Utilities Department
8850 North 79th Avenue, Peoria, AZ 85345

Director **Bill Mattingly** .... (623) 773-5150

Municipal Court
10100 N. 83rd Ave., Peoria, AZ 85345
Fax: (623) 773-7407

Presiding Judge **The Honorable George T. Anagnost** ... (623) 773-7400

City of Peoria, Illinois
City Hall, 419 Fulton St., Peoria, IL 61602

County: Peoria **Election Type:** Nonpartisan **Population:** 115,070 (2015)

Office of the Mayor
City Hall, 419 Fulton Street, Suite 207, Peoria, IL 61602
Fax: (309) 494-8556

★Mayor **Jim E. Ardis** .... (309) 494-8519
Began Service: 2005
Term Expires: May 3, 2017
E-mail: jardis@peoriagov.org
Education: Illinois State 1982 BS

Secretary **Brenda Hopwood** .... (309) 494-8519
E-mail: bhopwood@peoriagov.org

Office of the City Council
City Hall, 419 Fulton St., Peoria, IL 61602
Fax: (309) 494-8559

★Council Member **Denise Moore** (District 1) .... (309) 494-8994
Term Expires: May 2017
E-mail: dmoore@peoriagov.org

★Council Member **Charles V. Grayeb** (District 2) .... (309) 494-8995
Term Expires: May 2017
E-mail: bvanauken@peoriagov.org
Education: Bradley 1972 BA, 1979 MA

★Council Member **Timothy Riggenbach** (District 3) ...... (309) 494-8991
Term Expires: May 3, 2017
E-mail: triggenbach@peoriagov.org

Office of the City Council *continued*

★Council Member **Jim Montelongo** (District 4) .... (309) 494-8992
Term Expires: May 2017
E-mail: jmontelongo@peoriagov.org

★Council Member **Casey Johnson** (District 5) .... (309) 369-8391
Term Expires: May 2017
E-mail: cjohnson@peoriagov.org

★Council Member **Beth Akeson** (At-Large) .... (309) 454-8981
Term Expires: May 3, 2019
E-mail: bakeson@peoriagov.org

★Council Member **Elizabeth "Beth" Jensen** (At-Large) ... (309) 863-0160
Term Expires: May 3, 2019
E-mail: jensen@peoriagov.org
Education: Albion 1990 BA; Loyola U (Chicago) 1993 JD

★Council Member **Sid Ruckriegel** (At-Large) .... (309) 494-8696
Term Expires: May 3, 2019

★Council Member **Ryan Spain** (At-Large) .... (309) 494-8982
Term Expires: May 3, 2019
E-mail: rspain@peoriagov.org

★Council Member **W. Eric Turner** (At-Large) .... (309) 253-2489
Term Expires: May 3, 2019
E-mail: weturner@peoriagov.org
Education: Illinois BA; DePaul MA

Office of the City Manager
City Hall, 419 Fulton Street, Suite 207, Peoria, IL 61602
Fax: (309) 494-8556 E-mail: citymanager@peoriagov.org

City Manager **Patrick Urich** .... (309) 494-8524
E-mail: citymanager@peoriagov.org

Office of the City Clerk
City Hall, 419 Fulton Street, Suite 401, Peoria, IL 61602
Fax: (309) 494-8574

★City Clerk **Beth Ball** .... (309) 494-8565
Term Expires: May 3, 2017
E-mail: bball@peoriagov.org

Office of the City Treasurer
City Hall, 419 Fulton Street, Suite 100, Peoria, IL 61602
Fax: (309) 494-8495

★City Treasurer **Patrick A. Nichting** .... (309) 494-8545
Term Expires: May 3, 2017
E-mail: treasurer@peoriagov.org
Education: Bradley BS, MBA

Office of Emergency Management
3615 N. Grandview Dr., Peoria, IL 61614-8018
Fax: (309) 494-8080 Tel: (309) 494-8083

Coordinator **Duane Deppolder** .... (309) 494-8077
E-mail: ddeppolder@peoriagov.org

Community Development Department
Twin Towers Mall, 456 Fulton St., Suite 402, Peoria, IL 61602
Fax: (309) 494-8680

Director **Ross Black** .... (309) 494-8600
E-mail: planning@peoriagov.org

Inspections Department
Twin Towers Mall, 456 Fulton Street, Suite 401, Peoria, IL 61602
Fax: (309) 494-8674

Assistant Director **Joe Dulin** .... (309) 494-8620

Equal Opportunity Office
City Hall, 419 Fulton Street, Suite 200, Peoria, IL 61602
Tel: (309) 494-8532 Fax: (309) 494-8658

Manager **David Watkins** .... (309) 494-8530

★Elected Official ▲Appointed by Legislature ▼Appointed by Governor ▶Appointed by Board or Commission ●Appointed by Judge
■Appointed by Mayor △Appointed by Freeholders ▽Appointed by Supervisor ▷Appointed by County Executive ○Appointed by Council

Finance Department
City Hall, 419 Fulton Street, Suite 106, Peoria, IL 61602
Fax: (309) 494-8510

Director **Jim Scroggins** .... (309) 494-8550

Fire Department
505 NE Monroe St., Peoria, IL 61603
Fax: (309) 494-8777

Fire Chief **Chuck Lauss** .... (309) 494-8700
E-mail: clauss@peoriagov.org

Human Resources Department
City Hall, 419 Fulton Street, Suite 302, Peoria, IL 61602
Fax: (309) 494-8587 E-mail: humanresources@peoriagov.org

Director **Mary Ann Stalcup** .... (309) 494-8575
E-mail: mstalcup@peoriagov.org
Education: Minnesota 1979 BS

Information Systems Department
542 SW Adams, Peoria, IL 61602
Fax: (309) 494-8116

Director **Sam Rivera** .... (309) 494-8100
E-mail: srivera@peoriagov.org

Legal Department
City Hall, 419 Fulton Street, Suite 207, Peoria, IL 61602
Fax: (309) 494-8559

Corporation Counsel **Donald B. Leist** .... (309) 494-8590
Deputy Corporation Counsel **Sonni C. Williams** .... (309) 494-8590
Senior Staff Attorney **Ronald O'Neil** .... (309) 494-8590

Police Department
600 SW Adams, Peoria, IL 61602
Fax: (309) 494-8336

Chief of Police **Jerry Mitchell** .... (309) 494-8335

Public Works Department
City Hall, 419 Fulton Street, Suite 307, Peoria, IL 61602
Fax: (309) 494-8658

Director **Mike Rogers** .... (309) 494-8800
Traffic Operations Supervisor **Irv Dubois** .... (309) 494-8800

Peoria Public Schools
3202 North Wisconsin Avenue, Peoria, IL 61603
Fax: (309) 672-6708 Internet: www.psd150.org E-mail: info@psd150.org

Superintendent **Dr. Sharon Desmoulin-Kherat** .... (309) 672-6768

City of Philadelphia, Pennsylvania

City Hall, Philadelphia, PA 19107
Tel: (215) 686-1776 (Information) Internet: http://www.phila.gov
Internet: http://www.phila.gov/recovery/

County: Philadelphia **Election Type:** Partisan **Population:** 1,567,442 (2015)

Form of Municipal Government: City and county governments are combined.

Office of the Mayor
City Hall, Room 215, Philadelphia, PA 19107
Tel: (215) 686-2181 Fax: (215) 686-2180

★ Mayor **James F. "Jim" Kenney** (D) .... (215) 686-2181
Began Service: January 4, 2016
Term Expires: January 2020
Education: La Salle U 1980 BA

■ Chief of Staff **Jane Slusser** .... (215) 686-2181
■ Deputy Chief of Staff **Vaughn Ross** .... (215) 686-2181
■ Deputy Mayor of Intergovernmental Affairs **Deborah "Debbie" Mahler** .... (215) 686-2181
■ Deputy Mayor for Labor **Richard Lazer** .... (215) 686-2181
■ Deputy Mayor for Policy and Legislation **Jim Engler** .... (215) 686-2181
■ Deputy Mayor for Public Engagement **N. Nina Ahmad** .... (215) 686-2181
■ Chief Administrative Officer **Rebecca Rhynhart** .... (215) 686-2181
E-mail: rebecca.rhynhart@phila.gov
Education: Middlebury BA; Columbia MPA
■ Director of Performance Management **Liza Rodriguez** .... (215) 686-2181
Education: Duke BA; Texas MA; Temple PhD
■ Chief Diversity and Inclusion Officer **Nolan N. Atkinson, Jr.** .... (215) 686-2181
Education: Boston U 1964 AB; Howard U 1967 LLB; Pennsylvania 1969 LLM
■ Chief Education Officer **Otis Hackney** .... (215) 686-2181
■ Pre-K Director **Anne Gemmell** .... (215) 686-2181
■ Chief Integrity Officer **Ellen Mattleman Kaplan** .... (215) 686-2181
■ Director of Communications **Lauren Hitt** .... (215) 686-6210
■ Digital Director **Stephanie Waters** .... (215) 686-6210
■ Lesbian, Gay, Bisexual and Transgender Liaison **Helen "Nellie" Fitzpatrick** .... (215) 686-2194
Education: Florida BA; Florida Coastal JD
■ Director of Immigrant Affairs and Services **Miriam Enriquez** .... (215) 686-2181
■ Deputy Director of Immigrant Affairs and Services **Hani White** .... (215) 686-2181

Office of Arts, Culture and the Creative Economy
City Hall, Room 708, Philadelphia, PA 19107

■ Chief Cultural Officer **Kelly Lee** .... (215) 686-3989
E-mail: kelly.lee@phila.gov
■ Cultural Advisory Council Head **Joseph H. "Joe" Kluger** .... (215) 686-2181
E-mail: joseph.kluger@phila.gov
Education: Trinity Col (CT) 1977 BM; NYU 1979 MA

Mayor's Commission on Literacy
990 Spring Garden Street, Suite 200, Philadelphia, PA 19123

■ Executive Director **Judith Rényi** .... (215) 686-5250
E-mail: judith.renyi@phila.gov
Education: Pennsylvania AB; Warwick (UK) MA; Pennsylvania 1973 PhD

Mayor's Commission on People with Disabilities
Municipal Services Bldg., 1401 JFK Boulevard, Room 900, Philadelphia, PA 19102

Director **Charles Horton** .... (215) 686-2762

★ Elected Official ▲ Appointed by Legislature ▼ Appointed by Governor ► Appointed by Board or Commission ● Appointed by Judge
■ Appointed by Mayor △ Appointed by Freeholders ▽ Appointed by Supervisor ▷ Appointed by County Executive ○ Appointed by Council

Mayor's Commission on Services for the Aging
100 South Broad Street, 4th Floor, Philadelphia, PA 19110

Assistant Deputy Mayor **Lydia Hernandez Velez** .... (215) 686-8416

Mayor's Office of Empowerment and Opportunity
990 Spring Garden Street, 7th Floor, Philadelphia, PA 19123
Fax: (215) 685-3601

Executive Director **(Vacant)** .... (215) 685-3645

Mayor's Office of Grants
City Hall, Philadelphia, PA 19107

■ Chief Grants Officer **Ashley Del Bianco** .... (215) 686-2181
E-mail: ashley.bianco@phila.gov
Deputy Chief Grants Officer **Christine Piven** .... (215) 686-9022
Grant Officer **Jocelyn J. Arnold** .... (215) 686-9022

Mayor's Office of Sustainability
1515 Arch Street, NWC 13th Floor, Philadelphia, PA 19102
Fax: (215) 686-4477 Internet: www.phila.gov/green/

■ Director **Christine Knapp** .... (215) 686-4471
E-mail: christine.knapp@phila.gov

Office of the Inspector General
601 Walnut Street, Suite 300 East, Philadelphia, PA 19106
Fax: (215) 686-1757 E-mail: oig@phila.gov Internet: www.phila.gov/oig/

■ Inspector General **Amy L. Kurland** .... (215) 686-1770
E-mail: amy.kurland@phila.gov
First Deputy Inspector General **Kathleen McAfee** .... (215) 686-1771
Deputy Inspector General **Alex F. DeSantis** .... (215) 686-1770

Finance Department
1330 Municipal Services Bldg., 1401 JFK Blvd.,
Philadelphia, PA 19102-1693
Fax: (215) 568-1947 Internet: www.phila.gov/finance/

Chief Financial Officer **Robert "Rob" Dubow** .... (215) 686-6140
Education: Pennsylvania 1981 BA; Wharton 1987 MBA
Chief of Staff **Jacqueline Dunn** .... (215) 686-5604
Assistant to the Director of Finance
Tarlton David Williams .... (215) 686-3499
E-mail: tarlton.williams@phila.gov
Finance First Deputy Director **Catherine Paster** .... (215) 686-6160
■ Budget Director **Anna Wallace Adams** .... (215) 686-6147
Grants Accounting and Administration Manager
Carl Coin .... (215) 686-5627
E-mail: carl.coin@phila.gov
Human Resources Manager **Tamika McCray** .... (215) 686-5614
E-mail: tamika.mccray@phila.gov Fax: (215) 686-6202
Accounting Director **Josefine Arevalo** .... (215) 686-6164
E-mail: josefine.arevalo@phila.gov

Office of the City Treasurer
640 Municipal Services Bldg., 1401 JFK Blvd.,
Philadelphia, PA 19102-1681
Tel: (215) 686-2300 Fax: (215) 686-3815
Internet: www.phila.gov/treasurer/

■ Treasurer **Rasheia Johnson** .... (215) 686-2300
Executive Assistant to the City Treasurer
Eleanor Avery .... (215) 686-2301
E-mail: eleanor.avery@phila.gov
Assistant City Treasurer **Mark Disilvestro** .... (215) 686-3816
Deputy Treasurer **(Vacant)** .... (215) 686-2145
Executive Assistant **(Vacant)** .... (215) 686-3819

Revenue Department
630 Municipal Services Bldg., 1401 JFK Blvd.,
Philadelphia, PA 19102-1697
Tel: (215) 686-6400 Fax: (215) 686-6537 E-mail: revenue@phila.gov
Internet: www.phila.gov/revenue/

Revenue Commissioner **Frank Breslin** .... (215) 686-6400
Deputy Revenue Commissioner-Water **Michelle Bethel** ... (215) 686-6900

Revenue Department *continued*

Deputy Revenue Commissioner **Dave Dorman** .... (215) 686-6404
E-mail: dave.dorman@phila.gov
Deputy Revenue Commissioner **Marco A. Muniz** .... (215) 686-6626
Deputy Revenue Commissioner, Tax Policy and
Research **Marisa Waxman** .... (215) 686-6558
E-mail: marisa.waxman@phila.gov

Risk Management Division
1515 Arch St., 14th Floor, Philadelphia, PA 19102-1579
Fax: (215) 683-1718 Internet: www.phila.gov/risk/

Deputy Finance Director/Risk Manager **Barry Scott** ..... (215) 683-1710
E-mail: Barry.Scott@phila.gov

Law Department
One Parkway, 1515 Arch Street, 15th Floor, Philadelphia, PA 19102-1595

■ City Solicitor-Designate **Sozi P. Tulante** .... (215) 683-5003
Education: Harvard 1997 AB, 2001 JD
First Deputy City Solicitor **Craig M. Straw** .... (215) 683-5005
E-mail: craig.straw@phila.gov Fax: (215) 683-5069
Corporate and Tax Law Chair
Daniel W. Cantú-Hertzler .... (215) 683-5061
E-mail: daniel.cantu-hertzler@phila.gov Fax: (215) 683-5069
Education: Goshen BA; Harvard 1988 JD
Litigation Group Chair **Jane Lovitch Istvan** .... (215) 683-5014
E-mail: jane.istvan@phila.gov Fax: (215) 683-5296
Appeals and Legislation Chief Deputy City Solicitor
Richard G. Feder .... (215) 683-5013
E-mail: richard.feder@phila.gov Fax: (215) 683-5296
Civil Rights Chief Deputy City Solicitor **(Vacant)** .... (215) 683-5442
Fax: (215) 683-5397
Claims Chief Deputy City Solicitor **Ken Butensky** ...... (215) 683-5419
E-mail: ken.butensky@phila.gov Fax: (215) 683-5398
Code Enforcement Chief Deputy City Solicitor
Andrew Ross .... (215) 683-5118
E-mail: andrew.ross@phila.gov Fax: (215) 683-5097
Commercial Law Chief Deputy City Solicitor
Michael Athay .... (215) 683-5062
E-mail: michael.athay@phila.gov Fax: (215) 683-5069
Health and Adult Services Chief Deputy
Lynda H. Moore .... (215) 683-5219
E-mail: lynda.moore@phila.gov Fax: (215) 683-5346
Labor and Employment Chief Deputy City Solicitor
Nicole Morris .... (215) 683-5075
E-mail: nicole.morris@phila.gov Fax: (215) 683-5099
Regulatory Affairs Chief Deputy City Solicitor
J. Barry Davis .... (215) 683-5186
E-mail: j.barry.davis@phila.gov Fax: (215) 683-5175
Tax Chief Deputy City Solicitor **Frank Paiva** .... (215) 686-0503
E-mail: frank.paiva@phila.gov Fax: (215) 686-0582
Director of Administration **Suki Kazahaya** .... (215) 683-5235
E-mail: suki.kazahaya@phila.gov Fax: (215) 683-5297
Human Resources Manager **Angela Johnson-Lowe** ..... (215) 683-5236
E-mail: angela.johnson-lowe@phila.gov Fax: (215) 683-5452

Office of the Managing Director
1401 JFK Blvd, Room 1430, Philadelphia, PA 19102
Fax: (215) 686-3479 Internet: www.phila.gov/mdo/

■ Managing Director **Michael DiBerardinis** .... (215) 686-3480
E-mail: michael.diberardinis@phila.gov
Education: St Joseph's U 1971 BA
■ First Deputy Managing Director **Brian Abernathy** .... (215) 686-3641
Deputy Managing Director for Children and Families
Eva Gladstein .... (215) 686-3689
E-mail: eva.gladstein@phila.gov
■ Deputy Managing Director for Community and Culture
David G. Wilson .... (215) 686-3641
E-mail: david.g.wilson@phila.gov
Education: Bethany (WV) BA; Marquette MBA
■ Deputy Managing Director for Community Services
Joanna Otero-Cruz .... (215) 686-3480

★ Elected Official ▲ Appointed by Legislature ▼ Appointed by Governor ► Appointed by Board or Commission ● Appointed by Judge
■ Appointed by Mayor △ Appointed by Freeholders ▽ Appointed by Supervisor ▷ Appointed by County Executive ○ Appointed by Council

Office of the Managing Director *continued*

■ Deputy Managing Director for Criminal Justice **Benjamin Lerner** . . . . . (215) 686-3480
■ Deputy Managing Director for Infrastructure and Transportation **Clarena I. W. Tolson** . . . . . (215) 686-3641
Chief of Staff **(Vacant)** . . . . . (215) 686-2134

Managing Director's Office of Emergency Management

1401 JFK Boulevard, Philadelphia, PA 19102-1666
Fax: (215) 686-1117 E-mail: oem@phila.gov
Internet: http://oem.readyphiladelphia.org/

■ Deputy Managing Director for Emergency Management **Samantha Phillips** . . . . . (215) 686-4465
E-mail: samantha.phillips@phila.gov
■ Assistant Managing Director **(Vacant)** . . . . . (215) 686-4465
Deputy Director for External Affairs/Public Information Officer **Joan Przybylowicz** . . . . . (215) 686-4474
E-mail: joan.przybylowicz@phila.gov

Office of the City Commissioners

City Hall, Room 130, Philadelphia, PA 19107
Fax: (215) 587-9107 Internet: www.phila.gov/commissioners/

★ Chairman **Anthony Clark** (D) . . . . . (215) 686-3462
Term Expires: December 31, 2019
E-mail: Anthony.Clark@phila.gov
★ Co-Chair **Al Schmidt** (R) . . . . . (215) 686-3464
Term Expires: December 31, 2019
E-mail: al.schmidt@phila.gov
★ Commissioner **Lisa M. Deeley** (D) . . . . . (215) 686-3460
Term Expires: December 31, 2019

Office of the City Controller

Municipal Services Bldg., 1401 JFK Blvd., Room 1230, Philadelphia, PA 19102-1679
Fax: (215) 686-3832 E-mail: info@philadelphiacontroller.org
Internet: www.philadelphiacontroller.org/

★ City Controller **Alan L. Butkovitz** (D) . . . . . (215) 686-6680
Term Expires: December 31, 2017
E-mail: Alan.Butkovitz@phila.gov
Education: Temple 1973 BA, 1976 JD
First Deputy Controller **Bill Rubin** . . . . . (215) 686-6696
Deputy City Controller **Gerald V. Micciulla** . . . . . (215) 686-6684
Deputy City Controller **John H. Thomas** . . . . . (215) 686-6682

Office of the District Attorney

Three South Penn Square, Philadelphia, PA 19107-3499
Tel: (215) 686-8000 Fax: (215) 686-8024
Internet: www.phila.gov/districtattorney/

★ District Attorney **R. Seth Williams** (D) . . . . . (215) 686-8703
Term Expires: December 31, 2017
E-mail: seth.williams@phila.gov
Education: Penn State BA; Georgetown 1992 JD

Office of Economic Opportunity [OEO]

One Parkway Building, 1515 Arch Street, 12th Floor, Philadelphia, PA 19102
Tel: (215) 683-2057 Fax: (215) 683-2085 Internet: http://oeo.phila.gov/

Executive Director **Angela Dowd-Burton** . . . . . (215) 683-2055
E-mail: angela.dowd-burton@phila.gov
Education: Drexel 1974, 1979
Assistant Director **Alice Dungee-James** . . . . . (215) 683-2052
E-mail: alice.dungee@phila.gov

Office of Fleet Management [OFM]

100 South Broad Street, 3rd Floor, Philadelphia, PA 19102
Fax: (215) 686-1829 Internet: www.phila.gov/fleet/

■ Director **Christopher Cocci** . . . . . (215) 686-1825
E-mail: christopher.cocci@phila.gov

Office of Human Resources

1530 Municipal Services Building, 1401 JFK Boulevard, 15th Floor, Philadelphia, PA 19102-1675
Tel: (215) 686-0880 Fax: (215) 686-2317
Internet: www.phila.gov/personnel/

▶ Director **Albert "Al" D'Attilio** . . . . . (215) 686-2331
E-mail: albert.dattilio@phila.gov
Education: Temple JD

Office of Planning and Development

City Hall, Philadelphia, PA 19107

■ Director of Planning and Development **Anne Fadullon** . . . (215) 686-6210
Deputy Director **Frederick S. Purnell, Sr.** . . . . . (215) 686-9749

Division of Housing and Community Development

1234 Market Street, 17th Floor, Philadelphia, PA 19107-3701
Tel: (215) 686-9749 Fax: (215) 686-9853 E-mail: info.ohcd@phila.gov
Internet: http://www.phila.gov/ohcd

■ Director **(Vacant)** . . . . . (215) 686-9750
Deputy Director **Melissa Long** . . . . . (215) 686-9789
E-mail: melissa.long@phila.gov
Director of Policy and Planning **Katrina Pratt-Roebuck** . . (215) 686-9823
Compliance Department Director **Lynn Newsome** . . . . . (215) 683-3006
Contract Administration Department Director **Laura Taylor** . . . . . (215) 686-9711
Legal Department Director **Linda Medley** . . . . . (215) 686-9788
Information Technology Manager **Stephen Cavicchio** . . . . (215) 686-9748
E-mail: stephen.cavicchio@phila.gov
Monitoring Department Director **Wayne Stokes** . . . . . (215) 686-9784
E-mail: wayne.stokes@phila.gov
Neighborhood Program Coordination and Community Development Department Director **Belinda Mayo** . . . . . (215) 686-9763
E-mail: belinda.mayo@phila.gov
Office Services Director **Maurice Broaddus** . . . . . (215) 686-9835
Human Resources Department Manager **Karla Hill** . . . . . (215) 686-9724
E-mail: karla.hill@phila.gov
Director of Communications **Paul D. Chrystie** . . . . . (215) 686-9721
E-mail: paul.chrystie@phila.gov
Real Estate Department Director **Susie Jarmon** . . . . . (215) 448-3170

Historical Commission

576 City Hall, Philadelphia, PA 19107
Fax: (215) 686-7674 Internet: www.phila.gov/historical/

Historic Preservation Executive Director **Jon Farnham** . . . (215) 686-7660

Philadelphia City Planning Commission [PCPC]

1515 Arch St., 13th Floor, Philadelphia, PA 19102-1583
Fax: (215) 683-4630 E-mail: info@philaplanning.org

Executive Director **Gary Jastrzab** . . . . . (215) 683-4602
Education: SUNY (Buffalo) 1976 BA; Pennsylvania 1983 MCP
Development Planning Division Chief **Martin Gregorski** . . . . . (215) 683-4634
Deputy Planning Director **Alan Urek** . . . . . (215) 683-4628
Urban Design Division Chief **R. David Schaaf** . . . . . (215) 683-4658
Chairman **Alan Greenberger** . . . . . (215) 683-4600
■ Vice Chairman **Joseph R. Syrnick** . . . . . (215) 683-4615
Commissioner **Robert "Rob" Dubow** . . . . . (215) 683-4615
Education: Pennsylvania 1981 BA; Wharton 1987 MBA
■ Commissioner **Patrick J. Eiding** . . . . . (215) 683-4615
■ Commissioner **Bernard Lee** . . . . . (215) 683-4615
Education: Lake Forest Col 1972 BA; Pennsylvania 1977 JD
■ Commissioner **Elizabeth Miller** . . . . . (215) 683-4615
■ Commissioner **Richard Negrin** . . . . . (215) 683-4615
Education: Rutgers JD; Wagner BA
■ Commissioner **Nilda Iris Ruiz** . . . . . (215) 683-4615
Commissioner **Nancy Rogo Trainer** . . . . . (215) 683-4615

★ Elected Official ▲ Appointed by Legislature ▼ Appointed by Governor ▶ Appointed by Board or Commission ● Appointed by Judge
■ Appointed by Mayor △ Appointed by Freeholders ▽ Appointed by Supervisor ▷ Appointed by County Executive ○ Appointed by Council

Office of the Register of Wills

City Hall, Room 180, Philadelphia, PA 19107
Tel: (215) 686-6250 Fax: (215) 686-6268 E-mail: rowonline@phila.gov

★ Register of Wills **Ronald R. Donatucci** (D) .... (215) 686-6250
Term Expires: December 31, 2019
E-mail: Ronald.Donatucci@phila.gov
Chief Deputy (Acting) **Alba Collazo-Irwin** .... (215) 686-6267
First Deputy **(Vacant)** .... (215) 686-6254
Litigation Deputy **John F. Raimondi** .... (215) 686-6266
Inheritance Tax Deputy **Matthew Myers** .... (215) 686-6271
Probate Deputy **Louis DiRenzo** .... (215) 686-6257
Administrative Services Director **Emilio DiGregorio** ..... (215) 686-6253
E-mail: emilio.digregorio@phila.gov

Office of the Sheriff

Land Title Building, 100 South Broad Street, 5th Floor,
Philadelphia, PA 19110
Tel: (215) 686-3531 Fax: (215) 686-3579
Internet: www.phillysheriff.com/

★ Sheriff **Jewell Williams** (D) .... (215) 686-3530
Term Expires: December 31, 2019
E-mail: jewell.williams@phila.gov
Chief Deputy Sheriff **Kevin Lamb** .... (215) 686-3576
E-mail: benjamin.hayllar@phila.gov
Undersheriff **Joseph Vignola** .... (215) 686-3533
E-mail: joseph.vignola@phila.gov

Office of Supportive Housing [OSH]

1401 John F. Kennedy Boulevard, Suite 1030, Philadelphia, PA 19102
Fax: (215) 686-7126

Director **Marie Nahikian** .... (215) 686-7106
Deputy Director **Leticia Egea-Hinton** .... (215) 686-7190
Education: Pennsylvania 2000 MSW
Deputy Director **Roberta Cancellier** .... (215) 686-7105

Department of Behavioral Health and Intellectual Disability Services

1101 Market Street, 7th Floor, Philadelphia, PA 19107
Fax: (215) 685-4751 Internet: www.dbhids.org/

Commissioner **Dr. Arthur C. Evans, Jr.** .... (215) 685-4736

Department of Commerce

One Parkway, 1515 Arch St., 12th Floor, Philadelphia, PA 19102
Fax: (215) 683-2097

■ Director **Harold T. Epps** .... (215) 683-4600
Education: North Carolina Central BS; Western New England MBA
Senior Deputy Director of Commerce **Duane Bumb** ..... (215) 683-2005
E-mail: duane.bumb@phila.gov
Deputy Commerce Director **Karen Fegley** .... (215) 683-2109
Deputy Director of Finance and Administration
Cintya Ramos .... (215) 683-2020
E-mail: cintya.ramos@phila.gov
Senior Director, Office of Business Services
Curtis Gregory .... (215) 683-2092
E-mail: curtis.gregory@phila.gov
City Representative for Ceremonial and Special Events
Sheila Hess .... (215) 683-2060
Chief of Staff **Sylvie Gallier-Howard** .... (215) 683-2009

Office of Innovation and Technology

1234 Market Street, 18th Floor, Suite 1850, Philadelphia, PA 19107

■ Chief Technology Officer **Charles Brennan** .... (215) 686-8103
First Deputy Chief Information Officer **(Vacant)** .... (215) 686-8103
Chief Data Officer **Tim Wisniewski** .... (215) 686-8101
E-mail: Tim.Wisniewski@phila.gov
Director of Civic Technology **(Vacant)** .... (215) 686-8103

Fire Department

Fire Administration Bldg., 240 Spring Garden St.,
Philadelphia, PA 19123-2991
Fax: (215) 922-3952
Internet: www.phila.gov/fire/about/index_homepage.html

■ Fire Commissioner **Adam K. Thiel** .... (215) 686-1300
Education: North Carolina BA; Maryland BA; George Mason MPA
Administrative Services Deputy Commissioner **(Vacant)** .. (215) 686-1370
Operations Deputy Commissioner **Jesse Wilson** .... (215) 686-1302
Philadelphia Fire Academy, Fax: (215) 331-4097
5200 Pennypack St., Philadelphia, PA 19136
E-mail: jesse.wilson@phila.gov
Technical Services Deputy Commissioner
Robert W. Corrigan .... (215) 686-1304
Medical Director of EMS **C. Crawford Mechem** .... (215) 685-4201
E-mail: crawford.mechem@uphs.upenn.edu
Fire Marshal/Deputy Chief **Harry Bannan** .... (215) 686-1362
E-mail: harry.bannan@phila.gov Fax: (215) 686-1162
Executive Chief for Strategic Planning
Yolanda Stallings .... (215) 686-1300
Administrative Support Specialist II **Nancy Danczak** ..... (215) 686-1395
E-mail: nancy.danczak@phila.gov Fax: (215) 686-1374
Executive Chief/Media Inquiries **Clifford Gilliam** .... (215) 686-1384
E-mail: executive.firechief@phila.gov

Department of Human Services [DHS]

1515 Arch St., 8th Floor, Philadelphia, PA 19102
Internet: www.phila.gov/dhs/

■ Commissioner (Acting) **Jess Shapiro** .... (215) 683-6000
■ Children and Youth Division Deputy Commissioner
Gary D. Williams .... (215) 683-6014
E-mail: Gary.D.Williams@phila.gov Fax: (215) 683-6049
Finance Deputy Commissioner **Chanell Hanns** .... (215) 683-6060
Fax: (215) 683-6026
Juvenile Justice Services Deputy Commissioner
Timene L. Farlow .... (215) 683-9111
91 North 48th Street, Philadelphia, PA 19139 Fax: (215) 683-9285
Director, Communications **(Vacant)** .... (215) 683-6012
Fax: (215) 683-6107
Director, Family and Community Support Center
Patricia L. Erwin-Blue .... (215) 683-6707
Fax: (215) 683-6721

Department of Licenses and Inspections [L&I]

Municipal Services Center, 11th Fl., 1401 JFK Blvd.,
Philadelphia, PA 19102
Fax: (215) 686-2403 Internet: www.phila.gov/li/

■ Commissioner **David J. Perri** .... (215) 686-2400
E-mail: david.perri@phila.gov
Executive Assistant **Carlene Wyche** .... (215) 686-2616
Director of Development **Danny Rodriguez** .... (215) 686-3371
Fax: (215) 685-3711
Deputy Commissioner for Operations **Ralph DiPietro** .... (215) 686-2510
E-mail: ralph.dipietro@phila.gov Fax: (215) 686-2403
Executive Director of Development Services
Elizabeth Baldwin .... (215) 686-2473
Administrative Services Director **Kirk McClarren** .... (215) 686-2407
E-mail: kirk.mcclarren@phila.gov
Emergency Services Director **Scott Mulderig** .... (215) 686-2574
Zoning Administrator **Tanya Sunkett** .... (215) 686-2476
Chief of Staff **(Vacant)** .... (215) 686-2536
Policy Engagement and Civic Coordinator
Rebecca Corcoran Swanson .... (215) 686-2536
E-mail: rebecca.swanson@phila.gov

Police Department

Police Headquarters, 750 Race Street, Philadelphia, PA 19106-1587
Fax: (215) 625-0612 Internet: www.phillypolice.com/

■ Commissioner **Richard J. Ross, Jr.** .... (215) 686-3367
E-mail: richard.ross@phila.gov
Education: Penn State BA; St Joseph's U 2004 MS

Police Department *continued*

Deputy Commissioner, Office of Professional Responsibility **Denise M. Turpin** . . . . (215) 686-5000
Education: Chestnut Hill BA; St Joseph's U MS

Deputy Commissioner, Organizational Services **Christine M. Coulter** . . . . (215) 686-3313
Education: St Joseph's U 2004 MS

Deputy Commissioner, Patrol Operations **Myron Patterson** . . . . (215) 686-1270

Procurement Department

120 Municipal Services Bldg., 1401 JFK Blvd., Philadelphia, PA 19102-1685
Tel: (215) 686-4720 (Public Information Unit) Fax: (215) 686-4728

■ Procurement Commissioner (Acting) **Trevor Day** . . . . (215) 686-4750
E-mail: trevor.day@phila.gov
Education: Bates BA; Eastern U MBA

Procurement Operations Support Manager **Jackie Broomer** . . . . (215) 686-4733
E-mail: jackie.broomer@phila.gov Fax: (215) 686-4716

Director of Services, Supplies and Equipment **Sonia Lee** . . . . (215) 686-4770
E-mail: sonia.lee@phila.gov

Department of Public Health [PDPH]

1401 JFK Boulevard, MSB 600, Philadelphia, PA 19102
Tel: (215) 686-9009 Internet: www.phila.gov/health/

■ Health Commissioner **Thomas A. Farley** . . . . (215) 686-9009
Education: Haverford 1977 BA; Tulane MPH, MD Fax: (215) 686-5212

Chief of Staff **(Vacant)** . . . . (215) 686-5202

Financial Administration Deputy Commissioner **Tara Mohr** . . . . (215) 686-5207

Deputy Commissioner **Nan Feyler** . . . . (215) 686-5206
Fax: (215) 686-5209

Director of Policy and Planning **Dr. Giridhar Mallya** . . . . (215) 686-5230

Information Services **Mike Harris** . . . . (215) 685-5376
E-mail: mike.harris@phila.gov

Human Resources Director **Karen Hyers** . . . . (215) 685-5207
E-mail: karen.hyers@phila.gov Fax: (215) 685-5212

Department of Public Property

City Hall, Room 790, Philadelphia, PA 19107
Tel: (215) 686-4430 Fax: (215) 686-4498
Internet: www.phila.gov/property/

■ Commissioner **Bridget Collins-Greenwald** . . . . (215) 686-4430
E-mail: bridget.greenwald@phila.gov Fax: (215) 686-4498

Deputy Commissioner for Capital Projects **Gary F. Knappick** . . . . (215) 683-4402
One Parkway Building, 1515 Arch Street, 11th Floor, Philadelphia, PA 19102 Fax: (215) 683-4499

Deputy Commissioner for Facilities **Leonard Gipson** Room 794 . . . . (215) 686-4580
E-mail: leonard.gipson@phila.gov Fax: (215) 686-4520

Deputy Commissioner for Real Estate **John S. Herzins** Room 792 . . . . (215) 686-4434
Fax: (215) 686-4466

Deputy Chief of Staff **Thomas McDade** . . . . (215) 686-4442

Capital Projects Division

One Parkway, 1515 Arch St., 11th Floor, Philadelphia, PA 19102
Tel: (215) 683-4400 Fax: (215) 683-4499

Deputy Commissioner **Gary F. Knappick** . . . . (215) 683-4402

Recreation Project Director **Aparna Palantino** . . . . (215) 683-3655

Health and Human Services Project Director **James Lowe** . . . . (215) 683-4422

Controls and Quality Assurance Project Director **Jason Stevens** . . . . (215) 683-4406
Fax: (215) 683-4499

Department of Records

City Hall, Room 154, Philadelphia, PA 19107
Tel: (215) 686-2268 Fax: (215) 686-2273
Internet: www.phila.gov/records/ E-mail: records.info@phila.gov

■ Commissioner/Recorder of Deeds **Joan T. Decker** . . . . (215) 686-2268
E-mail: Joan.Decker@phila.gov
Education: Drexel 1980 MSLS; Temple 1995 MPA

■ Deputy Commissioner **(Vacant)** . . . . (215) 686-2260

Administrative Services Director **Jeanne Reedy** . . . . (215) 686-2267
E-mail: jeanne.reedy@phila.gov
Education: Penn State 1974 BS

City Archivist **David Baugh** . . . . (215) 685-9401

Title Recording Officer **(Vacant)** . . . . (215) 686-1482

Department of Recreation

1515 Arch St., 10th Floor, Philadelphia, PA 19102-1587
Tel: (215) 683-3600 Fax: (215) 683-3598
Internet: www.phila.gov/recreation/

■ Commissioner of Parks and Recreation **Kathryn Ott Lovell** . . . . (215) 683-3666
E-mail: kathryn.ott.lovell@phila.gov

First Deputy Commissioner **(Vacant)** . . . . (215) 683-0202

First Deputy Commissioner, Recreation **Lt. Susan Slawson** . . . . (215) 683-3601

Deputy Commissioner for Administration **Marissa Washington** . . . . (215) 683-3630
E-mail: marissa.washington@phila.gov

Deputy Commissioner of Operations **Chris Palmer** . . . . (215) 683-0220
E-mail: chris.palmer@phila.gov

Deputy Commissioner for Programs **(Vacant)** . . . . (215) 683-3690

Human Resources Manager **Linda Turner** . . . . (215) 683-3670
E-mail: Linda.Turner@phila.gov Fax: (215) 683-3698

Director of Operations **Mike Mecchella** . . . . (215) 683-3635
E-mail: mike.mecchella@phila.gov

The Free Library of Philadelphia

1901 Vine Street, Philadelphia, PA 19103
Tel: (215) 686-5322 Internet: www.freelibrary.org

Year Founded: 1891

Administration

President and Director **Siobhan A. Reardon** . . . . (215) 686-5300
E-mail: reardons@freelibrary.org Fax: (215) 686-5368
Education: SUNY (Purchase) BA; Fordham MA; Long Island MLS

Deputy Director of Customer Engagement **Joseph "Joe" Benford** . . . . (215) 686-5325
E-mail: benfordj@freelibrary.org

Chief of Staff **Indira C. Scott** . . . . (215) 686-5306
E-mail: scotti@freelibrary.org Fax: (215) 686-5368

Vice President of Development **Melissa Greenberg** . . . . (215) 567-7710
E-mail: melissa@freelibrary.org Fax: (215) 567-7850

Vice President of External Affairs **Sandra A. Horrocks** . . . . (215) 567-7710
E-mail: horrockss@freelibrary.org Fax: (215) 567-7850

Vice President, Strategic Initiatives **Sara S. Moran** . . . . (215) 686-5420
E-mail: morans@freelibrary.org Fax: (215) 686-5368

Vice President of Property Management **James Pecora** . . . . (215) 686-5312
E-mail: pecoraj@freelibrary.org

Chief, Neighborhood Library Services Division **Lynn Williamson** . . . . (215) 686-5310
E-mail: williamsonl@freelibrary.org Fax: (215) 686-5419

Philbrick Lending Library Department Head Assistant **Dena Heilik** . . . . (215) 686-5429
E-mail: heilikd@freelibrary.org

General Information Department Head **Lori Morse** . . . . (215) 686-5299
E-mail: morsel@freelibrary.org

Children's Department Head **Patricia McLaughlin** . . . . (215) 686-5369
E-mail: mclaughlinp@freelibrary.org

Interlibrary Loan Department Head **Sandra Miller** . . . . (215) 686-5360
E-mail: millers@freelibrary.org Fax: (215) 563-3628

Central Public Services Division Chief **Donald Root** . . . . (215) 686-5400
E-mail: rootd@freelibrary.org

(continued on next page)

★ Elected Official ▲ Appointed by Legislature ▼ Appointed by Governor ▶ Appointed by Board or Commission ● Appointed by Judge
■ Appointed by Mayor △ Appointed by Freeholders ▽ Appointed by Supervisor ▷ Appointed by County Executive ○ Appointed by Council

Administration *continued*

Public Service Support Office (Interim) **Chris Caputo** .... (215) 686-5372
E-mail: caputoc@freelibrary.org Fax: (215) 686-5374
Computer Information Systems Director **Laura Moore** ... (215) 686-5334
E-mail: moorel@freelibrary.org Fax: (215) 567-4352
Library Security Services Head (Acting)
Harolyn Holton .... (215) 686-5319
E-mail: holtonh@freelibrary.org Fax: (215) 686-5434

Department of Streets

Municipal Services Building, 1401 JFK Boulevard, 7th Floor, Philadelphia, PA 19102
Fax: (215) 686-5452 E-mail: csstreets@phila.gov
Internet: http://www.phila.gov/streets

■ Commissioner **Donald D. Carlton** .... (215) 686-5460
Note: On leave
E-mail: donald.carlton@phila.gov
■ Commissioner (Acting) **Michael A. "Mike" Carroll** ...... (215) 686-5460
E-mail: michael.carroll@phila.gov
■ Sanitation Deputy Commissioner **(Vacant)** .... (215) 686-5470
Transportation Deputy Commissioner
Michael A. "Mike" Carroll .... (215) 686-5681
Bridge Section Chief Engineer **(Vacant)** .... (215) 686-5542
Engineering Division Chief Engineer/Surveyor
Darin Gatti .... (215) 686-5537
E-mail: darin.gatti@phila.gov
Highways Division Chief Engineer **Stephen Lerrenz** ..... (215) 686-5498
E-mail: stephen.lerrenz@phila.gov
Chief of Traffic and Street Lighting **Richard Montanez** .. (215) 686-5515
E-mail: richard.montanez@phila.gov
Administrative Deputy Commissioner
Christopher Newman .... (215) 686-5465
E-mail: christopher.newman@phila.gov
■ Information Technology Director **Marion Storey** .... (215) 686-5030
E-mail: marion.storey@phila.gov
■ Planning and Public Affairs Supervisor **Keisha McCarty** .. (215) 686-5499
E-mail: keisha.mccarty@phila.gov
Training and Development Officer **Donna Felder** .... (215) 686-5490
E-mail: donna.felder@phila.gov Fax: (215) 686-5949
■ Recycling Director **Phil Bresee** .... (215) 686-5504
E-mail: phil.bresee@phila.gov

Philadelphia Water Department

Aramark Tower, 1101 Market Street, 5th Floor, Philadelphia, PA 19107-2994
Fax: (215) 685-4915

■ Commissioner **Debra A. McCarty** .... (215) 685-6103
E-mail: debra.mccarty@phila.gov
Compliance Deputy Commissioner **David Katz** .... (215) 685-6118
Planning and Environmental Services Deputy
Commissioner **Chris Crockett** .... (215) 685-6112
Finance Deputy Commissioner **Melissa LaBuda** .... (215) 685-6177
Operations Deputy Commissioner and General Manager
of Operations **(Vacant)** .... (215) 685-6102
Human Resources and Administration Deputy
Commissioner **Gerald Leatherman** .... (215) 685-6177
E-mail: gerald.leatherman@phila.gov
Planning and Engineering General Manager
Steve Furtek .... (215) 685-6108
E-mail: Steve.Furtek@phila.gov
Environmental Education and Public Affairs General
Manager **Joanne Dahme** .... (215) 685-6110
E-mail: Joanne.Dahme@phila.gov
Deputy Chief of Staff and Director of Government
Affairs **(Vacant)** .... (215) 685-6111
Chief of Staff **Mami Hara** .... (215) 685-6105
E-mail: mami.hara@phila.gov
General Counsel **Scott Schwarz** .... (215) 685-6135

Philadelphia Board of Ethics

One Parkway Building, 1515 Arch Street, 18th Floor, Philadelphia, PA 19102
Fax: (215) 686-9453 Internet: www.phila.gov/ethicsboard/

Chairman **Michael H. Reed** .... (215) 686-9450
Education: Temple 1969 BA; Yale 1972 JD
Vice Chair **Phyllis W. Beck** .... (215) 686-9450
Education: Brown U 1949 AB; Temple 1967 JD
Board Member **JoAnne A. Epps** .... (215) 686-9450
Education: Trinity Col (CT) 1973; Yale 1976 JD
Board Member **Sanjuanita Gonzalez** .... (215) 686-9450
Board Member **Brian J. McCormick, Jr.** .... (215) 686-9450
Executive Director **J. Shane Creamer, Jr.** .... (215) 686-9450

Philadelphia Commission on Human Relations

The Curtis Center Building, 601 Walnut Street, 3rd Floor, Suite 300 South, Philadelphia, PA 19106
Tel: (215) 686-4670 TTY: (215) 686-3238 Fax: (215) 686-4684
Internet: www.phila.gov/humanrelations/

■ Chairman **Thomas Earle** .... (215) 686-4670
■ Commissioner **Rebecca Alpert** .... (215) 686-4670
■ Commissioner **Regina Austin** .... (215) 686-4670
■ Commissioner **Alfredo Calderon** .... (215) 686-4670
■ Commissioner **Wei Chen** .... (215) 686-4670
■ Commissioner **Marshall E. Freeman** .... (215) 686-4670
■ Commissioner **Saadiq Abdul-Jabbar Garner** .... (215) 686-4670
■ Commissioner **Sarah Ricks** .... (215) 686-4670
■ Commissioner **Shalimar Thomas** .... (215) 686-4670
■ Executive Director **Rue Landau** .... (215) 686-4673
E-mail: rue.landau@phila.gov
Education: Temple 1998 JD
Deputy Director of Community Relations Division
Randy Duque .... (215) 686-4676
E-mail: randy.duque@phila.gov
Deputy Director of Discrimination and Enforcement
Pamela Gwaltney .... (215) 686-4698

Fair Housing Commission

■ Chairperson **Ralph E. Blanks** .... (215) 686-4670
■ Commissioner **James S. Allen** .... (215) 686-4670
■ Commissioner **Anthony Lewis, Jr.** .... (215) 686-4670
■ Commissioner **(Vacant)** .... (215) 686-4670
Executive Director **Rue Landau** .... (215) 686-4673
Education: Temple 1998 JD

Philadelphia Housing Authority [PHA]

12 South 23rd St., Philadelphia, PA 19103
Tel: (215) 684-4000 Internet: http://pha.phila.gov/

President and Chief Executive Officer **Kelvin Jeremiah** .. (215) 684-4174
Senior Executive Vice President of Finance and Chief
Financial Officer **Keith Daviston** .... (215) 684-4248
General Counsel **Barbara Adams** .... (215) 684-4127
Education: Smith; Temple 1978 JD

Philadelphia International Airport

Philadelphia International Airport, Terminal E Executive Offices, Philadelphia, PA 19153
Fax: (215) 937-6759 Internet: www.phl.org/

■ Chief Executive Officer
Rochelle L. "Chellie" Cameron .... (215) 937-6760
E-mail: rochelle.cameron@phila.gov
Chief Operating Officer **(Vacant)** .... (215) 937-5499

Philadelphia Parking Authority

701 Market Street, Suite 5400, Philadelphia, PA 19104
Internet: www.philapark.org

Executive Director **Vincent J. Fenerty** .... (215) 683-9600

★ Elected Official ▲ Appointed by Legislature ▼ Appointed by Governor ▶ Appointed by Board or Commission ● Appointed by Judge
■ Appointed by Mayor △ Appointed by Freeholders ▽ Appointed by Supervisor ▷ Appointed by County Executive ○ Appointed by Council

Philadelphia Prison System
7901 State Road, Philadelphia, PA 19136
Tel: (215) 685-8201 Fax: (215) 685-8577
Internet: www.phila.gov/prisons/

■ Commissioner **Blanche Carney** . . . . . (215) 685-8201

Philadelphia Redevelopment Authority [PRA]
SEPTA Building, 1234 Market Street, 16th Floor,
Philadelphia, PA 19107-3701
Tel: (215) 854-6500 Fax: (215) 854-6732
Internet: www.phila.gov/pra/index.html

Executive Director **Gregory Heller** . . . . . (215) 209-8720
Special Assistant to the Executive Director
Peilin Chen . . . . . (215) 209-8643
E-mail: peilin.chen@pra.phila.gov
Deputy Executive Director of Operations
David Thomas . . . . . (215) 209-8688
E-mail: david.thomas@pra.phila.gov
Deputy Executive Director, Development **Tania Nikolic** . . . (215) 209-8662
E-mail: tania.nikolic@pra.phila.gov
Director of Government Relations and Special Projects
Mary Fogg . . . . . (215) 209-8679
E-mail: mary.fogg@pra.phila.gov
Finance Director **Angela Chandler** . . . . . (215) 209-8717
Housing Construction Director **Ronald Peters** . . . . . (215) 209-8693
General Counsel **Ryan Harmon** . . . . . (215) 209-8624
Relocation and Real Estate Director **Melvis Dunbar** . . . . . (215) 209-8627
E-mail: melvis.dunbar@pra.phila.gov

Office of the City Council
City Hall, Room 494, Philadelphia, PA 19107
Fax: (215) 563-3162 Internet: www.phila.gov/citycouncil/

★ Council President **Darrell L. Clarke** (D-District 5) . . . . . (215) 686-3442
Term Expires: December 31, 2019 Fax: (215) 686-1901
E-mail: Darrell.Clarke@phila.gov
★ Council Member **Mark F. Squilla** (D-District 1) . . . . . (215) 686-3458
Term Expires: December 31, 2019 Fax: (215) 686-1931
E-mail: mark.squilla@phila.gov
★ Council Member **Kenyatta Johnson** (D-District 2) . . . . . (215) 686-3412
Term Expires: December 31, 2019 Fax: (215) 686-1932
E-mail: kenyatta.johnson@phila.gov
★ Council Member **Jannie L. Blackwell** (D-District 3) . . . . . (215) 686-3418
Term Expires: December 31, 2019 Fax: (215) 686-1933
E-mail: jannie.l.blackwell@phila.gov
Education: Cheyney BS; St Joseph's U MEd
★ Council Member **Curtis J. Jones, Jr.** (D-District 4) . . . . . (215) 686-3416
Term Expires: December 31, 2019 Fax: (215) 686-1934
E-mail: curtis.jones.jr@phila.gov
★ Council Member **Bobby Henon** (D-District 6) . . . . . (215) 686-3444
Term Expires: December 31, 2019 Fax: (215) 686-1935
E-mail: bobby.henon@phila.gov
★ Council Member
Maria D. Quiñones-Sánchez (D-District 7) . . . . . (215) 686-3448
Term Expires: December 31, 2019 Fax: (215) 686-1936
E-mail: maria.q.sanchez@phila.gov
★ Council Member **Cindy Bass** (D-District 8) . . . . . (215) 686-3424
Term Expires: December 31, 2019 Fax: (215) 686-1937
E-mail: cindy.bass@phila.gov
★ Council Member **Cherelle L. Parker** (D-District 9) . . . . . (215) 686-1776
Term Expires: December 31, 2019
★ Council Member **Brian J. O'Neill** (R-District 10) . . . . . (215) 686-3422
Term Expires: December 31, 2019 Fax: (215) 686-1939
E-mail: brian.o'neill@phila.gov
★ Council Member **Allan Domb** (D-At-Large) . . . . . (215) 686-1776
Term Expires: December 31, 2019
★ Council Member **Derek Green** (D-At-Large) . . . . . (215) 686-1776
Term Expires: December 31, 2019
★ Council Member **William K. Greenlee** (D-At-Large) . . . . . (215) 686-3446
Term Expires: December 31, 2019 Fax: (215) 686-1927
E-mail: Bill.Greenlee@phila.gov

Office of the City Council *continued*

★ Council Member **Helen Gym** (D-At-Large) . . . . . (215) 686-1776
Term Expires: December 31, 2019
★ Council Member **David Oh** (R-At-Large) . . . . . (215) 686-3452
Term Expires: December 31, 2019 Fax: (215) 686-1925
E-mail: david.oh@phila.gov
★ Council Member
Blondell Reynolds Brown (D-At-Large) . . . . . (215) 686-3438
Term Expires: December 31, 2019 Fax: (215) 686-1926
E-mail: blondell.reynolds.brown@phila.gov
Education: Penn State BS, MEd
★ Council Member **Al Taubenberger** (R-At-Large) . . . . . (215) 686-1776
Term Expires: December 31, 2019
Chief Clerk **Michael Decker** . . . . . (215) 686-3410

School District of Philadelphia
Education Center, 440 North Broad Street, Suite 301,
Philadelphia, PA 19130
Tel: (215) 400-4100 Internet: www.philasd.org

Superintendent **William R. Hite, Jr.** . . . . . (215) 400-4100
Education: Virginia Tech 1984 BS; Virginia 1989 MEd; Virginia Tech 2001 EdD
Chief Financial Officer **Uri Z. Monson** . . . . . (215) 400-4500
Chief Talent Officer (Acting) **Kendra-Lee Rosati** . . . . . (215) 400-6131
E-mail: krosati@phila.k12.pa.us
Chief Academic Support Officer **Cheryl Logan** . . . . . (215) 400-4100
General Counsel **Michael A. Davis** . . . . . (215) 400-4100

Philadelphia School Reform Commission
Education Center, 440 North Broad Street, Suite 101,
Philadelphia, PA 19130
Tel: (215) 400-4010 Internet: http://www.phila.k12.pa.us/src

■ Chair **Marjorie Neff** . . . . . (215) 400-6862
▼ Commissioner **Bill Green** (D) . . . . . (215) 400-6956
▼ Commissioner **Feather O'Connor Houstoun** . . . . . (215) 400-6791
▼ Commissioner **Farah M. Jimenez** . . . . . (215) 400-4010
■ Commissioner **Sylvia P. Simms** . . . . . (215) 400-4010
Chief of Staff **Claire Landau** . . . . . (215) 400-4010

City of Phoenix, Arizona
City Hall, 200 W. Washington St., Phoenix, AZ 85003
Tel: (602) 262-7111 (Information) Internet: http://phoenix.gov

County: Maricopa **Election Type:** Nonpartisan **Year Incorporated:** 1881 **Population:** 1,563,025 (2015)

Office of the Mayor
City Hall, 200 W. Washington St., 11th Floor, Phoenix, AZ 85003-1611
Fax: (602) 495-5583 Internet: http://phoenix.gov/mayor/

★ Mayor **Gregory "Greg" Stanton** . . . . . (602) 262-7111
Began Service: January 3, 2012
Term Expires: January 1, 2020
E-mail: mayor.stanton@phoenix.gov
Education: Marquette 1992 BA; Michigan 1995 JD
Assistant to the Mayor **Cindy Salazar** . . . . . (602) 262-7111
Chief of Staff, Policy **Seth Scott** . . . . . (602) 262-7111
Chief of Staff, Operations **Ruben Alonzo** . . . . . (602) 262-7111
E-mail: ruben.alonzo@phoenix.gov
Deputy Chief of Staff **Tracee Crockett** . . . . . (602) 262-7111
Press Secretary **Robbie Sherwood** . . . . . (602) 262-7111
E-mail: robbie.sherwood@phoenix.gov
Education: Arizona State 1993 BJ
Public Information Officer **Tamra Ingersoll** . . . . . (602) 262-7111
Assistant to the Mayor **Julie Cruz** . . . . . (602) 262-7111

★ Elected Official ▲ Appointed by Legislature ▼ Appointed by Governor ▶ Appointed by Board or Commission ● Appointed by Judge
■ Appointed by Mayor △ Appointed by Freeholders ▽ Appointed by Supervisor ▷ Appointed by County Executive ○ Appointed by Council

Office of the City Council

City Hall, 200 W. Washington St., 11th Floor, Phoenix, AZ 85003-1611
Tel: (602) 262-7029 Fax: (602) 495-2036

★Vice Mayor **Daniel Valenzuela** (District 5) .... (602) 262-7446
Term Expires: January 1, 2020 Fax: (602) 495-0628
E-mail: council.district.5@phoenix.gov

★Council Member **Thelda Williams** (District 1) .... (602) 262-7444
Term Expires: January 1, 2020 Fax: (602) 534-4793
E-mail: council.district.1@phoenix.gov

★Council Member **Jim Waring** (District 2) .... (602) 262-7445
Term Expires: January 1, 2018 Fax: (602) 495-0527
E-mail: council.district.2@phoenix.gov
Education: Northern Illinois 1990 BS; Arizona State 1992 MA, 1994 MPA, 1998 PhD

★Council Member **Bill Gates** (District 3) .... (602) 262-7441
Note: Resigning May 31, 2016 Fax: (602) 534-4190
Term Expires: January 1, 2020
E-mail: council.district.3@phoenix.gov
Education: Harvard 1996 JD

★Council Member **Laura A. Pastor** (District 4) .... (602) 262-7447
Term Expires: January 1, 2018 Fax: (602) 534-5438
E-mail: council.district.4@phoenix.gov
Education: Arizona State BA; Baruch Col 2006 MPA

★Council Member **Sal DiCiccio** (District 6) .... (602) 262-7491
Term Expires: January 1, 2018 Fax: (602) 534-3574
E-mail: council.district.6@phoenix.gov
Education: Arizona State BSBA

★Council Member **Michael Nowakowski** (District 7) .... (602) 262-7492
Term Expires: January 1, 2020 Fax: (602) 534-4816
E-mail: council.district.7@phoenix.gov

★Council Member **Kate Gallego** (District 8) .... (602) 262-7493
Term Expires: January 1, 2018 Fax: (602) 495-0587
E-mail: council.district.8@phoenix.gov

Executive Assistant to the City Council **Penny Parrella** ... (602) 262-4687
E-mail: penny.parrella@phoenix.gov

Office of the City Manager

City Hall, 200 West Washington Street, 12th Floor, Phoenix, AZ 85003
Tel: (602) 262-6941 Fax: (602) 261-8327

City Manager **Ed Zuercher** .... (602) 262-7958
E-mail: ed.zuercher@phoenix.gov
Education: Goshen 1987 BA; Kansas 1994 MPA

Deputy City Manager **Paul Blue** .... (602) 262-7941
E-mail: paul.blue@phoenix.gov

Deputy City Manager **Deanna Jonovich** .... (602) 495-0127
E-mail: deanna.jonovich@phoenix.gov

Deputy City Manager **Mario Paniagua** .... (602) 534-9803
E-mail: mario.paniagua@phoenix.gov

Deputy City Manager **Karen Peters** .... (602) 534-9803
E-mail: karen.peters@phoenix.gov

Environmental Programs Manager **Joe Giudice** .... (602) 256-5654
Fax: (602) 534-0795

Water Advisor **Clifford Neal** .... (602) 261-8532

Assistant City Manager

City Hall, 200 West Washington Street, 12th Floor, Phoenix, AZ 85003-1611

Assistant City Manager **Milton Dohoney, Jr.** .... (602) 262-7915
E-mail: milton.dohoney@phoenix.gov

Office of Arts and Culture

200 West Washington Street, 10th Floor, Phoenix, AZ 85003
Fax: (602) 262-6914 Internet: https://www.phoenix.gov/arts

Director of Cultural Affairs **Gail Browne** .... (602) 262-4637

Budget and Research Department

City Hall, 200 W. Washington St., 14th Floor, Phoenix, AZ 85003-1611
Tel: (602) 262-4800 Fax: (602) 534-3918
Internet: http://phoenix.gov/BUDGET/
E-mail: budget.research@phoenix.gov

Director (Acting) **Jeffrey "Jeff" Barton** .... (602) 262-4805
E-mail: jeffrey.barton@phoenix.gov

Deputy Budget and Research Director **Aaron Avila** .... (602) 262-4851
E-mail: Aaron.avila@phoenix.gov

Deputy Budget and Research Director **Rick Freas** .... (602) 262-4843
E-mail: rick.freas@phoenix.gov

Deputy Budget and Research Director **Tracy Reber** .... (602) 262-6960
E-mail: tracy.reber@phoenix.gov

Human Services Department

City Hall, 200 W. Washington St., 18th Floor, Phoenix, AZ 85003-1611
Tel: (602) 262-6666 Fax: (602) 534-3722

Director **Moises Gallegos** .... (602) 262-6668

Community Services Deputy Director **Jeff Jamison** .... (602) 262-4520
E-mail: jeff.jamison@phoenix.gov

Education Deputy Director **Amy Corriveau** .... (602) 262-4040

Management Services Deputy Director **Lisa Esquivel** .... (602) 262-6666
E-mail: lisa.esquivel@phoenix.gov

Parks and Recreation Department

City Hall, 200 West Washington Street, 16th Floor, Phoenix, AZ 85003
Tel: (602) 262-6862 Fax: (602) 732-2326
Internet: http://phoenix.gov/parks

Director (Acting) **Inger Erickson** .... (602) 262-4986

Assistant Director **Inger Erickson** .... (602) 534-1870

Deputy Director **Judy Weiss** .... (602) 262-4987

Public Information Officer **Gregg Bach** .... (602) 262-4994
E-mail: gregg.bach@phoenix.gov

Phoenix Public Library

1221 North Central Avenue, Phoenix, AZ 85004-1867
Tel: (602) 262-4636 Fax: (602) 261-8836 Internet: www.phxlib.org

Administration

City Librarian **Rita Hamilton** .... (602) 262-7930
E-mail: rita.hamilton@phoenix.gov

Deputy Director, Collections **Karl Kendall** .... (602) 534-9152
E-mail: karl.kendall@phoenix.gov

Deputy Director, Information Technology
Aimee Fifarek .... (602) 262-6250
E-mail: aimee.fifarek@phoenix.gov

Deputy Director, Public Services **Paula Fortier** .... (602) 262-5027
E-mail: paula.fortier@phoenix.gov

Police Department

620 W. Washington St., Phoenix, AZ 85003
Tel: (602) 262-7626 Fax: (602) 534-4831
Internet: www.phoenix.gov/police

Police Chief **Joseph "Joe" Yahner** .... (602) 262-6747
Note: Retiring October 2016
Assistant to the Chief **Marchelle Franklin** .... (602) 262-7626
E-mail: marchelle.franklin@phoenix.gov

Executive Assistant Chief **Dave Harvey** .... (602) 262-7626

Investigations Division Assistant Chief **Mary Roberts** .... (602) 262-7626

Reserve Division Assistant Chief **Scott Finical** .... (602) 262-7626

Patrol Division Assistant Chief **Harry Markley** .... (602) 262-7626

Support Services Division Assistant Chief
Sandra Renteria .... (602) 262-7626

Strategic Services Division Assistant Chief
Dave Harvey .... (602) 262-7626
E-mail: dave.harvey@phoenix.gov

Public Affairs Bureau Commander **Lt. Sal Freni** .... (602) 262-5050
E-mail: sal.freni@phoenix.gov

★Elected Official ▲Appointed by Legislature ▼Appointed by Governor ▶Appointed by Board or Commission ●Appointed by Judge
■Appointed by Mayor △Appointed by Freeholders ▽Appointed by Supervisor ▷Appointed by County Executive ○Appointed by Council

Public Transit Department
302 North First Avenue, Suite 900, Phoenix, AZ 85003-1621
Fax: (602) 495-2002 E-mail: pubtrans@phoenix.gov
Internet: http://phoenix.gov/publictransit/

Director **Maria Hyatt** .... (602) 262-7242
Deputy Director, Facilities **(Vacant)** .... (602) 262-7242
Deputy Director, Regional Information Technology **(Vacant)** .... (602) 262-7242
Deputy Director, Street Transportation **Jenny L. Grote** ... (602) 262-7242
E-mail: jenny.grote@phoenix.gov
Administrative Aide (Acting) **Aarti Cua** .... (602) 262-7614
Public Information Officer **Brenda Yanez** .... (602) 262-7242
E-mail: brenda.yanez@phoenix.gov

Public Works Department
200 West Washington Street, 7th Floor, Phoenix, AZ 85003
Tel: (602) 262-7251 Fax: (602) 534-1766
Internet: http://phoenix.gov/PUBLICWORKS/

Director **John A. Trujillo** .... (602) 495-7274
Assistant Director **Christine Smith** .... (602) 495-7274
Facilities Management Division, Deputy Director **Janice Stroud** .... (602) 256-5673
200 West Washington, 14th Floor, Phoenix, AZ 85003 Fax: (602) 534-1519
E-mail: janice.stroud@phoenix.gov
Fleet Management Division, Deputy Director **Brandy Barrett** .... (602) 262-7030
2441 S. 22nd Ave., Phoenix, AZ 85009
Solid Waste Diversion and Disposal Division, Deputy Director **Chuck Hamstra** .... (602) 256-0496
Solid Waste Field Services Division, Deputy Director **Fellipe Moreno** .... (602) 256-5625

Street Transportation Department
City Hall, 200 W. Washington St., 5th Floor, Phoenix, AZ 85003
Fax: (602) 495-2016 Internet: http://phoenix.gov/STREETS/

Street Transportation Director **Ray Dovalina, Jr.** .... (602) 262-6136
E-mail: ray.dovalina@phoenix.gov
Education: Texas A&I BS; Northern Arizona MPA

Aviation Department
3400 Sky Harbor Blvd., Ste. 3300 E. Mezzanine, Phoenix, AZ 85034-4420
Fax: (602) 273-4084 Internet: www.skyharbor.com

Aviation Director **James Bennett** .... (602) 273-3321
Assistant Aviation Director **Tamie Fisher** .... (602) 273-3316
Assistant Aviation Director **Deborah Ostreicher** .... (602) 273-3316
Deputy Aviation Director, Public Relations (Acting) **Julie Rodriguez** .... (602) 273-4303
E-mail: julie.rodriguez@phoenix.gov Fax: (602) 683-3678
Deputy Aviation Director, Financial Management **Jay Dewitt** .... (602) 273-3363
Deputy Aviation Director, Facilities and Services (Acting) **Bobbi Reid** .... (602) 273-3466
Deputy Aviation Director, Operations **Steve Grubbs** .... (602) 273-3466
E-mail: stephen.grubbs@phoenix.gov
Airport Police Unit Commander **Tracy Montgomery** .... (602) 683-3653
Aviation Fire Deputy Chief **Elizabeth Hendel** .... (602) 534-9999
E-mail: elizabeth.hendel@phoenix.gov
Noise Information Manager **(Vacant)** .... (602) 273-4300
Security Coordinator **Shawna Holton** .... (602) 273-2766
E-mail: shawna.holton@phoenix.gov Fax: (602) 273-2183
Training **Anita Clock** .... (602) 273-3325
E-mail: anita.clock@phoenix.gov

City Auditor Department
17 South Second Avenue, Suite 200, Phoenix, AZ 85003-2228
Tel: (602) 262-6641 Fax: (602) 534-1533
Internet: http://phoenix.gov/auditor/index.html

City Auditor **Bill Greene** .... (602) 262-6641
Deputy City Auditor **Diane Artrip** .... (602) 262-6641

City Auditor Department *continued*

Deputy City Auditor **Aaron Cook** .... (602) 262-6641
Deputy City Auditor **Barbara Coppage** .... (602) 262-6641
Deputy City Auditor **Irene Larkin** .... (602) 262-6641

City Clerk Department
City Hall, 200 West Washington Street, 15th Floor, Phoenix, AZ 85003-1611
Tel: (602) 262-6811 Fax: (602) 495-5847
Internet: http://phoenix.gov/CITYCLERK/

City Clerk **Cris Meyer** .... (602) 262-6558
E-mail: cris.meyer@phoenix.gov
Deputy City Clerk, Council, License and Management Services **Elizabeth Martin Parker** .... (602) 262-1874
E-mail: elizabeth.martin.parker@phoenix.gov
Deputy City Clerk, Records and Elections **Ben Lane** ..... (602) 262-7665
E-mail: ben.lane@phoenix.gov

Community and Economic Development Department
City Hall, 200 West Washington Street, 20th Floor, Phoenix, AZ 85003
Tel: (602) 262-5040 Fax: (602) 495-5097
E-mail: phx.business@phoenix.gov
Internet: http://phoenix.gov/ECONDEV/

Director **Christine Mackay** .... (602) 261-8709
E-mail: christine.mackay@phoenix.gov
Deputy Director **Cynthia Spell Tweh** .... (602) 262-5040
E-mail: cynthia.tweh@phoenix.gov
Technology Support **Ken Valencia** .... (602) 534-8722
E-mail: ken.valencia@phoenix.gov

Equal Opportunity Department
200 West Washington Sreet, 15th Floor, Phoenix, AZ 85003
Tel: (602) 262-7716 Fax: (602) 534-1124
Internet: http://phoenix.gov/EOD/

Director **Donald R. Logan** .... (602) 262-6258
Business Relations Division Deputy Director **Trevor Bui** .. (602) 262-6790
Compliance and Enforcement Division Director **Marquita Beene** .... (602) 262-7486

Finance Department
Calvin C. Goode Bldg., 251 W. Washington St., 9th Floor, Phoenix, AZ 85003-2201
Fax: (602) 495-5605 Internet: http://phoenix.gov/FINANCE/

Chief Financial Officer **Denise Olson** .... (602) 262-7166
City Treasurer **Kathleen Gitkin** .... (602) 262-7166
Assistant Finance Director **(Vacant)** .... (602) 262-7166
Lead User Technology Specialist **Mike Schultz** .... (602) 534-6096
E-mail: mike.schultz@phoenix.gov Fax: (602) 495-5605
Personnel Officer **Renee Gillison** .... (602) 495-0264
E-mail: renee.gillison@phoenix.gov

Fire Department
150 S. 12th St., Phoenix, AZ 85034
Tel: (602) 262-6002 Fax: (602) 262-4429
Internet: http://phoenix.gov/FIRE/

Fire Chief **Kara Kalkbrenner** .... (602) 256-3189
E-mail: kara.kalkbrenner@phoenix.gov
Deputy Chief, Physical Resources **Ken Leake** .... (602) 256-3189
Assistant Fire Chief, Training **Todd Harms** .... (602) 256-3149
E-mail: todd.harms@phoenix.gov
Assistant Fire Chief, Operations **Ron Jamison** .... (602) 256-3149
E-mail: ron.jamison@phoenix.gov
Executive Assistant Chief, Human Resources Bureau **Mark Angle** .... (602) 256-3189
E-mail: mark.angle@phoenix.gov
Information Technology Assistant Chief **(Vacant)** .... (602) 256-3149
Fire Prevention Assistant Chief **Scott A. Krushak** .... (602) 256-3149
E-mail: scott.krushak@phoenix.gov

★ Elected Official ▲ Appointed by Legislature ▼ Appointed by Governor ▶ Appointed by Board or Commission ● Appointed by Judge
■ Appointed by Mayor △ Appointed by Freeholders ▽ Appointed by Supervisor ▷ Appointed by County Executive ○ Appointed by Council

Government Relations

200 West Washington Street, 12th Floor, Phoenix, AZ 85003
Fax: (602) 534-3644 Internet: http://phoenix.gov/INTERGOV

Government Relations Director **Tom Remes** .... (602) 256-4257
E-mail: thomas.remes@phoenix.gov
Management Assistant **James Orloski** .... (602) 256-4257
E-mail: james.orloski@phoenix.gov

Housing Department

Calvin C. Goode Building, 251 West Washington Street, 4th Floor, Phoenix, AZ 85003-1611
Tel: (602) 262-6794 Fax: (602) 534-5345
Internet: http://phoenix.gov/HOUSING/

Director **Cindy Stotler** .... (602) 495-6945

Human Resources Department

135 N. Second Ave., Phoenix, AZ 85003-2018
Tel: (602) 262-6608 Fax: (602) 534-2602 E-mail: hrcenter@phoenix.gov

Director **Blair Johnson** .... (602) 262-6608
E-mail: blair.johnson@phoenix.gov

Information Technology Services

Calvin C. Goode Bldg., 251 W. Washington St., 6th Floor, Phoenix, AZ 85003-2295
Fax: (602) 534-1488 Internet: http://phoenix.gov/its/index.html

Chief Information Officer **Debbie Cotton** .... (602) 262-4481
E-mail: debbie.cotton@phoenix.gov
Education: Western Illinois 1978 BS; Arizona State 2003 MPA

Law Department

City Hall, 200 W. Washington St., Suite 1300, Phoenix, AZ 85003-1611
Internet: http://phoenix.gov/LAW/index.html

City Attorney **Brad Holm** .... (602) 262-6761
Fax: (602) 534-9866
Chief Assistant City Attorney **Daniel L. Brown** .... (602) 262-6761
Fax: (602) 534-9866
Transportation Section Assistant Chief Counsel
Jo Ellen McBride .... (602) 262-6761
E-mail: jo.ellen.mcbride@phoenix.gov
Public Safety Section Assistant Chief Counsel
(Vacant) .... (602) 262-6761
Fax: (602) 534-9866
Litigation Section Assistant Chief Counsel
Sharon K. Haynes .... (602) 262-6761
Fax: (602) 534-2487
Finance and Development Assistant Chief Counsel
Patricia "Pat" Boland .... (602) 262-6761
Fax: (602) 534-2476
Public Safety Section Assistant Chief Counsel
Sandra Hunter .... (602) 262-6761
Fax: (602) 534-9866
Development Section Assistant Chief Counsel **(Vacant)** ... (602) 262-6761
Fax: (602) 534-9866
Management Services Administrator **Mike Roberts** ...... (602) 262-6761
E-mail: mike.roberts@phoenix.gov Fax: (602) 534-9866

Criminal Division

300 W. Washington Street, 8th Floor, Phoenix, AZ 85003-2103
PO Box 4500, Phoenix, AZ 85030-4500
Fax: (602) 534-9806

City Prosecutor (Acting) **Vicki A. Hill** .... (602) 262-4781
Fax: (602) 534-9806
Chief Assistant City Prosecutor (Acting)
Will Gonzalez .... (602) 262-4781
Fax: (602) 534-9806
Appeals Assistant Bureau Chief **(Vacant)** .... (602) 256-3506
Charging Bureau Chief **Diana Hinz** .... (602) 262-7768
Fax: (602) 534-6151
Trial Bureau Chief **Will Gonzalez** .... (602) 262-6403
Fax: (602) 262-7052

Criminal Division *continued*

Diversion Programs Administrator **(Vacant)** .... (602) 262-6031
Fax: (602) 256-3509
Training and Technology **Sharon Stolpen** .... (602) 262-7058
E-mail: sharon.stolpen@phoenix.gov Fax: (602) 262-1633
Victim Services Administrator **(Vacant)** .... (602) 495-5846
Fax: (602) 534-4540
Community Prosecution Assistant Bureau Chief
Esteban Gomez .... (602) 256-3506
Fax: (602) 534-2693

Neighborhood Services Department [NSD]

City Hall, 200 W. Washington St., 4th Floor, Phoenix, AZ 85003-1611
Fax: (602) 534-1555 Internet: http://phoenix.gov/NSD/

Director **Chris Hallett** .... (602) 534-6176
E-mail: chris.hallett@phoenix.gov
Education: Arizona State 1986 BS, 1996 MBA
Revitalization Deputy Director **Aubrey Gonzalez** .... (602) 534-2393
E-mail: aubrey.gonzalez@phoenix.gov
Preservation Deputy Director **Darcy Kober** .... (602) 534-2393
E-mail: darcy.kober@phoenix.gov
Neighborhood Engagement Deputy Director
Lynda Dodd .... (602) 495-3789
E-mail: lynda.dodd@phoenix.gov

Phoenix Convention Center and Venues

100 North Third Street, Phoenix, AZ 85004
Fax: (602) 495-3642 Internet: http://www.phoenixconventioncenter.com/

Director **John Chan** .... (602) 262-6225
Education: Arizona State 1982 BSBA
Deputy Director **Jerry Harper** .... (602) 262-6795
Marketing Manager **Kevin Hill** .... (602) 534-9567

Planning and Development Department

City Hall, 200 W. Washington St., 3rd Floor, Phoenix, AZ 85003
Fax: (602) 534-0846 Internet: http://phoenix.gov/pdd/

Director **Alan Stephenson** .... (602) 495-5411
Assistant Director, Development (Acting) **Mo Glancy** .... (602) 495-7347
E-mail: mo.glancy@phoenix.gov
Deputy Director, Planning **Sandra Hoffman** .... (602) 256-3555
Historic Preservation Officer **Michelle Dodds** .... (602) 262-7468

Public Information Office

City Hall, 200 West Washington Sreet, 12th Floor, Phoenix, AZ 85003
Tel: (602) 262-7177 Fax: (602) 495-2432
Internet: http://phoenix.gov/PIO/

Director **Julie Watters** .... (602) 262-7177
Public Information Officer **Tammy Vo** .... (602) 261-8512
E-mail: tammy.vo@phoenix.gov
Public Information Officer **(Vacant)** .... (602) 262-6213
Phoenix Channel Eleven Station Manager
Deborah Sedillo Dugan .... (602) 262-7177
E-mail: deborah.sedillo.dugan@phoenix.gov
Emergency Management Coordinator
Kevin C. Kalkbrenner .... (602) 495-2077
E-mail: kevin.c.kalkbrenner@phoenix.gov

Water Services Department

City Hall, 200 W. Washington St., 9th Floor, Phoenix, AZ 85003
Fax: (602) 534-1090 Internet: www.phoenix.gov/waterservices

Director **Kathryn Sorensen** .... (602) 262-6627
Wastewater Assistant Director **Ron Serio** .... (602) 262-6627
Environmental Services Administrator **Randy Gottler** .... (602) 262-6627
Public Information Officer **Stephanie Bracken** .... (602) 534-1209

★ Elected Official ▲ Appointed by Legislature ▼ Appointed by Governor ▶ Appointed by Board or Commission ● Appointed by Judge
■ Appointed by Mayor △ Appointed by Freeholders ▽ Appointed by Supervisor ▷ Appointed by County Executive ○ Appointed by Council

City of Pierre, South Dakota

222 East Dakota, Pierre, SD 57501
P.O. Box 1253, Pierre, SD 57501
Internet: www.pierre.sd.gov/

County: Hughes **Election Type:** Nonpartisan **Population:** 14,002 (2015)

Office of the Mayor and City Commission

222 E. Dakota, Pierre, SD 57501
P.O. Box 1253, Pierre, SD 57501
Fax: (605) 773-7406

★ Mayor **Laurie R. Gill** . . . . . (605) 773-7407
Began Service: July 2008
Term Expires: July 2, 2017
E-mail: laurie.gill@ci.pierre.sd.us

★ Commissioner **Jeanne Goodman** . . . . . (605) 773-7407
Term Expires: July 1, 2016
E-mail: jeanne.goodman@ci.pierre.sd.us

★ Commissioner **Steve Harding** . . . . . (605) 773-7407
Term Expires: July 2, 2017
E-mail: steve.harding@ci.pierre.sd.us

★ Commissioner **Jamie Huizenga** . . . . . (605) 773-7407
Term Expires: July 1, 2018
E-mail: jamie.huizenga@ci.pierre.sd.us

★ Commissioner **James "Jim" Mehlhaff** . . . . . (605) 773-7407
Term Expires: July 1, 2018
E-mail: jim.mehlhaff@ci.pierre.sd.us

City Attorney **Lindsey Riter Rapp** . . . . . (605) 224-5825

▶ Finance Officer and Clerk to the Board **Twila Hight** . . . . . (605) 773-7407
E-mail: twila.hight@ci.pierre.sd.us

Office of the City Administrator

P.O. Box 1253, Pierre, SD 57501
Fax: (605) 773-7406

▶ City Administrator **Leon Schochenmaier** . . . . . (605) 773-7341
Education: South Dakota State 1974 BS

Building Department-Planning and Zoning

222 E. Dakota Ave., Pierre, SD 57501
P.O. Box 1253, Pierre, SD 57501
Fax: (605) 773-7406

Building Official **John Irvine** . . . . . (605) 773-3072
Building Inspector **Kirby Welch** . . . . . (605) 773-3071
City Planner **Sharon Pruess** . . . . . (605) 773-3062

City Landfill

2800 E. Park St., Pierre, SD 57501
P.O. Box 1253, Pierre, SD 57501
Fax: (605) 773-7436 Internet: http://ci.pierre.sd.us/landfill.htm

Superintendent **Val Keller** . . . . . (605) 773-7434

Community Development Department

222 East Dakota, Pierre, SD 57501

Government Community Services Coordinator
Brooke Bohnenkamp . . . . . (605) 773-3069
E-mail: brooke.bohnenkamp@ci.pierre.sd.us

Engineering and Planning Services

222 E. Dakota Ave., Pierre, SD 57501
P.O. Box 1253, Pierre, SD 57501
Fax: (605) 773-7406

City Engineer and Planning Director **John Childs** . . . . . (605) 773-3056
E-mail: john.childs@ci.pierre.sd.us

Engineering and Planning Services *continued*

Senior Engineering Technician **Derek Gray** . . . . . (605) 773-7341
E-mail: derek.gray@ci.pierre.sd.us

Staff Engineer **Kyle Kurth** . . . . . (605) 773-3066
E-mail: kyle.kurth@ci.pierre.sd.us

Administrative Assistant **Lauren Laird** . . . . . (605) 773-7341
E-mail: lauren.laird@ci.pierre.sd.us

Finance Office

222 E. Dakota Ave., Pierre, SD 57501
P.O. Box 1253, Pierre, SD 57501
Fax: (605) 773-7406 E-mail: finance.office@ci.pierre.sd.us

Business Manager/Finance Officer **Twila Hight** . . (605) 773-3063 ext. 122
Deputy Finance Officer **Erin Barnum** . . . . . (605) 773-3065 ext. 125

Fire Department

215 W. Dakota Ave., Pierre, SD 57501
P.O. Box 1253, Pierre, SD 57501
Fax: (605) 773-7400

▶ Fire Chief **Ian Paul** . . . . . (605) 773-7401
E-mail: ian.paul@ci.pierre.sd.us

Deputy Chief **Cory Hoffrogge** . . . . . (605) 773-7401
E-mail: cory.hoffrogge@ci.pierre.sd.us

First Assistant Chief **Leon Ellis** . . . . . (605) 773-7401
E-mail: leon.ellis@state.sd.us

Hillsview Golf Course

4125 E. Highway 34, Pierre, SD 57501
P.O. Box 1253, Pierre, SD 57501
E-mail: golfsupt@dtgnet.com

Golf Manager **Carin Hayn** . . . . . (605) 773-6191
Greens Superintendent **Dean Heymans** . . . . . (605) 773-7443

Human Resources Department

222 E. Dakota, Pierre, SD 57501
P.O. Box 1253, Pierre, SD 57501
Fax: (605) 773-7406

▶ Director **Laurie Gronlund** . . . . . (605) 773-7429
E-mail: laurie.gronlund@ci.pierre.sd.us

Library Department

Rawlins Municipal Library, 1000 E. Church St., Pierre, SD 57501
P.O. Box 1253, Pierre, SD 57501
Fax: (605) 773-7423

Director **Robin Schrupp** . . . . . (605) 773-7421
E-mail: robin.schrupp@ci.pierre.sd.us

Maintenance Operations Department

P.O. Box 1253, Pierre, SD 57501

Construction and Operations Manager **Lynn Patton** . . . . . (605) 773-7341
E-mail: lynn.patton@ci.pierre.sd.us

Street Superintendent **Mark Metzinger** . . . . . (605) 773-7439
Water Department Superintendent **Dane Brewer** . . . . . (605) 773-7448
Wastewater Department Superintendent
Nathan McCombs . . . . . (605) 773-7449

Parks and Recreation Department

1201 E. Missouri Ave., Pierre, SD 57501
P.O. Box 1253, Pierre, SD 57501

Park and Recreation Commissioner **Jeanne Goodman** . . . (605) 773-7437
Park and Recreation Director **Tom Farnsworth** . . . . . (605) 773-7437
Park Superintendent **Todd Kelly** . . . . . (605) 773-7437
Recreation Superintendent **Mindy Cheap** . . . . . (605) 773-7445

★ Elected Official ▲ Appointed by Legislature ▼ Appointed by Governor ▶ Appointed by Board or Commission ● Appointed by Judge
■ Appointed by Mayor △ Appointed by Freeholders ▽ Appointed by Supervisor ▷ Appointed by County Executive ○ Appointed by Council

Pierre City Utilities
P.O. Box 1253, Pierre, SD 57501
Internet: http://ci.pierre.sd.us/Department.aspx?id=21

Utilities Director **Brad Palmer** .... (605) 773-7341 ext. 115
Electricity Superintendent **Ryan Grant** .... (605) 295-0607

Police Department
State Correctional Facility, 3200 E. Highway 34, Pierre, SD 57501
P.O. Box 1253, Pierre, SD 57501
Tel: (605) 773-7413 Fax: (605) 773-7417

► Police Chief **Dave Panzer** .... (605) 773-7413
E-mail: dave.panzer@ci.pierre.sd.us
Administrative Captain **Capt. Elton Blemaster** .... (605) 773-7413
Communications Supervisor **Cindy Gross** .... (605) 773-7410
Fax: (605) 773-7417
Animal Control Officer **John Waggoner** .... (605) 773-7410

City of Pittsburgh, Pennsylvania

City-County Bldg., 414 Grant Street, Pittsburgh, PA 15219
Tel: (412) 255-2100 (Information)

County: Allegheny **Election Type:** Partisan **Population:** 304,391 (2015)

Office of the Mayor
512 City-County Bldg., 414 Grant St., Pittsburgh, PA 15219
Tel: (412) 255-2626 Fax: (412) 255-2687
Internet: www.pittsburghpa.gov/mayor/

★ Mayor **William "Bill" Peduto** (D) .... (412) 255-2626
Began Service: January 6, 2014
Term Expires: December 31, 2017
■ Chief of Staff **Kevin Acklin** .... (412) 255-2636
Fax: (412) 255-2687
■ Chief Administrative Officer **Debbie Lestitian** .... (412) 255-2619
■ Director of Policy **(Vacant)** .... (412) 255-2618
■ Chief Operations Officer **Guy Costa** .... (412) 255-2626
■ Non-Profit and Faith Based Manager **Betty Cruz** .... (412) 255-2626
■ Sustainability Manager/Chief Resilience Officer **Grant Ervin** .... (412) 255-2626
E-mail: Grant.ervin@pittsburghpa.gov
■ Communications Manager **Timothy McNulty** .... (412) 255-2626
■ Assistant Communications Manager **Katie O'Malley** .... (412) 255-2626

Office of Management and Budget
526 City-County Bldg., 414 Grant St., Pittsburgh, PA 15219
Fax: (412) 255-4899

Director of Management and Budget **Sam Ashbaugh** .... (412) 255-2640
E-mail: sam.ashbaugh@pittsburghpa.gov
Assistant Director **Jennifer Presutti** .... (412) 255-2640
E-mail: jennifer.presutti@pittsburghpa.gov
Assistant Director **Rea Price** .... (412) 255-2640
E-mail: rea.price@pittsburghpa.gov
Senior Budget Analyst **Kevin Pawlos** .... (412) 255-2640
Budget Administrator **Kim Osterman** .... (412) 255-2640
E-mail: kim.osterman@pittsburghpa.gov
Budget Analyst **Sheri Rolewski** .... (412) 255-2640
E-mail: sheri.rolewski@pittsburghpa.gov
Grants Officer **Sara DeRoy** .... (412) 255-2640
Budget/Accounts Technician **Laurie Lover** .... (412) 255-2640
E-mail: laurie.lover@omb.ri.gov
Fleet Contract Manager **Chuck O'Neill** .... (412) 255-2770
51 29th Street, Pittsburgh, PA 15201
Grants Officer **Daniel Barrett** .... (412) 255-6782
Senior Grants Officer **Melanie Ondek** .... (412) 255-2640

Pittsburgh Commission on Human Relations [PCHR]
City-County Building, 414 Grant Street, 9th Floor, Pittsburgh, PA 15219
Fax: (412) 255-2288

Executive Director **Carlos Torres** .... (412) 255-2600

Mayor's Office of Sustainability and Energy Efficiency
City-County Building, 414 Grant Street, Room 512, Pittsburgh, PA 15219
Tel: (412) 255-2626 Fax: (412) 255-2687

Sustainability Coordinator **Aftyn Giles** .... (412) 255-2626
Education: Carnegie Mellon BARCH, BA, MS; Keller Grad School MA

Office of the City Council
510 City-County Bldg., 414 Grant St., Pittsburgh, PA 15219-2404
Tel: (412) 255-2142 Fax: (412) 255-2821
Internet: www.city.pittsburgh.pa.us/council/

★ Council President **Bruce A. Kraus** (D-District 3) .... (412) 255-2130
Term Expires: December 31, 2019
★ Council Member **Darlene M. Harris** (D-District 1) .... (412) 255-2135
Term Expires: December 31, 2019
★ Council Member **Theresa Kail-Smith** (D-District 2) .... (412) 255-8963
Term Expires: December 31, 2017
★ Council Member **Natalia Rudiak** (D-District 4) .... (412) 255-2131
Term Expires: December 31, 2017
★ Council Member **Corey O'Connor** (D-District 5) .... (412) 255-8965
Term Expires: December 31, 2019
Education: Duquesne 2006 BA
★ Council Member **R. Daniel Lavelle** (D-District 6) .... (412) 255-2134
Term Expires: December 31, 2017
★ Council Member **Deborah "Deb" Gross** (D-District 7) .... (412) 255-2140
Term Expires: December 31, 2019
★ Council Member **Dan Gilman** (D-District 8) .... (412) 255-2133
Term Expires: December 31, 2017
★ Council Member **Rev. Ricky V. Burgess** (D-District 9) .... (412) 255-2137
Term Expires: December 31, 2019

Office of the City Clerk
510 City-County Building, 414 Grant Street, Pittsburgh, PA 15219
Tel: (412) 255-2138 Fax: (412) 255-2821

○ City Clerk **Mary Beth Doheny** .... (412) 255-2132
E-mail: mary.doheny@pittsburghpa.gov
○ Deputy City Clerk **Kimberly D. Clark-Baskin** .... (412) 255-2138
E-mail: kim.clark@pittsburghpa.gov

Office of the City Controller
City-County Building, 414 Grant Street, Pittsburgh, PA 15219
Tel: (412) 255-2054 Fax: (412) 255-8990

★ Controller **Michael E. Lamb** (D) .... (412) 255-2055
Term Expires: December 31, 2019
E-mail: michael.lamb@pittsburghpa.gov
Education: Penn State BA; Carnegie Mellon MA; Duquesne JD
Deputy Controller **Douglas W. Anderson** .... (412) 255-2055

Innovation and Performance [I&P]
City-County Building, 414 Grant Street, Room 604, Pittsburgh, PA 15219
Fax: (412) 255-2355

■ Chief and Director **Debra Lam** .... (412) 255-2152
E-mail: debra.lam@pittsburghpa.gov
Deputy Director **Sylvia Harris** .... (412) 255-2152
E-mail: sylvia.harris@pittsburghpa.gov
Deputy Director **James Sloss** .... (412) 255-2152

Department of City Planning
John P. Robin Civic Bldg., 200 Ross St., 4th Floor, Pittsburgh, PA 15219
Fax: (412) 255-2838

■ Planning Director **Raymond Gastil** .... (412) 255-2201
E-mail: ray.gastil@pittsburghpa.gov

★ Elected Official ▲ Appointed by Legislature ▼ Appointed by Governor ► Appointed by Board or Commission ● Appointed by Judge
■ Appointed by Mayor △ Appointed by Freeholders ▽ Appointed by Supervisor ▷ Appointed by County Executive ○ Appointed by Council

Department of City Planning *continued*

Assistant Director for Community Development
Michael Petrucci . . . . . (412) 255-2211
E-mail: mike.petrucci@pittsburghpa.gov
Assistant Director for Development and Design
Andrew Dash . . . . . (412) 255-2256
E-mail: andrew.dash@pittsburghpa.gov

Zoning Board of Adjustment

Zoning Administrator **Corey Layman** . . . . . (412) 255-2241

Finance Department

City-County Bldg., 414 Grant Street, Pittsburgh, PA 15219
Tel: (412) 255-2825 Fax: (412) 255-8649

Director of Finance **Paul Leger** . . . . . (412) 255-2825
Treasurer **Margaret L. Lanier** . . . . . (412) 255-2954
Assistant Treasurer **(Vacant)** . . . . . (412) 255-8664
Assistant Director **(Vacant)** . . . . . (412) 255-2899

Housing Authority of the City of Pittsburgh

John P. Robin Civic Bldg., 200 Ross St., Pittsburgh, PA 15219
Tel: (412) 456-5000 Fax: (412) 456-5068 Internet: www.hacp.org/

Executive Director **Caster D. Binion** . . . . . (412) 456-5012
Chief Community Affairs and Resident Relations Officer
Michelle Jackson . . . . . (412) 456-5058
E-mail: washingm@hacp.org
Chief Administrative Officer **Yasmin Shaheed** . . . . . (412) 456-5012
Chief Operating Officer **David Weber** . . . . . (412) 456-5020
E-mail: david.weber@hacp.org
Chief Financial Officer **Ber McGinley** . . . . . (412) 456-5022
Development and Modernization Director **Nate Boe** . . . . . (412) 456-5020
Director, Real Estate Asset Management
Michelle Ralston . . . . . (412) 456-5075
Real Estate Manager **Frank O'Leary** . . . . . (412) 456-5075
Public Safety **Joy Pekar-Miller** . . . . . (412) 456-5058
Section 8 Director **Heather Gaines** . . . . . (412) 456-4090
Human Resources Director **Steven Leonard** . . . . . (412) 456-5085
E-mail: steven.leonard@hacp.org
General Counsel **James Harris** . . . . . (412) 456-5015

Law Department

313 City-County Bldg., 414 Grant St., Pittsburgh, PA 15219
Tel: (412) 255-2015 Fax: (412) 255-2285

■ City Solicitor **Lourdes Sanchez-Ridge** . . . . . (412) 255-2010
E-mail: lourdes.sanchezridge@pittsburghpa.gov

Labor Relations Division

Assistant City Solicitor **Stephanie Eggar** . . . . . (412) 255-2004
E-mail: stephanie.eggar@pittsburghpa.gov
Assistant City Solicitor **Wendy Kobee** . . . . . (412) 255-2018
E-mail: wendy.kobee@pittsburghpa.gov
Assistant City Solicitor **Owen Sullivan** . . . . . (412) 255-2011
E-mail: owen.sullivan@pittsburghpa.gov

Office of Municipal Investigations [OMI]

City County Building, 414 Grant Street, Room 901, Pittsburgh, PA 15219
Fax: (412) 255-2952

Director **Deborah Walker** . . . . . (412) 255-2804

Pittsburgh Parking Authority

232 Blvd. of the Allies, Pittsburgh, PA 15222-1616
Fax: (412) 560-7200 Internet: http://www.pittsburghparking.com/

Executive Director **David G. Onorato** . . . . . (412) 560-2511
Administration and Pittsburgh Parking Court Director
Anthony Boule . . . . . (412) 560-2514
E-mail: aboule@pittsburghparking.com
Project Management Director **Chris Holt** . . . . . (412) 560-2523
Meter Services Director **Wes Pollard** . . . . . (412) 560-2557
E-mail: wpollard@pittsburghparking.com

Pittsburgh Parking Authority *continued*

Finance Director **Jo-Ann Williams** . . . . . (412) 560-2541
Parking Services Director **Christopher Speers** . . . . . (412) 560-2558
Director of Enforcement and Parking Court
Judi DeVito . . . . . (412) 560-2550

Parks and Recreation Department

City-County Building, 414 Grant St., Room 459, Pittsburgh, PA 15219
Tel: (412) 255-2362 Fax: (412) 255-2368
Internet: http://pittsburghpa.gov/citiparks/

■ Director **Jim Griffin** . . . . . (412) 255-2362
E-mail: jim.griffin@pittsburghpa.gov
Deputy Director **Jamie Beechey** . . . . . (412) 255-2372

Personnel Department and Civil Service Commission

City-County Bldg., 414 Grant St., Suite 431, Pittsburgh, PA 15219
Fax: (412) 255-4736 Internet: http://pittsburghpa.gov/personnel/

■ Director **Todd C. Siegel** . . . . . (412) 255-2717
E-mail: todd.siegel@pittsburghpa.gov
Assistant Director, Employee Compensation
Michele Burch . . . . . (412) 255-8887
E-mail: michele.burch@pittsburghpa.gov
Assistant Director, Pittsburgh Partnership
Ross Chapman . . . . . (412) 255-0716
E-mail: ross.chapman@pittsburghpa.gov
Employment Manager **Paula Kellerman** . . . . . (412) 255-2042
E-mail: paula.kellerman@pittsburghpa.gov
Assistant Director, Employment and Training/Chief
Examiner **Jenifer Matson** . . . . . (412) 255-2384
E-mail: jenifer.Matson@pittsburghpa.gov

Public Safety Department

414 Grant St., Pittsburgh, PA 15219

■ Director of Public Safety **Wendell Hissrich** . . . . . (412) 255-8615
Deputy Director of Public Safety **Michael "Mike" Huss** . . (412) 255-8615
Education: Point Park Col BA; Carnegie Mellon MA
Public Information Officer **Sonya Toler** . . . . . (412) 255-2626
E-mail: sonya.toler@pittsburghpa.gov

Animal Control Bureau

Animal Control Supervisor **Taylor Sumansky** . . . . . (412) 255-2036

Building Inspection Bureau

200 Ross Street, 3rd Floor, Pittsburgh, PA 15219
Fax: (412) 255-2974

■ Chief **Maura Kennedy** . . . . . (412) 255-2179
E-mail: maura.kennedy@pittsburghpa.gov

Emergency Medical Services Bureau

700 Filbert St., Pittsburgh, PA 15232
Tel: (412) 622-6930 Fax: (412) 622-6941

Chief **Mark A. Bocian** . . . . . (412) 622-6932

Fire Bureau

200 Ross St., Fifth Floor, Pittsburgh, PA 15219
Tel: (412) 255-2860 Fax: (412) 255-8839

■ Fire Chief **Darryl E. Jones** . . . . . (412) 255-2860
E-mail: darryl.jones@pittsburghpa.gov
Education: Carlow Col BS; Carnegie Mellon MPM
Deputy Chief, Fire Prevention **(Vacant)** . . . . . (412) 255-2822
Assistant Chief **Thomas Cook** . . . . . (412) 255-2860
E-mail: thomas.cook@pittsburghpa.gov

Police Headquarters

1203 Western Avenue, Pittsburgh, PA 15233
Tel: (412) 323-7800 Fax: (412) 323-7820

■ Chief of Police **Cameron McLay** . . . . . (412) 323-7814
E-mail: cameron.mclay@pittsburghpa.gov

★ Elected Official ▲ Appointed by Legislature ▼ Appointed by Governor ▶ Appointed by Board or Commission ● Appointed by Judge
■ Appointed by Mayor △ Appointed by Freeholders ▽ Appointed by Supervisor ▷ Appointed by County Executive ○ Appointed by Council

Pittsburgh Water and Sewer Authority

1200 Penn Avenue, Pittsburgh, PA 15222
Tel: (412) 255-8800 Fax: (412) 255-2475 Internet: http://www.pgh2o.com

■ Chairman **Alex W. Thomson** .... (412) 255-8937
■ Vice Chairman **Margaret L. Lanier** .... (412) 255-8937
■ Secretary **Caren Glotfelty** .... (412) 255-8937
Education: U Pacific BA; Pennsylvania 1973 MRP
■ Treasurer **Paul Leger** .... (412) 255-8937
■ Board Member **Andrea Geraghty** .... (412) 255-8937
■ Board Member **Deborah "Deb" Gross** (D) .... (412) 255-8937
■ Board Member **Michael Weber** .... (412) 255-8937

Administration

Fax: (412) 393-0522

Executive Director (Interim) **David Donahoe** .... (412) 255-8937
Director of Engineering **Robert Christian** .... (412) 255-2579
Director of Finance **Kent Lindsay** .... (412) 255-8943
Director of Field Services (Acting) **Rick Obermeier** ..... (412) 255-8938
Manager of External Affairs **Brendan Schubert** .... (412) 255-2099
E-mail: BSchubert@pgh2o.com
Solicitor **Mark F. Nowak** .... (412) 255-8937
Education: Franklin & Marshall 1979 BA; Emory 1982 JD

Public Works Department

301 City County Building, 414 Grant Street, Pittsburgh, PA 15219
Fax: (412) 255-8847 Internet: http://pittsburghpa.gov/dpw/

■ Director **Michael Gable** .... (412) 255-2726

Environmental Services Bureau

3001 Railroad St., Pittsburgh, PA 15201
Fax: (412) 255-2452

Assistant Director **William Klimovich** .... (412) 255-2778
Recycling Supervisor **Kyle Winkler** .... (412) 255-2345

Transportation and Engineering Bureau

301 City-County Building, 414 Grant Street, Pittsburgh, PA 15219-2455
Tel: (412) 255-8850 Fax: (412) 255-8847

Assistant Director **Patrick Hassett** .... (412) 255-2883
E-mail: patrick.hassett@pittsburghpa.gov

Bureau of Operations

Superintendent-Streets **William Crean** .... (412) 255-0923
611 Second Avenue, Pittsburgh, PA 15219
Superintendent-Parks **Tom Paulin** .... (412) 255-2594
301 City-County Bullding, 414 Grant St., Pittsburgh, PA 15219

Urban Redevelopment Authority of Pittsburgh [URA]

John P. Robin Civic Bldg., 200 Ross St., Pittsburgh, PA 15219
Tel: (412) 255-6600 Fax: (412) 255-6617 Internet: http://www.ura.org

Executive Director (Acting) **Robert Rubinstein** .... (412) 255-6663
E-mail: rrubinstein@ura.org Fax: (412) 255-6617
MBE/WBE Development Director **(Vacant)** .... (412) 255-6611
Fax: (412) 255-6617
Finance Director **Thomas Short** .... (412) 255-6675
Fax: (412) 255-6661
Center for Innovation and Entrepreneurship Director
Thomas Link .... (412) 255-6540
E-mail: tlink@ura.org Fax: (412) 255-6542
Engineering and Construction Director
Martin R. Kaminski .... (412) 255-6648
E-mail: mkaminski@ura.org Fax: (412) 255-6678
Housing Director **Thomas E. Cummings** .... (412) 255-6670
Fax: (412) 255-6645
Real Estate Director **Kyra Straussman** .... (412) 255-6418
Fax: (412) 255-6645
General Counsel **(Vacant)** .... (412) 255-6655
Fax: (412) 255-6617

Pittsburgh Public Schools

341 S. Bellefield Ave., Pittsburgh, PA 15213
Fax: (412) 622-3624 Internet: http://www.pps.k12.pa.us

▶ Superintendent of Schools **Linda Lane** .... (412) 622-3600
Note: Retiring June 30, 2016 Fax: (412) 622-3604
E-mail: superintendentoffice@pghboe.net
Education: Iowa BA; Drake MSE, EdD
▶ Superintendent of Schools **Dr. Anthony Hamlet** .... (412) 622-3600
Note: Effective July 1, 2016
Education: Miami 1992 BS
Webmaster **Christina DiLorenzo** .... (412) 622-3619
E-mail: christina.dilorenzo@pps.k12.pa.us Fax: (412) 622-3624
■ School Board President **Regina Holley** (D-District 2) .... (412) 622-3770
Term Expires: December 7, 2019
E-mail: boardoffice@pghboe.net
★ First Vice President **Sylvia C. Wilson** (D-District 1) ..... (412) 622-3770
Term Expires: December 2, 2017
★ School Board Member
Thomas H. Sumpter, Jr. (D-District 3) .... (412) 622-3770
Term Expires: December 2, 2017
E-mail: boardoffice@pghboe.net
★ School Board Member **Lynda Wrenn** (D-District 4) ..... (412) 622-3770
Term Expires: December 7, 2019
★ School Board Member **Terry Kennedy** (District 5) .... (412) 622-3770
Term Expires: December 2, 2017
★ School Board Member **Moira Kaleida** (D-District 6) ..... (412) 622-3770
Term Expires: December 7, 2019
★ School Board Member
Cynthia Ann Falls (D-District 7) .... (412) 622-3770
Term Expires: December 2, 2017
★ School Board Member **Kevin L. Carter** (D-District 8) .... (412) 622-3770
Term Expires: December 7, 2019
★ School Board Member **Carolyn Klug** (D-District 9) ...... (412) 622-3770
Term Expires: December 2, 2017

City of Plano, Texas

1520 K Avenue, Plano, TX 75074
P.O. Box 860358, Plano, TX 75086-0358
TTY: (972) 941-7000 (Information) TTY: (972) 941-7000 ext. 5600
Fax: (972) 423-9587 Internet: www.plano.gov

County: Collin **Election Type:** Nonpartisan **Population:** 283,558 (2015)

Office of the Mayor and City Council

P.O. Box 860358, Plano, TX 75086-0358
Fax: (972) 423-9587

★ Mayor **Harry LaRosiliere** (District 6) .... (972) 941-7107
Began Service: May 20, 2013
Term Expires: May 13, 2017
E-mail: mayor@plano.gov
Assistant to the Mayor and City Council
Dee Dee Falls .... (972) 941-7747
E-mail: deedee@plano.gov
★ Council Member **Angela Miner** (Place 1) .... (972) 941-7107
Term Expires: May 20, 2019
E-mail: angelaminer@plano.gov
★ Council Member **Ben Harris** (Place 2) .... (972) 941-7107
Term Expires: May 13, 2017
E-mail: benharris@plano.gov
Education: Texas BA
★ Council Member **Rick Grady** (Place 3) .... (972) 941-7107
Term Expires: May 20, 2019
E-mail: rickgrady@plano.gov
★ Council Member **Lissa Smith** (Place 4) .... (972) 941-7107
Term Expires: May 13, 2017
E-mail: lissasmith@plano.gov
★ Council Member **Ron Kelley** (Place 5) .... (972) 941-7107
Term Expires: May 20, 2019
E-mail: ronkelley@plano.gov

★ Elected Official ▲ Appointed by Legislature ▼ Appointed by Governor ▶ Appointed by Board or Commission ● Appointed by Judge
■ Appointed by Mayor △ Appointed by Freeholders ▽ Appointed by Supervisor ▷ Appointed by County Executive ○ Appointed by Council

Office of the Mayor and City Council *continued*

★Council Member **Tom Harrison** (Place 7) .... (972) 941-7107
Term Expires: May 20, 2019
E-mail: tomharrison@plano.gov

★Council Member **David Downs** (Place 8) .... (972) 941-7107
Term Expires: May 2017
E-mail: daviddowns@plano.gov

Office of the City Attorney

P.O. Box 860358, Plano, TX 75086-0358
Fax: (972) 424-0099

○City Attorney **Paige Mims** .... (972) 941-7125
E-mail: paigem@plano.gov

Office of the City Manager

P.O. Box 860358, Plano, TX 75086-0358
Tel: (972) 941-7121 Fax: (972) 423-9587

○City Manager **Bruce Glasscock** .... (972) 941-7121
E-mail: bruceg@plano.gov
Education: Metro State Col Denver BA; Colorado MPA
Executive Assistant **Cindy Pierce** .... (972) 941-7121
E-mail: cindyp@plano.gov

Deputy City Manager **Jim D. Parrish** .... (972) 941-7107
E-mail: jimpa@plano.gov

Deputy City Manager **LaShon D. Ross** .... (972) 941-7122
E-mail: lashonr@plano.gov

Deputy City Manager **Jack Carr** .... (972) 941-7122
E-mail: jackc@plano.gov

Assistant City Manager **Mark Israelson** .... (972) 941-5112
E-mail: marki@plano.gov

Office of the City Secretary

P.O. Box 860358, Plano, TX 75086-0358
Fax: (972) 423-9587

City Secretary **Lisa Henderson** .... (972) 941-7120
E-mail: lisah@plano.gov

Building Inspection

P.O. Box 860358, Plano, TX 75086-0358

Chief Building Official **Selso Mata** .... (972) 941-7212
E-mail: selsom@plano.gov

Customer and Utility Services

P.O. Box 860358, Plano, TX 75086-0358
Tel: (972) 941-7105 Fax: (972) 941-7441

Customer and Utility Services Director
Stephanie Foster .... (972) 941-7105

Engineering Department

P.O. Box 860358, Plano, TX 75086-0358

Director **B. Caleb Thornhill** .... (972) 941-7152
E-mail: calebt@plano.gov

Environmental Health Department

P.O. Box 860358, Plano, TX 75086-0358

Director **Rachel Patterson** .... (972) 941-7143
Fax: (972) 941-7142

Finance Department

1520 K Avenue, Suite 370, Plano, TX 75074
Tel: (972) 941-7479

Finance Director **Denise Tacke** .... (972) 941-7479

Fire-Rescue Department

P.O. Box 860358, Plano, TX 75086-0358

Fire Chief **Sam Greif** .... (972) 941-7159
E-mail: samg@plano.gov

Fire Marshal **David Kerr** .... (972) 941-7427
E-mail: davidk@plano.gov

Human Resources Department

P.O. Box 860358, Plano, TX 75086-0358

Director of Human Resources **Shante' Akafia** .... (972) 941-7115
E-mail: shantea@plano.gov

Library

2401 Coit Road, Plano, TX 75075

Director **Cathy Ziegler** .... (972) 769-4208
E-mail: cathyz@plano.gov

Marketing and Community Engagement Department

1520 K Avenue, Suite 220, Plano, TX 75074
Tel: (972) 941-7324

Director **Shannah Hayley** .... (972) 941-7324
E-mail: Shannah@plano.gov
Education: Missouri State U MA

Parks and Recreation Department

P.O. Box 860358, Plano, TX 75086-0358
Tel: (972) 941-7255

Director **Amy Fortenberry** .... (972) 941-7255

Planning Department

P.O. Box 860358, Plano, TX 75086-0358

Planning Director **Christina Day** .... (972) 941-7151

Police Department

P.O. Box 860358, Plano, TX 75086-0358
Tel: (972) 941-2135

Chief of Police **Gregory W. Rushin** .... (972) 941-2410

Public Works Department

P.O. Box 860358, Plano, TX 75086-0358

Director **Gerald Cosgrove** .... (972) 769-4264

Public Works Operations Manager **David Falls** .... (972) 769-4141
E-mail: davidf@plano.gov

Sustainability Director **Robert Smouse** .... (972) 769-4199

Purchasing

P.O. Box 860358, Plano, TX 75086-0358
Tel: (972) 941-7557

Chief Purchasing Officer **Diane Palmer-Boeck** .... (972) 941-7557
E-mail: purchasing@plano.gov

Technology Services Department

P.O. Box 860358, Plano, TX 75086-0358

Director (Acting) **Carlos Oregon** .... (972) 941-7342
E-mail: carloso@plano.gov

★Elected Official ▲Appointed by Legislature ▼Appointed by Governor ▶Appointed by Board or Commission ●Appointed by Judge
■Appointed by Mayor △Appointed by Freeholders ▽Appointed by Supervisor ▷Appointed by County Executive ○Appointed by Council

CITIES AND TOWNS

City of Pomona, California

505 S. Garey Ave., Pomona, CA 91766
P.O. Box 660, Pomona, CA 91769
Internet: http://www.ci.pomona.ca.us/

County: Los Angeles **Election Type:** Nonpartisan **Population:** 153,266 (2015)

Office of the Mayor and City Council

505 S. Garey Ave., Pomona, CA 91766
P.O. Box 660, Pomona, CA 91769
Fax: (909) 620-3707

★Mayor **Elliott Rothman** .... (909) 620-2053
Began Service: December 2008
Term Expires: December 2016
E-mail: elliott_rothman@ci.pomona.ca.us

★Vice Mayor **Paula Lantz** (District 4) .... (909) 620-2053
Term Expires: December 2016
E-mail: paula_lantz@ci.pomona.ca.us

★Council Member **John Nolte** (District 1) .... (909) 620-2053
Term Expires: December 2016
E-mail: John_Nolte@ci.pomona.ca.us

★Council Member **Adriana Robledo** (District 2) .... (909) 620-2053
Term Expires: December 2018
E-mail: Adriana_Robledo@ci.pomona.ca.us

★Council Member **Cristina Carrizosa** (District 3) .... (909) 620-2053
Term Expires: December 2018
E-mail: cristina_carrizosa@ci.pomona.ca.us

★Council Member **Debra Martin** (District 6) .... (909) 620-2053
Term Expires: December 2016
E-mail: Debra_Martin@ci.pomona.ca.us

★Council Member **Ginna E. Escobar** (District 5) .... (909) 620-2053
Term Expires: December 2018
E-mail: ginna_escobar@ci.pomona.ca.us

Senior Administrative Assistant **AnnMarie Acosta** .... (909) 620-2376
E-mail: annemarie_acosta@ci.pomona.ca.us

Office of the City Manager

P.O. Box 660, Pomona, CA 91769
Tel: (909) 620-2051 Fax: (909) 620-3707

○City Manager **Linda Lowry** .... (909) 620-3740
E-mail: linda_lowry@ci.pomona.ca.us

Public Information Officer **Mark Gluba** .... (909) 620-2448
E-mail: mark_gluba@ci.pomona.ca.us Fax: (909) 620-3707

Office of the City Clerk

P.O. Box 660, Pomona, CA 91769
Tel: (909) 620-2341 Fax: (909) 620-3710

City Clerk **Eva M. Buice** .... (909) 620-2341
E-mail: eva_buice@ci.pomona.ca.us

Deputy City Clerk **Candice Alvarez** .... (909) 620-2582
E-mail: candice_flom_alvarez@ci.pomona.ca.us

Office of the Treasurer

P.O. Box 660, Pomona, CA 91769
Fax: (909) 620-2432

Treasurer **Paula Chamberlain** .... (909) 620-2406

Community Development Department

P.O. Box 660, Pomona, CA 91769
Fax: (909) 620-3703

Community Development Director **Mark Lazzarretto** .... (909) 620-2421
E-mail: mark_lazzarretto@ci.pomona.ca.us

Housing Manager **Benita DeFrank** .... (909) 620-2094

Planning Manager **Brad Johnson** .... (909) 620-2436

Finance Department

P.O. Box 660, Pomona, CA 91769
Tel: (909) 620-2406 Fax: (909) 620-3711

Director **Paula Chamberlain** .... (909) 620-2406

Purchasing Manager **Keri Hinojos** .... (909) 620-2039
E-mail: keri_hinojos@ci.pomona.ca.us

Human Resources Department

505 S. Garey Ave., Pomona, CA 91766
Tel: (909) 620-2291 Fax: (909) 620-2295

Director **Linda Matthews** .... (909) 620-2491
E-mail: linda_matthews@ci.pomona.ca.us

Library Department

625 S. Garey Ave., Pomona, CA 91769
Tel: (909) 620-2043 Fax: (909) 620-3713

Director **(Vacant)** .... (909) 620-2043

Parks, Recreation, and Community Services

P.O. Box 660, Pomona, CA 91769
Tel: (909) 620-3671 Fax: (909) 620-4471

Director **Mike Osoff** .... (909) 620-2321
E-mail: mike_osoff@ci.pomona.ca.us

Police Department

P.O. Box 660, Pomona, CA 91769
Tel: (909) 620-2155

Chief of Police **Paul J. Capraro** .... (909) 620-2141

Public Works Department

P.O. Box 660, Pomona, CA 91769
Tel: (909) 620-2261 Fax: (909) 620-2269

Public Works Director **Rene Salas** .... (909) 620-2261

Utility Services

P.O. Box 660, Pomona, CA 91769
Tel: (909) 620-2173 Fax: (909) 620-2030

Director **(Vacant)** .... (909) 620-2283

Water/Waste Water Operations Director **Darron Poulson** .. (909) 620-2253
E-mail: darron_poulson@ci.pomona.ca.us

Equipment Superintendent **Albert Salcido** .... (909) 620-2361

City of Pompano Beach, Florida

100 West Atlantic Boulevard, Pompano Beach, FL 33060
Tel: (954) 786-4600 Internet: http://pompanobeachfl.gov/

County: Broward **Election Type:** Nonpartisan **Year Incorporated:** 1947 **Population:** 107,762 (2015)

Office of the Mayor and City Commission

100 West Atlantic Boulevard, Pompano Beach, FL 33060
Tel: (954) 786-4601 Fax: (954) 786-4504

★Mayor **Lamar Fisher** (At-Large) .... (954) 786-4623
Term Expires: November 2016
E-mail: lamar.fisher@copbfl.com

★Vice Mayor **Charlotte Burrie** (District 2) .... (954) 786-4625
Term Expires: November 4, 2016
E-mail: charlotte.burrie@copbfl.com

★Commissioner **Barry Dockswell** (District 1) .... (954) 786-4619
Term Expires: November 4, 2016
E-mail: barry.dockswell@copbfl.com

★Elected Official ▲Appointed by Legislature ▼Appointed by Governor ►Appointed by Board or Commission ●Appointed by Judge
■Appointed by Mayor △Appointed by Freeholders ▽Appointed by Supervisor ▷Appointed by County Executive ○Appointed by Council

Office of the Mayor and City Commission *continued*

★Commissioner **Rex Hardin** (District 3) .... (954) 786-4649
Term Expires: November 4, 2016
E-mail: rex.hardin@copbfl.com

★Commissioner **Edward Phillips** (District 4) .... (954) 786-4624
Term Expires: November 4, 2016
E-mail: ed.phillips@copbfl.com

★Commissioner **Barry Moss** (District 5) .... (954) 786-4618
Term Expires: November 4, 2016
E-mail: barry.moss@copbfl.com

Office of the City Manager

100 West Atlantic Boulevard, 4th Floor, Pompano Beach, FL 33060
Fax: (954) 786-4504

○City Manager **Dennis Beach** .... (954) 786-4601
E-mail: dennis.beach@copbfl.com

Assistant City Manager **Greg Harrison** .... (954) 786-4601
E-mail: greg.harrison@copbfl.com
Education: Northeastern State BS; Oklahoma MPA

Assistant City Manager **Phyllis Korab** .... (954) 786-4601
E-mail: phyllis.korab@copbfl.com

Deputy City Manager **Brian Donovan** .... (954) 786-4601

Public Communications Director **Sandra King** .... (954) 786-4527
E-mail: sandra.king@copbfl.com

Office of the City Attorney

100 West Atlantic Boulevard, Pompano Beach, FL 33060
Fax: (954) 786-4617

City Attorney **Mark Berman** .... (954) 786-4614

Assistant City Attorney **Carrie Sarver** .... (954) 786-4614

Office of the City Clerk

100 West Atlantic Boulevard, Second Floor, Pompano Beach, FL 33060
Fax: (954) 786-4095

City Clerk **Asceleta Hammond** .... (954) 786-4611
E-mail: asceleta.hammond@copbfl.com

Deputy City Clerk **Kevin Alfred** .... (954) 786-4611
E-mail: kervin.alfred@copbfl.com

Finance Department

100 West Atlantic Boulevard, Pompano Beach, FL 33060
Fax: (954) 786-4687

Director **Suzette Sibble** .... (954) 786-4680

Development Services Department

100 West Atlantic Boulevard, Third Floor, Pompano Beach, FL 33060
Fax: (954) 786-4666

Director **Robin Bird** .... (954) 786-4634

Assistant Director **Jennifer Gomez** .... (954) 786-4640
Fax: (954) 786-4044

Principal Planner **Paola West** .... (954) 786-7780
Fax: (954) 786-4044

Building Inspection Division

100 West Atlantic Boulevard, Suite 360, Pompano Beach, FL 33060
Fax: (954) 786-4677

Building Official **Miguel Nunez** .... (954) 786-7774

Fire Department

120 SW 3rd Street, Pompano Beach, FL 33060
Fax: (954) 786-4510

Fire Chief **John Jurgle** .... (954) 786-4327
E-mail: john.jurgle@copbfl.com

Human Resources Department

100 West Atlantic Boulevard, First Floor, Pompano Beach, FL 33060
Fax: (954) 786-5553

Human Resources Director **Michael Smith** .... (954) 786-4626
E-mail: michael.smith@copbfl.com

Senior Analyst **Bobby Bush** .... (954) 786-4626
E-mail: bobby.bush@copbfl.com

Information Technologies Department

100 West Atlantic Boulevard, Pompano Beach, FL 33060
Fax: (954) 786-4532

Information Technologies Director **Eugene Zamoski** ..... (954) 786-4530
E-mail: eugene.zamoski@copbfl.com

Internal Auditing

100 West Atlantic Boulevard, Pompano Beach, FL 33060
Fax: (954) 786-5550

Internal Auditor **Barbara Deleon** .... (954) 786-4689

Parks and Recreation Department

1801 NE 6 Street, Pompano Beach, FL 33060
Fax: (954) 786-4113

Recreation Programs Administrator **Mark Beaudreau** .... (954) 786-4111

Public Works Department

1201 NE 5 Avenue, Pompano Beach, FL 33060
Fax: (954) 786-4028

Director **Robert McCaughan** .... (954) 786-4061

Streets/Grounds Maintenance Division

1190 NE 3 Avenue, Pompano Beach, FL 33060
Fax: (954) 786-4011

Superintendent **Michael Carter** .... (954) 786-4107

Building Maintenance Division

1190 NE 3 Avenue, Pompano Beach, FL 33060
Fax: (954) 786-4014

Superintendent **Roger Palermo** .... (954) 786-4108
E-mail: roger.palermo@copbfl.com

Pompano Beach Cemetery

400 SE 23 Avenue, Pompano Beach, FL 33062
Fax: (954) 784-4937

Supervisor **Terrance Nelson, Jr.** .... (954) 786-4138

Engineering Division

1201 NE 5 Avenue, Pompano Beach, FL 33060
Fax: (954) 786-4028

City Engineer **Alessandra Delfico** .... (954) 786-4144
E-mail: alessandra.delfico@copbfl.com

Utilities Department

1205 NE 5 Avenue, Pompano Beach, FL 33060
Fax: (954) 545-7046

Director **Randolph Brown** .... (954) 545-7044

★ Elected Official ▲ Appointed by Legislature ▼ Appointed by Governor ► Appointed by Board or Commission ● Appointed by Judge
■ Appointed by Mayor △ Appointed by Freeholders ▽ Appointed by Supervisor ▷ Appointed by County Executive ○ Appointed by Council

City of Port St. Lucie, Florida

City Hall, 121 S.W. Port St. Lucie Boulevard, Port St. Lucie, FL 34984
Internet: www.cityofpsl.com

County: St. Lucie **Election Type:** Nonpartisan **Population:** 179,413 (2015)

Office of the Mayor and City Council

City Hall, 121 S.W. Port St. Lucie Boulevard, Port St. Lucie, FL 34984
Fax: (772) 871-7382

★Mayor **Gregory J. Oravec** .... (772) 871-5159
Began Service: November 17, 2014
Term Expires: November 2018
E-mail: mayor@cityofpsl.com

★Vice Mayor **Linda Bartz** (District 1) .... (772) 871-5159
Term Expires: November 2018
E-mail: district1@cityofpsl.com

★Councilwoman **Michelle Berger** (District 2) .... (772) 871-5159
Term Expires: November 2016
E-mail: district2@cityofpsl.com

★Councilwoman **Shannon Martin** (District 3) .... (772) 871-5159
Term Expires: November 2018
E-mail: district3@cityofpsl.com

★Councilman **Ron Bowen** (District 4) .... (772) 871-5159
Term Expires: November 2016
E-mail: district4@cityofpsl.com

Office of the City Manager

City Hall, 121 S.W. Port St. Lucie Boulevard, Port St. Lucie, FL 34984
Tel: (772) 871-5163 (TDD)

City Manager **Jeffrey Bremer** .... (772) 871-5163
E-mail: jbremer@cityofpsl.com

Office of the City Attorney

City Hall, 121 S.W. Port St. Lucie Boulevard, Port St. Lucie, FL 34984

City Attorney (Interim) **John J. Fumero** .... (772) 871-5294
City Attorney (Interim) **Azlina Goldstein Siegel** .... (772) 871-5294
E-mail: asiegel@cityofpsl.com
Assistant City Attorney **Stephanie Beskovoyne** .... (772) 871-5294
Assistant City Attorney **Chris DeLorenzo** .... (772) 871-5294
Staff Attorney **Ella Gilbert** .... (772) 871-5294
Staff Attorney **Keri Norbraten** .... (772) 871-5294

Office of the City Clerk

City Hall, 121 S.W. Port St. Lucie Boulevard, Port St. Lucie, FL 34984
Fax: (772) 871-7325

City Clerk **Karen A. Phillips** .... (772) 871-5157
E-mail: karenp@cityofpsl.com

Animal Control Division

1133 S.W. South Macedo Boulevard, Port St. Lucie, FL 34983

Supervisor **Bryan Lloyd** .... (772) 871-5042
Supervisor **Todd Wallace** .... (772) 871-5042

Building Department

Building B, 121 S.W. Port St. Lucie Boulevard, Port St. Lucie, FL 34984

Building Official **Joel Dramis** .... (772) 871-5132

Civic Center

9221 S.E. Civie Center Place, Port St. Lucie, FL 34952
Tel: (772) 807-4488 Fax: (772) 398-2944

Facility Administrator (Interim) **Sherman Conrad** .... (772) 871-5092
Recreation Manager **Kelly Tiger** .... (772) 807-4467
Administrative Assistant **Diane White** .... (772) 807-4484
E-mail: dwhite@cityofpsl.com

Communications Department

City Hall, 121 S.W. Port St. Lucie Boulevard, Port St. Lucie, FL 34984
Tel: (772) 871-5219 Fax: (772) 344-4111

Communications Director **Ed Cunningham** .... (772) 873-6329
E-mail: ecunningham@cityofpsl.com

Community Redevelopment Agency

City Hall, 121 S.W. Port St. Lucie Boulevard, Port St. Lucie, FL 34984

Assistant City Manager/Community Redevelopment Agency Director **Bridget Kean** .... (772) 873-6489
E-mail: bkean@cityofpsl.com

Community Services Department

City Hall, 121 S.W. Port St. Lucie Boulevard, Port St. Lucie, FL 34984

Director **Patricia Selmer** .... (772) 344-4084
E-mail: pselmer@cityofpsl.com

Emergency Management Department

121 S.W. Port St. Lucie Boulevard, Port St. Lucie, FL 34984

Emergency Management Coordinator **Carmen A. Capezzuto** .... (772) 871-5100
E-mail: ccapezzuto@cityofpsl.com

Finance Department

City Hall, 121 S.W. Port St. Lucie Boulevard, Port St. Lucie, FL 34984
Tel: (772) 344-4390 Fax: (772) 344-4137

Finance Director/Treasurer **Edwin M. Fry, Jr.** .... (772) 344-4390
E-mail: efry@cityofpsl.com

Human Resources Department

City Hall, 121 S.W. Port St. Lucie Boulevard, Port St. Lucie, FL 34984
Fax: (772) 871-5274

Director **Jerome Post** .... (772) 871-5207
E-mail: jpost@cityofpsl.com

Management Information Services Department

City Hall, 121 S.W. Port St. Lucie Boulevard, Port St. Lucie, FL 34984

Director **Bill Jones** .... (772) 344-4339
E-mail: bjones@cityofpsl.com
Assistant Director, MIS **Chris Valure** .... (772) 344-4339
E-mail: cvalure@cityofpsl.com

Office of Management and Budget

City Hall, 121 S.W. Port St. Lucie Boulevard, Port St. Lucie, FL 34984

Director **David K. Pollard** .... (772) 871-7391
E-mail: davep@cityofpsl.com
Senior Management Analyst **Ivy Ladyko** .... (772) 871-5233
E-mail: iladyko@cityofpsl.com
Management Analyst II **Margie Manfredi** .... (772) 344-4383
E-mail: mmanfredi@cityofpsl.com

Parks and Recreation Department

2195 S.E. Airoso Boulevard, Port St. Lucie, FL 34984
Fax: (772) 871-5290

Director **Sherman Conrad** .... (772) 878-2277
Assistant Director **Brad Keen** .... (772) 878-2277
Recreation Administrator **Jay Liss** .... (772) 878-2277
Building Maintenance Administrator **Mark Olsen** .... (772) 878-2277
E-mail: molsen@cityofpsl.com
Golf Course Administrator **Curtis Wichern** .... (772) 878-2277
E-mail: cwichern@cityofpsl.com

★Elected Official ▲Appointed by Legislature ▼Appointed by Governor ►Appointed by Board or Commission ●Appointed by Judge
■Appointed by Mayor △Appointed by Freeholders ▽Appointed by Supervisor ▷Appointed by County Executive ○Appointed by Council

Planning and Zoning Department
City Hall, 121 S.W. Port St. Lucie Boulevard, Port St. Lucie, FL 34984
Fax: (772) 871-5124

Director **Patti Tobin** .... (772) 871-5212
E-mail: ptobin@cityofpsl.com

Police Department
Building C, 121 S.W. Port St. Lucie Boulevard, Port St. Lucie, FL 34984

Chief of Police **John A. Bolduc** .... (772) 871-5000

Public Works Department
City Hall, 121 S.W. Port St. Lucie Boulevard, Port St. Lucie, FL 34984

City Engineer **Jim Angstadt** .... (772) 871-5100
E-mail: jangstadt@cityofpsl.com
Assistant City Engineer **(Vacant)** .... (772) 871-5177

Utility Systems Department
900 S.E. Ogden Lane, Port St. Lucie, FL 34983

Utility Director **Jesus A. Merejo** .... (772) 873-6400

City of Portland, Oregon

City Hall, 1221 SW Fourth Ave., Portland, OR 97204
Tel: (503) 823-4000 (Information)
Internet: http://www.portlandoregon.gov/

County: Multnomah **Election Type:** Nonpartisan **Year Incorporated:** 1851 **Population:** 632,309 (2015) **Employees:** 5,494 **Fiscal Year:** 2016 **Budget:** $3,705,197,000

Office of the Mayor
City Hall, 1221 SW Fourth Avenue, Suite 340, Portland, OR 97204
Tel: (503) 823-4120 Fax: (503) 823-3588

Employees: 18 **Fiscal Year:** 2016 **Budget:** $3,294,000

★ Mayor **Charlie Hales** .... (503) 823-4120
Began Service: January 1, 2013
Term Expires: December 31, 2016
■ Executive Assistant to the Mayor **Susan Dietz** .... (503) 823-1121
E-mail: susan.dietz@portlandoregon.gov
■ Chief of Staff **Josh Alpert** .... (503) 823-4120
E-mail: josh.alpert@portlandoregon.gov
■ Deputy Chief of Staff **Tera Pierce** .... (503) 823-4120
E-mail: tera.pierce@portlandoregon.gov
■ Policy Director **Zach Klonoski** .... (503) 823-4120
E-mail: zach.klonoski@portlandoregon.gov
■ Policy Director **Jillian Detweiler** .... (503) 823-4290
E-mail: jillian.detweiler@portlandoregon.gov
■ Policy Director **Deanna Wesson-Mitchell** .... (503) 823-4125
E-mail: deanna.wesson-mitchell@portlandoregon.gov
■ Constituent Services **Mustafa Washington** .... (503) 823-4120
E-mail: mustafa.washington@portlandoregon.gov
■ Special Assistant to the Mayor **William McMillen** .... (503) 823-4120
E-mail: William.McMillen@portlandoregon.gov
■ Community Outreach Director **Diana Nuñez** .... (503) 823-4120
E-mail: diana.nunez@portlandoregon.gov
■ Communications Director **Sara Hottman** .... (503) 823-4120
E-mail: sara.hottman@portlandoregon.gov
■ Project Management/Policy Assistant **Chad Stover** .... (503) 823-4120
E-mail: chad.stover@portlandoregon.gov
■ Policy Advisor **Camille Trummer** .... (503) 823-4120
■ Council and Special Appropriations Grant Manager
Rachael Wiggins .... (503) 823-4120
E-mail: rachael.wiggins@portlandoregon.gov

Office of Youth Violence Prevention
City Hall, 1221 SW Fourth Avenue, Portland, OR 97204

■ Director **Antoinette Edwards** .... (503) 823-3584
E-mail: antoinette.edwards@portlandoregon.gov

Office of the City Council
City Hall, 1221 SW Fourth Ave., Portland, OR 97204

★ Council President/Commissioner of Public Utilities
Amanda Fritz (Position 1) .... (503) 823-3008
Term Expires: December 31, 2016 Fax: (503) 823-3017
Chief of Staff **Tim Crail** .... (503) 823-3990
E-mail: tim.crail@portlandoregon.gov
★ Council Member/Commissioner of Public Works
Nick Fish (Position 2) .... (503) 823-3589
Term Expires: December 31, 2018 Fax: (503) 823-3596
Chief of Staff **Sonia Schmanski** .... (503) 823-3599
Fax: (503) 823-3596
★ Council Member/Commissioner of Public Affairs
Daniel R. "Dan" Saltzman (Position 3) .... (503) 823-4151
Term Expires: December 31, 2018 Fax: (503) 823-3036
E-mail: dan@portlandoregon.gov
Education: Cornell 1977 BS; MIT MS
Chief of Staff **Brendan Finn** .... (503) 823-4151
Education: SUNY (Buffalo) BSBA; Portland State MURP
★ Council Member/Commissioner of Public Safety
Steve Novick (Position 4) .... (503) 823-4682
Term Expires: December 31, 2016 Fax: (503) 823-4019
Chief of Staff **Chris Warner** .... (503) 823-4682
E-mail: chris.warner@portlandoregon.gov

Office of the City Attorney
City Hall, 1221 SW Fourth Avenue, Suite 430, Portland, OR 97204
Fax: (503) 823-3089

Employees: 63 **Fiscal Year:** 2016 **Budget:** $11,800,000

City Attorney **Tracy Reeve** .... (503) 823-4047
E-mail: tracy.reeve@portlandoregon.gov
Chief Deputy City Attorney **Mark Amberg** .... (503) 823-4047
Chief Deputy City Attorney **Harry Auerbach** .... (503) 823-4047
E-mail: harry.auerbach@portlandoregon.gov
Chief Deputy City Attorney **Kathryn Beaumont** .... (503) 823-4047
Chief Deputy City Attorney **Scott Moede** .... (503) 823-4047
Chief Deputy City Attorney **Ben Walters** .... (503) 823-4047
Office Manager **Kim Sneath** .... (503) 823-4047
E-mail: kim.sneath@portlandoregon.gov

Bureau of Emergency Management [BEM]
9911 SE Bush Street, Portland, OR 97266
Fax: (503) 823-3903 Internet: www.portlandonline.com/bem/

Employees: 131 **Fiscal Year:** 2016 **Budget:** $5,750,000

Director **Carmen Merlo** .... (503) 823-4375
E-mail: carmen.merlo@portlandoregon.gov
Education: SUNY (Albany) BA, MA
Public Information Officer **Dan Douthit** .... (503) 823-3928
E-mail: dan.douthit@portlandoregon.gov

Office for Community Technology
111 SW Columbia Street, Portland, OR 97201
Fax: (503) 823-5370

Manager **Mary Beth Henry** .... (503) 823-5385 ext. 7
E-mail: marybeth.henry@portlandoregon.gov

★ Elected Official ▲ Appointed by Legislature ▼ Appointed by Governor ► Appointed by Board or Commission ● Appointed by Judge
■ Appointed by Mayor △ Appointed by Freeholders ▽ Appointed by Supervisor ▷ Appointed by County Executive ○ Appointed by Council

Office of Government Relations

City Hall, 1221 SW Fourth Avenue, Room 410, Portland, OR 97204
Tel: (503) 823-4130 Fax: (503) 823-3014
E-mail: govrel@portlandoregon.gov

Employees: 9 **Fiscal Year:** 2016 **Budget:** $1,567,000

■ Director **Martha Pellegrino** .... (503) 823-4130
E-mail: Martha.pellegrino@portlandoregon.gov
Education: Oregon 2005 JD

Office of Management and Finance [OMF]

Portland Bldg., 1120 SW Fifth Avenue, Room 1250, Portland, OR 97204
Tel: (503) 823-5288 Fax: (503) 823-5384

Employees: 620 **Fiscal Year:** 2016 **Budget:** $467,599,000

■ Chief Administrative Officer **Fred Miller** .... (503) 823-1182
E-mail: fred.miller@portlandoregon.gov
Senior Business Operations Manager **Jane Braaten** ...... (503) 823-5665
E-mail: jane.braaten@portlandoregon.gov
Enterprise Business Solution Manager **Satish Hath** ...... (503) 823-7459
Senior Policy Analyst **Betsy Ames** .... (503) 823-4269

Bureau of Financial Services

1120 SW Fifth Avenue, Room 1250, Portland, OR 97204

Director **Kenneth L. Rust** .... (503) 823-5288
City Treasurer **Jennifer Cooperman** .... (503) 823-6851
City Economist **Josh Harwood** .... (503) 823-6954
Debt Manager **(Vacant)** .... (503) 823-4222
City Controller **Michelle Kirby** .... (503) 823-4358

Human Resources Bureau

1120 SW Fifth Avenue, Suite 404, Portland, OR 97204
Tel: (503) 823-3572 Fax: (503) 823-4156

Director **Anna Kanwit** .... (503) 823-3506
E-mail: anna.kanwit@portlandoregon.gov
Assistant Human Resources Director **David Rhys** .... (503) 823-5219
E-mail: david.rhys@portlandoregon.gov
Benefits/Wellness Manager **Cathy Bless** .... (503) 823-5207
E-mail: cathy.bless@portlandoregon.gov
Diversity, Outreach, and Employment Resources Manager **Lynda Lewis** .... (503) 823-3514
E-mail: lynda.lewis@portlandoregon.gov
Classification/Compensation Manager **Elizabeth Nunes** .. (503) 823-3507
Human Resources and Payroll Services System Manager **Tom Schneider** .... (503) 823-7138
E-mail: tom.schneider@portlandoregon.gov
Labor Relations Manager **Jarrell Gaddis** .... (503) 823-4170
E-mail: jarrell.gaddis@portlandoregon.gov

Internal Business Services Bureau

Portland Bldg., 1120 SW Fifth Avenue, Room 1250, Portland, OR 97204-1912
Tel: (503) 823-5288 Fax: (503) 823-5384

Director **Bryant Enge** .... (503) 823-6962
Education: Eastern Oregon State 1984 BS; Oregon 2000 MS
Facilities Manager **(Vacant)** .... (503) 823-2039
Printing and Distribution Services Manager **Matthew Spitulski** .... (503) 823-4449
124 SW Madison, Portland, OR 97204-3204
E-mail: matthew.spitulski@portlandoregon.gov
Risk Manager **Kate Wood** .... (503) 823-5277
E-mail: kate.wood@portlandoregon.gov
CityFleet Manager **John Hunt** .... (503) 823-4302
2835 N. Kerby, Portland, OR 97227-1610
Spectator Facilities Manager **Susan Gibson-Hartnett** .... (503) 823-6958
E-mail: susan.gibson-hartnett@portlandoregon.gov
Chief Procurement Officer **Christine Moody** .... (503) 823-1095

Revenue Division

111 SW Columbia Street, Suite 600, Portland, OR 97201
Tel: (503) 823-5157 Fax: (503) 823-5192

Director **Thomas Lannom** .... (503) 823-5154
E-mail: thomas.lannom@portlandoregon.gov

Revenue Division *continued*

License and Tax Division Manager **Terri Williams** .... (503) 865-2469
E-mail: terri.williams@portlandoregon.gov
Regulatory Program Administrator **Anne Holm** .... (503) 865-2488
Business Solutions Division Manager **Julie Shervey** ..... (503) 823-4973

Bureau of Technology Services

1120 SW Fifth Avenue, Suite 450, Portland, OR 97204

Chief Technology Officer **Jeffrey B. "Jeff" Baer** .... (503) 823-5198

Office of Neighborhood Involvement [ONI]

City Hall, 1221 SW Fourth Avenue, Suite 110, Portland, OR 97204
Tel: (503) 823-4519 Fax: (503) 823-3050

Employees: 43 **Fiscal Year:** 2016 **Budget:** $9,096,000

Director **Amalia Alarcon de Morris** .... (503) 823-4134
E-mail: amalia.morris@portlandoregon.gov
Neighborhood Resource Center Program Manager **Brian Hoop** .... (503) 823-3075
E-mail: brian.hoop@portlandoregon.gov
Crime Prevention Program Director **Stephanie Reynolds** .... (503) 823-2030
E-mail: stephanie.reynolds@portlandoregon.gov Fax: (503) 823-3050

Bureau of Development Services

1900 SW 4th Avenue, Suite 5000, Portland, OR 97201
Tel: (503) 823-7300 Fax: (503) 823-7250

Employees: 253 **Fiscal Year:** 2016 **Budget:** $66,674,000

Director **Paul L. Scarlett** .... (503) 823-7308
Director's Executive Assistant **Leanne Torgerson** ...... (503) 823-7937
E-mail: leanne.torgerson@portlandoregon.gov
Customer Service and Communications Public Information Officer **Ross Caron** .... (503) 823-4268
E-mail: ross.caron@portlandoregon.gov
ITAP Technology Capital Project Manager **Rebecca Sponsel** .... (503) 823-7056
E-mail: rebecca.sponsel@portlandoregon.gov

Bureau of Emergency Communications

P.O. Box 1927, Portland, OR 97207
Fax: (503) 823-4630

Employees: 131 **Fiscal Year:** 2016 **Budget:** $24,678,000

Director **Lisa Turley** .... (503) 823-0911
E-mail: oni@portlandoregon.gov

Bureau of Environmental Services

Portland Building, 1120 SW Fifth Avenue, Room 1000, Portland, OR 97204-1972
Tel: (503) 823-7740 Fax: (503) 823-6995

Employees: 505 **Fiscal Year:** 2016 **Budget:** $898,828,000

Director **Michael J. Jordan** .... (503) 823-7769
Public Information Manager **Megan Callahan** .... (503) 823-4759
E-mail: megan.callahan@portlandoregon.gov
Environmental Intergovernmental Relations **Kim Cox** .... (503) 823-5313
E-mail: kim.cox@portlandoregon.gov

Bureau of Planning and Sustainability [BPS]

1900 SW Fourth Ave., Suite 7100, Portland, OR 97201
Tel: (503) 823-7700 Fax: (503) 823-7800
E-mail: bps@portlandoregon.gov Internet: www.portlandoregon.gov/bps/

Employees: 93 **Fiscal Year:** 2016 **Budget:** $18,658,000

Director **Susan Anderson** .... (503) 823-7700
Green Building Division Manager **Alisa Kane** .... (503) 823-7082
Planning and Sustainability Commission Coordinator **Julie Ocken** .... (503) 823-6041
E-mail: julie.ocken@portlandoregon.gov
Solid Waste and Recycling Division Manager **Bruce Walker** .... (503) 823-7772

★ Elected Official ▲ Appointed by Legislature ▼ Appointed by Governor ► Appointed by Board or Commission ● Appointed by Judge
■ Appointed by Mayor △ Appointed by Freeholders ▽ Appointed by Supervisor ▷ Appointed by County Executive ○ Appointed by Council

Bureau of Transportation [PBOT]

Portland Bldg., 1120 SW Fifth Avenue, Suite 800, Portland, OR 97204
Tel: (503) 823-5185 Fax: (503) 823-7576

Employees: 700 **Fiscal Year:** 2016 **Budget:** $324,306,000

Director **Leah Treat** .... (503) 823-9194
Education: New Mexico 1994 MPA
Assistant Director **Maurice Henderson** .... (503) 823-5185
Senior Business Operations Manager **Alissa Mahar** .... (503) 823-6188
Planning Manager **Art Pearce** .... (503) 823-7736

Parks and Recreation

Portland Building, 1120 SW Fifth Avenue, Room 1302, Portland, OR 97204
Tel: (503) 823-7529 Fax: (503) 823-6007
Internet: http://www.portlandoregon.gov/parks/35300?

Employees: 445 **Fiscal Year:** 2016 **Budget:** $141,297,000

Director **Mike Abbaté** .... (503) 823-5379
Assistant Director **Warren Jimenez** .... (503) 823-5123
Finance Manager **Jeff Shaffer** .... (503) 823-5107
Portland Golf Manager **John Zoller** .... (503) 823-5104
Portland International Raceway Manager **E.C. Mueller** .... (503) 823-5899
1940 N. Victory Blvd., Portland, OR 97204
Workforce Support and Development Manager **Margaret Evans** .... (503) 823-5230
E-mail: mary.strayhand@portlandoregon.gov
Planning, Development and Asset Manager **Kia Selley** .. (503) 823-5590
Community Relations Manager **Jennifer Yocom** .... (503) 823-5592
E-mail: jennifer.yocom@portlandoregon.gov

Police Bureau

1111 SW Second Ave., Portland, OR 97204-3232
Fax: (503) 823-0342 E-mail: mail@portlandpolicebureau.com
Internet: www.portlandpolicebureau.com

Employees: 1,156 **Fiscal Year:** 2016 **Budget:** $190,133,000

■ Chief of Police **Larry O'Dea** .... (503) 823-0000
Note: On administrative leave
■ Chief of Police (Acting) **Donna Henderson** .... (503) 823-0000

Portland Development Commission [PDC]

222 NW Fifth Avenue, Portland, OR 97209
Tel: (503) 823-3200 Fax: (503) 823-3368 Internet: www.pdc.us

Executive Director **(Vacant)** .... (503) 823-3355
Deputy Director for Strategy and Operations **Kimberly Branam** .... (503) 823-3794
E-mail: branamk@pdc.us
Chief Financial Officer **Faye Brown** .... (503) 823-3346
Director of Business and Social Equity **John Jackley** .... (503) 823-3315
E-mail: john.jackley@portlandoregon.gov
Public Affairs Manager **Shawn Uhlman** .... (503) 823-7994
E-mail: shawn.uhlman@portlandoregon.gov
General Counsel **Eric Iverson** .... (503) 823-3221

Portland Fire and Rescue

55 SW Ash Street, Portland, OR 97204
Tel: (503) 823-3700 Fax: (503) 823-3710
Internet: http://www.portlandoregon.gov/fire/

Employees: 725 **Fiscal Year:** 2016 **Budget:** $117,918,000

Fire Chief **Erin Janssens** .... (503) 823-3730
E-mail: chief@portlandoregon.gov
Executive Assistant **Janice Moore** .... (503) 823-3730
E-mail: janice.moore@portlandoregon.gov
Special Operations Deputy Chief **Leo Krick** .... (503) 823-3049
E-mail: leo.krick@portlandoregon.gov
Emergency Operations Division Chief **John Nohr** .... (503) 823-4390
E-mail: john.nohr@portlandoregon.gov
Logistics Section Deputy Chief **Marco Benetti** .... (503) 823-3700
E-mail: marco.benetti@portlandoregon.gov
Training and Safety Division Chief **Merrill Gonterman** .. (503) 823-3892
E-mail: merril.gonterman@portlandoregon.gov

Portland Fire and Rescue *continued*

Fire Marshal **Nate Takara** .... (503) 823-3724
E-mail: nate.takara@portlandoregon.gov
Management Services Division Director **Jay Guo** .... (503) 823-3726
E-mail: jay.guo@portlandoregon.gov
Personnel Manager **Jim Fairchild** .... (503) 823-3753
E-mail: jim.fairchild@portlandoregon.gov
Public Information Officer **Rich Tyler** .... (503) 823-3700
E-mail: rich.tyler@portlandoregon.gov

Portland Housing Bureau [PHB]

421 Southwest Sixth Avenue, Suite 500, Portland, OR 97204
Tel: (503) 823-2375 Fax: (503) 823-2387

Employees: 53 **Fiscal Year:** 2016 **Budget:** $96,697,000

Director **Kurt Creager** .... (503) 823-2380
Assistant Housing Director **Javier Mena** .... (503) 823-6017
Administrative Services Manager **Letimya Clayton** .... (503) 823-3489
E-mail: letimya.clayton@portlandoregon.gov
Portland Housing Advisory Committee Program Manager **(Vacant)** .... (503) 823-3607
Housing Program Manager **Andrea Matthiessen** .... (503) 823-2379
Management Analyst **Antoinette Pietka** .... (503) 823-2394
E-mail: antoinette.pietka@portlandoregon.gov

Portland Water Bureau

Portland Bldg., 1120 SW Fifth Avenue, Room 600, Portland, OR 97204-1926
Tel: (503) 823-7404 Fax: (503) 823-6133

Employees: 538 **Fiscal Year:** 2016 **Budget:** $474,522,000

Bureau Director **Michael Stuhr** .... (503) 823-1517
Director, Maintenance and Construction Services **Ty Kovatch** .... (503) 823-1508
Director, Financial and Support Services **Cecelia Huynh** .. (503) 823-7417
Director, Resource Protection and Planning **Edward Campbell** .... (503) 823-2794
Director, Water Operations **Chris Wanner** .... (503) 823-4050
E-mail: chris.wanner@portlandoregon.gov
Chief Engineer **Teresa Elliott** .... (503) 823-7622
Communications Director **Gabriel Solmer** .... (503) 823-6926
Business Operations Supervisor **Susan Bailey** .... (503) 823-1956

Regional Arts and Culture Council [RACC]

411 NW Park, Suite 101, Portland, OR 97209
Tel: (503) 823-5111 Fax: (503) 823-5432 E-mail: info@racc.org
Internet: www.racc.org

Executive Director **Eloise Damrosch** .... (503) 823-5111
Community Engagement Director **Jeff Hawthorne** .... (503) 823-5258
E-mail: jhawthorne@racc.org
Operations Director **Cindy Knapp** .... (503) 823-5403
E-mail: cknapp@racc.org
Finance and Human Resources Specialist **Jennifer Matsumura** .... (503) 823-4627
E-mail: jmatsumura@racc.org
Arts Education Director **Marna Stalcup** .... (503) 823-4698
Work for Art Manager **Kathryn Jackson** .... (503) 823-5424

Office of the City Auditor

City Hall, 1221 SW Fourth Avenue, Room 140, Portland, OR 97204
Tel: (503) 823-4078 Fax: (503) 823-4571

Employees: 49 **Fiscal Year:** 2016 **Budget:** $25,844,000

★ City Auditor **Mary Hull Caballero** .... (503) 823-4078
Term Expires: December 31, 2018
E-mail: mary.caballero@portlandoregon.gov
Chief Deputy Auditor **Sarah Landis** .... (503) 823-4567
Audit Services Division Director **Drummond Kahn** .... (503) 823-4005
Council Contracts Manager **Toni Anderson** .... (503) 823-4022
Council Clerk **Karla Moore-Love** .... (503) 823-4086
Elections Officer **Deborah Scroggin** .... (503) 823-3546

★ Elected Official ▲ Appointed by Legislature ▼ Appointed by Governor ▶ Appointed by Board or Commission ● Appointed by Judge
■ Appointed by Mayor △ Appointed by Freeholders ▽ Appointed by Supervisor ▷ Appointed by County Executive ○ Appointed by Council

Office of the Ombudsman

City Hall, 1221 SW Fourth Avenue, Room 140, Portland, OR 97204-1987
Fax: (503) 823-4571

■ Ombudsman **Margie Sollinger** .... (503) 823-4503
E-mail: ombudsman@portlandoregon.gov

Portland Public Schools

501 North Dixon Street, Portland, OR 97227-1804
Fax: (503) 916-2724 Internet: www.pps.k12.or.us/

Superintendent of Schools **Carole Smith** .... (503) 916-3200
Fax: (503) 916-3110

★ Chair **Tom Koehler** (Zone 6) .... (503) 916-2000
Term Expires: June 30, 2017
E-mail: tkoehler@pps.net

★ Vice Chair **Amy Kohnstamm** (Zone 3) .... (503) 916-2000
Term Expires: June 2019
E-mail: akohnstamm@pps.net

★ School Board Member **Julie Esparza Brown** (Zone 1) ... (503) 916-2000
Term Expires: June 2019
E-mail: jebrown@pps.net

★ School Board Member **Paul D. Anthony** (Zone 2) .... (503) 916-2000
Term Expires: June 2019
E-mail: panthony@pps.net

★ School Board Member **Steve Buel** (Zone 4) .... (503) 916-3570
Term Expires: June 30, 2017
E-mail: sbuel@pps.net

★ School Board Member **Pam Knowles** (Zone 5) .... (503) 916-5710
Term Expires: June 30, 2017
E-mail: pknowles@pps.net

★ School Board Member **Mike Rosen** (Zone 7) .... (503) 916-2000
Term Expires: June 2019
E-mail: mrosen@pps.net

City of Portsmouth, Virginia

801 Crawford St., Portsmouth, VA 23704
P.O. Box 820, Portsmouth, VA 23705
Internet: www.portsmouthva.gov

County: None **Election Type:** Nonpartisan **Population:** 96,201 (2015)

Office of the Mayor and City Council

P.O. Box 820, Portsmouth, VA 23705
Fax: (757) 393-5378 E-mail: council@portsmouthva.gov

★ Mayor **Kenneth I. Wright** .... (757) 393-8746
Began Service: November 4, 2010
Term Expires: December 31, 2016
E-mail: mayor@portsmouthva.gov

★ Vice Mayor **Elizabeth M. Psimas** .... (757) 393-8639
Term Expires: December 31, 2016
E-mail: psimase@portsmouthva.gov

★ Council Member **Paige D. Cherry** .... (757) 393-8639
Term Expires: December 31, 2018
E-mail: cherryp@portsmouthva.gov

★ Council Member **Curtis E. Edmonds, Sr.** .... (757) 393-8639
Term Expires: December 31, 2016
E-mail: edmondsc@portsmouthva.gov

★ Council Member **Danny W. Meeks** .... (757) 393-8639
Term Expires: December 31, 2016
E-mail: meeksd@portsmouthva.gov

★ Council Member **William E. Moody, Jr.** .... (757) 393-8639
Term Expires: December 31, 2018
E-mail: moodyw@portsmouthva.gov

★ Council Member **Mark M. Whitaker** .... (757) 393-8639
Term Expires: December 31, 2018
E-mail: whitakerm@portsmouthva.gov

Office of the Assessor

P.O. Box 820, Portsmouth, VA 23705
Fax: (757) 393-8177

○ Assessor **Janey Culpepper** .... (757) 393-8631
E-mail: assessor@portsmouthva.gov

Office of the City Clerk

P.O. Box 820, Portsmouth, VA 23705
Fax: (757) 393-5378

○ City Clerk **Debra Y. White** .... (757) 393-8639
E-mail: whited@portsmouthva.gov

Chief Deputy Clerk **Anita Y. Sharrod** .... (757) 393-8639
E-mail: sherroda@portsmouthva.gov

Senior Deputy Clerk **Keia D. Waters** .... (757) 393-8639
E-mail: watersk@portsmouthva.gov

Deputy City Clerk **Monika B. Johnson** .... (757) 393-8639
E-mail: mbjohnson@portsmouthva.gov

Office of the Commissioner of Revenue

P.O. Box 820, Portsmouth, VA 23705

★ Commissioner of Revenue **Franklin Edmondson** .... (757) 393-8771
Term Expires: December 31, 2017
E-mail: edmondsonf@portsmouthva.gov

Office of the Commonwealth's Attorney

P.O. Box 820, Portsmouth, VA 23705

★ Commonwealth's Attorney **Stephanie Morales** .... (757) 393-8581
Term Expires: December 31, 2017
E-mail: moraless@portsmouthva.gov

Office of the Sheriff

P.O. Box 820, Portsmouth, VA 23705

★ Sheriff **Bill Watson** .... (757) 393-8210
Term Expires: December 31, 2017
E-mail: watsonb@portsmouthva.gov

Office of the Treasurer

P.O. Box 820, Portsmouth, VA 23705

★ Treasurer **James L. Williams** .... (757) 393-8651
Term Expires: December 31, 2017
E-mail: williamsjl@portsmouthva.gov

Office of the City Manager

P.O. Box 820, Portsmouth, VA 23705

○ City Manager **Dr. Lydia Pettis Patton** .... (757) 393-8641
E-mail: manager@portsmouthva.gov

Director of Information Technology **Daniel L. Jones** ..... (757) 393-8641

Economic Development Department

800 Crawford Street, 5th Floor, Portsmouth, VA 23704
Fax: (757) 393-8293

Director **Mallory C. Butler** .... (757) 393-8804
E-mail: butlerm@portsmouthva.gov

Finance Department

P.O. Box 820, Portsmouth, VA 23705

Chief Financial Officer **Alice M. Kelly** .... (757) 393-8831

Fire Department

P.O. Box 820, Portsmouth, VA 23705
Fax: (757) 393-5161

Fire Chief **Dwayne Bonnette** .... (757) 393-8765

★ Elected Official ▲ Appointed by Legislature ▼ Appointed by Governor ▶ Appointed by Board or Commission ● Appointed by Judge
■ Appointed by Mayor △ Appointed by Freeholders ▽ Appointed by Supervisor ▷ Appointed by County Executive ○ Appointed by Council

Department of General Services
2005 Frederick Boulevard, Portsmouth, VA 23704
Tel: (757) 393-8621 Fax: (757) 393-5178

Director **(Vacant)** .... (757) 393-8621

Department of Human Resource Management
801 Crawford Street, Portsmouth, VA 23704-3822
Tel: (757) 393-8626 Fax: (757) 393-8697

Director of Human Resource Management
Elizabeth Gooden .... (757) 393-8626
E-mail: hrm@portsmouthva.gov

Parks, Recreation and Leisure Services
801 Crawford St., Portsmouth, VA 23704
Fax: (757) 393-8265

Director **Mark W. Furlo** .... (757) 393-8481 ext. 4125

Police Department
P.O. Box 820, Portsmouth, VA 23705

Chief of Police **Tonya D. Chapman** .... (757) 393-8257

Portsmouth Public Library
601 Court St., Portsmouth, VA 23704
Fax: (757) 393-5107

Director **Todd Elliott** .... (757) 393-8501
E-mail: library@portsmouthva.gov

Public Works Department
P.O. Box 820, Portsmouth, VA 23705
Fax: (757) 393-8976

Director **Erin K Trimyer** .... (757) 393-8691 ext. 2202

Purchasing Department
801 Crawford St., Portsmouth, VA 23704-3822
Fax: (757) 393-8103

Purchasing Agent **Michael Ammons** .... (757) 393-8831
E-mail: ammonsm@portsmouthva.gov

Department of Social Services
1701 High Street, Suite 101, Portsmouth, VA 23704
Tel: (757) 405-1800

Director of Social Services **Pamela T. Little-Hill** .... (757) 405-1800

Portsmouth City Public Schools
P.O. Box 998, Portsmouth, VA 23705-0998
Fax: (757) 393-5238

Superintendent **Dr. Elie Bracy III** .... (757) 393-8742

City of Providence, Rhode Island

City Hall, 25 Dorrance Street, Providence, RI 02903
Tel: (401) 421-7740 (Information) Internet: www.providenceri.com

County: Providence **Election Type:** Partisan **Population:** 179,207 (2015)

Office of the Mayor
City Hall, 25 Dorrance St., Providence, RI 02903
Fax: (401) 455-8823

★ Mayor **Jorge O. Elorza** (D) .... (401) 421-2489
Began Service: January 6, 2015
Term Expires: January 5, 2019
Chief of Staff **Tony Simon** .... (401) 421-2489
Deputy Chief of Staff **Theresa Agonia** .... (401) 421-7740 ext. 345
Deputy Chief of Staff **Marisa O'Gara** .... (401) 421-7740 ext. 750
■ Chief Operating Officer **Brett P. Smiley** .... (401) 421-7740 ext. 750
E-mail: bsmiley@providenceri.com
Press Secretary **Evan England** .... (401) 426-8101
Education: Northeastern 2011 BS
■ Chief Innovation Officer **Nicole Pollock** .... (401) 421-2489
E-mail: npollock@providenceri.com
Director of Policy **Shelia Dormody** .... (401) 421-2489
Director of Sustainability **Leah Bamberger** .... (401) 421-2489

Office of the Recorder of the Deeds
City Hall, 25 Dorrance St., 5th Floor, Providence, RI 02903

■ Recorder of Deeds (Acting) **John A. Murphy** ... (401) 421-7740 ext. 547
E-mail: jmurphy@providenceri.com
Education: SUNY (Albany) BA; Columbus Law JD

Office of the City Solicitor
444 Westminster Street, Providence, RI 02903
Fax: (401) 680-5520

■ City Solicitor **Jeffrey Dana** .... (401) 680-5333
E-mail: jdana@providenceri.com

Community Action Partnership of Providence [PROCAP]
518 Hartford Avenue, Providence, RI 02909

■ Director **Melissa Husband** .... (401) 273-2000

Economic Development Department
444 Westminster Street, Providence, RI 02903

■ Economic Development Director **Mark Huang** .... (401) 680-8541
E-mail: mhuang@providenceri.com

Planning and Development Department
444 Westminster Street, Providence, RI 02903
Fax: (401) 351-9533 E-mail: planning@ids.net

■ Director **Bonnie Nickerson** .... (401) 680-8400
E-mail: bnickerson@providenceri.com
Deputy Director **Robert E. Azar** .... (401) 680-8400
Associate Director of Special Projects
Martina Haggerty .... (401) 680-8400

Inspections and Standards Department
444 Westminster Street, Providence, RI 02903
Fax: (401) 680-5482

■ Director **Jeff Lykins** .... (401) 680-5201
E-mail: jlykins@providenceri.com

★ Elected Official ▲ Appointed by Legislature ▼ Appointed by Governor ▶ Appointed by Board or Commission ● Appointed by Judge
■ Appointed by Mayor △ Appointed by Freeholders ▽ Appointed by Supervisor ▷ Appointed by County Executive ○ Appointed by Council

Finance Department
City Hall, 25 Dorrance St., 3rd Floor, Providence, RI 02903
Fax: (401) 621-8102

■ Director **Lawrence Mancini** . . . . . (401) 421-7740 ext. 536
E-mail: lmancini@providenceri.com
Education: Bryant U BS

■ Deputy Director **Sara Silveria** . . . . . (401) 421-7740 ext. 5531

Office of the City Controller
797 Westminster Street, Providence, RI 02903

City Controller **Michael D'Antuono** . . . . . (401) 465-9100 ext. 11142
E-mail: michael.d'antuono@ppsd.org

Office of the City Collector
City Hall, 25 Dorrance St., 2nd Floor, Providence, RI 02903
Fax: (401) 454-8247

■ City Collector **John A. Murphy** . . . . . (401) 331-5252 ext. 698
E-mail: jmurphy@providenceri.com
Education: SUNY (Albany) BA; Columbus Law JD

Tax Department
City Hall, 25 Dorrance St., 2nd Floor, Providence, RI 02903

■ Tax Assessor **David Quinn** . . . . . (401) 421-5900
E-mail: dquinn@providenceri.com

Deputy Assessor **Janesse Muscatelli** . . . . . (401) 421-5900
E-mail: jmuscatelli@providenceri.com

Human Resources Department
25 Dorrance Street, Room 401, Providence, RI 02903
Tel: (401) 421-2489 Fax: (401) 273-9510

Director **Sybil Bailey** . . . . . (401) 421-2489 ext. 240
E-mail: sbailey@providenceri.com

Parks and Recreation Department
1000 East Elmwood Avenue, Providence, RI 02905

■ Superintendent **Wendy Nilsson** . . . . . (401) 785-9450

■ Director of Recreation **Michael Stephens** . . . . . (401) 421-7740 ext. 323

Providence Public Library
Central Library, 225 Washington St., Providence, RI 02903
Tel: (401) 455-8000

Executive Director **Jack Martin** . . . . . (401) 455-8100
E-mail: jmartin@provlib.org

Public Property Department
City Hall, 25 Dorrance Street, Room 407, Providence, RI 02903

■ Director of Purchasing **Allen Sepe** . . . . . (401) 421-7740 ext. 300

Public Safety Department
325 Washington St., Providence, RI 02903

■ Commissioner **Col. Steven M. Paré** . . . . . (401) 272-3121
E-mail: spare@providenceri.com
Education: Bryant Col BS

Communications Department
One Communications Place, Providence, RI 02903
Fax: (401) 243-6445

Director **Caroline Arias** . . . . . (401) 243-6000

Fire Department
325 Washington St., Providence, RI 02903

■ Fire Chief (Acting) **Scott Mello** . . . . . (401) 243-6060
E-mail: smello@providenceri.com

Police Department
325 Washington St., Providence, RI 02903
E-mail: providencepolice@hotmail.com
Internet: http://www.providencepolice.com

■ Chief of Police **Hugh T. Clements, Jr.** . . . . . (401) 272-3121
E-mail: hclements@providenceri.com

Providence Emergency Management Agency
591 Charles Street, Providence, RI 02904

■ Director **COL Michael Borg** . . . . . (401) 228-8000
E-mail: mborg@providenceri.com
Education: Metro State Col Denver BA; American Military U MA; Naval War MA

Public Works Department
700 Allens Ave., Providence, RI 02905

■ Director **CAPT Russell P. Knight** . . . . . (401) 467-7950 ext. 377
E-mail: rknight@providenceri.com

Deputy Superintendent **Kevin Holt** . . . . . (401) 467-7950

Highways Superintendent **Sal Solomon** . . . . . (401) 467-7950

Sewer Superintendent **William Randall** . . . . . (401) 467-7950

Traffic Engineering Department
60 Ernest St., Providence, RI 02905

■ Director **William C. Bombard** . . . . . (401) 781-4045
E-mail: wbombard@providenceri.com

Vital Statistics Department
City Hall, 25 Dorrance St., Room 104, Providence, RI 02903

■ Registrar **Serena Conley** . . . . . (401) 421-7740 ext. 701
E-mail: sconley@providenceri.com

Workforce Solutions of Providence and Cranston [JPTA]
180 Westminster St., Providence, RI 02903

■ Administrator **Robert Ricci** . . . . . (401) 680-8585
E-mail: rricci@providenceri.com

Office of the City Council
City Hall, 25 Dorrance St., Providence, RI 02903
Fax: (401) 521-3928

★ Council President **Luis A. Aponte** (D-Ward 10) . . . . . (401) 421-7740
Term Expires: January 1, 2019
E-mail: ward10@providenceri.com

★ Council President Pro Tem **Sabina Matos** (D-Ward 15) . . (401) 421-7740
Term Expires: January 1, 2019
E-mail: ward15@providenceri.com

★ Council Member **Seth Yurdin** (D-Ward 1) . . . . . (401) 421-7740
Term Expires: January 1, 2019
E-mail: ward1@providenceri.com

★ Council Member **Samuel D. Zurier** (D-Ward 2) . . . . . (401) 421-7740
Term Expires: January 1, 2019
E-mail: ward2@providenceri.com

★ Council Member **Kevin Jackson** (D-Ward 3) . . . . . (401) 421-7740
Term Expires: January 1, 2019
E-mail: ward3@providenceri.com

★ Council Member **Nicholas J. Narducci** (D-Ward 4) . . . . . (401) 421-7740
Term Expires: January 1, 2019
E-mail: ward4@providenceri.com

★ Council Member **Jo Ann Ryan** (D-Ward 5) . . . . . (401) 421-7740
Term Expires: January 1, 2019
E-mail: jryan@providenceri.com

★ Council Member **Michael J. Correia** (D-Ward 6) . . . . . (401) 421-7740
Term Expires: January 1, 2019
E-mail: ward6@providenceri.com

★ Council Member **John J. Igliozzi** (D-Ward 7) . . . . . (401) 421-7740
Term Expires: January 1, 2019
E-mail: ward7@providenceri.com

★ Elected Official ▲ Appointed by Legislature ▼ Appointed by Governor ▶ Appointed by Board or Commission ● Appointed by Judge
■ Appointed by Mayor △ Appointed by Freeholders ▽ Appointed by Supervisor ▷ Appointed by County Executive ○ Appointed by Council

Office of the City Council *continued*

★Council Member **Wilbur W. Jennings, Jr.** (D-Ward 8) . . . (401) 421-7740
Term Expires: January 1, 2019
E-mail: ward8@providenceri.com

★Council Member **Carmen Castillo** (D-Ward 9) . . . (401) 421-7740
Term Expires: January 1, 2019
E-mail: ward9@providenceri.com

★Council Member **Mary Kay Harris** (D-Ward 11) . . . (401) 421-7740
Term Expires: January 1, 2019
E-mail: ward11@providenceri.com

★Majority Leader **Terrence M. Hassett** (D-Ward 12) . . . (401) 421-7740
Term Expires: January 1, 2019
E-mail: ward12@providenceri.com

★Council Member **Bryan Principe** (D-Ward 13) . . . (401) 421-7740
Term Expires: January 1, 2019
E-mail: ward13@providenceri.com

★Council Member **David A. Salvatore** (D-Ward 14) . . . (401) 421-7740
Term Expires: January 1, 2019
E-mail: ward14@providenceri.com

○Chief of Staff **Cyd McKenna** . . . (401) 421-7740 ext. 272
E-mail: cmckenna@providenceri.com

Office of the City Clerk

City Hall, 25 Dorrance St., 3rd Floor, Providence, RI 02903
Fax: (401) 421-6492

○City Clerk **Lori L. Hagen** . . . (401) 421-7740 ext. 256
E-mail: lhagen@providenceri.com

1st Deputy City Clerk **(Vacant)** . . . (401) 421-7740 ext. 249

2nd Deputy City Clerk **(Vacant)** . . . (401) 421-7740 ext. 249

Office of the City Treasurer

City Hall, 25 Dorrance St., 4th Floor, Providence, RI 02903

○City Treasurer **James J. Lombardi III** . . . (401) 421-7740 ext. 271
E-mail: jlombardi@providenceri.com

Board of Canvassers and Voter Registration

City Hall, 25 Dorrance St., 1st Floor, Providence, RI 02903

■Administrator of Elections **Kathy Palencia** . . . (401) 421-0495 ext. 203
E-mail: kplacencia@providenceri.com

Dunkin' Donuts Center

One LaSalle Square, Providence, RI 02903

General Manager **Lawrence J. Lepore** . . . (401) 331-0700

Office of the City Sergeant

City Hall, 25 Dorrance St., 1st Floor, Providence, RI 02903

■City Sergeant **David Tassoni** . . . (401) 421-7740 ext. 272
E-mail: dtassoni@providenceri.com

Housing Authority

100 Broad Street, Providence, RI 02903

■Executive Director **Paul J. Tavares** (D) . . . (401) 709-1101
E-mail: ptavares@providenceri.com

Licensing Board

City Hall, 25 Dorrance St., Providence, RI 02903

■Chairman (Acting) **Juan M. Pichardo** (D) . . . (401) 421-7740
E-mail: jpichardo@providenceri.com

Administrator **Serena Conley** . . . (401) 421-7740 ext. 207

School Department

797 Westminster Street, Providence, RI 02903

Superintendent (Interim) **Christopher Ndeki Maher** . . . (401) 456-9211

City of Provo, Utah

351 West Center Street, Provo, UT 84601
Internet: www.provo.org

County: Utah **Election Type:** Nonpartisan **Population:** 115,264 (2015)

Office of the Mayor

351 West Center Street, Provo, UT 84601
Tel: (801) 852-6105 Fax: (801) 852-6107

★Mayor **John Curtis** . . . (801) 852-6108
Began Service: January 5, 2010
Term Expires: January 3, 2018
E-mail: jcurtis@provo.utah.gov

Administrative Assistant **Gina Robie** . . . (801) 852-6108
E-mail: grobie@provo.utah.gov

Deputy Mayor **Corey Norman** . . . (801) 852-6103
E-mail: cnorman@provo.utah.gov

Chief Administrative Officer **Wayne C. Parker** . . . (801) 852-6102
E-mail: wparker@provo.utah.gov

Community Relations and Public Information Officer **Whitney Booth** . . . (801) 852-6104
E-mail: wbooth@provo.utah.gov

City Recorder **Janene Weiss** . . . (801) 852-6524
Fax: (801) 852-6530

Office of the Municipal Council

351 West Center Street, Provo, UT 84601
Fax: (801) 852-6121

★Chair **Kim Santiago** (District 2) . . . (801) 852-6120
Term Expires: January 9, 2018

★Council Member **Gary Winterton** (District 1) . . . (801) 852-6120
Term Expires: January 7, 2020

★Council Member **Dave Knecht** (District 3) . . . (801) 852-6120
Term Expires: January 7, 2020

★Council Member **Kay Van Buren** (District 4) . . . (801) 852-6120
Term Expires: January 7, 2020

★Council Member **David Harding** (District 5) . . . (801) 852-6120
Term Expires: January 7, 2020

★Council Member **David S. Sewell** (At-Large) . . . (801) 852-6120
Term Expires: January 9, 2018

★Council Member **George Stewart** (At-Large) . . . (801) 852-6120
Term Expires: January 7, 2020

Office of the City Attorney

351 West Center, Provo, UT 84061
Tel: (801) 852-6149 (Information) Fax: (801) 852-6150

City Attorney **Robert West** . . . (801) 852-6140
E-mail: rwest@provo.utah.gov

Assistant Attorney **Bob Trombly** . . . (801) 852-6140
E-mail: rtrombly@provo.utah.gov

Community Development Department

351 West Center Street, Provo, UT 84601
Fax: (801) 852-6417

Director **Gary McGinn** . . . (801) 852-6401
E-mail: gmcginn@provo.utah.gov

Assistant Director **Bill Peperone** . . . (801) 852-6402
E-mail: bpeperone@provo.utah.gov

Planner Supervisor **Brian Maxfield** . . . (801) 852-6404

Zoning Administrator **Carrie Walls** . . . (801) 852-6406

Chief Building Official **Dan Stubbs** . . . (801) 852-6465

★Elected Official ▲Appointed by Legislature ▼Appointed by Governor ▶Appointed by Board or Commission ●Appointed by Judge
■Appointed by Mayor △Appointed by Freeholders ▽Appointed by Supervisor ▷Appointed by County Executive ○Appointed by Council

Economic Development Department
351 West Center Street, Provo, UT 84601
Fax: (801) 375-1469

Deputy Mayor of Economic Development
Dixon Holmes .... (801) 852-6166
E-mail: dholmes@provo.utah.gov

Energy Department
251 West, 800 North, Provo, UT 84603
Fax: (801) 852-6947

Director **Travis Ball** .... (801) 852-6802

Finance Department
351 West Center Street, Provo, UT 84601

Director of Finance **Dan Follett** .... (801) 852-6503

Fire Department
80 South, 300 West, Provo, UT 84601
Fax: (801) 852-6330

Fire Chief **Gary Jolley** .... (801) 852-6318
E-mail: gary.jolley@provo.org Fax: (801) 852-6309

Housing Authority
650 W. 100th North, Provo, UT 84603
Fax: (801) 673-6560

Director **Jeremy Runia** .... (801) 900-5671

Human Resources Department
351 West Center Street, Provo, UT 84601
Tel: (801) 852-6184 Fax: (801) 852-6190

Human Resources Director **Gary Bushman** .... (801) 852-6184
E-mail: gbushman@provo.utah.gov

Police Department
351 West Center Street, Provo, UT 84601
Fax: (801) 377-7315

Chief of Police **John King** .... (801) 852-6200

Provo City Library
550 North University Avenue, Provo, UT 84601
Fax: (801) 852-6688

Director **Gene Nelson** .... (801) 852-6663

Public Works Department
1377 South, 350 East, Provo, UT 84606
Fax: (801) 852-6778

Director **David Decker** .... (801) 852-6770
City Engineer **Dave Graves** .... (801) 852-6741
E-mail: dgraves@provo.utah.gov

Redevelopment Agency
351 West Center, Provo, UT 84601
Fax: (801) 375-1469

Director **David Walter** .... (801) 852-6160
E-mail: dwalter@provo.utah.gov

City of Pueblo, Colorado
City Hall, 200 South Main, Pueblo, CO 81003
Internet: www.pueblo.us

County: Pueblo **Election Type:** Nonpartisan **Population:** 109,412 (2015)

Office of the City Council
City Hall, 200 South Main, Pueblo, CO 81003
Internet: http://www.pueblo.us/index.aspx?NID=585

Note: The Council President serves as Mayor.

★ Council President **Steve Nawrocki** (At-Large) .... (719) 553-2655
Began Service: January 1, 2010
Term Expires: December 31, 2017
E-mail: snawrocki@pueblo.us

★ Vice President **Ed Brown** (District 3) .... (719) 553-2655
Term Expires: December 31, 2017
E-mail: ebrown@pueblo.us

★ Council Member **Robert D. Schilling, Jr.** (District 1) .... (719) 250-4520
Term Expires: December 31, 2017
E-mail: bobschilling@juno.com

★ Council Member
Lawrence "Larry" Atencio (District 2) .... (719) 553-2655
Term Expires: December 31, 2019
Affiliation: Owner, LA Distributing
Education: Southern Colorado State 1970 BS; Northern Colorado 1977 MPA

★ Council Member **Ray Aguilera** (District 4) .... (719) 553-2655
Term Expires: December 31, 2019

★ Council Member **Lori Winner** (At-Large) .... (719) 553-2655
Term Expires: December 31, 2019

★ Council Member **Chris Nicoll** (At-Large) .... (719) 924-5449
Term Expires: December 31, 2019
E-mail: cnicoll@pueblo.us

Office of the City Manager
City Hall, 200 South Main, Pueblo, CO 81003

○ City Manager **Sam Azad** .... (719) 553-2655
E-mail: cityadmin@pueblo.us

Office of the City Attorney
Thatcher Building, Pueblo, CO 81003

City Attorney **Dan Kogovsek** .... (719) 562-3899
E-mail: dkogovsek@co.pueblo.co.us

Office of the City Clerk
City Hall, 200 South Main, 1st Floor, Pueblo, CO 81003
Fax: (719) 553-2697

City Clerk **Gina Dutcher** .... (719) 553-2669
E-mail: gdutcher@pueblo.us

Aviation Department
Pueblo Memorial Airport, 31201 Bryan Circle, Pueblo, CO 81001
E-mail: aviation@pueblo.us Fax: (719) 553-2761

Director (Interim) **Pat Cullen** .... (719) 553-2760

Civil Service Department
301 West B Street, Pueblo, CO 81003
Fax: (719) 553-2696

Director (Interim) **Lynne Huskins** .... (719) 553-2635

Finance Department
150 Central Main, 1st Floor, Pueblo, CO 81003
Fax: (719) 583-2617

Finance Director **Roni Kimbrel** .... (719) 553-2625

★ Elected Official ▲ Appointed by Legislature ▼ Appointed by Governor ▶ Appointed by Board or Commission ● Appointed by Judge
■ Appointed by Mayor △ Appointed by Freeholders ▽ Appointed by Supervisor ▷ Appointed by County Executive ○ Appointed by Council

Fire Department
1551 Bonforte Blvd., Pueblo, CO 81001
Fax: (719) 553-2831

Fire Chief **Shawn Shelton** .... (719) 553-2830
E-mail: sshelton@pueblo.us

Fleet Maintenance Department
300 East D Street, Pueblo, CO 81003

Director of Fleet Maintenance **Sam Ingo** .... (719) 553-2335

Housing and Citizen Services Department
2631 E. 4th St., Pueblo, CO 81001
Fax: (719) 553-2855

Director **Ada Clark** .... (719) 553-2850
E-mail: adaclark@pueblo.us

Human Resources
301 West B Street, Pueblo, CO 81003
Fax: (719) 553-2696

Director **Marisa Pacheco** .... (719) 553-2633
E-mail: mpacheco@pueblo.us

Information Technology Department
150 Central Main, Pueblo, CO 81003

Director **Lori Pinz** .... (719) 553-2424
E-mail: lpinz@pueblo.us
Webmaster **Bobby Cuomo** .... (719) 553-2444
E-mail: bcuomo@pueblo.us

Parks and Recreation Department
800 Goodnight Ave., Pueblo, CO 81005
Fax: (719) 553-2791

Director **Steve Meier** .... (719) 553-2790

Planning and Community Development Department
211 East D Street, Pueblo, CO 81003
Fax: (719) 553-2359

Director **Steve Meier** .... (719) 553-2259
E-mail: planninglanduse@pueblo.us

Police Department
200 South Main Street, Pueblo, CO 81003
E-mail: ppd@pueblo.us

Police Chief **Luis Velez** .... (719) 553-2420

Public Information Department
City Hall, 200 South Main, 2nd Floor, Pueblo, CO 81003

Director **Debra Hill** .... (719) 553-2549
E-mail: djhill@pueblo.us

Public Works Bureau
211 E. D St., Pueblo, CO 81003
Fax: (719) 553-2294

Director **Earl Wilkinson** .... (719) 553-2295
Assistant Director **Mickey Beyer** .... (719) 553-2295
Stormwater Director **(Vacant)** .... (719) 553-2299

Purchasing Department
230 S. Mechanic, Pueblo, CO 81003
Fax: (719) 553-2351

Director **Naomi Hedden** .... (719) 553-2350

Wastewater Department
211 East D Street, Pueblo, CO 81003
Fax: (719) 553-2294

Director **Gene Michael** .... (719) 553-2298

City of Raleigh, North Carolina

Raleigh Municipal Building, 222 West Hargett Street, Raleigh, NC 27601
P.O. Box 590, Raleigh, NC 27602
Internet: http://raleighnc.gov

County: Wake **Election Type:** Nonpartisan **Population:** 451,066 (2015)

Office of the Mayor and City Council
Raleigh Municipal Building, 222 West Hargett Street, Room 209, Raleigh, NC 27601
P.O. Box 590, Raleigh, NC 27602
Fax: (919) 996-7622

★ Mayor **Nancy McFarlane** .... (919) 996-3050
Began Service: December 5, 2011
Term Expires: November 30, 2017
E-mail: nancy.mcfarlane@raleighnc.gov
Staff Assistant **(Vacant)** .... (919) 996-3050
★ Council Member **Dickie Thompson** (District A) .... (919) 996-3050
Term Expires: November 30, 2017
★ Council Member **David Cox** (District B) .... (919) 996-3050
Term Expires: November 30, 2017
★ Council Member **Corey Branch** (District C) .... (919) 996-3050
Term Expires: November 30, 2017
★ Council Member **Kay C. Crowder** (District D) .... (919) 996-3050
Term Expires: November 30, 2017
E-mail: kay.crowder@raleighnc.gov
★ Council Member **Bonner Gaylord** (District E) .... (919) 996-3050
Term Expires: November 30, 2017
E-mail: bonner.gaylord@raleighnc.gov
★ Council Member **Mary-Ann Baldwin** (At-Large) .... (919) 996-3050
Term Expires: November 30, 2017
E-mail: mary-ann.baldwin@raleighnc.gov
★ Council Member **Russ Stephenson** (At-Large) .... (919) 996-3050
Term Expires: November 30, 2017
E-mail: russ.stephenson@raleighnc.gov

Office of the City Attorney
One Exchange Plaza, Suite 1020, Raleigh, NC 27601
Fax: (919) 857-4453

○ City Attorney **Thomas A. McCormick, Jr.** .... (919) 996-6560
E-mail: tom.mccormick@raleighnc.gov
Deputy City Attorney **Ira J. Botvinick** .... (919) 996-6560
E-mail: ira.botvinick@raleighnc.gov
Deputy City Attorney **Hunt K. Choi** .... (919) 996-6560
E-mail: hunt.choi@raleighnc.gov
Deputy City Attorney **Dorothy K. Leapley** .... (919) 996-6560
E-mail: dottie.leapley@raleighnc.gov

Office of the City Clerk/Treasurer
Raleigh Municipal Bldg., 222 West Hargett Street, Room 207, Raleigh, NC 27602
Fax: (919) 996-7620

○ City Clerk/Treasurer **Gail G. Smith** .... (919) 996-3040
E-mail: gail.smith@raleighnc.gov
Deputy City Clerk **Leslie H. Eldredge** .... (919) 996-3040
E-mail: leslie.eldredge@raleighnc.gov
Assistant Deputy Clerk **Cassidy R. Pritchard** .... (919) 996-3040
E-mail: cassidy.pritchard@raleighnc.gov
Assistant Deputy Clerk **Ralph Puccini** .... (919) 996-3040
E-mail: ralph.puccini@raleighnc.gov

★ Elected Official ▲ Appointed by Legislature ▼ Appointed by Governor ▶ Appointed by Board or Commission ● Appointed by Judge
■ Appointed by Mayor △ Appointed by Freeholders ▽ Appointed by Supervisor ▷ Appointed by County Executive ○ Appointed by Council

Office of the City Manager

Raleigh Municipal Building, 222 West Hargett Street, Suite 224, Raleigh, NC 27601
P.O. Box 590, Raleigh, NC 27602
Tel: (919) 996-3070 Fax: (919) 996-7598

○City Manager **Ruffin Hall** .... (919) 996-3070
E-mail: ruffin.hall@raleighnc.gov
Staff Assistant **Diane Smith** .... (919) 996-3070
E-mail: diane.smith@raleighnc.gov
Assistant City Manager **Tansy Hayward** .... (919) 996-3070
E-mail: tansy.hayward@raleighnc.gov
Assistant City Manager **James S. Greene, Jr.** .... (919) 996-3070
E-mail: james.greene@raleighnc.gov
Assistant City Manager **Marchell Adams David** .... (919) 996-3070
E-mail: marchell.adams-david@raleighnc.gov

Public Affairs

Tel: (919) 996-3100 Fax: (919) 996-7621

Communications Director **Damien Graham** .... (919) 996-3100
E-mail: damien.graham@raleighnc.gov
Assistant Director **Michael Williams** .... (919) 996-3100
E-mail: michael.williams@raleighnc.gov

Community Development Department

310 W. Martin St., Suite 101, Raleigh, NC 27601

Director **Michele Grant** .... (919) 996-4330
E-mail: michele.grant@raleighnc.gov

Community Services Department

310 W. Martin St., Suite 201, Raleigh, NC 27601
P.O. Box 590, Raleigh, NC 27602
Fax: (919) 831-6123

Director **Dwayne Patterson** .... (919) 996-6100
E-mail: dwayne.patterson@raleighnc.gov
Education: North Carolina State BA
Administrative Assistant **Anitra Wiggins** .... (919) 996-6100
E-mail: anitra.wiggins@raleighnc.gov

Finance Department

Raleigh Municipal Bldg., 222 West Hargett Street, Room 114, Raleigh, NC 27602
Fax: (919) 996-7625 E-mail: finance.info@raleighnc.gov

Chief Financial Officer **Perry E. James III** .... (919) 931-4930
Education: North Carolina BS
Assistant Chief Financial Officer **Robin Rose** .... (919) 996-3215
Accounting and Financial Reporting Manager **Brian Leden** .... (919) 966-4995
E-mail: brian.leden@raleighnc.gov
Controller **Allison Bradsher** .... (919) 996-4970
Assistant Controller **David P. Erwin** .... (919) 996-3571
Debt Manager **Todd Taylor** .... (919) 996-4939
Risk Management **Dennis Paren** .... (919) 996-2240
E-mail: dennis.paren@raleighnc.gov
Administrative Office Manager **(Vacant)** .... (919) 996-3215
Payroll Manager **(Vacant)** .... (919) 996-3235
Treasury Manager **(Vacant)** .... (919) 996-4938

Fire Department

310 W. Martin St., Suite 200, Raleigh, NC 27602
P.O. Box 590, Raleigh, NC 27602
Fax: (919) 831-6180 Internet: www.raleighnc.gov/fire

Fire Chief **John T. McGrath** .... (919) 996-6115
E-mail: john.mcgrath@raleighnc.gov
Secretary **Marissa Broome** .... (919) 996-5950
E-mail: marissa.broome@raleighnc.gov
Fire Marshall Assistant Chief **Keith Tessinear** .... (919) 996-5984
E-mail: keith.tessinear@raleighnc.gov
Operations Assistant Chief **Brad R. Harvey** .... (919) 996-5956
E-mail: bradley.harvey@raleighnc.gov

Fire Department *continued*

Services Assistant Chief **James D. Poole** .... (919) 996-5191
E-mail: james.poole@raleighnc.gov
Training Assistant Chief **Kendall Hocutt** .... (919) 996-5185
E-mail: kendall.hocutt@raleighnc.gov
Fire Systems Technology Manager **Paul Roberts** .... (919) 996-5186
E-mail: paul.roberts@raleighnc.gov

Housing Authority

900 Haynes St., Raleigh, NC 27604-1462
Fax: (919) 831-6160

Director **Wayne Felton** .... (919) 831-8300
Executive Administrative Assistant **Gwen Wall** .... (919) 831-8300
E-mail: gwall@rhaonline.com

Human Resources Department

Raleigh Municipal Building, 222 West Hargett Street, Room 101, Raleigh, NC 27602-0590
Fax: (919) 996-7611

Director **C. Stephen Jones** .... (919) 996-3315
E-mail: c.stephen.jones@raleighnc.gov
Administrative Assistant **Sandra Burke** .... (919) 996-3315
E-mail: sandra.burke@raleighnc.gov
Deputy Director **Gloria Hartsfield** .... (919) 996-3315
E-mail: gloria.hartsfield@raleighnc.gov
City Safety Program Administrator **Marty Molnar** .... (919) 996-3320
E-mail: martin.molnar@raleighnc.gov
Nurse Supervisor **Sandra Perry** .... (919) 996-3320
E-mail: sandra.perry@raleighnc.gov
Workplace Health Care Specialist **Jacqueline Brown** .... (919) 996-3315
Compensation Analyst **Teresa Pavlic** .... (919) 996-3315
E-mail: teresa.pavlic@raleighnc.gov

Information Technology

1 Exchange Plaza, Suite 900, Raleigh, NC 27602

Chief Information Officer **D. Darnell Smith** .... (919) 996-4645
Education: North Carolina A&T BS; North Carolina MBA

Inspections Department

One Exchange Plaza, Suite 504, Raleigh, NC 27601
Tel: (919) 996-2444 Fax: (919) 516-2172

Deputy Inspections Director **Curt Willis** .... (919) 996-2701
Chief Building Official **Jerzy Z. Hubert** .... (919) 996-2455
Housing and Environmental Inspection Administrator **Ashley Glover** .... (919) 996-2450

Parks and Recreation

2401 Wade Avenue, Raleigh, NC 27607
Tel: (919) 996-3285 Fax: (919) 996-7618

Director **Diane Sauer** .... (919) 996-3285
Design Development Administrator **Dick Bailey** .... (919) 946-4774
Marketing and Program Administrator **Kellee Beach** .... (919) 996-3285
Parks Superintendent **Wayne Schindler** .... (919) 996-3285
Recreation Superintendent **Scott Payne** .... (919) 996-3285
Recreation Superintendent **Ken Hisler** .... (919) 996-3285

Department of City Planning

One Exchange Plaza, Third Floor, Suite 304, Raleigh, NC 27601
E-mail: planning@raleighnc.gov Internet: www.raleighnc.gov/planning

Director (Interim) **Ken Bowers** .... (919) 996-2633
E-mail: kenneth.bowers@raleighnc.gov
Executive Assistant **Willa Brandon** .... (919) 996-2627
Deputy Director **Ken Bowers** .... (919) 996-2633
E-mail: kenneth.bowers@raleighnc.gov
Administration Senior Planner **Greg Hallam** .... (919) 996-2636
Transportation Planning Manager **Eric J. Lamb** .... (919) 996-2161
Development Services Manager **Christine Darges** .... (919) 996-2634

★Elected Official ▲Appointed by Legislature ▼Appointed by Governor ►Appointed by Board or Commission ●Appointed by Judge
■Appointed by Mayor △Appointed by Freeholders ▽Appointed by Supervisor ▷Appointed by County Executive ○Appointed by Council

CITIES AND TOWNS

Department of City Planning *continued*

Current Planning Services Senior Planner
Stacy Barbour . . . . . (919) 996-2631
Raleigh Urban Design Center and Communications Planning Manager **Grant Meacci** . . . . . (919) 996-8441
E-mail: grant.meacci@raleighnc.gov
Raleigh Urban Design Center and Communications Assistant Planning Manager **Roberta Fox** . . . . . (919) 996-5220
E-mail: roberta.fox@raleighnc.gov
City and Regional Planning Manager/Raleigh Historic Districts Commission **Daniel Becker** . . . . . (919) 996-2632
Zoning Enforcement Administrator **Walt Fulcher** . . . . . (919) 996-2555
Office of Economic Development Director **James Sauls** . . (919) 996-2626
E-mail: James.Sauls@raleighnc.gov

Police Department

6716 Six Forks Road, Raleigh, NC 27617
P.O. Box 590, Raleigh, NC 27602
Tel: (919) 996-3385 Fax: (919) 870-2838

Police Chief **Cassandra Deck-Brown** . . . . . (919) 996-3385
Deputy Chief **Major J.C. Perry** . . . . . (919) 996-1008
Police Attorney **Ashby Ray** . . . . . (919) 996-3340
Education: Emory & Henry BA; Campbell 2003 JD
Administration **Robert Council** . . . . . (919) 996-1108
Field Operations **A.C. Davis** . . . . . (919) 996-1185
Internal Affairs **Karen Riggsbee** . . . . . (919) 996-3385
Investigations **D. Regentin** . . . . . (919) 996-3555
Special Operations **Major S. Deans** . . . . . (919) 807-5135

Public Utilities Department

P.O. Box 590, Raleigh, NC 27602
Fax: (919) 996-1866

Director **Robert Massengill** . . . . . (919) 996-4540
Assistant Director **Kenny Waldroup** . . . . . (919) 996-3489

Public Works

Raleigh Municipal Building, 222 West Hargett Street, Room 400, Raleigh, NC 27601
Fax: (919) 996-7638

Director **Carl Dawson** . . . . . (919) 996-4093
Staff Analyst **Joy Sumner** . . . . . (919) 996-4092
City Construction Management Manager **Richard Kelly** . . . (919) 807-5575
Design and Construction Manager **Chris Johnson** . . . . . (919) 996-3030
Stormwater Manager **Danny Bowden** . . . . . (919) 996-4011
Street Maintenance Superintendent
Christopher W. McGee . . . . . (919) 996-6446
Traffic Services Supervisor **Greg Hooper** . . . . . (919) 996-4334
Traffic Signals Manager **H. P. Humphries** . . . . . (919) 996-4061
Transportation Operations Manager **Mike Kennon** . . . . . (919) 996-4037
Vehicle Fleet Services Supervisor **Travis Brown** . . . . . (919) 996-6407
Parking Administrator **Gordon Dash** . . . . . (919) 996-4041

Raleigh Convention Center

500 South Salisbury Street, Raleigh, NC 27601
Fax: (919) 996-8550

Director **(Vacant)** . . . . . (919) 996-8505
Assistant Director **Douglas Grissom** . . . . . (919) 996-8503
General Manager **Jamie Jenkins** . . . . . (919) 996-8708

City of Rancho Cucamonga, California

City Hall, 10500 Civic Center Dr., Rancho Cucamonga, CA 91730
Tel: (909) 477-2700 (Information) Internet: www.cityofrc.us/

County: San Bernardino **Election Type:** Nonpartisan **Year Incorporated:** 1977 **Population:** 175,236 (2015)

Office of the Mayor and City Council

City Hall, 10500 Civic Center Drive, Rancho Cucamonga, CA 91730
Fax: (909) 477-2846

★ Mayor **L. Dennis Michael** . . . . . (909) 477-2700
Began Service: December 1, 2010
Term Expires: December 5, 2018
E-mail: council@cityofrc.us
Executive Assistant **Donna Kendrena** . . . . . (909) 477-2700
E-mail: donna.kendrena@cityofrc.us
★ Mayor Pro Tem **Sam Spagnolo** . . . . . (909) 477-2700
Term Expires: December 5, 2016
E-mail: council@cityofrc.us
★ Council Member **William J. Alexander** . . . . . (909) 477-2700
Term Expires: December 5, 2018
E-mail: council@cityofrc.us
★ Council Member **Lynne Kennedy** . . . . . (909) 477-2700
Term Expires: December 5, 2016
E-mail: lynne.kennedy@cityofrc.us
★ Council Member **Diane Williams** . . . . . (909) 477-2700
Term Expires: December 5, 2018
E-mail: council@cityofrc.us

Office of the City Manager

City Hall, 10500 Civic Center Drive, Rancho Cucamonga, CA 91730
Fax: (909) 477-2846

○ City Manager **John Gillison** . . . . . (909) 477-2700 ext. 2000
E-mail: john.gillison@cityofrc.us
Assistant City Manager **Linda Daniels** . . . . . (909) 477-2700 ext. 2050
E-mail: linda.daniels@cityofrc.us
Executive Assistant **Donna Kendrena** . . . . . (909) 477-2700 ext. 2015
E-mail: donna.kendrena@cityofrc.us

Office of the City Clerk

City Hall, 10500 Civic Center Dr., Rancho Cucamonga, CA 91730
Fax: (909) 919-2905

★ City Clerk **Jan Reynolds** . . . . . (909) 477-2700
Term Expires: November 30, 2016
E-mail: jan.reynolds@cityofrc.us
Director of City Clerk Services **Linda Troyan** . . (909) 477-2700 ext. 2005
E-mail: linda.troyan@CityofRC.us

Administrative Services Department

City Hall, 10500 Civic Center Dr., Rancho Cucamonga, CA 91730
Fax: (909) 477-2845

Deputy City Manager **Lori Sassoon** . . . . . (909) 477-2700 ext. 2400
E-mail: lori.sassoon@cityofrc.us
Finance Officer **Tamara Layne** . . . . . (909) 477-2700
GIS/Special Districts Manager **Ingrid Y. Bruce** . . . . . (909) 477-2700
Fax: (909) 477-2849
Human Resources Director **Robert Neiuber** . . . . . (909) 477-2700
E-mail: robert.neiuber@cityofrc.us
DoIT Manager **Darryl Polk** . . . . . (909) 477-2700
E-mail: darryl.polk@CityofRC.us
Purchasing Manager **Ruth Cain** . . . . . (909) 477-2700
E-mail: ruth.cain@cityofrc.us

Animal Care and Services Department
11780 Arrow Route, Rancho Cucamonga, CA 91730
Fax: (909) 919-2698

Animal Services Director **Veronica Fincher** . . . . (909) 466-7387

Building and Safety Services Department
City Hall, 10500 Civic Center Dr., Rancho Cucamonga, CA 91730
Fax: (909) 477-2711

Director **Trang Huynh** . . . . (909) 477-2711

Community Services Department
City Hall, 10500 Civic Center Dr., Rancho Cucamonga, CA 91730
Fax: (909) 477-2761

Director **Nettie Nielsen** . . . . (909) 477-2760
E-mail: nettie.nielsen@cityofrc.us

Engineering Services Department
City Hall, 10500 Civic Center Dr., Rancho Cucamonga, CA 91730
Fax: (909) 477-2741

City Engineer **(Vacant)** . . . . (909) 477-2740

Fire Protection District
City Hall, 10500 Civic Center Dr., Rancho Cucamonga, CA 91730
Fax: (909) 477-2772

Fire Chief **Mike Costello** . . . . (909) 477-2770
E-mail: mike.costello@cityofrc.us

Planning Division
City Hall, 10500 Civic Center Dr., Rancho Cucamonga, CA 91730
Fax: (909) 477-2847

Planning Director **Candyce Burnett** . . . . (909) 477-4301
Deputy City Manager **Jeff Bloom** . . . . (909) 477-4301
E-mail: jeff.bloom@cityofrc.us

Public Works Services
9153 9th Street, Rancho Cucamonga, CA 91730
Fax: (909) 477-2731

Director **Bill Wittkopf** . . . . (909) 477-2730

Rancho Cucamonga Public Library
7368 Archibald Ave., Rancho Cucamonga, CA 91730
Fax: (909) 477-2721

Library Director **Michelle Perera** . . . . (909) 477-2720
E-mail: michelle.perera@cityofrc.us

City of Reno, Nevada

One East First Street, 15th Floor, Reno, NV 89501
P.O. Box 1900, Reno, NV 89505
Tel: (775) 334-4636 (Information) Internet: www.reno.gov

County: Washoe **Election Type:** Nonpartisan **Population:** 241,445 (2015)

Office of the Mayor and City Council
One East First Street, 15th Floor, Reno, NV 89501
P.O. Box 1900, Reno, NV 89505
Fax: (775) 334-2097

★ Mayor **Hillary Schieve** . . . . (775) 334-2001
Began Service: November 12, 2014
Term Expires: November 2018
E-mail: schieveh@reno.gov
Community Liaison **Barbara Dicianno** . . . . (775) 334-3112
E-mail: diciannob@reno.gov

Office of the Mayor and City Council *continued*

★ Council Member **Jenny Brekhus** (Ward 1) . . . . (775) 334-2011
Term Expires: November 2016
E-mail: brekhusj@reno.gov

★ Council Member **Naomi Duerr** (Ward 2) . . . . (775) 334-2017
Term Expires: November 2018
E-mail: duerrn@reno.gov

★ Council Member **Oscar Delgado** (Ward 3) . . . . (775) 334-2012
Term Expires: November 2016
E-mail: delgadoo@reno.gov

★ Council Member **Paul McKenzie** (Ward 4) . . . . (775) 334-2015
Term Expires: November 2018
E-mail: mckenziep@reno.gov

★ Council Member **Neoma Jardon** (Ward 5) . . . . (775) 334-2016
Term Expires: November 2016
E-mail: jardonn@reno.gov

★ Council Member **David Bobzien** (At-Large) . . . . (775) 334-2014
Term Expires: November 2016
E-mail: bobziend@reno.gov
Education: George Mason BA; Boise State MPA

Office of the City Attorney
One East First Street, 3rd Floor, Reno, NV 89501
P.O. Box 1900, Reno, NV 89505
Fax: (775) 334-2420

★ City Attorney **Karl S. Hall** . . . . (775) 334-2050
Term Expires: November 2018
E-mail: hallk@reno.gov

Office of the City Clerk
One East First Street, 2nd Floor, Reno, NV 89501
P.O. Box 7, Reno, NV 89504
Fax: (775) 334-2432

○ City Clerk **Ashley D. Turney** . . . . (775) 348-6916

Office of the City Manager
One East First Street, 15th Floor, Reno, NV 89501
P.O. Box 1900, Reno, NV 89505
Fax: (775) 334-2097

■ City Manager **Andrew K. Clinger** . . . . (775) 334-2020
E-mail: clingera@reno.gov
Education: Nevada (Reno) 1995 BSBA

Assistant City Manager **Maureen McKissick** . . . . (775) 334-2020
E-mail: mckissickm@reno.gov

Assistant City Manager **Kate Thomas** . . . . (775) 334-2020
E-mail: renodirect@reno.gov
Education: Michigan State; U Phoenix MBA

Assistant City Manager **William Thomas** . . . . (775) 334-2020
E-mail: renodirect@reno.gov

Public Relations Coordinator **Mary-Sarah Kinner** . . . . (775) 326-6664
Communications Program Manager
Matthew B. Brown . . . . (775) 785-5855
E-mail: brownm@reno.gov
Education: Cal State (Chico) 2003 BA
Communication and Community Engagement Director
Deanna Gescheider . . . . (775) 348-3909
E-mail: gescheiderd@reno.gov

Department of Communication and Technology
One East First Street, 5th Floor, Reno, NV 89501
P.O. Box 1900, Reno, NV 89505

Information Technology Manager **Daniel Johnson** . . . . . . (775) 334-2301
E-mail: johnsond@reno.gov Fax: (775) 334-2409

★ Elected Official ▲ Appointed by Legislature ▼ Appointed by Governor ▶ Appointed by Board or Commission ● Appointed by Judge
■ Appointed by Mayor △ Appointed by Freeholders ▽ Appointed by Supervisor ▷ Appointed by County Executive ○ Appointed by Council

Community Development and Redevelopment Agency
P.O. Box 1900, Reno, NV 89505

Community Development Director (Interim)
Alex Woodley . . . . (775) 334-3814
E-mail: woodleya@reno.gov
Planning Manager **Claudia Hanson** . . . . (775) 334-2381
Senior Civil Engineer **Bill Gall** . . . . (775) 334-2028
E-mail: GallW@reno.gov
Building and Safety Manager **Dan Holly** . . . . (775) 334-2063
Code Enforcement Manager **Alex Woodley** . . . . (775) 334-3814
Economic Development Manager **(Vacant)** . . . . (775) 334-3814
Senior Planner Community Housing **Des Craig** . . . . (775) 334-2578

Finance Department
One East First Street, 2nd Floor, Reno, NV 89501
P.O. Box 1900, Reno, NV 89505

Director of Finance and Administration **Robert Chisel** . . . (775) 334-2080
Education: Nevada (Reno) BSBA
Assistant Finance Director **Jill Olsen** . . . . (775) 334-2080

Fire Department
P.O. Box 1900, Reno, NV 89505

Fire Chief **David "Dave" Cochran** . . . . (775) 334-2300
E-mail: cochrand@reno.gov
Fire Marshal **Jenniver Donahue** . . . . (775) 813-8120
E-mail: donohueje@reno.gov

Human Resources
One East First Street, 4th Floor, Reno, NV 89501
P.O. Box 1900, Reno, NV 89505
Tel: (775) 334-2285 Fax: (775) 334-2045

Director **Kelly Leerman** . . . . (775) 334-2285
E-mail: leermank@reno.gov

Parks. Recreation and Community Services Department
1301 Valley Road, Reno, NV 89512
P.O. Box 1900, Reno, NV 89505

Director **Andy Bass** . . . . (775) 334-2260

Police Department
455 East Second Street, Reno, NV 89502
P.O. Box 1900, Reno, NV 89505

Chief of Police **Jason Soto** . . . . (775) 334-2100

Public Works Department
One East First Street, Suite 800, Reno, NV 89501
Fax: (775) 334-2490

Director/City Engineer **John Flansberg** . . . . (775) 334-2350
E-mail: flansbergj@reno.gov
Maintenance and Operations Division Manager
Erich Strunge . . . . (775) 334-2243
1640 East Commercial Row, Reno, NV 89512 Fax: (775) 334-2243
E-mail: strungee@reno.gov
Engineering Manager **Charla Honey** . . . . (775) 334-2191
E-mail: honeyc@reno.gov Fax: (775) 334-2490

City of Richardson, Texas
411 West Arapaho Road, Richardson, TX 75080-4100
Tel: (972) 744-4100 Internet: www.cor.net/

County: Collin; Dallas **Election Type:** Nonpartisan **Charter:** 1873
Population: 110,815 (2015)

Office of the Mayor and City Council
411 West Arapaho Road, Richardson, TX 75080-4100

★Mayor **Paul Voelker** . . . . (972) 744-4203
Began Service: May 2015
Term Expires: May 2017
E-mail: paul.voelker@cor.gov
★Mayor Pro Tem **Mark Solomon** (Place 2) . . . . (972) 744-4203
Term Expires: May 2017
Education: Southeastern Louisiana BA; Southern Mississippi MA
★Council Member **Bob Townsend** (Place 1) . . . . (972) 744-4203
Term Expires: May 2017
E-mail: bob.townsend@cor.gov
Education: Southern Methodist MA
★Council Member **Scott Dunn** (Place 3) . . . . (972) 744-4203
Term Expires: May 2017
E-mail: scott.dunn@cor.gov
Date of Birth: October 28, 1962
Education: Amber 1988
★Council Member **Mabel Simpson** (Place 4) . . . . (972) 744-4203
Term Expires: May 18, 2017
★Council Member **Marta Gómez Frey** (Place 5) . . . . (972) 744-4203
Term Expires: May 2017
E-mail: marta.frey@cor.gov
★Council Member **Steve Mitchell** (Place 6) . . . . (972) 744-4203
Term Expires: May 2017
E-mail: steve.mitchell@cor.gov
Education: North Texas BS, MS

City Manager's Office
411 West Arapaho Road, Richardson, TX 75080-4100

City Manager **Dan Johnson** . . . . (972) 744-4201
E-mail: dan.johnson@cor.gov
First Assistant City Manager **Don Magner** . . . . (972) 744-4202
E-mail: don.magner@cor.gov
Assistant City Manager, Development Services
Cliff Miller . . . . (972) 744-4206
E-mail: cliff.miller@cor.gov
Assistant City Manager, Administrative Services
Shanna Sims-Bradish . . . . (972) 744-4210
E-mail: shanna.sims-bradish@cor.gov
Chief Financial Officer **Kent Pfeil** . . . . (972) 744-4202

Office of the City Secretary
411 West Arapaho Road, Richardson, TX 75080-4100

City Secretary **Aimee Nemer** . . . . (972) 744-4292
E-mail: aimee.nemer@cor.gov
Deputy City Secretary **Vickie Schmid** . . . . (972) 744-4292
E-mail: vickie.schmid@cor.gov
Records Coordinator **Patti Tschirhart** . . . . (972) 744-4292

Office of Emergency Management
136 North Greenville Avenue, Richardson, TX 75081

Emergency Management Coordinator **Mistie Gardner** . . . . (972) 744-4212
E-mail: mistie.gardner@cor.gov

Capital Projects/Engineering Department
411 West Arapaho Road, Richardson, TX 75080-4100
Fax: (972) 744-5804

Director of Engineering **Steve Spanos** . . . . (972) 744-4280
E-mail: steve.spanos@cor.gov

(continued on next page)

★Elected Official ▲Appointed by Legislature ▼Appointed by Governor ▶Appointed by Board or Commission ●Appointed by Judge
■Appointed by Mayor △Appointed by Freeholders ▽Appointed by Supervisor ▷Appointed by County Executive ○Appointed by Council

Capital Projects/Engineering Department *continued*

Assistant Director of Engineering **Jim Lockart** . . . . (972) 744-4280
E-mail: jim.lockart@cor.gov
Assistant Director of Engineering **Jim Dulac** . . . . (972) 744-4280
E-mail: jim.dulac@cor.gov
Facilities Maintenance Manager **Jeff Savage** . . . . (972) 744-4280
E-mail: jeff.savage@cor.gov

Civic Center
411 West Arapaho Road, Suite 102, Richardson, TX 75080-4100
Tel: (972) 744-4090 Fax: (972) 744-5816

Manager **Donna Leach** . . . . (972) 744-4092

Community Services Department
411 West Arapaho Road, Richardson, TX 75080-4100

Administrator **Lindsay Truman** . . . . (972) 744-4168

Convention and Visitors Bureau
411 West Arapaho Road, Suite 105, Richardson, TX 75080-4100
Fax: (972) 744-5834 Internet: www.richardsontexas.org/Default.aspx

Director **Geoff Wright** . . . . (972) 744-4035

Development Services Department
411 West Arapaho Road, Richardson, TX 75080-4100
Fax: (972) 744-4320

Director **Michael Spicer** . . . . (972) 744-4240

Finance Department
411 West Arapaho Road, Richardson, TX 75080-4100

Director of Finance **Keith Dagen** . . . . (972) 744-4146
Tax Assessor/Collector **Pam Gidney** . . . . (972) 744-4146
E-mail: pam.gidney@cor.gov
Controller **Vicki McCarthy** . . . . (972) 744-4062
Purchasing Manager **(Vacant)** . . . . (972) 744-4146
Fleet and Materials Manager **Ernie Ramos** . . . . (972) 744-4420
1260 Columbia Drive, Richardson, TX 75081

Fire Department
136 North Greenville Avenue, Richardson, TX 75081

Fire Chief **Alan Palomba** . . . . (972) 744-5700
E-mail: alan.palomba@cor.gov

Health Department
411 West Arapaho Road, Room 107, Richardson, TX 75080-4100

Director of Health **Bill Alsup** . . . . (972) 744-4079

Human Resources Department
411 West Arapaho Road, Suite 103, Richardson, TX 75080-4100

Director **Jose Moreno** . . . . (972) 744-4000
E-mail: jose.moreno@cor.gov
Assistant Director **(Vacant)** . . . . (972) 744-4000

Parks and Recreation Department
411 West Arapaho Road, Richardson, TX 75080-4100

Director **Lori Smeby** . . . . (972) 744-4300
Assistant Director of Parks and Planning **Roger Scott** . . . . (972) 744-4300

Police Department [RPD]
140 North Greenville Avenue, Richardson, TX 75081
Internet: http://www.cor.net/index.aspx?page=16

Chief of Police **Jim Spivey** . . . . (972) 744-4800

Public Library
900 Civic Center Drive, Richardson, TX 75080

Director **Susan Allison** . . . . (972) 744-4350
E-mail: susan.allison@cor.gov

Public Services Department
411 West Arapaho Road, Richardson, TX 75080-4100

Director **Darryl Fourte** . . . . (972) 744-4224
E-mail: darryl.fourte@cor.gov
Assistant Director (Interim) **Hunter Stephens** . . . . (972) 744-4495
E-mail: hunter.stephens@cor.gov

City of Richmond, California

450 Civic Center Plaza, Richmond, CA 94804
Tel: (510) 620-6512 Fax: (510) 620-6542
Internet: www.ci.richmond.ca.us

County: Contra Costa **Year Founded:** 1905 **Year Incorporated:** 1905
Population: 109,708 (2015)

Office of the Mayor and City Council
450 Civic Center Plaza, Richmond, CA 94804
Fax: (510) 620-6861 Internet: www.ci.richmond.ca.us/index.aspx?NID=29

★ Mayor **Thomas K "Tom" Butt** . . . . (510) 620-6503
Began Service: January 13, 2015 Fax: (510) 412-2070
Term Expires: January 8, 2019
E-mail: tom.butt@intres.com
Education: UCLA MAUD
★ Vice Mayor **Eduardo Martinez** . . . . (510) 620-6861
Term Expires: January 8, 2019
E-mail: eduardo_martinez@ci.richmond.ca.us
★ Council Member **Nathaniel "Nat" Bates** . . . . (510) 620-6861
Term Expires: January 10, 2017
E-mail: natbates@comcast.net
Education: San Francisco State U BA
★ Council Member **Jovanka Beckles** . . . . (510) 620-6861
Term Expires: January 8, 2019
E-mail: jovanka_beckles@ci.richmond.ca.us
★ Council Member **Gayle McLaughlin** . . . . (510) 620-6861
Term Expires: January 8, 2019
E-mail: gayle_mclaughlin@ci.richmond.ca.us
★ Council Member **Jael Myrick** . . . . (510) 620-6861
Term Expires: January 8, 2017
E-mail: jael_myrick@ci.richmond.ca.us
★ Council Member **Vinay Pimplé** . . . . (510) 620-6861
Term Expires: January 14, 2017

Office of the City Manager
450 Civic Center Plaza, Richmond, CA 94804
Fax: (510) 620-6542

○ City Manager **Bill Lindsay** . . . . (510) 620-6512
E-mail: bill_lindsay@ci.richmond.ca.us

City Attorney's Office
450 Civic Center Plaza, Richmond, CA 94804
Fax: (510) 620-6518

City Attorney **Bruce Reed Goodmiller** . . . . (510) 620-6509
E-mail: city_attorney@ci.richmond.ca.us
Education: UC Berkeley 1971 BA; John F Kennedy 1984 JD

★ Elected Official ▲ Appointed by Legislature ▼ Appointed by Governor ► Appointed by Board or Commission ● Appointed by Judge
■ Appointed by Mayor △ Appointed by Freeholders ▽ Appointed by Supervisor ▷ Appointed by County Executive ○ Appointed by Council

City Clerk's Office
450 Civic Center Plaza, Richmond, CA 94804
Fax: (510) 620-6542

City Clerk **Pamela Christian** .... (510) 620-6513
E-mail: Pamela_Christian@ci.richmond.ca.us

Community Redevelopment Agency
450 Civic Center Plaza, Richmond, CA 94804
Fax: (510) 307-8149

Manager **Chadrick Smalley** .... (510) 307-8134

Richmond Housing Authority [RHA]
440 Civic Center Plaza, Richmond, CA 94804
Fax: (510) 237-5230

Executive Director **Tim Jones** .... (510) 621-1300

Employment and Training Department
330 25th Street, Richmond, CA 94804
Fax: (510) 307-8072

Director **Sal Vaca** .... (510) 307-8014
E-mail: sal_vaca@ci.richmond.ca.us

Community Services Department
440 Civic Center Plaza, Richmond, CA 94804
Fax: (510) 620-6583

Community Services Director **DeVone Boggan** .... (510) 620-6793
E-mail: devone_boggan@ci.richmond.ca.us

Engineering Services Department
450 Civic Center Plaza, Richmond, CA 94804
Fax: (510) 307-8116

City Engineer **(Vacant)** .... (510) 307-8137
E-mail: engineering@ci.richmond.ca.us

Finance Department
450 Civic Center Plaza, Richmond, CA 94804
Fax: (510) 620-6522

Finance Director **Belinda Warner** .... (510) 620-6740

Fire Department
440 Civic Center Plaza, Richmond, CA 94804
Fax: (510) 307-8048

Fire Chief **Adrian Sheppard** .... (510) 307-8031
E-mail: adrian_sheppard@ci.richmond.ca.us

Human Resources Management Department
450 Civic Center Plaza, Suite 310, Richmond, CA 94804
Internet: http://www.ci.richmond.ca.us/index.aspx?nid=60

Human Resources Management Director (Interim)
Lisa Stephenson .... (510) 620-6602
E-mail: lisa_stephenson@ci.richmond.ca.us

Information Technology Department
450 Civic Center Plaza, Richmond, CA 94804
Fax: (510) 620-6528

Information Technology Director **Sue Hartman** .... (510) 620-6970
E-mail: sue_hartman@ci.richmond.ca.us

Richmond Public Library
325 Civic Center Plaza, Richmond, CA 94804
Internet: http://www.ci.richmond.ca.us/index.aspx?NID=105

Library Director **Katy Curl** .... (510) 620-6555
E-mail: katy_curl@ci.richmond.ca.us

Planning and Building Services Department
450 Civic Center Plaza, Richmond, CA 94804

Director **Richard Mitchell** .... (510) 620-6868

Police Department
1701 Regatta Boulevard, Richmond, CA 94804
Fax: (510) 620-6880

Chief of Police **Allwyn Brown** .... (510) 620-6655
Code Enforcement Manager **Tim Higares** .... (510) 621-1279

Port of Richmond
1411 Harbour Way South, Richmond, CA 94804
Fax: (510) 233-3105

Executive Director **Jim Matzorkis** .... (510) 620-6784

Public Works Department
#6 - 13th Street, Richmond, CA 94801
Fax: (510) 231-3014

Director **Yader A. Bermudez** .... (510) 231-3008

City of Richmond, Virginia
City Hall, 900 East Broad Street, Richmond, VA 23219
Tel: (804) 646-7000 (Information) Internet: www.richmondgov.com

County: None **Election Type:** Nonpartisan **Population:** 217,853 (2015)

Office of the Mayor
900 East Broad Street, Suite 201, Richmond, VA 23219
Tel: (804) 646-7970 Fax: (804) 646-7987
Internet: http://www.richmondgov.com/Mayor/index.aspx

★ Mayor **Dwight Clinton Jones** .... (804) 646-7970
Began Service: January 1, 2009
Term Expires: December 31, 2016
E-mail: askthemayor@richmondgov.com
Education: Virginia Union 1970 BA, 1973 MDiv
Executive Assistant to the Mayor **Cheryl Green** ...... (804) 646-7970
E-mail: cheryl.green@richmondgov.com

■ Chief of Staff **(Vacant)** .... (804) 646-7970
■ Deputy Chief of Staff **Don Mark** .... (804) 646-7970
E-mail: don.mark@richmondgov.com

■ Senior Policy Analyst **David M. Hicks** .... (804) 646-7970
E-mail: david.hicks@richmondgov.com
Education: Virginia BA, JD

■ Press Secretary **Tammy Hawley** .... (804) 646-7985
E-mail: tammy.hawley@richmondgov.com Fax: (804) 646-5945
Education: VCU 1983 BS

Office of the Chief Administrative Officer
City Hall, 900 East Broad Street, 2nd Floor, Richmond, VA 23219
Tel: (804) 646-7978 Fax: (804) 646-3027

■ Chief Administrative Officer **Selena Cuffee-Glenn** ...... (804) 646-7978
Deputy Chief Administrative Officer for Economic Development **Lee Downey** .... (804) 646-4848
E-mail: lee.downey@richmondgov.com

■ Deputy Chief Administrative Officer for Finance and Administration **Lenora Reid** .... (804) 646-0485
E-mail: lenora.reid@richmondgov.com

Deputy Chief Administrative Officer for Human Services **Debra D. Gardner** .... (804) 646-3144
E-mail: debra.gardner@richmondgov.com

Deputy Chief Administrative Officer for Operations (Interim) **John J. Buturla** .... (804) 646-5361

(continued on next page)

★ Elected Official ▲ Appointed by Legislature ▼ Appointed by Governor ► Appointed by Board or Commission ● Appointed by Judge
■ Appointed by Mayor △ Appointed by Freeholders ▽ Appointed by Supervisor ▷ Appointed by County Executive ○ Appointed by Council

Office of the Chief Administrative Officer *continued*

Chief Service Officer **Paul Manning** .... (804) 646-6528
Education: Virginia Tech BSEE

Budget and Strategic Planning Department

900 East Broad Street, Room 1100, Richmond, VA 23219
Tel: (804) 646-7913 Fax: (804) 646-7927
Internet: www.richmondgov.com/Budget/index.aspx

Director **Jay Brown** .... (804) 646-3193
E-mail: jay.brown@richmondgov.com

Department of Economic and Community Development

Main Street Station, 1500 East Main Street, Suite 400, Richmond, VA 23219
Fax: (804) 646-6793 Internet: http://yesrichmondva.com/

Director (Interim) **Douglas Dunlap** .... (804) 646-5633
E-mail: douglas.dunlap@richmondgov.com
Deputy Director, Neighborhood Revitalization **Denise Lawus** .... (804) 646-3975
E-mail: Denise.Lawus@richmondgov.com
Chief Credit Officer, Financial Strategies **Ron Johnson** .. (804) 646-7489
E-mail: Ron.Johnson@richmondgov.com
Chief Operating Officer **Jane C. Ferrara** .... (804) 646-5633
E-mail: Jane.Ferrara@richmondgov.com
Tourism Coordinator **Anedra Bourne** .... (804) 646-1795
E-mail: anedra.bourne@richmondgov.com
Program Manager, Transportation Development **Viktoria Badger** .... (804) 646-5871
E-mail: Viktoria.Badger@richmondgov.com
Program Administrator, Business Attraction and Expansion **Betty-Anne Teter** .... (804) 646-1823
E-mail: Betty-Anne.Teter@richmondgov.com
Program Administrator, Real Estate Development **Paul McClellan** .... (804) 646-3061
E-mail: Paul.McClellan@richmondgov.com
Program Administrator, Workforce Development **Jamison Manion** .... (804) 646-6374
E-mail: Jamison.Manion@richmondgov.com

Finance Department

900 East Broad Street, Richmond, VA 23219
Tel: (804) 646-7000 Internet: www.richmondgov.com/Finance/

Finance Director (Acting) **James Duval** .... (804) 646-5829
City Controller **(Vacant)** .... (804) 646-5829

Fire and Emergency Services Department

201 East Franklin Street, Richmond, VA 23219
Tel: (804) 646-2500 Fax: (804) 646-3324
Internet: www.richmondgov.com/Fire/

Chief of Fire and Emergency Services **Robert A. Creecy** .... (804) 646-5451
E-mail: robert.creecy@richmondgov.com Fax: (804) 646-6671

Human Resources Department

City Hall, 900 East Broad Street, Room 902, Richmond, VA 23219
Tel: (804) 646-5660 Fax: (804) 646-6856
Internet: www.richmondgov.com/HumanResources/index.aspx

Director **Johnny McLean** .... (804) 646-6630
E-mail: johnny.mclean@richmondgov.com

Social Services Department

900 E. Marshall, Richmond, VA 23219
Fax: (804) 646-7441
Internet: www.richmondgov.com/SocialServices/index.aspx

Social Services Department Director **Shunda Giles** Room 330 .... (804) 646-7337
Fax: (804) 646-7441

Social Services Department *continued*

Deputy Director, Children, Families and Adults **Brinette Jones** .... (804) 646-1835
Deputy Director, Economic Support and Independence **Patrice Carpenter** .... (804) 646-6875
Deputy Director, Finance and Administration **Myrtle Brown** .... (804) 646-7337

Information Technology

900 East Broad Street, Room G-2, Richmond, VA 23219
Tel: (804) 646-5639 Fax: (804) 646-7048
Internet: www.richmondgov.com/InformationTechnology/

Director **(Vacant)** .... (804) 646-6539
Deputy Director/Information Technology Manager, Application Solutions **Charles Todd** .... (804) 646-6615
E-mail: charles.todd@richmondgov.com
Information Technology Manager, Infrastructure **Paul Florenz** .... (804) 646-3605
E-mail: paul.florenz@richmondgov.com
Information Technology Manager, User Services **Bernard Hanzer** .... (804) 646-5975
E-mail: bernard.hanzer@richmondgov.com

Parks, Recreation and Community Facilities

1209 Admiral Street, Richmond, VA 23220
Tel: (804) 646-5733 Fax: (804) 646-6931
E-mail: askparkrec@richmondgov.com
Internet: www.richmondgov.com/parks

Director **Dr. Norman C. Merrifield** .... (804) 646-5717
Deputy Director **Deborah E. Morton** .... (804) 645-5714
E-mail: deborah.morton@richmondgov.com
Education: Brooklyn 1979 BA; VCU 1982 MURP
Marketing and Public Relations **Tamara Jenkins** .... (804) 646-1087
E-mail: tamara.jenkins@richmondgov.com
Systems Developer **(Vacant)** .... (804) 646-5702
Fax: (804) 646-6931

Planning and Development Review [DPDR]

900 East Broad Street, Room 511, Richmond, VA 23219
Fax: (804) 646-5789

Director **Mark A. Olinger** .... (804) 646-6305
E-mail: mark.olinger@richmondgov.com
Education: NYU 1979 BA; Cincinnati 1981 MCP

Police Department

Police Headquarters, 200 West Grace Street, Richmond, VA 23220
Fax: (804) 646-3974 Internet: www.richmondgov.com/Police/

■ Chief of Police **Alfred Durham** .... (804) 646-6700
E-mail: durhama@ci.richmond.va.us
Deputy Chief of Police **Steve Drew** .... (804) 646-6700
Deputy Chief of Police **Eric English** .... (804) 646-6700
Deputy Chief of Police (Acting) **Michael Shamus** ...... (804) 646-6700

Department of Procurement Services

900 East Broad Street, Room 1104, Richmond, VA 23219
Fax: (804) 646-5989 Internet: www.richmondgov.com/Procurement/

Director **Edward C. Gibbs** .... (804) 646-5798
E-mail: edward.gibbs@richmondgov.com

Richmond Public Library

101 E. Franklin St., Richmond, VA 23219-2107
Tel: (804) 646-4256 Fax: (804) 646-7685
Internet: http://www.richmondpubliclibrary.org

Library Director **(Vacant)** .... (804) 646-2547
Deputy Director **Clayton Dishon** .... (804) 646-2548
E-mail: clay.dishon@richmondgov.com

Public Utilities

730 East Broad Street, 6th Floor, Richmond, VA 23219
Tel: (804) 646-7000 Fax: (804) 646-2870
Internet: www.richmondgov.com/PublicUtilities/

Director **Robert "Bob" Steidel** . . . . . (804) 646-5200
Deputy Director, Natural Gas Distribution **Al Scott** . . . . . (804) 646-8307
Deputy Director, Engineering Services, Capital Improvement Projects **Rosemary H. Green** . . . . . (804) 646-5217
E-mail: rosemary.green@richmondgov.com
Deputy Director, Water and Wastewater Treatment Plant and Stormwater Utility **(Vacant)** . . . . . (804) 646-7000
Energy Services Manager/Natural Gas Marketing **Mike Kearns** . . . . . (804) 646-5215
Public Information Manager **Angela Fountain** . . . . . (804) 646-7323
E-mail: angela.fountain@richmondgov.com

Public Works [DPW]

Tel: (804) 646-6430 Fax: (804) 646-6629

Director **Emmanuel Adediran** . . . . . (804) 646-6430
900 E. Broad St., Room 701, Richmond, VA 23219-1907
Executive Assistant to the Director **Jacqueline Howie** . . (804) 646-3702
900 East Broad Street, Room 704, Richmond, VA 23219-1907
E-mail: jacqueline.howie@richmondgov.com
Deputy Director, General Services **Lynne Lancaster** . . . . . (804) 646-0440
900 E. Broad St., Richmond, VA 23219-1907
Deputy Director, Finance Administration **(Vacant)** . . . . . (804) 646-6621
900 E. Broad St., Room 701, Richmond, VA 23219-1907
Deputy Director, Operations **Bobby Vincent** . . . . . (804) 646-6444
900 E. Broad St., Room 701, Richmond, VA 23219-1907
E-mail: bobby.vincent@richmondgov.com
Deputy Director-City Engineer **M.S. Khara** . . . . . (804) 646-5413
900 E. Broad St., Room 704, Richmond, VA 23219-1907
Public Information Manager **Sharon North** . . . . . (804) 646-5607
E-mail: sharon.north@richmondgov.com Fax: (804) 646-6629
Education: Youngstown State BA; Akron MA
City Transportation Engineer **Michael B. Sawyer** . . . . . (804) 646-3435
900 E. Broad St., Room 704, Richmond, VA 23219-1907
E-mail: michael.sawyer@richmondgov.com

Redevelopment and Housing Authority

901 Chamberlayne Parkway, Richmond, VA 23220
P.O. Box 26887, Richmond, VA 23261-6887
Fax: (804) 780-0009 E-mail: info@rrha.com Internet: www.rrha.com

Chief Executive Officer **T.K. Somanath** . . . . . (804) 780-4246
E-mail: tk.somanath@rrha.com

Richmond City Sustainability

900 East Broad Street, Room 1105, Richmond, VA 23219
Internet: http://www.richmondgov.com/sustainability/

■ Sustainability Project Manager **Alicia Zatcoff** . . . . . (804) 646-3055
E-mail: green@richmondgov.com

Richmond Retirement System

730 East Broad Street, Suite 900, Richmond, VA 23219
Fax: (804) 646-5299 Internet: www.richmondgov.com/Retirement/

▶ Executive Director **Leo Griffin** . . . . . (804) 646-5958
E-mail: leo.griffin@richmondgov.com

Office of the City Council

City Hall, 900 E. Broad St., Suite 200, Richmond, VA 23219
Tel: (804) 646-7955 Fax: (804) 646-7736
Internet: www.richmondgov.com/CityCouncil/

★ Council President **Michelle R. Mosby** (District 9) . . . . . (804) 646-5497
Term Expires: December 31, 2016 Fax: (804) 646-5468
E-mail: michelle.mosby@richmondgov.com
★ Vice President **Christopher A. Hilbert** (District 3) . . . . . (804) 646-0070
Term Expires: December 31, 2016 Fax: (804) 646-5468
E-mail: chris.hilbert@richmondgov.com
Education: Tennessee BS, MBA

Office of the City Council *continued*

★ Council Member **Jonathan Baliles** (District 1)
Term Expires: December 31, 2016
E-mail: jonathan.beliles@richmondgov.com
★ Council Member **Charles R. Samuels** (District 2) . . . . . (804) 646-6531
Term Expires: December 31, 2016 Fax: (804) 646-5468
E-mail: charles.samuels@richmondgov.com
★ Council Member **Katherine C Graziano** (District 4) . . . . . (804) 320-2454
Term Expires: December 31, 2016 Fax: (804) 320-2030
E-mail: kathy.graziano@richmondgov.com
Education: SUNY (Cortland) BA
★ Council Member **Parker C. Agelasto** (District 5) . . . . . (804) 646-7736
Term Expires: December 31, 2016 Fax: (804) 646-5468
E-mail: parker.agelasto@richmondgov.com
★ Council Member **Ellen F. Robertson** (District 6) . . . . . (804) 646-5348
Term Expires: December 31, 2016 Fax: (804) 646-5468
E-mail: ellen.robertson@richmondgov.com
Education: VCU BS
○ Council Member **Cynthia I. Newbille** (District 7) . . . . . (804) 646-5429
Term Expires: December 31, 2016 Fax: (804) 646-5468
E-mail: cynthia.newbille@richmondgov.com
Education: SUNY (Stony Brook) BA, MA
★ Council Member **Reva M. Trammell** (District 8) . . . . . (804) 646-6592
Term Expires: December 31, 2016 Fax: (804) 646-5468
E-mail: reva.trammell@richmondgov.com
○ Council Chief of Staff **Lou Brown Ali** . . . . . (804) 646-7955
E-mail: lou.ali@richmondgov.com
Education: South Carolina BA; VCU MSW; Richmond JD

Office of the City Assessor

City Hall, 900 East Broad Street, Room 802, Richmond, VA 23219
Fax: (804) 646-5686 Internet: www.richmondgov.com/Assessor/index.aspx

○ City Assessor **James D. Hester** . . . . . (804) 646-7500
E-mail: james.hester@richmondgov.com Fax: (804) 646-7655

Office of the City Attorney

City Hall, 900 East Broad Street, Suite 400, Richmond, VA 23219
Fax: (804) 646-6653
Internet: www.richmondgov.com/CityAttorney/index.aspx

○ City Attorney **Allen L. Jackson** . . . . . (804) 646-7940
E-mail: allen.l.jackson@richmondgov.com
Deputy City Attorney **Bonnie M. Ashley** . . . . . (804) 646-7940
Deputy City Attorney **Haskell C. Brown III** . . . . . (804) 646-7940
Deputy City Attorney **Laura K. Drewry** . . . . . (804) 646-7940
Deputy City Attorney **Kate D. O'Leary** . . . . . (804) 646-7940
E-mail: kate.o'leary@richmondgov.com
Deputy City Attorney **Stephen M. Hall** . . . . . (804) 646-7940

Office of the City Auditor

City Hall, 900 East Broad Street, Suite 806, Richmond, VA 23219-1907
Tel: (804) 646-5616 Fax: (804) 646-2230
Internet: www.richmondgov.com/Auditor/index.aspx

○ City Auditor **Umesh Dalal** . . . . . (804) 646-5640
E-mail: umesh.dalal@richmondgov.com

Office of the City Clerk

City Hall, 900 East Broad Street, Suite 200, Richmond, VA 23219
Tel: (804) 646-7955 Fax: (804) 646-7736
Internet: www.richmondgov.com/CityClerk/

○ City Clerk **Jean V. Capel** . . . . . (804) 646-7955
E-mail: jean.capel@richmondgov.com
Deputy City Clerk **Candice D. Reid** . . . . . (804) 646-7955
E-mail: candice.reid@richmondgov.com

Office of the Commonwealth's Attorney

John Marshall Courts Building, 400 North Ninth Street, Room 100, Richmond, VA 23219

★ Commonwealth's Attorney **Michael N. Herring** . . . . . (804) 646-3500
Term Expires: December 31, 2017 Fax: (804) 646-0506
E-mail: michael.herring@richmondgov.com

Office of the Registrar

City Hall, 900 East Broad Street, Room 105, Richmond, VA 23219
Fax: (804) 646-7848 E-mail: voterregistration@richmondgov.com
Internet: www.richmondgov.com/Registrar/index.aspx

General Registrar **J. Kirk Showalter** .... (804) 646-5950

Office of the Sheriff

1701 Fairfield Way, Richmond, VA 23223
Fax: (804) 646-0950 E-mail: sheriff@richmondgov.com
Internet: www.richmondgov.com/Sheriff/

★Sheriff **C.T. Woody, Jr.** .... (804) 646-0930
Term Expires: December 31, 2017
E-mail: ct.woody@richmondgov.com
Chief of Staff **Delores Anderson** .... (804) 646-0228
Fax: (804) 646-4291

Training Manager **Christopher Overby** .... (804) 646-0067
E-mail: christopher.overby@richmondgov.com Fax: (804) 646-4430
Public Affairs **Major Jerry Baldwin** .... (804) 646-0222
E-mail: jerry.baldwin@richmondgov.com Fax: (804) 646-4750
Investigations **Col. Joel Lawson** .... (804) 646-0979
Fax: (804) 646-0195

General Counsel **Tony Pham** .... (804) 646-0229
Fax: (804) 646-4291

Office of the Treasurer

City Hall, 900 East Broad Street, Suite 107, Richmond, VA 23219
Fax: (804) 646-3904

★Treasurer **Eunice Wilder** .... (804) 646-6474 ext. 3852
Term Expires: December 31, 2017
E-mail: eunice.wilder@richmondgov.com
Education: Howard U 1959 BA

Richmond Public Schools

301 N. Ninth St., 17th Floor, Richmond, VA 23219-1927
Tel: (804) 780-7710 Internet: http://www.richmond.k12.va.us

Superintendent of Schools **Dr. Dana Bedden** .... (804) 780-8320
Fax: (804) 780-4122

Executive Director for Elementary Education
Dr. Anthony Leonard .... (804) 780-7515
Fax: (804) 780-5414

Executive Director for Secondary Education
Abe Jeffers .... (804) 780-7720
Fax: (804) 780-7115

Assistant Superintendent, Support Services
Thomas Kranz .... (804) 780-7707
Fax: (804) 780-6208

Human Resources Executive Director
Dandridge Billups .... (804) 780-7325
Fax: (804) 780-8594

Chief Auditor **(Vacant)** .... (804) 780-7628
Fax: (804) 780-7099

Chief of Safety and Security **Timothy Mallory** .... (804) 780-8550

School Board

Fax: (804) 780-8133

★Chairman **Donald L. Coleman** (District 7) .... (804) 780-7719
Term Expires: December 31, 2016
E-mail: dcoleman2@richmond.k12.va.us

★Vice Chairman **Kristen N. Larson** (District 4) .... (804) 780-7719
Term Expires: December 31, 2016
E-mail: klarson@richmond.k12.va.us

★Member **(Vacant)** (District 1) .... (804) 780-7719
Term Expires: December 31, 2016

★Member **Kimberly B. Gray** (District 2) .... (804) 780-7719
Term Expires: December 31, 2016
E-mail: kgray@richmond.k12.va.us

★Member **Jeffrey M. Bourne** (District 3) .... (804) 780-7719
Term Expires: December 31, 2016
E-mail: jbourne@richmond.k12.va.us
Education: William & Mary 1999 BA

School Board *continued*

★Member **Mamie L. Taylor** (District 5) .... (804) 780-7719
Term Expires: December 31, 2016
E-mail: mtaylor4@richmond.k12.va.us

★Member **Shonda M. Harris-Muhammed** (District 6) .... (804) 780-7719
Term Expires: December 31, 2016
E-mail: smuhamme@richmond.k12.va.us

★Member **Derik E. Jones** (District 8) .... (804) 780-7719
Term Expires: December 31, 2016
E-mail: djones15@richmond.k12.va.us

★Member **Tichi L. Pinkney Eppes** (District 9) .... (804) 780-7719
Term Expires: December 31, 2016
E-mail: teppes@richmond.k12.va.us

City of Riverside, California

3900 Main Street, Riverside, CA 92522
Tel: (951) 826-5311 (Information) Internet: www.riversideca.gov

County: Riverside **Election Type:** Nonpartisan **Year Incorporated:** 1883 **Charter:** 1953 **Population:** 322,424 (2015)

Office of the Mayor and City Council

3900 Main St., Riverside, CA 92522
Fax: (951) 826-2543 E-mail: council@riversideca.gov

★Mayor **William "Rusty" Bailey** .... (951) 826-5551
Began Service: December 11, 2012 Fax: (951) 826-2543
Term Expires: June 2016
Chief of Staff **Cheryl-Marie Hansberger** .... (951) 826-5551

★Council Member **Mike Gardner** (Ward 1) .... (951) 826-5991
Term Expires: June 7, 2019

★Council Member **Andy Melendrez** (Ward 2) .... (951) 826-5991
Term Expires: June 4, 2017

★Council Member **Mike Soubirous** (Ward 3) .... (951) 826-5991
Term Expires: June 7, 2019

★Council Member **Paul Davis** (Ward 4) .... (951) 826-5991
Term Expires: June 4, 2017

★Council Member **Chris MacArthur** (Ward 5) .... (951) 826-5991
Term Expires: June 7, 2019

★Council Member **Jim Perry** (Ward 6) .... (951) 826-5991
Term Expires: June 4, 2017

★Council Member **John Burnard** (Ward 7) .... (951) 826-5991
Term Expires: June 7, 2019

Office of the City Attorney

3900 Main St., Riverside, CA 92522

○City Attorney **Gary Geuss** .... (951) 826-5567

Office of the City Clerk

3900 Main St., Riverside, CA 92522
Fax: (951) 826-5470 E-mail: city_clerk@riversideca.gov

○City Clerk **Colleen J. Nicol** .... (951) 826-5557
E-mail: city_clerk@riversideca.gov
Intergovernmental and Communications Officer
Phil Pitchford .... (951) 826-5975

Office of the City Manager

3900 Main St., Riverside, CA 92522
Fax: (951) 826-5470 E-mail: city_manager@riversideca.gov

○City Manager **John A. Russo** .... (951) 826-5553
Education: Yale 1981 BA; NYU JD
Assistant City Manager **Al Zelinka** .... (951) 826-5552
Education: Northern Arizona BS; Cornell MRP
Assistant City Manager
Marianna Marysheva-Martinez .... (951) 826-5552
Education: San Francisco State U BA; UC Berkeley MPP

★Elected Official ▲Appointed by Legislature ▼Appointed by Governor ▶Appointed by Board or Commission ●Appointed by Judge
■Appointed by Mayor △Appointed by Freeholders ▽Appointed by Supervisor ▷Appointed by County Executive ○Appointed by Council

Office of the City Manager *continued*

Assistant City Manager **Alex Nguyen** . . . . (951) 826-5190
Fleet Operations Manager **Carl Carey** . . . . (951) 351-6157
Real Property Services Manager **David Welch** . . . . (951) 826-5461

Finance Department

3900 Main St., Riverside, CA 92522
Internet: http://www.riversideca.gov/finance

Finance Director (Interim) **Scott Miller** . . . . (951) 826-5660
Controller **Edward Enriquez** . . . . (951) 826-5466
Purchasing Services Manager/Risk Manager **Art Torres** . . . (951) 826-5561
E-mail: atorres@riversideca.gov

Community and Economic Development Department

3900 Main St., Riverside, CA 92522

Director **Rafael Guzman** . . . . (951) 826-5658
E-mail: RGuzman@riversideca.gov

Office of Economic Development

3900 Main Street, 6th Floor, Riverside, CA 92522

Economic Development Manager (Interim) **Gregory Lee** . . (951) 826-5145
E-mail: glee@riversideca.gov
Business Liaison **Sherry Shimshock** . . . . (951) 826-2433
E-mail: sshimshock@riversideca.gov

Fire Department

3775 Fairmont Blvd., Riverside, CA 92501
Fax: (951) 826-5585 Internet: http://www.riversideca.gov/fire

Fire Chief **Michael Moore** . . . . (951) 826-5321
E-mail: mmoore@riversideca.gov

Human Resources Department

3780 Market St., Riverside, CA 92501
Fax: (951) 826-5943 E-mail: jobs@riversideca.gov
Internet: http://www.riversideca.gov/human

Director **Brenda Diederichs** . . . . (951) 826-5808
E-mail: bdiederichs@riversideca.gov

Innovation and Technology Department

3900 Main Street, Riverside, CA 92522

Chief Innovation Officer **Lea Deesing** . . . . (951) 826-5734
E-mail: ldeesing@riversideca.gov
Education: U Redlands BS; Cal State (Dominguez) MPA

Parks, Recreation and Community Services Department

6927 Magnolia Avenue, Riverside, CA 92501
Fax: (951) 826-2010 E-mail: parks@riversideca.gov
Internet: http://www.riversideca.gov/park_rec

Director **Adolfo Cruz** . . . . (951) 826-2000
Park Superintendent **Patricia Solano** . . . . (951) 826-2000
Recreation Superintendent **Robin Metz** . . . . (951) 826-2000

Police Department

4102 Orange St., Riverside, CA 92501
Internet: http://www.riversideca.gov/rpd

Police Chief **Sergio G. Diaz** . . . . (951) 826-5700
Deputy Police Chief **John Wallace** . . . . (951) 826-5700
Assistant Police Chief **Christopher O. Vicino** . . . . (951) 826-5700
Education: Claremont Men's Col BA; Naval Postgrad MA

Public Utilities Department

3901 Orange Street, Riverside, CA 92501
Tel: (951) 826-5485 (Programs and Services) TTY: (951) 826-5439
Fax: (951) 826-2450 Internet: http://www.riversideca.gov/utilities

General Manager **Girish Balachandran** . . . . (951) 826-8912
Chief Operating Officer (Interim) **Kevin Milligan** . . . . (951) 826-5485

Public Works Department

3900 Main St., Riverside, CA 92522
Fax: (951) 826-5542 Internet: http://www.riversideca.gov/pworks

Public Works Director/City Engineer **Kristine Martinez** . . (951) 826-5341
Traffic Engineer **Gilbert Hernandez** . . . . (951) 826-5366
Solid Waste Collections Supervisor **Archie Washington** . . . (951) 351-6103
8095 Lincoln Ave., Riverside, CA 92504

Riverside Metropolitan Museum

3580 Mission Inn Avenue, Riverside, CA 92501

Museum Director **Sarah Suverkrup Mundy** . . . . (951) 826-5273

Riverside Municipal Airport

6951 Flight Rd., Riverside, CA 92504
Fax: (951) 359-3570 E-mail: airport@riversideca.gov

Manager **Kim Ellis** . . . . (951) 351-6113

Riverside Public Library

3581 Mission Inn Ave., Riverside, CA 92501
Fax: (951) 826-5407 Internet: http://www.riversideca.gov/library

Director **Tonya Kennon** . . . . (951) 826-5373
E-mail: tkennon@riversideca.gov
Education: California Baptist U BA; San José State MS

City of Roanoke, Virginia

215 Church Avenue, SW, Roanoke, VA 24011-1536
Internet: www.roanokeva.gov

County: Roanoke **Election Type:** Partisan **Population:** 99,897 (2015)

Office of the Mayor and City Council

215 Church Avenue, SW, Room 452, Roanoke, VA 24011-1536
Fax: (540) 853-1145

★ Mayor-Elect **Sherman P. Lea** (D) . . . . (540) 853-2444
Began Service: July 1, 2016
Term Expires: June 30, 2020
E-mail: sherman.lea@roanokeva.gov
Assistant to the Mayor **Elizabeth Watson** . . . . (540) 853-2444
E-mail: elizabeth.watson@roanokeva.gov
★ Vice Mayor **Dr. David B. "Dave" Trinkle** (D) . . . . (540) 853-2541
Term Expires: June 30, 2018
E-mail: david.trinkle@roanokeva.gov
Education: Virginia MD
★ Council Member **William D. "Bill" Bestpitch** (I) . . . . (540) 853-2541
Term Expires: June 30, 2018
E-mail: bill.bestpitch@roanokeva.gov
★ Council Member-Elect **Michelle L. Dykstra** (I) . . . . (540) 853-2541
Term Expires: June 30, 2020
★ Council Member **Ray Ferris** (I) . . . . (540) 853-2541
Term Expires: June 30, 2018
E-mail: ray.ferris@roanokeva.gov
★ Council Member-Elect **John A. Garland** (I) . . . . (540) 853-2541
Term Expires: June 30, 2020
★ Council Member **Anita Price** (D) . . . . (540) 853-2541
Term Expires: June 30, 2020
E-mail: anita.price@roanokeva.gov

★ Elected Official ▲ Appointed by Legislature ▼ Appointed by Governor ▶ Appointed by Board or Commission ● Appointed by Judge
■ Appointed by Mayor △ Appointed by Freeholders ▽ Appointed by Supervisor ▷ Appointed by County Executive ○ Appointed by Council

Office of the City Attorney
215 Church Avenue, SW, Room 464, Roanoke, VA 24011-1595
Fax: (540) 853-1221 E-mail: cityatty@roanokeva.gov

○City Attorney **Daniel J. "Dan" Callaghan** . . . . (540) 853-2431
E-mail: daniel.callaghan@roanokeva.gov
Education: Villanova 1976 BA, 1979 JD

Office of the City Clerk
215 Church Avenue, SW, Room 456, Roanoke, VA 24011-1536
Fax: (540) 853-1145 E-mail: clerk@roanokeva.gov

○City Clerk **Stephanie M. Reynolds** . . . . (540) 853-2541
E-mail: clerk@roanokeva.gov
Deputy City Clerk **Susie McCoy** . . . . (540) 853-2541
E-mail: susie.mccoy@roanokeva.gov
Assistant Deputy City Clerk **Cecelia Tyree Webb** . . . . (540) 853-2541
E-mail: cecelia.webb@roanokeva.gov

Office of the Commissioner of the Revenue
215 Church Avenue, SW, Room 251, Roanoke, VA 24011-1536
Fax: (540) 853-1115 E-mail: revenue@roanokeva.gov

★Commissioner of the Revenue
Sherman A. Holland (D) . . . . (540) 853-2524
Term Expires: December 31, 2017
E-mail: sherman.holland@roanokeva.gov

Office of the Commonwealth's Attorney
315 Church Ave., SW, Room 218, Roanoke, VA 24016
Fax: (540) 853-1201 E-mail: commatty@roanokeva.gov

★Commonwealth's Attorney **Donald S. Caldwell** (D) . . . . . (540) 853-2626
Term Expires: December 31, 2017
E-mail: donald.caldwell@roanokeva.gov

Office of the Municipal Auditor
215 Church Avenue, SW, Room 502, Roanoke, VA 24011-1536
Fax: (540) 853-6395 E-mail: auditor@roanokeva.gov

○Municipal Auditor **Troy A. "Drew" Harmon** . . . . (540) 853-2644
E-mail: drew.harmon@roanokeva.gov
Assistant Municipal Auditor **Dawn Hope Mullins** . . . . (540) 853-5237

Office of the Sheriff
340 W. Campbell Ave., Roanoke, VA 24016
PO Box 494, Roanoke, VA 24003
Tel: (540) 853-2331 (Booking/Intake) Tel: (540) 853-2721 (Civil Process)
Tel: (540) 853-2621 (Jail) Fax: (540) 853-5353
E-mail: sheriff@roanokeva.gov

★Sheriff **Tim Allen** (D) . . . . (540) 853-2941
Term Expires: December 31, 2017
E-mail: tim.allen@roanokeva.gov

Office of the Treasurer
215 Church Avenue, SW, Room 254, Roanoke, VA 24011-1536
Fax: (540) 853-1019 E-mail: treasurer@roanokeva.gov

★Treasurer **Evelyn Powers** (D) . . . . (540) 853-2561
Term Expires: December 31, 2017
E-mail: evelyn.powers@roanokeva.gov

Finance Department
215 Church Avenue, Southwest, Room 461, Roanoke, VA 24011-1536
Tel: (540) 853-2824 (Accounts Payable) Tel: (540) 853-2038 (Payroll)
Tel: (540) 853-2062 (Retirement) Fax: (540) 853-2940
E-mail: finance@roanokeva.gov

Director **Barbara A. Dameron** . . . . (540) 853-2821
Administrative Secretary **Cindy Ayers** . . . . (540) 853-2821
E-mail: cindy.ayers@roanokeva.gov
Assistant Director **Andrea Trent** . . . . (540) 853-2970
Accounting Services Manager **Rene Satterwhite** . . . . (540) 853-2821
E-mail: rene.satterwhite@roanokeva.gov

Real Estate Valuation
215 Church Avenue, S.W., Room 250, Roanoke, VA 24011-1536
Tel: (540) 853-2771 Fax: (540) 853-2796
E-mail: realestate@roanokeva.gov

Director **Susan Lower** . . . . (540) 853-1812
E-mail: susan.lower@roanokeva.gov
Deputy Director **Steven Staker** . . . . (540) 853-2771
E-mail: steven.staker@roanokeva.gov

Registrar's Office
215 Church Avenue, SW, Room 109, Roanoke, VA 24011
Tel: (540) 853-2261 Fax: (540) 853-1025
E-mail: registrar@roanokeva.gov

Registrar **Andrew Cochran** . . . . (540) 853-2281

Office of the City Manager
215 Church Ave., SW, Room 364, Roanoke, VA 24011-1536
Fax: (540) 853-1138 E-mail: citymgr@roanokeva.gov

○City Manager **Christopher P. Morrill** . . . . (540) 853-2333
E-mail: citymgr@roanokeva.gov
Education: Holy Cross Col 1984 BA; North Carolina 1985 MPA
Communications and Media Officer **Melinda B. Mayo** . . . (540) 853-6357
E-mail: melinda.mayo@roanokeva.gov

Assistant City Manager for Community Development
215 Church Ave. SW, Room 364, Roanoke, VA 24011

Assistant City Manager **R. Brian Townsend** . . . . (540) 853-2333
E-mail: brian.townsend@roanokeva.gov

Human Services Department
1510 Williamson Road, Roanoke, VA 24012
Tel: (540) 853-2591 Fax: (540) 853-2027
E-mail: humanservices@roanokeva.gov

Director **Jane R. Conlin** . . . . (540) 853-2507

Parks and Recreation
215 Church Avenue, SW, Room 303, Roanoke, VA 24011
Fax: (540) 853-1287 E-mail: parksrec@roanokeva.gov

Director **Steve Buschor** . . . . (540) 853-2494

Planning, Building and Development
215 Church Ave. SW, Room 166, Roanoke, VA 24011
Tel: (540) 853-1730 Fax: (540) 853-1230
E-mail: planning@roanokeva.gov

Director **Chris Chittum** . . . . (540) 853-2356
E-mail: chris.chittum@roanokeva.gov
Building Commissioner **Neil Holland** . . . . (540) 853-1891
Planning Administrator **Ian Shaw** . . . . (540) 853-5808
Planning Coordinator **Tina Carr** . . . . (540) 853-1330

Police Department
348 Campbell Avenue, SW, Roanoke, VA 24011
Tel: (540) 853-2203 Fax: (540) 853-6043 E-mail: police@roanokeva.gov

Chief of Police **Christopher C. Perkins** . . . . (540) 853-2203
Secretary to the Chief **(Vacant)** . . . . (540) 853-2203

Roanoke Public Libraries
706 South Jefferson Street, Roanoke, VA 24011
Tel: (540) 853-2473 Fax: (540) 853-1781
E-mail: mainlibrary@roanokeva.gov

Director **Sheila Umberger** . . . . (540) 853-2476
E-mail: sheila.umberger@roanokeva.gov

★Elected Official ▲Appointed by Legislature ▼Appointed by Governor ▶Appointed by Board or Commission ●Appointed by Judge
■Appointed by Mayor △Appointed by Freeholders ▽Appointed by Supervisor ▷Appointed by County Executive ○Appointed by Council

Assistant City Manager for Operations
215 Church Avenue SW, Room 364, Roanoke, VA 24011

Assistant City Manager **Sherman Stovall** .... (540) 853-2333
E-mail: sherman.stovall@roanokeva.gov

Civic Facilities Department
710 Williamson Road, Roanoke, VA 24016
Fax: (540) 853-2748 Internet: http://www.theberglundcenter.com/

General Manager **Robyn Schon** .... (540) 853-2241

Fire-Emergency Medical Services Department
713 Third Street SW, Roanoke, VA 24016
Fax: (540) 853-1172 E-mail: fire-ems@roanokeva.gov

Fire/EMS Chief **David Hoback** .... (540) 853-2327
E-mail: david.hoback@roanokeva.gov
Deputy Chief **Billy Altman** .... (540) 853-1353
E-mail: billy.altman@roanoke.com
Fire Marshal **Daniel Rakes** .... (540) 853-2327
E-mail: daniel.rakes@roanokeva.gov
Emergency Services Coordinator **Marci Stone** .... (540) 853-2426
E-mail: marci.stone@vdem.virginia.gov

General Services Department
215 Church Ave. SW, Room 353, Roanoke, VA 24011
E-mail: general@roanokeva.gov Fax: (540) 853-1513

Director **Mike Shockley** .... (540) 853-1805
E-mail: michael.shockley@roanokeva.gov

Building Inspections Division
215 Church Avenue, SW, Room 170, Roanoke, VA 24011-1536
Tel: (540) 853-1090 (Development Assistance Center)
Fax: (540) 853-1594 E-mail: building@roanokeva.gov

Building Commissioner **Neil Holland** .... (540) 853-1325

Facilities Management
1802 Courtland Rd., NE, Roanoke, VA 24012
Fax: (540) 853-1270 E-mail: facilities@roanokeva.gov

Manager **John McGhee** .... (540) 853-2593
E-mail: john.mcghee@roanokeva.gov

Fleet Management
1802 Courtland Rd., NE, Roanoke, VA 24012
Tel: (540) 853-2423 Fax: (540) 853-6845 E-mail: fleet@roanokeva.gov

Manager **Michael Cosby** .... (540) 853-2108

Purchasing
215 Church Avenue, SW, Room 202, Roanoke, VA 24011-1536
Fax: (540) 853-1513 E-mail: purchasing@roanokeva.gov

Manager **Simone Knowles** .... (540) 853-2871
E-mail: simone.knowles@roanokeva.gov

Human Resources Department
215 Church Ave. SW, Room 207, Roanoke, VA 24011
Fax: (540) 853-1218 E-mail: hr@roanokeva.gov

Director **Michele Vineyard** .... (540) 853-5811
E-mail: michele.vineyard@roanokeva.gov

Management and Budget Department
215 Church Avenue, SW, Room 357, Roanoke, VA 24011
Tel: (540) 853-6800 Fax: (540) 853-2773 E-mail: dmb@roanokeva.gov

Director **Amelia Merchant** .... (540) 853-6805
E-mail: amelia.merchant@roanokeva.gov
Budget Administrator **R.B. Lawhorn** .... (540) 853-6403
E-mail: rb.lawhorn@roanokeva.gov

Division of Neighborhood Services
215 Church Avenue, SW, Room 312, Roanoke, VA 24011
Tel: (540) 853-2344 Fax: (540) 853-6597
E-mail: housing@roanokeva.gov

Director **Chris Chittum** .... (540) 853-2346
Codes Compliance Coordinator **Dan Webb** .... (540) 853-1046
Housing Development Specialist **Karl Kleinhenz** .... (540) 853-5647
Neighborhood Services Coordinator **Bob Clement** .... (540) 853-1286

Public Works Department
215 Church Avenue, SW, Room 357, Roanoke, VA 24011-1536
Fax: (540) 853-1270 E-mail: publicworks@roanokeva.gov

Director **Robert K. Bengtson** .... (540) 853-2741

Engineering
215 Church Avenue, SW, Room 350, Roanoke, VA 24011-1536
Tel: (540) 853-2731 Fax: (540) 853-1364
E-mail: engineer@roanokeva.gov

City Engineer **Phil Schirmer** .... (540) 853-2731
E-mail: phil.schirmer@roanokeva.gov

Environmental Management Division
215 Church Avenue, SW, Room 354, Roanoke, VA 24011

Environmental Administrator **Christopher Blakeman** .... (540) 853-2425

Solid Waste Management
1802 Courtland Rd., NE, Roanoke, VA 24012
Fax: (540) 853-1270 E-mail: solidwaste@roanokeva.gov

Manager **Frank W. "Skip" Decker III** .... (540) 853-6848

Transportation
1802 Courtland Road, NW, Roanoke, VA 24012
Fax: (540) 853-1270 E-mail: streets@roanokeva.gov

Manager **Mark Jamison** .... (540) 853-2676

Technology Department
215 Church Avenue, SW, 4th Floor North, Roanoke, VA 24011
Tel: (540) 853-2144 Fax: (540) 853-6044
E-mail: technology@roanokeva.gov

Director **Roy Mentkow** .... (540) 853-2105
E-mail: roy.mentkow@roanokeva.gov

E-911 Control Center
Tel: (540) 853-2411 Fax: (540) 853-1356 E-mail: e911@roanokeva.gov

Manager **Sonya Roman** .... (540) 853-2945
E-mail: sonya.roman@roanokeva.gov

Roanoke City Public Schools [RCPS]
40 Douglass Ave., Roanoke, VA 24012-4611
Internet: www.rcps.info

Superintendent of Schools **Dr. Rita Bishop** .... (540) 853-2381
School Board Clerk/Executive Assistant to the Superintendent **Cynthia H. Poulton** .... (540) 853-2381
E-mail: cpoulton@rcps.info
Assistant Superintendent for Teaching and Learning **Stephanie Hogan** .... (540) 853-6113
Deputy Superintendent for Operations **Steve Barnett** .... (540) 853-2382
E-mail: sbarnett@rcps.info
Director of Data and Analysis **Jean Pollock** .... (540) 853-2101
E-mail: jpollock@rcps.info
Human Resources Executive Director **Sandra Burks** ..... (540) 853-2502
E-mail: sburks@rcps.info
Community Relations Coordinator **Justin McLeod** ...... (540) 853-2816
E-mail: jmcleod@rcps.info
Student Support Services Executive Director **Yolanda Conaway Wood** .... (540) 853-1393

School Board
Chairman **Suzanne P. Moore** .... (540) 853-2381

(continued on next page)

★ Elected Official ▲ Appointed by Legislature ▼ Appointed by Governor ▶ Appointed by Board or Commission ● Appointed by Judge
■ Appointed by Mayor △ Appointed by Freeholders ▽ Appointed by Supervisor ▷ Appointed by County Executive ○ Appointed by Council

School Board *continued*

Vice Chairman **Lori E. Vaught** . . . . . (540) 853-2381
Member **Mark Kenneth Cathey** . . . . . (540) 853-2381
Member **William B. Hopkins** . . . . . (540) 853-2381
Member **Annette Lewis** . . . . . (540) 853-2381
Member **Laura Rottenborn** . . . . . (540) 853-2381
Member **Dick Willis** . . . . . (540) 853-2381

City of Rochester, Minnesota

201 4th Street SE, Rochester, MN 55904
Tel: (507) 328-2000 Fax: (507) 328-2727 Internet: www.rochestermn.gov

County: Olmsted **Election Type:** Nonpartisan **Year Founded:** 1854
Year Incorporated: 1858 **Population:** 112,225 (2015)

Office of the Mayor and City Council

201 4th Street SE, Rochester, MN 55904
Internet: www.rochestermn.gov/departments/mayor/

★Mayor **Ardell F. Brede** . . . . . (507) 328-2700
Began Service: January 6, 2003
Term Expires: December 31, 2018
E-mail: abrede@rochestermn.gov
★Council President **Randy Staver** . . . . . (507) 288-9034
Term Expires: December 31, 2016
★Council Member **Ed Hruska** (Ward 1) . . . . . (507) 328-2700
Term Expires: December 31, 2018
★Council Member **Michael Wojcik** (Ward 2) . . . . . (507) 269-8606
Term Expires: December 31, 2016
E-mail: votewojcik@gmail.com
Education: North Dakota BSEE; Minnesota 1999 MSEE, 2002 MBA
★Council Member **Nick Campion** (Ward 3) . . . . . (507) 328-2700
Term Expires: December 31, 2018
★Council Member **Mark Bilderback** (Ward 4) . . . . . (507) 328-2700
Term Expires: December 31, 2016
Education: Winona State 2007 BA
★Council Member **Mark Hickey** (Ward 5) . . . . . (507) 285-0295
Term Expires: December 31, 2018
★Council Member **Sandra Means** (Ward 6) . . . . . (507) 328-2700
Term Expires: December 31, 2016
Education: Concordia Col St Paul MN BA

Office of the City Administrator

201 4th Street SE, Rochester, MN 55904
Fax: (507) 328-2727
Internet: www.rochestermn.gov/departments/administration/

City Administrator **Stevan Kvenvold** . . . . . (507) 328-2000
E-mail: skvenvold@rochestermn.gov
Assistant City Administrator **Gary Neumann** . . . . . (507) 328-2000
E-mail: gneumann@rochestermn.gov
Development Administrator **Terry Spaeth** . . . . . (507) 328-2008
E-mail: tspaeth@rochestermn.gov

Office of the City Attorney

201 4th Street SE, Room 247, Rochester, MN 55904
Fax: (507) 328-2727
Internet: www.rochestermn.gov/departments/attorney/

City Attorney **Terry Adkins** . . . . . (507) 328-2100
E-mail: tadkins@rochestermn.gov
Deputy City Attorney **Dave Goslee** . . . . . (507) 328-2104

Office of the City Clerk

201 4th Street SE, Room 135, Rochester, MN 55904
Fax: (507) 328-2901
Internet: www.rochestermn.gov/departments/cityclerk/

City Clerk **Aaron Reeves** . . . . . (507) 328-2900
E-mail: areeves@rochestermn.gov
Deputy City Clerk **Valori Langseth** . . . . . (507) 328-2900
E-mail: vlangseth@rochestermn.gov

Building Safety Department

2122 Campus Drive, SE, Suite 300, Rochester, MN 55904
Fax: (507) 328-2601
Internet: www.rochestermn.gov/departments/bldgsafety/

Director **Randy Johnson** . . . . . (507) 328-2602

Finance Department

201 4th Street SE, Room 204, Rochester, MN 55904
Fax: (507) 328-2876

Director of Finance and Information Systems
Dale Martinson . . . . . (507) 328-2850
E-mail: dmartinson@rochestermn.gov
Assistant Finance Director **Cary McNallan** . . . . . (507) 328-2863
Information Systems Manager **Teryl Apel** . . . . . (507) 328-2850
E-mail: tapel@rochestermn.gov
Risk Manager/Purchasing Officer **Jennifer King** . . . . . (507) 328-2860
E-mail: jking@rochestermn.gov

Fire Department

201 4th Street SE, Room 10, Rochester, MN 55904
Fax: (507) 328-2829

Fire Chief **Greg K. Martin** . . . . . (507) 328-2800
E-mail: gmartin@rochestermn.gov

Human Resources Department

201 4th Street SE, Room 295, Rochester, MN 55904
Fax: (507) 328-2565 Internet: www.rochestermn.gov/departments/hr/

Director of Human Resources **Linda K. Hillenbrand** . . . . . (507) 328-2555
E-mail: lhillenbrand@rochestermn.gov

Music Department

201 4th Street SE, Suite 170, Rochester, MN 55904
Fax: (507) 328-2202 Internet: www.riversideconcerts.com/

General Manager **Steve Schmidt** . . . . . (507) 328-2201
E-mail: steve@riversideconcerts.com

Park and Recreation Department

201 4th Street SE, Room 160, Rochester, MN 55904
Fax: (507) 328-2535 Internet: www.rochestermn.gov/departments/park/

Director of Park and Recreation **Paul Widman** . . . . . (507) 328-2527
Park and Forestry Division Head **Mike Nigbur** . . . . . (507) 328-2541

Police Department

101 4th Street, SE, Rochester, MN 55904
Fax: (507) 328-6975
Internet: http://www.rochestermn.gov/departments/police/

Chief of Police **Roger Peterson** . . . . . (507) 328-6902

Public Works Department

201 4th Street SE, Room 108, Rochester, MN 55904
Fax: (507) 328-2401
Internet: www.rochestermn.gov/departments/publicworks/

Director **Richard Freese** . . . . . (507) 328-2400

★Elected Official ▲Appointed by Legislature ▼Appointed by Governor ►Appointed by Board or Commission ●Appointed by Judge
■Appointed by Mayor △Appointed by Freeholders ▽Appointed by Supervisor ▷Appointed by County Executive ○Appointed by Council

Rochester Public Utilities
4000 East River Road NE, Rochester, MN 55906
Internet: www.rpu.org/

General Manager **Mark Kotschevar** . . . . . (507) 280-1500

Rochester Public Library
101 2nd Street, SE, Rochester, MN 55904
Internet: www.rochesterpubliclibrary.org/

Director **Audrey S. Betcher** . . . . . (507) 328-2320
E-mail: audrey@rochester.lib.mn.us

City of Rochester, New York

City Hall, 30 Church St., Rochester, NY 14614
Tel: (585) 428-5990 (Information) TTY: (585) 232-3260
Internet: www.cityofrochester.gov

County: Monroe **Election Type:** Partisan **Population:** 209,802 (2015)

Office of the Mayor
City Hall, 30 Church St., Room 308A, Rochester, NY 14614
Tel: (585) 428-7045 Fax: (585) 428-6059

★ Mayor **Lovely A. Warren** (D) . . . . . (585) 428-7045
Began Service: January 1, 2014
Term Expires: December 31, 2017

■ Chief of Staff **Jeremy A. Cooney** . . . . . (585) 428-6271
E-mail: jeremy.cooney@cityofrochester.gov

■ Deputy Mayor **Leonard E. Redon** . . . . . (585) 428-7163
E-mail: redonl@cityofrochester.gov
Education: Worcester Polytech 1973 BS

■ Director of Special Projects and Educational Initiatives **Allen Williams** (D) . . . . . (585) 428-7192
E-mail: allen.williams@cityofrochester.gov

■ Assistant to the Mayor **Tracey Miller** . . . . . (585) 428-6684
E-mail: millertr@cityofrochester.gov

■ Executive Staff Assistant **Bridget Monroe** . . . . . (585) 428-6140
E-mail: bridget.monroe@cityofrochester.gov

Office of Public Integrity
85 Allen Street, Suite 100, Rochester, NY 14608
Tel: (585) 428-7245 Fax: (585) 428-7972
Internet: www.cityofrochester.gov/article.aspx?id=8589936098

Director **Timothy Weir** . . . . . (585) 428-7245

Manager of Internal Audit and Review **Daniel Mastrella** . . . . . (585) 428-6121

Information Technology Department
185 Exchange Blvd., Rochester, NY 14614-2124
Tel: (585) 428-7026 Fax: (585) 428-7280

Chief Information Officer **Lisa Bobo** . . . . . (585) 428-7026
E-mail: lisab@cityofrochester.gov

Office of the Corporation Counsel
City Hall, 30 Church Street, Room 400A, Rochester, NY 14614-1224
Fax: (585) 428-6950

■ Corporation Counsel **Brian F. Curran** (D) . . . . . (585) 428-6986
E-mail: Brian.Curran@cityofrochester.gov
Education: Harvard JD

Office of Management and Budget
30 Church Street, Room 200A, Rochester, NY 14614-1264
Fax: (585) 428-6865

■ Director **Christopher M. Wagner** . . . . . (585) 428-6186
E-mail: wagnerc@cityofrochester.gov

Bureau of Communications and Special Events
City Hall, 30 Church Street, Room 202A, Rochester, NY 14614
Tel: (585) 428-7135 TTY: (585) 428-6054 Fax: (585) 428-7069
E-mail: info@cityofrochester.gov

■ Director **James P. "Jim" Smith** . . . . . (585) 428-7405
E-mail: james.smith@cityofrochester.gov

Assistant to the Director **Ted Capuano** . . . . . (585) 428-7405
E-mail: capuanot@cityofrochester.gov

Deputy Director **Donald Starver** . . . . . (585) 428-6064
E-mail: starverd@cityofrochester.gov

Press Officer **Jessica Alaimo** . . . . . (585) 428-6064
E-mail: alaimoj@cityofrochester.gov

Department of Neighborhood and Business Development
30 Church Street, Room 0224B, Rochester, NY 14614
Tel: (585) 428-6550 Fax: (585) 428-7899
Internet: www.cityofrochester.gov/nbd/

■ Commissioner **Baye' Muhammad** . . . . . (585) 428-6883

Deputy Commissioner **Kathleen Washington** . . . . . (585) 428-6150

Emergency Communications Department
321 W. Main St., Rochester, NY 14608
Fax: (585) 528-2265 Internet: http://www.911Rochester.com

■ Director **John M. Merklinger** . . . . . (585) 528-2207
E-mail: Jmerklinger@monroecounty.gov
Education: Roberts Wesleyan 2000 MS

Deputy Director **Stephen Cusenz** . . . . . (585) 528-2200
E-mail: cusenzs@cityofrochester.gov

Executive Assistant **Allan Wenner** . . . . . (585) 528-2200
E-mail: wennera@cityofrochester.gov

Department of Environmental Services [DES]
City Hall, 30 Church Street, Room 300B, Rochester, NY 14614-1290
Fax: (585) 428-6010 Internet: www.cityofrochester.gov/DES/

■ Commissioner **Norman H. Jones** . . . . . (585) 428-6855
E-mail: norman@cityofrochester.gov

Assistant Commissioner **Mary Gaudioso** . . . . . (585) 428-6855

Bureau of Architecture and Engineering
414 Andrews St., Rochester, NY 14604
Fax: (585) 428-6004

City Engineer **James R. McIntosh** . . . . . (585) 428-6828
E-mail: jim.mcintosh@cityofrochester.gov

Managing Architect **Holly Barrett** . . . . . (585) 428-7357

Bureau of Operations and Parks
945 Mt. Read Blvd., Rochester, NY 14606
Fax: (585) 428-5996

Director **Karen St. Aubin** . . . . . (585) 428-6881

Assistant Director **(Vacant)** . . . . . (585) 428-7409

Building Services Division Manager **Tom Graves** . . . . . (585) 425-6535

Equipment Services Manager **Joel LaDelfa** . . . . . (585) 428-7550

Bureau of Water
10 Felix Street, Rochester, NY 14608
Tel: (585) 428-7500 Fax: (585) 428-6353
Internet: www.cityofrochester.gov/waterbureau/

Director **Patrick O'Connor** . . . . . (585) 428-7500

Water Distribution Manager **John Bonaldi** . . . . . (585) 428-7024

Water Production Manager **Patricia Bedard** . . . . . (585) 428-7882
Fax: (585) 367-3250

Department of Finance
City Hall, 30 Church Street, Room 109A, Rochester, NY 14614-1290
Fax: (585) 428-7533

■ Director **Charles Benincasa** . . . . . (585) 428-7151
E-mail: benincc@cityofrochester.gov

★ Elected Official ▲ Appointed by Legislature ▼ Appointed by Governor ► Appointed by Board or Commission ● Appointed by Judge
■ Appointed by Mayor △ Appointed by Freeholders ▽ Appointed by Supervisor ▷ Appointed by County Executive ○ Appointed by Council

Fire Department
185 Exchange Blvd., Suite 665, Rochester, NY 14614-2124
Fax: (585) 428-6069

■ Fire Chief **John P. Schreiber** .... (585) 428-7037
E-mail: fireweb@cityofrochester.gov
Executive Deputy Chief **Dennis Prevost** .... (585) 428-7485
E-mail: prevostd@cityofrochester.gov

Department of Human Resource Management
City Hall, 30 Church Street, Room 103A, Rochester, NY 14614
Tel: (585) 428-7115 Fax: (585) 428-6902

■ Director **Tassie R. Demps** .... (585) 428-6185
E-mail: dempst@cityofrochester.gov
Education: RIT BSBA, MBA
Labor Relations Manager **Jamie Warren** .... (585) 428-8851
Training and Safety Coordinator **Philip LaPorta** .... (585) 428-6508
107 Bridge View Drive, Rochester, NY 14615 Fax: (585) 428-7369
E-mail: laportap@cityofrochester.gov

Department of Recreation and Youth Services
City Hall, 30 Church Street, Room 222B, Rochester, NY 14614
Fax: (585) 428-6022

■ Commissioner **Marisol O. Ramos-Lopez** .... (585) 428-6749
Education: Barry 1992 BA

Police Department
185 Exchange Blvd., Rochester, NY 14614-2184
Tel: (585) 428-6720 Fax: (585) 428-6093
Internet: www.cityofrochester.gov/police/

■ Chief of Police **Michael Ciminelli** .... (585) 428-7033
Deputy Chief of Operations **Fred Bell** .... (585) 428-7055
E-mail: bellf@cityofrochester.gov
Deputy Chief of Administration **Wayne P. Harris** .... (585) 428-7296
Professional Development Section **Lt. David Gebhardt** ... (585) 428-7436
E-mail: gebhardtd@cityofrochester.gov Fax: (585) 428-7015
Research and Evaluation Section **Capt. Kevin Costello** ... (585) 428-1396
Public Information Officer **Sgt Jason Collins** .... (585) 428-7634

Office of the City Council
City Hall, 30 Church St., Room 301-A, Rochester, NY 14614-1265
Tel: (585) 428-7538 Fax: (585) 428-6347
E-mail: council@cityofrochester.gov

★ Council President **Loretta C. Scott** (D-At-Large) .... (585) 428-7538
Term Expires: December 31, 2017
E-mail: loretta.scott@cityofrochester.gov
★ Council Vice President **Dana K. Miller** (D-At-Large) ..... (585) 428-7538
Term Expires: December 31, 2017
E-mail: dana.miller@cityofrochester.gov
★ Council Member **Carolee A. Conklin** (D-At-Large) ...... (585) 428-7538
Term Expires: December 31, 2017
E-mail: carolee.conklin@cityofrochester.gov
★ Council Member **Adam C. McFadden** (D-South) .... (585) 428-7538
Term Expires: December 31, 2019
E-mail: adam.mcfadden@cityofrochester.gov
Education: Claflin BS
★ Council Member **Matt Haag** (D-At-Large) .... (585) 428-7538
Term Expires: December 31, 2017
E-mail: matt.haag@cityofrochester.gov
★ Council Member **Jacklyn Ortiz** (D-At-Large) .... (585) 428-7538
Term Expires: December 31, 2017
E-mail: jacklyn.ortiz@cityofrochester.gov
★ Council Member **Molly Clifford** (D-Northwest) .... (585) 428-7538
Term Expires: December 31, 2019
E-mail: Molly.Clifford@cityofrochester.gov
★ Council Member **Michael A. Patterson** (D-Northeast) ... (585) 451-2024
Term Expires: December 31, 2019
E-mail: Michael.Patterson@cityofrochester.gov

Office of the City Council *continued*

★ Council Member **Elaine M. Spaull** (D-East) .... (585) 428-7538
Term Expires: December 31, 2019
E-mail: elaine.spaull@cityofrochester.gov
○ Council Chief of Staff **Andrea Guzzetta** Room 301A .... (585) 428-7538
E-mail: andrea.guzzetta@cityofrochester.gov

Office of the City Clerk
○ City Clerk **Hazel Washington** Room 300A .... (585) 428-7421
E-mail: hazel.washington@cityofrochester.gov

Rochester City School District
131 W. Broad St., Rochester, NY 14614
Tel: (585) 262-8100 Fax: (585) 262-8381 Internet: www.rcsdk12.org

Superintendent (Interim) **Linda Cimusz** .... (585) 262-8100
Chief Financial Officer **Lauren Poehlman** .... (585) 262-8100
★ President **Van Henri White** (D) .... (585) 262-8525
Term Expires: December 31, 2017
E-mail: van.white@thelegalbrief.com
★ Vice President **Cynthia Elliott** (D) .... (585) 262-8525
Term Expires: December 31, 2017
E-mail: cynthiaelliott1938@yahoo.com
★ School Board Member **Mary B. Adams** (D) .... (585) 262-8525
Term Expires: December 31, 2019
E-mail: Mary.Adams@rcsdk12.org
★ School Board Member **Liz Hallmark** (D) .... (585) 262-8525
Term Expires: December 31, 2019
★ School Board Member **Jose A. Cruz** (D) .... (585) 262-8525
Term Expires: December 31, 2017
E-mail: countyleg@hotmail.com
★ School Board Member **Malik D. Evans** (D) .... (585) 262-8525
Term Expires: December 31, 2019
E-mail: malik@malikevans.org
Education: Rochester
★ School Board Member **Willa Powell** (D) .... (585) 262-8525
Term Expires: December 31, 2019
E-mail: Willa.Powell@rcsdk12.org

City of Rockford, Illinois
425 E. State St., Rockford, IL 61104
Tel: (779) 348-7300 (City Department Directory) Fax: (815) 967-6952
Internet: http://www.rockfordil.gov/

County: Winnebago **Election Type:** Nonpartisan **Year Incorporated:** 1839 **Population:** 148,278 (2015)

Lawrence J. "Larry" Morrissey
Mayor

Term Expires: April 25, 2017
Education: Notre Dame 1991 BA; Illinois 1995 JD

Office of the Mayor and City Council
425 E. State St., Rockford, IL 61104

★ Mayor **Lawrence J. "Larry" Morrissey** .... (779) 348-7300
E-mail: larry.morrissey@rockfordil.gov
Executive Coordinator to the Mayor **Susan Skinner** ..... (779) 348-7300
E-mail: susan.skinner@rockfordil.gov Fax: (815) 967-6952
★ Council Member **Tim Durkee** (Ward 1) .... (815) 637-6200
Term Expires: April 25, 2017
E-mail: tim.durkee@rockfordil.gov

★ Elected Official ▲ Appointed by Legislature ▼ Appointed by Governor ▶ Appointed by Board or Commission ● Appointed by Judge
■ Appointed by Mayor △ Appointed by Freeholders ▽ Appointed by Supervisor ▷ Appointed by County Executive ○ Appointed by Council

Office of the Mayor and City Council *continued*

★Council Member **Jamie Getchius** (Ward 2) .... (815) 713-7575
Term Expires: April 25, 2017
E-mail: jamie.getchius@rockfordil.gov

★Council Member **Thomas P. McNamara** (Ward 3) ...... (815) 262-6734
Term Expires: April 25, 2017
E-mail: thomas.mcnamara@rockfordil.gov

★Council Member **Kevin J. Frost** (Ward 4) .... (815) 978-0542
Term Expires: April 25, 2017
E-mail: kevin.frost@rockfordil.gov

★Council Member **Venita Hervey** (Ward 5) .... (815) 968-7682
Term Expires: April 25, 2017
E-mail: venita.hervey@rockfordil.gov

★Council Member **Pam Connell** (Ward 6)
Term Expires: April 25, 2017
E-mail: Pam.Connell@rockfordil.gov

★Council Member **Ann Thompson-Kelly** (Ward 7) .... (815) 968-8389
Term Expires: April 25, 2017
E-mail: ann.thompson@rockfordil.gov

★Council Member **Jeanne Oddo** (Ward 8) .... (815) 375-0457
Term Expires: April 25, 2017
E-mail: jeanne.oddo@rockfordil.gov

★Council Member **Teena M. Newburg** (Ward 9) .... (815) 654-8752
Term Expires: April 25, 2017
E-mail: teen.newburg@rockfordil.gov

★Council Member **Franklin C. Beach** (Ward 10) .... (815) 399-3737
Term Expires: April 25, 2017
E-mail: grandi123@aol.com

★Council Member **Karen Elyea** (Ward 11) .... (815) 961-1795
Term Expires: April 25, 2017
E-mail: karen.elyea@rockfordil.gov

★Council Member **John Beck** (Ward 12) .... (815) 289-4787
Term Expires: April 25, 2017
E-mail: john.beck@rockfordil.gov

★Council Member **Linda McNeely** (Ward 13) .... (815) 962-5424
Term Expires: April 25, 2017
E-mail: ald13mcneely@aol.com

★Council Member **Joseph V. Chiarelli** (Ward 14) .... (815) 721-2014
Term Expires: April 25, 2017
E-mail: joseph.chiarelli@rockfordil.gov

Office of the City Administrator

425 E. State St., Rockford, IL 61104
Fax: (815) 967-6952

■City Administrator **James R. Ryan** .... (779) 348-7300
E-mail: jim.ryan@rockfordil.gov

Community and Economic Development Department

425 E. State St., Rockford, IL 61104
Fax: (815) 967-6933

Director **Todd Cagnoni** .... (779) 348-7162
E-mail: todd.cagnoni@rockfordil.gov

Finance Department

425 E. State St., Rockford, IL 61104
Fax: (815) 987-5562

Director **Chris Black** .... (779) 348-7470

Fire Department

204 South First Street, Rockford, IL 61104
Fax: (815) 987-5565

Chief **Derek Bergsten** .... (779) 348-7171
E-mail: derek.bergsten@rockfordil.gov

Human Resources Department

425 E. State St., Rockford, IL 61104
Fax: (815) 967-6924

Director **Julia Valdez** .... (779) 348-7156
E-mail: julia.valdez@rockfordil.gov

Human Services Department

612 North Church Street, Rockford, IL 61103
Fax: (815) 987-5762

Executive Director **George Davis** .... (779) 348-7170

Information Technology Department

425 E. State St., Rockford, IL 61104
Fax: (815) 987-5562

Information Technology Director **Glenn Trommels** ...... (779) 348-7341
E-mail: glenn.trommels@rockfordil.gov

Legal Department

425 East State Street, 7th Floor, Rockford, IL 61104
Fax: (815) 967-6949

Director **Patrick Hayes** .... (779) 348-7154

Police Department

420 W. State St., Rockford, IL 61101
Fax: (815) 961-3208

Chief of Police **Dan O'Shea** .... (779) 500-6452

Public Works Department

425 E. State St., Rockford, IL 61104
Fax: (815) 967-6942

Director **Timothy Hanson** .... (779) 348-7646
E-mail: timothy.hanson@rockfordil.gov

City Engineer **Matt Vitner** .... (779) 348-7633
E-mail: matthew.vitner@rockfordil.gov

Traffic Engineer **Jeremy Carter** .... (779) 348-7656
E-mail: jeremy.carter@rockfordil.gov

Street Maintenance Supervisor **Mark Stockman** .... (779) 348-7631
523 South Central, Rockford, IL 61102

Water Superintendent **Tim Holdeman** .... (779) 348-7355

Rockford Housing Authority

223 South Winnebago Street, Rockford, IL 61102
Fax: (815) 987-3853

Executive Director **Ron Clewer** .... (815) 489-8750
E-mail: rclewer@rockfordha.org

City of Roseville, California

311 Vernon Street, Roseville, CA 95678
Tel: (916) 774-5200 Internet: http://www.roseville.ca.us/

County: Placer **Election Type:** Nonpartisan **Year Incorporated:** 1909
Population: 130,269 (2015)

Office of the Mayor and City Council

311 Vernon Street, Roseville, CA 95678
Fax: (916) 786-9175
Internet: http://www.roseville.ca.us/council/default.asp

★Mayor **Carol Garcia** .... (916) 774-5200
Began Service: January 10, 2007
Term Expires: December 2016
E-mail: citycouncil@roseville.ca.us

★Mayor Pro Tem **Susan Rohan** .... (916) 412-4796
Term Expires: December 2018
E-mail: citycouncil@roseville.ca.us

(continued on next page)

★Elected Official ▲Appointed by Legislature ▼Appointed by Governor ►Appointed by Board or Commission ●Appointed by Judge
■Appointed by Mayor △Appointed by Freeholders ▽Appointed by Supervisor ▷Appointed by County Executive ○Appointed by Council

Office of the Mayor and City Council *continued*

★ Council Member **Bonnie Gore** .... (916) 774-5200
Term Expires: December 2016
E-mail: citycouncil@roseville.ca.us

★ Council Member **Tim Herman** .... (916) 774-5200
Term Expires: December 2018
E-mail: citycouncil@roseville.ca.us

★ Council Member **Pauline Roccucci** .... (916) 782-2708
Term Expires: December 2016
E-mail: citycouncil@roseville.ca.us

Office of the City Manager

311 Vernon Street, Roseville, CA 95678
Internet: http://www.roseville.ca.us/citymanager/default.asp

City Manager **Rob Jensen** .... (916) 774-5362
E-mail: citymanager@roseville.ca.us

Assistant City Manager **Dominick Casey** .... (916) 774-5349
E-mail: dcasey@roseville.ca.us

Assistant City Manager **(Vacant)** .... (916) 774-5334

Communications Department

311 Vernon Street, Roseville, CA 95678

Public Information Officer **Brian Jacobson** .... (916) 774-5455
E-mail: bjacobson@roseville.ca.us

Public Affairs and Communications Director **Megan MacPherson** .... (916) 774-5455
E-mail: mmacpherson@roseville.ca.us

Government Relations Administrator **Mark Wolinski** .... (916) 774-5179
E-mail: mwolinski@roseville.ca.us

Office of the City Attorney

311 Vernon Street, Roseville, CA 95678

City Attorney **Rob R. Schmitt** .... (916) 774-5325
E-mail: attorney@roseville.ca.us

Office of the City Clerk

311 Vernon Street, Roseville, CA 95678
Fax: (916) 786-9175 Internet: http://www.roseville.ca.us/clerk/default.asp

City Clerk **Sonia Orozco** .... (916) 774-5263
E-mail: sorozco@roseville.ca.us

Development Services Department

311 Vernon Street, Roseville, CA 95678
Fax: (916) 774-5195

Development Services Director **Kevin Payne** .... (916) 774-5285
E-mail: kpayne@roseville.ca.us

Office of Economic Development

311 Vernon Street, Roseville, CA 95678
Internet: http://www.roseville.ca.us/ed/default.asp

Economic Development Director **Chris Robles** .... (916) 774-5362
E-mail: crobles@roseville.ca.us

Economic Development Manager **Laura Matteoli** .... (916) 774-5362
E-mail: lmatteoli@roseville.ca.us

Environmental Utilities Department

2005 Hilltop Circle, Roseville, CA 95747
Internet: http://www.roseville.ca.us/eu/default.asp

Director **Richard Plecker** .... (916) 774-5770

Finance Department

311 Vernon Street, Roseville, CA 95678
Internet: http://www.roseville.ca.us/gov/finance/default.asp

Finance Director **Monty Hanks** .... (916) 774-5319

Fire Department

401 Oak Street, Roseville, CA 95678
Fax: (916) 774-5810 Internet: http://www.roseville.ca.us/fire/default.asp

Fire Chief **Rick Bartee** .... (916) 774-5800
E-mail: rbartee@roseville.ca.us

Human Resources Department

311 Vernon Street, Roseville, CA 95678
Internet: http://www.roseville.ca.us/hr/default.asp

Human Resources Director **Gayle Satchwell** .... (916) 774-5475
E-mail: humanresources@roseville.ca.us

Parks, Recreation and Libraries Department

311 Vernon Street, Roseville, CA 95678

Director **Dion Louthan** .... (916) 774-5362
E-mail: parksandrec@roseville.ca.us

Roseville Public Library

225 Taylor Street, Roseville, CA 95678
Internet: http://www.roseville.ca.us/library/default.asp

Library Director **Natasha Casteel** .... (916) 774-5233
E-mail: library@roseville.ca.us

Planning Division

311 Vernon Street, Roseville, CA 95678
Fax: (916) 774-5129

Planning Manager **Greg Bitter** .... (916) 774-5276

Planning Manager **Cathy Pease** .... (916) 774-5276

Police Department

1051 Junction Boulevard, Roseville, CA 95678

Chief of Police **Daniel Hahn** .... (916) 774-5010
Education: Cal State (Sacramento) 1995 BABA; National U 2001 MPA

Public Works Department

311 Vernon Street, Roseville, CA 95678
Fax: (916) 746-1339 Internet: http://www.roseville.ca.us/pw/default.asp

Public Works Director **Rhon Herndon** .... (916) 774-5331
E-mail: publicworks@roseville.ca.us

Alternative Transportation Administration

401 Vernon Street, Roseville, CA 95678
Fax: (916) 746-1333

Alternative Transportation Manager **Michael Wixon** .... (916) 774-5293

Building Inspection Division

311 Vernon Street, Roseville, CA 95678
Fax: (916) 774-5394

Building Official **Scott Byrnes** .... (916) 774-5332

Engineering Division

311 Vernon Street, Roseville, CA 95678
Fax: (916) 746-1339

Engineering Manager **Jason Shykowski** .... (916) 774-1300
E-mail: jshykowski@roseville.ca.us

Street Maintenance Division

2005 Hilltop Circle, Roseville, CA 95747
Fax: (916) 774-5756

Superintendent **Jerry Dankbar** .... (916) 774-5790

Roseville Electric

2090 Hilltop Circle, Roseville, CA 95747
Fax: (916) 774-5583
Internet: http://www.roseville.ca.us/electric/default.asp

Electric Utility Director **Michelle Bertolino** .... (916) 797-6937

★ Elected Official ▲ Appointed by Legislature ▼ Appointed by Governor ▶ Appointed by Board or Commission ● Appointed by Judge
■ Appointed by Mayor △ Appointed by Freeholders ▽ Appointed by Supervisor ▷ Appointed by County Executive ○ Appointed by Council

City of Round Rock, Texas

221 East Main Street, Round Rock, TX 78664
Tel: (512) 218-5400 Internet: www.roundrocktexas.gov/

County: Travis; Williamson **Election Type:** Nonpartisan
Population: 115,997 (2015)

Office of the Mayor and City Council

221 East Main Street, Round Rock, TX 78664
Internet: www.roundrocktexas.gov/home/index.asp?page=200

★Mayor **Alan McGraw** .... (512) 218-5410
Began Service: May 2008
Term Expires: May 2017
E-mail: mayormcgraw@roundrocktexas.gov
Education: Austin State BS; Colorado State MS; Texas 1992 JD

★Council Member **Craig Morgan** (Place 1)............. (512) 218-5410
Term Expires: May 2017
E-mail: craigmorgan@roundrocktexas.gov

★Council Member **Renee Flores** (Place 2) .... (512) 218-5410
Term Expires: May 20, 2019

★Council Member **Frank Leffingwell** (Place 3) .... (512) 218-5410
Term Expires: May 2018
E-mail: frankleffingwell@roundrocktexas.gov

★Council Member **Will Peckham** (Place 4) .... (512) 218-5410
Term Expires: May 2017
E-mail: willpeckham@roundrocktexas.gov

★Council Member **Writ Baese** (Place 5) .... (512) 218-5410
Term Expires: May 2018
E-mail: writbaese@roundrocktexas.gov

★Council Member **Kris Whitfield** (Place 6) .... (512) 218-5410
Term Expires: May 20, 2019
E-mail: kriswhitfield@roundrocktexas.gov

Office of the City Manager

221 East Main Street, Round Rock, TX 78664
Fax: (512) 218-7097

City Manager **Laurie Hadley** .... (512) 218-5410
E-mail: citymanager@roundrocktexas.gov
Education: Arizona State BA; Northern Arizona MPA

Assistant City Manager **Brooks Bennett**................. (512) 218-5410
E-mail: bbennett@roundrocktexas.gov
Education: Texas BA; Texas Pan American MPA

Assistant City Manager **Bryan Williams** .... (512) 218-5410
E-mail: bwilliams@roundrocktexas.gov
Education: LeTourneau BABA

Emergency Management Coordinator **Dorothy Miller** .... (512) 218-3259
E-mail: dmiller@roundrocktexas.gov

Office of the City Clerk

221 East Main Street, Round Rock, TX 78664
Fax: (512) 218-7097

City Clerk **Sara White** .... (512) 218-5404
E-mail: swhite@roundrocktexas.gov

Communications Division

221 East Main Street, Round Rock, TX 78664
Fax: (512) 218-7097

Communications Director **Will Hampton** .... (512) 218-5409
E-mail: whampton@roundrocktexas.gov

Office of the City Attorney

309 East Main Street, Round Rock, TX 78664
Fax: (512) 255-8986

City Attorney **Stephan L. Sheets** .... (512) 255-8877
E-mail: steve@scrrlaw.com

Finance Department

221 East Main Street, Round Rock, TX 78664
Fax: (512) 218-5442
Internet: http://www.roundrocktexas.gov/departments/finance/

Chief Finance Officer **Susan Morgan** .... (512) 218-5445

Controller **Jerry D. Galloway** .... (512) 218-5432

Budget Supervisor **Jodi Rhodes** .... (512) 341-3338
E-mail: jrhodes@roundrocktexas.gov

Community Development Coordinator
Elizabeth Alvarado .... (512) 341-3328
E-mail: lalvarado@roundrocktexas.gov

Purchasing Department

231 East Main Street, Round Rock, TX 78664
Tel: (512) 671-2861 Fax: (512) 218-7028

Purchasing Manager **Ron Hunter** .... (512) 218-5457
E-mail: ronhunter@roundrocktexas.gov

Fire Department

203 Commerce Boulevard, Round Rock, TX 78664
Fax: (512) 218-5594

Fire Chief **David Coatney** .... (512) 218-5591
E-mail: dcoatney@roundrocktexas.gov
Education: San Antonio AS; Wayland Baptist BS, MA

Human Resources Department

231 East Main Street, Round Rock, TX 78664
Fax: (512) 218-5493

Director **Valerie Francois** .... (512) 218-5494
E-mail: vfrancois@roundrocktexas.gov

Risk Manager **Michael Bennett**....................... (512) 218-6643
E-mail: michaelbennett@roundrocktexas.gov

Round Rock Public Library

216 East Main Street, Round Rock, TX 78664
Tel: (512) 218-7000

Library Director **Michelle Cervantes** .... (512) 218-7010
E-mail: mcervantes@roundrocktexas.gov
Education: Concordia U (CA) BA; North Texas MS

Parks and Recreation Department

301 West Bagdad Street, Suite 250, Round Rock, TX 78664
Tel: (512) 218-5540

Parks and Recreation Director **Rick Atkins** .... (512) 341-3344

Planning and Development Services Department

301 West Bagdad Street, Round Rock, TX 78664
Tel: (512) 218-5428 Fax: (512) 218-3286

Director **Brad Wiseman** .... (512) 341-3321
E-mail: bwiseman@roundrocktexas.gov

Code Enforcement Supervisor **Rick Clark** .... (512) 218-5424

Building Inspection Division

2008 Enterprise Drive, Round Rock, TX 78664
Fax: (512) 218-5563

Chief Building Official **Mark Remmert** .... (512) 218-5550

Police Department

2701 North Mays, Round Rock, TX 78665
Tel: (512) 218-5500 Fax: (512) 218-7060

Chief of Police **Allen Banks** .... (512) 218-6650

Assistant Chief of Police **Alain Babin** .... (512) 218-6650

Assistant Chief of Police **Troy D. Evans** .... (512) 218-6650

★ Elected Official ▲ Appointed by Legislature ▼ Appointed by Governor ► Appointed by Board or Commission ● Appointed by Judge
■ Appointed by Mayor △ Appointed by Freeholders ▽ Appointed by Supervisor ▷ Appointed by County Executive ○ Appointed by Council

Transportation Department

2008 Enterprise Drive, Round Rock, TX 78664
Tel: (512) 218-5562 Fax: (512) 218-3242

Director **Gary Hudder** .... (512) 218-5562

Utilities and Environmental Services Department

2008 Enterprise Drive, Round Rock, TX 78664
Tel: (512) 671-2755 Fax: (512) 218-3242

Utilities Director **Michael Thane** .... (512) 218-3236

City of Sacramento, California

City Hall, 915 I Street, Sacramento, CA 95814
Tel: (916) 808-5011 (Information) Internet: www.cityofsacramento.org

County: Sacramento **Election Type:** Nonpartisan **Year Founded:** 1849
Charter: 1920 **Population:** 490,712 (2015)

Office of the Mayor and City Council

City Hall, 915 I Street, 5th Floor, Sacramento, CA 95814
Fax: (916) 264-7680

★Mayor **Kevin Johnson** .... (916) 808-5300
Note: Retiring 2016
Began Service: November 2, 2008
Term Expires: November 23, 2016
E-mail: mayor@cityofsacramento.org
Date of Birth: March 4, 1966
Education: UC Berkeley 1998 BA
Career: Professional Basketball Player, Phoenix Suns (1988-2000); Founder and Chief Executive Officer, St. HOPE Public Schools (2000-2008)

Chief of Staff **Crystal Strait** .... (916) 808-5300
Senior Advisor **Patti Bisharat** .... (916) 808-5300
Senior Advisor **Cassandra H. B. Jennings** .... (916) 808-5300
Education: Maryland 1978 BA; U San Francisco 1983 MPA
Press Secretary **Ben Sosenko** .... (916) 808-5300
E-mail: bsosenko@cityofsacramento.org
Executive Assistant to the Mayor **Adrianne Hall** .... (916) 808-5300
E-mail: aehall@cityofsacramento.org
Executive Assistant to the Mayor **Daniel Lopez** .... (916) 808-5300
E-mail: dlopez@cityofsacramento.org
Constituent Services Director and Senior Advisor **Helen Hewitt** .... (916) 808-5300

★Mayor Pro Tem **Larry Carr** (District 8) .... (916) 808-7008
Term Expires: November 2016
Education: Norfolk State BA; UCLA MBA

★Vice Mayor **Rick Jennings II** (District 7) .... (916) 808-7007
Term Expires: November 2018
E-mail: rjennings@cityofsacramento.org

★Council Member **Angelique Ashby** (District 1) .... (916) 808-7001
Term Expires: November 2018
E-mail: aashby@cityofsacramento.org

★Council Member **Allen Warren** (District 2) .... (916) 808-7002
Term Expires: November 23, 2016
E-mail: awarren@cityofsacramento.org

★Council Member **Jeff Harris** (District 3) .... (916) 808-7003
Term Expires: November 2018
E-mail: jsharris@cityofsacramento.org

★Council Member **Steve Hansen** (District 4) .... (916) 808-7004
Term Expires: November 23, 2016
E-mail: shansen@cityofsacramento.org

★Council Member **Jay Schenirer** (District 5) .... (916) 808-7005
Term Expires: November 2018
E-mail: jschenirer@cityofsacramento.org

★Council Member **Eric Guerra** (District 6) .... (916) 808-7006
Term Expires: November 23, 2016

Office of the Mayor and City Council *continued*

Mayor and Council Operations Manager **Stephanie Mizuno** .... (916) 808-7171
E-mail: smizuno@cityofsacramento.org

Office of the City Attorney

City Hall, 915 I Street, 4th Floor, Sacramento, CA 95814
Fax: (916) 808-7455

○City Attorney **James Sanchez** .... (916) 808-5346
E-mail: jsanchez@cityofsacramento.org
Assistant City Attorney **Matthew D. Ruyak** .... (916) 808-5346
E-mail: mruyak@cityofsacramento.org
Assistant City Attorney **Sandra Talbott** .... (916) 808-5346
E-mail: stalbott@cityofsacramento.org

Office of the City Clerk

City Hall, 915 I Street, 1st Floor, Sacramento, CA 95814
Fax: (916) 808-7672

○City Clerk **Shirley Concolino** .... (916) 808-7200
E-mail: sconcolino@cityofsacramento.org
Assistant City Clerk **Stephanie Mizuno** .... (916) 808-8093
E-mail: smizuno@cityofsacramento.org
Assistant City Clerk **Dawn Bullwinkel** .... (916) 808-7267
E-mail: dbullwinkel@cityofsacramento.org
Records Manager **Wendy Klock-Johnson** .... (916) 808-7509
915 I Street, Sacramento, CA 95314-2604 Fax: (916) 808-7672

Office of the City Treasurer

City Hall, 915 I Street, 3rd Floor, Sacramento, CA 95814
Fax: (916) 808-5171

○City Treasurer **Russell Fehr** .... (916) 808-5168
E-mail: rfehr@cityofsacramento.org
Debt Manager **Brian Wong** .... (916) 808-5811
Chief Investment Officer **John Coleville** .... (916) 808-5168

Office of the City Manager

City Hall, 915 I Street, 5th Floor, Sacramento, CA 95814
Fax: (916) 808-7618

○City Manager **John F. Shirey** .... (916) 808-5704
Note: Retiring November 18, 2016
E-mail: jfshirey@cityofsacramento.org
Assistant to the City Manager **Fran Halbakken** .... (916) 808-7194
E-mail: fhalbakken@cityofsacramento.org
Assistant City Manager **Howard Chan** .... (916) 808-7488
E-mail: HChan@cityofsacramento.org
Assistant City Manager **John Dangberg** .... (916) 808-1222
E-mail: JDangberg@cityofsacramento.org

Convention, Culture and Leisure Department

1030 15th Street, Suite 250, Sacramento, CA 95814
Tel: (916) 808-8225 Fax: (916) 808-7279

Director **Jody Ulich** .... (916) 808-8225
Convention Center General Manager **Matt Voreyer** ...... (916) 808-5630
1030 15th Avenue, Suite 100, Sacramento, CA 95814 Fax: (916) 808-7687
Crocker Art Museum Director **Lial A. Jones** .... (916) 808-5546
216 O St., Sacramento, CA 95814
Fairytale Town Director **Kathy Fleming** .... (916) 264-7060
3901 Land Park Dr., Sacramento, CA 95822 Fax: (916) 264-5356
History and Science Manager **Marcia Eymann** .... (916) 808-5960
551 Sequoia Pacific Blvd., Sacramento, CA 95814
Metropolitan Arts Executive Director **Shelly Willis** ...... (916) 808-3989
300 Richards Boulevard, 2nd Floor, Sacramento, CA 95815
Old City Cemetery Manager **Marcia Eymann** .... (916) 808-5960
922 Second Street, #220, Sacramento, CA 95818
Old Sacramento Management **Marcia Eymann** .... (916) 442-8575
1111 Second Street, Sacramento, CA 95814

★Elected Official ▲Appointed by Legislature ▼Appointed by Governor ▶Appointed by Board or Commission ●Appointed by Judge
■Appointed by Mayor △Appointed by Freeholders ▽Appointed by Supervisor ▷Appointed by County Executive ○Appointed by Council

Convention, Culture and Leisure Department *continued*

Sacramento Zoo Director/Chief Executive Officer
Dr. Kyle Burks .... (916) 808-5886
3930 West Land Park Dr., Sacramento, CA 95822

Economic Development Department

915 I Street, 3rd Floor, Sacramento, CA 95814
Fax: (916) 808-8161

Director **Larry Burkhardt** .... (916) 808-8196

Department of Finance

City Hall, 915 I Street, Sacramento, CA 95814
Tel: (916) 808-5845 Fax: (916) 808-5755

Finance Director **Leyne Milstein** .... (916) 808-5845

Accounting Division

City Hall, 915 I Street, 4th Floor, Sacramento, CA 95814
Fax: (916) 808-5444

Manager **Russ Robinson** .... (916) 808-5495
E-mail: rrobinson@cityofsacramento.org

Budget/Policy Division

City Hall, 915 I Street, Sacramento, CA 95814
Fax: (916) 808-5755

Manager **Dawn Holm** .... (916) 808-5832
E-mail: dholm@cityofsacramento.org

Procurement Services Division

City Hall, 915 I Street, 2nd Floor, Sacramento, CA 95814

Manager **Craig Lymus** .... (916) 808-5524
E-mail: clymus@cityofsacramento.org

Fire Department

5770 Freeport Blvd., #200, Sacramento, CA 95822
Tel: (916) 808-1300 Fax: (916) 808-1629

Fire Chief **Walt White** .... (916) 433-1300
E-mail: wwhite@sfd.cityofsacramento.org
Operations Deputy Chief **Lloyd Ogan** .... (916) 433-1300
E-mail: logan@sfd.cityofsacramento.org
Special Operations Assistant Chief **Ed Vasques** .... (916) 808-1300
E-mail: evasquez@sfd.cityofsacramento.org
Assistant Chief/Fire Marshal **Michael Bartley** .... (916) 433-1300
E-mail: mbartley@sfd.cityofsacramento.org
Chief of Training **Kim Iannucci** .... (916) 556-6590
E-mail: kiannucci@sfd.cityofsacramento.org

Human Resources Department

City Hall, 915 I Street, Sacramento, CA 95814
Fax: (916) 808-8567

Director **Melissa Chaney** .... (916) 808-7173
Americans with Disabilities (ADA) Coordinator
(Vacant) .... (916) 808-8795

Information Technology Department

1000 I Street, Suite 120, Sacramento, CA 95814
Fax: (916) 808-5087

Director **Maria MacGunigal** .... (916) 808-7998
E-mail: mmacgunigal@cityofsacramento.org

Neighborhood Services

Director **Vincene Jones** .... (916) 808-1406
E-mail: vjones@cityofsacramento.org
Area Manager **Derrick Lim** .... (916) 808-6172
E-mail: dlim@cityofsacramento.org

Parks and Recreation Department

City Hall, 915 I Street, Sacramento, CA 95814
Tel: (916) 808-8526

Director **Col Christopher C. Conlin** .... (916) 808-5200
Education: Rochester 1981 BA
Golf Division Manager **Barbara Collins** .... (916) 808-6316

Police Department

5770 Freeport Boulevard, Suite #100, Sacramento, CA 95822
Fax: (916) 433-0818 Internet: http://www.sacpd.org

Police Chief **Sam Somers, Jr.** .... (916) 808-0800
Deputy Chief **Brian Louie** .... (916) 808-0800

Public Works Department

City Hall, 915 I Street, 2nd Floor, Sacramento, CA 95814
Fax: (916) 808-5573

Director **Jerry Way** .... (916) 808-6381

Sacramento Public Library Authority

828 I Street, Sacramento, CA 95814-2589
Tel: (916) 264-2770 Fax: (916) 264-2755 Internet: www.saclibrary.org

Administration

Library Director **Rivkah Sass** .... (916) 264-2830
E-mail: director@saclibrary.org
Deputy Library Director **Denise Davis** .... (916) 264-2747
E-mail: ddavis@saclibrary.org
Finance Manager **Johnny Ea** .... (916) 264-2744
Human Resources Manager **Liane Lee** .... (916) 264-2868
E-mail: llee@saclibrary.org
Youth and Literary Services Manager **Christie Hamm** .... (916) 264-2978
E-mail: chamm@saclibrary.org

Utilities Department

1395 35th Avenue, Sacramento, CA 95822
Fax: (916) 808-1497 Internet: www.cityofsacramento.org/utilities/

Director **Bill Busath** .... (916) 808-1400
Integrated Waste Superintendent **(Vacant)** .... (916) 808-4900
Building A, 2812 Meadowview Road, Sacramento, CA 95832

City-County Office of Metropolitan Water Planning

Tel: (916) 808-1999 Fax: (916) 264-5286

Executive Director **Tom Gohring** .... (916) 808-1998
660 J Street, Suite 260, Sacramento, CA 95814
Senior Administrative Services Officer **Lilly Allen** .... (916) 808-1997
660 J Street, Suite 260, Sacramento, CA 95814
E-mail: lallen@waterforum.org

★ Elected Official ▲ Appointed by Legislature ▼ Appointed by Governor ► Appointed by Board or Commission ● Appointed by Judge
■ Appointed by Mayor △ Appointed by Freeholders ▽ Appointed by Supervisor ▷ Appointed by County Executive ○ Appointed by Council

City of St. Louis, Missouri

City Hall, 1200 Market St., St. Louis, MO 63103
Tel: (314) 622-4000 (Information) Internet: http://stlouis-mo.gov/

County: None **Election Type:** Partisan **Year Incorporated:** 1809
Charter: 1914 **Population:** 315,685 (2015)

Francis G. Slay (D)
Mayor

Began Service: April 2001
Term Expires: April 21, 2017
Date of Birth: March 18, 1955
Education: Quincy Col 1977 BA; Saint Louis U 1980 JD
Career: Alderman, Ward 23, City of St. Louis, Missouri (1985-1995); President, Board of Aldermen, City of St. Louis, Missouri (1995-2001)

Office of the Mayor

200 City Hall, 1200 Market St., St. Louis, MO 63103
Fax: (314) 622-4061
Internet: www.stlouis-mo.gov/government/departments/mayor/

★ Mayor **Francis G. Slay** (D) . . . . . (314) 622-3201
E-mail: mayorslay@stlouis-mo.gov
■ Chief of Staff **Mary Ellen Ponder** . . . . . (314) 622-3201
Deputy Chief of Staff **Patrick Brown** . . . . . (314) 622-3757
■ Communications Director **Maggie Crane** . . . . . (314) 622-4072
E-mail: cranem@stlouis-mo.gov
■ Director of Strategic Policy Initiatives **Carl Filler** . . . . . (314) 622-3746
Director of Operations **Todd Waelterman** . . . . . (314) 622-3201
E-mail: waeltermant@stlouis-mo.gov
Executive Assistant to the Mayor **Sherry Wibbenmeyer** . . (314) 622-3723
Scheduler **Josh Wiese** . . . . . (314) 622-3201
Special Assistant to the Mayor/Director of Diversity **Sable Campbell-Jones** . . . . . (314) 622-3201
Sustainability Director **Catherine Werner** . . . . . (314) 622-3733

Citizens Service Bureau

1520 Market Street, Room 4087, St. Louis, MO 63103
Tel: (314) 622-4800

Manager **Dotti Pennington** . . . . . (314) 622-4800

Office of the Board of Aldermen

230 City Hall, 1200 Market St., St. Louis, MO 63103-2871
Tel: (314) 622-3287 Fax: (314) 622-4273

★ President **Lewis E. Reed** (D) . . . . . (314) 622-4114
Term Expires: April 16, 2019
E-mail: reedl@stlouis-mo.gov
Secretary **Mary Cullins** . . . . . (314) 622-4114
E-mail: cullinsm@stlouis-mo.gov
★ Alderwoman **Sharon Tyus** (D-Ward 1) . . . . . (314) 622-3287
Term Expires: April 16, 2017
★ Alderwoman **Dionne Flowers** (D-Ward 2) . . . . . (314) 622-3287
Term Expires: April 16, 2019
E-mail: flowersd@stlouis-mo.gov
★ Alderman **Freeman M. Bosley, Sr.** (D-Ward 3) . . . . . (314) 622-3287
Term Expires: April 16, 2017
E-mail: bosleyf@stlouis-mo.gov
★ Alderman **Sam Moore** (D-Ward 4) . . . . . (314) 622-3287
Term Expires: April 16, 2019
E-mail: moores@stlouis-mo.gov
★ Alderwoman **Tammika Hubbard** (D-Ward 5) . . . . . (314) 622-3287
Term Expires: April 16, 2017
★ Alderwoman **Christine Ingrassia** (D-Ward 6) . . . . . (314) 622-3287
Term Expires: April 16, 2019

Office of the Board of Aldermen *continued*

★ Alderman **John "Jack" Coatar** (D-Ward 7) . . . . . (314) 622-3287
Term Expires: April 16, 2017
★ Alderman **Stephen J. Conway** (D-Ward 8) . . . . . (314) 622-3287
Term Expires: April 16, 2019
E-mail: conways@stlouis-mo.gov
★ Alderman **Kenneth Ortmann** (D-Ward 9) . . . . . (314) 622-3287
Term Expires: April 16, 2017
E-mail: ortmannk@stlouis-mo.gov
★ Alderman **Joseph Vollmer** (D-Ward 10) . . . . . (314) 622-3287
Term Expires: April 16, 2019
E-mail: vollmerj@stlouis-mo.gov
★ Alderman **Thomas Albert "Tom" Villa** (D-Ward 11) . . . . (314) 622-3287
Term Expires: April 16, 2017
E-mail: villat@stlouis-mo.gov
Education: Saint Louis U 1967 BS; Missouri (St Louis) 1971 MEd
★ Alderman **Larry Arnowitz** (D-Ward 12) . . . . . (314) 622-3287
Term Expires: April 16, 2019
E-mail: arnowitzl@stlouis-mo.gov
★ Alderwoman **Beth Murphy** (D-Ward 13) . . . . . (314) 622-3287
Term Expires: April 16, 2017
★ Alderwoman **Carol J. Howard** (D-Ward 14) . . . . . (314) 622-3287
Term Expires: April 16, 2019
★ Alderwoman **Megan Green** (D-Ward 15) . . . . . (314) 622-3287
Term Expires: April 16, 2017
★ Alderwoman **Donna Baringer** (D-Ward 16) . . . . . (314) 622-3287
Term Expires: April 16, 2019
E-mail: baringerd@stlouis-mo.gov
★ Alderman **Joseph D. Roddy** (D-Ward 17) . . . . . (314) 622-3287
Term Expires: April 19, 2017
E-mail: roddyj@stlouis-mo.gov
★ Alderman **Terry Kennedy** (D-Ward 18) . . . . . (314) 622-3287
Term Expires: April 16, 2019
E-mail: kennedyt@stlouis-mo.gov
★ Alderwoman **Marlene Davis** (D-Ward 19) . . . . . (314) 622-3287
Term Expires: April 19, 2017
E-mail: davism@stlouis-mo.gov
★ Alderwoman **Cara Spencer** (D-Ward 20) . . . . . (314) 622-3287
Term Expires: April 16, 2019
★ Alderman **Antonio French** (D-Ward 21) . . . . . (314) 622-3287
Term Expires: April 16, 2017
★ Alderman **Jeffrey L. Boyd** (D-Ward 22) . . . . . (314) 622-3287
Term Expires: April 16, 2019
E-mail: boydj@stlouis-mo.gov
★ Alderman **Joe Vaccaro** (D-Ward 23) . . . . . (314) 622-3287
Term Expires: April 19, 2017
★ Alderman **Scott Ogilvie** (I-Ward 24) . . . . . (314) 622-3287
Term Expires: April 19, 2019
E-mail: ogilvies@stlouis-mo.gov
★ Alderman **Shane Cohn** (D-Ward 25) . . . . . (314) 622-3287
Term Expires: April 16, 2017
★ Alderman **Frank A. Williamson** (D-Ward 26) . . . . . (314) 622-3287
Term Expires: April 16, 2019
E-mail: williamsonf@stlouis-mo.gov
★ Alderman **Chris Carter** (D-Ward 27) . . . . . (314) 622-3287
Term Expires: April 16, 2017
★ Alderwoman **Lyda Krewson** (D-Ward 28) . . . . . (314) 622-3287
Term Expires: April 16, 2019
E-mail: krewsonl@stlouis-mo.gov
▶ Clerk of the Board/Legal Counsel **Timothy O'Connell** . . . (314) 622-3287
Assistant Clerk **Donna Evans-Booker** . . . . . (314) 622-3287
E-mail: bookerd@stlouis-mo.gov
Administrative Assistant **Lisa R. McNichols** . . . . . (314) 622-3287
E-mail: mcnicholsl@stlouis-mo.gov

Office of the Assessor

120 City Hall, 1200 Market St., St. Louis, MO 63103
Fax: (314) 622-3619

■ Assessor **Freddie Dunlap** . . . . . (314) 622-4050
E-mail: dunlapf@stlouis-mo.gov

★ Elected Official ▲ Appointed by Legislature ▼ Appointed by Governor ▶ Appointed by Board or Commission ● Appointed by Judge
■ Appointed by Mayor △ Appointed by Freeholders ▽ Appointed by Supervisor ▷ Appointed by County Executive ○ Appointed by Council

Office of the Circuit Attorney
1114 Market Street, Room 401, St. Louis, MO 63101
Fax: (314) 622-3369 Internet: http://www.circuitattorney.org/
E-mail: caocommunications@stlouiscao.org

★ Circuit Attorney **Jennifer M. Joyce** (D) . . . . (314) 622-4941
Term Expires: December 31, 2016

Office of the City Counselor
City Hall, 1200 Market Street, Room 314, St. Louis, MO 63103-2806
Fax: (314) 622-4956

■ City Counselor **Winston Calvert** . . . . (314) 622-3361
E-mail: calvertw@stlouis-mo.gov
Deputy City Counselor **Nancy Kistler** . . . . (314) 622-3361
E-mail: kistlern@stlouis-mo.gov
Deputy City Counselor **(Vacant)** . . . . (314) 622-3361

Office of the Collector of Revenue
City Hall, 1200 Market Street, Room 110, St. Louis, MO 63103-2803
Tel: (314) 622-4111 Fax: (314) 622-4413
Internet: http://stlouis.missouri.org/citygov/collector/

★ Revenue Collector **Gregory F.X. Daly** (D) . . . . (314) 622-4111
Term Expires: March 1, 2019
E-mail: dalyg@stlouis-mo.gov
Executive Secretary **Jean Schuh** . . . . (314) 622-4111
E-mail: schuhj@stlouis-mo.gov
Deputy Collector **Thomas C. Vollmer** . . . . (314) 613-7357
E-mail: vollmert@stlouis-mo.gov
Earnings Tax Department Senior Assistant Collector
Jackie Whittier . . . . (314) 589-6031
E-mail: whittierj@stlouis-mo.gov Fax: (314) 622-4847
Finance Department Senior Assistant Collector
Robert A. Willner . . . . (314) 622-4784
E-mail: willnerr@stlouis-mo.gov Fax: (314) 622-4764
Water Rates and Support Services Department Senior
Assistant Collector **Rachel Bock** . . . . (314) 613-7412
E-mail: bockr@stlouis-mo.gov Fax: (314) 613-7041
Property Tax Department Assistant Collector
Pat Ortmann . . . . (314) 613-7248
E-mail: ortmannp@stlouis-mo.gov

Office of the Comptroller
City Hall, 1200 Market Street, Room 212, St. Louis, MO 63103-2806
Fax: (314) 622-4026

★ Comptroller **Darlene Green** (D) . . . . (314) 622-4389
Term Expires: April 19, 2017
E-mail: greend@stlouis-mo.gov
Education: Washington U (MO) BSBA
Deputy Comptroller **Bev Fitzsimmons** Room 311 . . . . (314) 589-6035
Fax: (314) 622-4354
Deputy Comptroller of Finance **(Vacant)** . . . . (314) 657-3431
1520 Market Street, St. Louis, MO 63103-2806 Fax: (314) 588-0550
Real Estate Property Specialist **(Vacant)** . . . . (314) 657-3421
1520 Market Street, St. Louis, MO 63103-2806 Fax: (314) 588-0550
Real Estate Records Clerk **Marsha Veal** . . . . (314) 657-3420
1520 Market Street, St. Louis, MO 63103-2806 Fax: (314) 588-0550

Office of the License Collector
1200 Market St., Room 102, St. Louis, MO 63103-2804
Fax: (314) 622-3275

★ License Collector **Mavis T. Thompson** . . . . (314) 622-4643
Term Expires: December 31, 2018
E-mail: licensecollectorsoffice@stlouis-mo.gov
Chief Deputy License Collector **Aaron Phillips** . . . . (314) 641-8322

Office of the Medical Examiner
1300 Clark Avenue, St. Louis, MO 63103
Tel: (314) 622-4971 Fax: (314) 622-4933

■ Chief Medical Examiner **Dr. Michael A. Graham** . . . . (314) 622-4972
Executive Assistant **Baxter W. Leisure, Jr.** . . . . (314) 622-4974
E-mail: leisureb@stlouis-mo.gov

Office of the Public Administrator
Civil Courts Bldg., 10 North Tucker Boulevard, Room 101,
St. Louis, MO 63101
Fax: (314) 621-7189

★ Public Administrator **Gerard A. Nester** (D) . . . . (314) 622-4394
Term Expires: December 31, 2016
Education: Saint Louis U 1984 BS, 1987 JD

Office of the Recorder of Deeds
126 City Hall, 1200 Market St., St. Louis, MO 63103
E-mail: info@stlouiscityrecorder.org

★ Recorder **Sharon Quigley Carpenter** (D) . . . . (314) 622-4610
Term Expires: December 31, 2018 Fax: (314) 622-4175
E-mail: carpentersh@stlouis-mo.gov
Chief Deputy Recorder **Georgie Simmons** . . . . (314) 622-4610
Fax: (314) 622-4175

Office of the Register
118 City Hall, 1200 Market St., St. Louis, MO 63103
Fax: (314) 622-4247

■ City Register **Parrie L. May** . . . . (314) 622-4306
E-mail: mayp@stlouis-mo.gov
City Deputy Register **Karen Jackson** . . . . (314) 622-4145

Office of the Sheriff
Civil Courts Building, 10 North Tucker Boulevard, Room 112,
St. Louis, MO 63101
Tel: (314) 622-4131 Fax: (314) 622-4839

★ Sheriff **James W. Murphy** (D) . . . . (314) 622-4131
Term Expires: December 31, 2016
E-mail: jmurphy@courts.mo.gov
Administrative Assistant **Michael Guzy** . . . . (314) 622-4255
E-mail: mguzy@mo.gov
Criminal Division Commander **Major Scott Lammert** . . . (314) 622-4699
E-mail: slammert@stlouisco.com
Security Commander Deputy **Capt. Dennis Pogue** . . . . . . (314) 622-4636
E-mail: dpogue@stlouisco.com
Training Director **Michael Guzy** . . . . (314) 622-4255
E-mail: mguzy@mo.gov
Administration **Major George Harsley** . . . . (314) 622-4958
E-mail: gharsley@stlouisco.com
Internal Affairs Deputy **Timothy Haill** . . . . (314) 622-4778
E-mail: thaill@stlouisco.com
Transportation **Lt. Lester Stewart** . . . . (314) 622-4660
E-mail: lstewart@stlouisco.com

Office of the Treasurer
1200 Market Street, Room 220, St. Louis, MO 63103-2805
Fax: (314) 622-4246

★ Treasurer **Tishaura O. Jones** (D) . . . . (314) 622-3434
Term Expires: December 31, 2016 Fax: (314) 622-4246
E-mail: jonestj@stlouis-mo.gov
Chief of Staff/Chief Counsel **Jared Boyd** . . . . (314) 612-1478
Assistant Treasurer **Judy Montgomery** . . . . (314) 622-3510
Chief Fiscal Officer **Michelle Smart** . . . . (314) 622-5678
Paymaster **Angela Gassel** . . . . (314) 622-5675
Cashier **Archell Dickerson** . . . . (314) 622-5672

St. Louis Agency on Training and Employment / SLATE American Job Center
1520 Market Street, St. Louis, MO 63103
Tel: (314) 589-8000 Internet: http://www.stlworks.com

■ Executive Director **Michael Holmes** . . . . (314) 589-8000
E-mail: mholmes@stlworks.com

★ Elected Official ▲ Appointed by Legislature ▼ Appointed by Governor ► Appointed by Board or Commission ● Appointed by Judge
■ Appointed by Mayor △ Appointed by Freeholders ▽ Appointed by Supervisor ▷ Appointed by County Executive ○ Appointed by Council

Brightside St. Louis

4646 Shenandoah, St. Louis, MO 63110-3424
Tel: (314) 772-4646 Fax: (314) 772-7444
E-mail: brightsidestl@gmail.com Internet: www.brightsidestl.org

Director **Mary Lou Green** .... (314) 772-4646 ext. 201
E-mail: brightsidestl@gmail.com

Civil Rights Enforcement Agency [CREA]

1114 Market Street, Suite 626, St. Louis, MO 63101
Fax: (314) 622-4190 E-mail: crea@stlouis-mo.gov

■ Director **Charles Bryson** .... (314) 622-3301
E-mail: brysonc@stlouis-mo.gov

Civil Service Commission

1114 Market Street, Room 700, St. Louis, MO 63101
Fax: (314) 622-3225

■ Chairman **Steven Barney** .... (314) 622-3403
■ Vice Chairman **Stanley Newsome, Sr.** .... (314) 622-3403
■ Member **Leo Donahue** .... (314) 622-3403

Community Development Administration [CDA]

1520 Market Street, Suite 2000, St. Louis, MO 63103
Tel: (314) 657-3700 Fax: (314) 613-7013
Internet: http://stlouis-mo.gov/cda/

■ Executive Director **Alfred J. Wessels, Jr.** (D) .... (314) 657-3835

St. Louis Convention and Visitors Commission [CVC]

701 Convention Plaza, Suite 300, St. Louis, MO 63101
Tel: (314) 421-1023 Fax: (314) 421-0039
Internet: www.explorestlouis.com/cvc/

President **Kathleen "Kitty" Ratcliffe** .... (314) 992-0604

St. Louis Development Corporation [SLDC]

1520 Market Street, Suite 2000, St. Louis, MO 63103
Tel: (314) 657-3700 Fax: (314) 613-7011
Internet: http://stlouis-mo.gov/government/departments/sldc/

Executive Director **Otis Williams** .... (314) 657-3703
E-mail: williamsot@stlouis-mo.gov
Director, New Markets Tax Credit **Bill Seddon** .... (314) 657-3705
E-mail: seddonb@stlouis-mo.gov
Commercial Development Director **Dale Ruthsatz** .... (314) 657-3732
E-mail: ruthsatzd@stlouis-mo.gov
Director, Major Projects **Rob Orr** .... (314) 657-3738
E-mail: orrr@stlouis-mo.gov
Real Estate Director **Laura Costello** .... (314) 657-3725
E-mail: costellol@stlouis-mo.gov
Director, Port Development **Susan Taylor** .... (314) 657-3740
E-mail: taylors@stlouis-mo.gov
Director, Minority Business Development
Howard Hayes .... (314) 657-3707
E-mail: hayesh@stlouis-mo.gov
Director, Human Resources and Administration
Melanie Pelletier .... (314) 657-3708

Office on the Disabled

City Hall, 1200 Market Street, Room 30, St. Louis, MO 63103
TTY: (314) 622-3693 Fax: (314) 622-4019

Commissioner **David Newburger** .... (314) 622-3686

Board of Election Commissioners

300 N. Tucker Blvd., St. Louis, MO 63101-1914
Tel: (314) 622-4336 Fax: (314) 622-4315
Internet: http://www.stlelections.com

▼ Chairman **Joan M. Burger** (D) .... (314) 622-4336
▼ Member **Paul Maloney** .... (314) 622-4336
▼ Member **Benjamin M. Phillips, Sr.** (D) .... (314) 622-4336

Board of Election Commissioners *continued*

▼ Member **Andrew L. Schwartz** (R) .... (314) 622-4336
▶ Democrat Director **Mary Wheeler-Jones** .... (314) 622-4336
E-mail: jonesm@stlelections.com
▶ Republican Director **Leo G. "Gary" Stoff** .... (314) 622-4336
E-mail: stoffg@stlelections.com

Department of Health

1520 Market Street, 4th Floor, St. Louis, MO 63103
Tel: (314) 612-5100 Fax: (314) 612-5105

Director (Acting) **Melba R. Moore** .... (314) 657-1528
Health Commissioner **Melba R. Moore** .... (314) 657-1528
Secretary to the Acting Director/Health Commissioner
Michelle Turner .... (314) 657-1528
E-mail: turnerm@stlouis-mo.gov

Department of Human Services

1520 Market Street, Suite 4065, St. Louis, MO 63103-2613
Fax: (314) 612-5909

■ Director **Eddie Roth** .... (314) 612-5900
E-mail: rothe@stlouis-mo.gov
Veterans Affairs Officer **Robert Crecelius** .... (314) 657-1656
Executive Secretary **LaJoyce Thomas** .... (314) 657-1653
E-mail: thomasla@stlouis-mo.gov

Housing Authority

3520 Page Boulevard, St. Louis, MO 63106
Tel: (314) 531-4770 TTY: (314) 286-4223 Fax: (314) 531-0184
Internet: www.slha.org/

Executive Director **Cheryl A. Lovell** .... (314) 286-4357
Vice President of Information Technology **Karl Hughes** .. (314) 286-4391
E-mail: khughes@slha.org

Lambert-St. Louis International Airport

10701 Lambert International Boulevard, St. Louis, MO 63145
P.O. Box 10212, St. Louis, MO 63145
Tel: (314) 426-8000 Fax: (314) 426-5733 Internet: www.flystl.com/

■ Director **Rhonda Hamm-Niebruegge** .... (314) 890-1356
E-mail: rkhamm-niebruegge@flystl.com
Deputy Director, Operations and Maintenance
Ron Stella .... (314) 426-8023
Deputy Director, Planning and Engineering
Jerry Beckmann .... (314) 551-5008
E-mail: gabeckmann@flystl.com
Finance and Administration Deputy Director
Antonio Strong .... (314) 890-1328
Information Systems Support Manager **Reed Glasener** ... (314) 890-1831
E-mail: rjglasener@flystl.com Fax: (314) 890-1844

Parks, Recreation and Forestry Department

5600 Clayton Ave., St. Louis, MO 63110
Fax: (314) 535-3901

■ Director **Greg Hayes** .... (314) 289-5310
Executive Assistant **Kathy Sullivan** .... (314) 289-5387
E-mail: sullivank@stlouis-mo.gov
Forestry Commissioner **Skip Kincaid** .... (314) 613-7200
Parks Commissioner **Daniel Skillman** .... (314) 289-5300
Recreation Commissioner **Evelyn Rice-Peebles** .... (314) 289-5320

Personnel Department

1114 Market Street, Room 700, St. Louis, MO 63101
Tel: (314) 622-4308 Fax: (314) 622-4293

Director **Richard R. Frank** .... (314) 622-3561
E-mail: frankr@stlouis-mo.gov Fax: (314) 641-8396
Deputy Director **Linda D. Thomas** .... (314) 622-3251
Fax: (314) 641-8396
Employee Benefits Manager **Karen Toal** .... (314) 622-3200
E-mail: toalk@stlouis-mo.gov Fax: (314) 436-7405

★ Elected Official ▲ Appointed by Legislature ▼ Appointed by Governor ▶ Appointed by Board or Commission ● Appointed by Judge
■ Appointed by Mayor △ Appointed by Freeholders ▽ Appointed by Supervisor ▷ Appointed by County Executive ○ Appointed by Council

Personnel Department *continued*

Recruitment and Examination Manager
Bryan Boeckelmann . . . . . (314) 622-4091
Training and Organizational Development Manager
Sylvia Donaldson . . . . . (314) 622-5763
E-mail: donaldsons@stlouis-mo.gov Fax: (314) 622-5768
Classification and Compensation Manager
John Unnerstall . . . . . (314) 622-3565
Employee Relations Manager **Carolyn Roston** . . . . . (314) 622-3563
E-mail: rostonc@stlouis-mo.gov
Personnel Services Supervisor **Theresa Dabrowski** . . . . . (314) 622-3251
E-mail: dabrowskit@stlouis-mo.gov Fax: (314) 641-8396
Employee Retirement System Manager
Denise Droege Room 900 . . . . . (314) 622-3560
E-mail: droeged@stlouis-mo.gov Fax: (314) 436-7405

Police Department

1915 Olive, St. Louis, MO 63103
Internet: http://slmpd.org/

Chief of Police **Doyle "Sam" Dotson** . . . . . (314) 444-5624
Emergency Management **Sgt Kyle West** . . . . . (314) 444-5624
E-mail: kylewest@slmpd.org
Police Academy Commander (Acting)
Sgt Angela Taylor . . . . . (314) 444-5572
E-mail: amtaylor@slmpd.org

St. Louis Public Library

1415 Olive Street, St. Louis, MO 63103
Tel: (314) 241-2288 Fax: (314) 241-3840 Internet: www.slpl.org

Administration

Executive Director **Waller F. McGuire** . . . . . (314) 539-0300
E-mail: wmcguire@slpl.org
Education: Earlham BA; Kentucky MLS
Deputy Director **Diane Freiermuth** . . . . . (314) 539-0394
E-mail: dfreiermuth@slpl.org
Associate Deputy Director **B. Kathy Leitle** . . . . . (314) 539-0378
E-mail: kleitle@slpl.org
Chief Financial Officer **William Jackson** . . . . . (314) 539-0311
Director, Branch Services **Judy Bruce** . . . . . (314) 539-0363
E-mail: jbruce@slpl.org
Director, Central Library **Brenda McDonald** . . . . . (314) 539-0348
E-mail: bmcdonald@slpl.org
Director, Human Resources and Support Services
Barry V. Berry . . . . . (314) 539-0308
E-mail: bberry@slpl.org
Director, Community Services **Gerald S. Brooks** . . . . . (314) 539-0315
E-mail: gbrooks@slpl.org
Director, Collection Management Services
Michelle Tooey . . . . . (314) 539-0321
E-mail: mtooey@slpl.org
Director, Technology Services **David "Dave" Halbeck** . . . (314) 539-0354
E-mail: dave.halbeck@mo.gov
Director, Youth Services **Patty Carleton** . . . . . (314) 539-0380
E-mail: pcarleton@slpl.org
Manager, Facilities and Maintenance **Alan Warfield** . . . . . (314) 241-8826
E-mail: awarfield@slpl.org
Director of Marketing **Cathy Heimberger** . . . . . (314) 539-0305
E-mail: cheimberger@mo.gov

Public Safety

401 City Hall, 1200 Market St., St. Louis, MO 63103
Fax: (314) 622-4392

■ Director **Col. Richard Gray** . . . . . (314) 622-3391
E-mail: grayr@stlouis-mo.gov
Deputy Director **Charlene Deeken** . . . . . (314) 622-3391
E-mail: deekenc@stlouis-mo.gov
Building Division Commissioner **Frank Oswald** . . . . . (314) 622-3318
Excise Division Commissioner **Robert Kraiberg** . . . . . (314) 622-4191
Commissioner of Corrections **Dale Glass** . . . . . (314) 621-5848
City Justice Center, 200 S. Tucker St., St. Louis, MO 63101

Public Safety *continued*

Public Information Officer **Cathy Smentkowski** . . . . . (314) 589-8132
E-mail: smentkowskic@stlouis-mo.gov

City Emergency Management Agency

1915 Olive Street, 6th Floor, St. Louis, MO 63103
Fax: (314) 622-3472

Commissioner **Gary Christmann** . . . . . (314) 444-5467
E-mail: christmang@stlouis-mo.gov
Office Manager **Lil Ezell** . . . . . (314) 444-5467
Communications Coordinator **Anthony Minden** . . . . . (314) 444-5467
E-mail: mindena@stlouis-mo.gov
Training Coordinator **Sarah Gamblin-Luig** . . . . . (314) 444-5469
E-mail: gamblin-luigs@stlouis-mo.gov

Fire Department

Headquarters Complex, 1421 N. Jefferson Ave., St. Louis, MO 63106
E-mail: stlfd@stlouis.missouri.org

Fire Chief **Dennis Jenkerson** . . . . . (314) 289-1953
E-mail: jenkersond@stlouis-mo.gov

Medium Security Institution

7600 N. Hall St., St. Louis, MO 63147

Commissioner **Dale Glass** . . . . . (314) 621-5848

Neighborhood Stabilization Team/Citizen Service Bureau

1520 Market Street, Room 4000, St. Louis, MO 63103

Manager **Dotti Pennington** . . . . . (314) 657-1391
E-mail: penningtond@stlouis-mo.gov

Office of Special Events

1200 Market St., Room 418, St. Louis, MO 63103

Director **Ann Chance** . . . . . (314) 589-6640
E-mail: chancea@stlouis-mo.gov

St. Louis Public School District

801 North 11th Street, St. Louis, MO 63101
Tel: (314) 231-3720 Internet: www.slps.org

Superintendent **Dr. Kelvin R. Adams** . . . . . (314) 345-2296
Education: Northeast Louisiana 1978 BA; Xavier (LA) 1991 MA; New Orleans 2005 PhD

Special Administrative Board [SAB]

President/Chief Executive Officer **Rick Sullivan** . . . . . (314) 345-2304
Vice President **Melanie Adams** . . . . . (314) 345-2304
Member **Richard Gaines** . . . . . (314) 345-2304

Board of Public Service

305 City Hall, 1200 Market Street, St. Louis, MO 63103
Tel: (314) 622-3535 Fax: (314) 622-4028
Internet: http://www.stl-bps.org/

■ President **Richard Bradley** . . . . . (314) 622-4143
E-mail: bradleyr@stlouis-mo.gov

Public Utilities

1640 South Kingshighway Boulevard, St. Louis, MO 63110
Fax: (314) 664-6786

■ Director **Curtis Skouby** . . . . . (314) 633-9000
Communications Commissioner
Donna Brooks-Sanders . . . . . (314) 552-2900
4971 Oakland Avenue, St. Louis, MO 63110 Fax: (314) 552-2985
E-mail: brooks-sandersd@stlouis-mo.gov

Soldiers Memorial Military Museum

1315 Chestnut St., St. Louis, MO 63103-2391
Fax: (314) 622-4237 Internet: www.stlsoldiersmemorial.org/

Superintendent **Lynnea Magnuson** . . . . . (314) 622-4550

★ Elected Official ▲ Appointed by Legislature ▼ Appointed by Governor ▶ Appointed by Board or Commission ● Appointed by Judge
■ Appointed by Mayor △ Appointed by Freeholders ▽ Appointed by Supervisor ▷ Appointed by County Executive ○ Appointed by Council

CITIES AND TOWNS

Department of Streets

1900 Hampton Avenue, St. Louis, MO 63139-2902
Fax: (314) 768-2888

■ Director **Stephen J. "Steve" Runde** . . . . . . (314) 647-3111
E-mail: rundes@stlouis-mo.gov
Refuse Division Commissioner **Nicholas Yung** . . . . . . (314) 647-3111
Fax: (314) 768-2888
Street Division Commissioner **Kent Flake** . . . . . . (314) 647-3111
Traffic and Lighting Commissioner **Deanna Venker** . . . . . (314) 647-3111

Supply Division

324 City Hall, 1200 Market St., St. Louis, MO 63103
Tel: (314) 622-4580 Fax: (314) 622-4141
Internet: www.stlouis-mo.gov/government/departments/supply/

■ Supply Commissioner **Carol Shepard** . . . . . . (314) 622-4330
E-mail: shepardc@stlouis-mo.gov

Saint Louis Zoo

One Government Drive, St. Louis, MO 63110-1395
Tel: (314) 781-0900 Fax: (314) 647-7969 E-mail: pr@stlzoo.org
Internet: www.stlzoo.org

President and Chief Executive Officer **Jeffrey P. Bonner** . . (314) 646-4619
Education: Missouri 1975 BA; Columbia 1977 MA, 1979 MPhil, 1982 PhD
Senior Vice President and Director of Zoological Operations **Eric Miller** . . . . . . (314) 646-4557

City of Saint Paul, Minnesota

City Hall, 15 West Kellogg Boulevard, Room 160, St. Paul, MN 55102
Tel: (651) 266-8989 (Information) Internet: http://www.stpaul.gov/

County: Ramsey **Election Type:** Nonpartisan **Charter:** 1900
Population: 300,851 (2015) **Employees:** 2,923 **Fiscal Year:** 2016
Budget: $548,277,000

Christopher B. "Chris" Coleman
Mayor

Began Service: January 2006
Term Expires: December 31, 2017
Education: Minnesota BA, 1987 JD

Office of the Mayor

City Hall, 15 West Kellogg Boulevard, Room 390, St. Paul, MN 55102
Tel: (651) 266-8510 Fax: (651) 266-8521
Internet: https://www.stpaul.gov/departments/mayors-office

Employees: 16 **Fiscal Year:** 2016 **Budget:** $2,371,000

★ Mayor **Christopher B. "Chris" Coleman** . . . . . . (651) 266-8510
E-mail: chris.coleman@ci.stpaul.mn.us
Assistant to the Mayor/Scheduler **Chris Rider** . . . . . . (651) 266-8535
E-mail: chris.rider@ci.stpaul.mn.us
Deputy Mayor **Kristin Beckmann** . . . . . . (651) 266-8569
E-mail: kristin.beckmann@ci.stpaul.mn.us
Education: Minnesota MPA
Policy Director **Nancy Homans** . . . . . . (651) 266-8568
■ Chief of Staff **Dana Bailey** . . . . . . (651) 266-8878
Education: Minnesota St (Mankato) 2000 BS
Communications Director **Tonya Tennessen** . . . . . . (651) 266-8518
E-mail: tonya.tennessen@ci.stpaul.mn.us
Education: Wisconsin BA
Press Secretary **Ashley Aram** . . . . . . (651) 266-8571

Office of the Mayor *continued*

Arts and Culture Policy Associate **Joe Spencer** . . . . . . (651) 266-8524
Education Policy Analyst **Peter Grafstrom** . . . . . . (651) 266-8516
Director of Outreach **Matt Freeman** . . . . . . (651) 266-8531
Governmental Relations **Katie Knutson** . . . . . . (651) 266-8519
E-mail: katie.knutson@ci.stpaul.mn.us
Events, Marketing and Communications Coordinator **Liz Xiong** . . . . . . (651) 266-8527
E-mail: liz.xiong@ci.stpaul.mn.us
Deputy Policy Director for Environment **Anne Hunt** . . . . . (651) 266-8520
Policy Associate **Ana Vang** . . . . . . (651) 266-8536
E-mail: ana.vang@ci.stpaul.mn.us
Communications Associate, Constituent Services **Fedha Abera** . . . . . . (651) 266-8512
E-mail: fedha.abera@ci.stpaul.mn.us
Volunteers in Service to America (VISTA) Manager **Morgan Weis** . . . . . . (651) 266-8582
E-mail: morgan.weis@ci.stpaul.mn.us
Office Manager **Jean Karpe** . . . . . . (651) 266-8526

Office of the City Council

City Hall, 15 West Kellogg Boulevard, Room 310, St. Paul, MN 55102
Tel: (651) 266-8560 Fax: (651) 266-8574

Employees: 28 **Fiscal Year:** 2016 **Budget:** $3,152,000

★ Council President **Russ Stark** (Ward 4) . . . . . . (651) 266-8640
Term Expires: December 31, 2019
E-mail: ward4@ci.stpaul.mn.us
★ Council Member **Dai Thao** (Ward 1) . . . . . . (651) 266-8610
Term Expires: December 31, 2019
E-mail: ward1@ci.stpaul.mn.us
★ Council Member **Rebecca Noecker** (Ward 2) . . . . . . (651) 266-8620
Term Expires: December 31, 2019
★ Council Member **Chris Tolbert** (Ward 3) . . . . . . (651) 266-8630
Term Expires: December 31, 2019
E-mail: ward3@ci.stpaul.mn.us
★ Council Member **Amy Brendmoen** (Ward 5) . . . . . . (651) 266-8650
Term Expires: December 31, 2019
E-mail: ward5@ci.stpaul.mn.us
★ Council Member **Dan Bostrom** (Ward 6) . . . . . . (651) 266-8660
Term Expires: December 31, 2019
E-mail: ward6@ci.stpaul.mn.us
★ Council Member **Jane Prince** (Ward 7) . . . . . . (651) 266-8670
Term Expires: December 31, 2019
○ City Council Operations Director **Trudy Moloney** . . . . . . (651) 266-8575
E-mail: trudy.moloney@ci.stpaul.mn.us

Office of the City Attorney

City Hall, 15 West Kellogg Boulevard, Room 400, St. Paul, MN 55102-1635
Fax: (651) 298-5619

Employees: 66 **Fiscal Year:** 2016 **Budget:** $9,299,000

■ City Attorney **Samuel "Sammy" Clark** . . . . . . (651) 266-8710
Deputy City Attorney, Civil Division **Jerry Hendrickson** . . . . . . (651) 266-8710
Deputy City Attorney, Criminal Division **Laura Pietan** . . . (651) 266-8740

Office of the City Clerk

City Hall, 15 West Kellogg Boulevard, Room 310, St. Paul, MN 55102-1635
Fax: (651) 266-8574 E-mail: cityclerk@ci.stpaul.mn.us
Internet: https://www.stpaul.gov/departments/city-clerk

○ City Clerk **Shari Moore** . . . . . . (651) 266-8686
E-mail: shari.moore@ci.stpaul.mn.us
Education: Mankato State ScB

★ Elected Official ▲ Appointed by Legislature ▼ Appointed by Governor ▶ Appointed by Board or Commission ● Appointed by Judge
■ Appointed by Mayor △ Appointed by Freeholders ▽ Appointed by Supervisor ▷ Appointed by County Executive ○ Appointed by Council

Emergency Management Department
357 Grove Street, 5th Floor, St. Paul, MN 55101
Fax: (651) 266-5493

Employees: 8 **Fiscal Year:** 2016 **Budget:** $1,392,000

■ Emergency Management Director **Rick Larkin** . . . . (651) 266-5494
E-mail: rick.larkin@ci.stpaul.mn.us
Emergency Coordinator **Terrance Sieben** . . . . (651) 266-5495
E-mail: terry.sieben@ci.stpaul.mn.us

Office of Financial Services [OFS]
City Hall, 15 West Kellogg Boulevard, Room 700, St. Paul, MN 55102
Tel: (651) 266-8800 Fax: (651) 266-8541

Employees: 46 **Fiscal Year:** 2016 **Budget:** $14,816,000

■ Director **Todd Hurley** . . . . (651) 266-8800
E-mail: Contact-OFS@ci.stpaul.mn.us

Contract and Analysis Services
Director **Jessica Kingston** Room 280 . . . . (651) 266-8900
E-mail: jessica.kingston@ci.stpaul.mn.us

Saint Paul Fire Department
645 Randolph Avenue, St. Paul, MN 55102
Fax: (651) 228-6255
Internet: https://www.stpaul.gov/departments/fire-paramedics

Employees: 479 **Fiscal Year:** 2016 **Budget:** $65,649,000

Fire Chief **Tim Butler** . . . . (651) 222-0477
E-mail: tim.butler@ci.stpaul.mn.us
Assistant Fire Chief **Butch Inks** . . . . (651) 228-6212
Assistant Fire Chief **Matt Simpson** . . . . (651) 228-6270
E-mail: matt.simpson@ci.stpaul.mn.us
Building and Maintenance Supervisor **Dave Hiveley** . . . . . (651) 771-7840
E-mail: dave.hiveley@ci.stpaul.mn.us
Equipment Services Supervisor **Glen Kadrlik** . . . . (651) 645-0648
E-mail: glen.kadrlik@ci.stpaul.mn.us
Fire Communications Liaison **Don Smiley** . . . . (651) 266-7716
E-mail: don.smiley@ci.stpaul.mn.us
Fire Prevention Fire Marshal **Steve Zaccard** . . . . (651) 228-6201
E-mail: steve.zaccard@ci.stpaul.mn.us
Training Chief **Ken Gilliam** . . . . (651) 224-9133
E-mail: ken.gilliam@ci.stpaul.mn.us
Information Systems Manager **Chin-Ming Yin** . . . . (651) 266-6767
E-mail: chin-ming.yin@ci.stpaul.mn.us

Human Resources
City Hall Annex, 25 West Fourth Street, Room 200, St. Paul, MN 55102
Fax: (651) 292-7656

Employees: 37 **Fiscal Year:** 2016 **Budget:** $8,969,000

■ Director **Angie Nalezny** . . . . (651) 266-6500
E-mail: angie.nalezny@ci.stpaul.mn.us

Office of Labor Relations
City Hall Annex, 25 West Fourth Street, Suite 200, St. Paul, MN 55102
Tel: (651) 266-6500 Fax: (651) 266-6495

Manager **Jason Schmidt** . . . . (651) 266-6503

Risk Management
25 West Fort Street, Suite 200, St. Paul, MN 55102
Fax: (651) 266-8886

Manager **Sandra Bodensteiner** . . . . (651) 266-6500
E-mail: sandra.bodensteiner@ci.stpaul.mn.us

Human Rights and Equal Economic Opportunity Department
City Hall, 15 West Kellogg Boulevard, Room 240, St. Paul, MN 55102
Fax: (651) 266-8919

Employees: 26 **Fiscal Year:** 2016 **Budget:** $4,090,000

■ Director **Jessica Kingston** . . . . (651) 266-8903
E-mail: jessica.kingston@ci.stpaul.mn.us

Human Rights and Equal Economic Opportunity Department *continued*

■ Deputy Director **Readus Fletcher** . . . . (651) 266-8976
E-mail: readus.fletcher@ci.stpaul.mn.us

Parks and Recreation Department
25 West Fourth Street, Suite 400, St. Paul, MN 55102
Tel: (651) 266-6400 Fax: (651) 292-7311

Employees: 555 **Fiscal Year:** 2016 **Budget:** $53,926,000

Director **Michael Hahm** . . . . (651) 266-6400
Education: U St Thomas (MN) BABA

Planning and Economic Development Department [PED]
City Hall Annex, 25 West Fourth Street, St. Paul, MN 55102
Tel: (651) 266-6700 Tel: (651) 266-6600 (Business Resource Center)
Fax: (651) 266-6549

Employees: 74 **Fiscal Year:** 2016 **Budget:** $25,444,000

■ Director **Jonathan Sage-Martinson** . . . . (651) 266-6628
E-mail: jonathan.sage-martinson@ci.stpaul.mn.us
Economic Development Manager **Ellen Muller** . . . . (651) 266-6605
E-mail: ellen.muller@ci.stpaul.mn.us
Grants and Administrative Management **Bob Hammer** . . . (651) 266-6693
E-mail: bob.hammer@ci.stpaul.mn.us
Housing/Invest Saint Paul **Patricia Lilledahl** . . . . (651) 266-6593
E-mail: patty.lilledahl@ci.stpaul.mn.us
Economic Development Director **Martin Schieckel** . . . . . . (651) 266-6616
E-mail: martin.schieckel@ci.stpaul.mn.us

Police Department
367 Grove Street, St. Paul, MN 55101-2296
Tel: (651) 291-1111 Fax: (651) 266-5850

Employees: 771 **Fiscal Year:** 2016 **Budget:** $107,655,000

■ Police Chief (Interim) **Kathleen Wuorinen** . . . . (651) 266-5588
Note: Effective June 2016
E-mail: kathy.wuorinen@ci.stpaul.mn.us
Operations Division Assistant Chief **Todd D. Axtel** . . . . . . (651) 266-5500
Support Services Division Assistant Chief
Kathleen Wuorinen . . . . (651) 266-5545
Major Crimes Division Assistant Chief
William "Bill" Martinez . . . . (651) 266-5500

Department of Safety and Inspections
375 Jackson Street, Suite 220, St. Paul, MN 55101
Tel: (651) 266-8989 Fax: (651) 266-9099

Employees: 145 **Fiscal Year:** 2016 **Budget:** $18,895,000

Director **Ricardo X. Cervantes** . . . . (651) 266-9101
Fax: (651) 266-9122
License Deputy Director **Dan Niziolek** . . . . (651) 266-9108
Animal Control Manager **Molly Lunaris** . . . . (651) 266-1110
Education: Dordt 2001 BA Fax: (651) 266-1120
Building Official **Steve Ubl** . . . . (651) 266-9071
Fax: (651) 266-9099
Fire Safety Division Director **Phillip Owens** . . . . (651) 266-9014
E-mail: phil.owens@ci.stpaul.mn.us Fax: (651) 266-9099
Web Coordinator **Carrie Grengs** . . . . (651) 266-9056
E-mail: carrie.grengs@ci.stpaul.mn.us Fax: (651) 266-9099
Zoning Manager **Wendy Lane** . . . . (651) 266-9081
Fax: (651) 266-9099

Code Enforcement Division
375 Jackson Street, Suite 220, St. Paul, MN 55101
Fax: (651) 266-1926

Manager **Steven Magner** . . . . (651) 266-1928
E-mail: steve.magner@ci.stpaul.mn.us
Deputy Director **(Vacant)** . . . . (651) 266-1928

★ Elected Official ▲ Appointed by Legislature ▼ Appointed by Governor ► Appointed by Board or Commission ● Appointed by Judge
■ Appointed by Mayor △ Appointed by Freeholders ▽ Appointed by Supervisor ▷ Appointed by County Executive ○ Appointed by Council

Saint Paul Public Library
90 West Fourth Street, St. Paul, MN 55102
Tel: (651) 266-7000 Fax: (651) 266-7060 Internet: www.sppl.org

Employees: 174 **Fiscal Year:** 2016 **Budget:**

■ Director **Jane Eastwood** .... (651) 266-7073
E-mail: jane.eastwood@ci.stpaul.mn.us
Education: Macalester BS; Hamline MA
Deputy Director **Tony Yang** .... (651) 266-7085
E-mail: tony.yang@ci.stpaul.mn.us
Facilities Manager **Lee Williamson** .... (651) 266-7425
E-mail: lee.williamson@ci.stpaul.mn.us Fax: (651) 266-7410

Public Works Department
City Hall Annex, 25 West 4th Street, 1500, St. Paul, MN 55102-1660
Tel: (651) 266-6134 Fax: (651) 292-6315

Employees: 385 **Fiscal Year:** 2016 **Budget:** $135,474,000

■ Director **Kathy Lantry** .... (651) 266-6099
City Engineer **John Maczko** .... (651) 266-6137
Capital Planning and Programming Director **Paul Kurtz** .. (651) 266-6137
Equipment Maintenance Manager **Ron Mundal** .... (651) 266-9815
Finance Manager **Larry Michalitsch** .... (651) 266-6070
Bridge Engineer **Glenn Pagel** .... (651) 266-6180
Right-of-Way Engineer **David Kuebler** .... (651) 266-9808
E-mail: david.kuebler@ci.stpaul.mn.us
Sewer Engineering and Maintenance Engineer
Bruce Elder .... (651) 266-6248
Street Design and Construction Engineer **Dan Haak** ...... (651) 266-6080
E-mail: Dan.haak@ci.stpaul.mn.us
Street Maintenance Engineer **Joe Spah** .... (651) 266-9714
Traffic and Lighting Engineer **Paul St. Martin** .... (651) 266-6118

Department of Technology and Communications
City Hall Annex, 25 West 4th Street, Suite 600, St. Paul, MN 55102
Fax: (651) 266-6755

Employees: 75 **Fiscal Year:** 2016 **Budget:** $11,776,000

■ Chief Information Officer **Tarek Tomes** .... (651) 266-6767
E-mail: tarek.tomes@ci.stpaul.mn.us
Education: Maryland BS

Cable Communications
15 West Kellogg Boulevard, Room 68, St. Paul, MN 55102
Tel: (651) 266-8870 Fax: (651) 266-8871

Cable Communications Officer **Mike Reardon** .... (651) 266-8870
E-mail: city18@ci.stpaul.mn.us

Port Authority
1900 Landmark Tower, 345 St. Peter Street, St. Paul, MN 55102
Fax: (651) 223-5198 Internet: http://sppa.com/

President and Chief Executive Officer **Lee Krueger** ...... (651) 224-5686

Capital Improvement Budget Committee
City Hall, 15 West Kellogg Boulevard, Room 700, St. Paul, MN 55102
Fax: (651) 266-8541

Chief Budget Analyst **John McCarthy** .... (651) 266-8554
E-mail: john.mccarthy@ci.stpaul.mn.us
Budget Analyst **Daley Lehmann** .... (651) 266-8825
E-mail: daley.lehmann@ci.stpaul.mn.us

Public Housing Agency
555 Wabasha Street North, Suite 600, St. Paul, MN 55102
Fax: (651) 298-5666

Executive Director **Jon Gutzmann** .... (651) 298-5664

Saint Paul Public Schools
360 Colborne Street, St. Paul, MN 55102
E-mail: communications.office@spps.org Internet: www.spps.org

Superintendent of Schools **Valeria Silva** .... (651) 767-8152
Education: St Cloud State BA; Pontifical Catholic (Chile) BA; Minnesota MA, EdS
Chief Executive Officer **Michelle Walker** .... (651) 767-8145
Ombudsman **Dana Abrams** .... (651) 767-8394
Fax: (651) 290-8386
Chief Operations Officer **Jean Ronnei** .... (651) 603-4958
E-mail: jean.ronnei@spps.org

Board of Education
Tel: (651) 767-8149

★ Chair **Jon Schumacher** .... (651) 767-8149
Term Expires: December 31, 2019
E-mail: Jon.Schumacher@spps.org
★ Vice Chair **Zuki Ellis** .... (651) 328-1443
Term Expires: December 31, 2019
E-mail: Zuki.Ellis@spps.org
★ Clerk **Chue Vue** .... (651) 767-8149
Term Expires: December 31, 2017
E-mail: chue.vue@spps.org
★ Director **John Brodrick** .... (651) 767-8149
Term Expires: December 31, 2017
E-mail: john.brodrick@spps.org
★ Director **Steve Marchese** .... (651) 767-8149
Term Expires: December 31, 2019
E-mail: Steven.Marchese@spps.org
★ Director **Jean O'Connell** .... (651) 767-8149
Term Expires: December 31, 2017
E-mail: jean.oconnell@spps.org
★ Director **Mary Vanderwent** .... (651) 767-8149
Term Expires: December 31, 2019
E-mail: Mary.Vanderwert@spps.org

Saint Paul River Centre Convention and Visitors Authority
175 West Kellogg Boulevard, Suite 502, St. Paul, MN 55102-1299
Fax: (651) 265-4899 E-mail: info@rivercenter.org

President and Chief Executive Officer **Terry Mattson** .... (651) 265-4902

Water Commissioners Board
1900 Rice Street, St. Paul, MN 55113
Fax: (651) 266-6350

General Manager **Steve Schneider** .... (651) 266-6274

City of St. Petersburg, Florida

City Hall, 175 Fifth St. North, St. Petersburg, FL 33701
P.O. Box 2842, St. Petersburg, FL 33731
Tel: (727) 893-7111 (Information) Internet: http://www.stpete.org

County: Pinellas **Election Type:** Nonpartisan **Population:** 257,083 (2015)

Office of the Mayor
City Hall, 175 Fifth St. North, St. Petersburg, FL 33701
P.O. Box 2842, St. Petersburg, FL 33731
Fax: (727) 892-5365

★ Mayor **Rick Kriseman** .... (727) 893-7201
Began Service: January 2, 2014
Term Expires: January 2, 2018
E-mail: mayor@stpete.org
Education: Florida 1984 BS; Stetson 1987 JD
Deputy Mayor **Dr. Kanika Jelks-Tomalin** .... (727) 893-7201
E-mail: kanika.tomalin@stpete.org

★ Elected Official ▲ Appointed by Legislature ▼ Appointed by Governor ▶ Appointed by Board or Commission ● Appointed by Judge
■ Appointed by Mayor △ Appointed by Freeholders ▽ Appointed by Supervisor ▷ Appointed by County Executive ○ Appointed by Council

Office of the Mayor *continued*

Chief of Staff **Kevin King** . . . . (727) 893-7201
Education: South Florida 2002 BA

Fire and Rescue

400 Dr. Martin Luther King, Jr. St., South, St. Petersburg, FL 33701
Fax: (727) 893-7935

■ Fire Chief **James D. Large** . . . . (727) 893-7694
E-mail: james.large@stpete.org
Operations Assistant Chief **Robert Bassett** . . . . (727) 893-7694
E-mail: robert.bassett@stpete.org
Division Chief/Rescue Division **Ian Womack** . . . . (727) 893-7694
E-mail: ian.womack@stpete.org
Safety and Training Division Chief **Joseph Bruni** . . . . (727) 893-7694
E-mail: joe.bruni@stpete.org

Legal Department

City Attorney **Jacqueline Kovilaritch** . . . . (727) 893-7401
E-mail: jacqueline.kovilaritch@stpete.org
Chief Assistant City Attorney **Jeannine Williams** . . . . (727) 893-7401

Police Department

1300 First Ave. North, St. Petersburg, FL 33705-1509
Fax: (727) 892-5040 Internet: www.stpete.org/police

■ Chief of Police **Anthony "Tony" Holloway** . . . . (727) 893-7563
E-mail: anthony.holloway@stpete.org
Administrative Services Bureau Assistant Chief (Acting)
Michael Kovacsev . . . . (727) 893-4016
Investigative Services Bureau Assistant Chief
James Previtera . . . . (727) 893-7908
Uniform Services Bureau Assistant Chief
Luke C. Williams . . . . (727) 893-7729

Office of the City Administrator

City Hall, 175 Fifth Street North, St. Petersburg, FL 33701

■ City Administrator **Gary G. Cornwell** . . . . (727) 893-7201
E-mail: gary.cornwell@stpete.org

Audit Services Department

P.O. Box 2842, St. Petersburg, FL 33731
Fax: (727) 893-4200

■ City Auditor **Brad Scott** . . . . (727) 893-7978
E-mail: brad.scott@stpete.org

Budget and Management Department

City Hall, 175 Fifth St. North, St. Petersburg, FL 33701
Tel: (727) 893-7436 Fax: (727) 892-5143
Internet: http://www.stpete.org/budget/

Director **Tom Greene** . . . . (727) 893-7435
E-mail: tom.greene@stpete.org
Budget Manager **Denise Labrie** . . . . (727) 893-7891
E-mail: denise.labrie@stpete.org
Grants Officer **Shrimatee Ojah-Maharaj** . . . . (727) 892-5180

Finance Department

Municipal Services Center, 1 Fourth St. North, St. Petersburg, FL 33701
Tel: (727) 893-7304 Fax: (727) 893-7120

Director **Anne Fritz** . . . . (727) 892-5113
Treasurer **Tom Hoffman** . . . . (727) 893-4170

Office of the City Clerk

175 Fifth St., North, St. Petersburg, FL 33701
Tel: (727) 893-7448 Fax: (727) 892-5102

City Clerk **Chandrahasa "Chan" Srinivasa** . . . . (727) 893-7202
E-mail: Chandrahasa.Srinivasa@stpete.org

Community Services Department

P.O. Box 2842, St. Petersburg, FL 33731

Director **Susan P. Ajoc** . . . . (727) 892-5141
E-mail: susan.ajoc@stpete.org

Billing and Collections Department

Municipal Services Center, 1 Fourth St. North, St. Petersburg, FL 33701
Tel: (727) 892-5278 Fax: (727) 892-5245

Director **Tammy Jerome** . . . . (727) 893-7977
Utility Accounts Manager **Jacinta Jackson** . . . . (727) 893-8037
Fax: (727) 893-7993

The Greenhouse

P.O. Box 2842, St. Petersburg, FL 33731
44 2nd Avenue North, St. Petersburg, FL 33701
Fax: (727) 551-3360

Manager **Sophia Sorolis** . . . . (727) 893-7787
E-mail: sophia.sorolis@stpete.org

Code Compliance Assistance

P.O. Box 2842, St. Petersburg, FL 33731
Fax: (727) 892-5558

Director **Robert Gerdes** . . . . (727) 893-7373
E-mail: robert.gerdes@stpete.org

Housing and Community Development

P.O. Box 2842, St. Petersburg, FL 33731
Fax: (727) 893-4100

Director **Joshua Johnson** . . . . (727) 893-7247
E-mail: joshua.johnson@stpete.org

City Development Administration

City Hall, 175 Fifth Street North, St. Petersburg, FL 33701
P.O. Box 2842, St. Petersburg, FL 33731
Tel: (727) 892-5400 Fax: (727) 892-5369

Administrator **Alan DeLisle** . . . . (727) 892-5024
E-mail: alan.delisle@stpete.org
City Development and Finance Managing Director
Joseph F. "Joe" Zeoli . . . . (727) 892-5065
E-mail: joe.zeoli@stpete.org
Development Coordination Managing Director
Chris Ballestra . . . . (727) 892-5960
Education: USC BA; U Phoenix MBA

Downtown Enterprise Facilities

City Hall, 175 Fifth Street North, St. Petersburg, FL 33701
Tel: (727) 892-5779 Fax: (727) 892-5719

Director **Clay Smith** . . . . (727) 892-5065
E-mail: clay.smith@stpete.org Fax: (727) 892-5719
Downtown Enterprise Facilities Assistant Director
(Vacant) . . . . (727) 892-5705
Coliseum/Sunken Gardens Manager **Lauren Kleinfeld** . . . . (727) 892-5708
E-mail: lauren.kleinfeld@stpete.org
Tropicana Field Manager **Rick Nafe** . . . . (727) 825-3195
Fax: (727) 825-3167

Albert Whitted Municipal Airport

107 Eighth Avenue, SE, St. Petersburg, FL 33701
Tel: (727) 893-7654

Manager **Rich Lesniak** . . . . (727) 893-7657
Fax: (727) 822-4767

Coliseum

535 Fourth Ave. North, St. Petersburg, FL 33701

Manager **Lauren Kleinfeld** . . . . (727) 892-5708
Fax: (727) 892-5525

★ Elected Official ▲ Appointed by Legislature ▼ Appointed by Governor ► Appointed by Board or Commission ● Appointed by Judge
■ Appointed by Mayor △ Appointed by Freeholders ▽ Appointed by Supervisor ▷ Appointed by County Executive ○ Appointed by Council

St. Petersburg Municipal Marina
400 Second Ave. NE, St. Petersburg, FL 33701
Tel: (727) 893-7820

Manager **Walt Miller** .... (727) 893-7820
Fax: (727) 551-3223

Port of St. Petersburg
250 Eighth Ave. SE, St. Petersburg, FL 33701
Tel: (727) 224-9640 (Port Security) Fax: (727) 893-7428
E-mail: port@stpete.org

Manager **Walt Miller** .... (727) 893-7820
Fax: (727) 551-3223

Planning and Economic Development
Municipal Services Center, 1 Fourth Street North, 9th Floor, St. Petersburg, FL 33701
Tel: (727) 893-7100

Director **Dave Goodwin** .... (727) 893-7171
E-mail: dave.goodwin@stpete.org
Economic Development Manager **Sophia Sorolis** .... (727) 893-7787
Zoning Official **Elizabeth Abernethy** .... (727) 892-5344
Fax: (727) 892-5557
Building Official **Rick Dunn** .... (727) 551-3391
E-mail: rick.dunn@stpete.org Fax: (727) 893-7428

Marketing and Communications Department
City Hall, 175 Fifth St., North, St. Petersburg, FL 33701
Tel: (727) 893-7465 Fax: (727) 892-5372

Director **Robert A. Danielson** .... (727) 893-7466
E-mail: robert.danielson@stpete.org
Web Master **Nicholas Stees** .... (727) 893-7468
E-mail: nicholas.stees@stpete.org

Real Estate and Property Management Department
Director **Bruce Grimes** .... (727) 892-5571
Fax: (727) 893-4134

Transportation and Parking Department
One Fourth Street North, 8th Floor, St. Petersburg, FL 33701
Fax: (727) 551-3326

Director **Evan Mory** .... (727) 892-5274
Fax: (727) 551-3326
Transportation Manager **Cheryl Stacks** .... (727) 892-5328
Neighborhood Manager **Michael Frederick** .... (727) 893-7843

Legislative, Education and Intergovernmental Affairs Department

■ Governmental Services Manager **Sally Everett** .... (727) 893-7884
E-mail: sally.everett@stpete.org

Human Resources Department

Municipal Services Center, 1 Fourth St. North, St. Petersburg, FL 33701
P.O. Box 2842, St. Petersburg, FL 33731
Tel: (727) 893-7481 Fax: (727) 893-7712

Director **Chris Guella** .... (727) 893-7032
E-mail: chris.guella@stpete.org
Employment, Staffing and Development Manager **Richard E. Anderson** .... (727) 893-7349
E-mail: richard.anderson@stpete.org
Labor Relations and Training Manager **Kristen Mory** .... (727) 893-7407
E-mail: christine.ward@stpete.org

Community Affairs Division
One 4th Street. North, St. Petersburg, FL 33701
P.O. Box 2842, St. Petersburg, FL 33731
Fax: (727) 892-5064

■ Coordinator **Lendel Bright** .... (727) 893-7229
E-mail: lendel.bright@stpete.org

Leisure Services Administration

P.O. Box 2842, St. Petersburg, FL 33731
Tel: (727) 893-7207 Fax: (727) 893-7901
Internet: www.stpete.org/leisure_and_community_services/

■ Administrator **Sherry McBee** .... (727) 892-7350
E-mail: sherry.mcbee@stpete.org Fax: (727) 893-7901
Public Information Specialist **Alexis Shuder** .... (727) 893-7918
E-mail: alexis.shuder@stpete.org Fax: (727) 892-5868

Golf Courses Department
Tel: (727) 893-7800 Fax: (727) 893-7805 E-mail: golf@stpete.org

Director **Jeffery G. Hollis** .... (727) 893-7807
Manager **Ken Betz** .... (727) 893-7804
Superintendent **(Vacant)** .... (727) 893-7907

Parks and Recreation Department
Tel: (727) 893-7441 Fax: (727) 892-5103

Director **Michael Jefferis** .... (727) 893-7890
Superintendent **Rick Craft** .... (727) 892-5103
Fax: (727) 893-7343
Superintendent **Phil Whitehouse** .... (727) 892-5490
Fax: (727) 893-7343
Manager **Thomas Jackson** .... (727) 893-7494
Manager **Linda Seufert** .... (727) 893-7317
Manager **Michael Vineyard** .... (727) 892-5233

St. Petersburg Public Library System
Main Library, 3745 Ninth Ave. North, St. Petersburg, FL 33713
Fax: (727) 892-5432 Internet: www.splibraries.org

Director **Mika Nelson** .... (727) 893-7736
E-mail: mika.nelson@stpete.org
Library Coordinator **Linda Branson** .... (727) 893-7318
E-mail: linda.branson@stpete.org

Veteran, Social and Homeless Services
P.O. Box 2842, St. Petersburg, FL 33731
Tel: (727) 893-7627 Fax: (727) 892-5102

Manager **Clifford "Cliff" Smith** .... (727) 893-7627

Public Works Administration

P.O. Box 2842, St. Petersburg, FL 33731
Fax: (727) 893-7901

■ Public Works Administrator **Claude Tankersley** .... (727) 893-7841
E-mail: claude.tankersley@stpete.org

Engineering and Capital Improvements Division
One, Fourth St. North, St. Petersburg, FL 33701
Fax: (727) 892-5476

Director **Thomas B. "Tom" Gibson** .... (727) 892-5206
E-mail: thomas.gibson@stpete.org

Fleet Management Department
1800 Seventh Ave., North, St. Petersburg, FL 33713
Fax: (727) 893-7086

Fleet Operations Director **Joe Krizen** .... (727) 893-7255
E-mail: joe.krizen@stpete.org

Sanitation Department
2001 28th St., North, St. Petersburg, FL 33713
Fax: (727) 893-7125

Director **Benjamin F. Shirley** .... (727) 893-7960
Assistant Director **Lynn Arthur** .... (727) 893-7960

Stormwater, Pavement and Traffic Operations Department
P.O. Box 2842, St. Petersburg, FL 33731
Fax: (727) 892-5686

Director **John Norris** .... (727) 893-7620

★ Elected Official ▲ Appointed by Legislature ▼ Appointed by Governor ▶ Appointed by Board or Commission ● Appointed by Judge
■ Appointed by Mayor △ Appointed by Freeholders ▽ Appointed by Supervisor ▷ Appointed by County Executive ○ Appointed by Council

Water Resources Department
1635 Third Avenue North, Saint Petersburg, FL 33713
Fax: (727) 823-9152

Director **Steve Leavitt** .... (727) 892-5600

Purchasing and Materials Management Department
Municipal Services Center, 1 Fourth St. North, St. Petersburg, FL 33701
Tel: (727) 893-7220 Fax: (727) 892-5325

Director **Louis Moore** .... (727) 893-7220
E-mail: louis.moore@stpete.org

Purchasing Manager **Barbara Grilli** .... (727) 893-7224
E-mail: barbara.grilli@stpete.org

Technology Services Department
Municipal Services Center, 1 Fourth St. North, St. Petersburg, FL 33701
Tel: (727) 893-7305 Fax: (727) 893-7173

Chief Information Officer **Muslim A. Gadiwalla** .... (727) 893-7909
E-mail: muslim@stpete.org

Oracle e-Business Solutions Manager **Christine West** .... (727) 892-5186
E-mail: christine.west@stpete.org Fax: (727) 893-7173

Office of the City Council
City Hall, 175 Fifth St. North, St. Petersburg, FL 33701
P.O. Box 2842, St. Petersburg, FL 33731
Fax: (727) 892-5360 E-mail: council@stpete.org
Internet: www.stpete.org/council/

★Chair **Amy Foster** (District 8) .... (727) 893-7117
Term Expires: January 2018
E-mail: amy.foster@stpete.org

★Vice Chair **Darden Rice** (District 4) .... (727) 893-7117
Term Expires: January 2018
E-mail: darden.rice@stpete.org

★Council Member **Charlie Gerdes** (District 1) .... (727) 893-7117
Term Expires: January 2, 2020
E-mail: charlie.gerdes@stpete.org

★Council Member
James R. "Jim" Kennedy, Jr. (District 2) .... (727) 893-7117
Term Expires: January 2, 2018
E-mail: james.kennedy@stpete.org

★Council Member **Ed Montanari** (District 3) .... (727) 893-7117
Term Expires: January 2, 2020
E-mail: ed.montanari@stpete.org

★Council Member **Steve Kornell** (District 5) .... (727) 893-7117
Term Expires: January 2, 2020
E-mail: steve.kornell@stpete.org

★Council Member **Karl Nurse** (District 6) .... (727) 893-7117
Term Expires: January 2, 2018
E-mail: karl.nurse@stpete.org

★Council Member **Lisa Wheeler-Brown** (District 7) ...... (727) 893-7117
Term Expires: January 2, 2020

○Administrative Services Officer **Cindy Sheppard** .... (727) 893-7118
E-mail: cynthia.sheppard@stpete.org

City of Salem, Oregon
555 Liberty St., SE, Salem, OR 97301-3503
Internet: www.cityofsalem.net

County: Marion **Election Type:** Nonpartisan **Year Incorporated:** 1857
Population: 164,549 (2015)

Office of the Mayor and City Council
555 Liberty St., SE, Room 220, Salem, OR 97301
Tel: (503) 588-6159 Fax: (503) 588-6354
E-mail: citycouncil@cityofsalem.net

★Mayor **Anna M. Peterson** .... (503) 588-6255
Began Service: January 11, 2011 Fax: (503) 588-6354
Term Expires: December 31, 2016
E-mail: ampeterson@cityofsalem.net

★Council Member **Chuck Bennett** (Ward 1) .... (503) 399-7801
Term Expires: December 31, 2016
E-mail: crbennett@cityofsalem.net

★Council Member **Tom Andersen** (Ward 2) .... (503) 399-7802
Term Expires: December 31, 2018
E-mail: tandersen@cityofsalem.net

★Council Member **Brad Nanke** (Ward 3) .... (503) 399-7803
Term Expires: December 31, 2016
E-mail: bnanke@cityofsalem.net

★Council Member **Steven McCoid** (Ward 4) .... (503) 399-7804
Term Expires: December 31, 2018
E-mail: smccoid@cityofsalem.net

★Council Member **Diana Dickey** (Ward 5) .... (503) 399-7905
Term Expires: December 31, 2016
E-mail: ddickey@cityofsalem.net

★Council Member **Daniel Benjamin** (Ward 6) .... (503) 399-7806
Term Expires: December 31, 2018
E-mail: dbenjamin@cityofsalem.net

★Council Member **Warren Bednarz** (Ward 7) .... (503) 399-7907
Term Expires: December 31, 2016
E-mail: wbednarz@cityofsalem.net

★Council Member **Jim Lewis** (Ward 8) .... (503) 399-7808
Term Expires: December 31, 2018
E-mail: jlewis@cityofsalem.net

Office of the City Manager
555 Liberty St., SE, Room 220, Salem, OR 97301
Fax: (503) 588-6354 E-mail: manager@cityofsalem.net

City Manager **Steven D. "Steve" Powers** .... (503) 588-6255
E-mail: spowers@cityofsalem.net
Education: Augustana (IL) BA; Kansas MPA

Deputy City Manager **Kacey Duncan** .... (503) 588-6255

Public Information Officer **Mike Gotterba** .... (503) 588-6255
E-mail: mgotterba@cityofsalem.net

Administrative Services
555 Liberty St., SE, Room 230, Salem, OR 97301
Fax: (503) 588-6251

Director **(Vacant)** .... (503) 588-6040

Community Development Department
555 Liberty St., SE, Room 305, Salem, OR 97301
Fax: (503) 588-6005

Director **Glenn Gross** .... (503) 588-6173 ext. 7506
E-mail: ggross@cityofsalem.net

Office Assistant **Casey Prock** .... (503) 588-6173 ext. 7500
E-mail: cprock@cityofsalem.net

★ Elected Official ▲Appointed by Legislature ▼Appointed by Governor ▶Appointed by Board or Commission ●Appointed by Judge
■Appointed by Mayor △Appointed by Freeholders ▽Appointed by Supervisor ▷Appointed by County Executive ○Appointed by Council

Fire Department
370 Trade St., SE, Salem, OR 97301
Fax: (503) 588-6371 E-mail: salemfire@cityofsalem.net

Fire Chief **Mike Niblock** .... (503) 588-6245
E-mail: mniblock@cityofsalem.net

Human Resources Department
555 Liberty St., SE, Room 225, Salem, OR 97301
Fax: (503) 588-6170 E-mail: HR@cityofsalem.net

Director **Mina Hanssen** .... (503) 588-6162
E-mail: mhanssen@cityofsalem.net

Legal Department
555 Liberty St., SE, Room 205, Salem, OR 97301-3503
Fax: (503) 588-6057 E-mail: legal@cityofsalem.net

City Attorney **Dan Atchison** .... (503) 588-6085
E-mail: datchison@cityofsalem.net Fax: (503) 361-2202
City Recorder **Amber Mathiesen** .... (503) 588-6091
E-mail: amathiesen@cityofsalem.net Fax: (503) 361-2202

Library
585 Liberty St., SE, Salem, OR 97301
Fax: (503) 588-6055 E-mail: library@cityofsalem.net

Library Manager (Interim) **Julie Sowles** .... (503) 588-6084
E-mail: JSowles@cityofsalem.net Fax: (503) 588-6055

Police Department
555 Liberty St., SE, Room 130, Salem, OR 97301
E-mail: police@cityofsalem.net

Chief of Police **Gerald Moore** .... (503) 588-6080
Fax: (503) 589-2019

Public Works Department
555 Liberty St., SE, Room 325, Salem, OR 97301
Fax: (503) 588-6025 E-mail: publicworks@cityofsalem.net

Director **Peter Fernandez** .... (503) 588-6211

City of Salinas, California

200 Lincoln Avenue, Salinas, CA 93901
Internet: www.ci.salinas.ca.us

County: Monterey **Election Type:** Nonpartisan **Year Incorporated:** 1874 **Population:** 157,380 (2015)

Office of the Mayor and City Council
200 Lincoln Ave., Salinas, CA 93901
Fax: (831) 758-7368

★ Mayor **Joe Gunter** .... (831) 758-7201
Began Service: December 2012
Term Expires: December 7, 2016
E-mail: salinasmayor@ci.salinas.ca.us
★ Council Member **Jose Castaneda** (District 1) .... (831) 206-6691
Term Expires: December 7, 2016
E-mail: district1@ci.salinas.ca.us
★ Council Member **Tony Barrera** (District 2) .... (831) 206-7563
Term Expires: December 7, 2018
E-mail: district2@ci.salinas.ca.us
★ Council Member **Steve McShane** (District 3) .... (831) 970-4141
Term Expires: December 7, 2018
E-mail: stevem@ci.salinas.ca.us
★ Council Member **Gloria De La Rosa** (District 4) .... (831) 206-8907
Term Expires: December 7, 2016
E-mail: district4@ci.salinas.ca.us

Office of the Mayor and City Council *continued*

★ Council Member **Kimbly Craig** (District 5) .... (831) 206-6495
Term Expires: December 7, 2018
E-mail: kimbly@ci.salinas.ca.us
★ Council Member **Jyl Lutes** (District 6) .... (831) 235-1432
Term Expires: December 7, 2016
E-mail: district6@ci.salinas.ca.us

Office of the City Manager
200 Lincoln Ave., Salinas, CA 93901
Fax: (831) 758-7368

City Manager **Ray E. Corpuz, Jr.** .... (831) 758-7201
E-mail: ray.corpuz@ci.salinas.ca.us
Education: St Martin's Col 1969 BA

Office of the City Clerk
200 Lincoln Ave., Salinas, CA 93901
Fax: (831) 758-7368

City Clerk **Patricia Barajas** .... (831) 758-7381
E-mail: cclerk@ci.salinas.ca.us

Human Resources and Risk Management
200 Lincoln Ave., Salinas, CA 93901
Fax: (831) 758-7941

Human Resources Officer **Marina Gallegos** .... (831) 758-7254
E-mail: marinah@ci.salinas.ca.us

Office of the City Attorney
200 Lincoln Ave., Salinas, CA 93901
Fax: (831) 758-7257

City Attorney **Christopher Callihan** .... (831) 758-7256
E-mail: chrisc@ci.salinas.ca.us

Community and Economic Development Department
65 West Alisal Street, Salinas, CA 93901

Director **Megan Hunter** .... (831) 758-7387
E-mail: meganh@ci.salinas.ca.us

Current Planning Division
65 West Alisal Street, Salinas, CA 93901
Fax: (831) 758-7215

Planning Manager **Courtney Grossman** .... (831) 758-7206

Finance Department
200 Lincoln Ave., Salinas, CA 93901
Fax: (831) 758-7937

Finance Director **Matt Pressey** .... (831) 758-7211
Education: UC Santa Barbara BA

Fire Department
65 W. Alisal St., Salinas, CA 93901
Fax: (831) 758-7265

Fire Chief **Edmond Rodriguez** .... (831) 758-7261
E-mail: edmond.rodriguez@ci.salinas.ca.us
Deputy Chief **Brett Loomis** .... (831) 758-7261
E-mail: brettl@ci.salinas.ca.us

Information Systems Division
200 Lincoln Ave., Salinas, CA 93901

Information Systems Manager (Acting) **Gina Moore** ..... (831) 758-7154
E-mail: gina@ci.salinas.ca.us
Network Administrator **Michael Elliot** .... (831) 758-7448
E-mail: michael@ci.salinas.ca.us Fax: (831) 758-7937

★ Elected Official ▲ Appointed by Legislature ▼ Appointed by Governor ▶ Appointed by Board or Commission ● Appointed by Judge
■ Appointed by Mayor △ Appointed by Freeholders ▽ Appointed by Supervisor ▷ Appointed by County Executive ○ Appointed by Council

Library and Community Services Department
200 Lincoln Ave., Salinas, CA 93901
Fax: (831) 758-7336

Director **Cary Siegfried** .... (831) 758-7311

Police Department
222 Lincoln Ave., Salinas, CA 93901
Fax: (831) 758-7934

Police Chief **Kelly McMillin** .... (831) 758-7286

Public Works Department
200 Lincoln Avenue, Salinas, CA 93901

Director **Gary Petersen** .... (831) 758-7241

Engineering and Transportation Division
200 Lincoln Ave., Salinas, CA 93901
Fax: (831) 758-7935

Deputy Public Works Director **Robert Russell** .... (831) 758-7241
E-mail: robr@ci.salinas.ca.us

Salinas Municipal Airport
30 Mortensen Ave., Salinas, CA 93901
Fax: (831) 759-2518

Airport Manager **Brett Godown** .... (831) 758-7214

Salt Lake City, Utah
City and County Building, 451 South State Street,
Salt Lake City, UT 84111
P.O. Box 145474, Salt Lake City, UT 84114-5474
Internet: www.slcgov.com/

County: Salt Lake **Election Type:** Nonpartisan **Population:** 192,672 (2015) **Employees:** 2,877 **Fiscal Year:** 2016 **Budget:** $1,772,082,000

Office of the Mayor
City and County Bldg., 451 South State Street, Room 306,
Salt Lake City, UT 84111
Fax: (801) 535-6331 Internet: http://mayor.slcgov.com/

Employees: 25 **Fiscal Year:** 2016 **Budget:** $2,646,000

★ Mayor **Jackie Biskupski** .... (801) 535-7704
Began Service: January 4, 2016
Term Expires: December 31, 2019
Education: Arizona State BS

■ Executive Assistant to the Mayor **Simone Butler** .... (801) 535-7704
E-mail: simone.butler@slcgov.com

■ Chief of Staff **Patrick Leary** .... (801) 535-7732
Education: Utah State 1991 BA; Utah 2011 MPA

■ Deputy Chief of Staff **David Litvack** .... (801) 535-7704
Education: Westminster (UT) BS; Chicago MA

Senior Advisor, Intergovernmental Affairs **Lynn Pace** .... (801) 535-7788
E-mail: lynn.pace@slcgov.com

■ Director of Community Relations **Jennifer M. Seelig** .... (801) 535-7117
E-mail: jennifer.seelig@slcgov.com
Education: Louisville BA; Utah MPA

■ Director of Communications **Matthew Rojas** .... (385) 228-2365
E-mail: matthew.rojas@slcgov.com

■ Deputy Director of Communications **Holly Mullen** .... (801) 535-6103
E-mail: holly.mullen@slcgov.com

■ Special Projects Manager **Christine Passey** .... (801) 535-7710
E-mail: christine.passey@slcgov.com

■ Office Manager **Robin Pratt** .... (801) 535-7705
E-mail: robin.pratt@slcgov.com

■ Office of Diversity and Human Rights Coordinator
Yolanda Francisco-Nez .... (801) 535-7734
E-mail: yolanda.francisco-nez@slcgov.com

Office of the City Attorney
City and County Bldg., 451 South State Street, Room 505,
Salt Lake City, UT 84111
P.O. Box 145478, Salt Lake City, UT 84114-5478
Fax: (801) 535-7640 E-mail: slcattorney@slcgov.com
Internet: www.slcgov.com/attorney

Employees: 61 **Fiscal Year:** 2016 **Budget:** $10,722,000

City Attorney **Margaret Plane** .... (801) 535-7788
E-mail: slcattorney@slcgov.com
Education: Utah 2002 JD

Deputy City Attorney **Rusty Vetter** .... (801) 535-7788

Risk Manager **Tamra Turpin** .... (801) 535-7788
E-mail: slcrisk@slcgov.com

City Recorder
451 South State Street, Suite 415, Salt Lake City, UT 84111
P.O. Box 145515, Salt Lake City, UT 84114-5515
Fax: (801) 535-7681

■ City Recorder **Cindi Mansell** .... (801) 535-7671
E-mail: recorder@slcgov.com

Department of Airports
P.O. Box 145550, Salt Lake City, UT 84114-5550
Tel: (801) 575-2400 Fax: (801) 575-2679 Internet: www.slcairport.com/

Employees: 555 **Fiscal Year:** 2016 **Budget:** $1,089,281,000

■ Executive Director **Maureen S. Riley** .... (801) 575-2408
E-mail: maureen.riley@slcgov.com
Education: Wharton 1981 BBA

Director of Finance **Ryan Tesch** .... (801) 575-2721

Community and Economic Development
City and County Bldg., 451 South State Street, Room 404,
Salt Lake City, UT 84111
Tel: (801) 535-6230 Fax: (801) 535-6005 Internet: www.slcgov.com/ced

Employees: 200 **Fiscal Year:** 2016 **Budget:** $21,287,000

■ Director **Mike Reberg** .... (801) 535-7707
E-mail: mike.reberg@slcgov.com
Education: Utah State 1985 BS

Deputy Director **Mary DeLaMare-Schaefer** .... (801) 535-6230
E-mail: mary.ds@slcgov.com

Finance and Administrative Services Director
Brent Beck .... (801) 535-6230
E-mail: brent.beck@slcgov.com

Arts Council
54 Finch Lane, Salt Lake City, UT 84102
Fax: (801) 530-0547

Arts Council Director **Karen Krieger** .... (801) 596-5000

Office of Economic Development
451 South State Street, Room 404, Salt Lake City, UT 84111
Fax: (801) 535-6005 Internet: www.slcgov.com/ed

Economic Development Deputy Director
Jill Remington Love .... (801) 535-7273

Building Services and Zoning Enforcement
City and County Building, 451 South State Street, Room 218,
Salt Lake City, UT 84111
Fax: (801) 535-7750 E-mail: buildzone@slcgov.com

Director **Orion Goff** .... (801) 535-7752
E-mail: orion.goff@slcgov.com

Housing and Neighborhood Development Division
City and County Building, 451 South State Street, Room 425,
Salt Lake City, UT 84111
Fax: (801) 535-6131

Director **Michael Akerlow** .... (801) 535-7228
E-mail: michael.akerlow@slcgov.com

★ Elected Official ▲ Appointed by Legislature ▼ Appointed by Governor ► Appointed by Board or Commission ● Appointed by Judge
■ Appointed by Mayor △ Appointed by Freeholders ▽ Appointed by Supervisor ▷ Appointed by County Executive ○ Appointed by Council

Planning and Zoning Enforcement Division
City and County Building, 451 South State Street, Room 406, Salt Lake City, UT 84111
Fax: (801) 535-6174

Planning Director **Nora L. Shepard** .... (801) 535-7757
Deputy Director **Cheri Coffey** .... (801) 535-7759

Transportation Division
349 South 200 East, Suite 450, Salt Lake City, UT 84111
Fax: (801) 535-6019

Director **Robin Hutcheson** .... (801) 535-6630

Department of Finance
451 South State Street, Room 248, Salt Lake City, UT 84111
Fax: (801) 535-7682

Employees: 63 **Fiscal Year:** 2016 **Budget:** $7,379,000

■ Finance Director **(Vacant)** .... (801) 535-7676

City Treasurer
451 South State Street, Room 228, Salt Lake City, UT 84111
Fax: (801) 535-6082

■ City Treasurer **Marina Scott** .... (801) 535-7946
E-mail: marina.scott@slcgov.com
Special Assessments **Garth Limburg** .... (801) 535-7719

Purchasing, Contracts and Property Management Division
451 South State Street, Room 235, Salt Lake City, UT 84111
P.O. Box 145455, Salt Lake City, UT 84114-5455

■ Chief Procurement Officer **R. Bryan Hemsley** .... (801) 535-7944
E-mail: bryan.hemsley@slcgov.com Fax: (801) 535-6637
Contracts **Dave Secrist** .... (801) 535-6309
Fax: (801) 535-6680

Fire Department
Public Safety Complex, 315 East 200 South, Salt Lake City, UT 84114
P.O. Box 145520, Salt Lake City, UT 84114-5520
Tel: (801) 799-3473 Fax: (801) 799-3038 Internet: www.slcfire.com

Employees: 340 **Fiscal Year:** 2016 **Budget:** $38,014,000

■ Fire Chief **Brian Dale** .... (801) 799-4101
E-mail: brian.dale@slcgov.com

Fire Prevention Bureau
Division Chief **Ryan Mellor** .... (801) 799-4150
E-mail: ryan.mellor@slcgov.com

Operations Bureau
Deputy Chief **Karl Lieb** .... (801) 799-4203
E-mail: karl.lieb@slcgov.com

Logistics
Deputy Chief **Martha Ellis** .... (801) 799-4202
E-mail: martha.ellis@slcgov.com

Department of Human Resources
451 South State Street, Room 115, Salt Lake City, UT 84111
Fax: (801) 535-6614

Employees: 26 **Fiscal Year:** 2016 **Budget:** $39,123,000

■ Director **Debra Alexander** .... (801) 535-7900
E-mail: debra.alexander@slcgov.com
Compensation Manager **David Salazar** .... (801) 535-7906
E-mail: david.salazar@slcgov.com
Employee Benefits **Jodi Langford** .... (801) 535-6610
E-mail: jodi.langford@slcgov.com

Information Management Services Department
349 South 200 East, Suite 200, Salt Lake City, UT 84111
Tel: (801) 535-7634

Employees: 70 **Fiscal Year:** 2016 **Budget:** $12,335,000

Director/Chief Information Officer **William Haight** ...... (801) 535-7948
E-mail: bill.haight@slcgov.com

Police Department
Public Safety Complex, 475 South 300 East, Salt Lake City, UT 84114-5497
Tel: (801) 799-3100 Fax: (801) 799-3640 Internet: www.slcpd.com/

Employees: 558 **Fiscal Year:** 2016 **Budget:** $61,398,000

■ Police Chief **Mike Brown** .... (801) 799-3802
E-mail: mike.brown@slcgov.com
Administrative Assistant **Laura Nygaard** .... (801) 799-3801
E-mail: laura.nygaard@slcgov.com
Administration Bureau Deputy Chief **Tim Doubt** .... (801) 799-3812
Patrol Bureau Deputy Chief **Terry A. Fritz** .... (801) 799-3805
Professional Standards Deputy Chief **Dave Askerlund** .... (801) 799-4603
Special Operations Deputy Chief **Isaac Atencio** .... (801) 799-3016
Strategic Deployment Deputy Chief (Acting)
Josh Scharman .... (801) 799-3652
Administrative Assistant **(Vacant)** .... (801) 799-3802

Department of Public Services
City and County Building, 451 South State Street, Room 138, Salt Lake City, UT 84111
P.O. Box 5469, Salt Lake City, UT 84114-5469
Fax: (801) 535-7789

Employees: 430 **Fiscal Year:** 2016 **Budget:** $93,731,000

■ Director **Richard Graham** .... (801) 535-7774
E-mail: rick.graham@slcgov.com Fax: (801) 535-6175
Administrative Services Director **Lisa Shaffer** .... (801) 535-7753
E-mail: lisa.shaffer@slcgov.com
Finance Director **Greg Davis** .... (801) 535-6123
Operations Division Director **Alden Breinholt** .... (801) 535-7778
E-mail: alden.breinholt@slcgov.com

Compliance Division
212 E. 600 South, Salt Lake City, UT 84111
Fax: (801) 535-6580

Manager **(Vacant)** .... (801) 535-6585

Facilities Division
248 E. 600 South, Salt Lake City, UT 84111
Fax: (801) 535-6483

Manager **Jim Cleland** .... (801) 535-6631
E-mail: jim.cleland@slcgov.com

Fleet Management
210 W. 500 S., Salt Lake City, UT 84104
Fax: (801) 535-6906

Manager **George Kucher** .... (801) 535-6914

Gallivan Center and Events
1965 West 500 South, Salt Lake City, UT 84111
Fax: (801) 535-6100

Manager **Talitha Day** .... (801) 535-6133

Golf Division
2375 S. 900 East, Salt Lake City, UT 84106
Fax: (801) 466-6705

Manager **(Vacant)** .... (801) 485-7831

Parks and Public Lands
1965 W. 500 South, Salt Lake City, UT 84104
Fax: (801) 972-7847

Manager **(Vacant)** .... (801) 972-7804

★ Elected Official ▲ Appointed by Legislature ▼ Appointed by Governor ► Appointed by Board or Commission ● Appointed by Judge
■ Appointed by Mayor △ Appointed by Freeholders ▽ Appointed by Supervisor ▷ Appointed by County Executive ○ Appointed by Council

Streets
210 W. 500 S., Salt Lake City, UT 84104
Fax: (801) 535-6988

Manager **Parviz Rokhva** .... (801) 535-6969

Youth and Family Programs
210 East 600 South, Salt Lake City, UT 84111
Fax: (801) 535-6098

Director **Kim Thomas** .... (801) 535-6129

Department of Public Utilities

1530 SW Temple St., Salt Lake City, UT 84115
Tel: (801) 483-6770 Fax: (801) 483-6855
Internet: www.ci.slc.ut.us/utilities/ E-mail: slcpu@slcgov.com

Employees: 392 **Fiscal Year:** 2016 **Budget:** $123,642,000

■ Director **Laura Briefer** .... (801) 483-6785
Deputy Director **Tom Ward** .... (801) 483-6768
Deputy Director **(Vacant)** .... (801) 483-6770
Chief Engineer **Chuck Call** .... (801) 483-6840
E-mail: chuck.call@slcgov.com
Finance Administrator **Kurt Spjute** .... (801) 483-6773
Water Quality Administrator **Jessie Stewart** .... (801) 483-6864
Operations and Maintenance Superintendent
Mark Stanley .... (801) 483-6717
E-mail: mark.stanley@slcgov.com
Water Reclamation Manager **Dale Christensen** .... (801) 799-4001

Salt Lake City Library System

210 East 400 South, Salt Lake City, UT 84111

Director (Acting) **Deborah Ehrman** .... (801) 524-8204
E-mail: dehrman@slcpl.org

Office of the City Council

City and County Building, 451 South State Street, Room 304,
Salt Lake City, UT 84114-5476
P.O. Box 145476, Salt Lake City, UT 84114-5476
Tel: (801) 535-7600 Fax: (801) 535-7651
E-mail: council.comments@slcgov.com Internet: www.slcgov.com/council/

Employees: 28 **Fiscal Year:** 2016 **Budget:** $2,882,000

★ Chair **James Rogers** (District 1) .... (801) 535-7600
Term Expires: December 31, 2017
E-mail: james.rogers@slcgov.com
★ Vice Chair **Stan Penfold** (District 3) .... (801) 535-7600
Term Expires: December 31, 2017
E-mail: stan.penfold@slcgov.com
★ Council Member **Andrew Johnston** (District 2) .... (801) 535-7600
Term Expires: December 31, 2019
★ Council Member **Derek Kitchen** (District 4) .... (801) 535-7600
Term Expires: December 31, 2019
★ Council Member **Erin Mendenhall** (District 5) .... (801) 535-7600
Term Expires: December 31, 2017
E-mail: erin.mendenhall@slcgov.com
★ Council Member **Charlie Luke** (District 6) .... (801) 535-7600
Term Expires: December 31, 2019
E-mail: charlie.luke@slcgov.com
★ Council Member **Lisa Ramsey Adams** (District 7) .... (801) 535-7600
Term Expires: December 31, 2017
E-mail: lisa.adams@slcgov.com
○ Executive Director **Cindy Gust-Jenson** .... (801) 535-7600
E-mail: cindy.gust-jenson@slcgov.com
○ Budget Policy Analyst **Lehua Weaver** .... (801) 535-7653
E-mail: lehua.weaver@slcgov.com
○ Constituent Liaison **Amber McClellan** .... (801) 535-7612
E-mail: amber.mcclellan@slcgov.com
○ Budget Analyst **Nick Tarbet** .... (801) 535-7603
E-mail: nick.tarbet@slcgov.com
○ Community Facilitator **Jan Aramaki** .... (801) 535-7607
E-mail: jan.aramaki@slcgov.com

Office of the City Council *continued*

○ Deputy Director **Jennifer Bruno** .... (801) 535-6295
E-mail: jennifer.bruno@slcgov.com
Education: Yale 2002 BA
○ Senior Public Policy Analyst **Russell Weeks** .... (801) 535-6206
E-mail: russell.weeks@slcgov.com
○ Staff Assistant **Becky Dangerfield** .... (801) 535-7621
E-mail: becky.dangerfield@slcgov.com
○ Staff Assistant **Tracey Fletcher** .... (801) 535-7626
E-mail: tracey.fletcher@slcgov.com
○ Staff Assistant **Kira Luke** .... (801) 535-7615
E-mail: kira.luke@slcgov.com
○ Agenda Coordinator **Priscilla Tuuao** .... (801) 535-7611
E-mail: priscilla.tuuao@slcgov.com

Salt Lake City School District

440 East 100 South, Salt Lake City, UT 84111-1898
Fax: (801) 578-8685 Internet: www.slcschools.org/

Superintendent **McKell Withers** .... (801) 578-8349
Associate Superintendent **Patrick Garcia** .... (801) 578-8344
Public Information Officer **Jason Olsen** .... (801) 578-8352
E-mail: jason.olsen@slcschools.org
Director of Education Technology **Julie Atwood** .... (801) 578-8391
E-mail: julie.atwood@slcschools.org
★ Board of Education President
Heather Bennett (Precinct 5) .... (801) 583-1012
Term Expires: December 31, 2016
E-mail: heather.bennett@slcschools.org
★ Board of Education Vice President
Tiffany Sandberg (Precinct 1) .... (801) 595-8599
Term Expires: December 31, 2016
★ Board of Education Member **Michael Clara** (Precinct 2) .... (801) 578-8599
Term Expires: December 31, 2016
★ Board of Education Member
Katherine Kennedy (Precinct 3) .... (801) 532-5457
Term Expires: December 31, 2018
★ Board of Education Member
Rosemary Emery (Precinct 4) .... (801) 578-8349
Term Expires: December 31, 2018
★ Board of Education Member
Melissa H. Ford (Precinct 6) .... (801) 582-4165
Term Expires: December 31, 2018
★ Board of Education Member **Kristi Swett** (Precinct 7) .... (801) 485-0681
Term Expires: December 31, 2016
E-mail: kristi.swett@slcschools.org

Salt Lake City Justice Court

333 South 200 East, Salt Lake City, UT 84111
P.O. Box 145499, Salt Lake City, UT 84114-5499
Tel: (801) 535-6300 Fax: (801) 535-6302

Employees: 47 **Fiscal Year:** 2016 **Budget:** $4,164,000

City Courts Director **Curtis Preece** .... (801) 535-7173
Civil Court Manager **Claudia Sundbeck** .... (801) 535-6314
Criminal Section Manager **Tammy Shelton** .... (801) 535-6326

★ Elected Official ▲ Appointed by Legislature ▼ Appointed by Governor ► Appointed by Board or Commission ● Appointed by Judge
■ Appointed by Mayor △ Appointed by Freeholders ▽ Appointed by Supervisor ▷ Appointed by County Executive ○ Appointed by Council

City of San Antonio, Texas

100 Military Plaza, San Antonio, TX 78205
P.O. Box 839966, San Antonio, TX 78283-3966
Tel: (210) 207-7080 (Information) Internet: www.sanantonio.gov

County: Bexar **Election Type:** Nonpartisan **Population:** 1,469,845 (2015)

Office of the Mayor and City Council

P.O. Box 839966, San Antonio, TX 78283-3966
Fax: (210) 207-4168

★Mayor **Ivy R. Taylor** .... (210) 207-7060
Began Service: July 22, 2014
Term Expires: May 31, 2017
E-mail: Mayor.IvyTaylor@sanantonio.gov
Education: Yale 1992 BA; North Carolina 1992 MURP
Chief of Staff **Jill DeYoung** .... (210) 207-7067
Chief of Policy **Leilah H. Powell** .... (210) 207-9889
Liaison to Council **Andrew Solano** .... (210) 207-8980
Communications Director/Senior Policy Analyst **Leslie Garza** .... (210) 207-8448
E-mail: leslie.garza@sanantonio.gov
Constituent Services **(Vacant)** .... (210) 207-7083
Special Projects Manager **Ruben Lizalde** .... (210) 207-7060
Executive Assistant to the Mayor **Yolanda Oden** .... (210) 207-7069
E-mail: yolanda.oden@sanantonio.gov
★Council Member **Robert Treviño** (District 1) .... (210) 207-7279
Term Expires: May 31, 2017
E-mail: district1@sanantonio.gov
★Council Member **Alan Warrick** (District 2) .... (210) 207-7278
Term Expires: May 31, 2017
★Council Member **Rebecca Viagran** (District 3) .... (210) 207-7064
Term Expires: May 31, 2017
E-mail: district3@sanantonio.gov
★Council Member **Rey Saldaña** (District 4) .... (210) 207-7281
Term Expires: May 31, 2017
E-mail: district4@sanantonio.gov
Education: Stanford 2009, 2010 MA
★Council Member **Shirley Gonzales** (District 5) .... (210) 207-7043
Term Expires: May 31, 2017
E-mail: district5@sanantonio.gov
★Council Member **Ray Lopez** (District 6) .... (210) 207-7065
Term Expires: May 31, 2017
E-mail: district6@sanantonio.gov
★Council Member **Cris Medina** (District 7) .... (210) 207-7044
Term Expires: May 31, 2017
E-mail: district7@sanantonio.gov
Education: Palo Alto 2004 AA; Texas (San Antonio) 2006 BA
★Council Member **Ron Nirenberg** (District 8) .... (210) 207-7086
Term Expires: May 31, 2017
E-mail: district8@sanantonio.gov
★Council Member **Joe Krier** (District 9) .... (210) 207-7325
Term Expires: May 31, 2017
E-mail: district9@sanantonio.gov
★Council Member **Mike Gallagher** (District 10) .... (210) 207-7276
Term Expires: May 31, 2017
E-mail: district10@sanantonio.gov
Assistant to the City Council **Christopher D. Callanen** .... (210) 207-7040
E-mail: chris.callanen@sanantonio.gov

Office of the City Auditor

P.O. Box 839966, San Antonio, TX 78283-3966
Fax: (210) 223-0173 Internet: http://www.sanantonio.gov/cityauditor

○City Auditor **Kevin W. Barthold** .... (210) 207-2853
E-mail: kevin.barthold@sanantonio.gov

Office of the City Clerk

P.O. Box 839966, San Antonio, TX 78283-3966
Fax: (210) 207-7032 Internet: www.sanantonio.gov/clerk

○City Clerk **Leticia M. Vacek** .... (210) 207-7253
E-mail: leticia.vacek@sanantonio.gov

Municipal Courts

401 South Frio, San Antonio, TX 78207
Internet: www.sanantonio.gov/court

○Municipal Judge **Judge John Bull** .... (210) 207-8970
E-mail: john.bull@sanantonio.gov

Office of the City Manager

P.O. Box 839966, San Antonio, TX 78283-3966
Fax: (210) 207-4127 Internet: www.sanantonio.gov/manager

○City Manager **Sheryl L. Sculley** .... (210) 207-7080
E-mail: citymanager@sanantonio.gov
Education: Ball State 1974 BS; Western Michigan 1980 MPA
Chief of Staff **Edward Benavides** .... (210) 207-7080
Deputy City Manager **Erik J. Walsh** .... (210) 207-4484
E-mail: erik.walsh@sanantonio.gov
Education: Trinity U 1991 BA, 1994 MS
Deputy City Manager **Peter Zanoni** .... (210) 207-2066
E-mail: peter.zanoni@sanantonio.gov
Education: Jacksonville U BA; Florida State MPA
Assistant City Manager **Carlos Contreras** .... (210) 207-6912
E-mail: carlos.contreras@sanantonio.gov
Education: St Mary's U (TX) BA; Texas MPA, JD
Assistant City Manager **Lori Houston** .... (210) 207-6912
E-mail: lori.houston@sanantonio.gov
Assistant City Manager **Maria D. Villagomez** .... (210) 207-8480
E-mail: maria.villagomez@sanantonio.gov
Chief Financial Officer **Ben Gorzell** .... (210) 207-4478
Education: Texas (San Antonio) 1989 BBA

Office of the City Attorney

P.O. Box 839966, San Antonio, TX 78283-3966

City Attorney (Acting) **Martha G. Sepeda** .... (210) 207-8940
E-mail: martha.sepeda@sanantonio.gov
First Assistant City Attorney **Ed Guzman** .... (210) 207-8940

Office of Emergency Management

P.O. Box 839966, San Antonio, TX 78283-3966
Fax: (210) 206-8570

Emergency Management Coordinator **Lawrence Trevino** .... (210) 206-8580
E-mail: lawrence.trevino@sanantonio.gov

Office of Historic Preservation

P.O. Box 839966, San Antonio, TX 78283-3966
Fax: (210) 207-7897

Historic Preservation Officer **Shanon Shea Miller** .... (210) 207-8316

Office of Management and Budget

P.O. Box 839966, San Antonio, TX 78283-3966
Fax: (210) 207-4144

Director (Interim) **Chad Tustison** .... (210) 207-8360
E-mail: chad.tustison@sanantonio.gov

Office of Military Affairs [OMA]

P.O. Box 839966, San Antonio, TX 78283-3966

Director **MajGen Juan G. Ayala** .... (210) 207-2712
Education: Texas (El Paso) 1979

★Elected Official ▲Appointed by Legislature ▼Appointed by Governor ▶Appointed by Board or Commission ●Appointed by Judge
■Appointed by Mayor △Appointed by Freeholders ▽Appointed by Supervisor ▷Appointed by County Executive ○Appointed by Council

Office of Sustainability [OEP]
P.O. Box 839966, San Antonio, TX 78283-3966
Fax: (210) 207-6934

Chief Sustainability Officer **Doug R. Melnick** .... (210) 207-6103

Animal Care Services
P.O. Box 839966, San Antonio, TX 78283-3966

Director **Kathy Davis** .... (210) 207-3338

Aviation Department/San Antonio International Airport
P.O. Box 839966, San Antonio, TX 78283-3966
Fax: (210) 207-3500 E-mail: aviation@sanantonio.gov

Director **LtGen Noel T. "Tom" Jones** .... (210) 207-7242
Education: Air Force Acad 1980 BS; Embry-Riddle 1987 MS; Naval War 2000 MNSSS

Building and Equipment Services
P.O. Box 839966, San Antonio, TX 78283-3966
Tel: (210) 207-7858

Director **Jorge A. Pérez** .... (210) 207-7858
Fleet Acquisitions Administrator **Maggie Metzner** ...... (210) 207-2079

Information Technology Services Department
P.O. Box 839966, San Antonio, TX 78283-3966
Fax: (210) 207-4040

Chief Technology Officer **Hugh Miller** .... (210) 207-8301
E-mail: hugh.miller@sanantonio.gov

Department for Culture and Creative Development [DCCD]
115 Plaza de Armas, Suite 102, San Antonio, TX 78205

Director **Felix Padron** .... (210) 207-6968

Development Services Department
1901 South Alamo, San Antonio, TX 78204
Internet: www.sanantonio.gov/dsd/

Director **Roderick Sanchez** .... (210) 207-0171
E-mail: roderick.sanchez@sanantonio.gov
Assistant Director **Michael Shannon** .... (210) 207-8259
E-mail: michael.shannon@sanantonio.gov
Assistant Director **Terry Kannawin** .... (210) 207-8259
E-mail: terry.kannawin@sanantonio.gov

Finance Department
P.O. Box 839966, San Antonio, TX 78283-3966
Fax: (210) 207-4072

Finance Director **Troy Elliott** .... (210) 207-5734

Fire Department [SAFD]
P.O. Box 839966, San Antonio, TX 78283-3966
Internet: www.sanantonio.gov/safd

Fire Chief **Charles Hood** .... (210) 207-8400
E-mail: charles.n.hood@sanantonio.gov
Education: Ottawa U BS
Deputy Fire Chief **Yvette Granato** .... (210) 207-8400
Deputy Fire Chief **Vance Meade** .... (210) 207-8400
E-mail: vance.meade@sanantonio.gov
Deputy Fire Chief **Carl Wedige** .... (210) 207-8400
E-mail: carl.wedige@sanantonio.gov

Human Resources Department
P.O. Box 839966, San Antonio, TX 78283-3966

Chief Human Resources Officer **Lori Steward** .... (210) 207-8705
E-mail: lori.steward@sanantonio.gov

Department of Government and Public Affairs
P.O. Box 839966, San Antonio, TX 78283-3966

Director **Jeff Coyle** .... (210) 207-8109
E-mail: jeff.coyle@sanantonio.gov
Education: Florida State

Economic Development Department
P.O. Box 839966, San Antonio, TX 78283-3966
Fax: (210) 207-8151

Director **Rene Dominguez** .... (210) 207-8080
E-mail: rene.dominguez@sanantonio.gov

Parks and Recreation Department
P.O. Box 839966, San Antonio, TX 78283-3966

Director **Xavier Urrutia** .... (210) 207-8480

Planning and Community Development Department
P.O. Box 839966, San Antonio, TX 78283-3966

Director **John M. Dugan** .... (210) 207-0147
E-mail: john.dugan@sanantonio.gov
Education: Tulane 1969 BA; Harvard 1971 MCP

Police Department [SAPD]
315 South Santa Rosa, San Antonio, TX 78207

Police Chief **William McManus** .... (210) 207-7360
Education: Villanova; Johns Hopkins MS; JFK School Govt

Solid Waste Management Department [SWMD]
P.O. Box 839966, San Antonio, TX 78283-3966

Director **David W. McCary** .... (210) 207-6470

Department of Transportation and Capital Improvements
P.O. Box 839966, San Antonio, TX 78283-3966

Director **Michael X. Frisbie** .... (210) 207-8022

Center City Development and Operations Department
P.O. Box 839966, San Antonio, TX 78283-3966

Director **John Jacks** .... (210) 207-3914
E-mail: john.jacks@sanantonio.gov

Convention and Sports Facilities
P.O. Box 839966, San Antonio, TX 78283-3966
Fax: (210) 223-1495 Internet: http://www.sahbgcc.com/

Director **Michael Sawaya** .... (210) 207-8500

Convention and Visitors Bureau
P.O. Box 839966, San Antonio, TX 78283-3966
Internet: http://www.visitsanantonio.com Fax: (210) 207-6768

Director **Casandra Matej** .... (210) 207-6700

Metropolitan Health District
332 West Commerce, Suite 307, San Antonio, TX 78205-2489
Fax: (210) 207-8999 Internet: www.sanantonio.gov/health

Health Director (Interim) **Vincent Nathan** .... (210) 207-8730

San Antonio Housing Authority
818 South Flores Street, San Antonio, TX 78204
E-mail: customer_care@saha.org Internet: www.saha.org/

President and Chief Executive Officer (Interim)
David Nisivoccia .... (210) 477-6047

(continued on next page)

★ Elected Official ▲ Appointed by Legislature ▼ Appointed by Governor ► Appointed by Board or Commission ● Appointed by Judge
■ Appointed by Mayor △ Appointed by Freeholders ▽ Appointed by Supervisor ▷ Appointed by County Executive ○ Appointed by Council

San Antonio Housing Authority *continued*

Director of Communications and Public Affairs
Rosario Neaves . . . . (210) 477-6131
E-mail: communications@saha.org

San Antonio Public Library [SAPL]

P.O. Box 839966, San Antonio, TX 78283-3966

Director **Ramiro Salazar** . . . . (210) 207-2644
E-mail: ramiro.salazar@sanantonio.gov
Education: Texas A&I 1978 BA; Texas Woman's 1979 MLS

San Antonio Independent School District

141 Lavaca St., San Antonio, TX 78210
Fax: (210) 299-5580 Internet: http://www.saisd.net

Superintendent of Schools **Pedro Martinez** . . . . (210) 554-2200
Deputy Superintendent **Emilio Castro** . . . . (210) 554-2200
★President **Patti Radle** (District 5) . . . . (210) 554-2200
Term Expires: May 2019
E-mail: PRADLE1@saisd.net
★Vice President **Arthur V. Valdez, Jr.** (District 4) . . . . (210) 554-2200
Term Expires: May 2017
E-mail: AVALDEZ1@saisd.net
★Secretary **Debra Guerrero** (District 3) . . . . (210) 554-2200
Term Expires: May 2017
E-mail: dguerrero1@saisd.net
★Board of Trustees Member **Steve Lecholop** (District 1) . . (210) 554-2200
Term Expires: May 2017
E-mail: SLECHOLOP1@saisd.net
★Board of Trustees Member **James Howard** (District 2) . . (210) 554-2200
Term Expires: May 2019
E-mail: howard8@swbell.net
★Board of Trustees Member **Olga Hernandez** (District 6) . . (210) 554-2200
Term Expires: May 2019
E-mail: olgahernandez@satx.rr.com
★Board of Trustees Member **Ed Garza** (District 7) . . . . (210) 554-2200
Term Expires: May 2017
E-mail: EGARZA8@saisd.net
Education: Texas A&M 1992 BLA, 1994 MS

City of San Bernardino, California

300 North D St., San Bernardino, CA 92418
Tel: (909) 384-5211 (Information)
Internet: http://www.ci.san-bernardino.ca.us

County: San Bernardino **Election Type:** Nonpartisan
Population: 216,108 (2015)

Office of the Mayor and City Council

300 North D St., San Bernardino, CA 92418
Fax: (909) 384-5067 (Mayor's Fax) Fax: (909) 384-5105 (Council Fax)

★Mayor **Carey Davis** . . . . (909) 384-5133
Began Service: March 2014
Term Expires: March 1, 2018
E-mail: frazier_ju@sbcity.org
Chief of Staff **Christopher Lopez** . . . . (909) 384-5133
Executive Assistant to the Mayor **Evelyn Estrada** . . . . . . (909) 384-5133
★Council Member **Virginia Marquez** (Ward 1) . . . . (909) 384-5188
Term Expires: March 1, 2018
★Council Member **Benito Barrios** (Ward 2) . . . . (909) 384-5222
Term Expires: March 1, 2018 Fax: (909) 384-5105
★Council Member **John Valdivia** (Ward 3) . . . . (909) 384-5188
Term Expires: March 1, 2020

Office of the Mayor and City Council *continued*

★Council Member **Fred Shorett** (Ward 4) . . . . (909) 384-5188
Term Expires: March 1, 2018
★Council Member **Henry Nickel** (Ward 5) . . . . (909) 384-5188
Term Expires: March 1, 2020
★Council Member **Bessine Littlefield-Richard** (Ward 6) . . . (909) 384-5188
Term Expires: March 1, 2020
★Council Member **Jim Mulvihill** (Ward 7) . . . . (909) 384-5188
Term Expires: March 1, 2020

Office of the City Attorney

300 North D St., San Bernardino, CA 92418
Fax: (909) 384-5238

★City Attorney **Gary Saenz** . . . . (909) 384-5355
Term Expires: March 1, 2020

Office of the City Clerk

300 North D St., San Bernardino, CA 92418
Fax: (909) 384-5158

★City Clerk **Georgeann "Gigi" Hanna** . . . . (909) 384-5002
Term Expires: March 1, 2020

Office of the Treasurer

300 North D St., San Bernardino, CA 92418

★Treasurer **David Kennedy** . . . . (909) 384-5021
Term Expires: March 1, 2020

Office of the City Manager

300 North D St., San Bernardino, CA 92418
Fax: (909) 384-5138

■City Manager **Mark Scott** . . . . (909) 384-5122
E-mail: Scott_Ma@SBCity.org
Executive Assistant to the City Manager **Tanya Romo** . . . . (909) 384-5122
E-mail: romo_ta@sbcity.org
Deputy City Manager **Nita McKay** . . . . (909) 384-5122
E-mail: McKay_Ni@sbcity.org
Deputy City Manager **Bill Manis** . . . . (909) 384-5122
E-mail: Manis_Bi@sbcity.org

Animal Control Department

333 Chandler Pl., San Bernardino, CA 92408-2097
Fax: (909) 384-5483

Operations Manager **Capt. Paul Williams** . . . . (909) 384-1304

Civil Service Department

300 North D St., San Bernardino, CA 92418
Fax: (909) 384-5918

Chief Examiner **Rebekah Kramer** . . . . (909) 384-5062

Finance Department

300 North D St., San Bernardino, CA 92418
Fax: (909) 384-5043

Director of Finance (Acting) **Nita McKay** . . . . (909) 384-5242

Fire Department

200 E. Third St., San Bernardino, CA 92410
Fax: (909) 384-5281

Fire Chief **Thomas Hannemann** . . . . (909) 384-5286

Human Resources

300 North D St., San Bernardino, CA 92418
Fax: (909) 384-5397

Manager **Helen Tran** . . . . (909) 384-5161

★Elected Official ▲Appointed by Legislature ▼Appointed by Governor ▶Appointed by Board or Commission ●Appointed by Judge
■Appointed by Mayor △Appointed by Freeholders ▽Appointed by Supervisor ▷Appointed by County Executive ○Appointed by Council

Parks, Recreation and Community Services Department
547 N. Sierra Way, San Bernardino, CA 92410
Fax: (909) 384-5160

Director **Mickey Valdivia** .... (909) 384-5233

Police Department
710 North D St., San Bernardino, CA 92401

Police Chief **Jarrod Burguan** .... (909) 384-5742
Education: U Redlands MA Fax: (909) 388-4950

San Bernardino Public Library
555 W. Sixth St., San Bernardino, CA 92410
Fax: (909) 381-8229

Director **Edward Erjavek** .... (909) 381-8201
E-mail: erjavek.ed@sbpl.org

Public Works Department
300 North D St., San Bernardino, CA 92418
Fax: (909) 384-5190

Director (Acting) **Marlene Miyoshi** .... (909) 384-5045

Water Department
300 North D St., San Bernardino, CA 92418
Fax: (909) 384-5215

General Manager **Stacey Aldstadt** .... (909) 384-5141

City of San Diego, California
City Administration Bldg., 202 C Street, San Diego, CA 92101
Tel: (619) 236-5555 (Information) Internet: www.sandiego.gov

County: San Diego **Election Type:** Nonpartisan **Population:** 1,394,928 (2015)

Office of the Mayor
City Administration Building, 202 C Street, 11th Floor,
San Diego, CA 92101
Tel: (619) 236-6330 Fax: (619) 236-7228
Internet: www.sandiego.gov/mayor

★ Mayor **Kevin L. Faulconer** .... (619) 236-6330
Began Service: March 3, 2014
Term Expires: December 3, 2016
E-mail: kevinfaulconer@sandiego.gov
Date of Birth: 1967
Education: San Diego State 1990 BA
Executive Assistant to the Mayor **Tanya J. Lundy** .... (619) 236-6330
E-mail: tlundy@sandiego.gov
Chief of Staff **Stephen "Steve" Puetz** .... (619) 236-6330
Deputy Chief of Staff for Communications
Matt Awbrey .... (619) 236-6330
E-mail: mawbrey@sandiego.gov
Deputy Chief of Staff for Policy **Jaymie Bradford** .... (619) 236-6330
Deputy Chief of Staff **Felipe Monroig** .... (619) 236-6330
Director of Administration **Sara Cavataio** .... (619) 236-6330
E-mail: scavataio@sandiego.gov
Assistant to Director of Administration
Caroline Garcia .... (619) 236-6330
E-mail: cledesma@sandiego.gov
Director of Outreach **John Ly** .... (619) 236-6330
E-mail: jly@sandiego.gov
Director of Protocol **Don Giaquinto** .... (619) 236-6330
Director of Scheduling **Michelle Porras** .... (619) 236-6330
Director of Appointments **Francis Barraza** .... (619) 236-6330

Office of the Mayor *continued*
Press Secretary/Director of Media Relations
Craig Gustafson .... (619) 236-6330
E-mail: cgustafson@sandiego.gov
Press Secretary **Jen Lebron Kuhney** .... (619) 236-6330
E-mail: jkuhney@sandiego.gov
Press Secretary/Senior Advisor **Charles Chamberlayne** .. (619) 236-6330
E-mail: chamberlayne@sandiego.gov
Education: Howard U 2002 BA
Community Representative/Veterans Advocate
Darnisha Hunter .... (619) 236-6330
Director of Federal Government Affairs
Alejandra Gavaldon .... (619) 236-6330
Deputy Director of Government Affairs
Katherine Johnston .... (619) 236-6330
Director of State Government Affairs **Kristin Tillquist** .... (619) 236-6330

Community and Legislative Services
City Administration Building, 202 C Street, 11th Floor,
San Diego, CA 92101
Fax: (619) 236-7228

■ Chief of Staff **Stephen "Steve" Puetz** .... (619) 236-6249
E-mail: spuetz@sandiego.gov

Performance and Analytics Department [P&A]
202 C Street, 8th Floor, San Diego, CA 92101
Fax: (619) 236-7228

Director **Almis Udrys** .... (619) 236-5929
E-mail: audrys@sandiego.gov
Chief Data Officer **Maksim Pecherskiy** .... (619) 235-5252
E-mail: maksimp@sandiego.gov
Education: DePaul BS

Special Events
World Trade Center Bldg., 1250 Sixth Avenue, 7th Floor,
San Diego, CA 92101
Fax: (619) 685-1334 Internet: www.sandiego.gov/specialevents/

Special Events Director **Carolyn E. Wormser** .... (619) 685-1332

Office of the Chief Operating Officer
Tel: (619) 236-6207 Fax: (619) 236-7153

■ Chief Operating Officer **Scott Chadwick** .... (619) 236-6207
Confidential Secretary **Jacqueline Palmer** .... (619) 236-6207

Assistant Chief Operating Officer
City Administration Building, 202 C Street, San Diego, CA 92101

■ Assistant Chief Operating Officer **Stacey LoMedico** ..... (619) 533-6207
E-mail: slomedico@sandiego.gov
Education: San Diego State BA

Department of Information Technology
1010 Second Avenue, Suite 500 East, San Diego, CA 92101
Fax: (619) 533-3254 E-mail: DeptOfIT@sandiego.gov
Internet: www.sandiego.gov/it/

Chief Information Officer **Jonathan Behnke** .... (619) 533-3750
E-mail: jbehnke@sandiego.gov
Deputy Director, Security Compliance and Risk Management **Gary Hayslip** .... (619) 533-4840
E-mail: ghayslip@sandiego.gov
Citywide Technologies and Applications Manager
Christopher Bennett .... (619) 533-3034
E-mail: cwbennett@sandiego.gov
Web Services Manager **Ron Vazquez** .... (619) 236-6164
E-mail: rvasquez@sandiego.gov

★ Elected Official ▲ Appointed by Legislature ▼ Appointed by Governor ▶ Appointed by Board or Commission ● Appointed by Judge
■ Appointed by Mayor △ Appointed by Freeholders ▽ Appointed by Supervisor ▷ Appointed by County Executive ○ Appointed by Council

Personnel Department
1200 3rd Avenue, Suite 300, San Diego, CA 92101-4195
Internet: www.sandiego.gov/empopp/ Fax: (619) 236-5515

Personnel and Human Resources Manager
Hadi Dehgani .... (619) 236-6400
E-mail: personnel@sandiego.gov

Purchasing and Contracting Department
1200 3rd Avenue, Suite 200, San Diego, CA 92101-4195
Fax: (619) 236-5904 Internet: www.sandiego.gov/purchasing/index.shtml

Director **Kristina Peralta** .... (619) 236-6000
E-mail: purchasing@sandiego.gov

Chief Financial Officer
CIty Administration Building, 202 C Street, MS-9A,
San Diego, CA 92101
Tel: (619) 236-5941 Fax: (619) 236-6606

■ Deputy Chief Operating Officer/Chief Financial Officer
Mary Lewis .... (619) 236-5941
E-mail: mlewis@sandiego.gov

Office of the City Comptroller
City Administration Building, 202 C Street, Mail Stop 6 A,
San Diego, CA 92101
Fax: (619) 533-3998 E-mail: comptroller@sandiego.gov
Internet: www.sandiego.gov/comptroller/

■ City Comptroller **Rolando Charvel** .... (619) 236-6162
E-mail: rcharvel@sandiego.gov

Financial Management
202 C Street, Suite 800, MS 8A, San Diego, CA 92101
Fax: (619) 533-3215 Internet: www.sandiego.gov/fm/

Director **Tracy McCraner** .... (619) 236-6060

Treasurer's Department
1200 3rd Avenue, Suite 100, San Diego, CA 92101-4195
Fax: (619) 236-7134 Internet: http://www.sannet.gov/treasurer/

City Treasurer **Gail Granewich** .... (619) 236-6112

Communications Department
City Administration Building, 202 C Street, San Diego, CA 92101

■ Communications Director **Amelia Brazell** .... (619) 236-6330
E-mail: abrazell@sandiego.gov

Development Services Department
1222 First Avenue, MS 301, San Diego, CA 92101-4154
Fax: (619) 446-5490 Internet: www.sandiego.gov/development-services/

Director **Robert A. Vacchi** .... (619) 446-5423
E-mail: ravacchi@sandiego.gov
Assistant Deputy Director, Information Technology and
Records **Jim Myers** .... (619) 236-5007
E-mail: jmyers@sandiego.gov
Executive Assistant **MIchelle Frick** .... (619) 446-5423
E-mail: mfrick@sandiego.gov

Building Construction and Safety Division
1222 First Avenue, MS 301, San Diego, CA 92101-4101

Chief Building Official **Afsaneh Ahmadi** .... (619) 557-7998
E-mail: aahmadi@sandiego.gov
Assistant Deputy Director, Inspections
William Barrañón .... (858) 573-1216
E-mail: wbarranon@sandiego.gov
Assistant Deputy Director, Permits **Leslie Goossens** ..... (619) 446-4331
E-mail: lgoossens@sandiego.gov

Civic San Diego
401 B Street, Suite 400, San Diego, CA 92101
Tel: (619) 235-2200 Fax: (619) 236-9148

President **Reese Jarrett** .... (619) 235-2200
E-mail: jarrett@civicsd.com

Civic San Diego *continued*

Assistant Vice President, Planning **Brad Richter** .... (619) 235-2200
Assistant Vice President, Human Resources and
Compliance **Lisa M. Greeson** .... (619) 235-2200
E-mail: greeson@ccdc.com
Assistant Vice President, Neighborhood Investment
Kendy Li .... (619) 235-2200
E-mail: li@civicsd.com

Code Enforcement Division
1222 First Avenue, MS 301, San Diego, CA 92101-4101

Code Enforcement Officer **Michael S. Richmond** .... (619) 533-6302
E-mail: mrichmond@sandiego.gov

Engineering Division
1222 First Avenue, MS 301, San Diego, CA 92101-4101

Deputy Director **Greg Hopkins** .... (619) 446-5291
E-mail: ghopkins@sandiego.gov

Land Development Review Division
1222 First Avenue, San Diego, CA 92101-4101

Deputy Director (Interim) **Kerry Santoro** .... (619) 446-5121

Project Management Division
1222 First Avenue, MS 301, San Diego, CA 92101-4101

Deputy Director **Elyse Lowe** .... (619) 446-5127
Assistant Deputy Director **Mike Westlake** .... (619) 446-5220

San Diego Housing Commission
1122 Broadway, San Diego, CA 92101
Tel: (619) 578-7531 Internet: http://www.sdhc.org/

○ President and Chief Executive Officer
Richard C. Gentry .... (619) 578-7531
E-mail: rgentry@sandiego.gov Fax: (619) 578-7360
Education: Wake Forest BA; Florida State MA
Safety Officer **Trevor Abney** .... (619) 578-7479
E-mail: tabney@sandiego.gov
Vice President, Human Resources Department
Michael McKenna .... (619) 578-7739
Fax: (619) 578-7351

Fire-Rescue Department
1010 Second Avenue, Suite 400, San Diego, CA 92101
Tel: (619) 533-4300 Fax: (619) 544-9351 E-mail: fire@sandiego.gov
Internet: www.sandiego.gov/fire/

■ Fire Chief **Brian Fennessy** .... (619) 533-4301
E-mail: bfennessy@sandiego.gov Fax: (619) 533-4377
Emergency Medical Services Deputy Chief
Christopher Heiser .... (619) 533-4306
E-mail: cheiser@sandiego.gov Fax: (619) 533-4499
Assistant Chief of Operations **Colin Stowell** .... (619) 533-4401
E-mail: cstowell@sandiego.gov Fax: (619) 544-9351
Assistant Chief, Support Services **Ken Barnes** .... (619) 533-4302
E-mail: kbarnes@sandiego.gov
Battalion Chief, Training Division **James Gaboury** ...... (619) 692-4983
E-mail: jgaboury@sandiego.gov Fax: (619) 523-2923
Fire Marshal **Doug Perry** .... (619) 533-4304
E-mail: dperry@sandiego.gov Fax: (619) 544-6806
Human Resource Manager **Curt Glaser** .... (619) 533-4413
E-mail: cglaser@sandiego.gov Fax: (619) 533-4376
Human Resources Director **Joy Freeman** .... (619) 533-4307
E-mail: jfreeman@sandiego.gov Fax: (619) 544-9351
Lifeguard Chief **Rick Wurts** .... (619) 221-8832
2581 Quivira Court, Fax: (619) 221-8858
Mail Stop 32A, San Diego, CA 92109
E-mail: rwurts@sandiego.gov
Emergency Medical Services Medical Director
Dr. James V. "Jim" Dunford .... (619) 533-4300
E-mail: jdunford@sandiego.gov
Fiscal Services Manager **Michelle Yamamoto** .... (619) 533-4303
E-mail: myamamoto@sandiego.gov

★ Elected Official ▲ Appointed by Legislature ▼ Appointed by Governor ▶ Appointed by Board or Commission ● Appointed by Judge
■ Appointed by Mayor △ Appointed by Freeholders ▽ Appointed by Supervisor ▷ Appointed by County Executive ○ Appointed by Council

Office of Homeland Security
1010 Second Avenue, Suite 1500, San Diego, CA 92101
Internet: www.sandiego.gov/ohs/

Program Manager **John Valencia** .... (619) 533-6763
E-mail: jvalencia@sandiego.gov

Park and Recreation Department
202 C Street, San Diego, CA 92101
Fax: (619) 525-8220 Internet: www.sandiego.gov/park-and-recreation/

Director **Herman Parker** .... (619) 236-6643
Assistant Director **Andrew Field** .... (619) 236-6643
Community Parks I Deputy Director **Kathy Ruiz** .... (619) 235-1130
Community Parks II Deputy Director **David Monroe** ..... (619) 525-8235
Developed Regional Parks Deputy Director
Bruce Martinez .... (619) 235-1157
Open Space Deputy Director **Chris Zirkle** .... (619) 685-1323
Golf Operations Deputy Director **Mark Marney** .... (858) 552-1634
E-mail: mmarney@sandiego.gov
Maintenance Assessment District Assistant Deputy
Director **Paul Sirois** .... (619) 685-1307

Police Department
1401 Broadway, San Diego, CA 92101
Tel: (619) 531-2000 Fax: (619) 531-2530
Internet: http://www.sandiego.gov/police/

Chief of Police **Shelley Zimmerman** .... (619) 531-2777
Executive Assistant Chief **David Ramirez** .... (619) 531-2730
Assistant Chief, Centralized Investigations
Terry McManus .... (619) 531-2720
Assistant Chief, Neighborhood Policing
Albert Guaderrama .... (619) 531-2745
E-mail: aguaderrama@pd.sandiego.gov
Assistant Chief, Patrol Operations **Todd Jarvis** .... (619) 531-2734
Fax: (619) 531-2977
Assistant Chief, Traffic, Youth and Event Services
Mark Jones .... (619) 531-2770
Assistant Chief, Training and Employee Development
Sarah Creighton .... (619) 531-2740
E-mail: screighton@pd.sandiego.gov
Program Manager/Communications **Gerardo Gurrola** .... (619) 531-2365
E-mail: ggurrola@pd.sandiego.gov Fax: (619) 531-2977
Program Manager/Information Services **Chris Haley** ..... (619) 531-2401
E-mail: chaley@pd.sandiego.gov Fax: (619) 531-2101

San Diego Public Library
820 E Street, San Diego, CA 92101-6478
Tel: (619) 236-5800 Fax: (619) 238-6639
E-mail: weblibrary@sandiego.gov
Internet: www.sandiego.gov/public-library

Year Founded: 1882

Administration
Library Director **Misty Jones** .... (619) 236-5870
E-mail: LibraryDirector@sandiego.gov Fax: (619) 236-5878
Executive Secretary **Nicole Spriggs** .... (619) 236-5870
E-mail: nspriggs@sandiego.gov
Deputy Director, Branches **Bruce Johnson** .... (619) 236-5845
E-mail: bjohnson@sandiego.gov
Public Information Officer **Marion Moss Hubbard** ...... (619) 236-5848
E-mail: mhubbard@sandiego.gov
Senior Management Analyst **Bert Salamida** .... (619) 236-5893
E-mail: bsalamida@sandiego.gov

Public Works Department
City Administration Building, 202 C Street, 9th Floor,
San Diego, CA 92101
Fax: (619) 533-4736

■ Director **James Nagelvoort** .... (619) 533-4207

Capital Improvements Program
202 C Street, Mail Stop 9A, San Diego, CA 92101-3869
Internet: http://www.sannet.gov/engineering-cip/
E-mail: engineering@sandiego.gov

Director **James Nagelvoort** .... (619) 533-5110
E-mail: jnagelvoort@sandiego.gov Fax: (619) 533-4736
Assistant Director **Marnell Gibson** .... (619) 533-5213
E-mail: mgibson@sandiego.gov
Assistant Director **Luis Schaar** .... (858) 627-3220
E-mail: lschaar@sandiego.gov

Environmental Services Department
9601 Ridgehaven Ct., Suite 210, San Diego, CA 92123-1636
Tel: (858) 573-1200 Fax: (858) 492-5021
Internet: www.sannet.gov/environmental-services/

Director **Mario X. Sierra** .... (858) 573-1212
Executive Secretary **Stefanie Wenceslao** .... (858) 492-5014
E-mail: swenceslao@sandiego.gov
Assistant Director **Darren Greenhalgh** .... (858) 573-1214

Qualcomm Stadium
9449 Friars Rd., MS 34, San Diego, CA 92108
Tel: (619) 641-3100 Fax: (619) 283-0460

General Manager **Mike McSweeney** .... (619) 641-3100

Real Estate Assets
1200 3rd Avenue, Suite 1700, San Diego, CA 92101-4195
Tel: (619) 236-6020 Fax: (619) 236-6706
Internet: www.sandiego.gov/real-estate-assets/

Director **Cybele Thompson** .... (619) 236-6145
Deputy Director **Kristi Geitz** .... (619) 236-5548

San Diego City Employees' Retirement System
401 West A Street, Suite 400, San Diego, CA 92101-4298
Tel: (619) 525-3650 Fax: (619) 595-0357 Internet: www.sdcers.org

Chief Executive Officer **Mark A. Hovey** .... (619) 525-3650
Chief of Staff/Human Resources Manager
Lourdes Silva .... (619) 525-3643
E-mail: lsilva@sandiego.gov Fax: (619) 234-5314
Director of Member Services **Cynthia Jorner** .... (619) 525-3634
Fax: (619) 234-5314

San Diego Convention Center Corporation [SDCCC]
111 West Harbor Dr., San Diego, CA 92101
Tel: (619) 525-5000 Fax: (619) 525-5132
Internet: www.visitsandiego.com

President and Chief Executive Officer
Clifford "Rip" Rippetoe .... (619) 525-5101
Executive Vice President **Thomas Mazzocco** .... (619) 525-5150
E-mail: tom.mazzocco@visitsandiego.com
Senior Vice President, Centerplate **John Vingas** .... (619) 525-5823
Vice President, Finance **Mark Emch** .... (619) 525-5301
Vice President, Public Affairs **Steven Johnson** .... (619) 525-5251
E-mail: steven.johnson@visitsandiego.com
General Manager, Centerplate **Nancy Murgello** .... (619) 525-5855
General Manager, Event Management **Deanne Snyder** ... (619) 525-5429
Procurement Manager **(Vacant)** .... (619) 525-5381

Public Utilities Department
9192 Topaz Way, San Diego, CA 92123
Tel: (858) 292-6401 Fax: (858) 292-6310
Internet: www.sandiego.gov/publicutilities/

■ Director **Halla Razak** .... (858) 292-6401
Business Support Assistant Director
Lee Ann Jones-Santos .... (858) 292-6401
Strategic Programs Assistant Director **Tom Crane** .... (858) 292-6412
Water Operations Assistant Director **Stan Griffith** .... (619) 527-7431
2797 Caminito Chollas, San Diego, CA 92105-5097

(continued on next page)

★ Elected Official ▲ Appointed by Legislature ▼ Appointed by Governor ▶ Appointed by Board or Commission ● Appointed by Judge
■ Appointed by Mayor △ Appointed by Freeholders ▽ Appointed by Supervisor ▷ Appointed by County Executive ○ Appointed by Council

Public Utilities Department *continued*

Wastewater Operations Assistant Director
Robert Mulvey . . . . . (858) 292-6402
E-mail: rmulvey@sandiego.gov
Customer Support Deputy Director **Mike Vogl** . . . . . (619) 533-5153
600 B Street, Suite 1100, San Diego, CA 92101
Employee Services and Quality Assurance Deputy Director **Susan LaNier** . . . . . (858) 292-6466
Engineering and Program Management Deputy Director
Rania Amen . . . . . (858) 292-6476
Environmental Monitoring and Technical Services Division Deputy Director **Peter Vroom** . . . . . (619) 758-2301
NTC Laboratory, Fax: (619) 758-2309
2392 Kincaid Road, San Diego, CA 92101
Finance and Information Technology Deputy Director
Seth Gates . . . . . (858) 614-4042
LRP and Water Resources Deputy Director **Lan Wiborg** . . (619) 533-4112
600 B Street, Suite 600, San Diego, CA 92101-4518
Wastewater Treatment and Disposal Deputy Director
Agnes Generoso . . . . . (858) 292-6447
9191 Kearny Villa Road, San Diego, CA 92123
System Operations Division Deputy Director
Jesus Meda . . . . . (858) 292-6300
2797 Caminito Chollas, San Diego, CA 92105-5097
Water Construction and Maintenance Deputy Director
Isam Hireish . . . . . (619) 527-7434
2797 Caminito Chollas, San Diego, CA 92105-5097
Pure Water Assistant Director **John Helminski** . . . . . (859) 292-6401
600 B Street, San Diego, CA 92101-4518

San Diego Workforce Partnership, Inc.

3910 University Avenue, Suite 400, San Diego, CA 92105
Fax: (619) 228-2901 E-mail: info@workforce.org
Internet: http://workforce.org/

President and Chief Executive Officer **Peter Callstrom** . . . (619) 228-2906

Transportation and Storm Water Department

202 C Street, MS 9A, San Diego, CA 92101

Director **Kris McFadden** . . . . . (619) 236-6594
Fax: (619) 236-6570

Office of the City Auditor

1010 Second Avenue, 5th Floor, West Tower, MS 605B, San Diego, CA 92101
Fax: (619) 533-3036 E-mail: cityauditor@sandiego.gov
Internet: www.sandiego.gov/auditor/

City Auditor **Eduardo Luna** . . . . . (619) 533-3165
Education: Santa Clara U BS; Texas MPA

Office of the City Attorney

1200 3rd Avenue, Suite 1620, San Diego, CA 92101
Tel: (619) 236-6220 Fax: (619) 236-7215
Internet: www.sandiego.gov/city-attorney/

★City Attorney **Jan Goldsmith** . . . . . (619) 236-6220
Term Expires: December 4, 2016
E-mail: jgoldsmith@sandiego.gov
Education: San Diego 1976 JD
Executive Assistant City Attorney **Paul E. Cooper** . . . . . (619) 236-6220
Assistant City Attorney-Litigation **Dan Bamberg** . . . . . (619) 533-5800
Assistant City Attorney-Advisory **Mary T. Nuesca** . . . . . (619) 236-6220
Criminal Division Assistant City Attorney (Interim)
John Hemmerling . . . . . (619) 533-5500
Director of Communications **Gerry Braun** . . . . . (619) 236-6220
E-mail: gbraun@sandiego.gov

Office of the City Council

City Administration Building, 202 C Street, San Diego, CA 92101
Tel: (619) 236-6440 Fax: (619) 236-6529
Internet: www.sandiego.gov/citycouncil/

★Council President **Sherri S. Lightner** (District 1) . . . . . (619) 236-6611
Term Expires: December 3, 2016 Fax: (619) 236-6999
E-mail: sherrilightner@sandiego.gov
★Council President Pro Tem **Marti Emerald** (District 9) . . . (619) 236-6677
Term Expires: December 3, 2016 Fax: (619) 238-1360
E-mail: martiemerald@sandiego.gov
★Council Member **Lorie Zapf** (District 2) . . . . . (619) 236-6616
Term Expires: December 6, 2018 Fax: (619) 236-7329
E-mail: loriezapf@sandiego.gov
★Council Member **Todd Gloria** (District 3) . . . . . (619) 236-6633
Term Expires: December 3, 2016 Fax: (619) 595-1481
E-mail: toddgloria@sandiego.gov
Education: San Diego 2000 BA
★Council Member **Myrtle Cole** (District 4) . . . . . (619) 236-6644
Term Expires: December 6, 2018 Fax: (619) 236-7273
E-mail: myrtlecole@sandiego.gov
★Council Member **Mark Kersey** (District 5) . . . . . (619) 236-6655
Term Expires: December 3, 2016 Fax: (619) 238-0915
E-mail: mkersey@sandiego.gov
★Council Member **Chris Cate** (District 6) . . . . . (619) 236-6616
Term Expires: December 6, 2018 Fax: (619) 236-6529
E-mail: chriscate@sandiego.gov
★Council Member **Scott Sherman** (District 7) . . . . . (619) 236-6688
Term Expires: December 6, 2016 Fax: (619) 231-7918
E-mail: ssherman@sandiego.gov
★Council Member **David Alvarez** (District 8) . . . . . (619) 236-6688
Term Expires: December 6, 2018 Fax: (619) 231-7918
E-mail: davidalvarez@sandiego.gov

Office of the City Clerk

City Administration Bldg., 202 C Street, 2nd Floor, San Diego, CA 92101
Tel: (619) 533-4000 Fax: (619) 533-4045
Internet: http://www.sandiego.gov/city-clerk/

○City Clerk **Elizabeth Maland** . . . . . (619) 533-4080
E-mail: cityclerk@sandiego.gov
Legislative Services Deputy Director **George Biagi** . . . . . (619) 533-4024
Elections and Information Services Deputy Director
Bonnie Stone . . . . . (619) 533-4060
E-mail: bstone@sandiego.gov
Records Management Deputy Director **Sheila Beale** . . . . . (619) 235-5247

San Diego Unified School District

Board of Education Office, 4100 Normal Street, Room 2231, San Diego, CA 92103-2682
Tel: (619) 725-5550 Fax: (619) 297-5624 E-mail: board@sandi.net
Internet: www.sandi.net

Superintendent of Public Education **Cindy Marten** . . . . . (619) 725-5506
Education: Wisconsin (La Crosse) BA; UC San Diego MA
★President **Marne Foster** (District E) . . . . . (619) 725-5550
Term Expires: December 5, 2016
E-mail: mfoster@sandi.net
★Vice President **John Lee Evans** (District A) . . . . . (619) 725-5550
Term Expires: December 5, 2016
E-mail: johnleeevans@sandi.net
★School Board Member **Kevin Beiser** (District B) . . . . . (619) 725-5550
Term Expires: December 6, 2018
E-mail: kevinbeiser@sandi.net
★School Board Member
Michael G. McQuary (District C) . . . . . (619) 725-5550
Term Expires: December 6, 2018
★School Board Member **Richard Barrera** (District D) . . . . . (619) 725-5550
Term Expires: December 5, 2016
E-mail: rbarrera1@sandi.net

★Elected Official ▲Appointed by Legislature ▼Appointed by Governor ▶Appointed by Board or Commission ●Appointed by Judge
■Appointed by Mayor △Appointed by Freeholders ▽Appointed by Supervisor ▷Appointed by County Executive ○Appointed by Council

City and County of San Francisco, California

City Hall, One Dr. Carlton B. Goodlett Place, San Francisco, CA 94102
Tel: (415) 554-4000 (Information) Internet: www.sfgov.org

County: San Francisco **Election Type:** Nonpartisan
Population: 864,816 (2015)

Office of the Mayor

City Hall, 1 Dr. Carlton B. Goodlett Place, Room 200, San Francisco, CA 94102
Tel: (415) 554-6141 Fax: (415) 554-6160

★ Mayor **Edwin M. "Ed" Lee** . . . . . (415) 554-6141
Began Service: January 11, 2011
Term Expires: January 2020
E-mail: mayoredwinlee@sfgov.org
Date of Birth: May 5, 1952
Education: Bowdoin 1974 BA; Boalt Hall 1978 JD

■ Special Assistant to the Mayor **(Vacant)** . . . . . (415) 554-6654

■ Chief of Staff **Steve Kawa** . . . . . (415) 554-6603
E-mail: steve.kawa@sfgov.org

■ Budget Director **Kate Howard** . . . . . (415) 554-6486
E-mail: kate.howard@sfgov.org

■ Legislative Analyst **Andrew Dayton** . . . . . (415) 554-6971
E-mail: andrew.dayton@sfgov.org

■ Communications Director **Christine Falvey** . . . . . (415) 554-6131
E-mail: christine.falvey@sfgov.org

■ Board of Supervisors Liaison **Jason Elliott** . . . . . (415) 554-5262
E-mail: jason.elliott@sfgov.org

■ Government Affairs Assistant **Jason Elliott** . . . . . (415) 554-5975
E-mail: jason.elliott@sfgov.org

■ Policy Advisor for Public Safety **Paul Henderson** . . . . . (415) 554-6141

■ Chief of Protocol **Charlotte Mailliard Shultz** . . . . . (415) 554-6141
Education: Arkansas BA

Mayor's Office on Disability

401 Van Ness Avenue, Room 300, San Francisco, CA 94104
Tel: (415) 554-6789 Fax: (415) 554-6159 TTY: (415) 554-6799
E-mail: mod@sfgov.org Internet: http://www.sfgov.org/sfmod

■ Director (Interim) **Carla Johnson** . . . . . (415) 554-6789
E-mail: carla.johnson@sfgov.org

Mayor's Office of Housing

25 Van Ness Ave., Suite 600, San Francisco, CA 94102
Tel: (415) 701-5500 Fax: (415) 701-5501
Internet: http://www.sfgov.org/moh

■ Director **Olson Lee** . . . . . (415) 701-5500

Mayor's Office of Neighborhood Services [MONS]

1 Dr. Carlton B. Goodlett Place, Room 160, San Francisco, CA 94102
Tel: (415) 554-5977 Fax: (415) 554-4864
Internet: http://www.sfgov.org/mons/

■ Chief Deputy Director **Derick Brown** . . . . . (415) 554-5977
E-mail: derick.brown@sfgov.org

■ Deputy Community Manager **Ashley Cheng** . . . . . (415) 554-5977
E-mail: ashley.cheng@sfgov.org

Mayor's Office of Public Policy and Finance

City Hall, One Dr. Carlton B. Goodlett Place, Room 336, San Francisco, CA 94102-4645
Fax: (415) 554-4864

■ Director **Nadia Sesay** . . . . . (415) 554-5956
E-mail: nadia.sesay@sfgov.org

Office of the City Administrator

City Hall, One Dr. Carlton B. Goodlett Place, Room 362, San Francisco, CA 94102
Fax: (415) 554-4849 Internet: http://www.sfgov.org/cao/

■ City Administrator **Naomi Kelly** . . . . . (415) 554-4852
E-mail: city.administrator@sfgov.org

Office of Community Investment and Infrastructure Commission

One South Van Ness, 5th Floor, San Francisco, CA 94103
Fax: (415) 749-2525

■ Chairperson **Mara E. Rosales** . . . . . (415) 749-2457
Education: Hastings 1982

■ Commissioner **Miguel Bustos** . . . . . (415) 749-2457

■ Commissioner **Marily Mondejar** . . . . . (415) 749-2457

■ Commissioner **Leah Pimentel** . . . . . (415) 749-2457

■ Commissioner **Darshan Singh** . . . . . (415) 749-2457
Education: Golden Gate BBA; San Francisco State U MS

Office of Community Investment and Infrastructure [SFRA]

One South Van Ness, 5th Floor, San Francisco, CA 94103
Tel: (415) 749-2400 Fax: (415) 749-2525

Executive Director **Tiffany Bohee** . . . . . (415) 749-2458
E-mail: tiffany.bohee@sfgov.org

Deputy Director/Agency General Counsel **Jim Morales** . . (415) 749-2454
E-mail: james.morales@sfgov.org

Deputy Director, Finance and Administration **Bree Mawhorter** . . . . . (415) 749-2465
E-mail: Bree.Mawhorter@sfgov.org

Deputy Director, Projects and Programs **Sally Oerth** . . . . . (415) 749-2580
E-mail: Sally.Oerth@sfgov.org

Project Manager **Shane Hart** . . . . . (415) 749-2510
E-mail: shane.hart@sfgov.org

Assistant Manager, Real Estate **Christine Maher** . . . . . (415) 749-2481
E-mail: Christine.Maher@sfgov.org

Office of Economic and Workforce Development [OEWD]

1 Dr. Carlton B. Goodlett Place, Room 448, San Francisco, CA 94102
Internet: www.oewd.org

■ Director **Todd Rufo** . . . . . (415) 554-5694
E-mail: Todd.Rufo@sfgov.org

Managing Deputy Director **Joaquin Torres** . . . . . (415) 554-6969
E-mail: joaquin.torres@sfgov.org

Workforce Development Director **Michael Carr** . . . . . (415) 581-2351
E-mail: pat.mulligan@sfgov.org

Adult Probation Department

880 Bryant Street, Room 200, San Francisco, CA 94103

Chief of Adult Probation **Karen Fletcher** . . . . . (415) 553-1706

Airport Commission

P.O. Box 8097, San Francisco, CA 94128-8097
Tel: (650) 821-5000 Fax: (650) 821-5005 Internet: http://www.flysfo.com

■ President **Larry Mazzola, Jr.** . . . . . (650) 821-5042

■ Vice President **Linda S. Crayton** . . . . . (650) 821-5042

■ Commission Member **Richard J. Guggenhime** . . . . . (650) 821-5042
Education: Stanford 1961 AB; Harvard 1964 JD

■ Commission Member **Eleanor Johns** . . . . . (650) 821-5042

■ Commission Member **Peter A. Stern** . . . . . (650) 821-5042

Commission Secretary **Jean Caramatti** . . . . . (650) 821-5042
E-mail: jean.caramatti@flysfo.com

★ Elected Official ▲ Appointed by Legislature ▼ Appointed by Governor ▶ Appointed by Board or Commission ● Appointed by Judge
■ Appointed by Mayor △ Appointed by Freeholders ▽ Appointed by Supervisor ▷ Appointed by County Executive ○ Appointed by Council

San Francisco International Airport
P.O. Box 8097, San Francisco, CA 94128-8097
Tel: (650) 821-8211

■ Airport Director **John L. Martin** .... (650) 821-5000
Note: Until July 17, 2016
E-mail: john.martin@flysfo.com
■ Airport Director **Ivar C. Satero** .... (650) 821-5000
Note: Effective July 17, 2016

Board of Appeals
1650 Mission St., Room 304, San Francisco, CA 94103-2414
Fax: (415) 575-6885 Internet: www.sfgov.org/boa

■ President **Ann Blumlein Lazarus** .... (415) 575-6880
Education: Stanford 1971 BA, 1980 MBA
■ Vice President **Darryl Honda** .... (415) 575-6880
■ Commissioner **Frank Fung** .... (415) 575-6880
Education: UC Berkeley BARCH, MArch
▶ Commissioner **Rick Swig** .... (415) 575-6880
Education: Stanford 1973 AB
▶ Commissioner **Bobbie Wilson** .... (415) 575-6880
▶ Executive Director **Cynthia Goldstein** .... (415) 575-6880
E-mail: cynthia.goldstein@sfgov.org

Building Inspection Commission [BIC]
1660 Mission St., 6th Floor, San Francisco, CA 94103
Fax: (415) 558-6509 Internet: www.sfdbi.org/index.aspx?page=21

■ President **Angus McCarthy** .... (415) 558-6164
▽ Vice President **Warren Mar** .... (415) 558-6164
■ Commissioner **Kevin Clinch** .... (415) 558-6164
■ Commissioner **Frank Lee** .... (415) 558-6164
Education: UC Berkeley 1993 BA
■ Commissioner **Dr. James McCray, Jr.** .... (415) 558-6164
▽ Commissioner **Myrna Melgar** .... (415) 558-6164
▽ Commissioner **Debra Walker** .... (415) 558-6164
Commission Secretary **Sonya Harris** .... (415) 558-6164

Department of Building Inspection
1660 Mission St., San Francisco, CA 94103
Tel: (415) 558-6131 Internet: www.sfgov.org/dbi

Director **Tom Hui** .... (415) 558-6131
E-mail: tom.hui@sfgov.org Fax: (415) 558-6225
Deputy Director, Permit Services **Edward Sweeney** .... (415) 558-6139
E-mail: edward.sweeney@sfgov.org
Deputy Director, Inspection Services **Dan Lowrey** .... (415) 558-6127
E-mail: daniel.lowrey@sfgov.org
Deputy Director, Administrative Services
Taras Madison .... (415) 558-6239
E-mail: taras.madison@sfgov.org

Department of Child Support Services
617 Mission St., San Francisco, CA 94105

Director **Karen Roye** .... (415) 356-2919

Department of Children, Youth, and Their Families
Fox Plaza Bldg., 1390 Market St., Suite 900, San Francisco, CA 94102
Tel: (415) 934-4879 (TTY) Fax: (415) 554-8965 E-mail: info@dcyf.org
Internet: http://www.dcyf.org

■ Director **Maria Su** .... (415) 554-3547
E-mail: Maria.Su@dcyf.org

Civil Service Commission
25 Van Ness Ave., Room 720, San Francisco, CA 94102
Fax: (415) 252-3260

■ President **Douglas S. Chan** .... (415) 252-3247
■ Vice President **Gina M. Roccanova** .... (415) 252-3247
■ Commissioner **Kate Favetti** .... (415) 252-3247
■ Commissioner **Scott Heldfond** .... (415) 252-3247
■ Commissioner **(Vacant)** .... (415) 252-3247

Civil Service Commission *continued*

Executive Officer **Michael Brown** .... (415) 252-3247
E-mail: jennifer.johnston@sfgov.org

Elections Commission
1 Dr. Carlton B. Goodlett Place, Room 48, San Francisco, CA 94102
Tel: (415) 554-7457 Internet: www.sfgov2.org/index.aspx?page=319

President **Jill Battilega Rowe** .... (415) 554-4305
Term Expires: January 2021
Education: San Diego 1990 BA; U Washington 1998 JD
Vice President **Christopher Jerdonek** .... (415) 554-4305
Term Expires: January 2019
Member **Roger Donaldson** .... (415) 554-4305
Term Expires: January 2020
Member **Charles Jung** .... (415) 554-4305
Term Expires: January 2018
Member **Dominic Paris** .... (415) 554-4305
Term Expires: January 2018
Member **Rosabella Safont** .... (415) 554-4305
Term Expires: January 2019
Member **Winnie Yu** .... (415) 554-4305
Term Expires: January 2017
Commission Secretary **Nadya Hewitt** .... (415) 554-4305
E-mail: nadya.hewitt@sfgov.org

Department of Elections
City Hall, Rm. 48, 1 Dr. Carlton B. Goodlett Place,
San Francisco, CA 94102-4634
Tel: (415) 554-4375 Fax: (415) 554-7344 E-mail: sfvote@sfgov.org
Internet: www.sfelections.org

Director **John Arntz** .... (415) 554-4375
Deputy Director **Nataliya Kuzina** .... (415) 554-4375
E-mail: nataliya.kuzina@sfgov.org

Department of Emergency Management [DEM]
1011 Turk Street, San Francisco, CA 94102
Fax: (415) 431-7500 Internet: http://www.sfdem.org/

Executive Director **Anne Kronenberg** .... (415) 558-2745
E-mail: anne.kronenberg@sfgov.org
Education: U Washington BA; U San Francisco MPA
Assistant to Executive Director **David Ebarle** .... (415) 558-3810
E-mail: david.ebarle@sfgov.org

Division of Emergency Services
1011 Turk Street, San Francisco, CA 94102
Tel: (415) 487-5000 Fax: (415) 487-5043

Deputy Director **Rob Dudgeon** .... (415) 487-5000
E-mail: rob.dudgeon@sfgov.org

Environment Commission
1455 Market Street, Suite 1200, San Francisco, CA 94103
E-mail: environment@sfgov.org Internet: http://www.sfenvironment.org

■ President **Jacquelyn Omotalade** .... (415) 355-3709
■ Vice President **Elmy Bermejo** .... (415) 355-3709
■ Commissioner **Lisa Hoyos** .... (415) 355-3709
■ Commissioner **Heather Stephenson** .... (415) 355-3709
■ Commissioner **Johanna Wald** .... (415) 355-3709
■ Commissioner **Sarah Ching-Ting Wan** .... (415) 355-3709
■ Commissioner **(Vacant)** .... (415) 355-3709
Commission Affairs Manager **Guillermo Rodriguez** .... (415) 355-3709
E-mail: guillermo.rodriguez@sfgov.org Fax: (415) 554-6393

Environment Department
Fax: (415) 554-6393 E-mail: environment@sfgov.org
Internet: http://www.sfenviroment.com

■ Director **Deborah O. Raphael** .... (415) 355-3701
E-mail: deborah.raphael@sfgov.org
Deputy Director **Jennifer Kass** .... (415) 355-3762
Environmental Justice Program Manager **(Vacant)** .... (415) 355-3700
Public Outreach Program Manager **Donald Oliveira** .... (415) 355-3700

★ Elected Official ▲ Appointed by Legislature ▼ Appointed by Governor ▶ Appointed by Board or Commission ● Appointed by Judge
■ Appointed by Mayor △ Appointed by Freeholders ▽ Appointed by Supervisor ▷ Appointed by County Executive ○ Appointed by Council

Environment Department *continued*

Transportation Clean Air Program Manager **(Vacant)** . . . . (415) 355-3700
Recycling Manager **Robert Haley** . . . . (415) 355-3700
Climate and Energy Program Manager **Cal Broomhead** . . (415) 355-3700
Environmental Health and Safety Manager **Jen Jackson** . . (415) 554-6141
Toxics Materials Reduction Manager **Jennifer Jackson** . . (415) 355-3758
Urban Forestry Associate **Mei Ling Hui** . . . . (415) 355-3700
Policy and Communications Director
Guillermo Rodriguez . . . . (415) 355-3756
E-mail: guillermo.rodriguez@sfgov.org

Fine Arts Museums of San Francisco

Golden Gate Park, 50 Hagiwara Tea Garden Drive,
San Francisco, CA 94118
Tel: (415) 750-3600 (Museum Information) Fax: (415) 750-7686
Internet: www.famsf.org

President, Board of Trustees **Diane "Dede" Wilsey** . . . . (415) 750-3600
Education: Connecticut Col 1965 BA
Museums Director (Acting) **Richard Benefield** . . . . (415) 750-3662
Deputy Director and Chief Operating Officer
Richard Benefield . . . . (415) 750-3600
E-mail: richard.benefield@sfgov.org
Chief Curator **Julian Cox** . . . . (415) 750-3600
Education: Manchester (UK) 1987 BA; U Wales (UK) 1990 MPhil
Chief Administrative Officer/Chief Financial Officer
Michele Gutierrez . . . . (415) 750-3662

Fire Commission

698 Second St., San Francisco, CA 94107-2015
Fax: (415) 558-3413 Internet: www.sf-fire.org/index.aspx?page=248

■ President **Francee Covington** . . . . (415) 558-3451
■ Vice President **Ken Cleveland** . . . . (415) 558-3451
■ Commissioner **Michael Hardeman** . . . . (415) 558-3451
■ Commissioner **Stephen A. Nakajo** . . . . (415) 558-3451
■ Commissioner **(Vacant)** . . . . (415) 558-3451
Commission Secretary **Maureen Conefrey** . . . . (415) 558-3451
E-mail: maureen.conefrey@sfgov.org

Fire Department

Internet: www.sf-fire.org/

■ Fire Chief **Joanne Hayes-White** . . . . (415) 558-3401
E-mail: joanne.hayes-white@sfgov.org
Fire Marshal **Daniel DeCossio** . . . . (415) 558-3320
E-mail: dan.decossio@flysfo.com
Administration Deputy Chief **Raemona Williams** . . . . (415) 558-3411
E-mail: raemona.williams@sfgov.org
Operations Deputy Chief **Mark Gonzales** . . . . (415) 558-3402
E-mail: mark.gonzales@sfgov.org
Public Information Officer **Jon Baxter** . . . . (415) 558-3403
E-mail: fireadministration@sfgov.org

General Services Agency

Office of the County Clerk

1 Dr. Carlton B. Goodlett Place, Room 168, San Francisco, CA 94102
Tel: (415) 554-4950 Fax: (415) 554-4951
Internet: www.sfgov.org/countyclerk

County Clerk **Catherine Stefani** . . . . (415) 554-4955
E-mail: county.clerk@sfgov.org

Animal Care and Control Department

1200 - 15th St., San Francisco, CA 94103-4208
Tel: (415) 554-6364 Fax: (415) 557-9950 E-mail: acc@sfgov.org
Internet: www.sfgov.org/acc/

Director **Virginia Donohue** . . . . (415) 554-9413
Education: Northwestern BA; Kellogg MA
Operations **Vicky Guldbech** . . . . (415) 554-9402
E-mail: vicky.guldbech@sfgov.org Fax: (415) 864-2866
Volunteer/Outreach Coordinator **Deb Campbell** . . . . (415) 554-9427
E-mail: acc@sfgov.org

Office of Contract Administration

City Hall, Rm. 430, 1 Dr. Carlton B. Goodlett Place,
San Francisco, CA 94102-4685
Fax: (415) 554-6717 E-mail: oca@sfgov.org
Internet: http://www.sfgov.org/oca

Director and Purchaser **Jaci Fong** . . . . (415) 554-6743
E-mail: oca@sfgov.org
Assistant Director **Cameron Langner** . . . . (415) 554-7799
E-mail: cameron.langner@sfgov.org
Assistant Director **Kofo Domingo** . . . . (415) 554-6714
E-mail: kofo.domingo@sfgov.org
Supervising Purchaser **Darlene Frohm** . . . . (415) 695-2124
E-mail: oca.records@sfgov.org
Supervising Purchaser **Ben Kawamura** . . . . (650) 554-3166
E-mail: ben.kawamura@flysfo.com Fax: (650) 821-2820
Supervising Purchaser **Galen Leung** . . . . (415) 701-2465
E-mail: galen.leung@sfmta.com Fax: (415) 701-4729
Supervising Purchaser **Greg Pustelnik** . . . . (415) 554-6264

Convention Facilities Department

747 Howard Street, 5th Floor, San Francisco, CA 94103
Tel: (415) 978-5925 Fax: (415) 978-5913

Director **John T. Noguchi** . . . . (415) 974-4027

Fleet Management Division

Tel: (415) 550-4600 Fax: (415) 550-4611
Internet: www.sfgov.org/fleetmanagement

Fleet Manager **Dave Del Grande** . . . . (415) 550-4603

Medical Examiner

850 Bryant St., San Francisco, CA 94103-4603
Fax: (415) 553-1650 Internet: www.sfgov.org/med_examiner

Chief Medical Examiner **Dr. Michael D. Hunter** . . . . (415) 553-1694

Public Works Department

City Hall, Rm. 348, 1 Dr. Carlton B. Goodlett Place,
San Francisco, CA 94102-4645
Tel: (415) 554-6920 Fax: (415) 554-6944 E-mail: info@sfdpw.org
Internet: http://www.sfgov.org/dpw

Director **Mohammed Nuru** . . . . (415) 554-6920
Executive Assistant **Frank Lee** . . . . (415) 554-6919
E-mail: frank.lee@sfdpw.org
Director of Policy and Communications **Rachel Gordon** . . (415) 554-6931
E-mail: rachel.gordon@sfdpw.org
Deputy Director for Buildings and City Architect
Edgar Lopez . . . . (415) 557-4700
E-mail: edgar.lopez@sfgov.org
City Engineer, Deputy Director for Design and
Construction **Fuad Sweiss** . . . . (415) 554-6920
E-mail: fuad.sweiss@sfgov.org
Finance and Administration Deputy Director
Julia Dawson . . . . (415) 554-4831
E-mail: julia.dawson@sfdpw.org
Operations Deputy Director **Larry Stringer** . . . . (415) 695-2003
2323 Cesar Chavez St., San Francisco, CA 94124
E-mail: larry.stringer@sfdpw.org

Real Estate Division

25 Van Ness Ave., Suite 400, San Francisco, CA 94102
Fax: (415) 552-9216 Internet: www.sfgov.org/realestate

Director **John Updike** . . . . (415) 554-9850

Alemany Farmer's Market and Flea Market

100 Alemany Blvd., San Francisco, CA 94110
Fax: (415) 643-9514

Office Staff Supervisor **Wayne Giang** . . . . (415) 647-9423
E-mail: wayne.giang@sfgov.org
Office Staff Supervisor **Amalia Martinez** . . . . (415) 647-9423
E-mail: amalia.martinez@sfgov.org
Office Staff Supervisor **Barbara Meskunas** . . . . (415) 647-9423
E-mail: barbara.meskunas@sfgov.org

(continued on next page)

★ Elected Official ▲ Appointed by Legislature ▼ Appointed by Governor ▶ Appointed by Board or Commission ● Appointed by Judge
■ Appointed by Mayor △ Appointed by Freeholders ▽ Appointed by Supervisor ▷ Appointed by County Executive ○ Appointed by Council

Real Estate Division *continued*

Office Staff Supervisor **Sharie Canja** (415) 647-9423
E-mail: sharie.canja@sfgov.org

Risk Management

25 Van Ness Avenue, Suite 750, San Francisco, CA 94102

Director of Risk Management **Matt Hansen** (415) 554-2302
E-mail: matt.hansen@sfgov.org

Department of Technology

1 South Van Ness Avenue, 2nd Floor, San Francisco, CA 94103
Tel: (415) 581-7100 Fax: (415) 581-4002
Internet: www.sfgov3.org/index.aspx?page=1421

■ Chief Information Officer **Miguel A. Gamiño, Jr.** (415) 581-4082
E-mail: miguel.gamino@sfgov.org
Education: Texas (El Paso) BABA

Chief Data Officer **Joy Ellyn Bonaguro** (415) 554-6588
E-mail: joy.bonaguro@sfgov.org

Deputy Director of Finance and Administration **Leo Levenson** (415) 581-4001

Deputy Director, Public Communications **Ron Vinson** (415) 581-4003
E-mail: ron.vinson@sfgov.org

Deputy Director of Service Delivery **Ashley Amjad** (415) 581-4096

Chief Technology Officer **Joe Voje** (415) 581-4014
E-mail: joe.voje@sfgov.org

Health Commission

101 Grove Street, Room 300, San Francisco, CA 94102
Tel: (415) 554-2666 Fax: (415) 554-2665

■ President **Dr. Edward Chow** (415) 554-2666
■ Vice President **David Singer** (415) 554-2666
■ Commissioner **Cecilia Chung** (415) 554-2666
Education: Golden Gate 1987 BA
■ Commissioner **Dr. Judith F. Karshmer** (415) 554-2666
■ Commissioner **David R. Pating** (415) 554-2666
■ Commissioner **David J. Sanchez, Jr.** (415) 554-2666
■ Commissioner **Belle Taylor-McGhee** (415) 554-2666

Executive Secretary to the Commission **Mark Morewitz** (415) 554-2633
E-mail: mark.morewitz@sfgov.org

Department of Public Health [DPH]

101 Grove Street, Room 308, San Francisco, CA 94102
Fax: (415) 554-2888 Internet: www.sfdph.org/dph/

Director of Health **Barbara Garcia** (415) 554-2610
Education: UC Santa Cruz BS; U San Francisco MPA

Chief Financial Officer **Greg Wagner** (415) 554-2610
E-mail: greg.wagner@sfdph.org

Chief Information Officer **Bill Kim** (415) 554-2610
E-mail: bill.kim@sfdph.org

Planning and Administration Deputy Director **Colleen Chawla** (415) 554-2769

Planning and Administration Assistant Director **(Vacant)** (415) 554-2633

Housing Authority Commission

Internet: http://www.sfha.org/

■ President **Joaquin Torres** (415) 715-3280
■ Vice President **Jaci Fong** (415) 715-3280
■ Member **Phil Arnold** (415) 715-3280
■ Member **Leroy Lindo** (415) 715-3280
■ Member **Lotti Titus** (415) 715-3280
■ Member **Ted Yamasaki** (415) 715-3280
■ Member **(Vacant)** (415) 715-3280

San Francisco Housing Authority [SFHA]

1815 Egbert Avenue, San Francisco, CA 94124
Fax: (415) 241-1038 Internet: http://www.sfgov.org/sfha/

■ Executive Director (Acting) **Barbara Smith** (415) 715-3280
E-mail: smithb@sfha.org

Deputy Director/Chief Operating Officer **Dariush Kayhan** (415) 715-3280

San Francisco Housing Authority *continued*

Chief Procurement Officer **Solomon Gebala** (415) 715-3280
E-mail: gebalas@sfha.org
Education: UC Santa Cruz BA

Director of Public Housing Operations **Twima Earley** (415) 715-3280
E-mail: earleyt@sfha.org

Client Placement Director **Nicole T. McCray-Dickerson** (415) 715-3280

Human Resources Manager **Phyllis Moore-Lewis** (415) 715-3280
E-mail: phyllis.moore-lewis@sfgov.org
Education: National U BA

Director of Information Systems **David Rosario** (415) 715-3280
E-mail: rosariod@sfha.org
Education: CUNY BS

Director of Government Affairs and Policy **Linda Martin-Mason** (415) 715-3280
Education: San Francisco Law JD

Chief Strategic Planning and Budgeting Officer **(Vacant)** (415) 715-3280

Department of Human Resources

44 Gough Street, 2nd Floor, San Francisco, CA 94103
Tel: (415) 557-4800

■ Director **Micki Callahan** (415) 557-4845
E-mail: micki.callahan@sfgov.org
Education: UMass (Amherst) BA

Human Rights Commission

25 Van Ness Avenue, Suite 800, San Francisco, CA 94102
Fax: (415) 431-5764 E-mail: hrc.info@sfgov.org Internet: www.sf-hrc.org

■ Chair **Susan Belinda Christian** (415) 252-2500
■ Vice Chair **Sheryl Evans Davis** (415) 252-2500
■ Commissioner **Mark Kelleher** (415) 252-2500
■ Commissioner **Michael Pappas** (415) 252-2500
■ Commissioner **Abigail Porth** (415) 252-2500
■ Commissioner **Richard Pio Roda** (415) 252-2500
■ Commissioner **Michael Sweet** (415) 252-2500
■ Commissioner **(Vacant)** (415) 252-2500
■ Commissioner **(Vacant)** (415) 252-2500

Director **Theresa Sparks** (415) 252-2500

Human Services Commission

P.O. Box 7988, San Francisco, CA 94120-7988
Tel: (415) 557-6431 Tel: (415) 557-5214 (TTY) Fax: (415) 431-9270
Internet: www.sfgov.org/dhs/

■ President **Dr. Pablo Stewart** (415) 557-6431
■ Vice President **Scott L. Kahn** (415) 557-6431
■ Commissioner **Dr. James McCray, Jr.** (415) 557-6431
■ Commissioner **Dr. Rita Semel** (415) 557-6431
■ Commissioner **George Yamasaki, Jr.** (415) 557-6431
Education: Stanford 1957 AB, 1959 JD

Secretary **Louise Rainey** (415) 557-6431
E-mail: louise.rainey@sfgov.org

Human Services Agency

Tel: (415) 557-6541

■ Executive Director **Trent Rhorer** (415) 557-6541
E-mail: trent.rhorer@sfgov.org
Education: UCLA BA; JFK School Govt 1996 MPP

Deputy Director of Welfare to Work **Tony Lugo** (415) 557-6348

Chief Financial Officer **Daniel Kaplan** (415) 557-5641

Family and Children's Services Deputy Director **Sylvia Deporto** (415) 557-6348

Policy and Planning Director **Noelle Simmons** (415) 557-5404

Innovation Office Design Anthropologist **Marc Hebert** (415) 557-6541

Aging and Adult Services Commission

1650 Mission Street, 5th Floor, San Francisco, CA 94103
Fax: (415) 355-6785 Internet: http://www.sfgov.org/

■ President **Edna James** (415) 355-3555
■ Vice President **Gustavo Serina** (415) 355-3555
■ Commissioner **Samer Itani** (415) 355-3555

★ Elected Official ▲ Appointed by Legislature ▼ Appointed by Governor ▶ Appointed by Board or Commission ● Appointed by Judge
■ Appointed by Mayor △ Appointed by Freeholders ▽ Appointed by Supervisor ▷ Appointed by County Executive ○ Appointed by Council

Aging and Adult Services Commission *continued*

■ Commissioner **Katie Loo** .... (415) 355-3555
■ Commissioner **Richard G. Ow** .... (415) 355-3555
■ Commissioner **Neil Sims** .... (415) 355-3555
■ Commissioner **(Vacant)** .... (415) 355-3555
Commission Secretary **Bridget Badasow** .... (415) 335-3509

Aging and Adult Services Department
1650 Mission Street, 5th Floor, San Francisco, CA 94103
Fax: (415) 355-6785

■ Executive Director **Shireen McSpadden** .... (415) 355-3555
E-mail: shireen.mcspadden@sfgov.org

Office on Aging
1650 Mission Street, 5th Floor, San Francisco, CA 94103

Director **Denise Cheung** .... (415) 355-3555

Office of the Public Administrator
1650 Mission Street, San Francisco, CA 94103
Tel: (415) 355-3555 Fax: (415) 355-3554

Public Administrator **Michelle Lewis** .... (415) 355-3568

Office of the Public Conservator
1650 Mission Street, 4th Floor, San Francisco, CA 94103

Public Conservator **Mary Anne Warren** .... (415) 355-3555

San Francisco County Veterans Service Office
2 Gough Street, San Francisco, CA 94103
Tel: (415) 934-4200 Fax: (415) 934-4240
Internet: www.sfhsa.org/134.htm

County Veterans Service Officer **Wallace Levin** .... (415) 934-4200
Assistant County Veterans Service Officer **Shan Yue** .... (415) 934-4293

Law Library
401 Van Ness Avenue, Room 400, San Francisco, CA 94102
Fax: (415) 554-6820 Internet: http://www.sfgov.org/sfll

Director **Marcia R. Bell** .... (415) 554-6821
E-mail: marcia.bell@sfgov.org

Library Commission
Main Library, 100 Larkin Street, San Francisco, CA 94102-4733

Note: The Public Library Commission is a seven-member commission appointed by the Mayor of San Francisco. The commission sets policy for the San Francisco Public Library System, approves the library budget, and appoints the City Librarian. Commissioners serve a four-year term.

■ President **Dr. Mary J. Wardell Ghirarduzzi** .... (415) 557-4400
■ Vice President **Susan Mall** .... (415) 557-4400
■ Commissioner **Zoe Dunning** .... (415) 557-4400
■ Commissioner **Luis Herrera** .... (415) 557-4400
Education: Texas (El Paso) BS; Arizona 1976 MLS; Cal State (Long Beach) MPA
■ Commissioner **John Lee** .... (415) 557-4400
■ Commissioner **Michael Nguyen** .... (415) 557-4400
■ Commissioner **Teresa Ono** .... (415) 557-4400

San Francisco Public Library [SFPL]
Main Library, 100 Larkin Street, San Francisco, CA 94102-4733
Tel: (415) 557-4400 Fax: (415) 557-4205 E-mail: info@sfpl.org
Internet: www.sfpl.org

Administration
City Librarian **Luis Herrera** .... (415) 557-4236
E-mail: luis.herrera@sfpl.org
Education: Texas (El Paso) BS; Arizona 1976 MLS; Cal State (Long Beach) MPA
Secretary, Library Commission **Sue Blackman** .... (415) 557-4233
E-mail: sblackman@sfpl.org

San Francisco Municipal Transportation Agency [SFMTA]
1 South Van Ness Avenue, 7th Floor, San Francisco, CA 94103
Fax: (415) 701-4502 Internet: www.sfmta.com

Board of Directors
1 South Van Ness Avenue, 7th Floor, San Francisco, CA 94103

■ Chairman **Tom Nolan** .... (415) 701-4505
E-mail: mtaboard@sfmta.com
■ Vice Chair **Cheryl Brinkman** .... (415) 701-4505
E-mail: mtaboard@sfmta.com
■ Director **Gwyneth Borden** .... (415) 701-4505
■ Director **Malcolm A. Heinicke** .... (415) 701-4505
E-mail: mtaboard@sfmta.com
■ Director **Joél Ramos** .... (415) 701-4505
E-mail: mtaboard@sfmta.com
■ Director **Cristina Rubke** .... (415) 701-4505
E-mail: mtaboard@sfmta.com
■ Director **(Vacant)** .... (415) 701-4505
E-mail: mtaboard@sfmta.com
Board Secretary **Roberta Boomer** .... (415) 701-4500
E-mail: roberta.boomer@sfmta.com

Staff
Director of Transportation **Edward D. Reiskin** .... (415) 701-4500
Education: MIT BS; NYU MBA; Harvard MPA
Capital Programs and Construction Director **Vincent Harris** .... (415) 701-4500
Finance and Information Technology Director **Sonali Bose** .... (415) 701-4500
E-mail: sonali.bose@sfmta.com
Safety, Training, Security and Enforcement Director **Melvyn Henry** .... (415) 701-4500
E-mail: melvyn.henry@sfgov.org
Sustainable Streets Director **Tom Maguire** .... (415) 701-4500
Transit Director **John J. Haley, Jr.** .... (415) 701-4500
City Traffic Engineer **Ricardo Olea** .... (415) 701-4500
E-mail: ricardo.olea@sfgov.org
Press Officer **Paul Rose** .... (415) 701-4500
E-mail: paul.rose@sfmta.com

Planning Commission
1650 Mission Street, Suite 400, San Francisco, CA 94103

■ President **Rodney Fong** .... (415) 558-6309
E-mail: planning@rodneyfong.com
▶ Vice President **Dennis Richards** .... (415) 558-6309
E-mail: dennis.richards@sfgov.org
■ Commissioner **Michael Antonini** .... (415) 558-6309
E-mail: wordweaver21@aol.com
■ Commissioner **Rich Hillis** .... (415) 558-6309
E-mail: richhillissf@yahoo.com
■ Commissioner **Christine Johnson** .... (415) 558-6309
E-mail: christine.johnson@sfgov.org
▶ Commissioner **Kathrin Moore** .... (415) 558-6309
E-mail: mooreurban@aol.com
▶ Commissioner **Cindy Wu** .... (415) 558-6306
E-mail: cwu.planning@gmail.com
Commission Secretary **Jonas P. Ionin** .... (415) 558-6309
E-mail: commissions.secretary@sfgov.org

Planning Department
1650 Mission St., Suite 400, San Francisco, CA 94103

Director **John Rahaim** .... (415) 558-6411
Zoning Administrator **Scott Sanchez** .... (415) 558-6350

Historic Preservation Commission
Fax: (415) 558-6409

■ President **Andrew Wolfram** .... (415) 901-4912
E-mail: andrew@tefarch.com
■ Vice President **Aaron Jon Hyland** .... (415) 558-6309
E-mail: aaron.hyland.hpc@gmail.com
■ Commissioner **Karl Hasz** .... (415) 558-6309
E-mail: karl@haszinc.com

(continued on next page)

★ Elected Official ▲ Appointed by Legislature ▼ Appointed by Governor ▶ Appointed by Board or Commission ● Appointed by Judge
■ Appointed by Mayor △ Appointed by Freeholders ▽ Appointed by Supervisor ▷ Appointed by County Executive ○ Appointed by Council

Historic Preservation Commission *continued*

■ Commissioner **Ellen Johnck** (415) 558-6309
E-mail: ellen.hpc@ellenjohnckconsulting.com
■ Commissioner **Richard S.E. Johns** (415) 781-8494
E-mail: rsejohns@yahoo.com
■ Commissioner **Diane Matsuda** (415) 348-0011
E-mail: diane@johnburtonfoundation.org
■ Commissioner **Jonathan Pearlman** (415) 558-6309
E-mail: jonathan.pearlman.hpc@gmail.com
Historic Preservation Officer **Tim Frye** (415) 575-6822
Fax: (415) 558-6409
Commission Secretary **Jonas P. Ionin** (415) 558-6309
E-mail: commissions.secretary@sfgov.org

Police Commission

1245 3rd Street, San Francisco, CA 94158
Tel: (415) 837-7070 Fax: (415) 575-6083

▶ President **Suzy Loftus** (415) 837-7070
▶ Vice President **L. Julius Turman** (415) 837-7070
Affiliation: Partner, San Francisco, CA Office, Reed Smith LLP
Education: Michigan 1987 BGS; Rutgers 1992 JD
■ Commissioner **Petra DeJesus** (415) 837-7070
▶ Commissioner **Victor Hwang** (415) 837-7070
■ Commissioner **Dr. Joe Marshall** (415) 837-7070
■ Commissioner **Tom Mazzucco** (415) 837-7070
■ Commissioner **Sonia Melara** (415) 837-7070

Police Department

Fax: (415) 553-1554

■ Chief of Police (Acting) **Toney Chaplin** (415) 553-1551
E-mail: Toney.Chaplin@sfgov.org
Deputy Chief, Administration Bureau **Mikail Ali** (415) 837-7250
Deputy Chief, Airport Bureau **Denise Schmitt** (650) 821-7100
P.O. Box 8097, San Francisco, CA 94128-8097
Deputy Chief, Chief of Staff **Hector Sainea** (415) 837-7000
Deputy Chief, Operations Bureau **Michael Redmond** (415) 575-7142
E-mail: michael.redmond@sfgov.org
Deputy Chief, Professional Standards and Principled Policing Bureau **Toney Chaplin** (415) 837-7000
Deputy Chief, Special Operations Bureau **Garret Tom** (415) 832-8424
Public Affairs **Sgt Michael Andraychak** (415) 553-1651
E-mail: michael.andraychak@sfgov.org

Port Commission

Pier One, San Francisco, CA 94111
Tel: (415) 274-0400 Fax: (415) 274-0412 Internet: http://www.sfport.com

■ President **William Adams** (415) 274-0406
■ Vice President **Kimberly Brandon** (415) 274-0406
Education: San Francisco State U BA
■ Commissioner **Leslie Katz** (415) 274-0406
■ Commissioner **Doreen Woo Ho** (415) 274-0406
■ Commissioner **(Vacant)** (415) 274-0406
Commission Secretary **Amy Quesada** (415) 274-0406
E-mail: amy.quesada@sfport.com
Communications Manager **Renee Martin** (415) 274-0488
E-mail: renee.martin@sfgov.org

Port of San Francisco

Pier One, San Francisco, CA 94111
Fax: (415) 274-0412

■ Executive Director (Interim) **Elaine Forbes** (415) 274-0401
E-mail: elaine.forbes@sfport.com
Deputy Director, Finance and Administration (Interim) **John Woo** (415) 274-0445
E-mail: john.woo@sfgov.org
Deputy Director, Maintenance **Thomas Carter** (415) 597-7903
E-mail: tom_carter@sfport.com
Deputy Director, Maritime **Peter Dailey** (415) 274-0517
Education: Col St Mary BS; Golden Gate MBA

Port of San Francisco *continued*

Deputy Director, Planning and Development **Byron Rhett** (415) 274-0546
Education: Cincinnati BS
Deputy Director, Real Estate **Susan Reynolds** (415) 274-0501
Director of Homeland Security **Sidonie Sansom** (415) 274-0579
E-mail: Sidonie.Sansom@sfport.com Fax: (415) 274-0586
Chief Harbor Engineer **Eunejune Kim** (415) 274-0570
E-mail: eunejune@gmail.com

San Francisco Public Utilities Commission [SFPUC]

525 Golden Gate Avenue, 13th Floor, San Francisco, CA 94102
Tel: (415) 554-3155 Fax: (415) 554-3424 Internet: http://www.sfwater.org

■ President **Francesca Vietor** (415) 554-3165
■ Vice President **Anson Moran** (415) 554-3165
■ Commissioner **Ann Moller Caen** (415) 554-3165
Education: Golden Gate 1988 MBA
■ Commissioner **Vince Courtney** (415) 554-3165
Education: UC Santa Cruz BA; San Francisco Law 1999 JD
■ Commissioner **Ike Kwon** (415) 554-3165
Commission Secretary **Donna Hood** (415) 554-3163
General Manager **Harlan L. Kelly, Jr.** (415) 554-3160
Assistant General Manager, Infrastructure **Kathy How** (415) 554-3409
Assistant General Manager, Wastewater Enterprise **Tommy Moala** (415) 554-2465
Communications Director **Tyrone Jue** (415) 554-3247
Human Resource Services Director **Cindy Charan** (415) 554-2404
Information Technology Services Director **Ken Salmon** (415) 551-4302
Local and Regional Water **David Briggs** (650) 872-5901
Assistant General Manager of Water **Steve Ritchie** (415) 554-3155
Assistant General Manager of Business Services/Chief Financial Officer **Eric L. Sandler** (415) 554-3155
Assistant General Manager of External Affairs **Juliet Ellis** (415) 554-3155
Assistant General Manager of Power **Barbara Hale** (415) 554-3155
Education: San Francisco State U 1986 BA
Land and Resources Management Manager **Tim Ramirez** (415) 554-3265
Water Quality Bureau Manager **Andrew DeGraca** (415) 554-3155
Deputy General Services Manager **Michael Carlin** (415) 554-3155

Recreation and Park Commission

McLaren Lodge, Golden Gate Park, 501 Stanyan St., San Francisco, CA 94117-1898
Fax: (415) 224-8034

■ President **Mark Buell** (415) 831-2750
■ Vice President **Allan E. Low** (415) 831-2750
Education: UC Berkeley 1983 BS; Hastings 1986 JD
■ Commissioner **Gloria Bonilla** (415) 831-2750
Education: U San Francisco BA
■ Commissioner **Tom Harrison** (415) 831-2750
■ Commissioner **Meagan Levitan** (415) 831-2750
Education: Stanford 1987 AB
■ Commissioner **Eric McDonnell** (415) 831-2750
■ Commissioner **(Vacant)** (415) 831-2750
Commission Liaison **Margaret McArthur** (415) 831-2752

Golden Gate Park Concourse Authority

McLaren Lodge, Golden Gate Park, 501 Stanyan Street, San Francisco, CA 94117-1898
Fax: (415) 831-2099

■ Commissioner **Lily Chan** (415) 581-2542
■ Commissioner **Murat Eskicioglu** (415) 581-2542
■ Commissioner **Dung Hoa Nguyen** (415) 581-2542
■ Commissioner **Anderson Pugash** (415) 581-2542
■ Commissioner **Stephen Revetria** (415) 581-2542
■ Commissioner **Stephanie Roumeliotes** (415) 581-2542
■ Commissioner **(Vacant)** (415) 581-2542
Executive Director **Dan Mauer** (415) 581-2542

★ Elected Official ▲ Appointed by Legislature ▼ Appointed by Governor ▶ Appointed by Board or Commission ● Appointed by Judge
■ Appointed by Mayor △ Appointed by Freeholders ▽ Appointed by Supervisor ▷ Appointed by County Executive ○ Appointed by Council

Recreation and Parks Department
McLaren Lodge, Golden Gate Park, 501 Stanyan Street,
San Francisco, CA 94117-1898
Fax: (415) 831-2096

General Manager **Philip A. Ginsburg** .... (415) 831-2700
Outreach, Education and Customer Services Manager
Elton Pon .... (415) 831-2700
Director of Finance and Administration
Katharine Petrucione .... (415) 831-2700
E-mail: katharine.petrucione@sfgov.org
Education: Pomona BA; Texas MPA
Director of Operations **Dennis Kern** .... (415) 831-2700
E-mail: dennis.kern@sfgov.org
Education: Miami U (OH) BA; Fletcher Law & Diplomacy MA
Director of Planning and Capital Management
Dawn Kamalanathan .... (415) 581-2559

Relocation Appeals Board
One Van Ness Avenue, Suite 500, San Francisco, CA 94103
Fax: (415) 701-5501 Internet: http://sf-moh.org/index.aspx?page=659

■ Board Member **Natividad Ramirez** .... (415) 701-5598
■ Board Member **(Vacant)** .... (415) 701-5598
■ Board Member **(Vacant)** .... (415) 701-5598
■ Board Member **(Vacant)** .... (415) 701-5598
Executive Secretary **Eugene Flannery** .... (415) 701-5598
E-mail: eugene.flannery@sfgov.org

Retirement System Board [SFERS]
30 Van Ness Avenue, Suite 3000, San Francisco, CA 94102
Tel: (415) 487-7020 Fax: (415) 487-7023 Internet: http://mysfers.org/

★ President **Malia Cohen** .... (415) 487-7020
Term Expires: January 20, 2017
★ Vice President **Herb Meiberger** .... (415) 487-7020
Term Expires: February 20, 2017
■ Commissioner **Leona Bridges** .... (415) 487-7020
Term Expires: February 20, 2018
★ Commissioner **Joseph D. Driscoll** .... (415) 487-7020
Term Expires: February 20, 2021
■ Commissioner **Victor Makras** .... (415) 487-7020
Term Expires: February 20, 2019
■ Commissioner **Wendy Paskin-Jordan** .... (415) 487-7020
Term Expires: February 20, 2019
Education: Stanford 1977 AB; Wharton MBA
▽ Commissioner **Brian Stansbury** .... (415) 487-7020
Term Expires: February 20, 2020
E-mail: brian.stansbury@sfgov.org

Retirement System
30 Van Ness Avenue, Suite 3000, San Francisco, CA 94102

Executive Director **Jay Huish** .... (415) 487-7020
Deputy Director **Caryn Bortnick** .... (415) 487-7015
Chief Investment Officer **William J. Coaker, Jr.** .... (415) 487-7015
Managing Director, Public Markets **Robert Shaw** .... (415) 487-7001
E-mail: robert.shaw@sfgov.org
Commission Secretary **Norm Nickens** .... (415) 487-7025
E-mail: norm.nickens@sfgov.org

Small Business Commission
City Hall, 1 Dr. Carlton B. Goodlett Place, Room 110,
San Francisco, CA 94102
Tel: (415) 554-6134 Fax: (415) 558-7844
Internet: http://www.sfgov.org/sbc

■ President **Mark Dwight** .... (415) 554-6134
■ Commissioner **Stephen "Steve" Adams** .... (415) 554-6134
▽ Commission Member **Kathleen Dooley** .... (415) 554-6134
▽ Commission Member **William Ortiz-Cartagena** .... (415) 554-6134
■ Commission Member **Paul Tour-Sarkissian** .... (415) 554-6134
■ Commission Member **Irene Yee Riley** .... (415) 554-6134
▽ Commissioner **Miriam Zouzounis** .... (415) 554-6134

Small Business Commission *continued*

Policy Analyst/Commission Secretary **(Vacant)** .... (415) 554-6408
E-mail: sbac@sfgov.org Fax: (415) 558-7844

Office of Small Business
City Hall, 1 Dr. Carlton B. Goodlett Place, Room 110,
San Francisco, CA 94102
Fax: (415) 558-7844

■ Executive Director **Regina Dick-Endrizzi** .... (415) 554-6481
E-mail: regina.dick-endrizzi@sfgov.org

Commission on the Status of Women
25 Van Ness Ave., Suite 240, San Francisco, CA 94102-6061
Tel: (415) 252-2570 Fax: (415) 252-2575 E-mail: dosw@sfgov.org
Internet: http://www.sfgov.org/cosw

■ President **Andrea Shorter** .... (415) 252-2570
■ Vice President **Deborah "Debbie" Mesloh** .... (415) 252-2570
Education: Kansas BSJ
■ Commissioner **Nancy Kirshner-Rodriguez** .... (415) 252-2570
■ Commissioner **Olga A. Ryerson** .... (415) 252-2570
■ Commissioner **Julie Soo** .... (415) 252-2570
■ Commissioner **Breanna Nicole Zwart** .... (415) 252-2570
Education: Carnegie Mellon 2008 BA
■ Commissioner **(Vacant)** .... (415) 252-2570
Commission Secretary **Herschell Larrick** .... (415) 252-3216
E-mail: herschell.larrick@sfgov.org

Department on the Status of Women
25 Van Ness Avenue, Suite 240, San Francisco, CA 94102

■ Executive Director **Dr. Emily M. Murase** .... (415) 252-2570
E-mail: emily.murase@sfgov.org
Education: Bryn Mawr 1987 AB; UC San Diego 1990 MA;
Stanford 2003 PhD

War Memorial and Performing Arts Center, San Francisco
401 Van Ness Avenue, Suite 110, San Francisco, CA 94102-4521
Fax: (415) 621-5091

Board of Trustees
■ President **Thomas E. Horn** .... (415) 621-6600
■ Vice President **Nancy Hellman Bechtle** .... (415) 621-6600
Education: Stanford 1959 BA
■ Member **Belva Davis** .... (415) 621-6600
■ Member **Edwin M. "Ed" Lee** .... (415) 621-6600
Date of Birth: May 5, 1952
Education: Bowdoin 1974 BA; Boalt Hall 1978 JD
■ Member **Gorretti Lo Lui** .... (415) 621-6600
■ Member **Gina Moscone** .... (415) 621-6600
■ Member **MajGen James M. "Mike" Myatt** .... (415) 621-6600
■ Member **Paul F. Pelosi** .... (415) 621-6600
■ Member **Charlotte Mailliard Shultz** .... (415) 621-6600
Education: Arkansas BA
■ Member **Vaughn R. Walker** .... (415) 621-6600
Date of Birth: 1944
Education: Michigan 1966 AB; Stanford 1970 JD
■ Member **Diane "Dede" Wilsey** .... (415) 621-6600
Education: Connecticut Col 1965 BA

War Memorial Staff
Managing Director **Elizabeth Murray** .... (415) 621-6600
Assistant Managing Director **Jennifer E. Norris** .... (415) 554-6308
Booking Manager **Rob Levin** .... (415) 554-6317
Communications and Events Manager **John Caldon** .... (415) 554-6321
E-mail: john.caldon@sfgov.org
Green Room Booking Manager **Elizabeth Soberanes** .... (415) 554-6313

★ Elected Official ▲ Appointed by Legislature ▼ Appointed by Governor ▶ Appointed by Board or Commission ● Appointed by Judge
■ Appointed by Mayor △ Appointed by Freeholders ▽ Appointed by Supervisor ▷ Appointed by County Executive ○ Appointed by Council

Office of the Board of Supervisors

City Hall, 1 Dr. Carlton B. Goodlett Place, Room 244,
San Francisco, CA 94102-4689
Tel: (415) 554-5184 Fax: (415) 554-5163
E-mail: board.of.supervisors@sfgov.org Internet: www.sfgov.org/bos

★ President **London Breed** (District 5) .... (415) 554-5184
Term Expires: January 8, 2017
E-mail: london.breed@sfgov.org

★ Supervisor **Eric L. Mar** (District 1) .... (415) 554-7410
Term Expires: January 8, 2017 Fax: (415) 554-7415
E-mail: eric.l.mar@sfgov.org

★ Supervisor **Mark Farrell** (District 2) .... (415) 554-7752
Term Expires: January 8, 2019 Fax: (415) 554-7843
E-mail: mark.farrell@sfgov.org

★ Supervisor **Aaron Peskin** (District 3) .... (415) 554-5184
Term Expires: January 8, 2017

★ Supervisor **Katy Tang** (District 4) .... (415) 554-7460
Term Expires: January 8, 2019 Fax: (415) 554-7432
E-mail: katy.tang@sfgov.org

★ Supervisor **Jane Kim** (District 6) .... (415) 554-7970
Term Expires: January 8, 2019 Fax: (415) 554-7974
E-mail: jane.kim@sfgov.org

★ Supervisor **Norman Yee** (District 7) .... (415) 554-5184
Term Expires: January 8, 2017
E-mail: norman.yee@sfgov.org

★ Supervisor **Scott Wiener** (District 8) .... (415) 554-6968
Term Expires: January 8, 2019 Fax: (415) 554-6909
E-mail: scott.wiener@sfgov.org

★ Supervisor **David Campos** (District 9) .... (415) 554-5144
Term Expires: January 8, 2017 Fax: (415) 554-6255
E-mail: david.campos@sfgov.org

★ Supervisor **Malia Cohen** (District 10) .... (415) 554-7670
Term Expires: January 8, 2019 Fax: (415) 554-7674
E-mail: malia.cohen@sfgov.org

★ Supervisor **John Avalos** (District 11) .... (415) 554-6975
Term Expires: January 8, 2017 Fax: (415) 554-6979
E-mail: john.avalos@sfgov.org

Office of the Clerk to The Board of Supervisors

City Hall, 1 Dr. Carlton B. Goodlett Place, Room 244,
San Francisco, CA 94102
Internet: http://www.sfbos.org/index.aspx?page=36

▽ Clerk of the Board **Angela Calvillo** .... (415) 554-5184
E-mail: board.of.supervisors@sfgov.org Fax: (415) 554-5163

San Francisco County Transportation Authority

1455 Market Street, Floor 22, San Francisco, CA 94103
Fax: (415) 522-4800 E-mail: info@sfcta.org
Internet: http://www.sfcta.org

Chair **Scott Wiener** .... (415) 554-6968
Vice Chair **Eric L. Mar** .... (415) 554-7410
Board Member **John Avalos** .... (415) 554-6975
Board Member **London Breed** .... (415) 554-7360
Board Member **David Campos** .... (415) 554-5144
Board Member **Malia Cohen** .... (415) 554-7670
Board Member **Mark Farrell** .... (415) 554-7752
Board Member **Jane Kim** .... (415) 554-7970
Board Member **Aaron Peskin** .... (415) 554-6516
Board Member **Katy Tang** .... (415) 554-7460
Board Member **Norman Yee** .... (415) 554-7630
Executive Director **Tilly Chang** .... (415) 522-4800
Clerk of the Authority **Steve Stamos** .... (415) 522-4817
E-mail: steve.stamos@sfcta.org

Office of the Assessor/Recorder

City Hall, Rm. 190, 1 Dr. Carlton B. Goodlett Place,
San Francisco, CA 94102
Fax: (415) 554-7915 E-mail: assessor@sfgov.org

★ Assessor/Recorder **Carmen Chu** .... (415) 554-5502
Term Expires: January 2018
E-mail: assessor@sfgov.org
Education: Occidental 2000 BA; UC Berkeley 2003 MA

Recording Division Manager **Kurt Fuchs** .... (415) 554-5502
E-mail: kurt.fuchs@sfgov.org

Chief Appraiser **Matt Thomas** .... (415) 554-5583
E-mail: matt.thomas@sfgov.org

Office of the City Attorney

City Hall, Rm. 234, 1 Dr. Carlton B. Goodlett Place,
San Francisco, CA 94102
Fax: (415) 554-4745 E-mail: cityattorney@sfgov.org
Internet: http://www.sfgov.org/cityattorney/

★ City Attorney **Dennis Herrera** .... (415) 554-4700
Term Expires: January 2018
E-mail: dennis.herrera@sfgov.org
Education: George Washington 1988 JD

Chief Assistant City Attorney **Jesse C. Smith** .... (415) 554-4709
E-mail: jesse.smith@sfgov.org

Deputy City Attorney **Christine B. Van Aken** .... (415) 554-4633
Education: NYU JD

Public Information Officer **Matt Dorsey** .... (415) 554-4662
E-mail: matt.dorsey@sfgov.org

Investigator **David Pfieffer** .... (415) 554-4700

Office of the Controller

City Hall, Rm. 316, 1 Dr. Carlton B. Goodlett Place,
San Francisco, CA 94102-4694
Fax: (415) 554-7466 Internet: http://www.sfgov.org/controller/

■ Controller **Ben Rosenfield** .... (415) 554-7500
E-mail: controller@sfgov.org

Deputy Controller **Todd Rydstrom** .... (415) 554-7500
Education: Iowa State BS; UC Berkeley MPP

Office of the District Attorney

850 Bryant Street, 3rd Floor, San Francisco, CA 94103
Tel: (415) 553-1741 Fax: (415) 553-1737
Internet: http://www.sfdistrictattorney.org

★ District Attorney **George Gascón** .... (415) 553-1741
Term Expires: January 2020
E-mail: districtattorney@sfgov.org
Education: Cal State (Long Beach) 1978 BA;
Western State U San Diego 1996 JD

Chief of Staff **Cristine DeBerry** .... (415) 553-1744
Chief Assistant District Attorney **Sharon Woo** .... (415) 553-1744
Chief of the White Collar Division **June Cravett** .... (415) 551-9500
Chief of Investigations **James Kerrigan** .... (415) 553-1030
Chief of the Criminal Division, Horizontal Units
Marshall Khine .... (415) 553-1744
Chief of the Criminal Division, Vertical Units
David Merin .... (415) 553-1744

Office of the Public Defender

555 Seventh St., 2nd Floor, San Francisco, CA 94103-4672
Tel: (415) 553-1671 Fax: (415) 553-9810
Internet: http://sfpublicdefender.org/

★ Public Defender **Jeff Adachi** .... (415) 553-1671
Term Expires: January 7, 2019
E-mail: jeff.adachi@sfgov.org

★ Elected Official ▲ Appointed by Legislature ▼ Appointed by Governor ► Appointed by Board or Commission ● Appointed by Judge
■ Appointed by Mayor △ Appointed by Freeholders ▽ Appointed by Supervisor ▷ Appointed by County Executive ○ Appointed by Council

Sheriff's Department

City Hall, Rm. 456, 1 Dr. Carlton B. Goodlett Place,
San Francisco, CA 94102
Internet: http://www.sfsheriff.com

★ Sheriff **Vicki Hennessy** .... (415) 554-7225
Term Expires: January 2020
Undersheriff **Carl Koehler** .... (415) 554-7225
E-mail: carl.koehler@sfgov.org
Assistant Sheriff **(Vacant)** .... (415) 554-7225
Chief Deputy **Matthew Freeman** .... (415) 575-4392
E-mail: matthew.freeman@sfgov.org
Chief Deputy **Kathy Gorwood** .... (415) 554-7225
E-mail: kathy.gorwood@sfgov.org
Chief Deputy **Al Waters** .... (415) 734-2323
E-mail: al.waters@sfgov.org

Office of the Treasurer/Tax Collector

City Hall, One Dr. Carlton B. Goodlett Place, Room 140,
San Francisco, CA 94102
Tel: (415) 554-4478 Fax: (415) 554-4672
E-mail: treasurer.taxcollector@sfgov.org Internet: http://www.sfgov.org/tax

★ Treasurer **José Cisneros** .... (415) 554-4478
Term Expires: January 15, 2018
E-mail: jose.cisneros@sfgov.org
Chief Assistant Treasurer **Pauline Marx** .... (415) 554-5260
Education: Yale 1979 MBA
Tax Collector **David P. Augustine** .... (415) 554-7601
E-mail: david.augustine@sfgov.org
Education: Stanford 2002 JD
Delinquent Revenue Bureau Director
Margarita Rodriguez .... (415) 554-4413
E-mail: margarita.rodriguez@sfgov.org
Tax Investigator **Phil De La Cruz** .... (415) 554-5309

San Francisco Unified School District [SFUSD]

555 Franklin Street, San Francisco, CA 94102
Internet: www.sfusd.edu

Superintendent of Schools **Richard A. Carranza** .... (415) 241-6121
Education: Arizona BA; Northern Arizona MEd Fax: (415) 241-6012

Board of Education

555 Franklin St., Room 106, San Francisco, CA 94102
Tel: (415) 241-6427 Fax: (415) 241-6429 Internet: http://www.sfusd.edu

★ President **Matt Haney** .... (415) 241-6427
Term Expires: January 2017
E-mail: matthaney@sfusd.edu
★ Vice President **Shamann Walton** .... (415) 241-6427
Term Expires: January 8, 2019
E-mail: ShamannWalton@sfusd.edu
★ Board Member **Sandra Lee Fewer** .... (415) 241-6427
Term Expires: January 2017
E-mail: sandrafewer@sfusd.edu
★ Board Member **Hydra B. Mendoza-McDonnell** .... (415) 241-6427
Term Expires: January 8, 2019
E-mail: hydra.mendoza@sfusd.edu
★ Board Member **Dr. Emily M. Murase** .... (415) 241-6427
Term Expires: January 8, 2019
E-mail: emilymurase@sfusd.edu
Education: Bryn Mawr 1987 AB; UC San Diego 1990 MA; Stanford 2003 PhD
★ Board Member **Rachel Norton** .... (415) 241-6427
Term Expires: January 2017
E-mail: rachelnorton@sfusd.edu
★ Board Member **Jill Wynns** .... (415) 241-6427
Term Expires: January 2017
E-mail: jillwynns@sfusd.edu

City of San Jose, California

200 East Santa Clara Street, San Jose, CA 95113
Tel: (408) 535-3500 (Information) Internet: www.sanjoseca.gov

County: Santa Clara **Election Type:** Nonpartisan **Population:** 1,026,908 (2015)

Office of the Mayor and City Council

200 East Santa Clara Street, San Jose, CA 95113
Fax: (408) 292-6422

★ Mayor **Sam Liccardo** .... (408) 535-4800
Began Service: January 1, 2015
Term Expires: December 31, 2018
Chief of Staff **Jim Reed** .... (408) 535-4800
Director of Policy **Ragan Henninger** .... (408) 535-4800
Education: Santa Clara U BA
Public Information Officer **David Low** .... (408) 535-4800
E-mail: david.low@sanjoseca.gov
Director of Land use and Economic Development
Ru Weerakoon .... (408) 535-4800
Education: San José State BS, MS
Policy Advisor **(Vacant)** .... (408) 535-4800
Policy Advisor **Ruth Cueto** .... (408) 535-4800
Policy Advisor **Paul Pereira** .... (408) 535-4800
Executive Assistant/Scheduler **Barbara Howard** .... (408) 535-4800
Executive Assistant/Scheduler **Chris Marcoida** .... (408) 535-4800
Communications Specialist **Ahmad Chapman** .... (408) 535-4800
★ Vice Mayor **Rose Herrera** (District 8) .... (408) 535-4908
Term Expires: December 31, 2016 Fax: (408) 292-6469
E-mail: rose.herrera@sanjoseca.gov
★ Council Member **Charles "Chappie" Jones** (District 1) .... (408) 535-4901
Term Expires: December 31, 2018
★ Council Member **Ash Kalra** (District 2) .... (408) 535-4902
Term Expires: December 31, 2016
E-mail: district2@sanjoseca.gov
Tel: (408) 292-6451
★ Council Member **Raul Peralez** (District 3) .... (408) 535-4903
Term Expires: December 31, 2018 Fax: (408) 292-6456
★ Council Member **Manh Nguyen** (District 4) .... (408) 535-4904
Term Expires: December 31, 2016 Fax: (408) 292-6459
★ Council Member **Magdalena Carrasco** (District 5) .... (408) 535-4905
Term Expires: December 31, 2018 Fax: (408) 292-6462
★ Council Member **Pierluigi Oliverio** (District 6) .... (408) 535-4906
Term Expires: December 31, 2016 Fax: (408) 292-6465
E-mail: pierluigi.oliverio@sanjoseca.gov
★ Council Member **Tam Nguyen** (District 7) .... (408) 535-4907
Term Expires: December 31, 2018 Fax: (408) 292-6468
★ Council Member **Don Rocha** (District 9) .... (408) 535-4909
Term Expires: December 31, 2018 Fax: (408) 292-6471
E-mail: district9@sanjoseca.gov
★ Council Member **Johnny Khamis** (District 10) .... (408) 535-4910
Term Expires: December 31, 2016 Fax: (408) 292-6478

Office of the City Manager

200 East Santa Clara Street, San Jose, CA 95113
Fax: (408) 920-7007

○ City Manager **Norberto Dueñas** .... (408) 535-8111
E-mail: norberto.duenas@sanjoseca.gov
Assistant City Manager **David Sykes** .... (408) 535-8185
E-mail: david.sykes@sanjoseca.gov
Senior Deputy City Manager/Budget Director
Jennifer A. Maguire .... (408) 535-8100
E-mail: jennifer.maguire@sanjoseca.gov
Director of Communications **David Vossbrink** .... (408) 535-8170
E-mail: david.vossbrink@sanjoseca.gov
Education: Stanford AB

★ Elected Official ▲ Appointed by Legislature ▼ Appointed by Governor ▶ Appointed by Board or Commission ● Appointed by Judge
■ Appointed by Mayor △ Appointed by Freeholders ▽ Appointed by Supervisor ▷ Appointed by County Executive ○ Appointed by Council

Budget Office
E-mail: budget.office@ci.san-jose.ca.us
Internet: http://www.sanjoseca.gov/index.aspx?nid=183

Budget Director/Senior Deputy City Manager
Jennifer A. Maguire .... (408) 535-8144
E-mail: jennifer.maguire@sanjoseca.gov

Office of Economic Development
Internet: http://www.do-biz-here.com/

Director **Kim Walesh** .... (408) 535-8177
E-mail: kim.walesh@sanjoseca.gov Fax: (408) 292-6719
Office of Cultural Affairs Special Events Program
Director **Kerry Adams Hapner** .... (408) 793-4344
Fax: (408) 277-3160

Office of Employee Relations
Director **Jennifer Schembri** .... (408) 535-8154
E-mail: jennifer.schembri@sanjoseca.gov

Intergovernmental Relations
Director **Betsy Shotwell** .... (408) 535-8270
E-mail: betsy.shotwell@sanjoseca.gov

Environmental Services Department
200 East Santa Clara Street, Tenth Floor, San Jose, CA 95113
Tel: (408) 535-8550 Fax: (408) 292-6211

Director **Kerrie Romanow** .... (408) 535-8552
Assistant Director **Ashwini Kantak** .... (408) 535-8557
Integrated Waste Management Deputy Director
Jo Zientek .... (408) 975-2511
Public Information Manager **Jennie Loft** .... (408) 535-8554
E-mail: jennie.loft@sanjoseca.gov

Finance Department
200 East Santa Clara Street, 13th Floor, San Jose, CA 95113
Fax: (408) 292-6482

Director **Julia H. Cooper** .... (408) 535-7011
Assistant Director **Derek Hansel** .... (408) 535-7041
Deputy Director of Accounting **Grace Martinez** .... (408) 535-7028
E-mail: grace.martinez@sanjoseca.gov
Purchasing Division Manager **Mark Giovannetti** .... (408) 535-7052
E-mail: mark.giovannetti@sanjoseca.gov
Revenue Management Division Manager
Wendy Sollazzi .... (408) 535-7005
E-mail: wendy.sollazzi@sanjoseca.gov
Deputy Director, Treasury **(Vacant)** .... (408) 535-7045

Fire Department
Building A, 1661 Senter Road, 3rd Floor, San Jose, CA 95112

Fire Chief (Interim) **Curtis Jacobson** .... (408) 794-7000
E-mail: curtis.jacobson@sanjoseca.gov

Housing Department
200 East Santa Clara Street, 12th Floor, San Jose, CA 95113
E-mail: housing@sanjoseca.gov Internet: www.sjhousing.org

Director **Jacqueline "Jacky" Morales-Ferrand** .... (408) 535-3855
Assistant to the Director **Maria Haase** .... (408) 975-4413
E-mail: maria.haase@sanjoseca.gov
Assistant Director (Interim) **Dave Bopf** .... (408) 535-3854
Administrative Assistant **Patricia Amii** .... (408) 535-8233
E-mail: patricia.amii@sanjoseca.gov Fax: (408) 292-6203

Human Resources Department
200 East Santa Clara Street, San Jose, CA 95113
Tel: (408) 535-1285 Fax: (408) 993-0139

Director **Joe Angelo** .... (408) 535-1285
E-mail: joe.angelo@sanjoseca.gov

Information Technology Department
200 East Santa Clara Street, 11th Floor, San Jose, CA 95113
Fax: (408) 292-6034 E-mail: websubmittal@sanjoseca.gov
Internet: www.sanjoseca.gov/itd/

Chief Information Officer **Vijay Sammeta** .... (408) 535-3566
E-mail: vijay.sammeta@sanjoseca.gov
Telecom Manager **George Salcido** .... (408) 793-6886
E-mail: george.salcido@sanjoseca.gov

Department of Parks, Recreation and Neighborhood Services [PRNS]
200 East Santa Clara Street, 9th Floor, San Jose, CA 95113
Tel: (408) 535-3570 Fax: (408) 292-6299
Internet: www.sanjoseca.gov/prns/

Director **Angel Rios, Jr.** .... (408) 535-5553
E-mail: angel.rios@sanjoseca.gov
Assistant Director **Matt Cano** .... (408) 535-3580
Community Services Director **Suzanne Wolff** .... (408) 535-3571
E-mail: suzanne.wolf@sanjoseca.gov
Parks Deputy Director **Steve Hammack** .... (408) 535-3373

Planning, Building and Code Enforcement Department
200 East Santa Clara Street, San Jose, CA 95113
Tel: (408) 535-3555 Fax: (408) 292-6055
Internet: www.sanjoseca.gov/planning/

Director **Harry Freitas** .... (408) 535-7900
E-mail: steve.mcharris@sanjoseca.gov
Planning, Building and Code Enforcement Assistant
Director **Steven McHarris** .... (408) 535-7819
Chief Building Official **Chu Chang** .... (408) 535-7791
E-mail: chu.chang@sanjoseca.gov Fax: (408) 292-6214
Code Enforcement Official **Diane Buchanan** .... (408) 535-7770
E-mail: diane.buchanan@sanjoseca.gov Fax: (408) 294-7832

Police Department [SJPD]
201 W. Mission St., San Jose, CA 95110
Tel: (408) 277-8900 (Non-Emergency Call Center) Fax: (408) 286-0923
Internet: http://www.sjpd.org/

Police Chief **Edgardo "Eddie" Garcia** .... (408) 277-4212
Assistant Chief of Police **Dave Knopf** .... (408) 277-4214
Fax: (408) 453-6131

Bureau of Technical Services Deputy Chief
Jeff Marozick .... (408) 277-5322
Fax: (408) 277-3880

Public Works Department
5th Floor Tower, 200 East Santa Clara Street, San Jose, CA 95113
Fax: (408) 292-6296

Director **Barry Ng** .... (408) 535-8300
Assistant Director **Jon Cicirelli** .... (408) 535-8300
Deputy Director **Joe Garcia** .... (408) 535-1298
E-mail: joe.garcia@sanjoseca.gov
Administrative Officer **Steve McCollum** .... (408) 535-8300
E-mail: steve.mccollum@sanjoseca.gov
Equality Assurance/Labor Compliance Manager
Nina Grayson .... (408) 535-8300
Technology Manager **Matt Loesch** .... (408) 975-7381
E-mail: matt.loesch@sanjoseca.gov

Engineering Services Division
Building A, 1661 Senter Road, First Floor, San Jose, CA 95112
Tel: (408) 975-7444 Fax: (408) 971-4883

Deputy Director **Michael "Mike" Liw** .... (408) 535-6835
E-mail: michael.liw@sanjoseca.gov

Development Services
Division Manager **Michael "Mike" Liw** .... (408) 535-6835
E-mail: michael.liw@sanjoseca.gov
City Geologist **Mike Shimamoto** .... (408) 535-3555

★ Elected Official ▲ Appointed by Legislature ▼ Appointed by Governor ▶ Appointed by Board or Commission ● Appointed by Judge
■ Appointed by Mayor △ Appointed by Freeholders ▽ Appointed by Supervisor ▷ Appointed by County Executive ○ Appointed by Council

Development Services *continued*

Floodplain Manager **(Vacant)** . . . . (408) 535-7803

Transportation and Hydraulics Services Division

Deputy Director **Michael O'Connell** . . . . (408) 975-7333
E-mail: michael.oconnell@sanjoseca.gov

Retirement Services Department

200 East Santa Clara Street, San Jose, CA 95113

Director **Roberto Pena** . . . . (408) 794-1000

Department of Transportation

200 East Santa Clara Street, 8th Floor, San Jose, CA 95113
Fax: (408) 292-6092

Director **Jim Ortbal** . . . . (408) 535-3845
Assistant Director **Kevin O'Connor** . . . . (408) 535-3830

Norman Y. Mineta San Jose International Airport

1701 Airport Bouleverd, Suite B-1130, San Jose, CA 95110
Fax: (408) 441-4591

Aviation Director **Kimberly J. Becker** . . . . (408) 392-3610
Assistant Director of Aviation **John Aitken** . . . . (408) 392-3600
Airport Operations Deputy Director **Bob Lockhart** . . . . . . (408) 392-3600
Facilities and Engineering Deputy Director
Patrick Tonna . . . . (408) 392-3600
E-mail: ptonna@sjc.org
Finance and Administration Deputy Director **Kim Hawk** . . (408) 392-3600
E-mail: khawk@sjc.org
San Jose Police Department, Airport Division
Alex Nguyen . . . . (408) 392-3600
Airport Technology Services Division Manager **(Vacant)** . . (408) 392-3600
Public Information Manager **Rosemary Barnes** . . . . (408) 392-3608
Marketing and Customer Services Director **Vicki L. Day** . . (408) 392-3600
Government and Legislative Affairs Director
James E. Webb . . . . (408) 392-3600
E-mail: jwebb@sjc.org

San Jose Convention and Visitors Bureau

408 Almaden Boulevard, San Jose, CA 95110-2715
Tel: (408) 295-9600 Fax: (408) 295-3937

Chief Executive Officer **Karolyn Kirchgesler** . . . . (408) 792-4107
Director of Sales **Mark McMinn** . . . . (408) 792-4521
Fax: (408) 277-3535

San Jose Public Library [SJPL]

150 East San Fernando Street, San Jose, CA 95112-3580
Fax: (408) 808-2133 Internet: http://www.sjlibrary.org

Library Director **Jill Bourne** . . . . (408) 808-2150
Note: Until Summer 2016
E-mail: jill.bourne@sjlibrary.org
Education: NYU BA; U Washington MSLIS
Assistant Library Director **Heidi Dolamore** . . . . (408) 808-2151
E-mail: heidi.dolamore@sjlibrary.org
Administrative Officer **Neil Rufino** . . . . (408) 808-2152
E-mail: neil.rufino@sjlibrary.org

Office of the City Attorney

200 East Santa Clara Street, 16th Floor, San Jose, CA 95113
Fax: (408) 998-3131

○ City Attorney **Richard Doyle** . . . . (408) 535-1950
E-mail: richard.doyle@sanjoseca.gov
Assistant City Attorney **Ed Moran** . . . . (408) 535-1900
E-mail: ed.moran@sanjoseca.gov
Assistant City Attorney **Nora Frimann** . . . . (408) 535-1900
E-mail: nora.frimann@sanjoseca.gov

Office of the City Auditor

200 East Santa Clara Street, San Jose, CA 95113
Fax: (408) 292-6071

○ City Auditor **Sharon Winslow Erickson** . . . . (408) 535-1250
E-mail: sharon.erickson@sanjoseca.gov

Office of the City Clerk

200 East Santa Clara Street, Tower 14th Floor, San Jose, CA 95113
Fax: (408) 292-6207

○ City Clerk **Toni Taber** . . . . (408) 535-1260
E-mail: city.clerk@sanjoseca.gov
Assistant City Clerk **Christina Guttierez** . . . . (408) 535-1260

Office of the Independent Police Auditor

75 East Santa Clara Street, Suite 93, San Jose, CA 95113
Fax: (408) 977-1053

Independent Police Auditor **Walter Katz** . . . . (408) 794-6226

Redevelopment Agency

200 East Santa Clara Street, 14th Floor Tower, San Jose, CA 95113
Internet: www.sjredevelopment.org/

■ Managing Director **Richard Keit** . . . . (408) 795-1849
E-mail: richard.keit@sanjoseca.gov
Chief Financial Officer **Abe Andrade** . . . . (408) 795-1821

City of Santa Ana, California

20 Civic Center Plaza, Santa Ana, CA 92701
P.O. Box 1988, Santa Ana, CA 92702
Tel: (714) 647-5400 (Information) Internet: www.santa-ana.org

County: Orange **Election Type:** Nonpartisan **Population:** 335,400 (2015)

Office of the Mayor and City Council

20 Civic Center Plaza, Santa Ana, CA 92701
P.O. Box 1988, Santa Ana, CA 92702
Fax: (714) 647-6954 E-mail: council@santa-ana.org

★ Mayor **Miguel A. Pulido** . . . . (714) 647-6900
Began Service: November 1994
Term Expires: December 11, 2018
E-mail: mpulido@santa-ana.org
Education: Cal State (Fullerton) BA
Career: Mayor Pro Tem, Office of the Mayor and City Council, City of Santa Ana, California; Member, Board of Directors, Orange County Water District (1998-1999)
Executive Assistant **Becky Magallon** . . . . (714) 647-6900
E-mail: bmagallon@santa-ana.org
★ Council Member **Vincent Sarmiento** (Ward 1) . . . . (714) 647-6900
Term Expires: December 11, 2016
E-mail: vsarmiento@santa-ana.org
★ Council Member **Michele Martinez** (Ward 2) . . . . (714) 647-6900
Term Expires: December 11, 2018
E-mail: mimartinez@santa-ana.org
★ Council Member **Angelica Amezcua** (Ward 3) . . . . (714) 647-6900
Term Expires: December 11, 2016
E-mail: aamezcua@santa-ana.org
★ Council Member **David Benavides** (Ward 4) . . . . (714) 647-6900
Term Expires: December 11, 2018
E-mail: dbenavides@santa-ana.org
★ Council Member **Roman Reyna** (Ward 5) . . . . (714) 647-6900
Term Expires: December 11, 2016
E-mail: rreyna@santa-ana.org
★ Council Member **Sal Tinajero** (Ward 6) . . . . (714) 647-6900
Term Expires: December 11, 2018
E-mail: stinajero@santa-ana.org

Office of the City Attorney
20 Civic Center Plaza, Santa Ana, CA 92701-4058
P.O. Box 1988, Santa Ana, CA 92702
Fax: (714) 647-6515 Internet: www.ci.santa-ana.ca.us/cao/default.asp

○ City Attorney **Sonia R. Carvalho** .... (714) 647-5201
E-mail: scarvalho@santa-ana.org
Education: UC Irvine 1989 BA; UCLA 1992 JD

Chief Assistant City Attorney **Jose Sandoval** .... (714) 647-5213

Office of the Clerk of the Council
20 Civic Center Plaza, Santa Ana, CA 92701
P.O. Box 1988 (M-30), Santa Ana, CA 92702
Fax: (714) 647-6956 Internet: www.santa-ana.org/coc/

○ Clerk of the Council **Maria D. Huizar** .... (714) 647-6520
E-mail: mhuizar@santa-ana.org

Office of the City Manager
20 Civic Center Plaza, Santa Ana, CA 92701
P.O. Box 1988, Santa Ana, CA 92702
Fax: (714) 647-6954 Internet: www.ci.santa-ana.ca.us/cm/

○ City Manager **David Cavazos** .... (714) 647-5200
E-mail: dcavazos@santa-ana.org
Education: Western Illinois 1983 BS; Carnegie Mellon 1987 MA

Assistant City Manager **(Vacant)** .... (714) 647-5200

Public Information Officer **Alma Flores** .... (714) 647-5200
E-mail: aflores@santa-ana.org Fax: (714) 647-6954

Community Development Agency
20 Civic Center Plaza, M25, Santa Ana, CA 92701
P.O. Box 1988 (M-25), Santa Ana, CA 92702
Tel: (714) 647-5360 Fax: (714) 647-6549
Internet: www.santa-ana.org/cda/

Executive Director **Kelly Reenders** .... (714) 647-5360
E-mail: kreenders@santa-ana.org

Economic Development Manager **Marc Morley** .... (714) 647-5360

Housing Manager **Sidney Stone** .... (714) 667-2200

Finance and Management Services Agency
20 Civic Center Plaza, Santa Ana, CA 92701
P.O. Box 1988, Santa Ana, CA 92702
Tel: (714) 647-5400 Fax: (714) 647-5414
Internet: www.ci.santa-ana.ca.us/finance/

Executive Director **Francisco Gutierrez** .... (714) 647-5420

Assistant Director of Finance **Sergio Vidal** .... (714) 647-5295

Fleet Services Manager (Acting) **John Aguilar** .... (714) 647-5008

Information Services Manager **Jim Lentz** .... (714) 647-6909

Treasury Manager **Will Holt** .... (714) 647-5456

Facilities Maintenance Superintendent **John Aguilar** .... (714) 647-5008
E-mail: jaguilar@santa-ana.org

Accounting Manager **Bich Ta** .... (714) 647-5434

Parks, Recreation and Community Services Agency
26 Civic Center Plaza, Santa Ana, CA 92701
Tel: (714) 571-4200 Fax: (714) 571-4211
Internet: www.ci.santa-ana.ca.us/parks/

Executive Director **Gerardo Mouet** .... (714) 571-4204
E-mail: gmouet@santa-ana.org

Administrative Services Manager **Ron Ono** .... (714) 571-4220
E-mail: rono@santa-ana.org

Santa Ana Zoo Manager **Kent Yamaguchi** .... (714) 647-6522
1801 E. Chestnut Ave., Santa Ana, CA 92701

Senior Park Maintenance Supervisor **Mike Lopez** .... (714) 647-3324

Community Services Manager **Jenny Jurado** .... (714) 571-4228
E-mail: jjurado@santa-ana.org

Santa Ana Public Library
26 Civic Center Plaza, Santa Ana, CA 92701
P.O. Box 1988/M-75, Santa Ana, CA 92702
Tel: (714) 647-5250 Internet: www.ci.santa-ana.ca.us/library/

Library Operations Manager **Heather Folmar** .... (714) 647-5296
E-mail: hfolmar@santa-ana.org

Personnel Services Agency
20 Civic Center Plaza, Santa Ana, CA 92702
P.O. Box 1988, Santa Ana, CA 92702
Fax: (714) 647-6930 Internet: www.ci.santa-ana.ca.us/personnel/

Executive Director **Ed Raya** .... (714) 647-5340
E-mail: eraya@santa-ana.org

Executive Secretary **Cindi Sangenito** .... (714) 647-5374
E-mail: csangenito@santa-ana.org

Planning and Building Agency [PBA]
Ross Annex, 20 Civic Center Plaza, Santa Ana, CA 92701
Fax: (714) 973-1461 Internet: www.santa-ana.org/pba

Planning and Building Agency Executive Director
Hassan Haghani .... (714) 667-2706
Education: UCLA BA, MAUP

Planning Manager **Candida Neal** .... (714) 647-2728

Principal Planner **Vince Fregoso** .... (714) 647-2713

Police Department
60 Civic Center Plaza, Santa Ana, CA 92702
P.O. Box 1981, Santa Ana, CA 92702
Tel: (714) 245-8665 Fax: (714) 245-8007
Internet: www.ci.santa-ana.ca.us/pd/

Police Chief **Carlos Rojas** .... (714) 245-8003
Education: Cal State (Long Beach) BA; Chapman MA

Public Works Agency
20 Civic Center Plaza, M21, Santa Ana, CA 92701
P.O. Box 1988, M21, Santa Ana, CA 92702
Tel: (714) 647-5690 Fax: (714) 647-5622
Internet: http://www.ci.santa-ana.ca.us/pwa/

Executive Director **Fred Mousavipour** .... (714) 647-5654

City Engineer **William Galvez** .... (714) 647-5659

Administrative Services Manager **Margaret Mercer** .... (714) 647-5050
E-mail: mmercer@santa-ana.org

Maintenance Manager **Pedro Guillen** .... (714) 647-3301

Water Resources Manager **Nabil Saba** .... (714) 647-3317

Transportation and Traffic Engineering Division
Principal Engineer **Taig Higgins** .... (714) 647-5645
E-mail: thiggins@santa-ana.org Fax: (714) 647-5616

City of Santa Clara, California
City Hall, 1500 Warburton Avenue, Santa Clara, CA 95050
Internet: http://santaclaraca.gov/

County: Santa Clara **Election Type:** Nonpartisan **Year Incorporated:** July 1852 **Population:** 126,215 (2015)

Office of the Mayor and City Council
City Hall, 1500 Warburton Avenue, Santa Clara, CA 95050
Fax: (408) 241-6771 E-mail: mayorandcouncil@santaclaraca.gov

★ Mayor **Lisa M. Gillmor** .... (408) 615-2250
Began Service: February 2016 Fax: (408) 241-6771
Term Expires: December 2018
E-mail: mayorandcouncil@santaclaraca.gov
Executive Assistant **Jashma Kadam** .... (408) 615-2250

★ Vice Mayor **Teresa O'Neill** (Seat 7) .... (408) 615-2250
Term Expires: December 2016
E-mail: mayorandcouncil@santaclaraca.gov

★ Elected Official ▲ Appointed by Legislature ▼ Appointed by Governor ► Appointed by Board or Commission ● Appointed by Judge
■ Appointed by Mayor △ Appointed by Freeholders ▽ Appointed by Supervisor ▷ Appointed by County Executive ○ Appointed by Council

Office of the Mayor and City Council *continued*

★ Council Member **Patrick Kolstad** (Seat 2) . . . . (408) 615-2250
Term Expires: December 2018
E-mail: mayorandcouncil@santaclaraca.gov

★ Council Member **Debi Davis** (Seat 3) . . . . (408) 615-2250
Term Expires: December 2016
E-mail: mayorandcouncil@santaclaraca.gov

★ Council Member **Jerry Marsalli** (Seat 4) . . . . (408) 615-2250
Term Expires: December 2016
E-mail: mayorandcouncil@santaclaraca.gov

★ Council Member **Dominic J. Caserta** (Seat 5) . . . . (408) 615-2250
Term Expires: December 2018

★ Council Member **Kathy Watanabe** (Seat 6) . . . . (408) 615-2250
Term Expires: December 2016
E-mail: mayorandcouncil@santaclaraca.gov

Office of the City Manager

City Hall, 1500 Warburton Ave., Santa Clara, CA 95050
Fax: (408) 241-6771 E-mail: manager@santaclaraca.gov
Internet: http://santaclaraca.gov/index.aspx?page=117

City Manager (Acting) **Rajeev Batra** . . . . (408) 615-2210
E-mail: Manager@santaclaraca.gov

Assistant City Manager/Chief Operating Officer of Utilities **Alan Kurotori** . . . . (408) 615-6600
E-mail: akurotori@santaclaraca.gov

Assistant City Manager **Sheila Tucker** . . . . (408) 615-2210
E-mail: stucker@santaclaraca.gov

Assistant City Manager/Economic Development Officer **Ruth Shikada** . . . . (408) 615-2210
E-mail: rshikada@santaclaraca.gov

Office of the City Clerk/City Auditor

City Hall, 1500 Warburton Ave., Santa Clara, CA 95050
E-mail: clerk@santaclaraca.gov
Internet: http://santaclaraca.gov/index.aspx?page=116

★ City Clerk/City Auditor **Rod Diridon, Jr.** . . . . (408) 615-2220
Term Expires: December 20, 2016
E-mail: clerk@santaclaraca.gov
Education: San José State BA

Assistant City Clerk (Acting) **Bernadette DeSousa** . . . . . (408) 615-2220
E-mail: bdesousa@santaclaraca.gov

Office of the City Attorney

City Hall, 1500 Warburton Ave., Santa Clara, CA 95050
Internet: http://santaclaraca.gov/index.aspx?page=115

○ City Attorney **Richard E. "Ren" Nosky, Jr.** . . . . (408) 615-2230
E-mail: cityattorney@santaclaraca.gov Fax: (408) 249-7846

Electric Utilities-Silicon Valley Power

City Hall, 1500 Warburton Ave., Santa Clara, CA 95050
E-mail: siliconvalleypower@santaclaraca.gov
Internet: http://www.siliconvalleypower.com/

Director **John C. Roukema** . . . . (408) 616-6600
Fax: (408) 249-0217

Finance Department

City Hall, 1500 Warburton Ave., Santa Clara, CA 95050
Fax: (408) 243-8687 E-mail: finance@santaclaraca.gov
Internet: http://santaclaraca.gov/index.aspx?page=118

Director of Finance/Assistant City Manager **Gary Ameling** . . . . (408) 615-2340
E-mail: gameling@santaclaraca.gov Fax: (408) 243-8687

Assistant Director **Marcelo Penha** . . . . (408) 615-2340
Fax: (408) 243-8687

Fire Department

City Hall, 1500 Warburton Ave., Santa Clara, CA 95050
Tel: (408) 615-4900 Fax: (408) 246-8652 E-mail: fire@santaclaraca.gov
Internet: http://santaclaraca.gov/index.aspx?page=119

Fire Chief **William Kelly** . . . . (408) 615-4900
E-mail: wkelly@santaclaraca.gov

Deputy Fire Chief **John Madden** . . . . (408) 615-4900
E-mail: jmadden@santaclaraca.gov Fax: (408) 296-1748

Human Resources Department

City Hall, 1500 Warburton Ave., Santa Clara, CA 95050
E-mail: humanresources@santaclaraca.gov
Internet: http://santaclaraca.gov/index.aspx?page=120

Director **Elizabeth Brown** . . . . (408) 615-2080
E-mail: lizbrown@santaclaraca.gov Fax: (408) 985-0667

Human Resources Division Manager/Training and Safety Officer **Greg Harris** . . . . (408) 615-2080
E-mail: gharris@santaclaraca.gov Fax: (408) 985-0667

Information Technology Department

City Hall, 1500 Warburton Ave., Santa Clara, CA 95050
Tel: (408) 615-2022 Fax: (408) 241-3479
E-mail: itdepartment@santaclaraca.gov
Internet: http://santaclaraca.gov/index.aspx?page=121

Director **Gaurav Garg** . . . . (408) 615-2022
E-mail: ggarg@santaclaraca.gov

Web and Digital Media Manager **Laura Lee** . . . . (408) 615-2022
E-mail: llee@santaclaraca.gov

Parks and Recreation Department

City Hall, 1500 Warburton Ave., Santa Clara, CA 95050
E-mail: parksandrecreation@santaclaraca.gov
Internet: http://santaclaraca.gov/index.aspx?page=123

Director **James Teixeira** . . . . (408) 615-2260
Fax: (408) 260-9719

Planning and Inspection Department

City Hall, 1500 Warburton Ave., Santa Clara, CA 95050
E-mail: planning@santaclaraca.gov
E-mail: buildinginspection@santaclaraca.gov

Director **(Vacant)** . . . . (408) 615-2450
Fax: (408) 247-9857

Police Department

601 El Camino Real, Santa Clara, CA 95050
Fax: (408) 248-0276 E-mail: police@santaclaraca.gov
Internet: www.scpd.org

★ Chief of Police **Michael Sellers** . . . . (408) 615-4700
Term Expires: November 2016 Fax: (408) 261-9165
E-mail: police@santaclaraca.gov

Public Works Department

City Hall, 1500 Warburton Ave., Santa Clara, CA 95050
E-mail: engineering@santaclaraca.gov
Internet: http://santaclaraca.gov/index.aspx?page=126

Director of Public Works/City Engineer **Rajeev Batra** . . . . (408) 615-3000
E-mail: rbatra@santaclaraca.gov Fax: (408) 985-7936

Santa Clara City Library

Central Park Library, 2635 Homestead Road, Santa Clara, CA 95051
E-mail: library@santaclaraca.gov
Internet: http://library.santaclaraca.gov/index.aspx?page=8

City Librarian **Hilary Keith** . . . . (408) 615-2930
E-mail: library@santaclaraca.gov Fax: (408) 247-9657

★ Elected Official ▲ Appointed by Legislature ▼ Appointed by Governor ► Appointed by Board or Commission ● Appointed by Judge
■ Appointed by Mayor △ Appointed by Freeholders ▽ Appointed by Supervisor ▷ Appointed by County Executive ○ Appointed by Council

Water and Sewer Utilities
City Hall, 1500 Warburton Ave., Santa Clara, CA 95050
E-mail: sewer@santaclaraca.gov E-mail: water@santaclaraca.gov
Internet: http://santaclaraca.gov/index.aspx?page=257

Director of Water and Sewer Utilities
Christopher L. de Groot . . . . (408) 615-2000
Fax: (408) 247-0784

City of Santa Clarita, California

City Hall, 23920 Valencia Blvd., Santa Clarita, CA 91355-2196
Internet: www.santa-clarita.com

County: Los Angeles **Election Type:** Nonpartisan **Year Incorporated:** 1987 **Population:** 182,371 (2015)

Office of the Mayor and City Council
City Hall, 23920 Valencia Boulevard, Suite 300,
Santa Clarita, CA 91355-2196
Tel: (661) 259-2489 Fax: (661) 259-8125

★Mayor **Bob Kellar** . . . . (661) 255-4395
Term Expires: November 2016
E-mail: bkellar@santa-clarita.com

★Mayor Pro Tem **Dante Acosta** . . . . (661) 255-4395
Term Expires: November 2018
E-mail: dacosta@santa-clarita.com

★Council Member **TimBen Boydston** . . . . (661) 255-4395
Term Expires: November 2016
E-mail: tboydston@santa-clarita.com
Education: Cal State (Northridge) BA

★Council Member **Marsha McLean** . . . . (661) 255-4395
Term Expires: November 2018
E-mail: mmclean@santa-clarita.com

★Council Member **Laurene Weste** . . . . (661) 255-4395
Term Expires: November 2018
E-mail: lweste@santa-clarita.com

Office of the City Manager
City Hall, 23920 Valencia Boulevard, Suite 300,
Santa Clarita, CA 91355-2196

City Manager **Ken Striplin** . . . . (661) 255-4905
E-mail: kstriplin@santa-clarita.com
Education: Cal State (Northridge) 1995 BA, MPA; Pepperdine PhD

Assistant City Manager and Personnel Officer
Frank Oviedo . . . . (661) 255-4901
E-mail: foviedo@santa-clarita.com

Office of the City Attorney
City Hall, 23920 Valencia Blvd., Santa Clarita, CA 91355-2196

City Attorney **Joseph M. Montes** . . . . (661) 255-4315
E-mail: jmontes@bwslaw.com
Education: Santa Clara U 1990 BA; Loyola Marymount 1994 JD

Office of the City Clerk
City Hall, 23920 Valencia Boulevard, Suite 120,
Santa Clarita, CA 91355-2196

City Clerk **Kevin Tonoian** . . . . (661) 255-4391
E-mail: ktonoian@santa-clarita.com

Administrative Services Department
City Hall, 23920 Valencia Boulevard, Suite 295,
Santa Clarita, CA 91355-2196

Deputy City Manager and Director of Administrative Services **Darren Hernández** . . . . (661) 255-4922
E-mail: dhernandez@santa-clarita.com

Community Development Department
City Hall, 23920 Valencia Boulevard, Suite 302,
Santa Clarita, CA 91355-2196

Director **Tom Cole** . . . . (661) 255-4367
E-mail: tcole@santa-clarita.com

Communications Division
City Hall, 23920 Valencia Boulevard, Suite 300,
Santa Clarita, CA 91355-2196
Fax: (661) 259-8125

Communications Manager **Gail Morgan** . . . . (661) 255-4314

Parks, Recreation, and Community Services Department
City Hall, 23920 Valencia Boulevard, Suite 120,
Santa Clarita, CA 91355-2196

Director **Rick Gould** . . . . (661) 255-4945
E-mail: rgould@santa-clarita.com

Public Works Department
City Hall, 23920 Valencia Blvd., Suite 225, Santa Clarita, CA 91355-2196

Director **Robert Newman** . . . . (661) 255-4345
E-mail: rnewman@santa-clarita.com

City of Santa Fe, New Mexico

200 Lincoln, Santa Fe, NM 87501
P.O. Box 909, Santa Fe, NM 87504-0909
Internet: www.santafenm.gov

County: Santa Fe **Election Type:** Nonpartisan **Population:** 84,099 (2015)

Office of the Mayor and City Council
P.O. Box 909, Santa Fe, NM 87504-0909
Fax: (505) 955-6695 Internet: www.santafenm.gov/index.aspx?nid=72

★Mayor **Javier M. Gonzales** . . . . (505) 955-6590
Began Service: March 2014 Fax: (505) 955-6695
Term Expires: March 2018
E-mail: jmgonzales@santafenm.gov
Date of Birth: 1966
Education: New Mexico State 1989 BA
Executive Assistant **Xochitl Campos Biggs** . . . . (505) 955-6590
Fax: (505) 955-6695

★Mayor Pro Tem **Peter Ives** (District 2) . . . . (505) 955-6818
Term Expires: March 2020

★Council Member **Signe Lidell** (District 1) . . . . (505) 955-6812
Term Expires: March 2018
E-mail: silindell@santafenm.gov

★Council Member **Renee Villarreal** (District 1) . . . . (505) 955-2345
Term Expires: March 2020

★Council Member **Joseph Maestas** (District 2) . . . . (505) 955-6815
Term Expires: March 2018
E-mail: jmaestas@santafenm.gov
Education: New Mexico 1983 BSCE; Arizona State 1983 MSCE

★Council Member **Carmichael Dominguez** (District 3) . . . (505) 955-6814
Term Expires: March 2018
E-mail: cadominguez@santafenm.gov

★Council Member **Chris Rivera** (District 3) . . . . (505) 955-6818
Term Expires: March 2020

★Council Member **Mike Harris** (District 4) . . . . (505) 955-6818
Term Expires: March 2020

★Council Member **Ronald Trujillo** (District 4) . . . . (505) 955-6811
Term Expires: March 2018
E-mail: rstrujillo@santafenm.gov

★Elected Official ▲Appointed by Legislature ▼Appointed by Governor ▶Appointed by Board or Commission ●Appointed by Judge
■Appointed by Mayor △Appointed by Freeholders ▽Appointed by Supervisor ▷Appointed by County Executive ○Appointed by Council

Office of the City Manager

P.O. Box 909, Santa Fe, NM 87504-0909
Fax: (505) 955-6683 Tel: (505) 955-6848

■ City Manager **Brian Snyder** .... (505) 955-6848
E-mail: bksnyder@santafenm.gov
Education: Drexel BSCE

Public Information Multimedia Administrator
Matt Ross .... (505) 955-6045
E-mail: mross@santafenm.gov

Executive Administrative Assistant **Celeste Valentine** .... (505) 955-6848
E-mail: cmvalentine@santafenm.gov

Office of the City Attorney

P.O. Box 909, Santa Fe, NM 87504-0909
Fax: (505) 955-6748

City Attorney (Interim) **Kelley Brennan** .... (505) 955-6511
E-mail: kabrennan@santafenm.gov

Office of the City Clerk

P.O. Box 909, Santa Fe, NM 87504-0909
Fax: (505) 955-6910

City Clerk **Yolanda Vigil** .... (505) 955-6520
E-mail: yyvigil@santafenm.gov

Community Services Department

P.O. Box 909, Santa Fe, NM 87504-0909
Fax: (505) 955-6671

Director **Issac Pino** .... (505) 955-6568
E-mail: ijpino@santafenm.gov

Constituent Services

P.O. Box 909, Santa Fe, NM 87504-0909
Tel: (505) 955-6949 Fax: (505) 955-6683

Division Director **Sevastian E. Gurule** .... (505) 955-6047

Finance Division

P.O. Box 909, Santa Fe, NM 87504-0909
Fax: (505) 955-6745

Director **Oscar S. Rodriguez** .... (505) 955-6531
Education: Harvard BA; MIT MA

Fire Department

P.O. Box 909, Santa Fe, NM 87504-0909
Fax: (505) 955-3115

Fire Chief **Erik J. Litzenberg** .... (505) 955-3110
E-mail: ejlitzenberg@santafenm.gov

Fire Marshal **Rey Gonzales** .... (505) 955-3316
E-mail: rdgonzales@santafenm.gov Fax: (505) 955-3315

Human Resources Department

P.O. Box 909, Santa Fe, NM 87504-0909
Fax: (505) 955-6810

Director **Lynette Trujillo** .... (505) 955-6691
E-mail: latrujillo@santafenm.gov

Information Technology and Telecommunications Division

P.O. Box 909, Santa Fe, NM 87504

Director **Renee Martinez** .... (505) 955-5580
E-mail: rjmartinez@santafenm.gov

Library

145 Washington St., Santa Fe, NM 87501
P.O. Box 909, Santa Fe, NM 87504-0909
Fax: (505) 955-6676 Internet: http://www.santafelibrary.org/

Director **Pat Hodapp** .... (505) 955-6780
E-mail: library@santafenm.gov

Land Use Department

P.O. Box 909, Santa Fe, NM 87504-0909
Fax: (505) 955-6829

Land Use Director **Lisa Martinez** .... (505) 955-6925

Police Department

P.O. Box 909, Santa Fe, NM 87504-0909
Fax: (505) 955-5052

Chief of Police (Interim) **Patrick Gallagher** .... (505) 955-5010

Deputy Chief of Police **Mario Salbidrez** .... (505) 955-5267

Public Utilities Department

P.O. Box 909, Santa Fe, NM 87504-0909
Fax: (505) 955-5645 Internet: http://www.santafenm.gov/public_utilities

Director (Acting) **Nick Schiavo** .... (505) 955-5640

Public Works Department

P.O. Box 909, Santa Fe, NM 87504-0909
Fax: (505) 955-6627

Director **Issac Pino** .... (505) 955-6621

Parks, Open Spaces and Trails

P.O. Box 909, Santa Fe, NM 87504-0909
Fax: (505) 955-2111

Parks Division Director **Rob Carter** .... (505) 955-5921

Recreation Division

P.O. Box 909, Santa Fe, NM 87504-0909
Fax: (505) 955-2525

Director **Rob Carter** .... (505) 955-5921

Traffic Engineering/Operations

P.O. Box 909, Santa Fe, NM 87504-0909
Fax: (505) 955-6476

Director **John Romero** .... (505) 955-6638
E-mail: jjromero1@ci.santa-fe.nm.us

Aviation Division/Santa Fe Municipal Airport

P.O. Box 909, Santa Fe, NM 87504-0909
Fax: (505) 955-2905

Director/Airport Manager **Cam Humphres** .... (505) 955-2900

Parking Division

P.O. Box 909, Santa Fe, NM 87504-0909
Fax: (505) 955-6430

Director **Noel P. Correia** .... (505) 955-6611

Storm Water Management

P.O. Box 909, Santa Fe, NM 87504-0909
Fax: (505) 955-3135

Director (Interim) **Bryan Romero** .... (505) 955-4650

Streets and Drainage Maintenance Division

Fax: (505) 955-2413

Director **David R. Catanach** .... (505) 955-3000
E-mail: drcatanach@santafenm.gov

★ Elected Official ▲ Appointed by Legislature ▼ Appointed by Governor ▶ Appointed by Board or Commission ● Appointed by Judge
■ Appointed by Mayor △ Appointed by Freeholders ▽ Appointed by Supervisor ▷ Appointed by County Executive ○ Appointed by Council

Santa Fe Convention and Visitors Bureau
201 West Marcy Street, Santa Fe, NM 87504-0909
P.O. Box 909, Santa Fe, NM 87504
Fax: (505) 955-6623 E-mail: sccenter@santafe.org
Internet: www.santafe.org

Executive Director **Randy Randall** .... (505) 955-6209

Santa Fe Public Schools
610 Alta Vista St., Santa Fe, NM 87505
Fax: (505) 995-3300 Internet: www.sfps.info

Superintendent of Schools **Joel Boyd** .... (505) 467-2003

★President **Linda M. Trujillo** (District 4) .... (505) 795-4324
Term Expires: March 1, 2019
E-mail: lindat@sfps.info
Education: Seattle JD

★Vice President **Lorraine Price** (District 5) .... (505) 470-8247
Term Expires: March 1, 2017
E-mail: lprice@sfps.info

★School Board Member **Steven J. Carrillo** (District 1) .... (505) 699-7478
Term Expires: March 1, 2019
E-mail: scarrillo@sfps.info

★School Board Member **Maureen Cashmon** (District 2) .. (505) 690-8937
Term Expires: March 1, 2019

★School Board Member **Susan Duncan** (District 3) ...... (505) 470-8863
Term Expires: March 1, 2017
E-mail: sduncan@sfps.info

City of Santa Rosa, California

City Hall, 100 Santa Rosa Ave., Santa Rosa, CA 95404-4906
Internet: http://www.srcity.org

County: Sonoma **Election Type:** Nonpartisan **Year Incorporated:** 1868
Population: 174,972 (2015)

Office of the Mayor and City Council
City Hall, 100 Santa Rosa Ave., Room 10, Santa Rosa, CA 95404
Fax: (707) 543-3030

★Mayor **John Sawyer** .... (707) 543-3010
Began Service: December 2, 2014
Term Expires: December 2018
E-mail: jsawyer@srcity.org

★Vice Mayor **Tom Schwedhelm** .... (707) 543-3010
Term Expires: December 2018
E-mail: tschwedhelm@srcity.org

★Council Member **Erin Carlstrom** .... (707) 543-3010
Term Expires: December 2016
E-mail: ecarlstrom@srcity.org

★Council Member **Julie Combs** .... (707) 543-3010
Term Expires: December 2016
E-mail: jcombs@srcity.org

★Council Member **Chris Coursey** .... (707) 543-3010
Term Expires: December 2018
E-mail: ccoursey@srcity.org

★Council Member **Ernesto Olivares** .... (707) 543-3010
Term Expires: December 2016
E-mail: eolivares@srcity.org

★Council Member **Gary Wysocky** .... (707) 543-3010
Term Expires: December 2016
E-mail: gwysocky@srcity.org

Office of the City Manager
City Hall, 100 Santa Rosa Avenue, Room 10, Santa Rosa, CA 95404
Fax: (707) 543-3030

○City Manager **Sean McGlynn** .... (707) 543-3010
E-mail: smcglynn@srcity.org

Deputy City Manager **Gloria Hurtado** .... (707) 543-3010
E-mail: ghurtado@srcity.org

Office of the City Manager *continued*

Assistant City Manager **Chuck Regalia** .... (707) 543-3010
E-mail: cregalia@srcity.org

Chief Technology Officer **Eric McHenry** .... (707) 543-3097
E-mail: emchenry@srcity.org
Education: MIT BSEE

Office of the City Attorney
City Hall, 100 Santa Rosa Avenue, Room 8, Santa Rosa, CA 95404
Fax: (707) 543-3055

City Attorney **Caroline Fowler** .... (707) 543-3040
E-mail: cfowler@srcity.org

Office of the City Clerk
City Hall, 100 Santa Rosa Avenue, Room 10, Santa Rosa, CA 95404
Fax: (707) 543-3030

City Clerk (Interim) **Stephanie Williams** .... (707) 543-3015
E-mail: swilliams@srcity.org

Community Development Department
City Hall, 100 Santa Rosa Avenue, Room 3, Santa Rosa, CA 95404
E-mail: askcd@srcity.org Fax: (707) 543-3269

Director (Acting) **David Guhin** .... (707) 543-3189
E-mail: dguhin@srcity.org

Economic Development and Housing Department
City Hall Annex, 90 Santa Rosa Ave., Santa Rosa, CA 95404
Fax: (707) 543-3317

Director **David Gouin** .... (707) 543-3300
E-mail: dgouin@srcity.org

Finance Department
City Hall Annex, 90 Santa Rosa Ave., Santa Rosa, CA 95404

Chief Financial Officer **Deborah Lauchner** .... (707) 543-3089
E-mail: dlauchner@srcity.org Fax: (707) 543-3139

Fire Department
2373 Circadian Way, Santa Rosa, CA 95407
Tel: (707) 543-3500 Fax: (707) 543-3520 E-mail: srfd@srcity.org

Fire Chief **Anthony "Tony" Gossner** .... (707) 543-3531
E-mail: agossner@srcity.org

Deputy Chief (Acting) **Bill Shubin** .... (707) 543-3531
E-mail: bshubin@santarosafd.com

Training Division Chief **(Vacant)** .... (707) 543-3533

Fire Marshal (Acting) **Mark Pedroia** .... (707) 543-3500
E-mail: mpedroia@santarosafd.com

Human Resources Department
100 Santa Rosa Avenue, Room 1, Santa Rosa, CA 95404
Fax: (707) 543-3064

Director (Interim) **Rhonda McKinnon** .... (707) 543-3070
E-mail: rmckinnon@srcity.org

Police Department
955 Sonoma Ave., Santa Rosa, CA 95404
Internet: http://srcity.org

Police Chief **Robert "Hank" Schreeder** .... (707) 543-3600
Fax: (707) 543-3557

Recreation, Parks and Community Services
55 Stony Point Road, Santa Rosa, CA 95401
Fax: (707) 543-3288 Internet: http://srcity.org/rp

Director **Nanette Smejkal** .... (707) 543-3292

★Elected Official ▲Appointed by Legislature ▼Appointed by Governor ▶Appointed by Board or Commission ●Appointed by Judge
■Appointed by Mayor △Appointed by Freeholders ▽Appointed by Supervisor ▷Appointed by County Executive ○Appointed by Council

Santa Rosa City Schools
211 Ridgway Avenue, Santa Rosa, CA 95401
Fax: (707) 528-5440

Superintendent (Interim) **Diann Kitamura** .... (707) 528-5181

Transportation and Public Works Department
Municipal Services Center South, 69 Stony Circle, Santa Rosa, CA 95401
Fax: (707) 543-3801

Director of Transportation and Public Works
Jason Nutt .... (707) 543-3800

Water Department
Municipal Services Center, 69 Stony Circle, Santa Rosa, CA 95401
Fax: (707) 543-3936

Director **David Guhin** .... (707) 543-4299

City of Savannah, Georgia
2 E. Bay, Savannah, GA 31401
P.O. Box 1027, Savannah, GA 31402
Tel: (912) 651-6565 (Information) Internet: www.savannahga.gov

County: Chatham **Election Type:** Nonpartisan **Population:** 145,674 (2015)

Office of the Mayor and City Council
P.O. Box 1027, Savannah, GA 31402
Tel: (912) 651-6444 Fax: (912) 651-6805

★Mayor **Eddie DeLoach** .... (912) 651-6444
Began Service: January 5, 2016
Term Expires: December 31, 2019
Chief of Staff **Martin Sullivan** .... (912) 651-6444

★Mayor Pro Tem **Van R. Johnson II** (District 1) .... (912) 236-9494
Term Expires: December 31, 2019 Fax: (912) 238-9596
E-mail: aldermanjohnson1@aol.com
Education: Savannah State 1990 BBA, 1992 MPA; Georgia Southern 1992 MPA

★Chairman **Tony Thomas** (District 6) .... (912) 349-0386
Term Expires: December 31, 2019 Fax: (912) 927-7170
E-mail: tthomas@savannahga.gov

★Council Member **Bill Durrence** (District 2) .... (912) 651-6444
Term Expires: December 31, 2019

★Council Member **John Hall** (District 3) .... (912) 596-1807
Term Expires: December 31, 2019
E-mail: jhall@savannahga.gov

★Council Member **Julian Miller** (District 4) .... (912) 659-0103
Term Expires: December 31, 2019

★Council Member **Estella Edwards Shabazz** (District 5) . . (912) 213-6444
Term Expires: December 31, 2019
E-mail: eshabazz@savannahga.gov

★Council Member **Carolyn Bell** (At-Large, Post 1) .... (912) 663-7907
Term Expires: December 31, 2019
E-mail: cbell@savannahga.gov
Education: Shaw 1971 BS; Georgia 1976 MPA

★Council Member **Brian Foster** (At-Large, Post 2) .... (912) 651-6441
Term Expires: December 31, 2019

○Clerk of the Council **Dyanne C. Reese** .... (912) 651-6441
E-mail: dreese@savannahga.gov Fax: (912) 651-4260

Office of the City Attorney
P.O. Box 1027, Savannah, GA 31402
Fax: (912) 525-3267

○City Attorney **W. Brooks Stillwell** .... (912) 525-3092
E-mail: bstillwell@savannahga.gov
Education: Wake Forest 1968 BA; Georgia 1971 JD

Office of the City Manager
P.O. Box 1027, Savannah, GA 31402
Internet: www.savannahga.gov/index.aspx?nid=394

City Manager **Stephanie S. Cutter** .... (912) 651-6415
Education: Savannah State BS, MPA

Assistant City Manager for Utilities, Development and Construction Services **Peter Shonka** .... (912) 651-6420

Director of Council and Legislative Affairs (Interim)
Bret Bell .... (912) 651-6414

Deputy Assistant to the City Manager **Marty Johnston** . . (912) 651-6419

Community and Economic Development Bureau
P.O. Box 1027, Savannah, GA 31402
Fax: (912) 651-6816

Chief **Taffanye Young** .... (912) 651-2363
E-mail: tyoung@savannahga.gov

Coastal Workforce Services Department
Executive Director **Michael Tucker** .... (912) 351-6379
E-mail: mtucker@savannahga.gov

Community Planning and Development Department
Internet: www.savannahga.gov/cityweb/CommServ.nsf

Director **Kerri Reid** .... (912) 651-6520
E-mail: kreid@savannahga.gov

Development Services
Director **Julie McLean** .... (912) 651-6510
E-mail: julie_mclean@savannahga.gov

Economic Development Department
Director **Manul Dominguez** .... (912) 651-3653

Housing Department
P.O. Box 1027, Savannah, GA 31402
Fax: (912) 651-6853

Director **Martin Fretty** .... (912) 651-6926

Real Property Services Department
Department Head **David Keating** .... (912) 651-6524

Fire Department
121 E. Oglethorpe Ave., Savannah, GA 31401
Fax: (912) 651-3195 Internet: www.savannahfire.org

Fire Chief **Charles G. Middleton** .... (912) 651-6756
E-mail: charles_middleton@savannahga.gov

Assistant Fire Chief, Logistics **Curtis Wallace** .... (912) 651-6756
E-mail: cwallace@savannahga.gov

Assistant Fire Chief, Operations **Elzie Kitchen, Jr.** .... (912) 651-6756
E-mail: ekitchen@savannahga.gov

Emergency Management Director **Daniel Stowers** .... (912) 651-6754

Management Services Bureau
P.O. Box 1027, Savannah, GA 31402
Fax: (912) 525-1511

Management Services Bureau Chief **Sean Brandon** ..... (912) 651-2201
E-mail: sbrandon@savannahga.gov
Education: Hampton 1999 BA; North Carolina 2001 MPA

Director of Purchasing **Molly Huhn** .... (912) 651-6425
E-mail: mhuhn@savannahga.gov

Auditing Department
Director **Megan Duffy** .... (912) 651-6496
Fax: (912) 651-3683

Finance Department
Fax: (912) 644-5962

Chief Financial Officer **David Maxwell** .... (912) 651-6434

★ Elected Official ▲ Appointed by Legislature ▼ Appointed by Governor ▶ Appointed by Board or Commission ● Appointed by Judge
■ Appointed by Mayor △ Appointed by Freeholders ▽ Appointed by Supervisor ▷ Appointed by County Executive ○ Appointed by Council

Human Resources Department
Human Resources Director **(Vacant)** . . . . . . (912) 651-6484
Fax: (912) 651-6706

Information Technology Department
Director **Cam Mathis** . . . . . . (912) 651-6906
E-mail: cmathis@savannahga.gov Fax: (912) 525-1506

Parking and Mobility Division
Director **Veleeta McDonald** . . . . . . (912) 651-6470

Recorders Court
Fax: (912) 652-7413

Clerk of Court **Angela Barnes** . . . . . . (912) 652-7425

Research and Budget Department
Director **Melissa Carter** . . . . . . (912) 651-6490
E-mail: mcarter01@savannahga.gov Fax: (912) 651-4250

Research Library Department
Director **Luciana Spracher** . . . . . . (912) 651-6412
E-mail: lspracher@savannahga.gov Fax: (912) 233-1992

Revenue Department
Director **Cindy Landolt** . . . . . . (912) 651-6450
E-mail: clandolt01@savannahga.gov Fax: (912) 651-6957

Vehicle Maintenance Department
Director **Iris Ellsberry-Smith** . . . . . . (912) 351-3891
Fax: (912) 351-3896

Savannah Chatham Metropolitan Police Department
P.O. Box 8032, Savannah, GA 31412
Fax: (912) 651-6675 Internet: http://scmpd.org/

Chief of Police **Joseph "Jack" Lumpkin, Sr.** . . . . . . (912) 651-6664
Assistant Chief **Juliette Tolbert** . . . . . . (912) 651-6664
E-mail: jtolbert@savannahga.gov
Director of Training **Gary Taylor** . . . . . . (912) 921-5451
E-mail: gtaylor@savannahga.gov Fax: (912) 921-5453

Leisure Services Bureau
P.O. Box 1027, Savannah, GA 31402
Tel: (912) 351-3837 Fax: (912) 651-3848

Bureau Chief **Joseph C. Shearouse** . . . . . . (912) 351-3837
E-mail: jshearouse@savannahga.gov

Parks and Recreation Services Bureau
P.O. Box 1027, Savannah, GA 31402
Fax: (912) 351-3423

Director **Barry Baker** . . . . . . (912) 351-3841
Maintenance Administrator **Jim Shirley** . . . . . . (912) 351-3847
E-mail: jim_shirley@savannahga.gov Fax: (912) 351-3843
Civic Center Director (Acting) **Joseph C. Shearouse** . . . . (912) 651-6550
Fax: (912) 651-6552

Department of Cemeteries
300 Bonaventure Road, Savannah, GA 31404
Tel: (912) 651-6843

Cemeteries Division Director **Richard Gerbasi** . . . . . . (912) 651-6843

Public Information Office
P.O. Box 1027, Savannah, GA 31402
Tel: (912) 651-6410 Fax: (912) 651-6408

Public Information Director **Bret Bell** . . . . . . (912) 651-6410
E-mail: bbell@savannahga.gov

Public Works and Water Resources Bureau
706 Stiles Ave., Savannah, GA 31415-5325

Water Resources/Public Works Director **John Sawyer** . . . (912) 651-4241
Fax: (912) 651-3681

Public Works and Water Resources Bureau *continued*

Conveyance and Distribution Director
James Laplander . . . . . . (912) 651-6584
Water Reclamation Department Director (Interim)
Lester Hendrix . . . . . . (912) 651-6620
Water and Sewer Planning Director **Heath Lloyd** . . . . . . (912) 651-0698
Water Supply and Treatment Director **Heath Lloyd** . . . . . . (912) 964-0698
Streets Maintenance Director **Richard Spivey** . . . . . . (912) 651-6571
Fax: (912) 650-7832
Traffic Engineering Director **Michael J. Weiner** . . . . . . (912) 651-6600
Fax: (912) 525-1535

Sanitation Bureau
P.O. Box 1027, Savannah, GA 31402
Tel: (912) 651-6579 Fax: (912) 651-6497

Bureau Chief **Gene Prevatt** . . . . . . (912) 651-6581
Commercial Refuse/Recycling and Litter Abatement
Director **Jimmy Rhodes** . . . . . . (912) 651-1967
Refuse Disposal Director **Travis Dawn** . . . . . . (912) 651-6625
Residential Collection Director **John Denion** . . . . . . (912) 651-6580
Street Cleaning Administrator **Willie London** . . . . . . (912) 651-6579

Property Maintenance Department
Fax: (912) 651-6975

Director **Kimberly Corbin** . . . . . . (912) 651-6770

City of Scottsdale, Arizona
3939 North Drinkwater Boulevard, Scottsdale, AZ 85251
Tel: (480) 312-3111 (Information) Fax: (480) 312-2738
Tel: (480) 312-0961 (City Court TTY)
Internet: http://www.scottsdaleaz.gov

County: Maricopa **Election Type:** Nonpartisan **Year Incorporated:** 1951 **Population:** 236,839 (2015)

W.J. "Jim" Lane
Mayor

Began Service: January 13, 2009
Term Expires: December 31, 2016
Education: St Joseph's U BA

Office of the Mayor
3939 N. Drinkwater Blvd., Scottsdale, AZ 85251
Fax: (480) 312-2738

★Mayor **W.J. "Jim" Lane** . . . . . . (480) 312-2433
E-mail: jlane@scottsdaleaz.gov
Chief of Staff **Rachel Smetana** . . . . . . (480) 312-7806
Executive Secretary **Charlene Penfold** . . . . . . (480) 312-2466
Communications and Public Affairs Director
Kelly Corsette . . . . . . (480) 312-2336

Office of the City Manager
3939 N. Drinkwater Blvd., Scottsdale, AZ 85251
Fax: (480) 312-9055 Internet: http://www.scottsdaleaz.gov/city-manager

○City Manager (Acting) **Brian Biesemeyer** . . . . . . (480) 312-2800
E-mail: citymanager@scottsdaleaz.gov
Assistant City Manager **Brent Stockwell** . . . . . . (480) 312-7288
E-mail: bstockwell@scottsdaleaz.gov

Office of the City Manager *continued*

Government Relations Director **Brad Lundahl** . . . . (480) 312-2683
E-mail: blundahl@scottsdaleaz.gov Fax: (480) 312-9055
Management Assistant **MarJan Hill-Enriquez** . . . . (480) 312-2800
E-mail: mhill@scottsdaleaz.gov

Office of Communications

3939 North Drinkwater Boulevard, Scottsdale, AZ 85251
Tel: (480) 312-7825

Public Affairs Manager **Mike Phillips** . . . . (480) 312-7825
E-mail: mphillips@scottsdaleaz.gov

Community Services Department

7447 East Indian School Road, Suite 300, Scottsdale, AZ 85251
Fax: (480) 312-2337

Executive Director **Bill Murphy** . . . . (480) 312-7954
E-mail: bmurphy@scottsdaleaz.gov Fax: (480) 312-2337

Human Services Department

6535 East Osborn Road, Suite 8, Scottsdale, AZ 85251-6029

Human Services Director **Greg Bestgen** . . . . (480) 312-0104

Parks and Recreation Department

7447 East Indian School Road, Suite 300, Scottsdale, AZ 85251
Tel: (480) 312-1011

Parks and Recreation Director **Reed Pryor** . . . . (480) 312-1011
Fax: (480) 312-2337

Preservation Department

7447 East Indian School Road, Suite 300, Scottsdale, AZ 85251
Fax: (480) 312-2337

Strategic Projects and Preserve Director **Kroy Ekblaw** . . . . (480) 312-7064

Scottsdale Public Library System

3839 N. Drinkwater Blvd., Scottsdale, AZ 85251
Tel: (480) 312-2474 Fax: (480) 312-7993
Internet: www.scottsdalelibrary.org

Director **Kathleen M. Wade** . . . . (480) 312-2691
E-mail: kwade@scottsdaleaz.gov

Economic Development Department

4021 North 75th Street, #102, Scottsdale, AZ 85251
Fax: (480) 312-2672

Director **Danielle Casey** . . . . (480) 312-7601
E-mail: dcasey@scottsdaleaz.gov

Human Resources Department

9191 East San Salvador Drive, Scottsdale, AZ 85258
Tel: (480) 312-2491 Fax: (480) 312-7960

Director of Human Resources **Donna B. Brown** . . . . (480) 312-2491
E-mail: dbrown@scottsdaleaz.gov

Information Technology Department

7384 East Second Street, Scottsdale, AZ 85251-5604
Fax: (480) 312-2623 Internet: www.scottsdaleaz.gov/departments/IT.asp

Chief Information Officer **Brad Hartig** . . . . (480) 312-7615
E-mail: bhartig@scottsdaleaz.gov
Communications Director **Shannon Tolle** . . . . (480) 312-7631
E-mail: stolle@scottsdaleaz.gov
Information Technology Director **Robert Fisher** . . . . (480) 312-7688
E-mail: rfisher@scottsdaleaz.gov
Applications Development Manager **Dean Schmidt** . . . . . . (480) 312-7838
E-mail: dschmidt@scottsdaleaz.gov
Applications and GIS Director **Eric Wood** . . . . (480) 312-7871
E-mail: ewood@scottsdaleaz.gov
Chief Information Security Officer **Don Thelander** . . . . . . (480) 312-2712
E-mail: dthelander@scottsdaleaz.gov

Information Technology Department *continued*

Enterprise Systems Engineering Manager **Felix Ortiz** . . . . . (480) 312-2351
E-mail: fortiz@scottsdaleaz.gov
GIS Manager **Chris Lechner** . . . . (480) 312-7792
E-mail: clechner@scottsdaleaz.gov
Office Manager **Anne Carroll** . . . . (480) 312-7963
E-mail: acarroll@scottsdaleaz.gov
Web and Design Services Manager **Amy Davison** . . . . (480) 312-7310
E-mail: adavison@scottsdaleaz.gov
Telecom Policy Coordinator **Kevin Sonoda** . . . . (480) 312-4138
E-mail: ksonoda@scottsdaleaz.gov
Senior Management Analyst **Jennifer Jensen** . . . . (480) 312-4137
E-mail: jjensen@scottsdaleaz.gov

Planning and Development Services

7447 East Indian School Road, Scottsdale, AZ 85251-3915
Tel: (480) 312-7000 Fax: (480) 312-7088
E-mail: planninginfo@scottsdaleaz.gov
Internet: http://www.scottsdaleaz.gov/planning

Planning and Development Director **Randy Grant** . . . . (480) 312-2664
E-mail: rgrant@scottsdaleaz.gov Fax: (480) 312-7781
Chief Development Officer and Building Official
Michael Clack . . . . (480) 312-7629
E-mail: mclack@scottsdaleaz.gov Fax: (480) 312-7781
Advance Planning Manager **Erin Perreault** . . . . (480) 312-7093
Fax: (480) 312-7088
Current Planning Director **Tim Curtis** . . . . (480) 312-2500
Fax: (480) 312-7088
Inspections Manager **Ralph Noriega** . . . . (480) 312-5769
9191 East San Salvador Drive, Fax: (480) 312-5704
Scottsdale, AZ 85258
Neighborhood Director **Raun Keagy** . . . . (480) 312-2373
7506 East Indian School Road, Fax: (480) 312-2455
Scottsdale, AZ 85251
E-mail: rkeagy@scottsdaleaz.gov
Stormwater Manager **Ashley Couch** . . . . (480) 312-4317

Police Department

8401 East Indian School Road, Scottsdale, AZ 85251
Fax: (480) 312-1969 Internet: www.scottsdalepd.com

Chief of Police **Alan Rodbell** . . . . (480) 312-1900
Public Information Supervisor **Ben Hoster** . . . . (480) 312-1910
E-mail: pio@ScottsdaleAZ.gov

Public Works Department

9191 East San Salvador Drive, Scottsdale, AZ 85258
Tel: (480) 312-5550 Fax: (480) 312-5539

Executive Director **Dan Worth** . . . . (480) 312-5555

Asset Management Division

7447 East Indian School Road, Scottsdale, AZ 85251
Tel: (480) 312-7250 Fax: (480) 312-7971

Coordinator **Maria Muiser** . . . . (480) 312-7853

Solid Waste Management Division

9191 East San Salvador Drive, Scottsdale, AZ 85258
Tel: (480) 312-5600 Fax: (480) 312-8115

Director **Frank Moreno** . . . . (480) 312-5605
Solid Waste Management Systems Coordinator
Gabriel Fragoso . . . . (480) 312-5608

Purchasing Department

9191 East San Salvador Drive, Scottsdale, AZ 85258
Tel: (480) 312-5700 Fax: (480) 312-5701

Purchasing Director **Jim Flanagan** . . . . (480) 312-5706
E-mail: jflanagan@ScottsdaleAZ.gov

★ Elected Official ▲ Appointed by Legislature ▼ Appointed by Governor ▶ Appointed by Board or Commission ● Appointed by Judge
■ Appointed by Mayor △ Appointed by Freeholders ▽ Appointed by Supervisor ▷ Appointed by County Executive ○ Appointed by Council

Scottsdale Fire Department
8401 E. Indian School Rd., Scottsdale, AZ 85251
Tel: (480) 312-8000 (Fire Department Main Administrative Phone Line)
Tel: (480) 312-1855 (Fire Prevention Inspection Scheduling)
Fax: (480) 312-1887 (Main Fire Department Administrative Fax Line)
E-mail: fire@scottsdaleaz.gov Internet: www.scottsdaleaz.gov/fire

Fire Chief **Tom Shannon** .... (480) 312-1802
E-mail: tshannon@scottsdaleaz.gov
Executive Assistant Chief **Ryan Freeburg** .... (480) 312-1802
E-mail: rfreeburg@scottsdaleaz.gov
Fire Marshal **Jim Ford** .... (480) 312-1852
E-mail: jford@scottsdaleaz.gov

Scottsdale Airport
15000 N. Airport Dr., Scottsdale, AZ 85260
Fax: (480) 312-8480 Internet: www.scottsdaleaz.gov/airport/

Aviation Director **Gary Mascaro** .... (480) 312-7735
Operations Manager **Chris Read** .... (480) 312-2674
E-mail: cread@scottsdaleaz.gov

Tourism and Events Department
7506 East Indian School Road, Scottsdale, AZ 85251
Tel: (480) 312-7177 Fax: (480) 312-7088

Tourism and Events Director **Karen Churchard** .... (480) 312-7177

Transportation Department
7447 East Indian School Road, Suite 205, Scottsdale, AZ 85251
Fax: (480) 312-4000

Transportation Director **Paul Basha** .... (480) 312-7651
Office Coordinator **Frances Cookson** .... (480) 312-7637
Public Information Officer **Jennifer Banks** .... (480) 312-7517
E-mail: jbanks@scottsdaleaz.gov
Senior Transportation Representative **Rose Arballo** .... (480) 312-7650
Senior Transportation Representative **Joan Freeman** .... (480) 312-7519
Senior Transportation Planner **Susan Conklu** .... (480) 312-2308
Senior Transportation Planner **Greg Davies** .... (480) 312-7829

Traffic Engineering
Tel: (480) 312-7696 Fax: (480) 312-4000

Traffic Engineering and Operations Manager
Phillip Kercher .... (480) 312-7645
E-mail: pkercher@scottsdaleaz.gov

Transportation Planning and Transit
Tel: (480) 312-7696 Fax: (480) 312-4000

Transportation Planning and Transit Operations Manager
Madeline Clemann .... (480) 312-2732
E-mail: mclemann@scottsdaleaz.gov
Transit Manager **Ratna Korepella** .... (480) 312-7630
Transit Operations Coordinator **John Kelley** .... (480) 312-7626
E-mail: jkelley@ScottsdaleAZ.gov
Transportation Planner **Mercedes McPherson** .... (480) 312-7802

Water Resources Department
9379 East San Salvador, Scottsdale, AZ 85258-5503
Tel: (480) 312-5685 Fax: (480) 312-5615

Executive Director **Brian Biesemeyer** .... (480) 312-5685
Training **Jeff Fritsch** .... (480) 312-5687
9312 North 94th Street, Scottsdale, AZ 85258-3503
E-mail: jfritsch@scottsdaleaz.gov
Water Operations Systems Integrator **Dave Petty** .... (480) 312-5699
9312 North 94th Street, Scottsdale, AZ 85258-3503
E-mail: dpetty@scottsdaleaz.gov

Office of the City Treasurer
7447 E. Indian School Rd., Scottsdale, AZ 85251
Tel: (480) 312-2427 Fax: (480) 312-7897

City Treasurer/Chief Financial Officer
Jeffrey M. Nichols .... (480) 312-2364 ext. 2234

Office of the City Attorney
3939 N. Drinkwater Blvd., Scottsdale, AZ 85251
Fax: (480) 312-2548

○ City Attorney **Bruce Washburn** .... (480) 312-2405
E-mail: bwashburn@scottsdaleaz.gov
Education: Wisconsin BA; Iowa JD
Deputy City Attorney **Joseph "Joe" Padilla** .... (480) 312-2405
E-mail: jpadilla@scottsdaleaz.gov
Deputy City Attorney **Sherry R. Scott** .... (480) 312-2405
E-mail: sscott@scottsdaleaz.gov

Office of the City Auditor
4021 North 75th Street, Suite 105, Scottsdale, AZ 85251
Fax: (480) 312-2634 Internet: http://www.scottsdaleaz.gov/auditor

○ City Auditor **Sharron Walker** .... (480) 312-7867
E-mail: swalker@scottsdaleaz.gov
Education: Southeast Missouri State BSBA; Southwest Missouri State MBA

Office of the City Clerk
3939 N. Drinkwater Blvd., Scottsdale, AZ 85251
Fax: (480) 312-7797

○ City Clerk **Carolyn Jagger** .... (480) 312-2411
E-mail: cjagger@scottsdaleaz.gov
City Records Manager **Karen Dingman** .... (480) 312-2413

Office of the City Council
3939 North Drinkwater Boulevard, Scottsdale, AZ 85251
Fax: (480) 312-7885 E-mail: citycouncil@scottsdaleaz.gov
Internet: www.scottsdaleaz.gov/council

★ Vice Mayor **David N. Smith** .... (480) 312-2550
Term Expires: January 2019
E-mail: dnsmith@scottsdaleaz.gov
★ Councilwoman **Suzanne Klapp** .... (480) 312-2550
Term Expires: January 2017
E-mail: sklapp@scottsdaleaz.gov
★ Councilwoman **Virginia Korte** .... (480) 312-2550
Term Expires: January 2017
E-mail: vkorte@scottsdaleaz.gov
★ Councilwoman **Kathy Littlefield** .... (480) 312-2550
Term Expires: January 2019
E-mail: klittlefield@scottsdaleaz.gov
★ Councilwoman **Linda Milhaven** .... (480) 312-2550
Term Expires: January 2019
E-mail: lmilhaven@scottsdaleaz.gov
★ Councilman **Guy Phillips** .... (480) 312-2550
Term Expires: January 2017
E-mail: gphillips@scottsdaleaz.gov

★ Elected Official ▲ Appointed by Legislature ▼ Appointed by Governor ► Appointed by Board or Commission ● Appointed by Judge
■ Appointed by Mayor △ Appointed by Freeholders ▽ Appointed by Supervisor ▷ Appointed by County Executive ○ Appointed by Council

City of Seattle, Washington

Seattle City Hall, 600 Fifth Avenue, Seattle, WA 98104-1900
Tel: (206) 684-2489 (Information) Internet: http://www.seattle.gov
Internet: http://data.seattle.gov

County: King **Election Type:** Nonpartisan **Year Incorporated:** 1865
Population: 684,451 (2015) **Employees:** 12,068 **Fiscal Year:** 2016
Budget: $5,050,582,000

Office of the Mayor

Seattle City Hall, 600 Fourth Avenue, 7th Floor, Seattle, WA 98104
P.O. Box 94749, Seattle, WA 98124-4749
Tel: (206) 684-4000 Fax: (206) 684-8390 TTY: (206) 615-0476
Internet: www.seattle.gov/mayor

Employees: 45 **Fiscal Year:** 2016 **Budget:** $5,833,000

★ Mayor **Edward B. Murray** .... (206) 684-4000
Began Service: January 6, 2014
Term Expires: December 31, 2017
E-mail: ed.murray@seattle.gov
Education: Portland BA
Executive Assistant to the Mayor **Alison Warner** .... (206) 615-0753
E-mail: alison.warner@seattle.gov

■ Chief of Staff **Mike Fong** .... (206) 727-8760
E-mail: michael.fong@seattle.gov

■ Intergovernmental Relations Director **Nick Harper** .... (206) 684-9202
E-mail: nick.harper@seattle.gov Fax: (206) 684-8267
Education: U Washington BA; Seattle JD

Communications Director (Acting) **Jason Kelly** .... (206) 684-8379
E-mail: jason.w.kelly@seattle.gov

Deputy Mayor, External Affairs **Hyeok Kim** .... (206) 727-8760
E-mail: hyeok.kim@seattle.gov
Education: William Smith BA

Deputy Mayor, Operations **Kate Joncas** .... (206) 684-3790
E-mail: kate.joncas@seattle.gov

External Relations Manager **Austin Miller** .... (206) 615-0391
E-mail: austin.miller@seattle.gov

■ Special Advisor for Strategic Initiatives **Chris Gregorich** .. (206) 684-4000
E-mail: chris.gregorich@seattle.gov
Education: U Washington BA

Office of Arts and Cultural Affairs

700 5th Avenue, Suite 1766, Seattle, WA 98104
P.O. Box 94748, Seattle, WA 98124-4748
Tel: (206) 684-7171 Fax: (206) 684-7172
E-mail: arts.culture@seattle.gov Internet: http://www.seattle.gov/Arts/

Employees: 30 **Fiscal Year:** 2016 **Budget:** $338,116,000

■ Director **Randy Engstrom** .... (206) 684-7173
E-mail: randy.engstrom@seattle.gov

Communications and Outreach Manager
Calandra Childres .... (206) 684-7306
E-mail: calandra.childers@seattle.gov

Public Art Program Director **Ruri Yampolsky** .... (206) 684-7309

Finance and Administration Manager **Jane Morris** .... (206) 684-8362
E-mail: jane.morris@seattle.gov

Cultural Partnerships Program Manager **Kathy Hsieh** .... (206) 733-9926

Accountant **Steven Eng** .... (206) 615-1825
E-mail: steven.eng@seattle.gov

Office for Civil Rights [SOCR]

Central Building, 810 Third Avenue, Suite 750, Seattle, WA 98104-1627
Tel: (206) 684-4500 Fax: (206) 684-0332
Internet: www.seattle.gov/civilrights

Employees: 36 **Fiscal Year:** 2016 **Budget:** $6,162,000

■ Director **Patricia C. "Patty" Lally** .... (206) 684-4500
E-mail: patricia.lally@seattle.gov

Operations Manager **Latrice Ybarra** .... (206) 684-4539
E-mail: latrice.ybarra@seattle.gov

Office for Civil Rights *continued*

Public Information Officer **Elliott Bronstein** .... (206) 684-4507
E-mail: elliott.bronstein@seattle.gov

Information Technology Systems Analyst **Amie Thao** .... (206) 684-4534
E-mail: amie.thao@seattle.gov

Office of Economic Development [OED]

Seattle Municipal Tower, 700 Fifth Avenue, Suite 5752,
Seattle, WA 98104-5072
P.O. Box 94708, Seattle, WA 98124-4708
Fax: (206) 684-0379 Internet: www.seattle.gov/EconomicDevelopment/

Employees: 31 **Fiscal Year:** 2016 **Budget:** $11,486,000

■ Director **Brian K. Surratt** .... (206) 684-8090
E-mail: brian.surratt@seattle.gov

Deputy Director **(Vacant)** .... (206) 684-3348

Communications Director **Joe Mirabella** .... (206) 733-9810
E-mail: joe.mirabella@seattle.gov

Senior Policy Advisor **Nancy Yamamoto** .... (206) 684-8189
E-mail: nancy.yamamoto@seattle.gov

Office of Housing

700 Fifth Avenue, Suite 5700, Seattle, WA 98104-5032 (Delivery Address)
P.O. Box 94725, Seattle, WA 98124-4725 (Mailing Address)
Tel: (206) 684-0721 Fax: (206) 233-7117
Internet: www.seattle.gov/housing/ E-mail: housing@seattle.gov

Employees: 45 **Fiscal Year:** 2016 **Budget:** $52,489,000

■ Director **Steve Walker** .... (206) 684-0721
E-mail: steve.walker@seattle.gov

Office of Sustainability and Environment [OSE]

700 Fifth Avenue, Suite 2748, Seattle, WA 98124-4023
P.O. Box 94729, Seattle, WA 98124-4729
Fax: (206) 684-3013 E-mail: ose@seattle.gov
Internet: www.seattle.gov/environment

Employees: 23 **Fiscal Year:** 2016 **Budget:** $3,375,000

■ Director **Jess Finn Coven** .... (206) 615-0817

Customer Service Bureau

P.O. Box 94669, Seattle, WA 98124-4669
Fax: (206) 684-8286

■ Director **Fred Podesta** .... (206) 386-0041
E-mail: fred.podesta@seattle.gov

City Budget Office [CBO]

600 Fourth Avenue, 6th Floor, Seattle, WA 98104
P.O. Box 94747, Seattle, WA 98124-4747
Fax: (206) 233-0022 Internet: www.seattle.gov/financedepartment/

Employees: 35 **Fiscal Year:** 2016 **Budget:** $5,895,000

■ Director **Ben Noble** .... (206) 615-1962
E-mail: ben.noble@seattle.gov
Education: Michigan 1989 BA; U Washington 1994 PhD
Assistant to the Director **Mark Palermo** .... (206) 684-8155
E-mail: mark.palermo@seattle.gov

Department of Education and Early Learning

700 5th Avenue, Suite 1700, Seattle, WA 98104-6965
Tel: (206) 233-5118 Fax: (206) 386-1900

Director (Acting) **Dwane Chappelle** .... (206) 233-5118

Finance and Administrative Services

Seattle Municipal Tower, 700 Fifth Avenue, Suite 5200,
Seattle, WA 98124
P.O. Box 94689, Seattle, WA 98124-4689
Tel: (206) 684-2489 Fax: (206) 684-0188

Employees: 651 **Fiscal Year:** 2016 **Budget:** $277,639,000

Director **Fred Podesta** .... (206) 684-2489

(continued on next page)

★ Elected Official ▲ Appointed by Legislature ▼ Appointed by Governor ► Appointed by Board or Commission ● Appointed by Judge
■ Appointed by Mayor △ Appointed by Freeholders ▽ Appointed by Supervisor ▷ Appointed by County Executive ○ Appointed by Council

Finance and Administrative Services *continued*

Senior Executive Assistant **Mickey Bannister-Mingo** .... (206) 615-0996
E-mail: mickey.bannister-mingo@seattle.gov
Finance Director **Glen Lee** .... (206) 615-0996

Fire Department

301 Second Ave., South, Seattle, WA 98104
Fax: (206) 386-1412 Internet: www.seattle.gov/fire/

Employees: 1,189 **Fiscal Year:** 2016 **Budget:** $183,523,000

■ Fire Chief **Harold Scoggins** .... (206) 386-1423
Executive Assistant **Debbie Brooks** .... (206) 386-1401
E-mail: debbie.brooks@seattle.gov
Executive Director of Administration **Helen Fitzpatrick** .. (206) 386-1404
E-mail: helen.fitzpatrick@seattle.gov
Assistant Chief, Operations **Jay Hagan** .... (206) 386-1489
E-mail: jay.hagan@seattle.gov
Fire Marshal **John Nelson** .... (206) 386-1064
220 Third Avenue South, Seattle, WA 98104
E-mail: john.nelson@seattle.gov
Deputy Chief, Training Division **Mark Lawson** .... (206) 386-1481
E-mail: mark.lawson@seattle.gov
Communications Director **Michael Teffre** .... (206) 386-1463
E-mail: michael.teffre@seattle.gov
Public Information Officer **Corey Orvold** .... (206) 386-1679
E-mail: corey.orvold@seattle.gov
Resource Management **A. D. Vickery** .... (206) 386-1474
E-mail: alan.vickery@seattle.gov
Information Systems Manager **Jim Hominiuk** .... (206) 386-1186

Department of Human Resources

700 Fifth Avenue, Suite 5500, Seattle, WA 98124
Fax: (206) 615-1634

Employees: 151 **Fiscal Year:** 2016 **Budget:** $16,572,000

■ Director **Susan Coskey** .... (206) 615-1622
E-mail: susan.coskey@seattle.gov
Executive Assistant **Anne Davis** .... (206) 684-0529
E-mail: anne.davis@seattle.gov
Director of Talent Acquisition and Development
Justin Natali .... (206) 684-0544
E-mail: justin.natali@seattle.gov
Labor Relations Director **David Bracilano** .... (206) 684-7874
E-mail: david.bracilano@seattle.gov

Human Services Department

700 Fifth Avenue, Suite 5800, Seattle, WA 98124-4215
P.O. Box 34215, Seattle, WA 98124-4215
Tel: (206) 386-1001 Fax: (206) 233-5119
Internet: www.seattle.gov/humanservices/

Employees: 343 **Fiscal Year:** 2016 **Budget:** $142,172,000

■ Director **Catherine Lester** .... (206) 386-1143
E-mail: catherine.lester@seattle.gov
Public Information Officer **Katherine Jolly** .... (206) 684-0253
E-mail: katherine.jolly@seattle.gov
Human Resource Manager **Christine Scarlett** .... (206) 233-5173
E-mail: christine.scarlett@seattle.gov

Department of Information Technology [DoIT]

Seattle Municipal Tower, 700 Fifth Avenue, Suite 2700,
Seattle, WA 98104
P.O. Box 94709, Seattle, WA 98124-4709
Tel: (206) 684-0600 Fax: (206) 684-0911 Internet: www.seattle.gov/doit/

Employees: 208 **Fiscal Year:** 2016 **Budget:** $83,423,000

■ Director **Michael Mattmiller** .... (206) 684-0600
E-mail: michael.mattmiller@seattle.gov
Communications Technologies Director
Robert William "Bill" Norris .... (206) 684-0600
E-mail: bill.norris@seattle.gov

Department of Information Technology *continued*

Director of Financing and Contracting Services
Patti DeFazio .... (206) 733-9962
E-mail: patti.defazio@seattle.gov
Technology Program Management Office Director
Ryan Meeks .... (206) 684-0600
E-mail: Ryan.Meeks@seattle.gov
Office of Electronic Communication Director
John Giamberso .... (206) 684-8588
E-mail: john.giamberso@seattle.gov
Human Resources Manager **Andre Nellams** .... (206) 733-9833
E-mail: andre.nellams@seattle.gov
Public Information Advisor **LaTonya Brown** .... (206) 233-8736
E-mail: LaTonya.Brown@seattle.gov

Department of Neighborhoods

700 Fifth Avenue, Suite 1700, Seattle, WA 98104
P.O. Box 94649, Seattle, WA 98124-4649
Tel: (206) 684-0464 Fax: (206) 233-5142
Internet: www.seattle.gov/neighborhoods/
Internet: www.facebook.com/SeattleNeighborhoods

Employees: 47 **Fiscal Year:** 2016 **Budget:** $7,041,000

■ Director **Kathy Nyland** .... (206) 684-0464
E-mail: kathy.nyland@seattle.gov
Executive Assistant **Melia Brooks** .... (206) 684-0303
E-mail: melia.brooks@seattle.gov
Human Resources **Pat Hairston** .... (206) 684-0710
E-mail: pat.hairston@seattle.gov Fax: (206) 233-5142
Public Information Officer **Lois Maag** .... (206) 615-0950
E-mail: lois.maag@seattle.gov

Office of Planning and Community Development

700 5th Avenue, 19th Floor, Seattle, WA 98104
Tel: (206) 684-8880

Employees: 46 **Fiscal Year:** 2016 **Budget:** $8,027,000

Director **Samuel Assefa** .... (206) 233-3882
Note: Effective June 1, 2016

Seattle Parks and Recreation

100 Dexter Ave., North, Seattle, WA 98109-5199
Fax: (206) 233-7023 Internet: http://www.seattle.gov/parks

Employees: 1,008 **Fiscal Year:** 2016 **Budget:** $209,807,000

■ Superintendent **Jesús Aguirre** .... (206) 684-8022
E-mail: jesus.aguirre@seattle.gov
Education: Texas 1990 BA; Arizona State 2006 MBA
Deputy Superintendent **Christopher Williams** .... (206) 684-2629
Education: Columbia BBA; Seattle MBA
Communications Manager **David Takami** .... (206) 684-8020
E-mail: david.takami@seattle.gov

Police Department

610 5th Ave., Seattle, WA 98104
P.O. Box 34986, Seattle, WA 98124-4986
Tel: (206) 684-5577 Fax: (206) 684-5525
Internet: www.seattle.gov/police/

Employees: 2,047 **Fiscal Year:** 2016 **Budget:** $299,838,000

■ Chief of Police **Kathleen M. O'Toole** .... (206) 684-5577
E-mail: kathleen.otoole@seattle.gov
Deputy Chief **Carmen Best** .... (206) 684-5577
Education: Western Illinois BA
Assistant Chief **Lesley Cordner** .... (206) 684-5577
Assistant Chief **Robert Merner** .... (206) 684-5577
Assistant Chief **Perry Tarrant** .... (206) 386-0061
Assistant Chief **Steve Wilske** .... (206) 684-5577
Director of Human Resources (Interim) **Mike Fields** ..... (206) 684-5464
E-mail: michael.fields@seattle.gov
Chief Information Officer **(Vacant)** .... (206) 684-5577
Chief Operating Officer **Brian Maxey** .... (206) 684-5577

★ Elected Official ▲ Appointed by Legislature ▼ Appointed by Governor ► Appointed by Board or Commission ● Appointed by Judge
■ Appointed by Mayor △ Appointed by Freeholders ▽ Appointed by Supervisor ▷ Appointed by County Executive ○ Appointed by Council

Police Department *continued*

Director of Transparency and Privacy **Mary Perry** . . . . (206) 684-5577
Education: St Mary's Col (IN) BA; Seattle JD

Seattle Department of Transportation [SDOT]

700 5th Ave., Suite 3900, Seattle, WA 98104-5043
P.O. Box 34996, Seattle, WA 98124-4996
Fax: (206) 684-5180 Internet: www.seattle.gov/transportation/

Employees: 844 **Fiscal Year:** 2016 **Budget:** $491,035,000

■ Director **Scott Kubly** . . . . (206) 684-7623
E-mail: scott.kubly@seattle.gov
Deputy Director **Barbara Gray** . . . . (206) 684-7623
Deputy Director **Jon Layzer** . . . . (206) 684-7623
Deputy Director **Karen Melanson** . . . . (206) 684-7623
Deputy Director **Michael "Mike" Terrell** . . . . (206) 684-3078
Human Resources Director **(Vacant)** . . . . (206) 386-1139
Policy Director **Tracy Krawczyk** . . . . (206) 733-9329
Maintenance Operations Director **Rodney Maxie** . . . . (206) 684-5319
Traffic Operations Director **Mark Bandy** . . . . (206) 684-5097
Council Liaison **Cheryl Swab** . . . . (206) 386-1831
E-mail: cheryl.swab@seattle.gov
Street Use Director **Brian de Place** . . . . (206) 684-5572

Seattle City Employees' Retirement Office [SCERS]

720 Third Avenue, Suite 900, Seattle, WA 98104-1829
Fax: (206) 386-1506 Internet: www.seattle.gov/retirement/

Employees: 20 **Fiscal Year:** 2016 **Budget:** $20,490,000

Executive Director (Interim) **Kenneth J. Nakatsu** . . . . (206) 386-1293

Seattle Center

305 Harrison St., Seattle, WA 98109-4645
Tel: (206) 684-7200 (Customer Service) Fax: (206) 233-3950
Internet: www.seattlecenter.com

Employees: 260 **Fiscal Year:** 2016 **Budget:** $45,261,000

■ Director **Robert L. Nellams** . . . . (206) 684-7334
E-mail: robert.nellams@seattle.gov
Education: Central Washington BA
Director of Finance and Administration **Thomas Israel** . . . (206) 684-7298
E-mail: tom.israel@seattle.gov
Web Master **Dennis McCoy** . . . . (206) 684-0995
E-mail: dennis.mccoysc@seattle.gov

Seattle City Light

700 Fifth Avenue, Seattle, WA 98104
P.O. Box 34023, Seattle, WA 98124-4023
Fax: (206) 684-3158 Internet: www.seattle.gov/light/

Employees: 1,875 **Fiscal Year:** 2016 **Budget:** $1,369,595,000

■ General Manager and Chief Executive Officer
Larry Weis . . . . (206) 684-3260
E-mail: larry.weiss@seattle.gov
Assistant to the General Manager **(Vacant)** . . . . (206) 684-3519
Chief Financial Officer (Interim) **Paula Laschober** . . . . . . (206) 684-4649
Account Services/Customer Relations Director
Kelly Enright . . . . (206) 684-3111
Environmental Affairs Division Director **Lynn Best** . . . . . . (206) 386-4586
Utility Support Services Division Director
Bernie O'Donnell . . . . (206) 684-3359
Information Systems Director **Dirk Mahling** . . . . (206) 386-4634
E-mail: dirk.mahling@seattle.gov
Energy Delivery Operation **Tuan Tran** . . . . (206) 386-4565
Officer for Customer Service and Energy Delivery
(Interim) **Mike Haynes** . . . . (206) 684-3618
Customer Service Officer **(Vacant)** . . . . (206) 684-3718
Human Resources Officer **DaVonna Johnson** . . . . (206) 684-3125
Power Supply and Environment Officer **Michael Jones** . . . (206) 684-3243
Procurement and Contracting Manager **Nelson S. Park** . . . (206) 386-1760
E-mail: nelson.park@seattle.gov

Seattle Planning Commission

700 Fifth Ave., Suite 2000, Mail Stop 34019, Seattle, WA 98124-4019
Tel: (206) 684-0433 Fax: (206) 233-0085

► Executive Director **Vanessa Murdock** . . . . (206) 684-0431
E-mail: vanessa.murdock@seattle.gov

Seattle Public Library

1000 4th Avenue, Seattle, WA 98104
Tel: (206) 386-4636 Fax: (206) 386-4108 E-mail: infospl@spl.org
Internet: www.spl.org/

Employees: 664 **Fiscal Year:** 2016 **Budget:** $71,750,000

City Librarian/Chief Executive Officer
Marcellus "M.T." Turner . . . . (206) 386-4636
E-mail: city.librarian@spl.org
Executive Assistant **Amy Lawson** . . . . (206) 386-4636
E-mail: amy.lawson@spl.org

Seattle Public Utilities [SPU]

Seattle Municipal Tower, 700 Fifth Avenue, Seattle, WA 98124-5004
(Physical Address, Deliveries)
P.O. Box 34018, Seattle, WA 98124-4018 (U.S. Mail)
Tel: (206) 684-5851 Fax: (206) 684-4631
E-mail: respond.spu@seattle.gov Internet: www.seattle.gov/util/

Employees: 1,467 **Fiscal Year:** 2016 **Budget:** $1,023,537,000

■ Director **Ray Hoffman** . . . . (206) 684-5852
E-mail: ray.hoffman@seattle.gov
Education: Illinois 1978 BS, 1980 MS; U Washington 1984 PhD
Executive Assistant **Phuong Nguyen** . . . . (206) 684-5850
E-mail: phuong.nguyen@seattle.gov
Director of Corporate Strategies and Communications
Office **(Vacant)** . . . . (206) 684-5984
Environmental Engineer **Henry Friedman** . . . . (206) 684-5852
115 110th Place, SE, Bellevue, WA 98004 Fax: (206) 684-4631
E-mail: henry.friedman@seattle.gov

Field Operations and Maintenance Branch

Deputy Director **Rick Scott** . . . . (206) 233-2613
E-mail: rick.scott@seattle.gov Fax: (206) 386-1911
Solid Waste Operations Director **Ken Snipes** . . . . (206) 684-5832
E-mail: ken.snipes@seattle.gov Fax: (206) 233-2632
Drainage and Wastewater Operations Director
John Holmes . . . . (206) 386-1264
E-mail: john.holmes@seattle.gov
Water Operations Director **Tony Blackwell** . . . . (206) 386-1264
E-mail: tony.blackwell@seattle.gov Fax: (206) 233-2632
Planning and Systems Support **Andy Strong** . . . . (206) 684-5826
E-mail: andy.strong@seattle.gov

Finance and Administration Branch

Deputy Director **Melina S. Thung** . . . . (206) 684-0958
E-mail: melina.thung@seattle.gov Fax: (206) 233-7867
Finance Division Deputy Director **Sherri Crawford** . . . . . . (206) 615-1372
Fax: (206) 233-7867
Technology Program Office **Vicki Evans** . . . . (206) 684-8857
E-mail: vicki.evans@seattle.gov
Seattle Public Utilities Information Technology
Division Director **Thomas J. Nolan** . . . . (206) 684-8937
E-mail: tom.nolan@seattle.gov
Facilities and Real Property **Judith Cross** . . . . (206) 386-1814
E-mail: judith.cross@seattle.gov

Project Delivery Branch

Tel: (206) 684-5950

Deputy Director (Interim) **Henry Chen** . . . . (206) 615-0563
E-mail: henry.chen@seattle.gov
Construction Management Division Director
Jeff Fowler . . . . (206) 684-5960
E-mail: jeff.fowler@seattle.gov
Engineering and Technical Services Director
Henry Chen . . . . (206) 615-0563
E-mail: henry.chen@seattle.gov

★ Elected Official ▲ Appointed by Legislature ▼ Appointed by Governor ► Appointed by Board or Commission ● Appointed by Judge
■ Appointed by Mayor △ Appointed by Freeholders ▽ Appointed by Supervisor ▷ Appointed by County Executive ○ Appointed by Council

Human Resources and Service Equity
Human Resources Director **Kimberly Collier** .... (206) 233-7927
Fax: (206) 233-7867

Civil Service Commission [CSC]
700 Fifth Avenue, P.O. Box 94729, Suite 1670, Seattle, WA 98124-4729
Fax: (206) 684-0755 E-mail: csc@seattle.gov
Internet: www.seattle.gov/csc/

Employees: 3 **Fiscal Year:** 2016 **Budget:** $507,000

○ Chair **Steven Jewell** .... (206) 233-7118
E-mail: commissioner.steven.jewell@seattle.gov
○ Commissioner **Angelique M. Davis** .... (206) 233-7118
E-mail: angelique.davis@seattle.gov
■ Commissioner **Eric de los Santos** .... (206) 233-7118
Affiliation: Corporate Counsel, TrueBlue, Inc.
Executive Director **Jennifer Greenlee** .... (206) 233-7118
E-mail: jennifer.greenlee@seattle.gov
Administrative Staff Assistant **Teresa R. Jacobs** .... (206) 386-1301
E-mail: teresa.jacobs@seattle.gov

Ethics and Elections Commission [SEEC]
P.O. Box 94729, Seattle, WA 98124-4729
Fax: (206) 684-8590 Internet: www.seattle.gov/ethics/default.htm

Employees: 6 **Fiscal Year:** 2016 **Budget:** $654,000

Executive Director **Wayne Barnett** .... (206) 684-8577

Public Safety Civil Service Commission
700 Fifth Avenue, Suite 1670, Seattle, WA 98104
Fax: (206) 684-0755 Internet: www.seattle.gov/pscsc

Chair **Joel A. Nark** .... (206) 386-1301
■ Commissioner **Christian M. Halliburton** .... (206) 386-1301
○ Commissioner **Sam Pailca** .... (206) 386-1301
Executive Director **Jennifer Greenlee** .... (206) 233-7118
E-mail: jennifer.greenlee@seattle.gov

City Council
Legislative Department, 600 Fourth Avenue, 2nd Floor, Seattle, WA 98104 (Delivery Address)
P.O. Box 34025, Seattle, WA 98124-4025 (Mailing Address)
Tel: (206) 684-8888 Fax: (206) 684-8587 E-mail: council@seattle.gov
Internet: www.seattle.gov/council

Employees: 89 **Fiscal Year:** 2016 **Budget:** $14,316,000

★ President **Bruce A. Harrell** (District 2) .... (206) 684-8804
Term Expires: December 31, 2019
E-mail: bruce.harrell@seattle.gov
★ Council Member **Lisa Herbold** (District 1) .... (206) 684-8888
Term Expires: December 31, 2019
★ Council Member **Kshama Sawant** (District 3) .... (206) 684-8816
Term Expires: December 31, 2019
E-mail: kshama.sawant@seattle.gov
★ Council Member **Rob Johnson** (District 4) .... (206) 684-8888
Term Expires: December 31, 2019
★ Council Member **Debora Juarez** (District 5) .... (206) 684-8888
Term Expires: December 31, 2019
★ Council Member **Michael "Mike" O'Brien** (District 6) ... (206) 684-8800
Term Expires: December 31, 2019
E-mail: mike.obrien@seattle.gov
★ Council Member **Sally Bagshaw** (District 7) .... (206) 684-8801
Term Expires: December 31, 2019
E-mail: sally.bagshaw@seattle.gov
★ Council Member **Tim Burgess** (At-Large) .... (206) 684-8806
Term Expires: December 31, 2017
★ Council Member **Lorena Gonzalez** (At-Large) .... (206) 684-8802
Term Expires: December 31, 2017
E-mail: Lorena.Gonzalez@seattle.gov

Office of City Auditor
Seattle Municipal Tower, 700 Fifth Avenue, Suite 2410, Seattle, WA 98124-4729
P.O. Box 94729, Seattle, WA 98124-4729
Tel: (206) 233-3801 Fax: (206) 684-0900 Internet: www.seattle.gov/audit/

Employees: 10 **Fiscal Year:** 2016 **Budget:** $1,792,000

○ City Auditor **David Jones** .... (206) 233-1095
E-mail: davidg.jones@seattle.gov
Education: Haverford BA; Harvard MPP
Deputy City Auditor **Cindy Drake** .... (206) 684-8158

Office of the City Clerk
Legislative Department, 600 Fourth Avenue, 3rd Floor, Seattle, WA 98104 (Delivery)
P.O. Box 94728, Seattle, WA 98124-4728 (Mailing)
Fax: (206) 386-9025

○ City Clerk **Monica Martinez Simmons** .... (206) 684-8344
E-mail: monica.simmons@seattle.gov
City Archivist **Scott Cline** .... (206) 684-8353
Education: Portland State 1972 BS, 1982 MA
Information Technology Manager **Ian Smith** .... (206) 684-5474
E-mail: ian.smith@seattle.gov
City Records Manager **Jennifer Winkler** .... (206) 684-8154
Education: Western Washington MA
Public Records Act Officer **Kimberly Ferreiro** .... (206) 684-7566
Public Records Act Officer **Sharon D. Johnson** .... (206) 733-9597

Office of the Hearing Examiner
Seattle Municipal Tower, 700 Fifth Avenue, Suite 4000, Seattle, WA 98124-4729
Fax: (206) 684-0536

Hearing Examiner **Sue Tanner** .... (206) 684-0521
Internet: www.seattle.gov/examiner/

Central Staff Division (Policy Analysis)
Director **Kirstan Arestad** .... (206) 684-8160
E-mail: kirstan.arestad@seattle.gov

Office of the City Attorney/Law Department
600 Fourth Avenue, 4th Floor, Seattle, WA 98104
P.O. Box 94769, Seattle, WA 98124-4769
Fax: (206) 684-8284 Internet: www.seattle.gov/law/

Employees: 180 **Fiscal Year:** 2016 **Budget:** $24,348,000

★ City Attorney **Peter Holmes** .... (206) 684-8288
Term Expires: December 31, 2017
E-mail: peter.holmes@seattle.gov
Education: Virginia 1984 JD
Chief of Staff **Darby DuComb** .... (206) 684-8228
Special Assistant **Gina Lantino** .... (206) 684-8288
E-mail: gina.lantino@seattle.gov
Government Affairs Director **Carlton Seu** .... (206) 733-9390
E-mail: carlton.seu@seattle.gov
Contracts Director **Engel Lee** .... (206) 233-2157
Employment Director **Paul Olsen** .... (206) 684-8218
E-mail: paul.olsen@seattle.gov
Environmental Protection Director **Laura Wishik** .... (206) 684-8199
Land Use Director **Roger Wynne** .... (206) 233-2177
Torts Director **Marcia Nelson** .... (206) 684-8221
Utilities Director **Engel Lee** .... (206) 233-2157
Civil Division Chief **Jean Boler** .... (206) 684-8207
Criminal Division Chief (Acting) **Kevin Kilpatrick** .... (206) 684-7757
Fax: (206) 684-4648
System Administrator **Ken Carlstedt** .... (206) 233-2682
E-mail: ken.carlstedt@seattle.gov Fax: (206) 684-7900
Department Administrator **Dana Anderson** .... (206) 684-7761
E-mail: dana.anderson@seattle.gov

★ Elected Official ▲ Appointed by Legislature ▼ Appointed by Governor ▶ Appointed by Board or Commission ● Appointed by Judge
■ Appointed by Mayor △ Appointed by Freeholders ▽ Appointed by Supervisor ▷ Appointed by County Executive ○ Appointed by Council

Seattle Public Schools

2445 3rd Ave. S., Seattle, WA 98134-1923
P.O. Box 34165, Seattle, WA 98124-1165
Tel: (206) 252-0040 Fax: (206) 252-0101
Internet: www.seattleschools.org

Superintendent of Schools **Dr. Larry Nyland** . . . . (206) 252-0167
Education: U Washington BA, MA, DEd Fax: (206) 252-0209
Assistant Superintendent of Operations **Pegi McEvoy** . . . . (206) 252-0707
E-mail: pmcevoy@seattleschools.org Fax: (206) 252-0626
Chief Communications Officer **Jacque Coe** . . . . (206) 252-0198
E-mail: jacoe@seattleschools.org
★School Board President **Betty Patu** (District VII) . . . . (206) 252-0040
Term Expires: November 2017
E-mail: betty.patu@seattleschools.org
★School Board Vice President **Sue Peters** (District IV) . . . . (206) 252-0040
Term Expires: November 2017
E-mail: sue.peters@seattleschools.org
★School Board Member **Scott S. Pinkham** (District I) . . . . (206) 252-0040
Term Expires: November 2019
★School Board Member **Rick Burke** (District II) . . . . (206) 252-0040
Term Expires: November 2019
★School Board Member **Jill Geary** (District III) . . . . (206) 252-0040
Term Expires: November 2019
Education: UC Berkeley 1988 BA; Seattle 1993 JD
★School Board Member **Stephen Blanford** (District V) . . . (206) 252-0040
Term Expires: November 2017
E-mail: stephan.blanford@seattleschools.org
★School Board Member **Leslie Harris** (District VI) . . . . (206) 252-0040
Term Expires: November 2019

City of Shreveport, Louisiana

Government Plaza, 505 Travis Street, Shreveport, LA 71101
P.O. Box 31109, Shreveport, LA 71130
Tel: (318) 673-2489 (Information) Internet: www.shreveportla.gov/

County: Caddo Parish **Election Type:** Partisan **Population:** 197,204 (2015)

Office of the Mayor

City Hall, 505 Travis Street, Suite 200, Shreveport, LA 71101
Tel: (318) 673-5050 Fax: (318) 673-5099

★Mayor **Ollie S. Tyler** (D) . . . . (318) 673-5050
Began Service: December 27, 2014
Term Expires: November 26, 2018
E-mail: mayor@shreveportla.gov
Education: Grambling State BS; LSU MS
■Director of Communications **Africa Price** . . . . (318) 673-5050
E-mail: africa.price@shreveportla.gov Fax: (318) 673-5087
■Chief Executive Assistant to the Mayor **Pam Raines** . . . . . (318) 673-5050
E-mail: pam.raines@shreveportla.gov Fax: (318) 673-5087

Office of the Chief Administrative Officer

City Hall, 505 Travis Street, Shreveport, LA 71101

■Chief Administrative Officer **Brian Crawford** . . . . (318) 673-5000
E-mail: brian.crawford@shreveportla.gov
■Assistant Chief Administrative Officer **Sherricka Fields** . . (318) 673-5010
E-mail: sherricka.fields@shreveportla.gov
Education: Centenary (LA) 2005 BS; LSU 2012 MS

Airports Department

5103 Hollywood, Suite 300, Shreveport, LA 71109

■Director **Henry L. Thompson** . . . . (318) 673-5370
Deputy Director **Bill Cooksey** . . . . (318) 673-5370

Office of the City Marshal

1244 Texas Avenue, Shreveport, LA 71101
Tel: (318) 673-6800 Fax: (318) 673-6816

★City Marshal **Charlie Caldwell, Jr.** (D) . . . . (318) 673-6800
Term Expires: December 2020
E-mail: charlie.caldwell@shreveportla.gov

Community Development

P.O. Box 31109, Shreveport, LA 71130
E-mail: community@ci.shreveport.la.us

■Director **Bonnie Moore** . . . . (318) 673-5900
E-mail: bonnie.moore@shreveportla.gov

Department of Engineering and Environmental Services

Government Plaza, 505 Travis Street, Suite 300, Shreveport, LA 71101

City Engineer (Acting) **Robert Westerman** . . . . (318) 673-6038
E-mail: robert.westerman@shreveportla.gov
Environmental Services Manager **Wes Wyche** Suite 580 . . (318) 673-6072

Finance Department

Government Plaza, 505 Travis Street, Shreveport, LA 71101

■Director **Charles Madden** . . . . (318) 673-5400
E-mail: finance@shreveportla.gov
Controller **John Pistorius** . . . . (318) 673-5600
E-mail: john.pistorius@shreveportla.gov
Data Services Administrator **Dan Thomas** . . . . (318) 673-5700
E-mail: dan.thomas@shreveportla.gov
Purchasing Agent (Interim) **Wendy Wagnon** . . . . (318) 673-5450
E-mail: wendy.wagnon@shreveportla.gov
■Revenue Administrator **Angela Duncan** . . . . (318) 673-5585
E-mail: angela.duncan@shreveportla.gov

Fire Department

Central Fire Station, 263 North Common, Shreveport, LA 71101
Fax: (318) 673-6656

■Fire Chief **Scott Wolverton** . . . . (318) 673-6655
E-mail: fire@shreveportla.gov
Deputy Chief **Ronald Jones** . . . . (318) 673-6658
E-mail: ronald.jones@shreveportla.gov
Chief of Fire Prevention **Patricia Dyas** . . . . (318) 673-6740
Chief Training Officer **John Lane** . . . . (318) 673-6766
E-mail: john.lane@shreveportla.gov
Chief of Communications **Kathy Rushworth** . . . . (318) 673-2200
E-mail: kathy.rushworth@shreveportla.gov
Chief of EMS **Nathan Tabor** . . . . (318) 673-6720
E-mail: nathan.tabor@shreveportla.gov

Metropolitan Planning Commission

Government Plaza, 505 Travis Street, Shreveport, LA 71101
Fax: (318) 673-6461

■Director **Mark Sweeney** . . . . (318) 673-6480
E-mail: mark.sweeney@shreveportla.gov

Human Resources Department

Government Plaza, 505 Travis Street, Shreveport, LA 71101
Fax: (318) 673-5161 E-mail: personnel@ci.shreveport.la.us

■Director **Angelita Jackson** . . . . (318) 673-5150
E-mail: angelita.jackson@shreveportla.gov
Tel: (318) 673-5199

Police Department

1234 Texas Avenue, Shreveport, LA 71101

■Police Chief **Willie Shaw** . . . . (318) 673-6900
E-mail: police@shreveportla.gov
Investigations Assistant Police Chief **Travis Hayes** . . . . . . (318) 673-7210
Support Assistant Police Chief **Wayne Smith** . . . . (318) 673-7079
Uniform Service Division Assistant Chief-East Side
David Kent . . . . (318) 673-7202
Uniform Service Division Assistant Chief-West Side
Robert Dowell . . . . (318) 673-7204

★Elected Official ▲Appointed by Legislature ▼Appointed by Governor ▶Appointed by Board or Commission ●Appointed by Judge
■Appointed by Mayor △Appointed by Freeholders ▽Appointed by Supervisor ▷Appointed by County Executive ○Appointed by Council

Public Assembly and Recreation/Public Buildings
Government Plaza, 505 Travis Street, Shreveport, LA 71101
Fax: (318) 673-7858

■ Director **Shelly Ragle** .... (318) 673-5109
E-mail: spar@shreveportla.gov
Assistant to the Director **Ronnie Hammond** .... (318) 673-5143
E-mail: ronnie.hammond@shreveportla.gov
Assistant Director **Patrick Wesley** .... (318) 673-7838
E-mail: patrick.wesley@shreveportla.gov
Environmental Services Division Manager
Reginald Hodge .... (318) 673-5149
E-mail: reginald.hodge@shreveportla.gov
Maintenance Division Manager **Joe Brown** .... (318) 673-7895
Event Services Division Manager **Catherine Kennedy** ... (318) 673-7892

Office of Public Works
1731 Kings Highway, Shreveport, LA 71103

Director **Michael Wood** .... (318) 673-6300
Deputy Director/Chief Building Official **(Vacant)** .... (318) 673-6100
505 Travis Street, Suite 130, Shreveport, LA 71101
City Traffic Engineer **Michael Erlund** .... (318) 673-6181
2123 Lakeshore Drive, Shreveport, LA 71103
Fleet Services Superintendent **Chris Wilder** .... (318) 673-6361
Solid Waste Superintendent **Fred Williams** .... (318) 673-6300
Streets and Drainage Superintendent (Interim)
Ernie Negrete .... (318) 673-6330
1935 Claiborne Avenue, Shreveport, LA 71103

Sportran
1115 Jack Wells Boulevard, Shreveport, LA 71107
Fax: (318) 673-7424

General Manager/Director **Dinero Washington** .... (318) 673-7400

Department of Water and Sewerage
505 Travis Street, Suite 580, Shreveport, LA 71101
Tel: (318) 673-7660 Fax: (318) 673-7663

Director **Barbara Featherston** .... (318) 673-7660
Customer Service Manager **Lashaun Wheeler** .... (318) 673-5510
Field Operations Superintendent **James Kennedy** .... (318) 673-6551
Water Purification Superintendent **Quiana Maple** .... (318) 673-7656
Wastewater Assistant Director **Robert Campbell** .... (318) 673-7660

Office of the City Council
Government Plaza, 505 Travis Street, Shreveport, LA 71101
Tel: (318) 673-5262 E-mail: council@ci.shreveport.la.us

★ Council Member **Willie Bradford** (D-District A) .... (318) 673-5262
Term Expires: November 26, 2018 Fax: (318) 673-5270
★ Council Member **Jeff Everson** (D-District B) .... (318) 673-5262
Term Expires: November 26, 2018 Fax: (318) 673-5279
E-mail: jeff.everson@shreveportla.gov
Education: Centenary (LA) 2001 BA
★ Council Member **Oliver Jenkins** (R-District C) .... (318) 673-5262
Term Expires: November 26, 2018 Fax: (318) 673-5270
E-mail: oliver.jenkins@shreveportla.gov
Education: Dartmouth 1988 BA
★ Council Member **Michael Corbin** (R-District D) .... (318) 673-5262
Term Expires: November 26, 2018 Fax: (318) 673-5270
E-mail: michael.corbin@shreveportla.gov
★ Council Member **James Flurry** (R-District E) .... (318) 673-5262
Term Expires: November 26, 2018 Fax: (318) 673-5270
E-mail: james.flurry@shreveportla.gov
★ Council Member **Stephanie Lynch** (D-District F) .... (318) 673-5262
Term Expires: November 26, 2018 Fax: (318) 673-5270
★ Council Member **Jerry Bowman, Jr.** (D-District G) .... (318) 673-5262
Term Expires: November 26, 2018 Fax: (318) 673-5270
E-mail: jerry.bowman@shreveportla.gov
○ Clerk of Council **Arthur G. Thompson** .... (318) 673-5262
E-mail: council@shreveportla.gov
○ City Internal Auditor **Leanis Steward** .... (318) 673-7900
E-mail: leanis.graham@shreveportla.gov

Office of the City Attorney
Government Plaza, 505 Travis Street, Shreveport, LA 71101
Tel: (318) 673-5200 Fax: (318) 673-5230

■ City Attorney **William Bradford, Jr.** .... (318) 673-5200
E-mail: william.bradford@shreveportla.gov

City of Simi Valley, California
City Hall, 2929 Tapo Canyon Rd., Simi Valley, CA 93063
Internet: www.simivalley.org

County: Ventura **Election Type:** Nonpartisan **Population:** 126,788 (2015)

Office of the Mayor and City Council
City Hall, 2929 Tapo Canyon Rd., Simi Valley, CA 93063-2117

★ Mayor **Bob Huber** .... (805) 583-6703
Began Service: November 29, 2010
Term Expires: December 1, 2016
E-mail: bhuber@simivalley.org
★ Mayor Pro Tem **Keith Mashburn** .... (805) 583-6703
Term Expires: December 1, 2016
E-mail: kmashburn@simivalley.org
★ Council Member **Glen T. Becerra** .... (805) 583-6703
Term Expires: December 1, 2018
E-mail: gbecerra@simivalley.org
Education: UC Berkeley 1993 BA
★ Council Member **Mike Judge** .... (805) 583-6703
Term Expires: December 1, 2018
E-mail: mjudge@simivalley.org
★ Council Member **Steven T. Sojka** .... (805) 583-6703
Term Expires: December 1, 2016
E-mail: ssojka@simivalley.org

Office of the City Manager/Clerk
City Hall, 2929 Tapo Canyon Rd., Simi Valley, CA 93063-2117
Fax: (805) 526-2489

○ City Manager/Clerk **Eric J. Levitt** .... (805) 583-6701
E-mail: elevitt@simivalley.org
Assistant City Manager/Economic Development
Brian Gabler .... (805) 583-6701
E-mail: bgabler@simivalley.org
Assistant City Manager/Government Affairs **(Vacant)** .... (805) 583-6701
Deputy City Clerk **Ky Spangler** .... (805) 583-6813
E-mail: kspangler@simivalley.org

Office of the City Attorney
City Hall, 2929 Tapo Canyon Rd., Simi Valley, CA 93063-2117

○ City Attorney **Lonnie J. Eldridge** .... (805) 583-6714
E-mail: leldridge@simivalley.org
Deputy City Attorney **Sonia Hehir** .... (805) 583-6714

Administrative Services Department
City Hall, 2929 Tapo Canyon Rd., Simi Valley, CA 93063-2117
Fax: (805) 583-6302

Director (Interim) **Ken Al-Imam** .... (805) 583-6749
E-mail: kalimam@simivalley.org

Community Services Department
3855-A Alamo St., Simi Valley, CA 93063
Fax: (805) 583-6301

Director **Sommer Barwick** .... (805) 583-6754
E-mail: sbarwick@simivalley.org

★ Elected Official ▲ Appointed by Legislature ▼ Appointed by Governor ► Appointed by Board or Commission ● Appointed by Judge
■ Appointed by Mayor △ Appointed by Freeholders ▽ Appointed by Supervisor ▷ Appointed by County Executive ○ Appointed by Council

Environmental Services Department
3855-A Alamo St., Simi Valley, CA 93063
Fax: (805) 583-7922
Director **Peter Lyons** .... (805) 583-6875

Police Department
3901 Alamo St., Simi Valley, CA 93063-2102
Fax: (805) 583-6201
Police Chief **Mitch McCann** .... (805) 583-6901

Public Works Department
City Hall, 2929 Tapo Canyon Rd., Simi Valley, CA 93063-2117
Fax: (805) 583-6300
Director **Ron Fuchiwaki** .... (805) 583-6808

City of Sioux Falls, South Dakota
City Hall, 224 West Ninth Street, Sioux Falls, SD 57104-7402
Tel: (605) 376-8800 (Information) Internet: www.siouxfalls.org

County: Minnehaha **Election Type:** Nonpartisan **Population:** 171,544 (2015)

Office of the Mayor
City Hall, 224 West Ninth Street, Sioux Falls, SD 57104-7402
Fax: (605) 367-8490

★ Mayor **Mike T. Huether** .... (605) 367-8800
Began Service: May 17, 2010
Term Expires: May 16, 2018
E-mail: mhuether@siouxfalls.org

Chief Project Manager **Kendra Siemonsma** .... (605) 367-8800
E-mail: ksiemonsma@siouxfalls.org
Education: South Dakota BS

Finance Department
■ Finance Director **Tracy Turbak** .... (605) 367-8270
E-mail: tturbak@siouxfalls.org Fax: (605) 367-7700

Office of the City Attorney
100 South Dakota Avenue, Suite 200, Sioux Falls, SD 57117-7402
Fax: (605) 367-7330 E-mail: cityattorney@siouxfalls.org

■ City Attorney **David Pfeifle** .... (605) 367-8880
E-mail: dpfeifle@siouxfalls.org

Office of the City Clerk
235 West 10th Street, Sioux Falls, SD 57104
Fax: (605) 367-7801 E-mail: cityclerk@siouxfalls.org

○ City Clerk **LTC Thomas M. Greco** .... (605) 367-8081
E-mail: tgreco@siouxfalls.org Fax: (605) 367-7801
Education: West Point 1985 BS

Central Services
132 North Dakota Avenue, Sioux Falls, SD 57104
Fax: (605) 367-8113 E-mail: centralservices@siouxfalls.org

■ Director **Sue Quanbeck Etten** .... (605) 367-8828
E-mail: squanbecketten@siouxfalls.org Fax: (605) 367-8736

Multimedia Manager **Brett Mathison** .... (605) 367-8856
E-mail: bmathison@siouxfalls.org Fax: (605) 367-8113

Community Development/Public Parking Department
City Hall, 224 West Ninth Street, Sioux Falls, SD 57104-6407
Fax: (605) 367-4599 E-mail: development@siouxfalls.org

■ Director **Darrin Smith** .... (605) 367-8180
E-mail: dsmith@siouxfalls.org

Economic Development Manager **Brent O'Neil** .... (605) 367-8180
E-mail: boneil@siouxfalls.org

Economic Development Coordinator **Dustin Powers** ..... (605) 367-8847
E-mail: dpowers@siouxfalls.org

Neighborhood Development Coordinator **Adam Roach** ... (605) 367-8179
E-mail: aroach@siouxfalls.org

Fire Rescue
2820 S. Minnesota Ave., Sioux Falls, SD 57105-4735
E-mail: firerescue@siouxfalls.org Fax: (605) 367-8101

■ Fire Chief **Jim Sideras** .... (605) 367-8092
E-mail: jsideras@siouxfalls.org

Human Resources
City Hall, 224 W. Ninth St., Sioux Falls, SD 57104-6407
Fax: (605) 367-7865 E-mail: hr@siouxfalls.org

■ Director **Bill O'Toole** .... (605) 367-8740
E-mail: botoole@siouxfalls.org Fax: (605) 367-7865

Parks and Recreation Department
100 East Sixth Street, Sioux Falls, SD 57104
E-mail: parksandrec@siouxfalls.org

■ Director **Donald Kearney** .... (605) 367-8222
E-mail: dkearney@siouxfalls.org Fax: (605) 367-4326

Planning and Building Services
City Hall, 224 W. Ninth St., Sioux Falls, SD 57104-6407
E-mail: planning@siouxfalls.org

■ Director **Mike Cooper** .... (605) 367-8888
E-mail: mcooper@siouxfalls.org Fax: (605) 367-8863

Police Department
320 West 4th Street, Sioux Falls, SD 57104
E-mail: policedept@siouxfalls.org

■ Police Chief **Matt Burns** .... (605) 367-7261
E-mail: mburns@siouxfalls.org Fax: (605) 367-7316

Public Health Department
521 North Maine Avenue, Suite 101, Sioux Falls, SD 57104-5963
E-mail: healthdept@siouxfalls.org

■ Director **Jill Franken** .... (605) 367-8761
E-mail: jfranken@siouxfalls.org Fax: (605) 367-8246

Public Works
City Hall, 224 W. Ninth St., Sioux Falls, SD 57104-6407
E-mail: publicworks@siouxfalls.org

■ Director **Mark Cotter** .... (605) 367-8600
E-mail: mcotter@siouxfalls.org Fax: (605) 367-4605

Siouxland Libraries
Main Library, 201 N. Main Ave., Sioux Falls, SD 57104-6002
E-mail: circ@siouxland.lib.sd.us Internet: http://www.siouxland.lib.sd.us

■ Director **Mary Johns** .... (605) 367-8702
E-mail: mjohns@siouxfalls.org Fax: (605) 367-4312

★ Elected Official ▲ Appointed by Legislature ▼ Appointed by Governor ▶ Appointed by Board or Commission ● Appointed by Judge
■ Appointed by Mayor △ Appointed by Freeholders ▽ Appointed by Supervisor ▷ Appointed by County Executive ○ Appointed by Council

Office of the City Council

235 West 10th Street, Sioux Falls, SD 57104
Fax: (605) 367-8085

★ Chair **Rex Rolfing** .... (605) 367-8085
Term Expires: May 1, 2018
E-mail: rrolfing@siouxfalls.org

★ Council Member **Christine M. Erickson** .... (605) 367-8085
Term Expires: May 2018
E-mail: cerickson@siouxfalls.org
Education: National American U ABA; U Sioux Falls 2005 BA

★ Council Member **Michelle Erpenbach** .... (605) 367-8085
Term Expires: May 1, 2018
E-mail: merpenbach@siouxfalls.org

★ Council Member **Rick Kiley** .... (605) 367-8085
Term Expires: May 2018
E-mail: rkiley@siouxfalls.org

★ Council Member **Greg Neitzert** .... (605) 367-8085
Term Expires: May 2020

★ Council Member **Marshall Selberg** .... (605) 367-8085
Term Expires: May 2020

★ Council Member **Pat Starr** .... (605) 367-8085
Term Expires: May 2020

★ Council Member **Theresa Stehly** .... (605) 367-8085
Term Expires: May 2020

Sioux Falls School District

201 East 38th Street, Sioux Falls, SD 57105-5898
Tel: (605) 367-7900 Fax: (605) 367-4637

Superintendent **Dr. Brian Maher** .... (605) 367-7900

City of South Bend, Indiana

227 W. Jefferson Blvd., South Bend, IN 46601
Internet: www.southbendin.gov

County: St. Joseph **Election Type:** Partisan **Population:** 101,516 (2015)

Office of the Mayor and City Council

227 W. Jefferson Blvd., South Bend, IN 46601

★ Mayor **Pete Buttigieg** (D) .... (574) 235-9261
Began Service: January 1, 2012
Term Expires: December 31, 2019
E-mail: mayorpete@southbendin.gov
Education: Harvard
Chief of Staff **James Mueller** .... (574) 235-9261

★ Council Member **Tim Scott** (D-District 1) .... (574) 235-9321
Term Expires: December 31, 2019
E-mail: tscott@southbendin.gov

★ Council Member **Regina W. Preston** (D-District 2) .... (574) 235-9321
Term Expires: December 31, 2019

★ Council Member **Randy Kelly** (D-District 3) .... (574) 235-9321
Term Expires: December 31, 2019

★ Council Member **Jo M. Broden** (D-District 4) .... (574) 235-9321
Term Expires: December 31, 2019

★ Council Member **Dr. David A. Varner** (R-District 5) .... (574) 235-9321
Term Expires: December 31, 2019
E-mail: dvarner@southbendin.gov
Education: Indiana BS, DDS

★ Council Member **Oliver Davis** (D-District 6) .... (574) 235-9321
Term Expires: December 31, 2019
E-mail: odavis@southbendin.gov

★ Council Member **Gavin Ferlic** (D-At-Large) .... (574) 235-9321
Term Expires: December 31, 2019
E-mail: gferlic@southbendin.gov

★ Council Member **John Voorde** (D-At-Large) .... (574) 235-9321
Term Expires: December 31, 2019

Office of the Mayor and City Council *continued*

★ Council Member **Karen L. White** (D-At-Large) .... (574) 235-9321
Term Expires: December 31, 2019
E-mail: kwhite@southbendin.gov
Education: Indiana State BA; Indiana MA

Administration and Finance Department

227 W. Jefferson Blvd., South Bend, IN 46601
Fax: (574) 235-9928

■ Controller **John Murphy** .... (574) 235-9742
E-mail: jmurphy@ci.south-bend.in.us

Human Resources Director **Janet Cardotte** .... (574) 235-9482
E-mail: jcardotte@ci.south-bend.in.us

Information Technology Director **Shawn Delahanty** .... (574) 245-6000
E-mail: sdelahanty@southbendin.gov

Safety and Risk Director **Rob Yeary** .... (574) 235-9483
E-mail: ryeary@ci.south-bend.in.us

Building Department

125 South Lafayette Boulevard, Suite 100, South Bend, IN 46601

Building Commissioner **Charles C. Bulot** .... (574) 235-9554
Education: Texas BS

Community Investment Department

227 W. Jefferson Blvd., South Bend, IN 46601
Fax: (574) 235-9021

■ Executive Director **Scott Ford** .... (574) 235-9371
E-mail: sford@ci.south-bend.in.us

Fire Department

1222 South Michigan, South Bend, IN 46601
Fax: (574) 235-9305

■ Fire Chief **Stephen Cox** .... (574) 235-9255
E-mail: scox@ci.south-bend.in.us

Legal Department

227 W. Jefferson Blvd., South Bend, IN 46601

Corporation Counsel **Cristal Brisco** .... (574) 235-9241

■ City Attorney **Aladean De Rose** .... (574) 235-9241
E-mail: cleone@southbendin.gov

Parks and Recreation Department

321 East Walter Street, South Bend, IN 46614

■ Superintendent **Aaron Perri** .... (574) 299-4765
E-mail: aperri@southbendin.gov

Maintenance Superintendent **Michael Dyszkiewicz** .... (574) 235-9414

Park Administrator **Betsy Harriman** .... (574) 235-5596
E-mail: bharrima@southbendin.gov

Golf Director **(Vacant)** .... (574) 271-9180

Recreation Director **Susan O'Connor** .... (574) 299-4768 ext. 244

Zoo Director **Greg Bockheim** .... (574) 235-9800

Fiscal Officer **Bill Carleton** .... (574) 299-4765

City Forester **Brent Thompson** .... (574) 299-4768 ext. 249

Police Department

701 West Sample Street, South Bend, IN 46601
Fax: (574) 288-0268

■ Chief of Police **Scott Ruszkowski** .... (574) 235-9311
E-mail: sbpd@southbendin.gov

Public Works Department

1316 County-City Building, South Bend, IN 46601

■ Director of Public Works **Eric Horvath** .... (574) 235-9251

Engineering Division

City Engineer **Kara Boyles** .... (574) 235-9251

★ Elected Official ▲ Appointed by Legislature ▼ Appointed by Governor ▶ Appointed by Board or Commission ● Appointed by Judge
■ Appointed by Mayor △ Appointed by Freeholders ▽ Appointed by Supervisor ▷ Appointed by County Executive ○ Appointed by Council

Environmental Services Division
3113 Riverside Drive, South Bend, IN 46628
Director **Al Greek** .... (574) 277-8515
Solid Waste Bureau Superintendent **(Vacant)** ..... (574) 277-8823 ext. 61
Wastewater Director **(Vacant)** .... (574) 277-8515

Equipment Services Division
Director **Matthew L. Chlebowski** .... (574) 235-9316

Transportation Division
731 South Lafayette Boulevard, South Bend, IN 46601
■ Director **(Vacant)** .... (574) 235-9444

Water Works Division
224 North Main Street, South Bend, IN 46601
Director **(Vacant)** .... (574) 235-9322

Weights and Measures
142 South Olive Street, South Bend, IN 46609
Director **Kenneth J. Hintz** .... (574) 235-9751

Office of the City Clerk
227 W. Jefferson Blvd., South Bend, IN 46601
★ City Clerk **Kareemah N. Fowler** (D) .... (574) 235-9221
Term Expires: December 31, 2019

City of Spokane, Washington

West 808 Spokane Falls Boulevard, Spokane, WA 99201
Internet: www.spokanecity.org

County: Spokane **Election Type:** Nonpartisan **Year Incorporated:** 1881
Population: 213,272 (2015)

Office of the Mayor
808 West Spokane Falls Boulevard, Spokane, WA 99201
Fax: (509) 625-6563

★ Mayor **David Anthony Condon** .... (509) 625-6250
Began Service: January 1, 2012
Term Expires: December 31, 2019
E-mail: mayor@spokanecity.org
Receptionist **Katie Ross** .... (509) 625-6276
E-mail: kross@spokanecity.org
Mayor's Office Director **Brandy Cote** .... (509) 625-6250
Director of Local Governmental and Multicultural Affairs **Gloria Ochoa** .... (509) 625-6250
E-mail: gochoa@spokanecity.org

Office of the City Administrator
West 808 Spokane Falls Boulevard, Spokane, WA 99201
Fax: (509) 625-6217

■ City Administrator **Theresa Sanders** .... (509) 625-6250
E-mail: tsanders@spokanecity.org

Office of the City Clerk
W. 808 Spokane Falls Blvd., Spokane, WA 99201
Fax: (509) 625-6217

City Clerk **Terri Pfister** .... (509) 625-6350
E-mail: tpfister@spokanecity.org

Office of the Treasurer
808 West Spokane Falls Boulevard, Spokane, WA 99201
Fax: (509) 625-6939

Treasurer **Kim Bustos** .... (509) 625-6032

Accounting Department
W. 808 Spokane Falls Blvd., Spokane, WA 99201
Fax: (509) 625-6939

Director **Kim Bustos** .... (509) 625-6034
E-mail: kbustos@spokanecity.org

Building Services
W. 808 Spokane Falls Blvd., Spokane, WA 99201
Fax: (509) 625-6124

Building Official **John Halsey** .... (509) 625-6300

Business and Development Services
West 808 Spokane Falls Boulevard, Spokane, WA 99201

Director (Acting) **Scott Simmons** .... (509) 625-6584
Historic Preservation Officer **Megan Duvall** .... (509) 625-6543

City Cable Channel 5
W. 808 Spokane Falls Blvd., Spokane, WA 99201

Director **John Delay** .... (509) 625-6355
E-mail: jdelay@spokanecity.org

Civil Service Department
W. 808 Spokane Falls Blvd., Spokane, WA 99201
Fax: (509) 625-6077

Chief Examiner **Gita George-Hatcher** .... (509) 625-6160
E-mail: ggeorge-hatcher@spokanecity.org

Communications Department
West 808 Spokane Falls Boulevard, Spokane, WA 99201

Communications Director **Brian Coddington** .... (509) 625-6740
E-mail: bcoddington@spokanecity.org

Community, Housing and Human Services Department
W. 808 Spokane Falls Blvd., Spokane, WA 99201
Fax: (509) 625-6315

Director (Interim) **Jennifer Stapleton** .... (509) 625-6091

Community and Neighborhood Services Division
West 808 Spokane Falls Boulevard, Spokane, WA 99201

Director **Jonathan Mallahan** .... (509) 625-6730
E-mail: jmallahan@spokanecity.org

Engineering Services Department
City Hall, 808 West Spokane Falls Boulevard, 2nd Floor, Spokane, WA 99201-3343
Fax: (509) 625-6349

Operations Manager **Kyle Twohig** .... (509) 625-6700
E-mail: ktwohig@spokanecity.org

Finance Division
West 808 Spokane Falls Boulevard, Spokane, WA 99201
Fax: (509) 625-6939

Chief Financial Officer **Gavin Cooley** .... (509) 625-6586

Information Technology Department
W. 808 Spokane Falls Blvd., Spokane, WA 99201
Fax: (509) 625-6550

Director **Eric Finch** .... (509) 625-6455
E-mail: efinch@spokanecity.org

★ Elected Official ▲ Appointed by Legislature ▼ Appointed by Governor ▶ Appointed by Board or Commission ● Appointed by Judge
■ Appointed by Mayor △ Appointed by Freeholders ▽ Appointed by Supervisor ▷ Appointed by County Executive ○ Appointed by Council

Fire Department
W. 44 Riverside, Spokane, WA 99201
Fax: (509) 625-7039

Fire Chief **Bobby Williams** .... (509) 625-7030
E-mail: bwilliams@spokanecity.org

Fleet Services
N. 1410 Normandie St., Spokane, WA 99201
Fax: (509) 625-7999

Director **Gene Jakubczak** .... (509) 625-7777

Hearing Examiner's Office
W. 808 Spokane Falls Blvd., Spokane, WA 99201

Hearing Examiner **Brian T. McGinn** .... (509) 625-6010

Human Resources Department
W. 808 Spokane Falls Blvd., Spokane, WA 99201
Fax: (509) 625-6379

Director **Heather Lowe** .... (509) 625-6363
E-mail: hlowe@spokanecity.org

Legal Department
W. 808 Spokane Falls Blvd., Spokane, WA 99201
Fax: (509) 625-6277

City Attorney **Nancy Isserlis** .... (509) 625-6225
E-mail: nisserlis@spokanecity.org

Neighborhood Services and Code Enforcement Department
City Hall, 808 West Spokane Falls Boulevard, 6th Floor, Spokane, WA 99201
Fax: (509) 625-6817

Director **Heather Trautman** .... (509) 625-6730
E-mail: htrautman@spokanecity.org

Parks and Recreation Department
W. 808 Spokane Falls Blvd., Spokane, WA 99201
Fax: (509) 625-6205

Director **Leroy Eadie** .... (509) 625-6200

Planning and Building Services Department
808 West Spokane Falls Boulevard, Spokane, WA 99201
Fax: (509) 625-6013

Director (Interim) **Louis Meuler** .... (509) 625-6300

Police Department
West 1100 Mallon Avenue, Spokane, WA 99260-0001
Fax: (509) 625-4066

■ Police Chief (Interim) **Rick Dobrow** .... (509) 625-4063

Public Defender
N. 824 Monroe St., Spokane, WA 99201

Public Defender **Kathy Knox** .... (509) 835-5955

Risk Management
W. 808 Spokane Falls Blvd., Spokane, WA 99201
Fax: (509) 625-6836

Risk Manager **Tim Dunivant** .... (509) 625-6845
E-mail: tdunivant@spokanecity.org

Spokane Employees' Retirement System [SERS]
808 West Spokane Falls Boulevard, 6th Floor, Spokane, WA 99201
Fax: (509) 625-6861

Director (Interim) **Tim Dunivant** .... (509) 625-6330

Spokane Public Library
906 West Main Street, Spokane, WA 99201
Fax: (509) 444-5365

Director **Andrew Chanse** .... (509) 444-5300
E-mail: achanse@spokanelibrary.org

Street Department
901 North Nelson Street, Spokane, WA 99202
Fax: (509) 232-8830

Director **Mark Serbousek** .... (509) 232-8800
Traffic Operations Division Engineer **Bob Turner** .... (509) 232-8800
E-mail: bturner@spokanecity.org

Public Works and Utilities Department
W. 808 Spokane Falls Blvd., Spokane, WA 99201
Fax: (509) 625-6274

Director **Rick Romero** .... (509) 625-6270
Communications Director **Marlene Feist** .... (509) 625-6505
E-mail: mfeist@spokanecity.org

Environmental Programs
Fax: (509) 625-6573

Manager **Lloyd Brewer** .... (509) 625-6968

Solid Waste Collection Department
1225 E. Marietta, Spokane, WA 99207
Fax: (509) 625-7899

Director **Scott Windsor** .... (509) 625-7878

Solid Waste Disposal Department
Fax: (509) 456-7409

Director **Chuck Conklin** .... (509) 625-6524

Wastewater Management
4401 N. Aubrey L. White Pkwy., Spokane, WA 99205
Fax: (509) 625-7940

Director **(Vacant)** .... (509) 625-7900

Water Department
914 E. North Foothills Dr., Spokane, WA 99207
Fax: (509) 625-7816

Director **Dan Kegley** .... (509) 625-7800
Utilities Billing Division Credit Supervisor **Ron Nicodemus** .... (509) 625-6000

Office of City Council
W. 808 Spokane Falls Blvd., Spokane, WA 99201
Fax: (509) 625-6059

★ Council President **Ben Stuckart** (At-Large) .... (509) 625-6252
Term Expires: December 31, 2019
E-mail: bstuckart@spokanecity.org
Assistant to Council President **Adam McDaniel** .... (509) 625-6255
E-mail: amcdaniel@spokanecity.org

★ Council Member **Mike Fagan** (District 1) .... (509) 625-6255
Term Expires: December 31, 2019
E-mail: mfagan@spokanecity.org

★ Council Member **Amber Waldref** (District 1) .... (509) 625-6255
Term Expires: December 31, 2017
E-mail: awaldref@spokanecity.org

★ Council Member **Breean Beggs** (District 2) .... (509) 625-6255
Term Expires: December 31, 2017
E-mail: bbeggs@spokanecity.org

★ Council Member **Lori Kinnear** (District 2) .... (509) 625-6255
Term Expires: December 31, 2019

★ Council Member **Candace Mumm** (District 3) .... (509) 625-6255
Term Expires: December 31, 2017
E-mail: cmumm@spokanecity.org

★ Elected Official ▲ Appointed by Legislature ▼ Appointed by Governor ► Appointed by Board or Commission ● Appointed by Judge
■ Appointed by Mayor △ Appointed by Freeholders ▽ Appointed by Supervisor ▷ Appointed by County Executive ○ Appointed by Council

Office of City Council *continued*

★ Council Member **Karen Stratton** (District 3) .... (509) 625-6255
Term Expires: December 31, 2019
E-mail: kstratton@spokanecity.org

Spokane Public Schools

200 North Bernard Street, Spokane, WA 99201
Tel: (509) 354-5900

Superintendent **Shelley Redinger** .... (509) 354-7364

City of Springfield, Illinois

300 South Seventh Street, Springfield, IL 62701
Internet: http://www.springfield.il.us

County: Sangamon **Election Type:** Nonpartisan **Population:** 116,565 (2015)

Office of the Mayor

800 East Monroe Street, Room 300, Springfield, IL 62701
Fax: (217) 789-2109

★ Mayor **James Langfelder** .... (217) 789-2200
Began Service: May 7, 2015
Term Expires: April 30, 2019
E-mail: j.langfelder@springfield.il.us
Executive Assistant **Bonnie Drew** .... (217) 789-2200
■ Communication Director **Julia Frevert** .... (217) 789-2235

Office of the City Council

300 South Seventh Street, Room 305, Springfield, IL 62701
Fax: (217) 789-2153

★ Alderman **Chuck Redpath** (Ward 1) .... (217) 789-2151
Term Expires: May 7, 2019
★ Alderman **Herman Senior** (Ward 2) .... (217) 789-2151
Term Expires: May 7, 2019
★ Alderman **Doris Turner** (Ward 3) .... (217) 789-2151
Term Expires: April 30, 2019
★ Alderman **John Fulgenzi** (Ward 4) .... (217) 789-2151
Term Expires: May 7, 2019
★ Alderman **Andrew Proctor** (Ward 5) .... (217) 789-2151
Term Expires: May 7, 2019
★ Alderman **Cory Jobe** (Ward 6) .... (217) 789-2151
Term Expires: April 30, 2019
★ Alderman **Joseph McMenamin** (Ward 7) .... (217) 789-2151
Term Expires: April 30, 2019
★ Alderman **Kristofer D. Theilen** (Ward 8) .... (217) 789-2151
Term Expires: April 30, 2019
★ Alderman **James Donelan** (Ward 9) .... (217) 789-2151
Term Expires: May 7, 2019
★ Alderman **Ralph Hanauer** (Ward 10) .... (217) 789-2151
Term Expires: May 7, 2019
○ Council Coordinator **Tim Griffin** .... (217) 789-2151

Office of the City Clerk

300 South Seventh Street, Room 106, Springfield, IL 62701
Fax: (217) 789-2144 Internet: http://www.springfieldcityclerk.com/

★ City Clerk **Frank Lesko** .... (217) 789-2216
Term Expires: May 7, 2019
E-mail: city.clerk@springfield.il.us

Office of the Treasurer

300 South Seventh Street, Room 104, Springfield, IL 62701
Fax: (217) 789-2297

★ Treasurer **Misty Buscher** .... (217) 789-2224
Term Expires: May 7, 2019
E-mail: m.buscher@springfield.il.us

Office of the Corporation Counsel

Municipal Center East, 800 East Monroe Street, Room 313, Springfield, IL 62701
Fax: (217) 789-2397

○ Corporation Counsel **Jim Zerkle** .... (217) 789-2393
E-mail: j.zerkle@springfield.il.us

Airport Authority

Abraham Lincoln Capitol Airport, 1200 Capitol Airport Drive, Springfield, IL 62707
Fax: (217) 788-8056

○ Executive Director **Mark Hanna** .... (217) 788-1060
E-mail: m.hanna@springfield.il.us

City Water, Light and Power [CWLP]

Municipal Center East, 800 East Monroe Street, Springfield, IL 62757
Fax: (217) 789-2136 Internet: http://www.cwlp.com

○ General Manager (Acting) **Doug Brown** .... (217) 789-2116 ext. 2659
Chief Utility Engineer **Doug Brown** .... (217) 789-2116 ext. 2659
Finance Director **(Vacant)** .... (217) 789-2116 ext. 2641
Regulatory Affairs Manager **Christine Zeman** .. (217) 789-2116 ext. 2628
Water Division Director **Ted Meckes** .... (217) 789-2116 ext. 2612

Office of Budget and Management

800 East Monroe Street, Springfield, IL 62701

■ Director **Bill McCarty** .... (217) 789-2191
E-mail: William.McCarty@cwlp.com
Chief Accountant **Ramona Metzger** .... (217) 789-2191
E-mail: Ramona.Metzger@cwlp.com
Payroll **Patty Connolly** .... (217) 789-2195
Purchasing Agent **Jay Wavering** .... (217) 789-2205
E-mail: Jay.Wavering@cwlp.com

Community Relations

231 South Sixth Street, Springfield, IL 62701

Director **Juan Huerta** .... (217) 789-2270 ext. 224
E-mail: Juan.Huerta@cwlp.com
Community Program Specialist **Carla Rowles** .... (217) 789-2270
E-mail: Carla.Rowles@cwlp.com
Community Relations Commissioner **(Vacant)** .... (217) 789-2270

Building and Zoning

300 South Seventh Street, Springfield, IL 62701

Zoning Administrator **Mat McLaughlin** .... (217) 789-2171

Fire Department

825 East Capitol Street, Springfield, IL 62701

Chief **Barry Helmerichs** .... (217) 788-8474

Human Resources

300 South Seventh Street, Springfield, IL 62701
Fax: (217) 789-2118

Director **Melina Tomaras-Colllins** .... (217) 789-2446
E-mail: m.tomaras-colllins@springfield.il.us
Benefits Division Manager **Brooke Jones** .... (217) 789-2193
E-mail: b.jones@springfield.il.us
Labor Relations Manager **Stephanie Barton** .... (217) 789-2446
E-mail: s.barton@springfield.il.us
Benefits Specialist **Sara Taylor** .... (217) 789-2193
E-mail: s.taylor@springfield.il.us

(continued on next page)

★ Elected Official ▲ Appointed by Legislature ▼ Appointed by Governor ► Appointed by Board or Commission ● Appointed by Judge
■ Appointed by Mayor △ Appointed by Freeholders ▽ Appointed by Supervisor ▷ Appointed by County Executive ○ Appointed by Council

Human Resources *continued*

Human Resources Manager **Jim Kuizin** . . . . (217) 789-2446
E-mail: j.kuizin@springfield.il.us

Lincoln Library

326 South Seventh Street, Springfield, IL 62701
Fax: (217) 788-8310

Director **Nancy Huntley** . . . . (217) 753-4900
E-mail: nancy.huntley@lincolnlibrary.info

Office of Planning and Economic Development

800 East Monroe Street, Suite 107, Springfield, IL 62701
Fax: (217) 789-2380

■ Director **Mike Farmer** . . . . (217) 789-2377 ext. 470
E-mail: michael.farmer@cwlp.com
City Planner **Paul O'Shea** . . . . (217) 789-2377 ext. 472
Supervisor of Fiscal Services **John Rogers** . . . . . (217) 789-2377 ext. 471
E-mail: John.Rogers@cwlp.com
Senior Business Projects Manager
Teri Whitfield . . . . (217) 789-2377 ext. 475
E-mail: teri.whitfield@cwlp.com
Rehabilitation Construction Specialist
Richard Willms . . . . (217) 789-2377 ext. 453

Police Department

800 East Monroe Street, Springfield, IL 62701
Fax: (217) 788-8310

○ Chief of Police **Ken Winslow** . . . . (217) 788-8360
E-mail: k.winslow@springfield.il.us

Public Works Department

300 South Seventh Street, Springfield, IL 62701

■ Director **Mark Mahoney** . . . . (217) 789-2255
City Engineer **Nathan Bottom** . . . . (217) 789-2255 ext. 5223
City Traffic Engineer **Lori Williams** . . . . (217) 789-2255 ext. 5225

City of Springfield, Massachusetts

City Hall, 36 Court St., Springfield, MA 01103
Tel: (413) 787-6000 (Information) Internet: www.springfieldcityhall.com

County: Hampden **Election Type:** Nonpartisan **Year Incorporated:** 1852 **Population:** 154,341 (2015)

Office of the Mayor

Administration Bldg., 36 Court St., Springfield, MA 01103

★ Mayor **Domenic J. Sarno** . . . . (413) 787-6100
Began Service: January 2008
Term Expires: January 1, 2018
E-mail: dsarno@springfieldcityhall.com
Administrative Assistant **Carolyn Jackson** . . . . (413) 787-6100
E-mail: cjackson@springfieldcityhall.com
Aide to the Mayor **Minnie Marrero** . . . . (413) 787-6100
E-mail: mmarrero@springfieldcityhall.com
Aide to the Mayor **Darryl E. Moss** . . . . (413) 787-6100
E-mail: dmoss@springfieldcityhall.com
■ Chief of Staff **Denise Jordan** . . . . (413) 787-6107
E-mail: djordan@springfieldcityhall.com
■ Communications Director **Marian Sullivan** . . . . (413) 787-6100
E-mail: msullivan@springfieldcityhall.com
Constituent Services Director **William Baker** . . . . (413) 787-6100
E-mail: wbaker@springfieldcityhall.com

Office of the Assessors

Administration Bldg., 36 Court St., Springfield, MA 01103
Tel: (413) 787-6160

■ Chairman **Richard Allen** . . . . (413) 787-6164
E-mail: rallen@springfieldcityhall.com
■ Assessor **Patrick Greenhaigh** . . . . (413) 787-6164
■ Assessor **(Vacant)** . . . . (413) 787-6164

Office of the City Attorney

Administration Bldg., 36 Court St., Springfield, MA 01103

■ City Solicitor **Edward M. Pikula** . . . . (413) 787-6085
E-mail: epikula@springfieldcityhall.com
Deputy City Solicitor **Kathleen Breck** . . . . (413) 787-6085
E-mail: kbreck@springfieldcityhall.com

Office of Management and Budget

Administration Bldg., 36 Court St., Springfield, MA 01103

■ Chief Administrative and Financial Officer
Timothy J. "T.J." Plante . . . . (413) 886-5288
Education: Stonehill BS; Suffolk MPA
■ City Collector/Treasurer **Stephen Lonergan** . . . . (413) 787-6130
E-mail: slonergan@springfieldcityhall.com

Code Enforcement Department

Administration Bldg., 70 Tapley Street, Springfield, MA 01104

■ Commissioner **Steven T. Desilets** . . . . (413) 787-6030
E-mail: sdesilets@springfieldcityhall.com

Community Development Department

Administration Bldg., 36 Court St., Springfield, MA 01103

■ Chief Development Officer **Kevin Kennedy** . . . . (413) 787-6050
E-mail: kkennedy@springfieldcityhall.com

Election Office

Administration Bldg., 36 Court St., Springfield, MA 01103
Tel: (413) 787-6190

■ Elections Commissioner **Gladys Oyola** . . . . (413) 787-6189
E-mail: goyola@springfieldcityhall.com

Emergency Preparedness Office

1212 Carew Street, Springfield, MA 01104

■ Director **Robert Hassetts** . . . . (413) 787-6720
E-mail: rhassett@springfieldcityhall.com

Facilities Management Department

233 Allen St., Springfield, MA 01108

■ Superintendent **Patrick Sullivan** . . . . (413) 787-6280
E-mail: psullivan@springfieldcityhall.com

Fire Department

605 Worthington St., Springfield, MA 01103
Tel: (413) 787-6400

Fire Commissioner **Joseph A. Conant** . . . . (413) 787-6411
E-mail: jconant@springfieldcityhall.com

Health and Human Services Department

95 State Street, Springfield, MA 01103

■ Commissioner **Helen R. Caulton-Harris** . . . . (413) 787-6740
E-mail: hcaulton@springfieldcityhall.com

Housing Authority

25 Saab Court, Springfield, MA 01104

Director **William H. Abrashkin** . . . . (413) 785-4513

★ Elected Official ▲ Appointed by Legislature ▼ Appointed by Governor ▶ Appointed by Board or Commission ● Appointed by Judge
■ Appointed by Mayor △ Appointed by Freeholders ▽ Appointed by Supervisor ▷ Appointed by County Executive ○ Appointed by Council

Human Resources Department
Administration Bldg., 36 Court St., Springfield, MA 01103
Tel: (413) 787-6055

■ Director **William E. Mahoney** .... (413) 787-6068
E-mail: wmahoney@springfieldcityhall.com
Retirement/Systems Supervisor **Anne C. Leduc** .... (413) 787-6090
70 Tapley Street, Springfield, MA 01104
E-mail: aleduc@springfieldcityhall.com

Housing and Neighborhood Services
1600 East Columbus Avenue, Springfield, MA 01103

Director **Geraldine "Gerry" McCafferty** .... (413) 787-6500

Labor Relations Department
Administrative Building, 36 Court Street, Springfield, MA 01103

■ Director **William E. Mahoney** .... (413) 787-6085
E-mail: wmahoney@springfieldcityhall.com

Municipal Information Systems Department
Administration Bldg., 36 Court St., Springfield, MA 01103

■ Chief Information Officer **Andrew Doty** .... (413) 750-2400
E-mail: adoty@springfieldcityhall.com

Parks and Recreation Department
Forest Park Administration Bldg., 200 Trafton Rd., Springfield, MA 01108

■ Superintendent **Patrick Sullivan** .... (413) 787-6440
E-mail: psullivan@springfieldcityhall.com

Planning and Economic Development Department
Administration Bldg., 36 Court St., Springfield, MA 01103

■ Director **Kevin Kennedy** .... (413) 787-6020
E-mail: kkennedy@springfieldcityhall.com
Deputy Director **Phillip Dromey** .... (413) 787-6020
E-mail: pdromey@springfieldcityhall.com

Police Department
130 Pearl St., Springfield, MA 01105
Tel: (413) 787-6310 E-mail: spd@spfldpd.org
Internet: http://www.spfldpd.org

■ Commissioner **John R. Barbieri** .... (413) 787-6313
E-mail: jbarbieri@springfieldpolice.net

Office of Procurement
36 Court Street, Springfield, MA 01103

■ Chief Procurement Officer **Lauren Stabilo** .... (413) 787-6284
E-mail: lstabilo@springfieldcityhall.com

Public Works Department
70 Tapley Street, Springfield, MA 01104

■ Director **Christopher M. Cignoli** .... (413) 787-6224
E-mail: ccignoli@springfieldcityhall.com
Engineer **Christopher M. Cignoli** .... (413) 787-6213
E-mail: ccignoli@springfieldcityhall.com

Veterans Department
Administration Bldg., 36 Court St., Springfield, MA 01103
Tel: (413) 787-6144

■ Director **Tom Belton** .... (413) 787-6148
E-mail: tbelton@springfieldcityhall.com

Office of the City Council
Administration Bldg., 36 Court St., Springfield, MA 01103
E-mail: council@springfieldcityhall.com

★ Council President **Michael A. Fenton** (Ward 2) .... (413) 787-6170
Term Expires: January 1, 2018
E-mail: mfenton@springfieldcityhall.com
★ Vice President **Orlando Ramos** (Ward 8) .... (413) 342-9232
Term Expires: January 1, 2018
E-mail: oramos108@aol.com
★ Council Member **Adam Gomez** (Ward 1) .... (413) 787-6170
Term Expires: January 1, 2018
★ Council Member **Melvin A. Edwards** (Ward 3) .... (413) 348-8036
Term Expires: January 1, 2018
E-mail: melvinspeaks@msn.com
★ Council Member **E. Henry Twiggs** (Ward 4) .... (413) 737-7306
Term Expires: January 1, 2018
E-mail: ehenry2@aol.com
★ Council Member **Marcus J. Williams** (Ward 5) .... (413) 787-6170
Term Expires: January 1, 2018
★ Council Member **Ken Shea** (Ward 6) .... (413) 787-6170
Term Expires: January 1, 2018
E-mail: kshea@springfieldcityhall.com
★ Council Member **Timothy C. Allen** (Ward 7) .... (413) 427-4650
Term Expires: January 1, 2018
E-mail: timallen1951@hotmail.com
★ Council Member **Thomas Ashe** (At-Large) .... (413) 505-9289
Term Expires: January 1, 2018
E-mail: tomashe318@gmail.com
★ Council Member **Justin Hurst** (At-Large) .... (413) 374-5844
Term Expires: January 1, 2018
E-mail: jhurst@springfieldcityhall.com
★ Council Member **Timothy J. Rooke** (At-Large) .... (413) 787-6170
Term Expires: January 1, 2018
E-mail: trooke@springfieldcityhall.com
★ Council Member **Kateri B. Walsh** (At-Large) .... (413) 787-6170
Term Expires: January 1, 2018
E-mail: kwalsh@springfieldcityhall.com
★ Council Member **Bud L. Williams** (At-Large) .... (413) 787-6170
Term Expires: January 1, 2018
E-mail: budl3@comcast.net
Aide **Susan Kacoyannakis** .... (413) 787-6170
E-mail: skacoyannakis@springfieldcityhall.com
Aide **Kelley Mickiewicz** .... (413) 787-6170

Office of the City Clerk
Administration Bldg., 36 Court St., Springfield, MA 01103
Fax: (413) 787-6205

○ City Clerk **Anthony Wilson** .... (413) 787-6095
E-mail: awilson@springfieldcityhall.com
Deputy City Clerk **Camile Nelson Campbell** .... (413) 787-6095
E-mail: cnelson@springfieldcityhall.com

Springfield Public Schools
1550 Main Street, Springfield, MA 01103
Tel: (413) 787-7100 Internet: www.sps.springfield.ma.us

Superintendent **Daniel J. Warwick** .... (413) 787-7087

★ Elected Official ▲ Appointed by Legislature ▼ Appointed by Governor ▶ Appointed by Board or Commission ● Appointed by Judge
■ Appointed by Mayor △ Appointed by Freeholders ▽ Appointed by Supervisor ▷ Appointed by County Executive ○ Appointed by Council

CITIES AND TOWNS

City of Springfield, Missouri

840 Boonville Avenue, Springfield, MO 65802
P.O. Box 8368, Springfield, MO 65801-8368
Tel: (417) 864-1000 (Information) E-mail: city@springfieldmo.gov
Internet: www.springfieldmo.gov

County: Greene **Election Type:** Nonpartisan **Year Incorporated:** 1838
Charter: 1953 **Population:** 166,810 (2015)

Office of the Mayor and City Council

P.O. Box 8368, Springfield, MO 65801-8368
Fax: (417) 864-1649 E-mail: citycouncil@springfieldmo.gov

★Mayor **Bob Stephens** .... (417) 864-1651
Began Service: May 9, 2012
Term Expires: April 2017
E-mail: rstephens@springfieldmo.gov
Education: Southwest Missouri State BS; Drury U 2001 MA

★Council Member **Phyllis Ferguson** (Zone 1) .... (417) 864-1651
Term Expires: April 2017
E-mail: pferguson@springfieldmo.gov

★Council Member **Justin Burnett** (Zone 2) .... (417) 864-1651
Term Expires: April 2019
E-mail: jburnett@springfieldmo.gov

★Council Member **Mike Schilling** (Zone 3) .... (417) 864-1651
Term Expires: April 2019
E-mail: mschilling@springfieldmo.gov

★Council Member **Craig Fishel** (Zone 4) .... (417) 864-1651
Term Expires: April 2017
E-mail: cfishel@springfieldmo.gov

★Council Member **Jan Fisk** (At-Large A) .... (417) 864-1651
Term Expires: April 2017
E-mail: jfisk@springfieldmo.gov

★Council Member **Craig Hosmer** (At-Large B) .... (417) 864-1651
Term Expires: April 2017
E-mail: chosmer@springfieldmo.gov

★Council Member **Kristi Fulnecky** (At-Large C) .... (417) 864-1651
Term Expires: April 2019
E-mail: kfulnecky@springfieldmo.gov

★Council Member **Ken McClure** (At-Large D) .... (417) 864-1651
Term Expires: April 2019
E-mail: kmcclure@springfieldmo.gov
Education: Missouri State U 1972 BA; Missouri 1974 MA

Office of the City Clerk

P.O. Box 8368, Springfield, MO 65801-8368
Fax: (417) 864-1649

○City Clerk **Anita Cotter** .... (417) 864-1651
E-mail: acotter@springfieldmo.gov

Assistant City Clerk **Tom Smith** .... (417) 864-1650
E-mail: tomsmith@springfieldmo.gov

Office of the City Manager

P.O. Box 8368, Springfield, MO 65801-8368
Fax: (417) 864-1912

○City Manager **Gregory L. "Greg" Burris** .... (417) 864-1006
E-mail: gburris@springfieldmo.gov
Education: Missouri State U 1983 BS, MBA

Deputy City Manager **Timothy W. Smith** .... (417) 864-1004
E-mail: twsmith@springfieldmo.gov

Assistant City Manager **Collin Quigley** .... (417) 864-1116
E-mail: cquigley@springfieldmo.gov

Executive Assistant **Sharon Smith** .... (417) 864-1006
E-mail: sdsmith@springfieldmo.gov

Airport, Springfield/Branson Regional

2300 North Airport Boulevard, Suite 100, Springfield, MO 65802
Internet: www.flyspringfield.com/

Director of Aviation **Brian Weiler** .... (417) 868-0500 ext. 2001
Education: Embry-Riddle BS; Central Missouri MS Fax: (417) 868-0501

Assistant Director **Shawn Schroeder** .... (417) 868-0500 ext. 2002
Fax: (417) 868-0501

Art Museum, Springfield City

1111 East Brookside Drive, Springfield, MO 65807
P.O. Box 8368, Springfield, MO 65801-8368

Director **Nick Nelson** .... (417) 837-5700
Fax: (417) 837-5704

Building Development Services Department

840 Boonville Avenue, Springfield, MO 65802
P.O. Box 8368, Springfield, MO 65801-8368
Fax: (417) 864-1109

Director **Chris Straw** .... (417) 864-1059
Education: Missouri State U

911 Communications

P.O. Box 8368, Springfield, MO 65801-8368
330 West Scott Street, Springfield, MO 65802
Fax: (417) 864-1824

Director of Emergency Communications
Zim Schwartze .... (417) 829-6000
E-mail: zschwartze@springfieldmo.gov Fax: (417) 829-6100

Environmental Services Department

P.O. Box 8368, Springfield, MO 65801-8368
Fax: (417) 864-1929

Director **Stephen A. "Steve" Meyer** .... (417) 864-1919
Education: Missouri (Rolla) 1975 MS

Assistant Director **Errin Kemper** .... (417) 864-1910
E-mail: ekemper@springfieldmo.gov Fax: (417) 864-1983

Finance Department

840 Boonville Avenue, Springfield, MO 65802
P.O. Box 8368, Springfield, MO 65801-8368

Director **Mary Mannix-Decker** .... (417) 864-1625
Education: Trinity U BA Fax: (417) 864-1880

Fire Department

P.O. Box 8368, Springfield, MO 65801-8368
830 Boonville Avenue, Springfield, MO 65802

Fire Chief **David Hall** .... (417) 864-1500
E-mail: dhall@springfieldmo.gov Fax: (417) 864-1505
Education: Missouri State U BA, MBA

Human Resources Department

840 Boonville Avenue, Springfield, MO 65802
P.O. Box 8368, Springfield, MO 65801-8368

Director **Sheila Maerz** .... (417) 864-1607
E-mail: smaerz@springfieldmo.gov Fax: (417) 864-2041
Education: Arkansas 1984 BSBA; Pittsburg State 1999 MA

Information Systems Department

840 Boonville Avenue, Springfield, MO 65802
P.O. Box 8368, Springfield, MO 65801-8368
Fax: (417) 864-1122

Director **Jeff Coiner** .... (417) 864-1628
E-mail: jcoiner@springfieldmo.gov Fax: (417) 864-1122

★Elected Official ▲Appointed by Legislature ▼Appointed by Governor ▶Appointed by Board or Commission ●Appointed by Judge
■Appointed by Mayor △Appointed by Freeholders ▽Appointed by Supervisor ▷Appointed by County Executive ○Appointed by Council

Law Department
840 Boonville Avenue, Springfield, MO 65802
P.O. Box 8368, Springfield, MO 65801-8368

City Attorney **Dan Wichmer** .... (417) 864-1645
E-mail: dwichmer@springfieldmo.gov Fax: (417) 864-1551
Education: Northeast Missouri State BA; Missouri JD

Parks and Recreation Department
1923 North Weller, Springfield, MO 65803
P.O. Box 8368, Springfield, MO 65801-8368
Internet: http://www.springfieldmo.gov/623/Parks-Recreation

Director **Bob Belote** .... (417) 864-1327
Fax: (417) 837-5811

Planning and Development Department
840 Boonville Avenue, Springfield, MO 65802
P.O. Box 8368, Springfield, MO 65801-8368
Fax: (417) 864-1030

Director **Mary Lilly Smith** .... (417) 864-1031
E-mail: mlsmith@springfieldmo.gov Fax: (417) 864-1030

Police Department
321 East Chestnut Expressway, Springfield, MO 65802
P.O. Box 8368, Springfield, MO 65801

Police Chief **Paul F. Williams** .... (417) 864-1780
Education: Northern Michigan BSCrimJ; Fax: (417) 864-2052
Northeastern State MSc

Public Information Department
840 Boonville Avenue, Springfield, MO 65802
P.O. Box 8368, Springfield, MO 65801

Director of Public Information and Civic Engagement
Cora Scott .... (417) 864-1009
E-mail: cscott@springfieldmo.gov Fax: (417) 864-1114

Public Works Department
P.O. Box 8368, Springfield, MO 65801
840 Boonville Avenue, Springfield, MO 65802
Fax: (417) 864-1929

Director **Dan Smith** .... (417) 864-1902
Assistant Director **Martin Gugel** .... (417) 864-1902
Assistant Director **Kirk Juranas** .... (417) 864-1902

Springfield-Greene County Health Department [SGCHD]
227 East Chestnut Expressway, Springfield, MO 65802
P.O. Box 8368, Springfield, MO 65801-8368
Tel: (417) 864-1658 Fax: (417) 864-1099

Director **Kevin Gipson** .... (417) 864-1657
Education: Drury Col BA; Webster MA Fax: (417) 864-1099

Workforce Development Department
2900 East Sunshine, Springfield, MO 65804
P.O. Box 8368, Springfield, MO 65801
Internet: www.ozarksjobpath.org/

Director **Mary Ann Rojas** .... (417) 887-4343
E-mail: mrojas@springfieldmo.gov Fax: (417) 887-1892

City of Stamford, Connecticut
Government Center, 888 Washington Blvd., Stamford, CT 06901
P.O. Box 10152, Stamford, CT 06904-2152

County: Fairfield **Election Type:** Partisan **Year Incorporated:** 1893
Population: 128,874 (2015)

Office of the Mayor and Board of Representatives
Government Center, 888 Washington Boulevard, 10th Floor, Stamford, CT 06901
P.O. Box 10152, Stamford, CT 06904-2152
Tel: (203) 977-4150 Fax: (203) 977-5845 E-mail: bdreps@stamfordct.gov

★ Mayor **David R. Martin** (D) .... (203) 977-4150
Began Service: December 1, 2013
Term Expires: November 30, 2017
E-mail: mayorsoffice@stamfordct.gov
Education: MIT 1975 SB, 1976 BSE; Stanford 1979 MBA

■ Chief of Staff **Michael Pollard** .... (203) 977-4150
E-mail: mpollard@stamfordct.gov

★ President and Deputy Mayor
Randall M. Skigen (D-District 19) .... (203) 977-5032
Term Expires: November 30, 2017
E-mail: rskigen@stamfordct.gov

★ Board Member **Kieran Ryan** (R-District 1) .... (203) 977-5032
Term Expires: November 30, 2017
E-mail: kryan@stamfordct.gov

★ Board Member **David Watkins** (R-District 1) .... (203) 977-5032
Term Expires: November 30, 2017
E-mail: dwatkins1@stamfordct.gov

★ Board Member **Virgil de la Cruz** (D-District 2) .... (203) 977-5032
Term Expires: November 30, 2017
E-mail: vdelacruz@stamfordct.gov

★ Board Member **Elaine Mitchell** (D-District 2) .... (203) 977-5032
Term Expires: November 30, 2017
E-mail: emitchell@stamfordct.gov

★ Board Member **Terry B. Adams** (D-District 3) .... (203) 977-5032
Term Expires: November 30, 2017
E-mail: tadams@stamfordct.gov

★ Board Member **Elise Coleman** (D-District 3) .... (203) 977-5032
Term Expires: November 30, 2017
E-mail: ecoleman@stamfordct.gov

★ Board Member **Willy Giraldo** (D-District 4) .... (203) 977-5032
Term Expires: November 30, 2017
E-mail: wgiraldo@stamfordct.gov

★ Board Member **Mary Savage** (D-District 4) .... (203) 977-5032
Term Expires: November 30, 2017
E-mail: msavage@stamfordct.gov

★ Board Member **Gloria G. DePina** (D-District 5) .... (203) 977-5032
Term Expires: November 30, 2017
E-mail: gdepina@stamfordct.gov

★ Board Member **Lila Wallace** (D-District 5) .... (203) 977-5032
Term Expires: November 30, 2017
E-mail: lwallace@stamfordct.gov

★ Board Member **Denis W. Patterson** (D-District 6) .... (203) 977-5032
Term Expires: November 30, 2016

★ Board Member **Annie M. Summerville** (D-District 6) .... (203) 977-5032
Term Expires: November 30, 2017
E-mail: asummerville@stamfordct.gov

★ Board Member **Monica Di Costanzo** (D-District 7) .... (203) 977-5032
Term Expires: November 30, 2017
E-mail: mdicostanzo@stamfordCT.gov

★ Board Member **LIndsey C. Miller** (D-District 7) .... (203) 977-5032
Term Expires: November 30, 2017

★ Board Member **Anabel Diaz Figueroa** (D-District 8) .... (203) 977-5032
Term Expires: November 30, 2017
E-mail: afigueroa@stamfordct.gov

★ Board Member **Eileen Heaphy** (D-District 8) .... (203) 977-5032
Term Expires: November 30, 2017
E-mail: eheaphy@stamfordct.gov

(continued on next page)

★ Elected Official ▲ Appointed by Legislature ▼ Appointed by Governor ▶ Appointed by Board or Commission ● Appointed by Judge
■ Appointed by Mayor △ Appointed by Freeholders ▽ Appointed by Supervisor ▷ Appointed by County Executive ○ Appointed by Council

Office of the Mayor and Board of Representatives *continued*

★ Board Member **Valerie McNeil** (D-District 9) . . . . (203) 977-5032
Term Expires: November 30, 2017
E-mail: vmcneil@stamfordct.gov

★ Board Member **Rodney Pratt** (D-District 9) . . . . (203) 977-5032
Term Expires: November 30, 2017
E-mail: rpratt@stamfordCT.gov

★ Board Member **Philip J. Giordano** (D-District 10) . . . . . . (203) 977-5032
Term Expires: November 30, 2017
E-mail: pgiordano@stamfordct.gov

★ Board Member
Sister Mavina Felicia Moore (D-District 10) . . . . (203) 862-9823
Term Expires: November 30, 2017
E-mail: mmoore@stamfordct.gov

★ Board Member **Alice R. Liebson** (D-District 11) . . . . (203) 977-5032
Term Expires: November 30, 2017
E-mail: aliebson@stamfordct.gov

★ Board Member **John R. Zelinsky, Jr.** (D-District 11) . . . . (203) 977-5032
Term Expires: November 30, 2017
E-mail: jzelinsky@stamfordct.gov

★ Board Member **Brien T. Buckman** (D-District 12) . . . . (203) 977-5032
Term Expires: November 30, 2017
E-mail: bbuckman@stamfordct.gov

★ Board Member **Marion McGarry** (D-District 12) . . . . (203) 977-5032
Term Expires: November 30, 2017
E-mail: mmcgarry@stamfordCT.gov

★ Board Member **Harry Dale Day** (R-District 13) . . . . (203) 977-5032
Term Expires: November 30, 2017
E-mail: hday@stamfordCT.gov
Education: Yale 1970 BA; Cornell 1973 JD

★ Board Member **Keith Silver** (D-District 13) . . . . (203) 977-5032
Term Expires: November 30, 2017
E-mail: ksilver@stamfordct.gov

★ Board Member **Robert "Gabe" DeLuca** (R-District 14) . . (203) 977-5032
Term Expires: November 30, 2017
E-mail: rdeluca@stamfordCT.gov

★ Board Member **Carl J. Franzetti** (R-District 14) . . . . (203) 977-5032
Term Expires: November 30, 2017
E-mail: cfranzetti@stamfordct.gov

★ Board Member **Frank D. Cerasoli** (R-District 15) . . . . (203) 977-5032
Term Expires: November 30, 2017
E-mail: fcerasoli@stamfordct.gov

★ Board Member **Joseph G. Coppola, Jr.** (R-District 15) . . (203) 977-5032
Term Expires: November 30, 2017
E-mail: jcoppola@stamfordCT.gov

★ Board Member **Steven Kolenberg** (R-District 16) . . . . (203) 977-5032
Term Expires: November 30, 2017
E-mail: skolenberg@stamfordct.gov

★ Board Member **Matthew Quinones** (D-District 16) . . . . . (203) 977-5032
Term Expires: November 30, 2017
E-mail: mquinones@stamfordct.gov

★ Board Member **Jonathan T. Hoch** (R-District 17) . . . . . . (203) 977-5032
Term Expires: November 30, 2017

★ Board Member **Mary Lisa Fedeli** (R-District 17) . . . . (203) 977-5032
Term Expires: November 30, 2017
E-mail: mfedeli@stamfordCT.gov

★ Board Member **James F. Caterbone** (R-District 18) . . . . . (203) 977-5032
Term Expires: November 30, 2017
E-mail: jcaterbone@stamfordct.gov

★ Board Member **J.R. McMullen** (R-District 18) . . . . (203) 977-5032
Term Expires: November 30, 2017
E-mail: jmcmullen@stamfordCT.gov

★ Board Member **Gail Okun** (R-District 19) . . . . (203) 977-5032
Term Expires: November 30, 2017
E-mail: gokun@stamfordct.gov

★ Board Member **Dennis Mahoney** (R-District 20) . . . . (203) 977-5032
Term Expires: November 30, 2017
E-mail: dmahoney@stamfordct.gov

★ Board Member **Susan Nabel** (D-District 20) . . . . (203) 977-5032
Term Expires: November 30, 2017
E-mail: snabel@stamfordct.gov

Secretary **Angie Staley** . . . . (203) 977-2069

Office of Economic Development

Government Center, 888 Washington Boulevard, 10th Floor, Stamford, CT 06901
Fax: (203) 977-5845

■ Director **Thomas Madden** . . . . (203) 977-5168
E-mail: tmadden@stamfordct.gov

Office of the Town Clerk

P.O. Box 10152, Stamford, CT 06904-2152
Fax: (203) 977-4943

★ Town Clerk **Donna Loglisci** (R) . . . . (203) 977-4054
Term Expires: November 30, 2017
E-mail: dloglisci@stamfordct.gov

Office of Administration

P.O. Box 10152, Stamford, CT 06904-2152

■ Administration Director **Michael Handler** . . . . (203) 977-4183
E-mail: mhandler@stamfordct.gov

Office of Assessment and Tax Collection

P.O. Box 10152, Stamford, CT 06904-2152
Fax: (203) 977-5898

Assessment and Collection Director **William A. Forker** . . . (203) 977-4021
Assessor **Greg Stackpole** . . . . (203) 977-4018

Office of the Controller

P.O. Box 10152, Stamford, CT 06904-2152
Fax: (203) 977-5683

Controller **David Yanik** . . . . (203) 977-4186
888 Washington Boulevard, 10th Floor, Stamford, CT 06904-2152
E-mail: dyanik@stamfordct.gov

Community Development Department

P.O. Box 10152, Stamford, CT 06904-2152
Tel: (203) 977-4053

Grants Officer **Karen Cammarota** . . . . (203) 977-5709

Purchasing Department

P.O. Box 10152, Stamford, CT 06904
Fax: (203) 977-5253

Purchasing Agent **Beverly Aveni** . . . . (203) 977-4107
E-mail: baveni@stamfordct.gov

Technology Management Services Department

P.O. Box 10152, Stamford, CT 06904
Tel: (203) 977-4936 Fax: (203) 977-5060

Director **Michael Pensiero** . . . . (203) 977-4936
E-mail: mpensiero@stamfordct.gov Fax: (203) 977-4115

Ferguson Library

P.O. Box 10152, Stamford, CT 06904
Tel: (203) 964-1000 Fax: (203) 357-9098

President **Alice Knapp** . . . . (203) 964-1000 ext. 8200

Finance Board

P.O. Box 10152, Stamford, CT 06904
Fax: (203) 977-5030 E-mail: lgilden@stamfordct.gov

Chairman **Dr. Richard M. Freedman** . . . . (203) 977-4699
Clerk **(Vacant)** . . . . (203) 977-4699

Housing Authority

P.O. Box 1376, Stamford, CT 06904-1376

Executive Director **Vincent Tufo** . . . . (203) 977-1400

★ Elected Official ▲ Appointed by Legislature ▼ Appointed by Governor ► Appointed by Board or Commission ● Appointed by Judge
■ Appointed by Mayor △ Appointed by Freeholders ▽ Appointed by Supervisor ▷ Appointed by County Executive ○ Appointed by Council

Office of Legal Affairs
P.O. Box 10152, Stamford, CT 06904-2152
Fax: (230) 977-5560

■ Corporation Counsel **Kathryn Emmett** .... (203) 977-4082
E-mail: kemmett@stamfordct.gov

Human Resources Division
P.O. Box 10152, Stamford, CT 06904
Tel: (203) 977-4070 Fax: (203) 977-4075

Human Resources Director **Clemon Williams** .... (203) 977-4073
E-mail: cwilliams@stamfordct.gov

Office of Operations
P.O. Box 10152, Stamford, CT 06904
Tel: (203) 977-4141

■ Operations Director **Ernie Orgera** .... (203) 977-4140
E-mail: eorgera@stamfordct.gov
Solid Waste Supervisor **Dan Colleluori** .... (203) 977-4117

Building Inspections Department
888 Washington Blvd., 7th Floor, Stamford, CT 06901
Fax: (203) 977-4163

Chief Building Official **Robert "Bob" DeMarco** .... (203) 977-5700

Engineering Department
888 Washington Boulevard, 7th Floor, Stamford, CT 06904-2152
Tel: (203) 977-4189 Fax: (203) 977-4137

City Engineer **Louis Casolo** .... (203) 977-5796
E-mail: lcasolo@stamfordct.gov

Environmental Protection Board
888 Washington Blvd., Stamford, CT 06901
Fax: (203) 977-4100

Executive Director **Richard H. Talamelli** .... (203) 977-4965

Land Use Bureau
P.O. Box 10152, Stamford, CT 06904

Chief **Norman Cole** .... (203) 977-4714

Water Pollution Control Authority
Harbor View Avenue, Stamford, CT 06902
Tel: (203) 977-4590 Fax: (203) 977-5081

Executive Director **William Brink** .... (203) 977-5809
E-mail: wbrink@stamfordct.gov
Administration Manager **Rhudean Bull** .... (203) 977-4590
E-mail: rbull@stamfordct.gov
Supervising Engineer **Prakash Chakravarti** .... (203) 977-4590
E-mail: pchakravarti@stamfordct.gov

Zoning Board of Appeals
888 Washington Blvd., 7th Floor, Stamford, CT 06901
Tel: (203) 977-5704 Fax: (203) 977-4100

Chairperson **Claire Friedlander** .... (203) 977-4160

Office of Public Safety, Health and Welfare
P.O. Box 10152, Stamford, CT 06904-2152

○ Director **Thaddeus K. Jankowski** .... (203) 977-4151
E-mail: tjankowski@stamfordct.gov
Social Services **Ellen Bromley** .... (203) 977-4112

Office of Emergency Management
P.O. Box 10152, Stamford, CT 06904
Tel: (203) 977-5900

Director **Thomas Lombardo** .... (203) 977-5900
E-mail: tlombardo@stamfordct.gov

Environmental Health and Inspection Services
P.O. Box 10152, Stamford, CT 06904
Tel: (203) 977-4382 Fax: (203) 977-5882

Director **Ronald Miller** .... (203) 977-4363

Fire and Rescue Department
629 Main Street, 3rd Floor, Stamford, CT 06901
P.O. Box 10152, Stamford, CT 06904
Internet: http://www.stamfordfire.com

■ Fire Chief **Trevor Roach** .... (203) 977-4763
E-mail: troach@stamfordct.gov
Chief Fire Marshal **Charles Spaulding** .... (203) 977-4651
888 Washington Blvd., Stamford, CT 06901 Fax: (203) 977-5475
E-mail: cspaulding@stamfordct.gov

Health and Social Services Department
P.O. Box 10152, Stamford, CT 06904
Tel: (203) 977-5889 (Health Department Hotline) Fax: (203) 977-5882

■ Director (Interim) **David Knauf** .... (203) 977-4396
E-mail: dknauf@stamfordct.gov
Medical Director **Henry H. Yoon** .... (203) 977-4366
Education: Emory BS; Rush MD

Police Department
805 Bedford Street, Stamford, CT 06901-1194
Tel: (203) 977-4444 Fax: (203) 977-5583

■ Chief of Police **Jon Fontneau** .... (203) 977-4681
E-mail: jfontneau@stamfordct.gov

Registrars of Voters
P.O. Box 10152, Stamford, CT 06904-4070
888 Washington Blvd., 6th Floor, Stamford, CT 06901
Tel: (203) 977-4011 Tel: (203) 977-4012 Fax: (203) 977-5563

Democratic Registrar **Ron Malloy** .... (203) 977-4009
Republican Registrar **Lucy F. Corelli** .... (203) 977-4010

Stamford Public Schools
P.O. Box 10152, Stamford, CT 06904-2152

Superintendent of Schools (Interim) **James Connelly** .... (203) 977-4543

City of Sterling Heights, Michigan

40555 Utica Road, Sterling Heights, MI 48313
Internet: www.sterling-heights.net

County: Macomb **Election Type:** Nonpartisan **Year Incorporated:** 1968
Population: 132,052 (2015)

Office of the Mayor and City Council
40555 Utica Rd., Sterling Heights, MI 48313
P.O. Box 8009, Sterling Heights, MI 48311-8009
Fax: (586) 276-4060

★ Mayor **Michael C. Taylor** .... (586) 446-2489
Began Service: 2009
Term Expires: November 2017
E-mail: mctaylor@sterling-heights.net
Education: Kalamazoo 2005 BA; Wayne State U 2008 JD
★ Mayor Pro Tem **Joseph V. Romano** .... (586) 446-2489
Term Expires: November 2017
E-mail: cityhall@sterling-heights.net
★ Council Member **Deanna E. Koski** .... (586) 446-2489
Term Expires: November 2017
E-mail: dkoski@sterling-heights.net

(continued on next page)

★ Elected Official ▲ Appointed by Legislature ▼ Appointed by Governor ▶ Appointed by Board or Commission ● Appointed by Judge
■ Appointed by Mayor △ Appointed by Freeholders ▽ Appointed by Supervisor ▷ Appointed by County Executive ○ Appointed by Council

Office of the Mayor and City Council *continued*

★Council Member **Maria Schmidt** . . . . . (586) 446-2489
Term Expires: November 2017
E-mail: mgschmidt@sterling-heights.net

★Council Member **Nate B. Shannon** . . . . . (586) 446-2489
Term Expires: November 2017
E-mail: nshannon@sterling-heights.net

★Council Member **Doug Skrzyniarz** . . . . . (586) 446-2489
Term Expires: November 2017
E-mail: dskrzyniarz@sterling-heights.net

★Council Member **Barbara Ziarko** . . . . . (586) 446-2489
Term Expires: November 2017
E-mail: bziarko@sterling-heights.net

Office of the City Manager

40555 Utica Rd., Sterling Heights, MI 48313
P.O. Box 8009, Sterling Heights, MI 48311-8009

City Manager **Mark D. Vanderpool** . . . . . (586) 446-2305
E-mail: mvanderpool@sterling-heights.net
Education: Augustana (IL) BPA; Northern Illinois MPA

Office of the City Attorney

12900 Hall Rd., Suite 350, Sterling Heights, MI 48313
Fax: (586) 726-1560

City Attorney **Jeffrey Bahorski** . . . . . (586) 726-1000
E-mail: jbahorski@orlaw.com
Education: Michigan BA; Detroit JD

Office of the City Clerk

40555 Utica Rd., Sterling Heights, MI 48313
Fax: (586) 276-4077

City Clerk **Mark Carufel** . . . . . (586) 446-2421
E-mail: mcarufel@sterling-heights.net

Office of the Controller

40555 Utica Rd., Sterling Heights, MI 48313

Controller **Nick Makie** . . . . . (586) 446-2322
E-mail: nmakie@sterling-heights.net

Office of the Assessor

40555 Utica Rd., Sterling Heights, MI 48313

City Assessor **Dwayne McLachlan** . . . . . (586) 446-2341
E-mail: dmclachlan@sterling-heights.net

Office of Building Services

40555 Utica Rd., Sterling Heights, MI 48313
P.O. Box 8009, Sterling Heights, MI 48311
Tel: (586) 446-2360

Building Official **Mike Viazanko** . . . . . (586) 446-2361
E-mail: mviazanko@sterling-heights.net

Office of Business Development

40555 Utica Rd., Sterling Heights, MI 48313

City Development Director **Denice Gerstenberg** . . . . . (586) 446-2386
E-mail: dgerstenberg@sterling-heights.net

Office of Engineering

40555 Utica Rd., Sterling Heights, MI 48313
P.O. Box 8009, Sterling Heights, MI 48311
Tel: (586) 446-2580

City Engineer **Brent Beshaw** . . . . . (586) 446-2581
E-mail: bbashaw@sterling-heights.net

Office of Financial Services

40555 Utica Rd., Sterling Heights, MI 48313
P.O. Box 8009, Sterling Heights, MI 48311

Finance and Budget Director **Brian Baker** . . . . . (586) 446-2302
E-mail: bbaker@sterling-heights.net

Office of Information Technology

40555 Utica Rd., Sterling Heights, MI 48313
P.O. Box 8009, Sterling Heights, MI 48311

Director **Steve Deon** . . . . . (586) 446-2621
E-mail: sdeon@sterling-heights.net

Office of Planning

40555 Utica Rd., Sterling Heights, MI 48313
P.O. Box 8009, Sterling Heights, MI 48311
Tel: (586) 446-2720

City Planner **Christopher McLeod** . . . . . (586) 446-2360

Office of Purchasing

40555 Utica Rd., Sterling Heights, MI 48313
P.O. Box 8009, Sterling Heights, MI 48311
Tel: (586) 446-2740 Fax: (586) 276-4062

Purchasing Manager **James Buhlinger** . . . . . (586) 446-2741
E-mail: jbuhlinger@sterling-heights.net
Education: Walsh 1984 BSBA; Wayne State U 1996 MBA

Office of the Treasury

40555 Utica Rd., Sterling Heights, MI 48313
P.O. Box 8009, Sterling Heights, MI 48311
Tel: (586) 446-2780 Fax: (586) 276-4075

City Treasurer **Jennifer Varney** . . . . . (586) 446-2781

Community Relations Department

40555 Utica Rd., Sterling Heights, MI 48313
P.O. Box 8009, Sterling Heights, MI 48311

Director **Bridget Doyle** . . . . . (586) 446-2489
E-mail: bdoyle@sterling-heights.net Fax: (586) 446-4065

Fire Department

41625 Ryan Rd., Sterling Heights, MI 48314
Tel: (586) 446-2950 (Non Emergency)

Fire Chief **Chris Martin** . . . . . (586) 446-2951
E-mail: cmartin@sterling-heights.net

Police Department

40333 Dodge Park Rd., Sterling Heights, MI 48313
Tel: (586) 446-2800 (Non Emergency)

Chief of Police (Interim) **John Berg** . . . . . (586) 446-2810

Public Works Department

7200 Eighteen-Mile Rd., Sterling Heights, MI 48314
Tel: (586) 446-2440

Director **Michael Moore** . . . . . (586) 446-2441

Sterling Heights Public Library

40255 Dodge Park Rd., Sterling Heights, MI 48313-4140
Tel: (586) 446-2640

Director **Tammy Turgeon** . . . . . (586) 446-2641
E-mail: turgeont@libcoop.net

City of Stockton, California

425 North El Dorado Street, Stockton, CA 95202
Tel: (209) 937-8212 Internet: http://www.stocktongov.com

County: San Joaquin **Election Type:** Nonpartisan **Population:** 305,658 (2015)

Office of the Mayor and City Council

425 N. El Dorado St., Stockton, CA 95202
Fax: (209) 937-7194 Internet: www.stocktongov.com/government/council/

★Mayor **Anthony Silva** .... (209) 937-8499
Began Service: January 1, 2013
Term Expires: December 31, 2016
Executive Assistant **Sharon Simas** .... (209) 937-8499
E-mail: sharon.simas@stocktonca.gov

★Vice Mayor **Christina Fugazi** (District 5) .... (209) 937-8244
Term Expires: December 31, 2018

★Council Member **Elbert H. Holman, Jr.** (District 1) ..... (209) 937-8279
Term Expires: December 31, 2018
E-mail: dist1@stocktonca.gov

★Council Member **Daniel Wright** (District 2) .... (209) 937-8244
Term Expires: December 31, 2016
E-mail: dist2@stocktonca.gov

★Council Member **Susan Lofthus** (District 3) .... (209) 937-8279
Term Expires: December 31, 2018

★Council Member **Michael Blower** (District 4) .... (209) 937-8279
Term Expires: December 31, 2016

★Council Member **Michael Tubbs** (District 6) .... (209) 937-8279
Term Expires: December 31, 2016

Office of the City Attorney

425 North El Dorado Street, Stockton, CA 95202-1997
Fax: (209) 937-8898

○City Attorney **John M. Luebberke** .... (209) 937-8000
E-mail: john.luebberke@stocktonca.gov

Assistant City Attorney **Susana Alcala Wood** .... (209) 937-8009

Executive Assistant to the City Attorney
Paula Gonzalez .... (209) 937-8319
E-mail: joanne.montanez@stocktonca.gov

Office of the City Clerk

425 N. El Dorado St., Stockton, CA 95202
Tel: (209) 937-8458 Fax: (209) 937-8447

○City Clerk **Bonnie Paige** .... (209) 937-8458
E-mail: bonnie.paige@stocktonca.gov

Assistant City Clerk **Bret Hunter** .... (209) 937-7121
E-mail: bret.hunter@stocktonca.gov

Office of the City Manager

425 N. El Dorado St., Stockton, CA 95202
Tel: (209) 937-8212 Fax: (209) 937-7149

○City Manager **Kurt O. Wilson** .... (209) 937-8212
E-mail: city.manager@stocktonca.gov
Executive Assistant to the City Manager **Karen Costa** .. (209) 937-8212
E-mail: karen.costa@stocktonca.gov
Assistant to the City Manager **Christian Clegg** .... (209) 937-8212
E-mail: christian.clegg@stocktonca.gov

Deputy City Manager **Laurie Montes** .... (209) 937-8212
E-mail: laurie.montes@stocktonca.gov
Education: Cal State (Stanislaus) BSBA, MPA

Deputy City Manager **Scott Carney** .... (209) 937-8212
E-mail: scott.carney@stocktonca.gov

Public Information Officer **Connie Cochran** .... (209) 937-8827
E-mail: connie.cochran@stocktonca.gov

Administrative Services

425 N. El Dorado St., Stockton, CA 95202
Tel: (209) 937-8460 Fax: (209) 937-8844

Chief Financial Officer **Matt Paulin** .... (209) 937-8460
E-mail: matt.paulin@stocktonca.gov

Accounting Division

425 North El Dorado Street, Stockton, CA 95202
Tel: (209) 937-8571 Fax: (209) 937-8822

Accounting Manager **Ed Gato** .... (209) 937-5435
E-mail: ed.gato@stocktonca.gov

Information Technology Division

Fax: (209) 937-8897

Director **Nabil Fares** .... (209) 937-8550

Purchasing Division

Tel: (209) 937-8357 Fax: (209) 937-8855

Purchasing Agent **Concepcion Gayotin** .... (209) 937-8712
E-mail: concepcion.gayotin@stocktonca.gov

Community Development Department

345 N. El Dorado St., Stockton, CA 95202-1997
Tel: (209) 937-8444 Fax: (209) 937-8893

Director **David Kwong** .... (209) 937-8444

Building and Life Safety Division Deputy Director
Carl Hessner .... (209) 937-8561
E-mail: carl.hessner@stocktonca.gov

Planning and Engineering Services Division Deputy
Director **(Vacant)** .... (209) 937-8266

Community Services Department

6 E. Lindsay St., Stockton, CA 95202-1997
Tel: (209) 937-8206 Fax: (209) 937-8260

Director **John Alita** .... (209) 937-8373

Recreation Deputy Director **Craig Bronzan** .... (209) 937-8285

Executive Assistant **Kendra Stockwell** .... (209) 937-8419
E-mail: kendra.stockwell@stocktonca.gov

Library Services

605 N. El Dorado St., Stockton, CA 95202
Tel: (209) 937-8362 Fax: (209) 937-8683 Internet: http://www.ssjcpl.org/

Library Director **John Alita** .... (209) 937-8364
E-mail: john.alita@stocktonca.gov
Executive Assistant **Kendra Stockwell** .... (209) 937-8257
E-mail: kendra.stockwell@stocktonca.gov

Deputy Director **(Vacant)** .... (209) 937-8362

Economic Development Department

425 North El Dorado Street, Suite 317, Stockton, CA 95202
Tel: (209) 937-8539 Fax: (209) 937-5099
E-mail: economic.development@stocktonca.gov

Director **Micah Runner** .... (209) 937-8810
E-mail: micah.runner@stocktonca.gov

Fire Department

425 N. El Dorado St., Stockton, CA 95202
Tel: (209) 937-8801 Fax: (209) 937-8836
Internet: www.stocktongov.com/government/departments/fire/

Fire Chief **Erik Newman** .... (209) 937-8801

Deputy Chief/Fire Marshal **Mario McArn** .... (209) 937-8801
E-mail: mario.mcarn@stocktonca.gov

Division Chief/Training Director **Ken Johnson** .... (209) 937-8528
E-mail: ken.johnson@stocktonca.gov Fax: (209) 937-7280

★Elected Official ▲Appointed by Legislature ▼Appointed by Governor ▶Appointed by Board or Commission ●Appointed by Judge
■Appointed by Mayor △Appointed by Freeholders ▽Appointed by Supervisor ▷Appointed by County Executive ○Appointed by Council

Human Resources Department
22 East Weber Avenue, Suite 150, Stockton, CA 95202
Tel: (209) 937-8233 Fax: (209) 937-8558

Director (Interim) **Deanna Solina** . . . . (209) 937-8233
E-mail: deanna.solina@stocktonca.gov
Assistant Director/Employee Benefits **Deanna Solina** . . . . (209) 937-8617
E-mail: deanna.solina@stocktonca.gov
Executive Assistant **Sherri Asakawa** . . . . (209) 937-7557
E-mail: sherri.asakawa@stocktonca.gov

Municipal Utilities
2500 Navy Dr., Stockton, CA 95206
Tel: (209) 937-8750 E-mail: mud@stocktonca.gov

Director (Acting) **Robert Granberg** . . . . (209) 937-8700
Assistant Director **Robert Granberg** . . . . (209) 937-8734
Wastewater Deputy Director **Margaret P. Orr** . . . . (209) 937-5125
Water Resources Planning Deputy Director **(Vacant)** . . . . . (209) 937-8779

Police Department
22 E. Market St., Stockton, CA 95202-2876
Tel: (209) 937-8377 Fax: (209) 937-8894

Chief of Police **Eric Jones** . . . . (209) 937-8218
Program Manager, Telecommunications Supervisor
Melissa Murray . . . . (209) 937-8887
E-mail: melissa.murray@stocktonca.gov

Public Works Department
22 East Weber Avenue, Room 301, Stockton, CA 95202-2317
Tel: (209) 937-8411 Fax: (209) 937-7115

Director **Gordon MacKay** . . . . (209) 937-8400
Education: British Columbia BSCE
Executive Assistant **Cheryle Lawson** . . . . (209) 937-8531
E-mail: cheryle.lawson@stocktonca.gov

Engineering Division
Tel: (209) 937-8411 Fax: (209) 937-8277

Deputy Director/City Engineer **Eric Alvarez** . . . . (209) 937-8228
E-mail: eric.alvarez@stocktonca.gov

Operations/Maintenance Division
1465 South Lincoln, Stockton, CA 95206
Tel: (209) 937-8341 Fax: (209) 937-8883

Deputy Director **John Abrew** . . . . (209) 937-8438
E-mail: john.abrew@stocktonca.gov
Fleet Maintenance Supervisor **Douglas Smith** . . . . (209) 937-7144

Solid Waste and Recycling Division
Fax: (209) 937-7115

Solid Waste Manager **Gretchen Olsen** . . . . (209) 937-8826

City of Suffolk, Virginia

442 West Washington Street, Suffolk, VA 23434
P.O. Box 1858, Suffolk, VA 23439
Internet: www.suffolkva.us/

County: None **Election Type:** Nonpartisan **Population:** 88,161 (2015)

Office of the Mayor and City Council
442 West Washington Street, Suffolk, VA 23434
P.O. Box 1858, Suffolk, VA 23439
Fax: (757) 514-4027 E-mail: council@suffolkva.us

★ Mayor **Linda T. Johnson** . . . . (757) 514-4018
Began Service: July 5, 2000
Term Expires: December 31, 2016
E-mail: mayor@suffolkva.us
Career: City Council Liaison, State Corporation Commission, Commonwealth of Virginia; City Council Member, City of Suffolk, Virginia (2000-2006)
★ Vice Mayor **Leroy Bennett** (Cypress) . . . . (757) 514-4018
Term Expires: December 31, 2018
E-mail: cypress@suffolkva.us
★ Council Member **Michael Duman** (Chuckatuck) . . . . (757) 514-4018
Term Expires: December 31, 2018
E-mail: chuckatuck@suffolkva.us
★ Council Member **Roger Fawcett** (Sleepy Hole) . . . . (757) 514-4018
Term Expires: December 31, 2016
E-mail: sleepyhole@suffolkva.us
★ Council Member **Don Goldberg** (Suffolk) . . . . (757) 514-4018
Term Expires: December 31, 2018
E-mail: suffolk@suffolkva.us
★ Council Member **Timothy J. Johnson** (Holy Neck) . . . . . (757) 514-4018
Term Expires: December 31, 2018
E-mail: holyneck@suffolkva.us
★ Council Member **Curtis R. Milteer, Sr.** (Whaleyville) . . . . (757) 514-4018
Term Expires: December 31, 2016
E-mail: whaleyville@suffolkva.us
★ Council Member **Lue Ward** (Nansemond) . . . . (757) 514-4018
Term Expires: December 31, 2016
E-mail: nansemond@suffolkva.us

Office of the City Manager
442 West Washington Street, Suffolk, VA 23434
P.O. Box 1858, Suffolk, VA 23439
Fax: (757) 514-4010

○ City Manager **Patrick Roberts** . . . . (757) 514-4012
E-mail: citymanager@suffolkva.us
Voter Registrar **Susan Saunders** . . . . (757) 514-7750
Fax: (757) 514-7759
Deputy City Manager **Durrell "Scott" Mills** . . . . (757) 514-4011

Capital Programs and Buildings Department
442 West Washington Street, Suffolk, VA 23434
P.O. Box 1858, Suffolk, VA 23439

Director **Gerry L. Jones** . . . . (757) 514-4030

Economic Development Department
442 West Washington Street, Suffolk, VA 23434

Director **Kevin Hughes** . . . . (757) 514-4043
E-mail: khughes@suffolkva.us

Finance Department
P.O. Box 1858, Suffolk, VA 23439

Director **Tealen Hansen** . . . . (757) 514-7500

★ Elected Official ▲ Appointed by Legislature ▼ Appointed by Governor ► Appointed by Board or Commission ● Appointed by Judge
■ Appointed by Mayor △ Appointed by Freeholders ▽ Appointed by Supervisor ▷ Appointed by County Executive ○ Appointed by Council

Fire and Rescue Department
P.O. Box 1858, Suffolk, VA 23439

Fire Chief **Cedric Scott** .... (757) 514-4530
E-mail: firechief@suffolkva.us

Emergency Management Coordinator
Coordinator **CAPT James T. Judkins** .... (757) 514-4536
E-mail: jjudkins@suffolkva.us

Human Resources Department
P.O. Box 1858, Suffolk, VA 23439

Director **Nancy N. Olivo** .... (757) 514-4120
E-mail: nolivo@suffolkva.us
Assistant Director **Jessica Stallings** .... (757) 514-4115
E-mail: jstallings@suffolkva.us

Information Technology Department
P.O. Box 1858, Suffolk, VA 23439

Department Director **Kenneth R. Beam, Jr.** .... (757) 514-7241
E-mail: kbeam@suffolkva.us

Suffolk Public Library
P.O. Box 1858, Suffolk, VA 23439
Internet: http://www.suffolkpubliclibrary.com/

Director **Clint Rudy** .... (757) 514-7323
E-mail: crudy@suffolkva.us

Parks and Recreation
P.O. Box 1858, Suffolk, VA 23439

Director **Lakita S. Watson** .... (757) 514-7250
E-mail: lwatson@suffolkva.us

Planning and Community Development Department
442 West Washington Street, Suffolk, VA 23434

Director (Acting) **Robert Goumas** .... (757) 514-4060

Police Department
P.O. Box 1858, Suffolk, VA 23439

Chief of Police **Thomas E. Bennett** .... (757) 514-7900
Education: St Leo Col BA; Old Dominion MPA

Public Utilities Department
442 West Washington Street, Suffolk, VA 23434
Internet: www.suffolkva.us/pub_utl/ E-mail: publicutil@suffolkva.us

Director **Albert S. Moor II** .... (757) 514-7000

Public Works Department
P.O. Box 1858, Suffolk, VA 23439

Director **Eric T. Nielsen, Jr.** .... (757) 514-4356

Fleet Management Department
Fax: (757) 539-4303

Fleet and Equipment Services Manager **Jason Lalonde** .. (757) 514-4426

Redevelopment and Housing Authority
530 E. Pinner St., Suffolk, VA 23439

Executive Director **Clarissa McAdoo** .... (757) 539-2100
E-mail: cmcadoo@suffolkrha.org

Social Services Department
P.O. Box 1858, Suffolk, VA 23439

Director **Azeez Felder** .... (757) 514-7333

Suffolk Executive Airport
1200 Gene Bolton Drive, Suffolk, VA 23434
Tel: (757) 514-4411 Fax: (757) 538-0240

Airport Manager **Kent Marshall** .... (757) 514-4411

Western Tidewater Community Services Board
5268 Godwin Boulevard, Suffolk, VA 23434
Fax: (757) 255-7142 Internet: www.wtcsb.org/welcome/

Executive Director **Demetrios N. Peratsakis** .... (757) 255-7136

Office of the City Assessor
442 West Washington Street, Suffolk, VA 23434

○ Assessor of Real Estate **Jean Jackson** .... (757) 514-7479
E-mail: cityassessor@suffolkva.us
Deputy Assessor **Timothy H. "Tim" Lamb** .... (757) 514-7479

Office of the City Attorney
442 West Washington Street, Suffolk, VA 23434
P.O. Box 1858, Suffolk, VA 23439

○ City Attorney **Helivi Holland** .... (757) 514-7130
E-mail: cityattorney@suffolkva.us

Office of the City Clerk
442 West Washington Street, Suffolk, VA 23434
P.O. Box 1858, Suffolk, VA 23439

○ City Clerk **Erika S. Dawley** .... (757) 514-4020
E-mail: edawley@suffolkva.us

Office of the Commissioner of the Revenue
P.O. Box 1459, Suffolk, VA 23439

★ Commissioner of the Revenue **Susan L. Draper** .... (757) 514-4260
Term Expires: December 31, 2017
E-mail: sdraper@suffolkva.us

Office of the Commonwealth's Attorney
Godwin Courts Building, 150 North Main Street, Suffolk, VA 23434
Tel: (757) 514-4365

★ Commonwealth's Attorney **C. Phillips Ferguson** .... (757) 514-4369
Term Expires: December 31, 2017
E-mail: cwattorney@suffolkva.us

Office of the Sheriff
P.O. Box 1632, Suffolk, VA 23439

★ Sheriff **Raleigh H. Isaacs, Sr.** .... (757) 514-7847
Term Expires: December 31, 2017
E-mail: risaacs@suffolkva.us

Office of the Treasurer
P.O. Box 1583, Suffolk, VA 23439
Fax: (757) 514-7299

★ Treasurer **Ronald H. Williams** .... (757) 514-4285
Term Expires: December 31, 2017
E-mail: rwilliams@suffolkva.us

Suffolk Public Schools
100 North Main Street, Suffolk, VA 23434
Tel: (757) 925-6750 Fax: (757) 925-6751 Internet: www.spsk12.net/

Superintendent of Schools **Deran R. Whitney** .... (757) 925-6750

★ Elected Official ▲ Appointed by Legislature ▼ Appointed by Governor ▶ Appointed by Board or Commission ● Appointed by Judge
■ Appointed by Mayor △ Appointed by Freeholders ▽ Appointed by Supervisor ▷ Appointed by County Executive ○ Appointed by Council

City of Sunnyvale, California

P.O. Box 3707, Sunnyvale, CA 94088-3707
Internet: www.sunnyvale.ca.gov

County: Santa Clara **Population:** 151,754 (2015)

Office of the Mayor and City Council

P.O. Box 3707, Sunnyvale, CA 94088-3707
Fax: (408) 730-7699 E-mail: council@sunnyvale.ca.gov

★Mayor **Glenn Hendricks** (Seat 2) . . . . . (408) 730-7473
Began Service: January 2014
Term Expires: January 2019
E-mail: ghendricks@sunnyvale.ca.gov

★Vice Mayor **Gustav Larsson** (Seat 1) . . . . . (408) 730-7473
Term Expires: January 2019

★Council Member **Jim Davis** (Seat 6) . . . . . (408) 730-7473
Term Expires: January 2017

★Council Member **James R. Griffith** (Seat 3) . . . . . (408) 730-7473
Term Expires: January 2019

★Council Member **Tara Martin-Milius** (Seat 7) . . . . . (408) 730-7473
Term Expires: January 2017

★Council Member **Patrick Meyering** (Seat 5) . . . . . (408) 730-7473
Term Expires: January 2017

★Council Member **David Whittum** (Seat 4) . . . . . (408) 730-7473
Term Expires: January 2017
E-mail: dwhittum@sunnyvale.ca.gov

Office of the City Manager

P.O. Box 3707, Sunnyvale, CA 94088-3707
Fax: (408) 730-7699

City Manager **Deanna J. Santana** . . . . . (408) 730-7480
E-mail: citymgr@sunnyvale.ca.gov
Education: UC Berkeley 1992; MIT 1995

Assistant City Manager **Walter C. Rossmann** . . . . . (408) 730-7480
E-mail: wrossmann@sunnyvale.ca.gov

Second Assistant City Manager **Kent Steffens** . . . . . (408) 730-7480
E-mail: ksteffens@sunnyvale.ca.gov

Office of the City Clerk

P.O. Box 3707, Sunnyvale, CA 94088-3707
Fax: (408) 730-7619

City Clerk **Kathleen Franco Simmons** . . . . . (408) 730-7483
E-mail: cityclerk@sunnyvale.ca.gov Fax: (408) 730-7619

Office of the City Attorney

P.O. Box 3707, Sunnyvale, CA 94088-3707
Fax: (408) 730-7468

City Attorney **John Nagel** . . . . . (408) 730-7464

Community Development Department

P.O. Box 3707, Sunnyvale, CA 94088-3707
Fax: (408) 730-7715

Director **Trudi Ryan** . . . . . (408) 730-7444
E-mail: tryan@sunnyvale.ca.gov Fax: (408) 730-7715

NOVA Workforce Services

505 West Olive Avenue, Suite 550, Sunnyvale, CA 94086
Fax: (408) 730-7643

Director **Kris Stadelman** . . . . . (408) 730-7232
E-mail: webmaster@novaworks.org

Environmental Services Department

P.O. Box 3707, Sunnyvale, CA 94088-3707

Director **John Stufflebean** . . . . . (408) 730-7900
Fax: (408) 730-7286

Finance Department

P.O. Box 3707, Sunnyvale, CA 94088-3707
Fax: (408) 737-4950

Director (Acting) **Tim Kirby** . . . . . (408) 730-7380

Human Resources Department

505 West Olive Avenue, Suite 200, Sunnyvale, CA 94086

Director **Teri Silva** . . . . . (408) 730-7490
Fax: (408) 720-1497

Information Technology Department

650 West Olive Avenue., Sunnyvale, CA 94086

Director **David Jensen** . . . . . (408) 730-7540
E-mail: djensen@sunnyvale.ca.gov

Library and Community Services Department

665 W. Olive Ave., Sunnyvale, CA 94086

Library Director **Cynthia Bojorquez** . . . . . (408) 730-7314
Fax: (408) 735-8767

Public Safety Department

700 All America Way, Sunnyvale, CA 94086
Fax: (408) 749-0166

Director **Frank Grgurina** . . . . . (408) 730-7100
E-mail: pubsfty@sunnyvale.ca.gov Fax: (408) 730-5713

Public Works Department

P.O. Box 3707, Sunnyvale, CA 94088-3707

Director **Manuel Pineda** . . . . . (408) 730-7415
Fax: (408) 730-7286

Purchasing Division

P.O. Box 3707, Sunnyvale, CA 94088-3707

Purchasing Officer **Pete Gonda** . . . . . (408) 730-7405
E-mail: purchasing@sunnyvale.ca.gov Fax: (408) 730-7710

City of Syracuse, New York

City Hall, 233 E. Washington St., Syracuse, NY 13202
Tel: (315) 448-2489 (Information) TTY: (315) 448-8525
Internet: www.syrgov.net

County: Onondaga **Election Type:** Partisan **Population:** 144,142 (2015)

Office of the Mayor

City Hall, 233 East Washington Street, Syracuse, NY 13202
Fax: (315) 448-8067 Internet: http://www.syrgov.net/City_Hall.aspx

★Mayor **Stephanie Miner** (D) Room 203 . . . . . (315) 448-8005
Began Service: January 1, 2010
Term Expires: December 31, 2017
E-mail: mayor@syrgov.net
Date of Birth: April 30, 1970
Education: Syracuse 1992 BA; SUNY (Buffalo) 1999 JD

■Chief of Staff **William M. Ryan** (D) . . . . . (315) 448-8005
E-mail: wryan@syrgov.net

■Assistant Director, Intergovernmental Affairs
Michael "Mick" Sicchio . . . . . (315) 448-8005
E-mail: msicchio@syrgov.net

■Director of Mayoral Initiatives **Tim Carroll** . . . . . (315) 448-8005

■Press Secretary **Alexander Marion** Room 203 . . . . . (315) 448-8005
E-mail: amarion@syrgov.net
Education: St John's U (NY) 2012 BA

■Director of Constituent Services **Maria Ferrara** . . . . . (315) 448-8005
E-mail: MFerrara@SyrGov.net

★Elected Official ▲Appointed by Legislature ▼Appointed by Governor ▶Appointed by Board or Commission ●Appointed by Judge
■Appointed by Mayor △Appointed by Freeholders ▽Appointed by Supervisor ▷Appointed by County Executive ○Appointed by Council

Finance Department
City Hall, 233 East Washington Street, Room 128, Syracuse, NY 13202
Fax: (315) 448-8424 E-mail: finance@syrgov.net

■ Commissioner of Finance **David Delvecchio** . . . . (315) 448-8310
E-mail: ddelvecchio@syrgov.net

Information Systems Bureau
Fax: (315) 448-8030

■ Director **David Prowak** . . . . (315) 448-8250
E-mail: dprowak@syrgov.net

Personnel and Labor Relations Department
City Hall, 233 East Washington Street, Room 312, Syracuse, NY 13202
Fax: (315) 448-8761

■ Director **Derrick Thomas** . . . . (315) 448-8780
E-mail: dthomas@syrgov.net

Research Bureau
City Hall, 233 E. Washington St., Rm. 419, Syracuse, NY 13202-1421
Tel: (315) 448-8020 Fax: (315) 448-8008

■ Director **Janet Burke** . . . . (315) 448-8020
E-mail: jburke@syrgov.net

Office of Management and Budget
City Hall, 233 E. Washington St., Room 213, Syracuse, NY 13202
Tel: (315) 448-8252 Fax: (315) 448-8116 E-mail: budget@syrgov.net

■ Budget Director **Mary Vossler** . . . . (315) 448-8080
E-mail: mvossler@syrgov.net

Assessment Department
City Hall, 233 East Washington Street, Room 130, Syracuse, NY 13202
Tel: (315) 448-8280 E-mail: assessment@syrgov.net

■ Commissioner **David Clifford** . . . . (315) 448-8286
E-mail: dclifford@syrgov.net
First Deputy Commissioner **Ann Gallagher** . . . . (315) 448-8280
E-mail: agallagher@syrgov.net

Aviation Department
Hancock International Airport, 1000 Colonel Eileen Collins Blvd., Syracuse, NY 13212
Fax: (315) 454-8757 E-mail: realec@syrairport.org

■ Commissioner **Christina Callahan** . . . . (315) 454-3263
E-mail: callahanc@syrairport.org

Department of Neighborhood and Business Development
333 West Washington Street, Suite 130, Syracuse, NY 13202
Fax: (315) 448-8036

■ Director **Paul Driscoll** . . . . (315) 448-8100
E-mail: PDriscoll@SyrGov.net
Deputy Director **Ben Walsh** . . . . (315) 473-3275
E-mail: bwalsh@syrgov.net
Deputy Director **(Vacant)** . . . . (315) 448-8100
Code Enforcement Director **Ken Towsley** . . . . (315) 448-8706
E-mail: CodeEnforcement@SyrGov.net Fax: (315) 448-8764

Fire Department
Public Safety Bldg., 511 S. State St., Syracuse, NY 13202
Fax: (315) 422-7766

■ Fire Chief **Paul Linnertz** . . . . (315) 473-5525
E-mail: plinnertz@syrgov.net
First Deputy Chief **Kent Young** . . . . (315) 473-5525
E-mail: kyoung@syrgov.net

Law Department
City Hall, 233 East Washington Street, Room 300, Syracuse, NY 13202
Fax: (315) 448-8381 E-mail: law@syrgov.net

■ Corporation Counsel **Robert P. Stamey** . . . . (315) 448-8400
E-mail: law@syrgov.net

Leadership Greater Syracuse
5703 Enterprise Parkway, East Syracuse, NY 13057
Tel: (315) 422-5471 Fax: (315) 422-6455 E-mail: lgs@leadsyr.org
Internet: http://www.leadsyr.org

Executive Director **Pam Brunet** . . . . (315) 422-5471
E-mail: pam@leadsyr.org

Parks and Recreation Department
412 Spencer St., Syracuse, NY 13204
Fax: (315) 428-8513

Commissioner **Lazarus Sims** . . . . (315) 473-4330
Deputy Commissioner **Mary Beth Roach** . . . . (315) 473-4330

Police Department
Public Safety Bldg., 511 S. State St., Syracuse, NY 13202
Fax: (315) 442-5198 E-mail: police@syrgov.net

■ Chief of Police **Frank Fowler** . . . . (315) 442-5250
E-mail: ffowler@syrgov.net
First Deputy Chief of Police **Dave Barrette** . . . . (315) 442-5250

Public Works Department
1200 Canal St. Extension, Syracuse, NY 13210
Tel: (315) 448-2489 Fax: (315) 448-8531 E-mail: dpw@syrgov.net

■ Commissioner **Pete O'Connor** . . . . (315) 448-8515
E-mail: poconnor@syrgov.net
First Deputy Commissioner **Tom Simone** . . . . (315) 448-8515

Water Department
101 N. Beech St., Syracuse, NY 13210
Tel: (315) 473-2609 Fax: (315) 473-2608 E-mail: syrwater@syrgov.net

■ Commissioner **Deborah Somers** . . . . (315) 473-2609

Office of the Common Council
City Hall, 233 East Washington Street, Room 314, Syracuse, NY 13202
Fax: (315) 448-8423 Internet: www.syracuse.ny.us/Common_Council.aspx

★ President **Van B. Robinson** (D) . . . . (315) 448-8466
Term Expires: December 31, 2017
E-mail: vrobinson@syrgov.net
Administrative Assistant **Morgan Striggles** . . . . (315) 448-8466
E-mail: mstriggles@syrgov.net
★ Council Member **Joseph G. Carni** (R-District 1) . . . . (315) 448-8466
Term Expires: December 31, 2017
★ Council Member **Chad Ryan** (D-District 2) . . . . (315) 448-8466
Term Expires: December 31, 2017
E-mail: cryan@syrgov.net
★ Council Member **Susan C. Boyle** (D-District 3) . . . . (315) 448-8466
Term Expires: December 31, 2017
★ Council Member **Khalid Bey** (D-District 4) . . . . (315) 448-8466
Term Expires: December 31, 2017
E-mail: kbey@syrgov.net
★ Council Member **Nader Maroun** (D-District 5) . . . . (315) 448-8466
Term Expires: December 31, 2017
E-mail: nmaroun@syrgov.net
★ Council Member **Helen Hudson** (D-At-Large) . . . . (315) 448-8466
Term Expires: December 31, 2019
E-mail: hhudson@syrgov.net
★ Council Member **Jean Kessner** (D-At-Large) . . . . (315) 448-8466
Term Expires: December 31, 2017
E-mail: jkessner@syrgov.net
★ Council Member **Joseph Nicoletti** (D-At-Large) . . . . (315) 448-8466
Term Expires: December 31, 2017

(continued on next page)

★ Elected Official ▲ Appointed by Legislature ▼ Appointed by Governor ▶ Appointed by Board or Commission ● Appointed by Judge
■ Appointed by Mayor △ Appointed by Freeholders ▽ Appointed by Supervisor ▷ Appointed by County Executive ○ Appointed by Council

Office of the Common Council *continued*

★Council Member **Steven P. Thompson** (D-At-Large) .... (315) 448-8466
Term Expires: December 31, 2019
Secretary to the Council **Amanda Gusman** .... (315) 448-8466
Secretary to the Council **Carmelita Sapp-Walker** .... (315) 448-8466
E-mail: csapp-walker@syrgov.net
Research Assistant **James Conroy** .... (315) 448-8466
E-mail: jconroy@syrgov.net

Office of the City Clerk

City Hall, 233 East Washington Street, Room 231, Syracuse, NY 13202
Tel: (315) 448-8216 Fax: (315) 448-8489
Internet: www.syracuse.ny.us/City_Clerk.aspx

○City Clerk **John P. Copanas** .... (315) 448-8218
E-mail: jcopanas@syrgov.net
Deputy City Clerk **Patricia McBride** .... (315) 448-8388
E-mail: jparker@syrgov.net

Office of the City Auditor

City Hall, 233 East Washington Street, Room 433, Syracuse, NY 13202
Fax: (315) 448-8475 Internet: www.syracuse.ny.us/city_auditor.aspx

★City Auditor **Martin D. Masterpole** (D).............. (315) 448-8477
Term Expires: December 31, 2019
E-mail: mmasterpole@syrgov.net
Education: SUNY (Oswego) 1998 BA

Syracuse City School District

725 Harrison St., Syracuse, NY 13210-2325
Tel: (315) 435-4499 Internet: http://www.syracusecityschools.com

Superintendent of Schools **Sharon L. Contreras** .... (315) 435-4161
Chief of Staff **Monique Wright-Williams** .... (315) 435-4161
Fax: (315) 435-4015
Director of Facilities, Maintenance and Operations
Thomas Ferrara .... (315) 435-4292
E-mail: tferrara@scsd.us Fax: (315) 425-5225
Chief Operations Officer **Jaime Alicea** .... (315) 435-4161
E-mail: jalicea@scsd.us
Chief Accountability Officer **Dr. Brandan Keaveny** ...... (315) 435-4281
Chief Talent Officer **Christopher Miller** .... (315) 435-4212
E-mail: Cmiller@scsd.us Fax: (315) 435-4163
Chief Financial Officer **Suzanne Slack** .... (315) 435-4826
Chief Academic Officer **Linda Mulvey** .... (315) 435-5844

City of Tacoma, Washington

Tacoma Municipal Bldg., 747 Market St., Tacoma, WA 98402-3768
Internet: www.cityoftacoma.org

County: Pierce **Election Type:** Nonpartisan **Year Incorporated:** 1884
Population: 207,948 (2015)

Office of the Mayor and City Council

Tacoma Municipal Bldg., 747 Market St., Room 1200,
Tacoma, WA 98402-3766
Tel: (253) 591-5100 Fax: (253) 591-5123

★Mayor **Marilyn Strickland** .... (253) 594-7848
Began Service: January 1, 2010
Term Expires: December 31, 2017
E-mail: marilyn.strickland@cityoftacoma.org
Mayor and Council Support **Ann Chambers** .... (253) 594-7848
E-mail: ann.chambers@cityoftacoma.org
★Deputy Mayor **Ryan Mello** (At-Large 8).............. (253) 591-5470
Term Expires: December 31, 2019
E-mail: ryan.mello@cityoftacoma.org
★Council Member **Anders Ibsen** (District 1) .... (253) 591-5470
Term Expires: December 31, 2019
E-mail: anders.ibsen@cityoftacoma.org

Office of the Mayor and City Council *continued*

★Council Member **Robert Thoms** (District 2) .... (253) 594-7848
Term Expires: December 31, 2017
Education: SUNY Col (Buffalo) BA; Gonzaga MA
★Council Member **Keith Blocker** (District 3) .... (253) 591-5470
Term Expires: December 31, 2019
★Council Member **Marty Campbell** (District 4).......... (253) 591-5470
Term Expires: December 31, 2017
E-mail: marty.campbell@cityoftacoma.org
★Council Member **Joe Lonergan** (District 5) .... (253) 591-5470
Term Expires: December 31, 2017
E-mail: joe.lonergan@cityoftacoma.org
★Council Member **Victoria Woodards** (At-Large 6) ...... (253) 591-5470
Term Expires: December 31, 2017
E-mail: victoria.woodards@cityoftacoma.org
★Council Member **Conor McCarthy** (At-Large 7) .... (253) 591-5470
Term Expires: December 31, 2019
E-mail: conor.mccarthy@cityoftacoma.org
Council Support **Rosheida Myers** .... (253) 591-5470
E-mail: rmyers@cityoftacoma.org

Office of the City Manager

Tacoma Municipal Building, 747 Market Street, Room 1200,
Tacoma, WA 98402-3766
Tel: (253) 591-5125 Fax: (253) 591-5123

City Manager **T. C. Broadnax** .... (253) 591-5134
E-mail: tc.broadnax@cityoftacoma.org
Education: Washburn BA, BA; North Texas MPA
Assistant City Manager **Mark R. Lauzier** .... (253) 591-5125
Assistant to the City Manager **Nadia Chandler Hardy** ... (253) 591-5125
E-mail: nchandler2@cityoftacoma.org
Government Relations Officer **Randy Lewis** .... (253) 591-5122

Office of the City Attorney

Tacoma Municipal Bldg., 747 Market St., Room 1120,
Tacoma, WA 98402-3768
Tel: (253) 591-5885 Fax: (253) 591-5755

City Attorney **Elizabeth Pauli** .... (253) 591-5627
E-mail: epauli@cityoftacoma.org
City Clerk **Doris Sorum** .... (253) 591-5361
E-mail: dsorum@cityoftacoma.org

Community and Economic Development Department

Tacoma Municipal Building, 747 Market Street, Room 900,
Tacoma, WA 98402-3793
Tel: (253) 591-5624 Fax: (253) 591-5232

Director **Ricardo Noguera** .... (253) 591-5139
E-mail: rnoguera@cityoftacoma.org

Environmental Services

747 Market Street, Room 408, Tacoma, WA 98402
Tel: (253) 591-5525 Fax: (253) 591-5097

Director **Michael P. "Mike" Slevin III** .... (253) 591-5528
Assistant Director **John O'Loughlin** .... (253) 502-2175
E-mail: joloughl@cityoftacoma.org
Science and Engineering Division Manager
Geoffrey M. Smyth .... (253) 502-2111
326 East D Street, Tacoma, WA 98421-1801
E-mail: gsmyth@cityoftacoma.org
Solid Waste Management Division Manager **Gary Kato** .. (253) 593-7713
3510 South Mullen Street, Tacoma, WA 98409
Operations and Maintenance Division Manager
Judith Scott .... (253) 502-2154
2201 East Portland Avenue, Tacoma, WA 98421
E-mail: jscott5@cityoftacoma.org

★Elected Official ▲Appointed by Legislature ▼Appointed by Governor ▶Appointed by Board or Commission ●Appointed by Judge
■Appointed by Mayor △Appointed by Freeholders ▽Appointed by Supervisor ▷Appointed by County Executive ○Appointed by Council

Environmental Services *continued*

Business Operations Division Manager
Daniel C. Thompson .... (253) 502-2191
2201 East Portland Avenue, Tacoma, WA 98421
E-mail: dthompso@cityoftacoma.org

Finance Department

Tacoma Municipal Bldg., 747 Market St., Room 132,
Tacoma, WA 98402-3768
Tel: (253) 591-5800 Fax: (253) 591-5757

Director **Andy Cherullo** .... (253) 591-5803
Fax: (253) 591-5757
City Treasurer **Teresa Sedmak** .... (253) 591-5841
Fax: (253) 573-2327
Procurement and Payables Division Manager
Patsy Best .... (253) 502-8252
E-mail: pbest@cityoftacoma.org Fax: (253) 502-8372
Tax and License Division Manager **Danielle Larson** ..... (253) 591-5251
E-mail: dlarson@cityoftacoma.org Fax: (253) 591-5512

Fire Department

901 Fawcett Ave., Tacoma, WA 98402
Tel: (253) 591-5737 Fax: (253) 591-5746

Fire Chief **James "Jim" Duggan** .... (253) 591-5737
E-mail: jduggan@cityoftacoma.org
Administration Bureau Deputy Chief **Toryono Green** .... (253) 591-5010
E-mail: tgreen@cityoftacoma.org
Operations Bureau Deputy Chief **Faith Mueller** .... (253) 591-5011
E-mail: fmueller@cityoftacoma.org

Hearing Examiner

Tacoma Municipal Bldg., 747 Market Street, Room 720,
Tacoma, WA 98402-3768
Tel: (253) 591-5195 Fax: (253) 591-2003

Hearing Examiner **Phyllis K. Macleod** .... (253) 591-5195
Education: U Puget Sound 1980 JD

Human Resources Department

Tacoma Municipal Bldg., 747 Market St., Room 1336,
Tacoma, WA 98402-3768
Tel: (253) 591-5400 Fax: (253) 591-5793

Director **Joy St. Germain** .... (253) 591-5400
E-mail: jstgermain@cityoftacoma.org

Information Technology Department

733 Market Street, Room 50, Tacoma, WA 98402
Tel: (253) 382-2600 Fax: (253) 382-2654

Director **Jack Kelanic** .... (253) 502-2630
E-mail: jkelanic@cityoftacoma.org
Assistant Director **Paul Federighi** .... (253) 382-2606
E-mail: pfederig@cityoftacoma.org

Neighborhood and Community Services Department

Tacoma Municipal Building, 747 Market Street, Room 836,
Tacoma, WA 98402-3779
Tel: (253) 591-5012 Fax: (253) 591-5050

Director **Nadia Chandler Hardy** .... (253) 591-5012

Planning and Development Services Department

747 Market Street, Room 408, Tacoma, WA 98402-3766

Director **Peter Huffman** .... (253) 591-5056

Police Department

3701 South Pine, Tacoma, WA 98409
Tel: (253) 591-5900 E-mail: info@TacomaPolice.org
Internet: http://www.tacomapolice.org

Chief of Police **Donald Ramsdell** .... (253) 591-5905
Investigations Bureau Assistant Chief **Pete Cribbin** ...... (253) 830-6513
E-mail: pcribbin@cityoftacoma.org
Administrative Services Bureau Assistant Chief
Kathy McAlpine .... (253) 591-5889
Operations Bureau Assistant Chief **Michael Ake** .... (253) 591-5942
E-mail: make@cityoftacoma.org
Public Information Officer **Loretta Cool** .... (253) 591-5968
E-mail: lcool@cityoftacoma.org

Public Assembly Facilities

Greater Tacoma Convention & Trade Center

1500 Broadway, Tacoma, WA 98402
Tel: (253) 830-6601 Fax: (253) 573-2363

Deputy Director **Kim Bedier** .... (253) 593-7600

Tacoma Dome

2727 East D Street, Tacoma, WA 98421
Tel: (253) 272-3663 Fax: (253) 593-7620

Public Assembly Facilities Deputy Director **Jon Houg** ... (253) 593-7626
E-mail: jhoug@cityoftacoma.org

Tacoma Public Library

1102 Tacoma Ave. South, Tacoma, WA 98402
Tel: (253) 292-2001 Fax: (253) 344-5584

Director **Susan Odencrantz** .... (253) 292-2001 ext. 1111
E-mail: sodencrantz@tacomalibrary.org

Public Utility Board

P.O. Box 11007, Tacoma, WA 98411
Internet: www.mytpu.org/

Chair **Bryan Flint** .... (253) 502-8205
Vice Chair **Mark Patterson** .... (253) 502-8205
Secretary **Monique Trudnowski** .... (253) 502-8205
Member **Woodrow Jones** .... (253) 502-8205
Member **Karen J. Larkin** .... (253) 502-8205

Tacoma Public Utilities

3628 South 35th Street, Tacoma, WA 98409
P.O. Box 11007, Tacoma, WA 98411
Tel: (253) 502-8600 Internet: http://www.mytpu.org/

Director and Chief Executive Officer
William A. "Bill" Gaines .... (253) 502-8205
Customer Service Manager **Steve Hatcher** .... (253) 502-8650

Tacoma Power

3628 South 35th Street, Tacoma, WA 98409
P.O. Box 11007, Tacoma, WA 98411
Tel: (253) 502-8000 Fax: (253) 502-8378
E-mail: power@cityoftacoma.org Internet: www.mytpu.com

Power Superintendent **Chris Robinson** .... (253) 502-8282
Click! Network Manager **Tenzin Gyaltsen** .... (253) 502-8148
Generation Manager **Pat McCarty** .... (253) 502-8445
Transmission and Distribution Manager
Dolores Stegeman .... (253) 502-8115

Tacoma Rail

2601 SR 509 North Frontage Road, Tacoma, WA 98421
P.O. Box 11007, Tacoma, WA 98411
Tel: (253) 502-8819 Fax: (253) 922-9088
E-mail: railoperations@cityoftacoma.org
Internet: http://www.mytpu.org/tacomarail/

Rail Superintendent **Dale King** .... (253) 502-8894
Fax: (253) 922-9088

(continued on next page)

★ Elected Official ▲ Appointed by Legislature ▼ Appointed by Governor ▶ Appointed by Board or Commission ● Appointed by Judge
■ Appointed by Mayor △ Appointed by Freeholders ▽ Appointed by Supervisor ▷ Appointed by County Executive ○ Appointed by Council

Tacoma Public Utilities *continued*

Assistant Rail Superintendent **Alan Hardy** . . . . (253) 502-8896
Fax: (253) 502-8908

Terminal Superintendent **Tim Flood** . . . . (253) 502-8675
E-mail: tim.flood@cityoftacoma.org Fax: (253) 502-8908

Chief Mechanical Officer **Alan Matheson** . . . . (253) 502-8934
Fax: (253) 396-3378

Road Foreman of Engines/Safety Manager
Marc Robertson . . . . (253) 396-3393
Fax: (253) 922-9088

Chief Information/Financial Officer **Dan McCabe** . . . . (253) 396-3040
E-mail: dmccabe@cityoftacoma.org Fax: (253) 922-9088

Manager of Operating Practices **Josh Banks** . . . . (253) 396-3282
E-mail: jbanks@cityoftacoma.org Fax: (253) 922-9088

Chief Administrative Officer **Lori Daniels** . . . . (253) 396-3037
E-mail: ldaniels@cityoftacoma.org Fax: (253) 922-9088

Tacoma Water
3628 South 35th Street, Tacoma, WA 98409
P.O. Box 11007, Tacoma, WA 98411
Tel: (253) 502-8247 E-mail: water@cityoftacoma.org
Internet: www.mytpu.org/tacomawater/

Water Superintendent **Linda McCrea** . . . . (253) 502-8188

Deputy Water Superintendent/Water Quality
Chris McMeen . . . . (253) 502-8210

Deputy Water Superintendent/Asset and Information Management Manager **Heather Pennington** . . . . (253) 502-8199
E-mail: hpenning@cityoftacoma.org

Water Distribution Engineering Manager **Tony Lindgren** . . (253) 502-8745

Water Distribution Operations Manager **Ray West** . . . . (253) 502-8394
E-mail: rwest@cityoftacoma.org

Water Rates and Financial Planning Manager
Sean Senescall . . . . (253) 502-8913

Water Supply Manager **Glen George** . . . . (253) 502-8737

Public Works Department

Tacoma Municipal Building, 747 Market Street, Room 408, Tacoma, WA 98402-3769
Tel: (253) 591-5525 Fax: (253) 591-5097

Director/City Engineer **Kurtis D. Kingsolver** . . . . (253) 591-5525

Assistant Director **Jeffrey A. Jenkins** . . . . (253) 591-5525

Engineering

Division Manager **Chris Larson** . . . . (253) 591-5538
E-mail: clarson@cityoftacoma.org

Facilities Management Division

Division Manager **Justin Davis** . . . . (253) 591-5449
E-mail: justin.davis@cityoftacoma.org

Facilities Maintenance - Operations **Jeff Paradee** . . . . (253) 591-5466
E-mail: jparadee@cityoftacoma.org

Real Property Services, Assistant Division Manager
Jennifer Hines . . . . (253) 591-5320

Facilities Project Manager **Josh Clarke** . . . . (253) 591-5395
E-mail: jclarke@cityoftacoma.org

Fleet Services Manager **Fred Chun** . . . . (253) 591-5553

Street Operations Division

2324 South C Street, Tacoma, WA 98402

Division Manager **Rae Bailey** . . . . (253) 591-5495

Tacoma Employees' Retirement System [TERS]

TPU Administration Building North, 3628 South 35th Street, Ground Floor, Tacoma, WA 98409
Tel: (253) 502-8200 Fax: (253) 502-8660

Retirement Director **Tim Allen** . . . . (253) 502-8605

City of Tallahassee, Florida

City Hall, 300 South Adams Street, Tallahassee, FL 32301
Tel: (850) 891-0010 (Information) Fax: (850) 891-8210
Internet: www.talgov.com

County: Leon **Election Type:** Nonpartisan **Population:** 189,907 (2015)
Employees: 2,874 **Fiscal Year:** 2016 **Budget:** $706,765,000

Office of the Mayor and City Commission

City Hall, 300 S. Adams St., Tallahassee, FL 32301
Fax: (850) 891-8542 E-mail: ccoffice@talgov.com

Employees: 13 **Fiscal Year:** 2016 **Budget:** $1,533,000

★ Mayor **Andrew D. Gillum** (Seat 4) . . . . (850) 891-8181
Began Service: November 21, 2014
Term Expires: November 2018
Date of Birth: July 26, 1979

Chief of Staff **Dustin Daniels** . . . . (850) 891-8181

Internal Affairs Coordinator **Angie Whitaker** . . . . (850) 891-8503

★ Commissioner **Scott C. Maddox** (Seat 1) . . . . (850) 891-8181
Term Expires: November 5, 2016

★ Commissioner **Curtis B. Richardson** (Seat 2) . . . . (850) 891-8181
Term Expires: November 2016
Education: Florida State 1978 BS; West Florida 1979 MA; Florida State 1983 MS

★ Commissioner **Nancy Miller** (Seat 3) . . . . (850) 891-8181
Term Expires: November 10, 2018

★ Commissioner **Gil David Ziffer** (Seat 5) . . . . (850) 891-8181
Term Expires: November 5, 2018

Office of the City Attorney

City Hall, 300 S. Adams St., Tallahassee, FL 32301
Fax: (850) 891-8973 E-mail: kirkpatn@talgov.com

Employees: 21 **Fiscal Year:** 2016 **Budget:** $3,175,000

▶ City Attorney **Lewis Shelley** . . . . (850) 891-8554
E-mail: lewis.shelley@talgov.com

Deputy City Attorney **Cassandra Jackson** . . . . (850) 891-8554

Office of the City Auditor

City Hall, 300 S. Adams St., Tallahassee, FL 32301
Fax: (850) 891-0912

Employees: 7 **Fiscal Year:** 2016 **Budget:** $934,000

▶ City Auditor **T. Bert Fletcher** . . . . (850) 891-8397
E-mail: bert.fletcher@talgov.com

Office of the City Treasurer-Clerk

City Hall, 300 S. Adams St., Tallahassee, FL 32301
Fax: (850) 891-8210

Employees: 56 **Fiscal Year:** 2016 **Budget:** $21,110,000

▶ City Treasurer-Clerk **Jim Cooke** . . . . (850) 891-8131
E-mail: cookej@talgov.com
Education: Florida State BS, MSA

Office of the City Manager

City Hall, 300 S. Adams St., Tallahassee, FL 32301
Fax: (850) 891-8669 E-mail: citymanager@talgov.com

Employees: 36 **Fiscal Year:** 2016 **Budget:** $5,549,000

▶ City Manager **Ricardo "Rick" Fernandez** . . . . (850) 891-8200

Assistant to the City Manager/Communications Director (Interim) **Alison Faris** . . . . (850) 891-8533

Assistant City Manager/Development and Transportation Services **Lonnie Ballard** . . . . (850) 891-8208

Assistant City Manager/Safety and Neighborhood Services (Interim) **Cynthia Barber** . . . . (850) 891-8328

Assistant City Manager/Utility Services **Reese Goad** . . . . (850) 891-8200

★ Elected Official ▲ Appointed by Legislature ▼ Appointed by Governor ▶ Appointed by Board or Commission ● Appointed by Judge
■ Appointed by Mayor △ Appointed by Freeholders ▽ Appointed by Supervisor ▷ Appointed by County Executive ○ Appointed by Council

Office of the City Manager *continued*

Environmental Policy and Energy Resources Director (Interim) **John Powell** . . . . (850) 891-8200

Aviation Department

Tallahassee Regional Airport, 3300 Capital Circle SW, Tallahassee, FL 32310
Fax: (850) 891-7837

Employees: 55 **Fiscal Year:** 2016 **Budget:** $9,499,000

Director **Thomas C. "Chris" Curry** . . . . (850) 891-7808

Economic and Community Development

City Hall, 300 S. Adams St., Tallahassee, FL 32301
Fax: (850) 891-2051

Employees: 36 **Fiscal Year:** 2016 **Budget:** $5,233,000

Director **Michael Parker** . . . . (850) 891-6500
E-mail: parkerm@talgov.com

Community Redevelopment

City Hall, 300 S. Adams St., Tallahassee, FL 32301
Fax: (850) 891-8734 E-mail: dma@talgov.com

Planning Manager **Roxanne Manning** . . . . (850) 891-8551
Manager of Procurement Services **Andre Libroth** . . . . (850) 891-8551

Electric Operations

2602 Jackson Bluff Rd., Tallahassee, FL 32304
Fax: (850) 891-5162

Employees: 303 **Fiscal Year:** 2016 **Budget:** $300,556,000

General Manager **Rob McGarrah** . . . . (850) 891-4968
Electric System Integrated Planning Manager **David Byrne** . . . . (850) 891-3126

Equity and Workforce Development

City Hall, 300 S. Adams St., Tallahassee, FL 32301
Fax: (850) 891-8733

Director **Angela Hendrieth** . . . . (850) 891-8290
E-mail: hendrietha@talgov.com

Fire Department

911 Easterwood Drive, Tallahassee, FL 32311
Fax: (850) 891-6621

Employees: 296 **Fiscal Year:** 2016 **Budget:** $41,962,000

Fire Chief **Jerome Gaines** . . . . (850) 891-6600
E-mail: jerome.gaines@talgov.com

Gas Operations

2602 Jackson Bluff Rd., Tallahassee, FL 32304
Tel: (850) 891-5100 Fax: (850) 891-5161

General Manager **Stephen Mayfield** . . . . (850) 891-5108

Growth Management Department

City Hall, 300 S. Adams St., Tallahassee, FL 32301
Fax: (850) 891-7184 E-mail: gm@talgov.com

Employees: 63 **Fiscal Year:** 2016 **Budget:** $6,870,000

Director **Karen Jumonville** . . . . (850) 891-7001
E-mail: jumonvillek@talgov.com
Education: Florida State BA, MURP

Human Resources Department

City Hall, 300 S. Adams St., Tallahassee, FL 32301
Fax: (850) 891-5388

Manager **Ellen Blair** . . . . (850) 891-8538
E-mail: ellen.blair@talgov.com

Management and Administration Department

300 South Adams Street, Tallahassee, FL 32301

Employees: 184 **Fiscal Year:** 2016 **Budget:** $56,134,000

Director **Raoul Lavin** . . . . (850) 891-8149
E-mail: raoul.lavin@talgov.com

Office of Budget and Policy

300 South Adams Street, Tallahassee, FL 32301
Internet: http://www.talgov.com/fm/fm-budget-home.aspx

Budget Manager **Robert Wigen** . . . . (850) 891-8533
E-mail: robert.wigen@talgov.com

Parks, Recreation and Neighborhood Affairs Department

912 Myers Park Dr., Tallahassee, FL 32301
Fax: (850) 891-3850 E-mail: pennywej@talgov.com

Employees: 173 **Fiscal Year:** 2016 **Budget:** $22,016,000

Director **Ashley Edwards** . . . . (850) 891-3899

Police Department

234 E. Seventh Ave., Tallahassee, FL 32303
Fax: (850) 891-4242 E-mail: tpdpublicinformation@talgov.com

Employees: 466 **Fiscal Year:** 2016 **Budget:** $55,951,000

Chief of Police **Michael DeLeo** . . . . (850) 891-4341

Public Works Department

City Hall, 300 S. Adams St., Tallahassee, FL 32301
Fax: (850) 891-8733

Employees: 286 **Fiscal Year:** 2016 **Budget:** $25,981,000

Director **Gabriel Menendez** . . . . (850) 891-8197

Solid Waste Operations

2727 Municipal Way, Tallahassee, FL 32304
Fax: (850) 891-5550

Employees: 83 **Fiscal Year:** 2016 **Budget:** $25,812,000

Manager **Reginald Ofuani** . . . . (850) 891-5252

Star Metro Transit System

555 Appleyard Dr., Tallahassee, FL 32304
Fax: (850) 891-5385

Employees: 148 **Fiscal Year:** 2016 **Budget:** $15,339,000

Director **Ivan Maldonado** . . . . (850) 891-5200

Utility Services

408 North Adams Street, Tallahassee, FL 32301
Fax: (850) 891-6194

Employees: 148 **Fiscal Year:** 2016 **Budget:** $167,248,000

Director **Reese Goad** . . . . (850) 891-4968

Underground Utilities

City Hall, 300 S. Adams St., Tallahassee, FL 32301
Fax: (850) 891-5100 Internet: www.talgov.com/you/

Employees: 362 **Fiscal Year:** 2016 **Budget:** $136,768,000

General Manager **Mike Tadros** . . . . (850) 891-6806

City of Tampa, Florida

City Hall, 315 East Kennedy Boulevard, Tampa, FL 33602
Tel: (813) 274-8211 (Information) Internet: www.tampagov.net

County: Hillsborough **Election Type:** Nonpartisan **Population:** 369,075 (2015)

Office of the Mayor

306 East Jackson Street, Tampa, FL 33602
Fax: (813) 274-7050

★ Mayor **Bob Buckhorn** .... (813) 274-8251
Began Service: April 1, 2011
Term Expires: March 31, 2019
E-mail: bob.buckhorn@tampagov.net
Education: Penn State 1980 BA

■ Assistant to the Mayor **Bridgett McCormick** .... (813) 274-8251
E-mail: bridgett.mccormick@tampagov.net

■ Chief of Staff **Dennis Rogero** .... (813) 274-7360
E-mail: dennis.rogero@tampagov.net Fax: (813) 274-8127
Executive Aide **Debra Rotolo** .... (813) 274-7360
E-mail: debra.rotolo@tampagov.net

■ Internal Audit Director **Christine Glover** .... (813) 274-7167
Date of Birth: December 15, 1961
Education: South Carolina State 1984 BSAcc; Webster 2000 MBA; Army War Col 2007 SM

■ Public Affairs Director **Ashley Bauman** .... (813) 274-8262
E-mail: ashley.bauman@tampagov.net

Intergovernmental Relations Office

306 East Jackson Street, 8th Floor East, Tampa, FL 33602
Tel: (813) 274-8162 Fax: (813) 274-8127

Manager **Deborah Hummer Stevenson** .... (813) 274-8162
E-mail: deborah.stevenson@tampagov.net

Office of the City Council

City Hall, 3rd Fl., 315 E. Kennedy Blvd., Tampa, FL 33602
Tel: (813) 274-8131 Fax: (813) 274-7076

★ Council Chair **Mike Suarez** (District 1) .... (813) 274-7072
Term Expires: March 31, 2019
E-mail: mike.suarez@tampagov.net
Legislative Aide **Lorena Hardwick** .... (813) 274-7072

★ Chair Pro Tem **Harry Cohen** (District 4) .... (813) 274-8134
Term Expires: March 31, 2019
E-mail: harry.cohen@tampagov.net
Education: Gettysburg BA; New York Law JD
Legislative Aide **CJo Ford** .... (813) 274-8134

★ Council Member **Charlie Miranda** (District 2) .... (813) 274-7074
Term Expires: March 31, 2019
E-mail: charlie.miranda@tampagov.net
Education: Tampa 1977 BA
Legislative Aide **Mary Bryan** .... (813) 274-7074

★ Council Member **Yvonne Yolie Capin** (District 3) .... (813) 274-8133
Term Expires: March 31, 2019
E-mail: yvonne.capin@tampagov.net
Legislative Aide **Cynthia L. Sarff** .... (813) 274-8133
E-mail: cynthia.sarff@tampagov.net

★ Council Member **Frank Reddick** (District 5) .... (813) 274-8189
Term Expires: March 31, 2019
E-mail: frank.reddick@tampagov.net
Legislative Aide **Cedric McCray** .... (813) 274-8189

★ Council Member **Guido Maniscalco** (District 6) .... (813) 274-7071
Term Expires: March 31, 2019
E-mail: guido.maniscalco@tampagov.net
Legislative Aide **Carrie Henriquez** .... (813) 274-7071
E-mail: carrie.henriquez@tampagov.net

★ Council Member **Lisa Montelione** (District 7) .... (813) 274-7073
Term Expires: March 31, 2019
E-mail: lisa.montelione@tampagov.net

Office of the City Council *continued*

Legislative Aide **Christopher Berg** .... (813) 274-7073
E-mail: Christopher.Berg@tampagov.net

Office of the City Attorney

City Hall, 315 E. Kennedy Blvd., 5th Floor, Tampa, FL 33602
Tel: (813) 274-8996 Fax: (813) 274-8809
Internet: www.tampagov.net/dept_City_Attorney/

■ City Attorney **Julia Mandell** .... (813) 274-7312
E-mail: julia.mandell@tampagov.net

Office of the City Clerk

City Hall, 315 East Kennedy Boulevard, 3rd Floor, Tampa, FL 33602
Fax: (813) 274-8306

■ City Clerk **Shirley Foxx-Knowles** .... (813) 274-8397
E-mail: shirley.foxxknowles@tampagov.net
Education: Florida A&M BS

Deputy City Clerk **Stephanie Thomas** .... (813) 274-7064
E-mail: stephanie.thomas@tampagov.net

Deputy City Clerk **Sandra S. "Sandy" Marshall** .... (813) 274-7077
E-mail: sandy.marshall@tampagov.net

Archivist/Records Manager **Jennifer Dietz** .... (813) 274-8030

Community Affairs Division

306 East Jackson Street 3N, Tampa, FL 33602

Human Rights Investigation Supervisor
Patricia Newton .... (813) 274-5856
Fax: (813) 274-5854

Convention Center, Tourism, Recreation and Cultural Arts

306 East Jackson Street, Tampa, FL 33602
Fax: (813) 274-8127

Director **Rick J. Hamilton** .... (813) 274-5624
E-mail: rick.hamilton@tampagov.net

Tampa Convention Center

333 South Franklin Street, Tampa, FL 33602
Fax: (813) 274-7430 Internet: www.tampaconventioncenter.com

■ Convention Center and Tourism Director
Rick J. Hamilton .... (813) 274-5624
E-mail: rick.hamilton@tampaconventioncenter.com

■ Convention Facilities Director **Robert Rose** .... (813) 274-7751
E-mail: robert.rose@tampaconventioncenter.com

Economic and Urban Development Department

306 East Jackson Street, Tampa, FL 33602
Fax: (813) 274-7410

Administrator **Bob McDonaugh** .... (813) 274-8245
E-mail: bob.mcdonaugh@tampagov.net

Minority Business Development Department

Fax: (813) 274-5544

Manager **Greg Hart** .... (813) 274-5522
E-mail: gregory.hart@tampagov.net

Tampa Fire Rescue

808 East Zack Street, Tampa, FL 33602
Fax: (813) 274-7026
Internet: www.tampagov.net/dept_fire_rescue/index.asp

Fire Chief **Thomas "Tom" Forward** .... (813) 274-7527
E-mail: tom.forward@tampagov.net
Education: Northwood BA; U Phoenix MA

Assistant Chief of Administration **Milton Jenkins** .... (813) 274-7013
E-mail: milt.jenkins@tampagov.net

Assistant Chief of Operations **A. Nick Locicero** .... (813) 274-7013
E-mail: nick.locicero@tampagov.net

★ Elected Official ▲ Appointed by Legislature ▼ Appointed by Governor ► Appointed by Board or Commission ● Appointed by Judge
■ Appointed by Mayor △ Appointed by Freeholders ▽ Appointed by Supervisor ▷ Appointed by County Executive ○ Appointed by Council

Tampa Fire Rescue *continued*

Airport Fire Chief **Daniel Olegario** .... (813) 348-6520
E-mail: danny.olegario@tampagov.net
Fire Training Chief **Jason Dougherty** .... (813) 242-5410
Personnel Chief **(Vacant)** .... (813) 274-7008
Rescue Operations Chief **Bryan Riley** .... (813) 274-7005
E-mail: bryan.riley@tampagov.net
Fire Marshal **(Vacant)** .... (813) 274-7000
Emergency Coordinator **Chauncia Willis** .... (813) 274-8088
E-mail: chauncia.willis@tampagov.net
Education: Loyola U (New Orleans) BA

Human Resources Department

306 East Jackson Street, Tampa, FL 33602
Tel: (813) 274-8041 Fax: (813) 274-8365

Human Resources Director **Kimberly Crum** .... (813) 274-8041
E-mail: kimberly.crum@tampagov.net

Community Partnerships and Neighborhood Engagement

306 East Jackson Street, Tampa, FL 33602
Fax: (813) 274-7410

Manager **Miray Holmes** .... (813) 274-7574
E-mail: miray.holmes@tampagov.net

Neighborhood Enhancement

2105 North Nebraska Avenue, Tampa, FL 33602
Fax: (813) 274-5567
Internet: http://www.tampagov.net/neighborhood-enhancement

Manager **Sal Ruggiero** .... (813) 274-5545
E-mail: sal.ruggiero@tampagov.net

Parks and Recreation Department

3402 West Columbus Drive, Tampa, FL 33607
Fax: (813) 274-5749
Internet: www.tampagov.net/dept_parks_and_recreation/

■ Director **Gregory Bayor** .... (813) 274-8615
E-mail: greg.bayor@tampagov.net
Education: Baltimore 1971 BA
Communications and Events Superintendent **(Vacant)** .... (813) 274-7723

Planning and Development Department

1400 North Boulevard, Tampa, FL 33607
Fax: (813) 274-7410

Director **Thomas "Tom" Snelling** .... (813) 274-8577
E-mail: thomas.snelling@tampagov.net
Deputy Director **(Vacant)** .... (813) 274-8577
Land Development Coordination Division Manager
Gloria Moreda .... (813) 274-8405
Housing and Community Development Manager
Vanessa McCleary .... (813) 274-7954
E-mail: vanessa.mccleary@tampagov.net
Education: Springfield (MA) BS
Real Estate Division Manager **Monica Ammann** .... (813) 274-8845

Construction Services Center

1400 North Boulevard, Tampa, FL 33607

Construction Services Manager **John Barrios** .... (813) 274-3100

Ybor Service Center

2015 East 7th Avenue, Tampa, FL 33605

Ybor City Development Corporation President
Courtney Orr .... (813) 274-7937
E-mail: courtney.orr@tampagov.net
East Tampa Development and Community Lending
Manager **Ed Johnson** .... (813) 242-3806
3808 North 22nd Street, Tampa, FL 33610
E-mail: ed.johnson@tampagov.net

Police Department

One Police Center, 411 North Franklin Street, Tampa, FL 33602
Tel: (813) 276-3200 Fax: (813) 276-3776
Internet: http://www.tampagov.net/police

Police Chief **Eric Ward** .... (813) 276-3788
Assistant Chief of Special Support and Investigations
Brian Dugan .... (813) 276-3798
Assistant Chief of Operations **Marc Hamlin** .... (813) 276-3200
E-mail: marc.hamlin@tampagov.net

Public Works and Utility Services Department

306 East Jackson Street, Tampa, FL 33602

■ Administrator **Brad L. Baird** .... (813) 274-8121
Education: Florida 1982 BS

Contract Administration

306 East Jackson Street, 4th Floor, Tampa, FL 33602
Fax: (813) 274-8080

Director **LCDR Michael W. Chucran** .... (813) 274-8568

Transportation

306 E. Jackson St., Room 6N, Tampa, FL 33602
Fax: (813) 274-5830

■ Director **Jean Duncan** .... (813) 274-8333
E-mail: jean.duncan@tampagov.net
Fleet Maintenance Division Manager **(Vacant)** .... (813) 348-1010
1508 North Clark Avenue, Tampa, FL 33607 Fax: (813) 348-1042
Parking Manager **(Vacant)** .... (813) 274-8182
107 North Franklin Street, Tampa, FL 33602 Fax: (813) 274-8482
Special Projects Manager/Riverwalk Development
Manager **Lee Hoffman** .... (813) 274-7439
306 E. Jackson Street, 5th Floor, Tampa, FL 33602

Wastewater Department

2545 Guy N. Verger Boulevard, Tampa, FL 33605
Fax: (813) 274-8448

■ Director **Eric A. Weiss** .... (813) 274-8070
Chief Engineer **Charlie Lynch** .... (813) 274-8916
Wastewater Treatment Plant Manager **Erik Garwell** .... (813) 247-3451
2700 Maritime Boulevard, Tampa, FL 33605 Fax: (813) 248-5269
Wastewater Collections System Manager
Francis "Eddy" Drovie .... (813) 259-1693
2609 North Rome Avenue, Tampa, FL 33607 Fax: (813) 259-1628

Water Department

306 East Jackson Street, 5E, Tampa, FL 33602
Tel: (813) 274-7105 Fax: (813) 274-7435
Internet: www.tampagov.net/water

Director **Chuck Weber** .... (813) 274-8663
Distribution and Consumer Services Manager
Elias J. Franco .... (813) 259-1637
2603 North Rome Avenue, Tampa, FL 33607 Fax: (813) 259-1645
Engineering Division Chief Engineer **Seung Park** .... (813) 274-7095
E-mail: seung.park@tampagov.net
Production Division Manager **John Rañon** .... (813) 231-5255
7125 North 30th Street, Tampa, FL 33610 Fax: (813) 231-5283

Solid Waste Department

4010 W. Spruce St., Tampa, FL 33607
Fax: (813) 348-1076 Internet: www.tampagov.net/dept_Solid_Waste/

Director **Mark C. Wilfalk** .... (813) 348-1151
E-mail: mark.wilfalk@tampagov.net
Operations Chief **Daryl L. Stewart** .... (813) 348-1104
E-mail: daryl.stewart@tampagov.net
Administrative Chief **Adriana Colina** .... (813) 348-1148
Commercial Services Manager **Michael Laverty** .... (813) 348-1135
Residential Services Manager **Kiana D. Romeo** .... (813) 348-6513

★ Elected Official ▲ Appointed by Legislature ▼ Appointed by Governor ▶ Appointed by Board or Commission ● Appointed by Judge
■ Appointed by Mayor △ Appointed by Freeholders ▽ Appointed by Supervisor ▷ Appointed by County Executive ○ Appointed by Council

Purchasing Department
City Hall Annex, 306 East Jackson Street, 2nd Floor, East, Tampa, FL 33602
Tel: (813) 274-8351 Fax: (813) 274-8355

Director **Gregory K. Spearman** .... (813) 274-8855
E-mail: gregory.spearman@tampagov.net
Procurement Manager **Kevin Frye** .... (813) 274-8833
E-mail: kevin.frye@tampagov.net
Purchasing System Manager **DeAnna Marshall** .... (813) 274-8838
E-mail: deanna.marshall@tampagov.net

Department of Revenue and Finance
306 East Jackson Street, Tampa, FL 33602
Fax: (813) 274-8127

■ Chief Financial Officer **Sonya C. Little** .... (813) 274-8151
E-mail: sonya.little@tampagov.net
Budget Officer **Michael Perry** .... (813) 274-8552
E-mail: michael.perry@tampagov.net
Chief Accountant **Lee Huffstutler** .... (813) 274-7171
E-mail: lee.huffstutler@tampagov.net
Grants Specialist **Cherrise Wilks** .... (813) 274-3325
Education: North Florida MPA

Technology and Innovation Department
411 North Franklin Street, 7th Floor, Tampa, FL 33602
Fax: (813) 274-7302

Director/Chief Information Officer **Russell Haupert** .... (813) 274-8670
E-mail: russell.haupert@tampagov.net
Enterprise Change Management Manager **Diane Jamai** ... (813) 274-7437
E-mail: diane.jamai@tampagov.net
Manager of Enterprise Application Integration **(Vacant)** .. (813) 274-5541

City of Tempe, Arizona

31 East Fifth Street, Tempe, AZ 85281
P.O. Box 5002, Tempe, AZ 85280
Tel: (480) 967-2001 (Information) Internet: www.tempe.gov/

County: Maricopa **Election Type:** Nonpartisan **Year Founded:** 1871
Year Incorporated: 1894 **Population:** 175,826 (2015)

Office of the Mayor and City Council
P.O. Box 5002, Tempe, AZ 85280
Tel: (480) 350-8110 Fax: (480) 350-8996

★ Mayor **Mark Mitchell** .... (480) 350-8959
Began Service: July 2012
Term Expires: December 31, 2020
E-mail: mark_mitchell@tempe.gov
Education: Arizona State
Chief of Staff **Elizabeth Higgins** .... (480) 350-8965
Assistant to the Mayor **Tony Cani** .... (480) 350-8959
E-mail: tony_cani@tempe.gov
★ Council Member **Robin Arredondo-Savage** .... (480) 350-8792
Term Expires: December 31, 2018
E-mail: robin_arredondo-savage@tempe.gov
★ Council Member **Kolby W. Granville** .... (480) 350-8796
Term Expires: December 31, 2020
E-mail: kolby_granville@tempe.gov
★ Council Member-Elect **Randy Keating** .... (480) 350-8110
Term Expires: December 31, 2020
★ Council Member **Lauren Kuby** .... (480) 350-8507
Term Expires: December 31, 2018
E-mail: lauren_kuby@tempe.gov
★ Council Member **Joel Navarro** .... (480) 350-8795
Term Expires: December 31, 2020
E-mail: joel_navarro@tempe.gov

Office of the Mayor and City Council *continued*

★ Council Member **David Schapira** .... (480) 350-8510
Term Expires: December 31, 2018
E-mail: david_schapira@tempe.gov
Date of Birth: February 17, 1980
Education: George Washington BA
Council Aide **Parrish Spisz** .... (480) 350-8816
E-mail: parrish_spisz@tempe.gov
Council Aide **Kristin Gwinn** .... (480) 350-8916
E-mail: kristin_gwinn@tempe.gov

Office of the City Attorney
P.O. Box 5002, Tempe, AZ 85280
Fax: (480) 350-8645

○ City Attorney **Judith R. "Judi" Baumann** .... (480) 350-8227
E-mail: judi_baumann@tempe.gov

Office of the City Clerk
31 East Fifth Street, 2nd Floor, Tempe, AZ 85281
P.O. Box 5002, Tempe, AZ 85280
Tel: (480) 350-8241 Fax: (480) 858-2012

○ City Clerk **Brigitta Kuiper** .... (480) 350-8241
E-mail: brigitta_kuiper@tempe.gov
Education: Arizona State BA

Office of the City Manager
P.O. Box 5002, Tempe, AZ 85280
Tel: (480) 350-8221 Fax: (480) 350-8915

○ City Manager **Andrew Ching** .... (480) 350-8221
E-mail: Andrew_ching@tempe.gov
Education: Arizona 1991 BA; Arizona State 1994 JD
Deputy City Manager - Chief Financial Officer
Ken Jones .... (480) 350-8504
E-mail: ken_jones@tempe.gov
Deputy City Manager - Chief Operating Officer
Steven Methvin .... (480) 350-8221
E-mail: steven_methvin@tempe.gov

Community Development Department
31 East Sixth Street, Suite 208, Tempe, AZ 85281

Director **David Nakagawara** .... (480) 350-8023
E-mail: david_nakagawara@tempe.gov
Planning Deputy Director **Ryan Levasque** .... (480) 858-2393

Housing Services
3500 South Rural Road, 2nd Floor, Tempe, AZ 85282
Tel: (480) 350-8950 Fax: (480) 858-7703

Housing and Revitalization Manager **Craig Hittie** .... (480) 350-8960

Code Compliance Department
21 East Sixth Street, Suite 208, Tempe, AZ 85281
Tel: (480) 350-4311 Fax: (480) 858-2070

Code Enforcement Manager **Jeff Tamulevich** .... (480) 350-8441
E-mail: jeffrey_tamulevich@tempe.gov

Redevelopment Division
31 East Sixth Street, Suite 208, Tempe, AZ 85281

Redevelopment Manager **Larry Schmalz** .... (480) 350-8924
E-mail: larry_schmalz@tempe.gov

Tempe Town Lake
620 North Mill Avenue, Tempe, AZ 85281
P.O. Box 5002, Tempe, AZ 85280

Director **David Nakagawara** .... (480) 350-8023
E-mail: david_nakagawara@tempe.gov

★ Elected Official ▲ Appointed by Legislature ▼ Appointed by Governor ▶ Appointed by Board or Commission ● Appointed by Judge
■ Appointed by Mayor △ Appointed by Freeholders ▽ Appointed by Supervisor ▷ Appointed by County Executive ○ Appointed by Council

Communications and Media Relations
P.O. Box 5002, Tempe, AZ 85280
Tel: (480) 350-8909 Fax: (480) 350-8996

Communications and Media Relations Director
Nikki Ripley . . . . (480) 350-8846
E-mail: nikki_ripley@tempe.gov
Neighborhood Programs Director **Shauna Warner** . . . . (480) 350-8883
E-mail: shauna_warner@tempe.gov

Community Services Department
3500 South Rural Road, Suite 203, Tempe, AZ 85282
Tel: (480) 350-5000

Community Services Director **Shelley Hearn** . . . . (480) 350-8906
E-mail: shelley_hearn@tempe.gov
Deputy Community Services Director, Recreation
Kelly Rafferty . . . . (480) 350-5182
History Museum Manager **Brenda Abney** . . . . (480) 350-5105
809 East Southern Avenue, Tempe, AZ 85282
Deputy Library Manager **Barbara Roberts** . . . . (480) 350-5237
E-mail: barbara_roberts@tempe.gov
Human Services Director **Naomi Farrell** . . . . (480) 350-5428
Volunteer Coordinator **Jodie Garth** . . . . (480) 350-5276
E-mail: jodie_garth@tempe.gov

Economic Development
P.O. Box 5002, Tempe, AZ 85280

Director **Donna Kennedy** . . . . (480) 858-2395
E-mail: donna_kennedy@tempe.gov

Fire Medical Rescue Department
P.O. Box 5002, Tempe, AZ 85280

Fire Medical Rescue Chief **Greg Ruiz** . . . . (480) 858-7212
E-mail: greg_ruiz@tempe.gov
Assistant Chief, Administrative Services
Craig Fredricks . . . . (480) 858-7202
E-mail: craig_fredricks@tempe.gov
Assistant Chief, Emergency Services
Hans Silberschlag . . . . (480) 858-7201
E-mail: hans_silberschlag@tempe.gov

Internal Services Department
P.O. Box 5002, Tempe, AZ 85280
Tel: (480) 350-8576

Internal Services Director **Renie A. Broderick** . . . . (480) 350-8276
E-mail: renie_broderick@tempe.gov
Education: Carnegie Mellon MPM

Finance Division
20 East Sixth Street, 2nd Floor, Tempe, AZ 85281
Tel: (480) 350-8505 Fax: (480) 350-8915

Deputy Director, Finance **Jerry Hart** . . . . (480) 350-8505
Budget Manager **Cecilia Velasco-Robles** . . . . (480) 350-8881
E-mail: cecilia_velasco-robles@tempe.gov
Central Services Manager **Michael Greene** . . . . (480) 350-8516
E-mail: michael_greene@tempe.gov
Customer Services Manager **Tarja Nummela** . . . . (480) 350-8637
Risk Manager **Christopher Hansen** . . . . (480) 350-2904
E-mail: christopher_hanson@tempe.gov
License and Collections Supervisor **Bruce Smith** . . . . (480) 350-2955
E-mail: bruce_smith@tempe.gov

Human Resources Division
20 East Sixth Street, 1st Floor, Tempe, AZ 85281
Internet: http://www.tempe.gov/hr

Deputy Internal Services Director - Human Resources
Jon O'Connor . . . . (480) 350-8423
E-mail: jon_oconnor@tempe.gov
Employee Benefits Manager **Suzanne Olson** . . . . (480) 350-2975
Training and Organizational Development Supervisor
Aaron Peterson . . . . (480) 350-5311

Human Resources Division *continued*

Employment Services Manager **Lawrence LaVictoire** . . . . (480) 350-8277
E-mail: lawrence_lavictoire@tempe.gov

Information Technology Division
P.O. Box 5002, Tempe, AZ 85280

Deputy Internal Services Director - Information
Technology **Dave Heck** . . . . (480) 350-8777
E-mail: david_heck@tempe.gov

Police Department
120 East 5th Street, Tempe, AZ 85281
Fax: (480) 350-8337 Internet: http://www.tempe.gov/police

Chief of Police **Sylvia Moir** . . . . (480) 350-8306
Assistant Police Chief **Brenda Buren** . . . . (480) 350-8991
Assistant Police Chief **Angel Carbajal, Jr.** . . . . (480) 350-8880
Assistant Police Chief **John Rush** . . . . (480) 350-8274
Special Investigations Bureau Commander **Kim Hale** . . . . . (480) 350-8322

Public Works Department
31 East Fifth Street, Garden Level, Tempe, AZ 85281
P.O. Box 5002, Tempe, AZ 85280
Tel: (480) 350-8371 Fax: (480) 350-8815
Internet: www.tempe.gov/publicworks/

Director **Don Bessler** . . . . (480) 350-8205
Parks Manager **Oliver Ncube** . . . . (480) 350-5234

Engineering Division
31 East Fifth Street, Garden Level, Tempe, AZ 85281
P.O. Box 5002, Tempe, AZ 85280
Tel: (480) 350-8200 Fax: (480) 350-8591
Internet: www.tempe.gov/engineering/

Deputy Public Works Manager/City Engineer
Andy Goh . . . . (480) 350-8896
E-mail: andy_goh@tempe.gov
Principal Civil Engineer, Private Development and
Private Utility **Tom Wilhite** . . . . (480) 350-2921
E-mail: tom_wilhite@tempe.gov
Engineering Services Manager **Wendy Springborn** . . . . . . (480) 350-8250
E-mail: wendy_springborn@tempe.gov

Field Operations Division
P.O. Box 5002, Tempe, AZ 85280

Deputy Public Works Director, Field Operations
John Osgood . . . . (480) 350-8949

Fleet Services Division
Building D, 53 South Priest Drive, Tempe, AZ 85281

Fleet Director **Kevin Devery** . . . . (480) 350-8088

Transportation Division
200 East Fifth Street, Tempe, AZ 85281
Tel: (480) 350-4311 Fax: (480) 858-2097

Transportation Maintenance Manager **Isaac Chavira** . . . . . (480) 350-8349
Transit Manager **Mike Nevarez** . . . . (480) 858-2209
Public Information Officer **Amanda Nelson** . . . . (480) 350-2707
E-mail: amanda_nelson@tempe.gov
Principal Planner **Bonnie Richardson** . . . . (480) 350-8628
Principal Planner **Robert Yabes** . . . . (480) 350-2734

Water Utilities
255 East Marigold Lane, Tempe, AZ 85281
P.O. Box 5002, Tempe, AZ 85280
Fax: (480) 350-8336
Internet: http://www.tempe.gov/city-hall/public-works/water

Deputy Public Works Director/Water Utilities
Marilyn DeRosa . . . . (480) 350-2660
Deputy Manager/Operations **Bradley Fuller** . . . . (480) 350-2601
E-mail: bradley_fuller@tempe.gov
Environmental Compliance Supervisor **Richard Dalton** . . . (480) 350-2851

(continued on next page)

★ Elected Official ▲ Appointed by Legislature ▼ Appointed by Governor ► Appointed by Board or Commission ● Appointed by Judge
■ Appointed by Mayor △ Appointed by Freeholders ▽ Appointed by Supervisor ▷ Appointed by County Executive ○ Appointed by Council

CITIES AND TOWNS

Water Utilities *continued*

Water Resources Manager **Eric Kamienski** . . . . (480) 350-2608
Environmental Services Manager **David McNeil** . . . . (480) 350-2844

City of Thornton, Colorado

9500 Civic Center Drive, Thornton, CO 80229
Internet: www.cityofthornton.net

County: Adams **Election Type:** Nonpartisan **Year Incorporated:** 1956
Population: 133,451 (2015)

Office of the Mayor and City Council

9500 Civic Center Drive, Thornton, CO 80229

★Mayor **Heidi K. Williams** . . . . (303) 538-7531
Began Service: November 15, 2011
Term Expires: November 2019
E-mail: heidi.williams@cityofthornton.net

★Mayor Pro Tem **Eric Montoya** (Ward 2) . . . . (303) 538-7536
Term Expires: November 2019
E-mail: eric.montoya@cityofthornton.net

★Council Member **Mack Goodman** (Ward 1) . . . . (303) 538-7534
Term Expires: November 2017
E-mail: mack.goodman@cityofthornton.net

★Council Member **Jacque Phillip** (Ward 1) . . . . (303) 538-7200
Term Expires: November 2019

★Council Member **Valentin J. "Val" Vigil** (Ward 2) . . . . . . (303) 538-7535
Term Expires: November 2017
E-mail: val.vigil@cityofthornton.net
Education: Adams State 1970 BA

★Council Member **Sam Nizam** (Ward 3) . . . . (303) 538-7533
Term Expires: November 2017
E-mail: sam.nizam@cityofthornton.net

★Council Member **Josh Zygielbaum** (Ward 3) . . . . (303) 538-7200
Term Expires: November 2019

★Council Member **Jennifer Kulmann** (Ward 4) . . . . (303) 538-7201
Term Expires: November 2017
E-mail: jan.kulmann@cityofthornton.net

★Council Member **Adam Matkowsky** (Ward 4) . . . . (303) 538-7200
Term Expires: November 2019

Office of the City Attorney

9500 Civic Center Drive, Thornton, CO 80229

○City Attorney **Margaret Emerich** . . . . (303) 538-7210
E-mail: margaret.emerich@cityofthornton.net

Office of the City Manager

9500 Civic Center Drive, Thornton, CO 80229

○City Manager **Jack Ethredge** . . . . (303) 538-7200
E-mail: jack.ethredge@cityofthornton.net

Office of the City Clerk

9500 Civic Center Drive, Thornton, CO 80229

City Clerk **Nancy A. Vincent** . . . . (303) 538-7200
E-mail: nancy.vincent@cityofthornton.net

Communications Office

9500 Civic Center Drive, Thornton, CO 80229

Communications Director **Todd Barnes** . . . . (303) 538-7279
E-mail: todd.barnes@cityofthornton.net

Office of Management and Budget

9500 Civic Center Drive, Thornton, CO 80229

Assistant City Manager **Joyce Hunt** . . . . (303) 538-7200
E-mail: joyce.hunt@cityofthornton.net

City Development Department

9500 Civic Center Drive, Thornton, CO 80229

Deputy City Manager, City Development **Jeff Coder** . . . . . (303) 538-7295
E-mail: jeff.coder@cityofthornton.net

Economic Development Division

9500 Civic Center Drive, Thornton, CO 80229
Fax: (303) 538-7244

Economic Development Director **John Cody** . . . . (303) 538-7448
E-mail: business@cityofthornton.net

Thornton Development Authority

9500 Civic Center Drive, Thornton, CO 80229

Commissioner **(Vacant)** . . . . (303) 538-7532

Community Services Department

2211 Eppinger Boulevard, Thornton, CO 80229

Executive Director **Mike Soderberg** . . . . (303) 255-7832
E-mail: mike.soderberg@cityofthornton.net

Parks Division

Parks and Forestry Manager
Andrew P. "Andy" Jennings . . . . (303) 255-7832
E-mail: andy.jennings@cityofthornton.net

Recreation Division

Recreation Manager **Jan Kiehl** . . . . (720) 977-5906
E-mail: jan.kiehl@cityofthornton.net

Fire Department

9500 Civic Center Drive, Third Floor, Thornton, CO 80229
Fax: (303) 538-7660

Fire Chief **Gordon "Gordie" Olson** . . . . (303) 538-7602
E-mail: gordon.olson@cityofthornton.net

Infrastructure Department

9500 Civic Center Drive, Thornton, CO 80229

Deputy City Manager, Infrastructure **Bud Elliot** . . . . (720) 977-6200
E-mail: bud.elliot@cityofthornton.net

Management Services Department

9500 Civic Center Drive, Thornton, CO 80229

Deputy City Manager, Management Services
Charlie Long . . . . (303) 538-7200
E-mail: charlie.long@cityofthornton.net

Contract Administration Division

9500 Civic Center Drive, Thornton, CO 80229
Fax: (303) 538-7556

Contracts Manager **Alberto Mezarina** . . . . (303) 538-7466
Purchasing Manager **Dan Galanaugh** . . . . (303) 538-7375
E-mail: Dan.Galanaugh@cityofthornton.net

Police Department

9500 Civic Center Drive, Thornton, CO 80229

Chief of Police **Randy Nelson** . . . . (720) 977-5150

★Elected Official ▲Appointed by Legislature ▼Appointed by Governor ▶Appointed by Board or Commission ●Appointed by Judge
■Appointed by Mayor △Appointed by Freeholders ▽Appointed by Supervisor ▷Appointed by County Executive ○Appointed by Council

City of Thousand Oaks, California

City Hall, 2100 Thousand Oaks Blvd., Thousand Oaks, CA 91362
Internet: www.toaks.org

County: Ventura **Population:** 129,339 (2015)

Office of the Mayor and City Council

City Hall, 2100 Thousand Oaks Blvd., Thousand Oaks, CA 91362
Tel: (805) 449-2121 Fax: (805) 449-2125 E-mail: city@toaks.org

★Mayor **Joel Price** .... (805) 449-2105
Began Service: March 22, 2012
Term Expires: December 2018
E-mail: jprice@toaks.org

★Mayor Pro Tem **Claudia Bill-de la Peña** .... (805) 449-2103
Term Expires: December 2018
E-mail: claudia4slowgrowth@roadrunner.com

★Council Member **Al Adam** .... (805) 449-2102
Term Expires: December 2016
E-mail: albertcadam@gmail.com

★Council Member **Andrew P. Fox** .... (805) 449-2101
Term Expires: December 2018
E-mail: cnclmanfox@aol.com

★Council Member **Rob McCoy** .... (805) 449-2104
Term Expires: December 2016
E-mail: rmccoy@toaks.org

Office of the City Manager

City Hall, 2100 Thousand Oaks Blvd., Thousand Oaks, CA 91362
Tel: (805) 449-2121 Fax: (805) 449-2125 E-mail: citymanager@toaks.org

City Manager **Scott Mitnick** .... (805) 449-2121
E-mail: smitnick@toaks.org

Assistant City Manager **Andrew Powers** .... (805) 449-2399
E-mail: apowers@toaks.org

Office of the City Attorney

City Hall, 2100 Thousand Oaks Blvd., Thousand Oaks, CA 91362
E-mail: cityattorney@toaks.org

○City Attorney **Tracy Noonan** .... (805) 449-2170
E-mail: tnoonan@toaks.org
Education: Southwestern JD

City Clerk Department

City Hall, 2100 Thousand Oaks Blvd., Thousand Oaks, CA 91362
Fax: (805) 449-2150 E-mail: cityclerk@toaks.org

City Clerk **Cynthia Rodriguez** .... (805) 449-2151
E-mail: crodriguez@toaks.org

Deputy City Clerk **Antoinette Mann** .... (805) 449-2165
E-mail: amann@toaks.org

Community Development Department

City Hall, 2100 Thousand Oaks Blvd., Thousand Oaks, CA 91362
Fax: (805) 449-2350 E-mail: communitydevelopment@toaks.org

Director **John Prescott** .... (805) 449-2323
E-mail: jprescott@toaks.org

Cultural Affairs Department

2100 Thousand Oaks Blvd., Thousand Oaks, CA 91362
Tel: (805) 449-2700

Director **Barry McComb** .... (805) 449-2707
Deputy Director **Stacy Park** .... (805) 449-2767

Finance Department

City Hall, 2100 Thousand Oaks Blvd., Thousand Oaks, CA 91362
Fax: (805) 449-2250 E-mail: finance@toaks.org

Finance Director/City Treasurer **John Adams** .... (805) 449-2235

Accounting Manager **Fay Menkin** .... (805) 449-2828
E-mail: fmenkin@toaks.org

Facilities Manager **Elizabeth Perez** .... (805) 449-2225
E-mail: eperez@toaks.org

Information Technology Manager **Ed Hughes** .... (805) 449-2231
E-mail: ehughes@toaks.org

Deputy Finance Director **Jamie Boscarino** .... (805) 449-2220

Purchasing Division **Allison Fochler** .... (805) 449-2239
E-mail: afochler@toaks.org

Building Maintenance Supervisor **Tim Coates** .... (805) 449-2238
E-mail: tcoates@toaks.org

Human Resources Department

City Hall, 2100 Thousand Oaks Blvd., Thousand Oaks, CA 91362
Fax: (805) 449-2149 E-mail: humanresources@toaks.org

Human Resources Director **Gary Rogers** .... (805) 449-2144
E-mail: grogers@toaks.org

Human Resources Deputy Director **Libby White** .... (805) 449-2146
E-mail: lwhite@toaks.org

Police Department

2100 Thousand Oaks Blvd., Thousand Oaks, CA 91362
Tel: (805) 494-8200 Fax: (805) 494-8295 E-mail: police@toaks.org

Police Chief **Tim Hagel** .... (805) 494-8265
Administrative Services **Capt. Jim Fryhoff** .... (805) 494-8248

Public Library

Grant R. Brimhall Library, 1401 E. Janss Rd., Thousand Oaks, CA 91362
Fax: (805) 373-6858 Internet: http://www.toaks.org/library
E-mail: library@toaks.org

Director **Nancy Schram** .... (805) 381-7300 ext. 7351
E-mail: nschram@tolibrary.org

Public Works Department

City Hall, 2100 Thousand Oaks Blvd., Thousand Oaks, CA 91362
Fax: (805) 449-2475 E-mail: publicworks@toaks.org

Director **Jay Spurgin** .... (805) 449-2444

Deputy Public Works Director **Cliff Finley** .... (805) 449-2444
E-mail: cfinley@toaks.org

Engineering Division Manager **(Vacant)** .... (805) 449-2430

Engineering Division Manager, Water/Wastewater **(Vacant)** .... (805) 449-2462

Deputy Public Works Director **John Smallis** .... (805) 449-2499 ext. 340
1993 Rancho Conejo Boulevard, Fax: (805) 498-4941
Thousand Oaks, CA 91320-1425

Traffic Division Manager **(Vacant)** .... (805) 449-2412

Wastewater Treatment Plant Superintendent **(Vacant)** .... (805) 498-4011
Fax: (805) 498-5727

Thousand Oaks Civic Arts Plaza

City Hall, 2100 Thousand Oaks Blvd, Thousand Oaks, CA 91362
Fax: (805) 449-2750 Internet: http://www.civicartsplaza.com
E-mail: theatres@toaks.org E-mail: info@civicartsplaza.com

Theatres Director **Barry McComb** .... (805) 449-2707

★Elected Official ▲Appointed by Legislature ▼Appointed by Governor ►Appointed by Board or Commission ●Appointed by Judge
■Appointed by Mayor △Appointed by Freeholders ▽Appointed by Supervisor ▷Appointed by County Executive ○Appointed by Council

City of Toledo, Ohio

One Government Center, Toledo, OH 43604
Tel: (419) 245-1001 (Information) Internet: www.toledo.oh.gov/

County: Lucas **Election Type:** Nonpartisan **Population:** 279,789 (2015)

Office of the Mayor

One Government Center, Suite 2200, Toledo, OH 43604
Fax: (419) 245-1370

★Mayor **Paula Hicks-Hudson** . . . . (419) 245-1001
Began Service: February 1, 2015
Term Expires: December 31, 2019
E-mail: mayor@toledo.oh.gov
Education: Spelman BA; Colorado State 1975 MA; Iowa 1982 JD

Chief of Staff **Mark Sobczak** . . . . (419) 245-1007

Chief Operating Officer **Eileen Granata** . . . . (419) 245-1007
E-mail: eileen.granata@toledo.oh.gov

Executive Assistant **Alan Bannister** . . . . (419) 245-1041
E-mail: alan.bannister@toledo.oh.gov

Public Information Officer **Janet Schroeder** . . . . (419) 245-1895
E-mail: janet.schroeder@toledo.oh.gov

Office of the City Auditor

Fax: (419) 245-1610

○City Auditor **John Jaksetic** Suite 2150 . . . . (419) 245-1080
E-mail: john.jaksetic@toledo.oh.gov

Office of Affirmative Action/Contract Compliance

One Government Center, Suite 1900, Toledo, OH 43604
Tel: (419) 245-1198 Fax: (419) 245-1058

Affirmative Action Director **Calvin Brown** . . . . (419) 245-1198

Department of Development

One Government Center, Suite 2250, Toledo, OH 43604-2295
Tel: (419) 245-1600 Fax: (419) 245-1462
Internet: http://toledo.oh.gov/services/development/

Director (Interim) **Calvin J. Lawshe** . . . . (419) 245-1600
Education: Toledo BBA, MBA

Commissioner **Bill Burkett** . . . . (419) 245-1692
E-mail: bill.burkett@toledo.oh.gov

Manager of Development **Steven Powell** . . . . (419) 245-1286

Real Estate Records Clerk **Terri King** . . . . (419) 245-1452
E-mail: terri.king@toledo.oh.gov

Real Estate Specialist **Paul Kwapich** . . . . (419) 245-1431
E-mail: paul.kwapich@toledo.oh.gov

Department of Finance

One Government Center, Ste. 2050, Toledo, OH 43604
Fax: (419) 245-1863

■Director (Acting) **George Sarantou** . . . . (419) 245-1648
E-mail: george.sarantou@toledo.oh.gov

Accounts Division Commissioner **Richard Jackson** . . . . (419) 245-1602

Budget Commissioner **Melanie Campbell** . . . . (419) 245-1252
E-mail: melanie.campbell@toledo.oh.gov

■Purchasing Commissioner (Acting) **Bryan Benner** . . . . (419) 245-1194
E-mail: bryan.benner@toledo.oh.gov Fax: (419) 245-1013

Treasury/Taxation Division Commissioner
Clarence Coleman . . . . (419) 245-1662
Fax: (419) 936-2320

Fire and Rescue Department

545 N. Huron, Toledo, OH 43604
Fax: (419) 245-1296

Fire Chief **Luis Santiago** . . . . (419) 245-1125
E-mail: luis.santiago@toledo.oh.gov

Fire and Rescue Department *continued*

Assistant Chief, Fire Prevention, Training and Safety
Karen Marquardt . . . . (419) 245-3507
E-mail: karen.marquardt@toledo.oh.gov

Deputy Chief, Communications and Emergency Medical Services **Brian Byrd** . . . . (419) 245-1275
E-mail: brian.byrd@toledo.oh.gov

Deputy Chief **Thomas Jaksetic** . . . . (419) 245-3587
E-mail: thomas.jaksetic@toledo.oh.gov

Deputy Chief **Richard Syroka** . . . . (419) 245-1125
E-mail: richard.syroka@toledo.oh.gov

Toledo-Lucas County Health Department

635 North Erie Street, Toledo, OH 43604
Tel: (419) 213-4100 (Information) Fax: (419) 213-4017

Health Commissioner **David L. Grossman** . . . . (419) 213-4018

Deputy Health Commissioner **(Vacant)** . . . . (419) 213-4018

Chief Financial Officer/Director of Administrative Services **Joanne Melamed** . . . . (419) 213-4018
E-mail: melamedj@co.lucas.oh.us

Environmental Health

635 North Erie Street, Suite 366, Toledo, OH 43604
Tel: (419) 213-4100 Fax: (419) 213-4141

Director **Eric Zgodzinski** . . . . (419) 213-4046

Health Services

635 North Erie Street, Toledo, OH 43604
Tel: (419) 213-4113 Fax: (419) 213-4017

Director **(Vacant)** . . . . (419) 213-4113

Human Resources Department

One Government Center, Suite 1920, Toledo, OH 43604
Fax: (419) 245-1511

Commissioner **Michael Niedzielski** . . . . (419) 245-1500
E-mail: mike.Niedzielski@toledo.oh.gov

Department of Information Communication and Technology

One Government Center, Toledo, OH 43604
Fax: (419) 245-1475

Director **David Scherting** . . . . (419) 245-1493
E-mail: david.scherting@toledo.oh.gov

Law Department

One Government Center, Suite 2250, Toledo, OH 43604-2293
Fax: (419) 245-1752

■Director **Adam W. Loukx** . . . . (419) 245-1020
E-mail: adam.loukx@toledo.oh.gov

General Counsel **Paul F. Syring** . . . . (419) 245-1020

Labor and Employment Chief **Ellen Grachek** . . . . (419) 245-1020

Litigation Chief **Jeffrey Charles** . . . . (419) 245-1020

Chief Prosecutor **David L. Toska** . . . . (419) 936-2385
555 N. Erie St., Toledo, OH 43624

Toledo-Lucas County Plan Commissions

One Government Center, Ste. 1620, Toledo, OH 43604
Fax: (419) 936-3730 E-mail: toledo.plancommission@toledo.oh.gov

▶Director **Thomas C. Gibbons** . . . . (419) 245-1200
E-mail: thomas.gibbons@toledo.oh.gov

Police Department

525 N. Erie, Toledo, OH 43604
Fax: (419) 936-3706 Internet: www.toledopolice.com/

■Chief of Police **George Kral** . . . . (419) 245-3200
E-mail: george.kral@toledo.oh.gov

★Elected Official ▲Appointed by Legislature ▼Appointed by Governor ▶Appointed by Board or Commission ●Appointed by Judge
■Appointed by Mayor △Appointed by Freeholders ▽Appointed by Supervisor ▷Appointed by County Executive ○Appointed by Council

Police Department *continued*

Administrative Services Division Deputy Chief
Benjamin Tucker . . . . . (419) 245-3200
E-mail: benjamin.tucker@toledo.oh.gov
Investigative Services Division Deputy Chief
James O'Bryant . . . . . (419) 245-3200
Operations Division Deputy Chief **Tom Wiegand** . . . . . (419) 245-3200

Public Service Department

110 North Westwood Avenue, Toledo, OH 43607-1219
Fax: (419) 936-7299

■ Director **William H. Franklin** . . . . . (419) 245-1835
E-mail: william.franklin@toledo.oh.gov Fax: (419) 936-7299
Administrative Assistant **Pamela A. Knight** . . . . . (419) 245-1835
E-mail: pam.knight@toledo.oh.gov
Landfill Operations Manager **Dan Pittman** . . . . . (419) 936-2640
3962 Hoffman Road, Toledo, OH 43611 Fax: (419) 245-1399
E-mail: dan.pittman@toledo.oh.gov

Facility and Fleet Division

Fax: (419) 245-1019

Commissioner **Kevin McCarthy** . . . . . (419) 936-2550
E-mail: kevin.mccarthy@toledo.oh.gov Fax: (419) 936-2561
Facility Administrator **Rick Akeman** . . . . . (419) 936-2560
E-mail: rick.akeman@toledo.oh.gov Fax: (419) 936-2560
Fleet Administrator **Mike Bombrys** . . . . . (419) 936-2556
Fax: (419) 936-2561

Division of Parks Recreation and Forestry

2201 Ottawa Parkway, Toledo, OH 43606-4338
Fax: (419) 936-2878

Commissioner, Parks Recreation & Forestry (Acting)
Lisa Ward . . . . . (419) 245-3357
Parks and Recreation Manager **Curtis Cotton** . . . . . (419) 936-2700
Forestry and Cemetery Manager **Jody Prude** . . . . . (419) 936-2896

Streets, Bridges and Harbor Division

Fax: (419) 245-1544

■ Streets, Bridges, and Harbor Commissioner
David Welch . . . . . (419) 245-1526
1189 West Central Avenue, Toledo, OH 43610 Fax: (419) 245-1544
E-mail: david.welch@toledo.oh.gov
Streets Superintendent **Mark Marzec** . . . . . (419) 245-1539
Fax: (419) 245-1546
Manager **Jerry Mikolajczyk** . . . . . (419) 245-1537
Manager **Amy J. Wood** . . . . . (419) 245-1538

Transportation Division

Fax: (419) 245-1310

■ Transportation Commissioner (Acting)
Sherri L. Frederick . . . . . (419) 245-1301
110 N. Westwood, Toledo, OH 43607
E-mail: sherri.frederick@toledo.oh.gov
Sign Shop Superintendent **Joe Whitten** . . . . . (419) 245-1300
Instrumentation Supervisor **Greg Wilson** . . . . . (419) 245-1453

Public Utilities Department

420 Madison Avenue, Suite 100, Toledo, OH 43604-1219
Tel: (419) 245-1800 Fax: (419) 245-1853

■ Director **Edward A. Moore** . . . . . (419) 245-1318
E-mail: ed.moore@toledo.oh.gov Fax: (419) 245-1853
Public Utilities Administrator **Donald M. Moline** . . . . . (419) 245-1318
Engineering Services Division Commissioner
Douglas Stephens . . . . . (419) 936-2710
One Lake Erie Center, Fax: (419) 936-3737
3rd Floor, Toledo, OH 43604
E-mail: douglas.stephens@toledo.oh.gov
Environmental Services Division Commissioner
E. Jeanette Ball . . . . . (419) 936-3950
348 South Erie Street, Toledo, OH 43604-1633 Fax: (419) 936-3959

Public Utilities Department *continued*

Water Distribution Commissioner **Christy Sonerant** . . . . . (419) 936-2826
420 Madison Ave., Fax: (419) 936-2828
Suite 100, Toledo, OH 43604-1219
Utilities Administration Commissioner **Abby Arnold** . . . . . (419) 936-2338
E-mail: abby.arnold@toledo.oh.gov
Utilities Administration Manager **Jenny Gogol** . . . . . (419) 936-2472
420 Madison Ave., Toledo, OH 43604-1219 Fax: (419) 245-1853
E-mail: jennifer.gogol@toledo.oh.gov
Sewer and Drainage Services Division Manager
Calvin Harris . . . . . (419) 936-2694
4032 Creekside, Toledo, OH 43612 Fax: (419) 936-2716
Water Reclamation Division Plant Administrator
Alan Ruffell . . . . . (419) 727-2602
3900 N. Summit St., Toledo, OH 43611 Fax: (419) 936-2161
Water Treatment Commissioner (Acting)
Chuck Campbell . . . . . (419) 245-1846
Fax: (419) 245-1853
Sewer and Drainage Services Commissioner
David E. Pratt . . . . . (419) 936-2172
4032 Creekside, Toledo, OH 43612 Fax: (419) 936-2716
E-mail: david.pratt@toledo.oh.gov
Administrative Analyst **Stacy Weber** . . . . . (419) 245-1800

Office of the City Council

One Government Center, Suite 2120, Toledo, OH 43604
Fax: (419) 245-1072

★ Council President **Steve Steel** (At-Large) . . . . . (419) 245-1050
Term Expires: December 31, 2017
E-mail: steve.steel@toledo.oh.gov
★ Council Member **Tyrone Riley** (District 1) . . . . . (419) 245-1050
Term Expires: December 31, 2019
E-mail: tyrone.riley@toledo.oh.gov
★ Council Member
Matthew A "Matt" Cherry (District 2) . . . . . (419) 245-1050
Term Expires: December 31, 2019
★ Council Member **Peter S. Ujvagi** (District 3) . . . . . (419) 245-1050
Term Expires: December 31, 2019
E-mail: Peter.Ujvagi@toledo.oh.gov
★ Council Member **Yvonne Harper** (District 4) . . . . . (419) 245-1050
Term Expires: December 31, 2019
E-mail: Yvonne.Harper@toledo.oh.gov
★ Council Member **Tom Waniewski** (District 5) . . . . . (419) 245-1050
Term Expires: December 31, 2019
E-mail: tom.waniewski@toledo.oh.gov
★ Council Member **Lindsay M. Webb** (District 6) . . . . . (419) 245-1050
Term Expires: December 31, 2019
E-mail: lindsay.webb@toledo.oh.gov
★ Council Member **Cecelia Adams** (At-Large) . . . . . (419) 245-1050
Term Expires: December 31, 2019
E-mail: Cecelia.Adams@toledo.oh.gov
★ Council Member **Theresa M. Gabriel** (At-Large) . . . . . (419) 245-1050
Term Expires: December 31, 2017
★ Council Member **Rob Ludeman** (At-Large) . . . . . (419) 245-1050
Term Expires: December 31, 2017
E-mail: rob.ludeman@toledo.oh.gov
★ Council Member **Sandy Spang** (At-Large) . . . . . (419) 245-1050
Term Expires: December 31, 2017
★ Council Member **Larry Sykes** (At-Large) . . . . . (419) 245-1050
Term Expires: December 31, 2017
E-mail: Larry.Sykes@toledo.oh.gov

Office of the Clerk of Council

Fax: (419) 245-1610

○ Clerk of Council **Gerald E. "Jerry" Dendinger**
Suite 2140 . . . . . (419) 245-1065
E-mail: gerald.dendinger@toledo.oh.gov
Date of Birth: September 22, 1951
Education: Toledo 1973 BBA
Secretary to the Clerk **JoAnne Bell-Carr** . . . . . (419) 245-1060
E-mail: joanne.bell-carr@toledo.oh.gov

★ Elected Official ▲ Appointed by Legislature ▼ Appointed by Governor ▶ Appointed by Board or Commission ● Appointed by Judge
■ Appointed by Mayor △ Appointed by Freeholders ▽ Appointed by Supervisor ▷ Appointed by County Executive ○ Appointed by Council

City of Topeka, Kansas

215 SE Seventh Street, Topeka, KS 66603-3914
Tel: (785) 368-3940 Internet: www.topeka.org

County: Shawnee **Election Type:** Nonpartisan **Population:** 127,265 (2015)

Office of the Mayor

215 SE Seventh Street, Room 352, Topeka, KS 66603-3914
Fax: (785) 368-3850 (Mayor's Fax) Internet: www.topeka.org/mayor/

★ Mayor **Larry Wolgast** . . . . . . (785) 368-3895
Began Service: April 2013
Term Expires: April 2017
E-mail: lwolgast@topeka.org
Education: Kansas State BA; Kansas MA, PhD
Assistant to the Mayor **Margo Rangel** . . . . . . (785) 368-3895
E-mail: mrangel@topeka.org

Office of the City Council

215 SE Seventh Street, Room 255, Topeka, KS 66603-3914
Tel: (785) 368-3710 Fax: (785) 368-3958 E-mail: council@topeka.org
Internet: www.topeka.org/cityofficials/index.shtml

★ Deputy Mayor **Karen Hiller** (District 1) . . . . . . (785) 368-3710
Term Expires: April 1, 2017
E-mail: khiller@topeka.org
★ Council Member **Sandra Clear** (District 2) . . . . . . (785) 368-3710
Term Expires: April 2019
E-mail: sclear@topeka.org
★ Council Member **Sylvia Ortiz** (District 3) . . . . . . (785) 368-3710
Term Expires: April 1, 2017
E-mail: sortiz@topeka.org
★ Council Member **(Vacant)** (District 4) . . . . . . (785) 368-3710
Term Expires: April 2019
★ Council Member **Michelle De La Isla** (District 5) . . . . . . (785) 368-3710
Term Expires: April 2017
E-mail: mdelaisla@topeka.org
★ Council Member **Brendan Jensen** (District 6) . . . . . . (785) 368-3710
Term Expires: April 2019
E-mail: bjensen@topeka.org
★ Council Member **Elaine Schwartz** (District 7) . . . . . . (785) 368-3710
Term Expires: April 1, 2017
E-mail: eschwartz@topeka.org
★ Council Member **Jeff Coen** (District 8) . . . . . . (785) 368-3710
Term Expires: April 2019
E-mail: jcoen@topeka.org
★ Council Member **Richard Harmon** (District 9) . . . . . . (785) 368-3710
Term Expires: April 1, 2017
E-mail: rharmon@topeka.org
Assistant to the City Council **Angela Horn** . . . . . . (785) 368-3710

Office of the City Manager

215 SE Seventh Street, Room 355, Topeka, KS 66603-3914
Fax: (785) 368-3909
Internet: http://www.topeka.org/citymanager/index.shtml

City Manager **Jim Colson** . . . . . . (785) 368-3725
E-mail: jcolson@topeka.org
Education: Northwood BA; Western Sem MA; Michigan MURP
City Clerk **Brenda Younger** . . . . . . (785) 368-3940
E-mail: byounger@topeka.org Fax: (785) 368-3943
Deputy City Manager **Douglas Gerber** . . . . . . (785) 368-3725
E-mail: dgerber@topeka.org

City Communications Division

Internet: http://www.topeka.org/communications/index.shtml

City Communications Manager **Aly Van Dyke** . . . . . . (785) 368-0991
620 SE Madison, Topeka, KS 66603
E-mail: avandyke@topeka.org

Office of the City Attorney

215 SE Seventh Street, Room 353, Topeka, KS 66603-3914
Fax: (785) 368-3901 Internet: www.topeka.org/cityattorney/contacts.shtml

City Attorney **Lisa Robertson** . . . . . . (785) 368-3883
E-mail: lrobertson@topeka.org

Finance and Administrative Services

215 SE Seventh Street, Room 358, Topeka, KS 66603-3914
Tel: (785) 368-3970 Fax: (785) 368-3975
Internet: www.topeka.org/administrative/index.shtml

Director **(Vacant)** . . . . . . (785) 368-3970
Finance Director **Brandon Kauffman** . . . . . . (785) 368-0919
Budget Manager **Nickie Lee** . . . . . . (785) 368-3970
E-mail: nlee@topeka.org
Contracts and Procurement Director **Jay Oyler** . . . . . . (785) 368-3749
E-mail: joyler@topeka.org Fax: (785) 368-4499

Fleet Services

215 SE 7th, Room 358, Topeka, KS 66603-3914
Fax: (785) 368-3983 Internet: www.topeka.org/fleetservices/index.shtml

Manager **Brian Bigenwalt** . . . . . . (785) 368-3735

Fire Department

324 SE Jefferson Street, Topeka, KS 66607-1133
Fax: (785) 368-4030 Internet: http://www.topeka.org/tfd/index.shtml

Fire Chief (Interim) **Tim Wayne** . . . . . . (785) 368-4000
E-mail: twwayne@topeka.org
Advisor **Greg Bailey** . . . . . . (785) 368-4000
Note: Retiring June 20, 2016
E-mail: gbailey@topeka.org
Deputy Chief **Greg Moody** . . . . . . (785) 368-4111
E-mail: gmoody@topeka.org
Fire Marshal **Michael Martin** . . . . . . (785) 368-4000
E-mail: mmartin@Topeka.org

Human Resources Department

215 SE Seventh Street, Room 170, Topeka, KS 66603-3914
Fax: (785) 368-3605
Internet: www.topeka.org/humanresources/index.shtml

Director **Jacque Russell** . . . . . . (785) 368-3867
E-mail: jrussell@topeka.org
Benefits Manager **Mishelle Wilcox** . . . . . . (785) 368-2580
Wellness Program Manager **Samantha Griffin** . . . . . . (785) 368-3602
E-mail: sgriffin@topeka.org

Information Technology Department

215 SE Seventh Street, Room 52, Topeka, KS 66603-3914
Fax: (785) 368-3719 Internet: http://www.topeka.org/it/index.shtml

Director **Mark Biswell** . . . . . . (785) 368-3718

Department of Neighborhood Relations

620 Southeast Madison, Topeka, KS 66607
Fax: (785) 368-2546 Internet: www.topeka.org/hnd/index.shtml

Director **Sasha Haehn** . . . . . . (785) 368-4461
E-mail: sstiles@topeka.org
Director of Housing Services **Cori Wright** . . . . . . (785) 368-4490

Planning Department

620 Southeast Madison, Topeka, KS 66607
Fax: (785) 368-2535 Internet: www.topeka.org/planning/

Director **Bill Fiander** . . . . . . (785) 368-3728

Police Department

320 S. Kansas Ave., Suite 100, Topeka, KS 66603
Fax: (785) 368-9458 Internet: www.topeka.org/tpd/index.shtml

Chief of Police **James L. Brown** . . . . . . (785) 368-9551
Animal Control Manager **Linda Halford** . . . . . . (785) 368-9256

★ Elected Official ▲ Appointed by Legislature ▼ Appointed by Governor ▶ Appointed by Board or Commission ● Appointed by Judge
■ Appointed by Mayor △ Appointed by Freeholders ▽ Appointed by Supervisor ▷ Appointed by County Executive ○ Appointed by Council

Public Works Department
620 Southeast Madison, Topeka, KS 66607
Fax: (785) 368-3805 Internet: www.topeka.org/publicworks/index.shtml

Director of Public Works **Jason Peek** .... (785) 368-3949
City Engineer **Shawn Bruns** .... (785) 368-3842
E-mail: sbruns@topeka.org Fax: (785) 368-3881
Development Services Director **Richard Faulkner** .... (785) 368-1606
Fax: (785) 368-3915
Utilities and Transportation Operations **(Vacant)** .... (785) 368-3803
Fax: (785) 368-3814
Street Maintenance and Traffic Operations **Ron Raines** ... (785) 368-3803
200 North Topeka, Topeka, KS 66603 Fax: (785) 368-3814
E-mail: rraines@topeka.org
Evaluation and Planning Manager **Carlos Salazar** ...... (785) 368-3920
927 NW Harrison Street, Topeka, KS 66608 Fax: (785) 368-3936
Traffic Engineer **(Vacant)** .... (785) 368-3842
Water Pollution Control Director **Bob Sample** .... (785) 368-4233
3245 Waterworks Drive, Topeka, KS 66606 Fax: (785) 368-3825
Water System General Manager **Riley Vittitoe** .... (785) 368-2424
Fax: (785) 368-3869
Facility Maintenance **Vincent Schuetz** .... (785) 368-3959
E-mail: vschuetz@topeka.org Fax: (785) 368-3806

Topeka City Zoo
635 SW Gage Ave., Topeka, KS 66606
Tel: (785) 368-9180 (Information) Fax: (785) 368-9152
Internet: http://topekazoo.org/

Director **Brendan Wiley** .... (785) 368-9131

Topeka Public Schools
624 SW 24th Street, Topeka, KS 66611-1294
Fax: (785) 575-6160 Internet: www.topekapublicschools.net/

Superintendent of Schools **Dr. Julie Ford** .... (785) 295-3000
★ Board President **C. Patrick Woods** .... (785) 295-3000
Term Expires: June 30, 2019
E-mail: pwoods@tps501.org
★ Board Vice President **Dr. Michael R. Morrison** .... (785) 295-3000
Term Expires: June 30, 2017
E-mail: mmorrison@tps501.org
★ Board Member **Janel Johnson** .... (785) 295-3000
Term Expires: June 30, 2019
E-mail: jjohnson2@tps501.org
★ Board Member **Nancy Kirk** .... (785) 295-3000
Term Expires: June 30, 2019
E-mail: nkirk@tps501.org
★ Board Member **Dr. Peg McCarthy** .... (785) 295-3000
Term Expires: June 30, 2019
E-mail: pmccarthy@tps501.org
★ Board Member **Scott Mickelsen** .... (785) 295-3000
Term Expires: June 30, 2017
E-mail: smickelsen@tps501.org
★ Board Member **John R. Williams** .... (785) 295-3000
Term Expires: June 30, 2017
E-mail: jwilliams2@tps501.org
Clerk of the Board **Carleen Lister** .... (785) 295-3000
E-mail: clister@tps501.org

City of Torrance, California
3031 Torrance Blvd., Torrance, CA 90503
Tel: (310) 328-5310 (Information) Fax: (310) 618-5891
Internet: www.torranceca.gov

County: Los Angeles **Election Type:** Nonpartisan **Year Founded:** 1912
Year Incorporated: 1921 **Population:** 148,475 (2015)

Office of the Mayor and City Council
3031 Torrance Blvd., Torrance, CA 90503
Fax: (310) 618-5841

★ Mayor **Patrick J. "Pat" Furey** .... (310) 618-2801
Began Service: July 15, 2014
Term Expires: June 6, 2018
E-mail: pfurey@torranceca.gov
★ Council Member **Heidi Ann Ashcraft** .... (310) 618-2801
Term Expires: June 6, 2018
E-mail: hashcraft@torranceca.gov
★ Council Member **Gene Barnett** .... (310) 618-2801
Term Expires: June 3, 2016
E-mail: gbarnett@torranceca.gov
★ Council Member **Tim Goodrich** .... (310) 618-2801
Term Expires: June 2018
E-mail: tgoodrich@torranceca.gov
★ Council Member **Mike Griffiths** .... (310) 618-2801
Term Expires: June 7, 2016
E-mail: mgriffiths@torranceca.gov
★ Council Member **Geoff Rizzo** .... (310) 618-2801
Term Expires: June 2018
E-mail: grizzo@torranceca.gov
★ Council Member **Kurt Weideman** .... (310) 618-2801
Term Expires: June 6, 2016
E-mail: kweideman@torranceca.gov

Office of the City Attorney
3031 Torrance Blvd., Torrance, CA 90503
Fax: (310) 618-5813

○ City Attorney **John L. Fellows III** .... (310) 618-5810
E-mail: jfellows@torranceca.gov

Office of the City Clerk
3031 Torrance Blvd., Torrance, CA 90503
Fax: (310) 618-2931

★ City Clerk **Rebecca Poirier** .... (310) 618-2870
Term Expires: June 6, 2018
E-mail: RPoirier@torranceca.gov

Office of the City Treasurer
3031 Torrance Blvd., Torrance, CA 90503
Fax: (310) 781-7615

★ City Treasurer **Dana Cortez** .... (310) 618-5801
Term Expires: June 6, 2018
E-mail: dcortez@torranceca.gov

Office of the City Manager
3031 Torrance Blvd., Torrance, CA 90503
Fax: (310) 618-5891

○ City Manager **LeRoy J. Jackson** .... (310) 618-5880
E-mail: ljackson@torranceca.gov

Office of Cable and Community Relations
3350 Civic Center Drive, Torrance, CA 90503
Fax: (310) 781-7132

Manager **Michael D. Smith** .... (310) 618-5762
E-mail: msmith@torranceca.gov

★ Elected Official ▲ Appointed by Legislature ▼ Appointed by Governor ▶ Appointed by Board or Commission ● Appointed by Judge
■ Appointed by Mayor △ Appointed by Freeholders ▽ Appointed by Supervisor ▷ Appointed by County Executive ○ Appointed by Council

Civil Service Commission
3231 Torrance Blvd., Torrance, CA 90503
Fax: (310) 618-2927 E-mail: cvs@torranceca.gov

Manager **Kelli Lee** .... (310) 618-2967
E-mail: klee@torranceca.gov

Communications and Information Technology
3031 Torrance Blvd., Torrance, CA 90503
Fax: (310) 618-5879

Director **Richard Shigaki** .... (310) 618-2880
E-mail: rshigaki@torranceca.gov

Community Development Department
3031 Torrance Blvd., Torrance, CA 90503
Fax: (310) 618-5829

Director **Jeff Gibson** .... (310) 618-5990
E-mail: jgibson@torranceca.gov

Community Services Department
3031 Torrance Blvd., Torrance, CA 90503
Tel: (310) 618-2930 Fax: (310) 781-7598

Director **John Jones** .... (310) 618-2930

Finance Department
3031 Torrance Blvd., Torrance, CA 90503
Tel: (310) 618-5850 Fax: (310) 618-5852

Director **Eric Tsao** .... (310) 618-5850

Fire Department
1701 Crenshaw Blvd., Torrance, CA 90503
Fax: (310) 781-7030

Chief **(Vacant)** .... (310) 781-7000

General Services Department
3350 Civic Center Drive, Torrance, CA 90503
Fax: (310) 781-7199

Director **Sheryl Ballew** .... (310) 781-7140
E-mail: sballew@torranceca.gov

Police Department
3300 N. Civic Center Dr., Torrance, CA 90503
Tel: (310) 328-3456 Fax: (310) 618-5532
E-mail: torrancepd@torranceca.gov

Chief of Police **Mark Matsuda** .... (310) 618-5641

Public Works Department
20500 Madrona Avenue, Torrance, CA 90503
Fax: (310) 781-6902 E-mail: publicworkinfo@torranceca.gov

Director **Rob Beste** .... (310) 781-6900
Deputy Director, Operations **Craig Bilezerian** .... (310) 781-6900

Sanitation Division
Manager **Matt Knapp** .... (310) 781-6900
Refuse and Recycling **Tony Mullikin** .... (310) 781-6900
Street Sweeping **Tom Cook** .... (310) 781-6900
Wastewater **Tom Cook** .... (310) 781-6900

Transit Department
20500 Madrona Avenue, Torrance, CA 90503
Fax: (310) 618-6229

Director **Kim Turner** .... (310) 618-6266

City of Trenton, New Jersey
319 East State Street, Trenton, NJ 08608
Internet: www.trentonnj.org

County: Mercer **Election Type:** Nonpartisan **Population:** 84,225 (2015)

Office of the Mayor
319 E. State St., Trenton, NJ 08608
Fax: (609) 989-3939

★ Mayor **Eric E. Jackson** .... (609) 989-3030
Began Service: July 1, 2014
Term Expires: June 30, 2018
E-mail: mayorsoffice@trentonnj.org
Chief of Staff **Francis Blanco** .... (609) 989-3344
Public Information Officer **Michael Walker** .... (609) 989-3033
E-mail: mwalker@trentonnj.org

Business Administration
319 E. State St., Trenton, NJ 08608
Fax: (609) 989-4250

■ Business Administrator **Terry McEwen** .... (609) 989-3807
E-mail: tmcewen@trentonnj.org
Information Technology Division Director **(Vacant)** ...... (609) 989-3964
Personnel Division Director **Steven R. Ponella** .... (609) 989-3115
Purchasing Division Director **Isabel Garcia** .... (609) 989-3135
E-mail: igarcia@trentonnj.org
Budget Examiner **Alphonso Jones** .... (609) 989-3104
E-mail: ajones@trentonnj.org

Finance Department
319 E. State St., Trenton, NJ 08608
Fax: (609) 989-4280

■ Comptroller and Chief Financial Officer
Janet Schoenhaar .... (609) 989-3041
E-mail: jschoenhaar@trentonnj.org

Fire Department
244 Perry Street, Trenton, NJ 08618
Fax: (609) 989-4035

■ Fire Director (Acting) **Quareeb Bashir** .... (609) 989-4038
E-mail: qbashir@trentonnj.org
Emergency Management Deputy Chief
Leonard Carmichael, Jr. .... (609) 989-4031
E-mail: lcarmichael@trentonnj.org
Training Battalion Chief **Robert Tharp** .... (609) 989-4096
E-mail: rtharp@trentonnj.org
Communications Officer **Mark Robotin** .... (609) 989-3992
E-mail: mrobotin@trentonnj.org

Health and Human Services Department
319 E. State St., Trenton, NJ 08608
Fax: (609) 989-4245

■ Director (Acting) **James A. Brownlee** .... (609) 989-3332
E-mail: jbrownlee@trentonnj.org
Community Relations and Social Services Division
Director **Ruth Carter** .... (609) 989-3345
Education: Penn State BA; Temple MSW

Housing and Economic Development Department
319 E. State St., Trenton, NJ 08608
Fax: (609) 989-4243

■ Director (Acting) **Diana R. Rogers** .... (609) 989-3518
E-mail: drogers@trentonnj.org
Economic Development Division Director
Diana R. Rogers .... (609) 989-3512
E-mail: drogers@trentonnj.org

★ Elected Official ▲ Appointed by Legislature ▼ Appointed by Governor ► Appointed by Board or Commission ● Appointed by Judge
■ Appointed by Mayor △ Appointed by Freeholders ▽ Appointed by Supervisor ▷ Appointed by County Executive ○ Appointed by Council

Housing and Economic Development Department *continued*

Chief of Housing Production **Marc Leckington** . . . . (609) 989-3536
Principal Planner **Jeffrey Wilkerson** . . . . (609) 989-3502

Inspections Department

319 E. State St., Trenton, NJ 08608
Fax: (609) 989-4241

■ Director (Acting) **Leslie O. Graham** . . . . (609) 989-3545
E-mail: lgraham@trentonnj.org

Law Department

319 E. State St., Trenton, NJ 08608
Fax: (609) 989-4242

■ Director of Law (Acting) **Marc McKithen** . . . . (609) 989-3011
E-mail: mmckithen@trentonnj.org

Police Department

225 North Clinton Avenue, Trenton, NJ 08609

■ Police Director **Ernest Parrey** . . . . (609) 989-4055
E-mail: eparrey@trentonnj.org Fax: (609) 989-4270

Public Works Department

319 E. State St., Trenton, NJ 08608
Fax: (609) 989-4287

■ Director (Acting) **Sean Semple** . . . . (609) 989-3152
E-mail: ssemple@trentonnj.org
General Superintendent and Chief Engineer, Sewer and Water **Dilip Patel** . . . . (609) 989-3214
E-mail: dpatel@trentonnj.org
Public Property Division Director **Harold Hall** . . . . (609) 989-3165
Traffic and Transportation Division Director **Hoggarth Stephen** . . . . (609) 989-3615
Bureau of Streets Supervisor **Garland Barber** . . . . (609) 989-3200
Bureau of Sewers Superintendent **Joseph McIntyre** . . . . . . (609) 989-3151
Sanitation Inspector **Gregory Addye** . . . . (609) 989-3175

Recreation, Natural Resources and Culture Department

319 East State Street, Trenton, NJ 08608
Tel: (609) 989-3635 Fax: (609) 989-4290

Director **Fiah Gussin** . . . . (609) 989-3635

Office of the City Council

319 E. State St., Trenton, NJ 08608
Fax: (609) 989-3190

★ Council President **Zachary A. Chester** (West Ward) . . . . . (609) 989-3146
Term Expires: June 30, 2018
E-mail: zac.chester@gmail.com
★ Council Member **Alex Bethea** (At-Large) . . . . (609) 989-3146
Term Expires: June 30, 2018
E-mail: abethea@trenton.k12.nj.us
★ Council Member **Marge Caldwell-Wilson** (North Ward) . . . . (609) 989-3146
Term Expires: June 30, 2018
E-mail: marge1515@verizon.net
★ Council Member **Duncan W. Harrison, Jr.** (At-Large) . . . (609) 989-3146
Term Expires: June 30, 2018
E-mail: duncanwharrison@gmail.com
★ Council Member **Phyllis Holly-Ward** (At-Large) . . . . (609) 989-3146
Term Expires: June 30, 2018
E-mail: pholly1@verizon.net
★ Council Member **George Muschal** (South Ward) . . . . (609) 989-3146
Term Expires: June 30, 2018
E-mail: georgemuschal@aol.com
★ Council Member **Verlina Reynolds-Jackson** (East Ward) . . . . (609) 989-3146
Term Expires: June 30, 2018
E-mail: vreynolds-jackson@trentonnj.org

Office of the City Clerk

319 E. State St., Trenton, NJ 08608
Fax: (609) 989-3190

○ City Clerk **Richard M. Kachmar** . . . . (609) 989-3187
Term Expires: October 2016
E-mail: rkachmar@trentonnj.org

City of Tucson, Arizona

255 West Alameda, Tucson, AZ 85701
P.O. Box 27210, Tucson, AZ 85726-7210
Fax: (520) 791-5198 Internet: www.tucsonaz.gov

County: Pima **Election Type:** Partisan **Year Incorporated:** 1877
Population: 531,641 (2015) **Employees:** 4,782 **Fiscal Year:** 2016
Budget: $1,367,212,000

Office of the Mayor and City Council

P.O. Box 27210, Tucson, AZ 85726-7210
E-mail: mcweb@mail.ci.tucson.az.us

Employees: 43 **Fiscal Year:** 2016 **Budget:** $2,559,000

★ Mayor **Jonathan Rothschild** (D) . . . . (520) 791-4201
Began Service: December 5, 2011 Fax: (520) 791-5348
Term Expires: December 1, 2019
Communications Director **Lisa Markkula** . . . . (520) 791-4201
E-mail: Lisa.Markkula@tucsonaz.gov
★ Council Member **Regina Romero** (D-Ward 1) . . . . (520) 791-4040
Term Expires: December 1, 2019 Fax: (520) 791-5393
E-mail: ward1@tucsonaz.gov
★ Council Member **Paul Cunningham** (D-Ward 2) . . . . (520) 791-4687
Term Expires: December 1, 2019 Fax: (520) 791-5380
E-mail: ward2@tucsonaz.gov
★ Council Member **Karin Uhlich** (D-Ward 3) . . . . (520) 791-4711
Term Expires: December 3, 2017
E-mail: ward3@tucsonaz.gov
★ Council Member **Shirley C. Scott** (D-Ward 4) . . . . (520) 791-3199
Term Expires: December 1, 2019 Fax: (520) 791-4717
E-mail: ward4@tucsonaz.gov
Education: Drew BA; Cincinnati MA
★ Council Member **Richard Fimbres** (D-Ward 5) . . . . (520) 791-4231
Term Expires: December 3, 2017 Fax: (520) 791-3188
E-mail: ward5@tucsonaz.gov
★ Council Member **Steve Kozachik** (D-Ward 6) . . . . (520) 791-4601
Term Expires: December 3, 2017 Fax: (520) 791-3211
E-mail: ward6@tucsonaz.gov

Office of the City Attorney

P.O. Box 27210, Tucson, AZ 85726-7210
Fax: (520) 623-9803

Employees: 93 **Fiscal Year:** 2016 **Budget:** $8,638,000

○ City Attorney **Michael G. Rankin** . . . . (520) 791-4221
Chief Deputy City Attorney **David Deibel** . . . . (520) 791-4221
E-mail: dave.deibel@tucsonaz.gov
Criminal Division Deputy City Attorney **Baird Greene** . . . (520) 791-4104
E-mail: baird.greene@tucsonaz.gov

Office of the City Clerk

P.O. Box 27210, Tucson, AZ 85726-7210
Fax: (520) 791-4017

Employees: 43 **Fiscal Year:** 2016 **Budget:** $4,300,000

○ City Clerk **Roger Randolph** . . . . (520) 791-4213
E-mail: roger.randolph@tucsonaz.gov
Chief Deputy City Clerk **Deborah Rainone** . . . . (520) 791-4213
E-mail: deborah.rainone@tucsonaz.gov
Assistant City Clerk **Suzanne Mesich** . . . . (520) 791-4213
E-mail: suzanne.mesich@ci.tracy.ca.us

★ Elected Official ▲ Appointed by Legislature ▼ Appointed by Governor ▶ Appointed by Board or Commission ● Appointed by Judge
■ Appointed by Mayor △ Appointed by Freeholders ▽ Appointed by Supervisor ▷ Appointed by County Executive ○ Appointed by Council

CITIES AND TOWNS

Office of the City Manager
P.O. Box 27210, Tucson, AZ 85726-7210
Fax: (520) 791-5198

Employees: 33 **Fiscal Year:** 2016 **Budget:** $5,426,000

○City Manager **Michael Ortega** .... (520) 791-4204
E-mail: citymanager@tucsonaz.gov
Deputy City Manager **Martha Durkin** .... (520) 791-4204
E-mail: martha.durkin@tucsonaz.gov
Assistant City Manager **Albert Elias** .... (520) 791-4204
E-mail: albert.elias@tucsonaz.gov
Assistant City Manager **Julie Hughes** .... (520) 791-4204
Assistant City Manager **Ron Lewis** .... (520) 791-4204
E-mail: ron.lewis@tucsonaz.gov

Office of Intergovernmental Relations
City Hall, 255 West Alameda, Tucson, AZ 85701
Fax: (520) 791-4555

Intergovernmental Relations Coordinator
Adriana Marinez .... (520) 791-5200
E-mail: adriana.marinez@ci.tracy.ca.us

Office of Economic Initiatives
City Hall 4E, 255 West Alameda, Tucson, AZ 85701

Economic Development Specialist for International Trade **Juan Francisco Padres** .... (520) 837-4079
E-mail: Juan.Padres@tucsonaz.gov
Economic Development Specialist **Andrew Squire** .... (520) 837-4094
E-mail: andrew.squire@tucsonaz.gov
Economic Development Specialist **Camila Bekat** .... (520) 837-4078
E-mail: Camila.Bekat@tucsonaz.gov
Annexation Manager **Mike Czechowski** .... (520) 837-6576
Management Assistant **Nick Ross** .... (520) 837-6576

Budget and Internal Audit
P.O. Box 27210, Tucson, AZ 85726-7210
Fax: (520) 791-4973

Employees: 15 **Fiscal Year:** 2016 **Budget:** $1,482,000

Director **Joyce Garland** .... (520) 791-4551

Environmental Services Department
P.O. Box 27210, Tucson, AZ 85726-7210
Fax: (520) 791-4155

Employees: 214 **Fiscal Year:** 2016 **Budget:** $46,713,000

Director **Andrew H. Quigley** .... (520) 791-3175

Finance Department
P.O. Box 27210, Tucson, AZ 85726-7210
Fax: (520) 791-4941

Employees: 112 **Fiscal Year:** 2016 **Budget:** $19,620,000

Finance Director/Chief Financial Officer
Silvia M. Amparano .... (520) 791-4893
Deputy Finance Director **Karen Tenace** .... (520) 791-4893
Accounting Operations Administrator **Shane Oman** .... (520) 791-4561
Fax: (520) 791-4364
Revenue Administrator **Joel M. Peterson** .... (520) 791-4080
Fax: (520) 791-5136
Treasury Administrator **Silvia Navarro** .... (520) 791-4273
Fax: (520) 791-5082
Risk Manager **Allie Matthews** .... (520) 791-4728
E-mail: allie.matthews@ci.tracy.ca.us Fax: (520) 791-4941

Fire Department
P.O. Box 27210, Tucson, AZ 85726-7210
Fax: (520) 791-3231 E-mail: tfd_web_mail@mail.ci.tucson.az.us

Employees: 766 **Fiscal Year:** 2016 **Budget:** $99,156,000

Fire Chief **Jim Critchley** .... (520) 791-4828
E-mail: jim.critchley@tucsonaz.gov
Education: Arizona State; Arizona MBA

General Services Department
P.O. Box 27210, Tucson, AZ 85726-7210
Fax: (520) 791-3190 Internet: http://cms3.tucsonaz.gov/generalservices

Employees: 222 **Fiscal Year:** 2016 **Budget:** $58,484,000

Director (Interim) **Joan Stauch** .... (520) 791-3101
E-mail: joan.stauch@tucsonaz.gov
Deputy Director (Interim) **Amber Kerwin** .... (520) 791-3101
E-mail: amber.kerwin@tucsonaz.gov
Architecture and Engineering Administrator
Vinnie Hunt .... (520) 837-6311
E-mail: vinnie.hunt@tucsonaz.gov
Facilities and Communications Maintenance Division Administrator **Ross Adelmen** .... (520) 837-6331
E-mail: Ross.Adelman@tucsonaz.gov
Fleet Services Administrator **Tammy Smith** .... (520) 837-6325

Housing and Community Development Department
P.O. Box 27210, Tucson, AZ 85726-7210
Fax: (520) 791-5407

Employees: 146 **Fiscal Year:** 2016 **Budget:** $77,459,000

Director **Sally Stang** .... (520) 791-4171
E-mail: sally.stang@tucsonaz.gov
Deputy Director **Teresa Williams** .... (520) 791-4171
E-mail: teresa.williams@ci.tracy.ca.us
Planning and Development Services Director
Ernie Duerte .... (520) 791-4171
E-mail: ernie.duerte@ci.tracy.ca.us

Human Resources Department
P.O. Box 27210, Tucson, AZ 85726-7210
Fax: (520) 791-4236

Employees: 29 **Fiscal Year:** 2016 **Budget:** $9,702,000

Director (Interim) **Curry C. Hale** .... (520) 837-4156
E-mail: curry.hale@tucsonaz.gov

Information Technology Department
P.O. Box 27210, Tucson, AZ 85726-7210
Fax: (520) 791-4595 Internet: http://cms3.tucsonaz.gov/it/

Employees: 105 **Fiscal Year:** 2016 **Budget:** $19,436,000

Director/Chief Information Officer **Dave Scheuch** .... (520) 791-4747
E-mail: dave.scheuch@ci.tracy.ca.us
Deputy Director **Howell Herring** .... (520) 791-4747
Application Administrator **D. J. Parslow** .... (520) 791-4747
E-mail: djparslow@tucsonaz.gov
Network Services **Chong Cornn** .... (520) 791-4747
Technical Administrator **(Vacant)** .... (520) 791-4747
Information Technology Manager **(Vacant)** .... (520) 791-4747
Customer Service Information Technology Manager
(Vacant) .... (520) 791-4747
Information Technology Manager Applications **(Vacant)** .. (520) 791-4747
Information Technology Manager Applications **(Vacant)** .. (520) 791-4747
Information Technology Manager Network Services
(Vacant) .... (520) 791-4747
TV Production Manager **Gene Einfrank** .... (520) 791-2582 ext. 2
Telephone Services Coordinator **David Frye** .... (520) 791-4747
E-mail: david.frye@tucsonaz.gov
Emergency Communication Data Services Community Systems **(Vacant)** .... (520) 791-4747

Parks and Recreation Department
900 South Randolph Way, Tucson, AZ 85716
Tel: (520) 791-4873 Fax: (520) 791-4008
Internet: http://www.tucsonaz.gov/parks

Employees: 478 **Fiscal Year:** 2016 **Budget:** $37,891,000

Director **Fred H. Gray, Jr.** .... (520) 791-4225
Deputy Director/Golf **Mike Hayes** .... (520) 791-5853
East District Administrator **Glenna Overstreet** .... (520) 791-5930

★ Elected Official ▲ Appointed by Legislature ▼ Appointed by Governor ▶ Appointed by Board or Commission ● Appointed by Judge
■ Appointed by Mayor △ Appointed by Freeholders ▽ Appointed by Supervisor ▷ Appointed by County Executive ○ Appointed by Council

Parks and Recreation Department *continued*

West District Administrator **Peg Weber** . . . . (520) 791-5909
Zoo Administrator **Jason Jacobs** . . . . (520) 791-3204 ext. 13
E-mail: jason.jacobs@tucsonaz.gov

Planning and Development Services [PDSD]

201 North Stone, Tucson, AZ 85701
Fax: (520) 791-4340 Internet: http://cms3.tucsonaz.gov/pdsd

Employees: 99 **Fiscal Year:** 2016 **Budget:** $8,953,000

Director (Interim) **James Mazzocco** . . . . (520) 837-4904
Deputy Director and Zoning Administrator
James Mazzocco . . . . (520) 791-4505
Building Official (Interim) **Clayton Trevillyan** . . . . (520) 837-4913
City Engineer **Jim Vogelsberg** . . . . (520) 837-4926
E-mail: jim.vogelsberg@tucsonaz.gov
Rezoning and Signs Administrator **Glenn Moyer** . . . . (520) 837-4954

Police Department

270 S. Stone Ave., Tucson, AZ 85701-1917
Tel: (520) 791-4444 Fax: (520) 791-5491 Tel: (520) 791-4484 (Records)
Fax: (520) 791-5418 (Records Fax)

Employees: 1,319 **Fiscal Year:** 2016 **Budget:** $167,648,000

Police Chief **Chris Magnus** . . . . (520) 791-4441
Deputy Chief of Police **Chad Kasmar** . . . . (520) 791-4441
Field Services Bureau Assistant Chief **Ramon Batista** . . . (520) 791-4441
Investigative Services Bureau Assistant Chief
John Leavitt . . . . (520) 791-4441
E-mail: john.leavitt@tucsonaz.gov
Administrative Services Bureau Assistant Chief
Carla Johnson . . . . (520) 791-4441
Support Services Bureau Assistant Chief **Mark Timpf** . . . . (520) 791-4441

Procurement Department

P.O. Box 27210, Tucson, AZ 85726-7210
Fax: (520) 791-4735

Employees: 39 **Fiscal Year:** 2016 **Budget:** $3,156,000

Director **Marcheta E. Gillespie** . . . . (520) 791-4347
E-mail: marcheta.gillespie@tucsonaz.gov
Deputy Director **Laura Jestings** . . . . (520) 791-4135
E-mail: laura.jestings@tucsonaz.gov

Transportation Department

201 North Stone, Tucson, AZ 85701
Fax: (520) 791-4608

Employees: 287 **Fiscal Year:** 2016 **Budget:** $125,078,000

Director **Daryl Cole** . . . . (520) 791-4371
Parking Administrator **Donovan Durband** . . . . (520) 791-5071
110 East Pennington Street, Suite 150, Tucson, AZ 85726

Tucson Convention Center

260 South Church Avenue, Tucson, AZ 85701
Fax: (520) 791-5572

Employees: 45 **Fiscal Year:** 2016 **Budget:** $7,713,000

General Manager **Glenn Grabski** . . . . (520) 791-4101

Tucson Water

P.O. Box 27210, Tucson, AZ 85726-7210
Fax: (520) 791-3293 Internet: http://cms3.tucsonaz.gov/water

Employees: 547 **Fiscal Year:** 2016 **Budget:** $172,069,000

Director **(Vacant)** . . . . (520) 791-2666
Deputy Director **Sandy Elder** . . . . (520) 791-2666
Business Services **(Vacant)** . . . . (520) 791-2666
Customer Service **Christine Rodriguez** . . . . (520) 791-2666
Maintenance Administrator **Britt Klein** . . . . (520) 791-2666
E-mail: brit.klein@tucsonaz.gov
Planning Administrator **Pat Eisenberg** . . . . (520) 791-2666

Tucson Water *continued*

Water Resource Management Administrator
Wally Wilson . . . . (520) 791-2666
Water Quality Management **Ray Wilson** . . . . (520) 791-2666
Engineering Administrator **Melodee Loyer** . . . . (520) 791-2666
Strategic Initiatives Division Manager **Jeff B. Biggs** . . . . . (520) 791-2666

Office of the Zoning Examiner

City Hall, 255 West Alameda, 9th Floor, Tucson, AZ 85701
Fax: (520) 791-4555

Zoning Examiner **Linus Kafka** . . . . (520) 791-4174

Tucson Unified School District

1010 East Tenth Street, Tucson, AZ 85719
Tel: (520) 225-6000 Fax: (520) 225-6174 Internet: www.tusd.k12.az.us/

Superintendent **Dr. Heliodoro Torres "H.T." Sanchez** . . . . (520) 225-6060

City of Tulsa, Oklahoma

City Hall, 175 East 2nd Street, Tulsa, OK 74103
Tel: (918) 596-2100 (Information) Internet: http://www.cityoftulsa.org

County: Tulsa **Election Type:** Nonpartisan **Population:** 403,505 (2015)

Office of the Mayor

City Hall, 175 East 2nd Street, Tulsa, OK 74103
Fax: (918) 596-9010 Internet: http://www.cityoftulsa.org/OurCity/Mayor/

★ Mayor **Dewey F. Bartlett, Jr.** . . . . (918) 596-7411
Began Service: December 7, 2009
Term Expires: December 7, 2017
E-mail: mayor@cityoftulsa.org
Chief of Staff **Jarred Brejcha** . . . . (918) 596-7411
City Manager **Jim Twombly** . . . . (918) 596-7411
E-mail: jtwombly@cityoftulsa.org
Director of Community Development and Transportation
Dwain Midget . . . . (918) 596-7411
E-mail: dmidget@cityoftulsa.org
■ Chief Economic Development Officer **Clay Bird** . . . . (918) 596-7411
E-mail: cbird@cityoftulsa.org
Press Secretary **Lloyd Wright** . . . . (918) 596-7411
E-mail: lwright@cityoftulsa.org
Video Services Specialist **Brian Nutt** . . . . (918) 596-7411
Chief Resilience Officer **Mary Kell** . . . . (918) 596-2100

Office of the City Council

City Hall, 175 East 2nd Street, Tulsa, OK 74103
Tel: (918) 596-1990 Fax: (918) 596-1964 Internet: www.tulsacouncil.org

★ Chair **Jeannie Cue** (District 2) . . . . (918) 596-1922
Term Expires: December 7, 2016
E-mail: dist2@tulsacouncil.org
★ Vice Chair **Anna America** (District 7) . . . . (918) 596-1927
Term Expires: December 7, 2016
E-mail: Dist7@tulsacouncil.org
★ Councilor **Jack Henderson** (District 1) . . . . (918) 596-1921
Term Expires: December 7, 2016
E-mail: dist1@tulsacouncil.org
★ Councilor **David Patrick** (District 3) . . . . (918) 596-1923
Term Expires: December 7, 2016
E-mail: dist3@tulsacouncil.org
★ Councilor **Blake Ewing** (District 4) . . . . (918) 596-1924
Term Expires: December 7, 2016
E-mail: dist4@tulsacouncil.org
★ Councilor **Karen Gilbert** (District 5) . . . . (918) 596-1925
Term Expires: December 7, 2016
E-mail: dist5@tulsacouncil.org

(continued on next page)

★ Elected Official ▲ Appointed by Legislature ▼ Appointed by Governor ▶ Appointed by Board or Commission ● Appointed by Judge
■ Appointed by Mayor △ Appointed by Freeholders ▽ Appointed by Supervisor ▷ Appointed by County Executive ○ Appointed by Council

Office of the City Council *continued*

★Councilor **Connie Dodson** (District 6) . . . . (918) 596-1926
Term Expires: December 7, 2016
E-mail: Dist6@tulsacouncil.org

★Chairman **Phil Lakin, Jr.** (District 8) . . . . (918) 596-1928
Term Expires: December 7, 2016
E-mail: dist8@tulsacouncil.org

★Councillor **G.T. Bynum** (District 9) . . . . (918) 596-1929
Term Expires: December 7, 2016
E-mail: dist9@tulsacouncil.org

Council Senior Staff

Council Administrator/Chief of Staff **Drew Rees** . . . . (918) 596-1965

Policy Administrator **Jack Blair** . . . . (918) 596-1969
E-mail: jblair@tulsacouncil.org

Secretary of the Council **Keith Madden** . . . . (918) 596-1965
E-mail: KeithMadden@tulsacouncil.org

Office of the City Auditor

City Hall, 175 East 2nd Street, Tulsa, OK 74103
Fax: (918) 699-3023

★City Auditor **Cathy Criswell** . . . . (918) 596-7505
Term Expires: December 7, 2016
E-mail: cathycriswell@cityoftulsa.org

Internal Auditing Department

City Hall, 175 East 2nd Street, Tulsa, OK 74103
Tel: (918) 596-7844

Chief Internal Auditor **Ronald Maxwell** . . . . (918) 596-7845
Fax: (918) 596-7846

Office of the City Attorney

City Hall, 175 East 2nd Street, Tulsa, OK 74103
Fax: (918) 596-9700

City Attorney **David E. O'Meilia** . . . . (918) 596-7717
E-mail: domeilia@cityoftulsa.org
Education: Oklahoma State 1973 BA; Tulsa 1976 JD

Deputy City Attorney **Jean Ann Hudson** . . . . (918) 596-7717
E-mail: jhudson@cityoftulsa.org

Office of the City Clerk

City Hall, 175 East 2nd Street, Tulsa, OK 74103
Tel: (918) 596-7514

City Clerk **Nora Thierry** . . . . (918) 596-7514
E-mail: nthierry@cityoftulsa.org

Asset Management Department

490 West 23rd Street, Tulsa, OK 74107-3006
Tel: (918) 596-9838 Fax: (918) 596-1498

Director **Mark Hogan** . . . . (918) 596-9838

Administrative Manager **Brian Franklin** . . . . (918) 596-9838
E-mail: bfranklin@cityoftulsa.org

Maintenance Manager **Michael Wallace** . . . . (918) 596-9838
E-mail: mwallace@cityoftulsa.org

Finance Department

City Hall, 175 East 2nd Street, Tulsa, OK 74103-3827

Director **Mike Kier** . . . . (918) 596-7522
Fax: (918) 576-5650

Senior Administrative Services Officer **Melissa Stice** . . . (918) 596-7508

Budget Manager **Keith Eldridge** . . . . (918) 596-7589
E-mail: keldridge@cityoftulsa.org Fax: (918) 699-3187

Controller **David Bryant** . . . . (918) 596-7620
E-mail: dbryant@cityoftulsa.org Fax: (918) 596-7231

Treasury Division Manager **Stan Jones** . . . . (918) 596-7632
Fax: (918) 596-7224

Grants Administration and Capital Planning Manager (Acting) **Gary Hamer** . . . . (918) 596-7573
Fax: (918) 699-3240

Utilities Services Manager **Mark Weathers** . . . . (918) 596-9550
Education: Tulsa 1996 MBA Fax: (918) 699-3358

Finance Department *continued*

Records Manager **Wendy Z. Martin** . . . . (918) 596-2489
Education: Northeastern State 1999 BS; St Gregory's 2011 MSM Fax: (918) 699-5650

Purchasing Office

175 East 2nd Street, Suite 865, Tulsa, OK 74103
Fax: (918) 596-7560

Purchasing Agent **Larry Hood** . . . . (918) 596-7550
E-mail: lhood@cityoftulsa.org

Fire Department

1760 Newblock Park Drive, Tulsa, OK 74127
Fax: (918) 596-1297

■Fire Chief **Ray Driskell** . . . . (918) 596-9444
E-mail: rdriskell@cityoftulsa.org

Senior Systems Analyst **Jill Goforth** . . . . (918) 596-9203
E-mail: jgoforth@cityoftulsa.org

Gilcrease Museum

1400 N. Gilcrease Museum Rd., Tulsa, OK 74127-2100
Fax: (918) 596-2770 E-mail: gilcrease@utulsa.edu
Internet: http://gilcrease.utulsa.edu/

■Executive Director **James Pepper Henry** . . . . (918) 596-2710
E-mail: jph@utulsa.edu

Director of Museum Science and Management **Bob Pickering** . . . . (918) 596-2706

Security Coordinator **Paul Downe** . . . . (918) 596-2718

Communications Manager **Melani Hamilton** . . . . (918) 596-2752
E-mail: melani-hamilton@utulsa.edu

Communications Department

City Hall, 175 East 2nd Street, Tulsa, OK 74103

Director **Kimberly MacLeod** . . . . (918) 596-2100
E-mail: kmacleod@cityoftulsa.org

Human Resources Department

City Hall, 175 East 2nd Street, Tulsa, OK 74103
Fax: (918) 596-7145

Director **Erica Felix-Warwick** . . . . (918) 596-7442
E-mail: efelix-warwick@cityoftulsa.org

Human Rights Department

City Hall, 175 East 2nd Street, Suite 675, Tulsa, OK 74103
Fax: (918) 596-7826

Director **Jackson Landrum** . . . . (918) 596-7824

Office Assistant III **Rod Wade** . . . . (918) 596-7692
E-mail: rwade@cityoftulsa.org

Information Technology Department

City Hall, 175 East 2nd Street, Suite 0660, Tulsa, OK 74103
Fax: (918) 596-7142

■Chief Information Officer **Michael Dellinger** . . . . (918) 596-2470
E-mail: mdellinger@cityoftulsa.org

Park and Recreation Department

175 East 2nd Street, # 570, Tulsa, OK 74103
Tel: (918) 596-7275 Fax: (918) 596-2530 (Customer Service)

Director **Lucy Dolman** . . . . (918) 596-7275

Oxley Nature Center Director **Eddie Reese** . . . . (918) 669-6640

Streets and Stormwater Department

City Hall, 175 East 2nd Street, Suite 1584, Tulsa, OK 74103
Fax: (918) 596-7397

Director, Streets and Stormwater **Terry Ball** . . . . (918) 596-9715

Director, Water and Sewer **Clayton Edwards** . . . . (918) 596-7810

Engineering Services Division Director **Paul Zachary** . . . . (918) 596-9565
2317 S. Jackson, Tulsa, OK 74107
E-mail: pzachary@cityoftulsa.org

★Elected Official ▲Appointed by Legislature ▼Appointed by Governor ▶Appointed by Board or Commission ●Appointed by Judge
■Appointed by Mayor △Appointed by Freeholders ▽Appointed by Supervisor ▷Appointed by County Executive ○Appointed by Council

Tulsa Airports
7777 East Apache, Suite A217, Tulsa, OK 74115
P.O. Box 581838, Tulsa, OK 74158-1838
Fax: (918) 838-5199 Internet: http://www.tulsaairports.com/
Internet: http://www.tulsaairports.com/about-tait/staff/

Airports Director **Jeffrey "Jeff" Mulder** .... (918) 838-5000
Airports Marketing Deputy Director **Alexis Higgins** ..... (918) 838-5000
Facilities and Engineering Deputy Director **Jeff Hough** ... (918) 838-5000
Note: Until June 2016
E-mail: jeffhough@tulsaairports.com
Finance and Administration Deputy Airports Director
Carl E. Remus .... (918) 838-5000
E-mail: carlremus@tulsaairports.com
Operations Deputy Airports Director **Chuck Hannum** .... (918) 838-5000
E-mail: chuckhannum@tulsaairports.com

Tulsa Performing Arts Center
110 E. Second St., Tulsa, OK 74103
Fax: (918) 596-7144 Internet: http://tulsapac.com/index.asp

Director **John E. Scott** .... (918) 596-7122
Education: Drake 1969 BMusEd; Michigan State 1974 MMus

Tulsa Area Emergency Management Agency [TAEMA]
600 Civic Center EOC, Tulsa, OK 74103
Tel: (918) 596-9899 Fax: (918) 596-9888

Director **Roger Jolliff** .... (918) 596-9898
E-mail: rjolliff@cityoftulsa.org

Housing Authority
415 East Independence Street, Tulsa, OK 74106
Fax: (918) 582-0645
Internet: http://www.tulsahousing.org/Home/Staff.aspx

President and Chief Executive Officer
Chea Redditt .... (918) 582-0021 ext. 5910
Education: Arkansas 1980 BA

Police Department
600 Civic Center, Suite 303, Tulsa, OK 74103
Fax: (918) 596-9330 Internet: www.tulsapolice.org

■ Police Chief **Chuck Jordan** .... (918) 596-9328
E-mail: tpdchief@cityoftulsa.org

Tulsa Public Schools
3027 S. New Haven Ave., Tulsa, OK 74114
P.O. Box 470208, Tulsa, OK 74147-0208
Fax: (918) 746-6850

Superintendent **Deborah A. Gist** .... (918) 746-6800
Education: Oklahoma BS; South Florida MA; Harvard MPA
★ President **Dr. Lana Turner-Addison** (District 3) .... (918) 746-6800
Term Expires: February 1, 2017
E-mail: board3@tulsaschools.org
★ School Board Vice President
Suzanne Schreiber (District 7) .... (918) 746-6800
Term Expires: February 1, 2018
E-mail: board7@tulsaschools.org
Education: Tulsa 1999 JD
★ School Board Member **Gary Percefull** (District 1) .... (918) 746-6800
Term Expires: February 1, 2019
E-mail: board1@tulsaschools.org
★ School Board Member **Wilbert Collins, Sr.** (District 2) ... (918) 746-6800
Term Expires: February 1, 2017
E-mail: board2@tulsaschools.org
★ School Board Member **Shawna Keller** (District 4) ...... (918) 746-6800
Term Expires: February 1, 2018
E-mail: board4@tulsaschools.org
★ School Board Member **Cindy Decker** (District 5) .... (918) 746-6800
Term Expires: February 1, 2020
E-mail: board5@tulsaschools.org

Tulsa Public Schools *continued*
★ School Board Member **Ruth Ann Fate** (District 6) ...... (918) 746-6800
Term Expires: February 1, 2020
E-mail: board6@tulsaschools.org
Clerk of the Board **Cindy Hutchings** .... (918) 746-6393
E-mail: hutchci@tulsaschools.org

City of Vallejo, California
City Hall, 555 Santa Clara Street, Vallejo, CA 94590
Internet: http://www.cityofvallejo.net/

County: Solano **Election Type:** Nonpartisan **Population:** 121,253 (2015)

Office of the Mayor and City Council
City Hall, 555 Santa Clara St., Vallejo, CA 94590
Fax: (707) 649-3479

★ Mayor **Osby Davis** .... (707) 648-4377
Term Expires: January 2017
E-mail: mayor@cityofvallejo.net
Education: Cal State (Fresno) BSME; Boalt Hall 1973 JD
Career: Supervisor, Board of Supervisors, County of Solano, California (1979-1993)
★ Council Member **Pippin Dew-Costa** .... (707) 648-4132
Term Expires: January 2019
E-mail: Pippin.Dew-Costa@cityofvallejo.net
★ Council Member **Jesus "Jess" Malgapo** .... (707) 648-4131
Term Expires: January 2019
E-mail: jesus.malgapo@cityofvallejo.net
★ Council Member **Robert McConnell** .... (707) 648-4135
Term Expires: January 2017
E-mail: robert.mcconnell@cityofvallejo.net
★ Council Member **Katy Miessner** .... (707) 648-4133
Term Expires: January 2019
E-mail: Katy.Miessner@cityofvallejo.net
★ Council Member **Bob Sampayan** .... (707) 648-4130
Term Expires: January 2017
E-mail: bob.sampayan@cityofvallejo.net
★ Council Member **Rozzana Verder-Aliga** .... (707) 648-4134
Term Expires: January 2017
E-mail: rozzana.verder-aliga@cityofvallejo.net

Office of the City Manager
City Hall, 555 Santa Clara St., Vallejo, CA 94590
Fax: (707) 648-4426

○ City Manager **Daniel E. Keen** .... (707) 648-4576
E-mail: city.manager@cityofvallejo.net
Assistant City Manager **Craig Whittom** .... (707) 648-4579
E-mail: craig.whittom@cityofvallejo.net

Code Enforcement Division
Fax: (707) 649-3540
Manager **Kenny Park** .... (707) 648-4469

Information Technology Division
555 Santa Clara Street, Vallejo, CA 94590
Tel: (707) 648-4468
Chief Information Officer **Gregory Taylor** .... (707) 648-4468
E-mail: gregory.taylor@cityofvallejo.net

Office of the City Clerk
City Hall, 555 Santa Clara St., Vallejo, CA 94590
Fax: (707) 648-4535

City Clerk **Dawn Abrahamson** .... (707) 648-4527
E-mail: dawn.abrahamson@cityofvallejo.net
Deputy City Clerk **Tarienne Grover** .... (707) 648-4527
E-mail: tarienne.grover@cityofvallejo.net

★ Elected Official ▲ Appointed by Legislature ▼ Appointed by Governor ► Appointed by Board or Commission ● Appointed by Judge
■ Appointed by Mayor △ Appointed by Freeholders ▽ Appointed by Supervisor ▷ Appointed by County Executive ○ Appointed by Council

Office of the City Attorney
City Hall, 555 Santa Clara St., 3rd Floor, Vallejo, CA 94590
P.O. Box 3068, Vallejo, CA 94590
Fax: (707) 648-4687

City Attorney **Claudia Quintana** .... (707) 648-4545
E-mail: claudia.quintana@cityofvallejo.net
Chief Assistant City Attorney **Donna Mooney** .... (707) 648-4545
Assistant City Attorney **Khadijah Hargett** .... (707) 648-4456

Economic Development Department
City Hall, 555 Santa Clara St., Vallejo, CA 94590
Fax: (707) 648-4499

Director **Andrea Ouse** .... (707) 648-4326
E-mail: andrea.ouse@cityofvallejo.net

Building Division
Fax: (707) 552-0163

Chief Building Official **Lonell Butler** .... (707) 648-4374

Economic Development Division
City Hall, 555 Santa Clara St., Vallejo, CA 94590
E-mail: econdev@cityofvallejo.net

Director **Kathleen Diohep** .... (707) 649-5452
E-mail: kathleen.diohep@cityofvallejo.net

Housing and Community Development Division
200 Georgia Street, Vallejo, CA 94590
Fax: (707) 648-5249

Program Manager **Anne Putney** .... (707) 648-4508
E-mail: anne.putney@cityofvallejo.net

Planning Division
Manager **Dina Tasini** .... (707) 648-4326

Finance Department
City Hall, 555 Santa Clara St., Vallejo, CA 94590
Fax: (707) 649-5406

Director **Ron Millard** .... (707) 648-4592

Fire Department
970 Nimitz Avenue, Vallejo, CA 94592

Fire Chief **Jack McArthur** .... (707) 648-4526
E-mail: Jack.McArthur@cityofvallejo.net

Human Resources Department
City Hall, 555 Santa Clara St., Vallejo, CA 94590
P.O. Box 3068, Vallejo, CA 94590
Fax: (707) 648-5292

Human Resources Director **Jasmin Loi** .... (707) 648-4363
E-mail: jasmin.loi@cityofvallejo.net

Police Department
111 Amador St., Vallejo, CA 94590
Fax: (707) 648-4390 E-mail: vpd_community@cityofvallejo.net

Chief of Police **Andrew Bidou** .... (707) 648-4540

Public Works Department
Fax: (707) 648-4691

Director **David Kleinschmidt** .... (707) 648-4433
City Engineer **Jill Mercurio** .... (707) 648-5251
E-mail: jill.mercurio@cityofvallejo.net

Water Division
Fax: (707) 648-4060

Water Superintendent **Martin Querin** .... (707) 648-4307

City of Vancouver, Washington
City Hall, 415 West 6th Street, Vancouver, WA 98660
Internet: www.cityofvancouver.us

County: Clark **Year Incorporated:** 1857 **Charter:** 1952
Population: 172,860 (2015)

Office of the Mayor and City Council
City Hall, 415 West 6th Street, Vancouver, WA 98660
P.O. Box 1995, Vancouver, WA 98668-1995
Fax: (360) 487-8625

★ Mayor **Tim Leavitt** .... (360) 487-8629
Began Service: January 1, 2010
Term Expires: December 31, 2017
E-mail: tim.leavitt@cityofvancouver.us
Education: Washington State 1994 BSCE, 1997 MSCE

★ Council Member **Jack Burkman** .... (360) 487-8629
Term Expires: December 31, 2017
E-mail: jack.burkman@cityofvancouver.us

★ Council Member **Bart Hansen** .... (360) 487-8629
Term Expires: December 31, 2019
E-mail: bart.hansen@cityofvancouver.us
Education: Washington State 1998 BA; Marylhurst 2009 MBA

★ Council Member **Anne McEnerny-Ogle** .... (360) 487-8629
Term Expires: December 31, 2017
E-mail: anne.mcenerny-ogle@cityofvancouver.us

★ Council Member **Ty Stober** .... (360) 487-8629
Term Expires: December 31, 2019

★ Council Member **Alisha Topper** .... (360) 487-8629
Term Expires: December 31, 2017
E-mail: alisha.topper@cityofvancouver.us

★ Council Member **Bill Turlay** .... (360) 487-8629
Term Expires: December 31, 2019
E-mail: bill.turlay@cityofvancouver.us
City Council Secretary **Amanda Delapena** .... (360) 487-8605

Office of the City Attorney
City Hall, 415 West 6th Street, Vancouver, WA 98668
P.O. Box 1995, Vancouver, WA 98668
Fax: (360) 696-8250 E-mail: vanlaw@cityofvancouver.us

○ City Attorney **E. Bronson Potter** .... (360) 487-8500
Education: UC Berkeley BA; Lewis & Clark JD

Office of the City Manager
City Hall, 415 West 6th Street, Vancouver, WA 98668
Fax: (360) 487-8625

○ City Manager **Eric Holmes** .... (360) 487-8000
E-mail: eric.holmes@cityofvancouver.us
Education: Oregon BS; Lewis & Clark MPA
Administrative Assistant to the City Manager **Jill Brown** .... (360) 487-8609
E-mail: jill.brown@cityofvancouver.us
Deputy City Manager **David R. Mercier** .... (360) 487-8060
E-mail: dave.mercier@cityofvancouver.us
Program Development and Policy Manager **Jan Bader** .... (360) 487-8606
Public Information Officer **Carol Bua** .... (360) 487-8611
Staff Assistant to Office of Neighborhood and Boards and Commissions **Kerry Peck** .... (360) 487-8612
E-mail: kerry.peck@cityofvancouver.us
Staff Assistant to Government Relations, Program Development and Policy Manager **Kerry Peck** .... (360) 487-8616
E-mail: kerry.peck@cityofvancouver.us
Neighborhood Services Coordinator **Judi Bailey** .... (360) 487-8608
E-mail: judi.bailey@cityofvancouver.us
Airport Manager **Willie Williamson** .... (360) 487-8619

★ Elected Official ▲ Appointed by Legislature ▼ Appointed by Governor ► Appointed by Board or Commission ● Appointed by Judge
■ Appointed by Mayor △ Appointed by Freeholders ▽ Appointed by Supervisor ▷ Appointed by County Executive ○ Appointed by Council

Community and Economic Development Department
P.O. Box 1995, Vancouver, WA 98668-1995
Tel: (360) 487-7800 Fax: (360) 487-7807

Director **Chad Eiken** . . . . . (360) 487-7800
E-mail: chad.eiken@cityofvancouver.us Fax: (360) 487-7807
Building Official/Inspection Supervisor
Sree Thirunagari . . . . . (360) 487-7800
Fax: (360) 487-7805
Development Review Division Manager
Larry Vasquez . . . . . (360) 487-7800
E-mail: larry.vasquez@cityofvancouver.us Fax: (360) 487-7805
Parking Manager **Mike Merrill** . . . . . (360) 735-8879
Fax: (360) 619-1294
Community Development Block Grant Program
Manager **Peggy Sheehan** . . . . . (360) 487-7952
E-mail: peggy.sheehan@cityofvancouver.us
Long Range Planning Manager **Sandra Towne** . . . . . (360) 487-7707
E-mail: sandra.towne@cityofvancouver.us
Economic Development Division Manager **Teresa Brum** . . (360) 487-7800
E-mail: teresa.brum@cityofvancouver.us
Land Chief Manager **Greg Turner** . . . . . (360) 487-7800
E-mail: greg.turner@cityofvancouver.us

Financial and Management Services
610 Esther St., Vancouver, WA 98660

Chief Financial Officer **Lloyd Tyler** . . . . . (360) 487-7200
Accounting Manager **Christine Smith** . . . . . (360) 619-1044
E-mail: christine.smith@cityofvancouver.us
Treasurer **Carrie Lewellen** . . . . . (360) 619-1082

Procurement Services
P.O. Box 1995, Vancouver, WA 98668
City Hall, 415 West 6th Street, Vancouver, WA 98660
Fax: (360) 619-1033

Manager **Kevin Yin** . . . . . (360) 487-8429
E-mail: kevin.yin@cityofvancouver.us
Commodities Buying **Elma Malloy** . . . . . (360) 487-8427
E-mail: elma.malloy@cityofvancouver.us
Senior Procurement Specialist **Matt Hausman** . . . . . (360) 487-8432
E-mail: matt.hausman@cityofvancouver.us
Professional Service Agreements **Scott Cramer** . . . . . (360) 487-8426
E-mail: scott.cramer@cityofvancouver.us
Professional Services **(Vacant)** . . . . . (360) 487-8435
Procurement Specialist **Mike Wolfson** . . . . . (360) 487-8428
E-mail: mike.wolfson@cityofvancouver.us

Fire Department
7110 NE 63rd St., Vancouver, WA 98661
Fax: (360) 487-7227

Fire Chief **Joe Molina** . . . . . (360) 487-7212
E-mail: joe.molina@cityofvancouver.us
Deputy Chief **Dan Olson** . . . . . (360) 487-7204
E-mail: dan.olson@cityofvancouver.us
Emergency Services Division Chief **Steve Eldred** . . . . . (360) 487-7212
E-mail: steve.eldred@cityofvancouver.us
Training Chief **Ward Knable** . . . . . (360) 487-7207
E-mail: ward.knable@cityofvancouver.us
Fire Marshall **Heidi Scarpelli** . . . . . (360) 487-7212
E-mail: heidi.scarpelli@cityofvancouver.us
Education: U Washington BA

Human Resources Department
City Hall, 415 West 6th Street, Vancouver, WA 98660
Fax: (360) 619-1018 Tel: (866) 886-2847 (Toll Free)
E-mail: hr@vanhr.org

Director **Suzi Schwabe** . . . . . (360) 487-8408
E-mail: Suzi.Schwabe@cityofvancouver.us

Media Services
202 East Mill Plain Blvd., Vancouver, WA 98660
Fax: (360) 696-8298 E-mail: vaninfo@cityofvancouver.us

Manager **(Vacant)** . . . . . (360) 696-8233
Web Content Manager **Jim Reed** . . . . . (360) 696-8016
E-mail: jim.reed@cityofvancouver.us Fax: (360) 696-8942

Operations Center
P.O. Box 1995, Vancouver, WA 98668
Fax: (360) 696-8002

Manager **Terry McClure** . . . . . (360) 696-8177

Parks and Recreation Department
415 West 6th Street, Vancouver, WA 98660
Tel: (360) 487-8311

Director **Julie Hannon** . . . . . (360) 487-8311

Police Department
P.O. Box 1995, Vancouver, WA 98668-1995
Tel: (360) 487-7355 Fax: (360) 695-3530

Chief of Police **James McElvain** . . . . . (360) 487-7475

Port of Vancouver USA
3103 NW Lower River Road, Vancouver, WA 98660
Tel: (360) 693-3611 Fax: (360) 735-1565 E-mail: info@portvanusa.com

Executive Director and Chief Executive Officer (Interim)
Julianna Marler . . . . . (360) 693-3611
E-mail: jmarler@portvanusa.com

Public Works Administration
4500 SE Columbia Way, Vancouver, WA 89661
Tel: (360) 487-7130 Fax: (360) 487-7139

Director **Brian Carlson** . . . . . (360) 487-7130
Capital Planning, Finance and Asset Management
Manager **Bill Whitcomb** . . . . . (360) 487-7130
Design and Construction Engineering Manager
Dan Swensen . . . . . (360) 487-7750
Environmental Resources Manager **Rich McConaghy** . . . . (360) 487-7111

City of Ventura, California

City Hall, 501 Poli St., Ventura, CA 93001
Internet: www.cityofventura.net

County: Ventura **Year Incorporated:** 1866 **Population:** 109,708 (2015)

Note: The city's full name is San Buenaventura

Office of the Mayor and City Council
City Hall, 501 Poli St., Ventura, CA 93001
P.O. Box 99, Ventura, CA 93002

★ Mayor **Erik Nasarenko** . . . . . (805) 654-7827
Began Service: December 2013
Term Expires: December 3, 2018
E-mail: enasarenko@cityofventura.net
★ Deputy Mayor **Neal Andrews** . . . . . (805) 654-7827
Term Expires: December 3, 2018
E-mail: nandrews@cityofventura.net
★ Council Member **Cheryl Heitmann** . . . . . (805) 654-7827
Term Expires: December 3, 2016
E-mail: cheitmann@cityofventura.net
★ Council Member **James L. Monahan** . . . . . (805) 654-7827
Term Expires: December 3, 2018
E-mail: jmonahan@cityofventura.net

(continued on next page)

★ Elected Official ▲ Appointed by Legislature ▼ Appointed by Governor ▶ Appointed by Board or Commission ● Appointed by Judge
■ Appointed by Mayor △ Appointed by Freeholders ▽ Appointed by Supervisor ▷ Appointed by County Executive ○ Appointed by Council

Office of the Mayor and City Council *continued*

★Council Member **Carl E. Morehouse** . . . . (805) 654-7827
Term Expires: December 5, 2016
E-mail: cmorehouse@cityofventura.net
Education: Purdue BA; Indiana MPA

★Council Member **Mike Tracy** . . . . (805) 654-7827
Term Expires: December 3, 2018
E-mail: mike.tracy@cityofventura.net

★Council Member **Christy Weir** . . . . (805) 654-7827
Term Expires: December 5, 2016
E-mail: cweir@cityofventura.net

Office of the City Manager

City Hall, 501 Poli St., Ventura, CA 93001

City Manager **Mark D. Watkins** . . . . (805) 654-7740
E-mail: mwatkins@cityofventura.net

Assistant City Manager **Dan Paranick** . . . . (805) 276-3446
E-mail: dparanick@cityofventura.net

Office of the City Clerk

City Hall, 501 Poli St., Ventura, CA 93001

City Clerk **(Vacant)** . . . . (805) 658-4787
E-mail: cityclerk@cityofventura.net

Assistant City Clerk **Roxanne Fiorillo** . . . . (805) 658-4787
E-mail: rfiorillo@cityofventura.net

Community Development Department

City Hall, 501 Poli Street, Room 133, Ventura, CA 93001

Director **Jeffrey J. Lambert** . . . . (805) 677-3921
E-mail: jlambert@cityofventura.net

Planning Manager **Dave Ward** . . . . (805) 654-3964
E-mail: dward@cityofventura.net

Chief Building Official **Yolanda Bundy** . . . . (805) 654-7869

Finance and Technology

City Hall, 501 Poli St., Ventura, CA 93001
Fax: (805) 648-2961

Chief Financial Officer **Gilbert Garcia** . . . . (805) 654-7812

Fire Department

1425 Dowell Drive, Ventura, CA 93003
Internet: http://www.cityofventura.net/fire

Fire Chief **David Endaya** . . . . (805) 339-4340
E-mail: dendaya@cityofventura.net

Assistant Fire Chief of Operations **Matt Brock** . . . . (805) 339-4340
E-mail: mbrock@cityofventura.net

Fire Marshal **Brian Clark** . . . . (805) 654-7794
E-mail: bclark@cityofventura.net

Administrative Secretary **Jeannie McGovern** . . . . (805) 339-4310
E-mail: jmcgovern@cityofventura.net

Human Resources Department

City Hall, 501 Poli St., Room 210, Ventura, CA 93001

Director **Elizabeth Foushee** . . . . (805) 654-7853
E-mail: efoushee@cityofventura.net

Parks, Recreation and Community Partnerships Department

City Hall, 501 Poli St., Room 226, Ventura, CA 93001

Director **Elena Brokaw** . . . . (805) 658-4726
E-mail: ebrokaw@cityofventura.net

Parks Division

P.O. Box 99, Ventura, CA 93002

Manager **Nancy O'Connor** . . . . (805) 652-4550

Police Department

1425 Dowell Drive, Ventura, CA 93003

Chief of Police **Ken Corney** . . . . (805) 339-4400

Public Works Department

City Hall, 501 Poli St., Ventura, CA 93001

Public Works Director and City Engineer **Rick Raives** . . . . (805) 654-7808
E-mail: rraives@cityofventura.net

Office of the City Attorney

City Hall, 501 Poli St., Ventura, CA 93001

City Attorney **Gregory Diaz** . . . . (805) 654-7818
E-mail: gdiaz@cityofventura.net
Education: Cal State (Long Beach) BA; Western State U San Diego JD

City of Victorville, California

14343 Civic Drive, Victorville, CA 92392
Tel: (760) 955-5000 Internet: http://ci.victorville.ca.us

County: San Bernardino **Election Type:** Nonpartisan **Year Incorporated:** 1962 **Population:** 122,225 (2015)

Office of the Mayor and City Council

14343 Civic Drive, Victorville, CA 92392
Internet: http://ci.victorville.ca.us/council.aspx

★Mayor **Gloria Garcia** . . . . (760) 955-5026
Began Service: December 2012
Term Expires: November 2016
E-mail: ggarcia@victorvilleca.gov

★Mayor Pro Tem **James L. "Jim" Cox** . . . . (760) 955-5026
Term Expires: December 7, 2016
E-mail: jcox@victorvilleca.gov

★Council Member **Jim Kennedy** . . . . (760) 955-5026
Term Expires: December 7, 2018
E-mail: jkennedy@victorvilleca.gov

★Council Member **Ryan McEachron** . . . . (760) 955-5026
Term Expires: November 2016
E-mail: rmceachron@victorvilleca.gov
Education: Arizona State 1995 BS

★Council Member **Eric Negrete** . . . . (760) 955-5026
Term Expires: December 2, 2018

Office of the City Manager

14343 Civic Drive, Victorville, CA 92392

○City Manager **Douglas B. "Doug" Robertson** . . . . (760) 955-5029

Executive Assistant **Charlene Robinson** . . . . (760) 955-5029

Office of the City Clerk

14343 Civic Drive, Victorville, CA 92392
Internet: http://ci.victorville.ca.us/cityclerk.aspx

City Clerk **Carolee Bates** . . . . (760) 955-5188
E-mail: cbates@ci.victorville.ca.us

Assistant City Clerk **Marcie Wolters** . . . . (760) 955-5035
E-mail: mwolters@ci.victorville.ca.us

Deputy City Clerk **Heidi Roche** . . . . (760) 955-5188
E-mail: hroche@ci.victorville.ca.us

Records Division

14343 Civic Drive, Victorville, CA 92392

Records Management Coordinator **Loraine Stevens** . . . . . (760) 955-2807
E-mail: lstevens@ci.victorville.ca.us

★Elected Official ▲Appointed by Legislature ▼Appointed by Governor ▶Appointed by Board or Commission ●Appointed by Judge
■Appointed by Mayor △Appointed by Freeholders ▽Appointed by Supervisor ▷Appointed by County Executive ○Appointed by Council

Community Services Department
14343 Civic Drive, Victorville, CA 92392

Director of Community Services **Christian Guntert** ..... (760) 955-5257
E-mail: cguntert@ci.victorville.ca.us
Assistant Director **(Vacant)** ..... (760) 955-5257
Facilities Manager **(Vacant)** ..... (760) 955-5263
Golf and Grounds Manager **(Vacant)** ..... (760) 955-5271
Recreation Services Manager **Glenn Salas** ..... (760) 951-3812

Library Services Division
15011 Circle Drive, Victorville, CA 92395

Librarian **Karen Everett** ..... (760) 245-4222
E-mail: keverrett@ci.victorville.ca.us

Development Department
14343 Civic Drive, Victorville, CA 92392
Internet: http://ci.victorville.ca.us/development.aspx

Director of Development **Chris Borchert** ..... (760) 955-5132
Administrative Secretary **Tessa Tate** ..... (760) 955-5132
E-mail: ttate@ci.victorville.ca.us

Building Division
14343 Civic Drive, Victorville, CA 92392
Internet: http://ci.victorville.ca.us/building.aspx

Building and Fire Official **Kevin Collins** ..... (760) 955-5100
E-mail: kcollins@ci.victorville.ca.us

Code Enforcement Division
14343 Civic Drive, Victorville, CA 92392
Internet: http://ci.victorville.ca.us/codeenforcement2.aspx

Code Enforcement Manager **Jorge Duran** ..... (760) 955-5104

Planning Division
14343 Civic Drive, Victorville, CA 92392
Internet: http://ci.victorville.ca.us/planning.aspx

City Planner **Scott Webb** ..... (760) 955-5135
Senior Planner **Michael Szarzynski** ..... (760) 955-5135

Fire Department
14343 Civic Drive, Victorville, CA 92392
Internet: http://ci.victorville.ca.us/fire.aspx

Fire Chief **Dan Munsey** ..... (760) 955-5227
E-mail: dmunsey@sbcfire.org
Emergency Services Coordinator **Dana Wellborn** ..... (760) 243-6344
E-mail: oes@victorvilleca.gov

Police Department
14200 Amargosa Road, Victorville, CA 92392
Tel: (760) 241-2911

Captain **Sam Lucia** ..... (760) 241-2911
Public/Media Relations and Crime Prevention Officer
Stella Hodson ..... (760) 241-1841

Public Works Department
14343 Civic Drive, Victorville, CA 92392

Assistant Director **Doug Matthews** ..... (760) 955-6332
Solid Waste Manager **Dana Armstrong** ..... (760) 955-5086

Engineering Department
14343 Civic Drive, Victorville, CA 92392
Fax: (760) 955-5159 Internet: http://ci.victorville.ca.us/engineering.aspx

City Engineer **Brian Gengler** ..... (760) 955-5158
Administrative Secretary **Linda St. Louis** ..... (760) 955-5157
E-mail: lstlouis@ci.victorville.ca.us

Capital Improvements Division
14343 Civic Drive, Victorville, CA 92392

Associate Civil Engineer **Stephan Longoria** ..... (760) 955-5158
E-mail: slongoria@victorvilleca.gov

Development Support Division
14343 Civic Drive, Victorville, CA 92392

Junior Engineer **Carlos Seanez** ..... (760) 955-5158
E-mail: cseanez@ci.victorville.ca.us

Survey Division
14343 Civic Drive, Victorville, CA 92392

City Surveyor **David Cockrum** ..... (760) 243-6339

Traffic Division
14343 Civic Drive, Victorville, CA 92392

City Engineer **Brian Gengler** ..... (760) 955-5158
E-mail: bgengler@victorvilleca.gov

Victorville Water District
14343 Civic Drive, Victorville, CA 92392
Fax: (760) 269-0088

Director **Doug Matthews** ..... (760) 955-6332

Assistant City Manager
14343 Civic Drive, Victorville, CA 92392

Assistant City Manager **Keith C. Metzler** ..... (760) 243-4773
E-mail: kmetzler@ci.victorville.ca.us
Education: UC Riverside BSBA; Cal State (San Bernardino) MBA

Southern California Logistics Airport [SCLA]
18374 Phanton Street, Victorville, CA 92394
Fax: (760) 243-1900 Internet: http://ci.victorville.ca.us/scla.aspx

Director **Keith C. Metzler** ..... (760) 243-1901
Education: UC Riverside BSBA; Cal State (San Bernardino) MBA

Economic Development Department
14343 Civic Drive, Victorville, CA 92392
Internet: http://ci.victorville.ca.us/eda.aspx
Internet: http://www.victorvillecity.com/

Economic Development Administrator **Sophie Smith** ..... (760) 955-5032
E-mail: ssmith@ci.victorville.ca.us
Housing Senior Management Analyst **Lesyenia Marin** ..... (760) 955-5032
E-mail: lmarin@ci.victorville.ca.us

Assistant City Manager
14343 Civic Drive, Victorville, CA 92392

Assistant City Manager **Bill Webb** ..... (760) 955-5029

Information Technology Division
14343 Civic Drive, Victorville, CA 92392

Manager **Joe Haggard** ..... (760) 955-5000
E-mail: jhaggard@ci.victorville.ca.us

Human Resources Department
14343 Civic Drive, Victorville, CA 92392
Internet: http://ci.victorville.ca.us/hr.aspx

Personnel Officer **Josie Trevino** ..... (760) 955-5051
E-mail: jtrevino@ci.victorville.ca.us

Finance Department
14343 Civic Drive, Victorville, CA 92392
Fax: (760) 269-0052 Internet: http://ci.victorville.ca.us/finance.aspx

City Treasurer **Bill Webb** ..... (760) 955-5012
Management Analyst **(Vacant)** ..... (760) 243-6312
Finance Manager **Patricia Rosenberg** ..... (760) 955-5057
Finance Supervisor **Carolyn Contreras** ..... (760) 955-2656
Purchasing Manager **John Mendiola** ..... (760) 955-5079
E-mail: jmendiola@ci.victorville.ca.us Fax: (760) 269-0045

City Attorney
14343 Civic Drive, Victorville, CA 92392

City Attorney **Andre de Bortnowsky** . . . . (760) 955-5029

City of Virginia Beach, Virginia
Municipal Center, City Hall Building, 2401 Courthouse Drive, Virginia Beach, VA 23456-9120
Tel: (757) 385-3111 (Information) Internet: www.vbgov.com

County: None **Election Type:** Nonpartisan **Population:** 452,745 (2015)
Employees: 16,970 **Fiscal Year:** 2016 **Budget:** $1,872,230,000

Office of the Mayor and City Council
Municipal Center, City Hall Building, 2401 Courthouse Drive, Virginia Beach, VA 23456-9000
Tel: (757) 385-4581 Fax: (757) 385-5699 E-mail: rhfraser@vbgov.com

Employees: 11 **Fiscal Year:** 2016 **Budget:** $562,000

★Mayor **William D. Sessoms, Jr.** . . . . (757) 385-4581
Began Service: January 1, 2009
Term Expires: December 31, 2016
Secretary **Debbie Collins** . . . . (757) 385-4581
E-mail: mayorsassistant@vbgov.com
Secretary **Judy Faro** . . . . (757) 385-4581
E-mail: jfaro@vbgov.com

★Vice Mayor **Louis R. Jones** (Bayside) . . . . (757) 385-4303
Term Expires: December 31, 2018
E-mail: lrjones@vbgov.com
Education: Old Dominion 1958 BS

★Council Member **M. Ben Davenport** (At-Large) . . . . (757) 385-4303
Term Expires: December 31, 2018

★Council Member **Robert M. "Bob" Dyer** (Centerville) . . . (757) 385-4303
Term Expires: December 31, 2016
E-mail: bdyer@vbgov.com

★Council Member **Barabara M. Henley** (Princess Anne) . . . (757) 385-4303
Term Expires: December 31, 2018
E-mail: bhenley@vbgov.com

★Council Member **Shannon D.S. Kane** (Rose Hall) . . . . . . (757) 385-4303
Term Expires: December 31, 2018

★Council Member **John D. Moss** (At-Large) . . . . (757) 385-4303
Term Expires: December 31, 2018

★Council Member **Amelia Ross-Hammond** (Kempsville) . . (757) 385-4303
Term Expires: December 31, 2016

★Council Member **John E. Uhrin** (Beach) . . . . (757) 385-4303
Term Expires: December 31, 2018
E-mail: juhrin@vbgov.com

★Council Member **Rosemary A. Wilson** (At-Large) . . . . . . (757) 422-0733
Term Expires: December 31, 2016
E-mail: rcwilson@vbgov.com
Education: Old Dominion 1974 BS

★Council Member **James L. "Jim" Wood** (Lynnhaven) . . . (757) 385-4303
Term Expires: December 31, 2018
E-mail: jlwood@vbgov.com
Education: Washington and Lee 1985 BS

Office of the City Attorney
Municipal Center, Buliding 1, 2401 Courthouse Drive, Room 260, Virginia Beach, VA 23456-9004
Fax: (757) 385-5687

Employees: 40 **Fiscal Year:** 2016 **Budget:** $4,012,000

○City Attorney **Mark Stiles** . . . . (757) 385-4531
E-mail: mstiles@vbgov.com

Office of the City Auditor
Municipal Center, Bldg. 1, 2401 Courthouse Drive, Virginia Beach, VA 23456-9003
Fax: (757) 385-5875

Employees: 7 **Fiscal Year:** 2016 **Budget:** $761,000

○City Auditor **Lyndon S. Remias** . . . . (757) 385-5870
E-mail: lremias@vbgov.com

Office of the City Clerk
Municipal Center, Bldg. 1, 2401 Courthouse Drive, Virginia Beach, VA 23456
Tel: (757) 385-4303 Fax: (757) 385-5669

Employees: 6 **Fiscal Year:** 2016 **Budget:** $581,000

○City Clerk **Ruth Hodges-Fraser** . . . . (757) 385-4303
E-mail: rhfraser@vbgov.com

Office of the City Treasurer
Municipal Center, Bldg. 1, 2401 Courthouse Drive, Virginia Beach, VA 23456-9018
Fax: (757) 385-6399

Employees: 74 **Fiscal Year:** 2016 **Budget:** $5,691,000

★City Treasurer **John T. Atkinson** . . . . (757) 385-4445
Term Expires: December 31, 2017
E-mail: jatkinso@vbgov.com

Office of the Commissioner of the Revenue
Municipal Center, Bldg. 1, 2401 Courthouse Drive, Virginia Beach, VA 23456-9002
Fax: (757) 385-5685

Employees: 65 **Fiscal Year:** 2016 **Budget:** $4,350,000

★Commissioner **Philip J. Kellam** . . . . (757) 385-4251
Term Expires: December 31, 2017
E-mail: coradmin@vbgov.com

Office of the Commonwealth's Attorney
Building 10B, 2425 Nimmo Parkway, Virginia Beach, VA 23456-9050
Fax: (757) 385-9647

Employees: 87 **Fiscal Year:** 2016 **Budget:** $8,595,000

★Commonwealth's Attorney **Colin D. Stolle** . . . . (757) 385-4401
Term Expires: December 31, 2017 Fax: (757) 385-9647
E-mail: cstolle@vbgov.com

Office of the General Registrar
Municipal Center, Bldg. 14, 2449 Princess Anne Road, Virginia Beach, VA 23456-9116
Fax: (757) 385-5632 E-mail: voter@vbgov.com

Employees: 12 **Fiscal Year:** 2016 **Budget:** $1,392,000

▶General Registrar **Donna Patterson** . . . . (757) 385-8683
E-mail: dpatterson@vbgov.com
Education: VCU BS; National-Louis MS

Office of the Real Estate Assessor
Municipal Center, Bldg. 18, 2424 Courthouse Drive, Virginia Beach, VA 23456-9054
Fax: (757) 385-5727

Employees: 34 **Fiscal Year:** 2016 **Budget:** $4,350,000

○Assessor **Jerald Banagan** . . . . (757) 385-4601
E-mail: assessor@vbgov.com

★Elected Official ▲Appointed by Legislature ▼Appointed by Governor ▶Appointed by Board or Commission ●Appointed by Judge
■Appointed by Mayor △Appointed by Freeholders ▽Appointed by Supervisor ▷Appointed by County Executive ○Appointed by Council

Office of the Sheriff
Municipal Center, Bldg. 7, 2501 James Madison Boulevard, Virginia Beach, VA 23456-9107
Fax: (757) 385-5037

Employees: 514 **Fiscal Year:** 2016 **Budget:** $43,022,000

★ Sheriff **Kenneth W. Stolle** .... (757) 385-4555
Term Expires: December 31, 2017
E-mail: kstolle@vbgov.com
Education: Berry BS

Office of the City Manager
Municipal Center, Bldg. 1, 2401 Courthouse Drive, Virginia Beach, VA 23456-9001
Fax: (757) 427-5626

Employees: 34 **Fiscal Year:** 2016 **Budget:** $3,859,000

City Manager **David Hansen** .... (757) 385-4242
E-mail: dhansen@vbgov.com
Communications Administrator **Julie Hill** .... (757) 385-4242
Education: Emerson BA; Bowling Green State MA, PhD

Emergency Medical Services Department
477 Viking Drive, Virginia Beach, VA 23452
Fax: (757) 431-3019 E-mail: ems@vbgov.com

Employees: 75 **Fiscal Year:** 2016 **Budget:** $10,045,000

EMS Chief (Interim) **Edward Brazle** .... (757) 385-1999

Fire Department
Municipal Center, Bldg. 21, 2408 Courthouse Drive, Virginia Beach, VA 23456-9065
Fax: (757) 385-5676 E-mail: vbfire@vbgov.com

Employees: 485 **Fiscal Year:** 2016 **Budget:** $48,786,000

Fire Chief **Steven Cover** .... (757) 385-4228
E-mail: scover@vbgov.com

Police Department
Municipal Center, Bldg. 11, 2509 Princess Anne Road, Virginia Beach, VA 23456-9117
Fax: (757) 427-9163 E-mail: vbpd@vbgov.com

Employees: 1,015 **Fiscal Year:** 2016 **Budget:** $96,941,000

Chief of Police **James A. "Jim" Cervera** .... (757) 385-4141
Education: St Leo Col BA; Old Dominion MPA

Deputy City Manager
Municipal Center, Building 1, 2401 Courthouse Drive, Virginia Beach, VA 23456-9120

Deputy City Manager (Acting) **Regina S. Hilliard** .... (757) 385-4242
E-mail: rhilliard@vbgov.com
Education: Old Dominion MPA

Human Resources Department
Municipal Center, Bldg. 18, 2424 Courthouse Drive, Virginia Beach, VA 23456-9056
Fax: (757) 427-2731 E-mail: hrcareers@vbgov.com

Employees: 47 **Fiscal Year:** 2016 **Budget:** $4,308,000

Director **Regina S. Hilliard** .... (757) 385-8374
E-mail: rhilliard@vbgov.com
Education: Old Dominion MPA

Human Services
3432 Virginia Beach Blvd., Virginia Beach, VA 23452-4420
Fax: (757) 437-3466

Employees: 1,091 **Fiscal Year:** 2016 **Budget:** $125,578,000

Deputy Director **Dannette R. Smith** .... (757) 437-3613
Education: Eastern Michigan BS; Illinois (Chicago) MSW
Deputy Director **Alexis Zoss** .... (757) 437-3613

Developmental Services Division
Pembroke Six, 297 Independence Boulevard, Suite 208, Virginia Beach, VA 23462-2837

Director (Interim) **Francis Fox** .... (757) 385-0601

Parks and Recreation
Municipal Center, Bldg. 21, 2408 Courthouse Drive, Virginia Beach, VA 23456-9016
Fax: (757) 385-1130 E-mail: fun@vbgov.com

Employees: 830 **Fiscal Year:** 2016 **Budget:** $50,112,000

Director **Michael J. Kalvort** .... (757) 385-1100
Education: Florida BA; Nova Southeastern MPA

Public Libraries Administration
Municipal Center, Bldg. 19, 2416 Courthouse Drive, Virginia Beach, VA 23456-9068
Fax: (757) 385-4220

Employees: 253 **Fiscal Year:** 2016 **Budget:** $18,204,000

Director **Eva Poole** .... (757) 385-4321
E-mail: epoole@vbgov.com

Municipal Reference Services
Meyera E. Oberndorf Central Library, 4100 Virginia Beach Boulevard, Virginia Beach, VA 23452-1767
Fax: (757) 431-4134 E-mail: muniref@vbgov.com

Municipal Reference Librarian
Stephanie Klinkenberger .... (757) 385-4644
E-mail: muniref@vbgov.com

Wahab Law Library
Judicial Center Building 10B, 2425 Nimmo Parkway, Virginia Beach, VA 23456-9062
Tel: (757) 385-4419 Fax: (757) 385-8742 E-mail: llstaff@vbgov.com

Law Librarian Supervisor **Jean Tancredi** .... (757) 385-4419
E-mail: jtancredi@vbgov.com

Volunteer Resources Office
Municipal Center, Building 1, 2401 Courthouse Drive, Room 201, Virginia Beach, VA 23456-9021
Fax: (757) 427-5626 E-mail: volunteer@vbgov.com

Director **Rev. James A. Parke** .... (757) 385-4722
E-mail: jparke@vbgov.com

Deputy City Manager
Municipal Center, Building 1, 2401 Courthouse Drive, Virginia Beach, VA 23456-9120

Deputy City Manager (Acting) **Thomas M. Leahy III** .... (757) 385-4242
E-mail: tleahy@vbgov.com

Communications and Information Technology
Municipal Center, Bldg. 2, 2405 Courthouse Drive, Virginia Beach, VA 23456-9027
Fax: (757) 385-5782

Employees: 168 **Fiscal Year:** 2016 **Budget:** $21,685,000

Chief Information Officer **Matthew B. Arvay** .... (757) 385-4121
E-mail: marvay@vbgov.com

Finance
Municipal Center, Bldg. 1, 2401 Courthouse Drive, Virginia Beach, VA 23456-9009
Fax: (757) 385-4302

Employees: 57 **Fiscal Year:** 2016 **Budget:** $4,754,000

Director of Finance **Patricia A. Phillips** .... (757) 385-4681

CITIES AND TOWNS

Management Services Office
Municipal Center, Bldg. 1, 2401 Courthouse Drive,
Virginia Beach, VA 23456-9012
Fax: (757) 385-1857

Director **Catheryn Whitesell** .... (757) 385-8234
E-mail: budget@vbgov.com

Public Utilities
Municipal Center, Bldg. 2, 2405 Courthouse Drive,
Virginia Beach, VA 23456-9041
Fax: (757) 427-3183 Internet: www.vbgov.com/pu

Employees: 417 **Fiscal Year:** 2016 **Budget:** $103,751,000

Director **Thomas M. Leahy III** .... (757) 385-4171

Public Works
Municipal Center, Bldg. 2, 2405 Courthouse Drive,
Virginia Beach, VA 23456-9030
Fax: (757) 385-5783 E-mail: pworks@vbgov.com

Employees: 903 **Fiscal Year:** 2016 **Budget:** $156,390,000

Director **Phil Davenport** .... (757) 385-4167

Deputy City Manager
Municipal Center, Building 1, 2401 Courthouse Drive,
Virginia Beach, VA 23456-9120

Deputy City Manager **Douglas L. Smith** .... (757) 385-4242

Department of Agriculture
2837 Court Plaza Drive, Virginia Beach, VA 23456-3443
Fax: (757) 385-5684

Employees: 12 **Fiscal Year:** 2016 **Budget:** $4,148,000

Director **David Trimmer** .... (757) 385-5775

Convention and Visitors Bureau
2101 Parks Avenue, Suite 500, Virginia Beach, VA 23451-4160

Employees: 106 **Fiscal Year:** 2016 **Budget:** $20,346,000

Director **Brad Van Dommelen** .... (757) 385-4700

Office of Cultural Affairs
Sandler Center for the Performing Arts, 201 Market Street, Suite 204,
Virginia Beach, VA 23462
Tel: (757) 385-2526 Fax: (757) 493-5450

Employees: 3 **Fiscal Year:** 2016 **Budget:** $2,380,000

Director **Emily Labows** .... (757) 385-0226

Economic Development
222 Central Park Avenue, Suite 1000, Virginia Beach, VA 23462-3022
Tel: (800) 989-4567 Tel: (757) 385-6464 (Local) Fax: (757) 499-9894
E-mail: ecdev@vbgov.com

Employees: 18 **Fiscal Year:** 2016 **Budget:** $3,819,000

Director **Warren Harris** .... (757) 385-6464
E-mail: wharris@vbgov.com

Housing and Neighborhood Preservation
Municipal Center, Bldg. 18A, 2424 Courthouse Drive,
Virginia Beach, VA 23456-9083
Fax: (757) 385-5766

Employees: 61 **Fiscal Year:** 2016 **Budget:** $27,468,000

Director **Andrew Friedman** .... (757) 385-5750

Department of Museums
717 General Booth Blvd., Virginia Beach, VA 23451-4811
Fax: (757) 437-4976

Employees: 164 **Fiscal Year:** 2016 **Budget:** $12,018,000

Manager of Historic Houses **(Vacant)** .... (757) 385-5105

Planning & Community Department
Municipal Center, Bldg. 2, 2405 Courthouse Drive,
Virginia Beach, VA 23456-9040
Fax: (757) 385-5667

Employees: 115 **Fiscal Year:** 2016 **Budget:** $10,498,000

Director **Barry Frankenfield** .... (757) 385-4621

Strategic Growth Area Office
Municipal Center, Building 1, 2401 Courthouse Drive,
Virginia Beach, VA 23456

Director **(Vacant)** .... (757) 385-2901

City of Visalia, California
425 East Oak Avenue, Suite 301, Visalia, CA 93291
Internet: www.ci.visalia.ca.us

County: Tulare **Election Type:** Nonpartisan **Year Incorporated:** 1874
Population: 130,104 (2015)

Office of the Mayor and City Council
425 East Oak Avenue, Visalia, CA 93291

★ Mayor **Steven Nelsen** .... (559) 713-4512
Term Expires: November 2018
E-mail: snelsen@ci.visalia.ca.us
Date of Birth: January 3, 1949
Education: Cal State (Fullerton) 1972 BA

★ Vice Mayor **E. Warren Gubler** .... (559) 713-4512
Term Expires: November 2018
E-mail: wgubler@ci.visalia.ca.us
Date of Birth: March 4, 1957
Education: BYU 1980 BA; J Reuben Clark Law 1983 JD

★ Council Member **Greg Collins** .... (559) 713-4512
Term Expires: November 2018
E-mail: greg.collins@ci.visalia.ca.us

★ Council Member **Robert R. "Bob" Link** .... (559) 713-4512
Term Expires: November 2016
E-mail: blink@ci.visalia.ca.us
Date of Birth: July 1, 1937
Education: U Redlands 1955 BA

★ Council Member **Amy Shuklian** .... (559) 713-4512
Term Expires: November 2016
E-mail: ashuklian@ci.visalia.ca.us
Education: Cal State (Fresno) 1987 BS

Office of the City Manager
425 East Oak Avenue, Visalia, CA 93291

City Manager **Michael Olmos** .... (559) 713-4312
E-mail: molmos@ci.visalia.ca.us

Chief Deputy City Clerk **Michelle Nicholson** .... (559) 713-4512
E-mail: cityclerk@ci.visalia.ca.us

Communications Manager **Allison Lambert** .... (559) 713-4535
E-mail: allison.lambert@visalia.city

Assistant City Manager **Leslie Caviglia** .... (559) 713-4317
E-mail: lcaviglia@ci.visalia.ca.us

Deputy City Manager **Eric Frost** .... (559) 713-4317
E-mail: efrost@ci.visalia.ca.us

Community Development Department
315 East Acequia Avenue, Visalia, CA 93291
Fax: (559) 713-4813

Community Development Director **Nick Mascia** .... (559) 713-4444
E-mail: nick.mascia@ci.visalia.ca.us

★ Elected Official ▲ Appointed by Legislature ▼ Appointed by Governor ► Appointed by Board or Commission ● Appointed by Judge
■ Appointed by Mayor △ Appointed by Freeholders ▽ Appointed by Supervisor ▷ Appointed by County Executive ○ Appointed by Council

Building Safety Division
315 East Acequia Avenue, Visalia, CA 93291
Fax: (559) 713-4814

Building Official **Chuck Clark** . . . . (559) 713-4495
E-mail: chuck.clark@ci.visalia.ca.us

Engineering Division
315 East Acequia Avenue, Visalia, CA 93291

Engineering Manager **Jason Huckleberry** . . . . (559) 713-4359
E-mail: jhuckleberry@ci.visalia.ca.us

GIS Division
315 East Acequia Avenue, Visalia, CA 93291
Fax: (559) 713-4812

GIS Manager **Jason Huckleberry** . . . . (559) 713-4495

Planning Division
315 East Acequia Avenue, Visalia, CA 93291
Fax: (559) 713-4814

Assistant Director/City Planner **Josh McDonnell** . . . . . . (559) 713-4364

Finance Department
707 West Acequia Avenue, Visalia, CA 93291

Finance Director **Renee Nagel** . . . . (559) 713-4298
Financial Analyst **Yolanda Gonzales** . . . . (559) 713-4298

Fire Department
707 West Acequia Avenue, Visalia, CA 93291
Internet: http://www.ci.visalia.ca.us/depts/fire/default.asp

Fire Chief **Doug McBee** . . . . (559) 713-4266
E-mail: doug.mcbee@ci.visalia.ca.us

Housing Services
315 East Acequia Avenue, Visalia, CA 93291

Housing Specialist **Rhonda Haynes** . . . . (559) 713-4460
E-mail: rhaynes@ci.visalia.ca.us
Building Inspector **Doug Elliott** . . . . (559) 713-4462
E-mail: delliott@ci.visalia.ca.us

Human Resources Department
707 West Acequia Avenue, Visalia, CA 93291
Fax: (559) 713-4803

Human Resources Manager **Diane Davis** . . . . (559) 713-4575
E-mail: ddavis@ci.visalia.ca.us

Risk Management Division
707 West Acequia Avenue, Visalia, CA 93291

Insurance and Benefits Manager **Charlotte Dunn** . . . . (559) 713-4335
E-mail: cdunn@ci.visalia.ca.us

Information Services
707 West Acequia Avenue, Visalia, CA 93291

Information Services Manager **Mike Allen** . . . . (559) 713-4515
E-mail: mallen@ci.visalia.ca.us

Natural Resource Conservation Department
425 East Oak Avenue, Visalia, CA 93291

Manager **Kim Loeb** . . . . (559) 713-4531

Parks and Recreation Department
345 North Jacob Street, Visalia, CA 93291

Director **Vincent A. Elizondo** . . . . (559) 713-4367

Police Department
303 South Johnson Street, Visalia, CA 93291

Chief of Police **Jason Salazar** . . . . (559) 713-4215

Public Works Department
315 East Acequia Avenue, Visalia, CA 93291

Director **Adam Ennis** . . . . (559) 713-4428
Solid Waste Manager **Earl Nielsen** . . . . (559) 713-4533

Transportation and General Services Division
425 East Oak Avenue, Visalia, CA 93291

Transit Manager **Monty Cox** . . . . (559) 713-4591

Visalia Convention Center
303 East Acequia Avenue, Visalia, CA 93291

Manager **Shelley Ellis** . . . . (559) 713-4004

Visalia Municipal Airport
9501 Airport Drice, Visalia, CA 93277
Fax: (559) 713-4827

Airport Manager **Mario Cifuentez II** . . . . (559) 713-4480

City of Waco, Texas
P.O. Box 2570, Waco, TX 76702-2570
Internet: www.waco-texas.com

County: McLennan **Election Type:** Nonpartisan **Year Incorporated:** 1856 **Population:** 132,356 (2015)

Office of the Mayor and City Council
P.O. Box 2570, Waco, TX 76702-2570
Fax: (254) 750-5748 Internet: www.waco-texas.com/council.asp

★ Mayor **Kyle Deaver** . . . . (254) 548-4846
Began Service: May 18, 2016 Fax: (254) 750-5748
Term Expires: May 2018
E-mail: wacomayor@waco-texas.com

★ Council Member **Wilbert Austin, Sr.** (District 1) . . . . . . (254) 752-2128
Term Expires: May 13, 2018 Fax: (254) 750-5748
E-mail: ccouncil1@waco-texas.com

★ Council Member **Alice Rodriguez** (District 2) . . . . (254) 235-2458
Term Expires: May 2017 Fax: (254) 750-5748
E-mail: ccouncil2@waco-texas.com

★ Council Member **John Kinnaird** (District 3) . . . . (254) 307-1023
Term Expires: May 13, 2018 Fax: (254) 750-5748
E-mail: ccouncil3@waco-texas.com

★ Council Member **Dillon Meek** (District 4) . . . . (254) 755-7417
Term Expires: May 19, 2017 Fax: (254) 750-5748

★ Council Member **(Vacant)** (District 5) . . . . (254) 755-7417
Term Expires: May 2017 Fax: (254) 750-5748
E-mail: ccouncil5@waco-texas.com

Office of the City Manager
P.O. Box 2570, Waco, TX 76702-2570
Fax: (254) 750-5880

○ City Manager **Dale A. Fisseler** . . . . (254) 750-5640
E-mail: dalef@ci.waco.tx.us
Education: Texas A&M BSCE

Deputy City Manager **Wiley Stem III** . . . . (254) 750-5640
E-mail: wileys@ci.waco.tx.us

Assistant City Manager **Deidra Emerson** . . . . (254) 750-5640
Assistant City Manager **Cynthia Garcia** . . . . (254) 750-5640
Assistant City Manager **Jack Harper II** . . . . (254) 750-5640

★ Elected Official ▲ Appointed by Legislature ▼ Appointed by Governor ▶ Appointed by Board or Commission ● Appointed by Judge
■ Appointed by Mayor △ Appointed by Freeholders ▽ Appointed by Supervisor ▷ Appointed by County Executive ○ Appointed by Council

City Attorney
P.O. Box 2570, Waco, TX 76702-2570
Fax: (254) 750-5888

○City Attorney **Jennifer Richie** .... (254) 750-5888
E-mail: jenniferr@ci.waco.tx.us

City Secretary
P.O. Box 2570, Waco, TX 76702-2570
Fax: (254) 750-5748

○City Secretary **Esmeralda Hudson** .... (254) 750-5750
E-mail: esmeraldac@ci.waco.tx.us

Budget Department
P.O. Box 2570, Waco, TX 76702-2570
Fax: (254) 750-5880

Program Manager, Budget/Audit **Laura Chiota** .... (254) 750-5694

Building Inspections/Construction/Code Enforcement Department
P.O. Box 2570, Waco, TX 76702-2570
Fax: (254) 750-5624 (Code fax)

Director **Randall Childers** .... (254) 750-5612

Convention and Visitor Services Department
P.O. Box 2570, Waco, TX 76702-2570
Fax: (254) 750-5801

Director (Interim) **Rusty Black** .... (254) 750-5810

Economic Development Department
P.O. Box 2570, Waco, TX 76702-2570
Fax: (254) 750-5880

Deputy Director **Melett Harrison** .... (254) 750-5643

Emergency Management Services
P.O. Box 2570, Waco, TX 76702-2570
Fax: (254) 750-5938

Coordinator **Frank Patterson** .... (254) 750-5911
E-mail: frankp@ci.waco.tx.us

Engineering Department
P.O. Box 2570, Waco, TX 76702-2570

Director **Octavio Garza** .... (254) 750-5440
Fax: (254) 750-5844

Traffic Operations Program Administrator **(Vacant)** .... (254) 750-6638
Fax: (254) 750-6641

Street Services Program Administrator **(Vacant)** .... (254) 750-8690
Fax: (254) 750-8694

Solid Waste Services Director **Charles Dowdell** .... (254) 299-2612
Fax: (254) 299-2609

Recycling Services Program Coordinator
Anna Dunbar .... (254) 751-8536
Fax: (254) 299-2609

Finance Department
P.O. Box 2570, Waco, TX 76702-2570
Fax: (254) 750-5772

Director **Janice Andrews** .... (254) 750-5758

Fire Department
P.O. Box 2570, Waco, TX 76702-2570
Fax: (254) 750-1769

Fire Chief (Interim) **Paul Simmons** .... (254) 750-1740

Housing and Community Development Department
P.O. Box 2570, Waco, TX 76702-2570
Fax: (254) 750-5604

Director **Jeff Wall** .... (254) 750-5656
E-mail: jwall@ci.waco.tx.us

Human Resources Department
P.O. Box 2570, Waco, TX 76702-2570
Fax: (254) 750-5737

Director **Missie Pustejovsky** .... (254) 750-5740

Information Technology Department
P.O. Box 2570, Waco, TX 76702-2570
Fax: (254) 750-5718

Director **James Brown** .... (254) 750-5700

Library Services
P.O. Box 2570, Waco, TX 76702-2570
Fax: (254) 750-5940

Library Director **Essy Day** .... (254) 750-5941

Municipal Information Services
P.O. Box 2570, Waco, TX 76702-2570
Fax: (254) 750-5634

Director **Larry Holze** .... (254) 750-5638
E-mail: larryh@ci.waco.tx.us

Neighborhood Services
P.O. Box 2570, Waco, TX 76702-2570
Fax: (254) 750-5880

Program Administrator **Melett Harrison** .... (254) 750-5640
E-mail: meletth@ci.waco.tx.us

Parks and Recreation
P.O. Box 2570, Waco, TX 76702-2570
Fax: (254) 750-8087

Director **John Williams** .... (254) 750-8080

Planning Department
P.O. Box 2570, Waco, TX 76702-2570
Fax: (254) 750-1605

Director **Clint Peters** .... (254) 750-5650

Police Department
P.O. Box 2570, Waco, TX 76702-2570
Fax: (254) 750-7676

Police Chief **Brent Stroman** .... (254) 750-7500

Purchasing Services
P.O. Box 2570, Waco, TX 76702-2570
Fax: (254) 750-8063

Director of General Services **Kelly Holocek** .... (254) 750-8433
E-mail: kellyh@ci.waco.tx.us

Facilities (Building Maintenance)
P.O. Box 2570, Waco, TX 76702-2570
Fax: (254) 750-8014

Program Administrator **Vince Tobola** .... (254) 750-8082
E-mail: vincentt@ci.waco.tx.us

Fleet Services
P.O. Box 2570, Waco, TX 76702-2570
Fax: (254) 750-8053

Director **Thomas Auston** .... (254) 750-8059

★ Elected Official ▲ Appointed by Legislature ▼ Appointed by Governor ▶ Appointed by Board or Commission ● Appointed by Judge
■ Appointed by Mayor △ Appointed by Freeholders ▽ Appointed by Supervisor ▷ Appointed by County Executive ○ Appointed by Council

Risk Management Department
P.O. Box 2570, Waco, TX 76702-2570
Fax: (254) 750-5780

Risk Manager **Melissa Sullinger** . . . . (254) 750-5730

Water Utilities Services
P.O. Box 2570, Waco, TX 76702-2570
Fax: (254) 750-8032

Director **Lisa Tyer** . . . . (254) 750-8040

Waco Regional Airport
P.O. Box 2570, Waco, TX 76702-2570
Fax: (254) 750-8659

Director **Joel Martinez** . . . . (254) 750-8655

Waco Transit Services
P.O. Box 2570, Waco, TX 76702-2570
Fax: (254) 750-1901

General Manager **John Hendrickson** . . . . (254) 750-1900

City of Warren, Michigan

One City Square, Warren, MI 48093
Tel: (586) 574-4500 (Information) Internet: www.cityofwarren.org

County: Macomb **Election Type:** Nonpartisan **Population:** 135,358 (2015)

Office of the Mayor
One City Square, Warren, MI 48093
Fax: (586) 574-4524

★ Mayor **James R. Fouts** . . . . (586) 574-4520
Began Service: 2007
Term Expires: November 2019
E-mail: mayor@cityofwarren.org

Office of the City Council
5460 Arden Street, Warren, MI 48092
Fax: (586) 268-0606

★ President **Cecil D. St. Pierre, Jr.** (District 3) . . . . (586) 457-1800
Term Expires: November 2019
E-mail: cdspjr@yahoo.com

★ Vice President **Patrick Green** (District 1) . . . . (586) 524-1315
Term Expires: November 2019
E-mail: pgreen@cityofwarren.org

★ Mayor Pro Tem **Kelly Colegio** (At-Large) . . . . (586) 216-7437
Term Expires: November 2019
E-mail: kcolegio4@aol.com

★ Council Member **Keith Sadowski** (District 2) . . . . (586) 216-6377
Term Expires: November 2019
E-mail: ksadowski@cityofwarren.org

★ Council Member **Steven Warner** (District 4) . . . . (586) 296-9894
Term Expires: November 2019
E-mail: sgwarner1@yahoo.com

★ Council Member **Robert Boccomino** (District 5) . . . . (586) 850-5221
Term Expires: November 2019
E-mail: boccomino2007@wowway.com

★ Council Member **Scott Stevens** (At-Large) . . . . (586) 468-4438
Term Expires: November 2019
E-mail: scs425@wowway.com

Office of the Assessor
One City Square, Suite 310, Warren, MI 48093
Fax: (586) 574-0793

■ Assessor **Marcia Smith** . . . . (586) 574-4627
E-mail: msmith@cityofwarren.org

Office of the City Attorney
One City Square, Suite 400, Warren, MI 48093
Fax: (586) 574-4530

■ City Attorney (Acting) **Mary Michaels** . . . . (586) 574-4671
E-mail: mmichaels@cityofwarren.org

Office of the City Clerk
One City Square, Suite 205, Warren, MI 48093
Fax: (586) 574-4556

★ City Clerk **Paul Wojno** . . . . (586) 574-4557
Term Expires: November 2019
E-mail: clerk@cityofwarren.org

Office of the Controller
One City Square, Suite 425, Warren, MI 48093
Fax: (586) 574-4614

■ Controller **Rob Maleszyk** . . . . (586) 574-4600
E-mail: rmaleszyk@cityofwarren.org

Office of the Treasurer
One City Square, Suite 200, Warren, MI 48093
Fax: (586) 574-4698

★ Treasurer **Lorie Barnwell** . . . . (586) 574-4542
Term Expires: November 2019
E-mail: treasurer@cityofwarren.org

Building Department
One City Square, Suite 305, Warren, MI 48093
Fax: (586) 574-4577

■ Director **Greg Paliczuk** . . . . (586) 574-4662
E-mail: gpaliczuk@cityofwarren.org

Communications Department
5460 Arden Street, Warren, MI 48092
Fax: (586) 258-2001

■ Communications Director **Tracey Perry** . . . . (586) 258-2012
E-mail: tperry@cityofwarren.org

Community and Economic Development Department
One City Square, Suite 215, Warren, MI 48093
Fax: (586) 574-4524

■ Economic Development Director **Lark Samouelian** . . . . . . (586) 574-4519
E-mail: lsamouelian@cityofwarren.org

Downtown Development Authority Director
Lark Samouelian . . . . (586) 574-4529

Fire Department
23295 Schoenherr, Warren, MI 48089
Fax: (586) 774-2120

■ Fire Commissioner **Wilburt "Skip" McAdams, Jr.** . . . . . . (586) 756-2800
E-mail: wmcadams@cityofwarren.org

Human Resources Department
One City Square, Suite 410, Warren, MI 48093
Fax: (586) 582-9999

■ Director **A. Philip "Phil" Easter** . . . . (586) 574-4670
E-mail: peaster@cityofwarren.org

★ Elected Official ▲ Appointed by Legislature ▼ Appointed by Governor ▶ Appointed by Board or Commission ● Appointed by Judge
■ Appointed by Mayor △ Appointed by Freeholders ▽ Appointed by Supervisor ▷ Appointed by County Executive ○ Appointed by Council

Parks and Recreation Department
5460 Arden Street, Warren, MI 48092
Fax: (586) 268-8409

■ Director **Henry Bowman** . . . . (586) 268-8400
E-mail: hbowman@cityofwarren.org

Planning Department
One City Square, Suite 315, Warren, MI 48093
Fax: (586) 574-4685

■ Director (Acting) **Ron Wuerth** . . . . (586) 574-4532
E-mail: rwuerth@cityofwarren.org

Police Department
29900 Civic Center Boulevard, Warren, MI 48093
Fax: (586) 574-4862

■ Police Commissioner **Jere Green** . . . . (586) 574-4800
E-mail: jgreen@warrenpd.org
■ Deputy Commissioner **(Vacant)** . . . . (586) 574-4800

Warren Public Library
One City Square, Suite 100, Warren, MI 48093
Fax: (586) 264-2811 E-mail: wplweb@libcoop.net
Internet: http://www.libcoop.net/warren

■ Library Director (Acting) **Oksana Urban** . . . . (586) 574-5001
E-mail: ourban@cityofwarren.org

Public Service Department
One City Square, Suite 320, Warren, MI 48093
Fax: (586) 574-4517

■ Director **Richard Sabaugh** . . . . (586) 574-4604
E-mail: rsabaugh@cityofwarren.org

Purchasing Department
One City Square, Suite 425, Warren, MI 48093
Fax: (586) 574-4614

Purchasing Agent **Craig Treppa** . . . . (586) 574-4636
E-mail: ctreppa@cityofwarren.org

City of Warwick, Rhode Island

3275 Post Road, Warwick, RI 02886
Internet: www.warwickri.gov

County: Kent **Election Type:** Partisan **Population:** 81,699 (2015)

Scott Avedisian (R)
Mayor

Began Service: 2000
Term Expires: January 2017
Education: Providence 1987

Office of the Mayor
3275 Post Rd., Warwick, RI 02886
Fax: (401) 738-6639 E-mail: mayorsoffice@warwickri.com

★ Mayor **Scott Avedisian** (R) . . . . (401) 738-2000 ext. 6200
E-mail: mayorsoffice@warwickri.com
■ Chief of Staff (Interim) **David Picozzi** . . . . (401) 738-2000 ext. 6200
Press Secretary **Courtney Marciano** . . . . (401) 738-2000 ext. 6205

Office of the City Council
3275 Post Rd., Warwick, RI 02886
Fax: (401) 738-0845 Tel: (401) 738-2000 ext. 6475

★ Council President
Donna M. Travis (D-Ward 6) . . . . (401) 738-2000 ext. 6475
Term Expires: January 2017
E-mail: donna.m.travis@warwickri.com

★ Council Member
Steven A. Colantuono (R-Ward 1) . . . . (401) 738-2000 ext. 6475
Term Expires: January 2017
E-mail: colantuonolaw@gmail.com

★ Council Member
Thomas H. Chadronet (D-Ward 2) . . . . (401) 738-2000 ext. 6475
Term Expires: January 2017
E-mail: tcwardtwo@gmail.com

★ Council Member
Camile F. Vella-Wilkinson (D-Ward 3) . . . . . . (401) 738-2000 ext. 6475
Term Expires: January 2017
E-mail: camilleV-W@mail.com

★ Council Member
Joseph J. Solomon, Sr. (D-Ward 4) . . . . (401) 738-2000 ext. 6475
Term Expires: January 20, 2017
E-mail: joseph.j.solomon@warwickri.com

★ Council Member
Edgar N. Ladouceur (D-Ward 5) . . . . (401) 738-2000 ext. 6475
Term Expires: January 2017
E-mail: edgar.ladouceur@warwickri.com

★ Council Member
Kathleen M. Usler (D-Ward 7) . . . . (401) 738-2000 ext. 6475
Term Expires: January 2017
E-mail: uslerward7@gmail.com

★ Council Member
Joseph Gallucci (D-Ward 8) . . . . (401) 738-2000 ext. 6475
Term Expires: January 5, 2017
E-mail: joseph.gallucci@warwickri.com

★ Council Member
Steven B. Merolla (D-Ward 9) . . . . (401) 738-2000 ext. 6475
Term Expires: January 2017
E-mail: steven.b.merolla@warwickri.com

Council Liaison **Joanne M. Cournoyer** . . . . (401) 738-2000 ext. 6475
E-mail: joanne.m.cournoyer@warwickri.com

Office of the Assessor
3275 Post Rd., Warwick, RI 02886

Assessor **Christopher Celeste** . . . . (401) 738-2000 ext. 6016
Fax: (401) 732-1252

Office of the Board of Canvassers
City Hall, 3275 Post Road, 1st Floor, Warwick, RI 02886
Fax: (401) 732-3439

Director of Elections **Patty Aylesworth** . . . . (401) 738-2000 ext. 6224

Office of the City Clerk
3275 Post Rd., Warwick, RI 02886
Fax: (401) 738-6639 E-mail: cityclerk@warwickri.com

■ City Clerk **Judy Wild** . . . . (401) 738-2000 ext. 6212

Office of the City Engineer
3275 Post Rd., Warwick, RI 02886

■ City Engineer **Eric Hindinger** . . . . (401) 738-2000 ext. 6537

Office of the City Solicitor
3275 Post Rd., Warwick, RI 02886

■ City Solicitor **Peter Ruggiero** . . . . (401) 737-8700

★ Elected Official ▲ Appointed by Legislature ▼ Appointed by Governor ► Appointed by Board or Commission ● Appointed by Judge
■ Appointed by Mayor △ Appointed by Freeholders ▽ Appointed by Supervisor ▷ Appointed by County Executive ○ Appointed by Council

Office of the Treasurer
3275 Post Rd., Warwick, RI 02886
E-mail: treasury@warwickri.com

■ Treasurer **David C. Olsen** .... (401) 738-2000 ext. 6228
E-mail: david.c.olsen@warwickri.com

Building Inspection Department
3275 Post Rd., Warwick, RI 02886

■ Building Official **Al DeCourt** .... (401) 738-2000 ext. 6299
E-mail: war.build@warwickri.com

Civil Defense Department
111 Veterans Memorial Drive, Warwick, RI 02886

■ Director/Chief (Acting) **Edmund B. Armstrong** .... (401) 468-4040
E-mail: edmund.armstrong@warwickri.com

Finance Department
3275 Post Rd., Warwick, RI 02886
E-mail: finance@warwickri.com

■ Director **Ernie Zmyslinski** .... (401) 738-2000 ext. 6207
E-mail: ernest.m.zmyslinski@warwickri.com

Purchasing Division
3275 Post Rd., Warwick, RI 02886
E-mail: purchasing@warwickri.com

■ Purchasing Agent **Patricia A. Peshka** .... (401) 738-2000 ext. 6242
E-mail: purchasing@warwickri.com

Human Services Department
3027 West Shore Road, Warwick, RI 02886

■ Director **Patricia St. Amant** .... (401) 468-4108
E-mail: human.serv@warwickri.com

Parks and Recreation Department
975 Sandy Lane, Warwick, RI 02889
E-mail: parks-rec@warwickri.com

■ Deputy Director **Michael Rooney** .... (401) 738-2000 ext. 6504
E-mail: warwick-rec@warwickri.com

Planning Department
3275 Post Rd., Warwick, RI 02886
E-mail: war.plan@warwickri.com

■ City Planner **William DePasquale, Jr.** .... (401) 738-2000 ext. 6289
E-mail: william.depasquale@warwickri.com

Warwick Public Library
600 Sandy Lane, Warwick, RI 02889
Internet: http://wpl.lib.ri.us

Library Director **Chris LaRoux** .... (401) 739-5440 ext. 223
E-mail: laroux.chris@gmail.com

Public Safety Department
99 Veterans Memorial Drive, Warwick, RI 02886

■ Chair **Leslie Walaska-Baxter** .... (401) 468-4217

Fire Department
111 Veterans Memorial Drive, Warwick, RI 02886
E-mail: wfd-admin@warwickri.com

■ Fire Chief **James McLaughlin** .... (401) 468-4000
Assistant Chief **David E. Morse** .... (401) 468-4000
Fire Marshal **Peter Marietti** .... (401) 468-4000
E-mail: peter.marietti@warwickri.com
Assistant Fire Marshal **Michael Matteson** .... (401) 468-4000
E-mail: michael.matteson@warwickri.com
Deputy Chief, Training Division **Francis Colantonio** .... (401) 468-4000
E-mail: francis.colantonio@warwickri.com

Fire Department *continued*

Emergency Management Services Coordinator
Joseph Pfeiler .... (401) 468-4000
E-mail: joseph.pfeiler@warwickri.com

Police Department
99 Veterans Memorial Drive, Warwick, RI 02886

■ Chief of Police **Col. Stephen McCartney** .... (401) 468-4200
Deputy Police Chief **Michael Babula** .... (401) 468-4200
Operations Commander **Christine Kelley** .... (401) 468-4200

Public Works Department
925 Sandy Lane, Warwick, RI 02889

Director (Acting) **David Picozzi** .... (401) 738-2000 ext. 6500

Department of Tourism, Culture, and Development
3275 Post Rd., Warwick, RI 02886
TTY: (401) 739-9150 Fax: (401) 738-6639 E-mail: info@warwickri.com
Internet: http://www.warwickri.gov/tourism.htm

■ Director **Karen Jedson** .... (401) 738-2000 ext. 6402
E-mail: karen.jedson@warwickri.com

Weights and Measures Department
925 Sandy Lane, Warwick, RI 02886

Sealer of Weights and Measures
David Picozzi .... (401) 738-2000 ext. 6500

Warwick Public Schools
34 Warwick Lake Ave., Warwick, RI 02889
Internet: http://www.warwickschools.org

Superintendent **Philip Thornton** .... (401) 734-3100
Fax: (401) 734-3105

City of Waterbury, Connecticut
City Hall, 235 Grand Street, Waterbury, CT 06702
Tel: (203) 574-6890 (Information) Internet: www.waterburyct.org

County: New Haven **Election Type:** Partisan **Year Incorporated:** 1853
Population: 108,802 (2015)

Office of the Mayor and Board of Aldermen
City Hall, 235 Grand Street, Waterbury, CT 06702
Fax: (203) 574-6804

★ Mayor **Neil O'Leary** (D) .... (203) 574-6712
Began Service: December 1, 2011
Term Expires: November 2019
E-mail: noleary@waterburyct.org

★ Alderman **Ernest Brunelli** (D-District 1) .... (203) 574-6741
Term Expires: November 30, 2017
E-mail: ebrunelli@waterburyct.org

★ Alderman **Paul V. Ciochetti** (R-District 1) .... (203) 574-6741
Term Expires: November 30, 2017

★ Alderman **Jerry P. Padula** (R-District 1) .... (203) 574-6741
Term Expires: November 30, 2017
E-mail: jpadula@waterburyct.org

★ Alderman **Francis Guerrera** (R-District 2) .... (203) 574-6741
Term Expires: November 30, 2017

★ Alderman **Gregory Hadley** (D-District 2) .... (203) 574-6741
Term Expires: November 30, 2017
E-mail: ghadley@waterburyct.org

(continued on next page)

★ Elected Official ▲ Appointed by Legislature ▼ Appointed by Governor ► Appointed by Board or Commission ● Appointed by Judge
■ Appointed by Mayor △ Appointed by Freeholders ▽ Appointed by Supervisor ▷ Appointed by County Executive ○ Appointed by Council

Office of the Mayor and Board of Aldermen *continued*

★ Alderman **Victor Lopez, Jr.** (D-District 2) . . . . (203) 574-6741
Term Expires: November 30, 2017
E-mail: vlopez@waterburyct.org

★ Alderman **Steven Giacomi** (R-District 3) . . . . (203) 574-6741
Term Expires: November 30, 2017
E-mail: sgiacomi@waterburyct.org

★ Alderman **Ronald Napoli, Jr.** (D-District 3) . . . . (203) 574-6741
Term Expires: November 30, 2017

★ Alderman **Paul K. Pernerewski, Jr.** (D-District 3) . . . . (203) 574-6741
Term Expires: November 30, 2017
E-mail: ppernerewski@comcast.net

★ Alderman **Frank A. Burgio, Sr.** (D-District 4) . . . . (203) 574-6741
Term Expires: November 30, 2017

★ Alderman **Stephanie Cummings** (R-District 4) . . . . (203) 574-6741
Term Expires: November 30, 2017
E-mail: scummings@waterburyct.org

★ Alderman **Michael DiGiovancarlo** (D-District 4) . . . . (203) 574-6741
Term Expires: November 30, 2017

★ Alderman **Abdalla A. Johnson** (D-District 5) . . . . (203) 574-6741
Term Expires: November 30, 2017

★ Alderman **Sandra Martinez-McCarthy** (D-District 5) . . . . (203) 574-6741
Term Expires: November 30, 2017

★ Alderman **Roger Sherman** (R-District 5) . . . . (203) 574-6741
Term Expires: November 30, 2017

Office of the City Assessor

City Hall, 235 Grand Street, Courtyard Level, Waterbury, CT 06702

▶ City Assessor **David Dietsch** . . . . (203) 574-6821
E-mail: ddietsch@waterburyct.org

Office of the City Clerk

City Hall, 235 Grand Street, 1st Floor, Waterbury, CT 06702
Tel: (203) 574-6741 Fax: (203) 574-6745

★ City Clerk **Michael J. Dalton** (D) . . . . (203) 574-6741
Term Expires: November 30, 2017
E-mail: mdalton@waterburyct.org

Office of the Town Clerk

235 Grand Street, Waterbury, CT 06702

★ Town Clerk **Antoinette C. Spinelli** (D) . . . . (203) 574-6806
Term Expires: November 30, 2019
E-mail: aspinelli@waterburyct.org

Office of Finance

City Hall, 235 Grand Street, 2nd Floor, Waterbury, CT 06702
Fax: (203) 753-6831

Director of Finance **Michael LeBlanc** . . . . (203) 574-6840

Office of the Tax Collector

City Hall, 235 Grand Street, Waterbury, CT 06702

■ Deputy Tax Collector **Frank Caruso** . . . . (203) 574-6810
E-mail: fcaruso@waterburyct.org

Corporation Counsel

City Hall, 235 Grand Street, Waterbury, CT 06702
Tel: (203) 574-6731 Fax: (203) 574-8340

Corporation Counsel **Linda Wihbey** . . . . (203) 574-6732

Waterbury Public Schools

City Hall, 236 Grand Street, 3rd Floor, Waterbury, CT 06702

Superintendent of Schools **Dr. Kathleen M. Ouellette** . . . (203) 574-8001

Fire Department

City Hall, 235 Grand Street, 4th Floor, Waterbury, CT 06702

Fire Chief **David Martin** . . . . (203) 597-3450
E-mail: dmartin@waterburyct.org

Health Department

95 Scovill Street, Suite 100, Waterbury, CT 06706

Director **William Quinn** . . . . (203) 574-6780
Education: Yale 1975 MPH

Assistant Director **Shane Lockwood** . . . . (203) 574-6780

Housing Authority

2 Lakewood Rd., Waterbury, CT 06704

Director **Ron Dubuque** . . . . (203) 596-2640

Office of Human Resources

235 Grand Street, 2nd Floor, Waterbury, CT 06702
Tel: (203) 574-6761 Fax: (203) 574-8087

Human Resources Director (Acting) **Scott P. Morgan** . . . . (203) 574-6761
E-mail: smorgan@waterburyct.org

Planning Department

26 Kendrick Avenue, 2nd Floor, Waterbury, CT 06702

City Planner **James Sequin** . . . . (203) 574-6817

Police Department

255 E. Main St., Waterbury, CT 06702

Chief of Police **Vernon Riddick, Jr.** . . . . (203) 574-6906
Deputy Chief of Police **Fernando Spagnolo** . . . . (203) 574-6911
Deputy Chief of Police **William Covel** . . . . (203) 574-6911

Public Works Department

236 Grand Street, Waterbury, CT 06702
Fax: (203) 574-8277

Public Works Director **Dave B. Simpson** . . . . (203) 574-6851
Deputy Public Works Director **(Vacant)** . . . . (203) 574-6851
Water Pollution Control General Manager
Dennis Cuevas . . . . (203) 574-8265
Municiple Road, Waterbury, CT 06708
Bureau of Water Superintendent **Chris Bogucki** . . . . (203) 574-8251
21 East Aurora Street, Waterbury, CT 06708
Fleet Supervisor **Pat Mulvehill** . . . . (203) 574-6965
181A East Aurora Street, Waterbury, CT 06708
City Engineer **Paul Bellagamba** . . . . (203) 574-6851
26 Kendrick Avenue, Fax: (203) 574-8277
2nd Floor, Waterbury, CT 06702
Purchasing Agent **Rocco Orso** . . . . (203) 574-6740
235 Grand Street, 1st Floor, Waterbury, CT 06702
E-mail: rorso@waterburyct.org

Bureau of Parks

26 Kendrick Avenue, 2nd Floor, Waterbury, CT 06702

Supervisor of Parks **Mark Lombardo** . . . . (203) 574-6793

Sheriff's Office

17 Congress Avenue, Waterbury, CT 06708

Sheriff **Stephen M. Conway** . . . . (203) 574-6741
Term Expires: November 30, 2017

★ Elected Official ▲ Appointed by Legislature ▼ Appointed by Governor ▶ Appointed by Board or Commission ● Appointed by Judge
■ Appointed by Mayor △ Appointed by Freeholders ▽ Appointed by Supervisor ▷ Appointed by County Executive ○ Appointed by Council

City of West Covina, California

1444 W. Garvey Ave., West Covina, CA 91790
Internet: http://www.westcovina.org

County: Los Angeles **Year Incorporated:** 1923 **Population:** 108,484 (2015)

Office of the Mayor and City Council

1444 W. Garvey Ave., Room 305, West Covina, CA 91790
Fax: (626) 939-8406

★Mayor **James Toma** .... (626) 939-8401
Began Service: November 2013
Term Expires: November 1, 2017
E-mail: james.toma@westcovina.org

★Mayor Pro Tem **Corey Warshaw** .... (626) 939-8401
Term Expires: November 1, 2017
E-mail: corey.warshaw@westcovina.org

★Council Member **Lloyd A. Johnson** .... (626) 939-8401
Term Expires: November 2019

★Council Member **Mike Spence** .... (626) 939-8401
Term Expires: November 1, 2017
E-mail: westcovina@mikespence.com

★Council Member **Tony Wu** .... (626) 939-8401
Term Expires: November 2019

Office of the City Attorney

1444 West Garvey Ave., Room 305, West Covina, CA 91790
Fax: (626) 939-8406

○City Attorney **Kim Hall Barlow** .... (626) 939-8401
E-mail: khb@jones-mayer.com

Office of the City Clerk

1444 W. Garvey Ave., Room 317, West Covina, CA 91790

★City Clerk **Nickolas S. Lewis** .... (626) 939-8433
Term Expires: November 2017
E-mail: nickolas.lewis@westcovina.org

Assistant City Clerk **Rosalia Conde** .... (626) 939-8433
E-mail: rosalia.conde@westcovina.org

Office of the City Manager

1444 West Garvey Ave., Room 305, West Covina, CA 91790

○City Manager **Chris Freeland** .... (626) 939-8401
E-mail: chris.freeland@westcovina.org

Assistant City Manager **(Vacant)** .... (626) 939-8401

Community and Economic Development Commission

1444 W. Garvey Ave., Room 218, West Covina, CA 91790

Director **(Vacant)** .... (626) 939-8417

Community and Recreation Services Department

1444 West Garvey Avenue, Room 316, West Covina, CA 91790

Director **Nikole Bresciani** .... (626) 939-8489
E-mail: Nikole.Bresciani@westcovina.org

Finance Department

1444 West Garvey Avenue South, Room 308, West Covina, CA 91790

Finance Director **Christa Buhagiar** .... (626) 939-8450

Human Resources Director **Tom Bokosky** .... (626) 939-8438
E-mail: tom.bokosky@westcovina.org

Fire Department

1444 West Garvey Avenue, 205, West Covina, CA 91790
Internet: http://www.westcovina.org/departments/fire-

Fire Chief **Larry Whithorn** .... (626) 939-8824
E-mail: larry.whithorn@westcovina.org

Planning Department

1444 W. Garvey Ave., Room 208, West Covina, CA 91790

Director **Jeff Anderson** .... (626) 939-8422

Police Department

1444 W. Garvey Ave., West Covina, CA 91790

Chief of Police **David Faulkner** .... (626) 939-8501
Education: Columbia Southern BS

Public Works Department

1444 W. Garvey Ave., Room 215, West Covina, CA 91790

Director **Chino Consunji** .... (626) 939-8425

City of West Jordan, Utah

8000 South Redwood Road, West Jordan, UT 84088
Tel: (801) 569-5000 Internet: www.wjordan.com/

County: Salt Lake **Election Type:** Nonpartisan **Year Incorporated:** 1941 **Population:** 111,946 (2015)

Office of the Mayor and City Council

8000 South Redwood Road, West Jordan, UT 84088
Internet: www.wjordan.com/Government.aspx?pgID=2.1.1

★Mayor **Kim V. Rolfe** .... (801) 569-5105
Began Service: January 8, 2014
Term Expires: January 1, 2018
E-mail: kimr@wjordan.com

★Council Member **Chris McConnehey** (District 1) .... (801) 569-5105
Term Expires: January 6, 2020
E-mail: chrism@wjordan.com

★Council Member **Dirk Burton** (District 2) .... (801) 569-5105
Term Expires: January 6, 2020

★Council Member **Zach Jacob** (District 3) .... (801) 569-5105
Term Expires: January 6, 2020

★Council Member **Sophie Rice** (District 4) .... (801) 450-4822
Term Expires: January 6, 2020
E-mail: sophier@wjordan.com

★Council Member **Jeff Haaga** (At-Large) .... (801) 569-5105
Term Expires: January 1, 2018
E-mail: jeffreyh@wjordan.com

★Council Member **Chad Nichols** (At-Large) .... (801) 569-5105
Term Expires: January 1, 2018
E-mail: chadn@wjordan.com
Education: BYU BS

Office of the City Manager

8000 South Redwood Road, West Jordan, UT 84088
Internet: www.wjordan.com/CManager.aspx?pgID=3.2
Fax: (801) 565-8978

○City Manager **Mark R. Palesh** .... (801) 569-5100
E-mail: mpalesh@wjordan.com

Assistant City Manager **(Vacant)** .... (801) 569-5100

★Elected Official ▲Appointed by Legislature ▼Appointed by Governor ▶Appointed by Board or Commission ●Appointed by Judge
■Appointed by Mayor △Appointed by Freeholders ▽Appointed by Supervisor ▷Appointed by County Executive ○Appointed by Council

CITIES AND TOWNS

Office of the City Attorney
8000 South Redwood Road, Suite 1000, West Jordan, UT 84088
Fax: (801) 569-5149
Internet: www.wjordan.com/CAttorney.aspx?pgID=3.3

○City Attorney **David R. Brickey** .... (801) 569-5140
Education: Utah BS; Willamette JD

Office of the City Clerk
8000 South Redwood Road, 3rd Floor, West Jordan, UT 84088
Fax: (801) 569-5115
Internet: www.wjordan.com/CityClerk.aspx?pgID=3.4

City Clerk **Melanie Briggs** .... (801) 569-5117
E-mail: melanieb@wjordan.com
Deputy City Clerk **Carol Herman** .... (801) 569-5115
E-mail: carolh@wjordan.com
Deputy City Clerk **Jamie Lyn Vincent** .... (801) 569-5115
E-mail: jamiev@wjordan.com

Community Development Department
8000 South Redwood Road, West Jordan, UT 84088
Internet: www.wjordan.com/CD.aspx?pgID=3.6

Community Development Director **David Oka** .... (801) 569-5060

Engineering Department
8000 South Redwood Road, 2nd Floor, West Jordan, UT 84088
Fax: (801) 569-5099
Internet: www.wjordan.com/Engineering.aspx?pgID=3.7

Director **Wendell T. Rigby** .... (801) 569-5070
E-mail: wendellr@wjordan.com
Education: BYU 1979 BSCE, 1980 MSCE

Finance Department
City Hall, 8000 South Redwood Road, 1st Floor, West Jordan, UT 84088

Finance Manager/Controller **Ryan Bradshaw** .... (801) 569-5021
Purchasing Agent **Paul Wellington** .... (801) 569-5107
E-mail: pwellington@wjordan.com

Fire Department
7602 South Jordan Landing Boulevard, West Jordan, UT 84084
Fax: (801) 260-7320 E-mail: infowjfd@wjordan.com
Internet: www.wjordan.com/Fire.aspx?pgID=3.9

Fire Chief **Marc McElreath** .... (801) 569-7300
E-mail: marcm@wjordan.com
Education: Utah Valley State BS

Human Resources Department
8000 South Redwood Road, 3rd Floor, West Jordan, UT 84088
Fax: (801) 563-4747 Internet: www.wjordan.com/HR.aspx?pgID=3.10

Manager **Jon Gardner** .... (801) 569-5030
E-mail: jong@wjordan.com

Information Technology Department
8000 South Redwood Road, West Jordan, UT 84088
Internet: http://www.wjordan.com/IT.aspx?pgID=3.16 Fax: (801) 569-5127

Information Technology Manager **Michael Oliver** .... (801) 569-5200
E-mail: michaelo@wjordan.com

Police Department
8040 South Redwood Road, West Jordan, UT 84088
Fax: (801) 562-2105 Internet: www.wjordan.com/Police.aspx?pgID=3.13

Police Chief **Doug Diamond** .... (801) 569-2000

Public Works Department
8000 South Redwood Road, West Jordan, UT 84088
Fax: (801) 569-5127 Internet: www.wjordan.com/PW.aspx?pgID=3.14

Director **Wendell T. Rigby** .... (801) 569-5070
Education: BYU 1979 BSCE, 1980 MSCE

City of West Palm Beach, Florida

401 Clematis Street, West Palm Beach, FL 33401
Tel: (561) 822-2222 Internet: www.wpb.org

County: Palm Beach **Population:** 106,779 (2015)

Office of the City Commission
401 Clematis Street, West Palm Beach, FL 33401
Tel: (561) 822-1390 Fax: (561) 822-1399

★Mayor **Geraldine "Jeri" Muoio** .... (561) 822-1400
Began Service: March 31, 2011
Term Expires: March 2019
E-mail: gmuoio@wpb.org
Education: Syracuse PhD
Economic Development Director **Christopher Roog** .... (561) 822-1400
E-mail: croog@wpb.org
★Commissioner **Sylvia Moffett** (District 1) .... (561) 822-1390
Term Expires: March 2018
E-mail: smoffett@wpb.org
★Commissioner **Cory Neering** (District 2) .... (561) 822-1390
Term Expires: March 2017
E-mail: cneering@wpb.org
★Commissioner **Paula Ryan** (District 3) .... (561) 822-1390
Term Expires: March 2018
E-mail: pryan@wpb.org
★Commissioner **Keith A. James** (District 4) .... (561) 822-1390
Term Expires: March 31, 2017
E-mail: kjames@wpb.org
Education: Harvard 1979 BA, 1982 JD
★Commissioner **Shanon Materio** (District 5) .... (561) 822-1390
Term Expires: March 2018
E-mail: smaterio@wpb.org

Office of the City Administrator
401 Clematis Street, West Palm Beach, FL 33401
Tel: (561) 822-1400

City Administrator **Jeff Green** .... (561) 822-1400
E-mail: jgreen@wpb.org
Deputy City Administrator **Dorritt Miller** .... (561) 822-1400
E-mail: dmiller@wpb.org
Assistant City Administrator **Scott Kelly** .... (561) 822-2060
Assistant City Administrator **Danielle Slaterpryce** ...... (561) 822-2060
E-mail: dslaterpryce@wpb.org
Assistant to the City Administrator **Millie Figueroa** ...... (561) 822-1400
E-mail: mfigueroa@wpb.org

Office of the City Attorney
401 Clematis Street, 5th Floor, West Palm Beach, FL 33401
Tel: (561) 822-1350

City Attorney **Kimberly Rothenburg** .... (561) 822-1350
E-mail: krothenburg@wpb.org

★Elected Official ▲Appointed by Legislature ▼Appointed by Governor ▶Appointed by Board or Commission ●Appointed by Judge
■Appointed by Mayor △Appointed by Freeholders ▽Appointed by Supervisor ▷Appointed by County Executive ○Appointed by Council

Office of the City Clerk
401 Clematis Street, West Palm Beach, FL 33401
Tel: (561) 822-1210 E-mail: cityclerk@wpb.org
Internet: www.wpb.org/clerk/

City Clerk **Hazeline F. Carson** .... (561) 822-1210
E-mail: cityclerk@wpb.org

Youth and Family Services Division
811 Palm Beach Lake Boulevard, West Palm Beach, FL 33401 (North)
3801 Georgia Avenue, West Palm Beach, FL 33405
Tel: (561) 804-4970 (North) Tel: (561) 804-4975 (South)
Fax: (561) 835-7150 (North) Fax: (561) 835-7183 (South)
Internet: www.wpb.org/vickers/

Director **Lisa Kemp** .... (561) 804-4975

Development Services Department
401 Clematis Street, 1st Floor, West Palm Beach, FL 33401
Tel: (561) 805-6700 Internet: www.wpb.org/construction/

Director **Richard Greene** .... (561) 805-6650
E-mail: rgreene@wpb.org
Chief Building Official **Robert Brown** .... (561) 805-6654
Planning and Zoning Administrator **Angella Jones** ...... (561) 822-1435

Finance Department
200 2nd Street, 4th Floor, West Palm Beach, FL 33401
Tel: (561) 822-1310 Internet: www.wpb.org/finance/admin.php

Director **Mark A. Parks, Jr.** .... (561) 822-1310

Fire Rescue Department
500 North Dixie Highway, West Palm Beach, FL 33401
Tel: (561) 804-4700 Internet: www.wpbfr.com

Fire Chief **Carlos Cabrera** .... (561) 804-4700
E-mail: ccabrera@ieee.org

Human Resources Department
401 Clematis Street, 3rd Floor, West Palm Beach, FL 33401
Tel: (561) 494-1000 Internet: www.wpb.org/hr/

Director **Jose-Luis Rodriguez** .... (561) 494-1000
E-mail: jrodriguez@wpb.org

Parks and Recreation Department
401 Clematis Street, 4rd Floor, West Palm Beach, FL 33401
Tel: (561) 804-4900

Director **Leah Rockwell** .... (561) 804-4904
Assistant Director **(Vacant)** .... (561) 804-4904

Police Department
600 Banyan Boulevard, West Palm Beach, FL 33401
Tel: (561) 822-1900 Internet: www.wpbpolice.org/main.php

Police Chief **Bryan Kummerlen** .... (561) 822-1900
Assistant Chief **Sarah Mooney** .... (561) 822-1900

Public Library
411 Clematis Street, West Palm Beach, FL 33401
Tel: (561) 868-7700 Fax: (561) 868-7706
Internet: www.mycitylibrary.org

Director **Christopher Murray** .... (561) 868-7700
E-mail: cmurray@wpb.org

Public Works Department
1045 Charlotte Avenue, West Palm Beach, FL 33401
Tel: (561) 822-2060 Internet: www.wpb.org/public_works/index.htm

Director **(Vacant)** .... (561) 822-2060

Code Compliance Division
401 Clematis Street, West Palm Beach, FL 33401
Fax: (561) 822-1486 Internet: www.wpb.org/cc/

Community Improvement Manager **Mark Joyce** .... (561) 822-1473
E-mail: mjoyce@wpb.org

West Valley City, Utah

City Hall, 3600 South Constitution Blvd.,
West Valley City, UT 84119-3720
Internet: www.wvc-ut.gov

County: Salt Lake **Year Incorporated:** 1980 **Population:** 136,208 (2015)

Office of the Mayor and City Council
City Hall, 3600 South Constitution Blvd.,
West Valley City, UT 84119-3720
Tel: (801) 963-3220 Fax: (801) 966-8455

★ Mayor **Ron Bigelow** .... (801) 963-3373
Began Service: January 1, 2014
Term Expires: December 31, 2017
E-mail: rbigelow@wvc-ut.gov
Education: Utah BS
★ Council Member **Tom Huynh** (District 1) .... (801) 963-3370
Term Expires: December 31, 2019
E-mail: tom.huynh@wvc-ut.gov
★ Council Member **Steve Buhler** (District 2) .... (801) 963-3374
Term Expires: December 31, 2017
E-mail: steve.buhler@wvc-ut.gov
★ Council Member **Karen Lang** (District 3) .... (801) 963-3371
Term Expires: December 31, 2019
E-mail: karen.lang@wvc-ut.gov
★ Council Member **Steve Vincent** (District 4) .... (801) 963-3372
Term Expires: December 31, 2017
E-mail: steve.vincent@wvc-ut.gov
★ Council Member **Don Christensen** (At-Large) .... (801) 963-3220
Term Expires: December 31, 2019
★ Council Member **Lars Nordfelt** (At-Large) .... (801) 963-3373
Term Expires: December 31, 2017
E-mail: lnordfelt@wvc-ut.gov

Office of the City Manager
City Hall, 3600 South Constitution Blvd., West Valley City, UT 84119
Fax: (801) 966-8455

○ City Manager **Wayne T. Pyle** .... (801) 963-3438
E-mail: wayne.pyle@wvc-ut.gov
Assistant City Manager **Nicole Cottle** .... (801) 963-3203
E-mail: nicole.cottle@wvc-ut.gov
Administrative Assistant **DeAnn Varney** .... (801) 963-3438
E-mail: deann.varney@wvc-ut.gov
Assistant City Manager **Paul D. Isaac** .... (801) 963-3438
E-mail: paul.isaac@wvc-ut.gov

City Recorder
3600 South Constitution Blvd., West Valley City, UT 84119-3720

City Recorder **(Vacant)** .... (801) 963-3207

Office of the City Attorney
3600 Constitution Boulevard, West Valley City, UT 84119

City Attorney **J. Eric Bunderson** .... (801) 966-3600
E-mail: ebunderson@wvc-ut.gov
Education: Utah State BA; Utah JD

Community and Economic Development Department
City Hall, 3600 Constitution Boulevard, West Valley City, UT 84119

Director **Nicole Cottle** .... (801) 963-3286
E-mail: nicole.cottle@wvc-ut.gov

(continued on next page)

★ Elected Official ▲ Appointed by Legislature ▼ Appointed by Governor ▶ Appointed by Board or Commission ● Appointed by Judge
■ Appointed by Mayor △ Appointed by Freeholders ▽ Appointed by Supervisor ▷ Appointed by County Executive ○ Appointed by Council

Community and Economic Development Department *continued*

Executive Administrative Assistant **Margo Hoyt** . . . . (801) 963-3286
E-mail: margo.hoyt@wvc-ut.gov

Building Inspection
City Hall, 3600 Constitution Boulevard, Suite 220,
West Valley City, UT 84119

Chief Building Official **Ed Domian** . . . . (801) 963-3276
E-mail: ed.domian@wvc-ut.gov
Building Inspector **Tex Couch** . . . . (801) 963-5445
Building Inspector **Troy Glines** . . . . (801) 963-3328
E-mail: troy.glines@wvc-ut.gov
Building Inspector **Jeff Pankow** . . . . (801) 963-3530
E-mail: jeff.pankow@wvc-ut.gov
Plans Examiner **David Warnick** . . . . (801) 963-3487
E-mail: dwarnick@wvc-ut.gov
Executive Secretary **Misty Jenkins** . . . . (801) 963-3475
E-mail: misty.jenkins@wvc-ut.gov
Executive Secretary **Michelle Robinson** . . . . (801) 963-3283
E-mail: michelle.robinson@wvc-ut.gov

Economic Development
City Hall, 3600 Constitution Blvd., West Valley City, UT 84119
Tel: (801) 963-3321 Fax: (801) 963-3559

Economic Development Director **Mark Nord** . . . . (801) 963-3322
E-mail: mark.nord@wvc-ut.gov
Business Development Director **Jeff Jackson** . . . . (801) 963-3473
E-mail: jeff.jackson@wvc-ut.gov
Business Retention Manager **(Vacant)** . . . . (801) 955-3605
Economic Development/RDA Financial Analyst
Pauline Davies . . . . (801) 963-3321
E-mail: pauline.davies@wvc-ut.gov

Planning and Zoning
City Hall, 3600 Constitution Boulevard, Suite 240,
West Valley City, UT 84119
Fax: (801) 963-3559

Planning Director **Steve Pastorik** . . . . (801) 963-3545
E-mail: steve.pastorik@wvc-ut.gov
Zoning Administrator **Jody Knapp** . . . . (801) 963-3497
Current Planning Manager **Steve Lehman** . . . . (801) 963-3311
Planner **Brock Anderson** . . . . (801) 963-3361
Planner **Ryan Harris** . . . . (801) 965-7991
Long Range Planner **Lee Logston** . . . . (801) 963-3321
Administrative Assistant **Nichole Camac** . . . . (801) 963-3282
E-mail: nichole.camac@wvc-ut.gov

Community Preservation Department
4522 West 3500 South, West Valley City, UT 84120
Tel: (801) 963-3420

Community Preservation Director **Layne Morris** . . . . (801) 963-3329
E-mail: layne.morris@wvc-ut.gov
Administrative Assistant **Jennifer Siebach** . . . . (801) 963-3420
E-mail: jennifer.siebach@wvc-ut.gov

Housing Authority
3600 Constitution Boulevard, West Valley City, UT 84119
Tel: (801) 963-3320 Fax: (801) 963-3518

Assistant Grants Administrator **Heather Royall** . . . . (801) 963-3280
Assistant Housing Administrator **Cheryl Syme** . . . . (801) 963-3524

Animal Services
4522 West 3500 South, West Valley City, UT 84120
Tel: (801) 965-5800

Animal Services Director **Chris Curtis** . . . . (801) 965-3364
Animal Services Field Supervisor **Nathan Beckstead** . . . . (801) 965-5806

Finance Department
3600 South Constitution Blvd., West Valley City, UT 84119-3720
Tel: (801) 963-3238 Fax: (801) 963-3365

Director of Finance **James D. Welch** . . . . (801) 963-3238

Fire Department
City Hall, 3600 South Constitution Blvd., West Valley City, UT 84119

Fire Chief **John Evans** . . . . (801) 963-3336
E-mail: john.evans@wvc-ut.gov
Deputy Fire Chief **(Vacant)** . . . . (801) 963-3336
Fire Marshal **Bob Fitzgerald** . . . . (801) 963-3336
E-mail: bfitzgerald@wvc-ut.gov

Parks and Recreation Department
5415 West 3100 South, West Valley City, UT 84120

Director **Kevin Astill** . . . . (801) 955-4000
Assistant to the Director **Nancy Day** . . . . (801) 955-4000
Harman Home Director **Zenda Rogers** . . . . (801) 965-5822
Golf Pro **Mike Richards** . . . . (801) 963-3387

Police Department
City Hall, 3600 South Constitution Blvd., West Valley City, UT 84119

Chief of Police **Lee Russo** . . . . (801) 963-3300
Patrol Division **Capt. Anita Schwemmer** . . . . (801) 963-3300

Public Works Department
City Hall, 3600 South Constitution Blvd., Ste. 280,
West Valley City, UT 84119

Director **Russ Willardson** . . . . (801) 963-3448
City Engineer **Daniel Johnson** . . . . (801) 963-3318
E-mail: daniel.johnson@wvc-ut.gov
Sanitation Coordinator **Jeff Nosack** . . . . (801) 955-3720

City of Westminster, Colorado

4800 West 92nd Avenue, Westminster, CO 80031
Internet: www.cityofwestminster.us

County: Adams; Jefferson **Charter:** 1958 **Population:** 113,130 (2015)

Office of the Mayor and City Council
4800 West 92nd Avenue, Westminster, CO 80031

★ Mayor **Herb Atchison** . . . . (303) 658-2006
Began Service: November 11, 2013
Term Expires: November 2017
E-mail: herb.atchison@netzero.com
★ Mayor Pro Tem **Alberto Garcia** . . . . (303) 658-2006
Term Expires: November 2017
★ Councillor **Bruce Baker** . . . . (303) 658-2006
Term Expires: November 2017
★ Councillor **Shannon Bird** . . . . (303) 658-2006
Term Expires: November 2019
Education: Colorado; Colorado (Denver) MBA, MS; Denver JD
★ Councillor **Maria De Cambra** . . . . (303) 658-2006
Term Expires: November 2019
Education: Ohio State BA
★ Councillor **Emma Pinter** . . . . (303) 658-2006
Term Expires: November 2017
★ Councillor **Anita Seitz** . . . . (303) 658-2006
Term Expires: November 4, 2019

Office of the City Manager
4800 West 92nd Ave., Westminster, CO 80031
Fax: (303) 706-3921

City Manager **Donald Tripp** . . . . (303) 658-2006
E-mail: dtripp@cityofwestminster.us
Deputy City Manager **Jody Andrews** . . . . (303) 658-2006
E-mail: jandrews@cityofwestminster.us
Deputy City Manager **Steve Smithers** . . . . (303) 658-2006
E-mail: ssmithers@ci.westminster.co.us

★ Elected Official ▲ Appointed by Legislature ▼ Appointed by Governor ▶ Appointed by Board or Commission ● Appointed by Judge
■ Appointed by Mayor △ Appointed by Freeholders ▽ Appointed by Supervisor ▷ Appointed by County Executive ○ Appointed by Council

Economic Development Division
E-mail: econdevo@cityofwestminster.us

Manager **John Hall** . . . . . (303) 658-2113
E-mail: jhall@ci.westminster.co.us

Office of the City Attorney
Fax: (303) 650-0158 E-mail: caoadminstaff@cityofwestminster.us

City Attorney **David Frankel** . . . . . (303) 658-2231
E-mail: dfrankel@cityofwestminster.us

Community Development Department
4800 West 92nd Avenue, Westminster, CO 80031

Director **John Carpenter** . . . . . (303) 658-2121
E-mail: jcarpenter@cityofwestminster.us

Building Division
Chief Building Official **Dave Horras** . . . . . (303) 658-2077

Engineering Division
City Engineer **Dave Downing** . . . . . (303) 658-2116
E-mail: ddowning@cityofwestminster.us

Housing Assistance Programs
Community Development Programs Coordinator
Heather Ruddy . . . . . (303) 658-2111
E-mail: hruddy@cityofwestminster.us

Planning Division
Manager **Mac Cummins** . . . . . (303) 658-2093

Finance Department
4800 West 92nd Avenue, Westminster, CO 80031
Tel: (303) 430-2041 ext. 2041

Finance Director **Tammy Hitchens** . . . . . (303) 658-2036

Fire Department
Westminster Public Safety Center, 9110 Yates St., Westminster, CO 80031

Fire Chief **Doug Hall** . . . . . (303) 658-4500
E-mail: fire@cityofwestminster.us

General Services Department
4800 West 92nd Avenue, Westminster, CO 80031
Tel: (303) 658-2150

Director **Debbie Mitchell** . . . . . (303) 658-2360
E-mail: dmitchell@cityofwestminster.us

Office of the City Clerk
City Clerk **Linda Yeager** . . . . . (303) 658-2161

Building Operations and Maintenance Division
Facilities Manager **Mark Ruse** . . . . . (303) 658-2449
E-mail: bo&m@cityofwestminster.us

Fleet Maintenance Division
Municipal Service Center, 6405 West 88th Ave., Westminster, CO 80031

Fleet Manager **Jeff Bowman** . . . . . (303) 658-2511

Human Resources Division
Employee Development and Benefits Manager
Lisa Chrisman . . . . . (303) 658-2151
E-mail: lchrisman@ci.westminster.co.us

Workforce Planning and Compensation Manager
Dee Martin . . . . . (303) 658-2154
E-mail: dmartin@ci.westminster.co.us

Risk Manager **Martee Erichson** . . . . . (303) 658-2156
E-mail: merichson@ci.westminster.co.us

Municipal Court Division
3030 Turnpike Drive, Westminster, CO 80030
E-mail: municipalcourtfunctions@cityofwestminster.us

Court Administrator **Patricia Kmitta** . . . . . (303) 658-2241

Municipal Court Division *continued*
Presiding Judge **John A. Stipech** . . . . . (303) 658-2240

Parks, Recreation and Libraries Department
4800 West 92nd Avenue, Westminster, CO 80031
E-mail: prl@cityofwestminster.us

Administrative Division Director **Jason Genck** . . . . . (303) 658-2198
Library Services Division Manager **Kate Skarbek** . . . . . (303) 658-2640
3705 West 112th Avenue, Westminster, CO 80031
E-mail: kskarbek@ci.westminster.co.us
Park Services Division Manager **Lance Johnson** . . . . . (303) 658-2854

Police Department
Westminster Public Safety Center, 9110 Yates Street, Westminster, CO 80031
Fax: (303) 487-4181 E-mail: police@cityofwestminster.us

Chief of Police **Lee Birk** . . . . . (303) 658-4200

Deputy Chief, Investigations and Technical Services
Mike Cressman . . . . . (303) 658-4221
Fax: (303) 487-4154

Deputy Chief, Patrol, Traffic and Special Operations
Tim Carlson . . . . . (303) 658-4281
Fax: (303) 487-1129

Public Works and Utilities Department
4800 West 92nd Avenue, Westminster, CO 80031

Director of Public Works **Max Kirschbaum** . . . . . (303) 658-2175
Street Operations Division Manager **Dave Cantu** . . . . . (303) 658-2501
6575 West 88th Avenue, Westminster, CO 80031
E-mail: streets@cityofwestminster.us
Utilities Operations Division Manager **Stephen Gay** . . . . . (303) 658-2500
6575 West 88th Avenue, Westminster, CO 80031
E-mail: utilops@cityofwestminster.us
Water Resources and Treatment Division Manager
Mike Happe . . . . . (303) 658-2176

City of Wichita Falls, Texas
1300 7th Street, Wichita Falls, TX 76301
Internet: www.wichitafallstx.gov/

County: Wichita **Election Type:** Nonpartisan **Year Founded:** 1882
Population: 104,710 (2015)

Office of the Mayor and City Council
1300 7th St., Wichita Falls, TX 76301
Fax: (940) 761-8833

★ Mayor **Glenn Barham** . . . . . (940) 761-7404
Began Service: May 11, 2010
Term Expires: November 8, 2016
E-mail: glenn.barham@wichitafallstx.gov

★ Council Member **Stephen Santellana** (District 1) . . . . . (940) 761-7404
Term Expires: November 7, 2017

★ Council Member **DeAndra Chenault** (District 2) . . . . . (940) 761-7404
Term Expires: November 7, 2017

★ Council Member **Brian Hooker** (District 3) . . . . . (940) 761-7404
Term Expires: November 8, 2016
E-mail: brian.hooker@wichitafallstx.gov

★ Council Member **Timothy Ingle** (District 4) . . . . . (940) 761-7404
Term Expires: November 8, 2016
E-mail: tim.ingle@wichitafallstx.gov

★ Council Member **Tom Quintero** (District 5) . . . . . (940) 761-7404
Term Expires: November 8, 2016
E-mail: tom.quintero@wichitafallstx.gov

★ Council Member **Michael Smith** (At-Large) . . . . . (940) 761-7404
Term Expires: November 7, 2017
E-mail: michael.smith@wichitafallstx.gov

★ Elected Official ▲ Appointed by Legislature ▼ Appointed by Governor ▶ Appointed by Board or Commission ● Appointed by Judge
■ Appointed by Mayor △ Appointed by Freeholders ▽ Appointed by Supervisor ▷ Appointed by County Executive ○ Appointed by Council

CITIES AND TOWNS

Office of the City Attorney
1300 7th St., Room 108, Wichita Falls, TX 76301
Fax: (940) 761-7626

City Attorney **Kinley Hegglund** .... (940) 761-7625
E-mail: kinley.hegglund@wichitafallstx.gov

Office of the City Clerk
1300 7th St., Wichita Falls, TX 76301
Fax: (940) 761-7499

City Clerk **Tracy Norr** .... (940) 761-7409
E-mail: tracy.norr@wichitafallstx.gov

Office of the City Manager
1300 7th St., Wichita Falls, TX 76301
Fax: (940) 761-8833

City Manager **Darron Leiker** .... (940) 761-7404
E-mail: darron.leiker@wichitafallstx.gov

Aviation, Traffic and Transportation
2100 Seymour Hwy., Wichita Falls, TX 76301
Fax: (940) 761-7949

Director **John Burrus** .... (940) 761-7640

Fire Department
1005 Bluff St., Wichita Falls, TX 76301
Fax: (940) 761-7900

Fire Chief **Jon Reese** .... (940) 761-7901
E-mail: jon.reese@wichitafallstx.gov

Health Department
1700 3rd St., Wichita Falls, TX 76301
Fax: (940) 767-5242

Director **Lou Kreidler** .... (940) 761-7804

Parks and Recreation
1300 7th St., Wichita Falls, TX 76301
Fax: (940) 767-1090

Director **Jack Murphy** .... (940) 761-7490

Wichita Falls Public Library
600 Eleventh St., Wichita Falls, TX 76301-4604
Fax: (940) 720-6659

Administrator **Lesley Daly** .... (940) 767-0868
E-mail: lesley.daly@wfpl.net

Police Department
610 Holliday, Wichita Falls, TX 76301
Fax: (940) 761-6848

Police Chief **Manuel Borrego** .... (940) 761-7732

Department of Public Works
1300 7th Street, Wichita Falls, TX 76301
Tel: (940) 761-7477 Fax: (940) 761-6873

Director of Public Works **Russell Schreiber** .... (940) 761-7477

Deputy City Manager
1300 7th Street, Wichita Falls, TX 76301

Deputy City Manager **Jim Dockery** .... (940) 761-7404
E-mail: jim.dockery@wichitafallstx.gov

Community Development
1300 7th St., Wichita Falls, TX 76301
Fax: (940) 761-7419

Assistant Director of Community Development
Bob Teague .... (940) 761-7459
E-mail: bobby.teague@wichitafallstx.gov

Finance
1300 7th St., Wichita Falls, TX 76301
Fax: (940) 761-7470

Finance Director **Patrick Halverson** .... (940) 761-7462

Human Resources Department
1300 7th Street, Suite 100, Wichita Falls, TX 76301
Fax: (940) 761-7613
Internet: http://www.wichitafallstx.gov/index.aspx?nid=18

Manager **Christi Klyn** .... (940) 761-7633
E-mail: christi.klyn@wichitafallstx.gov

Building Maintenance
1300 7th St., Wichita Falls, TX 76301
Fax: (940) 761-8870

Manager **Rodney Busby** .... (940) 761-8820

Public Information Office
1300 7th St., Room 109, Wichita Falls, TX 76301
Fax: (940) 761-7486

Communications Specialist **Barry Levy** .... (940) 761-7406
E-mail: barry.levy@wichitafallstx.gov
Audio Visual Producer **Eric Crosslin** .... (940) 761-7402
E-mail: eric.crosslin@wichitafallstx.gov

City of Wichita, Kansas
City Hall, 455 N. Main St., Wichita, KS 67202
Internet: www.wichita.gov

County: Sedgwick **Election Type:** Nonpartisan **Population:** 389,965 (2015)

Office of the Mayor and City Council
City Hall, 455 North Main Street, 1st Floor, Wichita, KS 67202
Fax: (316) 858-7743 Internet: www.wichita.gov/Government/CityCouncil/

★ Mayor **Jeff Longwell** .... (316) 268-4331
Began Service: April 14, 2015
Term Expires: April 2019
E-mail: jlongwell@wichita.gov
★ Vice Mayor **James Clendenin** (District 3) .... (316) 268-4331
Term Expires: April 10, 2017
★ Council Member **Lavonta K. Williams** (District 1) .... (316) 268-4331
Term Expires: April 14, 2017
E-mail: lkwilliams@wichita.gov
★ Council Member **Pete Meitzner** (District 2) .... (316) 268-4331
Term Expires: April 10, 2019
E-mail: pmeitzner@wichita.gov
★ Council Member **Jeff Blubaugh** (District 4) .... (316) 268-4331
Term Expires: April 10, 2019
★ Council Member **Bryan Frye** (District 5) .... (316) 268-4331
Term Expires: April 10, 2019
★ Council Member **Janet Miller** (District 6) .... (316) 268-4331
Term Expires: April 14, 2017
E-mail: jmiller@wichita.gov

Office of the City Manager
City Hall, 455 North Main Street, 13th Floor, Wichita, KS 67202
Fax: (316) 858-7712

City Manager **Robert Layton** .... (316) 268-4351
E-mail: rlayton@wichita.gov
Education: Drake BA; Syracuse MPA
Assistant City Manager **Catherine Holdeman** .... (316) 268-4351
E-mail: choldeman@wichita.gov
Assistant City Manager and Director of Development
Scott Rigby .... (316) 268-4351
Education: BYU BA; Arizona State 2003 MPA

★ Elected Official ▲ Appointed by Legislature ▼ Appointed by Governor ▶ Appointed by Board or Commission ● Appointed by Judge
■ Appointed by Mayor △ Appointed by Freeholders ▽ Appointed by Supervisor ▷ Appointed by County Executive ○ Appointed by Council

Century II/Expo Hall
225 W. Douglas, Wichita, KS 67202
Fax: (316) 268-9268

Manager **John D'Angelo** .... (316) 303-8600

Human Resources Department
City Hall, 2nd Fl., 455 N. Main St., Wichita, KS 67202
Fax: (316) 268-4286

Director **Chris Bezruki** .... (316) 268-4531
E-mail: cbezruki@wichita.gov

Information Technology
City Hall, 455 North Main Street, 9th Floor, Wichita, KS 67202
Fax: (316) 858-7550

Director **Mike Mayta** .... (316) 268-4318
E-mail: mmayta@wichita.gov

Intergovernmental Relations
Manager **Dale Goter** .... (316) 268-4351
E-mail: dgoter@wichita.gov

Internal Audit Office
Internal Auditor **Laurie Wolf** .... (316) 268-4351
Education: Emporia State BS

Communications Division
Strategic Communications Director **Ken Evans** .... (316) 268-4351
Public Information Officer **Van Williams** .... (316) 268-4351
E-mail: vwilliams@wichita.gov

Office of Urban Development
City Hall, 455 North Main Street, 13th Floor, Wichita, KS 67202
Fax: (316) 268-4656 Internet: www.wichita.gov/CityOffices/Urban/

Economic Development Director **Allen Bell** .... (316) 268-4524
E-mail: abell@wichita.gov

Finance Department
City Hall, 12th Fl., 455 N. Main St., Wichita, KS 67202
Fax: (316) 268-4656

Director **Shawn Henning** .... (316) 268-4300
Program Manager **Rob Raine** .... (316) 268-4324
City Controller **Michelle Law** .... (316) 268-4651
E-mail: mnlaw@wichita.gov
City Treasurer (Interim) **Rob Raine** .... (316) 268-4324
Budget Officer **Mark Manning** .... (316) 268-4145
E-mail: mmanning@wichita.gov
Purchasing Manager **Melinda Walker** .... (316) 268-4636
E-mail: mwalker@wichita.gov

Fire Department
City Hall, 11th Fl., 455 N. Main St., Wichita, KS 67202
Fax: (316) 858-7702

Fire Chief **Ronald D. Blackwell** .... (316) 268-4451
E-mail: rblackwell@wichita.gov
Operations Deputy Fire Chief **Elizabeth Snow** .... (316) 268-4451
E-mail: esnow@wichita.gov
Support Services Deputy Fire Chief **Ronald L. Aaron** .... (316) 268-4451
E-mail: raaron@wichita.gov
Division Chief of Training and Safety **Mark Hahn** .... (316) 268-4451
Fire Marshal **Brad Crisp** .... (316) 268-4451
E-mail: bcrisp@wichita.gov

Housing and Community Services Department
332 N. Riverview Street, Wichita, KS 67203
Fax: (316) 462-3719

Director **Mary K. Vaughn** .... (316) 462-3700
E-mail: mkvaughn@wichita.gov
Assistant Director **Brad Snapp** .... (316) 462-3700
E-mail: bsnapp@wichita.gov

Department of Law
City Hall, 13th Fl., 455 N. Main St., Wichita, KS 67202
Fax: (316) 268-4335

City Attorney **Jennifer Magana** .... (316) 268-4681 ext. 4
E-mail: jmagana@wichita.gov
Education: Arkansas State 1990 BA; Kansas 1992 JD
Deputy City Attorney **Jay Hinkel** .... (316) 268-4681 ext. 3
E-mail: jhinkel@wichita.gov
Deputy City Attorney **Brian McLeod** .... (316) 268-4681 ext. 9
E-mail: bmcleod@wichita.gov

Wichita Public Library
223 S. Main St., Wichita, KS 67202
Fax: (316) 262-4540 Internet: http://www.wichita.lib.ks.us

Director of Libraries **Cynthia Berner** .... (316) 261-8500
E-mail: admin@wichita.lib.ks.us

Park and Recreation Department
City Hall, 11th Fl., 455 N. Main St., Wichita, KS 67202-1690
Fax: (316) 858-7768

Director **Troy Houtman** .... (316) 268-4628
Recreation Superintendent **Greg Olmer** .... (316) 268-4130
Forestry and Maintenance Superintendent
David McGuire .... (316) 268-4361
Marketing and Development Manager **Stacey Hamm** .... (316) 268-4124

Police Department
City Hall, 4th Fl., 455 N. Main St., Wichita, KS 67202-1679
Fax: (316) 858-7704 Internet: www.wichitapolice.com

Police Chief **Gordon Ramsay** .... (316) 268-4158
Education: Minnesota (Duluth) BA; Col St Scholastica MA
Field Services Deputy Chief **Gavin Seiler** .... (316) 268-4239
Investigations Deputy Chief **Hassan Ramzah** .... (316) 268-4270
Support Services Deputy Chief **Troy Livingston** .... (316) 268-4165
Information Services Officer **Mike Leiber** .... (316) 268-4149
E-mail: mleiber@wichita.gov

Public Works and Utilities Department
City Hall, 8th Fl., 455 N. Main St., Wichita, KS 67202-1685
Fax: (316) 337-9027

Director **Alan King** .... (316) 268-4422
Assistant Director, Environment **Don Henry** .... (316) 268-4422
Assistant Director, Maintenance **Joseph T. Pajor** .... (316) 268-4422
City Engineer **Gary Janzen** .... (316) 268-4266
E-mail: gjanzen@wichita.gov
Maintenance Engineer **Aaron Henning** .... (316) 268-4081
Storm Water Utility Engineer (Interim) **Joe Hickle** .... (316) 268-4624
E-mail: jhickle@wichita.gov
Fleet Manager **Jay Newton** .... (316) 268-4016
Water Distribution Superintendent **Elizabeth Owens** .... (316) 268-4578
Sewer Maintenance Superintendent **Bill Perkins** .... (316) 268-4073
Sewage Treatment Superintendent **Becky Lewis** .... (316) 303-8702

Metropolitan Transit Authority
777 East Waterman, Wichita, KS 67202

General Manager **Stephen "Steve" Spade** .... (316) 352-4802

Wichita Mid-Continent Airport
2173 Air Cargo Road, Wichita, KS 67209
Fax: (316) 946-4793 Internet: http://www.flywichita.com

Director of Airports **Victor White** .... (316) 946-4700

Wichita Art Museum
1400 West Museum Boulevard, Wichita, KS 67203
Fax: (316) 268-4980 E-mail: info@wichitaartmuseum.org
Internet: http://wichitaartmuseum.org

Director **Patricia McDonnell** .... (316) 268-4921

★ Elected Official ▲ Appointed by Legislature ▼ Appointed by Governor ▶ Appointed by Board or Commission ● Appointed by Judge
■ Appointed by Mayor △ Appointed by Freeholders ▽ Appointed by Supervisor ▷ Appointed by County Executive ○ Appointed by Council

Wichita Public Schools
Alvin Morris Administrative Center, 201 North Water Street, Wichita, KS 67202
Fax: (316) 973-4595 Internet: www.usd259.org

Superintendent **John Allison** . . . . (316) 973-4580
Education: Kansas BS; Emporia State MS

City of Wilmington, North Carolina

102 North Third Street, Wilmington, NC 28401
Tel: (910) 341-7800 Internet: www.wilmingtonnc.gov

County: New Hanover **Election Type:** Nonpartisan **Year Incorporated:** 1739 **Population:** 115,933 (2015)

Office of the Mayor and City Council
102 North Third Street, Wilmington, NC 28401
Tel: (910) 341-7815 Fax: (910) 341-4628
E-mail: council@wilmingtonnc.gov

★ Mayor **Bill Saffo** . . . . (910) 341-7815
Began Service: November 2007
Term Expires: December 2017
E-mail: bill.saffo@wilmingtonnc.gov

Executive Staff Assistant **Dawn Grants** . . . . (910) 341-7815
E-mail: dawn.grants@wilmingtonnc.gov

★ Mayor Pro Tem **Margaret Haynes** . . . . (910) 341-7815
Term Expires: December 2019
E-mail: margaret.haynes@wilmingtonnc.gov

★ Council Member **Neil Anderson** . . . . (910) 341-7815
Term Expires: December 2019
E-mail: neil.anderson@wilmingtonnc.gov

★ Council Member **Paul Lawler** . . . . (910) 341-7815
Term Expires: December 2019
E-mail: paul.lawler@wilmingtonnc.gov
Education: North Carolina State 1978 BA

★ Council Member **Kevin O'Grady** . . . . (910) 352-8058
Term Expires: December 2017
E-mail: kevin.ogrady@wilmingtonnc.gov

★ Council Member **Charles H. "Charlie" Rivenbark, Jr.** . . . (910) 791-0400
Term Expires: December 2017
E-mail: charlie.rivenbark@wilmingtonnc.gov

★ Council Member **Earl Sheridan** . . . . (910) 799-5541
Term Expires: December 2017
E-mail: earl.sheridan@wilmingtonnc.gov

Office of the City Manager
102 North Third Street, Wilmington, NC 28401
Tel: (910) 341-7810 Fax: (910) 341-5839

City Manager **Sterling B. Cheatham** . . . . (910) 341-7810
E-mail: sterling.cheatham@wilmingtonnc.gov

Executive Support Specialist **Tracy Corle** . . . . (910) 341-7810
E-mail: tracy.corle@wilmingtonnc.gov

Deputy City Manager **Tony Caudle** . . . . (910) 341-7800
E-mail: tony.caudle@wilmingtonnc.gov

Executive Staff Assistant **Chris Compton** . . . . (910) 341-7800
E-mail: chris.compton@wilmingtonnc.gov

Communications Division
102 North Third Street, Wilmington, NC 28401
Fax: (910) 341-5839

Communications Manager/Public Information Officer **Malissa Talbert** . . . . (910) 342-2736
E-mail: malissa.talbert@wilmingtonnc.gov

Communications Specialist **Rebecca Blue** . . . . (910) 341-0061
E-mail: rebecca.blue@wilmingtonnc.gov

Internal Audit Division
102 North Third Street, Wilmington, NC 28401
Fax: (910) 341-5839

City Auditor **Allison Collins** . . . . (910) 341-5828

Parking Management Division
305 Chestnut Street, 3rd Floor, Wilmington, NC 28401
Fax: (910) 341-3264

Parking Manager **Betty Gurganus** . . . . (910) 342-2786

Administrative Support Assistant **Genna Porter** . . . . (910) 341-0831
E-mail: Genna.Porter@wilmingtonnc.gov

Community Services Department
305 Chestnut Street, Wilmington, NC 28401
Fax: (910) 341-7802

Director **Steve Harrell** . . . . (910) 341-7836
E-mail: steve.harrell@wilmingtonnc.gov

Community Development Division
305 Chestnut Street, Wilmington, NC 28401

Director **Teresa Campo** . . . . (910) 341-3236
E-mail: teresa.campo@wilmingtonnc.gov

Parks and Landscaping Division
1702 Burnett Boulevard, Wilmington, NC 28401
Fax: (910) 341-4663

Superintendent **Ryan O'Reilly** . . . . (910) 342-2795

Recreation Division
301 Willard Street, Wilmington, NC 28401
Tel: (910) 341-7855 Fax: (910) 341-7854

Superintendent (Interim) **Amy Beatty** . . . . (910) 341-4604

Planning, Development, and Transportation Department
305 Chestnut Street, Wilmington, NC 28401
Tel: (910) 341-3258 Fax: (910) 341-7801

Director **Glenn Harbeck** . . . . (910) 341-5808

GIS Planner **Liz Penley** . . . . (910) 341-5893

Planning Division
305 Chestnut Street, Wilmington, NC 28401
Tel: (910) 254-0900 Fax: (910) 341-3264

Planning Manager **Ron Satterfield** . . . . (910) 341-3255

Traffic Engineering Division
206 Operations Center Drive, Wilmington, NC 28412
Tel: (910) 341-7888 Fax: (910) 341-7801

Manager **Don Bennett** . . . . (910) 341-4696
E-mail: don.bennett@wilmingtonnc.gov

Finance Department
305 Chestnut Street, Wilmington, NC 28401
Tel: (910) 341-7822 Fax: (910) 254-0906
Internet: www.wilmingtonnc.gov/finance.aspx

Director **Debra Mack** . . . . (910) 341-7822

Assistant Finance Director/Controller **Stephanie Jacobs** . . . . (910) 341-7822

Assistant Finance Director/Treasurer **Byron Dorey** . . . . (910) 341-7822

Budget Director **Lynn Heim** . . . . (910) 341-5886
E-mail: lynn.heim@wilmingtonnc.gov

Fleet Manager **John Fortuin** . . . . (910) 341-7812

Purchasing Manager **Daryle Parker** . . . . (910) 342-2735
E-mail: daryle.parker@wilmingtonnc.gov

★ Elected Official ▲ Appointed by Legislature ▼ Appointed by Governor ▶ Appointed by Board or Commission ● Appointed by Judge
■ Appointed by Mayor △ Appointed by Freeholders ▽ Appointed by Supervisor ▷ Appointed by County Executive ○ Appointed by Council

Fire Department
801 Market Street, Wilmington, NC 28401
Tel: (910) 341-7846 Fax: (910) 343-4772
Internet: www.wilmingtonnc.gov/fire_department.aspx

Fire Chief **Cecil V. "Buddy" Martinette** . . . . (910) 341-7846
E-mail: buddy.martinette@wilmingtonnc.gov

Human Resources Department
305 Chestnut Street, Wilmington, NC 28401
Tel: (910) 341-7840 Fax: (910) 341-5841
Internet: www.wilmingtonnc.gov/human_resources.aspx

Director **Jeanne Sexton** . . . . (910) 341-5842
E-mail: jeanne.sexton@wilmingtonnc.gov

Information Technology Department
305 Chestnut Street, Wilmington, NC 28401
Fax: (910) 341-4624

Director **Keith Green** . . . . (910) 341-5848
E-mail: keith.green@wilmingtonnc.gov

Police Department
615 Bess Street, Wilmington, NC 28402
Internet: http://www.wilmingtonnc.gov/police_department

Chief of Police **Ralph Evangelous** . . . . (910) 343-3610

Public Services Department
209 Coleman Drive, Wilmington, NC 28412
Tel: (910) 343-4777 Fax: (910) 341-0099
Internet: http://www.wilmingtonnc.gov/public_services

Director **Richard King** . . . . (910) 343-4777

Solid Waste Division
209 Coleman Drive, Wilmington, NC 28412

Superintendent **Dave Bundick** . . . . (910) 341-0081

Engineering Division
209 Coleman Drive, Wilmington, NC 28412

City Engineer **David Cowell** . . . . (910) 341-5879
E-mail: david.cowell@wilmingtonnc.gov

Buildings Management Division
209 Coleman Drive, Wilmington, NC 28412

Facilities Manager **Donald McLamb** . . . . (910) 341-7853
E-mail: donald.mclamb@wilmingtonnc.gov

Stormwater Division
209 Coleman Drive, Wilmington, NC 28412
Fax: (910) 341-0099

Manager **Dave Mayes** . . . . (910) 341-5880

Streets Division
209 Coleman Drive, Wilmington, NC 28412

Manager **Jay Carter** . . . . (910) 341-7879

Office of the City Attorney
305 Chestnut Street, 2nd Floor, Annex, Wilmington, NC 28401
Fax: (910) 341-5824 Internet: http://www.wilmingtonnc.gov/city_attorney

City Attorney **William Wolak** . . . . (910) 343-3629
E-mail: bill.wolak@wilmingtonnc.gov

Office of the City Clerk
102 North Third Street, Wilmington, NC 28401
Fax: (910) 341-5823 Internet: http://www.wilmingtonnc.gov/city_clerk

○ City Clerk **Penny Spicer-Sidbury** . . . . (910) 341-7816
E-mail: penny.spicer-sidbury@wilmingtonnc.gov

Office of the City Clerk *continued*

Assistant City Clerk **Tracy Manning** . . . . (910) 341-7816
E-mail: tracy.manning@wilmingtonnc.gov

City of Winston-Salem, North Carolina

City Hall, 101 North Main Street, Winston-Salem, NC 27101
P.O. Box 2511, Winston-Salem, NC 27102
Tel: (336) 727-8000 (Information) Internet: www.cityofws.org

County: Forsyth **Election Type:** Partisan **Population:** 241,218 (2015)

Allen Joines (D)
Mayor

Began Service: 2001
Term Expires: December 5, 2016
Education: Appalachian State 1969 BS; Georgia MPA
Career: Deputy City Manager, City of Winston-Salem, North Carolina (1992-2000); President, Winston-Salem Alliance, City of Winston-Salem, North Carolina (2001-2002)

Office of the Mayor and City Council
City Hall, 101 North Main Street, Suite 150, Winston-Salem, NC 27101

★ Mayor **Allen Joines** (D) . . . . (336) 727-2058
E-mail: allenj@cityofws.org Fax: (336) 748-3241
Assistant **Linda Jackson-Barnes** . . . . (336) 727-2058

★ Mayor Pro Tem **Vivian H. Burke** (D) . . . . (336) 727-2224
Term Expires: December 5, 2016
E-mail: vivianb@cityofws.org

★ Council Member **Denise D. Adams** (D) . . . . (336) 727-2224
Term Expires: December 5, 2016
E-mail: denisea@cityofws.org

★ Council Member **Dan Besse** (D) . . . . (336) 727-2224
Term Expires: December 5, 2016
E-mail: danbesse@danbesse.org

★ Council Member **Robert C. Clark** (R) . . . . (336) 727-2224
Term Expires: December 5, 2016
E-mail: robertc@cityofws.org

★ Council Member **Molly Leight** (D) . . . . (336) 727-2224
Term Expires: December 5, 2016
E-mail: mollyl@cityofws.org

★ Council Member **Jeff MacIntosh** (D) . . . . (336) 727-2224
Term Expires: December 5, 2016
E-mail: jeffm@cityofws.org

★ Council Member **Derwin L. Montgomery** (D) . . . . (336) 727-2224
Term Expires: December 5, 2016
E-mail: derwinm@cityofws.org

★ Council Member **James Taylor, Jr.** (D) . . . . (336) 727-2224
Term Expires: December 5, 2016
E-mail: jamestjr@cityofws.org

Office of the City Attorney
City Hall, 101 North Main Street, Winston-Salem, NC 27101
Fax: (336) 727-3816

▶ City Attorney **Angela I. Carmon** . . . . (336) 747-7404
E-mail: angelac@cityofws.org
Education: Howard U BA; North Carolina JD

★ Elected Official ▲ Appointed by Legislature ▼ Appointed by Governor ▶ Appointed by Board or Commission ● Appointed by Judge
■ Appointed by Mayor △ Appointed by Freeholders ▽ Appointed by Supervisor ▷ Appointed by County Executive ○ Appointed by Council

Office of the City Manager
City Hall, 101 North Main Street, Winston-Salem, NC 27101
Fax: (336) 748-3060

▶ City Manager **Lee Garrity** . . . . . . (336) 747-7380
E-mail: leeg@cityofws.org
Education: George Mason 1983 BS, 1990 MPA

Assistant Manager **Derwick Paige** . . . . . . (336) 747-7473
E-mail: derwickp@cityofws.org

Assistant City Manager **Gregory Turner** . . . . . . (336) 747-6866
E-mail: gregt@cityofws.org

Office of the City Secretary
City Hall, 101 North Main Street, Winston-Salem, NC 27101
Fax: (336) 727-2880

City Secretary **Renée L. Phillips** . . . . . . (336) 727-2224

Deputy Secretary **Melanie Johnson** . . . . . . (336) 727-2224
E-mail: melaniej@cityofws.org

Black-Phillips-Smith Neighborhood Center
2301 N. Patterson Ave., Winston-Salem, NC 27105
Fax: (336) 748-9388

Assistant Director **(Vacant)** . . . . . . (336) 734-1211

Budget and Evaluation Department
City Hall, 101 North Main Street, Winston-Salem, NC 27101
Fax: (336) 734-1224 Internet: www.cityofws.org/departments/budget

Director **Trevor Minor** . . . . . . (336) 747-7090
E-mail: trevorm@cityofws.org

Lawrence Joel Veterans Memorial Coliseum
2825 University Pkwy., Winston-Salem, NC 27105
Tel: (336) 774-8880 Fax: (336) 727-2922 Internet: www.ljvm.com

Administrative Assistant **Cary Hester** . . . . . . (336) 724-1569
E-mail: caryh@cityofws.org

Dixie Classic Fair
421 West 27th Street, Winston-Salem, NC 27102
Fax: (336) 727-2799 E-mail: feedback@dcfair.com
Internet: www.dcfair.com

Director **David L. Sparks** . . . . . . (336) 727-2236

Emergency Management Department
Smith-Reynolds Airport, Room 104, Winston-Salem, NC 27105
Fax: (336) 727-2200

Director **Melton J. Sadler** . . . . . . (336) 661-6440
E-mail: meltons@cityofws.org

Hazardous Materials Coordinator **Robert Reece** . . . . . . (336) 661-6440
E-mail: rreece@cityofwsfire.org

Emergency Management Officer (Logistics and Public Education) **Michelle Brock** . . . . . . (336) 661-6440
E-mail: michelleb@cityofwsfire.org

Emergency Management Officer (Plans and Operations) **Leigha Cordell** . . . . . . (336) 661-6440
E-mail: leighac@cityofwsfire.org

Finance Department
City Hall, 101 North Main Street, Winston-Salem, NC 27101
Fax: (336) 727-2566 E-mail: financeinfo@cityofws.org

Chief Financial Officer **Lisa Saunders** . . . . . . (336) 747-6911
E-mail: lisas@cityofws.org

Assistant Financial Officer **Donna Hull** . . . . . . (336) 747-6903
E-mail: donnah@cityofws.org

Fire Department
725 N. Cherry St., Winston-Salem, NC 27101
Fax: (336) 773-7974 Internet: www.cityofws.org/departments/fire

Fire Chief **William "Trey" Mayo** . . . . . . (336) 773-7979
E-mail: williamm@cityofws.org

Assistant Fire Chief **Harry Brown** . . . . . . (336) 773-7963
E-mail: harryb@cityofwsfire.org

Property and Facilities Management
City Hall, 101 North Main Street, Winston-Salem, NC 27101

Director **James Mitchell** . . . . . . (336) 747-7366
E-mail: jamestm@cityofws.org

Fleet Services Manager **James Mitchell** . . . . . . (336) 747-7366
Building 3, 650 Stadium Drive, Fax: (336) 747-8431
Winston-Salem, NC 27101
E-mail: jamestm@cityofws.org

Central Warehouse Supervisor **Shanita Wright** . . . . . . (336) 734-1523
E-mail: shanitaw@cityofws.org

Building Maintenance Supervisor **Chris Stewart** . . . . . . (336) 727-8260
E-mail: chriss@cityofws.org

Community and Business Development Department
100 East First Street, Winston-Salem, NC 27101
Fax: (336) 727-2878

Director **D. Ritchie Brooks** . . . . . . (336) 734-1250

Housing Development Division
100 East First Street, Winston-Salem, NC 27102
Fax: (336) 727-2878

Director **Mellin Parker** . . . . . . (336) 734-1310
E-mail: mellinp@cityofws.org

Human Relations Department
101 North Main Street, Winston-Salem, NC 27101
Fax: (336) 748-3002

Director **Wanda E. Allen-Abraha** . . . . . . (336) 727-1226

Human Resources
100 East First Street, Suite 131, Winston-Salem, NC 27101
Fax: (336) 748-3053 Internet: http://www.cityofws.org/hr

Director **Carmen Caruth** . . . . . . (336) 747-6802
E-mail: carmenc@cityofws.org

Information Systems
100 East First Street, Suite 520, Winston-Salem, NC 27101
Fax: (336) 727-2874

Chief Information Officer (Interim) **Tom Kureczka** . . . . . . (336) 747-7005
E-mail: tomk@cityofws.org

Infrastructure Services Coordinator **Todd Porter** . . . . . . (336) 747-7006
E-mail: toddp@cityofws.org

Internal Auditing
City Hall, 101 North Main Street, Winston-Salem, NC 27101
Fax: (336) 727-2878

Special Projects Coordinator **H.P. Higgins** . . . . . . (336) 734-1203

Marketing and Communications Department
City Hall, 101 North Main Street, Winston-Salem, NC 27101
Fax: (336) 748-3237

Director **Eddie McNeal** . . . . . . (336) 747-7361

★ Elected Official ▲ Appointed by Legislature ▼ Appointed by Governor ▶ Appointed by Board or Commission ● Appointed by Judge
■ Appointed by Mayor △ Appointed by Freeholders ▽ Appointed by Supervisor ▷ Appointed by County Executive ○ Appointed by Council

Minority/Women's Business Enterprise Program [M/WBE]

City Hall, 101 North Main Street, Winston-Salem, NC 27101
Fax: (336) 748-3819

Coordinator **Tiesha Hinton** .... (336) 734-1262

City-County Planning and Development Services Department

City Hall, 100 East First Street, Room 201, Winston-Salem, NC 27101
Fax: (336) 748-3163 E-mail: planning@cityofws.org

Director **A. Paul Norby** .... (336) 747-7061
Deputy Director **Chris Murphy** .... (336) 747-7049

Police Department

725 N. Cherry St., Winston-Salem, NC 27101
Fax: (336) 773-7996

Police Chief **Barry Rountree** .... (336) 773-7760
Public Safety Attorney/Assistant City Attorney
Lori Sykes .... (336) 773-7764
Public Safety Communications Director **Rebecca Boles** .. (336) 773-7866
E-mail: rboles@wspd.org
Assistant Police Chief, Field Services Bureau
Wilson S. Weaver II .... (336) 773-7755
Education: Gardner-Webb BS; Appalachian State MPA
Assistant Police Chief, Investigative Services Bureau
Catrina A. Thompson .... (336) 773-7709
Assistant Police Chief, Support Services Bureau
Scott Bricker .... (336) 773-7863

Public Works Department

City Hall, 101 North Main Street, Winston-Salem, NC 27101
Fax: (336) 727-2361

Director and Assistant City Manager **Gregory Turner** .... (336) 747-6866
E-mail: gregt@cityofws.org
Sanitation Director **Johnnie F. Taylor** .... (336) 747-6986

Streets Division

Fax: (336) 727-8169

Assistant Director of Transportation **Myra Stafford** ...... (336) 734-1550

Utilities Division

Internet: www.cityofws.org/departments/utilities

Director **Ron Hargrove** .... (336) 727-7312
Fax: (336) 727-8432
Deputy Director **(Vacant)** .... (336) 747-7315
Cemeteries Superintendent **Scotty Speas** .... (336) 747-8877
Capital Project Engineer **Mike Patton** .... (336) 771-5121
E-mail: mikep@cityofws.org

Engineering Division

Internet: www.cityofws.org/departments/engineering

City Engineer **Robert J. Prestwood** .... (336) 747-6985
E-mail: robertp@cityofws.org

Purchasing Department, City/County

City Hall, 101 North Main Street, Winston-Salem, NC 27101
Fax: (336) 727-2443

Director **Jerry Bates** .... (336) 747-6939
E-mail: jerryjb@cityofws.org

Real Estate Office

100 East First Street, Winston-Salem, NC 27101
Fax: (336) 727-2878

Administrator **Kirk Bjorling** .... (336) 734-1291

Recreation and Parks Department

100 East First Street, Suite 407, Winston-Salem, NC 27101
Fax: (336) 727-2066 Internet: http://www.cityofws.org/recreation

Director **Timothy A. Grant** .... (336) 734-1210

Risk Management

City Hall, 101 North Main Street, Winston-Salem, NC 27101
Fax: (336) 727-8299

Administrator **Anthony "Tony" Baker** .... (336) 734-1320
E-mail: anthonyb@cityofws.org

Transportation Department

City Hall, 100 East First Street, Room 307, Winston-Salem, NC 27101
P.O. Box 2511, Winston-Salem, NC 27102
Fax: (336) 748-3370
Internet: www.cityofws.org/departments/transportation

Director **Toneq McCullough** .... (336) 747-6867
Deputy Director **Connie James** .... (336) 747-6872
Transit Authority General Manager **Arthur Barnes** ...... (336) 727-2648
Fax: (336) 727-8106
Traffic Maintenance Supervisor **Dale Hester** .... (336) 727-8202

TV 13

City Hall, 101 North Main Street, Winston-Salem, NC 27101
Fax: (336) 748-3237

Manager **Eddie McNeal** .... (336) 747-7361

City of Worcester, Massachusetts

City Hall, 455 Main St., Worcester, MA 01608
Internet: www.worcesterma.gov

County: Worcester **Election Type:** Partisan **Year Incorporated:** 1722
Population: 184,815 (2015)

Office of the Mayor and City Council

City Hall, 455 Main Street, Room 112, Worcester, MA 01608
Tel: (508) 799-1049 E-mail: council@ci.worcester.ma.us

★Mayor **Joseph M. Petty** (D) .... (508) 799-1153
Began Service: January 2, 2012
Term Expires: January 2018
E-mail: mayor@worcesterma.gov
Education: Nichols BS; New England JD
Chief of Staff **Daniel J. Racicot** .... (508) 799-1153
★Council Member **Tony Economou** (D-District 1) .... (508) 799-1049
Term Expires: January 2018
★Council Member **Candy F. Mero-Carson** (D-District 2) .. (508) 799-1049
Term Expires: January 2018
★Council Member **George Russell** (D-District 3) .... (508) 799-1049
Term Expires: January 2018
★Council Member **Sarai Rivera** (D-District 4) .... (508) 799-1049
Term Expires: January 2018
★Council Member **Gary Rosen** (D-District 5) .... (508) 799-1049
Term Expires: January 2018
Education: Worcester Polytech BS; Worcester State Col MA
★Council Member **Morris A. Bergman** (I-At-Large) .... (508) 799-1049
Term Expires: January 2018
★Council Member **Michael T. Gaffney** (I-At-Large) .... (508) 799-1049
Term Expires: January 2018
★Council Member **Khrystian E. King** (C-At-Large) .... (508) 799-1049
Term Expires: January 2018
★Council Member **Konstantina B. Lukes** (D-At-Large) ... (508) 799-1049
Term Expires: January 2018
E-mail: lukesk@worcesterma.gov
Education: Simmons 1964 BS; Connecticut JD

(continued on next page)

★Elected Official ▲Appointed by Legislature ▼Appointed by Governor ▶Appointed by Board or Commission ●Appointed by Judge
■Appointed by Mayor △Appointed by Freeholders ▽Appointed by Supervisor ▷Appointed by County Executive ○Appointed by Council

Office of the Mayor and City Council *continued*

★ Council Member **Kathleen Toomey** (D-At-Large) . . . . (508) 799-1049
Term Expires: January 2018
E-mail: toomeyk@worcesterma.gov
Education: Regis Col (MA) BA

City Manager's Office

City Hall, 455 Main Streeet, Room 309, Worcester, MA 01608
Fax: (508) 799-1208

City Manager **Edward M. Augustus, Jr.** (D) . . . . (508) 799-1175
E-mail: citymanager@worcesterma.gov
Education: Suffolk 1987 BA; Johns Hopkins MA

City Auditor

City Hall, 455 Main Street, Room 102, Worcester, MA 01608

City Auditor **Robert Stearns** . . . . (508) 799-1053

City Clerk

City Hall, 455 Main Street, Room 206, Worcester, MA 01608

City Clerk **David J. Rushford** . . . . (508) 799-1121
E-mail: clerk@worcesterma.gov

Administration and Finance

City Hall, 455 Main Street, Room 201, Worcester, MA 01608
Fax: (508) 799-1203 Internet: http://www.worcesterma.gov/finance

Chief Financial Officer **Thomas F. Zidelis** . . . . (508) 799-1180

Assessing Division

City Hall, 455 Main Street, Room 209, Worcester, MA 01608

City Assessor **William Ford** . . . . (508) 799-1098
E-mail: assessing@worcesterma.gov

Budget Division

City Hall, 455 Main St., Room 201, Worcester, MA 01608

Director **Jarrett Conner** . . . . (508) 799-1180
E-mail: budget@worcesterma.gov

Purchasing Division

City Hall, 455 Main Street, Room 201, Worcester, MA 01608

Director **Christopher Gagliastro** . . . . (508) 799-1220
E-mail: purchasing@worcesterma.gov

Technical Services Division

Building A, 1 Skyline Drive, Worcester, MA 01605

Chief Information Officer **Paul R. Covello** . . . . (508) 799-1272
E-mail: techservices@worcesterma.gov

Treasurer and Collector of Taxes Division

City Hall, 455 Main Street, Room 203, Worcester, MA 01608

Treasurer **Mariann Castelli Hier** . . . . (508) 799-1095
E-mail: treasurer@worcesterma.gov

Worcester Regional Airport

Worcester Municipal Airport, 375 Airport Dr., Worcester, MA 01602

Airport Director **Andrew B. Davis** . . . . (508) 799-1350

Economic Development Department

44 Front St., Suite 530, Worcester, MA 01608

Chief Development Officer **Michael Traynor** . . . . (508) 799-1400 ext. 240
E-mail: traynorm@wilmingtonde.gov

Neighborhood Development Division

44 Front St., Suite 520, Worcester, MA 01608

Director **Gregory Baker** . . . . (508) 799-1400
E-mail: eons@worcesterma.gov

Elder Affairs and Senior Center

128 Providence St., Worcester, MA 01604

Director **Amy Vogel Waters** . . . . (508) 799-1232

Election Commission

City Hall, 455 Main Street, Room 208, Worcester, MA 01608

Assistant Director of Elections **Nikolin Vangjeli** . . . . (508) 799-1134

Emergency Communications Department

9-11 Lincoln Square, Worcester, MA 01608
Tel: (508) 799-1776 Fax: (508) 799-1718
E-mail: communications@worcesterma.gov

Director **Richard H. Fiske III** . . . . (508) 799-1776

Fire Department

141 Grove St., Worcester, MA 01605

Fire Chief **Gerard A. Dio** . . . . (508) 799-1822
E-mail: wfd@worcesterma.gov

Human Resources Department

City Hall, 455 Main Street, Room 109, Worcester, MA 01608

Director **Kathleen G. Johnson** . . . . (508) 799-1030
E-mail: HR@worcesterma.gov

Human Rights

City Hall, 455 Main Street, Room 303, Worcester, MA 01608

Director **Jayna Turchek** . . . . (508) 799-1152

Inspectional Services

25 Meade Street, Worcester, MA 01610
Fax: (508) 799-1198

Commissioner **John R. Kelly** . . . . (508) 799-1198

Law Department

City Hall, 455 Main Street, Room 301, Worcester, MA 01608

City Solicitor **David M. Moore** . . . . (508) 799-1161
E-mail: law@worcesterma.gov

Worcester Public Library

Salem Square, Worcester, MA 01608

Head Librarian **Geoffrey Dickinson** . . . . (508) 799-1724
E-mail: dickinsong@worcesterma.gov

Police Department

Police Headquarters, 9-11 Lincoln Square, Worcester, MA 01608
E-mail: wpd@worcesterma.gov

Chief of Police **Steven M. Sargent** . . . . (508) 799-8611 ext. 28320
Deputy Chief **Sean J. Fleming** . . . . (508) 799-8611 ext. 28316
Deputy Chief **Edward J. McGinn, Jr.** . . . . (508) 799-8611 ext. 28308
Education: Notre Dame 1981 BA; Duquesne 1984 JD; Temple 1988 LLM
Deputy Chief **Mark Roche** . . . . (508) 799-8611 ext. 28314
Deputy Chief **(Vacant)** . . . . (508) 799-8611 ext. 28320

Public Health

25 Meade Street, Worcester, MA 01610

Medical Director **Michael P. Hirsh** . . . . (508) 799-8531
Director of Public Health **Derek Brindisi** . . . . (508) 799-8531

Public Works and Parks Department

20 E. Worcester St., Worcester, MA 01604
E-mail: dpw@ci.worcester.ma.us

Commissioner **Paul J. Moosey** . . . . (508) 799-1430

★ Elected Official ▲ Appointed by Legislature ▼ Appointed by Governor ▶ Appointed by Board or Commission ● Appointed by Judge
■ Appointed by Mayor △ Appointed by Freeholders ▽ Appointed by Supervisor ▷ Appointed by County Executive ○ Appointed by Council

Public Works and Parks Department *continued*

Engineering Director **Joseph Borbone** . . . . (508) 799-1454
E-mail: borbonej@worcesterma.gov
Trash and Recycling Division Manager
James M. Kempton . . . . (508) 929-1300
Water and Sewer Division Director **Philip D. Guerin** . . . . . (508) 799-1485
E-mail: guerinp@worcesterma.gov

Parks, Recreation and Cemetery Department

50 Skyline Dr., Worcester, MA 01605-2515
Assistant Commissioner **Robert Antonelli** . . . . (508) 799-1190

Veterans' Services

455 Main Street, Room 402, Worcester, MA 01608
Fax: (508) 799-1018
Veterans Agent **(Vacant)** . . . . (508) 799-1041

Worcester Public Schools

20 Irving St., Worcester, MA 01609
Superintendent of Schools (Interim)
Dr. Marco Rodrigues . . . . (508) 799-3115

Workforce Development

44 Front St., Worcester, MA 01608
Director **Jamice Weekes** . . . . (508) 799-1600
E-mail: weekesj@worcesterma.gov
Director **Jeffrey Turgeon** . . . . (508) 799-1600
E-mail: turgeonj@worcesterma.gov

City of Yonkers, New York

City Hall, 40 S. Broadway, Yonkers, NY 10701
Tel: (914) 377-6000 (Information) Internet: www.yonkersny.gov

County: Westchester **Election Type:** Partisan **Population:** 201,116 (2015)

Office of the Mayor

City Hall, 40 S. Broadway, Suite 200, Yonkers, NY 10701
E-mail: cityhall@yonkersny.gov

★ Mayor **Mike Spano** (D) . . . . (914) 377-6300
Began Service: January 1, 2012
Term Expires: December 31, 2019
E-mail: mike.spano@yonkersny.gov
Date of Birth: April 22, 1964

Office of the City Council

City Hall, 40 South Broadway, 4th Floor, Yonkers, NY 10701

★ President **Liam McLaughlin** (R) . . . . (914) 377-6060
Term Expires: December 31, 2017
E-mail: liam.mclaughlin@yonkersny.gov
★ Council Member **Christopher Johnson** (D-District 1) . . . (914) 377-6311
Term Expires: December 31, 2019
E-mail: christopher.johnson@yonkersny.gov
★ Council Member **Corazon Pineda Isaac** (D-District 2) . . . (914) 377-6312
Term Expires: December 31, 2017
E-mail: corazon.pineda.isaac@yonkersny.gov
★ Minority Leader **Michael Sabatino, Jr.** (D-District 3) . . . . (914) 377-6313
Term Expires: December 31, 2019
E-mail: michael.sabatino@yonkersny.gov
Education: St John's U (NY) 1972 BS; Long Island 1979 MS
★ Council Member **Dennis E. Shepherd** (R-District 4) . . . . (914) 377-6314
Term Expires: December 31, 2017
E-mail: dennis.shepherd@yonkersny.gov

Office of the City Council *continued*

★ Council Member **Michael Breen** (R-District 5) . . . . (914) 377-6315
Term Expires: December 31, 2019
E-mail: mike.breen@yonkersny.gov
★ Majority Leader **John J. Larkin** (R-District 6) . . . . (914) 377-6316
Term Expires: December 31, 2017
E-mail: john.larkin@yonkersny.gov

Office of the City Clerk

City Hall, 40 South Broadway, Room 107, Yonkers, NY 10701
Fax: (914) 377-6029

○ City Clerk **Vincent Spano** . . . . (914) 377-6022
E-mail: vincent.spano@yonkersny.gov

Office of Constituent Services

City Hall, 40 South Broadway, Suite 210, Yonkers, NY 10701
Fax: (914) 377-6009

■ Director **Euthimios Theotokatos** . . . . (914) 377-6010
E-mail: Euthimios.Theotokatos@yonkersny.gov
■ Veterans' Services **Louis Navarro** . . . . (914) 377-6700
120 New Main Street, Yonkers, NY 10701 Fax: (914) 377-6703
E-mail: louis.navarro@yonkersny.gov

Office of the Inspector General

40 South Broadway, Yonkers, NY 10701
Tel: (914) 377-6107 Fax: (914) 377-6990
Inspector General **Brendan J. McGrath** . . . . (914) 377-6107

Code Enforcement Bureau

City Hall Annex, 87 Nepperhan Ave., Room 228, Yonkers, NY 10701
Director **Anita Morck** . . . . (914) 377-6610
Fax: (914) 377-6669

Corporation Counsel Department

City Hall, 40 South Broadway, Room 300, Yonkers, NY 10701
Corporation Counsel **Michael Curti** . . . . (914) 377-6250
■ Deputy Corporation Counsel **Karen Ramos** . . . . (914) 377-6250
E-mail: karen.ramos@yonkersny.gov

Engineering Department

City Hall, 40 S. Broadway, Yonkers, NY 10701
Fax: (914) 377-6215

■ City Engineer **Paul Summerfield** . . . . (914) 377-6210
E-mail: paul.summerfield@yonkersny.gov
Traffic Engineering Director **Dominic Micka** . . . . (914) 377-6777
E-mail: dominic.micka@yonkersny.gov

Finance and Management Services Department

City Hall, 40 South Broadway, Yonkers, NY 10701

■ Commissioner **John A. Liszewski** . . . . (914) 377-6160
One Larkin Center, 3rd Floor, Yonkers, NY 10701
E-mail: john.liszewski@yonkersny.gov
■ Budget Director **Andrew Lenney** Room 416 . . . . (914) 377-6103
E-mail: andrew.lenney@yonkersny.gov
■ Payroll Administrator **John Breheny** . . . . (914) 377-6115
One Larkin Center, 3rd Floor, Yonkers, NY 10701
E-mail: john.breheny@yonkersny.gov
■ City Assessor **David B. Jackson** Room 100 . . . . (914) 377-6200
E-mail: david.jackson@yonkersny.gov
Purchasing Director **Thomas Collich** . . . . (914) 377-6035
One Larkin Center, 3rd Floor, Yonkers, NY 10701
E-mail: thomas.collich@yonkersny.gov

Fire Department

470 Nepperhan Avenue, # 201, Yonkers, NY 10701

■ Commissioner **John Darcy** . . . . (914) 377-7500
E-mail: john.darcy@yonkersny.gov

★ Elected Official ▲ Appointed by Legislature ▼ Appointed by Governor ▶ Appointed by Board or Commission ● Appointed by Judge
■ Appointed by Mayor △ Appointed by Freeholders ▽ Appointed by Supervisor ▷ Appointed by County Executive ○ Appointed by Council

Housing and Buildings Department

City Hall Annex, 87 Nepperhan Avenue, Room 500, Yonkers, NY 10701
Tel: (914) 377-6500 Fax: (914) 377-6545

■ Commissioner **William Schneider** .... (914) 377-6544
E-mail: william.schneider@yonkersny.gov
■ Deputy Commissioner **James Flandreau** .... (914) 377-6542

Department of Human Resources

One Larkin Center, 2nd Floor, Yonkers, NY 10701
Tel: (914) 377-6180 Fax: (914) 377-6940

■ Commissioner **Carlos Moran** .... (914) 377-6176
E-mail: carlos.moran@yonkersny.gov
■ Deputy Commissioner (Acting) **Christine Dodge** .... (914) 377-6186
E-mail: christine.dodge@yonkersny.gov

Industrial Development Agency

87 Nepperhan Avenue, 2nd Floor, Yonkers, NY 10701

■ President and Chief Executive Officer **Ken Jenkins** ...... (914) 509-8651
E-mail: info@yonkersida.com Fax: (914) 509-8650

Department of Information Technology

87 Nepperhan Avenue, Suite 120, Yonkers, NY 10701

Chief Information Officer **Robert "Bob" Cacace** .... (914) 377-6591
E-mail: bob.cacace@yonkersny.gov
Deputy Commissioner **Cheryl Green** .... (914) 377-6582
E-mail: cheryl.green@yonkersny.gov
■ Deputy Commissioner **Tor Soderquist** .... (914) 377-6564
E-mail: tor.soderquist@yonkersny.gov
Director **Helen Henkel** .... (914) 377-6220
E-mail: helen.henkel@yonkersny.gov

Parks, Recreation and Conservation

285 Nepperhan Ave., Yonkers, NY 10701

■ Commissioner **Yvette Hartsfield** .... (914) 377-6450
E-mail: yvette.hartsfield@yonkersny.gov
■ Deputy Commissioner **Steve Sansone** .... (914) 377-6450
E-mail: Steve.Sansone@YonkersNY.gov
Recreation Director **Jennifer Kearins** .... (914) 377-6450

Planning and Development Department

87 Nepperhan Avenue, Room 307, Yonkers, NY 10701

■ Commissioner **Wilson Kimball** .... (914) 377-6150
E-mail: wilson.kimball@yonkersny.gov

Downtown/Waterfront Development

City Hall Annex, 87 Nepperhan Avenue, Room 309, Yonkers, NY 10701

■ Planning Commissioner **Wilson Kimball** .... (914) 377-6080
E-mail: wilson.kimball@yonkersny.gov

Police Department

104 S. Broadway, Yonkers, NY 10701
Fax: (914) 377-7213 E-mail: police@ypd.yonkersny.gov

■ Commissioner **Charles Gardner** .... (914) 377-7200
E-mail: charles.gardner@ypd.yonkersny.gov
■ Deputy Chief **Frank Cariello** .... (914) 377-7206
E-mail: frank.cariello@ypd.yonkersny.gov
■ Deputy Chief **Francis Intervallo** .... (914) 377-7209
■ Deputy Chief **Timothy Hodges** .... (914) 377-7935
E-mail: tim.hodges@ypd.yonkersny.gov

Public Works Department

City Hall, 40 South Broadway, Room 311, Yonkers, NY 10701
Tel: (914) 377-6271 Fax: (914) 377-6273

■ Commissioner **Thomas Meier** .... (914) 377-6271
E-mail: thomas.meier@yonkersny.gov
Deputy Commissioner **Sam Borelli** .... (914) 377-6283
Deputy Commissioner **Anthony M. Landi** .... (914) 377-6271
Deputy Commissioner **Thomas Tiedemann** .... (914) 377-6717

Public Works Department *continued*

Water Superintendent **John Speight** .... (914) 377-6761

Yonkers Public Schools

One Larkin Center, Yonkers, NY 10701
Fax: (914) 376-8584 Internet: http://www.yonkerspublicschools.org

Superintendent **Dr. Edwin M. Quezada** .... (914) 376-8000

★ Elected Official ▲ Appointed by Legislature ▼ Appointed by Governor ▶ Appointed by Board or Commission ● Appointed by Judge
■ Appointed by Mayor △ Appointed by Freeholders ▽ Appointed by Supervisor ▷ Appointed by County Executive ○ Appointed by Council

Counties

County of Ada, Idaho

200 West Front Street, Boise, ID 83702

County Seat: Boise **Election Type:** Nonpartisan **Population:** 434,211 (2015)

Office of the Board of Commissioners

200 West Front Street, 3rd Floor, Boise, ID 83702
Fax: (208) 287-7009 E-mail: bocc1@adaweb.net
Internet: www.adaweb.net/commissioners.aspx

★ Chair **Jim Tibbs** (District 1) .... (208) 287-7000
Term Expires: January 1, 2019
E-mail: BOCC1@adaweb.net
Education: Boise State BA

★ Commissioner **Richard L. "Rick" Yzaguirre** (District 2) .. (208) 287-7000
Term Expires: January 1, 2017
Education: Boise State 1984 BS

★ Commissioner **Dave Case** (District 3) .... (208) 287-7000
Term Expires: January 1, 2017

Chief of Staff to the Board **Larry Maneely** .... (208) 287-7006

Office Manager **Judy Morris** .... (208) 287-7011

Office of the Public Defender

200 W. Front St., Boise, ID 83702
Fax: (208) 287-7409

▶ Public Defender **Alan Trimming** .... (208) 287-7400

Department of Administration

200 West Front Street, Boise, ID 83702
Tel: (208) 287-7123 Fax: (208) 287-6999
Internet: https://adacounty.id.gov/administration

Human Resources Manager **Bethany Calley-Green** ...... (208) 287-7123
E-mail: bcalley@adaweb.net

Development Services Department

200 West Front Street, Boise, ID 83702
Fax: (208) 287-7909

▶ Director **Meg Leatherman** .... (208) 287-7922

County Engineer **Angela Gilman** .... (208) 287-7925

County Surveyor **Jerry Hastings** .... (208) 287-7912

Ada City-County Emergency Management [ACCEM]

7200 Barrister Drive, Boise, ID 83704
Fax: (208) 577-4759

▶ Director **Doug Hardman** .... (208) 577-4750

Information Technology Department

200 West Front Street, Suite 3269, Boise, ID 83702

▶ Director **Stephen Patrick O'Meara** .... (208) 287-7022

Operations Department

200 W. Front St., Boise, ID 83702
Fax: (208) 287-7109

▶ Director (Interim) **Scott Williams** .... (208) 287-7100
E-mail: swilliams@adaweb.net

Parks and Waterways

4049 South Eckert Road, Boise, ID 83706
Fax: (208) 577-4579 E-mail: parks@adaweb.net

▶ Director **Scott Koberg** .... (208) 577-4577
E-mail: skoberg@adaweb.net

Solid Waste Management Department

200 West Front Street, Boise, ID 83702
E-mail: solidwaste@adaweb.net

▶ Director **Scott Williams** .... (208) 577-4725
E-mail: swilliams@adaweb.net

Weed, Pest and Mosquito Abatement Department

975 East Pine Avenue, Meridian, ID 83642
Fax: (208) 577-4631 E-mail: weedandpest@adaweb.net

▶ Director **Brian Wilbur** .... (208) 577-4646
E-mail: wpwilbbk@adaweb.net

Ada County Indigent Services

252 East Front Street, Suite 199, Boise, ID 83702
Fax: (208) 287-7969

▶ Director **Jesse Barcroft** .... (208) 287-7967

Ada County Paramedics [ACP]

70 Benjamin Street, Boise, ID 83704
Tel: (208) 287-2962

▶ Director **Darby Weston** .... (208) 287-2975
E-mail: darby@adaweb.net

Office of the Assessor

200 West Front Street, Boise, ID 83702
Fax: (208) 287-7209

★ Assessor **Robert H. "Bob" McQuade** .... (208) 287-7200
Term Expires: January 13, 2019
E-mail: asmcqurh@adaweb.net
Education: George Mason 1979 BA; Boise State 1995 MBA

Chief Deputy **Tim Tallman** .... (208) 287-7202
E-mail: ttallman@adaweb.net

Office of the Clerk/Auditor/Recorder

200 West Front Street, Room 1196, Boise, ID 83702
Tel: (208) 287-6000 (Clerk) Tel: (208) 287-6860 (Elections)
Tel: (208) 287-6840 (Recorder) Fax: (208) 287-6909

★ Clerk/Auditor/Recorder **Christopher D. "Chris" Rich** .... (208) 287-6886
Term Expires: January 13, 2019
E-mail: aurichcd@adaweb.net

Chief Deputy **Phil McGrane** .... (208) 287-6886

Office of the Coroner

5550 Morris Hill Rd., Boise, ID 83705
Fax: (208) 287-5579

★ Coroner **Dotti Owens** .... (208) 287-5556
Term Expires: January 13, 2019

Chief Deputy Coroner **Val Brisbin** .... (208) 287-5556

Office of the Prosecuting Attorney

200 West Front Street, 3rd Floor, Boise, ID 83702
Fax: (208) 287-7709

★ Prosecuting Attorney **Jan Bennetts** .... (208) 287-7700
Term Expires: January 8, 2017
E-mail: prbennet@adaweb.net

Chief Civil Deputy **Theodore E. Argyle** .... (208) 287-7700

Chief Criminal Deputy **(Vacant)** .... (208) 287-7700

COUNTIES

★ Elected Official ▲ Appointed by Legislature ▼ Appointed by Governor ▶ Appointed by Board or Commission ● Appointed by Judge
■ Appointed by Mayor △ Appointed by Freeholders ▽ Appointed by Supervisor ▷ Appointed by County Executive ○ Appointed by Council

COUNTIES

Office of the Sheriff
7200 Barrister Drive, Boise, ID 83704
Tel: (208) 577-3000 Fax: (208) 377-6535
E-mail: mailbox@adasheriff.org Internet: www.adasheriff.org

★Sheriff **Stephen Bartlett** . . . . (208) 577-3000
Term Expires: January 8, 2017
E-mail: sbartlett@adaweb.net
Chief Deputy **Major Ron Freeman** . . . . (208) 377-3305
E-mail: rfreeman@adaweb.net

Office of the Treasurer
200 W. Front St., Boise, ID 83701-2868
Fax: (208) 287-6809

★Treasurer/Tax Collector/Public Administrator
Vicky Oleksey McIntyre . . . . (208) 287-6800
Term Expires: January 13, 2019
E-mail: vmcintyre@adaweb.net
Chief Deputy Treasurer **Kimberlee Irby** . . . . (208) 287-6800

County of Adams, Colorado
450 South Fourth Avenue, Brighton, CO 80601-3193
Tel: (303) 659-2120 Internet: www.co.adams.co.us

County Seat: Brighton **Election Type:** Partisan **Population:** 491,337 (2015)

Board of Commissioners
450 South Fourth Avenue, Brighton, CO 80601-3193
Tel: (720) 523-6100 Fax: (303) 659-0577

★Chair **Charles "Chaz" Tedesco** (D-District 2) . . . . (720) 523-6100
Term Expires: January 2017
E-mail: ctedesco@adcogov.org
★Vice Chair **Eva "J." Henry** (D-District 1) . . . . (720) 523-6100
Term Expires: January 2017
E-mail: ehenry@adcogov.org
★Commissioner **Erik Hansen** (R-District 3) . . . . (303) 523-6867
Term Expires: January 13, 2019
E-mail: ehansen@adcogov.org
Education: Truman State 1992 BA; Denver 1995 MBA
★Commissioner **Steve O'Dorisio** (D-District 4) . . . . (303) 523-6100
Term Expires: January 13, 2019
★Commissioner **Jan Pawlowksi** (R-District 5) . . . . (303) 523-6100
Term Expires: January 13, 2019

Office of the County Attorney
4430 South Adams County Parkway, 5th Floor, Brighton, CO 80601
Fax: (720) 523-6114

▶County Attorney **Heidi Miller** . . . . (720) 523-6116
E-mail: hmiller@adcogov.org

Office of the County Manager
4430 South Adams County Parkway, 5th Floor, Brighton, CO 80601-8204
Fax: (720) 523-6045

▶County Manager **Todd Leopold** . . . . (720) 523-6100
E-mail: tleopold@adcogov.org
▶Deputy County Manager, External Services
Raymond Gonzales . . . . (720) 523-6829
E-mail: rgonzales@adcogov.org
▶Deputy County Manager, Internal Services
Edward M. "Ed" Finger . . . . (720) 523-6792
E-mail: efinger@adcogov.org
Education: Denver BBA, MS
Deputy Clerk of the Board **(Vacant)** . . . . (720) 523-6100

Office of Emergency Management [OEM]
4201 East 72nd Avenue, Commerce City, CO 80022
Tel: (720) 523-6600

Director **Heather McDermott** . . . . (720) 523-6600
E-mail: hmcdermott@adcogov.org
Education: Gonzaga JD
Public Education and Outreach Coordinator **(Vacant)** . . . . (720) 523-6602
Training and Exercise Coordinator
Jeffrey "Jeff" Newsome . . . . (720) 523-6603
E-mail: jnewsome@adcogov.org
Emergency Management Coordinator **Richard Atkins** . . . . (720) 523-6600

Veterans Service Office
4430 South Adams County Parkway, 1st Floor, Brighton, CO 80601-8220
Fax: (303) 227-2651

Veterans Service Officer **Robert J. Sheetz** . . . . (303) 227-2107

Finance Department
4430 South Adams County Parkway, 4th Floor, Brighton, CO 80601-8212
Fax: (720) 523-6300

Director **Benjamin J. "Ben" Dahlman** . . . . (720) 523-6050
E-mail: bdahlman@adcogov.org
Assistant Director **(Vacant)** . . . . (720) 523-6050
Purchasing/Accounts Payable Manager **Kim Roland** . . . . (720) 523-6050
E-mail: kroland@adcogov.org

Human Resources Department
4430 South Adams County Parkway, 4th Floor, Brighton, CO 80601-8213
Fax: (720) 523-6069

Director **Bryan Ostler** . . . . (720) 523-6070
E-mail: hr@adcogov.org

Human Services Department
7190 Colorado Boulevard, Commerce City, CO 80022
Tel: (303) 287-8831 Fax: (303) 227-2106

Director **Chris Kline** . . . . (303) 227-2100
Deputy Director **Herb Covey** . . . . (303) 227-2216
Human Resources Manager **Amy Jones** . . . . (303) 227-6106
E-mail: amy.burger@dss.co.adams.co.us Fax: (303) 227-2114

Division of Children and Family Services
7401 North Broadway, Denver, CO 80221
Tel: (303) 412-8121 Fax: (303) 412-5335

Director **Jan James** . . . . (303) 412-5085
Manager of Client Services **Ellen Sandoval** . . . . (303) 412-5088
Manager of Intake **Kris Cowperthwaite** . . . . (303) 412-5086
Manager of Permanency **Edie Winters** . . . . (303) 412-5091
Fax: (303) 412-5325
Manager of Quality Assurance **Cisco Maez** . . . . (303) 412-5200

Self Sufficiency and Adult Services Division
7190 Colorado Boulevard, Commerce City, CO 80022
Tel: (303) 227-2348 Fax: (303) 227-2106

Director **Monica Sorenson** . . . . (303) 227-2102
Contract Manager **Sally Ten Eyck** . . . . (303) 227-2116
Manager of Child Support Enforcement **Velta Straube** . . . (303) 227-2225
Specialty Programs Director **Sue Bozinovski** . . . . (303) 227-2283

Supportive Services Division
7190 Colorado Boulevard, Sixth Floor, Commerce City, CO 80022
Tel: (303) 227-2233 Fax: (303) 227-2239

Director **Brian Kenna** . . . . (303) 227-2727
Manager of Accounting and Finance **(Vacant)** . . . . (303) 227-6291
Manager of Information Systems **Steve Hartley** . . . . (303) 227-2133
Manager of Investigation and Recovery **Gerald Garcia** . . . (303) 227-2121

★Elected Official ▲Appointed by Legislature ▼Appointed by Governor ▶Appointed by Board or Commission ●Appointed by Judge
■Appointed by Mayor △Appointed by Freeholders ▽Appointed by Supervisor ▷Appointed by County Executive ○Appointed by Council

Information Technology Department
4430 South Adams County Parkway, Third Floor, Suite C3000,
Brighton, CO 80601-8212
Tel: (720) 523-6066 Fax: (720) 523-6150

Director **Kevin Beach** . . . . . (303) 227-6066
E-mail: kbeach@adcogov.org

Parks and Community Resources Department
9755 Henderson Road, Brighton, CO 80601
Tel: (303) 637-8000 Fax: (303) 637-8015

Director **Nathan Mosley** . . . . . (303) 637-8000

Planning and Development Department
4430 South Adams County Parkway, 1st Floor, Brighton, CO 80601-8216
Fax: (720) 523-6998

Director **Nana Appiah** . . . . . (720) 523-6819
E-mail: nappiah@adcogov.org

Neighborhood Services Department
4430 South Adams County Parkway, Brighton, CO 80601
Tel: (720) 523-6880

Director **Norman Wright** . . . . . (720) 523-6880

Building Safety Division
4430 South Adams County Parkway, 1st Floor, Brighton, CO 80601
Tel: (720) 523-6825 Fax: (720) 523-6967

Chief Building Official **Justin Blair** . . . . . (720) 523-6843
E-mail: jblair@adcogov.org

Transportation Department
4430 South Adams County Parkway, Brighton, CO 80601
Tel: (720) 523-6875 Fax: (720) 523-6996

Director **(Vacant)** . . . . . (720) 523-6875

Office of the County Assessor
450 South Fourth Avenue, Brighton, CO 80601-3193
Tel: (720) 523-6038 Fax: (720) 523-6037

★County Assessor **Patsy Melonakis** (R) . . . . . (720) 523-6038
Term Expires: January 2019
E-mail: assessor@adcogov.org

Office of the County Clerk and Recorder
4430 South Adams County Parkway, Brighton, CO 80601-8203
Tel: (720) 523-6020 Fax: (720) 523-6059

★County Clerk and Recorder **Stan Martin** (R) . . . . . (720) 523-6015
Term Expires: January 2019

Office of the County Coroner
330 North 19th Avenue, Brighton, CO 80601
Tel: (303) 659-1027 Fax: (303) 659-4718

★County Coroner **Monica Broncucia-Jordan** (D) . . . . . (303) 659-1027
Term Expires: January 2019
E-mail: mbroncucia-jordan@adcogov.org

Office of the County Surveyor
450 South Fourth Avenue, Brighton, CO 80601-3193
Tel: (720) 523-6875

★County Surveyor **Timothy "Tim" Thoms** (D) . . . . . (720) 523-6875
Term Expires: January 2019
E-mail: surveyor@adcogov.org

Office of the County Treasurer
450 South Fourth Avenue, Brighton, CO 80601-3193
Tel: (720) 523-6160 Fax: (720) 523-6175

★County Treasurer **Brigitte Grimm** (R) . . . . . (720) 523-6160
Term Expires: January 2019
E-mail: bgrimm@adcogov.org

Office of the District Attorney
1000 Judicial Center Drive, Suite 100, Brighton, CO 80601
Tel: (303) 659-7720 Fax: (303) 835-5522

★District Attorney **David Young** (D) . . . . . (303) 659-1161
Term Expires: January 2019

Office of the Public Trustee
1000 Judicial Center Drive, Brighton, CO 80601
Tel: (720) 523-6250 Fax: (720) 523-6548

▼Public Trustee **Susan A. Orecchio** . . . . . (720) 523-6250
Term Expires: February 1, 2019
E-mail: sorecchio@adcogov.org

Office of the Sheriff
332 North 19th Avenue, Brighton, CO 80601
Tel: (303) 654-1850 Tel: (720) 322-1313 (Records Information)

★Sheriff **Michael McIntosh** (R) . . . . . (303) 654-1850
Term Expires: January 2019
E-mail: mmcintosh@adcogov.org

County of Alameda, California
County Administration Bldg., 1221 Oak St., Oakland, CA 94612
Tel: (510) 272-6984 (Information) TTY: (510) 834-6754
Fax: (510) 272-3784 Internet: www.acgov.org

County Seat: Oakland **Election Type:** Nonpartisan
Population: 1,638,215 (2015)

Office of the Board of Supervisors
County Administration Building, 1221 Oak Street, Room 536,
Oakland, CA 94612

★President **Scott Haggerty** (District 1) . . . . . (510) 272-6691
Term Expires: January 4, 2017 Fax: (510) 208-3910
E-mail: district1@acgov.org

★Vice President **Wilma Chan** (District 3) . . . . . (510) 272-6693
Term Expires: January 4, 2019 Fax: (510) 268-8004
E-mail: district3@acgov.org
Education: Wellesley BA; Stanford MA

★Supervisor **Richard Valle** (District 2) . . . . . (510) 272-6692
Term Expires: January 2019 Fax: (510) 271-5115
E-mail: district2@acgov.org
Education: Cal State (East Bay) BA, MPA

★Supervisor **Nate Miley** (District 4) . . . . . (510) 272-6694
Term Expires: January 4, 2017 Fax: (510) 465-7628
E-mail: district4@acgov.org
Education: Franklin & Marshall 1973 BA; Maryland 1976 JD

★Supervisor **Keith Carson** (District 5) . . . . . (510) 272-6695
Term Expires: January 4, 2017 Fax: (510) 271-5151
E-mail: dist5@acgov.org
Education: UC Berkeley 1971 BA; Cal State (East Bay) 1973 MPA

Clerk of the Board **Anika Campbell-Belton** . . . . . (510) 272-6347

★Elected Official ▲Appointed by Legislature ▼Appointed by Governor ►Appointed by Board or Commission ●Appointed by Judge
■Appointed by Mayor △Appointed by Freeholders ▽Appointed by Supervisor ▷Appointed by County Executive ○Appointed by Council

COUNTIES

Office of the County Administrator

County Administration Bldg., 1221 Oak Street, Room 555,
Oakland, CA 94612
Tel: (510) 272-3862 Fax: (510) 272-3784 Internet: www.acgov.org/cao

▽County Administrator **Susan S. Muranishi** .... (510) 272-3862
E-mail: countyadministrator@acgov.org
Assistant County Administrator **(Vacant)** .... (510) 272-3862
Public Information Officer **Ludmyrna Lopez** .... (510) 272-3882
Education: Carnegie Mellon MS

Office of the County Counsel

County Administration Building, 1221 Oak Street, Suite 450,
Oakland, CA 94612-4296
Tel: (510) 272-6700 Fax: (510) 272-5020
Internet: www.acgov.org/counsel

▽County Counsel **Donna R. Ziegler** .... (510) 272-6706

Extension Office

1131 Harbor Bay Parkway, Suite 131, Alameda, CA 94502-6577
Tel: (510) 670-5650 Fax: (510) 670-5671

Director **Robert Bennaton** .... (510) 670-5621
Management Services Officer **Zoya Khalaf-Kirkman** ..... (510) 639-1367
E-mail: zhkhalaf@ucanr.edu

Office of the Public Defender

1401 Lakeside Drive, Suite 400, Oakland, CA 94612
Fax: (510) 272-6610 Internet: www.acgov.org/defender

▽Public Defender **Brendon D. Woods** .... (510) 272-6600 ext. 22
E-mail: brendon.woods@acgov.org
Senior Assistant Public Defender
Robert Shipway .... (510) 272-6600 ext. 34

Office of the Registrar of Voters

County Courthouse, 1225 Fallon Street, Room G-1,
Oakland, CA 94612-4283
TTY: (510) 208-4967 Fax: (510) 272-6982

Registrar **Tim Dupuis** .... (510) 272-6933
Deputy Registrar **Cynthia Cornejo** .... (510) 272-6933
E-mail: cynthia.cornejo@acgov.org

Community Development Agency

224 West Winton Avenue, Room 110, Hayward, CA 94544
Fax: (510) 670-6374 Internet: http://www.co.alameda.ca.us/cda/

Director **Chris Bazar** .... (510) 670-5333
E-mail: chris.bazar@acgov.org

Agriculture, Weights and Measures Department

224 West Winton Avenue, Room 184, Hayward, CA 94544
Fax: (510) 783-3928

Agricultural Commissioner/Sealer of Weights and
Measures **Scott T. Paulsen** .... (510) 670-5232
Assistant Agriculture Commissioner **(Vacant)** .... (510) 783-3928

Housing and Community Development

224 West Winton Avenue, Room 108, Hayward, CA 94544
Fax: (510) 670-6378

Housing Director **Linda Gardner** .... (510) 670-6417
E-mail: linda.gardner@acgov.org

Healthy Homes

2000 Embarcadero, Suite 300, Oakland, CA 94606
Fax: (510) 567-8272

Director **Maricela Foster** .... (510) 567-8282

Planning Department

224 West Winton Avenue, Suite 111, Hayward, CA 94544
Fax: (510) 785-8793

Planning Director **Albert Lopez** .... (510) 670-5400
E-mail: albert.lopez@acgov.org
Assistant Planning Director, Code Enforcement
Tona Marie Henninger .... (510) 670-5400
E-mail: tona.henninger@acgov.org
Assistant Planning Director, Development Planning
Sandra Rivera .... (510) 670-5400
Planning Director, Policy Planning **Liz McEllig** .... (510) 670-5400

Economic and Civic Development Agency

224 West Winton Avenue, Suite 110, Hayward, CA 94544
Tel: (510) 670-6509 Fax: (510) 670-6374

Director **Eileen Dalton** .... (510) 670-6509
E-mail: eileen.dalton@acgov.org

Surplus Property

224 West Winton Avenue, Hayward, CA 94544
Fax: (510) 670-6374

Director **Stuart Cook** .... (510) 670-5333
Manager **(Vacant)** .... (510) 670-5333

Alameda County Fire Department [ACFD]

6363 Clark Avenue, Dublin, CA 94568
Fax: (925) 875-9387 Internet: www.acgov.org/fire

Fire Chief **David A. Rocha** .... (925) 833-3473 ext. 1110
Deputy Chief of Operations **Dan Benfield** ..... (925) 833-3473 ext. 1111

General Services Agency

1401 Lakeside Drive, 10th Floor, Oakland, CA 94612
Fax: (510) 208-9711

Director (Acting) **Caroline Judy** .... (510) 208-9700
E-mail: caroline.judy@acgov.org

Purchasing Department

1401 Lakeside Drive, Suite 907, Oakland, CA 94612
Tel: (510) 208-9600

Deputy Director **Pedro Valencia** .... (510) 208-9625 ext. 29625
E-mail: pedro.valencia@acgov.org Fax: (510) 208-9626
Purchasing Manager **John Glann** .... (510) 208-9625 ext. 29627
E-mail: john.glann@acgov.org Fax: (510) 208-9626

Health Care Services Agency

1000 San Leandro Boulevard, Suite 300, San Leandro, CA 94577
Tel: (510) 618-3452 Fax: (510) 351-1367 Internet: www.acgov.org/health

Director **Alex Briscoe** .... (510) 618-3452
Finance Director **Rebecca Gebhart** .... (510) 618-3452

Human Resource Services Department

Lakeside Plaza Bldg., 1405 Lakeside Dr., Oakland, CA 94612-4305
TTY: (510) 272-3703 Fax: (510) 272-6424

Director (Interim) **Mary Welch** .... (510) 272-6435
Deputy Director **Stephen Amano** .... (510) 272-6435
E-mail: stephen.amano@acgov.org
Training and Education Center Director **Elsie Lum** ...... (510) 272-6467
E-mail: elsie.lum@acgov.org Fax: (510) 208-4848

Information Technology Department

1106 Madison Street, Room 336, Oakland, CA 94612
Tel: (510) 481-3700 Fax: (510) 272-3608 E-mail: itd@acgov.org
Internet: www.acgov.org/itd

Director/Chief Information Officer **Tim Dupuis** .... (510) 272-3730
E-mail: tim.dupuis@acgov.org
Chief Technology Officer **Tobin Broadhurst** .... (510) 272-3730
E-mail: tobin.broadhurst@acgov.org
Assistant Director **Sybil Gurney** .... (510) 481-3700
E-mail: sybil.gurney@acgov.org

★Elected Official ▲Appointed by Legislature ▼Appointed by Governor ▶Appointed by Board or Commission ●Appointed by Judge
■Appointed by Mayor △Appointed by Freeholders ▽Appointed by Supervisor ▷Appointed by County Executive ○Appointed by Council

Information Technology Department *continued*

Administrative Services Officer **Mary Williams** .... (510) 481-3700
E-mail: mary.williams@acgov.org

Probation Department

400 Broadway, P.O. Box 2059, Oakland, CA 94604-2059
Tel: (510) 268-7050 Fax: (510) 268-7274
Internet: www.acgov.org/probation

Chief Probation Officer **LaDonna Harris** .... (510) 268-7233
Fax: (510) 839-2776

Public Works Agency

399 Elmhurst St., Hayward, CA 94544
Fax: (510) 670-5541

▽ Director and County Engineer **Daniel Woldesenbet** ..... (510) 670-5455
Administrative Secretary **Leslie Robertson** .... (510) 670-5455
E-mail: leslie@acpwa.org

Construction and Development Services Department

Fax: (510) 670-5269

Deputy Director **Bill Lepere** .... (510) 670-5431
Building Inspector **Allen Lang** .... (510) 670-5440

Engineering Department

Deputy Director **(Vacant)** .... (510) 670-5457
Principal Civil Engineer-Flood Control **Hank Ackerman** .. (510) 670-5553
E-mail: hank@acpwa.org
Principal Civil Engineer-Roads **Art Carrera** .... (510) 670-5581

Management Services Department

Fax: (510) 670-5541

Administrator **Keith Whitaker** .... (510) 670-5456
Senior Departmental Personnel Officer **Denise Fetty** .... (510) 670-5414
Fiscal Services Manager **Jan Bass** .... (510) 670-5471
Program and Policy Development Office Administrator
Lupe Serrano .... (510) 670-5593

Maintenance and Operation Department

951 Turner Court, Hayward, CA 94545
Fax: (510) 670-5251

Deputy Director **John Medlock, Jr.** .... (510) 670-5506
Supervising Civil Engineer-Project Management and
Inspection **Tom Hinderlie** .... (510) 670-5619
Homeland Security Safety Officer
Richard A. "Rick" Ruiz .... (510) 670-5500
Fleet Operations Manager **Keith LaHaie** .... (925) 803-7006
4825 Gleason Drive, Dublin, CA 94568 Fax: (925) 829-8167

Social Services Agency

2000 San Pablo Avenue, 4th Floor, Oakland, CA 94612
Fax: (510) 271-9120 E-mail: ssaplan@co.alameda.ca.us
Internet: www.alamedasocialservices.org

Director **Lori Cox** .... (510) 271-9103
Assistant Agency Director **Don R. Edwards** .... (510) 645-9350
Media Relations Officer **Sylvia Soublet** .... (510) 271-9100

Department of Adult, Aging, and Medi-Cal Services

6955 Foothill Boulevard, Suite 300, Oakland, CA 94605
Fax: (510) 577-1965

Assistant Agency Director **Randy Morris** .... (510) 577-1968

Children and Family Services Department

Tel: (510) 667-7714 Fax: (510) 667-3937

Assistant Agency Director **Michelle Love** .... (510) 667-7714

Workforce and Benefits Department

24100 Amador Street, Hayward, CA 94544-1203
Fax: (510) 259-3810

Assistant Agency Director **Andrea Ford** .... (510) 259-3812

Workforce and Investment Board [WIB]

24100 Amador Street, 6th Floor, Hayward, CA 94544-1203

Assistant Director (Acting) **Patti Castro** .... (510) 259-3843

Alameda County Library

2450 Stevenson Boulevard, Fremont, CA 94538-2326
Fax: (510) 793-2987 Internet: www.aclibrary.org

▽ County Librarian (Acting) **Carmen Martinez** .... (510) 745-1504
E-mail: cmartinez@aclibrary.org
Deputy County Librarian **Cynthia Chadwick** .... (510) 745-1504
E-mail: cchadwick@aclibrary.org

Office of the Assessor

County Administration Bldg., 1221 Oak Street, Room 145,
Oakland, CA 94612-4288
Fax: (510) 891-8911 Internet: www.acgov.org/assessor

★ County Assessor **Ron Thomsen** .... (510) 272-3755
Term Expires: January 6, 2019
E-mail: ron.thomsen@acgov.org

Auditor-Controller Agency

County Administration Building, 1221 Oak Street, Room 249,
Oakland, CA 94612
Fax: (510) 272-6502 (Auditor-Controller)
Fax: (510) 272-6382 (Clerk-Recorder) Internet: www.acgov.org/auditor

★ Auditor-Controller/Clerk-Recorder **Steve Manning** ...... (510) 272-6565
Term Expires: 2018
E-mail: steve.manning@acgov.org
Chief Deputy Auditor **Melissa Wilk** .... (510) 272-6565
Assistant Controller **Kevin Hing** .... (510) 272-6565
Assistant Controller **Carol Gloria** .... (510) 272-6565
Assistant Controller **Malinda Jones-Williams** .... (510) 272-6565

Office of the District Attorney

County Courthouse, 1225 Fallon Street, Suite 900, Oakland, CA 94612
Fax: (510) 208-3965 Internet: www.alcoda.org

★ District Attorney **Nancy E. O'Malley** .... (510) 272-6222
Term Expires: January 3, 2018
E-mail: nancy.omalley@acgov.org
Education: Cal State (Hayward) 1977 BA; Golden Gate 1983 JD
Executive Assistant **Towanda Lee** .... (510) 272-6222
E-mail: towanda.lee@acgov.org
Chief Assistant District Attorney **Kevin E. Dunleavy** .... (510) 272-6222
E-mail: kevin.dunleavy@acgov.org
Inspectors Chief **Robert Chenault** .... (510) 272-6222
Assistant Chief **Craig Chew** .... (510) 272-6222

Office of the Sheriff-Coroner Bureau

480 4th Street, Oakland, CA 94607
Tel: (510) 268-7300 Fax: (510) 208-1153
Internet: www.alamedacountysheriff.org

★ Sheriff/Coroner **Gregory J. Ahern** .... (510) 272-6878
Term Expires: December 31, 2018
E-mail: gahern@acgov.org
Undersheriff **Richard T. "Rich" Lucia** .... (510) 268-7300
E-mail: rlucia@acgov.org
Assistant Sheriff **Casey Nice** .... (510) 268-7300
Assistant Sheriff **Brett Keteles** .... (510) 268-7300

COUNTIES

★ Elected Official ▲ Appointed by Legislature ▼ Appointed by Governor ▶ Appointed by Board or Commission ● Appointed by Judge
■ Appointed by Mayor △ Appointed by Freeholders ▽ Appointed by Supervisor ▷ Appointed by County Executive ○ Appointed by Council

Office of the Treasurer-Tax Collector

#131 County Administration Building, 1221 Oak Street, Oakland, CA 94612-4285
Fax: (510) 268-5377

★ Treasurer-Tax Collector **Donald R. White** . . . . (510) 272-6803
Term Expires: 2018
E-mail: donald.white@acgov.org
Education: Cal State (Hayward) BS

Chief Deputy Tax Collector **Karen Poe** . . . . (510) 272-6803
E-mail: karen.poe@acgov.org

Assistant Treasurer **Melani Munoz** . . . . (510) 272-6803

Alameda County Employees' Retirement Association [ACERA]

475-14th Street, 10th Floor, Suite 1000, Oakland, CA 94612
Tel: (510) 628-3000 Fax: (510) 268-9574 E-mail: info@acera.org
Internet: www.acera.org

Chief Executive Officer (Interim) **Kathy Foster** . . . . (510) 628-3001

Assistant Chief Executive Officer **Kathy Foster** . . . . (510) 628-3062
E-mail: kfoster@acera.org Fax: (510) 287-5411

Financial Services Officer **Margo Allen** . . . . (510) 628-3127
E-mail: mallen@acera.org Fax: (510) 287-5394

Chief Investment Officer **Betty Tse** . . . . (510) 628-3027
E-mail: btse@acera.org Fax: (510) 834-6425

Human Resource Officer **Victoria Arruda** . . . . (510) 628-3039
E-mail: varruda@acera.org Fax: (510) 287-5414

Alameda County Office of Education [ACOE]

313 West Winton Avenue, Hayward, CA 94544-1198
Tel: (510) 887-0152 Fax: (510) 670-3747 Internet: www.acoe.org

★ Superintendent **L. Karen Monroe** . . . . (510) 670-4140
Term Expires: January 1, 2019

Associate Superintendent **Gary Jones** . . . . (510) 670-4270
E-mail: gjones@acoe.org

Executive Director of Technology **Rob van Herk** . . . . (510) 337-7140
E-mail: rvanherk@alameda.k12.ca.us

Chief Human Resources Officer **Movetia Salter** . . . . (510) 670-4265
E-mail: msalter@acoe.org

Public Information Officer **Patrick Gannon** . . . . (510) 670-7754
E-mail: pgannon@acoe.org

County of Allegheny, Pennsylvania

County Courthouse, 436 Grant St., Pittsburgh, PA 15219
Tel: (412) 350-5313 (Information) Internet: www.alleghenycounty.us

County Seat: Pittsburgh **Election Type:** Partisan **Population:** 1,230,459 (2015)

Office of the County Executive

County Courthouse, 436 Grant Street, Room 101, Pittsburgh, PA 15219-2499
Tel: (412) 350-6500 Fax: (412) 350-6512
E-mail: executive@alleghenycounty.us
Internet: www.alleghenycounty.us/welcome

★ County Executive **Rich Fitzgerald** (D) . . . . (412) 350-6500
Term Expires: December 31, 2019
E-mail: executive@alleghenycounty.us
Education: Carnegie Mellon 1981 BS

Chief of Staff **Jennifer Liptak** . . . . (412) 350-1349
E-mail: jennifer.liptak@alleghenycounty.us

Office of the County Solicitor/Law Department

445 Fort Pitt Boulevard, Suite 300, Pittsburgh, PA 15219
Tel: (412) 350-1120 Fax: (412) 350-1174

Solicitor **Andrew F. Szefi** . . . . (412) 350-1128
Education: Richmond; Pittsburgh JD

First Assistant Solicitor **George Janocsko** . . . . (412) 350-1132

Office of the County Manager

119 County Courthouse, 436 Grant St., Pittsburgh, PA 15219-2403
Tel: (412) 350-5300 Fax: (412) 350-3581

▷ County Manager **William D. "Willy" McKain** . . . . (412) 350-5300
E-mail: william.mckain@alleghenycounty.us

Deputy County Manager **Barbara M. Parees** . . . . (412) 350-5300
E-mail: barbara.parees@alleghenycounty.us

Deputy County Manager **Steve Pilarski** . . . . (412) 350-5300
E-mail: steve.pilarski@alleghenycounty.us

Communications Division

101 County Courthouse, 436 Grant Street, Pittsburgh, PA 15219-2499
Fax: (412) 350-6512 Internet: www.alleghenycounty.us/comm

Director **Amie Downs** . . . . (412) 350-3711
E-mail: Amie.Downs@alleghenycounty.us

Office of Budget and Finance

225 County Courthouse, 436 Grant St., Pittsburgh, PA 15219
Tel: (412) 350-5131 Fax: (412) 350-3041
Internet: www.alleghenycounty.us/budget

▷ Director **Mary C. Soroka** . . . . (412) 350-5131
E-mail: mary.soroka@alleghenycounty.us
Education: Robert Morris Col (PA) MA

Penn State Center, Pittsburgh

1435 Bedford Avenue, Suite A, Pittsburgh, PA 15219
Tel: (412) 263-1000 Fax: (412) 482-3470 E-mail: alleghenyext@psu.edu
Internet: www.extension.psu.edu/allegheny

Director **Deno Deciantis** . . . . (412) 263-1000

Office of the Medical Examiner

1520 Penn Avenue, Pittsburgh, PA 15222
Tel: (412) 350-4800 Fax: (412) 350-4899
Internet: www.alleghenycounty.us/me

► Medical Examiner **Karl E. Williams** . . . . (412) 350-4800
E-mail: karl.williams@alleghenycounty.us

Manager of Administration **Robert Huston** . . . . (412) 350-4800

Educational Coordinator **Annie Marbury** . . . . (412) 350-4800
E-mail: annie.marbury@alleghenycounty.us

Forensic Laboratory Division

1520 Penn Avenue, Pittsburgh, PA 15222
Tel: (412) 350-4800 Fax: (412) 350-6167

Director **Robert Huston** . . . . (412) 350-3741

Evidence Submission Manager **Paul McGlumphy** . . . . (412) 350-4800

Environmental Chemistry, Arson, and Firearms **Deborah Tator** . . . . (412) 350-4800

Latent Prints **Deborah Tator** . . . . (412) 350-4800

Serology and DNA **Sara Bitner** . . . . (412) 350-4800

Toxicology **Jennifer K. Janssen** . . . . (412) 350-4800

Trace and Drug Chemistry **Joshua Yohannan** . . . . (412) 350-4800

Office of Property Assessments

400 North Lexington Street, Suite LL115, Pittsburgh, PA 15208-2566
Tel: (412) 473-4285 Fax: (412) 473-4395
E-mail: opa@alleghenycounty.us

Manager **(Vacant)** . . . . (412) 473-4285

★ Elected Official ▲ Appointed by Legislature ▼ Appointed by Governor ► Appointed by Board or Commission ● Appointed by Judge
■ Appointed by Mayor △ Appointed by Freeholders ▽ Appointed by Supervisor ▷ Appointed by County Executive ○ Appointed by Council

Retirement Office of Allegheny County
County Office Bldg., 542 Forbes Ave,, Room 106, Pittsburgh, PA 15219
Tel: (412) 350-4674 Fax: (412) 350-3923

Executive Director **Tim Johnson** .... (412) 350-4679

Administrative Services Department
County Courthouse, 436 Grant Street, Room 202,
Pittsburgh, PA 15219-2489

▷ Director **Jerry Tyskiewicz** .... (412) 350-6109
E-mail: jerry.tyskiewicz@alleghenycounty.us

Office of the Public Defender
400 County Office Bldg., 542 Forbes Ave., Pittsburgh, PA 15219-2946
Tel: (412) 350-2401 Fax: (412) 350-2390

▷ Public Defender **Elliot J. Howsie** .... (412) 350-2401
E-mail: elliot.howsie@alleghenycounty.us

Office of Veterans' Services
4141 Fifth Avenue, Pittsburgh, PA 15213-3547
Tel: (412) 621-4357 Fax: (412) 621-3622

▷ Director **Ronald F. Conley** .... (412) 621-4357
E-mail: rconley@alleghenycounty.us
Executive Assistant **Michael D. Murphy III** .... (412) 621-4357
E-mail: mmurphy@alleghenycounty.us
Administrative Secretary **Debra Presutti** .... (412) 621-4357
E-mail: dpresutti@alleghenycounty.us

Computer Services Division
621 County Office Bldg., 542 Forbes Avenue, Room 621,
Pittsburgh, PA 15219-2952
Fax: (412) 350-4754

▷ Chief Information Officer **Joseph W. Gavlik** .... (412) 350-4760

Elections Division
604 County Office Building, 542 Forbes Avenue, Suite 604,
Pittsburgh, PA 15219-2953
Tel: (412) 350-4500 Fax: (412) 350-5697

▷ Division Manager **Mark Wolosik** .... (412) 350-4509

Purchasing Division
206 County Courthouse, 436 Grant Street, Pittsburgh, PA 15219

▷ Chief Purchasing Officer **John Deighan** .... (412) 350-4495
E-mail: jdeighan@alleghenycounty.us

Soldiers and Sailors Memorial Hall and Museum Trust, Incorporated
4141 Fifth Avenue, Pittsburgh, PA 15213-3547
Fax: (412) 683-9339 Internet: www.soldiersandsailorshall.org

President and Chief Executive Officer **John F. McCabe** ... (412) 621-4253
Executive Assistant and Director of Public Relations **Jamie Pavlot** .... (412) 621-4253 ext. 226
E-mail: jamie@soldiersandsailorshall.org
Vice President and Director of Operations **James "Jim" Gubash** .... (412) 621-4253 ext. 209
Director of Education and Curatorial Services **Tim E. Neff** .... (412) 621-4253 ext. 219

Department of Court Records
Allegheny County Court House, 436 Grant Street, Room 114,
Pittsburgh, PA 15219
Internet: http://www.alleghenycounty.us/Civil/index.aspx

▷ Director **Kate Barkman** .... (412) 350-5729
E-mail: civil@alleghenycounty.us
Deputy Director **(Vacant)** .... (412) 350-4200

Economic Development Department
Chatham One, 112 Washington Place, Suite 900, Pittsburgh, PA 15219
Tel: (412) 350-1000 Fax: (412) 471-1032
E-mail: director.ed@alleghenycounty.us
Internet: www.alleghenycounty.us/economic

▷ Executive Director **Robert Hurley** .... (412) 350-1083
E-mail: director.ed@alleghenycounty.us
Senior Deputy Director **John J. Exler, Jr.** .... (412) 350-1020
E-mail: jack.exler@alleghenycounty.us
Deputy Director **Patrick Earley** .... (412) 350-1036
E-mail: john.earley@alleghenycounty.us

Authority for Improvements in Municipalities [AIM]
Manager **John J. Exler, Jr.** .... (412) 350-1036
E-mail: jack.exler@alleghenycounty.us

Allegheny County Residential Finance Authority [ACRFA]
Manager **John J. Exler, Jr.** .... (412) 350-1036
E-mail: jexler@alleghenycounty.us

Department of Emergency Services
400 North Lexington Street, Suite 200, Pittsburgh, PA 15208-2521
Tel: (412) 473-2550 Fax: (412) 473-2623
E-mail: ems@county.allegheny.pa.us
Internet: www.alleghenycounty.us/emerserv

▷ Chief **Alvin Henderson, Jr.** .... (412) 473-2550
E-mail: ahenderson@alleghenycounty.us
Education: Columbia Southern
Assistant Chief for Administration and Support **Rebecca Frazier** .... (412) 473-2550
Assistant Chief for Operations and Training **(Vacant)** .... (412) 473-2550

911 Communications
400 North Lexington Street, Pittsburgh, PA 15208-2521
Tel: (412) 473-1000 Fax: (412) 473-2589
Internet: www.alleghenycounty.us/emerserv/911

Assistant Chief/911 Coordinator **Gary J. Thomas** .... (412) 473-1412
911 Communications Manager **Marissa Williams** .... (412) 473-1000
911 Communications Manager **Donald Sand** .... (412) 473-1000
911 Communications Manager **Tom McDough** .... (412) 473-1000

Emergency Management Agency
400 North Lexington Street, Pittsburgh, PA 15208-2566
Fax: (412) 473-2623

▷ Coordinator **Steven J. Wilharm** .... (412) 473-2550
E-mail: swilharm@alleghenycounty.us

Allegheny County Fire Academy [ACFA]
700 West Ridge Road, Allison Park, PA 15101-1798
Fax: (724) 935-6099

Administrator **Steve Imbarlina** .... (412) 931-3158

Fire Marshal Office
400 North Lexington Street, Pittsburgh, PA 15208-2566
Fax: (412) 241-6941

Fire Marshal **Alvin Henderson, Jr.** .... (412) 473-2552
E-mail: ahenderson@alleghenycounty.us
Education: Columbia Southern
Chief Deputy Fire Marshal **Donald "Don" Brucker** ..... (412) 473-2552
E-mail: dbrucker@alleghenycounty.us
Deputy Fire Marshal **Michael D. Liko** .... (412) 473-2552
E-mail: mliko@alleghenycounty.us
Deputy Fire Marshal **Mike Shawley** .... (412) 473-2552
E-mail: mshawley@alleghenycounty.us
Deputy Fire Marshal **Gene Stouffer** .... (412) 473-2552
E-mail: gstouffer@alleghenycounty.us

Human Resources Department
County Office Building, 542 Forbes Avenue, Room 102, Pittsburgh, PA 15219-2946
Tel: (412) 350-6830 Fax: (412) 350-5230

Director **Laura Zaspel** .... (412) 350-6830
E-mail: laura.zaspel@alleghenycounty.us

Department of Human Services
One Smithfield Street, Suite 400, Pittsburgh, PA 15222-2225
Tel: (412) 350-5701 Fax: (412) 350-4004
Internet: www.alleghenycounty.us/dhs

▷ Director **Marc Cherna** .... (412) 350-5701
E-mail: marc.cherna@alleghenycounty.us
Administrative Assistant **Terry Lane** .... (412) 350-3692
E-mail: terry.lane@alleghenycounty.us

Area Agency on Aging [AAA]
2100 Wharton Street, 2nd Floor, Pittsburgh, PA 15203
Tel: (412) 350-4234 (Business) Tel: (412) 350-5460 (Senior Line)
Fax: (412) 350-4330

▷ Administrator **Mildred E. Morrison** .... (412) 350-4234
E-mail: mmorrison@alleghenycounty.us

Office of Administration and Information Management Services
One Smithfield Street, Suite 500, Pittsburgh, PA 15222-2225
Tel: (412) 350-3536 Fax: (412) 350-6390

Deputy Director **Randolph W. Brockington** .... (412) 350-5203
E-mail: randolph.brockington@alleghenycounty.us

Office of Behavioral Health
One Smithfield Street, 3rd Floor, Pittsburgh, PA 15222-2225
Tel: (412) 350-4457 Fax: (412) 350-3880

Deputy Director **Denise Macerelli** .... (412) 350-5212

Office of Children, Youth and Families
Tel: (412) 350-5701 Fax: (412) 350-4004

Deputy Director **Walter H. Smith, Jr.** .... (412) 350-3424
Fax: (412) 350-3702

Office of Community Relations
One Smithfield Street, Pittsburgh, PA 15222-2225
Fax: (412) 350-5891

Deputy Director **Karen L. Blumen** .... (412) 350-5707
E-mail: karen.blumen@alleghenycounty.us

Office of Community Services
One Smithfield Street, 2nd Floor, Pittsburgh, PA 15222-2225
Tel: (412) 350-6611 Fax: (412) 350-2785

Deputy Director **Reginald B. Young** .... (412) 350-5709

Office of Intellectual Disability
2020 Ardmore Boulevard, Room 380, Pittsburgh, PA 15221
Tel: (412) 436-2750 Fax: (412) 436-1392

Deputy Director **Donald "Don" Clark** .... (412) 436-2803

Office of Data Analysis, Research and Evaluation
One Smithfield Street, Fourth Floor, Pittsburgh, PA 15222-2225
Tel: (412) 350-5701 Fax: (412) 350-4004

Deputy Director **Erin Dalton** .... (412) 350-1110

Parks Department
542 Forbes Avenue, Room 211, Pittsburgh, PA 15219-2946
Tel: (412) 350-7275 Fax: (412) 350-2682
Internet: www.alleghenycounty.us/parks

▷ Director **Andrew G. "Andy" Baechle** .... (412) 350-7275
E-mail: andrew.baechle@alleghenycounty.us

Office of Special Events
542 Forbes Avenue, Room 515C, Pittsburgh, PA 15219
Tel: (412) 350-2528 Fax: (412) 350-5386
E-mail: specevents@alleghenycounty.us
Internet: www.alleghenycounty.us/spev

Manager **William "Bill" Deasy** .... (412) 350-3790

Allegheny County Police Department
400 North Lexington Street, Suite 201, Pittsburgh, PA 15208
Tel: (412) 473-1200 Fax: (412) 473-1205
Internet: www.alleghenycounty.us/police

Superintendent **Charles Moffatt** .... (412) 473-1201

Police Training Academy
700 West Ridge Dr., Allison Park, PA 15101
Fax: (724) 935-6522

Director/Inspector **Wayne Gaffron** .... (724) 935-5566

Public Works Department
501 County Office Building, 542 Forbes Avenue, Pittsburgh, PA 15219-2904
Tel: (412) 350-4005 Fax: (412) 350-5386

▷ Director **Stephen Shanley** .... (412) 350-4005
Administration Deputy Director **Joseph A. Hrabik** .... (412) 350-4005
Road Engineering Deputy Director **Michael Dillon** .... (412) 350-7131
E-mail: mdillon@alleghenycounty.us
Bridge Engineer **Richard Connors** .... (412) 350-5877
E-mail: rconnors@alleghenycounty.us
Architecture **Carlton Bolton** .... (412) 350-5447
Construction Manager **Michael Dillon** .... (412) 350-2517
Fleet Management **Michael McCarlton** .... (412) 350-6969
Geotechnical **Steve Smallhover** .... (412) 350-5923

Department of Facilities Management
542 Forbes Avenue, Pittsburgh, PA 15219-2946
Tel: (412) 350-4005

Director (Interim) **Douglas Nolfi** .... (412) 350-4005

Allegheny County Airport Authority [ACAA]
Pittsburgh International Airport, Landside Terminal, P.O. Bo, Pittsburgh, PA 15231-0370
1000 Airport Boulevard, Pittsburgh, PA 15231
Tel: (412) 472-3500 Fax: (412) 472-3505

Chairman, Board of Directors **David Minnotte** .... (412) 472-3500
▷ Chief Executive Officer **Christina Cassotis** .... (412) 472-3511
Chief Operating Officer **James R. Gill** .... (412) 472-3669
E-mail: jgill@pitairport.com
Director, Air Service Development **Bryan Dietz** .... (412) 472-3503
Director, Communications **Robert Kerlik** .... (412) 472-3840
E-mail: bkerlik@flypittsburgh.com
Director, Planning and Environmental Programming
Richard C. "Rich" Belotti .... (412) 472-3545
Fax: (412) 472-3636
Director, Safety and Security **Kurt Sopp** .... (412) 472-3610
E-mail: ksopp@pitairport.com Fax: (412) 472-3628
Principal Architect **(Vacant)** .... (412) 472-3701
Fax: (412) 472-3690

Allegheny County Board of Health
542 Fourth Avenue, Pittsburgh, PA 15219
E-mail: boh@achd.net Internet: www.achd.net/board

▷ Chair **Lee Harrison** .... (412) 687-2243

Allegheny County Health Department [ACHD]
955 Rivermont Dr., Pittsburgh, PA 15207
Tel: (412) 578-8103 Fax: (412) 578-8144 Internet: www.achd.net

▶ Director **Dr. Karen Hacker** .... (412) 578-8008
Deputy Director **Ron Sugar** .... (412) 578-8005

★ Elected Official ▲ Appointed by Legislature ▼ Appointed by Governor ▶ Appointed by Board or Commission ● Appointed by Judge
■ Appointed by Mayor △ Appointed by Freeholders ▽ Appointed by Supervisor ▷ Appointed by County Executive ○ Appointed by Council

Allegheny County Housing Authority [ACHA]

625 Stanwix Street, 12th Floor, Pittsburgh, PA 15222
Fax: (412) 232-0281 Internet: www.achsng.com

▷ Chair, Board of Directors **Austin Davis** . . . . (412) 402-2450
Executive Director **Frank Aggazio** . . . . (412) 402-2450

Allegheny County Jail

950 Second Avenue, Pittsburgh, PA 15219-3100
Tel: (412) 350-2000 Fax: (412) 350-2186
Internet: www.alleghenycounty.us/jail

Warden **Orlando Harper** . . . . (412) 350-2000

Allegheny League of Municipalities

Regional Enetrprise Tower, 425 Sixth Avenue, Suite 2710,
Pittsburgh, PA 15219
Tel: (412) 261-2521 Fax: (412) 261-7606
Internet: www.alleghenycounty.us/alom

Executive Director **Jason Davidek** . . . . (412) 261-2521
E-mail: jason@alleghenyleague.org

Community College of Allegheny County [CCAC]

800 Allegheny Avenue, Pittsburgh, PA 15233-1895
Tel: (412) 323-2323 Internet: www.ccac.edu

President **Quintin B. Bullock** . . . . (412) 237-4413
Education: Prairie View A&M; Texas (Houston) DDS; Rochester (Attended)

Executive Director, Human Resources
Paul Schwarzmiller . . . . (412) 237-3001
Fax: (412) 237-3164

John J. Kane Regional Centers

955 Rivermont Dr., Pittsburgh, PA 15207
Fax: (412) 422-6966

▷ Executive Director **Dennis R. Biondo** . . . . (412) 422-6050
E-mail: dbiondo@alleghenycounty.us

Shuman Juvenile Detention Center

7150 Highland Dr., Pittsburgh, PA 15206
Tel: (412) 661-6806 Fax: (412) 661-6471
Internet: www.alleghenycounty.us/shuman

▷ Director **Earl F. Hill** . . . . (412) 661-6806

Office of the County Council

County Courthouse, 436 Grant Street, Room 119,
Pittsburgh, PA 15219-2499
Tel: (412) 350-6490 Fax: (412) 350-6499
E-mail: council@alleghenycounty.us
Internet: www.alleghenycounty.us/council

★ President **John P. DeFazio** (D-At-Large) . . . . (412) 350-6516
Term Expires: December 31, 2019
E-mail: jdefazio@alleghenycounty.us

★ Vice President **Nicholas "Nick" Futules** (D-District 7) . . . (412) 350-6555
Term Expires: December 31, 2019
E-mail: nfutules@alleghenycounty.us

★ Council Member **Tom Baker** (R-District 1) . . . . (412) 350-6525
Term Expires: December 31, 2017

★ Council Member **Cindy Kirk** (R-District 2) . . . . (412) 350-6490
Term Expires: December 31, 2019

★ Council Member **Edward J. Kress** (R-District 3) . . . . (412) 350-6535
Term Expires: December 31, 2017

★ Council Member **Michael J. Finnerty** (D-District 4) . . . . . (412) 350-6540
Term Expires: December 31, 2017
E-mail: mfinnerty@alleghenycounty.us

★ Council Member **Sue Means** (R-District 5) . . . . (412) 350-6545
Term Expires: December 31, 2019

Office of the County Council *continued*

★ Council Member **John F. Palmiere** (D-District 6) . . . . (412) 350-6550
Term Expires: December 31, 2019
E-mail: jpalmiere@alleghenycounty.us

★ Council Member **Dr. Charles J. Martoni** (D-District 8) . . . (412) 350-6560
Term Expires: December 31, 2017
E-mail: cmartoni@alleghenycounty.us
Education: Pittsburgh EdD

★ Council Member
Robert J. "Bob" Macey (D-District 9) . . . . (412) 350-6565
Term Expires: December 31, 2017
E-mail: bmacey@alleghenycounty.us

★ Council Member **DeWitt Walton** (D-District 10) . . . . (412) 350-6490
Term Expires: December 31, 2019

★ Council Member **Paul Klein** (D-District 11) . . . . (412) 350-6490
Term Expires: December 31, 2019

★ Council Member **Jim Ellenbogen** (D-District 12) . . . . (412) 350-6580
Term Expires: December 31, 2017
E-mail: jellenbogen@alleghenycounty.us
Education: Pittsburgh

★ Council Member
Denise Ranalli-Russell (D-District 13) . . . . (412) 350-6585
Term Expires: December 31, 2019

★ Council Member **Sam DeMarco** (R-At-Large) . . . . (412) 350-6520
Term Expires: December 31, 2019

○ Budget Director **Walter Szymanski** . . . . (412) 350-5742
Education: Rutgers 1963 BS

○ Director of Constituent Services and Government
Relations **Joe Catanese** . . . . (412) 350-6492
E-mail: jcatanese@alleghenycounty.us

○ Director of Legislative Services and Chief Clerk
Jared Barker . . . . (412) 350-6523
E-mail: jbarker@alleghenycounty.us
Education: Pittsburgh 1992 BA; George Washington 1995 JD

Council Clerk **Jared Barker** . . . . (412) 350-6490
Education: Pittsburgh 1992 BA; George Washington 1995 JD

Office of the Controller

104 County Courthouse, 436 Grant St., Pittsburgh, PA 15219-2498
Tel: (412) 350-4660 Fax: (412) 350-3006

★ Controller **Chelsa Wagner** (D) . . . . (412) 350-4660
Term Expires: December 31, 2019
Education: Chicago 1999 BA; Pittsburgh JD

Deputy Controller **Amy B. Griser** . . . . (412) 350-3078

Office of the District Attorney

303 County Courthouse, 436 Grant Street, Pittsburgh, PA 15219-2489
Tel: (412) 350-4400 Fax: (412) 350-3311
Internet: www.da.allegheny.pa.us

★ District Attorney **Stephen A. Zappala, Jr.** (D) . . . . (412) 350-4400
Term Expires: December 31, 2019
E-mail: szappala@alleghenycountyda.us
Education: Pittsburgh 1979 BA; Duquesne 1984 JD

First Assistant District Attorney and Chief of Staff
Rebecca Spangler . . . . (412) 350-4401
Education: West Virginia 1978 BA; Pittsburgh 1992 JD

First Assistant District Attorney **(Vacant)** . . . . (412) 350-4406

Chief of Detectives **Dennis Logan** . . . . (412) 388-5300
E-mail: dlogan@alleghenycountyda.us

Office of the Sheriff

111 County Courthouse, 436 Grant Street, Pittsburgh, PA 15219-2496
Tel: (412) 350-4700 Fax: (412) 350-6388
Internet: www.sheriffalleghenycounty.com

★ Sheriff **William P. "Bill" Mullen** (D) . . . . (412) 350-4711
Term Expires: December 31, 2017
E-mail: wmullen@court.allegheny.pa.us

(continued on next page)

COUNTIES

★ Elected Official ▲ Appointed by Legislature ▼ Appointed by Governor ▶ Appointed by Board or Commission ● Appointed by Judge
■ Appointed by Mayor △ Appointed by Freeholders ▽ Appointed by Supervisor ▷ Appointed by County Executive ○ Appointed by Council

Office of the Sheriff *continued*

Chief Deputy **Kevin Kraus** . . . . . (412) 350-4717
E-mail: kevin.kraus@alleghenycourts.us
Education: La Roche
Administrative Assistant **Marianne Di Vecchio** . . . . . (412) 350-4713
E-mail: marianne.divecchio@court.allegheny.pa.us

Office of the Treasurer

108 County Courthouse, 436 Grant Street, Pittsburgh, PA 15219-2497
Tel: (412) 350-4100 Fax: (412) 350-5649

★ Treasurer **John K. Weinstein** (D) . . . . . (412) 350-4120
Term Expires: December 31, 2019
E-mail: jweinstein@alleghenycounty.us

COUNTIES

County of Anne Arundel, Maryland

Arundel Center, 44 Calvert Street, Annapolis, MD 21401
P.O. Box 2700, Annapolis, MD 21404
Tel: (410) 222-7000 (Information) Internet: www.aacounty.org

County Seat: Annapolis **Election Type:** Partisan **Population:** 564,195 (2015)

Office of the County Executive

Arundel Center, 44 Calvert Street, Annapolis, MD 21401
P.O. Box 2700, Annapolis, MD 21404
Tel: (410) 222-1821 (Information) Fax: (410) 222-1155
Internet: www.aacounty.org/countyexec

★ County Executive **Steven R. "Steve" Schuh** (R) . . . . . (410) 222-1312
Term Expires: November 30, 2018
E-mail: exschu00@aacounty.org
Education: Dartmouth AB; Harvard 1987 MBA; Johns Hopkins MSEd
▷ Chief of Staff **Diane Croghan** . . . . . (410) 222-1182 ext. 1386
▷ Director of Community and Constituent Services
Nancy Schrum . . . . . (410) 222-1795
Fax: (410) 222-1244
▷ Director of Government Relations **Bernie Marczyk** . . . . . (410) 222-1756
Special Assistant for Minority Affairs
Yevola S. Peters Room 330 . . . . . (410) 222-1220
Fax: (410) 222-1198

Administrative Hearings Office

P.O. Box 2700, Annapolis, MD 21404
Fax: (410) 222-1268 Internet: www.aacounty.org/adminhear

▷ Administrative Hearings Officer
Douglas Clark "Doug" Hollmann . . . . . (410) 222-1266 ext. 1145

Office of Law

Heritage Office Complex, 2660 Riva Road, 4th Floor, Annapolis, MD 21401
Fax: (410) 222-7835 Internet: www.aacounty.org/law

▷ County Attorney **Nancy Duden** . . . . . (410) 222-7888
E-mail: nduden@aacounty.org

Office of the Chief Administrative Officer

Arundel Center, 44 Calvert Street, Annapolis, MD 21401
P.O. Box 2700, Annapolis, MD 21404
Fax: (410) 222-1155

▷ Chief Administrative Officer **Mark Hartzell** . . . . (410) 222-1312 ext. 1074

Office of Budget

44 Calvert Street, Annapolis, MD 21401
Fax: (410) 222-1108 Internet: www.aacounty.org/budget

Budget Officer **John R. Hammond** . . . . . (410) 222-1222 ext. 2352
E-mail: jhammond@aacounty.org Fax: (410) 222-1108

Office of Central Services

2660 Riva Road, 3rd Floor, Annapolis, MD 21401
Fax: (410) 222-7623

Director **Doug Jones** . . . . . (410) 222-7644
E-mail: djones@aacounty.org
Purchasing Agent **William L. "Bill" Schull** . . . . . (410) 222-7672

Office of Finance

44 Calvert Street, Annapolis, MD 21401
Fax: (410) 222-1354 Internet: www.aacounty.org/finance

▷ Controller **Julie Mussog** . . . . . (410) 222-1166 ext. 2368
Education: Michigan BABA, MBA

Office of Information Technology [OIT]

44 Calvert Street, Annapolis, MD 21401
Fax: (410) 222-1272 Internet: www.aacounty.org/oit

Information Technology Officer
Rick Napolitano . . . . . (410) 222-1159 ext. 1115

Office of Personnel

2660 Riva Road, 1st Floor, Annapolis, MD 21401
Fax: (410) 222-7650

▷ Personnel Officer **Andrea M. Fulton Rhodes** . . . . . (410) 222-7595

Office of Planning and Zoning

2664 Riva Road, Annapolis, MD 21401
Fax: (410) 222-7255 Internet: www.aacounty.org/planzone

▷ Planning and Zoning Officer **Larry R. Tom** . . . . . (410) 222-7450
E-mail: ltom@aacounty.org

Office of Public Information

44 Calvert Street, Annapolis, MD 21401
Tel: (410) 222-1288

Public Information Officer **Owen McAvoy** . . . . . (410) 222-1261
E-mail: owen.mcevoy@aacounty.org

Department of Aging and Disabilities

2666 Riva Road, 4th Floor, Annapolis, MD 21401
P.O. Box 6675, Annapolis, MD 21401
Fax: (410) 222-4360 Internet: www.aacounty.org/aging

▷ Director **Pamela A. Jordan** . . . . . (410) 222-4464
E-mail: pjordan@aacounty.org
Education: Maryland BS

Department of Detention Facilities

131 Jennifer Road, Annapolis, MD 21401
Fax: (410) 222-7208

▷ Superintendent **Terry Kokolis** . . . . . (410) 222-7084
E-mail: tkokolis@aacounty.org

Anne Arundel County Fire Department

8501 Veterans Highway, Millersville, MD 21108
Fax: (410) 987-2904

Chief **Allan Graves** . . . . . (410) 222-8200
E-mail: firechief@aacounty.org

★ Elected Official ▲ Appointed by Legislature ▼ Appointed by Governor ▶ Appointed by Board or Commission ● Appointed by Judge
■ Appointed by Mayor △ Appointed by Freeholders ▽ Appointed by Supervisor ▷ Appointed by County Executive ○ Appointed by Council

Office of Emergency Management [OEM]
7480 Baltimore and Annapolis Boulevard, Suite 102, Glen Burnie, MD 21061
Fax: (410) 222-0690 E-mail: oem@aacounty.org
Internet: www.aacounty.org/oem

Director **Michael O'Connell** (410) 222-0600

Department of Health [DOH]
J. Howard Beard Health Services Building, 3 Harry S. Truman Parkway, Annapolis, MD 21401-7085
Tel: (410) 222-7095 (Information) Fax: (410) 222-7294
Internet: www.aahealth.org

▷ Health Officer **Jinlene Chan** (410) 222-7375
E-mail: hdchan22@aacounty.org

Department of Inspections and Permits
2664 Riva Road, Annapolis, MD 21401
Fax: (410) 222-7970 E-mail: ipmailbox@aacounty.org
Internet: www.aacounty.org/ip

▷ Director **Daniel L. Kane** (410) 222-7790

Anne Arundel County Police Department [AACOPD]
8495 Veterans Highway, Millersville, MD 21108
Fax: (410) 987-9087

▷ Chief of Police **Timothy Altomare** (410) 222-8503
Communications Section Manager **Lt. Sara Schriver** (410) 222-8600

Department of Public Works [DPW]
Heritage Complex, 2662 Riva Road, Annapolis, MD 21401
Fax: (410) 222-4374 Internet: www.aacounty.org/dpw

▷ Director **Christopher J. Phipps** (410) 222-7092
E-mail: cphipps@aacounty.org
Education: Virginia Tech BSCE

Department of Recreation and Parks
1 Harry S Truman Parkway, Annapolis, MD 21401
Fax: (410) 222-4509 Internet: www.aacounty.org/recparks

▷ Director **Rick Anthony** (410) 222-7300
E-mail: ranthony@aacounty.org

Anne Arundel County Department of Social Services [AADSS]
80 West Street, Annapolis, MD 21401
Tel: (410) 269-4500 (Information)
Fax: (410) 974-8566 E-mail: aacodss@dhr.state.md.us
Internet: www.dhr.state.md.us/county/ann

▷ Director **Carnitra White** (410) 269-4600
Deputy Director **Sharon Hargrove** (410) 269-4612
Deputy Director, FIA **Edith Harrison** (410) 269-4603
Assistant Director, Child Welfare Intake **Susan Tyzack** (410) 269-4607

Anne Arundel Community College
101 College Parkway, Arnold, MD 21012
Tel: (410) 777-2222 (Information) Internet: www.aacc.edu

President **Dr. Dawn Lindsay** (410) 777-1177 ext. 1266
Education: McDaniel BA, BSW, MA; Pepperdine PhD
Chair, Board of Trustees **Arthur Ebersberger** (410) 777-1177
Vice President for Learner Support Services
Felicia L. Patterson (410) 777-2718
Vice President for Learning (Interim) **Michael Gavin** (410) 777-2332
Dean of Student Services **Dr. Jacqueline Jackson** (410) 777-7044
Fax: (410) 777-1323

Anne Arundel County Mental Health Agency, Inc. [AACMHA]
1 Harry S Truman Parkway, Suite 101, Annapolis, MD 21401
P.O. Box 6675, Annapolis, MD 21401
Fax: (410) 222-7881 E-mail: info@aamentalhealth.org
Internet: www.aamentalhealth.org

Executive Director **Adrienne Mickler** (410) 222-7858
Office Manager **Leanne Sorrells** (410) 222-7858

Anne Arundel County Public Library [AACPL]
Five Harry S. Truman Pkwy., Annapolis, MD 21401
Fax: (410) 222-7188 Internet: www.aacpl.net

President, Board of Trustees **M. Hall Worthington** (410) 222-7371
Chief Executive Officer **Hampton "Skip" Auld** (410) 222-7234
E-mail: sauld@aacpl.net
Education: Davidson 1973; North Carolina 1979 MSLS

Anne Arundel Partnership for Children, Youth and Families
1 Harry S Truman Parkway, Suite 103, Annapolis, MD 21401
Fax: (410) 222-7674 Internet: www.aacounty.org/partnership

Executive Director **Dr. Pamela Brown** (410) 222-7423 ext. 1

Anne Arundel Workforce Development Corporation [AAWDC]
401 Headquarters Drive, Suite 205, Millersville, MD 21108
Fax: (410) 987-3896 Internet: www.aawdc.org

President and Chief Executive Officer
Kirkland J. Murray (410) 987-3890
E-mail: kmurray@aawdc.org

Arundel Community Development Services, Inc. [ACDS]
2666 Riva Road, Suite 210, Annapolis, MD 21401
Fax: (410) 222-7619 E-mail: info@acdsinc.org Internet: www.acdsinc.org

Executive Director **Kathleen Koch** (410) 222-7600 ext. 110
E-mail: kkoch@acdsinc.org

Housing Commission of Anne Arundel County [HCAAC]
7477 Baltimore-Annapolis Boulevard, Glen Burnie, MD 21061-3574
Tel: (410) 222-6200 (Information) Fax: (410) 222-6214
E-mail: pha@hcaac.org Internet: www.hcaac.org

Chief Executive Officer
Clifton C. "Clif" Martin (410) 222-6200 ext. 1040

Office of the County Council
Arundel Center, 44 Calvert Street, Annapolis, MD 21401
P.O. Box 2700, Annapolis, MD 21404
Tel: (410) 222-1401 Fax: (410) 222-1755
Internet: www.aacounty.org/countycouncil

★ Council Member **Pete Smith** (D-District 1) (410) 222-1401
Term Expires: December 2018
★ Vice Chairman **John Joseph Grasso** (R-District 2) (410) 222-1401
Term Expires: November 31, 2018
E-mail: john.grasso@aacounty.org
★ Chairman **Derek Fink** (R-District 3) (410) 222-1401
Term Expires: November 30, 2018
E-mail: dfink@aacounty.org
★ Council Member **Andrew C. Pruski** (D-District 4) (410) 222-1401
Term Expires: November 30, 2018
Education: Niagara 2000 BA, 2001 MS
★ Council Member **Michael A. Petrouka** (R-District 5) (410) 222-1401
Term Expires: November 30, 2018

(continued on next page)

★ Elected Official ▲ Appointed by Legislature ▼ Appointed by Governor ▶ Appointed by Board or Commission ● Appointed by Judge
■ Appointed by Mayor △ Appointed by Freeholders ▽ Appointed by Supervisor ▷ Appointed by County Executive ○ Appointed by Council

Office of the County Council *continued*

★Council Member **The Honorable Christopher J. Trumbauer** (D-District 6) .... (410) 222-1401
Term Expires: November 30, 2018
E-mail: ctrumbauer@aacounty.org

★Council Member **Jerry Walker** (R-District 7) .... (410) 222-1401
Term Expires: November 30, 2018
E-mail: jerry.walker@aacounty.org

○Administrative Officer **Elizabeth E. "Beth" Jones** ...... (410) 222-1401
E-mail: beth.jones@aacounty.org

Office of the County Auditor

P.O. Box 1768, Annapolis, MD 21404-1768
Fax: (410) 222-1346 Internet: www.aacounty.org/auditor

○County Auditor (Acting) **Jodee Dickinson** .... (410) 222-1138

Office of the Register of Wills

Circuit Courthouse, Church Circle, Annapolis, MD 21404
P.O. Box 2368, Annapolis, MD 21404-2368
Fax: (410) 222-1467

★Register of Wills **Lauren M. Parker** (R) .... (410) 222-1430
Term Expires: November 30, 2018
E-mail: row.aacounty@registers.maryland.gov

Office of the Sheriff

8 Church Circle, P.O. Box 507, Annapolis, MD 21404
Fax: (410) 222-1583 E-mail: shwebmail@aacounty.org
Internet: www.aacounty.org/sheriff

★Sheriff **Ronald S. Bateman** (D) .... (410) 222-1571
Term Expires: November 30, 2018
Education: Baltimore 1997 BSCrimJ

Office of the State's Attorney

8 Church Circle, Suite 200, Annapolis, MD 21401-1935
Fax: (410) 222-1196 E-mail: aacsao@aacounty.org
Internet: http://www.statesattorney-annearundel.com

★State's Attorney **Wes Adams** (R) .... (410) 222-1740
Term Expires: January 2, 2019

Public Information Officer **(Vacant)** .... (410) 222-1740 ext. 3845

Anne Arundel County Board of Elections

6740 Baymeadow Drive, Glen Burnie, MD 21060
Fax: (410) 222-6833 Internet: www.aacounty.org/elections

Director **Joseph A. Torre III** .... (410) 222-6600

Anne Arundel County Public Schools [AACPS]

2644 Riva Road, Annapolis, MD 21401
Tel: (410) 222-5000 E-mail: info@aacps.org Internet: www.aacps.org

Board of Education

2644 Riva Road, Annapolis, MD 21401
Tel: (410) 222-5311 Fax: (410) 222-5629

▼President **Stacy Korbelak** (District 21) .... (443) 603-5205
Term Expires: June 30, 2017
E-mail: stacy.korbelak@aacps.org
Education: Michigan BA; Johns Hopkins MS

▼Vice President **Patricia Nalley** (At-Large) .... (410) 757-0454
Term Expires: June 30, 2017
E-mail: patricia.nalley@aacps.org

Board of Education *continued*

▼Member **Teresa Milio Birge** (District 32) .... (410) 674-5354
Term Expires: June 30, 2018
E-mail: teresa.birge@aacps.org
Education: Towson U 1993 BS; Delaware 1995 MPA

▼Member **Tom Frank** (At-Large) .... (301) 261-6181
Term Expires: June 30, 2018
E-mail: Thomas.Frank@aacps.org

▼Member **Julie Hummer** (At-Large) .... (410) 693-7458
Term Expires: June 30, 2019
E-mail: Julie.Hummer@aacps.org

▼Member **Allison Pickard** (District 33A-District 33B) ..... (410) 570-0361
Term Expires: June 30, 2016
E-mail: Allison.Pickard@aacps.org

▼Member **Terrill R. "Terry" Gilleland, Jr.** (R-District 31) .. (443) 534-2660
Term Expires: June 30, 2020
E-mail: terry.gilleland@aacps.org
Education: Loyola Col (MD) 1999 BA; Baltimore 2001 MBA

▼Member **Maria Delores Sasso** (District 30) .... (410) 267-0326
Term Expires: June 30, 2020
E-mail: maria.sasso@aacps.org

▼Student Member **Jacob Horstkamp** .... (410) 271-2944
Term Expires: June 30, 2016
E-mail: jacob.horstkamp@aacps.org

Executive Assistant to the Board **Molly Connolly** .... (410) 222-5311
E-mail: mconnolly@aacps.org

Office of the Superintendent

2660 Riva Road, Annapolis, MD 21401

Superintendent of Schools **Dr. George Arlotto** .... (410) 222-5303
Deputy Superintendent **Arlen Liverman** .... (410) 222-5192
Deputy Superintendent **Maureen McMahon** .... (410) 222-5304

County of Arapahoe, Colorado

5334 South Prince Street, Littleton, CO 80120-1136
Tel: (303) 795-4400 (Information) E-mail: info@co.arapahoe.co.us
Internet: www.co.arapahoe.co.us

County Seat: Littleton **Election Type:** Partisan **Population:** 631,096 (2015)

Board of County Commissioners

5334 South Prince Street, Littleton, CO 80120-1136
Fax: (303) 738-7894 E-mail: commissioners@co.arapahoe.co.us
Internet: www.co.arapahoe.co.us/departments/cm

★Chair **Nancy A. Doty** (R-District 1) .... (303) 795-4630
Term Expires: January 14, 2019

★Commissioner **Nancy N. Sharpe** (R-District 2) .... (303) 795-4630
Term Expires: January 14, 2019
E-mail: nsharpe@co.arapahoe.co.us

★Commissioner **Rod Bockenfeld** (R-District 3) .... (303) 795-4630
Term Expires: January 14, 2017
Date of Birth: December 9, 1955
Education: Western Illinois 1978 BSCrim; Colorado MA

★Commissioner **Nancy Jackson** (D-District 4) .... (303) 795-4630
Term Expires: January 14, 2019
E-mail: njackson@co.arapahoe.co.us

★Commissioner **Bill Lee Holen** (D-District 5) .... (303) 795-4630
Term Expires: January 14, 2017
Date of Birth: December 13, 1945
Education: Minnesota BA

Office of the County Attorney

5334 South Prince Street, Littleton, CO 80120-1136
Fax: (303) 738-7836 E-mail: attorney@arapahoegov.com

►County Attorney **Ron Carl** .... (303) 795-4680
E-mail: rcarl@arapahoegov.com

★Elected Official ▲Appointed by Legislature ▼Appointed by Governor ►Appointed by Board or Commission ●Appointed by Judge
■Appointed by Mayor △Appointed by Freeholders ▽Appointed by Supervisor ▷Appointed by County Executive ○Appointed by Council

Office of the Public Trustee
2329 West Main Street, Suite 100, Littleton, CO 80120
Fax: (303) 730-0076 Internet: www.co.arapahoe.co.us/departments/pt

▼Public Trustee **Cynthia D. Mares** .... (303) 730-0071
E-mail: eforeclosures@ArapahoeGov.com

Board of County Commissioners Administration
Administration Building, 5334 South Prince Street,
Littleton, CO 80120-1136
Fax: (303) 738-7894

▶Manager **Diana Maes** .... (303) 795-4530
E-mail: lbosanko@arapahoegov.com
Special Assistant to the Board of Commissioners
Shannon Carter .... (303) 795-4464
E-mail: scarter@co.arapahoe.co.us

Communication Services Department
5334 South Prince Street, Suite 440, Littleton, CO 80120-1136
Fax: (303) 734-5470 Internet: www.co.arapahoe.co.us/departments/cms

▶Director **Andrea Rasizer** .... (303) 795-4284
E-mail: arasizer@arapahoegov.com

Community Resources Department
1690 West Littleton Boulevard, Suite 300, Littleton, CO 80120
Fax: (303) 738-8099 E-mail: communityresources@co.arapahoe.co.us
Internet: www.co.arapahoe.co.us/departments/cs

▶Director **Don Klemme** .... (303) 738-8040
E-mail: communityresources@arapahoegov.com

Arapahoe/Douglas Works!
6974 South Lima Street, Centennial, CO 80111
Fax: (303) 636-1250 Internet: www.adworks.org

▶Manager **Joseph "Joe" Barela** .... (303) 636-1225
E-mail: jbarela@arapahoegov.com

Colorado State University Extension - Arapahoe County
5804 South Datura Street, Littleton, CO 80120-2192
Fax: (303) 730-2764 Internet: www.coopext.colostate.edu/arapahoe

Manager **Tim Aston** .... (303) 730-1920

Veterans Service Office
1690 West Littleton Boulevard, Suite 103, Littleton, CO 80120
Fax: (303) 738-7929

Veterans' Service Officer **Tim Westphal** .... (303) 738-8045

Facilities and Fleet Management Department
1690 West Littleton Boulevard, Littleton, CO 80120
Fax: (303) 734-5452 E-mail: ffm@co.arapahoe.co.us
Internet: www.co.arapahoe.co.us/departments/fm

▶Director **Dick Hawes** .... (303) 734-5489
E-mail: dhawes@arapahoegov.com

Finance Department
5334 South Prince Street, Littleton, CO 80120-1136
Fax: (303) 738-7929 E-mail: finance@co.arapahoe.co.us
Internet: www.co.arapahoe.co.us/departments/fi

▶Director **Janet Kennedy** .... (303) 795-4620
E-mail: jkennedy@arapahoegov.com
▶Budget Manager **Todd Weaver** .... (303) 795-4620
E-mail: tweaver@arapahoegov.com
Purchasing Manager **Keith Ashby** .... (303) 795-4435
E-mail: kashby@arapahoegov.com

Human Resources Department
5334 South Prince Street, Littleton, CO 80120-1136
Fax: (303) 738-7878 E-mail: humanresources@co.arapahoe.co.us
Internet: www.co.arapahoe.co.us/departments/hr

▶Director **Patrick L. Hernandez** .... (303) 795-4482
E-mail: phernandez@arapahoegov.com

Human Services Department
14980 East Alameda Drive, Aurora, CO 80012
Fax: (303) 636-1906 E-mail: humanservices@co.arapahoe.co.us
Internet: www.co.arapahoe.co.us/departments/hs

Director **Cheryl Ternes** .... (303) 636-1130

Information Technology Department
5334 South Prince Street, Littleton, CO 80120-1136
Fax: (303) 738-7899 Internet: www.co.arapahoe.co.us/departments/it

▶Director **David Bessen** .... (303) 795-4462
E-mail: dbessen@co.arapahoe.co.us

Public Works and Development
Lima Plaza Campus, 6924 South Lima Street, Centennial, CO 80112
Fax: (720) 874-6611 E-mail: publicworks@co.arapahoe.co.us
Internet: www.co.arapahoe.co.us/departments/pw

▶Director **David M. Schmit** .... (720) 874-6500
E-mail: pwd@arapahoegov.com
Building Division Manager **Steve Byer** .... (720) 874-6600
Planning and Zoning Division Manager **Jan Yeckes** ...... (720) 874-6500

Arapahoe County Animal Control
6924 South Lima Street, Centennial, CO 80112
E-mail: pwdanimalcontrol@arapahoegov.com
Internet: www.co.arapahoe.co.us/departments/pw/animalcontrol

Supervisor **Caitlyn Cahill** .... (720) 874-6750

Arapahoe Library District
5500 South Quebec Street, Suite 175, Greenwood, CO 80111
Fax: (303) 798-2485 E-mail: ask@ald.lib.co.us
Internet: www.arapahoelibraries.org

▶Executive Director **Nicole Davies** .... (303) 542-7279

Office of the Assessor
5334 South Prince Street, Littleton, CO 80120-1136
Fax: (303) 797-1295 E-mail: assessor@co.arapahoe.co.us
Internet: www.co.arapahoe.co.us/departments/as

★Assessor **Corbin Sakdol** (R) .... (303) 795-4600
Term Expires: January 14, 2019
E-mail: csakdol@co.arapahoe.co.us
Deputy Assessor of Administration (Interim)
Monica Babbitt .... (303) 795-4610
E-mail: mbabbitt@co.arapahoe.co.us
Deputy Residential Property Appraiser
Stephen T. Bonner .... (303) 795-4510
E-mail: sbonner@co.arapahoe.co.us
Deputy Commercial Property Assessor **Marcus Scott** .... (303) 795-4661

Office of the Clerk and Recorder
5334 South Prince Street, Littleton, CO 80120-1136
Fax: (303) 794-4625 E-mail: clerk@co.arapahoe.co.us
Internet: www.co.arapahoe.co.us/departments/cr

★Clerk and Recorder **Matthew Crane** (R) .... (303) 795-4200
Term Expires: January 14, 2019
E-mail: clerk@arapahoegov.com

★Elected Official ▲Appointed by Legislature ▼Appointed by Governor ▶Appointed by Board or Commission ●Appointed by Judge
■Appointed by Mayor △Appointed by Freeholders ▽Appointed by Supervisor ▷Appointed by County Executive ○Appointed by Council

Office of the Coroner

13101 East Broncos Parkway, Centennial, CO 80112
Fax: (720) 874-3627 E-mail: coroner@arapahoegov.com
Internet: www.co.arapahoe.co.us/departments/co

★Coroner **Dr. Kelly Lear-Kaul** (R) .... (720) 874-3625
Term Expires: January 14, 2019
E-mail: Coroner@arapahoegov.com

Office of the District Attorney

6450 South Revere Parkway, Centennial, CO 80111
Fax: (720) 874-8501

★District Attorney **George Butler** .... (720) 874-8500
Term Expires: January 14, 2019

Office of the Sheriff

13101 E. Broncos Parkway, Centennial, CO 80112
Fax: (720) 874-4158 E-mail: sheriff@co.arapahoe.co.us
Internet: www.arapahoesheriff.org

Sheriff **David C. Walcher** .... (720) 874-4176
E-mail: dwalcher@arapahoegov.com
Education: Metro State Col Denver BS; Colorado (Denver)
Undersheriff **Louie Perea** .... (720) 874-4179
E-mail: lperea@arapahoegov.com

Office of the Treasurer

5334 South Prince Street, Littleton, CO 80120-1136
Fax: (303) 347-2597 E-mail: treasurer@co.arapahoe.co.us
Internet: www.co.arapahoe.co.us/departments/tr

★Treasurer **Susan "Sue" Sandstrom** (D) .... (303) 795-4550
Term Expires: January 2019
E-mail: ssandstrom@co.arapahoe.co.us

County of Arlington, Virginia

2100 Clarendon Boulevard, Arlington, VA 22201-5445
Tel: (703) 228-3000 (Information) Internet: www.arlingtonva.us

County Seat: Arlington **Election Type:** Partisan **Population:** 229,164 (2015)

Office of the County Board

2100 Clarendon Boulevard, Suite 300, Arlington, VA 22201-5445
Fax: (703) 228-7430 E-mail: countyboard@arlingtonva.us

★Chair **E.T. "Libby" Garvey** .... (703) 228-3130
Term Expires: December 31, 2016
Education: Mount Holyoke 1977 BA
★Board Member **Kate Cristol** .... (703) 228-3130
Term Expires: December 31, 2019
★Board Member **Christian Dorsey** .... (703) 228-3130
Term Expires: December 31, 2019
★Board Member **Jay Fisette** (D) .... (703) 228-3130
Term Expires: December 31, 2017
E-mail: jfisette@arlingtonva.us
Education: Bucknell 1978 BA; Pittsburgh 1983 MA
★Board Member **John Vihstadt** (R) .... (703) 228-3130
Term Expires: December 31, 2018
Education: Nebraska BA, JD
►Clerk to the County Board **Hope Halleck** .... (703) 228-3130
County Auditor **Jessica Tucker** .... (703) 228-3000

Office of the County Attorney

2100 Clarendon Boulevard, Suite 403, Arlington, VA 22201
Fax: (703) 228-7106

►County Attorney **Stephen A. MacIsaac** .... (703) 228-3100
E-mail: smacisaac@arlingtonva.us
Deputy County Attorney **Ara L. Tramblian** .... (703) 228-3100
E-mail: atramblian@arlingtonva.us

Office of the County Manager

2100 Clarendon Boulevard, Suite 302, Arlington, VA 22201
Tel: (703) 228-3120 Fax: (703) 228-3295
E-mail: countymanager@arlingtonva.us

►County Manager **Mark Schwartz** .... (703) 228-3120
E-mail: mschwartz@arlingtonva.us
Education: Harvard 1982 AB; Pennsylvania 1985 JD
Assistant County Manager **Shannon Flanagan-Watson** .. (703) 228-3911
Education: Buffalo BA; Syracuse MPA
Assistant County Manager **Raul A. Torres** .... (703) 228-7045
E-mail: rtorre@arlingtonva.us
Education: George Washington 1998 MLaw
Assistant County Manager and Director of Communications **Diana Sun** .... (703) 228-3247
Education: Virginia 1975 BA; Pace MBA
Chief of Staff **Lynne Porfiri** .... (703) 228-0599

Office of the Deputy County Manager

Deputy County Manager **Carol J. Mitten** .... (703) 228-3120

Arlington Economic Development [AED]

1100 North Glebe Road, Suite 1500, Arlington, VA 22201
Tel: (703) 228-0808 E-mail: aed@arlingtonva.us

Director **Victor L. Hoskins** .... (703) 228-0850
Education: Dartmouth; MIT 1981 MCP

Department of Environmental Services [DES]

2100 Clarendon Boulevard, Suite 900, Arlington, VA 22201
Tel: (703) 228-4488 E-mail: des@arlingtonva.us

Director **Greg Emanuel** .... (703) 228-5022

Office of the Deputy County Manager

Deputy County Manager **James H. Schwartz** .... (703) 228-3120

Department of Technology Services [DTS]

2100 Clarendon Boulevard, Suite 612, Arlington, VA 22201
Fax: (703) 228-3304
Internet: www.arlingtonva.us/Departments/TechnologyServices/TechnologyServicesMain.aspx

Chief Information Officer **Jack Belcher** .... (703) 228-3220
E-mail: cio@arlingtonva.us

Office of Emergency Management

1400 North Uhle Street, Arlington, VA 22201
E-mail: oem@arlingtonva.us

Director **Jack Brown** .... (703) 228-7935
E-mail: jjbrown@arlingtonva.us

Arlington County Police Department

1425 N. Court House Rd., 7th Floor, Arlington, VA 22201
Fax: (703) 228-4127 E-mail: police@arlingtonva.us

Police Chief **M. Jay Farr** .... (703) 228-4040

Arlington County Fire Department

2100 Clarendon Boulevard, Suite 400, Arlington, VA 22201
Tel: (703) 228-3362 E-mail: fire@arlingtonva.us
Internet: www.arlingtonva.us/Departments/Fire/FireMain.aspx

Fire Chief **James Bonzano** .... (703) 228-3395
Assistant Chief **Joseph M. Reshetar** .... (703) 228-3362
E-mail: jreshe@arlingtonva.us

★Elected Official ▲Appointed by Legislature ▼Appointed by Governor ►Appointed by Board or Commission ●Appointed by Judge
■Appointed by Mayor △Appointed by Freeholders ▽Appointed by Supervisor ▷Appointed by County Executive ○Appointed by Council

Office of the Deputy County Manager

Deputy County Manager (Acting) **Michelle Cowan** . . . . . . (703) 228-3415
E-mail: mcowan@arlingtonva.us
Education: Eastern Michigan BA

Arlington Public Library

1015 North Quincy Street, Arlington, VA 22201
Fax: (703) 228-3354 E-mail: libraries@arlingtonva.us
Internet: http://library.arlingtonva.us/

Director **Diane Nester Kresh** . . . . (703) 228-3348

Department of Parks and Recreation

2100 Clarendon Boulevard, Suite 414, Arlington, VA 22201
E-mail: dpr@arlingtonva.us

Director **Jane Rudolph** . . . . (703) 228-3913

Human Resources Department

2100 Clarendon Boulevard, Suite 511, Arlington, VA 22201
TTY: (703) 228-4613 Fax: (703) 228-3265
E-mail: benefits@arlingtonva.us
Internet: www.arlingtonva.us/Departments/HumanResources/HumanResourcesMain.aspx

Director **Marcy Foster** . . . . (703) 228-3442
E-mail: mfoster@arlingtonva.us

Department of Management and Finance [DMF]

2100 Clarendon Boulevard, Suite 501, Arlington, VA 22201
Fax: (703) 228-3401 E-mail: dmf@arlingtonva.us

Director and Chief Financial Officer (Acting)
Maria Meredith . . . . (703) 228-3415
Budget Director **Richard Stephenson** . . . . (703) 228-3412
E-mail: rstephenson@arlingtonva.us
Comptroller **Barbara Wiley** . . . . (703) 228-3415
E-mail: bwiley@arlingtonva.us

Department of Human Services [DHS]

2100 Washington Boulevard, Arlington, VA 22204
Tel: (703) 228-1300 TTY: (703) 228-1788 Fax: (703) 228-1146
E-mail: dhs@arlingtonva.us

Director **Anita Friedman** . . . . (703) 228-1790

Office of the Deputy County Manager

Deputy County Manager **Gabriela Acurio** . . . . (703) 228-3120
E-mail: gacurio@arlingtonva.us
Education: Catholic U BS

Department of Community Planning, Housing and Development [CPHD]

2100 Clarendon Boulevard, Suite 700, Arlington, VA 22201
Fax: (703) 228-7495 E-mail: cphd@arlingtonva.us

Director **Steven R. Cover** . . . . (703) 228-3525
Education: Georgia Tech MA
Housing Director **David Cristeal** . . . . (703) 228-0761
E-mail: dcristeal@arlingtonva.us
Planning Director **Robert J. Duffy** . . . . (703) 228-3525
Education: Cincinnati BA
Zoning Administrator **Norma Cozart** . . . . (703) 228-3893
Chief Building Official **Shahriar Amiri** . . . . (703) 228-3848

Office of the Commissioner of Revenue

2100 Clarendon Boulevard, Suite 200, Arlington, VA 22201-5445
Fax: (703) 228-7048 E-mail: revenue@arlingtonva.us

★ Commissioner of Revenue **Ingrid H. Morroy** (D) . . . . (703) 228-3033
Term Expires: December 31, 2019
E-mail: imorroy@arlingtonva.us
Education: UDC BSBA; Averett U MBA
Chief Deputy **Anne M. Biedscheid** . . . . (703) 228-3025
E-mail: abiedscheid@arlingtonva.us

Office of the Commonwealth's Attorney

1425 N. Court House Rd., Suite 5200, Arlington, VA 22201
Fax: (703) 228-7116 Internet: http://www.vacao.com/

★ Commonwealth's Attorney **Theophani "Theo" Stamos** . . (703) 228-4410
Term Expires: December 31, 2019
Education: Northern Illinois BA; American U JD
Chief Deputy Commonwealth's Attorney
Molly Newton . . . . (703) 228-4410

Office of the Registrar of Voters

2100 Clarendon Blvd., Suite 320, Arlington, VA 22201
Fax: (703) 228-3659 E-mail: voters@arlingtonva.us

Registrar of Voters **Linda Lindberg** . . . . (703) 228-3456

Office of the Sheriff

1425 N. Court House Rd., 9th Floor, Arlington, VA 22201
Fax: (703) 228-7022
Internet: www.arlingtonva.us/Departments/Sheriff/SheriffMain.aspx

★ Sheriff **Beth Arthur** (D) . . . . (703) 228-4460
Term Expires: December 31, 2019
E-mail: barthur@arlingtonva.us
Chief Deputy **Paul Larson** . . . . (703) 228-7148
E-mail: plarson@arlingtonva.us

Office of the Treasurer

2100 Clarendon Boulevard, Suite 201, Arlington, VA 22201
Fax: (703) 228-7436 E-mail: treasurer@arlingtonva.us
Internet: www.arlingtonva.us/Departments/Treasurer/TreasurerMain.aspx

★ Treasurer (Interim) **Carla de la Pava** . . . . (703) 228-3255
Term Expires: December 31, 2019
E-mail: cdelapava@arlington.com
Chief Deputy Treasurer **(Vacant)** . . . . (703) 228-3255

Arlington Public Schools [APS]

1426 N. Quincy St., Suite 105, Arlington, VA 22207
Tel: (703) 228-6000 Fax: (703) 228-7640 Internet: www.apsva.us

★ Chair **James S. Lander** . . . . (703) 228-6015
Term Expires: December 31, 2017
★ Vice Chair **Dr. Emma Violand-Sánchez** . . . . (703) 228-6015
Term Expires: December 31, 2016
★ Board Member **Ried S. Goldstein** . . . . (703) 228-6015
Term Expires: December 31, 2019
★ Board Member **Barbara Kanninen** . . . . (703) 228-6015
Term Expires: December 31, 2018
★ Board Member **Nancy Van Doren** . . . . (703) 228-6015
Term Expires: December 31, 2016
Clerk of the Board **Melanie Elliott** . . . . (703) 228-6015
Superintendent of Schools **Dr. Patrick K. "Pat" Murphy** . . (703) 228-8634
Education: James Madison BS; Virginia Tech MA, EdD

County of Atlantic, New Jersey

County Office Building, 1333 Atlantic Avenue, Atlantic City, NJ 08401
Tel: (609) 343-2201 Fax: (609) 343-2194 Internet: www.aclink.org

County Seat: Mays Landing **Election Type:** Partisan **Year Founded:** 1837 **Population:** 274,219 (2015)

Office of the County Executive

1333 Atlantic Avenue, Atlantic City, NJ 08401
Tel: (609) 343-2201 Fax: (609) 343-2194
Internet: www.aclink.org/countyexecutive

★County Executive **Dennis Levinson** (R) . . . . (609) 343-2201
Term Expires: January 1, 2020
Education: Rowan U BA
Chief of Staff **Howard J. Kyle** . . . . (609) 343-2368

Office of the County Administrator

1333 Atlantic Avenue, Atlantic City, NJ 08401
Tel: (609) 343-2203 Fax: (609) 343-2194

▷County Administrator **Gerald "Jerry" DelRosso** . . . . (609) 343-2203
E-mail: delrosso_jerry@aclink.org
Education: Villanova 1969; Rutgers 1972 MSW
Deputy County Administrator **Diana Rutala** . . . . (609) 343-2223
E-mail: rutala_diana@aclink.org

Office of Cultural and Heritage Affairs

40 Farragut Avenue, Mays Landing, NJ 08330
Tel: (609) 625-2776 ext. 6314 Fax: (609) 625-8143
Internet: www.aclink.org/culturalaffairs

Administrator
Cynthia "Cindy" Mason Purdie . . . . (609) 625-2776 ext. 6314

Office of Extension Services

6260 Old Harding Highway, Mays Landing, NJ 08330-1533
Tel: (609) 625-0056 Fax: (609) 625-3646
Internet: http://rutgers-atlantic.org/

Director **Richard W. VanVranken** . . . . (609) 625-0056

Office of Internal Audit

1333 Atlantic Avenue, Atlantic City, NJ 08401
Tel: (609) 343-2166

Internal Auditor **Joseph McDermott** . . . . (609) 343-2166

Office of the Treasurer

1333 Atlantic Avenue, 6th Floor, Atlantic City, NJ 08401
Tel: (609) 343-2257 Fax: (609) 343-2189
Internet: www.aclink.org/treasurer

Treasurer/Chief Financial Officer **Bonnie Lindaw** . . . . (609) 343-2221
Comptroller **Julie Sharkey** . . . . (609) 343-2258
E-mail: gallagher_julie@aclink.org

Office of Veterans Services

Atlantic County Vet's Center, 6601 Ventor Avenue, Suite 307, Ventnor City, NJ 08406
Tel: (609) 677-5700 Fax: (609) 487-6783
Internet: www.aclink.org/veterans

Veterans Services Officer **Robert L. Frolow** . . . . (609) 487-6932

Department of Administrative Services

1333 Atlantic Avenue, Atlantic City, NJ 08401
Tel: (609) 343-2289 Fax: (609) 343-2204

Department Head **Diana Rutala** . . . . (609) 343-2289
E-mail: rutala_diana@aclink.org

Office of Communications

1333 Atlantic Avenue, Atlantic City, NJ 08401
Tel: (609) 343-2313 Fax: (609) 343-2194

Public Information Officer **Linda Gilmore** . . . . (609) 343-2313

Division of Budget and Purchasing

1333 Atlantic Avenue, 6th Floor, Atlantic City, NJ 08401
Tel: (609) 343-2268 Fax: (609) 343-2193
Internet: www.aclink.org/adminserv/purchasing

Purchasing Agent **Palma Conover** . . . . (609) 343-2268
E-mail: conover_palma@aclink.org

Division of Human Resources

1333 Atlantic Avenue, Atlantic City, NJ 08401
Tel: (609) 343-2211 Fax: (609) 343-2202
Internet: www.aclink.org/adminserv/hr

Division Director **Audrey McCant** . . . . (609) 343-2211
E-mail: mccant_audrey@aclink.org

Office of Equal Employment Opportunity

1333 Atlantic Avenue, Atlantic City, NJ 08401
Tel: (609) 343-2283 Fax: (609) 343-2373

Equal Employment Opportunity Officer **Edward Kyle** . . . . (609) 343-2241

Division of Information Technologies

1333 Atlantic Avenue, Atlantic City, NJ 08401
Tel: (609) 343-2321 Fax: (609) 343-2204

Director **Brian Ruh** . . . . (609) 343-2321
E-mail: ruh_brian@aclink.org
Records Manager **Donna Lenzi** . . . . (609) 343-2220

Department of Family and Community Development

1333 Atlantic Avenue, Atlantic City, NJ 08401
Tel: (609) 343-2377 Fax: (609) 343-2374 Internet: www.aclink.org/fcd

Department Head **J. Forrest Gilmore** . . . . (609) 343-2377
E-mail: gilmore_forrest@aclink.org

Department of Human Services

235 Dolphin Avenue, Northfield, NJ 08225
Tel: (609) 645-5930 Fax: (609) 645-5904

▷Department Head **Patricia Diamond** . . . . (609) 645-5930
E-mail: diamond_patricia@aclink.org
Education: Trenton State 1975; Temple

Office of Support Services

201 South Shore Road, Northfield, NJ 08225
Tel: (609) 645-5944

Director **Alan Knudsen** . . . . (609) 645-5944
E-mail: knudsen_alan@aclink.org

Division of Intergenerational Services

Shoreview Building, 101 South Shore Road, Northfield, NJ 08225
Tel: (888) 426-9243 (In County) Tel: (609) 645-5843 (Out of County)
Fax: (609) 645-5940 Internet: www.aclink.org/intergenerational

Director **Marilu Gagnon** . . . . (609) 645-5843

Division of Public Health

Stillwater Building, 201 South Shore Road, Northfield, NJ 08225
Tel: (609) 645-5935 Fax: (609) 645-5931
Internet: www.aclink.org/publichealth

Public Health Officer **Patricia Diamond** . . . . (609) 645-5935
Education: Trenton State 1975; Temple

★Elected Official ▲Appointed by Legislature ▼Appointed by Governor ▶Appointed by Board or Commission ●Appointed by Judge
■Appointed by Mayor △Appointed by Freeholders ▽Appointed by Supervisor ▷Appointed by County Executive ○Appointed by Council

Division of Public Health *continued*

Community Health and Clinical Services Unit Coordinator **Barbara Kennedy** . . . . (609) 645-5933
Environmental Health Unit Coordinator **Patrick Dillon** . . (609) 645-5971
Substance Abuse Unit Coordinator **Robert Widitz** . . . . . (609) 645-5932

Meadowview Nursing and Rehabilitation Center
235 Dolphin Avenue, Northfield, NJ 08225
Tel: (609) 645-5955 Fax: (609) 645-5939
Internet: www.aclink.org/meadowview

Administrator **Michelle Savage** . . . . (609) 645-5955
Assistant Administrator **Charlene Barr** . . . . (609) 645-5955

Department of Law
1333 Atlantic Avenue, Atlantic City, NJ 08401
Tel: (609) 343-2279 Fax: (609) 343-2373 Internet: www.aclink.org/law

▷ County Counsel **James F. "Jim" Ferguson** . . . . (609) 343-2310
E-mail: ferguson_james@aclink.org
Education: St Joseph's U; Villanova JD

Office of the Adjuster
1333 Atlantic Avenue, Atlantic City, NJ 08401
Tel: (609) 343-2361 Fax: (609) 343-2322

County Adjuster **Lillian Cross** . . . . (609) 343-2378

Department of Public Safety
Gerard L. Gormley Justice Facility, 5060 Atlantic Avenue, Mays Landing, NJ 08330
Tel: (609) 645-5855 Fax: (609) 909-7451
Internet: www.aclink.org/publicsafety

▷ Department Head **(Vacant)** . . . . (609) 909-7577

Office of Emergency Preparedness [OEP]
Anthony "Tony" Canale Training Center, 5033 English Creek Avenue, Egg Harbor Township, NJ 08234
Tel: (609) 407-6742 Fax: (609) 407-6745 Internet: www.aclink.org/oep

Emergency Management Coordinator **Vincent J. Jones III** . . . . (609) 407-6742
E-mail: jones_vincent@aclink.org
Deputy Emergency Management Coordinator **Edward "Ed" Conover** . . . . (609) 407-6735
E-mail: conover_edward@aclink.org

Office of Fire Safety
Anthony "Tony" Canale Training Center, 5033 English Creek Avenue, Egg Harbor Township, NJ 08234
Tel: (609) 407-6741

Fire Marshal **David Buzby** . . . . (609) 407-6741
E-mail: buzby_david@aclink.org

Office of Fire Training
Anthony "Tony" Canale Training Center, 5033 English Creek Avenue, Egg Harbor Township, NJ 08234
Tel: (609) 407-6728

Director **Michael Corbo** . . . . (609) 407-6728
E-mail: corbo_michael@aclink.org

Office of Highway Safety
Anthony "Tony" Canale Training Center, 5033 English Creek Avenue, Egg Harbor Township, NJ 08234
Tel: (609) 407-6739 Fax: (609) 407-6718
Internet: www.aclink.org/publicsafety/highwaysafety

Coordinator **Christine Zeltman** . . . . (609) 407-6739
E-mail: zeltman_christine@aclink.org

Division of Adult Detention
Gerard L. Gormley Justice Facility, 5060 Atlantic Avenue, Mays Landing, NJ 08330
Tel: (609) 645-5855 Fax: (609) 909-7451

Warden **Geraldine Cohen** . . . . (609) 909-7433

Division of Adult Detention *continued*

Deputy Warden **David Cohen** . . . . (609) 909-7433

Division of Youth Detention
Harborfields Juvenile Detention Center, 800 Buffalo Avenue, Egg Harbor City, NJ 08215
Tel: (609) 965-3583 Fax: (609) 965-7962

Superintendent **Kimery Lewis** . . . . (609) 965-3583
Assistant Superintendent **Wayne Ford** . . . . (609) 965-3583

Atlantic County Firearms Training Facility
175 Betsey Scull Road, Egg Harbor Township, NJ 08234
Tel: (609) 926-3491 Fax: (609) 926-5274
Internet: www.aclink.org/publicsafety/ftf

Range Manager **David Daniels** . . . . (609) 926-3491

Atlantic County Police Training Center
Anthony "Tony" Canale Training Center, 5033 English Creek Avenue, Egg Harbor Township, NJ 08234
Tel: (609) 407-6727 Fax: (609) 407-6717 Internet: www.aclink.org/ptc

Police School Director **Sidney Terrell** . . . . (609) 407-6727

Department of Regional Planning and Development
Route 9 and Dolphin Avenue, Northfield, NJ 08225
P.O. Box 719, Northfield, NJ 08225
Tel: (609) 645-5898 Fax: (609) 645-5836
Internet: www.aclink.org/planning

▷ Department Head **John Peterson** . . . . (609) 645-5898
E-mail: peterson_john@aclink.org
Supervising Planner **Robert B. "Bob" Lindaw, Jr.** . . . . . (609) 645-5898
E-mail: lindaw_robert@aclink.org

Office of Geographic Information Systems
Route 9 and Dolphin Avenue, Northfield, NJ 08225
Tel: (609) 645-5898 Fax: (609) 645-5836

Director **Barry Hackett** . . . . (609) 645-5898

Office of Policy, Planning and Development
Route 9 and Dolphin Avenue, Northfield, NJ 08225
Tel: (609) 645-5898 Fax: (609) 645-5836
Internet: www.aclink.org/planning/mainpages/oppd.asp

Director **John Peterson** . . . . (609) 645-5898
E-mail: peterson_john@aclink.org

Office of Land Acquisition
Route 9 and Dolphin Avenue, Northfield, NJ 08225

Open Space Acquisition Program Manager **Ranae Fehr** . . (609) 645-5898
E-mail: fehr_ranae@aclink.org

Division of Engineering
Route 9 and Dolphin Avenue, Northfield, NJ 08225
Tel: (609) 645-5898 Fax: (609) 645-5836

County Engineer **Mark Shourds** . . . . (609) 645-5898
E-mail: shourds_mark@aclink.org

Department of Public Works
Route 9 and Dolphin Avenue, Northfield, NJ 08225
Tel: (609) 645-5831 Fax: (609) 645-5873
Internet: www.aclink.org/publicworks

▷ Department Head **Clayton Ingersoll** . . . . (609) 645-5831
E-mail: Ingersoll_Clayton@aclink.org
Deputy Department Head **(Vacant)** . . . . (609) 645-5831

Atlantic County Animal Shelter
240 Old Turnpike Road, Pleasantville, NJ 08232
Tel: (609) 485-2345 Fax: (609) 484-0767
Internet: www.aclink.org/animalshelter

Manager **Kathy Kelsey** . . . . (609) 485-2345

★ Elected Official ▲ Appointed by Legislature ▼ Appointed by Governor ▶ Appointed by Board or Commission ● Appointed by Judge
■ Appointed by Mayor △ Appointed by Freeholders ▽ Appointed by Supervisor ▷ Appointed by County Executive ○ Appointed by Council

COUNTIES

Office of Fleet Management
Route 9 and Dolphin Avenue, Northfield, NJ 08225
Tel: (609) 645-5812

Director **Gregory "Greg" Brookins** . . . . . . (609) 645-5812

Office of Mosquito Control
Route 9 and Dolphin Avenue, Northfield, NJ 08225
Tel: (609) 645-5948 Fax: (609) 645-5846
Internet: www.aclink.org/publicworks/mosquito

Superintendent **John "Doug" Abdill** . . . . . . (609) 645-5948

Division of Facilities, Capital Planning and Property Management
1227 Drexel Avenue, Atlantic City, NJ 08404
P.O. Box 1107, Atlantic City, NJ 08404
Tel: (609) 343-2284 Fax: (609) 344-3654
Internet: www.aclink.org/facilities

Director **Glen Mawby** . . . . . . (609) 343-2284
E-mail: mawby_glen@aclink.org

Division of Parks and Recreation
109 State Highway 50, Mays Landing, NJ 08330
Tel: (609) 625-1897 Fax: (609) 645-5960 Internet: www.aclink.org/parks

Park Superintendent **Eric Husta** . . . . . . (609) 645-5960

Division of Roads and Bridges
Route 9 and Dolphin Avenue, Northfield, NJ 08225
Tel: (609) 645-5830 Fax: (609) 645-5845

Director **Fred Worlock** . . . . . . (609) 645-5830
E-mail: worlock_fred@aclink.org

Atlantic County Library System
40 Farragut Avenue, Mays Landing, NJ 08330
Tel: (609) 625-2776 Fax: (609) 625-8143 E-mail: contactus@aclsys.org
Internet: www.atlanticlibrary.org

Director **Karen L. George** . . . . . . (609) 625-2776
E-mail: kgeorge@aclsys.org

Board of Chosen Freeholders
201 South Shore Road, Northfield, NJ 08225
Tel: (609) 645-5900 Fax: (609) 645-5922 E-mail: freeholders@aclink.org
Internet: www.aclink.org/freeholders

★Freeholder **Ernest D. Coursey** (D-District 1) . . . . . . (609) 645-5900
Term Expires: December 31, 2016
E-mail: coursey_ernest@aclink.org

★Freeholder **Maureen Kern** (R-District 2) . . . . . . (609) 645-5900
Term Expires: December 31, 2018

★Freeholder **John Carman** (R-District 3) . . . . . . (609) 645-5900
Term Expires: December 31, 2017
E-mail: carman_john@aclink.org

★Freeholder **Richard "Rich" Dase** (R-District 4) . . . . . . (609) 645-5900
Term Expires: December 31, 2016
E-mail: dase_richard@aclink.org

★Freeholder **James A. "Jimmy" Bertino** (R-District 5) . . . (609) 645-5900
Term Expires: December 31, 2018
E-mail: bertino_james@aclink.org

★Freeholder **Frank D. Formica** (R-At-Large) . . . . . . (609) 645-5900
Term Expires: December 31, 2019

★Freeholder **Alexander C. Marino** (R-At-Large) . . . . . . (609) 645-5900
Term Expires: December 31, 2017
E-mail: marino_alex@aclink.org

★Freeholder **William Pauls** (R-At-Large) . . . . . . (609) 645-5900
Term Expires: December 31, 2016
E-mail: pauls_will@aclink.org

★Freeholder **John W. Risley** (R-At-Large) . . . . . . (609) 645-5900
Term Expires: December 31, 2017
E-mail: risley_john@aclink.org

Clerk to the Board **Sonya G. Harris** . . . . . . (609) 645-5909

Legislative Counsel **Roger C. Steedle** . . . . . . (609) 641-6800
Fax: (609) 641-2325

Office of the County Clerk
5901 Main Street, Mays Landing, NJ 08330
County Office Building, 1333 Atlantic Avenue, 1st Floor, Atlantic City, NJ 08401 (Atlantic City Satellite Office)
Tel: (609) 641-7867 Tel: (609) 343-2358 (Atlantic City Satellite Office)
Fax: (609) 909-5111 Fax: (609) 343-2167 (Atlantic City Satellite Office)
Internet: www.atlanticcountyclerk.org

★County Clerk **Edward P. "Ed" McGettigan** (D) . . . . . . (609) 645-5858
Term Expires: December 31, 2016
E-mail: mcgettigan_ed@aclink.org
Education: Villanova

Chief County Clerk **Frank R. Borino** . . . . . . (609) 645-5839
E-mail: borino_frank@aclink.org

Deputy County Clerk **Antoinette Flath** . . . . . . (609) 625-4011 ext. 5285
E-mail: flath_antoinette@aclink.org

Deputy County Clerk **Michael Sommers** . . . . . . (609) 625-4011 ext. 5241
E-mail: sommers_mike@aclink.org

Elections Department Office Manager
Jacob Austin . . . . . . (609) 625-4011 ext. 5231

Office of the County Prosecutor
4997 Unami Boulevard, Mays Landing, NJ 08330
Tel: (609) 909-7800 Fax: (609) 909-7802 Internet: www.acpo.org

▼County Prosecutor **James P. McClain** . . . . . . (609) 909-7800
Education: LaSalle Col (Canada) 1979 BA; Rutgers 1982 JD

First Assistant Prosecutor **Diane Ruberton** . . . . . . (609) 909-7800

Chief of County Detectives **Daren J. Dooley** . . . . . . (609) 909-7800
Education: Salisbury U BS; St Joseph's U MS

Public Information Officer **Jay McKeen** . . . . . . (609) 909-7881

Office of the County Surrogate
Atlantic County Civil Court House, 1201 Bacharch Boulevard, Atlantic City, NJ 08401
Mays Landing Criminal Court House, 5911 Main Street, Mays Landing, NJ 08330
Tel: (609) 343-2341 (Atlantic County Civil Court House)
Tel: (609) 645-5800 (Mays Landing Criminal Court House)
Fax: (609) 343-2197 (Atlantic County Civil Court House)
Fax: (609) 645-5805 (Mays Landing Criminal Court House)
Internet: www.aclink.org/surrogate

★County Surrogate **James "Jim" Curcio** (R) . . . . . . (609) 343-2341
Term Expires: December 31, 2018
E-mail: curcio_james@aclink.org
Tel: (609) 645-5800
Education: Rutgers BA; William & Mary 1985 JD

Deputy Surrogate **Maureen S. Krause** Civil Courthouse . . . . . . (609) 343-2341
Fax: (609) 343-2197

Special Deputy Surrogate **Mary Lou Latorre** County Government Complex . . . . . . (609) 645-5800
Fax: (609) 645-5805

Atlantic County Sheriff's Office
4997 Unami Boulevard, Mays Landing, NJ 08330
Tel: (609) 909-7200 Fax: (609) 909-7292
E-mail: oprarequest@acsheriff.org (Public Records Requests)
Internet: www.acsheriff.org

★Sheriff **Frank X. Balles** (R) . . . . . . (609) 909-7211
Term Expires: December 31, 2016
E-mail: balles_frank@aclink.org
Confidential Aide **(Vacant)** . . . . . . (609) 909-7214

Undersheriff **Michael Petuskey** . . . . . . (609) 909-7216
E-mail: petuskey_michael@aclink.org

Undersheriff **Stephen J. "Steve" Caldwell** . . . . . . (609) 909-7288
E-mail: caldwell_stephen@aclink.org

Chief Warrant Officer **Keith J. Fane** . . . . . . (609) 909-7265
E-mail: fane_keith@aclink.org

★Elected Official ▲Appointed by Legislature ▼Appointed by Governor ►Appointed by Board or Commission ●Appointed by Judge
■Appointed by Mayor △Appointed by Freeholders ▽Appointed by Supervisor ▷Appointed by County Executive ○Appointed by Council

Board of Elections

Historic Court House Complex, 5903 Main Street,
Mays Landing, NJ 08330
Tel: (609) 645-5867 Fax: (609) 645-5875

▼Chairman **Evelynn "Lynn" Caterson** .... (609) 645-5867
Note: Reappointed on March 8, 2016 by Governor Christie, pending New Jersey Senate approval.
▼Commissioner **Ernest Aponte** .... (609) 645-5867
▼Commissioner **Mary Jo Counts** .... (609) 645-5867
▼Commissioner **John Mooney** .... (609) 645-5867
Note: Reappointed on March 8, 2016 by Governor Christie, pending New Jersey Senate approval.

Administrative Staff

Clerk of the Board **Susan Sandman** .... (609) 645-5867
E-mail: sandman_susan@aclink.org
Clerk of the Board **Bill Sacchinelli** .... (609) 645-5867
E-mail: sacchinelli_bill@aclink.org

County of Baltimore, Maryland

Old Courthouse, 400 Washington Avenue, Towson, MD 21204
Internet: www.baltimorecountymd.gov

County Seat: Towson **Election Type:** Partisan **Population:** 831,128 (2015)

Office of the County Executive

Old Courthouse, 400 Washington Ave., Towson, MD 21204
Fax: (410) 887-5781

★County Executive **Kevin Kamenetz** (D) .... (410) 887-2450
Term Expires: November 30, 2018
E-mail: kevin@baltimorecountymd.gov
Date of Birth: 1957
Education: Johns Hopkins 1979 BS; Baltimore 1982 JD
Chief of Staff **Donald I. "Don" Mohler III** .... (410) 887-2460
Director of Government Affairs **Yolanda G. Winkler** ..... (410) 887-2450
E-mail: ywinkler@baltimorecountymd.gov
Education: Towson State U 1989 BS; Morgan State 1995 MBA

Office of Budget and Finance

Old Courthouse, 400 Washington Avenue, Room 100, Towson, MD 21204
Fax: (410) 887-3097 E-mail: financeinfo@baltimorecountymd.gov

▷Director **Keith Dorsey** .... (410) 887-3313
E-mail: kdorsey@baltimorecountymd.gov

Office of Communications

Old Courthouse, Mezzanine Level, 400 Washington Ave.,
Towson, MD 21204
Fax: (410) 337-8496 E-mail: communications@baltimorecountymd.gov

Chief of Staff and Communications Director
Donald I. "Don" Mohler III .... (443) 865-8772
E-mail: dmohler@baltimorecountymd.gov
Deputy Communications Director **Ellen L. Kobler** .... (410) 365-2834
E-mail: ekobler@baltimorecountymd.gov

Office of Homeland Security and Emergency Management

700 East Joppa Road, Baltimore, MD 21286-5500
Fax: (410) 832-8515
E-mail: emergencymanagement@baltimorecountymd.gov

Director **Mark F. Hubbard** .... (410) 887-8114
E-mail: mhubbard@baltimorecountymd.gov

Office of Human Resources

308 Allegheny Avenue, Towson, MD 21204
Tel: (410) 887-3135 Fax: (410) 887-8475
E-mail: ohr@baltimorecountymd.gov

Director **George E. Gay** .... (410) 887-3139
E-mail: ohr@baltimorecountymd.gov
Deputy Director **Suzanne Berger** .... (410) 887-3122
Classification and Compensation Division Chief
Regina Charles .... (410) 887-2004
E-mail: rcharles@baltimorecountymd.gov
Records Management Chief **Julie Guilbault** .... (410) 887-3121
Training Division Chief **Virginia Story** .... (410) 887-8713
E-mail: vstory@baltimorecountymd.gov
Employment Manager **Shannon Powell** .... (410) 887-3135
E-mail: spowell@baltimorecountymd.gov

Office of Information Technology

Old Courthouse Building, 400 Washington Avenue, Room 33, MS 2007,
Towson, MD 21204
Tel: (410) 887-2441 Fax: (410) 821-8024
E-mail: infotech@baltimorecountymd.gov
Internet: www.baltimorecountymd.gov/agencies/infotech

Director **Robert R. "Rob" Stradling** .... (410) 887-2441
E-mail: rstradling@baltimorecountymd.gov

Office of Law

Old Courthouse, 400 Washington Avenue, 2nd Floor, Towson, MD 21204
Fax: (410) 296-0931

County Attorney **Michael E. Field** .... (410) 887-4420
E-mail: mefield@baltimorecountymd.gov
Deputy County Attorney **Gregory E. Gaskins** .... (410) 887-4420

Baltimore County Department of Aging [BCDA]

611 Central Avenue, Towson, MD 21204
Tel: (410) 887-2594 (Information and Referral)
Fax: (410) 887-2159 E-mail: aginginfo@baltimorecountymd.gov
Internet: www.baltimorecountymd.gov/aging
Internet: www.takingcareofmomanddad.net (Caregiver Information)

▷Director **Joanne E. Williams** .... (410) 887-2109
E-mail: jwilliams@baltimorecountymd.gov
Deputy Director **Laura Riley** .... (410) 887-2109

Department of Corrections

720 Bosley Avenue, Towson, MD 21204
Tel: (410) 512-3200 Fax: (410) 512-3424
E-mail: corrections@baltimorecountymd.gov

▷Director **Deborah J. Richardson** .... (410) 512-3400
E-mail: djrichardson@baltimorecountymd.gov Fax: (410) 512-3406
Education: Maryland Baltimore 1979 BA, 2003 MA
Deputy Director **Thomas G. Fitzgerald** .... (410) 512-3400
Fax: (410) 512-3406
Detention Center **Major Robert Airey** .... (410) 512-3400
Fax: (410) 512-3406
Human Services Program Manager **Sharon M. Tyler** ..... (410) 512-3400
Education: Baltimore 1985 BA Fax: (410) 512-3406

Department of Economic and Workforce Development

Historic Courthouse, 400 Washington Ave., Suite 100,
Towson, MD 21204-4606
Fax: (410) 887-8017 E-mail: businesshelp@baltimorecountymd.gov
Internet: www.baltimorecountymd.gov/business

▷Director **Will Anderson** .... (410) 887-8000
E-mail: wanderson@baltimorecountymd.gov

★Elected Official ▲Appointed by Legislature ▼Appointed by Governor ►Appointed by Board or Commission ●Appointed by Judge
■Appointed by Mayor △Appointed by Freeholders ▽Appointed by Supervisor ▷Appointed by County Executive ○Appointed by Council

Department of Environmental Protection and Sustainability [EPS]

111 West Chesapeake Avenue, Third Floor, Room 319,
Towson, MD 21204
Fax: (410) 887-4804 E-mail: eps@baltimorecountymd.gov
Internet: www.baltimorecountymd.gov/agencies/environment

▷ Director **Vincent J. "Vince" Gardina** (D) . . . . (410) 887-3776
E-mail: vgardina@baltimorecountymd.gov
Education: Maryland Baltimore BA; Babson 1986 BS

Baltimore County Fire Department [BCFD]

Public Safety Building, 700 East Joppa Road, 4th Floor,
Baltimore, MD 21286-5500
Tel: (410) 887-4500 Fax: (410) 853-1883
Internet: www.baltimorecountymd.gov/fire

▷ Fire Chief **John J. Hohman** . . . . (410) 887-4511
E-mail: jhohman@baltimorecountymd.gov
Assistant Chief **Kyrle Preis III** . . . . (410) 887-8108
E-mail: kpreis@baltimorecountymd.gov

Department of Health

6401 York Road, 3rd Floor, Baltimore, MD 21212
Tel: (410) 887-2243 E-mail: hhs@baltimorecountymd.gov
Internet: www.baltimorecountymd.gov/health

▷ Health Officer **Gregory Wm. Branch** . . . . (410) 887-2773
E-mail: gbranch@baltimorecountymd.gov
Deputy Health Officer **Della J. Leister** . . . . (410) 887-2702

Department of Permits, Approvals and Inspections

County Office Building, 111 West Chesapeake Avenue,
Towson, MD 21204
Fax: (410) 887-5708
Internet: www.baltimorecountymd.gov/agencies/permits

▷ Director **Arnold E. Jablon** . . . . (410) 887-3353
E-mail: ajablon@baltimorecountymd.gov
Education: SUNY (Albany) 1965 BA; Maryland 1968 JD, 1971 MA

Department of Planning

The Jefferson Building, 105 West Chesapeake Avenue, Suite 101,
Towson, MD 21204
Fax: (410) 887-5862 E-mail: planning@baltimorecountymd.gov
Internet: www.baltimorecountymd.gov/agencies/planning

▷ Director **Andrea Van Arsdale** . . . . (410) 887-3211
E-mail: avanarsdale@baltimorecountymd.gov
Education: Rutgers; Ohio State MCRP
Deputy Director of Community Development
Jeff Mayhew . . . . (410) 887-3480
E-mail: jmayhew@baltimorecountymd.gov
Education: Delaware BS; Baltimore MPA
Deputy Director of Neighborhood Improvement
Elizabeth S. "Liz" Glenn . . . . (410) 887-3317
E-mail: eglenn@baltimorecountymd.gov
Education: Maryland Inst Art 1976 BFA; Baltimore BBA

Baltimore County Police Department [BCoPD]

Public Safety Bldg., 700 E. Joppa Rd., Towson, MD 21286
Fax: (410) 887-4958 E-mail: bcpd@baltimorecountymd.gov
Internet: www.baltimorecountymd.gov/police

▷ Police Chief **James W. Johnson** . . . . (410) 887-2201
E-mail: jwjohnson@baltimorecountymd.gov
Administrative and Technical Services Bureau Chief
Col. Joseph Burris . . . . (410) 887-2220
Community Resources Bureau Chief **(Vacant)** . . . . (410) 887-2206
Operations Bureau Chief **Col. Alexander Jones** . . . . (410) 887-6010
Operations Bureau Chief **Col. Evan Cohen** . . . . (410) 887-6010

Department of Public Works

County Office Building, 111 West Chesapeake Avenue, Room 307,
Towson, MD 21204
Fax: (410) 887-3406 E-mail: publicworks@baltimorecountymd.gov
Internet: www.baltimorecountymd.gov/agencies/publicworks

▷ Director **Edward C. Adams, Jr.** . . . . (410) 887-3306
E-mail: eadams@baltimorecountymd.gov
Deputy Director **(Vacant)** . . . . (410) 887-3302

Department of Recreation and Parks

105 West Chesapeake Avenue, Suite 302, Towson, MD 21204
Tel: (410) 887-3871 Fax: (410) 825-3305
E-mail: recparks@baltimorecountymd.gov

▷ Director **Barry F. Williams** . . . . (410) 887-3806
E-mail: bfwilliams@baltimorecountymd.gov
Education: Maryland 1976 BA
Chief of Recreation Services **Beahta Davis** . . . . (410) 887-3082

Department of Social Services

6401 York Road, Third Floor, Baltimore, MD 21212
Tel: (410) 853-3000 Fax: (410) 853-3955

▷ Director **Gregory Wm. Branch** . . . . (410) 853-3000
E-mail: gbranch@baltimorecountymd.gov

Baltimore County Commission on Disabilities

105 West Chesapeake Avenue, Suite 201, Towson, MD 21204

Chair **(Vacant)** . . . . (410) 887-3580
Administrator **Hal Franklin** . . . . (410) 887-3580

Baltimore County Public Library [BCPL]

320 York Road, Towson, MD 21204
Tel: (410) 887-6100 Fax: (410) 887-6103 E-mail: bcpl@bcpl.info
Internet: www.bcpl.info

Year Founded: 1948

Administration

Director **Paula J. Miller** . . . . (410) 887-6160
E-mail: pmiller@bcpl.net
Assistant Director, Public Services **(Vacant)** . . . . (410) 887-6121
Assistant Director, Support Services **James Cooke** . . . . . . (410) 887-6122
Information Services Coordinator **Jim DeArmey** . . . . (410) 887-6100
E-mail: jdearmey@bcpl.net

Office of the County Council

Court House, 400 Washington Avenue, Room 205,
Towson, MD 21204-4606
Tel: (410) 887-3196 Fax: (410) 887-5791
E-mail: countycouncil@baltimorecountymd.gov
Internet: www.baltimorecountymd.gov/countycouncil

★ Chairwoman **Vicki Almond** (D-District 2) . . . . (410) 887-3385
Term Expires: December 2018
E-mail: council2@baltimorecountymd.gov
★ Council Member **Tom Quirk** (D-District 1) . . . . (410) 887-0896
Term Expires: December 2018
E-mail: council1@baltimorecountymd.gov
★ Council Member **A. Wade Kach** (R-District 3) . . . . (410) 887-3387
Term Expires: December 2018
E-mail: council3@baltimorecountymd.gov
Education: Western Maryland 1970 BA
★ Council Member **Julian Earl Jones, Jr.** (D-District 4) . . . (410) 887-3389
Term Expires: December 2018
E-mail: council4@baltimorecountymd.gov
★ Council Member **David Marks** (R-District 5) . . . . (410) 887-3384
Term Expires: December 2018
E-mail: council5@baltimorecountymd.gov
★ Council Member **Cathy Bevins** (D-District 6) . . . . (410) 887-3388
Term Expires: December 2018
E-mail: council6@baltimorecountymd.gov

★ Elected Official ▲ Appointed by Legislature ▼ Appointed by Governor ► Appointed by Board or Commission ● Appointed by Judge
■ Appointed by Mayor △ Appointed by Freeholders ▽ Appointed by Supervisor ▷ Appointed by County Executive ○ Appointed by Council

Office of the County Council *continued*

★Council Member **Todd Crandell** (R-District 7) . . . . (410) 887-3383
Term Expires: December 2018
E-mail: council7@baltimorecountymd.gov
Legislative Counsel/Secretary
Thomas J. Peddicord, Jr. . . . . (410) 887-3196
Administrator **Chris Belcastro** . . . . (410) 887-3196

Office of the County Auditor
400 Washington Avenue, Room 221, Towson, MD 21204-4672
Fax: (410) 887-4621 E-mail: auditor@baltimorecountymd.gov

○Auditor **Lauren Smelkinson** . . . . (410) 887-3193
E-mail: auditor@baltimorecountymd.gov

Office of the District Public Defender
Fax: (410) 769-7882

District Public Defender **Donald E. Zaremba** . . . . (410) 324-8963
Deputy District Public Defender **Gayle L. Robinson** . . . . . (410) 324-8911

Office of the Register of Wills
County Courts Building, 401 Bosley Avenue, Suite 500, Towson, MD 21204
Tel: (410) 887-6680 Fax: (410) 583-2517

★Register of Wills **Grace G. Connolly** (D) . . . . (410) 887-6691
Term Expires: November 30, 2018
E-mail: gconnolly@baltimorecountymd.gov

Sheriff's Office
County Courts Bldg., 401 Bosley Ave., Towson, MD 21204
Fax: (410) 887-3870

★Sheriff **R. Jay Fisher** (D) . . . . (410) 887-3151
Term Expires: November 30, 2018
E-mail: rjfisher@baltimorecountymd.gov
Education: Baltimore BA
Undersheriff **Col. Robert Haukdal** . . . . (410) 887-8698
E-mail: rhaukdal@baltimorecountymd.gov

State's Attorney's Office
401 Bosley Avenue, Room 511, Towson, MD 21204
Fax: (410) 828-1078

★State's Attorney **Scott D. Shellenberger** (D) . . . . (410) 887-6600
Term Expires: December 31, 2018
Education: Loyola U (Maryland) 1981 BA; Baltimore 1984 JD

Baltimore County Board of Elections
106 Bloomsbury Avenue, Catonsville, MD 21228-5220
Fax: (410) 887-0894 E-mail: elections@baltimorecountymd.gov
Internet: www.baltimorecountymd.gov/agencies/elections

Director **Katie Brown** . . . . (410) 887-0902
Deputy Director **Rena Waggoner** . . . . (410) 887-0888
E-mail: rwaggoner@baltimorecountymd.gov

Baltimore County Public Schools
6901 Charles St., Towson, MD 21204-3711
Tel: (410) 887-4554 Fax: (410) 887-4309 Internet: www.bcps.org

Board of Education
President **Charles McDaniels** . . . . (410) 887-4554

Office of the Superintendent
Superintendent of Schools **Dr. S. Dallas Dance** . . . . (410) 887-4281
Education: Virginia Union BA; VCU MEd, PhD

County of Bergen, New Jersey
One Bergen County Plaza, Hackensack, NJ 07601
Tel: (201) 336-6000 (Information) Fax: (201) 336-7304
Internet: www.co.bergen.nj.us

County Seat: Hackensack **Election Type:** Partisan **Population:** 938,506 (2015)

Office of the County Executive
One Bergen County Plaza, Room 580, Hackensack, NJ 07601
Tel: (201) 336-7300

★County Executive **James J. "Jim" Tedesco III** (D) . . . . . . (201) 336-7300
Term Expires: December 31, 2018
E-mail: countyexecutive@co.bergen.nj.us
Chief of Staff **Michele Dilorgi** . . . . (201) 336-7311
Deputy Chief of Staff **Marc Schrieks** . . . . (201) 336-7313
Communications Director **Alicia D'Alessandro** . . . . (201) 336-6979
Education: Notre Dame 2005; Johns Hopkins 2008

Department of Administration and Finance
One Bergen County Plaza, Room 580, Hackensack, NJ 07601-7076
Fax: (201) 336-7304

County Administrator/Director **Dominic J. Novelli** . . . . . . (201) 336-7335
Senior Policy and Planning Advisor **Peter C. Botsolas** . . . (201) 336-7307

Information Technology
One Bergen County Plaza, 5th Floor, Hackensack, NJ 07601
Fax: (201) 336-6650

Director **Benjamin "Ben" Kezmarsky** . . . . (201) 336-6600
E-mail: bkezmarsky@co.bergen.nj.us
Supervisor of Programming **Evelyn Guzman** . . . . (201) 336-6600
E-mail: eguzman@co.bergen.nj.us
Supervisor of Systems **Wayne Atkins** . . . . (201) 336-6600
E-mail: watkins@co.bergen.nj.us

Division of Fiscal Operations
One Bergen County Plaza, 5th Floor, Hackensack, NJ 07601
Fax: (201) 336-6529

Chief Financial Officer **Joseph Luppino** . . . . (201) 336-6550
E-mail: jluppino@co.bergen.nj.us
Budget Officer **Marlene Golden** . . . . (201) 336-6571
E-mail: mgolden@co.bergen.nj.us

Division of Personnel
One Bergen County Plaza, Room 321, Hackensack, NJ 07601
Fax: (201) 336-6384

Director **Ralph W. Kornfeld** . . . . (201) 336-6375
E-mail: rkornfeld@co.bergen.nj.us
Assistant Director **Michele Popkin** . . . . (201) 336-6378
E-mail: mpopkin@co.bergen.nj.us
Affirmative Action Officer **Dr. Margaret Haynes** . . . . (201) 336-6377
One Bergen County Plaza, Fax: (201) 336-6289
Room 320, Hackensack, NJ 07601-7076
E-mail: mhaynes@co.bergen.nj.us

Division of Purchasing
One Bergen County Plaza, Room 331, Hackensack, NJ 07601-7076
Tel: (201) 336-7100 Fax: (201) 336-7105

Purchasing Director **Dominic J. Novelli** . . . . (201) 336-7111
E-mail: dnovelli@co.bergen.nj.us
Senior Buyer **(Vacant)** Room 308W . . . . (201) 336-7110
Chief Clerk and Bid Supervisor **Linda Campanaro** . . . . . . (201) 336-7102
E-mail: lcampanaro@co.bergen.nj.us

★Elected Official ▲Appointed by Legislature ▼Appointed by Governor ▶Appointed by Board or Commission ●Appointed by Judge
■Appointed by Mayor △Appointed by Freeholders ▽Appointed by Supervisor ▷Appointed by County Executive ○Appointed by Council

COUNTIES

Division of Treasury
One Bergen County Plaza, 5th Floor, Hackensack, NJ 07601
Treasurer **Joseph Luppino** .... (201) 336-6555

Bergen County Department of Health Services [BCDHS]
One Bergen County Plaza, Hackensack, NJ 07601
Tel: (201) 634-2600 Fax: (201) 336-6086
E-mail: healthdept@co.bergen.nj.us Internet: www.bergenhealth.org
▷ Director/Health Officer **Nancy Mangieri** .... (201) 634-2600
E-mail: nmangieri@co.bergen.nj.us

Office of Alcohol and Drug Dependency [OADD]
Tel: (201) 634-2740 Fax: (201) 336-6086
Internet: www.bergenhealth.org/oadd
Coordinator **Sue A. Marchese-Debiak** .... (201) 634-2740
Employee Assistance Coordinator **Susan Boggia** .... (201) 634-2753
Municipal Alliance Program Coordinator **Judy Forman** .. (201) 634-2744
Spring House for Women Coordinator
Sue A. Marchese-Debiak .... (201) 261-3582
East Ridgewood Avenue, Paramus, NJ 07652

Office of Health Promotion
One Bergen County Plaza, Fourth Floor, Hackensack, NJ 07601
Tel: (201) 634-2693 Fax: (201) 336-6068
Administrator **Marla Klein** .... (201) 634-2693

Office of Public Health Nursing
One Bergen County Plaza, Hackensack, NJ 07601
Tel: (201) 634-2655 (Communicable Disease Control)
Tel: (201) 634-2660 (Cancer Education and Early Detection)
Tel: (201) 634-2653 (Chronic/Interlocal Contracts)
Tel: (201) 634-2647 (Immunization Management)
Tel: (201) 634-2654 (In-Service/Non-Public Schools)
Tel: (201) 634-2620 (Special Child Health Services) Fax: (201) 986-1068
Director **(Vacant)** .... (201) 634-2646

Mental Health Division
Tel: (201) 634-2750 Fax: (201) 336-6068
Internet: www.bergenhealth.org/mental
Administrator **Michele Hart-Loughlin** .... (201) 634-2745
Mental Health Law Project **Jose Ortiz** .... (201) 634-2763

Environmental Protection Program
327 East Ridgewood Avenue, Paramus, NJ 07652-4895
Fax: (201) 599-6270
Program Administrator **Thomas Longo, Jr.** .... (201) 634-2780

Planning and Epidemiology
Assistant Director of Administrative Services
Cathy Vacirca .... (201) 634-2603

Bergen County Animal Shelter and Adoption Center
100 United Lane, Teterboro, NJ 07608
Tel: (201) 229-4600 Fax: (201) 440-4358
E-mail: shelter@co.bergen.nj.us Internet: www.co.bergen.nj.us/bcas
Manager **Deborah Yankow** .... (201) 229-4606

Bergen County Health Care Center
35B Piermont Rd., Rockleigh, NJ 07647
Fax: (201) 784-3590 Internet: www.bergenhealth.org/bchcc
Administrator **Harvey Silberstein** .... (201) 750-8310

Department of Human Services
One Bergen County Plaza, 2nd Floor, Hackensack, NJ 07601-7076
Fax: (201) 336-7450 Internet: www.co.bergen.nj.us/bcdhs
▷ Director **Jane C. Linter** .... (201) 336-7474
E-mail: jlinter@co.bergen.nj.us
Planning and Program Development Officer
Sarah Onello .... (201) 336-7458

Department of Human Services *continued*
Homeless Services Coordinator **Susan Nottingham** .... (201) 336-7461

Office for Children
One Bergen County Plaza, 2nd Floor, Hackensack, NJ 07601
Fax: (201) 336-7155 E-mail: ofc@co.bergen.nj.us
Director **Julie O'Brien** (D) .... (201) 336-7150

Division of Alternatives to Domestic Violence [ADV]
One Bergen County Plaza, 2nd Floor, Hackensack, NJ 07601
Fax: (201) 336-7555 E-mail: adv@co.bergen.nj.us
Director **David Cohen** .... (201) 336-7575

Division of Community Transportation
178 Essex Street, Lodi, NJ 07644
Fax: (201) 845-4683
Director **Jo Marie Sacchinelli** .... (201) 368-5955

Division of Disability Services
One Bergen County Plaza, 2nd Floor, Hackensack, NJ 07601
Tel: (201) 336-6500 TTY: (201) 336-6505 Fax: (201) 336-6510
Director **James Thebery** .... (201) 336-6500

Division of Family Guidance
One Bergen County Plaza, 2nd Floor, Hackensack, NJ 07601
Fax: (201) 336-7370 E-mail: fgintake@co.bergen.nj.us
Director **Nicholas A. Montello** .... (201) 336-7350

Division of Senior Services
One Bergen County Plaza, 2nd Floor, Hackensack, NJ 07601
Tel: (201) 336-7400 Fax: (201) 336-7424
E-mail: seniors@co.bergen.nj.us
Internet: www.co.bergen.nj.us/bcdhs/divisions/senior.htm
Director **Lorraine Joewono** .... (201) 336-7400

Division of Veterans Services
One Bergen County Plaza, 2nd Floor, Hackensack, NJ 07601
Fax: (201) 336-6327 E-mail: veterans@co.bergen.nj.us
Director **A.J. Luna** .... (201) 336-6325

Department of Law
One Bergen County Plaza, Room 580, Hackensack, NJ 07601-7076
Fax: (201) 336-6966 Internet: www.co.bergen.nj.us/departments/cc
▷ Director/County Counsel **Julien Xavier Neals** .... (201) 336-6950
E-mail: jneals@co.bergen.nj.us
Education: Morehouse Col BA; Emory JD

Office of the County Adjuster
One Bergen County Plaza, Room 340, Hackensack, NJ 07601
Fax: (201) 336-6176
County Adjuster **John TenHoeve, Jr.** .... (201) 336-6175

Department of Planning and Engineering
One Bergen County Plaza, 4th Floor, Hackensack, NJ 07601-7076
Fax: (201) 336-6449 Internet: www.co.bergen.nj.us/planning
▷ Director **(Vacant)** .... (201) 336-6437

Community Development Division
One Bergen County Plaza, Hackensack, NJ 07601
Tel: (201) 646-2559 (Small Business/1st Time Buyers Mortgage Program)
Director **Robert G. Esposito** .... (201) 336-7200

Data Resources and Technology
Division Director **Shujun Zhang** .... (201) 336-6447
E-mail: szhang@co.bergen.nj.us

Land Use and Development Review
Principal Planner **Eric Timsak** .... (201) 336-6434
E-mail: etimsak@co.bergen.nj.us

★ Elected Official ▲ Appointed by Legislature ▼ Appointed by Governor ► Appointed by Board or Commission ● Appointed by Judge
■ Appointed by Mayor △ Appointed by Freeholders ▽ Appointed by Supervisor ▷ Appointed by County Executive ○ Appointed by Council

Division of Open Space
One Bergen County Plaza, Hackensack, NJ 07601
Division Director **Adam Strobel** .... (201) 336-6458

Regional Planning and Transportation
Division Director **Donna Orbach** .... (201) 336-6438

Construction Board of Appeals
▷ Chairman **Richard Bolan** .... (201) 336-6453
Board Counsel **John Libretti** .... (201) 336-6950
Board Secretary **Maizie Patterson** .... (201) 336-6453

Planning Board
Chairperson **Joseph Valente** .... (201) 336-6436
Board Counsel **John Libretti** .... (201) 336-6950
Board Secretary **Maizie Patterson** .... (201) 336-6436

Department of Parks
One Bergen County Plaza, 4th Floor, Hackensack, NJ 07601-7000
Fax: (201) 336-7262 Internet: www.co.bergen.nj.us/bcparks
Director **James Koth** .... (201) 336-7275
Superintendent of Parks **Todd Cochran** .... (201) 336-7284

Division of Cultural and Historic Affairs
One Bergen County Plaza, Room 425, Hackensack, NJ 07601
Fax: (201) 336-7262
Director **Cynthia Forster** .... (201) 336-7276

Probation Division
39 Hudson Street, Hackensack, NJ 07601
Tel: (201) 527-4000
Internet: www.judiciary.state.nj.us/bergen/probation.htm
Chief Probation Officer **John A. Fuhrman** .... (201) 527-4000
Fax: (201) 527-4090
Administration/Juvenile Supervision Assistant Chief
Ron Nowakowski .... (201) 527-4000
Fax: (201) 527-4050
Adult Supervision Assistant Chief **Roy A. Friedman** ..... (201) 527-4000
Fax: (201) 527-1223
Child Support Enforcement Assistant Chief **Lori Tirri** ..... (201) 527-4000
Fax: (201) 527-1222
Community Service Program Principal Probation
Officer **Susan Calandriello** .... (201) 527-4059
Fax: (201) 527-4050
Pre-Trial Intervention Principal Probation Officer
Brenda Patterson .... (201) 527-4053
Fax: (201) 527-4050

Department of Public Safety
Bergen County Law and Public Safety Institute, 281 Campgaw Road, Mahwah, NJ 07430
Tel: (201) 785-8500 Fax: (201) 785-6036
▷ Director **Ralph Rivera, Jr.** .... (201) 785-8550
Assistant to the Director **Maria Toscano** .... (201) 785-5705

Office of Consumer Affairs and Protection
One Bergen County Plaza, Room 324, Hackensack, NJ 07601
Tel: (201) 336-6400 Fax: (201) 336-6415
Coordinator **John V. Bentz** .... (201) 336-6400

Office of Emergency Management [OEM]
285 Campgaw Road, Mahwah, NJ 07430
Tel: (201) 785-5757 Fax: (201) 785-8571 Internet: www.bcoem.org
Coordinator **Matthew Tiedemann** .... (201) 634-5757
Director **Thomas Metzler** .... (201) 785-5757

Office of Fire Marshal
Law & Public Safety Institute, 281 Campgaw Road, Mahwah, NJ 07430
Fax: (201) 785-6036
Fire Marshal **Bryan Hennig** .... (201) 785-5718

Office of Highway Safety
66 Zabriskie Street, Hackensack, NJ 07601
Fax: (201) 646-3344
Director **(Vacant)** .... (201) 336-6420

Office of the Medical Examiner
351 E. Ridgewood Ave., Paramus, NJ 07652
Tel: (201) 634-2940 Fax: (201) 634-2950
△ County Medical Examiner **Dr. Frederick Decarlo** .... (201) 634-2940
E-mail: fdecarlo@co.bergen.nj.us
Assistant County Medical Examiner **Jennifer L. Swatz** .. (201) 634-2940

Division of Weights and Measures
327 East Ridgewood Avenue, Room 207, Paramus, NJ 07652
Tel: (201) 336-7921 Fax: (201) 599-2912
County Superintendent **Michael Alpher** .... (201) 336-7921

Bergen County Law and Public Safety Institute [BCLPSI]
Law and Public Safety Institute, 281 Campgaw Rd., Mahwah, NJ 07430
Tel: (201) 785-6000 Fax: (201) 785-6036
Internet: www.co.bergen.nj.us/bclpsi
Director **Richard C. Blohm** .... (201) 785-5702
Fax: (201) 785-6036
Chief Fire Instructor **Larry Rauch** .... (201) 785-5710
E-mail: rauch@bclpsi.net
Chief of Police Training **(Vacant)** .... (201) 785-6009
EMS Training Coordinator **(Vacant)** .... (201) 785-6026

Bergen County Police Department [BCPD]
32 East Ridgewood Avenue, Paramus, NJ 07652
Tel: (201) 336-7801 Fax: (201) 646-2723 Internet: www.bcpd.org
▷ Police Chief (Acting) **Mark Lepinski** .... (201) 336-7801

Department of Public Works
One Bergen County Plaza, 4th Floor, Hackensack, NJ 07601
Tel: (201) 336-6800 Fax: (201) 336-6845
Internet: www.co.bergen.nj.us/departments/publicworks.html
Director **Raymond W. Dressler** .... (201) 336-6800
Assistant Director/County Engineer **Joseph A. Femia** .... (201) 336-6800
E-mail: jfemia@co.bergen.nj.us

General Services Division
Tel: (201) 336-6767 Fax: (201) 336-6751
Director **Raymond W. Dressler** .... (201) 336-6752
E-mail: rdressler@co.bergen.nj.us

Mosquito Control Division
P.O. Box 236, Paramus, NJ 07652
Tel: (201) 599-6141 Fax: (201) 599-6143
Director **Peter Pluchino, Jr.** .... (201) 634-2880

Operations Division
70 Zabriskie St., Hackensack, NJ 07601
Tel: (201) 646-2808 Fax: (201) 646-3111
Supervisor of Roads **Thomas "Tom" Connolly** .... (201) 646-2808
E-mail: tconnolly@co.bergen.nj.us
Assistant Supervisor of Roads **Russell G. Martin** .... (201) 646-2808
E-mail: rmartin@co.bergen.nj.us

Bergen Community College [BCC]
400 Paramus Road, Paramus, NJ 07652-1595
Tel: (201) 447-7200 Internet: www.bergen.edu
President **Dr. B. Kaye Walter** .... (201) 447-7237
Fax: (201) 447-9042
Vice President, Academic Affairs
Dr. William Mullaney .... (201) 447-7104
Fax: (201) 612-8225
Vice President, Institutional Effectiveness **Dr. Yun Kim** ... (201) 493-3619

(continued on next page)

COUNTIES

★ Elected Official ▲ Appointed by Legislature ▼ Appointed by Governor ► Appointed by Board or Commission ● Appointed by Judge
■ Appointed by Mayor △ Appointed by Freeholders ▽ Appointed by Supervisor ▷ Appointed by County Executive ○ Appointed by Council

Bergen Community College *continued*

Vice President, Student Affairs
Dr. Naydeen Gonzalez "Nancy" De Jesus .... (201) 447-7491
Fax: (201) 447-3730

Executive Director, Human Resources **Jim Miller** .... (201) 447-7124

Executive Director, Information Technology **(Vacant)** ..... (201) 447-7433
Fax: (201) 612-6710

Managing Director of Continuing Education
Paul Ragusa .... (201) 612-5233
Fax: (201) 612-8225

Bergen County Board of Taxation

One Bergen County Plaza, Room 370, Hackensack, NJ 07601-7076
Tel: (201) 336-6300 Fax: (201) 336-6310
Internet: www.co.bergen.nj.us/taxboard

▼Tax Administrator **Robert F. Layton** .... (201) 336-6303

Bergen County Improvement Authority [BCIA]

One Bergen County Plaza, Room 480, Hackensack, NJ 07601
Fax: (201) 336-6352 E-mail: bcia@co.bergen.nj.us Internet: www.bcia.us

Chairperson **Philip Wilson** .... (201) 336-6350

Executive Director (Acting) **Mauro D. Raguseo** (D) ..... (201) 336-6350
E-mail: mraguseo@co.bergen.nj.us
Education: Rutgers 2000 BA, 2009 MPA

Deputy Executive Director **Mauro D. Raguseo** (D) ...... (201) 336-6350
E-mail: mraguseo@co.bergen.nj.us
Education: Rutgers 2000 BA, 2009 MPA

Bergen County Technical Schools [BCTS]

327 East Ridgewood Avenue, Paramus, NJ 07652
Fax: (201) 225-9692 Internet: www.bergen.org

Superintendent of Technical Schools
Dr. Howard Lerner .... (201) 343-6000 ext. 4005

Business Administrator **John Susino** .... (201) 343-6000 ext. 4056

Bergen County Utilities Authority [BCUA]

Foot of Mehrhof Road, P.O. Box 9, Little Ferry, NJ 07643
Tel: (201) 641-2552 Fax: (201) 641-6407 Internet: www.bcua.org

►Executive Director **Robert E. Laux** .... (201) 807-5801
E-mail: rlaux@bcua.org Fax: (201) 641-5356

Solid Waste Management Division

Foot of Mehrhof Road, Little Ferry, NJ 07643
P.O. Box 9, Little Ferry, NJ 07643

Director **Richard Wierer** .... (201) 807-5818
Fax: (201) 641-3509

Water Pollution Control Division

Foot of Mehrhof Road, P.O. Box 9, Little Ferry, NJ 07643

Director and Chief Engineer **Eric Andersen** .... (201) 807-8634
E-mail: eandersen@bcua.org Fax: (201) 807-8633

Housing Authority of Bergen County

1 Bergen County Plaza, Second Floor, Hackensack, NJ 02701
Tel: (201) 336-7600 TTY: (201) 336-7669 Fax: (201) 336-7660

▷Executive Director **Lynn Bartlett** .... (201) 336-7600
E-mail: info@habcnj.org

Office of the Board of Chosen Freeholders

One Bergen County Plaza, Floor 5, Room 520,
Hackensack, NJ 07601-7076
Tel: (201) 336-6200 Fax: (201) 336-6290
Internet: www.co.bergen.nj.us/freeholders

★Chairman **Steven A. Tanelli** (D) .... (201) 336-6200
Term Expires: December 31, 2018

Office of the Board of Chosen Freeholders *continued*

★Vice Chairwoman **Tracy Silna Zur** (D) .... (201) 336-6200
Term Expires: December 31, 2018

★Freeholder **Maura R. DeNicola** (R) .... (201) 336-6200
Term Expires: December 31, 2016
E-mail: mdenicola@co.bergen.nj.us
Education: Boston Col 1978 BA; Columbia 1980 MA

★Freeholder **John A. Felice** (R) .... (201) 336-6200
Term Expires: December 31, 2016
E-mail: jfelice@co.bergen.nj.us

★Freeholder **David L. Ganz** (D) .... (201) 336-6200
Term Expires: December 31, 2017
E-mail: dganz@co.bergen.nj.us

★Freeholder **Thomas Sullivan** (D) .... (201) 336-6200
Term Expires: December 31, 2016

★Freeholder **Joan M. Voss** (D) .... (201) 336-6200
Term Expires: December 31, 2017
Education: Montclair State U BA, MA; Fordham EdD

△Clerk to the Board **(Vacant)** .... (201) 336-6526

△Director of Communications and Policy **Peter Berthelis** .. (201) 336-6530

Office of the County Clerk

One Bergen County Plaza, Room 122, Hackensack, NJ 07601
Tel: (201) 336-7000 Fax: (201) 336-7002
Internet: www.co.bergen.nj.us/countyclerk

★County Clerk **John S. Hogan** (D) .... (201) 336-7000
Term Expires: November 2016
E-mail: countyclerk@co.bergen.nj.us

Deputy County Clerk (Interim) **Lauren Zyriek** .... (201) 336-7043
E-mail: lzyriek@co.bergen.nj.us Fax: (201) 336-7010

Elections Deputy Clerk **Lauren Zyriek** .... (201) 336-7043
Fax: (201) 336-7005

Passports and Naturalization **Liliana Otalvaro** .... (201) 336-7054

Registry Records Supervisor **Carlos Soto** .... (201) 336-7034

Trade Names and Notary Public Supervisor
Mark Tomko .... (201) 336-7016

Systems Programmer **Ahae Cho** .... (201) 336-7067
E-mail: acho@co.bergen.nj.us

Record Manager **Christina Napolitano** .... (201) 336-7072

Office of the County Prosecutor

Bergen County Justice Center, 10 Main Street, Hackensack, NJ 07601
Fax: (201) 646-3794

▼Prosecutor (Acting) **Gurbir S. Grewal** .... (201) 646-2300
Education: Georgetown 1995 BSFS; William & Mary 1999 JD

Surrogate's Court

Bergen County Justice Center, 10 Main Street, Room 211,
Hackensack, NJ 07601-7000

★Surrogate **Michael R. Dressler** (D) .... (201) 646-2252
Term Expires: December 31, 2016
Education: Fairleigh Dickinson 1976 BA; Seton Hall 1979 JD

Office of the Bergen Executive County Superintendent of Schools

One Bergen County Plaza, Room 350, Hackensack, NJ 07601
Tel: (201) 336-6875 Fax: (201) 336-6880

▼Executive County Superintendent (Interim) **Norah Peck** .. (201) 336-6875

★Elected Official ▲Appointed by Legislature ▼Appointed by Governor ►Appointed by Board or Commission ●Appointed by Judge
■Appointed by Mayor △Appointed by Freeholders ▽Appointed by Supervisor ▷Appointed by County Executive ○Appointed by Council

Office of the Sheriff

Bergen County Justice Center, 10 Main Street,
Hackensack, NJ 07601-7692
Tel: (201) 336-3519 Tel: (201) 646-2222 (24-hour Line)
Fax: (201) 752-4164 Internet: www.bcsd.us

★ Sheriff **Michael Saudino** (D) .... (201) 336-3545
Term Expires: December 31, 2017
E-mail: msaudino@bcsd.us
Executive Undersheriff **Joseph Hornyak** .... (201) 336-3541
E-mail: jhornyak@bcsd.us
Undersheriff **Brian Smith** .... (201) 336-3542
E-mail: bsmith@bcsd.us
Undersheriff **Harry Shortway, Jr.** .... (201) 527-3543
E-mail: hshortway@bcsd.us
Undersheriff **Bob Colaneri** .... (201) 336-3519
Public Information **Anthony Cureton** .... (201) 336-3516
E-mail: acureton@bcsd.us

Bergen County Board of Elections

One Bergen County Plaza, Room 310, Hackensack, NJ 07601
Tel: (201) 336-6230 Fax: (201) 336-6230

▼ Chairman **Eileen K. DeBari** .... (201) 336-6230
Note: Reappointed on March 8, 2016 by Governor Christie, pending New Jersey Senate approval.
▼ Commissioner **Paul A. Juliano** .... (201) 336-6230
Term Expires: March 1, 2018
▼ Commissioner **Richard L. "Rich" Miller** .... (201) 336-6230
Note: Reappointed on March 8, 2016 by Governor Christie, pending New Jersey Senate approval.
▼ Commissioner **Jamie Sheehan-Willis** .... (201) 336-6230
Term Expires: March 1, 2017

Office of the Superintendent of Elections

One Bergen County Plaza, Room 380, Hackensack, NJ 07601
Tel: (201) 336-6100 Fax: (201) 336-6111
Internet: www.co.bergen.nj.us/elections

▼ Superintendent of Elections/Commissioner of Registration **Patricia DiCostanzo** .... (201) 336-6100
E-mail: bcsuptelection@aol.com
▼ Deputy Superintendent of Elections/Deputy Commissioner of Registration **Theresa M. O'Connor** ... (201) 336-6118
Voting Machine Division Director **David Ursprung** ...... (201) 896-6932
Fax: (201) 896-6935

County of Bernalillo, New Mexico

One Civic Plaza, NW, Albuquerque, NM 87102
Tel: (505) 468-7000 (Information) Fax: (505) 462-9813
Internet: www.bernco.gov

County Seat: Albuquerque **Election Type:** Partisan
Population: 676,685 (2015)

Office of the County Commission

One Civic Plaza, NW, 10th Floor, Suite 10111, Albuquerque, NM 87102
Fax: (505) 468-7329 E-mail: info@bernco.gov
Internet: www.bernco.gov/county-commissioners

★ Chair **Art De La Cruz** (D-District 2) .... (505) 468-7448
Term Expires: December 31, 2016
E-mail: adelacruz@bernco.gov
Education: New Mexico; U Phoenix MA
★ Vice Chair **Wayne A. Johnson** (R-District 5) .... (505) 468-7212
Term Expires: December 31, 2018
E-mail: wjohnson@bernco.gov

Office of the County Commission *continued*

★ Commissioner **M. Debbie O'Malley** (D-District 1) ...... (505) 468-7027
Term Expires: December 31, 2018
★ Commissioner **Maggie Hart Stebbins** (R-District 3)..... (505) 468-7108
Term Expires: December 31, 2016
★ Commissioner **Lonnie C. Talbert** (R-District 4) .... (505) 468-7010
Term Expires: December 31, 2016
Commission Administrator **(Vacant)** .... (505) 468-7083

Office of the County Attorney

520 Lomas, NW, 4th Floor, Albuquerque, NM 87102
Fax: (505) 242-0828 Internet: www.bernco.gov/county-attorneys-office

▶ County Attorney **W. Ken Martinez** (D) .... (505) 314-0180
E-mail: kenmartinez@bernco.gov Fax: (505) 242-0828
Education: New Mexico BA; Notre Dame JD

Office of the County Manager

One Civic Plaza, NW, 10th Floor, Suite 10111, Albuquerque, NM 87102
Fax: (505) 462-9813 E-mail: info@bernco.gov

▶ County Manager **Julie Morgas Baca** .... (505) 468-7000
E-mail: jbaca@bernco.gov

Economic Development

Tel: (505) 468-7185

Director **Mayling Armijo** .... (505) 468-7185
E-mail: marmijo@bernco.gov

Human Resources Department

One Civic Plaza, NW, 4th Fl., Albuquerque, NM 87102
Tel: (505) 468-1500 Fax: (505) 468-1527 E-mail: hr@bernco.gov
Internet: www.bernco.gov/human-resources

Director **Renetta Torres** .... (505) 468-1500
E-mail: rtorres@bernco.gov
Administrative Officer III **Candace M. Sanchez** .... (505) 468-1513
E-mail: csanchez@bernco.gov
Human Resources Employee Relations Administrator **Matt Marquez** .... (505) 468-1512

Metropolitan Detention Center/Corrections

100 Deputy Dean Miera Drive Southwest, Albuquerque, NM 87151
Fax: (505) 462-9806 E-mail: mdc@bernco.gov
Internet: www.bernco.gov/metropolitan-detention-center

Chief of Corrections (Interim) **Thomas E. "Tom" Swisstack** (D) .... (505) 839-8700
Education: Albuquerque BA

Community Services Division

One Civic Plaza, 10th Floor, Albuquerque, NM 87102
Fax: (505) 462-9816

Deputy County Manager **Vincent C. Murphy** .... (505) 468-7000

Communications Services [PID]

One Civic Plaza, NW, 10th Floor, Albuquerque, NM 87102
Tel: (505) 468-7026 Fax: (505) 768-4444

Director **Tia Bland** .... (505) 468-7026
E-mail: tbland@bernco.gov
Communications Services Coordinator **Tiffany Chamblee** .... (505) 468-7438
E-mail: tchamblee@bernco.gov
Communication Services Administrator **Andrew Lenderman** .... (505) 314-0403
E-mail: alenderman@bernco.gov
Website Administrator **Tracy Dingmann** .... (505) 468-1276
E-mail: tdingmann@bernco.gov

★ Elected Official ▲ Appointed by Legislature ▼ Appointed by Governor ▶ Appointed by Board or Commission ● Appointed by Judge
■ Appointed by Mayor △ Appointed by Freeholders ▽ Appointed by Supervisor ▷ Appointed by County Executive ○ Appointed by Council

Cooperative Extension Office
1510 Menaul, NW, Albuquerque, NM 87107
Fax: (505) 243-1545 E-mail: bernalil@nmsu.edu
Internet: http://bernalilloextension.nmsu.edu

Director **Cynthia Davies** .... (505) 243-1386

Environmental Health Office
111 Union Square, SE, Suite 300, Albuquerque, NM 87102
Fax: (505) 314-0470 E-mail: eh@bernco.gov

Director **Enrico Gradi** .... (505) 314-0384
Administrative Officer II **Miriam Aguilar** .... (505) 314-0316
E-mail: maguilar@bernco.gov
Urban Biologist **Paul Smith** .... (505) 314-0310

Bernalillo County Housing Department [BCHD]
1900 Bridge Boulevard Southwest, Albuquerque, NM 87105
Tel: (505) 314-0200 Fax: (505) 462-9737 E-mail: housing@bernco.gov
Internet: www.bernco.gov/housing

Director **Betty Valdez** .... (505) 314-0235
Assistant Director **(Vacant)** .... (505) 314-0225

Parks and Recreation Department
111 Union Square St., Southeast, Suite 200, Albuquerque, NM 87102
Fax: (505) 314-0436 E-mail: parks@bernco.gov
Internet: www.bernco.gov/fun

Director **Debbie Jo Almager** .... (505) 314-0402
Assistant Director **(Vacant)** .... (505) 314-0400
Parks and Open Space Administrator
Colleen McRoberts .... (505) 314-0400
Community Fitness Section Manager **Laura Kennedy** .... (505) 314-0400
Land Managing Section Manager **Ed Martinez** .... (505) 224-2119
Sports Program Specialist **Rick Espinoza** .... (505) 314-0400
Budget and Planning Officer **Corina Cortez-Ali** .... (505) 314-0400
E-mail: ccortez@bernco.gov

Planning and Development Services
111 Union Square Street, SE, Suite 100, Albuquerque, NM 87102
Fax: (505) 314-0480 E-mail: zoning@bernco.gov
Internet: www.bernco.gov/zoning-building-and-planning

Director **Enrico Gradi** .... (505) 314-0350
Community Development Manager **(Vacant)** .... (505) 314-0350
Building Official **Jeff Senseney** .... (505) 314-0382
Senior Administrative Officer **Miriam Aguilar** .... (505) 314-0350
E-mail: maguilar@bernco.gov
Zoning Enforcement Manager **Tom Kay** .... (505) 314-0396
Land Use Planner **Robert D. Peirson** .... (505) 314-0350
Land Use Planner **Catherine Ver Eecke** .... (505) 314-0350

Finance Division
One Civic Plaza, NW, 10th Floor, Albuquerque, NM 87102
Fax: (505) 768-4201 E-mail: financedivision@bernco.gov

Deputy County Manager **Shirley Ragin** .... (505) 468-7020

Information Technology Department
One Civic Center Plaza, NW, 2nd Floor, Albuquerque, NM 87102
Tel: (505) 468-7999 Internet: www.bernco.gov/information-technology

Chief Information Officer/Director **Paul Roybal** .... (505) 468-7999
E-mail: proybal@bernco.gov
Assistant to the Director **Rose Silva** .... (505) 468-7999

Accounting and Budget Department
415 Tijeras Avenue N.W., Albuquerque, NM 87102
Fax: (505) 468-1411

Accounting and Budget Director **Pamela Moon** .... (505) 468-1694
E-mail: budget@bernco.gov

Procurement and Business Services
One Civic Center Plaza, NW, Albuquerque, NM 87102
Fax: (505) 768-4067 E-mail: purchasing@bernco.gov
Internet: www.bernco.gov/purchasing

Director **Dinah Esquivel** .... (505) 468-7013

Risk Management Department
111 Union Square, SE, Suite 201, Albuquerque, NM 87102
E-mail: risk@bernco.gov

Director/Loss Control Administrator **Kevin Kinzie** .... (505) 314-0443
E-mail: kkinzie@bernco.gov

Public Safety Division
One Civic Plaza, NW, Tenth Floor, Albuquerque, NM 87102
Fax: (505) 468-7329

Deputy County Manager
Thomas E. "Tom" Swisstack (D) .... (505) 468-7000
E-mail: publicsafety@bernco.gov
Education: Albuquerque BA

Animal Care Services Department
P.O. Box 12156, Albuquerque, NM 87195-2156
Fax: (505) 462-9745 E-mail: animal@bernco.gov
Internet: www.bernco.gov/animal-care

Director **Misha Goodman** .... (505) 314-0284

Fire and Rescue Department [BCFD]
Atrium Bldg., 6840 Second St., NW, Albuquerque, NM 87107
Fax: (505) 462-9746 E-mail: fire@bernco.gov
Internet: www.bernco.gov/fire-and-rescue

Fire and Rescue Chief **Christopher "Chris" Celaya** .... (505) 468-1310
Deputy Chief of Operations **Scott Aragon** .... (505) 468-1310
E-mail: saragon@bernco.gov
Deputy Chief of Administration **Greg Perez** .... (505) 468-1310
E-mail: gperez@bernco.gov
Deputy Chief of Training **Brian Kadle** .... (505) 468-1312
E-mail: bkadle@bernco.gov
Tel: (505) 468-1302

Department of Substance Abuse Programs [DSAP]
5901 Zuni Southeast, Albuquerque, NM 87108
Fax: (505) 266-3726 Internet: www.bernco.gov/substance-abuse-programs

Director **Katrina C. Hotrum** .... (505) 468-1553

Bernalillo County Youth Services Center [BCYSC]
5100 Second Street, NW, Albuquerque, NM 87107
Tel: (505) 761-6600 Fax: (505) 462-9917
Internet: www.bernco.gov/youth-services-center

Director **Craig Sparks** .... (505) 468-7122
Assistant Director of Administration **Anne Martinez** .... (505) 468-7157
E-mail: asmartinez@bernco.gov
Assistant Director of Operations **Michael A. Ferstl** .... (505) 468-7143
E-mail: mferstl@bernco.gov
Administrative Officer **Denise Sandoval** .... (505) 468-7133
E-mail: desandoval@bernco.gov

Public Works Division
2400 Broadway Blvd., SE, Albuquerque, NM 87102
Fax: (505) 848-1510 E-mail: publicworks@bernco.gov

Deputy County Manager **Roger Paul** .... (505) 848-1500
E-mail: publicworks@bernco.gov

Fleet and Facilities Management Department
Building B, 2400 Broadway, Albuquerque, NM 87102
Fax: (505) 224-1619

Director **Mary Murnane** .... (505) 224-1610
Facilities Administrator **Ruth Lott** .... (505) 224-1634
Facilities Administrator **(Vacant)** .... (505) 224-1634

★ Elected Official ▲ Appointed by Legislature ▼ Appointed by Governor ▶ Appointed by Board or Commission ● Appointed by Judge
■ Appointed by Mayor △ Appointed by Freeholders ▽ Appointed by Supervisor ▷ Appointed by County Executive ○ Appointed by Council

Operations and Maintenance Department
2400 Broadway Boulevard, SE, Albuquerque, NM 87102
Director **David Mitchell** . . . . (505) 848-1543

Solid Waste Department
2400 Broadway Blvd., SE, Albuquerque, NM 87102
Director **Adrienne Candelaria** . . . . (505) 224-1639

Technical Services Department
2400 Broadway Blvd., SE, Albuquerque, NM 87102
Director **Roger Paul** . . . . (505) 848-1515

Office of the Assessor

501 Tijeras Avenue, Northwest, Albuquerque, NM 87102
P.O. Box 27108, Albuquerque, NM 87125
Tel: (505) 222-3700 Fax: (505) 222-3771 E-mail: assessor@bernco.gov
Internet: www.bernco.gov/assessor-office

★Assessor **Tanya R. Giddings** . . . . (505) 222-3700
Term Expires: December 31, 2018
E-mail: tgiddings@bernco.gov
Deputy Assessor/Chief Administrative Officer
Michelle Salas . . . . (505) 222-3700
Deputy Assessor/Chief Information Officer
Damian Lara . . . . (505) 222-3700

Office of the District Attorney

520 Lomas Boulevard, NW, Albuquerque, NM 87102
Fax: (505) 241-1302

★District Attorney **Kari E. Brandenburg** (D) . . . . (505) 222-1099
Term Expires: December 31, 2016
E-mail: kbrandenburg@da2nd.state.nm.us
Education: Trinity U 1976 BA; Southern Methodist 1979 JD
Chief Deputy District Attorney **Sylvia Martinez** . . . . (505) 222-1045
Chief Deputy District Attorney **Deborah DePalo** . . . . (505) 222-1304
E-mail: ddepalo@da2nd.state.nm.us
Chief Deputy District Attorney **Troy Davis** . . . . (505) 222-1211

Office of the County Clerk

One Civic Center Plaza, NW, 6th Floor, Albuquerque, NM 87102
P.O. Box 542, Albuquerque, NM 87102
Tel: (505) 468-1290 (Recording & Filing) Fax: (505) 468-1293
Fax: (505) 468-1294 (Recording and Filing) E-mail: clerk@bernco.gov
Internet: www.bernco.gov/clerk

★County Clerk **Maggie Toulouse Oliver** (D) . . . . (505) 468-1231
Term Expires: December 31, 2016
Education: New Mexico 2001 BA, 2004 MA
Deputy Clerk, Bureau of Elections **Roman Motoya** . . . . . . (505) 468-1202
Deputy Clerk, Recording and Filing **Michael A. Garcia** . . (505) 468-1202
E-mail: michaelg@bernco.gov
Administrative Officer **Patricia Nicasio** . . . . (505) 468-1231

Office of the Sheriff

Law Enforcement Center, 400 Roma Avenue Northwest,
Albuquerque, NM 87102
P.O. Box 25927, Albuquerque, NM 87125-5927
Tel: (505) 468-7100 Fax: (505) 468-7299 E-mail: sheriff@bernco.gov
Internet: www.bernco.gov/sheriffs-office

★Sheriff **Manuel Gonzales III** (D) . . . . (505) 468-7100
Term Expires: December 31, 2018
Assistant to the Sheriff **Mickie Segotta** . . . . (505) 468-7100
Undersheriff **Greg Rees** . . . . (505) 468-7100
Undersheriff **Rudy Mora** . . . . (505) 468-7100
Field Services Division Commander **(Vacant)** . . . . (505) 468-7249
Administrative Services Bureau Chief
Shureke Sid Covington . . . . (505) 468-7324

Office of the Sheriff *continued*

Internal Affairs Unit Commander **(Vacant)** . . . . (505) 468-7061
Commander, Bernalillo County Regional Training
Academy **Lt. Broderick Sharp** . . . . (505) 468-1363
415 Tijeras Avenue N.W., Albuquerque, NM 87102
Crossing Guard Supervisor **Joe Girardin** . . . . (505) 314-0010
E-mail: jgirardin@bernco.gov
Legal Technician **(Vacant)** . . . . (505) 468-7100

Office of the Treasurer

One Civic Center Plaza, NW, Room B 2090, Albuquerque, NM 87102
Tel: (505) 468-7031 Fax: (505) 468-7115
Internet: www.bernco.gov/treasurers-office

★Treasurer **Manny Ortiz** . . . . (505) 468-7161
Term Expires: December 31, 2016
Administrative Officer **Margaret Duran** . . . . (505) 468-7339
Chief Deputy Treasurer **Isabelle Purcella** . . . . (505) 468-7931
Accounting Manager **Christopher Sanchez** . . . . (505) 468-7381
Cashiering Manager **Bennie Romero** . . . . (505) 468-7353
Delinquent Tax Manager **Pamela "Pam" Klenck** . . . . (505) 468-7576
E-mail: pklenck@bernco.gov
Special Accounts Manager **Vicki Lucero** . . . . (505) 468-7327
E-mail: vlucero@bernco.gov
Treasury Customer Service Manager
Rosemary A. Apodaca . . . . (505) 468-7363
Compliance Officer **Dennis C. Chavez** . . . . (505) 468-7360
Investment Banking Officer **(Vacant)** . . . . (505) 468-7031
Special Projects & Investment Officer **(Vacant)** . . . . (505) 468-7359

County of Bexar, Texas

County Courthouse, 100 Dolorosa, San Antonio, TX 78205-3036
Tel: (210) 335-2011 (Information) Internet: www.bexar.org

County Seat: San Antonio **Election Type:** Partisan
Population: 1,897,753 (2015)

Office of the County Judge

Paul Elizondo Tower, 101 West Nueva Street, Suite 1019,
San Antonio, TX 78205
Fax: (210) 335-2926 Internet: www.bexar.org/countyjudge

★County Judge **Nelson W. Wolff** (D) . . . . (210) 335-2626
Term Expires: December 31, 2018
E-mail: nwolff@bexar.org
Education: St Mary's U (TX) BA, 1966 JD
Career: Council Member, San Antonio City Council, City of San Antonio, Texas (1987-1990); Mayor (D), City of San Antonio, Texas (1991-1995)
Assistant to the County Judge **Linda Sue Guajardo** . . . . (210) 335-1326
E-mail: lguajardo@bexar.org
Chief of Staff **Marcie Ripper** . . . . (210) 335-2280
Public Information Officer **Laura Jesse** . . . . (210) 335-0073
Education: Texas State (San Marcos) 2003 BA

Commissioners Court

Paul Elizondo Tower, 101 West Nueva Street, 10th Floor,
San Antonio, TX 78205
Tel: (210) 335-2626 Fax: (210) 335-2926

★County Commissioner
Sergio "Chico" Rodriguez (D-Precinct 1) . . . . (210) 335-2611
Term Expires: December 31, 2016
E-mail: chico@bexar.org
★County Commissioner **Paul Elizondo** (D-Precinct 2) . . . . . (210) 335-2612
Term Expires: December 31, 2018
E-mail: pelizondo@bexar.org
Education: St Mary Col 1957 BA

(continued on next page)

★Elected Official ▲Appointed by Legislature ▼Appointed by Governor ▶Appointed by Board or Commission ●Appointed by Judge
■Appointed by Mayor △Appointed by Freeholders ▽Appointed by Supervisor ▷Appointed by County Executive ○Appointed by Council

Commissioners Court *continued*

★County Commissioner **Kevin A. Wolff** (R-Precinct 3) . . . . (210) 335-2613
Term Expires: December 31, 2016
E-mail: kwolff@bexar.org
Education: St Mary's U (TX) BBA, MBA

★County Commissioner **Tommy Calvert** (D-Precinct 4) . . . . (210) 335-2614
Term Expires: December 31, 2018
E-mail: tc@bexar.org

Economic Development Department

101 West Nueva Street, Suite 944, San Antonio, TX 78205
Tel: (210) 335-0667 Fax: (210) 335-0665 Internet: www.bexar.org/ed

Executive Director **David E. Marquez** . . . . (210) 335-0661
E-mail: dmarquez@bexar.org
Education: Trinity U 1998

Economic Development Manager **Melissa Shannon** . . . . (210) 335-2271
E-mail: mshannon@bexar.org
Education: Wayland Baptist 2002 BSOE, 2009 MPA

COUNTIES

Office of the County Manager

101 West Nueva Street, Suite 1023, San Antonio, TX 78205

County Manager **David L. Smith** . . . . (210) 335-0179
E-mail: david.smith@bexar.org
Education: Texas (San Antonio) 1991 BBA; LSU 1993 MS

Chief of Staff **Thomas Guevara** Suite 1021 . . . . (210) 335-0326

Fire Marshal

662 Dolorosa Street, San Antonio, TX 78207-4535
Fax: (210) 335-0330 Internet: www.bexar.org/bcfmo

●Fire Marshal **Chris Lopez** . . . . (210) 335-0300

Government Relations Office

101 West Nueva Street, Suite 901, San Antonio, TX 78205
Tel: (210) 335-0485 Fax: (210) 335-2683
Internet: http://home.bexar.org/GR/index.html

Government Relations Manager **Manuel Leal III** . . . . (210) 335-0485
Government Relations Coordinator **(Vacant)** . . . . (210) 335-0688

Medical Examiner's Office

7337 Louis Pasteur Drive, San Antonio, TX 78229
Tel: (210) 335-4000 Fax: (210) 335-4052
Internet: www.bexar.org/medicalexaminer

Chief Medical Examiner **Randall E. Frost** . . . . (210) 335-4053
Deputy Chief Medical Examiner **D. Kimberly Molina** . . . . (210) 335-4053
Chief Medical Investigator **Jimmy Holguin** . . . . (210) 335-4010

Veterans Service Office

233 N. Pecos, Suite 320, San Antonio, TX 78207
Fax: (210) 335-3632

●Veterans Service Officer **Queta Marquez** . . . . (210) 335-6737
E-mail: vets@bexar.org

Detention Health Care Services

200 N. Comal Street, San Antonio, TX 78207-3573
Fax: (210) 335-6193

Director **Katherine Whiteley** . . . . (210) 335-6260
Administrative Director **Martha Rodriguez** . . . . (210) 335-6260

Elections Department

11103 South Frio Street, San Antonio, TX 78207
Fax: (210) 335-0371 Internet: www.co.bexar.tx.us/elections

▶Elections Administrator **Jacquelyn F. Callanen** . . . . (210) 335-0362
E-mail: jcallanen@bexar.org

Bexar County Information Technology Department [BCIT]

203 West Nueva, Suite 200, San Antonio, TX 78207-4507
Internet: www.bexar.org/it

●Chief Information Officer **Catherine Maras** . . . . (210) 335-0200
E-mail: cmaras@bexar.org

Department of Management and Finance

Heritage Plaza, 410 South Main, Suite 208, San Antonio, TX 78204
Tel: (210) 335-2405 Fax: (210) 335-2683 Internet: www.bexar.org/prm

Executive Director/Budget Officer **Seth McCabe** . . . . (210) 335-2405
E-mail: smccabe@bexar.org

Budget Division

410 South Main, Suite 208, San Antonio, TX 78204
Tel: (210) 335-2656 Fax: (210) 335-2683
Internet: www.bexar.org/prm/budgetdivision.html

Manager **Seth McCabe** . . . . (210) 335-2405
E-mail: smccabe@bexar.org
Senior Analyst **(Vacant)** . . . . (210) 335-1220
Analyst **Tonya Gaitan** . . . . (210) 335-0514
E-mail: tgaitan@bexar.org
Analyst **(Vacant)** . . . . (210) 335-0733

Human Resources Division

400 South Main, 1st Floor, San Antonio, TX 78204-1114
Tel: (210) 335-2545 Fax: (210) 335-2558
Internet: www.bexar.org/prm/human%20resources.html

Manager **Janet Guadarrama** . . . . (210) 335-2645
E-mail: jguadarrama@bexar.org Fax: (210) 335-2857
Benefits Administrator **(Vacant)** . . . . (210) 335-2849
Civil Service Coordinator **(Vacant)** . . . . (210) 335-2688
Compensation Coordinator **(Vacant)** . . . . (210) 335-2049
Training and Development Specialist **(Vacant)** . . . . (210) 335-2643
Workers' Compensation Specialist **Pearl Jauregui** . . . . (210) 335-3374
E-mail: pjauregui@bexar.org
Senior Analyst **Ana Bernal** . . . . (210) 335-3371
E-mail: abernal@bexar.org
Analyst **(Vacant)** . . . . (210) 335-2848

Management and Financial Services Division

Heritage Plaza, 410 South Main, Suite 208, San Antonio, TX 78204
Fax: (210) 335-2683 Internet: www.bexar.org/prm/mfsdivision.html

Manager **Tina Smith-Dean** . . . . (210) 335-2455
Operations Manager **John Diaz** . . . . (210) 335-0309
E-mail: jdiaz@bexar.org
Court Collections Coordinator **(Vacant)** . . . . (210) 335-8407

Bexar County Civil Service Commission

Heritage Plaza Building, 400 South Main, San Antonio, TX 78204-1114
Fax: (210) 335-2545 Internet: www.bexar.org/prm/civilservice.html

Director **Adam Leos** . . . . (210) 335-2545
E-mail: aleos@bexar.org

Public Works

233 N. Pecos, Suite 420, San Antonio, TX 78207
Tel: (210) 335-6700 Fax: (210) 335-6713

Director of Public Works/County Engineer
K. Renee Green . . . . (210) 335-6700
E-mail: rgreen@bexar.org
Fiscal and Administrative Manager **Linda Rios** . . . . (210) 335-6700
E-mail: lrios@bexar.org
Asset Manager **Joe Newton** . . . . (210) 335-6700
Facilities Manager **Betty Bueché** . . . . (210) 335-6684
E-mail: bbueche@bexar.org
Facilities Maintenance Manager **Jose Torralva** . . . . (210) 335-6732
E-mail: joset@bexar.org Fax: (210) 335-6717
County Architect **Oscar J. Cervantes** . . . . (210) 335-6729
E-mail: ojcervantes@bexar.org
Fleet Maintenance Director **Pat Crossno** . . . . (210) 475-9910

★Elected Official ▲Appointed by Legislature ▼Appointed by Governor ▶Appointed by Board or Commission ●Appointed by Judge
■Appointed by Mayor △Appointed by Freeholders ▽Appointed by Supervisor ▷Appointed by County Executive ○Appointed by Council

Purchasing Department
233 N. Pecos, Suite 320, San Antonio, TX 78207-3178
Fax: (210) 335-2219

County Purchasing Agent (Interim) **Mary Salas** .... (210) 335-2211
E-mail: msalas@bexar.org

Texas A&M AgriLife Extension Service
3355 Cherry Ridge Drive, Suite 212, San Antonio, TX 78230-4818
Fax: (210) 631-0429 Internet: http://bexar-tx.tamu.edu

County Extension Director **Nelda Speller** .... (210) 631-0400
E-mail: nlspeller@ag.tamu.edu

County Extension Agent (4-H and Youth Development)
Natalie Cervantes .... (210) 631-0400

County Extension Agent (Family and Consumer Sciences) **(Vacant)** .... (210) 631-0400

County Extension Agent (Horticulture)
David Rodriguez .... (210) 631-0400

Program Coordinator, Water and Natural Resources
(Vacant) .... (210) 631-0400

County Extension Agent (Agriculture) **(Vacant)** .... (210) 631-0400

Extension Agent (4-H and Youth Development)
Melinda Garcia .... (210) 631-0400

Extension Agent (Family and Consumer Sciences)
Grace Guerra-Gonzalez .... (210) 467-6575

Bexar County Dispute Resolution Center
Cadena-Reeves Justice Center, 300 Dolorosa, Suite 1102,
San Antonio, TX 78205-3009
Tel: (210) 335-2128 Fax: (210) 335-2941 E-mail: bcdrc@bexar.org
Internet: www.co.bexar.tx.us/drc

Director **Alfred A. Cortez** .... (210) 335-2128
E-mail: acortez@bexar.org

Law Library/Bar Association
Bexar County Courthouse, 100 Dolorosa, 5th Floor,
San Antonio, TX 78205-3036
Fax: (210) 271-9614

Director **Jimmy Allison** .... (210) 227-8822 ext. 21
E-mail: jimmya@sabar.org

Office of the County Auditor
101 West Nueva Street, Suite 800, San Antonio, TX 78205
Fax: (210) 335-2996 Internet: www.bexar.org/auditor

● Auditor **Susan Yeatts** .... (210) 335-2301
E-mail: aufrontdesk@bexar.org

First Assistant Auditor **Leo Caldera** .... (210) 335-2301

Office of the County Clerk
County Courthouse, 100 Dolorosa, Suite 104,
San Antonio, TX 78205-3883
Fax: (210) 335-2197

★ County Clerk **Gerard C. "Gerry" Rickhoff** (R) .... (210) 335-2216
Term Expires: December 31, 2018
E-mail: grickhoff@bexar.org

Chief Deputy **Thomas Koenig** .... (210) 335-2124
E-mail: tkoenig@bexar.org

Chief Deputy **Betty Aguilar** .... (210) 335-2247
E-mail: baguilar@bexar.org

Office of the Criminal District Attorney
101 West Nueva Street, Fourth Floor, San Antonio, TX 78205
Tel: (210) 335-2311 Internet: www.bexar.org/da2

★ Criminal District Attorney
Nicholas "Nico" LaHood (D) .... (210) 335-2342
Term Expires: December 31, 2018
E-mail: lydia.oconnell@bexar.org

First Assistant Criminal District Attorney
Woodrow Halstead .... (210) 335-2342
E-mail: whalstead@bexar.org

Chief Administrative Attorney
Juanita Vasquez-Gardner .... (210) 335-2342
E-mail: jvasquez.gardner@bexar.org

Chief Investigator **Willie Ng** .... (210) 335-2342

Office of the District Clerk
Paul Elizondo Tower, 101 West Nueva Street, Suite 217,
San Antonio, TX 78205
Tel: (210) 335-2113 Fax: (210) 335-3424 Internet: www.bexar.org/dc

★ District Clerk **Donna Kay McKinney** (R) .... (210) 335-2113
Term Expires: December 31, 2018

Chief Deputy **Brady Satcher** .... (210) 335-2113

Office of the Sheriff
200 N. Comal, San Antonio, TX 78207-3505
Fax: (210) 335-6019 Internet: www.bexar.org/bcsheriff

★ Sheriff **MajGen Susan Pamerleau** (R) .... (210) 335-6010
Term Expires: December 31, 2016

Chief Deputy **Manuel Longoria** .... (210) 335-6010
E-mail: mlongoria@bexar.org

Public Safety Communications Manager
Robert M. Adelman .... (210) 335-4601
Fax: (210) 335-4609

Jail Administrator **Raul S. Banasco** .... (210) 335-6219
Fax: (210) 335-6199

Chief Communications Officer **James Keith** .... (210) 335-5106
E-mail: james.keith@bexar.org

Webmaster **Cruz Castillo** .... (210) 335-6825
E-mail: cruz.castillo@bexar.org

Office of the Tax Assessor/Collector
233 North Pecos-La Trinidad, San Antonio, TX 78207
Fax: (210) 335-6573 Internet: www.bexar.org/tax

★ Tax Assessor/Collector **Albert Uresti** .... (210) 335-6585
Term Expires: December 31, 2016

Chief Deputy of Operations **Stephen W. Palacios** .... (210) 335-6585
E-mail: splacios@bexar.org

Chief of Administration **Lisa Anderson** .... (210) 335-6585
E-mail: lisaanderson@bexar.org

COUNTIES

★ Elected Official ▲ Appointed by Legislature ▼ Appointed by Governor ▶ Appointed by Board or Commission ● Appointed by Judge
■ Appointed by Mayor △ Appointed by Freeholders ▽ Appointed by Supervisor ▷ Appointed by County Executive ○ Appointed by Council

County of Brevard, Florida

Government Center, 2725 Judge Fran Jamieson Way, Viera, FL 32940
P.O. Box 999, Titusville, FL 32781-0239
Tel: (321) 633-2000 (Information) Internet: www.brevardcounty.us

County Seat: Titusville **Election Type:** Partisan **Population:** 568,088 (2015)

Office of the County Commission

Government Center, 2725 Judge Fran Jamieson Way, Viera, FL 32940
Tel: (321) 633-2001 Internet: www.brevardcounty.us/commission

★Chair **Jim Barfield** (R-District II) .... (321) 454-6601
Term Expires: November 20, 2018 Fax: (321) 454-6602
E-mail: jim.barfield@brevardcounty.us

★Vice Chair **Curt Smith** (R-District IV) .... (321) 633-2044
Term Expires: November 20, 2018 Fax: (321) 633-2121
E-mail: curt.smith@brevardcounty.us

★Commissioner **Robin L. Fisher** (D-District I) .... (321) 264-6750
Term Expires: November 17, 2016 Fax: (321) 264-6751
E-mail: robin.fisher@brevardcounty.us

★Commissioner **Trudie Infantini** (R-District III) .... (321) 952-6300
Term Expires: November 17, 2016 Fax: (321) 952-6340
E-mail: trudie.infantini@brevardcounty.us

★Commissioner **Andy Anderson** (R-District V) .... (321) 253-6611
Term Expires: November 17, 2016 Fax: (321) 253-6620
E-mail: andy.anderson@brevardcounty.us

Office of the County Attorney

Government Center, 2725 Judge Fran Jamieson Way, Viera, FL 32940
Fax: (321) 633-2096

▶County Attorney **Scott Knox** .... (321) 633-2090
E-mail: scott.knox@brevardcounty.us

Office of the County Manager

Government Center, Building C, 2725 Judge Fran Jamieson Way, Room C-301, Viera, FL 32940
Fax: (321) 633-2115

▶County Manager **Stockton Whitten** .... (321) 633-2001
E-mail: stockton.whitten@brevardcounty.us
Education: Florida
Administrative Assistant to the County Manager **Pamela Barrett** .... (321) 633-2001
E-mail: pamela.barrett@brevardcounty.us

Agenda Coordinator **Sally Lewis** .... (321) 633-2010

Budget Office

2725 Judge Fran Jamieson Way, Viera, FL 32940
Tel: (321) 633-2153 Fax: (321) 690-6821
Internet: www.brevardcounty.us/budgetoffice/budget

Director **Tom Rosenberg** .... (321) 633-2153
E-mail: thomas.rosenberg@brevardcounty.us

Assistant County Manager, Development and Public Services

Government Center, Building C, 2725 Judge Fran Jamieson Way, Viera, FL 32940

Assistant County Manager **(Vacant)** .... (321) 633-2002

Natural Resources Management Department

Government Center, 2725 Judge Fran Jamieson Way, Viera, FL 32940
Fax: (321) 633-2029 Internet: www.brevardcounty.us/naturalresources

Director **Virginia Barker** .... (321) 633-2016
Fax: (321) 633-2029

Environmental Resources Program Manager **Amanda Elmore** .... (321) 633-2016

Watershed Program Manager **(Vacant)** .... (321) 633-2016

Remediation and Compliance Programs and Local Program Manager **P. Douglas "Doug" Divers** .... (321) 633-2017

Natural Resources Management Department *continued*

Support Services Manager **Paul Bessler** .... (321) 265-2016
E-mail: paul.bessler@brevardcounty.us

Beach Project Manager **Mike McGarry** .... (321) 633-2016
Education: North Carolina Wilmington; Florida Tech

Mosquito Control Department

Space Coast Regional Airport, 800 Perimeter Road, Titusville, FL 32780
Fax: (321) 264-5034 E-mail: mosquito.control@brevardcounty.us
Internet: www.brevardcounty.us/mosquito

Director **Chris Richmond** .... (321) 264-5032

Operations Manager **Chris Richmond** .... (321) 264-5032

Planning and Development Department

Brevard County Government Center, Building A, 2725 Judge Fran Jamieson Way, Viera, FL 32940
Tel: (321) 633-2069 (Planning) Tel: (321) 633-2070 (Zoning)
Fax: (321) 633-2074 (Planning) Fax: (321) 633-2152 (Zoning)
Internet: http://www.brevardcounty.us/PlanningDev

Planning and Zoning Director **Robin M. DiFabio** .... (321) 633-2069

Planning, Zoning and Enforcement Manager **Cynthia Fox** .... (321) 633-2070
Fax: (321) 633-2152

Public Works Department

Building A, 2725 Judge Fran Jamieson Way, Room 201, Viera, FL 32940-6605
Fax: (321) 617-7208 Internet: www.brevardpublicworks.org

Director **John Denninghoff** .... (321) 617-7202
E-mail: john.denninghoff@brevardcounty.us

County Surveyor **Mike Sweeney** .... (321) 633-2080

Traffic Manager **Corrina Gumm** .... (321) 633-2077
E-mail: corrina.gumm@brevardcounty.us

Finance Manager **Tammy Thomas-Wood** .... (321) 617-7202
Fax: (321) 617-7208

Landscape Operations Manager **Jason Kelly** .... (321) 433-4440
E-mail: Jason.kelly@brevardcounty.us Fax: (321) 433-4445

Road and Bridge Construction Manager **Susan Jackson** .... (321) 690-6840
E-mail: Susan.jackson@brevardcounty.us Fax: (321) 617-7208

Floodplain Administrator **Frank N. Skarvelis** .... (321) 617-7340
E-mail: frank.skarvelis@brevardcounty.us

Land Acquisition/Right-of-Way **Dan Jones** .... (321) 690-6847

Map Reproduction **Shane Lyons** .... (321) 633-2174

Right Of Way and Easements **Marc Cazessus** .... (321) 617-7315

Engineering Manager **Andrew Holmes** .... (321) 633-7202

Solid Waste Management Department

2725 Judge Fran Jamieson Way, Viera, FL 32940
Tel: (321) 633-2042 Fax: (321) 633-2038
Internet: www.brevardcounty.us/swr

Director **Euripides Rodriguez** .... (321) 633-2042

Operations **Richard Dees** .... (321) 633-1888
E-mail: richard.dees@brevardcounty.us

Pick-ups/Complaints/Inquiries **Mandy Guppenberger** .... (321) 633-2042

Questions on Hazardous Wastes **Deborah Lugar** .... (321) 633-2042

Questions on Household Hazardous Wastes **Rita Perini** ... (321) 635-7954

Recycling Coordinator **Hillary Arena** .... (321) 633-2043

Utility Services Department [USD]

Government Center, 2725 Judge Fran Jamieson Way, Viera, FL 32940
Fax: (321) 633-2095 Internet: www.brevardcounty.us/usd

Director **James Helmer** .... (321) 633-2091

Assistant Director **(Vacant)** .... (321) 633-2092
Internet: www.brevardcounty.us/utilityservices

Water/Wastewater Manager **Steve Harrell** .... (321) 633-2093
E-mail: steve.harrell@brevardcounty.us

Construction Management **Craig Helpling** .... (321) 633-2089

★Elected Official ▲Appointed by Legislature ▼Appointed by Governor ▶Appointed by Board or Commission ●Appointed by Judge
■Appointed by Mayor △Appointed by Freeholders ▽Appointed by Supervisor ▷Appointed by County Executive ○Appointed by Council

Valkaria Airport
2865 Greenbrooke Street, Valkaria, FL 32950
Fax: (321) 952-4592 Internet: www.brevardcounty.us/valkaria_airport
Airport Manager **Stephen "Steve" Borowski** .... (321) 952-4590

Assistant County Manager, Community Services
Government Center, Building C, 2725 Judge Fran Jamieson Way, Viera, FL 32940
Tel: (321) 633-2001 Fax: (321) 633-2115
Assistant County Manager **Venetta Valdengo-Blevins** ... (321) 633-2003
E-mail: venetta.valdengo@brevardcounty.us

Office of Extension Services (University of Florida)
Agricultural Center, 3695 Lake Dr., Cocoa, FL 32926
Tel: (321) 633-1702 (Cocoa Office) Fax: (321) 633-1890
Tel: (321) 952-4536 (Palm Bay Office) Fax: (321) 952-4539
E-mail: brevard@ifas.ufl.edu Internet: http://brevard.ifas.ufl.edu/
Director **Linda Seals** .... (321) 633-1702 ext. 236

Brevard County Tourism Development Council
430 Brevard Avenue, Suite 150, Cocoa, FL 32922
Tel: (321) 433-4470 Fax: (321) 433-4476
Internet: www.brevardcounty.us/tdc
▶ Chairperson **Tom Williamson** .... (321) 433-4470
Executive Director **Eric Garvey** .... (321) 433-4470
Director of Sales, Marketing, and Film **Bonnie King** ..... (321) 433-4470

Housing and Human Services Department [HHS]
Government Center, Building B, 2725 Judge Fran Jamieson Way, Suite 106, Viera, FL 32940
Tel: (321) 633-2007 Fax: (321) 633-2170
Internet: www.brevardcounty.us/human_services
Director **Ian Golden** .... (321) 633-2007
Assistant Director **Juanita Davis** .... (321) 633-2076
Finance Manager (Acting) **Juanita Davis** .... (321) 633-2007
Veterans Service Officer **Dennis Zannorsdall** .... (321) 633-2012
School Crossing Guards Supervisor
Deborah "Debbie" Morancie .... (321) 633-2007

Office of the Medical Examiner
1750 Cedar Street, Rockledge, FL 32955
Fax: (321) 633-1986
▼ Medical Examiner **Sajid Qaiser** .... (321) 633-1981
E-mail: sajid.qaiser@brevardcounty.us

Library Services Department
308 Forrest Avenue, Cocoa, FL 32922
Fax: (321) 633-1798
Director **Jeff Thompson** .... (321) 633-1801
Information Technology Manager **Tina Hare** .... (321) 633-1789

Parks and Recreation Department
2725 Judge Fran Jamieson Way, Viera, FL 32940
Tel: (321) 633-2046 (Information) Fax: (321) 633-2198
E-mail: info@brevardparks.com Internet: http://www.brevardparks.com
Director **Jack Masson** .... (321) 633-2046
Education: Florida 1970 BA
Assistant Director **Hector Lopez** .... (321) 633-2046
Environmentally Endangered Lands Program Manager
Mike Knight .... (321) 255-4466
91 East Drive, Melbourne, FL 32940
Education: Vermont 1987 BS
Parks Finance Manager **(Vacant)** .... (321) 633-2046
Parks Golf Manager **(Vacant)** .... (321) 633-2046
Central Area Parks Operations **Terry Lane** .... (321) 633-1874
840 Forrest Avenue, Cocoa, FL 32922
North Area Parks Operations **Jeff Davis** .... (321) 264-5105
475 North Williams Avenue, Titusville, FL 32796
E-mail: jdavis@brevardparks.com

Parks and Recreation Department *continued*
South Area Parks Operations **Greg Minor** .... (321) 255-4400
E-mail: gminor@brevardparks.com
Education: Central Florida 1992 MA
Parks Support Services **(Vacant)** .... (321) 633-2046

Transit Services Department
401 S. Varr Ave., Cocoa, FL 32922
Tel: (321) 633-1878 (Information Bus Operations)
Tel: (321) 952-4563 (Information Commuter Assistance)
Fax: (321) 633-1905
Director **James Liesenfelt** .... (321) 635-7815
North Operations **Pat Ryan** .... (321) 635-7815
E-mail: pat.ryan@brevardcounty.us
South Operations **Joseph Lammon** .... (321) 952-4561
Operations and Maintenance **Scott Nelson** .... (321) 635-7815
E-mail: scott.nelson@brevardcounty.us
Volunteers-In-Motion **Lori Hamilton** .... (321) 635-7999
Customer Service **Carmen Baez** .... (321) 633-1878

COUNTIES

Assistant County Manager, Public Safety and Support Services
Tel: (321) 633-2002
Assistant County Manager **Frank Abbate** .... (321) 633-2004
E-mail: Frank.Abbate@brevardcounty.us

Human Resources Office
Fax: (321) 633-2036
Director **Jerry Visco** .... (321) 633-2034
E-mail: gerard.visco@brevardcounty.us
Risk Manager **Julie Jones** .... (321) 637-5446
E-mail: julie.jones@brevardcounty.us Fax: (321) 637-5364

Information Technology Department [ITD]
2725 Judge Fran Jamieson Way, Viera, FL 32940
Tel: (321) 617-7395 Fax: (321) 617-7396
Internet: www.brevardcounty.us/icsd
Director (Interim) **Frank Abbatte** .... (321) 617-7395
E-mail: frank.abbatte@brevardcounty.us

Fire Rescue Department
1040 South Florida Avenue, Rockledge, FL 32955
Tel: (321) 633-2056 Fax: (321) 633-2057
Internet: www.brevardcounty.us/fire_rescue
Fire Chief **Mark Schollmeyer** .... (321) 633-2056
E-mail: mark.schollmeyer@brevardcounty.us
Deputy Chief **Dennis Neterer** .... (321) 633-2056
E-mail: dennis.neterer@brevardcounty.us
Education: Central Florida
Medical Director **John McPherson** .... (321) 633-2056
Assistant Chief, Professional Development
Michael Zocchi .... (321) 633-2056
E-mail: michael.zocchi@brevardcounty.us
Division Chief, Emergency Medical Services
Orlando Dominguez .... (321) 633-2056
Education: National-Louis 2000 BS
Chief, Ocean Lifeguards **Jeffrey "Jeff" Scabarozi** ...... (321) 633-2056
Division Chief, Support Services **Fred Jodts** .... (321) 633-2056
E-mail: fred.jodts@brevardcounty.us
Fire Marshal **Frank Scates** .... (321) 637-5660
E-mail: frank.scates@brevardcounty.us
Public Information Officer **Mark Schollmeyer** .... (321) 633-2056
Assistant Chief, Fire Operations **Scott Gold** .... (321) 633-2056
E-mail: scott.gold@brevardcounty.us

Central Services Department
2725 Judge Fran Jamieson Way, A-207, Viera, FL 32940
Fax: (321) 633-2051
Director **Teresa Camarata** .... (321) 633-2050
E-mail: teresa.camarata@brevardcounty.us Fax: (321) 633-2051

★ Elected Official ▲ Appointed by Legislature ▼ Appointed by Governor ▶ Appointed by Board or Commission ● Appointed by Judge
■ Appointed by Mayor △ Appointed by Freeholders ▽ Appointed by Supervisor ▷ Appointed by County Executive ○ Appointed by Council

Brevard County Emergency Management Office
1746 Cedar Street, Rockledge, FL 32955
Tel: (321) 637-6670 Fax: (321) 633-1738

Director **Kimberly Prosser** .... (321) 637-6670
E-mail: Kimberly.Prosser@brevardcounty.us

Office of the Clerk of the Circuit Court
400 South St., Titusville, FL 32780
Tel: (321) 637-5413 Fax: (321) 264-6940 Internet: www.brevardclerk.us

★Clerk of the Circuit Court **Scott Ellis** (R) .... (321) 637-5413
Term Expires: January 2, 2017 Fax: (321) 267-6940
E-mail: scott.ellis@brevardclerk.us
Chief Deputy Clerk **Laurie Rice** .... (321) 637-6512
Clerk to the Board **Tammy Rowe** .... (321) 637-2001
Finance Director **Steve Burdett** .... (321) 637-2002
Court Administration **Mark Van Bever** .... (321) 633-2171
Fax: (321) 633-2172

Office of the Property Appraiser
400 South Street, 5th Floor, Titusville, FL 32780
Fax: (321) 264-5187 Internet: www.brevardpropertyappraiser.com

★Property Appraiser **Dana Blickley** (R) .... (321) 264-6700
Term Expires: January 2, 2017

Office of the Public Defender
Government Center, Bldg. E, 2725 Judge Fran Jamieson Way, Viera, FL 32940
Tel: (321) 617-7373 Fax: (321) 617-7353
E-mail: publicdefender@pubdef-18.brevard.fl.us
Internet: www.brevardcounty.us/publicdefender

★Public Defender **Robert Blaise Trettis** (R) .... (321) 617-7373
Term Expires: January 2, 2017

Office of the Sheriff
700 South Park Avenue, Titusville, FL 32780
Fax: (321) 264-5360 Internet: http://brevardsheriff.com

★Sheriff **Wayne Ivey** (R) .... (321) 264-5201
Term Expires: January 9, 2017
Chief Deputy **Cdr. Douglas "Doug" Waller** .... (321) 264-5201
Chief Financial Officer **Gregory "Greg" Pelham** .... (321) 264-7753
Fax: (321) 264-5324
Staff Services **Cdr. Jimmy Donn** .... (321) 264-5216
Fax: (321) 264-5287

Animal Services and Enforcement Department
2725 Judge Fran Jamieson Way, A119, Viera, FL 32940
Fax: (321) 633-2011 Internet: www.brevardanimalservices.com

Animal Services Operations Manager **Lacie Davis** .... (321) 633-2105
Community Outreach Coordinator **Tracy Wisner** .... (321) 253-6608
Animal Services Enforcement **Lt. Tom Young** .... (321) 633-2105
North Animal Care and Adoption Center **Kurt Hanling** ... (321) 264-5119
South Animal Care and Adoption Center **Paula Hunter** ... (321) 253-6608

Office of the State Attorney
Government Center, 2725 Judge Fran Jamieson Way, Viera, FL 32940
Tel: (321) 617-7510 Fax: (321) 617-7542 Internet: www.sa18.state.fl.us

★State Attorney **Phil Archer** (R) .... (321) 617-7510
Term Expires: January 2, 2017

Office of the Supervisor of Elections
2725 Judge Fran Jamieson Way, Suite C-105, Viera, FL 32940
Fax: (321) 633-2130

★Supervisor of Elections **Lori Scott** .... (321) 633-2124
Term Expires: January 2, 2017
E-mail: soe@votebrevard.com
Executive Assistant **Judy Moran** .... (321) 690-6833
E-mail: jmoran@votebrevard.com
Chief Deputy of Operations **Karen Graham** .... (321) 633-2131
E-mail: kgraham@votebrevard.com
Chief Deputy of Information Systems **Tim Bobanic** ..... (321) 633-2175
E-mail: tbobanic@votebrevard.com

Office of the Tax Collector
400 South Street, 6th Floor, Titusville, FL 32780
P.O. Box 2500, Titusville, FL 32781-2500
Fax: (321) 264-6919 (Administration)
Fax: (321) 264-5149 (Current and Delinquent Taxes)
Fax: (321) 264-6792 (Business, Tangible, and Tourist Tax)
Internet: www.brevardtaxcollector.com

★Tax Collector **Lisa Cullen** .... (321) 264-6930
Term Expires: January 7, 2017
E-mail: lisa.cullen@brevardtc.com

Brevard Public Schools
2700 Judge Fran Jamieson Way, Viera, FL 32940
Tel: (321) 633-1000 ext. 500 Fax: (321) 633-3432

Superintendent **Dr. Desmond Blackburn** .... (321) 633-1000 ext. 402

County of Bristol, Massachusetts

Superior Courthouse, Nine Court Street, Taunton, MA 02780
Tel: (508) 824-9681 (Information) Internet: www.countyofbristol.net

County Seat: Taunton **Election Type:** Partisan **Population:** 556,772 (2015)

Office of the County Commissioners
Superior Courthouse, Nine Court Street, Taunton, MA 02780
P.O. Box 208, Taunton, MA 02780

★Chair **Paul B. Kitchen** (D) .... (508) 824-9681
Term Expires: January 2, 2017
E-mail: commissioners@countyofbristol.net
★Commissioner **John R. Mitchell** (D) .... (508) 824-9681
Term Expires: January 2, 2017
E-mail: commissioners@countyofbristol.net
Education: UMass (Amherst) 1975; Georgetown 1978 JD
★Commissioner **John T. Saunders** (D) .... (508) 824-9681
Term Expires: January 2019
Administrator **Jaye M. Cioper** .... (508) 824-9681
E-mail: jcioper@countyofbristol.net Fax: (508) 821-3101

Office of the County Treasurer
Superior Courthouse, Nine Court Street, Taunton, MA 02780

★County Treasurer **Christopher T. Saunders** (D) .... (508) 824-4028
Term Expires: January 7, 2017
E-mail: csaunders@bctreasurer.org
Education: Salve Regina U 1993 BA; New England 1996 JD

★Elected Official ▲Appointed by Legislature ▼Appointed by Governor ►Appointed by Board or Commission ●Appointed by Judge
■Appointed by Mayor △Appointed by Freeholders ▽Appointed by Supervisor ▷Appointed by County Executive ○Appointed by Council

Office of the Sheriff
400 Faunce Corner Rd., North Dartmouth, MA 02747
Tel: (508) 995-1311

★Sheriff **Thomas M. Hodgson** .... (508) 995-1311
Term Expires: January 1, 2017

Bristol County Jail and House of Corrections
226 Ash St., New Bedford, MA 02740

Superintendent **Thomas M. Hodgson** ....(508) 995-1311

Retirement Board
County Crossing, 645 County Street, Unit 5, Taunton, MA 02780

Chairman **Christopher T. Saunders** (D) ....(508) 824-4029
Education: Salve Regina U 1993 BA; New England 1996 JD
Member **Roxanne Donovan** ....(508) 824-4029
Member **William M. Downey** ....(508) 824-4029
Member **Paul B. Kitchen** (D) ....(508) 824-4029
Member **Stephen J. Rivard** ....(508) 824-4029
Director of Operations **Roxanne Donovan** ....(508) 824-4029

County of Broward, Florida
Governmental Center, 115 South Andrews Avenue,
Fort Lauderdale, FL 33301
Tel: (954) 831-4000 (Information) Internet: www.broward.org

County Seat: Fort Lauderdale **Election Type:** Partisan
Population: 1,896,425 (2015)

Office of the Board of Commissioners
Governmental Center, 115 South Andrews Avenue, Room 421,
Fort Lauderdale, FL 33301
Tel: (954) 357-7000 Fax: (954) 357-7295
Internet: www.broward.org/commission

★Mayor **Martin David "Marty" Kiar** (D-District 1) .... (954) 357-7001
Term Expires: November 18, 2016
E-mail: mkiar@broward.org
Education: Palm Beach Atlantic 1999 BA; Nova Southeastern 2002 JD
★Commissioner **Mark D. Bogen** (D-District 2) .... (954) 357-7002
Term Expires: November 16, 2018
★Commissioner **Stacy J. Ritter** (D-District 3) .... (954) 357-7003
Term Expires: November 18, 2016
E-mail: sritter@broward.org
Date of Birth: June 8, 1960
Education: Rollins 1982 BA; Nova 1985 JD
★Commissioner **Charles "Chip" LaMarca** (R-District 4) ... (954) 357-7004
Term Expires: November 16, 2018
E-mail: clamarca@broward.org
★Commissioner **Lois Wexler** (D-District 5) .... (954) 357-7005
Term Expires: November 18, 2016
E-mail: lwexler@broward.org
Education: Florida Atlantic
★Commissioner **Quentin Beam Furr** (D-District 6) .... (954) 357-7006
Term Expires: November 16, 2018
Education: Trinity Col (FL) BA; South Florida MA
★Commissioner **Timothy M. Ryan** (D-District 7) .... (954) 357-7007
Term Expires: November 16, 2016
E-mail: tryan@broward.org
Education: Florida 1978 BS, 1981 JD
★Commissioner **Barbara Sharief** (D-District 8) .... (954) 357-7008
Term Expires: November 16, 2016
E-mail: bsharief@broward.org
★Commissioner **Dale V. C. Holness** (D-District 9) .... (954) 357-7009
Term Expires: November 16, 2016
E-mail: dholness@broward.org

Office of the County Attorney
Governmental Center, 115 South Andrews Avenue, Room 423,
Fort Lauderdale, FL 33301
Fax: (954) 357-7641 Internet: www.broward.org/legal

County Attorney **Joni Armstrong Coffey** .... (954) 357-7600
E-mail: jacoffey@broward.org
Education: Florida State 1976 BA; Florida 1979 JD
Chief Deputy County Attorney **Andrew J. Meyers** ...... (954) 357-7600
Deputy County Attorney **Maite Azcoitia** .... (954) 357-7600
E-mail: mazcoitia@broward.org
Deputy County Attorney **Michael J. Kerr** .... (954) 357-7600
E-mail: mkerr@broward.org
Deputy County Attorney **Angela J. Wallace** .... (954) 357-7600
E-mail: ajwallace@broward.org
Legal Administrator **Jackie Jackson** .... (954) 357-7600
County Attorney Administrative Assistant
Gillian Fairclough .... (954) 357-7600
E-mail: gfairclough@broward.org

Office of the County Auditor
Governmental Center, 115 South Andrews Avenue, Room 520,
Fort Lauderdale, FL 33301
Fax: (954) 357-7592 Internet: www.broward.org/auditor

County Auditor **Evan A. Lukic** .... (954) 357-7590
Deputy County Auditor **Kathie Ulett** .... (954) 357-7590
Audit Supervisor **Dirk Hansen** .... (954) 357-7590

Office of the County Administrator
Governmental Center, 115 South Andrews Avenue, Room 409,
Fort Lauderdale, FL 33301
Tel: (954) 357-7000 Fax: (954) 357-7360
Internet: www.broward.org/administrator

►County Administrator **Bertha Henry** .... (954) 357-7362
E-mail: bhenry@broward.org
Education: Florida State 1977 BS, 1978 MS
Assistant to the County Administrator
Gretchen Cassini .... (954) 357-7579
E-mail: gcassini@broward.org
Assistant to the County Administrator
Alphonso Jefferson, Jr. .... (954) 357-7352
E-mail: ajefferson@broward.org

Office of the Deputy County Administrator
115 South Andrews Avenue, Room 409, Fort Lauderdale, FL 33301
Tel: (954) 357-7357 Fax: (954) 357-7360

Deputy County Administrator **Rob Hernandez** .... (954) 357-7375
E-mail: rhernandez@broward.org

Office of Economic and Small Business Development
Governmental Center, 115 South Andrews Avenue, Room A680,
Fort Lauderdale, FL 33301
Fax: (954) 357-5674 Internet: www.broward.org/smallbusiness

Director **Sandy-Michael McDonald** .... (954) 357-6155
Assistant Director **Chris Atkinson** .... (954) 357-6400
E-mail: catkinson@broward.org
Economic Development Manager **Steven Tinsley** .... (954) 357-6400

Cultural Division
100 South Andrews Avenue, 6th Floor, Fort Lauderdale, FL 33301-1829
Tel: (954) 357-7457 Tel: (800) 249-2787 (Arts Line)
Tel: (954) 357-7979 (Cultural Information Center) Fax: (954) 357-5769
Fax: (954) 357-7978 (Cultural Information Center)
E-mail: culturaldiv@broward.org Internet: www.broward.org/arts

Director **Earl Bosworth** .... (954) 357-7456
Administrative Coordinator **Rowena Nocom** .... (954) 357-7503
E-mail: rnocom@broward.org
Grants Administrator **James Shermer** .... (954) 357-7502
Assistant Director/Marketing Administrator
Jody Horne-Leshinsky .... (954) 357-7463

(continued on next page)

★Elected Official ▲Appointed by Legislature ▼Appointed by Governor ►Appointed by Board or Commission ●Appointed by Judge
■Appointed by Mayor △Appointed by Freeholders ▽Appointed by Supervisor ▷Appointed by County Executive ○Appointed by Council

COUNTIES

Cultural Division *continued*

Public Art and Design Administrator **Leslie Fordham** .... (954) 357-7532
Arts, Education and Community Development Manager
Grace Kewl-Durfey .... (954) 357-7869
E-mail: gkewl@broward.org

Parks and Recreation Division

950 Northwest 38th Street, Oakland Park, FL 33309
Tel: (954) 357-8100 TTY: (954) 537-2844 Fax: (954) 357-5991
Internet: www.broward.org/parks

Director **Dan West** .... (954) 357-8106
Administrative Manager **Cathy Hagen** .... (954) 357-8107
E-mail: chagen@broward.org
Security Manager **Cherise Williams** .... (954) 357-8142
E-mail: cwilliams@broward.org
Community Partnerships and Outreach Manager
Chester Pruitt .... (954) 577-8181
E-mail: cpruitt@broward.org
Information Technology Manager **Adrian Anghel** .... (954) 357-7852
E-mail: canghel@broward.org
Business Operations Manager **Cheryl Cayer** .... (954) 357-8111
E-mail: ccayer@broward.org
Planning And Development/Environmental Section
Manager **Carol Morgenstern** .... (954) 357-8124
Human Resources Representative **Mary Noe** .... (954) 357-8175
E-mail: mnoe@broward.org
Marketing and Public Relations **Cyndy Baker** .... (954) 357-8117
E-mail: cybaker@broward.org
Marketing Development Associate **Michael Mills** .... (954) 357-8115
Special Populations **Dori Horowitz** .... (954) 357-8170
Volunteer Coordinator **Anita Ziegler** .... (954) 357-8153
Planning and Engineering Superintendent **Tina Murto** .... (954) 357-8184
E-mail: tmurto@broward.org
Superintendent **Gayle Preston** .... (954) 957-8704
Superintendent **Sarah Perkins** .... (954) 357-8802
Swim Central **Jay Sanford** .... (954) 357-8123
Urban Horticulture Extension Agent
John Pipoly .... (954) 357-5280 ext. 227

Broward County Library

100 South Andrews Avenue, Fort Lauderdale, FL 33301
Tel: (954) 357-7377 Fax: (954) 357-6542

Year Founded: 1974

Administration

Director, Libraries Division **(Vacant)** .... (954) 357-7559
Senior Division Administrative Assistant
Christopher Flynn .... (954) 357-7559
E-mail: cflynn@broward.org

Law Library

Broward County Courthouse, 201 South East Sixth Street, Room 1800, Fort Lauderdale, FL 33301

Director **Arlene Elias** .... (954) 831-6226
E-mail: aelias@broward.org

Greater Fort Lauderdale Convention and Visitors Bureau

101 North East Third Avenue, Suite 100, Fort Lauderdale, FL 33301
Fax: (954) 765-4467 E-mail: gflcvb@broward.org
Internet: www.sunny.org

President **Nicki E. Grossman** .... (954) 765-4466 ext. 250
Note: Until June 1, 2016
Assistant **Sophia Jones** .... (954) 767-2450
E-mail: sjones@broward.org
Public Relations/Communications Vice President
Kim Butler .... (954) 767-2442
E-mail: kbutler@broward.org

Convention Center, Greater Fort Lauderdale/Broward County

1950 Eisenhower Blvd., Fort Lauderdale, FL 33316
Tel: (954) 765-5900 Fax: (954) 763-9551
Internet: http://www.ftlauderdalecc.com

General Manager **Mark Gatley** .... (954) 765-5920

Greater Fort Lauderdale Convention and Visitors Bureau *continued*

Deputy Director **Carlos Puentes** .... (954) 765-5925

Finance and Administrative Services Department

Governmental Center, 115 South Andrews Avenue, Fort Lauderdale, FL 33301-4803
Tel: (954) 357-7130 Internet: http://www.broward.org/finance.htm
Fax: (954) 357-7134 E-mail: finance@broward.org

Chief Financial Officer/Director **Robert R. Miracle**
Room 513 .... (954) 357-7130
Deputy Chief Financial Officer/Deputy Director
(Vacant) Room 513 .... (954) 357-7132
Executive Assistant **Rose Johnson** Room 513 .... (954) 357-7130
E-mail: rjohnson@broward.org
Assistant to the Department Director **Stephen Farmer**
Room A430 .... (954) 357-7246
E-mail: sfarmer@broward.org
Investment and Finance Coordinator **Lori Fortenberry**
Room A430 .... (954) 357-7201
E-mail: lfortenberry@broward.org
Value Adjustment Board Administrative Coordinator I
Madeline Ayala Room 120 .... (954) 357-7300
Fax: (954) 357-5573
Investment and Finance Coordinator **(Vacant)**
Room A430 .... (954) 357-7133

Accounting Division

115 South Andrews Avenue, Fort Lauderdale, FL 33301
Fax: (954) 357-7148 E-mail: accounting@broward.org
Internet: www.broward.org/accounting

Director **Susan Friend** .... (954) 357-7140
115 South Andrews Avenue, Room 221, Fort Lauderdale, FL 33301-4803
E-mail: sfriend@broward.org
Assistant Director **Paul Cissell** .... (954) 357-7242
115 South Andrews Avenue, Room 221, Fort Lauderdale, FL 33301-4803
E-mail: pcissell@broward.org
Senior Division Administrative Assistant
Jennifer Pezzella .... (954) 357-7140
115 South Andrews Avenue, Room 221, Fort Lauderdale, FL 33301-4803
E-mail: jpezzella@broward.org

Enterprise Technology Services Division

Broward County Government Center, West Building, One North University Drive, Suite 4003A, Plantation, FL 33324
Tel: (954) 357-8500 Fax: (954) 357-5601 Internet: www.broward.org/ets

Chief Information Officer **John Bruno** .... (954) 357-8821
Assistant Director **(Vacant)** .... (954) 357-7911
Fax: (954) 357-5601
Director of Infrastructure Services **Keith Wolf** .... (954) 357-5918
E-mail: kwolf@broward.org Fax: (954) 357-5601
Business Operations Manager **Benjamin Sanchez** .... (954) 357-8502
Fax: (954) 357-5601

Human Resources Division

115 South Andrews Avenue, Room 508, Fort Lauderdale, FL 33301
Tel: (954) 357-6001 Fax: (954) 357-8414
Internet: www.broward.org/humanresources

Director **Kevin B. Kelleher** .... (954) 357-6005
115 South Andrews Avenue, Room 508, Fort Lauderdale, FL 33301-4803
E-mail: kkelleher@broward.org
Assistant Director **Mary McDonald** .... (954) 357-6044
115 South Andrews Avenue, Room 514, Fort Lauderdale, FL 33301-4803
E-mail: mmcdonald@broward.org
Compensation and Records Manager **Sharon Woods** .... (954) 357-6437
115 South Andrews Avenue, Room 508, Fort Lauderdale, FL 33301-4803

★ Elected Official ▲ Appointed by Legislature ▼ Appointed by Governor ▶ Appointed by Board or Commission ● Appointed by Judge
■ Appointed by Mayor △ Appointed by Freeholders ▽ Appointed by Supervisor ▷ Appointed by County Executive ○ Appointed by Council

Human Resources Division *continued*

Employee Benefits Manager **Lisa Morrison** Room 514 . . . (954) 357-6700
Labor Relations Manager **Allen Wilson** . . . . . (954) 357-6090
115 South Andrews Avenue, Room 508,
Fort Lauderdale, FL 33301-4803
E-mail: awilson@broward.org
Learning and Organizational Development Manager
John Pelkey . . . . . (954) 357-6588
115 South Andrews Avenue, Room 516,
Fort Lauderdale, FL 33301-4803
E-mail: jpelkey@broward.org
Staffing Services Manager **Sharon Liebowitz** Annex B . . . . . (954) 357-6434
E-mail: sliebowitz@broward.org Fax: (954) 357-5782

Purchasing Division

115 South Andrews Avenue, Room 212, Fort Lauderdale, FL 33301
Tel: (954) 357-6065 Fax: (954) 357-8535
Internet: www.broward.org/purchasing

Director **Brenda J. Billingsley** . . . . . (954) 357-6070
E-mail: bbillingsley@broward.org
Assistant Director **Glenn Marcos** . . . . . (954) 357-6072
E-mail: gmarcos@broward.org
Purchasing Manager **Connie Mangan** . . . . . (954) 357-6009
E-mail: cmangan@broward.org
Administrative Coordinator I **Sharon Rock** . . . . . (954) 357-6224
E-mail: srock@broward.org
Administrative Coordinator I **Lucy Garcia** . . . . . (954) 357-6071
E-mail: lugarcia@broward.org
Central Warehouse Supervisor **Joel Mariani** . . . . . (954) 537-2850
E-mail: jmariani@broward.org Fax: (954) 537-2855

Records, Taxes and Treasury Division

Tel: (954) 831-4000 Fax: (954) 357-5573
Internet: www.broward.org/records

Director **Thomas "Tom" Kennedy** Room 120 . . . . . (954) 357-5777
Assistant Director **Gary Mehringer** A-430 . . . . . (954) 357-5440
Fax: (954) 357-5569
Document Control Section Supervisor **André Morrell** . . . . (954) 357-7298
115 South Andrews Avenue, Fax: (954) 357-5569
Room 336U, Fort Lauderdale, FL 33301
Records Center Supervisor **Susan Kluck** . . . . . (954) 577-4626
Fax: (954) 831-1438
Accounting Manager, CPA, Treasury and Tax Administration **Aecha Schot** . . . . . (954) 357-7245
115 South Andrews Avenue, Fax: (954) 357-5731
A-400, Fort Lauderdale, FL 33301
E-mail: aschot@broward.org
Value Adjustment Board and Documents Manager
Josephine Bieber Room 120 . . . . . (954) 357-5444
Recording Manager **Jeannie Terwilliger** . . . . . (954) 357-7274
Customer Service: (954) 356-6716
Tax and Licenses OPS **Dana Buker** . . . . . (954) 357-5378
E-mail: revenue@broward.org Fax: (954) 468-3429
RTT Senior Manager **Claudio Manicone** Room 100 . . . . . (954) 357-8638
E-mail: cmanicone@broward.org Fax: (954) 468-3429
Vehicle and Vessel Registration/Titling Manager
Paul Rowe . . . . . (954) 797-8779
1800 NW 66 Avenue, Room 100, Plantation, FL 33313
Customer Service: (954) 797-8733
Systems Network Analyst IV **Mark Lichtenberg** Room 121 . . . . . (954) 357-8272
E-mail: mlichtenberg@broward.org Fax: (954) 357-7676
Senior Division Administrative Assistant **Eva Rose** . . . . . (954) 357-7276
E-mail: erose@broward.org
Customer Service: (954) 357-8455
Tourist Tax Revenue **Randy Luechauer** . . . . . (954) 357-6172
E-mail: rluechauer@broward.org Fax: (954) 357-6524

Risk Management Division

115 South Andrews Avenue, Room 210, Fort Lauderdale, FL 33301
Tel: (954) 357-7200 Fax: (954) 357-6545
Internet: www.broward.org/riskmanagement

Director **John Burkholder** . . . . . (954) 357-7203
E-mail: jburkholder@broward.org Fax: (954) 357-7180
Assistant Director **Roger Moore** . . . . . (954) 357-7219
Safety and Occupational Health Manager **Jim Litrides** . . . (954) 357-8037
E-mail: jlitrides@broward.org Fax: (954) 468-3566
Workers Compensation Manager **Jeffrey O'Connor** . . . . . (954) 357-7230
Investigative Services Coordinator **Tony Lorini** . . . . . (954) 357-7208
E-mail: tlorini@broward.org Fax: (954) 357-3566
Liability Claims Manager **Mitch Weinstein** . . . . . (954) 357-7225
Safety and Health Specialist **Merry Giovachino** . . . . . (954) 357-5583
115 South Andrews Avenue, Fax: (954) 357-6132
Room A510, Fort Lauderdale, FL 33301-4803
Systems Network Analyst IV **Karen Gaither** . . . . . (954) 357-7238
E-mail: kgaither@broward.org Fax: (954) 357-6545
Senior Division Administrative Assistant **(Vacant)** . . . . . (954) 357-7029
Fax: (954) 357-6027

COUNTIES

Public Works Department

115 South Andrews Avenue, Room A600, Fort Lauderdale, FL 33301
Tel: (954) 357-6410 Fax: (954) 357-6340
Internet: www.broward.org/publicworks

Director **Thomas J. Hutka** . . . . . (954) 357-6410
Deputy Director **Anthony "Tony" Hui** . . . . . (954) 357-6308
E-mail: thui@broward.org

Transportation Department

1 North University Drive, Plantation, FL 33324
Tel: (954) 357-8300 Fax: (954) 357-8305 Internet: www.broward.org/bct

Director **Chris Walton** . . . . . (954) 357-8361
Assistant to the Division Director
Cynthia Corbett-Elder . . . . . (954) 357-8451
E-mail: celder@broward.org
Executive Assistant **Denise Martinez** . . . . . (954) 357-8301
Deputy Director **Timothy S. "Tim" Garling** . . . . . (954) 357-8424
Grants Manager **Traci Miller** . . . . . (954) 357-6780
Transit Manager Operations **Corwin Gibbs** . . . . . (954) 357-8555
E-mail: cgibbs@broward.org Fax: (954) 357-8378
Compliance and Administrative Services Manager
Oscar Figueroa . . . . . (954) 357-8481
Customer Relations and Communications Manager
Mary Shaffer . . . . . (954) 357-8366
Fax: (954) 357-8371
Information Systems Manager **Carlos Alvarado** . . . . . (954) 357-8360
Fax: (954) 357-7719
Maintenance Manager (Acting) **Alex Bengochea** . . . . . (954) 357-8324
Paratransit Services Manager **Paul Strobis, Jr.** . . . . . (954) 357-8321
Fax: (954) 357-8345
Service and Capital Planning Manager **Barney McCoy** . . . (954) 357-8369
Fax: (954) 357-8342
Human Resources Officer **Dorothy Powell** . . . . . (954) 357-8307
E-mail: dpowell@broward.org
Community Bus Program **Irvin Minney** . . . . . (954) 357-7713
Fax: (954) 357-8342
Fleet Manager **David DellaPenta** . . . . . (954) 357-6499

Office of the Assistant County Administrator

115 South Andrews Avenue, Room 409, Fort Lauderdale, FL 33301
Tel: (954) 357-7354 Fax: (954) 357-7360

Assistant County Administrator **Monica Cepero** . . . . . (954) 357-7354
E-mail: mcepero@broward.org
Education: Florida State BS, 1992 MPA

★ Elected Official ▲ Appointed by Legislature ▼ Appointed by Governor ▶ Appointed by Board or Commission ● Appointed by Judge
■ Appointed by Mayor △ Appointed by Freeholders ▽ Appointed by Supervisor ▷ Appointed by County Executive ○ Appointed by Council

Office of Intergovernmental Affairs and Professional Standards
Governmental Center, 115 South Andrews Avenue, Room 426, Fort Lauderdale, FL 33301
Fax: (954) 357-6573 Internet: www.broward.org/intergovernmental

Director **Edward G. Labrador** .... (954) 357-7575
Legislative Counsel **C. Marty Cassini** .... (954) 357-7575
Legislative Coordinator **Sean Kolaskar** .... (954) 357-7575
Legislative Coordinator **Daphnee Sainvil** .... (954) 357-7575

Office of the Medical Examiner and Trauma Services
5301 SW 31st Ave., Fort Lauderdale, FL 33312
Tel: (954) 327-5200 Fax: (954) 327-6580
Internet: www.broward.org/medical

▼Chief Medical Examiner and Director **CAPT Craig T. Mallak** .... (954) 357-5200

Office of Public Communications
115 South Andrews Avenue, Room 506, Fort Lauderdale, FL 33301
Tel: (954) 357-6990 Fax: (954) 357-6936
E-mail: publicinfo@broward.org

Director **Margaret Stapleton** .... (954) 357-6990
E-mail: mstapleton@broward.org
Webmaster **Rob Nadeau** .... (954) 357-7462
E-mail: rnadeau@broward.org
Assistant Director **Ric Barrick** .... (954) 357-8541

Environmental Protection and Growth Management Department
115 South Andrews Avenue, Fort Lauderdale, FL 33301
Fax: (954) 357-8655 Internet: www.broward.org/environmentandgrowth

Director **Cynthia Chambers** .... (954) 357-6613
Deputy Director **Henry Swiezek** .... (954) 357-6666
Housing and Community Development Division Director **Ralph Stone** .... (954) 765-5320
E-mail: rstone@broward.org
Planning and Redevelopment Division Director **Josie Sesodia** .... (954) 357-6666
Environmental Licensing Building and Permit Division Director **Leonard Vialpando** .... (954) 519-1473
E-mail: lvialpando@broward.org

Human Services Department
Governmental Center, 115 South Andrews Avenue, Room 303, Fort Lauderdale, FL 33301-1817
Tel: (954) 357-6385 Fax: (954) 468-3592
Internet: www.broward.org/humanservices

Director **Michael Elwell** .... (954) 357-6748

Office of Evaluation and Planning
115 S. Andrews Ave., Room 318, Fort Lauderdale, FL 33301
Tel: (954) 357-6978 Fax: (954) 468-3578 E-mail: bcgrants@broward.org

Director **Robin Floyd** .... (954) 357-7895
Assistant Director **(Vacant)** .... (954) 357-5697

Broward Addiction and Recovery Center Division [BARC]
1000 Southwest 2nd Court, Fort Lauderdale, FL 33312
Tel: (954) 357-4880 Fax: (954) 357-4853

Director **Paul Faulk** .... (954) 357-4860
Clinical Director **Jasmine Bascombe** .... (954) 357-5082

Community Partnership Division
115 South Andrews Avenue, Room A-330, Fort Lauderdale, FL 33301
Tel: (954) 357-6101 Fax: (954) 468-3591

Director **Mandy Wells** .... (954) 357-6101 ext. 6398
E-mail: mwells@broward.org

Children Services Administration Section

Community Partnership Division *continued*

Tel: (954) 357-6202 Fax: (954) 468-3591

Administrator **Linda L. Raybin** .... (954) 357-6396 ext. 7249
Education: NYU BA; Barry MSW
Child Care Licensing Section Manager **(Vacant)** .... (954) 537-2800
Fax: (954) 537-2922

Health Care Services Section
115 South Andrews Avenue, Room A-330, Fort Lauderdale, FL 33301

Administrator **(Vacant)** .... (954) 357-5390

Homeless Initiative Partnership Section
115 South Andrews Avenue, Room A-370, Fort Lauderdale, FL 33301
Tel: (954) 357-6101 Fax: (954) 357-5521

Administrator (Acting) **Michael Wright** .... (954) 357-6101 ext. 6167

Elderly and Veterans Services Division
2995 N. Dixie Hwy., Fort Lauderdale, FL 33334
Tel: (954) 357-6622 Fax: (954) 357-8815
Internet: www.broward.org/eldervets

Director **Andrew Busade** .... (954) 537-2936
Assistant Director **Joseph Ciamataro** .... (954) 537-2936
Veterans' Service Officer **Owen Walker** .... (954) 537-2936
Fax: (954) 537-2804

Family Success Administration Division
115 S. Andrews Ave., Room 311, Fort Lauderdale, FL 33301
Tel: (954) 357-6367 Fax: (954) 468-3579

Director **Patricia G. West** .... (954) 357-6466

Office of Management and Budget
Governmental Center, 115 South Andrews Avenue, Room 404, Fort Lauderdale, FL 33301
Tel: (954) 357-6345 Fax: (954) 357-6364
Internet: www.broward.org/budget

Director **Kayla Olsen** .... (954) 357-6346
E-mail: kolsen@broward.org
Assistant Director **Marci Gelman** .... (954) 357-6354
E-mail: mgelman@broward.org
Program Manager **Jennifer Stillman** .... (954) 357-6353
Program Manager **Maureen Shields** .... (954) 357-6358
E-mail: mshields@broward.org

Broward County Aviation Department [BCAD]
2200 Southwest 45th Street, Dania Beach, FL 33312
Tel: (954) 359-6100 Fax: (954) 359-0027
Internet: www.broward.org/airport

Director of Aviation **Mark Gale** .... (954) 359-6214
Education: Embry-Riddle 1987 BS
Assistant to the Director **Mayra Lecusay** .... (954) 359-1329
E-mail: mlecusay@broward.org
Deputy Director **(Vacant)** .... (954) 359-6188
Assistant Director of Airport Development **Steve Wiesner** .... (954) 359-6148
Director of Administration **Andrea "Celina" Saucedo** .... (954) 359-6176
E-mail: asaucedo@broward.org
Director of Business **Yasmi Govin** .... (954) 359-6145
E-mail: ygovin@broward.org
Director of Finance **Helena James-Rendleman** .... (954) 359-6128
Director of Maintenance **Richard Waskiewicz** .... (954) 359-1250
Director of Operations **Michael "Mike" Nonnemacher** .... (954) 359-1213
E-mail: mnonnemacher@broward.org Fax: (954) 359-6198
Director of Planning **Michael Pacitto** .... (954) 359-2583
Director of Capital Improvement Project **Marc Gambrill** .... (954) 359-2343
Director of Airport Expansion **Trevor Fisher** .... (954) 359-6866

Office of the Property Appraiser

Governmental Center, 115 South Andrews Avenue, Room 111, Fort Lauderdale, FL 33301
Tel: (954) 357-6830 Fax: (954) 357-8474 Internet: www.bcpa.net

★ Property Appraiser **Lori Parrish** (D) .... (954) 357-6904
Term Expires: January 3, 2017
E-mail: lori@bcpa.net
General Counsel and Director of Administration **Jerrod Mathias** .... (954) 357-6934
E-mail: jmathias@bcpa.net
Deputy General Counsel **Mila Schwartzreich** .... (954) 357-6031

Office of the Public Defender

Broward County Courthouse, 201 SE Sixth Street, Room 3872, Fort Lauderdale, FL 33301
Internet: http://www.browarddefender.org

★ Public Defender **Howard Finkelstein** (D) .... (954) 831-8650
Term Expires: November 30, 2016

Office of the Sheriff

2601 West Broward Boulevard, Fort Lauderdale, FL 33312-1308
Tel: (954) 831-8900 Fax: (954) 797-0936 Internet: www.sheriff.org

★ Sheriff **Scott J. Israel** .... (954) 831-8901
Term Expires: December 31, 2016
E-mail: scott_israel@sheriff.org

Department of Fire Rescue and Emergency Services [DFRES]

Public Safety Building, 2601 West Broward Boulevard, Fort Lauderdale, FL 33312-1308
Tel: (954) 831-8200 Fax: (954) 831-8265 Internet: www.sheriff.org

Chief **Anthony P. Stravino** .... (954) 831-8201
E-mail: anthony_stravino@sheriff.org
Deputy Chief of Administration **Frank Porcella** .... (954) 831-8214
E-mail: frank_porcella@sheriff.org
Deputy Chief of Operations **Joseph Fernandez** .... (954) 321-4592
E-mail: joseph_fernandez@sheriff.org
Fire Marshal **Michael Cassano** .... (954) 831-8280
E-mail: michael_cassano@sheriff.org
Medical Director **(Vacant)** .... (954) 560-1900
Deputy Chief of Logistics and Special Services **Miriam Erdman** .... (954) 321-4624

Office of the State Attorney

Broward County Courthouse, 201 SE Sixth Street, Room 640, Fort Lauderdale, FL 33301
Internet: www.sao17.state.fl.us

★ State Attorney **Michael J. Satz** .... (954) 831-6955
Term Expires: November 30, 2016 Fax: (954) 831-7321
Education: Miami 1968 JD

Office of the Supervisor of Elections

Governmental Center, 115 South Andrews Avenue, Room 102, Fort Lauderdale, FL 33301
Tel: (954) 357-7050 Fax: (954) 357-7070 Internet: www.browardsoe.org

★ Supervisor of Elections **Dr. Brenda C. Snipes** (D) .... (954) 712-1951
Term Expires: January 5, 2017
E-mail: bsnipes@browardsoe.org
Education: Talladega 1964 BA; Florida Atlantic 1975 MA; Nova Southeastern 1998 PhD
Executive Assistant **Fred S. Bellis** .... (954) 712-1953
E-mail: fbellis@browardsoe.org

Broward County Public Schools [BCPS]

600 Southeast Third Avenue, Fort Lauderdale, FL 33301
Internet: www.browardschools.com

School Board of Broward County

Fax: (754) 321-2700 E-mail: schoolboard@browardschools.com

Chair **Rosalind Osgood** .... (754) 321-2001
Fax: (754) 321-2700

Office of the Superintendent

Fax: (754) 321-2701

Superintendent **Robert W. Runcie** .... (754) 321-2600
Education: Harvard BA; Northwestern 1991 MM

County of Bucks, Pennsylvania

Courthouse, Broad and Court Streets, Doylestown, PA 18901
Tel: (215) 348-6000 (Information) Internet: www.buckscounty.org

County Seat: Doylestown **Election Type:** Partisan **Population:** 627,367 (2015)

Office of the County Commission

Administration Bldg., 55 East Court Street, 5th Floor, Doylestown, PA 18901
Tel: (215) 348-6000
Internet: www.buckscounty.org/government/commissioners

★ Chairman **Robert G. Loughery** (R) .... (215) 348-6424
Term Expires: December 31, 2019 Fax: (215) 348-6146
E-mail: comm.loughery@co.bucks.pa.us
Date of Birth: 1969
Education: Dickinson Col 1991 BA
Executive Assistant **Karen M. Nagy** .... (215) 348-6424
E-mail: knagy@co.bucks.pa.us
★ Vice Chairman **Charles H. Martin** (R) .... (215) 348-6426
Term Expires: December 31, 2019 Fax: (215) 340-8204
E-mail: chmartin@co.bucks.pa.us
Education: Lebanon Valley 1964 BA
Executive Assistant **Theresa DeSantis** .... (215) 348-6426
E-mail: tdesantis@co.bucks.pa.us
★ Commissioner **Diane Ellis-Marseglia** (D) .... (215) 348-6425
Term Expires: December 31, 2019 Fax: (215) 340-8169
E-mail: dmellismarseglia@co.bucks.pa.us
Education: Delaware; Pennsylvania 1984 MSW
Executive Assistant **Robin Rosenthal** .... (215) 348-6425
E-mail: rrrosenthal@co.bucks.pa.us

Office of the Chief Operating Officer

Administration Building, 55 East Court Street, 5th Floor, Doylestown, PA 18901
Tel: (215) 348-6433 Fax: (215) 348-6769

▶ Chief Operating Officer **Brian Hessenthaler** .... (215) 348-6433
E-mail: bhessenthaler@co.bucks.pa.us
Education: Bloomsburg BSBA; Philadelphia U MBA
Executive Secretary **Judith A. Faunce** .... (215) 348-6433
E-mail: jafaunce@co.bucks.pa.us
▶ Chief County Clerk **Lynn T. Bush** .... (215) 348-6433
E-mail: ltbush@co.bucks.pa.us

COUNTIES

★ Elected Official ▲ Appointed by Legislature ▼ Appointed by Governor ▶ Appointed by Board or Commission ● Appointed by Judge
■ Appointed by Mayor △ Appointed by Freeholders ▽ Appointed by Supervisor ▷ Appointed by County Executive ○ Appointed by Council

Office of Public Information

Administration Building, 55 East Court Street, 5th Floor, Doylestown, PA 18901
Tel: (215) 348-6414

Director **Christopher T. "Chris" Edwards** . . . . (215) 348-6413
E-mail: ctedwards@co.bucks.pa.us

Office of the Solicitor

Administration Bldg., 55 E. Court St., Doylestown, PA 18901
Fax: (267) 885-1654

▶ Solicitor **Michael A. Klimpl** . . . . (215) 348-6464
E-mail: maklimpl@buckscounty.org
Assistant County Solicitor **Sean M. Corr** . . . . (215) 348-6464
Litigation Solicitor **Tina Mazaheri** . . . . (215) 348-6464
Senior Assistant County Solicitor **Donna L. Snyder** . . . . . (215) 348-6464
Assistant County Solicitor **Donald E. Williams** . . . . (215) 348-6464

Community Services Division

1260 Almshouse Road, Doylestown, PA 18901

Division Leader **Lynn T. Bush** . . . . (215) 348-6433

Bucks County Planning Commission [BCPC]

The Almshouse, Neshaminy Manor Center, 1260 Almshouse Road, Doylestown, PA 18901
Tel: (215) 345-3400 Fax: (215) 345-3886 E-mail: bcpc@co.bucks.pa.us

▶ Executive Director **Lynn T. Bush** . . . . (215) 345-3402
E-mail: ltbush@co.bucks.pa.us
Director, Agricultural Land Preservation Program **Richard B. Harvey** . . . . (215) 345-3409
Director, GIS/Transportation and Coordinator of Open Space Program **David P. Johnson** . . . . (215) 345-3883
Director, Planning Services **Timothy A. Koehler** . . . . (215) 345-3410
Office Supervisor **Donna Byers** . . . . (215) 345-3403
E-mail: dwbyers@co.bucks.pa.us

Bucks County Board of Elections

Administration Bldg., 55 East Court Street, 2nd Floor, Doylestown, PA 18901
Tel: (215) 348-6154 Fax: (215) 348-6387
E-mail: elections@co.bucks.pa.us

▶ Director **Deena K. Dean** . . . . (215) 348-6154
E-mail: dkdean@co.bucks.pa.us

Department of Housing and Community Development

Neshaminy Manor Center, 1260 Almshouse Rd., Doylestown, PA 18901
Tel: (215) 345-3840 Fax: (215) 345-3865

▶ Director **Roger Collins** . . . . (215) 345-3840
HOME Program Administrator **Martha Woglom** . . . . (215) 345-3842

Military Affairs Office

1260 Almshouse Road, 4th Floor, Doylestown, PA 18901
Fax: (215) 345-3278

▶ Director **Dan Fraley** . . . . (215) 345-3307
E-mail: dhfraley@co.bucks.pa.us
Veterans Aide **Betty Carleo** . . . . (215) 345-3885
Quakertown Government Services Center, 261 California Road, Quakertown, PA 18951
Veterans Assistant **Karen L. Mayer** . . . . (267) 580-3560
Bucks County Government Services Center, Branch Office, 7321 New Falls Road, Levittown, PA 19055

Office of Consumer Protection/Weights and Measures

1260 Almshouse Road, Fourth Floor, Doylestown, PA 18901
Fax: (267) 885-1420

▶ Director/Chief Sealer **Michael D. Bannon** . . . . (215) 348-6060
E-mail: mdbannon@buckscounty.org
Office Manager/Coordinator **Sally A. Carr** . . . . (215) 348-6060

Office of the Public Defender

Justice Center, 100 North Main Street, Doylestown, PA 18901
Tel: (215) 348-6473 Fax: (215) 348-6499

▶ Public Defender **Christina A. King** . . . . (215) 348-6511
E-mail: caking@co.bucks.pa.us
Education: Villanova JD
1st Deputy Public Defender **Peter C. Hall** . . . . (215) 348-6252
Chief Deputy Public Defender **(Vacant)** . . . . (215) 348-6474
Administrative Deputy **Ann P. Russavage-Faust** . . . . (215) 348-6487
Office Manager **Debbie J. Meier** . . . . (215) 348-6475

Department of Corrections [DOC]

1730 S. Easton Rd., Doylestown, PA 18901-2885
Tel: (215) 345-3700 Fax: (215) 345-3846
E-mail: bucksdoc@co.bucks.pa.us

▶ Director **William F. Plantier** . . . . (215) 340-8480
E-mail: wfplantier@co.bucks.pa.us
Administrative Assistant **Michelle McLaughlin** . . . . (215) 340-8481
Deputy Director, Facility Operations **Christopher A. "Chris" Pirolli** . . . . (215) 340-8483
E-mail: capirolli@co.bucks.pa.us
Warden **Terrance P. Moore** . . . . (215) 345-3701
Deputy Warden **Clifton Mitchell** . . . . (215) 345-3702
Assistant Warden, Inmate Services **Lillian Budd** . . . . (215) 345-3740
Administrative Affairs Captain **Clarke Fulton** . . . . (215) 340-8482
Finance Director **Mary Jo Pellegrino** . . . . (215) 345-3741
Correctional Mental Health Services Executive Director **Dr. John Markey** . . . . (215) 345-3735
Dispensary Supervisor **Joseph Lynch** . . . . (215) 345-3752
Drug/Alcohol Supervisor **James Cunningham** . . . . (215) 345-3742
Records Supervisor **David Kratz** . . . . (215) 345-3774
Librarian **Richard Dittman** . . . . (215) 345-3746

Men's and Women's Community Corrections Centers

Superintendent **Kevin Rousset** . . . . (215) 345-3923
Deputy Superintendent **David Galione** . . . . (215) 345-3902

Emergency Services Division

911 Freedom Way, Ivyland, PA 18974

Director **Scott T. Forster** . . . . (215) 340-8700

Office of the Fire Marshal

911 Freedom Way, Ivyland, PA 18974
Fax: (215) 957-0765 E-mail: buckscountyfiremarshal@buckscounty.org

▶ Fire Marshal **Mark Kramer** . . . . (215) 340-8730
E-mail: makramer@buckscounty.org
Assistant Fire Marshal **Kevin T. Flanagan** . . . . (215) 340-8730
E-mail: ktflanagan@buckscounty.org

Department of Emergency Communications

Bucks County Emergency Services Complex, 911 Freedom Way, Ivyland, PA 18974
Tel: (888) 245-7210 Fax: (267) 885-1323

▶ Director and 9-1-1 Coordinator **Audre Kenney** . . . . (888) 245-7210
E-mail: arkenny@co.bucks.pa.us
Superintendent of Operations **Dennis R. Forsyth** . . . . (215) 328-5192
E-mail: drforsyth@co.bucks.pa.us
Superintendent of Training **Stephen H. Reichman** . . . . . . (215) 328-5154
E-mail: shreichman@co.bucks.pa.us
Director of Technology **Tracy Carl** . . . . (215) 345-8112
E-mail: tacarl@co.bucks.pa.us
Computer-Aided Dispatch (CAD) Coordinator **Jon R. Stoughton** . . . . (215) 348-5156
E-mail: jrstoughton@co.bucks.pa.us

Bucks County Emergency Health Services [BCEHS]

911 Freedom Way, Ivyland, PA 18974
Tel: (215) 340-8735 Fax: (215) 957-0765 E-mail: info@bcehs.com
Internet: www.bcehs.com

▶ Director **Jeryl DeGideo** . . . . (215) 340-8735
E-mail: jldegideo@buckscounty.org

★ Elected Official ▲ Appointed by Legislature ▼ Appointed by Governor ▶ Appointed by Board or Commission ● Appointed by Judge
■ Appointed by Mayor △ Appointed by Freeholders ▽ Appointed by Supervisor ▷ Appointed by County Executive ○ Appointed by Council

Emergency Management Agency
911 Freedom Way, Ivyland, PA 18974
Fax: (215) 957-0765

▶ Coordinator **Scott T. Forster** .... (215) 340-8700
E-mail: stforster@buckscounty.org
Deputy Coordinator **(Vacant)** .... (215) 340-8700

Finance and Administration Division
55 East Court Street, 3rd Floor, Doylestown, PA 18901

Director **David P. Boscola** .... (215) 348-6564
E-mail: dpboscola@co.bucks.pa.us
Education: Bloomsburg 1989 BS

Board of Assessment
Administration Building, 55 East Court Street, 3rd Floor, Doylestown, PA 18901
Tel: (215) 348-6219 Fax: (215) 348-6225

Director of Assessments **Richard L. Brosius** .... (215) 348-6226
Chief Appraiser **Robert Bozena** .... (215) 340-8175

Finance Department
Administration Building, 55 East Court Street, 3rd Floor, Doylestown, PA 18901
Fax: (215) 348-6227

Director **David P. Boscola** .... (215) 348-6564
Education: Bloomsburg 1989 BS
Deputy Finance Director **Russell G. Rice III** .... (215) 348-6564

Department of Human Resources
50 North Main Street, 1st Floor, Doylestown, PA 18901-3730
Tel: (215) 348-6544

Director **Travis Monroe** .... (215) 348-6418

Information Technology Department
Court House, 55 East Court Street, 7th Floor, Doylestown, PA 18901
Fax: (215) 348-6574 E-mail: cio@co.bucks.pa.us

▶ Chief Information Officer **Donald W. Jacobs** .... (215) 348-6195
E-mail: dwjacobs@co.bucks.pa.us
Deputy Chief Information Officer **William F. "Bill" Waterbury** .... (215) 340-8289
E-mail: wfwaterbury@co.bucks.pa.us
Finance and Administration Manager **Susan L. "Sue" Conrad** .... (215) 340-8045
E-mail: slconrad@co.bucks.pa.us
Training Coordinator **Randall S. "Randy" Miller** .... (215) 348-6874
E-mail: rsmiller@co.bucks.pa.us

Purchasing Department
Administration Building, 55 East Court Street, Doylestown, PA 18901-4318
Fax: (215) 348-6379 E-mail: purchasing@co.bucks.pa.us

▶ Director **Maureen Wilson McIlvaine** .... (215) 348-6372

Tax Claims Bureau
Administration Building, 55 East Court Street, 3rd Floor, Doylestown, PA 18901
Fax: (215) 340-8113

▶ Director **Marguerite C. Genesio** .... (215) 348-6280
E-mail: mcgenesio@co.bucks.pa.us

General Services Division
Neshaminy Manor Warehouse, Route 611 and Almshouse Road, Doylestown, PA 18901
Fax: (215) 345-3967

▶ Director of Operations **Gerald "Jerry" Anderson** .... (215) 345-3950
E-mail: gbanderson@co.bucks.pa.us
Administrative Assistant **Cathy A. Barton** .... (215) 345-3950
E-mail: cabarton@co.bucks.pa.us

Asset Management
Neshaminy Manor Center, Route 611 and Almshouse Road, Doylestown, PA 18901

County Asset Manager **Peter J. "Pete" McElroy** .... (215) 345-3914

County Facilities
Administration Building, 55 East Court Street, 1st Floor, Doylestown, PA 18901
Fax: (215) 348-6121

County Facilities Manager **Barry Snyder** .... (215) 348-6217
Administrative Assistant **(Vacant)** .... (215) 348-6363

Department of Parks and Recreation
901 E. Bridgetown Pike, Langhorne, PA 19047-1597
Tel: (215) 348-6114 Fax: (215) 752-1421
E-mail: parksandrecreation@co.bucks.pa.us

▶ Executive Director **William M. Mitchell** .... (215) 757-0571
E-mail: wmmitchell@co.bucks.pa.us
Historic Properties Manager **Charles J. Yeske** .... (215) 348-6627
152 East Swamp Road, Doylestown, PA 18901

Human Services Division
Administration Bldg., 55 E. Court St., Fourth Floor, Doylestown, PA 18901
Tel: (215) 348-6201 Fax: (267) 885-7655

▶ Director **Jonathan Rubin** .... (215) 348-6203
E-mail: jerubin@buckscounty.org
Education: Temple MSW
Administrative Assistant **Victoria Harris** .... (215) 348-6201
E-mail: vlharris@buckscounty.org
Deputy Director **Christina Finello** .... (215) 340-8801

Area Agency on Aging
30 East Oakland Avenue, Doylestown, PA 18901
Tel: (267) 880-5700 Fax: (215) 348-0356
E-mail: aging@buckscounty.org

▶ Director **Najja R. Orr** .... (267) 880-5700
E-mail: nrorr@buckscounty.org
Deputy Director **Carol Boyle** .... (267) 880-5700
Care Management Deputy Director **Lois Tobin** .... (267) 880-5700

Children and Youth Social Services Agency
Heritage Center, Building 500, 2325 Heritage Center Drive, Furlong, PA 18925
Tel: (215) 348-6900 Fax: (215) 348-6989

Executive Director **Lynne Kallus-Rainey** .... (215) 348-6942
Assistant Director **Marjorie McKeone** .... (215) 348-6928
Adoption Manager **Karen Robos** .... (215) 348-6936
Intake Manager **Nancy Morgan** .... (215) 348-6912
Placement Manager **Virginia Trea** .... (215) 348-6942
Adolescent Services Manager **Christine Lilley** .... (215) 348-6982
Protective Services Manager **Sara Miller** .... (215) 348-6953

Bucks County Drug and Alcohol Commission, Inc. [BCDAC, Inc.]
600 Louis Drive, Suite 102-A, Warminster, PA 18974
Tel: (215) 773-9313 Fax: (215) 956-9939

▶ Executive Director **Diane W. Rosati** .... (215) 773-9313
E-mail: dwrosati@co.bucks.pa.us
Associate Director **Margie Rivera** .... (215) 773-9313
Clinical Director **Ana Rosado** .... (215) 773-9313
Human Resources Manager **Pam Leutze** .... (215) 773-9313 ext. 2705
E-mail: pleutze@co.bucks.pa.us

Bucks County Health Department
Health Building, 1282 Almshouse Road, Doylestown, PA 18901
Tel: (215) 345-3318 Fax: (215) 345-3833

Director **David C. Damsker** .... (215) 345-3320

★ Elected Official ▲ Appointed by Legislature ▼ Appointed by Governor ▶ Appointed by Board or Commission ● Appointed by Judge
■ Appointed by Mayor △ Appointed by Freeholders ▽ Appointed by Supervisor ▷ Appointed by County Executive ○ Appointed by Council

Department of Mental Health/Developmental Programs
600 Louis Drive, Suite 101, Warminster, PA 18974
Fax: (215) 444-2890

► Administrator **Donna Duffy-Bell** .... (215) 444-2801
E-mail: ddduffybell@buckscounty.org
Deputy Administrator, Mental Health Services
Dawn Seader .... (215) 444-2870
Emergency and Court Services Director **Carol Bamford** .. (215) 444-2880
Children's Services Director **Barbara J. Miller** .... (215) 444-2885
Supports Coordinator Supervisor **Cindy Kowalewski** .... (215) 444-2850
Financial Director **Joseph McMichael** .... (215) 444-2815
Early Intervention Director **Pat Erario** .... (215) 444-2825
Deputy Administrator, Intellectual Disabilities
Mary Dunn .... (215) 444-2840

Neshaminy Manor
1660 Easton Road, Warrington, PA 18976
Tel: (215) 345-3205 Fax: (215) 345-3213

► Administrator **Margaret Zigler** .... (215) 345-3205
Assistant Administrator **J. C. Bailey** .... (215) 345-3205

COUNTIES

Authorities and Operating Affiliates

Bucks County Airport Authority [BCAA]
P.O. Box 1185, Doylestown, PA 18901
Tel: (215) 345-1970 Fax: (215) 348-5354 E-mail: bcaa@bellatlantic.net
Internet: www.bcaanet.org

Administrator **Colleen B. Raterman** .... (215) 345-1970
Financial Administrator **Linda Landis** .... (215) 345-1970

Bucks County Community College
275 Swamp Rd., Newtown, PA 18940
Tel: (215) 968-8000 Fax: (215) 968-8129 Internet: www.bucks.edu

President **Dr. Stephanie H. Shanblatt** .... (215) 968-8221
Executive Assistant to the President
Kathleen Fedorko .... (215) 968-8220
E-mail: kathleen.fedorko@bucks.edu
Chief Financial Officer and Vice President,
Administrative Affairs **Dennis Matthews** .... (215) 968-8301
E-mail: dennis.matthews@bucks.edu
Vice President, Student Affairs **Barbara Yetman** .... (215) 968-8105
Vice President, Information Technology Services
(Vacant) .... (215) 968-8400
Provost **Clayton Railey** .... (215) 968-8048
Associate Provost, Academic Affairs
Catherine McElroy .... (215) 968-8212
Strategic Liaison for Presidential Initiatives
Jason Mayland .... (215) 968-8414
E-mail: jason.mayland@bucks.edu

Bucks County Conference and Visitors Bureau, Inc.
3207 Street Rd., Bensalem, PA 19020-2032
Fax: (215) 642-3276 Internet: www.visitbuckscounty.com

Executive Director **Jerry Lepping** .... (215) 639-0300 ext. 234
Marketing Director **Paul Bencivengo** .... (215) 639-0300 ext. 230
Director of Marketing and Sales
Heather Walter .... (215) 639-0300 ext. 228
Marketing Services and Partnership Manager
Kathi Lacomchik .... (215) 639-0300 ext. 225
Operations Director **Linda Dougherty** .... (215) 639-0300 ext. 222
E-mail: ldougherty@visitbuckscounty.com

Bucks County Conservation District
1456 Ferry Road, Suite 704, Doylestown, PA 18901
Fax: (215) 345-7584 Internet: www.bucksccd.org

Manager **Gretchen Schatschneider** .... (215) 345-7577 ext. 106
Environmental Educator **Mary Ellen Noonan** ... (215) 345-7577 ext. 101

Bucks County Economic Development Corporation [BCEDC]
2 East Court Street, Doylestown, PA 18901
Tel: (215) 348-9031 Fax: (215) 348-8829 Internet: www.bcedc.com

Executive Director **Robert F. Cormack** .... (215) 348-9031
E-mail: rfc@bcedc.com

Bucks County Free Library
150 South Pine Street, Doylestown, PA 18901-4932
Tel: (215) 348-0332 Fax: (215) 348-4760 Internet: www.buckslib.org

► Executive Director **Martina Kominiarek** ...... (215) 348-0332 ext. 1101
E-mail: kominiarekm@buckslib.org
Education: Michigan MLS
Chief Financial Officer **John Doran** .... (215) 348-0332 ext. 1104
Collection Management Director **(Vacant)** ..... (215) 348-0332 ext. 1102
Administrative Services Manager
Joe Thompson .... (215) 348-9083 ext. 1181
E-mail: thompsonj@buckslib.org
Technical Services Manager **Ceil Hedrick** ...... (215) 348-9083 ext. 1171
District Consultant **Christina M. Snyder** ...... (215) 348-0332 ext. 1171
E-mail: snyderc@buckslib.org
Education: Drexel MSLS

Bucks County Redevelopment Authority [BCRDA]
One North Wilson Avenue, Suite 1, Bristol, PA 19007
Tel: (215) 781-8711 Fax: (215) 781-8716 E-mail: bcrda@bcrda.com
Internet: www.bcrda.com

Executive Director **Robert White** .... (215) 781-8711 ext. 14
Deputy Director **Jeff Darwak** .... (215) 781-8714 ext. 13
General Manager **Joe D'Adamo** .... (215) 781-8711
Neighborhood Conservation Specialist
James Kozak .... (215) 781-8711 ext. 11
Office Manager **Midge Wagner** .... (215) 781-8711
Administrative Assistant **Yaritza Maldonado** ..... (215) 781-8711 ext. 10

Bucks County Water and Sewer Authority [BCWSA]
1275 Almshouse Road, Warrington, PA 18976
Tel: (800) 222-2068 (Toll Free) Fax: (267) 200-0324
E-mail: email@bcwsa.net Internet: www.bcwsa.net

Chief Executive Officer
Benjamin W. "Ben" Jones .... (215) 343-2538 ext. 104
Executive Assistant **Anne O'Toole** .... (215) 343-2538
Chief Operations Officer **John Butler** .... (215) 343-2538
Chief Financial Officer **Arthur J. Hass** .... (215) 343-2538
Chief Information Officer **Patrick W. Cleary** .... (215) 343-2538
Director of Information Services **Nathaniel Rafalski** ..... (215) 343-2538
Engineering Manager **Glenn D. Argue** .... (215) 343-2538
Human Resources Manager **Mike Smith** .... (215) 343-2538
Corporate Counsel **Melissa Fiala** .... (215) 343-2538

Bucks County Workforce Investment Board, Inc. [BC-WIB]
1268 Veterans Highway, Bristol, PA 19007
Tel: (215) 874-2800 Fax: (215) 874-2804 Internet: www.bc-wib.org

Executive Director **Elizabeth Walsh** .... (215) 874-2800 ext. 109
Director of Finance **Thom Lord** .... (215) 874-2800 ext. 103

James A. Michener Art Museum
138 South Pine Street, Doylestown, PA 18901
Fax: (215) 340-9807 Internet: www.michenerartmuseum.org

Director **Lisa Tremper Hanover** .... (215) 340-9800 ext. 114
Director of Operations **Hollie Brown** .... (215) 340-9800 ext. 151

Office of the Controller

Administration Bldg., 55 E. Court St., Doylestown, PA 18901
Tel: (215) 348-6435 Fax: (215) 348-6107

★ Controller (Acting) **Kimberly S. Doran** .... (215) 348-6781
Term Expires: December 31, 2017
Deputy Controller **Kimberly S. Doran** .... (215) 348-6781
Audit Supervisor **Denise M. Rimby** .... (215) 348-6435

★ Elected Official ▲ Appointed by Legislature ▼ Appointed by Governor ► Appointed by Board or Commission ● Appointed by Judge
■ Appointed by Mayor △ Appointed by Freeholders ▽ Appointed by Supervisor ▷ Appointed by County Executive ○ Appointed by Council

Office of the Controller *continued*

Payroll Supervisor **(Vacant)** . . . . (215) 348-6435
Pre-Audit Supervisor **Joan Keightly** . . . . (215) 348-6435
Solicitor **Joseph A. "Joe" Cullen, Jr.** . . . . (267) 907-9612
Education: St Bonaventure 1995 BA; Villanova 1998 JD

Office of the Coroner

850 Eagle Boulevard, Warminster, PA 18974
Fax: (267) 880-5656 E-mail: coroner@co.bucks.pa.us

★Coroner **Dr. Joseph P. Campbell** (R) . . . . (267) 880-5040
Term Expires: December 31, 2019
Executive Secretary and Deputy Coroner
Janette M. Crompton . . . . (267) 880-5040
Chief Deputy Coroner **Keith T. Preston** . . . . (267) 880-5040
First Deputy Coroner **Richard Kuntz** . . . . (267) 880-5040
Solicitor **Charles O. Marte, Jr.** . . . . (267) 880-5040

Office of the District Attorney

100 North Main Street, Suite 2300, Doylestown, PA 18901
Tel: (215) 348-6344 Fax: (215) 348-6299

★District Attorney **David W. Heckler** (R) . . . . (215) 348-6345
Term Expires: December 31, 2017
E-mail: dwheckler@co.bucks.pa.us
Chief of Staff **Daniel B. Sweeney** . . . . (215) 348-6328
E-mail: dbsweeney@co.bucks.pa.us
Chief Deputy District Attorney
Matthew D. "Matt" Weintraub . . . . (215) 348-8159
First Assistant District Attorney **Michelle A. Henry** . . . . . . (215) 348-6343
Chief of Appeals **Stephen B. Harris** . . . . (215) 348-6295
Chief of Trials **Robert D. James** . . . . (215) 348-6343
E-mail: rdjames@co.bucks.pa.us
Chief County Detective **Christopher McAteer** . . . . (215) 348-6354
Office Manager **Michele Cevasco** . . . . (215) 348-6302

Office of the Prothonotary

Bucks County Justice Center, 100 North Main Street, Doylestown, PA 18901
Tel: (215) 348-6191 Fax: (215) 348-6184

★Prothonotary **Patricia L. Bachtle** (R) . . . . (215) 348-6191
Term Expires: December 31, 2017
E-mail: plbachtle@buckscounty.org
1st Deputy Prothonotary **Nicole L. Waltman** . . . . (215) 348-8046
2nd Deputy Prothonotary **Patricia A. Zimmerman** . . . . . . (215) 348-6111

Office of the Recorder of Deeds

Administration Building, 55 East Court Street, 2nd Floor, Doylestown, PA 18901
Fax: (215) 340-8157 E-mail: recorderdeeds@co.bucks.pa.us

★Recorder **Joseph J. Szafran, Jr.** (R) . . . . (215) 348-6209
Term Expires: December 31, 2017
First Deputy Recorder **Christine Ferrara** . . . . (215) 348-6213
Second Deputy Recorder **Steven "Steve" Pizzollo** . . . . . . (215) 348-6214

Office of the Register of Wills

Administration Bldg., 55 E. Court St., 3rd Floor, Doylestown, PA 18901
Fax: (215) 348-6156 E-mail: registerofwills@buckscounty.org
E-mail: orphanscourt@buckscounty.org

★Register **Donald Petrille, Jr.** (R) . . . . (215) 348-6265
Term Expires: December 31, 2019
1st Deputy Register **Colleen Strunk** . . . . (215) 348-6263

Office of the Sheriff

Administration Building, 55 East Court Street, 1st Floor, Doylestown, PA 18901-4327
Tel: (215) 348-6124 Fax: (215) 348-6289

★Sheriff **Edward J. Donnelly** (R) . . . . (215) 348-6124
Term Expires: December 31, 2017
E-mail: ejdonnelly@co.bucks.pa.us

Office of the Treasurer

Administration Building, 55 East Court Street, 3rd Floor, Doylestown, PA 18901
Tel: (215) 348-6244 Fax: (215) 348-6291

★Treasurer **Tom Panzer** (R) . . . . (215) 348-6249
Term Expires: December 31, 2019
Chief Deputy Treasurer **Amy M. Crosson** . . . . (215) 348-6251

County of Burlington, New Jersey

49 Rancocas Road, Mount Holly, NJ 08060
P.O. Box 6000, Mount Holly, NJ 08060
Tel: (609) 265-5000 (Information) Internet: www.co.burlington.nj.us

County Seat: Mt. Holly **Election Type:** Partisan **Population:** 450,226 (2015)

Office of the Board of Chosen Freeholders

49 Rancocas Road, Mount Holly, NJ 08060
Fax: (609) 702-7000 E-mail: freeholders@co.burlington.nj.us

★Director **Bruce D. Garganio** (R) . . . . (609) 265-5020
Term Expires: December 31, 2017
★Freeholder **Joe Donnelly** (R) . . . . (609) 265-5020
Term Expires: December 31, 2016
E-mail: jdonnelly@co.burlington.nj.us
★Freeholder **Kate Gibbs** (R) . . . . (609) 265-5020
Term Expires: December 31, 2018
★Freeholder **Mary Ann O'Brien** (R) . . . . (609) 265-5020
Term Expires: December 31, 2017
★Freeholder **Ryan Peters** (R) . . . . (609) 265-5020
Term Expires: December 31, 2018
Clerk of the Board **Gina Wheatley** . . . . (609) 265-5020
E-mail: gwheatley@co.burlington.nj.us

Office of the County Administrator

49 Rancocas Rd., Mount Holly, NJ 08060
Fax: (609) 265-5022

△County Administrator **Eve A. Cullinan** . . . . (609) 265-5020
E-mail: clerkoftheboard@co.burlington.nj.us
Public Information Officer **Eric Arpert** . . . . (609) 265-5028
Fax: (609) 265-5151

Aging and Disability Resource Center

Human Services Facility, 795 Woodlane Road, Westampton, NJ 08060
Fax: (609) 265-3725 E-mail: bcofficeonaging@co.burlington.nj.us
Internet: www.co.burlington.nj.us/aging

Director **Linda J. Cushing** . . . . (609) 265-5069

Office of the County Solicitor

49 Rancocas Road, Room 225, Mount Holly, NJ 08060

△County Solicitor **Kendall J. Colins** . . . . (609) 265-5289
Senior Assistant Solicitor **Carl V. Buck III** . . . . (609) 265-5200

(continued on next page)

★Elected Official ▲Appointed by Legislature ▼Appointed by Governor ►Appointed by Board or Commission ●Appointed by Judge
■Appointed by Mayor △Appointed by Freeholders ▽Appointed by Supervisor ▷Appointed by County Executive ○Appointed by Council

Office of the County Solicitor *continued*

Senior Assistant Solicitor **Jeffrey Rabin** . . . . (609) 265-5200
First Assistant Solicitor **Dina Rocco** . . . . (609) 265-5289

Office of the County Engineer

1900 Briggs Road, Mount Laurel, NJ 08054
Fax: (609) 642-3710 E-mail: engineering@co.burlington.nj.us

△ County Engineer **Joseph T. Brickley** . . . . (856) 642-3700
E-mail: jbrickley@co.burlington.nj.us

Office of the Medical Examiner

Westampton Complex, 4 Academy Drive, Westampton, NJ 08060
Fax: (609) 265-5989 E-mail: medicalexaminer@co.burlington.nj.us

△ Chief Medical Examiner **Dr. Ian C. Hood** . . . . (609) 702-7030
E-mail: ihood@co.burlington.nj.us

Veterans' Service Office

Human Services Facility, 795 Woodlane Rd., Westampton, NJ 08060
Fax: (609) 265-3184

△ Veterans' Service Officer **Walt Tafe** . . . . (609) 265-5008
E-mail: wtafe@co.burlington.nj.us

Division of Extension Services

49 Rancocas Rd., Mount Holly, NJ 08060
Fax: (609) 265-5613

County Agricultural Agent **Raymond J. Samulis** . . . . (609) 265-5051

Division of Fire Investigations and Inspections

Emergency Services Training Center, 53 Academy Drive, Westampton, NJ 08060
Fax: (609) 702-7100

△ Chief Fire Marshal **Michael J. Reed** . . . . (609) 702-7158
E-mail: mreed@co.burlington.nj.us
Assistant Fire Marshal **Robert W. "Bob" Carr, Jr.** . . . . (609) 702-7158
E-mail: bcarr@co.burlington.nj.us

Division of Parks

Six Park Avenue, Eastampton, NJ 08060
Fax: (609) 265-5797 E-mail: parks@co.burlington.nj.us

△ Superintendent **John Smith** . . . . (609) 265-5858
E-mail: jsmith@co.burlington.nj.us
△ County Historian **(Vacant)** . . . . (609) 265-5068

Probation Division

Courts Facility, Mount Holly, NJ 08060
Fax: (609) 518-2792

Division Manager **(Vacant)** . . . . (609) 518-2750

Building and Grounds

Basement-Courts Facility, Mount Holly, NJ 08060
Fax: (609) 265-3778

△ Superintendent **Timothy J. "Tim" Lutz** . . . . (609) 265-5011
E-mail: tlutz@co.burlington.nj.us

Department of Community Development

Human Services Facility, 795 Woodlane Road, Westampton, NJ 08060
Fax: (609) 265-5500

Coordinator **Karen Trommelen** . . . . (609) 265-5072
E-mail: ktrommelen@co.burlington.nj.us

Department of Economic Development and Regional Planning

1900 Briggs Road, Mount Laurel, NJ 08054
Fax: (609) 265-5006

△ Director **Mark A. Remsa** . . . . (609) 265-5055
E-mail: mremsa@co.burlington.nj.us

Finance Department

49 Rancocas Road, Room 101, Mount Holly, NJ 08060
Fax: (609) 265-5438

△ Chief Financial Officer **Marc Krassan** . . . . (609) 265-5018
△ Treasurer **Edward J. Troy** . . . . (609) 265-5018

Burlington County Health Department [BCHD]

Raphael Meadow Health Center, 15 Pioneer Boulevard, Westampton, NJ 08060
Fax: (609) 265-3152 Internet: www.co.burlington.nj.us/health

Director of Health **Holly Cucuzzella** . . . . (609) 265-5548

Highways Department

624 Pemberton-Browns Mills Rd., Pemberton, NJ 08068
Fax: (609) 726-7333

△ Supervisor **Jeffrey Kerchner** . . . . (609) 726-7300
E-mail: jkerchner@co.burlington.nj.us

Department of Information Technology

49 Rancocas Road, Room 111, Mount Holly, NJ 08060
Fax: (609) 265-3721 E-mail: it@co.burlington.nj.us

Chief Information Officer/Director **Nicholas J. Behmke** . . (609) 265-5125
E-mail: nbehmke@co.burlington.nj.us
Assistant Director **Glenn F. Tighe** . . . . (609) 265-5125
E-mail: gtighe@co.burlington.nj.us
Principal Clerk **Kim Kleszics** . . . . (609) 265-5125

Public Safety Department

49 Rancocas Rd., Mount Holly, NJ 08060
Fax: (609) 265-1323

△ Director (Acting) **Howard Black** . . . . (609) 261-3900
E-mail: hblack@co.burlington.nj.us
Emergency Management Coordinator **Kevin H. Tuno** . . . . . (609) 261-3900
E-mail: ktuno@co.burlington.nj.us
Forensic Science Laboratory Chief Forensic Chemist **John Drinkard** . . . . (609) 261-3900
E-mail: jdrinkard@co.burlington.nj.us

Purchasing Department

49 Rancocas Road, Room 104, Mount Holly, NJ 08060
Fax: (609) 265-5438 E-mail: purchasing@co.burlington.nj.us

Purchasing Agent **Sharon Brauckmann** . . . . (609) 265-5012
E-mail: sbrauckmann@co.burlington.nj.us

Resource Conservation Department

1900 Briggs Rd., Mount Laurel, NJ 08054

△ Director **Mary Pat Robbie** . . . . (856) 642-3850
E-mail: mrobbie@co.burlington.nj.us

Department of Solid Waste

49 Rancocas Rd., Mount Holly, NJ 08060
Fax: (609) 499-5212

Director **Jerome P. Sheehan** . . . . (609) 499-1001

Board of Social Services

Human Services Facility, 795 Woodlane Rd., Westampton, NJ 08060

Director **Ronald Yulick** . . . . (609) 261-1000

★ Elected Official ▲ Appointed by Legislature ▼ Appointed by Governor ▶ Appointed by Board or Commission ● Appointed by Judge
■ Appointed by Mayor △ Appointed by Freeholders ▽ Appointed by Supervisor ▷ Appointed by County Executive ○ Appointed by Council

COUNTIES

Burlington County Bridge Commission
1300 Route 73 North, Palmyra, NJ 08065
Tel: (856) 829-1900 Internet: www.bcbridges.org

Chairman **John B. Comegno II** (R) .... (856) 829-1900
Term Expires: October 22, 2018
Vice Chair **James D. Fattorini** (R) .... (856) 829-1900
Term Expires: October 22, 2016
Commissioner **Troy E. Singleton** (D) .... (856) 829-1900
Term Expires: October 22, 2017
Education: Rowan
Secretary **Kathleen M. Wiseman** .... (856) 829-1900
E-mail: kwiseman@bcbridges.org
Treasurer **Christine J. Nociti** .... (856) 829-1900
Executive Director **John D. Jeffers** .... (856) 829-1900
E-mail: jjeffers@bcbridges.org

Burlington County College [BCC]
601 Pemberton-Browns Mills Road, Pemberton, NJ 08068
Fax: (609) 894-0183 Internet: www.bcc.edu

President **Paul Drayton, Jr.** .... (609) 894-9311
Education: Delaware 1982; Villanova 1986 JD

Burlington County Jail
54 Grant St., Mount Holly, NJ 08060
Fax: (609) 265-5804

△ Administrator/Warden **Mildred Scholtz** .... (609) 265-5042
E-mail: mscholtz@co.burlington.nj.us

Burlington County Juvenile Detention Center [BCJDC]
620 Pemberton-Browns Mills Rd., Mount Holly, NJ 08060
Fax: (609) 726-7213

△ Director **Mildred Scholtz** .... (609) 726-7150
E-mail: mscholtz@co.burlington.nj.us

Burlington County Library
5 Pioneer Blvd., Westampton, NJ 08060
Fax: (609) 267-4091 Internet: http://www.burlco.lib.nj.us/

Library Director **Ranjna Das** .... (609) 267-9660
E-mail: rdas@bcls.lib.nj.us

Office of the County Clerk
Courts Facility, 49 Rancocas Road, Room 104, Mount Holly, NJ 08060
Fax: (609) 265-0696

★ County Clerk **Timothy Tyler** (D) .... (609) 265-5122
Term Expires: December 31, 2016
E-mail: ttyler@co.burlington.nj.us
Deputy County Clerk **Wade Hale** .... (609) 265-5122
E-mail: whale@co.burlington.nj.us

Office of the Executive Superintendent of Schools
Two Academy Drive, Westampton, NJ 08060
Fax: (609) 265-5922

Superintendent **(Vacant)** .... (609) 265-5060

Office of the Prosecutor
Courts Facility, 49 Rancocas Road, 2nd Floor, Mount Holly, NJ 08060
Fax: (609) 265-5586 E-mail: prosecutor@co.burlington.nj.us

▼ Prosecutor **Robert D. Bernardi** .... (609) 265-5035
E-mail: prosecutor@co.burlington.nj.us

Office of the Sheriff
49 Rancocas Road, Room 202, Mount Holly, NJ 08060
Fax: (609) 265-5767

★ Sheriff **Jean Stanfield** (R) .... (609) 265-5046
Term Expires: December 31, 2016
E-mail: jstanfield@co.burlington.nj.us

Office of the Surrogate
Courts Facility, Mount Holly, NJ 08060
Fax: (609) 261-4511

★ Surrogate **George Kotch** .... (609) 265-5005
Term Expires: December 31, 2016
E-mail: gkotch@co.burlington.nj.us
Deputy Surrogate **Bonnie Nutt Madara** .... (609) 265-5581

Board of Elections
Tel: (609) 265-5062 Tel: (609) 265-5161 Fax: (609) 265-3131
E-mail: electionboard@co.burlington.nj.us

▼ Chairperson **Joseph P. Dugan**
▼ Secretary **Christopher Baxter**
Note: Reappointed on March 8, 2016 by Governor Christie, pending New Jersey Senate Approval
▼ Member **Alice Furia**
Note: Reappointed on March 8, 2016 by Governor Christie, pending New Jersey Senate Approval
▼ Member **Michael A. Eaton**

County of Camden, New Jersey
Courthouse, 520 Market Street, Camden, NJ 08102-1375
Internet: www.camdencounty.com

County Seat: Camden **Election Type:** Partisan **Population:** 510,923 (2015)

Office of the Board of Freeholders
Courthouse, 520 Market Street, Camden, NJ 08102-1375
Tel: (856) 225-5451 E-mail: freeholders@camdencounty.com

★ Director **Louis Cappelli, Jr.** (D) .... (856) 225-5454
Term Expires: December 31, 2017 Fax: (856) 968-2348
E-mail: louc@camdencounty.com
Education: Albright BS; Rutgers (Camden) 1987 JD
Confidential Assistant **Anthony Bianco** .... (856) 216-2133
E-mail: abianco@camdencounty.com
★ Deputy Director **Edward T. McDonnell** (D) .... (856) 225-5458
Term Expires: December 31, 2016 Fax: (856) 225-5555
E-mail: mcdonnel@camdencounty.com
Education: Glassboro State BA, MA, MA; Nova Southeastern EdD
★ Freeholder **William "Bill" Moen** (D) .... (856) 225-5563
Term Expires: December 31, 2018
E-mail: william.moen@camdencounty.com
★ Freeholder **Jeffrey Nash** (D) .... (856) 225-5468
Term Expires: December 31, 2018 Fax: (856) 968-2348
E-mail: jnash@camdencounty.com
Education: George Washington 1981 BA; Hofstra 1983 JD
★ Freeholder **Carmen Rodriguez** (D) .... (856) 225-5575
Term Expires: December 31, 2016 Fax: (856) 225-5336
E-mail: carmenr@camdencounty.com
★ Freeholder **Susan Shin Angulo** (D) .... (856) 225-5305
Term Expires: December 31, 2018
E-mail: susan.shinangulo@camdencounty.com
★ Freeholder **Jonathan L. Young, Sr.** (D) .... (856) 225-5562
Term Expires: December 31, 2017
E-mail: jonathan.young@camdencounty.com

★ Elected Official ▲ Appointed by Legislature ▼ Appointed by Governor ▶ Appointed by Board or Commission ● Appointed by Judge
■ Appointed by Mayor △ Appointed by Freeholders ▽ Appointed by Supervisor ▷ Appointed by County Executive ○ Appointed by Council

COUNTIES

Office of the Clerk of the Board
Courthouse, 520 Market St., 8th Floor, Camden, NJ 08102-1375
Fax: (856) 968-2348

△Clerk of the Board **Marianne DiPiero** . . . . (856) 225-5586
E-mail: mdipiero@camdencounty.com
Secretary **Anna Wawrzyniak** . . . . (856) 225-5468
E-mail: annaw@camdencounty.com

Administration Department
Courthouse, 520 Market St., 16th Floor, Camden, NJ 08102-1375
Tel: (856) 225-5354 Fax: (856) 225-5319
E-mail: admin@camdencounty.com

△County Administrator **Ross G. Angilella** . . . . (856) 225-5354
E-mail: admin@camdencounty.com
Executive Assistant **Mary Dorazo** . . . . (856) 225-5354
Deputy County Administrator **Holly Cass** . . . . (856) 225-5358
E-mail: hcass@camdencounty.com
Deputy County Administrator (Communications and Health and Human Services) **James H. Rhodes** . . . . . . (856) 225-2130
E-mail: jrhodes@camdencounty.com
Deputy County Administrator (Public Services)
Dominic J. Vesper, Jr. . . . . (856) 225-2130
Custodian of Records **Maria Efstratiades** . . . . (856) 225-2131
Courthouse, 520 Market Street, 11th Floor, Camden, NJ 08102-1375 Fax: (856) 580-5702
E-mail: mariae@camdencounty.com

Office of Archives and Records Management
Courthouse, 520 Market Street, 11th Floor, Camden, NJ 08102-1375
Fax: (856) 580-5702

Director **Maria Efstratiades** . . . . (856) 225-2131
E-mail: mariae@camdencounty.com Fax: (856) 580-5702

Office of the County Counsel
Courthouse, 520 Market Street, 14th Floor, Camden, NJ 08102
Fax: (856) 756-2244 E-mail: counsel@camdencounty.com

△County Counsel **Christopher A. "Chris" Orlando** . . . . (856) 225-5543

Office of the Executive Superintendent of Schools
PO Box 200, College Drive, Blackwood, NJ 08012
Tel: (856) 401-2400 Fax: (856) 401-2410
E-mail: camden@doe.state.nj.us

Executive County Superintendent (Interim)
Dr. Lovell Pugh-Bassett . . . . (856) 401-2400

Office of the Medical Examiner
254 County House Road, Clarksboro, NJ 08020
Fax: (856) 384-6915

Medical Examiner **Dr. Gerald Feigin** . . . . (856) 384-6910

Office of Hispanic Affairs
Courthouse, 520 Market Street, Suite 306, Camden, NJ 08102-1375
Fax: (856) 225-5591 E-mail: hispanic@camdencounty.com

△Director **Nilsa J. Cruz-Perez (D)** . . . . (856) 225-5312
Date of Birth: January 21, 1961
Education: Puerto Rico BA

Office of Public Affairs
Courthouse, 520 Market Street, 15th Floor, Camden, NJ 08102-1375
Fax: (856) 225-5430

△Director **Dan Keashen** . . . . (856) 225-5431
Public Information Officer **Ron Tomasello** . . . . (856) 225-5431

Office of Veterans' Affairs
315 S. White Horse Pike, Magnolia, NJ 08049
Fax: (856) 374-5402

Director **Floyd White** . . . . (856) 374-5801

Human Resources Division
Courthouse, 520 Market St., 11th Floor, Camden, NJ 08102

△Director **Frank Cirii** . . . . (856) 225-5373
E-mail: fcirii@camdencounty.com

Camden County College [CCC]
Main Campus, Little Gloucester Road, Blackwood, NJ 08012
Tel: (856) 227-7200 Internet: www.camdencc.edu

President **Dr. Raymond Yannuzzi** . . . . (856) 374-4937
Fax: (856) 374-4894

Camden County Police Department
6 Collier Drive, Blackwood, NJ 08012
Tel: (856) 757-7474

Police Director **Edward J. Fanelle** . . . . (856) 401-2484

Metro Division
Chief **John Scott Thomson** . . . . (856) 757-7474

Community Development Office
512 Lakeland Road, Suite 211, Blackwood, NJ 08012-0088
Tel: (856) 374-2580 Fax: (856) 374-2585

△Director **Gino A. Lewis** . . . . (856) 374-2580
E-mail: glewis@camdencounty.com

Cultural and Heritage Commission
P.O. Box 200, Blackwood, NJ 08012
Fax: (856) 374-4913

Executive Director **Sandra Turner-Barnes** . . . . . (856) 227-7200 ext. 4063

Finance Department
Courthouse, 520 Market Street, 9th Floor, Camden, NJ 08102-1375
Fax: (856) 225-5298

△Chief Financial Officer **David McPeak** . . . . (856) 225-5383
E-mail: davem@camdencounty.com Fax: (856) 225-5298
Accounting Manager **Michael Kwasizur** . . . . (856) 225-5397
E-mail: michaelk@camdencounty.com Fax: (856) 225-5519
Accounts Payable **Sandy Hall** . . . . (856) 225-5391
Fax: (856) 225-5519
△Budget Director **David McPeak** . . . . (856) 225-5386
E-mail: davem@camdencounty.com Fax: (856) 225-5298
△Comptroller **Steven M. "Steve" Williams** . . . . (856) 225-5396
E-mail: stevew@camdencounty.com Fax: (856) 225-5519

Division of Purchasing
520 Market Street, 17th Floor, Camden, NJ 08102
Fax: (856) 225-5444

△Purchasing Agent **Anna Marie Wright** . . . . (856) 225-5447
E-mail: annamarie@camdencounty.com

Department of Health and Human Services
Di Piero Center, 512 Lakeland Road, Suite 637, Blackwood, NJ 08012-0088
Tel: (856) 374-6000 Fax: (856) 374-6324
Internet: www.camdencounty.com/health

△Director **Ann Biondi** . . . . (856) 374-6319
E-mail: abiondi@camdencounty.com
Deputy Director **Robert Jakubewski** . . . . (856) 401-6443
Medical Director **Michael DeShields** . . . . (856) 374-6162
Public Health Officer **Paschal Nwakl** . . . . (856) 374-6032
Fax: (856) 374-6034

Alcohol and Substance Abuse Unit
512 Lakeland Road, Suite 501, Blackwood, NJ 08012-0088

△Director **John Pellicane** . . . . (856) 374-6320
E-mail: jpellicane@camdencounty.com
County Municipal Alliance Coordinator
Betty Ann Cowling-Carson . . . . (856) 374-6315

★Elected Official ▲Appointed by Legislature ▼Appointed by Governor ▶Appointed by Board or Commission ●Appointed by Judge
■Appointed by Mayor △Appointed by Freeholders ▽Appointed by Supervisor ▷Appointed by County Executive ○Appointed by Council

Administrative Support and Finance Division
512 Lakeland Road, Suite 601, Blackwood, NJ 08012
Tel: (856) 374-6300 Fax: (856) 374-6374

Director **(Vacant)** .... (856) 374-6310
Grants **Diana Comisky** .... (856) 374-6325
E-mail: dianac@camdencounty.com
Personnel **(Vacant)** .... (856) 374-6304

Division of Community Health Services
Di Piero Center, 512 Lakeland Road, Suite 501, Blackwood, NJ 08012
Tel: (856) 374-6300 Fax: (856) 374-6354

Director **Paschal Nwakl** .... (856) 374-6318

Division of Environmental Health
Di Piero Center, 512 Lakeland Road, Suite 301, Blackwood, NJ 08012
Tel: (856) 374-6000 Tel: (800) 999-9045 (Toll Free) Fax: (856) 374-6211

Director **Paschal Nwakl** .... (856) 374-6022
Administrative Assistant **Deborah Hall** .... (856) 374-6037
E-mail: dhall@camdencounty.com

Division of Senior and Disabled Citizen Services
Parkview Terrace, 700 Browning Rd., Suite 11,
West Collingswood, NJ 08107
Tel: (877) 222-3737 E-mail: seniors@camdencounty.com

Director **Maureen Bergeron** .... (856) 858-3312
Administrative Assistant **(Vacant)** .... (856) 858-3312

Department of Children Services
Di Piero Center, 512 Lakeland Road, Suite 200, Blackwood, NJ 08012
(P.O. Box 88)
Tel: (856) 374-6376 Fax: (856) 374-6394

△ Director **Sister Donna Minster** .... (856) 374-6378
E-mail: children@camdencounty.com
Administrative Assistant **Ester Falcone** .... (856) 374-6317

Senior Citizens Day Care Center
Di Piero Center, 512 Lakeland Road, Suite 144, Blackwood, NJ 08012
Fax: (856) 374-5197

Program Director **Joan Connell** .... (856) 374-6005

Parks Department

1301 Park Blvd., Cherry Hill, NJ 08002
Fax: (856) 216-2146

△ Director **Francisco "Frank" Moran** (D) .... (856) 216-2117
E-mail: fmoran@camdencounty.com

Camden County Boathouse
7050 North Park Drive, Pennsauken, NJ 08109
Tel: (856) 661-3188 Fax: (856) 661-3187
E-mail: boathouse@comcast.net

Director **Jamie Stack** .... (856) 661-3188

Rutgers Cooperative Extension
152 Ohio Avenue, Clementon, NJ 08021
Fax: (856) 225-6493

Director **Robin Waddell** .... (856) 225-6169

Division of Environmental Affairs
520 North Newton Lake Drive, Collingswood, NJ 08107
Fax: (856) 858-3470

Director **Jack Sworaski** .... (856) 858-5211

Division of Open Space and Farmland Preservation
520 North Newton Lake Drive, Collingswood, NJ 08107
Fax: (856) 858-3470

Director **Jack Sworaski** .... (856) 858-5211

Camden County Golf Academy
8001 South Route 130, Pennsauken, NJ 08109
Tel: (856) 661-3636 Fax: (856) 661-3635

Manager **Bob Cardea** .... (856) 661-3636

Department of Public Safety

Charles J. DePalma Complex, Building 18, 2311 Egg Harbor Road,
Lindenwold, NJ 08021
Fax: (856) 435-2760 Internet: www.camdencounty.com/public-safety

△ Director **Robin J. Blaker** .... (856) 783-4808 ext. 5400
E-mail: robin.blaker@publicsafetycc.com

Office of Emergency Management
Charles J. DePalma Complex Buildiong 18, 2311 Egg Harbor Road,
Lindenwold, NJ 08021

Coordinator **Samuel M. "Sam" Spino** .... (856) 783-4808 ext. 5202
E-mail: samuel.spino@publicsafetycc.com

Office of the Fire Marshal
420 Woodbury-Turnersville Rd., Blackwood, NJ 08012

Chief Fire Marshal **Paul Sandrock** .... (856) 374-6191
E-mail: paul.sandrock@publicsafetycc.com

Communications Division
Charles J. DePalma Complex Building 18, 2311 Egg Harbor Road,
Lindenwold, NJ 08021

Chief **James Jankowski** .... (856) 783-4808 ext. 5052
E-mail: james.jankowski@publicsafetycc.com

911 Telecommunications Division
Charles DePalma Building 18, 2311 Egg Harbor Road,
Lindenwold, NJ 08021

911 Coordinator **Anthony Sirolli** .... (856) 783-4808
E-mail: anthony.sirolli@publicsafetycc.com

Camden County Youth Center
Eight South Woodbury-Turnersville Road, Blackwood, NJ 08012
Internet: www.camdencounty.com/public-safety/youth-center

Administrator **Edward J. Fanelle** .... (856) 401-2484

Department of Public Works

Charles J. DePalma Complex, 2311 Egg Harbor Road,
Lindenwold, NJ 08021
Fax: (856) 566-2929 E-mail: ccdpw@camdencounty.com

△ Director **Simeon Martello** .... (856) 566-2980
△ Roads Supervisor **Joe Esposrto** .... (856) 566-2980
△ Assistant Supervisor **(Vacant)** .... (856) 566-2980

Division of Engineering
△ County Engineer **Kevin Becica** .... (856) 566-2980

Division of Planning
△ Director **Andrew Levecchia** .... (856) 566-2980

Camden County Board of Social Services

600 Market Street, Camden, NJ 08102-1255
Tel: (856) 225-8800 Fax: (856) 225-7797
E-mail: ccbss-info@camdenbss.org

Director **Shawn B. Sheekey** .... (856) 225-8800

Workforce Investment Board [WIB]

1111 Marlkress Road, Suite 101, Cherry Hill, NJ 08003
Tel: (856) 751-1500 Fax: (856) 751-4495 E-mail: ccwib@ccwib.com
Internet: www.ccwib.com

Director **Jeffrey S. Swartz** .... (856) 751-1500
E-mail: jeff@ccwib.com

★ Elected Official ▲ Appointed by Legislature ▼ Appointed by Governor ▶ Appointed by Board or Commission ● Appointed by Judge
■ Appointed by Mayor △ Appointed by Freeholders ▽ Appointed by Supervisor ▷ Appointed by County Executive ○ Appointed by Council

COUNTIES

Camden County Improvement Authority [CCIA]

1909 Rt. 70 East, Suite 300, Cherry Hill, NJ 08003-4501
Fax: (856) 751-2242 Fax: (856) 566-3105
E-mail: justask@camdencounty.com
Internet: http://ccia.camdencounty.com/

Executive Director **James P. Blanda** . . . . (856) 751-2242
E-mail: jblanda@camdencounty.com

Camden County Library System

203 Laurel Road, Voorhees, NJ 08043
Fax: (856) 772-6105 Internet: www.camdencountylibrary.org

△ Director **Linda Devlin** . . . . (856) 772-1636 ext. 7344
E-mail: ldevlin@camdencountylibrary.org
President, Library Commission **Nancy D. Costantino** . . . . (856) 772-1636

Camden County Municipal Utilities Authority

1645 Ferry Avenue, Camden, NJ 08104
Tel: (856) 541-3700 Fax: (856) 964-1829 E-mail: mail@ccmua.org
Internet: www.ccmua.org

Executive Director/Chief Engineer
Andrew H. "Andy" Kricun . . . . (856) 583-1223
E-mail: andy@ccmua.org

Office of the County Clerk

Courthouse, 520 Market Street, Room 102, Camden, NJ 08102-1375
Tel: (856) 225-5300 Fax: (856) 225-7100

★ County Clerk **Joseph Ripa** (D) . . . . (856) 225-7211
Term Expires: December 31, 2017
E-mail: jripa@camdencounty.com
Deputy County Clerk **John Schmidt** . . . . (856) 225-5316
Deputy County Clerk **Christopher T. Morris** . . . . (856) 225-7213

Office of the Prosecutor

25 North Fifth Street, Camden, NJ 08102-1231
Fax: (856) 963-0080

▼ Prosecutor **Mary Eva Colalillo** . . . . (856) 225-8400
E-mail: mcolalillo@ccprosecutor.org
Education: Vermont Law 1976 JD
First Assistant Prosecutor **Mark K. Chase** . . . . (856) 225-8400
Chief of Investigators **Ron Moten** . . . . (856) 225-8400
Public Information Officer **Andy McNeil** . . . . (856) 225-8555
E-mail: amcneil@ccprosecutor.org

Office of the Sheriff

Courthouse, 520 Market St., Camden, NJ 08102
Tel: (856) 225-5470 Fax: (856) 225-5595
Internet: www.camdencounty.com/sheriff

★ Sheriff **Gilbert L. "Whip" Wilson** (D) . . . . (856) 225-5473
Term Expires: December 31, 2018
E-mail: sheriff@camdencounty.com
Undersheriff **Robert Turner** . . . . (856) 225-5540
Chief Sheriff's Officer **Thomas Macauley** . . . . (856) 225-5560
Captain **John Fetzer** . . . . (856) 225-5470

Office of the Superintendent of Elections

7250 Westfield Avenue, Suite C, Pennsauken, NJ 08110
Fax: (856) 661-3556 E-mail: soe@camdencounty.com

▼ Superintendent of Elections **Phyllis Pearl** (D) . . . . (856) 661-3570
E-mail: ppearl@camdencounty.com

Board of Elections

Elections and Archive Center, 100 University Court,
Blackwood, NJ 08012
Tel: (856) 401-8683 Tel: (856) 401-8689
E-mail: boardofelections@camdencounty.com

▼ Chairperson **Robert Venuti**
▼ Secretary **Donna Marie Robinson**
Note: Reappointed on March 8, 2016 by Governor Christie, pending New Jersey Senate Approval
▼ Member **Novella Starks Hinson**
▼ Member **Richard A. Ambrosino, Jr.**
Note: Reappointed on March 8, 2016 by Governor Christie, pending New Jersey Senate Approval

Office of the Surrogate

600 Market Street, Camden, NJ 08102
Fax: (856) 225-7389 Internet: www.camdencounty.com/surrog.htm

★ Surrogate **Michelle Gentek-Mayer** (D) . . . . (856) 225-7282
Term Expires: December 31, 2018
E-mail: mgentek@camdencounty.com

County of Cameron, Texas

964 East Harrison Street, Brownsville, TX 78520
Tel: (956) 544-0815 Internet: www.co.cameron.tx.us

County Seat: Brownsville **Election Type:** Partisan **Population:** 422,156 (2015)

Office of the County Judge

1100 East Monroe Street, Brownsville, TX 78520
Tel: (956) 544-0830 Fax: (956) 544-0801

★ County Judge **Pedro "Pete" Sepulveda, Jr.** . . . . (956) 544-0830
Term Expires: December 31, 2018
E-mail: psepulveda@co.cameron.tx.us

Office of the County Administrator

1100 East Monroe Street, Brownsville, TX 78520
Tel: (956) 982-5414 Fax: (956) 983-5099
Internet: www.co.cameron.tx.us/administrator.htm

County Administrator **David Garcia** . . . . (956) 982-5414
E-mail: dagarcia@co.cameron.tx.us
Deputy County Administrator **(Vacant)** . . . . (956) 982-5414
Treasurer **David A. Betancourt** . . . . (956) 544-0819

Department of Elections and Voter Registration

964 East Harrison Street, Brownsville, TX 78520
Tel: (956) 544-0809 Fax: (956) 550-7298
Internet: www.co.cameron.tx.us/election

Elections Administrator (Interim) **Remi Garza** . . . . (956) 544-0809

Emergency Management Department

1100 East Monroe Street, Suite B45, Brownsville, TX 78520
Tel: (956) 547-7000 Fax: (956) 547-7006
Internet: www.co.cameron.tx.us/emergency

Chief Emergency Officer and Homeland Security
Director **Tom Husen** . . . . (956) 547-7000
Deputy Emergency Management Coordinator
Charles D. "Chuck" Hoskins . . . . (956) 547-7000
E-mail: charles.hoskins@co.cameron.tx.us
Fire Marshal **Armando Lucio** . . . . (956) 547-7000
E-mail: armando.lucio@co.cameron.tx.us

★ Elected Official ▲ Appointed by Legislature ▼ Appointed by Governor ► Appointed by Board or Commission ● Appointed by Judge
■ Appointed by Mayor △ Appointed by Freeholders ▽ Appointed by Supervisor ▷ Appointed by County Executive ○ Appointed by Council

Health and Human Services Department
1390 West Expressway 83, San Benito, TX 78586
Tel: (956) 247-3685 Fax: (956) 361-8230
E-mail: health@co.cameron.tx.us Internet: www.co.cameron.tx.us/health

Health Administrator **Esmeralda Guajardo** . . . . (956) 247-3685
Assistant Health Administrator (Acting)
Veronica Ramirez . . . . (956) 247-3685

Human Resources Department
1100 East Monroe Street, Brownsville, TX 78520
Tel: (956) 544-0827 Fax: (956) 550-1373
Internet: www.co.cameron.tx.us/hr

Director **Arnold Flores** . . . . (956) 544-0827
Assistant Director **Susana "Susie" Marfileno** . . . . (956) 544-0827
E-mail: smarfileno@co.cameron.tx.us

Parks and Recreation Department
1100 East Monroe Street, Brownsville, TX 78520
Tel: (956) 761-3700 Fax: (956) 761-5317
Internet: www.co.cameron.tx.us/parks

Director **Joe E. Vega** . . . . (956) 761-3700
Deputy Director **(Vacant)** . . . . (956) 761-3700
Administrative Aid **Cynthia A. Escobedo** . . . . (956) 761-3701
E-mail: caescobedo@co.cameron.tx.us

Computer Information Services
964 East Harrison Street, Suite 320, Brownsville, TX 78520
Tel: (956) 544-0818 Tel: (956) 550-1326

Chief Technology Officer **Joe Reyes** . . . . (956) 550-1332
E-mail: ccsup@co.cameron.tx.us

Office of the Commissioner's Court
1100 East Monroe Street, Brownsville, TX 78520
Tel: (956) 982-5414 Fax: (956) 983-5099

★Commissioner **Sofia C. Benavides** (Precinct 1) . . . . (956) 574-8167
Term Expires: December 31, 2016 Fax: (956) 544-0820
E-mail: sofia.benavides@co.cameron.tx.us
★Commissioner **Alex Dominguez** (Precinct 2) . . . . (956) 983-5091
Term Expires: December 31, 2018 Fax: (956) 983-5090
E-mail: alex.dominguez@co.cameron.tx.us
★Commissioner **David A. Garza** (Precinct 3) . . . . (956) 361-8209
Term Expires: December 31, 2016 Fax: (956) 361-8211
1390 West Expressway 83, San Benito, TX 78586
E-mail: dgarza@co.cameron.tx.us
★Commissioner **Dan Sanchez** (Precinct 4) . . . . (956) 427-8069
Term Expires: December 31, 2018 Fax: (956) 427-8071
201 North T Street, Harlingen, TX 78550
E-mail: dan.sanchez@co.cameron.tx.us

Office of the County Auditor
1100 East Monroe Street, Brownsville, TX 78520
Tel: (956) 544-0822 Fax: (956) 548-9527
Internet: www.co.cameron.tx.us/auditor

County Auditor **Martha Galarza** . . . . (956) 544-0822

Office of the County Clerk
964 East Harrison Street, Brownsville, TX 78520
Tel: (956) 544-0815 Internet: www.co.cameron.tx.us/countyclerk

★County Clerk **Sylvia Garza Perez** (D) . . . . (956) 544-0815
Term Expires: December 31, 2018

Office of the District Attorney
964 East Harrison Street, Brownsville, TX 78520
Tel: (956) 544-0849 Fax: (956) 544-0869
E-mail: district.attorney@co.cameron.tx.us
Internet: www.co.cameron.tx.us/district_attorney

★District Attorney **Luis V. Saenz** . . . . (956) 544-0849
Term Expires: December 31, 2016

Office of the County Sheriff
7300 Old Alice Road, Olmito, TX 78575
Tel: (956) 554-6700 Fax: (956) 554-6780
Internet: www.co.cameron.tx.us/sheriffs/sheriffsoffice.html

★County Sheriff **Omar Lucio** . . . . (956) 554-6700
Term Expires: December 31, 2016
Chief Deputy **Gus Reyna, Jr.** . . . . (956) 554-6700
E-mail: greyna1@co.cameron.tx.us

Office of the Tax Assessor-Collector
964 East Harrison Street, Brownsville, TX 78520
Tel: (956) 544-0800 Fax: (956) 544-0808
E-mail: assessorcollector@co.cameron.tx.us
Internet: www.co.cameron.tx.us/tax

★Tax Assessor-Collector **Tony Yzaguirre, Jr.** . . . . (956) 544-0800
Term Expires: December 31, 2016
E-mail: tyzaguirre@co.cameron.tx.us

County of Cass, North Dakota
P.O. Box 2806, Fargo, ND 58108
Tel: (701) 241-5601 (Information) TTY: (701) 239-6784
Fax: (701) 241-5728 Internet: www.casscountynd.gov

County Seat: Fargo **Election Type:** Nonpartisan **Population:** 171,512 (2015)

Office of the Board of Commissioners
211 9th Street South, Fargo, ND 58103
P.O. Box 2806, Fargo, ND 58108
Tel: (701) 241-5609 TTY: (701) 239-6784 Fax: (701) 241-5728

★Chairwoman **Mary Scherling** (District 5) . . . . (701) 241-5609
Term Expires: December 5, 2016
E-mail: scherlingm@casscountynd.gov
★Vice Chairman **Chad Peterson** (District 1) . . . . (701) 241-5609
Term Expires: December 5, 2016
E-mail: petersonc@casscountynd.gov
★Commissioner **Rick Steen** (District 2) . . . . (701) 241-5609
Term Expires: December 3, 2018
E-mail: steenr@casscountynd.gov
★Commissioner **Ken Pawluk** (District 3) . . . . (701) 241-5609
Term Expires: December 5, 2016
E-mail: pawlukk@casscountynd.gov
★Commissioner **Arland Rasmussen** (District 4) . . . . (701) 241-5609
Term Expires: December 1, 2018
E-mail: rasmussena@casscountynd.gov

Office of the County Administrator
211 9th Street South, Fargo, ND 58103
Fax: (701) 297-6020

▶County Administrator **Keith Berndt** . . . . (701) 241-5770
E-mail: berndtk@casscountynd.gov

COUNTIES

★Elected Official ▲Appointed by Legislature ▼Appointed by Governor ▶Appointed by Board or Commission ●Appointed by Judge
■Appointed by Mayor △Appointed by Freeholders ▽Appointed by Supervisor ▷Appointed by County Executive ○Appointed by Council

Personnel Office
P.O. Box 2806, Fargo, ND 58108
Fax: (701) 297-6020

Director **Keith Berndt** .... (701) 241-5725
E-mail: berndtk@casscountynd.gov

Extension Office (North Dakota State University)
1010 2nd Avenue South, Fargo, ND 58108
P.O. Box 2806, Fargo, ND 58108-2806
Fax: (701) 241-5935 E-mail: ndsu.cass.extension@ndsu.edu
Internet: www.ag.ndsu.edu/casscountyextension

► County Extension Agent **John Kringler** .... (701) 241-5700
E-mail: kringler@casscountynd.gov

Planning Office
1201 West Main Avenue, West Fargo, ND 58078
Fax: (701) 298-2395

County Planner **Hali Durand** .... (701) 298-2375

Tax Equalization Office
P.O. Box 2806, Fargo, ND 58108
Fax: (701) 241-5728

► Director **Frank Klein** .... (701) 241-5616
E-mail: kleinf@casscountynd.gov

Veterans Service Office
P.O. Box 2806, Fargo, ND 58108
Fax: (701) 239-6821

► Service Officer **Dan Thorstad** .... (701) 241-5756
E-mail: thorstadd@casscountynd.gov

Highway Department
1201 West Main Avenue, West Fargo, ND 58078
Fax: (701) 298-2395

► County Engineer **Jason Benson** .... (701) 298-2370
E-mail: bensonj@casscountynd.gov
Education: North Dakota State 1996 BS; U Mary 2005 MM

Information Technology Department [ITD]
P.O. Box 2806, Fargo, ND 58108
Fax: (701) 241-5728

► Director **Terry Schmaltz** .... (701) 241-5723
E-mail: schmaltzt@casscountynd.gov

Social Services Department
P.O. Box 3106, Fargo, ND 58108
Fax: (701) 241-5775

► Director **Chip Ammerman** .... (701) 239-6700
E-mail: ammermanc@casscountynd.gov

Office of the Auditor
P.O. Box 2806, Fargo, ND 58108
Fax: (701) 241-5728

★ Auditor **Michael Montplaisir** .... (701) 241-5601
Term Expires: April 1, 2019
E-mail: montplaisirm@casscountynd.gov

Office of the Recorder
P.O. Box 2806, Fargo, ND 58108
Fax: (701) 241-5621

★ Recorder **Jewel Spies** .... (701) 241-5620
Term Expires: December 31, 2018
E-mail: spiesj@casscountynd.gov

Office of the Sheriff
P.O. Box 488, Fargo, ND 58107
Fax: (701) 241-5805 E-mail: sheriff@casscountynd.gov

★ Sheriff **Paul Laney** .... (701) 241-5800
Term Expires: December 31, 2018

Office of the State's Attorney
P.O. Box 2806, Fargo, ND 58108
Fax: (701) 241-5838

★ State's Attorney **Birch Burdick** .... (701) 241-5850
Term Expires: December 31, 2018
E-mail: burdickb@casscountynd.gov

Office of the Treasurer
P.O. Box 2806, Fargo, ND 58108
Fax: (701) 241-5728

★ Treasurer **Charlotte Sandvik** .... (701) 241-5611
Term Expires: May 1, 2019
E-mail: sandvikc@casscountynd.gov

County of Chester, Pennsylvania

313 West Market Street, Suite 6202, West Chester, PA 19380-0991
Tel: (610) 344-6000 (Information) Internet: www.chesco.org

County Seat: West Chester **Election Type:** Partisan
Population: 515,939 (2015)

Office of the Board of Commissioners
313 West Market Street, Suite 6202, West Chester, PA 19380-0991
Fax: (610) 344-5995

★ Chairman **Terence Farrell** (R) .... (610) 344-6100
Term Expires: December 31, 2019
E-mail: tfarrell@chesco.org
Education: Carleton 1969 BA; Indiana State 2006

★ Vice-Chair **Kathi Cozzone** (D) .... (610) 344-6100
Term Expires: December 31, 2019
E-mail: kcozzone@chesco.org
Education: Col New Jersey 1984 BS

★ Commissioner **Michelle Kichline** .... (610) 344-6100
Term Expires: December 31, 2019

Chief Operating Officer **Mark J. Rupsis** .... (610) 344-6025
E-mail: mrupsis@chesco.org

Domestic Relations Office
201 West Market Street, Suite 3400, West Chester, PA 19380
P.O. Box 2748, West Chester, PA 19380-0991
Fax: (610) 344-6977

Director **Joseph M. Waters** .... (610) 344-6215
Deputy Director **Robin Kelly** .... (610) 344-6215
Deputy Director **William R. Whitehead** .... (610) 344-6215

Office of the Public Defender
201 West Market Street, Suite 2325, West Chester, PA 19380
P.O. Box 2748, West Chester, PA 19380-0991
Fax: (610) 344-6120

Public Defender **John R. Merrick** .... (610) 344-6940

★ Elected Official ▲ Appointed by Legislature ▼ Appointed by Governor ► Appointed by Board or Commission ● Appointed by Judge
■ Appointed by Mayor △ Appointed by Freeholders ▽ Appointed by Supervisor ▷ Appointed by County Executive ○ Appointed by Council

Office of Public Information
313 West Market Street, Suite 6202, West Chester, PA 19380-0991
P.O. Box 2748, West Chester, PA 19380-0991
Fax: (610) 344-5995

Communications Coordinator **Rebecca Brain** . . . . (610) 344-6100
E-mail: rbrain@chesco.org

Office of the Solicitor
313 West Market Street, Suite 6702, West Chester, PA 19380-0991
P.O. Box 2748, West Chester, PA 19380-0991
Fax: (610) 344-5471

Solicitor **Thomas J. Whiteman** . . . . (610) 344-6195

Office of Veterans' Affairs
Government Services Center, 601 Westtown Road, Suite 385,
West Chester, PA 19380-0990
P.O. Box 2747, West Chester, PA 19380-0990
Fax: (610) 344-4552

Director **Lawrence Davidson** . . . . (610) 344-6375

Voter Services Office
Government Services Center, 601 Westtown Road, Suite 150,
West Chester, PA 19380-0990
P.O. Box 2747, West Chester, PA 19380-0990
Fax: (610) 344-5682

Director **Kara Rahn** . . . . (610) 344-6410

Adult Probation Department
201 West Market Street, Suite 2100, West Chester, PA 19380
P.O. Box 2746, West Chester, PA 19380-0989
Fax: (610) 344-6321

Director **Christopher J. Murphy** . . . . (610) 344-6290

Department of Assessment
313 West Market Street, Suite 4202, West Chester, PA 19380-0991
Fax: (610) 344-5902

Director **Jonathan Schuck** . . . . (610) 344-6105
E-mail: jschuck@chesco.org

Department of Children, Youth and Family Services
Government Services Center, 601 Westtown Road, Suite 310,
West Chester, PA 19380-0990
P.O. Box 2747, West Chester, PA 19380-0990
Fax: (610) 344-5858

Director **Keith Hayes** . . . . (610) 344-5800

Department of Community Development [DCD]
601 Westtown Road, Suite 365, West Chester, PA 19380
P.O. Box 2747, West Chester, PA 19380-0990
Fax: (610) 344-6925

Director **Patrick Bokovitz** . . . . (610) 344-6900
E-mail: pbokovitz@chesco.org

Department of Computing and Information Services [DCIS]
313 West Market Street, Suite 5302, West Chester, PA 19380-0991
Fax: (610) 344-6794

Chief Information Officer/Director **Glenn E. Angstadt** . . . (610) 344-6475
E-mail: gangstadt@chesco.org

Department of Drug and Alcohol Services
Government Services Center, 601 Westtown Road, Suite 325,
West Chester, PA 19380-0990
P.O. Box 2747, West Chester, PA 19380-0990
Fax: (610) 344-5743 Internet: www.chesco.org/drugandalcohol

Executive Director **Vincent H. Brown** . . . . (610) 344-6620

Department of Emergency Services
Government Services Center, 601 Westtown Road, Suite 12,
West Chester, PA 19380-0990
P.O. Box 2747, West Chester, PA 19380-0990
TTY: (610) 344-6440 Fax: (610) 344-5050 Internet: www.chesco.org/des

Director **Robert Kagel** . . . . (610) 344-5000
E-mail: rkagel@chesco.org

Facilities and Parks and Recreation Department
313 West Market Street, Suite 5402, West Chester, PA 19380-0991
P.O. Box 2748, West Chester, PA 19380-0991
Fax: (610) 344-5984

Director **Steve Fromnick** . . . . (610) 344-6220
E-mail: sfromnick@chesco.org

Finance Department
P.O. Box 2748, West Chester, PA 19380-0991
313 West Market Street, Suite 6902, West Chester, PA 19380-0991
Fax: (610) 344-5998

Financial Services Director **Julie Bookheimer** . . . . (610) 344-6190

General Services Department
601 Westtown Road, Suite 030, West Chester, PA 19380
P.O. Box 2747, West Chester, PA 19380-0990
Fax: (610) 344-5599

Manager **Shane Colburn** . . . . (610) 344-5700
E-mail: scolburn@chesco.org

Human Resources Department
313 West Market Street, Suite 4302, West Chester, PA 19380-0991
P.O. Box 2748, West Chester, PA 19380-0991
Fax: (610) 344-5489

Director **Michelle Achenbach** . . . . (610) 344-6280
E-mail: machenbach@chesco.org

Human Services Department
Government Services Center, 601 Westtown Road, Suite 330,
West Chester, PA 19380-0990
P.O. Box 2747, West Chester, PA 19380-0990
Fax: (610) 344-5736

Director **Kim Bowman** . . . . (610) 344-6640

Juvenile Probation Department
201 West Market Street, Suite 3100, West Chester, PA 19380
P.O. Box 2746, West Chester, PA 19380-0989
Fax: (610) 344-5443

Director **Don Corry** . . . . (610) 344-6295

Law Library
201 West Market Street, Suite 2400, West Chester, PA 19380
P.O. Box 2746, West Chester, PA 19380-0989
Fax: (610) 344-6994 E-mail: lawlibrary@chesco.org

Library Assistant **Ritza Hazen** . . . . (610) 344-6166
Library Assistant **Judith Roccaro** . . . . (610) 344-6167

Department of Mental Health/Intellectual and Developmental Disabilities [MH/IDD]

Government Services Center, 601 Westtown Road, Suite 340, West Chester, PA 19380-0990
P.O. Box 2747, West Chester, PA 19380-0990
Fax: (610) 344-5997 Internet: www.chesco.org/mhidd

Administrator **Gary Entrekin** . . . . (610) 344-6265

Penn State Cooperative Extension of Chester County

Government Services Center, 601 Westtown Road, Suite 370, West Chester, PA 19380-0990
P.O. Box 2747, West Chester, PA 19380-0990
Fax: (610) 696-4831

Director **Leon Ressler** . . . . (610) 696-3500

Planning Commission

Government Services Center, 601 Westtown Road, Suite 270, West Chester, PA 19380-0990
P.O. Box 2747, West Chester, PA 19380-0990
Fax: (610) 344-6515

Executive Director **Brian O'Leary** . . . . (610) 344-6285
Assistant Director **David Ward** . . . . (610) 344-6285

Department of Procurement

P.O. Box 2748, West Chester, PA 19380-0991
313 West Market Street, Suite 4402, West Chester, PA 19380-0991
Fax: (610) 344-5503 E-mail: procurement@chesco.org

Director **Peter T. Navarro** . . . . (610) 344-6325
E-mail: pnavarro@chesco.org

Tax Claim Bureau

313 West Market Street, Suite 3602, West Chester, PA 19380-0991
P.O. Box 2748, West Chester, PA 19380-0991
Fax: (610) 344-4722 E-mail: taxclaimdept@chesco.org

Director **Jonathan Schuck** . . . . (610) 344-6360

Chester County Archives and Record Services

601 Westtown Road, Suite 080, West Chester, PA 19380-0990
P.O. Box 2747, West Chester, PA 19380-0990
Fax: (610) 344-5616

Director **Laurie Rofini** . . . . (610) 344-6760

Chester County Board of Health

601 Westtown Road, West Chester, PA 19380-0990
Tel: (610) 344-6233

Chester County Health Department [CCHD]

601 Westtown Road, Suite 290, West Chester, PA 19380-0990
P.O. Box 2747, West Chester, PA 19380-0990
Tel: (610) 344-6225 Fax: (610) 344-6727 E-mail: cchd@chesco.org
Internet: www.chesco.org/health

Director **Jeanne E. Casner** . . . . (610) 344-6233

Bureau of Administrative and Support Services

601 Westtown Road, Suite 290, West Chester, PA 19380-0990
Fax: (610) 344-6727

Deputy Public Health Administrator **Mary R. Johnson** . . . (610) 344-6225
E-mail: mjohnson@chesco.org

Bureau of Environmental Health Protection

601 Westtown Road, Suite 295, West Chester, PA 19380-0990
Fax: (610) 344-4705

Director **Richard M. Johnson** . . . . (610) 344-6238

Bureau of Personal Health Services

601 Westtown Road, Suite 180, West Chester, PA 19380-0990
Fax: (610) 344-5405

Director **(Vacant)** . . . . (610) 344-6252

Chester County Conference and Visitors Bureau

17 Wilmont Mews, Suite 400, West Chester, PA 19382
Tel: (610) 719-1730 Fax: (610) 719-1736

Executive Director **Susan Hamley** . . . . (610) 280-6145

Chester County Library System [CCLS]

450 Exton Square Parkway, Exton, PA 19341-2496
Fax: (610) 280-2688

Director **Joseph L. "Joe" Sherwood** . . . . (610) 280-2600
E-mail: jsherwood@ccls.org
Education: Drexel 1999 MS

Chester County Prison

501 S. Wawaset Rd., West Chester, PA 19382-6776
Fax: (610) 793-3902 Internet: www.chesco.org/prison

Warden **D. Edward McFadden** . . . . (610) 793-1510

Correctional Center

503 S. Wawaset Rd., West Chester, PA 19382-6782
Fax: (610) 793-0223

Manager **George Roberts** . . . . (610) 793-9993

Chester County Youth Center

505 South Wawaset Road, West Chester, PA 19382-6762
Fax: (610) 793-4538

Director **Gary Blair** . . . . (610) 793-5910

Pocopson Home

1695 Lenape Rd., West Chester, PA 19382-6800
Fax: (610) 793-2493 Internet: www.chesco.org/pocopson

Administrator **Jackie McKenna** . . . . (610) 793-1212

Office of the Controller

313 West Market Street, Suite 6302, West Chester, PA 19380-0991
P.O. Box 2748, West Chester, PA 19380

★ Controller **Norman MacQueen** (R) . . . . (610) 344-6155
Term Expires: January 1, 2018
E-mail: nmacqueen@chesco.org

Office of the Coroner

313 West Market Street, Suite 4102, West Chester, PA 19380-0991
P.O. Box 2748, West Chester, PA 19380
Fax: (610) 344-6018 Internet: www.chesco.org/coroner

★ Coroner **Gordon Eck** (R) . . . . (610) 344-6165
Term Expires: January 1, 2018

Office of the District Attorney

201 West Market Street, Suite 4450, West Chester, PA 19380
P.O. Box 2746, West Chester, PA 19380-0989
Fax: (610) 344-5905 Internet: www.chesco.org/da

★ District Attorney **Thomas P. "Tom" Hogan** (R) . . . . (610) 344-6801
Term Expires: December 31, 2019
E-mail: thogan@chesco.org
Education: Dartmouth 1989; Virginia 1992 JD

★ Elected Official ▲ Appointed by Legislature ▼ Appointed by Governor ▶ Appointed by Board or Commission ● Appointed by Judge
■ Appointed by Mayor △ Appointed by Freeholders ▽ Appointed by Supervisor ▷ Appointed by County Executive ○ Appointed by Council

Office of the Prothonotary

201 West Market Street, Suite 1425, West Chester, PA 19380
P.O. Box 2746, West Chester, PA 19380-0989
Fax: (610) 344-5903

★ Prothonotary **Matt Holliday** (R) ....(610) 344-6300
Term Expires: December 31, 2019

Office of the Recorder of Deeds

313 West Market Street, Suite 3302, West Chester, PA 19380-0991
P.O. Box 2748, West Chester, PA 19380-0991
Tel: (610) 344-6330 Fax: (610) 344-6408
Internet: www.chesco.org/recorder

★ Recorder of Deeds **Rick Loughery** ....(610) 344-6330
Term Expires: December 31, 2019
Education: West Chester 2006 BA, 2010 MPA

Office of the Register of Wills

201 West Market Street, Suite 2200, West Chester, PA 19380
P.O. Box 2746, West Chester, PA 19380-0989
Fax: (610) 344-6218 E-mail: rwills@chesco.org

★ Register of Wills **Terri Clark** (R).......................(610) 344-6335
Term Expires: December 31, 2019

Office of the Sheriff

201 West Market Street, Suite 1201, West Chester, PA 19380
P.O. Box 2746, West Chester, PA 19380-0984
Fax: (610) 344-6099

★ Sheriff **The Honorable Carolyn "Bunny" Welsh** (R) ... (610) 344-6850
Term Expires: December 31, 2019
E-mail: cwelsh@chesco.org

Office of the Treasurer

313 West Market Street, Suite 3202, West Chester, PA 19380-0991
P.O. Box 2748, West Chester, PA 19380-0991
Fax: (610) 344-6359

★ Treasurer **Ann Duke** ....(610) 344-6370
Term Expires: January 1, 2018
E-mail: aduke@chesco.org

County of Chittenden, Vermont

175 Main St., Burlington, VT 05402
P.O. Box 187, Burlington, VT 05402
Tel: (802) 863-3467 (Information)

County Seat: Burlington **Election Type:** Nonpartisan
Population: 161,382 (2015)

Office of the County Judges

175 Main St., Burlington, VT 05402

★ Assistant Judge **Charles L. Delaney** ....(802) 951-5121
Term Expires: January 31, 2019
★ Assistant Judge **Constance C. "Connie" Ramsey**.......(802) 651-1720
Term Expires: January 31, 2019
E-mail: conniecainramsey@chittendencountyvt.org

Office of the High Bailiff

P.O. Box 1426, Burlington, VT 05402

★ High Bailiff **Daniel L. Gamelin**......................(802) 863-4341
Term Expires: January 31, 2019

Office of the Sheriff

70 Ethan Allen Dr., South Burlington, VT 05403
P.O. Box 1426, Burlington, VT 05402

★ Sheriff **Kevin M. McLaughlin** ....(802) 863-4341
Term Expires: January 31, 2019

Office of the State's Attorney

32 Cherry St., Suite 305, Burlington, VT 05401

★ State's Attorney **Thomas J. Donovan, Jr.** ....(802) 863-2865
Term Expires: January 31, 2019

Office of the County Clerk

175 Main Street, Burlington, VT 05402

County Clerk **Anne Williams**.........................(802) 951-5106
E-mail: anne.william@state.vt.us

County of Clackamas, Oregon

2051 Kaen Road, Oregon City, OR 97045
Tel: (503) 655-8581 Internet: www.co.clackamas.or.us

County Seat: Oregon City **Election Type:** Nonpartisan
Population: 401,515 (2015)

Board of County Commissioners

2051 Kaen Road, Oregon City, OR 97045
Tel: (503) 655-8581 Fax: (503) 742-5919
E-mail: bcc@co.clackamas.or.us Internet: www.co.clackamas.or.us/bcc

★ Chair **John Ludlow** (Position 1) ....(503) 655-8581
Term Expires: December 31, 2016
★ Commissioner **Paul Savas** (Position 2) ....(503) 655-8581
Term Expires: December 31, 2018
★ Commissioner **Martha Schrader** (Position 3)...........(503) 655-8581
Term Expires: December 31, 2016
★ Commissioner **Tootie Smith** (Position 4) ....(503) 655-8581
Term Expires: December 31, 2016
Education: Concordia Col (OR) BS
★ Commissioner **Jim Bernard** (Position 5)...............(503) 655-8581
Term Expires: December 31, 2018

Office of the County Counsel

2051 Kaen Road, Oregon City, OR 97045
Tel: (503) 655-8362 Fax: (503) 742-5397

County Counsel **Stephen L. Madkour** ....(503) 742-5391
Assistant County Counsel **Nathan Boderman** ....(503) 655-8364
Assistant County Counsel **Scott C. Ciecko** ....(503) 742-5391
Assistant County Counsel **Alexander Gordon** ....(503) 742-5392
Assistant County Counsel **Kathleen J. Rastetter**........(503) 742-5395
Assistant County Counsel **Christopher B. Storey** ....(503) 742-4623
Assistant County Counsel **Christina Thacker** ....(503) 655-8363

Office of the County Administrator

2051 Kaen Road, Oregon City, OR 97045
Tel: (503) 655-8581

County Administrator **Donald D. "Don" Krupp**.........(503) 655-8581
E-mail: dkrupp@clackamas.us
Deputy County Administrator **Laurel Butman** ....(503) 655-8893
E-mail: lbutman@co.clackamas.or.us

(continued on next page)

★ Elected Official ▲ Appointed by Legislature ▼ Appointed by Governor ▶ Appointed by Board or Commission ● Appointed by Judge
■ Appointed by Mayor △ Appointed by Freeholders ▽ Appointed by Supervisor ▷ Appointed by County Executive ○ Appointed by Council

Office of the County Administrator *continued*

Deputy County Administrator **Nancy Newton** .... (503) 742-5918
E-mail: nancynew@co.clackamas.or.us
Clerk to the Board of Commissioners **Mary Raethke** .... (503) 742-5912

Department of Employee Services [DES]

2051 Kaen Road, Oregon City, OR 97045
Tel: (503) 655-8459 Fax: (503) 742-5468
E-mail: jobs@co.clackamas.or.us

Director **Evelyn Minor-Lawrence** .... (503) 655-8812

Finance Department

2051 Kaen Road, Oregon City, OR 97045
Tel: (503) 742-5400 Fax: (503) 742-5401

Director **Marc Gonzales** .... (503) 742-5405
Budget Manager **Diane Padilla** .... (503) 742-5425
E-mail: dianep@co.clackamas.or.us
Payroll Manager **Vicky Anderson** .... (503) 742-5404

COUNTIES

Health, Housing, and Human Services Department [H3S]

2051 Kaen Road, Oregon City, OR 97045
Tel: (503) 650-5697 Fax: (503) 655-8677
Internet: www.clackamas.us/h3s

Director **Richard F. "Rich" Swift, Jr.** .... (503) 650-5696
Assistant Director of Operations **Jill Archer** .... (503) 650-5694

Public and Government Affairs Department [PGA]

2051 Kaen Road, Oregon City, OR 97045
Tel: (503) 655-8751 Fax: (503) 655-8898
Internet: www.clackamas.us/pga

Director **Gary Schmidt** .... (503) 655-8751
E-mail: gschmidt@co.clackamas.or.us
Cable Communications Manager **Debbie McCoy** .... (503) 742-5903
Government Affairs Manager **Chris Lyons** .... (503) 742-5909
E-mail: clyons@clackamas.us

Technology Services Department

121 Library Court, Oregon City, OR 97045
Tel: (503) 655-8322

Chief Information Officer **David Cummings** .... (503) 655-8322
E-mail: davidcu@co.clackamas.or.us
Deputy Information Officer **David DeVore** .... (503) 655-8322
E-mail: daviddev@co.clackamas.or.us
Technology Procurement **Debbie Paxson** .... (503) 655-8322
E-mail: debbiepax@co.clackamas.or.us
GIS Manager **Eric Bohard** .... (503) 723-4814
Fax: (503) 655-8255

Department of Transportation and Development [DTD]

150 Beavercreek Road, Oregon City, OR 97045
Tel: (503) 742-4400

Director **Barbara Cartmill** .... (503) 742-4339

Office of the County Surveyor

9101 Southeast Sunnybrooke Boulevard, Suite 428, Clackamas, OR 97015-6612
Tel: (503) 353-4475 Fax: (503) 353-4481

County Surveyor **Carl Clinton** .... (503) 353-4499

Office of the County Assessor

150 Beavercreek Road, Oregon City, OR 97045
Tel: (503) 655-8671 Fax: (503) 655-8313
E-mail: propertytaxinfo@co.clackamas.or.us

★ County Assessor **Bob Vroman** .... (503) 655-8671
Term Expires: December 31, 2016
E-mail: bobv@co.clackamas.or.us
Assessment and Taxation Manager **Tami Little** .... (503) 655-8671
Appraisal Manager **Joe Honl** .... (503) 655-8671

Office of the County Clerk

2051 Kaen Road, Second Floor, Oregon City, OR 97045
Tel: (503) 650-5686 Fax: (503) 650-5687
Internet: www.clackamas.us/clerk

★ County Clerk **Sherry Hall** .... (503) 655-8698
Term Expires: December 31, 2018
E-mail: sherryhal@co.clackamas.or.us

Office of the County Treasurer

2051 Kaen Road, #470, Oregon City, OR 97045
Tel: (503) 742-5990

★ County Treasurer **Shari Anderson** .... (503) 742-5995
Term Expires: December 31, 2018
E-mail: shariand@co.clackamas.or.us

Office of the District Attorney

807 Main Street, Oregon City, OR 97045
Tel: (503) 655-8431 E-mail: districtattorney@co.clackamas.or.us

★ District Attorney **John S. Foote** .... (503) 655-8431
Term Expires: December 31, 2016
E-mail: johnfoote@co.clackamas.or.us

Office of the Sheriff

12800 Southeast 82nd Avenue, Clackamas, OR 97015
Tel: (503) 722-6790 Fax: (503) 353-8060
Internet: www.clackamas.us/sheriff

★ Sheriff **Craig Roberts** .... (503) 722-6790
Term Expires: December 31, 2016
E-mail: craigrob@co.clackamas.or.us
Undersheriff **Matt Ellington** .... (503) 722-6790
Chief Deputy **Chris Hoy** .... (503) 722-6790

County of Clark, Nevada

Clark County Government Center, 500 South Grand Central Parkway, Las Vegas, NV 89155
Tel: (702) 455-3500 (Information) Internet: www.accessclarkcounty.com

County Seat: Las Vegas **Election Type:** Partisan
Population: 2,114,801 (2015)

Office of the Board of Commissioners

Clark County Government Center, 500 South Grand Central Parkway, Las Vegas, NV 89106-1601
P.O. Box 551601, Las Vegas, NV 89155-1601
Fax: (702) 383-6041

★ Chair **Steve Sisolak** (D-District A) .... (702) 455-3501
Term Expires: December 31, 2016
E-mail: ccdista@clarkcountynv.gov
Date of Birth: December 26, 1953
Education: Wisconsin (Milwaukee) 1974 BS; UNLV 1978 MBA

★ Elected Official ▲ Appointed by Legislature ▼ Appointed by Governor ► Appointed by Board or Commission ● Appointed by Judge
■ Appointed by Mayor △ Appointed by Freeholders ▽ Appointed by Supervisor ▷ Appointed by County Executive ○ Appointed by Council

Office of the Board of Commissioners *continued*

★ Vice-Chair
Lawrence L. "Larry" Brown III (D-District C) . . . . (702) 455-3501
Term Expires: December 31, 2016
E-mail: ccdistc@clarkcountynv.gov

★ Commissioner **Marilyn Kirkpatrick** (D-District B) . . . . . (702) 455-3501
Term Expires: January 31, 2017
E-mail: ccdistb@clarkcountynv.gov

★ Commissioner **Lawrence Weekly** (D-District D) . . . . (702) 455-3501
Term Expires: December 31, 2016
E-mail: ccdistd@clarkcountynv.gov
Education: Grambling State BA

★ Commissioner
Christina R. "Chris" Giunchigliani (D-District E) . . . . . (702) 455-3501
Term Expires: January 7, 2019
E-mail: ccdiste@clarkcountynv.gov
Education: Avila Col BA; UNLV MEd

★ Commissioner **Susan Brager** (D-District F) . . . . (702) 455-3501
Term Expires: January 7, 2019
E-mail: ccdistf@clarkcountynv.gov

★ Commissioner **Mary Beth Scow** (D-District G) . . . . (702) 455-3501
Term Expires: January 7, 2019
E-mail: ccdistg@clarkcountynv.gov

Las Vegas Metropolitan Police Department

400 South Martin Luther King Boulevard, Las Vegas, NV 89106
Fax: (702) 828-0144 E-mail: sheriff@lvmpd.com
Internet: www.lvmpd.com

★ Sheriff **Joseph Lombardo** . . . . (702) 828-3231
Term Expires: December 31, 2018
Undersheriff **Kevin McMahill** . . . . (702) 828-3438
Assistant Sheriff for Law Enforcement Services Group
Todd Fasulo . . . . (702) 828-1526
Assistant Sheriff for Law Enforcement Operations
Group **Kirk Primas** . . . . (702) 828-8380
Deputy Chief for Homeland Security and Investigations
Group **Patrick Neville** . . . . (702) 828-3370
Deputy Chief for Administrative and Sciences Division
Barbara Doran . . . . (702) 828-0150
Deputy Chief for Professional Standards Division
Tim Kelly . . . . (702) 828-3520
Deputy Chief for Technology and Support Division
Brett Zimmerman . . . . (702) 828-5755
Deputy Chief for Detention Services **Charles Hank** . . . . . . (702) 828-8220
Deputy Chief and Investigative Services Division
Thomas Roberts . . . . (702) 828-5699
Deputy Chief for Community Police **Jim Owens** . . . . (702) 828-5699
Chief Financial Officer **Richard Hoggan** . . . . (702) 828-1365
Captain, Office of Internal Oversight **Matt McCarthy** . . . . (702) 828-8460
General Counsel **Liesi Freedman** . . . . (702) 828-3310
Director, Office of Intergovernmental Services
Chuck Callaway . . . . (702) 828-5537
Director, Office of Public Information **Carla Alston** . . . . . . (702) 828-2741

Office of the County Manager

Clark County Government Center, 500 South Grand Central Parkway, 6th Floor, Las Vegas, NV 89155-1111
Fax: (702) 455-3558

► County Manager **Donald G. "Don" Burnette** . . . . (702) 455-3530
E-mail: dgb@clarkcountynv.gov
Education: Northern Arizona BS; New Mexico State MPA
Public Communications Director **Erik Pappa** . . . . (702) 455-3530
E-mail: epappa@clarkcountynv.gov

Office of the Assistant County Manager

500 South Grand Central Parkway, Las Vegas, NV 89155-3530
Tel: (702) 455-3530

Assistant County Manager **Jeffrey M. "Jeff" Wells** . . . . . . (702) 455-3530
E-mail: jmwells@clarkcountynv.gov

Office of the Public Defender

309 S. Third St., 2nd Fl., P.O. Box 552610, Las Vegas, NV 89155-2610
Fax: (702) 455-5112

Public Defender **Philip J. Kohn** . . . . (702) 455-4685

Office of the Coroner

1704 Pinto Lane, Las Vegas, NV 89106
Fax: (702) 455-3101

Coroner **John Fudenberg** . . . . (702) 455-3210

Department of Juvenile Justice Services

601 N. Pecos Rd., Las Vegas, NV 89101
Tel: (702) 455-5200 Fax: (702) 455-5216

Director **John "Jack" Martin** . . . . (702) 455-5210

Law Library

309 South Third Street, #400, Las Vegas, NV 89101
Tel: (702) 455-4696 Fax: (702) 455-5120

Director **Karen Byrd** . . . . (702) 455-6956
Office Services Manager **Chanteyl Newman** . . . . (702) 455-4582

Office of the Assistant County Manager

500 South Grand Central Parkway, Las Vegas, NV 89106
Tel: (702) 455-3530

Assistant County Manager **Randall J. "Randy" Tarr** . . . . . (702) 455-3530
E-mail: rtarr@clarkcountynv.gov

Air Quality

4701 West Russell Road, Suite 200, Las Vegas, NV 89118-2231
Tel: (702) 455-5942 Tel: (702) 383-9994
E-mail: airquality@ClarkCountyNV.gov

Director **Marci Henson** . . . . (702) 455-5942

Building Department and Fire Prevention Bureau

4701 West Russell Road, Las Vegas, NV 89118
Tel: (702) 455-3000 Fax: (702) 221-0630

Director **Ronald L. Lynn** . . . . (702) 455-2794
Assistant Director, Building **Samuel D. Palmer** . . . . (702) 455-2794

Business License Department

Clark County Government Center, 500 South Grand Central Parkway, 3rd Floor, Las Vegas, NV 89106
Tel: (702) 455-4252 Fax: (702) 386-2168

Director **Jacqueline R. Holloway** . . . . (702) 455-3568

Comprehensive Planning Department

Clark County Government Center, 500 South Grand Central Parkway, Suite 3012, Las Vegas, NV 89106
P.O. Box 551741, Las Vegas, NV 89155-1741
Tel: (702) 455-4314 E-mail: zoning@ClarkCountyNV.gov

Director **Nancy Amundsen** . . . . (702) 455-3113

Nuclear Waste Program

P.O. Box 551751, Las Vegas, NV 89155-1751
Fax: (702) 382-4593

Planning Manager **Phil Klevorick** . . . . (702) 455-6933

Department of Public Works

Clark County Government Center, 500 S. Grand Central Pkwy., Las Vegas, NV 89155-4000
Tel: (702) 455-6000 Fax: (702) 455-6040

► Director **Denis Cederburg** . . . . (702) 455-6020
E-mail: dlc@clarkcountynv.gov
Deputy Director **Robert Thompson** . . . . (702) 455-4600
E-mail: rbt@clarkcountynv.gov Fax: (702) 455-6113
► County Surveyor **James L. "Jim" Marlett, Jr.** . . . . (702) 455-6150
E-mail: jmx@clarkcountynv.gov
Construction Management Division Assistant Manager
Mike Mamer . . . . (702) 455-4600
E-mail: mmamer@clarkcountynv.gov

(continued on next page)

★ Elected Official ▲ Appointed by Legislature ▼ Appointed by Governor ► Appointed by Board or Commission ● Appointed by Judge
■ Appointed by Mayor △ Appointed by Freeholders ▽ Appointed by Supervisor ▷ Appointed by County Executive ○ Appointed by Council

Department of Public Works *continued*

Design Engineering Division Manager **Joe Yatson** ...... (702) 455-6050
E-mail: jyatson@clarkcountynv.gov
Road Division (Maintenance) **Angelo Santorino** .... (702) 455-7540
E-mail: angelo@clarkcountynv.gov
Traffic Management Division Manager **Kaizad Yazdani** ... (702) 455-6000
Development Review Division **Erik Denman** .... (702) 455-4600

Parks and Recreation

2601 East Sunset Road, Las Vegas, NV 89120-3515
Tel: (702) 455-8200 Fax: (702) 455-8260
Internet: www.clarkcountynv.gov/parks

Director **Jane Pike** .... (702) 455-8822
E-mail: jepx@clarkcountynv.gov
Assistant Director **Mindy Meyers** .... (702) 455-8214
E-mail: meyersm@clarkcountynv.gov Fax: (702) 455-8260
Manager **Cliff Fields** .... (702) 455-8839
Fax: (702) 263-5284
Assistant Manager **Kevin J. Parker** .... (702) 455-8294
E-mail: kjp@clarkcountynv.gov Fax: (702) 455-8234
Manager of Recreation **Patrick Almeido** .... (702) 455-8134
Fax: (702) 455-8275
Principal Analyst **Jeffrey Sherwood** .... (702) 455-8118
Fax: (702) 455-8153
Webmaster **Stacey Fuqua** .... (702) 455-8803
E-mail: sfuqua@clarkcountynv.gov

Real Property Management [RPM]

Clark County Government Center, 500 South Grand Central Parkway, 4th Floor, Las Vegas, NV 89155-1825
Tel: (702) 455-4616 Fax: (702) 455-4055
Internet: www.clarkcountynv.gov/depts/real_property

▶ Director **Jerry Stueve** .... (702) 455-6462
E-mail: jerry.stueve@clarkcountynv.gov

Clark County Water Reclamation District

5857 E. Flamingo Rd., Las Vegas, NV 89122-5598
Tel: (702) 668-8888 Fax: (702) 435-5435
Internet: www.cleanwaterteam.com

General Manager **Tom Minwegan** .... (702) 668-8060
Fax: (702) 435-5435
Assistant General Manager, Collection System and Maintenance Service Center **Rick Donahue** .... (702) 668-8351
E-mail: rdonahue@cleanwaterteam.com Fax: (702) 668-9275
Assistant General Manager, Engineering and Construction Service Center **Sam Scire** .... (702) 668-8140
E-mail: sscire@cleanwaterteam.com Fax: (702) 668-9140
Assistant General Manager, Finance and Technology **Mark Binney** .... (702) 668-8266
E-mail: mbinney@cleanwaterteam.com Fax: (702) 668-9266
Assistant General Manager, Plant Operations and Laboratory Service Center **Dan Fisher** .... (702) 668-8455
E-mail: dfisher@cleanwaterteam.com Fax: (702) 668-9455
Laughlin Services Manager **Dan Fisher** .... (702) 668-9140
450 Bruce Woodbury, Laughlin, NV 89029 Fax: (702) 668-9455
E-mail: dfisher@cleanwaterteam.com

Department of Finance

Clark County Government Center, 500 S. Grand Central Pkwy., Las Vegas, NV 89155-1211
Fax: (702) 455-6298 Internet: www.clarkcountynv.gov/depts/finance

Chief Financial Officer **Yolanda T. King** .... (702) 455-3543

Comptroller's Office

Clark County Government Center, 500 S. Grand Central Pkwy., Las Vegas, NV 89155-1210
Fax: (702) 455-5794

Comptroller **Jessica Colvin** .... (702) 455-3895

Automotive Services Division

4241 Stephanie St., Las Vegas, NV 89122
Tel: (702) 455-8513 Fax: (702) 455-8555

Manager **David Johnson** .... (702) 455-8556

Budget and Financial Planning Division

500 South Grand Central Parkway, 6th Floor, Las Vegas, NV 89155-1120
Fax: (702) 455-6298

Assistant Director **David Dobrzynski** .... (702) 455-3543
E-mail: ddo@clarkcountynv.gov

Enterprise Resource Planning Division [ERP]

500 South Grand Central Parkway, Las Vegas, NV 89106-1601
Fax: (702) 868-6466

Director **Susan Laveway** .... (702) 868-6407

Human Resources Department

Clark County Government Center, 500 South Grand Central Parkway, 3rd Floor, Las Vegas, NV 89155-1791
Tel: (702) 455-4565 Tel: (702) 455-3174 (Information Job Hotline)
Fax: (702) 384-1405
Internet: www.clarkcountynv.gov/depts/human_resources

Director **Sandy Jeantete** .... (702) 455-3514
Employment Manager **Diane Koksha** .... (702) 455-3176
Employee Assistance/Wellness Information Manager **Felice Lipkint** .... (702) 455-3066
Employee/Labor Relations Manager **Angela White** ...... (702) 455-5598

Clark County Fire Department [CCFD]

575 East Flamingo Road, Las Vegas, NV 89119
Fax: (702) 734-6111 (Administration)
Fax: (702) 455-8349 (Training Center)
Fax: (702) 455-7347 (Fire Prevention) Internet: http://fire.co.clark.nv.us/

▶ Fire Chief **Gregory D. Cassell** .... (702) 455-7311
Senior Deputy Chief, Fire Administration **(Vacant)** ...... (702) 455-7311
Deputy Chief, Support Services **Jeff Buchanan** .... (702) 455-7311
Emergency Medical Services Coordinator **Troy Tuke** .... (702) 455-7311
Education: BYU 1989
Assistant Chief, Investigations/Community Outreach **Sandra J. Baker** .... (702) 455-7316
E-mail: sjr@clarkcountynv.gov
Assistant Chief, Rural Services **Larry Haydu** .... (702) 455-7311
Senior Deputy Chief, Operations **Roy Session** .... (702) 455-7311
Deputy Chief, Homeland Security **John Steinbeck** .... (702) 455-7311
Deputy Chief, Training **(Vacant)** .... (702) 455-7311
Airport Training Officer **Bill Hutfilz** .... (702) 261-5218
E-mail: billh@clarkcountynv.gov

Office of the Chief Administrative Officer

500 South Grand Central Parkway, Las Vegas, NV 89106
Tel: (702) 455-3530

Chief Administrative Officer **Sabra Smith-Newby** ...... (702) 455-3530

Election Department

Clark County Election Center, 965 Trade Drive, Suite A, North Las Vegas, NV 89030-7802
Tel: (702) 455-8683 Fax: (702) 455-2793

▶ Registrar of Voters **Joseph Paul Gloria** .... (702) 455-2784
E-mail: jpg@ClarkCountyNV.gov

Information Technology Department [IT]

500 South Grand Central Parkway, Las Vegas, NV 89155-1761
Fax: (702) 455-4932 Internet: www.clarkcountynv.gov/depts/it

▶ Chief Information Officer **Louis Carr, Jr.** .... (702) 455-4000
Education: Stanford 1987 BEE

★ Elected Official ▲ Appointed by Legislature ▼ Appointed by Governor ▶ Appointed by Board or Commission ● Appointed by Judge
■ Appointed by Mayor △ Appointed by Freeholders ▽ Appointed by Supervisor ▷ Appointed by County Executive ○ Appointed by Council

Office of the Public Guardian
515 Shadow Lane, Las Vegas, NV 89106
Fax: (702) 455-4797

Public Guardian **Kathleen Buchanan** . . . . . (702) 455-4332
Fax: (702) 455-4772

Purchasing and Contracts Division
Clark County Government Center, 500 South Grand Central Parkway, 4th Floor, Las Vegas, NV 89155-1217
Fax: (702) 386-4914 E-mail: countypurchasing@clarkcountynv.gov

Purchasing Manager **Adleen Stidhum** . . . . . (702) 455-2897
E-mail: abs@clarkcountynv.gov

Social Service Department
1600 Pinto Lane, Las Vegas, NV 89106
Tel: (702) 455-4270 Fax: (702) 455-5950
Internet: www.clarkcountynv.gov/depts/social_service

Director **Tim Burch** . . . . . (702) 455-5596
Assistant Director **Bobby J. Gordon** . . . . . (702) 455-5722
Social Service Manager **Randy Reinoso** . . . . . (702) 455-5722
Administrative Secretary **Jasmine Cook** . . . . . (702) 455-4270

Administrative Services
Community Resources Management Division
500 South Grand Central Parkway, Fifth Floor, Las Vegas, NV 89155-1212
Tel: (702) 455-5025 Fax: (702) 455-5038

Manager **Michael Pawlak** . . . . . (702) 455-5025

Audit Department
Clark County Government Center, 5th Fl., 500 South Grand Central Parkway, Las Vegas, NV 89155-1120
Fax: (702) 455-3893 E-mail: countyauditor@clarkcountynv.gov
Internet: www.clarkcountynv.gov/depts/internal_audit

Director **Angela M. Darragh** . . . . . (702) 455-3269
Education: DePaul 1997 MBA
Principal Auditor **Rachael H. Bernal** . . . . . (702) 455-5704
Principal Auditor **Cynthia Birney** . . . . . (702) 455-5575

Las Vegas-Clark County Library District
7060 West Windmill Lane, Las Vegas, NV 89113
Tel: (702) 734-7323 (Information) Fax: (702) 507-6187
Internet: www.lvccld.org

Executive Director **Dr. Ronald R. Heezen** . . . . . (702) 507-6184
E-mail: heezenr@lvccld.org
Deputy Director/Chief Operating Officer **Jennifer Schember** . . . . . (702) 507-6290
Deputy Director/Chief Financial Officer **Fred James** . . . . . (702) 507-6168

McCarran International Airport
5757 Wayne Newton Boulevard, Las Vegas, NV 89119
P.O. Box 11005, Las Vegas, NV 89111-1005
Tel: (702) 261-5211 Fax: (702) 597-9553
Internet: http://www.mccarran.com

Director **Rosemary A. Vassiliadis** . . . . . (702) 261-4525
Fax: (702) 261-4111

Deputy Director of Aviation, Operations **James Chrisley** . . . . . (702) 261-5321
E-mail: DeputyDirector@mccarran.com Fax: (702) 261-4111
Deputy Director, Support Services **Saeed Bonabian** . . . . . (702) 261-4540
Fax: (702) 261-4111

Airside Operations Assistant Director **Dennis Anderson** . . . . . (702) 261-5321
Fax: (702) 261-3157

Employee Services and Risk Management Assistant Director **Christine Santiago** . . . . . (702) 261-5311
E-mail: chrissa@mccarran.com Fax: (702) 261-5096
Airport Chief Financial Director **Joseph Piurkowski** . . . . . (702) 261-6029
Fax: (702) 261-5562

McCarran International Airport *continued*

General Aviation Assistant Director **Benedict "Ben" Czyzewski** . . . . . (702) 261-3802
Fax: (702) 261-5137

Information Systems Assistant Director **Samuel Ingalls** . . . . . (702) 261-5281
E-mail: sami@mccarran.com Fax: (702) 261-3755
Landside Operations Assistant Director **Freddie Kirtley** . . . (702) 261-3256
E-mail: freddiek@mccarran.com Fax: (702) 261-5320
Terminal Operations Assistant Director **Ralph LePore** . . . . (702) 261-3250
E-mail: ralphlp@mccarran.com Fax: (702) 261-3255
Airport Chief Marketing Officer **Chris Jones** . . . . . (702) 261-5290
E-mail: chrisjo@mccarran.com Fax: (702) 261-5288
Airport Enterprise Resource Planning Manager **Majed Khater** . . . . . (702) 261-5746
Fax: (702) 261-5137

Office of the Assessor
Clark County Government Center, 500 South Grand Central Parkway, 2nd Floor, Las Vegas, NV 89155-1212
Fax: (702) 455-5553 Internet: www.clarkcountynv.gov/assessor

★ Assessor **Michele W. Shafe** (D) . . . . . (702) 455-3891
Term Expires: January 7, 2019
E-mail: mls@clarkcountynv.gov
Education: UNLV BSBA, MBA
Assistant Director **Doug Scott** . . . . . (702) 455-3891
E-mail: dts@clarkcountynv.gov

Office of the County Clerk
200 Lewis Avenue, 5th Floor, Las Vegas, NV 89101
Tel: (702) 671-0500 Fax: (702) 382-3611
Internet: www.clarkcountynv.gov/depts/clerk

★ County Clerk **Lynn Goya** (D) . . . . . (702) 671-0710
Term Expires: December 31, 2019
Executive Assistant **Robin Delaney** . . . . . (702) 671-0708
E-mail: delaneyr@clarkcountynv.gov

Office of the District Attorney
Regional Justice Center, 200 Lewis Avenue, Las Vegas, NV 89101
Fax: (702) 471-6615 E-mail: dainfo@clarkcountyda.com
Internet: www.clarkcountynv.gov/depts/district_attorney

★ District Attorney **Steve Wolfson** . . . . . (702) 671-2700
Term Expires: January 7, 2019
Fiscal Services Administrator **Patricia L. Cummings** . . . . (702) 671-0988
Personnel Director **Gregory Smith** . . . . . (702) 671-0987

Civil Division
Clark County Government Center, 500 South Grand Central Parkway, Suite 507, Las Vegas, NV 89155-2215
Fax: (702) 382-5178

County Counsel **Mary-Anne Miller** . . . . . (702) 455-4761

Criminal Division
Regional Justice Center, 200 Lewis Avenue, Las Vegas, NV 89101

Assistant District Attorney **Christopher Lalli** . . . . . (702) 671-2800
Assistant District Attorney **Robert Daskas** . . . . . (702) 671-2800

Family Support Division
1900 East Flamingo Road, Las Vegas, NV 89919
Tel: (702) 671-9200 Fax: (702) 366-2400

Assistant Director **Jeffrey "Jeff" Witthun** . . . . . (702) 671-9499

Juvenile Division
601 N. Pecos Rd., Las Vegas, NV 89101-2408
Tel: (702) 455-5320 Fax: (702) 455-5878

Chief Deputy District Attorney **Christopher Lalli** . . . . . (702) 455-5320

COUNTIES

★ Elected Official ▲ Appointed by Legislature ▼ Appointed by Governor ▶ Appointed by Board or Commission ● Appointed by Judge
■ Appointed by Mayor △ Appointed by Freeholders ▽ Appointed by Supervisor ▷ Appointed by County Executive ○ Appointed by Council

Office of the Public Administrator

515 Shadow Lane, Las Vegas, NV 89106
Fax: (702) 455-4717 Internet: www.clarkcountynv.gov/depts/pa
E-mail: pubadm@clarkcountynv.gov

★Public Administrator **John J. Cahill** (D) . . . . (702) 455-4332
Term Expires: January 7, 2019
E-mail: jjcahill@clarkcountynv.gov

Office of the Recorder

Clark County Government Center, 500 South Grand Central Parkway, 2nd Floor, Las Vegas, NV 89155-1510
Tel: (702) 455-4336 Fax: (702) 455-5644
E-mail: recweb@clarkcountynv.gov
Internet: www.clarkcountynv.gov/recorder

★Recorder **Deborah Conway** (D) . . . . (702) 455-4336
Term Expires: January 7, 2019
E-mail: djc@clarkcountynv.gov

Treasurer's Office

Clark County Government Center, 500 South Grand Central Parkway, Las Vegas, NV 89106
Tel: (702) 455-4323 Fax: (702) 385-3905
Internet: www.clarkcountynv.gov/depts/treasurer

★Treasurer **Laura B. Fitzpatrick** (D) . . . . (702) 455-5531
Term Expires: January 7, 2019
E-mail: lbf@clarkcountynv.gov

Clark County School District [CCSD]

5100 West Sahara Avenue, Las Vegas, NV 89146
Internet: www.ccsd.net

Board of School Trustees

5100 West Sahara Avenue, Las Vegas, NV 89146
Fax: (702) 799-1082

★President **Erin Cranor** (District F) . . . . (702) 799-1072
Term Expires: December 31, 2016

Office of the Superintendent

5100 West Sahara Avenue, Las Vegas, NV 89146

Superintendent **Pat Skorkowsky** . . . . (702) 799-5307

County of Clark, Washington

1300 Franklin Street, Vancouver, WA 98660
Tel: (360) 397-2000 Internet: www.co.clark.wa.us

County Seat: Vancouver **Election Type:** Partisan **Population:** 459,495 (2015)

Office of the Board of County Councilors

1300 Franklin Street, Vancouver, WA 98660
Tel: (360) 397-2232 Internet: www.co.clark.wa.us/bocc

★Chair **Marc Boldt** (R-At-Large) . . . . (360) 397-2232
Term Expires: January 2020
E-mail: marc.boldt@clark.wa.gov
Date of Birth: 1954

★Councilor **Jeanne Stewart** (R-District 1) . . . . (360) 397-2232
Term Expires: January 2019

★Councilor **Julie Olson** (R-District 2) . . . . (360) 397-2232
Term Expires: January 2020
E-mail: julie.olson2@clark.wa.gov

Office of the Board of County Councilors *continued*

★Councilor **David Madore** (R-District 3) . . . . (360) 397-2232
Term Expires: December 31, 2016

★Councilor **Thomas M. "Tom" Mielke** (R-District 4) . . . . . (360) 397-2232
Term Expires: December 31, 2016
E-mail: tom.mielke@clark.wa.gov
Date of Birth: 1942
Education: Eastern Washington State 1961 BA; Columbia Basin

Office of the County Manager

1300 Franklin Street, Vancouver, WA 98660
Tel: (360) 397-2232

○County Manager **Mark McCauley** . . . . (360) 397-2232
○Deputy County Manager **(Vacant)** . . . . (360) 397-6097

Budget Office

1300 Franklin Street, 6th Floor, Vancouver, WA 98660
Tel: (360) 397-6097

Manager **Robert Stevens** . . . . (360) 397-6097

Office of the Medical Examiner

900 West 13th Street, Vancouver, WA 98660
Tel: (360) 397-8405 Fax: (360) 397-6120
E-mail: medical.examiner@clark.wa.gov

Medical Examiner **Dennis Wickham** . . . . (360) 397-8405

Community Development Department

1300 Franklin Street, Vancouver, WA 98660
Tel: (360) 397-2375 Fax: (360) 397-2011

Director **Marty Snell** . . . . (360) 397-2375 ext. 4101

Community Planning Department

1300 Franklin Street, Vancouver, WA 98660
Tel: (360) 397-2280 Fax: (360) 759-6762
E-mail: commplanning@clark.wa.gov

Director **Oliver Orjiako** . . . . (360) 397-2280 ext. 4112
Administrative Assistance **Marilee McCall** . . . (360) 397-2280 ext. 4558
E-mail: marilee.mccall@clark.wa.gov

Community Services Department

Building 17, 1601 East Fourth Plain Boulevard, Suite A419, Vancouver, WA 98661
Tel: (360) 397-2130 Fax: (360) 397-6028
E-mail: community.services@clark.wa.gov

Director **Vanessa R. Gaston** . . . . (360) 397-2130
E-mail: vanessa.gaston@clark.wa.gov
Education: U Washington MPA

Environmental Services Department

1300 Franklin Street, 1st Floor, Vancouver, WA 98660
Tel: (360) 397-2121 Fax: (360) 397-2062

Director **Don Benton** (R) . . . . (360) 397-2121 ext. 5358
Date of Birth: April 8, 1957
Education: Concordia U (CA) BSBusMgt
Administrative Assistant **Susan Rice** . . . . (360) 397-2121 ext. 4314
E-mail: susan.rice@clark.wa.gov

General Services Department

1300 Franklin Street, Suite 650, Vancouver, WA 98660
Tel: (360) 397-2323 Fax: (360) 397-6027
E-mail: general.services@clark.wa.gov

Director **Mark Wilsdon** . . . . (360) 397-2323
E-mail: mark.wilsdon@clark.wa.gov

★Elected Official ▲Appointed by Legislature ▼Appointed by Governor ►Appointed by Board or Commission ●Appointed by Judge
■Appointed by Mayor △Appointed by Freeholders ▽Appointed by Supervisor ▷Appointed by County Executive ○Appointed by Council

Human Resources Department
1300 Franklin Street, 5th Floor, Vancouver, WA 98660
Tel: (360) 397-2456 Fax: (360) 397-2457 E-mail: hradmin@clark.wa.gov

Director **Francine Reis** . . . . . (360) 397-2456
E-mail: francine.reis@clark.wa.gov

Information Services Department
1300 Franklin Street, 5th Floor, Vancouver, WA 98660
Tel: (360) 397-6121 Internet: www.co.clark.wa.us/is

Director **(Vacant)** . . . . . (360) 397-4577

Public Information and Outreach Department
1300 Franklin Street, Floor 6, Vancouver, WA 98660
Tel: (360) 397-6012 Fax: (360) 397-6015 E-mail: pio@clark.wa.gov

Director **Mary Keltz** . . . . . (360) 397-6012
E-mail: mary.keltz@clark.wa.gov

Public Works Department
1300 Franklin Street, 1st Floor, Vancouver, WA 98660
Tel: (360) 397-2446 Fax: (360) 397-6051
E-mail: pubwks.cservice@clark.wa.gov

Director **Heath Henderson** . . . . . (360) 397-2446 ext. 4944
E-mail: heath.henderson@clark.wa.gov

Department of Assessment
1300 Franklin Street, 2nd Floor, Vancouver, WA 98660
Tel: (360) 397-2391 Fax: (360) 397-6046 E-mail: asrgis@clark.wa.gov
Internet: www.co.clark.wa.us/assessor

★ Assessor **Peter Van Nortwick** (R) . . . . . (360) 397-2391
Term Expires: December 31, 2018
E-mail: peter.vannortwick@clark.wa.gov
Chief Deputy Assessor **Linda Latto** . . . . . (360) 397-2391

Office of the County Auditor
1300 Franklin Street, 5th Floor, Vancouver, WA 98660
Tel: (360) 397-2241 Fax: (360) 397-6007 E-mail: auditor@clark.wa.gov
Internet: www.clark.wa.gov/auditor

★ County Auditor **Greg Kimsey** (R) . . . . . (360) 397-2241
Term Expires: December 31, 2018
E-mail: greg.kimsey@clark.wa.gov
Education: U Washington BABA; Portland State MBA
Director, Finance **Mark Gassaway** . . . . . (360) 397-2241 ext. 4839

Office of the County Clerk
1200 Franklin Street, Vancouver, WA 98660
Tel: (360) 397-2292 Fax: (360) 397-6099
E-mail: countyclerk@clark.wa.gov
Internet: https://www.clark.wa.gov/clerk

★ County Clerk **Scott G. Weber** (R) . . . . . (360) 397-2292
Term Expires: December 31, 2018
E-mail: scott.weber@clark.wa.gov
Chief Deputy Clerk **Baine Wilson** . . . . . (360) 397-2292

Office of the County Treasurer
1300 Franklin Street, 2nd Floor, Vancouver, WA 98660
Tel: (360) 397-2252 Fax: (360) 397-6042 E-mail: treasoff@clark.wa.gov
Internet: www.clark.wa.gov/treasurer

★ County Treasurer **Doug Lasher** (D) . . . . . (360) 397-2252
Term Expires: December 31, 2018
E-mail: doug.lasher@clark.wa.gov
Education: Lewis & Clark BA, MPA
Deputy Treasurer **Sara Lowe** . . . . . (360) 397-2252

Office of the Prosecuting Attorney
1013 Franklin Street, Vancouver, WA 98660
Tel: (360) 397-2261 Fax: (360) 397-2230 Internet: www.clark.wa.gov/pa

★ Prosecuting Attorney **Tony Golik** (D) . . . . . (360) 397-2261
Term Expires: December 31, 2018
E-mail: tony.golik@clark.wa.gov
Chief Deputy **(Vacant)** . . . . . (360) 397-2261

Office of the Sheriff
707 West 13th Street, Vancouver, WA 98660
Tel: (360) 397-2211 E-mail: sheriff@clark.wa.gov
Internet: www.clark.wa.gov/sheriff

★ Sheriff **Chuck E. Atkins** (R) . . . . . (360) 397-2211
Term Expires: December 31, 2018
Undersheriff **Mike Cooke** . . . . . (360) 397-2211

COUNTIES

County of Cobb, Georgia
100 Cherokee Street, Marietta, GA 30090
Tel: (770) 528-1000 Internet: www.cobbcounty.org

County Seat: Marietta **Election Type:** Partisan **Population:** 741,334 (2015)

Office of the Board of Commissioners
100 Cherokee Street, Suite 300, Marietta, GA 30090-9680
Tel: (770) 528-3000 Fax: (770) 528-2606
Internet: www.cobbcountyga.gov/boc

★ Chairman **Tim Lee** (R-At-Large) . . . . . (770) 528-3300
Term Expires: December 31, 2016
E-mail: tlee@cobbcounty.org
Education: Fordham (Attended)
Commission Assistant **Charlotte Collins** . . . . . (770) 528-3319
E-mail: charlotte.collins@cobbcounty.org
★ Commissioner **Bob Weatherford** (R-District 1) . . . . . (770) 528-3313
Term Expires: December 31, 2018
Commission Assistant **Shannon Woody** . . . . . (770) 528-3313
E-mail: shannon.woody@cobbcounty.org
★ Commissioner **Bob Ott** (R-District 2) . . . . . (770) 528-3316
Term Expires: December 31, 2016
E-mail: bob.ott@cobbcounty.org
Education: Bucknell 1979 BA; USC 1990 MS
Commission Assistant **Kim Swanson** . . . . . (770) 528-3315
★ Commissioner **JoAnn Birrell** (R-District 3) . . . . . (770) 528-3317
Term Expires: December 31, 2018
E-mail: joann.birrell@cobbcounty.org
Commission Assistant **Inger Eberhart** . . . . . (770) 528-3317
E-mail: inger.eberhart@cobbcounty.org
★ Commissioner **Lisa Cupid** (D-District 4) . . . . . (770) 528-3312
Term Expires: December 31, 2016
Commission Assistant **Bianca Keaton** . . . . . (770) 528-3311

Office of the County Attorney
100 Cherokee Street, Suite 595, Marietta, GA 30090-9689
Fax: (770) 528-4010

▶ County Attorney **Deborah Dance** . . . . . (770) 528-4000

Office of the County Clerk
100 Cherokee Street, Suite 355, Marietta, GA 30090-9680
Tel: (770) 528-3307 Fax: (770) 528-3325

County Clerk **Pamela Mabry** . . . . . (770) 528-3309
E-mail: pmabry@cobbcounty.org

★ Elected Official ▲ Appointed by Legislature ▼ Appointed by Governor ▶ Appointed by Board or Commission ● Appointed by Judge
■ Appointed by Mayor △ Appointed by Freeholders ▽ Appointed by Supervisor ▷ Appointed by County Executive ○ Appointed by Council

COUNTIES

Office of the County Manager
100 Cherokee Street, Suite 300, Marietta, GA 30090-9605
Tel: (770) 528-2600 Fax: (770) 528-2606

▶ County Manager **David Hankerson** .... (770) 528-2612
E-mail: dhankerson@cobbcounty.org
Education: Fort Valley State BS; Woodrow Wilson JD

Communications Office
100 Cherokee Street, Suite 130, Marietta, GA 30090
Tel: (770) 528-2480 Fax: (770) 528-2490
E-mail: information@cobbcounty.org

Director **Sheri Kell** .... (770) 528-2485

Office of Internal Audit
100 Cherokee Street, Suite 550, Marietta, GA 30090
Tel: (770) 528-2559 Fax: (770) 528-1506

Director **Latona Thomas** .... (770) 528-2559

Office of the Medical Examiner
150 N. Marietta Pkwy., Marietta, GA 30060
Tel: (770) 528-2200 Fax: (770) 528-2207

Medical Examiner **Cristopher Gulledge** .... (770) 528-2200

Community Development Agency
1150 Powder Springs Road, Marietta, GA 30064
Tel: (770) 528-2120 Fax: (770) 528-2049
E-mail: comdev@cobbcounty.org

Director **Dana Johnson** .... (770) 528-2125
E-mail: Dana.johnson@cobbcounty.org
Manager, Business License Division
Sandra Richardson .... (770) 528-8410
Manager, Code Enforcement Division **Cathey Pickett** .... (770) 528-2180
Fax: (770) 528-2092
Manager, Development and Inspections Division
Lee McClead .... (770) 528-2039
Manager, Planning Division **Jason Gaines** .... (770) 528-2018
Manager, Zoning Division **John Pederson** .... (770) 528-2025
Manager, Administration Division **(Vacant)** .... (770) 528-2125

Office of Finance and Economic Development
100 Cherokee Street, Suite 400, Marietta, GA 30090-9610
Fax: (770) 528-1501

▶ Director **James "Jim" Pehrson** .... (770) 528-1505
E-mail: jpehrson@cobbcounty.org

Human Resources Department
100 Cherokee Street, Suite 200, Marietta, GA 30090-7006
Tel: (770) 528-2541 Fax: (770) 528-2590

Director **Tony Hagler** .... (770) 528-2541
E-mail: thagler@cobbcounty.org

Public Safety Agency
100 Cherokee Street, Suite 460, Marietta, GA 30090
Tel: (770) 528-3800 Fax: (770) 528-3820

Director **Samuel "Sam" Heaton** .... (770) 528-3801
E-mail: sheaton@cobbcounty.org

Fire and Emergency Services Department
1595 County Services Pkwy., Marietta, GA 30008
Fax: (770) 528-8015 Internet: http://fire.cobbcountyga.gov/

Fire Chief **Randy Crider** .... (770) 528-8000
E-mail: randal.crider@cobbcounty.org

Cobb County Police Department
140 N. Marietta Pkwy., Marietta, GA 30060
Fax: (770) 499-4197 Internet: http://police.cobbcountyga.gov/

Chief of Police **John R. Houser** .... (770) 499-3902

Public Services Agency
100 Cherokee Street, Suite 300, Marietta, GA 30090
Tel: (770) 528-2610 Fax: (770) 528-2606

Director **Dr. Jackie McMorris** .... (770) 528-2610
E-mail: jackie.mcmorris@cobbcounty.org

Office of Cooperative Extension (University of Georgia)
678 South Cobb Drive, Marietta, GA 30060
Fax: (770) 528-4086 Internet: www.cobbextension.com

County Coordinator **Hope Warren** .... (770) 528-4095

Parks, Recreation and Cultural Affairs Department [PARKS]
1792 County Services Pkwy., Marietta, GA 30008
Fax: (770) 528-8813 Internet: http://prca.cobbcountyga.gov/

Director **Eddie Canon** .... (770) 528-8800

Cobb Senior Services Department [CSS]
1150 Powder Springs Road, Suite 100, Marietta, GA 30064
Tel: (770) 528-5355 Fax: (770) 528-5378
Internet: http://seniors.cobbcountyga.gov/

Director **Jessica Gill** .... (770) 528-5365

Public Library System
266 Roswell Street, Marietta, GA 30060
Tel: (770) 528-2320 Fax: (770) 528-2349 E-mail: contactus@cobbcat.org
Internet: www.cobbcat.org

Director **Helen D. Poyer** .... (770) 528-2320

Cobb County Board of Elections and Registration
736 Whitlock Avenue SW, Suite 400, Marietta, GA 30064
Tel: (770) 528-2581 Fax: (770) 528-2519
Internet: http://elections.cobbcountyga.gov/

Director of Elections **Janine Eveler** .... (770) 528-2312

Support Services Agency
100 Cherokee Street, Marietta, GA 30090
Tel: (770) 528-2608 Fax: (770) 528-1506
Internet: http://supportservices.cobbcountyga.gov

Director **(Vacant)** .... (770) 528-2608

Office of the Tax Assessor
736 Whitlock Avenue SW, Suite 200, Marietta, GA 30064
P.O. Box 649, Marietta, GA 30090-0649
Fax: (770) 528-3118 E-mail: cobbtaxassessor@cobbcounty.org
Internet: www.cobbassessor.org

▶ Director/Chief Appraiser **Stephen D. White** .... (770) 528-3100

Fleet Management Department
1940 County Services Parkway, Marietta, GA 30008
Fax: (770) 528-1115

Fleet Manager **Al Curtis** .... (770) 528-1110

Information Services Department
100 Cherokee Street, Marietta, GA 30090-9700
Fax: (770) 528-8706

Director **Sharon Stanley** .... (770) 528-8700

★ Elected Official ▲ Appointed by Legislature ▼ Appointed by Governor ▶ Appointed by Board or Commission ● Appointed by Judge
■ Appointed by Mayor △ Appointed by Freeholders ▽ Appointed by Supervisor ▷ Appointed by County Executive ○ Appointed by Council

Property Management Department
57 Waddell Street, Marietta, GA 30060
Tel: (770) 528-2100 Fax: (770) 528-2148

Director **John Reida** . . . . . . (770) 528-2105
E-mail: jreida@cobbcounty.org

Purchasing Department
1772 County Services Pkwy., Marietta, GA 30008-4012
Tel: (770) 528-8400 Fax: (770) 528-8428
E-mail: purchasing@cobbcounty.org
Internet: http://purchasing.cobbcountyga.gov/

Director **Joe Tommie** . . . . . . (770) 528-8416

Department of Transportation [DOT]
1890 County Services Parkway, Marietta, GA 30008
Tel: (770) 528-1600 Fax: (770) 528-1611
E-mail: cobbdot@cobbcounty.org Internet: http://dot.cobbcountyga.gov/

Director (Interim) **Jim Wilgus** . . . . . . (770) 528-1600
Deputy Director/Chief Engineer **Jim Wilgus** . . . . . . (770) 528-1650
E-mail: jim.wilgus@cobbcounty.org

Airport Division
1723 McCollum Pkwy., Kennesaw, GA 30144
Fax: (770) 528-1655

Manager **Karl Von Hagel** . . . . . . (770) 528-1615

Engineering Division
1890 County Services Parkway, Marietta, GA 30008
Fax: (770) 528-1620

Transportation Division Manager **(Vacant)** . . . . . . (770) 528-1670

Planning Division
1890 County Services Pkwy., Marietta, GA 30008

Manager **Eric Meyer** . . . . . . (770) 528-1539

Transit Division
463 Commerce Park Drive, Suite 112, Marietta, GA 30060
Fax: (770) 528-4360

Manager **Gail Franklin** . . . . . . (770) 427-4444

Traffic Operations Division
1890 County Services Parkway, Marietta, GA 30008
Fax: (770) 528-3679

Manager **David Montanye** . . . . . . (770) 528-1684
E-mail: david.montanye@cobbcounty.org

Road Maintenance Division
1890 County Services Parkway, Marietta, GA 30008

Manager **Bill Shelton** . . . . . . (770) 528-3686
E-mail: bill.shelton@cobbcounty.org

Cobb County Water System
660 South Cobb Drive, Marietta, GA 30060
Fax: (770) 419-6224 Internet: http://water.cobbcountyga.gov/

Director **Stephen D. "Steve" McCullers** . . . . . . (770) 419-6225

Office of the District Attorney
70 Haynes Street, Marietta, GA 30090
Fax: (770) 528-3030 E-mail: cobbdistrictattorney@cobbcounty.org

★ District Attorney **D. Victor Reynolds** . . . . . . (770) 528-3080
Term Expires: December 31, 2016

Office of the Sheriff
185 Roswell Street, Marietta, GA 30090-9650
Fax: (770) 499-4796 Internet: www.cobbsheriff.org

★ Sheriff **Neil Warren** (R) . . . . . . (770) 499-4609
Term Expires: December 31, 2016
E-mail: nwarren@cobbcounty.org

Office of the Solicitor General
10 East Park Square, Suite 300, Marietta, GA 30090
Fax: (770) 528-8578 Internet: http://www.cobbsolicitorgeneral.com

★ Solicitor General **Barry E. Morgan** (R) . . . . . . (770) 528-8500
Term Expires: December 31, 2016
E-mail: barry.morgan@cobbcounty.org

Office of the Surveyor
3569 Cobb Drive, Smyrna, GA 30090

★ Surveyor **Donald L. Perryman** (R) . . . . . . (770) 444-9736
Term Expires: December 31, 2016

Office of the Tax Commissioner
736 Whitlock Avenue SW, Marietta, GA 30064
Tel: (770) 528-8600 Fax: (770) 528-8679
Internet: http://www.cobbtax.org

★ Tax Commissioner **Carla Jackson** . . . . . . (770) 528-8600
Term Expires: December 31, 2016
Education: North Carolina State BA
Deputy Tax Commissioner **Chelly McDuffie** . . . . . . (770) 528-8600
Education: Florida State 1986 BS

Cobb County School District [CCSD]
514 Glover Street, Marietta, GA 30060
Tel: (770) 426-3300 Internet: www.cobbk12.org

Board of Education
514 Glover Street, Marietta, GA 30060
Internet: www.cobbk12.org/board

★ Chair **Randy Scamihorn** (R-Post 1) . . . . . . (770) 337-8553
Term Expires: December 31, 2016 Fax: (678) 594-8559
★ Member **Susan Thayer** (R-Post 2) . . . . . . (678) 773-1877
Term Expires: December 31, 2018
★ Member **David Morgan** (R-Post 3) . . . . . . (404) 702-1857
Term Expires: December 31, 2016
E-mail: dmorgan.boardmember@cobbk12.org
★ Member **David Chastain** (R-Post 4) . . . . . . (678) 896-6399
Term Expires: December 31, 2018
★ Member **David Banks** (R-Post 5) . . . . . . (404) 725-3394
Term Expires: December 31, 2016
E-mail: dbanks.boardmember@cobbk12.org
★ Member **Scott Sweeney** (R-Post 6) . . . . . . (678) 646-2470
Term Expires: December 31, 2018
★ Member **Brad Wheeler** (R-Post 7) . . . . . . (770) 335-5982
Term Expires: December 31, 2016 Fax: (678) 594-8559
E-mail: bwheeler.boardmember@cobbk12.org

Office of the Superintendent
514 Glover Street, Marietta, GA 30060
Fax: (678) 594-8559

Superintendent **Chris Ragsdale** . . . . . . (770) 426-3452
Education: Kennesaw State U BS
Chief of Staff **Dr. Angela Huff** . . . . . . (770) 426-3452

COUNTIES

★ Elected Official ▲ Appointed by Legislature ▼ Appointed by Governor ▶ Appointed by Board or Commission ● Appointed by Judge
■ Appointed by Mayor △ Appointed by Freeholders ▽ Appointed by Supervisor ▷ Appointed by County Executive ○ Appointed by Council

County of Collin, Texas

Administration Building, 2300 Bloomdale Road, McKinney, TX 75071
Courthouse, 2100 Bloomdale Road, McKinney, TX 75071
Tel: (972) 548-4100 Internet: www.co.collin.tx.us

County Seat: McKinney **Election Type:** Partisan **Year Founded:** 1846
Population: 914,127 (2015)

Commissioners' Court

2300 Bloomdale Road, Suite 4192, McKinney, TX 75071
Tel: (972) 424-1460 ext. 4631 Fax: (972) 548-4699
E-mail: commcourt@collincountytx.gov
Internet: www.co.collin.tx.us/commissioners_court/index.jsp

★County Judge **Keith Self** (R) . . . . (972) 548-4623
Term Expires: December 31, 2018
E-mail: keith.self@collincountytx.gov
Education: West Point 1975; USC

★Commissioner **Susan Fletcher** (R-Precinct 1) . . (972) 424-1460 ext. 4631
Term Expires: December 31, 2016

★Commissioner **Cheryl Williams** (R-Precinct 2) . . . . (972) 548-4626
Term Expires: December 31, 2018

★Commissioner **Chris Hill** (R-Precinct 3) . . . . (972) 548-4625
Term Expires: December 31, 2016

★Commissioner **Duncan Webb** (R-Precinct 4) . . . . (972) 548-4627
Term Expires: December 31, 2018

Administrative Services

2300 Bloomdale Road, Suite 4192, McKinney, TX 75071
Tel: (972) 548-4675 E-mail: adminser@collincountytx.gov
Internet: www.co.collin.tx.us/administrative_services

Director **Bill Bilyeu** . . . . (972) 548-4675
E-mail: bbilyeu@collincountytx.gov

Budget and Finance Department

2300 Bloomdale Road, Suite 4100, McKinney, TX 75071
Tel: (972) 548-4650 E-mail: budget@collincountytx.gov

Director **Mónika Arris** . . . . (972) 548-4650
E-mail: marris@collincountytx.gov

Law Library

2100 Bloomdale Road, Suite 10216, McKinney, TX 75071
Tel: (972) 424-1460 ext. 4255 E-mail: lawlib@collincountytx.gov
Internet: www.co.collin.tx.us/law_library

Law Librarian **Diane Roberts** . . . . (972) 424-1460 ext. 4255

Engineering Department

4690 Community Avenue, Suite 200, McKinney, TX 75071
Tel: (972) 548-3727 E-mail: engineer@collincountytx.gov
Internet: www.co.collin.tx.us/engineering/index.jsp

County Engineer **Clarence Daugherty** . . . . (972) 548-3727
E-mail: Cdaugherty@collincountytx.gov

Parks and Open Space Program

Myers Park and Event Center, 7117 County Road 166,
McKinney, TX 75071
Tel: (972) 424-1460 ext. 4792 Fax: (972) 542-2265
E-mail: mpec@collincountytx.gov

Manager **Judy Florence** . . . . (972) 424-1460 ext. 4792

Facilities Maintenance Department

4600 Community Avenue, McKinney, TX 75071
Tel: (972) 547-5300 Fax: (972) 547-5498
E-mail: facilities@collincountytx.gov

Director **Dan C. James** . . . . (972) 547-5331
E-mail: djames@collincountytx.gov

Health Care Services

825 North McDonald Street, McKinney, TX 75069
Tel: (972) 548-5500 Fax: (972) 548-5550 E-mail: hc@collincountytx.gov

Director **Candy Blair** . . . . (972) 548-5500
Health Authority **Muriel Marshall** . . . . (972) 548-5500
Chief Epidemiologist **Jawaid Asghar** . . . . (972) 548-5534

Substance Abuse Program

900 East Park Boulevard, Suite 170, Plano, TX 75074
Tel: (972) 548-5570 Fax: (972) 548-5579

Manager **Grace Raulston** . . . . (972) 548-5570

Department of Homeland Security

4300 Community Avenue, McKinney, TX 75071
Tel: (972) 548-5537 Fax: (972) 548-4747
E-mail: homelandsecurity@collincountytx.gov
Internet: www.co.collin.tx.us/homeland_security/index.jsp

Director **Kelley Stone** . . . . (972) 548-5537
E-mail: kstone@collincountytx.gov

Office of the Fire Marshal

825 North McDonald Street, Suite 140, McKinney, TX 75069
Tel: (972) 548-5576 Fax: (972) 548-5574
E-mail: fmadmin@collincountytx.gov
Internet: www.co.collin.tx.us/fire_marshal

Fire Marshal **Jason Browning** . . . . (972) 548-5576

Human Resources Department

2300 Bloomdale Road, Suite 4117, McKinney, TX 75071
Tel: (972) 548-4606 Fax: (972) 548-4509
E-mail: humanresources@collincountytx.gov

Director **Cynthia Jacobson** . . . . (972) 548-4606
E-mail: cjacobson@collincountytx.gov
Assistant Director **Lisa Meyer** . . . . (972) 548-4606
E-mail: lmeyer@collincountytx.gov
Risk Manager **Erica Johnson** . . . . (972) 548-4782
E-mail: ejohnson@collincountytx.gov

Office of the Medical Examiner

700 B. Wilmeth Road, McKinney, TX 75069
Tel: (972) 548-3775 Fax: (972) 548-3760
E-mail: medicalexam@collincountytx.gov
Internet: www.co.collin.tx.us/medical_examiner/index.jsp

Medical Examiner **William Rohr** . . . . (972) 548-3775

Department of Information Technology

2300 Bloomdale Road, Suite 3198, McKinney, TX 75071
Tel: (972) 424-1460 E-mail: is@collincountytx.gov
Internet: www.co.collin.tx.us/information_services/index.jsp

Director **Caren Skipworth** . . . . (972) 424-1460
E-mail: cskipworth@collincountytx.gov

GIS/Rural Addressing Department

2300 Bloomdale Road, Suite 3198, McKinney, TX 75071
Tel: (972) 424-1460 ext. 4192 E-mail: gisra@collincountytx.gov
Internet: www.co.collin.tx.us/gis_rural_addressing/index.jsp

Manager **Tim Nolan** . . . . (972) 424-1460 ext. 4192

Records Management Department

825 North McDonald Street, McKinney, TX 75069
Tel: (972) 424-1460 ext. 5560 E-mail: records@collincountytx.gov
Internet: www.co.collin.tx.us/records/index.jsp

Manager **L'Cena Parsons** . . . . (972) 424-1460 ext. 5560

★Elected Official ▲Appointed by Legislature ▼Appointed by Governor ►Appointed by Board or Commission ●Appointed by Judge
■Appointed by Mayor △Appointed by Freeholders ▽Appointed by Supervisor ▷Appointed by County Executive ○Appointed by Council

Public Information Office
2300 Bloomdale Road, Suite 4192, McKinney, TX 75071
Tel: (972) 548-4673 Fax: (972) 548-4699
E-mail: publicrelations@collincountytx.gov
Internet: www.co.collin.tx.us/public_information/index.jsp

Public Information Officer **Eric Nishimoto** .... (972) 548-4772
E-mail: enishimoto@collincountytx.gov
Public Information Officer **Tim Wyatt** .... (972) 548-4673
E-mail: twyatt@collincountytx.gov

Public Works Department
700 A. Wilmeth Road, McKinney, TX 75069
Tel: (972) 548-3700 Fax: (972) 548-3754
E-mail: pubworks@collincountytx.gov
Internet: www.co.collin.tx.us/public_works/index.jsp

Director **Jon Kleinheksel** .... (972) 548-3700
Assistant Director **Gary Enna** .... (972) 548-3700
Utilities Coordinator **Tony Cook** .... (972) 548-3743

Purchasing Department
2300 Bloomdale Road, Suite 3160, McKinney, TX 75071
Tel: (972) 548-4165 Fax: (972) 548-4694
Internet: www.co.collin.tx.us/purchasing/index.jsp

Director **Michalyn Rains** .... (972) 548-4111

County Clerk's Office
2300 Bloomdale Road, Room 2106, McKinney, TX 75071
Tel: (972) 548-4185 Fax: (972) 547-5731
E-mail: ctyclerks@collincountytx.gov
Internet: www.co.collin.tx.us/county_clerk/index.jsp

★ County Clerk **Stacey Kemp** (R) .... (972) 548-4133
Term Expires: December 31, 2018
E-mail: ctyclerks@collincountytx.gov

Sheriff's Office
4300 Community Avenue, McKinney, TX 75071
Tel: (972) 547-5100 Fax: (972) 547-5304
E-mail: sheriff@collincountytx.gov
Internet: www.co.collin.tx.us/sheriff/index.jsp

★ Sheriff **Terry G. Box** (R) .... (972) 547-5100
Term Expires: January 2017
E-mail: sheriffbox@collincountytx.gov
Assistant Chief **Charles Adams** .... (972) 547-5100
E-mail: cadams@collincountytx.gov

Tax Assessor and Collector's Office
2300 Bloomdale Road, Suite 2324, McKinney, TX 75071
P.O. Box 8006, McKinney, TX 75071
Tel: (972) 547-5020 E-mail: taxassessor@collincountytx.gov
Internet: www.co.collin.tx.us/tax_assessor/index.jsp

★ Tax Assessor and Collector **Kenneth Maun** (R) .... (972) 547-5020
Term Expires: January 2017

County of Contra Costa, California
County Administration Building, 651 Pine Street, Martinez, CA 94553
Internet: www.cccounty.us

County Seat: Martinez **Election Type:** Nonpartisan
Population: 1,126,745 (2015)

Office of the Board of Supervisors
County Administration Building, 651 Pine Street, Room 107, Martinez, CA 94553
Tel: (925) 335-1900 Fax: (925) 335-1913

★ Chair **Candace Andersen** (District 2) .... (925) 957-8860
Term Expires: December 31, 2016 Fax: (925) 820-3785
E-mail: supervisorandersen@bos.cccounty.us
Education: BYU 1982 BA; J Reuben Clark Law 1985 JD
Chief of Staff **Gayle Israel** .... (925) 957-8860
Education: San Diego State BAJ
★ Vice Chair **Mary Nejedly Piepho** (District 3) .... (925) 252-4500
Term Expires: December 31, 2016 Fax: (925) 240-7261
E-mail: mary.piepho@bos.cccounty.us
Chief of Staff **Tomi Riley** .... (925) 252-4500
★ Supervisor **John Gioia** (District 1) .... (510) 231-8686
Term Expires: December 31, 2019 Fax: (510) 374-3429
11780 San Pablo Avenue, Suite D, El Cerrito, CA 94530
E-mail: john.gioia@bos.cccounty.us
Education: UC Berkeley BA; Boalt Hall JD
Chief of Staff **Sonia Bustamante** .... (510) 231-8689
★ Supervisor **Karen Mitchoff** (District 4) .... (925) 521-7100
Term Expires: December 31, 2019
E-mail: karen.mitchoff@bos.cccounty.us
Education: Cal State (East Bay) 2002 BA
★ Supervisor **Federal D. Glover** (District 5) .... (925) 355-8200
Term Expires: January 6, 2017 Fax: (925) 427-8142
315 E. Leland Rd., Pittsburg, CA 94565
E-mail: federal.glover@bos.cccounty.us
Chief of Staff **David E. Fraser** .... (925) 355-8200
Chief Clerk (Interim) **Theresa B. "Terry" Speiker**
Room 106 .... (925) 335-1900
E-mail: theresa.speiker@cob.cccounty.us Fax: (925) 335-1913

Office of the County Administrator
County Administration Bldg., 651 Pine Street, 10th Floor, Martinez, CA 94553
Fax: (925) 335-1098

▽ County Administrator **David J. Twa** .... (925) 335-1080
E-mail: david.twa@cao.cccounty.us
Education: Minnesota JD
Chief Assistant County Administrator **Allison Picard** .... (925) 335-1080
Chief Assistant County Administrator **Eric Angstadt** ..... (925) 335-1080

Office of Finance
651 Pine Street, 10th Floor, Martinez, CA 94553
Tel: (925) 335-1023 Fax: (925) 335-1098

Finance Director **Lisa Driscoll** .... (925) 335-1023
E-mail: lisa.driscoll@cao.cccounty.us

Office of Risk Management
2530 Arnold Drive, Suite 140, Martinez, CA 94553
Tel: (925) 335-1400 Fax: (925) 335-1454

Risk Manager **Sharon Hymes-Offord** .... (925) 335-1442
E-mail: sharon.hymes-offord@riskm.cccounty.us

★ Elected Official ▲ Appointed by Legislature ▼ Appointed by Governor ▶ Appointed by Board or Commission ● Appointed by Judge
■ Appointed by Mayor △ Appointed by Freeholders ▽ Appointed by Supervisor ▷ Appointed by County Executive ○ Appointed by Council

Health and Human Services
651 Pine Street, 10th Floor, Martinez, CA 94553
Tel: (925) 335-1009 Fax: (925) 335-1098

Senior Deputy County Administrator **Dorothy Sansoe** . . . (925) 335-1009
E-mail: dorothy.sansoe@cao.cccounty.us

Department of Child Support Services [DCSS]
50 Douglas Drive, Suite 100, Martinez, CA 94553
Tel: (925) 957-7300 Fax: (925) 335-3636
E-mail: childsupport@dcss.cccounty.us

▽Director **Linda Dippel** . . . . (925) 313-4455
E-mail: linda.dippel@dcss.cccounty.us

Employment and Human Services Department [EHSD]
40 Douglas Drive, Martinez, CA 94553
Tel: (925) 313-1500 Fax: (925) 313-1575

▽Director **Kathy Gallagher** . . . . (925) 313-1579
E-mail: kgallagher@ehsd.cccounty.us

Aging and Adult Services Bureau
40 Douglas Drive, Martinez, CA 94553
Fax: (925) 313-1575

Director **Victoria Tolbert** . . . . (925) 313-1605

Children and Family Services Bureau
40 Douglas Drive, Martinez, CA 94553
Fax: (925) 313-1575

Director (Interim) **Joan Miller** . . . . (925) 313-1583

Community Services Bureau
40 Douglas Drive, Martinez, CA 94553
Fax: (925) 313-1511

▽Director **Camilla Rand** . . . . (925) 313-1771
E-mail: crand@ehsd.cccounty.us

Workforce Development Board [WDB]
300, Ellinwood Way, Third Floor, Pleasant Hill, CA 94523
Tel: (925) 602-6800 Fax: (925) 602-6802

Executive Director **Stephen Baiter** . . . . (925) 602-6820
E-mail: sbaiter@ehsd.cccounty.us

Workforce Services Bureau
40 Douglas Drive, Martinez, CA 94553
Fax: (925) 313-1575

Director **Wendy Therrian** . . . . (925) 313-1593
E-mail: wtherria@ehsd.cccounty.us

Contra Costa Health Services [CCHS]
50 Douglas Drive, Suite 310-A, Martinez, CA 94553
Tel: (925) 957-5400 Fax: (925) 957-5401 Internet: www.cchealth.org

▽Director and Health Officer **Dr. William B. Walker** . . . . . . (925) 957-5400
E-mail: wwalker@hsd.cccounty.us

Veterans Services Office
10 Douglas Drive, Suite 100, Martinez, CA 94553
Tel: (925) 313-1481 Fax: (925) 313-1490

▽Veterans Service Officer **Nathan Johnson** . . . . (925) 313-1481
E-mail: nathan.johnson@vs.cccounty.us

Municipal Services
651 Pine Street, 10th Floor, Martinez, CA 94553
Tel: (925) 335-1077 Fax: (925) 335-1098

Senior Deputy County Administrator **Julie Enea** . . . . (925) 335-1077
E-mail: julie.enea@cao.cccounty.us
Education: Cal State (Hayward) 1984 BSBA

Department of Conservation and Development
30 Muir Road, Martinez, CA 94553
Fax: (925) 674-7250

▽Director (Interim) **John Kopchik** . . . . (925) 674-7865
E-mail: john.kopcik@dcd.cccounty.us

Cooperative Extension
75 Santa Barbara Rd., 2nd Floor, Pleasant Hill, CA 94523
Fax: (925) 646-6708 E-mail: contracosta@ucdavis.edu

Director **Robert Bennaton** . . . . (925) 646-6124

County Counsel
County Administration Bldg., 651 Pine Street, 9th Floor, Martinez, CA 94553
Fax: (925) 646-1078

▽County Counsel **Sharon L. Anderson** . . . . (925) 335-1800
E-mail: sharon.anderson@cc.cccounty.us

General Services Department
255 Glacier Dr., Martinez, CA 94553
Fax: (925) 313-2333

Deputy Director **(Vacant)** . . . . (925) 313-2114

Fleet Services Division
2467 Waterbird Way, Martinez, CA 94553
Tel: (925) 313-7071 Fax: (925) 313-7088

Fleet Manager **Carlos Velasquez** . . . . (925) 313-7076

Purchasing Services Division
255 Glacier Dr., Martinez, CA 94553
Tel: (925) 313-2000 Fax: (925) 313-2150

Purchasing Manager **David Gould** . . . . (925) 313-2151
E-mail: dgould@pw.cccounty.us

Human Resources Department
County Administration Bldg., 651 Pine Street, 3rd Floor, Martinez, CA 94553
Tel: (925) 335-1700 Fax: (925) 335-1797

Director (Interim) **Kathy Ito** . . . . (925) 335-1754
E-mail: kathy.ito@hsd.cccounty.us

Department of Information Technology
30 Douglas Drive, Martinez, CA 94553
Tel: (925) 313-1200 Fax: (925) 313-1459

Chief Information Officer **Edward G. Woo** . . . . (925) 313-1200
E-mail: ed.woo@doit.cccounty.us

Public Works Department
255 Glacier Dr., Martinez, CA 94553
Tel: (925) 313-2000 Fax: (925) 313-2333

▽Director **Julie Bueren** . . . . (925) 313-2202
E-mail: julie.bueren@pw.cccounty.us

Contra Costa County Airports
550 Sally Ride Dr., Concord, CA 94520-5550
Tel: (925) 646-5722 Fax: (925) 646-5731

Director **Keith Freitas** . . . . (925) 646-5722

Contra Costa County Library [CCCL]
1750 Oak Park Blvd., Pleasant Hill, CA 94523
Tel: (925) 646-6423 Fax: (925) 646-6461 E-mail: libadmin@ccclib.org
Internet: www.ccclib.org

▽Director/County Librarian **Jessica Hudson** . . . . (925) 927-3216
E-mail: jhudson@ccclib.org
Public Information Officer **Brooke Converse** . . . . (925) 927-3213
E-mail: bconvers@ccclib.org

Public Protection
651 Pine Street, 10th Floor, Martinez, CA 94553
Tel: (925) 335-1036 Fax: (925) 646-1353

Senior Deputy County Administrator
Timothy "Tim" Ewell . . . . (925) 335-1036
E-mail: timothy.ewell@cao.cccounty.us

Department of Agriculture
2366-A Stanwell Circle, Concord, CA 94520
Fax: (925) 646-5732

▽ Agricultural Commissioner/Director of Weights and Measures **Chad Godoy** . . . . (925) 646-5250
E-mail: cgodo@ag.cccounty.us

Animal Services Department
4849 Imhoff Place, Martinez, CA 94553
Tel: (925) 335-8300 Fax: (925) 335-8371

▽ Director **Glenn Howell** . . . . (925) 335-8300
E-mail: glenn.howell@asd.cccounty.us

Probation Department
50 Douglas Drive, Suite 201, Martinez, CA 94553-8500
Tel: (925) 313-4000 Fax: (925) 313-4191

Chief Probation Officer **Philip Kader** . . . . (925) 313-4188
Fax: (925) 313-4191

Office of the Public Defender
800 Ferry Street, Martinez, CA 94553
Tel: (925) 335-8000 Fax: (925) 335-8030
Internet: www.contracostapublicdefender.us

Public Defender **Robin Lipetzky** . . . . (925) 335-8000
Education: UC Berkeley 1982 BA; Boalt Hall 1986 JD

Special Districts and Authorities
Contra Costa Fire Protection District [CCFPD]
2010 Geary Road, Pleasant Hill, CA 94523
Tel: (925) 941-3300 Fax: (925) 941-3309 E-mail: cccfd@fd.cccounty.us
Internet: www.cccfpd.org

Chief **Jeff Carman** . . . . (925) 941-3599
E-mail: jcarm@cccfpd.org

Housing Authority of the County of Contra Costa
3133 Estudillo Street, Martinez, CA 94553
Tel: (925) 957-8000 Fax: (925) 372-3678
Internet: www.contracostahousing.org

▽ Executive Director **Joseph E. Villarreal** . . . . (925) 957-8011

Office of the Assessor
2530 Arnold Drive, Suite 400, Martinez, CA 94553
Fax: (925) 313-7660

★ Assessor **Gus S. Kramer** . . . . (925) 313-7500
Term Expires: January 4, 2019
E-mail: gus.kramer@assr.cccounty.us

Office of the Auditor/Controller
625 Court Street, Room 103, Martinez, CA 94553
Fax: (925) 646-2649

★ Auditor/Controller **Robert Campbell** . . . . (925) 646-2181
Term Expires: January 4, 2019
E-mail: bob.campbell@ac.cccounty.us

Office of the County Clerk/Recorder
555 Escobar Street, Martinez, CA 94553
Fax: (925) 335-7893

★ Clerk/Recorder **Joseph Canciamilla** . . . . (925) 335-7899
Term Expires: January 4, 2019
E-mail: joe.canciamilla@cr.cccounty.us

Office of the District Attorney
900 Ward Street, Martinez, CA 94553
Fax: (925) 957-2240

★ District Attorney **Mark A. Peterson** . . . . (925) 957-2200
Term Expires: January 4, 2019
E-mail: mpeterson@contracostada.org
Education: Colorado BA; Denver JD

Office of the Sheriff/Coroner
County Administration Building, 651 Pine Street, 7th Floor, Martinez, CA 94553
Tel: (925) 335-1500 Fax: (925) 335-1691 Internet: www.cocosheriff.org

★ Sheriff/Coroner **David O. Livingston** . . . . (925) 335-1500
Term Expires: January 4, 2019
E-mail: dlivi@so.cccounty.us
Education: U San Francisco JD

Dispatch Center Director **Gale Bowen** . . . . (925) 313-2454
E-mail: gbowe@so.cccounty.us Fax: (925) 313-2479

Director of Emergency Services **Bani Kollo** . . . . (925) 646-4461
50 Glacier Drive, Martinez, CA 94553
E-mail: bkoll@so.cccounty.us

Public Information Officer **Jimmy Lee** . . . . (925) 313-2643
E-mail: jlee@so.cccounty.us

Office of the Treasurer/Tax Collector
625 Court Street, Room 100, Martinez, CA 94553
P.O. Box 631, Martinez, CA 94553-0063
Fax: (925) 957-2898

★ Treasurer/Tax Collector **Russell Watts** . . . . (925) 957-5280
Term Expires: January 4, 2019
E-mail: russell.watt@tax.cccounty.us

Contra Costa County Employees' Retirement Association [CCCERA]
1355 Willow Way, Suite 221, Concord, CA 94520
Tel: (925) 521-3960 Fax: (925) 646-5747 Internet: www.cccera.org

Chief Executive Officer **Gail Strohl** . . . . (925) 521-3977

County of Cook, Illinois
Cook County Building, 118 North Clark Street, Chicago, IL 60602-1304
Tel: (312) 603-6400 (Information) Internet: www.cookcountyil.gov

County Seat: Chicago **Election Type:** Partisan **Population:** 5,238,216 (2015)

Office of the President
118 North Clark Street, Room 537, Chicago, IL 60602-1304
Tel: (312) 603-4600 Fax: (312) 443-4397

★ President **Toni R. Preckwinkle** . . . . (312) 603-4600
Term Expires: November 30, 2018
Education: Chicago 1969 AB, 1977 MA

Chief of Staff **Brian A. Hamer** . . . . (312) 603-4600

Office of the County Auditor
69 West Washington Street, Suite 2200, Chicago, IL 60602
Fax: (312) 603-9972

▶ Auditor **Shelly A. Banks** . . . . (312) 603-1500

★ Elected Official ▲ Appointed by Legislature ▼ Appointed by Governor ▶ Appointed by Board or Commission ● Appointed by Judge
■ Appointed by Mayor △ Appointed by Freeholders ▽ Appointed by Supervisor ▷ Appointed by County Executive ○ Appointed by Council

COUNTIES

Office of the Independent Inspector General [OIIG]

69 West Washington Street, Suite 1160, Chicago, IL 60602
Fax: (312) 603-9948

Inspector General **Patrick M. Blanchard** . . . . . (312) 603-0350
E-mail: patrick.blanchard@cookcountyil.gov

Law Office of the Public Defender

69 West Washington Street, 16th Floor, Chicago, IL 60602
Fax: (312) 603-9878

▶ Public Defender **Amy P. Campanelli** . . . . . (312) 603-0600
E-mail: amy.campanelli@cookcountyil.gov
First Assistant Public Defender **Keith Ahmad** . . . . . (312) 603-0600
Chief of Staff **Lester Finkle** . . . . . (312) 603-0600
Deputy of Administrative Operations **Rhonda Berryhill** . . (312) 603-0600
E-mail: rhonda.berryhill@cookcountyil.gov
Deputy of Employment Litigation and Financial Development **Karen Dimond** . . . . . (312) 603-0600
Chief Financial Officer **Andrew Jatico** . . . . . (312) 603-0600
Deputy of Community and Media Relations **Kim Sorrells** . . . . . (312) 603-0600
E-mail: kim.sorrells@cookcountyil.gov
Deputy Assistant Public Defender, Trial Support Service Division **Amy Thompson** . . . . . (312) 603-0600
Legislative Liaison **Stephen Baker** . . . . . (312) 603-0600
Deputy of Central Operations **Michael Morrissey** . . . . . (773) 674-3230
2650 South California Avenue, Seventh Floor, Chicago, IL 60608
Deputy Academic and Professional Development, Countywide **Peter Parry** . . . . . (312) 433-7046
2245 West Ogden, 7th Floor, Chicago, IL 60612 Fax: (312) 433-5282
E-mail: peter.parry@cookcountyil.gov
Deputy of Suburban Operations **Crystal Gray** . . . . . (708) 974-6470
10220 South 76th Avenue, Room 141, Bridgeview, IL 60455 Fax: (708) 974-6057
E-mail: crystal.gray@cookcountyil.gov

Bureau of Administration

Cook County Building, 118 North Clark Street, Room 820, Chicago, IL 60602
Tel: (312) 603-3055 Fax: (312) 603-4479

▶ Chief Administrative Officer (Acting) **Martha Martinez** . . (312) 603-3055
Special Assistant to the Chief Administrative Officer **Noel Nehf** . . . . . (312) 603-3698
E-mail: noel.nehf@cookcountyil.gov
Deputy Chief Administrative Officer **Martha Martinez** . . . (312) 603-3055
E-mail: martha.martinez@cookcountyil.gov

Office of the Medical Examiner

2121 West Harrison Street, Chicago, IL 60612
Fax: (312) 997-4516

▶ Chief Medical Examiner **Dr. Stephen J. Cina** . . . . . (312) 997-4500

Department of Adoption and Child Custody Advocacy

69 West Washington Street, Suite 818, Chicago, IL 60602
Tel: (312) 603-0550 Fax: (312) 603-9909

Director **Margaret LaReviere** . . . . . (312) 603-0558

Department of Animal and Rabies Control

10220 South 76th Avenue, Bridgeview, IL 60455
Fax: (708) 974-6046

▶ Administrator **Dr. Donna Alexander** . . . . . (708) 974-6140
E-mail: donna.alexander@cookcountyil.gov

Department of Environmental Control

69 West Washington Street, Suite 1900, Chicago, IL 60602-3004
Fax: (312) 603-9828

▶ Director and Chief Sustainability Officer **Deborah "Debbie" Stone** . . . . . (312) 603-8200
E-mail: deborah.stone@cookcountyil.gov
Education: Beloit 1979 BA; Chicago 1981 MA

Department of Transportation and Highways

69 West Washington Street, Suite 2300, Chicago, IL 60602-1369
Fax: (312) 603-9945

▶ Superintendent (Acting) **John Yonan** . . . . . (312) 603-1600
E-mail: john.yonan@cookcountyil.gov

Cook County Law Library

Richard J. Daley Center, 50 West Washington Street, Room 2900, Chicago, IL 60602
TTY: (312) 603-7706 Fax: (312) 603-4716

Executive Law Librarian **Montell Davenport** . . . . . (312) 603-5423
E-mail: montell.davenport@cookcountyil.gov
Deputy Law Librarian **Jean M. Wenger** . . . . . (312) 603-5423
Education: St Mary's Col (MN) BA; Illinois JD; Rosary MLIS
Technical Services Librarian **(Vacant)** . . . . . (312) 603-5423
Branch Services Chief **(Vacant)** . . . . . (312) 603-5423
Fiscal Chief **(Vacant)** . . . . . (312) 603-5423
Systems Chief **Keith Caldwell** . . . . . (312) 603-4268

Veterans Assistance Commission

1100 South Hamilton Avenue, Chicago, IL 60612
Fax: (312) 433-6015

Superintendent **Abundio Zaragoza** . . . . . (312) 433-6010
Director **Bill Browne** . . . . . (312) 433-6016

Bureau of Economic Development

69 West Washington Street, Suite 3000, Chicago, IL 60602-1380
Tel: (312) 603-1077 Fax: (312) 603-9970

Bureau Chief **Michael Jasso** . . . . . (312) 603-1077
Deputy Director **James Wilson** . . . . . (312) 603-1000

Department of Building and Zoning

69 West Washington Street, Suite 2830, Chicago, IL 60602-3007
Tel: (312) 603-0500 Fax: (312) 603-9940

▶ Commissioner **Timothy Bleuher** . . . . . (312) 603-0504

Department of Capital Planning and Policy

69 West Washington, Suite 3000, Chicago, IL 60602
Fax: (312) 603-9997

Director **Phillip Boothby** . . . . . (312) 603-0300 ext. 2

Division of Real Estate Management

69 West Washington Street, Suite 3000, Chicago, IL 60602

Director **Anna Ashcraft** . . . . . (312) 603-0305

Department of Planning and Development

69 West Washington Street, Suite 2900, Chicago, IL 60602
Fax: (312) 603-9970

Deputy Director **Jane Hornstein** . . . . . (312) 603-1009

Cook County Works

69 West Washington Street, Suite 2800, Chicago, IL 60602
Fax: (312) 603-9994

Director **Karin M. Norington-Reaves** . . . . . (312) 603-0200
E-mail: karinnorington.reaves@cookcountyil.gov Fax: (312) 603-9930
Education: Northwestern 1991 BA; Southern Methodist 1996 JD

Bureau of Finance

Cook County Building, 118 North Clark Street, Room 1127, Chicago, IL 60602
Tel: (312) 603-6846 Fax: (312) 603-3681
Internet: www.cookcountyil.gov/finance

Chief Financial Officer **Ivan Samstein** . . . . . (312) 603-6669
Deputy Chief Financial Officer **Ammar Rizki** . . . . . (312) 603-4458

★ Elected Official ▲ Appointed by Legislature ▼ Appointed by Governor ▶ Appointed by Board or Commission ● Appointed by Judge
■ Appointed by Mayor △ Appointed by Freeholders ▽ Appointed by Supervisor ▷ Appointed by County Executive ○ Appointed by Council

Office of the Comptroller
Cook County Bldg., 118 North Clark Street, Room 500,
Chicago, IL 60602
Fax: (312) 603-6122

▶ Comptroller **Lawrence Wilson** . . . . . (312) 603-5601
E-mail: lawrence.wilson@cookcountyil.gov

Office of Contract Compliance
118 North Clark Street, Room 1020, Chicago, IL 60602
Tel: (312) 603-5503 Fax: (312) 603-4547
Internet: www.cookcountyil.gov/contractcompliance

Director **Jacqueline Gomez** . . . . . (312) 603-5502

Office of the Purchasing Agent
Cook County Bldg., 118 North Clark Street, Room 1018,
Chicago, IL 60602
Fax: (312) 603-4477 Internet: www.cookcountyil.gov/purchasing

▶ Director **Shannon E. Andrews** . . . . . (312) 603-6129
E-mail: shannon.andrews@cookcountyil.gov
Deputy Purchasing Agent **Cynthia Parks** . . . . . (312) 603-5370
E-mail: cynthia.parks@cookcountyil.gov

Department of Revenue
118 North Clark Street, Room 1160, Chicago, IL 60602
Internet: www.cookcountyil.gov/revenue

Director **Zahra Ali** . . . . . (312) 603-6870
E-mail: zahra.ali@cookcountyil.gov

Bureau of Human Resources
Cook County Building, 118 North Clark Street, Room 840,
Chicago, IL 60602-1304
Tel: (312) 603-3300 Fax: (312) 603-5404

▶ Chief **(Vacant)** . . . . . (312) 603-3300
Deputy Chief **(Vacant)** . . . . . (312) 603-3824
Deputy Chief **Rebecca Strisko** . . . . . (312) 603-4661
E-mail: rebecca.strisko@cookcountyil.gov
Manager of Training and Development
Liu Montsho Room 834 . . . . . (312) 603-4372

Bureau of Technology
69 West Washington Street, Suite 2700, Chicago, IL 60602
Tel: (312) 603-1400 Fax: (312) 603-9905

Chief Information Officer **Simona Rollinson** . . . . . (312) 603-1400
Education: Tech U Sofia BS; Southern Illinois BS, MS
Deputy Chief Information Officer for Shared Services
Adam Clement . . . . . (312) 603-1400
E-mail: adam.clement@cookcountyil.gov

Department of Geographic Information Systems
69 West Washington Street, Suite 2700, Chicago, IL 60602
Fax: (312) 603-6713

Director **Amber Knapp** . . . . . (312) 603-1370

Department of IT Solutions and Services
118 North Clark Street, 7th Floor, Chicago, IL 60602-1304
Fax: (312) 603-3452

Chief Technology Officer **(Vacant)** . . . . . (312) 603-4629

Application and Management Systems
69 West Washington Street, Suite 2700, Chicago, IL 60602
Fax: (312) 603-9905

Director **Derrick Thomas** . . . . . (312) 603-1400

Department of Facilities Management
Cook County Administration Bldg., 69 W. Washington St., Room 3015,
Chicago, IL 60602
Tel: (312) 603-0340 Fax: (312) 603-9990

Director **BilQis Jacobs-El** . . . . . (312) 603-0340

Department of Facilities Management *continued*

Deputy Director **Michael J. Carberry** (D) . . . . . (312) 603-9990
2600 South California Avenue, Chicago, IL 60608
Business Manager IV, Purchasing and Bids
Belinda Henderson . . . . . (312) 603-0340
2245 West Ogden, Chicago, IL 60612

Department of Homeland Security and Emergency Management [DHSEM]
69 West Washington, Suite 2630, Chicago, IL 60602
Tel: (312) 603-8180 Fax: (312) 603-9883
Internet: www.cookcountyhomelandsecurity.org

Executive Director **Ernest Brown** . . . . . (312) 603-8180
E-mail: Ernest.brown@cookcountyil.gov

Cook County Health and Hospitals System [CCHHS]
1900 West Polk Street, Suite 220, Chicago, IL 60612-3714
Tel: (312) 864-6000 Fax: (312) 864-9994
Internet: www.cookcountyhhs.org

▶ Chief Executive Officer **Dr. John J. "Jay" Shannon** . . . . (312) 864-6000
Education: Spring Hill; Rush 1986 MD

Cermak Health Services of Cook County
2800 S. California Ave., Chicago, IL 60608
Tel: (773) 869-7000 Fax: (773) 869-7177

Chief Operating Officer **(Vacant)** . . . . . (773) 869-7000

John H. Stroger, Jr. Hospital of Cook County
1901 West Harrison, Chicago, IL 60612-3714
Tel: (312) 864-6000 Internet: www.cchil.org

Chief Operating Officer **(Vacant)** . . . . . (312) 864-5500
Chief Financial Officer **John R. Morales** . . . . . (312) 864-6000
Medical Director **(Vacant)** . . . . . (312) 864-5100

Oak Forest Health Center
15900 South Cicero Avenue, Oak Forest, IL 60452-4006
Tel: (708) 687-7200

Chief Operating Officer **(Vacant)** . . . . . (312) 687-7200

Provident Hospital of Cook County
500 East 51st Street, Chicago, IL 60615-2400
Tel: (312) 572-2000 Fax: (312) 572-1216

Chief Operating Officer **Tom Dohm** . . . . . (312) 572-2000
E-mail: tdohm@cookcountyhhs.org
Medical Director **Aaron Hamb** . . . . . (312) 572-2370

Cook County Department of Public Health [CCDPH]
1010 Lake Street, Suite 300, Oak Park, IL 60301-1133
Tel: (708) 633-4000 Internet: www.cookcountypublichealth.org

Chief Operating Officer **Dr. Terry Mason** . . . . . (708) 633-4000
E-mail: tmason@cookcountyhhs.org
Education: Loyola U (Chicago) 1974 MD

Office of the Board of Commissioners
Cook County Bldg., 118 North Clark Street, Room 567,
Chicago, IL 60602
Tel: (312) 603-6398 Fax: (312) 603-4678

★ Commissioner **Richard R. Boykin** (D-District 1) . . . . . (312) 603-4566
Term Expires: November 30, 2018 Fax: (312) 603-3696
Date of Birth: September 9, 1968
Education: Central State 1990 BA; Dayton 1994 JD

★ Commissioner **Robert B. Steele** (D-District 2) . . . . . (312) 603-3019
Term Expires: November 30, 2018 Fax: (312) 603-4055
E-mail: robert.steele@cookcountyil.gov
Education: Morgan State 1983 BS

(continued on next page)

Office of the Board of Commissioners *continued*

★Commissioner **Jerry "Iceman" Butler** (D-District 3) .... (312) 603-6391
Term Expires: November 30, 2018 Fax: (312) 603-5671
E-mail: jerry.butler@cookcountyil.gov
Date of Birth: December 8, 1939
Education: Governors State BS, 1993 MA

★Commissioner **Stanley Moore** (D-District 4) .... (312) 603-2065
Term Expires: November 30, 2018 Fax: (312) 603-2039

★Commissioner **Deborah Sims** (D-District 5) .... (312) 603-6381
Term Expires: November 30, 2018 Fax: (312) 603-3693
E-mail: deborah.sims@cookcountyil.gov
Education: Chicago City

★Commissioner **Joan Patricia Murphy** (D-District 6) ..... (312) 603-4216
Term Expires: November 30, 2018 Fax: (312) 603-3759
E-mail: joan.murphy@cookcountyil.gov
Education: Boston State Col

★Commissioner **Jesus G. "Chuy" Garcia** (D-District 7) ... (312) 603-5443
Term Expires: November 30, 2018 Fax: (312) 603-3759
E-mail: jesus.garcia@cookcountyil.gov
Date of Birth: April 12, 1956
Education: Illinois (Chicago) 1980 BA, MUP

★Commissioner **Luis Arroyo, Jr.** (D-District 8) .... (312) 603-6386
Term Expires: November 30, 2018 Fax: (312) 603-9531

★Commissioner **Peter N. Silvestri** (R-District 9) .... (312) 603-4393
Term Expires: November 30, 2018 Fax: (312) 603-1154
E-mail: cookcty9@aol.com
Education: DePaul BA, JD

★Commissioner **Bridget Gainer** (D-District 10) .... (312) 603-4210
Term Expires: November 30, 2018 Fax: (312) 603-3695
E-mail: info@bridgetgainer.com
Education: Illinois BA; Chicago MBA

★Commissioner **John P. Daley** (D-District 11) .... (312) 603-4400
Term Expires: November 30, 2018 Fax: (312) 603-6688
E-mail: john.daley@cookcountyil.gov
Education: Loyola U (Chicago) BA

★Commissioner **John Alden Fritchey IV** (D-District 12) ... (312) 603-6380
Term Expires: November 30, 2018 Fax: (312) 603-1265
E-mail: commish@fritchey.com
Education: Michigan 1986 BA; Northwestern 1989 JD

★Commissioner
Lawrence J. "Larry" Suffredin, Jr. (D-District 13) .... (312) 603-6383
Term Expires: November 30, 2018 Fax: (312) 603-3622
E-mail: lsuffredin@aol.com
Education: Loyola U (Chicago) 1969 BA; Georgetown 1972 JD

★Commissioner **Gregg Goslin** (R-District 14) .... (312) 603-4932
Term Expires: November 30, 2018 Fax: (312) 603-3686
E-mail: commissioner.goslin@cookcountyil.gov
Education: Southern Illinois 1975 BS

★Commissioner
Timothy O. "Tim" Schneider (R-District 15) .... (312) 603-6388
Term Expires: November 30, 2018 Fax: (312) 603-6500
E-mail: tim.schneider@cookcountyil.gov
Education: Illinois BS

★Commissioner
Jeffrey R. "Jeff" Tobolski (D-District 16) .... (312) 603-6384
Term Expires: November 30, 2018 Fax: (312) 603-4744
E-mail: jeffrey.tobolski@cookcountyil.gov
Education: Knox (IL) BA

★Commissioner **Sean Morrison** (R-District 17) .... (312) 603-4215
Term Expires: November 30, 2018 Fax: (312) 603-2014

Secretary to the Board **Matthew B. DeLeon** .... (312) 603-6127
E-mail: matthew.deleon@cookcountyil.gov Fax: (312) 603-4683

Office of the Public Guardian

69 West Washington Street, Suite 700, Chicago, IL 60602
Fax: (312) 603-9946 E-mail: opg@cookcountyil.gov
Internet: www.publicguardian.org

▶Public Guardian **Robert F. Harris** .... (312) 603-0800

Cook County Commission on Human Rights

69 West Washington Street, Suite 3040, Chicago, IL 60602
Tel: (312) 603-1100 Fax: (312) 603-9988

Executive Director **Ranjit J. Hakim** .... (312) 603-1100
Education: Northwestern 2002 BA, 2002 MA; Chicago 2005 JD

Forest Preserve of Cook County [FPDCC]

536 North Harlem Avenue, River Forest, IL 60305
Tel: (708) 366-9420 Tel: (800) 870-3666 TTY: (708) 771-1190
Fax: (708) 771-1181 Internet: www.forestpreservedistrict.com

General Superintendent **Arnold L. Randall** .... (708) 771-1510
Education: Chicago 1994

Deputy General Superintendent **Eileen Figel** .... (312) 603-8960

Chief Financial Officer **Stephen Hughes** .... (312) 603-8950

Comptroller **Troy Alin** .... (312) 603-8951

Chief Attorney **Dennis White** .... (312) 603-0020

Chief of Police **John Roberts** .... (708) 836-9037

Maintenance Superintendent **Lee Stephenson** .... (708) 771-1059

Superintendent of Permits and Recreational Activities
Karen Vaughan .... (708) 771-1550
Education: Illinois 2001 BS; DePaul 2006 MA

Director of Human Resources **Michelle Gage** .... (312) 603-5296
E-mail: michelle.gage@cookcountyil.gov

Director of Planning and Development
Christine "Chris" Slattery .... (708) 771-1572

Resource Management Director **John McCabe** .... (708) 771-1138

Public Information Officer **Lambrini Lukidis** .... (708) 771-1019
E-mail: lambrini.lukidis@cookcountyil.gov

Purchasing Agent **Thomas J. "Tom" Conlon** .... (312) 603-8968
E-mail: tom.conlon@cookcountyil.gov

Office of the Cook County Assessor

Cook County Building, 118 North Clark Street, Room 314,
Chicago, IL 60602
Tel: (312) 443-7550 Fax: (312) 603-3167
Internet: www.cookcountyassessor.com

★County Assessor **Joseph "Joe" Berrios** (D) .... (312) 603-7800
Term Expires: December 31, 2018
E-mail: taxinfo@cookcountyassessor.com
Date of Birth: February 14, 1952
Education: Illinois BS

Chief Deputy Assessor **Christopher Crawley** .... (312) 603-7800

Communications Director **Mark Bretz** .... (312) 603-7301
E-mail: mbretz@cookcountyassessor.com

Appraisal and Education Manager **(Vacant)** .... (312) 603-5115
118 North Clark Street, Fax: (312) 603-4789
Room 320, Chicago, IL 60602-1304

Deputy Communications Director **Tom Shaer** .... (312) 603-7322

Office of the County Clerk

Cook County Administration Building, 69 West Washington Street,
5th Floor, Chicago, IL 60602-1380
Tel: (312) 603-5656 Fax: (312) 603-9788
Internet: www.cookcountyclerk.com

★County Clerk **David Orr** (D) .... (312) 603-0996
Term Expires: November 30, 2018
E-mail: clerk.david@cookcountyil.gov
Education: Simpson (IA) 1966 BA; Case Western 1968 MA

Deputy County Clerk **Courtney Greze** .... (312) 603-0925

Office of the Public Administrator

69 West Washington Street, Suite 2220, Chicago, IL 60602
Tel: (312) 603-0100 Fax: (312) 603-9999

▼Public Administrator **David A. Epstein** .... (312) 603-0100
E-mail: david.epstein@cookcountyil.gov

★Elected Official ▲Appointed by Legislature ▼Appointed by Governor ▶Appointed by Board or Commission ●Appointed by Judge
■Appointed by Mayor △Appointed by Freeholders ▽Appointed by Supervisor ▷Appointed by County Executive ○Appointed by Council

Office of the Recorder of Deeds

Cook County Building, 118 North Clark Street, Room 120, Chicago, IL 60602
Fax: (312) 603-4597 Internet: www.cookrecorder.com

★ Recorder of Deeds **Karen A. Yarbrough** (D) .... (312) 603-5050
Term Expires: December 31, 2020
Education: Chicago State BA; Northeastern Illinois MA
Chief Deputy Recorder **Cedric Giles** .... (312) 603-5050

Office of the Sheriff

Richard J. Daley Center, 50 West Washington Street, Chicago, IL 60602-1305
Tel: (312) 603-3365 (Civil Process)
Tel: (708) 865-4915 (Fugitive Warrants)
Fax: (773) 674-7292 (Inmate Records)
Fax: (708) 865-6151 (Police Records)
Internet: www.cookcountysheriff.org

★ Sheriff **Thomas J. "Tom" Dart** (D) .... (312) 603-6444
Term Expires: November 30, 2018 Fax: (312) 603-4420
E-mail: sheriff.dart@cookcountyil.gov
Education: Providence BA; Loyola U (Chicago) 1987 JD
Undersheriff **Zelda Whittler** .... (312) 603-6444
E-mail: zelda.whittler@cookcountyil.gov
Chief of Staff **(Vacant)** .... (773) 674-7710
Chief Legal Officer **Helen Burke** .... (773) 674-6444
E-mail: helen.burke@cookcountyil.gov
Chief Strategy Officer **Cara Smith** .... (773) 674-7710
E-mail: cara.smith@cookcountyil.gov
Chief Operating Officer **Joellen Bailey** .... (773) 674-7710
E-mail: joellen.bailey@cookcountyil.gov

Department of Communications

Fax: (312) 603-7692

Director **Benjamin Breit** .... (773) 674-8054
E-mail: benjamin.breit@cookcountyil.gov

Cook County Department of Corrections [CCDOC]

2700 South California Avenue, Chicago, IL 60608
Tel: (773) 674-6810 (Records) Fax: (773) 674-7292 (Records)

Executive Director **Dr. Nneka Jones** .... (773) 674-7710

Court Services Department

50 West Washington Street, Room 705, Chicago, IL 60602-1305

► Chief Deputy Sheriff **Kevin Connelly** .... (312) 603-6100
E-mail: kevinconnelly@cookcountyil.gov

Cook County Sheriff's Police Department [CCSPD]

1401 South Maybrook Drive, Maywood, IL 60153
Fax: (708) 865-6151 (Records Department Fax)

First Deputy Chief of Police **Dana Wright** .... (708) 865-4710

Office of the State's Attorney

69 West Washington Street, Room 3200, Chicago, IL 60602
Fax: (312) 603-4708 E-mail: statesattorney@cookcountyil.gov
Internet: www.statesattorney.org

★ State's Attorney **Anita Alvarez** (D) .... (312) 603-3035
Term Expires: November 30, 2016
E-mail: statesattorney@cookcountyil.gov
Date of Birth: January 16, 1960
Education: Loyola U (Chicago); Chicago-Kent 1986 JD
First Assistant State's Attorney **Daniel Kirk** .... (312) 603-5526

Office of the Treasurer

Cook County Bldg., 118 North Clark Street, Room 112, Chicago, IL 60602
Tel: (312) 443-5100 Fax: (312) 603-2113

★ Treasurer **Maria Pappas** (D) .... (312) 603-6202
Term Expires: November 30, 2018
E-mail: mpappas@cookcountytreasurer.com
Education: West Virginia MA; Chicago-Kent JD; Loyola U (Chicago) PhD
Chief Deputy Treasurer **Joseph M. Fratto** .... (312) 603-6210
Chief Deputy Treasurer **Bill Kouruklis** .... (312) 603-3050

Board of Review (Tax Review)

Cook County Building, 118 North Clark Street, Room 601, Chicago, IL 60602
Fax: (312) 603-3479 Internet: www.cookcountyboardofreview.com

★ District 1 Commissioner **Dan Patlak** (R) .... (312) 603-3644
Term Expires: December 7, 2016
Education: Valparaiso
★ District 2 Commissioner
Michael M. "Mike" Cabonargi .... (312) 603-5560
Term Expires: December 7, 2016
Education: Illinois 2000 JD; Miami U (OH) 1993 BA
★ District 3 Commissioner **Larry R. Rogers, Jr.** .... (312) 603-5540
Term Expires: December 7, 2018
E-mail: larry.rogers@cookcountyil.gov

County of Cuyahoga, Ohio

2079 East Ninth Street, Cleveland, OH 44115
Tel: (216) 443-7000 (Information) Internet: www.cuyahogacounty.us

County Seat: Cleveland **Election Type:** Partisan **Population:** 1,255,921 (2015)

Office of the County Executive

2079 East Ninth Street, Eighth Floor, Cleveland, OH 44115
Tel: (216) 698-2100 E-mail: contacted@cuyahogacounty.us
Internet: http://executive.cuyahogacounty.us/

★ County Executive **Armond D. Budish** (D) .... (216) 443-8088
Term Expires: December 31, 2018
Date of Birth: June 2, 1953
Education: Swarthmore BA; NYU JD
Chief of Staff **Sharon Sobol Jordan** .... (216) 443-7372
Education: Indiana 1981 BPA; Ohio State 1984 JD
Deputy Chief of Staff for Economic Development
Nathan "Nate" Kelly .... (216) 263-4605
E-mail: nkelly@cuyahogacounty.us
Deputy Chief of Staff for Health and Human Services
Dave Merriman .... (216) 698-2064
Deputy Chief of Staff for Operations **(Vacant)** .... (216) 698-2100
Chief Communications Officer **Eliza Wing** .... (216) 348-4395
E-mail: ewing@cuyahogacounty.us
Director of Communications **Mary Louise Madigan** ... (216) 698-5637
Director of Regional Collaboration **Edward Kraus** .... (216) 698-3022
E-mail: ekraus@cuyahogacounty.us
▷ Director of Law **Robert J. Triozzi** .... (216) 698-6549
E-mail: rtriozzi@cuyahogacounty.us

Office of the Fiscal Officer

2079 East Ninth Street, Cleveland, OH 44115
Tel: (216) 443-7010 Fax: (216) 443-5090
Internet: http://fiscalofficer.cuyahogacounty.us/

▷ Fiscal Officer **Dennis Kennedy** .... (216) 443-7010
Education: Cleveland State BA
Deputy Fiscal Officer **(Vacant)** .... (216) 443-7010

★ Elected Official ▲ Appointed by Legislature ▼ Appointed by Governor ► Appointed by Board or Commission ● Appointed by Judge
■ Appointed by Mayor △ Appointed by Freeholders ▽ Appointed by Supervisor ▷ Appointed by County Executive ○ Appointed by Council

Office of Budget and Management
2079 East Ninth Street, Third Floor, Cleveland, OH 44115
Fax: (216) 443-7256

▶ Director (Interim) **Chris Murray** . . . . (216) 443-7220
E-mail: cmurray@cuyahogacounty.us

Treasurer's Office
2079 East Ninth Street, First Floor, Cleveland, OH 44115
Fax: (216) 443-7463 Internet: www.treasurer.cuyahogacounty.us

▷ Treasurer **Chris Murray** . . . . (216) 443-7400
Administrator/Human Resources **Bruce L. Nimrick** . . . . . . (216) 443-7409
Tax Administrator **Michael M. Sweeney** . . . . . . (216) 443-5872
E-mail: msweeney@cuyahogacounty.us
Supervisor of Investments **Rebecca Ruffing** . . . . . . (216) 443-7567
Director of Community Programs and Outreach
Patricia Cooney . . . . (216) 443-2149
E-mail: pcooney@cuyahogacounty.us
Facilities Manager **Gerald P. Murphy** . . . . . . (216) 443-7408
E-mail: gmurphy@cuyahogacounty.us

Cuyahoga County Board of Revision
2079 East Ninth Street, Second Floor, Cleveland, OH 44115
Fax: (216) 443-8282 E-mail: bor@cuyahogacounty.us
Internet: http://bor.cuyahogacounty.us/

Administrator **Shelley Davis** . . . . (216) 443-7195

Cuyahoga County Budget Commission
2079 East Ninth Street, Cleveland, OH 44115
Fax: (216) 698-5790

Director **Bryan Dunn** . . . . (216) 443-2134
E-mail: bdunn@cuyahogacounty.us

Department of Consumer Affairs
2079 East Ninth Street, Cleveland, OH 44115
Tel: (216) 443-7010

Director **Sheryl Harris** . . . . (216) 443-7010

Office of Health and Human Services
2079 East Ninth Street, Suite 4-200, Cleveland, OH 44115
Fax: (216) 443-5884

▷ Director of Human Services (Interim) **Matt Carroll** . . . . (216) 443-7032
E-mail: mpcarroll@cuyahogacounty.us
Education: Brown U 1986 BA; Georgetown 1989 JD

Division of Children and Family Services [DCFS]
Jane Edna Hunter Building, 3955 Euclid Avenue, Cleveland, OH 44115
Fax: (216) 432-5047 Internet: http://cfs.cuyahogacounty.us/

Director **Thomas Pristow** . . . . (216) 432-2273
Education: Maryland MSW

Cuyahoga Job and Family Services
Virgil E. Brown Center, 1641 Payne Avenue, Cleveland, OH 44114
Fax: (216) 987-8183 Internet: http://cjfs.cuyahogacounty.us/

Director **David Merriman** . . . . (216) 987-6640

Department of Senior and Adult Services [DSAS]
Mount Pleasant NFSC, 13815 Kinsman Road, Cleveland, OH 44120
Fax: (216) 420-6600 Internet: http://dsas.cuyahogacounty.us/

Director **Richard Jones** . . . . (216) 420-6755

Cuyahoga Job and Family Services, Office of Child Support Services
1640 Superior Avenue, Cleveland, OH 44114
P.O. Box 93318, Cleveland, OH 44101-5318
Fax: (216) 515-8484 E-mail: cuycsea@odjfs.state.oh.us

▷ Administrator **Dave Merriman** . . . . (216) 443-5100

Department of Human Resources
2079 East Ninth Street, Suite 7-200, Cleveland, OH 44115
Tel: (216) 443-7190 Fax: (216) 443-5858
E-mail: humanresources@cuyahogacounty.us
Internet: http://hr.cuyahogacounty.us/

▷ Director (Interim) **Ed Morales** . . . . (216) 443-6984
E-mail: emorales@cuyahogacounty.us

Office of the Inspector General
2079 East Ninth Street, Sixth Floor, Cleveland, OH 44115

▷ Inspector General **Mark Griffin** . . . . (216) 698-2101
Education: Case Western 1994 JD

Office of the Medical Examiner
Gerber Building, 11001 Cedar Avenue, Cleveland, OH 44106
Tel: (216) 721-5610 Fax: (216) 721-2559
Internet: http://medicalexaminer.cuyahogacounty.us/

▷ Medical Examiner **Dr. Thomas P. "Tom" Gilson** . . . . . . (216) 721-5610
Education: Medical Col (PA) 1988 MD

Office of Procurement and Diversity [OPD]
1219 Ontario Street, Room 110, Cleveland, OH 44113
Tel: (216) 443-7200 Fax: (216) 443-7206
E-mail: opd@cuyahogacounty.us Internet: www.opd.cuyahogacounty.us

Director **Lenora M. Lockett** . . . . (216) 443-7487
E-mail: llockett@cuyahogacounty.us
Purchasing Manager **Richard Opre** . . . . (216) 443-7203
E-mail: ropre@cuyahogacounty.us

Office of the Sheriff
Justice Center, 1215 West Third Street, Cleveland, OH 44113
Tel: (216) 443-6000 Fax: (216) 348-4353
E-mail: shcuy@cuyahogacounty.us
Internet: http://sheriff.cuyahogacounty.us/

▷ Sheriff **Clifford "Cliff" Pinkney** . . . . (216) 443-6000
E-mail: cpinkney@cuyahogacounty.us

Cuyahoga County Archives
2905 Franklin Blvd. NW, Cleveland, OH 44113
Fax: (216) 443-3636 E-mail: archive@cuyahogacounty.us

Manager **Dr. Judith G. Cetina** . . . . (216) 443-7250

Department of Development
2079 East Ninth Street, Seventh Floor, Cleveland, OH 44115
Tel: (216) 443-7260 Fax: (216) 443-7258
Internet: http://development.cuyahogacounty.us/

▶ Director **Ted Carter** . . . . (216) 443-7275
E-mail: tcarter@cuyahogacounty.us

Cuyahoga County Airport - Robert D. Shea Field
26300 Curtiss Wright Parkway, Cleveland, OH 44143
Fax: (216) 289-4113 E-mail: ccairport@cuyahogacounty.us

Manager (Acting) **Bonita G. "Bonnie" Teeuwen** . . . . . . (216) 289-4111

Public Safety and Justice Services Department
2079 East Ninth Street, Fifth Floor, Cleveland, OH 44115
Tel: (216) 443-7265 Fax: (216) 443-5656
Internet: http://ja.cuyahogacounty.us/

Director (Acting) **Brandy Carney** . . . . (216) 443-7265
E-mail: bcarney@cuyahogacounty.us
Deputy Chief of Staff for Public Safety and Justice
Services **(Vacant)** . . . . (216) 698-2701
Assistant Deputy Chief **(Vacant)** . . . . (216) 443-3761
Manager, Cuyahoga County Emergency Management
Agency **Brandy Carney** . . . . (216) 443-5691
E-mail: bcarney@cuyahogacounty.us

★ Elected Official ▲ Appointed by Legislature ▼ Appointed by Governor ▶ Appointed by Board or Commission ● Appointed by Judge
■ Appointed by Mayor △ Appointed by Freeholders ▽ Appointed by Supervisor ▷ Appointed by County Executive ○ Appointed by Council

Public Safety and Justice Services Department *continued*

Manager, Cuyahoga Regional Information System (CRIS) **(Vacant)** .... (216) 443-7940
Business Services Manager **Mary Beth Vaughn** .... (216) 443-5906
Grants and Training Manager **(Vacant)** .... (216) 443-7265
Fax: (216) 443-5681
Witness/Victim Services Manager **Jill Smialek** .... (216) 443-7347
Human Resources Administrator **Emina Pauneskü** ...... (216) 348-3993

Educational Service Center of Cuyahoga County [ESC]

6393 Oak Tree Boulevard, Independence, OH 44130
Tel: (216) 524-3000 Fax: (216) 524-3683 E-mail: info@esc-cc.org
Internet: www.esc-cc.org

Superintendent **Dr. Robert A. "Bob" Mengerink** .... (216) 524-3000
Education: Edinboro BSEd; Cleveland State MSEd; Akron DEd

Cuyahoga County Department of Information Technology

2079 East Ninth Street, Sixth Floor, Cleveland, OH 44115
Tel: (216) 443-8010 Fax: (216) 443-7363
Internet: http://isc.cuyahogacounty.us/

▷ Chief Information Officer **Jeff B. Mowry** ...... (216) 443-8010 ext. 8011
E-mail: jmowry@cuyahogacounty.us
Education: Ashland 1989 BS; Central Michigan 1992 MS

Cleveland Metroparks

4101 Fulton Parkway, Cleveland, OH 44144-1923
Fax: (216) 635-3286 Internet: www.clemetparks.com

President, Board of Park Commissioners **Dan T. Moore** .. (216) 635-3200
Executive Director/Secretary **Brian M. Zimmerman** ..... (216) 635-3200
Education: Wisconsin BS

Cuyahoga County Public Library

2111 Snow Road, Parma, OH 44134-2728
Tel: (216) 398-1800 Tel: (800) 749-5560 Fax: (216) 749-9500
Internet: www.cuyahogalibrary.org

Year Founded: 1923

Administration

Executive Director **Sari Feldman** .... (216) 749-9490
E-mail: sfeldman@cuyahogalibrary.org
Education: SUNY (Binghamton) BA; Wisconsin 1977 MLS
Deputy Director **Tracy Strobel** .... (216) 749-9419
E-mail: tstrobel@cuyahogalibrary.org

Cuyahoga Metropolitan Housing Authority [CMHA]

1441 W. 25th St., Cleveland, OH 44113
Tel: (216) 348-5000 Fax: (216) 348-4925 Internet: www.cmha.net

Chairperson **Ronnie A. Dunn** .... (216) 348-5000
Chief Executive Officer **Jeffrey K. Patterson** .... (216) 348-5031
Education: Mount Union; Baldwin-Wallace MBA

The MetroHealth System (MetroHealth Medical Center)

2500 MetroHealth Drive, Cleveland, OH 44109-1998
Tel: (216) 778-5700 Fax: (216) 778-1166 Internet: www.metrohealth.org

President and Chief Executive Officer **Dr. Akram Boutros** .... (216) 778-7800

Board of Trustees

2500 MetroHealth Drive, Cleveland, OH 44109-1998
Tel: (216) 778-2020 Fax: (216) 778-5900

Chairman **Thomas M. McDonald** .... (216) 778-2020
Term Expires: 2020

The Elisabeth Severance Prentiss Center - Skilled Nursing Care at MetroHealth

3525 Scranton Road, SW, Cleveland, OH 44109
Fax: (216) 957-8096

Administrator **Christina Szatala** .... (216) 957-8898

Department of Sustainability

2079 East Ninth Street, Cleveland, OH 44115
Tel: (216) 443-3055

Director **Mike Foley** (D) .... (216) 443-3055
Education: Dayton BA; Cleveland-Marshall JD
Deputy Director **Shanelle Smith** .... (216) 443-3785

Department of Public Works

2079 East Ninth Street, Fifth Floor, Cleveland, OH 44115
Tel: (216) 443-6992 Fax: (216) 443-7663
Internet: http://publicworks.cuyahogacounty.us/

▶ Director **Michael W. Dever** .... (216) 698-2058
E-mail: mdever@cuyahogacounty.us
Maintenance Administrator **John Myers** .... (216) 348-3800
E-mail: jmyers@cuyahogacounty.us
Planning and Fiscal Administrator **Stanley D. Kosilesky** .... (216) 348-3800
Fleet Services Manager **John Pinter** .... (216) 661-2800

Office of the County Engineer

2079 East Ninth Street, Fifth Floor, Cleveland, OH 44115
Fax: (216) 348-3896 E-mail: county@cuyctyengineers.org
Internet: www.cuyctyengineers.org

▷ County Engineer **David E. Marquard** .... (216) 348-3808
E-mail: marquard1@cuyahogacounty.us
MIS Coordinator **Joe Conway** .... (216) 348-3875
E-mail: jconway@cuyahogacounty.us

Alcohol, Drug Addiction and Mental Health Services Board of Cuyahoga County [ADAMHSCC]

2012 West 25th Street, 6th Floor, Cleveland, OH 44113
Fax: (216) 861-5067 Internet: www.adamhscc.org

Chair **Eugenia Cash** .... (216) 241-3400

Board Staff

Chief Executive Officer **William M. Denihan** .... (216) 241-3400
Director of External Affairs **Scott Osiecki** ...... (216) 241-3400 ext. 814
E-mail: osiecki@adamhscc.org

Cuyahoga County Board of Developmental Disabilities [CCBDD]

Michael A. Donzella Administration Building, 1275 Lakeside Avenue, Cleveland, OH 44114
Tel: (216) 241-8230 Fax: (216) 861-0253 Internet: www.cuyahogabdd.org

President **Ara A. Bagdasarian** .... (216) 241-8230
Vice President **Steven M. Licciardi**
Secretary **Tania Younkin** .... (216) 241-8230
Member **David Crampton** .... (216) 241-8230

Board Staff

Superintendent **Kelly Connor Petty** .... (216) 241-8230

Cuyahoga County Board of Elections

2925 Euclid Avenue, Cleveland, OH 44115
Tel: (216) 443-3200 Fax: (216) 443-6633
Internet: http://boe.cuyahogacounty.us/

Chairwoman **Inajo Davis Chappell** .... (216) 443-6436
Term Expires: February 28, 2017
Education: Yale 1982 BA; Columbia 1985 JD
Director **Pat McDonald** .... (216) 443-6411

★ Elected Official ▲ Appointed by Legislature ▼ Appointed by Governor ▶ Appointed by Board or Commission ● Appointed by Judge
■ Appointed by Mayor △ Appointed by Freeholders ▽ Appointed by Supervisor ▷ Appointed by County Executive ○ Appointed by Council

Cuyahoga County Board of Health [CCBH]
5550 Venture Drive, Parma, OH 44130
Fax: (216) 676-1311

President **Debbie Moss** ....(216) 201-2000

Administration
Health Commissioner
Terrence M. "Terry" Allan ....(216) 201-2001 ext. 1100

Planning Commission
2079 East Ninth Street, Fifth Floor, Cleveland, OH 44115
Fax: (216) 443-3737 E-mail: cpc@planning.co.cuyahoga.oh.us
Internet: http://planning.co.cuyahoga.oh.us/

Director **Glenn Coyne** .... (216) 443-3700

Public Defender Commission
Courthouse Square Building, 310 West Lakeside Avenue, Suite 400, Cleveland, OH 44113
Fax: (216) 443-3632 Internet: www.publicdefender.cuyahogacounty.us

▶ Chief Public Defender **Robert L. Tobik** ....(216) 443-7223
E-mail: rtobik@cuyahogacounty.us

Office of the County Council
2079 East Ninth Street, Eighth Floor, Cleveland, OH 44115
Tel: (216) 698-2010 Fax: (216) 698-2040
Internet: http://council.cuyahogacounty.us/

★ President **Daniel R. "Dan" Brady** (D-District 3) .... (216) 698-2014
Term Expires: December 31, 2018
E-mail: dbrady@cuyahogacounty.us
Education: Ohio 1976 BA

★ Vice President **Pernel Jones, Jr.** (D-District 8) .... (216) 698-2019
Term Expires: December 31, 2020
E-mail: pjones@cuyahogacounty.us

★ Council Member **Dave Greenspan** (R-District 1)........(216) 698-2047
Term Expires: December 31, 2018
E-mail: dgreenspan@cuyahogacounty.us

★ Council Member **Dale Miller** (D-District 2) .... (216) 698-2011
Term Expires: December 31, 2016
E-mail: damiller@cuyahogacounty.us
Date of Birth: September 16, 1949
Education: Case Western 1971 BS; Utah 1976 PhD

★ Council Member
Charles M. "Chuck" Germana (D-District 4) .... (216) 698-2013
Term Expires: December 31, 2016
E-mail: cgermana@cuyahogacounty.us
Date of Birth: October 23, 1946
Education: Ohio 1968 AB

★ Council Member **Michael J. Gallagher** (R-District 5)....(216) 698-2015
Term Expires: December 31, 2018
E-mail: mjgallagher@cuyahogacounty.us
Education: Cleveland State BA

★ Council Member **Jack H. Schron, Jr.** (R-District 6) ..... (216) 698-2016
Term Expires: December 31, 2020
E-mail: jschron@cuyahogacounty.us
Education: Florida Southern 1970 BS; Ohio Northern 1975 JD

★ Council Member **Yvonne M. Conwell** (D-District 7).....(216) 698-2017
Term Expires: December 31, 2018
E-mail: yconwell@cuyahogacounty.us

★ Council Member **Shontel M. Brown** (D-District 9)......(216) 698-2023
Term Expires: December 31, 2018
E-mail: sbrown@cuyahogacounty.us

★ Council Member **Anthony T. Hairston** (D-District 10) ... (216) 698-2022
Term Expires: December 31, 2020
E-mail: ahairston@cuyahogacounty.us

★ Council Member **Sunny M. Simon** (D-District 11)...... (216) 698-2035
Term Expires: December 31, 2018
E-mail: ssimon@cuyahogacounty.us

Chief of Staff **Joseph A. Nanni** .... (216) 698-2520
Education: Ohio State

Office of the County Council *continued*

○ Clerk of the Council **Jeanne M. Schmotzer** .... (216) 698-2020
E-mail: jschmotzer@cuyahogacounty.us

Deputy Clerk of the Council **Janine D. Carter** ....(216) 698-7208
E-mail: jdcarter@cuyahogacounty.us

Research and Policy Analyst/Special Counsel
Michael W. King .... (216) 443-6118

Office of the Prosecutor
Justice Center–Courts Tower, 1200 Ontario St., 9th Floor, Cleveland, OH 44113
Tel: (216) 443-7800 Fax: (216) 698-2270
E-mail: prosecutor@cuyahogacounty.us
Internet: http://prosecutor.cuyahogacounty.us/

★ Prosecuting Attorney **Timothy J. McGinty** (D) ....(216) 443-7800
Term Expires: December 31, 2016
Education: Heidelberg 1972 BA; Cleveland-Marshall 1981 JD; Nevada (Reno) 2000 MA

First Assistant Prosecuting Attorney **Duane J. Deskins**...(216) 443-7800
Civil Division Litigation Manager **Charles Hannan** ......(216) 443-7800
Special Investigations Division Chief **Richard Bell** ....(216) 443-7800
Criminal Division Chief **Andrew Nichol** ....(216) 443-7800

County of Dakota, Minnesota
1590 Highway 55, Hastings, MN 55033-2343
Tel: (651) 437-3191

County Seat: Hastings **Election Type:** Nonpartisan
Population: 414,686 (2015)

Board of Commissioners
1590 Highway 55, Hastings, MN 55033-2343
Tel: (651) 438-4418

★ Chair **Nancy Schouweiler** (District 4) ....(651) 438-4430
Term Expires: December 2016
E-mail: nancy.schouweiler@co.dakota.mn.us

★ Commissioner **Mike Slavik** (District 1) ....(651) 438-4427
Term Expires: December 2018
E-mail: mike.slavik@co.dakota.mn.us

★ Commissioner **Kathleen A. Gaylord** (District 2)........(651) 438-4428
Term Expires: December 31, 2018
E-mail: kathleen.gaylord@co.dakota.mn.us

★ Commissioner **Thomas A. Egan** (District 3) .... (651) 438-4429
Term Expires: December 2016
E-mail: thomas.egan@co.dakota.mn.us

★ Commissioner **Liz Workman** (District 5)...............(651) 438-4431
Term Expires: December 2016
E-mail: liz.workman@co.dakota.mn.us

★ Commissioner **Mary Liz Holberg** (District 6)...........(651) 438-4418
Term Expires: December 2018

★ Commissioner **Chris Gerlach** (District 7) .... (651) 438-4411
Term Expires: December 2016
E-mail: chris.gerlach@co.dakota.mn.us
Education: U St Thomas (MN) BA; South Dakota MBA

County Manager
Tel: (651) 438-4418

▶ County Manager **Brandt Richardson** .... (651) 438-4418
E-mail: brandt.richardson@co.dakota.mn.us

Deputy County Manager **Matt Smith** .... (651) 438-4418
E-mail: matt.smith@co.dakota.mn.us

Senior Administrative Coordinator to the Board
Kelly Olson...(651) 438-4417
E-mail: kelly.olson@co.dakota.mn.us

★ Elected Official ▲ Appointed by Legislature ▼ Appointed by Governor ▶ Appointed by Board or Commission ● Appointed by Judge
■ Appointed by Mayor △ Appointed by Freeholders ▽ Appointed by Supervisor ▷ Appointed by County Executive ○ Appointed by Council

Communications Office
Tel: (651) 438-8179

Director **Mary Beth Schubert** . . . . . (651) 438-8179

Employee Relations Department
Tel: (651) 438-4435 Fax: (651) 438-8178

Director **Nancy Hohbach** . . . . . (651) 438-4435

Financial Services Department
Tel: (651) 438-4585

Director **Stephanie Shawback** . . . . . (651) 438-4585

Community Services Division
One Mendota Road West, Suite 500, Saint Paul, MN 55118-4473
Tel: (651) 554-5742 Fax: (651) 554-5948

Director **Kelly Harder** . . . . . (651) 554-5742
E-mail: Kelly.harder@co.dakota.mn.us

Community Corrections
1560 Highway 55, Hastings, MN 55033-2343
Tel: (651) 438-8288 Fax: (651) 438-8340

Director **Barbara J. Illsley** . . . . . (651) 554-6060
E-mail: barbara.illsley@co.dakota.mn.us

Department of Employment and Economic Assistance
One Mendota Road West, Suite 100, Saint Paul, MN 55118-4473
Tel: (651) 554-5611

Director **Martha "Marti" Fischbach** . . . . . (651) 554-5611
Fax: (651) 554-5709

Dakota County Public Health Department
One Mendota Road West, Suite 410, Saint Paul, MN 55118-4473
Tel: (651) 554-6100 Fax: (651) 554-6130

Director **Bonnie Brueshoff** . . . . . (651) 554-6100

Social Services
14955 Galaxie Avenue West, Apple Valley, MN 55124
Tel: (952) 891-7400 Fax: (952) 891-7473

Director **Andrea Zuber** . . . . . (952) 891-7400
E-mail: andrea.zuber@co.dakota.mn.us

Veterans Services
Tel: (651) 554-5601 Fax: (651) 554-5839

Director **Lisa Thomas** . . . . . (651) 554-5601

Information Technology Department
Tel: (651) 438-4270 Fax: (651) 438-8832

Director **Dan Cater** . . . . . (651) 438-4270
E-mail: dan.cater@co.dakota.mn.us

Office of Performance and Analysis
Manager **Jessica Parker-Carlson** . . . . . (651) 438-4529
Planning Supervisor **Kurt Chatfield** . . . . . (952) 891-7022

Physical Development Division
14955 Galaxie Avenue West, Apple Valley, MN 55124
Tel: (952) 891-7000 Fax: (952) 891-7031

Director **Steve Mielke** . . . . . (952) 891-7000
E-mail: steven.mielke@co.dakota.mn.us

Office of Geographic Information Systems
Tel: (952) 891-7081

Manager **Randy Knippel** . . . . . (952) 891-7081

Surveyor's Office
Tel: (952) 891-7087 Fax: (952) 891-7097

County Surveyor **Todd B. Tollefson** . . . . . (952) 891-7087

Environmental Resources Office
Tel: (952) 891-7000

Director **Georg Fischer** . . . . . (952) 891-7000

Parks Department
Tel: (952) 891-7000 Fax: (952) 891-7031

Director **Steven Sullivan** . . . . . (952) 891-7000

Transportation Department
Tel: (952) 891-7100 Fax: (952) 891-7127

Director and County Engineer **Mark Krebsbach** . . . . . (952) 891-7100
E-mail: mark.krebsbach@co.dakota.mn.us

Public Services and Revenue Division
Tel: (651) 438-4576 Fax: (651) 438-8260

Director **Thomas V. "Tom" Novak** . . . . . (651) 438-4366
Deputy Director **Jean Erickson** . . . . . (651) 438-4286

Assessing Services Department
Tel: (651) 438-4200 Fax: (651) 438-4469

Assessor **Teresa Mitchell** . . . . . (651) 438-4200

Property Taxation and Records Department
Tel: (651) 438-4576

Director **Joel Beckman** . . . . . (651) 438-4576
E-mail: joel.beckman@co.dakota.mn.us

Service and License Center Department
14955 Galaxie Avenue West, Apple Valley, MN 55124
Tel: (952) 891-7570

Director **Kathy Jensen** . . . . . (952) 891-7570

County Attorney's Office
1560 Highway 55, Hastings, MN 55033-2343
Tel: (651) 438-4438 Fax: (651) 438-4499
Internet: www.co.dakota.mn.us/departments/attorney

★ County Attorney **James C. Backstrom** . . . . . (651) 438-4438
Term Expires: December 31, 2018
E-mail: attorney@co.dakota.mn.us

Sheriff's Office
Law Enforcement Center, 1580 Highway 55, Hastings, MN 55033-2343
Tel: (651) 438-4700 Fax: (651) 438-4709

★ Sheriff **Tim Leslie** . . . . . (651) 438-4710
Term Expires: December 2018
E-mail: tim.leslie@co.dakota.mn.us
Chief Deputy **Joseph "Joe" Leko** . . . . . (651) 438-4710
Emergency Preparedness Coordinator **Dan Carlson** . . . . . (651) 438-4703
Administrative Captain **Patrick "Pat" Enderlein** . . . . . (651) 438-4710
E-mail: patrick.enderlein@co.dakota.mn.us

Detention Services
Commander **Daniel "Dan" Scheuermann** . . . . . (651) 438-4800
Jail Administrator **Richard "Rick" Schroeder** . . . . . (651) 438-4800

Operations
Commander **John Grant** . . . . . (651) 438-4720
E-mail: john.grant@co.dakota.mn.us
Supervisor, Investigation Division
James "Jim" Rogers . . . . . (651) 438-4720
Supervisor, Patrol Division **Daniel "Dan" Bianconi** . . . . . (651) 438-4750

COUNTIES

★ Elected Official ▲ Appointed by Legislature ▼ Appointed by Governor ▶ Appointed by Board or Commission ● Appointed by Judge
■ Appointed by Mayor △ Appointed by Freeholders ▽ Appointed by Supervisor ▷ Appointed by County Executive ○ Appointed by Council

COUNTIES

County of Dallas, Texas

County Administration Bldg., 411 Elm Street, Dallas, TX 75202
Tel: (214) 653-7361 (Information) Internet: www.dallascounty.org

County Seat: Dallas **Election Type:** Partisan **Population:** 2,553,385 (2015)

Office of the County Judge and Commissioners

County Administration Bldg., 411 Elm St., Dallas, TX 75202
Tel: (214) 653-7363

★ County Judge **Clay Lewis Jenkins** (D) .... (214) 653-7949
Term Expires: December 31, 2018
E-mail: cjenkins@dallascounty.org
Education: Baylor, 1987 JD
Chief of Staff **Lauren Mish** .... (214) 653-7949

★ Commissioner **Dr. Theresa Daniel** (D-District 1) .... (214) 653-7552
Term Expires: December 31, 2016
E-mail: theresa.danielphd@dallascounty.org

★ Commissioner
Michael E. "Mike" Cantrell (R-District 2) .... (214) 653-6100
Term Expires: December 31, 2016
E-mail: mcantrell@dallascounty.org
Education: Abilene Christian BS; Southern Methodist 1982 JD
Chief of Staff **Traci Enna** .... (214) 589-7060

★ Commissioner **John Wiley Price** (D-District 3) .... (214) 653-6671
Term Expires: December 31, 2016
E-mail: jprice@dallascounty.org

★ Commissioner **Dr. Elba Garcia** (D-District 4) .... (214) 653-6670
Term Expires: December 31, 2018 Fax: (214) 653-7057
E-mail: elba.garciadds@dallascounty.org
Education: U A Metropolitana 1984; Baylor Col Dentistry 1990 DDS

▶ Administrator **Darryl Martin** .... (214) 653-7328
E-mail: darryl.martin@dallascounty.org
Education: SUNY (Albany) BSW, MSW

▶ Assistant Administrator for Governmental Affairs
Charles Reed .... (214) 653-7363
E-mail: charles.reed@dallascounty.org

▶ Assistant Administrator for Operations **Gordon Hikel** ... (214) 653-7650
E-mail: gordon.hikel@dallascounty.org

Office of the Auditor

Records Bldg., 509 Main Street, Room 407, Dallas, TX 75202
Fax: (214) 653-6440

● County Auditor **Darryl Thomas** .... (214) 653-7221

Office of Budget and Evaluation

County Administration Bldg., 411 Elm St., Dallas, TX 75202
Fax: (214) 653-6517 E-mail: budget@dallascounty.org

▶ Budget Officer **Ryan Brown** .... (214) 653-6384
E-mail: rbrown@dallascounty.org

Office of Extension Services (Texas A&M University)

N. Dallas Government Center, 10056 Marsh Lane, Suite B-10, Dallas, TX 75229
Fax: (214) 904-3080

Director **Dale Groom** .... (214) 904-3050

Office of the Public Defender

Frank Crowley Courts Bldg., 133 N. Industrial Blvd, 9th Floor, Dallas, TX 75207
Fax: (214) 653-3539

▶ Chief Public Defender **Lynn Pride Richardson** .... (214) 653-3554
E-mail: lrichardson@dallascounty.org
Education: Florida 1982 JD

Alternative Dispute Resolution

George L. Allen Courts Bldg., 600 Commerce Street, 4th Floor, Room 681, Dallas, TX 75202
Fax: (214) 653-7891

Director **(Vacant)** .... (214) 653-7898

Child Support

Allen Courts Bldg., 600 Commerce St., Suite 128, Dallas, TX 75202
Fax: (214) 653-7574

Director **Angela Igrisan** .... (214) 653-7584

Communication and Information Services Department

County Administration Building, 411 Elm Street, Room 504, Dallas, TX 75202
Fax: (214) 653-6708

▶ Director/Chief Information Officer **Stanley Victrum** ..... (214) 653-7339
Education: Citadel 1982 BA; Naval Postgrad 1987 MS

Community Supervision and Corrections Department [CSCD]

Frank Crowley Courts Bldg., 133 N. Industrial Blvd., 9th Floor, Dallas, TX 75207
Fax: (214) 653-5217

● Director **Javed Syed** .... (214) 653-5183
E-mail: jsyed@dallascounty.org

Elections Department

2377 North Stemmons, Suite 820, Dallas, TX 75207
Fax: (214) 819-6301

▶ Elections Administrator **Toni Pippins-Poole** .... (214) 819-6335
E-mail: tpippins@dallascounty.org

Forensic Sciences Institute

5230 Medical Center Dr., Dallas, TX 75235

▶ Director **Dr. Jeffrey J. Barnard** .... (214) 920-5900
E-mail: jbarnard@dallascounty.org

Dallas County Fire Marshal's Office

Old Criminal Courts Building, 509 Main Street, Dallas, TX 75202
Fax: (214) 904-3080

▶ Fire Marshal **Robert De Los Santos** .... (214) 653-7980
E-mail: robert.delossantos@dallascounty.org

Dallas County Health and Human Services Department [DCHHS]

2377 North Stemmons Freeway, Dallas, TX 75207
Fax: (214) 819-2107 Internet: www.dallascounty.org/department/hhs

▶ Director **Zachary S. Thompson** .... (214) 819-2100
E-mail: zthompson@dallascounty.org
Medical Director **Christopher Perkins** .... (214) 819-2023

Human Resources/Civil Service Department

Records Building, 509 Main Street, Room 103, Dallas, TX 75202
Fax: (214) 653-7616

▶ Director **Mattye Mauldin-Taylor** .... (214) 653-7668
E-mail: mmauldin-taylor@dallascounty.org

Juvenile Services Department

2600 Lone Star Drive, Dallas, TX 75212
Fax: (214) 698-5508

Director **Dr. Terry Smith** .... (214) 698-2200

★ Elected Official ▲ Appointed by Legislature ▼ Appointed by Governor ▶ Appointed by Board or Commission ● Appointed by Judge
■ Appointed by Mayor △ Appointed by Freeholders ▽ Appointed by Supervisor ▷ Appointed by County Executive ○ Appointed by Council

Metrocare Services
1345 River Bend Drive, Suite 200, Dallas, TX 75247-6945
Tel: (214) 743-1200 Fax: (214) 630-3469
Internet: www.metrocareservices.org

▶ Chief Executive Officer **Dr. John Burruss** .... (214) 743-1200

Planning and Development Department
County Administration Building, 411 Elm Street, Dallas, TX 75202
Fax: (214) 653-7057

Director **Rick Loessberg** .... (214) 653-7601
E-mail: rloessberg@dallascounty.org

Public Works Department
County Administration Bldg., 411 Elm St., Dallas, TX 75202
Fax: (214) 653-6445

▶ Director **Alberta L. Blair** .... (214) 653-6400
E-mail: alberta.blair@dallascounty.org
Education: Texas A&M (Corpus Christi) 1983 BS

Administrative Assistant/Office Manager
Lacey Freeman .... (214) 653-7541
E-mail: lacey.freeman@dallascounty.org

Purchasing Department
Records Building, 509 Main Street, Room 623, Dallas, TX 75202
Tel: (214) 653-7431 Fax: (214) 653-7449
Internet: www.dallascounty.org/department/purchasing

▶ Purchasing Agent **Daniel R. Garza** .... (214) 653-7431

Dallas Central Appraisal District [DCAD]
2949 N. Stemmons Freeway, Dallas, TX 75247

Chief Tax Appraiser **Ken Nolan** .... (214) 631-0520
E-mail: nolank@dcad.org

Veterans' Services Office
2377 Stemmons Freeway, 6th Floor, Dallas, TX 75207-2710
Fax: (214) 819-2880

▶ Director **Tracy Y. Little** .... (972) 692-4939
E-mail: tlittle@dallascounty.org

Office of the County Clerk
Records Bldg., 509 Main Street, 2nd Floor, Dallas, TX 75202
Fax: (214) 653-7176 Tel: (214) 653-7099

★ County Clerk **John Warren** (D) .... (214) 653-7131
Term Expires: December 31, 2018
E-mail: jwarren@dallascounty.org

Office of the County Tax Assessor/ Collector
Records Bldg., 500 Main Street, 1st floor, Dallas, TX 75202
Fax: (214) 653-7887

★ County Tax Assessor/Collector **John R. Ames** (D) .... (214) 653-7811
Term Expires: December 31, 2016
E-mail: jrames@dallascounty.org

Office of the County Treasurer
Records Bldg., 509 Main Street, Room 303, Dallas, TX 75202
Fax: (214) 653-7705

★ County Treasurer **Pauline Medrano** (D) .... (214) 653-7321
Term Expires: December 31, 2018
Education: Texas (Arlington) 1976 BA

Office of the County Sheriff
Frank Crowley Courts Bldg., 133 N. Industrial Blvd., Suite LB-31, Dallas, TX 75207-4399
Fax: (214) 653-3420

★ County Sheriff **Lupe Valdez** (D) .... (214) 749-8641
Term Expires: December 31, 2016
E-mail: lvaldez@dallascounty.org

Office of the District Attorney
Frank Crowley Courts Building, 133 North Riverfront Boulevard, Suite LB-19, Dallas, TX 75207-4399
Fax: (214) 653-2924 Internet: www.dallasda.com

★ District Attorney **Susan Hawk** (R) .... (214) 653-3600
Term Expires: December 31, 2018
E-mail: districtattorney@dallascounty.org

First Assistant District Attorney **Messina Madson** ...... (214) 653-3600

Office of the District Clerk
Allen Courts Bldg., 600 Commerce St., Dallas, TX 75202
Fax: (214) 653-7966

★ District Clerk **Felicia Pitre** (D) .... (214) 653-7421
Term Expires: December 31, 2018

County of Dane, Wisconsin
City-County Building, 210 Martin Luther King, Jr. Boulevard, Madison, WI 53703
Tel: (608) 266-4114 (Information) Internet: www.countyofdane.com

County Seat: Madison **Election Type:** Partisan **Population:** 523,643 (2015)

Office of the County Executive
City-County Building, 210 Martin Luther King, Jr. Boulevard, Room 421, Madison, WI 53703
Tel: (608) 266-4114 Fax: (608) 266-2643
Internet: www.countyofdane.com/exec

★ County Executive **Joseph T. "Joe" Parisi** (D) .... (608) 266-4114
Term Expires: April 2017
Date of Birth: October 24, 1960
Education: Wisconsin BA

Chief of Staff **Josh Wescott** .... (608) 266-9069
Education: Wisconsin (Stevens Point) BA

Cultural Affairs Director **Mark J. Fraire** .... (608) 266-5915
Equal Opportunity Director **Isadore Knox, Jr.** .... (608) 266-4192
Legislative Lobbyist **Mary Ann "Mickey" Beil** .... (608) 266-4576
Social Media Director **(Vacant)** .... (608) 267-8823
Community Relations Director **(Vacant)** .... (608) 266-4296

Corporation Counsel's Office
City-County Building, 210 Martin Luther King, Jr. Boulevard, Room 419, Madison, WI 53703
Tel: (608) 266-4355 Fax: (608) 267-1556
Internet: www.countyofdane.com/corpcnsl

Corporation Counsel **Marcia A. MacKenzie** .... (608) 266-4355

Extension Office
5201 Fen Oak Drive, Room 138, Madison, WI 53718
Fax: (608) 224-3727 Internet: http://dane.uwex.edu/

Director **Carrie Edgar** .... (608) 224-3706

★ Elected Official ▲ Appointed by Legislature ▼ Appointed by Governor ▶ Appointed by Board or Commission ● Appointed by Judge
■ Appointed by Mayor △ Appointed by Freeholders ▽ Appointed by Supervisor ▷ Appointed by County Executive ○ Appointed by Council

COUNTIES

Medical Examiner's Office
115 West Doty Street, Room 2144, Madison, WI 53703
Internet: www.countyofdane.com/examiner

Chief Medical Examiner **Dr. Vincent Tranchida** .... (608) 284-6000

Veterans Service Office
1919 Alliant Energy Center Way, Madison, WI 53713
E-mail: vets@countyofdane.com
Internet: www.countyofdane.com/veterans

Veterans Service Officer **Daniel Connery** .... (608) 266-4158

Department of Administration
City-County Building, 210 Martin Luther King, Jr. Boulevard, Room 425, Madison, WI 53703
Tel: (608) 266-4941 Fax: (608) 266-4425
Internet: www.countyofdane.com/admin

▷ Director (Interim) **Carlos Pabellon** .... (608) 266-4941

Controller's Office
210 Martin Luther King, Jr. Boulevard, Room 426, Madison, WI 53703

Controller **Charles Hicklin** .... (608) 266-4109
E-mail: hicklin@countyofdane.com
Assistant Controller **Meg Krohn** .... (608) 266-4110
E-mail: krohn@countyofdane.com
Enterprise Budget Analyst **Helen Anderson** .... (608) 266-4570
Enterprise Budget Analyst **Joe Kroll** .... (608) 266-4171

Division of Information Management
210 Martin Luther King, Jr. Boulevard, Room 524, Madison, WI 53703

Applications Services Manager (Interim) **John Mueller** .. (608) 266-9047
Applications Services Manager (Interim) **Jon Hatley** ..... (608) 266-9047
Customer Service Manager **Peter Scott** .... (608) 266-4627
Technical Services Manager **Marvin Klang** .... (608) 266-4392

Purchasing Division
210 Martin Luther King, Jr. Boulevard, Room 425, Madison, WI 53703
E-mail: purchasing@countyofdane.com

Purchasing Agent **Carolyn Ninedorf** .... (608) 266-4966
E-mail: ninedorf.carolyn@countyofdane.com
Purchasing Agent **Peter Patten** .... (608) 267-3523
E-mail: patten.peter@countyofdane.com

Division of Risk Management
210 Martin Luther King, Jr. Boulevard, Room 425, Madison, WI 53703
Fax: (608) 283-2973

Risk Manager **Dan Lowndes** .... (608) 266-4134
E-mail: lowndes@countyofdane.com

Department of Emergency Management
115 West Doty Street, Room 2107, Madison, WI 53703-3202
Fax: (608) 266-4500 E-mail: emergency.management@countyofdane.com

▷ Director **Charles A. Tubbs** .... (608) 266-4330

Department of Human Services [DCDHS]
1202 Northport Drive, Madison, WI 53704
Tel: (608) 242-6200 Fax: (608) 242-6293
Internet: www.danecountyhumanservices.org

▷ Director **Lynn Green** .... (608) 242-6200
Education: Wisconsin MSW
Deputy Director **G.P. Foster** .... (608) 242-6431

Adult Community Services Division
1202 Northport Drive, Madison, WI 53704

Division Administrator **Fran Genter** .... (608) 242-6481
Fax: (608) 242-6531

Children, Youth and Families Division
1202 Northport Drive, 4th Floor, Madison, WI 53704

Division Administrator **Bob Lee** .... (608) 242-6474

Economic Assistance and Work Services Division
1819 Aberg Avenue, Suite D, Madison, WI 53704
Tel: (888) 794-5556 Internet: www.danejobs.com

Division Administrator **Shawn Tessmann** .... (608) 242-7463

Badger Prairie Health Care Center [BPHCC]
1100 East Verona Road, Madison, WI 53704
Fax: (608) 845-9271
Internet: www.danecountyhumanservices.org/badgerprairie

Administrator **William "Bill" Brotzman** .... (608) 845-1264

Land and Water Resources Department [LWRD]
Lyman F. Anderson Agriculture and Conservation Center, 5201 Fen Oak Drive, Room 208, Madison, WI 53718
Fax: (608) 224-3745 E-mail: lwrd@countyofdane.com

Director **Kevin Connors** .... (608) 224-3730
Deputy Director **Laura Hicklin** .... (608) 224-3765
Real Estate Coordinator **Jan Zimmermann** .... (608) 224-3761

Office of Lakes and Watersheds
5201 Fen Oak Drive, Room 234, Madison, WI 53718
E-mail: lakes@countyofdane.com

Watershed Management Coordinator **Susan Jones** ...... (608) 224-3730
Strategic Engagement Coordinator **Susan Sandford** ..... (608) 224-3730

Land Conservation Division
5201 Fen Oak Drive, Room 208, Madison, WI 53718
Fax: (608) 224-3745

County Conservationist **Amy Callis** .... (608) 224-3730

Parks Division
5201 Fen Oak Drive, Room 234, Madison, WI 53718
Fax: (608) 224-3774 E-mail: dane-parks@countyofdane.com

Director **Darren Marsh** .... (608) 224-3730
Acquisition and Planning Specialist **Sara Rigelman** ..... (608) 224-3611

Water Resource Engineering Division
5201 Fen Oak Drive, Room 208, Madison, WI 53718
Fax: (608) 224-3745

Manager **Jeremy Balousek** .... (608) 224-3730

Department of Planning and Development [DPD]
City-County Building, 210 Martin Luther King, Jr. Boulevard, Room 116, Madison, WI 53703
Fax: (608) 267-1540

▷ Director **Todd Violante** .... (608) 266-4251
▽ County Surveyor **Dan Frick** .... (608) 266-4252
Zoning Administrator **Roger Lane** .... (608) 266-9083
Land Division Review Officer **Daniel "Dan" Everson** ... (608) 267-1541

Community Analysis and Planning Division
30 West Mifflin Street, Suite 402, Madison, WI 53703

▷ Executive Director **Michael King** .... (608) 266-4137

Department of Public Works, Highway, and Transportation [PWHT]
2302 Fish Hatchery Road, Madison, WI 53713 (Highway / Transportation)
1919 Alliant Energy Center Way, Madison, WI 53713 (Public Works)
Fax: (608) 266-4269 (Highway / Transportation)
Fax: (608) 267-1533 (Public Works)
Internet: www.countyofdane.com/pwht

▷ Commissioner/Director **Gerald J. "Jerry" Mandli** .... (608) 266-4039
Deputy Commissioner **Pamela J. Dunphy** .... (608) 266-4036
Assistant Director of Public Works **Rob Nebel** .... (608) 267-0119

★ Elected Official ▲ Appointed by Legislature ▼ Appointed by Governor ▶ Appointed by Board or Commission ● Appointed by Judge
■ Appointed by Mayor △ Appointed by Freeholders ▽ Appointed by Supervisor ▷ Appointed by County Executive ○ Appointed by Council

Department of Public Works, Highway, and Transportation *continued*

Engineering Manager **Scott Carlson** .... (608) 266-4179
E-mail: carlson.scott@countyofdane.com
Solid Waste Engineer **John Welch** .... (608) 266-4139

Alliant Energy Center of Dane County

1919 Alliant Energy Center Way, Madison, WI 53713
Tel: (608) 267-3976 Fax: (608) 267-0146
E-mail: aec@alliantenergycenter.com
Internet: www.alliantenergycenter.com

Director **Mark Clarke** .... (608) 267-3982

Board of Health of Madison and Dane County

210 Martin Luther King, Jr. Boulevard, Room 507, Madison, WI 53703
Internet: www.publichealthmdc.com/about/board

Chair **Judith M. "Judy" Wilcox** .... (608) 243-0300
Term Expires: April 18, 2017

Public Health - Madison and Dane County [PHMDC]

210 Martin Luther King, Jr. Boulevard, Room 507,
Madison, WI 53703-3346
Tel: (608) 266-4821 Fax: (608) 266-4858
E-mail: health@publichealthmdc.com Internet: www.publichealthmdc.com

Director **Janel Heinrich** .... (608) 243-0300
Operations Director **Shawnee Parens** .... (608) 242-6521
Community Health Director **Carl Meyer** .... (608) 243-0425
Emergency Preparedness Coordinator **Tristen Jordan** .... (608) 243-0352
E-mail: tjordan@publichealthmdc.com
Environmental Health and Laboratories Director
Doug Voegeli .... (608) 243-0360
Communications Manager **Sarah Mattes** .... (608) 242-6414
E-mail: smattes@publichealthmdc.com

Dane County Housing Authority [DCHA]

2001 West Broadway, Suite 1, Monona, WI 53713-3707
Tel: (608) 224-3636 Fax: (608) 224-3632 E-mail: info@dcha.net
Internet: www.dcha.net

▷ Director **Rob Dicke** .... (608) 224-3636 ext. 23

Dane County Library Service [DCLS]

201 West Mifflin Street, Madison, WI 53703
Internet: www.scls.lib.wi.us/dcl

▷ Director **Tracy Herold** .... (608) 266-6388

Dane County Regional Airport

4000 International Lane, Madison, WI 53704
Tel: (608) 246-3380 Internet: www.msnairport.com

Director **Chris Ladell** .... (608) 246-3380

Public Safety Communications Center

City-County Bldg., 210 Martin Luther King, Jr. Blvd., Room 109,
Madison, WI 53703
Internet: www.dane911.com

▷ Director **John DeJung** .... (608) 267-1911

Henry Vilas Zoo

702 South Randall Avenue, Madison, WI 53715-1665
Tel: (608) 266-4732 Internet: www.vilaszoo.org

Director **Ronda Schwetz** .... (608) 266-4732
Deputy Director **Jeff Halter** .... (608) 266-4732
Office Manager **Karen Berendes** .... (608) 266-4943

Office of Economic and Workforce Development

Director **David B. Phillips** .... (608) 266-4006

Office of the Board of Supervisors

City-County Building, 210 Martin Luther King, Jr. Boulevard,
Room 106B, Madison, WI 53703
Fax: (608) 266-4361 Internet: www.countyofdane.com/board

★ Chair **Sharon Corrigan** (District 26) .... (608) 333-2285
Term Expires: April 2018
★ First Vice Chair **Carousel Andrea Bayrd** (District 8) .... (608) 442-6294
Term Expires: April 2018
★ Supervisor **Mary Kolar** (District 1) .... (608) 886-2640
Term Expires: April 2018
★ Supervisor **Heidi Wegleitner** (District 2) .... (608) 333-3676
Term Expires: April 2018
E-mail: wegleitner.heidi@countyofdane.com
★ Supervisor **Nick Zweifel** (District 3) .... (608) 318-1309
Term Expires: April 2018
★ Supervisor **Richard Kilmer** (District 4) .... (608) 255-9131
Term Expires: April 2018
E-mail: kilmer.richard@countyofdane.com
★ Supervisor **Hayley Young** (District 5) .... (414) 915-4529
Term Expires: April 2018
E-mail: young.hayley@countyofdane.com
★ Supervisor **John Hendrick** (District 6) .... (608) 446-4842
Term Expires: April 2018
★ Supervisor **Matt Veldran** (District 7) .... (608) 271-0722
Term Expires: April 2018
★ Supervisor **Paul Nelson** (District 9) .... (608) 831-3514
Term Expires: April 2018
★ Supervisor **Jeremy Levin** (District 10) .... (608) 577-9335
Term Expires: April 2018
★ Supervisor **Alfred "Al" Matano** (District 11) .... (608) 238-3045
Term Expires: April 2018
★ Supervisor **Paul Rusk** (District 12) .... (608) 249-9667
Term Expires: April 2018
★ Supervisor **Chuck Erickson** (District 13) .... (608) 212-8753
Term Expires: April 2018
★ Supervisor **George Gillis** (District 14) .... (608) 852-4160
Term Expires: April 2018
★ Supervisor **Ronn G. Ferrell** (District 15) .... (608) 695-1231
Term Expires: April 2018
E-mail: ronnferrell15@charter.net
★ Supervisor **Dave de Felice** (District 16) .... (608) 556-3738
Term Expires: April 2018
★ Supervisor **Jeff Pertl** (District 17) .... (608) 772-2907
Term Expires: April 2018
Education: Wisconsin; UC Berkeley MPP
★ Supervisor **Michele Ritt** (District 18) .... (608) 335-6827
Term Expires: April 2018
★ Supervisor **Bill Clausius** (District 19) .... (608) 825-1465
Term Expires: April 2018
Education: Wisconsin 1975 BA
★ Supervisor **Dennis O'Loughlin** (District 20) .... (608) 846-1851
Term Expires: April 2018
★ Supervisor **Andrew Schauer** (District 21) .... (608) 630-5427
Term Expires: April 2018
E-mail: schauer.andrew@countyofdane.com
★ Supervisor **Maureen McCarville** (District 22) .... (608) 576-4056
Term Expires: April 2018
★ Supervisor **Shelia Stubbs** (District 23) .... (608) 345-6961
Term Expires: April 2018
★ Supervisor **Robin R. Schmidt** (District 24) .... (608) 221-0514
Term Expires: April 2018
★ Supervisor **Tim Kiefer** (District 25) .... (608) 358-7213
Term Expires: April 2018
★ Supervisor **Dorothy Krause** (District 27) .... (608) 271-7532
Term Expires: April 2018
★ Supervisor **Nikole Jones** (District 28) .... (608) 798-1249
Term Expires: April 2018
E-mail: jones.nikole@countyofdane.com
★ Supervisor **David J. Ripp** (District 29) .... (608) 849-7643
Term Expires: April 2018
★ Supervisor **Patrick Downing** (District 30) .... (608) 527-2472
Term Expires: April 2018

(continued on next page)

COUNTIES

★ Elected Official ▲ Appointed by Legislature ▼ Appointed by Governor ▶ Appointed by Board or Commission ● Appointed by Judge
■ Appointed by Mayor △ Appointed by Freeholders ▽ Appointed by Supervisor ▷ Appointed by County Executive ○ Appointed by Council

Office of the Board of Supervisors *continued*

★ Supervisor **Jerome Bollig** (District 31) . . . . (608) 835-7520
Term Expires: April 2018
★ Supervisor **Mike Willett** (District 32) . . . . (608) 845-8503
Term Expires: April 2018
★ Supervisor **Jenni Dye** (District 33) . . . . (608) 492-2454
Term Expires: April 2018
★ Supervisor **Patrick Miles** (District 34) . . . . (608) 886-9167
Term Expires: April 2018
★ Supervisor **Carl Chenoweth** (District 35) . . . . (608) 873-4483
Term Expires: April 2018
★ Supervisor **Danielle Williams** (District 36) . . . . (608) 839-0752
Term Expires: April 2018
E-mail: williams.danielle@countyofdane.com
★ Supervisor **Bob Salov** (District 37) . . . . (608) 423-4358
Term Expires: April 2018
Chief of Staff **Karin Peterson Thurlow** . . . . (608) 266-4533
Legislative Services Director **(Vacant)** . . . . (608) 267-1529

Office of the Clerk of the Circuit Court

215 South Hamilton Street, Madison, WI 53703

Clerk of the Circuit Court **Carlo Esqueda** . . . . (608) 266-4311

Office of the County Clerk

City-County Building, 210 Martin Luther King, Jr. Boulevard, Room 106A, Madison, WI 53703
Tel: (608) 266-4121 E-mail: county.clerk@co.dane.wi.us
Internet: www.countyofdane.com/clerk

★ County Clerk **Scott McDonnell** (D) . . . . (608) 266-4121
Term Expires: January 7, 2017

Office of the District Attorney

215 South Hamilton Street, Madison, WI 53703
Fax: (608) 267-2545 Internet: www.countyofdane.com/da

★ District Attorney **Ismael R. Ozanne** . . . . (608) 266-4211
Term Expires: January 2, 2017
E-mail: ismael.ozanne@da.wi.gov
Education: Wisconsin 1994 BS, 1998 JD

Office of the Register of Deeds

City-County Bldg., 210 Martin Luther King, Jr. Blvd., Room 110, Madison, WI 53703
Fax: (608) 266-3110

★ Register of Deeds **Kristi Chlebowski** (D) . . . . (608) 266-4141
Term Expires: January 2, 2017

Office of the Sheriff

115 West Doty Street, Room 2002, Madison, WI 53703
Fax: (608) 284-6163 Internet: www.danesheriff.com

★ Sheriff **David J. "Dave" Mahoney** (D) . . . . (608) 284-6800
Term Expires: January 2, 2019

Office of the Treasurer

City-County Bldg., 210 Martin Luther King, Jr. Blvd., Room 114, Madison, WI 53703
Fax: (608) 266-4154

★ Treasurer **Adam Gallagher** . . . . (608) 266-4151
Term Expires: January 2, 2017

County of DeKalb, Georgia

Clark Harrison Building, 330 West Ponce de Leon Avenue, Decatur, GA 30030
Tel: (404) 371-2000 (Information) Fax: (404) 371-7004
Internet: www.co.dekalb.ga.us

County Seat: Decatur **Election Type:** Partisan **Population:** 734,871 (2015)

Office of the Chief Executive Officer

Clark Harrison Building, 330 West Ponce de Leon Avenue, Decatur, GA 30030
Tel: (404) 371-2881 Fax: (404) 371-4751 E-mail: ceo@co.dekalb.ga.us
Internet: www.co.dekalb.ga.us/portals/ceo

★ Chief Executive Officer (Interim) **Lee N. May II** (D) . . . . . (404) 371-4745
Term Expires: December 31, 2016
E-mail: lmay@dekalbcountyga.gov
Education: Clark Atlanta 1998
Special Assistant to the Chief Executive Officer
Karren Yarbrough . . . . (404) 371-2881
Special Projects Coordinator **Margaret Britton** . . . . (404) 371-2895

Office of the Chief Operating Officer

1300 Commerce Drive, 6th Floor, Decatur, GA 30030
Tel: (404) 371-2326 Fax: (404) 687-3585

Chief Operating Officer/Executive Assistant
Zachary Williams . . . . (404) 371-2881

Office of the Deputy Chief Operating Officer for Development

330 West Ponce de Leon Avenue, 5th Floor, Decatur, GA 30030
Tel: (404) 371-2155 Fax: (404) 371-4556

Deputy Chief Operating Officer **Luz Borrero** . . . . (404) 371-2155

Development Authority Office of DeKalb [OED]

125 Clairemont Avenue, Suite 150, Decatur, GA 30030
Tel: (404) 687-2730

Chair **Tyrone Rachal** . . . . (404) 687-2730
Vice Chair **Don Bolia** . . . . (404) 687-2730

Community Development Department

150 East Pone de Leon Avenue, Suite 330, Decatur, GA 30030
Tel: (404) 371-2727 Fax: (404) 371-2642
Internet: www.dekalbcountyga.gov/commdev

Director **Chris H. Morris** . . . . (404) 286-3308
E-mail: chmorris@dekalbcountyga.gov
Education: Mercer 1973 BA; Georgia State 1976 MS
Assistant Director **Allen Mitchell** . . . . (404) 286-3351
E-mail: amitchell@dekalbcountyga.gov

Department of Planning and Sustainability

330 West Ponce de Leon Avenue, Suite 500, Decatur, GA 30030
Tel: (404) 371-2155 Fax: (404) 371-4556

Director **Andrew A. Baker** . . . . (404) 371-2155
Associate Director of Planning **Philip Etiwe** . . . . (404) 371-2155
Land Development Manager **Lee Azimi** . . . . (404) 371-2169
Strategic Planning Administrator **Cedric Hudson** . . . . (404) 371-2155
Zoning Administrator **Marian Eisenberg** . . . . (404) 371-2155
Code Compliance Administrator **Marcus Kellum** . . . . (404) 687-3700

★ Elected Official ▲ Appointed by Legislature ▼ Appointed by Governor ► Appointed by Board or Commission ● Appointed by Judge
■ Appointed by Mayor △ Appointed by Freeholders ▽ Appointed by Supervisor ▷ Appointed by County Executive ○ Appointed by Council

DeKalb Workforce Development Department
774 Jordan Lane, Decatur, GA 30030
Tel: (404) 687-3400 Fax: (404) 687-3443
Internet: www.dekalbworkforce.org

Director **Sheryl Stone** . . . . (404) 687-3400
E-mail: sstone@dekalbcountyga.gov

Office of the Deputy Chief Operating Officer for Infrastructure
330 West Ponce de Leon Avenue, 4th Floor, Decatur, GA 30030
Tel: (404) 371-4778 Fax: (404) 371-7083

Deputy Chief Operating Officer **Luz Borrero** . . . . (404) 371-4778

Facilities Operation and Maintenance
Building D, 3681 Chestnut Street, Scottdale, GA 30079
Internet: www.co.dekalb.ga.us/facilities

Deputy Director **George Smith** . . . . (404) 297-2575

Public Works Department
330 West Ponce de Leon, 4th Floor, Decatur, GA 30030
Tel: (404) 371-4778 Fax: (404) 371-4761
Internet: www.co.dekalb.ga.us/publicwrks

Director **(Vacant)** . . . . (404) 371-4778

Department of Recreation, Parks and Cultural Affairs
Manuel J. Maloof Center, 1300 Commerce Dr., Room 200, Decatur, GA 30030-3222
Fax: (404) 371-3088 Internet: www.dekalbcountyga.gov/parks

Director **Roy E. Wilson** . . . . (404) 371-3005
Education: Tennessee State 1970 BS
Parks Operation General Manager **Ed Venson** . . . . (404) 371-7040
Deputy Director, Recreation Services Division
Marvin F. Billups, Jr. . . . . (404) 371-4925
Special Events Coordinator **Erica Brooks** . . . . (404) 371-3695

Department of Watershed Management [DWM]
1580 Roadhaven Drive, Stone Mountain, GA 30083
Internet: www.dekalbwatershed.com

Director **Scott Towler** . . . . (770) 621-7200

DeKalb County Public Library
215 Sycamore Street, Decatur, GA 30030
Tel: (404) 508-7190 Fax: (404) 370-8469 Internet: www.dekalblibrary.org

Director **Alison Weissinger** . . . . (404) 508-7190
Education: UC Davis 1992 BA; Florida State 1996 MLIS

DeKalb-Peachtree Airport
Administration Building, 2000 Airport Road, Room 212, Atlanta, GA 30341
Fax: (770) 936-5446 Internet: www.pdkairport.org

Director (Interim) **Mario A. Evans** . . . . (770) 936-5440
Assistant Director **Mario A. Evans** . . . . (770) 936-5440

Board of Registrations and Elections
4380 Memorial Drive, Suite 300, Decatur, GA 30032-1239
Tel: (404) 298-4020 Fax: (404) 298-4038
E-mail: voterreg@dekalbcountyga.gov Internet: www.dekalbvotes.com

Director **Maxine Daniels** . . . . (404) 298-4022
E-mail: mwdaniel@dekalbcountyga.gov
Education: Spelman BA

Cooperative Extension
4380 Memorial Dr., Decatur, GA 30032
Tel: (404) 298-4080 Fax: (404) 298-3084 E-mail: uge1089@uga.edu
Internet: http://www.caes.uga.edu/extension/dekalb/

Director **Jessica E. Hill** . . . . (404) 298-4080

Family and Children Services
178 Sams Street, Decatur, GA 30030-4134
Fax: (404) 370-5499

Director **Laurence D. Nelson** . . . . (404) 370-5076
Administrative Assistant **Gloria White** . . . . (404) 370-5076
E-mail: gmwhite@dhr.state.ga.us

Human Resources and Merit System Department
Manuel J. Maloof Center, 1300 Commerce Drive, Suite 100, Decatur, GA 30030-3222
Tel: (404) 371-2719 Fax: (404) 371-4993

▷ Director **Benita C. Ransom** . . . . (404) 371-2719
E-mail: bcransom@dekalbcountyga.gov
Administrative Assistant **Jonquil Harris** . . . . (404) 371-2719
Assistant Director **Margaret Richwagen** . . . . (404) 371-2719

Information Systems Department
Callaway Bldg., 120 W. Trinity Place, Room L-8, Decatur, GA 30030
Fax: (404) 371-2413

Director **John A. Matelski** . . . . (404) 371-2181
Education: Arizona State 1988 MBA

Property Appraisal Department
Callaway Bldg., 120 West Trinity Place, Room 208, Decatur, GA 30030
Fax: (404) 687-7143

Chief Appraiser **Calvin C. Hicks, Jr.** . . . . (404) 371-2468
E-mail: cchicks@dekalbcountyga.gov

Purchasing and Contracting Department
Manuel J. Maloof Center, 1300 Commerce Dr., Room 202, Decatur, GA 30030
Fax: (404) 371-7006 Internet: www.co.dekalb.ga.us/purchasing

Director **Scott Callan** . . . . (404) 687-3478
E-mail: scallan@dekalbcountyga.gov

Law Department
Manuel J. Maloof Center, 1300 Commerce Dr., 5th Floor, Decatur, GA 30030
Fax: (404) 371-3024

▷ Chief Legal Officer/County Attorney
Overtis Hicks "O.V." Brantley . . . . (404) 371-3011
Education: Arkansas (Little Rock) BA; Vanderbilt JD
Deputy County Attorney **Viviane H. Ernstes** . . . . (404) 371-3011
E-mail: vernstes@dekalbcountyga.gov
Education: Georgia 1988 JD
Deputy County Attorney **Laura K. Johnson** . . . . (404) 371-3011
E-mail: lkjohnson@dekalbcountyga.gov
Education: Georgia 1993 JD

Office of the Chief of Staff
Clark Harrison Center, 330 West Ponce de Leon Avenue, 6th Floor, Decatur, GA 30030
Tel: (404) 371-2881 Fax: (404) 371-6291

Chief of Staff **(Vacant)** . . . . (404) 371-2881
Deputy Chief of Staff **(Vacant)** . . . . (404) 371-3689

★ Elected Official ▲ Appointed by Legislature ▼ Appointed by Governor ▶ Appointed by Board or Commission ● Appointed by Judge
■ Appointed by Mayor △ Appointed by Freeholders ▽ Appointed by Supervisor ▷ Appointed by County Executive ○ Appointed by Council

Communications Office
Clark Harrison Center, 330 West Ponce de Leon Avenue, 6th Floor, Decatur, GA 30030
Tel: (404) 371-2881 Fax: (404) 371-4751

▷ Press Secretary **Burt Brenan** .... (404) 371-6305

Department of Finance [DoF]
Manuel J. Maloof Center, 1300 Commerce Dr., Decatur, GA 30030
Fax: (404) 371-2750 Internet: www.co.dekalb.ga.us/finance

▷ Director/Chief Financial Officer **(Vacant)** .... (404) 371-2861

Public Safety Office
1960 West Exchange Place, Tucker, GA 30084
Tel: (770) 508-3500 Fax: (770) 724-7555

▷ Deputy Chief Operating Officer
Dr. Cedric L. Alexander .... (404) 371-2881
Education: St Thomas U; Wright State 1997 PhD

DeKalb County Police Department
1960 West Exchange Place, 4th Floor, Tucker, GA 30084
Internet: www.dekalbpolice.com

Police Chief (Interim) **James Conroy** .... (770) 724-7670
Assistant Chief, Uniform Division **Dale A. Holmes** .... (770) 724-7493
Assistant Chief, Criminal Investigations Division
Michael Yarbrough .... (770) 724-7592
Assistant Chief, Special Operations Division
Brian Harris .... (770) 724-7805

Fire and Rescue Department
1950 West Exchange Place, Tucker, GA 30084
Tel: (678) 406-7750

Fire Chief **Darnell D. Fullum** .... (678) 406-7731
Community Education Unit **Capt. Kelly Sizemore** .... (678) 406-7735
Fax: (678) 414-2126

DeKalb County Medical Examiner
3550 Kensington Road, Decatur, GA 30032
Fax: (404) 508-3504

Chief Medical Examiner **Gerald T. Gowitt** .... (404) 508-3500
Director **(Vacant)** .... (404) 508-3500

Office of the Board of Commissioners
Manuel J. Maloof Center, 1300 Commerce Drive, 5th Floor, Decatur, GA 30030
Tel: (404) 371-2886 Fax: (404) 371-7004

★ Presiding Officer **Larry Johnson** (D-District 3) .... (404) 371-2425
Term Expires: December 31, 2018
E-mail: larryjohnson@dekalbcountyga.gov
Education: Illinois BS; Northern Colorado MPH

★ Commissioner **Nancy Jester** (R-District 1) .... (404) 371-2844
Term Expires: December 31, 2016
E-mail: njester@dekalbcountyga.gov

★ Commissioner **Jeff Rader** (D-District 2) .... (404) 371-2863
Term Expires: December 31, 2018
E-mail: jrader@dekalbcountyga.gov
Education: Georgia

★ Commissioner **Sharon Barnes-Sutton** (D-District 4) .... (404) 371-4907
Term Expires: December 31, 2016
E-mail: sbsutton@dekalbcountyga.gov
Education: Alabama BS; Mercer MBA

★ Commissioner **Mereda Davis Johnson** (D-District 5) .... (404) 371-2410
Term Expires: December 31, 2016

★ Commissioner **Kathie Gannon** (D-District 6) .... (404) 371-4909
Term Expires: December 31, 2016
E-mail: kgannon@dekalbcountyga.gov
Education: Marquette 1971 BA; Georgia MSW

Office of the Board of Commissioners *continued*

★ Commissioner **(Vacant)** (District 7) .... (404) 371-3681
Note: A special election will be held to fill this position on November 8, 2016.
Term Expires: December 31, 2018

Office of the District Attorney
Courthouse, 556 North McDonough Street, Room 700, Decatur, GA 30030-3308
Fax: (404) 371-2670 Internet: www.dekalbda.org

★ District Attorney **Robert D. James, Jr.** (D) .... (404) 371-2561
Term Expires: December 31, 2016
E-mail: rdjames@dekalbcountyga.gov
Education: Mid Tennessee State 1995 BA; Georgetown 1999 JD

Chief Assistant District Attorney **Nicole D. Golden** .... (404) 371-2561
E-mail: ndmarchand@dekalbcountyga.gov
Education: Xavier (LA) 2000 BS; Emory 2003 JD

Administrative Operation Manager **Karen Fordham** .... (404) 371-2469

Office of the Sheriff
4415 Memorial Dr., Decatur, GA 30032
Fax: (404) 298-8101 Internet: www.dekalbsheriff.org

★ Sheriff **Jeffrey Mann** .... (404) 298-8166
Term Expires: December 31, 2016

Chief Deputy **Reginald Scandrett** .... (404) 298-8148
Civil Process Section Coordinator **N. Bates** .... (404) 371-2428
Chief of Administration **Xernia Fortson** .... (404) 298-8148

Office of the Solicitor-General
Courthouse, 556 North McDonough Street, Room 500, Decatur, GA 30030
Tel: (404) 371-2201 Fax: (404) 371-7048
Internet: www.dekalbsolicitorgeneral.org

★ Solicitor-General **Sherry Boston** (D) .... (404) 371-2232
Term Expires: December 31, 2016
E-mail: sboston@dekalbcountyga.gov
Education: Villanova 1996 BA; Emory 1999 JD

Office of the Tax Commissioner
4380 Memorial Dr., Decatur, GA 30032-1239
Tel: (404) 298-4000 (Property Tax Inquiries)
Tel: (404) 298-4000 (Vehicle Registration Inquiries)
Fax: (404) 298-3040 (Administration)
Fax: (404) 298-3104 (Property Tax Inquiries)
Fax: (404) 298-3093 (Vehicle Registration Inquiries)
Internet: http://co.dekalb.ga.us/taxcommissioner

★ Tax Commissioner **Claudia G. Lawson** (D) .... (404) 298-4000
Term Expires: December 31, 2016

DeKalb County School System
3770 North Decatur Road, Decatur, GA 30032
Tel: (678) 676-1200 Fax: (678) 676-0785 Internet: www.dekalb.k12.ga.us

Board of Education
★ Chair **Dr. Melvin Johnson** (District 6) .... (678) 676-0027
E-mail: melvin_johnson@dekalbschoolsga.org

★ Vice Chair **Michael Erwin** (District 3) .... (678) 676-1200
E-mail: michael_erwin@dekalbschoolsga.org
Education: South Carolina 2008 PhD

★ Member **Stan O. Jester** (District 1) .... (678) 676-1200
E-mail: stan_jester@dekalbschoolsga.org

★ Member **Marshall Orson** (District 2) .... (678) 676-1200
E-mail: marshall_orson@dekalbschoolsga.org

★ Elected Official ▲ Appointed by Legislature ▼ Appointed by Governor ▶ Appointed by Board or Commission ● Appointed by Judge
■ Appointed by Mayor △ Appointed by Freeholders ▽ Appointed by Supervisor ▷ Appointed by County Executive ○ Appointed by Council

Board of Education *continued*

★Member **James L. "Jim" McMahan** (District 4) . . . . (678) 676-1200
E-mail: jim_mcmahan@dekalbschoolsga.org
★Member **Vickie Turner** (District 5) . . . . (678) 676-1200
E-mail: vickie_turner@dekalbschoolsga.org
★Member **Joyce Morley** (District 7) . . . . (678) 676-1200
E-mail: joyce_a_morley@dekalbschoolsga.org
★Member **Karen Carter** (District 8) . . . . (678) 676-1200
★Member **Thaddeus Mayfield** (District 9) . . . . (678) 676-1200

Office of the Superintendent

▶Superintendent **Dr. R. Stephen Green** . . . . (678) 676-1200

County of Delaware, Pennsylvania

Government Center Building, 201 West Front Street, Media, PA 19063
Tel: (610) 891-4000 (Information) Internet: www.co.delaware.pa.us

County Seat: Media **Election Type:** Partisan **Population:** 563,894 (2015)

Office of the County Council

Government Center Bldg., 201 W. Front St., Media, PA 19063
Tel: (610) 891-4270 Fax: (610) 892-9788
Internet: www.co.delaware.pa.us/council1.html

★Chairman **Mario J. Civera, Jr.** (R) . . . . (610) 891-4264
Term Expires: December 31, 2017
E-mail: civeram@co.delaware.pa.us
★Vice Chair **Colleen Morrone** (D) . . . . (610) 891-4264
Term Expires: December 31, 2019
★Council Member **Michael Culp** (R) . . . . (610) 891-4269
Term Expires: December 31, 2019
★Council Member **John McBlain** (R) . . . . (610) 891-4264
Term Expires: December 31, 2019
★Council Member **David J. White** (R) . . . . (610) 891-4270
Term Expires: December 31, 2017

Office of the County Clerk

Government Center Bldg., 201 W. Front St., Media, PA 19063

○County Clerk **Anne M. Coogan** . . . . (610) 891-4260
E-mail: coogana@co.delaware.pa.us

Office of Workforce Development

9 South 69th Street, Upper Darby, PA 19082
Fax: (610) 713-2224

Executive Director **Francis J. Carey** . . . . (610) 713-2200
E-mail: careyf@co.delaware.pa.us

Office of the Executive Director

Government Center Bldg., 201 W. Front St., Media, PA 19063
Fax: (610) 891-0647

○Executive Director **Marianne Grace** . . . . (610) 891-4453
E-mail: gracem@co.delaware.pa.us
Education: Temple BS; St Joseph's U MS

Office of Housing and Community Development

600 N. Jackson St., Rm. 101, Media, PA 19063-2561
Fax: (610) 566-0532

Director **Linda Hill** . . . . (610) 891-5425
E-mail: hilll@co.delaware.pa.us

Office of Judicial Support

Courthouse, 210 West Front Street, Media, PA 19063

Director **Angela L. Martinez** . . . . (610) 891-4370
E-mail: martineza@co.delaware.pa.us

Office of the Medical Examiner

Fair Acres Center, Lima, PA 19037
Tel: (610) 891-5953

Medical Examiner **Fredric N. Hellman** . . . . (610) 891-5953

Office of the Public Defender

313 West Front Street, Media, PA 19063
Tel: (610) 891-4100 Fax: (610) 892-8065

○Director **Douglas C. Roger** . . . . (610) 891-4084
E-mail: rogerd@co.delaware.pa.us
First Assistant **Francis Zarrilli** . . . . (610) 891-4100
E-mail: zarrillif@co.delaware.pa.us

Office of the Recorder of Deeds

Government Center Bldg., 201 West Front Street, Room 107, Media, PA 19063
Tel: (610) 891-4152

○Recorder **Thomas J. Judge, Sr.** . . . . (610) 891-4152
E-mail: judget@co.delaware.pa.us
Chief Deputy **(Vacant)** . . . . (610) 891-4146

Office of the Solicitor

Government Center Bldg., 201 W. Front St., Media, PA 19063

Solicitor **Michael P. Maddren** . . . . (610) 891-4072

Office of the Treasurer

Government Center Bldg., 201 W. Front St., Media, PA 19063

○Treasurer **John A. Dowd** . . . . (610) 891-4273
E-mail: dowdj@co.delaware.pa.us

Board of Assessment and Appeals

Government Center Bldg., 201 W. Front St., Media, PA 19063
Tel: (610) 891-4879 Fax: (610) 891-4883

Assessment Manager **John Van Zelst** . . . . (610) 891-5137

Administrative Services Department

Government Center Building, 201 West Front Street, Media, PA 19063

○Director **George Troilo** . . . . (610) 891-4427

Adult Probation and Parole

Government Center Bldg., 201 W. Front St., Media, PA 19063
Tel: (610) 891-4591 Fax: (610) 891-7294

Director **Michael W. Raith** . . . . (610) 891-4591

Budget Management Department

Government Center Bldg., 201 W. Front St., Media, PA 19063

○Budget Director **James Hayes** . . . . (610) 891-4449
E-mail: hayesj@co.delaware.pa.us

Buildings and Maintenance Department

Government Center Bldg., 201 W. Front St., Room G-55, Media, PA 19063
Fax: (610) 891-4501

○Director **Joe DeVuono** . . . . (610) 891-4061
E-mail: devuonoj@co.delaware.pa.us

Central Purchasing Department

Government Center Bldg., 201 W. Front St., Media, PA 19063
Tel: (610) 891-4426 Fax: (610) 566-8565

○Director **George Troilo** . . . . (610) 891-4427

(continued on next page)

★Elected Official ▲Appointed by Legislature ▼Appointed by Governor ▶Appointed by Board or Commission ●Appointed by Judge
■Appointed by Mayor △Appointed by Freeholders ▽Appointed by Supervisor ▷Appointed by County Executive ○Appointed by Council

Central Purchasing Department *continued*

Buyer **Stephen Lucas** .... (610) 891-4426

Department of Community Corrections

Second & Orange Streets, Ground Floor, Media, PA 19063
Fax: (610) 891-5304

Director **Walter R. "Walt" Omlor, Jr.** .... (610) 891-4461

Consumer Affairs Department

Government Center Bldg., 201 W. Front St., Media, PA 19063
Tel: (610) 891-4865

○ Director **Evelyn Yancoskie** .... (610) 891-4872
E-mail: yancoskiee@co.delaware.pa.us

Cooperative Extension Services Department

Smedley Park, 20 Paper Mill Rd., Springfield, PA 19064
Fax: (610) 690-2676

Director **Nancy Stevens** .... (610) 489-4315

Information Technology Department

Government Center Bldg., 201 W. Front St., Media, PA 19063
Fax: (610) 566-4076

○ Director **Jerry O'Connor** .... (610) 891-4675
E-mail: oconnorj@co.delaware.pa.us

Department of Domestic Relations

P.O. Box 543, Media, PA 19063
Fax: (610) 891-1959

Director **Mimi Bradley Walker** .... (610) 891-4314

Office of Support Enforcement

Second & Orange Streets, Media, PA 19063
Fax: (610) 891-5128

Chief Counsel **Daniel Vanwyk** .... (610) 891-4233

Election Bureau

Government Center Bldg., 201 W. Front St., Media, PA 19063
Tel: (610) 891-4673 Fax: (610) 892-0641

Chief Clerk **Laureen Hagan** .... (610) 891-4673

Department of Emergency Services

360 North Middletown Road, Media, PA 19063
Fax: (610) 892-9583

○ Director **Edwin J. Truitt** .... (610) 565-8700

Human Services Department

20 South 69th Street, Upper Darby, PA 19082
Fax: (610) 713-2326 Internet: www.delcohsa.org

○ Director **Joseph T. "Joe" Dougherty** .... (610) 713-2323
E-mail: doughertyj@delcohsa.org

Office of Behavioral Health [OBH]

20 South 69th Street, Upper Darby, PA 19082
Tel: (610) 713-2365 Fax: (610) 713-2378

Administrator **Jonna L. DiStefano** .... (610) 713-2365

Office of Children and Youth Services

20 South 69th Street, 3rd Floor, Upper Darby, PA 19082

Director **Deirdre Gordon** .... (610) 713-2000

Department of Intercommunity Health

Government Center Bldg., 201 West Front Street, Room 117, Media, PA 19063
Tel: (610) 891-5311 Fax: (610) 891-6966
E-mail: delcoich@co.delaware.pa.us
Internet: www.co.delaware.pa.us/intercommunity

Director **Maureen Hennessey** .... (610) 891-5310

Motor Vehicle Management Department

County Garage, 201 W. Front St., Media, PA 19063
Fax: (610) 891-4327

○ Director **Brian Hudak** .... (610) 891-4157

Parks and Recreation Department

1671 North Providence Road, Media, PA 19063

○ Supervisor **Marc J. Manfre** .... (610) 891-4663
E-mail: manfrem@co.delaware.pa.us

Personnel Department

Government Center Building, 201 West Front Street, Room 220, Media, PA 19063
Fax: (610) 565-0687

○ Director **Robert J. White** .... (610) 891-4852

Planning Department

201 W. Front St., Media, PA 19063
Fax: (610) 891-5203

○ Director **Linda Hill** .... (610) 891-5200
E-mail: hilllj@co.delaware.pa.us

Public Relations Department

Government Center Bldg., 201 W. Front St., Media, PA 19063
Fax: (610) 566-3947

○ Director **Trish Cofiell** .... (610) 891-4934
E-mail: delcopr@co.delaware.pa.us

Public Works Department

Government Center Bldg., 201 West Front Street, Room 207, Media, PA 19063
Fax: (610) 891-4482

○ Director (Acting) **Dennis J. Carey** .... (610) 891-4668

Special Events Department

Government Center Bldg., 201 W. Front St., Media, PA 19063

○ Director **Marc J. Manfre** .... (610) 565-7410
E-mail: manfrem@co.delaware.pa.us

Tax Claim Bureau

Government Center Building, 201 West Front Street, Ground Floor, Media, PA 19063-2768
Fax: (610) 891-4115

Manager **Kathy Wike** .... (610) 891-4293

Veterans' Affairs Department

Government Center Bldg., 201 W. Front St., Media, PA 19063
Fax: (610) 566-8366

○ Director **William A. Lovejoy** .... (610) 891-4646
E-mail: lovejoyw@co.delaware.pa.us

Voter Registration Commission

Government Center Bldg., 201 W. Front St., Media, PA 19063

Chief Clerk **Mary Jo Headley** .... (610) 891-4659

★ Elected Official ▲ Appointed by Legislature ▼ Appointed by Governor ► Appointed by Board or Commission ● Appointed by Judge
■ Appointed by Mayor △ Appointed by Freeholders ▽ Appointed by Supervisor ▷ Appointed by County Executive ○ Appointed by Council

Voting Machines Department
403 East 24th Street, Chester, PA 19013

○ Director **James Kerns** .... (610) 874-8780

Workforce Investment Board
9 South 69th Street, Upper Darby, PA 19082

Chairman **Albert Danish** .... (610) 713-2200

Delaware County Conservation District
Rose Tree Park - Hunt Club, 1521 North Providence Road, Media, PA 19063
Fax: (610) 892-9484 Internet: www.delcocd.org

Director **Edward Magargee** .... (610) 892-9484

Delaware County Housing Authority [DCHA]
1855 Constitution Avenue, Woodlyn, PA 19094
Internet: www.dcha1.org

○ Executive Director **Lawrence E. Hartley** .... (610) 876-2521
E-mail: leh@dcha1.org

Delaware County Library System [DCLS]
Four Acres Building 19, 340 North Middletown Rd., Media, PA 19063-5597
Tel: (610) 891-8622 Fax: (610) 891-8641
Internet: www.delcolibraries.org

Director **David Belanger** .... (610) 891-8622
E-mail: dbelanger@delcolibraries.org

Delaware County Prison
500 Cheyney Road, Thornton, PA 19373
Fax: (610) 361-9689

Superintendent **John A. Reilly, Jr.** .... (610) 361-3282

Risk Management Department
Government Center Building, 201 W. Front St., Room 220, Media, PA 19063

Director **Thomas N. Micozzie** .... (610) 891-5233

Francis J. Catania Law Library
Court House, 201 West Front Street, 4th Floor, Media, PA 19063
Fax: (610) 891-4480

Librarian **Susan Perretta** .... (610) 891-4462
E-mail: perrettas@co.delaware.pa.us
Education: Temple JD; Drexel MLIS

Office of the Controller
Government Center Bldg., 201 W. Front St., Media, PA 19063
Fax: (610) 566-3256

★ Controller **Edward E. O'Lone** (R) .... (610) 891-5333
Term Expires: December 31, 2017

Office of the District Attorney
Courthouse, 201 West Front Street, Room 102, Media, PA 19063
Tel: (610) 891-4161 Fax: (610) 892-0677

★ District Attorney **John J. "Jack" Whelan** (R) .... (610) 891-4161
Term Expires: December 31, 2019

Office of the Register of Wills
Government Center Bldg., 201 W. Front St., Media, PA 19063
Fax: (610) 891-4812

★ Register of Wills **Jennifer Holsten Maddaloni** (R) .... (610) 891-4400
Term Expires: December 31, 2017

Office of the Sheriff
Government Center Bldg., 201 W. Front St., Media, PA 19063
Fax: (610) 891-1765

★ Sheriff **Marry McFall Hopper** (R) .... (610) 891-4296
Term Expires: December 31, 2017

County of Denton, Texas
110 West Hickory Street, Denton, TX 76201-4168
Tel: (940) 349-3110 Tel: (800) 807-4685
Internet: http://dentoncounty.com/

County Seat: Denton **Election Type:** Partisan **Population:** 780,612 (2015)

Office of the County Judge
110 West Hickory Street, Second Floor, Denton, TX 76201-4168
Tel: (940) 349-2820 Tel: (972) 434-8805 Fax: (940) 349-2821
Internet: www.dentoncounty.com/court/judge

★ County Judge **Mary Horn** (R) .... (940) 349-2820
Term Expires: December 31, 2018
E-mail: mary.horn@dentoncounty.com

Director of Administration **Kate Lynass** .... (972) 434-8805
E-mail: kate.lynass@dentoncounty.com

Administrative Specialist II **Teresa Farnam** .... (940) 349-2820
E-mail: teresa.farnam@dentoncounty.com

Office of the County Auditor
401 West Hickory, Denton, TX 76201-9026
Tel: (940) 349-3100 Fax: (940) 349-3101

County Auditor **James Wells** .... (940) 349-3100

Chief Assistant County Auditor **Natalie Riegelman** .... (940) 349-3100

Accounts Payable Supervisor **Diana Phillips** .... (940) 349-3100

Data Processing Manager **Leila Timmis** .... (940) 349-3100
E-mail: leila.timmis@dentoncounty.com

Budget Office
401 West Hickory, Suite 609, Denton, TX 76201-9026
Tel: (940) 349-3060 Fax: (940) 349-3061

Budget Director **Donna Stewart** .... (940) 349-3060
E-mail: donna.stewart@dentoncounty.com

Assistant Director **Jona Macsas** .... (940) 349-3060
E-mail: jona.macsas@dentoncounty.com

Budget Systems Analyst **(Vacant)** .... (940) 349-3060

Budget Analyst **LaDawn Fitzgerald** .... (940) 349-3060

Financial Support Specialist III **Donna Henrikson** .... (940) 349-3060
E-mail: donna.henrikson@dentoncounty.com

Office of Elections Administration
401 West Hickory, Suite 125, Denton, TX 76201-9026
Tel: (940) 349-3200 Fax: (940) 349-3201

Elections Administrator **Lannie Noble** .... (940) 349-3200

Deputy Elections Administrator **Kerry Martin** .... (940) 349-3200

Department of Emergency Services
9060 Teasley Lane, Denton, TX 76210-4010
Tel: (940) 349-2840 Fax: (940) 349-2841

Chief Fire Marshal/Emergency Management Coordinator
Joseph A. "Jody" Gonzalez .... (940) 349-2840
Education: Southwest Texas State BA

Assistant Chief Fire Marshal **Roland Asebedo** .... (940) 349-2840
E-mail: roland.asebedo@dentoncounty.com

Assistant Emergency Management Coordinator
Mark Wilkins .... (940) 349-2840
E-mail: mark.wilkins@dentoncounty.com

★ Elected Official ▲ Appointed by Legislature ▼ Appointed by Governor ► Appointed by Board or Commission ● Appointed by Judge
■ Appointed by Mayor △ Appointed by Freeholders ▽ Appointed by Supervisor ▷ Appointed by County Executive ○ Appointed by Council

Denton County Health Department [DCHD]
535 South Loop 288, Denton, TX 76205
Tel: (940) 349-2900 Fax: (940) 349-2905
Internet: www.dentoncounty.com/health

Director **Matt Richardson** .... (940) 349-2913

Historical Commission
110 West Hickory Street, Denton, TX 76201-4168
Tel: (940) 349-2860 Fax: (940) 349-2851

Chairman **Beth Stribling** .... (940) 349-2860

Human Resources Department
401 West Hickory, Suite 516, Denton, TX 76201-9026
Tel: (940) 349-3080 Fax: (940) 349-3081

Director **Amy Phillips** .... (940) 349-3080
E-mail: amy.phillips@dentoncounty.com

Juvenile Probation Department
210 South Woodrow Lane, Denton, TX 76205-6304
Tel: (940) 349-2400 Fax: (940) 349-2401

Director **Ken Metcalf** .... (940) 349-2400
Assistant Director **Matt Marick** .... (940) 349-2400

Local Emergency Planning Committee
9060 Teasley Lane, Denton, TX 76210-4010
Tel: (940) 349-2840 Fax: (940) 349-2481

Chairperson **Mark Wilkins** .... (940) 349-2840

Department of Public Facilities
306 North Loop 288, Suite 237, Denton, TX 76209
Tel: (940) 349-2970 Fax: (940) 349-2971

Director **Danny Brumley** .... (940) 349-2970
E-mail: danny.brumley@dentoncounty.com

Department of Public Works and Engineering
1505 West McKinney Street, Denton, TX 76209-4525
Tel: (940) 349-3250 Fax: (940) 349-3251

City Engineer **Bennett Howell** .... (940) 349-3520
E-mail: bennett.howell@dentoncounty.com
Construction Manager **Robert Musgrove** .... (940) 349-3520
E-mail: robert.musgrove@dentoncounty.com

Purchasing Department
401 West Hickory, Denton, TX 76201-9026
Tel: (940) 349-3130 Fax: (940) 349-3131

Director **Beth Fleming** .... (940) 349-3130
E-mail: beth.fleming@dentoncounty.com
Assistant Director **Scott Arledge** .... (940) 349-3130
E-mail: scott.arledge@dentoncounty.com
Contract Administrator **Annet Warzwick** .... (940) 349-3130
E-mail: annet.warzwick@dentoncounty.com

Technology Services Department
401 West Hickory, Denton, TX 76201-9026
Tel: (940) 349-3001 Fax: (940) 349-3003

Chief Information Officer **Kevin Carr** .... (940) 349-3001
E-mail: kevin.carr@dentoncounty.com
Assistant Director **Brian King** .... (940) 349-3001
E-mail: brian.king@dentoncounty.com

Office of the County Commission
110 West Hickory Street, Denton, TX 76201-4168
Tel: (940) 349-2010 Internet: www.dentoncounty.com/court

★Commissioner **Hugh Coleman** (R-Precinct 1) .... (940) 249-2810
Term Expires: December 31, 2016 Fax: (940) 349-2811
E-mail: hugh.coleman@dentoncounty.com
★Commissioner **Ron Marchant** (R-Precinct 2) .... (940) 434-7140
Term Expires: December 31, 2018 Fax: (940) 434-7141
E-mail: ron.marchant@dentoncounty.com
Education: Southern Nazarene 1977 BS
★Commissioner **Bobbie J. Mitchell** (R-Precinct 3) .... (940) 434-4780
Term Expires: December 31, 2016 Fax: (940) 434-4781
E-mail: bobbie.mitchell@dentoncounty.com
★Commissioner **Andy Eads** (R-Precinct 4) .... (940) 349-2801
Term Expires: December 31, 2018 Fax: (940) 349-2803
E-mail: andy.eads@dentoncounty.com

Office of the Constables
★Constable **Johnny Hammons** (R-Precinct 1) .... (940) 349-3160
Term Expires: December 31, 2016
★Constable **Michael A. Truitt** (Precinct 2) .... (972) 434-7220
Term Expires: December 31, 2016 Fax: (972) 434-7221
E-mail: michael.truitt@dentoncounty.com
★Constable **Jerry Raburn** (Precinct 3) .... (972) 434-4770
Term Expires: December 31, 2016 Fax: (972) 434-4771
E-mail: jerry.raburn@dentoncounty.com
★Constable **Tim Burch** (Precinct 4) .... (972) 434-3980
Term Expires: December 31, 2016 Fax: (972) 434-3981
E-mail: tim.burch@dentoncounty.com
★Constable **Doug Boydston** (Precinct 5) .... (940) 349-3480
Term Expires: December 31, 2016 Fax: (940) 349-3481
★Constable **Ron Smith** (Precinct 6) .... (972) 434-7120
Term Expires: December 31, 2016 Fax: (972) 434-7121
E-mail: ron.smith@dentoncounty.com

Office of the County Clerk
1450 East McKinney Street, Denton, TX 76209-4524
Tel: (940) 349-2012 Fax: (940) 349-2013

★County Clerk **Juli Anne Luke** (R) .... (940) 349-2012
Term Expires: December 31, 2018
Chief Deputy County Clerk **Tracy Jones** .... (940) 349-2012
Administration Department Supervisor
Ronnie Anderson .... (940) 349-2012
E-mail: ronnie.anderson@dentoncounty.com
Recording Department Supervisor **Stacy Welch** .... (940) 349-2010
Criminal Misdemeanor Courts Department Supervisor
Debra Wilson .... (940) 349-2014

Office of the County Treasurer
401 West Hickory, Suite 309, Denton, TX 76201-9026
Tel: (940) 349-3150 Fax: (940) 349-3151
E-mail: countytreasurer@dentoncounty.com

★County Treasurer **Cindy Yeatts Brown** (R) .... (940) 349-3150
Term Expires: December 31, 2018
Assistant County Treasurer **Mark Price** .... (940) 349-3150
Financial Analyst **Jay Vanatta** .... (940) 349-3150
Payroll Supervisor **Jana Bullock** .... (940) 349-3150
Financial Support Specialist II **Teresa Huerta** .... (940) 349-3150
Administrative Specialist **Judy Muller** .... (940) 349-3150
E-mail: judy.muller@dentoncounty.com

★Elected Official ▲Appointed by Legislature ▼Appointed by Governor ▶Appointed by Board or Commission ●Appointed by Judge
■Appointed by Mayor △Appointed by Freeholders ▽Appointed by Supervisor ▷Appointed by County Executive ○Appointed by Council

Office of the District Attorney

1450 East McKinney Street, Third Floor, Denton, TX 76209-4524
Tel: (940) 349-2600 Fax: (940) 349-2601

★ District Attorney **Paul Johnson** (R) .... (940) 349-2600
Term Expires: December 31, 2018
E-mail: paul.johnson@dentoncounty.com
Director of Administration **Kim Guertler** .... (940) 349-2612
Office Administrator **Fran Middleton** .... (940) 349-2610

Office of the District Clerk

1450 East McKinney Street, First Floor, Denton, TX 76209-4524
Tel: (940) 349-2200 Fax: (940) 349-2201

★ District Clerk **Sherri Adelstein** (R) .... (940) 349-2200
Term Expires: December 31, 2018
E-mail: sherri.adelstein@dentoncounty.com
Chief Deputy District Clerk **Mark Yarbrough** .... (940) 349-2200
E-mail: mark.yarbrough@dentoncounty.com

Office of the Tax Assessor/Collector

1505 West McKinney Street, Denton, TX 76209-4525
Tel: (940) 349-3500 Fax: (940) 349-3501

★ Tax Assessor/Collector **Michelle French** (R) .... (940) 349-3500
Term Expires: December 31, 2016

Office of the Sheriff

127 North Woodrow Lane, Denton, TX 76205-6397
Tel: (940) 349-1600 Fax: (940) 349-1604

★ Sheriff **William B. Travis** (R) .... (940) 349-1600
Term Expires: December 31, 2016
Communication Manager **Holly Rodriguez** .... (940) 349-1641
E-mail: holly.rodriguez@dentoncounty.com

County of Douglas, Nebraska

Civic Center, 1819 Farnam Street, Omaha, NE 68183
Tel: (402) 444-7000 (Information) Internet: www.douglascounty-ne.gov

County Seat: Omaha **Election Type:** Partisan **Population:** 550,064 (2015)

Office of the Board of Commissioners

Civic Center, 1819 Farnam St., Suite LC2, Omaha, NE 68183-0100
Fax: (402) 444-6559

★ Chairman **Mary Ann Borgeson** (R-District 6) .... (402) 444-7025
Term Expires: January 1, 2019
E-mail: maryann.borgeson@douglascounty-ne.gov
★ Commissioner **Mike Boyle** (D-District 1) .... (402) 444-7025
Term Expires: January 1, 2017
E-mail: mike.boyle@douglascounty-ne.gov
★ Commissioner **James P. Cavanaugh** (D-District 2) ...... (402) 444-7025
Term Expires: January 2019
★ Commissioner
Christopher T. "Chris" Rodgers (D-District 3) .... (402) 444-7025
Term Expires: January 1, 2017
E-mail: chris.rodgers@douglascounty-ne.gov
Education: Creighton 1992 BA, 1999 MBA; Nebraska (Omaha) 2002 MPA
★ Commissioner **Paul J. "P.J." Morgan, Jr.** (R-District 4) .. (402) 444-7025
Term Expires: January 1, 2019
E-mail: pj.morgan@douglascounty-ne.gov
Date of Birth: April 9, 1940
★ Commissioner **Marc Kraft** (D-District 5) .... (402) 444-7025
Term Expires: January 1, 2017
E-mail: marc.kraft@douglascounty-ne.gov

Office of the Board of Commissioners *continued*

★ Commissioner **Clare Duda** (R-District 7) .... (402) 444-7025
Term Expires: January 1, 2017
E-mail: clare.duda@douglascounty-ne.gov

Administrative Services Office

Omaha-Douglas Civic Center, 1819 Farnam Street, LC2, Omaha, NE 68183
Fax: (402) 444-6559

Chief Administrative Officer **Patrick Bloomingdale** ..... (402) 444-7025
E-mail: patrick.bloomingdale@douglascounty-ne.gov
Budget and Finance Director **Joseph "Joe" Lorenz** ..... (402) 444-6825
E-mail: joseph.lorenz@douglascounty-ne.gov

Corrections Department

710 South 17th Street, Omaha, NE 68102
Tel: (402) 444-7400 Fax: (402) 599-2264

▶ Director of Corrections **Mark Foxall** .... (402) 599-2265

Emergency Management Agency

Civic Center, 1819 Farnam St., Room 114EOC, Omaha, NE 68183
Fax: (402) 354-2060 E-mail: paul.johnson@douglascounty-ne.gov

▶ Director **Paul W. Johnson** .... (402) 444-5040
E-mail: paul.johnson@douglascounty-ne.gov

Environmental Services

3015 Menke Circle, Omaha, NE 68134
Fax: (402) 444-4963

▶ Director **Kent Holm** .... (402) 444-6181
E-mail: kent.holm@douglascounty-ne.gov

General Assistance Department

1111 South 41st Street, Suite 220, Omaha, NE 68105
Tel: (402) 444-6215 Fax: (402) 444-6696

▶ Director **Deb Redding** .... (402) 444-7232
E-mail: deb.redding@douglascounty-ne.gov

Douglas County Health Department

1111 South 41st Street, Omaha, NE 68105
Tel: (402) 444-7476 Fax: (402) 444-6267
Internet: www.douglascountyhealth.com

▶ Director **Dr. Adi Pour** .... (402) 444-7471
E-mail: adi.pour@douglascounty-ne.gov

Human Resources Department [DCHR]

Civic Center, 1819 Farnam Street, Room 505, Omaha, NE 68183
Tel: (402) 444-6188 Fax: (402) 444-6678

Director **Karen Buche** .... (402) 444-6123
E-mail: karen.buche@douglascounty-ne.gov
Deputy Director **Tim McNally** .... (402) 444-6125
E-mail: tim.mcnally@douglascounty-ne.gov
Benefits Administration Manager **Kathy Adair** .... (402) 444-6099
Human Resources Analyst **Mark Williams** .... (402) 444-6189
Employee Development and Relations Coordinator
Carol Donnelly .... (402) 444-6553
E-mail: carol.donnelly@douglascounty-ne.gov

Public Properties

Civic Center, 1819 Farnam Street, Room 1212, Omaha, NE 68183
Tel: (402) 444-7878 Fax: (402) 444-7879

▶ Director (Interim) **Jerry Leahy** .... (402) 444-7858
E-mail: jerry.leahy@douglascounty-ne.gov

★ Elected Official ▲ Appointed by Legislature ▼ Appointed by Governor ▶ Appointed by Board or Commission ● Appointed by Judge
■ Appointed by Mayor △ Appointed by Freeholders ▽ Appointed by Supervisor ▷ Appointed by County Executive ○ Appointed by Council

Purchasing Department
Civic Center, 1819 Farnam Street, Room 902, Omaha, NE 68183
Fax: (402) 444-4992

▶ Purchasing Agent **Eric J. Carlson** .... (402) 444-7158
E-mail: eric.carlson@douglascounty-ne.gov

Risk Management and Labor Relations
Civic Center, 1819 Farnam Street, Room LC2, Omaha, NE 68183
Fax: (402) 444-6559

▶ Deputy Administrator **Diane Carlson** .... (402) 444-7138
E-mail: diane.carlson@douglascounty-ne.gov

Veterans' Service Office
1111 South 41st Street, Suite 110, Omaha, NE 68105
Fax: (402) 444-4114 Internet: www.douglascounty-ne.gov/veterans

Veterans Service Officer **Allan Jackson** .... (402) 444-7180

Douglas County Community Mental Health Center [CMHC]
4102 Woolworth, Omaha, NE 68105
Tel: (402) 444-7449 Fax: (402) 444-4542
Internet: www.douglascounty-ne.gov/cmhc

Director **Sherry Glasnapp** .... (402) 444-7608

Douglas County Health Center [DCHC]
4102 Woolworth Avenue, Omaha, NE 68105
Tel: (402) 444-7000 Fax: (402) 444-6287
Internet: www.dchc.douglascounty-ne.gov

▶ Administrator **James C. Tourville** .... (402) 444-3946
E-mail: james.tourville@douglascounty-ne.gov

Douglas County Juvenile Assessment Center [JAC]
1111 South 41st Street, Suite 120, Omaha, NE 68105
Fax: (402) 444-6475

Director **Shawne Coonfare** .... (402) 444-5413

Douglas County Youth Center
1301 S. 41st St., Omaha, NE 68105
Fax: (402) 444-4252 Internet: www.douglascounty-ne.gov/youthcenter

Director **Brad Alexander** .... (402) 444-1924

Douglas County Election Commission
225 North 115th Street, Omaha, NE 68154
Fax: (402) 444-4181 Internet: www.votedouglascounty.com

▼ Election Commissioner **Brian S. Kruse** .... (402) 444-7141
Term Expires: December 31, 2019

Public Building Commission
Omaha-Douglas Civic Center, 1819 Farnam Street, Room 1205, Omaha, NE 68183
Fax: (402) 444-5088

Administrator **Paul Cohen** .... (402) 444-5345
Office Manager **Mary Svajgl** .... (402) 444-5345

Douglas-Omaha Technology Commission [DOT.Comm]
408 South 18th Street, Omaha, NE 68102
Tel: (402) 444-4869 Fax: (402) 444-6276 Internet: www.dotcomm.org

Director **Derek Kruse** .... (402) 444-6053

Office of the County Assessor/ Register of Deeds
Omaha Douglas Civic-Center, 1819 Farnam Street, Fourth Floor, Omaha, NE 68183
Tel: (402) 444-7060 Fax: (402) 444-3973
Internet: http://www.dcassessor.org

★ Assessor/Register of Deeds **Diane L. Battiato** (D) .... (402) 444-7060
Term Expires: January 2019
Chief Deputy Assessor **Barry D. Couch** .... (402) 444-6729
E-mail: barry.couch@douglascounty-ne.gov

Office of the County Attorney
100 Hall of Justice, 17th FarnamStreet, Omaha, NE 68183
Fax: (402) 444-6787

★ Attorney **Donald "Don" Kleine** (D) .... (402) 444-6132
Term Expires: January 1, 2019
E-mail: donald.kleine@douglascounty-ne.gov

Office of the County Clerk/ Comptroller
Civic Center, 1819 Farnam Street, Room H08, Omaha, NE 68183
Tel: (402) 444-7143 Fax: (402) 444-6456
Internet: www.douglascountyclerk.org

★ County Clerk/Comptroller **Dan Esch** .... (402) 444-6767
Term Expires: January 1, 2017

Office of the County Engineer
15505 West Maple Road, Omaha, NE 68116-5173
Tel: (402) 444-6372 Fax: (402) 444-6244

★ Engineer **Thomas D. "Tom" Doyle** (D) .... (402) 444-6465
Term Expires: January 1, 2019
E-mail: tom.doyle@douglascounty-ne.gov

Office of the Public Defender
Hall of Justice, 1701 Farnam Street, Room 306, Omaha, NE 68183
Fax: (402) 444-6017

★ Public Defender **Thomas "Tom" Riley** (D) .... (402) 444-7687
Term Expires: January 1, 2017
E-mail: thomas.riley@douglascounty-ne.gov

Office of the Sheriff
3601 North 156th Street, Omaha, NE 68116
Tel: (402) 444-6641 Fax: (402) 444-7342

★ Sheriff **Timothy F. "Tim" Dunning** (R) .... (402) 444-6627
Term Expires: January 1, 2019
E-mail: timothy.dunning@douglascounty-ne.gov
Chief Deputy **Tom Wheeler** .... (402) 444-6632
E-mail: thomas.wheeler@douglascounty-ne.gov
Administrative Services Bureau **Kevin Conlon** .... (402) 444-7976
E-mail: kevin.conlon@douglascounty-ne.gov
Court Service Bureau **Lt. Wayne Hudson** .... (402) 444-7076
E-mail: wayne.hudson@douglascounty-ne.gov

Office of the Treasurer
Civic Center, 1819 Farnam Street, Room H03, Omaha, NE 68183
Fax: (402) 444-6453

★ Treasurer **John W. Ewing, Jr.** (D) .... (402) 444-3224
Term Expires: January 1, 2019
E-mail: john.ewing@douglascounty-ne.gov
Date of Birth: April 18, 1961
Education: Nebraska (Omaha) BS, 1986 MS

★ Elected Official ▲ Appointed by Legislature ▼ Appointed by Governor ▶ Appointed by Board or Commission ● Appointed by Judge
■ Appointed by Mayor △ Appointed by Freeholders ▽ Appointed by Supervisor ▷ Appointed by County Executive ○ Appointed by Council

County of DuPage, Illinois

Jack T. Knuepfer Administration Building, 421 North County Farm Road, Wheaton, IL 60187
Tel: (630) 407-6500 (Information) Internet: www.dupageco.org

County Seat: Wheaton **Election Type:** Partisan **Population:** 933,736 (2015)

Office of the County Board

Jack T. Knuepfer Administration Building, 421 N. County Farm Rd., Wheaton, IL 60187
Tel: (630) 407-6023 Fax: (630) 407-6001

★ Chairman **Daniel J. "Dan" Cronin** (R) .... (630) 407-6060
Term Expires: November 30, 2018
E-mail: daniel.cronin@dupageco.org
Date of Birth: November 7, 1959
Education: Northwestern BA; Loyola U (Chicago) 1986 JD
Chief of Staff **Thomas "Tom" Cuculich** .... (630) 407-6060
Deputy Chief of Staff **Sheryl Markay** .... (630) 407-6012
E-mail: sheryl.markay@dupageco.org

★ Vice Chairman **John Curran** (R-District 3) .... (630) 407-6023
Term Expires: November 30, 2018
E-mail: john.curran@dupageco.org

★ Board Member **Paul Fichtner** (R-District 1) .... (630) 407-6023
Term Expires: November 30, 2018
E-mail: pfichtner@dupageco.org
Education: Illinois 1983 BS; DePaul 1991 MBA

★ Board Member **Donald E. Puchalski** (R-District 1) .... (630) 407-6023
Term Expires: November 30, 2016
E-mail: dpuchalski@dupageco.org
Education: DePaul BS; John Marshall JD

★ Board Member **Salvatore "Sam" Tornatore** (R-District 1) .... (630) 407-6023
Term Expires: November 30, 2016
E-mail: sam.tornatore@dupageco.org

★ Board Member **Elizabeth Chapin** (D-District 2) .... (630) 407-6023
Term Expires: November 30, 2016
E-mail: elizabeth.chapin@dupageco.org

★ Board Member **Peter P. DiCianni** (R-District 2) .... (630) 407-6023
Term Expires: November 30, 2018

★ Board Member **Sean Noonan** (R-District 2) .... (630) 407-6023
Term Expires: November 30, 2016
E-mail: sean.noonan@dupageco.org

★ Board Member **Gary A. Grasso** (R-District 3) .... (630) 407-6023
Term Expires: November 30, 2016
E-mail: gary.grasso@dupageco.org

★ Board Member **Brian Krajewski** (R-District 3) .... (630) 407-6023
Term Expires: November 30, 2016
E-mail: brian.krajewski@dupageco.org

★ Board Member **Grant Eckhoff** (R-District 4) .... (630) 407-6023
Term Expires: November 30, 2018
E-mail: grant.eckhoff@dupageco.org

★ Board Member **Amy L. Grant** (R-District 4) .... (630) 407-6023
Term Expires: November 30, 2016
E-mail: amy.grant@dupageco.org

★ Board Member **Karyn Romano** (R-District 4) .... (630) 407-6023
Term Expires: November 30, 2016
E-mail: karyn.romano@dupageco.org

★ Board Member **James D. Healy** (R-District 5) .... (630) 407-6023
Term Expires: November 30, 2016
E-mail: jhealey@dupageco.org
Education: Elmhurst 1982 BA; John Marshall 1993 JD

★ Board Member **Tonia Jane Khouri** (R-District 5) .... (630) 407-6023
Term Expires: November 30, 2018
E-mail: tonia.khouri@dupageco.org

★ Board Member **Anthony "Tony" Michelassi** (D-District 5) .... (630) 407-6023
Term Expires: November 30, 2016
E-mail: anthony.michelassi@dupageco.org

★ Board Member **Robert Larsen** (R-District 6) .... (630) 407-6023
Term Expires: November 30, 2016
E-mail: robert.larsen@dupageco.org

Office of the County Board *continued*

★ Board Member **Kevin Wiley** (R-District 6) .... (630) 407-6023
Term Expires: November 30, 2018
E-mail: kevin.wiley@dupageco.org

★ Board Member **James F. Zay, Jr.** (R-District 6) .... (630) 407-6023
Term Expires: November 30, 2016
E-mail: jzay@dupageco.org

Office of Homeland Security and Emergency Management [OHSEM]

Jack T. Knuepfer Administration Building, 421 North County Farm Road, Wheaton, IL 60187
E-mail: oem@dupageco.org

▶ Director **William "Bill" Babyar** .... (630) 682-7925
E-mail: oem@dupageco.org

Office of the Public Defender

Judicial Office Facility, 505 N. County Farm Rd., Wheaton, IL 60187
Tel: (630) 407-8300

Public Defender **Jeffrey R. "Jeff" York** .... (630) 407-8300

Supervisor of Assessments Office

Jack T. Knuepfer Administration Building, 421 N. County Farm Rd., Wheaton, IL 60187
Fax: (630) 407-5860

▶ Supervisor of Assessments **Craig Dovel** .... (630) 407-5858
E-mail: craig.dovel@dupageco.org

Animal Care and Control Department

120 N. County Farm Rd., Wheaton, IL 60187
Tel: (630) 407-2800 Fax: (630) 407-2801
E-mail: animalcontrol@dupageco.org
Internet: www.dupageco.org/animalcontrol

Veterinary Administrator **Mary Karr** .... (630) 407-2800

Department of Community Services

Jack T. Knuepfer Administration Building, 421 N. County Farm Rd., Wheaton, IL 60187
Tel: (630) 407-6500 E-mail: csprograms@dupageco.org
Internet: www.dupageco.org/community

Director **Mary Keating** .... (630) 407-6500
E-mail: mary.keating@dupageco.org

Building and Zoning Department

Jack T. Knuepfer Administration Building, 421 N. County Farm Rd., Wheaton, IL 60187
Tel: (630) 682-7230 Internet: www.dupageco.org/edp

Director **(Vacant)** .... (630) 407-6700
Stormwater Director **Anthony J. Charlton** .... (630) 407-6700
Workforce Development Director **Sue Clark** .... (630) 955-2030
2525 Cabot Drive, Suite 302, Lisle, IL 60532
E-mail: sclark@worknetdupage.org
Regulatory Services Manager **James "Jim" Stran** .... (630) 407-6700
Zoning Administrative Coordinator **Paul Hoss** .... (630) 407-6700

Finance Department

Jack T. Knuepfer Administration Building, 421 N. County Farm Rd., Wheaton, IL 60187
Internet: www.co.dupage.il.us/finance

Chief Financial Officer **Paul Rafac** .... (630) 407-6161

Procurement Division

Jack T. Knuepfer Administration Building, 421 County Farm Road, Wheaton, IL 60187

Procurement Officer **John Meneghini** .... (630) 407-6183
E-mail: john.meneghini@dupageco.org

★ Elected Official ▲ Appointed by Legislature ▼ Appointed by Governor ▶ Appointed by Board or Commission ● Appointed by Judge
■ Appointed by Mayor △ Appointed by Freeholders ▽ Appointed by Supervisor ▷ Appointed by County Executive ○ Appointed by Council

Human Resources Department
Jack T. Knuepfer Administration Building, 421 N. County Farm Rd., Wheaton, IL 60187
Fax: (630) 407-6301 E-mail: DPCHumanResources@dupageco.org
Internet: www.dupageco.org/hr

Director **Margaret Ewing** .... (630) 407-6300
Benefits Specialist **Tatia Hegranes** .... (630) 407-6300
Payroll Supervisor **Joanne Uitto** .... (630) 407-6300
E-mail: joanne.uitto@dupageco.org
Security **Keith Briggs** .... (630) 407-5225

Information Technology Department
Jack T. Knuepfer Administration Building, 421 N. County Farm Rd., Wheaton, IL 60187
Fax: (630) 407-5001

Chief Information Officer/Director
Donald "Don" Carlsen .... (630) 407-5000
E-mail: dcarlsen@dupageco.org

Division of Transportation [DuDOT]
Jack T. Knuepfer Administration Building, 421 N. County Farm Rd., Wheaton, IL 60187
Fax: (630) 640-6901 E-mail: dot@dupageco.org

Director **Christopher C. Snyder** .... (630) 407-6900
Deputy Director **(Vacant)** .... (630) 407-6900
County Engineer **Christopher C. Snyder** .... (630) 407-6900
E-mail: christopher.snyder@dupageco.org
Deputy Director of Facilities Management
Timothy "Tim" Harbaugh .... (630) 407-5700
E-mail: tim.harbaugh@dupageco.org
Director of Public Works
Nicholas N. "Nick" Kottmeyer .... (630) 407-6800

DuPage Convalescent Center [DPCC]
400 North County Farm Road, Wheaton, IL 60187
Fax: (630) 784-4203 E-mail: dpcc@dupageco.org

Director **Jennifer Ulmer** .... (630) 665-6400

DuPage County Board of Health
111 North County Farm Road, Lower Level Conference Room #1, Wheaton, IL 60187
Internet: www.dupagehealth.org/board-of-health

President **Linda A. Kurzawa** (R) .... (630) 682-7400

DuPage County Health Department [DCHD]
111 North County Farm Road, Wheaton, IL 60187
Tel: (630) 682-7400 TTY: (630) 932-1447
Internet: www.dupagehealth.org

▶ Executive Director **Karen Ayala** .... (630) 682-7400
Communications Manager **David Hass** .... (630) 221-7374
E-mail: dhass@dupagehealth.org

DuPage County Law Library
Judicial Office Facility, 503 North County Farm Road, Wheaton, IL 60187
Internet: www.dupageco.org/lawlibrary

Director **Liz Cooper** .... (630) 407-8798
E-mail: elizabeth.cooper@dupageco.org

DuPage County Election Commission
Jack T. Knuepfer Administration Building, 421 N. County Farm Rd., Wheaton, IL 60187
Tel: (630) 407-5600 Fax: (630) 407-5630
E-mail: ecommission@dupageco.org Internet: www.dupageelections.com

Chairman **Cathy Ficker Terrill** .... (630) 407-5697
Vice Chairman **Jamie Lowe** .... (630) 407-5699
Secretary **Arthur Ludwig** .... (630) 407-5698

DuPage County Election Commission *continued*

▶ Executive Director **Robert T. "Bob" Saar** .... (630) 407-5625
E-mail: rsaar@dupageco.com

Office of the County Auditor
Jack T. Knuepfer Administration Building, 421 N. County Farm Rd., Wheaton, IL 60187
Fax: (630) 407-6076 E-mail: auditor@dupageco.org

★ Auditor **Bob Grogan** (R) .... (630) 407-6095
Term Expires: November 30, 2016
E-mail: auditor@dupageco.org
Deputy Auditor **Peter Balgemann** .... (630) 407-6090

Office of the County Clerk
Jack T. Knuepfer Administration Building, 421 N. County Farm Rd., Wheaton, IL 60187
E-mail: coclerk@dupageco.org

★ County Clerk **Paul Hinds** .... (630) 407-5500
Term Expires: November 30, 2018
E-mail: paul.hinds@dupageco.org
Chief Deputy County Clerk **Kathy King** .... (630) 407-5500
E-mail: kathy.king@dupageco.org

Office of the County Coroner
414 N. County Farm Rd., Wheaton, IL 60187
Fax: (630) 407-2601

★ Coroner **Dr. Richard Jorgensen** .... (630) 407-2600
Term Expires: November 30, 2016
E-mail: rjorgensen@dupageco.org
Chief Deputy Coroner **Charles J. "Charlie" Dastych** .... (630) 407-2600

Office of the County Recorder of Deeds
Jack T. Knuepfer Administration Building, 421 N. County Farm Rd., Wheaton, IL 60187
E-mail: recorder@dupageco.org

★ County Recorder **Fred Bucholz** (R) .... (630) 407-5400
Term Expires: November 30, 2016
E-mail: fbucholz@dupageco.org
Chief Deputy Recorder **Anthony Manzzullo** .... (630) 407-5400

Office of the County Sheriff
501 North County Farm Road, Wheaton, IL 60187
Tel: (630) 682-7256 Fax: (630) 682-7747
E-mail: sheriff@dupagesheriff.org

★ Sheriff **John E. Zaruba** (R) .... (630) 407-2000
Term Expires: November 30, 2018
E-mail: jzaruba@dupagesheriff.org
Education: Western Illinois; Lewis U
Administrative Bureau Chief **James "Jim" Kruse** .... (630) 407-2000
E-mail: james.kruse@dupageco.org
Corrections Bureau Chief **Al Angus** .... (630) 407-2000
Law Enforcement Bureau Chief **Daniel Bilodeau** .... (630) 407-2000
E-mail: dan.bilodeau@dupagesheriff.org

★ Elected Official ▲ Appointed by Legislature ▼ Appointed by Governor ▶ Appointed by Board or Commission ● Appointed by Judge
■ Appointed by Mayor △ Appointed by Freeholders ▽ Appointed by Supervisor ▷ Appointed by County Executive ○ Appointed by Council

Office of the Treasurer

Jack T. Knuepfer Administration Building, 421 N. County Farm Rd., Wheaton, IL 60187
Tel: (630) 407-5900 Fax: (630) 407-5991

★Treasurer/Collector **Gwen S. Henry** (R) . . . . . (630) 407-5990
Term Expires: November 30, 2016
E-mail: gwen.henry@dupageco.org

Chief Deputy Treasurer, Collection **Leann Stahelin** . . . . . (630) 407-5990
E-mail: leann.stahelin@dupageco.org

Chief Deputy Treasurer, Treasury **Venessa Lopatka** . . . . . (630) 407-5990

Office of the State's Attorney

503 North County Farm Road, Wheaton, IL 60187
Fax: (630) 407-8151 E-mail: sao@dupageco.org

★State's Attorney **Robert B. "Bob" Berlin** (R) . . . . . (630) 407-8000
Term Expires: November 30, 2016
E-mail: sao@dupageco.org
Education: Dickinson Col BA; Washington U (MO) 1987 JD

DuPage Regional Office of Education

Jack T. Knuepfer Administration Building, 421 North County Farm Road, Wheaton, IL 60187
Tel: (630) 407-5800 Internet: www.dupage.k12.il.us

★Regional Superintendent of Schools
Dr. Darlene J. Ruscitti (R) . . . . . (630) 407-5770
Term Expires: June 2019
E-mail: druscitti@dupageroe.org
Education: Northeastern Illinois 1976 BA, 1988 MA; Loyola U (Chicago) 2002 EdD

Assistant Regional Superintendent **(Vacant)** . . . . . (630) 407-5772

County of El Paso, Colorado

200 S. Cascade Ave., Colorado Springs, CO 80903
Tel: (719) 520-7276 (Information) Internet: www.elpasoco.com

County Seat: Colorado Springs **Election Type:** Partisan
Population: 674,471 (2015)

Office of the Board of Commissioners

200 S. Cascade Ave., Suite 500, Colorado Springs, CO 80903
Tel: (719) 520-7276 Fax: (719) 520-6397

★Chair **Amy Lathen** (R-District 2) . . . . . (719) 520-7276
Term Expires: January 13, 2017
E-mail: amylathen@elpasoco.com

★Vice Chair **Dennis Hisey** (R-District 4) . . . . . (719) 520-7276
Term Expires: January 13, 2017

★Commissioner **Darryl Glenn** (R-District 1) . . . . . (719) 520-7276
Term Expires: January 9, 2019
Education: Air Force Acad BS; Western New England MBA; New England JD

★Commissioner **Sallie Clark** (R-District 3) . . . . . (719) 520-7276
Term Expires: January 13, 2017

★Commissioner **Peggy Littleton** (R-District 5) . . . . . (719) 520-7276
Term Expires: January 9, 2019
Education: Regent U BS

Clerk to the Board **Vicki Ratterree** . . . . . (719) 520-6432
E-mail: vickiratterree@elpasoco.com Fax: (719) 520-7326

Office of the County Attorney

27 E. Vermijo Ave., Colorado Springs, CO 80903-2208
Fax: (719) 520-6487 E-mail: cat@elpasoco.com

►County Attorney **Amy R. Folsom** . . . . . (719) 520-6485
E-mail: amyfolsom@elpasoco.com

Public Defender

415 S. Sahwatch, Colorado Springs, CO 80903
Fax: (719) 475-1476 E-mail: cosprings.defenders@state.co.us

Colorado Springs Office Head/Deputy Public Defender
Carrie Lynn Thompson . . . . . (719) 475-1235

Office of the Public Trustee

105 East Vermijo Avenue, Suite 101, Colorado Springs, CO 80903
Fax: (719) 520-6781

▼Public Trustee **Thomas S. Mowle** . . . . . (719) 520-6780
E-mail: thomasmowle@elpasopublictrustee.com Fax: (719) 520-6781

El Paso County Board of Health

Regional Development Center, 2880 International Circle, Colorado Springs, CO 80910
Tel: (719) 578-3101 Internet: www.elpasocountyhealth.org/pages/boh.aspx

President **Kari Kilroy** . . . . . (719) 578-3101

El Paso County Public Health

1675 West Garden of the Gods Road, Colorado Springs, CO 80907
Tel: (719) 578-3199 Fax: (719) 578-3192
E-mail: healthinfo@epchealth.org Internet: www.elpasocountyhealth.org

Executive Director **Dan Martindale** . . . . . (719) 578-3266
Medical Director **Dr. Bill Leston** . . . . . (719) 578-3199

Office of the County Administrator

200 S. Cascade Ave., Suite 200, Colorado Springs, CO 80903
Fax: (719) 520-6397 E-mail: adm@elpasoco.com

►County Administrator **(Vacant)** . . . . . (719) 520-7276
Deputy County Administrator **Monnie L. Gore, Jr.** . . . . . (719) 520-6900
E-mail: monniegore@elpasoco.com

Budget Administration Department

200 S. Cascade Ave., Colorado Springs, CO 80903
Tel: (719) 520-6486
Internet: http://adm.elpasoco.com/budgetadministration/

County Budget Officer **Nicola Sapp** . . . . . (719) 520-6400

Budget Division

27 East Vermijo Avenue, 5th Floor, Colorado Springs, CO 80903-2208
Fax: (719) 520-6428

Manager **Elaine Johnsen** . . . . . (719) 520-6400
E-mail: elainejohnsen@elpasoco.com

Economic Development Division

27 East Vermijo Avenue, 5th Floor, Colorado Springs, CO 80903
Fax: (719) 520-6486 E-mail: bnfweb@elpasoco.com

Manager **DeAnne McCann** . . . . . (719) 520-6481

Finance Division

200 S. Cascade Ave., Suite 500, Colorado Springs, CO 80903
Fax: (719) 520-6428

Manager **Nikki S. Simmons** . . . . . (719) 520-6498

Public Information Division

200 S. Cascade Ave., Suite 500, Colorado Springs, CO 80903
Fax: (719) 520-6397
Internet: http://adm.elpasoco.com/publiccommunications/

Chief Public Information Officer **Dave Rose** . . . . . (719) 520-6540
E-mail: daverose@elpasoco.com

Community Services Department

2002 Creek Crossing, Colorado Springs, CO 80906

Director **Tim Wolken** . . . . . (719) 520-7529

COUNTIES

★Elected Official ▲Appointed by Legislature ▼Appointed by Governor ►Appointed by Board or Commission ●Appointed by Judge
■Appointed by Mayor △Appointed by Freeholders ▽Appointed by Supervisor ▷Appointed by County Executive ○Appointed by Council

Office of Cooperative Extension (Colorado State University)
305 South Union Boulevard, Colorado Springs, CO 80910
Tel: (719) 520-7684 Fax: (719) 520-7699 E-mail: csue@elpasoco.com
Internet: http://elpasoco.colostate.edu/

County Extension Director **Barbara Bates** .... (719) 520-7690

Environmental Division
3255 Akers Drive, Colorado Springs, CO 80922
Fax: (719) 520-7827

Manager **Kathy Andrew** .... (719) 520-7879

Parks Operations Division
2002 Creek Crossing, Colorado Springs, CO 80906
Fax: (719) 520-6389 E-mail: prkweb@elpasoco.com
Internet: http://adm.elpasoco.com/parks/

Manager **Brad Bixler** .... (719) 520-7529

El Paso County Fair and Event Complex
366 10th Street, Calhan, CO 80808
Fax: (719) 520-7883 E-mail: events@elpasoco.com
Internet: www.elpasocountyfair.com

Special Events Coordinator **Suzan McCoy** .... (719) 520-7880

Development Services Department
2880 International Circle, Suite 110, Colorado Springs, CO 80910
Tel: (719) 520-6300 Fax: (719) 520-6695

Executive Director **Craig Dossey** .... (719) 520-6300

Development Services Division
2880 International Circle, Colorado Springs, CO 80910
Fax: (719) 520-6322 E-mail: plnweb@elpasoco.com

Manager **Mike Hrebenar** .... (719) 520-6300

Department of Human Services [DHS]
1675 West Garden of the Gods Road, Colorado Springs, CO 80907
Tel: (719) 636-0000 Fax: (719) 444-5598
Internet: www.dhs.elpasoco.com

▶ Director **Richard Bengtsson** .... (719) 444-5535
E-mail: richardbengtsson@elpasoco.com

Senior Services Division
Fountain Valley Senior Center, 5745 Southmoor Drive, Fountain, CO 80817
Fax: (719) 392-2994

Transportation and Operations Supervisor and Executive Director **Dennis A. Crosser** .... (719) 520-6473
E-mail: denniscrosser@elpasoco.com

Veteran Services Division
105 East Vermijo Avenue, Suite 103, Colorado Springs, CO 80903
Fax: (719) 520-7751 Internet: http://adm.elpasoco.com/veteranservices/

Manager **Jim Tackett** .... (719) 520-7756

Public Services Department
3275 Akers Drive, Colorado Springs, CO 80922
Fax: (719) 520-6879 Internet: http://adm.elpasoco.com/publicservices/

Deputy County Administrator **Monnie L. Gore, Jr.** .... (719) 520-6900
County Engineer **Andre Brackin** .... (719) 520-6460
Operations Manager **(Vacant)** .... (719) 520-6460
Construction Services Section Manager **Carl McClillan** ... (719) 520-6460
E-mail: carlmcclillan@elpasoco.com

Contracts and Procurement Division
200 S. Cascade Ave., Suite 150, Colorado Springs, CO 80903
Fax: (719) 520-6396

Contracts Manager **Eileen Gonzales** .... (719) 520-6398
E-mail: eileengonzales@elpasoco.com

Office of Emergency Management
3755 Mark Dabling Bouldevard, Colorado Springs, CO 80907
Tel: (719) 575-8424

Executive Director **James A. Reid** .... (719) 575-8424
Operations Manager and Recovery Coordinator **R. C. Smith** .... (719) 575-8400
E-mail: rcsmith@elpasoco.com
Emergency Management Coordinator **Caroline Joy** ...... (719) 575-8424
E-mail: carolinejoy@elpasoco.com

Support Services Department
2880 International Circle, Suite N060, Colorado Springs, CO 80910
Fax: (719) 520-7406

▶ Director **Imad Karaki** .... (719) 520-6424
E-mail: imadkaraki@elpasoco.com

Employment, Benefits and Medical Services Division [EBMS]
2880 International Circle, Colorado Springs, CO 80910
Fax: (719) 520-7406

Workman's Compensation Division Manager **Andrea McGee** .... (719) 520-7420

Information Technologies Division
325 South Cascade Avenue, Colorado Springs, CO 80903
Fax: (719) 520-6755 E-mail: isvweb@elpasoco.com

Chief Information Officer **Bill Miller** .... (719) 520-6435
Education: BYU 1972 BS; Utah 1973 MBA

Pikes Peak Library District
5550 North Union Boulevard, Colorado Springs, CO 80918
Internet: http://library.ppld.org

Director **John Spears** .... (719) 531-6333 ext. 2300
E-mail: paulamiller@elpasoco.com
Associate Director (Community Engagement) **Dee Vasquez Sabol** .... (719) 531-9828
E-mail: deevasquez@elpasoco.com
Associate Director (Public Services) **(Vacant)** .... (719) 531-6333

Law Library
20 North Cascade Avenue, Colorado Springs, CO 80903
Fax: (719) 632-5744

Law Librarian **Emilie Satterwhite** .... (719) 531-6333 ext. 2309
E-mail: emiliesatterwhite@elpasoco.com

Office of the Assessor
1675 West Garden of the Gods Road, Colorado Springs, CO 80907
Fax: (719) 520-6635 E-mail: asrweb@elpasoco.com

★ Assessor **Steve Schleiker** (R) .... (719) 520-6600
Term Expires: January 2019

Office of the Clerk and Recorder
1675 West Garden of the Gods Road, Colorado Springs, CO 80907
Fax: (719) 520-6212

★ Clerk and Recorder **Chuck Broerman** (R) .... (719) 520-6202
Term Expires: January 2019

Office of the Coroner
2743 E. Las Vegas St., Colorado Springs, CO 80906
Fax: (719) 390-2462 E-mail: cor@elpasoco.com
Internet: http://cor.elpasoco.com

★ Coroner **Dr. Robert C. Bux** (R) .... (719) 390-2410
Term Expires: January 9, 2019
Education: U A Guadalajara 1974 MD

★ Elected Official ▲ Appointed by Legislature ▼ Appointed by Governor ▶ Appointed by Board or Commission ● Appointed by Judge
■ Appointed by Mayor △ Appointed by Freeholders ▽ Appointed by Supervisor ▷ Appointed by County Executive ○ Appointed by Council

Office of the District Attorney

105 E. Vermijo Ave., Colorado Springs, CO 80903
Fax: (719) 520-6185 E-mail: dao@elpasoco.com

★ District Attorney **Dan May** .... (719) 520-6000
Term Expires: January 13, 2017
E-mail: districtattorney@elpasoco.com

Office of the Sheriff

101 West Castilla Street, Colorado Springs, CO 80903
Fax: (719) 520-7259 E-mail: shrweb@elpasoco.com

★ Sheriff **Bill Elder** (R) .... (719) 520-7100
Term Expires: January 2019

Office of Emergency Management

101 West Castilla Street, Colorado Springs, CO 80903
Fax: (719) 575-8591

Director **Jim Reid** .... (719) 575-8400

Office of the Surveyor

2610 Northridge Drive, Colorado Springs, CO 80918

★ County Surveyor **G. Lawrence Burnett** (R) .... (719) 271-1601
Term Expires: January 2019

Office of the Treasurer

1675 West Garden of the Gods Road, Colorado Springs, CO 80907
Fax: (719) 635-3115 E-mail: trsweb@elpasoco.com

★ Treasurer **Mark Lowderman** (R) .... (719) 520-6666
Term Expires: January 2019

County of El Paso, Texas

County Courthouse, 500 E. San Antonio Ave., El Paso, TX 79901
Tel: (915) 546-2000 (Information) Internet: www.epcounty.com

County Seat: El Paso **Election Type:** Partisan **Population:** 835,593 (2015)

Office of the County Judge

County Courthouse, 500 East San Antonio Avenue, Room 301, El Paso, TX 79901
Tel: (915) 546-2098 Fax: (915) 543-3888
Internet: www.epcounty.com/judge

★ County Judge **Veronica Escobar** (D) .... (915) 546-2098
Term Expires: December 31, 2018
E-mail: countyjudge@epcounty.com
Education: Texas (El Paso) 1991 BA; NYU 1993 MA
Executive Assistant **Celeste A. Varela** .... (915) 546-2098
E-mail: cvarela@epcounty.com
Public Policy Director **Ruben John Vogt** .... (915) 546-2098

Office of the County Commission

County Courthouse, 500 East San Antonio Avenue, Room 301, El Paso, TX 79901
Fax: (915) 543-3885

★ Commissioner **Carlos Leon** (D-Precinct 1) .... (915) 546-2014
Term Expires: December 31, 2016
E-mail: commissioner1@epcounty.com
Administrative Assistant **Mayela Mejia** .... (915) 546-2111
E-mail: mmejia@epcounty.com Fax: (915) 543-3817

Office of the County Commission *continued*

★ Commissioner **David Stout** (D-Precinct 2) .... (915) 546-2111
Term Expires: December 31, 2018 Fax: (915) 543-3817
E-mail: commissioner2@epcounty.com
Administrative Assistant **Joshua Acevedo** .... (915) 546-2111
E-mail: joacevedo@epcounty.com Fax: (915) 543-3817
★ Commissioner **Vincent M. Perez** (D-Precinct 3) .... (915) 546-2144
Term Expires: December 31, 2016 Fax: (915) 543-3809
E-mail: commissioner3@epcounty.com
Public Policy Advisor **Jose Landeros** .... (915) 546-2144
E-mail: jlanderos@epcounty.com Fax: (915) 543-3809
★ Commissioner **Andrew Haggerty** (R-Precinct 4) .... (915) 546-2044
Term Expires: December 31, 2018 Fax: (915) 543-3854
E-mail: commissioner4@epcounty.com
Administrative Assistant **Candance E. McCann** .... (915) 546-2044
E-mail: cmccann@epcounty.com Fax: (915) 543-3845

Office of the County Auditor

800 East Overland Street, Room 406, El Paso, TX 79901
Fax: (915) 546-8172 Internet: www.epcounty.com/auditor

County Auditor **Edward A. Dion** .... (915) 546-2040 ext. 3482
Director of Financial Operations **Victor Perez** .. (915) 546-2040 ext. 3477

Office of the Medical Examiner

4505 Alberta Avenue, El Paso, TX 79905
Fax: (915) 532-6630 Internet: www.epcounty.com/medicalexaminer

▶ Chief Medical Examiner/Forensic Pathologist
Mario Rascon .... (915) 532-1447
E-mail: mrascon@epcounty.com
Deputy Medical Examiner **Juan U. Contin** .... (915) 532-1447
Deputy Medical Examiner **Janice Cavalliery** .... (915) 532-1447

Office of the Public Defender

County Courthouse, 500 East San Antonio Avenue, Room 501, El Paso, TX 79901
Fax: (915) 546-8186 E-mail: publicdefender@epcounty.com
Internet: www.epcounty.com/pdefender

▶ Public Defender **Jaime Gandara** .... (915) 546-8185
Education: Texas 1983 JD

Communications Department

500 East San Antonio Street, Room 304, El Paso, TX 79901
Fax: (915) 543-3847 Internet: www.epcounty.com/communications

Director **Victor Montes** .... (915) 546-2000
E-mail: vmontes@epcounty.com

Elections Department

County Courthouse, 500 East San Antonio Avenue, Room 314, El Paso, TX 79901
Fax: (915) 546-2220 Internet: www.epcounty.com/elections

● Administrator **Lisa Wise** .... (915) 546-2154
E-mail: lwise@epcounty.com
Assistant Administrator **Antonio Rivera** .... (915) 546-2154
Elections Generalist, Sr. **Vanessa Ruiz** .... (915) 546-2154

Facilities Management Department

County Courthouse, 500 East San Antonio Avenue, Room M-1, El Paso, TX 79901
Fax: (915) 543-3820 Internet: www.epcounty.com/facilities

Administrative Support Manager (Interim)
Gilbert Mijarez .... (915) 546-2009
E-mail: gmijarez@epcounty.com

COUNTIES

COUNTIES

Family and Community Services Department
800 East Overland Street, Room 208, El Paso, TX 79901
Tel: (915) 546-8167 (Congregate Program Meals)
Tel: (915) 546-8168 (Homebound Delivery Program) Fax: (915) 532-4563

▶ Director **(Vacant)** .... (915) 546-8167
Program Accountant **Grace Condardo** .... (915) 546-8167
E-mail: gcondardo@epcounty.com

General Assistance Agency
800 East Overland Street, Suite 301, El Paso, TX 79901
Fax: (915) 544-6259
Internet: www.epcounty.com/famcom/generalassist.htm

▶ Manager **Michael Flores** .... (915) 546-8150
E-mail: miflores@epcounty.com
Senior Caseworker/Supervisor **Lucino Martinez** .... (915) 546-8150

Veterans' Assistance Office
4641 Cohen Avenue, Suite D, El Paso, TX 79924
Fax: (915) 759-0217 Internet: www.epcounty.com/veterans

Manager **Michael Flores** .... (915) 759-7990

Robert J. Galvan Law Library
County Courthouse, 500 East San Antonio Avenue, Room 1202, El Paso, TX 79901
Fax: (915) 546-2250 Internet: www.epcounty.com/lawlibrary

Librarian/Director **Lynn E. Sanchez** .... (915) 546-2245
E-mail: lsanchez@epcounty.com
Assistant Librarian **Sandra Andrade** .... (915) 546-2245
E-mail: sandrade@epcounty.com

Human Resources Department
800 East Overland Street, Room 223, El Paso, TX 79901
Fax: (915) 546-8126 Internet: www.epcounty.com/hr

▶ Chief Human Resources Officer **Melissa Carrillo** .... (915) 546-2218
E-mail: melcarrillo@epcounty.com
Deputy Human Resources Officer **Michele Cochrane** .... (915) 887-3420
E-mail: mcochrane@epcounty.com
Deputy Human Resources Officer **Sam Trujillo** .... (915) 546-2218
E-mail: strujillo@epcounty.com
Deputy Human Resources Officer **Elsie West** .... (915) 546-2218
E-mail: elwest@epcounty.com
Human Resources Manager **Natalia Chaparro** .... (915) 849-2536
E-mail: nachaparro@epcounty.com
Human Resources Manager **Melissa Laibinis** .... (915) 538-2179
E-mail: mlaibinis@epcounty.com
Human Resources Manager **Reginal Powe** .... (915) 849-2521
E-mail: rpowe@epcounty.com
Personnel Manager **(Vacant)** .... (915) 546-2218
Human Resources Supervisor **(Vacant)** .... (915) 538-2218
Human Resources Supervisor **Valeria Fernandez** .... (915) 538-2218
E-mail: vfernandez@epcounty.com
Human Resources Supervisor **Ludy Velo** .... (915) 546-2218
E-mail: lvelo@epcounty.com
Workers Compensation Specialist **Kathleen Amparan** .... (915) 546-2218
E-mail: kamparan@epcounty.com
Americans with Disabilities (ADA) Coordinator
Amanda Proffitt .... (915) 546-2218
E-mail: aproffitt@epcounty.com

Civil Service Commission
▶ Chairperson **Selena Solis** .... (915) 546-2218
▶ Commissioner **Carlos Gomez** .... (915) 546-2218
▶ Commissioner **Grace Munoz** .... (915) 546-2218

Information Technology Department
800 East Overland Street, Suite 400, El Paso, TX 79901
Tel: (915) 546-2041 Fax: (915) 546-2042
Internet: www.epcounty.com/itd

▶ Chief Technology Officer
Christopher Stathis .... (915) 546-2041 ext. 3384

Information Technology Department *continued*

Director of Information Technology
David Garcia .... (915) 546-2041 ext. 3768
E-mail: dgarcia@epcounty.com
Internet/Intranet Applications Manager
Luke Gilpin .... (915) 546-2041 ext. 3842
E-mail: lgilpin@epcounty.com
Office and Administrative Support Manager
Cathy Rice .... (915) 546-2041 ext. 3555
Server and Systems Manager **Suzi Esquivel** .... (915) 546-2041 ext. 3573
Help Desk/Tech Support Manager
Nanette Olivas .... (915) 546-2041 ext. 3002
E-mail: olivas@epcounty.com
Telecommunications/Project Manager **(Vacant)** .. (915) 546-2041 ext. 2169

Parks and Recreation Department
6900 Delta Dr., El Paso, TX 79905-5500
Fax: (915) 771-9358 Internet: www.epcounty.com/parksandrec

▶ Director **Eric Storrie** .... (915) 772-5605 ext. 23
E-mail: estorrie@epcounty.com
Administrative Assistant **Lupe Leyva** .... (915) 772-5605
E-mail: lleyva@epcounty.com

Purchasing Department
800 East Overland Street, Suite 300, El Paso, TX 79901
Fax: (915) 546-8180 Internet: www.epcounty.com/purchasing

Purchasing Agent **Kennie Downing** .... (915) 546-2048
E-mail: kdowning@epcounty.com
Assistant Purchasing Agent **Jose Lopez, Jr.** .... (915) 546-2068
E-mail: jlopez@epcounty.com

Road and Bridge Department
800 East Overland Street, Room 407, El Paso, TX 79901
Fax: (915) 546-8194 Internet: www.epcounty.com/rb

▶ Director of Public Works/County Engineer
Patricia D. Adauto .... (915) 546-2015
Administrative Assistant **Dolores Reyes** .... (915) 546-2015
E-mail: dreyes@epcounty.com
Assistant Public Works Director **Norma Palacios** .... (915) 546-2015
E-mail: npalacios@epcounty.com

West Texas Community Supervision and Corrections Department [WTCSCD]
800 East Overland Street, Suite 100, El Paso, TX 79901
Fax: (915) 546-8130 Internet: www.epcounty.com/wtc

● Director **Magdalena "Maggie" Morales-Aina** .... (915) 546-8120
E-mail: senders@epcounty.com

Texas AgriLife Extension Service
301 Manny Martinez Sr. Drive, Second Floor, El Paso, TX 79905
Tel: (915) 771-2354 Fax: (915) 771-2356 E-mail: el-paso-tx@tamu.edu
Internet: http://el-paso-tx.tamu.edu/

County Extension Director **Raymond Bader** ... (915) 771-2354 ext. 2357

Office of the County Attorney
County Courthouse, 500 East San Antonio Avenue, Room 503, El Paso, TX 79901
Fax: (915) 546-2133 E-mail: comments@ca.epcounty.com
Internet: www.epcounty.com/ca

★ County Attorney **Jo Anne Bernal** (D) .... (915) 546-2050
Term Expires: December 31, 2016
E-mail: joanne.bernal@epcounty.com
Education: Texas, 1986 JD
Executive Assistant to the County Attorney
Melissa Watt .... (915) 546-2050
First Assistant County Attorney **Eddie Sosa** .... (915) 546-2050

★ Elected Official ▲ Appointed by Legislature ▼ Appointed by Governor ▶ Appointed by Board or Commission ● Appointed by Judge
■ Appointed by Mayor △ Appointed by Freeholders ▽ Appointed by Supervisor ▷ Appointed by County Executive ○ Appointed by Council

Office of the County Clerk

County Courthouse, 500 East San Antonio Avenue, Room 105, El Paso, TX 79901-2496
Fax: (915) 546-2012 E-mail: countyclerk@epcounty.com
Internet: www.epcounty.com/clerk

★ County Clerk **Delia Briones** (D) .... (915) 546-2071
Term Expires: December 31, 2018
Chief Deputy **Carol Sagaribay** .... (915) 546-2071
E-mail: csagaribay@epcounty.com
Office Manager **Anthony E. "Tony" Bedoya** .... (915) 546-2071

Records Management and Archives Department

500 East San Antonio Avenue, Suite 105, El Paso, TX 79901
Tel: (915) 546-8101 (Information) Fax: (915) 546-8125

▶ Administrator **Gabriel Escandon** .... (915) 546-8110
E-mail: gescandon@epcounty.com

Office of the District Attorney

County Courthouse, 500 East San Antonio Avenue, Room 203, El Paso, TX 79901
Fax: (915) 533-5520 Internet: www.epcounty.com/da

★ District Attorney **Jaime Eloy Esparza** (D) .... (915) 546-2059
Term Expires: December 31, 2016
E-mail: daesparza@epcounty.com
Education: Texas 1979 BBA; Houston 1983 JD
First Assistant District Attorney **Karen LaRose** .... (915) 546-2059
E-mail: klarose@epcounty.com

Office of the Sheriff

3850 Justice Drive, El Paso, TX 79938
Tel: (915) 538-2000 Fax: (915) 538-2028
E-mail: epsheriff@epcounty.com Internet: http://shr.elpasoco.com/

★ Sheriff **Richard D. Wiles** .... (915) 538-2006
Term Expires: December 31, 2016
E-mail: rwiles@epcounty.com
Executive Chief Deputy **Sylvia Aguilar** .... (915) 538-2105
E-mail: saguilar@epcounty.com
Chief, Detention Bureau **Sylvia Aguilar** .... (915) 538-2105
Chief, Law Enforcement Bureau **Tom Whitten** .... (915) 538-2081
E-mail: twhitten@epcounty.com

Office of the Tax Assessor/Collector

301 Manny Martinez Sr. Drive, First Floor, El Paso, TX 79905
Tel: (915) 771-2300 Fax: (915) 771-2301
E-mail: ctaxassessor@epcounty.com
Internet: www.epcounty.com/taxoffice

★ Tax Assessor-Collector **Ruben P. Gonzalez** .... (915) 546-2097
Term Expires: December 31, 2016
E-mail: ctaxassessor@epcounty.com
Chief Deputy Tax Assessor-Collector **Arturo Pastrana** ... (915) 546-2096
Director, Motor Vehicle Registration and Titling Division **Barbara Banks** .... (915) 546-2150
Enforcement Director **Sergio H. Garcia** .... (915) 755-3535
E-mail: segarcia@epcounty.com
Accounting Manager **Letty Ramos** .... (915) 543-3875
E-mail: lramos@epcounty.com

County of Erie, New York

Rath Bldg., 95 Franklin Street, Buffalo, NY 14202
Tel: (716) 858-6000 (Information) Internet: www.erie.gov

County Seat: Buffalo **Election Type:** Partisan **Population:** 922,578 (2015)

Office of the County Executive

Rath Building, 95 Franklin Street, Buffalo, NY 14202
Fax: (716) 858-8411 Internet: www.erie.gov/exec

★ County Executive **Mark C. Poloncarz** (D) .... (716) 858-8500
Term Expires: December 31, 2019
▷ Deputy County Executive (Interim) **Maria R. Whyte** (D) .. (716) 858-8500

Division of Budget and Management

Rath Building, 95 Franklin Street, Room 1601, Buffalo, NY 14202
Fax: (716) 858-8837 Internet: www.erie.gov/exec/budget_info.asp

▷ Director **Robert W. Keating** .... (716) 858-8515

Office of the County Attorney

95 Franklin Street, Room 1634, Buffalo, NY 14202-3972
Tel: (716) 858-2200 Fax: (716) 858-2281

▷ County Attorney **Michael A. Siragusa** .... (716) 858-2200
E-mail: michael.siragusa@erie.gov
Education: Rutgers JD
First Assistant County Attorney **Michelle M. Parker** ..... (716) 858-2209

Erie County Office for the Disabled [ECOD]

Rath Bldg., 95 Franklin Street, Room 625, Buffalo, NY 14202
Fax: (716) 858-6411 Internet: www.erie.gov/ecod

▷ Executive Director **Frank A. Cammarata III** .... (716) 858-6215
E-mail: frank.cammarata@erie.gov

Office of Equal Employment Opportunity [EEO]

Rath Building, 95 Franklin Street, Room 625, Buffalo, NY 14202
Tel: (716) 858-7542 Fax: (716) 858-8311

▷ Director **Jesse L. Burnett** .... (716) 858-7542
E-mail: jesse.burnette@erie.gov

Erie County Central Police Services

Public Safety Building, 45 Elm Street, Buffalo, NY 14203
Tel: (716) 858-8219 Fax: (716) 858-6039 Internet: www2.erie.gov/cps

▷ Commissioner **John A. Glascott** .... (716) 858-6365

Department of Emergency Services

45 Elm Street, Buffalo, NY 14203
Fax: (716) 858-7937 Internet: www.erie.gov/emergency

▷ Commissioner **Daniel Neaverth, Jr.** .... (716) 858-6578
E-mail: daniel.neaverth@erie.gov
▷ Deputy Commissioner, Civil Defense/Disaster Preparedness **Greg Butcher** .... (716) 858-2944
E-mail: gregory.butcher@erie.gov
▷ Deputy Commissioner, Fire Safety **James McCullough** .. (716) 681-7111
3359 Broadway, Cheektowaga, NY 14227
E-mail: james.mccullough@erie.gov

Department of Environment and Planning [DEP]

Edward A. Rath Building, 95 Franklin Street, Room 1053, Buffalo, NY 14202
Tel: (716) 858-8390 Fax: (716) 858-7248
Internet: www.erie.gov/environment

▷ Commissioner **Thomas J. Dearing** .... (716) 858-8390
E-mail: thomas.dearing@erie.gov

COUNTIES

★ Elected Official ▲ Appointed by Legislature ▼ Appointed by Governor ▶ Appointed by Board or Commission ● Appointed by Judge
■ Appointed by Mayor △ Appointed by Freeholders ▽ Appointed by Supervisor ▷ Appointed by County Executive ○ Appointed by Council

Office of Planning and Economic Development [OED]
Edward A. Rath County Office Building, 95 Franklin Street, 10th Floor, Buffalo, NY 14202
Tel: (716) 858-8390 Fax: (716) 858-7248

Deputy Commissioner **Michael J. LoCurto** (D) . . . . (716) 858-7256
Business Assistance Director **Kenneth J. Swanekamp**
Room 1060 . . . . (716) 858-6170
E-mail: kenneth.swanekamp@erie.gov
Industrial Assistance Program Coordinator
Christopher S. Pawenski Room 1056 . . . . (716) 858-2950
E-mail: christopher.pawenski@erie.gov

Division of Planning and Environmental Compliance
Edward A. Rath County Office Building, 95 Franklin Street, 10th Floor, Buffalo, NY 14202
Tel: (716) 858-6370 Fax: (716) 858-7713

Deputy Commissioner **Thomas R. Hersey** . . . . (716) 858-6370

Erie County Department of Health [ECDOH]
Rath Bldg., 95 Franklin Street, Room 910, Buffalo, NY 14202
Fax: (716) 858-8701

▷Commissioner **Dr. Gail R. Burstein** . . . . (716) 858-6976
Education: Buffalo DM
Executive Assistant to the Commissioner
Benjamin Swane Kamp . . . . (716) 858-6000
Administration Director **Cheryll Moore** . . . . (716) 858-4941
Disease Control Director **Janinne Blank** . . . . (716) 858-6462
Environmental Health Director **Dolores Funke** . . . . (716) 858-6105
▷Regional Public Health Laboratory Director
Carlene Pope . . . . (716) 898-6105
Public Information Officer **Mary St. Mary** . . . . (716) 858-8688
E-mail: stmarym@erie.gov
Senior Medical Care Administrator **Jacquelyn Andula** . . . (716) 858-7731

Office of the Medical Examiner
501 Kensington Avenue, Buffalo, NY 14214
Tel: (716) 961-7591 Fax: (716) 961-7581

Director **Janinne Blank** . . . . (716) 961-7591
Chief Medical Examiner **Dr. Tara J. Mahar** . . . . (716) 961-7591

Division of Information and Support Services [DISS]
Rath Building, 95 Franklin Street, Room 1500, Buffalo, NY 14202-3963
Fax: (716) 858-8072

▷Chief Information Officer **Michael C. Breeden** . . . . (716) 858-6266
E-mail: michael.breeden@erie.gov
▷Director of Information Technology **Lori Stilwell** . . . . (716) 858-2688
E-mail: lori.stilwell@erie.gov

Department of Labor Relations
Rath Building, 95 Franklin Street, Room 604, Buffalo, NY 14202

▷Commissioner **Steven M. Miller** . . . . (716) 858-8476
E-mail: steven.miller@erie.gov
▷Deputy Commissioner **Mary Thomas Scott** . . . . (716) 858-8476
Secretary **Mary Dickey** . . . . (716) 858-8476
E-mail: dickeym@erie.gov

Department of Mental Health
Rath Building, 95 Franklin Street, Room 1237, Buffalo, NY 14202-3966
Fax: (716) 858-6592 Internet: http://www2.erie.gov/mentalhealth/

▷Commissioner **Michael Ranney** . . . . (716) 858-8530

Department of Parks Recreation, and Forestry
Rath Building, 95 Franklin Street, Room 1254, Buffalo, NY 14202
Fax: (716) 858-8314 Internet: www.erie.gov/parks

Commissioner **Daniel Rizzo** . . . . (716) 858-6000
▷Deputy Commissioner **Gregory B. Olma** . . . . (716) 858-7037

Department of Personnel
Rath Bldg., 95 Franklin Street, Room 604A, Buffalo, NY 14202
Fax: (716) 858-8445

▷Commissioner **David A. Palmer** . . . . (716) 858-8460

Department of Probation
One Niagra Plaza, Buffalo, NY 14202-3492
Fax: (716) 858-8194 Internet: www2.erie.gov/probation

Commissioner **Brian McLaughlin** . . . . (716) 858-8205
Deputy Commissioner **Ysaias Feliz** . . . . (716) 858-8205

Department of Public Works [DPW]
95 Franklin Street, 14th Floor, Buffalo, NY 14202
Tel: (716) 858-8300 Fax: (716) 858-8303 Internet: www.erie.gov/dpw

▷Commissioner **John C. Loffredo** . . . . (716) 858-8300
E-mail: john.loffredo@erie.gov
Secretary **Diane Bukowski** . . . . (716) 858-8301
Highway Deputy Commissioner **William Geary** . . . . (716) 858-7372
Fax: (716) 858-8228

Department of Purchasing
Rath Bldg., 95 Franklin Street, Room 1254, Buffalo, NY 14202
Tel: (716) 858-6315 Fax: (716) 858-6465
Internet: www.erie.gov/depts/purchasing

▷Director **Vallie M. Ferraraccio** . . . . (716) 858-6315
E-mail: Vallie.Ferraraccio@erie.gov

Department of Senior Services
Rath Building, 95 Franklin Street, Room 1329, Buffalo, NY 14202
Tel: (716) 858-8526 Fax: (716) 858-7259 E-mail: seniorinfo@erie.gov
Internet: www.erie.gov/depts/seniorservices

▷Commissioner **Randy Hoak** . . . . (716) 858-8526
Fax: (716) 858-6597

Department of Social Services
Rath Building, 95 Franklin Street, Buffalo, NY 14202
Fax: (716) 858-8812

▷Commissioner **Al Dirschberger** . . . . (716) 858-7511
E-mail: dirscha2@erie.gov
First Deputy Commissioner **Judith Shanley** . . . . (716) 858-8000

Buffalo and Erie County Public Library
One Lafayette Square, Buffalo, NY 14203-1887
Tel: (716) 858-8900 Fax: (716) 858-6211 Internet: www.buffalolib.org

Administration
Director **Mary Jean Jakubowski** . . . . (716) 858-7180
E-mail: jakubowskim@buffalolib.org
Education: Buffalo 1991 MLS
Deputy Director and Chief Financial Officer
Kenneth H. Stone . . . . (716) 858-7170
E-mail: stonek@buffalolib.org
Deputy Director and Chief Operating Officer
Carol Ann Batt . . . . (716) 858-7191
E-mail: battc@buffalolib.org

Erie Community College [ECC]
121 Ellicott St., Buffalo, NY 14203
Tel: (716) 851-1001 Fax: (716) 851-1129 Internet: www.ecc.edu

President **John F. "Jack" Quinn, Jr.** (R) . . . . (716) 851-1200
Date of Birth: April 13, 1951 Fax: (716) 851-1029
Education: Siena Col 1973 BA; SUNY (Buffalo) 1978 MA
Chief Administrative Financial Officer **William Reuter** . . . (716) 851-1700
Fax: (716) 851-1703
Chief Information Officer **Joseph W. Stewart** . . . . (716) 851-1977
E-mail: stewart@ecc.edu Fax: (716) 270-2824

★ Elected Official ▲ Appointed by Legislature ▼ Appointed by Governor ► Appointed by Board or Commission ● Appointed by Judge
■ Appointed by Mayor △ Appointed by Freeholders ▽ Appointed by Supervisor ▷ Appointed by County Executive ○ Appointed by Council

Erie Community College *continued*

Executive Vice President for Academic Affairs
Richard Washousky . . . . (716) 851-1500
Fax: (716) 851-1418

Erie County Medical Center Corporation [ECMC]

462 Grider Street, Buffalo, NY 14215
Tel: (716) 898-3000 Fax: (716) 898-5178 Internet: www.ecmc.edu

▶Chief Executive Officer **Thomas J. Quatroche, Jr.** . . . . (716) 898-5975
E-mail: tquatroc@ecmc.edu
President **(Vacant)** . . . . (716) 898-5503
Chief Financial Officer **Stephen M. Gary** . . . . (716) 898-6291
Education: St John Fisher; RIT MBA
Chief Information Officer **Leslie Feidt** . . . . (716) 898-4641
E-mail: lfeidt@ecmc.edu
Chief Medical Officer **Brian M. Murray** . . . . (716) 898-3936
Chief Operations Officer **(Vacant)** . . . . (716) 898-5273
Chief People Officer **Julia Culkin-Jacobia** . . . . (716) 898-5598
Senior Vice President, Nursing **Karen Ziemianski** . . . . (716) 898-5888
Senior Vice President of Operations **Jarrod Johnson** . . . . (716) 898-5273
Associate Hospital Administrator **Donna M. Brown** . . . . (716) 898-5847
E-mail: dbrownml@ecmc.edu
Education: D'Youville 1983 BS
Vice President of Post-Acute Care **Christopher Koenig** . . (716) 551-7110
Legal Counsel **Anthony Colucci III** . . . . (716) 898-5975

Terrace View Long Term Care Facility

462 Girder Street, Buffalo, NY 14215
Tel: (716) 551-7100 Fax: (716) 937-5729

Administrator **Charles Rice** . . . . (716) 551-7100
Administrative Assistant **Mary Ann Fix** . . . . (716) 551-7100
Operations Manager **Deborah Bernier** . . . . (716) 551-7100
E-mail: dbernier@ecmc.edu

Erie County Veterans' Services Agency

Rath Bldg., 95 Franklin Street, Room 1659, Buffalo, NY 14202
Fax: (716) 858-6363 Internet: http://www2.erie.gov/veterans/

▷Veterans Services Officer **Carlos Benitez** . . . . (716) 858-6000
Assistant Veteran Service Officer **Felice Krycia** . . . . (716) 858-4834
Assistant Veteran Service Officer **David Shenk** . . . . (716) 858-4834

Commission of the Status of Women

Rath Bldg., 95 Franklin Street, Room 625, Buffalo, NY 14202
Tel: (716) 858-8307 Fax: (716) 858-8311 E-mail: csw@erie.gov

▷Executive Director **Sawrie Becker** . . . . (716) 858-8307
E-mail: sawrie.becker@erie.gov

Office of the County Legislature

Fourth Floor, 92 Franklin Street, Buffalo, NY 14202

★Chairman **John J. Mills** (R-District 11) . . . . (716) 858-8850
Term Expires: December 31, 2017
E-mail: John.Mills@erie.gov
★Minority Leader **Betty Jean Grant** (R-District 2) . . . . (716) 894-0914
Term Expires: December 31, 2017
E-mail: bjg@erie.gov
★Legislator **Barbara Miller-Williams** (D-District 1) . . . . (716) 842-0490
Term Expires: December 31, 2017
E-mail: bmw@erie.gov
★Legislator **Peter J. Savage III** (D-District 3) . . . . (716) 832-0493
Term Expires: December 31, 2017
E-mail: peter.savage@erie.gov
★Legislator **Kevin R. Hardwick** (R-District 4) . . . . (716) 858-8672
Term Expires: December 31, 2017
E-mail: kevin.hardwick@erie.gov
★Legislator **Thomas A. Loughran** (D-District 5) . . . . (716) 836-0198
Term Expires: December 31, 2017
E-mail: loughran@erie.gov

Office of the County Legislature *continued*

★Legislator **Edward A. Rath III** (R-District 6) . . . . (716) 858-8676
Term Expires: December 31, 2017
E-mail: edward.rath@erie.gov
Education: Canisius 2005 MBA
★Legislator **Patrick B. Burke** (D-District 7) . . . . (716) 858-8480
Term Expires: December 31, 2017
E-mail: patrick.burke@erie.gov
★Legislator **Ted B. Morton** (R-District 8) . . . . (716) 858-8856
Term Expires: December 31, 2017
E-mail: ted.morton@erie.gov
★Legislator **Lynne M. Dixon** (R-District 9) . . . . (716) 858-8671
Term Expires: December 31, 2017
E-mail: lynne.dixon@erie.gov
Education: West Virginia 1988 BA
★Legislator **Joseph C. Lorigo** (R-District 10) . . . . (716) 858-8922
Term Expires: December 31, 2017
E-mail: joseph.lorigo@erie.gov
Legislature Clerk **Karen M. McCarthy** . . . . (716) 858-8738

Office of the Comptroller

Rath Bldg., 95 Franklin Street, 11th Floor, Buffalo, NY 14202-3972
Tel: (716) 858-8400 Fax: (716) 858-8507
Internet: www.erie.gov/comptroller

★Comptroller **Stefan I. Mychajliw** . . . . (716) 858-8400
Term Expires: December 31, 2017
Deputy Comptroller **Gregory G. "Greg" Gach** . . . . (716) 858-8132
Deputy Comptroller-Audit **Scott Kroll** . . . . (716) 858-8430

Office of the County Clerk

92 Franklin Street, Buffalo, NY 14202
Fax: (716) 858-6550 E-mail: eriecountyclerkoffice@erie.gov
Internet: www2.erie.gov/clerk

★County Clerk **Christopher L. Jacobs** . . . . (716) 858-8866
Term Expires: December 31, 2018
Education: Boston Col BA; American U MBA; Buffalo JD

Office of the District Attorney

25 Delaware Avenue, Buffalo, NY 14202
Fax: (716) 858-7922 Internet: www.erie.gov/da

★District Attorney (Acting) **Michael J. Flaherty, Jr.** . . . . (716) 858-2467
Term Expires: December 31, 2016
E-mail: flahertm@erie.gov
First Assistant District Attorney **Donna A. Milling** . . . . (716) 858-2466
E-mail: millingd@erie.gov
Education: SUNY Col (Buffalo) JD; Pace BA
Chief Trial Counsel **Christopher Belling** . . . . (716) 858-6000
Chief of Homicide **Colleen Curtin Gable** . . . . (716) 858-6000
Chief, Special Investigations Unit/ Public Integrity Unit
Paul E. Bonanno . . . . (716) 858-6000
Chief, Buffalo City Court Bureau **Mara L. McCabe** . . . . (716) 858-6000
Chief, Animal Cruelty Unit **Justin Wallens** . . . . (716) 858-6000
Chief, Domestic Violence Bureau **Lynette M. Reda** . . . . (716) 858-6000
Chief, Administration Division **Amy C. Hughes** . . . . (716) 858-6000
Chief, Special Victims Bureau **Rosanne E. Johnson** . . . . (716) 858-6000
Chief, Tactical Prosecution Unit **Michael Felicetta** . . . . (716) 858-6000
Chief, Appeals Bureau **Michael Hillery** . . . . (716) 858-6000
Chief, Felony Trials Bureau **Paul J. Glascott** . . . . (716) 858-6000
Chief, Felony Trials Bureau **Rachel L. Newton** . . . . (716) 858-6000
Chief, Felony Trials Bureau **John Schoemick** . . . . (716) 858-6000

★ Elected Official ▲ Appointed by Legislature ▼ Appointed by Governor ▶ Appointed by Board or Commission ● Appointed by Judge
■ Appointed by Mayor △ Appointed by Freeholders ▽ Appointed by Supervisor ▷ Appointed by County Executive ○ Appointed by Council

Office of the Sheriff

10 Delaware Avenue, Buffalo, NY 14202
Fax: (716) 858-7680

★ Sheriff **Timothy B. Howard** (R) .... (716) 858-7608
Term Expires: December 31, 2017
E-mail: timothy.howard@erie.gov
Education: SUNY (Albany) 1986 MA

Undersheriff **Mark Wipperman** .... (716) 858-6168
E-mail: mark.wipperman@erie.gov

Chief, Administrative Division **John Greenan** .... (716) 858-6869
E-mail: john.greenan@erie.gov

Chief, Police Services Division **Scott Joslyn** .... (716) 858-3944
E-mail: scott.joslyn@erie.gov Fax: (716) 858-3277

Chief, Special Services Division **Scott Patronik** .... (716) 858-6889
E-mail: scott.patronik@erie.gov Fax: (716) 858-6039

Jail Management Division

40 Delaware Avenue, Buffalo, NY 14202
Fax: (716) 858-8645

Superintendent **Thomas Diina** .... (716) 858-7635
Fax: (716) 858-8645

Deputy Superintendent **John Rodriguez** .... (716) 858-7022
Fax: (716) 937-3083

Deputy Superintendent **Michael Reardon** .... (716) 937-3083
11581 Walden Avenue, Walden, NY 14004

Erie County Board of Elections

134 W. Eagle St., Buffalo, NY 14202-3896
Tel: (716) 858-8891 Fax: (716) 858-8282
Internet: http://elections.erie.gov/

Democrat Commissioner **Leonard R. Lenihan** .... (716) 858-7787
Republican Commissioner **Ralph M. Mohr** .... (716) 858-7786

County of Essex, New Jersey

Hall of Records, 465 Dr. Martin Luther King, Jr. Boulevard,
Newark, NJ 07102
Tel: (973) 621-5000 (Information) Internet: www.essexcountynj.org

County Seat: Newark **Election Type:** Partisan **Population:** 797,434 (2015)

Office of the County Executive

Hall of Records, 465 Dr. Martin Luther King, Jr. Boulevard, Room 405,
Newark, NJ 07102
Tel: (973) 621-4400 Fax: (973) 621-6343

★ County Executive **Joseph N. DiVincenzo, Jr.** (D) .... (973) 621-4400
Term Expires: December 31, 2018 Fax: (973) 621-6343
E-mail: joedi@admin.essexcountynj.org
Education: Jersey City State 1975 BS
Career: Member, Board of Chosen Freeholders, County of Essex, New Jersey (1990-2002)

▷ Chief of Staff **Philip B. Alagia** .... (973) 621-5200
E-mail: palagia@essexcountynj.org Fax: (973) 621-6345

Secretary for the Chief of Staff
Asmeret Ghebremichel .... (973) 621-5200

▷ Deputy Chief of Staff **William D. Payne** .... (973) 621-5200
E-mail: wpayne@essexcountynj.org Fax: (973) 621-6345

▷ Deputy Chief of Staff **M. Teresa Ruiz** (D) .... (973) 621-4400
E-mail: mruiz@essexcountynj.org Fax: (973) 621-6343

Constituent Services Director **Joyce Goldman** .... (973) 621-4400
E-mail: jgoldman@admin.essexcountynj.org

Scheduler/Executive Assistant **Ana Santos** .... (973) 621-4400

Office of the County Administrator

Hall of Records, 465 Dr. Martin Luther King, Jr. Boulevard, Room 510,
Newark, NJ 07102
Fax: (973) 621-6650

▷ County Administrator **Ralph J. Ciallella** .... (973) 621-4432
465 Dr. Martin L. King, Jr. Blvd., Room 510, Newark, NJ 07102
E-mail: rciallella@essexcountynj.org

▷ Deputy County Administrator **Allen Abramowitz** .... (973) 621-4432

▷ Assistant County Administrator **Sheila Y. Oliver** (D) .... (973) 621-4432
E-mail: soliver@essexcountynj.org
Education: Lincoln U (PA) BA; Columbia 1976 MS

Office of Accounts and Controls

Hall of Records, 465 Dr. Martin L. King, Jr. Blvd., Room 542,
Newark, NJ 07102
Fax: (973) 621-6670

▷ Chief Financial Officer **Kim Browne-Smeraldo** .... (973) 621-4368
E-mail: kbrowne-smeraldo@admin.essexcountynj.org

Office of Human Resources

Hall of Records, 465 Dr. Martin Luther King, Jr. Boulevard, Room 340,
Newark, NJ 07102
Fax: (973) 621-4993

▷ Director **Alan Abramowitz** .... (973) 621-4977
E-mail: aabramowitz@admin.essexcountynj.org

Deputy Director **Robert Jackson** .... (973) 621-4977
E-mail: rjackson@admin.essexcountynj.org

Office of Public Information

465 Dr. Martin Luther King, Jr. Boulevard, Room 408, Newark, NJ 07102
Fax: (973) 621-6136

Director **Anthony Puglisi** .... (973) 621-2542
E-mail: apuglisi@admin.essexcountynj.org

Office of Purchasing

Hall of Records, 465 Dr. Martin Luther King, Jr. Boulevard, Room 325,
Newark, NJ 07102
Fax: (973) 621-5109

▷ Director **Julius Coltre** .... (973) 621-5100
E-mail: jcoltre@admin.essexcountynj.org

Office of the Treasurer

Hall of Records, 465 Dr. Martin Luther King, Jr. Boulevard, Room 510,
Newark, NJ 07102
Fax: (973) 621-5209

▷ Treasurer **Mark E. Acker** .... (973) 621-4443
E-mail: macker@admin.essexcountynj.org

Office of the County Counsel

Hall of Records, 465 Dr. Martin L. King, Jr. Blvd., Room 535,
Newark, NJ 07102-1730
Tel: (973) 621-5003 Fax: (973) 621-4599

County Counsel/County Adjuster
Courtney M. Gaccione .... (973) 621-2703

Director, Office of Labor Relations
L. Grace Spencer (D) .... (973) 621-4428

Chief, Mental Health and Governmental Affairs Section
Thomas Bachman .... (973) 621-2538
E-mail: tbachman@counsel.essexcountynj.org

Chief, Welfare and Support Section **Elissa Testa** .... (973) 286-2996

Department of Citizen Services

50 South Clinton Street, Suite 3200, East Orange, NJ 07018
18 Rector Street, Suite 3100, Newark, NJ 07102
Tel: (973) 395-8684 Tel: (973) 733-3325 (Newark) Fax: (973) 395-8493
Fax: (973) 504-9316 (Newark)

Director **Anibal Ramos, Jr.** .... (973) 395-3400
Deputy Director **(Vacant)** .... (973) 733-3325

★ Elected Official ▲ Appointed by Legislature ▼ Appointed by Governor ▶ Appointed by Board or Commission ● Appointed by Judge
■ Appointed by Mayor △ Appointed by Freeholders ▽ Appointed by Supervisor ▷ Appointed by County Executive ○ Appointed by Council

Office of Investigational Services
18 Rector Street, Newark, NJ 07102

Investigations Coordinator **Frank Eagan** .... (973) 733-5551
Chief Investigator **Frank Egan** .... (973) 733-5551

Office of Medicaid Services
18 Rector Street, Newark, NJ 07102

Administrator **Lisa Upshur** .... (973) 645-7030

Office of Special Services
18 Rector Street, 5th Floor, Newark, NJ 07102
Fax: (973) 642-4960

Administrator **Debra Edmoson** .... (973) 645-8340

Division of Community Action
50 South Clinton Street, 3rd Floor, Suite 3201, East Orange, NJ 07018
Fax: (973) 395-8433

▷ Director **Maurice J. Brown** .... (973) 395-8350
E-mail: mjbrown@communityaction.essexcountynj.org
Consumer Advocate **Melvin Williams** .... (973) 395-8360
Weights and Measures Superintendent **Louis Turco** ...... (973) 395-8363

Division of Senior Services
900 Bloomfield Avenue, Verona, NJ 07044
Fax: (973) 228-6892

▷ Director **Jaklyn DeVore** .... (973) 395-8375

Division of Welfare
18 Rector Street, Newark, NJ 07102
Fax: (973) 504-9316

Director **Jeanette Page-Hawkins** .... (973) 733-3325
Education: Rutgers 1974 BA, 1979 MSW
Administrative Services Chief **MaLeater Skipper** .... (973) 733-5505
Administrative Supervisor of Family Services
Cassandra Smalls-Nicholson .... (973) 733-2518
Food Stamp Program Administrator **Carla Tention** .... (973) 395-8132
50 South Clinton Street, 1st Floor, East Orange, NJ 07018

Division of Youth Services
80 Duryea St., Newark, NJ 07103
Tel: (973) 497-4735 Fax: (973) 497-4747

▷ Administrator **Dennis Hughes** .... (973) 497-2227
Director, Youth Services Commission **Lee B. Fisher** ..... (973) 733-4667
18 Rector St., Newark, NJ 07102 Fax: (973) 824-2306
Family Crises Supervisor **Richard Browne** .... (973) 693-6750

Department of Corrections
Essex County Correctional Facility, 354 Doremus Avenue, Newark, NJ 07105
Tel: (973) 274-7800 Tel: (973) 274-7597 Fax: (973) 274-6969

Director **Alfaro Ortiz, Jr.** .... (973) 274-7818
Deputy Director, Administration **David Boyd** .... (973) 274-7818
E-mail: dboyd@eccorrections.org
Warden **Charles Green** .... (973) 274-7670

Department of Economic Development, Training and Employment
50 South Clinton Street, 5th Floor, Suite 5400, East Orange, NJ 07018
Fax: (973) 395-8493

Director **Anibal Ramos, Jr.** .... (973) 395-8400

Training and Employment Division
50 South Clinton Street, Suite 3100, East Orange, NJ 07018
Fax: (973) 395-5798

Director **Samuel "Sam" Okparaeke** .... (973) 395-5827
▷ Workforce Investment Board Executive Director
Samuel "Sam" Okparaeke 4th Floor .... (973) 395-8409
Fax: (973) 395-8483

Department of Health and Rehabilitation
204 Grove Avenue, Cedar Grove, NJ 07009
Tel: (973) 571-2800 Fax: (973) 571-2864

▷ Director **Frank Del Gaudio** .... (973) 571-2801
Fax: (973) 571-2864

Essex County Hospital Center
204 Grove Avenue, Cedar Grove, NJ 07009
Tel: (973) 571-2800 Fax: (973) 571-2864

Director **Frank Del Gaudio** .... (973) 571-2801
Medical Director **Bolivar Pascal** .... (973) 571-2863

Department of Management and Budget
465 Dr. Martin Luther King, Jr. Boulevard, Newark, NJ 07102

Director **Mark E. Acker** .... (973) 621-4443
E-mail: macker@admin.essexcountynj.org

Department of Parks, Recreation, and Cultural Affairs
115 Clifton Avenue, Newark, NJ 07104
Tel: (973) 268-3500 Fax: (973) 481-5302

▷ Director **Daniel K. Salvante** .... (973) 268-3517
E-mail: dsalvante@essexcountynj.org
▷ Assistant Director **Kate Hartwyk** .... (973) 418-5423
E-mail: khartwyk@essexcountynj.org
Golf Director **Tim Christ** .... (973) 751-0384

Department of Public Works
900 Bloomfield Avenue, Verona, NJ 07044
Tel: (973) 226-8500
Tel: (973) 239-3366 (Information Emergency Assistance)

▷ Director **Sanjeev Varghese** .... (973) 226-8500 ext. 2660
E-mail: svarghese@essexcountynj.org
Executive Assistant **Lillian Malanga** .... (973) 226-8500 ext. 2280
E-mail: lmalanga@essexcountynj.org

Building and Grounds Division
Fax: (973) 403-9572

Director **Frank Pascucci** .... (973) 226-8500 ext. 2340
E-mail: fpascucci@essexcountynj.org

Engineering Division
County Engineer **Sanjeev Varghese** .... (973) 226-8500 ext. 2660
E-mail: svarghese@essexcountynj.org
Assistant County Engineer
Dennis R. Sedaille .... (973) 226-8506 ext. 2670
E-mail: dsedaille@essexcountynj.org

Mosquito Control Division
99 West Bradford Avenue, Cedar Grove, NJ 07009
Fax: (973) 239-8637

Director **William Clark** .... (973) 239-3366 ext. 2390

Planning Division
Fax: (973) 226-7469

Director **David Antonio** .... (973) 226-8500 ext. 2580

Roads and Transportation Division
Director **William Clark** .... (973) 239-3366 ext. 2390

Board of Taxation
50 South Clinton Street, Suite 5200, East Orange, NJ 07018

Administrator **Joan Codey Durkin** .... (973) 395-8525
President **Mary Devon O'Brien** .... (973) 395-8525

★ Elected Official ▲ Appointed by Legislature ▼ Appointed by Governor ▶ Appointed by Board or Commission ● Appointed by Judge
■ Appointed by Mayor △ Appointed by Freeholders ▽ Appointed by Supervisor ▷ Appointed by County Executive ○ Appointed by Council

Essex County College [ECC]

303 University Ave., Newark, NJ 07102
Tel: (973) 877-3000 Fax: (973) 877-3044 Internet: www.essex.edu

President (Acting) **A. Zachary Yamba** . . . . (973) 877-4462

Essex County Improvement Authority

155 Passaic Avenue, Fairfield, NJ 07004
Fax: (973) 808-0528

Executive Director **Steven Rother** . . . . (973) 621-2701
E-mail: srother@counsel.essexcountynj.org

Essex County College Public Safety Academy

250 Grove Avenue, Cedar Grove, NJ 07009
Tel: (973) 877-4350 Fax: (973) 239-8842
Internet: www.essex.edu/pacademy

Director **Rocco L. Miscia, Jr.** . . . . (973) 877-4352
Associate Director **Paul Costello** . . . . (973) 877-4353
Commanding Officer **Lori Apicelli** . . . . (973) 877-4354

Essex County Utilities Authority [ECUA]

Leroy F. Smith Jr. Public Safety Building, 60 Nelson Place, 6th Floor, Fairfield, NJ 07012
Fax: (973) 857-9066 E-mail: info@ecuanj.com Internet: www.ecuanj.com

▷ Executive Director (Acting) **Elmer Herrmann, Jr.** . . . . (973) 792-9069
E-mail: eherrmann@essexcountynj.org

Office of the Board of Chosen Freeholders

Hall of Records, 465 Dr. Martin L. King, Jr. Blvd., Room 558, Newark, NJ 07102
Tel: (973) 621-4486 Fax: (973) 621-5695
Internet: http://freeholders.essexcountynj.org

★ President **Britnee N. Timberlake** (D-District 3) . . . . (973) 621-5680
Term Expires: December 31, 2017

★ Vice President **Brendan W. Gill** (D-At-Large) . . . . (973) 621-4467
Term Expires: December 31, 2017
Education: Seton Hall 1996 BA

★ Freeholder **Rolando Bobadilla** (D-District 1) . . . . (973) 621-4477
Term Expires: December 31, 2017
E-mail: rbobadilla@freeholders.essexcountynj.org
Education: CUNY BS

★ Freeholder **Wayne Richardson** (D-District 2) . . . . (973) 621-6457
Term Expires: December 31, 2017

★ Freeholder **Leonard M. Luciano** (D-District 4) . . . . (973) 621-4481
Term Expires: December 31, 2017
E-mail: lluciano@freeholders.essexcountynj.org
Education: Montclair State U BA; Thomas Edison State MA

★ Freeholder **Cynthia Toro** (D-District 5) . . . . (973) 621-4479
Term Expires: December 31, 2017

★ Freeholder **Rufus I. Johnson** (D-At-Large) . . . . (973) 621-4483
Term Expires: December 31, 2017
E-mail: rjohnson@freeholders.essexcountynj.org
Education: Essex County; Wilberforce

★ Freeholder **Lebby Jones** (D-At-Large) . . . . (973) 621-4473
Term Expires: December 31, 2017

★ Freeholder **Patricia Sebold** (D-At-Large) . . . . (973) 621-4484
Term Expires: December 31, 2017
E-mail: psebold@freeholders.essexcountynj.org
Education: Upsala

△ Clerk of the Board **Deborah Davis Ford** . . . . (973) 621-4492
E-mail: ddavisford@freeholders.essexcountynj.org

△ Freeholder Board Counsel **Michael J. Parlavecchio** . . . . . (973) 621-5075
E-mail: mparlavecchio@freeholders.essexcountynj.org

Office of the County Clerk

Hall of Records, 465 Dr. Martin L. King, Jr. Blvd., Room 247, Newark, NJ 07102
Tel: (973) 621-4921 Fax: (973) 621-2537 E-mail: info@essexclerk.com
Internet: www.essexclerk.com

★ County Clerk
Christopher J. "Chris" Durkin (D) . . . . (973) 621-4921 ext. 223
Term Expires: December 31, 2020
E-mail: cdurkin@essexcountynj.org
Education: Rutgers BA; Seton Hall 2001 MA

Deputy County Clerk **Anthony Jackson** . . . . (973) 621-4921 ext. 224

Office of the Prosecutor

Essex Veterans Courthouse., 50 West Market Street, 3rd Floor, Newark, NJ 07102
Tel: (973) 621-4700 Fax: (973) 621-4560 Internet: www.njecpo.org

▼ Prosecutor (Acting) **Carolyn A. Murray** . . . . (973) 621-4700
E-mail: carolyn.murray@njecpo.org
Education: Georgetown 1984; NYU 1987 JD

First Assistant Prosecutor (Acting) **Robert D. Laurino** . . . . (973) 621-4700

Chief Executive Assistant Prosecutor
Thomas S. Fennelly . . . . (973) 621-4602
Fax: (973) 242-4271

Chief Executive Assistant Prosecutor **Michael Morris** . . . . (973) 621-4712
Fax: (973) 621-4560

Chief Executive Assistant Prosecutor **Debra Simms** . . . . . (973) 621-4623

Chief Executive Assistant Prosecutor
Clara M. Rodriguez . . . . (973) 266-4252
Fax: (973) 395-3790

Chief of Investigators **Quovella Spruill** . . . . (973) 621-4998
Fax: (973) 621-2833

Office of the Register of Deeds and Mortgages

Hall of Records, 465 Dr. Martin L. King, Jr. Blvd., Room 130, Newark, NJ 07102
Tel: (973) 621-4960 Fax: (973) 621-2590
Internet: www.essexregister.com

★ Register **Dana Rone** . . . . (973) 621-4960 ext. 6201
Term Expires: December 31, 2019

Deputy Register **(Vacant)** . . . . (973) 621-4960 ext. 6216

Office of the Sheriff

Essex County Veterans Courthouse, 50 West Market Street, Room 204, Newark, NJ 07102
Fax: (973) 621-4066 Internet: www.essexsheriff.com

★ Sheriff **Armando B. Fontoura** (D) . . . . (973) 621-4105
Term Expires: December 31, 2016
E-mail: afontoura@essexsheriff.com

Chief Warrant Officer **John D. Dough** . . . . (973) 621-4171
E-mail: jdough@essexsheriff.com Fax: (973) 621-6097

Undersheriff **Kevin Ryan** . . . . (973) 324-9750
E-mail: kryan@essexsheriff.com

Undersheriff **Jesus A. Padilla** . . . . (973) 621-4160
E-mail: jpadilla@essexsheriff.com

Undersheriff **James Pitts** . . . . (973) 621-4134
E-mail: jpitts@essexsheriff.com

Director of Homeland Security **Garey S. Chin** . . . . (973) 621-7792
E-mail: gchin@essexsheriff.com

Deputy Sheriffs Division Director **David Berkowitz** . . . . . (973) 621-4105
E-mail: dberkowitz@essexsheriff.com

Internal Affairs Division Director
Capt. John Napolitano . . . . (973) 621-4135

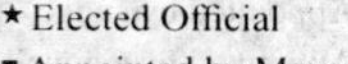

★ Elected Official ▲ Appointed by Legislature ▼ Appointed by Governor ► Appointed by Board or Commission ● Appointed by Judge
■ Appointed by Mayor △ Appointed by Freeholders ▽ Appointed by Supervisor ▷ Appointed by County Executive ○ Appointed by Council

Office of the Superintendent of Schools

Leroy F. Smith Public Safety Building, 60 Nelson Place, 1st Floor, Newark, NJ 07102
Fax: (973) 621-1603

Executive County Superintendent (Interim)
Joseph Zarra .... (973) 621-2750

Essex County Board of Elections

465 Dr. Martin Luther King, Jr. Boulevard, Room 417A, Newark, NJ 07102
Tel: (973) 621-5071 Fax: (973) 621-6464

Clerk of the Board **Linda von Nessi** .... (973) 621-5071
Superintendent-Designate **Edna Y. Baugh** .... (973) 621-5061
Education: Hartwick BA; Vermont JD
Deputy Superintendent **Patricia Spango** .... (973) 621-5679

County of Fairfax, Virginia

12000 Government Center Parkway, Fairfax, VA 22035-0001
Tel: (703) 324-2000 (Information) Internet: www.fairfaxcounty.gov

County Seat: Fairfax **Election Type:** Partisan **Population:** 1,142,234 (2015)

Office of the Board of Supervisors

12000 Government Center Parkway, Fairfax, VA 22035-0072
Tel: (703) 324-3151 Fax: (703) 324-3926

★ Chairman **Sharon Bulova** (D) .... (703) 324-2321
Term Expires: December 31, 2019 Fax: (703) 324-3955
12000 Government Center Parkway, Suite 530, Fairfax, VA 22035-0001
E-mail: chairman@fairfaxcounty.gov

★ Vice Chairman
Penelope A. "Penny" Gross (D-Mason) .... (703) 256-7717
Term Expires: December 31, 2019 Fax: (703) 354-8419
6507 Columbia Pike, Annandale, VA 22003
E-mail: mason@fairfaxcounty.gov
Education: Oregon 1965 BS

★ Supervisor **John C. Cook** (R-Braddock) .... (703) 425-9300
Term Expires: December 31, 2019
9002 Burke Lake Road, Burke, VA 22015
E-mail: braddock@fairfaxcounty.gov
Education: George Washington 1988 JD

★ Supervisor **John W. Foust** (D-Dranesville) .... (703) 356-0551
Term Expires: December 31, 2019 Fax: (703) 821-4275
1437 Balls Hill Road, McLean, VA 22101-3428
E-mail: dranesville@fairfaxcounty.gov
Education: Pittsburgh

★ Supervisor **Patrick S. "Pat" Herrity** (R-Springfield) .... (703) 451-8873
Term Expires: December 31, 2019 Fax: (703) 451-3047
West Springfield Government Center, 6140 Rolling Road, Springfield, VA 22152-1579
E-mail: springfield@fairfaxcounty.gov
Education: Virginia Tech 1982 BS

★ Supervisor **Catherine M. Hudgins** (D-Hunter Mill) .... (703) 478-0283
Term Expires: December 31, 2019 Fax: (703) 471-6847
12000 Bowman Towne Drive, Reston, VA 20190-3378
E-mail: hntrmill@fairfaxcounty.gov
Education: Arkansas (Pine Bluff) BS; George Mason 1994 MPA

★ Supervisor **Jeffrey C. "Jeff" McKay** (D-Lee) .... (703) 971-6262
Term Expires: December 31, 2019 Fax: (703) 971-3032
Franconia Government Center, 6121 Franconia Road, Alexandria, VA 22310-2508
E-mail: leedist@fairfaxcounty.gov
Education: James Madison BA

Office of the Board of Supervisors *continued*

★ Supervisor **Kathy L. Smith** (R-Sully) .... (703) 814-7100
Term Expires: December 31, 2019
E-mail: sully@fairfaxcounty.gov
Education: Muhlenberg BA

★ Supervisor **Linda Q. Smyth** (D-Providence) .... (703) 560-6946
Term Expires: December 31, 2019 Fax: (703) 207-3541
8739 Lee Highway, Fairfax, VA 22031-2013
E-mail: provdist@fairfaxcounty.gov
Education: Washington U (MO) 1970 BA; Virginia 1971 MA, 1978 PhD

★ Supervisor **Daniel G. Storck** (D-Mount Vernon) .... (703) 324-3151
Term Expires: December 31, 2019
E-mail: mtvernon@fairfaxcounty.gov
Education: Miami BS, MBA

▶ Clerk to the Board **Catherine A. Chianese** Suite 533 .... (703) 324-3151
E-mail: catherine.chianese@fairfaxcounty.gov Fax: (703) 324-3926

Office of the County Attorney

12000 Government Center Parkway, Fairfax, VA 22035-0001
Tel: (703) 324-3956

County Attorney **David P. Bobzien** .... (703) 324-2421
E-mail: david.bobzien@fairfaxcounty.gov

Office of the Financial and Programs Audit [OFPA]

12000 Government Center Parkway, Fairfax, VA 22035-0001

Auditor of the Board **Jim Shelton** .... (703) 324-4005

Office of the County Executive

12000 Government Center Parkway, Suite 552, Fairfax, VA 22035
Tel: (703) 324-2531 Fax: (703) 324-3956

▶ County Executive **Edward L. Long, Jr.** .... (703) 324-2531
E-mail: edward.long@fairfaxcounty.gov
Administrative Associate **Sue Robinson** .... (703) 324-2536
E-mail: sue.robinson@fairfaxcounty.gov
Assistant County Executive **Catherine A. Chianese** .... (703) 324-2531

Office of the Deputy County Executive

County Executive Deputy **Robert A. Stalzer** .... (703) 324-3440
E-mail: rob.stalzer@fairfaxcounty.gov

Department of Code Compliance

12000 Government Center Parkway, Fairfax, VA 22035-0001

Director **Jeffrey Blackford** .... (703) 324-1300
Management Analyst (Operations) **Tammy Avren** .... (703) 324-4044
Management Analyst (Administration)
Sandra Harrington .... (703) 324-8239

Department of Planning and Zoning [DPZ]

12055 Government Center Parkway, Suite 775, Fairfax, VA 22035-5550
Fax: (703) 324-3056 Internet: www.fairfaxcounty.gov/dpz

Director **Fred R. Selden** .... (703) 324-1325
Planning Division Director **Marianne Gardner** .... (703) 324-1380
Zoning Administrator Division Director **Leslie Johnson** .. (703) 324-1314
Zoning Evaluation Division Director **Barbara Berlin** .... (703) 324-1290

Department of Transportation

4050 Legato Road, Suite 400, Fairfax, VA 22033-2895
Fax: (703) 877-5623

Director **Tom Biesiadny** .... (703) 877-5695
Education: Saint Louis U 1985 BS Fax: (703) 877-5697
Administrative Assistant **Pam Martin** .... (703) 877-5696
E-mail: pam.martin@fairfaxcounty.gov

COUNTIES

★ Elected Official ▲ Appointed by Legislature ▼ Appointed by Governor ▶ Appointed by Board or Commission ● Appointed by Judge
■ Appointed by Mayor △ Appointed by Freeholders ▽ Appointed by Supervisor ▷ Appointed by County Executive ○ Appointed by Council

Public Works and Environmental Services Department
12055 Government Center Parkway, Suite 659, Fairfax, VA 22035-5502
Tel: (703) 323-1211 (After Hours Sewers)
Tel: (703) 324-1200 (Planning and Zoning)
Tel: (703) 324-5015 (Sewer Information)
Tel: (703) 802-3322 (Trash Collection and Recycling)
Tel: (703) 383-8368 (VDOT) Fax: (703) 324-1818

Director **James Patteson** . . . . . (703) 324-1716
Administrative Assistant **Rona Courtney** . . . . . (703) 324-5581

Capital Facilities
Branch Manager **Seema Ajrawat** . . . . . (703) 324-5197
E-mail: seema.ajrawat@fairfaxcounty.gov Fax: (703) 631-0842
Building, Designing, and Construction Division Director **Carey Needham** . . . . . (703) 324-5114
E-mail: carey.needham@fairfaxcounty.gov Fax: (703) 324-3943
Land Acquisition Division Director **Julie Cline** . . . . . (703) 324-5106
Fax: (703) 631-0842
Deputy Director **Ronald N. Kirkpatrick** . . . . . (703) 324-5366
Fax: (703) 324-4365
Utilities Division Director **Melton Brad** . . . . . (703) 324-5114
E-mail: melton.brad@fairfaxcounty.com

Land Development Services
Director **William Hicks** . . . . . (703) 324-1780
Fax: (703) 324-1847
Code Services Director **Paul Shirey** . . . . . (703) 324-1780
Building Plan Review and Permits Director **Brian Foley** . . (703) 324-1695
Commercial Inspections Division Director **Brian Foley** . . . (703) 324-1910
Site Development and Facilities Inspections Director **Jack Weyant** . . . . . (703) 324-1995
Residential Inspections Director **Guy Tomberlin** . . . . . (703) 324-1972
Urban Forest Management Director **Keith Klein** . . . . . (703) 324-1729
Financial Management Branch Manager **(Vacant)** . . . . . (703) 324-1880
Human Resources Branch Manager **Barbara Brock** . . . . . (703) 324-1834
IT Services Branch Manager **Blair Burkholder** . . . . . (703) 324-1774
E-mail: blair.burkholder@fairfaxcounty.gov

Solid Waste Management
Solid Waste Disposal and Resource Recovery Assistant Division Director **(Vacant)** . . . . . (703) 324-5230
Fax: (703) 324-3950
Operations Division Deputy Director **Steven Aitcheson** . . . . . (703) 324-5046
Fax: (703) 802-3949

Stormwater
Tel: (703) 877-2800 (Complaints)
Maintenance and Stormwater Management Division Director **Ellie Codding** . . . . . (703) 877-2868
Fax: (703) 934-2868
Stormwater and Waterwaster Programs Director **Randy Bartlett** . . . . . (703) 324-5732
Stormwater Planning Director **Craig A. Carinci** . . . . . (703) 324-5500
Fax: (703) 802-5955

Wastewater Management
6000 Freds Oak Road, Burke, VA 22015
Wastewater Collection Division Director **Tom Russell** . . . . (703) 250-2700
Fax: (703) 324-1818
Wastewater Planning and Monitoring Division Director **Shahram Mohsenin** . . . . . (703) 324-5026
Fax: (703) 803-3297
Wastewater Treatment Division Director **Michael McGrath** . . . . . (703) 550-9740 ext. 225
9399 Richmond Hwy., Lorton, VA 22079 Fax: (703) 339-5070

Office of the Deputy County Executive
Deputy County Executive **David M. "Dave" Rohrer** . . . . . (703) 324-3440

Fairfax County Police Department
4100 Chain Bridge Road, Fairfax, VA 22030-7002
Internet: www.fairfaxcounty.gov/police
Police Chief **Edwin C. Roessler, Jr.** . . . . . (703) 246-2195
Administrative Support Bureau Chief **Major Joe Hill** . . . . (703) 246-7560
Deputy Chief in Charge of Patrol **Lt. Col. Erin Schaible** . . (703) 246-4488
Deputy Chief of Administration **Lt. Col. Thomas Ryan** . . (703) 246-2558
Operations Deputy Chief/Investigations and Operations Support **Ted Arnn** . . . . . (703) 246-3396

Fairfax County Animal Shelter
4500 West Ox Rd., Fairfax, VA 22030-6122
Fax: (703) 830-0318
Animal Control Director **Tony Matos** . . . . . (703) 330-1100
Shelter Director **Barbara Hutcherson** . . . . . (703) 830-1100

Fire and Rescue Department
4100 Chain Bridge Road, Fairfax, VA 22030-7001
Tel: (703) 246-2126 Internet: http://www.fairfaxcounty.gov/fire
Fire Chief **Richard R. "Richie" Bowers, Jr.** . . . . . (703) 246-2546
Fax: (703) 273-1049
Assistant Chief **Garrett Dyer** . . . . . (703) 246-3957
Fax: (703) 273-1049
Fire Prevention Deputy Chief **Michael Reilly** . . . . . (703) 246-4753
Fax: (703) 691-0209
Safety and Personnel Services Division Deputy Chief **Danny Gray** . . . . . (703) 246-3800
Fax: (703) 691-1514
Special Operations Deputy Chief **Reginald T. Johnson** . . . . . (703) 246-2823
Fax: (703) 273-4830

Department of Public Safety Communications
12000 Government Center Parkway, Fairfax, VA 22035-0001
Director **Stephen Souder** . . . . . (571) 350-1709
Administrative Assistant **Shanica Taylor** . . . . . (571) 350-1709

Office of Emergency Management
4890 Alliance Drive, Fairfax, VA 22030
Tel: (571) 350-1000 Fax: (571) 350-1050
Internet: www.fairfaxcounty.gov/oem
Coordinator **David M. "Dave" McKernan** . . . . . (571) 350-1000
E-mail: david.mckernan@fairfaxcounty.gov
Education: George Mason 2002 BIS

Office of Partnerships
12000 Government Center Pkwy., Suite 432, Fairfax, VA 22035-0001
Fax: (703) 222-9198
Director **Patricia Stevens** . . . . . (703) 324-5282
E-mail: patti.stevens@fairfaxcounty.gov
Program Manager **Ingrid Abernathy** . . . . . (703) 324-5022

Office of the Deputy County Executive
County Executive Deputy **Patricia Harrison** . . . . . (703) 324-2531
E-mail: patricia.harrison@fairfaxcounty.gov

Department of Administration for Human Services [DAHS]
12011 Government Center Pkwy., Suite 942, Fairfax, VA 22035-1100
Fax: (703) 324-7572 Internet: www.fairfaxcounty.gov/admin
Director **M. Gail Ledford** . . . . . (703) 324-5630
E-mail: gail.ledford@fairfaxcounty.gov
Administrative Assistant **Dwight Curtis** . . . . . (703) 324-5630
E-mail: dwight.curtis@fairfaxcounty.gov

Department of Housing and Community Development
3700 Pender Drive, Suite 300, Fairfax, VA 22030-6039
Fax: (703) 246-5115
Director-Elect **Thomas E. Fleetwood** . . . . . (703) 246-5105
Administrative Assistant **Jodi Cienki** . . . . . (703) 246-5105

★ Elected Official ▲ Appointed by Legislature ▼ Appointed by Governor ▶ Appointed by Board or Commission ● Appointed by Judge
■ Appointed by Mayor △ Appointed by Freeholders ▽ Appointed by Supervisor ▷ Appointed by County Executive ○ Appointed by Council

Department of Neighborhood and Community Services
12011 Government Center Parkway, Suite 1050, Fairfax, VA 22035-1118
Fax: (703) 222-9792

Director **Christopher A. Leonard** .... (703) 324-5501
E-mail: christopher.leonard@fairfaxcounty.gov
Administrative Assistant **Marian Matthews** .... (703) 324-5640

Family Services Department
12011 Government Center Parkway, Suite 500, Fairfax, VA 22035-1100
Fax: (703) 222-9487

Director **Nannette M. Bowler** .... (703) 324-7749
Administrative Assistant **Mary Medina** .... (703) 324-7749
E-mail: mary.medina@fairfaxcounty.gov

Office for Children
12011 Government Center Parkway, Suite 920, Fairfax, VA 22035-1100
Fax: (703) 803-0116

Director **Anne-Marie Twohie** .... (703) 324-8103

Fairfax Area Agency on Aging
12011 Government Center Parkway, Suite 708, Fairfax, VA 22035-1100
Tel: (703) 324-5411 Fax: (703) 449-8689

Director **Sharon Lynn** .... (703) 324-5411

Office for Women and Domestic and Sexual Violence Services
12000 Government Center Pkwy., Suite 339, Fairfax, VA 22035
Fax: (703) 324-3959

Executive Director **Ina G. Fernandez** .... (703) 324-5730
Office Manager **Amy Kegley** .... (703) 324-5721

Health Department
10777 Main Street, Suite 203, Fairfax, VA 22030-2903
Fax: (703) 273-0825 Internet: www.fairfaxcounty.gov/hd

Director **Gloria Addo-Ayensu** .... (703) 246-2479
Administrative Assistant **Hope Segar** .... (703) 246-2479

Office of the Deputy County Executive
Deputy County Executive and Chief Information Officer
David J. Molchany .... (703) 324-4775
E-mail: david.molchany@fairfaxcounty.gov
Education: Juniata 1983 BS

Cable Communications and Consumer Protection Department
12000 Government Center Pkwy., Suite 433, Fairfax, VA 22035-0045
Fax: (703) 324-3016

Director **Michael S. Liberman** .... (703) 324-5949
Administrative Assistant **Robin Dove** .... (703) 324-5998
E-mail: robin.dove@fairfaxcounty.gov

Department of Vehicle Services [DVS]
12000 Government Center Parkway, Suite 417, Fairfax, VA 22035-0015
Fax: (703) 324-3936

Director **Mark G. Moffatt** .... (703) 324-3525
Administrative Assistant **Dorothy Halligan** .... (703) 324-3525
E-mail: dorothy.halligan@fairfaxcounty.gov

Facilities Management Department
12000 Government Center Pkwy., Suite 424, Fairfax, VA 22035-0011
Fax: (703) 324-3930

Director **Jose A. Comayagua** .... (703) 324-2801
E-mail: jose.comayagua@fairfaxcounty.gov
Administrative Assistant **Rachel Campbell** .... (703) 324-2801
E-mail: rachel.campbell@fairfaxcounty.gov

Fairfax County Public Library [FCPL]
12000 Government Center Pkwy., Suite 324, Fairfax, VA 22035-0095
Fax: (703) 222-3193 Internet: www.fairfaxcounty.gov/library

Director **Edwin S. Clay III** .... (703) 324-8308
E-mail: edwin.clay@fairfaxcounty.gov
Administrative Assistant **Karen Gates** .... (703) 324-8324

Information Technology Department
12000 Government Center Parkway, Suite 527, Fairfax, VA 22035-0063
Tel: (703) 324-3380 Fax: (703) 324-4573

Director and Chief Technology Officer
Wanda M. Gibson .... (703) 324-4521
E-mail: wanda.gibson@fairfaxcounty.gov
Education: Howard U BA, MA
Administrative Assistant **Lucy Flores** .... (703) 324-4521
12000 Government Center Parkway, Suite 527, Fairfax, VA 22035-0074
Chief Information Security Officer **Michael Dent** .... (703) 324-4006

Office of Human Rights and Equity Programs
12000 Government Center Parkway, Suite 318, Fairfax, VA 22035-0093
Fax: (703) 324-3570

Director **Kenneth L. Saunders** .... (703) 324-2220
Administrative Assistant **Jenal Mickens** .... (703) 324-2220

Office of the Chief Financial Officer
Chief Financial Officer **Joe Mondoro** .... (703) 324-2531

Department of Management and Budget
12000 Government Center Parkway, Suite 561, Fairfax, VA 22035-0074
Fax: (703) 324-3940

Director **Joe Mondoro** .... (703) 324-4096
Administrative Assistant **Patricia Walker** .... (703) 324-3571
E-mail: patricia.walker@fairfaxcounty.gov

Department of Purchasing and Supply Management
12000 Government Center Parkway, Suite 427, Fairfax, VA 22035-0017
Fax: (703) 324-3587

Director **Cathy A. Muse** .... (703) 324-3206
E-mail: cathy.muse@fairfaxcounty.gov
Administrative Assistant **Michelle Fowler** .... (703) 324-3206
E-mail: michelle.fowler@fairfaxcounty.gov

Department of Tax Administration
12000 Government Center Parkway, Suite 261, Fairfax, VA 22035-0076
Fax: (703) 324-4935

Director **Kevin C. Greenlief** .... (703) 324-4804
E-mail: kevin.greenlief@fairfaxcounty.gov
Administrative Assistant **Andie O'Dell** .... (703) 324-4804
E-mail: andie.odell@fairfaxcounty.gov
Personal Property and Business License Division
Juan Rengel .... (703) 324-3803
E-mail: juan.rengel@fairfaxcounty.gov Fax: (703) 324-3103
Administrative Assistant **Delores Lashley** .... (703) 324-3857
E-mail: delores.lashley@fairfaxcounty.gov Fax: (703) 324-4171
Real Estate Director **Howard Goodie** Room 357 .... (703) 324-4802
Administrative Assistant **Milagres Woolson** .... (703) 324-4802
Revenue Collection Director **Scott Sizemore**
Suite 223 .... (703) 324-2555
Fax: (703) 324-3935
Administrative Assistant **Amanda Trinh** .... (703) 324-2550
Fax: (703) 324-3935

Finance Department
12000 Government Center Pkwy., Suite 214, Fairfax, VA 22035-0016
Fax: (703) 324-4767

Director **Christopher Pietsch** .... (703) 324-3126
Administrative Assistant **Kristina Overton** .... (703) 324-3126
E-mail: kristina.overton@fairfaxcounty.gov

Office of the Internal Auditor
12000 Government Center Parkway, Suite 533, Fairfax, VA 22035-0074

Director **Sharon Pribadi** .... (703) 324-4218
Auditor Manager **Andrea Goutam** .... (703) 324-4211
Deputy Director **(Vacant)** .... (703) 324-4211
Administrative Assistant **(Vacant)** .... (703) 324-4218
Deputy Auditor **(Vacant)** .... (703) 324-2531

COUNTIES

★ Elected Official ▲ Appointed by Legislature ▼ Appointed by Governor ► Appointed by Board or Commission ● Appointed by Judge
■ Appointed by Mayor △ Appointed by Freeholders ▽ Appointed by Supervisor ▷ Appointed by County Executive ○ Appointed by Council

Department of Human Resources
12000 Government Center Parkway, Suite 270, Fairfax, VA 22035-0038
Fax: (703) 324-3945

Director **Susan Woodruff** Suite 258 .... (703) 324-3448
E-mail: susan.woodruff@fairfaxcounty.gov Fax: (703) 324-3945
Administrative Assistant **Edith C. Johnson** Suite 258 .... (703) 324-3448
E-mail: edith.johnson2@fairfaxcounty.gov
Assistant Director **Catherine "Cathy" Spage** .... (703) 324-3448
E-mail: catherine.spage@fairfaxcounty.gov

Office of Public Affairs
12000 Government Center Parkway, Fairfax, VA 22035-0001
Tel: (703) 324-3956

Public Affairs Director **Tony Castrilli** .... (703) 324-3189
E-mail: tony.castrilli@fairfaxcounty.gov

Planning Commission
12000 Government Center Parkway, Suite 330, Fairfax, VA 22035-0042
Fax: (703) 324-3948

Chairman **Peter F. Murphy, Jr.** .... (703) 324-2865
Executive Director **Jill Cooper** .... (703) 324-2869
Assistant Director **Kim Bassarab** .... (703) 324-2865

Fairfax-Falls Church Community Services Board
12011 Government Center Parkway, Suite 836, Fairfax, VA 22035-1100
Fax: (703) 324-7092 E-mail: wwwcsb@fairfaxcounty.gov
Internet: www.fairfaxcounty.gov/csb

Chairman **Gary Ambrose** .... (703) 324-7000
Vice Chair **Suzette C. Kern** .... (703) 324-7000
Member **(Vacant)** .... (703) 324-7000

Executive Staff
Executive Director **Tisha Deeghan** .... (703) 324-7015

Administrative Operations
Clinical Operations
Deputy Director **Daryl Washington** .... (703) 324-7089
E-mail: daryl.washington@fairfaxcounty.gov
Medical Director **Dr. Colton Hand** .... (703) 324-7000
Director of Nursing **Louella Meachem** .... (703) 799-2737

Fairfax County Park Authority
12055 Government Center Parkway, Suite 927, Fairfax, VA 22035-5550
Tel: (703) 324-8700 Fax: (703) 324-3974

Director **Kirk Kincannon** .... (703) 324-8733
Administrative Assistant **Barbara Gorski** .... (703) 324-8734
E-mail: barbara.gorski@fairfaxcounty.gov

McLean Community Center
1234 Ingleside Avenue, McLean, VA 22101-2817
Fax: (703) 556-0547 Internet: http://www.mcleancenter.org

Executive Director **George Sachs** .... (703) 790-0123

Reston Community Center
2310 Colts Neck Road, Reston, VA 20191-2888
Fax: (703) 476-8617

Executive Director **Leila Gordon** .... (703) 390-6142
E-mail: leila.gordon@fairfaxcounty.gov
Administrative Assistant **Barbara Wylmer** .... (703) 390-6147

Office of the Commonwealth's Attorney
4110 Chain Bridge Rd., #114, Fairfax, VA 22030

★ Commonwealth's Attorney
Raymond F. "Ray" Morrogh .... (703) 246-2776
Term Expires: December 31, 2019
Chief of Administrative Services **Debbie Thorpe** ...... (703) 246-2776
Chief Deputy Commonwealth's Attorney
Casey M. Lingan .... (703) 246-2776

Office of Elections
12000 Government Center Parkway, Suite323, Fairfax, VA 22035-0001
Fax: (703) 324-4735 (Electoral Board)
Fax: (703) 222-0776 (General Registrar)
Internet: www.fairfaxcounty.gov/eb

Chairman **Stephen M. Hunt** .... (703) 324-4735
Secretary **Katherine K. Hanley** .... (703) 324-4735
Education: Missouri 1965 BS, 1965 BA; Harvard 1966 MAT
Vice-Chairman **Seth Stark** (D) .... (703) 324-4735
General Registrar **Cameron Sasnett** .... (703) 222-0776
Deputy Registrar **Gary Scott** .... (703) 222-0776
Election Manager **Judy Flaig** .... (703) 222-0776

Office of the Sheriff
4110 Chain Bridge Rd., Fairfax, VA 22030-4041
Fax: (703) 359-4192 Internet: www.fairfaxcounty.gov/ps/sheriff

★ Sheriff **Stacey Ann Kincaid** (D) .... (703) 246-3260
Term Expires: December 31, 2019
Administrative Assistant **Kelly Hartle** .... (703) 246-3260

Fairfax County Public Schools
8115 Gatehouse Road, Falls Church, VA 22042
Tel: (571) 423-1000 E-mail: fcpsinfo@fcps.edu Internet: www.fcps.edu

Fairfax County School Board
8115 Gatehouse Road, Suite 5400, Falls Church, VA 22042
Fax: (571) 423-1067 E-mail: fairfaxcountyschoolboard@fcps.edu
Tel: (571) 423-1075

★ Chairman **Pat M. Hynes** (Hunter Mill) .... (571) 423-1082
Term Expires: December 31, 2019
E-mail: Pat.Hynes@fcps.edu
★ Vice Chair **Sandra S. "Sandy" Evans** (Mason) .... (571) 423-1083
Term Expires: December 31, 2019
E-mail: ssevans@fcps.edu
★ Member **Karen L. Corbett Sanders** (Mount Vernon) .... (571) 423-1075
Term Expires: December 31, 2019
★ Member **Jeanette Hough** (At-Large) .... (571) 423-1091
Term Expires: December 31, 2019
★ Member **Tamara Derenak Kaufax** (Lee) .... (571) 423-1081
Term Expires: December 31, 2019
E-mail: tdkaufax@fcps.edu
★ Member **Ryan L. McElveen** (At-Large) .... (571) 423-1089
Term Expires: December 31, 2019
E-mail: Ryan.McElveen@fcps.edu
★ Member **Megan O. McLaughlin** (Braddock) .... (571) 423-1088
Term Expires: December 31, 2019
E-mail: Megan.McLaughlin@fcps.edu
★ Member **Ilryong Moon** (At-Large) .... (571) 423-1090
Term Expires: December 31, 2019
E-mail: ilryong.moon@fcps.edu
Education: Harvard 1981 AB; William & Mary 1984 JD
★ Member **Dalia Palchik** (Providence) .... (571) 423-1084
Term Expires: December 31, 2019
★ Member **Elizabeth L. Schultz** (Springfield) .... (571) 423-1080
Term Expires: December 31, 2019
E-mail: elizabeth.schultz@fcps.edu
★ Member **Jane K. Strauss** (Dranesville) .... (571) 423-1087
Term Expires: December 31, 2019
E-mail: jane.strauss@fcps.edu
Education: George Washington 1969 BA; Harvard 1971 MAT
★ Member **Thomas Wilson** (Sully) .... (571) 423-1075
Term Expires: December 31, 2019
Clerk to the Board **Ilene Muhlberg** .... (571) 423-1060
E-mail: ilene.muhlberg@fcps.edu

★ Elected Official ▲ Appointed by Legislature ▼ Appointed by Governor ▶ Appointed by Board or Commission ● Appointed by Judge
■ Appointed by Mayor △ Appointed by Freeholders ▽ Appointed by Supervisor ▷ Appointed by County Executive ○ Appointed by Council

Office of the Superintendent
8115 Gatehouse Road, Falls Church, VA 22042
Tel: (571) 423-1010 Fax: (571) 423-1007

▶ Superintendent of Schools **Karen Garza** . . . . (571) 423-1010
E-mail: superintendentgarza@fcps.edu
Education: Houston BS, MEd; Texas EdD

Deputy Superintendent **Steven Lockard** . . . . (571) 423-1020

Director of Communications and Congressional Relations **Matthew Guilfoyle** . . . . (571) 423-1200
E-mail: matthew.guilfoyle@fcps.edu

County of Fort Bend, Texas
301 Jackson Street, Richmond, TX 77469

County Seat: Fairfax **Election Type:** Partisan **Population:** 716,087 (2015)

Office of the County Judge
301 Jackson Street, Richmond, TX 77469
Fax: (281) 341-8609

★ County Judge **Robert E. "Bob" Hebert** (R) . . . . (281) 341-8608
Term Expires: December 31, 2018
E-mail: hebertb@co.fort-bend.tx.us
Education: Pepperdine MA; California Coast PhD
Executive Assistant **Ann Werlein** . . . . (281) 341-8608
E-mail: werleann@co.fort-bend.tx.us

Budget Office
309 South 4th Street, Suite 515, Richmond, TX 77469
Fax: (281) 344-3954 E-mail: budget@co.fort-bend.tx.us

Director of Finance and Investments **Pamela "Pam" Gubbels** . . . . (281) 344-3938

Office of the County Auditor
309 South 4th St., 5th Floor, Richmond, TX 77469
Fax: (281) 341-3774

County Auditor **Robert Ed Sturdivant** . . . . (281) 341-3760

Office of Emergency Management
307 Fort Street, Richmond, TX 77469
Fax: (281) 342-4798

Emergency Management Coordinator **Jeff Braun** . . . . (281) 342-6185
E-mail: braunjef@co.fort-bend.tx.us

Deputy Emergency Management Coordinator **Alan L. Spears** . . . . (281) 342-6185
E-mail: alan.spears@co.fort-bend.tx.us

Community Development Department
4520 Reading Road, Suite A, Rosenberg, TX 77471
Fax: (281) 341-3762

Director **Marilynn Kindell** . . . . (281) 341-4410

Engineering Department
1124 Blume Road, Rosenberg, TX 77471
Fax: (281) 342-7366

County Engineer **Richard Stolleis** . . . . (281) 633-7500

Facilities Management and Planning Department
1517 Eugene Heimann Circle, Suite 500, Richmond, TX 77469
Fax: (281) 633-7022

Director **James Knight** . . . . (281) 633-7045
E-mail: james.knight@fortbendcountytx.gov

Department of Health and Human Services [HHS]
4520 Reading Road, Suite A-100, Rosenberg, TX 77471
Tel: (281) 238-3233 Fax: (281) 238-3355
E-mail: hhs@fortbendcountytx.gov

Director **Dr. Mary desVignes-Kendrick** . . . . (281) 238-3233

Human Resources Department
4520 Reading Road, Rosenberg, TX 77471
Fax: (281) 238-3322

Human Resources Director **Kent Edwards** . . . . (281) 341-8617
E-mail: hrdept@co.fort-bend.tx.us

Information Technology Department
500 Liberty Street, Suite 212, Richmond, TX 77469
Fax: (281) 341-4526

Director **Ray Webb** . . . . (281) 341-4570
E-mail: ray.webb@co.fort-bend.tx.us

Parks and Recreation Department
2725 F.M. 521 North, Fresno, TX 77545
Fax: (281) 431-3079

Parks Director **Michel E. Davis** . . . . (281) 835-9419
Assistant Parks Director **Mike Reyes** . . . . (281) 835-9419

Public Transportation Department
12550 Emily Court, Suite 400, Sugar Land, TX 77478
Fax: (281) 243-6710 E-mail: transit@co.fort-bend.tx.us

Director **Paulette Shelton** . . . . (281) 633-7433

Purchasing Department
4520 Reading Road, Suite A, Rosenberg, TX 77471

Purchasing Agent **Gilbert Jalomo** . . . . (281) 341-8640
E-mail: jalomgil@co.fort-bend.tx.us

Risk Management Department
4520 Reading Road, Suite A, Rosenberg, TX 77471
Fax: (281) 341-3751

Director **Wyatt O. Scott** . . . . (281) 341-8630
E-mail: wyatt.scott@co.fort-bend.tx.us

Road and Bridge Department
201 Payne Lane, Richmond, TX 77469
Fax: (281) 238-3635

Road and Bridge Commissioner **Marc S. Grant** . . . . (281) 342-4513
E-mail: grantmar@co.fort-bend.tx.us

Social Services Department
4520 Reading Road, Suite A, Rosenberg, TX 77471
Fax: (281) 342-0557

Director **Anna Gonzalez** . . . . (281) 342-7300

Fort Bend County Drainage District
1004 Blume Road, Rosenberg, TX 77471
P.O. Box 1028, Rosenberg, TX 77471
Fax: (281) 342-9130

General Manager/Chief Engineer **Mark Vogler** . . . . (281) 342-2863
E-mail: voglemar@co.fort-bend.tx.us

Fort Bend County Libraries [FBCL]
1001 Golfview Drive, Richmond, TX 77469

Library Director **Clara Russell** . . . . (281) 633-4770

Veterans Service Office
4520 Reading Road, Suite A, Rosenberg, TX 77471
Fax: (281) 238-3581 E-mail: veteranservices@co.fort-bend.tx.us

Veterans Service Officer **Dwight Marshall** . . . . (281) 341-4550

Office of the Commissioners
301 Jackson Street, Richmond, TX 77469

★Commissioner **Richard Morrison** (D-Precinct 1) . . . . (281) 344-9400
Term Expires: December 31, 2016 Fax: (281) 342-0587
E-mail: commpct1@co.fort-bend.tx.us

★Commissioner **Grady Prestage** (D-Precinct 2) . . . . (281) 403-8000
Term Expires: December 31, 2018 Fax: (281) 403-8009
Education: Southern U (New Orleans) 1980 BSCE

★Commissioner **W. A. "Andy" Meyers** (R-Precinct 3) . . . . . (281) 494-1199
Term Expires: December 31, 2016 Fax: (281) 242-9060
E-mail: meyersan@co.fort-bend.tx.us
Education: LSU BS, MBA

★Commissioner **James Patterson** (R-Precinct 4) . . . . (281) 980-2235
Term Expires: December 31, 2018
E-mail: commpct4@co.fort-bend.tx.us
Education: Sam Houston State BA; Houston MA

Office of the County Attorney
301 Jackson Street, Suite 728, Richmond, TX 77469
Fax: (281) 341-4557

★County Attorney **Roy L. Cordes, Jr.** (R) . . . . (281) 341-4555
Term Expires: December 31, 2016
E-mail: corderoy@co.fort-bend.tx.us

Office of the County Clerk
301 Jackson Street, Suite 101, Richmond, TX 77469
Fax: (281) 341-8697

★County Clerk **Laura Richard** (R) . . . . (281) 341-8652
Term Expires: December 31, 2018

Office of the District Attorney
301 Jackson Street, 2nd Floor, Richmond, TX 77469
Fax: (281) 238-3340

★District Attorney **John F. Healey, Jr.** (R) . . . . (281) 341-4460
Term Expires: December 31, 2018

Office of the District Clerk
301 Jackson Street, Richmond, TX 77469
Fax: (281) 341-4519 E-mail: distclerk@co.fort-bend.tx.us

★District Clerk **Annie R. Elliott** (R) . . . . (281) 341-4513
Term Expires: December 31, 2018

Office of the Tax Assessor and Collector
500 Liberty Street, Suite 101, Richmond, TX 77469

★Tax Assessor/Collector **Patsy Schultz** (R) . . . . (281) 341-3741
Term Expires: December 31, 2016

Office of the Treasurer
309 South 4th Street, Suite 514, Richmond, TX 77469
Fax: (281) 341-3757

★Treasurer **Jeff Council** (R) . . . . (281) 341-3750
Term Expires: December 31, 2018

Office of the Sheriff
1410 Ransom Road, Richmond, TX 77469
Fax: (281) 341-4701

★Sheriff **Troy E. Nehls** . . . . (281) 341-4700
Term Expires: December 31, 2016

County of Franklin, Ohio

County Courthouse, 373 South High Street, Columbus, OH 43215
Tel: (614) 525-3000 (Information) Internet: www.franklincountyohio.gov

County Seat: Columbus **Election Type:** Partisan
Population: 1,251,722 (2015)

Office of the Board of Commissioners
County Courthouse, 373 South High Street, 26th Floor,
Columbus, OH 43215
Tel: (614) 525-3322 (Information)
TTY: (614) 525-7588 Fax: (614) 525-5999
Internet: http://commissioners.franklincountyohio.gov/

★President **John O'Grady** (D) . . . . (614) 525-5589
Term Expires: January 1, 2017
Policy Director **Lauren Rummel** . . . . (614) 525-5589
E-mail: laurenrummel@franklincountyohio.gov

★Commissioner **Paula L. Brooks** (D) . . . . (614) 525-5729
Term Expires: January 1, 2017
E-mail: plbrooks@franklincountyohio.gov
Education: Youngstown State 1975 BA; Capital U 1983 JD
Policy Manager **Brook Kohn** . . . . (614) 525-6638
E-mail: brookkohn@franklincountyohio.gov

★Commissioner **Marilyn Brown** (D) . . . . (614) 525-3461
Term Expires: January 1, 2019
Policy Director **Michael Daniels** . . . . (614) 525-3461
E-mail: michael.daniels@franklincountyohio.gov

Office of the County Administrator
373 South High Street, 26th Floor, Columbus, OH 43215
Tel: (614) 525-5337 Fax: (614) 525-5940

▶County Administrator **Kenneth Wilson** . . . . (614) 525-3324
Executive Assistant **Carla Wallace** . . . . (614) 525-4132
E-mail: cmwallac@franklincountyohio.gov

Deputy County Administrator **Kris Long** . . . . (614) 525-4263
Education: Hope 1991 BA; SUNY (Buffalo) 1998 JD

Deputy County Administrator **Erik J. Janas** . . . . (614) 525-4263
Education: Dayton BA; Cleveland State 2002 MPA

Office on Aging
280 East Broad Street, 3rd Floor, Columbus, OH 43215
Fax: (614) 525-5300 Internet: www.officeonaging.org

Director **Antonia M. Carroll** . . . . (614) 525-5230

Office of Homeland Security and Justice Programs [OHS&JP]
373 South High Street, 25th Floor, Columbus, OH 43215
Fax: (614) 525-5549 E-mail: jpu@franklincountyohio.gov
Internet: www.franklincountyohio.gov/commissioners/hsjp

Director **Kathy Crandall** . . . . (614) 525-5570
E-mail: kbcrandall@franklincountyohio.gov

Office of Management and Budget
Franklin County Courthouse, 373 South High Street, 26th Floor,
Columbus, OH 43215
E-mail: budget@franklincountyohio.gov

Director **Zak Talarek** . . . . (614) 525-5774
E-mail: zttalare@franklincountyohio.gov

★Elected Official ▲Appointed by Legislature ▼Appointed by Governor ▶Appointed by Board or Commission ●Appointed by Judge
■Appointed by Mayor △Appointed by Freeholders ▽Appointed by Supervisor ▷Appointed by County Executive ○Appointed by Council

Human Resources Department
373 South High Street, 25th Floor, Columbus, OH 43215
Tel: (614) 525-6224 Fax: (614) 525-6273

Director **Robert J. Young** . . . . (614) 525-6224

Animal Care and Control Department
4340 Tamarack Boulevard, Columbus, OH 43229
Tel: (614) 525-3647 Fax: (614) 525-6658
Internet: www.franklincountydogs.com

Director **(Vacant)** . . . . (614) 525-3485

Child Support Enforcement Agency [CSEA]
80 E. Fulton St., Columbus, OH 43215
TTY: (614) 525-7697 Fax: (614) 525-6409
Internet: www.franklincountyohio.gov/commissioners/csea

Director **Susan A. Brown** . . . . (614) 525-6030

Economic Development and Planning Department
150 South Front Street, Suite 10, Columbus, OH 43215
Fax: (614) 525-7155
Internet: www.franklincountyohio.gov/commissioners/edp

Director **James R. Schimmer** . . . . (614) 525-3094
E-mail: jrschimmer@franklincountyohio.gov

Fleet Management Department
1721 Alum Creek Drive, Columbus, OH 43207
Fax: (614) 443-1132 Internet: http://fleet.franklincountyohio.gov/

Director **Charlotte Ashcraft** . . . . (614) 525-3412

Department of Job and Family Services
1721 Northland Park Avenue, Columbus, OH 43229
Fax: (614) 233-2398
Internet: www.franklincountyohio.gov/commissioners/jafs

Director **Joy Bivens** . . . . (614) 233-2000

Department of Public Facilities Management [PFM]
County Courthouse, 373 South High Street, 2nd Floor, Columbus, OH 43215
Fax: (614) 525-3180
Internet: www.franklincountyohio.gov/commissioners/pfm

Director **James Goodenow** . . . . (614) 525-3800
E-mail: jagooden@franklincountyohio.gov
Assistant Director, Administration **Darla Reardon** . . . . (614) 525-6322
E-mail: dreardon@franklincountyohio.gov
Assistant Director, Property Management
Richard E. "Dick" Myers . . . . (614) 525-3800
E-mail: remyers@franklincountyohio.gov

Purchasing Department
County Courthouse, 373 South High Street, 25th Floor, Columbus, OH 43215
Fax: (614) 525-3144
Internet: www.franklincountyohio.gov/commissioners/prch

Director **Karl H. Kuespert** . . . . (614) 525-3750

Department of Sanitary Engineering
280 East Broad Street, 2nd Floor, Columbus, OH 43215
Fax: (614) 525-5210
Internet: www.franklincountyohio.gov/commissioners/seng

Director **Stephen A. Renner** . . . . (614) 525-3940

Franklin County Children Services
855 West Mound Street, Columbus, OH 43223
Tel: (614) 275-2571 TTY: (614) 275-2686
Internet: www.franklincountyohio.gov/children_services

Executive Director **Charles M. "Chip" Spinning** . . . . (614) 275-2649

Franklin County Convention Facilities Authority [FCFCA]
Greater Columbus Convention Center, 400 North High Street, Columbus, OH 43215

Executive Director **Don L. Brown** . . . . (614) 827-2800

Franklin County Emergency Management and Homeland Security
5300 Strawberry Farms Boulevard, Columbus, OH 43230
Fax: (614) 882-3209 E-mail: fcem&hs@franklincountyohio.gov

Director **Col Michael R. Pannell** . . . . (614) 794-0213
E-mail: mrpannel@franklincountyohio.gov
Deputy Director **Darrel Koerber** . . . . (614) 794-0213
E-mail: dlkoerbe@franklincountyohio.gov

Franklin County Data Center
Tel: (614) 525-3208

Chief Information Officer **Terri Bettinger** . . . . (614) 525-3208

Alcohol, Drug Addiction and Mental Health Board of Franklin County [ADAMH]
447 East Broad Street, Columbus, OH 43215
Tel: (614) 224-1057 Fax: (614) 224-0991
Internet: www.adamhfranklin.org

Board Staff
Chief Executive Officer **David A. Royer** . . . . (614) 222-3760

Franklin County Board of Elections
280 E. Broad St., 1st Floor, Columbus, OH 43215
Fax: (614) 525-3489 E-mail: boe@franklincountyohio.gov
Internet: http://vote.franklincountyohio.gov/

Director **William A. Anthony, Jr.** (D) . . . . (614) 525-3100
Deputy Director **David Payne** . . . . (614) 525-3100

Franklin County Board of Developmental Disabilities [FCBDD]
2879 Johnstown Road, Columbus, OH 43219
Tel: (614) 475-6440 Fax: (614) 342-5001 Internet: www.fcbdd.org

President **Renée Stein** . . . . (614) 475-6440
Vice President **Linda Craig** . . . . (614) 475-6440

Board Staff
Superintendent **Jed W. Morison** . . . . (614) 475-6440

Franklin County Board of Health
Memorial Hall, 280 East Broad Street, Columbus, OH 43215
Internet: www.myfcph.org/board.php

President **Jerry L. Lupfer** . . . . (614) 525-3160
Term Expires: 2019

Franklin County Public Health
280 East Broad Street, 2nd Floor, Columbus, OH 43215
Tel: (614) 525-3160 Fax: (614) 525-6672
E-mail: fcph@franklincountyohio.gov Internet: www.myfcph.org

Health Commissioner **Susan A. Tilgner** . . . . (614) 525-3670
Medical Director **Miller Sullivan** . . . . (614) 525-3670

COUNTIES

★ Elected Official ▲ Appointed by Legislature ▼ Appointed by Governor ▶ Appointed by Board or Commission ● Appointed by Judge
■ Appointed by Mayor △ Appointed by Freeholders ▽ Appointed by Supervisor ▷ Appointed by County Executive ○ Appointed by Council

Franklin Soil and Water Conservation District
1328 Dublin Road, Suite 101, Columbus, OH 43215
Tel: (614) 486-9613 Fax: (614) 486-9614 E-mail: info@franklinswcd.org
Internet: www.franklinswcd.org

Director **Jennifer Fish** . . . . (614) 486-9613 ext. 119

Solid Waste Authority of Central Ohio [SWACO]
4239 London-Groveport Road, Grove City, OH 43123
E-mail: info@swaco.org Internet: www.swaco.org

Executive Director **Ty D. Marsh** . . . . (614) 871-5100
Education: Ohio Wesleyan
Assistant Executive Director **Jeffrey "Jeff" Cahill** . . . . . . (614) 645-5100

Veterans Service Commission [VSC]
250 West Broad Street, Columbus, OH 43215
Fax: (614) 525-2505 E-mail: veteransservice@franklincountyohio.gov
Internet: www.franklincountyohio.gov/vets

Director **(Vacant)** . . . . (614) 525-2500

Office of the Auditor
County Courthouse, 373 South High Street, 21st Floor,
Columbus, OH 43215
Tel: (614) 525-7399 TTY: (614) 525-7593
Internet: www.franklincountyauditor.com

★ Auditor **Clarence E. Mingo II** (R) . . . . (614) 525-7399
Term Expires: January 2019
E-mail: franklincountyauditor@franklincountyohio.gov
Education: Ohio State BA, JD
Chief of Staff **Cindi Becker** . . . . (614) 525-7358
Consumer Services Division Administrator
Sharon James . . . . (614) 525-7375
Data Center Information Technology Director
Terri Bettinger . . . . (614) 525-5668
Estate Tax Division Administrator **Julie Dixon** . . . . . . (614) 525-7371
Fiscal Services Division Administrator **Robert Caldwell** . . (614) 525-7520
Real Estate Division Administrator **Larry McQuain** . . . . . . (614) 525-4683
E-mail: lgmcquai@franklincountyohio.gov

Office of the Coroner
520 King Avenue, Columbus, OH 43201
Fax: (614) 525-6002 Internet: www.franklincountyohiocoroner.com

★ Coroner **Dr. Anahi Ortiz** . . . . (614) 525-5290
Term Expires: January 7, 2017
Chief Investigator **Amanda Alvarez** . . . . (614) 525-5290
Chief Pathologist **Dr. J Scott Somerset** . . . . (614) 525-5290
Chief Toxicologist **Daniel Baker** . . . . (614) 525-5290

Office of the County Engineer
970 Dublin Road, Columbus, OH 43215
Fax: (614) 525-3359 Internet: www.franklincountyengineer.org

★ Engineer **Dean C. Ringle** (R) . . . . (614) 525-3030
Term Expires: January 1, 2017
E-mail: dringle@franklincountyengineer.org
Education: Ohio State BS
Chief Deputy Engineer **Mark Sherman** . . . . (614) 525-3900
E-mail: msherman@franklincountyengineer.org
Chief Deputy Engineer **Cornell Robertson** . . . . (614) 525-3080
E-mail: crobertson@franklincountyengineer.org

Office of the County Recorder
County Courthouse, 373 South High Street, 18th Floor,
Columbus, OH 43215
Tel: (614) 525-3930 Fax: (614) 525-4299
E-mail: recorder@franklincountyohio.gov
Internet: www.franklincountyohio.gov/recorder

★ Recorder **Terry J. Brown** (D) . . . . (614) 525-3980
Term Expires: January 1, 2017

Office of the Prosecuting Attorney
County Courthouse, 373 South High Street, 14th Floor,
Columbus, OH 43215
TTY: (614) 525-7698 Fax: (614) 525-6103
Internet: www.franklincountyohio.gov/prosecuting_attorney

★ Prosecuting Attorney **Ron O'Brien** (R) . . . . (614) 525-3555
Term Expires: December 31, 2016
E-mail: rjobrien@franklincountyohio.gov
Education: Ohio Dominican Col BBA; Ohio State 1974 JD
First Assistant Attorney, Civil Division
Nick A. Soulas, Jr. . . . . (614) 525-3520
E-mail: nasoulas@franklincountyohio.gov Fax: (614) 525-6012
First Assistant Attorney, Criminal Division
Douglas P. "Doug" Stead . . . . (614) 525-3555
Fax: (614) 525-6103

Office of the Public Defender
County Courthouse, 373 South High Street, 12th Floor,
Columbus, OH 43215-6302
Fax: (614) 461-6470

Public Defender **Yeura R. Venters** . . . . (614) 525-3194

Office of the Sheriff
Hall of Justice, 369 South High Street, 2nd Floor, Columbus, OH 43215
TTY: (614) 525-7699 Internet: www.sheriff.franklin.oh.us

★ Sheriff **Zach Scott** (D) . . . . (614) 525-3360
Term Expires: January 1, 2017
E-mail: zxscott@franklincountyohio.gov

Office of the Treasurer
County Courthouse, 373 South High Street, 17th Floor,
Columbus, OH 43215-6306
Fax: (614) 221-8124 Internet: http://treasurer.franklincountyohio.gov/

★ Treasurer **Edward "Ed" Leonard** . . . . (614) 525-3438
Term Expires: September 3, 2017
E-mail: ed_leonard@franklincountyohio.gov

Educational Service Center of Central Ohio [ESCCO]
2080 Citygate Drive, Columbus, OH 43219
TTY: (614) 445-3771 Fax: (614) 445-3767
Internet: www.escofcentralohio.org

Superintendent (Acting) **Tom Goodney** . . . . (614) 445-3750
Deputy Superintendent/Chief of Staff **Michael Trego** . . . . . (614) 445-3750

★ Elected Official ▲ Appointed by Legislature ▼ Appointed by Governor ▶ Appointed by Board or Commission ● Appointed by Judge
■ Appointed by Mayor △ Appointed by Freeholders ▽ Appointed by Supervisor ▷ Appointed by County Executive ○ Appointed by Council

County of Fresno, California

Hall of Records, 2281 Tulare Street, Room 301, Fresno, CA 93721
Tel: (559) 600-3529 (Information) Fax: (559) 600-1608
Internet: www.co.fresno.ca.us

County Seat: Fresno **Election Type:** Nonpartisan **Population:** 974,861 (2015)

Office of the Board of Supervisors

Hall of Records, 2281 Tulare Street, Room 301, Fresno, CA 93721-2198
Tel: (559) 600-3529 Fax: (559) 600-1608

★ Chairman **Buddy Mendes** (District 4) .... (559) 600-4000
Term Expires: January 7, 2019
E-mail: district4@co.fresno.ca.us
Assistant **Vickie Day** .... (559) 600-4000
E-mail: vday@co.fresno.ca.us

★ Vice Chairman **Brian Pacheco** (District 1) .... (559) 600-3529
Term Expires: December 2018
Assistant **Kathy Burrows** .... (559) 600-1000
E-mail: kburrows@co.fresno.ca.us

★ Supervisor **Andreas Borgeas** (District 2) .... (559) 600-2000
Term Expires: January 9, 2017
Education: Georgetown 1999 JD
Assistant **Heather Elkins** .... (559) 600-2000
E-mail: helkins@co.fresno.ca.us

★ Supervisor **Henry P. Perea** (District 3) .... (559) 600-3000
Term Expires: January 9, 2017
Education: Cal State (Fresno) 1974 BS; USC 1995 MPA
Assistant **Patricia Pinedo** .... (559) 600-3000
E-mail: ppinedo@co.fresno.ca.us

★ Supervisor **Deborah A. Poochigian** (District 5) .... (559) 600-5000
Term Expires: January 9, 2017
E-mail: district5@co.fresno.ca.us
Education: Cal State (Fresno) 1973 BA
Assistant **Sue Garabedian** .... (559) 600-5000

Clerk to the Board **Bernice E. Seidel** .... (559) 600-3529
E-mail: clerk/bos@co.fresno.ca.us
Deputy Clerk to the Board **Sherrie Evans** .... (559) 600-3529
E-mail: sevans@co.fresno.ca.us
Chief of Security **Jerry Morris** .... (559) 600-6785
2220 Tulare Street, Suite 1600, Fresno, CA 93721

Office of the County Counsel

Fresno County Plaza, 2220 Tulare Street, 5th Floor, Fresno, CA 93721-2106
Tel: (559) 600-3479 Fax: (559) 600-3480

▽ County Counsel **Daniel C. Cederborg** .... (559) 600-3479
Administrative Secretary **Joan Cuadres** .... (559) 600-3479
Chief Deputy County Counsel **Brian Lee Melikian** .... (559) 600-3479
E-mail: bmelikian@co.fresno.ca.us
Education: Cal State (Fresno); Santa Clara U JD
Assistant County Counsel **Janelle E. Kelley** .... (559) 600-3479

Office of the County Administrative Officer

Hall of Records, 2281 Tulare Street, Room 304, Fresno, CA 93721
Fax: (559) 600-1230

▽ County Administrative Officer **Jean Rousseau** .... (559) 600-1710
E-mail: jrousseau@co.fresno.ca.us
Assistant County Administrative Officer **Kathleen Donawa** .... (559) 600-1223
E-mail: kdonawa@co.fresno.ca.us

Office of Cooperative Extension (University of California)

550 E. Shaw Avenue, Suite 210-B, Fresno, CA 93710
Tel: (559) 241-7515 Fax: (559) 241-7539 E-mail: cefresno@ucdavis.edu
Internet: http://cefresno.ucdavis.edu/

County Director **Dr. Shannon C. Mueller** .... (559) 241-7515

Office of the Public Defender

Fresno County Plaza, 2220 Tulare Street, 3rd Floor, Fresno, CA 93721
Tel: (559) 488-3546 Fax: (559) 600-1570

Public Defender **Elizabeth Diaz** .... (559) 488-3546

Veterans' Service Office

3845 North Clark Street, Suite 103, Fresno, CA 93726-4812
Tel: (559) 600-5436 Fax: (559) 600-4080

Veterans' Services Officer **Charles Hunnicutt** .... (559) 600-5436

Department of Agriculture

1730 South Maple Avenue, Fresno, CA 93702-4516
Fax: (559) 600-2415 E-mail: fresnoag@co.fresno.ca.us

▽ Agricultural Commissioner/Sealer of Weights and Measures (Acting) **Les Wright** .... (559) 600-7510
E-mail: lwright@co.fresno.ca.us
Chief Deputy Commissioner, Environmental Protection and Weights and Measures Division **Les Wright** .... (559) 600-7510
Deputy Commissioner, Pest Detection and Exclusion Division **Melissa Cregan** .... (559) 600-7510
Deputy Commissioner, Pest Management, Standardization and Statistics Division **Fred Rinder** .... (559) 600-7510

Department of Behavioral Health

4441 East Kings Canyon, Fresno, CA 93702
Tel: (559) 600-9180 Fax: (559) 600-7674
Internet: www.co.fresno.ca.us/behavioralhealth

Director **Dawan Utecht** .... (559) 600-9193

Internal Services Department

2048 North Fine Avenue, Fresno, CA 93727
Tel: (559) 600-5800 Fax: (559) 600-5927

Director/Chief Information Officer **Robert Bash** .... (559) 600-5800
E-mail: rbash@co.fresno.ca.us

Facility Services Division

4590 East Kings Canyon Road, Fresno, CA 93702
Fax: (559) 600-7739

Manager **Fenix Batista** .... (559) 600-7242
E-mail: fbatista@co.fresno.ca.us

Fleet Services Division

4551 East Hamilton Street, Fresno, CA 93702
Fax: (559) 600-7508

Manager **Allen Moore** .... (559) 600-7530

Purchasing Services Division

4525 E. Hamilton Ave., Fresno, CA 93702
Fax: (559) 600-7126

Manager **Gary Cornuelle** .... (559) 600-7110
E-mail: gcornuelle@co.fresno.ca.us

Personnel Services Department

Fresno County Plaza, 2220 Tulare Street, 16th Floor, Fresno, CA 93721
Fax: (559) 455-4790 Internet: www.co.fresno.ca.us/personnel

Director **Beth Bandy** .... (559) 600-1800

COUNTIES

★ Elected Official ▲ Appointed by Legislature ▼ Appointed by Governor ▶ Appointed by Board or Commission ● Appointed by Judge
■ Appointed by Mayor △ Appointed by Freeholders ▽ Appointed by Supervisor ▷ Appointed by County Executive ○ Appointed by Council

COUNTIES

Probation Department
P.O. Box 453, Fresno, CA 93709
Tel: (559) 600-3420 E-mail: fresnocoprobation@co.fresno.ca.us
Internet: www.co.fresno.ca.us/probation

Chief Probation Officer **Mike Elliott** .... (559) 600-1298
Deputy Chief Probation Officer **Rosalinda Acosta** ...... (559) 600-1295
Chief Secretary **Christina Young** .... (559) 600-3996
Human Resources Manager **Vicki Passmore** .... (559) 600-1299
E-mail: vpassmore@co.fresno.ca.us
Training Manager **Melissa Madsen** .... (559) 600-3420
E-mail: mmadsen@co.fresno.ca.us
Automation Services **David Touma** .... (559) 600-4735

Department of Public Health
1221 Fulton Mall, Fresno, CA 93721
Tel: (559) 600-3200 Fax: (559) 445-3370 E-mail: dph@co.fresno.ca.us
Internet: www.co.fresno.ca.us/publichealth

Director **Dave Pomaville** .... (559) 600-3204

Department of Public Works and Planning
Fresno County Plaza, 2220 Tulare Street, 6th Floor, Fresno, CA 93721
Fax: (559) 600-4548

Director **Alan Weaver** .... (559) 600-4078

Capital Projects Division
Fresno County Plaza, 2220 Tulare Street, 6th Floor, Fresno, CA 93721
Fax: (559) 600-4548

Manager **Stuart Seiden** .... (559) 600-5206

Community Development Division
Fresno County Plaza, 2220 Tulare Street, 6th Floor, Fresno, CA 93721
Fax: (559) 600-4573

Manager **Gigi Gibbs** .... (559) 600-4292
E-mail: ggibbs@co.fresno.ca.us

Construction Management Division
Fresno County Plaza, 2220 Tulare Street, 6th Floor, Fresno, CA 93721
Fax: (559) 600-4544

Manager **Robert Palacios** .... (559) 600-4154
E-mail: rpalacios@co.fresno.ca.us
Materials Engineer **Steve Deis** .... (559) 600-7884
E-mail: sdeis@co.fresno.ca.us

Design Division
Fresno County Plaza, 2220 Tulare Street, 6th Floor, Fresno, CA 93721
Fax: (559) 600-4548

Design Engineer **Mohammad Alimi** .... (559) 600-4109
E-mail: malimi@co.fresno.ca.us

Development Services Division
Fresno County Plaza, 2220 Tulare Street, Suite A, Fresno, CA 93721
Fax: (559) 600-4200

Manager **Will Kettler** .... (559) 600-4497

Maintenance and Operations Division
Fresno County Plaza, 2220 Tulare Street, Suite B, Fresno, CA 93721
Fax: (559) 600-4203

Maintenance and Operations Engineer **(Vacant)** .... (559) 600-4240
Supervising Engineer **Frank Daniele** .... (559) 600-4240
E-mail: fdaniele@co.fresno.ca.us

Resources Division
Fresno County Plaza, 2220 Tulare Street, 6th Floor, Fresno, CA 93721
Fax: (559) 600-4552

Division Manager **John Thompson** .... (559) 600-4259
E-mail: jothompson@co.fresno.ca.us

Department of Social Services [DSS]
2135 Fresno Street, Suite 100, Fresno, CA 93702
Tel: (559) 600-2300 Fax: (559) 600-2310

Director **Delfino Neira** .... (559) 600-2300

Fresno County Public Library
2420 Mariposa Street, Fresno, CA 93721
Tel: (559) 600-3184 Fax: (559) 600-7628 Internet: www.fresnolibrary.org

Librarian **Laurel Prysiazny** .... (559) 600-6237
E-mail: laurel.prysiazny@fresnolibrary.org
Associate County Librarian **Kelley Worman** .... (559) 600-6237
E-mail: kelley.worman@fresnolibrary.org
Business Manager **Steve Nitta** .... (559) 600-6235
E-mail: steve.nitta@fresnolibrary.org
Training Coordinator **Bill Secrest, Jr.** .... (559) 600-6269
E-mail: bill.secrest@fresnolibrary.org

Office of the Assessor/Recorder
Hall of Records, 2281 Tulare Street, Room 201, Fresno, CA 93721
Fax: (559) 600-1482

★ Assessor/Recorder **Paul A. Dictos** .... (559) 600-6879
Term Expires: January 1, 2019
Education: Cal State (Fresno) BS
Assistant Assessor/Recorder **Timothy Leming** .... (559) 600-6879
Recording Manager **Georgina Luna** .... (559) 600-3471

Office of the Auditor-Controller/ Treasurer-Tax Collector
Hall of Records, 2281 Tulare Street, Room 105, Fresno, CA 93721-1247
P.O. Box 1247, Fresno, CA 93715-1247
Fax: (559) 600-1444

★ Auditor-Controller/Treasurer-Tax Collector **Vicki Crow** ... (559) 600-3496
Term Expires: December 31, 2018
E-mail: vcrow@co.fresno.ca.us
Deputy Auditor-Controller **Alan Cade** .... (559) 600-3496
Deputy Treasurer-Tax Collector **Kimberly Lamanuzzi** .... (559) 600-3496
E-mail: klamanuzzi@co.fresno.ca.us

Office of the County Clerk/Registrar of Voters
2221 Kern Street, Fresno, CA 93721-2613
Tel: (559) 600-2575 (Clerk) Tel: (559) 600-8683 (Elections)
Fax: (559) 488-3279 E-mail: clerk-elections@co.fresno.ca.us
Internet: www.co.fresno.ca.us/elections

★ County Clerk/Registrar of Voters **Brandi L. Orth** .... (559) 600-2575
Term Expires: January 6, 2019
E-mail: borth@co.fresno.ca.us

Office of the District Attorney
Fresno County Plaza, 2220 Tulare Street, Suite 1000, Fresno, CA 93721
Tel: (559) 600-3141 Fax: (559) 600-4400
E-mail: damail@co.fresno.ca.us

★ District Attorney-Public Administrator
Lisa A. Smittcamp .... (559) 600-3141
Term Expires: January 7, 2019
Assistant District Attorney **Jeffrey Dupras** .... (559) 600-3141
E-mail: jdupras@co.fresno.ca.us
Assistant District Attorney **Blake J. Gunderson** .... (559) 600-3141
E-mail: bgunderson@co.fresno.ca.us
Assistant District Attorney **Stephen Wright** .... (559) 600-3141
E-mail: swright@co.fresno.ca.us

★ Elected Official ▲ Appointed by Legislature ▼ Appointed by Governor ▶ Appointed by Board or Commission ● Appointed by Judge
■ Appointed by Mayor △ Appointed by Freeholders ▽ Appointed by Supervisor ▷ Appointed by County Executive ○ Appointed by Council

Office of the Sheriff-Coroner

P.O. Box 1788, Fresno, CA 93717
Tel: (559) 600-8400 Fax: (559) 262-4032 Internet: www.fresnosheriff.org

★ Sheriff-Coroner **Margaret Mims** .... (559) 600-8800
Term Expires: January 4, 2019
E-mail: margaret.mims@fresnosheriff.org
Education: National U MPA
Undersheriff **Steve Wilkins** .... (559) 600-8146

Fresno County Office of Education [FCOE]

1111 Van Ness, Fresno, CA 93721-2000
Tel: (559) 265-3000 Fax: (559) 237-0733 Internet: www.fcoe.org

★ Superintendent **Jim A. Yovino** .... (559) 265-3010
Term Expires: December 31, 2018
E-mail: jyovino@fcoe.org
Executive Assistant to the Superintendent
Teresa M. Trevino .... (559) 265-3010
E-mail: ttrevino@fcoe.org
Deputy Superintendent, Business Services and Chief Financial Officer **Richard A. Martin** .... (559) 265-3083
E-mail: rmartin@fcoe.org Fax: (559) 237-3251
Deputy Superintendent, Educational Services
Dr. Kathryn Catania .... (559) 265-3090
Fax: (559) 497-3739
Communications and Public Relations Administrator
Lisa Birrell .... (559) 265-3012
E-mail: lbirrell@fcoe.org
Human Resources Administrator **Laurie Gabriel** .... (559) 265-3008
Fax: (559) 497-3949
Information Systems Administrator **Raj Sra** .... (559) 265-3017
Fax: (559) 497-3707

County of Fulton, Georgia

Fulton County Government Center, 141 Pryor Street, SW, Atlanta, GA 30303-3485
Tel: (404) 612-4000 (Information Customer Service) Fax: (404) 730-8254
Internet: www.fultoncountyga.gov

County Seat: Atlanta **Election Type:** Nonpartisan
Population: 1,010,562 (2015)

Office of the Board of Commissioners

Fulton County Government Center, 141 Pryor St., SW, Suite 10035, Atlanta, GA 30303-3444
Tel: (404) 612-8200 Fax: (404) 730-8254
Internet: www.fultoncountyga.gov/commissioners

★ Chairman **John H. Eaves** (At-Large, District 7) .... (404) 612-8232
Term Expires: January 1, 2019
E-mail: john.eaves@fultoncountyga.gov
Education: Morehouse Col 1984; Yale 1987 MAR; South Carolina 1999 PhD
★ Vice Chair **Liz Hausmann** (District 1) .... (404) 612-8232
Term Expires: January 1, 2019
E-mail: liz.hausmann@fultoncountyga.gov
★ Commissioner **Bob Ellis** (District 2) .... (404) 612-8232
Term Expires: January 1, 2017
★ Commissioner **E. Lee Morris III** (District 3) .... (404) 612-8232
Term Expires: January 1, 2019
Education: Duke BA; Emory JD
★ Commissioner **Joan P. Garner** (District 4) .... (404) 612-8232
Term Expires: January 1, 2017
E-mail: joan.garner@fultoncountyga.gov
Education: UDC 1975 BA; Howard U 1977 MA
★ Commissioner **Marvin S. Arrington, Jr.** (District 5) .... (404) 612-8232
Term Expires: January 1, 2019

Office of the Board of Commissioners *continued*

★ Commissioner **Emma I. Darnell** (District 6) .... (404) 612-8232
Term Expires: January 1, 2017
E-mail: emma.darnell@fultoncountyga.gov
Education: Fisk 1953 BA; Columbia MEd; Howard U JD
▶ Clerk **Mark Massey** .... (404) 612-8232
E-mail: mark.massey@fultoncountyga.gov
Chief Deputy Clerk **Tonya Grier** .... (404) 612-8242
E-mail: tonya.grier@fultoncountyga.gov

Office of the County Attorney

Fulton County Government Center, 141 Pryor Street, SW, Suite 4038, Atlanta, GA 30303
Fax: (404) 740-6324 Internet: www.fultoncountyga.gov/county-attorney

▶ County Attorney (Interim) **Jerolyn Ferrari** .... (404) 612-0246
Office Manager/Administrative Coordinator
Helen Barrow .... (404) 612-0246
Deputy County Attorney **Kaye Woodard Burwell** .... (404) 612-0246
E-mail: kaye.burwell@fultoncountyga.gov
Education: Arizona State 1985 JD; Emory 1986 LLM
Deputy County Attorney **(Vacant)** .... (404) 612-0246

Office of the County Manager

Fulton County Government Center, 141 Pryor St., SW, 10th Floor, Suite 10061, Atlanta, GA 30303
Tel: (404) 612-8320 Fax: (404) 893-6511
Internet: www.fultoncountyga.gov/county-manager-home

▶ County Manager **Richard Anderson** .... (404) 612-8320
Executive Assistant to the County Manager
Rosemary Shedrick .... (404) 612-6205
Assistant to the County Manager **(Vacant)** .... (404) 612-8758
Assistant County Manager **Lisa Rushin** .... (404) 612-8758
Director of Boards of Equalization **Melvin Richardson** .... (404) 612-6950
E-mail: melvin.richardson@fultoncountyga.gov
Director of Broadcasting and Cable **Shaunya Chavis** .... (404) 612-8310
E-mail: shaunya.chavis@fultoncountyga.gov
Director of Customer Service **(Vacant)** .... (404) 612-4000
Internal Audit Manager **Anthony Nicks** .... (404) 612-4233

Communications Division

Fulton County Government Center, 141 Pryor Street, SW, Suite 3090, Atlanta, GA 30303-3485
Tel: (404) 612-8300 Fax: (404) 730-6642

Director of External Affairs **Jessica Corbitt** .... (404) 612-8303
E-mail: jessica.corbitt@fultoncountyga.gov
Public Affairs Manager, Special Services District
Jolene Butts-Freeman .... (404) 612-2209
E-mail: jolene.freeman@fultoncountyga.gov
Public Affairs Manager **Felecia Church** .... (404) 612-5570
E-mail: felecia.church@fultoncountyga.gov
Public Information Officer II, Probate and Juvenile Courts, Board of Assessors **Bob Giordano** .... (404) 612-8397
E-mail: bob.giordano@fultoncountyga.gov
Senior Public Information Officer, Health and Wellness
April Majors .... (404) 612-1282
E-mail: april.majors@fultoncountyga.gov
Senior Public Information Officer **Claudia Strange** .... (404) 612-2206
E-mail: claudia.strange@fultoncountyga.gov
Division Manager, Communications **Darryl Carver** .... (404) 612-8305

Office of Diversity and Civil Rights Compliance [OEEODA]

141 Pryor Street, SW, Room 5042, Atlanta, GA 30303
Fax: (404) 893-6544

Director (Acting) **Dr. Ann Faith Harris** .... (404) 612-3735

COUNTIES

★ Elected Official ▲ Appointed by Legislature ▼ Appointed by Governor ▶ Appointed by Board or Commission ● Appointed by Judge
■ Appointed by Mayor △ Appointed by Freeholders ▽ Appointed by Supervisor ▷ Appointed by County Executive ○ Appointed by Council

COUNTIES

Office of the Medical Examiner
430 Pryor Street SW, Atlanta, GA 30312-2716
Fax: (404) 730-4405 Internet: www.fcmeo.org

▶ Chief Medical Examiner **Randy L. Hanzlick** .... (404) 730-4400
E-mail: randy.hanzlick@fultoncountyga.gov
Deputy Director **John Cross** .... (404) 730-4400
Operations Chief **Paul Desamours** .... (404) 730-4400
Administrative Coordinator **Barbara Pringle-Smalls** ..... (404) 730-4400
E-mail: barbara.pringle-smalls@fultoncountyga.gov

Office of the Public Defender, Atlanta Judicial Circuit
100 Peachtree Street NW,, Suite 100, Atlanta, GA 30303
Tel: (404) 612-5200 Fax: (404) 893-1789

Director **Vernon S. Pitts, Jr.** .... (404) 612-5210
Deputy Director **D'Andre J. Berry** .... (404) 612-5180
Training Supervisor **Luana K. Walsh** .... (404) 612-5332
E-mail: luana.walsh@fultoncountyga.gov

Cooperative Extension Service
Fulton County Government Center, 141 Pryor St., SW, Suite 1031, Atlanta, GA 30303
Fax: (404) 730-4121 E-mail: uge1121@uga.edu

County Extension Coordinator **Menia Chester** .... (404) 332-2400
Administrative Coordinator **Trina Chaney** .... (404) 332-2400

Planning and Community Services Department
5440 Fulton Industrial Boulevard, Suite 2085, Atlanta, GA 30336
Fax: (404) 730-7818 Internet: www.fultonecd.org

Director **Randy Beck** .... (404) 612-8102
Deputy Director, Zoning and Planning **(Vacant)** .... (404) 612-8053
Assistant Director, Building Plan Review and Inspections **Lee Peek** .... (404) 612-3011
Administration and Budget Manager **(Vacant)** .... (404) 612-8062
Permits Manager **Michelle Macaley** .... (404) 612-8094
Lead Engineer **Dick Wilcox** .... (404) 612-7474
E-mail: dick.wilcox@fultoncountyga.gov

Family and Children Services Department
1249 Donald L. Hollowell Parkway, Atlanta, GA 30318
Tel: (404) 206-5300 Fax: (404) 206-5786

Director **Glenene Lanier** .... (404) 206-5778
Fax: (770) 306-6514
Deputy Director **Julius Wilson** .... (404) 206-5300
Administrative Coordinator **Sheryl Charleston** .... (404) 206-5300
Financial Services Director **Greg Hicks** .... (404) 206-5772
Human Resources Director **Kaneisha Harris** .... (404) 206-5700
E-mail: Kaneisha.harris@fultoncountyga.gov

Finance Department
Fulton County Government Center, 141 Pryor St., SW, Suite 7001, Atlanta, GA 30303
Tel: (404) 612-7600

▶ Director **Patrick J. O'Connor** .... (404) 612-7688
E-mail: patrick.oconnor@fultoncountyga.gov
Assistant Director **Sharon Whitmore** .... (404) 612-7385
Comptroller **Ray Turner** .... (404) 612-7737
E-mail: ray.turner@fultoncountyga.gov
Budget Division Manager **Hakeem Oshikoya** .... (404) 612-7641
E-mail: hakeem.oshikoya@fultoncountyga.gov
Investment Officer **Tammy Goebeler** .... (404) 612-7698
Employee Benefits Manager **Melissa Harriott** .... (404) 612-7674
Water and Sewer/Collection and Billing Manager **Lee Poolmar** .... (404) 612-7697

Risk Management Division
Tel: (404) 612-6708

Risk Manager **Eldridge Morris** .... (404) 222-0556
E-mail: eldridge.morris@fultoncountyga.gov
Assistant Risk Manager **Denise McHam-Pinto** .... (404) 612-7663
E-mail: denise.pinto@fultoncountyga.gov
Workers Compensation Supervisor **Valerie J. Howard** .... (404) 612-6749

Fulton County Fire and Rescue Department [FCFRD]
5440 Fulton Industrial Boulevard, Atlanta, GA 30336
Tel: (404) 612-5711 Fax: (404) 893-6714
Internet: www.fultoncountyga.gov/fcfrd

▷ Fire Chief **Chief Larry Few** .... (404) 612-3755
E-mail: larry.few@fultoncountyga.gov Fax: (404) 893-6767
Date of Birth: December 9, 1953
Education: Shorter Col (GA) 1996 BSMS
Deputy Fire Chief, Fire and EMS **Charles Wesley Stubbs** .... (404) 612-5700
Fax: (404) 612-5713
Deputy Fire Chief, Safety and Member Services **Jack Butler, Jr.** .... (404) 612-5700
E-mail: jack.butler@fultoncountyga.gov Fax: (404) 699-8947
Fire Marshal **Lt. Martin Salamanca** .... (404) 612-5700
Fax: (404) 893-6532

Department of Facilities and Transportation Services
Fulton County Government Center, 141 Pryor Street, SW, Suite G119, Atlanta, GA 30303
Tel: (404) 730-5900 Fax: (404) 730-5897

▶ Director **(Vacant)** .... (404) 612-5900
Assistant Director **Shelia Benefield** .... (404) 612-5929
Financial Systems Manager (Acting) **Shelia Benefield** ... (404) 612-5919
Human Resources Manager **April L. Pye** .... (404) 612-5900
Network Administrator **Nanette Troutman** .... (404) 612-5523
E-mail: nanette.troutman@fultoncountyga.gov
Emergency Evacuation Training Coordinator **Brenda Walker** .... (404) 612-9098
E-mail: brenda.walker@fultoncountyga.gov

Central Fulton Service Area
Fax: (404) 730-7897

Area Manager **Jenny Williams** .... (404) 730-5900
Fax: (404) 730-7897

Fulton County Airport - Brown Field
3952 Aviation Circle, Room 200, Atlanta, GA 30336
Fax: (404) 699-4259

Manager **Douglas "Doug" Barrett** .... (404) 699-4200

Fleet Management
Tel: (404) 612-9494

Fleet Maintenance Division Assistant Director **Keith Staley** .... (404) 612-6519
Fleet Maintenance Manager (Acting) **Keir Freeman** ...... (404) 612-9494

Greater Fulton Service Area
Fax: (404) 730-7897

Area Manager **Jerry Williams** .... (404) 612-3739

Jail Services
Fax: (404) 335-5985

Assistant Director **Michael Ross** .... (404) 612-3772

Land Division
141 Pryor Street, SW, Suite 8021, Atlanta, GA 30303

Land Administrator **Charles "Mike" Yeargin** .... (404) 612-7870
E-mail: charles.yeargin@fultoncountyga.gov Fax: (404) 730-7877

★ Elected Official ▲ Appointed by Legislature ▼ Appointed by Governor ▶ Appointed by Board or Commission ● Appointed by Judge
■ Appointed by Mayor △ Appointed by Freeholders ▽ Appointed by Supervisor ▷ Appointed by County Executive ○ Appointed by Council

Materials Management Group
3929 Aviation Circle, Atlanta, GA 30336

Manager **Calvin Gamble** .... (404) 612-2254
E-mail: calvin.gamble@fultoncountyga.gov

Zonal Maintenance
Manager - Central **Vijay Nair** .... (404) 612-6586
Justice Center Building, 160 Pryor Street, SW, Suite B-4, Atlanta, GA 30303

Department of Health and Wellness
99 Jesse Hill Jr. Drive, South East, Atlanta, GA 30303
Tel: (404) 612-1211 Fax: (404) 730-1283
Internet: www.fultoncountyga.gov/dhw-home

Director (Interim) **Dr. David A Sarnow** .... (404) 613-1202
Education: South Florida MD
Deputy Director of Administration **Linda Jefferson** ...... (404) 612-9390
E-mail: linda.jefferson@fultoncountyga.gov
Environmental Health Director **Ellis "Eli" Jones** .... (404) 613-1337
Medical Director **Matthew McKenna** .... (404) 613-1201
Bioterrorism/Emergency Preparedness Program Director (Acting) **Matthew McKenna** .... (404) 613-1287
Board of Health/Community Liaison **Charles Releford** ... (404) 613-1202
E-mail: charles.releford@fultoncountyga.gov

Administrative and Support Services
Facility Management Supervisor **Richie Carter** .... (404) 613-1246
Fiscal Services Manager **Dorothy Robinson** .... (404) 612-1215
Grants and Contracts Manager **(Vacant)** .... (404) 613-1238
Human Resources Manager **Gidget McCrimon** .... (404) 612-1569
E-mail: gidget.mccrimon@fultoncountyga.gov
Material Management Manager **Deirdre Chambers** ...... (404) 613-1288
E-mail: deirdre.chambers@fultoncountyga.gov
Vital Records Manager **Tina Atkinson** .... (404) 613-1306

Department of Housing and Human Services
115 Martin Luther King, Jr. Drive, Suite 400, Atlanta, GA 30303
Fax: (404) 730-6889 E-mail: housing.humanservices@fultoncountyga.gov
Internet: http://hs.myfultoncountyga.us/

Director **Frankie Atwater** .... (404) 613-7944
Manager, Children and Youth Division **Melinda Pruitt** ... (404) 612-3726
Manager, Emergency Transitional Housing Division **Leonard Westmoreland** .... (404) 874-0412
Aging Program Manager **Sarah Hilton** .... (404) 332-7944

Department of Information Technology [DoIT]
Fulton County Government Center, 141 Pryor St., SW, 9th Floor, Atlanta, GA 30303
Tel: (404) 612-2000 E-mail: technology@fultoncountyga.gov
Internet: www.fultoncountyga.gov/county/it

Chief Information Officer/Director **Sally Wright** .... (404) 612-2000
E-mail: sally.wright@fultoncountyga.gov
Deputy Director/Chief Technology Officer **Shin Kim** ..... (404) 612-2000
E-mail: Shin.Kim@fultoncountyga.gov
Assistant Director/Chief Information Security Officer **Namarr Strickland, Sr.** .... (404) 612-2000
E-mail: namarr.strickland@fultoncountyga.gov

Law Library
Justice Center Tower, 185 Central Avenue, Suite JCT 7000, Atlanta, GA 30303
Tel: (404) 612-4544 Fax: (404) 730-4565
Internet: http://sca.fultoncourt.org/lawlibrary/

Librarian/Manager **Jeannie R. Ashley** .... (404) 612-4559
E-mail: jeannie.ashley@fultoncountyga.gov

Department of Parks and Recreation
Fulton County Government Center, 141 Pryor St., SW, Suite 8031, Atlanta, GA 30303
Fax: (404) 730-6206
Internet: www.fultoncountyga.gov/parks-and-recreation

▶ Director **Frankie Smith** .... (404) 612-4058
E-mail: frankie.smith@fultoncountyga.gov
Assistant Director **Tony Phillips** .... (404) 612-5347

Personnel Department
Fulton County Government Center, 141 Pryor St., SW, Suite 3030, Atlanta, GA 30303
Tel: (404) 730-6700 Fax: (404) 730-6326
Internet: www.fultoncountyga.gov/personnel

Director **Kenneth L. Hermon, Jr.** .... (404) 613-0923
E-mail: Kenneth.Hermon@fultoncountyga.gov
Deputy Director **(Vacant)** .... (404) 613-0880

Classification and Compensation Division
Personnel Manager **Stacey Jones** .... (404) 613-0898
E-mail: stacey1.jones@fultoncountyga.gov

Employee and Labor Relations Division
Fax: (404) 730-7942

Personnel Manager **Serena Brooks-Thomas** .... (404) 613-0885
E-mail: serena.brooks@fultoncountyga.gov

Personnel Administration and Payroll Division
Personnel Manager **Kimberly Flowers** .... (404) 613-0904

Recruiting Division
Fax: (404) 730-6217

Personnel Manager **Amorette Williams** .... (404) 613-0902
E-mail: amorette.williams@fultoncountyga.gov

Training and Career Development Division
Training Chief **Danny Parrish** .... (404) 613-0886
E-mail: danny.parrish@fultoncountyga.gov

COUNTIES

Fulton County Police Department [FCPD]
5440 Fulton Industrial Boulevard, Atlanta, GA 30336
Tel: (404) 613-5711 Fax: (404) 893-6570 Internet: www.fultonpolice.org

Police Chief **Gary D. Stiles** .... (404) 613-5705
Assistant Chief **(Vacant)** .... (404) 613-5712

Public Safety Training Center
3025 Merk Road, College Park, GA 30349
Tel: (404) 346-7940 Fax: (404) 346-7941
E-mail: fulton@fultoncountyga.gov

Director **Capt. Tina Johnson** .... (404) 346-7940
E-mail: tina.johnson@fultoncountyga.gov
Assistant Director **Capt. Marcus Woods** .... (404) 346-7945
E-mail: marcus.woods@fultoncountyga.gov
Range Master **Lt. Breylan Hicks** .... (404) 346-8396
5301 Aldredge Drive, College Park, GA 30349
E-mail: breylan.hicks@fultoncountyga.gov

Department of Public Works [DPW]
Fulton County Government Center, 141 Pryor St., SW, Suite 6001, Atlanta, GA 30303
Tel: (404) 612-7400 Fax: (404) 730-6325
Internet: www.fultoncountyga.gov/publicworks-home

Director **(Vacant)** .... (404) 612-8102
Administrative Coordinator **Mabel Green** .... (404) 612-7451
E-mail: mabel.green@fultoncountyga.gov

Administration Division
Deputy Director **Jerome Noble** .... (404) 612-2957
E-mail: jerome.noble@fultoncountyga.gov
Financial Systems Manager **Tony Moore** .... (404) 612-7527

(continued on next page)

★ Elected Official ▲ Appointed by Legislature ▼ Appointed by Governor ▶ Appointed by Board or Commission ● Appointed by Judge
■ Appointed by Mayor △ Appointed by Freeholders ▽ Appointed by Supervisor ▷ Appointed by County Executive ○ Appointed by Council

Administration Division *continued*

General Information Systems Manager **Colin Gowens** . . . (404) 612-0638
E-mail: colin.gowens@fultoncountyga.gov
Human Resources Manager **Alysia Shands** . . . . (404) 612-7424
E-mail: alysia.shands@fultoncountyga.gov
Safety Manager **Romano White** . . . . (404) 612-1001

Transportation Division

Fax: (912) 893-6206

Assistant Director **(Vacant)** . . . . (404) 612-7468
Deputy Director **Ernest Slaughter** . . . . (404) 612-8325

Water and Sewer Services Division

Assistant Director **Kun Suwanarpa** . . . . (404) 612-7394
Deputy Director **Paul V. Williams** . . . . (404) 612-7547
E-mail: paul.williams@fultoncountyga.gov
Engineer Administrator **Lamar Lambert** . . . . (404) 612-7470
E-mail: lamar.lambert@fultoncountyga.gov

Department of Purchasing and Contract Compliance

Public Safety Building, 130 Peachtree Street, Southwest, Suite 1168, Atlanta, GA 30303
Tel: (404) 612-5800 Fax: (404) 893-0894

Director (Interim) **Felicia Strong-Whitaker** . . . . (404) 612-7981
Deputy Director **Felicia Strong-Whitaker** . . . . (404) 612-4204
E-mail: felicia.strong-whitaker@fultoncountyga.gov
Contract Administrator **Donna Jenkins** . . . . (404) 612-4213
E-mail: donna.jenkins@fultoncountyga.gov
Chief Assistant Purchasing Agent (Team A)
Cheryl Cochran . . . . (404) 612-4203
E-mail: cheryl.cochran@fultoncountyga.gov
Chief Assistant Purchasing Agent (Team B)
William Long . . . . (404) 612-5823
E-mail: william.long@fultoncountyga.gov
Chief Assistant Purchasing Agent (Team C)
Charles Leonard . . . . (404) 612-7660
Administrative Coordinator **Marylan James** . . . . (404) 612-7981
E-mail: marylan.james@fultoncountyga.gov

Contract Compliance

130 Peachtree St. SW, Suite 1167, Atlanta, GA 30303
Tel: (404) 612-6300 Fax: (404) 730-6311

Administrator **Rholanda M. Stanberry** . . . . (404) 612-6304

Registration and Elections Department

Fulton County Government Center, 130 Peachtree Street SW, Suite 2186, Atlanta, GA 30303
Tel: (404) 612-7020 Fax: (404) 730-7024
Internet: www.fultoncountyga.gov/registration-elections

Director **Rick Barron** . . . . (404) 612-7020
Administrative Coordinator II **Brenda McCloud** . . . . (404) 612-7020
E-mail: brenda.mccloud@fultoncountyga.gov
Elections Chief **Dwight Brower** . . . . (404) 612-7033
Registration Chief **Shauna Dozier** . . . . (404) 612-7072
Elections Preparation Manager
Nadine Etienne Williams . . . . (404) 612-3130
Administrative Coordinator (Elections)
Sharon Benjamin . . . . (404) 612-7020
E-mail: sharon.benjamin@fultoncountyga.gov
Secretary to the Director and Board **Shirley Arnold** . . . . . . (404) 612-7020
E-mail: shirley.arnold@fultoncountyga.gov
Registration Manager **Ralph Jones** . . . . (404) 612-7072
E-mail: ralph.jones@fultoncountyga.gov

Atlanta-Fulton County Emergency Management Agency [AFCEMA]

Public Safety Building, 130 Peachtree Street SW, Suite G-157, Atlanta, GA 30303
Tel: (404) 730-5600 Fax: (404) 730-5625 Internet: www.afcema.com

Director **Matthew "Matt" Kallmyer** . . . . (404) 730-5600
E-mail: matthew.kallmyer@fultoncountyga.gov
Deputy Director **Pansy Ricks** . . . . (404) 730-5600
E-mail: pansy.ricks@fultoncountyga.gov
Operations Officer **Donnie Reece** . . . . (404) 730-5600
E-mail: donnie.reece@fultoncountyga.gov
Administrative Services Manager **Wanda Floyd** . . . . (404) 730-5600
E-mail: wanda.floyd@fultoncountyga.gov
Education: Georgia State MPA

Atlanta-Fulton Public Library System [AFPLS]

One Margaret Mitchell Square, Atlanta, GA 30303-1089
Tel: (404) 730-1700 Fax: (404) 730-1990 Internet: www.afpls.org

Administration

Director of Libraries, Arts, and Culture (Interim)
Gayle Holloman . . . . (404) 730-1972
E-mail: gayle.holloman@fultoncountyga.gov
Library Deputy Director (Interim) **Dr. Gabriel Morley** . . . . (404) 730-1700
Public Relations and Marketing Director
Claudia Strange . . . . (404) 730-1865
E-mail: claudia.strange@fultoncountyga.gov

Fulton County Arts Council [FCAC]

Fulton County Government Center, 141 Pryor St., SW, Suite 2030, Atlanta, GA 30303
Fax: (404) 730-5798 E-mail: contact@fultonarts.org
Internet: www.fultonarts.org

Director **Tae Earl-Jackson** . . . . (404) 612-5780
Marketing Specialist **Carole Sykes** . . . . (404) 612-5780

Abernathy Arts Center

254 Johnson Ferry Rd., Atlanta, GA 30328
Fax: (404) 303-6135

Arts Program Coordinator **Laura Martin** . . . . (404) 303-6172

Johns Creek Art Center

Building #700, 6290 Abbots Bridge Road, Duluth, GA 30097
Fax: (770) 623-6695

Executive Director **D. Stuart Miller** . . . . (770) 623-8448

South Fulton Arts Center

4645 Butner Rd., College Park, GA 30349
Fax: (770) 306-3100

Arts Program Coordinator **Narviar Griffin-Watson** . . . . . . (770) 306-3087

Southwest Arts Center

915 New Hope Road, Atlanta, GA 30331
Fax: (404) 505-3224

Arts Program Coordinator **Cheryl Odelye** . . . . (404) 613-3220

West End Performing Arts Center

945 Ralph David Abernathy Blvd., Atlanta, GA 30310
Fax: (404) 756-6470

Arts Program Coordinator **Mary Cannon** . . . . (404) 756-6465

Fulton County Emergency Communications Center

Public Safety Building, 130 Peachtree Street, Suite 3147, Atlanta, GA 30303
Tel: (404) 730-7900

Director **Joseph Barasoain** . . . . (404) 730-7903
Support Services Manager **Latisha Schofield** . . . . (404) 730-7902
E-mail: latisha.schofield@fultoncountyga.gov

★ Elected Official ▲ Appointed by Legislature ▼ Appointed by Governor ▶ Appointed by Board or Commission ● Appointed by Judge
■ Appointed by Mayor △ Appointed by Freeholders ▽ Appointed by Supervisor ▷ Appointed by County Executive ○ Appointed by Council

Fulton County Emergency Communications Center *continued*

Deputy Director **Treachous "Tony" Bailey** ....(404) 612-7900
IT Operations Manager **Jonathan Reich** ....(404) 730-7908
E-mail: jonathan.reich@fultoncountyga.gov
Communications Systems Specialist **Marcus Traylor** .....(404) 730-7910
E-mail: marcus.traylor@fultoncountyga.gov

Housing Authority of Fulton County [HAFC]

4273 Wendell Drive, Atlanta, GA 30336-2913
Tel: (404) 588-4950 Fax: (404) 472-3438 Internet: www.hafc.org

Executive Director **Larry Haqq** ....(404) 588-4950
Office Manager/Executive Assistant
Taqua Clay ....(404) 588-4950 ext. 7002
E-mail: tclay@hafc.org
Director of Finance **Calixto Garcia** ....(404) 588-4950

Office of the District Attorney

Courthouse, 136 Pryor St., SW, 3rd Floor, Atlanta, GA 30303
Tel: (404) 730-4980 Fax: (404) 893-2769 Internet: www.atlantada.org

★ District Attorney **Paul L. Howard, Jr.** ....(404) 613-4984
Term Expires: December 31, 2016
E-mail: paul.howard@fultoncountyga.gov
Education: Morehouse Col; Emory 1976 JD
Administrative Assistant **Luz Sanchez** ....(404) 612-2565
E-mail: luz.tellez@fultoncountyga.gov

Office of the Sheriff

185 Central Avenue, SW, Suite 9100, Atlanta, GA 30303
Tel: (404) 612-5100 Fax: (404) 224-8826 E-mail: info@fultonsheriff.org
Internet: www.fultonsheriff.org

★ Sheriff **Theodore "Ted" Jackson** ....(404) 612-5108
Term Expires: December 31, 2016 Fax: (404) 224-8821
E-mail: ted.jackson@fultoncountyga.gov
Chief Deputy **Jimmy Carter** ....(404) 612-5122
E-mail: jimmy.carter@fultoncountyga.gov
Chief of Staff **Col. Leighton Graham** ....(404) 612-5100

Fulton County Jail

901 Rice Street, NW, Atlanta, GA 30318
Tel: (404) 613-2000 Fax: (404) 853-2045

Chief Jailer **Col. Mark Adger** ....(404) 613-2000
Assistant Chief **Lt. Col. Kirt Beasley** ....(404) 613-2000
Administrative Officer **Lt. Col. Rueben Wingfield** ......(404) 613-2000
Records **Lt. Col. Kirt Beasley** ....(404) 613-2000

Office of the Solicitor General

160 Pryor St., SW, Room J-301, Atlanta, GA 30303
Tel: (404) 612-4800 Fax: (404) 730-6968

★ Solicitor General **Carmen D. Smith** ....(404) 612-4800
Term Expires: December 31, 2016
E-mail: carmen.smith@fultoncountyga.gov
Education: Fisk; NYU JD

Office of the Tax Commissioner

Fulton County Government Center, 141 Pryor Street SW,
Atlanta, GA 30303
Tel: (404) 730-6100 Fax: (404) 730-6154

★ Tax Commissioner **Arthur E. Ferdinand** ....(404) 613-0114
Term Expires: December 31, 2016 Fax: (404) 893-0606
E-mail: arthur.ferdinand@fultoncountyga.gov
Education: U London BS, PhD
Chief Deputy Tax Commissioner **(Vacant)** ....(404) 613-0111
Fax: (404) 893-0606

Office of the Tax Commissioner *continued*

Tax Administrator, Accounting Division **Matthew Buff**...(404) 613-0014
E-mail: matthew.buff@fultoncountyga.gov
Tax Administrator, Current Tax Division
Gladys Bradfield ....(404) 613-0079
Tax Administrator, Delinquent Tax Division
Terry Noble ....(404) 613-0116
E-mail: terry.noble@fultoncountyga.gov
Tax Administrator, Motor Vehicles Division **(Vacant)** ....(404) 613-0105
Tax Administrator, Satellite Operations Division
Rodney Floyd ....(404) 613-0680
Administrative Coordinator III **Sharon Feltner** ....(404) 613-0115
E-mail: sharon.feltner@fultoncountyga.gov
Administrative Coordinator III **(Vacant)** ....(404) 613-0115

Fulton County Board of Tax Assessors

Fulton County Government Center, 141 Pryor St., SW, Suite 2052,
Atlanta, GA 30303
Fax: (404) 893-6612 Internet: www.fultonassessor.org

Chair **Dillon H. Fries** ....(404) 612-6440
Vice Chair **Frank Lewandowski** ....(404) 612-6440
Assessor **Salma H. Ahmed** ....(404) 612-6440
Assessor **E. Gayle Barnett** ....(404) 612-6440
Assessor **Brandi Hunter** ....(404) 612-6440
Secretary to the Board **S. DeWayne Pinkney** ....(404) 612-6401
Chief Appraiser **David Fitzgibbon** ....(404) 612-6440

Fulton County School System [FCS]

6201 Powers Ferry Road, Atlanta, GA 30339
Tel: (470) 254-3600 Internet: www.fultonschools.org

Board of Education

6201 Powers Ferry Road, Atlanta, GA 30339
Tel: (470) 254-3600

★ President **Linda McCain** ....(470) 254-6890
Term Expires: December 31, 2018
E-mail: mccainl@fultonschools.org

Office of the Superintendent

6201 Powers Ferry Road, Atlanta, GA 30339
Fax: (470) 254-1246 E-mail: superintendent@fultonschools.org

Superintendent (Interim) **Kenneth Zeff** ....(470) 254-6890
Note: Until May 31, 2016
Superintendent **Jeff Rose** ....(470) 254-6890
Note: Effective June 1, 2016
Education: Lewis & Clark EdD
Executive Manager **Vijay Prugulla** ....(404) 254-6890
Deputy Superintendent of Academics and Instruction
Rob Anderson ....(470) 254-4578
Deputy Superintendent of Organizational Advancement
(Vacant)..(470) 254-4922
Assistant Superintendent, Learning and Teaching
Amy Barger ....(470) 254-4943
Chief Financial Officer (Interim) **Marvin Dereef** ....(470) 254-6841
Chief Human Resources Officer **Ron Wade** ....(470) 254-4585
E-mail: waderonnie@fultonschools.org
Deputy Superintendent of Operations **Patrick Burke**......(470) 254-8998
E-mail: burkep@fultonschools.org
Director of Safety and Security **Shannon Flounnory** ....(470) 254-8988

COUNTIES

★ Elected Official ▲ Appointed by Legislature ▼ Appointed by Governor ▶ Appointed by Board or Commission ● Appointed by Judge
■ Appointed by Mayor △ Appointed by Freeholders ▽ Appointed by Supervisor ▷ Appointed by County Executive ○ Appointed by Council

County of Genesee, Michigan

County Administration Bldg., 1101 Beach St., Flint, MI 48502
Tel: (810) 257-3020 (Information) TTY: (810) 257-3027
Internet: www.gc4me.com

County Seat: Flint **Election Type:** Partisan **Population:** 410,849 (2015)

Office of the Board of Commissioners

County Administration Building, 1101 Beach Street, Room 312, Flint, MI 48502-1417
Fax: (810) 257-3008 Internet: www.gc4me.com

★Chairman **Jamie W. Curtis** (D-District 3) .... (810) 257-3020
Term Expires: December 31, 2016
E-mail: jcurtis@co.genesee.mi.us

★Commissioner **Bryant W. Nolden** (D-District 1) .... (810) 257-3020
Term Expires: December 31, 2016

★Commissioner **Brenda J. Clack** (D-District 2) .... (810) 257-3020
Term Expires: December 31, 2016
E-mail: bclack@co.genesee.mi.us
Education: Tennessee State 1969 BS

★Commissioner **John Northrup** (D-District 4) .... (810) 257-3020
Term Expires: December 31, 2016
E-mail: jnorthrup@co.genesee.mi.us

★Commissioner **Mark Young** (D-District 5) .... (810) 257-3020
Term Expires: December 31, 2016

★Commissioner **Tony Brown** (R-District 6) .... (810) 257-3020
Term Expires: December 31, 2016

★Commissioner **Mike Lynch** (D-District 7) .... (810) 257-3020
Term Expires: December 31, 2016

★Commissioner **Ted Henry** (D-District 8) .... (810) 257-3020
Term Expires: December 31, 2016
E-mail: thenry@co.genesee.mi.us

★Commissioner **Pegge Adams** (D-District 9) .... (810) 257-3020
Term Expires: December 31, 2016

Office of the Controller

County Administration Building, 1101 Beach Street, Flint, MI 48502
Tel: (810) 257-3040 Fax: (810) 257-3560
Internet: www.co.genesee.mi.us/controller

Controller **Keith Francis** .... (810) 257-2627
E-mail: kfrancis@co.genesee.mi.us

Assistant Controller **Jauneysa Dorsey** .... (810) 257-3857

Assistant Controller- Fiscal Services **Kristie Primeau** .... (810) 257-3857

Assistant Controller- Financial Operations
Joy Haynes-Hawkins .... (810) 257-3851

Risk Manager/Worker's Compensation **Terrie Dunn** .... (810) 257-2628
E-mail: tdunn@co.genesee.mi.us Fax: (810) 257-3502

Office of Corporation Counsel

County Administration Bldg., 1101 Beach Street, Room 317, Flint, MI 48502-1417
Tel: (810) 257-3050 Fax: (810) 257-2715

Corporation Counsel **Celeste D. Bell** .... (810) 257-3050

Assistant Corporation Counsel **Andrew C. Thompson** .... (810) 257-3050

Legal Secretary **(Vacant)** .... (810) 257-3050

Genesee County Probation Office

816 Beach St., Flint, MI 48502
Tel: (810) 257-3524 Fax: (810) 257-3810
Internet: www.co.genesee.mi.us/probation.htm

Region Manager **Stephanie Musser** .... (810) 257-3524

Supervisor **Martha Bamford** .... (810) 257-3524

Supervisor **Robert W. Standal, Jr.** .... (810) 257-3524

Supervisor **Tika Tyson** .... (810) 257-3524

Valley Area Agency on Aging

225 East Fifth Street, Suite 200, Flint, MI 48502
Fax: (810) 239-8869 Internet: www.valleyareaaging.org

Executive Director **Kathryn Boles** .... (810) 239-7671

Animal Control Department

G-4351 W. Pasadena Ave., Flint, MI 48504
Fax: (810) 732-1493

▶Chief Officer **Paul Wallace** .... (810) 732-1661

Bishop International Airport Authority

G-3425 West Bristol Road, Flint, MI 48507
Fax: (810) 233-3065 Internet: www.bishopairport.org

Chairperson **Winfield L. Cooper III** .... (810) 235-6560

Vice Chairperson **Loyst Fletcher, Jr.** .... (810) 235-6560

Treasurer **Jay Freeman** .... (810) 235-6560

Secretary **Mark Yonan** .... (810) 235-6560

Airport Director **Craig Williams** .... (810) 235-6560

Genesee County Community Action Resource Department [GCCARD]

601 North Saginaw Street, Suite 1B, Flint, MI 48502-2009
Tel: (810) 232-2185 Fax: (810) 768-4667

Executive Director **Matthew Purcell** .... (810) 232-2185

Deputy Executive Director **Stephanie Howard** .... (810) 232-2185

Special Projects Director **Veonca Johnson** .... (810) 232-2185

Document Control Director **(Vacant)** .... (810) 232-2185

Document Control Assistant Director **Andre Strater** .... (810) 232-2185

Head Start - Child Development Services Program
Director **Kelli Webb** .... (810) 235-5613
719 Harrison St., Flint, MI 48502

Neighborhood Services Center Director
Veronica Johnson .... (810) 768-4675

Senior Nutrition Program Director **Laura Rahmaad** .... (810) 235-3567

Weatherization Director **Matthew Purcell** .... (810) 232-2185

Work First (PATH) Program Director **(Vacant)** .... (810) 257-3154

Home Maintenance Assistant Director
Daniel Newcombe .... (810) 232-2185

Genesee Health System

420 West Fifth Avenue, Flint, MI 48503
Tel: (810) 257-3705 TTY: (810) 257-1346
Tel: (810) 257-3740 (Access Center) Tel: (810) 257-3797 (Jobline)
Fax: (810) 257-1328 Internet: www.genhs.org

Chief Executive Officer **Danis Russell** .... (810) 257-3707
Fax: (810) 257-3770

Genesee County Circuit Court, Court Services

Genesee County Courthouse, 900 South Saginaw Street, Flint, MI 48502-1529
Fax: (810) 239-9280

▶Court Administrator **Barbara Menear** .... (810) 424-4355
E-mail: bmenear@co.genesee.mi.us

Emergency Management and Homeland Security Office

1002 S. Saginaw St., Flint, MI 48502
Fax: (810) 237-6169

Emergency Management Director **Jenifier Boyer** .... (810) 257-3064
E-mail: jboyer@co.genesee.mi.us

Office of Equity and Diversity

County Administration Bldg., 1101 Beach Street, Room 343, Flint, MI 48502-1417
Fax: (810) 768-7943

▶Director **Stephanie Howard** .... (810) 257-3028
E-mail: showard@co.genesee.mi.us

★ Elected Official ▲ Appointed by Legislature ▼ Appointed by Governor ▶ Appointed by Board or Commission ● Appointed by Judge
■ Appointed by Mayor △ Appointed by Freeholders ▽ Appointed by Supervisor ▷ Appointed by County Executive ○ Appointed by Council

Employees Retirement System
County Administration Building, 1101 Beach Street, Flint, MI 48502-1453
Tel: (810) 257-2626 Fax: (810) 768-7097
Internet: www.co.genesee.mi.us/retirement

▶ Chairperson **Jeffery Cyphert** (810) 257-2626
▶ Retirement Services Administrator **Tracy Khan** (810) 257-2626
E-mail: tkhan@co.genesee.mi.us

Equalization Department
County Administration Bldg., 1101 Beach Street, Room 206,
Flint, MI 48502-1468
Fax: (810) 768-7954

▶ Director **Peggy Nolde** (810) 257-3017

Department of Human Services
125 East Union Street, Flint, MI 48502
Tel: (810) 760-2200 Fax: (810) 760-2984 (Central Administration Fax)

▶ Director **Sandi Mose** (810) 760-2645
Administrative Assistant **Tamika January** (810) 760-2651
Children's Services Director **Mike Milks** (810) 760-2361
Administrative Assistant **Eron Schoolcraft** (810) 760-2651

Genesee County 911
G-4481 Corunna Rd., Flint, MI 48532
Fax: (810) 732-7986 Internet: www.geneseecounty911.org

Director **David Ackley** (810) 732-4720
Deputy Director **Tim Jones** (810) 732-4720
Administrative Assistant **Robin Bush** (810) 732-4720

Genesee District Library [GDL]
G-4195 W. Pasadena Ave., Flint, MI 48504
Tel: (810) 732-0110 Fax: (810) 732-1161 Internet: www.thegdl.org

Library Director **David Conklin** (810) 732-5570
E-mail: dconklin@thegdl.org
Branch Operations Manager **Mary Higginbottom** (810) 732-5570
Finance Manager **Amy Goldyn** (810) 732-5570
Human Resources Manager **Jerilyn Schwartz** (810) 732-5570
Technical Services Manager **Darwin McGuire** (810) 732-5570
Information Technology Manager **Chris Wells** (810) 732-5570
Community Relations Officer **Eileen Button** (810) 732-5570

Genesee County Health Department
Floyd J. McCree Courts and Human Services Building,
630 South Saginaw Street, Suite 4, Flint, MI 48502-1540
Tel: (810) 257-3612 Fax: (810) 257-3147 Internet: www.gchd.us

▶ Health Officer/Director **Mark Valacak** (810) 257-3588
E-mail: mvalacak@gchd.us
Medical Director **Gary K. Johnson** (810) 257-3155
Community Health Director **Tamara Brickey** (810) 257-3202
Health Accounts Supervisor **Ingrid Fink** (810) 237-6167

Human Resources Department
County Administration Bldg., 1101 Beach Street, Room 337,
Flint, MI 48502-1454
Fax: (810) 768-7097

▶ Director **Anita Galajda** (810) 257-3034
E-mail: agalajda@co.genesee.mi.us
Assistant Director **(Vacant)** (810) 257-3034

Information Technology
Tel: (810) 257-3007

Chief Information Officer **Christopher Newell** (810) 237-6103

Law Library
Courthouse, 900 South Saginaw Street, Room 204, Flint, MI 48502
Fax: (810) 239-9280

Law Librarian **Janet Patsy** (810) 257-3253
E-mail: jpatsy@co.genesee.mi.us

Metropolitan Planning Commission
County Administration Building, 1101 Beach Street, Room 223,
Flint, MI 48502
Fax: (810) 257-3185 E-mail: gcmpc@co.genesee.mi.us

▶ Director **Derek Bradshaw** (810) 257-3010
E-mail: dbradshaw@co.genesee.mi.us
Assistant Director **Christine A. Durgan** (810) 257-3010
Principal Planner **Jason Nordberg** (810) 766-6543
Principal Planner **Sheila Taylor** (810) 766-6547

Michigan State University Extension, Genesee County
605 North Saginaw Street, Suite 1-A, Flint, MI 48502
Tel: (989) 244-8500 Fax: (810) 341-1729
E-mail: msue.genesee@county.msu.edu
Internet: http://msue.anr.msu.edu/county/info/genesee

Director **Diane Smith** (517) 526-7895
E-mail: dismith@anr.msu.edu

Parks and Recreation Commission
5045 Stanley Road, Flint, MI 48506
Fax: (810) 736-7220 Internet: www.geneseecountyparks.org

▶ Director **Amy M. McMillan** (810) 736-7100 ext. 814
E-mail: amcmillan@gcparks.org
Secretary **Deborah Wilkes** (810) 736-7100 ext. 812
E-mail: dwilkes@gcparks.org
Deputy Director **Barry June** (810) 736-7100 ext. 817
E-mail: bjune@gcparks.org

Purchasing Department
County Administration Bldg., 1101 Beach Street, Room 343,
Flint, MI 48502
Fax: (810) 257-3380

Purchasing Manager **Cindy Carnes** (810) 257-3030 ext. 2

Genesee County Road Commission [GCRC]
211 West Oakley Street, Flint, MI 48503
Fax: (810) 767-5373 Internet: www.gcrc.org

▶ Manager/Director **John H. Daly III** (810) 767-4920
E-mail: jdaly@gcrc.org
▶ Director of Engineering/County Highway Engineer
Fred F. Peivandi (810) 767-4920
E-mail: fpeivandi@gcrc.org
Director of Equipment and Facilities **John Bennett** (810) 767-4920
E-mail: jbennett@gcrc.org
Director of Finance **Melissa Williams** (810) 767-4920
Director of Maintenance **Anthony Branch** (810) 767-4920
E-mail: abranch@gcrc.org
Director of Personnel (Interim) **John H. Daly III** (810) 767-4920

Department of Veterans Services
Genesee County Administration Building, 1101 Beach Street, 2nd Floor,
Flint, MI 48502
Fax: (810) 237-6172 Tel: (810) 257-3068
Internet: www.co.genesee.mi.us/veterans

Director **Jeanne C. Thick** (810) 257-3068
Deputy Director **John Nelson** (810) 257-3068

COUNTIES

★ Elected Official ▲ Appointed by Legislature ▼ Appointed by Governor ▶ Appointed by Board or Commission ● Appointed by Judge
■ Appointed by Mayor △ Appointed by Freeholders ▽ Appointed by Supervisor ▷ Appointed by County Executive ○ Appointed by Council

Office of the County Clerk

Courthouse, 900 South Saginaw Street, 2nd Floor, Flint, MI 48502-1517
Tel: (810) 257-3282 Fax: (810) 257-3464
Internet: www.geneseecountyclerk.com

★County Clerk **John J. Gleason** (D) .... (810) 257-3224
Term Expires: December 31, 2016
Administrative Assistant County Clerk **Leslie Raleigh** .... (810) 257-3224
Elections and Vital Records Supervisor
Doreen D. Fulcher .... (810) 257-3283
E-mail: dfulcher@co.genesee.mi.us
Legal Division Supervisor **Cynthia Grossbauer** .... (810) 257-3220

Board of Canvassers

Courthouse, 900 South Saginaw Street, 2nd Floor, Flint, MI 48502-1517
▸Democrat Canvasser **Alexander Isaac** (D) .... (810) 257-3283
▸Democrat Canvasser **Sharon Reeves** (D) .... (810) 257-3283
▸Republican Canvasser **Edward Goggins** (R) .... (810) 257-3283
▸Republican Canvasser **Michelle Voorheis** (R) .... (810) 257-3283

Office of the Drain Commissioner

4608 Beecher Rd., Flint, MI 48532
Fax: (810) 732-1474

★Drain Commissioner **Jeffrey "Jeff" Wright** (D) .... (810) 732-1590
Term Expires: December 31, 2016
E-mail: jwright@co.genesee.mi.us
Chief Deputy Drain Commissioner **Warren Vyvyan** ..... (810) 732-1590

A. Ragnone Waste Water Treatment Plant

G-9290 Farrand Road, Montrose, MI 48457
Fax: (810) 232-3280

Plant Superintendent **Joseph M. Goergen** .... (810) 232-7662

District 3 & 7 Treatment Plant

14412 Hogan Road, Linden, MI 48451
Fax: (810) 735-1346

Plant Superintendent **Brian Ross** .... (810) 735-7135

Water Department

G-4608 Beecher Rd., Flint, MI 48532
Fax: (810) 732-1474

Superintendent **Rich Bysko** .... (810) 732-7870

Water and Waste Services Division

G-4610 Beecher Rd., Flint, MI 48532
Fax: (810) 732-9773

Director **John O'Brien** .... (810) 732-7870

Operation and Maintenance

G-4612 Beecher Road, Flint, MI 48532
Fax: (810) 732-9773

Operations and Maintenance Chief **Mark Horgan** .... (810) 732-7870
E-mail: mhorgan@gcdcwws.com

Office of the Prosecuting Attorney

900 South Saginaw Street, Flint, MI 48502
Tel: (810) 257-3210 Fax: (810) 257-3219
Internet: www.co.genesee.mi.us/prosecutors

★Prosecuting Attorney **David Leyton** (D) .... (810) 257-3210
Term Expires: December 31, 2016
E-mail: dleyton@co.genesee.mi.us
Administrative Secretary **Tamara S. Johns** .... (810) 257-3210
E-mail: tjohns@co.genesee.mi.us
Chief Assistant Prosecutor **Randall Petrides** .... (810) 257-3210
Special Assistant Prosecutor **John Potbury** .... (810) 257-3210

Office of the Register of Deeds

County Administration Building, 1101 Beach Street, Room 138, Flint, MI 48502
Tel: (810) 257-3060 Fax: (810) 768-7965
Internet: www.co.genesee.mi.us/registerdeeds

★Register of Deeds **John J. Gleason** (D) .... (810) 257-3060
Term Expires: December 31, 2016
Chief Deputy Register of Deeds **Roberta Sacharski** ..... (810) 257-1285
Deputy Register of Deeds **Sheila House** .... (810) 257-3334

Office of the Sheriff

1002 S. Saginaw St., Flint, MI 48502
Tel: (810) 257-3406
Tel: (810) 257-3426 (County Jail - Inmate Information)
Fax: (810) 257-3077 Internet: www.co.genesee.mi.us/sheriff

★Sheriff **Robert J. Pickell** (D) .... (810) 257-3406
Term Expires: December 31, 2016
E-mail: rpickell@co.genesee.mi.us
Undersheriff **Chris Swanson** .... (810) 257-3406
E-mail: cswanson@co.genesee.mi.us
Corrections Administrator **Jason Gould** .... (810) 257-3439
Law Enforcement Division **Robert Heath** .... (810) 257-3406
E-mail: mheath@co.genesee.mi.us
Paramedic Division **Casey Tafoya** .... (810) 257-3406

Office of the Surveyor

5370 Miller Rd., Suite 13, Swartz Creek, MI 48473
Fax: (810) 230-7844

★Surveyor **Kim R. Carlson** (D) .... (810) 230-1333
Term Expires: December 31, 2016
E-mail: kimcarlson@fse.us

Office of the Treasurer

County Administration Bldg., 1101 Beach St., Flint, MI 48502
Fax: (810) 257-3885

★Treasurer **Deborah H. Cherry** (D) .... (810) 257-3054
Term Expires: December 31, 2016
Education: Michigan (Flint) 1993 MPA
Chief Deputy Treasurer **Kelly Rau** .... (810) 257-3481

County of Greenville, South Carolina

301 University Ridge, Greenville, SC 29601
Tel: (864) 467-7115 Fax: (864) 467-7358
Internet: www.greenvillecounty.org

County Seat: Greenville **Election Type:** Partisan **Year Founded:** 1831
Population: 491,863 (2015)

Office of the County Council

301 University Ridge, Suite 2400, Greenville, SC 29601
Tel: (864) 467-7115 Fax: (864) 467-7358
Internet: www.greenvillecounty.org/county_council

★Chair **Dr. Bob Taylor** (R-District 22) .... (864) 414-7219
Term Expires: November 2016
E-mail: btaylor@greenvillecounty.org
Education: Bob Jones U BS; Penn State MA; Clemson PhD; South Carolina MBA
★Vice Chair **H. G. "Butch" Kirven** (R-District 27) .... (864) 963-7616
Term Expires: November 2016
E-mail: bkirven@greenvillecounty.org
Education: Presbyterian Col BA; Army War Col

★Elected Official ▲Appointed by Legislature ▼Appointed by Governor ▸Appointed by Board or Commission ●Appointed by Judge
■Appointed by Mayor △Appointed by Freeholders ▽Appointed by Supervisor ▹Appointed by County Executive ○Appointed by Council

Office of the County Council *continued*

★Council Member **Joe Dill** (R-District 17) . . . . (864) 895-7387
Term Expires: November 2018
E-mail: jdill@greenvillecounty.org

★Council Member
Joseph R. "Joe" Baldwin (R-District 18) . . . . (864) 968-1420
Term Expires: November 2016
E-mail: jbaldwin@greenvillecounty.org

★Council Member **Willis H. Meadows** (R-District 19) . . . . (864) 294-4807
Term Expires: November 2018
E-mail: wmeadows@greenvillecounty.org

★Council Member **Sid Cates** (R-District 20) . . . . (864) 268-2725
Term Expires: November 2016
E-mail: scates@greenvillecounty.org
Education: Bob Jones U 1969 BS; Clemson 1971 MS; Bob Jones U 1984 EdD

★Council Member **Jim Burns** (R-District 21) . . . . (864) 288-5712
Term Expires: November 2016
E-mail: jburns@greenvillecounty.org
Education: Clemson

★Council Member
Xanthene Sayles Norris (D-District 23) . . . . (864) 271-6798
Term Expires: November 2018
E-mail: xnorris@greenvillecounty.org
Education: Clark Atlanta; Furman

★Council Member **Liz Seman** (R-District 24) . . . . (864) 294-3474
Term Expires: November 2016
E-mail: lseman@greenvillecounty.org
Education: Miami U (OH) BS

★Council Member **Lottie Beal Gibson** (D-District 25) . . . . (864) 277-1796
Term Expires: November 2016
E-mail: lgibson@greenvillecounty.org
Education: West Virginia State Col BA

★Council Member **Lynn Ballard** (R-District 26) . . . . (864) 243-0014
Term Expires: November 2018
E-mail: lballard@greenvillecounty.org

★Council Member **Fred Payne** (R-District 28) . . . . (864) 963-1564
Term Expires: November 2018
E-mail: fpayne@greenvillecounty.org

Office of the Clerk to Council

301 University Ridge, Suite 2400, Greenville, SC 29601
Tel: (864) 467-7115

Clerk to Council **Theresa B. Kizer** . . . . (864) 467-7117
E-mail: tkizer@greenvillecounty.org

Deputy Clerk **Regina McCaskill** . . . . (864) 467-7118
E-mail: rmccaskill@greenvillecounty.org

Office of the County Attorney

301 University Ridge, Suite 2400, Greenville, SC 29601
Tel: (864) 467-7110 Internet: www.greenvillecounty.org/County_Attorney/

County Attorney **Mark W. Tollison** . . . . (864) 467-7110
E-mail: mtollison@greenvillecounty.org
Education: Clemson 1984 BA; North Carolina 1988 MCRP

Deputy County Attorney **Dean Campbell** . . . . (864) 467-7110
E-mail: dcampbell@greenvillecounty.org

Assistant County Attorney **Jeffrey D. Wile** . . . . (864) 467-7110
E-mail: jwile@greenvillecounty.org

Assistant County Attorney **Kimberly Wunder** . . . . (864) 467-7110
E-mail: kwunder@greenvillecounty.org

Office of the County Administrator

301 University Ridge, Suite 2400, Greenville, SC 29601
Internet: www.greenvillecounty.org/county_administrator

County Administrator **Joseph Kernell** . . . . (864) 467-7105
E-mail: jkernell@greenvillecounty.org

Governmental Affairs Coordinator **Bob Mihalic** . . . . (864) 467-7105
E-mail: bmihalic@greenvillecounty.org

General Services

301 University Ridge, Greenville, SC 29601
Tel: (864) 467-7020 Internet: www.greenvillecounty.org/General_Services/

Deputy County Administrator **John Hansley** . . . . (864) 467-7105
E-mail: jhansley@greenvillecounty.org

Office of Management and Budget

301 University Ridge, Suite 200, Greenville, SC 29601
Tel: (864) 467-7020 Fax: (864) 467-7340
Internet: www.greenvillecounty.org/management_and_budget

Director **Ruth Parris** . . . . (864) 467-7020
E-mail: rparris@greenvillecounty.org

Tax Collector's Office

301 University Ridge, Suite 700, Greenville, SC 29601
Tel: (864) 467-7050 Fax: (864) 467-7189
Internet: www.greenvillecounty.org/tax_collector

Director **Kevin Hunter** . . . . (864) 467-7050
E-mail: khunter@greenvillecounty.org

Financial Operations Division

301 University Ridge, Suite 200, Greenville, SC 29601
Tel: (864) 467-7020 Fax: (864) 467-7049
Internet: www.greenvillecounty.org/finance_division

Director **Angela E. Roache** . . . . (864) 467-7020

Fleet Management Division

657 Keith Drive, Greenville, SC 29607
Tel: (864) 467-2650 Fax: (864) 467-2654
Internet: www.greenvillecounty.org/Fleet_Management/

Director **Alan Fairfield** . . . . (864) 467-2650

Geographic Information Systems Division

301 University Ridge, Suite 1000, Greenville, SC 29601
E-mail: gis@greenvillecounty.org Internet: www.gcgis.org

Director **Richard B. "Rich" Hanning** . . . . (864) 467-7328

Information Systems Division

301 University Ridge, Suite 1800, Greenville, SC 29601
Tel: (864) 467-7488 Fax: (864) 467-7456
Internet: www.greenvillecounty.org/Information_Systems/

Director **Dale Rice** . . . . (864) 467-7488
E-mail: drice@greenvillecounty.org

Procurement Services Division

301 University Ridge, Suite 100, Greenville, SC 29601
Tel: (864) 467-7200 Internet: www.greenvillecounty.org/Purchasing_Dept/

Director **G. Nadine Chasteen** . . . . (864) 467-7300
E-mail: nchasteen@greenvillecounty.org

Human Resources

301 University Ridge, Suite 500, Greenville, SC 29601
Tel: (864) 467-7150
Internet: www.greenvillecounty.org/Human_Resources/

Director **Debra Ham** . . . . (864) 467-7150

Planning and Code Compliance Division

301 University Ridge, Suite 400, Greenville, SC 29601
Tel: (864) 467-7357 Fax: (864) 467-7222
Internet: www.greenvilleplanning.com

Director **Eric Vinson** . . . . (864) 467-7281

Zoning Division

301 University Ridge, Suite 4100, Greenville, SC 29601
Tel: (864) 467-7425 Fax: (864) 467-7222

Administrator **Kris Kurjiaka** . . . . (864) 467-7282

COUNTIES

★ Elected Official ▲ Appointed by Legislature ▼ Appointed by Governor ▶ Appointed by Board or Commission ● Appointed by Judge
■ Appointed by Mayor △ Appointed by Freeholders ▽ Appointed by Supervisor ▷ Appointed by County Executive ○ Appointed by Council

Public Safety
Four McGee Street, Greenville, SC 29601
Tel: (864) 467-5257 Fax: (864) 467-5278
Internet: www.greenvillecounty.org/Public_Safety/

Assistant County Administrator **John Vandermosten** . . . . (864) 467-5257
E-mail: jvandermosten@greenvillecounty.org

Community Planning, Development, and Public Works
301 University Ridge, Suite 3800, Greenville, SC 29601
Tel: (864) 467-7007 Fax: (864) 467-7161
Internet: www.greenvillecounty.org/public_works

Assistant County Administrator **Paula Gucker** . . . . (864) 467-7007
E-mail: pgucker@greenvillecounty.org

Code Enforcement Division
301 University Ridge, Suite 4100, Greenville, SC 29601
Tel: (864) 467-7090

Building Official **Herb Yingling** . . . . (864) 467-7070

Engineering and Maintenance Division
301 University Ridge, Suite 3800, Greenville, SC 29601
Tel: (864) 467-7016
Internet: www.greenvillecounty.org/Public_Works/Eng.asp

County Engineer **Hesha Gamble** . . . . (864) 467-7010
E-mail: hgamble@greenvillecounty.org

Land Development Division
301 University Ridge, Suite 3900, Greenville, SC 29601
Tel: (864) 467-4610 Fax: (864) 467-7518

Director **Judith F. "Judy" Wortkoetter** . . . . (864) 467-4610

Solid Waste Management Division
Tel: (864) 243-9672 Fax: (864) 243-5276
Internet: www.greenvillecounty.org/solid_waste

Solid Waste Manager **Marcia L. Papin** . . . . (864) 243-9672

Greenville County Emergency Medical Services [GCEMS]
301 University Ridge, Greenville, SC 29601
Tel: (864) 467-7005

Director (Interim) **David T. "Tim" Gault** . . . . (864) 467-7005
Deputy Director - Administration
Sarah Warwick "Sally" Clark . . . . (864) 467-7005
E-mail: sclark@greenvillecounty.org
Deputy Director - Operations **David T. "Tim" Gault** . . . . . (864) 467-7005
E-mail: tgault@greenvillecounty.org

Animal Care Services
328 Furman Hall Road, Greenville, SC 29609
Tel: (864) 467-3953

Manager **Shelly Simmons** . . . . (864) 467-3953

Coroner's Office
Memorial Medical Office Building, 1190 West Faris Road, Greenville, SC 29605
Tel: (864) 522-1870 Fax: (864) 522-1879

★ County Coroner **B. Parks Evans, Jr.** (R) . . . . (864) 522-1870
Term Expires: December 31, 2016
E-mail: pevans@greenvillecounty.org
Chief Deputy Coroner **Mike Ellis** . . . . (864) 522-1870

Office of the County Auditor
301 University Ridge, Suite 800, Greenville, SC 29601
Tel: (864) 467-7040 Internet: www.greenvillecounty.org/County_Auditor/

★ County Auditor **Scott Case** (R) . . . . (864) 467-7056
Term Expires: December 31, 2018
E-mail: scase@greenvillecounty.org

Office of the County Treasurer
301 University Ridge, Suite 600, Greenville, SC 29601
Tel: (864) 467-7210 Fax: (864) 467-7077
Internet: www.greenvillecounty.org/County_Treasurer/

★ Treasurer **Jill Rees Kintigh** (R) . . . . (864) 467-7210
Term Expires: July 2019
E-mail: jkintigh@greenvillecounty.org

Register of Deeds Office
301 University Ridge, Suite 1300, Greenville, SC 29601
Tel: (864) 467-7240 Fax: (864) 467-7107
Internet: www.greenvillecounty.org/rod

★ Register of Deeds **Timothy "Tim" Nanney** (R) . . . . (864) 467-7240
Term Expires: December 31, 2016
E-mail: tnanney@greenvillecounty.org

Sheriff's Office
Four McGee Street, Greenville, SC 29601
Tel: (864) 467-5100 Internet: www.gcso.org

★ Sheriff **Steve Loftis** (R) . . . . (864) 467-5280
Term Expires: December 31, 2016
E-mail: sloftis@greenvillecounty.org
Chief Deputy **John Eldridge** . . . . (864) 467-5174
E-mail: jeldridge@greenvillecounty.org

Office of the Solicitor
Greenville County Court House, 305 East North Street, Greenville, SC 29601
Tel: (864) 467-8647 Internet: www.greenvillecounty.org/solicitor

★ Solicitor **William Walter "Walt" Wilkins III** . . . . (864) 467-8647
Term Expires: December 31, 2018
E-mail: wwilkins@greenvillecounty.org
Education: Wofford 1996; South Carolina 1999 JD

County of Guilford, North Carolina

301 West Market Street, Greensboro, NC 27401
Post Office Box 3427, Greensboro, NC 27402
Tel: (336) 641-3383 Fax: (336) 641-6833
Internet: http://www.myguilford.com/

County Seat: Greensboro **Election Type:** Partisan **Population:** 517,600 (2015)

Office of the Board of County Commissioners
301 West Market Street, Greensboro, NC 27401
P.O. Box 3427, Greensboro, NC 27402
Tel: (336) 641-4893 Fax: (336) 641-6833

★ Chair **Jeff Phillips** (R-District 5) . . . . (336) 641-3383
Term Expires: November 30, 2016
E-mail: jphillips@myguilford.com

★ Elected Official ▲ Appointed by Legislature ▼ Appointed by Governor ► Appointed by Board or Commission ● Appointed by Judge
■ Appointed by Mayor △ Appointed by Freeholders ▽ Appointed by Supervisor ▷ Appointed by County Executive ○ Appointed by Council

Office of the Board of County Commissioners *continued*

★ Vice Chair **Jerry Allen Branson** (R-District 4) .... (336) 641-3383
Term Expires: November 30, 2016
E-mail: jbranson@myguilford.com

★ Commissioner **J. Carlvena Foster** (D-District 1) .... (336) 641-3383
Term Expires: December 6, 2018
E-mail: jfoster@myguilford.com

★ Commissioner **Alan W. Perdue** (R-District 2) .... (336) 641-3383
Term Expires: November 30, 2018
E-mail: aperdue@myguilford.com

★ Commissioner **Justin Conrad** (R-District 3) .... (336) 641-7717
Term Expires: November 30, 2018
E-mail: Jconrad@myguilford.com

★ Commissioner **Hank Henning** (R-District 6) .... (336) 641-3383
Term Expires: November 30, 2016
E-mail: hhenning@myguilford.com

★ Commissioner **Carolyn Coleman** (D-District 7) .... (336) 641-3383
Term Expires: November 30, 2016
E-mail: ccoleman@myguilford.com
Education: Savannah State BS; North Carolina State MS

★ Commissioner **Raymond Trapp** (D-District 8) .... (336) 641-3383
Term Expires: November 30, 2016
E-mail: rtrapp@myguilford.com

★ Commissioner **Katie S. "Kay" Cashion** (D-At-Large) .... (336) 641-3383
Term Expires: November 30, 2016
E-mail: kcashion@myguilford.com

▶ Clerk to the Board **Robin Keller** .... (336) 641-4893

Office of the County Attorney

301 W. Market St., Suite 301, Greensboro, NC 27401
P.O. Box 3427, Greensboro, NC 27402
Fax: (336) 641-3642

▶ County Attorney **J. Mark Payne** .... (336) 641-3852
E-mail: mpayne@myguilford.com
Education: North Carolina 1979 BA, 1983 JD

Chief Deputy County Attorney **James Secor** .... (336) 641-3161
E-mail: jsecor@myguilford.com

Office of the County Manager

301 W. Market St., Greensboro, NC 27401
P.O. Box 3427, Greensboro, NC 27402
Tel: (336) 641-3383 Fax: (336) 641-6833

▶ County Manager **Marty K. Lawing** .... (336) 641-3383
E-mail: mlawing@co.guilford.nc.us

Deputy County Manager **Clarence Grier** .... (336) 641-3383
E-mail: cgrier@co.guilford.nc.us

Guilford County Animal Shelter

4525 West Wendover Avenue, Greensboro, NC 27409
Fax: (336) 297-5023 E-mail: info@adoptshelterpets.org
Internet: www.adoptshelterpets.org

Director **Logan D. Rustan** .... (336) 641-5990

Budget Evaluation and Management Department

P.O. Box 3427, Greensboro, NC 27402

Director **Michael Halford** .... (336) 641-3275
E-mail: mhalfor@co.guilford.nc.us

Cooperative Extension Office (North Carolina State University)

3309 Burlington Rd., Greensboro, NC 27405
Tel: (336) 641-2400 Fax: (336) 641-2402

Director (Interim) **Karen Neill** .... (336) 641-2400

Emergency Services Department

1002 Meadowood Street, Greensboro, NC 27409
Fax: (336) 641-6538

Director **James Albright** .... (336) 641-7565
Deputy Director/EMS **Kyle Paschal** .... (336) 641-7565
Operations Deputy Director **(Vacant)** .... (336) 641-7565

Finance Department

201 South Greene Street, Greensboro, NC 27402
Fax: (336) 641-6692

▶ Finance Director **N. Reid Baker** .... (336) 644-3949
E-mail: rbaker@co.guilford.nc.us
Administrative Assistant **(Vacant)** .... (336) 641-3300

Assistant Finance Director **(Vacant)** .... (336) 641-4574
Cash and Debt Manager **Calvin Clay Hicks** .... (336) 641-3299
Treasurer **Shannon Bridges** .... (336) 641-3303

Department of Health and Human Services [DHHS]

1203 Maple Street, Greensboro, NC 27405
Tel: (336) 641-7777 Fax: (336) 641-6971

Director **Merle C. Green** .... (336) 641-3283
Administrative Assistant **Tamara Clarke** .... (336) 641-3283
E-mail: tclarke@co.guilford.nc.us

Assistant Director **Ken Carter** .... (336) 641-6026
Allied Health Program Manager **Cindy Toler** .... (336) 641-6904
1100 East Wendover Avenue, Greensboro, NC 27405
Clinical Services Program Manager **Judy Southern** .... (336) 641-3712
1100 East Wendover Avenue, Greensboro, NC 27405
Community Services Program Manager **Felicia Reid** .... (336) 641-3768
1100 East Wendover Avenue, Greensboro, NC 27405
E-mail: freid@co.guilford.nc.us
Environmental Health Program Manager **David South** .... (336) 641-3566
Media Relations Manager **Sandy Ellington** .... (336) 641-6667
1100 East Wendover Avenue, Greensboro, NC 27405
Public Health Preparedness Manager **Alyson E. Best** .... (336) 641-4728
E-mail: abest@co.guilford.nc.us

Division of Social Services

1203 Maple Street, Greensboro, NC 27405
P.O. Box 3388, Greensboro, NC 27402-3388
Tel: (336) 641-3000 Fax: (336) 641-6868

Director **Heather Skeens** .... (336) 641-6086
Administrative Assistant **Denise Hayes** .... (336) 641-6086
E-mail: dhayes@co.guilford.nc.us
Staff Development Training Coordinator
Gregory Bush .... (336) 641-4918
E-mail: glbush@myguilford.com Fax: (336) 641-6868

Aging and Adult Services Division [AASD]

Fax: (336) 641-5405

Aging and Adult Services Division Director
Jenise Davis .... (336) 641-3380
Fax: (336) 641-5405

Administrative Assistant **Karen Thompson** .... (336) 641-3143
E-mail: kthomps@myguilford.com

Program Manager **Cheryl Millmore** .... (336) 641-3818
Program Manager **(Vacant)** .... (336) 641-2927

Children Welfare Services Division [CWSD]

Child Welfare Services Division Director
Sharon Barlow .... (336) 641-7618
Fax: (336) 641-6868

Administrative Assistant **Moneca Allen** .... (336) 641-3034
E-mail: mallen2@myguilford.com

Program Manager **Robert Lee** .... (336) 641-6701
Fax: (336) 641-6285

Program Manager **Brenden Hargett** .... (336) 641-3019
Fax: (336) 641-5405

Program Manager **Karen Williamson** .... (336) 641-3739
Fax: (336) 641-6285

(continued on next page)

★ Elected Official ▲ Appointed by Legislature ▼ Appointed by Governor ▶ Appointed by Board or Commission ● Appointed by Judge
■ Appointed by Mayor △ Appointed by Freeholders ▽ Appointed by Supervisor ▷ Appointed by County Executive ○ Appointed by Council

Division of Social Services *continued*

Program Manager **Laurie Jones** . . . . . . (336) 641-5729
Fax: (336) 641-6285

Economic Services Division [ES]

Economic Services Division Director **Elizabeth White** . . . (336) 641-3007
Fax: (336) 641-6868

Program Manager **Chris Crawford** . . . . . . (336) 641-7829
Tel: (336) 641-4588 Fax: (336) 641-4885

Program Manager **Shantele Williams** . . . . . . (336) 641-7327
E-mail: swillia6@myguilford.com Fax: (336) 641-6067

Human Resources Department

201 South Greene Street, Greensboro, NC 27401
Tel: (336) 641-4710 Fax: (336) 641-6906

Director **John Dean** . . . . . . (336) 641-3324

Information Services Department

201 North Eugene Street, Greensboro, NC 27401
P.O. Box 3427, Greensboro, NC 27402
Fax: (336) 641-4504

Chief Information Officer/Director **Hemant Desai** . . . . . . (336) 641-3371
E-mail: hdesai@myguilford.com

Deputy Chief Information Officer/Chief Technology Officer **Bridget Lindsay** . . . . . . (336) 641-3371
E-mail: blindsa@co.guilford.nc.us

Facilities, Parks, and Property Management

301 West Market Street, Greensboro, NC 27401
P.O. Box 3427, Greensboro, NC 27402
Fax: (336) 641-3802

Director **Robert McNiece** . . . . . . (336) 641-3340
E-mail: rmcniece@myguilford.com

Purchasing Department

301 W. Market St., Greensboro, NC 27401
P.O. Box 3427, Greensboro, NC 27402
Tel: (336) 641-3383 Fax: (336) 641-3317

Purchasing Director **Bonnie Stellfox** . . . . . . (336) 641-3226
E-mail: bstellf@co.guilford.nc.us

Tax Department

400 West Market Street, Greensboro, NC 27401
P.O. Box 3138, Greensboro, NC 27402
Fax: (336) 641-7908

Director **Ben Chavis** . . . . . . (336) 641-3379
E-mail: tax@co.guilford.nc.us
Administrative Assistant **Dare Rice** . . . . . . (336) 641-4882

Guilford County Transportation and Mobility Services [TAMS]

1203 Maple Street, Greensboro, NC 27405

Director **Myra Thompson** . . . . . . (336) 641-4848

Regional Juvenile Detention Center

15 Lockheed Ct., Greensboro, NC 27409

Director **Douglas Logan** . . . . . . (336) 641-2600
Administrative Officer **Emilia Caldwell** . . . . . . (336) 641-2609

Office of the Register of Deeds

201 West Market Street, Greensboro, NC 27401
P.O. Box 3427, Greensboro, NC 27402
Tel: (336) 641-7556 Fax: (336) 641-5778

★Register of Deeds **Jeff L. Thigpen** (D) . . . . . . (336) 641-7556
Term Expires: November 30, 2016
E-mail: jthigpe@co.guilford.nc.us

Office of the Sheriff

400 W. Washington St., Greensboro, NC 27401
P.O. Box 3427, Greensboro, NC 27402
Tel: (336) 641-3694 Fax: (336) 641-6729

★Sheriff **B.J. Barnes** (R) . . . . . . (336) 641-3694
Term Expires: November 30, 2018
E-mail: bbarnes@co.guilford.nc.us

Administrative Director **Debbie Lemonds** . . . . . . (336) 641-3272
E-mail: dlemond@co.guilford.nc.us

Chief Deputy **Col. T. R. "Randy" Powers** . . . . . . (336) 641-3694
E-mail: rpowers@co.guilford.nc.us

Court Services Bureau **Major Chuck Williamson** . . . . . . (336) 641-6108
Fax: (336) 641-6729

Operations Bureau **Major Jonathan S. "Jon" Jacobs** . . . (336) 641-2495
E-mail: jjacobs@co.guilford.nc.us

Guilford County Board of Elections

301 West Market Street, Greensboro, NC 27401
Fax: (336) 641-7676 Internet: http://www.myguilford.com/elections/

Director **Charlie Collicut** . . . . . . (336) 641-3836
Deputy Director **Tim Tsujii** . . . . . . (336) 641-3836

Guilford County Schools

712 North Eugene Street, Greensboro, NC 27402
Tel: (336) 370-8100 E-mail: goodnews@gcsnc.com
Internet: www.gcsnc.com

Co-Superintendent (Interim) **Nora Carr** . . . . . . (336) 370-8992
Co-Superintendent (Interim) **Terrance Young** . . . . . . (336) 370-8992

County of Gwinnett, Georgia

75 Langley Drive, Lawrenceville, GA 30046-6935
Tel: (770) 822-8000 (Information) Internet: www.gwinnettcounty.com

County Seat: Lawrenceville **Election Type:** Partisan
Population: 895,823 (2015)

Office of the Board of Commissioners

75 Langley Drive, Lawrenceville, GA 30046-6935
Tel: (770) 822-7000 Fax: (770) 822-7097

★Chairman **Charlotte J. Nash** (R-At-Large) . . . . . . (770) 822-7009
Term Expires: December 31, 2016
E-mail: charlotte.nash@gwinnettcounty.com
Education: Georgia 1971 BBA

★Commissioner **Jace Brooks** (R-District 1) . . . . . . (770) 822-7001
Term Expires: December 31, 2016
Education: Louisiana Tech U BS; Georgia State MBA; New Orleans Baptist MA

★Commissioner **Lynette Howard** (R-District 2) . . . . . . (770) 822-7002
Term Expires: December 31, 2018
E-mail: lynette.howard@gwinnettcounty.com

★Commissioner **Tommy Hunter** (R-District 3) . . . . . . (770) 822-7003
Term Expires: December 31, 2016

★Commissioner **John Wilson Heard** (R-District 4) . . . . . . (770) 822-7004
Term Expires: December 31, 2018
E-mail: john.heard@gwinnettcounty.com

County Clerk **Diane Kemp** . . . . . . (770) 822-7017
E-mail: diane.kemp@gwinnettcounty.com

Deputy County Clerk **Tina King** . . . . . . (770) 822-7000
E-mail: tina.king@gwinnettcounty.com

★Elected Official ▲Appointed by Legislature ▼Appointed by Governor ▶Appointed by Board or Commission ●Appointed by Judge
■Appointed by Mayor △Appointed by Freeholders ▽Appointed by Supervisor ▷Appointed by County Executive ○Appointed by Council

Office of the County Administrator

75 Langley Drive, Lawrenceville, GA 30046-6935
Tel: (770) 822-7000 Fax: (770) 822-7097

▶ County Administrator **Glenn Stephens** . . . . . (770) 822-7008
E-mail: glenn.stephens@gwinnettcounty.com

▶ Deputy County Administrator **Phil Hoskins** . . . . . (770) 822-7134
E-mail: phil.hoskins@gwinnettcounty.com

Communications Department

75 Langley Drive, Lawrenceville, GA 30046-6935
Tel: (770) 822-7180 Fax: (770) 822-7189

▶ Director **Joe Sorenson** . . . . . (770) 822-7123
E-mail: joe.sorenson@gwinnettcounty.com

Internet Services Manager **Bob Thompson** . . . . . (770) 822-7181
E-mail: bob.thompson@gwinnettcounty.com Fax: (770) 822-7189

Community Services Department

75 Langley Drive, Lawrenceville, GA 30046-6935
Tel: (770) 822-8880 Fax: (770) 822-8795

▶ Director **Phil Hoskins** . . . . . (770) 822-8890
E-mail: phil.hoskins@gwinnettcounty.com

Parks and Recreation Division

75 Langley Drive, Lawrenceville, GA 30046-6935

Director **Tina Fleming** . . . . . (770) 822-8819
Fax: (770) 822-8835

Corrections Department

750 Hi-Hope Road, Lawrenceville, GA 30043-4540
Tel: (678) 407-6000 Fax: (678) 407-6003

▶ Warden **Darrell Johnson** . . . . . (678) 407-6006

Financial Services Department

75 Langley Drive, Lawrenceville, GA 30046-6935
Tel: (770) 822-7850 Fax: (770) 822-7818

▶ Chief Financial Officer/Director **Maria Woods** . . . . . (770) 822-7197
E-mail: Maria.Woods@gwinnettcounty.com
Education: Georgia

Purchasing Division

75 Langley Drive, Lawrenceville, GA 30046-6935
Tel: (770) 822-8720 Fax: (770) 822-8735 Fax: (770) 822-8728

▶ Purchasing Director **Bryant Davis** . . . . . (770) 822-8725
E-mail: bryant.davis@gwinnettcounty.com

Fire and Emergency Services

Gwinnett Fire Headquarters, 408 Hurricane Shoals Road, NE,
Lawrenceville, GA 30046
Tel: (678) 518-4800 Fax: (678) 518-4806

Fire Chief **Casey Snyder** . . . . . (678) 518-4800

Human Resources Department

75 Langley Drive, Lawrenceville, GA 30046-6935
Tel: (770) 822-7940 Fax: (770) 822-7947

Director **Scott Fuller** . . . . . (770) 822-7915
E-mail: scott.fuller@gwinnettcounty.com

Deputy Director **Sandra Sheppard** . . . . . (770) 822-7920
E-mail: sandra.sheppard@gwinnettcounty.com

Information Technology Services

Tel: (770) 822-8900

Chief Information Officer **Abe A. Kani** . . . . . (770) 822-8900
Education: Utah State 1983 BS; Oklahoma State 1998 MBA

Law Department

75 Langley Drive, Lawrenceville, GA 30046-6935
Tel: (770) 822-8700 Fax: (770) 822-8790

▶ County Attorney **Bill Linkous** . . . . . (770) 822-8707

Planning and Development Department

446 West Crogan Street, Lawrenceville, GA 30046
Tel: (678) 518-6001 Fax: (678) 518-6275

▶ Director **Bryan Lackey** . . . . . (770) 518-6030
E-mail: bryan.lackey@gwinnettcounty.com

Police Department

P.O. Box 602, Lawrenceville, GA 30046-0602
Tel: (770) 513-5000 Fax: (770) 513-5005

▶ Police Chief **A.A. "Butch" Ayers** . . . . . (770) 513-5208
E-mail: Butch.Ayers@gwinnettcounty.com

Emergency Management

P.O. Box 602, Lawrenceville, GA 30046-0602

Director **Greg Swanson** . . . . . (770) 513-5060
E-mail: gregory.swanson@gwinnettcounty.com

Water Resources Department

684 Winder Hwy., Lawrenceville, GA 30045-5012
Tel: (678) 376-6700 Fax: (678) 376-7162

▶ Director **Ron Seibenhener** . . . . . (678) 376-7114
E-mail: ron.seibenhener@gwinnettcounty.com

Support Services Department

75 Langley Drive, Lawrenceville, GA 30046-6935
Tel: (770) 822-8010 Fax: (770) 822-8017

▶ Director **Angelia Parham** . . . . . (770) 822-8011

Transportation Department

75 Langley Drive, Lawrenceville, GA 30046-6935
Tel: (770) 822-7400 Fax: (770) 822-7478

▶ Director **Alan Chapman** . . . . . (770) 822-7417
E-mail: Alan.Chapman@gwinnettcounty.com

Deputy Director **David Tucker** . . . . . (770) 822-7407
E-mail: david.tucker@gwinnettcounty.com

Gwinnett County Public Library [GCPL]

1001 Lawrenceville Highway, Lawrenceville, GA 30045-4707
Tel: (770) 822-4522 Internet: www.gwinnettpl.org

Executive Director **Charles L. Pace** . . . . . (770) 822-4522
Education: North Texas BLS, MLS

Office of the District Attorney

75 Langley Drive, Lawrenceville, GA 30046-6935
Tel: (770) 822-8400 Fax: (770) 822-8465

★ District Attorney **Danny Porter** (R) . . . . . (770) 822-8400
Term Expires: December 31, 2016
E-mail: danny.porter@gwinnettcounty.com

Office of the Sheriff

2900 University Parkway, Lawrenceville, GA 30043-4588
Tel: (770) 822-3100 Fax: (770) 822-3115

★ Sheriff **Butch Conway** (R) . . . . . (770) 822-3122
Term Expires: December 31, 2016
E-mail: butch.conway@gwinnettcounty.com

★ Elected Official ▲ Appointed by Legislature ▼ Appointed by Governor ▶ Appointed by Board or Commission ● Appointed by Judge
■ Appointed by Mayor △ Appointed by Freeholders ▽ Appointed by Supervisor ▷ Appointed by County Executive ○ Appointed by Council

Office of the Supervisor of Elections

455 Grayson Highway, Suite 200, Lawrenceville, GA 30046
Tel: (678) 226-7210 Fax: (678) 226-7208

Supervisor of Elections **Lynn Ledford** .... (678) 226-7231

Office of the Tax Commissioner

75 Langley Drive, Lawrenceville, GA 30046-6935
Tel: (770) 822-8808 Fax: (770) 822-7295
E-mail: taxcommissioner@gwinnettcounty.com
Internet: www.gwinnetttaxcommissioner.manatron.com

★ Tax Commissioner **Richard Steele** (R) .... (770) 822-7394
Term Expires: December 31, 2016
E-mail: richard.steele@gwinnettcounty.com
Education: Georgia 1996 BS

COUNTIES

County of Hamilton, Ohio

County Administration Building, 138 East Court Street,
Cincinnati, OH 45202
Tel: (513) 946-4400 (Information) Internet: www.hamilton-co.org

County Seat: Cincinnati **Election Type:** Partisan **Population:** 807,598 (2015)

Office of the Board of Commissioners

County Administration Building, 138 East Court Street, Room 603,
Cincinnati, OH 45202
Tel: (513) 946-4400 Fax: (513) 946-4444

★ President **Chris R. Monzel** (R) .... (513) 946-4409
Term Expires: January 1, 2017
E-mail: chris.monzel@hamilton-co.org
Education: Purdue 1990; Cincinnati; Harvard 1998 MPP

★ Commissioner **Dennis Deters** (R) .... (513) 946-4406
Term Expires: January 3, 2017

★ Commissioner **Todd B. Portune** (D) .... (513) 946-4401
Term Expires: January 1, 2017 Fax: (513) 946-4446
E-mail: todd.portune@hamilton-co.org
Date of Birth: 1958
Education: Oberlin 1980; Cincinnati 1983 JD

► Clerk of the Board **Jacqueline Panioto** .... (513) 946-4414
E-mail: jacqueline.panioto@hamilton-co.org

Office of the County Administrator

County Administration Building, 138 East Court Street, Room 603,
Cincinnati, OH 45202
Tel: (513) 946-4400 Fax: (513) 946-4444

► County Administrator (Acting)
Jeffrey W. "Jeff" Aluotto .... (513) 946-4420
E-mail: jeff.aluotto@hamilton-co.org
Education: Miami U (OH) 1992 BS, 1994 MS;
Xavier (OH) 2002 MBA
Assistant to the County Administrator
Mary Gruber Neil .... (513) 946-4439
E-mail: mary.gruber@hamilton-co.org

Assistant County Administrator
Jeffrey W. "Jeff" Aluotto .... (513) 946-4436
E-mail: jeff.aluotto@hamilton-co.org
Education: Miami U (OH) 1992 BS, 1994 MS;
Xavier (OH) 2002 MBA

Property Manager **Ralph W. Linne** .... (513) 946-5026
E-mail: rwl@cms.hamilton-co.org
Education: Cincinnati 1971 AAS, 1974 SB; Lake Erie 1989 MBA

Receptionist and Administrative Assistant
Traci Paquette .... (513) 946-4438
E-mail: maryhgruber@gmail.com

Office of Cooperative Extension (Ohio State University)

110 Boggs Lane, Suite 315, Cincinnati, OH 45246
Tel: (513) 946-8989 Fax: (513) 772-6126
Internet: http://hamilton.osu.edu/

Director **Chris Olinsky** .... (513) 946-8975
4-H Youth Development Educator **(Vacant)** .... (513) 946-8996
Family and Consumer Sciences Extension Educator
Betsy DeMatteo .... (513) 946-8987
Family and Consumer Sciences Extension Educator
Jenny Even .... (513) 946-8987
Horticulture Extension Educator **Joseph Boggs** .... (513) 946-8989
Horticulture Extension Educator **Julie Crook** .... (513) 946-8998

Law Office of the Public Defender

William Howard Taft Center, 230 East Ninth Street, 2nd Floor,
Cincinnati, OH 45202
Fax: (513) 946-3707

Public Defender **Raymond Faller** .... (513) 946-3880
Deputy Public Defender **Daniel James** .... (513) 946-3663

Adult Probation Department

800 Broadway, Cincinnati, OH 45202
Tel: (513) 946-9666 Fax: (513) 946-9805

Chief Probation Officer **Patrick Dressing** .... (513) 946-5900
Assistant Chief Probation Officer **Joseph Elfers** .... (513) 946-9631
Assistant Chief Probation Officer - Municipal
Jerry Campbell .... (513) 946-9669
Fax: (513) 946-5808

Communication Center

2377 Civic Center Dr., Cincinnati, OH 45231-1305
Fax: (513) 595-8457

► Director **(Vacant)** .... (513) 825-2170
Operations Manager **Debra Stockelman** .... (513) 825-2170
Telecommunications Manager **Ron Bien** .... (513) 825-2170
E-mail: ron.bien@hamilton-co.org

County Facilities Department

County Courthouse, 1000 Main Street, Room B-95, Cincinnati, OH 45202
Tel: (513) 946-5000 Fax: (513) 946-5031
Internet: www.hamiltoncountyohio.gov/facilities

► Director **Ralph W. Linne** .... (513) 946-5025
E-mail: rwl@cms.hamilton-co.org
Education: Cincinnati 1971 AAS, 1974 SB; Lake Erie 1989 MBA
Office Manager **Inger Rothering** .... (513) 946-5075
Assistant Director for Facilities Management
Anthony K. Matre .... (513) 946-5030
E-mail: akm@cms.hamilton-co.org
Assistant Director for Facilities Support Services
Diana Supe .... (513) 946-5060
E-mail: dew@cms.hamilton-co.org
Construction/Trades Manager **(Vacant)** .... (513) 946-5058
Safety and Security Manager **(Vacant)** .... (513) 946-5059
Systems Administrator **(Vacant)** .... (513) 946-5002

Hamilton County Educational Service Center [HCESC]

11083 Hamilton Avenue, Cincinnati, OH 45231
Fax: (513) 742-5525 Internet: www.hcesc.org

Superintendent and Chief Executive Officer
David L. "Dave" Distel .... (513) 674-4236
Assistant Superintendent **(Vacant)** .... (513) 674-4240
Treasurer **Donald F. "Don" Rabe** .... (513) 674-4237

★ Elected Official ▲ Appointed by Legislature ▼ Appointed by Governor ► Appointed by Board or Commission ● Appointed by Judge
■ Appointed by Mayor △ Appointed by Freeholders ▽ Appointed by Supervisor ▷ Appointed by County Executive ○ Appointed by Council

Hamilton County Emergency Management Agency
2000 Radcliff Drive, Cincinnati, OH 45204
Fax: (513) 263-8222 Internet: www.hamiltoncountyohioema.org

Director **Nick Crossley** . . . . . (513) 263-8200
E-mail: nick.crossley@hamilton-co.org

Department of Environmental Services [DOES]
250 William Howard Taft Road, 1st Floor, Cincinnati, OH 45219-2660
Tel: (513) 946-7777 Tel: (800) 889-0474 (Toll Free In-State)
Fax: (513) 946-7778 Fax: (513) 946-7779 Internet: www.hcdoes.org

Director **Holly F. Christmann** . . . . . (513) 946-7705
Assistant Director **Bradley M. Miller** . . . . . (513) 946-7731
Monitoring and Analysis Supervisor **Anna L. Kelley** . . . . . (513) 946-7725
Permits and Enforcement Section Supervisor
Michael B. Kramer . . . . . (513) 946-7727
Solid Waste Program Manager **Michelle E. Balz** . . . . . (513) 946-7789
Operations Manager **Ali A. Khodadad** . . . . . (513) 946-7726
E-mail: ali.khodadad@hamilton-co.org
Public Relations Coordinator **Megan Hummel** . . . . . (513) 946-7748
E-mail: megan.hummel@hamilton-co.org
Systems Administrator **Edward C. Moser** . . . . . (513) 946-7717
E-mail: ed.moser@hamilton-co.org

Hamilton County Job and Family Services Department [HCJFS]
222 East Central Parkway, Cincinnati, OH 45202
Tel: (513) 946-1000 Fax: (513) 946-2451 Internet: www.hcjfs.org

► Director **Moira Weir** . . . . . (513) 946-1000
E-mail: weirm@jfs.hamilton-co.org
Chief Operating Officer **Tim McCartney** . . . . . (513) 946-1000
E-mail: mccart04@jfs.hamilton-co.org

Human Resources Department
County Administration Building, 138 East Court Street, Room 707, Cincinnati, OH 45202
Fax: (513) 946-4720

► Director **Cheryl A. Keller** . . . . . (513) 946-4704
E-mail: cheryl.keller@hamilton-co.org

Planning and Development Department
County Administration Building, 138 East Court Street, Room 801, Cincinnati, OH 45202-1235
Tel: (513) 946-4550 Fax: (513) 946-4475
Internet: www.hamilton-co.org/pd

► Director **Todd M. Kinskey** . . . . . (513) 946-4454
E-mail: Todd.Kinskey@hamilton-co.org
Administrative Secretary **(Vacant)** . . . . . (513) 946-4451
Operations Manger **Sherry Baker** . . . . . (513) 946-4748
E-mail: sherry.baker@hamilton-co.org

Building Inspections Division
County Administration Building, 138 East Court Street, Room 801, Cincinnati, OH 45202
Tel: (513) 946-4545 Fax: (513) 946-4511

► Chief Building Official **Gerry Stoker** . . . . . (513) 946-4545
Administrative Assistant **(Vacant)** . . . . . (513) 946-4545

Community Development Division
138 East Court Street, Room 1002, Cincinnati, OH 45202
Tel: (513) 946-8230 Fax: (513) 946-8240

► Division Manager **Joy Pierson** . . . . . (513) 946-8235

Board of Zoning Appeals [BZA]
County Administration Building, 138 East Court Street, Room 801, Cincinnati, OH 45202
Tel: (513) 946-4550 Fax: (513) 946-4475

Zoning Services Administrator **Bryan Snyder** . . . . . (513) 946-4464

Hamilton County Regional Planning Commission [HCRPC]
138 East Court Street, Cincinnati, OH 45202

Executive Director **Todd M. Kinskey** . . . . . (513) 946-4454

Hamilton County Public Health [HCPH]
250 William Howard Taft Road, 2nd Floor, Cincinnati, OH 45219-2612
Tel: (513) 946-7800 Fax: (513) 946-7890
Internet: www.hamiltoncountyhealth.org

Health Commissioner **Timothy I. "Tim" Ingram** . . . . . (513) 946-7822

Purchasing Department
County Administration Bldg., 138 E. Court St., Room 507, Cincinnati, OH 45202
Tel: (513) 946-4310 Fax: (513) 946-4335

Purchasing Director **JoAnn Cramer** . . . . . (513) 946-4310
E-mail: joann.cramer@hamilton-co.org
Purchasing Agent **Gina Richmond** . . . . . (513) 946-4321
E-mail: gina.richmond@hamilton-co.org
Purchasing Agent **Jill Williams** . . . . . (513) 946-4337
E-mail: jill.williams@hamilton-co.org
Purchasing Agent **(Vacant)** . . . . . (513) 946-4347
Surplus Auction Manager **Sharon Maloney** . . . . . (513) 946-4354
E-mail: sharon.maloney@hamilton-co.org

Hamilton County Developmental Disabilities Services [HCDDS]
1520 Madison Road, Cincinnati, OH 45206
Tel: (513) 794-3300 Fax: (513) 559-6608 Internet: www.hamiltondds.org

President **Nestor Melnyk** . . . . . (513) 794-3300
Vice President **Andrew Magenheim** . . . . . (513) 794-3300
Secretary **Dr. Cindy Molloy** . . . . . (513) 794-3300

Board Staff
Superintendent **Alice Pavey** . . . . . (513) 794-3300
Administrative Assistant **Beth Luensman** . . . . . (513) 559-6687
E-mail: beth.luensman@hamiltondds.org
Director of Service and Support Administration
Melissa Hamilton . . . . . (513) 559-6886
Director of Planning Innovation and Quality **(Vacant)** . . . . (513) 559-6768

Board of Elections
824 Broadway Street, Cincinnati, OH 45202-1345
Tel: (513) 632-7000 Fax: (513) 579-0988
Internet: www.hamilton-co.org/boe

Director **Sherry L. Poland** . . . . . (513) 632-7077
E-mail: sherry.poland@hamilton-co.org
Deputy Director **Sally J. Krisel** . . . . . (513) 632-7011

Hamilton County Mental Health and Recovery Services Board [MHRSB]
2350 Auburn Avenue, Cincinnati, OH 45219
Tel: (513) 946-8600 Fax: (513) 946-8610
E-mail: hccmhb@hamilton.mhrsb.state.oh.us

Chairman **Thomas L. "Tom" Gabelman** . . . . . (513) 946-8600

Staff
President and Chief Executive Officer **Patrick Tribbe** . . . . . (513) 946-8601

The Public Library of Cincinnati and Hamilton County
800 Vine Street, Cincinnati, OH 45202-2071
Tel: (513) 369-6900 Fax: (513) 369-6993
E-mail: comments@cincinnatilibrary.org
Internet: www.cincinnatilibrary.org

Year Founded: 1853

★ Elected Official ▲ Appointed by Legislature ▼ Appointed by Governor ► Appointed by Board or Commission ● Appointed by Judge
■ Appointed by Mayor △ Appointed by Freeholders ▽ Appointed by Supervisor ▷ Appointed by County Executive ○ Appointed by Council

Administration
Executive Director **Kimber L. "Kim" Fender** .... (513) 369-6972
E-mail: Kimber.Fender@cincinnatilibrary.org
Education: Northern Kentucky BS; Kentucky 1983 MLS
Database/Unix Administrator **Dave Menninger** .... (513) 369-6970
E-mail: dave.menninger@cincinnatilibrary.org Fax: (513) 369-3188

Hamilton County Law Library [HCLL]
County Courthouse, Rm. 601, 1000 Main St., Cincinnati, OH 45202
Tel: (513) 946-5300 (Reference Desk) Fax: (513) 946-5252
Internet: www.hamilton-co.org/cinlawlib

Director **Mary Jenkins** .... (513) 946-5263
E-mail: mjenkins@cms.hamilton-co.org
Assistant Law Librarian - Systems **Julie Koehne** .... (513) 946-5266
E-mail: jkoehne@cms.hamilton-co.org

COUNTIES

Great Parks of Hamilton County
10245 Winton Rd., Cincinnati, OH 45231
Tel: (513) 521-7275 Fax: (513) 521-2606 Internet: www.greatparks.org

▶ Executive Director **Jack Sutton** .... (513) 521-7275
E-mail: jsutton@greatparks.org
Executive Assistant **Donna Weber** .... (513) 245-7449 ext. 250
E-mail: dweber@greatparks.org
Deputy Director of Business **Rebecca Mcdonough** ...... (513) 521-7275
Chief Financial Officer **Thomas Lowe** .... (513) 521-7275
Human Resources Director **Rebecca Mcdonough** .... (513) 521-7275
Outdoor Education Director **Amy Roell** .... (513) 521-7275
Park Services Director **(Vacant)** .... (513) 521-7275
Planning Director **Ross Hamre** .... (513) 521-7275
Recreation Services Director **Bill Mowery** .... (513) 521-7275
Ranger Chief **Thomas E. Doyle** .... (513) 521-7275
Facility Management Superintendent **Todd Palmeter** ..... (513) 521-7275
E-mail: tpalmeter@greatparks.org
Public Affairs Manager **Jennifer Sivak** .... (513) 521-7275

Hamilton County Soil and Water Conservation District
22 Triangle Park Drive, Cincinnati, OH 45246
Tel: (513) 772-7645 Fax: (513) 772-7656 Internet: www.hcswcd.org

District Administrator **Holly Utrata-Halcomb** .... (513) 772-7645 ext. 12
Urban Conservationist **Dan Taphorn** .... (513) 772-7645 ext. 16

Hamilton County Veterans Service Commission
230 E. Ninth Street, Cincinnati, OH 45202-2174
Tel: (513) 946-3300 Fax: (513) 946-3320 Internet: http://www.hcvsc.org/

▶ Executive Director/Service Officer
William A. Boettcher .... (513) 946-3301
E-mail: william.boettcher@hamilton-co.org
Administrative Assistant
Barbara G. "Barb" Esterkamp .... (513) 946-3313
E-mail: barb.esterkamp@hamilton-co.org

Office of the Auditor
County Administration Bldg., 138 E. Court St., Room 304, Cincinnati, OH 45202
Tel: (513) 946-4000 Fax: (513) 946-4043
Internet: www.hamiltoncountyauditor.org

★ Auditor **Dusty Rhodes** (D) .... (513) 946-4047
Term Expires: March 1, 2019
E-mail: dusty.rhodes@auditor.hamilton-co.org
Education: Syracuse 1961 BS
Administration Director **Susan Silver** .... (513) 946-4047
E-mail: susan.silver@auditor.hamilton-co.org Fax: (513) 946-4043
Computer Systems and Information Service Director
David Barnes .... (513) 946-4135
E-mail: david.barnes@auditor.hamilton-co.org Fax: (513) 946-4139

Office of the Coroner
3159 Eden Ave., Cincinnati, OH 45219
Fax: (513) 946-8730

★ Coroner **Lakshmi K. Sammarco** .... (513) 946-8700
Term Expires: January 2017
Administrator **Andrea Hatten** .... (513) 946-8700
E-mail: andrea.hatten@hamilton-co.org

Office of the County Engineer
County Administration Building, 138 E. Court Street, Room 700, Cincinnati, OH 45202-1224
Tel: (513) 946-4250 Fax: (513) 946-4288
Internet: www.hamiltoncountyohio.gov/engineer

★ County Engineer **Theodore B. "Ted" Hubbard** .... (513) 946-8903
Term Expires: January 1, 2017
E-mail: ted.hubbard@hamilton-co.org
Education: Cincinnati 1979 BSCE
Chief Deputy Engineer **Timothy Gilday** .... (513) 946-8914
E-mail: tim.gilday@hamilton-co.org

Office of the Prosecuting Attorney
230 E. 9th St., Ste. 4000, Cincinnati, OH 45202
Fax: (513) 946-3017

★ Prosecutor **Joseph T. Deters** (R) .... (513) 946-3000
Term Expires: January 1, 2017
Education: Cincinnati 1979 BS, 1982 JD
Systems Administrator **Debi Holthaus** .... (513) 946-3085

Office of the Recorder
County Administration Building, 138 East Court Street, Room 209, Cincinnati, OH 45202-1236
Fax: (513) 946-4577 E-mail: recordersoffice@hamilton-co.org

★ Recorder **Wayne Coates** (D) .... (513) 946-4561
Term Expires: January 1, 2017
E-mail: wayne.coates@hamilton-co.org

Office of the Sheriff
Justice Center, 1000 Sycamore Street, Room 110, Cincinnati, OH 45202
Tel: (513) 946-6400 Fax: (513) 946-6402 Internet: www.hcso.org

★ Sheriff **James Neil** .... (513) 946-6400
Term Expires: January 4, 2017
Chief Deputy **Mark Schoonover** .... (513) 946-6400

Office of the Treasurer
County Administration Building, 138 East Court Street, Room 402, Cincinnati, OH 45202-1226
Tel: (513) 946-4800 Fax: (513) 946-4818
E-mail: county.treasurer@hamilton-co.org
Internet: www.hamilton-co.org/treasurer

★ Treasurer **Robert A. Goering** (R) .... (513) 946-4800
Term Expires: September 4, 2017

★ Elected Official ▲ Appointed by Legislature ▼ Appointed by Governor ▶ Appointed by Board or Commission ● Appointed by Judge
■ Appointed by Mayor △ Appointed by Freeholders ▽ Appointed by Supervisor ▷ Appointed by County Executive ○ Appointed by Council

County of Harris, Texas

Administration Building, 1001 Preston, Houston, TX 77002
Tel: (713) 755-5000 (Information) Internet: www.co.harris.tx.us

County Seat: Houston **Election Type:** Partisan **Population:** 4,538,028 (2015)

Office of the County Judge

1001 Preston, Suite 911, Houston, TX 77002
Tel: (713) 755-4000 Fax: (713) 755-8379 Internet: www.judgeemmett.org

★County Judge **Edward M. "Ed" Emmett** (R) . . . . (713) 755-4000
Term Expires: January 15, 2019
E-mail: judge.emmett@cjo.hctx.net
Education: Rice 1971 BA; Texas 1974 MPA
Career: President, The National Industrial Transportation League
Executive Assistant **Leanna Abbott** . . . . (713) 755-4011
Chief of Staff **Kathy Luhn** . . . . (713) 755-4024

Office of County Auditor

1001 Preston, Suite 800, Houston, TX 77002
Fax: (713) 755-8932 Internet: www.co.harris.tx.us/auditor

▶Auditor **Barbara J. Schott** . . . . (713) 755-6505
E-mail: auditor@co.harris.tx.us

Domestic Relations Office

1310 Prairie Street, Suite 700, Houston, TX 77002
Tel: (713) 755-6757 (Information) Fax: (713) 755-8856
Internet: www.dro.hctx.net

▶Executive Director **David W. Simpson** . . . . (713) 755-6757

Texas A&M AgriLife Extension Service

3033 Bear Creek Drive, Houston, TX 77084
Tel: (281) 855-5600 Fax: (281) 855-5638 E-mail: harris-tx@tamu.edu
Internet: http://harris.agrilife.org/

▶Director **Allen Malone** . . . . (281) 855-5600
E-mail: amalone@ag.tamu.edu

Office of the Fire Marshal [HCFMO]

7701 Wilshire Place Drive, Houston, TX 77040
Fax: (281) 436-8005 Internet: www.hcfmo.net/

▶Fire Marshal **Michael "Mike" Montgomery** . . . . (281) 436-8121
E-mail: tom.petty@fmo.hctx.net

Office of Homeland Security and Emergency Management [OHSEM]

6922 Katy Road, Houston, TX 77024
Tel: (713) 881-3100 Fax: (713) 881-3007 Internet: www.hcoem.org

Director **Edward M. "Ed" Emmett** (R) . . . . (713) 755-4000
Education: Rice 1971 BA; Texas 1974 MPA
●Emergency Management Coordinator **Mark Sloan** . . . . (713) 881-3100
E-mail: mark.sloan@oem.hctx.net Fax: (713) 881-3077
Deputy Emergency Management Coordinator
Bill Wheeler . . . . (713) 881-3100

Office of the Public Defender

1310 Prairie Street, Suite 980, Houston, TX 77002
Tel: (713) 368-0016 Fax: (713) 368-9278

○Public Defender **Alexander "Alex" Bunin** . . . . (713) 368-0016
E-mail: alex.bunin@pdo.hctx.net
Education: Bowdoin AB; South Texas 1985 JD
Administrative Officer **Carmen Mireles** . . . . (713) 368-0016
E-mail: carmen.mireles@pdo.hctx.net
Chief, Appellate Division **Bob Wicoff** . . . . (713) 368-0016
Chief, Mental Health Division **Floyd Jennings** . . . . (713) 368-0016
Receptionist **Jacqueline Yii** . . . . (713) 368-0016
E-mail: jacqueline.yii@pdo.hctx.net

Purchasing Agent's Office

1001 Preston Street, Room 670, Houston, TX 77002
Fax: (713) 755-6695 Internet: www.co.harris.tx.us/purchasing

▶Purchasing Agent **DeWight M. Dopslauf** . . . . (713) 274-4400
E-mail: dewight.dopslauf@pur.hctx.net
Assistant Purchasing Agent, Industrial Division
Damon Harris . . . . (713) 274-4400
Assistant Purchasing Agent, Medical and Technology Division **Vivian Groce** . . . . (713) 274-4400
E-mail: vivian.groce@pur.hctx.net

Community Supervision and Corrections Department [CSCD]

49 San Jacinto Street, 6th Floor, Houston, TX 77002
Fax: (713) 437-4035 Internet: www.hctx.net/cscd

Director **Teresa May** . . . . (713) 755-2711

Community Services Department

8410 Lantern Point Drive, Houston, TX 77054
Fax: (713) 578-2090 Internet: www.csd.hctx.net

▶Director **David B. Turkel** . . . . (713) 578-2708
E-mail: david_turkel@co.harris.tx.us
Assistant II **Madeline Santa** . . . . (713) 578-2000

Office of Administrative Services

8410 Lantern Point Drive, Houston, TX 77054
Fax: (713) 578-2190

Director **Jessica Deculus** . . . . (713) 578-2000
E-mail: jessica.deculus@csd.hctx.net

Office of Economic Development

8410 Lantern Point Drive, Houston, TX 77054
Fax: (713) 578-2250

Director **Annie Yang** . . . . (713) 578-2254
E-mail: annie.yang@csd.hctx.net

Office of Financial Services

8410 Lantern Point Drive, Houston, TX 77054
Fax: (713) 692-3963

Finance Director **Craig Atkins** . . . . (713) 578-2266

Office of Housing and Community Development

8410 Lantern Point Drive, Houston, TX 77054
Fax: (713) 578-2090

Director **Daphne Lemelle** . . . . (713) 578-2000
E-mail: daphne.lemelle@csd.hctx.net

Office of Social Services

9418 Jensen Drive, Houston, TX 77093

Director **Ellen Seaton** . . . . (713) 696-1948

Veterans' Service Office

9418 Jensen, Houston, TX 77093
Fax: (713) 692-3963 Internet: www.vso.hctx.net

Veterans Service Officer **Vincent "Vince" Morrison** . . . . . (281) 876-6600

Office of Transit Services

8410 Lantern Point Drive, Houston, TX 77054
Fax: (713) 697-3164 Internet: www.harriscountytransit.com

Director **Kenton R. Fickes, Jr.** . . . . (713) 578-2000

Juvenile Probation Department

1200 Congress, Houston, TX 77002
Internet: www.hcjpd.org

▶Executive Director **Thomas D. "Tom" Brooks** . . . . (713) 222-4801
E-mail: thomas.brooks@hcjpd.hctx.net
Assistant Executive Director **Henry Gonzales** . . . . (713) 222-4878

★Elected Official ▲Appointed by Legislature ▼Appointed by Governor ▶Appointed by Board or Commission ●Appointed by Judge
■Appointed by Mayor △Appointed by Freeholders ▽Appointed by Supervisor ▷Appointed by County Executive ○Appointed by Council

Budget Management Department
1001 Preston Street, Suite 938, Houston, TX 77002

► Executive Director/County Budget Officer
William J. Jackson . . . . . (713) 755-5113
E-mail: william.jackson@bmd.hctx.net
Director of Operations **Judith Marshall** . . . . . (713) 755-5034
E-mail: judith.marshall@bmd.hctx.net
Director, Budget Services and Planning **Frank Bruce** . . . . . (713) 755-3287
E-mail: frank.bruce@bmd.hctx.net
Director, Financial Management **Mike Austin** . . . . . (713) 755-8171
Director, Human Resources and Risk Management
David Kester . . . . . (713) 755-5586
E-mail: david.kester@bmd.hctx.net
Director, Applied Technology Services **Jeff Goalen** . . . . . (713) 368-3283
E-mail: jeff.goalen@bmd.hctx.net

COUNTIES

Mental Health and Mental Retardation Authority of Harris County [MHMRA]
7011 SW Freeway, Houston, TX 77074
Tel: (713) 970-7000 Fax: (713) 970-7105 Internet: www.mhmraharris.org

► Executive Director **Dr. Steven B. "Steve" Schnee** . . . . . (713) 970-7190
E-mail: steven.schnee@mhmraharris.org
Education: Texas Tech 1972 PhD
Executive Administrative Assistant **Carolyn Taylor** . . . . . (713) 970-7160
E-mail: carolyn.taylor@mhmraharris.org
Chief Operating Officer **Dr. Scott P. Strange** . . . . . (713) 970-7170
E-mail: scott.strange@mhmraharris.org

Parks Department
Internet: www.co.harris.tx.us/parks

Superintendent (Precinct 1) **Chamber Washington** . . . . . (713) 991-6881
Superintendent (Precinct 2) **Gilbert Smith** . . . . . (281) 457-0694
16003 Lorenzo Channel View, Houston, TX 77530
Superintendent (Precinct 3) **Steve Dorman** . . . . . (281) 531-1592
3535 War Memorial Drive, Houston, TX 77084
Superintendent (Precinct 4) **Dennis Johnston** . . . . . (281) 353-8100
22540 Aldine Westfield, Houston, TX 77373

Harris County Pollution Control Services
101 South Richey, Suite H, Pasadena, TX 77506
Tel: (713) 920-2831 Fax: (713) 274-6475

Director **Robert "Bob" Allen** . . . . . (713) 274-6416
Compliance Manager **Jennifer Wheeler** . . . . . (713) 274-6355
Emergency Response Manager **Craig Hill** . . . . . (713) 274-6425
E-mail: craig.hill@pcs.hctx.net
Environmental Toxicologist Manager **Dr. Latrice Babin** . . . (713) 274-6415
Administrative Services Manager **Sandee L. Wilson** . . . . . (713) 274-6309
E-mail: sandee.wilson@pcs.hctx.net
Laboratory Manager **Michael Cantu** . . . . . (713) 274-6323
Permit and Technical Manager **Stuart Mueller** . . . . . (713) 274-6414

Harris County Public Health and Environmental Services [HCPHES]
2223 West Loop South, Houston, TX 77027
Fax: (713) 439-6080 Tel: (713) 439-6000 Internet: www.hcphes.org

► Executive Director **Umair A. Shah** . . . . . (713) 439-6016
Deputy Director **Leslie "Les" Becker** . . . . . (713) 439-6184

Engineering Department
1001 Preston Street, 5th Floor, Houston, TX 77002
Fax: (713) 755-4459 Internet: www.hcpid.org

County Engineer **John Blount** . . . . . (713) 755-5370
1001 Preston, 7th Floor, Houston, TX 77002
Construction Programs Division Director **Rich Elwood** . . . (713) 274-1531
1310 Prairie Street, Suite 1104, Houston, TX 77002
Right of Way Division Director **Shannon Watson** . . . . . (713) 274-3725
10555 Northwest Freeway, Suite 210, Houston, TX 77092
E-mail: shannon.watson@hcpid.org

General Services
10555 Northwest Freeway, Suite 220, Houston, TX 77092

Manager **Josh Stuckey** . . . . . (713) 274-3743
E-mail: josh.stuckey@hcpid.org
Chief, Fleet Services **Dave Martin** . . . . . (713) 274-3711

Harris County Information Technology Center [ITC]
406 Caroline Street, 4th Floor, Houston, TX 77002
Fax: (713) 755-8930 Internet: www.co.harris.tx.us/itc

► Chief Information Officer **Bruce High** . . . . . (713) 755-6685
E-mail: bruce.high@itc.hctx.net
Deputy Director **Kevin Russell** . . . . . (713) 755-6977
E-mail: kevin.russell@itc.hctx.net
Chief Technology Officer **Steve Higgenbotham** . . . . . (713) 755-7548
E-mail: steve.higgenbotham@itc.hctx.net

Harris County Institute of Forensic Sciences [HCIFS]
1885 Old Spanish Trail, Houston, TX 77054
Fax: (713) 796-6828 Internet: www.co.harris.tx.us/ifs

► Chief Medical Examiner **Luis A. Sanchez** . . . . . (713) 796-9292
E-mail: luis.sanchez@meo.hctx.net
Education: UMass (Boston) BS; UMass (Worcester) MD

Harris County Pretrial Services
1201 Franklin Street, 12th Floor, Houston, TX 77002
Fax: (713) 755-2929 Internet: www.co.harris.tx.us/pretrial

► Director (Interim) **Dennis Potts** . . . . . (713) 755-5440
E-mail: dennis_potts@dca.hctx.net
Assistant Director **Dennis Potts** . . . . . (713) 755-5440

Harris County Protective Services for Children and Adults [HCPS]
2525 Murworth Drive, Houston, TX 77054
Fax: (713) 394-4150 Internet: www.hc-ps.org

► Executive Director **George Ford** . . . . . (713) 394-4000
E-mail: george.ford@cps.hctx.net

Harris County Public Library [HCPL]
8080 El Rio Street, Houston, TX 77054
Fax: (713) 749-9090 Internet: www.hcpl.net

► Director **Edward Melton** . . . . . (713) 749-9000
E-mail: emelton@hcpl.net
Assistant Director, Support Services **Ron Lucik** . . . . . (713) 749-9050
E-mail: rlucik@hcpl.net
Assistant Director, Technology **Gene Rollins** . . . . . (713) 749-9020
E-mail: grollins@hcpl.net

Law Library
1019 Congress, First Floor, Houston, TX 77002
Internet: www.harriscountylawlibrary.org

► Director **Mariann Sears** . . . . . (713) 274-5211
► Deputy Director **Joseph D. Lawson** . . . . . (713) 274-5212
Associate Law Librarian **Judith A. Jackson** . . . . . (713) 755-5183

Office of the County Commissioners
1001 Preston, 9th Floor, Suite 950, Houston, TX 77002
Fax: (713) 755-6114

★ Commissioner **Gene L. Locke** (Precinct 1) . . . . . (713) 755-6111
Term Expires: December 31, 2016 Fax: (713) 755-6114
Education: Houston 1965 BA; Texas 1981 JD
★ Commissioner **Jack Morman** (R-Precinct 2) . . . . . (713) 755-6220
Term Expires: December 31, 2018 Fax: (713) 755-8810
E-mail: jack.morman@pct2.hctx.net

★ Elected Official ▲ Appointed by Legislature ▼ Appointed by Governor ► Appointed by Board or Commission ● Appointed by Judge
■ Appointed by Mayor △ Appointed by Freeholders ▽ Appointed by Supervisor ▷ Appointed by County Executive ○ Appointed by Council

Office of the County Commissioners *continued*

★ Commissioner **Steve Radack** (R-Precinct 3) . . . . (713) 755-6306
Term Expires: December 31, 2016

★ Commissioner **R. Jack "Cactus" Cagle** (R-Precinct 4) . . . (713) 755-6444
Term Expires: December 31, 2018 Fax: (713) 755-8801
Education: Rice

Office of the Assessor and Collector of Taxes

1001 Preston Street, 1st Floor, Houston, TX 77002
Fax: (713) 368-2509 E-mail: tax_office@co.harris.tx.us
Internet: www.tax.co.harris.tx.us

★ Assessor and Collector of Taxes **Mike Sullivan** . . . . (713) 368-2000
Term Expires: December 31, 2016

Office of the County Attorney

1019 Congress Street, 15th Floor, Houston, TX 77002
Tel: (713) 755-5101 Fax: (713) 755-8924 Internet: www.hctx.net/coatty

★ County Attorney **Vince Reed Ryan, Jr.** (D) . . . . (713) 755-5101
Term Expires: December 31, 2016
E-mail: vince.ryan@cao.hctx.net
Education: Houston 1969 BA, 1974 JD; Rice MA
Executive Assistant to County Attorney **Nancy Hock** . . . (713) 274-5104
E-mail: nancy.hock@cao.hctx.net

Special Council **Terence "Terry" O'Rourke** . . . . (713) 755-7880
First Assistant **Robert Soard** . . . . (713) 274-5103

Office of the County Clerk

201 Caroline Street, 4th Floor, Houston, TX 77002
P.O. Box 1525, Houston, TX 77251-1525
Fax: (713) 755-4977 Internet: www.cclerk.hctx.net

★ County Clerk **Stan Stanart** (R) . . . . (713) 755-6411
Term Expires: December 31, 2018
E-mail: sstanart@cco.hctx.net

Chief Deputy **George Hammerlein** . . . . (713) 755-6411
E-mail: ghammerlein@cco.hctx.net

Office of the County Constables

★ Constable **Alan Rosen** (D-Precinct 1) . . . . (713) 755-5200
Term Expires: December 31, 2016
1302 Preston, Houston, TX 77002

★ Constable **Christopher Diaz** (D-Precinct 2) . . . . (713) 477-2766
Term Expires: December 31, 2016
109 E. Shaw, Pasadena, TX 77506

★ Constable **Ken Jones** (D-Precinct 3) . . . . (281) 427-4792
Term Expires: December 31, 2016
701 Baker Road, Baytown, TX 77521
E-mail: ken_jones@co.harris.tx.us

★ Constable **Mark Herman** (R-Precinct 4) . . . . (281) 401-6205
Term Expires: December 31, 2016
6831 Cypresswood Dr., Spring, TX 77379

★ Constable **Phil Camus** (R-Precinct 5) . . . . (281) 492-3500
Term Expires: December 31, 2016
17423 Katy Freeway, Houston, TX 77094

★ Constable **Heliodoro Martinez, Jr.** (D-Precinct 6) . . . . (713) 923-9156
Term Expires: December 31, 2016
333 Lockwood, Houston, TX 77011

★ Constable **May Walker** (D-Precinct 7) . . . . (713) 643-6118
Term Expires: December 31, 2016
5300 Griggs Road, Houston, TX 77021

★ Constable **Phil Sandlin** (R-Precinct 8) . . . . (281) 479-2525
Term Expires: December 31, 2016
7330 Spencer Highway, Pasadena, TX 77505

Office of the County Treasurer

1001 Preston, Room 652, Houston, TX 77002
Fax: (713) 755-8842 Internet: www.hctx.net/treasurer

★ County Treasurer **Orlando Sanchez** (R) . . . . (713) 755-5120
Term Expires: December 31, 2018
E-mail: osanchez@hctx.net
Education: Houston BA

First Assistant County Treasurer **Greg Lueb** . . . . (713) 755-5120

Office of the District Attorney

1201 Franklin, Suite 600, Houston, TX 77002
Fax: (713) 755-6865 Internet: http://app.dao.hctx.net/

★ District Attorney **Devon Anderson** . . . . (713) 755-5800
Term Expires: December 31, 2016
Education: Texas JD

First Assistant District Attorney **Belinda Hill** . . . . (713) 755-5800

Office of the Sheriff

1200 Baker Street, Houston, TX 77002
Tel: (713) 755-6044 Fax: (713) 755-6228
Internet: www.harriscountyso.org

★ Sheriff (Interim) **Ron Hickman** (R) . . . . (713) 755-6044
Term Expires: December 31, 2016

Harris County Department of Education [HCDE]

6300 Irvington Blvd., Houston, TX 77022
Fax: (713) 696-0730 Internet: www.hcde-texas.org

Board of Trustees

President **Angie Chesnut** . . . . (713) 694-6300

Office of the Superintendent

Superintendent of Schools **James Colbert** . . . . (713) 696-0715

County of Hennepin, Minnesota

Government Center, 300 South Sixth Street, Minneapolis, MN 55487
Tel: (612) 348-3000 (Information) TTY: (612) 348-6646
Internet: www.hennepin.us

County Seat: Minneapolis **Election Type:** Nonpartisan
Population: 1,223,149 (2015)

Office of the Board of Commissioners

Government Center, 300 South Sixth Street, Room A-2400,
Minneapolis, MN 55487
TTY: (612) 348-7708 Fax: (612) 348-8701

★ Chairman **Janis "Jan" Callison** (District 6) . . . . (612) 348-7886
Term Expires: December 31, 2016
E-mail: janis.callison@hennepin.us

★ Commissioner **Michael "Mike" Opat** (District 1) . . . . (612) 348-7881
Term Expires: December 31, 2018
E-mail: mike.opat@hennepin.us
Education: Minnesota 1983 BS; Harvard 1989 MPP

★ Commissioner **Linda Higgins** (District 2) . . . . (612) 348-7882
Term Expires: December 31, 2018
Education: Mankato State 1972 BS

★ Commissioner **Marion Greene** (District 3) . . . . (612) 348-7883
Term Expires: December 31, 2018
Education: Swarthmore BA; Texas MBA

(continued on next page)

★ Elected Official ▲ Appointed by Legislature ▼ Appointed by Governor ▶ Appointed by Board or Commission ● Appointed by Judge
■ Appointed by Mayor △ Appointed by Freeholders ▽ Appointed by Supervisor ▷ Appointed by County Executive ○ Appointed by Council

Office of the Board of Commissioners *continued*

★ Commissioner **Peter McLaughlin** (District 4) . . . . (612) 348-7884
Term Expires: December 31, 2018
E-mail: peter.mclaughlin@hennepin.us
Education: Princeton 1971 AB; Minnesota 1977 MA

★ Commissioner
Randall David "Randy" Johnson (District 5) . . . . (612) 348-7885
Term Expires: December 31, 2016
E-mail: randy.johnson@hennepin.us
Date of Birth: September 10, 1963
Education: Macalester 1968 BA; Minnesota 1974 JD

★ Commissioner **Jeff Johnson** (District 7) . . . . (612) 348-7887
Term Expires: December 31, 2016
E-mail: jeff.johnson@hennepin.us
Education: Concordia Col Moorhead MN 1989 BA; Georgetown 1992 JD

Clerk of the Board **Kelly Allen** . . . . (612) 348-3081

COUNTIES

Office of the County Administrator

Government Center, 300 South Sixth Street, Room A2303,
Minneapolis, MN 55487
Fax: (612) 348-8228

▶ County Administrator **David J. Hough** . . . . (612) 348-4260
E-mail: david.hough@hennepin.us

Administrative Assistant **Sarah Lawler** . . . . (612) 348-4447
E-mail: sarah.lawler@hennepin.us

Office of the Assistant County Administrator for Human Services and Public Health

Government Center, 300 South Sixth Street, Room A2303,
Minneapolis, MN 55487
Tel: (612) 348-8228

Assistant County Administrator **Rex Holzemer** . . . . (612) 348-3456
E-mail: rex.holzemer@hennepin.us

Administrative Assistant **Carol Schroeder** . . . . (612) 348-3342
E-mail: carol.schroeder@hennepin.us

Hennepin County Medical Center

701 Park Avenue South, Minneapolis, MN 55415-1600
Tel: (612) 873-3000 TTY: (612) 873-5663 Fax: (612) 904-4214
Internet: www.hcmc.org

Chief Executive Officer **Dr. Jon L. Pryor** . . . . (612) 873-2352
Director, Public Policy and Strategy **David Godfrey** . . . . . . (612) 873-3317
Director of Facilities, Life Safety, and Space Planning
Facilities Management **Gary L. Hempeck** . . . . (612) 873-9128
E-mail: gary.hempeck@hcmed.org
Chief Analytics Officer **Nancy Garrett** . . . . (612) 873-9049
Chief Nursing Officer **Kathy Wilde** . . . . (612) 873-2993
Vice President, Professional and Support Services
(Vacant) . . . . (612) 873-9082
Hennepin Health Foundation Vice President
Suzanne M. Begin . . . . (612) 873-9041
Admissions Director **Karoline Pierson** . . . . (612) 873-2238
Medical Director and Chief Medical Officer
Michael B. Belzer . . . . (612) 873-2979
Poison Information Center Director **Deb Anderson** . . . . . . (612) 873-2107
Public Relations/Marketing Director **Tom Hayes** . . . . (612) 873-3337
Fax: (612) 904-4656
Sexual Assault Resource Service Director
Andrea Olson . . . . (612) 873-5832
Social Service Director **Sharon Carlson** . . . . (612) 873-2244
Behavioral Health and Rehabilitation Director
Megen Cullen . . . . (612) 873-3364
Critical Care and Emergency Director **Andrea Olson** . . . . (612) 873-9393
Director of Women and Children **Mary L. Peterson** . . . . . (612) 873-2585
Financial Planning and Budget Division Director
Larry Kryzaniak . . . . (612) 873-2350
Revenue Cycle Management Director **Kim Parrish** . . . . (612) 873-3642
Chief Compliance Officer and Senior Director of
Internal Audit **Warren Simpson** . . . . (612) 873-5774

Hennepin County Medical Center *continued*

Media Relations **Christine A. Hill** . . . . (612) 873-5719
Fax: (612) 904-4656

Primary Care, NorthPoint Health and Wellness Center

North Point Health Center, 1313 Penn Avenue North,
Minneapolis, MN 55411-3094
Tel: (612) 302-4600 Fax: (612) 302-4870

Chief Executive Officer **Stella Whitney-West** . . . . (612) 302-4762

Office of the Medical Examiner

530 Chicago Ave., Minneapolis, MN 55415-1518
Fax: (612) 466-9970

▶ Medical Examiner **Dr. Andrew Baker** . . . . (612) 215-6300
E-mail: andrew.baker@hennepin.us

Metropolitan Health Plan [MHP]

400 South Fourth Street, Suite 201, Minneapolis, MN 55415
Tel: (612) 596-1036 Fax: (612) 904-4266
E-mail: hennepinhealth@hennepin.us Internet: www.hennepinhealth.org

Chief Executive Officer **Shannon Mayer** . . . . (800) 647-0550
Chief Operating Officer **(Vacant)** . . . . (800) 647-0550
Chief Financial Officer **Brian Bergs** . . . . (800) 647-0550
Chief Information Officer/Director, Claims
Sandra L. "Sandy" Hvizdos . . . . (800) 647-0550
Medical Director **Tamiko Morgan** . . . . (800) 647-0550

Human Services and Public Health Department [HSPHD]

Government Center, 300 South Sixth Street, Room A2303,
Minneapolis, MN 55487
Fax: (612) 348-8228

Director **Jennifer DeCubellis** . . . . (612) 596-9416
Education: Wisconsin

Office of the Assistant County Administrator for Public Works

Government Center, 300 South Sixth Street, Room A-2303,
Minneapolis, MN 55487
Fax: (612) 348-8228

Assistant County Administrator (Acting) **Carl Michaud** . . . (612) 348-4306
E-mail: carl.michaud@hennepin.us

Administrative Secretary **Kimberly Lanoux** . . . . (612) 348-4077
E-mail: kimberly.lanoux@hennepin.us

Emergency Management Director **Eric Waage** . . . . (612) 596-0252
E-mail: eric.waage@hennepin.us Fax: (763) 478-4001

Department of Environmental Services

417 North Fifth Street, Suite 200, Minneapolis, MN 55401
Tel: (612) 348-3777 Fax: (612) 348-8532
E-mail: desmail@co.hennepin.mn.us

Director **Carl Michaud** . . . . (612) 348-3054
Assistant Director, Environmental Protection Division
Rosemary Lavin . . . . (612) 348-8596
Assistant Director, Solid Waste Division
David "Dave" McNary . . . . (612) 348-5906

Housing, Community Works and Transit Department [HCWT]

417 North Fifth Street, Suite 320, Minneapolis, MN 55401
Tel: (612) 348-9260 Fax: (612) 348-9170

Director **John Doàn** . . . . (612) 348-6445
Community Works Manager **Patricia Fitzgerald** . . . . (612) 348-2215
E-mail: patricia.fitzgerald@co.hennepin.mn.us
Housing Development Manager **Kevin Dockry** . . . . (612) 348-2270
Leasing and Land Management Manager
J. Michael Noonan . . . . (612) 348-8537
Engineering and Transit Planning Engineer **Joe Gladke** . . (612) 348-2134
HCRRA Properties **Jessica Galatz** . . . . (612) 348-2691

★ Elected Official ▲ Appointed by Legislature ▼ Appointed by Governor ▶ Appointed by Board or Commission ● Appointed by Judge
■ Appointed by Mayor △ Appointed by Freeholders ▽ Appointed by Supervisor ▷ Appointed by County Executive ○ Appointed by Council

Public Works Management Support Department
417 North Fifth Street, Suite 200, Minneapolis, MN 55401
Fax: (612) 348-9710

Director **Maurice Gieske** (612) 348-9330
E-mail: maurice.gieske@co.hennepin.mn.us

Property Services Department
Government Center, 300 South Sixth Street, Room A-2208, Minneapolis, MN 55487-0228
Fax: (612) 348-3492

Director **Mike Sayler** Room A2208 (612) 348-3897

Transportation Department
1600 Prairie Drive, Medina, MN 55340-5421

Director/County Engineer **James Grube** (612) 596-0307
E-mail: james.grube@co.hennepin.mn.us
Education: Iowa State 1976 BA
Construction Engineer **Harlan Hanson** (612) 596-0340
Design Engineer **(Vacant)** (612) 596-0360
Traffic and ITS Engineer **(Vacant)** (612) 596-0330
Road and Bridge Engineer **Brian Langseth** (612) 596-0330
Transportation Planning Engineer **(Vacant)** (612) 596-0350
Strategic Planning and Resources **(Vacant)** (612) 348-0624

Office of the Assistant County Administrator for Operations
300 South Sixth Street, Room A2303, Minneapolis, MN 55487
Fax: (612) 348-8228

Assistant County Administrator for Operations
Judy Regenscheid (612) 348-3392
E-mail: judy.regenscheid@hennepin.us
Administrative Assistant **Sarah Lawler** (612) 348-4447
E-mail: sarah.lawler@hennepin.us

Hennepin County Library
12601 Ridgedale Drive, Minnetonka, MN 55305
Tel: (612) 543-8500 Fax: (612) 847-8600 Internet: www.hclib.org

Year Founded: 1922

History: On January 1, 2008, the Hennepin County Library system merged with the Minneapolis Library system.

Administration
Library Director **Lois Langer Thompson** (612) 543-8541
Education: Gustavus Adolphus 1983 BA; Denver 1985 MA
Manager, Operations **Nancy Palmer** (612) 543-8611
E-mail: nancy.palmer@co.hennepin.mn.us
Manager, Library Services **Janet Mills** (612) 543-8558
E-mail: jmills@hclib.org

Information Technology Department
Government Center, 300 South Sixth Street, Room A-1900, Minneapolis, MN 55487-0190
Fax: (612) 348-9505

Chief Information Officer **Jerome Driessen** (612) 596-7409
Chief Technology Officer **Glen Gilbertson** (612) 348-2080
Chief Financial Officer **Colleen Livermore** (612) 348-6507
Chief Enterprise Architect **Craig Troska** (612) 348-2080
E-mail: craig.troska@co.hennepin.mn.us
Contracts and Vendor Management **Bob Kelly** (612) 348-9308

Internal Audit Department
Government Center, 300 South Sixth Street, Room A-2102, Minneapolis, MN 55487
Tel: (612) 348-8330 Fax: (612) 348-8486

Director **Karen Marquardt** (612) 348-2690

Communications Department
Government Center, Northeast Street Level, 300 S. Sixth St., Minneapolis, MN 55487-0011
Tel: (612) 348-3848 Fax: (612) 348-9857

Public Relations Officer **Carolyn Marinan** (612) 348-5969
E-mail: carolyn.marinan@hennepin.us
Strategic Communications Officer **Jamie Zwilling** (612) 596-8337
E-mail: jamie.zwilling@hennepin.us
Special Projects **Diana Houston** (612) 348-5130
E-mail: diana.houston@hennepin.us

Residence and Realtor Services
Government Center, 300 South Sixth Street, Room A-600, Minneapolis, MN 55487
Tel: (612) 348-3000 Fax: (612) 348-9677

Director, County Auditor and County Treasurer
Mark V. Chapin (612) 348-5297
E-mail: mark.chapin@co.hennepin.mn.us

Elections Division
300 South Sixth Street, Minneapolis, MN 55487
E-mail: hc.vote@co.hennepin.mn.us

Manager **Ginny Gelms** (612) 348-9289

Financial Analysis/Support Division
Manager **Paul Buschmann** (612) 596-7407

Property Tax Division
300 South Sixth Street, A-600, Minneapolis, MN 55487

Manager **Scott Loomer** (612) 348-5100
E-mail: scott.loomer@co.hennepin.mn.us

Public Records Division
300 South Sixth Street, Room A-500, Minneapolis, MN 55487
Fax: (612) 348-4948

Recorder and Registrar of Titles **Marty McCormick** (612) 348-3893

Service Center Division
300 South Sixth Street, Suite A025, Minneapolis, MN 55487-0501
E-mail: license.gc@co.hennepin.mn.us

Director of Licensing **Kathy Schons** (612) 348-4961

Survey Division
Fax: (612) 348-2837

County Surveyor/Manager **Chris Mavis** (612) 348-2618

Office of the Assistant County Administrator for Public Safety
300 South Sixth Street, Room A2303, Minneapolis, MN 55487
Fax: (612) 348-8228

Assistant County Administrator **Mark Thompson** (612) 348-9050
E-mail: mark.thompson@hennepin.us
Administrative Assistant **Cherie Nelson** (612) 543-2819
E-mail: cherie.nelson@hennepin.us

Office of Budget and Finance
Government Center, 300 South Sixth Street, Room A-2301, Minneapolis, MN 55487
Tel: (612) 348-5125 Fax: (612) 348-7970
E-mail: obf.internet@co.hennepin.mn.us

Director **David Lawless** (612) 348-4860
E-mail: david.lawless@co.hennepin.mn.us Fax: (612) 348-7970
Controller **Cindy Twistol** (612) 348-3949
E-mail: cindy.twistol@co.hennepin.mn.us Fax: (612) 348-9991
Investment/Debt Manager **John Villerius** (612) 543-0448
E-mail: john.villerius@co.hennepin.mn.us Fax: (612) 348-7970
Payroll Manager **Ray Hirte** (612) 348-3251
Fax: (612) 348-9991

COUNTIES

★ Elected Official ▲ Appointed by Legislature ▼ Appointed by Governor ▶ Appointed by Board or Commission ● Appointed by Judge
■ Appointed by Mayor △ Appointed by Freeholders ▽ Appointed by Supervisor ▷ Appointed by County Executive ○ Appointed by Council

Purchasing and Contract Services Division
A-1705 Government Center, 300 South Sixth Street,
Minneapolis, MN 55487-0225
Fax: (612) 348-3886 E-mail: selling2hennepin@co.hennepin.mn.us

Purchasing Manager **Christopher O. Gran** . . . . (612) 348-3181
E-mail: christopher.gran@co.hennepin.mn.us

Human Resources Department
A-400 Government Center, 300 S. Sixth St.,
Minneapolis, MN 55487-0040
Tel: (612) 348-2163 Fax: (612) 348-6224 TTY: (612) 348-5467
E-mail: HR.Dept@co.hennepin.mn.us

Director **Michael Rossman** . . . . (612) 348-6761
E-mail: michael.rossman@hennepin.us Fax: (612) 348-6689

Intergovernmental Relations Department
Government Center, 300 South Sixth Street, Room A-2305,
Minneapolis, MN 55487-0235
Tel: (612) 348-3233 Fax: (612) 348-8394

Director **Mary Beth Davidson** . . . . (612) 348-5120
E-mail: mary.davidson@co.hennepin.mn.us
Deputy Director **Kareem Murphy** . . . . (612) 596-9711
E-mail: kareem.murphy@hennepin.us
Coordinator **Ellen Hacker** . . . . (612) 348-3233
E-mail: ellen.hacker@co.hennepin.mn.us

Labor Relations Department
Government Center, 300 South Sixth Street, Minneapolis, MN 55487
Fax: (612) 348-6689 E-mail: lr.dept@hennepin.us

Director **Katherine Megarry** . . . . (612) 348-5010

Hennepin County Law Library
Government Center, 300 South Sixth Street, C-2451,
Minneapolis, MN 55487-0540
Fax: (612) 348-4230 Internet: http://hclaw.co.hennepin.mn.us

Director **Lois Llanger-Thompson** . . . . (612) 348-8860
Administrator **Karen Westwood** . . . . (612) 348-7977
E-mail: karen.westwood@hennepin.us

Department of Community Corrections and Rehabilitation [DOCCR]
C2353 Government Center, 300 South Sixth Street, Mail Code 533,
Minneapolis, MN 55487-0533
Fax: (612) 348-6488

Department Director **Chester Cooper** . . . . (612) 348-5762
Corrections Area Director- Adult **Fred Bryan** . . . . (612) 348-9720
Corrections Area Director- Juvenile **Karen Kuglar** . . . . (612) 348-0594
C2353 Government Center, 300 South 6th Street,
Mail Code 533, Minneapolis, MN 55487-0533
Corrections Area Director- Organizational Change
Management **Julie Rud** . . . . (612) 596-0594
Adult Corrections Facility **Sean Chapman** . . . . (612) 596-0072
1145 Shenandoah Lane, Fax: (763) 475-4266
Mail Code W734, Plymouth, MN 55447-3292
Adult Probation and Parole **Brian Kopperud** . . . . (612) 348-5041
A-302 Government Center, 300 South Sixth Street, Fax: (612) 348-8757
Mail Code 032, Minneapolis, MN 55487
County Home School (Acting) **Randy Bacon** . . . . (612) 596-0550
14300 County Road 62, Fax: (952) 949-4552
Mail Code W736, Minnetonka, MN 55345-6797
Juvenile Detention Center **Craig Riggs** . . . . (612) 348-8806
510 Park Avenue, South, Fax: (612) 348-2296
Mail Code L873, Minneapolis, MN 55415-1597
Juvenile Probation and Parole **James Libera** . . . . (612) 348-3711
510 Park Avenue, South, Fax: (612) 348-6598
Minneapolis, MN 55415-1597
Family Court Services and Adult Probation and Parole
Renee Meerkins . . . . (612) 348-8768
Family Justice Center, 110 South 4th Street, Fax: (612) 348-6332
Mail Code L892, Minneapolis, MN 55401

Department of Community Corrections and Rehabilitation *continued*

Organizational and Employee Development
Mindy Manninen . . . . (612) 348-0213
2600 East 25th Street, Fax: (612) 728-1409
Seward Neighborhood Probation, mail code S636,
Minneapolis, MN 55406
E-mail: mindy.manninen@hennepin.us
Information Technology Manager **Bret Wiske** . . . . (612) 348-2935
Government Center, 300 South Sixth Street, Fax: (612) 348-2276
Suite A2104, Mail Code 214, Minneapolis, MN 55487
Community Offender Management **Chris Owens** . . . . (612) 348-3817
3000 Second Street North, Fax: (612) 321-3429
Mail Code L702, Minneapolis, MN 55417

Office of the Examiner of Titles
Government Center, 300 South Sixth Street, A-701,
Minneapolis, MN 55487
Fax: (612) 348-3872

Examiner **Susan Ledray** . . . . (612) 348-3191

Office of the County Assessor
Government Center, 300 South Sixth Street, Room A-2103,
Minneapolis, MN 55487-0213
Fax: (612) 348-8751

County Assessor **James Atchison** . . . . (612) 348-3046
E-mail: james.atchison@co.hennepin.mn.us

Hennepin County Sheriff's Office
Courthouse, 350 South Fifth Street, Room 6,
Minneapolis, MN 55415-1369
Tel: (612) 348-3744 TTY: (612) 348-6480 Fax: (612) 348-4208
Internet: www.hennepinsheriff.org

★County Sheriff **Richard W. "Rich" Stanek** . . . . (612) 348-3740
Term Expires: December 31, 2018
E-mail: rich.stanek@co.hennepin.mn.us
Chief Deputy **Michael D. Carlson** . . . . (612) 596-9895
E-mail: michael.d.carlson@co.hennepin.mn.us
Administrative Services Bureau **Major Tracey Martin** . . . . (612) 596-9759
E-mail: tracey.martin@co.hennepin.mn.us
Enforcement Services Bureau **Major Jeff Storms** . . . . (612) 596-4870
E-mail: jeff.storms@co.hennepin.mn.us
Investigations Bureau **Major Pete Dietzman** . . . . (612) 596-2015
E-mail: pete.dietzman@co.hennepin.mn.us
Enforcement Services Bureau **Major Darrell Huggett** . . . . (612) 596-9817
E-mail: darrell.huggett@co.hennepin.mn.us
IT Manager **Scott Busche** . . . . (612) 348-6371
Senior Administrative Manager **Julianne Ortman** . . . . (612) 596-9828

Office of the County Attorney
Government Center, 300 South Sixth Street, C-2000,
Minneapolis, MN 55487-0501
Tel: (612) 348-5550 Fax: (612) 348-9712
Internet: www.hennepinattorney.org

★County Attorney **Mike Freeman** . . . . (612) 348-5540
Term Expires: December 31, 2018
Deputy County Attorney **Charlene Hatcher** . . . . (612) 348-4222
E-mail: charlene.hatcher@hennepin.us
Deputy County Attorney **David Brown** . . . . (612) 348-8406
Managing Attorney, Special Litigation
Marlene Senechal . . . . (612) 348-5161
Child Protection Division Chief **Lori Whittier** . . . . (612) 348-3027
Child Support Division Chief **Julie Harris** . . . . (612) 348-6392
Civil Law Division Chief **Dan Rogan** . . . . (612) 348-5529
Community Prosecution Division Chief **Andy Lefevour** . . (612) 348-8595
Juvenile Prosecution Division Chief **Tom Arneson** . . . . . . (612) 348-7916
Mental Health Division Chief **Dan Rogan** . . . . (612) 348-5529
Adult Prosecution Division Chief **Al Harris** . . . . (612) 348-5527
Victim Services Division Chief **Lolita Ulloa** . . . . (612) 348-5355

★Elected Official ▲Appointed by Legislature ▼Appointed by Governor ►Appointed by Board or Commission ●Appointed by Judge
■Appointed by Mayor △Appointed by Freeholders ▽Appointed by Supervisor ▷Appointed by County Executive ○Appointed by Council

Office of the Public Defender (4th Judicial District)

701 Fourth Avenue South, Suite 1400, Minneapolis, MN 55415-1600
Tel: (612) 348-7530 Fax: (612) 348-6179
E-mail: pd.info@co.hennepin.mn.us

Chief Public Defender **Mary Moriarty** . . . . (612) 348-7530
First Assistant to the Chief Public Defender
Jeanette Boerner . . . . (612) 348-7530

County of Hidalgo, Texas

302 West University Drive, Edinburg, TX 78539
Internet: www.co.hidalgo.tx.us

County Seat: Edinburg **Election Type:** Partisan **Population:** 842,304 (2015)

Office of the County Judge

P.O. Box 1356, Edinburg, TX 78539-1356
100 East Cano, Suite 201, Edinburg, TX 78539
Fax: (956) 318-2699

★ County Judge **Ramon Garcia** (D) . . . . (956) 318-2600
Term Expires: December 31, 2018
E-mail: ramon.garcia@co.hidalgo.tx.us
Chief of Staff **Yolanda Chapa** . . . . (956) 318-2600
County Manager **Bobby Villarreal** . . . . (956) 318-2600

Office of the Auditor

2818 South Business Highway 281, Edinburg, TX 78539
P.O. Box 689, Edinburg, TX 78540-0689
Fax: (956) 318-2577

► Auditor **Ray Eufracio** . . . . (956) 318-2511

Veterans' Service Office

2816 South Business Highway 281, Edinburg, TX 78539
Fax: (956) 318-2439 E-mail: hcveterans@co.hidalgo.tx.us

► Director **Emilo De Los Santos** . . . . (956) 318-2436

Community Supervision and Corrections Department [CSCD]

3100 South Bus. Highway 281, Edinburg, TX 78539
P.O. Box 970, Edinburg, TX 78539
Fax: (956) 318-2488

► Executive Director **Arnold K. Patrick** . . . . (956) 587-6000

Drainage Department

902 North Doolittle Road, Edinburg, TX 78541
Fax: (956) 292-7089

Manager **Raul Sesin** . . . . (956) 292-7080 ext. 5801

Elections Department

1001 South Tenth Avenue, Edinburg, TX 78539
Fax: (956) 318-2569

Administrator **Yvonne Ramon** . . . . (956) 318-2570

Extension Office (Texas A&M University)

410 North 13th Avenue, Edinburg, TX 78541
Fax: (956) 383-1735 E-mail: hidalgo-tx@tamu.edu
Internet: http://hidalgo-tx.tamu.edu/

County Coordinator **Barbara A. Storz** . . . . (956) 383-1026

Facilities Management Department

2100 South Highway 281, Edinburg, TX 78539
Fax: (956) 318-2648

► Director **Daniel Flores** . . . . (956) 289-7854
E-mail: daniel.flores@co.hidalgo.tx.us

Health and Human Services Department

1304 South 25th Street, Edinburg, TX 78539
Fax: (956) 383-3229 Internet: www.hchd.org

► Director **Eduardo "Eddie" Olivarez** . . . . (956) 383-6221 ext. 223

Human Resources Department

208 West Cano, Edinburg, TX 78539
Fax: (956) 318-2669

Director **Esther Cortez** . . . . (956) 318-2660
E-mail: esther.cortez@co.hidalgo.tx.us

Information Technology Department

100 East Cano, Edinburg, TX 78539
Fax: (956) 318-2152

► Director **Renan Ramirez** . . . . (956) 292-7010
E-mail: renan@co.hidalgo.tx.us

Juvenile Probation Department

1001 North Doolittle Road, Edinburg, TX 78540
Fax: (956) 383-4280

► Director/Chief Juvenile Probation Officer
Israel "Buddy" Silva, Jr. . . . . (956) 587-6200

Planning Department

1304 South 25th Street, Edinburg, TX 78539
Fax: (956) 318-2844

► Director **T.J. Arredondo** . . . . (956) 318-2840

Purchasing Department

2802 South Highway 281, Edinburg, TX 78539
Fax: (956) 318-2629 Internet: www.co.hidalgo.tx.us/purchasing

► County Purchasing Agent **Martha L. "Marty" Salazar** . . . (956) 318-2626
E-mail: martha.salazar@co.hidalgo.tx.us

Safety Department

9805 N. 10th Street, McAllen, TX 78504
Fax: (956) 318-2658

► Safety Director **Roy Quintanilla** . . . . (956) 292-7030

Housing Authority of the County of Hidalgo [HACH]

1800 N. Texas Blvd., Weslaco, TX 78596
Fax: (956) 969-5863 Internet: www.hidalgocha.org

Director **Mike Lopez** . . . . (956) 969-5865

Office of the County Commissioners

P.O. Box 1356, Edinburg, TX 78540

★ Commissioner **A.C. Cuellar** (D-Precinct 1) . . . . (956) 968-8733
Term Expires: December 31, 2016 Fax: (956) 969-1417
1902 Joe Stephans Avenue, Suite 301, Edinburg, TX 78596
★ Commissioner **Eduardo "Eddie" Cantu** (D-Precinct 2) . . . (956) 787-1891
Term Expires: December 31, 2018 Fax: (956) 787-4683
300 West Hall Acres, Edinburg, TX 78577
★ Commissioner **Joe M. Flores** (D-Precinct 3) . . . . (956) 585-4509
Term Expires: December 31, 2016 Fax: (956) 585-7816
724 North Breyfogle, Edinburg, TX 78574
E-mail: joe.flores@co.hidalgo.tx.us

(continued on next page)

★ Elected Official ▲ Appointed by Legislature ▼ Appointed by Governor ► Appointed by Board or Commission ● Appointed by Judge
■ Appointed by Mayor △ Appointed by Freeholders ▽ Appointed by Supervisor ▷ Appointed by County Executive ○ Appointed by Council

Office of the County Commissioners *continued*

★ Commissioner **Joseph Palacios** (D-Precinct 4) .... (956) 383-3112
Term Expires: December 31, 2018 Fax: (956) 381-5905
1051 North Doolittle Road, Edinburg, TX 78542

Office of the County Clerk

100 North Closner, 1st Floor, Edinburg, TX 78539
P.O. Box 58, Edinburg, TX 78540
Fax: (956) 318-2105 Internet: www.hidalgocountyclerk.us

County Clerk **Arturo Guajardo, Jr.** .... (956) 318-2100
Term Expires: December 31, 2018
E-mail: aguajardo@hidalgocountyclerk.us

Office of the District Attorney

Courthouse, 100 North Closner, Third Floor, Edinburg, TX 78539
Fax: (956) 381-1511 (Civil) Fax: (956) 318-2301 (Felony)

★ District Attorney **Ricardo Rodriguez** (D) .... (956) 318-2300
Term Expires: December 31, 2018

Office of the Sheriff

P.O. Box 228, Edinburg, TX 78540
711 El Cibdo Road, Edinburg, TX 78541
Fax: (956) 393-6179

★ Sheriff (Interim) **J.E. "Eddie" Guerra** .... (956) 393-8114
Term Expires: December 31, 2016

Office of the Tax Assessor-Collector

P.O. Box 178, Edinburg, TX 78540
2804 U.S. Highway 281, Edinburg, TX 78539
Fax: (956) 318-2733 Tel: (956) 318-2157

★ Tax Assessor-Collector **Paul Villarreal** (D) .... (956) 318-2157
Term Expires: December 31, 2016

Office of the Treasurer

2810 South Highway 281, Edinburg, TX 78539-6243
Fax: (956) 318-2507

★ Treasurer **Norma G. Garcia** (D) .... (956) 318-2506
Term Expires: December 31, 2018

County of Hillsborough, Florida

County Center, 601 E. Kennedy Blvd., Tampa, FL 33602
Internet: www.hillsboroughcounty.org

County Seat: Tampa **Election Type:** Partisan **Population:** 1,349,050 (2015)

Board of County Commissioners [BOCC]

County Center, 601 East Kennedy Boulevard, 2nd Floor, Tampa, FL 33602
Tel: (813) 272-5660 Fax: (813) 273-3732
E-mail: info@hillsboroughcounty.org

★ Chair **Lesley "Les" Miller, Jr.** (D-District 3) .... (813) 272-5720
Term Expires: November 21, 2016 Fax: (813) 272-7048
E-mail: millerlj@hillsboroughcounty.org
Education: South Florida 1978 BA, MPA

Board of County Commissioners *continued*

★ Vice Chair **Victor D. Crist** (R-District 2) .... (813) 272-5452
Term Expires: November 3, 2018 Fax: (813) 272-7047
E-mail: cristv@hillsboroughcounty.org
Date of Birth: 1961
Education: South Florida 1983 BA

★ Commissioner **Sandra L. Murman** (R-District 1) .... (813) 272-5470
Term Expires: November 21, 2016 Fax: (813) 272-7046
E-mail: murmans@hillsboroughcounty.org
Date of Birth: August 9, 1950
Education: Indiana 1972 BS

★ Commissioner **Stacy White** (R-District 4) .... (813) 272-5740
Term Expires: November 21, 2018 Fax: (813) 272-7049
E-mail: whites@hillsboroughcounty.org

★ Commissioner **Ken Hagan** (R-District 5) .... (813) 272-5725
Term Expires: November 3, 2018 Fax: (813) 272-7052
E-mail: hagank@hillsboroughcounty.org
Education: Florida; Tampa MBA

★ Commissioner **Kevin Beckner** (D-District 6) .... (813) 272-5730
Term Expires: November 3, 2016 Fax: (813) 272-7053
E-mail: becknerk@hillsboroughcounty.org

★ Commissioner **Al Higginbotham** (R-District 7) .... (813) 272-5735
Term Expires: November 20, 2018 Fax: (813) 272-7054
E-mail: higginbothama@hillsboroughcounty.org

Office of the County Attorney

County Center, 601 East Kennedy Boulevard, 27th Floor, Tampa, FL 33602
P.O. Box 1110, Tampa, FL 33601
Fax: (813) 272-5231

▶ County Attorney **Charles "Chip" Fletcher** .... (813) 272-5670
Education: Florida Tech 1991 BSc; Florida State 1996 JD

Office of the County Administrator

County Center, 601 East Kennedy Boulevard, 26th Floor, Tampa, FL 33602
Tel: (813) 272-5750 Fax: (813) 272-5248
Internet: www.hillsboroughcounty.org/administrator

▶ County Administrator **Michael S. "Mike" Merrill** .... (813) 276-2843
E-mail: merillm@hillsboroughcounty.org
Education: Marquette 1975 BS
Executive Assistant **Michelle Sekouri** .... (813) 276-2843
E-mail: sekourim@hillsboroughcounty.org

Chief Financial Administrator **Bonnie M. Wise** .... (813) 272-7418
E-mail: wiseb@hillsboroughcounty.org Fax: (813) 272-5248
Education: Florida 1984 BS, 1986 MBA

Deputy County Administrator **Greg Horwedel** .... (813) 272-1175
E-mail: horwedelg@hillsboroughcounty.org

Chief Communications Administrator **Liana Lopez** ...... (813) 276-1141
E-mail: lopezlia@hillsboroughcounty.org
Education: South Florida 1996 BA

Chief Development and Information Administrator **Lucia E. Garsys** .... (813) 276-8785
E-mail: garsysl@hillsboroughcounty.org
Education: Illinois Tech BS; Illinois MUP

Chief Human Services Administrator **Carl S. Harness** .... (813) 272-1153

Chief Information and Innovation Officer **Ramin Kouzehkanani** .... (813) 272-5244
E-mail: ramink@hillsboroughcounty.org

Operations and Legislative Affairs Officer **Brandon Wagner** .... (813) 276-2640
E-mail: wagnerb@hillsboroughcounty.org

Office of Cooperative Extension (University of Florida)

5339 County Road 579, Seffner, FL 33584-3334
Fax: (813) 744-5776

Director and Agriculture Development Manager **Stephen Gran** .... (813) 744-5519 ext. 54113

4-H Program Leader **Brent Broaddus** .... (813) 744-5519 ext. 54132

★ Elected Official ▲ Appointed by Legislature ▼ Appointed by Governor ▶ Appointed by Board or Commission ● Appointed by Judge
■ Appointed by Mayor △ Appointed by Freeholders ▽ Appointed by Supervisor ▷ Appointed by County Executive ○ Appointed by Council

Office of Cooperative Extension (University of Florida) *continued*

Agriculture Program Leader **Alicia Whidden** . . (813) 744-5519 ext. 54134
Family and Consumer Sciences Program
Leader **Lisa Leslie** . . . . (813) 744-5519 ext. 54143
E-mail: lmleslie@ufl.edu
Urban Horticulture Program Leader
Nicole Pinson . . . . (813) 744-5519 ext. 54145

Equal Opportunity Administrator's Office

700 Twiggs St., Suite 830, Tampa, FL 33602
Fax: (813) 276-2217 Internet: www.hillsboroughcounty.org/equalopp

Equal Opportunity Administrator **(Vacant)** . . . . (813) 272-6554

Office of the Medical Examiner

11025 North 46th Street, Tampa, FL 33617
Fax: (813) 276-2049 Internet: www.hillsboroughcounty.org/medexam

Chief Medical Examiner/Director **Mary K. Mainland** . . . . (813) 914-4500
Assistant Manager **Robert Salmon** . . . . (813) 914-4500

Hillsborough County 9-1-1 Administration

601 East Kennedy Boulevard, Tampa, FL 33602
Tel: (813) 744-5911 Fax: (813) 744-5857

Director **Ira U. Pyles** . . . . (813) 744-5911
E-mail: pylesi@hillsboroughcounty.org
Administrative Assistant **Marcie Bryant** . . . . (813) 744-5911

Department of Pet Resources

440 Falkenburg Rd., Tampa, FL 33619
P.O. Box 89159, Tampa, FL 33689-0402
Tel: (813) 744-5660 Fax: (813) 744-5685

Director **Scott Trebatoski** . . . . (813) 744-5660
Education: Wisconsin BABA, MBA
Senior Administrative Assistant **Dana Vick** . . (813) 612-8425 ext. 53105
E-mail: vickd@hillsboroughcounty.org
Staff Veterinarian **Lisa Centonze** . . . . (813) 612-5366 ext. 51583
Operations Manager **John Paige** . . . . (813) 612-8442
Community Relations Coordinator **Michelle Van Dyke** . . . (813) 272-5305

Strategic Planning and Grant Management

601 East Kennedy Boulevard, 26th Floor, Tampa, FL 33602
Fax: (813) 272-5248

Director **Eric R. Johnson** . . . . (813) 272-6582
E-mail: johnsone@hillsboroughcounty.org

Department of Procurement Services

County Center, 601 East Kennedy Boulevard, 18th Floor,
Tampa, FL 33602
Fax: (813) 272-6290

Director **Scott P. Stromer** . . . . (813) 724-6878
E-mail: stromers@hillsboroughcounty.org

Human Resources Group

County Center, 601 East Kennedy Boulevard, 17th Floor,
Tampa, FL 33602
Fax: (813) 272-7142

Director **Lori Krieck** . . . . (813) 272-5130
E-mail: krieckl@hillsboroughcounty.org

Grants Management

Grants Administrator **M. Wayne Finley** . . . . (813) 276-2720

Code Enforcement Department

10119 Windhorst Road, Tampa, FL 33619
Fax: (813) 274-6691 Internet: www.hillsboroughcounty.org/hcce

Director **Ron Spillers** . . . . (813) 274-6600
Administrative Assistant **Jane Angelo** . . . . (813) 274-6600
E-mail: angeloj@hillsboroughcounty.org

Code Enforcement Department *continued*

Community Action Program Manager **Artie Fryer** . . . . (813) 273-3747
601 East Kennedy Boulevard, 25th Floor, Tampa, FL 33602
E-mail: fryera@hillsboroughcounty.org

Communications Department

601 East Kennedy Boulevard, Tampa, FL 33602
Fax: (813) 276-5495
Internet: www.hillsboroughcounty.org/communications

Director, Citizen and Communications Support
Gema Alvare . . . . (813) 276-2676
E-mail: alvareg@hillsboroughcounty.org
Communications and Digital Media Manager
Annette Spina . . . . (813) 301-7239
E-mail: spinaa@hillsboroughcounty.org

Consumer Protection Agency

1101 East 139th Avenue, Tampa, FL 33613-3420
Fax: (813) 903-3432
Internet: www.hillsboroughcounty.org/consumerprotection

Chief Investigator **Eric Olsen** . . . . (813) 903-3430

Economic Development Department

County Center, 601 East Kennedy Boulevard, 20th Floor,
Tampa, FL 33602
Fax: (813) 276-2638

Director **Lindsey Kimball** . . . . (813) 273-3684
E-mail: kimballl@hillsboroughcounty.org
Entrepreneur Collaborative Center Manager
Lynn Kroesen . . . . (813) 204-9267
E-mail: kroesenl@hillsboroughcounty.org
Competitive Sites and Redevelopment Manager
Eric Lindstrom . . . . (813) 276-2747
E-mail: lindstrome@hillsboroughcounty.org
Workforce Development Manager **Ken Jones** . . . . (813) 272-1143
E-mail: jonesk@hillsboroughcounty.org
Technology and Innovation Manager **Jennifer Whelihan** . . (813) 272-6217
E-mail: whelihanj@hillsboroughcounty.org
Entrepreneur Services Manager **Carol Johns** . . . . (813) 204-9267
E-mail: johnsc@hillsboroughcounty.org

Department of Family and Aging Services

County Center, 601 East Kennedy Boulevard, 25th Floor,
Tampa, FL 33602
Tel: (813) 272-5040 Fax: (813) 276-6648

Director **Venerria "Ven" Thomas** . . . . (813) 301-7344

Aging Services Division

County Center, 601 East Kennedy Boulevard, 25th Floor,
Tampa, FL 33602
P.O. Box 1110, Tampa, FL 33601
Tel: (813) 272-5250 Fax: (813) 272-6862

Director **Tracy Gogichaishvili** . . . . (813) 272-5525
Case Management Services Section Manager
Karla Munoz . . . . (813) 272-6956
In-Home Services Section Manager **Yolanda Gaskin** . . . . . (813) 272-6315
Nutrition Services Section Manager **Mary Jo McKay** . . . . (813) 272-2450
Education: Florida BS
Senior Adult Day Care Manager **Anika Coney** . . . . (813) 272-6263

Children's Services Division

3191 Clay Mangum Lane, Tampa, FL 33618
Fax: (813) 264-3874

Director **JoAnn Rollins** . . . . (813) 264-3821
Clinical Services Director **Rhonda Rhodes** . . . . (813) 264-3807
Child Care Licensing Program Manager
Angela Chowning . . . . (813) 264-3925
Fax: (813) 264-2118

COUNTIES

Head Start Division

Fountain Oaks Business Center, 3639 Waters Avenue, Suite 500, Tampa, FL 33614-2783
Tel: (813) 272-5140 Fax: (813) 975-2161
Internet: www.hillsboroughcounty.org/headstart

Director **Dr. Jacquelyn Jenkins** . . . . (813) 272-5140 ext. 52711
Deputy Director of Program Operations **(Vacant)** . . . . (813) 272-5140 ext. 52743
Assistant Director, Child Outcomes **Melania Kesoglou** . . . . (813) 272-5140 ext. 52709
Assistant Director, Family Outcomes and Manager of Quality Assurance and Accountability **LaVonne Malphuf-Nelson** . . (813) 272-5140 ext. 52743

Social Services Division

County Center, 601 East Kennedy Boulevard, 25th Floor, Tampa, FL 33602-4932
Fax: (813) 276-8727 Internet: www.hillsboroughcounty.org/hss

Director **Audrey Ziegler** . . . . (813) 272-7416 Fax: (813) 276-2866
Financial Services Director **Debbie Denavidez** . . . . (813) 301-7348 Fax: (813) 272-7038
Community Action Program Manager **Faith Pullen** . . . . . . (813) 276-2342 Fax: (813) 272-7203
Ryan White Program Director **Gene Earley** . . . . (813) 272-6935 Fax: (813) 276-8593
Sunshine Line Manager **Scott Clark** . . . . (813) 276-8999 Fax: (813) 801-6823
Veterans Affairs Manager **Kevin Jackson** . . . . (813) 975-2181 Fax: (813) 272-5002

Fire Rescue Department [HCFR]

2709 East Hanna Avenue, Tampa, FL 33619
Fax: (813) 272-6692 Internet: www.hillsboroughcounty.org/firerescue

Fire Chief **Dennis W. Jones** . . . . (813) 272-6600
Deputy Fire Chief - Administration **Jason Dougherty** . . . (813) 272-6600

Emergency Dispatch Center

2711 East Hanna, Tampa, FL 33619
Fax: (813) 276-2039

Manager **Margaret Hamrick** . . . . (813) 272-6408
Administrative Assistant **(Vacant)** . . . . (813) 272-6408

Office of Emergency Management

2711 East Hanna, Tampa, FL 33619
Fax: (813) 272-6878 Internet: www.hillsboroughcounty.org/emergency

Emergency Manager **Preston D. Cook** . . . . (813) 276-2364

Fleet Management Department

410 S. 78th St., Tampa, FL 33619
Fax: (813) 744-5566

Director **Bob Stine** . . . . (813) 744-5580 ext. 63230

Information and Technology Services Department

County Center, 601 East Kennedy Boulevard, 28th Floor, Tampa, FL 33602
Fax: (813) 272-6292 Internet: www.hillsboroughcounty.org/its

Director **Earl Williams** . . . . (813) 276-2405
E-mail: williamsel@hillsboroughcounty.org

Parks, Recreation and Conservation Department [PRC]

10119 Windhorst Road, Tampa, FL 33619
Tel: (813) 635-3500 Fax: (813) 635-3527

Director **Dale "Doc" Dougherty** . . . . (813) 635-3510
Administrative Services Manager **(Vacant)** . . . . (813) 635-3501
Athletics Services Section Manager **Billy Graham** . . . . (813) 635-3500
Recreation Services Section Manager **Rick Valdez** . . . . (813) 744-5948

Parks, Recreation and Conservation Department *continued*

Therapeutics Section Manager **Eric Hothem** . . . . (813) 744-5936

Development Services Department

County Center, 601 East Kennedy Boulevard, 20th Floor, Tampa, FL 33602
Tel: (813) 272-5600 Fax: (813) 272-6068

Director **Michael Rimoldi** . . . . (813) 272-5600 ext. 41800
Director, Administrative Services Division **Mark Karet** . . . (813) 276-8307
E-mail: karetm@hillsboroughcounty.org
Director, Building Services Division **Wayne A. Francis** . . (813) 272-8334
Director, Planning and Zoning Services Division **Joe Moreda** . . . . (813) 276-8351
Director, Transportation and Land Development Review Division (Acting) **Gene Boles** . . . . (813) 272-5170

Public Utilities Department

925 East Twiggs Street, Tampa, FL 33602
Fax: (813) 272-5589

Director **George Cassady** . . . . (813) 272-5977 ext. 43394

Public Works Department

601 East Kennedy Boulevard, 22nd Floor, Tampa, FL 33602
Fax: (813) 272-5811 Internet: www.hillsboroughcounty.org/publicworks

Director **John W. Lyons** . . . . (813) 307-4754

Transportation Maintenance Division

601 East Kennedy Boulevard, 22nd Floor, Tampa, FL 33602
Fax: (813) 272-7059

Director **Robert "Rob" Suess** . . . . (813) 307-1854
E-mail: suessr@hillsboroughcounty.org

Real Estate and Facilities Services Department

County Center, 601 East Kennedy Boulevard, 23rd Floor, Tampa, FL 33602
Fax: (813) 272-5597 Internet: www.hillsboroughcounty.org/realestate

Director **Joshua Bellotti** . . . . (813) 272-5810
Real Property Section Manager **Swati Bose** . . . . (813) 272-5810
Manager, Geomatics **Erick Sumner** . . . . (813) 272-5810

Law Library

701 East Twiggs Street, Tampa, FL 33602
Fax: (813) 272-5226

Director **Norma Wise** . . . . (813) 272-5818
E-mail: wisen@hillsboroughcounty.org

Tampa-Hillsborough County Public Library System

900 North Ashley Drive, Tampa, FL 33602
Fax: (813) 273-3707 Internet: www.hcplc.org

Director **Andrew Breidenbaugh** . . . . (813) 273-3652

Office of the Clerk of the Circuit Court

George E. Edgecomb Courthouse, 800 Twiggs Street, Tampa, FL 33602
Tel: (813) 276-8100 Fax: (813) 272-6518
E-mail: clerkadmin@hillsclerk.com

★ Clerk of the Circuit Court **Pat Collier Frank** (D) . . . . (813) 276-8100
Term Expires: November 2016
E-mail: frankp@hillsclerk.com
Education: Florida 1951 BSBA; Georgetown (Attended)

★ Elected Official ▲ Appointed by Legislature ▼ Appointed by Governor ▶ Appointed by Board or Commission ● Appointed by Judge
■ Appointed by Mayor △ Appointed by Freeholders ▽ Appointed by Supervisor ▷ Appointed by County Executive ○ Appointed by Council

Office of the Property Appraiser

County Center, 601 East Kennedy Boulevard, 15th Floor, Tampa, FL 33602
Fax: (813) 272-5519 E-mail: custserv@hcpafl.org
Internet: http://www.hcpafl.org

★ Property Appraiser **Bob "Coach" Henriquez** (D) . . . . (813) 272-6100
Term Expires: November 3, 2016
Education: Princeton 1986 BA

Office of the Public Defender

700 East Twiggs Street, Fifth Floor, Tampa, FL 33602
Fax: (813) 388-4267

★ Public Defender **Julianne Holt** (D) . . . . (813) 272-5980
Term Expires: January 5, 2017
E-mail: pd13@pd13.state.fl.us
Education: South Texas JD

Office of the Sheriff

2008 E. Eighth Ave., Tampa, FL 33605
E-mail: hcso@hcso.tampa.fl.us Internet: http://www.hcso.tampa.fl.us

★ Sheriff **David Gee** (R) . . . . (813) 247-8008
Term Expires: November 3, 2016 Fax: (813) 247-8246
E-mail: geed@hillsboroughcounty.org

Office of the Supervisor of Elections

County Center, 601 East Kennedy Boulevard, 16th Floor, Tampa, FL 33602
Fax: (813) 272-7043 E-mail: info@votehillsborough.org
Internet: www.votehillsborough.org

★ Supervisor of Elections **Craig Latimer** . . . . (813) 272-5850
Term Expires: November 3, 2016
E-mail: latimerc@hillsboroughcounty.org

Office of the Tax Collector

County Center, 601 East Kennedy Boulevard, 14th Floor, Tampa, FL 33602-4931
Fax: (813) 612-6762 E-mail: admin@hillstax.org
Internet: http://www.hillstax.org

★ Tax Collector **Doug Belden** (R) . . . . (813) 635-5200
Term Expires: November 3, 2016
E-mail: beldend@hillsboroughcounty.org
Education: South Florida BA

Hillsborough County Aviation Authority

P.O. Box 22287, Tampa, FL 33622
Tel: (813) 870-8700

Chief Executive Officer **Joseph W. Lopano** . . . . (813) 870-8701
Education: Pace 1978 BBA Fax: (813) 875-6670

Board of Directors

Chairman **Robert I. Watkins** . . . . (813) 254-3369
Education: South Florida 1973
Vice Chairman **Gary Harrod** . . . . (813) 229-1500
Term Expires: July 1, 2017
Treasurer **(Vacant)** . . . . (813) 754-1665
Secretary **Victor D. Crist** (R) . . . . (813) 272-5452
Date of Birth: 1961
Education: South Florida 1983 BA
Assistant Secretary/Assistant Treasurer **Bob Buckhorn** . . . (813) 274-8251
Education: Penn State 1980 BA

Hillsborough County Public Schools [HCPS]

901 East Kennedy Boulevard, Tampa, FL 33602
Tel: (813) 272-4000 Fax: (813) 272-4991
E-mail: informationcenter@sdhc.k12.fl.us Internet: www.sdhc.k12.fl.us

Hillsborough County School Board

★ Chair **April Griffin** . . . . (813) 272-4000
Term Expires: November 2016

Office of the Superintendent

Superintendent of Schools (Acting) **Jeff Eakins** . . . . (813) 272-4050
Communications Officer **Tanya Arja** . . . . (813) 272-4060

Office of the County Comptroller

County Center, 601 East Kennedy Boulevard, Tampa, FL 33602
Tel: (813) 276-8100 Fax: (813) 272-6518
E-mail: clerkadmin@hillsclerk.com

★ Clerk of Circuit Court/Comptroller
Pat Collier Frank (D) . . . . (813) 276-8100
E-mail: frankp@hillsclerk.com
Education: Florida 1951 BSBA; Georgetown (Attended)

County of Hillsborough, New Hampshire

329 Mast Road, Suite 114, Goffstown, NH 03045
Internet: www.hillsboroughcountynh.org

County Seat: Nashua **Election Type:** Nonpartisan **Population:** 406,678 (2015)

Commissioner's Office of Administration and Finance

329 Mast Road, Suite 114, Goffstown, NH 03045
Tel: (603) 627-5602 Fax: (603) 627-5603

★ Chair **Sandra Ziehm** (District 2) . . . . (603) 627-5600
Term Expires: December 31, 2016
E-mail: sziehm@hcnh.org
★ Clerk **Antonia H. "Toni" Pappas** (District 1) . . . . (603) 627-5600
Term Expires: December 31, 2016
E-mail: tpappas@hcnh.org
Education: Rutgers BA
★ Commissioner-Elect **Robert H. Rowe** (District 3) . . . . (603) 627-5600
Term Expires: December 31, 2016

Computer Information Systems Department

329 Mast Road, Goffstown, NH 03045
Fax: (603) 621-1444

Network Administrator **Chip Roach** . . . . (603) 627-5613
E-mail: croach@hcnh.org
Systems Administrator **David Kearsly** . . . . (603) 625-0689

Cooperative Extension Service

329 Mast Road, Suite 101, Goffstown, NH 03045
Fax: (603) 645-5252

▶ Extension Coordinator **Daniel Reidy** . . . . (603) 641-6060
E-mail: daniel.reidy@unh.edu
Education: Plymouth State Col 1976 BS, 1977 MEd

COUNTIES

★ Elected Official ▲ Appointed by Legislature ▼ Appointed by Governor ▶ Appointed by Board or Commission ● Appointed by Judge
■ Appointed by Mayor △ Appointed by Freeholders ▽ Appointed by Supervisor ▷ Appointed by County Executive ○ Appointed by Council

Corrections Department
445 Willow Street, Manchester, NH 03103-6216
Fax: (603) 627-5618 Internet: http://www.hillsboroughcountydoc.org/

▶ Superintendent **David Dionne** . . . . (603) 627-5620 ext. 14
E-mail: ddionne@hillsboroughcountydoc.org

Administration and Finance
329 Mast Road, Suite 114, Goffstown, NH 03045
Fax: (603) 627-5603

▶ County Administrator **Gregory J. Wenger** . . . . (603) 627-5629
E-mail: gwenger@hcnh.org

County Conservation District
Chappell Professional Center, Rt. 13 South, Milford, NH 03055
Fax: (603) 673-0597

▶ Secretary **Kerry Rickrode** . . . . (603) 673-2409
E-mail: kerry.rickrode@nh.nacdnet.net

Delegation Office
329 Mast Road, Suite 104, Goffstown, NH 03045
Fax: (603) 621-1462

Chair **Larry Gagne** . . . . (603) 627-5631
Coordinator **Marcia Rusch-Castonguay** . . . . (603) 627-5631
E-mail: mrusch@hillsboroughcountynh.org

Human Resources Department
329 Mast Road, Suite 112, Goffstown, NH 03045
Tel: (603) 627-5604 Fax: (603) 624-4263

▶ Director **Denise Boyd** . . . . (603) 627-5633
E-mail: dboyd@hcnh.org

Hillsborough County Nursing Home [HCNH]
400 Mast Road, Goffstown, NH 03045
Tel: (603) 627-5540 Fax: (603) 627-5547 Internet: www.hcnh.org

▶ Administrator **Bruce Moorehead** . . . . (603) 627-5540
E-mail: bmoorehead@hcnh.org

Office of the County Attorney
19 Temple Street, Nashua, NH 03060
Fax: (603) 627-5624

★ County Attorney **Dennis C. Hogan** . . . . (603) 627-5605
Term Expires: December 31, 2018
E-mail: dhogan@hcao.net

Office of the Registrar of Deeds
19 Temple Street, Nashua, NH 03060
Fax: (603) 882-7527

★ Registrar **Pam Coughlin** . . . . (603) 882-6933
Term Expires: December 31, 2016
E-mail: pcoughlin@nhdeeds.com

Office of the Sheriff
329 Mast Road, Goffstown, NH 03045
Internet: http://www.hcsonh.us

★ Sheriff **James Hardy** . . . . (603) 627-5610
Term Expires: December 31, 2018
E-mail: jhardy@hcsonh.us

Office of the Treasurer
329 Mast Road, Goffstown, NH 03045

★ Treasurer **David Fredette** . . . . (603) 627-5602
Term Expires: December 31, 2016

County of Hudson, New Jersey
Hudson County Administration Bldg., 595 Newark Ave.,
Jersey City, NJ 07306
Tel: (201) 795-6000 (Information) Internet: www.hudsoncountynj.org

County Seat: Jersey City **Election Type:** Partisan **Population:** 674,836 (2015)

Office of the County Executive
Justice Brennan Court House, 583 Newark Ave., Jersey City, NJ 07306
Tel: (201) 795-6200 Fax: (201) 714-4825
Tel: (201) 795-6000 (Information)

★ County Executive **Thomas A. "Tom" DeGise** (D) . . . . (201) 795-6200
Term Expires: December 31, 2018
E-mail: hcexec@hcnj.us
Education: St Peter's Col 1973 BA

Chief of Staff **Craig Guy** . . . . (201) 795-6200
Constituent Services Director **William La Rosa** . . . . (201) 795-6295
▷ Policy and Communications Director
James "Jim" Kennelly . . . . (201) 795-6060

Office of the County Administrator
Administration Bldg. Annex, 567 Pavonia Ave., Jersey City, NJ 07306
Fax: (201) 795-6520

▷ County Administrator **Abraham "Abe" Antun** . . . . (201) 795-6100
Deputy County Administrator **Laurie Cotter** . . . . (201) 795-6100

Office of Consumer Affairs and Constituent Services
Hudson County Administration Bldg., 583 Newark Ave.,
Jersey City, NJ 07306
Fax: (201) 795-6462

▷ Director (Acting) **Lynda Kennedy** . . . . (201) 795-6295
E-mail: lkennedy@hudsoncountynj.org

Office of Emergency Management [OEM]
595 County Ave., Secaucus, NJ 07094
Fax: (201) 319-3875

▷ Director **James Woods** . . . . (201) 319-3871

Office of the Medical Examiner
325 Norfolk St., Newark, NJ 07103
Fax: (973) 648-3692

▷ Medical Examiner **(Vacant)** . . . . (973) 648-7259

Office of Cultural Affairs and Tourism
583 Newark Ave., Jersey City, NJ 07306
Fax: (201) 792-0729

▷ Director **William "Bill" LaRosa** . . . . (201) 459-2070
E-mail: blarosa@hcnj.us

Office of Weights and Measures
595 County Ave., Secaucus, NJ 07094

Director **Frank Alonso** . . . . (201) 369-4323

Department of Corrections [HCDOC]
30-35 South Hackensack Avenue, Kearny, NJ 07032-4690
Tel: (201) 395-5600 Fax: (201) 395-5630

Director **Oscar Aviles** . . . . (201) 395-5600
Deputy Director **Tish Nalls-Castillo** . . . . (201) 395-5600

★ Elected Official ▲ Appointed by Legislature ▼ Appointed by Governor ▶ Appointed by Board or Commission ● Appointed by Judge
■ Appointed by Mayor △ Appointed by Freeholders ▽ Appointed by Supervisor ▷ Appointed by County Executive ○ Appointed by Council

Department of Finance and Administration

Administration Annex Bldg., 567 Pavonia Ave., 2nd Floor,
Jersey City, NJ 07306
Tel: (201) 795-6077 Fax: (201) 795-3512

▷ Director **Cheryl G. Fuller** .... (201) 795-6068
Accounts and Controls Division Chief **(Vacant)** .... (201) 795-6077
Budget Director **(Vacant)** .... (201) 795-6062
Central Services Division Chief **Arnold Bettinger** .... (201) 795-6272
Purchasing Agent Division Chief **Maria Mercurio** .... (201) 795-6280
E-mail: purchasing@hcnj.us
Minority/Women Business Enterprise
Frances Thompson .... (201) 395-6267
Tax Assessments/County Tax Administrator
Donald Kenny .... (201) 395-6260
Data Processing **Robert Sparrock** .... (201) 795-6066

Department of Health and Human Services

Building 2, 595 County Avenue, Secaucus, NJ 07094
Tel: (201) 369-5280 Fax: (201) 271-4357

▷ Director **Darice Toon** .... (201) 369-5280
E-mail: dtoon@hcnj.us
Addiction Services Coordinator **Robin James** .. (201) 369-5280 ext. 4248
Municipal Alliance Coordinator
Derron Palmer .... (201) 368-5280 ext. 4245

Office on Aging

Building 2, 595 County Rd., Secaucus, NJ 07094

Director **Brian Poffel** .... (201) 369-4313
Veterans Affairs Coordinator
JoAnn Northgrave .... (201) 369-5280 ext. 4258

Veterans Interments Office

257 Cornelison Avenue, Jersey City, NJ 07302
Fax: (201) 369-3431

Director **JoAnn Northgrave** .... (201) 369-3430

Law Department

Administration Bldg. Annex, 567 Pavonia Ave., Jersey City, NJ 07306
Tel: (201) 795-6250 Fax: (201) 795-6428

▷ County Counsel **Don Battista** .... (201) 795-6250
Deputy County Counsel **Mark Morchel** .... (201) 795-6250
County Adjuster **Neil Carroll** .... (201) 795-6001
Risk Management **Edmond Shea** .... (201) 558-7081
595 County Ave., Secaucus, NJ 07094

Office of the County Prosecutor

Hudson County Administration Bldg., 595 Newark Ave.,
Jersey City, NJ 07306
Fax: (201) 795-3365 Internet: www.hcpo.org/

▼ County Prosecutor **Esther Suarez** .... (201) 795-6400
Deputy First Assistant Prosecutor **Peter Stoma** .... (201) 795-6400
Chief of Investigations (Acting) **Gennaro Rubino** .... (201) 795-6400
Chief of Staff **Carol Lamparello** .... (201) 795-6400
Director of Business Operations and Human Resources
(Acting) **Anna P. Pereira** .... (201) 795-6400

Department of Parks and Community Services

595 County Avenue, Secaucus, NJ 07094
Fax: (201) 558-7044

▷ Director **Michelle E. Richardson** .... (201) 369-4300

Division of Housing and Community Development

Justice Brennan Court House, 583 Newark Ave., Jersey City, NJ 07306

Chief **Randi Moore** .... (201) 369-4520
E-mail: rmoore@hcnj.us

Division of Parks

595 County Avenue, Secaucus, NJ 07094
Tel: (201) 915-1388 Fax: (201) 915-1385
Internet: www.hudsoncountynj.org/county-park-system.aspx

Director **Joseph Cecchini** .... (201) 915-1388
Administration Building, Fax: (201) 915-1387
Lincoln Park, Jersey City, NJ 07304

Division of Planning

Bergen Square Center, 830 Bergen Avenue, Suite 6A,
Jersey City, NJ 07306
Tel: (201) 217-5137 Fax: (201) 795-7856
Internet: www.hudsoncountynj.org/division-of-planning.aspx

▷ Director **Massiel Medina Ferrara** .... (201) 217-5137
E-mail: mferrara@hcnj.us

Department of Roads and Public Property

257 Cornelison Avenue, Jersey City, NJ 07302
Fax: (201) 319-3722

Director **(Vacant)** .... (201) 369-2777
549 Duncan Ave., Jersey City, NJ 07306
Central Garage Chief **Ed Latour** .... (201) 915-1373
Roads and Bridges Division Chief **Wally Wolfe** .... (201) 915-1373

Hudson County Community College [HCCC]

70 Sip Avenue, 4th Floor, Jersey City, NJ 07306
Tel: (201) 714-7100 Fax: (201) 656-1799 Internet: www.hccc.edu

President **Glen Gabert** .... (201) 714-7100
Education: Benedictine U BA; Notre Dame 1968 MA;
Loyola U (Chicago) PhD; Rockhurst U MBA

Hudson County Improvement Authority [HCIA]

574 Summit Ave., Jersey City, NJ 07306
Fax: (201) 795-0240 Internet: www.hcia.org

Chief Executive Officer **Norman M. Guerra** .... (201) 795-4555
E-mail: norman@hcia.org

Hudson County Mosquito Control

595 County Avenue, Secaucus, NJ 07094
Tel: (201) 223-1133 Fax: (201) 223-0122
Internet: www.hudsonregional.org/mosquito

Superintendent **Gregory Williams** .... (201) 223-1133

Office of the Board of Chosen Freeholders

Administration Bldg. Annex, 567 Pavonia Ave., Jersey City, NJ 07306
Tel: (201) 795-6001 Fax: (201) 217-0404

★ Chair **Tilo Rivas** (D-District 6) .... (201) 795-6001
Term Expires: December 31, 2017
★ Vice Chair **Anthony P. Vainieri, Jr.** (D-District 8) .... (201) 795-6001
Term Expires: December 31, 2017
★ Freeholder **Kenneth Kopacz** (D-District 1) .... (201) 795-6001
Term Expires: December 31, 2017
★ Freeholder **William O'Dea** (D-District 2) .... (201) 795-6001
Term Expires: December 31, 2017
★ Freeholder **Gerard Balmir** (D-District 3) .... (201) 795-6001
Term Expires: December 31, 2017
★ Freeholder **E. Junior Maldonado** (D-District 4) .... (201) 795-6001
Term Expires: December 31, 2017
★ Freeholder **Anthony L. "Stick" Romano** (D-District 5) .. (201) 795-6001
Term Expires: December 31, 2017
★ Freeholder **Caridad Rodriguez** (D-District 7) .... (201) 795-6001
Term Expires: December 31, 2017
★ Freeholder **Albert Cifelli** (D-District 9) .... (201) 795-6001
Term Expires: December 31, 2017
△ Counsel to the Board **Ed Florio** .... (201) 795-6001
△ Clerk to the Board **Alberto Santos** .... (201) 795-6001

COUNTIES

★ Elected Official ▲ Appointed by Legislature ▼ Appointed by Governor ▶ Appointed by Board or Commission ● Appointed by Judge
■ Appointed by Mayor △ Appointed by Freeholders ▽ Appointed by Supervisor ▷ Appointed by County Executive ○ Appointed by Council

Office of the County Clerk

257 Cornelison Avenue, Fourth Floor, Jersey City, NJ 07302
Tel: (201) 369-3470 Fax: (201) 369-3478

★County Clerk **Barbara A. Netchert** .... (201) 369-3470
Term Expires: December 31, 2016 Fax: (201) 369-3478
E-mail: countyclerk@hcnj.us
Deputy Clerk **Janet Larwa** .... (201) 369-3470
Special Deputy Clerk **Susan Antun** .... (201) 369-3470

Office of the County Register/Deeds and Mortgages

257 Cornelison Avenue, Jersey City, NJ 07302
Fax: (201) 795-5179

★County Register **Pamela Gardner** .... (201) 395-4760
Term Expires: December 31, 2016
Deputy County Register **Lorraine Senerchia** .... (201) 395-4760

Office of the Sheriff

Hudson County Administration Bldg., Ground Fl., 595 Newark Ave., Jersey City, NJ 07306
Tel: (201) 795-6300 Fax: (201) 369-4336
Internet: www.hudsoncountynj.org/sheriffs-office.aspx

★Sheriff **Frank X. Schillari** (D) .... (201) 369-7262
Term Expires: December 31, 2016
E-mail: fschillari@hcnj.us
Executive Assistant to the Sheriff **Robert Taino** .... (201) 795-6300
E-mail: rtaino@hcnj.us
Undersheriff **Francine Shelton** .... (201) 795-6300
Undersheriff **James Sharrock** .... (201) 795-6300
E-mail: jsharrock@hcnj.us

Office of the Superintendent of Schools

595 County Avenue, 1st Floor, Secaucus, NJ 07094
Fax: (201) 369-5288

▶Executive Superintendent (Interim) **Monica M. Tone** .... (201) 369-5290

Office of the Surrogate

Hudson County Administration Bldg., 595 Newark Avenue, Room 107, Jersey City, NJ 07306
Fax: (201) 795-5488 Internet: www.hudsonsurrogate.com

★Surrogate-Judge **Joseph Ryglicki** (D) .... (201) 795-6378
Term Expires: December 31, 2017
E-mail: jryglicki@hcnj.us

Probation Department

595 Newark Avenue, Jersey City, NJ 07306
Tel: (201) 795-6800 Fax: (201) 217-5117

Chief Probation Officer **Kimberly Cicala** .... (201) 795-6827
Assistant Chief, Adult Supervision **Claribel Bautista** .... (201) 795-6839
Assistant Chief, Child Support Division **(Vacant)** .... (201) 295-7660
Assistant Chief, Special Programs **(Vacant)** .... (201) 795-6839

County of Jackson, Mississippi

P.O. Box 998, Pascagoula, MS 39568
Internet: www.co.jackson.ms.us

County Seat: Pascagoula **Election Type:** Nonpartisan
Population: 141,425 (2015)

Office of the Board of Supervisors

P.O. Box 998, Pascagoula, MS 39568

★President **Melton Harris, Jr.** (District 2) .... (228) 769-3170
Term Expires: December 31, 2019 Fax: (228) 762-6578
E-mail: melton_harris@co.jackson.ms.us
★Vice President **Troy Ross** (District 4) .... (228) 769-3457
Term Expires: December 31, 2019
E-mail: troy_ross@co.jackson.ms.us
★Supervisor **Barry Cumbest** (District 1) .... (228) 769-3403
Term Expires: December 31, 2019 Fax: (228) 769-3475
E-mail: barry_cumbest@co.jackson.ms.us
★Supervisor **Ken Taylor** (District 3) .... (228) 762-7641
Term Expires: December 31, 2019
Education: North Texas State 1963 BSC
★Supervisor **Randy Bosarge** (District 5) .... (228) 769-3378
Term Expires: December 31, 2019
E-mail: Randy_Bosarge@co.jackson.ms.us

Office of the County Administrator

P.O. Box 998, Pascagoula, MS 39568
Fax: (228) 769-3348

▽County Administrator **Brian Fulton** .... (228) 769-3088
E-mail: brian_fulton@co.jackson.ms.us

Office of the County Board Attorney

P.O. Box 998, Pascagoula, MS 39568
Fax: (228) 769-3119

▽Board Attorney **Gary Evans** .... (228) 769-3371
E-mail: gevans@jcboardatty.com

Office of the Public Defender

P.O. Box 998, Pascagoula, MS 39568
Fax: (228) 769-3058

Public Defender **Amanda Galle** .... (228) 769-3058

Office of Emergency Services

P.O. Box 998, Pascagoula, MS 39568
Fax: (228) 769-3108

▽Director **Earl Etheridge** .... (228) 769-3111
E-mail: earl_etheridge@co.jackson.ms.us

Information Systems

P.O. Box 998, Pascagoula, MS 39568
Fax: (228) 769-3314

Systems Manager **Paul Tristani** .... (228) 769-3458
E-mail: paul_tristani@co.jackson.ms.us

Cooperative Extension Service

P.O. Box 1248, Pascagoula, MS 39568-1248
Fax: (228) 769-3347

County Agent/Coordinator **Terri Thompson** .... (228) 769-3217

★Elected Official ▲Appointed by Legislature ▼Appointed by Governor ▶Appointed by Board or Commission ●Appointed by Judge
■Appointed by Mayor △Appointed by Freeholders ▽Appointed by Supervisor ▷Appointed by County Executive ○Appointed by Council

Finance Department
P.O. Box 998, Pascagoula, MS 39568
Fax: (228) 769-3357
Internet: www.co.jackson.ms.us/departments/finance.php

▽ Finance Director **Samantha Wells** .... (228) 769-3155
E-mail: samantha_wells@co.jackson.ms.us

Human Resources Department
P.O. Box 998, Pascagoula, MS 39568
Fax: (228) 769-3379

Director **Janet Krebs** .... (228) 769-3380
E-mail: Janet_Krebs@co.jackson.ms.us

Planning Department
P.O. Box 998, Pascagoula, MS 39568
Fax: (228) 769-3116 E-mail: michele_coats@co.jackson.ms.us

Director **Michele L. Coats** .... (228) 769-3919
Education: Southern Mississippi BA

Public Information
P.O. Box 998, Pascagoula, MS 39568
Fax: (228) 769-3100

Public Information Officer **Nicole Grundel** .... (228) 769-3260
E-mail: nicole_grundel@co.jackson.ms.us

Purchasing Department
P.O. Box 998, Pascagoula, MS 39568
Fax: (228) 769-3291

Purchasing Agent **Jennifer Pry** .... (228) 769-3121
E-mail: jennifer_pry@co.jackson.ms.us

Recreation Department
5400 Ball Park Rd., Vancleave, MS 39565
P.O. Box 998, Pascagoula, MS 39568
Fax: (228) 826-5779

Director **Jack Hamilton** .... (228) 826-5330

Roads Department
P.O. Box 998, Pascagoula, MS 39568
Fax: (228) 826-5918

▽ Road Manager **Joe O'Neil** .... (228) 826-2547
Education: Southern Mississippi BS

Solid Waste Department
P.O. Box 998, Pascagoula, MS 39568
Fax: (228) 872-8341

Coordinator **Ronda Powell** .... (228) 872-8340

Trent Lott International Airport
8301 Saracennia Rd., Box 11, Moss Point, MS 39563
Fax: (228) 475-8066

Director **Carol Snapp** .... (228) 475-1371

Veteran's Service Office
P.O. Box 998, Pascagoula, MS 39569
Fax: (228) 769-2578

Veteran's Officer **Robert Whipple** .... (228) 769-3075

Office of the Assessor
P.O. Box 998, Pascagoula, MS 39568
Fax: (228) 769-3133

★ Tax Assessor **Nick Elmore** .... (228) 769-3070
Term Expires: December 31, 2019

Office of the Chancery Clerk
P.O. Box 998, Pascagoula, MS 39568
Fax: (228) 769-3397

★ Chancery Clerk **Joshua Eldridge** .... (228) 769-3124
Term Expires: December 31, 2019

Office of the Constables
P.O. Box 998, Pascagoula, MS 39568

★ Constable **Ty Thompson** (District 1) .... (228) 769-3080
Term Expires: December 31, 2019

★ Constable **Calvin Hutchins** (District 2) .... (228) 769-3080
Term Expires: December 31, 2019

★ Constable **K. Shane Langfitt** (District 3) .... (228) 769-3080
Term Expires: December 31, 2019

★ Constable **Kerry B. Fountain** (District 4) .... (228) 769-3080
Term Expires: December 31, 2019

Office of the Coroner/Medical Examiner
P.O. Box 998, Pascagoula, MS 39568
Fax: (228) 769-3489

★ Coroner/Medical Examiner **Vicki Broadus** .... (228) 769-3197
Term Expires: December 31, 2019
E-mail: vicki_broadus@co.jackson.ms.us

Office of the County Prosecuting Attorney
3102 Canty St., Pascagoula, MS 39567
Fax: (228) 769-1417

★ County Prosecuting Attorney **Mark Watts** .... (228) 762-2373
Term Expires: December 31, 2019

Office of the District Attorney
P.O. Box 998, Pascagoula, MS 39568
Fax: (228) 769-3345

★ District Attorney **Anthony "Tony" Lawrence III** .... (228) 769-3045
Term Expires: December 31, 2019
E-mail: anthony_lawrence@co.jackson.ms.us

Office of the Election Commissioners
P.O. Box 998, Pascagoula, MS 39568
Tel: (228) 769-3261 Fax: (228) 769-3009

★ Chairman **Danny Glaskox** (District 1) .... (228) 588-3771
Term Expires: December 31, 2016
E-mail: danny_glaskox@co.jackson.ms.us

★ Commissioner **Jerry Sims** (District 2) .... (228) 475-6646
Term Expires: December 31, 2016
E-mail: jerry.sims@co.jackson.ms.us

★ Commissioner **Debrah Hodges** (District 3) .... (228) 762-3622
Term Expires: December 31, 2016

★ Commissioner **Michael Dickinson** (District 4) .... (228) 875-6784
Term Expires: December 31, 2016

★ Commissioner **Tamara Vidrine** (District 5) .... (228) 818-1994
Term Expires: December 31, 2016

Office of the Sheriff
P.O. Box 998, Pascagoula, MS 39568
Fax: (228) 769-6168

★ Sheriff **Mike Ezell** .... (228) 769-3024
Term Expires: December 31, 2019
E-mail: Mike_Ezell@co.jackson.ms.us

(continued on next page)

COUNTIES

★ Elected Official ▲ Appointed by Legislature ▼ Appointed by Governor ► Appointed by Board or Commission ● Appointed by Judge
■ Appointed by Mayor △ Appointed by Freeholders ▽ Appointed by Supervisor ▷ Appointed by County Executive ○ Appointed by Council

Office of the Sheriff *continued*

Chief Deputy **Ray Bates** .... (228) 769-3064

Office of the Superintendent of Education

P.O. Box 5069, Vancleave, MS 39565-5069
Fax: (228) 826-1757

★ School Superintendent **Dr. Barry Amacker** ...... (228) 826-1757 ext. 332
Term Expires: December 31, 2019

Office of the Tax Collector

P.O. Box 998, Pascagoula, MS 39568
Fax: (228) 769-3270

★ Tax Collector **Joe Tucker** .... (228) 769-3200
Term Expires: December 31, 2019
E-mail: joe_tucker@co.jackson.ms.us

County of Jackson, Missouri

Jackson County Courthouse, 415 East 12th Street,
Kansas City, MO 64106
Tel: (816) 881-3000 (Information) Internet: www.jacksongov.org

County Seat: Independence **Election Type:** Partisan
Population: 687,623 (2015)

Office of the County Executive

Jackson County Courthouse, 415 East 12th Street, 2nd Floor,
Kansas City, MO 64106
Fax: (816) 881-3133 E-mail: countyexecutive@jacksongov.org
Internet: www.jacksongov.org/executive

★ County Executive (Acting) **Frank White, Jr.** .... (816) 881-3333
Note: A special election will be held in November 2016 to fill this position for the remainder of the term ending in 2018.
Term Expires: December 31, 2018

Office of the County Counselor

Jackson County Courthouse, 415 East 12th Street, 2nd Floor,
Kansas City, MO 64106
Tel: (816) 881-3355 E-mail: cocounselor@jacksongov.org

▷ County Counselor **W. Stephen Nixon** .... (816) 881-3355
Education: Missouri (Kansas City) BS, 1975 JD

Office of Human Relations and Citizens Complaints [OHRCC]

Jackson County Courthouse, 415 East 12th Street, 7th Floor,
Kansas City, MO 64106
Fax: (816) 881-6338 E-mail: ohrcc@jacksongov.org
Internet: www.jacksongov.org/ohrcc

▷ Director **Dawna Shumate** .... (816) 881-3670
E-mail: dshumate@jacksongov.org

Office of the Medical Examiner [JCMEO]

950 East 21st Street, Kansas City, MO 64108
Fax: (816) 404-1345

▷ Chief Medical Examiner (Interim) **Dr. Diane Peterson** ... (816) 881-6600
E-mail: dpeterson@jacksongov.org

Office of the Chief Administrative Officer

Jackson County Courthouse, 415 East 12th Street, 2nd Floor,
Kansas City, MO 64106

▷ Chief Administrative Officer **Mary Lou Brown** .... (816) 881-3333
E-mail: mlbrown@jacksongov.org
Public Information Officer **Mark Siettmann** .... (816) 881-3449

Collections Department

415 East 12th Street, 1st Floor, Kansas City, MO 64106
E-mail: collections@jacksongov.org
Internet: www.jacksongov.org/collections

▷ Director **V. Edwin "Ed" Stoll** Room 100 .... (816) 881-3187

Finance and Purchasing Department

415 East 12th Street, Room 105, Kansas City, MO 64106
Fax: (816) 881-3877 E-mail: finance@jacksongov.org
Internet: www.jacksongov.org/finance

▷ Director **Q. Troy Thomas** .... (816) 881-3176
E-mail: qtthomas@jacksongov.org

Human Resources Department

Jackson County Courthouse, 415 East 12th Street, 1st Floor,
Kansas City, MO 64106

▷ Director **Dennis Dumovich** .... (816) 881-3135
E-mail: ddumovich@jacksongov.org

Information Technology Department [IT]

415 East 12th Street, Kansas City, MO 64106
E-mail: webmaster@jacksongov.org Internet: www.jacksongov.org/it

▷ Director **Michael Erickson** .... (816) 881-3155
E-mail: merickson@jacksongov.org

Office of the Deputy Chief Administrative Officer

Jackson County Courthouse, 415 East 12th Street, 2nd Floor,
Kansas City, MO 64106

Chief Operating Officer **Gary Panethiere** .... (816) 881-3333
E-mail: gpanethiere@jacksongov.org

Department of Corrections

Jackson County Detention Facility, 1300 Cherry, Kansas City, MO 64106
E-mail: corrections@jacksongov.org
Internet: www.jacksongov.org/corrections

▷ Director (Acting) **Joseph Piccinini** .... (816) 881-4231
E-mail: jpiccinini@jacksongov.org

Parks and Recreation Department

22807 Woods Chapel Road, Blue Springs, MO 64105
E-mail: parksrec@jacksongov.org Internet: www.jacksongov.org/recreation

▷ Director **Michele Newman** .... (816) 503-4820
E-mail: mnewman@jacksongov.org

Public Works Department

303 West Walnut Street, Independence, MO 64050
E-mail: pubworks@jacksongov.org
Internet: www.jacksongov.org/publicworks

▷ Public Works Director/Chief Engineer **Brian Gaddie** ..... (816) 881-4538
E-mail: bgaddie@jacksongov.org

Office of the Chief of Staff

Jackson County Courthouse, 415 East 12th Street, 2nd Floor,
Kansas City, MO 64106

Chief of Staff **Calvin Williford** .... (816) 881-3333
E-mail: cwilliford@jacksongov.org

★ Elected Official ▲ Appointed by Legislature ▼ Appointed by Governor ▶ Appointed by Board or Commission ● Appointed by Judge
■ Appointed by Mayor △ Appointed by Freeholders ▽ Appointed by Supervisor ▷ Appointed by County Executive ○ Appointed by Council

Assessment Department
416 East 12th Street, 1M, Kansas City, MO 64106
Tel: (816) 881-3530 E-mail: assessment@jacksongov.org

▷ Director (Acting) **V. Edwin "Ed" Stoll** .... (816) 881-3239
Assistant Director/Senior Statistician **(Vacant)** .... (816) 881-3307

Recorder of Deeds Department
415 East 12th Street, Room 104, Kansas City, MO 64106
E-mail: records@jacksongov.org Internet: www.jacksongov.org/recorder

▷ Recorder of Deeds **Bob Kelly** .... (816) 881-3191
E-mail: rtkelly@jacksongov.org

Office of the County Legislature
Jackson County Courthouse, 415 East 12th Street, 2nd Floor, Kansas City, MO 64106

★ Chair **Crystal Williams** (D-At-Large, District 2) .... (816) 881-3464
Term Expires: January 1, 2019 Fax: (816) 881-3340
E-mail: crystalwilliams@jacksongov.org

★ Vice Chair **Theresa Galvin** (R-District 6) .... (816) 881-4423
Term Expires: January 1, 2019 Fax: (816) 881-4473

★ Legislator **Scott Burnett** (D-District 1) .... (816) 881-3076
Term Expires: January 1, 2019 Fax: (816) 881-3340
E-mail: sburnett@jacksongov.org
Education: Kansas State BA

★ Legislator **Alfred Jordan** (D-District 2) .... (816) 881-3163
Term Expires: January 16, 2018

★ Legislator **Dennis Waits** (D-District 3) .... (816) 881-4441
Term Expires: January 1, 2019 Fax: (816) 881-4473
E-mail: dwaits@jacksongov.org
Education: Missouri (Kansas City) 1971 BS, 1986 JD

★ Legislator **Dan Tarwater** (D-District 4) .... (816) 881-3362
Term Expires: January 1, 2019 Fax: (816) 881-3340
E-mail: dtarwater@jacksongov.org
Education: Rockhurst Col BS

★ Legislator **Gregory O. "Greg" Grounds** (R-District 5) ... (816) 881-4476
Term Expires: January 1, 2019
E-mail: ggrounds@jacksongov.org

★ Legislator **Garry Baker** (D-At-Large, District 1) .... (816) 881-3132
Term Expires: January 1, 2019
E-mail: gbaker@jacksongov.org

★ Legislator **Tony Miller** (D-At-Large, District 3) .... (816) 881-4477
Term Expires: January 1, 2019 Fax: (816) 881-4473
E-mail: tmiller@jacksongov.org

Clerk of the Legislature **Mary Jo Spino** .... (816) 881-3242
E-mail: mspino@jacksongov.org

Legislative Auditor **Crissy Wooderson** .... (816) 881-3069

Office of the Prosecuting Attorney
Jackson County Courthouse, 415 East 12th Street, 11th Floor, Kansas City, MO 64106
Fax: (816) 881-3843

★ Prosecuting Attorney **Jean Peters-Baker** (D) .... (816) 881-3555
Term Expires: December 31, 2016
Education: Columbia Col (MO) 1991 BS; Missouri 1995 MPA; Missouri (Kansas City) 1998 JD

Family Support Division
417 East 13th Street, Suite 200, Kansas City, MO 64106

Director **Melissa Mauer-Smith** .... (816) 881-3181

Office of the Sheriff
4001 NE Lakewood Court, Lees Summit, MO 64064

★ Sheriff **Mike Sharp** .... (816) 524-4302
Term Expires: December 31, 2016
E-mail: msharp@jacksongov.org

Jackson County Election Board
215 North Liberty, Independence, MO 64051
Fax: (816) 325-4609 Internet: www.jcebmo.org

Democrat Director **Robert "Bob" Nichols** .... (816) 325-4600
Republican Director **Tammy Brown** .... (816) 325-4600
E-mail: tbrown@jcebmo.org

County of Jefferson, Alabama
County Courthouse, 716 Richard Arrington, Jr. Boulevard, North, Birmingham, AL 35203
Tel: (205) 325-5311 (Information) Internet: http://jeffconline.jccal.org

County Seat: Birmingham **Election Type:** Nonpartisan
Population: 660,367 (2015)

Office of the County Commissioners
County Courthouse, 716 Richard Arrington Jr Blvd. North, Room 230, Birmingham, AL 35203
Fax: (205) 325-5950

★ President **James A. "Jimmie" Stephens** (District 3) .... (205) 325-5555
Term Expires: November 2, 2018
E-mail: stephensj@jccal.org

★ President Pro Tempore
Sandra Little-Brown (District 2) .... (205) 325-5074
Term Expires: November 2, 2018
E-mail: browns@jccal.org

★ Commissioner **George F. Bowman** (District 1) .... (205) 325-5504
Term Expires: November 2, 2018
E-mail: bowmang@jccal.org

★ Commissioner **Joe Knight** (District 4) .... (205) 325-5070
Term Expires: November 2, 2018
E-mail: knightjoe@jccal.org

★ Commissioner **David Carrington** (District 5) .... (205) 325-5503
Term Expires: November 2, 2018
E-mail: carringtond@jccal.org

Office of the County Manager
County Manager **Tony Petelos** .... (205) 731-2880
E-mail: petelost@jccal.org
Education: Alabama Birmingham 1981 BA

Office of the Coroner/Medical Examiner
Jefferson County Coroner, 1515 Sixth Avenue, South Room 220, Birmingham, AL 35233
Fax: (205) 930-3595

▶ Chief Coroner/Medical Examiner **Gregory G. Davis** ..... (205) 930-3603
E-mail: davisg@jccal.org

Associate Coroner/Medical Examiner **Dr. Daniel Dye** .... (205) 930-3603
Associate Coroner/Medical Examiner **Gary Simmons** .... (205) 930-3603

Office of the County Attorney
County Courthouse, 716 Richard Arrington Jr. Blvd. North, Room 280, Birmingham, AL 35203
Fax: (205) 325-5840

▶ County Attorney **Carol Sue Nelson** .... (205) 325-5688
E-mail: nelsonc@jccal.org

Office of Senior Citizens Services [OSCS]
2601 South Highland Avenue, Birmingham, AL 35205
Tel: (205) 325-1416 Fax: (205) 325-1429

▶ Executive Director (Acting) **Frederick Hamilton** .... (205) 325-1416
E-mail: frederick.hamilton@adss.alabama.gov

★ Elected Official ▲ Appointed by Legislature ▼ Appointed by Governor ▶ Appointed by Board or Commission ● Appointed by Judge
■ Appointed by Mayor △ Appointed by Freeholders ▽ Appointed by Supervisor ▷ Appointed by County Executive ○ Appointed by Council

COUNTIES

COUNTIES

Community Development
County Courthouse, 716 Richard Arrington, Jr. Boulevard, Suite A430, Birmingham, AL 35203

Director **Frederick Hamilton** . . . . (205) 325-5761
E-mail: hamiltonf@jccal.org

Finance Department
County Courthouse, 716 Richard Arrington, Jr. Blvd. North, Room 810, Birmingham, AL 35203
Fax: (205) 325-5222 Internet: http://jeffconline.jccal.org/finance

▶ Chief Financial Officer/Director **George Tablack** . . . . (205) 583-8338
E-mail: tablackg@jccal.org
Chief Accountant **Barry Doss** . . . . (205) 325-5041
Budget Management Director **Tracie Hodge** . . . . (205) 325-8709
716 Richard Arrington, Jr. Boulevard, North, 6th Floor Annex, Birmingham, AL 35203

Purchasing Office
County Courthouse, 716 Richard Arrington Jr. Blvd. North, Room 830, Birmingham, AL 35203
Fax: (205) 325-5841

▶ Purchasing Agent **Michael D. Matthews** . . . . (205) 325-5381
E-mail: matthewsm@jccal.org

General Services Department
716 Richard Arrington Jr. Blvd. North, Room 1, Birmingham, AL 35203
Fax: (205) 325-5144

Director **Jeffrey S. Smith** . . . . (205) 325-5504
E-mail: smithjs@jccal.org

Human Resources Department
County Courthouse, 716 Richard Arrington Jr. Blvd. North, Room A610, Birmingham, AL 35203
Fax: (205) 325-5598

Court Appointed Receiver **Ronald Sims** . . . . (205) 325-5249

Information Services Department
716 Richard Arrington Jr. Blvd. North, Suite 700 A, Birmingham, AL 35203

Chief Information Officer **Roosevelt Butler** . . . . (205) 325-5301
E-mail: butlerr@jccal.org
Deputy Chief Information Officer **(Vacant)** . . . . (205) 325-5301

Land Development Department
716 Richard Arrington, Jr. Boulevard, Room 260, Birmingham, AL 35203
Fax: (205) 325-5224

▶ Director **(Vacant)** . . . . (205) 325-5640

Retirement/Pension Department
County Courthouse, 716 Richard Arrington Jr. Blvd. North, Room 430, Birmingham, AL 35203
Fax: (205) 325-5054

▶ Pension Coordinator **Cathy Crumley** . . . . (205) 325-5354
E-mail: crumleyc@jccal.org

Revenue Department
County Courthouse, 716 Richard Arrington Jr. Blvd. North, Room A-100, Birmingham, AL 35203

▶ Director **Travis Hulsey** . . . . (205) 325-5171
E-mail: hulseyt@jccal.org

Department of Roads and Transportation
County Courthouse, 716 Richard Arrington Jr. Blvd. North, Room A 200, Birmingham, AL 35203
Fax: (205) 325-5156

▶ Director/County Engineer **Tracy Pate** . . . . (205) 325-5794
E-mail: patet@jccal.org

Tax Department
County Courthouse, 716 Richard Arrington Jr. Blvd. North, Birmingham, AL 35203
Fax: (205) 325-4884

★ Tax Assessor **Gaynell Hendricks** Suite 170 . . . . (205) 325-5505
Term Expires: November 2, 2020
E-mail: hendricksg@jccal.org
★ Tax Collector **J.T. Smallwood** Suite 160 . . . . (205) 325-5500
Term Expires: November 2020
E-mail: smallwoodjt@jccal.org

Jefferson County Board of Registrars
County Courthouse, 716 Richard Arrington, Jr. Boulevard, Suite A410, Birmingham, AL 35203
Fax: (205) 325-5369 Internet: http://jeffconline.jccal.org/bor

▶ Chair **Barry Stephenson** . . . . (205) 325-5550
E-mail: stephensonb@jccal.org

Jefferson County Emergency Management Agency
709 North 19th Street, Birmingham, AL 35203
Fax: (205) 328-9162 Internet: www.impactalabama.com

Coordinator **James A. Coker** . . . . (205) 254-2039
E-mail: cokerj@jccal.org
Training Officer **Michael Harter** . . . . (205) 254-2039
E-mail: harterm@jccal.org

Jefferson County Law Library
Jefferson County Courthouse, 716 Richard Arrington Jr. Blvd. North, Suite 530, Birmingham, AL 35203
Fax: (205) 322-5915

Law Librarian **Linda M. Hand** . . . . (205) 325-5628

Office of the District Attorney
Criminal Justice Center, 801 Richard Arrington Jr. Blvd. North, Room L-01, Birmingham, AL 35203
Fax: (205) 325-5266

★ District Attorney **Brandon K. Falls** . . . . (205) 325-5252
Term Expires: January 2017
E-mail: fallsb@jccal.org
Chief Deputy District Attorney **Doug Davis** . . . . (205) 325-5252

Sheriff's Office
2200 8th Ave. N, Birmingham, AL 35203
Tel: (205) 325-5900 Fax: (205) 325-5822 Internet: www.jeffcosheriff.org

★ Sheriff **Mike Hale** . . . . (205) 325-1450
Term Expires: January 7, 2019
E-mail: halem@jccal.org

Office of the Treasurer
County Courthouse, 716 Richard Arrington Jr. Blvd. North, Room 300, Birmingham, AL 35203
Fax: (205) 325-5978

★ Treasurer **Mike Miles** . . . . (205) 325-5373
Term Expires: November 30, 2016
★ Deputy Treasurer **Sherry McClain** . . . . (205) 481-4192
Term Expires: November 30, 2016

★ Elected Official ▲ Appointed by Legislature ▼ Appointed by Governor ▶ Appointed by Board or Commission ● Appointed by Judge
■ Appointed by Mayor △ Appointed by Freeholders ▽ Appointed by Supervisor ▷ Appointed by County Executive ○ Appointed by Council

Jefferson County School System
2100 18th Street South, Birmingham, AL 35209
Fax: (205) 379-2311 Internet: www.jefcoed.com

Board of Education
2100 18th Street South, Birmingham, AL 35209
Internet: www.jefcoed.com/board

President **Jacqueline Smith** .... (205) 379-2000

Office of the Superintendent
2100 18th Street South, Birmingham, AL 35209

Superintendent **Dr. Warren Craig Pouncey** .... (205) 379-2000
Deputy Superintendent for School and Community Support **Dr. Anna Bacca** .... (205) 325-5311
Deputy Superintendent for School and Community Support **Rebecca "Becky" Lee** .... (205) 325-5311

County of Jefferson, Colorado
100 Jefferson County Parkway, Golden, CO 80419
Tel: (303) 279-6511 (Information) Internet: www.jeffco.us

County Seat: Golden **Election Type:** Partisan **Population:** 565,524 (2015)

Office of the Board of Commissioners
100 Jefferson County Pkwy., Golden, CO 80419-5550
E-mail: commish@jeffco.us Tel: (303) 271-8166

★ Chair **Libby Szabo** (R-District 1) .... (303) 271-8525
Term Expires: December 31, 2016
E-mail: commish1@jeffco.us

★ Commissioner **Casey P. Tighe** (D-District 2) .... (303) 271-8525
Term Expires: December 31, 2016
E-mail: commish2@jeffco.us

★ Commissioner **Donald Rosier** (R-District 3) .... (303) 271-8525
Term Expires: January 7, 2019
E-mail: commish3@jeffco.us

Office of the County Attorney
100 Jefferson County Parkway, Suite 5500, Golden, CO 80419
Fax: (303) 271-8901

► County Attorney **Ellen G. Wakeman** .... (303) 271-8900
E-mail: ewakeman@jeffco.us
Education: UC Davis BA; Boalt Hall JD

Jefferson County Board of Health
Jefferson County Courts and Administration Building, 100 Jefferson County Parkway, Hearing Room 2, Golden, CO 80419
Tel: (303) 271-5716

► President **Bonnie McNulty** .... (303) 271-5716

Jefferson County Public Health [JCPH]
645 Parfet Street, Lakewood, CO 80215
Tel: (303) 232-6301 Fax: (303) 271-5702
Internet: www.co.jefferson.co.us/public-health

Executive Director **Dr. Mark B. Johnson** .... (303) 271-5701

Vital Records
800 Jefferson County Parkway, Golden, CO 80419
Tel: (303) 271-6450

Supervisor **Bernadette Berger** .... (303) 271-5707

Jefferson County Public Library [JCPL]
10200 West 20th Avenue, Lakewood, CO 80215
Tel: (303) 235-5275 Internet: http://jefferson.lib.co.us

Executive Director **Pam Nissler** .... (303) 275-2201
E-mail: pam.nissler@jeffcolibrary.org

Office of the County Manager
100 Jefferson County Parkway, Golden, CO 80419-2520
Tel: (303) 271-8500 E-mail: countymanager@jeffco.us

► County Manager **Ralph Schell** .... (303) 271-8508
E-mail: rschell@jeffco.us
Public Engagement Director **Kate McIntire** .... (303) 271-8515
E-mail: kmcintir@jeffco.us

Office of Public Information
100 Jefferson County Parkway, Golden, CO 80419
Tel: (303) 271-8512 Fax: (303) 271-8232

Web Content and Social Media Director **Julie Story** ..... (303) 271-8541
E-mail: jstory@jeffco.us

Office of the Deputy County Manager
100 Jefferson County Parkway, Golden, CO 80419
Fax: (303) 271-8232

Deputy County Manager **Kate Newman** .... (303) 271-8508
E-mail: knewman@jeffco.us

Fleet Services Division
21401 Golden Gate Canyon Rd., Golden, CO 80403
Fax: (303) 271-5281

Director **Buck Benke** .... (303) 271-5236

Facilities and Construction Management Division
700 Jefferson County Parkway, Suite 300, Golden, CO 80401
Fax: (303) 271-5055

Director **Mark A. Danner** .... (303) 271-5000
E-mail: mdanner@jeffco.us

Jefferson County Archives
3500 Illinois Street, Suite 2350, Golden, CO 80401
Fax: (303) 271-8452 E-mail: archivist@jeffco.us

County Archivist **Ronda Frazier** .... (303) 271-8448

Department of Jefferson County Parks
700 Jefferson County Parkway, Golden, CO 80401
Fax: (303) 271-5955

Director **Tom Hoby** .... (303) 271-5925
E-mail: thoby@jeffco.us
Education: Colorado State BS

Boettcher Mansion
900 Colorow Road, Golden, CO 80401
Fax: (303) 526-5519

Director **Cynthia Shaw** .... (720) 497-7632

Jefferson County Extension (Colorado State University)
15200 West Sixth Avenue, Unit C, Golden, CO 80401
Fax: (303) 271-6644

Director **Jacki Paone** .... (303) 271-6620

Jefferson County Fairgrounds
15200 W. Sixth Ave., Golden, CO 80401
Fax: (303) 271-6606

Director **Scott Gales** .... (303) 271-6600

COUNTIES

★ Elected Official ▲ Appointed by Legislature ▼ Appointed by Governor ► Appointed by Board or Commission ● Appointed by Judge
■ Appointed by Mayor △ Appointed by Freeholders ▽ Appointed by Supervisor ▷ Appointed by County Executive ○ Appointed by Council

Jefferson County Open Space
700 Jefferson County Pkwy., Suite 100, Golden, CO 80401
Fax: (303) 271-5955 Internet: www.jeffco.us/parks

Director **Tom Hoby** .... (303) 271-5925
Education: Colorado State BS

Department of Development and Transportation
100 Jefferson County Parkway, Golden, CO 80419
Fax: (303) 271-8232

Director **Jeanie Rossillon** .... (303) 271-8545
Education: Colorado State BS; Colorado (Denver)

Division of Building Safety
800 Jefferson County Parkway, Golden, CO 80419
Fax: (303) 271-8282

Director **Rebecca "Becky" Baker** .... (303) 271-8260

Planning and Zoning Division
100 Jefferson County Parkway, Suite 3550, Golden, CO 80419
Fax: (303) 271-8744

Director **John Wolforth** .... (303) 271-8700

Road and Bridge Division
21401 Golden Gate Canyon Road, Golden, CO 80403

Director **Larry Benshoof** .... (303) 271-5200
E-mail: lbenshoo@jeffco.us

Transportation and Engineering Division
100 Jefferson County Parkway, Suite 3500, Golden, CO 80419
Fax: (303) 271-8490

Director **Steve Durian** .... (303) 271-8495
E-mail: sdurian@co.jefferson.co.us

Rocky Mountain Metropolitan Airport
Terminal Building, 11755 Airport Way, Broomfield, CO 80021
Fax: (303) 271-4875

Airport Manager **Bryan Jonson** .... (303) 241-4850

Department of Human Resources
100 Jefferson County Parkway, Suite 4530, Golden, CO 80419

Director **Jennifer Fairweather** .... (303) 271-8400
E-mail: jfairwea@jeffco.us
Education: Colorado 1990 BS; Webster 2000 MA

Department of Human Services
900 Jefferson County Parkway, Golden, CO 80401

Director **Lynn Johnson** .... (303) 271-1388

Division of Children, Youth and Families [CYF]
900 Jefferson County Parkway, Golden, CO 80401

Deputy Director **Mary Berg** .... (303) 271-1388

Community Assistance Division
900 Jefferson County Parkway, Suite 110, Golden, CO 80401

Director **Lynnae Flora** .... (303) 271-1388

Community Development Division
3500 Illinois Street, Golden, CO 80401
Fax: (303) 271-4708

Director **Kat Douglas** .... (303) 271-8372
E-mail: kdouglas@jeffco.us

Aging and Adult Services
900 Jefferson County Parkway, Suite 110, Golden, CO 80401
Tel: (303) 271-1388

Director **Rena Kuberski** .... (303) 271-1388

Justice Services Division
3500 Illinois Street, Suite 2800, Golden, CO 80401

Director **Kathy Otten** .... (303) 271-4840

Jefferson County Head Start [JCHS]
5150 Allison Street, Arvada, CO 80002
Fax: (720) 898-0664

Director **Gayle Perryman** .... (720) 497-7900

Jefferson County Workforce Center
Laramie Building, 3500 Illinois Street, Suite 1600, Golden, CO 80401

Director **Kat Douglas** .... (303) 271-4701

Department of Finance and Information Technology
Director **Holly Bjorklund** .... (303) 271-8545

Accounting Division
100 Jefferson County Parkway, Golden, CO 80419
Fax: (303) 271-8524

Director **Deborah Freischlag** .... (303) 271-8532

Information Technology Services Division [ITS]
3500 Illinois Street, Golden, CO 80401
Fax: (303) 271-8001

Director/Chief Information Officer **Jim F. Smith** .... (303) 271-8800
E-mail: jfsmith@jeffco.us
Deputy Chief Information Officer **(Vacant)** .... (303) 271-8800

Budget and Risk Management
100 Jefferson County Parkway, Suite 4570, Golden, CO 80419

Director **Mary O'Neil** .... (303) 271-8520

Office of the Clerk and Recorder
100 Jefferson County Parkway, Golden, CO 80419
Fax: (303) 271-8197

★County Clerk and Recorder **Faye Griffin** (R) .... (303) 271-8168
Term Expires: January 7, 2019
Clerk to the Board **Teri Schmaedecke** .... (303) 271-8174

Office of the Coroner
800 Jefferson County Parkway, Golden, CO 80401
Fax: (303) 271-6488

★Coroner **John Graham** (R) .... (303) 271-6480
Term Expires: January 7, 2019
E-mail: jgraham@jeffco.us

Office of the County Assessor
100 Jefferson County Parkway, Suite 250, Golden, CO 80419
Fax: (303) 271-8616 E-mail: assessor@jeffco.us

★County Assessor **Ron Sandstrom** (R) .... (303) 271-8655
Term Expires: January 7, 2019
E-mail: assessor@jeffco.us
Deputy Assessor **Nancy Anders** .... (303) 271-8600
E-mail: nanders@jeffco.us

Office of the District Attorney
500 Jefferson County Pkwy., Golden, CO 80401
Fax: (303) 271-6888

★District Attorney **Peter A. Weir** .... (303) 271-6800
Term Expires: December 31, 2016
Education: Duke; Denver JD

★ Elected Official ▲ Appointed by Legislature ▼ Appointed by Governor ▶ Appointed by Board or Commission ● Appointed by Judge
■ Appointed by Mayor △ Appointed by Freeholders ▽ Appointed by Supervisor ▷ Appointed by County Executive ○ Appointed by Council

Office of the Public Trustee

100 Jefferson County Parkway, Suite 154, Golden, CO 80419-1540

▼Public Trustee **Margaret T. Chapman** . . . . (303) 271-8580
Term Expires: February 1, 2019
E-mail: mchapman@jeffco.us

Office of the Treasurer

100 Jefferson County Parkway, Suite 252, Golden, CO 80419-2025
Fax: (303) 271-8359

★Treasurer **Tim Kauffman** (R) . . . . (303) 271-8330
Term Expires: January 7, 2019
E-mail: tkauffman@jeffco.us

Office of the Sheriff

200 Jefferson County Parkway, Golden, CO 80401-2697
Fax: (303) 271-5307

★Sheriff **Jeff Shrader** (R) . . . . (303) 271-5305
Term Expires: January 7, 2019
E-mail: jshrader@jeffco.us

Undersheriff **Raymond "Ray" Fleer** . . . . (303) 271-5305
E-mail: rfleer@jeffco.us
Education: Western State Col BA

Animal Control Office

700 Jefferson County Parkway, Room 160, Golden, CO 80401
Fax: (303) 271-5075

Manager **Carla Zinanti** . . . . (303) 271-5070

Office of Emergency Management

800 Jefferson County Parkway, Golden, CO 80401
Fax: (303) 271-4905

Director **(Vacant)** . . . . (303) 271-4900

Jefferson Parish, Louisiana

General Government Building, 200 Derbigny Street, Gretna, LA 70053
Tel: (504) 736-6100 (Information) Internet: www.jeffparish.net

County Seat: Gretna **Election Type:** Nonpartisan **Population:** 436,275 (2015)

Office of the Parish President

200 Derbigny Street, 6th Floor, Gretna, LA 70053
Tel: (504) 736-6400 (Jefferson office) Tel: (504) 364-2700 (Gretna office)
Fax: (504) 736-6638

★Parish President **Michael S. "Mike" Yenni** . . . . (504) 736-6405
Term Expires: January 2020

Office of the Parish Attorney

200 Derbigny Street, Gretna, LA 70053
Fax: (504) 364-2673 E-mail: jpparishattorney@jeffparish.net

Parish Attorney **Michael Power** . . . . (504) 736-6305
Education: Loyola U (New Orleans) JD

Office of the Finance Director

New Government Building, 200 Derbigny Street, Suite 4200, Gretna, LA 70053
Fax: (504) 364-2815

Finance Director **Timothy J. Palmatier** . . . . (504) 364-2767

Accounting Department

General Government Building, 200 Derbigny Street, Suite 4200, Gretna, LA 70053
Fax: (504) 364-2797

Director **Tara Hazelbaker** . . . . (504) 364-2777
E-mail: jpaccounting@jeffparish.net

Budget Department

General Government Building, 200 Derbigny Street, Suite 4200, Gretna, LA 70053
Fax: (504) 364-2815

Director **Antoinette Scott** . . . . (504) 364-3833
E-mail: anscott@jeffparish.net

Purchasing Department

General Government Building, 200 Derbigny Street, Suite 4400, Gretna, LA 70053
Fax: (504) 364-2693

Director **Brenda J. Campos** . . . . (504) 364-2678
E-mail: bcampos@jeffparish.net
Education: Loyola U (New Orleans) BA; New Orleans MPA

COUNTIES

Office of the Chief Operating Officer

Joseph S. Yenni Building, 1221 Elmwood Park Boulevard, Jefferson, LA 70123
Fax: (504) 736-6420

▷Chief Operating Officer **Keith A. Conley** . . . . (504) 736-6403
Deputy Chief Operating Officer **Natalie Newton** . . . . (504) 736-6400

Public Information Office

Joseph S. Yenni Building, 1221 Elmwood Park Boulevard, Suite 1002, Jefferson, LA 70123
Tel: (504) 736-6410 Fax: (504) 736-6413

Public Information Officer **Antwan Harris** . . . . (504) 363-5521

Department of Emergency Management

1887 Ames Boulevard, Marrero, LA 70072
Fax: (504) 349-5366

Director **Joseph Valienete** . . . . (504) 349-5360

Office of the Chief Administrative Assistant for Administration

1221 Elmwood Park Boulevard, Jefferson, LA 70123
Fax: (504) 736-6638

Chief Administrative Assistant **Diane M. Roussel** . . . . (504) 736-6412

Electronic Information Systems Department [EIS]

Joseph S. Yenni Building, 1221 Elmwood Park Boulevard, Room 700, Jefferson, LA 70123
Fax: (504) 736-6123 E-mail: jpeis@jeffparish.net

Director **Ridley Boudreaux** . . . . (504) 736-6720
E-mail: rboudreaux@jeffparish.net

Human Resource Management Department

2000 Segnette Boulevard, Westwego, LA 70094
Fax: (504) 736-6125

Director **Peggy O. Barton** . . . . (504) 736-6175

Personnel Department

200 Derbigny Street, Suite 3100, Gretna, LA 70053
Fax: (504) 365-3320

Director **John Dumas** . . . . (504) 364-2730

★Elected Official ▲Appointed by Legislature ▼Appointed by Governor ▶Appointed by Board or Commission ●Appointed by Judge
■Appointed by Mayor △Appointed by Freeholders ▽Appointed by Supervisor ▷Appointed by County Executive ○Appointed by Council

Department of Risk Management
Joseph S. Yenni Building, 1221 Elmwood Park Boulevard, Suite 315, Jefferson, LA 70123
Fax: (504) 736-6828

Director **William "Bill" Fortenberry** .... (504) 736-6907
E-mail: wfortenberry@jeffparish.net

Office of the Chief Administrative Assistant for Community Programs
1221 Elmwood Park Boulevard, Jefferson, LA 70123
Fax: (504) 736-6420

Chief Administrative Assistant **Darryl Ward** .... (504) 731-4557
E-mail: dward@jeffparish.net

Citizens' Affairs Department
1221 Elmwood Park Boulevard, Suite 403, Jefferson, LA 70123
Fax: (504) 736-6778 E-mail: jpcitizensaffairs@jeffparish.net

Director **Sean Burke** .... (504) 736-6100
E-mail: sburke@jeffparish.net

Community Development Department
1221 Elmwood Park Boulevard, Suite 605, Jefferson, LA 70123
Fax: (504) 736-6425

Director **Tamithia P. Shaw** .... (504) 736-6262
E-mail: JPCommunityDevelopment@jeffparish.net

Department of Workforce Connection
1900 Lafayette Street, Suite 1, Gretna, LA 70053
Fax: (504) 365-3341

Director **Sharon Wegner** .... (504) 227-1283
E-mail: swegner@jeffparish.net

Department of Transit Administration
21 Westbank Expressway, Gretna, LA 70053
Fax: (504) 364-3453 E-mail: jptransit@jeffparish.net
Internet: www.jeffersontransit.org

Director **Ryan Brown** .... (504) 364-3450
E-mail: rbrown@jeffparish.net

Jefferson Community Action Programs [JEFFCAP]
Gretna Community Center, 1700 Monroe Street, Gretna, LA 70053
Fax: (504) 736-7093

Director **Jedidiah Bernell Jackson** .... (504) 736-6900

Office of the Chief Administrative Assistant for Development
1221 Elmwood Park Boulevard, Jefferson, LA 70123
Fax: (504) 736-6638

Chief Administrative Assistant **Loren M. Marino** .... (504) 736-6590
E-mail: lmarino@jeffparish.net

Department of Inspection and Code Enforcement
Joseph S. Yenni Building, 1221 Elmwood Park Boulevard, Room 205, Jefferson, LA 70123
Fax: (504) 736-6953

Director **Tiffany Scot Wilken** .... (504) 736-6950

Planning Department
Joseph S. Yenni Building, 1221 Elmwood Park Boulevard, Room 601, Jefferson, LA 70123-2337
Tel: (504) 736-6320 Fax: (504) 736-6343

Director **Terri Wilkinson** .... (504) 736-6337

Jefferson Parish Animal Shelter
#1 Humane Way, Jefferson, LA 70123-0640
P.O. Box 10640, Jefferson, LA 70121-0640
Fax: (504) 736-8729 E-mail: jpanimalshelter@jeffparish.net

Director **Robin Beaulieu** .... (504) 736-6111

Office of the Chief Administrative Assistant for Operations
1221 Elmwood Park Boulevard, Jefferson, LA 70123
Fax: (504) 736-6638

Director **Steve Caraway** .... (504) 736-6435

Department of Environmental Affairs
4901 Jefferson Highway, Suite E, Jefferson, LA 70121
Fax: (504) 731-4607

Director **Marnie Winter** .... (504) 736-6440

Department of Telecommunications
5698 Belle Terre Road, Marrero, LA 70072
Fax: (504) 349-5384

Director **Valerie Waguespack Brolin** .... (504) 349-5300

Department of Juvenile Services [DJS]
1546-B Gretna Boulevard, Harvey, LA 70058
Fax: (504) 364-3719

Director **Roy Junker** .... (504) 364-3750 ext. 225

Jefferson Parish Library [JPL]
4747 West Napoleon Avenue, Metairie, LA 70001
Tel: (504) 838-1100 Fax: (504) 838-1110
Internet: www.jefferson.lib.la.us

Director **Marylyn Palmisano Haddican** .... (504) 838-1133

East Bank Consolidated Fire Department
1221 Elmwood Park Boulevard, Suite 704, Jefferson, LA 70123
Fax: (504) 736-6209

Director **Joseph R. "Joe" Greco, Jr.** .... (504) 736-6200
E-mail: jgreco@jeffparish.net

Community Justice Agency [CJA]
3420 North Cause Way Boulevard, Metairie, LA 70002
E-mail: jpcommunityjustice@jeffparish.net Fax: (504) 736-8717

Director **Ronald E. Lampard** .... (504) 736-6844

Office of the Chief Administrative Assistant for Services
200 Derbigny Street, Gretna, LA 70053
Fax: (504) 364-2828

Chief Administrative Assistant **Royce J. Blanchard** ...... (504) 364-2700
E-mail: rblanchard@jeffparish.net
Education: New Orleans BS

Department of Fleet Management
4901 Jefferson Highway, Suite A, Jefferson, LA 70121
Fax: (504) 736-6883

Director **Nicholas "Nick" DiGerolamo** .... (504) 736-6877

Department of General Services
General Government Building, 200 Derbigny Street, Suite 3300, Gretna, LA 70053
Fax: (504) 365-3312 E-mail: jpgeneralservices@jeffparish.net

Director **Anthony L. Francis, Jr.** .... (504) 364-2675
E-mail: afrancis@jeffparish.net

Department of Parks and Recreation
6921 Saints Drive, Metairie, LA 70003
Fax: (504) 736-9524

Director **C. J. Gibson** .... (504) 736-6999

★ Elected Official ▲ Appointed by Legislature ▼ Appointed by Governor ► Appointed by Board or Commission ● Appointed by Judge
■ Appointed by Mayor △ Appointed by Freeholders ▽ Appointed by Supervisor ▷ Appointed by County Executive ○ Appointed by Council

John A. Alario Sr. Event Center
2000 Segnette Boulevard, Westwego, LA 70094
Fax: (504) 349-5533 Internet: www.alariocenter.com

General Manager **Lydia S. Folse** .... (504) 349-5525

Office of the Public Works Director
1221 Elmwood Park Boulevard, Jefferson, LA 70123
Fax: (504) 736-6739

Public Works Director **Kazem Alikhani** .... (504) 736-6512

Department of Capital Projects
Joseph S. Yenni Building, 1221 Elmwood Park Boulevard, Suite 906, Jefferson, LA 70123
Fax: (504) 736-6833

Director **Reda Youssef** .... (504) 736-6833

Department of Drainage
1561 Riverpark Road, Bridge City, LA 70094
E-mail: jpdrainage@jeffparish.net

Director **Mitchell T. "Mitch" Theriot** .... (504) 736-6751

Department of Engineering
Joseph S. Yenni Building, 1221 Elmwood Park Boulevard, Room 802, Jefferson, LA 70123
Fax: (504) 736-6526 E-mail: jpengineering@jeffparish.net

Director **Mark Drewes** .... (504) 736-6505
E-mail: mdrewes@jeffparish.net

Department of Sewerage
Joseph S. Yenni Building, 1221 Elmwood Park Boulevard, Room 803, Jefferson, LA 70123
Fax: (504) 736-6694

Director **Linda Daly** .... (504) 736-6661

Department of Streets
1901 Ames Boulevard, Marrero, LA 70072
Fax: (504) 349-5828 E-mail: jpstreets@jeffparish.net

Director **Randy Nicholson** .... (504) 349-5800

Parkways Department
1901 Ames Boulevard, Marrero, LA 70072
Fax: (504) 349-5828 E-mail: jpparkways@jeffparish.net

Director **Brook Burmaster** .... (504) 349-5800

Water Department
Joseph S. Yenni Building, 1221 Elmwood Park Boulevard, Suite 909, Jefferson, LA 70123
Fax: (504) 736-6835 Tel: (504) 736-6744 E-mail: jpwater@jeffparish.net

Director **Salvador Maffei, Jr.** .... (504) 736-6742

Office of the Parish Council
General Government Building, 200 Derbigny Street, Gretna, LA 70053
Tel: (504) 364-2600

★ Chairman **Christopher L. "Chris" Roberts** (At-Large, Division A) .... (504) 736-6615
Term Expires: January 6, 2020 Fax: (504) 731-4646
E-mail: croberts@jeffparish.net

★ Vice-Chairman **Paul D. Johnston** (District 2) .... (504) 736-6607
Term Expires: January 6, 2020 Fax: (504) 731-4433

★ Council Member **Ricky J. Templet** (District 1) .... (504) 364-2607
Term Expires: January 6, 2020 Fax: (504) 364-2615

★ Council Member **Mark Spears** (District 3) .... (504) 364-2603
Term Expires: January 6, 2020 Fax: (504) 364-3704

★ Council Member **E. B. "Ben" Zahn** (District 4) .... (504) 736-6622
Term Expires: January 6, 2020 Fax: (504) 736-6598

★ Council Member **Jennifer Van Vrancken** (District 5) .... (504) 736-6607
Term Expires: January 6, 2020
Education: Sophie Newcomb 1992 BA; Tulane 1995 JD

Office of the Parish Council *continued*

★ Council Member
Cynthia Lee-Sheng (At-Large, Division B) .... (504) 364-2600
Term Expires: January 6, 2020

Chief of Staff **Lowell C. "Sonny" Burmaster, Jr.** .... (504) 364-6600

Parish Clerk **Eula A. Lopez** .... (504) 364-2626
Fax: (504) 364-2633

Office of the Assessor
Courthouse Annex, 200 Derbigny Street, Gretna, LA 70053
Fax: (504) 366-4087 E-mail: assessor@jpassessor.com
Internet: www.jpassessor.com

★ Assessor **Thomas J. "Tom" Capella** .... (504) 362-4100
Term Expires: January 2019

Office of the Coroner
2018 8th Street, Harvey, LA 70058
Fax: (504) 365-1750 Internet: www.jpcoroner.com

★ Coroner **Gerry Cvitanovich** .... (504) 365-9100
Term Expires: March 27, 2020

Office of the District Attorney
200 Derbigny Street, Gretna, LA 70053
Fax: (504) 361-2585 Internet: www.jpda.org

★ District Attorney **Paul D. Connick, Jr.** .... (504) 368-1020
Term Expires: January 13, 2021

Office of the Registrar of Voters
1221 Elmwood Park Boulevard, Suite 502, Jefferson, LA 70123
P.O. Box 10494, Jefferson, LA 70181
Fax: (504) 736-6197

○ Registrar of Voters **Dennis DiMarco** .... (504) 736-6191
E-mail: ddimarco@jeffparish.net
Education: New Orleans 1969 BS; Loyola U (New Orleans) 1970 MBA

Chief Deputy **Philip Trupiano** .... (504) 349-5690
5001 Westbank Expressway, Suite C-2, Marrero, LA 70072 Fax: (504) 349-5695

Office of the Sheriff
Building B, 1233 Westbank Expressway, 5th Floor, Harvey, LA 70058
Tel: (504) 363-5500 Fax: (504) 363-5711 Internet: www.jpso.com

★ Sheriff **Newell D. Normand** .... (504) 363-5500
Term Expires: June 30, 2020
E-mail: sheriff@jpso.com

Jefferson Parish Public School System [JPPSS]
501 Manhattan Boulevard, Harvey, LA 70058
Tel: (504) 349-7600 Fax: (504) 349-7960 Internet: jpschools.org

Jefferson Parish School Board
501 Manhattan Boulevard, Harvey, LA 70058

★ President **Cedric Floyd** .... (504) 349-7804

Office of the Superintendent of Schools
501 Manhattan Boulevard, Harvey, LA 70058

Superintendent of Schools **Isaac Joseph** .... (504) 349-7600

★ Elected Official ▲ Appointed by Legislature ▼ Appointed by Governor ▶ Appointed by Board or Commission ● Appointed by Judge
■ Appointed by Mayor △ Appointed by Freeholders ▽ Appointed by Supervisor ▷ Appointed by County Executive ○ Appointed by Council

County of Johnson, Kansas

111 South Cherry Street, Olathe, KS 66061
Tel: (913) 715-0430 Internet: www.jocogov.org

County Seat: Olathe **Election Type:** Nonpartisan **Population:** 580,159 (2015)

Board of County Commissioners

111 South Cherry Street, Suite 3300, Olathe, KS 66061-3486
Tel: (913) 715-0430 Fax: (913) 715-0440
E-mail: bocc-commissioners@jocogov.org

★Chairman **Ed Eilert** . . . . . . (913) 715-0500
Term Expires: January 10, 2019 Fax: (913) 715-0440
E-mail: ed.eilert@jocogov.org
Education: Emporia State 1962 BSBA, 1963 MS

★Commissioner **Ronald L. "Ron" Shaffer** (District 1) . . . . (913) 715-0431
Term Expires: January 12, 2019
E-mail: ron.shaffer@jocogov.org

★Commissioner **James P. Allen** (District 2) . . . . (913) 715-0432
Term Expires: January 17, 2017
E-mail: jim.allen@jocogov.org
Education: Emporia State 1973 BA; Rockhurst Col 1973 MBA

★Commissioner **Steven C. Klika** (District 3) . . . . (913) 715-0433
Term Expires: January 14, 2017
E-mail: steve.kilka@jocogov.org

★Commissioner **Jason Osterhaus** (District 4) . . . . (913) 715-0434
Term Expires: January 10, 2019
E-mail: jason.osterhaus@jocogov.org

★Commissioner **Michael L. "Mike" Ashcraft** (District 5) . . (913) 715-0435
Term Expires: January 10, 2019
E-mail: michael.ashcraft@jocogov.org
Education: Indiana State BA; Alabama MPA

★Commissioner **John Toplikar** (District 6) . . . . (913) 715-0436
Term Expires: January 14, 2017
E-mail: john.toplikar@jocogov.org

Office of the County Auditor

111 South Cherry Street, Suite 3300, Olathe, KS 66061
Tel: (913) 715-1830 Fax: (913) 715-1831

County Auditor **Ken Kleffner** . . . . (913) 715-1825
Senior Auditor **Michelle Cleveland** . . . . (913) 715-1830
Auditor II **Lynn Smith** . . . . (913) 715-1830
Auditor I **(Vacant)** . . . . (913) 715-1830

Office of the County Manager

111 South Cherry Street, Suite 3300, Olathe, KS 66061
Tel: (913) 715-0725 Fax: (913) 715-0727
Internet: http://cmo.jocogov.org/

County Manager **Hannes Zacharias** . . . . (913) 715-0731
E-mail: hannes.zacharias@jocogov.org
Education: Wichita State; Kansas MPA

Assistant County Manager **Maury Thompson** . . . . (913) 715-0734
E-mail: maury.thompson@jocogov.org
Education: Mount Mercy 1984 BA; Park U 1998 MPA

Deputy County Manager **Penny Postoak Ferguson** . . . . (913) 715-0733
E-mail: penny.postoakferguson@jocogov.org
Education: Kansas 1992 BBA, 1994 MPA

Office Manager **Brittney Wray** . . . . (913) 715-0501

Bureau Chief **J. Joseph Waters** . . . . (913) 715-1105
E-mail: joe.waters@jocogov.org

Clerk of the Board of Commissioners (Interim)
Linda W. Barnes . . . . (913) 715-0426

Director of Public Affairs and Communications
Sharon L. Watson . . . . (913) 715-0730
E-mail: sharon.watson@jocogov.org

Office of the County Appraiser

11811 South Sunset Drive, Suite 2100, Olathe, KS 66061
Tel: (913) 715-9000 Fax: (913) 715-0010
Internet: http://appraiser.jocogov.org/

County Appraiser **Paul A. Welcome** . . . . (913) 715-0001
Education: Bowling Green State 1972 BSBA, 1974 MBA

Department of Corrections

206 West Loula Street, Olathe, KS 66061
Tel: (913) 715-4501 Internet: http://corrections.jocogov.org/

Director **Elizabeth M. "Betsy" Gillespie** . . . . (913) 715-4525
E-mail: betsy.gillespie@jocogov.org

Assistant Director **Susan Dougan** . . . . (913) 715-4504
E-mail: susan.dougan@jocogov.org

Emergency Management and Homeland Security

111 South Cherry Street, Suite 100, Olathe, KS 66061
Tel: (913) 782-3038 Fax: (913) 791-5002 Internet: www.jocoem.org

Deputy Director **Dan Robeson** . . . . (913) 715-1013
E-mail: drobeson@jocogov.org

Assistant Director, Community Preparedness
Trent Pittman . . . . (913) 715-1003

Assistant Director, Government Preparedness
Gerard McConaha . . . . (913) 715-1004
E-mail: gerard.mcconaha@jocogov.org

Assistant Director, Operations **(Vacant)** . . . . (913) 715-1002

Environmental Department [JCED]

11811 South Sunset Drive, Suite 2700, Olathe, KS 66061-7061
Tel: (913) 715-6900 Internet: http://jced.jocogov.org/

Director **Lougene Marsh** . . . . (913) 715-6900

Facilities Management Department

111 South Cherry Street, Suite 2100, Olathe, KS 66061
Tel: (913) 715-1100 Fax: (913) 715-1130
Internet: http://facilities.jocogov.org/

Director **Brad Reinhardt** . . . . (913) 715-1100
E-mail: brad.reinhardt@jocogov.org
Education: Kansas State BSME; Kansas MBA

Department of Human Resources

111 South Cherry Street, Suite 2600, Olathe, KS 66061
Tel: (913) 715-1400 Fax: (913) 715-1419 Internet: http://hr.jocogov.org/

Human Resources Director **Rebecca "Becky" Salter** . . . . (913) 715-1423
E-mail: rebecca.salter@jocogov.org

Legal Department

111 South Cherry Street, Suite 3200, Olathe, KS 66061
Tel: (913) 715-1900 Fax: (913) 715-1873
Internet: http://legal.jocogov.org/

Chief Counsel **Donald J. "Don" Jarrett** . . . . (913) 715-1840
Education: Kansas 1973 BA, 1976 JD

Deputy Director of Legal Services **Cindy Dunham** . . . . (913) 715-1852

Department of Planning and Development

111 South Cherry Street, Suite 3500, Olathe, KS 66061
Tel: (913) 715-2200 Fax: (913) 715-2222 Internet: planning.jocogov.org

Director **Dean Palos** . . . . (913) 715-2220
Deputy Director **Paul Greeley** . . . . (913) 715-2205

Department of Treasury and Financial Management

111 South Cherry Street, Suite 2400, Olathe, KS 66061
Tel: (913) 715-0525 Fax: (913) 715-0577
Internet: http://treasurer.jocogov.org/

Director and County Treasurer **Tom Franzen** . . . . (913) 715-0525

★Elected Official ▲Appointed by Legislature ▼Appointed by Governor ▶Appointed by Board or Commission ●Appointed by Judge
■Appointed by Mayor △Appointed by Freeholders ▽Appointed by Supervisor ▷Appointed by County Executive ○Appointed by Council

Department of Treasury and Financial Management *continued*

Chief Deputy Treasurer **Amy Meeker** . . . . (913) 715-2601

Johnson County Emergency Communications Center [ECC]

11880 South Sunset Drive, Olathe, KS 66061
Tel: (913) 826-1000 Fax: (913) 826-1019

Director **Ellen Wernicke** . . . . (913) 826-1004
E-mail: ewernicke@jocogov.org
Deputy Director, Operations **(Vacant)** . . . . (913) 826-1004

Johnson County Med-Act

11811 South Sunset Drive, Suite 1100, Olathe, KS 66061
Tel: (913) 715-1950 Fax: (913) 715-1959 E-mail: medact@jocoems.org
Internet: www.jocoems.org

EMS Chief **Ted McFarlane** . . . . (913) 715-1950
Education: Kansas
Deputy Chief of Operations **Mark Terry** . . . . (913) 715-1950
Education: Missouri (Kansas City)

Johnson County Museum

6305 Lackman Road, Shawnee, KS 66217
Tel: (913) 715-2550 Fax: (913) 715-2565 Internet: www.jocomuseum.org

Director **Mindi Love** . . . . (913) 715-2550
Executive Assistant **Audrea Griggs** . . . . (913) 715-2550
E-mail: audrea.griggs@jocogov.org

Johnson County Transit [The JO]

1800 West 56 Highway, Olathe, KS 66061
Tel: (913) 715-8300 Fax: (913) 715-2453 Internet: www.thejo.com

Director of Transportation **(Vacant)** . . . . (913) 715-8352

Johnson County Wastewater [JCW]

11811 South Sunset Drive, Suite 2500, Olathe, KS 66061
Tel: (913) 715-8500 Fax: (913) 715-8501 Internet: www.jcw.org

General Manager **John P. O'Neil** . . . . (913) 715-8570

Airport Commission

One New Century Parkway, New Century, KS 66031
Tel: (913) 715-6000 Fax: (913) 715-6008 Internet: jcac.jocogov.org

Executive Director **Colin McKee** . . . . (913) 715-6000
Deputy Director **Larry Peet** . . . . (913) 715-6000

Johnson County Developmental Supports [JCDS]

10501 Lackman Road, Lenexa, KS 66219
Tel: (913) 826-2626 Fax: (913) 826-2627 Internet: www.jcds.org

Executive Director **Chad VonAhnen** . . . . (913) 826-2626

Johnson County Library

9875 West 87th Street, Overland Park, KS 66212
Tel: (913) 495-2400 Internet: www.jocolibrary.org

County Librarian **Sean Casserley** . . . . (913) 495-2400
E-mail: sean.casserley@jocogov.org
Deputy County Librarian **Tricia Suellentrop** . . . . (913) 495-2488
E-mail: patricia.suellentrop@jocogov.org

Parks and Recreation District [JCPRD]

7904 Renner Road, Shawnee, KS 66219
Tel: (913) 438-7275 E-mail: info@jcprd.com Internet: www.jcprd.com

○ Chair **George J. Schlagel** . . . . (913) 438-7275
E-mail: chairman@jcprd.com
○ Vice Chair **Paul W. Snider** . . . . (913) 438-7275
E-mail: vicechair@jcprd.com
○ Secretary **Nancy Wallerstein** . . . . (913) 438-7275
E-mail: Secretary@jcprd.com

Parks and Recreation District *continued*

○ Treasurer **Michael Priner** . . . . (913) 438-7275
E-mail: treasurer@jcprd.com
○ Assistant Secretary **Steve Baru** . . . . (913) 438-7275
E-mail: assistant_Secretary@jcprd.com
○ Assistant Treasurer **Chris Carroll** . . . . (913) 438-7275
E-mail: assistant_treasurer@jcprd.com
○ Board Member **R. Eric Hughes** . . . . (913) 438-7275

District Attorney's Office

100 North Kansas, Olathe, KS 66061
Tel: (913) 715-3000 Fax: (913) 715-3050 Internet: http://da.jocogov.org/

★ District Attorney **Stephen M. "Steve" Howe** . . . . (913) 715-3000
Term Expires: November 6, 2016
E-mail: steve.howe@jocogov.org
Education: Washburn 1985 BA

Sheriff's Office

588 E Santa Fe, Olathe, KS 66061
Tel: (913) 715-5800 Internet: www.jocosheriff.org

★ Sheriff **Frank Denning** . . . . (913) 715-5505
Term Expires: November 6, 2016
E-mail: frank.denning@jocogov.org
Education: Ottawa U
Undersheriff **Kevin Cavanaugh** . . . . (913) 715-5800
E-mail: kevin.cavanaugh@jocogov.org

Johnson County Election Office

2101 East Kansas City Road, Olathe, KS 66061
Tel: (913) 782-3441 Fax: (913) 791-1753
E-mail: election@jocoelection.org Internet: www.jocoelection.org

Election Commissioner **Ronnie Metsker** . . . . (913) 715-6850
Term Expires: August 2016
Date of Birth: May 9, 1950
Deputy Election Commissioner **Debbie Tyrrel** . . . . (913) 715-6827
Assistant Election Commissioner **Kathy Spann** . . . . (913) 715-6841
Assistant Election Commissioner **Jessica White** . . . . (913) 715-6828

County of Kanawha, West Virginia

P.O. Box 3627, Charleston, WV 25336
Tel: (304) 357-0100 (Information) Fax: (304) 357-0788
Internet: www.kanawha.us

County Seat: Charleston **Election Type:** Partisan **Population:** 188,332 (2015)

Office of the County Commission

P.O. Box 3627, Charleston, WV 25336
Fax: (304) 357-0788

★ President **W. Kent Carper** (D) . . . . (304) 357-0109
Term Expires: December 31, 2018
E-mail: kentcarper@kanawha.us
Education: West Virginia State Col 1975 BA; Ohio Northern 1978 JD
★ Commissioner **David Hardy** (D) . . . . (304) 357-4673
Term Expires: December 31, 2016
E-mail: davidhardy@kanawha.us
Education: West Virginia Tech 1980 BS; Tennessee 1983 JD
★ Commissioner **Henry C. "Hoppy" Shores** (R) . . . . (304) 357-0139
Term Expires: December 31, 2020
E-mail: hoppyshores@kanawha.us
Education: West Virginia 1954 BS

(continued on next page)

★ Elected Official ▲ Appointed by Legislature ▼ Appointed by Governor ▶ Appointed by Board or Commission ● Appointed by Judge
■ Appointed by Mayor △ Appointed by Freeholders ▽ Appointed by Supervisor ▷ Appointed by County Executive ○ Appointed by Council

Office of the County Commission *continued*

▶ County Manager **Jennifer Sayre** . . . . . . (304) 357-0101
E-mail: jennifer@kanawha.us

▶ Chief Fiscal Officer **Kim Fleck** . . . . . . (304) 357-0179

Office of the Fiduciary Supervisor/Probate Office

P.O. Box 3627, Charleston, WV 25336
Fax: (304) 357-0426

▶ Fiduciary Supervisor **Andrew Gunnoe** . . . . . . (304) 357-0125
E-mail: andrewgunnoe@kanawha.us

Emergency Services Office

P.O. Box 3627, Charleston, WV 25336

▶ Director **Dale Petry** . . . . . . (304) 357-0117
E-mail: dalepetry@kanawha.us

Parks and Recreation Commission

2000 Coonskin Dr., Charleston, WV 25311
Fax: (304) 344-2696

Director **Jeff Hutchinson** . . . . . . (304) 341-8000

Planning and Community Development Office

P.O. Box 3627, Charleston, WV 25336
Fax: (304) 357-0572

▶ Director **Steve Neddo** . . . . . . (304) 357-0570
E-mail: steveneddo@kanawha.us

Purchasing Office

P.O. Box 3627, Charleston, WV 25336
Fax: (304) 357-0595 E-mail: purchasing@kancocomm.com

▶ Director **Jerie Whitehead** . . . . . . (304) 357-0118
E-mail: jeriewhitehead@kanawha.us

Office of the Assessor

409 Virginia, Suite E, Charleston, WV 25301
Fax: (304) 357-0551 E-mail: assessor@kanawha.us

★ Assessor **Sallie Robinson** (D) . . . . . . (304) 357-0250
Term Expires: December 31, 2016

Office of the County Clerk

P.O. Box 3226, Charleston, WV 25332-3226
Fax: (304) 357-0585 Fax: (304) 357-0588 (Voters' Registration Fax)

★ County Clerk **Vera McCormick** (R) . . . . . . (304) 357-0130
Term Expires: December 31, 2016
E-mail: veramccormick@kanawha.us

Office of the Prosecuting Attorney

W. Kent Carper Justice and Public Safety Complex,
301 Virginia Street, East, Charleston, WV 25301
Fax: (304) 357-0342

★ Prosecuting Attorney **Chuck Miller** . . . . . . (304) 357-0300
Term Expires: December 31, 2016
E-mail: cmiller@kanawhaprosecutor.com

Chief of Staff **(Vacant)** . . . . . . (304) 357-0777

Office of the Sheriff/County Treasurer

P.O. Box 75087, Charleston, WV 25375
Fax: (304) 357-0516

★ Sheriff/County Treasurer **John Rutherford** (D) . . . . . . (304) 357-0216
Term Expires: December 31, 2016

Chief Deputy, Law Enforcement Division
Mike Rutherford (D) . . . . . . (304) 357-0150

Office of the Sheriff/County Treasurer *continued*

Chief Deputy, Legal Process Division **Dave Ross** . . . . . . (304) 357-0200
E-mail: dave.ross@kanawha.us

Chief Deputy, Tax Division **Allen Bleigh** . . . . . . (304) 357-0290
E-mail: allenbleigh@kanawha.us

County of Kent, Michigan

County Bldg., 300 Monroe Ave., NW, Grand Rapids, MI 49503-2288
Tel: (616) 632-7570 (Information) Internet: www.accessKent.com

County Seat: Grand Rapids **Election Type:** Partisan
Population: 636,369 (2015)

Office of the Board of Commissioners

County Bldg., 300 Monroe Ave., NW, Grand Rapids, MI 49503-2288
Tel: (616) 632-7580 Fax: (616) 632-7585

★ Chair **Jim Saalfeld** (R-District 11) . . . . . . (616) 464-1939
Term Expires: December 31, 2016
E-mail: jim.saalfeld@kentcountymi.gov

★ Vice Chair **Shana Shroll** (R-District 19) . . . . . . (616) 292-4642
Term Expires: December 31, 2016
E-mail: shana.shroll@kentcountymi.gov

★ Vice Chair (Minority Party)
Carol M. Hennessy (D-District 14) . . . . . . (616) 453-9167
Term Expires: December 31, 2016

★ Commissioner **Theodore "Ted" Vonk** (R-District 1) . . . . . . (616) 874-2604
Term Expires: December 31, 2016
E-mail: ted.vonk@kentcountymi.gov

★ Commissioner **Thomas Antor** (R-District 2) . . . . . . (616) 887-7210
Term Expires: December 31, 2016
E-mail: tom.antor@kentcountymi.gov

★ Commissioner **Roger Morgan** (R-District 3) . . . . . . (616) 866-4264
Term Expires: December 31, 2016
E-mail: roger.morgan@kentcountymi.gov

★ Commissioner **Diane Jones** (R-District 4) . . . . . . (616) 874-8740
Term Expires: December 31, 2016
E-mail: diane.jones@kentcountymi.gov

★ Commissioner **Mandy Bolter** (R-District 5) . . . . . . (616) 295-7909
Term Expires: December 31, 2016
E-mail: mandy.bolter@kentcountymi.gov

★ Commissioner **Stan Stek** (R-District 6) . . . . . . (616) 776-6324
Term Expires: December 31, 2016
E-mail: stan.stek@kentcountymi.gov

★ Commissioner **Stan Ponstein** (R-District 7) . . . . . . (616) 726-2331
Term Expires: December 31, 2016
E-mail: stan.ponstein@kentcountymi.gov

★ Commissioner **Harold J. Voorhees** (R-District 8) . . . . . . (616) 534-1876
Term Expires: December 31, 2016
E-mail: harold.voorhees@kentcountymi.gov

★ Commissioner **Matt Kallman** (R-District 9) . . . . . . (616) 915-5098
Term Expires: December 31, 2016
E-mail: matt.kallman@kentcountymi.gov

★ Commissioner **Emily Post Brieve** (R-District 10) . . . . . . (616) 502-5010
Term Expires: December 31, 2016
E-mail: emily.brieve@kentcountymi.gov

★ Commissioner **Harold Mast** (R-District 12) . . . . . . (616) 532-5686
Term Expires: December 31, 2016
E-mail: harold.mast@kentcountymi.gov

★ Commissioner **Richard Vander Molen** (R-District 13) . . . (616) 455-1562
Term Expires: December 31, 2016
E-mail: dick.vandermolen@kentcountymi.gov

★ Commissioner **Jim Talen** (D-District 15) . . . . . . (616) 454-2243
Term Expires: December 31, 2016
E-mail: jim.talen@kentcountymi.gov
Education: Calvin Col 1976 BAEIEd

★ Commissioner **David Bulkowski** (D-District 16) . . . . . . (616) 560-2293
Term Expires: December 31, 2016
E-mail: dave.bulkowski@kentcountymi.gov

★ Elected Official ▲ Appointed by Legislature ▼ Appointed by Governor ▶ Appointed by Board or Commission ● Appointed by Judge
■ Appointed by Mayor △ Appointed by Freeholders ▽ Appointed by Supervisor ▷ Appointed by County Executive ○ Appointed by Council

Office of the Board of Commissioners *continued*

★Commissioner **Candace E. Chivis** (D-District 17) .... (616) 248-7896
Term Expires: December 31, 2016
E-mail: candace.chivis@kentcountymi.gov

★Commissioner **Dan Koorndyk** (R-District 18) .... (616) 458-8934
Term Expires: December 31, 2016
E-mail: dan.koorndyk@kentcountymi.gov

Executive Assistant to the Board **Pam Van Keuren** ...... (616) 632-7580
E-mail: pam.vankeuren@kentcountymi.gov

Office of the County Administrator

County Bldg., 300 Monroe Ave., NW, Grand Rapids, MI 49503-2288

▶County Administrator/Controller **Daryl Delabbio** .... (616) 632-7570
E-mail: daryl.delabbio@kentcountymi.gov

Assistant County Administrator **Wayman P. Britt** .... (616) 632-7570
E-mail: wayman.britt@kentcountymi.gov

Assistant County Administrator **Mary Swanson** .... (616) 632-7570
E-mail: mary.swanson@kentcountymi.gov

Community Liaison and Communications Director
Lisa LaPlante .... (616) 632-7182
E-mail: Lisa.LaPlante@kentcountymi.gov

Office of Community Corrections [OCC]

180 Ottawa NW, Grand Rapids, MI 49503
Tel: (616) 632-5350 Fax: (616) 632-5369

Director **Timothy "Tim" Bouwhuis** .... (616) 632-5327

Office of Cooperative Extension (Michigan State University)

775 Ball Avenue, NE, Grand Rapids, MI 49503-1992
Fax: (616) 336-3836

District Coordinator **Betty Blase** .... (616) 632-7887

Extension Administrator **Helen Gutierrez** .... (616) 632-7875
E-mail: helen.gutierrez@kentcountymi.gov

Office of the Register of Probate

Courthouse, 180 Ottawa NW, Suite 2500, Grand Rapids, MI 49503

Register of Probate **Susan Flakne** .... (616) 632-5422

Central Services Department

County Bldg., 300 Monroe Ave., NW, Grand Rapids, MI 49503

Director **P.J. Bevelacqua** .... (616) 632-7700

Community Development Department

82 Ionia Avenue, Northwest, Suite 390, Grand Rapids, MI 49503-3036
Tel: (616) 632-7400 Fax: (616) 632-7405

Director **Matthew Van Zetten** .... (616) 632-7404

Clerk **Courtney Hammond** .... (616) 632-7411
E-mail: courtney.hammond@kentcountymi.gov

Facilities Management Department

County Administration Building, 300 Monroe Ave. NW,
Grand Rapids, MI 49503-2206
Fax: (616) 632-7715

Director **Al Jano** .... (616) 262-3172

Fiscal Services Department

300 Monroe Avenue, N.W., Grand Rapids, MI 49503

Director **Stephen W. "Steve" Duarte** .... (616) 632-7570

Budget Director **Marvin Van Nortwick** .... (616) 632-7677
E-mail: marvin.vannortwick@kentcountymi.gov

Purchasing Manager **Calvin Brinks** .... (616) 632-7722

Department of Health and Human Services

121 Franklin Street SE, Suite 200, Grand Rapids, MI 49507
Tel: (616) 248-1000 Fax: (616) 248-1059

▼Board Chair **Bruce McCoy** .... (616) 248-1695

▼Vice Chair **Carla Sikkema** .... (616) 248-1695

▶Board Member **Jerry O. Kooiman** (R) .... (616) 248-1695

Director **Nancy Marshall** .... (616) 248-1002

Child Welfare Director **Salvator Selden-Johnson** ...... (616) 248-1682
Fax: (616) 248-1034

Kent County Health Department [KCHD]

700 Fuller, NE, Grand Rapids, MI 49503-1996
Tel: (616) 632-7100 Fax: (616) 632-7083
Internet: www.accesskent.com/health/healthdepartment/

Director/Health Officer **Adam London** .... (616) 632-7280

Kent County Animal Shelter [KCAS]

740 Fuller Avenue, NE, Grand Rapids, MI 49503-1996
Tel: (616) 632-7300 Fax: (616) 632-7324

Director **Carly Luttmann** .... (616) 632-7300

Human Resources Department

County Building, 300 Monroe Avenue, N.W., Grand Rapids, MI 49503
Tel: (616) 632-7440 (Information) Fax: (616) 632-7445
E-mail: jobs@kentcountymi.gov Internet: www.accesskent.com/hr

Director **Amy Rollston** .... (616) 632-7477
E-mail: amy.rollston@kentcountymi.gov

Information Technology Department [IT]

320 Ottawa Avenue, Northwest, Grand Rapids, MI 49503
Tel: (616) 632-6500 Fax: (616) 632-6505

▶Director **Craig Paull** .... (616) 632-6500
E-mail: craig.paull@kentcountymi.gov

Department of Public Works

1500 Scribner Avenue, NW, Grand Rapids, MI 49504-3233
Fax: (616) 632-7925

Director **Darwin Baas** .... (616) 632-7920

Department of Veterans' Affairs

836 Fuller Avenue, Grand Rapids, MI 49503
Fax: (616) 632-5723

Director **Carrie Jo Anderson** .... (616) 632-5722

Gerald R. Ford International Airport

Kent County Department of Aeronautics, 5500 44th St., SE,
Grand Rapids, MI 49512
Fax: (616) 233-6025 Internet: www.flyford.org

Executive Director **(Vacant)** .... (616) 233-6000

Deputy Executive Director **Phillip E. Johnson** .... (616) 233-6000
Education: Azusa Pacific BSBA; USC MSSM

Facilities Director **Thomas R. Ecklund** .... (616) 233-6000
E-mail: tecklund@grr.org

Finance and Administration Director **Brian Picardat** ..... (616) 233-6000
E-mail: bpicardat@grr.org

Marketing and Communications Manager
Tara Hernandez .... (616) 233-6053
E-mail: thernandez@grr.org

Public Safety and Operations Director **Lisa M. Carr** ..... (616) 233-6000
E-mail: lcarr@grr.org

Greater Grand Rapids Convention Bureau

Grand Center, Grand Rapids, MI 49503-2288
Fax: (616) 632-7585

County Representative **Jim Saalfeld** (R) .... (616) 632-7580

★Elected Official ▲Appointed by Legislature ▼Appointed by Governor ▶Appointed by Board or Commission ●Appointed by Judge
■Appointed by Mayor △Appointed by Freeholders ▽Appointed by Supervisor ▷Appointed by County Executive ○Appointed by Council

Kent County Road Commission

1500 Scribner Avenue, NW, Grand Rapids, MI 49504-3299
Fax: (616) 242-6968 Internet: www.kentcountyroads.net

Chairman **Mark E. Rambo** . . . . (616) 242-6960
Managing Director **Steven A. Warren** . . . . (616) 242-6960
Executive Secretary **Diane Martin** . . . . (616) 242-6960
E-mail: dmartin@kentcountyroads.net

Office of the County Clerk and Register of Deeds

County Bldg., 300 Monroe Ave., NW, Grand Rapids, MI 49503-2288
Fax: (616) 632-7645

★County Clerk and Register of Deeds
Mary Hollinrake (R) . . . . (616) 632-7640
Term Expires: December 31, 2016
E-mail: mary.hollinrake@kentcountymi.gov
Chief Deputy County Clerk **Jerome "Jerry" Czaja** . . . . . . (616) 632-7640
E-mail: jerome.czaja@kentcountymi.gov
Deputy County Clerk (Courts Division) **Nicholas Little** . . (616) 632-5480
E-mail: nicholas.little@kentcountymi.gov
Deputy Register of Deeds **Jerome "Jerry" Czaja** . . . . (616) 632-7610
Elections Director **Susan "Sue" de Steiguer** . . . . (616) 632-7640

COUNTIES

Office of the Drain Commissioner

1500 Scribner Avenue, NW, Grand Rapids, MI 49504-3233
Fax: (616) 336-3575

★Drain Commissioner **William R. "Bill" Byl** . . . . (616) 632-7910
Term Expires: December 31, 2016
E-mail: bill.byl@kentcountymi.gov
Deputy Drain Commissioner **Douglas "Doug" Sporte** . . . (616) 632-7910

Office of the Prosecuting Attorney

82 Ionia Avenue, NW, Suite 450, Grand Rapids, MI 49503
Fax: (616) 632-6714

★Chief Prosecuting Attorney **William A. Forsyth** (R) . . . . . (616) 632-6710
Term Expires: December 31, 2016

Office of the Treasurer

County Building, 300 Monroe Avenue, NW,
Grand Rapids, MI 49503-2288
P.O. Box Y, Grand Rapids, MI 49501
Fax: (616) 632-7505

★Treasurer **Kenneth D. Parrish** (R) . . . . (616) 632-7500
Term Expires: December 31, 2016
E-mail: ken.parrish@kentcountymi.gov
Education: Michigan State BA; Grand Valley State MBA

Sheriff Department

701 Ball Avenue, NE, Grand Rapids, MI 49503
Fax: (616) 632-6122

★Sheriff **Lawrence A. "Larry" Stelma** (R) . . . . (616) 632-6100
Term Expires: December 31, 2016

Office of Emergency Management and Homeland Security

701 Ball Ave., NE, Grand Rapids, MI 49503
Fax: (616) 632-6260

Director **Jack Stewart** . . . . (616) 632-6255
E-mail: jack.stewart@kentcountymi.gov

County of Kern, California

Administrative Center, 1115 Truxtun Avenue, Bakersfield, CA 93301

County Seat: Bakersfield **Election Type:** Nonpartisan
Population: 882,176 (2015)

Office of the Board of Supervisors

Administrative Center, 1115 Truxtun Avenue, 5th Floor,
Bakersfield, CA 93301
Internet: www.co.kern.ca.us/bos

★Chairman **Mick K. Gleason** (District 1) . . . . (661) 868-3650
Term Expires: January 2, 2017 Fax: (661) 868-3657
E-mail: district1@co.kern.ca.us
★Supervisor **Zack Scrivner** (District 2) . . . . (661) 868-3660
Term Expires: January 5, 2019 Fax: (661) 868-3666
E-mail: district2@co.kern.ca.us
Education: UC Santa Barbara BA
★Supervisor **Mike Maggard** (District 3) . . . . (661) 868-3670
Term Expires: January 5, 2019 Fax: (661) 868-3677
E-mail: district3@co.kern.ca.us
Education: Cal State (Bakersfield) BS
★Supervisor **David Couch** (District 4) . . . . (661) 868-3680
Term Expires: January 2, 2017 Fax: (661) 868-3688
E-mail: district4@co.kern.ca.us
★Supervisor **Leticia Perez** (District 5) . . . . (661) 868-3690
Term Expires: January 2, 2017 Fax: (661) 868-3645
E-mail: district5@co.kern.ca.us
▽Clerk of the Board **Kathleen Krause** . . . . (661) 868-3585
E-mail: clerkofboard@co.kern.ca.us Fax: (661) 868-3636

Administrative Office

Administrative Center, 1115 Truxtun Ave., Bakersfield, CA 93301-4617
Tel: (661) 868-3198 Fax: (661) 868-3190
Internet: www.co.kern.ca.us/cao

▽County Administrative Officer **John Nilon** . . . . (661) 868-3198
E-mail: jnilon@co.kern.ca.us
Education: Cal State (Bakersfield) BA, MPA
Assistant County Administrative Officer
Teresa Hitchcock . . . . (661) 868-3172
E-mail: thitchcock@co.kern.ca.us
Assistant County Administrative Officer for Fiscal and Administrative Services **Nancy M. Lawson** . . . . (661) 868-3170
E-mail: lawsonn@co.kern.ca.us
Employee Relations Officer **Devin Brown** . . . . (661) 868-3178

Office of the County Counsel

Administrative Center, 1115 Truxtun Avenue, 4th Floor,
Bakersfield, CA 93301
Fax: (661) 868-3809 Internet: www.co.kern.ca.us/cc

▽County Counsel **Theresa A. Goldner** . . . . (661) 868-3800
E-mail: tgoldner@co.kern.ca.us
Education: UC Davis 1979; UCLA 1982 JD
Chief Deputy County Counsel, Advisory
Gurujodha Khalasa . . . . (661) 868-3846
Chief Deputy County Counsel, Employment Law
Margo A. Raison . . . . (661) 868-3876
Chief Deputy County Counsel, Healthcare
Karen S. Barnes . . . . (661) 868-3817
Chief Deputy County Counsel, Litigation
Charles F. Collins . . . . (661) 868-3815
Assistant County Counsel **Mark L. Nations** . . . . (661) 868-3818

Office of the Public Defender

1315 Truxtun Avenue, Bakersfield, CA 93301
Fax: (661) 868-4788 Internet: www.co.kern.ca.us/pubdef

▶Public Defender **Konrad Moore** . . . . (661) 868-4799
Chief Deputy Public Defender **Dominic Eyherabide** . . . . . (661) 868-4799

★Elected Official ▲Appointed by Legislature ▼Appointed by Governor ▶Appointed by Board or Commission ●Appointed by Judge
■Appointed by Mayor △Appointed by Freeholders ▽Appointed by Supervisor ▷Appointed by County Executive ○Appointed by Council

Department of Aging and Adult Services
5357 Truxtun Avenue, Bakersfield, CA 93309
Fax: (661) 868-1001 Internet: www.co.kern.ca.us/aas

▽ Director **Lito Morillo** . . . . . (661) 868-1051
E-mail: morillom@co.kern.ca.us
Education: Cal State (Bakersfield) BA

Department of Agriculture and Measurement Standards
1001 S. Mt. Vernon Ave., Bakersfield, CA 93307-2851
Fax: (661) 868-6301 E-mail: agcomm@co.kern.ca.us
Internet: www.kernag.com

▽ Agricultural Commissioner/Sealer of Weights and Measures **Ruben J. Arroyo** . . . . . (661) 868-6300
E-mail: arroyor@co.kern.ca.us
Assistant Agricultural Commissioner/Sealer of Weights and Measures **Glenn Fankhauser** . . . . . (661) 868-6300

Employers' Training Resource [ETR]
1600 East Belle Terrace, Bakersfield, CA 93307
Fax: (661) 336-6855

Director **Teresa Hitchcock** . . . . . (661) 336-6956
Deputy Director **Bill Stevenson** . . . . . (661) 635-2758
E-mail: bills@co.kern.ca.us

Roads Department
2700 M Street, Room 400, Bakersfield, CA 93301-2370
Fax: (661) 862-8851 E-mail: roads@co.kern.ca.us

Director **Craig M. Pope** . . . . . (661) 862-8850
E-mail: cpope@co.kern.ca.us

Planning and Community Department
2700 M Street, Room 100, Bakersfield, CA 93301-2370
Fax: (661) 862-8601 E-mail: planning@co.kern.ca.us

Director **Lorelei H. Oviatt** . . . . . (661) 862-8600
E-mail: loreleio@co.kern.ca.us

Engineering, Surveying and Permit Services Department
2700 M Street, Suite 570, Bakersfield, CA 93301-2370
Tel: (661) 862-8650 (Building Inspection Division)
Tel: (661) 862-8603 (Code Compliance Division) Fax: (661) 862-5101
E-mail: ess@co.kern.ca.us

Director **Greg Fenton** . . . . . (661) 862-5100
E-mail: gregf@co.kern.ca.us

Kern County Fire Department [KCFD]
5642 Victor Street, Bakersfield, CA 93308-4056
Fax: (661) 391-7013 Internet: www.kerncountyfire.org

▶ Fire Chief **Brian Marshall** . . . . . (661) 391-7000
E-mail: bmarshall@co.kern.ca.us
Chief Deputy **Brent Moon** . . . . . (661) 391-7000
Deputy Chief **Mike Miller** . . . . . (661) 391-7000
E-mail: mmiller@co.kern.ca.us
Deputy Chief **John Silliman** . . . . . (661) 391-7000
Deputy Chief **Benny Wofford** . . . . . (661) 391-7000
Deputy Chief **(Vacant)** . . . . . (661) 391-7000
Network Systems Administrator **Michael Clark** . . . . . (661) 391-7195
Training Officer **Charles Truvillion** . . . . . (661) 391-7111
E-mail: ctruvillion@co.kern.ca.us Fax: (661) 399-5763

General Services Department
Administrative Center, 1115 Truxtun Avenue, 3rd Floor, Bakersfield, CA 93301-4639
Fax: (661) 868-3100 Internet: www.co.kern.ca.us/gsd

▽ Assistant County Administrative Officer **Jeff R. Frapwell** . . . . . (661) 868-3000
E-mail: jfrapwell@co.kern.ca.us
Division Director **Bret Haney** . . . . . (661) 868-3063
E-mail: haneyb@co.kern.ca.us
Division Director **Geoffrey Hill** . . . . . (661) 868-3029
Division Director **Sandi Formhals** . . . . . (661) 868-3000
E-mail: formhalss@co.kern.ca.us
Division Director **John Devlin** . . . . . (661) 868-2222
General Services Manager, Purchasing **Carol Cox** . . . . . (661) 868-3000
E-mail: coxc@co.kern.ca.us
General Services Manager, Fleet **Larry Wertz** . . . . . (661) 868-6910

Department of Human Services
100 East California Avenue, Bakersfield, CA 93307
Tel: (661) 631-6000 (Information)

▶ Director (Interim) **Dena Murphy** . . . . . (661) 631-6550
E-mail: murphyd@co.kern.ca.us Fax: (661) 631-6631
Chief Deputy Director **Cindy Uetz** . . . . . (661) 633-7257
Assistant Director, Administrative Services and Program Support **Ginny Krebs** . . . . . (661) 631-6646
Assistant Director, Child Protective Services **Antanette Reed** . . . . . (661) 631-6551
Assistant Director, Employment and Financial Services **Pam Holiwell** . . . . . (661) 631-6136
Assistant Director, Fiscal Support **Susan Casterline** . . . . . (661) 334-3482
E-mail: casters@co.kern.ca.us
Human Resources Manager **Debbie Davis** . . . . . (661) 633-7373
E-mail: davisd@co.kern.ca.us
Administrative Program Assistant Director **Doris Sons** . . . (661) 631-6549
Fax: (661) 631-6631
Office Services Coordinator **Misty Gray** . . . . . (661) 633-7412
Fax: (661) 631-6631

Information Technology Services [ITS]
1215 Truxtun Avenue, Basement, Bakersfield, CA 93301
Tel: (661) 868-2222 Fax: (661) 868-2100 Internet: www.co.kern.ca.us/its

▽ Director **John Devlin** . . . . . (661) 868-2000
E-mail: devlinj@co.kern.ca.us
Division Chief, Technology Services and Telecommunications **(Vacant)** . . . . . (661) 868-2000
Division Chief, Research and Development and Special Projects **(Vacant)** . . . . . (661) 868-2294
Technical Services Manager, Application Programming, Database Administration and Operations **Ron Nakagawa** . . . . . (661) 868-2287
E-mail: nakagawa@co.kern.ca.us

Kern County Mental Health Department [KCMH]
3300 Truxtun Avenue, Suite 100, Bakersfield, CA 93301
P.O. Box 1000, Bakersfield, CA 93302-1000
Fax: (661) 868-6847 Internet: www.co.kern.ca.us/kcmh

▽ Director **William P. Walker** . . . . . (661) 868-6609
E-mail: bwalker@co.kern.ca.us
Public Information Officer **Cindy Coe** . . . . . (661) 868-6608
E-mail: ccoe@co.kern.ca.us

Parks and Recreation Department
2820 M. Street, Bakersfield, CA 93301
TTY: (800) 735-2929 Fax: (661) 868-7001 Fax: (661) 868-7062
Internet: www.co.kern.ca.us/parks

▽ Director **Robert Lerude** . . . . . (661) 868-7000
E-mail: lerudeb@co.kern.ca.us
Administrative Coordinator **John Cove** . . . . . (661) 868-7041
E-mail: covej@co.kern.ca.us

(continued on next page)

COUNTIES

★ Elected Official ▲ Appointed by Legislature ▼ Appointed by Governor ▶ Appointed by Board or Commission ● Appointed by Judge
■ Appointed by Mayor △ Appointed by Freeholders ▽ Appointed by Supervisor ▷ Appointed by County Executive ○ Appointed by Council

Parks and Recreation Department *continued*

Business Manager **Laura Akey** ....(661) 868-7023
E-mail: akeyl@co.kern.ca.us
Park Planner **John Laybourn** ....(661) 868-7022
Parks Superintendent **Larry Swan** ....(661) 868-7010

Human Resources

Administrative Center, 1115 Truxtun Avenue, 1st Floor, Bakersfield, CA 93301
Fax: (661) 868-3928 E-mail: personnel@co.kern.ca.us

Director **Devin Brown** ....(661) 868-3480

Probation Department

2005 Ridge Road, Bakersfield, CA 93305
P.O. Box 3309, Bakersfield, CA 93385-3309
Tel: (661) 868-4100 Fax: (661) 868-4199
Internet: www.kernprobation.com

Chief Probation Officer **TR Merickel** ....(661) 868-4102

Department of Public Health

1800 Mt. Vernon Avenue, Bakersfield, CA 93306-3302
Tel: (661) 868-0502 (Information) Internet: www.kernpublichealth.com

▽ Director **Matthew "Matt" Constantine** ....(661) 868-0301
E-mail: mattc@co.kern.ca.us
Education: Cal State (Northridge) BS, MS
Deputy Director **Brynn Meek** ....(661) 868-0299
Health Officer **Claudia Jonah** ....(661) 868-0413

Emergency Medical Services Department [EMS]

1800 Mt. Vernon Avenue, Bakersfield, CA 93306-3302
Fax: (661) 868-0225 Internet: www.co.kern.ca.us/ems

Director **Edward "Ed" Hill** ....(661) 868-5210

Environmental Health Services Department

2700 M Street, Suite 300, Bakersfield, CA 93301-2370
Fax: (661) 862-8701 E-mail: eh@co.kern.ca.us
Internet: www.co.kern.ca.us/eh

Environmental Health Division Director **Donna Fenton** .. (661) 862-8726

Veterans' Services Department

1120 Golden State Ave., Bakersfield, CA 93301
Fax: (661) 631-0519 E-mail: kernvets@co.kern.ca.us
Internet: www.co.kern.ca.us/veterans

▽ Veterans Services Officer **Richard "Dick" Taylor** ....(661) 868-7300
E-mail: ktrich@co.kern.ca.us

Farm and Home Advisor/University of California Cooperative Extension

1031 S. Mt. Vernon Ave., Bakersfield, CA 93307
Fax: (661) 868-6200

▽ Director **Brian Marsh** ....(661) 868-6212
E-mail: bhmarsh@ucdavis.edu

Kern County Board of Trade

2101 Oak Street, Bakersfield, CA 93301
Fax: (661) 861-2017 E-mail: info@visitkern.com
Internet: www.visitkern.com

▶ Executive Director **Teresa Hitchcock** ....(661) 868-5376

Kern County Library [KCL]

701 Truxtun Avenue, Bakersfield, CA 93301
Fax: (661) 868-0799 Internet: www.kerncountylibrary.org

Director **Nancy Kerr** ....(661) 868-3198
Assistant Director, Support Services **Christie Kennedy** ... (661) 868-0700
Assistant Director, Public Services **Andrea Apple** .... (661) 868-0700

Kern County Museum

3801 Chester Avenue, Bakersfield, CA 93301
Fax: (661) 322-6415 Internet: www.kcmuseum.org

Director **(Vacant)** ....(661) 437-3330

Kern Medical Center

1700 Mount Vernon Avenue, Bakersfield, CA 93306
Tel: (661) 326-2000 Fax: (661) 326-2100
Internet: www.kernmedicalcenter.com

▽ Chief Executive Officer **Russell V. Judd** ....(661) 326-2000
Chief Financial Officer **Andrew Cantu** ....(661) 326-2000

Office of the Assessor-Recorder

Administrative Center, 1115 Truxtun Avenue, 3rd Floor, Bakersfield, CA 93301-4839
Fax: (661) 868-3209 Internet: www.recorder.co.kern.ca.us

★ Assessor/Recorder **Jon Lifquist** ....(661) 868-3485
Term Expires: January 2019
Assistant Assessor **Lee Smith** ....(661) 868-3260
Assistant Recorder **Brian Pace** ....(661) 868-6411
LAN Administrator **Aaron Deemer** ....(661) 868-3314
E-mail: deemera@co.kern.ca.us
Confidential Administrative Assistant **Heather Bullard** ... (661) 868-3382
E-mail: Bullardh@co.kern.ca.us

Office of the Auditor-Controller-County Clerk

Administrative Center, 1115 Truxtun Ave., Bakersfield, CA 93301-4617
Fax: (661) 868-3560 Internet: www.co.kern.ca.us/auditor

★ Auditor-Controller-County Clerk **Mary Bedard** ....(661) 868-3599
Term Expires: January 3, 2019
E-mail: bedardm@co.kern.ca.us
Administrative Assistant **Shawn DeSchutter** ....(661) 868-3510

Office of the District Attorney

1215 Truxtun Avenue, 4th Floor, Bakersfield, CA 93301
Fax: (661) 868-2700 E-mail: da@co.kern.ca.us
Internet: www.co.kern.ca.us/da

★ District Attorney **Lisa S. Green** ....(661) 868-2340
Term Expires: January 2019
Education: Cal State (Fresno) 1980; San Diego 1983 JD
Administrative Assistant **Christy King** ....(661) 868-2340
Assistant District Attorney **Scott J. Spielman** ....(661) 868-2340
Education: Cal State (Fresno); McGeorge 1993 JD

Office of the Sheriff-Coroner

1350 Norris Road, Bakersfield, CA 93308
Fax: (661) 391-7515 Internet: www.kernsheriff.com

★ Sheriff-Coroner **Donny Youngblood** ....(661) 391-7771
Term Expires: January 2019
E-mail: sheriff@kernsheriff.com
Undersheriff **RoseMary Wahl** ....(661) 391-7549
E-mail: wahlr@kernsheriff.com
Chief Deputy **Shelly Castaneda** ....(661) 391-7600
E-mail: castaneda@kernsheriff.com
Chief Deputy **Curtis Cornelison** ....(661) 391-7535
E-mail: cornelison@kernsheriff.com
Chief Deputy **Brian Wheeler** ....(661) 391-7539
Chief Deputy **Kevin Zimmermann** ....(661) 391-7533
E-mail: zimmermannk@kernsheriff.com
Technology Manager **Jeff Huot** ....(661) 391-7698
Fax: (661) 391-7674

★ Elected Official ▲ Appointed by Legislature ▼ Appointed by Governor ▶ Appointed by Board or Commission ● Appointed by Judge
■ Appointed by Mayor △ Appointed by Freeholders ▽ Appointed by Supervisor ▷ Appointed by County Executive ○ Appointed by Council

Coroner Section
1832 Flower Street, Bakersfield, CA 93305-4144
Fax: (661) 868-0149

Commander **Justin Fleeman** .... (661) 635-1323

Office of the Treasurer-Tax Collector
Administrative Center, 1115 Truxton Avenue, 2nd Floor, Bakersfield, CA 93301-4639
Fax: (661) 868-3409 E-mail: 2servu@co.kern.ca.us
Internet: http://www.kcttc.co.kern.ca.us

★ Treasurer-Tax Collector **Jordan Kaufman** .... (661) 868-3490
Term Expires: January 2019
E-mail: jkaufman@co.kern.ca.us
Education: Cal Poly San Luis Obispo 1992 BS
Administrative Assistant **Rocio Mosqueda** .... (661) 868-3417
E-mail: mosquedar@co.kern.ca.us
Assistant Treasurer-Tax Collector **Chase Nunneley** ...... (661) 868-3490
Financial Services Chief and Chief Investment Officer
Bret Black .... (661) 868-3490
E-mail: blackb@co.kern.ca.us
Information Technology Services Supervisor **Eric Pitts** ... (661) 868-3490
E-mail: pittse@co.kern.ca.us

Kern County Superintendent of Schools
1300 17th St., Bakersfield, CA 93301
Fax: (661) 636-4130 Internet: www.kern.org

Superintendent of Schools **Christine Lizardi Frazier** ..... (661) 636-4624
Education: Arizona State; Cal State (Bakersfield) 1985 MEd; U Pacific 2006 EdD

County of King, Washington
401 Fifth Avenue, Seattle, WA 98104
Tel: (206) 263-9600 (Information) Internet: www.kingcounty.gov

County Seat: Seattle **Election Type:** Nonpartisan
Population: 2,117,125 (2015)

Office of the County Executive
401 Fifth Avenue, Suite 800, Seattle, WA 98104
Tel: (206) 296-9600 Fax: (206) 296-0194
Internet: www.kingcounty.gov/exec

★ County Executive **Dow Constantine** .... (206) 296-4040
Term Expires: December 31, 2017
E-mail: kcexec@kingcounty.gov
Date of Birth: November 1961
Education: Washington U (MO) 1989 JD, 1992 MA
Executive Assistant to the County Executive
Jennifer Huston .... (206) 263-9625
E-mail: jennifer.huston@kingcounty.gov
Deputy County Executive **Fred Jarrett** .... (206) 263-9600
Education: Washington State; Seattle
Chief of Operations **Rhonda Berry** .... (206) 263-9661
E-mail: rhonda.berry@kingcounty.gov
Chief of Staff **Sung Yang** .... (206) 263-9613
E-mail: sung.yang@kingcounty.gov
Education: U Washington; U Ulster 1993 JD
Deputy Chief of Staff **(Vacant)** .... (206) 263-9615
▷ County Administrative Officer **Caroline L. Whalen** ...... (206) 263-9750
E-mail: caroline.whalen@kingcounty.gov Fax: (206) 296-3829
Communications Director **(Vacant)** .... (206) 263-9600
Customer Service Director **Natasha Jones** .... (206) 263-9623
Education: Pomona BA; U Phoenix MBA
Policy and Strategic Initiatives Director **Carrie S. Cihak** .. (206) 263-9634

Office of Labor Relations
401 Fifth Avenue, Suite 800, Seattle, WA 98104
Tel: (206) 263-8653 Fax: (206) 205-1395
Internet: www.kingcounty.gov/exec/laborrelations.aspx

Director (Interim) **Gerry Topping** .... (206) 263-8653

Office of Performance, Strategy and Budget [PSB]
401 Fifth Avenue, Suite 810, Seattle, WA 98104
Fax: (206) 296-3462 Internet: www.kingcounty.gov/exec/psb.aspx

▷ Director **Dwight D. Dively** .... (206) 263-9783
E-mail: dwight.dively@kingcounty.gov
Confidential Secretary **Sondra McCaw** .... (206) 263-8494
E-mail: sondra.mccaw@kingcounty.gov
Deputy Director **Jonathan Swift** .... (206) 263-9699
Deputy Director **Michael Jacobson** .... (206) 263-9622

Department of Adult and Juvenile Detention [DAJD]
500 Fifth Avenue, Seattle, WA 98104
Tel: (206) 477-2300 Fax: (206) 296-0570

▷ Director **William Hayes** .... (206) 477-2300
E-mail: william.hayes@kingcounty.gov
Deputy Director **Hikari Tamura** .... (206) 447-2351
Facility Commander (Kent) **Corinna Hyatt** .... (206) 477-2804
Facility Commander (Seattle) **Gordon Karlsson** .... (206) 477-5050
Chief of Administration **Steven Larsen** .... (206) 477-2339
E-mail: steven.larsen@kingcounty.gov
Community Corrections Division Director
Saudia Abdullah .... (206) 477-0652
Juvenile Detention Division Director **Pam Jones** .... (206) 205-9620
1211 E. Alder St., Seattle, WA 98122
Information Technology Service Delivery Manager
Mike Holland .... (206) 477-2365
E-mail: mike.holland@kingcounty.gov Fax: (206) 296-0570
Training Manager **Hikari Tamura** .... (206) 477-2351
E-mail: hikari.tamura@kingcounty.gov Fax: (206) 296-0570

Department of Community and Human Services [DCHS]
401 Fifth Avenue, Suite 10, Seattle, WA 98104
Tel: (206) 263-9100 Fax: (206) 296-5260 E-mail: dchs@kingcounty.gov
Internet: www.kingcounty.gov/dchs

▷ Director **Adrienne E. Quinn** Room 600 .... (206) 263-1491
E-mail: adrienne.quinn@kingcounty.gov
Deputy Director **Terry Mark** Room 600 .... (206) 263-9004
E-mail: terry.mark@kingcounty.gov
Deputy Director **Josephine Wong** .... (206) 263-9005
E-mail: josephine.wong@kingcounty.gov
Communications Manager **Sherry Hamilton** .... (206) 263-9010
E-mail: sherry.hamilton@kingcounty.gov

Behavioral Health and Recovery Division
Chinook Building, 401 Fifth Avenue, Suite 400, Seattle, WA 98104
Tel: (206) 263-9000 Fax: (206) 296-0583 E-mail: mhsa@kingcounty.gov
Internet: www.kingcounty.gov/healthservices/mhsa.aspx

Director **James R. Vollendroff** .... (206) 263-8903

Community Services Division [CSD]
Chinook Building, 401 Fifth Avenue, Suite 510, Seattle, WA 98104
Tel: (206) 263-9105 Fax: (206) 205-6565 E-mail: csd@kingcounty.gov
Internet: www.kingcounty.gov/socialservices/csd

Director **(Vacant)** .... (206) 263-9019
Aging Program Manager **Linda C. Wells** .... (206) 263-9069
Housing and Community Development Program
Manager **Kathy Tremper** .... (206) 263-9105
E-mail: kathy.Tremper@kingcounty.gov Fax: (206) 296-0229
Workforce Development Services Administration
Nancy Loverin .... (206) 263-1394
Fax: (206) 296-0298

(continued on next page)

★ Elected Official ▲ Appointed by Legislature ▼ Appointed by Governor ▶ Appointed by Board or Commission ● Appointed by Judge
■ Appointed by Mayor △ Appointed by Freeholders ▽ Appointed by Supervisor ▷ Appointed by County Executive ○ Appointed by Council

Community Services Division *continued*

Youth and Family Services Division Program Manager
Stephanie Moyes . . . . . . (206) 263-9064
Fax: (206) 296-0155

Women's Program Coordinator **Linda C. Wells** . . . . . . (206) 263-9069

Department of the Public Defender

Walthew Building, 123 Third Avenue, Suite 400, Seattle, WA 98104
Tel: (206) 296-7662 Fax: (206) 296-0587 E-mail: opd@kingcounty.gov
Internet: www.kingcounty.gov/opd

Director **Lorinda Youngcourt** . . . . . . (206) 296-7662

Developmental Disabilities Division [DDD]

Chinook Building, 401 Fifth Avenue, Suite 520, Seattle, WA 98104
Tel: (206) 263-9055 Fax: (206) 205-1632 E-mail: ddd@kingcounty.gov
Internet: www.kingcounty.gov/ddd

Director **Denise Rothleutner** . . . . . . (206) 263-8988

COUNTIES

Department of Executive Services [DES]

401 5th Avenue, Suite 135, Seattle, WA 98104
Tel: (206) 263-9750 Fax: (206) 205-0840

▷ Director/County Administrative Officer
Caroline L. Whalen . . . . . . (206) 263-9750
E-mail: caroline.whalen@kingcounty.gov

Deputy Director **Tom Koney** . . . . . . (206) 263-9755
E-mail: tom.koney@kingcounty.gov

Civil Rights Office

401 5th Avenue, Suite 215, Seattle, WA 98104
Tel: (206) 296-7592 Fax: (206) 296-4329
E-mail: civil-rights.ocr@kingcounty.gov

Division Director **Kelli Williams** . . . . . . (206) 296-7592

Emergency Management Office

3511 NE Second Street, Renton, WA 98056
Tel: (206) 205-4058 Fax: (206) 205-4056

Director **Walt Hubbard** . . . . . . (206) 205-4060
E-mail: walt.hubbard@kingcounty.gov

Facilities Management Division

King County Administrative Building, 500 Fourth Avenue, Room 800, Seattle, WA 98104-2384
Tel: (206) 477-9352 Fax: (206) 205-5070

▷ Division Director **Anthony Wright** . . . . . . (206) 477-9352
E-mail: anthony.wright@kingcounty.gov

Operations Manager **Dave Preugschat** . . . . . . (206) 477-9445
E-mail: dave.preugschat@kingcounty.gov

Deputy Division Director **Elissa Benson** . . . . . . (206) 477-9352

Building Services Manager **Ameer Faquir** . . . . . . (206) 477-9431
E-mail: ameer.faquir@kingcounty.gov

Real Estate Services Manager **Gail Hauser** . . . . . . (206) 477-9373

Major and Capital Projects Manager **Jim Burt** . . . . . . (206) 477-9355
E-mail: jim.burt@kingcounty.gov

Finance and Business Operations Division

CNK-ES-0300, 401 Fifth Avenue, Suite 300, Seattle, WA 98104
Tel: (206) 263-9258 Fax: (206) 684-2186

Division Director **Ken Guy** . . . . . . (206) 263-9258

Human Resources Management Division

500 4th Avenue, Suite 450, Seattle, WA 98104
Tel: (206) 296-7340 Fax: (206) 296-3904
E-mail: hrcentral@kingcounty.gov
Internet: www.kingcounty.gov/employees/humanresources

Division Director **Nancy Buonanno Grennan** . . . . . . (206) 296-7586
Education: Smith BA; U Washington JD

Records and Licensing Services Division

Records and Licensing Services Division, 500 Fourth Avenue, Seattle, WA 98104-2384
Tel: (206) 296-3185 Fax: (206) 296-4029

Director **Norm Alberg** . . . . . . (206) 296-1559

Deputy Director **Megan Pedersen** . . . . . . (206) 296-3188

Risk Management Office

900 Fourth Avenue, Suite 855, Seattle, WA 98164
Tel: (206) 263-2250 Fax: (206) 296-0949

Division Manager **Jennifer Hills** . . . . . . (206) 263-2250
E-mail: jennifer.hills@kingcounty.gov

King County Department of Information Technology [KCIT]

Chinook Building, 401 Fifth Avenue, Suite 600, Seattle, WA 98104
Tel: (206) 263-4357 Fax: (206) 263-6511

Director/Chief Information Officer **Bill Kehoe** . . . . . . (206) 263-7887
E-mail: bill.kehoe@kingcounty.gov

Chief Financial Officer **Christine Chou** . . . . . . (206) 263-7845

Department of Natural Resources and Parks [DNRP]

201 South Jackson Street, Suite 700, Seattle, WA 98104-3855
Fax: (206) 296-3749

▷ Director **Christie True** . . . . . . (206) 477-4700
E-mail: christie.true@kingcounty.gov
Education: Western Washington

Deputy Department Director **Bob Burns** . . . . . . (206) 477-4700
Fax: (206) 296-3749

KCGIS Center Manager **George Horning** . . . . . . (206) 477-4701
Fax: (206) 263-3145

Parks and Recreation Division Director **Kevin Brown** . . . . (206) 477-4527
Fax: (206) 296-8686

Parks and Recreation Division Assistant Director
Kathryn Terry . . . . . . (206) 477-4700
Fax: (206) 296-8686

Solid Waste Division Director
Patrick "Pat" McLaughlin . . . . . . (206) 477-4501
Fax: (206) 296-0197

Solid Waste Division Assistant Director
Kevin Kiernan . . . . . . (206) 477-4755
Fax: (206) 296-0197

Water and Land Resources Division Director
Mark Isaacson . . . . . . (206) 296-6585
Fax: (206) 296-0192

Wastewater Treatment Division Director (Acting)
Gunars Sreibers . . . . . . (206) 263-9473
Fax: (206) 684-1741

Wastewater Treatment Division Assistant Director
Sandy Kilroy . . . . . . (206) 684-1464
Fax: (206) 684-1741

Water and Land Resources Division Assistant Director
John Taylor . . . . . . (206) 477-4602

Department of Permitting and Environmental Review [DPER]

900 Oakesdale Ave., SW, Renton, WA 98055-1219
Tel: (206) 477-0353 Fax: (206) 296-6614
Internet: www.kingcounty.gov/property/permits.aspx

▷ Director **John Starbard** . . . . . . (206) 477-0385
E-mail: john.starbard@kingcounty.gov

Department of Transportation [DOT]

201 S. Jackson St., Seattle, WA 98104-3856
Tel: (206) 477-3800 Fax: (206) 684-1224
Internet: www.kingcounty.gov/transportation/kcdot.aspx

▷ Director **Harold S. Taniguchi** . . . . . . (206) 477-3809
E-mail: harold.taniguchi@kingcounty.gov Fax: (206) 684-1224

★ Elected Official ▲ Appointed by Legislature ▼ Appointed by Governor ► Appointed by Board or Commission ● Appointed by Judge
■ Appointed by Mayor △ Appointed by Freeholders ▽ Appointed by Supervisor ▷ Appointed by County Executive ○ Appointed by Council

Department of Transportation *continued*

Deputy Director **Laurie Brown** . . . . (206) 477-3856
Fax: (206) 684-1224

Fleet Administration Division Director
Jennifer Lindwall . . . . (206) 296-6521
Fax: (206) 296-0571

King County Airport Division Director
Randall D. "Randy" Berg . . . . (206) 296-7380
Fax: (206) 296-0190

Marine Division Director **Paul Brodeur** . . . . (206) 263-4248
Fax: (206) 684-1968

Metro Transit Division Director **Kevin Desmond** . . . . (206) 684-1619
Fax: (206) 684-1778

Road Services Division Director **Brenda Bauer** . . . . (206) 296-6590
Fax: (206) 205-0955

Communications Manager **Betty Gulledge-Bennett** . . . . (206) 263-3436
E-mail: betty.gulledge-bennett@kingcounty.gov Fax: (206) 263-3489

Grants Administrator **Lori Guerrero** . . . . (206) 477-3815

Public Health - Seattle and King County

401 5th Avenue, Suite 1300, Seattle, WA 98104
Tel: (206) 296-4600 Fax: (206) 296-0166
Internet: www.kingcounty.gov/health

▷ Director **Patty Hayes** . . . . (206) 263-8409
E-mail: patty.hayes@kingcounty.gov

Chief of Staff **Cyndi Schaeffer** . . . . (206) 477-3264

Chief of Assessment, Policy Development, and Evaluation **Marguerite Ro** . . . . (206) 263-8811

Director of External and Legislative Affairs
Jennifer Muhm . . . . (206) 263-8813
E-mail: jennifer.muhm@kingcounty.gov

King County Law Library [KCLL]

516 Third Avenue, Suite W-621, Seattle, WA 98104-2317
Tel: (206) 477-1305 (Seattle Branch)
Tel: (206) 477-1316 (Maleng Regional Justice Center)
Fax: (206) 205-0513 Internet: www.kcll.org

Director **Rita Dermody** . . . . (206) 296-0940
Education: DePaul 1973 BA; Illinois 1974 MLS

Office of the Metropolitan County Council

King County Courthouse, 516 Third Avenue, Room 1200, Seattle, WA 98104-2317
Tel: (206) 477-1000 Fax: (206) 296-0198
Internet: www.kingcounty.gov/council.aspx

★ Chair **J. Joseph "Joe" McDermott** (District 8) . . . . (206) 477-1008
Term Expires: December 31, 2019
E-mail: joe.mcdermott@kingcounty.gov
Education: Gonzaga 1989 BA; U Washington 1997 MPA
Chief of Staff **Shannon Braddock** . . . . (206) 477-1008

★ Vice Chair **Rod Dembowski** (District 1) . . . . (206) 477-1001
Term Expires: December 31, 2017
E-mail: rod.dembowski@kingcounty.gov
Chief of Staff **Kristina Logsdon** . . . . (206) 477-1001

★ Vice Chair **Reagan Dunn** (District 9) . . . . (206) 477-1009
Term Expires: December 31, 2017
E-mail: reagan.dunn@kingcounty.gov
Education: U Washington 1998 JD
Chief of Staff **Tom Goff** . . . . (206) 477-1009

★ Council Member **Larry Gossett** (District 2) . . . . (206) 477-1002
Term Expires: December 31, 2019
E-mail: larry.gossett@kingcounty.gov
Education: U Washington 1971 BA
Chief of Staff **Cindy Domingo** . . . . (206) 477-1002

★ Council Member **Kathy Lambert** (District 3) . . . . (206) 477-1003
Term Expires: December 31, 2017
E-mail: kathy.lambert@kingcounty.gov
Education: Washington U (MO) 1984 BA; Marin

Office of the Metropolitan County Council *continued*

Chief of Staff **Jeff McMorris** . . . . (206) 477-1003

★ Council Member **Jeanne E. Kohl-Welles** (District 4) . . . . (206) 477-1004
Term Expires: December 31, 2019
Education: Cal State (Northridge) 1965 BA, 1970 MA; UCLA MA, 1974 PhD

★ Council Member **Dave Upthegrove** (District 5) . . . . (206) 296-1005
Term Expires: December 31, 2017
Date of Birth: May 3, 1971
Education: Colorado BA
Chief of Staff **Jeff Muhm** . . . . (206) 477-0951

★ Council Member **Claudia Balducci** (District 6) . . . . (206) 477-1006
Term Expires: December 31, 2019
Education: Providence BA; Columbia 1994 JD

★ Council Member **Pete von Reichbauer** (District 7) . . . . (206) 477-1007
Term Expires: December 31, 2017
E-mail: pete.vonreichbauer@kingcounty.gov
Chief of Staff **Sara Smith** . . . . (206) 477-1007

Clerk of the Council **Anne Noris** . . . . (206) 477-1020
E-mail: anne.noris@kingcounty.gov Fax: (206) 205-8165

Office of the Auditor

King County Courthouse, 516 Third Avenue, Room W1033, Seattle, WA 98104-3272
Fax: (206) 296-0159 Internet: www.kingcounty.gov/auditor.aspx

○ Auditor **Kymber Waltmunson** . . . . (206) 477-1033
E-mail: kymber.waltmunson@kingcounty.gov

Office Manager **Rachel Baker** . . . . (206) 477-1033

Office of Citizen Complaints

516 Third Avenue, Room W1039, Seattle, WA 98104-2317
Tel: (206) 477-1050 Fax: (206) 296-0948
E-mail: ombudsman@kingcounty.gov
Internet: www.kingcounty.gov/operations/ombudsman

Ombudsman/Director **Amy Calderwood** . . . . (206) 477-1050

Office of the County Assessor

King County Administration Building, 500 Fourth Avenue, ADM-AS-0708, Seattle, WA 98104-2384
Fax: (206) 296-0595 Internet: http://www.kingcounty.gov/assessor/

★ County Assessor **John Wilson** . . . . (206) 296-7300
Term Expires: December 31, 2019
E-mail: assessor.info@kingcounty.gov

Office of the Prosecuting Attorney

King County Courthouse, 516 Third Ave., Room W-554, Seattle, WA 98104
Tel: (206) 296-9000 (Information) Fax: (206) 296-0955
Internet: www.kingcounty.gov/prosecutor.aspx

★ Prosecuting Attorney **Daniel T. Satterberg** . . . . (206) 477-1200
Term Expires: December 31, 2018 Fax: (206) 296-9013
E-mail: prosecuting.attorney@kingcounty.gov

Office of the Sheriff [KCSO]

King County Courthouse, 516 Third Ave., 1st Floor, Seattle, WA 98104-2312
Fax: (206) 296-0168 E-mail: sheriff@kingcounty.gov

★ Sheriff **John Urquhart** . . . . (206) 296-4155
Term Expires: December 31, 2017
E-mail: john.urquhart@kingcounty.gov

Chief Deputy **Jim Pugel** . . . . (206) 296-4156

Chief, Criminal Investigations Division **Robin Fenton** . . . . (206) 263-2100

Chief, Patrol Division **Dan Pingrey** . . . . (206) 296-7522

Chief, Technical Services Division **Patti Cole-Tindall** . . . . (206) 296-4170
E-mail: Patti.Cole-Tindall@kingcounty.gov

COUNTIES

★ Elected Official ▲ Appointed by Legislature ▼ Appointed by Governor ▶ Appointed by Board or Commission ● Appointed by Judge
■ Appointed by Mayor △ Appointed by Freeholders ▽ Appointed by Supervisor ▷ Appointed by County Executive ○ Appointed by Council

King County Elections

919 Southwest Grady Way, Renton, WA 98057-2906
Tel: (206) 296-8683 Fax: (206) 296-0108
E-mail: elections@kingcounty.gov
Internet: www.kingcounty.gov/elections.aspx

★ Elections Director **Julie Wise** .... (206) 477-4140
Term Expires: December 31, 2019
Deputy Director **Shannon Cortez** .... (206) 477-4176
Chief Communications Officer **(Vacant)** .... (206) 477-4100

County of Knox, Tennessee

Tel: (865) 215-2000 Internet: www.knoxcounty.org

County Seat: Knoxville **Election Type:** Partisan **Year Founded:** 1792
Population: 185,291 (2015)

Office of the County Mayor

City-County Building, 400 Main Street, Suite 615, Knoxville, TN 37902
Tel: (865) 215-2005 Internet: www.knoxcounty.org/countymayor

★ County Mayor **Tim Burchett** (R) .... (865) 215-2005
Term Expires: August 31, 2018
E-mail: county.mayor@knoxcounty.org
Education: Tennessee 1988 BS
Chief of Staff **Dean Rice** .... (865) 215-2005
Education: Tennessee 1994 BA
Communications Manager **Michael Grider** .... (865) 215-4750
E-mail: michael.grider@knoxcounty.org
Communications Manager **Jennifer Linginfelter** .... (865) 215-4579
Chief Administrative Officer **(Vacant)** .... (865) 215-2005

Code Administration

City-County Building, 400 Main Street, Room 547, Knoxville, TN 37902
Tel: (865) 215-2325 Fax: (865) 215-4255
E-mail: code.admin@knoxcounty.org Internet: www.knoxcounty.org/codes

Chief Building Official **Roy Braden** .... (865) 215-2325
Code Enforcement Officer **Tammy Harvey** .... (865) 215-4357
E-mail: tammy.harvey@knoxcounty.org
Code Enforcement Officer **Kim Jarnagin** .... (865) 215-4357
E-mail: kim.jarnagin@knoxcounty.org
Code Enforcement Officer **Jackie Paul** .... (865) 215-4357
E-mail: jackie.paul@knoxcounty.org

Department of Engineering and Public Works [EPW]

205 West Baxter Avenue, Knoxville, TN 37917
Tel: (865) 215-5800 Fax: (865) 215-5810
Internet: www.knoxcounty.org/epw

Senior Director **Dwight Van de Vate** .... (865) 215-5800
E-mail: dwight.vandevate@knoxcounty.org

Solid Waste Department

205 West Baxter Avenue, Knoxville, TN 37917
Tel: (865) 215-5865 Internet: www.knoxcounty.org/solid_waste

Director **Tom Salter** .... (865) 215-5865
E-mail: tom.salter@knoxcounty.org
Compliance Manager **Drew Thurman** .... (865) 215-5865
Recycling Coordinator **Zachary "Zach" Johnson** .... (865) 215-5865
E-mail: recycle@knoxcounty.org

Department of Finance

City-County Building, 400 Main Street, Suite 630, Knoxville, TN 37902
Tel: (865) 215-2350 Tel: (865) 215-2313 (Job Line)
TTY: (865) 215-2497 Fax: (865) 215-2352
Internet: www.knoxcounty.org/finance

Department Head **Chris Caldwell** .... (865) 215-2005

Department of Finance *continued*

Director, Community Development **Rebecca Gibson** .... (865) 215-3980

Purchasing Division

Tel: (865) 215-5777 Fax: (865) 215-5778
Internet: www.knoxcounty.org/purchasing

Director **Hugh Holt** .... (865) 215-5777
E-mail: hugh.holt@knoxcounty.org

Knox County Health Department [KCHD]

140 Dameron Avenue, Knoxville, TN 37917
Tel: (865) 215-5000 E-mail: health@knoxcounty.org
Internet: www.knoxcounty.org/health

Director/Chief Medical Officer **Martha Buchanan** .... (865) 215-5300
Deputy Director **Mark Miller** .... (865) 215-5300

Human Resources Department

400 Main Street, Suite 360, Knoxville, TN 37902
Tel: (865) 215-2321 Fax: (865) 215-3242
Internet: www.knoxcounty.org/hr

Director **Mark Jones** .... (865) 215-2321
Training Coordinator **Anthony Smith** .... (865) 215-2321
E-mail: anthony.smith@knoxcounty.org
Benefits Manager **Brian Barnard** .... (865) 215-2321
Benefits Coordinator **Samantha Chittum** .... (865) 215-2321
Human Resource Services Coordinator **Betty Penson** .... (865) 215-2321
E-mail: betty.penson@knoxcounty.org
Personnel Coordinator **Debbie Dew** .... (865) 215-2321
E-mail: debbie.dew@knoxcounty.org
Personnel Coordinator **Glenda Irwin** .... (865) 215-2321
E-mail: glenda.irwin@knoxcounty.org
Title VI, Americans with Disabilities Act (ADA), and Family and Medical Leave Act (FMLA) Coordinator
Pat Carson .... (865) 215-2321
E-mail: pat.carson@knoxcounty.org
Manager **Col Richard Julian** .... (865) 215-2321
E-mail: richard.julian@knoxcounty.org

Department of Information Technology

City-County Building, 400 Main Street, Suite L-114, Knoxville, TN 37902
Tel: (865) 215-4200 Internet: www.knoxcounty.org/it

Senior Director **Richard "Dick" Moran** .... (865) 215-4200
E-mail: dick.moran@knoxcounty.org
Education: SUNY Col (Buffalo) 1973

Department of Parks and Recreation

2447 Sutherland Avenue, Knoxville, TN 37919
Tel: (865) 215-6600 Internet: www.knoxcounty.org/parks

Senior Director **Doug Bataille** .... (865) 215-6600
Education: Ohio; Indiana
Deputy Director, Parks **Eric Hahn** .... (865) 215-6600
Deputy Director, Recreation **Jay Smelser** .... (865) 215-6600
Park Maintenance Superintendent
Charles "Chuck" James .... (865) 215-6600
Parks Coordinator **Joseph Inman** .... (865) 215-6600
Parks and Greenway Trails Coordinator
Shauna Godlevsky .... (865) 215-6600
Sports Operations Manager **Jennifer Gentry** .... (865) 215-6600
Office Manager **Sandra Burton** .... (865) 215-6600
Recreation Coordinator **Deana Dillon** .... (865) 215-6600

Knox County Public Library

500 West Church Avenue, Knoxville, TN 37902
Tel: (865) 215-8750

Director of Library Services **Myretta Black** .... (865) 215-8751
E-mail: director@knoxlib.org

★ Elected Official ▲ Appointed by Legislature ▼ Appointed by Governor ► Appointed by Board or Commission ● Appointed by Judge
■ Appointed by Mayor △ Appointed by Freeholders ▽ Appointed by Supervisor ▷ Appointed by County Executive ○ Appointed by Council

The Development Corporation of Knox County [TDC]

17 Market Square, Room 201, Knoxville, TN 37902
Tel: (865) 546-5887 Fax: (865) 546-6170
Internet: www.knoxdevelopment.org

President and Chief Executive Officer **Todd Napier** . . . . . . (865) 246-2648
E-mail: tanapier@knoxdevelopment.org
Executive Vice President **(Vacant)** . . . . (865) 546-5887

Veterans Service Office

1000 North Central Avenue, Knoxville, TN 37917
Tel: (865) 215-5645 Internet: www.knoxcounty.org/veterans

Veterans Service Officer **Tom Humphries** . . . . (865) 215-5645
Deputy Veterans Services Officer **Mark Lett** . . . . (865) 215-5645
Veterans Service Outreach Specialist **Tony Watley** . . . . (865) 594-6008

County Commission

City-County Building, 400 Main Street, Suite 603, Knoxville, TN 37902
Tel: (865) 215-2534 Fax: (865) 215-2038
E-mail: commission@knoxcounty.org
Internet: www.knoxcounty.org/commission

★ Chair **Dave Wright** (R-District 8) . . . . (865) 215-2534
Term Expires: August 2016
E-mail: dave.wright@knoxcounty.org
★ Commissioner
Samuel "Sam" McKenzie (D-District 1) . . . . (865) 215-2534
Term Expires: August 2016
E-mail: sam.mckenzie@knoxcounty.org
★ Commissioner **Amy Broyles** (D-District 2) . . . . (865) 224-6269
Term Expires: August 2016
E-mail: amy.broyles@knoxcounty.org
★ Commissioner **Randy Smith** (R-District 3) . . . . (865) 212-4516
Term Expires: August 2018
E-mail: randy.smith@knoxcounty.org
★ Commissioner **Jeff Ownby** (R-District 4) . . . . (865) 215-2534
Term Expires: August 2016
Date of Birth: April 12, 1967
★ Commissioner **John Schoonmaker** (R-District 5) . . . . (865) 632-5900
Term Expires: August 2016
★ Commissioner **Brad Anders** (D-District 6) . . . . (865) 215-2534
Term Expires: August 2016
E-mail: brad.anders@knoxcounty.org
Education: Tusculum 2006 BS
★ Commissioner **Charles Busler** (R-District 7) . . . . (865) 922-5433
Term Expires: August 2018
E-mail: charles.busler@knoxcounty.org
★ Commissioner **Michael "Mike" Brown** (R-District 9) . . . . (865) 577-3481
Term Expires: August 2016
E-mail: michael.brown@knoxcounty.org
★ Commissioner **Ed Brantley** (R-At-Large) . . . . (865) 215-2534
Term Expires: August 2018
E-mail: ed.Brantley@knoxcounty.org
★ Commissioner **Bob Thomas** (R-At-Large) . . . . (865) 215-2534
Term Expires: August 2018

Internal Audit Department

Tel: (865) 215-2892

○ Auditor **Richard Walls** . . . . (865) 215-2892
E-mail: richard.walls@knoxcounty.org

County Clerk's Office

Old Courthouse, 300 Main Street, Knoxville, TN 37902
Tel: (865) 215-2385 Fax: (865) 215-3655
Internet: www.knoxcounty.org/clerk

★ County Clerk **Foster D. Arnett, Jr.** (R) . . . . (865) 215-2385
Term Expires: August 5, 2018
E-mail: county.clerk@knoxcounty.org

Clerk of General Sessions Court - Civil Division

City-County Building, 400 Main Street, Room M30, Knoxville, TN 37902
Tel: (865) 215-2400 Fax: (865) 215-4251
Internet: www.knoxcounty.org/circuit

★ Clerk of Circuit Court Civil Sessions and Juvenile Court
Catherine F. "Cathy" Shanks (R) . . . . (865) 215-2518
E-mail: cathy.shanks@knoxcounty.org

Clerk of General Sessions Court - Criminal Division

City-County Building, 400 Main Street, Room 149, Knoxville, TN 37902
Tel: (865) 215-2492 Fax: (865) 215-2173
Internet: www.knoxcounty.org/criminalcourt

★ Criminal Court Clerk **Mike Hammond** (R) . . . . (865) 215-2375
Term Expires: August 5, 2018

Law Director's Office

City-County Building, 400 Main Street, Suite 612, Knoxville, TN 37902
Tel: (865) 215-2327 Fax: (865) 215-2936
Internet: www.knoxcounhty.org/law_director

★ Law Director **Richard "Bud" Armstrong** (R) . . . . (865) 215-2327
Term Expires: August 31, 2016

Property Assessor's Office

City-County Building, 400 Main Street, Suite 204, Knoxville, TN 37902
Tel: (865) 215-2360 Fax: (865) 215-3671
Internet: http://www.knoxcounty.org/property/index.php

★ Assessor of Property **Phil Ballard** (R) . . . . (865) 215-2360
Term Expires: August 2016
E-mail: county.assessor@knoxcounty.org
Chief Deputy Assessor **Jim Weaver** . . . . (865) 215-2360

Register of Deeds

City-County Building, 400 Main Street, Suite 225, Knoxville, TN 37902
Tel: (865) 215-2330 Tel: (865) 215-2329 (Record Room)
Fax: (865) 215-2332 Internet: www.knoxcounty.org/register

★ Register of Deeds **Sherry Witt** (R) . . . . (865) 215-2330
Term Expires: August 5, 2018
E-mail: sherry.witt@knoxcounty.org

Sheriff's Office [KCSO]

City-County Building, 400 Main Street, Suite L-165,
Knoxville, TN 37902
Tel: (865) 215-2243 Internet: www.knoxsheriff.org

★ Sheriff **Jimmy "J.J." Jones** (R) . . . . (865) 971-3901
Term Expires: August 31, 2018
Education: Tennessee MS
Chief Deputy **Eddie Biggs** . . . . (865) 971-3911

Animal Control Division

3201 Division Street, Knoxville, TN 37919
Tel: (865) 679-9698
Supervisor **Les Mullins** . . . . (865) 215-2444

★ Elected Official ▲ Appointed by Legislature ▼ Appointed by Governor ▶ Appointed by Board or Commission ● Appointed by Judge
■ Appointed by Mayor △ Appointed by Freeholders ▽ Appointed by Supervisor ▷ Appointed by County Executive ○ Appointed by Council

Trustee's Office

City-County Building, 400 Main Street, Suite 418, Knoxville, TN 37902
Tel: (865) 215-2305 Internet: www.knoxcounty.org/trustee

★Trustee **Ed Shouse** (R) .... (865) 215-2305
Term Expires: August 2018
E-mail: ed.shouse@knoxcounty.org

County of Lake, Illinois

Lake County Courthouse and Administrative Complex,
18 North County Street, Waukegan, IL 60085
Tel: (847) 377-2000 (Information) Internet: www.lakecountyil.gov

County Seat: Waukegan **Election Type:** Partisan **Population:** 703,910 (2015)

COUNTIES

County Board Office

County Bldg., 18 North County Street, 10th Floor,
Waukegan, IL 60085-4351
Tel: (847) 377-2300 Fax: (847) 360-7322
Internet: www.lakecountyil.gov/countyboard

★Chairman **Aaron Lawlor** (R-District 18) .... (224) 639-3138
Term Expires: November 30, 2016
E-mail: alawlor@lakecountyil.gov
Education: Lake Forest Col 2004

★Vice Chair **Carol Calabresa** (R-District 15) .... (847) 367-6640
Term Expires: November 30, 2016
E-mail: ccalabresa@lakecountyil.gov
Education: Wisconsin BS

★Board Member **Linda Pedersen** (R-District 1) .... (847) 395-1384
Term Expires: November 30, 2016
E-mail: lpedersen@lakecountyil.gov

★Board Member **Diane Hewitt** (D-District 2) .... (847) 244-2742
Term Expires: November 30, 2016
E-mail: dhewitt@lakecountyil.gov

★Board Member **Tom Weber** (R-District 3) .... (847) 377-2300
Term Expires: November 30, 2018
E-mail: tweber@lakecountyil.gov

★Board Member **Brent C. Paxton** (R-District 4) .... (847) 746-9542
Term Expires: November 30, 2016
E-mail: bpaxton@lakecountyil.gov
Education: National U Health Sciences 1985 BS, 1987 MD

★Board Member **Bonnie Thomson Carter** (R-District 5) .. (847) 546-2888
Term Expires: November 30, 2016
E-mail: bcarter@lakecountyil.gov

★Board Member **Jeff Werfel** (R-District 6) .... (847) 223-1438
Term Expires: November 30, 2018
E-mail: jwerfel@lakecountyil.gov

★Board Member **Steve Carlson** (R-District 7) .... (847) 356-4167
Term Expires: November 30, 2016
E-mail: scarlson@lakecountyil.gov
Education: Western Illinois 1971 BA

★Board Member **Bill Durkin** (D-District 8) .... (224) 456-9919
Term Expires: November 30, 2018
E-mail: bdurkin@lakecountyil.gov

★Board Member **Mary Ross Cunningham** (D-District 9) .. (847) 721-1563
Term Expires: November 30, 2018
E-mail: mcunningham@lakecountyil.gov

★Board Member **Chuck Bartels** (R-District 10) .... (847) 377-2300
Term Expires: November 30, 2018

★Board Member **Steve W. Mandel** (D-District 11) .... (847) 377-2300
Term Expires: November 30, 2016
E-mail: smandel@lakecountyil.gov

★Board Member **S. Michael Rummel** (R-District 12) ..... (847) 377-2300
Term Expires: November 30, 2016
E-mail: srummel@lakecountyil.gov

★Board Member **Sandra Hart** (D-District 13) .... (847) 377-2300
Term Expires: November 30, 2016
E-mail: shart@lakecountyil.gov

County Board Office *continued*

★Board Member **Audrey Nixon** (D-District 14) .... (847) 244-9517
Term Expires: November 30, 2016
E-mail: anixon@lakecountyil.gov

★Board Member **Terry Wilke** (D-District 16) .... (847) 546-9925
Term Expires: November 30, 2016
E-mail: twilke@lakecountyil.gov

★Board Member **Nick Sauer** (R-District 17) .... (847) 377-2300
Term Expires: November 30, 2018
E-mail: nsauer@lakecountyil.gov

★Board Member **Craig Taylor** (R-District 19) .... (224) 805-6027
Term Expires: November 30, 2018
E-mail: ctaylor@lakecountyil.gov

★Board Member **Sidney H. Mathias** (R-District 20) ...... (847) 377-2300
Term Expires: November 30, 2016
E-mail: smathias@lakecountyil.gov
Education: DePaul 1968 JD

★Board Member **Ann B. Maine** (R-District 21) .... (847) 374-9787
Term Expires: November 30, 2016
E-mail: amaine@lakecountyil.gov

County Administrator's Office

County Bldg., 18 North County Street, 9th Floor,
Waukegan, IL 60085-4304
Fax: (847) 360-6732 Internet: www.lakecountyil.gov/countyadministrator

►County Administrator **Barry A. Burton** .... (847) 377-2250
E-mail: bburton@lakecountyil.gov
Facilities Manager **Jeremiah Varco** .... (847) 377-2985
Fax: (847) 662-7370

Chief County Assessment Office

County Bldg., 18 N. County St., 7th Floor, Waukegan, IL 60085-4335
Fax: (847) 984-5931 E-mail: assessor@lakecountyil.gov
Internet: www.lakecountyil.gov/assessor

►Chief County Assessment Officer **Martin P. Paulson** ..... (847) 377-2050
E-mail: mpaulson@lakecountyil.gov

Public Defender's Office

15 South County Street, Waukegan, IL 60085
Fax: (847) 984-5751

Public Defender **Joy E. Gossman** .... (847) 377-3360

Lake County Board of Health

3010 Grand Avenue, 3rd Floor, Board Room, Waukegan, IL 60085-2399

President **Timothy Sashko** .... (847) 377-8000

Lake County Health Department and Community Health Center [LCHD]

3010 Grand Avenue, Waukegan, IL 60085-2399
Tel: (847) 377-8000 Fax: (847) 360-5957
Internet: www.lakecountyil.gov/health

►Executive Director **Tony Beltran** .... (847) 377-8073

Department of Finance and Administrative Services

County Building, 18 North County Street, 9th Floor,
Waukegan, IL 60085-4350
Fax: (847) 360-6592 Internet: www.lakecountyil.gov/finance

Director **Gary O. Gordon** .... (847) 377-2929
E-mail: ggordon@lakecountyil.gov
Purchasing Agent **Ruth Anne Hall** .... (847) 377-2929
E-mail: purchasing@lakecountyil.gov
Controller **Patrice Sutton-Burger** .... (847) 377-2929
E-mail: psuttonburger@lakecountyil.gov

★Elected Official ▲Appointed by Legislature ▼Appointed by Governor ►Appointed by Board or Commission ●Appointed by Judge
■Appointed by Mayor △Appointed by Freeholders ▽Appointed by Supervisor ▷Appointed by County Executive ○Appointed by Council

Human Resources Department
18 North County Street, 7th Floor, Waukegan, IL 60085-4355
Tel: (847) 377-2700 Fax: (847) 625-7045
E-mail: humanresources@lakecountyil.gov
Internet: www.lakecountyil.gov/hr

Director **Rodney Marion** .... (847) 377-2750
E-mail: rmarion@lakecountyil.gov
Assistant Director **Robert Szarzynski** .... (847) 377-2157
E-mail: rszarzynski@lakecountyil.gov
Human Resources Manager **Karla Hasty** .... (847) 377-2249
E-mail: khasty@lakecountyil.gov

Department of Information Technology
County Building, 18 North County Street, 8th Floor,
Waukegan, IL 60085-4357
Fax: (847) 360-6869 Internet: www.lakecountyil.gov/it

▶ Chief Information Officer (Interim) **Lora Nordstrom** .... (847) 377-2477
E-mail: lnordstrom@lakecountyil.gov

Planning, Building and Development Department
Lake County Central Permit Facility, 500 West Winchester Road,
Unit 101, Libertyville, IL 60048
Tel: (847) 377-2600 Fax: (847) 984-5854
E-mail: planning@lakecountyil.gov
Internet: www.lakecountyil.gov/planning

▶ Director **Eric Waggoner** .... (847) 377-2114
E-mail: ewaggoner@lakecountyil.gov
Deputy Director for Building and Code Enforcement
Steve Crivello .... (847) 377-2600
Deputy Director for Community Development
Jodi Gingiss .... (847) 377-2150

Department of Public Works
650 Winchester Rd., Libertyville, IL 60048-1391
Fax: (847) 377-7173 E-mail: publicworks@lakecountyil.gov
Internet: www.lakecountyil.gov/publicworks

Director **Peter Kolb** .... (847) 377-7500
Assistant Director **Phil Perna** .... (847) 377-7500
E-mail: pperna@lakecountyil.gov

Radio Department
1303 N. Milwaukee Ave., Libertyville, IL 60048-1308
Fax: (847) 377-7018 E-mail: radio@co.lake.il.us
E-mail: radio@lakecountyil.gov Internet: www.lakecountyil.gov/radio

▶ Director **(Vacant)** .... (847) 377-7115

Lake County Division of Transportation
600 West Winchester Road, Libertyville, IL 60048-1381
Fax: (847) 362-5290 E-mail: dot@lakecountyil.gov
Internet: www.lakecountyil.gov/transportation

▶ Director/County Engineer **Paula Trigg** .... (847) 377-7400

Lake County Forest Preserve District [LCFPD]
1899 West Winchester Road, Libertyville, IL 60048
Tel: (847) 367-6640 Internet: www.lcfpd.org

Executive Director **Ty Kovach** .... (847) 968-3338
Deputy Executive Director **(Vacant)** .... (847) 968-3338

William D. Block Memorial Law Library
18 North County Street, Waukegan, IL 60085

Supervisory Librarian **JoAnne Vandestreek** .... (847) 377-2800
E-mail: jvandestreek@lakecountyil.gov

Winchester House
1125 N. Milwaukee Ave., Libertyville, IL 60048-1399
Fax: (847) 816-5176

Administrator **Jacqueline Prestel** .... (847) 377-7200

Veterans' Assistance Commission
20 South Martin Luther King, Jr. Avenue, Waukegan, IL 60085-5571
Fax: (847) 360-3188 E-mail: veterans@lakecountyil.gov

Superintendent **Michael Peck** .... (847) 377-3344

Office of the Coroner
26 N. Martin Luther King Jr. Ave., Waukegan, IL 60085-8111
Tel: (847) 377-2200 Fax: (847) 662-5972
Internet: www.lakecountyil.gov/coroner

★ Coroner **Thomas Rudd** .... (847) 377-2200
Term Expires: November 30, 2016
E-mail: coroner@lakecountyil.gov

COUNTIES

Office of the County Clerk
County Bldg., 18 N. County St., Room 101, Waukegan, IL 60085-4364
Fax: (847) 984-5822

★ County Clerk **Carla N. Wyckoff** (R) .... (847) 377-2400
Term Expires: November 30, 2018
E-mail: countyclerk@lakecountyil.gov

Office of the Recorder of Deeds
County Bldg., 18 N. County St., 2nd Floor, Waukegan, IL 60085-4358
Fax: (847) 984-5860 E-mail: recorder@lakecountyil.gov
Internet: www.lakecountyil.gov/recorder

★ Recorder **Mary Ellen Vanderventer** (D) .... (847) 377-2575
Term Expires: December 4, 2016
E-mail: mvanderventer@lakecountyil.gov

Office of the Sheriff
25 South Martin Luther King, Jr. Avenue, Waukegan, IL 60085-5568
Fax: (847) 360-5796 Internet: www.lakecountyil.gov/sheriff

★ Sheriff **Mark C. Curran, Jr.** (R) .... (847) 377-4000
Term Expires: December 1, 2018
E-mail: mcurran@lakecountyil.gov
Training Coordinator **Sgt Anthony Parisi** .... (847) 377-4262
Fax: (847) 984-5736

Emergency Management Agency
1303 N. Milwaukee Ave., Libertyville, IL 60048-1308
Fax: (847) 377-7015

▶ Coordinator **Kent McKenzie** .... (847) 377-7100
E-mail: kmckenzie@lakecountyil.gov

Office of the State's Attorney
County Building, 18 North County Street, Third Floor,
Waukegan, IL 60085-4363
Fax: (847) 360-1538 Internet: http://lcsao.org/

★ State's Attorney **Michael G. Nerheim** (R) .... (847) 377-3000
Term Expires: December 4, 2016
E-mail: statesattorney@lakecountyil.gov

★ Elected Official ▲ Appointed by Legislature ▼ Appointed by Governor ▶ Appointed by Board or Commission ● Appointed by Judge
■ Appointed by Mayor △ Appointed by Freeholders ▽ Appointed by Supervisor ▷ Appointed by County Executive ○ Appointed by Council

COUNTIES

Office of the Treasurer

County Building, 18 North County Street, Room 102,
Waukegan, IL 60085-4361
Fax: (847) 625-7409 E-mail: treasurer@lakecountyil.gov
Internet: www.lakecountyil.gov/treasurer

★Treasurer **David B. Stolman** (R) .... (847) 377-2323
Term Expires: December 1, 2018
Education: Illinois BS; DePaul JD

Lake County Regional Office of Education

800 Lancer Lane, #E128, Grayslake, IL 60030-2656
Fax: (847) 543-7832

★Superintendent of Schools **Roycealee Wood** (R) .... (847) 543-7833
Term Expires: June 30, 2019
E-mail: rwood@lake.k12.il.us
Education: Northwestern BS, MA
Assistant Superintendent **Gary Pickens** .... (847) 665-0589

County of Lake, Indiana

County Government Center, 2293 North Main Street,
Crown Point, IN 46307
Internet: www.lakecountyin.org

County Seat: Crown Point **Election Type:** Partisan
Population: 487,865 (2015)

Office of the Board of Commissioners

County Government Center, 2293 N. Main St., Crown Point, IN 46307
Tel: (219) 755-3200 Fax: (219) 755-3064

★President **Gerry Scheub** (D-District 2) .... (219) 755-3200
Term Expires: December 31, 2016
★Commissioner **Kyle W. Allen, Sr.** (D-District 1) .... (219) 755-3204
Term Expires: December 31, 2018
★Commissioner **Michael Repay** (D-District 3) .... (219) 755-3200
Term Expires: December 31, 2016

Office of Cooperative Extension (Purdue University)

880 East 99 Court, Suite A, Crown Point, IN 46307
Fax: (219) 755-3251 Internet: www.ag.purdue.edu/counties/lake

Director **Janet Reed** .... (219) 755-3240

Office of the County Commission Attorney

County Government Center, 2293 N. Main St., Crown Point, IN 46307

▶County Attorney **John Steven Dull** .... (219) 755-3207 ext. 1
Assistant County Attorney **Joseph S. Irak** .... (219) 755-3207 ext. 2

Building Management Department

County Government Center, 2293 North Main Street, 1st Floor,
Crown Point, IN 46307
Fax: (219) 755-3053

▶Superintendent **Daniel "Dan" Ombac** .... (219) 755-3165

Economic Development Department

County Government Center, 2293 North Main Street, Room A-311,
Crown Point, IN 46307
Fax: (219) 736-5925 Internet: www.lakecountyin.com

Executive Director **Milan Grozdanich** .... (219) 755-3231
E-mail: mgrozdanich@lakecountyin.com

Health Department

County Government Center, 2293 N. Main St., Crown Point, IN 46307
Fax: (219) 755-3668

▶County Health Director **Susan W. Best** .... (219) 755-3655

Lake County Highway Department

Crown Point Facility, 1100 E. Monitor St., Crown Point, IN 46307-3521
Lowell Facility, 18211 Wicker Avenue, Lowell, IN 46356-9998
Tel: (219) 663-0525 Tel: (219) 696-0659 (Lowell Facility)
Fax: (219) 662-0497 (Crown Point Facility)
Fax: (219) 696-6174 (Lowell Facility)

▶Superintendent **Marcus W. Malczewski** .... (219) 663-0525
E-mail: malczmw@lakecountyin.org

Parks and Recreation Department

2293 North Main Street, Crown Point, IN 46307
Fax: (219) 755-3693

▶Director **Robert Nickovich** .... (219) 755-3885

Plan Commission

County Government Center, 2293 N. Main St., Crown Point, IN 46307
Fax: (219) 755-3712

▶Director **Ned Kovachevich** .... (219) 755-3700

Public Works Department

County Government Center, Bldg. B, 2293 N. Main St., 1st Floor,
Crown Point, IN 46307
Fax: (219) 755-3053

Director **William N. Henderson** .... (219) 755-3185

Purchasing Department

County Government Center, 2293 N. Main St., Crown Point, IN 46307
Fax: (219) 755-3216

▶Purchasing Agent **Brenda Koselke** .... (219) 755-3209

Veterans Service Office

County Government Center, 2293 N. Main St., Crown Point, IN 46307

▶Veterans Service Officer **Ray Guiden** .... (219) 755-3285
Assistant Veterans Service Officer **Daniel Archer** .... (219) 755-3285

Weights and Measures Department

2300 West 93rd Avenue, Crown Point, IN 46307
Fax: (219) 755-3739

▶Director **Christine Clay** .... (219) 755-3680

Office of the County Council

County Government Center, 2293 North Main Street,
Crown Point, IN 46307
Fax: (219) 755-3283

★Council Member **David Hamm** (D-District 1) .... (219) 755-3280
Term Expires: December 31, 2018
★Council Member **Elsie Brown Franklin** (D-District 2).... (219) 755-3280
Term Expires: December 31, 2018
★Council Member **Jamal Washington** (D-District 3) ...... (219) 755-3280
Term Expires: December 31, 2018
★Council Member **Dan Dernulc** (D-District 4) .... (219) 755-3280
Term Expires: December 31, 2018
★Council Member **Christine Cid** (D-District 5)........... (219) 755-3280
Term Expires: December 31, 2018
★Council Member **Ted F. Bilski** (D-District 6)........... (219) 755-3280
Term Expires: December 31, 2018
★Council Member **Eldon Strong** (R-District 7) .... (219) 755-3280
Term Expires: December 31, 2018

★ Elected Official ▲ Appointed by Legislature ▼ Appointed by Governor ▶ Appointed by Board or Commission ● Appointed by Judge
■ Appointed by Mayor △ Appointed by Freeholders ▽ Appointed by Supervisor ▷ Appointed by County Executive ○ Appointed by Council

Office of the Assessor

County Government Center, 2293 N. Main St., Crown Point, IN 46307
Fax: (219) 755-3022

★ Assessor **Jerome A. Prince** (D) ....(219) 755-3100
Term Expires: December 31, 2018

Office of the Auditor

County Government Center, 2293 N. Main St., Crown Point, IN 46307
Fax: (219) 755-3023

★ Auditor **John Petalas** (D) ....(219) 755-3120
Term Expires: December 31, 2018

Office of the County Clerk

County Government Center, 2293 N. Main St., Crown Point, IN 46307
Fax: (219) 755-3520

★ Clerk **Michael Brown** ....(219) 755-3465

Office of the County Coroner

2900 W. 93rd Ave., Crown Point, IN 46307-1854
Fax: (219) 755-3276

★ Coroner **Merrilee Frey** ....(219) 755-3265
Term Expires: December 31, 2016

Office of the County Prosecutor

County Government Center, 2293 N. Main St., Crown Point, IN 46307
Fax: (219) 755-3642

★ Prosecutor **Bernard A. Carter** (D) ....(219) 755-3720
Term Expires: December 31, 2018

Office of the Recorder

County Government Center, 2293 N. Main St., Crown Point, IN 46307
Fax: (219) 755-3257

★ Recorder **Mike Brown** (D) ....(219) 755-3730
Term Expires: December 31, 2016

Office of the Surveyor

County Government Center, 2293 N. Main St., Crown Point, IN 46307
Fax: (219) 755-3750

★ Surveyor **Bill Emerson, Jr.** ....(219) 755-3745
Term Expires: December 31, 2016

Office of the Sheriff

County Government Center, 2293 N. Main St., Crown Point, IN 46307
Fax: (219) 755-3371

★ Sheriff **John Buncich** (D) ....(219) 755-3333
Term Expires: December 31, 2018

Office of the Treasurer

County Government Center, 2293 N. Main St., Crown Point, IN 46307
Fax: (219) 755-3776

★ Treasurer **Peggy Holinga Katona** (D) ....(219) 755-3760
Term Expires: December 31, 2018

Lake County Board of Elections and Voter's Registration

County Government Center, 2293 N. Main St., Crown Point, IN 46307
Fax: (219) 755-3801

Chairperson **Mike Brown** ....(219) 755-3049
Board Member **Dana Dumezich** ....(219) 755-3795
Board Member **Dennis Hawrot** ....(219) 755-3795
Board Member **Michael Mellon** ....(219) 755-3795
Board Member **Kevin Smith** ....(219) 755-3795
Director **Michelle Freeman** ....(219) 755-3819
Assistant Director **Patrick E. Gabrione** (R) ....(219) 755-3795

County of Lancaster, Pennsylvania

Lancaster Government Center, 150 North Queen Street,
Lancaster, PA 17603
Tel: (717) 299-8000 (Information) Internet: www.co.lancaster.pa.us

County Seat: Lancaster **Election Type:** Partisan **Population:** 536,624 (2015)

Office of the Board of Commissioners

150 North Queen Street, Suite 715, Lancaster, PA 17603
Tel: (717) 299-8300 Fax: (717) 293-7208
E-mail: mccuea@co.lancaster.pa.us

★ Chairman **Dennis P. Stuckey** (R) ....(717) 299-8300
Term Expires: December 31, 2019
★ Commissioner **Craig Lehman** (D) ....(717) 299-8300
Term Expires: December 31, 2019
★ Commissioner **Joshua G. Parsons** (R) ....(717) 299-8300
Term Expires: December 31, 2019
▶ Chief Clerk **Robert Still** ....(717) 299-8300
E-mail: rstill@co.lancaster.pa.us

Office of Aging

150 North Queen Street, Suite 415, Lancaster, PA 17603
Fax: (717) 295-2070

▶ Director **Jackie Burch** ....(717) 299-7979
E-mail: aging@co.lancaster.pa.us

Office of the County Solicitor

150 North Queen Street, Suite 714, Lancaster, PA 17603
Tel: (717) 735-1584 Fax: (717) 293-7208

▶ Solicitor **(Vacant)** ....(717) 735-1584

Behavioral Health and Developmental Services [BHDS]

150 N. Queen St., Suite 610, Lancaster, PA 17603
Tel: (717) 299-8021 Fax: (717) 295-3680

▶ Executive Director **Lawrence George** ....(717) 299-8021
E-mail: georgel@co.lancaster.pa.us

Office of the Public Defender

150 North Queen Street, Suite 210, Lancaster, PA 17603
Tel: (717) 299-8131 Fax: (717) 295-2509

▶ Public Defender **Todd Brown** ....(717) 299-8131
E-mail: tbrown@co.lancaster.pa.us

Office of Tax Assessment

150 North Queen Street, Suite 310, Lancaster, PA 17603
Fax: (717) 299-8376

▶ Director of Property Assessment **John Mavrides** ....(717) 299-8381
E-mail: mavridesj@co.lancaster.pa.us

COUNTIES

★ Elected Official ▲ Appointed by Legislature ▼ Appointed by Governor ▶ Appointed by Board or Commission ● Appointed by Judge
■ Appointed by Mayor △ Appointed by Freeholders ▽ Appointed by Supervisor ▷ Appointed by County Executive ○ Appointed by Council

Board of Elections and Registration Commission
150 North Queen Street, Suite 117, Lancaster, PA 17603
Fax: (717) 209-3076

- ▶ Chief Clerk/Registrar **Randall O. Wenger** (R) .... (717) 299-8293
  E-mail: rwenger@co.lancaster.pa.us
- ▶ Voting Machine Director **William F. Paes III** .... (717) 299-8299

Building Maintenance and Facilities Department
150 North Queen Street, Suite 612, Lancaster, PA 17603
Fax: (717) 295-3508

- ▶ Facilities Management Engineer **Charles Douts** .... (717) 299-8323
  E-mail: cdouts@co.lancaster.pa.us

Human Resources Department
150 North Queen Street, Suite 312, Lancaster, PA 17603
Fax: (717) 293-7269

- ▶ Director **William Peters** .... (717) 299-8310
  E-mail: wpeters@co.lancaster.pa.us

Department of Information Technology and Budget Services
150 North Queen Street, Annex 3rd Floor, Suite 322, Lancaster, PA 17603
Tel: (717) 299-8252 Fax: (717) 299-8256

- ▶ Director **Maggie Weidinger** .... (717) 299-8252
  E-mail: ithelpdesk@co.lancaster.pa.us

Geographic Information Systems Division
150 North Queen Street, Annex 3rd Floor, Suite 322, Lancaster, PA 17603
Tel: (717) 391-7550 Fax: (717) 209-3118
Internet: www.co.lancaster.pa.us/gis

Manager **Glenn Mohler** .... (717) 391-7550

Department of Parks and Recreation
1050 Rockford Road, Lancaster, PA 17602
Tel: (717) 299-8215 Fax: (717) 295-5942
E-mail: parks@co.lancaster.pa.us Internet: www.co.lancaster.pa.us/parks

- ▶ Director **Paul Weiss** .... (717) 299-8215
  E-mail: weissp@co.lancaster.pa.us

Planning Commission
150 North Queen Street, Annex 3rd Floor, Suite 320, Lancaster, PA 17603
Fax: (717) 295-3659

- ▶ Director **James R. Cowhey** .... (717) 299-8333
  E-mail: planning@co.lancaster.pa.us

Probation Department
40 East King Street, Lancaster, PA 17602
Fax: (717) 391-7598

- ▶ Adult Probation Director **Mark Wilson** .... (717) 299-8181
  E-mail: mwilson@co.lancaster.pa.us
- ▶ Juvenile Probation Director **David H. Mueller** .... (717) 299-8161
  50 N. Duke St., Lancaster, PA 17608-3480
  E-mail: muellerd@co.lancaster.pa.us

Purchasing Department
150 North Queen Street, Suite 712, Lancaster, PA 17603
Fax: (717) 390-7739

- ▶ Director **Harry Klinger** .... (717) 299-8258
  E-mail: hklinger@co.lancaster.pa.us

Department of Veterans' Affairs
150 North Queen Street, Suite 115, Lancaster, PA 17603
Fax: (717) 209-3077

- ▶ Director **Daniel Tooth** .... (717) 299-7920
  E-mail: dtooth@co.lancaster.pa.us

Lancaster County Emergency Management Agency [LEMA]
P.O. Box 219, Manheim, PA 17545
Tel: (717) 664-1200 Fax: (717) 664-1235
Internet: www.lema.co.lancaster.pa.us

- ▶ Director **Randall Gockley** .... (717) 664-1200
  E-mail: rgockley@lema.co.lancaster.pa.us
- EMS Coordinator **Brenda Pittman** .... (717) 664-1208
  Education: National-Louis 1995 BAA

Lancaster County Housing and Redevelopment Authorities
202 North Prince Street, Suite 4001, Lancaster, PA 17603
Tel: (717) 394-0793 Fax: (717) 394-7635 E-mail: info@lchra.com
Internet: www.lchra.com

- ▶ Executive Director **Matthew Sternberg** .... (717) 394-0793

Lancaster County Law Library
50 North Duke Street, Lancaster, PA 17603
Tel: (717) 299-8090 Fax: (717) 295-2509

- ▶ Law Librarian **Eleanor Lloyd-Gerlott** .... (717) 299-8090

Lancaster County Prison
625 East King Street, Lancaster, PA 17602
Fax: (717) 299-7813 E-mail: prisonmail@co.lancaster.pa.us
Internet: www.co.lancaster.pa.us/lcprison

- ▶ Warden **Cheryl Steberger** .... (717) 299-7800
  E-mail: stebergerc@co.lancaster.pa.us

Lancaster Children and Youth Social Service Agency
900 East King Street, Lancaster, PA 17602
Fax: (717) 299-7929

- ▶ Executive Director **Crystal A. Natan** .... (717) 299-7925
  E-mail: cgingrich@co.lancaster.pa.us

Red Rose Transit Authority [RRTA]
45 Erick Road, Lancaster, PA 17601
Fax: (717) 397-4761 E-mail: info@redrosetransit.com
Internet: www.redrosetransit.com

- ▶ Executive Director **David Kilmer** .... (717) 397-5613
  E-mail: dkilmer@redrosetransit.com

Office of the Controller
150 North Queen Street, Suite 710, Lancaster, PA 17603
Tel: (717) 299-8262 Fax: (717) 293-7239

- ★ Controller **Brian Hurter** .... (717) 299-8262
  Term Expires: December 31, 2017

Office of the Coroner
Lancaster County Forensic Center, 2080 Spring Valley Road, Lancaster, PA 17601
Fax: (717) 735-2138

- ★ Coroner **Stephen G. Diamantoni** (R) .... (717) 735-2123
  Term Expires: December 31, 2019
  E-mail: SDiamantoni@co.lancaster.pa.us

Office of the District Attorney
50 N. Duke St., Lancaster, PA 17608-3480
Fax: (717) 295-3693 Internet: www.co.lancaster.pa.us/da

- ★ District Attorney **Craig Stedman** (R) .... (717) 735-8100
  Term Expires: December 31, 2019

★ Elected Official ▲ Appointed by Legislature ▼ Appointed by Governor ▶ Appointed by Board or Commission ● Appointed by Judge
■ Appointed by Mayor △ Appointed by Freeholders ▽ Appointed by Supervisor ▷ Appointed by County Executive ○ Appointed by Council

Investigative Division
50 N. Duke St., Lancaster, PA 17603
Fax: (717) 295-3693

▶ Chief **Michael Landis** .... (717) 299-8100
E-mail: landism@co.lancaster.pa.us

Office of the Prothonotary
50 N. Duke St., Lancaster, PA 17608-3480
Fax: (717) 293-7210

★ Prothonotary **The Honorable Katherine Wood-Jacobs** .. (717) 299-8282
Term Expires: December 31, 2019
E-mail: kwoodjacobs@co.lancaster.pa.us

Office of the Recorder of Deeds
150 North Queen Street, Suite 315, Lancaster, PA 17603
Fax: (717) 299-8393

★ Recorder of Deeds **Bonnie Bowman** (R) .... (717) 299-8238
Term Expires: December 31, 2017

Office of the Register of Wills
50 N. Duke St., Lancaster, PA 17608-3480
Fax: (717) 294-3522

★ Register of Wills **Anne L. Cooper** .... (717) 299-8243
Term Expires: December 31, 2019

Office of the Sheriff
50 North Duke Street, Lancaster, PA 17608-3480
Tel: (717) 299-8200 Fax: (717) 295-3656
Internet: www.co.lancaster.pa.us/sheriffs

★ Sheriff (Acting) **Mark Reese** .... (717) 299-8200
Term Expires: December 31, 2019
E-mail: reesem@co.lancaster.pa.us

Office of the Treasurer
150 North Queen Street, Suite 122 Annex, Lancaster, PA 17603
Fax: (717) 390-2319

★ Treasurer **Amber Green** .... (717) 299-8222
Term Expires: December 31, 2019

Lancaster County Solid Waste Management Authority
1299 Harrisburg Pike, Lancaster, PA 17604
Tel: (717) 397-9968 Fax: (717) 397-9973 Internet: www.lcswma.org

Chief Executive Officer **James D. "Jim" Warner** .... (717) 397-9968
Education: Shippensburg MS

County of Laramie, Wyoming
309 West 20th Street, Cheyenne, WY 82001
P.O. Box 608, Cheyenne, WY 82003
Internet: www.laramiecounty.com

County Seat: Cheyenne **Election Type:** Nonpartisan
Population: 97,121 (2015)

Office of the Board of Commissioners
310 West 19th Street, Suite 300, Cheyenne, WY 82001
TTY: (307) 633-4265 Fax: (307) 633-4267
E-mail: commissioners@laramiecounty.com

★ Chairman **Keith "Buck" Holmes** .... (307) 633-4260
Term Expires: January 5, 2017
E-mail: bholmes@laramiecounty.com

★ Vice Chair **Linda Heath** .... (307) 633-4260
Term Expires: January 2019

★ Commissioner **Amber Ash** .... (307) 633-4260
Term Expires: January 5, 2017
E-mail: aash@laramiecounty.com

★ Commissioner **Ron Kailey, Jr.** .... (307) 633-4260
Term Expires: January 2019

★ Commissioner **Troy Thompson** .... (307) 633-4260
Term Expires: January 5, 2019
E-mail: tthompson@laramiecounty.com

County Attorney
310 W. 19th St., Suite 320, Cheyenne, WY 82001
Fax: (307) 633-4329

▶ County Attorney **Mark Voss** .... (307) 633-4370
E-mail: mvoss@laramiecounty.com

Emergency Management Agency
3962 Archer Parkway, Cheyenne, WY 82009
Fax: (307) 633-4337

Director **Rob Cleveland** .... (307) 633-4333
E-mail: rcleveland@laramiecounty.com

Cheyenne-Laramie County Health Department
100 Central Avenue, Cheyenne, WY 82007
Tel: (307) 633-4000 Fax: (307) 633-4005

Director **Gus Lopez** .... (307) 633-4011
Environmental Health Director **Gary Hickman** .... (307) 633-4090
Fax: (307) 633-4038

Human Resources
310 W. 19th St., Suite 320, Cheyenne, WY 82001
Fax: (307) 633-4329

Director **Heather Rudy** .... (307) 633-4355

Information Technology Department
310 South 19th Street, Suite 410, Cheyenne, WY 82001

Director **Rick Fortney** .... (307) 633-4281
E-mail: rfortney@laramiecounty.com Fax: (307) 633-4527

Planning Department
3966 Archer Parkway, Cheyenne, WY 82009
Fax: (307) 633-4519

Director and Chief Planner **Dan Cooley** .... (307) 633-4303

Public Works
13797 Prairie Center, Cheyenne, WY 82009
Fax: (307) 633-4313

Director **Rob Geringer** .... (307) 633-4302

COUNTIES

★ Elected Official ▲ Appointed by Legislature ▼ Appointed by Governor ▶ Appointed by Board or Commission ● Appointed by Judge
■ Appointed by Mayor △ Appointed by Freeholders ▽ Appointed by Supervisor ▷ Appointed by County Executive ○ Appointed by Council

Office of the Assessor

309 W. 20th St., Cheyenne, WY 82001
Fax: (307) 633-4474 E-mail: assessor@laramiecounty.com

★Assessor **Ken Guille** .... (307) 633-4307
Term Expires: January 5, 2019
E-mail: kguille@laramiecounty.com
Assistant Assessor **Janet Knox** .... (307) 633-4412
E-mail: jknox@laramiecounty.com

Office of the Coroner

3964 Archer Parkway, Cheyenne, WY 82009
Fax: (307) 633-4524

★Coroner **Ronald J. "Ron" Sargent** .... (307) 633-4513
Term Expires: January 5, 2019
E-mail: rons@laramiecounty.com

Office of the County Clerk

309 W. 20th St., Cheyenne, WY 82001
Fax: (307) 633-4240 Internet: http://www.laramiecountyclerk.com

★County Clerk **Debbye Lathrop** .... (307) 633-4268
Term Expires: January 5, 2019
E-mail: dlathrop@laramiecountyclerk.com
Assistant County Clerk **Rhonda Bush** .... (307) 633-4266
E-mail: rhondar@laramiecountyclerk.com

Office of the District Attorney

310 West 19th Street, Suite 200, Cheyenne, WY 82001
Fax: (307) 633-4369

★District Attorney **Jeremiah Sandburg** .... (307) 633-4360
Term Expires: January 2019
Education: Cal State (San Bernardino) BA; Loyola U (Chicago) JD

Office of the Sheriff

1910 Pioneer, Cheyenne, WY 82001
Fax: (307) 633-4723

★Sheriff **Danny L. Glick** .... (307) 633-4700
Term Expires: January 5, 2019
E-mail: dglick@laramiecounty.com

Office of the Treasurer

309 West 20th Street, Cheyenne, WY 82001
Fax: (307) 633-4408

★Treasurer **Trudy Eisele** .... (307) 633-4222
Term Expires: January 3, 2019
E-mail: teisele@laramiecounty.com
Assistant Treasurer **Karen Fortney** .... (307) 633-4227

County of Lee, Florida

2115 Second Street, Fort Myers, FL 33901
Tel: (239) 533-2737 Internet: www.lee-county.com

County Seat: Fort Myers **Election Type:** Partisan **Year Founded:** 1887
Population: 701,982 (2015)

Board of County Commissioners

Old Lee County Courthouse, 2120 Main Street, Fort Myers, FL 33901
P.O. Box 398, Fort Myers, FL 33902-0398

★Chairman **Frank Mann** (R-District 5) .... (239) 533-2225
Term Expires: November 2016 Fax: (239) 485-2092
E-mail: dist5@leegov.com
Education: Vanderbilt BA
Executive Assistant **Chris Berry** .... (239) 533-2225
E-mail: cberry@leegov.com Fax: (239) 485-2092

★Vice Chair **John E. Manning** (R-District 1) .... (239) 533-2224
Term Expires: November 2016 Fax: (239) 485-2155
E-mail: dist1@leegov.com
Date of Birth: June 28, 1950
Education: Northeastern 1973 BS
Executive Assistant **Stacey Rohland** .... (239) 533-2224
Fax: (239) 485-2099

★Commissioner **Cecil Pendergrass** (District 2) .... (239) 533-2227
Term Expires: November 20, 2018 Fax: (239) 485-2099
E-mail: dist2@leegov.com
Executive Assistant **Christine Deramo** .... (239) 533-2227
Fax: (239) 485-2155

★Commissioner **Larry Kiker** (District 3) .... (239) 533-2223
Term Expires: November 2016 Fax: (239) 485-2021
E-mail: dist3@leegov.com
Executive Assistant **Antoinette Johnson** .... (239) 533-2223
Fax: (239) 485-2021

★Commissioner **Brian Hamman** (District 4) .... (239) 533-2226
Term Expires: November 20, 2018 Fax: (239) 485-2054
E-mail: dist4@leegov.com
Education: Florida Gulf Coast BA
Executive Assistant **Matt Spielman** .... (239) 533-2226
Fax: (239) 485-2054

Office of the County Attorney

2115 Second Street, 6th Floor, Fort Myers, FL 33901
Tel: (239) 533-2236 Fax: (239) 485-2118
Internet: www.lee-county.com/gov/dept/countyattorney

▶County Attorney **Richard Wesch** .... (239) 533-2236

Hearing Examiner's Office

1500 Monroe Street, Room 218, Fort Myers, FL 33901
Tel: (239) 533-8100 Fax: (239) 485-8406 E-mail: hex@leegov.com
Internet: www.lee-county.com/gov/dept/hearingexaminer

Chief Hearing Examiner **Donna Marie Collins** .... (239) 533-8100
Deputy Hearing Examiner **Laura B. Bellflower** .... (239) 533-8100

Office of the County Manager

2115 Second Street, 4th Floor, Fort Myers, FL 33901
Tel: (239) 533-2221 Fax: (239) 485-2262

○County Manager **Roger J. Desjarlais** .... (239) 533-2221
E-mail: rdesjarlais@leegov.com

Office of the Assistant County Manager for Administrative and Internal Services

Assistant County Manager **Peter "Pete" Winton** .... (239) 533-2221
E-mail: pwinton@leegov.com

★Elected Official ▲Appointed by Legislature ▼Appointed by Governor ▶Appointed by Board or Commission ●Appointed by Judge
■Appointed by Mayor △Appointed by Freeholders ▽Appointed by Supervisor ▷Appointed by County Executive ○Appointed by Council

Budget Services Division
Tel: (239) 533-2301
Internet: www.lee-county.com/gov/dept/budgetservices

Director **(Vacant)** .... (239) 533-2221

Division of County Lands
1500 Monroe Street, 4th Floor, Fort Myers, FL 33901
Tel: (239) 533-8505 Fax: (239) 485-8391

Director **Karen Wells** .... (239) 533-8888
Property Acquisition Assistant
Reneé L. M. Armstrong .... (239) 553-8855
E-mail: raarmstrong2@leegov.com
Senior Property Acquisition Agent **Teresa Mann** .... (239) 533-8742
Land Acquisition Manager **Robert G. Clemens** .... (239) 533-8747
E-mail: clemenrg@leegov.com
Real Estate Title Examiner **Sheila Bedwell** .... (239) 533-8746
Senior Geographic Information System (GIS) and
Inventory Technician **(Vacant)** .... (239) 533-8833

Facilities Services and Maintenance and Repair Service Division
1500 Monroe Street, 4th Floor, Fort Myers, FL 33901
Tel: (239) 533-8505 Internet: www.lee-county.com/gov/dept/facilities

Director **Damon Grant** .... (239) 533-8838
E-mail: dsgrant@leegov.com

Fleet Management Division
2955 Van Buren Street, Fort Myers, FL 33916
Tel: (239) 533-5300 Fax: (239) 533-5305

Fleet Manager **Marilyn Rawlings** .... (239) 533-5300

Department of Human Resources
2115 Second Street, 1st Floor, Fort Myers, FL 33901
Tel: (239) 533-2245 Fax: (239) 485-2077

Director (Interim) **Stephanie Figueroa** .... (239) 533-2006
E-mail: sfigueroa@leegov.com
Human Resources Manager **Lynne Peterson** .... (239) 533-2014
E-mail: hpeteson@leegov.com

Information Technology Division
Director **James "Jim" Desjarlais** .... (239) 533-2221
E-mail: jdesjarlais@leegov.com

Public Resources Division
2115 Second Street, Fort Myers, FL 33901
Tel: (239) 533-2737 Fax: (239) 485-2149

Director **(Vacant)** .... (239) 533-2737

Division of Procurement Management
1825 Hendry Street, 3rd Floor, Fort Myers, FL 33901
Tel: (239) 533-5450 Fax: (239) 485-5460

Procurement Director **Bob Franceschini** .... (239) 533-5450
E-mail: rfranceschini@leegov.com
Purchasing Agent **Kathryn "Kathy" Ciccarelli** .... (239) 533-5450
E-mail: kciccarelli@leegov.com

Office of the Assistant County Manager for Community Services
Assistant County Manager **Christine Brady** .... (239) 533-2221
E-mail: cbrady@leegov.com

Veterans Services Office
2072 Victoria Avenue, Fort Myers, FL 33901
Tel: (239) 533-8381 Fax: (239) 533-8382
Internet: www.lee-county.com/gov/dept/veteransservices

Director **Richard Beck** .... (239) 533-7978
E-mail: rbeck@leegov.com

Department of Community Development
1500 Monroe Street, Fort Myers, FL 33901
1825 Hendry Street, Fort Myers, FL 33901
Tel: (239) 533-8585 Fax: (239) 485-8386 Internet: www3.leegov.com/dcd

Director **David Loveland** .... (239) 533-8345
E-mail: dloveland@leegov.com

Department of Human Services
2440 Thompson Street, Fort Myers, FL 33901
Tel: (239) 533-7930 Fax: (239) 533-7960 Internet: http://dhs.leegov.com

Director **Ann M. Arnall** .... (239) 533-7930
E-mail: aarnall@leegov.com
Contracts Program Manager **Deanna Gilkerson** .... (239) 533-7918
Family Self-Sufficiency Program Manager **Kim Hustad** ... (239) 533-7916
E-mail: khustad@leegov.com
Eligibility Coordinator **Janeth B. Maldonado** .... (239) 533-7900
E-mail: jmaldonado@leegov.com
Housing Services Program Manager **Cyndy Cook** .... (239) 533-7941
Neighborhood Building Program Manager
Julie A. Boudreaux .... (239) 533-7911
Fiscal Manager **Barbara J. Hollis** .... (239) 533-7923
E-mail: bhollis@leegov.com
Geographic Information System (GIS) Coordinator
Jason Krejci .... (239) 533-7961
E-mail: jkrejci@leegov.com
Office Manager **Paula Allison** .... (239) 533-7927
Administrative Assistant **Laura L. Purks** .... (239) 533-7927

Transit Department [LeeTran]
6035 Landing View Road, Fort Myers, FL 33907
Tel: (239) 533-8726 Fax: (239) 277-5011 Internet: www.rideleetran.com

Director **Steve Myers** .... (239) 533-8726

Domestic Animal Services
5600 Banner Drive, Fort Myers, FL 33912
Tel: (239) 533-7387 Fax: (239) 432-2118 Internet: www.leelostpets.com

Director (Acting) **David W. Harner II** .... (239) 533-9200

Library System
2345 Union Street, Fort Myers, FL 33901
Tel: (239) 533-4800 Fax: (239) 485-1100
Internet: http://library.lee-county.com

Director **Sheldon Kaye** .... (239) 533-4800
E-mail: skaye@leegov.com

Parks and Recreation
Terry Park, 3410 Palm Beach Boulevard, Fort Myers, FL 33916
Tel: (239) 533-7275 Fax: (239) 485-2300 Internet: www.leeparks.org

Director **Dana Kasler** .... (239) 533-7412
Deputy Director **Alise Flanjack** .... (239) 533-7451

Division of Public Safety
14752 Six Mile Cypress Parkway, Fort Myers, FL 33912
Tel: (239) 533-3911 Fax: (239) 485-2605 Internet: www.lee-ems.com

Director **Robert Farmer** .... (239) 533-3905
E-mail: stuttle@leegov.com
Deputy Director and Emergency Medical Services
(EMS) Chief **Scott Tuttle** .... (239) 533-3961
Deputy Chief, Operations **Benjamin Abes** .... (239) 533-3916
E-mail: benjamin.abes@leegov.com

(continued on next page)

COUNTIES

★ Elected Official ▲ Appointed by Legislature ▼ Appointed by Governor ► Appointed by Board or Commission ● Appointed by Judge
■ Appointed by Mayor △ Appointed by Freeholders ▽ Appointed by Supervisor ▷ Appointed by County Executive ○ Appointed by Council

Division of Public Safety *continued*

Deputy Chief, Training and Continuous Quality Improvement (CQI) **Joseph Maguire** . . . . (239) 533-3917
E-mail: jmaguire@leegov.com

Office of the Assistant County Manager for Public Works

1500 Monroe Street, 4th Floor, Fort Myers, FL 33901
Internet: www3.leegov.com/publicworks

Assistant County Manager **Douglas "Doug" Meurer** . . . . (239) 533-2221

Facilities, Construction, and Management Department

1500 Monroe Street, Fort Myers, FL 33901
Fax: (239) 485-8307

Manager **Damon Grant** . . . . (239) 479-8505
E-mail: dgrant@leegov.com

Department of Transportation [DOT]

1500 Monroe Street, Fort Myers, FL 33901
Tel: (239) 553-8580 Fax: (239) 485-8520 Internet: www.leegov.com/dot

Director **Randy Cerchie** . . . . (239) 533-8573

Division of Natural Resources

1500 Monroe Street, Fort Myers, FL 33901
Tel: (239) 533-8109 Fax: (239) 485-8408
Internet: www.lee-county.com/gov/dept/NaturalResources

Director **Roland Ottolini** . . . . (239) 533-8127
Operations Manager **Kurt Harclerode** . . . . (239) 533-8146
E-mail: harclekd@leegov.com
Operations Manager, Environmental Section **Keith Kibbey** . . . . (239) 533-8129
Operations Manager, Marine Services **Steve Boutelle** . . . . (239) 533-8128
E-mail: boutelsj@leegov.com
Operations Manager, Water Resources **Anura Karuna-Muni** . . . . (239) 533-8131

Solid Waste Division

Resource Recovery Facility, 10500 Buckingham Road, Fort Myers, FL 33905
Tel: (239) 533-8000 Internet: www3.leegov.com/solidwaste

Director (Acting) **Keith Howard** . . . . (239) 533-8917
Deputy Director **(Vacant)** . . . . (239) 461-3043

Lee County Utilities [LCU]

1500 Monroe Street, 3rd Floor, Fort Myers, FL 33901
Tel: (239) 553-8181 Tel: (239) 936-0247 (Customer Service Center)
Fax: (239) 485-8385 Fax: (239) 936-0549 (Customer Service Center)
Internet: www.lee-county.com/utilities

Director **Pamela "Pam" Keyes** . . . . (239) 533-8181
Deputy Director **(Vacant)** . . . . (239) 533-5636
Operations Manager **Hank Barroso** . . . . (239) 567-2181
E-mail: hbarroso@leegov.com
Senior Wastewater Operations Manager **Dennis Lang** . . . . (239) 446-8039
E-mail: langdr@leegov.com
Senior Water Operations Manager **Hank Barroso** . . . . (239) 267-8228
E-mail: hbarroso@leegov.com
Senior Operations Manager **DeWayne Tagg** . . . . (239) 693-2992
E-mail: dtagg@leegov.com
Instrumentation and Electrical Manager **Doug Meyer** . . . . (239) 936-0247
E-mail: dmeyer@leegov.com
Maintenance and Cross Connection Control Manager **Larry Clifford** . . . . (239) 936-0247
Senior Manager for Development **Thom Osterhout** . . . . . (239) 533-8165
Sewer Assessments **Judy Raye** . . . . (239) 533-8725
Wastewater Collection System Manager **Rich Sims** . . . . (239) 693-2992 ext. 213
Water Distribution System Manager **Justin Dodd** . . . . (239) 693-2992

Lee County Utilities *continued*

Compliance and Legislative Manager/Public Information Officer **Patricia DiPiero** . . . . (239) 533-8534
E-mail: dipierpm@leegov.com
Customer Service Manager **Amanda Jobes** . . . . (239) 936-0247

Lee County Economic Development Office

2201 Second Street, Suite 500, Fort Myers, FL 33901
Tel: (239) 338-3161 Fax: (239) 338-3227

Director **John P. Boland** . . . . (239) 338-3161
E-mail: jboland@leegov.com
Business Assistance Specialist **Warren Baucom** . . . . (239) 533-6817
E-mail: wbaucom@leegov.com

Lee County Sports Authority

2201 Second Street, Suite 501, Fort Myers, FL 33901
Tel: (239) 533-5273 Tel: (866) 897-2002 (Toll Free) Fax: (239) 485-3111

Executive Director **Jeff Mielke** . . . . (239) 533-5273
Sports Development Manager **Gary Ewen** . . . . (239) 533-5273
E-mail: gewen@leegov.com
Administrative Specialist **Connie Keenan Buchanan** . . . . (239) 533-5273
E-mail: cbuchanan@leegov.com

Lee County Visitor and Convention Bureau [VCB]

12800 University Drive, Suite 550, Fort Myers, FL 33907
Tel: (239) 338-3500 Tel: (800) 237-6444 (Toll Free) Fax: (239) 334-1106
Internet: www.leevcb.com

Executive Director **Tamara Pigott** . . . . (239) 338-3500
Education: Florida State BS
Deputy Director **Pamela Johnson** . . . . (239) 338-3500
Fiscal Officer **Berta Maldonado** . . . . (239) 338-3500
E-mail: bmaldonado@leegov.com
Senior Account Clerk **Khandyce Mosely** . . . . (239) 338-3500
E-mail: kmosely@leegov.com
Office Manager **Fran Belasco** . . . . (239) 338-3500

Marketing and Communications Department

Director **Francesca Donlan** . . . . (239) 338-3500
Communications Manager **Lee Rose** . . . . (239) 338-3500
E-mail: lrose@leegov.com
Communications Coordinator **(Vacant)** . . . . (239) 338-3500

Product Development Department

Program Manager **Nancy MacPhee** . . . . (239) 338-3500

Sales Department

Director **Pamela Johnson** . . . . (239) 338-3500
Inside Sales Coordinator **Pam Brown** . . . . (239) 338-3500
Sales Manager and Meeting Planner **Kimball I. Mathews** . . . . (239) 338-3500
Tour & Travel **Shelley Crant** . . . . (239) 338-3500
International Sales Manager **Stefanie Zinke** . . . . (239) 338-3500
Travel Agent Help Desk Manager **Nancy "Jovina" Huber** . . . . (239) 338-3500

Visitor Services Department

Southwest Florida International Airport, 11000 Terminal Access Road, Suite 8640, Fort Myers, FL 33913
Tel: (239) 590-4855 Fax: (239) 590-4857

Director **Judi Durant** . . . . (239) 590-4855
Tourism Education Manager **Christine Davlin** . . . . (239) 590-4855
Visitor Services Coordinator **Simone Behr** . . . . (239) 590-4855
Visitor Services Coordinator **Sean Corey** . . . . (239) 590-4855

★ Elected Official ▲ Appointed by Legislature ▼ Appointed by Governor ▶ Appointed by Board or Commission ● Appointed by Judge
■ Appointed by Mayor △ Appointed by Freeholders ▽ Appointed by Supervisor ▷ Appointed by County Executive ○ Appointed by Council

Office of the Clerk of the Circuit Court

Justice Center, 1700 Monroe Street, 2nd Floor, Fort Myers, FL 33901
Tel: (239) 533-2555 Internet: www.leeclerk.org
E-mail: leeclerk_info@leeclerk.org

★ Clerk of the Circuit Court **Linda Doggett** . . . . (239) 533-2555
Term Expires: December 31, 2016

Office of the Property Appraiser

2480 Thompson Street, 4th Floor, Fort Myers, FL 33901
P.O. Box 1546, 4th Floor, Fort Myers, FL 33902
Tel: (239) 533-6100 Fax: (239) 533-6160 Internet: www.leepa.org

★ Property Appraiser **Kenneth M. Wilkinson** (R) . . . . (239) 339-6100
Term Expires: December 31, 2016
E-mail: wilkinsonk@leepa.org

Sheriff's Office

14750 Six Mile Cypress Parkway, Fort Myers, FL 33912
Tel: (239) 477-1000 Fax: (239) 477-1030 Internet: www.sheriffleefl.org

★ Sheriff **Mike Scott** . . . . (239) 477-1000
Term Expires: December 31, 2016
E-mail: sheriff@sheriffleefl.org

Supervisor of Elections Office

2480 Thompson Street, Fort Myers, FL 33901
Tel: (239) 533-8683 Fax: (239) 533-6310 Internet: www.leeelections.com

★ Supervisor of Elections **Sharon Harrington** . . . . (239) 533-8683
Term Expires: December 31, 2016

Tax Collector

2480 Thompson Street, 4th Floor, Fort Myers, FL 33901
Tel: (239) 533-6000 Fax: (239) 533-6065 Internet: www.leetc.com

★ Tax Collector **Larry Hart** (R) . . . . (239) 533-6000
Term Expires: December 31, 2016

County of Los Angeles, California

Kenneth Hahn Hall of Administration, 500 West Temple Street, Los Angeles, CA 90012
Tel: (213) 974-1311 (Information) Internet: http://lacounty.gov

County Seat: Los Angeles **Election Type:** Nonpartisan
Population: 10,170,292 (2015)

Office of the Board of Supervisors

Kenneth Hahn Hall of Administration, 500 West Temple Street, Los Angeles, CA 90012
Tel: (213) 974-1411 Fax: (213) 620-0636 Internet: bos.lacounty.gov

★ Chair **Hilda Lucia Solis** (District 1) . . . . (213) 974-4111
Term Expires: December 2018
E-mail: Hilda@hildasolis.com
Date of Birth: October 20, 1957
Education: Cal Poly (Pomona) 1979 BA; USC 1981 MPA

★ Supervisor **Mark Ridley-Thomas** (District 2) . . . . (213) 974-2222
Term Expires: December 1, 2016 Fax: (213) 680-3283
500 W. Temple St., Room 866, Los Angeles, CA 90012
E-mail: seconddistrict@bos.lacounty.gov
Date of Birth: November 6, 1954
Education: Immaculate Heart; USC 1989 PhD

Office of the Board of Supervisors *continued*

★ Supervisor **Sheila James Kuehl** (District 3) . . . . (213) 974-3333
Term Expires: December 2018 Fax: (213) 625-7360
Education: Harvard 1978 JD

★ Supervisor **Don Knabe** (District 4) Room 822 . . . . (213) 974-4444
Term Expires: December 1, 2016 Fax: (213) 626-6941
E-mail: don@bos.lacounty.gov
Date of Birth: August 15, 1943
Education: Graceland Col 1967 BA

★ Supervisor
Michael D. "Mike" Antonovich (District 5) . . . . (213) 974-5555
Term Expires: December 1, 2016 Fax: (213) 974-1010
500 West Temple Street, Los Angeles, CA 90012
E-mail: fifthdistrict@bos.lacounty.gov
Date of Birth: August 12, 1939
Education: Cal State (Los Angeles) 1963 BA, 1967 MA

Chief Executive Office

Kenneth Hahn Hall of Administration, 500 West Temple Street, Room 713, Los Angeles, CA 90012
Tel: (213) 974-1101 Fax: (213) 687-7130 E-mail: info@ceo.lacounty.gov
Internet: http://ceo.lacounty.gov/

▽ Chief Executive Officer **Sachi A. Hamai** . . . . (213) 974-1101
E-mail: shamai@bos.lacounty.gov Fax: (213) 687-7130
Chief Deputy **Jim Jones** . . . . (213) 974-1104
E-mail: jjones@ceo.lacounty.gov Fax: (213) 687-7130
Senior Assistant Chief Executive Officer, Countywide Budget **Sid Kikkawa** Room 726 . . . . (213) 974-6872
E-mail: skikkawa@ceo.lacounty.gov Fax: (213) 626-0892
Assistant Chief Executive Officer, Intergovernmental and External Affairs **Ryan Alsop** Room 723 . . . . (213) 974-1100
Fax: (213) 626-7836
Employee Relations Division Chief **Robinetta Mack** Room 493 . . . . (213) 974-2404
E-mail: rmack@ceo.lacounty.gov Fax: (213) 621-3172
Information Systems Manager **Denny Sunabe** Room 781 . . . . (213) 974-1255
Education: Cal Poly (Pomona) 1986 BS Fax: (213) 613-1001
Legislative Affairs and Intergovernmental Relations **Manuel Rivas, Jr.** . . . . (213) 974-1101

Office of Protocol

Fax: (213) 621-2084

Chief **Sandra Ausman** Room 375 . . . . (213) 974-1307
Deputy Chief **Lourdes Saab** Room 375 . . . . (213) 974-1307
E-mail: lsaab@ceo.lacounty.gov

Countywide Communications Office

500 West Temple Street, Room 358, Los Angeles, CA 90012
Fax: (213) 680-1122

Director **David Sommers** . . . . (213) 974-1363
500 West Temple Street, Room 358, Los Angeles, CA 90012
E-mail: dsommers@ceo.lacounty.gov

Office of Child Protection

500 West Temple Street, Room 726, Los Angeles, CA 90012
Tel: (213) 947-4530 Fax: (213) 626-0892

Deputy Chief Executive Officer **Fesia Davenport** . . . . (213) 974-7365
500 West Temple Street, Room 745, Los Angeles, CA 90012
E-mail: ajimenez@ceo.lacounty.gov

Department of Children and Family Services [DCFS]

425 Shatto Place, Los Angeles, CA 90020
Tel: (213) 351-5602 Fax: (213) 487-4431 Internet: http://lacdcfs.org

Director **Philip L. Browning** . . . . (213) 351-5600
Education: Auburn MBA; Alabama MSW
Executive Secretary **Veronica Martinez** . . . . (213) 739-6436
E-mail: marver@dcfs.lacounty.gov

★ Elected Official ▲ Appointed by Legislature ▼ Appointed by Governor ▶ Appointed by Board or Commission ● Appointed by Judge
■ Appointed by Mayor △ Appointed by Freeholders ▽ Appointed by Supervisor ▷ Appointed by County Executive ○ Appointed by Council

Department of Community and Senior Services [CSS]

3175 West Sixth Street, Los Angeles, CA 90020
Fax: (213) 380-8275 E-mail: info@css.lacounty.gov
Internet: http://css.lacounty.gov/

▽ Director **Cynthia D. Banks** .... (213) 637-0798
E-mail: cbanks@css.lacounty.gov
Chief Deputy Director **Otto Solórzano** .... (213) 738-2600
E-mail: osolorzano@css.lacounty.gov Fax: (213) 480-0926
Assistant Director, Administrative Services Branch
Joyce Washington .... (213) 738-2273
E-mail: jwashington@css.lacounty.gov
Education: U Phoenix 1993 MA
Assistant Director, Aging and Adult Services
Lorenza Sanchez .... (213) 738-2645
E-mail: lsanchez@css.lacounty.gov
Assistant Director, Workforce and Community Services
Josephine "Josie" Marquez .... (213) 738-3175
E-mail: jmarquez@css.lacounty.gov
Human Resource Director **Johnny Acosta** .... (213) 738-2604
E-mail: jacosta@css.lacounty.gov

Department of Public Social Services

12860 Crossroads Pkwy. South, City of Industry, CA 91746
Fax: (562) 908-0459

▽ Director **Sheryl Spiller** .... (562) 908-8400
Chief Deputy Director **Phil Ansell** .... (562) 908-8309
Special Assistant **Derrick Robinson** .... (562) 908-8311

Community Services and Capital Programs

500 West Temple Street, Room 723, Los Angeles, CA 90012
Tel: (213) 893-2477 Fax: (213) 626-0892

Deputy Chief Executive Officer **Rita L. Robinson** .... (213) 893-2477
500 West Temple Street, Room 723, Los Angeles, CA 90012
E-mail: rrobinson@ceo.lacounty.gov
Education: Scripps Col 1975

Department of Beaches and Harbors

13837 Fiji Way, Marina del Rey, CA 90292
Tel: (310) 305-9545 (Information) Fax: (310) 821-6345

▽ Director **Gary Jones** .... (310) 305-9523
Education: Southampton (UK) BS; De Montfort MS
Deputy Director **John Kelly** .... (310) 305-9523
Deputy Director **Brock Ladewig** .... (310) 305-9523
Education: Indiana (Indianapolis) BA, MBA; Santa Clara U JD
Public Information Officer **Carol Baker** .... (310) 305-9562
E-mail: cbaker@bh.lacounty.gov Fax: (310) 822-0119
Information Systems **Betsy Barker** .... (310) 305-9510
E-mail: bbarker@bh.lacounty.gov

Department of Parks and Recreation

433 S. Vermont Ave., Los Angeles, CA 90020
Tel: (213) 738-2961 (Information) Fax: (213) 738-6444
Internet: http://parks.lacounty.gov/

▽ Director (Acting) **John Wicker** .... (213) 738-2951
E-mail: jwicker@parks.lacounty.gov
Special Assistant **Kaye Michelson** .... (213) 738-2955
Chief Deputy **John Wicker** .... (213) 738-2953
Public Information Officer **(Vacant)** .... (213) 738-2963

Administrative Services Agency

433 S. Vermont Ave., Los Angeles, CA 90020

Administrative Deputy **Robert Maycumber** .... (213) 368-5823
E-mail: rmaycumber@parks.lacounty.gov
Administrative Services Manager II **Elizabeth Mendez** ... (213) 738-3040
Fax: (213) 637-9725
Contract Management/ Special Districts Chief
Kandy Hays .... (626) 821-4600
Fax: (626) 447-8573
Information Technology Services Director **(Vacant)** .... (213) 351-5070

Department of Parks and Recreation *continued*

Personnel Officer **David Waage** .... (213) 738-2993
E-mail: dwaage@parks.lacounty.gov Fax: (213) 386-6620

Planning and Development Agency

510 South Vermont Avenue, Los Angeles, CA 90020
Tel: (213) 351-5099 (Information) Fax: (213) 639-3959

Deputy Director **Norma E. Garcia** .... (213) 351-5198
Advanced Planning Chief **Kathline King** .... (213) 351-5098
Education: Northwestern 1983 BA; USC 1988 MPL
Project Management Division Chief **Jim Smith** .... (213) 639-6702
Fax: (213) 427-6158

Regional Facilities Agency

265 Cloverleaf Dr., Baldwin Park, CA 91706

Deputy Director **Hayden Sohm** .... (626) 369-8693
Regional Operations Manager **Hugo Maldonado** .... (626) 369-5147
E-mail: hmaldonado@parks.lacounty.gov
Regional Operations Manager **Roy Williams** .... (626) 333-7698
E-mail: rwilliams@parks.lacounty.gov

East County Community Services Agency

265 Cloverleaf Dr., Baldwin Park, CA 91706
Tel: (626) 369-8694 (Information) Fax: (626) 369-5809

Deputy Director **Frank Gonzales** .... (626) 369-8694
E-mail: fgonzales@parks.lacounty.gov
Agency Operations Manager **Manuel Escobar** .... (626) 369-5146
E-mail: mescobar@parks.lacounty.gov

North County Community Services Agency

31320 Castaic Rd., Castaic, CA 91384
Tel: (661) 294-3500 (Information) Fax: (661) 295-0920

Deputy Director **Jonathan E. "Jon" Gargin** .... (661) 294-3518
Agency Operations Manager **Joyce Gibson** .... (661) 294-3522

South County Community Services Agency

360 W. El Segundo Blvd., Los Angeles, CA 90061
Tel: (310) 965-8603 (Information) Fax: (310) 324-4869

Deputy Director **Joe Mendoza** .... (310) 965-8602
E-mail: jmendoza@parks.lacounty.gov
Agency Operations Manager **Mika Yamamoto** .... (310) 965-8605

Regional Park and Open Space District

510 South Vermont Avenue, Room 230, Los Angeles, CA 90020
Fax: (213) 385-0875

District Administrator **Jane Beesley** .... (213) 738-2981

Department of Public Works [DPW]

P.O. Box 1460, Alhambra, CA 91802-1460
Tel: (626) 458-5100 (Information) Fax: (626) 458-4022
Internet: http://dpw.lacounty.gov

Director **Gail Farber** .... (626) 458-4002
Education: San Diego State 1985 BSCE
Assistant Director **(Vacant)** .... (626) 458-4012
Chief Deputy Director **Mark Pestrella** .... (626) 458-4001
Assistant Director **Jacob Williams** .... (626) 458-4014
Deputy Director **Shari Afshari** .... (626) 458-4008
Deputy Director **Patrick V. "Pat" DeChellis** .... (626) 458-4004
Deputy Director **Massood Eftekhari** .... (626) 458-4016
E-mail: meftekhari@dpw.lacounty.gov
Deputy Director **Gary Hildebrand** .... (626) 458-4300
Deputy Director **Dennis Hunter** .... (626) 458-4006
Deputy Director **William "Bill" Winter** .... (626) 458-4018
Chief Information Officer **Jesse Juarros** .... (626) 458-4117
E-mail: jjuarros@dpw.lacounty.gov

Department of Regional Planning [DRP]

Hall of Records, 320 West Temple Street, Los Angeles, CA 90012-3225
Fax: (213) 626-0434 Internet: http://planning.lacounty.gov/

▽ Planning Director **Richard Bruckner** Room 1390 .... (213) 974-6401
E-mail: rbruckner@planning.lacounty.gov

★ Elected Official ▲ Appointed by Legislature ▼ Appointed by Governor ► Appointed by Board or Commission ● Appointed by Judge
■ Appointed by Mayor △ Appointed by Freeholders ▽ Appointed by Supervisor ▷ Appointed by County Executive ○ Appointed by Council

COUNTIES

Department of Regional Planning *continued*

▽Chief Deputy Director **Dennis Slavin** Room 1390 . . . . (213) 974-6405
E-mail: dslavin@planning.lacounty.gov
Deputy Director, Advance Planning **Mark Childs** Room 1351 . . . . (213) 974-6457
Deputy Director, Current Planning **Sorin Alexanian** Room 1351 . . . . (213) 974-6441
Deputy Director, Land Use Regulation **Jon Sanabria** Room 1386 . . . . (213) 974-6431
Administrative Deputy, Information and Fiscal Services **Ania G. Onley** Room 1390 . . . . (213) 974-6631

The County of Los Angeles Public Library

7400 East Imperial Highway, Downey, CA 90242-3375
Tel: (562) 940-8462 (Information) Fax: (562) 803-3032
Internet: www.colapublib.org

▽County Librarian **Skye Patrick** . . . . (562) 940-8400
E-mail: spatrick@library.lacounty.gov
Chief Deputy County Librarian **Yolanda De Ramos** . . . . . (562) 940-8418
E-mail: yderamos@library.lacounty.gov
Assistant Director, Capital Projects and Facilities Services **Pat McGee** . . . . (562) 940-4145
E-mail: pmcgee@library.lacounty.gov
Assistant Director, Finance and Planning **Tina Fanti** . . . . . (562) 940-8406
Assistant Director, Public Services **Barbara Custen** . . . . . . (562) 940-8409
E-mail: bcusten@library.lacounty.gov
Assistant Director, Department Chief Information Officer **Migell Acosta** . . . . (562) 940-8412
E-mail: macosta@library.lacounty.gov
Development Officer **(Vacant)** . . . . (562) 940-8403
Public Information Officer **Pamela Broussard** . . . . (562) 940-8415
E-mail: pbroussard@library.lacounty.gov
Public Affairs Coordinator **(Vacant)** . . . . (562) 940-8559
Assistant Director, Administrative Services **Amylen Clarke** . . . . (562) 940-4145
E-mail: aclarke@library.lacounty.gov

Health and Mental Health Services

500 West Temple Street, Room 726, Los Angeles, CA 90012
Tel: (213) 974-1160 Fax: (213) 620-1381

Deputy Chief Executive Officer **Gregory Polk** . . . . (213) 974-1160
500 West Temple Street, Room 726, Los Angeles, CA 90012

Department of Health Services [DHS]

313 North Figueroa Street, Room 912, Los Angeles, CA 90012
Fax: (213) 481-0503 E-mail: dhsportal@dhs.lacounty.gov
Internet: http://dhs.lacounty.gov

Director **Mitchell H. Katz** . . . . (213) 240-8101
Education: Yale BS; Harvard MD

Department of Mental Health [DMH]

550 South Vermont, Los Angeles, CA 90020
Tel: (213) 738-4601 Tel: (800) 854-7771 (Emergency Hotline)
Fax: (213) 386-1297 Internet: http://dmh.lacounty.gov

►Director (Acting) **Robin Kay** . . . . (213) 738-4601
E-mail: rkay@dmh.lacounty.gov
Chief Deputy Director **Robin Kay** . . . . (213) 738-4108
Medical Director **Roderick E. Shaner** . . . . (213) 738-4603
Education: UCLA 1976 MD
Chief Financial Officer **Kimberly Nall** . . . . (213) 738-4625
Chief Information Officer **Robert Greenless** . . . . (213) 251-6481
695 South Vermont, 7th Floor, Los Angeles, CA 90020 Fax: (213) 736-9360
E-mail: rgreenless@dmh.lacounty.gov

Department of Public Health [DPH]

313 North Figueroa Street, Room 806, Los Angeles, CA 90012
Fax: (213) 240-8626 Internet: http://publichealth.lacounty.gov/

Health Officer (Interim) **Dr. Jeffrey Gunzenhauser** . . . . . . (213) 240-8117
Executive Assistant **Maria Ojeda** . . . . (213) 240-8117
E-mail: mojeda@ph.lacounty.gov

Operations

500 West Temple Street, Room 726, Los Angeles, CA 90012
Tel: (213) 974-1186 Fax: (213) 687-7130

Deputy Chief Executive Officer **Santos H. Kreimann** . . . . (213) 974-1186
500 West Temple Street, Room 726, Los Angeles, CA 90012 Fax: (213) 687-7130

Chief Information Office

Los Angeles World Trade Center, 350 South Figureoa Street, Suite 188, Los Angeles, CA 90071

Chief Information Officer **Richard Sanchez** . . . . (213) 253-5600
E-mail: rsanchez@cio.lacounty.gov
Chief Information Security Officer **Robert Pittman** . . . . . (213) 253-5600
E-mail: rpittman@cio.lacounty.gov

Office of the Registrar-Recorder/County Clerk

12400 Imperial Highway, Norwalk, CA 90650-8357
Tel: (562) 466-1310 (Information) TTY: (562) 462-2259
Fax: (562) 929-4790 Internet: www.lavote.net

▽Registrar-Recorder/County Clerk **Dean C. Logan** . . . . (562) 462-2716
E-mail: dlogan@rrcc.lacounty.gov
Secretary **Frances Posadas** . . . . (562) 462-2720
E-mail: fposadas@rrcc.lacounty.gov
Chief Deputy **Debbie Martin** . . . . (562) 462-2883
Secretary **Cindy Cheng** . . . . (562) 462-2729
E-mail: ccheng@rrcc.lacounty.gov
Election Operations Assistant **Tim McNamara** . . . . (562) 462-2722
E-mail: tmcnamara@rrcc.lacounty.gov
Network and Voter Systems Division Manager **Ray Ching** . . . . (562) 462-2708
E-mail: rching@rrcc.lacounty.gov
Information Technology **Jeramy Gray** . . . . (562) 462-2714
E-mail: jgray@rrcc.lacounty.gov

Office of the Treasurer and Tax Collector

Kenneth Hahn Hall of Administration, 500 West Temple Street, Room 437, Los Angeles, CA 90012-2724
Tel: (213) 974-2101 Fax: (213) 626-1812 Internet: http://ttc.lacounty.gov/

▽Treasurer and Tax Collector **Joseph Kelly** . . . . (213) 974-2101
Chief Deputy Treasurer and Tax Collector **Keith Knox** . . . (213) 974-0703
Assistant Treasurer and Tax Collector/Administration **(Vacant)** . . . . (213) 974-0703
Assistant Treasurer and Tax Collector/Banking Operations **Mark Oune** . . . . (213) 974-7363
Assistant Treasurer and Tax Collector/Internal Controls **Nai Len Ishikawa** . . . . (213) 974-2139
Assistant Treasurer and Tax Collector/Public Finance and Investments **Glenn Byers** . . . . (213) 974-7175
E-mail: gbyers@ttc.lacounty.gov
Assistant Treasurer and Tax Collector/Tax Collections **Kathy Gloster** . . . . (213) 974-2077
E-mail: kgloster@ttc.lacounty.gov
Chief Information Officer **Ron Moskowitz** . . . . (213) 974-7618
E-mail: rmoskowitz@ttc.lacounty.gov

Department of Consumer and Business Affairs [DCA]

Kenneth Hahn Hall of Administration, 500 West Temple Street, Room B-96, Los Angeles, CA 90012-2706
Tel: (213) 974-1452 Tel: (800) 593-8222 (Toll-Free Los Angeles County)
Fax: (213) 687-0233 Internet: http://dca.lacounty.gov

▽Director **Brian J. Stiger** . . . . (213) 974-9750
Chief Deputy Director **(Vacant)** . . . . (213) 974-9774
Chief Consumer Affairs Representative **Rigoberto Reyes** . . . . (213) 974-9758
Consumer Affairs Specialist **(Vacant)** . . . . (213) 974-4615
Chief Consumer Affairs Representative **Maggie Becerra** . . (213) 974-0827
Counseling Services Coordinator **Dana Pratt** . . . . (213) 974-9769
E-mail: dpratt@dca.lacounty.gov
Public Information and Community Outreach Supervisor **Dawnnesha Smith** . . . . (213) 974-4120
E-mail: dsmith@dca.lacounty.gov

(continued on next page)

★ Elected Official ▲ Appointed by Legislature ▼ Appointed by Governor ► Appointed by Board or Commission ● Appointed by Judge
■ Appointed by Mayor △ Appointed by Freeholders ▽ Appointed by Supervisor ▷ Appointed by County Executive ○ Appointed by Council

Department of Consumer and Business Affairs *continued*

Real Estate Fraud Program **Rose Basmadzhyan** . . . . (213) 893-1263
133 NMorth Sunol Drive, Los Angeles, CA 90063
Small Claims Court Advisor Program **Nicholas Aquino** . . (213) 974-9769
Volunteer Program Coordinator **Esperanza Hernandez** . . . (213) 974-9740

Department of Human Resources

500 West Temple Street, Suite 579, Los Angeles, CA 90012
Tel: (213) 974-2406

Personnel Director **Lisa M. Garrett** . . . . (213) 974-2406
Executive Assistant **Daniel Kelleher** . . . . (213) 974-2406

Internal Services Department [ISD]

1100 N. Eastern Ave., Los Angeles, CA 90063-3200
Fax: (323) 264-7135 Internet: http://isd.lacounty.gov/

▶ Director **Jim Jones** . . . . (323) 267-2101
Chief Deputy Director **David Chittenden** . . . . (323) 267-2103
E-mail: dchittenden@isd.lacounty.gov
Administration and Finance Services Director
Dave Yamashita . . . . (323) 267-2136
E-mail: dyamashita@isd.lacounty.gov Fax: (323) 263-5286
Executive Services Management Division Manager
Celina Ortiz . . . . (323) 267-3111
Facilities Operations Service General Manager
Paul English . . . . (323) 267-2107
E-mail: penglish@isd.lacounty.gov Fax: (323) 881-0290
Information Technology Service General Manager
Tom Travis . . . . (562) 803-0724
9150 Imperial Highway, Downey, CA 90242 Fax: (562) 940-2901
E-mail: travist@isd.lacounty.gov
Purchasing and Contract Services General Manager
Joe Sandoval . . . . (323) 267-2109
E-mail: jsandoval@isd.lacounty.gov
Section Manager, Fleet Services **Randy Martin** . . . . (323) 881-3742

Natural History Museum of Los Angeles County

900 Exposition Blvd., Los Angeles, CA 90007
Tel: (213) 763-3466 Fax: (213) 746-2999 Fax: (213) 746-7538
E-mail: info@nhm.org Internet: www.nhm.org

▽ President and Director **Dr. Lori Bettison-Varga** . . . . (213) 763-3301
Education: UC Santa Barbara BA; UC Davis 1986 MS, 1991 PhD
Special Assistant **Martha M. Garcia** . . . . (213) 763-3302
E-mail: mgarcia@nhm.org

Los Angeles County Museum of Art [LACMA]

5905 Wilshire Boulevard, Los Angeles, CA 90036
Tel: (323) 857-6000 Fax: (323) 857-4702 Internet: www.lacma.org

Year Founded: 1910

Administration

Wallis Annenberg Director and Chief Executive Officer
Michael Govan . . . . (323) 857-6001
Education: Williams BA

Public Safety

500 West Temple Street, Room 754, Los Angeles, CA 90012
Tel: (213) 893-2374

Deputy Chief Executive Officer **Georgia Mattera** . . . . (213) 893-2374
500 West Temple Street, Room 766, Los Angeles, CA 90012
E-mail: gmattera@ceo.lacounty.gov

Agricultural Commissioner/Weights and Measures

12300 Lower Azusa Rd., Arcadia, CA 91006-5872
Fax: (626) 350-3243 Internet: http://acwm.lacounty.gov

▽ Commissioner **Kurt E. Floren** . . . . (626) 575-5451
E-mail: kfloren@acwm.lacounty.gov
Chief Deputy **Richard K. Iizuka** . . . . (626) 575-5453
Deputy Director, Environmental Protection Bureau
Greg Creekmur . . . . (626) 459-8886
Deputy Director, Pest Exclusion and Produce Quality
Bureau **Edmund Williams** . . . . (562) 622-0421
11012 Garfield Avenue, South Gate, CA 90280

Agricultural Commissioner/Weights and Measures *continued*

Deputy Director, Weed Hazard and Pest Management
Bureau **Ray Smith** . . . . (626) 575-4393
Deputy Director, Weights and Measures Bureau
Larry Nolan . . . . (562) 622-0403
11012 Garfield Ave., South Gate, CA 90280
Chief, Administrative Services Bureau **Alycia Araya** . . . . . (626) 575-5454
E-mail: aaraya@acwm.lacounty.gov

Office of the Public Defender

19-513 Clara Shortridge Foltz Criminal Justice Center,
210 West Temple Street, Los Angeles, CA 90012-3210
Tel: (213) 974-2811 Fax: (213) 625-5031 Internet: http://pd.co.la.ca.us/

▶ Public Defender **Ronald L. "Ron" Brown** . . . . (213) 974-2811
E-mail: rbrown@pubdef.lacounty.gov
Education: USC 1976 BA; UCLA 1979 JD
Chief Deputy (Acting) **Kelly Emling** . . . . (213) 974-2811
Assistant Public Defender, Administration and Central
Operations **Candis Glover** . . . . (213) 974-2923
Fax: (213) 633-5030
Assistant Public Defender, Branch and Area Operations
Carol Clem . . . . (213) 974-2928
Assistant Public Defender, Special Operations and
Litigation Support **Ruben Marquez** . . . . (213) 974-2901

Department of Animal Care and Control

5898 Cherry Ave., Long Beach, CA 90805
Tel: (562) 728-4882 Fax: (562) 422-3408
Internet: http://animalcare.lacounty.gov/

▽ Director **Marcia Mayeda** . . . . (562) 728-4610
E-mail: mmayeda@animalcare.lacounty.gov

Department of Coroner

1104 North Mission Road, Los Angeles, CA 90033
Tel: (323) 343-0714 Fax: (323) 221-9768
Internet: http://coroner.lacounty.gov/

▽ Director/Medical Examiner **Dr. Mark Fajardo** . . . . (323) 343-0778
Administrative Deputy **(Vacant)** . . . . (323) 343-0784
Coroner Investigations Chief **Kelly Yagerlener** . . . . (323) 343-0724
Forensic Medicine Division Chief **Christopher Rogers** . . . (323) 343-0715
Forensic Laboratories Division Chief **(Vacant)** . . . . (323) 343-0530
Public Services Division Chief **Vanessa Gastelum** . . . . . . (323) 343-0516
Departmental Human Resources Manager I
Marci Coromac . . . . (323) 343-0765
E-mail: mcoromac@coroner.lacounty.gov
Chief Deputy Director **Elaine Palaiologos** . . . . (323) 343-0714

Department of Military and Veterans Affairs

2615 South Grand Avenue, Suite 100, Los Angeles, CA 90007
Fax: (213) 744-4444

▽ Director **Ruth Wong** . . . . (213) 765-9680
Chief Deputy **Stephanie Stone** . . . . (213) 765-9680

Probation Department

9150 E. Imperial Hwy., Downey, CA 90242-2834
Fax: (562) 803-1855 E-mail: pic@probation.co.la.ca.us
Internet: http://probation.lacounty.gov

▽ Chief Probation Officer **Jerry Powers** . . . . (562) 940-2501

Executive Office of the Board of Supervisors

Kenneth Hahn Hall of Administration, 500 West Temple Street,
Los Angeles, CA 90012
Tel: (213) 974-1411

▽ Executive Officer (Acting) **Patrick Ogawa** Room 383 . . . . (213) 974-1401
E-mail: pogawa@bos.lacounty.gov Fax: (213) 620-0636

★ Elected Official ▲ Appointed by Legislature ▼ Appointed by Governor ▶ Appointed by Board or Commission ● Appointed by Judge
■ Appointed by Mayor △ Appointed by Freeholders ▽ Appointed by Supervisor ▷ Appointed by County Executive ○ Appointed by Council

Los Angeles County Arts Commission
1055 Wilshire Boulevard, Suite 800, Los Angeles, CA 90017
Fax: (213) 580-0017 Internet: www.lacountyarts.org

▽ Executive Director **Laura Zucker** .... (213) 202-5858
E-mail: lzucker@arts.lacounty.gov
Education: Barnard 1972 BA
Director of Development **Louanne Brazil** .... (213) 202-5858
Director of Civic Art (Interim) **Pauline Kamiyama** .... (213) 202-5858
Director of Communications and Marketing
Leticia Rhi Buckley .... (213) 202-5858
E-mail: lbuckley@arts.lacounty.gov
Director of Grants and Professional Development
Anji Gaspar-Milanovic .... (213) 202-5858
E-mail: amilanovic@arts.lacounty.gov
Director of Arts Education **Denise Grande** .... (213) 202-5858
Managing Director of Productions **Adam Davis** .... (213) 202-5858

Civil Service Commission
Kenneth Hahn Hall, 500 West Temple Street, Room 522,
Los Angeles, CA 90012
Fax: (213) 974-2534

Executive Director **Lawrence Crocker** .... (213) 974-2411

Employee Relations Commission [ERCOM]
Kenneth Hahn Hall of Administration, 500 West Temple Street,
Room 374, Los Angeles, CA 90012
Fax: (213) 687-3473

▽ Executive Officer **Tony Butka** .... (213) 974-2417
Secretary **Rose Henderson** .... (213) 974-2417

Commission on Human Relations
Hall of Records, 320 W. Temple St., Rm. 1184,
Los Angeles, CA 90012-3208
Fax: (213) 687-4251 Internet: www.lahumanrelations.org

President **Susanne Cumming** .... (213) 974-7611
Executive Director **Robin S. Toma** .... (213) 974-7611

Office of the County Counsel
Kenneth Hahn Hall of Administration, 500 West Temple Street, Suite 648,
Los Angeles, CA 90012
Tel: (213) 974-1811 Fax: (213) 617-1142
E-mail: contact_us@counsel.lacounty.gov
Internet: http://counsel.lacounty.gov/

► County Counsel **Mary C. Wickham** .... (213) 974-1801
Chief Deputy County Counsel (Acting) **Lester J. Tolnai** .. (213) 974-1822
Chief Deputy County Counsel, Board Services (Acting)
Lawrence L. Hafetz .... (213) 974-7546
Senior Assistant County Counsel
Rodrigo A. Castro-Silva .... (213) 974-1804
Senior Assistant County Counsel **Elizabeth M. Cortez** ... (213) 974-1810
Senior Assistant County Counsel **Thomas J. Faughnan** .. (213) 974-1838
Senior Assistant County Counsel **Roger H. Granbo** ...... (213) 974-1609
Senior Assistant County Counsel (Acting)
Dawyn Harrison .... (213) 974-1807
Managing Senior Assistant County Counsel
Patrick A. Wu .... (213) 974-1861
Litigation Cost Manager **Steven H. Estabrook** .... (213) 974-1762
Special Assistant **Brandon Nichols** .... (213) 974-0685
Contracts Division Assistant County Counsel
Manuel A. Valenzuela, Jr. .... (213) 974-1835
Dependency Division Assistant County Counsel (Acting)
Keith Davis .... (213) 526-6250
General Litigation Division Assistant County Counsel
Ruben Baeza, Jr. .... (213) 974-8216
Government Services Division Assistant County Counsel
Judy W. Whitehurst .... (213) 974-1921
Health Services Division Assistant County Counsel
Sharon H. Reichman .... (213) 974-1866
Labor and Employment Division Assistant County
Counsel **Joyce M. Aiello** .... (213) 974-1926

Office of the County Counsel *continued*

Law Enforcement Division Assistant County Counsel
Jennifer Lehman .... (213) 974-1908
Probate Division Assistant County Counsel
Leah D. Davis .... (213) 974-0663
Property Division Assistant County Counsel (Acting)
Elaine M. Lemke .... (213) 974-1930
Public Works Division Assistant County Counsel
Robert Cartwright .... (213) 974-1793
Social Services Division Assistant County Counsel
Lianne Edmonds .... (213) 974-9704
Transportation Division Assistant County Counsel
Charles M. Safer .... (213) 922-2511
Workers' Compensation Division Assistant County
Counsel **Ralph L. Rosato** .... (213) 974-6845
Law Librarian **Elizabeth Birnie** .... (213) 974-1982
E-mail: bbirnie@counsel.lacounty.gov

Auditor-Controller Department
Kenneth Hahn Hall of Administration, 500 West Temple Street,
Room 525, Los Angeles, CA 90012-2766
Tel: (213) 974-8301 Fax: (213) 626-5427
E-mail: constituent@auditor.lacounty.gov
Internet: http://auditor.lacounty.gov

► Auditor-Controller **John Naimo** .... (213) 974-8301
E-mail: constituent@auditor.lacounty.gov

Los Angeles County Fire Department [LACoFD]
1320 North Eastern Avenue, Los Angeles, CA 90063-3294
Tel: (323) 881-2411 Fax: (323) 265-9948 E-mail: info@fire.lacounty.gov
Internet: http://fire.lacounty.gov/

▽ Fire Chief **Daryl L. Osby** .... (323) 881-2401
E-mail: daryl.osby@fire.lacounty.gov
Education: Azusa Pacific BS
Chief Deputy, Business Operations **Dawnna Lawrence** ... (323) 881-2478
E-mail: dawnna.lawrence@fire.lacounty.gov
Chief Deputy, Emergency Operations (Acting)
David R. Richardson, Jr. .... (323) 881-6178
E-mail: david.richardson@fire.lacounty.gov
▽ Medical Director **Dr. Clayton Kazan** .... (323) 881-2471
E-mail: clayton.kazan@fire.lacounty.gov

Community Development Commission
700 West Main Street, Alhambra, CA 91801
Tel: (626) 262-4511 Internet: www.lacdc.org

► Executive Director **Sean Rogan** .... (626) 586-1500
E-mail: sean.rogan@lacdc.org
Deputy Executive Director **Monique King-Viehland** ..... (626) 586-1553
E-mail: monique.king-viehland@lacdc.org

Regional Planning Commission [RPC]
320 West Temple Street, Room 1350, Los Angeles, CA 90012-3225
Internet: http://planning.lacounty.gov/agenda/rpc

▽ Chair **Stephanie Pincetl** .... (213) 974-6409
▽ Vice Chair **Doug Smith** .... (213) 974-6409
▽ Commissioner **David W. Louie** .... (213) 974-6409
▽ Commissioner **Patrick J. "Pat" Modugno** .... (213) 974-6409
▽ Commissioner **Curt Pedersen** .... (213) 974-6409
Commission Secretary **Rosie Ruiz** .... (213) 974-6409
E-mail: rruiz@planning.lacounty.gov

Los Angeles County Office of Education [LACOE]
9300 Imperial Highway, Room 100, Downey, CA 90242-2890
Tel: (562) 922-6128 (Information) Fax: (562) 940-1727
Internet: www.lacoe.edu

COUNTIES

★ Elected Official ▲ Appointed by Legislature ▼ Appointed by Governor ► Appointed by Board or Commission ● Appointed by Judge
■ Appointed by Mayor △ Appointed by Freeholders ▽ Appointed by Supervisor ▷ Appointed by County Executive ○ Appointed by Council

Board of Education
9300 Imperial Highway, Downey, CA 90242-2890
Tel: (562) 922-6128 Fax: (562) 940-1727

▽President **Thomas A. Saenz** .... (562) 922-6128
E-mail: saenz_thomas@lacoe.edu
Education: Yale 1987 BA, 1991 JD
▽Board Member **Douglas Boyd** .... (562) 922-6128
E-mail: boyd_douglas@lacoe.edu
▽Board Member **Katie Braude** .... (562) 922-6128
E-mail: braude_katie@lacoe.edu
▽Board Member **Gabriella Holt** .... (562) 922-6128
▽Board Member **Alex Johnson** .... (562) 922-6128
E-mail: amj72180@aol.com
Education: Morehouse Col BA; American U JD
▽Board Member **Monte E. Perez** .... (562) 922-6128
▽Board Member **Rebecca J. Turrentine** .... (562) 922-6128
E-mail: turrentine_rebecca@lacoe.edu

Office of the Superintendent
9300 Imperial Highway, Downey, CA 90242-2890

▽Superintendent of Schools **Arturo Delgado** .... (562) 922-6111
E-mail: delgado_arturo@lacoe.edu
Education: East Los Angeles 1975 AA; Cal State (Los Angeles); La Verne 1997 EdD
Communications Director **Frank Kwan** .... (562) 922-6360
E-mail: kwan_frank@lacoe.edu Fax: (562) 803-6246

Office of the Assessor
Kenneth Hahn Hall of Administration, 500 West Temple Street, Room 320, Los Angeles, CA 90012
Fax: (213) 617-1493 Internet: http://assessor.lacounty.gov

★Assessor **Jeffrey Prang** .... (213) 974-3101
Term Expires: December 8, 2018
Chief Deputy Assessor **Santos H. Kreimann** .... (213) 974-3101
Assistant Assessor **George Renkei** .... (213) 974-3101
E-mail: grenkei@assessor.lacounty.gov
Administrative Deputy **Steve Hernandez** .... (213) 974-3182
Chief Information Officer **Tim Grizzle** .... (213) 974-2720
District Appraisals Director (Acting) **Jennifer Budzak** ... (213) 974-3400
Roll Services Director **Fred Chisholm** .... (213) 974-3121

Office of the District Attorney
Hall of Justice, 211 West Temple Street, Suite 1200, Los Angeles, CA 90012
Fax: (213) 933-1956 Internet: http://da.lacounty.gov

★District Attorney **Jackie Lacey** .... (213) 974-3500
Term Expires: December 6, 2016
E-mail: jlacey@da.lacounty.gov
Education: UC Irvine 1979 BA; USC 1982 JD
Executive Assistant **Karen Harris** .... (213) 257-2924
Executive Assistant **Letty Minjares** .... (213) 257-2925
Chief Deputy District Attorney **John Spillane** .... (213) 257-2928
Assistant District Attorney **Pamela Booth** .... (213) 257-3177
E-mail: pbooth@da.lacounty.gov
Assistant District Attorney **Joseph Esposito** .... (213) 257-2910
Assistant District Attorney **William Hodgman** .... (213) 257-2905

Media Relations Division
211 West Temple Street, Suite 1200, Los Angeles, CA 90012
Fax: (213) 257-2000

Communication **Jean Guccione** .... (213) 257-2949
Chief of Media Relations **Shiara Davila-Morales** .... (213) 257-2977
Senior Public Information Officer **Jane Robison** .... (213) 257-2978
E-mail: jrobison@da.lacounty.gov

Office of the Sheriff
211 West Temple Street, Los Angeles, CA 90012
Fax: (323) 267-6600

★Sheriff **Jim McDonnell** .... (323) 267-4800
Term Expires: December 31, 2018
Education: St Anselm BSCrimJ; USC MPA
Executive Officer **Neal Tyler** .... (323) 267-4800
Assistant Sheriff **Todd Rogers** .... (323) 267-4800
E-mail: trogers@lasd.org

County of Lucas, Ohio
One Government Center, Toledo, OH 43604
Internet: www.lucascountyoh.gov

County Seat: Toledo **Election Type:** Partisan **Population:** 433,689 (2015)

Office of the Board of Commissioners
One Government Center, Suite 800, Toledo, OH 43604-2259
Fax: (419) 213-4532

★President **Tina Skeldon Wozniak** (D) .... (419) 213-4817
Term Expires: January 2, 2017
E-mail: twozniak@co.lucas.oh.us
Education: Bowling Green State BSSW; Ohio State MSW
★Commissioner **Carol Contrada** (D) .... (419) 213-2155
Term Expires: December 31, 2018
E-mail: ccontrada@co.lucas.oh.us
★Commissioner **Pete Gerken** (D) .... (419) 213-4084
Term Expires: January 2, 2017
Education: Toledo 1991 BS
▶Clerk to the Board **Jody L. Balogh** .... (419) 213-4511
E-mail: jbalogh@co.lucas.oh.us

Office of the County Administrator
One Government Center, Suite 800, Toledo, OH 43604-2259
Fax: (419) 213-4532

County Administrator **Laura Lloyd-Jenkins** .... (419) 213-4542

Building Regulations
1115 S. McCord Rd, Holland, OH 43528-9596
Fax: (419) 213-2992

Chief Building Official **Phil Klocinski** .... (419) 213-2990

Child Support Enforcement Agency
701 Adams St., Toledo, OH 43604
Fax: (419) 213-3140

Director **Sophia Lloyd** .... (419) 213-3000

Canine Care and Control
410 South Erie Street, Toledo, OH 43604
Tel: (419) 213-2800 Fax: (419) 213-2803
Internet: www.co.lucas.oh.us/dogwarden

Dog Warden **Julie Lyle** .... (419) 213-2800

Department of Emergency Services
2144 Monroe Street, Toledo, OH 43604
Fax: (419) 213-6552

Director **Dennis Cole** .... (419) 213-6532
E-mail: dcole@co.lucas.oh.us

Emergency Management Agency
2144 Monroe St., Toledo, OH 43604
Fax: (419) 213-6520

Director (Interim) **Dennis Cole** .... (419) 213-6532
E-mail: dcole@co.lucas.oh.us

★Elected Official ▲Appointed by Legislature ▼Appointed by Governor ▶Appointed by Board or Commission ●Appointed by Judge
■Appointed by Mayor △Appointed by Freeholders ▽Appointed by Supervisor ▷Appointed by County Executive ○Appointed by Council

Facilities Management
1819 Canton Avenue, Toledo, OH 43604
Fax: (419) 241-7039 E-mail: ereid@co.lucas.oh.us

Facilities Manager **Doug Podiak** . . . . . (419) 213-6424

Human Resources Department
One Government Center, Suite 450, Toledo, OH 43604
Fax: (419) 213-2092

Director **James Meadows** . . . . . (419) 213-4543
E-mail: jmeadows@co.lucas.oh.us

Job and Family Services
3210 Monroe St., Toledo, OH 43699-0007
Fax: (419) 213-8820

Director **Sophia Lloyd** . . . . . (419) 213-8600

Lucas County Extension Office
One Government Center, Suite 550, Toledo, OH 43604
Tel: (419) 213-4254

County Extension Director **Amy Stone** . . . . . (419) 213-4254
Office Assistant **Gail Ritzler** . . . . . (419) 213-4254
E-mail: ritzler.2@osu.edu

Department of Planning and Development
Fax: (419) 213-4299

President and Chief Executive Officer
Megan Vahey Casiere . . . . . (419) 213-4545
E-mail: mvcasiere@co.lucas.oh.us

Lucas County Information Services Department [LCIS]
One Government Center, Suite 400, Toledo, OH 43604
Fax: (419) 213-4024

Director **Jason Gears** . . . . . (419) 213-4025

Office of Management and Budget
One Government Center, Suite 800, Toledo, OH 43604
Fax: (419) 213-2601

Director **Kelleigh Decker** . . . . . (419) 213-4649
E-mail: kdecker@co.lucas.oh.us

Risk Management Division
One Government Center, Suite 800, Toledo, OH 43604
Fax: (419) 213-4830

Director **Diane Robinson** . . . . . (419) 213-4522

Sanitary Engineer
1111 S. McCord Rd., Holland, OH 43528
Fax: (419) 865-1951

Sanitary Engineer **Jim Shaw** . . . . . (419) 213-4526
E-mail: jshaw@co.lucas.oh.us

Support Services Department
One Government Center, Suite 480, Toledo, OH 43604
Fax: (419) 213-4533

Director **Lynn DiPierro** . . . . . (419) 213-4509
E-mail: ldipierr@co.lucas.oh.us
Telecommunications Coordinator (Acting)
Lynn DiPierro . . . . . (419) 213-6424
E-mail: ldippierr@co.lucas.oh.us
Vehicle Maintenance Manager **Doug Podiak** . . . . . (419) 213-6424
Fax: (419) 213-3060

Toledo-Lucas County Public Library
325 N. Michigan St., Toledo, OH 43604-1628
Tel: (419) 259-5200 (Information) Fax: (419) 255-1332
Internet: www.toledolibrary.org

Director **Clyde S. Scoles** . . . . . (419) 259-5256
E-mail: clyde.scoles@toledolibrary.org
Executive Administrative Assistant **Susan Gannon** . . . . (419) 259-5256
E-mail: susan.gannon@toledolibrary.org

Toledo-Lucas County Public Library *continued*

Deputy Director **Jason Kucsma** . . . . . (419) 259-5256
E-mail: jason.kucsma@toledolibrary.org
Security Coordinator **Jeff Sabo** . . . . . (419) 259-5195
Facilities and Operations Division **Charlie Oswanski** . . . . (419) 259-5309
E-mail: charlie.oswanski@toledolibrary.org Fax: (419) 259-5125

Wastewater Treatment Plant
5758 North River Road, Waterville, OH 43566
Fax: (419) 878-0193

Plant Manager **Mickey Shank** . . . . . (419) 213-8740

Adult Probation Department
1100 Jefferson Street, 2nd Floor, Toledo, OH 43604
Fax: (419) 936-8151

Director **Donna Moore** . . . . . (419) 213-6140

Children Services Board
705 Adams Street, Toledo, OH 43604
Fax: (419) 327-3291 Tel: (419) 213-3200

▶ Executive Director **Robin Reese** . . . . . (419) 213-3255
E-mail: robin.reese@co.lucas.oh.us
Administrative Services Associate Director **Dave Sigler** . . (419) 213-3727
Quality Improvements Associate Director
John Hollingsworth . . . . . (419) 213-3658
Services Associate Director **Todd Spotts** . . . . . (419) 213-3255
Human Resources Director **(Vacant)** . . . . . (419) 213-3229

Elections Board
One Government Center, Suite 300, Toledo, OH 43604
Tel: (419) 213-4001 Fax: (419) 213-4069
Internet: www.lucascountyvotes.org

Director **Gina Kaczala** . . . . . (419) 213-2047
Deputy Director **LaVera Scott** . . . . . (419) 213-2044

Mental Health and Recovery Services Board of Lucas County [MHRSB]
701 Adams Street, Suite 800, Toledo, OH 43604
Tel: (419) 213-4600 Fax: (419) 244-4707
Internet: www.co.lucas.oh.us/mhrsb

Chair **Neema Bell** . . . . . (419) 213-4600
Vice Chair **Linda R. Howe** . . . . . (419) 213-4600
Secretary **Anthony "Tony" Pfeiffer** . . . . . (419) 213-4600
Treasurer **Dr. Tim R. Valko** . . . . . (419) 213-4600

Lucas County Board of Developmental Disabilities
1154 Larc Lane, Toledo, OH 43614
Tel: (419) 380-4000 Fax: (419) 380-5136
E-mail: comments@lucasmrdd.com

Superintendent **Deb Yenrick** . . . . . (419) 380-4000
Public Information Manager **London "Lon" Mitchell** . . . . (419) 380-4048

Pretrial-Presentence Department
1100 Jefferson, 1st Floor, Toledo, OH 43624

Director **Stacy Jarchow** . . . . . (419) 213-6028

Veterans Services Commission
1301 Monroe Street, Suite 180, Toledo, OH 43604
Fax: (419) 213-6099

Executive Director **Lee Armstrong** . . . . . (419) 213-6090

★ Elected Official ▲ Appointed by Legislature ▼ Appointed by Governor ▶ Appointed by Board or Commission ● Appointed by Judge
■ Appointed by Mayor △ Appointed by Freeholders ▽ Appointed by Supervisor ▷ Appointed by County Executive ○ Appointed by Council

Office of the Auditor

One Government Center, Suite 600, Toledo, OH 43604-2255
Fax: (419) 213-4399 Internet: www.co.lucas.oh.us/auditor

★ Auditor **Anita Lopez** (D) .... (419) 213-4322
Term Expires: March 2019
E-mail: alopez@co.lucas.oh.us
Education: Toledo 1994, 1997 JSD
Chief Deputy Auditor **Amy Petrus** .... (419) 213-4343

Office of the Coroner

2595 Arlington Ave., Toledo, OH 43614
Fax: (419) 213-3941

★ Coroner **James R. Patrick** (D) .... (419) 213-3900
Term Expires: January 5, 2017

COUNTIES

Office of the County Engineer

Tel: (419) 213-2860 E-mail: engineer@co.lucas.oh.us
Internet: www.co.lucas.oh.us/engineer

★ County Engineer **Keith G. Earley** (D) .... (419) 213-2860
Term Expires: January 5, 2017
Education: Ohio State BSCE
Administrative Deputy **Mark Drennen** .... (419) 213-2860

Road Maintenance Department

2504 Detroit Avenue, Maumee, OH 43537
Tel: (419) 893-2232 Fax: (419) 893-0111

Superintendent **Greg Wimberly** .... (419) 893-2232
E-mail: gwimberly@co.lucas.oh.us
Assistant Superintendent **Ryan Belinske** .... (419) 893-2232
E-mail: rbelinske@co.lucas.oh.us

Office of the Prosecuting Attorney

Lucas County Courthouse, 700 Adams Street, Suite 250,
Toledo, OH 43604
Fax: (419) 213-4595

★ Prosecutor **Julia R. Bates** (D) .... (419) 213-4700
Term Expires: January 5, 2017
E-mail: jbates@co.lucas.oh.us
Education: Toledo 1976 JD
Civil Division Chief **Steven J. Papadimos** .... (419) 213-2001
Education: Toledo 1983 JD
Criminal Division Chief **Jeffrey D. Lingo** .... (419) 213-4700
Special Units Division Chief **Robert A. Miller** .... (419) 213-4700

Office of the Recorder

One Government Center, Ste. 700, Toledo, OH 43604-2257
Tel: (419) 213-4400 Fax: (419) 213-4284

★ Recorder **Phillip Copeland** (D) .... (419) 213-4400
Term Expires: January 5, 2017
E-mail: pcopeland@co.lucas.oh.us

Office of the Sheriff

1622 Spielbusch Ave., Toledo, OH 43624
Tel: (419) 213-4924

★ Sheriff **John Tharp** (D) .... (419) 213-4900
Term Expires: January 5, 2017

Office of the Treasurer

One Government Center, Ste. 500, Toledo, OH 43604-2253
Fax: (419) 213-4499 E-mail: treasurer@co.lucas.oh.us
Internet: www.co.lucas.oh.us/treasurer

★ Treasurer **Wade Kapszukiewicz** (D) .... (419) 213-4305
Term Expires: September 7, 2017
E-mail: treasurer@co.lucas.oh.us
Date of Birth: October 30, 1972
Education: Marquette 1994 BA; Michigan 1996 MPP
Chief Deputy **Karen Poore** .... (419) 213-4303
Real Estate Director **Jim Moran** .... (419) 213-4294

Educational Service Center of Lake Erie West

2275 Collingwood Boulevard, Toledo, OH 43620
Fax: (419) 245-4186 Internet: www.lucas.k12.oh.us

Superintendent **Sandra C. Frisch** .... (419) 245-4150
Technology Coordinator **Chad Rex** .... (419) 246-3130

County of Macomb, Michigan

Macomb County Administration Bldg., One South Main Street, 9th Floor,
Mount Clemens, MI 48043
Tel: (586) 469-5100 (Information) Internet: www.macombcountymi.gov

County Seat: Mt. Clemens **Election Type:** Partisan
Population: 864,840 (2015)

Office of the County Executive

One South Main Street, 8th Floor, Mount Clemens, MI 48043
Tel: (586) 469-7001 Fax: (586) 469-7257
E-mail: executive@macombgov.org
Internet: http://executive.macombgov.org/

★ County Executive **Mark A. Hackel** (D) .... (586) 469-7001
Term Expires: December 31, 2018
E-mail: executive@macombgov.org
Education: Wayne State U 1991 BA; Central Michigan 1996 MSA
Deputy County Executive **Mark Deldin** .... (586) 469-0419
E-mail: deldin@macombgov.org
Assistant County Executive **Pamela J. "Pam" Lavers** .... (586) 493-4877
E-mail: lavers@macombgov.org
Assistant County Executive **Al Lorenzo** .... (586) 469-7278
E-mail: lorenzo@macombgov.org
Assistant County Executive **John Paul Rea** .... (586) 469-0781

Office of Cooperative Extension (Michigan State University)

VerKuilen Building, 21885 Dunham Road, Suite 12,
Clinton Township, MI 48036
Fax: (586) 469-6948

District Coordinator **Marie A. Ruemenapp** .... (586) 469-5180

Office of the Corporation Counsel

Macomb County Administration Bldg., One South Main Street, 8th Floor,
Mount Clemens, MI 48043
Fax: (586) 307-8286 Internet: http://corpcounsel.macombgov.org/

▷ Corporation Counsel **John A. Schapka** .... (586) 469-6346
E-mail: john.schapka@macombgov.org
Assistant Corporation Counsel **Robert S. Gazall** .... (586) 469-6346
Assistant Corporation Counsel **Frank Krycia** .... (586) 469-6346
Assistant Corporation Counsel **Jill K. Smith** .... (586) 469-6346

★ Elected Official ▲ Appointed by Legislature ▼ Appointed by Governor ▶ Appointed by Board or Commission ● Appointed by Judge
■ Appointed by Mayor △ Appointed by Freeholders ▽ Appointed by Supervisor ▷ Appointed by County Executive ○ Appointed by Council

Office of Emergency Management and Communications [OEM]
117 South Groesbeck Highway, Mount Clemens, MI 48043
Tel: (586) 469-5270 Fax: (586) 469-6439
Internet: http://oemc.macombgov.org/

▷ Director **Vicki Wolber** .... (586) 469-5270
E-mail: vicki.wolber@macombgov.org

Office of the Probate Court Administrator and Register
21850 Dunham Rd., Mount Clemens, MI 48043
Fax: (586) 783-0971

Register of Probate **John Brennan** .... (586) 469-5290

Office of Veterans' Services
VerKuilen Building, 21885 Dunham Road, Suite 3,
Clinton Township, MI 48036
Fax: (586) 469-5316 Internet: www.macombcountymi.gov/veterans

▶ Chief, Veteran Service Officer **Laura Rios** .... (586) 469-5315
E-mail: laura.rios@macombgov.org

Community Mental Health Services Department [MCCMH]
22550 Hall Road, Clinton Township, MI 48036
Tel: (586) 469-5275 Fax: (586) 469-7674 E-mail: ocr@mccmh.net
Internet: www.mccmh.net

▶ Executive Director **John Kinch** .... (586) 469-5275
E-mail: john.kinch@mccmh.net
Deputy Director **James "Jim" Losey** .... (586) 469-5765
Medical Director **Norma C. Josef** .... (586) 465-8323
Substance Abuse Services Director **Randy O'Brien** ...... (586) 469-5278

Facilities and Operations Department
44900 Vic Wertz Drive, Clinton Township, MI 48036
Fax: (586) 469-7770

▶ Director **Lynn M. Arnott-Bryks** .... (586) 469-5244
E-mail: lynn.arnott-bryks@macombgov.org

Finance Department
Macomb County Building, 10 North Main Street, 12th Floor,
Mount Clemens, MI 48043
Fax: (586) 469-5847 Internet: http://finance.macombgov.org/

▶ Director **Stephen L. Smigiel** .... (586) 469-5250
E-mail: stephen.smigiel@macombcountymi.gov
Assistant Finance Director, Fiscal Services
Michelle M. Mikytiak .... (586) 469-5250
Equalization Director **Steven Mellen** .... (586) 469-5260
Purchasing Manager **Polly A. Helzer** .... (586) 469-5255

Macomb County Health Department [MCHD]
43525 Elizabeth Road, Mount Clemens, MI 48043
Fax: (586) 469-5885 Tel: (586) 469-5235

▷ Director/Health Officer **William Ridella** .... (586) 469-5510
E-mail: bill.ridella@macombgov.org
Deputy Health Officer **Krista Willette** .... (586) 469-5512
Medical Director **Kevin P. Lokar** .... (586) 469-5511

Human Resources and Labor Relations Department
Macomb County Building, 120 North Main Street,
Mount Clemens, MI 48043
Tel: (586) 469-5280 Fax: (586) 469-6974
E-mail: human.resources@macombcountymi.gov
Internet: http://hrlr.macombgov.org/

▷ Director **Eric A. Herppich** .... (586) 469-5281
E-mail: eric.herppich@macombgov.org

Human Services Department
19700 Hall Road, Suite A, Clinton Township, MI 48038
Fax: (586) 412-6141

Director **Valerie Nunn** .... (586) 412-6143

Information Technology Department
Macomb County Building, 10 North Main Street, 7th Floor,
Mount Clemens, MI 48043
Fax: (586) 469-6547 Internet: http://it.macombgov.org/

▶ Chief Information Officer/Director **Sandra Jurek** .... (586) 469-0524

Planning and Economic Development Department
Macomb County Administration Bldg., 1 South Main Street, 7th Floor,
Mount Clemens, MI 48043
Fax: (586) 469-6787

Director **Stephen N. Cassin** .... (586) 469-5285
Deputy Director **Victoria "Vicki" Rad** .... (586) 469-5285
E-mail: vicky.rad@macombgov.org

Risk Management and Safety Department
Administration Building, One South Main Street, 8th Floor,
Mount Clemens, MI 48043
Fax: (586) 469-7902
Internet: www.macombcountymi.gov/riskmanagement

▶ Director **John P. Anderson** .... (586) 469-6349

Department of Roads [MCDOR]
117 South Groesbeck Highway, Mount Clemens, MI 48043
Tel: (586) 463-8671 Fax: (586) 463-8682 Internet: www.rcmcweb.org

Director **Robert P. "Bob" Hoepfner** .... (586) 463-0344

Senior Citizens' Services Department
VerKuilen Bldg., 21885 Dunham Rd., Suite 6,
Clinton Township, MI 48036
Fax: (586) 469-5578 Internet: www.macombcountymi.gov/seniorservices

▶ Director **Katherine R. Benford** .... (586) 469-5228

Office of the Board of Commissioners
Macomb County Administration Building, 1 South Main Street, 9th Floor,
Mount Clemens, MI 48043
Fax: (586) 469-5993 Internet: http://boc.macombgov.org/

★ Chair **David J. "Dave" Flynn** (D-District 4) .... (586) 469-5125
Term Expires: December 31, 2016
E-mail: dave.flynn10@gmail.com
Education: Michigan State 2008

★ Vice Chair **Kathleen E. "Kathy" Tocco** (D-District 11) .. (586) 469-5125
Term Expires: December 31, 2016
Education: Detroit JD

★ Sergeant-at-Arms **Steven Marino** (R-District 10) .... (586) 469-5125
Term Expires: December 31, 2016

★ Commissioner **Andrey Duzyj** (D-District 1) .... (586) 469-5125
Term Expires: December 31, 2016

★ Commissioner **Marvin E. Sauger** (D-District 2) .... (586) 469-5125
Term Expires: December 31, 2016

★ Commissioner **Veronica Klinefelt** (D-District 3) .... (586) 469-5125
Term Expires: December 31, 2016

★ Commissioner **Robert Mijac** (D-District 5) .... (586) 469-5125
Term Expires: December 31, 2016

★ Commissioner
James Louis "Jim" Carabelli (R-District 6) .... (586) 469-5125
Term Expires: December 31, 2016
E-mail: jimcarabelli@comcast.net
Date of Birth: June 7, 1965

★ Commissioner **Don Brown** (R-District 7) .... (586) 469-5125
Term Expires: December 31, 2016
E-mail: donbrownformacomb@gmail.com

(continued on next page)

★ Elected Official ▲ Appointed by Legislature ▼ Appointed by Governor ▶ Appointed by Board or Commission ● Appointed by Judge
■ Appointed by Mayor △ Appointed by Freeholders ▽ Appointed by Supervisor ▷ Appointed by County Executive ○ Appointed by Council

Office of the Board of Commissioners *continued*

★Commissioner **Kathy D. Vosburg** (R-District 8) . . . . (586) 469-5125
Term Expires: December 31, 2016

★Commissioner **Fred Miller** (D-District 9) . . . . (586) 469-5125
Term Expires: December 31, 2016

★Commissioner **Bob Smith, Jr.** (D-District 12) . . . . (586) 469-5125
Term Expires: December 31, 2016

★Commissioner **Joe Sabatini** (R-District 13) . . . . (586) 469-5125
Term Expires: December 31, 2016

Office of the County Clerk/Register of Deeds

Macomb County Court Building, 40 North Main Street, Mount Clemens, MI 48043
Fax: (877) 443-9505 Internet: clerk.macombgov.org

★County Clerk/Register of Deeds **Carmella Sabaugh** (D) . . (586) 469-7939
Term Expires: December 31, 2016
E-mail: carmella.sabaugh@macombgov.org

Chief Deputy Clerk **Todd Schmitz** . . . . (586) 469-5122
E-mail: todd.schmitz@macombgov.org

Chief Deputy Register of Deeds **Craig Jones** . . . . (586) 469-7953

Office of the Prosecutor

Macomb County Administration Bldg., One South Main Street, 3rd Floor, Mount Clemens, MI 48043
Fax: (586) 469-5609 Internet: http://prosecutorsmith.com/

★Prosecuting Attorney **Eric J. Smith** (D) . . . . (586) 469-5350
Term Expires: December 31, 2016
Education: Central Michigan BA; Detroit Law JD

Chief of Staff/Chief Assistant Prosecuting Attorney **Benjamin "Ben" Liston** . . . . (586) 469-5350
Education: Cambridge (UK) BA, MA; Georgetown 1990 JD

Chief Trial Attorney **Jean Cloud** . . . . (586) 496-4127

Chief of Homicide **William L. "Bill" Cataldo** . . . . (586) 469-5362
Education: Western Michigan BBA; Wayne State U JD

Chief of Operations **James Langtry** . . . . (586) 469-7325
Education: Michigan State 1983 BA; Thomas M Cooley 1987 JD

Office of the Public Works Commissioner

21777 Dunham Road, Clinton Township, MI 48036
Tel: (586) 469-5325 Fax: (586) 469-5933
Internet: www.macombcountymi.gov/publicworks

★Commissioner **Anthony V. Marrocco** (D) . . . . (586) 469-5325
Term Expires: December 31, 2016

Chief Deputy Commissioner **William W. Misterovich** . . . . (586) 307-8210

Office of the Sheriff

43565 Elizabeth Road, Mount Clemens, MI 48043
Fax: (586) 307-9621 E-mail: sheriff@macombsheriff.com
Internet: www.macombsheriff.com

★Sheriff **Anthony M. Wickersham** (D) . . . . (586) 307-9343
Term Expires: December 31, 2016
Education: Wayne State U BA

Undersheriff **Kent B. Lagerquist** . . . . (586) 307-9341

Office of the Treasurer

Macomb County Administration Building, 1 South Main Street, 2nd Floor, Mount Clemens, MI 48043
Fax: (586) 469-6770 E-mail: treasurer@macombcountymi.gov
Internet: www.macombcountymi.gov/treasurer

★Treasurer **Derek E. Miller** (D) . . . . (586) 469-5190
Term Expires: December 31, 2016
Education: Michigan State BA; Detroit Mercy JD

Chief Deputy Treasurer **Jerome T. "Jerry" Moffitt** . . . . . (586) 469-5190

County of Maricopa, Arizona

301 West Jefferson Street, Phoenix, AZ 85003
Tel: (602) 506-3011 (Information) Internet: www.maricopa.gov

County Seat: Phoenix **Election Type:** Partisan **Population:** 4,167,947 (2015)

Office of the Board of Supervisors

301 West Jefferson Street, 10th Floor, Phoenix, AZ 85003
Tel: (602) 506-3416 Fax: (602) 506-6362
Internet: www.maricopa.gov/bos

★Chairman **Steve Chucri** (R-District 2) . . . . (602) 506-7431
Term Expires: December 31, 2016
E-mail: chucris@mail.maricopa.gov
Date of Birth: August 6, 1970
Education: San Diego BBA
Chief of Staff **Page Gonzales** . . . . (602) 506-7431
Education: Arizona State BS

★Supervisor **Denny Barney** (R-District 1) . . . . (602) 506-1776
Term Expires: December 31, 2016
E-mail: barneyd@mail.maricopa.gov

★Supervisor **Andrew W. "Andy" Kunasek** (R-District 3) . . (602) 506-7562
Term Expires: December 31, 2016
E-mail: akunasek@mail.maricopa.gov
Date of Birth: December 16, 1962
Education: Arizona State 1986 BA
Chief of Staff **Kevin P. Tyne** . . . . (602) 506-7562
Education: USC BA

★Supervisor **Clint Hickman** (R-District 4) . . . . (602) 506-7642
Term Expires: December 31, 2016
E-mail: chickman@mail.maricopa.gov
Chief of Staff **Scott Isham** . . . . (602) 506-7642

★Supervisor **Steve Gallardo** (D-District 5) . . . . (602) 506-6524
Term Expires: December 31, 2016
Chief of Staff **Christina Arzaga-Williams** . . . . (602) 506-1368

▽Clerk of the Board **Fran McCarroll** . . . . (602) 506-3767
E-mail: fmccarroll@mail.maricopa.gov Fax: (602) 506-6402
Finance Business Analyst **Amy D. Gabaldon** . . . . (602) 372-1505

▽County Auditor **Ross L. Tate** . . . . (602) 506-1585
E-mail: rtate@mail.maricopa.gov Fax: (602) 506-8957
Education: BYU 1983 BS

Office of the County Manager

301 W. Jefferson St., 10th Floor, Phoenix, AZ 85003
Tel: (602) 506-3416 Fax: (602) 506-3328

▽County Manager **Joy Rich**
Note: Effective May 30, 2016

Chief of Staff **Valarie Beckett** . . . . (602) 506-1950

Deputy County Manager **Sandi Wilson** . . . . (602) 506-7280
E-mail: swilson@mail.maricopa.gov

Communications Director **Fields Moseley** . . . . (602) 506-7232
E-mail: moseleyf@mail.maricopa.gov
Communications Manager **Richard de Uriarte** . . . . (602) 506-3415
E-mail: deuriarter@mail.maricopa.gov

Government Relations Director **Richard Bohan** . . . . (602) 506-2798
E-mail: rbohan@mail.maricopa.gov

★Elected Official ▲Appointed by Legislature ▼Appointed by Governor ▶Appointed by Board or Commission ●Appointed by Judge
■Appointed by Mayor △Appointed by Freeholders ▽Appointed by Supervisor ▷Appointed by County Executive ○Appointed by Council

Office of Enterprise Technology [OET]

301 South Fourth Avenue, Suite 200, Phoenix, AZ 85003
Fax: (602) 506-5864 Internet: www.maricopa.gov/cio

Chief Information Officer **David L. Stevens** .... (602) 506-5934
Management Services Administrator **(Vacant)** .... (602) 372-4808
Web Department Team Supervisor **(Vacant)** .... (602) 506-7087

Office of Management and Budget [OMB]

301 West Jefferson Street, 10th Floor, Phoenix, AZ 85003
Fax: (602) 506-3063 Internet: www.maricopa.gov/budget

Budget Director **Sandi Wilson** .... (602) 506-7280
E-mail: swilson@mail.maricopa.gov
Executive Assistant **Kimberly Bonham** .... (602) 506-2468
Deputy Budget Director **Cindy Goelz** .... (602) 506-4010
E-mail: cgoelz@mail.maricopa.gov
Deputy Budget Director **Brian Hushek** .... (602) 506-6338
E-mail: bhushek@mail.maricopa.gov

Office of the Public Defender

620 West Jackson, Suite 4015, Phoenix, AZ 85003
Tel: (602) 506-7711 Fax: (602) 506-8377
E-mail: pdinfo@mail.maricopa.gov Internet: www.maricopa.gov/pdweb

▽ Public Defender **James J. Haas** .... (602) 506-7711
Education: Iowa State 1977 BA; Creighton 1980 JD
Training Director **Stephanie Conlon** .... (602) 506-7711
E-mail: conlons@mail.maricopa.gov

Emergency Management Department

5630 East McDowell Road, Phoenix, AZ 85008
Tel: (602) 273-1411 Fax: (602) 275-1638

▽ Director **Pete Weaver** .... (602) 273-1411
E-mail: peteweaver@mail.maricopa.gov
Education: U Phoenix BS
Operations and Communications Manager
Julie Symopoulos .... (602) 273-1411
E-mail: juliesyrmopoulos@mail.maricopa.gov
Education: Thunderbird International, MBA
Finance Manager **Sara Latin** .... (602) 273-1411
Education: Arizona BS; Western International MA

Environmental Services Department

1001 North Central, Suite 200, Phoenix, AZ 85004-1950
Tel: (602) 506-6623 Fax: (602) 506-5141
Internet: www.maricopa.gov/envsvc

Director **Steven Goode** .... (602) 506-6667
Business Operations Manager **Tom Maglio** .... (602) 506-6623
E-mail: tmaglio@mail.maricopa.gov
Water and Waste Management Division Manager
Kevin Chadwick .... (602) 506-6667
Fax: (602) 506-6925
Environmental Health Manager **Andrew Linton** .... (602) 506-6971
Vector Control Manager **John Townsend** .... (602) 506-0700

Facilities Management Department

401 W. Jefferson St., Phoenix, AZ 85003
Tel: (602) 506-1141 Fax: (602) 506-1556

Director **Reid H. Spaulding** .... (602) 506-8227
E-mail: reid.spaulding@fm.maricopa.gov
Assistant to the Director **Denise Goss** .... (602) 506-5914
E-mail: denise.goss@fm.maricopa.gov
Capital Facilities Director **Arno Leskinen** .... (602) 506-8188
E-mail: arno.leskinen@fm.maricopa.gov
Operations and Maintenance Division Chief **Ken Burt** .... (602) 506-5839
E-mail: ken.burt@fm.maricopa.gov
Protective Services Division Chief **Jordan Dacquisto** .... (602) 506-8350

Department of Finance

301 West Jefferson Street, Suite 960, Phoenix, AZ 85003-2115
Tel: (602) 506-3561 Fax: (602) 506-3439
E-mail: finance@mail.maricopa.gov Internet: www.maricopa.gov/finance

Chief Financial Officer/Director **Shelby L. Scharbach** ... (602) 506-3561
Deputy Director **John R. Lewis** .... (602) 506-3561

Forensic Science Center

701 W. Jefferson, Phoenix, AZ 85007-2908
Fax: (602) 506-1546 Internet: www.maricopa.gov/medex

Chief Medical Examiner **Dr. Jeffrey Johnston** .... (602) 506-3322
Director **David Boyer** .... (602) 506-3322
Administrative Assistant **Robyn McCraw** .... (602) 506-3322
E-mail: mccrawr@mail.maricopa.gov

Human Resources Department

301 West Jefferson Street, 2nd Floor, Suite 220, Phoenix, AZ 85003
Tel: (602) 506-3755 Fax: (602) 372-0277
Internet: www.maricopa.gov/human_resources

Director **Mary Ellen Sheppard** .... (602) 506-3755
Deputy Director **Andy Mesquita** .... (602) 506-3755
Fax: (602) 506-3313
Payroll and Records Manager **Portia Lomax** .... (602) 506-7188
E-mail: plomax@mail.maricopa.gov Fax: (602) 372-0277

Human Services Department

234 North Central, Suite 3201, Phoenix, AZ 85004
Tel: (602) 506-5911 Fax: (602) 506-8789
Internet: www.hsd.maricopa.gov

Director **Bruce Liggett** .... (602) 506-4137
Assistant Director, Administration, Policy, and Planning
Jacqueline Edwards .... (602) 506-4812
Assistant Director, Early Education
Alecia Jackson .... (602) 464-9669 ext. 201
Assistant Director, Community Services Division
Sandra Mendez .... (602) 506-2316
E-mail: mendezs002@mail.maricopa.gov
Assistant Director, Workforce Development Division
Patricia Wallace .... (602) 506-4146
E-mail: wallacep001@mail.maricopa.gov
Assistant Director, Community Development
Amy Jacobson .... (602) 372-1528
E-mail: jacobsona@mail.maricopa.gov
Assistant Director, Senior and Adult Services
Jeffrey Tourdot .... (602) 506-4936

Office of Procurement Services

320 West Lincoln Street, 2nd Floor, Phoenix, AZ 85003
Tel: (602) 506-3967 Fax: (602) 258-1573
Internet: http://www.maricopa.gov/procurement/

▶ Chief Procurement Officer **Wesley "Wes" Baysinger** .... (602) 506-3247
E-mail: wbaysing@maricopa.gov
Deputy Director **James E. Foley** .... (602) 506-8196
E-mail: james.foley@mail.maricopa.gov

Parks and Recreation Department

234 North Central Avenue, Suite 6400, Phoenix, AZ 85004
Tel: (602) 506-2930 Fax: (602) 506-4692
E-mail: maricopacountyparks@mail.maricopa.gov
Internet: www.maricopa.gov/parks

Director **R.J. Cardin** .... (602) 506-2930

Planning and Development Department

501 North 44th Street, Suite 200, Phoenix, AZ 85008
Fax: (602) 506-8510 Internet: www.maricopa.gov/planning

Deputy County Manager **Joy Rich** .... (602) 506-7167
Note: Until May 27, 2016
E-mail: joyrich@mail.maricopa.gov

(continued on next page)

★ Elected Official ▲ Appointed by Legislature ▼ Appointed by Governor ▶ Appointed by Board or Commission ● Appointed by Judge
■ Appointed by Mayor △ Appointed by Freeholders ▽ Appointed by Supervisor ▷ Appointed by County Executive ○ Appointed by Council

Planning and Development Department *continued*

Development Services Deputy Director **Lynn Favour** ..... (602) 506-8508
E-mail: lynnfavour@mail.maricopa.gov
Planning Services Deputy Director **Darren Gerard** .... (602) 506-7139
Planning Manager **Matthew Holm** .... (602) 506-7162
Director **Debra W. Stark** .... (602) 372-0688

Risk Management Department

222 North Central Avenue, Suite 1110, Phoenix, AZ 85004
Fax: (602) 506-6290 Internet: www.maricopa.gov/riskmgt

▶ Director **Pauline Hecker** .... (602) 506-7888
Deputy Director, Claims Division **Kathleen Kolm** .... (602) 506-6188
E-mail: kolmk@mail.maricopa.gov
Finance Manager **Samantha Wright** .... (602) 506-2827
Fax: (602) 506-6290
Manager, Environmental Division **Rita Neill** .... (602) 506-5063
E-mail: rneill@mail.maricopa.gov Fax: (602) 506-6290
Manager, Safety Division **James Tonda** .... (602) 723-7069
E-mail: tondaj@mail.maricopa.gov Fax: (602) 506-6290
Manager, Insurance and Volunteers **Christine Nobles** .... (602) 506-6087
Fax: (602) 506-6290

Transportation Department [MCDOT]

2901 West Durango Street, Phoenix, AZ 85009
Fax: (602) 506-4858

Director and County Engineer **Jennifer Toth** .... (602) 506-8600
E-mail: jennifertoth@mail.maricopa.gov
Education: Houston BSCE; New Mexico BSCE
Administrative Coordinator **Diane Rogers** .... (602) 506-4700

Flood Control District of Maricopa County

2801 West Durango Street, Phoenix, AZ 85009
Fax: (602) 506-4601 Internet: www.fcd.maricopa.gov

Chief Engineer/General Manager **William "Bill" Wiley** ... (602) 506-1501
Administrative Coordinator **Anna Medina** .... (602) 506-4708

Housing Authority of Maricopa County

8910 North 78th Avenue, Peoria, AZ 85345
Tel: (602) 744-4500 Fax: (602) 253-9268
E-mail: info@maricopahousing.org Internet: www.maricopahousing.org

▶ Director **Gloria Muñoz** .... (602) 744-4542
E-mail: g.munoz@maricopahousing.org

Maricopa County Board of Health

4041 North Central Avenue, Suite 1400, Phoenix, AZ 85012
Tel: (602) 506-6900 Internet: www.maricopa.gov/publichealth/board

President **(Vacant)** (District 3) .... (602) 506-6900
Term Expires: December 31, 2020

Maricopa County Department of Public Health [MCDPH]

4041 North Central Avenue, Suite 1400, Phoenix, AZ 85012
Tel: (602) 506-6900 Fax: (602) 506-6885
E-mail: phpio@mail.maricopa.gov Internet: www.wearepublichealth.org

Director **Dr. Bob England** .... (602) 506-6601
Education: Central Arizona AA; Arizona BS, MD; UCLA MPH
Deputy Director **Max Porter** .... (602) 506-6641

Clinical Services Division

Administrator **Corinne Velasquez** .... (602) 506-6657
Fax: (602) 506-4075

Community Health Transformation Division

Administrator (Acting) **Anna David** .... (602) 372-8436
Fax: (602) 506-6896

Disease Control Division

Administrator **Dr. Rebecca Sunenshine** .... (602) 568-2250

Maricopa County Library District [MCLD]

2700 North Central Avenue, Suite 700, Phoenix, AZ 85004
Tel: (602) 652-3000 Fax: (602) 652-3071 Internet: www.mcldaz.org

Director/County Librarian
Cynthia J. "Cindy" Kolaczynski .... (602) 652-3030
E-mail: cindykolaczynski@mcldaz.org
Education: Ithaca BS; SUNY (Buffalo) MLS

Office of the Assessor

301 West Jefferson Street, Suite 330, Phoenix, AZ 85003
Fax: (602) 506-3394

★ Assessor **The Honorable Paul D. Petersen** .... (602) 506-3877
Term Expires: December 31, 2016
Chief Deputy Assessor **Tim L. Boncoskey** (R) .... (602) 506-3877
E-mail: boncoskeyt@mail.maricopa.gov
Date of Birth: August 22, 1961
Education: Arizona 1983 BSc; Texas 1985 MPA

Office of the Clerk of Court

Downtown Justice Center, 520 West Jackson Street, Suite 3017, Phoenix, AZ 85003
Fax: (602) 506-7772 Internet: www.clerkofcourt.maricopa.gov

★ Clerk of Court **Michael K. Jeanes** (R) .... (602) 372-5375
Term Expires: December 21, 2018
Education: Loyola U (Chicago) BA; Arizona State MPA

Office of the County Attorney

301 West Jefferson Street, 8th Floor, Phoenix, AZ 85003
Fax: (602) 506-8102 Internet: www.maricopacountyattorney.org

★ County Attorney **William G. "Bill" Montgomery** (R) ... (602) 506-3411
Term Expires: December 31, 2016
E-mail: maricopacountyattorney@mcao.maricopa.gov
Date of Birth: March 2, 1967
Education: West Point 1989 BS; Arizona State 2001 JD
Chief Deputy **Mark C. Faull** .... (602) 506-3411
E-mail: faull@mcao.maricopa.gov

Office of the Sheriff

Wells Fargo Plaza, 100 West Washington, Suite 1900, Phoenix, AZ 85003
Fax: (602) 251-3877 Internet: www.mcso.org

★ Sheriff **Joseph M. "Joe" Arpaio** (R) .... (602) 876-1801
Term Expires: December 31, 2016
Chief Deputy **Gerard A. "Jerry" Sheridan** .... (602) 876-1801
E-mail: j_sheridan@mcso.maricopa.gov

Office of the Recorder

West Court Bldg., 111 South Third Avenue, Suite 103, Phoenix, AZ 85003
Fax: (602) 506-3273

★ Recorder **Helen Purcell** (R) .... (602) 506-3535
Term Expires: December 31, 2016
E-mail: hpurcell@risc.maricopa.gov
Elections Director **Karen Osborne** .... (602) 506-1511

Maricopa County Education Service Agency

4041 North Central Avenue, Suite 1100, Phoenix, AZ 85012
Fax: (602) 506-3753 Internet: http://www.maricopa.gov/schools
E-mail: contactus@schools.maricopa.gov

★ Superintendent of Schools **Donald "Don" Covey** (R) .... (602) 506-3661
Term Expires: December 31, 2016
E-mail: don.covey@mcesa.maricopa.gov

★ Elected Official ▲ Appointed by Legislature ▼ Appointed by Governor ▶ Appointed by Board or Commission ● Appointed by Judge
■ Appointed by Mayor △ Appointed by Freeholders ▽ Appointed by Supervisor ▷ Appointed by County Executive ○ Appointed by Council

Office of the Treasurer

301 West Jefferson Street, Room 100, Phoenix, AZ 85003-2199
Tel: (602) 506-8511 Fax: (602) 506-1102
Internet: https://treasurer.maricopa.gov/

★ Treasurer **Charles "Hos" Hoskins** .... (602) 506-3976
Term Expires: January 1, 2017
E-mail: treasurer@mail.maricopa.gov

Maricopa County Special Health Care District Board of Directors

Administration Building, Maricopa Medical Center,
2601 East Roosevelt Street, Phoenix, AZ 85004
Tel: (602) 344-5177 Fax: (602) 344-0892
Internet: www.mihs.org/board-of-directors

★ Chairman **Terence McMahon** (District 5) .... (602) 344-5177
Term Expires: 2016
E-mail: terence.mcmahon@mihs.org

Maricopa Integrated Health System [MIHS]

Maricopa Medical Center, 2601 East Roosevelt Street, Phoenix, AZ 85008
Tel: (602) 344-5011 Fax: (602) 344-5190 Internet: www.mihs.org

President and Chief Executive Officer
Stephen A. "Steve" Purves .... (602) 344-5011
Fax: (602) 344-1130

County of Mecklenburg, North Carolina

600 E. Fourth St., Charlotte, NC 28202
Tel: (704) 336-7600 (City/County Customer Service)
Internet: www.mecklenburgcountync.gov

County Seat: Charlotte **Election Type:** Partisan **Population:** 1,034,070 (2015)

Office of the Board of Commissioners

600 East Fourth Street, 11th Floor, Charlotte, NC 28202
Fax: (704) 336-5887

★ Chair **Trevor Fuller** (D-At-Large) .... (980) 314-2871
Term Expires: December 1, 2016
E-mail: trevor.fuller@mecklenburgcountync.gov

★ Vice Chair **Dumont Clarke** (D-District 4) .... (980) 314-2872
Term Expires: December 1, 2016
E-mail: dumontclarke@mvalaw.com
Education: Vassar 1974 BA; North Carolina 1978 JD

★ Commissioner **Jim Puckett** (R-District 1) .... (980) 314-2876
Term Expires: December 1, 2016
E-mail: jim.puckett@mecklenburgcountync.gov

★ Commissioner **Vilma D. Leake** (D-District 2) .... (980) 314-2877
Term Expires: December 1, 2016
E-mail: vilma.leake@mecklenburgcountync.gov
Education: Livingstone; Buffalo

★ Commissioner **George Dunlap** (D-District 3) .... (980) 314-2873
Term Expires: December 1, 2016
E-mail: george.dunlap@mecklenburgcountync.gov
Education: North Carolina Charlotte 1991 BS; North Carolina 2003 MPA

★ Commissioner **Matthew Ridenhour** (R-District 5) ...... (980) 314-2877
Term Expires: December 1, 2016
E-mail: matthew.ridenhour@mecklenburgcountync.gov

★ Commissioner **Bill James** (R-District 6) .... (980) 314-2878
Term Expires: December 1, 2016
E-mail: wjames@carolina.rr.com
Education: Florida Atlantic BS; Nova Southeastern MBA

Office of the Board of Commissioners *continued*

★ Commissioner **Pat Cotham** (D-At-Large) .... (980) 314-2874
Term Expires: December 1, 2016
E-mail: pat.cotham@mecklenburgcountync.gov

★ Commissioner **Ella B. Scarborough** (D-At-Large) .... (980) 314-2874
Term Expires: December 1, 2016
E-mail: ella.scarborough@mecklenburgcountync.gov

Clerk to the Board **Janice S. Paige** .... (980) 314-2912
E-mail: janice.paige@mecklenburgcountync.gov

Office of the County Manager

600 East Fourth Street, 11th Floor, Charlotte, NC 28202
P.O. Box 31787, Charlotte, NC 28231
Fax: (704) 336-5887

County Manager **Dena R. Diorio** .... (980) 314-2880
E-mail: dena.diorio@mecklenburgcountync.gov

Assistant County Manager **Leslie Johnson** .... (980) 314-2910
E-mail: leslie.johnson@mecklenburgcountync.gov

Assistant County Manager **Anthony S. Trotman** .... (980) 314-2911
Education: Bellevue U; Central Michigan

Deputy Assistant County Manager/Chief of Staff
Chris Peek .... (980) 314-2881
E-mail: chris.peek@mecklenburgcountync.gov

Assistant County Manager **Mark Foster** .... (980) 314-2930
E-mail: mark.foster@mecklenburgcountync.gov

Geospatial Information Services Director **Ron Bruzzese** .. (980) 314-6175

IT Manager **Keith Gregg** .... (980) 314-2350

Office of Cooperative Extension (North Carolina State University)

1418 Armory Drive, Charlotte, NC 28204
Fax: (704) 336-6876 Internet: http://mecklenburg.ces.ncsu.edu

Director (Interim) **Nelson McCaskill** .... (704) 336-2082

Office of the County Attorney

831 East Morehead Street, Suite 860, Charlotte, NC 28202

County Attorney **Marvin A. Bethune** .... (704) 377-1634
E-mail: marvin.bethune@mecklenburgcountync.gov Fax: (704) 342-3308
Date of Birth: March 6, 1948
Education: North Carolina JD

Deputy County Attorney **Tyrone C. Wade** .... (704) 336-2472
600 East Fourth Street, Charlotte, NC 28202

Managing County Attorney **James "Ed" Yeager** .... (704) 336-6661
720 East Fourth Street, Charlotte, NC 28202 Fax: (704) 336-7429
E-mail: edward.yeager@mecklenburgcountync.gov

Office of the Medical Examiner

3990 Rinoe Avenue, Charlotte, NC 28216
Fax: (704) 336-8353

Director **Thomas Owens** .... (704) 336-2005

Medical Examiner **Jonathan Privette** .... (704) 336-2005

Medical Examiner **Michael Sullivan** .... (704) 336-2005

Administrative Support **Stephanie Wooten** .... (704) 336-2005
E-mail: stephanie.wooten@mecklenburgcountync.gov

Office of the Tax Collector

700 E. Stonewall St., Charlotte, NC 28202
P.O. Box 71063, Charlotte, NC 28231-6077
Fax: (704) 336-6879

Tax Collector **Neal Dixon** .... (704) 336-4600
E-mail: neal.dixon@mecklenburgcountync.gov

Budget Department

600 East Fourth Street, 11th Floor, Charlotte, NC 28202
Fax: (704) 336-8494

Budget and Management Director (Acting)
Wanda Reeves .... (704) 336-2472

COUNTIES

★ Elected Official ▲ Appointed by Legislature ▼ Appointed by Governor ► Appointed by Board or Commission ● Appointed by Judge
■ Appointed by Mayor △ Appointed by Freeholders ▽ Appointed by Supervisor ▷ Appointed by County Executive ○ Appointed by Council

Child Support Enforcement Department [MCCSE]
5800 Executive Center Drive, Suite 200, Charlotte, NC 28212
Tel: (704) 432-9300

Director **Joan Kennedy** .... (704) 432-9300 ext. 7
Education: North Carolina

Community Support Services Department [CSS]
700 North Tryon Street, Charlotte, NC 28202
Fax: (704) 336-4198

Director **Stacy Lowry** .... (704) 336-3784

Veterans' Service Office
700 N. Tryon St., Charlotte, NC 28202
Fax: (704) 336-4449

Director **Jim Prosser** .... (704) 336-3135

Mecklenburg County Women's Commission
700 North Tryon Street, Charlotte, NC 28202
Fax: (704) 336-4198

Director **Marie White** .... (704) 336-8814
Program Coordinator **Jaqueline Fields** .... (704) 336-5053

Finance Department
600 East Fourth Street, 11th Floor, Charlotte, NC 28202
Tel: (704) 336-2108 Fax: (704) 336-2380

Director **Wanda Reeves** .... (980) 314-2979
Deputy Director **Patricia Gibson** .... (980) 314-2964

Insurance and Risk Management Division
Cameron Brown Building, 301 South McDowell Street, Suite 1100, Charlotte, NC 28204
Fax: (704) 336-7548

Risk Manager **Daniel Pliszka** .... (704) 336-3301

Mecklenburg County Health Department [MCHD]
249 Billingsley Road, Charlotte, NC 28211
Tel: (704) 336-6400 Fax: (704) 336-4709 Internet: www.meckhealth.org

Director **Marcus Plescia** .... (704) 336-6400
Education: North Carolina 1984 BS, 1989 MPH, 1990 MD

Human Resources Department
720 E. Fourth Street, Charlotte, NC 28202
Fax: (704) 336-5887

Senior Human Resources Director **Chris Peek** .... (704) 336-2931
E-mail: chris.peek@mecklenburgcountync.gov

Information Services and Technology Department
3205 Freedome Drive, Suite 107, Charlotte, NC 28208
Fax: (704) 336-7219

Director **Danny Diehl** .... (704) 336-2003
E-mail: daniel.diehl@mecklenburgcountync.gov

Internal Audit Department
600 East Fourth Street, 11th Floor, Charlotte, NC 28202
Fax: (704) 336-2380

Director **Joanne Prakapas** .... (704) 336-2575

Land Use and Environmental Services Agency [LUESA]
2145 Suttle Avenue, Charlotte, NC 28208
Fax: (704) 419-8961

Director **Ebenezer Gujjarlapudi** .... (704) 336-3725
Air Quality Director **Leslie Rhodes** .... (704) 336-5500

Land Use and Environmental Services Agency *continued*

Code Enforcement Director **Jim Bartl** .... (704) 336-3827
Solid Waste Director **Jeffrey "Jeff" Smithberger** .... (704) 336-2831
Support Services Director **Maia Setzer** .... (704) 336-3733
Water and Land Resources Director **Dave Canaan** .... (704) 336-3736
Senior Fiscal Administrator **Amy E. Johnson** .... (704) 432-0911
E-mail: amy.johnson@mecklenburgcountync.gov
Geospatial Information Services Director
Kurt Olmstead .... (704) 336-7600

Park and Recreation Department
5841 Brookshire Blvd., Charlotte, NC 28216-2403
Fax: (704) 336-5472

Director **James R. "Jim" Garges** .... (704) 336-3854
Administrative Support Coordinator **Kesha Meads** ...... (704) 336-5476

Public Service and Information Department
600 East Fourth Street, 2nd Floor, Charlotte, NC 28202-2838
Fax: (704) 336-6600

Director **Danny Diehl** .... (704) 336-2475
E-mail: daniel.diehl@mecklenburgcountync.gov

Department of Social Services
301 Billingsley Road, Charlotte, NC 28211
Tel: (704) 336-3000 Fax: (704) 353-1325

Director **Peggy Eagan** .... (704) 336-6279
Deputy Director **Rodney Adams** .... (980) 314-6475

Charlotte-Mecklenburg Community Relations Committee [CRC]
City Hall, 600 E. Trade St., Charlotte, NC 28202
Tel: (704) 336-2424 Fax: (704) 336-5176

Executive Director **Willie Ratchford** .... (704) 336-2424
E-mail: willie.ratchford@mecklenburgcountync.gov

Charlotte Mecklenburg Library
310 North Tryon Street, Charlotte, NC 28202-2176
Tel: (704) 416-0100 Fax: (704) 416-0130 Internet: www.cmlibrary.org

Administration
Chief Executive Officer **Lenoir C. "Lee" Keesler, Jr.** ..... (704) 416-0100
Director, Libraries **David Singleton** .... (704) 416-0100
Education: North Carolina BA, MLS

Mecklenburg County Emergency Medical Services [MEDIC]
4525 Statesville Road, Charlotte, NC 28269
Tel: (704) 943-6000 Fax: (704) 943-6001

Executive Director **Joe Penner** .... (704) 943-6000

Historic Landmark Commission
2100 Randolph Rd., Charlotte, NC 28207
Fax: (704) 372-4584 Internet: www.cmhpf.org

Consulting Director **Dr. Dan L. Morrill** .... (704) 999-3086

Office of the Tax Assessor
700 East Stonewall Street, Charlotte, NC 28202
Tel: (704) 336-6348

Assessor **Kenneth L. "Ken" Joyner** .... (980) 314-4288
Education: North Carolina State

★ Elected Official ▲ Appointed by Legislature ▼ Appointed by Governor ► Appointed by Board or Commission ● Appointed by Judge
■ Appointed by Mayor △ Appointed by Freeholders ▽ Appointed by Supervisor ▷ Appointed by County Executive ○ Appointed by Council

Office of the Register of Deeds

720 East Fourth Street, Room 103, Charlotte, NC 28202
Fax: (704) 336-7699
E-mail: beverly.buchanan@mecklenburgcountync.gov

★ Register of Deeds **David Granberry** (R) . . . . (704) 336-2443
Term Expires: November 30, 2016
E-mail: david.granberry@mecklenburgcountync.gov
Assistant Register **Carol Williams** . . . . (704) 336-2443

Office of the Sheriff

700 East Fourth Street, Charlotte, NC 28202
Tel: (704) 336-2543 Fax: (704) 336-6118

★ Sheriff **Irwin Carmichael** (D) . . . . (704) 336-2543
Term Expires: December 31, 2018

County Jail

700 East 4th Street, Charlotte, NC 28202
Chief Deputy Sheriff **Felicia H. McAdoo** . . . . (704) 336-2543

Charlotte-Mecklenburg Schools

701 East Martin Luther King, Jr. Boulevard, Charlotte, NC 28202
Tel: (980) 343-3000 Fax: (704) 343-7135 Internet: www.cms.k12.nc.us

Board of Education

Internet: www.cms.k12.nc.us/boe
Chairperson **Mary McCray** . . . . (980) 343-5139
Fax: (980) 343-7128

Office of the Superintendent

E-mail: superintendent@cms.k12.nc.us
Internet: www.cms.k12.nc.us/superintendent
Superintendent **Ann B. Clark** . . . . (980) 343-6270
Education: Davidson 1980
Deputy Superintendent **(Vacant)** . . . . (980) 343-1173

Mecklenburg County Board of Elections

741 Kenilworth Avenue, Suite 202, Charlotte, NC 28204
Tel: (704) 336-2133 Fax: (704) 343-0537 Internet: www.meckboe.org
Director of Elections **Michael G. Dickerson** . . . . (704) 336-2133

County of Merced, California

Administration Building, 2222 M Street, Merced, CA 95340
Tel: (209) 385-7434 (Information) Internet: www.co.merced.ca.us

County Seat: Merced **Election Type:** Nonpartisan **Population:** 268,455 (2015)

Office of the Board of Supervisors

Administration Building, 2222 M Street, Merced, CA 95340
Fax: (209) 726-7977

★ Chair **Hubert "Hub" Walsh** (District 2) . . . . (209) 385-7366
Term Expires: December 31, 2016
E-mail: dist2@co.merced.ca.us
Education: UC Berkeley BA; Pacific Lutheran MA
★ Supervisor **John Pedrozo** (District 1) . . . . (209) 385-7366
Term Expires: December 31, 2016
E-mail: dist1@co.merced.ca.us
★ Supervisor **Daron McDaniel** (District 3) . . . . (209) 385-7366
Term Expires: December 31, 2018

Office of the Board of Supervisors *continued*

★ Supervisor **Deidre Kelsey** (District 4) . . . . (209) 385-7366
Term Expires: December 31, 2016
E-mail: dist4@co.merced.ca.us
★ Supervisor **Jerry O'Banion** (District 5) . . . . (209) 385-7366
Term Expires: December 31, 2018
E-mail: dist5@co.merced.ca.us
Education: Cal State (Fresno) 1968 BS
Chief Clerk **James L. "Jim" Brown** . . . . (209) 385-7595

Office of the County Counsel

Administration Building, 2222 M Street, Merced, CA 95340
Fax: (209) 726-1337

▽ County Counsel **James N. Fincher** . . . . (209) 385-7564
E-mail: jfincher@co.merced.ca.us
Assistant County Counsel **Deanne Peterson** . . . . (209) 385-7564

COUNTIES

Office of the County Executive Officer

Administration Bldg., 2222 M St., Merced, CA 95340
Fax: (209) 385-7375

County Executive Officer **James "Jim" Brown** . . . . (209) 385-7637
E-mail: jbrown@co.merced.ca.us
Assistant County Executive Officer **Scott De Moss** . . . . . (209) 385-7637

Community and Economic Development Department

2222 M Street, Second Floor, Merced, CA 95340
Fax: (209) 726-1710

Director **Mark J. Hendrickson** . . . . (209) 385-7686
E-mail: mhendrickson@co.merced.ca.us
Assistant Director **Oksana Newmen** . . . . (209) 385-7654
E-mail: onewmen@co.merced.ca.us
Water Resources Coordinator **Lacey Kiriakou** . . . . (209) 385-7654
Education: Cal State (Stanislaus) 2002 BS

Castle Airport

1900 Airdrome Entry, Atwater, CA 95301
Airport Manager **Scott C. Malta** . . . . (209) 385-7686 ext. 4180

Child Support Services

3368 North Highway 59, Suite A, Merced, CA 95348
Tel: (866) 901-3212 Fax: (209) 381-1305 E-mail: dcss@co.merced.ca.us

Director **Sharon Wardale-Trejo** . . . . (866) 901-3212

Department of Administrative Services

Administration Bldg., 2222 M St., Merced, CA 95340
Fax: (209) 725-3535

Administrative Services Director/Chief Information Officer **Mark A. Cowart** . . . . (209) 385-7690
E-mail: mcowart@co.merced.ca.us

Department of Mental Health

480 East 13th Street, Merced, CA 95340
Fax: (209) 725-3676

▶ Director **Yvonnia Brown** . . . . (209) 381-6813
E-mail: yvonnia.brown@co.merced.ca.us
Assistant Mental Health Director **(Vacant)** . . . . (209) 381-6800

Department of Public Health

260 East 15th Street, Merced, CA 95340
Tel: (209) 381-1010 (Information) Fax: (209) 381-1215
Internet: www.co.merced.ca.us/publichealth

▽ Director **Kathleen Grassi** . . . . (209) 381-1200
E-mail: kgrassi@co.merced.ca.us
Assistant Director of Public Health **Michael Johnson** . . . . (209) 381-1227

★ Elected Official ▲ Appointed by Legislature ▼ Appointed by Governor ▶ Appointed by Board or Commission ● Appointed by Judge
■ Appointed by Mayor △ Appointed by Freeholders ▽ Appointed by Supervisor > Appointed by County Executive ○ Appointed by Council

Environmental Health
260 East 15th Street, Merced, CA 95340
Fax: (209) 384-1593

Director **Ron Rowe** .... (209) 381-1097
Supervising Environmental Health Specialist
Steven Lowe .... (209) 381-1100

Department of Workforce Investment
1020 West Main Street, Merced, CA 95340
Fax: (209) 725-3592

▽ Director **Robert Morris** .... (209) 724-2000
Assistant Director **(Vacant)** .... (209) 724-2000

Human Services Agency
2115 West Wardrobe Avenue, Merced, CA 95340
Fax: (209) 383-6925

▽ Director (Interim) **Scott Pettygrove** .... (209) 385-3000
E-mail: spettygrove@co.merced.ca.us

Area Agency on Aging
851 W. 23rd St., Merced, CA 95340
Fax: (209) 384-8102

▽ Director (Interim) **Scott Pettygrove** .... (209) 385-7550
E-mail: spettygrove@co.merced.ca.us

Veterans' Service Office
3605 Hospital Road, Suite E, Atwater, CA 95301
Tel: (209) 385-7588 Fax: (209) 725-3848

▽ Compliance Officer **Victor Nazario** .... (209) 385-7588
E-mail: vnazario@hsa.co.merced.ca.us
Veteran's Claim Representative Supervisor
Katherine Spears .... (209) 385-7588
Veteran's Services Officer **James D. "Jim" Kanaby** .... (209) 385-7588

Human Resources Division
Administration Bldg., 2222 M Street, 3rd Floor, Merced, CA 95340
Fax: (209) 385-7375

▽ Human Resources Director **Marci R. Barrera** .... (209) 385-7682
E-mail: mbarrera@co.merced.ca.us

Merced County Fire Department
735 Martin Luther King Jr. Way, Merced, CA 95340
Fax: (209) 725-0174

Fire Chief **Nancy B. Koerperich** .... (209) 385-7450
E-mail: nancy.koerperich@fire.ca.gov
Division Chief **Mark Lawson** .... (209) 385-7450
E-mail: mark.lawson@fire.ca.gov

Merced County Public Library
2100 O St., Merced, CA 95340
Tel: (209) 385-7643 Fax: (209) 726-7912

▽ Librarian **Amy Taylor** .... (209) 385-7443
E-mail: ataylor@co.merced.ca.us

Office of the Agricultural Commissioner-Sealer
2139 Wardrobe Ave., Merced, CA 95340-6495
Fax: (209) 725-3910

▽ Agricultural Commissioner-Sealer **David A. Robinson** .... (209) 385-7431
E-mail: drobinson@co.merced.ca.us
Assistant Agricultural Commissioner-Sealer
Sean Runyon .... (209) 385-7431

Probation Department
2150 M St., Merced, CA 95340
Fax: (209) 725-3999

Chief Probation Officer **Jeff Kettering** .... (209) 385-7560
Assistant Chief Probation Officer **(Vacant)** .... (209) 385-7560

Public Defender's Office
Kane Building, 2150 M Street, Merced, CA 95340
Fax: (209) 725-8873

Public Defender **David Elgin** .... (209) 385-7692 ext. 4123
Chief Deputy Public Defender
Vincent G. Andrade .... (209) 385-7692 ext. 4119
Education: UC San Diego; New Col California JD

Public Works Department
715 Martin Luther King, Jr. Way, Merced, CA 95340
Fax: (209) 725-3989

▽ Director **Dana Hertfelder** .... (209) 385-7602
E-mail: dhertfelder@co.merced.ca.us
Assistant Director **Richard A. Schwarz** .... (209) 385-7602
E-mail: rschwarz@co.merced.ca.us
Deputy Director, Administration **Yorel Ackerman** .... (209) 385-7602
E-mail: yackeman@co.merced.ca.us
Deputy Director, Parks **(Vacant)** .... (209) 385-7426
Deputy Director, Roads **Steve Rough** .... (209) 385-7601
Deputy Building Official **Lydia Clary** .... (209) 385-7477

University of California Cooperative Extension
2145 Wardrobe Avenue, Merced, CA 95341
Tel: (209) 385-7403 Fax: (209) 722-8856

County Director (Interim) **Maxwell Norton** .... (209) 385-7403

Office of the Assessor
Administration Bldg., 2222 M St., Merced, CA 95340

★ Assessor **Barbara "Barb" Levey** .... (209) 385-7631
Term Expires: November 30, 2018
E-mail: blevey@co.merced.ca.us
Assistant Assessor **Matt May** .... (209) 385-7346
Chief Deputy Recorder **Jennifer Padilla** .... (209) 385-7627
E-mail: jpadilla@co.merced.ca.us

Office of the Auditor-Controller
Administration Bldg., 2222 M St., Merced, CA 95340
Fax: (209) 725-3900

★ Auditor-Controller **Lisa Cardella-Presto** .... (209) 385-7511
Term Expires: November 30, 2018
Assistant Auditor-Controller-Recorder **Ron Kinchloe** .... (209) 385-7511

Office of the County Clerk
2222 M Street, Merced, CA 95340
Tel: (209) 385-7627 Fax: (209) 385-7626

★ County Clerk **Barbara "Barb" Levey** .... (209) 385-7627
Term Expires: November 30, 2018

Office of the District Attorney
550 West Main Street, Merced, CA 95340
Fax: (209) 725-3669

★ District Attorney **Larry D. Morse II** .... (209) 385-7381
Term Expires: December 31, 2018
E-mail: lmorse@co.merced.ca.us
Education: Arkansas 1979; McGeorge 1987 JD

Office of the Sheriff-Coroner
Administration Bldg., 2222 M St., Merced, CA 95340
Tel: (209) 385-7606 (Jail Division)

★ Sheriff-Coroner **Vern Warnke** .... (209) 385-7451
Term Expires: December 31, 2018

★ Elected Official ▲ Appointed by Legislature ▼ Appointed by Governor ► Appointed by Board or Commission ● Appointed by Judge
■ Appointed by Mayor △ Appointed by Freeholders ▽ Appointed by Supervisor ▷ Appointed by County Executive ○ Appointed by Council

Office of the Treasurer-Tax Collector

Administration Bldg., 2222 M St., Merced, CA 95340

★Treasurer-Tax Collector **Karen D. Adams** .... (209) 385-7307
Term Expires: November 30, 2018
E-mail: kadams@co.merced.ca.us
Treasurer/Tax Collector Administrative Services Manager **Shannon DeLouiz** .... (209) 385-7307
E-mail: sdelouiz@co.merced.ca.us

County of Miami-Dade, Florida

Stephen P. Clark Center, 111 NW First Street, Miami, FL 33128-1986
Tel: (305) 375-5071 (Information) TTY: (305) 547-5446
Internet: www.miamidade.gov

County Seat: Miami **Election Type:** Nonpartisan
Population: 2,693,117 (2015)

Carlos A. Gimenez
Mayor

Began Service: July 1, 2011
Term Expires: October 2016
Date of Birth: January 17, 1954
Education: Barry 1999 BPA

Office of the Mayor

Stephen P. Clark Center, 111 NW First St., 29th Floor, Miami, FL 33128
Fax: (305) 375-1262 Internet: www.miamidade.gov/mayor

★Mayor **Carlos A. Gimenez** .... (305) 375-5701
E-mail: mayor@miamidade.gov
Chief of Staff **Alex Ferro** .... (305) 375-1206
Deputy Mayor and Finance Director **Edward "Ed" Marquez** .... (305) 375-1451
E-mail: marquez@miamidade.gov
Education: Florida AA; Florida International BBA
Deputy Mayor **Russell Benford** .... (305) 375-5141
E-mail: benford@miamidade.gov
Deputy Mayor **Alina T. Hudak** .... (305) 375-2531
E-mail: ath2@miamidade.gov Fax: (305) 372-6082
Education: Miami 1982 BBA, 1984 MPA
Deputy Mayor **Jack Osterholt** .... (305) 375-3076
E-mail: josterholt@miamidade.gov
Deputy Mayor **(Vacant)** .... (305) 375-5311
Director of Policy and Legislative Affairs **Gabriela Lopez** .... (305) 375-5227
Communications Director **Michael A. Hernández** .... (305) 375-5322
E-mail: michael.hernandez@miamidade.gov
Education: Florida International 2004 BA, 2011 MPA
Press Secretary **Stephanie Severino** .... (305) 375-1224
E-mail: stephanie@miamidade.gov
Senior Advisor **Michael Spring** .... (305) 375-4634

Animal Services Department [ASD]

7401 Northwest 74 Street, Miami, FL 33166
Tel: (305) 884-1101 Fax: (305) 805-1619
Internet: www.miamidade.gov/animals

Director **Alex Munoz** .... (305) 884-1101
Education: Florida State 1990 BA, 1992 MSP

Audit and Management Services Department [AMS]

701 NW 1st Court, Eighth Floor, Miami, FL 33136
Tel: (786) 469-5900 Fax: (305) 349-6190
Internet: http://www.miamidade.gov/audit/

Director **Cathy Jackson** .... (786) 469-5900
Education: Miami BBA

Aviation Department [Miami International Airport]

P.O. Box 025504, Miami, FL 33102-5504
Tel: (305) 876-7000 Fax: (305) 876-7522
E-mail: marketing@miami-airport.com Internet: www.miami-airport.com

Director **Emilio T. Gonzalez** .... (305) 876-7077
Education: South Florida BA; Tulane MA; Naval War MA; Miami PhD
Deputy Aviation Director **Ken Pyatt** .... (305) 876-7129
Chief Financial Officer **Anne Lee** .... (305) 876-7730
Assistant Director, Administration **Barbara S. Jimenez** .. (305) 876-0458
E-mail: bjimenez@miami-airport.com
Assistant Director, Facilities Management and Engineering **Carlos E. Jose** .... (305) 876-8398
E-mail: cjose@miami-airport.com
Assistant Director, Public Safety and Security **Lauren Stover** .... (305) 876-7017
E-mail: lstover@miami-airport.com
Assistant Director, Operations **Dan Agostino** .... (305) 876-7138
E-mail: dagostino@miami-airport.com
Associate Director, Governmental Affairs **Tony Quintero** .... (305) 876-7533
E-mail: tquintero@miami-airport.com
Associate Director, Minority Affairs **Milton L. Collins** ... (305) 876-7221
Assistant Aviation Director, Business Retention and Development **Gregory C. Owens** .... (305) 869-1670

Community Action and Human Services Department

Tel: (786) 469-4600 Fax: (305) 514-6152
Internet: http://www.miamidade.gov/socialservices/

Director **Lucia Davis-Raiford** .... (786) 469-4600

Communications Department

111 N.W. First Street, Suite 2510, Miami, FL 33128
Tel: (305) 468-5900 Fax: (305) 375-3968
Internet: http://www.miamidade.gov/information/

Director **Inson Kim** .... (305) 375-5527

Corrections and Rehabilitation Department

2525 NW 62nd Street, Miami, FL 33147
Tel: (786) 263-6000 Fax: (786) 263-6135
Internet: www.miamidade.gov/corrections

Director **Marydell Guevara** .... (786) 263-6010
Executive Secretary **Sandra Loo** .... (786) 263-6010
Assistant Director, Custody Services **Daniel Junior** ...... (786) 263-6020
Assistant Director, Management Services **Jackie Berry** ... (786) 263-6049

Department of Cultural Affairs

Stephen P. Clark Center, 111 NW First Street, Suite 625, Miami, FL 33128
Tel: (305) 375-4634 Fax: (305) 375-3068
E-mail: culture@miamidade.gov Internet: www.miamidadearts.org

Director **Michael Spring** .... (305) 375-4634
Deputy Director **Deborah Margol** .... (305) 375-4634

COUNTIES

★ Elected Official ▲ Appointed by Legislature ▼ Appointed by Governor ► Appointed by Board or Commission ● Appointed by Judge
■ Appointed by Mayor △ Appointed by Freeholders ▽ Appointed by Supervisor ▷ Appointed by County Executive ○ Appointed by Council

Elections Department
2700 Northwest 87th Avenue, Miami, FL 33172
Tel: (305) 499-8500 Tel: (305) 499-8363 (Voter Registration)
Tel: (305) 499-8444 (Absentee Ballots) Fax: (305) 499-8501
E-mail: soedade@miamidade.gov Internet: www.miamidade.gov/elections

Supervisor of Elections **Penelope "Penny" Townsley** . . . (305) 499-8509
Education: Miami Dade Comm Col 1997 AA; Barry 2001 BPA Fax: (305) 468-2507

Finance Department
Stephen P. Clark Center, 111 NW First Street, Suite 2550, Miami, FL 33128-1995
Tel: (305) 375-5147 Fax: (305) 375-5659
Internet: www.miamidade.gov/finance

Deputy Mayor/Finance Director **Edward "Ed" Marquez** . . . (305) 375-1451
Education: Florida AA; Florida International BBA
Deputy Finance Director **Blanca Padron** . . . (305) 375-5149
Bond Administration Director **Frank P. Hinton** . . . (305) 375-5147
Cash Management Director **Mariela Gomez** . . . (305) 375-5134
Controller **Sandra Bridgeman** . . . (305) 375-5080
111 NW First Street, Suite 2620, Miami, FL 33128-1980 Fax: (305) 375-4966
Tax Collector **Marcus Saiz de la Mora** . . . (305) 375-5448
200 NW Second Avenue, Miami, FL 33128 Fax: (305) 375-4214
E-mail: jmp@miamidade.gov

Miami-Dade Fire Rescue Department [MDFR]
9300 NW 41st St., Miami, FL 33178
Fax: (786) 331-5100 E-mail: mdfrd@miamidade.gov
Internet: http://www.miamidade.gov/fire/

Fire Chief **David Downey** . . . (786) 331-5109
E-mail: downeyd@miamidade.gov
Assistant Fire Chief of Operations **Arthur Holmes** . . . (786) 331-5000
E-mail: holmesa@miamidade.gov
Assistant Fire Chief of Technical and Support Services **Louie Fernandez** . . . (786) 331-5000
E-mail: louief@miamidade.gov
Assistant Director of Finance and Administration **Scott Mendelsberg** . . . (786) 331-5000
E-mail: mendelsberg@miamidade.gov

Office of Emergency Management
9300 NW 41st St., Miami, FL 33178
Tel: (305) 468-5400 Fax: (305) 468-5401 E-mail: eoc@miamidade.gov
Internet: www.miamidade.gov/oem

Assistant Director, Emergency Management **Curtis Sommerhoff** . . . (305) 468-5403
E-mail: csomm@miamidade.gov
Division Director, Office of Emergency Management **(Vacant)** . . . (305) 468-5403

Information Technology Department
5680 S.W. 87th Avenue, Miami, FL 33173
Tel: (305) 596-8200 Fax: (305) 596-8088 Internet: www.miamidade.gov/

Director/Chief Information Officer **Angel Petisco** . . . (305) 596-8200
E-mail: apa@miamidade.gov
Education: Thomas Edison State BSBA
Assistant Director, Enterprise Application Services **Margaret Brisbane** . . . (305) 596-8320
E-mail: mbrisb@miamidade.gov
Assistant Director, Enterprise Computing and Network Infrastructure **Jose R. Otero** . . . (305) 596-8409
E-mail: jro@miamidade.gov
Chief Security Officer **Lars Schmekel** . . . (305) 596-8779
E-mail: lars@miamidade.gov

Internal Services Department
Stephen P. Clark Center, 111 NW First Street, Suite 2110, Miami, FL 33128
Tel: (305) 375-1364 Fax: (305) 375-2459
Internet: www.miamidade.gov/hr

Director **Tara Smith** . . . (305) 375-5289
E-mail: TASMITH@miamidade.gov
Director, Labor Relations, Human Resources **Tyrone W. Williams** . . . (305) 375-4171
Director, Design and Construction Services Division **Asael Marrero** . . . (305) 375-1101
Fax: (305) 375-1125
Director, Facilities and Utilities Management Division **Juan Silva** . . . (305) 375-3465
Fax: (305) 375-3914
Director, Fleet Management Division **Alex Alfonso** . . . (305) 375-2818
Fax: (305) 679-7722
Director, Real Estate Development Division **Jose Galan** . . . (305) 375-1150
Fax: (305) 375-1157

Department of Procurement Management [DPM]
Stephen P. Clark Center, 111 NW First Street, Suite 1300, Miami, FL 33128
Tel: (305) 375-5773 Fax: (305) 375-2316
E-mail: dpmdept@miamidade.gov

Assistant Director/Chief Procurement Officer **Miriam Singer** . . . (305) 375-5502
E-mail: singer@miamidade.gov
Education: Miami, MPA

Department of Small Business Development [SBD]
111 N.W. First Street, 19th Floor, Miami, FL 33128
Tel: (305) 375-3111 Fax: (305) 375-3160
E-mail: sbdmail@miamidade.gov Internet: www.miamidade.gov/sba

Director **Gary Hartfield** . . . (305) 375-3134
Fax: (305) 375-4751
Director, Administration and Financial Management Division **(Vacant)** . . . (305) 375-3183
Director, Business Opportunities Services Division **(Vacant)** . . . (305) 375-3123
Director, Contract Monitoring and Compliance Division **Alice Hidalgo-Gato** . . . (305) 375-3153

Juvenile Services Department [JSD]
275 Northwest 2nd Street, 2nd Floor, Miami, FL 33128
Tel: (305) 755-6200 Fax: (305) 755-6150 E-mail: jsd@miamidade.gov
Internet: www.miamidade.gov/jsd

Director **Morris Copeland** . . . (305) 755-6202
Education: Colorado Fax: (305) 755-6146

Miami-Dade Public Library System
Miami-Dade Cultural Center, 101 West Flagler Street, Miami, FL 33130-1523
Tel: (305) 375-2665 Fax: (305) 375-5545 Internet: www.mdpls.org

Administration
Director **Gia Arbogast** . . . (305) 375-5026
E-mail: director@mdpls.org
Education: Florida State 1986 MLS; Miami 1981 BA
Assistant Director, Public Services Operation **Kimberly Matthews** . . . (305) 375-5005
E-mail: matthewsk@mdpls.org
Public Affairs Officer **Jack Varela** . . . (305) 375-5291
Assistant Director, Fiscal Operations and Capital Development **Raymond Baker** . . . (305) 375-1089

★ Elected Official ▲ Appointed by Legislature ▼ Appointed by Governor ▶ Appointed by Board or Commission ● Appointed by Judge
■ Appointed by Mayor △ Appointed by Freeholders ▽ Appointed by Supervisor ▷ Appointed by County Executive ○ Appointed by Council

Office of Management and Budget [OMB]
Stephen P. Clark Center, 111 NW First Street, Suite 2210, Miami, FL 33128
Tel: (305) 375-5143 Fax: (305) 375-5168
Internet: www.miamidade.gov/omb

Director **Jennifer Moon** .... (305) 375-5143
E-mail: jgm@miamidade.gov
Education: Florida State 1992 BA
Deputy Director **Hugo D. Salazar** .... (305) 375-5143

Medical Examiner Department
One Bob Hope Rd., Miami, FL 33136-1133
Tel: (305) 545-2400 Fax: (305) 545-2412
Internet: www.miamidade.gov/medexam

Chief Medical Examiner/Director **Dr. Bruce A. Hyma** .... (305) 545-2425
Head Secretary **Leslie Cummings** .... (305) 545-2425
Deputy Chief Medical Examiner **Dr. Emma O. Lew** ..... (305) 545-2449
Operations Director **Larry Cameron** .... (305) 545-2487
Toxicology Director **Diane Boland** .... (305) 545-2454
Fax: (305) 545-2452

Miami-Dade Park and Recreation Department
275 Northwest 2nd Street, 5th Floor, Miami, FL 33128
Fax: (305) 755-7946 Internet: www.miamidade.gov/parks

Director **Jack C. Kardys** .... (305) 755-7903
Education: St Thomas U BA, MSM
Assistant Director for Administration **Carol J. Kruse** ..... (305) 755-7855
E-mail: jck@miamidade.gov
Assistant Director for Operations **(Vacant)** .... (305) 755-7950
Communications Manager **(Vacant)** .... (305) 755-7884
Fax: (305) 755-7857
Training and Development Manager **Juan Armas** .... (305) 755-7956
E-mail: jayc@miamidade.gov Fax: (305) 755-7962
Training Specialist and Safety Officer **Fred Williams** .... (305) 755-7869

Miami-Dade Police Department [MDPD]
9105 NW 25th Street, Room 3072, Miami, FL 33172
Fax: (305) 471-2163 Internet: www.miamidade.gov/mdpd

Director **Juan J. Perez** .... (305) 471-1780
Assistant Director, Investigative Services
Alfredo Ramirez .... (305) 471-2950
Fax: (305) 471-1864
Assistant Director, Police Services **Randy Heller** .... (305) 471-2625
Fax: (305) 471-2626
Deputy Director **(Vacant)** .... (305) 471-2059
Fax: (305) 471-2163

Department of Public Housing and Community Development [DHCD]
701 N.W. First Court, 14th Floor, Miami, FL 33136
Tel: (786) 469-2100 Fax: (786) 469-2170
Internet: www.miamidade.gov/ced

Executive Director **Michael Liu** .... (786) 469-4106
Assistant Director **Mari Saydal-Hamilton** .... (786) 469-2116
Director, Community and Housing Development Division **Clarence D. Brown** .... (786) 469-2221
E-mail: cdbrown@miamidade.gov
Director, Community Planning and Outreach Division **Selena Williams** .... (786) 469-2100
Director, Development and Loan Administration Division **Leyani Sosa** .... (786) 469-2110

Public Works and Solid Waste Management Department [PWWM]
2525 NW 62nd Street, Fifth Floor, Miami, FL 33147
Tel: (305) 514-6666 Fax: (305) 514-6219
E-mail: pwwm@miamidade.gov
Internet: www.miamidade.gov/publicworks

Director **Alina T. Hudak** .... (305) 375-2531
111 NW First Street, 29th Floor, Miami, FL 33128
Education: Miami 1982 BBA, 1984 MPA
Deputy Director and County Engineer
Antonio Cotarelo .... (305) 375-2787
111 NW First Street, 14th Floor, Miami, FL 33128 Fax: (305) 375-1918
E-mail: cotara@miamidade.gov
Education: South Florida 1985 BS
Assistant Director **Aneisha Daniel** .... (305) 514-6630
111 NW First Street, 16th Floor, Miami, FL 33128 Fax: (305) 375-3070
E-mail: adaniel@miamidade.gov
Assistant Director **Asok Ganguli** .... (786) 315-2597
Fax: (305) 514-6874
Deputy Director **Paul Mauriello** .... (305) 514-6623
E-mail: mauriel@miamidade.gov Fax: (305) 514-6874
Assistant Director **Gaspar Miranda** .... (305) 375-4437
111 NW First Street, 15th Floor, Miami, FL 33128 Fax: (305) 679-6638
E-mail: gxm@miamidade.gov
Assistant Director **Michael Fernandez** .... (305) 514-6621
E-mail: mfern@miamidade.gov Fax: (305) 514-6886
Assistant Director **Pamela Payne** .... (305) 514-6789
E-mail: pzp@miamidade.gov Fax: (305) 514-6886

Regulatory and Economic Resources Department
Director **Jack Osterholt** .... (305) 375-5071

Department of Planning
Stephen P. Clark Center, 111 NW First Street, 11th Floor, Miami, FL 33128-1972
Tel: (305) 375-2800 Fax: (305) 375-5862 E-mail: dpnz@miamidade.gov
Internet: www.miamidade.gov/planzone

Assistant Director **Mark Woerner** .... (305) 375-2835
Administrative Secretary **Shirley Pass** .... (305) 375-2835
E-mail: passs@miamidade.gov
Chief, Office of Sustainability **Nichole Hefty** .... (305) 375-5593
E-mail: heftyn@miamidade.gov
Long Range Planning Supervisor **Napoleon Somoza** .... (786) 375-3835
Chief, Planning Research **Manuel Armada** .... (305) 375-2845
Principal Geographic Planner **Dany Martinez** .... (305) 375-2845

Development Services Division
Stephen P. Clark Center, 111 N.W. First Street, Eleventh Floor, Miami, FL 33128
Tel: (305) 375-2800 Tel: (786) 315-2000 (Zoning Permits)

Assistant Director For Development Services
Nathan Kogon .... (305) 375-2842
Senior Zoning Chief **Amina Newsome** .... (305) 375-3565
Zoning Information Supervisor **Grisel Rodriguez** .... (305) 375-1806
Zoning Evaluation Supervisor **Nicholas Nitti** .... (305) 375-2566
Zoning Hearings and Administrative Review Supervisor
Ron Connally .... (305) 375-2141
Platting and Traffic Review Chief **Raul Pino** .... (305) 375-2141
Area Planning Implementation Supervisor
Gilbert Blanco .... (305) 375-2622
Planning Legislation Supervisor **Gianni Lodi** .... (305) 375-2341
Urban Design Center Supervisor **Shailendra Singh** ...... (305) 375-4446

COUNTIES

★ Elected Official ▲ Appointed by Legislature ▼ Appointed by Governor ▶ Appointed by Board or Commission ● Appointed by Judge
■ Appointed by Mayor △ Appointed by Freeholders ▽ Appointed by Supervisor ▷ Appointed by County Executive ○ Appointed by Council

Office of Economic Development and International Trade [OEDIT]
111 NW First Street, Suite 2200, Miami, FL 33128-1986
Fax: (305) 679-7895 E-mail: oedit@miamidade.gov

Director **Manuel Gonzalez** .... (305) 375-1879
E-mail: mjgz@miamidade.gov
Assistant Director **Dimitrios "Jimmy" Nares** .... (305) 375-4626
E-mail: nares@miamidade.gov

Permitting and Inspection Center [BNC]
11805 S.W. 26th Street, Miami, FL 33175
Tel: (786) 315-2000 Fax: (786) 315-2929
E-mail: bldgdept@miamidade.gov

Building Official **Juliana H. Salas** .... (786) 315-2332
Finance Division Director **Monica Boza** .... (786) 315-2393
Board and Code Administration Division Director
Michael Goolsby .... (305) 315-2509
Information and Permit Support Division Director
Angelique Bestard .... (786) 315-2335
Neighborhood Regulation and Legal Services Division
Director **Chaveli Moreno** .... (786) 315-2506

Miami-Dade Transit
Overtown Transit Village, 701 NW First Court, 17th Floor,
Miami, FL 33136
Tel: (786) 469-5475 Fax: (305) 469-5580
E-mail: mdtdirector@miamidade.gov Internet: www.miamidade.gov/transit

Director **Alice Bravo** .... (305) 469-5406
Assistant Director of Engineering, Planning and
Development **Albert A. Hernandez** .... (786) 469-5444
E-mail: aah@miamidade.gov
Deputy Director of Operations **Steven A. Feil** .... (786) 469-5675
E-mail: sfeil@miamidade.gov
Director of Rail Services **Jerry W. Blackman** .... (305) 884-7517
Assistant Director of Bus Services **Derrick Gordon** ...... (305) 637-3809
Senior Chief, Information Technology **Rosie Perez** ...... (786) 469-5072
E-mail: rdp@miamidade.gov
Education: Florida International 1986 BA
Chief, Civil Rights and Labor Relations **Cathy Lewis** .... (786) 469-5487
Education: Fort Valley State 1979 BA; St Thomas U 1987 MS
Chief, Quality Assurance **Lazaro Palenzuela** .... (786) 469-5465
Chief, Safety and Security **Eric Muntan** .... (305) 375-4240
E-mail: ejm@miamidade.gov

Miami-Dade Water and Sewer Department [WASD]
3071 SW 38th Avenue, Miami, FL 33146
Tel: (305) 665-7471 Fax: (786) 552-8647
Internet: www.miamidade.gov/water

Director **John W. Renfrow** .... (786) 552-8086
Education: Miami 1973 BS
Deputy Director of Operations **Joseph Ruiz** .... (786) 552-8102
E-mail: jruiz@miamidade.gov
Assistant Director, Administration **(Vacant)** .... (786) 552-8080
Assistant Director, Engineering **Eduardo A. Vega** .... (786) 552-8110
Assistant Director, Finance **Frances G. Morris** .... (786) 552-8104
Assistant Director, Planning Innovation and Compliance
Bertha M. Goldenberg .... (786) 552-8120
Assistant Director, Wastewater **Vicente Arrebola** .... (786) 552-8107
Education: Florida 1979 BS
Assistant Director, Water **Rafael A. Terrero** .... (786) 552-8112

Office of Human Rights and Fair Employment Practices [OHRFEP]
Stephen P. Clark Center, 111 NW First Street, Suite 2220,
Miami, FL 33128-2784
Tel: (305) 375-2784 Fax: (305) 375-2114 E-mail: ofep@miamidade.gov
Internet: www.miamidade.gov/ofep

Director **Arleene Cuellar** .... (305) 375-2784

Business Affairs Division
140 West Flagler Street, Room 903, Miami, FL 33130-1561
Tel: (305) 375-3677 Fax: (305) 375-4120
E-mail: consumer@miamidade.gov Internet: www.miamidade.gov/csd

Assistant Director, Business Affairs **(Vacant)** .... (305) 375-5952
Consumer Advocate **(Vacant)** .... (305) 375-4199
Consumer Protection Division Chief
Gregory "Greg" Baker .... (305) 375-5557
Cooperative Extension Director **Teresa Olczyk** . . . (305) 248-3311 ext. 241
18710 SW 288th St., Miami, FL 33030
Passenger Transportation Regulatory Division Chief
Joe Mora .... (305) 375-2460
Vehicle Inspection Station Manager **David Mattison** ..... (305) 375-3283

Department of Permitting, Environment and Regulatory Affairs [DERM]
701 NW 1st Court, Fourth Floor, Miami, FL 33136
Tel: (305) 372-6789 Fax: (305) 372-6760 E-mail: derm@miamidade.gov
Internet: www.miamidade.gov/development

Director **Jack Osterholt** .... (305) 375-5695
Senior Division Chief **José Gonzalez** .... (305) 372-6754
Education: NJIT 1973 BS
Assistant Director **Lee N. Hefty** .... (305) 372-6750
Education: Florida International 1986 BS
Chief, Office of Administrative Services
Christa Erml-Martinez .... (305) 372-6776
E-mail: e134311@miamidade.gov
Chief, Air Quality Management Division
H. Patrick Wong .... (305) 372-6934
Education: Southampton (UK) 1977 BS
Chief, Environmental Education and Communications
Office (Interim) **Craig Grossenbacher** .... (305) 372-6784
Chief, Environmentally Endangered Lands Division
Cynthia Guerra .... (305) 372-6781
Chief, Natural Resources Regulation and Restoration
Division **(Vacant)** .... (305) 372-6594
Chief, Plan Review and Development Approvals
Division **(Vacant)** .... (786) 315-2842
Chief, Pollution Control Division **Wilbur Mayorga** ...... (305) 372-6708
Education: Florida International 1990 MS
Chief, Pollution Regulation and Enforcement Division
Rashid Isdambouli .... (305) 372-6964

Housing Finance Authority of Miami-Dade County [HFA]
7855 North West 12th Street, Suite 102, Doral, FL 33126
Tel: (305) 594-2518 Fax: (305) 392-2722 Internet: http://hfamiami.com/

Executive Director **Cheree Gulley** .... (305) 594-2518
Multifamily Development Administrator
Giraldo Canales .... (305) 594-2518
E-mail: gcanales@hfamiami.com
Chief Financial Officer **Adela Suarez-Garcia** .... (305) 594-2518

Metropolitan Planning Organization [MPO]
Stephen P. Clark Center, 111 NW First Street, Suite 920,
Miami, FL 33128
Fax: (305) 375-4950

Executive Director (Interim) **Jesus Guerra** .... (305) 375-4507

Pérez Art Museum Miami [PAMM]
101 West Flagler Street, Miami, FL 33130
Fax: (305) 375-1725 E-mail: mamart@miamidade.gov
Internet: www.miamiartmuseum.org

Director **Franklin Sirmans** .... (305) 375-1701
Deputy Director for Curatorial Affairs/Chief Curator
Tobias Ostrander .... (305) 375-3000
Deputy Director for External Affairs **Leann Standish** .... (305) 375-3000
Director of Communications **Tracy Belcher** .... (305) 375-1705
E-mail: tbelcher@miamiartmuseum.org
Director of Cooperation **Christopher Pastor** .... (305) 375-2617

★ Elected Official ▲ Appointed by Legislature ▼ Appointed by Governor ▶ Appointed by Board or Commission ● Appointed by Judge
■ Appointed by Mayor △ Appointed by Freeholders ▽ Appointed by Supervisor ▷ Appointed by County Executive ○ Appointed by Council

Pérez Art Museum Miami *continued*

Director of Education and Public Programs **Emily Mello** . . (305) 375-3000
Chief Financial Officer **John Safranek** . . . . (305) 375-3000
Deputy Director for Legal and Government Affairs and
General Counsel **M. Thérèse "Terry" Vento** . . . . (305) 375-5071

Department of Human Resources

111 N.W. First Street, Twenty First Floor, Miami, FL 33128

Director **Arleene Cuellar** . . . . (305) 375-1589
E-mail: arleene.cuellar@miamidade.gov
Director, Recruitment, Testing and Career Development,
Human Resources **Virginia Washington** . . . . (305) 375-1793

Office of the Board of County Commissioners

Stephen P. Clark Center, 111 NW First Street, 2nd Floor,
Miami, FL 33128
Tel: (305) 375-5124 Internet: www.miamidade.gov/commiss

★ Chair **Jean Monestime** (District 2) . . . . (305) 375-4833
Term Expires: November 17, 2018 Fax: (305) 375-4843
E-mail: district2@miamidade.gov
Education: Florida International 1995 BA;
Nova Southeastern 2000 MBA
★ Commissioner **Barbara Jordan** (District 1) . . . . (305) 375-5694
Term Expires: November 19, 2016
E-mail: district1@miamidade.gov
Education: Morris Brown 1965 BS; Nova Southeastern 1986 MS
★ Commissioner **Audrey Edmonson** (District 3) . . . . (305) 375-5393
Term Expires: November 19, 2016 Fax: (305) 638-6906
E-mail: district3@miamidade.gov
Education: Florida International; Barry
★ Commissioner **Sally A. Heyman** (District 4) . . . . (305) 375-5128
Term Expires: November 17, 2018 Fax: (305) 372-6179
E-mail: district4@miamidade.gov
Date of Birth: October 10, 1954
Education: Florida 1975 BA; Nova 1975 MS; Miami 1992 JD
★ Commissioner **Bruno Barreiro** (District 5) . . . . (305) 643-8525
Term Expires: November 19, 2016 Fax: (305) 643-8528
E-mail: district5@miamidade.gov
Date of Birth: December 14, 1965
Education: Miami 1986 (Attended)
★ Commissioner **Rebeca Sosa** (District 6) . . . . (305) 375-5696
Term Expires: November 17, 2018 Fax: (305) 372-6090
E-mail: district6@miamidade.gov
Education: Biscayne; Puerto Rico
★ Commissioner **Xavier L. Suarez** (District 7) . . . . (305) 375-5680
Term Expires: November 19, 2016 Fax: (305) 372-6103
E-mail: district7@miamidade.gov
Education: Villanova 1971 BME; Harvard 1975 JD
★ Commissioner **Daniella Levine Cava** (District 8) . . . . (305) 375-5218
Term Expires: November 17, 2018 Fax: (305) 372-6073
★ Commissioner **Dennis C. Moss** (District 9) . . . . (305) 375-4832
Term Expires: November 19, 2016 Fax: (305) 372-6011
E-mail: dennismoss@miamidade.gov
Education: Grinnell 1974 BA
★ Commissioner **Javier D. Souto** (District 10) . . . . (305) 375-4835
Term Expires: November 17, 2018 Fax: (305) 375-3456
E-mail: javiersouto@miamidade.gov
Date of Birth: December 15, 1938
Education: Miami 1967 BA
★ Commissioner **Juan C. Zapata** (District 11) . . . . (305) 375-5511
Term Expires: November 19, 2016 Fax: (305) 375-5883
E-mail: district11@miamidade.gov
Education: Florida International 1994 BS
★ Commissioner **José "Pepe" Diaz** (District 12) . . . . (305) 375-4343
Term Expires: November 17, 2018 Fax: (305) 372-6109
E-mail: district12@miamidade.gov

Office of the Board of County Commissioners *continued*

★ Commissioner **Esteban L. Bovo, Jr.** (District 13) . . . . (305) 375-4831
Term Expires: November 19, 2016 Fax: (305) 375-2011
Date of Birth: June 12, 1962
Education: Miami Dade Comm Col 1983 BA;
Florida International 1987 BS
Division Chief **Christopher Agrippa** . . . . (305) 375-5124
111 N.W. First Street, Fax: (305) 275-2484
Suite 17-202, Miami, FL 33128

Miami-Dade Economic Advocacy Trust [MDEAT]

19 West Flagler Street, M-106, Miami, FL 33130
Tel: (305) 372-7600 Fax: (305) 579-3699
Internet: www.miamidade.gov/mmap

Executive Director **John E. Dixon, Jr.** . . . . (305) 372-7600 ext. 227
E-mail: jdixon@miamidade.gov
Public Information Officer **Susana Cortazar** . . . . (305) 372-7600 ext. 239
Marketing Administrator **Susana Cortazar** . . . . . (305) 372-7600 ext. 249
Teen Court Division Administrator
Ralph McCloud . . . . (305) 372-7600 ext. 253

Office of the Commission Auditor

Stephen P. Clark Center, 111 N.W. First Street, Miami, FL 33128-1963
Tel: (305) 375-4354 Fax: (305) 375-3096 E-mail: oca@miamidade.gov
Internet: www.miamidade.gov/auditor

▶ Commission Auditor **Charles Anderson** . . . . (305) 375-4354
Education: Florida A&M BS
Executive Secretary **Angie Martinez** . . . . (305) 375-2524
E-mail: anmr@miamidade.gov
Audit Manager **Neil R. Singh** . . . . (305) 375-1826
Budget Manager **Orky Rodriguez** . . . . (305) 375-1648
Research Supervisor **Bia Marsellos** . . . . (305) 375-1255

Office of Community Advocacy [OCA]

Stephen P. Clark Center, 111 NW First Street, Suite 620,
Miami, FL 33128
Tel: (305) 375-5730 Fax: (305) 375-4838
Internet: www.miamidade.gov/ocr

Executive Director **Rene Diaz** . . . . (305) 375-1799
E-mail: rened@miamidade.gov
Director, Commission for Women **Laura Morilla** . . . . (305) 375-4967
E-mail: morilla@miamidade.gov
Director, Community Relations Board **Amy K. Carswell** . . (305) 375-1406
E-mail: amy2@miamidade.gov
Director, Asian-American Advisory Board
Mohammad Shakir . . . . (305) 375-1570
E-mail: mshakir@miamidade.gov
Director, Black Affairs Advisory Board **Retha Boone** . . . . (305) 375-4606
E-mail: rboone@miamidade.gov
Director, Hispanic Affairs Advisory Board
Natalie Milian . . . . (305) 375-5098
E-mail: nmilian@miamidade.gov
Director, Military Affairs Board **Gustavo Cruz** . . . . (305) 375-4493
E-mail: guscruz@miamidade.gov
Coordinator, Goodwill Ambassadors **Yvans Morisseau** . . . (305) 375-3840
E-mail: moryva@miamidade.gov
Coordinator, Kids Aspire **Vanessa Ortega** . . . . (305) 375-4478
E-mail: ortegav@miamidade.gov

Office of the County Attorney

Stephen P. Clark Center, 111 NW First Street, Suite 2810,
Miami, FL 33128
Tel: (305) 375-5151 Fax: (305) 375-5634 E-mail: atty@miamidade.gov
Internet: http://attorney.miamidade.gov/

▶ County Attorney **Robert A. Cuevas, Jr.** . . . . (305) 375-5151
Education: Florida 1967 BA, 1970 JD
First Assistant County Attorney **Abigail Price-Williams** . . (305) 375-1319
E-mail: apw1@miamidade.gov
Education: Howard U 1981 BA; Miami 1984 JD

COUNTIES

★ Elected Official ▲ Appointed by Legislature ▼ Appointed by Governor ▶ Appointed by Board or Commission ● Appointed by Judge
■ Appointed by Mayor △ Appointed by Freeholders ▽ Appointed by Supervisor ▷ Appointed by County Executive ○ Appointed by Council

Office of the Inspector General [OIG]

19 West Flagler Street, Suite 220, Miami, FL 33130
Tel: (305) 375-1946 Fax: (305) 579-2656 Internet: www.miamidadeig.org

Inspector General **Mary T. Cagle** .... (305) 375-1946
Assistant Inspector General, Investigations
Felix Jimenez .... (305) 375-1946
Assistant Inspector General/Legal Counsel **Patra Liu** ..... (305) 375-1946
Education: U Washington BA, 1995 JD

Office of Intergovernmental Affairs

Stephen P. Clark Center, 111 NW First Street, Suite 1032, Miami, FL 33128
Tel: (305) 375-5600 Fax: (305) 375-5639
E-mail: intergov@miamidade.gov Internet: www.miamidade.gov/intergov

Director **Joe Rasco** .... (305) 375-5600
E-mail: jrasco@miamidade.gov
Administrative Coordinator **Tiffany Machado** .... (305) 375-5600
E-mail: tiff4@miamidade.gov
Federal Affairs Coordinator **Phillip Drujak** .... (305) 375-5600
Federal Affairs Coordinator **(Vacant)** .... (305) 375-5600
Legislative Delegation Coordinator **Erica Chanti** .... (305) 375-5600
State Affairs Coordinator **Alina Gonzalez** .... (305) 375-5600
Local Government Liaison **Alina Gonzalez** .... (305) 375-5600

Office of Communications

Stephen P. Clark Center, 111 NW First Street, 29th Floor, Miami, FL 33128-1986
Tel: (305) 375-1545 Fax: (305) 375-3304
Internet: www.miamidade.gov/communications

Director **Michael A. Hernández** .... (305) 375-1545
Education: Florida International 2004 BA, 2011 MPA

Office of the Clerk of the Courts

Dade County Courthouse, 73 W. Flagler St., Room 242, Miami, FL 33130
P.O. Box 011711, Miami, FL 33101
Fax: (305) 349-7403 Internet: www.miami-dadeclerk.com

★ Clerk **Harvey Ruvin** .... (305) 349-7333
Term Expires: January 2017
E-mail: clerk@miami-dadeclerk.com
Education: Florida 1959; Miami 1962 JD
Finance Director **Margaret Enciso** .... (305) 349-7333
Director, Strategic Management and Budget
Lisa Saboya-Fernandez .... (305) 349-7333

Office of the Property Appraiser

Stephen P. Clark Center, 111 NW First Street, Suite 710, Miami, FL 33128-1984
Tel: (786) 331-5321 Fax: (305) 679-7940
Internet: www.miamidade.gov/pa

★ Property Appraiser **Pedro J. Garcia** .... (305) 375-4008
Term Expires: December 31, 2016
Administration Director **Bobby Flevaris** .... (305) 375-1519
Information Division Director **Jose Nodàrse** .... (305) 375-4111
E-mail: nodarsej@miamidade.gov

Office of the Public Defender

1320 NW 14th St., Miami, FL 33125-1690
Tel: (305) 545-1600 Fax: (305) 545-1997 E-mail: info@pdmiami.com
Internet: www.pdmiami.com

★ Public Defender **Carlos J. Martinez** .... (305) 545-1900
Term Expires: December 31, 2016
E-mail: cmartinez@pdmiami.com
Executive Assistant **Rory Stein** .... (305) 545-1902
Director Support Services **Lattice McMorray** .... (305) 545-1913

Office of the State Attorney (11th Judicial Circuit of Florida)

1350 NW 12th Ave., Miami, FL 33136-2102
Internet: www.miamisao.com

★ State Attorney **Katherine Fernandez Rundle** .... (305) 547-0100
Term Expires: December 31, 2016 Fax: (305) 547-0811
Education: Miami 1973 BA, 1974; Cambridge (UK) 1976 JD

County of Middlesex, New Jersey

County Administration Building, 75 Bayard Street, New Brunswick, NJ 08903
P.O. Box 871, New Brunswick, NJ 08903
Tel: (732) 745-3000 (Information) Internet: www.co.middlesex.nj.us

County Seat: New Brunswick **Election Type:** Partisan
Population: 840,900 (2015)

Office of the Board of Chosen Freeholders

P.O. Box 871, New Brunswick, NJ 08903
Tel: (732) 745-3080 Fax: (732) 745-3110

★ Director **Ronald G. Rios** (D) .... (732) 745-5792
Term Expires: December 31, 2018
E-mail: ronald.rios@co.middlesex.nj.us
Date of Birth: 1952
Education: National Labor 2000 BA
★ Deputy Director **Carol Barrett Bellante** (D) .... (732) 296-6968
Term Expires: December 31, 2017
E-mail: carol.barrett@co.middlesex.nj.us
★ Freeholder **Kenneth Armwood** (D) .... (732) 745-4317
Term Expires: December 31, 2016
E-mail: kenneth.armwood@co.middlesex.nj.us
★ Freeholder **Charles Kenny** (D) .... (732) 745-4593
Term Expires: December 31, 2016
★ Freeholder **H. James Polos** (D) .... (732) 745-3852
Term Expires: December 31, 2018
E-mail: james.polos@co.middlesex.nj.us
★ Freeholder **Charles E. Tomaro** (D) .... (732) 745-4438
Term Expires: December 31, 2017
E-mail: charles.tomaro@co.middlesex.nj.us
★ Freeholder **Blanquita B. Valenti** (D) .... (732) 745-4153
Term Expires: December 31, 2016
E-mail: blanquita.valenti@co.middlesex.nj.us
Date of Birth: October 1936
Education: Rosemont 1955 BA; Rutgers
△ Clerk of the Board **Margaret E. Pemberton** .... (732) 745-3080
E-mail: clerkoftheboard@co.middlesex.nj.us

Office of the County Counsel

County Administration Bldg., John F. Kennedy Square, Room 230, New Brunswick, NJ 08901
Fax: (732) 745-4539

△ County Counsel **Thomas F. Kelso** .... (732) 745-3228
E-mail: thomas.kelso@co.middlesex.nj.us
Education: Rutgers 1972 BA; Brooklyn Law 1975 JD
Senior Deputy County Counsel **Niki Athanasopoulos** ... (732) 745-4149
Senior Deputy County Counsel **Benjamin D. Leibowitz** .. (732) 745-4195
Deputy County Counsel **Jeanne-Marie Scollo** .... (732) 745-4147
Deputy County Counsel **(Vacant)** .... (732) 745-3741

★ Elected Official ▲ Appointed by Legislature ▼ Appointed by Governor ► Appointed by Board or Commission ● Appointed by Judge
■ Appointed by Mayor △ Appointed by Freeholders ▽ Appointed by Supervisor ▷ Appointed by County Executive ○ Appointed by Council

Finance Department
P.O. Box 871, New Brunswick, NJ 08903
Fax: (732) 745-4356 E-mail: treasurer@co.middlesex.nj.us
Internet: www.co.middlesex.nj.us/treasurer

△Chief Financial Officer/Treasurer
Giuseppe "Joe" Pruiti . . . . . (732) 745-3173
E-mail: joe.pruiti@co.middlesex.nj.us

Office of the Tax Administrator
75 Bayard Street, Fourth Floor, New Brunswick, NJ 08901
Fax: (732) 745-3767 Internet: www.co.middlesex.nj.us/taxboard

Tax Administrator **Irving Verosloff** . . . . . (732) 745-3350
E-mail: irving.verosloff@co.middlesex.nj.us

Office of Purchasing
County Administration Building, 75 Bayard Street, 3rd Floor, New Brunswick, NJ 08901-2112
Fax: (732) 745-4432 Internet: www.co.middlesex.nj.us/purchasing

△Purchasing Agent **Ann Hartwick** . . . . . (732) 745-3277
E-mail: ann.hartwick@co.middlesex.nj.us

Office of the County Administrator
County Administration Bldg., 75 Bayard Street, 3rd Floor, New Brunswick, NJ 08901
Fax: (732) 745-3454

△County Administrator **John A. Pulomena** (D) . . . . . (732) 745-3040
E-mail: john.pulomena@co.middlesex.nj.us
Education: CUNY BS
Secretary **Erica Betti** . . . . . (732) 745-4085
Business Manager **Shannon Tambini** . . . . . (732) 745-3041

Human Resources Office
P.O. Box 871, New Brunswick, NJ 08903
Fax: (732) 745-4087

△Director **Dennis J. Cerami** . . . . . (732) 745-4201
E-mail: dennis.cerami@co.middlesex.nj.us
Secretary **Lori Ferrazzoli** . . . . . (732) 745-3854
E-mail: lori.ferrazzoli@co.middlesex.nj.us

Information Technology
75 Bayard St., New Brunswick, NJ 08901
Tel: (732) 745-3784 Fax: (732) 296-6934

Director of Information Technology **Silvio Casteluccio** . . . (732) 745-3784
E-mail: silvio.castelluccio@co.middlesex.nj.us

Middlesex County College
2600 Woodbridge Avenue, Edison, NJ 00818-3050
P.O. Box 3050, Edison, NJ 08818-3050
Tel: (732) 548-6000 Fax: (732) 494-8244 Internet: www.middlesexcc.edu

President **Joann La Perla-Morales** . . . . . (732) 906-2517

Community Services
75 Bayard Street, Second Floor, New Brunswick, NJ 08901
Tel: (732) 745-4230 Fax: (732) 745-7527

Department Head **Geraldine "Gerry" MacKenzie** . . . . . (732) 745-4230

George J. Otlowski, Sr. Center for Mental Health Care
George J. Otlowski, Sr. Center for Mental Health Care, 570 Lee St., Perth Amboy, NJ 08861
Tel: (732) 442-1666 Fax: (732) 442-9512

Executive Director **Richard L. Dixon** . . . . . (732) 376-6719
Medical Director **Dr. Dineshehandra G. Patel** . . . . . (732) 376-6737
Clinical Director **Sylvia Zanoni** . . . . . (732) 376-6721
Administrative Director **Alex Michals** . . . . . (732) 376-6725
E-mail: alex.michals@co.middlesex.nj.us
Outpatient Services Director **Stephen Sidorsky** . . . . . (732) 376-6701
Partial Care Director **Debra Klein** . . . . . (732) 376-6786

Office of Human Services
75 Bayard Street, New Brunswick, NJ 08903
Fax: (732) 296-7971 Internet: www.co.middlesex.nj.us/humanservices

△Executive Director **Melyssa Lewis** . . . . . (732) 745-4186
E-mail: melyssa.lewis@co.middlesex.nj.us
Secretary **Kathie Waite** . . . . . (732) 745-4186
E-mail: kathie.waite@co.middlesex.nj.us

Department of Housing, Community Development, and Social Services
County Administration Bldg., John F. Kennedy Square, Second Floor, New Brunswick, NJ 08901
Tel: (732) 745-3025 Fax: (732) 745-4117

△Director **Paul Buckley** . . . . . (732) 745-3950

Aging and Disabled Services Department
75 Bayard Street, 5th Floor, New Brunswick, NJ 08903
Tel: (732) 745-3295 Fax: (732) 246-5641
E-mail: answersonaging@co.middlesex.nj.us
Internet: www.co.middlesex.nj.us/aging

△Executive Director **Laila Caune** . . . . . (732) 745-3295

Office of the County Adjuster
County Administration Bldg., John F. Kennedy Square, 75 Bayard Street, Room 240, New Brunswick, NJ 08901
P.O. Box 469, New Brunswick, NJ 08903-0469
Fax: (732) 745-3496

County Adjuster **Sandra Y. Coleman** . . . . . (732) 745-3251

Business Development and Education
75 Bayard Street, Second Floor, New Brunswick, NJ 08903
Tel: (732) 745-3890 Fax: (732) 745-5911

Department Head **Kathaleen R. Shaw** . . . . . (732) 745-3890
E-mail: kathaleen.shaw@co.middlesex.nj.us

Office of Workforce Development
550 Jersey Avenue, New Brunswick, NJ 08901
Tel: (732) 745-3601 Fax: (732) 745-4050

△Director **Kevin Kurdziel** . . . . . (732) 745-3601
E-mail: kevin.kurdziel@dol.state.nj.us

Office of Economic and Business Development
County Administration Building, 75 Bayard Street, Second Floor, New Brunswick, NJ 08901
Fax: (732) 745-2568
Internet: www.co.middlesex.nj.us/economicdevelopment

Director **Kathaleen R. Shaw** . . . . . (732) 745-3890

Middlesex County Cultural and Heritage Commission
703 Jersey Ave., New Brunswick, NJ 08901-3605
Tel: (732) 745-4489 Fax: (732) 745-4524 TTY: (732) 745-3888
E-mail: culturalandheritage@co.middlesex.nj.us
Internet: http://co.middlesex.nj.us/culturalheritage

△Chairman **Reginald Johnson** . . . . . (732) 745-4489
E-mail: reginald.johnson@co.middlesex.nj.us
△Vice Chairman **Rob Becker** . . . . . (732) 745-4489
△Division Head **Isha Vyas** . . . . . (732) 745-4489

Infrastructure Management
75 Bayard Street, Third Floor, New Brunswick, NJ 08903
Tel: (732) 745-3995 Fax: (732) 296-6934

Department Head **Khalid Anjum** . . . . . (732) 745-3995

Department of Public Works
P.O. Box 7356, North Brunswick, NJ 08902
Fax: (732) 940-6934

△Director **Gary Vesce** . . . . . (732) 940-3805

★Elected Official ▲Appointed by Legislature ▼Appointed by Governor ▶Appointed by Board or Commission ●Appointed by Judge
■Appointed by Mayor △Appointed by Freeholders ▽Appointed by Supervisor ▷Appointed by County Executive ○Appointed by Council

Office of Planning
75 Bayard St., New Brunswick, NJ 08901
Fax: (732) 745-3201 Internet: www.co.middlesex.nj.us/planningboard

△Director **George M. Ververides** .... (732) 745-3013
E-mail: george.ververides@co.middlesex.nj.us
Education: Rutgers 1958 BA; Cornell 1961 MRP

Division of Solid Waste Management
100 Bayard Street, 2nd Floor, New Brunswick, NJ 08901
Fax: (732) 745-3010

△Division Head **Mickey Gross** .... (732) 745-4170
E-mail: mickey.gross@co.middlesex.nj.us

Office of Parks and Recreation
P.O. Box 661, New Brunswick, NJ 08903
Tel: (732) 745-3900 Fax: (732) 745-7351

△Director **Rick Lear** .... (732) 745-3995
E-mail: richard.lear@co.middlesex.nj.us

Office of the County Engineer
333 Townsend St., New Brunswick, NJ 08901
P.O. Box 871, New Brunswick, NJ 08903
Fax: (732) 937-4585 Internet: www.co.middlesex.nj.us/engineering

△County Engineer **Rich Wallner** .... (732) 745-3283
E-mail: rich.wallner@co.middlesex.nj.us
Education: North Carolina State 1974 BS
Secretary **Joshua Kamis** .... (732) 745-5719
E-mail: joshua.kamis@co.middlesex.nj.us
Assistant County Engineer **Valerio D'Aloia** .... (732) 745-4016
E-mail: valerio.d'aloia@co.middlesex.nj.us
Supervising Engineer, Transportation **Kenneth Preteroti** .... (732) 745-3994
E-mail: Kenneth.Preteroti@co.middlesex.nj.us
Senior Engineer, Bridges, Dams, and Site Plan **Joseph Donato** .... (732) 745-3245
E-mail: joseph.donato@co.middlesex.nj.us

Public Safety and Health
35 Kennedy Boulevard, East Brunswick, NJ 08816
Tel: (732) 745-3100 Fax: (732) 745-2568

Department Head **Joseph Krisza** .... (732) 745-3100

Probation Division
189 New Street, New Brunswick, NJ 08901
P.O. Box 789, New Brunswick, NJ 08903-0789
Fax: (732) 448-6204

Chief Probation Officer **Kathie DeFuria** .... (732) 448-6110

Office of Health Services
35 Kennedy Boulevard, East Brunswick, NJ 08816
Tel: (732) 745-3100

Director **Lester Jones** .... (732) 745-3121

Environmental Health Division
711 Jersey Avenue, New Brunswick, NJ 08901
Tel: (732) 745-8480 Fax: (732) 745-8484

Division Head **Mickey Gross** .... (732) 745-8480
Air Pollution Program Supervisor (Acting) **Sharad Trivedi** .... (732) 745-8865
GIS Program Supervisor **Gary Rojek** .... (732) 745-8859
Noise/Solid Waste Programs Supervisor **Joseph DiFillippo** .... (732) 745-8492
Recycling Program Supervisor **Joseph DiFillippo** .... (732) 745-8492
Environmental Health Coordinator **Sharon Martens** .... (732) 745-8481

Health Education Division
75 Bayard Street, 5th Floor, New Brunswick, NJ 08903
Fax: (732) 745-2568

Health Education Coordinator **John Dowd** .... (732) 745-8861
Health Educator **Twyla Paige** .... (732) 745-8864

Nursing Division
75 Bayard Street, 5th Floor, New Brunswick, NJ 08903
Fax: (732) 745-2568

Director of Nursing **Deborah "Debbie" Gash** .... (732) 745-3120

Office of the Medical Examiner
1490 Livingston Avenue, North Brunswick, NJ 08902
Fax: (732) 745-3491

△County Medical Examiner (Acting) **Dr. Dianne Karluk** .... (732) 745-3190
Assistant Medical Examiner **Dr. Diane Karluk** .... (732) 745-3190
Assistant Medical Examiner **Dr. Alex Zhang** .... (732) 745-3190
Assistant Medical Examiner **Dr. Lauren P. Thoma** .... (732) 745-3190

Department of Corrections and Youth Services
P.O. Box 266, New Brunswick, NJ 08903-0266
Fax: (732) 951-3322

△Director **Mark Cranston** .... (732) 951-3321
E-mail: mark.cranston@co.middlesex.nj.us
Chief of Staff **Brian Ferguson** .... (732) 951-3331
Business Manager **Patricia "Pat" Mondi** .... (732) 351-3430
Supervisor, Middlesex County Shelter **James F. White** .... (732) 297-8991 ext. 6252
Superintendent, Middlesex County Youth Detention Center **James F. White** .... (732) 297-8991 ext. 6263
PREA Coordinator **Bobby Danino** .... (732) 951-3440
Social Rehabilitation Services Director **Joyce Pirre** .... (732) 951-3380
Training Bureau **Dana Davis** .... (732) 951-3377
E-mail: dana.davis@co.middlesex.nj.us

Office of Consumer Affairs and Weights and Measures
711 Jersey Avenue, New Brunswick, NJ 08901
Fax: (732) 745-3815 E-mail: weightsmeasures@co.middlesex.nj.us

△Director **William Deinzer** .... (732) 745-3875
E-mail: deinzb@co.middlesex.nj.us
Assistant Director **Tom Reilly** .... (732) 745-3856
E-mail: tom.reilly@co.middlesex.nj.us

Office of Emergency Management
Tel: (732) 316-7100 Fax: (732) 727-8993

Office of Emergency Management Coordinator **John Ferguson** .... (732) 316-7100

Office of the County Clerk
County Administration Building, 75 Bayard Street, 4th Floor, New Brunswick, NJ 08903
Tel: (732) 745-3005 Fax: (732) 745-3642

★County Clerk **Elaine M. Flynn** (D) .... (732) 745-3005
Term Expires: December 31, 2020
E-mail: elaine.flynn@co.middlesex.nj.us
Education: Trenton State BA; Kean Col MA
△Deputy County Clerk **Zusette Dato** .... (732) 745-3828
E-mail: zusette.dato@co.middlesex.nj.us

Office of the County Prosecutor
25 Kirkpatrick Street, New Brunswick, NJ 08901
Fax: (732) 745-2791

▼County Prosecutor **Andrew C. Carey** .... (732) 745-3333
Term Expires: June 2019
E-mail: prosecutor@co.middlesex.nj.us
Secretary **Stephanie Kurowsky** .... (732) 745-3333
E-mail: stephanie.kurowsky@co.middlesex.nj.us
First Assistant Prosecutor **Christopher Kuberiet** .... (732) 745-3044

★Elected Official ▲Appointed by Legislature ▼Appointed by Governor ▶Appointed by Board or Commission ●Appointed by Judge
■Appointed by Mayor △Appointed by Freeholders ▽Appointed by Supervisor ▷Appointed by County Executive ○Appointed by Council

Office of the Sheriff

701 Livingston Avenue, New Brunswick, NJ 08901
Fax: (732) 745-4055

★Sheriff **Mildred S. "Millie" Scott** (D) .... (732) 745-3271
Term Expires: January 7, 2018
E-mail: sheriff@co.middlesex.nj.us
Undersheriff **Kevin Harris** .... (732) 745-3246
E-mail: kevin.harris@co.middlesex.nj.us

Office of the Surrogate

County Administration Bldg., 75 Bayard St., 1st Floor, New Brunswick, NJ 08901
P.O. Box 790, New Brunswick, NJ 08903
Fax: (732) 745-4125 E-mail: surrogate@co.middlesex.nj.us
Internet: http://co.middlesex.nj.us/surrogate.index.asp

★Surrogate **Kevin J. Hoagland** (D) .... (732) 745-3055
Term Expires: December 31, 2016
E-mail: kevin.hoagland@co.middlesex.nj.us
Deputy Surrogate **Eileen Weber** .... (732) 745-3055

Middlesex County Board of Elections

777 Jersey Avenue, New Brunswick, NJ 08901-3605
Tel: (732) 745-3471 Fax: (732) 214-1656
E-mail: elections@co.middlesex.nj.us

▼Chairman **Sylvia Engel** (R) .... (732) 745-3471
Note: Reappointed on March 8, 2016 by Governor Christie, pending New Jersey Senate approval.
Term Expires: March 1, 2016
▼Secretary/Commissioner of Registrations
Daniel E. "Dan" Frankel (D) .... (732) 745-3471
Note: Reappointed on March 8, 2016 by Governor Christie, pending New Jersey Senate approval.
Term Expires: March 1, 2016
▼Commissioner **Jason Hawrylak** (D) .... (732) 745-3471
Term Expires: March 1, 2016
▼Commissioner **Donald Katz** (R) .... (732) 745-3471
Term Expires: March 1, 2016
Administrator **James J. "Jim" Vokral** .... (732) 745-8005
E-mail: jim.vokral@co.middlesex.nj.us

Middlesex County Superintendent of Schools

Building 400, 1460 Livingston Avenue, 2nd Floor, North Brunswick, NJ 08902
Fax: (732) 296-0683 Internet: www.co.middlesex.nj.us/superintendent

Superintendent (Interim) **Laura Morana** .... (732) 249-2900

County of Milwaukee, Wisconsin

County Courthouse, 901 North Ninth Street, Milwaukee, WI 53233
Tel: (414) 278-4211 (Information) TTY: (414) 278-5228
Internet: www.milwaukeecounty.org

County Seat: Milwaukee **Election Type:** Nonpartisan
Population: 957,735 (2015)

Office of the County Executive

County Courthouse, 901 North Ninth Street, Room 306, Milwaukee, WI 53233-1548
Tel: (414) 278-4211 Fax: (414) 223-1375
E-mail: countyexec@milwcnty.com
Internet: http://county.milwaukee.gov/countyexecutive

★County Executive **Christopher S. "Chris" Abele** .... (414) 278-4346
Term Expires: April 2020
E-mail: chris.abele@milwaukeecountywi.gov
Date of Birth: January 28, 1967
Education: Lawrence U
Chief of Staff **Raisa Koltun** .... (414) 278-4221
E-mail: raisa.koltun@milwcnty.com
Deputy Chief of Staff **John Zapfel** .... (414) 278-5281
Director of Community Relations **Claire Zautke** .... (414) 278-4346
Director of Legislative Affairs **Jon Janowski** .... (414) 278-4338
Communications Director **Nate Holton** .... (414) 278-5281

Office of Corporation Counsel

County Courthouse, 901 North Ninth Street, Room 303, Milwaukee, WI 53233
Tel: (414) 278-4300 Fax: (414) 223-1249

▷Corporation Counsel **Paul Bargren** .... (414) 278-4300
Deputy Corporation Counsel **(Vacant)** .... (414) 278-4319
Office Coordinator **Jodi L. Giessel** .... (414) 278-4288
E-mail: jodi.giessel@milwcnty.com

Office of the Medical Examiner

933 West Highland Avenue, Milwaukee, WI 53233
Tel: (414) 223-1200 Fax: (414) 223-1237

▷Medical Examiner **Brian Peterson** .... (414) 223-1200
Deputy Medical Examiner **Wieslawa Tlomak** .... (414) 223-1200
Assistant Medical Examiner **Jessica Lelinski** .... (414) 223-1200
Assistant Medical Examiner **Brian Linert** .... (414) 223-1200
Assistant Medical Examiner **Jacob Smit** .... (414) 223-1200
Director, Forensic Toxicology Laboratory
Sarah Schriber .... (414) 223-1228
Forensic Investigator **Amy Michalack** .... (414) 223-1213
Forensic Autopsy Supervisor **Karen Komassa** .... (414) 223-1213
Operations Manager **Karen Domagalski** .... (414) 223-1207
E-mail: kdomagalski@milwcnty.com

Veteran's Service Office

6419 West Greenfield Avenue, West Allis, WI 53213
Fax: (414) 266-1233

▷Veterans' Service Officer **James "Jim" Duff** .... (414) 266-1234
E-mail: james.duff@milwaukeecountywi.gov

Department of Administrative Services

County Courthouse, 901 North Ninth Street, Room 308, Milwaukee, WI 53233-1458
Tel: (414) 278-5353 Fax: (414) 223-1245

▷Director **Teig Whaley-Smith** .... (414) 278-5353

★Elected Official ▲Appointed by Legislature ▼Appointed by Governor ▶Appointed by Board or Commission ●Appointed by Judge
■Appointed by Mayor △Appointed by Freeholders ▽Appointed by Supervisor ▷Appointed by County Executive ○Appointed by Council

Office for Persons with Disabilities [OPD]
901 North Ninth Street, Room 307B, Milwaukee, WI 53233
Tel: (414) 278-3932 TTY: (414) 278-3937 Fax: (414) 278-3939

▷ Director **Timothy "Tim" Ochnikowski** . . . . . (414) 278-3930
E-mail: timothy.ochnikowski@milwaukeecountywi.gov

Office of Performance Strategy and Budget
901 North Ninth Street, Room 308, Milwaukee, WI 53233

▷ Fiscal and Budget Administrator **Steven Kreklow** . . . . . (414) 278-4139
E-mail: Steven.kreklow@milwaukeecountywi.gov

Division of Human Resources
County Courthouse, 901 North Ninth Street, Room 210, Milwaukee, WI 53233-1425
Tel: (414) 278-4198 Fax: (414) 223-1379
Internet: http://county.milwaukee.gov/HumanResources

▷ Director **Kerry Mitchell** . . . . . (414) 278-4148
▷ Deputy Director **Rick Ceschin** . . . . . (414) 278-4148

Information Management Services Division [IMSD]
901 North Ninth Street, Room 307C, Milwaukee, WI 53233
Fax: (414) 223-1289

Chief Information Officer **Laurie Panella** . . . . . (414) 278-4944

Procurement Division
901 North Ninth Street, Room 308, Milwaukee, WI 53233
Fax: (414) 223-8107

Purchasing Administrator **Patrick Lee** . . . . . (414) 278-4137

Department on Aging
1220 West Vliet Street, Suite 302, Milwaukee, WI 53205
Fax: (414) 289-8590 Internet: http://county.milwaukee.gov/aging

▷ Director (Interim) **Jonette Arms** . . . . . (414) 289-6073
E-mail: jonette.arms@milwaukeecountywi.gov

Department of Child Support Services
John P. Hayes Center, 901 North Ninth Street, Room 101, Milwaukee, WI 53233
Fax: (414) 223-1865 E-mail: milwcse@milwaukeecountywi.gov

Director **James "Jim" Sullivan** . . . . . (414) 615-2593
Education: Wisconsin 1991 BA; Marquette 2001 JD

Department of Family Care [MCDFC]
901 North Ninth Street, Room 307C, Milwaukee, WI 53233
Fax: (414) 287-7704 Internet: www.familycaremilwaukeecounty.com

Executive Director **Maria E. Ledger** . . . . . (414) 287-7600
Contract Administration Manager **Don Sobczak** . . . . . (414) 287-7410

Department of Health and Human Services
1220 West Vliet Street, Milwaukee, WI 53205
Tel: (414) 289-6897

▷ Director **Hector Colón** . . . . . (414) 289-6817
E-mail: hector.colon@milwaukeecountywi.gov
Administrator, Delinquency and Court Services Division **Thomas Wanta** . . . . . (414) 257-7704
Fax: (414) 257-7660
Administrator, Disabilities Services Division **Geri Lyday** . . . . . (414) 289-6387
Fax: (414) 289-8570
Administrator, Housing Division **James Mathy** . . . . . (414) 278-5106

Behavioral Health Division
9455 Watertown Plank Road, Milwaukee, WI 53226
Tel: (414) 257-6995 Fax: (414) 257-8018

Administrator (Interim) **Alicia Modjeska** . . . . . (414) 257-6823
Chief Administrative Officer **(Vacant)** . . . . . (414) 257-5202
Chief Medical Officer **John Schneider** . . . . . (414) 257-7217
Chief Financial Officer **Randy Oleszak** . . . . . (414) 257-7088
Chief Nursing Officer **Linda Oczus** . . . . . (414) 257-7483

Behavioral Health Division *continued*

Chief Clinical Officer **Jennifer Bergersen** . . . . . (414) 257-7473

Department of Parks, Recreation and Culture
9480 Watertown Plank Road, Wauwatosa, WI 53226
Tel: (414) 257-7275 Fax: (414) 257-6466 E-mail: parks@milwcnty.com

▷ Director **John W. Dargle, Jr.** . . . . . (414) 257-7275
E-mail: Staci.Piontek@milwaukeecountywi.gov
Planning and Development Chief **(Vacant)** . . . . . (414) 257-6100
Operations Chief **Guy Smith** . . . . . (414) 257-7275
E-mail: guy.smith@milwcnty.com
Education: Wisconsin (Milwaukee) 2003 BS
Recreation Services Chief **Susie Devcich** . . . . . (414) 257-8075
Marketing Director **Jeff Baudry** . . . . . (414) 257-4575
Finance Manager **Sheree Marlow** . . . . . (414) 257-4780
E-mail: sheree.marlow@milwcnty.com

Milwaukee County Department of Transportation [MCDOT]
10320 West Watertown Plank Road, Second Floor, Wauwatosa, WI 53226
Fax: (414) 257-5950 Internet: http://county.milwaukee.gov/MCDOT

▷ Director **Brian Dranzik** . . . . . (414) 257-5992
E-mail: brian.dranzik@milwaukeecountywi.gov
Fleet Director **Daniel Goeden** . . . . . (414) 257-5992

General Mitchell International Airport
General Mitchell International Airport, 5300 S. Howell Ave., Milwaukee, WI 53207-6189
Fax: (414) 747-4525 E-mail: info@mitchellairport.com
Internet: www.mitchellairport.com

Director **Ismael "Izzy" Bonilla** . . . . . (414) 747-5331
Deputy Airport Director, Finance and Administration **(Vacant)** . . . . . (414) 747-5703
Deputy Airport Director, Operations and Maintenance **(Vacant)** . . . . . (414) 747-5328
Marketing and Public Relations Manager **Patricia "Pat" Rowe** . . . . . (414) 747-4545
E-mail: prowe@mitchellairport.com

Milwaukee County Transit System [MCTS]
1942 North 17th Street, Milwaukee, WI 53205
Fax: (414) 344-0148 Internet: www.ridemcts.com

▷ Managing Director **Dan Boehm** . . . . . (414) 937-3272
Education: Wisconsin 1988 BSCE

Milwaukee County UW Extension
9501 West Watertown Plank Road, Wauwatosa, WI 53226-3552
Fax: (414) 256-4646 Internet: http://milwaukee.uwex.edu

Director **Eloisa Gómez** . . . . . (414) 256-4640

Milwaukee County Zoological Gardens
10001 W. Bluemound Rd., Milwaukee, WI 53226
Fax: (414) 256-5410 Internet: www.milwaukeezoo.org

Director **Charles "Chuck" Wikenhauser** . . . . . (414) 771-3040
Administration and Finance Deputy Director **Vera Westphal** . . . . . (414) 771-3040
E-mail: vera.westphal@milwaukeecountywi.gov
Director of Animal Health **Elizabeth "Beth" Rich** . . . . . (414) 771-3040

Milwaukee County Economic Development [MCED]
Tel: (414) 278-4211

Director **Jim Tarantino** . . . . . (414) 278-4211

★ Elected Official ▲ Appointed by Legislature ▼ Appointed by Governor ► Appointed by Board or Commission ● Appointed by Judge
■ Appointed by Mayor △ Appointed by Freeholders ▽ Appointed by Supervisor ▷ Appointed by County Executive ○ Appointed by Council

Milwaukee Public Museum

800 West Wells Street, Milwaukee, WI 53233
Tel: (414) 278-2700 Fax: (414) 278-6100 Internet: www.mpm.edu

President and Chief Executive Officer **Dennis Kois** ...... (414) 278-2746

Office of the Board of Supervisors

Milwaukee County Courthouse, 901 North Ninth Street, Milwaukee, WI 53233
Tel: (414) 278-4222 Fax: (414) 223-1380 E-mail: cboard@milwcnty.com
Internet: http://county.milwaukee.gov/countyboard

★ Chairwoman **Marina Dimitrijevic** (District 4) .... (414) 278-4232
Term Expires: April 16, 2020
E-mail: marina.dimitrijevic@milwcnty.com
Education: Marquette 2003 BS
Chief of Staff **Kelly Bablitch** .... (414) 278-4169
E-mail: kelly.bablitch@milwcnty.com

★ Supervisor **Theodore A. "Theo" Lipscomb, Sr.** (District 1) ..... (414) 278-4280
Term Expires: April 2020
E-mail: theodore.lipscomb@milwcnty.com
Education: Wisconsin (Milwaukee) 1998 BS

★ Supervisor **Sequanna Taylor** (District 2) .... (414) 278-4278
Term Expires: April 2020
E-mail: sequanna.taylor@milwcnty.com

★ Supervisor **Sheldon A. Wasserman** (District 3) .... (414) 278-4237
Term Expires: April 2020
E-mail: sheldon.wasserman@milwcnty.com
Education: Wisconsin (Milwaukee) 1983 BS; Medical Col (WI) 1987 MD

★ Supervisor **Marcelia Nicholson** (District 5) .... (414) 278-4222
Term Expires: April 2020

★ Supervisor **James "Luigi" Schmitt** (District 6) .... (414) 278-4273
Term Expires: April 2020
E-mail: james.schmitt@milwcnty.com
Education: Wisconsin MA

★ Supervisor **Michael Mayo, Sr.** (District 7) .... (414) 278-4241
Term Expires: April 2020
E-mail: michael.mayo@milwcnty.com
Education: Wisconsin (Milwaukee) 1981 BA

★ Supervisor **David L. Sartori** (District 8) .... (414) 278-4231
Term Expires: April 2020

★ Supervisor **Steve F. Taylor** (District 9) .... (414) 278-4267
Term Expires: April 2020
E-mail: steve.taylor@milwcnty.com

★ Supervisor **Supreme Moore Omokunde** (District 10) ... (414) 278-4265
Term Expires: April 2020

★ Supervisor **Daniel Paul "Dan" Sebring** (District 11) .... (414) 278-4253
Term Expires: April 2020

★ Supervisor **Peggy A. Romo West** (District 12) .... (414) 278-5344
Term Expires: April 2020
E-mail: peggy.west@milwcnty.com

★ Supervisor **Willie Johnson, Jr.** (District 13) .... (414) 278-4233
Term Expires: April 2020
E-mail: willie.johnson@milwcnty.com
Date of Birth: March 22, 1951
Education: Northwestern BA

★ Supervisor **Jason Haas** (District 14) .... (414) 278-4252
Term Expires: April 2020
E-mail: jason.haas@milwcnty.com
Date of Birth: July 15, 1975
Education: Wisconsin (Milwaukee) 2009

★ Supervisor **Edward "Eddie" Cullen** (District 15) .... (414) 278-4263
Term Expires: April 2020

★ Supervisor **John F. Weishan, Jr.** (District 16) .... (414) 278-4255
Term Expires: April 2020
E-mail: john.weishan@milwcnty.com
Education: Wisconsin (Milwaukee) 2002 BBA

★ Supervisor **Anthony "Tony" Staskunas** (District 17) .... (414) 278-4247
Term Expires: April 2020
E-mail: anthony.staskunas@milwcnty.com
Education: Wisconsin (Milwaukee) 1983 BA; Wisconsin 1986 JD

Office of the Board of Supervisors *continued*

★ Supervisor **Deanna Alexander** (District 18) .... (414) 278-4259
Term Expires: April 2020

Comptroller's Office - Audit Services

633 West Wisconsin Avenue, Suite 904, Milwaukee, WI 53203
Fax: (414) 223-1895

▽ Director **Jerome J. Heer** .... (414) 278-4206
E-mail: jerome.heer@milwaukeecountywi.gov
Audit Compliance Manager **Paul A. Grant** .... (414) 278-4292

Office of the County Clerk

County Courthouse, 901 North Ninth Street, Room 105, Milwaukee, WI 53233
Tel: (414) 278-4067 Fax: (414) 278-4075
Internet: http://county.milwaukee.gov/countyclerk

★ County Clerk **Joseph J. Czarnezki** .... (414) 278-4067
Term Expires: January 1, 2017
E-mail: joseph.czarnezki@milwaukeecountywi.gov
Education: Wisconsin (Milwaukee) 1975 BA, 1977 MA
Deputy County Clerk **George Christenson** .... (414) 278-4625

Office of the County Comptroller

901 North Ninth Street, Room 301, Milwaukee, WI 53233
Tel: (414) 278-3001

★ Comptroller **Scott Manske** .... (414) 278-3001
Term Expires: April 2020

Office of the District Attorney

821 West State Street, Room 405, Milwaukee, WI 53233-1485
Tel: (414) 278-4646 Fax: (414) 223-1955

★ District Attorney **John T. Chisholm** .... (414) 278-4646
Term Expires: January 4, 2017
E-mail: milwaukee.da@da.wi.gov
Chief Deputy District Attorney **Kent Lovern** .... (414) 278-4646
E-mail: kent.lovern@da.wi.gov
Deputy District Attorney **Jeffrey Altenburg** .... (414) 278-4646
E-mail: jeffrey.altenburg@da.wi.gov
Deputy District Attorney **Lovell Johnson** .... (414) 278-4646
E-mail: lovell.johnson@da.wi.gov
Deputy District Attorney **Patrick J. Kenney** .... (414) 278-4646
E-mail: pat.kenney@da.wi.gov
Deputy District Attorney **James J. Martin** .... (414) 278-4646
E-mail: jim.martin@da.wi.gov

Office of the Register of Deeds

County Courthouse, 901 North Ninth Street, Room 103, Milwaukee, WI 53233
Fax: (414) 223-1257

★ Register of Deeds **John La Fave** .... (414) 278-4011
Term Expires: December 31, 2016
Education: Wisconsin BS
Deputy Register of Deeds **Larry Eckert** .... (414) 278-4009

Office of the Sheriff

821 West State Street, Room 107, Milwaukee, WI 53233-1488
Tel: (414) 278-4766 Fax: (414) 223-1386 Internet: www.mkesheriff.org

★ Sheriff **David A. Clarke, Jr.** .... (414) 278-4766
Term Expires: December 31, 2018
Education: Concordia U (WI) BA
Inspector/Senior Commander **Richard R. Schmidt** .... (414) 278-4766
Fax: (414) 223-1386

(continued on next page)

★ Elected Official ▲ Appointed by Legislature ▼ Appointed by Governor ▶ Appointed by Board or Commission ● Appointed by Judge
■ Appointed by Mayor △ Appointed by Freeholders ▽ Appointed by Supervisor ▷ Appointed by County Executive ○ Appointed by Council

Office of the Sheriff *continued*

Inspector/Adjutant to Sheriff **Edward H. Bailey** . . . . (414) 278-4766
Fax: (414) 223-1386

Office of the Treasurer

County Courthouse, 901 North Ninth Street, Room 102, Milwaukee, WI 53233-1462
Tel: (414) 278-4033 Fax: (414) 223-1383
Internet: www.county.milwaukee.gov
Internet: http://county.milwaukee.gov/CountyTreasurer

★ Treasurer **David A. Cullen** . . . . (414) 278-4033
Term Expires: December 31, 2016
Education: Wisconsin 1981 BS; Marquette 1984 JD

COUNTIES

County of Minnehaha, South Dakota

415 N. Dakota Ave., Sioux Falls, SD 57104-2465
Tel: (605) 367-4206 (Information) Fax: (605) 367-8314
Internet: www.minnehahacounty.org

County Seat: Sioux Falls **Election Type:** Nonpartisan
Population: 185,197 (2015)

Office of the County Commissioners

415 N. Dakota Ave., Sioux Falls, SD 57104-2465
Fax: (605) 367-8314 Internet: www.minnehahacounty.org/dept/co/co.aspx

★ Chair **Cindy Heiberger** . . . . (605) 367-4206
Term Expires: December 31, 2018
E-mail: cheiberger@minnehahacounty.org

★ Vice President **Gerald Beninga** . . . . (605) 367-4206
Term Expires: December 31, 2018
E-mail: gbeninga@minnehahacounty.org

★ Commissioner **Jeff Barth** . . . . (605) 367-4206
Term Expires: December 31, 2018
E-mail: jbarth@minnehahacounty.org

★ Commissioner **Jean Bender** . . . . (605) 367-4206
Term Expires: December 31, 2016

★ Commissioner **Dick Kelly** . . . . (605) 367-4206
Term Expires: December 31, 2016
E-mail: dkelly@minnehahacounty.org
Education: St Thomas U 1965 BA

▶ Commission Administrative Officer **Carol Muller** . . . . (605) 367-4206
E-mail: cmuller@minnehahacounty.org

Assistant Commission Administrative Officer
Robert Wilson . . . . (605) 367-4206
E-mail: rwilson@minnehahacounty.org

Commission Assistant **Marie Fox** . . . . (605) 367-4206

4H Extension Office

220 W. Sixth St., Sioux Falls, SD 57104
Fax: (605) 367-4609

4H Officer **Chuck Martinell** . . . . (605) 367-7877

Office of the Coroner

304 West 18th Street, Sioux Falls, SD 57717
Fax: (605) 333-1966 E-mail: fronsix@aol.com

▶ Coroner **Dr. Kenneth S. Snell** . . . . (605) 333-1730
E-mail: ksnell@lcmpath.com

Office of Emergency Management [OEM]

608 Sigler Ave., Sioux Falls, SD 57104-2040
Fax: (605) 367-4345 Internet: www.minnehahacounty.org/dept/em/em.aspx

▶ Director **Lynn DeYoung** . . . . (605) 367-4290
E-mail: ldeyoung@minnehahacounty.org

Office of the Public Advocate

415 N. Dakota Ave., Sioux Falls, SD 57104
Fax: (605) 367-7415 Internet: www.minnehahacounty.org/dept/pa/pa.php

▶ Public Advocate **Julie Hofer** . . . . (605) 367-7392
E-mail: jhofer@minnehahacounty.org

Public Defender's Office

413 North Main Avenue, Sioux Falls, SD 57104
Fax: (605) 367-6102 Internet: www.minnehahacounty.org/dept/pd/pd.aspx

▶ Public Defender **Traci Smith** . . . . (605) 367-4242

Veterans' Service Office

521 North Main Avenue, Sioux Falls, SD 57104
Fax: (605) 367-4235

▶ Veterans Service Officer **Patricia Kroupa** . . . . (605) 367-4201
E-mail: pkroupa@minnehahacounty.org

Board of Equalization

415 N. Dakota Ave., Sioux Falls, SD 57104-2465
Fax: (605) 367-7870

▶ Director **Kyle Helseth** . . . . (605) 367-4228
E-mail: khelseth@minnehahacounty.org

Facilities and Construction Department

500 N. Minnesota Ave., Sioux Falls, SD 57104
Fax: (605) 367-7425

▶ Director **Lloyd Olson** . . . . (605) 367-4241
E-mail: lolson@minnehahacounty.org

Highway Department

2124 E. 60th St. North, Sioux Falls, SD 57101
Fax: (605) 367-7255

▶ Superintendent **D.J. Buthe** . . . . (605) 367-4316

Human Resources Department

415 N. Dakota Ave., Sioux Falls, SD 57104-2465
Fax: (605) 367-4488 Internet: www.minnehahacounty.org/dept/hr/hr.aspx

▶ Director **CareyJo Deaver** . . . . (605) 367-4337
E-mail: cdeaver@minnehahacounty.org

Human Services Department

521 North Main Ave., Sioux Falls, SD 57104-6815
Fax: (605) 367-4235

▶ Director **Kari Bentz** . . . . (605) 367-4217

Information Technology Department

500 N. Minnesota Ave., Sioux Falls, SD 57104
Fax: (605) 367-8319

▶ Director **Monte Watembach** . . . . (605) 367-4320
E-mail: mwatembach@minnehahacounty.org

Planning and Zoning Department

415 N. Dakota Ave., Sioux Falls, SD 57104-2465
Fax: (605) 367-7413 Internet: www.minnehahacounty.org/dept/pl/pl.aspx

▶ Director **Scott Anderson** . . . . (605) 367-4204
E-mail: sanderson@minnehahacounty.org

★ Elected Official ▲ Appointed by Legislature ▼ Appointed by Governor ▶ Appointed by Board or Commission ● Appointed by Judge
■ Appointed by Mayor △ Appointed by Freeholders ▽ Appointed by Supervisor ▷ Appointed by County Executive ○ Appointed by Council

Metro Communications Agency
500 North Minnesota Avenue, Sioux Falls, SD 57104-2435
Fax: (605) 367-8319 E-mail: 911admin@911metro.org
Internet: www.911metro.org

▶ Director **Daren Ketcham** .... (605) 367-7218
Business Manager **Ona Reker** .... (605) 367-7218

Minnehaha County Regional Juvenile Detention Center
4200 S. West Ave., Sioux Falls, SD 57105
Fax: (605) 367-8386 Internet: www.minnehahacounty.org/dept/jdc/jdc.aspx

▶ Director **Jamie Gravett** .... (605) 367-4313

Siouxland Heritage Museums
200 W. 6th St., Sioux Falls, SD 57104
Fax: (605) 367-6004 E-mail: museum@minnehahacounty.org
Internet: www.minnehahacounty.org/museums

▶ Director **William J. "Bill" Hoskins** .... (605) 367-4210
E-mail: bhoskins@minnehahacounty.org

Office of the Auditor
415 North Dakota Avenue, Sioux Falls, SD 57104-2465
Fax: (605) 367-7409 Internet: www.minnehahacounty.org/dept/au/au.aspx

★ Auditor **Robert "Bob" Litz** .... (605) 367-4220
Term Expires: March 1, 2019
E-mail: blitz@minnehahacounty.org
Education: Augustana (SD) 1986 BA

Office of the Register of Deeds
415 N. Dakota Ave., Sioux Falls, SD 57104-2465
Fax: (605) 367-4832

★ Register of Deeds **Julie Risty** .... (605) 367-4223
Term Expires: December 31, 2018
E-mail: jristy@minnehahacounty.org

Office of the Sheriff
320 West 4th Street, Sioux Falls, SD 57104-2435
Fax: (605) 367-7319

★ Sheriff **Mike Milstead** .... (605) 367-4300
Term Expires: December 31, 2018
E-mail: mmilstead@minnehahacounty.org

Office of the State's Attorney
415 N. Dakota Ave., Sioux Falls, SD 57104-2465
Fax: (605) 367-4306

★ State's Attorney **Aaron McGowan** .... (605) 367-4226
Term Expires: December 31, 2016

Office of the Treasurer
415 N. Dakota Ave., Sioux Falls, SD 57104-2465
Fax: (605) 367-6091

★ Treasurer **Pam Nelson** .... (605) 367-4211
Term Expires: December 31, 2016
E-mail: pnelson@minnehahacounty.org

County of Mobile, Alabama
205 Government Street, Mobile, AL 36644-1001
Tel: (251) 574-4636 (Information) Internet: www.mobilecounty.org

County Seat: Mobile **Election Type:** Partisan **Population:** 415,395 (2015)

Office of the County Commission
205 Government Street, Mobile, AL 36644-1001
Tel: (251) 574-5077 Fax: (251) 574-4770

★ President **Jerry Carl** (R-District 3) .... (251) 574-3000
Term Expires: November 30, 2016
E-mail: jcarl@mobile-county.net
★ Commissioner **Connie Hudson** (R-District 2) .... (251) 574-2000
Term Expires: November 30, 2016
E-mail: chudson@mobile-county.net
★ Commissioner **Merceria L. Ludgood** (D-District 1) .... (251) 574-1000
Term Expires: November 30, 2016
E-mail: mludgood@mobile-county.net

Office of the County Administrator
P.O. Box 1443, Mobile, AL 33633-1443
Tel: (251) 574-5073 Fax: (251) 574-5080

▶ County Administrator **John F. Pafenbach** .... (251) 574-8606
E-mail: jpafenbach@mobile-county.net
▶ Deputy Administrator **Glenn L. Hodge** .... (251) 574-8605
E-mail: ghodge@mobile-county.net
Finance Director **Michelle Herman** .... (251) 574-8614
Director of General Services **Donna Jones** .... (251) 574-8719
E-mail: djones@mobile-county.net
Director of Public Affairs and Community Services
Nancy Johnson .... (251) 574-5088
E-mail: njohnson@mobile-county.net Fax: (251) 574-5070

Office of the General Administrator
215 South Cedar Street, Mobile, AL 36602
Fax: (251) 438-7073

General Administrator **Frank H. Kruse** .... (251) 574-8058
E-mail: frankkruse@att.net

Office of the Medical Examiner
P.O. Box 7925, Mobile, AL 36670

▶ Medical Examiner **Dr. Staci Turner** .... (251) 470-9912

Office of the Tobacco Tax Collector
1150 Government Street, Room 112, Mobile, AL 36604

▶ Tobacco Tax Collector **Kay Hart** .... (251) 574-8580

Building Maintenance
554 S. Royal St., Mobile, AL 36602
P.O. Box 1443, Mobile, AL 36633-1801
Fax: (251) 574-6440

Chief Building Engineer **George Oaks** .... (251) 574-4444
Building Inspector **Peter Olivero** .... (251) 574-3507
1150 Schillinger Rd. North, Mobile, AL 36608 Fax: (251) 574-3509

Cooperative Extension Service
1070 N. Schillinger Rd., Mobile, AL 36608
Fax: (251) 574-3245

County Agent Coordinator **Amelia Mitchell** .... (251) 574-8445

★ Elected Official ▲ Appointed by Legislature ▼ Appointed by Governor ▶ Appointed by Board or Commission ● Appointed by Judge
■ Appointed by Mayor △ Appointed by Freeholders ▽ Appointed by Supervisor ▷ Appointed by County Executive ○ Appointed by Council

Emergency Management Agency/Civil Defense
348 N. McGregor Avenue, Mobile, AL 36608-1949
Fax: (251) 460-8035

Director **Ron Adair** . . . . . (251) 460-8000

Parks and Wildlife
Internet: www.mobilecountyal.gov/living/parks.html

Chickasabogue Park Manager **Tom Hudson** . . . . . (251) 574-2267
760 Aldock Rd., Mobile, AL 36613 Fax: (251) 574-0542
West Mobile County Park Manager **Terri Frazier** . . . . . (251) 574-7275
2275 Leroy Stephens Rd., Mobile, AL 36695 Fax: (251) 574-3214

Personnel Board
P.O. Box 66794, Mobile, AL 36660-1794
Fax: (251) 470-1708

Director **Donald Dees** . . . . . (251) 470-7727

Public Law Library
205 Government Street, Room 308, Mobile, AL 36644-2308
Fax: (251) 574-4757

Librarian **Patricia B. Evans** . . . . . (251) 574-8436

Public Works and County Engineering
205 Government St., Mobile, AL 36644-1601
Fax: (251) 574-4722 Internet: www.mobilecountypublicworks.net

► County Engineer **Joe W. Ruffer** . . . . . (251) 574-8595
E-mail: jruffer@mobilecounty.net
Environmental Services Manager **G. "Bill" Melton** . . . . . (251) 574-3229
Traffic Engineering Manager **James Foster** . . . . . (251) 574-8595

Road and Bridge
1150 North Schillinger Road, Mobile, AL 36608
Fax: (251) 574-3513

Superintendent **Ted Lawson** . . . . . (251) 574-4030

Mobile County Board of Health
251 North Bayou Street, Mobile, AL 36603

Mobile County Health Department [MCHD]
251 North Bayou Street, Mobile, AL 36603
Tel: (251) 690-8158 Fax: (251) 432-7443 Internet: www.mchd.org

County Health Officer **Dr. Bernard H. Eichold III** . . . . . (251) 690-8158
Assistant Health Officer **Joel Tate** . . . . . (251) 690-8158

Mobile County Board of Registrars
151 Goverment Street, Suite 165, Mobile, AL 36602
Tel: (251) 574-8586

▼ Chair **Pat Tyrrell** . . . . . (251) 574-8586
Board Member **Virginia Delchamps** . . . . . (251) 574-8586
Board Member **Shirley Short** . . . . . (251) 574-8586

Office of the District Attorney
205 Government St., Mobile, AL 36644-2501
Fax: (251) 574-4848

★ District Attorney **Ashley Rich** (R) . . . . . (251) 574-8400
Term Expires: January 31, 2019

Office of the License Commission
P.O. Drawer 1867, Mobile, AL 36633
Fax: (251) 574-4819

★ License Commissioner **Nick Matranga** . . . . . (251) 574-8566
Term Expires: January 15, 2017

Office of the Revenue Commission
P.O. Box 1169, Mobile, AL 36633-1169
Fax: (251) 574-4788 Internet: http://www.mobilecopropertytax.com

★ Revenue Commissioner **Kim Hastie** . . . . . (251) 574-8545
Term Expires: September 30, 2017

Office of the Sheriff
P.O. Box 113, Mobile, AL 36601
Tel: (251) 574-8633

★ Sheriff **Samuel M. Cochran** . . . . . (251) 574-7827
Term Expires: December 31, 2018

Office of the Treasurer
P.O. Box 296, Mobile, AL 36601-0296
Tel: (251) 574-8606 Fax: (251) 574-5990

★ Treasurer **Phil Benson** (R) . . . . . (251) 574-8585
Term Expires: December 31, 2016

Mobile County Public School System [MCPSS]
One Magnum Pass, Mobile, AL 36618
Tel: (251) 221-4000 Internet: www.mcpss.com

Mobile County Public School Board
P.O. Box 1327, Mobile, AL 36633-1327
1 Magnum Pass, Mobile, AL 36618

★ President **Don Stringfellow** (District 2) . . . . . (251) 221-4387
Term Expires: November 2018
E-mail: jstout@mcpss.com
★ Vice President **Reginald A. Crenshaw** (District 3) . . . . . (251) 221-4387
Term Expires: November 2020
E-mail: rcrenshaw@mcpss.com
★ Commissioner **Doug Harwell** (District 1) . . . . . (251) 221-4387
Term Expires: November 2018
E-mail: kmegginson@mcpss.com
★ Commissioner
Robert Edward Battles, Sr. (D-District 4) . . . . . (251) 221-4387
Term Expires: November 2020
★ Commissioner **William Foster** (R-District 5) . . . . . (251) 221-4387
Term Expires: November 2016
E-mail: wmeredith@mcpss.com

Office of the Superintendent
One Magnum Pass, Mobile, AL 36618
Fax: (251) 221-4399

Superintendent **Martha L. Peek** . . . . . (251) 221-4394

★ Elected Official ▲ Appointed by Legislature ▼ Appointed by Governor ► Appointed by Board or Commission ● Appointed by Judge
■ Appointed by Mayor △ Appointed by Freeholders ▽ Appointed by Supervisor ▷ Appointed by County Executive ○ Appointed by Council

County of Monmouth, New Jersey

Hall of Records, One East Main Street, Freehold, NJ 07728
P.O. Box 1255, Freehold, NJ 07728-1255
Tel: (732) 431-7310 (Information) E-mail: contact@co.monmouth.nj.us
Internet: www.visitmonmouth.com

County Seat: Freehold **Election Type:** Partisan **Population:** 628,715 (2015)

Office of the Board of Chosen Freeholders

Hall of Records, One East Main Street, Freehold, NJ 07728
P.O. Box 1255, Freehold, NJ 07728-1255
Tel: (732) 431-7387 (Information) Fax: (732) 431-6519

★ Director **Thomas A. Arnone** (R) . . . . . (732) 431-7158
Term Expires: December 31, 2016
E-mail: tarnone@co.monmouth.nj.us

★ Deputy Director **Serena DiMaso** (R) . . . . . (732) 431-7411
Term Expires: December 31, 2016
E-mail: frida.mclaughlin@co.monmouth.nj.us

★ Freeholder **Lillian G. Burry** (R) . . . . . (732) 683-8855
Term Expires: December 31, 2017
E-mail: pam.chappell@co.monmouth.nj.us
Education: Wagner BA

★ Freeholder **John P. Curley** (R) . . . . . (732) 683-8838
Term Expires: December 31, 2018
E-mail: jcurley@co.monmouth.nj.us

★ Freeholder **Gary J. Rich** (R) . . . . . (732) 683-8559
Term Expires: December 31, 2017
E-mail: jennifer.gagnon@co.monmouth.nj.us

△ Clerk of the Board **Marion Masnick** . . . . . (732) 431-7387
E-mail: mmasnick@co.monmouth.nj.us

Office of the County Administrator

Hall of Records, One East Main Street, Freehold, NJ 07728
Fax: (732) 409-4820

△ County Administrator **Teri O'Connor** . . . . . (732) 431-7384
E-mail: toconnor@co.monmouth.nj.us

Office of the County Counsel

Hall of Records, One East Main Street, Freehold, NJ 07728
Fax: (732) 776-6901

△ County Counsel **Andrea I. Bazer** . . . . . (732) 683-8640
E-mail: abazer@co.monmouth.nj.us

Office of the County Treasurer

P.O. Box 1256, Freehold, NJ 07728-1256

△ Treasurer **Craig R. Marshall** . . . . . (732) 431-7391

Office of Cooperative Extension (Rutgers University)

4000 Kozloski Road, Freehold, NJ 07728
P.O. Box 5033, Freehold, NJ 07728
Tel: (732) 431-7260 Fax: (732) 409-4813

County Agricultural Agent **William Sciarappa** . . . . . (732) 431-7260
Family Consumer Health Sciences Associate
Rachel Tansey . . . . . (732) 431-7271

Office of Emergency Management [OEM]

300 Halls Mills Road, Freehold, NJ 07728
Tel: (732) 431-7911 (24 Hours) Fax: (732) 409-7532

△ Coordinator **Michael "Mike" Oppegaard** . . . . . (732) 431-7400
E-mail: moppegaa@co.monmouth.nj.us

Office of Emergency Management *continued*

Deputy Coordinator **Gary McTighe** . . . . . (732) 431-7400
E-mail: gmctighe@co.monmouth.nj.us

Deputy Coordinator **Robert Swannack** . . . . . (732) 431-7400

Office of the Fire Marshal

Fire Training Academy, 1027 Highway 33 East, Freehold, NJ 07728
Tel: (732) 683-8856 Fax: (732) 683-8864

△ County Fire Marshal **Henry A. "Hank" Stryker III** . . . . . (732) 683-8856
E-mail: hstryker@co.monmouth.nj.us

First Deputy Fire Marshal **Anthony Vecchio** . . . . . (732) 683-8856
E-mail: avecchio@co.monmouth.nj.us

Training Officer **Armand F. Guzzi, Jr.** . . . . . (732) 683-8856

Office of the Medical Examiner

CentraState Medical Center, W. Main St., Suite 267, Freehold, NJ 07728

Medical Examiner (Acting) **Dr. Diane Karluk** . . . . . (732) 577-8790

Department of Consumer Affairs

Hall of Records Annex, Freehold, NJ 07728

△ Director **Annmarie Howley** . . . . . (732) 431-7900
E-mail: annmarie.howley@co.monmouth.nj.us

Department of Economic Development

31 East Main Street, Freehold, NJ 07728
Fax: (732) 294-5930

△ Director **John Ciufo** . . . . . (732) 431-7470
E-mail: jciufo@co.monmouth.nj.us

Department of Finance

300 Halls Mill Road, Freehold, NJ 07728
Fax: (732) 409-4824

△ Director **Craig R. Marshall** . . . . . (732) 431-7391

Department of Human Resources

Hall of Records, One East Main Street, Freehold, NJ 07728
Fax: (732) 431-7924

Director **Frank J. Tragno, Jr.** . . . . . (732) 431-7300
E-mail: ftragno@co.monmouth.nj.us

Assistant Personnel Officer **(Vacant)** . . . . . (732) 431-7300

Benefits and Workers Compensation Manager
William H. McGuane . . . . . (732) 866-3622
E-mail: wmcguane@co.monmouth.nj.us

Management Assistant **Deana M. Valiante** . . . . . (732) 431-7300
E-mail: deana.valiant@co.monmouth.nj.us

Department of Human Services [MCDHS]

3000 Kozloski Road, Freehold, NJ 07728
P.O. Box 3000, Freehold, NJ 07728
Fax: (732) 431-7412 E-mail: mcdhs@co.monmouth.nj.us

Director (Acting) **Jeffrey R. Schwartz** . . . . . (732) 308-3770 ext. 1

Office of the County Adjuster

P.O. Box 3000, Freehold, NJ 07728
Fax: (732) 863-9154

Adjuster **William Bucco** . . . . . (732) 431-6302
E-mail: wbucco@co.monmouth.nj.us

Division of Aging, Disabilities and Veterans' Services

3000 Kozloski Road, Freehold, NJ 07728
Fax: (732) 303-7649

Director **Susan "Sue" Moleon** . . . . . (732) 431-7453

Division of Mental Health and Addiction Services

3000 Kozloski Road, Freehold, NJ 07728
Fax: (732) 866-3595

Director **Barry W. Johnson** . . . . . (732) 431-6451

★ Elected Official ▲ Appointed by Legislature ▼ Appointed by Governor ► Appointed by Board or Commission ● Appointed by Judge
■ Appointed by Mayor △ Appointed by Freeholders ▽ Appointed by Supervisor ▷ Appointed by County Executive ○ Appointed by Council

COUNTIES

Division of Planning and Contracting
3000 Kozloski Road, Freehold, NJ 07728
Fax: (732) 845-2054

Director **Jeffrey R. Schwartz** .... (732) 431-6585

Division of Social Services
3000 Kozloski Road, Freehold, NJ 07728
Fax: (732) 431-6266

Director **Kathleen M. Weir** .... (732) 431-6000

Division of Transportation [DOT]
250 Center Street, Freehold, NJ 07728
Fax: (732) 409-7592

△ Director **Kathleen Lodato** .... (732) 431-6485
E-mail: klodato@co.monmouth.nj.us

Workforce Investment Board [WIB]
145 Wyckoff Road, Suite 201, Eatontown, NJ 07724
Fax: (732) 544-5458

Chairman **Frances Kane** .... (732) 683-8850
Vice-Chairman **Wyatt Earp** .... (732) 683-8850
Executive Director **Eileen M. Higgins** .... (732) 683-8850

Department of Information Technology Services
Human Services Bldg., 3000 Kozloski Road, Freehold, NJ 07728
Fax: (732) 431-7847

△ Director **Gregory Putnam** .... (732) 431-7991
E-mail: gputnam@co.monmouth.nj.us

Probation Department
30 Mechanic St., P.O. Box 1259, Freehold, NJ 07728-1259

Chief Probation Officer **Cee Okuzu** .... (732) 677-4803

Department of Public Information and Tourism
Hall of Records Annex, One East Main Street, Freehold, NJ 07728
Tel: (732) 431-7310 Fax: (732) 866-3696

△ Director **Laura Kirkpatrick** .... (732) 431-7308
Public Information Officer **Laura Kirkpatrick** .... (732) 683-8843
E-mail: lkirkpat@co.monmouth.nj.us
Director of Tourism **Jeanne DeYoung** .... (732) 431-7308
E-mail: jeanne.deyoung@visitmonmouth.com

Department of Public Works and Engineering
250 Center Street, Freehold, NJ 07728
Fax: (732) 462-1863

△ Director **John W. Tobia** .... (732) 683-8757
E-mail: jwtobia@co.monmouth.nj.us
Assistant Director **James Cerreta** .... (732) 683-8758
Administrative Secretary **Susan Brodsky** .... (732) 683-8758
E-mail: sbrodsky@co.monmouth.nj.us
Executive Assistant **Victor Terwilliger III** .... (732) 431-6557

Division of Bridges
250 Center St., Freehold, NJ 07728
Fax: (732) 462-1863

△ Superintendent (Acting) **James Cerreta** .... (732) 577-5883

Division of Buildings and Grounds
250 Center St., Freehold, NJ 07728
Fax: (732) 409-7592

△ Superintendent **Robert W. Compton** .... (732) 431-7360
E-mail: rcompton@co.monmouth.nj.us
Management Assistant **David Krzyzanowski** .... (732) 431-7360
E-mail: dave.krzyzanowski@co.monmouth.nj.us

Division of Engineering
Hall of Records Annex, One E. Main St., Freehold, NJ 07728
Fax: (732) 431-7765

△ County Engineer **Joseph M. Ettore** .... (732) 431-7760
E-mail: jettore@co.monmouth.nj.us
Administrative Secretary **Rosanne Miller** .... (732) 431-7760
E-mail: rmiller@co.monmouth.nj.us
Assistant County Engineer **Ming Kao** .... (732) 431-7760

Division of Fleet Services
250 Center St., Freehold, NJ 07728
Fax: (732) 845-2059

Director (Acting) **Paul Grosselfinger** .... (732) 431-7830

Division of Highways
250 Center St., Freehold, NJ 07728
Fax: (732) 431-7833

△ Superintendent of Administration (Acting)
Joseph Santora .... (732) 431-6550
E-mail: jsantora@co.monmouth.nj.us
Superintendent of Operations (Acting) **Gary Fread** .... (732) 431-6550
Assistant Superintendent **(Vacant)** .... (732) 431-6550

Shade Tree Division
250 Center Street, Freehold, NJ 07728
Fax: (732) 866-3558

△ Superintendent (Acting) **Joseph Santora** .... (732) 431-7903
E-mail: jsantora@co.monmouth.nj.us
Chairman **Thomas Ritchie** .... (732) 431-7903

Reclamation Division
6000 Asbury Avenue, Tinton Falls, NJ 07753
Fax: (732) 922-6782

Superintendent **Richard Throckmorton** .... (732) 683-8686 ext. 5104
Fax: (732) 922-6782

Department of Purchasing
300 Halls Mill Road, Freehold, NJ 07728
P.O. Box 1262, Freehold, NJ 07728
Fax: (732) 431-7379

△ Director **Gerri C. Popkin** .... (732) 431-7370
Assistant Purchasing Agent **(Vacant)** .... (732) 431-7370

Department of Weights and Measures
1911 Wayside Road, Tinton Falls, NJ 07724

△ Superintendent **Benjamin S. Peluso** .... (732) 431-7362
E-mail: bpeluso@co.monmouth.nj.us
Administrative Clerk Typist **Melanie Belitsky** .... (732) 431-7362

Monmouth County Board of Agriculture [MCBOA]
4000 Kozloski Road, Freehold, NJ 07728-5033

President **Gary DeFelice** .... (732) 431-7260

Monmouth County Board of Health
3435 Route 9 North, Freehold, NJ 07728
Fax: (732) 409-7579

President **Judy Thorpe** .... (732) 431-7456
Term Expires: April 8, 2017
Director **Christopher Merkel** .... (732) 431-7456

Monmouth County Board of Taxation
Hall of Records, P.O. Box 1255, Freehold, NJ 07728
Fax: (732) 409-4890

President **James Stuart** .... (732) 431-7404
Vice President **Thomas J. Byrne** .... (732) 431-7404
Commissioner **Kathleen M. Cody Bjelka** .... (732) 431-7404
Education: North Carolina BA; U San Francisco MBA
Commissioner **Thomas B. "Tom" Considine** .... (732) 431-7404
▼ Commissioner **Clifford Moore** .... (732) 431-7404

★ Elected Official ▲ Appointed by Legislature ▼ Appointed by Governor ▶ Appointed by Board or Commission ● Appointed by Judge
■ Appointed by Mayor △ Appointed by Freeholders ▽ Appointed by Supervisor ▷ Appointed by County Executive ○ Appointed by Council

Monmouth County Board of Taxation *continued*

Commissioner **Wayne C. Pomanowski** . . . . (732) 431-7404
County Tax Administrator **Matthew S. Clark** . . . . (732) 431-7404
E-mail: mclark@co.monmouth.nj.us
Assistant County Tax Administrator **Veronica Shenk** . . . . (732) 431-7404

Monmouth County Historical Commission

Chairperson **Brooks Von Arx** Hall of Records Annex . . . . (732) 431-7413
Executive Director **Randall Gabrielan** Hall of Records Annex . . . . (732) 431-7413

Monmouth County Human Relations Commission [MCHRC]

Monmouth County Human Services Bldg., 3000 Kozloski Rd., Freehold, NJ 07728
E-mail: mchrc@co.monmouth.nj.us
Internet: www.monmouthcountyhrc.org

Chair **Dr. John P. Delaney** . . . . (732) 303-7666
Vice Chair **Sherri West** . . . . (732) 303-7666

Monmouth County Improvement Authority

Hall of Records, P.O. Box 1255, Freehold, NJ 07728
Fax: (732) 409-4821

Chairman **Al Rosenthal** . . . . (732) 308-2975
Secretary **Marion Masnick** . . . . (732) 308-2975
E-mail: mmasnick@co.monmouth.nj.us

Monmouth County Library

125 Symmes Dr., Manalapan, NJ 07726
Tel: (732) 431-7220

Director (Interim) **Judith Tolchin** . . . . (732) 431-7220

Monmouth County Park System

805 Newman Springs Rd., Lincroft, NJ 07738
Fax: (732) 842-4162 Internet: www.monmouthcountyparks.com

Chairman, Board of Recreation Commissioners **Edward J. Loud** . . . . (732) 842-4000 ext. 4215
△ Director/Board Secretary **James J. Truncer** . . . . (732) 842-4000 ext. 4215
E-mail: jjtruncer@monmouthcountyparks.com
Assistant Director (Acting) **Andrew J. Spears** . . . . (732) 842-4000 ext. 4216
Parks Superintendent **Thomas Forbes** . . . . (732) 842-4000 ext. 4220
Recreation Superintendent **Andrew J. Spears** . . (732) 842-4000 ext. 4247
Acquisition and Design Chief **Spencer H. Wickham** . . . . (732) 842-4000 ext. 4268
E-mail: swickham@monmouthcountyparks.com
Public Information Officer **Karen Livingstone** . . (732) 842-4000 ext. 4256

Monmouth County Planning Board [MCPB]

Hall of Records Annex, One East Main Street, Freehold, NJ 07728-1255
Tel: (732) 431-7460 Fax: (732) 409-7540

Chairman **Vincent Domidion** . . . . (732) 431-7460
Director of Planning **Edward Sampson** . . . . (732) 431-7460
Assistant Director of Planning **Joe Barris** . . . . (732) 431-7460
Community Development Director **Sharon Rafter** . . . . . . (732) 431-7460
E-mail: sharon.rafter@co.monmouth.nj.us

Monmouth County Police Academy

2000 Kozloski Road, Freehold, NJ 07728
Fax: (732) 577-8722

Director **David Morris** . . . . (732) 577-8710
E-mail: dmorris@co.monmouth.nj.us

Brookdale Community College

765 Newman Springs Road, Lincroft, NJ 07738-1597
Fax: (732) 224-2242 Internet: www.brookdalecc.edu

President **Dr. Maureen Murphy** . . . . (732) 224-2209

Brookdale Community College *continued*

Executive Vice President, Administration, Finance and Operations **Maureen Lawrence** . . . . (732) 224-2882
Executive Vice President, Educational Services (Interim) **Dr. Richard Fulton** . . . . (732) 224-2264
Vice President, Development, Governmental and Community Relations **(Vacant)** . . . . (732) 224-2258
Dean, Outreach, Business and Community Development **Marie Lucier-Woodruff** . . . . (732) 224-2719

Office of the County Clerk

33 Mechanic Street, Freehold, NJ 07728
Fax: (732) 409-7566

★ County Clerk **M. Claire French** (R) . . . . (732) 431-7324
Term Expires: December 31, 2017
Deputy County Clerk **Felicia Santaniello** . . . . (732) 431-7324
E-mail: fsantani@co.monmouth.nj.us
Passports and Naturalization Special Deputy County Clerk **(Vacant)** . . . . (732) 431-7353
Recording Special Deputy County Clerk **(Vacant)** . . . . (732) 431-7321
Archivist **Gary D. Saretzky** . . . . (732) 308-3772
Archives Records Manager **Mark J. Pizza** . . . . (732) 308-3773
125 Symmes Drive, Manalapan, NJ 07226

Office of the County Prosecutor

Monmouth County Court House, Freehold, NJ 07728
Fax: (732) 409-3673 Internet: http://prosecutor.co.monmouth.nj.us/

▼ County Prosecutor **Christopher J. Gramiccioni** . . . . (732) 431-7160
E-mail: cgramiccioni@co.monmouth.nj.us
Education: Towson U 1994 BS; Baltimore 1998 JD

Office of the County Sheriff

Veterans Memorial Bldg., 50 E. Main St., Freehold, NJ 07728
Fax: (732) 294-5965

★ Sheriff **Shaun Golden** (R) . . . . (732) 431-7139
Term Expires: December 31, 2016
E-mail: sgolden@co.monmouth.nj.us
Undersheriff **Ted Freeman** . . . . (732) 577-5748
E-mail: tfreeman@co.monmouth.nj.us
Law Enforcement Division Chief Sheriff's Officer **Michael Donovan** . . . . (732) 431-6160
E-mail: mdonovan@co.monmouth.nj.us Fax: (732) 294-5965

Department of Corrections

1 Waterworks Rd., Freehold, NJ 07728
PO Box 5007, Freehold, NJ 07728
Tel: (732) 431-7863 (Administration) Fax: (732) 294-5985

Warden (Acting) **Barry Nadrowski** . . . . (732) 431-7863
Business Manager **Jeffrey W. Sauter** . . . . (732) 294-5980

Office of the County Surrogate

Hall of Records, One E. Main St., Freehold, NJ 07728
P.O. Box 1265, Freehold, NJ 07728

★ Surrogate **Rosemarie D. Peters** (R) . . . . (732) 431-7330
Term Expires: December 31, 2016
E-mail: rpeters@co.monmouth.nj.us
Deputy Surrogate **Kathleen M. Reitsma** . . . . (732) 431-7330
Special Deputy Surrogate **Hazel L. Bove** . . . . . . (732) 431-7330 ext. 7346

COUNTIES

★ Elected Official ▲ Appointed by Legislature ▼ Appointed by Governor ▶ Appointed by Board or Commission ● Appointed by Judge
■ Appointed by Mayor △ Appointed by Freeholders ▽ Appointed by Supervisor ▷ Appointed by County Executive ○ Appointed by Council

Office of the Executive Superintendent of Schools
60 Neptune Boulevard, Neptune, NJ 07728-1264
Fax: (732) 776-7237

▼Executive County Superintendent **Lester Richens** . . . . (732) 431-7810
Executive County School Business Official (Interim)
Dr. Joan Saylor . . . . (732) 431-7824
General Education Specialist **Deborah Bleisnick** . . . . (732) 431-7810

Monmouth County Board of Elections
300 Halls Mill Road, Freehold, NJ 07728

Chairwoman/Commissioner **Leah Falk** . . . . (732) 431-7802
Secretary/Commissioner **Christine Giordano Hanlon** . . . . (732) 431-7802
Education: Barnard; Fordham 1992 JD
Commissioner **Jo-Ann Dinan** . . . . (732) 431-7802
Commissioner **Chantal Bouw** . . . . (732) 431-7802
Note: Reappointed on March 8, 2016 by Governor Christie, pending New Jersey Senate approval.
Commissioner-Designate **Allan C. Roth** . . . . (732) 431-7802
Note: Appointed on March 8, 2016 by Governor Christie, pending New Jersey Senate approval.

Superintendent of Elections
300 Halls Mill Road, Freehold, NJ 07728

△Superintendent of Elections and Commissioner of Registration **Hedra Siskel** . . . . (732) 431-7780 ext. 7785
E-mail: hsiskel@co.monmouth.nj.us
△Superintendent of Elections and Commissioner of Registration-Designate **Mary C. Desarno** . . . . (732) 431-7310
Deputy Commissioner **Dawn Hill** . . . . (732) 431-7780 ext. 7784
Chief Clerk **Patricia Fitzpatrick** . . . . (732) 431-7780 ext. 7782
E-mail: pfitzpat@shore.co.monmouth.nj.us
Secretary **Susan McRae** . . . . (732) 431-7780 ext. 7786
E-mail: smcrae@co.monmouth.nj.us

Monmouth County Vocational School District [MCVSD]
4000 Kozloski Road, Freehold, NJ 07728-5033
Fax: (732) 409-6736 Internet: www.mcvsd.org

President, Board of Education **Clement V. Sommers** . . . . (732) 431-7942
Superintendent **Timothy M. "Tim" McCorkell** . . . . (732) 431-7942

County of Monroe, New York
County Office Bldg., 39 West Main Street, Rochester, NY 14614
Internet: www.monroecounty.gov

County Seat: Rochester **Election Type:** Partisan **Population:** 749,600 (2015)

Office of the County Executive
County Office Building, 39 West Main Street, Room 110, Rochester, NY 14614
Tel: (585) 753-1000 Fax: (585) 753-1014
Internet: www.monroecounty.gov/executive-index.php

★County Executive **Cheryl Dinolfo** (R) . . . . (585) 753-1000
Term Expires: December 31, 2019
▷Deputy County Executive **Thomas VanStrydonck** . . . . . . (585) 753-1000
Assistant County Executive **Justin Roj** . . . . (585) 753-1000
Assistant County Executive **Michael A. Molinari** . . . . (585) 753-1000
E-mail: mmolinari@monroecounty.gov
Special Counsel **Patrick W. Pardyjack** . . . . (585) 753-1953

Cornell Cooperative Extension Monroe County (Cornell University)
2449 St. Paul Boulevard, Rochester, NY 14617
Fax: (585) 753-2560 E-mail: sam497@cornell.edu
Internet: www.cce.cornell.edu/monroe

Executive Director **Andrea Lista** . . . . (585) 753-2559

Office of the Historian
Lavery Library, St. John Fisher College, 3690 East Avenue, Rochester, NY 14618
Fax: (585) 428-8353 Internet: www.monroecounty.gov/history-index.php

▷County Historian **Carolyn Vacca** . . . . (585) 385-8244

Office of the Public Defender
Executive Office Building, 10 N. Fitzhugh Street, Rochester, NY 14614-1211
Tel: (585) 753-4210 Fax: (585) 753-4234

▲Public Defender **Timothy P. Donaher** . . . . (585) 753-4210
E-mail: tdonaher@monroecounty.gov

Board of Elections
County Office Building, 39 West Main Street, Room 106-108, Rochester, NY 14614-1490
Fax: (585) 753-1511 E-mail: mcboe@monroecounty.gov
Internet: www.monroecounty.gov/elections-index.php

▲Commissioner of Elections **Thomas F. Ferrarese** . . . . (585) 753-1560
E-mail: tferrarese@monroecounty.gov Fax: (585) 753-1531
▲Commissioner of Elections **David Van Varick** . . . . (585) 753-1500
E-mail: dvanvarick@monroecounty.gov Fax: (585) 753-1521
Education: Bowdoin AB; Boston U 1973 JD
Deputy Commissioner **Colleen D. Anderson** . . . . (585) 753-1524
E-mail: canderson@monroecounty.gov Fax: (585) 753-1531
Deputy Commissioner **Douglas E. French** . . . . (585) 753-1514
E-mail: dfrench@monroecounty.gov Fax: (585) 753-1521
Information Services Manager **Grant Hazelton** . . . . (585) 753-1505
E-mail: ghazelton@monroecounty.gov Fax: (585) 753-1531
Finance Analyst **David Reilich** . . . . (585) 753-1546
Fax: (585) 753-1521

Department of Communications
County Office Building, 39 West Main Street, Room 204, Rochester, NY 14614
Tel: (585) 753-1080 TTY: (585) 428-5491 Fax: (585) 753-1068
Internet: www.monroecounty.gov/communications-index.php

▷Director **William W. Napier** . . . . (585) 753-1080
Deputy Director **Heather Moffitt** . . . . (585) 753-1080

Department of Environmental Services [DES]
50 West Main Street, Suite 7100, Rochester, NY 14614-1228
Fax: (585) 324-1237 E-mail: mcdes@monroecounty.gov
Internet: www.monroecounty.gov/des-index.php

▷Director **Michael J. "Mike" Garland** . . . . (585) 753-7511
E-mail: mgarland@monroecounty.gov
Education: Villanova 1985 BSCE; SUNY (Buffalo) 1994 MSCE

Department of Finance
County Office Building, 39 West Main Street, Room 402, Rochester, NY 14614
Tel: (585) 753-1157 Fax: (585) 753-1133
Internet: www.monroecounty.gov/finance-index.php

▷Chief Financial Officer **Robert Franklin** . . . . (585) 753-1170
E-mail: robertfranklin@monroecounty.gov
Controller **Anthony "Tony" Feroce** . . . . (585) 753-1170
Senior Delinquent Tax Collector **Kevin Tubiolo**
Room B-2 . . . . (585) 753-1200
E-mail: ktubiolo@monroecounty.gov

★Elected Official ▲Appointed by Legislature ▼Appointed by Governor ►Appointed by Board or Commission ●Appointed by Judge
■Appointed by Mayor △Appointed by Freeholders ▽Appointed by Supervisor ▷Appointed by County Executive ○Appointed by Council

Department of Finance *continued*

Purchasing and Central Services Manager
Dawn Staub Room 200 . . . . (585) 753-1100
E-mail: dstaub@monroecounty.gov
Real Property Tax Service Director **Timothy Murphy**
Room 304 . . . . (585) 753-1125
E-mail: tmurphy@monroecounty.gov

Department of Human Services

111 Westfall Road, Room 660, Rochester, NY 14620-9985
Tel: (585) 753-6000 Fax: (585) 753-6296
E-mail: mcdss@monroecounty.gov

Commissioner **Kelly A. Reed** . . . . (585) 753-6298
Deputy Commissioner **Nancy Forgue** . . . . (585) 753-6635
Director, Child and Family Services Division
Amy Natale-McConnell . . . . (585) 753-6431
Director, Financial Assistance Division **Denise Read** . . . . . (585) 753-6519

Office for the Aging [OFA]

435 East Henrietta Road, 3rd Floor West, Faith Wing,
Rochester, NY 14620
Fax: (585) 753-6281 Internet: www.monroecounty.gov/aging-index.php

▷ Director **Julie Allen-Aldrich** . . . . (585) 753-6548

Monroe County Office of Mental Health [MCOMH]

Building J, 1099 Jay Street, Suite 305, Rochester, NY 14611
Tel: (585) 753-6047 Fax: (585) 753-6620
Internet: www.monroecounty.gov/mh-index.php

Director **David L. Putney** . . . . (585) 753-6047
Administrative Secretary **Anne Miller Jones** . . . . (585) 753-6047
E-mail: ajones@monroecounty.gov

Children's Detention Center

355 Westfall Road, Rochester, NY 14620

Director **Michael Marinan** . . . . (585) 753-5940

Rochester-Monroe County Youth Bureau

435 East Henrietta Rd., Rochester, NY 14620
Tel: (585) 753-6455

Executive Director **David Michael Barry, Jr.** . . . . (585) 753-6461
Fax: (585) 753-6465

Department of Human Resources

County Office Building, 39 West Main Street, Room 210,
Rochester, NY 14614
Tel: (585) 753-1700 Fax: (585) 753-1728
Internet: www.monroecounty.gov/hr-index.php

Director **Brayton M. Connard** . . . . (585) 753-1747
E-mail: bconnard@monroecounty.gov

Civil Service Commission

Fax: (585) 753-1728

Chairman **Jean Carrozzi** . . . . (585) 753-1747
Executive Director **Brayton M. Connard** . . . . (585) 753-1747
E-mail: bconnard@monroecounty.gov

Department of Information Services

CityPlace, 50 West Main Street, Suite 6151A, Rochester, NY 14614-1218
Fax: (585) 753-1850 E-mail: mcis@monroecounty.gov
Internet: www.monroecounty.gov/is-index.php

▷ Chief Information Officer/Director **Jennifer Kusse** . . . . . . (585) 753-1790
E-mail: jkusse@monroecounty.gov

Department of Law

County Office Building, 39 West Main Street, Room 307,
Rochester, NY 14614
Tel: (585) 753-1380 Fax: (585) 753-1331
E-mail: mclawdept@monroecounty.gov
Internet: www.monroecounty.gov/law-index.php

▷ County Attorney **Michael E. Davis** . . . . (585) 753-1380
E-mail: law@monroecounty.gov

Department of Parks

171 Reservoir Avenue, Rochester, NY 14620-2728
Tel: (585) 753-7275 (Reservations) Fax: (585) 753-7284
E-mail: mcparks@monroecounty.gov
Internet: www.monroecounty.gov/parks-index.php

▷ Director **Larry Staub** . . . . (585) 753-7275

Department of Planning and Development

50 West Main Street, Suite 8100, Rochester, NY 14614
Fax: (585) 753-2028
Internet: www2.monroecounty.gov/planning-index.php

▷ Director (Acting) **Paul Johnson** . . . . (585) 753-2000
E-mail: pjohnson@monroecounty.gov
Administrative Assistant **Delaine George** . . . . (585) 753-2006
E-mail: dgeorge@monroecounty.gov

Community Development Division

8100 City Place, 50 West Main Street, Rochester, NY 14614-1228
Fax: (585) 753-2028

▷ Manager **Jeffery L. "Jeff" McCann** (R) . . . . (585) 753-2000
E-mail: jefferymccann@monroecounty.gov

Economic Development Division

8100 City Place, 50 West Main Street, Rochester, NY 14614-1228
Fax: (585) 753-2028

▷ Manager **Chanh Quach** . . . . (585) 753-2000

Planning Division

8100 City Place, 50 West Main Street, Rochester, NY 14614-1228
Fax: (585) 753-2028 E-mail: mcplanning@monroecounty.gov
Internet: www2.monroecounty.gov/planning-planning.php

Manager **Thomas "Tom" Goodwin** . . . . (585) 753-2000
Chairperson, Monroe County Planning Board **(Vacant)** . . . (585) 753-2000

County of Monroe Industrial Development Agency [COMIDA]

CityPlace, 50 West Main Street, Suite 8100, Rochester, NY 14614
Fax: (585) 753-2002 Internet: www.growmonroe.org

▷ Executive Director (Acting) **Paul Johnson** . . . . (585) 753-2000
E-mail: pjohnson@monroecounty.gov

Monroe County Department of Public Health [MCDPH]

111 Westfall Road, Rochester, NY 14620
Tel: (585) 753-2991 Fax: (585) 753-5115
E-mail: mchealth@monroecounty.gov
Internet: www.monroecounty.gov/health-index.php

Commissioner of Public Health (Interim)
Dr. Jeremy T. Cushman . . . . (585) 753-2989
Deputy Director **(Vacant)** . . . . (585) 753-2989

Board of Health

111 Westfall Road, Room 950, Rochester, NY 14620
Fax: (585) 753-5115

President **Laura Markwick**
Vice President **John Lacek III**

COUNTIES

★ Elected Official ▲ Appointed by Legislature ▼ Appointed by Governor ▶ Appointed by Board or Commission ● Appointed by Judge
■ Appointed by Mayor △ Appointed by Freeholders ▽ Appointed by Supervisor ▷ Appointed by County Executive ○ Appointed by Council

Office of the Medical Examiner
740 East Henrietta Road, Rochester, NY 14623
Fax: (585) 753-5930

▷Medical Examiner **Nadia Granger** .... (585) 753-5905
Education: SUNY Downstate Med 2006 MD

Department of Public Safety
50 West Main Street, Rochester, NY 14614-1218
Fax: (585) 753-3023 Internet: www.monroecounty.gov/safety-index.php

Director **David T. Moore** .... (585) 753-3014
Education: Regis U BA, MA

Alternatives to Incarceration Program
50 West Main Street, Rochester, NY 14614-1218

Grant Manager **Guy Smith** .... (585) 753-3407
E-mail: guysmith@monroecounty.gov

Office of Emergency Management [OEM]
Public Safety Training Facility, 1190 Scottsville Road, Suite 200, Rochester, NY 14624
Fax: (585) 753-3810 Internet: www.monroecounty.gov/safety-oep.php

Emergency Preparedness Administrator
Frederick J. Rion, Jr. .... (585) 753-3810
E-mail: frion@monroecounty.gov

Office of the Fire Bureau
Public Safety Training Facility, 1190 Scottsville Road, Suite 203, Rochester, NY 14624
Fax: (585) 753-3867 Internet: www.monroecounty.gov/safety-fire.php

Fire Coordinator **Samuel J. DeRosa** .... (585) 753-3750
E-mail: sderosa@monroecounty.gov

Office of Probation-Community Corrections
33 North Fitzhugh Street, Suite 2000, Rochester, NY 14614
Fax: (585) 753-3552
Internet: www.monroecounty.gov/safety-probations.php

Chief Probation Officer **Robert J. Burns** .... (585) 753-3765

Monroe County Crime Laboratory
85 West Broad Street, Rochester, NY 14614

Administrator **John Clark** .... (585) 753-3535
E-mail: johnclark@monroecounty.gov

Public Safety Communications
1530 Highland Ave., Rochester, NY 14618

Director **Richard Verdouw** .... (585) 473-8989
E-mail: rverdouw@monroecounty.gov

Traffic Safety Board
CityPlace, 50 West Main Street, Suite 4111, Rochester, NY 14614
Internet: www.monroecounty.gov/safety-trafficsafety.php

▲Chairman **Ron Hinz** .... (585) 753-3011
Executive Secretary **Peggy Duffy** .... (585) 753-3011
E-mail: pduffy@monroecounty.gov

Weights and Measures Department
145 Paul Rd., Rochester, NY 14624

Administrator **Terrance Honan** .... (585) 753-7933

Department of Transportation [DOT]
CityPlace, 50 West Main Street, Suite 6100, Rochester, NY 14614
Fax: (585) 753-7730 E-mail: mcdot@monroecounty.gov
Internet: www.monroecounty.gov/dot-index.php

▷Director **Terrence J. Rice** .... (585) 753-7720
E-mail: trice@monroecounty.gov

Veterans' Service Agency
125 Westfall Road, Rochester, NY 14620
Tel: (585) 753-6040 Fax: (585) 753-6602
E-mail: mcveterans@monroecounty.gov
Internet: www.monroecounty.gov/vet-index.php

▷Director **Laura Stradley** .... (585) 753-6040 ext. 7
E-mail: lstradley@monroecounty.gov

Greater Rochester International Airport [GRIA]
1200 Brooks Avenue, Rochester, NY 14624
Tel: (585) 753-7020 Fax: (585) 753-7008
E-mail: mcairport@monroecounty.gov
Internet: www.monroecounty.gov/airport-index.php

▷Director of Aviation **CDR(Ret.) Michael A. Giardino** .... (585) 753-7020
E-mail: mgiardino@monroecounty.gov
Education: SUNY (Brockport) BS; Naval Postgrad MIMS; Naval War 2001 MNSSS

Monroe Community College [MCC]
1000 East Henrietta Road, Rochester, NY 14623-5780
Tel: (585) 292-2000 Internet: www.monroecc.edu

President **Dr. Anne M. Kress** .... (585) 292-2100
Education: Florida

▼Chairperson, Board of Trustees **John Bartolotta** .... (585) 292-2100

Monroe Community Hospital [MCH]
435 East Henrietta Rd., Rochester, NY 14620
Tel: (585) 760-6500 Fax: (585) 760-6066 E-mail: info@monroehosp.org
Internet: www.monroehosp.org

Executive Director **Gene Larrabee** .... (585) 760-6304
Administrative Secretary **Linda Seyba** .... (585) 760-6304
E-mail: lseyba@monroehosp.org
Hospital Board Chairperson **(Vacant)** .... (585) 760-6304

Monroe County Library System [MCLS]
115 South Avenue, Rochester, NY 14604
Tel: (585) 428-7300 Fax: (585) 428-8353 Internet: www.libraryweb.org

▲President, Board of Trustees **Laurence Guttmacher** ..... (585) 428-8045
Director **Patricia Uttaro** .... (585) 428-8045
E-mail: patricia.uttaro@libraryweb.org
Administrative Secretary **Gail Boldt** .... (585) 428-8046
E-mail: gail.boldt@libraryweb.org
Assistant Director **Sally Snow** .... (585) 428-8393

Monroe County Soil and Water Conservation District
The Towers, Building A, 1200 Scottsville Road, Suite 160, Rochester, NY 14624
Tel: (585) 753-7380 Fax: (585) 473-2124
Internet: www.monroecountyswcd.org

Chairperson **Rollin Pickering** .... (585) 753-7380
Executive Director **Kelly Emerick** .... (585) 753-7380
District Conservationist **(Vacant)** .... (585) 473-2120
Planning Technician **Tucker Kautz** .... (585) 753-7380

Monroe County Water Authority [MCWA]
475 Norris Drive, Rochester, NY 14610
Fax: (585) 442-0220 E-mail: information@mcwa.com
Internet: www.mcwa.com

Executive Director **Nicholas "Nick" Noce** .... (585) 442-2000

★Elected Official ▲Appointed by Legislature ▼Appointed by Governor ▶Appointed by Board or Commission ●Appointed by Judge
■Appointed by Mayor △Appointed by Freeholders ▽Appointed by Supervisor ▷Appointed by County Executive ○Appointed by Council

Office of the County Legislature

County Office Building, 39 West Main Street, Room 408, 409,
Rochester, NY 14614
Tel: (585) 753-1922 (Majority Office)
Fax: (585) 753-1960 (Majority Office)
Tel: (585) 753-1940 (Minority Office)
Fax: (585) 753-1946 (Minority Office)
Internet: www.monroecounty.gov/legislature-index.php

★President **Anthony J. Daniele** (R-District 10) .... (585) 753-1922
Term Expires: December 31, 2019
E-mail: monroe10@monroecounty.gov

★Majority Leader **Brian E. Marianetti** (R-District 7) ...... (585) 753-1922
Term Expires: December 31, 2019
E-mail: monroe7@monroecounty.gov

★Minority Leader **Cynthia W. Kaleh** (D-District 28) ...... (585) 753-1940
Term Expires: December 31, 2019
E-mail: cindy@kaltechsupport.com

★Legislator **Tina M. Brown** (R-District 1)............... (585) 753-1922
Term Expires: December 31, 2019
E-mail: monroe1@monroecounty.gov

★Legislator **Mike Rockow** (R-District 2)................ (585) 753-1922
Term Expires: December 31, 2019
E-mail: monroe2@monroecounty.gov

★Legislator **Tracy A. DiFlorio** (R-District 3) .... (585) 753-1922
Term Expires: December 31, 2019
E-mail: monroe3@monroecounty.gov

★Legislator **Frank Allkofer** (R-District 4) .... (585) 753-1922
Term Expires: December 31, 2019
E-mail: monroe4@monroecounty.gov

★Legislator **Karla F. Boyce** (R-District 5) .... (585) 753-1922
Term Expires: December 31, 2019
E-mail: monroe5@monroecounty.gov

★Legislator **Fred Ancello** (R-District 6)................. (585) 753-1922
Term Expires: December 31, 2019
E-mail: monroe6@monroecounty.gov

★Legislator **Matthew Terp** (R-District 8) .... (585) 753-1922
Term Expires: December 31, 2019
E-mail: monroe8@monroecounty.gov

★Legislator **Debbie Drawe** (R-District 9) .... (585) 753-1922
Term Expires: December 31, 2019
E-mail: monroe9@monroecounty.gov

★Legislator **Sean M. Delehanty** (R-District 11).......... (585) 753-1922
Term Expires: December 31, 2019
E-mail: monroe11@monroecounty.gov

★Legislator **Steve Brew** (R-District 12)................. (585) 753-1922
Term Expires: December 31, 2019
E-mail: monroe12@monroecounty.gov

★Legislator **John J. Howland** (R-District 13)............ (585) 753-1922
Term Expires: December 31, 2019
E-mail: monroe13@monroecounty.gov

★Legislator **Justin Wilcox** (D-District 14)............... (585) 753-1940
Term Expires: December 31, 2019
E-mail: jfwilcox@frontiernet.net

★Legislator **George J. Herbert** (R-District 15)........... (585) 753-1922
Term Expires: December 31, 2019
E-mail: monroe15@monroecounty.gov

★Legislator **Dr. Joe Carbone** (R-District 16) .... (585) 753-1922
Term Expires: December 31, 2019
E-mail: monroe16@monroecounty.gov

★Legislator **Joseph D. Morelle, Jr.** (D-District 17) .... (585) 753-1940
Term Expires: December 31, 2019
E-mail: jdmorellejr@gmail.com

★Legislator **Tanya Conley** (R-District 18) .... (585) 753-1922
Term Expires: December 31, 2019
E-mail: monroe18@monroecounty.gov

★Legislator **Kathleen A. Taylor** (R-District 19) .... (585) 753-1922
Term Expires: December 31, 2019
E-mail: monroe19@monroecounty.gov

★Legislator **Mike Zale** (R-District 20) .... (585) 753-1922
Term Expires: December 31, 2019
E-mail: monroe20@monroecounty.gov

Office of the County Legislature *continued*

★Legislator **Mark Muoio** (D-District 21)................ (585) 753-1940
Term Expires: December 31, 2019
E-mail: mark.muoio@gmail.com

★Legislator **Vincent R. Felder** (D-District 22) .... (585) 753-1940
Term Expires: December 31, 2019
E-mail: vincefelder22@gmail.com

★Legislator **James M. Sheppard** (D-District 23).......... (585) 753-1940
Term Expires: December 31, 2019
E-mail: jsheppar@rochester.rr.com

★Legislator **Joshua P. "Josh" Bauroth** (D-District 24).... (585) 753-1940
Term Expires: December 31, 2019
E-mail: jpbauroth@yahoo.com

★Legislator **John F. Lightfoot** (D-District 25)............ (585) 753-1940
Term Expires: December 31, 2019
E-mail: lightfootjohn16@gmail.com

★Legislator **Tony Micciche** (R-District 26) .... (585) 753-1922
Term Expires: December 31, 2019
E-mail: monroe26@monroecounty.gov

★Legislator **LaShay Harris** (D-District 27) .... (585) 753-1940
Term Expires: December 31, 2019
E-mail: lashayharris0@gmail.com

★Legislator **Ernest S. Flagler-Mitchell** (D-District 29) .... (585) 753-1940
Term Expires: December 31, 2019
E-mail: ernestflaglermitchell@gmail.com

Legislature Clerk's Office

Tel: (585) 753-1950 Fax: (585) 753-1932

▲Clerk of the Legislature **Jamie L. Slocum** .... (585) 753-1950
E-mail: jamieslocum@monroecounty.gov Fax: (585) 753-1932

▲Deputy Clerk of the Legislature **Heather D. Halstead**.... (585) 753-1950
E-mail: heatherhalstead@monroecounty.gov

▲Assistant Deputy Clerk of the Legislature **David Grant**... (585) 753-1950
E-mail: dgrant@monroecounty.gov

Chief of Staff (Republican) **Brett T. Walsh** .... (585) 753-1922
Fax: (585) 753-1960

Staff Director (Democratic) **Dennis O'Brien** .... (585) 753-1940
Fax: (585) 753-1946

Legislative Counsel **Patrick W. Pardyjak** .... (585) 753-1922

Legislature Clerk Assistant **(Vacant)** .... (585) 753-1950

Office of the County Clerk

County Office Building, 39 West Main Street, Room 101,
Rochester, NY 14614
Fax: (585) 753-1624 Internet: www.monroecounty.gov/clerk-index.php

★County Clerk **Adam Bello** .... (585) 753-1600
Term Expires: December 31, 2016
E-mail: mcclerk@monroecounty.gov

Deputy County Clerk **Michael A. Molinari**............. (585) 753-1600
E-mail: mmolinari@monroecounty.gov

Assistant Deputy Clerk **Diana M. Christodaro** .... (585) 753-1600
E-mail: dchristodaro@monroecounty.gov

Assistant Deputy Clerk, Auto License Bureau
Richard Turner .... (585) 753-1600
E-mail: rturner@monroecounty.gov

Office of the District Attorney

Ebenezer Watts Building, 47 South Fitzhugh Street, Rochester, NY 14614
Fax: (585) 753-4576 Internet: www.monroecounty.gov/da-index.php

★District Attorney **Sandra J. Doorley** (D) .... (585) 753-4500
Term Expires: December 31, 2019
E-mail: districtattorney@monroecounty.gov

★Elected Official ▲Appointed by Legislature ▼Appointed by Governor ►Appointed by Board or Commission ●Appointed by Judge
■Appointed by Mayor △Appointed by Freeholders ▽Appointed by Supervisor ▷Appointed by County Executive ○Appointed by Council

Office of the Sheriff

130 Plymouth Ave. South, Rochester, NY 14614-2209
Fax: (585) 753-4748 Internet: www.monroecounty.gov/sheriff-index.php

★Sheriff **Patrick M. O'Flynn** (R) .... (585) 753-4178
Term Expires: December 31, 2017
E-mail: poflynn@monroecounty.gov
Undersheriff **William Sanborn** .... (585) 753-4178
E-mail: wsanborn@monroecounty.gov

Monroe Correctional Facility

750 East Henrietta Road, Rochester, NY 14623
Fax: (585) 753-4051

Superintendent **Ronald M. Harling** .... (585) 753-3078

County of Monterey, California

P.O. Box 180, Salinas, CA 93902
Tel: (831) 755-5115 (Information) Internet: www.co.monterey.ca.us

County Seat: Salinas **Election Type:** Nonpartisan **Population:** 433,898 (2015)

Office of the Board of Supervisors

P.O. Box 1728, Salinas, CA 93902
Internet: www.co.monterey.ca.us/cob/supervisor.htm

★Chair **Jane Parker** (District 4) .... (831) 755-5044
Term Expires: January 2017
26161 First Avenue, Marina, CA 93933
E-mail: district4@co.monterey.ca.us
Education: UC Santa Cruz
Chief of Staff **Kristi Markey** .... (831) 755-5044
★Supervisor **Fernando Armenta** (District 1) .... (831) 755-5011
Term Expires: January 2017 Fax: (831) 755-5876
168 West Alisal Street, Salinas, CA 93901
E-mail: district1@co.monterey.ca.us
Education: San Diego 1976; San Jose Christian 1979 MSW
Chief of Staff **Alejandro Chávez** .... (831) 755-5011
★Supervisor **John Phillips** (District 2) .... (831) 755-5066
Term Expires: January 2019 Fax: (831) 755-5888
168 West Alisal Street, Salinas, CA 93901
Education: Boalt Hall JD
Chief of Staff **Josh Stratton** .... (831) 755-5022
★Supervisor **Simón Salinas** (District 3) .... (831) 755-5033
Term Expires: January 2019
E-mail: district3@co.monterey.ca.us
Education: Claremont McKenna BA; Santa Clara U 1984 JD
Chief of Staff **Christopher M. "Chris" Lopez** .... (831) 755-5033
★Supervisor **Dave Potter** (District 5) .... (831) 647-7755
Term Expires: January 2017 Fax: (831) 647-7695
1200 Aguajito Road, Monterey, CA 93940
E-mail: district5@co.monterey.ca.us
Chief of Staff **Kathleen Lee** .... (831) 755-5055
Clerk of the Board **Gail T. Borkowski** .... (831) 755-5066
E-mail: borkowskigt@co.monterey.ca.us Fax: (831) 755-5888

Office of the County Administrative Officer

168 West Alisal Street, Salinas, CA 93901
Tel: (831) 755-5115 Fax: (831) 757-5792
Internet: www.co.monterey.ca.us/admin

▽County Administrative Officer **Dr. Lew C. Bauman** .... (831) 755-5115
E-mail: baumanl@co.monterey.ca.us
Assistant County Administrative Officer **Nick Chiulos** .... (831) 755-5145
E-mail: chiulosn@co.monterey.ca.us

Office of the County Administrative Officer *continued*

Assistant County Administrative Officer
Manuel Gonzalez .... (831) 796-3593
E-mail: gonzalezmt@co.monterey.ca.us
Assistant County Administrative Officer
Dewayne Woods .... (831) 755-5309
E-mail: woodsd@co.monterey.ca.us

Office of the Agricultural Commissioner

1428 Abbott St., Salinas, CA 93901
Tel: (831) 754-7352 Fax: (831) 422-5003
E-mail: agcomm@co.monterey.ca.us Internet: http://ag.co.monterey.ca.us/

Commissioner **Eric Lauritzen** .... (831) 759-7325

Office of Cooperative Extension (University of California)

1432 Abbott Street, Salinas, CA 93901
Tel: (831) 759-7350 Fax: (831) 758-3018
Internet: http://cemonterey.ucdavis.edu/

County Director **Dr. Maria de la Fuente** .... (831) 759-7358

Elections Office

1370B South Main Street, Salinas, CA 93901
P.O. Box 4400, Salinas, CA 93912
Tel: (831) 796-1499 Fax: (800) 755-5485
E-mail: rov@montereycountyelections.us
Internet: www.montereycountyelections.us

Registrar of Voters (Interim) **Claudio Valenzuela** .... (831) 746-1499

Office of the Public Defender

P.O. Box 539, Salinas, CA 93902

Public Defender **James Samuel "Jim" Egar** .... (831) 755-5058
Education: UCLA; Loyola U (Los Angeles) 1975 JD

Department of Emergency Communications

P.O. Box 1883, Salinas, CA 93902
Internet: www.co.monterey.ca.us/911

Director **Bill Harry** .... (831) 755-5100

Monterey County Health Department

1270 Natividad Road, Salinas, CA 93906
Fax: (831) 755-4797 Internet: www.mtyhd.org

Director **(Vacant)** .... (831) 755-4526
Health Officer **Dr. Edward L. "Ed" Moreno** .... (831) 755-8942

Information Technology Department

1590 Moffett St., Salinas, CA 93905
Fax: (831) 759-6910 Internet: www.co.monterey.ca.us/iss

Director **Dianah L. Neff** .... (831) 759-6900

Parks Department

P.O. Box 5249, Salinas, CA 93915
Fax: (831) 755-4914 E-mail: parks@co.monterey.ca.us
Internet: www.co.monterey.ca.us/parks

Assistant Chief Administrative Officer **Nick Chiulos** .... (831) 755-4895

Resource Management Agency [RMA]

168 West Alisal Street, 2nd Floor, Salinas, CA 93901
Tel: (831) 755-4879 Fax: (831) 755-5877
Internet: www.co.monterey.ca.us/rma

Director **Carl Holm** .... (831) 755-4879
Deputy Director **(Vacant)** .... (831) 755-4879

★Elected Official ▲Appointed by Legislature ▼Appointed by Governor ▶Appointed by Board or Commission ●Appointed by Judge
■Appointed by Mayor △Appointed by Freeholders ▽Appointed by Supervisor ▷Appointed by County Executive ○Appointed by Council

Building Services Department
168 West Alisal Street, 2nd Floor, Salinas, CA 93901
Chief Building Official **Michael A. Rodriguez** .... (831) 784-5613

Planning Department
168 West Alisal Street, 2nd Floor, Salinas, CA 93901
Director **Mike Novo** .... (831) 755-5025

Public Works Department
168 West Alisal Street, Salinas, CA 93901
Director **(Vacant)** .... (831) 755-4800

Department of Social and Employment Services [DSES]
1000 South Main Street, Suite 208, Salinas, CA 93901
Internet: http://mcdses.co.monterey.ca.us/ Fax: (831) 755-8477
Director **Elliott Robinson** .... (831) 755-4400
Education: Stanford 1986 BA; UC Berkeley 1988 MSW

Office for Aging and Adults
1000 South Main Street, Suite 211-C, Salinas, CA 93901
Fax: (831) 757-9226
Director **Henry Espinosa** .... (831) 755-4466

Military and Veterans' Affairs Office [MVAO]
1200 Aguajito Road, Monterey, CA 93940
Internet: www.co.monterey.ca.us/va
Director **George Dixon** .... (831) 647-7610

Montgomery County Free Libraries
188 Seaside Circle, Marina, CA 93933
Fax: (831) 833-7574 Internet: www.co.monterey.ca.us/library
County Librarian **Jayanti Addleman** .... (831) 883-7573
E-mail: addlemanjg@co.monterey.ca.us

Office of the County Counsel
168 West Alisal Street, Salinas, CA 93901
Fax: (831) 755-5283 Internet: www.co.monterey.ca.us/countycounsel
▽ County Counsel **Charles J. McKee** .... (831) 755-5045
E-mail: mckeec@co.monterey.ca.us

Equal Opportunity Office
168 West Alisal Street, 3rd Floor, Salinas, CA 93901
Tel: (831) 755-5117 Fax: (831) 759-8070
Internet: www.co.monterey.ca.us/eqopp
Equal Opportunity Officer **Irma Ramirez-Bough** .... (831) 755-5117

Natividad Medical Center [NMC]
1441 Constitution Boulevard, Salinas, CA 93906
P.O. Box 81611, Salinas, CA 93902
Fax: (831) 755-6254 Internet: www.natividad.com
Chief Executive Officer **Gary Gray** .... (831) 755-4111

Probation Department
1422 Natividad Road, Salinas, CA 93906
Internet: www.co.monterey.ca.us/probation
Chief County Probation Officer **Manuel Real** .... (831) 755-3900

Water Resources Agency
P.O. Box 930, Salinas, CA 93902
General Manager **David Chardavoyne** .... (831) 755-4860

Office of the Assessor-County Clerk-Recorder
168 West Alisal Street, 1st Floor, Salinas, CA 93901
P.O. Box 570, Salinas, CA 93902
Fax: (831) 755-5435 E-mail: assessor@co.monterey.ca.us
Internet: www.co.monterey.ca.us/assessor (Assessor)
Internet: www.co.monterey.ca.us/recorder (Recorder-County Clerk)
★ Assessor-County Clerk-Recorder **Stephen L. Vagnini** .... (831) 755-5803
Term Expires: January 31, 2019
E-mail: vagninis@co.monterey.ca.us
Assistant County Clerk and Recorder **Alicia Sotelo** .... (831) 755-5874

Office of the Auditor-Controller
P.O. Box 390, Salinas, CA 93902
168 West Alisal Street, 3rd Floor, Salinas, CA 93901
Fax: (831) 755-5098 Internet: www.co.monterey.ca.us/auditor
★ Auditor-Controller **Michael J. Miller** .... (831) 755-5303
Term Expires: January 3, 2019
E-mail: millerm@co.monterey.ca.us
Chief Deputy Auditor-Controller **Ron Holly** .... (831) 755-5343
Chief Deputy Auditor-Controller **Gary Giboney** .... (831) 755-5343
Chief Deputy Auditor-Controller **Rupa Shah** .... (831) 755-5343

Office of the District Attorney
230 Church Street, Salinas, CA 93901
P.O. Box 1131, Salinas, CA 93902
Fax: (831) 755-5068 Internet: www.co.monterey.ca.us/da
★ District Attorney **Dean D. Flippo** .... (831) 755-5070
Term Expires: January 1, 2019
E-mail: flippodd@co.monterey.ca.us
Education: William & Mary BA; Wayne State U 1966 JD

Department of Child Support Services
752 La Guardia Street, Salinas, CA 93905
P.O. Box 2059, Salinas, CA 93902
Tel: (866) 901-3212 Fax: (831) 796-0232 Internet: www.mcdcss.org
Director (Acting) **Jody Holtzworth** .... (831) 769-8714

Office of the Sheriff-Coroner
1414 Natividad Rd., Salinas, CA 93906
Fax: (831) 755-3828 Internet: www.montereysheriff.org
★ Sheriff-Coroner **Steve Bernal** .... (831) 755-3700
Term Expires: 2019

Office of the Treasurer-Tax Collector
P.O. Box 1992, Salinas, CA 93902
Fax: (831) 424-6536 E-mail: taxcollector@co.monterey.ca.us
Internet: www.co.monterey.ca.us/taxcollector
★ Treasurer/Tax Collector **Mary A. Zeeb** .... (831) 755-5015
Term Expires: December 31, 2018
E-mail: zeebm@co.monterey.ca.us

Monterey County Office of Education [MCOE]
901 Blanco Circle, Salinas, CA 93901
P.O. Box 80851, Salinas, CA 93902
Tel: (831) 755-0301 Fax: (831) 755-6473 Internet: www.montereycoe.org
★ Superintendent **Dr. Nancy Kotowski** .... (831) 755-0301
Term Expires: December 31, 2018
E-mail: kotowski@monterey.k12.ca.us
Education: Dayton BS; Northwestern MA; USC 1992 PhD

COUNTIES

★ Elected Official ▲ Appointed by Legislature ▼ Appointed by Governor ► Appointed by Board or Commission ● Appointed by Judge
■ Appointed by Mayor △ Appointed by Freeholders ▽ Appointed by Supervisor ▷ Appointed by County Executive ○ Appointed by Council

County of Montgomery, Maryland

Executive Office Building, 101 Monroe Street, Rockville, MD 20850
Tel: (240) 777-0311 (Information) TTY: (240) 777-2545
Internet: www.montgomerycountymd.gov

County Seat: Rockville **Election Type:** Partisan **Population:** 1,040,116 (2015)

Office of the County Executive

Executive Office Bldg., 101 Monroe Street, 2nd Floor,
Rockville, MD 20850
Fax: (240) 777-2517 TTY: (240) 777-2544

★ County Executive **Isiah "Ike" Leggett** (D) . . . . (240) 777-2550
Term Expires: December 1, 2018
E-mail: ike.leggett@montgomerycountymd.gov
Date of Birth: July 25, 1945
Education: Southern U (New Orleans) 1967 BA; Howard U 1972 MA, 1974 JD; George Washington 1976 MLL
Career: At-Large Member, County Council, County of Montgomery, Maryland (1986-2002); Chairman, Democratic Party, State of Maryland (2002-2004)

Special Assistant **Constantia Latham** . . . . (240) 777-2528
E-mail: connie.latham@montgomerycountymd.gov

Special Assistant **Joy Nurmi** . . . . (240) 777-2522

Special Assistant **Charles Short** . . . . (240) 777-2522
E-mail: chuck.short@montgomerycountymd.gov

Office of the Chief Administrative Officer

101 Monroe Street, Rockville, MD 20850
Fax: (240) 777-2518

Chief Administrative Officer **Timothy L. Firestine** . . . . . . (240) 777-2519
E-mail: timothy.firestine@montgomerycountymd.gov

Assistant Chief Administrative Officer
Ramona Bell-Pearson . . . . (240) 777-2532
Education: Vanderbilt 1981; Howard U 1987 JD

Assistant Chief Administrative Officer **Bonnie Kirkland** . . (240) 777-2590

Assistant Chief Administrative Officer **Fariba Kassiri** . . . . (240) 777-2511
E-mail: fariba.kassiri@montgomerycountymd.gov
Education: Colorado (Denver) BS; Maryland MPP

Assistant Chief Administrative Officer **Lily Qi** . . . . (240) 777-2532
Education: Ohio 1993 MA; American U 2001 MBA

Office of Consumer Protection [OCP]

County Office Building, 100 Maryland Avenue, Room 330,
Rockville, MD 20850-2322
Fax: (240) 777-3768 E-mail: consumerprotection@montgomerymd.gov
Internet: www.montgomerycountymd.gov/consumer

▷ Director **Eric S. Friedman** . . . . (240) 777-3636
E-mail: eric.friedman@montgomerycountymd.gov

Management and Budget Specialist III
Marsha F. Carter . . . . (240) 777-3636
E-mail: marsha.carter@montgomerycountymd.gov

Executive Administrative Aide **Shaun Carew** . . . . (240) 777-3636
E-mail: shaun.carew@montgomerycountymd.gov

Office of the County Attorney

Executive Office Bldg., 101 Monroe Street, 3rd Floor,
Rockville, MD 20850-2540
Fax: (240) 777-6706

▷ County Attorney **Marc P. Hansen** . . . . (240) 777-6740
E-mail: marc.hansen@montgomerycountymd.gov
Education: MacMurray 1968 BA; Washington U (MO) 1969 MAT; Washington College of Law 1975 JD

Office of Emergency Management and Homeland Security [OEMHS]

P.O. Box 4117, Gaithersburg, MD 20878
Fax: (240) 777-2345
E-mail: mchomelandsecurity@montgomerycountymd.gov
Internet: www.montgomerycountymd.gov/oemhs

Director **Earl Stoddard** . . . . (240) 777-2300

Administration and Finance Division Chief
Michael Goldfarb . . . . (240) 777-2544

Operations Division Chief **Chuck Crisostomo** . . . . (240) 777-2544

Office of Human Resources

Executive Office Bldg., 101 Monroe Street, 7th Floor,
Rockville, MD 20850
Fax: (240) 777-5162

▷ Director **Shawn Stokes** . . . . (240) 777-5100
E-mail: ohr@Montgomerycountymd.gov
Education: Delaware State BS

Deputy Director of Labor and Employee Relations
Darryl Gorman . . . . (240) 777-5114
Education: Michigan BA; Harvard JD

Office of Human Rights

21 Maryland Avenue, Suite 330, Rockville, MD 20850
TTY: (240) 777-8480 Fax: (240) 777-8460

Director **James Stowe** . . . . (240) 777-8450

Compliance Manager **Loretta Garcia** . . . . (240) 777-8457
E-mail: loretta.garcia@montgomerycountymd.gov

Office of Intergovernmental Relations [OIR]

Executive Office Building, 101 Monroe Street, 4th Floor,
Rockville, MD 20850
E-mail: oir@montgomerycountymd.gov

▷ Director **Melanie L. Wenger** . . . . (240) 777-6556
E-mail: melanie.wenger@montgomerycountymd.gov
Education: Kansas State 1979 BS; George Washington 1985 MBA

Office of Management and Budget [OMB]

Executive Office Building, 101 Monroe Street, 14th Floor,
Rockville, MD 20850
Fax: (240) 777-2756 Internet: www.montgomerycountymd.gov/omb

▷ Director **Jennifer A. Hughes** . . . . (240) 777-2800
E-mail: jennifer.hughes@montgomerycountymd.gov
Education: Wellesley BA; Harvard MCRP

Public Information Office

Executive Office Building, 101 Monroe St., 4th Floor,
Rockville, MD 20850

▷ Director **Patrick Lacefield** . . . . (240) 777-6507
E-mail: patrick.lacefield@montgomerycountymd.gov
Education: Missouri 1977 BA

Deputy Director **Ohene Gyapong** . . . . (240) 777-6507
E-mail: Ohene.Gyapong@montgomerycountymd.gov

Correction and Rehabilitation Department

51 Monroe Street, Suite 1100, Rockville, MD 20850
Tel: (240) 777-9975 Fax: (240) 777-9992

▷ Director (Acting) **Robert Green** . . . . (240) 777-9976

Department of Economic Development [DED]

111 Rockville Pike, Suite 800, Rockville, MD 20850
Fax: (240) 777-2001 E-mail: ded.info@montgomerycountymd.gov
Internet: www.choosemontgomerymd.com

Note: Effective July 1, 2016, the functions of the Department of Economic Development will be assumed by the newly formed Montgomery County Economic Development Corporation.

▷ Director (Acting) **Sally Sternbach** . . . . (240) 777-2000

★ Elected Official ▲ Appointed by Legislature ▼ Appointed by Governor ▶ Appointed by Board or Commission ● Appointed by Judge
■ Appointed by Mayor △ Appointed by Freeholders ▽ Appointed by Supervisor ▷ Appointed by County Executive ○ Appointed by Council

Department of Economic Development *continued*

Deputy Director **Sally Sternbach** .... (240) 777-2000
E-mail: sally.sternbach@montgomerycountymd.gov

Department of Environmental Protection

255 Rockville Pike, Suite 120, Rockville, MD 20850
Tel: (240) 777-3867 (24-Hour Illegal Dumping Hotline)
Fax: (240) 777-7765 Internet: www.montgomerycountymd.gov/dep

▷ Director **Elisabeth "Lisa" Feldt** .... (240) 777-7700
Education: Union Col (NY) 1980 BSCE;
George Washington 1984 BSCE

Department of Finance

Executive Office Building, 101 Monroe Street, 15th Floor,
Rockville, MD 20850
Fax: (240) 777-8857 Internet: www.montgomerycountymd.gov/finance

▷ Director **Joseph F. Beach** .... (240) 777-8860

Montgomery County Fire and Rescue Service [MCFRS]

100 Edison Park Drive, Second Floor, Gaithersburg, MD 20878
Fax: (240) 777-2443 Internet: www.montgomerycountymd.gov/firerescue

Fire Chief **Scott Goldstein** .... (240) 777-2486

Department of General Services

101 Monroe Street, Rockville, MD 20850
Fax: (240) 777-6030

▷ Director **David E. Dise** .... (240) 777-6191
E-mail: david.dise@montgomerycountymd.gov

Fleet Management Services

Tel: (240) 777-5730 E-mail: fleet.mgmt@montgomerycountymd.gov

Division Chief **William "Bill" Griffiths** .... (240) 777-5776
Chief of Maintenance **Keith Stickley** .... (240) 777-5738

Department of Health and Human Services [HHS]

401 Hungerford Drive, 5th Floor, Rockville, MD 20850
Fax: (240) 777-1494 Internet: www.montgomerycountymd.gov/hhs
E-mail: hhsmail@montgomerycountymd.gov

▷ Director **Uma S. Ahluwalia** .... (240) 777-1266
E-mail: uma.ahluwalia@montgomerycountymd.gov
Education: U Delhi (India) MSW; George Washington
▷ Chief Operating Officer **Stuart Venzke** .... (240) 777-1151
E-mail: stuart.venzke@montgomerycountymd.gov
▷ Social Services Officer **Angela Cabellon** .... (240) 777-4580
E-mail: angela.cabellon@montgomerycountymd.gov

Aging and Disability Services

▷ Chief **John Jay Kenney** .... (240) 777-4565
E-mail: john.kenney@montgomerycountymd.gov

Behavioral Health and Crisis Services

▷ Chief **Raymond L. Crowel** .... (240) 777-1058
E-mail: raymond.crowel@montgomerycountymd.gov

Children, Youth and Family Services

▷ Chief **JoAnn Barnes** .... (240) 777-4580
E-mail: joann.barnes@montgomerycountymd.gov

Public Health Services [PHS]

▷ Health Officer/Chief **Ulder J. Tillmann** .... (240) 777-1603
E-mail: ulder.tillman@montgomerycountymd.gov
Deputy Health Officer **Helen Lettlow** .... (240) 777-1603

Special Needs Housing Services

▷ Special Housing Initiatives Chief **Nadim Khan** .... (240) 777-4565
E-mail: nadim.khan@montgomerycountymd.gov

Department of Housing and Community Affairs [DHCA]

100 Maryland Avenue, 4th Floor, Rockville, MD 20850
Tel: (240) 777-3677 Internet: www.montgomerycountymd.gov/dhca

▷ Director **Clarence J. Snuggs** .... (240) 777-3611
Education: Winston-Salem State BA; Howard U MBA

Department of Liquor Control

201 Edison Park Drive, Gaithersburg, MD 20878
Tel: (240) 777-1900 Fax: (240) 777-1962
E-mail: dlc@montgomerycountymd.gov

▷ Director (Interim) **Fariba Kassiri** .... (240) 777-1922
E-mail: fariba.kassiri@montgomerycountymd.gov Fax: (240) 777-1968
Education: Colorado (Denver) BS; Maryland MPP
Chief of Operations **Gus Montes de Oca** .... (240) 777-1914
Education: Maryland University Col BS
Chief of Administration **Sunil Pandya** .... (240) 777-1956
E-mail: sunil.pandya@montgomerycountymd.gov
Chief of Licensure, Regulation and Education
Kathie Durbin .... (240) 777-1917
Education: Maryland BA
Administrative Services Coordinator **Lynn Duncan** ...... (240) 777-1915
E-mail: lynn.duncan@montgomerycountymd.gov
Education: California U (PA) 1974 BA; Frostburg State U 1992 MBA

Board of Liquor License Commissioners

16650 Crabbs Branch Way, 2nd Floor, Rockville, MD 20855
Fax: (240) 777-1991

Chairman **Eugene M. Thirolf** .... (240) 777-1999
Education: Saint Louis U JD
Licensure, Regulation, and Education Division Chief
Kathie Durbin .... (240) 777-1917
Education: Maryland BA

Department of Parks

9500 Brunett Avenue, Silver Spring, MD 20901
Fax: (301) 495-9340 E-mail: mcp-parks@montgomeryparks.org
Internet: www.montgomeryparks.org

Director **Mike Riley** .... (301) 495-2553

Montgomery County Planning Department

8787 Georgia Avenue, Silver Spring, MD 20910-3760
Fax: (301) 495-1310 E-mail: mcp-cr@mncppc-mc.org
Internet: www.montgomeryplanning.org

Director **Gwen Wright** .... (301) 495-4500

Montgomery County Police Department [MCPD]

2350 Research Blvd., Rockville, MD 20850
Fax: (240) 773-5007 Internet: www.montgomerycountymd.gov/police

▷ Chief **J. Thomas "Tom" Manger** .... (240) 773-5000
E-mail: mcpdchief@montgomerycountymd.gov
Education: Maryland 1976 BA
Assistant Chief **Betsy Davis** .... (240) 773-5040
Assistant Chief **Russell E. "Russ" Hamill, Jr.** .... (240) 773-5200

Animal Services Division

7315 Muncaster Mill Road, Derwood, MD 20855
Fax: (301) 279-1063

Director **Thomas "Tom" Koenig** .... (240) 773-5928
Field Supervisor Manager **Paul D. Hibler** .... (240) 773-5929
Shelter Manager **Kate Walker** .... (240) 773-5640

Montgomery County Public Libraries [MCPL]

21 Maryland Avenue, Suite 310, Rockville, MD 20850
Tel: (240) 777-0002 Fax: (240) 777-0014
Internet: www.montgomerycountymd.gov/library

COUNTIES

★ Elected Official ▲ Appointed by Legislature ▼ Appointed by Governor ▶ Appointed by Board or Commission ● Appointed by Judge
■ Appointed by Mayor △ Appointed by Freeholders ▽ Appointed by Supervisor ▷ Appointed by County Executive ○ Appointed by Council

Administration

Director **B. Parker Hamilton** .... (240) 777-0012
E-mail: parker.hamilton@montgomerycountymd.gov

Public Services Administrator, Human Resource Management and Community Engagement
Carol Legarreta .... (240) 777-0030
E-mail: carol.legarreta@montgomerycountymd.gov

Public Services Administrator, Facilities and Strategic Management **Rita Gale** .... (240) 777-0022
E-mail: rita.gale@montgomerycountymd.gov

Public Services Administrator, Branch Operations and Customer Service **Chris Freeman** .... (240) 777-0002

Department of Recreation

4010 Randolph Road, Silver Spring, MD 20902
Tel: (240) 777-6800 Fax: (240) 777-6803
Internet: www.montgomerycountymd.gov/rec

▷ Director **Gabriel Albornoz** .... (240) 777-6800
E-mail: gabriel.albornoz@montgomerycountymd.gov

Division Chief **Jeffrey A. "Jeff" Bourne** .... (240) 777-6814
E-mail: jeffrey.bourne@montgomerycountymd.gov

Division Chief **Robin Riley** .... (240) 777-6824
E-mail: robin.riley@montgomerycountymd.gov

Department of Technology Services

Executive Office Bldg., 101 Monroe Street, 13th Floor, Rockville, MD 20850
Fax: (240) 777-2831

Chief Technology Officer **Harash "Sonny" Segal** .... (240) 777-2900
E-mail: sonny.segal@montgomerycountymd.gov

Chief Operating Officer **Dieter Klinger** .... (240) 777-2900
E-mail: dieter.klinger@montgomerycountymd.gov

Department of Transportation [MCDOT]

Executive Office Bldg., 101 Monroe Street, 10th Floor, Rockville, MD 20850-2540
Fax: (240) 777-7178 E-mail: mcdot.director@montgomerycountymd.gov
Internet: www.montgomerycountymd.gov/mcdot

▷ Director **Al R. Roshdieh** .... (240) 777-7170
E-mail: al.roshdieh@montgomerycountymd.gov

Deputy Director **Emil Wolanin** .... (240) 777-8788

Deputy Director for Transportation Policy (Acting)
Gary Erenrich .... (240) 777-7156

Montgomery County Ethics Commission

100 Maryland Avenue, Room 204, Rockville, MD 20850-2322
Fax: (240) 777-6672

▷ Chair **Kenita V. Barrow** .... (240) 777-6670

Chief Counsel/Staff Director **Robert W. Cobb** .... (240) 777-6674
E-mail: robert.cobb@montgomerycountymd.gov

Commission for Women [CFW]

401 Hungerford Drive, 1st Floor, Rockville, MD 20850
Internet: www.montgomerycountymd.gov/cfw

Executive Director **Jodi Finkelstein** .... (240) 777-8333

Revenue Authority

101 Monroe Street, 4th Floor, Rockville, MD 20850
Tel: (301) 762-9080 Fax: (301) 309-0652

Executive Director **Keith Miller** .... (301) 762-9080

Chief Financial Officer **Michael Boone** .... (301) 762-9080

Human Resources Manager **Gayle Jamison** .... (301) 762-9080
E-mail: gjamison@mcra-md.com

Information Technology and Program Manager
Gayle Jamison .... (301) 762-9080
E-mail: gjamison@mcra-md.com

Office of the County Council

Council Office Bldg., 100 Maryland Ave., Rockville, MD 20850
Tel: (240) 777-7900 Fax: (240) 777-7888
E-mail: county.council@montgomerycountymd.gov
Internet: www.montgomerycountymd.gov/council

★ President **Nancy Floreen** (D-At-Large) .... (240) 777-7959
Term Expires: December 7, 2018
E-mail: councilmember.floreen@montgomerycountymd.gov
Education: Smith 1973 BA; Rutgers 1976 JD
Chief of Staff **Patty Vitale** .... (240) 777-7900

★ Vice President **Roger Berliner** (D-District 1) .... (240) 777-7828
Term Expires: December 7, 2018
E-mail: councilmember.berliner@montgomerycountymd.gov
Chief of Staff **Cindy Gibson** .... (240) 777-7900

★ Council Member **Craig L. Rice** (D-District 2) .... (240) 777-7955
Term Expires: December 2018
E-mail: councilmember.rice@montgomerycountymd.gov
Education: Maryland BS
Chief of Staff **Steven "Steve" Goldstein** .... (240) 777-7900

★ Council Member **Sidney Katz** (D-District 3) .... (240) 777-7906
Term Expires: December 7, 2018

★ Council Member **Nancy Navarro** (D-District 4) .... (240) 777-7968
Term Expires: December 2018
E-mail: councilmember.navarro@montgomerycountymd.gov
Education: Missouri (St Louis) 1987 BA
Chief of Staff **Adam Fogel** .... (240) 777-7900

★ Council Member **Tom Hucker** (D-District 5) .... (240) 777-7960
Term Expires: December 2, 2018
Date of Birth: April 9, 1967
Education: Boston Col 1988 BS

★ Council Member **Marc Elrich** (D-At-Large) .... (240) 777-7966
Term Expires: December 2018
E-mail: councilmember.elrich@montgomerycountymd.gov
Chief of Staff **Dale Tibbitts** .... (240) 777-7900

★ Council Member **George L. Leventhal** (D-At-Large) .... (240) 777-7811
Term Expires: December 2018
E-mail: councilmember.leventhal@montgomerycountymd.gov
Education: UC Berkeley 1984 BA; Johns Hopkins 1987 MA

★ Council Member **Hans Riemer** (D-At-Large) .... (240) 777-7964
Term Expires: December 2018
E-mail: councilmember.riemer@montgomerycountymd.gov
Chief of Staff **Ken Silverman** .... (240) 777-7830
Education: Skidmore 2007 BA; William & Mary 2012 JD

○ Council Administrator **Stephen B. "Steve" Farber** .... (240) 777-7900
E-mail: steve.farber@montgomerycountymd.gov
Chief of Staff **Judy Jablow** .... (240) 777-7900

Legislative Information Officer **Neil Greenberger** .... (240) 777-7939
E-mail: neil.greenberger@montgomerycountymd.gov Fax: (240) 777-7882

Office of the Inspector General

51 Monroe Street, Suite 802, Rockville, MD 20850
Tel: (240) 777-7644 (Fraud Hotline) Fax: (240) 777-8254
E-mail: ig@montgomerycountymd.gov
Internet: www.montgomerycountymd.gov/ig

Inspector General **Edward L. Blansitt III** .... (240) 777-8240
Education: Texas (El Paso) 1971 BA; George Mason 1983 MBA

Office of Zoning and Administrative Hearings

Council Office Bldg., 100 Maryland Avenue, Room 200, Rockville, MD 20850
Fax: (240) 777-6665 E-mail: ozah@montgomerycountymd.gov

○ Director **Martin L. Grossman** .... (240) 777-6660
E-mail: martin.grossman@montgomerycountymd.gov

Board of Appeals

Council Office Building, 100 Maryland Avenue, Room 217, Rockville, MD 20850
E-mail: boa@montgomerycountymd.gov

○ Chair **David Perdue** .... (240) 777-6600

★ Elected Official ▲ Appointed by Legislature ▼ Appointed by Governor ▶ Appointed by Board or Commission ● Appointed by Judge
■ Appointed by Mayor △ Appointed by Freeholders ▽ Appointed by Supervisor ▷ Appointed by County Executive ○ Appointed by Council

Board of Appeals *continued*

Executive Director **Katherine Freeman** . . . . (240) 777-6600
E-mail: katherine.freeman@montgomerycountymd.gov

Merit System Protection Board

Council Office Bldg., 100 Maryland Avenue, Room 113,
Rockville, MD 20850

○ Chairman **Raul Chavera** . . . . (240) 777-6620
○ Associate Member **Charlotte Crutchfield** . . . . (240) 777-6620
○ Associate Member **Michael Kator** . . . . (240) 777-6620
Executive Director **Bruce P. Martin** . . . . (240) 777-6620
E-mail: bruce.martin@montgomerycountymd.gov
Education: Maryland BA; Chicago JD

Office of the Register of Wills

Judicial Center, 50 Maryland Avenue, Room 322,
Rockville, MD 20850-2397
Fax: (240) 777-9602
Internet: http://registers.maryland.gov/main/montgomery.html

★ Register of Wills **Joseph M. Griffin** (D) . . . . (240) 777-9600
Term Expires: December 1, 2018
E-mail: joseph.griffin@registers.maryland.gov
Education: St Francis Col (PA) 1988 BA
Chief Deputy Register of Wills **Margie Beatty** . . . . (240) 777-9600
Chief Deputy Register of Wills **Lynda Hawkins** . . . . (240) 777-9600
Systems Administrator Supervisor **Charles Keyser** . . . . . . (240) 777-9600

Office of the Sheriff

Circuit Court, 50 Maryland Avenue, North 4220, Rockville, MD 20850
Fax: (240) 777-7148
Internet: http://www.montgomerycountymd.gov/Sheriff/

★ Sheriff **Darren M. Popkin** (D) . . . . (240) 777-7000
Term Expires: November 30, 2018
E-mail: darren.popkin@montgomerycountymd.gov
Education: Maryland BA
Chief Deputy **Mark Bonanno** . . . . (240) 777-7000
E-mail: mark.bonanno@montgomerycountymd.gov

Office of the State's Attorney

Judicial Center, 50 Maryland Avenue, 5th Floor,
Rockville, MD 20850-2320
Fax: (240) 777-7413 Internet: www.montgomerycountymd.gov/sao

★ State's Attorney **John McCarthy** (D) . . . . (240) 777-7300
Term Expires: January 1, 2019
E-mail: states.attorney@montgomerycountymd.gov

Montgomery College

900 Hungerford Drive, Rockville, MD 20850-1195
Tel: (240) 567-5000 Internet: www.montgomerycollege.edu

President **DeRionne Pollard** . . . . (240) 567-5267
Chief of Staff **Stephen Cain** . . . . (240) 567-8015
Communications Director **Elizabeth Homan** . . . . (240) 567-7970
E-mail: elizabeth.homan@montgomerycollege.edu
Administrative Manager **Arlean Graham** . . . . (240) 567-5272
7362 Calhoun Place, Rockville, MD 20855
E-mail: arlean.graham@montgomerycollege.edu
Vice President of Communications **Ray Gilmer** . . . . (240) 567-7970

Montgomery County Board of Elections

18753 North Frederick Avenue, Suite 210, Gaithersburg, MD 20879
PO Box 4333, Rockville, MD 20849-4333
Tel: (240) 777-8683 (Registration/Voting Information)
Fax: (240) 777-8600 E-mail: elections@montgomerycountymd.gov
E-mail: absentee@montgomerycountymd.gov Internet: www.777vote.org
E-mail: voter.registration@montgomerycountymd.gov

President **James Shalleck** . . . . (240) 777-8525
Election Director **Margaret A. Jurgensen** . . . . (240) 777-8525

Montgomery County Public Schools [MCPS]

850 Hungerford Drive, Rockville, MD 20850
Tel: (301) 279-3617 Fax: (301) 279-3860
Internet: www.montgomeryschoolsmd.org

Board of Education

Tel: (301) 279-3617 Fax: (301) 279-3860 E-mail: boe@mcpsmd.org

★ President **Michael A. Durso** (District 5) . . . . (301) 924-3169
Term Expires: November 30, 2018
E-mail: michael_a_durso@mcpsmd.org
Education: Catholic U BA; American U
★ Vice President **Judith "Judy" Docca** (District 1) . . . . (301) 670-3234
Term Expires: November 30, 2018
E-mail: judy_docca@mcpsmd.org
★ Member **Rebecca Smondrwoski** (District 2) . . . . (301) 527-6070
Term Expires: November 30, 2016
★ Member **Patricia B. O'Neill** (District 3) . . . . (301) 320-7600
Term Expires: November 30, 2018
E-mail: patricia_o'neill@mcpsmd.org
Education: Southern Methodist BA
★ Member **Christopher S. "Chris" Barclay** (District 4) . . . . (301) 431-7736
Term Expires: November 30, 2016
E-mail: christopher_barclay@mcpsmd.org
Education: Columbia Col (IL) 1984
★ Member **Philip S. "Phil" Kauffman** (At-Large) . . . . (301) 924-3133
Term Expires: November 30, 2016
E-mail: phil_kauffman@mcpsmd.org
Education: Pennsylvania 1974 BA; Maryland 1977 JD
★ Member **Jill Ortman-Fouse** (At-Large) . . . . (301) 320-6564
Term Expires: December 2018
Student Member **Eric Guerci** . . . . (301) 279-3617
Term Expires: June 30, 2017
Chief of Staff **Roland Ikheloa** . . . . (301) 279-3301

Office of the Superintendent

Superintendent of Schools (Interim) **Larry A. Bowers** . . . . (301) 279-3381
Note: Until July, 1 2016
Superintendent of Schools **Jack R. Smith** . . . . (301) 279-3381
Note: Effective July 1, 2016 pending contract negotiations.
Education: Notre Dame PhD

★ Elected Official ▲ Appointed by Legislature ▼ Appointed by Governor ▶ Appointed by Board or Commission ● Appointed by Judge
■ Appointed by Mayor △ Appointed by Freeholders ▽ Appointed by Supervisor ▷ Appointed by County Executive ○ Appointed by Council

County of Montgomery, Ohio

Montgomery County Administration Bldg., 451 West Third Street, Dayton, OH 45422
P.O. Box 972, Dayton, OH 45422
Tel: (937) 225-4000 (Information) Internet: www.mcohio.org

County Seat: Dayton **Election Type:** Partisan **Population:** 532,258 (2015)

Office of the Board of Commissioners

Montgomery County Administration Bldg., 451 West Third Street, Dayton, OH 45422
Fax: (937) 496-7723

★President **Judy Dodge** (D) .... (937) 225-6470
Term Expires: December 31, 2016
E-mail: startzmanc@mcohio.org
Education: Wright State 1985 BA

★Commissioner **Daniel "Dan" Foley** (D) .... (937) 225-4912
Term Expires: December 31, 2018
E-mail: vangrovj@mcohio.org
Education: Bowling Green State 1987 BA; Wright State 1989 MA

★Commissioner **Deborah A. "Debbie" Lieberman** (D) ... (937) 225-4015
Term Expires: December 31, 2016
E-mail: oberert@mcohio.org
Education: Dayton 1986 JD

▶Clerk to the Board **Gayle L. Ingram** .... (937) 225-6491
E-mail: ingramg@mcohio.org Fax: (937) 496-6560

Office of the County Administrator

Montgomery County Administration Bldg., 451 West Third Street, 11th Floor, Dayton, OH 45422
P.O. Box 972, Dayton, OH 45422
Fax: (937) 496-7205

▶County Administrator **Joseph P. "Joe" Tuss** .... (937) 225-4693
E-mail: tussj@mcohio.org
Education: Arizona

Montgomery County Human Services Planning and Development Department

451 West Third Street, 9th Floor, Dayton, OH 45422-3100
Fax: (937) 496-7714

Director **Thomas "Tom" Kelley** .... (937) 225-4695

Office of Management and Budget [OMB]

Montgomery County Administration Bldg., 451 W. Third St., Dayton, OH 45422-1110
Tel: (937) 225-4735 Fax: (937) 225-4338
Internet: www.mcohio.org/services/omb

Director **Timothy S. Nolan** .... (937) 225-4735
E-mail: nolant@mcohio.org

Budget and Financial Planning Manager **Chris Neary** .... (937) 225-6289
E-mail: nearyc@mcohio.org

Law Offices of the Public Defender

117 South Main Street, Suite 400, Dayton, OH 45422
Fax: (937) 225-3449
Internet: www.mcohio.org/government/courts/public_defender

Public Defender **D.K. "Rudy" Wehner** .... (937) 496-7478
Education: Dayton 1973 BA; Cincinnati 1976 JD

Administrative Services Department

Montgomery County Administration Bldg., 451 West Third Street, 11th Floor, Dayton, OH 45422
P.O. Box 972, Dayton, OH 45422
Fax: (937) 496-7723

▶Assistant County Administrator **Amy S. Wiedeman** ..... (937) 225-5802

Office of Emergency Management

117 South Main Street, Suite 721, Dayton, OH 45422
Fax: (937) 224-8881

Director **Jeff Jordan** .... (937) 224-8934
E-mail: jordanj@mcohio.org

Communications Department

451 West Third Street, Dayton, OH 45422
Fax: (937) 496-7205

Director **Cathy Petersen** .... (937) 225-4693
E-mail: petersenc@mcohio.org

Human Resources Department

Montgomery County Administration Bldg., 451 West Third Street, 9th Floor, Dayton, OH 45422
P.O. Box 972, Dayton, OH 45422
Tel: (937) 225-4018 Tel: (937) 225-6128 (Job Line) Fax: (937) 496-7407

▶Director **Stephanie Echols** .... (937) 225-4018
E-mail: echolss@mcohio.org

Purchasing and Central Services Department

451 West Third Street, 9th Floor, Dayton, OH 45422
Fax: (937) 496-3006 Internet: www.mcohio.org/services/purchasing

▶Director **Tyler Small** .... (937) 225-4699
E-mail: smallt@mcohio.org

Animal Resource Center of Montgomery County [ARC]

6790 Webster Street, Dayton, OH 45414
Fax: (937) 454-8139 E-mail: animalshelter@mcohio.org

▶Director **Mark Kumpf** .... (937) 898-4457
E-mail: kumpfm@mcohio.org

Community and Economic Development Department

Montgomery County Administration Bldg., 451 West Third Street, 10th Floor, Dayton, OH 45422
P.O. Box 972, Dayton, OH 45422
Fax: (937) 225-6036

County Administrator **Bertha Henry** .... (937) 225-6140
Economic Development Specialist
Pamela "Pam" Fannin .... (937) 225-6140
E-mail: fanninp@mcohio.org

Building Regulations Office

451 West Third Street, 10th Floor, Dayton, OH 45422
Fax: (937) 225-6327

▶Chief Building Official/Manager **Maury Wyckoff** .... (937) 225-4586
E-mail: wyckoffm@mcohio.org

Community Development Office

451 West Third Street, 10th Floor, Dayton, OH 45422
Tel: (937) 225-6318 Fax: (937) 496-6629

Manager **Tawana Jones** .... (937) 225-6341

Economic Development Office

451 West Third Street, 10th Floor, Dayton, OH 45422-1350
Fax: (937) 225-6327

Director **Erik S. Collins** .... (937) 225-4642
E-mail: collinse@mcohio.org

★Elected Official ▲Appointed by Legislature ▼Appointed by Governor ▶Appointed by Board or Commission ●Appointed by Judge
■Appointed by Mayor △Appointed by Freeholders ▽Appointed by Supervisor ▷Appointed by County Executive ○Appointed by Council

Job and Family Services Department

Job Center, 1111 S. Edwin C. Moses Blvd., Dayton, OH 45422
P.O. Box 972, Dayton, OH 45422
Tel: (937) 496-6700 Tel: (937) 225-6164 (Customer Service)
Fax: (937) 225-6203

Director **Thomas "Tom" Kelley** .... (937) 225-4155
Fax: (937) 225-6256

Deputy Director **Robert Gruhl** .... (937) 225-4708
E-mail: bob.gruhl@jfs.ohio.gov Fax: (937) 225-6203

Deputy Director **Debra Downing** .... (937) 225-4155
Fax: (937) 225-6256

Assistant Director of Child Support Enforcement
Sarah E. Fields .... (937) 225-6004
Child Support Enforcement, Fax: (937) 225-5087
14 West Fourth Street, Dayton, OH 45422
E-mail: sarah.fields@jfs.ohio.gov

Assistant Director of Children Services **Jewell Good** .... (937) 276-1707
Children Services Division, Fax: (937) 276-6601
3304 N. Main St., Dayton, OH 45405
E-mail: jewell.good@jfs.ohio.gov

Assistant Director, Finance and Administrative Services
Thad Sargent .... (937) 276-1684
E-mail: thad.sargent@jfs.ohio.gov Fax: (937) 276-6601

Assistant Director, Social Services and Income Support
Deborah K. Hall .... (937) 496-6700
E-mail: deborah.hall@jfs.ohio.gov Fax: (937) 225-6203

Assistant Director, Workforce Development (Interim)
Robert Gruhl .... (937) 496-6700
E-mail: bob.gruhl@jfs.ohio.gov Fax: (937) 225-6203

Communications Coordinator **Kevin Lavoie** .... (937) 496-3305
E-mail: kevin.lavoie@jfs.ohio.gov Fax: (937) 225-6256

Human Resources Manager **Michelle Matthews** .... (937) 276-1720
E-mail: Michelle.Matthews@jfs.ohio.gov Fax: (937) 496-7520

Deputy Assistant Director, Social Services
Patrick Bailey .... (937) 496-6700
Fax: (937) 225-6203

Assistant County Administrator, Economic
Development/Workforce Development **(Vacant)** .... (937) 225-4645

Environmental Services Department

1850 Spaulding Rd., Kettering, OH 45432
Fax: (937) 781-2572 Internet: www.mcohio.org/water

Director **Patrick Turnbull** .... (937) 781-2576
E-mail: turnbullp@mcohio.org
Executive Assistant **Janel Regelski** .... (937) 781-2576
E-mail: regelskij@mcohio.org

Customer Services **Cathi Clements** .... (937) 781-2595
Fax: (937) 781-2687

Finance Services **Vijay Chitkara** .... (937) 225-4565
451 W. Third St., Dayton, OH 45422 Fax: (937) 225-5890

Information Technology Manager **Matt Hilliard** .... (937) 781-2618
E-mail: hilliardm@mcohio.org

Safety Officer **Jeremy Stockwell** .... (937) 781-2565

Engineering/Technical Services Office

1850 Spaulding Rd., Kettering, OH 45432
Fax: (937) 781-2686

▶ Engineering Manager **Nicole Diak** .... (937) 496-3080

Operations Office

1850 Spaulding Rd., Kettering, OH 45432
Fax: (937) 781-2685

▶ Deputy Director **(Vacant)** .... (937) 781-2577

Environmental Laboratory Manager **Jim Davis** .... (937) 781-3016
4257 Dryden Rd., Dayton, OH 45439

Field Operations Superintendent-Water and Wastewater
Nicole Diak .... (937) 781-2625

Maintenance Superintendent **David Hackett** .... (937) 781-2577

Wastewater Treatment Superintendent **Beth Moore** .... (937) 781-3032
E-mail: mooreb@mcohio.org

Stillwater Center

8100 North Main Street, Dayton, OH 45415
Fax: (937) 890-9579 Fax: (937) 890-7344

Director **Michelle Pierce-Mobley** .... (937) 890-0646
Education: Cincinnati 1984; Indiana Wesleyan 2007 MS, 2009 MA

Human Resources Manager **Catherine Bogan** .... (937) 890-0646

Nurse Manager **Pam Cooper** .... (937) 890-0646

Fiscal Manager **Lisa Leedy** .... (937) 890-0646

Emergency, Respite and Residential Program Manager
Carol O'Neill .... (937) 890-0646

Quality Assurance Coordinator **Doug Farmer** .... (937) 890-0646

Dayton and Montgomery County Board of Health

117 South Main Street, Dayton, OH 45422
Tel: (937) 225-4395 E-mail: boardagenda@phdmc.org
Internet: www.phdmc.org/about/board

Public Health – Dayton & Montgomery County [PHDMC]

Reibold Building, 117 South Main Street, Dayton, OH 45422-1280
Fax: (937) 496-3070 Internet: www.phdmc.org

Health Commissioner **Jeff A. Cooper** .... (937) 225-4395

Assistant Health Commissioner **Barbara Marsh** .... (937) 225-4395

Five Rivers MetroParks

1375 E. Siebenthaler Ave., Dayton, OH 45414
Tel: (937) 275-7275 Fax: (937) 278-8849 E-mail: email@metroparks.org
Internet: www.metroparks.org

Executive Director **Rebecca A. "Becky" Benná** .... (937) 275-7275

Deputy Director **Carrie Scarff** .... (937) 275-7275

Director of Marketing and Public Information
Trish Butler .... (937) 275-7275

Veterans' Service Commission

East Medical Plaza, 627 Edwin Moses Boulevard, 4th Floor,
Dayton, OH 45408
Fax: (937) 225-4854

▶ Executive Director **James Knowles** .... (937) 225-4801

Office of the Auditor

Montgomery County Administration Bldg., 451 West Third Street,
Dayton, OH 45422
P.O. Box 972, Dayton, OH 45422-1027
Tel: (937) 225-4333 Fax: (937) 496-7690 Internet: www.mcauditor.org

★ Auditor **Karl L. Keith** (D) .... (937) 225-4333
Term Expires: March 2019
E-mail: auditor@mcohio.org

Accounting Operations Manager **Tito Reynolds** .... (937) 225-4333

Director of Real Estate **Doug Trout** .... (937) 225-4333

Administrative Assistant **Matt Cox** .... (937) 225-5640

Office of the County Coroner

361 West Third Street, Dayton, OH 45402-1418
Fax: (937) 496-7916

★ Coroner **Dr. Kent Harshbarger** .... (937) 225-4156
Term Expires: December 31, 2016
E-mail: harshbargerk@mcohio.org

Director **Kenneth M. "Ken" Betz** .... (937) 225-4156

Webmaster **Tim Duerr** .... (937) 225-4990 ext. 2155
E-mail: duerrt@mcohio.org

COUNTIES

★ Elected Official ▲ Appointed by Legislature ▼ Appointed by Governor ▶ Appointed by Board or Commission ● Appointed by Judge
■ Appointed by Mayor △ Appointed by Freeholders ▽ Appointed by Supervisor ▷ Appointed by County Executive ○ Appointed by Council

Office of the County Engineer

Montgomery County Administration Building, 451 West Third Street, Dayton, OH 45422-1260
P.O. Box 972, Dayton, OH 45422-1260
Tel: (937) 225-4904 Fax: (937) 496-7441

County Engineer **Paul Gruner** .... (937) 225-4904
E-mail: grunerp@mcohio.org

Operations Engineer **W. Patrick "Pat" Timmons** .... (937) 837-2528
5625 Little Richmond Road, Dayton, OH 45426 Fax: (937) 854-3413
E-mail: timmonsp@mcohio.org

Safety Director **Kimberlee Beckner** .... (937) 837-2528
5625 Little Richmond Road, Dayton, OH 45426 Fax: (937) 854-3413
E-mail: becknerk@mcohio.org

Director of Finance **Chereese Loritts** .... (937) 225-4872

Office of the Prosecutor

301 West Third Street, Suite 500, Dayton, OH 45422
Fax: (937) 225-3470

★County Prosecutor **Mathias H. Heck, Jr.** (D) .... (937) 225-5599
Term Expires: December 31, 2016
E-mail: heckm@mcohio.org
Education: Marquette 1969 BS; Georgetown 1972 JD

Executive Assistant **Cara Sweet** .... (937) 225-5785
E-mail: sweetc@mcohio.org

First Assistant Prosecutor **Debra "Deb" Armanini** .... (937) 225-5751

Public Information Officer **Greg Flannagan** .... (937) 225-5610
E-mail: flannagang@mcohio.org

Office of the Recorder

Montgomery County Administration Bldg., 451 West Third Street, 5th Floor, Dayton, OH 45422
Fax: (937) 225-5980 E-mail: mcrecorder@mcohio.org
Internet: www.mcrecorder.org

★Recorder **Willis E. Blackshear** (D) .... (937) 225-4275
Term Expires: January 2, 2017
E-mail: blackshearw@mcohio.org

Office of the Sheriff

345 West Second Street, Dayton, OH 45422
P.O. Box 972, Dayton, OH 45422
Fax: (937) 225-4764

★Sheriff **Phil Plummer** .... (937) 225-4192
Term Expires: December 31, 2016

Chief Deputy **Robert Streck** .... (937) 224-8611

Office of the Treasurer

Montgomery County Administration Building, 451 West Third Street, Dayton, OH 45422-1475
Fax: (937) 496-7652

★Treasurer **Carolyn Rice** .... (937) 225-4010 ext. 105
Term Expires: September 4, 2017
E-mail: riceca@mcohio.org

Administrative Assistant **Angela Lilly** .... (937) 225-4010 ext. 104
E-mail: lillya@mcohio.org

Montgomery County Board of Elections [MCBOE]

451 W. Third St., Dayton, OH 45422
Fax: (937) 496-7798 E-mail: mcboe@mcohio.org
Internet: www.mcboe.org

Director **Jan Kelly** .... (937) 225-5670

Deputy Director **Steven P. Harsman** .... (937) 225-5674

Montgomery County Board of Elections *continued*

Finance Manager **Cathie Merkle** .... (937) 225-5660

Montgomery County Educational Service Center

200 S. Keowee St., Dayton, OH 45402
Fax: (937) 496-7426 Internet: www.montgomery.k12.oh.us

Superintendent of Schools **Frank DePalma** .... (937) 225-4598

County of Montgomery, Pennsylvania

P.O. Box 311, Norristown, PA 19404-0311
Tel: (610) 278-3000 Internet: www.montcopa.org

County Seat: Norristown **Election Type:** Partisan **Population:** 819,264 (2015)

Board of Commissioners

One Montgomery Plaza, Suite 800, Norristown, PA 19404
Fax: (610) 278-5943

★Chair **Joshua D. "Josh" Shapiro** (D) .... (610) 278-3024
Term Expires: December 31, 2019
E-mail: josh@montcopa.org
Education: Rochester 1995 BA; Georgetown 2002 JD

★Vice Chair **Dr. Valerie Ann Arkoosh** (D) .... (610) 278-3030
Term Expires: December 31, 2019
E-mail: val@montcopa.org
Education: Northwestern 1982 AB; Nebraska Medical 1986 MD; Johns Hopkins 2007 MPH

★Commissioner **Joe Gale** (R) .... (610) 278-3027
Term Expires: December 31, 2019

Chief Operating Officer/Chief Clerk

P.O. Box 311, Norristown, PA 19404-0311
Fax: (610) 278-5943

►Chief Clerk/Chief Operating Officer **Lauren Lambrugo** .. (610) 278-3020
E-mail: coo@montcopa.org

Aging and Adult Services [MCAAS]

Human Services Center, 1430 DeKalb St., Second Floor, Norristown, PA 19404
P.O. Box 311, Norristown, PA 19404-0311
Fax: (610) 278-3769

►Executive Director **Barbara O'Malley** ... (610) 278-3601 (Central Office)

Children and Youth

Human Services Center, 1430 DeKalb Street, Norristown, PA 19404
Fax: (610) 278-5898

►Executive Director **Laurie O'Connor** ...... (610) 278-5800 (Main Office)

Communications Office

P.O. Box 311, Norristown, PA 19404-0311
Fax: (610) 278-5943

►Director **Frank X. Custer** .... (610) 278-3062
E-mail: jwilling@montcopa.org

★Elected Official ▲Appointed by Legislature ▼Appointed by Governor ►Appointed by Board or Commission ●Appointed by Judge
■Appointed by Mayor △Appointed by Freeholders ▽Appointed by Supervisor ▷Appointed by County Executive ○Appointed by Council

Finance
P.O. Box 311, Norristown, PA 19404-0311
Fax: (610) 278-3069

▸ Chief Financial Officer **Dean Dortone** . . . . . (610) 278-3436
E-mail: Finance@montcopa.org

Public Defender
Montgomery County Courthouse, Second Floor,
Norristown, PA 19404-0311
P.O. Box 311, Norristown, PA 19404-0311
Fax: (610) 278-5941

▸ Public Defender **Keir Bradford-Grey** . . . . . (610) 278-3295

Solicitor
P.O. Box 311, Norristown, PA 19404-0311
Fax: (610) 278-3069

▸ Solicitor **Raymond McGarry** . . . . . (610) 278-3033
E-mail: rmcgarry@montcopa.org

Board of Assessment Appeals
P.O. Box 311, Norristown, PA 19404-0311
One Montgomery Plaza, Suite 301, Norristown, PA 19404
Fax: (610) 278-3560

▸ Chairman **Joseph S. Foster** . . . . . (610) 278-3761
Board Member **Patrick Costello** . . . . . (610) 278-3761
Board Member **Robert Adshead** . . . . . (610) 278-3761

Behavioral Health/Developmental Disabilities
P.O. Box 311, Norristown, PA 19404-0311
Human Services Center, 1430 DeKalb Street, Norristown, PA 19401-0311
Tel: (610) 278-3642 Fax: (610) 278-3683

▸ Administrator (Acting) **Penny Lafferty** . . . . . (610) 278-3642

Child Day Care Services
1430 DeKalb Street, Fifth Floor, Norristown, PA 19401-0311
P.O. Box 311, Norristown, PA 19401
Fax: (610) 278-5161 E-mail: mcccis@montcopa.org

▸ Executive Director **Elizabeth Adeyi** . . . . . (800) 278-3707

Commerce
Human Services Center, 1430 DeKalb Street, Fifth Floor,
Norristown, PA 19401
Fax: (610) 278-5944

▸ Director **Carolina C. DiGiorgio** . . . . . (610) 278-5950
E-mail: CDigiorg@montcopa.org
Education: Rutgers BA; Rutgers (Camden) JD

Montgomery County Correctional Facility
60 Eagleville Road, Eagleville, PA 19403
Fax: (610) 631-5909

▸ Warden **Julio Algarin** . . . . . (610) 631-7100 (Option 2)
E-mail: countyprison@montcopa.org

Domestic Relations
P.O. Box 311, Norristown, PA 19404-0311
Tel: (610) 278-3646 Fax: (610) 239-9637

▸ Director **Gary Kline** . . . . . (610) 278-3646

Voter Services
P.O. Box 311, Norristown, PA 19404-0311
Montgomery County Voter Services, One Montgomery Plaza,
425 Swede Street, Suite 602, Norristown, PA 19401
Tel: (610) 278-3275 (Election Board)
Tel: (610) 278-3280 (Voter Registration) Fax: (610) 292-4527

▸ Director **Kelly Green** . . . . . (610) 278-3275
E-mail: voters@montcopa.org

Montgomery County Health Department [MCHD]
Human Service Center, 1430 DeKalb St., Norristown, PA 19401-0311
P.O. Box 311, Norristown, PA 19404-0311
Tel: (610) 278-5117 Fax: (610) 278-5167

▸ Director (Interim) **Denise Wallin** . . . . . (610) 278-5117
E-mail: publichealth@montcopa.org
Health Director (Interim) **Dr. Valerie Ann Arkoosh** (D) . . (610) 278-5117
Education: Northwestern 1982 AB; Nebraska Medical 1986 MD;
Johns Hopkins 2007 MPH

Housing and Community Development
425 Swede Street, Suite 411, Norristown, PA 19404
P.O. Box 311, Norristown, PA 19404-0311
Tel: (610) 278-3540 TTY: (610) 631-1211 Fax: (610) 278-3636

▸ Director (Interim) **Carolyn Mayinja** . . . . . (610) 278-3540

Human Resources
One Montgomery Plaza, Suite 506, Norristown, PA 19404
P.O. Box 311, Norristown, PA 19404-0311
Fax: (610) 292-2160

▸ Director **Donna Pardieu** . . . . . (610) 278-3052

Information and Technology Solutions [ITS]
P.O. Box 311, Norristown, PA 19404-0311
Fax: (610) 270-0229

▸ Chief Technology Officer **Anthony Olivieri** . . . . . (610) 292-4931

Law Library
P.O. Box 311, Norristown, PA 19404-0311
Fax: (610) 278-5998

▸ Law Librarian **Jeanne M. Ottinger** . . . . . (610) 278-3806

Parks, Trails, and Historic Sites [PHS]
One Montgomery Plaza, 425 Swede Street, Suite 613,
Norristown, PA 19404
P.O. Box 311, Norristown, PA 19404-0311
Fax: (610) 278-3556

▸ Deputy Director **Ronald H. Ahlbrandt** . . . . . (610) 278-3555

Adult Probation
Main Office, 100 Ross Road, Suite 120, King of Prussia, PA 19406
Fax: (610) 992-7778

▸ Chief Adult Probation and Parole Officer
Michael P. Gordon . . . . . (610) 992-7777

Juvenile Probation
530 Port Indian Road, Norristown, PA 19403

▸ Chief Probation Officer, Juvenile **Steve Custer** . . . . . (610) 630-2252
Fax: (610) 630-1749

Public Property Division
P.O. Box 311, Norristown, PA 19404-0311
Fax: (610) 278-3563

▸ Deputy Director for Public Property in Assets and
Infrastructure Department **Mary Indiveri** . . . . . (610) 278-3519

COUNTIES

★ Elected Official ▲ Appointed by Legislature ▼ Appointed by Governor ▸ Appointed by Board or Commission ● Appointed by Judge
■ Appointed by Mayor △ Appointed by Freeholders ▽ Appointed by Supervisor ▹ Appointed by County Executive ○ Appointed by Council

Department of Public Safety

50 Eagleville Road, Eagleville, PA 19403
Tel: (610) 631-6500 Fax: (610) 631-6536

▶ Director **Thomas M. Sullivan** .... (610) 631-6500
▶ Deputy Director, Administration **Michelle Jackson** .... (610) 631-6500
▶ Deputy Director, Emergency Medical Services
David Paul Brown .... (610) 631-6500
▶ Deputy Director, Law Enforcement Liaison
Jesse Stemple .... (610) 631-6500
▶ Deputy Director, Fire Academy **Thomas J. Garrity** .... (610) 631-6500
Montgomery County Fire Academy,
1175 Conshohocken Road, Conshohocken, PA 19428
▶ Deputy Director, External Affairs **John Corcoran** .... (610) 631-6500

Purchasing

One Montgomery Plaza, 425 Swede Street, Seventh Floor, Suite 702,
Norristown, PA 19404
Fax: (610) 278-3086

▶ Director **Joseph Coco** .... (610) 278-3037

Roads and Bridges

One Montgomery Plaza, Airy and Swede Streets, Sixth Floor,
Norristown, PA 19401

Office Manager **Gretta Riley** .... (610) 278-3612
Fax: (610) 292-2032

Veterans Affairs

Human Service Center, 1430 DeKalb St., Norristown, PA 19401
P.O. Box 311, Norristown, PA 19404-0311
Fax: (610) 278-5935

▶ Director **Sean Halbom** .... (610) 278-3285

Youth Center

540-550 Port Indian Road, Norristown, PA 19403
Fax: (610) 631-2511

▶ Executive Director **Joseph Viti** .... (610) 631-1893

Montgomery County Planning Commission [MCPC]

One Montgomery County Plaza, 425 Swede Street, Suite 201,
Norristown, PA 19404
P.O. Box 311, Norristown, PA 19404-0311
Fax: (610) 278-3941

▶ Executive Director **Jody Holton** .... (610) 278-3722

Valley Forge Convention and Visitors Bureau

1000 First Avenue, Suite 101, King of Prussia, PA 19406
Fax: (610) 834-0202

▶ President **Paul R. Decker** .... (610) 834-7960
E-mail: decker@valleyforge.org

Assets and Infrastructure

One Montgomery Plaza, 425 Swede Street, Suite 800,
Norristown, PA 19404
Fax: (610) 278-3563

Director **Kenneth Starr** .... (610) 278-3044

Controller

P.O. Box 311, Norristown, PA 19404-0311
425 Swede Street, Suite 508, Norristown, PA 19404
Fax: (610) 278-3300

★ Controller **Karen Geld Sanchez** (D) .... (610) 278-3072
Term Expires: December 31, 2019

Coroner

P.O. Box 311, Norristown, PA 19404-0311
Fax: (610) 278-3547

★ Coroner **Michael Milbourne** (D) .... (610) 278-3057
Term Expires: December 31, 2019

District Attorney

Court House, P.O. Box 311, Norristown, PA 19404-0311
Fax: (610) 278-3095

★ District Attorney **Kevin R. Steele** (D) .... (610) 278-3090
Term Expires: December 31, 2019

Montgomery County Jury Selection Commission

P.O. Box 311, Norristown, PA 19404-0311
Maine and Swede Streets, Norristown, PA 19404
Fax: (610) 292-4968

★ Jury Commissioner **Joanne Olszewski** (D) .... (610) 278-3215
Term Expires: December 31, 2016
★ Jury Commissioner **Merry Woods** (R) .... (610) 278-3215
Term Expires: December 31, 2016

Office of the Prothonotary

Airy and Swede Streets, Norristown, PA 19404
Office of the Prothonotary, P.O. Box 311, Norristown, PA 19404-0311
Fax: (610) 278-5994

★ Prothonotary **Mark Levy** (D) .... (610) 278-3360
Term Expires: December 31, 2019

Recorder of Deeds

One Montgomery Plaza, 425 Swede Street, Third Floor,
Norristown, PA 19404
P.O. Box 311, Norristown, PA 19404-0311
Fax: (610) 278-3869

★ Recorder of Deeds **Jeanne Sorg** (D) .... (610) 278-3289
Term Expires: December 31, 2019

Register of Wills

One Montgomery Plaza, 425 Swede Street, Fourth Floor,
Norristown, PA 19404
P.O. Box 311, Norristown, PA 19404-0311
Tel: (610) 278-3414 (Marriage Licenses)
Tel: (610) 278-3400 (Register of Wills and Orphans' Court)
Fax: (610) 278-3240

★ Register of Wills/Clerk of Orphans' Court
D. Bruce Hanes (D) .... (610) 278-3400
Term Expires: December 31, 2019

Sheriff

P.O. Box 311, Norristown, PA 19404
Fax: (610) 278-3832

★ Sheriff **Sean P. Kilkenny** .... (610) 278-3331
Term Expires: December 31, 2019

Treasurer

P.O. Box 311, Norristown, PA 19404-0311
Fax: (610) 292-2191

★ Treasurer **Jason Salus** (D) .... (610) 278-3066
Term Expires: December 31, 2019

★ Elected Official ▲ Appointed by Legislature ▼ Appointed by Governor ▶ Appointed by Board or Commission ● Appointed by Judge
■ Appointed by Mayor △ Appointed by Freeholders ▽ Appointed by Supervisor ▷ Appointed by County Executive ○ Appointed by Council

County of Morris, New Jersey

Administration and Records Bldg., Morristown, NJ 07960
Tel: (973) 285-6000 (Information) Internet: www.co.morris.nj.us

County Seat: Morristown **Election Type:** Partisan **Population:** 499,509 (2015)

Office of the Board of Chosen Freeholders

Administration and Records Bldg., Morristown, NJ 07960
P.O. Box 900, Morristown, NJ 07963-0900
Tel: (973) 285-6010 Fax: (973) 539-6466

★Director **Kathryn DeFillippo** .... (973) 285-6010
Term Expires: December 31, 2016
E-mail: kdefillippo@co.morris.nj.us

★Deputy Director **William "Hank" Lyon** (R) .... (973) 285-6010
Term Expires: December 31, 2017
E-mail: hlyon@co.morris.nj.us
Education: Col Holy Cross

★Freeholder **Douglas R. Cabana** (R) .... (973) 285-6010
Term Expires: December 31, 2016
E-mail: dcabana@co.morris.nj.us

★Freeholder **John Cesaro** (R) .... (973) 285-6010
Term Expires: December 31, 2018
E-mail: jcesaro@co.morris.nj.us

★Freeholder **Thomas J. "Tom" Mastrangelo** (R) .... (973) 285-6010
Term Expires: December 31, 2016
E-mail: tmastrangelo@co.morris.nj.us

★Freeholder **Christine Myers** (R) .... (973) 285-6010
Term Expires: December 31, 2018

★Freeholder **Deborah Smith** (R) .... (973) 285-6010
Term Expires: December 31, 2018

△Clerk of the Board **Diane M. Ketchum** .... (973) 285-6010
E-mail: dketchum@co.morris.nj.us

Office of the County Counsel

Administration and Records Bldg., Morristown, NJ 07960
Fax: (973) 829-8045

△Counsel **Capt. John Napolitano** .... (973) 829-8060
E-mail: jnapolitano@co.morris.nj.us

Office of the County Administrator

Administration and Records Bldg., Morristown, NJ 07960
Fax: (973) 285-5266

△County Administrator **John Bonanni** .... (973) 285-6040
E-mail: jbonanni@co.morris.nj.us

Assistant County Administrator **Cathy Burd** .... (973) 285-6040
E-mail: cburd@co.morris.nj.us

Office of Labor Relations

Administration and Records Bldg., Morristown, NJ 07960
Fax: (973) 285-5266

Manager **Allison Stapleton** .... (973) 285-6051

Department of Finance

Administration and Records Building, 10 Court Street, Morristown, NJ 07960
Internet: www.co.morris.nj.us/services/finance.asp

Director **Joseph Kovalcik** .... (973) 829-6085

Office of the County Adjuster

Administration and Records Bldg., Morristown, NJ 07960

Adjuster (Acting) **Laurie Becker** .... (973) 285-6486

Medical Services

W. Hanover Ave., Morristown, NJ 07960

Director **William "Bill" Gluckman** .... (973) 998-7255
Education: Tufts BA; Bridgeport MS

Purchasing

Administration and Records Bldg., Morristown, NJ 07960
Fax: (973) 829-0304

Purchasing Agent (Acting) **Anthony Aponte** .... (973) 285-6332
E-mail: aaponte@co.morris.nj.us

Risk Management

One Court St., Morristown, NJ 07963
Fax: (973) 285-6360

Director **Staci Santucci** .... (973) 285-6353
E-mail: ssantucci@co.morris.nj.us

Assistant Director **Peter Gordon** .... (973) 285-6353
E-mail: pgordon@co.morris.nj.us

Mailing Services

Courthouse, Morristown, NJ 07960

Director **Robert Dorr** .... (973) 285-6331
E-mail: rdorr@co.morris.nj.us

Office of the Treasurer

Administration and Records Building, 10 Court Street, Morristown, NJ 07960

△Treasurer **Joseph Kovalcik** .... (973) 285-6085
E-mail: jkovalcik@co.morris.nj.us

Department of Human Services

30 Schuyler Place, Morristown, NJ 07960
Internet: www.morrishumanservices.org/hs

Director **Jennifer Carpinteri** .... (973) 285-6868

Office of Temporary Assistance

County Complex, Morristown, NJ 07963-0900
Tel: (973) 326-7800 Fax: (973) 326-7251
Internet: www.morrishumanservices.org/hs/ota.asp

Director **Gary Denamen** .... (973) 326-7240

Division of Aging, Disabilities and Community Programming

County Complex. Morris Township, Morristown, NJ 07960
Internet: www.morrishumanservices.org/dvs

Director **Ophelia Cruse** .... (973) 285-6846

Office for the Disabled

340 West Hanover Avenue, Morristown, NJ 07960
Tel: (973) 285-6855
Internet: www.morrishumanservices.org/dvs/disabled.asp

Coordinator **(Vacant)** .... (973) 285-6855

Office of Veterans Services

340 West Hanover Avenue, Morristown, NJ 07960
Tel: (973) 285-6866
Internet: www.morrishumanservices.org/dvs/veterans.asp

Veterans' Service Officer **Charles Jurgensen** .... (973) 285-6866

Division of Behavioral Health and Youth Services

30 Schuyler Place, Morristown, NJ 07960

Director **Laurie Becker** .... (973) 285-6852

Employment and Training Services

30 Schuyler Place, Morristown, NJ 07963
Internet: www.morrishumanservices.org/hs/employment.asp

Program Director **Donna Buchanan** .... (973) 285-6880

★Elected Official ▲Appointed by Legislature ▼Appointed by Governor ▶Appointed by Board or Commission ●Appointed by Judge
■Appointed by Mayor △Appointed by Freeholders ▽Appointed by Supervisor ▷Appointed by County Executive ○Appointed by Council

COUNTIES

Juvenile Detention Center
County Complex, Morristown, NJ 07960
Fax: (973) 285-2960
Internet: www.morrishumanservices.org/hs/juvenile.asp

Director **Tom Pollio** .... (973) 285-2959

Morris View Healthcare Center
540 W. Hanover Ave., Morristown, NJ 07960
Fax: (973) 285-6062
Internet: www.morrishumanservices.org/dvs/morrisview.asp

Administrator **Catherine Engler** .... (973) 285-2800

Youth Shelter
County Complex, Morristown, NJ 07960

Director **Jill Cerullo** .... (973) 285-2970

Community Development
30 Schuyler Place, 2nd Floor, Morristown, NJ 07963

Director **Tim Tansey** .... (973) 285-6060
E-mail: ttansey@co.morris.nj.us

Office of Information Technology
30 Schuyler Place, Morristown, NJ 07960
Internet: www.co.morris.nj.us/services/information.asp

Chief Information Officer **John Tugman** .... (973) 285-2869
E-mail: jtugman@co.morris.nj.us

Office of Public Information
Administration and Records Building, 10 Court Street, Morristown, NJ 07960

Communications and Social Media Manager
Lawrence "Larry" Ragonese .... (973) 285-6015
E-mail: lragonese@co.morris.nj.us

Office of Personnel
Administration and Records Bldg., Morristown, NJ 07960
Fax: (973) 993-9623

Director **Frank Corrente** .... (973) 285-6109
E-mail: fcorrente@co.morris.nj.us

Library Services
30 E. Hanover Ave., Whippany, NJ 07981
Fax: (973) 285-6982

Director **(Vacant)** .... (973) 285-6934

Department of Law and Public Safety
Morris County Public Safety Training Academy Complex, 500 West Hanover Avenue, Parsippany, NJ 07054
Fax: (973) 829-8604
Internet: www.co.morris.nj.us/services/lawpublicsafety.asp

Director **Scott DiGiralomo** .... (973) 829-8050
E-mail: sdigiralomo@co.morris.nj.us

Office of Emergency Management
Morris County Public Safety Training Academy Complex, 500 West Hanover Avenue, Parsippany, NJ 07054
P.O Box 900, Morristown, NJ 07963-0900
Tel: (973) 829-8600 Fax: (973) 829-8604 E-mail: oem@co.morris.nj.us
Internet: www.morrisoem.org

△ Coordinator **Jeffrey S. Paul** .... (973) 829-8600
E-mail: jpaul@co.morris.nj.us

Medical Examiner
P.O. Box 900, Morristown, NJ 07963-0900
Fax: (973) 829-8274

△ Medical Examiner **Dr. Ronald V. Suarez** .... (973) 829-8270
E-mail: rsuarez@co.morris.nj.us

Public Safety Training Academy
P.O. Box 900, Morristown, NJ 07963-0900
Fax: (973) 285-2971

△ Administrator **Daniel Colucci** .... (973) 285-2979
E-mail: dcolucci@co.morris.nj.us

Weights and Measures
101 Western Ave, Morristown, NJ 07960

Superintendent **Robert Alviene** .... (973) 285-2957

Department of Planning and Public Works
30 Schuyler Place, Morristown, NJ 07960
Fax: (973) 326-9025 Internet: www.co.morris.nj.us/services/planndevl.asp

Director **Deena Leary** .... (973) 829-8120
E-mail: dleary@co.morris.nj.us

Planning and Preservation
30 Schulyer Pl., Morristown, NJ 07960
Internet: www.morrisplanning.org

Coordinator **Christine Marion** .... (973) 829-8120

Roads, Bridges, and Shade Tree Management
W. Hanover Ave., Morristown, NJ 07960
P.O. Box 900, Morristown, NJ 07960

Superintendent **Michael D'Agostino** .... (973) 285-2928

Engineering and Transportation
Administration and Records Bldg., Morristown, NJ 07960
P.O. Box 900, Morristown, NJ 07960

County Engineer and Division Director
Christopher Vitz .... (973) 285-6750
E-mail: cvitz@co.morris.nj.us

Buildings and Grounds
Courthouse, Morristown, NJ 07960

Superintendent **Christopher Walker** .... (973) 285-6340
E-mail: cwalker@co.morris.nj.us

Office of the County Clerk
Administration and Records Bldg., 10 Court Street, Morristown, NJ 07963
Tel: (973) 285-6059 Fax: (973) 285-5233

★ County Clerk **Ann Grossi** (R) .... (973) 285-6125
Term Expires: December 31, 2018
E-mail: agrossi@co.morris.nj.us

Deputy County Clerk **John Wojtaszek** .... (973) 285-6132
E-mail: jwojtaszek@co.morris.nj.us

Office of the County Prosecutor
Administration and Records Bldg., Morristown, NJ 07960
Fax: (973) 285-6264 Internet: http://www.morrisnjpros.org

▼ Prosecutor **Fredric M. Knapp** .... (973) 285-6200
E-mail: fknapp@co.morris.nj.us

First Assistant Prosecutor **Thomas A. "Tom" Zelante** ... (973) 285-6200
Education: LaSalle Col (Canada) 1976 BA; Seton Hall 1979 JD

Chief of Investigations **John R. Speirs** .... (973) 285-6200

Office of the Executive Superintendent of Schools
P.O. Box 900, Morristown, NJ 07963-0900
Fax: (973) 285-8341

Superintendent of Schools (Interim) **Roger Jinks, Sr.** ..... (973) 285-8320

★ Elected Official ▲ Appointed by Legislature ▼ Appointed by Governor ► Appointed by Board or Commission ● Appointed by Judge
■ Appointed by Mayor △ Appointed by Freeholders ▽ Appointed by Supervisor ▷ Appointed by County Executive ○ Appointed by Council

Office of the Sheriff

Courthouse, Morristown, NJ 07960
Fax: (973) 605-8312 E-mail: sheriff@gti.net Internet: www.mcsheriff.org

★ Sheriff **Edward Rochford** (R) .... (973) 285-6600
Term Expires: December 31, 2016
E-mail: erochford@co.morris.nj.us
Education: John Jay Col BS

Office of the Surrogate

Administration and Records Bldg., Morristown, NJ 07963
Fax: (973) 993-5574 Internet: www.morrissurrogate.com

★ Surrogate **John Pecoraro** (R) .... (973) 285-6500
Term Expires: December 31, 2019
E-mail: jpecoraro@co.morris.nj.us
Deputy Surrogate **Christopher Luongo** .... (973) 285-6500

Authorities, Boards and Commissions

Board of Elections

Administration and Records Bldg., Morristown, NJ 07960
Tel: (973) 285-6720 Fax: (973) 285-5208
E-mail: info@morriselections.org

Administrator **Dale Kramer** .... (973) 285-6715

Office of the Tax Administrator

Administration and Records Bldg., Morristown, NJ 07960
Fax: (973) 993-9618

Tax Administrator **Ralph Meloro IV** .... (973) 285-6707
E-mail: rmeloro@co.morris.nj.us

Heritage Commission

300 Mendham Rd., Morristown, NJ 07963

Chairman **Larry Fast** .... (973) 829-8117
Archivist **Peg Shultz** .... (973) 829-8117

Division of Mosquito Control

P.O. Box 405, Morris Plains, NJ 07950
Fax: (973) 538-3857

Director **Kris McMorland** .... (973) 538-3200

Park Commission

53 E. Hanover Ave., Morristown, NJ 07962
Fax: (973) 644-2726

Director **David Helmer** .... (973) 326-7610

Morris County Housing Authority [MCHA]

99 Ketch Road, Morristown, NJ 07960
Fax: (973) 540-1914

Director **Roberta Strater** .... (973) 540-0389

Morris County Municipal Utilities Authority [MCMUA]

Courthouse, Morristown, NJ 07963
P.O. Box 370, Mendham, NJ 07945-0370
Fax: (973) 285-8397 E-mail: info@mcmua.com

Executive Director **Glenn Schweizer** .... (973) 285-8383
Chief Water Engineer **John P. Scarmozza** .... (973) 285-8386
E-mail: jscarmozza@co.morris.nj.us

County of Multnomah, Oregon

501 Southeast Hawthorne Boulevard, Portland, OR 97214-3501
Tel: (503) 823-4000 (Information) Internet: http://web.multco.us/

County Seat: Portland **Election Type:** Nonpartisan
Population: 790,294 (2015)

Office of the Board of Commissioners

Multnomah Building, 501 Southeast Hawthorne Boulevard, Suite 600, Portland, OR 97214
Internet: http://web.multco.us/board

★ Chair **Deborah Kafoury** .... (503) 988-3308
Term Expires: December 31, 2018 Fax: (503) 988-3093
E-mail: mult.chair@multco.us
Education: Whitman 1989 BA

★ Vice Chair **Jules Kopel Bailey** (District 1) .... (503) 988-5220
Term Expires: December 31, 2016 Fax: (503) 988-5440
E-mail: district1@multco.us
Education: Lewis & Clark 2001 BA; Princeton MA

★ Commissioner **Loretta J. Smith** (District 2) .... (503) 988-5219
Term Expires: December 31, 2018 Fax: (503) 988-5440
E-mail: district2@multco.us
Education: Oregon State 1987 BA

★ Commissioner **Judith C. "Judy" Shiprack** (District 3) ... (503) 988-5217
Term Expires: December 31, 2016 Fax: (503) 988-5262
E-mail: district3@multco.us
Education: Reed 1973 MA; Lewis & Clark 1980 JD

★ Commissioner **Diane McKeel** (District 4) .... (503) 988-5213
Term Expires: December 31, 2016 Fax: (503) 988-5262
E-mail: district4@multco.us
Education: Oregon BS

Clerk of the Board **Lynda J. Grow** .... (503) 988-5274
Fax: (503) 988-3013

Office of Multnomah County Attorney

Multnomah Bldg., 501 SE Hawthorne, Suite 500, Portland, OR 97214
Fax: (503) 988-3377

County Attorney **Jenny M. Madkour** .... (503) 988-3138
E-mail: jenny.m.madkour@multco.us
Deputy County Attorney
Jacqueline A. "Jacquie" Weber .... (503) 988-3138

Department of Community Justice [DCJ]

501 SE Hawthorne Boulevard, Suite 250, Portland, OR 97214
Tel: (503) 988-3701 Fax: (503) 988-3990

► Director **Scott M. Taylor** .... (503) 988-5590
E-mail: scott.m.taylor@multco.us
Education: Washington State; Portland State MPA

Deputy Director **Truls Neal** .... (503) 988-6131
Administrative Specialist **(Vacant)** .... (503) 988-6132
Budget/Policy Manager **Joyce Resare** .... (503) 988-3961
Human Resource Manager **Kevin Alamo** .... (503) 988-6100
Information Systems Manager **Michael Callaghan** .... (503) 988-3544
Communications Manager **Kathryn Sofich** .... (503) 988-4376

Adult Community Justice Administration

501 SE Hawthorne Blvd., Suite 250, Portland, OR 97214
Tel: (503) 988-3701 Fax: (503) 988-3990

Assistant Director **(Vacant)** .... (503) 988-8393
Administrative Analyst **Charlene M. Willett** .... (503) 988-6943

Juvenile Community Justice Administration

1401 NE 68th St., Portland, OR 97213
Tel: (503) 988-3460 Fax: (503) 988-3409

Assistant Director **Christina McMahon** .... (503) 988-4171
Administrative Specialist **Lisa Krzmarzick** .... (503) 988-3578

★ Elected Official ▲ Appointed by Legislature ▼ Appointed by Governor ► Appointed by Board or Commission ● Appointed by Judge
■ Appointed by Mayor △ Appointed by Freeholders ▽ Appointed by Supervisor ▷ Appointed by County Executive ○ Appointed by Council

Department of Community Services
1600 SE 190th Avenue, Portland, OR 97233
Tel: (503) 988-5000 Fax: (503) 988-3048

▶ Director **Kim Peoples** .... (503) 988-5880

Office of Emergency Management
501 Southeast Hawthorne Boulevard, 6th Floor, Portland, OR 97214-3501
Tel: (503) 988-6700 Fax: (503) 988-6095
E-mail: emergency.management@multco.us
Internet: http://web.multco.us/em

Director **Christopher "Chris" Voss** .... (503) 988-4649
E-mail: chris.voss@multco.us

Elections Division
1040 SE Morrison Street, Portland, OR 97214
Fax: (503) 988-3719

Director **Tim Scott** .... (503) 988-3720
Administrative Analyst **Cristabel Nichols** .... (503) 988-6824

Land Use Division
1600 SE 190th Avenue, Suite 116, Portland, OR 97233
Tel: (503) 988-3043 Fax: (503) 988-3389

Land Use Planning Manager
Michael Cerbone .... (503) 988-3043 ext. 29635
Administrative Analyst **Stuart Farmer** .... (503) 988-5276

Multnomah County Animal Services [MCAS]
1700 West Columbia River Highway, Troutdale, OR 97060
Fax: (503) 988-3002

Director **Jackie Rose** .... (503) 988-7387
Administrative Analyst **Gail Wilson** .... (503) 988-6274

Transportation Division
Tel: (503) 988-5050

County Engineer and Division Director **Ian Cannon** .... (503) 988-3595
E-mail: ian.b.cannon@multco.us
Bridge Engineering Services Manager **John Henrichsen** .. (503) 988-7126
1403 SE Waters Avenue, Portland, OR 97214
Bridge Design and Construction Manager (Interim)
Megan Neill .... (503) 360-6222
Bridge Maintenance Manager **Carl Morgan** .... (503) 988-3757
1403 SE Waters Avenue, Portland, OR 97214
Road Capital Improvement Manager **Riad Alharithi** .... (503) 988-0181
Transportation Planning and Development Manager
Joanna Valencia .... (503) 988-0219
Road Maintenance Manager **John Niiyama** .... (503) 988-5050
Road Operations Supervisor **Tim Burke** .... (503) 988-5050
Traffic Signals and Signs Supervisor **Greg Petesz** .... (503) 988-5171
Water Quality Program Specialist Senior **Roy Iwai** .... (503) 988-0195
County Surveyor **James S. "Jim" Clayton** .... (503) 988-5573

Department of County Assets
501 Southeast Hawthorne Boulevard, Portland, OR 97214-3501
Fax: (503) 988-3368

Director/Chief Information Officer
Sherry J. Swackhamer .... (503) 988-4183
E-mail: sherry.j.swackhamer@multco.us

Facilities and Property Management Division
401 North Dixon Street, Portland, OR 97227
Tel: (503) 988-3322 Fax: (503) 988-5082

Director **Henry Alaman** .... (503) 988-3322
E-mail: henry.alaman@multco.us

Fleet and Records Administration
1620 SE 190th Avenue, Portland, OR 97233
Tel: (503) 988-5050 Fax: (503) 988-5565

Fleet and Records Administration Manager
Garret R. Vanderzanden .... (503) 988-3424
E-mail: garret.vanderzanden@multco.us

Fleet and Records Administration *continued*

Records Officer **Jennifer Mundy** .... (503) 988-3741

Department of County Human Services
Lincoln Building, 421 SW Oak Street, Portland, OR 97204-1817
Fax: (503) 988-3379

▶ Director **Liesl Wendt** Suite 620 .... (503) 988-3691
Deputy Director **(Vacant)** .... (503) 988-3691
Domestic Violence Program Manager **Annie Neal** .... (503) 988-4113
421 SW Oak Street, Suite 230, Portland, OR 97204

Aging, Disability, and Veteran Services Division [ADS]
Lincoln Building, 421 Southwest Oak Street, Suite 510, Portland, OR 97204
Fax: (503) 988-3656 Internet: http://web.multco.us/ads

Division Director **Peggy Brey** .... (503) 988-3770
Education: Oakland U BA; Michigan MSW
Program Manager/Administrative Services **Dana Lloyd** ... (503) 988-4073

Developmental Disabilities Services Division [DDSD]
421 Southwest Oak Street, Suite 610, Portland, OR 97204
Fax: (503) 988-3648 Internet: http://web.multco.us/dd

Director **Muhammad Baber** .... (503) 988-6283

Mental Health and Addiction Services Division [MHASD]
421 Southwest Oak Street, Suite 520, Portland, OR 97204
Fax: (503) 988-5870 Internet: http://web.multco.us/mhas

Director **David A. Hidalgo** .... (503) 988-3076

Department of County Management
501 Southeast Hawthorne Boulevard, Suite 531, Portland, OR 97214-3501

Chief Operating Officer **Marissa Madrigal** .... (503) 988-2999
E-mail: marissa.d.madrigal@multco.us
Education: U Washington 1998 BS

Budget Office
501 Southeast Hawthorne Boulevard, Suite 531, Portland, OR 97214-3501
Fax: (503) 988-4570

▶ Budget Director **(Vacant)** .... (503) 988-3312
Economist **Michael D. "Mike" Jaspin** .... (503) 988-3312

Division of Assessment, Recording and Taxation [DART]
501 SE Hawthorne Boulevard, Suite 175, Portland, OR 97214
Tel: (503) 988-3326 Fax: (503) 988-3356

Director **Randy Walruff** .... (503) 988-3326

Finance and Risk Management Division
501 Southeast Hawthorne Boulevard, Suite 531, Portland, OR 97214-3501
Tel: (503) 988-3312 Fax: (503) 988-3292

Chief Financial Officer **Mark Campbell** .... (503) 988-3786
Purchasing Manager **Brian R. Smith** .... (503) 988-5111 ext. 24173
E-mail: brian.r.smith@multco.us Fax: (503) 988-3252

Human Resources Division
501 Southeast Hawthorne Boulevard, Suite 400, Portland, OR 97214-3501
Tel: (503) 988-5015 Fax: (503) 988-5670

▶ Director **Travis Graves** .... (503) 988-5135
E-mail: travis.r.graves@multco.us
Employee Health Benefits Manager **(Vacant)** .... (503) 988-5015
Training Manager **Wayne Scott** .... (503) 988-5015
E-mail: wayne.scott@multco.us

Multnomah County Health Department
426 SW Stark, 8th Floor, Portland, OR 97204
Fax: (503) 988-4117 E-mail: health.dept@multco.us
Internet: http://web.multco.us/health

▶ Director **Joanne Fuller** .... (503) 988-3674 ext. 22686
E-mail: joanne.fuller@multco.us
Education: Portland State 1996 MSW

★ Elected Official ▲ Appointed by Legislature ▼ Appointed by Governor ▶ Appointed by Board or Commission ● Appointed by Judge
■ Appointed by Mayor △ Appointed by Freeholders ▽ Appointed by Supervisor ▷ Appointed by County Executive ○ Appointed by Council

Multnomah County Health Department *continued*

Deputy Director **(Vacant)** .... (503) 988-3674 ext. 29122
Health Officer **Dr. Paul Lewis** .... (503) 988-3674
Deputy Health Officer **Jennifer Vines** .... (503) 988-3674
Education: Dartmouth BA
Senior Advisor of Public Health and Community Initiatives **Consuelo Saragoza** .... (503) 988-3674
E-mail: consuelo.c.saragoza@multco.us
Deputy Director, Business Services and Finance **Wendy R. Lear** .... (503) 988-3674 ext. 27574
Director, Community Health Services **Loreen Nichols** ... (503) 988-3674
Director, Human Resources and Workforce Development **(Vacant)** .... (503) 988-3674 ext. 26734
Director, Integrated Clinical Services **Vanetta M. Abdellatif** .... (503) 988-3674
Director, Policy and Planning **(Vacant)** .... (503) 988-3674

Multnomah County Library

Administration Building, 205 Northeast Russell Street, Portland, OR 97212
Fax: (503) 988-5441 Internet: www.multcolib.org

Director **Vailey Oehlke** .... (503) 988-5403
Education: Northern Illinois 1988; Illinois 1992 MLS
Deputy Director **Becky Cobb** .... (503) 988-5402
E-mail: beckyc@multcolib.org
Marketing and Communications Manager **Jeremy Graybill** .... (503) 988-5498
E-mail: jeremyg@multcolib.org
Director of Communications **Shawn Cunningham** ...... (503) 988-3097
E-mail: shawnc@multco.us

Office of the Auditor

501 SE Hawthorne, Room 601, Portland, OR 97214
E-mail: mult.auditor@multco.us

★ Auditor **Dr. Stephen "Steve" March** .... (503) 988-3320
Term Expires: December 31, 2016
E-mail: steve.march@multco.us
Education: Portland State 1991 MS, 1997 PhD

Office of the District Attorney

County Courthouse, 1021 SW Fourth Avenue, Room 600, Portland, OR 97204-1193
Fax: (503) 988-3643 E-mail: da@mcda.us Internet: www.mcda.us

★ District Attorney **Rodney D. "Rod" Underhill** .... (503) 988-3162
Term Expires: December 31, 2020
E-mail: rod.underhill@mcda.us
First Assistant **Jeffrey Howes** .... (503) 988-5260
Information Technology Manager **Karl Kosydar** .... (503) 988-6260
E-mail: karl.kosydar@mcda.us
Staff Services Manager **Jodi Erickson** .... (503) 988-3162
Fax: (503) 988-3643

Office of the Sheriff

501 SE Hawthorne Boulevard, Suite 350, Portland, OR 97214
Tel: (503) 988-4300 Fax: (503) 988-4316 Internet: www.mcso.us

★ Sheriff **Daniel Staton** .... (503) 988-4300
Term Expires: December 31, 2018
E-mail: sheriff@mcso.us
Chief Deputy **Timothy "Tim" Moore** .... (503) 988-0351
E-mail: timothy.moore@mcso.us
Chief Deputy, Business Services **Linda Yankee** .... (503) 988-4308
E-mail: linda.yankee@mcso.us
Chief Deputy, Corrections **Michael "Mike" Shults** ...... (503) 988-4349

County of Nassau, New York

One West Street, Mineola, NY 11501
Tel: (516) 571-3000 (Information) Internet: www.nassaucountyny.gov

County Seat: Mineola **Election Type:** Partisan **Population:** 1,361,350 (2015)

Office of the County Executive

1550 Franklin Avenue, Mineola, NY 11501
Tel: (516) 571-3131 Fax: (516) 571-4000

★ County Executive **Edward P. "Ed" Mangano** (R) .... (516) 571-3131
Term Expires: December 31, 2017
E-mail: emangano@nassaucountyny.gov
Date of Birth: March 24, 1962
Education: Hinds Com Col 1984 BA; Hofstra 1987 JD
Chief Deputy County Executive **Rob Walker** .... (516) 571-3140
Deputy County Executive, Economic Development (Acting) **Joseph J. Kearney** (R) .... (516) 571-3131
Education: St John's U (NY) 1975 JD
Deputy County Executive, Finance **Eric C. Naughton** .... (516) 571-3978
E-mail: enaughton@nassaucountyny.gov
Deputy County Executive, Health and Human Services **Lisa A. Murphy** .... (516) 571-6174
Deputy County Executive, Minority Affairs **Dr. Phillip E. Elliott** .... (516) 571-6174
Deputy County Executive, Public Safety **Chuck Ribando** .... (516) 571-4071
Deputy County Executive, Parks and Public Works **Brian Nugent** .... (516) 571-6027
Senior Policy Advisor and Communications Director **Brian Nevin** .... (516) 571-6105
E-mail: bnevin@nassaucountyny.gov
Constituent Affairs Director **Kim Collins** .... (516) 571-6000
E-mail: kcollins@nassaucountyny.gov
Counsel to the County Executive **Liz Loconsolo** .... (516) 571-1938
Executive Director, Coordinating Agency for Spanish Americans **Eldia Gonzalez** .... (516) 572-0750
E-mail: egonzalez@nassaucountyny.gov

Office of Consumer Affairs

200 County Seat Drive, Mineola, NY 11501-4807

▷ Commissioner (Acting) **Madalyn F. Farley** .... (516) 571-2600
E-mail: mfarley@nassaucountyny.gov

Office of the County Attorney

One West St., Mineola, NY 11501
Tel: (516) 571-3056 Fax: (516) 571-6604 Fax: (516) 571-6684

▷ County Attorney **Carnell T. Foskey** .... (516) 571-3056
Chief Deputy County Attorney **Lisa LoCurto** .... (516) 571-3056
E-mail: llocurto@nassaucountyny.gov

Office of the County Treasurer

1 West Street, Mineola, NY 11501
Tel: (516) 571-2090 Fax: (516) 571-1528
E-mail: nctreasurer@nassaucountyny.gov

Treasurer **Beaumont Jefferson** .... (516) 571-2090

Office of Emergency Management [OEM]

100 Carmen Avenue, East Meadow, NY 11554
Tel: (516) 573-0636 Fax: (516) 573-0673
E-mail: NCOEM@nassaucountyny.gov

▷ Commissioner **Craig J. Craft** .... (516) 573-0636
▷ First Deputy Commissioner **(Vacant)** .... (516) 573-0636

COUNTIES

★ Elected Official ▲ Appointed by Legislature ▼ Appointed by Governor ▶ Appointed by Board or Commission ● Appointed by Judge
■ Appointed by Mayor △ Appointed by Freeholders ▽ Appointed by Supervisor ▷ Appointed by County Executive ○ Appointed by Council

Office of Fire Marshal

1194 Prospect Avenue, Westbury, NY 11590-2723
Fax: (516) 573-9910

Chief Fire Marshal **Scott D. Tusa** .... (516) 573-9991

Housing Assistance

40 Main Street, First Floor, Hempstead, NY 11550
Tel: (516) 572-1900 Fax: (516) 572-2789

Executive Director **John Sarcone** .... (516) 572-1922
E-mail: jsarcone@nassaucountyny.gov

Office of Human Resources

One West Street, Room 127, Mineola, NY 11501
Fax: (516) 571-4384

Human Resources Director **Melissa Gallucci** .... (516) 571-3072
Administrative Aide **Andrea Plavnicky** .... (516) 571-3072

Office of Management and Budget [OMB]

One West St., Mineola, NY 11501
Fax: (516) 571-6164

▷ Director **Roseann D'Alleva** .... (516) 571-3122
Deputy Director **Robert Conroy** .... (516) 571-4273
E-mail: rconroy@nassaucountyny.gov
Deputy Director **Ann Hulka** .... (516) 571-4273
E-mail: ahulka@nassaucountyny.gov

Office of the Medical Examiner

Building R, 2251 Hempstead Turnpike, East Meadow, NY 11554-1856
Fax: (516) 572-5675

Chief Medical Examiner **Tamara Bloom** .... (516) 572-6400
Fax: (516) 572-5099

Office of Purchasing

1 West Street, Mineola, NY 11501
Fax: (516) 571-4263 Fax: (516) 571-6197

▷ Director **Michael Schlenoff** .... (516) 571-4060
E-mail: mschlenoff@nassaucountyny.gov

Office of the Public Administrator

240 Old Country Road, Mineola, NY 11501
Tel: (516) 571-5911 Fax: (516) 571-2924

Public Administrator **Jeffrey E. DeLuca** .... (516) 571-5911
E-mail: jdeluca2@nassaucountyny.gov
Deputy Public Administrator **Domenica Leone** .... (516) 571-5911

Office of the Sheriff

240 Old Country Road, Mineola, NY 11501
Fax: (516) 571-5086

▷ Sheriff **Michael J. Sposato** .... (516) 571-2113
E-mail: msposato@nassaucountyny.gov

Assessment Department

240 Old Country Road, Mineola, NY 11501
Fax: (516) 571-3549 E-mail: ncassessor@nassaucountyny.gov
Internet: www.nassaucountyny.gov/agencies/assessor

▷ County Assessor (Acting) **Jim Davis** .... (516) 571-1500

Office of Mental Health, Chemical Dependency and Developmental Disabilities Services

60 Charles Lindbergh Boulevard, 2nd Floor, Uniondale, NY 11553
Fax: (516) 227-7076

▷ Director **James R. Dolan, Jr.** .... (516) 227-7057
E-mail: james.dolanjr@hhsnassaucountyny.us

Department of Parks, Recreation and Museums

Administration Building, Eisenhower Park, East Meadow, NY 11554
Fax: (516) 572-0221 Internet: www.nassaucountyny.gov/parks

Commissioner **Brian Nugent** .... (516) 572-0272

Nassau County Police Department

1490 Franklin Ave., Mineola, NY 11501
Fax: (516) 573-7117 Internet: www.police.co.nassau.ny.us

▷ Commissioner (Acting) **Thomas C. Krumpter** .... (516) 573-7100
E-mail: tkrumpter@pdcn.org
Assistant **Joy C. Travaglia** .... (516) 573-7100
First Deputy Commissioner **Thomas C. Krumpter** .... (516) 573-7100
▷ Assistant Commissioner **Robert Hart** .... (516) 573-7100

Probation Department

101 County Seat Drive, Third Floor, Mineola, NY 11501-4823
Tel: (516) 571-5700 Tel: (516) 571-5491 (Fees Unit Tel)
Fax: (516) 571-5611

▷ Director **John D. Fowle** .... (516) 571-4676
▷ Assistant Probation Director **Stephen Goldberg** .... (516) 571-4673

Department of Public Works [DPW]

1194 Prospect Avenue, Westbury, NY 11590-2723
Fax: (516) 571-9657

▷ Commissioner **Shila Shah-Gavnoudias** .... (516) 571-9604
E-mail: sshahgavnoudias@nassaucountyny.gov
▷ Chief Deputy Commissioner **Richard Millet** .... (516) 571-9608
E-mail: rmillet@nassaucountyny.gov
Deputy Commissioner **William Nimmo** .... (516) 571-6810
E-mail: wnimmo@nassaucountyny.gov
▷ Deputy Commissioner for Engineering **Rakhal Maitra** .... (516) 571-9611
E-mail: rmaitra@nassaucountyny.gov

Nassau County Traffic Safety Board

1194 Prospect Avenue, Westbury, NY 11590-2723
Tel: (516) 571-6808 Fax: (516) 571-6874

Director **Christopher M. Mistron** .... (516) 571-6808
E-mail: cmistron@nassaucountyny.gov
Assistant Director **(Vacant)** .... (516) 571-7020
Traffic Safety Educator **Christopher M. Mistron** .... (516) 571-6808
E-mail: cmistron@nassaucountyny.gov

Department of Human Services [Area Agency on Aging]

60 Charles Lindbergh Boulevard, Suite 260, Uniondale, NY 11553-3691
Tel: (516) 227-8900 Fax: (516) 227-8972
E-mail: seniors@hhsnassaucountyny.us
Internet: www.nassaucountyny.gov/seniors

▷ Commissioner **Lisa A. Murphy** .... (516) 227-8900
E-mail: lisa.murphy@hhsnassaucountyny.us

Department of Social Services [DSS]

60 Charles Lindbergh Boulevard, Suite 160, Uniondale, NY 11553-3686
Fax: (516) 227-8432
Internet: www.nassaucountyny.gov/agencies/dss/dsshome.htm

Commissioner **John E. Imhof** .... (516) 227-7403
Education: Union Inst PhD
Deputy Commissioner of Social Services
Paul F. Broderick .... (516) 227-7412
AIDS Services Coordinator **Vivian Smalls** .... (516) 227-8488
Counsel **Rudolph Carmenaty** .... (516) 227-8576
Media Liaison **Karen Garber** .... (516) 227-7770

Nassau County Board of Health

200 County Seat Drive, Mineola, NY 11501-4807

Chair **Ellen J. Braunstein** .... (516) 227-9500

★ Elected Official ▲ Appointed by Legislature ▼ Appointed by Governor ► Appointed by Board or Commission ● Appointed by Judge
■ Appointed by Mayor △ Appointed by Freeholders ▽ Appointed by Supervisor ▷ Appointed by County Executive ○ Appointed by Council

Nassau County Department of Health
200 County Seat Drive, Mineola, NY 11501-4807
Fax: (516) 227-9696 Internet: www.nassaucountyny.gov/agencies/health

Commissioner **Dr. Lawrence E. Eisenstein** .... (516) 227-9500

Nassau County Youth Board
60 Charles Lindbergh Boulevard, Suite 220, Uniondale, NY 11553-3688
Tel: (516) 227-7134 Fax: (516) 227-7107

▷ Executive Director
Margaret "Maggie" Martinez-Malito .... (516) 227-7115
E-mail: maggie.malito@hhsnassaucountyny.us
Contract Management Director **Doris Hawthorne** .... (516) 227-7125
Development, Training and Legislative Advocacy
Director **Angela Zimmerman** .... (516) 227-7143
E-mail: angela.zimmerman@hhsnassaucountyny.us
Fiscal Management Director **Patricia Fowler** .... (516) 227-7124

Nassau County Assessment Review Commission [ARC]
240 Old Country Road, Mineola, NY 11501
Fax: (516) 571-1692

Chairperson **Robin Laveman** .... (516) 571-3214

Nassau County Civil Service Commission
40 Main Street, Hempstead, NY 11550
Fax: (516) 572-1863 Internet: www.nassaucivilservice.com

Executive Director **Karl Kampe** .... (516) 572-2697
E-mail: kkampe@nassaucountyny.gov

Nassau County Commission on Human Rights
240 Old Country Road, Room 606, Mineola, NY 11501
Tel: (516) 571-3662 Fax: (516) 571-1422

Executive Director **Rodney McRae** .... (516) 571-3662

Nassau County Planning Commission
100 County Seat Drive, Mineola, NY 11501-4841
Fax: (516) 571-3839

Chairman **Jeffrey H. Greenfield** .... (516) 571-9344
Deputy Commissioner of Planning **Satish Sood** .... (516) 571-9344

Nassau County Industrial Development Agency [NCIDA]
1550 Franklin Avenue, Suite 235, Mineola, NY 11501
Tel: (516) 571-1945 Fax: (516) 571-1076 Internet: www.nassauida.org

Executive Director **Joseph J. Kearney** (R) .... (516) 571-1945
E-mail: jkearney@nassauida.org
Education: St John's U (NY) 1975 JD

Nassau County Veterans Service Agency
Building Q, 2201 Hempstead Turnpike, East Meadow, NY 11554
Tel: (516) 572-6560 Internet: www.nassaucountyny.gov/veterans

▷ Director **Scott Castillo** .... (516) 572-6560

Nassau County Legislature
1550 Franklin Avenue, Mineola, NY 11501
Fax: (516) 571-4217

★ Presiding Officer **Norma L. Gonsalves** (R-District 13) ... (516) 571-6213
Term Expires: December 31, 2017 Fax: (516) 571-6746
E-mail: ngonsalves@nassaucountyny.gov
Education: St Joseph's Col (NY) BA; Hunter MA
★ Minority Leader **Kevan Abrahams** (D-District 1) .... (516) 571-6201
Term Expires: December 31, 2017 Fax: (516) 571-6187
E-mail: kabrahams@nassaucountyny.gov
Education: Queens Col (NY) BS

Nassau County Legislature *continued*

★ Legislator **Siela Bynoe** (D-District 2) .... (516) 571-6202
Term Expires: December 31, 2017 Fax: (516) 571-6761
E-mail: sbynoe@nassaucountyny.gov
★ Legislator **Carrie Solages** (D-District 3) .... (516) 571-6203
Term Expires: December 31, 2017 Fax: (516) 571-6732
E-mail: csolages@nassaucountyny.gov
★ Legislator **Denise A. Ford** (R-District 4) .... (516) 571-6204
Term Expires: December 31, 2017 Fax: (516) 571-6264
E-mail: dford@nassaucountyny.gov
★ Legislator **Laura Curran** (D-District 5) .... (516) 571-6205
Term Expires: December 31, 2017 Fax: (516) 571-0291
E-mail: lcurran@nassaucountyny.gov
★ Legislator **C. William Gaylor III** (R-District 6) .... (516) 571-6206
Term Expires: December 31, 2017
★ Legislator **Howard J. Kopel** (R-District 7) .... (516) 571-6207
Term Expires: December 31, 2017 Fax: (516) 571-4123
E-mail: hkopel@nassaucountyny.gov
★ Legislator **Vincent T. Muscarella** (R-District 8) .... (516) 571-6208
Term Expires: December 31, 2017 Fax: (516) 571-6268
E-mail: vmuscarella@nassaucountyny.gov
Education: St John's U (NY) 1979 JD
★ Legislator **Richard Nicolello** (R-District 9) .... (516) 571-6209
Term Expires: December 31, 2017 Fax: (516) 571-6166
E-mail: rnicolello@nassaucountyny.gov
Education: St John's U (NY) BA; Fordham JD
★ Legislator **Ellen W. Birnbaum** (D-District 10) .... (516) 571-6210
Term Expires: December 31, 2017 Fax: (516) 571-0405
E-mail: ebirnbaum@nassaucountyny.gov
★ Legislator **Delia DeRiggi-Whitton** (D-District 11) .... (516) 571-6211
Term Expires: December 31, 2017 Fax: (516) 571-6271
E-mail: dderiggiwhitton@nassaucountyny.gov
★ Legislator **James Kennedy** (R-District 12) .... (516) 571-6212
Term Expires: December 31, 2017 Fax: (516) 571-6734
★ Legislator **Laura M. Schaefer** (R-District 14) .... (516) 571-6214
Term Expires: December 31, 2017 Fax: (516) 571-6134
E-mail: lschaefer@nassaucountyny.gov
★ Legislator **Dennis Dunne, Sr.** (R-District 15) .... (516) 571-6215
Term Expires: December 31, 2017 Fax: (516) 571-0641
E-mail: ddunne@nassaucountyny.gov
Education: Hofstra 1979 BA
★ Legislator **Judith Jacobs** (D-District 16) .... (516) 571-6216
Term Expires: December 31, 2017 Fax: (516) 571-6287
E-mail: jjacobs@nassaucountyny.gov
★ Legislator **Rose Marie Walker** (R-District 17) .... (516) 571-6217
Term Expires: December 31, 2017 Fax: (516) 571-6277
E-mail: rwalker@nassaucountyny.gov
★ Legislator **Donald W. Mackenzie** (R-District 18) .... (516) 571-6218
Term Expires: December 31, 2017 Fax: (516) 571-6158
E-mail: dmackenzie@nassaucountyny.gov
★ Legislator **Steven Rhoads** (R-District 19) .... (516) 571-6219
Term Expires: December 31, 2017 Fax: (516) 571-3907
Clerk of the Legislature **William J. Muller III** .... (516) 571-4252
E-mail: wmuller@nassaucountyny.gov Fax: (516) 571-4217

Office of the County Clerk
240 Old Country Road, Mineola, NY 11501
Fax: (516) 742-4099

★ County Clerk **Maureen O'Connell** (R) .... (516) 571-2660
Term Expires: December 31, 2017
E-mail: moconnell@nassaucountyny.gov
Chief Deputy County Clerk **Barbara Brudie** .... (516) 571-2660
E-mail: bbrudie@nassaucountyny.gov
Deputy County Clerk **Eileen O'Donnell** .... (516) 571-2660
E-mail: eodonnell@nassaucountyny.gov

★ Elected Official ▲ Appointed by Legislature ▼ Appointed by Governor ▶ Appointed by Board or Commission ● Appointed by Judge
■ Appointed by Mayor △ Appointed by Freeholders ▽ Appointed by Supervisor ▷ Appointed by County Executive ○ Appointed by Council

Office of the County Comptroller

240 Old Country Road, Mineola, NY 11501-4247
Tel: (516) 571-2386 Fax: (516) 571-5900
E-mail: nccomptroller@nassaucountyny.gov

★Comptroller **George Maragos** (R) .... (516) 571-2386
Term Expires: December 31, 2017
E-mail: nccomptroller@nassaucountyny.gov
Counsel to the Comptroller **Sergio Blanco** .... (516) 571-2677
Chief Deputy Comptroller **James A. Garner** (R) .... (516) 571-2250
Deputy Comptroller for Audits and Special Projects
Raymond Averna .... (516) 571-1129
Director of Accounting **Lisa Tsikouras** .... (516) 571-2852
Director of Communications **Jostyn Hernandez** .... (516) 571-2383

Office of the District Attorney

262 Old Country Rd., Mineola, NY 11501
Fax: (516) 571-5065 Internet: www.nassauda.org

★District Attorney **Madeline Singas** .... (516) 571-3800
Term Expires: December 2019
E-mail: madeline.singas@nassauda.org
Education: Barnard; Fordham JD
Chief Assistant District Attorney **Albert Teichman** ...... (516) 571-3800
Education: John Marshall JD

Nassau County Board of Elections

240 Old Country Road, Mineola, NY 11501
Tel: (516) 571-8683 Fax: (516) 571-2058
Internet: www.nassaucountyny.gov/agencies/boe/index.html

Democratic Commissioner **David Gugerty** .... (516) 571-2413
Republican Commissioner **Louis G. Savinetti** (R) .... (516) 571-2300

County of New Castle, Delaware

New Castle County Building, 87 Reads Way, New Castle, DE 19720
Tel: (302) 395-5555 Internet: www.nccde.org

County Seat: Wilmington **Election Type:** Partisan **Population:** 556,779 (2015)

Office of the County Executive

87 Reads Way, New Castle, DE 19720
Tel: (302) 395-5101 Fax: (302) 395-5268
Internet: www2.nccde.org/executive

★County Executive **Tom Gordon** (D) .... (302) 395-5101
Term Expires: January 2017
Assistant to the County Executive **Angela Harris** ...... (302) 395-5118
▷Chief of Staff **James McDonald** .... (302) 395-5101
E-mail: jdmcdonald@nccde.org
▷Director of Communications **Antonio M. Prado** .... (302) 595-5129
E-mail: amprado@nccde.org

Office of the Chief Administrative Officer

New Castle County Government Center, 87 Reads Way,
New Castle, DE 19720
Fax: (302) 395-5268

▷Chief Administrative Officer **Timothy P. Mullaney** ...... (302) 395-5104
E-mail: TPMullaney@nccde.org
Deputy Chief Administrative Officer **Samuel L. Guy** .... (302) 395-5124
E-mail: slguy@nccde.org
Executive Assistant **Jillian Thomas** .... (302) 395-5103
E-mail: jmthomas@nccde.org

Office of Economic Development

87 Reads Way, New Castle, DE 19720
Tel: (302) 395-5959 Fax: (302) 395-5268
Internet: www2.nccde.org/redevelopment

▷Policy Director **Marcus Henry** .... (302) 395-5959
E-mail: mhenry@nccde.org
Education: Howard U 1996 BA; Delaware 2001 MPA

Office of Finance

New Castle County Government Center, 87 Reads Way,
New Castle, DE 19720
Tel: (302) 323-2600 Fax: (302) 395-5155
Internet: www2.nccde.org/finance

▷Financial Officer **Michael L. Coupe** .... (302) 395-8041
E-mail: mcoupe@nccde.org

Office of Human Resources

New Castle County Government Center, 87 Reads Way,
New Castle, DE 19720
Tel: (302) 395-5180 Fax: (302) 395-5190 Internet: www2.nccde.org/hr

▷Chief Human Resources Officer **Christine Dunning** ..... (302) 395-5184
E-mail: crdunning@nccde.org

Department of Administrative Services

New Castle County Government Center, 87 Reads Way,
New Castle, DE 19720
Fax: (302) 395-5252

▷Chief of Administrative Services **Tonney Gardner** .... (302) 395-5260
E-mail: tagardner@nccde.org

Department of Community Services

New Castle County Government Center, 87 Reads Way,
New Castle, DE 19720
Fax: (302) 395-5591

▷General Manager **Sophia Hanson** .... (302) 395-5605
E-mail: shanson@nccde.org

Department of Land Use

New Castle County Government Center, 87 Reads Way,
New Castle, DE 19720
Tel: (302) 395-5555 Fax: (302) 395-5443 E-mail: landuse@nccde.org
Internet: www.nccdelu.org

▷General Manager (Acting) **George O. Haggerty, Jr.** ..... (302) 395-5463

Department of Law

New Castle County Government Center, 87 Reads Way,
New Castle, DE 19720
Tel: (302) 395-5130 Fax: (302) 395-5150

County Attorney **Bernard Pepukayi** .... (302) 395-5146
▷County Solicitor **Darryl Parson** .... (302) 395-5132
E-mail: daparson@nccde.org

Department of Special Services

William J. Conner Building, 187A Old Churchmans Road,
New Castle, DE 19720
Tel: (302) 395-5700 Fax: (302) 395-5870
Internet: www2.nccde.org/specialservices

▷General Manager (Acting) **Wayne Merritt** .... (302) 395-5791

New Castle County Police

Public Safety Building, 3601 North DuPont Highway,
New Castle, DE 19720
Tel: (302) 573-2800 Fax: (302) 395-8039
Internet: www2.nccde.org/police

▷Chief of Police **Elmer Setting** .... (302) 395-8010

★Elected Official ▲Appointed by Legislature ▼Appointed by Governor ▶Appointed by Board or Commission ●Appointed by Judge
■Appointed by Mayor △Appointed by Freeholders ▽Appointed by Supervisor ▷Appointed by County Executive ○Appointed by Council

Office of the County Council

Louis L. Redding City County Building, 800 North French Street, 8th Floor, Wilmington, DE 19801
Fax: (302) 395-8385 Internet: www.nccde.org/countycouncil

★President **Christopher Bullock** (D) .... (302) 395-8340
Term Expires: November 6, 2016
★Council Member **(Vacant)** (District 1) .... (302) 395-8341
Note: A special election to fill this vacancy will be held on May 24, 2016.
Term Expires: November 12, 2018
★Council Member **Robert S. Weiner** (R-District 2) .... (302) 395-8342
Term Expires: November 12, 2018
Education: Delaware BA; Temple JD
★Council Member **Janet Kilpatrick** (R-District 3) .... (302) 395-8343
Term Expires: November 12, 2018
★Council Member **Penrose Hollins** (D-District 4) .... (302) 395-8344
Term Expires: November 12, 2018
★Council Member **Lisa Diller** (D-District 5) .... (302) 395-8345
Term Expires: November 12, 2018
★Council Member **William E. Powers, Jr.** (D-District 6) ... (302) 395-8346
Term Expires: November 12, 2018
★Council Member **George Smiley** (D-District 7) .... (302) 395-8347
Term Expires: November 6, 2016
★Council Member **John J. Cartier** (D-District 8) .... (302) 395-8348
Term Expires: November 6, 2016
★Council Member **Timothy P. Sheldon** (D-District 9) ..... (302) 395-8349
Term Expires: November 6, 2016
★Council Member **Jea P. Street** (D-District 10) .... (302) 395-8350
Term Expires: November 6, 2016
★Council Member **David L. Tackett** (D-District 11) .... (302) 395-8351
Term Expires: November 6, 2016
★Council Member **William "Bill" Bell** (D-District 12) ..... (302) 395-8352
Term Expires: November 6, 2016
○Clerk of Council **Betsy J. Gardner** .... (302) 395-8388
Deputy Clerk **Holly M. Shinn** .... (302) 395-8390
○Counsel to the Council **Carol J. Dulin** .... (302) 395-8389
Education: South Carolina BA; Widener JD

Office of the County Auditor

Tel: (302) 395-5279
County Auditor **Robert B. Wasserbach** .... (302) 395-5279

Office of the Clerk of the Peace

Louis L. Redding City County Bldg., 800 N. French St., Wilmington, DE 19801

★Clerk of the Peace **Kenneth W. Boulden, Jr.** (D) .... (302) 395-7782
Term Expires: December 31, 2016

Office of the Recorder of Deeds

Louis L. Redding City County Building, 800 North French Street, 4th Floor, Wilmington, DE 19801
Fax: (302) 395-7732

★Recorder of Deeds **Michael Kozikowski** (D) .... (302) 395-7700
Term Expires: December 31, 2018

Office of the Register of Wills

Louis L. Redding City County Building, 800 North French Street, 2nd Floor, Wilmington, DE 19801-3341
Fax: (302) 395-7801

Register of Wills **Ciro Poppiti III** (D) .... (302) 395-7800
Term Expires: December 31, 2018

Office of the Sheriff

Louis L. Redding City County Building, 800 North French Street, 5th Floor, Wilmington, DE 19801
Fax: (302) 395-8460

★Sheriff **Trinidad Navarro** .... (302) 395-8450
Term Expires: December 31, 2018

County of Niagara, New York

Courthouse, 175 Hawley Street, Lockport, NY 14094-2740
Internet: www.niagaracounty.com

County Seat: Lockport **Election Type:** Partisan **Population:** 212,652 (2015)

Office of the County Legislature

Courthouse, 175 Hawley Street, Lockport, NY 14094-2740
Fax: (716) 439-7124 Internet: www.niagaracounty.com/legislature.asp

★Chairman **William Keith McNall** (R-District 13) .... (716) 439-7000
Term Expires: December 31, 2017
★Vice Chairman **Clyde L. Burmaster** (R-District 1) .... (716) 439-7000
Term Expires: December 31, 2017
E-mail: clyde.burmaster@niagaracounty.com
★Majority Leader **Randy R. Brandt** (R-District 9) .... (716) 439-7000
Term Expires: December 31, 2017
★Minority Leader **Dennis F. Virtuoso** (D-District 6) ...... (716) 439-7000
Term Expires: December 31, 2017
E-mail: dennis.virtuoso@niagaracounty.com
★Legislator **Rebecca Wydysh** (R-District 2) .... (716) 439-7000
Term Expires: December 31, 2017
★Legislator **Mark J. Grozio** (D-District 3) .... (716) 439-7000
Term Expires: December 31, 2017
★Legislator **Owen T. Steed** (D-District 4) .... (716) 439-7000
Term Expires: December 31, 2017
★Legislator **Jason A. Zona** (D-District 5) .... (716) 439-7000
Term Expires: December 31, 2017
★Legislator **Kathryn Palka-Lance** (R-District 7) .... (716) 439-7000
Term Expires: December 31, 2017
★Legislator **Richard L. Andres, Jr.** (R-District 8) .... (716) 439-7000
Term Expires: December 31, 2017
★Legislator **David E. Godfrey** (R-District 10) .... (716) 439-7000
Term Expires: December 31, 2017
★Legislator **Anthony J. "Tony" Nemi** (R-District 11) ..... (716) 439-7000
Term Expires: December 31, 2017
★Legislator **William J. Collins, Sr.** (R-District 12) .... (716) 439-7000
Term Expires: December 31, 2017
★Legislator **John Syracuse** (R-District 14) .... (716) 439-7000
Term Expires: December 31, 2017
E-mail: john.syracuse@niagaracounty.com
★Legislator **Michael A. Hill** (R-District 15) .... (716) 439-7000
Term Expires: December 31, 2017
Clerk of the Legislature **Mary Jo Tamburlin** .... (716) 439-7177
E-mail: maryjo.tamburlin@niagaracounty.com

Office of the County Manager

Philo J. Brooks County Office Building, 59 Park Avenue, 1st Floor, Lockport, NY 14094
Fax: (716) 439-7212 Internet: www.niagaracounty.com/countymanager.asp

County Manager **Richard E. Updegrove** (R) .... (716) 439-7006

Office for the Aging [OFA]

111 Main Street, Suite 101, Lockport, NY 14094-3718
Tel: (716) 438-4020 Fax: (716) 438-4029
E-mail: ofa@niagaracounty.com Internet: www.niagaracounty.com/aging

Director **Kenneth M. "Ken" Genewick** .... (716) 438-4021
New York Connects Coordinator **(Vacant)** .... (716) 438-4023

COUNTIES

★Elected Official ▲Appointed by Legislature ▼Appointed by Governor ▶Appointed by Board or Commission ●Appointed by Judge
■Appointed by Mayor △Appointed by Freeholders ▽Appointed by Supervisor ▷Appointed by County Executive ○Appointed by Council

COUNTIES

Office of Management and Budget
59 Park Avenue, Lockport, NY 14094-2740
Tel: (716) 439-7004 Fax: (716) 439-7205

Director **Daniel Huntington** .... (716) 439-7036
E-mail: daniel.huntington@niagaracounty.com

Information Technology
59 Park Avenue, Room 249, Lockport, NY 14094-2740
Fax: (716) 439-7068

▲Director **Larry L. Helwig** .... (716) 439-7048
E-mail: larry.helwig@niagaracounty.com
Education: SUNY (Brockport) BS; SUNY (Buffalo) MS

Economic Development Department
Vantage Center, 6311- Inducon Corporate Drive, Suite 1,
Sanborn, NY 14132-9099
Tel: (716) 278-8750
Tel: (716) 278-8230 (Niagara County Business Assistance Hotline)
Fax: (716) 278-8757 Internet: www.nccedev.com

▲Commissioner **Samuel M. "Sam" Ferraro** .... (716) 278-8750
E-mail: sam.ferraro@niagaracounty.com
▲Deputy Commissioner of Business Development
Michael A. Casale .... (716) 278-8752
E-mail: michael.casale@niagaracounty.com
Senior Planner **Benjamin Bidell** .... (716) 278-8756
E-mail: benjamin.bidell@niagaracounty.com
Senior Planner **Amy E. Fisk** .... (716) 278-8754
E-mail: amy.fisk@niagaracounty.com

Niagara County Industrial Development Agency [NCIDA]
6311 Inducon Corporate Drive, Suite 1, Sanborn, NY 14132-9099
Tel: (716) 278-8230 (Niagara County Business Assistance Hotlline)
Fax: (716) 278-8769 Internet: www.nccedev.com

Executive Director **Samuel M. "Sam" Ferraro** .... (716) 278-8750
E-mail: sam.ferraro@niagaracounty.com
Director of Project Development **Susan Langdon** .... (716) 278-8764
E-mail: susan.langdon@niagaracounty.com
Chair, Board of Directors **(Vacant)** .... (716) 278-8760

Employment and Training Department
Trott Access Center, 1001 11th Street, 2nd Floor, Suite G,
Niagara Falls, NY 14301
Fax: (716) 278-8149

▲Director **Thomas M. "Tom" Jaccarino** .... (716) 278-8148
E-mail: thomas.jaccarino@niagaracounty.com

Fire and Emergency Services
5574 Niagara St. Extension, Lockport, NY 14094
P.O. Box 496, Lockport, NY 14095-0496
Fax: (716) 438-3173 Internet: www.niagaracounty.com/fire

▲Director of Emergency Services and Fire Coordinator
Jonathan Schultz .... (716) 438-3171
E-mail: jonathan.schultz@niagaracounty.com

Human Resources Department
111 Main Street, Suite G-2, Lockport, NY 14094
Tel: (716) 438-4070 Fax: (716) 438-4077

▲Director **Peter P. Lopes** .... (716) 438-4068
E-mail: peter.lopes@niagaracounty.com

Parks Department
59 Park Avenue, Lockport, NY 14094
Tel: (716) 439-7951 Fax: (716) 439-7955
Internet: www.niagaracounty.com/parks

Commissioner **(Vacant)** .... (716) 439-7951
General Foreman **Frank Rotella** .... (716) 439-7956
Senior Account Clerk **Lee Ann Cogar** .... (716) 439-7951

Probation Department
111 Main Street, Suite 201, Lockport, NY 14094

Director **John Cicchetti** .... (716) 438-4055
Lockport Supervisor (Adult) **William E. Collins** .... (716) 438-4055
Niagara Falls Supervisor (Adult) **Jeffrey Sheehan** .... (716) 278-8122
Niagara Falls Supervisor (Juvenile) **Deborah LaRock** .... (716) 278-8122
North Tonawanda Supervisor (Adult/Juvenile)
Deborah LaRock .... (716) 743-4526

Public Works Department
Philo J. Brooks Building, 59 Park Avenue, Lockport, NY 14094
Tel: (716) 439-7242 Fax: (716) 439-7245

Commissioner **Kevin P. O'Brien** .... (716) 439-7242
Building and Grounds Division Deputy Commissioner
Jeffrey Gaston .... (716) 439-7242
Engineering Deputy Commissioner **Richard W. Eakin** .... (716) 439-7250
E-mail: richard.eakin@niagaracounty.com Fax: (716) 439-7245

Highway Department
225 South Niagara Street, Lockport, NY 14094
Tel: (716) 439-7367 (Fleet Maintenance) Fax: (716) 439-7379

Deputy Commissioner **Michael F. Tracy** .... (716) 439-7360

Purchasing Department
59 Park Avenue, 1st Floor, Lockport, NY 14094
Tel: (716) 439-7200 Fax: (716) 439-7205
E-mail: purchasing@niagaracounty.com

Purchasing Agent **Maureen Watz** .... (716) 439-7203
E-mail: purchasing@niagaracounty.com

Real Property Tax Services
Philo J. Brooks Niagara County Office Buildings, 59 Park Ave.,
Lockport, NY 14094
Fax: (716) 439-7067 Internet: www.niagaracounty.com/realproperty

Director **John E. Shoemaker** .... (716) 439-7077
E-mail: john.shoemaker@niagaracounty.com

Risk and Insurance Services
111 Main Street, Suite 102, Lockport, NY 14094-2740
Tel: (716) 438-4080 Fax: (716) 438-4083

▲Director **Jennifer Pitarresi** .... (716) 438-3068
E-mail: jennifer.pitarresi@niagaracounty.com

Social Services Department
20 East Avenue, Lockport, NY 14905
Tel: (716) 439-7600 Fax: (716) 439-7609

▲Commissioner **Anthony J. Restaino** .... (716) 278-8630
E-mail: Anthony.Restaino@niagaracounty.com
▲Deputy Commissioner **Sharon M. Sloma** .... (716) 439-7604
E-mail: sharon.sloma-haberman@niagaracounty.com

Department of Weights and Measures
225 South Niagara Street, Lockport, NY 14094
Fax: (716) 439-7377

Director **Dean E. Lapp II** .... (716) 439-7371

Niagara County Youth Bureau
301 10th Street, Niagara Falls, NY 14302
Fax: (716) 278-6875

▲Director **Meghan Lutz** .... (716) 278-6872
E-mail: meghan.lutz@niagaracounty.com

Niagara County Department of Health
5467 Upper Mountain Road, Suite 100, Lockport, NY 14094-1894
Fax: (716) 439-7402 Internet: www.niagaracounty.com/health

Director **Daniel J. Stapleton** .... (716) 439-7435

★ Elected Official ▲ Appointed by Legislature ▼ Appointed by Governor ▶ Appointed by Board or Commission ● Appointed by Judge
■ Appointed by Mayor △ Appointed by Freeholders ▽ Appointed by Supervisor ▷ Appointed by County Executive ○ Appointed by Council

Niagara County Department of Health *continued*

Deputy Director/Director of Financial Operations
Victoria Pearson . . . . . (716) 439-7432
Director of Environmental Health **James J. Devald** . . . . . (716) 439-7453
Director of Patient Services **Kathleen Cavagnaro** . . . . . (716) 278-1933
Director, Children with Special Needs **Lisa Chester** . . . . . (716) 278-1991
Trott Center, Niagara Falls, NY 14303
Clinical Director, Children with Special Needs
Stacy Lampman . . . . . (716) 439-7463
Public Health Planning and Information Officer
Elaine Roman . . . . . (716) 439-7436
Fiscal Administrator **Jeffrey Beach** . . . . . (716) 439-7434

Civil Service Office

Golden Triangle Building, 111 Main Street, Suite G2,
Lockport, NY 14094-2740
Tel: (716) 438-4071 Fax: (716) 438-4077
E-mail: CivilService@niagaracounty.com

▲Personnel Officer **Malcolm A. Needler** (R) . . . . . (716) 438-4075
E-mail: malcolm.Needler@niagaracounty.com

Cornell Cooperative Extension Niagara County

4487 Lake Avenue, Lockport, NY 14094
Tel: (716) 433-8839 Fax: (716) 438-0275 E-mail: niagara@cornell.edu
Internet: www.cceniagaracounty.org

Executive Director **Cathy Lovejoy Maloney** . . . . (716) 433-8839 ext. 234

Office of the County Attorney

Courthouse, 175 Hawley Street, Lockport, NY 14094-2740
Fax: (716) 439-7114

▲County Attorney **Claude A. Joerg** . . . . . (716) 439-7105
E-mail: claude.joerg@niagaracounty.com
Education: Capital U 1976 BS; SUNY (Buffalo) 1979 JD

Office of the County Auditor

59 Park Ave., Lockport, NY 14094-2740
Fax: (716) 439-7205

▲Auditor **James B. "Jim" Sobczyk** . . . . . (716) 439-7336
E-mail: james.sobczyk@niagaracounty.com

Office of the Public Defender

Courthouse, 175 Hawley St., Lockport, NY 14094-2740
Fax: (716) 439-7076

▲Public Defender **David J. Farrugia** . . . . . (716) 439-7071
E-mail: david.farrugia@niagaracounty.com

Department of Mental Health [NCDMH]

5467 Upper Mountain Road, Suite 200, Lockport, NY 14094-1854
Fax: (716) 439-7418 E-mail: ncdmh@niagaracounty.com

Director **Laura J. Kelemen** . . . . . (716) 439-7410
Deputy Director **Michael A. White** . . . . . (716) 439-7410
Supervisor of Clinical Services **Timothy W. Deeks** . . . . . (716) 439-7410

Niagara County Community College [NCCC]

3111 Saunders Settlement Road, Sanborn, NY 14132
Tel: (716) 614-6222 Fax: (716) 614-6700
Internet: www.niagaracc.suny.edu

President **Dr. James P. Klyczek** . . . . . (716) 614-6222 ext. 5901

Environmental Solid Waste Management [NCRDD]

Courthouse, 175 Hawley St., Lockport, NY 14094-2740
Fax: (716) 439-7245 Internet: www.niagaracounty.com/landfill

Associate **Dawn Timm** . . . . . (716) 439-7240

Niagara County Sewer District No. 1

7346 Liberty Drive, Niagara Falls, NY 14304
Fax: (716) 693-8759

Director **Thomas Blodgett** . . . . . (716) 693-0001
Chief Operator **John Timkey** . . . . . (716) 693-0001

Niagara County Water District [NCWD]

5450 Ernest Road, Lockport, NY 14094
P.O. Box 315, Lockport, NY 14905-0315
Fax: (716) 434-8836

Administrative Director **Herbert A. Downs** . . . . . (716) 434-8835
Superintendent of Water Transmission **David K. Branch** . . (716) 434-8835

Office of the County Clerk

Courthouse, 175 Hawley Street, Lockport, NY 14094-2740
P.O. Box 461, Lockport, NY 14095-0461
Fax: (716) 439-7035 E-mail: niagaracounty.clerk@niagaracounty.com

★County Clerk **Joseph A. Jastrzemski** (R) . . . . . (716) 439-7022
Term Expires: December 31, 2020
E-mail: joseph.jastrzemski@niagaracounty.com
First Deputy County Clerk **Wendy J. Roberson** . . . . . (716) 439-7022
E-mail: wendy.roberson@niagaracounty.com

Office of the Historian

Civil Defense Building, 139 Niagara Street, Lockport, NY 14094-2740
Fax: (716) 439-7322

▲Historian **Catherine L. Emerson** . . . . . (716) 439-7324
E-mail: catherine.emerson@niagaracounty.com
Deputy Historian **Craig E. Bacon** . . . . . (716) 439-7324
Deputy Historian **Ronald F. Cary** . . . . . (716) 439-7324

Veterans Service Agency

111 Main Street, Suite 200, Lockport, NY 14094
Fax: (716) 438-4017 E-mail: veterans@niagaracounty.com

▲Director **Nina Cabrera** . . . . . (716) 438-4090
E-mail: nina.cabrera@niagaracounty.com
Veterans Service Officer **Al Thompson** . . . . . (716) 438-4090
Veterans Service Officer **Christopher Butler** . . . . . (716) 438-4090

Offices of the County Coroners

Courthouse, 175 Hawley St., Lockport, NY 14094-2740
Tel: (716) 439-7002 Fax: (716) 439-7124

★Coroner **James Carroll** (R-District 1) . . . . . (716) 791-3224
Term Expires: December 31, 2016
2744 Thornwoods Drive, Niagara Falls, NY 14304
★Coroner **Joseph Mantione** (R-District 2) . . . . . (716) 432-1061
Term Expires: December 31, 2017
240 Niagara Street, North Tonawanda, NY 14120
★Coroner **Kenneth Lederhouse** (R-District 3) . . . . . (716) 434-5414
Term Expires: December 31, 2017
138 Continental Drive, Lockport, NY 14094
★Coroner **Michael A. Ross** (R-District 4) . . . . . (716) 512-8857
Term Expires: December 31, 2017

Office of the District Attorney

Courthouse, 175 Hawley St., Lockport, NY 14094-2740
Fax: (716) 439-7102 E-mail: ncda@niagaracounty.com

★District Attorney **(Vacant)** . . . . . (716) 439-7085
Term Expires: December 31, 2019
Deputy District Attorney **Theodore A. Brenner** . . . . . (716) 439-7085
Deputy District Attorney **Doreen M. Hoffmann** . . . . . (716) 439-7085
Deputy District Attorney **Holly E. Sloma** . . . . . (716) 439-7085
E-mail: holly.sloma@niagaracounty.com

COUNTIES

★Elected Official ▲Appointed by Legislature ▼Appointed by Governor ►Appointed by Board or Commission ●Appointed by Judge
■Appointed by Mayor △Appointed by Freeholders ▽Appointed by Supervisor ▷Appointed by County Executive ○Appointed by Council

COUNTIES

Office of the Sheriff

5526 Niagara Street Extension, Lockport, NY 14094-2740
P.O. Box 496, Lockport, NY 14095-0496
Fax: (716) 438-3357 Internet: www.niagarasheriff.com

★Sheriff **James R. Voutour** .... (716) 438-3370
Term Expires: December 31, 2016
E-mail: james.voutour@niagaracounty.com
Undersheriff **Michael J. Filicetti** .... (716) 438-3333
Chief Deputy, Administrative Duties **Michael P. Dunn** .... (716) 438-3355
E-mail: michael.dunn@niagaracounty.com
Chief Deputy, Uniform Operations **Steven C. Preisch** .... (716) 438-3356
E-mail: steven.preisch@niagaracounty.com

Office of the Treasurer

59 Park Avenue, 1st Floor, Lockport, NY 14094
Fax: (716) 439-7021

★Treasurer **Kyle R. Andrews** (D) .... (716) 439-7018
Term Expires: December 31, 2018
E-mail: kyle.andrews@niagaracounty.com
Education: Niagara 2002 BA; Buffalo 2005 JD
Deputy Treasurer **Jennifer V. Kobrin** .... (716) 439-7019

Niagara County Board of Elections

111 Main Street, Suite 100, Lockport, NY 14094
Tel: (716) 438-4040 Tel: (716) 438-4054
Internet: www.elections.niagara.ny.us

Democrat Commissioner **Lora Allen** .... (716) 438-4041
Fax: (716) 438-4054
Republican Commissioner **Jennifer Fronczak** .... (716) 438-4040
Fax: (716) 438-4054

County of Norfolk, Massachusetts

614 High St., Dedham, MA 02026
P.O. Box 310, Dedham, MA 02026
Tel: (781) 461-6100 (Information) Internet: www.norfolkcounty.org

County Seat: Dedham **Election Type:** Partisan **Population:** 696,023 (2015)

Office of the Board of Commissioners

614 High St., Dedham, MA 02026
Fax: (781) 326-6480

★Chairman **Francis W. O'Brien** (D) .... (781) 461-6105
Term Expires: December 31, 2016
★Commissioner **Peter H. Collins** (D) .... (781) 461-6105
Term Expires: December 31, 2018
Education: Suffolk 1986 JD; UMass (Amherst) 1983 BA
★Commissioner **Joseph P. Shea** (D) .... (781) 461-6105
Term Expires: December 31, 2016

Office of the Sheriff

200 West St., Dedham, MA 02027
Fax: (781) 326-1079

★Sheriff **Michael Belotti** (D) .... (781) 329-3705
Term Expires: December 31, 2016

Office of the Treasurer

614 High St., Dedham, MA 02026
Fax: (781) 326-4527

★Treasurer **Joseph "Joe" Connolly** (D) .... (781) 461-6110
Term Expires: December 31, 2020
Education: Boston State Col BS; UMass (Boston) MPAff

Advisory Board

614 High St., Dedham, MA 02026
Fax: (781) 326-6480

Chair **Carl Balduf** .... (781) 461-6136
Vice Chair **Peter Padula** .... (781) 461-6136
Clerk **Helena M. Donohue** .... (781) 461-6136

County Operations Department

614 High Street, Dedham, MA 02026
Fax: (781) 326-6480

►Director **Frances Haggerty** .... (781) 461-6105
Administration/Budgets Manager **Philip R. Iantosca** .... (781) 461-6105
Data Processing Manager **Mark McDonald** .... (781) 461-6135
649 High St., Dedham, MA 02026
Personnel Services Manager **Ann Brown** .... (781) 461-6105
Purchasing Manager **Nancy McNealy** .... (781) 461-6139
Head Clerk **Jean F. McLeish** .... (781) 461-6105

Engineering Office

649 High St., Dedham, MA 02026
Fax: (781) 461-6148

►County Engineer **Joe McNichols** .... (781) 461-6128

Norfolk County Retired and Senior Volunteer Program [RSVP]

614 High St., Dedham, MA 02026
Fax: (781) 326-6480

►Director **Robert Pierson** .... (781) 329-5728

County of Oakland, Michigan

County Service Center, 1200 North Telegraph Road, Pontiac, MI 48341
Tel: (248) 858-1000 (Information) Internet: www.oakgov.com

County Seat: Pontiac **Election Type:** Partisan **Population:** 1,242,304 (2015)

L. Brooks Patterson (R)
County Executive

Began Service: 1992
Term Expires: December 31, 2016
Date of Birth: January 4, 1939
Education: Detroit 1967 JD

Office of the County Executive

Building 41W, 2100 Pontiac Lake Road, Waterford, MI 48328
Tel: (248) 858-0480 Fax: (248) 452-9215 Internet: www.oakgov.com/exec

★County Executive **L. Brooks Patterson** (R) .... (248) 858-0480
Executive Assistant **Kelly Sleva** .... (248) 858-5400
E-mail: slevak@oakgov.com
▷Chief Deputy County Executive **Gerald D. Poisson** .... (248) 858-2090
E-mail: poissong@oakgov.com

★Elected Official ▲Appointed by Legislature ▼Appointed by Governor ►Appointed by Board or Commission ●Appointed by Judge
■Appointed by Mayor △Appointed by Freeholders ▽Appointed by Supervisor ▷Appointed by County Executive ○Appointed by Council

Office of the County Executive *continued*

▷ Deputy County Executive and Chief Information Officer **Phil Bertolini** .... (248) 858-0815
E-mail: bertolinip@oakgov.com Fax: (248) 858-5130
Education: Michigan State 1985 BA

▷ Deputy County Executive **Malcolm Brown** .... (248) 858-0485
E-mail: brownm@oakgov.com
Education: Michigan State 1969 BA; Minnesota 1972 JD

▷ Deputy County Executive **Robert J. Daddow** .... (248) 858-1650
E-mail: daddowr@oakgov.com
Education: Central Michigan BSBA, 1975 MBA

▷ Deputy County Executive **Matthew A. "Matt" Gibb** .... (248) 975-9636
E-mail: gibbm@oakgov.com
Education: Alma BA; Kentucky JD

▷ Media and Communications Officer **William Mullan III** ... (248) 858-1048
E-mail: mullanw@oakgov.com
Secretary **Jaime Fenner** .... (248) 858-1049
E-mail: fennerj@oakgov.com

Adult Probation Department

North Office Bldg., 1200 North Telegraph Road, Pontiac, MI 48341-0407
Tel: (248) 858-0300 Fax: (248) 858-5167

Region Manager **Brock Dietrich** .... (248) 858-0303

Department of Central Services

2100 Pontiac Lake Road, Waterford, MI 48328
Tel: (248) 858-0516 Fax: (248) 452-9215

▷ Director **J. David VanderVeen** .... (248) 858-0516
E-mail: vanderveend@oakgov.com
Secretary **Doreen Pagel** .... (248) 858-1032
E-mail: pageld@oakgov.com

Aviation Division (Oakland County International Airport)

6500 Highland Rd., Waterford, MI 48327-1649
Tel: (248) 666-3900 Fax: (248) 666-3341 E-mail: ocia@oakgov.com
Internet: www.oakgov.com/aviation

Manager **Karl Randall** .... (248) 666-3901

Support Services Division

1200 N. Telegraph Rd., Department 043, Pontiac, MI 48341-0043
Tel: (248) 858-0928 Fax: (248) 858-4073

Manager **Todd T. Birkle** .... (248) 858-1036
E-mail: birklet@oakgov.com

Department of Corporation Counsel

1200 North Telegraph Road, Building 14 E, 3rd Floor, Pontiac, MI 48341-0419
Tel: (248) 858-0550 Fax: (248) 858-1003

▷ Corporation Counsel **Keith J. Lerminiaux** .... (248) 858-0553
E-mail: lerminiauxk@oakgov.com
Education: Michigan State 1976 BS; Detroit Mercy 1979 JD

▷ Deputy Corporation Counsel **Joellen Shortley** .... (248) 858-0557

Department of Economic Development and Community Affairs

Executive Office Building, 2100 Pontiac Lake Road, Building 41W, Waterford, MI 48328
Tel: (248) 858-0721 Fax: (248) 452-9215
Internet: www.advantageoakland.com

Director **Irene Spanos** .... (248) 858-9099
E-mail: spanose@oakgov.com
Education: Wayne State U 1993

Deputy Director **Dan Hunter** .... (248) 858-0764
E-mail: hunterd@oakgov.com

Marketing and Communications Officer **Steve Huber** .... (248) 858-1848
E-mail: hubers@oakgov.com

Community and Home Improvement Division

Oakland Pointe, 250 Elizabeth Lake Rd., Suite 1900, Pontiac, MI 48341-0431
Tel: (248) 858-0493 Internet: www.oakgov.com/chi

Manager **Karry L. Rieth** .... (248) 858-5403
E-mail: riethk@oakgov.com

Operations Chief **Gordon Lambert** .... (248) 858-5303
E-mail: lambertg@oakgov.com

Planner/Finance Officer **Carla Spradlin** .... (248) 858-5312
E-mail: spradlinc@oakgov.com

Planning and Economic Development Services Division

2100 Pontiac Lake Road, Building 41W, Waterford, MI 48328
Tel: (248) 858-0721 Fax: (248) 975-9555 Internet: www.oakgov.com/peds

Business Development Supervisor **Dave Schreiber** ...... (248) 858-0792
E-mail: schreiberd@oakgov.com

Financial Services Supervisor **Mary Langhauser** .... (248) 858-0879

Information Services Supervisor **Greg Doyle** .... (248) 858-2087
E-mail: doyleg@oakgov.com

Planning Supervisor **Bret C. Rasegan** .... (248) 858-5445
E-mail: raseganb@oakgov.com

Workforce Development Division

1200 North Telegraph Road, Department 437, Pontiac, MI 48341-0437
Tel: (248) 452-2256 Fax: (248) 452-2260

Manager **John W. Almstadt** .... (248) 452-2256
E-mail: almstadtj@oakgov.com

Department of Facilities Management

Public Works Building, One Public Works Drive, Waterford, MI 48328
Tel: (248) 858-0160 Fax: (248) 452-2250 Internet: www.oakgov.com/fm

▷ Director **William A. "Art" Holdsworth** .... (248) 858-0160
E-mail: holdswortha@oakgov.com
Education: Oakland U BS; Michigan State MBA
Secretary **Nan Chenoweth** .... (248) 858-0144
E-mail: chenowethn@oakgov.com

Facilities Planning and Engineering Division

Tel: (248) 858-0144 Fax: (248) 452-2250

Manager **Edward Joss** .... (248) 858-2111
E-mail: josse@oakgov.com

Facilities Maintenance and Operations Division

Tel: (248) 858-0169 Fax: (248) 452-2250

Manager **Joseph Murphy** .... (248) 858-0019
E-mail: murphyj@oakgov.com

Department of Health and Human Services

Building 34 East, 1200 North Telegraph Road, Pontiac, MI 48431
Tel: (248) 858-1293 Internet: www.oakgov.com/health

Director **George J. Miller, Jr.** .... (248) 858-1293

Children's Village

County Service Center, Bldg. 63W, 1200 North Telegraph Road, Department 444, Pontiac, MI 48341-0444
Tel: (248) 858-1150 Fax: (248) 858-5222

Manager **Joanna Overall** .... (248) 858-1164
Administrator **Greg Alessi** .... (248) 858-1135
Administrator **Heather Calcaterra** .... (248) 858-1160
Administrator **Patricia Lahar** .... (248) 858-1162

Homeland Security Division

Building 47 West, 1200 North Telegraph Road, Pontiac, MI 48341-0410
Tel: (248) 858-5300 Fax: (248) 858-5550

Manager **Theodore H. "Ted" Quisenberry** .... (248) 858-5300
E-mail: quisenberryt@oakgov.com

Chief of Emergency Management **Sara Stoddard** .... (248) 858-5080
E-mail: stoddards@oakgov.com

COUNTIES

★ Elected Official ▲ Appointed by Legislature ▼ Appointed by Governor ▶ Appointed by Board or Commission ● Appointed by Judge
■ Appointed by Mayor △ Appointed by Freeholders ▽ Appointed by Supervisor ▷ Appointed by County Executive ○ Appointed by Council

Oakland County Health Division [OCHD]

1200 North Telegraph Road, Pontiac, MI 48341-0432
Tel: (248) 858-1280 Fax: (248) 858-5428
Internet: www.oakgov.com/health

Manager/Health Officer **Kathleen "Kathy" Forzley** ..... (248) 858-1410
Chief of Medical Services
Dr. Pamela Beckstrom Hackert ..... (248) 858-1276
Education: Michigan 1981 BBA, 1984 JD, 1993 MD, 2008 MPH
Chief of Substance Abuse Services **Christina Nicholas** ... (248) 858-5107
Administrator, Administrative Services **Thomas Fockler** .. (248) 452-2151
E-mail: focklert@oakgov.com
Administrator, Community Health Promotion and Intervention Services **Lisa McKay-Chiasson** ..... (248) 858-1395
Administrator, Environmental Health Services
Anthony Drautz ..... (248) 858-1320
Administrator, Public Health Nursing Services
Jean Ulmer ..... (248) 858-1409
AIDS Coordinator **Rebecca Leach** ..... (248) 858-5476
Hearing and Vision Coordinator **Dianne Ferber** ..... (248) 424-7071
27725 Greenfield Road, Southfield, MI 48076
Immunization Action Plan Program Coordinator
Elaine Houser ..... (248) 858-1413
Infant Health Promotion Program Coordinator **(Vacant)** ... (248) 858-1380
Senior Citizen Services Coordinator **Mary Strobe** ..... (248) 858-0213
Vaccine Program Coordinator **Patricia White** ..... (248) 858-1300
WIC (Women, Infants and Children) Program
Coordinator **Jennifer Kirby** ..... (248) 858-5607
Education: Central Michigan 1998 BS, 2004 MSA
Children's Special Health Care Services Supervisor
Maggie Sherland ..... (248) 858-0726
Laboratory Services Supervisor
Barbara "Barb" Weberman ..... (248) 858-1310
Tuberculosis Control Unit Supervisor **Pat Brines** ..... (248) 858-1379
1200 N. Telegraph, Pontiac, MI 48341-0432
Epidemiologist **Shane Bies** ..... (248) 858-1540
Epidemiologist **Richard "Rick" Renas** ..... (248) 858-0009

Department of Human Resources

Building 41 West, 2100 Pontiac Lake Road, Waterford, MI 48328
Tel: (248) 858-0537 Fax: (248) 452-9172 Internet: www.oakgov.com/hr

▷ Director **Jordie Kramer** ..... (248) 858-0537
E-mail: kramerj@oakgov.com
Secretary **(Vacant)** ..... (248) 858-0537

Benefits Administration Division

Manager **Jennifer Hain** ..... (248) 858-5213
Employee Benefits Supervisor **Tina Ramey** ..... (248) 858-5212
Training and Development Supervisor **Melva Allen** ..... (248) 858-0018
Retirement Administrator **Judy Fandale** ..... (248) 858-5215

Labor Relations Division

Deputy Director **(Vacant)** ..... (248) 858-0546
Labor Relations Specialist **(Vacant)** ..... (248) 858-5351

Workforce Management Division

Manager **Lori Taylor** ..... (248) 858-5351
Employee Records and HRIS Supervisor
Kristy Slosson ..... (248) 858-5382
E-mail: slossonk@oakgov.com

Department of Information Technology [IT]

Building 49 West, 1200 North Telegraph Road, Pontiac, MI 48341-0421
Tel: (248) 858-0810 Fax: (248) 858-5130
Internet: www.oakgov.com/infotech

Chief Information Officer **Phil Bertolini** ..... (248) 858-0815
E-mail: bertolinip@oakgov.com
Education: Michigan State 1985 BA
▷ Director **Edwin Poisson** ..... (248) 858-0857
E-mail: poissone@oakgov.com

Department of Management and Budget [DMB]

2100 Pontiac Lake Road, Waterford, MI 48328
Fax: (248) 452-9172

▷ Director **Laurie Van Pelt** ..... (248) 858-2163
E-mail: vanpeltl@oakgov.com
Secretary **Lee Ann Ciecko** ..... (248) 975-4296

Equalization Division

Oakland Pointe, 250 Elizabeth Lake Rd., Suite 1000W, Pontiac, MI 48341-0431
Tel: (248) 858-0740 Fax: (248) 975-4407

Manager **David M. Hieber** ..... (248) 858-0760
Fax: (248) 858-9724
Administrator **Richard Vincent** ..... (248) 858-0754
Fax: (248) 858-1983

Fiscal Services Division

Building 41W, 2100 Pontiac Lake Road, Waterford, MI 48328
Tel: (248) 858-0375 Fax: (248) 975-9869

Manager **Lynn Sonkiss** ..... (248) 858-0807
Financial Services Chief **Penny Cremer** ..... (248) 858-0379
Financial Services Chief **Nancy Fournier** ..... (248) 858-0488
Financial Services Chief **(Vacant)** ..... (248) 858-0807

Purchasing Division

Building 41W, 2100 Pontiac Lake Road, Waterford, MI 48328
Tel: (248) 858-0511 Fax: (248) 858-1677

Manager **Jack Sato Smith** ..... (248) 858-0511
E-mail: hyllaj@oakgov.com
Chief Purchasing Officer **Scott Guzzy** ..... (248) 858-5481
E-mail: guzzys@oakgov.com

Reimbursement Division

Executive Office Bldg., 1200 North Telegraph Road, Department 455, Pontiac, MI 48341-0455
Tel: (248) 858-0500 Fax: (248) 975-4288

Manager **Lynn Sonkiss** ..... (248) 858-0807
Chief Reimbursement Supervisor **Judi Lockhart** ..... (248) 858-0502

Department of Public Services

2100 Pontiac Lake Road, Waterford, MI 48328
Tel: (248) 858-1074 Fax: (248) 452-9172

▷ Director **Mark Newman** ..... (248) 858-1074
E-mail: newmanm@oakgov.com

Office of Cooperative Extension (Michigan State University)

North Office Building, 1200 North Telegraph Road, Department 416, Pontiac, MI 48341-0416
Tel: (248) 858-0880 Fax: (248) 858-1477
E-mail: msue.oakland@county.msu.edu

District Coordinator **Julie Pioch** ..... (248) 657-8213

Office of the Medical Examiner

Building 28 East, 1200 North Telegraph Road, Pontiac, MI 48341-0438
Tel: (248) 858-5097 Fax: (248) 452-9173

Chief Forensic Pathologist/Medical Examiner
Dr. Ljubisa J. Dragovic ..... (248) 858-4046
Deputy Chief Forensic Pathologist
Dr. Kanubhai "Kanu" Virani ..... (248) 858-4044
Deputy Forensic Pathologist **Dr. Ruben Ortiz-Reyes** ..... (248) 452-9390
Deputy Forensic Pathologist **Bernardino Pacris** ..... (248) 858-1494
Administrator **Robert Gerds** ..... (248) 858-4045
Deputy Forensic Pathologist **Cheryl Loewe** ..... (248) 858-1910

Animal Control Division

1700 Brown Rd., Auburn Hills, MI 48326
Tel: (248) 391-4100 Fax: (248) 391-9266

Director **Bob Gatt** ..... (248) 391-0278 ext. 224

★ Elected Official ▲ Appointed by Legislature ▼ Appointed by Governor ▶ Appointed by Board or Commission ● Appointed by Judge
■ Appointed by Mayor △ Appointed by Freeholders ▽ Appointed by Supervisor ▷ Appointed by County Executive ○ Appointed by Council

Animal Control Division *continued*

Administrative Supervisor **Joanie M. Toole** . . . . . (248) 391-0278 ext. 222
E-mail: toolej@oakgov.com
Kennel Supervisor **Shelley Grey** . . . . . (248) 391-4100
Road/Dispatch Supervisor **(Vacant)** . . . . . (248) 391-4102 ext. 227

Community Corrections Division

250 Elizabeth Lake Rd., Suite 1520, Pontiac, MI 48341-0431
Tel: (248) 451-2310 Fax: (248) 451-2319

Manager **Barbara Hankey** . . . . . (248) 451-2306
Chief, Field Operations **Lawrence M. "Larry" Doyle** . . . . (248) 451-2305
E-mail: doylel@oakgov.com

Veterans' Services Division

Building 26E, 1200 North Telegraph Road, Pontiac, MI 48341
Tel: (248) 858-0785 Fax: (248) 452-2189
Internet: www.oakgov.com/veterans

Manager **Garth E. Wootten** . . . . . (248) 858-0785
Pontiac Counseling Office Supervisor
Lauren C. Chamberlin . . . . . (248) 858-0785
South Oakland Office Supervisor
Belinda Shelton Duggan . . . . . (248) 655-1250
1151 Crooks Road, Troy, MI 48084 Fax: (248) 655-1253

Department of Risk Management and Safety

Building 41W, 2100 Pontiac Lake Road, Waterford, MI 48328
Fax: (248) 452-9796

▷ Risk Manager **Dean Schultz** . . . . . (248) 858-1558
Education: Colgate 1969 AB; Georgetown 1972 JD
Insurance and Safety Coordinator **Bob Erlenbeck** . . . . . (248) 858-1694
Risk Management Claims Analyst **Julie Sweik** . . . . . (248) 858-1653
E-mail: sweikj@oakgov.com

Adams-Pratt Law Library

1200 North Telegraph Road, Department 450, Pontiac, MI 48341-0450
Fax: (248) 858-1536

Director **Laura Mancini** . . . . . (248) 858-0012
E-mail: asklaw@oakgov.com

Office of the Board of Commissioners

County Service Center, 1200 N. Telegraph Rd., Pontiac, MI 48341-0470
Fax: (248) 858-1572 Internet: www.oakgov.com/boc

★ Chairman **Michael J. "Mike" Gingell** (R-District 1) . . . . . (248) 728-7133
Term Expires: December 31, 2016
E-mail: gingellm@oakgov.com
Education: Oakland U 1993 BS; Wayne State U MBA
★ Commissioner **Robert J. "Bob" Hoffman** (R-District 2) . . (248) 858-1000
Term Expires: December 31, 2016
E-mail: hoffm2521@comcast.net
★ Commissioner **Michael Spisz** (R-District 3) . . . . . (248) 858-1000
Term Expires: December 31, 2016
E-mail: spiszm@oakgov.com
★ Commissioner **Thomas F. Middleton** (R-District 4) . . . . . (248) 858-1000
Term Expires: December 31, 2016
E-mail: middletont@oakgov.com
★ Commissioner **John A. Scott** (R-District 5) . . . . . (248) 858-1000
Term Expires: December 31, 2016
★ Commissioner **Eileen Kowall** (R-District 6) . . . . . (248) 858-1000
Term Expires: December 31, 2016
★ Commissioner **Christine A. Long** (R-District 7) . . . . . (248) 858-1000
Term Expires: December 31, 2016
E-mail: longc@oakgov.com
Education: Michigan State 1987 BS
★ Commissioner **Phillip J. Weipert** (R-District 8) . . . . . (248) 858-1000
Term Expires: December 31, 2016
E-mail: weipertpj@oakgov.com
Education: Michigan (Dearborn) 1983 BA; Thomas M Cooley 1988 JD
★ Commissioner **Hugh D. Crawford** (R-District 9) . . . . . (248) 858-1000
Term Expires: December 31, 2016

Office of the Board of Commissioners *continued*

★ Commissioner **David Bowman** (D-District 10) . . . . . (248) 858-1000
Term Expires: December 31, 2016
★ Commissioner **Robert Gosselin** (R-District 11) . . . . . (248) 858-1000
Term Expires: December 31, 2016
E-mail: gosselinr@oakgov.com
★ Commissioner **Shelley Taub** (R-District 12) . . . . . (248) 858-1000
Term Expires: December 31, 2016
E-mail: shelleytaub@comcast.net
★ Commissioner **Marcia Gershenson** (D-District 13) . . . . . (248) 858-1000
Term Expires: December 31, 2016
E-mail: gershensonm@oakgov.com
Education: Michigan 1971 BA
★ Commissioner **William "Bill" Dwyer** (R-District 14) . . . . . (248) 858-1000
Term Expires: December 31, 2016
E-mail: wdwyer@mi.rr.com
★ Commissioner **Adam Kochenderfer** (District 15) . . . . . (248) 858-1000
Term Expires: December 31, 2016
★ Commissioner **Wayde Flemming** (R-District 16) . . . . . (248) 858-1000
Term Expires: December 31, 2016
★ Commissioner **Nancy L. Quarles** (D-District 17) . . . . . (248) 858-1000
Term Expires: December 31, 2016
E-mail: quarlesn@oakgov.com
★ Commissioner **Helaine M. Zack** (D-District 18) . . . . . (248) 858-1000
Term Expires: December 31, 2016
E-mail: zackh@oakgov.com
★ Commissioner **David T. Woodward, Jr.** (D-District 19) . . (248) 858-1000
Term Expires: December 31, 2016
E-mail: woodwardd@oakgov.com
★ Commissioner **Gary R. McGillivray** (D-District 20) . . . . . (248) 858-1000
Term Expires: December 31, 2016
E-mail: mcgillivrayg@oakgov.com
★ Commissioner **Janet Jackson** (D-District 21) . . . . . (248) 858-1000
Term Expires: December 31, 2016
E-mail: jacksonj@oakgov.com
Administrative Director **Jim Ver Ploeg** . . . . . (248) 858-1701
Education: Grand Valley State 1983; Michigan State 1989 JD

Parks and Recreation Commission

2800 Watkins Lake Road, Waterford, MI 48328-1917
Tel: (248) 858-0906 Fax: (248) 858-1683
Internet: www.destinationoakland.com

Chairman **Gerald A. Fisher** . . . . . (888) 627-2757
Vice Chairman **J. David VanderVeen** . . . . . (888) 627-2757
Secretary **John Scott** . . . . . (888) 627-2757

Administration

Executive Officer **Daniel J. "Dan" Stencil** . . . . . (248) 858-4944
Manager - Parks and Recreation Operations **Sue Wells** . . . (248) 858-4634
Planning Supervisor **Jon Noyes** . . . . . (248) 760-8360
Business Development Representative for Internal
Services **Phil Castonia** . . . . . (248) 858-0909
Business Development Representative for Organizational
Management **Stephanie Mackey** . . . . . (248) 431-1268
Business Development Representative for Resource
Development **Melissa Prowse** . . . . . (248) 858-4630
Administrative Services Supervisor **Karen Kohn** . . . . . (248) 858-4606
E-mail: kohnk@oakgov.com
Communications/Marketing Supervisor
Desiree Stanfield . . . . . (248) 858-4627
E-mail: stanfieldd@oakgov.com
Supervisor of Golf Revenue and Operations
Darlene Rowley . . . . . (248) 431-1482
Chief of Recreation Programs and Services **Terry Fields** . . (248) 858-0914
Chief of Park Facilities, Maintenance and Development
Mike Donnellon . . . . . (248) 858-4623
Chief of Park Operations and Maintenance, North
District **Jim Dunleavy** . . . . . (248) 858-4647
Chief of Park Operations and Maintenance, South
District **Tom Hughes** . . . . . (248) 343-1011

★ Elected Official ▲ Appointed by Legislature ▼ Appointed by Governor ► Appointed by Board or Commission ● Appointed by Judge
■ Appointed by Mayor △ Appointed by Freeholders ▽ Appointed by Supervisor ▷ Appointed by County Executive ○ Appointed by Council

Office of the County Clerk/Register of Deeds

1200 North Telegraph Road, Department 415, Pontiac, MI 48341-0415
Tel: (248) 858-0597 Fax: (248) 858-1943 E-mail: clerk@oakgov.com
Internet: www.oakgov.com/clerkrod

★Clerk/Register **Lisa Anne Brown** (D) .... (248) 858-0560
Term Expires: December 31, 2016
Date of Birth: January 26, 1967
Education: Michigan State 1985 BA; Detroit Law 1993 JD
Deputy Clerk/Register **(Vacant)** .... (248) 452-9193
Deputy Clerk/Register **Sheila Cummings** .... (248) 452-2024
E-mail: cummingss@oakgov.com
Chief Deputy Clerk **Jennifer Howden** .... (248) 858-0586
E-mail: howdenj@oakgov.com Fax: (248) 452-9221
Chief Deputy Register **Laura Thierbach** .... (248) 858-0766
Fax: (248) 858-7466
Director of Elections **Joseph J. "Joe" Rozell** .... (248) 858-0563

Office of the Prosecuting Attorney

1200 North Telegraph Road, Pontiac, MI 48341
Tel: (248) 858-0656 Fax: (248) 452-2208
E-mail: info@oaklandprosecutor.org Internet: www.oaklandprosecutor.org

★Prosecutor **Jessica R. Cooper** (D) .... (248) 858-0656
Term Expires: December 31, 2016
E-mail: cooperj@oakgov.com
Date of Birth: 1946
Education: Wayne State U 1970 BA, 1973 JD
Chief Assistant Prosecutor **Paul T. Walton** .... (248) 858-0642

Office of the Sheriff

County Service Center, 1200 N. Telegraph Rd., Building 38 East, Pontiac, MI 48341-1044
Tel: (248) 858-5000 Fax: (248) 858-1806

★Sheriff **Michael J. "Mike" Bouchard** (R) .... (248) 858-5001
Term Expires: December 31, 2016
E-mail: ocso@oakgov.com
Date of Birth: April 12, 1956
Education: Michigan State 1979 BA
Undersheriff **Michael G. McCabe** .... (248) 858-0146
E-mail: mccabem@oakgov.com
Major, Correctional and Court Services Division
Chuck Snarey .... (248) 858-5017
Major, Law Enforcement Services Division
Robert Smith .... (248) 858-4970

Office of the Treasurer

County Service Center, 1200 North Telegraph Road, Department 479, Pontiac, MI 48341-0479
Tel: (248) 858-0611 Fax: (248) 858-1810
Internet: www.oakgov.com/treasurer

★Treasurer **Andrew E. "Andy" Meisner** (D) .... (248) 858-0624
Term Expires: June 30, 2017
E-mail: meisnera@oakgov.com
Date of Birth: March 30, 1973
Education: Michigan BS; Detroit Mercy 2006 JD
Chief Deputy Treasurer **Jody Weissler DeFoe** .... (248) 858-0625
Chief of Tax Administration **Laura Schmitt** .... (248) 858-0615
E-mail: lschmitt@oakgove.com
Investment Administrator **Natalie Neph** .... (248) 858-0626
E-mail: nephn@oakgov.com

Office of the Water Resources Commissioner [WRC]

Building 95 West, One Public Works Dr., Waterford, MI 48328
Tel: (248) 858-0958 Fax: (248) 858-1066 E-mail: wrc@oakgov.com
Internet: www.oakgov.com/water

★Water Resources Commissioner **Jim Nash** (D) .... (248) 858-0958
Term Expires: December 31, 2016
Administrative Assistant **Alyssa Atkinson** .... (248) 858-0967
E-mail: atkinsona@oakgov.com
Chief Deputy Commissioner **Phillip Sanzica** .... (248) 858-0981
Chief of Administrative Services **Sherri Gee** .... (248) 858-0108
E-mail: gees@oakgov.com

Engineering and Construction Division

Tel: (248) 858-0958 Fax: (248) 858-1066

Manager **Steven Korth** .... (248) 858-7598
E-mail: korths@oakgov.com
Chief Engineer **Glenn Appel** .... (248) 858-1031

Operations and Maintenance Division

Tel: (248) 858-1075 Fax: (248) 858-1066

Manager **Tim Prince** .... (248) 858-0937
E-mail: princet@oakgov.com
Chief Engineer **Amy Ploof** .... (248) 858-1069
E-mail: ploofa@oakgov.com

Oakland Schools

2111 Pontiac Lake Road, Waterford, MI 48328
Fax: (248) 209-2206 Internet: www.oakland.k12.mi.us

Superintendent **Dr. Wanda Cook-Robinson** .... (248) 209-2424
Deputy Superintendent of Finance and Operations
Robert F. Moore .... (248) 209-2368
E-mail: robert.moore@oakland.k12.mi.us
Deputy Superintendent of Instructional Services
Theresa Spencer .... (248) 209-2141

County of Ocean, New Jersey

Ocean County Administration Building, 101 Hooper Avenue, Toms River, NJ 08754-7605
P.O. Box 2191, Toms River, NJ 08754-2191
Tel: (732) 244-2121 Fax: (732) 506-5000 Internet: www.co.ocean.nj.us

County Seat: Toms River **Election Type:** Partisan **Population:** 588,721 (2015)

Board of Chosen Freeholders

101 Hooper Avenue, Toms River, NJ 08754
P.O. Box 2191, Toms River, NJ 08754-2191
Tel: (732) 506-5040 Fax: (732) 506-1918 E-mail: ocinfo@co.ocean.nj.us

★Director **John P. "Jack" Kelly** (R) .... (732) 929-2003
Term Expires: December 31, 2016
E-mail: ocinfo@co.ocean.nj.us
★Deputy Director **Gerry P. Little** (R) .... (732) 929-2001
Term Expires: December 31, 2018
E-mail: ocinfo@co.ocean.nj.us
Education: Bloomsburg BA
★Freeholder **John C. Bartlett, Jr.** (R) .... (732) 929-2116
Term Expires: December 31, 2018
E-mail: ocinfo@co.ocean.nj.us
Education: Western Maryland 1969 BA
★Freeholder **Virginia "Ginny" Haines** .... (732) 244-2121
Term Expires: December 31, 2016
E-mail: ocinfo@co.ocean.nj.us

★Elected Official ▲Appointed by Legislature ▼Appointed by Governor ▶Appointed by Board or Commission ●Appointed by Judge
■Appointed by Mayor △Appointed by Freeholders ▽Appointed by Supervisor ▷Appointed by County Executive ○Appointed by Council

Board of Chosen Freeholders *continued*

★ Freeholder **Joseph H. Vicari** (R) .... (732) 929-2002
Term Expires: December 31, 2017
E-mail: ocinfo@co.ocean.nj.us
Education: St Peter's Col 1969 BA; Fairleigh Dickinson 1972 MA
Clerk of the Board **Betty Vasil** .... (732) 929-2005
E-mail: bvasil@co.ocean.nj.us Fax: (732) 505-1918

Office of the Auditor

Building B, 680 Hooper Avenue, Suite 201, Toms River, NJ 08753
Fax: (732) 797-1022

△ Auditor **Robert Allison** .... (732) 797-1333

Office of Cooperative Extension (Rutgers University)

1623 Whitesville Road, Toms River, NJ 08755-1199
Fax: (732) 505-8941 Internet: http://ocean.njaes.rutgers.edu/

County Extension Department Head **Gef Flimlin** .... (732) 349-1152

Office of the County Adjuster

Building 2, 1027 Hooper Avenue, 2nd Floor, Toms River, NJ 08754-2191
Fax: (732) 288-7609

△ Adjuster **John C. Sahradnik** .... (732) 929-2084
△ Assistant County Adjuster **Michael H. Mathis** .... (732) 929-2084
Investigator **(Vacant)** .... (732) 506-5093

Office of the County Counsel

212 Hooper Ave., Toms River, NJ 08753-0757
P.O. Box 757, Toms River, NJ 08754
Fax: (732) 349-1983

► County Counsel **John C. Sahradnik** .... (732) 349-4800
E-mail: jsahradnik@bskb-law.com
Assistant County Counsel **Laura M. Benson** .... (732) 349-4800
Assistant County Counsel **Michael H. Mathis** .... (732) 296-1713

Office of the County Engineer

P.O. Box 2191, Toms River, NJ 08754-2191
Fax: (732) 506-5182 E-mail: ocengineering@co.ocean.nj.us

△ County Engineer **Frank S. Scarantino** .... (732) 929-2130
E-mail: fscarantino@co.ocean.nj.us

Office of the County Prosecutor

119 Hooper Ave., Toms River, NJ 08754
P.O. Box 2191, Toms River, NJ 08754-2191

▼ Prosecutor **Joseph D. Coronato** .... (732) 929-2027
First Assistant Prosecutor **John R. Corson, Jr.** .... (732) 929-2027

Office of the Medical Examiner

P.O. Box 2191, Toms River, NJ 08754-2191
Fax: (732) 341-9297

△ Medical Examiner **Donato Santangelo** .... (732) 341-3424
△ Assistant Medical Examiner **Dr. Neil A. Brodsky** .... (732) 241-3424
△ Assistant Medical Examiner **Leslie Cauvin** .... (732) 341-3424
△ Assistant Medical Examiner **Dr. Rocco Giliberti** .... (732) 341-3424
△ Assistant Medical Examiner **Dr. Harry Larkin** .... (732) 341-3424

Office of Senior Services

Bldg. 2, 1027 Hooper Ave., P.O. Box 2191, Toms River, NJ 08754-2191
Tel: (800) 668-4899 (Toll Free (New Jersey))
Tel: (877) 222-3737 (Toll Free Alternate) Fax: (732) 506-5019

△ Director **Jackie Rohan** .... (732) 929-2091

Office of the County Administrator

P.O. Box 2191, Toms River, NJ 08754-2191
Fax: (732) 506-5301

△ County Administrator **Carl W. Block** (R) .... (732) 929-2147
E-mail: cblock@co.ocean.nj.us

Bridge Department

Chestnut St. Garage, 152 Chestnut St., Toms River, NJ 08753
P.O. Box 2191, Toms River, NJ 08754-2191
Fax: (732) 506-5020

Superintendent of Bridges **Michael Reina** .... (732) 349-2480
Assistant Superintendent of Bridges **(Vacant)** .... (732) 349-2480

Buildings and Grounds Department

Building 5, 239 Washington Street, Toms River, NJ 08753
PO Box 2191, Toms River, NJ 08754-2191
Tel: (732) 929-2039 Fax: (732) 505-3262

Superintendent **Joseph Meyers, Jr.** .... (732) 929-2039

Consumer Affairs Department

1027 Hooper Ave., Bldg. 2, P.O. Box 2191, Toms River, NJ 08754-2191
Fax: (732) 506-5330

Director **Stephen Scaturro** .... (732) 929-2105

Weights and Measures Division

Fax: (732) 506-5330

Director **Stephen Scaturro** .... (732) 929-2105
Deputy Superintendent **Barry Wieck** .... (732) 929-2166
E-mail: bwieck@co.ocean.nj.us

Department of Corrections

Justice Complex, 114 Hooper Avenue, Toms River, NJ 08753
Tel: (732) 929-2043 Fax: (732) 506-5098

Warden **Sandra Mueller** .... (732) 929-2137
Fax: (732) 506-5027

Department of Employee Relations

P.O. Box 2191, Toms River, NJ 08754-2191
Fax: (732) 506-5303 E-mail: ocemployeerelations@co.ocean.nj.us

Director **Keith J. Goetting** .... (732) 929-2128
E-mail: kgoetting@co.ocean.nj.us
Education: Lycoming 1979 BA

Department of Finance

P.O. Box 2191, Toms River, NJ 08754-2191
Tel: (732) 929-2127 Fax: (732) 506-5129

△ Comptroller/Chief Financial Officer **Julie N. Tarrant** ..... (732) 929-2148
E-mail: jtarrant@co.ocean.nj.us

Ocean County Health Department [OCHD]

175 Sunset Avenue, Toms River, NJ 08754
P.O. Box 2191, Toms River, NJ 08754-2191
Tel: (732) 341-9700 TTY: (732) 914-9314 Fax: (732) 831-6495
E-mail: info@ochd.org Internet: www.ochd.org

Public Health Coordinator **Daniel E. Regenye** .. (732) 341-9700 ext. 7201

Department of Human Services

P.O. Box 2191, Toms River, NJ 08754-2191
Fax: (732) 341-4539 Internet: www.co.ocean.nj.us/ocdhs

△ Director **Tracy Maksel** .... (732) 506-5374
Assistant Director **Jamie Busch** .... (732) 506-5374

Office for Individuals with Disabilities

P.O. Box 2191, Toms River, NJ 08754-2191
Fax: (732) 341-4539

Coordinator **Maria La Face** .... (732) 506-5062

★ Elected Official ▲ Appointed by Legislature ▼ Appointed by Governor ► Appointed by Board or Commission ● Appointed by Judge
■ Appointed by Mayor △ Appointed by Freeholders ▽ Appointed by Supervisor ▷ Appointed by County Executive ○ Appointed by Council

COUNTIES

Ocean County Mental Health Board [MHB]
P.O. Box 2191, Toms River, NJ 08754-2191
Fax: (732) 341-4539 Internet: www.co.ocean.nj.us/ocdhs/mhb

Coordinator **Jamie Busch** .... (732) 506-5374

Information Technology Department
P.O. Box 2191, Toms River, NJ 08754-2191
Fax: (732) 288-7600

△ Director **Edward Bavais** .... (732) 929-2157
E-mail: ebavais@co.ocean.nj.us

Department of Juvenile Services
P.O. Box 2191, Toms River, NJ 08754-2191
Tel: (732) 341-1365 Fax: (732) 349-8563

Superintendent **Walter Hopson** .... (732) 288-7739
Director of Social Work Services **Dr. Barbara Barr** .... (732) 288-7716
RAISE Evening Program/Community Service Program **Jeff Reese** .... (732) 288-7740
School Mentoring Program **Richard Seitz** .... (732) 288-7726
Training Officer **Edward Turnbach** .... (732) 288-7780
E-mail: eturnbach@co.ocean.nj.us
Youth Services Coordinator **Shelby Voorhees** .... (732) 288-7792

Department of Management and Budget
P.O. Box 2191, Toms River, NJ 08754-2191
Fax: (732) 506-5333

△ Director **Michael J. Fiure** .... (732) 929-2099
E-mail: mfiure@co.ocean.nj.us

Parks and Recreation Department
1198 Bandon Road, Toms River, NJ 08753
Tel: (877) 627-2757 Fax: (732) 270-9464

Director **Michael T. Mangum** .... (732) 506-9090
General Supervisor of Parks **Kenneth F. Pullen** .... (732) 506-9090
Recreation Superintendent **Mary J. Bavais Mehorter** .... (732) 506-9090

Cultural and Heritage Commission
14 Hooper Avenue, Toms River, NJ 08754-2191
Fax: (732) 288-7871 E-mail: culturalheritage@co.ocean.nj.us
Internet: www.co.ocean.nj.us/cultural

△ Division Director **Timothy G. Hart** .... (732) 929-4779
E-mail: thart@co.ocean.nj.us
Assistant Director **(Vacant)** .... (732) 929-4779

Department of Planning
129 Hooper Avenue, Toms River, NJ 08754-2191
PO Box 2191, Toms River, NJ 08754-2191
Fax: (732) 244-8396 E-mail: ocplanning@co.ocean.nj.us
Internet: www.planning.co.ocean.nj.us

△ Board Chairman **Richard Work** .... (732) 929-2054
△ Board Vice Chairman **Donald Reed** .... (732) 929-2054
Planning Director **David J. McKeon** .... (732) 929-2054
Assistant Planning Director **Anthony M. "Tony" Agliata** .... (732) 929-2054

Robert J. Miller - Ocean County Airport
101 Airport Road, Berkeley Township, NJ 08721
P.O. Box 2191, Toms River, NJ 08754-2191
Tel: (732) 240-3520 Internet: www.planning.co.ocean.nj.us/rjmiller

Assistant Airpark Manager **(Vacant)** .... (732) 240-3520

Printing and Graphic Arts Department
162 Chestnut St., Toms River, NJ 08753
P.O. Box 2191, Toms River, NJ 08754-2191
Fax: (732) 929-4787

Director **Carmen F. Amato** .... (732) 929-4751

Office of Business Development and Tourism
101 Hooper Avenue, Room 109, Toms River, NJ 08754-2191
Tel: (732) 929-2000 (TTY) Fax: (732) 506-5000

Director **Dana Lancellotti** .... (732) 929-2000
E-mail: dlancellotti@co.ocean.nj.us
County Connection, Ocean County Mall **Leyla Wade** .... (732) 288-7777
Ocean County Mall, 1201 Hooper Avenue, Toms River, NJ 08753
E-mail: lwade@co.ocean.nj.us
Public Information Director **Donna E. Flynn** .... (732) 929-2000
E-mail: dflynn@co.ocean.nj.us

Mail Services Division
P.O. Box 2191, Toms River, NJ 08754-2191
Fax: (732) 506-5000

Supervisor **Thomas Coccia** .... (732) 929-4749
E-mail: thomascoccia@co.ocean.nj.us

Purchasing Department
P.O. Box 2191, Toms River, NJ 08754-2191
Fax: (732) 288-7636

△ Director **Michael J. Fiure** .... (732) 929-2101
E-mail: mfiure@co.ocean.nj.us

Roads Department
129 Hooper Ave., 2nd Floor, Toms River, NJ 08754
P.O. Box 2191, Toms River, NJ 08754-2191
Fax: (732) 506-5085

△ Road Supervisor **J. Thomas "Tom" Curcio** .... (732) 929-2133
Assistant County Road Supervisor **Scott J. Waters** .... (732) 929-2133

Department of Security
659 Ocean Avenue, Route 88, Lakewood, NJ 08701
Fax: (732) 363-1577

△ Director **Ronald Roma** .... (732) 929-4712
E-mail: ronroma@co.ocean.nj.us
Assistant Director **Robert Chadwick** .... (732) 929-4712

Department of Solid Waste Management
129 Hooper Ave., P.O. Box 2191, Toms River, NJ 08754-2191
Fax: (732) 244-8396 E-mail: ocrecycles@co.ocean.nj.us
Internet: www.co.ocean.nj.us/solidwaste

Director **Ernest J. Kuhlwein, Jr.** .... (732) 506-5047
Recycling Operations Superintendent **Arthur Burns** .... (732) 367-0802
E-mail: aburns@co.ocean.nj.us

Department of Transportation Services
1959 Route 9, Toms River, NJ 08754
PO Box 2191, Toms River, NJ 08754
Tel: (732) 736-8989 Fax: (732) 505-6963

△ Director **David L. Fitzgerald** .... (732) 736-8989
E-mail: dfitzgerald@co.ocean.nj.us
△ Operations Division Director **James A. Hand** .... (732) 736-8989

Veterans' Service Bureau
Bldg. 2, 1027 Hooper Ave., P.O. Box 2191, Toms River, NJ 08754-2191
Fax: (732) 506-5181

Director **John P. Dorrity** .... (732) 929-2096

Election Board of Ocean County
129 Hooper Avenue, Toms River, NJ 08754-2006
P.O. Box 2006, Toms River, NJ 08754
Fax: (732) 506-5110 E-mail: ocelectionboard@co.ocean.nj.us
Internet: www.co.ocean.nj.us/electionboard

Chairman **George R. Gilmore** .... (732) 929-2167

★ Elected Official ▲ Appointed by Legislature ▼ Appointed by Governor ▶ Appointed by Board or Commission ● Appointed by Judge
■ Appointed by Mayor △ Appointed by Freeholders ▽ Appointed by Supervisor ▷ Appointed by County Executive ○ Appointed by Council

Ocean County Board of Taxation

Court House, 118 Washington Street, Room 215, Toms River, NJ 08753
P.O. Box 2191, Toms River, NJ 08754-2191
Internet: www.tax.co.ocean.nj.us Fax: (732) 506-5197

Tax Administrator **Chelsea Skuby** .... (732) 929-2008

Ocean County Board of Social Services

1027 Hooper Ave., P.O. Box 547, Toms River, NJ 08754-0547
Tel: (732) 244-3812 (TDD) Fax: (732) 244-8075

Director **Linda Murtagh** .... (732) 349-1500
Deputy Director **Marisa Ligato** .... (732) 349-1500

Ocean County College

P.O. Box 2001, Toms River, NJ 08754-2001
Fax: (732) 255-0444 Internet: www.ocean.edu

President **Jon H. Larson** .... (732) 255-0400
Education: Norwich 1963 BA; Maryland 1971 MA, 1985 PhD

Ocean County Library

101 Washington Street, Toms River, NJ 08753
Fax: (732) 473-1356 Internet: www.theoceancountylibrary.org

Director **Susan Quinn** .... (732) 349-6200
E-mail: squinn@theoceancountylibrary.org
Education: Gettysburg 1980 BA; Rutgers
Librarian/Webmaster **David Evans** .... (732) 349-6200
E-mail: devans@theoceancountylibrary.org

Ocean County Vocational Technical School [OCVTS]

137 Bey Lea Road, Toms River, NJ 08753-2703
Fax: (732) 505-8929 Internet: www.ocvts.org

President, Board of Education **Nina Anuario** .... (732) 240-6414
Superintendent **William P. Hoey, Jr.** .... (732) 240-6414
Assistant Superintendent **Nancy Weber-Loeffert** .... (732) 240-6414

Office of the County Clerk

Court House, 118 Washington Street, Toms River, NJ 08754
P.O. Box 2191, Toms River, NJ 08754-2191
Tel: (732) 929-2018 Fax: (732) 349-4336
Internet: www.oceancountyclerk.com

★ County Clerk **Scott M. Colabella** (R) .... (732) 929-2018
Term Expires: December 31, 2020
E-mail: scolabella@co.ocean.nj.us
Date of Birth: August 1959
Education: Rider 1981 BA
Deputy County Clerk **Barbara Lanuto** (R) .... (732) 929-2018
E-mail: blanuto@co.ocean.nj.us
Confidential Assistant **Colleen M. Rivell** .... (732) 929-2018
E-mail: crivell@co.ocean.nj.us
Confidential Clerk **Kevin R. Toye** .... (732) 929-2018
E-mail: ktoye@co.ocean.nj.us

Office of the Executive County Superintendent of Schools

212 Washington Street, Toms River, NJ 08753
Fax: (732) 506-5336 Internet: www.co.ocean.nj.us/ocschools

Superintendent of Schools (Interim) **Todd C. Flora** ...... (732) 929-2079

Office of the Sheriff

Justice Complex, 120 Hooper Ave., P.O. Box 2191,
Toms River, NJ 08754-2191
Tel: (732) 929-2044 Tel: (732) 288-7841 (Sheriff's Sales)
Tel: (732) 929-2112 (Judicial Services)
Tel: (732) 929-2119 (CSI) Tel: (732) 929-2050 (Field Services)
Tel: (732) 929-2010 (Communications)
Tel: (732) 341-3451 (Emergency Management) Fax: (732) 349-1909
Internet: www.co.ocean.nj.us/ocsheriff

★ Sheriff **Michael G. Mastronardy** (R) .... (732) 929-2044
Term Expires: December 31, 2016
E-mail: mmastronardy@co.ocean.nj.us
Undersheriff **Brian J. Klimakowski** .... (732) 929-2044
E-mail: bklimakowski@co.ocean.nj.us
Chief Sheriff's Officer **Capt. David Schenk** .... (732) 349-2010
Communications Division **John Farnkopf** .... (732) 929-2112

Ocean County Police Academy

659 Ocean Avenue, Lakewood, NJ 08701
Fax: (732) 905-8345 Internet: www.ocpoliceacademy.com

Director **Brian J. Klimakowski** .... (732) 363-8710

Office of the Surrogate

Ocean County Courthouse, 118 Washington Street, Room 216,
Toms River, NJ 08754
Fax: (732) 506-5087 Internet: www.oceancountygov.com/surrogat

★ Surrogate **Jeffrey W. Moran** (R) .... (732) 929-2011
Term Expires: December 31, 2018
E-mail: jmoran@co.ocean.nj.us
Deputy Surrogate **Ashley Fiore** .... (732) 929-2011

County of Oklahoma, Oklahoma

County Office Bldg., 320 Robert S. Kerr Ave., Oklahoma City, OK 73102
Internet: www.oklahomacounty.org

County Seat: Oklahoma City **Election Type:** Partisan
Population: 776,864 (2015)

Office of the Board of County Commissioners

County Office Bldg., 320 Robert S. Kerr Ave., Oklahoma City, OK 73102

★ Chair **Brian Maughan** (R-District 2) .... (405) 713-1502
Term Expires: January 3, 2019
E-mail: brian@oklahomacounty.org
★ Vice Chair **Willa D. Johnson** (D-District 1) .... (405) 713-1501
Term Expires: January 2, 2019
E-mail: wjohnson@oklahomacounty.org
★ Commissioner
Raymond L. "Ray" Vaughn, Jr. (R-District 3) .... (405) 713-1503
Term Expires: January 1, 2019
E-mail: rvaughn@oklahomacounty.org
Education: Oklahoma Christian 1970 BA; Oklahoma City 1976 JD

Agricultural Extension Service

250 North East 63th Street, Oklahoma City, OK 73111

► Director and Extension Home Economist
Ladonna Dunlop .... (405) 713-1125

County Engineer

County Office Bldg., 320 Robert S. Kerr Ave., Oklahoma City, OK 73102

► County Engineer **Stacey Trumbo** .... (405) 713-1495
Planning Commission Director **Tyler Gammon, Jr.** ...... (405) 713-1361

★ Elected Official ▲ Appointed by Legislature ▼ Appointed by Governor ► Appointed by Board or Commission ● Appointed by Judge
■ Appointed by Mayor △ Appointed by Freeholders ▽ Appointed by Supervisor ▷ Appointed by County Executive ○ Appointed by Council

COUNTIES

Election Board
County Office Bldg., 4201 N. Lincoln, Oklahoma City, OK 73105
Fax: (405) 713-7191

Secretary **Doug Sanderson** .... (405) 713-1515
Assistant Secretary **Karla Durham** .... (405) 713-1515

Emergency Management
County Office Bldg., 320 Robert S. Kerr Ave., Room 101, Oklahoma City, OK 73102
Tel: (405) 713-1360

▶ Director **David Barnes** .... (405) 713-1369

Environmental Health and Safety Division
County Office Bldg., 320 Robert S. Kerr Ave., Oklahoma City, OK 73102

▶ Director **Dan Matthews** .... (405) 713-1371

Equalization Board
County Office Bldg., 320 Robert S. Kerr Ave., Oklahoma City, OK 73102

Board Member **Mevin Combs** .... (405) 713-1544
Board Member **Patrick Crawley** .... (405) 713-1544
Board Member **Randolph Shadid** .... (405) 713-1544
Secretary **Carolynn Caudill** (R) .... (405) 713-1544

Law Library
321 Park Ave., Oklahoma City, OK 73102
Fax: (405) 713-1852

Librarian **Venita Hoover** .... (405) 713-1353
E-mail: venhoo@oklahomacounty.org

Management Information Systems
County Office Bldg., 320 Robert S. Kerr Ave., Room 321, Oklahoma City, OK 73102

▶ Director **Mike Harman** .... (405) 713-1333

Metropolitan Library System
131 Dean A. McGee Ave., Oklahoma City, OK 73102

Executive Director **Tim Rodgers** .... (405) 606-3725
E-mail: trodgers@metrolibrary.org
Deputy Executive Director **Kay Bauman** .... (405) 231-8650
E-mail: kbauman@metrolibrary.org
Construction Management Director **Todd Olberding** .... (405) 606-3730
Development Director **Heather Zeoli** .... (405) 606-3760
E-mail: hzeoli@metrolibrary.org
Human Resources Coordinator **Elizabeth Kessler** .... (405) 606-3746
Marketing Director **Kim Terry** .... (405) 606-3755
E-mail: kterry@metrolibrary.org
Outreach Director **LaVetta Dent** .... (405) 606-3883
E-mail: ldent@metrolibrary.org
Headquarters Manager **(Vacant)** .... (405) 606-3728

Public Defender
County Office Bldg., 320 Robert S. Kerr Ave., Oklahoma City, OK 73102

Public Defender **Bob Ravitz** .... (405) 713-1550

Purchasing Department
County Office Bldg., 320 Robert S. Kerr Ave., Oklahoma City, OK 73102

Purchasing Agent **Jane Gaston** .... (405) 713-1485

Department of Training and General Assistance
Human Services Center, 7401 NE 23rd, Oklahoma City, OK 73141
Fax: (405) 713-1886

▶ Director **Christi Jernigan** .... (405) 713-1893

Oklahoma City-County Board of Health
2600 Northeast 63rd Street, Oklahoma City, OK 73111
Tel: (405) 425-4455 Internet: www.occhd.org/about/board-of-health

Oklahoma City-County Health Department [OCCHD]
2600 Northeast 63rd Street, Oklahoma City, OK 73111
Tel: (405) 427-8651 Fax: (405) 419-4279 Internet: www.occhd.org

Director **Gary R. Cox** .... (405) 425-4455
Education: Northeastern State 1968 BA; Tulsa 1973 JD
Medical Director **Dr. Lees** .... (405) 419-4036

Administrative Services Division
Deputy Director **Dave Cox** .... (405) 427-8651

Community Services Division
Deputy Director **Robert K. "Bob" Jamison** .... (405) 427-8651

Office of the County Assessor
County Office Bldg., 320 Robert S. Kerr Ave., Oklahoma City, OK 73102

★ County Assessor **Leonard E. Sullivan** (R) .... (405) 713-1200
Term Expires: December 31, 2018
Education: Oklahoma State BA
Chief Deputy County Assessor **Larry Stein** .... (405) 713-1200

Office of the County Clerk
County Office Bldg., 320 Robert S. Kerr Ave., Room 105, Oklahoma City, OK 73102
Fax: (405) 713-1810 Internet: http://countyclerk.oklahomacounty.org/

★ County Clerk/Registrar of Deeds **Carolynn Caudill** (R) .... (405) 713-7184
Term Expires: January 3, 2017
Chief Deputy Clerk **Danny Lambert** .... (405) 713-7188

Office of the County Sheriff
201 N. Shartel, Oklahoma City, OK 73102

★ Sheriff **John Whetsel** (D) .... (405) 713-1000
Term Expires: January 3, 2017
Undersheriff **P. D. Taylor** .... (405) 713-1000
Jail Administrator **Jack Herron** .... (405) 713-1000

Office of the County Treasurer
County Office Bldg., 320 Robert S. Kerr Ave., Room 307, Oklahoma City, OK 73102

★ Treasurer **Forrest "Butch" Freeman** (R) .... (405) 713-1300
Term Expires: January 2019
Education: Missouri 1965 BSJ, 1970 MBA
Chief Deputy Treasurer **Jerry Stone** .... (405) 713-1300

Office of the District Attorney
County Office Bldg., 320 Robert S. Kerr Ave., Oklahoma City, OK 73102

★ District Attorney **David Prater** (D) .... (405) 713-1600
Term Expires: January 2, 2019
Education: Oklahoma JD

Office of the District Clerk
320 Robert S. Kerr, Room 409, Oklahoma City, OK 73102

★ District Court Clerk **Rick Warren** .... (405) 713-1705
Term Expires: January 2, 2017

★ Elected Official ▲ Appointed by Legislature ▼ Appointed by Governor ▶ Appointed by Board or Commission ● Appointed by Judge
■ Appointed by Mayor △ Appointed by Freeholders ▽ Appointed by Supervisor ▷ Appointed by County Executive ○ Appointed by Council

County of Onondaga, New York

John H. Mulroy Civic Center, 421 Montgomery Street,
Syracuse, NY 13202
Tel: (315) 435-2222 (Information) Internet: www.ongov.net

County Seat: Syracuse **Election Type:** Partisan **Population:** 468,463 (2015)

Office of the County Executive

John H. Mulroy Civic Center, 421 Montgomery Street, 14th Floor,
Syracuse, NY 13202
Fax: (315) 435-8582 Internet: www.ongov.net/executive

★ County Executive **Joanne M. "Joanie" Mahoney** (R) . . . (315) 435-3516
Term Expires: December 31, 2019
Education: Syracuse BA, JD
Career: Prosecutor, Office of the District Attorney, County of Onondaga, New York; Council Member, Office of the Common Council, City of Syracuse, New York (2000-2004)
Senior Executive Assistant **Lesley B Dublin** . . . . (315) 435-3516
E-mail: lesleydublin@ongov.net
Deputy County Executive **William P. Fisher** . . . . (315) 435-3516
Executive Secretary **Mary Beth Rice** . . . . (315) 435-3516
E-mail: marybethrice@ongov.net
Deputy County Executive, Human Services
Ann Rooney . . . . (315) 435-3516
Executive Secretary **Karen Rein** . . . . (315) 435-3516
E-mail: karenrein@ongov.net
Deputy County Executive, Physical Services
Mary Beth Primo . . . . (315) 435-3516
Executive Secretary **Eloise Leflore** . . . . (315) 435-3516
E-mail: eloiseleflore@ongov.net
Chief of Staff **Martin Skahen** . . . . (315) 435-3516
Research and Communications Officer **Justin Sayles** . . . . (315) 435-3516
Confidential Information Aide **Pam Marsallo** . . . . (315) 435-3516
E-mail: pmarsallo@ongov.net

Adult and Longterm Care Service

John H. Mulroy Civic Center, 421 Montgomery Street, 13th Floor,
Syracuse, NY 13202
Tel: (315) 435-2362 Internet: www.ongov.net/ay

Department of Correction

6660 East Seneca Turnpike, Jamesville, NY 13078-9405
Fax: (315) 435-5596 Internet: www.ongov.net/correction

▷ Commissioner **Timothy H. Cowin** . . . . (315) 435-5581 ext. 1128
Education: SUNY (Empire State) 1988 BS; Syracuse 1991 JD
▷ Assistant Commissioner **Randy W. Blume** . . . . . (315) 435-5581 ext. 1136
E-mail: randyblume@ongov.net
Education: SUNY (Albany) 1979 BPS
▷ Assistant Commissioner **John Heisler III** . . . . . . (315) 435-5581 ext. 1139
Administrative Captain
Capt. George Manolis . . . . (315) 435-5581 ext. 1137
E-mail: georgemanolis@ongov.net
Security Captain **William T. Brush** . . . . (315) 435-5581 ext. 1243
Training Supervisor **Peter Battista** . . . . (315) 435-5581 ext. 1189
E-mail: peterbattista@ongov.net

Office of Economic Development

John H. Mulroy Civic Center, 421 Montgomery Street, 14th Floor,
Syracuse, NY 13202
Fax: (315) 435-3669 E-mail: info@syracusecentral.com
Internet: www.syracusecentral.com

Director **Julie A. Cerio** . . . . (315) 435-3770
E-mail: juliecerio@ongov.net
Secretary **Karen Doster** . . . . (315) 435-3770
E-mail: karendoster@ongov.net

Community Development Division

1100 Civic Center, Syracuse, NY 13202
Fax: (315) 435-3794 Internet: www.ongov.net/cd

Director **Robert S. DeMore** (R) . . . . (315) 435-3558
E-mail: robertdemore@ongov.net
Administrative Planning and Funding Coordinator
Nina Andon-McLane . . . . (315) 435-3558
E-mail: ninaandon-mclane@ongov.net
Housing Program Coordinator **Susan Grossman** . . . . (315) 435-3558
E-mail: susangrossman@ongov.net
Project Coordinator **Anthony Mueller** . . . . (315) 435-3558

Department of Emergency Communications

3911 Central Ave., Syracuse, NY 13215
Fax: (315) 435-8620 E-mail: E9ECOM1@ongov.net
Internet: www.ongov.net/911

▷ Commissioner **William R. Bleyle** . . . . (315) 435-7911
E-mail: wbleyle@ongov.net
Secretary **Lori Hable** . . . . (315) 435-7911
E-mail: LoriHable@ongov.net
Deputy Commissioner **Carl Loerzel, Jr.** . . . . (315) 435-7911
E-mail: carlloerzel@ongov.net

Office of the Environment

421 Montgomery Street, 14th Floor, Syracuse, NY 13202
Fax: (315) 435-8582 Internet: www.ongov.net/environment

▷ Director **Travis R. Glazier** . . . . (315) 435-2647
E-mail: Travisglazier@ongov.net

Department of Facilities Management

County Office Building, 600 South State, Room 100,
Syracuse, NY 13202-3022
Fax: (315) 435-3789 Internet: www.ongov.net/facilities

▷ Commissioner **Duane Owens** . . . . (315) 435-3451
Deputy Commissioner **Archie Wixson** . . . . (315) 435-3451
E-mail: archiewixson@ongov.net

Finance Department

John H. Mulroy Civic Center, 421 Montgomery Street, 15th Floor,
Syracuse, NY 13202-2998
Fax: (315) 435-2421 Internet: www.ongov.net/finance

▷ Chief Fiscal Officer **Steven Morgan** . . . . (315) 435-3346
Secretary **Cheryl Mahady** . . . . (315) 435-3346
Real Property/Tax Services Director **Donald Weber** . . . . . (315) 435-2426

Division of Management and Budget

John H. Mulroy Civic Center, 421 Montgomery St., 14th Fl.,
Syracuse, NY 13202-2998
Fax: (315) 435-3439

Deputy Director **Tara Venditti** . . . . (315) 435-3346
Loss Control Director **Robert J. Bratek** . . . . (315) 435-2856
E-mail: robertbratek@ongov.net
Risk Management Director **Mark A. Stanczyk** (D) . . . . . . (315) 435-3716
Employee Benefits Manager **Denise Downing** . . (315) 435-3498 ext. 4134

Department of Emergency Management

421 Montgomery Street, Syracuse, NY 13202
Fax: (315) 435-3309 E-mail: emweb01@ongov.net

▷ Commissioner **Dan Wears** . . . . (315) 435-2525
Director of Fire Bureau **Joe Rinefierd** . . . . (315) 435-2525
E-mail: jrinefierd@ongov.net
Director of EMS Bureau
Anthony M. "Tony" DiGregorio . . . . (315) 435-2525
Fax: (315) 435-5142
Program Assistant **Michael Huppmann** . . . . (315) 435-2525
E-mail: mhuppmann@ongov.net
Building/Fire Inspector **James Woods** . . . . (315) 435-2525

COUNTIES

★ Elected Official ▲ Appointed by Legislature ▼ Appointed by Governor ▶ Appointed by Board or Commission ● Appointed by Judge
■ Appointed by Mayor △ Appointed by Freeholders ▽ Appointed by Supervisor ▷ Appointed by County Executive ○ Appointed by Council

COUNTIES

Onondaga County Health Department [OCHD]
John H. Mulroy Civic Center, 421 Montgomery Street, 9th Floor, Syracuse, NY 13202-2903
Fax: (315) 435-5720 Internet: www.ongov.net/health

▷Commissioner **Indu Gupta** . . . . . (315) 435-3155
E-mail: indugupta@ongov.net
Secretary **Sheila Smith** . . . . . (315) 435-3155
E-mail: sheilasmith@ongov.net
Deputy Commissioner **Michelle Mignano** . . . . . (315) 435-3662
Medical Director **Quoc Nguyen** . . . . . (315) 435-3252
Public Health Administrator **(Vacant)** . . . . . (315) 435-3252
Fiscal Officer **(Vacant)** . . . . . (315) 435-3244

Office of the Medical Examiner
100 Elizabeth Blackwell St., Syracuse, NY 13210
Fax: (315) 435-3319

▷Chief Medical Examiner **Robert Stoppacher** . . . . . (315) 435-3163
E-mail: robertstoppacher@ongov.net
Operations Manager **Catherine Unger** . . . . . (315) 435-3163 ext. 4032
E-mail: catherineunger@ongov.net

Bureau of Community Environmental Health
421 Montgomery Street, 12th Floor, Syracuse, NY 13202
Fax: (315) 435-6606
Director **Kevin Zimmerman** . . . . . (315) 435-6623

Department of Information Technology
John H. Mulroy Civic Center, 421 Montgomery Street, 16th Floor, Syracuse, NY 13202
Fax: (315) 435-2208 Internet: www.ongov.net/it

▷Chief Information Officer **Kevin Sexton** . . . . . (315) 435-2441
E-mail: kevin.sexton@ongov.net
Secretary **Charlene Edwards** . . . . . (315) 435-2441
E-mail: charleneedwards@ongov.net
Deputy Chief Information Officer **Michele Clark** . . . . . (315) 435-2441
E-mail: micheleclark@ongov.net
Business Manager (Acting) **Denice Fire** . . . . . (315) 435-2441
E-mail: dfire@ongov.net

Law Department
John H. Mulroy Civic Center, 421 Montgomery Street, 10th Floor, Syracuse, NY 13202-2923
Fax: (315) 435-5729 Internet: www.ongov.net/law

▷County Attorney **Robert A. Durr** . . . . . (315) 435-2170

Department of Adult and Long Term Care Services
John H. Mulroy Civic Center, 421 Montgomery Street, 10th Floor, Syracuse, NY 13202
Fax: (315) 435-3279 Internet: www.ocdmh.net

▷Commissioner **Lisa D. Alford** . . . . . (315) 435-3355
E-mail: lalford@ongov.net
▷Deputy Commissioner and Executive Director **(Vacant)** . . . (315) 435-2362
Secretary **Nancy Lell** . . . . . (315) 435-3355 ext. 4967
E-mail: nancylell@ongov.net
▷Deputy Commissioner for Mental Health and Protective Services for Adults **Barry L. Beck** . . . . . (315) 435-3355
E-mail: barrybeck@ongov.net
Director of Contract Services **(Vacant)** . . . . . (315) 435-3355
Director of Planning and Quality Improvement **Mathew Roosa** . . . . . (315) 435-3355
Assisted Outpatient Treatment Coordinator **Helen Cosgrove** . . . . . (315) 435-3355
Director of Community Services Programs and Long Term Care **Joanne Spoto Decker** . . . . . (315) 435-2362
E-mail: joannedecker@ongov.net
Veterans Services Director **Corliss Dennis** . . . . . (315) 435-3217

Office for the Aging
Caregivers Resources Center Director **Cynthia Stevenson** . . . . . (315) 435-2362
Expanded In-Home Services to the Elderly Program (EISEP) Director **Deborah Jones** . . . . . (315) 435-2362
Home Energy Assistance Program (HEAP) and Transportation and Senior Employment Coordinator **Larry Mathews** . . . . . (315) 435-2362
Senior Nutrition Director **Maria Mahar** . . . . . (315) 435-2362

Department of Children and Family Services
John H. Mulroy Civic Center, 421 Montgomery Street, Eighth Floor, Syracuse, NY 13202
Tel: (315) 435-2884

Director of School Based Initiatives **Jennifer Parmalee** . . (315) 435-2884
Director of Day Treatment Services **Carol Yaeger-Rosario** . . . . . (315) 435-2884
Director of Outpatient Services **Erin Yudakatis** . . . . . (315) 435-2884

Parks and Recreation Department
106 Lake Drive, Liverpool, NY 13088
Fax: (315) 457-3681 E-mail: parks@ongov.net
Internet: www.onondagacountyparks.com

▷Commissioner **William J. "Bill" Lansley** . . . . . (315) 451-7275
E-mail: williamlansley@ongov.net
Administrative Director **Nathaniel "Nate" Stevens** . . . . . (315) 451-7275 ext. 107
Operations Director **George Boyle** . . . . . (315) 451-7275 ext. 114
Recreation Director **Leiko Benson** . . . . . (315) 435-3172 ext. 113
Director, Rosamond Gifford Zoo **Henry Fox** . . . . (315) 435-8511 ext. 104
One Conservation Place, Syracuse, NY 13204 Fax: (315) 435-8517
Deputy Commissioner **(Vacant)** . . . . . (315) 451-7275

Personnel Department
John H. Mulroy Civic Center, 421 Montgomery Street, 13th Floor, Syracuse, NY 13202-2959
Fax: (315) 435-8272 E-mail: peweb1@ongov.net
Internet: www.ongov.net/employment

▷Commissioner **Peter Troiano** . . . . . (315) 435-3537
E-mail: petertroiano@ongov.net
Education: SUNY (Oswego) 1976 BA; Syracuse 1977 MPA
Executive Assistant **Lorraine Bissi Greenlese** . . . . . (315) 435-3537
E-mail: lorrainebissi-greenlese@ongov.net
Civil Service Administration Director **(Vacant)** . . . . . (315) 435-3537
Employee Relations and Personnel Administration Director **Carl Hummel** . . . . . (315) 435-3537
E-mail: carlhummel@ongov.net

Department of Probation
John H. Mulroy Civic Center, 421 Montgomery Street, 6th Floor, Syracuse, NY 13202-2923
Tel: (315) 435-2321 Fax: (315) 435-3329
Internet: www.ongov.net/probation

▷Commissioner **Andrew Sicherman** . . . . . (315) 435-2380
E-mail: andysicherman@ongov.net

Hillbrook Juvenile Detention Center
4949 Velasko Rd., Syracuse, NY 13215-0237
Tel: (315) 435-1421 Fax: (315) 435-2671

Juvenile Justice and Detention Services Director **Troy Hopson** . . . . . (315) 435-1421
Administrative Officer **Vera Parsons** . . . . . (315) 435-1421
E-mail: veraparsons@ongov.net

Division of Purchase
John H. Mulroy Civic Center, 421 Montgomery Street, 13th Floor, Syracuse, NY 13202-2989
Fax: (315) 435-3424 Internet: www.ongov.net/purchase

▷Purchasing Director **Sean Carroll** . . . . . (315) 435-3458 ext. 2043

★ Elected Official ▲ Appointed by Legislature ▼ Appointed by Governor ▶ Appointed by Board or Commission ● Appointed by Judge
■ Appointed by Mayor △ Appointed by Freeholders ▽ Appointed by Supervisor ▷ Appointed by County Executive ○ Appointed by Council

Division of Purchase *continued*

Secretary **Elizabeth Canino** . . . . . . (315) 435-3458 ext. 2244
Assistant Director/Systems **Andrew Trombley** . . (315) 435-3458 ext. 5631

Department of Social Services [DSS]

John H. Mulroy Civic Center, 421 Montgomery Street, 12th Floor, Syracuse, NY 13202
Fax: (315) 435-8354 Internet: www.ongov.net/dss

▷Commissioner (Children's Services) **David A. Sutkowy** . . (315) 435-2985
E-mail: david.sutkowy@dfa.state.ny.us
Commissioner (Economic Security) **Sarah G. Merrick** . . . (315) 435-2985
Commissioner (Adult and Long Term Care)
Robert C. "Bob" Long . . . . . . (315) 435-3437
Education: Syracuse 1981 MPA
Assistant Commissioner, Medical Assistance
Brenda Streeter . . . . . . (315) 435-2928 ext. 4444
Assistant Commissioner, Personnel/Staff Development **Colleen A. Gunnip** . . . . . . (315) 435-2988 ext. 7150
E-mail: colleen.gunnip@dfa.state.ny.us
Assistant Commissioner, Temporary Assistance and Food Stamps **Ava Kerznowski** . . . . . . (315) 435-2700
Chief Welfare Attorney **Paula Mallory Engel** . . (315) 435-2585 ext. 7133
Welfare Management Systems Coordinator
Michael Torrick . . . . . . (315) 435-2348
Executive Deputy Commissioner **Monica Brown** . . . . . . (315) 435-2985

Transportation Department

John H. Mulroy Civic Center, 421 Montgomery Street, 11th Floor, Syracuse, NY 13202-2995
Fax: (315) 435-5744

▷Commissioner **Brian Donnelly** . . . . . . (315) 435-3205
E-mail: briandonnelly@ongov.net
Secretary to the Commissioner
Joyce Coburn . . . . . . (315) 435-3205 ext. 5786
E-mail: joycecoburn@ongov.net
Deputy Commissioner **Mark Premo** . . . . . . (315) 435-3205
Deputy Commissioner **Robert Petrovich** . . . . . . (315) 435-3205

Veterans Service Agency

John H. Mulroy Civic Center, 421 Montgomery Street, 10th Floor, Syracuse, NY 13202
Fax: (315) 435-3221 Internet: www.ongov.net/veterans/

Director **Corliss Dennis** . . . . . . (315) 435-3217

Department of Water Environment Protection [WEP]

650 Hiawatha Blvd. West, Syracuse, NY 13204-1194
Tel: (315) 435-2260 Fax: (315) 435-5023 Internet: www.ongov.net/wep

▷Commissioner **A. T. "Tom" Rhoads** . . . . . . (315) 435-2260
Deputy Commissioner **Michael J. Lannon** . . . . . . (315) 435-2260
Fiscal Officer **Bonnie Karasinski** . . . . . . (315) 435-2260
Training Officer **David Kenyon** . . . . . . (315) 435-2260
E-mail: davekenyon@ongov.net
Construction Supervisor **Paul McInerey** . . . . . . (315) 435-2260
E-mail: paulmcinerney@ongov.net
Sewer Maintenance Engineer **Nicholas A. Capozza** . . . . . . (315) 435-5402
E-mail: nickcapozza@ongov.net Fax: (315) 435-5458

CNY Works, Inc.

443 North Franklin Street, Syracuse, NY 13204
Fax: (315) 472-9492 Internet: www.cnyworks.com

Executive Director **Lenore Sealy** . . . . . . (315) 473-8250

Onondaga Community College [OCC]

4585 West Seneca Turnpike, Syracuse, NY 13215-4585
Fax: (315) 469-6775 E-mail: occinfo@sunyocc.edu
Internet: www.sunyocc.edu

President **Casey Crabill** . . . . . . (315) 498-2211

Onondaga Community College *continued*

Provost and Senior Vice President
Cathleen C. McColgin . . . . . . (315) 498-2790
Senior Vice President, College Affiliated Enterprises and Asset Management **David W. Murphy** . . . . . . (315) 498-2213

Onondaga County Public Library [OCPL]

Onondaga County Public Library, 447 South Salina Street, Syracuse, NY 13202-2494
Fax: (315) 435-8533 E-mail: reference@onlib.org
Internet: www.onlib.org

▷President, Board of Trustees **Virginia Biesiada** . . . . . . (315) 435-1900
Executive Director **Susan Mitchell** . . . . . . (315) 435-1900
E-mail: director@onlib.org
Administrative Director **Matt Delaney** . . . . . . (315) 435-1900
E-mail: mdelaney@onlib.org
Administrator for System and Member Services
Deb Lewis . . . . . . (315) 435-1900
E-mail: dlewis@onlib.org
City Libraries Administrator **Susan Reekhow** . . . . . . (315) 435-1900
E-mail: sreekhow@onlib.org

Onondaga County Resource Recovery Agency [OCRRA]

100 Elwood Davis Rd., North Syracuse, NY 13212
Fax: (315) 453-2872 E-mail: info@ocrra.org Internet: www.ocrra.org

Executive Director **Mark Donnelly** . . . . . . (315) 453-2866

Onondaga County Soil and Water Conservation District [OCSWCD]

6680 Onondaga Lake Parkway, Liverpool, NY 13088
Tel: (315) 457-0325 Fax: (315) 457-0410 Internet: www.ocswcd.org

Chairman of the Board **F. Spencer Givens III** . . . . . . (315) 457-0325
Vice Chairman of the Board **Craig Dennis** . . . . . . (315) 457-0325
Executive Director **Mark Burger** . . . . . . (315) 457-0325

Metropolitan Water Board/Onondaga County Water District

4170 Route 31, Clay, NY 13041
Fax: (315) 652-1977 Internet: www.ongov.net/mwb

▲Chairman **Robert J. Andrews** (R) . . . . . . (315) 652-8656
Vice Chair **Terrance Mannion** . . . . . . (315) 652-8656
Executive Director **I. Holly Rosenthal** . . . . . . (315) 652-8656

Syracuse-Onondaga County Planning Agency [SOCPA]

John H. Mulroy Civic Center, 421 Montgomery Street, 11th Floor, Syracuse, NY 13202
Fax: (315) 435-2439 Internet: www.ongov.net/planning

Director **(Vacant)** . . . . . . (315) 435-2611
GIS Services Manager **Ed Hart** . . . . . . (315) 435-8572
Syracuse Zoning Office Administrator
Heather Lamendola . . . . . . (315) 448-8640
201 East Washington Street, Room 512, Syracuse, NY 13202
Assistant Director for GIS Services **Megan Costa** . . . . . . (315) 435-8571

Office of the County Legislature

Court House, 401 Montgomery Street, Room 407, Syracuse, NY 13202
Tel: (315) 435-2070 Fax: (315) 435-8434
Internet: www.ongov.net/legislature

★Chairman **J. Ryan McMahon II** (R-District 15) . . . . . . (315) 415-2520
Term Expires: December 31, 2017
E-mail: r.mcmahon@tfsny.com
★Floor Leader **Linda R. Ervin** (D-District 17) . . . . . . (315) 449-1050
Term Expires: December 31, 2017
E-mail: ervinforcountyleg@gmail.com

(continued on next page)

★Elected Official ▲Appointed by Legislature ▼Appointed by Governor ►Appointed by Board or Commission ●Appointed by Judge
■Appointed by Mayor △Appointed by Freeholders ▽Appointed by Supervisor ▷Appointed by County Executive ○Appointed by Council

Office of the County Legislature *continued*

★Floor Leader **Patrick M. Kilmartin** (R-District 11) .... (315) 295-0810
Term Expires: December 31, 2017
E-mail: pkilmartin@oncountyleg.com

★Legislator **Brian F. May** (R-District 1) .... (315) 447-4914
Term Expires: December 31, 2017
E-mail: bfmay6@yahoo.com

★Legislator **John C. Dougherty** (R-District 2) .... (315) 944-0716
Term Expires: December 31, 2017
E-mail: john@johndougherty.org

★Legislator **Tim Burtis** (R-District 3) .... (315) 396-3300
Term Expires: December 31, 2017
E-mail: tburtis@hotmail.com

★Legislator **Judith A. Tassone** (R-District 4) .... (315) 457-5458
Term Expires: December 31, 2017
E-mail: tassone@twcny.rr.com

★Legislator **Kathleen A. Rapp** (R-District 5) .... (315) 451-5294
Term Expires: December 31, 2017
E-mail: rappkathleen5@gmail.com

★Legislator **Michael E. Plochocki** (R-District 6) .... (315) 263-3172
Term Expires: December 31, 2017
E-mail: mikeplochocki@hotmail.com

★Legislator **Danny J. Liedka** (R-District 7) .... (315) 405-0742
Term Expires: December 31, 2017
E-mail: legislatorliedka@gmail.com

★Legislator **Christopher Ryan** (D-District 8) .... (315) 484-9171
Term Expires: December 31, 2017
E-mail: cjryan1123@yahoo.com

★Legislator **Peggy Chase** (D-District 9) .... (315) 435-2035
Term Expires: December 31, 2017
E-mail: peggychase2013@twcny.rr.com

★Legislator **Kevin A. Holmquist** (R-District 10) .... (315) 256-7346
Term Expires: December 31, 2017
E-mail: kevinholmquist@reagan.com

★Legislator **David H. Knapp** (R-District 12) .... (315) 558-0154
Term Expires: December 31, 2017
E-mail: dknappmb@aol.com

★Legislator **Derek T. Shepard, Jr.** (R-District 13) .... (315) 352-0110
Term Expires: December 31, 2017
E-mail: shepard@twcny.rr.com

★Legislator **Casey E. Jordan** (R-District 14) .... (315) 474-2644
Term Expires: December 31, 2017
E-mail: cejordan@cnymail.com
Date of Birth: October 14, 1961

★Legislator **Monica Williams** (D-District 16) .... (315) 395-0642
Term Expires: December 31, 2017
E-mail: williamsmonica174@yahoo.com

▲Clerk of the Legislature **Deborah L. "Debbie" Maturo** .. (315) 435-2070
E-mail: debbiematuro@ongov.net

Deputy Clerk **Katherine M. French** .... (315) 435-2070

Assistant Clerk **Kimberly "Kim" Memory** .... (315) 435-2070

Legislative Analyst and Budget Review Director
Susan "Sue" Stanczyk .... (315) 435-2070
E-mail: suestanczyk@ongov.net

Legislative Aide **Darcie Lesniak** .... (315) 435-2070
E-mail: darcielesniak@ongov.net

Legislative Aide **William T. "Bill" Kinne** (D) .... (315) 435-2070
E-mail: williamkinne@ongov.net

Secretary **Mary Ellen Britt** .... (315) 435-2070
E-mail: maryellenbritt@ongov.net

Office of the Commissioner of Jurors

505 South State Street, Room 120, Syracuse, NY 13202
Fax: (315) 671-1161

Commissioner of Jurors **Sandra A. Schepp** (R) .... (315) 671-1000

Deputy Commissioner of Jurors **Susan Magari** .... (315) 671-1000

Office of the Comptroller

John H. Mulroy Civic Center, 421 Montgomery Street, 14th Floor, Syracuse, NY 13202-2998
Fax: (315) 435-2250 Internet: www.ongov.net/comptroller

★Comptroller **Robert E. Antonacci II** (R) .... (315) 435-2130
Term Expires: December 31, 2019
E-mail: rantonacci@ongov.net
Education: LeMoyne-Owen; Syracuse JD

Executive Secretary **Nancy Campolito** .... (315) 435-2130
E-mail: ncampolito@ongov.net

Accounting Deputy Comptroller **James V. Maturo** ...... (315) 435-2130
E-mail: jamesmaturo@ongov.net

Auditing Deputy Comptroller **T. R. Schepp** .... (315) 435-2130

Chief Governmental Accountant **Philip M. Britt** .... (315) 435-2130

Office of the County Clerk

Court House, 401 Montgomery Street, Room 200, Syracuse, NY 13202-2171
Fax: (315) 435-3455 Internet: www.ongov.net/clerk

★County Clerk **Lisa Dell** .... (315) 435-2229
Term Expires: December 31, 2016

Principal Deputy County Clerk **Rory Sweenie** .... (315) 435-2226
E-mail: rorysweenie@ongov.net

Principal Deputy County Clerk/Office Manager
Jackie Norfolk .... (315) 435-2229
E-mail: jackienorfolk@ongov.net

Office of the District Attorney

Onondaga County/City of Syracuse Criminal Courthouse, 505 South State Street, Syracuse, NY 13202
Fax: (315) 435-3969 Internet: www.ongovda.net

★District Attorney **William J. Fitzpatrick** (R) .... (315) 435-2470
Term Expires: December 31, 2019
Education: Syracuse 1974, 1976 JD

Executive Secretary **Michele Robbins** .... (315) 435-2470

First Chief Assistant District Attorney
Domenic F. "Rick" Trunfio .... (315) 435-2470
E-mail: ricktrunfio@ongov.net

Administrative Officer **Barry S. Weiss** .... (315) 435-2470
E-mail: barryweiss@ongov.net

Office of the Sheriff

407 S. State St., Syracuse, NY 13202
Fax: (315) 435-2942

★Sheriff **Eugene J. Conway** (R) .... (315) 435-3044
Term Expires: December 31, 2018 Fax: (315) 435-2942
E-mail: eugeneconway@ongov.net

Undersheriff **Jason M. Cassalia** .... (315) 435-3044
E-mail: jasoncassalia@ongov.net Fax: (315) 435-2942

Civil Department Chief Deputy **Kenneth C. Andrews** ... (315) 435-3060
E-mail: kennethcandrews@ongov.net Fax: (315) 435-3070

Custody Department Chief **Esteban M. Gonzalez** .... (315) 435-1778
Fax: (315) 435-1718

Police Department Chief **Joseph Ciciarelli** .... (315) 435-3052
E-mail: josephciciarelli@ongov.net Fax: (315) 435-1478

Office of the Surrogate

Court House, 401 Montgomery Street, Room 209, Syracuse, NY 13202
Fax: (315) 671-1162

Surrogate **Ava S. Raphael** .... (315) 671-2098

Chief Clerk **Ellen Weinstein** .... (315) 671-2100

Deputy Chief Clerk **Mary Ellen Sofinski** .... (315) 671-2100

Law Clerk **Deborah Barrer** .... (315) 671-2100

★Elected Official ▲Appointed by Legislature ▼Appointed by Governor ▶Appointed by Board or Commission ●Appointed by Judge
■Appointed by Mayor △Appointed by Freeholders ▽Appointed by Supervisor ▷Appointed by County Executive ○Appointed by Council

Onondaga County Board of Elections

1000 Erie Boulevard West, Syracuse, NY 13204
Fax: (315) 435-8451 Internet: www.ongov.net/elections

Democrat Commissioner **Dustin Czarny** . . . . (315) 435-3312
Republican Commissioner **Helen Kiggins Walsh** . . . . (315) 435-3312

County of Orange, California

P.O. Box 687, Santa Ana, CA 92701
333 West Santa Ana Boulevard, Santa Ana, CA 92701
Tel: (855) 886-5400 (Information) Internet: www.ocgov.com

County Seat: Santa Ana **Election Type:** Nonpartisan
Population: 3,169,776 (2015)

Office of the Board of Supervisors

333 West Santa Ana Boulevard, Santa Ana, CA 92701
Tel: (714) 834-3100

★ Chairman **Lisa Bartlett** (District 5) . . . . (714) 834-3550
Term Expires: January 2019 Fax: (714) 834-2670
★ Vice Chair **Michelle P. Steel** (District 2) . . . . (714) 834-3220
Term Expires: January 2019 Fax: (714) 834-6109
Education: Pepperdine BB
★ Supervisor **Andrew Do** (District 1) . . . . (714) 834-3110
Term Expires: January 7, 2017
E-mail: first.district@ocgov.com
★ Supervisor **Todd Spitzer** (District 3) . . . . (714) 834-3330
Term Expires: January 8, 2017 Fax: (714) 834-2786
★ Supervisor **Shawn Nelson** (District 4) . . . . (714) 834-3440
Term Expires: January 3, 2019 Fax: (714) 834-2045
Education: USC BA; Western State U San Diego JD

Office of Human Resources [OCHR]

333 West Santa Ana Boulevard, 2nd Floor, Santa Ana, CA 92701-4017
Tel: (714) 834-5315 Fax: (714) 834-5523 E-mail: ochr@ocgov.com

Human Resources Director **Terri Bruner** . . . . (714) 834-2836
Assistant Human Resources Director **(Vacant)** . . . . (714) 834-3194
Employee Benefits Assistant Director
Renee Catanzariti . . . . (714) 834-2564

County Executive Office

333 West Santa Ana Boulevard, 3rd Floor, Santa Ana, CA 92701
Fax: (714) 834-3018 Internet: www.ocgov.com/ceo

▽ County Executive Officer **Frank Kim** . . . . (714) 834-6200
E-mail: Frank.Kim@ocgov.com Fax: (714) 834-3018
Chief Real Estate Officer **Scott Mayer** . . . . (714) 834-3046
Fax: (714) 834-5607
Government and Community Relations Director
Cymantha Atkinson . . . . (714) 834-7219
Fax: (714) 834-7622

Office of the Registrar of Voters

Building C, 1300 South Grand Avenue, Santa Ana, CA 92705
PO Box 11298, Santa Ana, CA 92711-1298
Tel: (714) 567-7600 Fax: (714) 567-7556 Internet: www.ocvote.com

Registrar of Voters **Neal Kelley** . . . . (714) 567-5139

Office of the Chief Operating Officer

Chief Operating Officer **Mark R. Denny** . . . . (714) 834-3028
Education: Cal State (Fullerton) BA Fax: (714) 834-4790

Office of the County Counsel

333 West Santa Ana Boulevard, Suite 407, Santa Ana, CA 92701
P.O. Box 1379, Santa Ana, CA 92702
Tel: (714) 834-3300 Fax: (714) 834-2359

County Counsel **Leon Page** . . . . (714) 834-3303

Office of the Clerk of the Board

Fax: (714) 834-4439

▽ Clerk of the Board **(Vacant)** . . . . (714) 834-2206

Office of the Deputy Chief Operating Officer

Deputy Chief Operating Officer **Jessica Witt** . . . . (714) 834-2345

Social Services Agency [SSA]

500 North State College Boulevard, Orange, CA 92868
Tel: (714) 435-4626 (Information Case Inquiry) Fax: (714) 541-7811
E-mail: ocssa@ocgov.com Internet: www.ssa.ocgov.com

Director **Mike Ryan** . . . . (714) 541-7708
Chief Deputy Director **Carol Wiseman** . . . . (714) 541-7707

Administrative Services Division

500 North State College Boulevard, Orange, CA 92868

Director **An Tran** . . . . (714) 645-7712
E-mail: an.tran@ssa.ocgov.com

Adult Services and Assistance Programs Division [ASAP]

500 North State College Boulevard, Orange, CA 92868

Director **Wendy Aquin** . . . . (714) 541-7783

Children and Family Services Division [CFS]

500 North State College Boulevard, Orange, CA 92868

Director **Gary Taylor** . . . . (714) 541-7793

Family Self-Sufficiency Division [FSS]

500 North State College Boulevard, Orange, CA 92868

Director **Nathan Nishimoto** . . . . (714) 541-7810

OC Waste and Recycling

300 North Flower Street, Suite 400, Santa Ana, CA 92703-5000
Tel: (714) 834-4000 Fax: (714) 834-4001 E-mail: info@ocwr.ocgov.com
Internet: www.oclandfills.com

Director **Dylan Wright** . . . . (714) 834-4122
Public Information Officer **Julie Chay** . . . . (714) 834-4174

Orange County Public Works

300 North Flower, Suite 800, Santa Ana, CA 92703-5000
Tel: (714) 667-8800 Fax: (714) 834-2395

▷ Director **Shane L. Silsby** . . . . (714) 667-8800
Director, Administration **Becky Juliano** . . . . (714) 667-8800
Director/Chief Engineer, OC Engineering **Khalid Bazmi** . . (714) 667-8800
Director, OC Development Services **Colby Cataldi** . . . . . (714) 667-8800
Fax: (714) 834-2395
Manager, OC Facilities, Design and Construction
Phillip Cook . . . . (714) 667-8800
Manager, Information and Technology Services
Sheila Carter . . . . (714) 667-8800
Manager, Procurement Services **Maria Pirona** . . . . (714) 667-8800
Communications Officer **Shanon Widor** . . . . (714) 667-9759

Local Agency Formation Commission

12 Civic Center Plaza, Room 235, Santa Ana, CA 92701

Executive Officer **Carolyn Emery** . . . . (714) 834-2556

John Wayne Airport

3160 Airway Ave., Costa Mesa, CA 92626
Tel: (949) 252-5171 Fax: (949) 252-5178 Internet: www.ocair.com

Director **Barry A. Rondinella** . . . . (949) 252-5183
Education: Cal State (Los Angeles)
Assistant Airport Director **(Vacant)** . . . . (949) 252-5192

COUNTIES

★ Elected Official ▲ Appointed by Legislature ▼ Appointed by Governor ▶ Appointed by Board or Commission ● Appointed by Judge
■ Appointed by Mayor △ Appointed by Freeholders ▽ Appointed by Supervisor ▷ Appointed by County Executive ○ Appointed by Council

Office of the Deputy Chief Operating Officer
Tel: (714) 834-2345

Deputy Chief Operating Officer **Lilly Simmering** . . . . (714) 834-2345

Office of the Public Defender [OCPD]
14 Civic Center Plaza, Santa Ana, CA 92701-4029
Fax: (714) 834-2729 E-mail: pdinfo@pubdef.ocgov.com
Internet: www.pubdef.ocgov.com

Public Defender (Interim) **Sharon Petrosino** . . . . (714) 834-2144
Chief Deputy Public Defender **(Vacant)** . . . . (714) 834-2144

Probation Department
1535 East Orangewood Avenue, Anaheim, CA 92805
Tel: (714) 569-2000 Internet: http://egov.ocgov.com/ocgov/Probation

Chief Probation Officer **Steven J. Sentman** . . . . (714) 569-2000

Orange County Community Resources
1770 North Broadway, Santa Ana, CA 92706-2642

Director **Steve Franks** . . . . (714) 480-2877
E-mail: steve.franks@occr.ocgov.com
Orange County Animal Care Director
Jennifer Hawkins . . . . (714) 796-6417
561 The City Drive, Orange, CA 92868 Fax: (714) 935-6373
Orange County Community Services Director
Karen Roper . . . . (714) 480-2805
Building B, 1300 South Grand Avenue, Fax: (714) 480-2978
Santa Ana, CA 92705-4407
E-mail: karen.roper@occr.ocgov.com
Deputy Director for Housing and Community
Development **Julia Bidwell** . . . . (714) 480-2991
E-mail: julia.bidwell@occr.ocgov.com
Orange County Housing Authority Manager
John Hambuch . . . . (714) 480-2830
Homeless Prevention Programs Manager
Juanita Preciado . . . . (714) 480-2727

Office on Aging
Building B, 1300 South Grand Avenue, Santa Ana, CA 92705
Tel: (714) 480-6483 Fax: (714) 567-5021
E-mail: officeonaging@ocgov.com
Internet: www.officeonaging.ocgov.com

Executive Director **Renee Ramirez** . . . . (714) 480-6483

Human Relations Commission
Fax: (714) 567-7474 Internet: www.ochumanrelations.org

Executive Director **Rusty Kennedy** . . . . (714) 567-7470
E-mail: rusty.kennedy@occr.ocgov.com

Community Investment Division
Building B, 1300 South Grand Avenue, Santa Ana, CA 92705-4407
Tel: (714) 480-6449 Fax: (714) 834-7132

Executive Director **Andrew Munoz** . . . . (714) 480-6448
E-mail: andrew.munoz@occr.ocgov.com

Orange County Public Libraries [OCPL]
1501 East Saint Andrew Place, Santa Ana, CA 92705-4930
Tel: (714) 566-3000 E-mail: libraryadmin@occr.ocgov.com
Internet: www.ocpl.com

County Librarian **Helen Fried** . . . . (714) 566-3094
E-mail: helen.fried@occr.ocgov.com

Veterans Services Office
Building B, 1300 South Grand Avenue, Santa Ana, CA 92705-4407
Tel: (714) 567-7458 Fax: (714) 567-7450

Veterans Services Officer **Marco Martinez** . . . . (714) 480-6555

Orange County Parks
13042 Old Myford Road, Irvine, CA 92602
Tel: (714) 973-6865 E-mail: OCParks@ocparks.com
Internet: http://ocparks.com/

Orange County Parks Director **Stacy Blackwood** . . . . (949) 923-3743
Fax: (714) 667-6543

Orange County Parks *continued*

Senior Coastal Engineer **Susan Brodeur** . . . . (949) 585-6448
E-mail: susan.brodeur@ocparks.com
Education: Illinois Wesleyan; Florida Atlantic BSE

Orange County Health Care Agency [OCHCA]
405 West 5th Street, 7th Floor, Santa Ana, CA 92701
Fax: (714) 834-3660 Internet: www.ochealthinfo.com

Director **Mark A. Refowitz** . . . . (714) 834-6021
Assistant Agency Director **Richard Sanchez** . . . . (714) 834-6254

Office of Human Resources
Fax: (714) 834-4445

Manager **Robert Leys** . . . . (714) 834-2869
E-mail: rleys@ochca.com

Office of Information Technology
Fax: (714) 834-3632

Chief Information Officer **Christina Koslosky** . . . . (714) 834-5928
E-mail: akoslosky@ochca.com

Behavioral Health Services
Fax: (714) 834-5506

Deputy Agency Director **Mary R. Hale** . . . . (714) 834-6032

Correction Health Services
Deputy Agency Director **Kimberly Pearson** . . . . (714) 834-5404

Financial and Administrative Services
Fax: (714) 834-5506

Deputy Agency Director **Anna Peters** . . . . (714) 834-5101

Office of Health Policy and Communication
Chief **Donna Grubaugh** . . . . (714) 834-7652
Chief Compliance Officer **Thea Bullock** . . . . (714) 834-6254

Medical Services
Deputy Agency Director **Steve Thronson** . . . . (714) 834-4418

Health Disaster Management Division
Manager **(Vacant)** . . . . (714) 834-6167

Public Health Services
Fax: (714) 834-5506

Deputy Agency Director **David M. Souleles** . . . . (714) 834-3882
County Health Officer **Eric G. Handler** . . . . (714) 834-3155

Department of Child Support Services [CSS]
1055 N. Main St., Santa Ana, CA 92701
P.O. Box 22099, Santa Ana, CA 92702-2099
Tel: (866) 901-3212 (Toll-free) Fax: (714) 347-4811
Internet: www.css.ocgov.com

Director **Steven E. "Steve" Eldred** . . . . (714) 347-8115
E-mail: seldred@css.ocgov.com
Chief Deputy Director **Maria Arzola** . . . . (714) 347-8228
E-mail: marzola@css.ocgov.com
Deputy Director, Administration Services and
Information Technology **Rachael Vargas** . . . . (714) 347-8901
E-mail: rvargas@css.ocgov.com
Deputy Director, Case Management Operations
Dorothy Bond . . . . (714) 347-8926
Deputy Director, Policy and Process Management
(Vacant) . . . . (714) 347-8228
Customer Service Manager **Gloria Land** . . . . (714) 347-8107
Human Services Manager **Jennifer Canzoneri** . . . . (714) 347-5974
E-mail: jcanzoneri@css.ocgov.com
Marketing and Communications Manager
David Ruvalcaba . . . . (714) 347-8251
E-mail: druvalcaba@css.ocgov.com
Chief Attorney **Dee Dinnie** . . . . (714) 347-8130
Ombudsman **Maricela Siqueiros** . . . . (714) 347-8015

★ Elected Official ▲ Appointed by Legislature ▼ Appointed by Governor ▶ Appointed by Board or Commission ● Appointed by Judge
■ Appointed by Mayor △ Appointed by Freeholders ▽ Appointed by Supervisor ▷ Appointed by County Executive ○ Appointed by Council

Finance Office

333 West Santa Ana Boulevard, Third Floor, Santa Ana, CA 92701-4062
Tel: (714) 834-4304 Fax: (714) 834-3555

Chief Financial Officer **Michelle Aguirre** .... (714) 834-4304
Education: Cal State (Fullerton) MPA Fax: (714) 834-3555
Budget Director **(Vacant)** .... (714) 834-3530
Fax: (714) 834-6658
Public Finance Director **Suzanne Luster** .... (714) 834-3362
Fax: (714) 834-3346
Risk Manager **Tom Phillips** .... (714) 285-5510
E-mail: Tom.Phillips@ocgov.com Fax: (714) 285-5599

County Procurement Office

Bldg. A, 1300 South Grand Avenue, Santa Ana, CA 92705
Tel: (714) 567-7314 Fax: (714) 567-7307

County Procurement Officer **Rob Richardson** .... (714) 834-3481
E-mail: rob.richardson@ocgov.com Fax: (714) 567-5057

Chief Information Officer

333 West Santa Ana Boulevard, Second Floor, Santa Ana, CA 92701
Tel: (714) 834-3022 E-mail: cio.it@ocgov.com

Chief Information Officer **Christina Koslosky** .... (714) 834-7061
E-mail: christina.koslosky@ocgov.com Fax: (714) 834-7015

Office of the Assessor

Building 11, 625 North Ross Street, Room 142,
Santa Ana, CA 92702-5564
Fax: (714) 558-0681 Internet: www.ocgov.com/assessor

★ Assessor **Claude Parrish** .... (714) 834-2727
Term Expires: January 2019

Office of the Auditor-Controller

P.O. Box 567, Santa Ana, CA 92702-0567
Tel: (714) 834-2450 Fax: (714) 834-2569 Internet: www.ocgov.com/ac

★ Auditor-Controller **Eric Woolery** .... (714) 834-2457
Term Expires: December 31, 2018
Chief Deputy Auditor-Controller **(Vacant)** .... (714) 834-2458

Office of the County Clerk-Recorder

12 Civic Center Plaza, Room 101 and 106, Santa Ana, CA 92701
Tel: (714) 834-2500 Fax: (714) 834-2675 Internet: www.ocrecorder.com

★ Clerk-Recorder **Hugh Nguyen** .... (714) 834-2248
Term Expires: December 31, 2019
E-mail: hugh.nguyen@ocgov.com
Chief Deputy Clerk **Najeeb Siddiqui** .... (714) 834-2510
Chief Deputy Recorder **(Vacant)** .... (714) 834-2248

Office of the District Attorney-Public Administrator

401 Civic Center Drive West, Santa Ana, CA 92701
Tel: (714) 834-3600 Fax: (714) 834-5880
Internet: www.orangecountyda.com

★ District Attorney-Public Administrator
Anthony "Tony" Rackauckas .... (714) 834-3401
Term Expires: January 8, 2019
E-mail: tony.rackauckas@da.ocgov.com
Education: Cal State (Long Beach) 1968 BA; Loyola Law 1971 JD
Chief of Staff **Susan Kang Schroeder** .... (714) 347-8408
Education: USC BA; San Diego JD
Chief, Bureau of Investigation **Craig Hunter** .... (714) 347-8419
Senior Assistant District Attorney, Branch Court
Operations **Jaime Coulter** .... (714) 347-8404
Senior Assistant District Attorney, General Felonies/
Economic Crime **Joe D'Agostino** .... (714) 347-8403

Office of the District Attorney-Public Administrator *continued*

Senior Assistant District Attorney, Special Projects
Michael Lubinski .... (714) 347-8640
E-mail: Mike.Lubinski@da.ocgov.com Fax: (714) 834-5880
Senior Assistant District Attorney, Vertical Prosecution/
Violent Crimes **Jim Tanizaki** .... (714) 347-8402

Insurance Fraud Unit

P.O. Box 478, Santa Ana, CA 92702

Deputy-in-Charge **Tony Ferrentino** .... (714) 664-3933

Office of the Treasurer-Tax Collector

Building 11, 625 North Ross Street, Santa Ana, CA 92702-4515
PO Box 4515, Santa Ana, CA 92702-4515
Fax: (714) 834-2912 E-mail: treasurer@ttc.ocgov.com

★ Treasurer-Tax Collector **Shari L. Freidenrich** .... (714) 834-7625
Term Expires: January 1, 2019
E-mail: shari.freidenrich@ttc.ocgov.com
Education: Washington State 1982 BA
Chief Assistant Treasurer-Tax Collector **Paul Gorman** .... (714) 834-2288
E-mail: pgorman@ttc.ocgov.com
Assistant Treasurer-Tax Collector **Jennifer Burkhart** ..... (714) 834-6143
E-mail: jburkhart@ttc.ocgov.com
Assistant Treasurer-Tax Collector **Tomas Vargas** .... (714) 834-4774
E-mail: tvargas@ttc.ocgov.com

Orange County Department of Education [OCDE]

200 Kalmus Drive, Costa Mesa, CA 92628
P.O. Box 9050, Costa Mesa, CA 92628-9050
Fax: (714) 432-1916 Internet: www.ocde.us

Superintendent **Dr. Al Mijares** .... (714) 966-4001
Term Expires: January 2019
Executive Assistant **Darla Nunez** .... (714) 966-4003
E-mail: dnunez@ocde.us
Chief Academic Officer **Jeff Hittenberger** .... (714) 966-4010

Orange County Sheriff-Coroner Department [OCSD]

550 North Flower Street, Santa Ana, CA 92703
P.O. Box 449, Santa Ana, CA 92703
Fax: (714) 953-3092 Internet: www.ocsd.org

★ Sheriff-Coroner **Sandra Hutchens** .... (714) 647-1800
Term Expires: December 31, 2018
Education: La Verne 1996 BS
Undersheriff **Don Barnes** .... (714) 647-1815
Assistant Sheriff, Custody Operations and Court
Services Command **Steven Kea** .... (714) 647-1839
Assistant Sheriff, Field Operations and Investigative
Services Command **Lee Trujillo** .... (714) 647-1833
Assistant Sheriff, Professional Services Command
Linda Solorza .... (714) 647-1804
Senior Director, Administrative Services Command
Brian Wayt .... (714) 647-1802

COUNTIES

★ Elected Official ▲ Appointed by Legislature ▼ Appointed by Governor ▶ Appointed by Board or Commission ● Appointed by Judge
■ Appointed by Mayor △ Appointed by Freeholders ▽ Appointed by Supervisor ▷ Appointed by County Executive ○ Appointed by Council

County of Orange, Florida

201 South Rosalind Avenue, Orlando, FL 32802-1393
P.O. Box 1393, Orlando, FL 32802-1393
Tel: (407) 836-3111 (Information) Fax: (407) 836-7399
Internet: www.ocfl.net

County Seat: Orlando **Election Type:** Nonpartisan
Population: 1,288,126 (2015)

Office of the County Mayor

201 South Rosalind Avenue, 5th Floor, Orlando, FL 32802-1393
P.O. Box 1393, Orlando, FL 32802-1393
Tel: (407) 836-7370 Fax: (407) 836-7360

★County Mayor **Teresa Jacobs** .... (407) 836-7370
Term Expires: December 31, 2018
E-mail: mayor@ocfl.net
Education: Florida State 1980 BS
Chief of Staff **Graciela Noriega Jacoby** .... (407) 836-7370
Education: Central Florida 1998 BS, 2003 MPA
Office Manager (Interim) **Michelle Frank** .... (407) 836-7370

Office of the County Administrator

201 South Rosalind Avenue, 5th Floor, Orlando, FL 32802-1393
P.O. Box 1393, Orlando, FL 32802-1393
Fax: (407) 836-7399 E-mail: countyadmin@ocfl.net

▶County Administrator **Ajit Lalchandani** .... (407) 836-7370
E-mail: ajit.lalchandani@ocfl.net
▶Deputy County Administrator (Public Safety and Human Services) **George Ralls** .... (407) 836-5381
E-mail: george.ralls@ocfl.net

Office of the County Attorney

201 South Rosalind Avenue, 3rd Floor, Orlando, FL 32802-1393
P.O. Box 1393, Orlando, FL 32802-1393
Fax: (407) 836-5888

▶County Attorney **Jeffrey J. Newton** .... (407) 836-7320
E-mail: jeffrey.newton@ocfl.net
Education: Connecticut 1984 JD
Deputy County Attorney **Joel Prinsell** .... (407) 836-7320
E-mail: joel.prinsell@ocfl.net

Office of Accountability

201 South Rosalind Avenue, 5th Floor, Orlando, FL 32802-1393
Fax: (407) 836-7399

Chief Accountability Officer **Eric D. Gassman** .... (407) 836-7370

Office of Management and Budget

201 South Rosalind Avenue, 3nd Floor, Orlando, FL 32802-1393
Fax: (407) 836-2880

▶Manager **Kurt Petersen** .... (407) 836-7390
E-mail: kurt.petersen@ocfl.net
Assistant Manager **Ray Walls** .... (407) 836-7390
E-mail: ray.walls@ocfl.net

Office of Professional Standards

450 East South Street, Orlando, FL 32801
P.O. Box 1393, Orlando, FL 32802-1393
Fax: (407) 836-5399

Manager **John Petrelli** .... (407) 836-0016
E-mail: john.petrelli@ocfl.net

Human Resources Division

450 East South Street, 2nd Floor, Orlando, FL 32801
Fax: (407) 836-5369

▶Director **Ricardo Daye** .... (407) 836-5667
E-mail: ricardo.daye@ocfl.net

Information Systems and Services Division [ISS]

400 East South Street, 4th Floor, Orlando, FL 32801
P.O. Box 1393, Orlando, FL 32802-1393
Fax: (407) 836-5299

Chief Information Officer **Rafael Mena** .... (407) 836-5200
E-mail: rafael.mena@ocfl.net Fax: (407) 836-5298

Risk Management Division

109 East Church Street, Suite 200, Orlando, FL 32801
Fax: (407) 836-9630

Manager **John Petrelli** .... (407) 836-9640
E-mail: john.petrelli@ocfl.net

Administrative Services Department

IOC Building II, 400 East South Street, 5th Floor, Orlando, FL 32801
Fax: (407) 836-2911 E-mail: administrativesupport@ocfl.net

▶Director **Anne Kulikowski** .... (407) 836-7396
E-mail: john.kulikowski@ocfl.net
Deputy Director **Venetta Valdengo-Blevins** .... (407) 836-9559
E-mail: venetta.valdengo@ocfl.net

Business Development Division

IOC Building II, 400 East South Street, 2nd Floor, Orlando, FL 32801
Fax: (407) 836-5477

▶Manager **Sheena Ferguson** .... (407) 836-7345
E-mail: sheena.ferguson@ocfl.net

Capital Projects Department

One North Orange Avenue, Suite 900, Orlando, FL 32801
Fax: (407) 836-0051

▶Manager **Sara Flynn-Kramer** .... (407) 836-0033
E-mail: sara.flynnkramer@ocfl.net
Project Manager **(Vacant)** .... (407) 836-0033

Facilities Management Division

2010 E. Michigan St., Orlando, FL 32806
Fax: (407) 836-7484

▶Manager **Rich Steiger** .... (407) 836-7482
E-mail: rich.steiger@ocfl.net Fax: (407) 836-7477
Fiscal and Administration Coordinator **Reed Knowlton** .... (407) 836-7474
E-mail: reed.knowlton@ocfl.net Fax: (407) 836-7477

Fleet Management Division

4400 S. Vineland Rd., Orlando, FL 32839
Fax: (407) 836-8249

▶Manager **Bryan Lucas** .... (407) 836-8200
E-mail: bryan.lucas@ocfl.net

Purchasing and Contracts Division

IOC Building II, 400 East South Street, 2nd Floor, Orlando, FL 32801
Fax: (407) 836-5899

▶Chief of Purchasing and Contracts **Johnny Richardson** .. (407) 836-5633
E-mail: johnny.richardson@ocfl.net

Real Estate Management Division

109 East Church Street, 2nd Floor, Orlando, FL 32801
Fax: (407) 836-5969

▶Manager **Ann Caswell** .... (407) 836-7080
E-mail: ann.caswell@ocfl.net

Public Safety and Human Services

Deputy County Administrator (Acting) **George Ralls** .... (407) 836-2649
E-mail: george.ralls@ocfl.net

★Elected Official ▲Appointed by Legislature ▼Appointed by Governor ▶Appointed by Board or Commission ●Appointed by Judge
■Appointed by Mayor △Appointed by Freeholders ▽Appointed by Supervisor ▷Appointed by County Executive ○Appointed by Council

Family Services Department
2100 East Michigan Street, 2nd Floor, Orlando, FL 32806
P.O. Box 1393, Orlando, FL 32802-1393
Fax: (407) 836-7583

▶ Director **Lonnie C. Bell** ....(407) 836-7318
E-mail: lonnie.bell@ocfl.net
Executive Assistant **Diana Cadiz** ....(407) 836-6566
E-mail: diana.cadiz@ocfl.net

Cooperative Extension Division
2350 E. Michigan St., Orlando, FL 32806
Fax: (407) 836-7578

▶ County Extension Director **Richard Tyson** .... (407) 254-9201
E-mail: richard.tyson@ocfl.net

Animal Services Division
2769 Conroy Rd., Orlando, FL 32839
Fax: (407) 352-4388 E-mail: animalservices@ocfl.net

▶ Manager **Dil Luther** ....(407) 254-9145
E-mail: dil.luther@ocfl.net Fax: (407) 836-4378
Administrative Assistant **Shasman Robles** ....(407) 254-9144
E-mail: shasman.robles@ocfl.net

Citizens' Commission for Children
2002A E. Michigan St., 2nd Floor, Orlando, FL 32806
Fax: (407) 836-6556

Manager **Tyra Witsell** ....(407) 836-9504

Regional History Center
65 E. Central Blvd., Orlando, FL 32801
Fax: (407) 836-8550 Internet: http://www.thehistorycenter.org

▶ Museum Director **Michael Perkins** .... (407) 836-8500
E-mail: michael.perkins@ocfl.net

Health Services Department
101 S. Westmoreland Dr., Orlando, FL 32805
Fax: (407) 836-9206

▶ Manager **Christopher Hunter** .... (407) 836-2649
E-mail: christopher.hunter@ocfl.net
Executive Assistant **Stephanie Bologna** .... (407) 836-7611
E-mail: stephanie.bologna@ocfl.net

Fire and Rescue Department [OCFRD]
6590 Amory Court, Winter Park, FL 32792
Tel: (407) 836-9000 Tel: (407) 836-0070 (Inspections and Miscellaneous)
Tel: (407) 836-0004 (Plans Review)
Tel: (407) 836-9898 (Public Information Officer on Duty)

▶ Fire Chief **Otto Drozd III** ....(407) 836-9112
E-mail: otto.drozd@ocfl.net
Deputy Chief **James Fitzgerald** .... (407) 836-9061
E-mail: james.fitzgerald@ocfl.net
Planning and Technical Services Division Chief
David Rathbun ....(407) 836-9111
E-mail: david.rathbun@ocfl.net
Infrastructure Support Division Chief **Anthony Rios** ... (407) 836-9037
E-mail: anthony.rios@ocfl.net
Operations Division Chief **Michael Wajda** .... (407) 836-9107
E-mail: michael.wajda@ocfl.net
Manager, Office of Emergency Management
Ronald Plummer ....(407) 836-9140
E-mail: ronald.plummer@ocfl.net
Fire Marshal **Bruce Faust** ....(407) 836-9000
109 East Church Street, Lower Level, Orlando, FL 32801

Corrections Department
3723 Vision Boulevard, Orlando, FL 32839
P.O. Box 1393, Orlando, FL 32802-1393
Tel: (407) 836-3560

▶ Director (Interim) **Chief Cornita Riley** .... (407) 836-3564
E-mail: cornita.riley@ocfl.net
Executive Assistant **Ivonne San Inocencio** .... (407) 836-3564
E-mail: ivonne.saninocencio@ocfl.net

Corrections Department *continued*

Deputy Director **Chief Cornita Riley** ....(407) 836-3560

Regional Mobility
Tel: (407) 836-5610

Assistant County Administrator **James E. Harrison** ......(407) 836-5610
E-mail: jim.harrison@ocfl.net

Public Works Department
4200 S. John Young Parkway, 2nd Floor, Orlando, FL 32839-9205
P.O. Box 1393, Orlando, FL 32802-1393
Fax: (407) 836-7716 E-mail: publicworks@ocfl.net

▶ Director **Mark Massaro** .... (407) 836-7970
E-mail: mark.massaro@ocfl.net
Executive Assistant **Roxanne Young** .... (407) 836-7970
E-mail: roxanne.young@ocfl.net
▶ Deputy Director **Joe Kunkel** ....(407) 836-7972
E-mail: joe.kunkel@ocfl.net

Development Engineering Division
Fax: (407) 836-8003

▶ Manager **Diana Almodovar** ....(407) 836-7974
E-mail: diana.almodovar@ocfl.net

Highway Construction Division
Fax: (407) 836-7714

▶ Manager **Julie Naditz** ....(407) 836-7930
E-mail: julie.naditz@ocfl.net

Public Works Engineering Division
Fax: (407) 836-8024

▶ Manager **Robin Hammel** .... (407) 836-7909
E-mail: robin.hammel@ocfl.net

Roads and Drainage Division
Fax: (407) 836-7839

Manager **Deodat Budhu** ....(407) 836-7919
Chief Engineer **Micah Massaquoi** ....(407) 836-7875
E-mail: micah.massaquoi@ocfl.net

Stormwater Management Division
Fax: (407) 836-7770

▶ Manager **Rodney J. Lynn** ....(407) 836-7991
E-mail: rodney.lynn@ocfl.net

Traffic Engineering Division
Fax: (407) 836-7869

▶ Manager **Ruby D. Rozier** .... (407) 836-7890
E-mail: ruby.rozier@ocfl.net
Traffic Engineer **John Klimovitch** .... (407) 836-7890
E-mail: john.klimovitch@ocfl.net

Infrastructure Services
Assistant County Administrator **Chris Testerman** ....(407) 836-5883
E-mail: chris.testerman@ocfl.net
Education: Florida State 1979 BS

Utilities Department
9150 Curry Ford Road, Orlando, FL 32825
P.O. Box 1393, Orlando, FL 32802-1393
E-mail: utilitiesinformation@ocfl.net

▶ Director **Ray Hanson** ....(407) 254-9809
E-mail: ray.hanson@ocfl.net Fax: (407) 254-9899
Executive Assistant **Nicole Bell** ....(407) 836-9809
E-mail: nicole.bell@ocfl.net
Deputy Director **Teresa Remudo-Fries** ....(407) 254-9803
Deputy Director **Todd Swingle** ....(407) 254-9880
E-mail: todd.swingle@ocfl.net
Executive Assistant **Betty Herrera** ....(407) 254-9803
E-mail: betty.herrera@ocfl.net

COUNTIES

★ Elected Official ▲ Appointed by Legislature ▼ Appointed by Governor ▶ Appointed by Board or Commission ● Appointed by Judge
■ Appointed by Mayor △ Appointed by Freeholders ▽ Appointed by Supervisor ▷ Appointed by County Executive ○ Appointed by Council

Customer Service Division
9150 Curry Ford Road, Orlando, FL 32825
Manager **Timothy Armstrong** .... (407) 254-9947

Financial Services Division
9150 Curry Ford Road, Orlando, FL 32825
▶ Manager **Glenn Kramer** .... (407) 254-9882
E-mail: glenn.kramer@ocfl.net

Solid Waste Division
5901 Young Pine Rd., Orlando, FL 32829
Fax: (407) 836-6629
▶ Manager **Jim Becker** .... (407) 254-9660
E-mail: jim.becker@ocfl.net

Utilities Engineering Division
9150 Curry Ford Road, Orlando, FL 32825
Fax: (407) 254-9703
▶ Manager **Larry Tunnell** .... (407) 254-9703
E-mail: larry.tunnell@ocfl.net

Water Reclamation Division
9150 Curry Ford Road, Orlando, FL 32825
▶ Manager **Bill Hurley** .... (407) 254-9685
E-mail: bill.hurley@ocfl.net

Water Division
9150 Curry Ford Road, Orlando, FL 32825
▶ Manager **Jacqueline Torbert** .... (407) 254-9830
E-mail: jacqueline.torbert@ocfl.net
Executive Assistant **Cheryl Bobb** .... (407) 254-9832
E-mail: cheryl.bobb@ocfl.net

Community, Environmental and Development Services
201 South Rosalind Avenue, 2nd Floor, Orlando, FL 32802-1393
P.O. Box 1393, Orlando, FL 32802-1393
Fax: (407) 836-5862 E-mail: growthmanagement@ocfl.net
▶ Director **Jon V. Weiss** .... (407) 836-5312
E-mail: jon.weiss@ocfl.net Fax: (407) 836-6708
Executive Assistant **Elaine Parker** .... (407) 836-5312
E-mail: elaine.parker@ocfl.net Fax: (407) 836-6708

Parks and Recreation Division
4801 W. Colonial Dr., Orlando, FL 32808
Fax: (407) 836-6210 Internet: http://www.parks.onetgov.net
Manager **Matt Suedmeyer** .... (407) 836-6200

Housing and Community Development Division
525 E. South St., Orlando, FL 32802
Fax: (407) 836-5188 E-mail: cmcddb1@citizens-first.co.orange.fl.us
Manager **Mitchell L. Glasser** .... (407) 836-5150
E-mail: mitchell.glasser@ocfl.net Fax: (407) 836-5193

Environmental Protection Division
800 Mercy Dr., Ste. 4, Orlando, FL 32808
Fax: (407) 836-5188
▶ Manager **Lori Cunniff** .... (407) 836-1400
E-mail: lori.cunniff@ocfl.net Fax: (407) 836-1452

Code Enforcement Division
2450 33rd Street, Orlando, FL 32839
P.O. Box 1393, Orlando, FL 32802-1393
Fax: (407) 836-5507
Manager **Bob Spivey** .... (407) 836-4220
Fax: (407) 836-4240

Division of Building Safety
201 South Rosalind Avenue, 1st Floor, Orlando, FL 32802-1393
Fax: (407) 836-5510
▶ Director **Tim Boldig** .... (407) 836-5550
E-mail: tim.boldig@ocfl.net Fax: (407) 836-5463

Planning Division
201 South Rosalind Avenue, 2nd Floor, Orlando, FL 32802-1393
Fax: (407) 836-5862 E-mail: planning@ocfl.net
▶ Manager **Alberto Vargas** .... (407) 836-5600
E-mail: alberto.vargas@ocfl.net

Transportation Planning Division
Fax: (407) 836-8079
Manager **Renzo Nastasi** .... (407) 836-8072

Zoning Division
201 South Rosalind Avenue, 1st Floor, Orlando, FL 32802-1393
Fax: (407) 836-5507 E-mail: zoning@ocfl.net
Manager **Carol Hossfield** .... (407) 836-5525
Fax: (407) 836-5959

Office of Public Engagement and Citizen Advocacy
201 South Rosalind Avenue, 5th Floor, Orlando, FL 32802-1393
Fax: (407) 836-7399
▶ Mayor's Aide **Carol Clark** .... (407) 836-7370
E-mail: carol.clark@ocfl.net

Communications Division
201 South Rosalind Avenue, 5th Floor, Orlando, FL 32802-1393
Fax: (407) 836-7399
▶ Manager **Ann Marie Varga** .... (407) 836-5818
E-mail: annmarie.varga@ocfl.net
Assistant Manager **Sharnita Marshall** .... (407) 836-5361
E-mail: sharnita.marshall@ocfl.net

Government Relations Division
201 South Rosalind Avenue, 5th Floor, Orlando, FL 32802-1393
P.O. Box 1393, Orlando, FL 32802-1393
Fax: (407) 836-7399
Director **Chris Testerman** .... (407) 836-7370
E-mail: chris.testerman@ocfl.net
Education: Florida State 1979 BS

Neighborhood Preservation and Revitalization Division
450 East South Street, Orlando, FL 32801
P.O. Box 1393, Orlando, FL 32802-1393
Manager **Lavon Williams** .... (407) 836-5606
E-mail: lavon.williams@ocfl.net Fax: (407) 836-0920

Orange County Convention Center [OCCC]
9800 International Drive, Orlando, FL 32819
P.O. Box 1393, Orlando, FL 32802-1393
Fax: (407) 685-9876 Internet: www.occc.net
▶ Executive Director **Kathleen Canning** .... (407) 685-9843
E-mail: kathie.canning@occc.net Fax: (407) 685-8701
▶ General Manager **(Vacant)** .... (407) 685-5710

Office of the Board of Commissioners
201 South Rosalind Avenue, 5th Floor, Orlando, FL 32802-1393
P.O. Box 1393, Orlando, FL 32802-1393
Tel: (407) 836-7350 (Information) Fax: (407) 836-5879
★ Commissioner **S. Scott Boyd** (District 1) .... (407) 836-7350
Term Expires: January 3, 2017
E-mail: district1@ocfl.net
Administrative Aide **Laura Roberts** .... (407) 836-7350
E-mail: laura.roberts@ocfl.net
Administrative Aide **Diana Garcia** .... (407) 836-7350
★ Commissioner **Bryan Nelson** (District 2) .... (407) 836-7350
Term Expires: December 2018
Date of Birth: September 14, 1958
Education: Florida 1979 BS

★ Elected Official ▲ Appointed by Legislature ▼ Appointed by Governor ▶ Appointed by Board or Commission ● Appointed by Judge
■ Appointed by Mayor △ Appointed by Freeholders ▽ Appointed by Supervisor ▷ Appointed by County Executive ○ Appointed by Council

Office of the Board of Commissioners *continued*

★ Commissioner **Pete Clark** (District 3) . . . . (407) 836-7350
Term Expires: December 3, 2016
E-mail: pete.clark@ocfl.net

★ Commissioner **Jennifer Thompson** (District 4) . . . . (407) 836-7350
Term Expires: January 3, 2018
E-mail: district4@ocfl.net
Education: North Carolina Charlotte BA
Administrative Aide **Susan Makowski** . . . . (407) 836-7350
E-mail: susan.makowski@ocfl.net
Administrative Aide **Jason Russo** . . . . (407) 836-7350

★ Commissioner **Ted B. Edwards** (District 5) . . . . (407) 836-7350
Term Expires: January 3, 2017
E-mail: district5@ocfl.net
Education: Stetson 1978 BA; Duke 1981 JD
Administrative Aide **Edgar Robinson** . . . . (407) 836-7350
E-mail: edgar.robinson@ocfl.net
Administrative Aide **Lynette Rummel** . . . . (407) 836-7350
E-mail: lynette.rummel@ocfl.net

★ Commissioner **Victoria Siplin** (District 6) . . . . (407) 836-7350
Term Expires: December 2018

Commission Service Representative **Maria Cruz** . . . . (407) 836-7350
E-mail: maria.cardona@ocfl.net

Commission Service Representative **Lovon Shaw** . . . . (407) 836-7350
E-mail: lovon.shaw@ocfl.net

Office of the Clerk of the Courts

425 North Orange Avenue, Orlando, FL 32801
P.O. Box 4994, Orlando, FL 32802-4994
Tel: (407) 836-2000 Internet: www.myorangeclerk.com

★ Clerk of Courts **Tiffany Moore Russell** . . . . (407) 836-2000
Term Expires: January 3, 2017
E-mail: Tiffany.russell@ocfl.net

Office of the Comptroller

201 South Rosalind Avenue, 4th Floor, Orlando, FL 32802-1393
P.O. Box 1393, Orlando, FL 32802-1393
Fax: (407) 836-5599 Internet: www.occompt.com

★ Comptroller **Martha O. Haynie** . . . . (407) 836-5690
Term Expires: January 3, 2017
E-mail: martha.haynie@occompt.com

Chief Deputy Comptroller
Margaret A. "Peggy" McGarrity . . . . (407) 836-5690

Office of the Property Appraiser

200 S. Orange Ave., 17th Floor, Orlando, FL 32801-3410
P.O. Box 1393, Orlando, FL 32802-1393
Fax: (407) 836-5069 E-mail: postmaster@ocpafl.org
Internet: http://www.ocpafl.org

★ Property Appraiser **Rick Singh** . . . . (407) 836-5044
Term Expires: January 3, 2017

Office of the Public Defender

435 N. Orange Ave., Orlando, FL 32801
P.O. Box 1393, Orlando, FL 32802-1393
Fax: (407) 836-4819

★ Public Defender **Bob Wesley** . . . . (407) 836-4806
Term Expires: January 3, 2017
E-mail: wesley@circuit9.org

Office of the Sheriff

2500 West Colonial Drive, Orlando, FL 32804
Fax: (407) 836-4357 E-mail: ocso@magicnet.net Internet: www.ocso.com

★ Sheriff **Jerry Demings** . . . . (407) 254-7018
Term Expires: January 3, 2017

Office of the State Attorney

415 N. Orange Ave., Orlando, FL 32801
P.O. Box 1393, Orlando, FL 32802-1393
Fax: (407) 836-2499

★ State Attorney **Jeff Ashton** . . . . (407) 836-2400
Term Expires: January 3, 2017

Office of the Supervisor of Elections

119 W. Kaley St., Orlando, FL 32806
P.O. Box 1393, Orlando, FL 32802-1393
Fax: (407) 317-7633 Internet: http://www.ocfelections.com

★ Elections Supervisor **Bill Cowles** . . . . (407) 254-6535
Term Expires: January 3, 2017
E-mail: bill@ocfelections.com

Office of the Tax Collector

200 S. Orange Ave., Suite 1500, Orlando, FL 32801
P.O. Box 1393, Orlando, FL 32802-1393
Fax: (407) 836-2730 Internet: http://www.octaxcol.com

★ Tax Collector **Scott Randolphs** . . . . (407) 836-2700
Term Expires: January 3, 2017

Orange County Public Schools [OCPS]

445 West Amelia Street, Orlando, FL 32801
Tel: (407) 317-3200 Internet: www.ocps.net

Superintendent **Barbara M. Jenkins** . . . . (407) 317-3209

County of Orange, New York

County Government Center, 255 Main St., Goshen, NY 10924
Tel: (845) 291-3000 (Information) Internet: www.orangecountygov.com

County Seat: Goshen **Election Type:** Partisan **Population:** 377,647 (2015)

Office of the County Executive

County Government Center, 255 Main St., Goshen, NY 10924
Fax: (845) 291-2724

★ County Executive **Steven M. Neuhaus** (R) . . . . (845) 291-2700
Term Expires: December 31, 2017

Deputy County Executive **Wayne Booth** . . . . (845) 291-2700
Director of Operations and Cost Control **Harold Porr III** . . (845) 291-2700
Assistant to the County Executive for Communications and Media Relations **Justin Rodriguez** . . . . (845) 291-2700

Office for the Aging

18 Seward Avenue, Middletown, NY 10940
Fax: (845) 346-1191 E-mail: ofa@orangecountygov.com

▷ Director **Ann Marie Maglione** . . . . (845) 615-3700
E-mail: amaglione@orangecountygov.com

COUNTIES

★ Elected Official ▲ Appointed by Legislature ▼ Appointed by Governor ► Appointed by Board or Commission ● Appointed by Judge
■ Appointed by Mayor △ Appointed by Freeholders ▽ Appointed by Supervisor ▷ Appointed by County Executive ○ Appointed by Council

COUNTIES

Office of the County Attorney
County Government Center, 255 Main St., Goshen, NY 10924
Fax: (845) 291-3167

▷Attorney **Langdon C. Chapman** .... (845) 291-3150
E-mail: lchapman@orangecountygov.com

Office of Community Development
18 Seward Avenue, Middletown, NY 10940
Fax: (845) 344-1629

▷Director **Richard Mayfield** .... (845) 615-3820
E-mail: rmayfield@orangecountygov.com

Office of the Historian
101 Main St., Goshen, NY 10924
Fax: (845) 291-2027

▷County Historian **Johanna Porr** .... (845) 291-2388
E-mail: jporr@orangecountygov.com

Office of Real Property Tax Services
124 Main St., Goshen, NY 10924
Fax: (845) 291-2499

▷Director **John McCarey** .... (845) 291-2490
E-mail: jmccarey@orangecountygov.com

Division of Budget
County Government Center, 255 Main St., Goshen, NY 10924
Fax: (845) 291-2016

▷Director **J. Neil Blair** .... (845) 291-2020

Division of Risk Management
18 Seward Avenue, Middletown, NY 10940
Fax: (845) 346-1169

▷Risk Management Officer **Michael T. Morris** .... (845) 615-3600
E-mail: mmorris@orangecountygov.com

Department of Consumer Affairs
99 Main St., Goshen, NY 10924-1627
Fax: (845) 291-2385

▷Commissioner **Charles Mitchell** .... (845) 360-6700
E-mail: cmitchell@orangecountygov.com

Department of Emergency Services
22 Wells Farm Road, Goshen, NY 10924
Fax: (845) 291-2121

Commissioner **Walter C. Koury** .... (845) 615-0565
E-mail: wkoury@orangecountygov.com

Emergency Communications Division
22 Wells Farm Road, Goshen, NY 10924
Fax: (845) 291-2121

Deputy Commissioner **Allen Wierzbicki** .... (845) 615-0440
E-mail: awierzbicki@orangecountygov.com

Emergency Management Division
22 Wells Farm Road, Goshen, NY 10924
Fax: (845) 291-2121

Deputy Commissioner **Craig Cherry** .... (845) 615-0476
E-mail: ccherry@orangecountygov.com

Emergency Medical Services Division
22 Wells Farm Road, Goshen, NY 10924
Fax: (845) 291-2121

Deputy Commissioner **Frank Cassanite** .... (845) 615-0467

Fire Services Division
Nine Training Center Lane, New Hampton, NY 10958
Fax: (845) 374-1906

Deputy Commissioner **Vini Tankasali** .... (845) 374-1900

Police Liaison Division
22 Wells Farm Road, Goshen, NY 10924
Fax: (845) 291-2121

Deputy Commissioner **Craig Cherry** .... (845) 615-0564

Department of Finance
County Government Center, 255 Main St., Goshen, NY 10924
Fax: (845) 291-2516

▷Commissioner **Tawnya Muhlrad** .... (845) 291-2485
E-mail: tmuhlrad@orangecountygov.com

General Services
County Government Center, 255 Main Street, Goshen, NY 10924
Fax: (845) 291-2797

Commissioner **James "Jim" Burpoe** .... (845) 291-2792
E-mail: jburpoe@orangecountygov.com

Department of Health
124 Main Street, Goshen, NY 10924
Fax: (845) 291-2341

▷Commissioner **Eli N. Avila** .... (845) 291-2332

Office of the Medical Examiner
22 Wells Farm Road, Goshen, NY 10924
Tel: (845) 615-3870 Fax: (845) 291-4121

Medical Examiner (Acting) **Dr. Jennifer L. Roman** ...... (845) 615-3870

Department of Human Resources
County Government Center, 255 Main St., Goshen, NY 10924
Fax: (845) 291-2736

▷Commissioner **Steven M. Gross** .... (845) 291-2707
E-mail: sgross@orangecountygov.com

Department of Information Technology
75 Webster Ave., Goshen, NY 10924
Fax: (845) 291-2998

▷Commissioner **James "Jim" Burpoe** .... (845) 615-3750

Department of Mental Health
30 Harriman Drive, Goshen, NY 10924
Fax: (845) 291-2628

Department of Parks, Recreation and Conservation
211 Route 416, Montgomery, NY 12549
Fax: (845) 457-4906 E-mail: parks@orangecountygov.com
Internet: www.orangecountynyparks.com

▷Commissioner **Richard L. Rose, Jr.** .... (845) 615-3830

Department of Planning
124 Main St., Goshen, NY 10924
Fax: (845) 291-2533

▷Commissioner **David E. Church** .... (845) 615-3840
E-mail: dchurch@orangecountygov.com

Probation Department
County Government Center, 255 Main St., Goshen, NY 10924
Fax: (845) 291-4789

▷Director **Derek J. Miller** .... (845) 291-4750
E-mail: dmiller@orangecountygov.com

★Elected Official ▲Appointed by Legislature ▼Appointed by Governor ▶Appointed by Board or Commission ●Appointed by Judge
■Appointed by Mayor △Appointed by Freeholders ▽Appointed by Supervisor ▷Appointed by County Executive ○Appointed by Council

Department of Public Works
P.O. Box 509, Goshen, NY 10924
Fax: (845) 291-2778

▷ Commissioner **Christopher Viebrock** . . . . (845) 291-2750

Division of Environmental Facilities and Services [EFS]
P.O. Box 637, Goshen, NY 10924
Fax: (845) 291-2665

Deputy Commissioner **Peter S. Hammond** . . . . (845) 291-2640

Orange County Airport
500 Dunn Road, Montgomery, NY 12549-2402
Fax: (845) 291-4928

Director of Aviation **Edward Magryta** . . . . (845) 457-4925

Department of Social Services
Box Z, 11 Quarry Road, Goshen, NY 10924
Fax: (845) 291-4201

▷ Commissioner **Darcie M. Miller** . . . . (845) 291-4000

Department of Tourism
124 Main Street, Goshen, NY 10924
Fax: (845) 291-2137 Internet: http://www.orangetourism.org

Director **Susan Hawvermale-Cayea** . . . . (845) 615-3860

Orange County Board of Elections
25 Court Lane, Goshen, NY 10924
Fax: (845) 291-2437 E-mail: elections@orangecountygov.com

▲ Democrat Commissioner **Susan A. Bahren** . . . . (845) 291-2444
E-mail: sbahren@orangecountygov.com

▲ Republican Commissioner **David C. Green** . . . . (845) 291-2444
E-mail: dgreen@orangecountygov.com

Orange County Community College
115 South Street, Middletown, NY 10940
Fax: (845) 341-4998 Internet: www.sunyorange.edu

President **Kristine Young** . . . . (845) 341-4700

Orange County Employment and Training Administration [ETA]
18 Seward Avenue, Middletown, NY 10940
Fax: (845) 346-1173

▷ Director **Stephen "Steve" Knob** . . . . (845) 615-3630
E-mail: sknob@orangecountygov.com

Orange County Water Authority [OCWA]
99 Main Street, Goshen, NY 10924
Fax: (845) 291-4828 Internet: http://waterauthority.orangecountygov.com

Executive Director **David E. Church** . . . . (845) 615-3868

Orange County Youth Bureau
18 Seward Avenue, Middletown, NY 10940
Fax: (845) 346-1170 E-mail: youthbur@orangecountygov.com

▷ Executive Director **Rachel Wilson** . . . . (845) 615-3620

Valley View Center for Nursing Care and Rehabilitation
4 Glenmere Cove Road, Goshen, NY 10924
P.O. Box 59, Goshen, NY 10924
Fax: (845) 291-4715

▷ Administrator **Laurence Ladue** . . . . (845) 291-4740

Veterans Service Agency
11 Craigville Road, Goshen, NY 10924
P.O. Box 359, Goshen, NY 10924
Fax: (845) 291-2558

▷ Director **Christian Farrell** . . . . (845) 291-2470

Office of the County Legislature
County Government Center, 15 Matthews Street, Suite 203, Goshen, NY 10924
Fax: (845) 291-4809 E-mail: legislature@orangecountygov.com

★ Legislator **Michael Amo** (R-District 1) . . . . (845) 291-4800
Term Expires: December 31, 2017

★ Legislator **Melissa Bonacic** (R-District 2) . . . . (845) 291-4800
Term Expires: December 31, 2017

★ Legislator **Paul Ruszkiewicz** (R-District 3) . . . . (845) 291-4800
Term Expires: December 31, 2017

★ Legislator **Curlie W. Dillard** (D-District 4) . . . . (845) 291-4800
Term Expires: December 31, 2017

★ Legislator **Katherine E. Bonelli** (R-District 5) . . . . (845) 291-4800
Term Expires: December 31, 2017

★ Legislator **James M. Kulisek** (D-District 6) . . . . (845) 291-4800
Term Expires: December 31, 2017

★ Legislator **Myrna Kemnitz** (D-District 7) . . . . (845) 291-4800
Term Expires: December 31, 2017

★ Legislator **Barry J. Cheney** (R-District 8) . . . . (845) 291-4800
Term Expires: December 31, 2017

★ Legislator **L. Stephen Brescia** (R-District 9) . . . . (845) 291-4800
Term Expires: December 31, 2017

★ Legislator **John S. Vero** (R-District 10) . . . . (845) 291-4800
Term Expires: December 31, 2017

★ Legislator **Matthew A. Turnbull** (D-District 11) . . . . (845) 496-1813
Term Expires: December 31, 2017
E-mail: votematt2011@hotmail.com

★ Legislator **Kevin W. Hines** (R-District 12) . . . . (845) 291-4800
Term Expires: December 31, 2017

★ Legislator **Thomas Faggione** (R-District 13) . . . . (845) 551-5784
Term Expires: December 31, 2017
E-mail: tfaggione@orangecountygov.com

★ Legislator **James A. DiSalvo** (R-District 14) . . . . (845) 291-4800
Term Expires: December 31, 2017

★ Legislator **Christopher W. Eachus** (D-District 15) . . . . . . (845) 291-4800
Term Expires: December 31, 2017

★ Legislator **Leigh J. Benton** (R-District 16) . . . . (845) 291-4800
Term Expires: December 31, 2017

★ Legislator **Mike Anagnostakis** (R-District 17) . . . . (845) 291-4800
Term Expires: December 31, 2017

★ Legislator **Roseanne Sullivan** (D-District 18) . . . . (845) 744-2095
Term Expires: December 31, 2017

★ Legislator **Michael D. Paduch** (D-District 19) . . . . (845) 291-4800
Term Expires: December 31, 2017
E-mail: mrpaduch@citlink.net

★ Legislator **Jeffrey D. Berkman** (D-District 20) . . . . (845) 291-4800
Term Expires: December 31, 2017
E-mail: jeff@jeffberkman.com

★ Legislator **Philip Canterino** (R-District 21) . . . . (845) 291-4800
Term Expires: December 31, 2017
E-mail: philipcanterino@yahoo.com

▲ Legislative Clerk **Jean M. Ramppen** . . . . (845) 291-4800
E-mail: jramppen@orangecountygov.com

▲ Legislative Counsel **Antoinette Reed** . . . . (845) 291-4800
E-mail: areed@orangecountygov.com

Office of the County Clerk
Parry Building, 4 Glenmere Cove Road, Goshen, NY 10924
Fax: (845) 291-2691

★ County Clerk **Ann G. Rabbitt** (R) . . . . (845) 291-2690
Term Expires: December 31, 2017
E-mail: occrabbitt@orangecountygov.com

COUNTIES

★ Elected Official ▲ Appointed by Legislature ▼ Appointed by Governor ▶ Appointed by Board or Commission ● Appointed by Judge
■ Appointed by Mayor △ Appointed by Freeholders ▽ Appointed by Supervisor ▷ Appointed by County Executive ○ Appointed by Council

Office of the District Attorney
County Government Center, 255 Main St., Goshen, NY 10924
Fax: (845) 291-2085

★ District Attorney **David M. Hoovler** (R) . . . . . . (845) 291-2050
Term Expires: December 31, 2017

Office of the Sheriff
110 Wells Farm Rd., Goshen, NY 10924
Fax: (845) 294-1590

★ Sheriff **Carl E. Du Bois** (R) . . . . . . (845) 291-4033
Term Expires: December 31, 2018
E-mail: cdubois@orangecountygov.com

County of Palm Beach, Florida
301 North Olive Avenue, West Palm Beach, FL 33401
P.O. Box 1989, West Palm Beach, FL 33402-1989
Tel: (561) 355-2040 (Information) Internet: www.pbcgov.com

County Seat: West Palm Beach **Election Type:** Partisan
Population: 1,422,789 (2015)

Office of the Board of County Commissioners
301 North Olive Avenue, West Palm Beach, FL 33401
P.O. Box 1989, West Palm Beach, FL 33402-1989
Tel: (561) 355-2001 Fax: (561) 355-3990

★ Mayor **Mary Lou Berger** (D-District 5) . . . . . . (561) 355-2205
Term Expires: November 21, 2016
E-mail: mberger@pbcgov.org

★ Commissioner **Hal R. Valeche** (R-District 1) . . . . . . (561) 355-2201
Term Expires: November 21, 2016
E-mail: hvaleche@pbcgov.org

★ Commissioner **Paulette Burdick** (D-District 2) . . . . . . (561) 355-2202
Term Expires: November 20, 2018
E-mail: pburdick@pbcgov.org
Education: Northeastern

★ Commissioner **Shelley Vana** (D-District 3) . . . . . . (561) 355-2003
Term Expires: November 21, 2016 Fax: (561) 355-3990
E-mail: svana@pbcgov.org
Date of Birth: December 30, 1951
Education: Indiana (PA) 1973 BA

★ Commissioner **Steven L. Abrams** (R-District 4) . . . . . . (561) 355-2204
Term Expires: November 20, 2018
E-mail: sabrams@pbcgov.org
Education: Harvard 1980 BA; George Washington 1985 JD

★ Commissioner **Melissa McKinlay** (D-District 6) . . . . . . (561) 355-6300
Term Expires: November 20, 2018
E-mail: mmckinlay@pbcgov.org

★ Commissioner **Priscilla A. Taylor** (D-District 7) . . . . . . (561) 355-2207
Term Expires: November 20, 2018
E-mail: ptaylor@pbcgov.org
Education: Barry 1997; Palm Beach Atlantic 1999 MBA

Commission Administrative Assistant
Audrey Buchannon . . . . . . (561) 355-3346
E-mail: abuchann@pbcgov.org

Office of the County Attorney
301 North Olive Avenue, Suite 601, West Palm Beach, FL 33401
Fax: (561) 355-4398 Internet: www.pbcgov.com/countyattorney

▶ County Attorney **Denise M. Nieman** . . . . . . (561) 355-2225
E-mail: dnieman@pbcgov.org

Office of the Internal Auditor
2300 North Jog Road, West Palm Beach, FL 33411-2743
Fax: (561) 681-4490

▶ Internal Auditor **Joseph F. "Joe" Bergeron** . . . . . . (561) 681-4471
E-mail: jbergero@pbcgov.org

Audit Manager **David Zamora** . . . . . . (561) 681-4472

Office of the County Administrator
301 North Olive Avenue, Suite 1101, West Palm Beach, FL 33401
P.O. Box 1989, West Palm Beach, FL 33402-1989
Tel: (561) 355-2712 Fax: (561) 355-3982
Internet: www.pbcgov.com/administration

▶ County Administrator **Verdenia C. Baker** . . . . . . (561) 355-6726
E-mail: vbaker@pbcgov.org
Executive Assistant III **Theresa Lawrence** . . . . . . (561) 355-2712

Deputy County Administrator **Jon Van Arnam** . . . . . . (561) 355-6726
E-mail: jvanarna@pbcgov.org

Assistant County Administrator **Vincent J. Bonvento** . . . . . . (561) 335-2046
E-mail: vbonvent@pbcgov.org

Assistant County Administrator
Shannon R. LaRocque-Baas . . . . . . (561) 355-2428
E-mail: slarocqu@pbcgov.org

Assistant County Administrator **Brad Merriman** . . . . . . (561) 355-4019
E-mail: bmerrima@pbcgov.org

Assistant County Administrator **(Vacant)** . . . . . . (561) 355-2740

Legislative Affairs Office Director **Todd J. Bonlarron** . . . . (561) 355-3451
E-mail: tbonlarr@pbcgov.org

Agenda Coordinator **Patty Hindle** . . . . . . (561) 355-3229
E-mail: phindle@pbcgov.org

Office of Cooperative Extension (University of Florida)
559 North Military Trail, West Palm Beach, FL 33415
Tel: (561) 233-1700 Fax: (561) 233-1768

Director **Ronald Rice** . . . . . . (561) 233-1712

Office of Equal Opportunity [OEO]
301 North Olive Avenue, Tenth Floor, West Palm Beach, FL 33401
Fax: (561) 355-4932

Director **Pamela "Pam" Guerrier** . . . . . . (561) 355-4883

Office of Financial Management and Budget [OFMB]
301 North Olive Avenue, Suite 702.26, West Palm Beach, FL 33401
Tel: (561) 355-2580 Fax: (561) 355-2109
Internet: www.pbcgov.com/ofmb

Director **Elizabeth "Liz" Bloeser** . . . . . . (561) 355-4626
E-mail: lbloeser@pbcgov.org

Budget Division Director **John Wilson** . . . . . . (561) 355-2587
E-mail: jwilson@pbcgov.org

Contract Development and Control Division Director
Irwin Jacobowitz . . . . . . (561) 355-4150

Financial Management Division Director
Richard Iavarone . . . . . . (561) 355-4369
E-mail: riavarone@pbcgov.org

Office of the Medical Examiner
3126 Gun Club Road, West Palm Beach, FL 33406
Fax: (561) 688-4588

Chief Medical Examiner **Dr. Michael Bell** . . . . . . (561) 688-4575

Office of Small Business Assistance [OSBA]
50 South Military Trail, Suite 209, West Palm Beach, FL 33415
Fax: (561) 616-6850 Internet: www.pbcgov.com/osba

Director **Tonya Davis Johnson** . . . . . . (561) 616-6840

Airports Department
846, PBIA, West Palm Beach, FL 33406
Fax: (561) 471-7427 Internet: http://www.pbia.org

Director **Bruce V. Pelly** . . . . . . (561) 471-7420

★ Elected Official ▲ Appointed by Legislature ▼ Appointed by Governor ▶ Appointed by Board or Commission ● Appointed by Judge
■ Appointed by Mayor △ Appointed by Freeholders ▽ Appointed by Supervisor ▷ Appointed by County Executive ○ Appointed by Council

Airports Department *continued*

Deputy Director, Finance and Administration
C. Michael Simmons . . . . . (561) 471-7433
E-mail: csimmons@pbcgov.org
Business Affairs Deputy Director **Laura Beebe** . . . . . (561) 471-7403
Operations and Maintenance Deputy Director
Thomas K. Stewart . . . . . (561) 471-7404
E-mail: tstewart@pbcgov.org
Planning and Development Deputy Director
Jerry L. Allen . . . . . (561) 471-7423

Department of Community Services

810 Datura Street, West Palm Beach, FL 33401
Fax: (561) 355-3863 Internet: www.pbcgov.com/communityservices

Director **Channell Wilkins** . . . . . (561) 355-4700
E-mail: cwilkins@pbcgov.org
Education: Bucknell BS; Rutgers MPA
Head Start and Children's Services Division Director
Dr. Julian Serrano . . . . . (561) 233-1600
Human Services Division Director **Claudia Tuck** . . . . . (561) 355-4775
Senior Services Division Director **Faith Manfra** . . . . . (561) 355-4750

Engineering and Public Works Department

2300 North Jog Road, 3rd Floor, West Palm Beach, FL 33411-2745
Tel: (561) 684-4000 Fax: (561) 684-4050
Internet: www.pbcgov.com/engineering

County Engineer **George T. Webb** . . . . . (561) 355-2006
301 North Olive Avenue, Fax: (561) 656-7290
West Palm Beach, FL 33401
E-mail: gwebb@pbcgov.org
Deputy County Engineer **Tanya N. McConnell** . . . . . (561) 684-4019
E-mail: tmcconne@pbcgov.org Fax: (561) 684-4167
Assistant County Engineer **Steve Carrier** . . . . . (561) 684-4010
E-mail: scarrier@pbcgov.org Fax: (561) 684-4167
Administrative Services Director **Alexis Willhite** . . . . . (561) 684-4110
E-mail: awillhit@pbcgov.org Fax: (561) 684-4033
Construction Coordination Director **Mark Tomlinson** . . . . (561) 684-4180
E-mail: mtomlins@pbcgov.org Fax: (561) 684-4165
Land Development Director **Joanne Keller** . . . . . (561) 684-4090
Fax: (561) 684-4123
Road and Bridge Director **Daryl Dawson** . . . . . (561) 233-3950
2555 Vista Parkway, Fax: (561) 233-3986
West Palm Beach, FL 33411-5602
Roadway Production Director **Omelio Fernandez** . . . . . (561) 684-4150
Fax: (561) 684-4166
Traffic Division Director **(Vacant)** . . . . . (561) 684-4030
Fax: (561) 684-5770
Streetscape Section Manager **Carl Bengtson** . . . . . (561) 684-4100
E-mail: cbengtson@pbcgov.org Fax: (561) 684-5774
Survey Manager **Glenn Mark** . . . . . (561) 684-4054
Fax: (561) 684-4171

Environmental Resources Management Department

2300 North Jog Road, 4th Floor, West Palm Beach, FL 33411-2743
Fax: (561) 233-2414

Director **Robert Robbins** . . . . . (561) 233-2400
Fax: (561) 233-2414
Deputy Director **Daniel Bates** . . . . . (561) 233-2400
E-mail: dbates@pbcgov.org
Environmental Enhancement and Restoration Division
Director **Julie Bishop** . . . . . (561) 233-2400
E-mail: jbishop@pbcgov.org
Finance and Support Services Division Director
Laura Thompson . . . . . (561) 233-2400
Natural Resources Stewardship Division Director
Brenda Hovde . . . . . (561) 233-2400
E-mail: bhovde@pbcgov.org
Mosquito Control Division Director **Ed Bradford** . . . . . (561) 967-6480
9011 West Lantana Road, Lake Worth, FL 33467
Resources Protection Division Director
Bonnie Finneran . . . . . (561) 233-2400
E-mail: bfinnera@pbcgov.org

Facilities Development and Operations Department [FD&O]

2633 Vista Parkway, West Palm Beach, FL 33411
P.O. Box 1989, West Palm Beach, FL 33402-1989
Tel: (561) 233-0200 Fax: (561) 233-0206 Internet: www.pbcgov.com/fdo

Director **Audrey Wolf** . . . . . (561) 233-0204
E-mail: awolf@pbcgov.org
Director, Capital Improvements Division **John Chesher** . . (561) 233-0266
E-mail: jchesher@pbcgov.org
Director, Electronic Services and Security Division
Nancy Albert . . . . . (561) 233-0789
Director, Facilities Management Division
Garth Josephs . . . . . (561) 233-0217
E-mail: gjosephs@pbcgov.org
Director, Fleet Management Division **Doug Weichman** . . (561) 233-4550
2601 Vista Rockway, Palm Beach, FL 33400
Director, Property and Real Estate Management Division
Ross C. Herring . . . . . (561) 233-0217
Facilities Operations Director **Jimmy Beno** . . . . . (561) 233-0285
E-mail: jbeno@pbcgov.org
Facilities Services Director **Chauncey Taylor II** . . . . . (561) 233-0221
E-mail: ctaylor@pbcgov.org

Fire/Rescue Department

50 South Military Trail, Suite 101, West Palm Beach, FL 33415
Fax: (561) 616-7080 Internet: www.pbcgov.com/fire

Fire Chief **Jeffrey Collins** . . . . . (561) 616-7000
E-mail: jpcollin@pbcgov.org
Education: Maryland BS; Palm Beach Atlantic MS

Department of Economic Sustainability

100 Australian Avenue, Suite 500, West Palm Beach, FL 33406
Tel: (561) 233-3600 Fax: (561) 656-7589 Internet: www.pbcgov.com/des

Director **Edward W. Lowery** . . . . . (561) 233-3602
E-mail: elowery@pbcgov.org
Deputy Director **Sherry Howard** . . . . . (561) 233-3653
E-mail: showard@pbcgov.org Fax: (561) 656-7542
Capital, Real Estate, and Inspection Services Section
Manager **Bud Cheney** . . . . . (561) 233-3691
Mortgage and Housing Investments
Carol Eaddy-Langford . . . . . (561) 233-3660
Strategic Planning and External Operations Director
Carlos Serrano . . . . . (561) 233-3608
E-mail: cserrano@pbcgov.org

Human Resources Department

Airport Center Building #1, 100 Australian Avenue, Suite 300,
West Palm Beach, FL 33406
Tel: (561) 616-6888 Tel: (561) 616-6900 (Job Hotline)
Tel: (561) 616-6895 (TDD) Fax: (561) 616-6893
Internet: www.pbcgov.com/humanresources

Director **Wayne Condry** . . . . . (561) 616-6861
E-mail: wcondry@pbcgov.org
Fair Employment Programs **Karen Thompson** . . . . . (561) 616-6860
E-mail: kthompso@pbcgov.org
Compensation and Records Manager **Maria Figueroa** . . . . (561) 616-6873
Recruitment and Selection Manager **Leilani Yan** . . . . . (561) 616-6877
E-mail: lyan@pbcgov.org

Information Systems Services Department [ISS]

301 North Olive Avenue, 8th Floor, West Palm Beach, FL 33401
Fax: (561) 355-3538 Internet: www.pbcgov.com/iss

Director **Steve Bordelon** . . . . . (561) 355-2394
E-mail: sbordelon@pbcgov.org
Deputy Director, Information Technology Operations
Phil Davidson . . . . . (561) 355-3956
E-mail: pdavidso@pbcgov.org
Strategic Services and Finance Director **Irene Manning** . . (561) 355-6262
E-mail: imanning@pbcgov.org
Application Services Director **Archie Satchell** . . . . . (561) 355-3275
E-mail: asatchel@pbcgov.org
Network Services Director **Michael "Mike" Butler** . . . . . (561) 355-4601
E-mail: mbutler@pbcgov.org

(continued on next page)

★ Elected Official ▲ Appointed by Legislature ▼ Appointed by Governor ► Appointed by Board or Commission ● Appointed by Judge
■ Appointed by Mayor △ Appointed by Freeholders ▽ Appointed by Supervisor ▷ Appointed by County Executive ○ Appointed by Council

COUNTIES

Information Systems Services Department *continued*

Platform Services Director **Kelly Ratchinsky** (561) 355-4252
E-mail: kratchin@pbcgov.org

Law Library

County Courthouse, 205 North Dixie Highway, Room 12200,
West Palm Beach, FL 33401
Fax: (561) 355-1654

Manager **Holly Satterwhite** (561) 355-2928

Metropolitan Planning Organization [MPO]

2300 North Jog Road, 4th Floor, West Palm Beach, FL 33411-2749
Fax: (561) 233-5664 Internet: www.pbcgov.com/mpo

Director **Nick Uhren** (561) 684-4170

Parks and Recreation Department

2700 Sixth Avenue South, Lake Worth, FL 33461
Tel: (561) 966-6600 Fax: (561) 963-6734 E-mail: pbcparks@pbcgov.org
Internet: www.pbcparks.com

Director **Eric Call** (561) 966-6614
Assistant Director **Jennifer Cirillo** (561) 963-6732
Director, Aquatics Division **Laurie Schobelock** (561) 966-6629
Fax: (561) 966-7070
Director, Financial and Support Services Division
Rebecca Pine (561) 966-6650
E-mail: rpine@pbcgov.org Fax: (561) 966-6784
Director, Parks Division **Craig Murphy** (561) 966-6680
Fax: (561) 966-6678
Director, Recreation Services Division
Kathy Bolander (561) 966-6628
Fax: (561) 966-7050
Director, Special Facilities Division **Paul Connell** (561) 966-6626
Fax: (561) 966-7070
Director, Planning, Research, and Development Division
Bob Hamilton (561) 966-6651

Planning, Zoning and Building Department

2300 North Jog Road, West Palm Beach, FL 33411-2743
Internet: www.pbcgov.com/pzb

Executive Director **Rebecca Caldwell** (561) 233-5008
Fax: (561) 233-5212
Administration Division Director **Brenda Conner** (561) 233-5012
E-mail: bconner@pbcgov.org Fax: (561) 233-5167
Building Division Director **Douglas Wise** (561) 233-5100
Contractor's Certification Division Director
Oscar Alvarez (561) 233-5525
Code Enforcement **Ramsay Bulkeley** (561) 233-5525
Planning Division Director **Lorenzo Aghemo** (561) 233-5467
Zoning Division Director **Jon MacGillis** (561) 233-5234

Public Affairs Department

301 North Olive Avenue, Suite 1102, West Palm Beach, FL 33401
Tel: (561) 355-2754 Fax: (561) 355-3819
Internet: www.pbcgov.com/publicaffairs

Director **Lisa De La Rionda** (561) 355-2754
E-mail: ldelario@pbcgov.org Fax: (561) 355-3819
Education and Government Television (Channel 20)
Manager **Lester Williams** (561) 355-2282
Digital Marketing and Communications **Heather Shirm** (561) 355-3226
E-mail: hshirm@pbcgov.org
Media and Public Information **John Jamason** (561) 355-1891
E-mail: jjamason@pbcgov.org
Graphics Coordinator **John Johnson** (561) 691-3580
1701 South Jog Road, Greenacres, FL 33413 Fax: (561) 964-4076
E-mail: jdljohns@pbcgov.org

Public Safety Department

20 South Military Trail, West Palm Beach, FL 33415
Fax: (561) 712-6490 Internet: www.pbcgov.com/publicsafety

Director **Vincent J. Bonvento** (561) 712-6470
E-mail: vbonvent@pbcgov.org

Public Safety Department *continued*

Director, Animal Care and Control Division
Dianne Sauve (561) 233-1200
7100 Belvedere Rd., West Palm Beach, FL 33411
Director, Emergency Management Division
William "Bill" Johnson (561) 712-6400
E-mail: wpjohnso@pbcgov.org
Director, Justice Services Division **Nicole A. Bishop** (561) 355-1723
205 North Dixie Highway, Fax: (561) 355-6049
Suite 5.1100, West Palm Beach, FL 33401
Director, Victim Services Division **Nicole A. Bishop** (561) 355-2418
205 North Dixie, Suite 5.1100, West Palm Beach, FL 33401
Manager, Consumer Affairs Division **Eugene Reavis** (561) 712-6600
50 South Military Tr.,, Suite 201, West Palm Beach, FL 33415
Director, 911 Program Services **Charles Spalding** (561) 712-6486
E-mail: cspalding@pbcgov.org

Purchasing Department

50 South Military Trail, Suite 110, West Palm Beach, FL 33415
Fax: (561) 616-6811 Internet: www.pbcgov.com/purchasing

Director **Kathleen M. "Kathy" Scarlett** (561) 616-6805
E-mail: kscarlet@pbcgov.org

Risk Management Department

100 Australian Avenue, Suite 200, West Palm Beach, FL 33406
Fax: (561) 233-5420 Internet: www.pbcgov.com/riskmanagement

Director **Nancy Bolton** (561) 233-5400
E-mail: nbolton@pbcgov.org
Employee Assistance Program Manager
Dr. Marcy Weiss (561) 233-5461
E-mail: mweiss@pbcgov.org
Group Health and Life Insurance Manager
Andrea Mackey (561) 233-5405
E-mail: amackey@pbcgov.org
Loss Control Manager **Brian Berke** (561) 233-5430
E-mail: bberke@pbcgov.org
Occupational Health Clinic Manager **Annie Brewer** (561) 233-5454
Property and Liability Insurance Manager
Scott Marting (561) 233-5432
E-mail: smarting@pbcgov.org
Workers' Compensation Manager **Harry George** (561) 233-5417
E-mail: hgeorge@pbcgov.org

Surface Transportation Department [PalmTran]

3201 Electronics Way, West Palm Beach, FL 33407
Tel: (561) 841-4200 Fax: (561) 841-4291
Internet: www.pbcgov.com/palmtran

Executive Director **Clinton Forbes** (561) 841-4210
Education: St Thomas U 1994 BA
Assistant Director **Charles Frazier** (561) 841-4211
Finance Manager **(Vacant)** (561) 841-4263
Maintenance Manager **Jonathan Kavaliunas** (561) 841-4250
Marketing Manager **Paula Girard** (561) 841-4244
Operations Manager **Betty Jean Barrow** (561) 841-4212
E-mail: bjbarrow@pbcgov.org

Tourist Development Council [TDC]

1555 Palm Beach Lakes Boulevard, Suite 900,
West Palm Beach, FL 33401
Fax: (561) 233-3113 Internet: www.pbcgov.com/touristdevelopment

Director **Glenn Jergensen** (561) 233-3130

Water Utilities Department

8100 Forest Hill Boulevard, West Palm Beach, FL 33413
Tel: (561) 493-6000 Tel: (561) 740-4600 (Customer Service)
Fax: (561) 493-6008 E-mail: pbcwater@co.palm-beach.fl.us
Internet: www.pbcwater.com

Director **Jim Stiles** (561) 493-6000
Assistant Director **Debra West** (561) 493-6000
Assistant Director **Hassan Hadjimiry** (561) 493-6000

★ Elected Official ▲ Appointed by Legislature ▼ Appointed by Governor ▶ Appointed by Board or Commission ● Appointed by Judge
■ Appointed by Mayor △ Appointed by Freeholders ▽ Appointed by Supervisor ▷ Appointed by County Executive ○ Appointed by Council

Water Utilities Department *continued*

Finance and Administration Division Director
Debra West . . . . (561) 493-6000
E-mail: dwest@pbcwater.com
Operations and Maintenance Division Director
Juan Guevarez . . . . (561) 493-6000
E-mail: jguevarez@pbcwater.com
Utilities Engineering Division Director **Maurice Tobon** . . . (561) 493-6000
E-mail: mtobon@pbcwater.com

Palm Beach County Library System

3650 Summit Blvd., West Palm Beach, FL 33406
Fax: (561) 233-2692 Internet: www.pbclibrary.org

Director **Douglas Crane** . . . . (561) 233-2600
E-mail: craned@pbclibrary.org
Assistant Director **Aurora Arthay** . . . . (561) 233-2600
E-mail: arthaya@pbclibrary.org

Office of the Clerk and Comptroller

205 North Dixie Highway, West Palm Beach, FL 33401
E-mail: clerkweb@mypalmbeachclerk.com

★ Clerk and Comptroller **Sharon R. Bock** . . . . (561) 355-2996
Term Expires: December 2016

Property Appraiser's Office

301 North Olive Avenue, 5th Floor, West Palm Beach, FL 33401
Fax: (561) 355-3963 Internet: www.pbcgov.com/papa

★ Property Appraiser **Gary Nikolits** (R) . . . . (561) 355-3230
Term Expires: January 4, 2017
E-mail: gnikoli@pbcgov.org
Appraisal and Analysis Division Assistant Property
Appraiser **Thomas A. Barnhart** . . . . (561) 355-2862
E-mail: tbarnhar@pbcgov.org
Chief Deputy Property Appraiser **Dorothy Jacks** . . . . (561) 355-3233
E-mail: djacks@pbcgov.org
Educational Services Director **Mike Pratt** . . . . (561) 355-4021

Office of the Public Defender

421 3rd Street, West Palm Beach, FL 33401
Tel: (561) 355-7500 Fax: (561) 355-7737 E-mail: pdinfo@pd15.state.fl.us
Internet: www.pbcgov.com/opd

★ Public Defender **Carey Haughwout** (D) . . . . (561) 355-7651
Term Expires: January 4, 2017
E-mail: careypd@pd15.state.fl.us
Education: New Col Florida 1979; Florida State 1983 JD

Office of the Sheriff

3228 Gun Club Road, West Palm Beach, FL 33406
Fax: (561) 688-3033 Internet: www.pbso.org

★ Sheriff **Ric L. Bradshaw** . . . . (561) 688-3000
Term Expires: December 31, 2016
E-mail: bradshawr@pbso.org

Office of the State Attorney

401 North Dixie Highway, West Palm Beach, FL 33401
Fax: (561) 366-1800 E-mail: stateattorney@sa15.state.fl.us
Internet: www.sa15.state.fl.us

★ State Attorney **Dave Aronberg** (D) . . . . (561) 355-7100
Term Expires: January 8, 2017
Education: Harvard 1993 BA, 1996 JD

Office of the Supervisor of Elections

240 South Military Trail, West Palm Beach, FL 33415
Fax: (561) 656-6287 E-mail: mailbox@pbcelections.org
Internet: http://www.pbcelections.org

★ Supervisor of Elections **Susan Bucher** (D) . . . . (561) 656-6200
Term Expires: January 4, 2017
E-mail: susanbucher@pbcelections.org
Date of Birth: October 27, 1958
Education: Mira Costa (Attended)
Chief Deputy Supervisor of Elections **Charmaine Kelly** . . (561) 656-6200

Office of the Tax Collector

301 North Olive Avenue, 3rd Floor, West Palm Beach, FL 33401
P.O. Box 3715, West Palm Beach, FL 33402
Fax: (561) 355-4123 Internet: www.taxcollectorpbc.com

★ Tax Collector **Anne M. "Annie" Gannon** (D) . . . . (561) 355-2264
Term Expires: December 31, 2016
E-mail: clientadvocate@taxcollectorpbc.com
Date of Birth: December 23, 1947

County of Passaic, New Jersey

Administrative/Courthouse Complex, 401 Grand Street,
Paterson, NJ 07505
Tel: (973) 881-4000 (Information) Internet: www.passaiccountynj.org

County Seat: Paterson **Election Type:** Partisan **Population:** 510,916 (2015)

Office of the Board of Chosen Freeholders

Administrative/Courthouse Complex, 401 Grand St., Paterson, NJ 07505
Tel: (973) 881-4402 Fax: (973) 742-3746

★ Director **Theodore O. Best, Jr.** (D) . . . . (973) 881-4402
Term Expires: December 31, 2017
E-mail: tjbest@passaiccountynj.org
★ Deputy Director **John W. Bartlett** (D) . . . . (973) 881-4402
Term Expires: December 31, 2018
E-mail: jbartlett@passaiccountynj.org
★ Freeholder **Terry Duffy** (D) . . . . (973) 881-4402
Term Expires: December 31, 2016
E-mail: tduffy@passaiccountynj.org
Education: Marist 1972 BA
★ Freeholder **Bruce James** (D) . . . . (973) 881-4402
Term Expires: December 31, 2017
E-mail: bjames@passaiccountynj.org
Education: William Paterson Col
★ Freeholder **Cassandra Lazzara** (D) . . . . (973) 881-4402
Term Expires: December 31, 2018
E-mail: clazzara@passaiccountynj.org
★ Freeholder **Pat Lepore** (D) . . . . (973) 881-4402
Term Expires: December 31, 2016
E-mail: plepore@passaiccountynj.org
★ Freeholder **Hector C. Lora** (D) . . . . (973) 881-4402
Term Expires: December 31, 2018
E-mail: hlora@passaiccountynj.org
△ Clerk of the Board **Louis E. Imhof III** . . . . (973) 881-4412
E-mail: louisi@passaiccountynj.org

Office of the County Administrator

Administrative/Courthouse Complex, 401 Grand St., Paterson, NJ 07505
Tel: (973) 881-4405 Fax: (973) 881-2853
Internet: www.passaiccountynj.org/departments/administrator

△ County Administrator **Anthony J. Denova** . . . . (973) 881-4405
E-mail: adenova@passaiccountynj.org

(continued on next page)

★ Elected Official ▲ Appointed by Legislature ▼ Appointed by Governor ▶ Appointed by Board or Commission ● Appointed by Judge
■ Appointed by Mayor △ Appointed by Freeholders ▽ Appointed by Supervisor ▷ Appointed by County Executive ○ Appointed by Council

Office of the County Administrator *continued*

Deputy County Administrator **Matthew P. Jordan** .... (973) 881-4407
E-mail: mjordan@passaiccountynj.org

Office of the County Counsel

Administrative/Courthouse Complex, 401 Grand St., Paterson, NJ 07505
Fax: (973) 881-4072

△ County Counsel **William J. "Bill" Pascrell III** .... (973) 881-4477
E-mail: williamp@passaiccountynj.org
Education: Rutgers BA; Seton Hall 1989 JD

Assistant County Counsel **Monica Chacon** .... (973) 881-4471
Assistant County Counsel **Tracey Cosby** .... (973) 881-4405
Assistant County Counsel **Michael Glovin** .... (973) 881-4405
Assistant County Counsel **Joseph Greer** .... (973) 881-4405
Assistant County Counsel **John Pogorelec** .... (973) 881-4405
Assistant County Counsel **José Santiago** .... (973) 881-4405

Office of the County Adjuster

Administrative/Courthouse Complex, 401 Grand Street, Paterson, NJ 07505
Tel: (973) 881-4835 Fax: (973) 754-0249

△ Deputy County Counsel/Adjuster **(Vacant)** .... (973) 225-3813

Office of Weights and Measures

1310 Route 23 North, Wayne, NJ 07470
Tel: (973) 305-5881 Fax: (973) 628-1796

△ Superintendent **Ernest N. Salerno** .... (973) 305-5750
E-mail: ernests@passaiccountynj.org

Office of Emergency Management

Passaic County Community College Public Safety Academy, 300 Oldham Road, Wayne, NJ 07407
Fax: (973) 904-3843

△ Director **Robert Lyons** .... (973) 904-3630
E-mail: robertl@passaiccountynj.org

Deputy Coordinator **Maryann Trommelen** .... (973) 904-3621
E-mail: maryannt@passaiccountynj.org

Office of the Treasurer

Administrative/Courthouse Complex, 401 Grand St., Paterson, NJ 07505

△ County Treasurer **Flavio Rivera** .... (973) 881-4440
E-mail: flavior@passaiccountynj.org

Camp Hope of New Jersey

1792 Union Valley Road, West Milford, NJ 07480
Tel: (973) 728-8166 Fax: (973) 728-5902 Internet: www.camphopenj.com

△ Executive Director **Karen Cisco** .... (973) 728-8166
E-mail: karenc@passaiccountynj.org

Cooperative Extension of Passaic County, Rutgers

1310 Route 23 North, Wayne, NJ 07470
Fax: (973) 305-8865

Director **Marycarmen Kunicki** .... (973) 684-4786

Economic Development Department

930 Riverview Drive, Suite 250, Totowa, NJ 07512
Tel: (973) 569-4720 Fax: (973) 569-4725
E-mail: ecodev@passaiccountynj.org

△ Director **Deborah Hoffman** .... (973) 569-4720
E-mail: ecodev@passaiccountynj.org

Finance Department

Administrative/Courthouse Complex, 401 Grand St., Paterson, NJ 07505
Fax: (973) 881-0196

△ Director **Richard Cahill** .... (973) 881-4440

Department of Human Services

Administrative/Courthouse Complex, 401 Grand St., Paterson, NJ 07505
Fax: (973) 881-2733 Internet: www.passaiccountynj.org/human-services

△ Director **Pamela L. Owen** .... (973) 881-2834
E-mail: pamelao@passaiccountynj.org

Division of Mental Health and Addiction Services

401 Grand Street, Paterson, NJ 07505
Fax: (973) 881-2733

△ Director **Francine Vince** .... (973) 225-3188
E-mail: francinev@passaiccountynj.org

Para-Transit

1310 Route 23 North, Wayne, NJ 07470
Fax: (973) 305-9328

△ Director **John McGill** .... (973) 305-5756
E-mail: johnm@passaiccountynj.org

Personnel Department

Administrative/Courthouse Complex, 401 Grand St., Paterson, NJ 07505
Fax: (973) 881-4485

△ Personnel Director **Barbara De Spirito** .... (973) 881-4480
E-mail: barbrad@passaiccountynj.org

Planning Department

930 Riverview Drive, Totowa, NJ 07512
Fax: (973) 812-3450

△ Director **Michael LaPlace** .... (973) 569-4040
E-mail: mlaplace@passaiccountynj.org

Public Works Department

Administrative/Courthouse Complex, 401 Grand St., Paterson, NJ 07505
Fax: (973) 742-3936
Internet: www.passaiccountynj.org/public-works-department

△ Director/County Engineer **Steve Edmond** .... (973) 881-4456
E-mail: stevee@passaiccountynj.org

Buildings and Grounds Department

307 Pennsylvania Avenue, Paterson, NJ 07503
Fax: (973) 754-1988

△ Superintendent **Jack Nigro** .... (973) 881-4425
E-mail: jackn@passaiccountynj.org

Roads Department

311 Pennsylvania Ave., Paterson, NJ 07503
Fax: (973) 742-2498

△ Roads Supervisor **Kenneth Simpson** .... (973) 881-4500
E-mail: kenneths@passaiccountynj.org

Purchasing Department

Passaic County Procurement Center, 495 River Street, 2nd Floor, Paterson, NJ 07524
Fax: (973) 742-8295
Internet: www.passaiccountynj.org/departments/purchasing

△ Purchasing Agent **Michael Marinello** .... (973) 247-3300
E-mail: mmarinello@passaiccountynj.org

Department of Senior, Disability Services, and Veterans' Affairs

930 Riverview Drive, Totowa, NJ 07512
Fax: (973) 569-4060

△ Director **Mary Kuzinski** .... (973) 569-4060
E-mail: maryk@passaiccountynj.org

★ Elected Official ▲ Appointed by Legislature ▼ Appointed by Governor ▶ Appointed by Board or Commission ● Appointed by Judge
■ Appointed by Mayor △ Appointed by Freeholders ▽ Appointed by Supervisor ▷ Appointed by County Executive ○ Appointed by Council

Passaic County Board of Social Services [PCBSS]

80 Hamilton Street, Paterson, NJ 07505
Fax: (973) 881-3233 Internet: www.pcbss.org

Director **Anthony DeSimone** .... (973) 881-8546

Board of Taxation

435 Hamburg Turnpike, Wayne, NJ 07470

Tax Administrator **Jay Schwartz** .... (973) 720-7399
E-mail: jschwartz@passaiccountynj.org
Secretary **Patricia Meola** .... (973) 720-7399
E-mail: patriciam@passaiccountynj.org

Passaic County Community College [PCCC]

One College Blvd., Paterson, NJ 07505
Tel: (973) 684-5900 Fax: (973) 684-5843 Internet: www.pccc.edu

President **Steve Rose** .... (973) 684-5900

Passaic County Public Housing Agency

100 Hamilton Plaza, Suite 510, Paterson, NJ 07505
Tel: (973) 881-4369 Fax: (973) 684-0317
Internet: www.passaiccountynj.org/departments/housing

△ Executive Director **Janice De John** .... (973) 881-4369 ext. 505
E-mail: janicedj@passaiccountynj.org

Passaic County Workforce Development Center [PCWDC]

388 Lakeview Ave., Clifton, NJ 07011
Fax: (973) 340-7214

Executive Director **(Vacant)** .... (973) 340-3400

Preakness Healthcare Center

305 Oldham Road, Wayne, NJ 07407
Tel: (973) 317-7020 Fax: (973) 904-9843

Executive Director **Lucinda Corrado** .... (973) 585-2169

Office of the County Clerk

Administrative/Courthouse Complex, 401 Grand St., Room 130, Paterson, NJ 07505
Tel: (973) 225-3632 Fax: (973) 754-1920
Internet: www.passaiccountynj.org/countyclerk

★ County Clerk **Kristin Corrado** (R) .... (973) 225-3632
Term Expires: December 31, 2017
E-mail: kcorrado@passaiccountynj.org
Deputy County Clerk **Walter J. Davison** .... (973) 225-3631
E-mail: walterd@passaiccountynj.org

Office of the Executive County Superintendent of Schools

501 River Street, Paterson, NJ 07503
Fax: (973) 754-0241

▼ Executive County Superintendent (Interim)
Robert H. Davis .... (973) 569-2110
E-mail: robert.davis@doe.state.nj.us

Office of the Prosecutor

Passaic County Administration Building, 401 Grand Street, Paterson, NJ 07505
Fax: (973) 225-0155

▼ Prosecutor **Camelia M. Valdes** .... (973) 881-4800
E-mail: cvaldes@passaiccountynj.org
Education: Seton Hall 1993 BA; Rutgers 1996 JD; Temple 2001 LLM

Office of the Prosecutor *continued*

▼ First Assistant Prosecutor **Robert M. Holmsen** .... (973) 881-4800
E-mail: rholmsen@passaiccountynj.org
Education: Montclair State U 1982; Seton Hall 1985 JD

Office of the Sheriff

435 Hamburg Turnpike, Wayne, NJ 07470
Tel: (973) 389-5900 Fax: (973) 389-9350 Internet: www.pcsheriff.org

★ Sheriff **Richard H. Berdnik** (D) .... (973) 389-5919
Term Expires: December 31, 2017
Undersheriff **Joseph C. "Joe" Dennis** .... (973) 389-5900
Director of Business Administration **Gary Giardina** ...... (973) 389-9000

Office of the Superintendent of Elections

311 Pennsylvania Ave., Paterson, NJ 07503
Tel: (973) 881-4515 Fax: (973) 881-1634
Internet: www.passaiccountynj.org/elections

▼ Superintendent of Elections **Sherine El-Abd** .... (973) 881-4515
E-mail: sherinee@passaiccountynj.org
▼ Deputy Superintendent of Elections
Shona Mack-Pollack .... (973) 881-4515
E-mail: shonam@passaiccountynj.org

Office of the Surrogate

Surrogate Court, Courthouse, 77 Hamilton St., Paterson, NJ 07505
Tel: (973) 881-4760 Fax: (973) 523-3449

★ Surrogate **Bernice Toledo** (D) .... (973) 881-4760
Term Expires: December 31, 2016
E-mail: bernicet@passaiccountynj.org

Board of Elections

401 Grand St., Suite 123, Paterson, NJ 07505
Tel: (973) 881-4780 Fax: (973) 881-4780

Chairman **John Currie** .... (973) 881-4780
Note: Reappointed by Governor Christie on March 8, 2016, pending New Jersey Senate approval.
Secretary **Ricardo Farfan** .... (973) 881-4780
Note: Reappointed by Governor Christie on March 8, 2016, pending New Jersey Senate approval.
Commissioner **Rita Gernant** .... (973) 881-4780
Commissioner **Michael Ramaglia** .... (973) 881-4780

COUNTIES

★ Elected Official ▲ Appointed by Legislature ▼ Appointed by Governor ► Appointed by Board or Commission ● Appointed by Judge
■ Appointed by Mayor △ Appointed by Freeholders ▽ Appointed by Supervisor ▷ Appointed by County Executive ○ Appointed by Council

County of Pierce, Washington

County-City Building, 930 Tacoma Avenue South,
Tacoma, WA 98402-2100
Tel: (253) 798-7300 (Information) TTY: (253) 798-6080
Internet: www.piercecountywa.org

County Seat: Tacoma **Election Type:** Partisan **Population:** 843,954 (2015)

Office of the County Executive

County-City Bldg., 930 Tacoma Avenue South, Room 737,
Tacoma, WA 98402-2100
Tel: (253) 798-7477 Fax: (253) 798-6628
E-mail: pcexecutive@co.pierce.wa.us

★ County Executive **Pat McCarthy** (D) .... (253) 798-6602
Term Expires: December 31, 2016
E-mail: pcexecutive@co.pierce.wa.us
Date of Birth: 1970
Education: U Washington 1992 BA
Executive Secretary **Connie Perry** .... (253) 798-6602
E-mail: cperry@co.pierce.wa.us

Executive Director for Operations and Infrastructure

930 Tacoma Avenue South, Room 737, Tacoma, WA 98402-2100
Tel: (253) 798-7477 Fax: (253) 798-6628

▷ Deputy County Executive/Executive Director (Acting)
Ronald Klein .... (253) 798-7477
E-mail: rklein@co.pierce.wa.us
Executive Secretary **Danni Colo** .... (253) 798-2663
E-mail: dcolo@co.pierce.wa.us

Executive Director for External Affairs

930 Tacoma Avenue South, Room 737, Tacoma, WA 98402-2100
Tel: (253) 798-7477 Fax: (253) 798-6628

Executive Director **Keri Rooney** .... (253) 798-7186
E-mail: krooney@co.pierce.wa.us

Executive Director for Justice Services

930 Tacoma Avenue South, Room 737, Tacoma, WA 98402-2100
Tel: (253) 798-7477 Fax: (253) 798-6628

Executive Director **Allen P. "Al" Rose** .... (253) 798-2662
E-mail: arose@co.pierce.wa.us

Office of Assigned Counsel

949 Market Street, Suite 334, Tacoma, WA 98402
Fax: (253) 798-6715 E-mail: pcassgncnsel@co.pierce.wa.us

Director **Michael Kawamura** .... (253) 798-7069

Medical Examiner's Office

3619 Pacific Avenue, Tacoma, WA 98418
Fax: (253) 798-2893 E-mail: pcmedexam@co.pierce.wa.us

Director **Thomas B. Clark III** .... (253) 798-6494
Associate Medical Examiner **J. Matthew Lacy** .... (253) 798-6494
Service Program Manager **Sharon Johnson** .... (253) 798-6494

Department of Community Connections

1305 Tacoma Avenue South, Suite 104, Tacoma, WA 98402
Tel: (253) 798-4500 Fax: (253) 798-4470

Director **Peter Ansara** .... (253) 798-4500
E-mail: pansara@co.pierce.wa.us

Department of Emergency Management [DEM]

2501 South 35th Street, Suite D, Tacoma, WA 98409
Fax: (253) 798-3307 E-mail: pcemermgmt@co.pierce.wa.us

Director **Lowell M. Porter** .... (253) 798-7711

Parks and Recreation

9112 Lakewood Dr., SW, #121, Lakewood, WA 98499-3998
Tel: (253) 798-4176 Fax: (253) 582-7461
E-mail: pcparks@co.pierce.wa.us

Director **Tony Tipton** .... (253) 798-4250
Superintendent of Administrative Services **Janel Krilich** .. (253) 798-4008

Planning and Land Services [PALS]

2401 S. 35th, Tacoma, WA 98409-7494
Tel: (253) 798-7210 Fax: (253) 798-3131
E-mail: pcpals@co.pierce.wa.us

Director **Dennis Hanberg** .... (253) 798-2754

Public Works and Utilities

2702 South 42nd, Suite 201, Tacoma, WA 98409
Fax: (253) 798-2767 E-mail: pcpubworks@co.pierce.wa.us

Director **Brian J. Ziegler** .... (253) 798-7250
Deputy Director **Toby Rickman** .... (253) 798-3720
E-mail: toby.rickman@co.pierce.wa.us
County Engineer **Brian D. Stacy** .... (253) 798-7250
E-mail: bstacy@co.pierce.wa.us

Budget and Finance Department

615 South Ninth Street, Tacoma, WA 98405
Tel: (253) 798-7285 Fax: (253) 798-6699
E-mail: pcbudget@co.pierce.wa.us

Director **Gary Robinson** .... (253) 798-7450
E-mail: grobins@co.pierce.wa.us
Budget Manager **Jim Dickman** .... (253) 798-7512
E-mail: jdickma@co.pierce.wa.us

Department of Communications

930 Tacoma Avenue South, Room 737, Tacoma, WA 98402
Tel: (253) 798-6209 E-mail: pccomments@co.pierce.wa.us

▷ Director of Communications (Interim) **Ronald Klein** ..... (253) 798-6606
E-mail: rklein@co.pierce.wa.us

Facilities Management Department

Columbia Bank Building, 1102 Broadway Plaza, Suite 302,
Tacoma, WA 98402
Tel: (253) 798-7223 Fax: (253) 798-7401
E-mail: pcfacilities@co.pierce.wa.us

Director **Bret M. Carlstad** .... (253) 798-7223
E-mail: bcarlst@co.pierce.wa.us
Assistant Director **Ann Hibbert** .... (253) 798-7223
E-mail: ahibber@co.pierce.wa.us
Maintenance and Operations Division Manager
Bob Carr .... (253) 798-7223
E-mail: bcarr@co.pierce.wa.us
Resource Conservation Program Coordinator **(Vacant)** .... (253) 798-7223
Real Property Specialist **Rick Tackett** .... (253) 798-7223
E-mail: rtacket@co.pierce.wa.us
Real Property Specialist **Michael Gonzales** .... (253) 798-7223
E-mail: mgonzal@co.pierce.wa.us

Human Resources Department

615 South Ninth Street, Tacoma, WA 98405
Tel: (253) 798-7480 Fax: (253) 798-7489
E-mail: pcpersonnel@co.pierce.wa.us

Director **Virginia "Ginny" Dale** .... (253) 798-7469

Information Technology Department

Merit Bldg., 615 South Ninth Street, Suite 300, Tacoma, WA 98405
Tel: (253) 798-7476 Fax: (253) 798-6622
E-mail: pcinfosvcs@co.pierce.wa.us

Director **Linda Gerull** .... (253) 798-7472
E-mail: lgerull@co.pierce.wa.us
Fiscal Services Manager **Sandy Roberts** .... (253) 798-6788
Information Technology Operations Manager
Dawn Umstot .... (253) 798-7476
Software Development Manager **Larry Gezelius** .... (253) 798-7476

★ Elected Official ▲ Appointed by Legislature ▼ Appointed by Governor ▶ Appointed by Board or Commission ● Appointed by Judge
■ Appointed by Mayor △ Appointed by Freeholders ▽ Appointed by Supervisor ▷ Appointed by County Executive ○ Appointed by Council

Risk Management and Insurance Department
955 Tacoma Avenue, South, Suite 303, Tacoma, WA 98402-2160
Fax: (253) 798-3632 E-mail: pcriskmgmt@co.pierce.wa.us

Risk Manager **Mark Maenhout** .... (253) 798-6281
E-mail: mmaenho@co.pierce.wa.us

Pierce County Law Library
County-City Bldg., 930 Tacoma Avenue South, Room 1A-105,
Tacoma, WA 98402-2174
Fax: (253) 798-2989

Director **Laurie Miller** .... (253) 798-7493
E-mail: lmille2@co.pierce.wa.us
Assistant Librarian **(Vacant)** .... (253) 798-7494

Office of the County Council
County-City Bldg., 930 Tacoma Avenue South, Room 1046,
Tacoma, WA 98402-2176
Tel: (253) 798-7777 Tel: (800) 992-2456 (Toll Free) Fax: (253) 798-7509
E-mail: pccouncil@co.pierce.wa.us

★ Chair **Douglas G. Richardson** (R-District 6) .... (253) 798-7330
Term Expires: December 31, 2016
E-mail: drichar@co.pierce.wa.us
★ Vice Chair **Dan Roach** (R-District 1) .... (253) 798-3635
Term Expires: December 31, 2018
E-mail: droach@co.pierce.wa.us
★ Executive Pro Tempore **Joyce McDonald** (R-District 2) .. (253) 798-6694
Term Expires: December 31, 2016
E-mail: jmcdon2@co.pierce.wa.us
Education: Northwest U BA
★ Council Member **Jim McCune** (R-District 3) .... (253) 798-6626
Term Expires: December 31, 2016
E-mail: jmcune@co.pierce.wa.us
★ Council Member **Connie Ladenburg** (D-District 4) ...... (253) 798-7590
Term Expires: December 31, 2016
E-mail: cladenb@co.pierce.wa.us
★ Council Member **Rick Talbert** (D-District 5) .... (253) 798-6653
Term Expires: December 31, 2018
E-mail: rtalber@co.pierce.wa.us
★ Council Member **Derek Young** (D-District 7) .... (253) 798-6654
Term Expires: December 31, 2018
E-mail: dyoung2@co.pierce.wa.us
County Council Clerk **Denise D. Johnson** .... (253) 798-6065
E-mail: djohnso@co.pierce.wa.us

Office of the Assessor/Treasurer
2401 South 35th Street, Room 142, Tacoma, WA 98409
Tel: (253) 798-6111 Tel: (800) 992-2456 (Toll Free) Fax: (253) 798-3142
E-mail: pcatr@co.pierce.wa.us

★ Assessor/Treasurer **Mike Lonergan** .... (253) 798-7144
Term Expires: December 31, 2016
E-mail: mike.lonergan@co.pierce.wa.us

Office of the Auditor
Pierce County Annex, 2401 S. 35th St., Rm. 200,
Tacoma, WA 98409-7460
Fax: (253) 798-3182 E-mail: pcauditor@co.pierce.wa.us
Internet: www.piercecountyauditor.org

★ Auditor **Julie Anderson** .... (253) 798-3189
Term Expires: January 31, 2019
E-mail: julie.anderson@co.pierce.wa.us
Assistant to the Auditor **Whitney Rhodes** .... (253) 798-3189
E-mail: whitney.rhodes@co.pierce.wa.us
Deputy Auditor **Cindy Hartman** .... (253) 798-3217

Office of the Prosecuting Attorney
County-City Bldg., 930 Tacoma Avenue South, Room 946,
Tacoma, WA 98402-2171
Tel: (800) 992-2456 Tel: (253) 798-7400 Fax: (253) 798-6636
E-mail: pcprosatty@co.pierce.wa.us

★ Prosecuting Attorney **Mark Lindquist** .... (253) 798-7792
Term Expires: December 31, 2018
E-mail: mlindqu@co.pierce.wa.us
Education: USC BA; Seattle 1995 JD
Chief of Staff **Dawn Farina** .... (253) 798-7400

Office of the Sheriff
County-City Building, 930 Tacoma Avenue South,
Tacoma, WA 98402-2168
Tel: (253) 798-7530 Fax: (253) 798-6712
E-mail: pcsheriff@co.pierce.wa.us

★ Sheriff **Paul A. Pastor** .... (253) 798-7530
Term Expires: December 31, 2016
E-mail: ppastor@co.pierce.wa.us
Education: Pomona; Yale, PhD
Undersheriff **Robert "Rob" Masko** .... (253) 798-4221
E-mail: rmasko@co.pierce.wa.us
Chief of Administrative Services **Brent Bomkamp** ...... (253) 798-3884
E-mail: bbomkamp@co.pierce.wa.us
Chief of Operations **Nick Hausner** .... (253) 798-7530
E-mail: nhausner@co.pierce.wa.us
Media Relations and Public Information Officer
Edward C. Troyer .... (253) 798-7530

Corrections Bureau
910 Tacoma Ave. South, Tacoma, WA 98402
Tel: (253) 798-4590 Fax: (253) 798-3969

Chief of Corrections **Karen Daniels** .... (253) 798-7877

County of Pima, Arizona
130 W. Congress, Tucson, AZ 85701-1317
Tel: (520) 724-8661 (Information) Internet: www.pima.gov

County Seat: Tucson **Election Type:** Partisan **Population:** 1,010,025 (2015)

Office of the Board of Supervisors
130 West Congress, 11th Floor, Tucson, AZ 85701-1317
Fax: (520) 884-1152 Internet: www.pima.gov/bos

★ Chair **Sharon Bronson** (D-District 3) .... (520) 724-8051
Term Expires: December 31, 2016 Fax: (520) 884-1152
E-mail: district3@pima.gov
Education: Arizona BBA
★ Vice Chair **Richard Elias** (D-District 5) .... (520) 724-8126
Term Expires: December 31, 2016 Fax: (520) 884-1152
E-mail: District5@pima.gov
Education: Arizona 1988 BA
★ Supervisor **Ally Miller** (R-District 1) .... (520) 724-2738
Term Expires: December 31, 2016 Fax: (520) 740-8489
E-mail: district1@pima.gov
★ Supervisor **Ramón O. Valadez** (D-District 2) .... (520) 724-8126
Term Expires: December 31, 2016 Fax: (520) 884-1152
E-mail: district2@pima.gov
★ Supervisor **Raymond "Ray" Carroll** (R-District 4) ...... (520) 724-8094
Term Expires: December 31, 2016 Fax: (520) 884-1152
E-mail: district4@pima.gov

★ Elected Official ▲ Appointed by Legislature ▼ Appointed by Governor ▶ Appointed by Board or Commission ● Appointed by Judge
■ Appointed by Mayor △ Appointed by Freeholders ▽ Appointed by Supervisor ▷ Appointed by County Executive ○ Appointed by Council

Clerk of the Board of Supervisors

130 W. Congress, 5th Floor, Tucson, AZ 85701-1317
Fax: (520) 222-0448

▽County Clerk **Robin Brigode** .... (520) 724-8449
E-mail: robin.brigode@pima.gov
Deputy Clerk **Julie Castaneda** .... (520) 724-8007
E-mail: julie.castaneda@pima.gov

Office of the County Administrator

130 W. Congress, 10th Floor, Tucson, AZ 85701-1317
Fax: (520) 740-8171

▽County Administrator **C. H. Huckelberry** .... (520) 724-8661
E-mail: chh@pima.gov
Education: Arizona 1972 BS, 1976 MS
Deputy County Administrator **Tom Burke** .... (520) 724-8661
Deputy County Administrator for Medical and Health Services **Jan Lesher** .... (520) 724-8661
E-mail: jan.lesher@pima.gov
Education: Radford BS
Deputy County Administrator for Public Works **John M. Bernal** .... (520) 724-8480
E-mail: john.bernal@pima.gov
Executive Assistant **Nicole Fyffe** .... (520) 724-8661
E-mail: nicole.fyffe@pima.gov
Chief Administrative Assistant **Maura Kwiatkowski** .... (520) 724-8661
E-mail: maura.kwiatkowski@pima.gov
Special Staff Assistant **Diana Durazo** .... (520) 724-8661
E-mail: diana.durazo@pima.gov

Legal Defender's Office

32 North Stone Avenue, Suite 800, Tucson, AZ 85701
Tel: (520) 724-5775 Fax: (520) 724-7338
Internet: www.pima.gov/legaldef

Legal Defender **Isabel Garcia** .... (520) 724-5775

Public Defender's Office

33 North Stone Avenue, Suite 2100, Tucson, AZ 85701
Tel: (520) 243-6800 Fax: (520) 770-4168
Internet: www.pima.gov/publicdefender

Public Defender **Lori J. Lefferts** .... (520) 243-6800

Public Fiduciary's Office

32 North Stone Avenue, 4th Floor, Tucson, AZ 85701
Tel: (520) 740-5454 Fax: (520) 624-7190
Internet: www.pima.gov/depts/fiduc.html

Public Fiduciary **Philip Grant** .... (520) 740-5417

Department of Community Development and Neighborhood Conservation [CDNC]

Kino Service Center, 2797 East Ajo Way, Tucson, AZ 85713

Director **Margaret Kish** .... (520) 243-6745
E-mail: mkish@csd.pima.gov Fax: (520) 243-6797

Department of Community Resources

2500 East Ajo Way, Tucson, AZ 85713
Internet: www.pima.gov/ced/cr

Manager **Christopher "Chris" Bartos** .... (520) 434-1301

Department of Community Services, Employment and Training

Kino Service Center, 2797 East Ajo Way, Tucson, AZ 85713
Fax: (520) 243-6799

Director **Art Eckstrom** .... (520) 243-6741

Development Services Department

Public Works Building, 201 North Stone Avenue, 1st Floor, Tucson, AZ 85701
Fax: (520) 791-6553 E-mail: director@dsd.pima.gov
Internet: www.pimaxpress.com

Director **Carmine Debonis, Jr.** .... (520) 740-6490

Pima County Elections Department

6550 South Country Clud Road, Tucson, AZ 85756
Tel: (520) 351-6830 Fax: (520) 351-6870
Internet: www.pima.gov/elections

Director **Brad R. Nelson** .... (520) 351-6830

Department of Environmental Quality

33 North Stone Avenue, Suite 700, Tucson, AZ 85701

Director **Ursula Kramer** .... (520) 243-7454
Fax: (520) 838-7432

Facilities Management Department

150 W. Congress, 3rd Floor, Tucson, AZ 85701
Fax: (520) 740-3900 Internet: www.pima.gov/fm

Director **Michael Kirk** .... (520) 724-3085
E-mail: michael.kirk@pima.gov

Fleet Services

Tel: (520) 724-2670 Fax: (520) 724-7387

Director **Frank Samaniego** .... (520) 724-2670

Department of Finance and Risk Management

130 West Congress, 6th Floor, Tucson, AZ 85701
Fax: (520) 243-2329 Internet: www.pima.gov/finance

Director (Interim) **Ellen Moulton** .... (520) 724-3038

Risk Management Division

130 West Congress, Ninth Floor, Tucson, AZ 85701-1317
Fax: (520) 798-1407

Manager **Lauren Eib** .... (520) 243-8120

Fleet Services Department

1301 S. Mission, Tucson, AZ 85713
Fax: (520) 623-7387 Internet: www.pima.gov/fleet

Director **Frank Sameniego** .... (520) 740-5920
Fleet Maintenance Manager **Bob Charlton** .... (520) 740-2614

Communications Office

130 West Congress, First Floor, Tucson, AZ 85701-1317
Fax: (520) 740-2810 E-mail: graphics@pw.pima.gov
Internet: www.pima.gov/graphics

Director **Jeff Nordensson** .... (520) 724-8512

Pima County Health Department [PCHD]

3950 South Country Club Road, Suite 200, Tucson, AZ 85714
Tel: (520) 243-7770 Fax: (520) 623-1432 Internet: www.pimahealth.org

Director **Dr. Francisco Garcia** .... (520) 243-7770

Human Resources Department [HR]

150 West Congress Street, 5th Floor, Tucson, AZ 85701
Fax: (520) 620-1487 Internet: www.pima.gov/hr

Director **Allyn Bulzomi** .... (520) 740-8672
E-mail: allyn.bulzomi@pima.gov

★ Elected Official ▲Appointed by Legislature ▼Appointed by Governor ▶Appointed by Board or Commission ●Appointed by Judge
■Appointed by Mayor △Appointed by Freeholders ▽Appointed by Supervisor ▷Appointed by County Executive ○Appointed by Council

Natural Resources, Parks and Recreation Department [NRPR]
3500 West River Road, Tucson, AZ 85741
Fax: (520) 877-6000 E-mail: pcpr@pima.gov
Internet: www.pima.gov/nrpr

Director **Rafael Payan** .... (520) 877-6000

Procurement Department
130 W. Congress, 3rd Floor, Tucson, AZ 85701
Fax: (520) 798-1484 Internet: www.pima.gov/procure

Director **George Widugiris** .... (520) 724-8161
E-mail: george.widugiris@pima.gov Fax: (520) 798-1484

Regional Wastewater Reclamation Department [RWRD]
Public Works Bldg., 201 North Stone Avenue, 8th Floor, Tucson, AZ 85701
Internet: www.pima.gov/wwm

Director **Jackson Jenkins** .... (520) 724-6500

Department of Transportation
Public Works Building, 201 North Stone Avenue, 4th Floor, Tucson, AZ 85701
Internet: http://dot.pima.gov/

Director **Priscilla S. Cornelio** .... (520) 740-6775
Fax: (520) 740-6439
Deputy Director **Ana Olivares** .... (520) 740-6436

Law Library
Superior Court Building, 110 West Congress, Room 256, Tucson, AZ 85701
Fax: (520) 791-9122 E-mail: pcll@pima.gov
Internet: http://www.sc.pima.gov/lawlib

Director **Sol Gomez** .... (520) 740-8456

Pima County Public Library
101 North Stone Avenue, Tucson, AZ 85701
Internet: www.library.pima.gov

Director **Melinda S. Cervantes** .... (520) 594-5600
Deputy Director **Patrick C. Corella** .... (520) 594-5600

Pima County Regional Flood Control District [RFCD]
97 East Congress, Tucson, AZ 85701
Tel: (520) 243-1880

Regional Flood Control Director **Suzanne Shields**
Regional Flood Control District .... (520) 243-1800

Office of the County Assessor
County Courthouse, 115 North Church Avenue, 3rd Floor, Tucson, AZ 85701
Tel: (520) 740-8172 Fax: (520) 740-8013

★ Assessor **Bill Staples** (D) .... (520) 740-8172
Term Expires: December 31, 2016
E-mail: bill.staples@pima.gov
Chief Deputy Assessor **Monica Detaranto** .... (520) 740-8172
E-mail: monica.detaranto@pima.gov

Office of the County Attorney
32 North Stone Avenue, 14th Floor, Tucson, AZ 85701
Fax: (520) 791-3946

★ County Attorney **Barbara LaWall** (D) .... (520) 740-5622
Term Expires: December 31, 2016 Fax: (520) 791-3946
E-mail: pcao@pima.gov
Education: Arizona 1967 BA, 1976 JD
Administrative Chief Deputy **Amelia Craig Cramer** .... (520) 740-5598
E-mail: pimacounty.attorney@pcao.pima.gov Fax: (520) 791-3946
Civil Chief Deputy **Thomas Weaver** .... (520) 740-5750
E-mail: thomas.weaver@pcao.pima.gov Fax: (520) 620-6556
Criminal Chief Deputy **David Berkman** .... (520) 740-5600
E-mail: david.berkman@pcao.pima.gov Fax: (520) 620-1502

Office of the County Recorder
County Courthouse, 115 North Church Avenue, 1st Floor, Tucson, AZ 85701
Fax: (520) 623-1785

★ Recorder **F. Ann Rodriguez** (D) .... (520) 724-4350
Term Expires: December 31, 2016
E-mail: fann.rodriguez@recorder.pima.gov
Chief Deputy Recorder **Christopher Roads** .... (520) 740-4330
Registrar of Voters **Christopher Roads** .... (520) 740-4330

Office of the Sheriff
1750 East Benson Highway, Tucson, AZ 85714
Fax: (520) 351-4789 E-mail: pcsd@pimasheriff.net
Internet: www.pimasheriff.org

★ Sheriff **Chris Nanos** (D) .... (520) 351-4700
Term Expires: December 31, 2016
E-mail: pcsd@pimasheriff.net
Administrative Bureau Chief **Christopher Radtke** .... (520) 351-4700
E-mail: cradtke@pimasheriff.net
Correction Bureau Chief **Byron Gwaltney** .... (520) 351-8100
1270 West Silverlake Road, Tucson, AZ 85714
Operations Bureau Chief **Karl Woolridge** .... (520) 351-4700

Office of the Superintendent of Schools
200 North Stone Avenue, Tucson, AZ 85701
Fax: (520) 623-9308 E-mail: schools@schools.pima.gov
Internet: www.schools.pima.gov

★ Superintendent **Dr. Linda Lee Arzoumanian** (R) .... (520) 724-8451
Term Expires: December 31, 2016
E-mail: linda.arzoumanian@schools.pima.gov
Education: Ohio MEd; Nova EdD
Chief Deputy **Debbie D'Amore** .... (520) 724-8451

Office of the Treasurer
County Courthouse, 115 North Church Avenue, 1st Floor, Tucson, AZ 85701
Fax: (520) 740-2743

★ Treasurer **Beth Ford** (R) .... (520) 724-8775
Term Expires: December 31, 2016
Chief Deputy Treasurer **Patti Davidson** .... (520) 724-8775

Pima County Constable's Office
32 North Stone Avenue, Suite 111, Tucson, AZ 85701
Tel: (520) 740-5442 Fax: (520) 740-5445
Internet: www.pima.gov/depts/const.html

★ Constable 1 **David Lester** .... (520) 740-5442
Term Expires: December 31, 2016
E-mail: david.lester@pima.gov

(continued on next page)

★ Elected Official ▲ Appointed by Legislature ▼ Appointed by Governor ▶ Appointed by Board or Commission ● Appointed by Judge
■ Appointed by Mayor △ Appointed by Freeholders ▽ Appointed by Supervisor ▷ Appointed by County Executive ○ Appointed by Council

Pima County Constable's Office *continued*

★Constable 2 **Frank Fontes** (520) 740-5442
Term Expires: December 31, 2018

★Constable 3 **George Gradillas** (520) 387-5403
Term Expires: December 31, 2018

★Constable 4 **James "Jim" Driscoll** (520) 740-5442
Term Expires: December 31, 2016

★Constable 5 **Marge Cummings** (520) 740-5442
Term Expires: December 31, 2018

★Constable 6 **Bennett Bernal** (520) 740-5442
Term Expires: December 31, 2016
E-mail: bennett.bernal@pima.gov

★Constable 7 **R.C. Brown** (520) 740-5442
Term Expires: December 31, 2016
E-mail: r.brown@pima.gov

★Constable 8 **Mary C. Dorgan** (520) 740-5442
Term Expires: December 31, 2016
E-mail: mary.dorgan@pima.gov

★Constable 9 **Colette Philip** (520) 740-5442
Term Expires: December 31, 2016
E-mail: colette.phillip@pima.gov

★Constable 10 **Vince Roberts** (520) 740-5442
Term Expires: December 31, 2016
E-mail: vince.roberts@pima.gov

County of Pinellas, Florida

315 Court Street, Clearwater, FL 33756
Tel: (727) 464-3000 (County Connection)
Internet: www.pinellascounty.org

County Seat: Clearwater **Election Type:** Partisan **Population:** 949,827 (2015)

Office of the Board of County Commissioners

315 Court Street, Clearwater, FL 33756
Tel: (727) 464-3377 Fax: (727) 464-3022

★Chairman **Charles "Charlie" Justice** (D-District 3) (727) 464-3363
Term Expires: November 2016
E-mail: cjustice@pinellascounty.org
Education: South Florida 1993 BA

★Vice Chair **Janet C. Long** (D-District 1) (727) 464-3365
Term Expires: November 2016
E-mail: janetclong@pinellascounty.org

★Commissioner **Patricia Gerard** (D-District 2) (727) 464-3360
Term Expires: November 2018
E-mail: pgerard@pinellascounty.org
Education: South Florida BA, MA

★Commissioner **Dave Eggers** (R-District 4) (727) 464-3276
Term Expires: November 2018
E-mail: deggers@pinellascounty.org

★Commissioner **Karen Williams Seel** (R-District 5) (727) 464-3278
Term Expires: November 2016
E-mail: kseel@pinellascounty.org
Education: Florida 1979 BS; Thunderbird International 1981 MBA

★Commissioner **John Morroni** (R-District 6) (727) 464-3568
Term Expires: November 2018
E-mail: jmorroni@pinellascounty.org
Date of Birth: February 16, 1955
Education: Loyola U (Chicago) 1977 BA

★Commissioner **Kenneth T. "Ken" Welch** (D-District 7) (727) 464-3614
Term Expires: November 2016
E-mail: kwelch@pinellascounty.org
Education: South Florida 1985 BA; Florida A&M 1987 MBA

Office of Business Technology Services

400 South Fort Harrison Avenue, Clearwater, FL 33756
Tel: (727) 453-4357 Fax: (727) 464-4718
Internet: www.pinellascounty.org/bts

Director **Martin Rose** (727) 464-3395
E-mail: mrose@co.pinellas.fl.us

Office of the County Attorney

315 Court Street, Clearwater, FL 33756
Fax: (727) 464-4147

►County Attorney **James Lee "Jim" Bennett** (727) 464-3354
E-mail: jbennett@co.pinellas.fl.us
Education: Auburn; South Florida; Stetson JD

Office of Human Rights

400 South Fort Harrison Avenue, Room 500, Clearwater, FL 33756
Fax: (727) 464-4157

Human Rights/EEO Officer **Paul Valenti** (727) 464-4880

Office of the County Administrator

315 Court St., Clearwater, FL 33756
Fax: (727) 464-4384

County Administrator **Mark Woodard** (727) 464-3485
E-mail: mwoodard@pinellascounty.org

Chief Assistant County Administrator and Chief of Staff **Bruce Moeller** (727) 464-3485

►Assistant County Administrator **(Vacant)** (727) 464-3485

Animal Services

12450 Ulmerton Road, Largo, FL 33774
Fax: (727) 582-2637

Director **Maureen Freaney** (727) 582-2600

Communications

333 Chestnut St., Clearwater, FL 33756
Fax: (727) 464-4432

Director **Timothy Closterman** (727) 464-4600
Office Manager **Susan Morse** (727) 464-4600

Housing Finance Authority

600 Cleveland Street, Suite 800, Clearwater, FL 33755
Tel: (727) 223-6419 Fax: (727) 255-5562

Director **Kathryn Driver** (727) 223-6419
Program Administrator **Karmen Lemberg** (727) 223-6419

Construction Licensing Board

12600 Belcher Road, Suite 102, Largo, FL 33773
Fax: (727) 538-4797

Executive Director **Rodney Fischer** (727) 536-4720

County Extension Service

12175 - 125th St. North, Largo, FL 33774-3695
Fax: (727) 582-2149

Director **Mary Campbell** (727) 582-2100
Extension Program Coordinator **Spencer Curtis** (727) 582-2100
E-mail: scurtis@pinellascounty.org

Economic Development

13805 58th Street, N., Suite 1-200, Clearwater, FL 33760
Tel: (727) 464-7332 Fax: (727) 464-7053

Director **Mike Meidel** (727) 464-7332
E-mail: mmeidel@co.pinellas.fl.us

★Elected Official ▲Appointed by Legislature ▼Appointed by Governor ►Appointed by Board or Commission ●Appointed by Judge
■Appointed by Mayor △Appointed by Freeholders ▽Appointed by Supervisor ▷Appointed by County Executive ○Appointed by Council

Department of Emergency Management
400 South Fort Harrison Avenue, Suite 111, Clearwater, FL 33756
Tel: (727) 464-3800 Fax: (727) 464-4024
E-mail: ema@pinellascounty.org
Internet: www.pinellascounty.org/emergency

Director **Sally Bishop** .... (727) 464-3800
E-mail: sbishop@co.pinellas.fl.us

Department of Environment and Infrastructure [DEI]
14 South Fort Harrison Avenue, 5th Floor, Clearwater, FL 33756
Tel: (727) 464-3829 Fax: (727) 464-4152

Executive Director **(Vacant)** .... (727) 464-3829
Administrative Secretary **Angela E. Powell** .... (727) 464-3829
E-mail: apowell@pinellascounty.org

Administration and Business Support Division
14 South Fort Harrison Avenue, Clearwater, FL 33756

Director **Bob Peacock** .... (727) 464-3767

Solid Waste Division
3095 114th Avenue, St. Petersburg, FL 33716

Director **(Vacant)** .... (727) 464-7500

Public Works Division
Building 1, 22211 U.S. 19 North, Clearwater, FL 33765

Director **Richard L.V. Coates III** .... (727) 464-8913

Water and Sewer Division
1620 Ridge Road, Largo, FL 33778

Director **Bob Powell** .... (727) 582-2300

Department of Health and Human Services
2189 Cleveland Street, Clearwater, FL 33755
Fax: (727) 464-8454 Internet: www.pinellascounty.org/humanservices

Director **Lourdes Benedit** .... (727) 464-8400
Assistant Director **(Vacant)** .... (727) 464-8400

Heritage Village/Historical Museum
11909 - 125th St. North, Largo, FL 33774
Fax: (727) 582-2211

Museum Operations Manager **Ellen Babb** .... (727) 582-2123

Human Resources Department
400 S. Fort Harrison Ave., Clearwater, FL 33756-5113
Fax: (727) 464-3949

Director **Peggy Rowe** .... (727) 464-3367
E-mail: prowe@co.pinellas.fl.us
Education: Georgia 1979 BA; Georgia State 1995 MBA
Secretary **Peggy Sellards** .... (727) 464-3367
E-mail: psellards@co.pinellas.fl.us

Department of Justice and Consumer Services
15251 Roosevelt Blvd., Suite 209, Clearwater, FL 33760
Fax: (727) 453-7441

Director **Michael Cooksey** .... (727) 464-6200

Planning Department
600 Cleveland Street, Suite 750, Clearwater, FL 33755
Fax: (727) 464-8201

Director **(Vacant)** .... (727) 464-8200

Parks and Conservation Resources Department
12450 Ulmerton Road, Largo, FL 33774
Fax: (727) 582-2100

Director **Paul Cozzie** .... (727) 582-2100

Parks and Conservation Resources Department *continued*

P and R Operations Manager **(Vacant)** .... (727) 582-2100

Real Estate Management
509 East Avenue South, Clearwater, FL 33756
Fax: (727) 464-3374

Director **Paul Sacco** .... (727) 464-3494
E-mail: psacco@co.pinellas.fl.us
Manager, Lease Management **Sean Griffin** .... (727) 464-3496
E-mail: sgriffin@pinellascounty.org Fax: (727) 464-3374

Building and Development Review Services
310 Court St., Clearwater, FL 33756
Fax: (727) 464-3981

Director of Building Services **Larry Goldman** .... (727) 464-4252
Development Review Director **Blake Lyon** .... (727) 464-3888

Veterans' Service Office
2189 Cleveland Street, Clearwater, FL 33755
Fax: (727) 464-8407

Director **Michael Hill** .... (727) 464-8460

Pinellas County Young-Rainey STAR Center
7887 Bryan Dairy Rd., Suite 120, Largo, FL 33777
Fax: (727) 541-8251 E-mail: spcedc@co.pinellas.fl.us
Internet: http://www.stpete-clearwater-edc.com

Director **Paul Sacco** .... (727) 541-8942

Public Safety Services
12450 Ulmerton Road, Largo, FL 33774
Internet: www.pinellascounty.org/publicsafety/default.htm

Director **(Vacant)** .... (727) 582-2000

Emergency Communications/911
400 South Fort Harrison Avenue, Suite 140, Clearwater, FL 33756
Fax: (727) 464-3265

Director **Charles Freeman** .... (727) 464-3835

Emergency Medical Services and Fire Administration
12490 Ulmerton Rd., Largo, FL 33774
Fax: (727) 582-2039

Director **Craig Hare** .... (727) 582-2000
E-mail: chare@co.pinellas.fl.us
EMS Finance Manager **Jodie Sechler** .... (727) 582-2000
EMS Program Manager (Acting) **Craig Hare** .... (727) 582-2000
E-mail: chare@co.pinellas.fl.us
Fire Coordinator **Michael Cooksey** .... (727) 582-2000
E-mail: mcooksey@co.pinellas.fl.us

Purchasing
400 South Fort Harrison Avenue, 6th Floor, Clearwater, FL 33756
Fax: (727) 464-3925

Director (Interim) **Candy Mancuso** .... (727) 464-3311
E-mail: cmancuso@co.pinellas.fl.us
Assistant Director **Candy Mancuso** .... (727) 464-3311
E-mail: cmancuso@co.pinellas.fl.us

Risk Management
400 South Fort Harrison Avenue, 3rd Floor, Clearwater, FL 33756
Fax: (727) 464-3664

Director **Virginia Holscher** .... (727) 464-3664
Administrative Support Supervisor **(Vacant)** .... (727) 464-3513
Senior Claims Adjuster **Pam Grabo** .... (727) 464-3664
E-mail: pgrabo@co.pinellas.fl.us
Insurance Manager **Ginger White** .... (727) 464-3513

★ Elected Official ▲ Appointed by Legislature ▼ Appointed by Governor ► Appointed by Board or Commission ● Appointed by Judge
■ Appointed by Mayor △ Appointed by Freeholders ▽ Appointed by Supervisor ▷ Appointed by County Executive ○ Appointed by Council

St. Petersburg-Clearwater Area Convention and Visitors Bureau
8200 Bryan Dairy Road, Sute 200, Largo, FL 33777
Fax: (727) 464-7222 Internet: http://www.visitstpeteclearwater.com/

Executive Director **David Downing** . . . . (727) 464-7200
E-mail: david@visitspc.com
Deputy Director **(Vacant)** . . . . (727) 464-7200

St. Petersburg-Clearwater International Airport
14700 Terminal Blvd., Clearwater, FL 33762
Fax: (727) 536-3782

▶ Director **Tom Jewsbury** . . . . (727) 453-7800
E-mail: JEWSBURY@FLY2PIE.COM
Media and Public Relations Director **Michele Routh** . . . . . (727) 453-7800
E-mail: MROUTH@FLY2PIE.COM

Office of the Clerk of the Circuit Court and Comptroller
315 Court Street, 4th Floor, Clearwater, FL 33756
Tel: (727) 464-3341 Fax: (727) 453-3589
E-mail: clerkinfo@pinellascounty.org Internet: www.mypinellasclerk.org

★ Clerk of the Court **Ken Burke** . . . . (727) 464-3341
Term Expires: January 8, 2017
E-mail: kburke@pinellascounty.org

Office of the Property Appraiser
315 Court Street, Clearwater, FL 33756
Tel: (727) 464-3207 Fax: (727) 464-3448

★ Property Appraiser **Pam Dubov** (R) . . . . (727) 464-3207
Term Expires: January 1, 2017

Office of the Public Defender
Criminal Justice Center, 14250 49th Street North, Clearwater, FL 33762
Fax: (727) 464-6119 E-mail: pd6@wearethehope.org

★ Public Defender **Robert Henry "Bob" Dillinger** (R) . . . . . (727) 464-6516
Term Expires: December 31, 2016
E-mail: bdilling@co.pinellas.fl.us
Education: Columbia 1973; Stetson 1976 JD
Office Manager **Cassandra Hadad** . . . . (727) 464-6516

Office of the Sheriff
10750 Ulmerton Rd., Largo, FL 33778
Fax: (727) 582-6459

★ Sheriff **Bob Gualtieri** . . . . (727) 582-6200
Term Expires: December 31, 2016
E-mail: bgualtieri@pcsonet.com
Executive Administrative Assistant **Josephine Mattson** . . (727) 582-6200

Office of the State Attorney
Criminal Justice Center, 14250 - 49th St. North, Clearwater, FL 33762
Fax: (727) 464-7303 Internet: www.sao6.org

★ State Attorney **Bernard J. "Bernie" McCabe, Jr.** (R) . . . . (727) 464-6221
Term Expires: January 1, 2017
E-mail: bmccabe@co.pinellas.fl.us
Education: Stetson 1969 BA, 1972 JD

Office of the Supervisor of Elections
315 Court St., Clearwater, FL 33756
Fax: (727) 464-4158

★ Supervisor of Elections **Deborah Clark** (R) . . . . (727) 464-6108
Term Expires: January 1, 2017
E-mail: dclark@pinellascounty.org
Deputy Supervisor **Rick Becker** . . . . (727) 464-6108
E-mail: rbecker@pinellascounty.org
Deputy Supervisor **Julie Marcus** . . . . (727) 464-6108
E-mail: jmarcus@pinellascounty.org

Office of the Tax Collector
315 Court St., Clearwater, FL 33756
Fax: (727) 464-3727

★ Tax Collector **Diane Nelson** (R) . . . . (727) 464-7777
Term Expires: December 31, 2016

Pinellas County Health Department [PinCHD]
205 Dr. Martin Luther King Street North, St. Petersburg, FL 33701
Tel: (727) 824-6900 Fax: (727) 820-4275
E-mail: pinchd52info@doh.state.fl.us Internet: www.pinellashealth.com
Director **Ulyee Choe** . . . . (727) 824-6900

Pinellas County Schools [PCS]
301 Fourth Street, SW, Largo, FL 33770-2942
P.O. Box 2942, Largo, FL 33709
Tel: (727) 588-6000 Fax: (727) 588-6202 Internet: www.pcsb.org

Pinellas County School Board
E-mail: board@pcsb.org

★ Chairperson **Peggy L. O'Shea** . . . . (727) 588-6000
Term Expires: November 2016

Office of the Superintendent
E-mail: supt@pcsb.org

Superintendent of Schools **Michael Grego** . . . . (727) 588-6011
Deputy Superintendent/Chief of Staff **William Corbett** . . . (727) 588-6011

County of Plymouth, Massachusetts
44 Obery Street, Plymouth, MA 02360
Tel: (508) 830-9100 (Information) Fax: (508) 830-9106

County Seat: Plymouth **Election Type:** Nonpartisan
Population: 510,393 (2015)

Office of the Board of Commissioners
44 Obery Street, Plymouth, MA 02360
Fax: (508) 830-9106

★ Chairman **Daniel A. Pallotta** . . . . (508) 830-9100
Term Expires: January 2017
E-mail: dpallotta@plymouthcounty-ma.org
★ Commissioner **Gregory M. Hanley** . . . . (508) 830-9100
Term Expires: January 2017
E-mail: ghanley@plymouthcounty-ma.org
★ Commissioner **Sandra M. Wright** . . . . (508) 830-9100
Term Expires: January 2019
E-mail: swright@plymouthcounty-ma.org

Office of the Board of Commissioners *continued*

County Administrator **Frank Basler** . . . . (508) 830-9104
E-mail: fbasler@plymouthcounty-ma.org

Office of the Register of Probate/ Insolvency

52 Obery Street, Plymouth, MA 02360
Fax: (508) 746-6846

★ Register of Probate/Insolvency **Matthew McDonough** . . . (508) 747-6204
Term Expires: January 2017

Office of the Sheriff

Plymouth County Sheriff's Department, 24 Long Pond Road, Plymouth, MA 02360
Fax: (508) 830-6316 Internet: www.pcsdma.org

★ Sheriff **Joseph McDonald, Jr.** . . . . (508) 830-6200
Term Expires: January 2017

Office of the Treasurer

44 Obery Street, Plymouth, MA 02360
Fax: (508) 830-9135

Treasurer **Thomas J. O'Brien** . . . . (508) 830-9130
Term Expires: January 2019
E-mail: tobrien@plymouthcounty-ma.org

County of Polk, Florida

330 W. Church St., Bartow, FL 33830
P.O. Box 9005, Bartow, FL 33831
Tel: (863) 534-6000 (Information) Internet: www.polk-county.net

County Seat: Bartow **Election Type:** Partisan **Population:** 650,092 (2015)

Office of the Board of County Commissioners

330 West Church Street, Bartow, FL 33830
Drawer BC01, P.O. Box 9005, Bartow, FL 33831
Tel: (863) 534-6000 Fax: (863) 534-7655
E-mail: communications@polk-county.net

★ Chair **John Hall** (R-District 5) . . . . (863) 534-6049
Term Expires: November 30, 2016
E-mail: johnhall@polk-county.net
Executive Assistant **Chris Chila** . . . . (863) 534-6422
E-mail: chrischila@polk-county.net

★ Commissioner **George Lindsey** (R-District 1) . . . . (863) 534-6450
Term Expires: November 30, 2016
Executive Assistant **Chris Chilla** . . . . (863) 534-6422

★ Commissioner **Melony Bell** (R-District 2) . . . . (863) 534-6434
Term Expires: November 22, 2018
E-mail: melonybell@polk-county.net
Executive Assistant **Kay Hodgkins** . . . . (863) 534-6434
E-mail: kayhodgkins@polk-county.net

★ Commissioner **Edwin V. "Ed" Smith** (R-District 3) . . . . . (863) 534-6050
Term Expires: November 2016
E-mail: ed.smith@polk-county.net
Education: Regents 1977; Old Dominion 1992 MS
Executive Assistant **Kay Hodgkins** . . . . (863) 534-6050
E-mail: kayhodgkins@polk-county.net

★ Commissioner **R. Todd Dantzler** (R-District 4) . . . . (863) 534-6422
Term Expires: November 22, 2018
E-mail: todddantzler@polk-county.net
Date of Birth: November 20, 1959
Education: Florida BS

Office of the Board of County Commissioners *continued*

Executive Assistant **Chris Chila** . . . . (863) 534-6422
E-mail: chrischila@polk-county.net

County Attorney's Office

Drawer AT01, P.O. Box 9005, Bartow, FL 33831
Fax: (863) 534-7654

▶ County Attorney **Michael Craig** . . . . (863) 534-6786
E-mail: michaelcraig@polk-county.net

County Manager's Office

Drawer CA01, P.O. Box 9005, Bartow, FL 33831
Tel: (863) 534-6444 Fax: (863) 534-7069

▶ County Manager **Jim Freeman** . . . . (863) 534-6444
E-mail: jimfreeman@polk-county.net
Executive Secretary **Diane Pannebaker** . . . . (863) 534-6444
E-mail: dianepannebaker@polk-county.net

Deputy County Manager **William D. "Bill" Beasley** . . . . . (863) 534-6429
E-mail: billbeasley@polk-county.net
Secretary IV **Tabitha McGill** . . . . (863) 534-6444
E-mail: tabithamcgill@polk-county.net

Deputy County Manager **Lea Ann Thomas** . . . . (863) 534-6031
E-mail: leaannthomas@polk-county.net
Secretary IV **Donna Purvis** . . . . (863) 534-6444
E-mail: donnapurvis@polk-county.net

Deputy County Manager **Gary L. Hester** . . . . (863) 534-6428
E-mail: garyhester@polk-county.net
Executive Secretary **Diane Pannebaker** . . . . (863) 534-6444
E-mail: dianepannebaker@polk-county.net

Equal Opportunity Office [EO]

330 West Church Street, Bartow, FL 33830
Fax: (863) 534-7626

Director **Richard J. Bradford** . . . . (863) 534-6075
Administrative Secretary **Leah Wilson** . . . . (863) 534-5901
E-mail: leahwilson@polk-county.net

Office of Supplier Diversity

Drawer CA05 P.O. Box 9005, Bartow, FL 33831
Tel: (863) 534-5959 Fax: (863) 534-7521

Director **Cedric Joseph** . . . . (863) 534-5959

Social Services

1290 Golfview Avenue, Suite 116, Bartow, FL 33830
Fax: (863) 519-3709

Director **Marcia Andresen** . . . . (863) 534-5202

Cooperative Extension Services

1702 Hwy 17 South, Bartow, FL 33830
Fax: (863) 534-0001 Internet: http://polk.ifas.ufl.edu

Director **Nicole Walker** . . . . (863) 519-8677

Elderly Services

1290 Golfview Ave., Suite 116, Bartow, FL 33830
Fax: (863) 534-0314

Director **Hope Jones** . . . . (863) 534-5320

Housing and Neighborhood Development

Drawer HS04, P.O. Box 9005, Bartow, FL 33831
Fax: (863) 534-0349

Director **Greg Alpers** . . . . (863) 534-5240
E-mail: gregalpers@polk-county.net

Veteran Services

1290 Golfview Ave., Suite 116, Bartow, FL 33830
Fax: (863) 534-7378

Supervisor **Mike Mason** . . . . (863) 534-5220

COUNTIES

★ Elected Official ▲ Appointed by Legislature ▼ Appointed by Governor ▶ Appointed by Board or Commission ● Appointed by Judge
■ Appointed by Mayor △ Appointed by Freeholders ▽ Appointed by Supervisor ▷ Appointed by County Executive ○ Appointed by Council

COUNTIES

Facilities Management Division
Drawer PW05, P.O. Box 9005, Bartow, FL 33831
Fax: (863) 534-5542

Director **David R. Peach** .... (863) 534-5511
E-mail: davidpeach@polk-county.net

Parks and Natural Resources Division
4177 Ben Durrance Rd., Bartow, FL 33830
Fax: (863) 534-7374

Director **Jeff Spence** .... (863) 534-7377
Parks Manager **Michael "Mike" Callender** .... (863) 534-2508

Roads and Drainage Division
Drawer TR01, PO Box 9005, Bartow, FL 33831-9005
Fax: (863) 534-7339

Director **Jay Jarvis** .... (863) 535-2200
E-mail: jayjarvis@polk-county.net

Utilities Division
Drawer UT01 P.O. Box 9005, Bartow, FL 33831
Tel: (863) 298-4100 Fax: (863) 298-4111

Director **Margorie Craig** .... (863) 298-4135

Waste and Recycling Division
10 Environmental Loop, Winter Haven, FL 33880
Fax: (863) 284-4321

Director **Ana Wood** .... (863) 284-4319

Planning and Development Department
Drawer GM01, P.O. Box 9005, Bartow, FL 33831
Tel: (863) 534-6467 Fax: (863) 534-6543

Director **Tom Deardorff** .... (863) 534-6467
E-mail: thomasdeardorff@polk-county.net
Secretary **Sharon Yeck** .... (863) 534-6467
E-mail: sharonyeck@polk-county.net

Building Division
330 West Church Street, Bartow, FL 33830
Fax: (863) 534-6016

Director **Chandra Frederick** .... (863) 534-6080

Land Development Division
Drawer GM03, P.O. Box 9005, Bartow, FL 33831
Fax: (863) 534-6407

Director **John Bohde** .... (863) 534-6792

Code Enforcement Division
330 West Church Street, Bartow, FL 33830
Tel: (863) 534-6054

Administrator **Autumn Fenton** .... (863) 534-6054

Emergency Medical Services
PO Box 1458, Bartow, FL 33831
Fax: (863) 534-0010

Director **David Cash** .... (863) 519-7409

Polk County Fire Rescue
PO Box 1458, Bartow, FL 33831
Fax: (863) 534-0385

Chief **David Cash** .... (863) 519-7353
E-mail: davidcash@polkfl.com

Emergency Management
1295 Brice Boulevard, Bartow, FL 33830
Fax: (863) 534-5647

Director **Pete McNally** .... (863) 298-7023
E-mail: petemcnally@polkfl.com

Risk Management
Drawer AS07, P.O. Box 9005, Bartow, FL 33831
Fax: (863) 519-4726

Director **Michael "Mike" Kushner** .... (863) 534-5540
E-mail: mikekushner@polk-county.net

Information Technology Division
Drawer AS04, P.O. Box 9005, Bartow, FL 33831
Fax: (863) 534-7599

Director **Ed Wolfe** .... (863) 534-7500
E-mail: edwolfe@polk-county.net

Indigent Health Care
P.O. Box 9005 Drawer AS07, Bartow, FL 33831

Director **Joy Johnson** .... (863) 534-5204

Office of Equity and Human Resources
330 West Church Street, Bartow, FL 33831
PO Box 9005, Drawer CA03, Bartow, FL 33880
Fax: (863) 534-6534

Director **Kandis Buford** .... (863) 534-6030
E-mail: kandisbuford@polk.county.net

Fleet Management Division
Drawer AS03, P.O. Box 9005, Bartow, FL 33831
Fax: (963) 534-0390

Director **Charles Cheatham** .... (863) 534-5660

Communications Division
Drawer CA04 PO box 9005, Bartow, FL 33831-9005
Fax: (863) 534-6011

Director **Mianne Nelson** .... (863) 534-6083
E-mail: miannenelson@polk-county.net
Education: Iowa 1980 BGS

Budget and Procurement Division
330 West Church Street, Bartow, FL 33830-9005
Drawer AS05 PO Box 9005, Bartow, FL 33831-9005
Fax: (863) 534-7678

Director **Frances "Fran" McAskill** .... (863) 534-6430
E-mail: franmcaskill@polk-county.net
Budget Manager **Todd Bond** .... (863) 534-6430
E-mail: toddbond@polk-county.net

Central Florida Development Council [CFDC]
Drawer CF01, 2701 Lake Myrtle Park Road, Auburndale, FL 33823-9360
Fax: (863) 551-4739 Internet: www.cfdc.org

Staff
President and Chief Executive Officer **David Petr** .... (863) 551-4710
E-mail: david@cfdc.org
Senior Project Manager **Spiros Balntas** .... (863) 551-4719

Board of Directors
Chair **Greg Ruthven** .... (863) 551-4719
Vice Chair **Leonard Mass** .... (863) 551-4719
Secretary/Treasurer **Bud Strang** .... (863) 551-4719
Board Member **Trudy Block** .... (863) 551-4719
Board Member **R. Todd Dantzler** (R) .... (863) 551-4719
Date of Birth: November 20, 1959
Education: Florida BS
Board Member **Greg Littleton** .... (863) 551-4719
Board Member **Carl "Ed" Locke, Jr.** .... (863) 551-4719
Board Member **Larry Madrid** .... (863) 551-4719
Board Member **Amy Palmer** .... (863) 551-4719

★ Elected Official ▲ Appointed by Legislature ▼ Appointed by Governor ▶ Appointed by Board or Commission ● Appointed by Judge
■ Appointed by Mayor △ Appointed by Freeholders ▽ Appointed by Supervisor ▷ Appointed by County Executive ○ Appointed by Council

County Probation Division
1745 U.S. 17 South, Bartow, FL 33830
Fax: (863) 534-2140

Director **Lisa W. Ewing** . . . . (863) 534-4125

Polk County Law Library
Courthouse, Rm. 3076, 255 N. Broadway, Bartow, FL 33830
Fax: (863) 534-7443

Law Librarian **Irene Morris** . . . . (863) 534-4013

Office of the Clerk of the Circuit Court/County Comptroller's Office
P.O. Box 988, Bartow, FL 33831
Tel: (863) 534-4540 Fax: (863) 534-4089
Internet: www.polkcountyclerk.net

★ Clerk of Courts/Comptroller **Stacy Butterfield** . . . . (863) 534-4540
Term Expires: December 31, 2016

Office of the County Sheriff
1891 Jim Keene Boulevard, Winter Haven, FL 33880
Fax: (863) 298-6518 Internet: www.polksheriff.org

★ Sheriff **Grady Judd** (R) . . . . (863) 298-6200
Term Expires: November 30, 2016
E-mail: gjudd@polksheriff.org

Office of the Property Appraiser
255 N. Wilson Ave., Bartow, FL 33830
Fax: (863) 534-4753

★ Property Appraiser **Marsha Faux** (R) . . . . (863) 534-4777
Term Expires: December 31, 2016
E-mail: paoffice@polk-county.net

Office of the State's Attorney
P.O. Box 9000, Drawer SA, Bartow, FL 33831
Fax: (863) 534-4945

★ State's Attorney **Jerry Hill** (R) . . . . (863) 534-4800
Term Expires: December 31, 2016
E-mail: sao10.sao10@dsm.net

Office of the Supervisor of Elections
P.O. Box 1460, Bartow, FL 33831-1460
Fax: (863) 534-5899 Internet: http://www.polkelections.com

★ Supervisor of Elections **Lori Edwards** (D) . . . . (863) 534-5888
Term Expires: December 31, 2016
E-mail: loriedwards@polkelections.com

Office of the Tax Collector
P.O. Box 1189, Bartow, FL 33831
Fax: (863) 534-4717 E-mail: mail@taxcollector.polk-county.net
Internet: http://www.polktaxes.com

★ Tax Collector **Joe Tedder** (D) . . . . (863) 534-4700
Term Expires: December 31, 2016
E-mail: mail@polktaxes.com
Education: Florida Southern BS

County of Polk, Iowa
Administrative Office Bldg., 111 Court Ave., Des Moines, IA 50309
Tel: (515) 286-3000 (Information) TTY: (515) 286-2003
Fax: (515) 286-3436 Internet: www.polkcountyiowa.gov

County Seat: Des Moines **Election Type:** Partisan
Population: 467,711 (2015)

Board of Supervisors
111 Court Avenue, Des Moines, IA 50309
Tel: (515) 286-3120 Fax: (515) 323-5225
E-mail: countyboard@polkcountyiowa.gov
Internet: www.polkcountyiowa.gov/supervisors

★ Chair **Thomas Hockensmith** (D-District 4) . . . . (515) 286-3118
Term Expires: December 31, 2018

★ Supervisor **Robert Brownell** (R-District 1) . . . . (515) 286-3115
Term Expires: December 31, 2016
E-mail: robert.brownell@polkcountyiowa.gov
Education: Northern Iowa 1973 BA; Drake (Attended)

★ Supervisor **Angela Connolly** (D-District 2) . . . . (515) 286-3117
Term Expires: December 31, 2018
E-mail: angela.connolly@polkcountyiowa.gov

★ Supervisor **Steve Van Oort** (R-District 3) . . . . (515) 286-3120
Term Expires: December 31, 2016

★ Supervisor **John F. Mauro** (D-District 5) . . . . (515) 286-3118
Term Expires: December 31, 2016
E-mail: john.mauro@polkcountyiowa.gov

Secretary to the Board **Kelsie Christensen** Room 300 . . . (515) 286-3120
E-mail: kelsie.christensen@polkcountyiowa.gov

Secretary to the Board **Heather Ksiazek** . . . . (515) 286-3121
E-mail: heather.ksiazek@polkcountyiowa.gov

County Administrator **Mark F. Wandro** . . . . (515) 286-3120

Risk Manager **Bob Cataldo** . . . . (515) 286-3210
E-mail: bob.cataldo@polkcountyiowa.gov Fax: (515) 323-5318

Executive Assistant **Sarah Boese** . . . . (515) 286-3895

Office of the County Assessor
County Administration Building, 111 Court Avenue, Room 195, Des Moines, IA 50309
Tel: (515) 286-3014

County Assessor **Randy J. Ripperger** . . . . (515) 286-3013
Chief Deputy **Rodney Hervey** . . . . (515) 286-3011
Deputy Assessor **Amy Rasmussen** . . . . (515) 286-3326

Department of Community, Family and Youth Services [CFYS]
1900 Carpenter, Des Moines, IA 50314
Fax: (515) 286-2055 E-mail: cfsasu@co.polk.ia.us

▽ Director **Brian Boyer** . . . . (515) 286-3644
1548 Hull Ave., Des Moines, IA 50316
E-mail: brian.boyer@polkcountyiowa.gov

Assistant Director **Betty Devine** . . . . (515) 286-3202

Program Administrator **Joy Ihle** . . . . (515) 286-3556
Fax: (515) 286-2055

Program Administrator **Joyce Webb** . . . . (515) 286-2062

Youth Services Department
1548 Hull Ave., Des Moines, IA 50316

Director **Brian Boyer** . . . . (515) 286-3644
Assistant Director **Betty Devine** . . . . (515) 286-3202
Central Juvenile Intake and Detention Center
Dan Larson . . . . (515) 286-2100
Youth Shelter **Tony Rhoads** . . . . (515) 286-3725

★ Elected Official ▲ Appointed by Legislature ▼ Appointed by Governor ▶ Appointed by Board or Commission ● Appointed by Judge
■ Appointed by Mayor △ Appointed by Freeholders ▽ Appointed by Supervisor ▷ Appointed by County Executive ○ Appointed by Council

General Services Department

111 Court Avenue, Room 365, Des Moines, IA 50309
Fax: (515) 286-3082

▽Director **John Rowen** .... (515) 286-3215
E-mail: john.rowen@polkcountyiowa.gov

Building and Grounds Division

Building Engineering Division Chief **Rick Hutchins** ..... (515) 286-3230
E-mail: rick.hutchins@polkcountyiowa.gov
Building Service Manager **Tom Alessio** .... (515) 286-3228
E-mail: tom.alessio@polkcountyiowa.gov
Building Maintenance Manager **Kirk Winders** .... (515) 286-3620

Central Services Division

Director **John Rowen** .... (515) 286-3398
E-mail: john.rowen@polkcountyiowa.gov
Supervisor **Connie Boesen** .... (515) 286-3191
E-mail: connie.boesen@polkcountyiowa.gov
Archivist **Pam Giles** .... (515) 286-2188
Telecommunications Specialist **Roy Valgoi** .... (515) 286-2202
E-mail: roy.valgoi@polkcountyiowa.gov

COUNTIES

Polk County Health Department

1907 Carpenter Avenue, Des Moines, IA 50314
Tel: (515) 286-3798 (Information) Fax: (515) 286-2033
E-mail: healthdept@polkcountyiowa.gov
Internet: www.polkcountyiowa.gov/health

▽Public Health Director **Rick Kozin** .... (515) 286-3926
E-mail: rick.kozin@polkcountyiowa.gov

Human Resources Department

County Administration Building, 111 Court Avenue, Room 390, Des Moines, IA 50309
Tel: (515) 286-3200 Fax: (515) 286-3316

Director **Jim Nahas** .... (515) 286-3200
Labor Relations Manager **Mike Campbell** ..... (515) 286-3200 ext. 3033
Employment Manager **Gail Stevenson** .... (515) 286-3200 ext. 3360

Information Technology

111 Court Avenue, Room 373, Des Moines, IA 50309
Tel: (515) 286-3757 Fax: (515) 323-5301
Internet: www.polkcountyiowa.gov/it

▽Director **Tony Jefferson** .... (515) 286-3757
E-mail: tony.jefferson@polkcountyiowa.gov
Secretary **Andrea Zenor** .... (515) 286-3757
E-mail: andrea.zenor@polkcountyiowa.gov

Public Works and Engineering Department

5885 NE 14th St., Des Moines, IA 50313
Fax: (515) 286-3437

▽Public Works Director **Robert Rice** .... (515) 286-3705
E-mail: robert.rice@polkcountyiowa.gov
County Engineer **Kurt Bailey** .... (515) 286-3705
E-mail: kurt.bailey@polkcountyiowa.gov

Polk County Planning Division

5885 NE 14th St., Des Moines, IA 50313

Land Use Manager **Bret Vandelune** .... (515) 286-2290
Administrative Supervisor **Janna Colvin** .... (515) 286-3367
E-mail: janna.colvin@polkcountyiowa.gov
Land Use Planning Coordinator **Charlie Wong** .... (515) 286-3705
Development Services Manager **Bret Vandelune** .... (515) 286-3705

Polk County Conservation Board

Jester Park, Granger, IA 50109
Fax: (515) 323-5354 E-mail: pccb_info@polkcountyiowa.gov
Internet: www.conservationboard.org

▽Director (Interim) **Richard "Rich" Leopold** .... (515) 323-5300
E-mail: richard.leopold@polkcountyiowa.gov
Education: Minnesota St (Mankato) BS; Iowa State MS

Polk County Emergency Management Commission

111 Court Ave., Des Moines, IA 50309
Fax: (515) 323-5256
Internet: www.polkcountyiowa.gov/emergencymanagement

Director **A.J. Mumm** .... (515) 286-2107
E-mail: aj.mumm@polkcountyiowa.gov

Polk County Health Services, Inc.

Polk County River Place, 2309 Euclid Avenue, Des Moines, IA 50310
Tel: (515) 243-4545 Fax: (515) 243-8447
E-mail: polkdisabilityservices@pchsia.org Internet: www.pchsia.org

▽Executive Director **(Vacant)** .... (515) 243-0867 ext. 210

Commission on Veterans' Affairs

120 Second Avenue, 2nd Floor, Des Moines, IA 50309
Fax: (515) 286-2106 E-mail: veterans.affairs@polkcountyiowa.gov
Internet: www.polkcountyiowa.gov/veteranaffairs

Administrator **Rebecca "Becky" Buch** .... (515) 286-3670
Assistant Administrator **Nick Lemmo** .... (515) 286-3670

Office of the Auditor

111 Court Avenue, Room 230, Des Moines, IA 50309
Fax: (515) 286-3608

★Auditor **Jamie Fitzgerald** .... (515) 286-3080
Term Expires: December 31, 2016
E-mail: jamie.fitzgerald@polkcountyiowa.gov
Education: Iowa Central Com Col 1992 AA; Iowa State 1994 BA
First Deputy Auditor **Carl Wiederaenders** .... (515) 286-3995
Second Deputy Auditor **Becky Dewey** .... (515) 286-3080
Central Accounting Manager **Keith Olson** .... (515) 286-3075
E-mail: keith.olson@polkcountyiowa.gov Fax: (515) 323-5253
Elections Manager **John Chiodo** .... (515) 286-3247
E-mail: john.chiodo@polkcountyiowa.gov Fax: (515) 286-2099
GIMS (Geographical Information Management System) Manager **Ken Agey** ..... (515) 286-3003
E-mail: ken.agey@polkcountyiowa.gov
Tax Department Supervisor **Michael Albers** .... (515) 286-3097
E-mail: Michael.albers@polkcountyiowa.gov

Office of the County Attorney

206 Sixth Avenue, 2nd Floor, Des Moines, IA 50309
Tel: (515) 286-3737 Fax: (515) 286-3428

★County Attorney **John P. Sarcone** (D) .... (515) 286-3737
Term Expires: December 31, 2018
E-mail: john.sarcone@polkcountyiowa.gov
Education: Rockhurst Col 1972 AB; Drake 1975 JD
Office Supervisor **Roxanne Petersen** .... (515) 286-3737
E-mail: roxanne.petersen@polkcountyiowa.gov
First Assistant County Attorney **Roger Kuhle** .... (515) 286-3331
E-mail: roger.kuhle@polkcountyiowa.gov
Juvenile Court Bureau Chief **Jim Ward** .... (515) 286-2035
E-mail: jim.ward@polkcountyiowa.gov
General Trial Bureau Chief **Frank Severino** .... (515) 286-3737
E-mail: frank.severino@polkcountyiowa.gov
Intake and Screening Bureau Chief **Jeff Noble** .... (515) 286-3880
E-mail: jeff.noble@polkcountyiowa.gov
Major Offense Trial Bureau Chief **Nan Horvat** .... (515) 286-3680
E-mail: nan.horval@polkcountyiowa.gov

★ Elected Official ▲ Appointed by Legislature ▼ Appointed by Governor ▶ Appointed by Board or Commission ● Appointed by Judge
■ Appointed by Mayor △ Appointed by Freeholders ▽ Appointed by Supervisor ▷ Appointed by County Executive ○ Appointed by Council

Office of the County Attorney *continued*

Drug Prosecutor **Dan Voogt** . . . . . (515) 286-2121
E-mail: dan.voogt@polkcountyiowa.gov
Administrative Services Manager **Marsha Mills** . . . . . (515) 286-3737
Administrative Supervisor **Randi Radosevich** . . . . . (515) 286-3880
E-mail: randi.radosevich@polkcountyiowa.gov
Investigations Program Manager **Paul Houston** . . . . . (515) 286-3065
Restorative Justice Program Manager **Teri Mundell** . . . . . (515) 286-3057

Office of the Recorder

111 Court Avenue, Room 250, Des Moines, IA 50309-2251
Fax: (515) 323-5393 Internet: www.polkrecorder.com

★ Recorder **Julie Haggerty** (D) . . . . . (515) 286-3160
Term Expires: December 31, 2018
E-mail: julie.haggerty@polkcountyiowa.gov
First Deputy Recorder **Valeria J. Mason** . . . . . (515) 286-3166
Second Deputy Recorder **Nancy Albright Andrew** . . . . . (515) 286-3137
Second Deputy Recorder **Jason Connolly** . . . . . (515) 286-3161
Second Deputy Recorder **Jill Moon** . . . . . (515) 286-3168
Second Deputy Recorder **Patricia Umthun** . . . . . (515) 286-3183

Office of the Sheriff

206 Sixth Avenue, Suite 112, Des Moines, IA 50309
Tel: (515) 286-3800 Fax: (515) 286-3410

★ Sheriff **William "Bill" McCarthy** . . . . . (515) 286-3800
Term Expires: December 31, 2016
E-mail: bill.mccarthy@polkcountyiowa.gov
Executive Assistant **Tami Morton** . . . . . (515) 286-3814
E-mail: tami.morton@polkcountyiowa.gov
Chief Deputy Sheriff **Victor Munoz** . . . . . (515) 286-3245

Polk County Jail

1985 NE 51st place, Des Moines, IA 50313
Tel: (515) 323-5400
Chief Jailer **Tim Krum** . . . . . (515) 323-5400

Office of the Treasurer

111 Court Avenue, Room 140, Des Moines, IA 50309
Fax: (515) 286-2225

★ Treasurer **Mary Maloney** (D) . . . . . (515) 286-3041
Term Expires: December 31, 2018
E-mail: mary.malone@polkcountyiowa.gov
Education: Iowa State 1977 BS
Assistant Director **Ben Lacey** . . . . . (515) 286-3871
Second Deputy Treasurer, Motor Vehicles
Melisa Forbes . . . . . (515) 286-3053
Second Deputy Treasurer, Property Tax **Jodi Gjersvik** . . . . (515) 286-3050
Second Deputy Treasurer, Cash Management
Sarah Smith . . . . . (515) 286-3402
Second Deputy Treasurer, Administration **Kellie Phelps** . . (515) 286-3045
E-mail: kellie.phelps@polkcountyiowa.gov
Investment Administrator **Kyle Rice** . . . . . (515) 286-3042
E-mail: kyle.rice@polkcountyiowa.gov

County of Prince George's, Maryland

County Administration Building, 14741 Governor Oden Bowie Drive, Upper Marlboro, MD 20772
Tel: (301) 883-4748 (Information)
Internet: www.princegeorgescountymd.gov

County Seat: Upper Marlboro **Election Type:** Partisan
Population: 909,535 (2015)

Office of the County Executive

County Administration Building, 14741 Governor Oden Bowie Drive, 5th Floor, Upper Marlboro, MD 20772
Tel: (301) 952-4131 Fax: (301) 952-3784

★ County Executive **Rushern L. Baker III** (D) . . . . . (301) 952-4131
Term Expires: December 2, 2018
E-mail: countyexecutive@co.pg.md.us
Date of Birth: October 24, 1958
Education: Howard U 1982 BA, 1986 JD
▷ Chief of Staff **Glenda R. Wilson** . . . . . (301) 952-4431
E-mail: grwilson@co.pg.md.us
▷ Chief Administrative Officer **Nicholas A. Majett** . . . . . (301) 952-4547
E-mail: namajett@co.pg.md.us
Education: Howard U BS, 1985 JD
▷ Deputy Chief Administrative Officer for Budget, Finance and Administration **Thomas M. "Tom" Himler** . . . . . (301) 952-4441
E-mail: thimler@co.pg.md.us
Education: West Virginia BS, MPA
▷ Deputy Chief Administrative Officer for Public Infrastructure **Barry L. Stanton** . . . . . (301) 952-4227
E-mail: blstanton@co.pg.md.us
Education: Cheyney 1979 BA; U Phoenix
▷ Deputy Chief Administrative Officer for Health, Human Services and Education **Betty Hager Francis** . . . . . (301) 952-4450
E-mail: bhfrancis@co.pg.md.us
Education: Howard U BA; Suffolk JD
▷ Deputy Chief Administrative Officer for Public Safety
Mark A. Magaw . . . . . (301) 952-4758
E-mail: mamagaw@co.pg.md.us
Education: James Madison; Johns Hopkins 2008 MM
▷ Communications Director **Barry L. Hudson** . . . . . (301) 952-5980
E-mail: blhudson@co.pg.md.us
▷ Communications Deputy Director **Scott Peterson** . . . . . (301) 952-4620
E-mail: slpeterson@co.pg.md.us
▷ Manager of Intergovernmental Affairs **Lisa L. Jackson** . . . . (301) 952-3649
E-mail: lljackson@co.pg.md.us

Board of Appeals

County Administration Bldg., 14741 Governor Oden Bowie Dr., Upper Marlboro, MD 20772
Tel: (301) 952-3220

Administrator to the Board **Anne Carter** . . . . . (301) 952-3220
Education: Syracuse 1976 BA

Board of Elections

1100 Mercantile Lane, Suite 115A, Largo, MD 20772
Tel: (301) 341-7300

Elections Administrator **Alisha L. Alexander** . . . . . (301) 341-7300

Board of License Commissioners

9200 Basil Court, Room 420, Largo, MD 20774
Tel: (301) 583-9980 Fax: (301) 583-9978

Chief Liquor Inspector **Albert Fanelli** . . . . . (301) 583-9962
Deputy Chief Liquor Inspector
Christian Mendoza Munoz . . . . . (301) 583-9965
E-mail: cmendozamunoz@co.pg.md.us

COUNTIES

★ Elected Official ▲ Appointed by Legislature ▼ Appointed by Governor ▶ Appointed by Board or Commission ● Appointed by Judge
■ Appointed by Mayor △ Appointed by Freeholders ▽ Appointed by Supervisor ▷ Appointed by County Executive ○ Appointed by Council

COUNTIES

Prince George's County Personnel Board

1400 McCormick Drive, Suite 320, Largo, MD 20774-5313
Fax: (301) 883-6328

Chair **Carolyn F. Scriber** .... (301) 883-6320
Manager **Carol A. Rubino** .... (301) 883-6321
E-mail: carubino@co.pg.md.us

Office of County Audits and Investigations

County Administration Bldg., 14741 Governor Oden Bowie Dr., 1st Floor, Upper Marlboro, MD 20772

○ County Auditor **David H. "Dave" Van Dyke** .... (301) 952-3431
E-mail: dvandyke@co.pg.md.us

Assessment Office

Courthouse, 14735 Main Street, Upper Marlboro, MD 20772
Fax: (301) 952-2955

Supervisor **Daniel R. Puma** .... (301) 952-2500

Office of Central Services

1400 McCormick Drive, Room 336, Largo, MD 20774
Fax: (301) 883-6454

▷ Director **Roland L. Jones** .... (301) 883-6450
E-mail: rljones2@co.pg.md.us
Executive Administrative Aide **Deidra Walker** .... (301) 883-6450

Office of Child Support Enforcement

4235 28th Avenue, Suite 135, Temple Hills, MD 20748-1718
Fax: (301) 316-3350

Director **Jarnice Y. Johnson** .... (301) 316-3346

Office of Extension (University of Maryland)

6707 Groveton Drive, Clinton, MD 20735
Fax: (301) 599-6714 Internet: www.princegeorges.umd.edu

Director **Karol W. Dyson** .... (301) 868-9366

Office of Finance

County Administration Building, 14741 Governor Oden Bowie Drive, Room 3200, Upper Marlboro, MD 20772
Fax: (301) 952-3148

Director **Gail D. Francis** .... (301) 952-5025
Education: Howard U BS
Executive Administrative Aide **Ivy L. Kline** .... (301) 952-5025
E-mail: ilkline@co.pg.md.us
Deputy Director **Stephen J. "Steve" McGibbon** .... (301) 952-5025
Chief of Treasury **Linda Allen** .... (301) 952-4030
Revenue Manager **Gwen Yount** .... (301) 952-4606
Risk Manager **Steven Middleton** .... (301) 952-3563
Fax: (301) 574-0419

Office of Human Resources Management

1400 McCormick Drive, Suite 351, Largo, MD 20774
Tel: (301) 883-6330 Fax: (301) 883-6468

▷ Director **Stephanye Redd Maxwell** .... (301) 883-6344
E-mail: smaxwell@co.pg.md.us
Education: Boston Col 1984 BA; Columbus Law JD

Office of Information Technology

9201 Basil Ct., Suite 250, Largo, MD 20774
Fax: (301) 853-3143

Director **Vennard Wright** .... (301) 883-6575
E-mail: vwright@co.pg.md.us
Training Manager **(Vacant)** .... (301) 883-5992

Office of Law

County Administration Bldg., 14741 Governor Oden Bowie Dr., Room 5121, Upper Marlboro, MD 20772-3050
Fax: (301) 952-3071

▷ County Attorney **M. Andree Green** .... (301) 952-5225
E-mail: magreen@co.pg.md.us
Education: Southwestern Louisiana 1984 BA; Washington College of Law 1991 JD
Administrative Aide **Kristine Beck** .... (301) 952-4125
E-mail: krbeck@co.pg.md.us

Office of Management and Budget

County Administration Building, 14741 Governor Oden Bowie Drive, Room 3000, Upper Marlboro, MD 20772-3050
Fax: (301) 952-4783

▷ Director **Terri Bacote-Charles** .... (301) 952-3218
E-mail: tbcharles@co.pg.md.us
Secretary **Janice Marcellas** .... (301) 952-3218
E-mail: jmarcellas@co.pg.md.us
Budget Management Officer **(Vacant)** .... (301) 952-3300

Department of Corrections

13400 Dille Dr., Upper Marlboro, MD 20772
Tel: (301) 952-4800 (Information) Fax: (301) 952-7285

▷ Director **Mary Lou McDonough** .... (301) 952-7015
E-mail: mlmcdonough@co.pg.md.us
Assistant **Rebecca Chaney** .... (301) 952-7110
E-mail: rjchaney@co.pg.md.us
Deputy Director, Operations Bureau **Mark Person** .... (301) 952-7014
Deputy Director, Administration Bureau
Corenne D. Labbé .... (301) 952-7094
E-mail: cdlabbe@co.pg.md.us
Training Section Chief **Alecia Creighton** .... (301) 952-7075
E-mail: acreighton@co.pg.md.us
Public Information Officer **Yolonda Evans** .... (301) 952-7018
E-mail: yeevans@co.pg.md.us
Librarian **Beatrice McTernan** .... (301) 952-7089
E-mail: bwmcternan@co.pg.md.us

Department of the Environment [DER]

1801 McCormick Drive, Suite 500, Largo, MD 20774
Tel: (301) 883-5810 Fax: (301) 883-5444 E-mail: dercares@co.pg.md.us

Director **Adam Ortiz** .... (301) 883-5812
Administrative Assistant **Shirley Posten** .... (301) 883-5812

Animal Management Group

3750 Brown Station Road, Upper Marlboro, MD 20772
Fax: (301) 780-7258

Associate Director **Rodney Taylor** .... (301) 780-7200
Assistant Associate Director **Terri Littlejohn** .... (301) 780-7200

Department of Family Services

Harriet Hunter Building, 6420 Allentown Road, Camp Springs, MD 20748
Tel: (301) 265-8401 Fax: (301) 248-0716

▷ Director (Acting) **Elana T. Belon-Butler** .... (301) 265-8401
E-mail: etbelon@co.pg.md.us

Fire/EMS Department

Largo Government Center, 9201 Basil Court, Suite 452, Largo, MD 20774
Fax: (301) 883-5212

▷ Fire Chief **Marc S. Bashoor** .... (301) 883-5200
E-mail: msbashoor@co.pg.md.us

Prince George's County Health Department

1701 McCormick Dr., Largo, MD 20774
Tel: (301) 883-7834 Fax: (301) 883-7896

Health Officer/Director **Pamela Brown Creekmur** .... (301) 883-7834

★ Elected Official ▲ Appointed by Legislature ▼ Appointed by Governor ▶ Appointed by Board or Commission ● Appointed by Judge
■ Appointed by Mayor △ Appointed by Freeholders ▽ Appointed by Supervisor ▷ Appointed by County Executive ○ Appointed by Council

Prince George's County Health Department *continued*

Secretary **Audrea Spencer** .... (301) 883-7879
E-mail: pjcarolina@co.pg.md.us
Deputy Health Officer **Dr. Ernest Carter** .... (301) 883-7834

Department of Housing and Community Development [DHCD]

Inglewood Centre III, 9400 Peppercorn Place, Room 200, Largo, MD 20774
Tel: (301) 883-5531 Fax: (301) 883-9832 E-mail: dhcd@co.pg.md.us

Director **Eric C. Brown** .... (301) 883-5531
E-mail: ecbrown@co.pg.md.us
Education: Mississippi 1973 BPA, 1977 MURP

Human Relations Commission

RMS Building, 1400 McCormick Drive, Suite 245, Largo, MD 20774-5313
Fax: (301) 883-2649

Chair **Merrill Smith, Jr.** .... (301) 883-6170
▷ Executive Director **D. Michael Lyles** .... (301) 883-6170
E-mail: mlyles@co.pg.md.us
Education: Columbus Law 1994 JD

Prince George's County Police Department [PGPD]

7600 Barlowe Rd., Landover, MD 20785-4122
Fax: (301) 772-4788

▷ Chief of Police (Interim) **Hank Stawinski** .... (301) 772-4740
Assistant Chief of Police **Lt. Col. Craig A. Howard** ..... (301) 772-4740
Deputy Chief, Bureau of Administration
Gevonia R. Whittington .... (301) 772-4667
Fax: (301) 772-4838
Deputy Chief, Bureau of Investigation
Lt. Col. Hector Velez .... (301) 772-4770
Fax: (301) 772-4737
Deputy Chief, Bureau of Forensic Science and Intelligence **George Nader** .... (301) 772-4750
Fax: (301) 773-8659
Deputy Chief, Bureau of Patrol
Lt. Col. Henry P. Stawinski III .... (301) 772-4760
Fax: (301) 772-4737

Department of Permitting, Inspections, and Enforcement

9400 Peppercorn Place, First Floor, Largo, MD 20774

▷ Director **Haitham A. Hijazi** .... (301) 636-2000
E-mail: hahijazi@co.pg.md.us

Department of Public Works and Transportation [DPWT]

Inglewood Centre 3, 9400 Peppercorn Place, Room 300, Largo, MD 20774
Fax: (301) 883-5709

▷ Director **Darrell B. Mobley** .... (301) 883-5600
Executive Assistant (Acting) **Mary McClean** .... (301) 883-5600
E-mail: mkmcclean@co.pg.md.us
Deputy Director **Andre' Issayans** .... (301) 883-5600
Deputy Director **Martin L. Harris** .... (301) 883-5600

Department of Social Services

805 Brightseat Road, Landover, MD 20785-4723
Tel: (301) 209-5000 Fax: (301) 909-5008
E-mail: pgcdss@dhr.state.md.us

Director **Gloria Brown** .... (301) 909-7010
Chief of Staff **Stephen Liggett-Creel** .... (301) 909-7010
Assistant Director for Child, Adult and Family Services
Stacy Reid-Swain .... (301) 909-2008
925 Brightseat Road, Landover, MD 20785 Fax: (301) 909-2003

Department of Social Services *continued*

Assistant Director for Community Services
Renee Ensor-Pope .... (301) 909-6330
425 Brightseat Road, Landover, MD 20785 Fax: (301) 909-6331
E-mail: renee.pope@maryland.gov
Assistant Director for Family Investment **Evelyn Reed** ... (301) 909-7020
Assistant Director for Quality Assurance and Compliance **Kai Boggess-de Bruin** .... (301) 909-7004
425 Brightseat Road, Landover, MD 20785
E-mail: kboggess@dhr.state.md.us

Maryland-National Capital Park and Planning Commission [M-NCPPC]

County Administration Bldg., 14741 Governor Oden Bowie Dr., Upper Marlboro, MD 20772-3037
Tel: (301) 952-3560 Fax: (301) 952-5074 Internet: www.mncppc.org

Note: The Maryland-National Capital Park and Planning Commission is a bi-county agency that manages growth, stewards natural, cultural, and historic resources, and provides leisure and recreational experiences in Montgomery and Prince George's Counties.

▷ Chairman **Elizabeth M. Hewlett** (D) .... (301) 952-3561
E-mail: elizabeth.hewlett@mncppc.org
Education: Harvard; Boston Col 1979 JD
Executive Director **Patricia "Patti" Colihan-Barney** ..... (301) 454-1740
Secretary-Treasurer **Joseph C. "Joe" Zimmerman** ...... (301) 454-1740
Education: Frostburg State U 1979 BS; Baltimore 1991 MBA
General Counsel **Adrian R. Gardner** .... (301) 454-1740

Parks and Recreation Department

6600 Kenilworth Ave., Riverdale, MD 20737-2144
Tel: (301) 699-2255 TTY: (301) 699-2544

Director **Ronnie Gathers** .... (301) 699-2582
Fax: (301) 864-6941

Planning Department

County Administration Bldg., 14741 Governor Oden Bowie Dr., Upper Marlboro, MD 20772-3037
Tel: (301) 952-3594 Fax: (301) 952-5804 TTY: (301) 952-4366

Director **Fern V. Piret** .... (301) 952-3595

Prince George's Community College [PGCC]

301 Largo Road, Largo, MD 20774-2199
Tel: (301) 336-6000 Internet: www.pgcc.edu

President **Dr. Charlene Mickens Dukes** .... (301) 322-0400
Education: Indiana (PA) 1980 BS; Pittsburgh MEd, EdD Fax: (301) 353-1239
Chief of Staff **Alonia C. Sharps** .... (301) 322-0170
Vice President for Academic Affairs
Sandra A. Dunnington .... (301) 322-0406
Vice President for Administrative Services
Thomas Knapp .... (301) 322-0409
E-mail: knappte@pgcc.edu
Vice President for Student Services **Tyjaun A. Lee** .... (301) 322-0412
Vice President for Technology Services (Interim)
Rhonda Spells Fentry .... (301) 322-0987
Vice President for Workforce Development and Continuing Education **(Vacant)** .... (301) 322-0417
Chief Technology Officer **William L. Anderson** .... (301) 322-0622
E-mail: anderswl@pgcc.edu

Prince George's County Economic Development Corporation [EDC]

1801 McCormick Drive, Suite 350, Largo, MD 20774
Fax: (301) 772-8540

President/Chief Executive Officer
James "Jim" Coleman .... (301) 583-4650
Education: Howard U 1983 BA
Executive Vice President **Dr. Pradeep Ganguly** .... (301) 583-4650
E-mail: pganguly@co.pg.md.us
Education: U Delhi (India); Clemson PhD

(continued on next page)

★ Elected Official ▲ Appointed by Legislature ▼ Appointed by Governor ▶ Appointed by Board or Commission ● Appointed by Judge
■ Appointed by Mayor △ Appointed by Freeholders ▽ Appointed by Supervisor ▷ Appointed by County Executive ○ Appointed by Council

Prince George's County Economic Development Corporation *continued*

Director of Marketing and Communications **(Vacant)** .... (301) 583-4650
Chief Financial Officer **Brian Smith** .... (301) 583-4650

Prince George's County Memorial Library System [PGCMLS]

6532 Adelphi Road, Hyattsville, MD 20782-2098
Tel: (301) 699-3500 Fax: (301) 985-5494 Internet: www.pgcmls.info

Administration

Chief Executive Officer **Kathleen Rudden Teaze** .... (301) 699-3500
E-mail: kathleen.teaze@pgcmls.info
Education: Simmons 1991 MSLIS
Chief Financial Officer **Lamont Corprew** .... (301) 699-3500
Chief Operating Officer for Support Services
Michael B. Gannon .... (301) 699-3500
E-mail: michael.gannon@pgcmls.info
Director of Human Resources **Koven Roundtree** .... (301) 699-3500
E-mail: koven.roundtree@pgcmls.info
Chief Operating Officer for Public Services
Michelle Hamiel .... (301) 699-3500
Director of Community Engagement **Robin Jacobsen** .... (301) 699-3500
E-mail: Robin.Jacobsen@pgcmls.info

Office of the County Council

County Administration Bldg., 14741 Governor Oden Bowie Dr., 2nd Floor, Upper Marlboro, MD 20772
Tel: (301) 952-3700 Fax: (301) 952-3238

★ Chair **Derrick Leon Davis** (D-District 6) .... (301) 952-3426
Term Expires: December 3, 2018 Fax: (301) 952-3238
E-mail: councildistrict6@co.pg.md.us
Education: Maryland Eastern Shore 1989 BA
★ Council Member **Mary Angela Lehman** (D-District 1) ... (301) 952-3887
Term Expires: December 3, 2018 Fax: (301) 952-3238
E-mail: malehman@co.pg.md.us
★ Council Member **Deni Taveras** (D-District 2) .... (301) 952-4436
Term Expires: December 3, 2018 Fax: (301) 952-3238
★ Council Member **Dannielle M. Glaros** (D-District 3) .... (301) 952-3060
Term Expires: December 3, 2018 Fax: (301) 952-3238
★ Council Member **Todd Turner** (D-District 4) .... (301) 952-3094
Term Expires: December 3, 2018 Fax: (301) 952-3238
★ Council Member **Andrea C. Harrison** (D-District 5) .... (301) 952-3864
Term Expires: December 3, 2018 Fax: (301) 952-3238
E-mail: acharrison@co.pg.md.us
★ Council Member **Karen Renee Toles** (D-District 7) ...... (301) 952-3690
Term Expires: December 3, 2018 Fax: (301) 952-3238
E-mail: krtoles@co.pg.md.us
★ Council Member **Obie Patterson** (D-District 8) .... (301) 952-3860
Term Expires: December 3, 2018 Fax: (301) 952-3238
E-mail: opatterson@co.pg.md.us
Education: Johnson C Smith 1965 BS; Florida 1971 MA
★ Council Member **Mel Franklin** (D-District 9) .... (301) 952-3820
Term Expires: December 3, 2018 Fax: (301) 952-3238
E-mail: mfranklin@co.pg.md.us
○ Clerk to the County Council **Redis C. Floyd** .... (301) 952-3600
E-mail: rcfloyd@co.pg.md.us Fax: (301) 952-5178

Office of the Register of Wills

Courthouse 14735 Main Street, Suite 300, Upper Marlboro, MD 20773
Tel: (301) 952-3250 Fax: (301) 952-0908

★ Register of Wills **Cereta A. Lee** .... (301) 952-3250
Term Expires: December 3, 2018

Office of the Sheriff

5303 Chrysler Way, Upper Marlboro, MD 20772
Tel: (301) 780-8600 Fax: (301) 780-7355
E-mail: sheriffinfo@co.pg.md.us

★ Sheriff **Melvin C. High** (D) .... (301) 780-8600
Term Expires: December 3, 2018
E-mail: mchigh@co.pg.md.us
Executive Assistant **Dorothy M. Shavers** .... (301) 780-8602
E-mail: dmshavers@co.pg.md.us
Chief Assistant Sheriff **Darrin C. Palmer** .... (301) 780-8600
E-mail: dcpalmer@co.pg.md.us

Office of the State's Attorney

Courthouse, 14735 Main St., Suite M3403, Upper Marlboro, MD 20772
Tel: (301) 952-3500 Fax: (301) 952-3775

★ State's Attorney **Angela D. Alsobrooks** (D) .... (301) 952-3500
Term Expires: December 3, 2018
E-mail: adalsobrooks@co.pg.md.us
Education: Duke 1993 BA; Maryland 1996 JD

County of Pulaski, Arkansas

201 South Broadway, Little Rock, AR 72201
Internet: www.co.pulaski.ar.us

County Seat: Little Rock **Election Type:** Partisan **Year Founded:** 1818
Population: 392,664 (2015)

Office of the County Judge

201 South Broadway, Suite 400, Little Rock, AR 72201
Tel: (501) 340-8305 Fax: (501) 340-8282

★ County Judge **Barry Hyde** (D) .... (501) 340-8305
Term Expires: December 31, 2016
E-mail: cojudge@pulaskicounty.net
Administrative Coordinator **Sherry L. King** .... (501) 340-8305
E-mail: sking@co.pulaski.ar.us
Administrative Assistant **Felecia Williams** .... (501) 340-8305
E-mail: fwilliams@co.pulaski.ar.us

Quorum Court

201 South Broadway, Suite 410, Little Rock, AR 72201
Tel: (501) 340-8310 Fax: (501) 340-8329

★ Justice of the Peace **Doug Reed** (R-District 1) .... (501) 868-4742
Term Expires: December 31, 2016
E-mail: doug-reed@att.net
★ Justice of the Peace **Tyler Denton** (D-District 2) .... (501) 954-7243
Term Expires: December 31, 2016
★ Justice of the Peace **Kathy Lewison** (D-District 3) ...... (501) 663-1969
Term Expires: December 31, 2016
★ Justice of the Peace **Julie Blackwood** (D-District 4) ..... (501) 663-9504
Term Expires: December 31, 2016
E-mail: bodyshapepro@yahoo.com
★ Justice of the Peace
Lillie Ingram McMullen (D-District 5) .... (501) 565-2256
Term Expires: December 31, 2016
★ Justice of the Peace **Donna Massey** (D-District 6) .... (501) 660-4551
Term Expires: December 31, 2016
E-mail: jpdonna40@aol.com
★ Justice of the Peace **Teresa Coney** (D-District 7) .... (501) 407-0011
Term Expires: December 31, 2016
★ Justice of the Peace **Curtis Keith** (D-District 8) .... (501) 744-5477
Term Expires: December 31, 2016 Fax: (501) 663-3446
7817 Claybrook Road, Mablevale, AR 72103
★ Justice of the Peace **Judy Green** (D-District 9) .... (501) 340-8310
Term Expires: December 31, 2016

★ Elected Official ▲ Appointed by Legislature ▼ Appointed by Governor ► Appointed by Board or Commission ● Appointed by Judge
■ Appointed by Mayor △ Appointed by Freeholders ▽ Appointed by Supervisor ▷ Appointed by County Executive ○ Appointed by Council

Quorum Court *continued*

★ Justice of the Peace **Rev. Robert Green** (D-District 10) . . (501) 258-6921
Term Expires: December 31, 2016
★ Justice of the Peace **Aaron Robinson** (R-District 11) . . . . (501) 340-8310
Term Expires: December 31, 2016
★ Justice of the Peace **Luke McCoy** (R-District 12) . . . . (501) 340-8310
Term Expires: December 31, 2016
★ Justice of the Peace **Phil Stowers** (R-District 13) . . . . (501) 993-6165
Term Expires: December 31, 2016
E-mail: pstowers71@yahoo.com
★ Justice of the Peace **Paul Elliott** (R-District 14) . . . . (501) 851-7999
Term Expires: December 31, 2018
E-mail: pdelliottmail@gmail.com
★ Justice of the Peace **Staci Medlock** (D-District 15) . . . . . (501) 340-8310
Term Expires: December 31, 2016
Quorum Court Coordinator **Justin Blagg** . . . . (501) 340-8310

Office of Cooperative Extension (University of Arkansas)

2901 West Roosevelt Road, Little Rock, AR 72204
Fax: (501) 340-6669 E-mail: pulaski@uaex.edu

County Extension Agent/Staff Chair **Randy Forst** . . . . (501) 340-6650

Office of the Coroner

201 South Broadway, Suite 340, Little Rock, AR 72201
Fax: (501) 340-8358

● Coroner **Gerone Hobbs** . . . . (501) 340-8355
E-mail: ghobbs@co.pulaski.ar.us
Office Manager **Shantea Nelson** . . . . (501) 340-8355

Office of the Comptroller

201 South Broadway, Suite 440, Little Rock, AR 72201
Tel: (501) 340-8392 Fax: (501) 340-8804

Comptroller **Mike Hutchens** . . . . (501) 340-8392
E-mail: mhutchens@pulaskicounty.net
Assistant Comptroller for Purchasing **Jean Pope** . . . . (501) 340-8390
E-mail: jpope@pulaskicounty.net
Accounting Supervisor **Michelle Johnson** . . . . (501) 340-8381
Payroll Administrator **Chari Walker** . . . . (501) 340-8388

Office of the County Attorney

201 South Broadway, Suite 400, Little Rock, AR 72201
Fax: (501) 340-8282

County Attorney **Amanda Mitchell** . . . . (501) 340-8285
E-mail: amitchell@co.pulaski.ar.us
Chief Deputy Attorney **Chastity Scifres** . . . . (501) 340-8285
Staff Attorney **Cortney Cato** . . . . (501) 340-8285
E-mail: ccato@pulaskicounty.net
Staff Attorney II **Adam Fogleman** . . . . (501) 340-8285
E-mail: afogleman@pulaskicounty.net
Paralegal **Jamie Raleigh** . . . . (501) 340-8285

Office of the Public Defender

201 South Broadway, Suite 210, Little Rock, AR 72201-2321
Fax: (501) 340-6133

Public Defender **William R. "Bill" Simpson, Jr.** . . . . (501) 340-6120
Chief Deputy **Kent C. Krause** . . . . (501) 340-6120
Office Manager **Vernadean Webb** . . . . (501) 340-6120

Community Services and Housing Department

201 South Broadway, Suite 220, Little Rock, AR 72201
Fax: (501) 340-8951

● Director **Fredrick J. "Fred" Love** (D) . . . . (501) 340-3376
E-mail: flove@pulaskicounty.net
Administrative Assistant **Tiffany Meyers** . . . . (501) 340-3376
E-mail: tmeyers@pulaskicounty.net
Grant Fund Administrator **Debra Banks** . . . . (501) 340-8843
E-mail: dbarks@pulaskicounty.net

Community Services and Housing Department *continued*

Grants Manager **Marisha Collins** . . . . (501) 340-3433
Housing Choice Voucher Administrator
Shauntrae Taylor . . . . (501) 340-3384
E-mail: staylor@pulaskicounty.net
Self-Sufficiency Coordinator **Whitney Maralis** . . . . (501) 340-8212
Housing Technician **Dolores M. Couch** . . . . (501) 340-3321
Brownfields Program Administrator **Joshua Fout** . . . . (501) 340-8594

General Services Department

103 South Arch Street, Little Rock, AR 72201
Fax: (501) 340-8999

Director **Tod Creed** . . . . (501) 340-8326
E-mail: tcreed@co.pulaski.ar.us

Human Resources Department

201 South Broadway, Suite 100, Little Rock, AR 72201
Tel: (501) 340-6110 Fax: (501) 340-6033

● Director **Mary Ann Zakrzewski** . . . . (501) 340-6110
E-mail: mderamus@co.pulaski.ar.us
Compensation/Benefits Manager **Sonjia Persons** . . . . (501) 340-8797
E-mail: spersons@co.pulaski.ar.us
Employee Development Manager **Linda Lewis-Liddell** . . . (501) 340-6158
E-mail: lliddell@co.pulaski.ar.us

Information Systems Department

201 South Broadway, Suite 250, Little Rock, AR 72201

Director **Joseph "Joe" Musgrove** . . . . (501) 340-8319
E-mail: jmusgrove@co.pulaski.ar.us
Assistant Director **Dimple Patel** . . . . (501) 340-8919
E-mail: dpatel@co.pulaski.ar.us

Court Appointed Special Advocate for the Sixth Judicial District [CASA]

3001 W. Roosevelt, Little Rock, AR 72204
Tel: (501) 340-6946 Fax: (501) 340-6956

CASA Executive Director **Darryl Capps** . . . . (501) 340-6741
Advocate Supervisor **Tamara Keech** . . . . (501) 340-6946
Advocate Supervisor **Jeni Smith** . . . . (501) 340-6946

Probation Office (Arkansas Department of Community Correction, Area 7 Office)

2679 Pike Avenue, North Little Rock, AR 72114
Tel: (501) 837-3046 Fax: (501) 371-1566 Tel: (501) 682-9410 (Main)

Area Manager (Acting) **Violet Renee** . . . . (501) 371-1066

Pulaski County Election Commission

501 West Markham Street, Suite A, Little Rock, AR 72201
Tel: (501) 340-8383 Fax: (501) 340-6024 Internet: www.votepulaski.net

Chairman **Pat Hays** . . . . (501) 340-8383
Director **Bryan Poe** . . . . (501) 340-8383
E-mail: bpoe@votepulaski.net
Assistant Director **Shawn Camp** . . . . (501) 340-8383
E-mail: scamp@votepulaski.net
Administrative Assistant **Tonya S. Washington** . . . . (501) 340-8383

Pulaski County Juvenile Detention Center

3001 West Roosevelt Road, Little Rock, AR 72204
Fax: (501) 340-6888

Director **Carma Gardner** . . . . (501) 340-6697
Administrative Assistant **Amanda Skinner** . . . . (501) 340-6697

★ Elected Official ▲ Appointed by Legislature ▼ Appointed by Governor ► Appointed by Board or Commission ● Appointed by Judge
■ Appointed by Mayor △ Appointed by Freeholders ▽ Appointed by Supervisor ▷ Appointed by County Executive ○ Appointed by Council

Pulaski County Public Works

3200 Brown Street, Little Rock, AR 72204
Tel: (501) 340-6800 Fax: (501) 340-6820

● Director **Barbara Richard** .... (501) 340-6800
E-mail: brichard@co.pulaski.ar.us

Office of Emergency Management [OEM]

3200 Brown Street, Little Rock, AR 72204
Fax: (501) 340-6989

● Director **Andy Traffanstedt** .... (501) 340-6911
E-mail: atraffanstedt@co.pulaski.ar.us
Deputy Director/Fire Service Coordinator/Hazmat Team Chief **Terry Henson** .... (501) 340-6911
E-mail: thenson@co.pulaski.ar.us
Safety Officer **Catherine Arnold** .... (501) 340-6911
E-mail: carnold@co.pulaski.ar.us

Planning and Development Department

3200 Brown Street, Little Rock, AR 72204
Tel: (501) 340-8260 Fax: (501) 340-8274
Internet: www.co.pulaski.ar.us/planning.shtml

■ Director **Van McClendon** .... (501) 340-8263
E-mail: vmcclendon@co.pulaski.ar.us
Plan Review Coordinator **Jim Cranor** .... (501) 340-8265
Senior Addressing Coordinator **Maciej Jastrzebski** .... (501) 340-8265
E-mail: mjastrzebski@pulaskicounty.net
Administrative Coordinator **Angela Hadley** .... (501) 340-8260
E-mail: ahadley@pulaskicounty.net
GIF Technician **Kevin Tarkington** .... (501) 340-8269
E-mail: ktarkington@pulaskicounty.net
Watershed Inspector **Dave Miller** .... (501) 340-6881

Road and Bridge Department

3200 Brown St., Little Rock, AR 72204
Tel: (501) 340-6800 Fax: (501) 340-6820

Director **John Burton** .... (501) 340-6805

Pulaski County Sanitation and Animal Services

3403 W. 33rd St., Little Rock, AR 72204
Tel: (501) 210-7508 (Animal Services) Fax: (501) 603-9395
Internet: www.co.pulaski.ar.us/sanitation.shtml

● Director **Kathy Botsford** .... (501) 210-7500
E-mail: kbotsford@co.pulaski.ar.us
Education: Arkansas 1992 BA, 1994 BS

Pulaski County Youth Services

201 South Broadway, Suite 220, Little Rock, AR 72201
Tel: (501) 340-8250 Fax: (501) 340-8259

Director **Jamie Scott** .... (501) 340-8250
ACT Coordinator **Rhonda McBain** .... (501) 340-6671

Regional Recycling and Waste Reduction District [RR&WRD]

300 Spring Street, Suite 200, Little Rock, AR 72201
Tel: (501) 340-8787 Fax: (501) 340-8785

Executive Director **John Roberts** .... (501) 340-8787
Education: Arkansas BS, BA
Deputy Director/Recycling Coordinator **Carol Bevis** .... (501) 340-8787
Education: Central Arkansas BSE
Recycling Program Manager - Waste Tires **Stacy Edwards** .... (501) 340-8787
Public Outreach Specialist **Reita Miller** .... (501) 340-8787
E-mail: reita.miller@regionalrecycling.org
Comptroller and Human Resources Director **Desi Ledbetter** .... (501) 340-8787
E-mail: desi.ledbetter@regionalrecycling.org

Office of the Assessor

201 South Broadway, Suite 310, Little Rock, AR 72201
Fax: (501) 340-6009 E-mail: assessor@co.pulaski.ar.us
Internet: www.pulaskicountyassessor.net

★ Assessor **Janet T. Ward** (D) .... (501) 340-6170
Term Expires: December 31, 2016
E-mail: assessor@pulaskicountyassessor.net
Chief Deputy Assessor **Tom Ackerman** .... (501) 340-6160
E-mail: tackerman@pulaskicountyassessor.net
GIS Director **James Meyer** .... (501) 340-8382
Reappraisal Supervisor **Ron Campea** .... (501) 340-8524
Business Personal Property Chief Appraiser **Dewayne Sledge** .... (501) 340-6150
E-mail: dsledge@co.pulaski.ar.us

Office of the Circuit/County Clerk

Pulaski County Courthouse, 401 West Markham, Room 100, Little Rock, AR 72201
Tel: (501) 340-8500 Fax: (501) 340-8340 Internet: www.pulaskiclerk.com

★ Circuit County Clerk and Voter Registrar **Larry Crane** (D) .... (501) 340-8500
Term Expires: December 31, 2016
E-mail: admin@pulaskiclerk.com
Chief Deputy **Brandon Wood** .... (501) 340-8500
E-mail: bwood@pulaskiclerk.com
Court Administrator **Stephen C. "Steve" Sipes** .... (501) 340-8500
Central Receiving Supervisor **Nancy Sadler** .... (501) 340-5681
Fax: (501) 340-8420
Civil/Criminal Supervisor **Alisha Winkler** .... (501) 340-8431
Fax: (501) 340-8420
Juvenile Supervisor **Kendrick Turner** .... (501) 340-6767
Fax: (501) 340-7012
Marriage License Supervisor **Melissa Mofield** .... (501) 340-3567
E-mail: mmofield@pulaskiclerk.com Fax: (501) 340-3342
Real Estate Supervisor **Linda Johnson** .... (501) 340-8509
Fax: (501) 340-8889
Voter Registration Supervisor **Steve Sutterfield** .... (501) 340-3567
Fax: (501) 340-3556

Office of the Prosecuting Attorney

224 South Spring, Little Rock, AR 72201
Fax: (501) 340-3532 E-mail: pa@dist6pa.org
Internet: www.co.pulaski.ar.us/prosatty.shtml

★ Prosecuting Attorney **Larry Jegley** (D) .... (501) 340-8000
Term Expires: December 31, 2018
E-mail: larryj@dist6pa.org
Chief Deputy **John F. Johnson** .... (501) 340-8000
Senior Deputy **Terry Ball** .... (501) 340-8000
Senior Deputy **Melanie Martin** .... (501) 340-8000
Senior Deputy **Marianne Satterfield** .... (501) 340-8000

Office of the Sheriff

2900 S. Woodrow St., Little Rock, AR 72204
TTY: (501) 340-6987 Fax: (501) 340-7080 Internet: www.pcso.org

★ Sheriff **Doc Holladay** (D) .... (501) 340-6930
Term Expires: December 31, 2016
E-mail: docholladay@pcso.org
Chief Deputy **Mike Lowery** .... (501) 340-6902
E-mail: mlowery@pcso.org
Commander of Investigations/Warrants/Judicial Operations **Terry Ward** .... (501) 340-6991
E-mail: shaynes@co.pulaski.ar.us
Public Information Officer **Capt. Carl Minden** .... (501) 340-7055
Commander of Enforcement/Administrative Support Operations **Terry Ward** .... (501) 340-6966

★ Elected Official ▲ Appointed by Legislature ▼ Appointed by Governor ▶ Appointed by Board or Commission ● Appointed by Judge
■ Appointed by Mayor △ Appointed by Freeholders ▽ Appointed by Supervisor ▷ Appointed by County Executive ○ Appointed by Council

Office of the Treasurer and Collector

201 South Broadway, Suite 150, Little Rock, AR 72201
Fax: (501) 340-5663 E-mail: treasurer@pulaskicountytreasurer.net
Internet: www.pulaskicountytreasurer.net

★Treasurer/Collector **Debra Buckner** (D) . . . . . (501) 340-8345
Term Expires: December 31, 2016
E-mail: dbuckner@co.pulaski.ar.us
Chief Administrator **Debbye Wolter** . . . . . (501) 340-6055
Fax: (501) 340-5643

Pulaski County Special School District [PCSSD]

925 East Dixon Road, Little Rock, AR 72206
P.O. Box 8601, Little Rock, AR 72216
Tel: (501) 490-2000 Fax: (501) 490-0483 Internet: www.pcssd.org

Office of the Superintendent

Superintendent of Schools **Dr. Jerry Guess** . . . . . (501) 490-2001

County of Ramsey, Minnesota

Courthouse, 15 W. Kellogg Blvd., St. Paul, MN 55102
Tel: (651) 266-8500 (Information)
E-mail: contactramseycounty@co.ramsey.mn.us
Internet: www.co.ramsey.mn.us

County Seat: St. Paul **Election Type:** Nonpartisan **Population:** 538,133 (2015)

Office of the Board of County Commissioners

Courthouse, 15 W. Kellogg Blvd., Room 220, St. Paul, MN 55102
Tel: (651) 266-8350 Fax: (651) 266-8370
Internet: www.co.ramsey.mn.us/cb

★Board Chair **Victoria Reinhardt** (District 7) . . . . . (651) 266-8363
Term Expires: December 31, 2016
E-mail: victoria.reinhardt@co.ramsey.mn.us
Assistant **Darren Tobolt** . . . . . (651) 266-8368
E-mail: darren.tobolt@co.ramsey.mn.us
★Vice Chair **Janice Rettman** (District 3) . . . . . (651) 266-8360
Term Expires: December 31, 2018
E-mail: janice.rettman@co.ramsey.mn.us
Education: Abilene Christian BA
Assistant **Mark Voerding** . . . . . (651) 266-8378
E-mail: mark.voerding@co.ramsey.mn.us
★Commissioner **Blake C. Huffman** (District 1) . . . . . (651) 266-8362
Term Expires: December 31, 2016
Assistant **Trent Danielson** . . . . . (651) 266-8355
E-mail: trent.danielson@co.ramsey.mn.us
★Commissioner **Mary Jo McGuire** (District 2) . . . . . (651) 266-8356
Term Expires: December 31, 2016
Date of Birth: July 29, 1956
Education: Col St Catherine 1978 BA; Hamline 1988 JD; Harvard 1998 MPA
Assistant **Melissa Jamrock** . . . . . (651) 266-8359
E-mail: melissa.jamrock@co.ramsey.mn.us
★Commissioner **Toni Carter** (District 4) . . . . . (651) 266-8364
Term Expires: December 31, 2018
E-mail: toni.carter@co.ramsey.mn.us
Assistant **Noel Nix** . . . . . (651) 266-8366
E-mail: noel.nix@co.ramsey.mn.us
★Commissioner **Rafael E. Ortega** (District 5) . . . . . (651) 266-8361
Term Expires: December 31, 2018
E-mail: rafael.e.ortega@co.ramsey.mn.us
Education: Minnesota 1981 MSW
Assistant **Ken Iosso** . . . . . (651) 266-8367
E-mail: ken.iosso@co.ramsey.mn.us

Office of the Board of County Commissioners *continued*

★Commissioner **James "Jim" McDonough** (District 6) . . . (651) 266-8365
Term Expires: December 31, 2018
E-mail: jim.mcdonough@co.ramsey.mn.us
Assistant **JoAnn Ellis** . . . . . (651) 266-8357
E-mail: joann.ellis@co.ramsey.mn.us
►Chief Clerk **Bonnie Jackelen** . . . . . (651) 266-8014
E-mail: bonnie.jackelen@co.ramsey.mn.us Fax: (651) 266-8039

Office of the County Manager

Courthouse, 15 West Kellogg Boulevard, Room 250, St. Paul, MN 55102
Tel: (651) 266-8000 Fax: (651) 266-8039
Internet: www.co.ramsey.mn.us/cm/manager

►County Manager **Julie Kleinschmidt** . . . . . (651) 266-8009
E-mail: julie.kleinschmidt@co.ramsey.mn.us
Administrative Assistant **Pequita Jordan** . . . . . (651) 266-8008
E-mail: pequita.jordan@co.ramsey.mn.us
Deputy County Manager **Heather Worthington** . . . . . (651) 266-8010
E-mail: heather.worthington@co.ramsey.mn.us
Public Communications Manager **John Siqveland** . . . . . (651) 266-8017
Director of Policy Analysis and Planning
Ryan O'Connor . . . . . (651) 266-8011
Senior Intergovernmental Relations Specialist
Nicholas H. "Nick" Riley . . . . . (651) 266-8032
E-mail: nick.riley@co.ramsey.mn.us
Intergovernmental Relations Specialist
Claudia Brewington . . . . . (651) 266-8022
E-mail: claudia.brewington@co.ramsey.mn.us

Office of the Assessor

90 West Plato Boulevard, #400, St. Paul, MN 55107
P. O. Box 64097, St. Paul, MN 55164-0097
Fax: (651) 266-2001

►Assessor **Stephen L. Baker** . . . . . (651) 266-2131
E-mail: stephen.l.baker@co.ramsey.mn.us

Finance Department

15 West Kellogg Boulevard, Room 270, St. Paul, MN 55102-1659
Tel: (651) 266-8048 Fax: (651) 266-8066

Director **Lee Mehrkens** . . . . . (651) 266-8040
E-mail: lee.mehrkens@co.ramsey.mn.us
Deputy Director **Kathy Kapoun** . . . . . (651) 266-8059
E-mail: kathleen.kapoun@co.ramsey.mn.us
Financial Reporting Manager **Mike Webster** . . . . . (651) 266-8044
E-mail: mike.webster@co.ramsey.mn.us
Investment/Debt Manager **Mark Thompson** . . . . . (651) 266-8057
E-mail: mark.e.thompson@co.ramsey.mn.us
Payroll Manager **Katherine Reed** . . . . . (651) 266-1058
E-mail: kathryn.reed@co.ramsey.mn.us
Aspen/Hyperion Capability Manager **Peggy Vadnais** . . . . . (651) 266-8046
E-mail: peggy.vadnais@co.ramsey.mn.us
Procurement Manager **Dana Baker** . . . . . (651) 266-8075
E-mail: dana.baker@co.ramsey.mn.us
ERP Program Manager **Mike Piram** . . . . . (651) 266-8068

Office of the Medical Examiner

300 E. University Ave., St. Paul, MN 55101
Fax: (651) 266-1720

Medical Examiner **Michael McGee** . . . . . (651) 266-1700
Assistant Medical Examiner **Victor Froloff** . . . . . (651) 266-1700
Assistant Medical Examiner **Butch Huston** . . . . . (651) 266-1700
Principal Assistant Medical Examiner **Kelly Mills** . . . . . (651) 266-1700

Office of the Public Defender

101 Fifth Street East, Suite 1808, St. Paul, MN 55101
Fax: (651) 215-0673

Chief Public Defender **Pat Kittridge** . . . . . (651) 757-1600

★Elected Official ▲Appointed by Legislature ▼Appointed by Governor ►Appointed by Board or Commission ●Appointed by Judge
■Appointed by Mayor △Appointed by Freeholders ▽Appointed by Supervisor ▷Appointed by County Executive ○Appointed by Council

Community Corrections Department [RCCC]
121 Seventh Place East, Saint Paul, MN 55101
Fax: (651) 266-2293 Internet: www.co.ramsey.mn.us/cc

Director **John Klavins** .... (651) 266-2670
Deputy Director of Administrative Services
Jennifer Schuster-Jaeger .... (651) 266-2571
Management Analyst Supervisor **Connie Nowacki** ...... (651) 266-2388
E-mail: connie.nowacki@co.ramsey.mn.us

Adult Division
121 Seventh Place East, Saint Paul, MN 55101

Director **Andrew Erickson** .... (651) 266-2300

Boys Totem Town
398 Totem Road, St. Paul, MN 55119

Superintendent **Keith Lattimore** .... (651) 292-5012

Domestic Relations
Mediation/Investigation Supervisor **Robert Sierakowski** . . (651) 266-2671
50 W. Kellogg Blvd., Room 655, St. Paul, MN 55102

Juvenile Detention Center
25 W. 7th St., St. Paul, MN 55102

Superintendent **Peter Jessen-Howard** .... (651) 266-5230

Juvenile Service Center
25 W. 7th St., St. Paul, MN 55102

Director **Michelle Finstad** .... (651) 266-5300

Ramsey County Correctional Facility
297 S. Century Ave., St. Paul, MN 55119

Superintendent **Allen Carlson** .... (651) 266-1400

Community Human Services Department
160 East Kellogg Boulevard, St. Paul, MN 55101
Tel: (651) 266-4444 Fax: (651) 266-4439
Internet: www.co.ramsey.mn.us/hs

Director **Meghan Mohs** .... (651) 266-4429

Lake Owasso Residence [LOR]
210 N. Owasso Blvd., Shoreview, MN 55126
Fax: (651) 765-7722 Internet: www.co.ramsey.mn.us/hs/lor

Administrator **Dana Castonguay** .... (651) 765-7700

Ramsey County Care Center
2000 White Bear Avenue, St. Paul, MN 55109
Fax: (651) 777-1426 Internet: www.co.ramsey.mn.us/nh

Administrator **Frank Robinson** .... (651) 777-7486

Mental Health Center
1919 University Avenue W, St. Paul, MN 55104
Tel: (651) 266-7999 Fax: (651) 266-7851
Internet: www.co.ramsey.mn.us/hs

Director **Julie Duncan** .... (651) 266-7920

Emergency Management and Homeland Security
50 West Kellogg Boulevard, #913, St. Paul, MN 55102

Director **Judson Freed** .... (651) 266-1020
E-mail: judd.freed@co.ramsey.mn.us
Assistant Director **Karma Kumlin-Diers** .... (651) 266-1020
E-mail: Karma.Kumlin-Diers@co.ramsey.mn.us

Human Resources Department
121 Seventh Place East, Suite 2100, Saint Paul, MN 55101
Tel: (651) 266-2700 Fax: (651) 266-2727
Internet: www.co.ramsey.mn.us/hr

Director **Gail J. Blackstone** .... (651) 266-2730
E-mail: gail.blackstone@co.ramsey.mn.us

Human Resources Department *continued*

Secretary **Nancy Norstrem** .... (651) 266-2730
E-mail: nancy.norstrem@co.ramsey.mn.us
Training and Employee Development Manager
Shirley Pierce .... (651) 266-2769
E-mail: shirley.pierce@co.ramsey.mn.us

Department of Information Services
121 Seventh Place East, Suite 2300, Saint Paul, MN 55101
Tel: (651) 266-3400 Fax: (651) 266-3442
Internet: www.co.ramsey.mn.us/is

Chief Information Officer/Director **Jim Hall** .... (651) 266-3400
E-mail: jim.hall@co.ramsey.mn.us
Administration and Accounting Director **Dawn Siegling** . . (651) 266-3480
E-mail: dawn.siegling@co.ramsey.mn.us
Geographic Information Systems Division Manager
Matt Koukol .... (651) 266-3463
E-mail: matt.koukol@co.ramsey.mn.us
Compliance and Records Manager **(Vacant)** .... (651) 266-3427
Applications Services Division Manager **Tom Chow** ..... (651) 266-3424
Technical Services Division Manager **Tom Chow** .... (651) 266-3410

Parks and Recreation Department
2015 North Van Dyke Street, Maplewood, MN 55109
Fax: (651) 748-2508 E-mail: parks@co.ramsey.mn.us
Internet: www.co.ramsey.mn.us/parks

Director **Jon Oyanagi** .... (651) 748-2500
Administrative Assistant **Kara Coustry** .... (651) 748-2500
E-mail: kara.coustry@co.ramsey.mn.us Fax: (651) 748-2508

Property Management Administration
121 Seventh Place East, Suite 2200, Saint Paul, MN 55101
Fax: (651) 266-2264

Director **Bruce T. Thompson** .... (651) 266-2262
E-mail: bruce.thompson@co.ramsey.mn.us
Director of Administration **Dan Winek** .... (651) 266-2246

Department of Property Records and Revenue [PR&R]
90 West Plato Boulevard, St. Paul, MN 55107
Fax: (651) 266-2199 Internet: www.co.ramsey.mn.us/prr

Director **Mark Oswald** .... (651) 266-2196
E-mail: mark.oswald@co.ramsey.mn.us

Saint Paul - Ramsey County Department of Public Health
90 West Plato Boulevard, 2nd Floor, St. Paul, MN 55107
Tel: (651) 266-2400 Fax: (651) 266-2593
E-mail: askph@co.ramsey.mn.us Internet: www.co.ramsey.mn.us/ph

Director **Marina "Rina" McManus** .... (651) 266-2424
Administration Manager **Diane Holmgren** .... (651) 266-1221
E-mail: diane.holmgren@co.ramsey.mn.us
Correctional Health Manager **Diane Haugen** .... (651) 266-1263
Environmental Health Manager **Zack Hansen** .... (651) 266-1160
Family Health Manager **Joan Brandt** .... (651) 266-1826
Healthy Communities Manager **Don Gault** .... (651) 266-2404
Preventive Health and Correctional Health Manager
Diane Hougen .... (651) 266-1263
WIC Manager **Mary Peick** .... (651) 266-1315
Public Information Officer **Christopher "Chris" Burns** . . . (651) 266-2537
E-mail: christopher.burns@co.ramsey.mn.us

Public Works Department
1425 Paul Kirkwold Drive, Arden Hills, MN 55112

▶ Director and County Engineer **James "Jim" Tolaas** ..... (651) 266-7100
E-mail: james.tolaas@co.ramsey.mn.us

★ Elected Official ▲ Appointed by Legislature ▼ Appointed by Governor ▶ Appointed by Board or Commission ● Appointed by Judge
■ Appointed by Mayor △ Appointed by Freeholders ▽ Appointed by Supervisor ▷ Appointed by County Executive ○ Appointed by Council

University of Minnesota Extension
2020 White Bear Avenue, St. Paul, MN 55109
Tel: (651) 704-2080 Fax: (651) 704-2081

Cooking Matters Coordinator **CeAnn Klug** .... (651) 704-2074
Expanded Food and Nutrition Education Program Coordinator **Takayla Lightfield** .... (612) 704-2080
Office Support Manager **Jamie Aussendorf** .... (651) 704-2080

Workforce Solutions
Minnesota Workforce Center-Ramsey County, 2098 11th Ave. E, St. Paul, MN 55109
TTY: (651) 779-5223 Fax: (651) 779-5240

Director **Patricia Brady** .... (651) 770-4499
E-mail: patricia.brady@co.ramsey.mn.us

Ramsey County Law Library [RCLL]
1815 Courthouse, 15 West Kellogg Boulevard, St. Paul, MN 55102-1630
Fax: (651) 266-8399 Internet: www.co.ramsey.mn.us/ll

Director **Sara Galligan** .... (651) 266-8391
E-mail: sara.galligan@co.ramsey.mn.us

Ramsey County Public Library
4570 N. Victoria St., Shoreview, MN 55126-5863
Tel: (651) 486-2300 Fax: (651) 486-2220
Internet: http://www.rclreads.org/home

Director **Susan Nemitz** .... (651) 486-2200
E-mail: snemitz@rclreads.org

Ramsey County Veterans Services
90 Plato Boulevard W, Suite 210, St. Paul, MN 55107
Tel: (651) 266-2545 Fax: (651) 266-2546
E-mail: askveteransservice@co.ramsey.mn.us
Internet: www.co.ramsey.mn.us/vs

Director **Maria Wetherall** .... (651) 266-2545

Office of the County Attorney
345 Wabasha Street North, Suite 120, Saint Paul, MN 55102

★ County Attorney **John Jung-Hoon Choi** .... (651) 266-4000
Term Expires: December 31, 2018
E-mail: john.choi@co.ramsey.mn.us
Education: Marquette 1992 BA; Hamline 1995 JD

Office of the Sheriff
425 Grove Street, St. Paul, MN 55101
Tel: (651) 266-9333 Fax: (651) 266-9301
Internet: www.co.ramsey.mn.us/sheriff

★ Sheriff **Matt Bostrom** .... (651) 266-9333
Term Expires: December 31, 2018

County of Riverside, California
County Administrative Center, 4080 Lemon Street, Riverside, CA 92501
Tel: (951) 955-1000 (Information) Internet: www.countyofriverside.us

County Seat: Riverside **Election Type:** Nonpartisan
Population: 2,361,026 (2015)

Office of the Board of County Supervisors
County Administrative Center, 4080 Lemon Street, 1st Floor, Riverside, CA 92501
P.O. Box 1147, Riverside, CA 92502-1147
Tel: (951) 955-1060 Fax: (951) 955-1071

★ Chairman **John J. Benoit** (District 4) .... (951) 955-1040
Term Expires: January 4, 2019
E-mail: district4@rcbos.org
Date of Birth: December 1951
Education: Cal State (Los Angeles) 1978 BS; Cal State (San Bernardino) MPA

★ Supervisor **Kevin D. Jeffries** (District 1) .... (951) 955-1010
Term Expires: January 5, 2017

★ Supervisor **John F. Tavaglione** (District 2) .... (951) 955-1020
Term Expires: January 4, 2019 Fax: (951) 955-2362
E-mail: district2@rcbos.org
Date of Birth: July 10, 1948
Education: California Baptist Col 1987 BSBA

★ Supervisor **Chuck Washington** (District 3) .... (951) 955-1030
Term Expires: January 5, 2017
E-mail: district3@rcbos.org

★ Supervisor **Marion Ashley** (District 5) .... (951) 955-1050
Term Expires: January 4, 2019
E-mail: district5@rcbos.org

► Clerk of the Board **Kecia Harper-Ihem** .... (951) 955-1060
E-mail: kharper-ihem@rcbos.org

Office of the County Executive Officer
County Administrative Center, 4080 Lemon Street, 4th Floor, Riverside, CA 92501-3679
Fax: (951) 955-1034

▽ County Executive Officer **Jay E. Orr** .... (951) 955-1110
E-mail: jorr@rceo.org

Chief Assistant County Executive Officer **George A. Johnson** .... (951) 955-1110
E-mail: gajohnson@rceo.org

Chief Deputy County Executive Officer **Christopher Hans** .... (951) 955-1110
E-mail: chans@rceo.org

Deputy County Executive Officer **Ivan M. Chand** .... (951) 955-1110
E-mail: ichand@rceo.org

Deputy County Executive Officer **(Vacant)** .... (951) 955-1110
Deputy County Executive Officer **Alex Gann** .... (951) 955-1110
Deputy County Executive Officer **Brian Mespande** .... (951) 955-1110
Finance Director **Paul McDonnell** .... (951) 955-1110
Education: UC Berkeley BA; UCLA MBA
Public Information Officer **Ray Smith** .... (951) 955-1110

Office on Aging
6296 Rivercrest Drive, Suite K, Riverside, CA 92507
Tel: (951) 867-3800 Fax: (951) 697-4698 Internet: www.rcaging.org
E-mail: rcaging@rcaging.org

Director **Michele Haddock** .... (951) 867-3800
Deputy Director for Administration **Rachelle Román** .... (951) 867-3800
Deputy Director for Senior Programs **(Vacant)** .... (951) 867-3800
Web Manager **(Vacant)** .... (951) 867-3800

★ Elected Official ▲ Appointed by Legislature ▼ Appointed by Governor ► Appointed by Board or Commission ● Appointed by Judge
■ Appointed by Mayor △ Appointed by Freeholders ▽ Appointed by Supervisor ▷ Appointed by County Executive ○ Appointed by Council

Office of the County Counsel
Law Building, 3960 Orange Street, 5th Floor, Riverside, CA 92501-3674
Fax: (951) 955-6322

▶ County Counsel **Gregory P. "Greg" Priamos** . . . . (951) 955-6300
E-mail: gpriamos@co.riverside.ca.us
Education: USC 1985 BA; Loyola Law 1988 JD
Assistant County Counsel **Anita C. Willis** . . . . (951) 955-6300
Assistant County Counsel **James E. "Jeb" Brown** . . . . . . (951) 955-6300

Law Offices of the Public Defender
4200 Orange St., Riverside, CA 92501
Tel: (951) 955-6000 Fax: (951) 955-6025
Internet: http://publicdef.co.riverside.ca.us/

Chief Public Defender **Steven L. Harmon** . . . . (951) 955-6000
Assistant Public Defender **Brian Boles** . . . . (951) 955-6000
Assistant Public Defender **Thomas Cavanaugh** . . . . (760) 863-8231

Office of the Registrar of Voters
2724 Gateway Dr., Riverside, CA 92507
Tel: (951) 486-7200 Tel: (800) 773-8683 Fax: (951) 486-7272
Internet: www.voteinfo.net

▽ Registrar of Voters **Rebecca Spencer** . . . . (951) 486-7330
Assistant Registrar of Voters **Art Tinoco** . . . . (951) 486-7330

Agricultural Commissioner's Office
County Administration Center, 4080 Lemon Street, Room 19, Riverside, CA 92501
P.O. Box 1089, Riverside, CA 92502-1089
Fax: (951) 955-3047

Agricultural Commissioner/Sealer of Weights and Measures **John Snyder** . . . . (951) 955-3045
Assistant Commissioner/Sealer of Weights and Measures **G. Dustin Wiley** . . . . (951) 955-3004

Community Action Partnership of Riverside County
2038 Iowa Avenue, Suite B-102, Riverside, CA 92507
Fax: (951) 955-6506 Internet: www.capriverside.org

Executive Director **Brenda Freeman** . . . . (951) 955-4900
Human Resources Coordinator **Tamara Martin** . . . . (951) 955-4900
E-mail: tmartin@co.riverside.ca.us

Department of Public Health
4065 County Circle Dr., Suite 412, Riverside, CA 92503
Tel: (951) 358-5000 Fax: (951) 358-4529 Internet: www.rivcoph.org

Director/Health Officer **Sarah Mack** . . . . (951) 358-7036
Health Officer **Dr. Cameron Kaiser** . . . . (951) 358-5000

Cooperative Extension
21150 Box Springs Rd., Suite 202, Moreno Valley, CA 92557-8718
Fax: (951) 788-2615 E-mail: ceriverside@ucdavis.edu
Internet: http://ceriverside.ucdavis.edu/

Director **Etaferahu Takele** . . . . (951) 683-6491 ext. 221

Riverside County Economic Development Agency
3403 Tenth Street, Suite 400, Riverside, CA 92501
Tel: (951) 955-6662 Fax: (951) 955-9177 Internet: www.rivcoeda.org

Assistant County Executive Officer/EDA **Robert D. "Rob" Field** . . . . (951) 955-4860
E-mail: rfield@rivcoeda.org
Executive Assistant **Minnie Diaz** . . . . (951) 955-4861
E-mail: minnie.diaz@rivcoeda.org
Managing Director **Jeffrey Van Wagenen** . . . . (951) 955-1309
E-mail: jvanwagen@rivcoeda.org

Edward-Dean Museum And Gardens
9401 Oak Glen Rd., Cherry Valley, CA 92223
Tel: (951) 845-2626 Fax: (951) 845-2628
Internet: www.edward-deanmuseum.org

Senior Development Specialist **Stacy Chester** . . . . (951) 845-2626

Riverside County Fair and National Date Festival
82-503 Highway 111, Indio, CA 92201
Fax: (760) 863-8973 Tel: (760) 863-8247

Manager **Veronica Casper** . . . . (760) 863-8242

Workforce Development Center
1325 Spruce Street, Suite 110, Riverside, CA 92507
Tel: (951) 955-3100 Internet: www.rivcoworkforce.com

Assistant Director **Heidi Marshall** . . . . (951) 955-3100
Secretary **Valarie Jackson** . . . . (951) 955-7528
E-mail: vmjackson@rivcoeda.org

Housing Authority
5555 Arlington Avenue, Riverside, CA 92504
Tel: (951) 351-0700 Fax: (951) 688-6873 Internet: harivco.org

Assistant Director **Heidi Marshall** . . . . (951) 345-5466
Office Assistant **Kimberly Palay** . . . . (951) 351-5466

Riverside County Fire Department [RCOFD]
210 West San Jacinto Avenue, Perris, CA 92570
Tel: (951) 940-6900 Fax: (951) 940-6910 Internet: www.rvcfire.org

Fire Chief **John R. Hawkins** . . . . (951) 940-6900
Deputy Chief, Administration **Glenn Patterson** . . . . (951) 940-6900
Deputy Chief, East Operations **Dorian Cooley** . . . . (951) 940-6900
Deputy Chief, West Operations **Steve Curley** . . . . (951) 940-6900
Deputy Chief, Central Operations **Robert Michael** . . . . (951) 940-6900
Deputy Director of Administration **Diane Sinclair** . . . . (951) 940-6900

Human Resources Department
County Administrative Center, 4080 Lemon Street, Riverside, CA 92501
P.O. Box 1569, Riverside, CA 92502-1569
Tel: (951) 955-1000 (Information) Fax: (951) 955-3479
E-mail: hrdept@rc-hr.com Internet: www.rc-hr.com

Assistant County Executive Officer and Human Resources Director **Mike Stock** . . . . (951) 955-3510
E-mail: mstock@rc-hr.com
Executive Assistant **Abi Martin** . . . . (951) 955-3510
E-mail: amartin@rc-hr.com
Assistant Human Resources Director **John Mooney** . . . . . (951) 955-3510
E-mail: jmooney@rc-hr.com
Assistant Human Resources Director **Mike Bowers** . . . . . . (951) 955-3510
E-mail: mbowers@rc-hr.com

Information Technology Department [RCIT]
3450 Fourteenth Street, Riverside, CA 92501
Internet: www.riversidecountyit.org

Chief Information Officer **Steve Reneker** . . . . (951) 955-3700

Department of Mental Health
4095 County Circle Drive, Riverside, CA 92503
P.O. Box 7549, Riverside, CA 92513-7549
Tel: (951) 358-4500 Fax: (951) 358-4513 E-mail: mhweb@rcmhd.org
Internet: www.rcdmh.org

Director **Jerry A. Wengerd** . . . . (951) 358-4501
Assistant Director, Administration **Maria T. Mabey** . . . . . . (951) 358-4504
Assistant Director, Programs **Steve Steinburg** . . . . (951) 358-4511
Medical Director **Jerry L. Dennis** . . . . (951) 358-4500

Regional Park and Open-Space District
4600 Crestmore Road, Riverside, CA 92509-6858
Tel: (951) 955-4310 Fax: (951) 955-4305 Internet: www.rivcoparks.org

General Manager **Scott Bangle** . . . . (951) 955-4398

★ Elected Official ▲ Appointed by Legislature ▼ Appointed by Governor ▶ Appointed by Board or Commission ● Appointed by Judge
■ Appointed by Mayor △ Appointed by Freeholders ▽ Appointed by Supervisor ▷ Appointed by County Executive ○ Appointed by Council

Regional Park and Open-Space District *continued*

Parks and Recreation Bureau Chief **Kyla Brown** .... (951) 955-4346

Department of Public Social Services [DPSS]

4060 County Circle Dr., Riverside, CA 92503
Fax: (951) 358-3036 E-mail: dpssinquiry@riversidedpss.org
Internet: http://dpss.co.riverside.ca.us/

Director **Susan von Zabern** .... (951) 358-3000
Assistant Director, Administrative Services
Patricia Reynolds .... (951) 358-3000
Deputy Director, Planning and Evaluation
Rocio Aguiniga .... (951) 358-3000
Assistant Director, Child Protective Services
Tod Belonca .... (951) 358-3000
Assistant Director, Self Sufficiency **Anna Martinez** ...... (951) 358-3000
Deputy Director, CalWorks Gain and Child Care
Liz Solerd .... (951) 358-3000
Assistant Director, Adult Protective Services
Lisa Shiner .... (951) 358-3000
Internal Compliance Officer **Hillary Brown** .... (951) 358-3030
10281 Kidd Street, Riverside, CA 92503

Purchasing and Fleet Services Department

2980 Washington St., Riverside, CA 92504-4647
Fax: (951) 955-4948

▽ Director **Lisa Brandl** .... (951) 955-4936
Assistant Director **Teresa Summers** .... (951) 955-4928
Purchasing Manager **Lisa Boerner** .... (951) 955-4692
E-mail: dbaracz@co.riverside.ca.us

Transportation and Land Management Agency [TLMA]

County Administrative Center, 4080 Lemon Street, 14th Floor, Riverside, CA 92501
P.O. Box 1605, Riverside, CA 92502-1605
Tel: (951) 955-6838 Fax: (951) 955-6879 Internet: www.rctlma.org

▶ Agency Director **Juan C. Perez** .... (951) 955-6742
Deputy Director of Administrative Services **Ed Cooper** ... (951) 955-2027
Building and Safety Official **Mike Lara** .... (951) 955-2025
P.O. Box 1440, Riverside, CA 92502-1440 Fax: (951) 955-2023
Assistant Director of Transportation **Patricia Romo** ...... (951) 955-6740
P.O. Box 1090, Riverside, CA 92502-1090 Fax: (951) 955-3198

Department of Veterans Services

4360 Orange Street, Riverside, CA 92501
Tel: (951) 276-3060 Fax: (951) 276-3063
Internet: http://veteranservices.co.riverside.ca.us/

▽ Director **Grant Gautsche** .... (951) 276-3060
E-mail: gautsche@co.riverside.ca.us

Department of Waste Resources

14310 Frederick Street, Moreno Valley, CA 92553
Fax: (951) 486-3205 Internet: www.rcwaste.org

▶ General Manager/Chief Engineer **Hans Kernkamp** ...... (951) 486-3232
E-mail: hkernkam@co.riverside.ca.us
Executive Assistant **Frances Zamora** .... (951) 486-3204
E-mail: fzamora@co.riverside.ca.us
Assistant Chief Engineer **Joseph R. McCann** .... (951) 486-3341

Riverside County Flood Control and Water Conservation District

1995 Market Street, Riverside, CA 92501
Fax: (951) 788-9965 Internet: www.rcflood.org

▽ General Manager-Chief Engineer
Warren D. "Dusty" Williams .... (951) 955-1250
E-mail: dustyw@rcflood.org

Riverside County Regional Medical Center [RCRMC]

26520 Cactus Avenue, Moreno Valley, CA 92555
Tel: (951) 486-4450 Fax: (951) 486-4475 Internet: www.rcrmc.org

▽ Chief Executive Officer **Zareh Sarrafian** .... (951) 486-4450
Chief Operations Officer **Jennifer Cruikshank** .... (951) 486-4450

Office of the Assessor-County Clerk-Recorder

County Administrative Center, 4080 Lemon Street, First, Fifth, and Sixth Floors, Riverside, CA 92501
P.O. Box 751, Riverside, CA 92502-0751
Tel: (951) 955-6200 (Assessor)
Tel: (951) 486-7000 (County Clerk-Recorder)
E-mail: accrmail@asrclkrec.com Internet: http://riverside.asrclkrec.com

★ Assessor-County Clerk-Recorder **Peter Aldana** .... (951) 955-6200
Term Expires: December 31, 2018

Office of the Auditor-Controller

County Administrative Center, 4080 Lemon Street, 11th Floor, Riverside, CA 92502
P.O. Box 1326, Riverside, CA 92502-1326
Tel: (951) 955-3800 Fax: (951) 955-3802
Internet: www.auditorcontroller.org

★ Auditor-Controller **Paul Angulo** .... (951) 955-3800
Term Expires: December 31, 2018
E-mail: pangulo@co.riverside.ca.us
Assistant Auditor-Controller **Frankie Ezzat** .... (951) 955-3800

Office of the District Attorney

3960 Orange Street, Riverside, CA 92501-3674
Fax: (951) 955-5469 Internet: www.rivcoda.org

★ District Attorney **Michael A. Hestrin** .... (951) 955-5400
Term Expires: December 31, 2018
Chief Assistant District Attorney **John Aki** .... (951) 955-5400
Assistant District Attorney **Elaina Bentley** .... (951) 955-5400

Office of the Sheriff-Coroner-Public Administrator

Criminal Justice Building, 4095 Lemon Street, 2nd Floor, Riverside, CA 92501 (Sheriff)
P.O. Box 512, Riverside, CA 92502
800 South Redlands Avenue, Perris, CA 92570 (Coroner/Public Administrator)
Tel: (951) 955-2400 (Sheriff)
Tel: (951) 443-2300 (Coroner/Public Administrator)
Fax: (951) 955-2428 (Sheriff)
Fax: (951) 443-2370 (Coroner/Public Administrator)
Internet: www.riversidesheriff.org

★ Sheriff-Coroner-Public Administrator
Stanley "Stan" Sniff, Jr. .... (951) 955-2400
Term Expires: December 2018
E-mail: ssniff@riversidesheriff.org

COUNTIES

★ Elected Official ▲ Appointed by Legislature ▼ Appointed by Governor ▶ Appointed by Board or Commission ● Appointed by Judge
■ Appointed by Mayor △ Appointed by Freeholders ▽ Appointed by Supervisor ▷ Appointed by County Executive ○ Appointed by Council

Office of the Treasurer-Tax Collector

County Administrative Center, 4080 Lemon Street, 4th Floor, Riverside, CA 92501-3660
P.O. Box 12005, Riverside, CA 92502-2205
Fax: (951) 955-3923 E-mail: ttc@rivcottc.org
Internet: www.riversidetaxinfo.com

★ Treasurer-Tax Collector **Don Kent** .... (951) 955-3900
Term Expires: June 8, 2018
E-mail: dkent@rivcottc.org

Riverside County Office of Education [RCOE]

3939 Thirteenth Street, Riverside, CA 92501
P.O. Box 868, Riverside, CA 92502-0868
Tel: (951) 826-6530 Fax: (951) 826-6199 Internet: www.rcoe.k12.ca.us

Board of Education

★ President **Bruce N. Dennis** .... (951) 826-6530
Term Expires: December 31, 2016

Office of the Superintendent

★ Superintendent of Schools **Kenneth M. Young** .... (951) 826-6670
Term Expires: December 31, 2018
E-mail: kyoung@rcoe.us
Education: U Phoenix BS; American InterContinental

County of Sacramento, California

700 H Street, Sacramento, CA 95814-1280
Tel: (916) 875-5000 (Information) Fax: (916) 875-6692
Internet: www.saccounty.net

County Seat: Sacramento **Election Type:** Nonpartisan
Population: 1,501,335 (2015)

Office of the Board of Supervisors

700 H St., Room 2450, Sacramento, CA 95814-1280
Tel: (916) 874-5411 Fax: (916) 874-7593

★ Chair **Roberta MacGlashan** (District 4) .... (916) 874-5491
Term Expires: December 31, 2016
E-mail: macglashanr@saccounty.net
Education: Occidental 1973 BA; Cal State (Fresno)
Chief of Staff **Ted Wolter** .... (916) 874-5491

★ Vice Chair **Don Nottoli** (District 5) .... (916) 874-5465
Term Expires: December 31, 2018
E-mail: nottolid@saccounty.net
Education: Cal State (Sacramento) 1978 BA
Chief of Staff **Sheryll Venegas** .... (916) 874-5465

★ Supervisor **Phillip R. "Phil" Serna** (District 1) .... (916) 874-5485
Term Expires: December 31, 2018
E-mail: supervisorserna@saccounty.net
Education: Cal State (Sacramento) 1992 BA; Cal Poly San Luis Obispo 1994 MCRP
Chief of Staff **Lisa Nava** .... (916) 874-5485

★ Supervisor **Patrick Kennedy** (District 2) .... (916) 874-5481
Term Expires: December 31, 2018 Fax: (916) 874-7593
Chief of Staff **Susan McKee** .... (916) 874-5481

★ Supervisor **Susan Peters** (District 3) .... (916) 874-5471
Term Expires: December 31, 2016
E-mail: susanpeters@saccounty.net
Chief of Staff **Howard Schmidt** .... (916) 874-5471

Clerk of the Board **Cyndi Lee** .... (916) 874-5411
E-mail: leecyndi@saccounty.net

Office of the Board of Supervisors *continued*

Assistant Clerk **Florence "Flo" Evans** .... (916) 874-8150
E-mail: evansf@saccounty.net

Office of the County Counsel

700 H Street, Room 2650, Sacramento, CA 95814-1283
Fax: (916) 874-8207 Internet: www.countycounsel.saccounty.net

▶ County Counsel **John F. Whisenhunt** .... (916) 874-5544
E-mail: whisenhuntj@saccounty.net
Education: Occidental 1976 BA; UCLA 1979 JD

Assistant County Counsel **Traci F. Lee** .... (916) 875-6877

Probation Department

9750 Business Park Drive, Suite 220, Sacramento, CA 95827
Tel: (916) 875-0300 Fax: (916) 875-0203
E-mail: probationmail@saccounty.net
Internet: www.probation.saccounty.net

Chief Probation Officer **Lee E. Seale** .... (916) 875-0312
Assistant Chief Probation Officer **Michael Shores** .... (916) 875-0312
Assistant Chief Probation Officer **Marlon Yarber** .... (916) 875-0312

Office of the County Executive

700 H Street, Suite 7650, Sacramento, CA 95814-1280
Tel: (916) 874-5833 Fax: (916) 874-5885
Internet: www.ceo.saccounty.net

▶ County Executive **Bradley J. Hudson** .... (916) 874-7682
E-mail: hudsonb@saccounty.net
Education: Cal State (Fresno) BS; U San Francisco MPA

Assistant County Executive **Navdeep S. Gill** .... (916) 874-7682
E-mail: gilln@saccounty.net
Education: Missouri MA, MPA

Office of Financial Management

700 H Street, Room 7650, Sacramento, CA 95814-1280
Tel: (916) 874-9547 Fax: (916) 874-5885
Internet: www.ofm.saccounty.net E-mail: fergusonb@saccounty.net

Chief Financial Officer **Britt Ferguson** .... (916) 874-5473

Countywide Services Agency

700 H Street, Suite 7650, Sacramento, CA 95814
Fax: (916) 874-5885

Chief Deputy County Executive **Paul G. Lake** .... (916) 874-5886

Office of the Coroner

4800 Broadway, Suite 100, Sacramento, CA 95820-1530
Fax: (916) 874-9257 E-mail: coronerweb@saccounty.net
Internet: www.coroner.saccounty.net

Coroner **Kimberly D. Gin** .... (916) 874-9320

Office of the Public Defender

700 H St., Room 0270, Sacramento, CA 95814-1280
Tel: (916) 874-6411 Fax: (916) 874-8223

▶ Public Defender **Paulino G. Duran** .... (916) 874-6411
E-mail: duranp@saccounty.net

Department of Agriculture and Weights and Measures

4137 Branch Center Road, Sacramento, CA 95827-3823
Fax: (916) 875-6150 E-mail: agcomm@saccounty.net
Internet: www.agcomm.saccounty.net

▶ Agricultural Commissioner/Sealer of Weights and Measures **Juli Jensen** .... (916) 875-6603
Education: UC Davis 1979 BS

★ Elected Official ▲ Appointed by Legislature ▼ Appointed by Governor ▶ Appointed by Board or Commission ● Appointed by Judge
■ Appointed by Mayor △ Appointed by Freeholders ▽ Appointed by Supervisor ▷ Appointed by County Executive ○ Appointed by Council

Child Support Services Department
3701 Power Inn Road, Sacramento, CA 95826
Tel: (800) 901-3212

Director **E. Hardy "Terri" Porter** .... (916) 875-7277
E-mail: portert@saccounty.net

Conflict Criminal Defenders Department
901 H Street, Suite 409, Sacramento, CA 95814
Tel: (916) 874-6535 E-mail: ccd@saccounty.net

Executive Director **Fern Laethem** .... (916) 874-6898

Cooperative Extension Office
4145 Branch Center Rd., Sacramento, CA 95827
Fax: (916) 875-6233 E-mail: cesacramento@ucanr.edu
Internet: http://cesacramento.ucanr.edu/

Director **Morgan Doran** .... (530) 666-8738

Environmental Management Department [EMD]
10590 Armstrong Avenue, Mather, CA 95655
Tel: (916) 875-8484 (General Information) Fax: (916) 875-8588
E-mail: emdinfo@saccounty.net Internet: www.emd.saccounty.net

Director **Val F. Siebal** .... (916) 875-8444
Executive Secretary **Jan Koehn** .... (916) 875-8584
E-mail: jkoehn@saccounty.net

Department of Health and Human Services [DHHS]
7001-A East Parkway, Suite 1000, Sacramento, CA 95823-2501
Tel: (916) 875-6091 Fax: (916) 875-1283 (Administration)
E-mail: hhs-director@saccounty.net Internet: www.sacdhhs.com

Director **Sherri Z. Heller** .... (916) 875-2002
Health Officer **Dr. Olivia Kasirye** .... (916) 875-5881
Fax: (916) 875-5888

Administrator, Alcohol and Drug Services Division
Lori Vallone .... (916) 875-2046
Fax: (916) 875-2035

Deputy Director, Administration and Fiscal Services
Luis Villa .... (916) 875-0831
E-mail: villalx@saccounty.net

Deputy Director, Behavioral Health Services Division
Uma Zykofsky .... (916) 875-4904
Fax: (916) 875-6970

Deputy Director, Child Protective Services Division
Michelle Callejas .... (916) 875-0123
Fax: (916) 875-0187

Deputy Director, Primary Health Services Division
Sandy Damiano .... (916) 875-5701
Fax: (916) 875-6366

Chief, Senior and Adult Services Division
Debra J. Morrow .... (916) 876-7179
Fax: (916) 874-9682

Executive Director, Mental Health Treatment Center
Anthony Madariaga .... (916) 875-1010
Fax: (916) 875-1002

Human Assistance Department
2433 Marconi Avenue, Sacramento, CA 95821
Fax: (916) 875-3591 Internet: http://dhaweb.saccounty.net/

Director **Ann Edwards** .... (916) 875-3601
Veterans' Affairs Program Manager **Laurie Carriker** ...... (916) 874-6811
Volunteer Services Program Manager **Janine Brown** ..... (916) 874-2072

Voter Registration and Elections Department
7000 65th Street, Suite A, Sacramento, CA 95823-2315
Fax: (916) 876-5130 Internet: www.elections.saccounty.net

► Registrar of Voters **Jill LaVine** .... (916) 875-6558
E-mail: lavinej@saccounty.net
Assistant Registrar of Voters **Alice Jarboe** .... (916) 875-6761
E-mail: jarboea@saccounty.net

Internal Services Agency
700 H Street, Suite 7650, Sacramento, CA 95814
Fax: (916) 874-5885 Internet: www.isa.saccounty.net

Chief Deputy County Executive **David Villanueva** .... (916) 874-8515
E-mail: villanuevad@saccounty.net
Education: Cal State (Sacramento) BSBA
Executive Secretary **Leslie Iniguez** .... (916) 874-7804
Communications and Media Officer **Chris Andis** .... (916) 874-2691

Department of Technology [DTech]
799 G Street, Sacramento, CA 95814-1280
Tel: (916) 874-7752 Fax: (916) 874-9077
Internet: www.ocit.saccounty.net

▷ Director/Chief Information Officer **Rami Zakaria** .... (916) 874-7825
E-mail: zakariar@saccounty.net
Information Technology Division Chief **Steve Baird** ..... (916) 874-3636
E-mail: bairds@saccounty.net
Information Technology Division Chief **Debra Nadolna** .. (916) 875-6724
E-mail: nadolnad@saccounty.net
Information Technology Division Chief **(Vacant)** .... (916) 874-0175
Information Technology Division Chief **Rob Schultz** ..... (916) 874-7825
E-mail: SchultzRo@saccounty.net
Communications and Media Officer
Brenda Bongiorno .... (916) 874-7798
E-mail: bongiornob@saccounty.net Fax: (916) 874-5885

Office of the County Clerk/Recorder
600 8th Street, Sacramento, CA 95814
P.O. Box 839, Sacramento, CA 95812-0839
Tel: (916) 874-6334 Internet: www.ccr.saccounty.net

Clerk/Recorder **Donna Allred** .... (916) 874-6334
E-mail: sacrec@saccounty.net

Department of Finance
700 H St., Room 4650, Sacramento, CA 95814
Fax: (916) 874-8904 E-mail: finance-director@saccounty.net
Internet: www.finance.saccounty.net

▽ Director **Julie A. Valverde** .... (916) 874-6744
E-mail: valverdej@saccounty.net
Assistant Auditor/Controller **Ben Lamera** .... (916) 874-7450
Assistant Tax Collector **Angie Droszcz** .... (916) 874-6648
Assistant Treasurer **Peggy Marti** .... (916) 874-6368
Chief Investment Officer **Bernard Santo Domingo** ...... (916) 874-7320
E-mail: santodomingob@saccounty.net

Department of General Services [DGS]
9660 Ecology Lane, Sacramento, CA 95827
Tel: (916) 876-6170 Fax: (916) 876-6390
Internet: www.dgs.saccounty.net

Director **Michael M. Morse** .... (916) 876-6191
E-mail: morsem@saccounty.net Fax: (916) 854-9091

Department of Personnel Services [DPS]
700 H Street, Suite 4667, Sacramento, CA 95814
Tel: (916) 874-2020 Fax: (916) 874-4621
Internet: http://hra.co.sacramento.ca.us/

Director **David Devine** .... (916) 874-6388
E-mail: devined@saccounty.net

Office of Labor Relations
700 H Street, Suite 4667, Sacramento, CA 95814
Tel: (916) 874-7095 Fax: (916) 854-9444
Internet: www.laborrelations.saccounty.net

Director **Robert Bonner** .... (916) 874-7095

★ Elected Official ■ Appointed by Mayor ▲ Appointed by Legislature △ Appointed by Freeholders ▼ Appointed by Governor ▽ Appointed by Supervisor ► Appointed by Board or Commission ▷ Appointed by County Executive ● Appointed by Judge ○ Appointed by Council

Department of Revenue Recovery [DRR]
700 H Street, Suite 6720, Sacramento, CA 95814
4100 Branch Center Drive, Sacramento, CA 95827
Tel: (916) 875-7500 Fax: (916) 875-7664 E-mail: drrmail@saccounty.net
Internet: www.drr.saccounty.net

Director **Connie Ahmed** .... (916) 875-7500
E-mail: ahmedc@saccounty.net

Municipal Services
700 H Street, Suite 7650, Sacramento, CA 95814
Tel: (916) 874-6495 Fax: (916) 874-5885
Internet: www.municipalservices.saccounty.net

Chief Deputy County Executive **Robert Leonard** .... (916) 874-7876
E-mail: leonardr@saccounty.net
Education: San José State BSAE, MS

Department of Animal Care and Regulation
3839 Bradshaw Road, Sacramento, CA 95827
Fax: (916) 875-5519 E-mail: countyanimalcare@saccounty.net
Internet: www.saccountyshelter.net

▽ Director (Interim) **Dave Dickinson** .... (916) 368-7387
E-mail: dickinsond@saccounty.net

Department of Community Development
827 Seventh Street, Room 304, Sacramento, CA 95814-1280
Tel: (916) 874-1659 Internet: www.msa2.saccounty.net/ce

Director **Lori A. Moss** .... (916) 874-1659
E-mail: mossl@saccounty.net

Department of Regional Parks
9850 Goethe Road, Sacramento, CA 95827
Fax: (916) 875-6332 E-mail: parksinfo@saccounty.net
Internet: www.sacparks.net

▽ Director **Jeffrey Leatherman** .... (916) 875-6961
Education: Cal State (Chico) BS

Department of Transportation
906 G Street, Suite 510, Sacramento, CA 95814
Tel: (916) 874-6291 Fax: (916) 874-7831 E-mail: trdteam@saccounty.net
Internet: www.sacdot.com

Director **Michael J. Penrose** .... (916) 874-6291

Department of Waste Management and Recycling [WMR]
9850 Goethe Road, Sacramento, CA 95827
Tel: (916) 875-6789 Fax: (916) 875-6767
Internet: www.msa2.saccounty.net/wmr

Director **Paul Philleo** .... (916) 875-7011

Department of Water Resources
827 Seventh Street, Room 301, Sacramento, CA 95814-1280
Tel: (916) 874-6851 Fax: (916) 874-8693
E-mail: saccodwr@saccounty.net Internet: www.saccodwr.org

Director **Michael L. Peterson** .... (916) 874-6851

Sacramento County Airport System
6900 Airport Boulevard, Sacramento, CA 95837
Tel: (916) 929-5411 Fax: (916) 874-0636
E-mail: air-market@saccounty.net Internet: www.sacairports.org

Director **John Wheat** .... (916) 929-5411

Civil Service Commission
700 H Street, Room 2640, Sacramento, CA 95814
Tel: (916) 874-5586 Fax: (916) 854-9236
Internet: www.csc.saccounty.net

Executive Officer **Alice Dowdin-Calvillo** .... (916) 874-5586

First 5 Sacramento Commission
2750 Gateway Oaks Drive, Suite 330, Sacramento, CA 95833
Tel: (916) 876-5865 Fax: (916) 876-5877
Internet: www.first5sacramento.net

Chair **Phillip R. "Phil" Serna** .... (916) 874-5485
Education: Cal State (Sacramento) 1992 BA;
Cal Poly San Luis Obispo 1994 MCRP

Executive Director **Julie Gallelo** .... (916) 876-5867

Office of the Assessor
3701 Power Inn Road, Suite 3000, Sacramento, CA 95826
Fax: (916) 875-0765 Internet: www.assessor.saccounty.net

★ Assessor **Kathleen "Kathy" Kelleher** .... (916) 875-0760
Term Expires: December 31, 2019
Education: Cal State (Sacramento) 1987 BS

Office of the District Attorney
901 G St., Sacramento, CA 95814
Tel: (916) 874-6555 Fax: (916) 874-5340 Internet: www.sacda.org

★ District Attorney **Anne Marie Schubert** .... (916) 874-7000
Term Expires: December 31, 2018

Chief Deputy District Attorney **Steve Grippi** .... (916) 874-6556

Information Technology Division Chief
Bassam Amrou .... (916) 874-6577
Fax: (916) 874-5340

Office of the Sheriff
711 G St., Sacramento, CA 95814
Tel: (916) 874-5115 Fax: (916) 874-5332

★ Sheriff **Scott R. Jones** .... (916) 874-7146
Term Expires: December 31, 2019
E-mail: sheriff@sacsheriff.com

Undersheriff **James Lewis** .... (916) 874-7146
E-mail: jlewis@sacsheriff.com

Sacramento County Employees' Retirement System [SCERS]
980 9th Street, Suite 1800, Sacramento, CA 95814
P.O. Box 627, Sacramento, CA 95812-0627
Fax: (916) 874-6060

Chief Executive Officer **Richard Stensrud** .... (916) 874-9119
E-mail: stensrudr@saccounty.net

Sacramento County Office of Education [SCOE]
10474 Mather Boulevard, Mather, CA 95655
P.O. Box 269003, Sacramento, CA 95826-9003
Tel: (916) 228-2500 Fax: (916) 228-2403 E-mail: info@scoe.net
Internet: www.scoe.net

Superintendent of Schools **David W. Gordon** .... (916) 228-2410
Education: Brandeis BA; Harvard EdM

County of St. Louis, Missouri

41 South Central Avenue, Clayton, MO 63105
Tel: (314) 615-5000 (Information) Internet: www.stlouisco.com

County Seat: Clayton **Election Type:** Partisan **Population:** 1,003,362 (2015)

Office of the County Executive

41 S. Central Ave., Clayton, MO 63105-1719
Tel: (314) 615-7016 Fax: (314) 615-3727
Internet: www.stlouisco.com/yourgovernment/countyexecutive

★ County Executive **Steven "Steve" Stenger** (R) . . . . (314) 615-7016
Term Expires: December 31, 2018
E-mail: sstenger@stlouisco.com
Education: Saint Louis U 1996 JD
Chief Operating Officer **(Vacant)** . . . . (314) 615-7002
Senior Policy Advisor **Jeff R. Wagener** . . . . (314) 615-2502
Policy Advisor **Tom Curran** . . . . (314) 615-7007
Communications Director **Cordell Whitlock** . . . . (314) 615-7016
Communications Coordinator **Allison Blood** . . . . (314) 615-7016

Office of the County Counselor

Lawrence K. Roos County Government Center, 41 South Central Avenue, Clayton, MO 63105
Tel: (314) 615-7025 Fax: (314) 615-3732

County Counselor **Peter J. Krane** . . . . (314) 615-7025
Education: Colby 1979 BA; Washington U (MO) 1982 JD

Office of the Sheriff

7900 Carondelet Avenue, Room 551, Clayton, MO 63105-1719

Sheriff **Jim Buckles** . . . . (314) 615-4724
E-mail: jbuckles2@stlouisco.com

Administration Department

41 South Central Avenue, 8th Floor, Clayton, MO 63105-1719
Tel: (314) 615-7046 Fax: (314) 615-3707

▷ Director **Pamela J. "Pam" Reitz** . . . . (314) 615-7046
E-mail: preitz@stlouisco.com

Division of Personnel

41 South Central Avenue, 7th Floor, Clayton, MO 63105
Tel: (314) 615-5429 Fax: (314) 615-7703
E-mail: personnel@stlouisco.com Internet: www.stlouisco.com/personnel

▷ Director **Kirk McCarley** . . . . (314) 615-5410
E-mail: personnel@stlouisco.com

Division of Procurement and Administrative Services

41 South Central Avenue, 8th Floor, Clayton, MO 63105
Tel: (314) 615-7067 Fax: (314) 615-0197
Internet: www.stlouisco.com/procurement

Director **Toreen Parker** . . . . (314) 615-7070
E-mail: tparker@stlouisco.com

Department of Public Health

6121 North Hanley Road, Berkeley, MO 63134
Tel: (314) 615-0600 Fax: (314) 615-6435
Internet: www.stlouisco.com/healthandwellness

▷ Director **Faisal Khan** . . . . (314) 615-1627
E-mail: fkhan@stlouisco.com

Department of Transportation and Public Works

1050 North Lindbergh Boulevard, St. Louis, MO 63132
Fax: (314) 615-8156

▷ Director **Nicholas D. Gardner** . . . . (314) 615-5184
Deputy Director **Stephanie Leon-Streeter** . . . . (314) 615-5184

Department of Transportation and Public Works *continued*

Code Enforcement Division Manager
Daniel "Dan" Dreisewerd . . . . (314) 615-8190
41 South Central Avenue, Clayton, MO 63105
E-mail: ddreisewerd@stlouisco.com

Department of Human Services [DHS]

9666 Olive Boulevard, Suite 510, St. Louis, MO 63132
Tel: (314) 615-4453 Fax: (314) 615-4420 TTY: (314) 615-4425
Internet: www.stlouisco.com/healthandwellness/humanservices

▷ Director **Andrea Jackson-Jennings** . . . . (314) 615-4485
Education: Missouri (St Louis)
Director, Financial Services and Information Systems
Randee Fendelman . . . . (314) 615-4453
E-mail: rfendelman@stlouisco.com
Director, Lakeside Residential Treatment Center
Leonard McDonald . . . . (314) 615-4453
13044 Marine Avenue, St. Louis, MO 63146
Director, Office of Family and Community Services
Tom Fee . . . . (314) 615-2937
Director, Kathy J. Weinman Shelter **Leonard McDonald** . . (314) 615-4453
13044 Marine Avenue, St. Louis, MO 63146
County Veteran Programs Supervisor **Tom Fee** . . . . (314) 615-4453

Department of Justice Services

Buzz Westfall Justice Center, 100 South Central Avenue, 3rd Floor, Clayton, MO 63105-1719
Tel: (314) 615-5752 Fax: (314) 615-4329
Internet: www.stlouisco.com/justiceservices

▷ Director **Herbert Bernsen** . . . . (314) 615-4763
E-mail: hbernsen@stlouisco.com

Parks and Recreation Department

41 S. Central Ave., Clayton, MO 63105-1719
Tel: (314) 615-7275 Fax: (314) 615-4696

▷ Director **Gary Bess** . . . . (314) 615-5454
E-mail: gbess@stlouisco.com

Department of Planning

41 S. Central Ave., Clayton, MO 63105-1719
Tel: (314) 615-2520 Fax: (314) 615-3729 TTY: (314) 615-5467

▷ Director **Glenn Powers** . . . . (314) 615-2515
E-mail: gpowers@stlouisco.com

Community Development Division

41 South Central Avenue, Fifth Floor, Clayton, MO 63105
Fax: (314) 615-8674 TTY: (314) 615-5467

Director **Jim Holtzman** . . . . (314) 615-4414
E-mail: jholtzman@stlouisco.com

Police Department

7900 Forsyth Boulevard, Clayton, MO 63105-1719
Tel: (314) 889-2341

Police Chief **Jon Belmar** . . . . (314) 615-4260

Department of Revenue

41 South Central Avenue, Clayton, MO 63105-1719
Tel: (314) 615-7179 Fax: (314) 628-7121

▷ Director **Gregg Quinn** (R) . . . . (314) 615-7179
E-mail: gquinn@stlouisco.com

Office of the Recorder of Deeds

41 South Central Avenue, 4th Floor, Clayton, MO 63105
Tel: (314) 615-7100 E-mail: recorder@stlouisco.com

Recorder of Deeds **Gerald Smith** . . . . (314) 615-7189

COUNTIES

★ Elected Official ▲ Appointed by Legislature ▼ Appointed by Governor ▶ Appointed by Board or Commission ● Appointed by Judge
■ Appointed by Mayor △ Appointed by Freeholders ▽ Appointed by Supervisor ▷ Appointed by County Executive ○ Appointed by Council

Office of the Tax Collector
41 South Central Avenue, Clayton, MO 63105
Tel: (314) 615-5500 E-mail: collector@stlouisco.com

Tax Collector **Mark Devore** .... (314) 615-7192

Housing Authority of St. Louis County
8865 Natural Bridge, St. Louis, MO 63121
Fax: (314) 427-2937 Internet: www.haslc.com

▷ Executive Director **Susan C.J. Rollins** .... (314) 227-3114
E-mail: srollins@haslc.com

St. Louis Economic Development Partnership [SLCEC]
121 South Meramec Avenue, Suite 900, St. Louis, MO 63105-1719
Tel: (314) 615-7663 Tel: (314) 615-7666 E-mail: info@slcec.com
Internet: www.slcec.com

▷ Chief Executive Officer **Sheila Sweeney** .... (314) 615-7663
▷ President **Rodney Crim** .... (314) 615-7663
Executive Vice President **(Vacant)** .... (314) 615-3962

St. Louis County Library District [SLCL]
1640 South Lindbergh Boulevard, St. Louis, MO 63131-3598
Tel: (314) 994-3300 Internet: www.slcl.org

Administration
Library Director **Kristen Sorth** .... (314) 994-3300
E-mail: ksorth@slcl.org

Office of Community Empowerment
41 South Central Avenue, Fifth Floor, Clayton, MO 63105
Tel: (314) 615-7016

Director (Interim) **Ethel Byndom** .... (314) 615-7016

Office of Strategy and Innovation
41 South Central Avenue, Fifth Floor, Clayton, MO 63105
Tel: (314) 615-5186

Director of Strategy and Innovation **Lori Fiegel** .... (314) 615-5186

Office of the County Council
41 South Central Avenue, Clayton, MO 63105
Tel: (314) 615-5432 Fax: (314) 615-7890

★ Chairman **Michael "Mike" O'Mara** (D-District 4) .... (314) 615-5439
Term Expires: December 31, 2016
E-mail: mo'mara@stlouisco.com
Education: Saint Louis U 1983 BA

★ Vice Chair **Sam Page** (D-District 2) .... (314) 615-5437
Term Expires: December 31, 2016
E-mail: spage@stlouisco.com
Education: Missouri (Kansas City) BA, 1992 MD

★ Council Member **Hazel Erby** (D-District 1) .... (314) 615-5436
Term Expires: December 31, 2018
E-mail: herby@stlouisco.com

★ Council Member **Colleen Wasinger** (R-District 3) .... (314) 615-5438
Term Expires: December 31, 2018
E-mail: cwasinger@stlouisco.com

★ Council Member **Pat Dolan** (D-District 5) .... (314) 615-5441
Term Expires: December 31, 2018
E-mail: pdolan@stlouisco.com

★ Council Member **Kevin O'Leary** (D-District 6) .... (314) 615-0159
Term Expires: December 31, 2016

★ Council Member **Mark Harder** (R-District 7) .... (314) 615-5443
Term Expires: December 31, 2018
E-mail: mharder@stlouisco.com

Office of the County Auditor
Lawrence K. Roos County Government Center, 41 South Central Avenue, Clayton, MO 63105
Tel: (314) 615-5491 Fax: (314) 615-7890
Internet: www.stlouisco.com/auditor

○ County Auditor **David Makarewicz** .... (314) 615-5491
E-mail: dmakarewicz@stlouisco.com

Office of the County Clerk
Lawrence K. Roos County Government Center, 41 South Central Avenue, Clayton, MO 63105
Fax: (314) 615-7890 Internet: www.stlouisco.com/countyclerk

○ County Clerk/Council Administrative Director
Genevieve M. Frank .... (314) 615-5440
E-mail: gfrank@stlouisco.com

Chief Deputy County Clerk **Jeanette O. Hook** .... (314) 615-7171
E-mail: jhook@stlouisco.com

Office of the Assessor
41 South Central Avenue, Third Floor, Clayton, MO 63105
Tel: (314) 615-2555 Fax: (314) 615-8033
E-mail: assessor@stlouisco.com

★ Assessor **Jake Zimmerman** (D) .... (314) 615-5124
Term Expires: December 31, 2018
E-mail: assessor@stlouisco.com
Date of Birth: July 5, 1974
Education: Claremont McKenna 1996; Harvard 2000 JD

Deputy Assessor/Director of External Affairs
Crystal Ulett .... (314) 615-2573

Office of the Prosecuting Attorney
100 South Central Avenue, 2nd Floor, Clayton, MO 63105-1719
Tel: (314) 615-2600 Fax: (314) 615-2611 E-mail: pa@stlouisco.com
Internet: www.stlouiscopa.com

★ Prosecuting Attorney **Robert P. "Bob" McCulloch** (D) .... (314) 615-2600
Term Expires: December 31, 2018
E-mail: bmcculloch@stlouisco.com

First Assistant Prosecuting Attorney **John D. Evans** .... (314) 615-2600

St. Louis County Board of Elections
12 Sunnen Drive, St. Louis, MO 63143
Tel: (314) 615-1800 Tel: (314) 615-1999
Internet: www.stlouisco.com/elections

Director of Elections (Democratic) **Eric Fey** .... (314) 615-1851
Director of Elections (Republican) **Gary Fuhr** (R) .... (314) 615-1854

County of Salt Lake, Utah
Salt Lake County Government Center, 2001 South State Street, Salt Lake City, UT 84190

County Seat: Salt Lake City **Election Type:** Partisan
Population: 1,107,314 (2015)

Office of the Mayor
Salt Lake County Government Center, 2001 State Street, Suite N2100, Salt Lake City, UT 84190-1000
Fax: (385) 468-7001 Internet: www.mayor.slco.org

★ Mayor **Benjamin M. "Ben" McAdams** (D) .... (385) 468-7000
Term Expires: December 31, 2016
E-mail: mayor@slco.org
Education: Utah BA; Columbia 2003 JD

★ Elected Official ▲ Appointed by Legislature ▼ Appointed by Governor ▶ Appointed by Board or Commission ● Appointed by Judge
■ Appointed by Mayor △ Appointed by Freeholders ▽ Appointed by Supervisor ▷ Appointed by County Executive ○ Appointed by Council

Office of the Mayor *continued*

Executive Assistant **Stephanie Withers** . . . . (385) 468-7025
E-mail: swithers@slco.org
Deputy Mayor and Chief Administrative Officer
Lori G. Bays . . . . (385) 468-7005
E-mail: lbays@slco.org
Director of Communications **Alyson Heyrend** . . . . (385) 468-7027
Education: Utah BA
Government Relations Director **Patrick Reimherr** . . . . (385) 468-7028
E-mail: preimherr@slco.org
Diversity Affairs Director **Rebecca Sanchez** . . . . (385) 468-7014

Administrative Services Department

2001 South State Street, N4300, Salt Lake City, UT 84190-3100

Director **Sarah Brenna** . . . . (385) 468-7065
E-mail: SBrenna@slco.org
Associate Director **Megan Hillyard** . . . . (385) 468-7062
Administrative Coordinator **Ina Landry** . . . . (385) 468-7060
E-mail: ilandry@slco.org

Contracts and Procurement Division

Salt Lake County Government Center, 2001 South State Street, Suite N4500, Salt Lake City, UT 84190-3100
Fax: (385) 468-2476

Director **Jason E. Yocom** . . . . (385) 468-0304
E-mail: jyocom@slco.org
Education: Westminster (UT) 2004 MA

Facilities Services Division

Salt Lake County Government Center, 2001 South State Street, S3100, Salt Lake City, UT 84190-3300
Fax: (385) 468-3466

Director **Wayne Marion** . . . . (385) 468-0330
E-mail: wmarion@slco.org

Fleet Management Division

7125 South 600 West, Midvale, UT 84047
Tel: (385) 562-6411 Fax: (385) 562-6432 Internet: www.fleet.slco.org

Director **John Webster** . . . . (385) 562-6411

Human Resources Division

Salt Lake County Government Center, 2001 South State Street, Suite N4600, Salt Lake City, UT 84190-3150
Tel: (385) 468-0570 Tel: (385) 468-0580 (Benefits)
Tel: (385) 468-0570 (Employment Verification)
Tel: (385) 468-0560 (Payroll) Fax: (385) 468-2172 E-mail: jobs@slco.org

Director **Michael Ongkiko** . . . . (385) 465-0575
E-mail: mongkiko@slco.org
Education: Cincinnati BA, MLER
Associate Division Director **(Vacant)** . . . . (385) 468-0577
Benefits Manager **Michelle James** . . . . (385) 468-0593
Compensation, Classification, and Recruitment Manager
Kristin Jensen . . . . (385) 468-0554
Equal Employment Opportunity Manager **Nilsa Carter** . . . (385) 468-0585
Americans with Disabilities Act Coordinator
Alison Smith . . . . (385) 468-0583
E-mail: ALSmith@slco.org

Information Services Division

Salt Lake County Government Center, 2001 South State Street, Suite NL300, Salt Lake City, UT 84190-3050
Fax: (385) 468-2976

Director **Michael "Mike" Bailey** . . . . (385) 468-0700
E-mail: mbailey@slco.org
Chief Information Officer **Beth Overhuls** . . . . (385) 468-0700

Addressing Division

2001 South State Street, Suite N1400, Salt Lake City, UT 84190-1100
Internet: www.pw.slco.org/addressing

Property Addressing Manager **Teresa Curtis** . . . . (385) 468-6760
E-mail: tcurtis@slco.org

Records Management and Archives Division

4505 South 5600 West, West Valley, UT 84120
Fax: (385) 468-0819

Director (Interim) **Darrell Passey** . . . . (385) 468-0822

Community Services Department

Salt Lake County Government Center, 2001 South State Street, Suite N4300, Salt Lake City, UT 84190-3000
Tel: (385) 468-7060 Fax: (385) 468-3712

▶ Director **Erin Litvack** . . . . (385) 468-7060
E-mail: elitvack@slco.org
Associate Director **Holly Yocom** . . . . (385) 468-7052
E-mail: HYocom@slco.org
Office Coordinator **Michelle Roach** . . . . (385) 468-7060

Clark Planetarium

110 South 400 West, Salt Lake City, UT 84101-1145
Fax: (385) 456-4928 Internet: www.clarkplanetarium.org

Director **Seth Jarvis** . . . . (385) 456-4921

Discovery Gateway

444 West 100 South, Salt Lake City, UT 84101
Fax: (385) 456-5440 E-mail: info@discoverygateway.org

Executive Director **Maria S. Farrington** . . . . (385) 456-5437

Parks and Recreation

Salt Lake County Government Center, 2001 South State Street, Suite S4700, Salt Lake City, UT 84190-2300
Tel: (385) 468-1800 Fax: (385) 468-1798
Internet: www.recreation.slco.org

Director **Martin Jensen** . . . . (385) 468-1800

Salt Lake County Center for the Arts

Capitol Theatre, 50 West 200 South, Salt Lake City, UT 84101
Fax: (385) 538-2272

Director **Philip "Phil" Jordan** . . . . (385) 323-6800

Salt Palace Convention Center

100 South West Temple, Salt Lake City, UT 84101
Fax: (385) 534-6383

General Manager **Allyson Jackson** . . . . (385) 534-6325

Visit Salt Lake

90 South West Temple, Salt Lake City, UT 84101
Tel: (801) 534-4900

President and Chief Executive Officer **Scott Beck** . . . . (801) 534-4911

Zoo, Arts and Parks Program [ZAP]

2001 South State Street, Suite N4100, Salt Lake City, UT 84190

Program Manager **Victoria P. "Vicki" Bourns** . . . . (801) 468-3517

Human Services Department

Salt Lake County Government Center, 2001 South State Street, Suite N4300, Salt Lake City, UT 84190-2000
Internet: www.humanservices.slco.org

▶ Director **Karen Crompton** . . . . (385) 468-7060
E-mail: kcrompton@slco.org
Associate Director **Robin Chalhoub** . . . . (385) 468-7064

Aging and Adult Services

Salt Lake County Government Center, 2001 S. State St., Ste. S1500, Salt Lake City, UT 84190-2300
E-mail: slcoagingservices@slco.org

Director **Becky Capp** . . . . (385) 468-3200

★ Elected Official ▲ Appointed by Legislature ▼ Appointed by Governor ▶ Appointed by Board or Commission ● Appointed by Judge
■ Appointed by Mayor △ Appointed by Freeholders ▽ Appointed by Supervisor ▷ Appointed by County Executive ○ Appointed by Council

Community Resources and Development
Salt Lake County Government Center, 2001 South State Street, Suite S2100, Salt Lake City, UT 84190-2710
Fax: (385) 468-4881

Director **Michael R. Gallegos** . . . . (385) 468-4880
E-mail: mgallegos@slco.org

Criminal Justice Services
145 East 1300 South, Suite 501, Salt Lake City, UT 84115
Fax: (385) 468-3441

Director (Acting) **Kele Griffone** . . . . (385) 468-3500

Library Services
Whitmore Library, 2197 E. Fort Union Blvd., Salt Lake City, UT 84121
Fax: (385) 944-7572 Internet: www.slcolibrary.org

Director **James Cooper** . . . . (385) 944-7504
E-mail: jimcooper@slco.lib.ut.us Fax: (385) 942-6323

Salt Lake County Health Department [SLCoHD]
Salt Lake County Government Center, 2001 South State Street, Suite S-600, Salt Lake City, UT 84190-2150
Tel: (385) 468-4100 Fax: (385) 468-4106

Director **Gary Edwards** . . . . (385) 468-4117
Administrative Services Director **Dorothy Adams** . . . . (385) 468-4118
E-mail: dgadams@slco.org
Community Health Director **Beverly Hyatt** . . . . (385) 468-4061
Family Health Services Director **Audrey Stevenson** . . . . (385) 468-4084
Environmental Health Director **Royal DeLegge** . . . . (385) 468-3860
788 East Wood Oak Lane, Murray, UT 84107-6379
Medical Officer **Dr. Dagmar Vitek** . . . . (385) 468-4146

Substance Abuse Services
Salt Lake County Government Center, 2001 South State Street, Suite S2300, Salt Lake City, UT 84190-2250

Director **Tim Whalen** . . . . (385) 468-4727

Valley Behavioral Health
5965 S. 900 East, Salt Lake City, UT 84121
Internet: www.vmh.com

President and Chief Executive Officer **Gary Larcenaire** . . . (888) 949-4864

Youth Services Division
177 W. Price Ave., Salt Lake City, UT 84115-4345
Fax: (385) 468-4498 Internet: www.youth.slco.org

Director **Pat Berckman** . . . . (385) 468-4500
Associate Director **Roger D. Gisseman** . . . . (385) 468-4500
Youth Services Shelter Care Program Manager
Cara Stephens . . . . (801) 269-7500

Public Works Department

Salt Lake County Government Center, 2001 South State Street, Suite N3-200, Salt Lake City, UT 84190-4000
Internet: www.pw.slco.org

Director **Russ Wall** . . . . (385) 468-7055

Animal Services Division
511 W. 3900 S., Salt Lake City, UT 84123
Tel: (385) 468-7387 Fax: (385) 468-6028 E-mail: animal@slco.org
Internet: www.animalservices.slco.org

Director **(Vacant)** . . . . (385) 468-7387

Engineering and Flood Control Division
Salt Lake County Government Center, 2001 South State Street, Suite N3 120, Salt Lake City, UT 84190-4600
Tel: (385) 468-6600 Fax: (385) 468-6603 Internet: www.pweng.slco.org

Director **Scott Baird** . . . . (385) 468-6600
E-mail: sbaird@slco.org

Operations Division
7125 S. 600 West, Midvale, UT 84047
Tel: (385) 468-6101 E-mail: pwops-online@slco.org
Internet: www.pwops.slco.org

Director **Kevyn Smeltzer** . . . . (385) 468-6101
E-mail: ksmeltzer@slco.org

Sanitation Division and Solid Waste
604 West 6960 South, Midvale, UT 84047
Tel: (385) 468-6325 Fax: (385) 468-6330
Internet: www.sanitation.slco.org

Director **Yianni Ioannou** . . . . (385) 468-6325

Planning and Development Services Division
Salt Lake County Government Center, 2001 South State Street, Suite N3600, Salt Lake City, UT 84190-4050
Tel: (385) 468-6700 Fax: (385) 468-6674 Internet: www.pwpds.slco.org

Director **Rolen Yoshinaga** . . . . (385) 468-6675
E-mail: ryoshinaga@slco.org

Unified Fire Authority [UFA]

3380 South 900 West, Salt Lake City, UT 84119
Tel: (801) 743-7200 Fax: (801) 734-7211 Internet: www.unifiedfire.org

Fire Chief **Michael H. Jensen** (R) . . . . (801) 743-7200
E-mail: mjensen@ufa-slco.org
Education: Utah BS
Deputy Chief **Gaylord A. Scott** . . . . (801) 743-7200
E-mail: gscott@ufa-slco.org

Financial Administration

2001 South State Street, N4100, Salt Lake City, UT 84190-4575
Tel: (385) 468-7070 Fax: (385) 468-7071

Chief Financial Officer **Darrin Casper** . . . . (385) 468-7075
Fiscal Administrator **Greg Folta** . . . . (385) 468-7076
Accounting Director **(Vacant)** . . . . (385) 468-7118
Accounts Payable Administrator **Ryan Noyce** . . . . (385) 468-7107
E-mail: RNoyce@slco.org
Budget Administrator **Rodney Kitchens** . . . . (385) 468-7084
E-mail: rkitchens@slco.org
Capital Assets Administrator **LeAnne Sarver** . . . . (385) 468-7113
Payroll Administrator **JoAnn Buechler** . . . . (385) 468-7087
Web Administrator **Dirk Peterson** . . . . (385) 468-7081
E-mail: KDPeterson@slco.org

Office of the County Council

Salt Lake County Government Center, 2001 South State Street, Suite N2-200, Salt Lake City, UT 84190-1000
Tel: (385) 468-7500 Fax: (385) 468-7501 Internet: http://council.slco.org/

★ Chair **Max Burdick** (R-District 6) . . . . (385) 468-7459
Term Expires: December 31, 2018
E-mail: mburdick@slco.org
★ Council Member **Arlyn Bradshaw** (D-District 1) . . . . (385) 468-7454
Term Expires: December 31, 2018
E-mail: arbradshaw@slco.org
Education: Utah 2004 BA, 2010 MPA
★ Council Member **Michael H. Jensen** (R-District 2) . . . . . . (385) 468-7455
Term Expires: December 31, 2018
E-mail: mjensen@slco.org
Education: Utah BS
★ Council Member **Aimee Winder Newton** (District 3) . . . . (385) 468-7456
Term Expires: December 31, 2018
★ Council Member
Samuel Frank "Sam" Granato (D-District 4) . . . . (385) 468-7457
Term Expires: December 31, 2016
E-mail: sgranato@slco.org
★ Council Member **Steve DeBry** (R-District 5) . . . . (385) 468-7458
Term Expires: December 31, 2018
E-mail: sdebry@slco.org

★ Elected Official ▲ Appointed by Legislature ▼ Appointed by Governor ▶ Appointed by Board or Commission ● Appointed by Judge
■ Appointed by Mayor △ Appointed by Freeholders ▽ Appointed by Supervisor ▷ Appointed by County Executive ○ Appointed by Council

Office of the County Council *continued*

★Council Member
Jenny Wilson (D-At-Large, Position A) . . . . (385) 468-7451
Term Expires: December 31, 2020
Education: Utah 1988; Harvard 1998 MPA

★Council Member
Richard Snelgrove (R-At-Large, Position B) . . . . (385) 468-7452
Term Expires: December 31, 2016
E-mail: rsnelgrove@slco.org

★Council Member **Jim Bradley** (D-At-Large, Position C) . . (385) 468-7453
Term Expires: December 31, 2016
E-mail: jbradley@slco.org

Council Clerk **Gayelene Gudmundson** . . . . (385) 468-7360
E-mail: ggudmundson@slco.org

Office of the Assessor

Salt Lake County Government Center, 2001 South State Street, Suite N2300, Salt Lake City, UT 84190-1300
Internet: www.assessor.slco.org

★Assessor **Kevin Jacobs** . . . . (385) 468-7972
Term Expires: December 31, 2020
E-mail: kjacobs@slco.org
Administrative Assistant **Rebecca Adams** . . . . (385) 468-7972

Chief Deputy Assessor **Richard Burgi** . . . . (385) 468-8010
E-mail: rburgi@slco.org

Office of the Auditor

Salt Lake County Government Center, 2001 South State Street, Suite N3300, Salt Lake City, UT 84190-1100
Fax: (385) 468-7201 Internet: www.auditor.slco.org

★Auditor **Scott Tingley** . . . . (385) 468-7185
Term Expires: December 31, 2018

Chief Deputy **Lonn Litchfield** . . . . (385) 468-7186

Senior Advisor **Michael P. "Mike" Chabries** . . . . (385) 468-7187

Executive Assistant **Michael Anderson** . . . . (385) 468-7177
E-mail: mcanderson@slco.org

Director, Audit Division **Roger K. Larsen** . . . . (385) 468-7172

Director, Property Tax Compliance Division
Jodi Ann Martin . . . . (385) 468-7234
E-mail: jmartin@slco.org

Administrative and Fiscal Manager **Brad A. Rogers** . . . . . (385) 468-7188
E-mail: barogers@slco.org

Office of the County Clerk

Salt Lake County Government Center, 2001 South State Street, Suite S2200, Salt Lake City, UT 84190-1050
Tel: (385) 468-7399 Fax: (385) 468-7397 Internet: www.clerk.slco.org

★County Clerk **Sherrie Swensen** (D) . . . . (385) 468-7370
Term Expires: December 31, 2018
E-mail: sswensen@slco.org

Chief Deputy **Dahnelle Burton-Lee** . . . . (385) 468-7371
E-mail: dburton-lee@slco.org

Office of the District Attorney

Salt Lake County Government Center, 2001 South State Street, Suite S3500, Salt Lake City, UT 84190-1202
Tel: (385) 468-7600 Fax: (385) 468-2985
E-mail: districtattorney@slco.org Internet: www.districtattorney.slco.org

★District Attorney **Simarjit "Sim" Gill** (D) . . . . (385) 468-7600
Term Expires: December 31, 2018
E-mail: sgill@slco.org
Education: Utah BA; Lewis & Clark JD

Chief Deputy, Civil Division **Ralph Chamness** . . . . (385) 468-7600

Chief Deputy, Justice Division **Jeffrey W. "Jeff" Hall** . . . . (385) 468-7700

Chief Deputy, Justice Division **Blake A. Nakamura** . . . . . (385) 468-7700

Office of the Recorder

Salt Lake County Government Center, 2001 South State Street, Suite N1-600, Salt Lake City, UT 84190-1150
Fax: (385) 468-8170 E-mail: recorder@slco.org

★Recorder **Gary W. Ott** (R) . . . . (385) 468-8145
Term Expires: December 31, 2020
E-mail: gott@slco.org

Chief Deputy Recorder **Julie Dole** . . . . (385) 468-8147

Office of the Sheriff

Salt Lake County Government Center, 2001 South State Street, Suite S2700, Salt Lake City, UT 84190-1423
Fax: (385) 468-9760 Internet: www.slsheriff.org

★Sheriff **James M. "Jim" Winder** (D) . . . . (385) 468-9901
Term Expires: December 31, 2018

Undersheriff **Scott Carver** . . . . (385) 468-9901
E-mail: scarver@slco.org

Office of the Surveyor

P.O. Box 144575, Salt Lake City, UT 84114-4575
Fax: (385) 468-8258

★Surveyor **Reid J. Demman** (R) . . . . (385) 468-8240
Term Expires: December 31, 2020
E-mail: rdemman@slco.org

Chief Deputy **Phil G. Lanouette** . . . . (385) 468-8240

Office Operations Manager **Steve V. Keisel** . . . . (385) 468-8251
E-mail: skeisel@slco.org

Field Operations Manager **Byron M. Goff** . . . . (385) 468-8248
E-mail: bgoff@slco.org

Office of the Treasurer

Salt Lake County Government Center, 2001 South State Street, Suite N1-200, Salt Lake City, UT 84190-1250
P.O. Box 144575, Salt Lake City, UT 84114-4575
Fax: (385) 468-8298 Internet: www.treasurer.slco.org

★Treasurer **K. Wayne Cushing** . . . . (385) 468-8304
Term Expires: January 6, 2020
E-mail: slcotreasurer@slco.org

Deputy Treasurer **Randel L. Wightman** . . . . (385) 468-8304

County of San Bernardino, California

County Government Center, 385 North Arrowhead Avenue, San Bernardino, CA 92415-0130
Tel: (909) 387-2020 (Information) Internet: www.sbcounty.gov

County Seat: San Bernardino **Election Type:** Nonpartisan
Population: 2,128,133 (2015)

Office of the Board of Supervisors

County Government Center, 385 N. Arrowhead Ave., San Bernardino, CA 92415-0110

★Chair **James C. Ramos** (District 3) . . . . (909) 387-4855
Term Expires: December 5, 2016 Fax: (909) 387-3018
E-mail: supervisorramos@sbcounty.gov
Chief of Staff **Phil Paule** . . . . (909) 387-4855

★Vice Chair **Robert A. Lovingood** (District 1) . . . . (909) 387-4830
Term Expires: December 5, 2016 Fax: (909) 995-8105
E-mail: supervisorlovingood@sbcounty.gov

(continued on next page)

★Elected Official ▲Appointed by Legislature ▼Appointed by Governor ►Appointed by Board or Commission ●Appointed by Judge
■Appointed by Mayor △Appointed by Freeholders ▽Appointed by Supervisor ▷Appointed by County Executive ○Appointed by Council

Office of the Board of Supervisors *continued*

★ Supervisor **Janice Rutherford** (District 2) .... (909) 387-4833
Term Expires: December 1, 2016
E-mail: supervisorrutherford@sbcounty.gov
Education: UC Riverside BA; Claremont Grad 1993 MA

★ Supervisor **Curt Hagman** (District 4) .... (909) 387-4866
Term Expires: December 1, 2018 Fax: (909) 387-9090
Education: UCLA BA
Chief of Staff **Mike Spence** .... (909) 387-4866

★ Supervisor **Josie Gonzales** (District 5) .... (909) 387-4565
Term Expires: December 5, 2016 Fax: (909) 387-5392
E-mail: supervisorgonzales@sbcounty.gov
Chief of Staff **Daniel Flores** .... (909) 387-4565

▽ Clerk of the Board **Laura H. Welch** .... (909) 387-3848
E-mail: cob@sbcounty.gov Fax: (909) 387-4554

COUNTIES

Office of the County Administrative Officer

County Government Center, 385 North Arrowhead Avenue, 5th Floor, San Bernardino, CA 92415-0120
Fax: (909) 387-5430

▽ County Executive Officer
Gregory C. "Greg" Devereaux .... (909) 387-5417
E-mail: gdevereaux@cao.sbcounty.gov
Date of Birth: July 5, 1951
Education: West Virginia 1973 BFA, 1977 JD

Deputy Executive Officer **Dena M. Smith** .... (909) 387-5418
Public Information Officer **David Wert** .... (909) 387-4717

Office of the Public Defender

172 West Third Street, Second Floor, San Bernardino, CA 92415-0008
Fax: (909) 382-3965 Internet: www.sbcounty.gov/publicdefender

Public Defender **Phyllis K. Morris** .... (909) 382-3950

Arrowhead Regional Medical Center [ARMC]

400 North Pepper Avenue, Colton, CA 92324-1819
Tel: (909) 580-1000 Fax: (909) 580-6196
E-mail: info@armc.sbcounty.gov Internet: www.arrowheadmedcenter.org

Director and Chief Executive Officer **William L. Gilbert** .. (909) 580-6150
Chief Financial Officer **Frank Arambula** .... (909) 580-6170
Medical Director **Dr. Richard T. Pitts** .... (909) 580-6170
Associate Medical Director, Ambulatory and Medical Services **Dr. David Lanum** .... (909) 580-6240
Associate Medical Director, Ancillary Services
Dr. Mark Comunale .... (909) 580-2440
Associate Medical Director, Surgical Services
Dr. Guillermo Valenzuela .... (909) 580-3470
Associate Administrator, Ambulatory Services
Johnson Gill .... (909) 580-6145
Associate Administrator, Professional Services
Deborah "Debbie" Pease .... (909) 580-3170
E-mail: peased@armc.sbcounty.gov
Education Director **Erin McMeans** .... (909) 580-1200
Business Development and Marketing Director **(Vacant)** .. (909) 580-3290
Human Resources Director **Tim Rhyne** .... (909) 580-1320
E-mail: trhyne@hr.sbcounty.gov
Hospital Compliance and Ethics Officer
Deborah "Debbie" Pease .... (909) 580-3170
Material Management Manager **Terri Martinez** .... (909) 580-0070
E-mail: martinezte@armc.sbcounty.gov
Building Maintenance and Security Manager
Mick Zader .... (909) 580-0085
Chief Nursing Officer **Michelle Sayre** .... (909) 580-6180
Associate Hospital Administrator **Rhoda Vincent** .... (909) 580-3210

Economic Development Agency

215 North D Street, Suite 202, San Bernardino, CA 92415
Tel: (909) 387-4700 Fax: (909) 387-9815
Internet: www.sbcountyadvantage.com

Administrator **Larry Vaupel** .... (909) 387-9802
E-mail: lvaupel@eda.sbcounty.gov
Education: Liberty 1993 BS; Northern Illinois 1999 MPA
Assistant Administrator **Patricia M. Cole** .... (909) 387-4700
385 North Arrowhead Avenue, Fax: (909) 387-4415
3rd Floor, San Bernardino, CA 92415-0130
E-mail: pcole@sbcounty.gov

Department of Community Development and Housing

290 North D. Street, Suite 600, San Bernardino, CA 92415
Tel: (909) 388-0800 Fax: (909) 388-0858

Director **Dena Fuentes** .... (909) 387-4700

Human Resources Department

157 West Fifth Street, 1st Floor, San Bernardino, CA 92415-0440
Tel: (909) 387-8304 Fax: (909) 387-6075
Internet: www.co.san-bernardino.ca.us/hr

Director (Interim) **Dena M. Smith** .... (909) 387-5570
Chief, Employee Benefits and Services Division
Lori Goldman .... (909) 387-5787
Chief, Employment Division **Mark Deboer** .... (909) 387-8304
E-mail: mdeboer@hr.sbcounty.gov
Chief, Employee Relations Division **Victor Tordefillas** ... (909) 387-5564
E-mail: vtordefillas@hr.sbcounty.gov
Equal Opportunity Officer **Yvonne Johnson** .... (909) 387-5584
Deputy Director **Victor Tordefillas** .... (909) 387-8304
E-mail: vtordefillas@hr.sbcounty.gov

Human Services Administration

385 North Arrowhead Avenue, Fifth Floor,
San Bernardino, CA 92415-0182
Tel: (909) 387-4717 Fax: (909) 387-5430
Internet: http://hss.sbcounty.gov/

Assistant Executive Officer **Linda Haugan** .... (909) 387-4717
Executive Secretary **Nancy Hubbard** .... (909) 387-4717
E-mail: nhubbard@cao.sbcounty.gov
Deputy Executive Officer **Art Gomez** .... (909) 388-0252

Department of Aging and Adult Services [DAAS]

686 East Mill Street, San Bernardino, CA 92415-0640
Tel: (909) 891-3900 Fax: (909) 891-3940
Internet: http://hss.sbcounty.gov/daas

Director **Ron Buttram** .... (909) 891-3917

Department of Behavioral Health [DBH]

303 East Vanderbilt Way, San Bernardino, CA 92415-0026
Tel: (888) 743-1478 Fax: (909) 890-0435
Internet: www.sbcounty.gov/dbh

Director **CaSonya Thomas** .... (909) 388-0820
Executive Secretary **Debi Pasco** .... (909) 388-0820
E-mail: dpasco@dbh.sbcounty.gov
Assistant Director **Veronica Kelley** .... (909) 388-0814
Medical Director **Dr. Teresa Frausto** .... (909) 388-0810
Deputy Director of Administrative Services
Tanya Bratton .... (909) 388-0819
E-mail: tbratton@dbh.sbcounty.gov
Deputy Director of 24-Hour and Emergency Services
Sharon Nevins .... (909) 388-0815
Deputy Director of Regional Operations **Andy Gruchy** ... (909) 388-0817
Deputy Director of Children's and Recovery Support Services **Michael Schertell** .... (909) 388-0817
Deputy Director of Program Support Services
Sarah Eberhardt-Rios .... (909) 382-3037

★ Elected Official ▲ Appointed by Legislature ▼ Appointed by Governor ► Appointed by Board or Commission ● Appointed by Judge
■ Appointed by Mayor △ Appointed by Freeholders ▽ Appointed by Supervisor ▷ Appointed by County Executive ○ Appointed by Council

Department of Child Support Services [DCSS]
10417 Mountain View Avenue, Loma Linda, CA 92354-2030
Fax: (909) 478-7475 Internet: http://hss.sbcounty.gov/dcss

Director **Connie Brunn** .... (909) 478-7471
E-mail: cbrunn@hss.sbcounty.gov
Assistant Director **Victor Rea** .... (909) 478-6994

Children's Network of San Bernardino County
825 Hospitality Lane, Second Floor, San Bernardino, CA 92415-0049
Tel: (909) 383-9657 Fax: (909) 383-9688
Internet: http://hss.sbcounty.gov/childnet

Network Officer **Kathy Turnbull** .... (909) 383-9657

Children and Family Services Department [CFS]
150 South Lena Road, San Bernardino, CA 92415-0515
Fax: (909) 388-0233 Internet: http://hss.co.san-bernardino.ca.us/dcs

Director **Marlene Hagen** .... (909) 388-0242
Assistant Director **Jonathan Byers** .... (909) 387-2782

Preschool Services Department [PSD]
622 South Tippecanoe Avenue, San Bernardino, CA 92415-0630
Tel: (909) 383-2005 Fax: (909) 383-2080
Internet: http://hss.sbcounty.gov/psd

Director **Diana Alexander** .... (909) 383-2005

Department of Public Health [DPH]
351 North Mountain View Avenue, San Bernardino, CA 92415-0010
Tel: (800) 782-4264 Fax: (909) 387-6228
Internet: www.sbcounty.gov/dph

Public Health Director **Trudy Raymundo** .... (909) 387-9146
Assistant Director **Corwin Porter** .... (909) 387-9146
Health Officer **Maxwell Ohikhuare** .... (909) 387-6218

Transitional Assistance Department [TAD]
860 East Brier Drive, San Bernardino, CA 92415-0520
Fax: (909) 890-0515 Internet: http://hss.sbcounty.gov/hss/tad

Director **Nancy Swanson** .... (909) 388-0245
Assistant Director **Gilbert Ramos** .... (909) 388-0245

Department of Veterans' Affairs
175 West Fifth Street, 2nd Floor, San Bernardino, CA 92415-0470
Tel: (909) 387-5516 Fax: (909) 387-6090
Internet: http://hss.co.san-bernardino.ca.us/va

Director **Frank Guevara** .... (909) 387-5525

Probation Department
175 West Fifth Street, San Bernardino, CA 92415-0460
Tel: (909) 387-8310 Fax: (909) 387-5626
Internet: www.sbcounty.gov/probatn

Chief Probation Officer **Michelle Brown** .... (909) 387-5693

Public and Support Services Group

Office of the Registrar of Voters
777 E. Rialto Ave., San Bernardino, CA 92415-0770
Tel: (909) 387-8100 Fax: (909) 387-2022 Internet: www.sbcounty.gov/rov

Registrar **Michael J. "Mike" Scarpello** .... (909) 387-2100
Education: Nebraska (Omaha); Nebraska 1995 JD

Agriculture/Weights and Measures
777 E. Rialto Ave., San Bernardino, CA 92415-0720
Tel: (909) 387-2105 Fax: (909) 387-2449

Agricultural Commissioner/Sealer of Weights and Measures **Roberta Willhite** .... (909) 387-2115
Assistant Agricultural Commissioner/Sealer of Weights and Measures **Allen Lampman** .... (909) 387-2117
Cooperative Extension Director **Janet Hartin** .... (909) 387-2171
Cooperative Extension Director **Chris J. McDonald** .... (909) 387-2171

Facilities Management
200 South Lena Road, San Bernardino, CA 92415-0055
Tel: (909) 387-2227 Fax: (909) 387-3380

Director **Terry Thompson** .... (909) 387-2227

Fleet Management
210 North Lena Road, San Bernardino, CA 92415-0842
Tel: (909) 387-7881

Director **Roger G. Weaver** .... (909) 387-7870

Fire Department
157 West 5th Street, 2nd Floor, San Bernardino, CA 92415-0451
Tel: (909) 387-5974 Fax: (909) 387-5542 Internet: www.sbcfire.org

Fire Chief **Mark Hartwig** .... (909) 387-5948

Land Use Services Department
County Government Center, 385 North Arrowhead Avenue, 1st Floor, San Bernardino, CA 92415-0182
Tel: (760) 995-8140 (High Desert Region)
Tel: (909) 387-8311 (Valley Region) Fax: (909) 387-4288
Internet: www.sbcounty.gov/ehlus

Director **Tom Hudson** .... (909) 387-8311

Public Works Department
825 E. Third St., San Bernardino, CA 92415-0835
Tel: (909) 387-8104 Fax: (909) 387-7911

Director **Gerry Newcombe** .... (909) 387-7906

Regional Parks
777 East Rialto Avenue, San Bernardino, CA 92415-0763
Tel: (909) 387-2577 Fax: (909) 387-2052

Director (Interim) **Maureen Snelgrove** .... (909) 387-2757

Real Estate Services Department
385 North Arrowhead Avenue, 3rd Floor, San Bernardino, CA 92415
Tel: (909) 387-5252 Fax: (909) 387-5353

Director **Terry W. Thompson** .... (909) 387-5252
Education: UCLA BA

Project Management Division
385 North Arrowhead Avenue, 3rd Floor, San Bernardino, CA 94215-0184
Tel: (909) 387-5025 Fax: (909) 387-5050
E-mail: archeng@co.san-bernardino.ca.us

Director **Carl R. Alban** .... (909) 387-5000
E-mail: calban@ae.sbcounty.gov

San Bernardino County Library [SBCL]
777 E. Rialto Ave., San Bernardino, CA 92415-0720
Tel: (909) 387-2220 Fax: (909) 387-5724
Internet: www.sbcounty.gov/library

County Librarian **Leonard Hernandez** .... (909) 387-2220
E-mail: lhernandez@lib.sbcounty.gov

San Bernardino County Museum
2024 Orange Tree Lane, Redlands, CA 92374-4560
Tel: (909) 307-2669 E-mail: museum@sbcounty.gov
Internet: www.sbcounty.gov/museum

Director **Melissa Russo** .... (909) 798-8601

Purchasing Department
777 East Rialto Avenue, San Bernardino, CA 92415-0760
Tel: (909) 387-2060 Fax: (909) 387-2666
Internet: www.sbcounty.gov/purchasing

Director **Laurie Rozko** .... (909) 387-2074

★ Elected Official ▲ Appointed by Legislature ▼ Appointed by Governor ▶ Appointed by Board or Commission ● Appointed by Judge
■ Appointed by Mayor △ Appointed by Freeholders ▽ Appointed by Supervisor ▷ Appointed by County Executive ○ Appointed by Council

COUNTIES

Special Districts Department
157 W. Fifth St., San Bernardino, CA 92415-0450
Tel: (909) 387-5940 Fax: (909) 387-5542 E-mail: info@sdd.sbcounty.gov
Internet: www.specialdistricts.org

Director **Jeffrey O. Rigney** .... (909) 387-5967

Office of the County Counsel
County Government Center, 385 North Arrowhead Avenue, 4th Floor, San Bernardino, CA 92415-0140
Tel: (909) 387-5455 Fax: (909) 387-5462

▽County Counsel **Jean-Rene C. Basle** .... (909) 387-5455
E-mail: jbasle@cc.sbcounty.gov
Education: U Puget Sound; Seattle JD
Chief Assistant County Counsel
Michelle D. Blakemore .... (909) 387-5455

Civil Service Commission
175 W. Fifth St., 2nd Floor, San Bernardino, CA 92415-0410

▽Chairman **(Vacant)** .... (909) 387-5862

Local Agency Formation Commission [LAFCO]
215 North D Street, Suite 204, San Bernardino, CA 92415-0490
Fax: (909) 885-8170 E-mail: lafco@lafco.sbcounty.gov
Internet: www.sbclafco.org

Executive Officer **Kathleen Rollings-McDonald** .... (909) 388-0490
E-mail: kmcdonald@lafco.sbcounty.gov
Clerk **Rebecca Lowery** .... (909) 388-0484
E-mail: rlowery@lafco.sbcounty.gov
Administrative Assistant **Angela Schell** .... (909) 388-0483
E-mail: aschell@lafco.sbcounty.gov
Assistant Executive Officer **Samuel Martinez** .... (909) 388-0489
Project Manager **Michael Tuerpe** .... (909) 388-0488

Workforce Investment Board
215 North D Street, Suite 301, San Bernardino, CA 92415-0041

Director **Sandy Harmsen** .... (909) 387-9862
E-mail: sharmsen@wdd.sbcounty.gov

Office of the Assessor-Recorder-County Clerk
172 West Third Street, San Bernardino, CA 92415-0310
Tel: (909) 387-8306 Fax: (909) 387-6718
Internet: www.sbcounty.gov/assessor

★Assessor-Recorder-County Clerk **Bob Dutton** .... (909) 387-8306
Term Expires: January 2019
Assistant Assessor **Rhonda Pfeiffer** .... (909) 387-6730
Assistant Recorder **Joani Finwall** .... (909) 387-8306
Chief Appraiser **(Vacant)** .... (909) 387-6677
Chief of Assessment Services **(Vacant)** .... (909) 387-6730

Office of the Auditor-Controller/Treasurer/Tax Collector
222 West Hospitality Lane, San Bernardino, CA 92415-0018
Tel: (909) 387-8322 Tel: (866) 227-3880 (Toll Free)
Fax: (909) 386-8830 (Administration Fax) Internet: www.sbcounty.gov/atc

★Auditor-Controller/Treasurer/Tax Collector (Interim)
Oscar Valdez .... (909) 386-9000
Term Expires: January 7, 2019
E-mail: oscar.valdez@atc.sbcounty.gov
Assistant Auditor-Controller/Treasurer/Tax Collector
Matt Brown .... (909) 386-8818
Assistant Auditor-Controller/Treasurer/Tax Collector
Oscar Valdez .... (909) 386-8818
Chief Deputy Auditor **Denise Mejico** .... (909) 386-8821
Chief Deputy, Central Collections **Vanessa Doyle** .... (909) 387-5669
Chief Deputy Controller **Joon Cho** .... (909) 386-8973

Office of the Auditor-Controller/Treasurer/Tax Collector *continued*

Chief Deputy, Disbursements **Sonia Hermosillo** .... (909) 386-8856
E-mail: sonia.hermosillo@atc.sbcounty.gov
Chief Deputy, Information Technology **Jason Anderson** . . (909) 386-8714
E-mail: jason.anderson@atc.sbcounty.gov
Chief Deputy, Tax Collector **Diana Atkeson** .... (909) 387-6383
E-mail: diana.atkeson@atc.sbcounty.gov
Cash Manager/Investment Officer **John Johnson** .... (909) 387-6319

Office of the District Attorney
316 N. Mountain View Ave., San Bernardino, CA 92415-0004
Fax: (909) 382-7674

★District Attorney **Michael A. Ramos** .... (909) 382-3669
Term Expires: December 30, 2018
E-mail: da@sbcda.org
Education: UC Riverside 1980 BA; Citrus Belt 1988 JD

Criminal Division
316 N. Mt. View Ave., San Bernardino, CA 92415-0004

Assistant District Attorney **Gary Roth** .... (909) 387-8309
Administrative and Special Unit Division Assistant
District Attorney **Michael Fermin** .... (909) 387-8309

Office of the Sheriff/Coroner
655 E. Third St., San Bernardino, CA 92415-0061
Fax: (909) 387-3402 Internet: www.sbcounty.gov/sheriff
E-mail: paffairs@sbcsd.org

★Sheriff/Coroner **John McMahon** .... (909) 387-3400
Term Expires: January 4, 2019
E-mail: jmcmahon@sbcsd.org
Undersheriff **Joe Cusimano** .... (909) 387-3671
E-mail: jcusimano@sbcsd.org
Public Information **Lt. Brad Toms** .... (909) 387-3700
E-mail: ltoms@sbcsd.org
Security **Rob McCoy** .... (909) 387-3010
E-mail: rmccoy@sbcsd.org Fax: (909) 387-0617
Training **Capt. Darren Goodman** .... (909) 473-2604
E-mail: dgoodman@sbcsd.org Fax: (909) 473-2568
Technical Support **Mark Vandermeiden** .... (909) 387-0328
E-mail: mvandermeiden@sbcsd.org Fax: (909) 387-3666

San Bernardino County Employees' Retirement Association [SBCERA]
348 West Hospitality Lane, 3rd Floor, San Bernardino, CA 92408
Tel: (909) 885-7980 Fax: (909) 885-7446

Chief Executive Officer **Gary A. Amelio** .... (909) 885-7980
Date of Birth: November 24, 1956
Education: Pittsburgh 1978 BA, 1981 JD
Chief Investment Officer **Donald Pierce** .... (909) 885-7980

San Bernardino County Superintendent of Schools [SBCSS]
601 North East Street, San Bernardino, CA 92415-0020
Tel: (909) 888-3228 Fax: (909) 888-1235 Internet: www.sbcss.k12.ca.us

★County Superintendent **Ted Alajandre** .... (909) 386-2406
Term Expires: January 4, 2019
Assistant Superintendent, Business Services
Richard De Nava .... (909) 386-2459
Assistant Superintendent, Education Support Services
Beth Higbee .... (909) 386-2600
Assistant Superintendent, Student Services
Randy Elphic .... (909) 386-2704

★Elected Official ▲Appointed by Legislature ▼Appointed by Governor ►Appointed by Board or Commission ●Appointed by Judge
■Appointed by Mayor △Appointed by Freeholders ▽Appointed by Supervisor ▷Appointed by County Executive ○Appointed by Council

County of San Diego, California

County Administration Center, 1600 Pacific Highway,
San Diego, CA 92101
Tel: (858) 694-3900 (Information) Internet: www.sdcounty.ca.gov

County Seat: San Diego **Election Type:** Nonpartisan
Population: 3,299,521 (2015)

Office of the Board of Supervisors

County Administration Center, 1600 Pacific Highway, Room 335,
San Diego, CA 92101
Tel: (619) 531-5700 Internet: www.co.san-diego.ca.us/general/bos.html

★ Chairman **Ron Roberts** (District 4) .... (619) 531-5544
Term Expires: January 7, 2019 Fax: (619) 531-6262
E-mail: ron.roberts@sdcounty.ca.gov
Education: San Diego State BA; UC Berkeley 1968 MA

★ Supervisor **Gregory Cox** (District 1) .... (619) 531-5511
Term Expires: January 2, 2017 Fax: (619) 235-0644
E-mail: greg.cox@sdcounty.ca.gov
Education: San Diego State 1970 BA, 1977 MA

★ Supervisor **Dianne Jacob** (District 2) .... (619) 531-5522
Term Expires: January 2, 2017 Fax: (619) 696-7253
E-mail: dianne.jacob@sdcounty.ca.gov
Education: San Diego State 1961 BA

★ Supervisor **Dave W. Roberts** (District 3) .... (619) 531-5533
Term Expires: January 2, 2017 Fax: (619) 234-1559
E-mail: dave.roberts@sdcounty.ca.gov
Education: American U BA, MPA; Air Command Col

★ Supervisor **Bill Horn** (District 5) .... (619) 531-5555
Term Expires: January 7, 2019 Fax: (619) 685-2662
E-mail: bill.horn@sdcounty.ca.gov
Education: San Diego State 1966 BA

▽ Clerk of the Board of Supervisors **David Hall** .... (619) 531-5600
E-mail: david.hall@sdcounty.ca.gov Fax: (619) 595-4616

Office of the Chief Administrative Officer [CAO]

County Administration Center, 1600 Pacific Highway, Room 209,
San Diego, CA 92101-2472
Tel: (619) 531-5880 Fax: (619) 557-4060
E-mail: cao_mail@sdcounty.ca.gov

▽ Chief Administrative Officer **Helen N. Robbins-Meyer** .. (619) 531-5880
E-mail: helen.robbinsmeyer@sdcounty.ca.gov
Education: William & Mary 1980 BA
Chief of Staff **Andrew Strong** .... (619) 531-6271

Assistant Chief Administrative Officer/Chief Operating Officer **Donald F. Steuer** .... (619) 531-5880

Office of Ethics and Compliance

County Administration Center, 1600 Pacific Highway, Room 400,
San Diego, CA 92101
Tel: (619) 531-5174 Internet: www.sdcounty.ca.gov/cao/oia.html

Director **Joe Cordero** .... (619) 531-5174

Office of Strategy and Intergovernmental Affairs [SIA]

County Administration Center, 1600 Pacific Highway, Room 298,
San Diego, CA 92101-2422
Fax: (619) 557-4199 Internet: www.sdcounty.ca.gov/cao/osia.html

Director **Geoff Patnoe** .... (619) 531-5202
E-mail: geoff.patnoe@sdcounty.ca.gov
Education: UC Davis

Legislative Policy Advisor **Nadia Moshirian** .... (619) 531-5198
E-mail: nadia.moshirian@sdcounty.ca.gov

Legislative Policy Advisor **Caroline Smith** .... (619) 531-5198
E-mail: caroline.smith@sdcounty.ca.gov

Office of Strategy and Intergovernmental Affairs *continued*

Legislative Policy Advisor **Thomas Ledford** .... (619) 531-5198
E-mail: thomas.ledford@sdcounty.ca.gov

Community Services Group [CSG]

County Administration Center, 1600 Pacific Highway, Room 201,
San Diego, CA 92101
Tel: (619) 531-5274 Fax: (619) 531-6439

Deputy Chief Administrative Officer/General Manager
David R. Estrella .... (619) 531-5274
E-mail: david.estrella@sdcounty.ca.gov

Department of Animal Services

5480 Gaines Street, San Diego, CA 92110-2687
Fax: (619) 767-2706 Internet: www.sddac.com

Director **Dawn Danielson** .... (619) 767-2605

Department of General Services [DGS]

5555 Overland Avenue, Suite 2240, San Diego, CA 92123-1294
Fax: (858) 694-8929

Director **April F. Heinze** .... (858) 694-2527
E-mail: april.heinze@sdcounty.ca.gov
Education: Virginia 1982 BS; U Washington 1987 MS

Assistant Director **Lou Cavagnaro** .... (858) 694-2527
E-mail: lou.cavagnaro@sdcounty.ca.gov

Fleet Manager **Sharyl Blackington** .... (858) 694-2876

Department of Housing and Community Development [HCD]

3989 Ruffin Road, San Diego, CA 92123-1815
Fax: (858) 694-4871 Internet: www.sdhcd.org

Director **Todd Henderson** .... (858) 694-8750
Assistant Director **Kelly Duffek** .... (858) 694-8750

Purchasing and Contracting Department

5560 Overland Avenue, Suite 270, San Diego, CA 92123-1204
Tel: (858) 505-6367 Fax: (858) 715-6452

Director **Jack M. Pellegrino** .... (858) 505-6562
E-mail: jack.pellegrino@sdcounty.ca.gov

Chief, Procurement Services **Rochelle Lowe** .... (858) 505-6391
E-mail: rochelle.lowe@sdcounty.ca.gov Fax: (858) 715-6454

Assistant Director **Allen Hunsberger** .... (858) 505-6362
E-mail: allen.hunsberger@sdcounty.ca.gov

Senior Property and Salvage Worker **Daniel Lawson** ..... (858) 505-6352
4000 Ruffin Road, Suite 1, San Diego, CA 92123
E-mail: daniel.lawson@sdcounty.ca.gov

Office of the Registrar of Voters

5600 Overland Avenue, San Diego, CA 92123
P.O. Box 85656, San Diego, CA 92186-5656
Tel: (858) 505-7371 Fax: (858) 505-6876
E-mail: rovmail@sdcounty.ca.gov

Registrar **Michael Vu** .... (858) 505-7202

San Diego County Library [SDCL]

5560 Overland Avenue, Suite 110, San Diego, CA 92123-1204
Fax: (858) 495-5981 Internet: www.sdcl.org

▽ Director **José Antonio Aponte** .... (858) 694-2389
E-mail: jose.aponte@sdcounty.ca.gov
Education: Bard BA; Arizona 1976 MLS

Finance and General Government Group

County Administration Center, 1600 Pacific Highway, Room 166,
San Diego, CA 92101
Tel: (619) 531-5413

Deputy Chief Administrative Officer/General Manager
Tracy M. Sandoval .... (619) 531-5413
E-mail: tracy.sandoval@sdcounty.ca.gov

COUNTIES

★ Elected Official ▲ Appointed by Legislature ▼ Appointed by Governor ▶ Appointed by Board or Commission ● Appointed by Judge
■ Appointed by Mayor △ Appointed by Freeholders ▽ Appointed by Supervisor ▷ Appointed by County Executive ○ Appointed by Council

Office of the Auditor and Controller
County Administration Center, 1600 Pacific Highway, Room 166, San Diego, CA 92101-2478
Tel: (619) 531-5413 Fax: (619) 531-5219
E-mail: auditor@sdcounty.ca.gov

Assistant Chief Financial Officer/Auditor and Controller
Tracy M. Sandoval ... (619) 531-5413
E-mail: tracy.sandoval@sdcounty.ca.gov
Assistant Auditor and Controller **Tracy L. Drager** ... (619) 531-5413
Administrative Services Manager **James Bryant** ... (619) 531-5411
County Administration Center, Fax: (619) 531-5048
1600 Pacific Highway, Room 359, San Diego, CA 92101
E-mail: james.bryant@sdcounty.ca.gov
IT Management Services Chief **David Nickel** ... (619) 557-4122
County Administration Center, Fax: (619) 531-5163
1600 Pacific Highway, Room 256, San Diego, CA 92101
Deputy Controller for Financial Accounting and Reporting **(Vacant)** ... (619) 531-6166
Deputy Controller for Operations **(Vacant)** ... (619) 531-5338
Chief, Office of Audits and Advisory Services
Juan Perez ... (858) 495-5991
5500 Overland Avenue, Fax: (858) 495-5085
Suite 430, San Diego, CA 92123
Director, Office of Financial Planning
Ebony N. Shelton ... (619) 531-5177
1600 Pacific Highway, Fax: (619) 531-6261
Room 352, San Diego, CA 92101
Director, Office of Revenue and Recovery
Sean S. Sander ... (858) 637-5861
Fax: (858) 637-5858

Office of the County Counsel
County Administration Center, 1600 Pacific Highway, Room 355, San Diego, CA 92101-2469
Tel: (619) 531-4860 Fax: (619) 531-6005

▸ County Counsel **Thomas E. Montgomery** ... (619) 531-4847
E-mail: thomas.montgomery@sdcounty.ca.gov
Education: San Diego 1983 JD
Assistant County Counsel **Deborah McCarthy** ... (619) 531-4847
Chief Deputy **Timothy M. Barry** ... (619) 531-4847
Chief Deputy **George W. Brewster, Jr.** ... (619) 531-4847
Chief Deputy **C. Ellen Pilsecker** ... (619) 531-4847
Chief Deputy **David J. Smith** ... (619) 531-4847
Chief of Departmental Administrative Services
Rosana Legaspi ... (619) 531-4847
Juvenile Dependency Chief Deputy **John Philips** ... (858) 492-2500

County Communications Office
1600 Pacific Highway, Room 208, San Diego, CA 92101
Tel: (619) 595-4633

Director **Michael Workman** ... (619) 531-5450
E-mail: michael.workman@sdcounty.ca.gov

County Technology Office
County Administration Center, 1600 Pacific Highway, Room 306F, San Diego, CA 92101
Tel: (619) 531-5570 E-mail: webmaster@sdcounty.ca.gov

Chief Information Officer **Michael Haas** ... (619) 531-5570
Assistant Chief Information Officer **Susan Green** ... (619) 515-4337
E-mail: susan.green@sdcounty.ca.gov

Department of Human Resources
County Administration Center, 1600 Pacific Highway, Room 207, San Diego, CA 92101
Fax: (619) 531-6076 Internet: www.sdcounty.ca.gov/hr

Director **Susan Brazeau** ... (619) 531-5100
Education: Michigan State BA; Cal Western JD

Civil Service Commission
County Administration Center, 1600 Pacific Highway, Room 458, San Diego, CA 92101
Fax: (619) 685-2422

President **W. Dale Bailey** ... (619) 531-5751
Executive Officer **Todd Adams** ... (619) 531-5751
E-mail: todd.adams@sdcounty.ca.gov

Health and Human Services Agency [HHSA]
1600 Pacific Highway, Room 206, San Diego, CA 92101
Tel: (619) 515-6555

Agency Director/General Manager **Nick Macchione** ... (619) 515-6555
E-mail: nick.macchione@sdcounty.ca.gov Fax: (619) 515-6556
Chief Operations Officer **Dean Arabatzis** ... (619) 515-6555
E-mail: dean.arabatzis@sdcounty.ca.gov
Education: UC Riverside MBA
Executive Finance Director **Michael Van Mouwerik** ... (619) 515-6555
Human Resources Director **Donald Bradburn** ... (619) 338-2886
1255 Imperial Avenue, San Diego, CA 92101 Fax: (619) 338-2967
E-mail: donald.bradburn@sdcounty.ca.gov

Aging and Independence Services
9335 Hazard Way, San Diego, CA 92123-1222
Tel: (858) 495-5858 Fax: (858) 495-5080
Internet: www.sdcounty.ca.gov/hhsa/programs/ais

Director **Ellen Schmeding** ... (858) 495-5858

Public Administrator/Public Guardian's Office
5600 Overland Avenue, Suite 180, San Diego, CA 92123
Tel: (858) 694-3500 Fax: (858) 694-3987
Internet: www.sdcounty.ca.gov/hhsa/programs/papg

Public Administrator/Public Guardian **Ellen Schmeding** .. (858) 694-3500

Public Health Services [PHS]
1700 Pacific Highway, San Diego, CA 92101
Tel: (619) 531-5800 Fax: (619) 542-4186
Internet: www.sdcounty.ca.gov/hhsa/programs/phs

Public Health Officer **Dr. Wilma Wooten** ... (619) 542-4181

Commission on Children, Youth and Families [CCYF]
1255 Imperial Avenue, Suite 728, San Diego, CA 92101
Tel: (619) 338-2049

Executive Director **Tonya Torosian** ... (619) 338-2049
Administrative Secretary **Renee Rambus** ... (619) 338-2049
E-mail: renee.rambus@sdcounty.ca.gov
Administrative Analyst **Harold Randolph** ... (619) 338-2049

Land Use and Environmental Group
County Administration Center, 1600 Pacific Highway, Room 212, San Diego, CA 92101
Tel: (619) 531-6256 Internet: www.sdcounty.ca.gov/lueg

Deputy Chief Administrative Officer/General Manager
Sarah E. Aghassi ... (619) 531-6256
E-mail: sarah.aghassi@sdcounty.ca.gov

Farm and Home Advisor Office
9335 Hazard Way, Suite 201, San Diego, CA 92123-1219
Tel: (858) 822-7711 Fax: (858) 694-2849

Director **Jim Bethke** ... (858) 822-7711

Department of Agriculture, Weights and Measures [AWM]
9325 Hazard Way, Suite 100, San Diego, CA 92123-1217
Tel: (858) 694-2739 Fax: (858) 467-9697
E-mail: sdcawm@sdcounty.ca.gov

Agricultural Commissioner/Sealer of Weights and Measures **Ha Dang** ... (858) 694-2741
Administrative Secretary **Dawn D'aquisto** ... (858) 614-7704
E-mail: dawn.daquisto@sdcounty.ca.gov

★ Elected Official ▲ Appointed by Legislature ▼ Appointed by Governor ▸ Appointed by Board or Commission ● Appointed by Judge
■ Appointed by Mayor △ Appointed by Freeholders ▽ Appointed by Supervisor ▹ Appointed by County Executive ○ Appointed by Council

Department of Parks and Recreation
500 Overland Avenue, Suite 410, San Diego, CA 92123
Tel: (858) 694-3030 Fax: (858) 966-1391
E-mail: askparks.lue@sdcounty.ca.gov

Director **Brian Albright** .... (858) 966-1301
Deputy Director **Jason Hemmens** .... (858) 694-3030
Assistant Director **Renee Hilton** .... (858) 966-1301

Planning and Development Services
5510 Overland Avenue, San Diego, CA 92123-1295
Tel: (858) 694-2960 Fax: (858) 694-2555
Internet: www.sdcounty.ca.gov/dplu

Director **Mark Wardlaw** .... (858) 694-2962
Assistant Director **Darren Gretler** .... (858) 694-3765
Deputy Director **Clay Westling** .... (858) 694-3730
Code Compliance Chief **Pam Elias** .... (858) 495-5020
Advance Planning Chief **(Vacant)** .... (858) 694-3016
Building Chief **Vince Nicoletti** .... (858) 694-3730
Project Planning Chief **Cara Lacey** .... (858) 694-3722
Support Services Chief **Andrew Strong** .... (858) 694-3075
Land Development Chief **Ramin Abdi** .... (858) 495-5484

Department of Public Works [DPW]
5510 Overland Avenue, Suite 410, Mail Stop 0332,
San Diego, CA 92123-1295
Fax: (858) 694-3597 Internet: www.sdcounty.ca.gov/dpw

Director **Richard E. Crompton** .... (858) 694-2212
Engineering Services **Terrence "Terry" Rayback** .... (858) 694-8948
E-mail: terrence.rayback@sdcounty.ca.gov
Land Development **Ramin Abidi** .... (858) 694-2125
Fax: (858) 694-8928
Public Information Officer **(Vacant)** .... (858) 495-5736
Fax: (858) 505-6374
Training Coordinator **Kirsten Aaboe Hope** .... (858) 761-8976
E-mail: kirsten.aaboehope@sdcounty.ca.gov Fax: (858) 694-3597
Transportation **Derek Gade** .... (858) 694-3897
Fax: (858) 694-3928
Wastewater Management and Flood Control
Daniel Brogadir .... (858) 694-2714
Fax: (858) 505-6394

Public Safety Group [PSG]
1600 Pacific Highway, Room 205, San Diego, CA 92101
Tel: (619) 531-4535 Internet: www.sdcounty.ca.gov/public_safety

Deputy Chief Administrative Officer/General Manager
Ronald "Ron" Lane .... (619) 531-4535
E-mail: ronald.lane@sdcounty.ca.gov

Office of Emergency Services [OES]
5555 Overland Avenue, Suite 1911, San Diego, CA 92123
Fax: (858) 565-3499

Director **Holly Crawford** .... (858) 565-3490

Office of the Public Defender
450 B Street, Suite 900, San Diego, CA 92101
Tel: (619) 338-4700 Fax: (619) 338-4811
E-mail: yoursdpd@sdcounty.ca.gov

Public Defender **Henry C. Coker** .... (619) 338-4797
Education: Thomas Jefferson Law JD

Department of the Medical Examiner
Tel: (858) 694-2895 Fax: (858) 495-5956
Internet: www.sdcounty.ca.gov/me

Chief Medical Examiner **Glenn N. Wagner** .... (858) 694-2895
Administration Services Manager **Theresa Liget** .... (858) 694-2895
E-mail: theresa.liget@sdcounty.ca.gov

Probation Department
9444 Balboa Avenue, Suite 500, San Diego, CA 92123
Tel: (858) 514-3148 Fax: (858) 514-3121
E-mail: psg.probation@sdcounty.ca.gov
Internet: www.co.san-diego.ca.us/probation

Chief Probation Officer **Mack Jenkins** .... (858) 514-3200

Office of the Assessor-Recorder-County Clerk
County Administration Center, 1600 Pacific Highway,
Suite 103, Mail Stop A-4, San Diego, CA 92101-2480 (Assessor)
Tel: (619) 236-3771 (Assessor) Fax: (619) 557-4056 (Assessor)
Tel: (619) 237-0502 (Recorder/County Clerk)
Fax: (619) 557-4155 (Recorder/County Clerk)

Assessor-Recorder-County Clerk
Ernest J. Dronenburg, Jr. .... (619) 531-5507
Term Expires: January 5, 2019
E-mail: arcc.fgg@sdcounty.ca.gov

Office of the District Attorney
330 West Broadway, Suite 1300, San Diego, CA 92101
Tel: (619) 531-4040 Fax: (619) 237-1351
E-mail: publicaffairs@sdcda.org Internet: www.sdcda.org

★ District Attorney **Bonnie M. Dumanis** .... (619) 531-4114
Term Expires: December 1, 2018
E-mail: bonnie.dumanis@sdcda.org
Education: UMass (Amherst); Thomas Jefferson Law 1976 JD
Assistant District Attorney **Jesus Rodriguez** .... (619) 531-3875
Chief Deputy District Attorney
David P. "Dave" Greenberg .... (619) 531-4205
E-mail: david.greenberg@sdcda.org
Education: UCLA; San Diego JD
Chief Deputy District Attorney **David Hendren** .... (619) 531-4040
Chief Deputy District Attorney **Victor Nunez** .... (619) 531-4040
Chief Deputy District Attorney **Summer Stephan** .... (619) 531-4051
Chief of Investigations **(Vacant)** .... (619) 531-4303
Chief of Employee Relations **Cheryl Ruffier** .... (619) 531-4040
E-mail: cheryl.ruffier@sdcda.org

Sheriff's Department
9621 Ridgehaven Court, San Diego, CA 92123
P.O. Box 939062, San Diego, CA 92193-9062
Tel: (858) 974-2222 Fax: (858) 974-2244 Internet: www.sdsheriff.net

★ Sheriff **William D. "Bill" Gore** .... (858) 974-2240
Term Expires: January 8, 2018
E-mail: bill.gore@sdsheriff.org
Education: San Diego BA; Seattle MPA
Undersheriff **Mark Elvin** .... (858) 974-2250
E-mail: mark.elvin@sdsheriff.org Fax: (858) 974-2244
Assistant Sheriff, Courts and Human Resources
Bureaus **Timothy Curran** .... (858) 974-2277
E-mail: timothy.curran@sdsheriff.org Fax: (858) 974-2180
Courts: (858) 974-2133
Assistant Sheriff, Detentions Services Bureau
Rich Miller John Duffy Administration Center .... (858) 974-2278
Fax: (858) 974-2291
Assistant Sheriff, Law Enforcement Services Bureau
Mike Barnett .... (858) 974-2295
E-mail: mike.barnett@sdsheriff.org Fax: (858) 974-2304
Executive Director, Management Services Bureau
John C. "Chuck" Gaines .... (858) 974-2274
E-mail: chuck.gaines@sdsheriff.org Fax: (858) 974-2109

COUNTIES

★ Elected Official ▲ Appointed by Legislature ▼ Appointed by Governor ► Appointed by Board or Commission ● Appointed by Judge
■ Appointed by Mayor △ Appointed by Freeholders ▽ Appointed by Supervisor ▷ Appointed by County Executive ○ Appointed by Council

Office of the Treasurer-Tax Collector

County Administration Center, 1600 Pacific Highway, Room 112, San Diego, CA 92101
Tel: (877) 829-4732 (Tax Payment Information) Fax: (619) 595-4605
Internet: http://www.sdtreastax.com

★Treasurer-Tax Collector **Dan McAllister** . . . . (619) 531-5231
Term Expires: June 4, 2018
E-mail: dan.mcallister@sdcounty.ca.gov
Administrative Secretary **Susan Clapham** . . . . (619) 531-5231
Assistant Treasurer-Tax Collector **Dennis Gibson** . . . . (619) 531-5231
E-mail: dennis.gibson@sdcounty.ca.gov
Chief Deputy Tax Collector **Maria Pe** . . . . (619) 531-5731
E-mail: maria.pe@sdcounty.ca.gov
Chief Deputy Treasurer **Antoinette Chandler** . . . . (619) 531-5211
Special Projects Manager **(Vacant)** . . . . (619) 531-5231

COUNTIES

San Diego County Board of Education

6401 Linda Vista Road, San Diego, CA 92111
Internet: www.sdcoe.net/theboard.asp

★President **Gregg Robinson** (District 1) . . . . (858) 292-3609
Term Expires: January 7, 2017
E-mail: gregg.robinson@sdcoe.net
★Board Member **Guadalupe Gonzalez** (District 2) . . . . (858) 292-3609
Term Expires: January 5, 2017
E-mail: guadalupe.gonzalez@sdcoe.net
★Board Member **Alicia Muñoz** (District 3) . . . . (858) 292-3609
Term Expires: January 5, 2017
E-mail: alicia.munoz@sdcoe.net
★Board Member **Mark Anderson** (District 4) . . . . (858) 292-3609
Term Expires: January 5, 2017
E-mail: mark.anderson@sdcoe.net
★Board Member **Richard Shea** (District 5) . . . . (858) 292-3515
Term Expires: January 7, 2017
E-mail: rick.shea@sdcoe.net

San Diego County Office of Education

6401 Linda Vista Road, San Diego, CA 92111
Tel: (858) 292-3500 Fax: (858) 268-5864 Internet: www.sdcoe.net

Superintendent of Schools **Dr. Randolph E. Ward** . . . . (858) 292-3514
Education: Tufts 1978 BS; Harvard 1983 EdM; UMass (Boston) 1989 EdM; USC 1992 EdD

County of San Joaquin, California

Administration Building, 44 North San Joaquin Street, Stockton, CA 95202
Tel: (209) 468-3113 (Information) Internet: www.sjgov.org

County Seat: Stockton **Election Type:** Nonpartisan
Population: 726,106 (2015)

Office of the Board of County Supervisors

44 North San Joaquin Street, Suite 627, Stockton, CA 95202
Fax: (209) 468-3694

★Chair **Moses Zapien** (District 3) . . . . (209) 468-3113
Term Expires: December 31, 2016
★Vice Chair **Bob Elliott** (District 5) . . . . (209) 468-3113
Term Expires: December 31, 2016
★Supervisor **Carlos Villapudua** (District 1) . . . . (209) 468-3113
Term Expires: December 31, 2016
E-mail: cvillapudua@sjgov.org
Education: Cal State (Sacramento) BSW

Office of the Board of County Supervisors *continued*

★Supervisor **Katherine "Kathy" Miller** (District 2) . . . . (209) 468-3113
Term Expires: January 1, 2018
★Supervisor **Chuck Winn** (District 4) . . . . (209) 468-3113
Term Expires: January 1, 2018
Clerk of the Board **Mimi Duzenski** . . . . (209) 468-2350

Office of the County Administrator

44 North San Joaquin Street, Suite 640, Stockton, CA 95202
Fax: (209) 468-2875

▽County Administrator **Monica Nino** . . . . (209) 468-3203
E-mail: nino@sjgov.org
Assistant County Administrator **(Vacant)** . . . . (209) 468-3203
Assistant County Administrator **Deb West** . . . . (209) 468-3203

Office of Emergency Services

2101 East Earhart Avenue, Suite 300, Stockton, CA 95206
Fax: (209) 953-6268 E-mail: sjcoes@co.san-joaquin.ca.us
Internet: www.sjgov.org/oes

▽Director of Emergency Operations **Michael R. "Mike" Cockrell** . . . . (209) 953-6200
E-mail: mcockrell@co.san-joaquin.ca.us

Facilities Management Division

44 North San Joaquin Street, Suite 590, Stockton, CA 95202
Fax: (209) 468-2186 Internet: www.sjgov.org/facilitiesmgt

Director **Dennis Turner** . . . . (209) 468-3357
E-mail: dturner@sjgov.org

Human Resources Division

44 North San Joaquin Street, Suite 330, Stockton, CA 95202
Fax: (209) 468-0508 Internet: www.sjgov.org/hr

Director **Ted J. Cwiek** . . . . (209) 468-3370
E-mail: tcwiek@sjgov.org

Information Systems Division [ISD]

44 North San Joaquin Street, Suite 455, Stockton, CA 95202
Tel: (209) 468-3940 Fax: (209) 468-2178

Director/Chief Information Officer **Jerry Becker** . . . . (209) 468-3960
E-mail: jbecker@sjgov.org

Labor Relations Division

44 North San Joaquin Street, Suite 374, Stockton, CA 95202
Fax: (209) 468-9672 Internet: www.sjgov.org/labor_relations

Director **Ted J. Cwiek** . . . . (209) 468-9669

Purchasing and Support Services Division

44 North San Joaquin Street, Suite 540, Stockton, CA 95202
Fax: (209) 468-3393 Internet: www.sjgov.org/supportserv

Director **Jon Drake** . . . . (209) 468-3240
E-mail: jdrake@sjgov.org

Office of the Agricultural Commissioner

2101 East Earhart Avenue, Suite 100, Stockton, CA 95206
Fax: (209) 953-6022 Internet: www.sjgov.org/agcomm
E-mail: stocktonag2@sjgov.org

▽Agricultural Commissioner/Sealer of Weights and Measures **Tim Pelican** . . . . (209) 953-6000

Office of Cooperative Extension (University of California)

2101 East Earhart Avenue, Suite 200, Stockton, CA 95206
Fax: (209) 953-6128 E-mail: cesanjoaquin@ucdavis.edu
E-mail: stocktonag2@sjgov.org Internet: http://cesanjoaquin.ucdavis.edu/

County Director and Farm Advisor **Brent A. Holtz** . . . . . . (209) 953-6124

★Elected Official ▲Appointed by Legislature ▼Appointed by Governor ▶Appointed by Board or Commission ●Appointed by Judge
■Appointed by Mayor △Appointed by Freeholders ▽Appointed by Supervisor ▷Appointed by County Executive ○Appointed by Council

Office of the County Counsel
44 North San Joaquin Street, Suite 679, Stockton, CA 95202
Fax: (209) 468-0315 Internet: www.sjgov.org/counsel

▽County Counsel **Mark Myles** .... (209) 468-2980
E-mail: mmyles@sjgov.org
Assistant County Counsel **Richard Flores** .... (209) 468-2980

Public Defender Office
Human Services Agency, 102 South San Joaquin Street, Room 1, Stockton, CA 95202
Fax: (209) 468-2267 Internet: www.sjgov.org/pubdefender

▽Public Defender **Peter Fox** .... (209) 468-2730
E-mail: pfox@sjgov.org

Office of the Registrar of Voters
44 North San Joaquin Street, Suite 350, Stockton, CA 95202
Fax: (209) 468-2889 Internet: www.sjcrov.org

▶Registrar of Voters **Austin Erdman** .... (209) 468-2885
E-mail: aerdman@sjgov.org

Veterans' Services Office
105 South San Joaquin Street, Stockton, CA 95202
Fax: (209) 468-2918

▽Veterans Services Officer **Virginia Wimmer** .... (209) 468-2910
E-mail: vwimmer@sjgov.org

Community Development Department
1810 East Hazelton Avenue, Stockton, CA 95205-6298
Tel: (209) 468-3120 Fax: (209) 468-3163
Internet: www.sjgov.org/commdev

▽Director **Kerry Sullivan** .... (209) 468-3124
E-mail: ksullivan@sjgov.org

Employment and Economic Development Department
56 South Lincoln Street, Stockton, CA 95203
Fax: (209) 462-9063

▽Director **John Solis** .... (209) 468-3500
E-mail: jsolis@sjcworknet.org

Health Care Services Agency
500 West Hospital Road, French Camp, CA 95231
P.O. Box 1020, Stockton, CA 95201
Tel: (209) 468-6600 Fax: (209) 468-6136 Internet: www.sjhealthcare.com

▽Director **Greg Diederich** .... (209) 468-5610
E-mail: gdiederich@sjgh.org

Human Services Agency
P.O. Box 201056, Stockton, CA 95201-3006
333 East Washington Street, Stockton, CA 95201
Fax: (209) 468-1985

▽Director **Michael Miller** .... (209) 468-1000
E-mail: mmiller@sjgov.org

Parks and Recreation Department
11793 North Micke Grove Road, Lodi, CA 95240
E-mail: parks@sjgov.org Internet: www.sjgov.org/parks

Director **Duncan Jones** .... (209) 953-8800

Probation Department
575 W. Mathews Rd., French Camp, CA 95231
Fax: (209) 468-4012 E-mail: probation@sjgov.org

Chief Probation Officer **Stephanie James** .... (209) 468-4068

Department of Public Works
1810 E. Hazelton Ave., Stockton, CA 95205
Fax: (209) 468-2999 Internet: www.sjgov.org/pubworks

▽Director **Tom Gau** .... (209) 468-3000
E-mail: tgau@sjgov.org
Education: San José State BS

Stockton Metropolitan Airport
5000 S. Airport Way, Rm. 202, Stockton, CA 95206
Fax: (209) 468-4730 E-mail: sckmetro@inreach.com

▽Airport Manager **Harry S. Mavrogenes** .... (209) 468-4700
Education: San Francisco State U BS

Office of the Auditor-Controller
44 North San Joaquin Street, Suite 550, Stockton, CA 95202
Fax: (209) 468-3681

★Auditor/Controller **Jerome Wilverding** .... (209) 468-3925
Term Expires: December 31, 2018
E-mail: jwilverding@sjgov.org
Audits and Systems Chief **Jeffrey Woltkamp** .... (209) 468-3925
Budgeting and General Accounting Chief **Tod Hill** .... (209) 468-3925
E-mail: thill@sjgov.org
Property Taxes Chief **Sandra Chan** .... (209) 468-3925
E-mail: schan@sjgov.org

Office of the District Attorney
Courthouse, 222 E. Weber Ave., Room 202, Stockton, CA 95202
Fax: (209) 465-0371

★District Attorney **Tori Verber Salazar** .... (209) 468-2400
Term Expires: December 31, 2018

Office of the Assessor Recorder-County Clerk
44 North San Joaquin Street, Suite 230, Stockton, CA 95202
Fax: (209) 468-8040

★Assessor-Recorder-County Clerk **Steve J. Bestolarides** .. (209) 468-2630
Term Expires: December 31, 2018
E-mail: sbestolarides@sjgov.org
Date of Birth: April 25, 1956
Education: U Pacific; National U

Office of the Sheriff-Coroner-Public Administrator
7000 Canlis Blvd., French Camp, CA 95231
Fax: (209) 468-4597 Internet: www.sjgov.org/sheriff

★Sheriff-Coroner-Public Administrator **Steve Moore** ...... (209) 468-4310
Term Expires: December 31, 2018
E-mail: smoore@sjgov.org

Office of the Treasurer-Tax Collector
44 North San Joaquin Street, Suite 150, Stockton, CA 95202
Fax: (209) 468-2158

★Treasurer-Tax Collector **Shabbir A. Khan** .... (209) 468-2133
Term Expires: December 31, 2018
E-mail: skhan@sjgov.org
Chief Deputy Treasurer **Marc Young** .... (209) 468-2133
Assistant Treasurer-Tax Collector **Phonxay Keokham** .... (209) 468-2133
E-mail: pkeokham@sjgov.org
Education: Humphreys 2000 BS

COUNTIES

Revenue and Recovery Division

350 East Weber Avenue, Stockton, CA 95202
Fax: (209) 468-2277 E-mail: orr@sjgov.org
Internet: www.sjgov.org/revrec

Chief Deputy **(Vacant)** .... (209) 468-2133

San Joaquin County Office of Education [SJCOE]

Gaylord A. Nelson Education Center, 2901 Arch-Airport Road, Stockton, CA 95213-9030
Tel: (209) 468-4800 Internet: www.sjcoe.org

Board of Education

2901 Arch-Airport Road, Stockton, CA 95213-9030

★ President **Janet Dyk** .... (209) 468-4802
E-mail: jstanton@sjcoe.net

Office of the Superintendent of Schools

2901 Arch-Airport Road, Stockton, CA 95213-9030
Fax: (209) 468-4975

★ Superintendent of Schools **James Mousalimas** .... (209) 468-4802
Term Expires: December 31, 2018
E-mail: jmousalimas@sjcoe.net

County of San Mateo, California

400 County Center, Redwood City, CA 94063
Tel: (650) 363-4000 (Information)

County Seat: Redwood City **Election Type:** Nonpartisan
Population: 765,135 (2015)

Office of the Board of Supervisors

400 County Center, Redwood City, CA 94063
Tel: (650) 363-4653

★ President **Warren Slocum** (District 4) .... (650) 363-4570
Term Expires: January 6, 2017 Fax: (650) 366-6720

★ Vice President **Don Horsley** (District 3) .... (650) 363-4569
Term Expires: January 4, 2019 Fax: (650) 363-1856
E-mail: dhorsley@smcgov.org
Education: San Francisco State U 1969

★ Supervisor **David G. "Dave" Pine** (District 1) .... (650) 363-4571
Term Expires: January 6, 2017 Fax: (650) 368-3012
E-mail: dpine@smcgov.org
Date of Birth: 1958
Education: Dartmouth 1981 BA; Michigan 1985 JD

★ Supervisor **Carole Groom** (District 2) .... (650) 363-4568
Term Expires: January 4, 2019 Fax: (650) 366-6762
E-mail: cgroom@smcgov.org

★ Supervisor **Adrienne J. Tissier** (District 5) .... (650) 363-4572
Term Expires: January 6, 2017 Fax: (650) 701-0564
E-mail: atissier@smcgov.org
Education: UC Berkeley

Office of County Counsel

400 County Center, Sixth Floor, Redwood City, CA 94063
Tel: (650) 363-4250 Fax: (650) 363-4034
Internet: www.co.sanmateo.ca.us/countycounsel

▽ County Counsel **John C. Beiers** .... (650) 363-4775
E-mail: jbeiers@smcgov.org
Education: UC Santa Barbara 1983; Santa Clara U 1989 JD

Office of the County Manager-Clerk of the Board

400 County Center, Redwood City, CA 94063
Tel: (650) 363-4123 Fax: (650) 363-1916

▽ County Manager-Clerk of the Board **John L. Maltbie** .... (650) 363-4121
E-mail: jmaltbie@smcgov.org

Executive Assistant **Alicia Garcia** .... (650) 363-4634
E-mail: agarcia@smcgov.org

Assistant County Manager **(Vacant)** .... (650) 363-4131

Deputy County Manager **Reyna Farrales** .... (650) 363-4130
E-mail: rfarrales@smcgov.org

Deputy County Manager **Peggy Jensen** .... (650) 363-4598
E-mail: pjensen@smcgov.org

Deputy County Manager **Michael Callagy** .... (650) 363-4123
E-mail: mcallagy@smcgov.org

Budget Director **Jim Saco** .... (650) 363-4439
E-mail: jsaco@smcgov.org

Legislative Director **Connie Juarez-Diroll** .... (650) 599-1341

Chief Communications Officer **Michelle Durand** .... (650) 363-4123

Fire Protection Services

Fire Chief **Scott M. Jalbert** .... (831) 335-6700
E-mail: scotty.jalbert@fire.ca.gov

Real Property Services

455 County Center, 4th Floor, Redwood City, CA 94063

Manager **Freda Manuel** .... (650) 363-4047

Shared Services

455 County Center, 4th Floor, Redwood City, CA 94063
Fax: (650) 599-1702

Director **(Vacant)** .... (650) 363-4408

Lead Buyer **Charles Davenport** .... (650) 363-4406
E-mail: cdavenport@smcgov.org

Department of Agriculture/Weights and Measures

728 Heller Street, Redwood City, CA 94064
Fax: (650) 367-0130 E-mail: smateoag@co.sanmateo.ca.us
Internet: www.co.sanmateo.ca.us/agwm

Agricultural Commissioner/Sealer of Weights and Measures **Fred Crowder** .... (650) 363-4700

Department of Housing

262 Harbor Boulevard, Belmont, CA 94002
Fax: (650) 802-5049 Internet: www.co.sanmateo.ca.us/housingdepartment

Director **William Lowell** .... (650) 802-5050

Human Resources Department

455 County Center, Redwood City, CA 94063
Tel: (650) 363-4343 Fax: (650) 363-4219
Internet: www.co.sanmateo.ca.us/hr

Director **Donna Vaillancourt** .... (650) 363-4132
E-mail: dvaillancourt@smcgov.org

Assistant Director **(Vacant)** .... (650) 363-4393

Employee Benefits Services

Division Manager (Interim) **Jay Castellano** .... (650) 363-4676
E-mail: jcastellano@smcgov.org Fax: (650) 599-1573

Individual and Organizational Development

Division Manager **Teresa Henderson** .... (650) 363-4430
E-mail: thenderson@smcgov.org

Training Specialist **Noel Coloma** .... (650) 363-4948
E-mail: ncoloma@smcgov.org

Specialist **Rosemarie San Juan** .... (650) 363-4733
E-mail: rsanjuan@smcgov.org

★ Elected Official ▲ Appointed by Legislature ▼ Appointed by Governor ► Appointed by Board or Commission ● Appointed by Judge
■ Appointed by Mayor △ Appointed by Freeholders ▽ Appointed by Supervisor ▷ Appointed by County Executive ○ Appointed by Council

Public Safety Communications Division
400 County Center, Redwood City, CA 94063
Internet: http://www.smc911dispatch.org
Director **Jaime Young** . . . . . (650) 363-4949
E-mail: jyoung@smcgov.org

Revenue Services Division
555 County Center, Redwood City, CA 94063
Manager **Girdie Bernard** . . . . . (650) 363-4171
E-mail: gbernard@co.sanmateo.ca.us

Human Services Agency
1 Davis Drive, Belmont, CA 94002
Internet: www.co.sanmateo.ca.us/portal/site/humanservices
Director **Iliana Rodriguez** . . . . . (650) 802-7555
Economic Self Sufficiency Director **Clarisa Simon** . . . . . (650) 802-5026

Children and Family Services
Building B, 400 Harbor Boulevard, Belmont, CA 94002
Director **Loc Nguyen** . . . . . (650) 802-3390

Information Services Department
455 County Center, Redwood City, CA 94063-1663
Fax: (650) 363-7800
Chief Information Officer **Jon Walton** . . . . . (650) 363-4548
E-mail: jwalton@smcgov.org
Deputy Director **Kathleen Poutte-Foster** . . . . . (650) 599-1698
Financial Services Manager **Candi Clarno** . . . . . (650) 363-7878
E-mail: cclarno@smcgov.org
Infrastructure Deputy Director **Gordon Helms** . . . . . (650) 363-4548
E-mail: ghelms@smcgov.org

Department of Parks
555 County Center, Fifth Floor, Redwood City, CA 94063
Fax: (650) 599-1721 E-mail: parksandrecreation@co.sanmateo.ca.us
Internet: www.co.sanmateo.ca.us/parks
Chief Superintendent **Scott Lombardi** . . . . . (650) 363-1881
Director of Parks **Marlene Finley** . . . . . (650) 599-1394
Natural Resource Manager **Ramona Arechiga** . . . . . (650) 599-1394

Planning and Building Department
455 County Center, Redwood City, CA 94063
Fax: (650) 363-4849 E-mail: plngbldg@co.sanmateo.ca.us
Internet: www.co.sanmateo.ca.us/planning
Director **Steve Monowitz** . . . . . (650) 363-4161
Building Inspection Manager **Charles Clark** . . . . . (650) 599-7311

Probation Department
222 Paul Scannell Drive, San Mateo, CA 94402
Tel: (650) 312-8816 Fax: (650) 312-5597
Internet: www.co.sanmateo.ca.us/probation
Chief Probation Officer **John Keene** . . . . . (650) 312-8803

Department of Public Works
555 County Center, Redwood City, CA 94063
Fax: (650) 361-8220 Internet: www.co.sanmateo.ca.us/publicworks
Director **James C. Porter** . . . . . (650) 363-4100

Airports Division
Airport Manager **Gretchen Kelly** . . . . . (650) 573-3700

Engineering and Resource Protection Division
Manager **Ann Stillman** . . . . . (650) 599-1497

Facility Maintenance and Operations
455 County Center, Redwood City, CA 94063
Manager **Gary Behrens** . . . . . (650) 599-1875
E-mail: gbehrens@smcgov.org

Flood Control and Water Resources Division
Principal Civil Engineer **Vastal Patel** . . . . . (650) 599-1489
E-mail: vpatel@smcgov.org

Motor Vehicles Division
752 Chestnut Street, Redwood City, CA 94063
Manager **Tony Harwood** . . . . . (650) 599-1651

Road Maintenance Division
Deputy Director **Joe Lococo** . . . . . (650) 363-4102

San Mateo Cooperative Extension (University of California)
80 Stone Pine Road, Suite 100, Half Moon Bay, CA 94019
Fax: (650) 726-9267 E-mail: cesanmeto@ucdavis.edu
Internet: http://cesanmateo.ucdavis.edu/
Director **Virginia Bolshakova** . . . . . (650) 726-9059 ext. 102

San Mateo Health System
225 West 37th Avenue, San Mateo, CA 94403
Tel: (650) 372-8572 Fax: (650) 573-2116 E-mail: info@smhealth.org
Internet: www.smhealth.org
Chief of Health Systems **Jean Fraser** . . . . . (650) 573-2585

Aging and Adult Services Division
225 37th Avenue, San Mateo, CA 94403
Tel: (650) 573-3900 Fax: (650) 573-2310
Director **Lisa L. Mancini** . . . . . (650) 573-3904

Behavioral Health and Recovery Services
225 West 37th Street, San Mateo, CA 94403
Director **Steve Kaplan** . . . . . (650) 573-2544

Family Health Division
2000 Alameda De Las Pulgas, San Mateo, CA 94403
Tel: (650) 573-2346
Director **Brian Zamora** . . . . . (650) 573-3426

Animal Control and Licensing
225 37th Avenue, San Mateo, CA 94403
Program Manager **Pamela Machado** . . . . . (650) 573-3726

Food and Nutrition Services
2000 Alameda De Las Pulgas, San Mateo, CA 94403
Fax: (650) 577-9223
Director **Eliana Schultz** . . . . . (650) 573-3511

San Mateo Medical Center [SMMC]
222 West 39th Street, San Mateo, CA 94403
Internet: www.sanmateomedicalcenter.org
Chief Executive Officer **Susan P. Ehrlich** . . . . . (650) 573-2041

Office of the Assessor-County Clerk-Recorder
555 County Center, 3rd Floor, Redwood City, CA 94063
Tel: (650) 363-4500 Fax: (650) 363-1903 (Assessor's Office)
Fax: (650) 599-7458 (Clerk's Office)
Fax: (650) 363-4843 (Recorder's Office) Internet: www.smcare.org
★ Assessor-County Clerk-Recorder **Mark Church** . . . . . (650) 363-4988
Term Expires: December 31, 2018
E-mail: mchurch@smcare.org
Education: U Pacific BBA; McGeorge 1982 JD
Executive Assistant **Monica Carlisle** . . . . . (650) 599-1249
E-mail: mcarlisle@smcare.org
Deputy Assessor-Clerk-Recorder (Interim)
Julieta Fernandez . . . . . (650) 363-4988
E-mail: jfernandez@smcare.org

COUNTIES

★ Elected Official ▲ Appointed by Legislature ▼ Appointed by Governor ► Appointed by Board or Commission ● Appointed by Judge
■ Appointed by Mayor △ Appointed by Freeholders ▽ Appointed by Supervisor ▷ Appointed by County Executive ○ Appointed by Council

San Mateo County Elections Office
40 Tower Rd., San Mateo, CA 94402
Tel: (650) 312-5222 Fax: (650) 312-5348 E-mail: registrar@smcare.org
Internet: www.shapethefuture.org

★Chief Elections Officer **Mark Church** .... (650) 363-4988
Term Expires: December 31, 2018
E-mail: mchurch@smcare.org
Education: U Pacific BBA; McGeorge 1982 JD
Elections Manager **David Tom** .... (650) 312-5222

Office of the Coroner
50 Tower Road, San Mateo, CA 94402

★Coroner **Robert J. Foucrault** .... (650) 312-5233
Term Expires: December 31, 2018
E-mail: rfoucraulr@smcgov.org

Office of the County Controller-Auditor
555 County Center, 4th Floor, Redwood City, CA 94063

★Controller **Juan Raigoza** .... (650) 363-4777
Term Expires: December 31, 2018
Assistant Controller **(Vacant)** .... (650) 363-4853
Deputy Controller **Shirley Tourel** .... (650) 599-1149

Office of the District Attorney-Public Administrator
400 County Center, Redwood City, CA 94063
Tel: (650) 363-4636 Fax: (650) 363-4873

★District Attorney **Stephen M. "Steve" Wagstaffe** ...... (650) 363-4636
Term Expires: December 31, 2018
E-mail: swagstaffe@smcgov.org
Education: Notre Dame 1974 AB; Hastings 1977 JD
Chief Deputy District Attorney **Karen M. Guidotti** ...... (650) 363-4007

Office of the Sheriff
400 County Center, Redwood City, CA 94063
Internet: http://www.smcsheriff.com

★Sheriff **Greg Munks** .... (650) 599-1664
Term Expires: December 31, 2018
E-mail: gmunks@smcgov.org
Undersheriff **Carlos Bolanos** .... (650) 599-1662
E-mail: cbolanos@smcgov.org

Emergency Services Office
Emergency Command Center Area Coordinator
Edmund Barberini .... (650) 363-4790
E-mail: ebarberini@smcgov.org

Office of the Tax Collector-Treasurer
555 County Center, Redwood City, CA 94063
Tel: (650) 363-4142 Fax: (650) 363-4944
E-mail: taxmaster@co.sanmateo.ca.us
Internet: www.sanmateocountytaxcollector.org

★Tax Collector-Treasurer **Sandie Arnott** .... (650) 363-4580
Term Expires: December 31, 2018
E-mail: sarnott@co.sanmateo.ca.us
Assistant Tax Collector **Kelly A. Lawrence** .... (650) 363-4977
E-mail: klawrence@co.sanmateo.ca.us
Assistant Treasurer **Charles Tovstein** .... (650) 363-4228

San Mateo County Employees' Retirement Association
100 Marine World Parkway, Suite 125, Redwood Shores, CA 94065
Fax: (650) 599-1488

Chief Executive Officer **David Bailey** .... (650) 363-4930
E-mail: dbailey@smcgov.org
Information Technology Manager **Tariq Ali** .... (650) 363-4854
E-mail: tali@smcgov.org
Investment and Finance Manager **Michael R. Coultrip** ... (650) 599-7231
E-mail: mcoultrip@smcgov.org

County of Santa Barbara, California
105 East Anapamu Street, Santa Barbara, CA 93101
Tel: (805) 568-2190 (Information) Internet: www.countyofsb.org

County Seat: Santa Barbara **Election Type:** Nonpartisan
Population: 444,769 (2015)

Office of the Board of Supervisors
105 E. Anapamu St., Santa Barbara, CA 93101
Tel: (805) 568-2190 Internet: www.countyofsb.org/bos

★Chair **Peter Adam** (District 4) .... (805) 568-2190
Term Expires: January 2017
E-mail: peter.adam@countyofsb.org
★Vice Chair **Doreen Farr** (District 3) .... (805) 568-2192
Term Expires: January 2017 Fax: (805) 568-2883
E-mail: dfarr@countyofsb.org
★Supervisor **Salud Carbajal** (District 1) .... (805) 568-2186
Term Expires: January 2017 Fax: (805) 568-2534
E-mail: supervisorcarbajal@sbcbos1.org
Education: UC Santa Barbara 1990 BA; Fielding MA
★Supervisor **Janet Wolf** (District 2) .... (805) 568-2191
Term Expires: January 1, 2019
E-mail: jwolf@sbcbos2.org
★Supervisor **Steven J. "Steve" Lavagnino** (District 5) ... (805) 346-8400
Term Expires: January 2019 Fax: (805) 346-8404
E-mail: steve.lavagnino@countyofsb.org

Office of the Clerk of the Board of Supervisors
105 East Anapamu Street, Room 407, Santa Barbara, CA 93101
Fax: (805) 568-2249

▽Clerk of the Board **Mona Miyasato** .... (805) 568-3404
E-mail: cao@co.santa-barbara.ca.us
Chief Deputy Clerk of the Board **Michael Allen** .... (805) 568-2240
E-mail: allen@co.santa-barbara.ca.us

Office of the County Counsel
105 East Anapamu Street, Suite 201, Santa Barbara, CA 93101
Fax: (805) 568-2982 Internet: www.countyofsb.org/counsel

▽County Counsel **Michael Ghizzoni** .... (805) 568-2950
E-mail: mghizzoni@co.santa-barbara.ca.us
Chief Assistant County Counsel **Rachel Van Mullen** ..... (805) 568-2950
Chief Deputy **Martin G. McKenzie** .... (805) 568-2950
Chief Deputy **(Vacant)** .... (805) 568-2950

Office of the County Executive
105 East Anapamu Street, Room 406, Santa Barbara, CA 93101
Tel: (805) 568-3400 Fax: (805) 568-3414
E-mail: cao@co.santabarbara.ca.us Internet: www.countyofsb.org/ceo

▽County Executive Officer **Mona Miyasato** .... (805) 568-3404

★Elected Official ▲Appointed by Legislature ▼Appointed by Governor ▶Appointed by Board or Commission ●Appointed by Judge
■Appointed by Mayor △Appointed by Freeholders ▽Appointed by Supervisor ▷Appointed by County Executive ○Appointed by Council

Agricultural Commissioner's Office
263 Camino del Remedio, Santa Barbara, CA 93110-1335
Fax: (805) 681-5603

Agricultural Commissioner **Cathleen M. Fisher** . . . . (805) 681-5600

Cooperative Extension (University of California)
E-mail: cesantabarbara@ucdavis.edu
Internet: http://cesantabarbara.ucdavis.edu/

Division Director **Mary Bianchi** . . . . (805) 781-5940

Office of the Public Defender
1100 Anacapa Street, Santa Barbara, CA 93101
Tel: (805) 568-3470 Fax: (805) 568-3564
Internet: www.countyofsb.org/defender

Public Defender **Raimundo Montes De Oca** . . . . (805) 568-3470
Assistant Public Defender - North County
James K. Voysey . . . . (805) 346-7500
312 E. Cook St., Santa Maria, CA 93454 Fax: (805) 346-7670
Chief Trial Deputy **Jeff Chambliss** . . . . (805) 568-3470
Fax: (805) 568-3564
Chief Trial Deputy **Giovanni Giordani** . . . . (805) 737-7770
115 Civic Center Plaza, Lompoc, CA 93436 Fax: (805) 737-7881

Department of Alcohol, Drug and Mental Health Services [ADMHS]
300 North San Antonio Road, Santa Barbara, CA 93110-1316
Fax: (805) 681-5262 E-mail: admhsinfo@co.santa-barbara.ca.us
Internet: www.countyofsb.org/admhs

Director **Dr. Alice Gleghorn** . . . . (805) 681-5233
Assistant to the Director **Maria Xique** . . . . (805) 681-5232
E-mail: mxique@co.santa-barbara.ca.us
Medical Director **Ole Behrendtsen** . . . . (805) 681-5220
Alcohol and Drug Services Program Manager
John Doyel . . . . (805) 681-4907

Fire Department
4410 Cathedral Oaks Rd., Santa Barbara, CA 93110-1042
Fax: (805) 681-5563

▽ Fire Chief **Eric Peterson** . . . . (805) 681-5500

General Services Department
105 East Anapamu Street, Room 108, Santa Barbara, CA 93101
Tel: (805) 586-2625 Fax: (805) 568-2663
Internet: www.countyofsb.org/gs

Director **Matthew "Matt" Pontes** . . . . (805) 568-2626
Assistant Director, Financial Services **Karen Miles** . . . . . . (805) 884-6866
Fax: (805) 884-6861
Assistant Director, Support Services **Greg Chains** . . . . (805) 568-3096
E-mail: gchains@co.santa-barbara.ca.us Fax: (805) 568-3249

Purchasing Division
105 East Anapamu Street, Room 304, Santa Barbara, CA 93101
Fax: (805) 568-2705

Purchasing Manager **Mark Masoner** . . . . (805) 568-2692
E-mail: mmasone@co.santa-barbara.ca.us

Human Resources Department
1226 Anacapa Street, Santa Barbara, CA 93101
Fax: (805) 568-2833 Internet: www.countyofsb.org/hr

Director (Interim) **Bob MacLeod** . . . . (805) 568-2816
E-mail: bmacleod@sbcountyhr.org
Assistant Director **Melissa Grisales** . . . . (805) 568-2800
E-mail: mgrisales@sbcountyhr.org
Assistant Director **(Vacant)** . . . . (805) 568-3400

Community Services Division/Parks Department
123 E. Anapamu Street, Second Floor, Santa Barbara, CA 93101
Fax: (805) 568-2490 E-mail: contact@sbparks.org
Internet: www.sbparks.org

Director **George Chapjian** . . . . (805) 568-2461
Education: USC BA, MSW
Deputy Director **Paddy Langlands** . . . . (805) 568-2461

Planning and Development
123 East Anapamu Street, Santa Barbara, CA 93101
Fax: (805) 568-2030 E-mail: padstaff@co.santa-barbara.ca.us
Internet: www.sbcountyplanning.org

Director **Dr. Glenn Russell** . . . . (805) 568-2085
E-mail: grussell@co.santa-barbara.ca.us
Education: Wisconsin; UCLA
Assistant Director **Dianne Black** . . . . (805) 568-2086
E-mail: dianne@co.santa-barbara.ca.us
Assistant Director **Steve Mason** . . . . (805) 568-2070
E-mail: mason@co.santa-barbara.ca.us

Probation Department
117 East Carrillo Street, Santa Barbara, CA 93101
Fax: (805) 882-3651

Chief Probation Officer **Guadalupe Rabago** . . . . (805) 739-8603
Deputy Chief Probation Officer, Adult Services
Tanja Heitman . . . . (805) 739-8537
Deputy Chief Probation Officer, Juvenile Services
Steven DeLira . . . . (805) 739-8588
Deputy Chief Probation Officer, Institutions **Lee Bethel** . . (805) 882-3675
Administrative Deputy Director **Damon Fletcher** . . . . (805) 882-3654
E-mail: dfletch@co.santa-barbara.ca.us

Public Health Department [PHD]
300 North San Antonio Road, Santa Barbara, CA 93110-1316
Tel: (805) 681-5102 Fax: (805) 681-5191 Internet: www.sbcphd.org

Director/Health Officer **Takashi Michael Wada** . . . . (805) 681-5105
Education: UCLA 1994 MD, 2002 MPH
Deputy Director **Susan Klein-Rothschild** . . . . (805) 681-5102
Deputy Assistant Director **Dan Reid** . . . . (805) 681-5173

Public Works Department
123 E. Anapamu St., Santa Barbara, CA 93101
Fax: (805) 568-3019

Director **Scott D. McGolpin** . . . . (805) 568-3010
Executive Secretary **Michelle Garcia** . . . . (805) 568-3010
E-mail: mgarcia@cosbpw.net
Flood Control and Water Conservation Deputy Director
Thomas "Tom" Fayram . . . . (805) 568-3436
Fax: (805) 568-3434
Roads and Transportation Deputy Director
Chris Sneddon . . . . (805) 568-3064
Resource Recovery & Waste Management Deputy
Director **Mark Schleich** . . . . (805) 882-3605
130 East Victoria Street, Fax: (805) 882-3601
Suite 100, Santa Barbara, CA 93101
Surveyor **Alexsandar Jevremovic** . . . . (805) 568-3012
Fax: (805) 568-3318

Social Services Department
234 Camino del Remedio, Santa Barbara, CA 93110-1369
Fax: (805) 681-4403

Director **Daniel Nelson** . . . . (805) 681-4451
Administrative Deputy Director **Terri Consellos** . . . . (805) 681-4455
E-mail: tconsellos@co.santa-barbara.ca.us
Calworks Deputy Director **Ken Jensen** . . . . (805) 681-4485
Child Welfare Services Deputy Director **Devin Drake** . . . . (805) 681-7312

★ Elected Official ▲ Appointed by Legislature ▼ Appointed by Governor ▶ Appointed by Board or Commission ● Appointed by Judge
■ Appointed by Mayor △ Appointed by Freeholders ▽ Appointed by Supervisor ▷ Appointed by County Executive ○ Appointed by Council

COUNTIES

Air Pollution Control District [APCD]

260 North San Antonio Road, Suite A, Santa Barbara, CA 93110-1315
Tel: (805) 961-8800 (Front Desk) Fax: (805) 961-8801
E-mail: apcd@sbcapcd.org Internet: http://www.ourair.org/

Air Pollution Control Officer **Dave Van Mullem** .... (805) 961-8853

Office of the Auditor-Controller

105 East Anapamu Street, Room 303, Santa Barbara, CA 93101
P.O. Box 39, Santa Barbara, CA 93102-0039
Fax: (805) 568-2016 E-mail: auditor@co.santa-barbara.ca.us

★ Auditor-Controller **Robert W. Geis** .... (805) 568-2100
Term Expires: January 1, 2019
E-mail: geis@co.santa-barbara.ca.us

Assistant Auditor-Controller **Theo Fallati** .... (805) 568-2100

Department Administrator **Andrea Johnson** .... (805) 568-2454

Office of the County Clerk-Recorder-Assessor

105 East Anapamu Street, Room 204, Santa Barbara, CA 93101
P.O. Box 159, Santa Barbara, CA 93102-0159
Fax: (805) 568-3247 Internet: www.sbcvote.com

★ County Clerk-Recorder-Assessor
Joseph Edward Holland .... (805) 568-2550
Term Expires: January 6, 2019
E-mail: holland@co.santa-barbara.ca.us

Chief Deputy Clerk-Recorder **Melinda Greene** .... (805) 568-2574

Chief Deputy Assessor **Keith Taylor** .... (805) 568-2562
E-mail: taylor@co.santa-barbara.ca.us

Chief Deputy Registrar of Voters **Renee Bischof** .... (805) 696-8963
E-mail: rbischo@co.santa-barbara.ca.us

Office of the District Attorney

1112 Santa Barbara Street, Santa Barbara, CA 93101
Tel: (805) 568-2300 Fax: (805) 568-2398
Internet: www.countyofsb.org/da

★ District Attorney **Joyce Dudley** .... (805) 568-2306
Term Expires: January 8, 2019
E-mail: jdudley@co.santa-barbara.ca.us
Education: UC Santa Barbara 1975 BA, 1978 MEd

Office of the Sheriff-Coroner

4434 Calle Real, Santa Barbara, CA 93110
Fax: (805) 681-4322 Internet: www.sbsheriff.org

★ Sheriff-Coroner **Bill Brown** .... (805) 681-4100
Term Expires: January 1, 2019
E-mail: bbrown@co.santa-barbara.ca.us

Undersheriff **Bernard K. Melekian** .... (805) 681-4100
E-mail: bmelekian@co.santa-barbara.ca.us
Education: Cal State (Northridge) 1980 BA, 1994 MPA

Chief Deputy, Custody Operations **Julie McCammon** .... (805) 681-4245

Chief Deputy, Law Enforcement Operations (Acting)
Sam Gross .... (805) 681-4100

Chief Deputy, Support Services **(Vacant)** .... (805) 681-4100

Office of the Treasurer-Tax Collector

105 East Anapamu Street, Room 109, Santa Barbara, CA 93101
P.O. Box 579, Santa Barbara, CA 93102-0579
Fax: (805) 568-2488 Internet: www.countyofsb.org/ttcpapg

★ Treasurer-Tax Collector **Harry E. Hagen** .... (805) 568-2490
Term Expires: January 2019
E-mail: hhagen@co.santa-barbara.ca.us
Education: UC Santa Barbara

County of Santa Clara, California

Government Center, 70 West Hedding Street, San Jose, CA 95110-1705
Tel: (408) 299-5105 (Information) Internet: www.sccgov.org

County Seat: San Jose **Election Type:** Nonpartisan
Population: 1,918,044 (2015)

Board of Supervisors

Government Center, 70 West Hedding Street, 10th Floor,
San Jose, CA 95110-1705
Fax: (408) 298-8460

★ President **David D. "Dave" Cortese** (District 3)........ (408) 299-5030
Term Expires: January 31, 2017 Fax: (408) 298-6637
E-mail: dave.cortese@bos.sccgov.org
Education: UC Davis 1978 BS; Lincoln U (CA) 1995 JD

★ Supervisor **Mike Wasserman** (District 1).............. (408) 299-5010
Term Expires: January 31, 2017 Fax: (408) 295-6993
E-mail: mike.wasserman@bos.sccgov.org
Education: USC 1980 BA

★ Supervisor **Cindy Chavez** (District 2) .... (408) 299-5020
Term Expires: January 31, 2017 Fax: (408) 295-8642

★ Supervisor
Dr. Kenneth Eugene "Ken" Yeager (District 4)....... (408) 299-5040
Term Expires: January 31, 2017 Fax: (408) 299-2038
E-mail: ken.yeager@bos.sccgov.org
Date of Birth: December 12, 1952
Education: San José State BA; Stanford 1986 AM, 1991 PhD

★ Supervisor **Saren Joseph "Joe" Simitian** (District 5) ... (408) 299-5050
Term Expires: January 31, 2017 Fax: (408) 280-0418
Education: Colorado Col BA; Stanford MA; UC Berkeley JD

▶ Clerk of the Board **Megan Doyle** .... (408) 299-5001
E-mail: megan.doyle@bos.sccgov.org

Office of the County Executive

Government Center, East Wing, 70 W. Hedding Street, 11th Floor,
San Jose, CA 95110-1705
Tel: (408) 299-5105 Tel: (408) 229-5007 (Information)

▶ County Executive **Jeffrey Virgil "Jeff" Smith** .... (408) 299-5102
E-mail: jeff.smith@ceo.sccgov.org
Education: Loyola Marymount 1976 BS; USC 1980 MD;
Boalt Hall 1989 JD

Deputy County Executive **Leslie Crowell** .... (408) 299-5173
E-mail: leslie.crowell@ceo.sccgov.org

Deputy County Executive **Sylvia Gallegos** .... (408) 299-5106
E-mail: sylvia.gallegos@ceo.sccgov.org

Deputy County Executive **(Vacant)** .... (408) 299-5828

Deputy County Executive **René G. Santiago** .... (408) 885-6868

Chief Operating Officer **Gary A. Graves** .... (408) 299-5181
E-mail: gary.graves@ceo.sccgov.org

Deputy County Executive **James R. Williams** .... (408) 829-9510
Education: Princeton 2006 BA; Stanford 2010 JD

Deputy County Executive **John Mill** .... (408) 299-5105

Office of Budget and Analysis [OBA]

70 West Hedding Street, 11th Floor, San Jose, CA 95110-1705

Budget Director **Gregory Iturria** .... (408) 299-5174
E-mail: gregory.iturria@oba.sccgov.org

Printing Manager **Gary Roby** .... (408) 918-3300
Building 2, 1555 Berger Drive, San Jose, CA 95112-2716

Office of the County Counsel

Government Center, 70 W. Hedding St., 9th Floor,
San Jose, CA 95110-1770
Fax: (408) 292-7240

▶ County Counsel **Orry Korb** .... (408) 299-5902
Education: UCLA 1978 BA; Syracuse 1983 JD

★ Elected Official ▲ Appointed by Legislature ▼ Appointed by Governor ▶ Appointed by Board or Commission ● Appointed by Judge
■ Appointed by Mayor △ Appointed by Freeholders ▽ Appointed by Supervisor ▷ Appointed by County Executive ○ Appointed by Council

Office of Emergency Services [OES]
55 West Younger Avenue, Suite 450, San Jose, CA 95110-1721
Fax: (408) 294-4851 E-mail: oes@oes.sccgov.org

Director **Dana Reed** .... (408) 808-7801
E-mail: dana.reed@oes.sccgov.org
Deputy Director **David Flamm** .... (408) 808-7800
Senior Emergency Planning Coordinator **Ken Foot** .... (408) 808-7803
E-mail: ken.foot@oes.sccgov.org
Senior Emergency Planning Coordinator **Cindy Stewart** .. (408) 808-7808
E-mail: cindy.stewart@oes.sccgov.org
Emergency Planning Coordinator **Tammy Dunbar** .... (408) 808-7805
E-mail: tammy.dunbar@oes.sccgov.org
Program Manager- Grants Management
Michelle Sandoval .... (408) 808-7811
E-mail: michelle.sandoval@oes.sccgov.org
Battalion Chief- County Multidisciplinary Task Force
Doug Young .... (408) 808-7812
E-mail: doug.young@oes.sccgov.org

Office of the Medical Examiner-Coroner
850 Thornton Way, San Jose, CA 95128-4702
Fax: (408) 793-1934

Medical Examiner-Coroner **Dr. Michelle Jorden** .... (408) 793-1900

Office of Pretrial Services
Government Center, 70 West Hedding Street, West Wing, 1st Floor, San Jose, CA 95110
Tel: (408) 792-2460 Fax: (408) 299-7145

Director **Garry Herceg** .... (408) 792-2499
Education: San José State 1993 BA

Office of the Public Defender
120 W. Mission Street, San Jose, CA 95110-1715
Tel: (408) 299-7700 Fax: (408) 998-8265

▶ Public Defender **Molly O'Neal** .... (408) 299-7711
E-mail: moneal@pdo.sccgov.org

Office of the Registrar of Voters
Building 2, 1555 Berger Drive, San Jose, CA 95112-2716
Fax: (408) 998-7314 E-mail: registrar@rov.sccgov.org
Internet: www.sccvote.org

Registrar of Voters **Shannon Bushey** .... (408) 299-8683

Agriculture and Environmental Management Department
Building 1, 1553 Berger Drive, San Jose, CA 95112

Director **Greg Van Wassenhove** .... (408) 918-4646
Environmental Health Department Director **Ben Gale** .... (408) 918-1955

Department of Child Support Services
2851 Junction Avenue, San Jose, CA 95134
Fax: (408) 503-5252

▶ Director **Ralph Miller** .... (408) 503-5345
E-mail: rmiller@dcss.sccgov.org

Department of Correction
180 W. Hedding Street, San Jose, CA 95110-1772
Fax: (408) 288-8271

Chief (Acting) **John Hirokawa** .... (408) 808-3640

Santa Clara County Communications
2700 Carol Drive, San Jose, CA 95125-2032
Fax: (408) 279-2666

Director **Bert Hildebrand** .... (408) 977-3200

Employee Services Agency
Government Center, 70 W. Hedding Street, 8th Floor, San Jose, CA 95110-1705
Fax: (408) 279-5764 Internet: www.sccjobs.org

Deputy County Executive **(Vacant)** .... (408) 299-5828

Office of Labor Relations
70 W. Hedding Street, 8th Floor, East Wing, San Jose, CA 95110
Tel: (408) 299-5820 Fax: (408) 286-4813

Director **Sandra J. Poole** .... (408) 299-5814

Department of Equal Opportunity and Employee Development [EO/ED]
1641 North First Street, Suite 200, San Jose, CA 95112-4525
Fax: (408) 437-3040

Director **Sabahete Kraja** .... (408) 299-5864
2310 North First Street, Suite 101, San Jose, CA 95131
Financial and Administrative Services Manager
Quyen Nguyen .... (408) 299-5871
70 West Hedding Street, 8th Floor, East Wing, San Jose, CA 95110-1705 Fax: (408) 295-3012

Department of Human Resources
70 West Hedding Street, 8th Floor, East Wing, San Jose, CA 95110-1705
Tel: (408) 299-5830 Fax: (408) 295-3065

Director **John Dam** .... (408) 299-5835

Finance Agency
Government Center, 70 West Hedding Street, 2nd Floor, San Jose, CA 95110-1705
Tel: (408) 299-5200 Fax: (408) 289-8629
Internet: www.sccgov.org/portal/site/fin

Director **Emily Harrison** .... (408) 299-5205
Controller-Treasurer **Alan Minato** .... (408) 299-5202
Tax Collector **George Putris** .... (408) 808-7950
E-mail: george.putris@tax.sccgov.org

Facilities and Fleet Department
2310 North First Street, Suite 200, San Jose, CA 95131
Tel: (408) 993-4600 Fax: (408) 993-4777

Director **Jeffrey D. "Jeff" Draper** .... (408) 993-4600
E-mail: jeff.draper@faf.sccgov.org
Deputy Director, Capital Programs **Ken Rado** .... (408) 993-4600
E-mail: ken.rado@faf.sccgov.org
Deputy Director, Facilities and Fleet **Dave Snow** .... (408) 299-2357
E-mail: dave.snow@faf.sccgov.org

Santa Clara County Fire Department [SCCFD]
14700 Winchester Boulevard, Los Gatos, CA 95032-1818
Fax: (408) 378-9342 Internet: www.sccfd.org

Fire Chief **Kenneth R. "Ken" Kehmna** .... (408) 378-4010 ext. 4411
E-mail: ken.kehmna@cnt.sccgov.org
Education: Mission AS; St Mary's Col (CA) 1999 BA; Grand Canyon 2009 MS

Human Relations Commission
1880 Pruneridge Avenue, Santa Clara, CA 95050-6514
Fax: (408) 297-2463

Manager **Delorme McKee-Stovall** .... (408) 792-2300

Information Services Department [ISD]
1555 Berger Drive, 2nd Floor, San Jose, CA 95112-2716
Fax: (408) 918-7100

Chief Information Officer **Joyce Wing** .... (408) 918-7001
E-mail: joyce.wing@isd.sccgov.org

COUNTIES

★ Elected Official ▲ Appointed by Legislature ▼ Appointed by Governor ▶ Appointed by Board or Commission ● Appointed by Judge
■ Appointed by Mayor △ Appointed by Freeholders ▽ Appointed by Supervisor ▷ Appointed by County Executive ○ Appointed by Council

Department of Planning and Development

Government Center, 70 West Hedding Street, East Wing, 7th Floor, San Jose, CA 95110

Director **Kirk Girard** .... (408) 299-6740
Development Services Manager/Building Official
Michael "Mike" Harrison .... (408) 299-5709
Planning Manager (Acting) **Carolyn Walsh** .... (408) 299-5773

Department of Parks and Recreation

298 Garden Hill Drive, Los Gatos, CA 95032
Fax: (408) 355-2290 Internet: www.parkhere.org

Director **Robb Courtney** .... (408) 355-2244

Probation Department

840 Guadalupe Pkwy., San Jose, CA 95110-1714
Fax: (408) 294-6879 E-mail: public_information@pro.sccgov.org

Chief Probation Officer **Laura Garnette** .... (408) 278-5900
Education: UC Santa Cruz 1989 BA; San José State 2006 MPA

Procurement Department

2310 North First Street, Suite 201, San Jose, CA 95131
Tel: (408) 491-7400 Fax: (408) 491-7496
Internet: http://procurement.sccgov.org/

Director **Jenti Vandertuig** .... (408) 491-7434
E-mail: jenti.vandertuig@proc.sccgov.org

Roads and Airports Department

101 Skyport Dr., San Jose, CA 95110-1302
Fax: (408) 441-0142 Internet: http://countryroads.org

Director **Michael Murdter** .... (408) 573-2438
Administrative Services Manager **Tony Arata** .... (408) 573-2404
E-mail: tony.arata@rda.sccgov.org
Infrastructure Development Deputy Director
Dan Collen .... (408) 573-2480
Fax: (408) 441-0276
Fiscal Officer **Madhur Bagla** .... (408) 573-2418
Fax: (408) 441-0142
Road Maintenance Deputy Director **Ron Jackson** .... (408) 494-2760
1505 Schallenberger Road, San Jose, CA 95131-2434 Fax: (408) 297-0530

Santa Clara Valley Health and Hospital System [SCVHHS]

645 South Bascom Avenue, Suite 212, San Jose, CA 95128
Tel: (408) 885-4030 Fax: (408) 885-4051

Director **René G. Santiago** .... (408) 885-6868

Department of Alcohol and Drug Services [DADS]

976 Lenzen Avenue, San Jose, CA 95126-2737
Fax: (408) 947-8702

Director **Bruce Copley** .... (408) 792-5680

Santa Clara Valley Medical Center [SCVMC]

751 South Bascom Avenue, San Jose, CA 95128-2604
Tel: (408) 885-5000 Fax: (408) 793-1817 Internet: www.scvmed.org

Chief Executive Officer **Paul E. Lorenz** .... (408) 885-4010

Mental Health Department

828 South Bascom Avenue, Suite 200, San Jose, CA 95128-2600
Tel: (408) 885-5782 Fax: (408) 885-5788 Internet: www.sccmhd.org

Director **Toni Tullys** .... (408) 885-5782
Deputy Director **Deane Wiley** .... (408) 885-5773
Medical Director **Tiffany Ho** .... (408) 885-5767
Fax: (408) 885-4889

Public Health Department [SCCPHD]

976 Lenzen Avenue, 2nd Floor, San Jose, CA 95126-2737
Tel: (408) 792-5040 Fax: (408) 792-5041 Internet: www.sccphd.org

Director **Dr. Sara H. Cody** .... (408) 792-5040
Education: Stanford BS; Yale MD
Emergency Medical Services Agency Director
Jackie Lowther .... (408) 885-4250
645 South Bascom Avenue, San Jose, CA 95128 Fax: (408) 885-4262

Social Services Agency

333 West Julian Street, San Jose, CA 95110-2335
Fax: (408) 755-7960 Internet: www.sccgov.org/ssa

Director **Robert Menicocci** .... (408) 755-7700
Director, Department of Aging and Adult Services
James Ramoni .... (408) 755-7600
Fax: (408) 975-4850
Director, Department of Employment and Benefit Services **Denise Boland** .... (408) 755-7720
E-mail: denise.boland@ssa.sccgov.org Fax: (408) 755-7965
Director, Department of Family and Children Services
Lori Medina .... (408) 501-6800
Fax: (408) 792-1406

Housing Authority of the County of Santa Clara [HACSC]

505 West Julian Street, San Jose, CA 95110-2300
Fax: (408) 280-1929 Internet: www.hacsc.org

Executive Director **Katherine Harasz** .... (408) 993-2903
Director of Housing **Aleli Sangalang** .... (408) 993-2903

Santa Clara County Library

14600 Winchester Boulevard, Los Gatos, CA 95032
Fax: (408) 364-0161 Internet: www.santaclaracountylib.org

Executive Director/County Librarian
Nancy Howe .... (408) 293-2326 ext. 3001
E-mail: nhowe@sccl.org

Office of the Assessor

Government Center, East Wing, 70 W. Hedding Street, 5th Floor, San Jose, CA 95110-1705
Fax: (408) 298-9446

★ Assessor **Lawrence E. Stone** .... (408) 299-5588
Term Expires: December 31, 2018
E-mail: larry.stone@asr.sccgov.org
Assistant Assessor **Mary Fuentes** .... (408) 299-5568

Office of the Clerk-Recorder

70 West Hedding Street, San Jose, CA 95110-1705
Tel: (408) 299-5688

County Clerk/Recorder
Regina M. "Gina" Alcomendras .... (408) 299-5621
E-mail: gina.alcomendras@rec.sccgov.org

Office of the District Attorney

Government Center, West Wing, 70 W. Hedding Street, San Jose, CA 95110-1705
Tel: (408) 299-7400 Fax: (408) 286-5437
E-mail: webmaster@da.co.santa-clara.ca.us
Internet: www.santaclara-da.org

★ District Attorney **Jeffrey Francis "Jeff" Rosen** .... (408) 299-3099
Term Expires: December 31, 2016
E-mail: jrosen@da.sccgov.org
Education: UCLA 1989 BA; Boalt Hall 1992 JD
Chief Assistant District Attorney **Jay Steven Boyarsky** .. (408) 299-3099
Education: UC Santa Cruz 1987; Boalt Hall 1991 JD

★ Elected Official ▲ Appointed by Legislature ▼ Appointed by Governor ▶ Appointed by Board or Commission ● Appointed by Judge
■ Appointed by Mayor △ Appointed by Freeholders ▽ Appointed by Supervisor ▷ Appointed by County Executive ○ Appointed by Council

Office of the Sheriff

55 West Younger Avenue, San Jose, CA 95110-1721
Tel: (408) 808-4400 Fax: (408) 283-0562 Internet: www.sccsheriff.org

★Sheriff **Laurie Smith** .... (408) 808-4904
Term Expires: December 31, 2018
E-mail: laurie.smith@sheriff.sccgov.org
Undersheriff **John Hirokawa** .... (408) 808-4900
E-mail: john.hirokawa@sheriff.sccgov.org

County of Sedgwick, Kansas

525 N. Main St., Wichita, KS 67203
Tel: (316) 660-9000 (Information) Internet: www.sedgwickcounty.org

County Seat: Wichita **Election Type:** Partisan **Population:** 511,574 (2015)

Office of the Board of Commissioners

525 N. Main St., Suite 320, Wichita, KS 67203
Fax: (316) 383-8275 Internet: www.sedgwickcounty.org/commissioners

★Chair **Jim Howell** (R-District 5) .... (316) 660-9300
Term Expires: January 2019
Education: Southern Illinois BS; Friends BS
★Chair Pro Tem **Richard Ranzau** (R-District 4) .... (316) 660-9300
Term Expires: January 13, 2019
E-mail: rranzau@sedgwick.gov
★Commissioner **Dave Unruh** (R-District 1) .... (316) 660-9300
Term Expires: January 13, 2019
E-mail: dunruh@sedgwick.gov
★Commissioner **Tim R. Norton** (R-District 2) .... (316) 660-9300
Term Expires: January 8, 2017
E-mail: tnorton@sedgwick.gov
Education: Arkansas State BA; Newman U MEd
★Commissioner **Karl Peterjohn** (R-District 3) .... (316) 660-9300
Term Expires: January 8, 2017
E-mail: kpeterjo@sedgwick.gov

Office of the Appraiser

525 N. Main St., Suite 227, Wichita, KS 67203
Fax: (316) 383-7457 E-mail: appraiser@sedgwick.gov
Internet: www.sedgwickcounty.org/appraiser

►Appraiser **Michael S. Borchard** .... (316) 660-9110
E-mail: mborchar@sedgwick.gov

Sedgwick County Public Works

1144 South Seneca Street, Wichita, KS 67213
Internet: www.sedgwickcounty.org/public_works Tel: (316) 660-1777
Fax: (316) 263-9241

►Director/County Engineer **David C. Spears** .... (316) 660-1777
E-mail: dspears@sedgwick.gov

Office of the County Manager

525 N. Main St., Suite 343, Wichita, KS 67203
Fax: (316) 383-7946 Internet: www.sedgwickcounty.org/manager

County Manager **Michael Scholes** .... (316) 660-9393

Communications and Community Initiatives

Courthouse, 525 N. Main St., Wichita, KS 67203

Director **Kristi Zukovich** .... (316) 660-9370

Community Relations Division

Deputy Director **Jill Tinsley** .... (316) 660-9375

Extension Services

7001 W. 21st St. North, Wichita, KS 67205
Fax: (316) 722-7727 E-mail: sginform@oznet.ksu.edu
Internet: www.oznet.ksu.edu/sedgwick

Extension Director **Bev Dunning** .... (316) 660-0100

Finance Division

525 N. Main St., SUite 823, Wichita, KS 67203

Chief Financial Officer **Chris Chronis** .... (316) 660-7130

Accounting Department

525 N. Main St., Suite 823, Wichita, KS 67203
Fax: (316) 383-7729

Controller **Sara Jantz** .... (316) 660-7136
E-mail: sjantz@sedgwick.gov

Budget Department

525 N. Main St., 8th Floor, Wichita, KS 67203
Fax: (316) 383-7729

Director **Lindsay Rousseau** .... (316) 660-7141

Economic Development Department

Courthouse, 525 N. Main St., Room 343, Wichita, KS 67203
Tel: (316) 660-7591

Director **Sherdeill Breathett** .... (316) 268-1139
Education: Oklahoma 1982 BA

Purchasing

604 North Main Street, Suite F, Wichita, KS 67203
Fax: (316) 383-7055

Director (Acting) **Joe Thomas** .... (316) 660-7255
E-mail: jethomas@sedgwick.gov

Risk Management Department

510 N. Main St., Room 304, Wichita, KS 67203
Fax: (316) 383-7674

Manager **Mick A. McBride** .... (316) 660-9682
E-mail: mmcbride@sedgwick.gov

Human Resources Division

510 N. Main St., 3rd Floor, Wichita, KS 67203
Fax: (316) 383-7288

Director **Eileen McNichol** .... (316) 660-7050

Health and Human Services Division

635 N. Main St., Wichita, KS 67203
Internet: www.sedgwickcounty.org/human_services

Director **Tim Kaufman** .... (316) 660-7057

Comprehensive Community Care [COMCARE]

635 N. Main St., Wichita, KS 67203
Internet: www.sedgwickcounty.org/comcare

Director **Marilyn Cook** .... (316) 660-7665

Department on Aging

510 N. Main St., 5th Floor, Wichita, KS 67203
Fax: (316) 383-7757 Internet: www.sedgwickcounty.org/aging

Director **Annette Graham** .... (316) 660-5221

Sedgwick County Health Department [SCHD]

1900 East Ninth Street, Wichita, KS 67214-3115
Tel: (316) 660-7300 Fax: (316) 660-7310
Internet: www.sedgwickcounty.org/healthdept

Director **Adrienne Byrne-Lutz** .... (316) 660-7414
County Health Officer **Garold O. Minns** .... (316) 660-7300
Children and Family Health Director
Nicole Fox Phillips .... (316) 660-7312
Health Protection Director **Chris Steward** .... (316) 660-7339

(continued on next page)

★Elected Official ▲Appointed by Legislature ▼Appointed by Governor ►Appointed by Board or Commission ●Appointed by Judge
■Appointed by Mayor △Appointed by Freeholders ▽Appointed by Supervisor ▷Appointed by County Executive ○Appointed by Council

Sedgwick County Health Department *continued*

Preventive Health Division Director **Preston Goering** .... (316) 660-7324

Animal Control Department
1015 Stillwell, Wichita, KS 67213
Fax: (316) 383-7337

Administrative Officer **Cindy Pollard** .... (316) 660-1840

Information and Operations Division
538 N. Main Street, 1st Floor, Wichita, KS 67203
Fax: (316) 383-7673

Chief Information Officer (Acting) **Wes Ellington** ...... (316) 660-9825
E-mail: hellingt@sedgwick.gov
Geographic Information System (GIS) Manager
John F. Rogers .... (316) 660-9290
E-mail: jrogers@sedgwick.gov
Infrastructure **Wes Ellington** .... (316) 660-9825
Records Manager and Freedom of Information Officer
Douglas K. "Doug" King .... (316) 660-9846
E-mail: dking@sedgwick.gov

Office of the Assistant County Manager
Assistant County Manager **Ronald W. "Ron" Holt** ...... (316) 660-9393

Culture and Recreation Division
525 N. Main St., Suite 343, Wichita, KS 67203
Fax: (316) 383-7946

Director **Ronald W. "Ron" Holt** .... (316) 660-9393
Director of Exploration Place **Jan Luth** .... (316) 660-0670

Sedgwick County Zoo
5555 Zoo Blvd., Wichita, KS 67212-1698
Fax: (316) 942-3781 E-mail: info@scz.org Internet: http://www.scz.org

Director of Sedgwick County Zoo
Mark C. Reed .... (316) 660-8201 ext. 201

Environmental Resources and Household Hazardous Waste Department
2625 S. Tyler Rd., Wichita, KS 67215
Fax: (316) 721-9366

Director **Susan Erlenwein** .... (316) 660-7205

Public Safety Division
525 N. Main St., Suite 343, Wichita, KS 67203

Director of Public Safety **Marvin Duncan** .... (316) 660-9393
Director of the Regional Forensic Science Center
Tim Rohring .... (316) 660-4804

Department of Corrections
905 N. Main St., Wichita, KS 67203
Fax: (316) 660-1670 Internet: www.sedgwickcounty.org/corrections

Director of Corrections **Mark Masterson** .... (316) 660-7014

Emergency Communications
525 N. Main St., Suite B6, Wichita, KS 67203
Fax: (316) 383-8060 Internet: www.sedgwickcounty.org/dispatch

Director of Emergency Communications (Interim)
Kim Pennington .... (316) 660-4983

Emergency Management
535 N. Main St., Suite B-10, Wichita, KS 67203
Fax: (316) 383-7559 Internet: www.sedgwickcounty.org/emermgmt

Director of Emergency Management (Interim)
John Crosby .... (316) 660-5965
714 North Main, Wichita, KS 67203-3603

Emergency Medical Service
538 N. Main St., 1st Floor, Wichita, KS 67203
Fax: (316) 383-7338 Internet: www.sedgwickcounty.org/ems

Director of Emergency Medical Services **Scott Hadley** ... (316) 660-7994

Fire Department
4343 N. Woodlawn, Wichita, KS 67220
Fax: (316) 744-0944

Fire Chief **Tavis Leake** .... (316) 660-3473
E-mail: tleake@sedgwick.gov
Education: Barclay BA; Southwestern Col (KS) MA

Facilities, Fleets, and Parks
525 N. Main St., Room 135, Wichita, KS 67203

Facilities Director **Steve Claassen** .... (316) 660-9075
E-mail: claassen@sedgwick.gov
Director of Security **Darrel Haynes** .... (316) 660-7782

Lake Afton/Sedgwick County Park
6501 W. 21st St. North, Wichita, KS 67205
Fax: (316) 942-3127

Director **Mark Sroufe** .... (316) 794-2774

Department of Facilities
Facilities Maintenance Director **Greg Tuxhorn** .... (316) 660-9062

Project Services
Director of Project Services **Tania Cole** .... (316) 660-9854

Fleet Services
Fleet Manager **Penny Poland** .... (316) 660-7477

Housing
Tel: (316) 660-7276

Director **Dorsha Kirksey** .... (316) 660-7276

Metropolitan Area Building and Construction Department
Director **Thomas Stolz** .... (316) 660-1840

Wichita-Sedgwick County Metropolitan Area Planning Department [MAPD]
City Hall, 455 North Main Street, 10th Floor, Wichita, KS 67202
Tel: (316) 268-4425 Fax: (316) 268-4390
Internet: www.wichita.gov/cityoffices/planning

Director **John L. Schlegel** .... (316) 268-4425

Office of the County Counselor
525 N. Main St., 359, Wichita, KS 67203
Tel: (316) 660-9340

County Counselor-Designate **Eric Yost** .... (316) 660-9340
Education: Kansas 2015 JD

Office of the County Clerk
525 N. Main St., Room 211, Wichita, KS 67203
Tel: (316) 660-9249 Fax: (316) 383-7961

★ County Clerk **Kelly Arnold** (R) .... (316) 660-9222
Term Expires: January 8, 2017
E-mail: sgclerk@sedgwick.gov

Office of the District Attorney
525 N. Main St., 2nd Floor Annex, Wichita, KS 67203
Fax: (316) 660-3600 E-mail: da@feist.com
Internet: http://www.feist.com/da

★ District Attorney **Marc Bennett** (R) .... (316) 660-3600
Term Expires: January 8, 2017

Office of the Election Commissioner
510 N. Main St., Suite 101, Wichita, KS 67203
Fax: (316) 383-7388

Election Commissioner **Tabitha Lehman** .... (316) 660-7121

★ Elected Official ▲ Appointed by Legislature ▼ Appointed by Governor ▶ Appointed by Board or Commission ● Appointed by Judge
■ Appointed by Mayor △ Appointed by Freeholders ▽ Appointed by Supervisor ▷ Appointed by County Executive ○ Appointed by Council

Office of the Register of Deeds

525 N. Main St., Suite 415, Wichita, KS 67203
Fax: (316) 383-8066

★ Register of Deeds **Bill Meek** (R) .... (316) 660-9422
Term Expires: January 8, 2017

Office of the Sheriff

141 W. Elm, 2nd Floor, Wichita, KS 67203
Fax: (316) 383-7758

★ Sheriff **Jeff Easter** (R) .... (316) 660-3900
Term Expires: January 8, 2017

Office of the Treasurer

525 N. Main St., Room 107, Wichita, KS 67201
Fax: (316) 383-7113

★ Treasurer **Linda Kizzire** .... (316) 660-9127
Term Expires: January 8, 2017

County of Seminole, Florida

1101 East First Street, Sanford, FL 32771
Tel: (407) 665-0311 Internet: www.seminolecountyfl.gov

County Seat: Sanford **Election Type:** Partisan **Population:** 449,144 (2015)

Board of County Commissioners

1101 East First Street, Sanford, FL 32771
Fax: (407) 665-7958

★ Chair **Brenda Carey** (R-District 5) .... (407) 665-7209
Term Expires: November 2016
E-mail: bcarey@seminolecountyfl.gov

★ Vice Chair **John Horan** (R-District 2) .... (407) 665-7205
Term Expires: November 20, 2018
Education: Notre Dame 1974 AB, 1977 JD

★ Commissioner **Robert E. "Bob" Dallari** (R-District 1) .... (407) 665-7215
Term Expires: November 2016

★ Commissioner **D. Lee Constantine** (R-District 3) .... (407) 665-7207
Term Expires: November 2016
E-mail: lconstantine@seminolecountyfl.gov
Education: Central Florida 1974 BA

★ Commissioner **Carlton D. Henley** (R-District 4) .... (407) 665-7201
Term Expires: November 20, 2018
E-mail: chenley@seminolecountyfl.gov
Education: Memphis State BS, MA

Office of the County Attorney

1101 East First Street, Sanford, FL 32771
Tel: (407) 665-7254 Internet: www.seminolecountyfl.gov/ca

County Attorney **A. Bryant Applegate** .... (407) 665-7254
E-mail: bapplegate@seminolecountyfl.gov
Education: Davis & Elkins 1977 BA; Nova 1980 JD

Office of the County Manager

1101 East First Street, Sanford, FL 32771
Tel: (407) 665-7211 Fax: (407) 665-7958
Internet: www.seminolecountyfl.gov/cm

○ County Manager **Nicole Guillet** .... (407) 665-7211
E-mail: nguillet@seminolecountyfl.gov
County Manager Coordinator **Shani Beach** .... (407) 665-7211
E-mail: sbeach@seminolecountyfl.gov
Deputy County Manager **Bruce McMenemy** .... (407) 665-7224
E-mail: bmcmenemy@seminolecountyfl.gov

Office of the County Manager *continued*

Administrative Assistant **Shelly Brubaker** .... (407) 665-7224
E-mail: sbrubaker@seminolecountyfl.gov

Human Resources Division

1101 East First Street, Sanford, FL 32771-1468

Manager **Christina Brandolini** .... (407) 665-7944
E-mail: HR@seminolecountyfl.gov

Geographic Information Services Division [GIS]

1101 East First Street, Sanford, FL 32771
Tel: (407) 665-1105 Fax: (407) 665-7412
Internet: www.seminolecountyfl.gov/cs/gis

Program Manager **Melvin Barnes** .... (407) 665-1105

Fleet and Facilities Management Division

205 West County Home Road, Sanford, FL 32773
Tel: (407) 665-5282 Internet: www.seminolecountyfl.gov/cs/fleetfacil

Manager **Tim Marcopulos** .... (407) 665-5282

Community Services Department

534 West Lake Mary Boulevard, Sanford, FL 32773
Tel: (407) 665-2300 Internet: www.seminolecountyfl.gov/comsrvs

Director **Valmarie Turner** .... (407) 665-2300
E-mail: vturner@seminolecountyfl.gov

Environmental Services Department

500 West Lake Mary Boulevard, Sanford, FL 32773-7499
Tel: (407) 665-2000 Fax: (407) 665-2019
Internet: www.seminolecountyfl.gov/envsrvs

Director **Carol Hunter** .... (407) 665-2110
E-mail: chunter@seminolecountyfl.gov

Resource Management

1101 East First Street, Third Floor, Sanford, FL 32771
Tel: (407) 665-7176 Fax: (407) 665-7183
Internet: www.seminolecountyfl.gov/fs

Director **Edward Bass** .... (407) 665-7172

Purchasing and Contracts Office

1301 East Second Street, Sanford, FL 32771
Tel: (407) 665-7116 Fax: (407) 665-7956
E-mail: purch@seminolecountyfl.gov
Internet: www.seminolecountyfl.gov/cm/purchasing

Manager **Ray Hooper** .... (407) 665-7111
E-mail: rhooper@seminolecountyfl.gov

Leisure Services Department

845 Lake Markham Road, Sanford, FL 32771
Tel: (407) 665-2001 Internet: www.seminolecountyfl.gov/leisure

Director **Joseph R. Abel** .... (407) 665-2001
E-mail: jabel@seminolecountyfl.gov

Extension Services Division

250 West County Home Road, Sanford, FL 32773
Tel: (407) 665-5560 Internet: www.seminolecountyfl.gov/leisure/coopext

Manager **Barbara Hughes** .... (407) 665-5556

Greenways and Natural Lands Division

Ed Yarborough Nature Center, 3485 North County Road 426, Geneva, FL 32732
Tel: (407) 349-0959 Internet: www.seminolecountyfl.gov/leisure/natland

Program Manager **Jim Duby** .... (407) 349-0769

★ Elected Official ▲ Appointed by Legislature ▼ Appointed by Governor ► Appointed by Board or Commission ● Appointed by Judge
■ Appointed by Mayor △ Appointed by Freeholders ▽ Appointed by Supervisor ▷ Appointed by County Executive ○ Appointed by Council

Parks and Recreation Division
845 Lake Markham Road, Sanford, FL 32771
Tel: (407) 665-2001 Internet: www.seminolecountyfl.gov/leisure/parks

Manager **Shorty Robbins** . . . . (407) 665-2001

Seminole County Convention and Visitors Bureau
515 International Parkway, Suite 1013, Lake Mary, FL 32746
Tel: (407) 665-2900 Fax: (407) 665-2920
Internet: www.visitseminole.com

Executive Director **Danny Trosset** . . . . (407) 665-2913

Seminole County Public Library
Central Branch Library, 215 North Oxford Road, Casselberry, FL 32707
Tel: (407) 665-1500 Fax: (407) 665-1510
Internet: www.seminolecountyfl.gov/library

Manager **Christine Patten** . . . . (407) 665-1500
E-mail: cpatten@seminolecountyfl.gov

Development Services
1101 East First Street, Sanford, FL 32771
Tel: (407) 665-7432 Fax: (407) 665-7417
Internet: www.seminolecountyfl.gov/gm

Director **(Vacant)** . . . . (407) 665-7396

Public Safety Department
150 Bush Boulevard, Sanford, FL 32773
Tel: (407) 665-5000 Internet: www.seminolecountyfl.gov/dps

Director **Jean Jreij** . . . . (407) 665-5001
Adult Probation Manager **Derek J. Gallagher** . . . . (407) 665-4613
E-mail: dgallagher@seminolecountyfl.gov
Animal Services Manager **Bob Hunter** . . . . (407) 665-5202
E-911 Administrator **Marti Walker** . . . . (407) 665-5911
E-mail: mwalker@seminolecountyfl.gov
Program Manager **Robert Durant** . . . . (407) 665-5100
Emergency Manager **Alan S. Harris** . . . . (407) 665-5102
E-mail: aharris@seminolecountyfl.gov
Fire Chief **Leeanna R. Mims** . . . . (407) 665-5175
E-mail: lmims@seminolecountyfl.gov

Public Works Department
520 West Lake Mary Boulevard, Suite 200, Sanford, FL 32773
Tel: (407) 665-5768 Fax: (407) 665-5600
Internet: www.seminolecountyfl.gov/pw

Director **(Vacant)** . . . . (407) 665-5768
County Engineer **Brett Blackader** . . . . (407) 665-5674

Office of the Clerk of Courts
301 North Park Avenue, Sanford, FL 32771
Tel: (407) 665-4313 Fax: (407) 330-7193

Clerk of the Circuit Court **Maryanne Morse** (R) . . . . (407) 665-4313
Term Expires: November 2016

Office of the Property Appraiser
1101 East First Street, Sanford, FL 32771
Tel: (407) 665-7506 Internet: www.scpafl.org

★ Property Appraiser **David Johnson** . . . . (407) 665-7506
Term Expires: November 2016

Office of the Sheriff
100 North Bush Boulevard, Sanford, FL 32773-6706
Tel: (407) 665-6650 Fax: (407) 665-6654
E-mail: sheriff@seminolesheriff.org Internet: www.seminolesheriff.org

★ Sheriff **Donald F. Eslinger** . . . . (407) 665-6650
Term Expires: November 2016
E-mail: deslinger@seminolesheriff.org

Office of the Supervisor of Elections
1500 East Airport Boulevard, Sanford, FL 32773
Tel: (407) 708-7700 Internet: www.voteseminole.org
Fax: (407) 708-7705

★ Supervisor of Elections **Michael Ertel** . . . . (407) 708-7700
Term Expires: November 2016
E-mail: mertel@seminolecountyfl.gov
Chief Deputy of Election Services **Laurie White** . . . . (407) 708-7700
E-mail: lwhite@seminolecountyfl.gov
Chief Deputy of Voter Services **Rebecca Quinn** . . . . (407) 708-7700
E-mail: rquinn@seminolecountyfl.gov

Office of the Tax Collector
1101 East First Street, Sanford, FL 32771-1468
Tel: (407) 665-1000 Fax: (407) 665-7603 Internet: www.seminoletax.org

★ County Tax Collector **Ray Valdes** Room 1134 . . . . (407) 665-7601
Term Expires: November 2016
E-mail: rvaldes@seminoletax.org
Assistant Tax Collector **Robert Hagey** . . . . (407) 665-1000

Florida Department of Health in Seminole County
400 West Airport Boulevard, Sanford, FL 32773
Tel: (407) 665-3000 Fax: (407) 665-3213
Internet: www.seminolecohealth.com

Director **Dr. Swannie Jett** . . . . (407) 665-3200
Education: Tennessee State BS; Tennessee MSc; Kentucky DrPH

County of Shelby, Tennessee
160 North Main Street, Eleventh Floor, Memphis, TN 38103
Tel: (901) 222-2300 (Information) Internet: www.shelbycountytn.gov

County Seat: Memphis **Election Type:** Nonpartisan
Population: 938,069 (2015)

Office of the County Mayor
160 North Main Street, Eleventh Floor, Memphis, TN 38103-1876
Fax: (901) 222-2005

★ County Mayor **Mark H. Luttrell, Jr.** . . . . (901) 222-2000
Term Expires: August 31, 2018
Education: Union U 1969 BA; U Memphis 1974 MPA
Administrative Assistant **Brandon Whiteley** . . . . (901) 222-2004
E-mail: brandon.whitelely@shelbycountytn.gov
■ Quality Manager **Robin Harwell** . . . . (901) 222-2000
E-mail: Robin.Harwell@shelbycountytn.gov
Director of Legislative Affairs **David McKinney** . . . . (901) 222-2300

Public Affairs Office
160 North Main Street, Memphis, TN 38103
Tel: (901) 222-2047 Fax: (901) 222-2005

■ Public Affairs Officer **Steve Shular** . . . . (901) 222-2047
E-mail: steve.shular@shelbycountytn.gov

Mayor's Action Center
160 North Main Street, Suite 625, Memphis, TN 38103
Tel: (901) 222-2300 Fax: (901) 222-1065
E-mail: action@shelbycountytn.gov

■ Administrator **Steve Shular** . . . . (901) 222-2047
E-mail: steve.shular@shelbycountytn.gov

★ Elected Official ▲ Appointed by Legislature ▼ Appointed by Governor ▶ Appointed by Board or Commission ● Appointed by Judge
■ Appointed by Mayor △ Appointed by Freeholders ▽ Appointed by Supervisor ▷ Appointed by County Executive ○ Appointed by Council

Office of the County Attorney
160 North Main Street, Ninth Floor, Memphis, TN 38103
Fax: (901) 222-2105

■ County Attorney **(Vacant)** .... (901) 222-2100
Chief Administration Attorney **Marcy Ingram** .... (901) 222-2100
Chief Litigation Attorney **Kim Koratsky** .... (901) 222-2300

Divorce Referee's Office
140 Adams Avenue, Room 327, Memphis, TN 38103
Tel: (901) 222-2150 E-mail: dvrfdivorcereferee@shelbycountytn.gov

Divorce Referee **Cary C. Woods** .... (901) 222-2150

Office of the Public Defender
201 Poplar Avenue, Room 201, Memphis, TN 38103
Tel: (901) 222-2800 Fax: (901) 222-2801

■ Chief Public Defender **Stephen Bush** .... (901) 222-2800
E-mail: stephen.bush@shelbycountytn.gov

Office of the Chief Administrative Officer
160 North Main Street, Suite 850, Memphis, TN 38103
Fax: (901) 222-2051

■ Chief Administrative Officer **Harvey Kennedy** .... (901) 222-2050
E-mail: harvey.kennedy@shelbycountytn.gov
■ Deputy Chief Administrative Officer **Kim Hackney** .... (901) 222-2050
E-mail: kim.hackney@shelbycountytn.gov

Administration and Finance Division
160 North Main Street, Memphis, TN 38103

■ Director **Mike Swift** .... (901) 222-2249
E-mail: mike.swift@shelbycountytn.gov

Election Commission
Elections Operations Center, 980 Nixon Drive, Memphis, TN 38134
Tel: (901) 222-1200

Chairman **Robert Meyers** .... (901) 222-1200
▶ Administrator **Linda Phillips** .... (901) 222-1200

Finance Department
160 North Main Street, Suite 800, Memphis, TN 38103
Fax: (901) 222-2231

Finance Administrator **Raymond Pipkin** .... (901) 222-2200
Budget Manager **Wanda Richards** .... (901) 222-2200
E-mail: wanda.richards@shelbycountytn.gov

Human Resources Department
160 North Main Street, Suite 901, Memphis, TN 38103-1876
Fax: (901) 222-2364

■ Administrator **Michael "Mike" Lewis** .... (901) 222-2327
E-mail: mike.lewis@shelbycountytn.gov

Information Technology Department
160 N. Main St., Suite 7, Memphis, TN 38103
Tel: (901) 222-2600

■ Administrator **Lee Wessels** .... (901) 222-2605
E-mail: Lee.Wessels@ShelbyCountyTN.gov
■ Manager **Jeff Yallope** .... (901) 222-2675
E-mail: jeff.yallope@shelbycountytn.gov

Internal Audit Department
1075 Mullins Station Road, Room C112, Memphis, TN 38134

■ Chief Auditor **Tommy Cates** .... (901) 222-7350
E-mail: tommy.cates@shelbycountytn.gov

Purchasing Department
160 North Main Street, Suite 550, Memphis, TN 38103
Fax: (901) 222-2064

■ Administrator **Clifton Davis** .... (901) 222-2250
E-mail: clifton.davis@shelbycountytn.gov

Community Services Division
160 North Main Street, 2nd Floor, Memphis, TN 38103

■ Director **Martha Lott** .... (901) 222-2040
E-mail: martha.lott@shelbycountytn.gov

Aging Commission of the Mid-South
2670 Union Avenue Extended, 10th Floor, Suite 1000, Memphis, TN 38112
Tel: (901) 222-4100 (24 Hour) Fax: (901) 222-4199
Internet: www.agingcommission.org

Executive Director **Dora Ivey** .... (901) 222-4100

Community Services Agency
2470 Union Avenue Extended, 5th Floor, Memphis, TN 38112

Administrator **Louise Smith** .... (901) 222-4200
E-mail: louise.smith@shelbycountytn.gov

Crime Victims Assistance Center [CVC]
1750 Madison Avenue, Madison, TN 38105

■ Administrator **Anna Whalley** .... (901) 222-3952
E-mail: anna.whalley@shelbycountytn.gov

Office of Early Childhood and Youth [OECY]
160 North Main Street, 2nd Floor, Memphis, TN 38103
Fax: (901) 222-4316 Internet: www.shelbycountychildren.org

■ Administrator **Keisha Walker** .... (901) 222-3991
E-mail: keisha.walker@shelbycountytn.gov

Just Care Family Network
1750 Madison Avenue, Fifth Floor, Madison, TN 38105
Fax: (901) 222-4501

Project Director/Administrator **Dr. Altha J. Stewart** .... (901) 222-4525

Pre-Trial Services
201 Poplar, 8th Fl., Memphis, TN 38103
Fax: (901) 222-4078

■ Manager **Richard "Rick" Harrell** .... (901) 222-4000
E-mail: richard.harrell@shelbycountytn.gov

Corrections Division
1045 Mullins Station Road, Memphis, TN 38134
Fax: (901) 222-8581

■ Director **Bill Gupton** .... (901) 222-8580
Deputy Director/Finance Administrator **David Barber** .... (901) 222-8629
Operations Administrator **(Vacant)** .... (901) 222-6527

Health Division
814 Jefferson Avenue, Memphis, TN 38105
Tel: (901) 222-9000 Fax: (901) 544-7475
Internet: www.shelbycountytn.gov/health

■ Director **Alisa Haushaulter** Room 126 .... (901) 222-9000
E-mail: shelbytnhealth@shelbycountytn.gov
Health Officer **Dr. Helen Morrow** .... (901) 222-9000
Finance Administrator **Audrey Tipton** Room 121 .... (901) 222-9000
Environmental Health Services Administrator **Dr. Tyler Zerwekh** Room 125 .... (901) 222-9000
Education: Texas Tech BS; Texas MPH, 2003 DrPH
Environmental Sanitation Manager **Kasia Alexander** .... (901) 222-9000
Pollution Control Manager **Bob Rogers** .... (901) 222-9000
Vector Control Program Manager **Dr. Daniel Sprenger** .... (901) 222-9715
Fax: (901) 222-9746

COUNTIES

★ Elected Official ▲ Appointed by Legislature ▼ Appointed by Governor ▶ Appointed by Board or Commission ● Appointed by Judge
■ Appointed by Mayor △ Appointed by Freeholders ▽ Appointed by Supervisor ▷ Appointed by County Executive ○ Appointed by Council

Medical Examiner's Office
1060 Madison Avenue, Room 300, Memphis, TN 38103
Fax: (901) 544-7211

▶ Medical Examiner **Karen E. Chancellor** . . . . . . (901) 222-9000

Memphis/Shelby County Division of Planning and Development [DPD]
125 North Main Street, Suite 468, Memphis, TN 38103
Fax: (901) 576-6603

■ Director **Richard S. "Rick" Copeland** . . . . . . (901) 576-7197
E-mail: rick.copeland@memphistn.gov
Deputy Director **John Zeanah** . . . . . . (901) 576-7199
E-mail: john.zeanah@memphistn.gov

Office of Planning and Development/Land Use
125 North Main Street, Room 468, Memphis, TN 38103
Fax: (901) 576-7194

Administrator **Josh Whitehead** . . . . . . (901) 576-6602
Education: Cincinnati 2000 MCP; U Memphis 2005 JD

Office of Sustainability
125 North Main Street, Room 468, Memphis, TN 38103
Internet: www.sustainableshelby.com

Administrator **(Vacant)** . . . . . . (901) 576-7167

Department of Construction Code Enforcement
6465 Mullins Station Road, Memphis, TN 38134
Fax: (901) 222-8346

Administrator **Allen Medlock** . . . . . . (901) 222-8351
Deputy Administrator **Maurice Sargent** . . . . . . (901) 222-8350

Department of Housing
1075 Mullins Station Road, Memphis, TN 38134
Fax: (901) 222-7620

■ Administrator **Jim Vazquez** . . . . . . (901) 222-7602
E-mail: jim.vazquez@shelbycountytn.gov

Department of Regional Services / Transportation Planning
125 North Main Street, Suite 450, Memphis, TN 38103
Fax: (901) 576-7272

Administrator **Pragati Srivastava** . . . . . . (901) 576-7198

Office of Preparedness
P.O. Box 111249, Memphis, TN 38111-1249

▷ Director **Dale Lane** . . . . . . (901) 222-6700
E-mail: dale.lane@shelbycountytn.gov
Deputy Director **Levell Blanchard** . . . . . . (901) 222-6700
E-mail: levell.blanchard@shelbycountytn.gov
Planning Officer **Kimberlyn Bouler** . . . . . . (901) 222-6700
E-mail: kimberlyn.bouler@shelbycountytn.gov
Grant Coordinator **Patrina Chambers** . . . . . . (901) 222-6700
Procurement Officer **Shelby Logan** . . . . . . (901) 222-6700
E-mail: shelby.logan@shelbycountytn.gov
Preparedness Officer **Mike Brazzell** . . . . . . (901) 222-6700
E-mail: michael.brazzell@shelbycountytn.gov
Preparedness Officer **Terry Donald** . . . . . . (901) 222-6700
E-mail: terry.donald@shelbycountytn.gov
Preparedness Officer **Jesse Gammel** . . . . . . (901) 222-6700
E-mail: Jesse.Gammel@shelbycountytn.gov
Preparedness Officer **Eugene Jones** . . . . . . (901) 222-6700
E-mail: Eugene.jones@shelbycountytn.gov
Preparedness Officer **Shannon Towery** . . . . . . (901) 222-6700
E-mail: shannon.towery@shelbycountytn.gov

Public Works Division
160 N. Main St., Memphis, TN 38103
Fax: (901) 222-2090

■ Director/County Engineer **Tom Needham** Room 801 . . . . (901) 222-2036
E-mail: tom.needham@shelbycountytn.gov

Shelby County Fire Department
1115 Sycamore View Rd., Memphis, TN 38134

■ Fire Chief **Alvin Benson** . . . . . . (901) 222-8010
■ Assistant Fire Chief **(Vacant)** . . . . . . (901) 222-8010

Roads and Bridges Department
6449 Haley Road, Memphis, TN 38103
E-mail: roadsandbridges@shelbycountytn.gov

Administrator **Darren Sanders** . . . . . . (901) 222-7705
E-mail: darren.sanders@shelbycountytn.gov
Deputy Administrator **Charles Wood** . . . . . . (901) 222-7705
E-mail: charles.wood@shelbycountytn.gov

Support Services Department
584 Adams Avenue, Memphis, TN 38104

Administrator **Tom Moss** . . . . . . (901) 222-2432
E-mail: tom.moss@shelbycountytn.gov
Education: Tennessee BS

Office of the Board of Commissioners
160 North Main Street, Suite 450, Memphis, TN 38103
Fax: (901) 222-1002

★ Chairman **Terry Roland** (District 1) . . . . . . (901) 222-1000
Term Expires: August 31, 2018
E-mail: terry.roland@shelbycountytn.gov
★ Chair Pro Tem **Van Turner** (District 12) . . . . . . (901) 222-1000
Term Expires: August 31, 2018
Education: Tennessee 2002 JD
★ Commissioner **George Chism** (District 2) . . . . . . (901) 222-1000
Term Expires: August 31, 2018
★ Commissioner **David Reaves** (District 3) . . . . . . (901) 222-1000
Term Expires: August 31, 2018
★ Commissioner **Mark Billingsley** (District 4) . . . . . . (901) 222-1000
Term Expires: August 31, 2018
★ Commissioner **Heidi Shafer** (District 5) . . . . . . (901) 222-1000
Term Expires: August 31, 2018
E-mail: heidi.shafer@shelbycountytn.gov
★ Commissioner **Willie Brooks** (District 6) . . . . . . (901) 222-1000
Term Expires: August 31, 2018
★ Commissioner **Melvin Burgess** (District 7) . . . . . . (901) 222-1000
Term Expires: August 31, 2018
E-mail: melvin.burgess@shelbycountytn.gov
★ Commissioner **Walter L. Bailey, Jr.** (District 8) . . . . . . (901) 222-1000
Term Expires: August 31, 2018
E-mail: walter.bailey@shelbycountytn.gov
★ Commissioner **Justin Ford** (District 9) . . . . . . (901) 222-1000
Term Expires: August 31, 2018
E-mail: justin.ford@shelbycountytn.gov
★ Commissioner **Reginald Milton** (District 10) . . . . . . (901) 222-1000
Term Expires: August 31, 2018
★ Commissioner **Eddie Jones** (District 11) . . . . . . (901) 222-1000
Term Expires: August 31, 2018
★ Commissioner **Steve Basar** (District 13) . . . . . . (901) 222-1000
Term Expires: August 31, 2018
Chief Administrator **Quran Folsom** . . . . . . (901) 222-2300
E-mail: quran.folsom@shelbycountytn.gov
Deputy Administrator **Clay Perry** . . . . . . (901) 222-2300
E-mail: clay.perry@shelbycountytn.gov

Office of the Assessor
1075 Mullins Station Road, Memphis, TN 38134
Fax: (901) 379-7199 E-mail: assessor@assessor.shelby.tn.us
Internet: www.assessor.shelby.tn.us

★ Assessor of Property **Cheyenne Johnson** . . . . . . (901) 222-7001
Term Expires: August 31, 2016

★ Elected Official ▲ Appointed by Legislature ▼ Appointed by Governor ▶ Appointed by Board or Commission ● Appointed by Judge
■ Appointed by Mayor △ Appointed by Freeholders ▽ Appointed by Supervisor ▷ Appointed by County Executive ○ Appointed by Council

Office of the County Clerk

150 Washington Avenue, Memphis, TN 38103
Fax: (901) 545-3779 E-mail: shelbycountyclerk@shelbycountytn.gov

★ County Clerk **Wayne Mashburn** .... (901) 222-3000
Term Expires: August 31, 2018
E-mail: wayne.mashburn@shelbycountytn.gov

Office of the District Attorney General

Justice Center, 201 Poplar, 3rd Floor, Memphis, TN 38103
Internet: www.scdag.com

★ District Attorney General **Amy P. Weirich** .... (901) 222-1300
Term Expires: December 31, 2022
E-mail: info@scdag.com
Education: Tennessee (Martin) 1987; U Memphis 1990 JD

Office of the Register of Deeds

1075 Mullins Station Road, Suite W165, Memphis, TN 38134
Fax: (901) 379-7577 Internet: http://register.shelby.tn.us/

★ Register of Deeds **Tom Leatherwood** .... (901) 222-8100
Term Expires: August 31, 2018
E-mail: tom.leatherwood@shelbycountytn.gov

Office of the Sheriff

201 Poplar Avenue, 9th Floor, Memphis, TN 38103
Fax: (901) 222-5504 Internet: www.shelby-sheriff.org

★ Sheriff **William "Bill" Oldham** .... (901) 222-5500
Term Expires: August 31, 2018
E-mail: bill.oldham@shelby-sheriff.org

Office of the Trustee

157 Poplar Avenue, Memphis, TN 38101
P.O. Box 2751, Memphis, TN 38101
Fax: (901) 545-4421 Internet: www.shelbycountytrustee.com

★ Trustee **David C. Lenoir** .... (901) 432-4829
Term Expires: August 31, 2018
E-mail: dlenoir@shelbycountytrustee.com
Education: Alabama 1990 BS

Shelby County Schools [SCS]

160 South Hollywood Street, Memphis, TN 38112
Tel: (901) 321-2500 Internet: www.scsk12.org

Board of Education

160 South Hollywood Street, Memphis, TN 38112

★ Chairperson **Teresa Jones** (District 2) .... (901) 321-2525
Term Expires: August 31, 2020
Affiliation: Chief Prosecutor, Office of the City Prosecutor, Office of the City Attorney, City of Memphis, Tennessee

★ Vice Chair **Shante Avant** (District 6) .... (901) 321-2525
Term Expires: August 31, 2018

★ Member **Christopher Caldwell** (District 1) .... (901) 321-2525
Term Expires: August 31, 2018

★ Member **Stephanie P. Love** (District 3) .... (901) 321-2525
Term Expires: August 31, 2016

★ Member **Kevin Woods** (District 4) .... (901) 321-2525
Term Expires: August 31, 2020

★ Member **Scott McCormick** (District 5) .... (901) 321-2525
Term Expires: August 31, 2020
Education: U Memphis 1982 BBA

★ Member **Miska Bibbs** (District 7) .... (901) 321-2525
Term Expires: August 31, 2020

★ Member **Billy Orgel** (District 8) .... (901) 321-2525
Term Expires: August 31, 2018

Board of Education *continued*

★ Member **Michael L. "Mike" Kernell** (District 9) .... (901) 321-2525
Term Expires: August 31, 2018

Office of the Superintendent

160 South Hollywood Street, Memphis, TN 38112
E-mail: superintendent@scsk12.org

▶ Superintendent **Dorsey Hopson** .... (901) 416-5444
Deputy Superintendent **(Vacant)** .... (901) 321-2521
Human Resources Director **Trinette Small** .... (901) 321-2644
E-mail: smallt@scsk12.org
Student Services **Gerald Darling** .... (901) 473-2560
Chief Financial Officer **Lin Johnson** .... (901) 416-5461
Chief Information Officer **John Michael Williams** .... (901) 416-2100

County of Snohomish, Washington

3000 Rockefeller Ave., Everett, WA 98201
Tel: (425) 388-3411 (Information) TTY: (425) 388-3700
Internet: www.co.snohomish.wa.us

County Seat: Everett **Election Type:** Partisan **Population:** 772,501 (2015)

Office of the County Executive

3000 Rockefeller Avenue, Mail Stop 407, Everett, WA 98201
Tel: (425) 388-3312 Fax: (425) 388-3434
E-mail: county.executive@co.snohomish.wa.us

★ County Executive **David J. "Dave" Somers** (D) .... (425) 388-3312
Term Expires: December 31, 2019
Education: U Washington BS, MS

Office of the Medical Examiner

9509 29th Avenue West, Everett, WA 98204
Fax: (425) 438-6222

▷ Chief Medical Examiner **Dr. Daniel Selove** .... (425) 438-6200
E-mail: contact.medadmin@snoco.org

Office of Public Defense [OPD]

3000 Rockefeller Ave., Room C-103, Mail Stop 209, Everett, WA 98201
Tel: (425) 388-3500

▷ Attorney Administrator **Sara Bhagat** .... (425) 388-3500
E-mail: sara.bhagat@snoco.org

Airport (Paine Field)

3220 - 100th Street SW, Suite A, Everett, WA 98204
Fax: (425) 355-9883 E-mail: paine.field@co.snohomish.wa.us
Internet: http://www.painefield.com/homepage.htm

▷ Director **Arif Ghouse** .... (425) 388-5125

Department of Emergency Management [DEM]

3509 109th Street S.W., Everett, WA 98204
Tel: (425) 388-5060 Fax: (425) 423-9152

▷ Director (Interim) **Jason Biermann** .... (425) 388-5060
E-mail: jason.biermann@snoco.org
Deputy Director **Jason Biermann** .... (425) 388-5060
E-mail: jason.biermann@snoco.org

Facilities Management Department

3000 Rockefeller Avenue, Mail Stop 404, Everett, WA 98201
Tel: (425) 388-3221

▷ Director **Mark Thunberg** .... (425) 388-3035
E-mail: mark.thunberg@co.snohomish.wa.us

(continued on next page)

★ Elected Official ▲ Appointed by Legislature ▼ Appointed by Governor ▶ Appointed by Board or Commission ● Appointed by Judge
■ Appointed by Mayor △ Appointed by Freeholders ▽ Appointed by Supervisor ▷ Appointed by County Executive ○ Appointed by Council

COUNTIES

Facilities Management Department *continued*

Purchasing Manager **Bramby Tollen** .... (425) 388-3329

Finance Department

3000 Rockefeller Avenue, Mail Stop 610, Everett, WA 98201
Tel: (425) 388-3401 Fax: (425) 388-3744

▷ Controller **Sharyl Raines** .... (425) 388-3862
E-mail: Sharyl.Raines@co.snohomish.wa.us

Human Resources Department

3000 Rockefeller Avenue, Mail Stop 503, Everett, WA 98201
Tel: (425) 388-3411 Fax: (425) 388-3579
E-mail: human.resources@co.snohomish.wa.us

▷ Director **Bridget Clawson** .... (425) 388-3411
E-mail: bridget.clawson@co.snohomish.wa.us

COUNTIES

Human Services Department [HSD]

3000 Rockefeller Avenue, Mail Stop 305, Everett, WA 98201
Tel: (425) 388-7200 Fax: (425) 259-1444

▷ Director **Mary Jane "MJ" Brell Vujovic** .... (425) 388-7204
E-mail: maryjane.brell@snoco.org

Department of Information Services [DIS]

3000 Rockefeller Avenue, Mail Stop 709, Everett, WA 98201
Tel: (425) 388-3349 Fax: (425) 388-3985

▷ Director **Trever Esko** .... (425) 388-3349
E-mail: Trever.Esko@snoco.org

Parks and Recreation Department

6705 Puget Park Drive, Snohomish, WA 98296
Fax: (425) 388-6645

Director **Tom Teigen** .... (425) 388-6600

Planning and Development Services [PDS]

3000 Rockefeller Avenue, Mail Stop 604, Everett, WA 98201

Director **Clay White** .... (425) 388-3122
E-mail: clay.white@co.snohomish.wa.us
Education: Central Washington 1996 BA

Public Works Department

3000 Rockefeller Ave., M/S 607, Everett, WA 98201
Tel: (425) 388-3488 E-mail: public.works@co.snohomish.wa.us

▷ Director **Steve Thomsen** .... (425) 388-3488
E-mail: steve.thomsen@co.snohomish.wa.us

Snohomish County Law Library

3000 Rockefeller Avenue, Room 139, Mail Stop 703, Everett, WA 98201
Tel: (425) 388-3010 Fax: (425) 388-3020

Law Librarian **Lettice Parker** .... (425) 388-3010
E-mail: lettice.parker@co.snohomish.wa.us

Office of the County Council

3000 Rockefeller Avenue, Mail Stop 609, Everett, WA 98201
Tel: (425) 388-3494 Fax: (425) 388-3496
E-mail: county.council@co.snohomish.wa.us

★ Chair **Terry Ryan** (D-District 4) .... (425) 388-3494
Term Expires: December 31, 2017

★ Vice Chair **Brian Sullivan** (D-District 2) .... (425) 388-3494
Term Expires: December 31, 2019
E-mail: brian.sullivan@co.snohomish.wa.us
Date of Birth: March 26, 1958

★ Council Member **Ken Klein** (R-District 1) .... (425) 388-3494
Term Expires: December 31, 2017

Office of the County Council *continued*

★ Council Member **Stephanie Wright** (D-District 3) ...... (425) 388-3494
Term Expires: December 31, 2019
E-mail: stephanie.wright@co.snohomish.wa.us

★ Council Member **Hans Dunshee** (D-District 5) .... (425) 388-3494
Term Expires: December 31, 2017
E-mail: Hans.Dunshee@co.snohomish.wa.us
Date of Birth: October 26, 1953
Education: U Washington BS; Western Washington MA

○ Chief of Staff (Interim) **Stephen Clifton** .... (425) 388-3471
E-mail: stephen.clifton@co.snohomish.wa.us

Office of the Hearing Examiner

3000 Rockefeller Avenue, Mail Stop 405, Everett, WA 98201-4046
Tel: (425) 388-3538 Fax: (425) 388-3201
E-mail: hearing.examiner@snoco.org

○ Hearing Examiner **Peter Camp** .... (425) 388-3538

Office of the County Assessor

3000 Rockefeller Avenue, Mail Stop 510, Everett, WA 98201-4046
E-mail: contact.assessor@co.snohomish.wa.us
Internet: www.snohomishcountywa.gov/175/assessor

★ Assessor **Linda Hjelle** .... (425) 388-3433
Term Expires: December 31, 2019

Office of the County Auditor

3000 Rockefeller Avenue, Mail Stop 505, Everett, WA 98201-4046
Fax: (425) 259-2777 E-mail: county.auditor@co.snohomish.wa.us

★ Auditor **Carolyn Weikel** .... (425) 388-3693
Term Expires: December 31, 2019
E-mail: carolyn.weikel@co.snohomish.wa.us

Office of the County Clerk

3000 Rockefeller Avenue, Mail Stop 605, Everett, WA 98201
E-mail: county.clerk@co.snohomish.wa.us

★ County Clerk **Sonya Kraski** .... (425) 388-3466
Term Expires: December 31, 2019
E-mail: sonya.kraski@co.snohomish.wa.us

Office of the County Prosecuting Attorney

Admin. E., 3000 Rockefeller Ave, 7th FL, Mail Stop 504,
Everett, WA 98201-4046
Fax: (425) 388-7172 E-mail: prosecuting.attorney@co.snohomish.wa.us

★ Prosecuting Attorney **Mark Roe** .... (425) 388-3772
Term Expires: December 31, 2018
E-mail: prosecuting.attorney@co.snohomish.wa.us

Office of the Sheriff

3000 Rockefeller Avenue, Mail Stop 606, Everett, WA 98201-4046
Fax: (425) 388-3805 E-mail: contact.sheriff@co.snohomish.wa.us

★ Sheriff **Ty Trenary** .... (425) 388-3393
Term Expires: December 31, 2019

Undersheriff **Rob Beidler** .... (425) 388-3616
E-mail: rob.beidler@snoco.org

★ Elected Official ▲ Appointed by Legislature ▼ Appointed by Governor ▶ Appointed by Board or Commission ● Appointed by Judge
■ Appointed by Mayor △ Appointed by Freeholders ▽ Appointed by Supervisor ▷ Appointed by County Executive ○ Appointed by Council

Office of the Treasurer

3000 Rockefeller Avenue, M/S 501, Everett, WA 98201-4060
Tel: (425) 388-3366 Fax: (425) 388-3089
E-mail: treasurer@co.snohomish.wa.us

★ Treasurer **Kirke Sievers** (D) . . . . (425) 388-3179
Term Expires: December 31, 2019
E-mail: kirke.sievers@co.snohomish.wa.us

Snohomish Health District [SHD]

The Rucker Building, 3020 Rucker Avenue, Suite 306,
Everett, WA 98201-3900
Tel: (425) 339-5200 Fax: (425) 339-5216 E-mail: admin@snohd.org
Internet: www.snohd.org

Health Officer/Director **Gary M. Goldbaum** . . . . (425) 339-5210
Education: Colorado 1978 MD; U Washington 1989 MPH
Deputy Director **Pete Mayer** . . . . (425) 339-5210

County of Solano, California

675 Texas Street, Fairfield, CA 94533
Tel: (707) 784-6100 Internet: www.solanocounty.com

County Seat: Fairfield **Election Type:** Nonpartisan
Population: 436,092 (2015)

Office of the Board of Supervisors

675 Texas Street, Suite 6500, Fairfield, CA 94533
Tel: (707) 784-6100 Fax: (707) 784-6665

★ Chairwoman **Erin Hannigan** (District 1) . . . . (707) 784-6662
Term Expires: January 4, 2017
E-mail: ehannigan@solanocounty.com
★ Vice Chair **John M. Vasquez** (District 4) . . . . (707) 784-6129
Term Expires: January 4, 2019
E-mail: jmvasquez@solanocounty.com
★ Supervisor **Linda J. Seifert** (District 2) . . . . (707) 784-3031
Term Expires: January 4, 2017
E-mail: ljseifert@solanocounty.com
Education: Cal State (Fullerton) 1971; U Pacific 1984
★ Supervisor **James P. "Jim" Spering** (District 3) . . . . (707) 784-6136
Term Expires: January 4, 2019
E-mail: jpspering@solanocounty.com
★ Supervisor **Skip Thomson** (District 5) . . . . (707) 784-6130
Term Expires: January 4, 2017
E-mail: sthomson@solanocounty.com
Clerk of the Board **Birgitta E. Corsello** . . . . (707) 784-6108
Fax: (707) 784-7975

Office of the County Counsel

675 Texas Street, Suite 6600, Fairfield, CA 94533
Tel: (707) 784-6140 Fax: (707) 784-6862

County Counsel **Dennis Walter Bunting** . . . . (707) 784-6140
E-mail: dwbunting@solanocounty.com
Education: UC Davis, 1972 JD
Assistant County Counsel **Azniv Darbinian** . . . . (707) 784-6140
E-mail: adarbinian@solanocounty.com

Office of the County Administrator

675 Texas Street, Suite 6500, Fairfield, CA 94533
Tel: (707) 784-6100 Fax: (707) 784-7975
E-mail: cao-clerk@solanocounty.com

County Administrator **Birgitta E. Corsello** . . . . (707) 784-6100
E-mail: becorsello@solanocounty.com
Assistant County Administrator **Nancy Huston** . . . . (707) 784-6100
E-mail: nlhuston@solanocounty.com
Education: UC Davis BS; U San Francisco

Office of the Agricultural Commissioner

501 Texas Street, 2nd Floor, Fairfield, CA 94533
Tel: (707) 784-1310 Fax: (707) 784-1330

Agricultural Commissioner **Jim Allan** . . . . (707) 784-1310
Assistant Agricultural Commissioner **Simone Hardy** . . . . . (707) 784-1310

Office of the Public Defender

675 Texas Street, Suite 3500, Fairfield, CA 94533
Tel: (707) 784-6700 Fax: (707) 784-6747
E-mail: publicdefender@solanocounty.com

Public Defender **Lesli Michele Caldwell** . . . . (707) 784-6700
Education: UC Berkeley; Santa Clara U 1979 JD
Chief Deputy Public Defender **Elena D'Agustino** . . . . (707) 784-6700
Chief Deputy Public Defender **Oscar Bobrow** . . . . (707) 784-6700

Office of the Registrar of Voters

675 Texas Street, Suite 2600, Fairfield, CA 94533
Tel: (707) 784-6675 Fax: (707) 784-6678
E-mail: elections@solanocounty.com

Registrar of Voters **Ira Rosenthal** . . . . (707) 784-6675
Assistant Registrar of Voters **John Gardner** . . . . (707) 784-6675

Department of General Services

675 Texas Street, Suite 2500, Fairfield, CA 94533
Tel: (707) 784-7900 Fax: (707) 784-7912

Director **Mike Lango** . . . . (707) 784-7900
E-mail: mjlango@solanocounty.com
Deputy Director **Kanon R. Artiche** . . . . (707) 784-7900
E-mail: krartiche@solanocounty.com

Department of Health and Social Services [H&SS]

275 Beck Avenue, Fairfield, CA 94533
Tel: (707) 784-8400 Fax: (707) 421-3207
Internet: www.co.solano.ca.us/depts/hss

Director **Gerald Huber** . . . . (707) 784-8400
Fax: (707) 421-3207

Department of Human Resources

675 Texas Street, Suite 1800, Fairfield, CA 94533
Tel: (707) 784-6170 Fax: (707) 784-6014

Director **Marc A. Fox** . . . . (707) 784-2552
E-mail: mafox@solanocounty.com
Assistant Director **Jeannine Seher** . . . . (707) 784-3406
E-mail: jmseher@solanocounty.com

Department of Information Technology

675 Texas Street, Suite 3700, Fairfield, CA 94533
Tel: (707) 784-6340 Fax: (707) 784-4883
Internet: www.solanocounty.com

Chief Information Officer **Ira Rosenthal** . . . . (707) 784-3000
E-mail: ijrosenthal@solanocounty.com

Department of Probation

475 Union Avenue, Fairfield, CA 94533
Tel: (707) 784-7600 Fax: (707) 784-7605

Chief Probation Officer **Christopher Hansen** . . . . (707) 784-7600
E-mail: chansen@solanocounty.com
Assistant Probation Officer **Donna Robinson** . . . . (707) 784-7600
E-mail: dlrobinson@solanocounty.com

Department of Resource Management

675 Texas Street, Suite 5500, Fairfield, CA 94533
Tel: (707) 784-6765 Fax: (707) 784-4805
E-mail: rmhelp@solanocounty.com

Director **William F. "Bill" Emlen** . . . . (707) 784-6765

(continued on next page)

COUNTIES

★ Elected Official ▲ Appointed by Legislature ▼ Appointed by Governor ► Appointed by Board or Commission ● Appointed by Judge
■ Appointed by Mayor △ Appointed by Freeholders ▽ Appointed by Supervisor ▷ Appointed by County Executive ○ Appointed by Council

Department of Resource Management *continued*

Assistant Director of Resource Management
Terry Schmidtbauer . . . . . . (707) 784-6765

Department of Veteran Services

675 Texas Street, Suite 4700, Fairfield, CA 94533
Tel: (707) 784-6590 Fax: (707) 784-0927

Director **Ted Puntillo** . . . . . . (707) 784-6590

Solano County Library

1150 Kentucky Street, Fairfield, CA 94533
Tel: (866) 572-7587 Internet: www.solanolibrary.com

Director of Library Services **Bonnie Katz** . . . . . . (707) 784-1500
E-mail: bkatz@solanocounty.com Fax: (707) 421-7474
Assistant Director of Library Services **(Vacant)** . . . . . . (707) 784-1500

Office of the Assessor/Recorder

675 Texas Street, Suite 2700, Fairfield, CA 94533
Tel: (707) 784-6200 Fax: (707) 784-6209
E-mail: assessor@solanocounty.com

★ Assessor/Recorder **Marc C. Tonnesen** . . . . . . (707) 784-6203
Term Expires: January 2019
E-mail: mctonnesen@solanocounty.com
Assistant Assessor/Recorder **Kathy Dossa** . . . . . . (707) 784-6231
E-mail: kldossa@solanocounty.com

Office of the Auditor-Controller

675 Texas Street, Suite 2800, Fairfield, CA 94533
Tel: (707) 784-6280 Fax: (707) 784-3553

★ Auditor-Controller **Simona Padilla-Scholtens** . . . . . . (707) 784-6280
Term Expires: January 2019
E-mail: sjpadilla@solanocounty.com
Education: Cal State (Sacramento) BSBA
Assistant Auditor-Controller **Phyllis Taynton** . . . . . . (707) 784-6280
Education: Cal State (Sacramento) 1987 BSBA

Office of the District Attorney

675 Texas Street, Suite 4500, Fairfield, CA 94533-6340
Tel: (707) 784-6800 Fax: (707) 784-7986
E-mail: solanoda@solanocounty.com

★ District Attorney **Krishna Abrams** . . . . . . (707) 784-6800
Term Expires: January 1, 2019
E-mail: kabrams@solanocounty.com
Chief Deputy District Attorney **Terry Ray** . . . . . . (707) 784-6800
E-mail: taray@solanocounty.com
Chief Deputy District Attorney **John Daugherty** . . . . . . (707) 784-6800
E-mail: jmdaugherty@solanocounty.com
Chief Deputy District Attorney **Jeffrey Kauffman** . . . . . . (707) 784-6800
E-mail: jckauffman@solanocounty.com

Office of the Sheriff/Coroner

530 Union Avenue, Suite 100, Fairfield, CA 94533
Tel: (707) 784-7000 Fax: (707) 784-6412

★ Sheriff/Coroner **Thomas "Tom" Ferrara** . . . . . . (707) 784-7030
Term Expires: December 31, 2018
E-mail: taferrara@solanocounty.com
Education: San Joaquin Delta AA; Southern Illinois BS
Undersheriff **Gary Elliott** . . . . . . (707) 784-7030
E-mail: gelliott@solanocounty.com

Office of the Treasurer-Tax Collector-County Clerk

675 Texas Street, Suite 1900, Fairfield, CA 94533
Tel: (707) 784-7910 (Clerk's Office)
Tel: (707) 784-6295 (Treasurer's Office)
Tel: (707) 784-7485 ((Tax Collector)) Fax: (707) 784-6311
E-mail: ttccc@solanocounty.com

★ Treasurer/Tax Collector/County Clerk
Charles A. Lomeli . . . . . . (707) 784-6295
Term Expires: January 2019
E-mail: calomeli@solanocounty.com
Assistant Treasurer/Tax Collector/County Clerk
Michael R. Cooper . . . . . . (707) 784-6295
E-mail: mcooper@solanocounty.com

County of Sonoma, California

575 Administration Dr., Santa Rosa, CA 95403
Tel: (707) 565-2431 (Information) Internet: www.sonoma-county.org

County Seat: Santa Rosa **Election Type:** Nonpartisan
Population: 502,146 (2015)

Office of the Board of Supervisors

575 Administration Dr., Room 100A, Santa Rosa, CA 95403
Fax: (707) 565-3778 Internet: http://supervisors.sonoma-county.org/

★ Chair **Efren Carrillo** (District 5) . . . . . . (707) 565-2241
Term Expires: December 31, 2016
E-mail: efren.carrillo@sonoma-county.org
★ Supervisor **Susan Gorin** (District 1) . . . . . . (707) 565-2241
Term Expires: December 31, 2016
Education: Sonoma State 1991 BA
★ Supervisor **David Rabbitt** (District 2) . . . . . . (707) 565-2241
Term Expires: December 31, 2018
E-mail: drabbitt@sonoma-county.org
★ Supervisor **Shirlee Zane** (District 3) . . . . . . (707) 565-2241
Term Expires: December 31, 2017
E-mail: shirlee.zane@sonoma-county.org
★ Supervisor **James Gore** (District 4) . . . . . . (707) 565-2241
Term Expires: December 31, 2018
Clerk of the Board **Roxanne Epstein** . . . . . . (707) 565-2241

Office of the County Administrator

575 Administration Dr., Room 104A, Santa Rosa, CA 95403
Fax: (707) 565-3778

▽ County Administrator **Veronica Ferguson** . . . . . . (707) 565-2431

Office of the Agricultural Commissioner

133 Aviation Boulevard, Suite 110, Santa Rosa, CA 95403
Fax: (707) 565-3850 Internet: www.sonoma-county.org/agcomm

▽ Agricultural Commissioner/Sealer **Tony Linegar** . . . . . . (707) 565-2371

Agricultural Division

133 Aviation Boulevard, Suite 110, Santa Rosa, CA 95403
Fax: (707) 565-3850

Chief Deputy Agricultural Commissioner **Sue Ostrom** . . . (707) 565-2371

Weights and Measures Division

133 Aviation Boulevard, Suite 110, Santa Rosa, CA 95403
Fax: (707) 565-3850

Chief Deputy Sealer **Fernando Vasquez** . . . . . . (707) 565-2371

★ Elected Official ▲ Appointed by Legislature ▼ Appointed by Governor ► Appointed by Board or Commission ● Appointed by Judge
■ Appointed by Mayor △ Appointed by Freeholders ▽ Appointed by Supervisor ▷ Appointed by County Executive ○ Appointed by Council

Cooperative Extension Office
133 Aviation Boulevard, Suite 109, Santa Rosa, CA 95403
Fax: (707) 565-2623 Internet: http://cesonoma.ucdavis.edu/

▽ Director **Stephanie Larson** .... (707) 565-2621
E-mail: slarson@ucdavis.edu

Office of the County Counsel
575 Administration Drive, Room 105A, Santa Rosa, CA 95403
Fax: (707) 565-2624

▽ County Counsel **Bruce Goldstein** .... (707) 565-2421
E-mail: bgoldste@sonoma-county.org

Office of Education
5340 Skylane Blvd., Santa Rosa, CA 95403-8246

★ Superintendent **Steven Herrington** .... (707) 524-2600
Term Expires: December 31, 2018

Office of the Public Defender
Hall of Justice, 600 Administration Drive, Room 111J, Santa Rosa, CA 95403
Fax: (707) 565-3357 Internet: www.sonoma-county.org/pubdef

▽ Public Defender **(Vacant)** .... (707) 565-2791
▽ Chief Deputy Public Defender **Michael Perry** .... (707) 565-2791
E-mail: mperry@sonoma-county.org
Administrative Services Officer **Donna Gomes** .... (707) 565-2791
E-mail: dgomes2@sonoma-county.org

Veterans' Services Office
3725 Westwind Boulevard, Suite 101, Santa Rosa, CA 95403

Manager **Chris Bingham** .... (707) 565-5960

Community Development Commission
1440 Guerneville Rd., Santa Rosa, CA 95403
Fax: (707) 565-7583

▽ Executive Director **Kathleen H. Kane** .... (707) 565-7505
E-mail: kkane@sonoma-county.org
▽ Community Development Manager **Mark Krug** .... (707) 565-7509
E-mail: mkrug@sonoma-county.org

Economic Development
401 College Avenue, Suite D, Santa Rosa, CA 95401
Fax: (707) 565-7231

▽ Director **Ben Stone** .... (707) 565-7170
E-mail: bstone@sonoma-county.org

Emergency Services Department
2300 County Center Drive, Suite 221A, Santa Rosa, CA 95403
Fax: (707) 565-1172

Director **Mark Aston** .... (707) 565-1152
E-mail: maston@sonoma-county.org

Fire Services Division
Deputy Chief/Fire Marshal **Robert MacIntyre** .... (707) 565-1152

Emergency Management Department
Emergency Services Coordinator **Sandy Covall-Alves** .... (707) 565-1152
E-mail: scovall@sonoma-county.org

Hazardous Materials Division
Program Manager **Andy Parsons** .... (707) 565-1152
E-mail: aparsons@sonoma-county.org

General Services Department
2300 County Center Drive, A205, Santa Rosa, CA 95403
Fax: (707) 565-2358 Internet: www.sonoma-county.org/gs

▽ Director **José Obregón** .... (707) 565-2977
E-mail: jobregon@sonoma-county.org
Education: Texas A&M (Kingsville) 1974 BS

General Services Department *continued*

Deputy Director **Gene Clark** .... (707) 565-2977

County Architect
Fax: (707) 565-3240

▽ Architect **Robert Kambak** A220 .... (707) 565-3211

Real Estate Department
Fax: (707) 565-2358

▽ Manager **Mike Wagner** A200 .... (707) 565-2463
E-mail: mwagner@sonoma-county.org

Risk Management
575 Administration Dr., Suite 116B, Santa Rosa, CA 95403
Fax: (707) 565-1139

▽ Manager **Marcia Chadbourne** .... (707) 565-2942

Department of Health Services
3313 Chanate Road, Santa Rosa, CA 95404
Tel: (707) 565-4700 Fax: (707) 565-7849
E-mail: DHSDIR@sonoma-county.org

▽ Director **Stephan Betz** .... (707) 565-4700
E-mail: Stephan.Betz@sonoma-county.org
Health Officer **Dr. Karen Milman** .... (707) 565-8697

Behavioral Health Division
3322 Chanate Road, Santa Rosa, CA 95404
Tel: (707) 565-4850 Fax: (707) 565-4892

▽ Division Director **Michael "Mike" Kennedy** .... (707) 565-4850
E-mail: Michael.Kennedy@sonoma-county.org

Human Resources Department
575 Administration Drive, Suite 116B, Santa Rosa, CA 95403
Fax: (707) 565-3770 Internet: http://hr.sonoma-county.org/

▽ Director (Acting) **Christina Cramer** .... (707) 565-2331
E-mail: ccramer@sonoma-county.org
Assistant Director **Julee Murphy** .... (707) 565-2331

Human Services Department
2550 Paulin Dr., Santa Rosa, CA 95403-1539
Fax: (707) 565-5890 Internet: www.sonoma-county.org/human

▽ Director **Jo Weber** .... (707) 565-5855

Area Agency on Aging [AAA]
3725 Westwind Boulevard, Suite 101, Santa Rosa, CA 95403
Tel: (707) 565-5950 Fax: (707) 565-5957 E-mail: aaa@schsd.org
Internet: www.socoaaa.org

▽ Director **Diane Kaljian** .... (707) 565-5950

Information Systems Department [ISD]
2615 Paulin Dr., Santa Rosa, CA 95403
Fax: (707) 565-3009 Internet: www.sonoma-county.org/isd

Director **John Hartwig** .... (707) 565-2911

Communications Division
445 Fiscal Dr., Santa Rosa, CA 95403
Fax: (707) 565-1985

▽ Manager **Lou Maricle** .... (707) 565-1980
E-mail: lmaricle@sonoma-county.org

Permit and Resource Management Department
2550 Ventura Ave., Santa Rosa, CA 95403
Fax: (707) 565-1103

▽ Director **Pete Parkinson** .... (707) 565-1925
Deputy Director **Jennifer Barrett** .... (707) 565-1947

★ Elected Official ▲ Appointed by Legislature ▼ Appointed by Governor ▶ Appointed by Board or Commission ● Appointed by Judge
■ Appointed by Mayor △ Appointed by Freeholders ▽ Appointed by Supervisor ▷ Appointed by County Executive ○ Appointed by Council

Probation Department

Hall of Justice, 600 Administration Drive, Room 104J,
Santa Rosa, CA 95403
Fax: (707) 565-2878 Internet: www.sonoma-county.org/probation

▽Chief Probation Officer **Robert Ochs** .... (707) 565-2731
E-mail: rochs@sonoma-county.org
Administrative Services Officer **Carl Vanden Heuvel** .... (707) 565-2149
Deputy Chief Probation Officer, Institutional Services
Kim King .... (707) 565-6311
Deputy Chief Probation Officer, Probation Services
Sheralynn Freitas .... (707) 565-2149
Director, Adult Services Division **Gale Reeder** .... (707) 565-3372
Director, Juvenile Services Division **Maria Lopez** ...... (707) 565-6310
7425 Rancho Los Guilicos Rd., Santa Rosa, CA 95409

Transportation and Public Works Department

2300 County Center Drive, Suite 100B, Santa Rosa, CA 95403
Fax: (707) 565-2620 Internet: www.sonoma-county.org/tpw

Director **Philip Demery** .... (707) 565-2231

Charles M. Schulz - Sonoma County Airport

2290 Airport Boulevard, Santa Rosa, CA 95403
Fax: (707) 542-5303 Internet: www.sonomacountyairport.org

▽Airport Manager **Jon Stout** .... (707) 565-7243

Sonoma County Public Library

Third & E Sts., Santa Rosa, CA 95404
Fax: (707) 525-9563 Internet: www.sonomalibrary.org

▽Director **Sandra Cooper** .... (707) 545-0831
E-mail: scooper@sonoma-county.org

Sonoma County Regional Parks

2300 County Center Drive, Suite 120A, Santa Rosa, CA 95403-3009
Fax: (707) 579-8247 Internet: www.sonoma-county.org/parks

▽Director **Caryl O. Hart** .... (707) 565-2041
E-mail: chart@sonoma-county.org

Sonoma County Water Agency

404 Aviation Building, Santa Rosa, CA 95403
Fax: (707) 544-6123 Internet: www.scwa.ca.gov

▽General Manager **Grant Davis** .... (707) 526-5370

Office of the Auditor-Controller

585 Fiscal Drive, Room 101F, Santa Rosa, CA 95403-2871
Fax: (707) 565-3489

★Auditor-Controller, Tax Collector and Treasurer
David E. Sundstrom .... (707) 565-3285
Term Expires: December 31, 2018
E-mail: david.sundstrom@sonoma-county.org
Education: Sonoma State BA; UC Davis 1985 MBA
Executive Secretary **Terina Tracy** .... (707) 565-3285
E-mail: ttracy@sonoma-county.org
Assistant Auditor-Controller **Donna Dunk** .... (707) 565-3274
Administrative Services Officer **Julianne Kamplain** ..... (707) 565-3583
E-mail: jkamplai@sonoma-county.org

Office of the County Clerk-Recorder-Assessor-Registrar of Voters

585 Fiscal Drive, Room 104F, Santa Rosa, CA 95403
Fax: (707) 565-1364 Internet: www.sonoma-county.org/cra

★County Clerk-Recorder-Assessor-Registrar of Voters
William F. "Bill" Rousseau .... (707) 565-1877
Term Expires: December 31, 2018
E-mail: thecountyclerk@sonoma-county.org

Assessor Division

585 Fiscal Drive, Room 104F, Santa Rosa, CA 95403
Fax: (707) 565-1364 E-mail: assessor@sonoma-county.org
Internet: www.sonoma-county.org/assessor

Chief Deputy Assessor **Greg Walsh** .... (707) 565-1863

County Clerk Division

2300 County Center Drive, Suite B177, Santa Rosa, CA 95403
Tel: (707) 565-3800 Fax: (707) 565-3957
Internet: www.sonoma-county.org/clerk

Chief Deputy County Clerk **Deva Proto** .... (707) 565-3800
E-mail: deva.proto@sonoma-county.org

Recorder Division

585 Fiscal Drive, Room 103F, Santa Rosa, CA 95403-0124
Fax: (707) 565-3388 Internet: www.sonoma-county.org/recorder

▽Chief Deputy Recorder **Deva Proto** .... (707) 565-3246
E-mail: deva.proto@sonoma-county.org

Registrar of Voters Division

435 Fiscal Drive, Santa Rosa, CA 95403
P.O. Box 11485, Santa Rosa, CA 95406-1485
Fax: (707) 565-6843 Internet: http://vote.sonoma-county.org/

▽Assistant Registrar of Voters **Elizabeth Acosta** .... (707) 565-6800
E-mail: elizabeth.acosta@sonoma-county.org

Office of the District Attorney

Hall of Justice, 600 Administration Drive, Room 212J,
Santa Rosa, CA 95403
Fax: (707) 565-2762

★District Attorney **Jill Ravitch** .... (707) 565-2311
Term Expires: December 31, 2018
E-mail: jravitch@sonoma-county.org

Office of the Sheriff-Coroner

2796 Ventura Ave., Santa Rosa, CA 95403
Tel: (707) 565-2751 (Information Civil Division) Fax: (707) 526-0403
Internet: www.sonomasheriff.org

★Sheriff-Coroner **Steve Freitas** .... (707) 565-2781
Term Expires: December 31, 2018
E-mail: sfreitas@sonoma-county.org

Office of the Treasurer-Tax Collector

585 Fiscal Drive, Room 100F, Santa Rosa, CA 95403
Tel: (707) 565-2631 Fax: (707) 565-3489

★Treasurer-Tax Collector **David E. Sundstrom** .... (707) 565-2631
Term Expires: December 31, 2018
E-mail: david.sundstrom@sonoma-county.org
Education: Sonoma State BA; UC Davis 1985 MBA

★Elected Official ▲Appointed by Legislature ▼Appointed by Governor ▶Appointed by Board or Commission ●Appointed by Judge
■Appointed by Mayor △Appointed by Freeholders ▽Appointed by Supervisor ▷Appointed by County Executive ○Appointed by Council

County of Spokane, Washington

County Courthouse, 1116 W. Broadway Ave., Spokane, WA 99260
Internet: www.spokanecounty.org

County Seat: Spokane **Election Type:** Partisan **Population:** 490,945 (2015)

Office of the County Commission

County Courthouse, 1116 West Broadway Avenue, 1st Floor, Spokane, WA 99260-0100
Fax: (509) 477-2274

★ Chair **Shelly O'Quinn** (R-District 2) .... (509) 477-2265
Term Expires: December 31, 2016
★ Vice Chair **Al French** (R-District 3) .... (509) 477-2265
Term Expires: December 31, 2018
E-mail: afrench@spokanecounty.org
★ Commissioner **Nancy McLaughlin** (R-District 1) .... (509) 477-2265
Term Expires: December 31, 2016
Clerk of the Board **Ginna Vasquez** .... (509) 477-2265
E-mail: gvasquez@spokanecounty.org

Office of the Chief Executive Officer

Fax: (509) 477-2251

▶ Chief Executive Officer **Gerald L. "Gerry" Gemmill** .... (509) 477-2600
Education: Whitworth 1985 BA; Eastern Washington MA
▶ Chief Operating Officer **John Dickson** .... (509) 477-2600
Education: U Washington 1985 BSME; Washington State 2000 MS

Budget and Finance Office

County Courthouse, 1116 West Broadway Avenue, 2nd Floor, Spokane, WA 99260
Tel: (509) 477-2159 Fax: (509) 477-2251
Internet: www.spokanecounty.org/budget

▶ Budget and Finance Director
Robert W. "Bob" Wrigley .... (509) 477-4790
E-mail: bwrigley@spokanecounty.org
Education: Cal State (Long Beach) BS
Budget Analyst **Downs Paul** .... (509) 477-5799
E-mail: dpaul@spokanecounty.org
Budget Analyst **Margaret M. Smith** .... (509) 477-5789
E-mail: msmith@spokanecounty.org

Cooperative Extension Office (Washington State University)

Spokane County Extension Education Center, 222 North Havana, Spokane, WA 99202-4799
Tel: (509) 477-2048 Fax: (509) 477-2087
Internet: www.spokane-county.wsu.edu

County Director **Dori Babcock** .... (509) 477-2170
County Extension Educator **Steve McConnell** .... (509) 477-2175
County Extension Educator **Diana Roberts** .... (509) 477-2167
4-H County Extension Educator **Gary F. Varrella** .... (509) 477-2163

Medical Examiner's Office

5901 North Lidgerwood Street, Suite 24B, Spokane, WA 99208
Tel: (509) 477-2296 Fax: (509) 477-6327
Internet: www.spokanecounty.org/medexaminer

▶ Medical Examiner **Sally S. Aiken** .... (509) 477-2296
E-mail: saiken@spokanecounty.org
Education: U Washington 1982 MD
▶ Medical Examiner **John D. Howard** .... (509) 477-2296
E-mail: jhoward@spokanecounty.org
Education: U Washington MD

Public Defender's Office

1033 West Gardner Avenue, Spokane, WA 99260-0280
Tel: (509) 477-4246 Fax: (509) 477-2567
Internet: www.spokanecounty.org/pubdefender

▶ Public Defender **Thomas J. Krzyminski** .... (509) 477-4812
Chief Deputy Public Defender **Karen Lidholdt** .... (509) 477-4863
Office Manager **Julie Curtis** .... (509) 477-4803

Veteran Services Office

Secoma Building, 1102 West College Avenue, Spokane, WA 99201-2085
Tel: (509) 477-3690 Fax: (509) 477-2299
Internet: www.spokanecounty.org/veteran

▶ Director **Charles "Chuck" Elmore** .... (509) 477-3690
E-mail: celmore@spokanecounty.org
Staff Assistant **Dan Souts** .... (509) 477-3690

COUNTIES

Department of Building and Planning

Public Works Building, 1026 West Broadway Avenue, Spokane, WA 99260
Tel: (509) 477-3675 Fax: (509) 477-4703
E-mail: bphelp@spokanecounty.org Internet: www.spokanecounty.org/bp

Building Director **Randy Vissia** .... (509) 477-3675
E-mail: rvissia@spokanecounty.org
Planning Director **John C. Pederson** .... (509) 477-3675
Administrative Services Manager **Laurie Carber** .... (509) 477-3675

Division of Engineering and Roads

Public Works Building, 1026 West Broadway Avenue, Spokane, WA 99260-0170
Tel: (509) 477-3600 Fax: (509) 477-3478
Internet: www.spokanecounty.org/engineer

County Engineer **Mitch Reister** .... (509) 477-3600
Education: Washington State 1997 BSCE, 2005 MS

Utilities Division

Public Works Building, 1026 West Broadway Avenue, 4th Floor, Spokane, WA 99260
Tel: (509) 477-3604 Fax: (509) 477-4715
Internet: www.spokanecounty.org/utilities

Director **N. Bruce Rawls** .... (509) 477-3604

Community Services, Housing and Community Development

312 West 8th Avenue, Spokane, WA 99204-2506
Tel: (509) 477-5722 Fax: (509) 477-6827
Internet: www.spokanecounty.org/communitysvcs

▶ Director **Christine Barada** .... (509) 477-7561
E-mail: cbarada@spokanecounty.org
Secretary **Tami Landsiedel** .... (509) 477-2588
E-mail: tlandsiedel@spokanecounty.org
Housing and Community Development Manager
Tim Crowley .... (509) 477-4488
E-mail: tcrowley@spokanecounty.org
Mental Health Services Administrator **Suzie McDaniel** ... (509) 477-4512
Developmental Disabilities Coordinator **Brian Nichols** .... (509) 477-2029
Drugs/Alcohol Coordinator **Charisse Pope** .... (509) 477-4507
Substance Abuse Prevention Coordinator **Becky Swan** ... (509) 477-4540
Supportive Living Coordinator **Kim Longhofer** .... (509) 477-4383

Human Resources Department

1229 West Mallon Avenue, Spokane, WA 99260-0230
Tel: (509) 477-5750 Tel: (509) 477-5627 (Information Job Hotline)
Fax: (509) 477-5642 Internet: www.spokanecounty.org/hr

▶ Director **Cathy Malzahn** .... (509) 477-2120
E-mail: cmalzahn@spokanecounty.org

★ Elected Official ▲ Appointed by Legislature ▼ Appointed by Governor ▶ Appointed by Board or Commission ● Appointed by Judge
■ Appointed by Mayor △ Appointed by Freeholders ▽ Appointed by Supervisor ▷ Appointed by County Executive ○ Appointed by Council

COUNTIES

Information Systems Department [ISD]
815 N. Jefferson St., Spokane, WA 99260-0400
Tel: (509) 477-6020 Fax: (509) 477-4705
E-mail: isdhelp@spokanecounty.org
Internet: www.spokanecounty.org/infosystems

Director **Becky Gehret** .... (509) 477-4244
E-mail: bgehret@spokanecounty.org
GIS (Geographic Information System) Manager
Ian Von Essen .... (509) 477-6344
E-mail: ivonessen@spokanecounty.org
Programming Manager **Kevin Norris** .... (509) 477-4244
Programming Manager **Steve Nelson** .... (509) 477-4244
Technical Services Manager and Assistant Director
Pat Ferrell .... (509) 477-6308
E-mail: pferrell@spokanecounty.org

Parks, Recreation and Golf Department
404 N. Havana St., Spokane, WA 99202
Fax: (509) 477-2454 Internet: www.spokanecounty.org/parks

Director **Doug Chase** .... (509) 477-4730
Education: Eastern Washington 1991 BA, 2000 MA
Assistant Director **John Bottelli** .... (509) 477-4730
Parks Superintendent **Don Secor** .... (509) 926-4616
Recreation Coordinator **Joel Blackman** .... (509) 477-4730
Recreation Program Manager **Bekah Bennett** .... (509) 477-4730

Public Information and Communications Department
Public Works Building, 1026 West Broadway Avenue, 4th Floor, Spokane, WA 99260
Fax: (509) 477-4715

Manager **Martha Lou Wheatley-Billeter** .... (509) 477-7195
E-mail: mwheatleybilleter@spokanecounty.org

Purchasing Department
Monroe Court Building, 901 North Monroe Street, #350-B, Spokane, WA 99201-2103
Fax: (509) 477-6627

▶ Director **Béla G. Kovács** .... (509) 477-2301
E-mail: bkovács@spokanecounty.org

Risk Management Department
1033 West Gardner Avenue, Spokane, WA 99260-0280
Fax: (509) 477-2681 Internet: www.spokanecounty.org/riskmgmt

▶ Director of Risk Management **Steve Bartel** .... (509) 477-6113
E-mail: sbartel@spokanecounty.org

Law Library
1116 West Broadway Avenue, Second Floor, Spokane, WA 99260-0100
Tel: (509) 477-3680 Fax: (509) 477-4722
Internet: www.spokanecounty.org/lawlibrary

Librarian **Cynthia Lucas** .... (509) 477-3680
E-mail: clucas@spokanecounty.org

Board of Equalization [BOE]
Broadway Centre Building, 721 North Jefferson Street, Suite 201, Spokane, WA 99260
Fax: (509) 477-2568
Internet: www.spokanecounty.org/boardofequalization

Director **Linda M. Kovick** .... (509) 477-2250
E-mail: lkovick@spokanecounty.org
Specialist **Susan "Suzi" Castelo** .... (509) 477-2250
E-mail: scastelo@spokanecounty.org
Specialist **Niki Sanders** .... (509) 477-2250

Noxious Weed Control Board
Agricultural Center, N. 222 Havana St., Spokane, WA 99202
Fax: (509) 477-2675

Coordinator **David J. Mundt** .... (509) 477-5777

Spokane County Fair and Expo Center
404 North Havana St., Suite 1, Spokane Valley, WA 99202-4663
Fax: (509) 477-8926

Director **Rich Hartzell** .... (509) 477-2786
Fair Coordinator **Jessica "Jessie" McLaughlin** .... (509) 477-2772
Marketing and Sales Manager **Erin Gurtel** .... (509) 447-2785

Spokane County Library District [SCLD]
4322 North Argonne Road, Spokane, WA 99212-1868
Fax: (509) 893-8472 Internet: www.scld.org

Executive Director **Nancy Ledeboer** .... (509) 893-8200

Spokane County Regional Animal Protection Service [SCRAPS]
North 2521 Flora Road, Spokane Valley, WA 99216
Tel: (509) 477-2532 Fax: (509) 477-4745
Internet: www.spokanecounty.org/animal

▶ Director **Nancy Hill** .... (509) 477-1967
E-mail: nhill@spokanecounty.org
Office Operations Manager **Dianne Timoney** .... (509) 477-4221
E-mail: dtimoney@spokanecounty.org

Spokane Regional Health District Board of Health
1101 West College Avenue, Room 330, Spokane, WA 99201-2095
Tel: (509) 324-1501 Fax: (509) 324-1507 Internet: http://boh.srhd.org/

Spokane Regional Health District [SRHD]
1101 West College Avenue, Spokane, WA 99201-2095
Tel: (509) 324-1500 Fax: (509) 324-1507 Internet: www.srhd.org

▶ Health Officer **Dr. Joel E. McCullough** .... (509) 324-1501
E-mail: jmccullough@srhd.org
Administrator **Torney Smith** .... (509) 324-1518
Chief Deputy Registrar, Vital Statistics **Paula Maxwell** ... (509) 324-1523
Public Information Manager **Kimberly "Kim" Papich** .... (509) 324-1539
E-mail: kpapich@srhd.org

Community and Family Services Division
Tel: (509) 324-1640 Fax: (509) 324-1699

Director **Sheila Masteller** .... (509) 324-1617

Environmental Public Health Division
Tel: (509) 324-1560 Fax: (509) 324-3603

Director **David Swink** .... (509) 324-1590

Health Promotion Division
Director **Kyle Unland** .... (509) 324-1540

Office of the Assessor
County Courthouse, 1116 West Broadway Avenue, 1st Floor, Spokane, WA 99260-0100
Tel: (509) 477-3698 (Real Property Appraisal)
Tel: (509) 477-4787 (Personal and Business Property Appraisal)
Fax: (509) 477-3697 Internet: www.spokanecounty.org/assessor

★ Assessor **Vicki Horton** (R) .... (509) 477-5775
Term Expires: December 31, 2018
E-mail: vhorton@spokanecounty.org
Deputy Assessor **Byron Hodgson** .... (509) 477-3698

★ Elected Official ▲ Appointed by Legislature ▼ Appointed by Governor ▶ Appointed by Board or Commission ● Appointed by Judge
■ Appointed by Mayor △ Appointed by Freeholders ▽ Appointed by Supervisor ▷ Appointed by County Executive ○ Appointed by Council

Office of the Auditor

County Courthouse, 1116 West Broadway Avenue, Room 200,
Spokane, WA 99260-0100
Fax: (509) 477-6451

★ Auditor **Vicky Dalton** (D) .... (509) 477-2217
Term Expires: December 31, 2018
E-mail: vdalton@spokanecounty.org
Executive Assistant **Denise Toutloff** .... (509) 477-2217
E-mail: dtoutloff@spokanecounty.org

Elections and Voter Registrations

Gardner Center, 1033 W. Gardner, Spokane, WA 99260
Tel: (509) 477-2320 (General Information) Fax: (509) 477-6607
Internet: http://www.spokanecounty.org/elections

Elections Manager **Mike McLaughlin** .... (509) 477-6390

Financial Services Department

Accounting Manager **Jenny Stettler** .... (509) 477-4755
E-mail: jstettler@spokanecounty.org
Accounting Supervisor **Jill McBride** .... (509) 477-7275
E-mail: jmcbride@spokanecounty.org
Accounts Payable and Payroll Supervisor
Debbie Crocker .... (509) 477-2298

Motor Vehicle Department

Courthouse Annex, 1116 W. Broadway Ave., 1st Fl., Spokane, WA 99260
P.O. Box 2351, Spokane, WA 99210-2351
Tel: (509) 477-2222 (Licensing General Information)

Manager **Ellen Marsh** .... (509) 477-2215

Recording Department

P.O. Box 2353, Spokane, WA 99210-2353
Tel: (509) 477-2270 (General Information)

Records Manager **Melanie Muzatko** .... (509) 477-5959
Recording Supervisor **Kathy Cook** .... (509) 477-2270

Office of the County Clerk

County Courthouse, 1116 West Broadway Avenue, Room 300,
Spokane, WA 99260-0100
Tel: (509) 477-2211 E-mail: spococlerks@spokanecounty.org
Internet: www.spokanecounty.org/clerk

○ County Clerk **Col. Timothy W. Fitzgerald** .... (509) 477-2211
Term Expires: December 31, 2018
Executive Assistant **Leslie Lashbrook** .... (509) 477-2211
Chief Deputy **Gary D. Berg** .... (509) 477-2211
E-mail: gberg@spokanecounty.org
Records Manager **Karin Peterson** .... (509) 477-6429

Office of the Prosecuting Attorney

Public Safety Building, West 1100 Mallon Avenue, 1st Floor,
Spokane, WA 99260
Fax: (509) 477-3409 Internet: www.spokanecounty.org/prosecuting

★ Prosecuting Attorney **Lawrence H. Haskell** .... (509) 477-5838
Term Expires: December 31, 2018
E-mail: lhaskell@spokanecounty.org

Sheriff's Office

Public Safety Building, West 1100 Mallon Avenue, Spokane, WA 99260
Fax: (509) 477-5641 Internet: www.spokanecounty.org/sheriff

★ Sheriff **Ozzie Knezovich** (R) .... (509) 477-6917
Term Expires: December 31, 2018
E-mail: oknezovich@spokanesheriff.org
Undersheriff **Jeff Tower** .... (509) 477-4749
E-mail: jtower@spokanesheriff.org
Valley Precinct Chief **Rick VanLeuven** .... (509) 477-3300
E-mail: rvanleuven@spokanesheriff.org

Sheriff's Office *continued*

Jail Commander **Capt. John McGrath** .... (509) 477-2337
Investigative Services **John Nowels** .... (509) 477-4760
E-mail: jnowels@spokanesheriff.org
Patrol Services **Capt. Mark Werner** .... (509) 477-6549
E-mail: mwerner@spokanesheriff.org
Public Information Officer **Craig Chamberlain** .... (509) 477-6612
Training **Sgt Marty Tucker** .... (509) 477-3552
Chief Examiner **Nancy J. Paladino** .... (509) 477-4526
E-mail: npaladino@spokanecounty.org

911 Emergency Communications Center

1620 N. Rebecca Street, Spokane, WA 99217-7200
Tel: (509) 532-8911 Fax: (509) 535-6719

Director **Lorlee Mizell** .... (509) 532-8911
E-mail: lmizell@spokanecounty.org

Emergency Management Department

1680 N. Rebecca Street, Spokane, WA 99217-7200
Fax: (509) 477-5759

Deputy Director **Ed Lewis** .... (509) 477-7607
E-mail: elewis@spokanecounty.org

Geiger Corrections Center

3507 South Spotted Road, Spokane, WA 99224
Fax: (509) 477-3408

Captain **John McGrath** .... (509) 477-3259

Office of the Treasurer

County Courthouse, 1116 West Broadway Avenue, 2nd Floor,
Spokane, WA 99260-0100
Tel: (509) 477-4713 Fax: (509) 477-3674
E-mail: treasurer@spokanecounty.org
Internet: www.spokanecounty.org/treasurer

★ Treasurer **Rob Chase** (R) .... (509) 477-4786
Term Expires: December 31, 2018
E-mail: rchase@spokanecounty.org
Chief Deputy Treasurer **Mike Volz** .... (509) 477-2074
Finance Deputy **John Christina** .... (509) 477-5178
Senior Finance Manager **J. J. Hernandez** .... (509) 477-6393
Tax Collection Supervisor **Debbie Gehret** .... (509) 477-5769
E-mail: dgehret@spokanecounty.org
Tax Collection Supervisor **(Vacant)** .... (509) 477-4747
Executive Assistant **Debra Poindexter** .... (509) 477-4786
E-mail: dpoindexter@spokanecounty.org

Spokane International Airport

9000 West Airport Drive, Suite 204, Spokane, WA 99224
Tel: (509) 455-6455 Fax: (509) 624-6663
E-mail: info@spokaneairports.net Internet: www.spokaneairports.net

Chief Executive Officer and Executive Director
Lawrence J. "Larry" Krauter .... (509) 455-6419
Finance Director **Dave Armstrong** .... (509) 455-6448
Marketing and Public Affairs Director **Todd Woodard** .... (509) 455-6470
Operations and Maintenance Director **Ryan Sheehan** .... (509) 455-6418
E-mail: rsheehan@spokaneairports.net
Planning and Engineering Director (Interim)
Matt Breen .... (509) 455-6433
Properties and Contracts Director **Judy Gifford** .... (509) 455-6415
E-mail: judyg@spokaneairports.net
Airport Police Chief **Peter L. Troyer** .... (509) 455-6430

Spokane Regional Clean Air Agency

3104 East Augusta Avenue, Spokane, WA 99207-5384
Tel: (509) 477-4727 Fax: (509) 477-6828
E-mail: mail@spokanecleanair.org Internet: www.spokanecleanair.org

► Director **Julie Oliver** .... (509) 477-4727 ext. 121
E-mail: joliver@spokanecleanair.org

(continued on next page)

COUNTIES

★ Elected Official ▲ Appointed by Legislature ▼ Appointed by Governor ► Appointed by Board or Commission ● Appointed by Judge
■ Appointed by Mayor △ Appointed by Freeholders ▽ Appointed by Supervisor ▷ Appointed by County Executive ○ Appointed by Council

Spokane Regional Clean Air Agency *continued*

Finance and Personnel Administrator
Barbara Nelson . . . . . (509) 477-4727 ext. 116
E-mail: bnelson@spokanecleanair.org
Enforcement/Compliance Administrator
(Vacant) . . . . . (509) 477-4727 ext. 102
Engineering/Technical Services Chief
April Westby . . . . . (509) 477-4727 ext. 105
E-mail: awestby@spokanecleanair.org
Public Information **Lisa Woodard** . . . . . (509) 477-4727 ext. 115
E-mail: lwoodard@spokanecleanair.org

County of Stanislaus, California

1010 10th Street, Modesto, CA 95354
Tel: (209) 525-6333 (Information) Internet: www.stancounty.com

County Seat: Modesto **Election Type:** Nonpartisan
Population: 538,388 (2015)

Office of the Board of Supervisors

1010 10th Street, Suite 6500, Modesto, CA 95354
Fax: (209) 525-4420 Internet: www.stancounty.com/board

★ Chairman **Dick Monteith** (District 4) . . . . . (209) 525-4445
Term Expires: January 7, 2019
E-mail: monteithd@stancounty.com
★ Supervisor **William O'Brien** (District 1) . . . . . (209) 525-4440
Term Expires: December 31, 2016
E-mail: obrienw@stancounty.com
★ Supervisor **Vito Chiesa** (District 2) . . . . . (209) 525-6440
Term Expires: December 31, 2016
E-mail: vito.chiesa@stancounty.com
★ Supervisor **Terry Withrow** (District 3) . . . . . (209) 525-6560
Term Expires: January 7, 2019
E-mail: withrowt@stancounty.com
Education: Cal State (Stanislaus) 1982 BA
★ Supervisor **James "Jim" De Martini** (District 5) . . . . . (209) 525-4470
Term Expires: December 31, 2016
E-mail: demartinij@stancounty.com
▽ Clerk of the Board **Christine Ferraro Tallman** . . . . . (209) 525-4494
Assistant Clerk of the Board **Elizabeth A. King** . . . . . (209) 525-4494

Office of the Chief Executive Officer

1010 10th Street, Suite 6800, Modesto, CA 95354
Fax: (209) 544-6226 Internet: www.co.stanislaus.ca.us/ceo

Chief Executive Officer **Stan Risen** . . . . . (209) 525-6333
E-mail: risens@stancounty.com
Chief Operations Officer/Assistant Executive Officer
Patricia Hill Thomas . . . . . (209) 525-6333
E-mail: Thomasp@stancounty.com
Assistant Executive Officer **Keith D. Boggs** . . . . . (209) 525-6333
E-mail: boggsk@stancounty.com
Assistant Executive Officer **Jody Hayes** . . . . . (209) 525-6333
E-mail: hayesj@stancounty.com

Office of the County Counsel

1010 10th Street, Suite 6400, Modesto, CA 95354
Fax: (209) 525-4473 Internet: www.stancounty.com/counsel

▽ County Counsel **John P. Doering III** . . . . . (209) 525-6376
E-mail: john.doering@stancounty.com
Education: Cal State (Humboldt); McGeorge 1990 JD
Assistant County Counsel **Thomas E. Boze** . . . . . (209) 525-6376

Office of Emergency Services [OES]

3705 Oakdale Road, Modesto, CA 95357
Tel: (209) 552-3600 Fax: (209) 552-2512 Internet: www.stanoes.com

▽ Assistant Director/Fire Warden **Dale Skiles** . . . . . (209) 552-3600
Fire Marshal (Interim) **Jerry McDaniel** . . . . . (209) 552-3700

Department of Aging and Veterans Services

121 Downey Ave., Suite 102, Modesto, CA 95354
Fax: (209) 558-8648

▽ Director **Margie Palomino** . . . . . (209) 525-4601
E-mail: palminm@stancounty.com

Department of Agriculture/Weights and Measures

Agricultural Center, 3800 Cornucopia Way, Suite B, Modesto, CA 95358
E-mail: agcom50@mail.co.stanislaus.ca.us

▽ Agricultural Commissioner/Sealer **Milton O'Haire** . . . . . (209) 525-4730

Alliance Worknet

251 East Hackett Road, Room C-2, Modesto, CA 95358
Tel: (209) 558-2100 Fax: (209) 558-2164
Internet: www.allianceworknet.com

▽ Director **Jeff Rowe** . . . . . (209) 558-2150
E-mail: rowej@stanalliance.com

Behavioral Health and Recovery Services [BHRS]

800 Scenic Dr., Modesto, CA 95350
Tel: (209) 525-7423 Fax: (209) 525-6291
E-mail: dmhinfo@mail.co.stanislaus.ca.us
Internet: www.co.stanislaus.ca.us/bhrs

▽ Director **Madelyn Schlaepfer** . . . . . (209) 525-6225

Community Services Agency

251 E. Hackett Rd., Modesto, CA 95357
P.O. Box 42, Modesto, CA 95353-0042

▽ Director **Kathryn Harwell** . . . . . (209) 558-2500

Cooperative Extension (University of California)

3800 Cornucopia Way, Suite A, Modesto, CA 95358
Fax: (209) 525-6840 Internet: http://cestanislaus.ucdavis.edu/

▽ Director (Interim) **Theresa Spezzano** . . . . . (209) 525-6800

Emergency Dispatch Department/Regional 911

3705 Oakdale Road, Modesto, CA 95357
Internet: http://www.stan911.com

▽ Director **Joel Broumas** . . . . . (209) 552-3900

Environmental Resources Department

3800 Cornucopia Way, Suite C, Modesto, CA 95358
Fax: (209) 525-6773 E-mail: jaggers@stancounty.com

▽ Director **Jami Aggers** . . . . . (209) 525-6770

Health Services Agency [HSA]

830 Scenic Drive, Modesto, CA 95350
Fax: (209) 558-7123 Internet: www.schsa.org

▽ Director **Mary Ann Lee** . . . . . (209) 558-7163

Parks and Recreation Department

3800 Cornucopia Way, Suite C, Modesto, CA 95358-9492

▽ Director **Jami Aggers** . . . . . (209) 525-6770

★ Elected Official ▲ Appointed by Legislature ▼ Appointed by Governor ▶ Appointed by Board or Commission ● Appointed by Judge
■ Appointed by Mayor △ Appointed by Freeholders ▽ Appointed by Supervisor ▷ Appointed by County Executive ○ Appointed by Council

Department of Planning and Community Development
1010 - 10th Street, Suite 3400, Modesto, CA 95354
Fax: (209) 525-5911
▽Director **Angela Freitas** . . . . . (209) 525-6330

Probation Department
2215 Blue Gum Ave., Modesto, CA 95358-1097
▽Chief Probation Officer **Jill Sliva** . . . . . (209) 525-4598

Public Defender
1021 I Street, Suite 201, Modesto, CA 95354
Fax: (209) 525-4244
▽Public Defender **Timothy Bazar** . . . . . (209) 525-4200

Public Works Department
1010 10th Street, Suite 3500, Modesto, CA 95354
▽Director **Matt Machado** . . . . . (209) 525-6550
Chief Building Official **Dennis Wister** . . . . . (209) 525-6557

Purchasing Department
1010 10th Street, Suite 5400, Modesto, CA 95354
P.O. Box 3229, Modesto, CA 95353
Purchasing Agent **Keith D. Boggs** . . . . . (209) 525-7640
E-mail: boggsk@stancounty.com

Stanislaus Consolidated Fire Protection District [SCFPD]
3324 Topeka Street, Riverbank, CA 95367
Tel: (209) 869-7470 Fax: (209) 869-7475 Internet: www.scfpd.us
▽Fire Chief **(Vacant)** . . . . . (209) 869-7470

Stanislaus County Library
1500 I Street, Modesto, CA 95354
Fax: (209) 529-4779 Internet: www.stanislauslibrary.org
▽Librarian **Diane McDonnell** . . . . . (209) 558-7801

Office of the Assessor
1010 10th Street, Suite 2400, Modesto, CA 95354
Fax: (209) 525-6586 E-mail: assessor@stancounty.com
Internet: www.stancounty.com/assessor
★Assessor **Don Gaekle** . . . . . (209) 525-6461
Term Expires: January 3, 2019

Office of the Auditor-Controller
1010 10th Street, Suite 5100, Modesto, CA 95354
★Auditor-Controller **Lauren Parrill Klein** . . . . . (209) 525-6576
Term Expires: January 7, 2019
E-mail: lauren.klein@stancounty.com
Education: Dominican Col (NY); Cal State (Hayward)
Assistant Auditor-Controller **Kashmir Gill** . . . . . (209) 525-6579

Office of the Clerk-Recorder
1021 I Street, Suite 101, Modesto, CA 95354
P.O. Box 1008, Modesto, CA 95353
Fax: (209) 525-5804 (Clerk-Recorder)
Fax: (209) 525-5802 (Registrar of Voters)
Internet: www.stancounty.com/clerkrecorder Internet: www.stanvote.com
★Clerk-Recorder/Registrar of Voters **Lee Lundrigan** . . . . . (209) 525-5200
Term Expires: January 7, 2019
E-mail: stanvote@stancounty.com
Tel: (209) 525-5250

Office of the District Attorney
832 12th Street, Suite 300, Modesto, CA 95354
Fax: (209) 558-4027 Internet: www.stanislaus-da.org
★District Attorney **Birgit Ann Fladager** . . . . . (209) 525-5550
Term Expires: January 7, 2019
E-mail: birgit.fladager@standa.org
Education: St Olaf; McGeorge 1986 JD
Assistant District Attorney **Dave Harris** . . . . . (209) 525-5550

Office of the Sheriff-Coroner-Public Administrator
250 East Hackett Road, Modesto, CA 95358
Fax: (209) 525-7106 Internet: www.scsdonline.com
★Sheriff-Coroner-Public Administrator
Adam Christianson . . . . . (209) 525-7216
Term Expires: January 7, 2019
E-mail: chradam@stanislaussheriff.com
Education: Union Inst U 2006 BA

Office of the Treasurer-Tax Collector
1010 10th Street, Suite 2500, Modesto, CA 95354
P.O. Box 859, Modesto, CA 95358
Fax: (209) 525-7868 Internet: www.stancounty.com/tr-tax
★Treasurer-Tax Collector **Gordon B. Ford** . . . . . (209) 525-6388
Term Expires: January 7, 2019
E-mail: fordg@stancounty.com

Stanislaus County Office of Education
1100 H Street, Modesto, CA 95354
Fax: (209) 525-5147 Internet: www.stancoe.org
★Superintendent **Tom Changnon** . . . . . (209) 238-1700
Term Expires: January 7, 2019
E-mail: tchangnon@stancoe.org
Education: Stanford 1972 BA; U San Francisco

County of Stark, Ohio
County Administration Building, 110 Central Plaza South,
Canton, OH 44702
Internet: www.starkcountyohio.gov

County Seat: Canton **Election Type:** Partisan **Population:** 375,165 (2015)

Office of the Board of Commissioners
County Administration Bldg., 110 Central Plaza South, Suite 240,
Canton, OH 44702
Fax: (330) 451-7906
★President **Janet Weir Creighton** (R) . . . . . (330) 451-7371
Term Expires: January 1, 2019
E-mail: jwcreighton@starkcountyohio.gov
Education: Ohio
★Board Member **Richard S. Regula** (R) . . . . . (330) 451-7371
Term Expires: January 1, 2017
★Board Member **David Bridenstine** (R) . . . . . (330) 451-7065
Term Expires: January 2, 2017
E-mail: dmbridenstine@starkcountyohio.gov

★Elected Official ▲Appointed by Legislature ▼Appointed by Governor ▶Appointed by Board or Commission ●Appointed by Judge
■Appointed by Mayor △Appointed by Freeholders ▽Appointed by Supervisor ▷Appointed by County Executive ○Appointed by Council

COUNTIES

County Administrator
110 Central Plaza South, Canton, OH 44702
Fax: (330) 451-7906

▶ County Administrator **Brant Luther** (R) .... (330) 451-7581
E-mail: BLuther@starkcountyohio.gov

▶ County Clerk **Jean Young** .... (330) 451-7364
E-mail: bjyoung@starkcountyohio.gov

Dog Warden's Office
1801 Mahoning Rd., NE, Canton, OH 44705

▶ Dog Warden **Jon Barber** .... (330) 451-2343
E-mail: jsbarber@starkcountyohio.gov

Public Defender's Office
200 W. Tuscarawas St., Suite 200, Canton, OH 44702

▶ Public Defender **Tammi Johnson** .... (330) 451-7200
Fax: (330) 451-7227

Building Inspection Department
100 Central Plaza North, Canton, OH 44702
Fax: (330) 451-1779

▶ Building Inspector **Angela Cavanaugh** .... (330) 451-1770
E-mail: ajcavanaugh@starkcountyohio.gov Fax: (330) 451-1779

Building Maintenance Department
225 Fourth St., NE, Basement, Canton, OH 44702

▶ Building Manager **Lee Henderson** .... (330) 451-7500

Equal Employment Opportunity
201 Third Street, 2nd Floor, Canton, OH 44702
Fax: (330) 451-7990

▶ EEO Officer **David A. Thorley** .... (330) 451-7776

Information Technology Department
Data Building, 225 Fourth St., NE, Canton, OH 44702

▶ Manager **Anita Henderson** .... (330) 451-7432
Fax: (330) 451-7190

Department of Job and Family Services
221 Third Street, SE, Canton, OH 44702
Tel: (330) 452-4661 Internet: www.starkdjfs.org

Executive Director **Deborah Forkas** .... (330) 452-4661

Purchasing Department
110 Central Plaza South, Suite 240, Canton, OH 44702
Fax: (330) 451-7906

Purchasing Manager **Jean Young** .... (330) 451-7364
E-mail: bjyoung@starkcountyohio.gov
Purchasing Assistant **(Vacant)** .... (330) 451-7925

Sanitary Engineering Department
1701 Mahoning Road, NE, Canton, OH 44705
Fax: (330) 453-9044 E-mail: scse@co.stark.oh.us

▶ Sanitary Engineer **Jim Troike** .... (330) 451-2303
E-mail: jftroike@starkcountyohio.gov

Board of Elections
201 Third Street, NE, 1st Floor, Canton, OH 44702
Tel: (330) 451-8683 Fax: (330) 451-7000
E-mail: boe@starkcountyohio.gov

▶ Director **Jeanette Mullane** .... (330) 451-7001
▶ Deputy Director **Jeffrey Matthews** .... (330) 451-7002

Mental Health and Recovery Services Board [MHRSB]
121 Cleveland Avenue SW, Canton, OH 44702
Tel: (330) 455-6644 Fax: (330) 455-7424 E-mail: info@starkmhrsb.org
Internet: www.starkmhrsb.org

President **Elizabeth Bowen** .... (330) 455-6644
Term Expires: 2017

Administration
▶ Executive Director **John R. Aller** .... (330) 430-3930
E-mail: jaller@starkmhrsb.org
Marketing/ Administrative Specialist **(Vacant)** .... (330) 430-3941

Stark County Educational Service Center
2100 38th Street, NW, Canton, OH 44709-2300
Fax: (330) 492-6381 Internet: www.starkcountyesc.org

▶ Superintendent **Larry Morgan** .... (330) 492-8136

Stark County Emergency Management Agency
4500 Atlantic Boulevard, NE, Canton, OH 44711-9515
Fax: (330) 451-3934 E-mail: starkema@starkcountyohio.gov

▶ Director **Tim Warstler** .... (330) 451-3900
Fax: (330) 451-3934
Deputy Director **Rich Weber** .... (330) 451-3900
▶ Local Emergency Planning Committee (LEPC) Coordinator **Don McDonald** .... (330) 451-3907
Fax: (330) 451-3934
▶ 911 System Communications Director **Tim Warstler** .... (330) 451-3900
Fax: (330) 451-3934

Stark County Park District [SCPD]
5300 Tyner Street, NW, Canton, OH 44708
Tel: (330) 477-3552 Fax: (330) 477-1211
E-mail: information@starkparks.com Internet: www.starkparks.com

Director **Robert "Bob" Fonte** .... (330) 477-3552

Stark County Regional Planning Commission [SCRPC]
201 Third Street, Suite 201, Canton, OH 44702-1231
Tel: (330) 451-7389 Fax: (330) 451-7990

▶ Director **Robert Nau** .... (330) 451-7488

Office of the Auditor
County Administration Bldg., 110 Central Plaza South, Suite 220, Canton, OH 44702
Fax: (330) 451-7100 Internet: www.auditor.starkcountyohio.gov

★ Auditor **Alan C. Harold** (R) .... (330) 451-7357
Term Expires: March 2019 Fax: (330) 451-7630
Education: Mount Union 1998; Ohio State 2003 MBA

Office of the Coroner
Doctors Hospital of Stark County, 4500 Atlantic Blvd., NE, Canton, OH 44711
Tel: (330) 451-1368 Fax: (330) 451-1366

★ Coroner **P. S. Murthy** (D) .... (330) 451-1368
Term Expires: January 2017 Fax: (330) 837-3380

Office of the County Engineer
5165 Southway, SW, Canton, OH 44706
Fax: (330) 477-3926

★ County Engineer **Keith Bennett** .... (330) 477-6781
Term Expires: December 31, 2019

★ Elected Official ▲ Appointed by Legislature ▼ Appointed by Governor ▶ Appointed by Board or Commission ● Appointed by Judge
■ Appointed by Mayor △ Appointed by Freeholders ▽ Appointed by Supervisor ▷ Appointed by County Executive ○ Appointed by Council

Office of the Prosecuting Attorney

County Administration Bldg., 110 Central Plaza South, Suite 510,
Canton, OH 44702
Fax: (330) 451-7965

★ Prosecuting Attorney **John D. Ferrero** (D) . . . . (330) 451-7897
Term Expires: January 8, 2017

Office of the Recorder

Stark County Office Building, 110 Central Plaza, Suite 170,
Canton, OH 44702
Fax: (330) 451-7394

★ Recorder **Rick Campbell** (D) . . . . (330) 451-7443
Term Expires: January 8, 2017

Office of the Sheriff

4500 Atlantic Blvd., NE, Canton, OH 44711
Tel: (330) 430-3800 Fax: (330) 430-3807 E-mail: strkshrf@raex.com
Internet: http://www.sheriff.co.stark.oh.us

★ Sheriff **George T. Maier** . . . . (330) 430-3805
Term Expires: January 8, 2017 Fax: (330) 451-3844

Office of the Treasurer

County Administration Bldg., 110 Central Plaza South, Suite 250,
Canton, OH 44702
Fax: (330) 451-7815 Internet: http://www.starktaxes.com

★ Treasurer **Alexander Zumbar** . . . . (330) 451-7814
Term Expires: January 8, 2017

County of Suffolk, New York

H. Lee Dennison Building, 100 Veterans Memorial Highway,
Hauppauge, NY 11778-0099
P.O. Box 6100, Hauppauge, NY 11788-0099
Internet: www.co.suffolk.ny.us

County Seat: Riverhead **Election Type:** Partisan **Population:** 1,501,587 (2015)

Office of the County Executive

H. Lee Dennison Building, 12th Floor, Hauppauge, NY 11778
P.O. Box 6100, Hauppauge, NY 11788-0099
Tel: (631) 853-4000 Fax: (631) 853-4818
E-mail: county.executive@suffolkcountyny.gov

★ County Executive **Steve Bellone** (D) . . . . (631) 853-4000
Term Expires: December 31, 2019
E-mail: county.executive@suffolkcountyny.gov
Education: Webster MA; Fordham 1984 JD
Chief Deputy County Executive **Dennis Cohen** . . . . (631) 853-4018
Deputy County Executive **Jon Schneider** . . . . (631) 853-4000
Deputy County Executive **(Vacant)** . . . . (631) 853-4000
Assistant Deputy County Executive **(Vacant)** . . . . (631) 853-4000
▷ Communications Director **Vanessa Baird-Streeter** . . . . . . (631) 853-4018
Deputy Communications Director **(Vacant)** . . . . (631) 853-4018

Office for the Aging

H. Lee Dennison Building, 100 Veterans Memorial Highway, 3rd Floor,
Hauppauge, NY 11788-0099
Tel: (631) 853-8200 Fax: (631) 853-8225
E-mail: aging.office@suffolkcountyny.gov

Director **Holly Rhodes-Teague** . . . . (631) 853-8200

Office of Consumer Affairs

North County Complex, Building 340, Veterans Memorial Highway,
Hauppauge, NY 11788
Tel: (631) 853-4600 Fax: (631) 853-4825
E-mail: consumer.affairs@suffolkcountyny.gov

▷ Director **(Vacant)** . . . . (631) 853-4600

Office of Intergovernmental Relations

P.O. Box 6100, Hauppauge, NY 11788-0099
Tel: (631) 853-4000 Fax: (631) 853-4086

Chief of Staff **Eric A. Kopp** . . . . (631) 853-4000

Office of Labor Relations

P.O. Box 6100, Hauppauge, NY 11788-0099
Fax: (631) 853-4981

▷ Director **Jennifer K. McNamara** . . . . (631) 853-4900

Office of Minority Affairs

H. Lee Dennison Building, 100 Veterans Memorial Highway,
Hauppauge, NY 11778-0099
Tel: (631) 853-4738 Fax: (631) 853-8294
E-mail: minority.affairs@suffolkcountyny.gov

Director **Roderick Pearson** . . . . (631) 853-4738

Office for People with Disabilities

North County Complex, Building 158, Veterans Memorial Highway,
Hauppauge, NY 11788
Tel: (631) 853-8333 Fax: (631) 853-8339

Director **Frank Krotschinsky** . . . . (631) 853-8333

Office of Women's Services

H. Lee Dennison Building, 100 Veterans Memorial Highway, 3rd Floor,
Hauppauge, NY 11778-0099
Tel: (631) 853-8284 Fax: (631) 853-8295
E-mail: womens.services@suffolkcountyny.gov

Director **Grace Ioannidis** . . . . (631) 853-8284

Suffolk County Veterans Service Agency

H. Lee Dennison Building, 100 Veterans Memorial Highway, 3rd Floor,
Hauppauge, NY 11778-0099
Tel: (631) 853-8387 Fax: (631) 853-8295

Director **Thomas "Tom" Ronayne** . . . . (631) 853-8381

Suffolk County Youth Bureau

H. Lee Dennison Building, 100 Veterans Memorial Highway,
Hauppauge, NY 11778-0099
Tel: (631) 853-8270 E-mail: youth.services@suffolkcountyny.gov

Executive Director **Roderick Pearson** . . . . (631) 853-8270

Human Rights Commission

P.O. Box 6100, Hauppauge, NY 11788-0099

▷ Chairman **Rabbi Steven Moss** . . . . (631) 853-5480
▷ Executive Director **Jennifer Blaske** . . . . (631) 853-5480
Fax: (631) 853-5478

Office of the Public Administrator

300 Center Drive, Riverhead, NY 11901
Fax: (631) 852-2740

Public Administrator **Franklyn A. Farris** . . . . (631) 852-1753
E-mail: franklyn.farris@suffolkcountyny.gov
Deputy Public Administrator **Theresa Powell** . . . . (631) 852-1753
E-mail: theresa.powell@suffolkcountyny.gov

★ Elected Official ▲ Appointed by Legislature ▼ Appointed by Governor ► Appointed by Board or Commission ● Appointed by Judge
■ Appointed by Mayor △ Appointed by Freeholders ▽ Appointed by Supervisor ▷ Appointed by County Executive ○ Appointed by Council

COUNTIES

COUNTIES

Department of Civil Service
William J. Lindsay County Complex, Building 158,
725 Veterans Memorial Highway, Hauppauge, NY 11788-0099
P.O. Box 6100, Hauppauge, NY 11788-0099
Tel: (631) 853-5500 Fax: (631) 853-6074

Personnel Director **Alan Schneider** .... (631) 853-5794
E-mail: alan.schneider@suffolkcountyny.gov
Education: Wilkes U BA; Temple MA

Department of Fire, Rescue and Emergency Services [DFRES]
P.O. Box 127, Yaphank, NY 11980-0127
Tel: (631) 852-4855 Fax: (631) 852-4861
E-mail: scdfres@co.suffolk.ny.us

▷Commissioner **Joseph F. Williams** .... (631) 852-4850
E-mail: commissionerjoe.williams@suffolkcountyny.gov
Deputy Commissioner **John Jordan** .... (631) 852-4854
E-mail: john.jordan@suffolkcountyny.gov
Chief Fire Marshal **Edward K. Springer** .... (631) 852-4855
E-mail: edward.springer@suffolkcountyny.gov

Department of Health Services
Tel: (631) 854-0000 Fax: (631) 854-0108
E-mail: scdhsweb@suffolkcountyny.gov
Internet: www.suffolkcountyny.gov/health

Commissioner **James L. Tomarken** .... (631) 854-0100
Assistant to the Commissioner **Jennifer Culp** .... (631) 854-0096
Fax: (631) 854-0108
Chief Deputy Commissioner **Linda Mermelstein** .... (631) 854-0205
Fax: (631) 854-0236
Deputy Commissioner **Christina Capobianco** .... (631) 854-0098
Fax: (631) 854-0108
Executive Assistant for Finance and Administration
Barbara Marano .... (631) 854-0097
Fax: (631) 854-0108

Office of Minority Health
Fax: (631) 854-0383

Director **Gregson Pigott** .... (631) 854-0378

Division of Community Mental Hygiene Services
North County Complex Building C928, 725 Veterans Memorial Highway,
Hauppauge, NY 11788-9006
Fax: (631) 853-3117

Director **Arthur Flescher** .... (631) 853-8500

Division of Emergency Medical Services
360 Yaphank Avenue, Suite 1B, Yaphank, NY 11980
Tel: (631) 852-5080 Fax: (631) 852-5028

Director **Robert Delagi** .... (631) 852-5080

Division of Environmental Quality [DEQ]
360 Yaphank Avenue, Yaphank, NY 11980
Fax: (631) 852-5825

Director **Walter Dawydiak** .... (631) 852-5800

Office of the Medical Examiner
William J. Lindsay County Complex, Building 487,
725 Veterans Memorial Hwy., Hauppauge, NY 11788-2920
Fax: (631) 853-4673

Chief Medical Examiner **Dr. Michael J. Caplan** .... (631) 853-5555

Division of Patient Care Services
Fax: (631) 854-0234

Director **Shaheda Iftikhar** .... (631) 854-0200

Division of Preventive Medicine
H. Lee Dennison Building, 100 Veterans Memorial Hwy.,
Hauppauge, NY 11788
Fax: (631) 853-6208

Director **(Vacant)** .... (631) 853-3069

Division of Public Health
Fax: (631) 854-0346 Tel: (631) 854-0333

Director **Shaheda Iftikhar** .... (631) 854-0333

Division of Services for Children with Special Needs
50 Laser Court, Hauppauge, NY 11788-3958
Fax: (631) 853-2300

Director (Acting) **Ellen R. Ellis** .... (631) 853-3130

Department of Labor, Licensing and Consumer Affairs
725 Veterans Memorial Highway, Hauppauge, NY 11788
Fax: (631) 853-6510 E-mail: sc.dol@suffolkcountyny.gov
Internet: www.suffolkcounty.gov/labor

▷Commissioner **Frank Nardelli** .... (631) 853-6500
E-mail: admin@suffolkcountyny.gov
Administrative Director **Elizabeth M. Pearsall** .... (631) 853-6509
Chair, Workforce Development Board **James DiLiberto** .. (631) 853-6612

Department of Law
H. Lee Dennison Bldg., 100 Veterans Memorial Hwy., Sixth Floor,
Hauppauge, NY 11788
P.O. Box 6100, Hauppauge, NY 11788-0099
Fax: (631) 853-5169

▷County Attorney **Dennis M. Brown** .... (631) 853-4049
Chief Deputy County Attorney **Lynne A. Bizzarro** .... (631) 853-4049
E-mail: lynne.bizzarro@suffolkcountyny.gov
Education: Boston Col 1987 JD
Deputy County Attorney **Gail M. Lolis** .... (631) 853-4049
E-mail: gail.lolis@suffolkcountyny.gov

Department of Parks, Recreation and Conservation
P.O. Box 144, West Sayville, NY 11796-0144
Fax: (631) 854-4969 E-mail: scparks@suffolkcountyny.gov

▷Commissioner **Greg Dawson** .... (631) 854-4949
E-mail: greg.dawson@suffolkcountyny.gov

Department of Economic Development and Planning
H. Lee Dennison Bldg., 100 Veterans Memorial Hwy.,
Hauppauge, NY 11788
PO Box 6100, Hauppauge, NY 11788-0099
Tel: (631) 853-5191 Fax: (631) 853-4767
E-mail: planning@suffolkcountyny.gov

▷Commissioner **Joanne M. Minieri** .... (631) 853-4800
Education: Hofstra
▷Deputy Commissioner **Amy Keys** .... (631) 853-4800
▷Deputy Commissioner **Louis Bekofsky** .... (631) 853-4800
▷Director **Sarah Lansdale** .... (631) 853-5191
E-mail: sarah.lansdale@suffolkcountyny.gov
Education: NYU MUP

Division of Economic Development and Planning
H. Lee Dennison Building, 100 Veterans Memorial Highway,
Hauppauge, NY 11778-0099
P.O. Box 6100, Hauppauge, NY 11788
Fax: (631) 853-4888 E-mail: ecodev@suffolkcountyny.gov

Intergovernmental Relations Coordinator **(Vacant)** .... (631) 853-4833
Director of Real Estate **(Vacant)** .... (631) 853-5705
Cultural Affairs Program Coordinator
Diana Cherryholmes .... (631) 853-4834

★ Elected Official ▲ Appointed by Legislature ▼ Appointed by Governor ▶ Appointed by Board or Commission ● Appointed by Judge
■ Appointed by Mayor △ Appointed by Freeholders ▽ Appointed by Supervisor ▷ Appointed by County Executive ○ Appointed by Council

Francis G. Gabreski Airport
Administration Building #1, Westhampton Beach, NY 11978
Fax: (631) 852-8092 E-mail: gabreski@suffolkcountyny.gov

Airport Manager **Anthony C. Ceglio** . . . . (631) 852-8095

Suffolk County Police Department [SCPD]
30 Yaphank Avenue, Yaphank, NY 11980
E-mail: scpdinfo@suffolkcountyny.gov
Internet: www.co.suffolk.ny.us/police

▷ Commissioner **Timothy D. Sini** . . . . (631) 852-6080
Education: Brooklyn Law 2005 JD
Deputy Commissioner **Risco Mention-Lewis** . . . . (631) 852-6080
Public Information Director **Kevin Fallon** . . . . (631) 852-6308
Fax: (631) 852-6526

Probation Department
P.O. Box 188, Yaphank, NY 11980-0188
Tel: (631) 852-5000 Fax: (631) 852-5103
Internet: www.co.suffolk.ny.us/departments/probation.aspx

Director **Patrice Dlhopolsky** . . . . (631) 852-5100

Department of Public Works
335 Yaphank Ave., Yaphank, NY 11980-9744
Tel: (631) 852-4010 Fax: (631) 852-4165
E-mail: public.works@suffolkcountyny.us
Internet: www.co.suffolk.ny.us/departments/publicworks.aspx

▷ Commissioner **Gilbert Anderson** . . . . (631) 852-4011
E-mail: gilbert.anderson@suffolkcountyny.gov
General Service Manager **Charles Jaquin** . . . . (631) 852-4044
E-mail: charles.jaquin@suffolkcountyny.gov
Deputy Commissioner **Phil Berdolt** . . . . (631) 852-4010
Deputy Commissioner **Darnell Tyson** . . . . (631) 852-4012
Director of Buildings Operations and Maintenance
Craig Rhodes . . . . (631) 852-4095
E-mail: craig.rhodes@suffolkcountyny.gov
Director of Transportation Operations **Garry Lenberger** . . (631) 852-4880
Director of Vector Control **Dominick V. Ninivaggi** . . . . . . (631) 852-4270
Highway Maintenance Supervisor **Cliff Mitchell** . . . . (631) 852-4070
County Architect **James Ingenito** . . . . (631) 852-4690
Chief Engineer, Facilities **Michael Monaghan** . . . . (631) 852-4225
E-mail: michael.monaghan@suffolkcountyny.gov
Chief Engineer, Highways **William Hillman** . . . . (631) 852-4002
E-mail: william.hillman@suffolkcountyny.gov
Chief Engineer, Sanitation **John Donovan** . . . . (631) 852-4205
E-mail: john.donovan@suffolkcountyny.gov
Assistant Fleet Service Manager **Mike James** . . . . (631) 852-4258

Social Services Department
3085 Veterans Memorial Hwy., Ronkonkoma, NY 11779
P.O. Box 18100, Hauppauge, NY 11788-8900
Tel: (631) 854-9930 Fax: (631) 854-9996

Commissioner **John F. O'Neill** . . . . (631) 854-9930
Deputy Commissioner **(Vacant)** . . . . (631) 854-9931

Real Property Tax Service Agency
300 Center Dr., Riverhead, NY 11901-3398
Fax: (631) 852-1566

▷ Director **Penny Wells LaValle** . . . . (631) 852-1550
E-mail: penny.wellslavalle@suffolkcountyny.gov

Suffolk Cooperative Library System
627 North Sunrise Service Road, P.O. Box 9000,
Bellport, NY 11713-9000
Fax: (631) 286-1647 Internet: www.suffolklibrarysystem.org

Director **Kevin Verbesey** . . . . (631) 286-1600 ext. 1304
E-mail: kevin@suffolknet.org

Suffolk County Board of Elections
Yaphank Ave., P.O. Box 700, Yaphank, NY 11980
Fax: (631) 852-4590

▲ Democratic Commissioner **Anita S. Katz** (D) . . . . (631) 852-4500
▲ Republican Commissioner **Nick LaLota** . . . . (631) 852-4500
Democratic Deputy Commissioner
Jeanne C. O'Rourke (D) . . . . (631) 852-4500
Republican Deputy Commissioner **(Vacant)** . . . . (631) 852-4500

Suffolk County Community College [SCCC]
533 College Road, Selden, NY 11784
Tel: (631) 451-4000 Fax: (631) 451-4715 Internet: www.sunysuffolk.edu

President **Shaun L. McKay** . . . . (631) 451-4736
Education: Maryland BS; Notre Dame MA; Morgan State 2004 EdD
Assistant to the President **Sandra O'Hara** . . . . (631) 451-4736
E-mail: oharas@sunysuffolk.edu
Executive Vice President **(Vacant)** . . . . (631) 451-4611
Director of Communications **Drew Biondo** . . . . (631) 451-4776
E-mail: biondodr@sunysuffolk.edu
College General Counsel **Louis J. Petrizzo** . . . . (631) 451-4235
Education: Le Moyne BA; Toledo JD
Intergovernmental Relations Coordinator
Benjamin Zwirn . . . . (631) 451-4867
E-mail: zwirnb@sunysuffolk.edu

Suffolk County Water Authority [SCWA]
4060 Sunrise Hwy., Oakdale, NY 11769-0901
PO Box 38, Oakdale, NY 11769
Tel: (631) 589-5200 Fax: (631) 563-0370 E-mail: info@scwa.com
Internet: www.scwa.com

▲ Chairman **James F. Gaughran** . . . . (631) 563-0291
E-mail: jgaughran@scwa.com
Chief Executive Officer **Jeffrey W. "Jeff" Szabo** . . . . (631) 563-0353
Deputy Chief Executive Officer, Customer Service
Janice E. Tinsley (D) . . . . (631) 563-0365
Deputy Chief Executive Officer, Operations
Joseph Pokorny . . . . (631) 563-0203
E-mail: jpokorny@scwa.com

Suffolk County Cooperative Extension (Cornell University)
423 Griffing Avenue, Suite 100, Riverhead, NY 11901
Fax: (631) 727-7130 E-mail: suffolk@cornell.edu

Executive Director **Vito A. Minei** . . . . (631) 727-7850 ext. 306
Associate Executive Director (Interim)
Nora J. Catlin . . . . (631) 727-7850 ext. 214
Public Affairs and Development Director
Judith Lach "Judi" Veeck . . . . (631) 727-7850 ext. 372

Suffolk County Soil and Water Conservation District
423 Griffing Avenue, Suite 110, Riverhead, NY 11901
Fax: (631) 727-3160

District Manager **Paul TeNyenhuis** . . . . (631) 727-2315 ext. 3

Office of the County Legislature
P.O. Box 6100, Hauppauge, NY 11788-0099
Tel: (631) 853-4070 Fax: (631) 853-4899
Internet: http://legis.suffolkcountyny.gov/

★ Presiding Officer **DuWayne Gregory** (D-District 15) . . . . . (631) 854-1111
Term Expires: December 31, 2017 Fax: (631) 854-1114
E-mail: duwayne.gregory@suffolkcountyny.gov
Education: North Carolina Wesleyan 1991
★ Majority Leader **Robert T. Calarco** (D-District 7) . . . . . . (631) 854-1400
Term Expires: December 31, 2017 Fax: (631) 854-1403
★ Legislator **Al Krupski** (D-District 1) . . . . (631) 852-3200
Term Expires: December 31, 2017 Fax: (631) 852-3203

(continued on next page)

COUNTIES

★ Elected Official ▲ Appointed by Legislature ▼ Appointed by Governor ► Appointed by Board or Commission ● Appointed by Judge
■ Appointed by Mayor △ Appointed by Freeholders ▽ Appointed by Supervisor ▷ Appointed by County Executive ○ Appointed by Council

Office of the County Legislature *continued*

★Legislator **Bridget Fleming** (D-District 2) .... (631) 852-8400
Term Expires: December 31, 2017

★Legislator **Kate M. Browning** (DWF-District 3) .... (631) 852-1300
Term Expires: December 31, 2017 Fax: (631) 852-1303
E-mail: kate.browning@suffolkcountyny.gov

★Legislator **Thomas "Tom" Muratore** (R-District 4) ..... (631) 854-9292
Term Expires: December 31, 2017 Fax: (631) 854-9351
E-mail: tom.muratore@suffolkcountyny.gov

★Legislator **Kara Hahn** (D-District 5) .... (631) 854-1650
Term Expires: December 31, 2017 Fax: (631) 854-1653

★Legislator **Sarah Anker** (D-District 6) .... (631) 854-1600
Term Expires: December 31, 2017 Fax: (631) 854-1603
E-mail: sarah.anker@suffolkcountyny.gov
Education: St Leo U 1986 BFA

★Legislator **William J. "Bill" Lindsay** (D-District 8) ...... (631) 854-9611
Term Expires: December 31, 2017 Fax: (631) 854-9687
E-mail: william.lindsay@suffolkcountyny.gov

★Legislator **Monica R. Martinez** (D-District 9) .... (631) 853-3700
Term Expires: December 31, 2017 Fax: (631) 853-3568

★Legislator **Thomas "Tom" Cilmi** (R-District 10) .... (631) 854-0940
Term Expires: December 31, 2017 Fax: (631) 854-0943
E-mail: tom.cilmi@suffolkcountyny.gov

★Legislator **Thomas F. Barraga** (R-District 11) .... (631) 854-4100
Term Expires: December 31, 2017 Fax: (631) 854-4103
E-mail: thomas.barraga@suffolkcountyny.gov

★Legislator **Leslie Kennedy** (R-District 12) .... (631) 854-3735
Term Expires: December 31, 2017 Fax: (631) 854-3744
E-mail: Leslie.Kennedy@suffolkcountyny.gov

★Legislator **Robert Trotta** (R-District 13) .... (631) 854-3900
Term Expires: December 31, 2017 Fax: (631) 854-3903

★Legislator **Kevin J. McCaffrey** (R-District 14) .... (631) 854-1100
Term Expires: December 31, 2017 Fax: (631) 854-1103

★Legislator **Steven H. "Steve" Stern** (D-District 16) ..... (631) 854-5100
Term Expires: December 31, 2017 Fax: (631) 854-5103
E-mail: steven.stern@suffolkcountyny.gov

★Legislator **Louis "Lou" D'Amaro** (D-District 17) .... (631) 854-4433
Term Expires: December 31, 2017 Fax: (631) 854-4415
E-mail: lou.damaro@suffolkcountyny.gov

★Legislator **William "Doc" Spencer** (D-District 18) ...... (631) 854-4500
Term Expires: December 31, 2017 Fax: (631) 854-4503

▲Clerk of the Legislature **Jason Richberg** .... (631) 853-4074
E-mail: jason.richberg@suffolkcountyny.gov Fax: (631) 853-4899

▲Chief Deputy Clerk **Amy Ellis** .... (631) 853-6351
E-mail: Amy.Ellis@suffolkcountyny.gov

Office of Legislative Budget Review

W.H. Rogers Legislature Building, 725 Veterans Memorial Highway, Hauppauge, NY 11788-9006
Tel: (631) 853-4100 Fax: (631) 853-5496

▲Director (Acting) **Robert Lipp** .... (631) 853-4109
E-mail: robert.lipp@suffolkcountyny.gov

▲Deputy Director **Rosalind Gazes** .... (631) 853-5495

▲Administrative Assistant **Sharen Wagner** .... (631) 853-4903

Office of Legislative Counsel

W.H. Rogers Legislature Building, 725 Veterans Memorial Highway, Hauppauge, NY 11788-0099
Fax: (631) 853-4015

Counsel to the Legislature **George M. Nolan** .... (631) 853-4860
Assistant Counsel **Sarah Simpson** .... (631) 853-4860

Office of the Comptroller

H. Lee Dennison Building, 100 Veterans Memorial Highway, Ninth Floor, Hauppauge, NY 11788-0099
Fax: (631) 853-5057 E-mail: comptroller@suffolkcountyny.gov

★Comptroller **John M. Kennedy, Jr.** (R) .... (631) 853-5040
Term Expires: January 1, 2019

Chief Deputy Comptroller **Louis Necroto** .... (631) 853-5037

Office of the County Clerk

310 Center Dr., Riverhead, NY 11901-3392
Tel: (631) 852-2000 Fax: (631) 852-2004
E-mail: countyclerk@suffolkcountyny.gov

★County Clerk **Judith A. Pascale** (R) .... (631) 852-2000
Term Expires: December 31, 2018
E-mail: judith.pascale@suffolkcountyny.gov

Chief Deputy **Nicole DeLuca** .... (631) 852-2000
E-mail: nicole.deluca@suffolkcountyny.gov

Security Manager **Michael Schlosberg** .... (631) 852-2000

Office of the District Attorney

North County Complex, Building 77, Veterans Memorial Highway, Hauppauge, NY 11788
Fax: (631) 853-5820 E-mail: infoda@suffolkcountyny.gov

★District Attorney **Thomas J. Spota III** (D) .... (631) 853-4161
Term Expires: December 31, 2017
E-mail: thomas.spota@suffolkcountyny.gov
Education: Fairfield BA; St John's U (NY) 1966 JD

Chief Assistant District Attorney **Emily A. Constant** .... (631) 853-4161
Education: Marymount Col (NY); Pace JD

Office of the Sheriff

100 Center Dr., Riverhead, NY 11901
Fax: (631) 852-1898 E-mail: suffolk_sheriff@suffolkcountyny.gov
Internet: www.co.suffolk.ny.us/departments/sheriff.aspx

★Sheriff **Vincent F. DeMarco** (D) .... (631) 852-2200
Term Expires: December 31, 2017
E-mail: vincent.demarco@suffolkcountyny.gov

Undersheriff **Joseph T. Caracappa** (R) .... (631) 852-2200
E-mail: joseph.caracappa@suffolkcountyny.gov

Undersheriff **John P. Meyerricks, Jr.** .... (631) 852-2200
E-mail: john.meyerricks@suffolkcountyny.gov

Office of the Treasurer

330 Center Dr., Riverhead, NY 11901-3311
Tel: (631) 852-1500 Fax: (631) 852-1507
E-mail: treasurer@suffolkcountyny.gov

County Treasurer **(Vacant)** .... (631) 852-1504
Term Expires: December 31, 2017
Assistant to Treasurer **(Vacant)** .... (631) 852-1500

Chief Deputy **Douglas W. Sutherland** .... (631) 852-1505

Deputy **(Vacant)** .... (631) 852-1508

County of Summit, Ohio

Ohio Building, 175 South Main Street, Akron, OH 44308
Tel: (330) 643-2500 (Information) Internet: www.co.summit.oh.us

County Seat: Akron **Election Type:** Partisan **Population:** 541,968 (2015)

Office of the County Executive

Ohio Bldg., 175 South Main Street, 8th Floor, Akron, OH 44308-1314
Tel: (330) 643-2605 Fax: (330) 643-2507
Internet: www.co.summit.oh.us/executive

★County Executive **Russell M. Pry** (D) .... (330) 643-2624
Term Expires: December 31, 2016
E-mail: rpry@summitoh.net
Education: Kent State BA; Akron 1984 JD

Chief of Staff **Jason Dodson** .... (330) 643-2075

★Elected Official ▲Appointed by Legislature ▼Appointed by Governor ►Appointed by Board or Commission ●Appointed by Judge
■Appointed by Mayor △Appointed by Freeholders ▽Appointed by Supervisor ▷Appointed by County Executive ○Appointed by Council

Department of Administrative Services
2525 State Road, Cuyahoga Falls, OH 44223-1503
Tel: (330) 926-2405 Fax: (330) 926-2471
Internet: www.co.summit.oh.us/executive/adminsrvcs.htm

▷ Director **Craig Stanley** . . . . . (330) 926-2405
E-mail: cstanley@summitoh.net

Department of Communications
175 South Main Street, Akron, OH 44308
Tel: (330) 643-2627 Fax: (330) 643-2507
Internet: www.co.summit.oh.us/executive/communications.htm

▷ Director **Jill Hinig Skapin** . . . . . (330) 643-2627
E-mail: jskapin@summitoh.net

Department of Community and Economic Development
Ohio Bldg., 175 South Main Street, Room 207, Akron, OH 44308-1308
Tel: (330) 643-2893 Fax: (330) 643-2886
Internet: www.co.summit.oh.us/executive/dev.htm

▷ Director **Connie L. Krauss** . . . . . (330) 643-2893
E-mail: ckrauss@summitoh.net
Deputy Director **Robert Genet** . . . . . (330) 643-7769

Division of Building Standards
1030 E. Tallmadge Ave., Akron, OH 44310
Fax: (330) 630-7296

▷ Chief Building Official **John Labriola** . . . . . (330) 630-7298
E-mail: jlabriola@summitoh.net
Senior Administrator **Karen Brown** . . . . . (330) 630-7300
Senior Administrator **Mark Shenot** . . . . . (330) 630-7300

Department of Finance and Budget
175 South Main Street, Room 742, Akron, OH 44308
Tel: (330) 643-8065 Fax: (330) 643-8107
Internet: www.co.summit.oh.us/executive/finandbud.htm

▷ Director **Brian Nelsen** . . . . . (330) 643-8065
E-mail: bnelsen@summitoh.net Fax: (330) 643-8107
Education: Akron

Department of Environmental Services [DOES]
2525 State Road, Cuyahoga Falls, OH 44223-1503
Tel: (330) 926-2435 Fax: (330) 926-2471
Internet: www.co.summit.oh.us/executive/does.htm

▷ Director **Michael Weant** . . . . . (330) 926-2407
E-mail: mweant@does.summitoh.net

Department of Human Resources
Ohio Building, 175 South Main Street, Room 103, Akron, OH 44308-1308
Tel: (330) 643-2503 Fax: (330) 643-8562
Internet: www.co.summit.oh.us/executive/humsource.htm

▷ Director **Leonard M. Foster** . . . . . (330) 643-2426
E-mail: lfoster@summitoh.net

Department of Job and Family Services [DJFS]
47 North Main Street, Akron, OH 44308-1991
Tel: (330) 643-8200 Fax: (330) 643-7234 Internet: www.summitdjfs.org

▷ Director **Patricia L. Divoky** . . . . . (330) 643-7200
E-mail: pdivoky@summitoh.net
Deputy Director of Budget and Finance **Terri Burns** . . . . . (330) 643-7329

Division of Labor Relations
Ohio Building, 175 South Main Street, Room 103, Akron, OH 44308-1308
Tel: (330) 643-7786 Fax: (330) 643-8624

▷ Deputy Director **Yamini Adkins** . . . . . (330) 643-7786
E-mail: yadkins@summitoh.net

Department of Law, Insurance and Risk Management
Ohio Building, 175 South Main Street, 8th Floor, Akron, OH 44308-1313
Tel: (330) 643-2520 Fax: (330) 643-2507
Internet: www.co.summit.oh.us/executive/law.htm

▷ Director **Deborah S. "Deb" Matz** . . . . . (330) 643-2520
E-mail: dmatz@summitoh.net
Education: Kent State BSBA; Akron, 1992 JD
Deputy Director of Employee Benefits and Risk Management **Wendy Weaver** . . . . . (330) 643-2783
E-mail: wweaver@summitoh.net

Department of the Medical Examiner
85 North Summit Street, Akron, OH 44308-1948
Tel: (330) 643-2101 Fax: (330) 643-2100

▷ Chief Medical Examiner **Lisa J. Kohler** . . . . . (330) 643-2101
E-mail: lkohler@summitoh.net

Summit County Emergency Management Agency
175 South Main Street, Akron, OH 44308
Tel: (330) 643-2558 Fax: (330) 643-2889
Internet: www.co.summit.oh.us/executive/ema.htm

▷ Senior Administrator **Valerie De Rose** . . . . . (330) 643-2558
E-mail: vderose@summitoh.net

Office of the County Council
Ohio Building, 175 South Main Street, 7th Floor, Akron, OH 44308-1314
Tel: (330) 643-2725 Fax: (330) 643-2531
Internet: www.co.summit.oh.us/council

★ President **Ilene Shapiro** (D-At-Large) . . . . . (330) 643-2725
Term Expires: December 31, 2018
★ Council Member **Nick Kostandaras, Sr.** (D-District 1) . . . (330) 643-2725
Term Expires: December 31, 2016
E-mail: nkostandaras@summitoh.net
★ Council Member **John N. Schmidt** (D-District 2) . . . . . (330) 643-2725
Term Expires: December 31, 2016
E-mail: jschmidt@summitoh.net
Education: Akron BS; Kent State MA
★ Council Member **Gloria Rodgers** (R-District 3) . . . . . (330) 643-2725
Term Expires: December 31, 2016
E-mail: grodgers@summitoh.net
★ Council Member **Frank Comunale** (D-District 4) . . . . . (330) 643-2725
Term Expires: December 31, 2016
E-mail: fcomunale@summitoh.net
Education: Akron BA
★ Council Member **Tamala Lee** (D-District 5) . . . . . (330) 643-2725
Term Expires: December 31, 2016
E-mail: tlee@summitoh.net
★ Council Member **Jerry E. Feeman** (D-District 6) . . . . . (330) 643-2725
Term Expires: December 31, 2016
E-mail: jfeeman@summitoh.net
★ Council Member **Tim Crawford** (D-District 7) . . . . . (330) 643-2725
Term Expires: December 31, 2016
E-mail: tcrawford@summitoh.net
★ Council Member **Paula Prentice** (D-District 8) . . . . . (330) 643-2725
Term Expires: December 31, 2016
E-mail: pprentice@summitoh.net
★ Council Member **John A. Donofrio** (D-At-Large) . . . . . (330) 643-2725
Term Expires: December 31, 2016
E-mail: johndonofrio@summitoh.net
★ Council Member **Elizabeth "Liz" Walters** (D-At-Large) . . (330) 643-2725
Term Expires: December 31, 2016
○ Chief of Staff **Mark Potter** . . . . . (330) 643-2726
E-mail: mpotter@summitoh.net
Executive Assistant **Lucky Tisch** . . . . . (330) 643-2725
Clerk of Council **Jennifer Novakovic** . . . . . (330) 643-2727
E-mail: jnovakovic@summitoh.net

COUNTIES

★ Elected Official ▲ Appointed by Legislature ▼ Appointed by Governor ▶ Appointed by Board or Commission ● Appointed by Judge
■ Appointed by Mayor △ Appointed by Freeholders ▽ Appointed by Supervisor ▷ Appointed by County Executive ○ Appointed by Council

Adult Probation Department
Court of Common Pleas, 53 University Avenue, Akron, OH 44308-1680
Tel: (330) 643-2300 Fax: (330) 643-2691

Chief Probation Officer **Michael Rick** .... (330) 643-2300

Akron-Canton Airport
5400 Lauby Road, NW, North Canton, OH 44720-1598
Tel: (330) 499-4059 (Administration Office)
Tel: (330) 499-4221 (Information Center)
Tel: (330) 896-2385 (Information Center) Fax: (330) 499-5176
Internet: www.akroncantonairport.com

President and Chief Executive Officer
Richard B. "Rick" McQueen .... (330) 499-4059
Education: Walsh Col BA

Senior Vice President and Chief Marketing and Communications Officer **Kristie VanAuken** .... (330) 896-2376
E-mail: kvanauken@akroncantonairport.com
Education: Austin Col BA; Western Michigan MPA

Public Safety and Operations Manager **Todd Laps** .... (330) 499-4059
E-mail: tlaps@akroncantonairport.com

Akron-Summit County Public Library
60 South High Street, Akron, OH 44326
Tel: (330) 643-9000 Internet: www.ascpl.lib.oh.us

Director **David Jennings** .... (330) 643-9100
E-mail: djennings@akronlibrary.org

Alcohol, Drug Addiction and Mental Health Services Board [ADM]
1867 West Market Street, Suite B2, Akron, OH 44313-6914
Tel: (330) 762-3500 Fax: (330) 252-3024 E-mail: adm@admboard.org
Internet: www.admboard.org

Chair **Phillip J. Montgomery** (D) .... (330) 762-3500
Date of Birth: December 17, 1981
Education: DeVry U BBA; Ohio Dominican U MBA

Board Staff
Executive Director **Gerald A. "Jerry" Craig** .... (330) 564-4080

Children Services
264 S. Arlington St., Akron, OH 44306-1399
Tel: (330) 379-9094 Fax: (330) 379-1981

Executive Director **Julie Barnes** .... (330) 379-2009

Historical Society
550 Copley Rd., Akron, OH 44320
Fax: (330) 535-0250

President and Chief Executive Officer
Leianne Neff Heppner .... (330) 535-1120

Akron Law Library
Court House, 209 South High Street, 4th Floor, Akron, OH 44308-1675
Fax: (330) 535-0077 Internet: www.akronlawlib.org

Director **Alan Canfora** .... (330) 643-2804
E-mail: acanfora@akronlawlib.org
Reference Librarian **(Vacant)** .... (330) 643-2804

Legal Defender Office
One Cascade Plaza, Suite 1940, Akron, OH 44308
Fax: (330) 434-3371

Director **Joseph Kodish** .... (330) 434-3461
Fax: (330) 434-3371

Metro Parks, Serving Summit County
975 Treaty Line Rd., Akron, OH 44313-5898
Fax: (330) 867-4711 Internet: www.summitmetroparks.org

Director-Secretary **(Vacant)** .... (330) 867-5511

Summit County Extension Office (Ohio State University)
1100 Graham Road Circle, Stow, OH 44224-2992
Tel: (330) 928-4769 Fax: (330) 928-9418 Internet: http://summit.osu.edu/

County Extension Director and 4-H Educator
Jackie Krieger .... (330) 928-4769 ext. 2454

Summit Soil and Water Conservation District
1180 South Main Street, Akron, OH 44301
E-mail: staff@summitswcd.org Internet: www.summitswcd.org

District Program Administrator **Brian Prunty** .... (330) 926-2448
E-mail: bprunty@summitswcd.org
Administrative Assistant **Jeannine K. Royer** .... (330) 926-2445
E-mail: jroyer@summitswcd.org
Education Specialist **Sandy Barbic** .... (330) 926-2452
E-mail: sbarbic@summitswcd.org
Storm Water Specialist **Julie Berbari** .... (330) 926-2446
Storm Water Specialist **Stephanie Deibel** .... (330) 926-2455
Storm Water Specialist **Cindy Fink** .... (330) 926-2443

Veterans' Service Commission
1060 East Waterloo Road, Akron, OH 44306-3802
Fax: (330) 643-8779

Executive Director **Larry D. Moore** .... (330) 643-2835
Administrative Supervisor **Gail R. Warley** .... (330) 643-7575
E-mail: gwarley@eyesright.org Fax: (330) 643-8779

Office of the County Engineer
538 E. South St., Akron, OH 44311-1843
Tel: (330) 643-2850 Fax: (330) 762-7829
Internet: www.summitengineer.net

★ County Engineer **B. Alan Brubaker** (D) .... (330) 643-2850
Term Expires: January 5, 2017
E-mail: abrubaker@summitengineer.net
Executive Assistant to Engineer **Denise Longstreth** .... (330) 643-8168
E-mail: dlongstreth@summitengineer.net
Chief Deputy Engineer **Larry Fulton** .... (330) 643-8458
E-mail: lfulton@summitengineer.net
Administration/Finance Director **Steve Brunot** .... (330) 643-8103
E-mail: sbrunot@summitengineer.net
Budget/Management Director **Marie Newlove** .... (330) 643-8074
E-mail: mnewlove@summitengineer.net
Government Affairs Director **Heidi Swindell** .... (330) 643-8170
E-mail: hswindell@summitengineer.net
Training Coordinator **Lisa McGonigal** .... (330) 643-8054
E-mail: lmcgonigal@summitengineer.net Fax: (330) 762-7829

Maintenance Division
601 E. Crosier St., Akron, OH 44311-1808
Tel: (330) 643-2860 Fax: (330) 374-6961

Director **Gus Kabbara** .... (330) 643-8108
E-mail: gkabbara@summitengineer.net
Maintenance Deputy Director **Patrick Dobbins** .... (330) 643-2860
E-mail: pdobbins@summitengineer.net

Office of the County Prosecutor
City-County Safety Building, 53 University Avenue, 6th Floor, Akron, OH 44308-1680
Tel: (330) 643-2800 Fax: (330) 643-2137
Internet: www.co.summit.oh.us/prosecutor

★ County Prosecutor **Sherri Bevan Walsh** (D) .... (330) 643-2800
Term Expires: December 31, 2016
Chief Counsel **Brad Gessner** 7th Floor .... (330) 643-2788
Fax: (330) 643-8277

Assistant Prosecuting Attorney for Department of Delinquency, Juvenile Division **Deborah Pasternak** .... (330) 643-2943
650 Dan Street, Akron, OH 44310 Fax: (330) 379-3647

★ Elected Official ▲ Appointed by Legislature ▼ Appointed by Governor ▶ Appointed by Board or Commission ● Appointed by Judge
■ Appointed by Mayor △ Appointed by Freeholders ▽ Appointed by Supervisor ▷ Appointed by County Executive ○ Appointed by Council

Office of the County Prosecutor *continued*

Assistant Prosecuting Attorney for Department of Dependency/Neglect/Abuse, Juvenile Division
Christine Mastran . . . . . (330) 643-2943
650 Dan Street, Akron, OH 44310 Fax: (330) 379-3647

Child Support Enforcement Agency

Ohio Bldg., 175 S. Main St., 5th Floor, Akron, OH 44308-1312

Director **Jennifer Bheam** . . . . . (330) 643-2765

Office of the County Sheriff

City-County Safety Bldg., 53 University Ave., 4th Floor, Akron, OH 44308-1679
Tel: (330) 643-2154 Fax: (330) 434-2701
Internet: www.co.summit.oh.us/sheriff

★ Sheriff **Steve Barry** (D) . . . . . (330) 643-2111
Term Expires: January 5, 2017
Major of Corrections **Dale Soltis** . . . . . (330) 643-2114
E-mail: dsoltis@sheriff.summitoh.net Fax: (330) 643-7897
Major of Operations **Major Bradley Whitfield** . . . . . (330) 643-2117
E-mail: bwhitfield@sheriff.summitoh.net Fax: (330) 379-3694
Investigations Inspector **Chris Rhoades** . . . . . (330) 643-2152
E-mail: crhoades@sheriff.summitoh.net Fax: (330) 434-2701
Homeland Security **Bill Holland** . . . . . (330) 643-5091
E-mail: bholland@sheriff.summitoh.net Fax: (330) 434-2701

Office of the Fiscal Officer

Ohio Building, 175 South Main Street, 4th Floor, Akron, OH 44308-1306
Tel: (330) 643-2632 Fax: (330) 643-2622
E-mail: summittreas@summitoh.net
Internet: http://fiscaloffice.summitoh.net/

★ Fiscal Officer **Kristen M. Scalise** (D) . . . . . (330) 643-8091
Term Expires: January 2, 2017

Summit County Board of Elections

470 Grant Street, Akron, OH 44311-1157
Tel: (330) 643-5200 Fax: (330) 643-5422
Internet: www.summitcountyboe.com

Director **Joe Masich** . . . . . (330) 643-5200

Summit County Board of Health

1100 Graham Road Circle, Stow, OH 44224-2992

President **Leon Ricks** . . . . . (330) 923-4891

Summit County Combined General Health District [SCHD]

1867 West Market Street, Akron, OH 44313-6914
Tel: (330) 923-4891 Fax: (330) 923-7558 Internet: www.schd.org

Health Commissioner **Donna Skoda** . . . . . (330) 926-5601
Assistant Health Commissioner **(Vacant)** . . . . . (330) 926-5654
Medical Director **Dr. Marguerite A. Erme** . . . . . (330) 926-5603
Director of Administrative Services **Heather Pierce** . . . . . (330) 926-5605
E-mail: hpierce@schd.org
Director of Community Health Services **Tonya Block** . . . . . (330) 926-5604
Director of Environmental Health
Robert "Bob" Hasenyager . . . . . (330) 926-5625
Assistant Director **Donna Barrett** . . . . . (330) 926-5654
Assistant Director **Leanne Beavers** . . . . . (330) 926-5654
Assistant Director **(Vacant)** . . . . . (330) 926-5654
Assistant Director **Joanne Tate** . . . . . (330) 733-0730

Summit County Educational Service Center

420 Washington Avenue, Cuyahoga Falls, OH 44221
Fax: (330) 945-6222 Internet: http://cybersummit.org

Superintendent **Joe Iacano** . . . . . (330) 945-5600 ext. 513910
Education: Akron MEd

Human Resources Commission [HRC]

Ohio Bldg., 175 S. Main St., Room 708, Akron, OH 44308
Fax: (330) 643-8101
Internet: www.co.summit.oh.us/hrc/humrescommission.htm

Executive Director **Kasie L. Briggs-Pizarro** . . . . . (330) 643-2545
E-mail: kbriggs@summitoh.net

COUNTIES

County of Tarrant, Texas

100 E. Weatherford St., Fort Worth, TX 76196
Tel: (817) 884-1111 (Information) Internet: www.tarrantcounty.com

County Seat: Fort Worth **Election Type:** Partisan
Population: 1,982,498 (2015)

Office of the County Judge

100 East Weatherford Street, 5th Floor, Fort Worth, TX 76196-0101
Fax: (817) 884-2793

★ County Judge **B. Glen Whitley** (R) . . . . . (817) 884-1040
Term Expires: December 31, 2018
E-mail: gwhitley@tarrantcounty.com
Date of Birth: 1952
Education: Texas (Arlington) 1976 BBA
Community Outreach Coordinator **Natalie Rose** . . . . . (817) 884-1041
E-mail: nmrose@tarrantcounty.com
Executive Administrator **Neil Strassman** . . . . . (817) 884-1442
E-mail: nostrassman@tarrantcounty.com
Chief of Staff **Tom Stallings** . . . . . (817) 884-1043
Education: Texas Christian BS

Office of the County Administrator

100 East Weatherford Street, Suite 404, Fort Worth, TX 76196-0609

► County Administrator **G.K. Maenius** . . . . . (817) 884-1733
E-mail: gkmaenius@tarrantcounty.com
Public Information Officer **Marc Flake** . . . . . (817) 884-2535

Office of the County Auditor

100 East Weatherford Street, Suite 506, Fort Worth, TX 76196-0103

Auditor **S. Renee Tidwell** . . . . . (817) 884-1205
Education: Texas (Arlington) 1981 BBA

Office of the Chief Medical Examiner

200 Feliks Gwozdz Place, Fort Worth, TX 76104-4919
Fax: (817) 920-5713 Internet: www.tarrantcounty.com/emedicalexaminer

► Chief Medical Examiner **Nizam Peerwani** . . . . . (817) 920-5700
E-mail: npeerwani@tarrantcounty.com
Chief Forensic Investigator **Michael Floyd** . . . . . (817) 920-5700

Texas AgriLife Extension Services

200 Taylor Street, Suite 500, Fort Worth, TX 76196
Tel: (817) 884-1945 Fax: (817) 884-1941 E-mail: tarrant-tx@tamu.edu

County Extension Director **Joan Jacobsen** . . . . . (817) 884-1945

★ Elected Official ▲ Appointed by Legislature ▼ Appointed by Governor ► Appointed by Board or Commission ● Appointed by Judge
■ Appointed by Mayor △ Appointed by Freeholders ▽ Appointed by Supervisor ▷ Appointed by County Executive ○ Appointed by Council

Budget and Risk Management Department
100 East Weatherford Street, Room 305, Fort Worth, TX 76196-0102
Fax: (817) 850-2938 Internet: www.tarrantcounty.com/ebudget

▶ Director **Debbie Schneider** .... (817) 884-1002
E-mail: dschneider@tarrantcounty.com

Child Protective Services Office
2700 Ben Ave., Fort Worth, TX 76103-2947

Assistant District Attorney **Cindy Williams** .... (817) 255-8729

Community Development and Housing Department
1509-B S. University Dr., #276, Fort Worth, TX 76107-6568
Fax: (817) 850-7944

Director **Patricia Ward** .... (817) 850-7940
E-mail: pward@tarrantcounty.com

Community Supervision and Corrections Department
200 W. Belknap, Fort Worth, TX 76196-0255
Fax: (817) 884-1862

Director **Leighton Iles** .... (817) 884-1741
Assistant Director **Cobi Tittle** .... (817) 212-7555

Information Technology Department
200 Taylor Street, Fort Worth, TX 76102
Fax: (817) 212-3060

Chief Information Officer **Christopher Nchopa-Ayafor** .. (817) 884-3888

Dell Dehay Law Library
100 West Weatherford Street, Room 420, Fort Worth, TX 76196-0800
Tel: (817) 884-1481 Fax: (817) 884-1509

Director **Holly Gerber** .... (817) 884-1891 ext. 1
E-mail: hgerber@tarrantcounty.com
Assistant Director **Peggy Martindale** .... (817) 884-1508 ext. 2
E-mail: pmartindale@tarrantcounty.com

Domestic Relations Office
200 E. Weatherford Street, Fort Worth, TX 76196-0290
Fax: (817) 884-2591

Executive Director **Christina S. Glenn** .... (817) 884-1742
E-mail: cglenn@tarrantcounty.com
Child Support **Jessica Buchert** .... (817) 884-1475
E-mail: jbuchert@tarrantcounty.com Fax: (817) 884-3769
Community Supervision Unit **Donna Larson** .... (817) 884-1848
E-mail: dmlarson@tarrantcounty.com Fax: (817) 212-7020
Legal Enforcement Division **Clint Dupew** .... (817) 884-1879
Family Court Services **Janet Denton** .... (817) 884-1616
Fax: (817) 212-7063

Elections Administration Office
2700 Premier Street, Fort Worth, TX 76111
Fax: (817) 831-6475

Elections Administrator **Stephen Vickers** .... (817) 831-6480
Elections Administrator **Frank Phillips** .... (817) 831-6480

Facilities Management Department
100 West Weatherford Street, Suite 460B, Fort Worth, TX 76196
Tel: (817) 884-2878 Fax: (817) 884-3078

▶ Director **David Phillips** .... (817) 884-3344
E-mail: dphillips@tarrantcounty.com
Education: Texas Christian 1997 BBA
Secretary **Carla Savage** .... (817) 884-2878
E-mail: chsavage@tarrantcounty.com

Department of Human Resources
100 E. Weatherford St., Room 301, Fort Worth, TX 76196-0105
Fax: (817) 884-3250 Internet: www.tarrantcounty.com

▶ Director **Tina Glenn** .... (817) 884-1510
E-mail: tinaglenn@tarrantcounty.com
Assistant Director **Robin Worthy** .... (817) 884-1511
E-mail: rworthy@tarrantcounty.com
Benefits Manager **Joyce Kirk** .... (817) 212-7035
Organizational Development Officer
Jeannette Johnson .... (817) 884-3811
E-mail: jejohnson@tarrantcounty.com
Civil Service Coordinator **Ann Smith** .... (817) 884-3252
E-mail: asmith@tarrantcounty.com

Human Services Department
1200 Circle Drive, Suite 200, Fort Worth, TX 76119
Tel: (817) 531-5620 Fax: (817) 531-5648

▶ Director **Julie Parks** .... (817) 531-5620
E-mail: Jparks@tarrantcounty.com
Assistant Director **(Vacant)** .... (817) 531-5620

Juvenile Services
Scott D. Moore Juvenile Justice Center, 2701 Kimbo Rd., Fort Worth, TX 76111
Internet: www.tarrantcounty.com/ejuvenile

Director **Randy Turner** .... (817) 838-4600
Fax: (817) 838-4633

Public Health Department [TCPH]
1101 South Main Street, Room 2400, Fort Worth, TX 76104
Tel: (817) 321-4700 Fax: (817) 321-5302
Internet: www.tarrantcounty.com/ehealth

Public Health Director **Veerinder Taneja** .... (817) 321-5301
Health Authority/Medical Director **Catherine Colquitt** ... (817) 321-5305
Associate Director/Community and Public Health Nursing **Ann Salyer-Caldwell** .... (817) 321-5309
Associate Director/Disease Control and Environmental Health **Dr. Anita K. Kurian** .... (817) 321-5377
Business Manager **Marsha Gillespie** .... (817) 321-5335
Chronic Disease/Injury Prevention Manager
Glenda Redeemer .... (817) 321-5310
Environmental Health Promotion Division Manager
David Jefferson .... (817) 321-4969
Epidemiology/Health Information Division Manager
Russell Jones .... (817) 321-5333
Health Planning and Policy Development Division Manager **Jan Parker** .... (817) 321-5316
North Texas Regional Laboratory Division Manager
Guy Dixon .... (817) 321-4757
Prevention and Planning Associate Director **(Vacant)** ..... (817) 321-5300
Adult Health Services **Mark Wilson** .... (817) 321-4819
Tuberculosis Control Division Manager
Jeremy Gallups .... (817) 321-4900

Purchasing Department
100 East Weatherford Street, Suite 303, Fort Worth, TX 76196-0104
Fax: (817) 884-2629

▶ Purchasing Agent **Jack Beacham** .... (817) 884-1133
E-mail: jbeacham@tarrantcounty.com

Records Information Management Department
200 Taylor Street, Room 4200, Fort Worth, TX 76196
Fax: (817) 884-3363

Senior Manager **Sharon Coleman** .... (817) 884-1726

★ Elected Official ▲ Appointed by Legislature ▼ Appointed by Governor ▶ Appointed by Board or Commission ● Appointed by Judge
■ Appointed by Mayor △ Appointed by Freeholders ▽ Appointed by Supervisor ▷ Appointed by County Executive ○ Appointed by Council

Tarrant County 911 District

2600 Airport Freeway, Fort Worth, TX 76111
Internet: www.tc911.org

Executive Director **Greg Petrey** . . . . . (817) 820-1188
E-mail: greg@tc911.org
Chief Fiscal Officer/Business Manager **Melinda Oliver** . . . (817) 820-1181
E-mail: moliver@tc911.org
Geographic Information Systems Manager **Yui Skulpoonkitti** . . . . . (817) 820-1186
E-mail: yuis@tc911.org
Director of Operations **Wanda McCarley** . . . . . (817) 820-1185
E-mail: wanda@tc911.org
Technical Operations Manager **Kevin Kleck** . . . . . (817) 820-1170
E-mail: kkleck@tc911.org

Transportation Services Department

100 East Weatherford Street, Room 401, Fort Worth, TX 76196-0601
Fax: (817) 884-1178 Internet: www.tarrantcounty.com/etransportation

► Director **William Riley** . . . . . (817) 884-1173
County Engineer **Joe L. Trammel** . . . . . (817) 884-1153
E-mail: jltrammel@tarrantcounty.com
Environmental Specialist **Robert Berndt** . . . . . (817) 884-2634
Education: Tarleton State 1987 BS
Transportation Planning Manager **Randall V. Skinner** . . . . (817) 884-1653
Education: LeTourneau 2000 BA

Veterans Services Office

1200 Circle Drive, Suite 300, Fort Worth, TX 76119
Fax: (817) 531-5649 Internet: www.tarrantcounty.com/eveterans

► Director **Thomas Belton III** . . . . . (817) 531-5645
Counselor **Victor Diaz** . . . . . (817) 531-5645
Counselor **Ken Davis** . . . . . (817) 531-5645
Counselor **Juan Rios** . . . . . (817) 531-5645
Office Clerk **Natalie Juarez** . . . . . (817) 531-5645
E-mail: njuarez@tarrantcounty.com

Office of the County Commissioners

100 East Weatherford Street, Fort Worth, TX 76196-0609
Tel: (817) 884-1234 Fax: (817) 884-2793
Internet: www.tarrantcounty.com/ecommissioner

★ Commissioner **Roy Charles Brooks** (D-Precinct 1) . . . . . (817) 370-4500
Term Expires: December 31, 2016
E-mail: rcbrooks@tarrantcounty.com
★ Commissioner **Andy H. Nguyen** (R-Precinct 2) . . . . . (817) 548-3900
Term Expires: December 31, 2018
E-mail: ahnguyen@tarrantcounty.com
★ Commissioner **Gary Fickes** (D-Precinct 3) . . . . . (817) 581-3600
Term Expires: December 31, 2016
E-mail: ggfickes@tarrantcounty.com
★ Commissioner **J. D. Johnson** (R-Precinct 4) . . . . . (817) 238-4400
Term Expires: December 31, 2018 Fax: (817) 238-4403
E-mail: jdjohnson@tarrantcounty.com

Office of the County Clerk

100 W. Weatherford St., Fort Worth, TX 76196-0401

★ County Clerk **Mary Louise Garcia** (R) . . . . . (817) 884-1195
Term Expires: December 31, 2018 Fax: (817) 884-3295

Office of the Criminal District Attorney

401 West Belknap Street, Fort Worth, TX 76196-0201
Fax: (817) 884-1667

★ Criminal District Attorney **Sharen Wilson** (R) . . . . . (817) 884-1400
Term Expires: December 31, 2018
E-mail: swilson@tarrantcountytx.gov

Office of the Criminal District Attorney *continued*

First Assistant District Attorney **(Vacant)** . . . . . (817) 884-1233
Fax: (817) 884-1675
Executive Administrator **Deborah Falcone** . . . . . (817) 884-1400
E-mail: dfalcone@tarrantcountytx.gov
Appellate Chief **Charles Mallin** . . . . . (817) 884-1687
E-mail: cmallin@tarrantcountytx.gov Fax: (817) 884-1672
Civil Chief (Interim) **Russell Friemel** . . . . . (817) 884-1233
Education: Texas 1977 JD Fax: (817) 884-1675
Crimes Against Children Unit Chief **(Vacant)** . . . . . (817) 884-2800
Fax: (817) 884-1881
White Collar Crimes Chief **Harry White** . . . . . (817) 884-1661
E-mail: hwhite@tarrantcountytx.gov Fax: (817) 884-1881
Gang Unit Chief **Tim Bednarz** . . . . . (817) 884-3450
E-mail: tbednarz@tarrantcountytx.gov Fax: (817) 212-6973
Education: Texas Tech 1988 JD
Investigation Chief **Jim Rizy** . . . . . (817) 884-3434
E-mail: jrizy@tarrantcountytx.gov Fax: (817) 884-3333
Juvenile Chief **Riley Shaw** . . . . . (817) 838-4613
E-mail: rshaw@tarrantcountytx.gov Fax: (817) 838-4616
Misdemeanor Chief **Richard Alpert** . . . . . (817) 884-2488
E-mail: ralpert@tarrantcountytx.gov Fax: (817) 884-2499
Pre-Trial Services Chief **Dixie Bersano** . . . . . (817) 212-7046
E-mail: dbersano@tarrantcountytx.gov Fax: (817) 884-1189
Business Manager **Helen Giese** . . . . . (817) 884-1624
E-mail: hhgeise@tarrantcountytx.gov Fax: (817) 850-2300
Narcotics Commander **Herschel Tebay** . . . . . (817) 492-5222
Fax: (817) 492-5235
Narcotics Chief Prosecutor **Charlie Brandenberg** . . . . . (817) 492-5222
Fax: (817) 492-5235

Office of the District Clerk

401 W. Belknap St., Fort Worth, TX 76196-0402

★ District Clerk **Thomas A. Wilder** (R) . . . . . (817) 884-1574
Term Expires: December 31, 2018
E-mail: dclerk@tarrantcounty.com

Office of the Sheriff

200 Taylor Street, Fort Worth, TX 76102-2084
Fax: (817) 212-6987

★ Sheriff **Dee Anderson** (R) . . . . . (817) 884-3099
Term Expires: December 31, 2016
E-mail: sheriffanderson@tarrantcounty.com
Executive Chief Deputy, Confinement **Alan Dennis** . . . . . (817) 884-3736
Executive Chief Deputy, Operations **John M. Ray** . . . . . (817) 884-2187
E-mail: jmray@tarrantcounty.com
Chief Deputy, Courts **Tim Canas** . . . . . (817) 884-1304
Chief Deputy, Patrol **Jay Six** . . . . . (817) 238-4200
E-mail: ajsix@tarrantcounty.com
Chief Deputy, Warrants/CID/IAD **Mike Simonds** . . . . . (817) 884-1278
E-mail: msimonds@tarrantcounty.com
Director, Information Technology **Eric Metcalf** . . . . . (817) 884-1367

Office of the Tax Assessor/Collector

100 E. Weatherford St., Fort Worth, TX 76196-0301
Fax: (817) 884-1555 E-mail: taxoffice@tarrantcounty.com
Internet: www.tarrantcounty.com/etax

★ Tax Assessor/Collector **Ronald J. "Ron" Wright** . . . . . (817) 884-1100
Term Expires: December 31, 2016
Education: Texas (Arlington)

★ Elected Official ▲ Appointed by Legislature ▼ Appointed by Governor ► Appointed by Board or Commission ● Appointed by Judge
■ Appointed by Mayor △ Appointed by Freeholders ▽ Appointed by Supervisor ▷ Appointed by County Executive ○ Appointed by Council

County of Travis, Texas

Courthouse, 1000 Guadalupe St., Austin, TX 78701
Tel: (512) 854-9188 (Information)

County Seat: Austin **Election Type:** Partisan **Population:** 1,176,558 (2015)

Office of the County Judge

Travis County Administration Bldg., 314 W. 11th St., Suite 520, Austin, TX 78701
P.O. Box 1748, Austin, TX 78767-1748
Fax: (512) 854-9535

★County Judge **Sarah Eckhardt** (D) .... (512) 854-9555
Term Expires: December 31, 2018
E-mail: sarah.eckhard@traviscountytx.gov
Executive Assistant **Joe Hon** .... (512) 854-1123
E-mail: joe.hon@traviscountytx.gov
Chief of Staff **Peter Einhorn** .... (512) 854-9229

Office of the County Auditor

700 Lavaca Street, Suite 1200, Austin, TX 78701

County Auditor **Nicki Riley** .... (512) 854-9125
First Assistant County Auditor **Patti Smith** .... (512) 854-9125

Purchasing Office

Travis County Purchasing Office, 700 Lavaca Street, Suite 800, Austin, TX 78701
Tel: (512) 854-9700 Fax: (512) 854-9185

Purchasing Agent **Cyd V. Grimes** .... (512) 854-9700
E-mail: cyd.grimes@co.travis.tx.us

Administrative Operations

314 West 11th Street, Suite 535, Austin, TX 78701
Tel: (512) 854-9020 Fax: (512) 854-9542
Internet: www.co.travis.tx.us/administrative_operations

Executive Manager **(Vacant)** .... (512) 854-9020

Facilities Management Department

1010 Lavaca Street, Suite 400, Austin, TX 78701
P.O. Box 1748, Austin, TX 78767-1748
Fax: (512) 854-9226

Director **Roger A. El Khoury** .... (512) 854-9661
E-mail: roger.elkhoury@co.travis.tx.us
Division Director for Maintenance and Repair **(Vacant)** ... (512) 854-4772

Human Resources Management Department

1010 Lavaca Street, 2nd Floor, Austin, TX 78701
Fax: (512) 854-4827

▶Director **Debbie Maynor** .... (512) 854-9165

Information and Telecommunications Systems Department

700 Lavaca Street, 5th Floor, Austin, TX 78701
Fax: (512) 854-9633

Director/Chief Information Officer **Tanya Acevedo** ...... (512) 854-8685
E-mail: tanya.acevedo@co.travis.tx.us

Community Supervision and Corrections Department (Adult Probation)

P.O. Box 2245, Austin, TX 78768
Fax: (512) 854-4606 Internet: www.co.travis.tx.us/community_supervision

●Director **Charles Robinson** .... (512) 854-4600
Assistant Director **Rodolfo Perez, Jr.** .... (512) 854-4600
Division Director **Kim McConnell** .... (512) 854-4600

Community Supervision and Corrections Department (Adult Probation) *continued*

Division Director **Marsha Morgenroth** .... (512) 854-4600
Division Director **Dawn Tannous** .... (512) 854-4600
Operations Division Director **Robert Klepac** .... (512) 854-4600
E-mail: robert.klepac@co.travis.tx.us

Pretrial Services Division

411 West Thirteenth Street, Room 601, Austin, TX 78701
P.O. Box 1748, Austin, TX 78767-1748
Fax: (512) 854-9018 Internet: www.traviscountytx.gov/pretrial_services

Division Director **Irma Guerrero** .... (512) 854-9381
Manager **Stacy Brown** .... (512) 854-9381
Manager **Daniel McCoy-Bae** .... (512) 854-9381
E-mail: daniel.mccoy-bae@traviscountytx.gov
Manager **Sara Perez** .... (512) 854-9381
Manager **Gerald Rodriguez** .... (512) 854-9381
Office Manager **Rachel A. Flores** .... (512) 854-9381
E-mail: rachel.flores@traviscountytx.gov

Department of Family and Protective Services [DFPS]

14000 Summit Drive, Suite 100, Austin, TX 78728
Tel: (512) 834-3195 (Information) Fax: (512) 339-5915

Regional Director **Sheila Brown** .... (512) 834-3100
Investigations Program Administrator (North)
Marta Talbert .... (512) 834-3195
Investigations Program Administrator (South)
Matthew Gilbert .... (254) 750-9295
Conservatorship Program Director **Ingrid Vogel** .... (512) 834-3206
Fax: (512) 339-5910
Regional Deputy **Irina Meza** .... (512) 834-3195
Fax: (512) 339-5910
Foster Home/Adoption Program Director
Holly Benningfield .... (512) 834-3195
Program Director **Julie Branch** .... (512) 834-3195
Program Director **(Vacant)** .... (512) 834-3195
Administrative Director **Lindsey Van Buskirk** .... (512) 834-3195

Health and Human Services and Veterans Services

Palm Square Building, 100 North Interregional Highway 35, Suite 2000, Austin, TX 78701
P.O. Box 1748, Austin, TX 78767-1748
Tel: (512) 854-4100 Fax: (512) 279-2197
Internet: www.co.travis.tx.us/health_human_services

▶Executive Director **Sherri Fleming** .... (512) 854-4101
E-mail: sherri.fleming@co.travis.tx.us

Texas AgriLife Extension Service

1600-B Smith Rd., Austin, TX 78721
Tel: (512) 854-9600 Fax: (512) 854-9611 E-mail: travis-tx@tamu.edu

County Extension Director **Maggie Johnson** .... (512) 854-9600
E-mail: mmjohnson@ag.tamu.edu

Veterans Services Office

Palm Square Bldg., 100 North IH35, Suite 2400, Austin, TX 78701
P.O. Box 1748, Austin, TX 78767
Fax: (512) 854-4453

▶Veterans Services Officer **Olie L. Pope, Jr.** .... (512) 854-9340
E-mail: olie.pope@co.travis.tx.us

★Elected Official ▲Appointed by Legislature ▼Appointed by Governor ▶Appointed by Board or Commission ●Appointed by Judge
■Appointed by Mayor △Appointed by Freeholders ▽Appointed by Supervisor ▷Appointed by County Executive ○Appointed by Council

Transportation and Natural Resources Department [TNR]

P.O. Box 1748, Austin, TX 78767-1748
700 Lavaca Street, Fifth Floor, Austin, TX 78701
Tel: (512) 854-9383 Fax: (512) 854-4697
Internet: www.co.travis.tx.us/tnr

▶ County Executive **Steven M. Manilla** . . . . (512) 854-9383
E-mail: steven.manilla@co.travis.tx.us
Education: West Virginia 1978 BS

Chief Deputy **Cynthia McDonald** . . . . (512) 854-4239

Administrative Services Director **Donna Holt** . . . . (512) 854-9417
E-mail: donna.holt@co.travis.tx.us

Development Services and Long Range Planning Director **Anna Bowlin** . . . . (512) 854-7561

Financial Manager **Sydnia Crosbie** . . . . (512) 854-9383

Natural Resources and Environmental Quality Director **Jon White** . . . . (512) 854-7212

Parks Director **Charles Bergh** . . . . (512) 854-9408

Assistant Public Works Director - Road and Bridge **Don Ward** . . . . (512) 854-9317

Public Works Director **Morgan Cotten** . . . . (512) 854-9383

Safety Officer **Dennis Miller** . . . . (512) 854-4691
E-mail: dennis.miller@co.travis.tx.us

Assistant Public Works Director - CIP **Steve Sun** . . . . (512) 854-4660

Travis County Department of Emergency Services

5501 Airport Boulevard, Suite 203, Austin, TX 78751
Tel: (512) 854-9367 Fax: (512) 854-4786
Internet: www.co.travis.tx.us/emergency_services

County Executive Manager **Danny Hobby** . . . . (512) 854-9367

Office of Emergency Management

5010 Old Manor Road, Austin, TX 78723
Tel: (512) 974-0472

Emergency Management Coordinator (Acting) **Stacy Moore** . . . . (512) 974-0473
E-mail: stacy.moore@co.travis.tx.us

Fire Marshal's Office

5555 Airport Boulevard, Suite 400, Austin, TX 78751
Tel: (512) 854-4621 Fax: (512) 854-6471
Internet: www.co.travis.tx.us/fire_marshal

▶ Fire Marshal **Hershel Lee** . . . . (512) 854-4621
E-mail: hershel.lee@co.travis.tx.us

Travis County Medical Examiner's Office [TCMEO]

Forensic Center, 1213 Sabine St., Austin, TX 78701
P.O. Box 1748, Austin, TX 78767-1748
Tel: (512) 854-9599 Fax: (512) 854-9044
E-mail: merequests@co.travis.tx.us
Internet: www.co.travis.tx.us/medical_examiner

▶ Director **Dr. J. Keith Pinckard** . . . . (512) 854-9599
E-mail: keith.pinckard@co.travis.tx.us

Office of the County Commissioners

Travis County Administration Bldg., 314 West 11th Street, 5th Floor, Austin, TX 78701

★ Commissioner **Ron Davis** (D-Precinct 1) . . . . (512) 854-9111
Term Expires: December 31, 2016
E-mail: ron.davis@co.travis.tx.us

★ Commissioner **Brigid Shea** (Precinct 2) . . . . (512) 854-9222
Term Expires: December 31, 2018

★ Commissioner **Gerald Daugherty** (Precinct 3) . . . . (512) 854-9333
Term Expires: December 31, 2016
E-mail: gerald.daugherty@co.travis.tx.us

★ Commissioner **Margaret Gomez** (D-Precinct 4) . . . . (512) 854-9444
Term Expires: December 31, 2018
E-mail: commissioner.gomez@co.travis.tx.us

Offices of the Constables

★ Constable **Danny Thomas** (D-Precinct 1) . . . . (512) 854-7510
Term Expires: December 31, 2016 Fax: (512) 929-0981
1811 Springdale Rd., #120, Austin, TX 78721
E-mail: danny.thomas@co.travis.tx.us

★ Constable **Adan Ballesteros** (D-Precinct 2) . . . . (512) 854-9697
Term Expires: December 31, 2016 Fax: (512) 854-9196
10409 Burnet Rd., #150, Austin, TX 78758-4427
E-mail: adan.ballesteros@co.travis.tx.us

★ Constable **Sally Hernandez** (Precinct 3) . . . . (512) 854-7245
Term Expires: December 31, 2016
E-mail: sally.hernandez@co.travis.tx.us

★ Constable **Maria Canchola** (D-Precinct 4) . . . . (512) 854-9488
Term Expires: December 31, 2016 Fax: (512) 854-4452
4011 McKinney Falls Parkway, Suite 1100, Austin, TX 78744
E-mail: maria.canchola@co.travis.tx.us

★ Constable **Carlos Lopez** (Precinct 5) . . . . (512) 854-9100
Term Expires: December 31, 2016 Fax: (512) 854-4228
1003 Guadalupe Street, Austin, TX 78701
E-mail: carlos.lopez@co.travis.tx.us

COUNTIES

Office of the County Attorney

Travis County Administration Bldg., 314 W. 11th St., Suite 300, Austin, TX 78701
Fax: (512) 854-9316 Internet: www.co.travis.tx.us/county_attorney

★ County Attorney **David A. Escamilla** (D) . . . . (512) 854-9415
Term Expires: December 31, 2016
E-mail: david.escamilla@co.travis.tx.us
Education: Texas 1979 BA, 1982 JD
Office Manager **Chantelle Abruzzo** . . . . (512) 854-9415

First Assistant County Attorney **Steve Capelle** . . . . (512) 854-9415
E-mail: steve.capelle@co.travis.tx.us

Office of the County Clerk

5501 Airport Boulevard, Austin, TX 78751
P.O. Box 149325, Austin, TX 78714
Tel: (512) 854-9188 (Information) TTY: (512) 854-9069
Fax: (512) 854-3942 Fax: (512) 854-9075 (Elections)

★ County Clerk **Dana DeBeauvoir** (D) . . . . (512) 854-9188
Term Expires: December 31, 2018
E-mail: dana.debeauvoir@co.travis.tx.us

Chief Deputy County Clerk **Ronald Morgan** . . . . (512) 854-9587
E-mail: ron.morgan@co.travis.tx.us

Office of the County Treasurer

700 Lavaca Street, Suite 1.300, Austin, TX 78701
Fax: (512) 854-9361 Internet: www.traviscountytx.gov/county_treasurer

★ Treasurer **Dolores Ortega Carter** (D) . . . . (512) 854-9365
Term Expires: December 31, 2018
E-mail: dolores.ortega-carter@traviscountytx.gov
Education: Texas A&M 1976 BA, 1980 MA

Office of the District Attorney

Blackwell-Thurman Criminal Justice Center, 509 West 11th Street, Austin, TX 78701
Fax: (512) 854-9695 Internet: www.traviscountyda.com

★ District Attorney **Rosemary Lehmberg** . . . . (512) 854-9400
Term Expires: December 31, 2016
E-mail: rosemary.lehmberg@co.travis.tx.us
Education: Texas BA; St Mary's U (TX) 1974 JD

First Assistant District Attorney **John Neal** . . . . (512) 854-9400
E-mail: john.neal@co.travis.tx.us

Chief of Investigations **Dawn McLean** . . . . (512) 854-9400
E-mail: dawn.mclean@co.travis.tx.us

★ Elected Official ▲ Appointed by Legislature ▼ Appointed by Governor ▶ Appointed by Board or Commission ● Appointed by Judge
■ Appointed by Mayor △ Appointed by Freeholders ▽ Appointed by Supervisor ▷ Appointed by County Executive ○ Appointed by Council

Office of the Sheriff

P.O. Box 1748, Austin, TX 78767-1748
Tel: (512) 854-9770 Tel: (512) 974-0845 (Non-Emergency Dispatch)
Fax: (512) 854-3289 Internet: www.tcsheriff.org

★ Sheriff **Greg Hamilton** (D) . . . . . (512) 854-9788
Term Expires: December 31, 2016
E-mail: Greg.hamilton@traviscountytx.gov
Chief Deputy **James N. "Jim" Sylvester** . . . . . (512) 854-9787
E-mail: jim.sylvester@traviscountytx.gov
Administration and Support Bureau **Michael Gottner** . . . . (512) 854-9758
E-mail: michael.gottner@traviscountytx.gov
Corrections Bureau **Wes Priddy** . . . . . (512) 854-9348
Law Enforcement Bureau **Major William Poole** . . . . . (512) 854-9759
E-mail: william.poole@traviscountytx.gov
Finance Director **Paul D. Matthews** . . . . . (512) 854-9234
Public Information Officer **Roger Wade** . . . . . (512) 854-4986
E-mail: roger.wade@traviscountytx.gov

COUNTIES

Office of the Tax Assessor/Collector

5501 Airport Boulevard, Austin, TX 78751
P.O. Box 1748, Austin, TX 78767-1748
Fax: (512) 854-5868 Internet: www.traviscountytax.org

★ Tax Assessor/Collector **Bruce Elfant** (D) . . . . . (512) 854-9473
Term Expires: December 31, 2016
Administrative Assistant I **Kathleen Bellarose** . . . . . (512) 854-9473
Chief Deputy **Tina Morton** . . . . . (512) 854-9702

Travis County Domestic Relations Office

1010 Lavaca Street, Austin, TX 78701
P.O. Box 1495, Austin, TX 78767-1495
Fax: (512) 854-9294 Internet: www.co.travis.tx.us/dro

Director **Scot M. Doyal** . . . . . (512) 854-9696
Office Manager **Etta Jarmon** . . . . . (512) 854-9696

County of Tulare, California

2800 West Burrel Avenue, Visalia, CA 93291
Tel: (559) 635-5000 (Information) Internet: tularecounty.ca.gov

County Seat: Visalia **Election Type:** Nonpartisan **Population:** 459,863 (2015)

Office of the Board of Supervisors

2800 West Burrel Avenue, Visalia, CA 93291
Fax: (559) 733-6898

★ Chairman **Mike Ennis** (District 5) . . . . . (559) 636-5000
Term Expires: December 31, 2018
E-mail: mennis@co.tulare.ca.us
★ Vice Chairman **Allen Ishida** (District 1) . . . . . (559) 636-5000
Term Expires: January 2, 2017
★ Supervisor **Pete Vander Poel** (District 2) . . . . . (559) 636-5000
Term Expires: January 2, 2017
E-mail: pvanderpoel@co.tulare.ca.us
★ Supervisor **Phillip A. Cox** (District 3) . . . . . (559) 636-5000
Term Expires: January 2, 2017
★ Supervisor **J. Steven "Steve" Worthley** (District 4) . . . . (559) 636-5000
Term Expires: December 31, 2018
Date of Birth: June 23, 1953
Education: Occidental BA; McGeorge JD
Chief Clerk **Michelle Baldwin** . . . . . (559) 636-5000
E-mail: mbaldwin@co.tulare.ca.us
Program Administrator **Allison Pierce** . . . . . (559) 636-5000
E-mail: agpierce@co.tulare.ca.us

Office of the Board of Supervisors *continued*

Board Representative **Julieta Martinez** . . . . . (559) 636-5000
E-mail: jmartinez2@co.tulare.ca.us
Board Representative **Carrie Crane** . . . . . (559) 636-5000
E-mail: ccrane@co.tulare.ca.us

Office of the County Administrative Officer

2800 West Burrel Avenue, Visalia, CA 93291-4582
Fax: (559) 733-6318

▽ County Administrative Officer/Clerk of the Board
Michael C. "Mike" Spata . . . . . (559) 636-5005
E-mail: mspata@co.tulare.ca.us
Education: Maryland BA

Cooperative Extension Office

4437 S. Laspina, Tulare, CA 93274
Fax: (559) 733-6720 Internet: www.cetulare.ucdavis.edu

County Director **Kevin Day** . . . . . (559) 639-3300

Department of Child Support Services

8040 West Doe Avenue, Visalia, CA 93291
Tel: (866) 901-3212 Fax: (559) 730-2595

Director **Roger Dixon** . . . . . (866) 901-3212

General Services

Tel: (559) 624-7227 Fax: (559) 624-1022

General Services Manager (Interim) **John Hess** . . . . . (559) 624-7227
E-mail: jhess@co.tulare.ca.us

Health and Human Services Agency

5957 South Mooney Boulevard, Visalia, CA 93291
Tel: (559) 624-8000 Fax: (559) 737-4692 Internet: www.tularehhsa.org

▽ Director **Cheryl Duerksen** . . . . . (559) 624-8011
E-mail: cduerkse@tularehhsa.org

Department of Mental Health

5957 South Mooney Boulevard, Visalia, CA 93291
Fax: (559) 737-4693

▽ Director **Cheryl Duerskin** . . . . . (559) 624-7445

Human Resources and Development Department

2900 W. Burrel Ave., Visalia, CA 93291-4583
Fax: (559) 730-2597 Internet: www.co.tulare.ca.us/hrd

▽ Director **Rhonda Sjostrom** . . . . . (559) 636-4900
Assistant Director **Rachel Buckley** . . . . . (559) 636-4900

Information Technology Department

221 S. Mooney Blvd., Visalia, CA 93291-4593
Fax: (559) 730-2568

▽ Information Technology Director **Peg Yeates** . . . . . (559) 636-4805
E-mail: pyeates@co.tulare.ca.us

Law Library

221 South Mooney Boulevard, Room 1, Visalia, CA 93291
E-mail: lawlibrary@co.tulare.ca.us
Internet: www.co.tulare.ca.us/government/law

Director **Anne R. Bernardo** . . . . . (559) 636-4600
E-mail: abernard@co.tulare.ca.us
Education: UC Davis 1978 BS

★ Elected Official ▲ Appointed by Legislature ▼ Appointed by Governor ▶ Appointed by Board or Commission ● Appointed by Judge
■ Appointed by Mayor △ Appointed by Freeholders ▽ Appointed by Supervisor ▷ Appointed by County Executive ○ Appointed by Council

Office of the Agricultural Commissioner/Sealer of Weights and Measures

4437 S. Laspina, Tulare, CA 93274
Fax: (559) 713-3768

▽Commissioner/Sealer **Marilyn Kinoshita** . . . . (559) 685-3323
E-mail: mkinoshi@co.tulare.ca.us
Education: Arkansas State 1985 BS

Office of the County Counsel

2900 W. Burrel Ave., Visalia, CA 93291-4583
Fax: (559) 737-4319 Internet: www.tularecountycounsel.org

County Counsel **Kathleen Bales-Lange** . . . . (559) 636-4950
Education: Cal State (Hayward); Hastings 1980 JD

Office of the Public Defender

221 South Mooney Boulevard, Room G-35, Visalia, CA 93291-4593
Fax: (559) 733-6113

Public Defender **Lisa Bertolino** . . . . (559) 636-4500
Assistant Public Defender **Thomas "Tom" McGuire** . . . . . (559) 636-4500
Chief Public Defender, Porterville Office **Ben Smukler** . . . (559) 782-6960
633 North Westwood Street, Porterville, CA 93257 Fax: (559) 782-3936
Supervising Attorney **Angela Krueger** . . . . (559) 636-4500
Supervising Attorney **Nathan Leedy** . . . . (559) 636-4500
Supervising Attorney **Tim Rote** . . . . (559) 636-4500
Supervising Attorney **Patricia Stanley** . . . . (559) 636-4500

Probation Department

221 South Mooney Boulevard, Room 206, Visalia, CA 93291
Fax: (559) 730-2626 E-mail: tulprob@lightspeed.net

Chief Probation Officer **Christie Myer** . . . . (559) 713-2750
Adult Services Manager **(Vacant)** . . . . (559) 713-2750
Assistant Chief Probation Officer **Ollie Dimery-Ratliff** . . . (559) 713-2750
Juvenile Court and Central Records Manager
Michelle Gayden . . . . (559) 713-2750
Juvenile Detention Facility Manager **Tate Rankin** . . . . . . (559) 713-2750
Probation Youth Facility Manager **Le Anne Williams** . . . . (559) 713-2750

Purchasing Division

221 South Mooney Boulevard, Room 3G, Visalia, CA 93291
Fax: (559) 733-6759

Purchasing Agent **Lori Looney** . . . . (559) 636-5245
E-mail: llooney@co.tulare.ca.us

Resource Management Agency [RMA]

5961 South Mooney Boulevard, Visalia, CA 93291
Fax: (559) 624-7000 Internet: http://co.tulare.ca.us/government/rma

Director (Interim) **Benjamin Ruiz** . . . . (559) 624-7000
Assistant Director, Administration **Roger Hunt** . . . . . . (559) 624-7000
Associate Director, Planning Branch **Mike Washam** . . . . (559) 624-7000
E-mail: mwasham@co.tulare.ca.us
Assistant Director, Public Works Branch **(Vacant)** . . . . . . (559) 624-7000
Assistant Director, Transportation **Johnny Wong** . . . . . . (559) 624-7000
Parks and Recreation Division Manager **Neil Pilegard** . . . . (559) 624-7227
5953 South Mooney Boulevard, Visalia, CA 93277 Fax: (559) 642-1022
Community Development **(Vacant)** . . . . (559) 624-7000

Solid Waste

Tel: (559) 624-7195 E-mail: TCSolidWaste@co.tulare.ca.us

Solid Waste Director **Bryce Howard** . . . . (559) 624-7195

Tulare County Library

200 West Oak Avenue, Visalia, CA 93291
Fax: (559) 737-4586 E-mail: questions@tularecountylibrary.org
Internet: www.tularecountylibrary.org

▽Director **Darla Wegener** . . . . (559) 713-2723

Tulare County Fire Department [TCFD]

907 West Visalia Road, Farmersville, CA 93223
Fax: (559) 747-8242

▽Fire Chief **Charlie Norman** . . . . (559) 622-7600
E-mail: cnorman@co.tulare.ca.us

Tulare County Employees' Retirement Association [TCERA]

136 North Akers Street, Visalia, CA 93291
Fax: (559) 730-2631

Director **David Kehler** . . . . (559) 713-2900
Assistant Retirement Administrator **Leanne Malison** . . . . . (559) 713-2900

Workforce Investment Board

309 West Main Street, Suite 120, Visalia, CA 93291
Tel: (559) 713-5200 Fax: (559) 713-5263 E-mail: info@tularewib.org
Internet: www.tularewib.org

Director **Adam Peck** . . . . (559) 713-5200
E-mail: apeck@tularewib.org

COUNTIES

Office of the Auditor-Controller/Treasurer-Tax Collector/Registrar of Voters

221 South Mooney Boulevard, Room 101E, Visalia, CA 93291-4593
Fax: (559) 730-2547 (Auditor-Controller)
Fax: (559) 733-6988 (Tax Collector) Fax: (559) 730-2532 (Treasurer)

★Auditor-Controller/Treasurer-Tax Collector/Registrar of
Voters **Rita A. Woodard** . . . . (559) 636-5200
Term Expires: January 7, 2019
Assistant Auditor-Controller **Debbie Paolinelli** . . . . (559) 636-5200
Chief Deputy Treasurer-Tax Collector **Hiley R. Wallis** . . . . (559) 636-5265

Elections Division

5951 South Mooney Boulevard, Visalia, CA 93277
Fax: (559) 737-4498 Internet: www.tularecoelections.org

Manager **Ann Turner** . . . . (559) 624-7300
E-mail: aturner@co.tulare.ca.us

Office of the County Assessor/Clerk-Recorder

221 South Mooney Boulevard, Room 103, Visalia, CA 93291-4593
Tel: (559) 636-5051 (Clerk) Tel: (559) 636-5050 (Recorder)
Fax: (559) 740-4329

★County Assessor/Clerk-Recorder **Roland P. Hill** . . . . (559) 636-5050
Term Expires: January 31, 2019

Office of the District Attorney

2350 Burrell Avenue, Room 224, Visalia, CA 93291-4593
Fax: (559) 730-2658 Internet: http://www.da-tulareco.org

★District Attorney **Tim Ward** . . . . (559) 636-5494
Term Expires: December 31, 2018

Office of the Sheriff-Coroner

2404 W. Burrel Ave., Visalia, CA 93291-4580
Fax: (559) 733-2756 Internet: www.tularecounty.ca.us/government/sheriff

★Sheriff-Coroner **Mike Boudreaux** . . . . (559) 636-4716
Term Expires: December 31, 2018
Undersheriff **Robin Skiles** . . . . (559) 636-4716
Administrative Services Captain **Sheri Lehner** . . . . (559) 636-4716
Custody Captain **Tom Sigley** . . . . (559) 636-4716
Investigations Captain **Larry Micari** . . . . (559) 636-4716

(continued on next page)

★Elected Official ▲Appointed by Legislature ▼Appointed by Governor ▶Appointed by Board or Commission ●Appointed by Judge
■Appointed by Mayor △Appointed by Freeholders ▽Appointed by Supervisor ▷Appointed by County Executive ○Appointed by Council

Office of the Sheriff-Coroner *continued*

Patrol Captain **Keith Douglas** . . . . (559) 636-4716
Assistant Undersheriff **Scott Logue** . . . . (559) 636-4716
Fiscal and Planning **Mike Watson** . . . . (559) 636-4716

Office of the Treasurer/Tax Collector

221 S. Mooney Blvd., Visalia, CA 93291-4593

★Treasurer/Tax Collector **Rita A. Woodard** . . . . (559) 636-5250
Term Expires: January 7, 2019

Tulare County Office of Education

2637 W. Burrel Ave., Visalia, CA 93278
P.O. Box 5091, Visalia, CA 93278-5091
Fax: (559) 627-5219 Internet: www.tcoe.k12.ca.us

Board of Education

★President **Joe Enea** (Area 5) . . . . (559) 733-6300
Term Expires: November 30, 2016
E-mail: joee@tcoe.org
★Vice President **Chris Reed** (Area 6) . . . . (559) 733-6300
Term Expires: November 30, 2016
★Member **Celia Maldonado-Arroyo** (Area 1) . . . . (559) 733-6300
Term Expires: November 30, 2018
E-mail: celiama@tcoe.org
★Member **Deborah Lynn "Debby" Holguin** (Area 2) . . . . . (559) 733-6300
Term Expires: November 30, 2016
E-mail: debbyh@tcoe.org
★Member **Tom Link** (Area 3) . . . . (559) 733-6300
Term Expires: November 30, 2016
★Member **Judy Coble** (Area 4) . . . . (559) 733-6300
Term Expires: November 30, 2018
E-mail: judyc@tcoe.org
★Member **Patricia Ann "Pat" Hillman** (Area 7) . . . . (559) 733-6300
Term Expires: November 30, 2018

Office of the Superintendent

Superintendent of Schools **Jim Vidak** . . . . (559) 733-6301
Deputy Superintendent, Business Services
Craig Wheaton . . . . (559) 730-6474
Deputy Superintendent, Instructional Services
GEN Guadalupe Solis . . . . (559) 733-6328
Assistant Superintendent, Special Services
Tammy Bradford . . . . (559) 730-2910
Director, Human Resources **John Rodriguez** . . . . (559) 733-6306

County of Tulsa, Oklahoma

500 S. Denver Ave., Tulsa, OK 74103
Tel: (918) 596-5000 (Information) Fax: (918) 596-4647
Internet: www.tulsacounty.org

County Seat: Tulsa **Election Type:** Partisan **Population:** 639,242 (2015)

Office of the Board of County Commissioners

Administration Building, 500 South Denver Avenue, Tulsa, OK 74103
Tel: (918) 596-5000 Fax: (918) 596-4647

★Chairman **Karen Keith** (D-District 2) . . . . (918) 596-5015
Term Expires: December 31, 2016
E-mail: kkeith@tulsacounty.org
Education: Oklahoma State 1976
Secretary **Sherry Langston** . . . . (918) 596-5016
E-mail: slangston@tulsacounty.org

Office of the Board of County Commissioners *continued*

★Commissioner **John M. Smaligo, Jr.** (R-District 1) . . . . . . (918) 596-5020
Term Expires: December 31, 2018
E-mail: jsmaligo@tulsacounty.org
Date of Birth: September 17, 1975
Education: Central Oklahoma 1998 BA
Secretary **Deneice Arterburn** . . . . (918) 596-5021
E-mail: darterburn@tulsacounty.org
★Commissioner **Ron Peters** (R-District 3) . . . . (918) 596-5010
Term Expires: December 31, 2018
E-mail: rpeters@tulsacounty.org
Date of Birth: September 28, 1944
Education: Tulsa 1966 BS
Secretary **Pam Kinkade** . . . . (918) 596-5011
E-mail: pkinkade@tulsacounty.org
▶Fiscal Officer **Tom Gerrard** . . . . (918) 596-5220
E-mail: tgerard@tulsacounty.org
Public Information Officer/Director of Governmental Affairs and Chief Deputy **Michael Willis** . . . . (918) 596-5018
E-mail: mwillis@tulsacounty.org

Administrative Services Department

County Annex Bldg., 633 W. Third St., Tulsa, OK 74127-8942
Fax: (918) 596-5870

▶Director **Gary Fisher** . . . . (918) 596-5882
E-mail: gfisher@tulsacounty.org
Operations Manager **(Vacant)** . . . . (918) 596-5882

Building and Fleet Operations Department

500 South Denver Avenue, Suite B1, Tulsa, OK 74103
Tel: (918) 596-5501 Fax: (918) 596-4546

▶Director **Daniel Belding** . . . . (918) 596-5501
E-mail: dbelding@tulsacounty.org

Division of Court Services

Tulsa County Court Services, 500 South Denver, Room B3, Tulsa, OK 74103
Fax: (918) 596-8842

Director **Sherri Carrier** . . . . (918) 596-5790
Assistant Director **Chris Worsham** . . . . (918) 596-8844

Engineering Department

500 S. Denver Ave., Tulsa, OK 74103
Tel: (918) 596-5733 Fax: (918) 596-5743

▶County Engineer **Tom Rains** . . . . (918) 596-5736
E-mail: trains@tulsacounty.org
Assistant County Engineer **Harry Creech** . . . . (918) 596-5737
E-mail: hcreech@tulsacounty.org

Inspections Division

County Annex Bldg., 633 W. Third St., Tulsa, OK 74127
Fax: (918) 596-5209

Director **Tom Rains** . . . . (918) 596-5736
E-mail: trains@tulsacounty.org

Division of Human Resources

County Annex Bldg., 633 W. Third St., Tulsa, OK 74127
Tel: (918) 596-5095 Tel: (918) 596-5098 (Information Job Line)
Fax: (918) 596-5215

▶Director **Terry E. Tallent** . . . . (918) 596-5096
E-mail: ttallent@tulsacounty.org
Compensation and Benefits Manager **Clark Burbank** . . . . . (918) 596-5093
Benefits Specialist **Deepa Pollard** . . . . (918) 596-5090

★Elected Official ▲Appointed by Legislature ▼Appointed by Governor ▶Appointed by Board or Commission ●Appointed by Judge
■Appointed by Mayor △Appointed by Freeholders ▽Appointed by Supervisor ▷Appointed by County Executive ○Appointed by Council

Department of Information Technology
County Annex Building, 633 West Third Street, Tulsa, OK 74127
Fax: (918) 596-4703

▶ Director (Interim) **Dan Pease** (918) 596-5202
E-mail: dpease@tulsacounty.org
Telecommunications Administrator **Gary Cook** (918) 596-5252

Tulsa County Juvenile Bureau
315 S. Gilcrease Museum Rd., Tulsa, OK 74127
Fax: (918) 596-4523

▶ Director **Justin Jones** (918) 596-5971

Parks Department
2315 Charles Page Blvd., Tulsa, OK 74127-8424
Fax: (918) 596-5997 Internet: www.parks.tulsacounty.org

▶ Director **Richard Bales** (918) 596-5990
E-mail: rbales@tulsacounty.org

Purchasing Department
500 South Denver Avenue, Room 322A, Tulsa, OK 74103
Tel: (918) 596-5025 Fax: (918) 596-4647

▶ Purchasing Director **Linda R. Dorrell** (918) 596-5022
E-mail: ldorrell@tulsacounty.org
Assistant Purchasing Director **Terrisa Hardy** (918) 596-5023
E-mail: thardy@tulsacounty.org

Social Services Division
2401 Charles Page Blvd., Tulsa, OK 74127-8435
Fax: (918) 596-5568

▶ Director **Linda J. Johnston** (918) 596-5560
E-mail: ljohnston@tulsacounty.org

Tulsa City-County Health Department [THD]
James O. Goodwin Health Center, 5051 South 129 East Avenue, Tulsa, OK 74134-7004
Tel: (918) 582-9355 Fax: (918) 595-4586 E-mail: info@tulsa-health.org
Internet: www.tulsa-health.org

Director **Bruce D. Dart** (918) 595-4044
Chief Operating Officer **Reggie Ivey** (918) 582-9355
E-mail: rivey@tulsa-health.org

Tulsa City-County Library
400 Civic Center, Tulsa, OK 74103-3830
Tel: (918) 549-7323 Fax: (918) 549-7370 Internet: www.tulsalibrary.org

Chief Executive Officer and Strategic Initiative Officer
Gary Shaffer (918) 549-7366
E-mail: gshaffe@tulsalibrary.org
Education: Idaho 1986 BS; USC 2003; Pratt Inst 2005 MLIS
Chief Operating Officer **Kim Johnson** (918) 549-7362
E-mail: kjohnso@tulsalibrary.org
Deputy Director, Central Library **Suanne Wymer** (918) 549-7368
E-mail: swymer@tulsalibrary.org
Chief Financial Officer **Gail Morris** (918) 549-7373
Chief People and Commission Support Officer
Shauna McConnell (918) 549-7382
E-mail: smcconn@tulsalibrary.org
Chief Technology Officer **Monique Sendze** (918) 549-7369
Web and Integrated Library System Administrator
Shona Koehn (918) 549-7305
E-mail: skoehn@tulsalibrary.org
Literacy Services Manager **Jennifer Armistead** (918) 549-7401
E-mail: jarmist@tulsalibrary.org
Regional Director, Northwest **Barry Hensley** (918) 549-7686
E-mail: bhensle@tulsalibrary.org
Regional Director, Southeast **Amy Stevens** (918) 549-7599
E-mail: astephe@tulsalibrary.org
Research Wizard **Martha Gregory** (918) 549-7431
E-mail: wizard@tulsalibrary.org

Tulsa City-County Library *continued*

Communications Director **Larry Bartley** (918) 549-7365
E-mail: lbartle@tulsalibrary.org

Tulsa County Election Board
555 North Denver Avenue, Tulsa, OK 74103
Fax: (918) 596-5775

Chairman **Elaine Dodd** (918) 596-5780
Vice-Chairman **George Wiland** (918) 596-5780
Secretary **Patricia "Patty" Bryant** (918) 596-5780
Assistant Secretary **Martha Bales** (918) 596-5780
E-mail: electionboard@tulsacounty.org

Tulsa County Law Library
500 South Denver Avenue, Tulsa, OK 74103
Fax: (918) 596-4509 E-mail: lawlibrary@tulsacounty.org

Director **Joyce M. Pacenza** (918) 596-5404
E-mail: jpacenza@tulsacounty.org

Office of the County Assessor
500 South Denver Avenue, Room 215, Tulsa, OK 74103
Fax: (918) 596-4799

★ Assessor **Ken Yazel** (R) (918) 596-5100
Term Expires: December 31, 2018
E-mail: assessor@tulsacounty.org
Education: Oklahoma 1969 BS
Chief Deputy Assessor **Patrick Milton** (918) 596-5159

Office of the County Clerk
500 South Denver Avenue, Room 120, Tulsa, OK 74103-3832
Tel: (918) 596-5801 Fax: (918) 596-5865
Internet: www.countyclerk.tulsacounty.org

★ County Clerk **Pat Key** (918) 596-5851
Term Expires: December 31, 2016
E-mail: pkey@tulsacounty.org
First Deputy **Nancy Rothman** (918) 596-5831
E-mail: nrothman@tulsacounty.org
Second Deputy **Kathy Semler** (918) 596-5822
E-mail: ksemler@tulsacounty.org
MIS Director **Dan Pease** (918) 596-5202
E-mail: dpease@tulsacounty.org

Office of the County Sheriff
500 S. Denver Ave., Tulsa, OK 74103
303 West 1st, Tulsa, OK 74103
Tel: (918) 596-5601 (Main) Tel: (918) 596-5701 (Faulkner Building)
Fax: (918) 596-5697 E-mail: tcso@tcso.org Internet: http://www.tcso.org

★ County Sheriff **Vic Regalado** (R) (918) 596-5641
Term Expires: December 31, 2016
Undersheriff **(Vacant)** (918) 596-5634
Fax: (918) 596-4681
Chief Deputy **Michelle Robinette** (918) 596-8662
E-mail: mrobinette@tcso.org
Chief Deputy **(Vacant)** (918) 596-5661

Office of the County Treasurer
500 S. Denver Ave., 3rd Floor, Tulsa, OK 74103
Tel: (918) 596-5071 (Tax Information) Fax: (918) 596-5029
Internet: www.treasurer.tulsacounty.org

★ County Treasurer **J. Dennis Semler** (R) (918) 596-5071
Term Expires: June 30, 2019
E-mail: dsemler@tulsacounty.org
Education: Oral Roberts 1978 BA; Tulsa 1981 JD
Chief Deputy Treasurer **Steve Blue** (918) 596-5058

(continued on next page)

COUNTIES

COUNTIES

Office of the County Treasurer *continued*

Second Deputy Treasurer **Jamie Vos** . . . . (918) 596-5032

Office of the District Attorney

500 South Denver Avenue, Suite 900, Tulsa, OK 74103-3832
Fax: (918) 596-4830 E-mail: districtattorney@tulsacounty.org
Internet: www.da.tulsacounty.org

★ District Attorney **Steve Kunzweiler** (R) . . . . (918) 596-4864
Term Expires: December 31, 2018

First Assistant District Attorney **John D. Luton** . . . . (918) 596-4865
E-mail: jluton@tulsacounty.org
Education: Oklahoma 1946 BL, 1950 JD

County of Union, New Jersey

County Administration Building, 10 Elizabethtown Plaza, Elizabeth, NJ 07207
Tel: (908) 527-4000 (Information) Internet: www.ucnj.org

County Seat: Elizabeth **Election Type:** Partisan **Population:** 555,786 (2015)

Office of the Board of Chosen Freeholders

County Administration Building, 10 Elizabethtown Plaza, 6th Floor, Elizabeth, NJ 07207
Tel: (908) 527-4100 Fax: (908) 289-4143
E-mail: ucfreeholders@ucnj.org

★ Chairman **Bruce Bergen** (D) . . . . (908) 527-4110
Term Expires: December 31, 2018
E-mail: bbergen@ucnj.org

★ Vice Chairman **Sergio Granados** (D) . . . . (908) 527-4112
Term Expires: December 31, 2016
E-mail: sgranados@ucnj.org

★ Freeholder **Linda Carter** (D). . . . . (908) 527-4117
Term Expires: December 31, 2016
E-mail: linda.carter@ucnj.org

★ Freeholder **Angel G. Estrada** (D) . . . . (908) 527-4111
Term Expires: December 31, 2017
E-mail: aestrada@ucnj.org
Education: Kean Col 1982 BA

★ Freeholder **Christopher Hudak** (D). . . . . (908) 527-4116
Term Expires: December 31, 2017
E-mail: chudak@ucnj.org

★ Freeholder **Mohamed Jalloh** (D) . . . . (908) 527-4114
Term Expires: December 31, 2018
E-mail: mjalloh@ucnj.org

★ Freeholder **Bette Jane Kowalski** (D) . . . . (908) 527-4113
Term Expires: December 31, 2016
E-mail: bkowalski@ucnj.org
Education: Hunter BA; NYU MAJ

★ Freeholder **Alexander Mirabella** (D). . . . . (908) 527-4115
Term Expires: December 31, 2018
E-mail: amirabella@ucnj.org
Education: Hobart 1986 BA

★ Freeholder **Vernell Wright** (D) . . . . (908) 527-4109
Term Expires: December 31, 2017
E-mail: vwright@ucnj.org

△ Clerk of the Board **James E. Pellettiere** . . . . (908) 527-4141
E-mail: jpellettiere@ucnj.org

Director of Communications **Sebastian D'Elia** . . . . (908) 527-4419
E-mail: sdelia@ucnj.org Fax: (908) 527-4704

Office of the County Manager

Union County Administration Building 10, Elizabethtown Plaza, Elizabeth, NJ 07207
Fax: (908) 289-0180

△ County Manager **Alfred J. "Al" Faella** . . . . (908) 527-4200
E-mail: afaella@ucnj.org
Education: Kean U, MPA

△ Deputy County Manager/Director of Economic Development **William Reyes** . . . . (908) 527-4202

Department of Administrative Services

County Administration Bldg., Elizabethtown Plaza, Elizabeth, NJ 07207
Tel: (908) 527-4170 Fax: (908) 558-2566

Director **Norman W. Albert** . . . . (908) 527-4200
E-mail: nalbert@ucnj.org

Personnel Management and Labor Relations Division Director **Norman W. Albert** . . . . (908) 527-4160
E-mail: nalbert@ucnj.org Fax: (908) 558-2566

Purchasing Division Director **Michael Yuska** . . . . (908) 527-4130
E-mail: myuska@ucnj.org Fax: (908) 558-2548

Motor Vehicles Division Director **Chris Meehan** . . . . (908) 659-7470
Fax: (908) 659-7443

Corrections Department

15 Elizabethtown Plaza, Elizabeth, NJ 07207
Tel: (908) 558-2600 Fax: (908) 558-6944

Director (Acting) **George Blaskewicz** . . . . (908) 558-2610
E-mail: gblaskewicz@ucnj.org

Assistant Director **George Blaskewicz** . . . . (908) 558-6912
E-mail: gblaskewicz@ucnj.org

Administrative Captain **Robert Cesaro** . . . . (908) 558-2305
E-mail: rcesaro@ucnj.org

Security and Operations Captain **Jeffrey Barber** . . . . (908) 558-2352
E-mail: jbarber@ucnj.org

Environmental Health/Custody Management Captain **Anthony Bonito** . . . . (908) 558-2612
E-mail: abonito@ucnj.org

Engineering, Public Works and Facilities Department

2325 South Ave., Scotch Plains, NJ 07076
Tel: (908) 789-3653 Fax: (908) 789-3674

Director **Joseph A. Graziano, Sr.** . . . . (908) 789-3653
E-mail: jgraziano@ucnj.org

Engineering Division

2325 South Ave., Scotch Plains, NJ 07076
Fax: (908) 789-3674

County Engineer/Director **Thomas O. Mineo** . . . . (908) 789-3675
E-mail: tmineo@ucnj.org Fax: (908) 789-3674

Director, Bureau of Traffic Safety and Maintenance **Angelo Paparella** . . . . (908) 789-3353
E-mail: apaparella@ucnj.org Fax: (908) 789-9764

Director, Bureau of Information Technologies **Diego Otero** . . . . (908) 527-4731
E-mail: dotero@ucnj.org Fax: (908) 558-6949

Director, Bureau of Geographic Information Systems **Matt Mathan** . . . . (908) 789-3691
E-mail: mmathan@ucnj.org Fax: (908) 789-9764

Facilities Management Division

Courthouse, Two Broad Street, Elizabeth, NJ 07207
Tel: (908) 527-4218 Fax: (908) 558-2353

Director **Charles Chirafesi** . . . . (908) 527-4218

Bureau of Construction Management **Thomas MacDermant** . . . . (908) 527-4241

Bureau of Custodial Maintenance **Thomas Sullivan** . . . . . (908) 527-4243
E-mail: tsullivan@ucnj.org

Bureau of General Trades **Kevin Kolbeck** . . . . (908) 527-4240
E-mail: kkolbeck@ucnj.org

★ Elected Official ▲ Appointed by Legislature ▼ Appointed by Governor ▶ Appointed by Board or Commission ● Appointed by Judge
■ Appointed by Mayor △ Appointed by Freeholders ▽ Appointed by Supervisor ▷ Appointed by County Executive ○ Appointed by Council

Facilities Management Division *continued*

Bureau of Administrative Support **Vincent Paparella** .... (908) 659-7401
Bureau of Stationary Engineers **Philip "Phil" Triano** ..... (908) 527-4246
E-mail: ptriano@ucnj.org Fax: (908) 353-5124

Public Works Division

2371 South Ave., Scotch Plains, NJ 07076
Tel: (908) 789-3660 Fax: (908) 789-3227

Director **Joseph J. Policay, Jr.** .... (908) 789-3657
Inspections Bureau Chief **Arthur Kobitz** .... (908) 789-3658
Fax: (908) 789-3227
Mosquito Control Bureau Chief **Ralph Strano** .... (908) 654-9873
Fax: (908) 654-9874
Roads and Bridges Chief **Paul Fellner** .... (908) 789-3695
Fax: (908) 889-4065
Shade Tree and Conservation Bureau Chief
James Kelly, Sr. .... (908) 789-6027
Fax: (908) 889-4065

Department of Finance

County Administration Bldg., Elizabethtown Plaza, Elizabeth, NJ 07207
Tel: (908) 527-4055 Fax: (908) 558-3486

Director/County Treasurer **Bibi Taylor** .... (908) 527-4055
Education: West Florida 1998 BA; Rutgers 2001 MPA
Comptroller and Director, Division of the Comptroller
Erick Mesias .... (908) 527-4754
E-mail: emesias@ucnj.org
Director, Division of Reimbursement
Caterina Campanella .... (908) 527-4065
Director, Division of the Treasurer **Julie Origliato** .... (908) 527-4099

Department of Human Services [DHS]

County Administration Bldg., Elizabethtown Plaza, Elizabeth, NJ 07207
Fax: (908) 527-4875 Internet: http://ucnj.org/departments/human-services/

Director **Frank L. Guzzo** .... (908) 527-4808
Assistant Director **Karen Dinsmore** .... (908) 527-4809
Juvenile Detention Center Superintendent **Diana Youst** ... (908) 523-1583
1075 Edward Street, Linden, NJ 07036 Fax: (908) 523-7358
Shelter Home Program **Julia Leftwich** .... (908) 436-1955
640 Summer Street, 2nd Floor, Elizabeth, NJ 07202
Paratransit Unit **Kathleen Carmello** .... (908) 659-5001
79 W. Grand St., Elizabeth, NJ 07202 Fax: (908) 659-7443

Contracts Unit

Director **Maureen Glenn** .... (908) 527-4838
Fax: (908) 558-6680

Division on Aging

10 Elizabethtown Plaza, Elizabeth, NJ 07207
Fax: (908) 659-7410

Director **Frances A. Benson** .... (908) 527-4869

Division of Planning

Fax: (408) 558-2562

Director **Melissa Lespinasse** .... (908) 527-4883
Director of Behavioral Health/Mental Health
Administrator **Sara Thode** .... (908) 527-4844
Director, Office for the Disabled **Bill Smith** .... (908) 527-4840
Alcoholism, Drug Abuse and Municipal Alliance
Coordinator **Brenda Cruz** .... (908) 527-4844
Human Services Advisory Council (HSAC)
James Baker .... (908) 527-4843
Intoxicated Driver Resource Center (IDRC)
Cheryl Hathaway .... (908) 527-4804
Rape Crisis Center **Tamara Adelman** .... (908) 233-7273
300 North Ave. East, Westfield, NJ 07090

Social Services Division (County Welfare Agency)

342 Westminster Ave., Elizabeth, NJ 07208
Tel: (908) 965-3706 Fax: (908) 965-2752 (Elizabeth)
Fax: (908) 791-7098 (Plainfield)

Director **Charles Gillon** .... (908) 965-3706
Assistant Director **Alan McGarry** .... (908) 965-2895

Workforce Development Operations

Tel: (908) 791-2039 (One-Stop Operations Director)
Tel: (908) 558-8000 (Eastern One Stop Center)
Tel: (908) 757-9090 (Western One Stop Center)

Workforce Development and Business Initiatives
Director **Jean Koszulinski** .... (908) 527-4812
Fax: (908) 527-4885
Planning Unit **Perle Almeida** .... (908) 527-4887
Fax: (908) 527-4885

Youth Services Division

Director **Darrell C. Hatchett** .... (908) 558-2525
Fax: (908) 558-2540
Youth Services Commission **Monica Lallo** .... (908) 558-2381
Fax: (908) 527-4042

Office of Veteran Affairs

Union County Administration Building, 10 Elizabethtown Plaza,
4th Floor, Elizabeth, NJ 07207
Tel: (908) 659-7407 Tel: (866) 640-7115 (Toll-Free Veterans Hotline)
Fax: (908) 527-4172

Senior Veterans' Advocate **Richard Thompson** .... (908) 527-4719

Cornerstone Behavioral Health Hospital of Union County

40 Watchung Way, Berkeley Heights, NJ 07922
Fax: (908) 771-5820

Administrator **Michael Flemming** .... (908) 771-5720

Law Department

County Administration Bldg., Elizabethtown Plaza, Elizabeth, NJ 07207
Tel: (908) 527-4250 Fax: (908) 289-4230

△County Counsel **Robert E. Barry** .... (908) 527-4250
E-mail: rbarry@ucnj.org
First Deputy County Counsel **Rosalba Comas** .... (908) 527-4250

Department of Parks and Recreation

County Administration Bldg., Elizabethtown Plaza,
Elizabeth, NJ 07207-2204
Tel: (908) 527-4900 Fax: (908) 527-4901

Director **Ronald Zuber** .... (908) 527-4910
Deputy Director **(Vacant)** .... (908) 527-4291
Director of Recreational Facilities **Armando Sanchez** .... (908) 241-2042
E-mail: armando.sanchez@ucnj.org
Director, Division of Parks Planning and Environmental
Services **Daniel Bernier** .... (908) 789-3682
Director, Park Maintenance **Michael Brennan** .... (908) 789-6029

Probation Department

1143 E. Jersey St., Elizabeth, NJ 07201

Chief Probation Officer **Raymond U. Reynolds** .... (908) 659-4094
Fax: (908) 659-3770
Vicinage Assistant Chief Probation Officer - Adult
Supervision **Herbert K. Francis, Jr.** .... (908) 659-4097
Fax: (908) 659-3770
Vicinage Assistant Chief Probation Officer – Child
Support Enforcement and Juvenile Supervision
Jennifer L. Edwards .... (908) 659-4098
Fax: (908) 659-3770

★ Elected Official ▲ Appointed by Legislature ▼ Appointed by Governor ► Appointed by Board or Commission ● Appointed by Judge
■ Appointed by Mayor △ Appointed by Freeholders ▽ Appointed by Supervisor ▷ Appointed by County Executive ○ Appointed by Council

Public Safety Department
300 North Avenue East, Westfield, NJ 07090

Director **Andrew Moran** .... (908) 654-9816
E-mail: amoran@ucnj.org
Education: Rutgers BS

Division of Emergency Management
300 North Avenue East, Westfield, NJ 07090
Fax: (908) 654-9851

Emergency Management Coordinator
Christopher Scaturo .... (908) 654-9881
E-mail: cscaturo@ucnj.org

Division of Health
300 North Avenue East, Westfield, NJ 07090

Director **Annie McNair** .... (908) 518-5620
Fax: (908) 654-9252

Division of the Medical Examiner
300 North Avenue East, Westfield, NJ 07090
Fax: (908) 654-9898

Medical Examiner **Dr. Junaid Shaikh** .... (908) 654-9893

Division of Police
300 North Avenue East, Westfield, NJ 07090
Fax: (908) 518-7933

Officer in Charge **Capt. Chris Debbie** .... (908) 654-9825

Division of Weights and Measures and Office of Consumer Affairs
300 North Avenue East, Westfield, NJ 07090
Fax: (908) 654-3082

Weights and Measures Superintendent **Michael J. Florio** .. (908) 654-9845

Rutgers Cooperative Extension of Union County
300 North Avenue, East, Westfield, NJ 07090-1499
Tel: (908) 654-9854 Fax: (908) 518-7925

Department Head and Family and Community Health Sciences Educator **Karen M. Ensle** .... (908) 654-9854
E-mail: ensle@aesop.rutgers.edu
Associate Department Head and 4-H Agent
James Nichnadowicz .... (908) 654-9854
Office Administrative Assistant **Judi Laganga** .... (908) 654-9854
E-mail: jlaganga@ucnj.org

Taxation Board
271 N. Broad St., Elizabeth, NJ 07207
Tel: (908) 527-4775 Fax: (908) 527-4774

County Tax Administrator **Christopher R. Duryee** ...... (908) 527-4775
▼Commissioner **Christopher Kolibas** .... (908) 527-4775
Commissioner **Peter Lijoi** .... (908) 527-4775
▼Commissioner **Maureen McLeer Morin** .... (908) 527-4775
Commissioner **Melanie Selk** .... (908) 527-4775
Commissioner **Elizabeth Urquhart** .... (908) 527-4775
▼Commissioner **George T. Wagenhoffer** .... (908) 527-4775

Union County College [UCC]
1033 Springfield Ave., Cranford, NJ 07016-1599
Fax: (908) 709-0527 E-mail: info@ucc.edu Internet: www.ucc.edu

President **Margaret M. McMenamin** .... (908) 709-7000

Department of Economic Development
Tel: (908) 527-4802 Fax: (908) 352-3980

Deputy Director **Amy Wagner** .... (908) 527-4802
E-mail: awagner@ucnj.org

Bureau of Community Development
Tel: (908) 527-4086 Fax: (908) 527-4715

Bureau Chief **Thomas E. Connell** .... (908) 527-4086
E-mail: commdevinfo@ucnj.org

Workforce Development Board
Tel: (908) 527-4195 Fax: (908) 659-7406 Internet: http://ucnj.org/wdb

Director **Antonio Rivera** .... (908) 527-4195
E-mail: arivera@ucnj.org

Division of Strategic Planning and Intergovernmental
Bureau Chief, Transportation Planning **Liza Betz** .... (908) 558-2273
Fax: (908) 527-4715
Bureau Chief, Planning and Economic Development
Kamal Saleh .... (908) 527-4268
E-mail: ksaleh@ucnj.org Fax: (908) 527-4901

Bureau of Housing
Tel: (908) 527-4229 Fax: (908) 352-3980

Bureau Chief **James Heim** .... (908) 527-4229

Division of Information Technologies
Tel: (908) 527-4731 Fax: (908) 558-6949

Division Head **Diego Otero** .... (908) 527-4731
E-mail: dotero@ucnj.org

Office of the County Clerk
Court House, Two Broad Street, 1st Floor, Room 115, Elizabeth, NJ 07207
Fax: (908) 558-2589 Internet: clerk.ucnj.org

★County Clerk **Joanne Rajoppi** (D) .... (908) 527-4787
Term Expires: December 31, 2020
E-mail: jrajoppi@ucnj.org
Education: Case Western 1970 BA; Seton Hall MPA
Deputy County Clerk **Nicole L. DiRado** .... (908) 527-4786
E-mail: ndirado@ucnj.org

Office of the Prosecutor
32 Rahway Ave., Elizabeth, NJ 07202-2115
Tel: (908) 527-4500 Fax: (908) 289-1267 E-mail: ucpo@ucnj.org

▼Prosecutor (Acting) **Grace Park** .... (908) 527-4506
First Assistant Prosecutor **Thomas Isenhour** .... (908) 527-4505
Victim/Witness Program Coordinator **Maria Reynolds** .... (908) 527-4500
Director of Communications **Mark Spivey** .... (908) 527-4500

Office of the Sheriff
10 Elizabethtown Plaza, Elizabeth, NJ 07207
Tel: (908) 527-4450 Fax: (908) 527-4455 (Sheriff's personal fax)
Tel: (908) 527-4490 (General faxes)
Internet: www.ucnj.org/government/sheriff

★Sheriff **Joseph P. Cryan** (D) .... (908) 527-4450
Term Expires: January 1, 2018
E-mail: jcryan@ucnj.org
Education: Belmont Abbey BA
Undersheriff **Amilcar "Mickey" Colon** .... (908) 558-2315
E-mail: acolon@ucnj.org
Undersheriff **Michael Frank** .... (908) 527-4959
E-mail: mfrank@ucnj.org
Undersheriff **Gerald Green** .... (908) 558-4454
E-mail: ggreen@ucnj.org

★Elected Official ▲Appointed by Legislature ▼Appointed by Governor ▶Appointed by Board or Commission ●Appointed by Judge
■Appointed by Mayor △Appointed by Freeholders ▽Appointed by Supervisor ▷Appointed by County Executive ○Appointed by Council

Office of the Superintendent of Schools

300 North Avenue East, Westfield, NJ 07090
Tel: (908) 654-9860 Fax: (908) 654-9869

▼Superintendent of Schools (Interim) **Roger Jinks, Sr.** .... (908) 654-9865
School Business Administrator **Karen Dunn** .... (908) 654-9860
Certification **Marilyn Perez** .... (908) 654-9863
Child Study Supervisor (Interim) **Sandra Gogerty** ...... (908) 654-9867
Education Program Development Specialist
Maria Mendez .... (908) 654-9860

Office of the Surrogate

Court House, Two Broad Street, 2nd Floor, Elizabeth, NJ 07207
Fax: (908) 351-9212 Internet: www.ucnj.org/surrogate

★Surrogate **James S. LaCorte** (D) .... (908) 527-4280
Term Expires: December 31, 2017
E-mail: jlacorte@ucnj.org
Education: Fordham 1969 BS
Deputy Surrogate **Jo Ann Schwab** .... (908) 527-4280
Special Deputy Surrogate **(Vacant)** .... (908) 527-4280

Union County Board of Elections

271 North Broad Street, Elizabeth, NJ 07208-3702
Tel: (908) 527-4123 Fax: (908) 527-4127

▼Chair **John DeSimone** .... (908) 527-4121
Note: Reappointed on March 8, 2016 by Governor Christie, pending New Jersey Senate approval.
▼Secretary/Commissioner of Registration **Clara T. Harelik** .. (908) 527-4121
Note: Reappointed on March 8, 2016 by Governor Christie, pending New Jersey Senate approval.
Term Expires: 2016
▼Commissioner **Marie Oakie** .... (908) 527-4121
▼Commissioner **Mary Ellen Harris** .... (908) 527-4121
Term Expires: 2016
Administrator **Dennis S. Kobitz** .... (908) 527-4128
E-mail: dkobitz@ucnj.org
Deputy Administrator **Joanne "Joan" Arena** .... (908) 527-4279
E-mail: jarena@ucnj.org

County of Utah, Utah

100 East Center Street, Suite 2300, Provo, UT 84606
Tel: (801) 851-8000 E-mail: utahcnty@utahcounty.gov
Internet: utahcounty.gov

County Seat: Provo **Election Type:** Partisan **Year Founded:** 1852
Population: 575,205 (2015)

County Commission

100 East Center Street, Suite 2300, Provo, UT 84606
Tel: (801) 851-8100 Fax: (801) 851-8146
Internet: http://www.utahcounty.gov/Dept/commish/index.asp

★Chairman **Larry A. Ellertson** (R) .... (801) 851-8133
Term Expires: January 1, 2017
E-mail: larrye@utahcounty.gov
Education: Southern Utah BS
★Member **Greg James Graves** (R) .... (801) 851-8136
Term Expires: January 1, 2019
E-mail: GregG@utahcounty.gov
★Member **William "Bill" Lee** (R) .... (801) 851-8136
Term Expires: January 1, 2019
E-mail: WilliamL@utahcounty.gov

Agriculture Inspection Department

151 South University Avenue, Provo, UT 84601
Tel: (801) 851-7792 Fax: (801) 851-7797
Internet: http://www.utahcounty.gov/Dept/AgInsp/index.asp

Inspector **(Vacant)** .... (801) 851-7794

Community Development Department

51 South University Avenue, Suite 117, Provo, UT 84601
Tel: (801) 851-8343 Fax: (801) 851-8340
Internet: http://www.utahcounty.gov/Dept/comdev/index.asp

Director **Richard Nielson** .... (801) 851-8343

Building Inspection Division

51 South University Avenue, Suite 117, Provo, UT 84601
Tel: (801) 851-8342

Building Official **Steven D. Kitchen** .... (801) 851-8342

Fire Marshal

51 South University Avenue, Suite 120, Provo, UT 84601
Tel: (801) 851-8348

Fire Marshal **Jack Snow** .... (801) 851-8348
E-mail: jacks@utahcounty.gov

Planning and Zoning Division

51 South University Avenue, Suite 117, Provo, UT 84601
Tel: (801) 851-8343

Assistant Director **Bryce Armstrong** .... (801) 851-8343

Information Systems Department

100 East Center Street, Suite L100, Provo, UT 84606
Tel: (801) 851-8411
Internet: http://www.utahcounty.gov/Dept/IS/index.asp

Director **Neil Peterson** .... (801) 851-8411

Personnel Department

100 East Center Street, Suite 3800, Provo, UT 84606
Tel: (801) 851-8158 Fax: (801) 851-8166
Internet: http://www.utahcounty.gov/Dept/PubWrks/index.asp

Director **Lana Jensen** .... (801) 851-8158
E-mail: lanaj@utahcounty.gov
Assistant Director **Mark Brady** .... (801) 851-8158

Public Works Department

2855 South State Street, Provo, UT 84606
Tel: (801) 851-8600 Fax: (801) 851-8612
Internet: www.utahcountyonline.org/Dept/pubwrks/index.asp

Director **Richard Nielson** .... (801) 851-8600
Associate Director **Donald Nay** .... (801) 851-8062

Engineering and Parks Division

2855 South State Street, Provo, UT 84606
Tel: (801) 851-8261

Manager **John McMullin** .... (801) 851-8261

Roads Division

2855 South State Street, Provo, UT 84606
Tel: (801) 851-8605

Manager **Ken Bringhurst** .... (801) 851-8605

County Surveyor's Office

2855 South State Street, Provo, UT 84606
Tel: (801) 851-8669

★Surveyor **Gary Ratcliffe** .... (801) 851-8669
Term Expires: December 31, 2018
E-mail: gary@utahcounty.gov

COUNTIES

★Elected Official ▲Appointed by Legislature ▼Appointed by Governor ►Appointed by Board or Commission ●Appointed by Judge
■Appointed by Mayor △Appointed by Freeholders ▽Appointed by Supervisor ▷Appointed by County Executive ○Appointed by Council

Utah County Board of Health
Utah County Health and Justice Building, 151 South University Avenue, Suite 2500, Provo, UT 84601

Utah County Health Department [UCHD]
151 South University Avenue, Suite 2800, Provo, UT 84601
Tel: (801) 851-7012 Fax: (801) 851-7536
Internet: www.utahcountyonline.org/dept/health

Director/Health Officer **(Vacant)** .... (801) 851-7011
Deputy Director **Ralph L. Clegg** .... (801) 851-7016

Division of Environmental Health
151 South University Avenue, Suite 2600, Provo, UT 84601
Tel: (801) 851-7525 Fax: (801) 851-7521
Internet: www.utahcountyonline.org/dept/healthenvir

Director **Bryce Larsen** .... (801) 851-7519

Division of Health Promotion
151 South University Avenue, Suite 2700, Provo, UT 84601
Tel: (801) 851-7095 Fax: (801) 851-7508

Director **Eric Edwards** .... (801) 851-7097

County Assessor's Office
100 East Center Street, Room 1100, Provo, UT 84606
Tel: (801) 851-8244
Internet: http://www.utahcounty.gov/Dept/assess/index.asp

★County Assessor **Kris Poulson** (R).......... (801) 851-8275
Term Expires: January 1, 2019
E-mail: krisp@utahcounty.gov
Chief Deputy Assessor **Keven Ewell** .... (801) 851-8285

County Attorney's Office
100 East Center Street, Suite 2100, Provo, UT 84606
Tel: (801) 851-8026 Fax: (801) 851-8051
Internet: http://utahcounty.gov/dept/atty/index.asp

★County Attorney **Jeffrey R. "Jeff" Buhman** (R) .... (801) 851-8026
Term Expires: January 1, 2019
Education: BYU 1990; J Reuben Clark Law 1993 JD

County Clerk/Auditor's Office
100 East Center Street, Room 3600, Provo, UT 84606
Tel: (801) 851-8109 Fax: (801) 851-8232
Internet: http://www.utahcounty.gov/Dept/clerkaud/index.asp

★Clerk/Auditor **Bryan E. Thompson** (R) .... (801) 851-8109
Term Expires: January 1, 2019
E-mail: bryant@utahcounty.gov
Chief Deputy Clerk/Auditor **Scott C. Hogensen** .... (801) 851-8124
E-mail: scottch@utahcounty.gov

County Recorder's Office
100 East Center Street, Suite 1300, Provo, UT 84606
Tel: (801) 851-8179 Fax: (801) 851-8181
Internet: http://www.utahcounty.gov/Dept/Record/index.asp

★County Recorder **Jeff Smith** (R) .... (801) 851-8174
Term Expires: January 1, 2019
Chief Deputy Recorder **Andrea Allen** .... (801) 851-8202

County Sheriff's Office [UCSO]
3075 North Main, Spanish Fork, UT 84660
Tel: (801) 851-4000 Fax: (801) 851-4009
Internet: http://www.utahcounty.gov/Dept/Sheriff/Index.asp

★Sheriff **James O. "Jim" Tracy** (R) .... (801) 851-4000
Term Expires: January 1, 2019
E-mail: jimtr@utahcounty.gov
Under Sheriff **Mike Forshee** .... (801) 851-4000
E-mail: mikef@utahcounty.gov

Emergency Services Division
3075 North Main, Spanish Fork, UT 84660
Tel: (801) 851-4130

Commander **Wally Perschon** .... (801) 851-4130
E-mail: wallyp@utahcounty.gov

County Treasurer's Office
100 East Center Street, Suite 1200, Provo, UT 84606
Tel: (801) 851-8254 Fax: (801) 851-8265
Internet: http://www.utahcounty.gov/Dept/Treas/index.asp

★Treasurer **Kim Jackson** (R) .... (801) 851-8255
Term Expires: January 1, 2019
Deputy Treasurer **Cary McConnell** .... (801) 851-8254

County of Ventura, California

County Government Center, Administration Bldg., 800 S. Victoria Ave., Ventura, CA 93009
Tel: (805) 654-5000 (Information) Internet: www.ventura.org

County Seat: Ventura **Election Type:** Nonpartisan **Population:** 850,536 (2015)

Office of the Board of County Supervisors
County Government Center, Administration Bldg., 800 S. Victoria Ave., 4th Floor, Ventura, CA 93009

★Chair **Linda Parks** (District 2) .... (805) 214-2510
Term Expires: December 31, 2018 Fax: (805) 373-8396
E-mail: linda.parks@ventura.org
Education: Cal Poly San Luis Obispo 1980 BS
★Vice Chair **John C. Zaragoza** (District 5) .... (805) 654-2613
Term Expires: January 2, 2017 Fax: (805) 289-3215
E-mail: john.zaragoza@ventura.org
Education: La Verne 1978 BBA
★Supervisor **Steve Bennett** (District 1) .... (805) 654-2703
Term Expires: January 2, 2017 Fax: (805) 654-2226
E-mail: steve.bennett@ventura.org
★Supervisor **Kathy I. Long** (District 3) .... (805) 654-2276
Term Expires: January 2, 2017
E-mail: kathy.long@ventura.org
Education: Eastern Michigan BA
★Supervisor **Peter C. Foy** (District 4) .... (805) 955-2300
Term Expires: December 31, 2018
E-mail: supervisor.foy@ventura.org
Clerk to the Board **Brian Palmer** .... (805) 654-3398

Office of the County Counsel
County Government Center, Administration Bldg., 800 S. Victoria Ave., 4th Floor, Ventura, CA 93009-1830
Tel: (805) 654-2580 Fax: (805) 654-2185

▽County Counsel **Leroy Smith** .... (805) 654-2581
E-mail: leroy.smith@ventura.org
Education: San Diego 1982 JD
Chief Assistant County Counsel **Michael G. Walker** .... (805) 654-2596

★Elected Official ▲Appointed by Legislature ▼Appointed by Governor ▶Appointed by Board or Commission ●Appointed by Judge
■Appointed by Mayor △Appointed by Freeholders ▽Appointed by Supervisor ▷Appointed by County Executive ○Appointed by Council

Office of the County Counsel *continued*

Litigation Supervisor **Alberto Boada** . . . . (805) 654-2578

County Executive Office

County Government Center, Administration Building,
800 South Victoria Avenue, L#1940, Ventura, CA 93009
Fax: (805) 658-4500 E-mail: countyexecutiveofficer@ventura.org

▽County Executive Officer **Michael Powers** . . . . . . (805) 654-2681
E-mail: michael.powers@ventura.org
Education: UCLA 1986; Loyola Law 1989 JD

Executive Assistant **Veronica Gonzalez** . . . . . . (805) 654-2644
E-mail: veronica.gonzalez@ventura.org

Administration Division

County Government Center, Administration Building,
800 South Victoria Avenue, Ventura, CA 93009-2020
Tel: (805) 654-2864

Assistant County Executive Officer
J. Matthew "Matt" Carroll . . . . (805) 654-2864
E-mail: matt.carroll@ventura.org
Education: Cal State (Northridge) 1981 BS; USC 1985 MS

Finance Division

County Government Center, Administration Building,
800 South Victoria Avenue, Ventura, CA 93009-2020
Tel: (805) 662-6792

Assistant County Executive Officer/Chief Financial Officer **Catherine Rodriguez** . . . . (805) 654-5088
Education: UC Santa Barbara BA

Human Resources Division

County Government Center, Administration Building,
800 South Victoria Avenue, Suite 1970, Ventura, CA 93009-1940
Tel: (805) 654-5129 Fax: (805) 658-6244
Tel: (805) 654-2847 (Job Information Line) Internet: www.ventura.org/hr

Assistant County Executive Officer for Human Resources **Shawn Atin** . . . . (805) 654-2561
E-mail: shawn.atin@ventura.org

Office of the Agricultural Commissioner

555 Airport Way, Suite E, Camarillo, CA 93010
Tel: (805) 388-4343 Fax: (805) 388-4331

Agricultural Commissioner **Henry S. Gonzales** . . . . . (805) 388-4343
Chief Deputy Agricultural Commissioner **(Vacant)** . . . . (805) 388-4343
Deputy Agricultural Commissioner **Korinne Bell** . . . . (805) 388-4222
Deputy Agricultural Commissioner **Ryan Casey** . . . . (805) 933-2926
Deputy Agricultural Commissioner **Ellen Kragh** . . . . (805) 933-2926

Law Offices of the Public Defender

Hall of Justice, 800 S. Victoria Ave., Room 207, Ventura, CA 93009
Tel: (805) 654-2201 Fax: (805) 648-9220
Internet: www.pubdef.countyofventura.org

▽Public Defender **Stephen P. "Steve" Lipson** . . . . . (805) 654-2201
E-mail: steve.lipson@ventura.org
Education: UC Santa Barbara BA; Oregon 1984 JD

Assistant Public Defender **Todd Howeth** . . . . . . (805) 654-2844
Education: UCLA; Santa Clara U JD

Chief Deputy Public Defender, Appeals
Michael McMahon . . . . (805) 477-7114
Education: Hastings JD

Chief Deputy Public Defender, Felonies
John McNamara . . . . (805) 654-3022

Chief Deputy Public Defender, Juvenile/Mental Health
Rod Kodman . . . . (805) 654-3041

Chief Deputy Public Defender, Misdemeanors
Paul Drevenstedt . . . . (805) 654-2408

Chief Investigator **Ann Favor** . . . . (805) 654-3025

Fiscal/Administrative Manager **Aurora Lazaro** . . . . . (805) 654-2214
E-mail: aurora.lazaro@ventura.org

Area Agency on Aging

646 County Square Drive, Suite 100, Ventura, CA 93003
Tel: (805) 477-7300 Fax: (805) 477-7312
Internet: www.ventura.org/vcaaa

Director **Victoria Jump** . . . . (805) 477-7300
Grants Administrator **Marleen Canniff** . . . . . . (805) 477-7300

Airports Department

555 Airport Way, Suite B, Camarillo, CA 93010
Tel: (805) 388-4372 Fax: (805) 388-4366

Airports Director **Todd McNamee** . . . . . . (805) 388-4200
Airports Deputy Director **Jorge Rubio** . . . . . . (805) 388-4201
Camarillo Airport Manager **Nick Martino** . . . . . . (805) 388-4246
Oxnard Airport Manager **Brent Brown** . . . . . . (805) 382-3024
Fiscal Manager **Jamal Ghazaleh** . . . . . . (805) 388-4207
Projects Manager **Erin Powers** . . . . . . (805) 388-4205
Maintenance Supervisor **Col Louis J. Danner** . . . . . (805) 388-4206

Department of Animal Services

600 Aviation Dr., Camarillo, CA 93010-8594
Fax: (805) 388-4393 Internet: www.vcas.us

Director **Tara Diller** . . . . (805) 388-4355
Veterinarian **Heather Skogerson** . . . . . . (805) 388-4341

Ventura County Fire Department [VCFD]

Camarillo Airport, 165 Durley Ave., Camarillo, CA 93010-8586
Tel: (805) 389-9710 Fax: (805) 388-4364
Internet: http://fire.countyofventura.org/

Fire Chief **Mark Lorenzen** . . . . (805) 389-9704
E-mail: mark.lorenzen@ventura.org

Deputy Chief **Vaughan Miller** . . . . (805) 389-9703
E-mail: vaughan.miller@ventura.org

Assistant Chief, Emergency Services Bureau
Andy Ortega . . . . (805) 389-9708

Assistant Chief, Human Resources Bureau
Mike Milkovich . . . . (805) 389-9726
E-mail: mike.milkovich@ventura.org

Assistant Chief, Support Services Bureau **Steve Francis** . . (805) 389-9728
E-mail: steve.francis@ventura.org

Fire Marshal, Fire Prevention Bureau **Massoud Araghi** . . . (805) 389-9729
E-mail: massoud.araghi@ventura.org

Manager, Administrative and Fiscal Services Bureau
Tom Kasper . . . . (805) 389-9764

Fire Communications Manager **Steve McClellan** . . . . . (805) 389-9779

General Services Agency

County Government Center, 800 S. Victoria Ave., L#1000,
Ventura, CA 93009
Tel: (805) 654-3700 Fax: (805) 662-6537

Director **Paul S. Grossgold** . . . . (805) 654-3800
E-mail: paul.grossgold@ventura.org
Education: CUNY BS; Naval War MS

Chief Deputy Director/Facilities and Materials
Paul R. Young . . . . (805) 654-3806

Administrative Services Deputy Director
Greg Bergman . . . . (805) 654-3936
E-mail: greg.bergman@ventura.org Fax: (805) 662-6612

Fleet Services Manager **Peter Bednar** . . . . . . (805) 672-2040
E-mail: peter.bednar@ventura.org

Parks Deputy Director **Ronald L. "Ron" Van Dyck** . . . . . (805) 654-3945

Ventura County Harbor Department

3900 Pelican Way, Oxnard, CA 93035-4367
Tel: (805) 973-5950 Fax: (805) 382-3015

Director **Lyn Krieger** . . . . (805) 937-5950

COUNTIES

★ Elected Official ▲ Appointed by Legislature ▼ Appointed by Governor ▶ Appointed by Board or Commission ● Appointed by Judge
■ Appointed by Mayor △ Appointed by Freeholders ▽ Appointed by Supervisor ▷ Appointed by County Executive ○ Appointed by Council

COUNTIES

Health Care Agency [HCA]
2323 Knoll Dr., Ventura, CA 93003
Tel: (805) 677-5110 Fax: (805) 677-5116 Internet: www.vchca.org

Director **Barry Fisher** .... (805) 677-5272
Chief Deputy Director **(Vacant)** .... (805) 677-5280
Deputy Director and Ambulatory Care Administrator **(Vacant)** .... (805) 677-5290
Emergency Medical Services Administrator **Steve Carroll** .... (805) 981-5301
Chief Financial Officer/Fiscal Services **Catherine Rodriguez** .... (805) 677-5140
Education: UC Santa Barbara BA
Public Health Officer **Dr. Robert M. Levin** .... (805) 981-5101
Medical Examiner **(Vacant)** .... (805) 641-4400
Ventura County Medical Center Hospital Administrator **Kim Milstien** .... (805) 652-6058
Education: Western Ontario BA; La Sierra MBA
Alcohol and Drug Programs Director **Patrick Zarate** .... (805) 981-0016
Behavioral Health Director **Elaine Crandall** .... (805) 981-2214
Fax: (805) 981-6838
Public Health Director **Rigoberto Vargas** .... (805) 981-5101
Health Care Agency Information Technology Manager **Terry Theobald** .... (805) 652-5762
Human Resources Director **(Vacant)** .... (805) 677-5184

Human Services Agency [HSA]
855 Partridge Drive, Ventura, CA 93003
Fax: (805) 477-5385 Internet: www.vchsa.org

Director **Barry Zimmerman** .... (805) 477-5100

Information Technology Services
County Government Center, Hall of Administration, 800 S. Victoria Ave., L#1100, Ventura, CA 93009-1100
Tel: (805) 654-3540 Fax: (805) 654-3394

Chief Information Officer **Mike Pettit** .... (805) 654-2720
E-mail: mike.pettit@ventura.org
Assistant Chief Information Officer **Rodney Lanthier** .... (805) 654-3573
E-mail: rodney.lanthier@ventura.org
Deputy Chief Information Officer for Application Services **Kevin Coe** .... (805) 654-7658
E-mail: kevin.coe@ventura.org
Deputy Chief Information Officer for Network Services **Robert Connal** .... (805) 677-8777
Chief Information Security Officer **Robert Wood** .... (805) 654-5089
E-mail: robert.wood@ventura.org
Deputy Chief Information Officer for Technical Services **Kim Porter** .... (805) 654-3561
E-mail: kim.porter@ventura.org
Administrative Officer **Laura Barroso** .... (805) 654-5014
Deputy Chief Information Officer for Enterprise Systems and Services **Ed Altos** .... (805) 654-3122
Fiscal Manager **Rick Young** .... (805) 654-3896

Ventura County Probation Agency
County Government Center, Pre-Trial Detention Facility, 800 S. Victoria Ave., L#3200, Ventura, CA 93009-0001
Tel: (805) 654-2106 Fax: (805) 654-3544

▶ Director and Chief Probation Officer **Mark Varela** .... (805) 654-2100
E-mail: mark.varela@ventura.org
Program Assistant **Milane Acevedo** .... (805) 654-5003
E-mail: milane.acevedo@ventura.org
Chief Deputy, Business Services **Sandra Solorzano** .... (805) 654-2125
Chief Deputy, Institutions **Gina Johnson** .... (805) 654-2111
Chief Deputy, Probation Services **Patricia Olivares** .... (805) 654-2115
Homeland Security Contact **Cdr. JF Watch** .... (805) 981-5625
Chief Deputy, Administrative Services **Patrick Neil** .... (805) 654-2106

Public Works Agency
County Government Center, Administration Bldg., 800 S. Victoria Ave., L#1600, Ventura, CA 93009
Tel: (805) 654-2018 Fax: (805) 654-3952

Director **Jeff Pratt** .... (805) 654-2073
Central Services Director **Janice Turner** .... (805) 654-2084
E-mail: janice.turner@ventura.org
Engineering Director **Herbert Schwind** .... (805) 654-2096
E-mail: herbert.schwind@ventura.org
Transportation Director **David Fleisch** .... (805) 654-2077
Water and Sanitation Director **David J. Sasek** .... (805) 654-2075
E-mail: david.sasek@ventura.org
Watershed Protection District Director **Tully Clifford** .... (805) 654-2040
E-mail: tully.clifford@ventura.org

Resource Management Agency [RMA]
County Government Center, Administration Bldg., 800 S. Victoria Ave., LOC#1700, Ventura, CA 93009
Fax: (805) 654-2630 Internet: www.ventura.org/rma

Director **Christopher Stephens** .... (805) 654-2661
E-mail: chris.stephens@ventura.org Fax: (805) 654-2630
Building and Safety Building Official **Jim MacDonald** .... (805) 654-2787
Fax: (805) 648-9212
Environmental Health Director **William "Bill" Stratton** .... (805) 654-2818
Fax: (805) 654-2480
Planning Director **Kimberly L. "Kim" Prillhart** .... (805) 654-2481
Fax: (805) 654-2509
Code Compliance Director **Jim Delperdang** .... (805) 654-2446
Fax: (805) 654-5177

Ventura County Cooperative Extension
669 County Square Drive, Suite 100, Ventura, CA 93003-5401
Tel: (805) 645-1451 Fax: (805) 645-1474 E-mail: ceventura@ucdavis.edu
Internet: http://ceventura.ucdavis.edu/

County Director **Christopher Smith** .... (805) 662-6943

Ventura County Air Pollution Control District [VCAPCD]
669 County Square Drive, 2nd Floor, Ventura, CA 93003
Fax: (805) 645-1444 Internet: www.vcapcd.org

Air Pollution Control Officer **Michael Villegas** .... (805) 645-1400
Public Information Division Manager **Barbara L. Page** .... (805) 645-1415
E-mail: barbara@vcapcd.org

Ventura County Library [VCL]
646 County Square Drive, Suite 150, Ventura, CA 93003-0435
Fax: (805) 477-7340 Internet: www.vencolibrary.org

▶ Director **Jackie Y. Griffin** .... (805) 677-7150
E-mail: jackie.griffin@ventura.org
Education: Wisconsin MLIS

Law Library
County Government Center, Hall of Justice, 800 South Victoria Avenue, Ventura, CA 93009-2020
Fax: (805) 642-7177 E-mail: vcll@rain.org

Librarian **Dolly Moehrle** .... (805) 642-8982

Office of the Assessor
County Government Center, Administration Bldg., 800 S. Victoria Ave., Ventura, CA 93009-1270
Tel: (805) 654-2161 Fax: (805) 477-7144
Internet: http://assessor.countyofventura.org/

★ Assessor **Dan Goodwin** .... (805) 654-2161
Term Expires: January 8, 2019
E-mail: dan.goodwin@ventura.org

★ Elected Official ▲ Appointed by Legislature ▼ Appointed by Governor ▶ Appointed by Board or Commission ● Appointed by Judge
■ Appointed by Mayor △ Appointed by Freeholders ▽ Appointed by Supervisor ▷ Appointed by County Executive ○ Appointed by Council

Office of the Assessor *continued*

Chief Deputy Assessor **Frank Newell** . . . . (805) 447-1514
E-mail: frank.newell@ventura.org
Chief Deputy Assessor **Ken Kaiser** . . . . (805) 654-2220
E-mail: ken.kaiser@ventura.org

Office of the Auditor-Controller

800 S. Victoria Ave., Ventura, CA 93009-1540
Tel: (805) 654-3152 Internet: http://auditor.countyofventura.org
Fax: (805) 654-5081

★ Auditor-Controller **Jeffery S. Burgh** . . . . (805) 654-3151
Term Expires: January 5, 2019
E-mail: jeff.burgh@ventura.org
Assistant Auditor-Controller **Joanne McDonald** . . . . (805) 654-3191
E-mail: joanne.mcdonald@ventura.org
Chief Deputy Auditor-Controller **Valerie Barraza** . . . . (805) 654-3194
Chief Deputy Auditor-Controller **Barbara Beatty** . . . . (805) 654-3113
Chief Deputy Auditor-Controller **Jill Ward** . . . . (805) 654-3153
Chief Deputy Auditor-Controller **Michelle Yamaguchi** . . . (805) 654-3170

Office of the County Clerk and Recorder

County Government Center, Administration Bldg., 800 S. Victoria Ave., Main Plaza, Ventura, CA 93009-1260
Tel: (805) 654-2263 (County Clerk Division)
Tel: (805) 654-3665 (Recorder's Office)
Tel: (805) 654-2781 (Elections Division) Fax: (805) 654-2392
Internet: http://recorder.countyofventura.org/

★ County Clerk and Recorder **Mark A. Lunn** . . . . (805) 654-2266
Term Expires: January 5, 2019 Fax: (805) 654-2392
E-mail: mark.lunn@ventura.org
Assistant County Clerk and Recorder **Jim Becker** . . . . (805) 654-2293
E-mail: jim.becker@ventura.org
Assistant Registrar of Voters **Tracy D. Saucedo** . . . . (805) 654-2700
Fax: (805) 648-9200

Office of the District Attorney

Hall of Justice, 800 S. Victoria Ave., 3rd Floor, Ventura, CA 93009
Tel: (805) 654-2500 Fax: (805) 654-3850
Internet: http://da.countyofventura.org/

★ District Attorney **Gregory D. "Greg" Totten** . . . . (805) 654-2501
Term Expires: January 11, 2019
E-mail: greg.totten@ventura.org
Education: San Francisco State U; Pepperdine 1982 JD
Assistant District Attorney **Janice Maurizi** . . . . (805) 477-1638
Criminal Prosecutions Chief Deputy District Attorney
Michael K. "Mike" Frawley . . . . (805) 654-2548
Special Prosecutions Chief Deputy District Attorney
R. Miles Weiss . . . . (805) 662-1701
Bureau of Investigation Chief **Mike Baray** . . . . (805) 477-1614
E-mail: mike.baray@ventura.org
Deputy Chief Investigator **Kenneth Valentini** . . . . (805) 477-1614
E-mail: ken.valentini@ventura.org
Director of Fiscal, Administrative and Legislative Services **Stuart Gardner** . . . . (805) 477-1677
E-mail: stuart.gardner@ventura.org
Special Assistant District Attorney
Michael D. "Mike" Schwartz . . . . (805) 654-2719
Administrative Services Chief **Chuck Hughes** . . . . (805) 654-2532
E-mail: chuck.hughes@ventura.org

Office of the Sheriff

County Government Center, 800 South Victoria Avenue, L#3330, Ventura, CA 93009
Tel: (805) 654-2380 Fax: (805) 645-1391 Internet: www.vcsd.org

★ Sheriff **Geoff Dean** . . . . (805) 654-2315
Term Expires: January 6, 2019
Undersheriff, Detention Services/Special Services
Gary Pentis . . . . (805) 654-2701
E-mail: gary.pentis@ventura.org
Assistant Sheriff, Patrol Services/Support Services
Steve DeCesari . . . . (805) 494-8260
E-mail: steve.decesari@ventura.org
Human Resources Manager **Tracey Pirie** . . . . (805) 654-3637
E-mail: tracey.pirie@ventura.org

Office of the Treasurer-Tax Collector

County Government Center, Administration Building, 800 South Victoria Avenue, L#1290, Ventura, CA 93009-1290
Fax: (805) 654-2189

★ Treasurer-Tax Collector **Steven E. "Steve" Hintz** . . . . (805) 654-3744
Term Expires: January 6, 2019
E-mail: steven.hintz@ventura.org
Education: San Diego State 1968; Boalt Hall 1971 JD

Treasury and Tax Collections Department

County Government Center, Administration Bldg., 800 S. Victoria Ave., Main PLaza, Ventura, CA 93009-1290

Tax Collections Manager **Karen Carr** . . . . (805) 654-3741
E-mail: karen.carr@ventura.org
Assistant Treasurer-Tax Collector **Linda Catherine Le** . . . (805) 654-3771
E-mail: lindacatherine.le@ventura.org
Treasury Manager **Connie Mah** . . . . (805) 654-3746
Financial Analyst **Andrew Huey** . . . . (805) 654-3722

Ventura County Employees' Retirement Association [VCERA]

1190 S. Victoria Ave., Ste. 200, Ventura, CA 93003
Tel: (805) 339-4250 Fax: (805) 339-4269 E-mail: vcera.info@ventura.org

Administrator **Linda Webb** . . . . (805) 339-4250
Chief Financial Officer **Henry Solis** . . . . (805) 339-4250
Chief Operations Officer **Julie Stallings** . . . . (805) 339-4250
Retirement Benefits Manager **Shalini Nunna** . . . . (805) 339-4250
Retirement Benefits Manager **Vickie Williams** . . . . (805) 339-4250
Chief Investment Officer **Dan Gallagher** . . . . (805) 477-1553

Ventura County Office of Education

5189 Verdugo Way, Camarillo, CA 93012-8603
Tel: (805) 383-1900 Fax: (805) 383-1908 Internet: www.vcoe.org

★ Superintendent of Schools
Stanley C. "Stan" Mantooth . . . . (805) 383-1901
Term Expires: 2018
E-mail: mantooth@vcoe.org
Education: Cal State (Northridge) 1976 BA; Pepperdine 1991 MSBA
Fiscal and Administrative Services Associate Superintendent **Misty Key** . . . . (805) 383-1906
E-mail: mkey@vcoe.org
Deputy Superintendent **Roger Rice** . . . . (805) 383-1921
Technology Services Director **Steve Carr** . . . . (805) 383-1978
Fax: (805) 383-1997

★ Elected Official ▲ Appointed by Legislature ▼ Appointed by Governor ▶ Appointed by Board or Commission ● Appointed by Judge
■ Appointed by Mayor △ Appointed by Freeholders ▽ Appointed by Supervisor ▷ Appointed by County Executive ○ Appointed by Council

Ventura County Transportation Commission [VCTC]

950 County Square Drive, Suite 207, Ventura, CA 93003
Tel: (805) 642-1591 Fax: (805) 642-4860 Internet: www.goventura.org

Chair **Peter C. Foy** .... (805) 955-2300
Vice Chair **Keith Millhouse** .... (805) 517-6222
Executive Director **Darren Kettle** .... (805) 642-1591 ext. 123
Bus Transit Director **Martin Erickson** .... (805) 642-1591 ext. 110
Planning and Technology Director
Steve DeGeorge .... (805) 642-1591 ext. 103
E-mail: sdegeorge@goventura.org
Programming Director **Peter De Haan** .... (805) 642-1591 ext. 106
Finance Director **Sally DeGeorge** .... (805) 642-1591 ext. 112
Clerk of the Board/Public Information Officer
Donna Cole .... (805) 642-1591 ext. 101
E-mail: dcole@goventura.org

County of Volusia, Florida

Thomas C. Kelly Administration Center, 123 West Indiana Avenue,
DeLand, FL 32720-4612
Internet: www.volusia.org

County Seat: DeLand **Election Type:** Nonpartisan
Population: 517,887 (2015)

Office of the County Council

Thomas C. Kelly Administration Center, 123 W. Indiana Ave., Room 301,
DeLand, FL 32720-4612
Tel: (386) 736-5920 Fax: (386) 822-5707
Internet: www.volusia.org/countycouncil

★ Chair **Jason Davis** (At-Large) .... (386) 736-5920
Term Expires: December 31, 2016 Fax: (386) 943-7028
E-mail: jdavis@volusia.org
★ Vice Chair **Pat Patterson** (District 1) .... (386) 740-5224
Term Expires: December 31, 2016 Fax: (386) 626-6557
E-mail: ppatterson@volusia.org
Education: Florida Atlantic 1976 BA, 1978 MEd
★ Member **Joshua Wagner** (District 2) .... (386) 304-5535
Term Expires: December 31, 2016 Fax: (386) 304-5536
E-mail: jwagner@volusia.org
★ Member **Deborah Denys** (District 3) .... (386) 740-5224
Term Expires: December 31, 2018 Fax: (386) 626-6557
E-mail: ddenys@volusia.org
★ Member **Doug Daniels** (District 4) .... (386) 736-5920
Term Expires: December 31, 2016 Fax: (386) 626-6557
E-mail: ddaniels@volusia.org
★ Member **Fred Lowry, Jr.** (District 5) .... (386) 736-5920
Term Expires: December 31, 2018 Fax: (386) 943-7028
★ Member **Joyce Cusack** (At-Large) .... (386) 740-5224
Term Expires: December 31, 2018 Fax: (386) 626-6557
E-mail: jcusack@volusia.org
Education: St Leo Col 1984 BA

Office of the County Attorney

Thomas C. Kelly Administration Center, 123 West Indiana Avenue,
Suite 301, DeLand, FL 32720
Fax: (386) 736-5990

○ County Attorney **Daniel D. Eckert** .... (386) 736-5950
E-mail: deckert@volusia.org

Office of the County Manager

Thomas C. Kelly Administration Center, 123 W. Indiana Ave., Room 301,
DeLand, FL 32720-4612
Tel: (386) 736-5920 Fax: (386) 822-5707

○ County Manager/Clerk of the Council
James T. "Jim" Dinneen .... (386) 740-5133
E-mail: jdinneen@volusia.org Fax: (386) 822-5707
Education: Dayton BPA, MPA; Virginia Tech MURP
Executive Assistant **Marja Kolomyski** .... (386) 740-5133
E-mail: mkolomyski@volusia.org Fax: (386) 943-7020
Deputy County Manager **Mary Anne Connors** .... (386) 822-5060
E-mail: mconnors@volusia.org Fax: (386) 822-5707
Deputy County Manager **Donna de Peyster** .... (386) 943-7054
E-mail: ddepeyster@volusia.org Fax: (386) 822-5780
Deputy Clerk of the Council **Marcy A. Zimmerman** ..... (386) 736-5920
E-mail: mzimmerman@volusia.org Fax: (386) 822-5707
Community Information Director
Joanne Magley .... (386) 822-5062 ext. 12689
E-mail: jmagley@volusia.org Fax: (386) 822-5072
Internal Auditor **(Vacant)** .... (386) 736-5920
Fax: (386) 822-5707

Office of the Deputy County Manager and Chief Financial Officer

Tel: (386) 943-7054

Deputy County Manager and Chief Financial Officer
Donna de Peyster .... (386) 943-7054

Community Services Department

Thomas C. Kelly Administration Center, 123 W. Indiana Ave.,
DeLand, FL 32720-4612
Fax: (386) 740-5101

Director **Dona Butler** .... (386) 943-7029
E-mail: ddbutler@volusia.org

Office of Extension (University of Florida)

3100 East New York Avenue, DeLand, FL 32724-6497
Fax: (386) 822-5767 Internet: www.volusia.org/extension

Director **David T. Griffis** .... (386) 822-5778

Community Assistance Division

110 West Rich Avenue, DeLand, FL 32720
Fax: (386) 740-5112

Director **Dona DeMarsh Butler** .... (386) 943-7039
E-mail: ddemarshbutler@volusia.org
Manager, Housing and Grants Administration
Diana Phillips .... (386) 736-5955 ext. 2566

Library Services

Library Operations Center, 1290 Indian Lake Rd.,
Daytona Beach, FL 32124
Fax: (386) 248-1746

Director **Lucinda Colee** .... (386) 248-1745
E-mail: llcolee@volusia.org

Parks, Recreation and Culture Division

202 North Florida Avenue, DeLand, FL 32720-4618
Fax: (386) 943-7012

Director **Tim Baylie** .... (386) 736-5953

Transportation/VOTRAN Services

950 Big Tree Rd., South Daytona, FL 32119
Fax: (386) 756-7487 Internet: www.volusia.org/votran

General Manager **Steven Sherrer** .... (386) 756-7496
Assistant General Manager, Operations and Maintenance
Elizabeth "Liz" Suchsland .... (386) 756-7496
E-mail: esuchsland@co.volusia.fl.us
Assistant General Manager, Planning, Marketing and
Customer Services **Heather Blanck** .... (386) 756-7496

★ Elected Official ▲ Appointed by Legislature ▼ Appointed by Governor ▶ Appointed by Board or Commission ● Appointed by Judge
■ Appointed by Mayor △ Appointed by Freeholders ▽ Appointed by Supervisor ▷ Appointed by County Executive ○ Appointed by Council

Veterans' Services Division
123 West Indiana Avenue, Room 100, DeLand, FL 32720-4612

Director **Jeffrey L. Bumb** .... (386) 740-5102
123 West Indiana Avenue, Room 100, DeLand, FL 32720 Fax: (386) 740-5101

Senior Veterans Counselor **Tim Algiere** .... (386) 775-5205
775 Harley Strickland Boulevard, Suite 104, Orange City, FL 32763 Fax: (386) 775-5207

Senior Veterans Counselor **Raymond Allen** .... (386) 254-4646
250 North Beach Street, Room 102, Daytona Beach, FL 32114 Fax: (386) 239-7764

Counselor **Aly Rivers** .... (386) 740-5102
123 W. Indiana Ave., Room 100, DeLand, FL 32720 Fax: (386) 740-5101

Counselor **Frederick Spano** .... (386) 740-5102
123 W. Indiana Ave., DeLand, FL 32720 Fax: (386) 740-5101

Counselor **Pantos Ellis-Pettus** .... (386) 254-4646
250 North Beach Street, Room 102, Daytona Beach, FL 32114 Fax: (386) 239-7764

Volusia County Ocean Center
101 N. Atlantic Ave., Daytona Beach, FL 32118
Tel: (800) 858-6444 (Information) Tel: (386) 254-4500 (Information)
Fax: (386) 254-4512 Internet: www.oceancenter.com

Director **Donald C. Poor** .... (386) 254-4500

Financial and Administrative Services
Thomas C. Kelly Administration Center, 123 West Indiana Avenue, Room 300, DeLand, FL 32720
Fax: (386) 822-5780

Business Services Director **Rhonda C. Orr** .... (386) 736-5938

Accounting Director **Ryan Ossowski** .... (386) 736-5933 ext. 2687
Fax: (386) 822-5042

Central Services Director **George Baker** .... (386) 254-1595
Fax: (386) 254-1504

Information Technology Director **Kim Westberry** .... (386) 736-5922
Fax: (386) 822-5728

Investments **Myriam Lemay** .... (386) 736-5933 ext. 2261
Education: Florida 1981 BA; Texas 1983 MPA Fax: (386) 822-5042

Management and Budget Director **Tammy Bong** .... (386) 736-5934
Fax: (386) 822-5707

Human Resources Director **Tom Motes** .... (386) 736-5951
Fax: (386) 740-5149

Purchasing Director **Jeaniene Jennings** .... (386) 736-5935
Fax: (386) 736-5972

Revenue Director **Rhonda C. Orr** .... (386) 736-5938
Fax: (386) 822-5729

Office of the Deputy County Manager
123 West Indiana Avenue, DeLand, FL 32720

Deputy County Manager **George Recktenwald** .... (386) 736-5920
E-mail: grecktenwald@volusia.org

Public Protection Department
125 West New York Avenue, Room 282, DeLand, FL 32724
Fax: (386) 740-5283

Director **Terry Sanders** .... (386) 258-4025
Education: Central Florida BA, MPA

Office of the Medical Examiner
1360 Indian Lake Rd., Daytona Beach, FL 32124-1001
Fax: (386) 258-4061

Director **Marie A. Herrmann** .... (386) 258-4060 ext. 1118

Animal Services Division
29 Keyton Dr., Daytona Beach, FL 32124

Director **Sergio Pacheco** .... (386) 740-5241

Beach Safety Division
515 South Atlantic, Daytona Beach, FL 32114
Tel: (386) 239-6414 Fax: (386) 239-6420

Director **Mark Swanson** .... (386) 239-6414

Corrections Division
1300 Red John Dr., Daytona Beach, FL 32124
Fax: (386) 323-3504

Director **Marilyn Chandler Ford** .... (386) 323-3505

Emergency Management Services Division
Emergency Operations Center, 49 Keyton Dr., Daytona Beach, FL 32124
Fax: (386) 248-1742

Director **James A. "Jim" Judge** .... (386) 252-4900
E-mail: jjudge@volusia.org

Fire Services Division
125 West New York Avenue, DeLand, FL 32720
Fax: (386) 822-5025

Director **Jeff Smith** .... (386) 258-4025

Public Works Department
Thomas C. Kelly Administration Center, 123 West Indiana Avenue, DeLand, FL 32720
Tel: (386) 736-5965 Fax: (386) 740-5184

Director **John Angiulli** .... (386) 736-5965

Operations Manager **John Gamble** .... (386) 736-5965
E-mail: jgamble@volusia.org

Activity Project Manager **Arden Fontaine** .... (386) 736-5965

Coastal Division
700 Catalina Drive, Suite 121, Daytona Beach, FL 32114
Fax: (386) 248-8075

Director **Jessica Winterwerp** .... (386) 248-8072

Engineering and Construction Division
123 West Indiana Avenue, DeLand, FL 32720

Director/County Engineer **Gerald Brinton** .... (386) 736-5967
E-mail: gbrinton@volusia.org

Mosquito Control Division
801 South Street, New Smyrna Beach, FL 32168
Tel: (386) 424-2920 Fax: (386) 424-2924

Director **Jim McNelly** .... (386) 424-2920

Road and Bridge Division
2560 West State Road 44, DeLand, FL 32720
Fax: (386) 736-5145

Director **Judy Grim** .... (386) 822-6422
E-mail: jgrim@volusia.org

Solid Waste Division [SWD]
3151 East New York Avenue, DeLand, FL 32724
Tel: (386) 947-2952 Fax: (386) 947-2955

Director **Leonard Marion** .... (386) 943-7889

Recycling Coordinator **Regina Montgomery** .... (386) 943-7889

Traffic Engineering Division
123 West Indiana Avenue, DeLand, FL 32720
Tel: (386) 736-5968 Fax: (386) 740-5242

Traffic Engineer **Jon Cheney** .... (386) 736-5968
E-mail: jcheney@volusia.org

Water Resources and Utilities Division
Thomas C. Kelly Administration Center, 123 W. Indiana Ave., DeLand, FL 32720
Tel: (386) 943-7027 Fax: (386) 740-5162

Director **Michael Ulrich** .... (386) 943-7027

Growth and Resource Management Department
Thomas C. Kelly Administration Center, 123 W. Indiana Ave., DeLand, FL 32720-4604

Director **Kelli McGee** .... (386) 740-5210
E-mail: kmcgee@co.volusia.fl.us Fax: (386) 822-5727
Education: Virginia 1988 BA; George Washington 1997 JD

(continued on next page)

★ Elected Official ▲ Appointed by Legislature ▼ Appointed by Governor ▶ Appointed by Board or Commission ● Appointed by Judge
■ Appointed by Mayor △ Appointed by Freeholders ▽ Appointed by Supervisor ▷ Appointed by County Executive ○ Appointed by Council

Growth and Resource Management Department *continued*

Building and Zoning Director **Mike Nelson** . . . (386) 626-6591 ext. 12083
Fax: (386) 740-5297

Code Administration Manager **Bryan Jiles** . . . . (386) 736-5925
Fax: (386) 626-6549

Comprehensive Planning Manager **Susan Jackson** . . . . . . (386) 736-5959
Fax: (386) 740-5148

Planning and Development Services Director
Palmer M. Panton . . . . (386) 736-5942
Fax: (386) 740-5121

Operations Manager **Tara Boujoulian** . . . . (386) 736-5924
Fax: (386) 943-7096

Building Official **Joe Levrault** . . . . (386) 822-5739
Fax: (386) 626-6560

Environmental Management Department
Thomas C. Kelly Administration Center, 123 W. Indiana Ave., DeLand, FL 32720
Tel: (386) 736-5927 Fax: (386) 740-5193

Director **Ginger Adair** . . . . (386) 736-5927

Aviation and Economic Resources
Daytona Beach International Airport, 700 Catalina Drive, Suite 300, Daytona Beach, FL 32114
Tel: (386) 248-8069 (Operations/Security) Fax: (386) 248-8038

Director **Fredrick Brennan "Rick" Karl, Jr.** . . . . (386) 248-8030 ext. 8318
Education: Florida State 1977 BS; Florida 1981 JD

Aviation Division
700 Catalina Drive, Daytona Beach, FL 32114
Fax: (386) 248-8038 Internet: www.flydaytonafirst.com

Director of Airport Services **Pat O'Brien** . . . . (386) 248-8069

Department of Economic Development
700 Catalina Drive, Suite 200, Daytona Beach, FL 32114
Fax: (386) 328-4761 E-mail: doed@volusia.org
Internet: www.floridabusiness.org

Director **Rob Ehrhardt** . . . . (386) 248-8048
E-mail: rehrhardt@volusia.org

Office of the Clerk of the Circuit Court

101 North Alabama Avenue, DeLand, FL 32724
Fax: (386) 822-5711 E-mail: clerk@clerk.org

Clerk of the Circuit Court **Diane M. Matousek** . . . . (386) 736-5915
Term Expires: November 2016
E-mail: clerk@clerk.org

Office of the Elections Supervisor

125 West New York Avenue, DeLand, FL 32720-4208
Fax: (386) 943-7073 E-mail: elections@co.volusia.fl.us
Internet: www.volusia.org/elections

★Elections Supervisor **Ann McFall** . . . . (386) 736-5930
Term Expires: December 31, 2016
E-mail: amcfall@volusia.org

Office of the Property Appraiser

Thomas C. Kelly Administration Center, 123 W. Indiana Ave., Room 102, DeLand, FL 32720-4270
Fax: (386) 822-5063 Internet: www.volusia.org/property

★Property Appraiser **Morgan B. Gilreath, Jr.** . . . . (386) 736-5901
Term Expires: January 5, 2017
E-mail: mgilreath@co.volusia.fl.us

Chief Deputy **Janice K. Cornelius** . . . . (386) 736-5901
E-mail: jcornelius@co.volusia.fl.us

Office of the Property Appraiser *continued*

Operations Manager **Mary Ellen Chiarelli** . . . . (386) 736-5901
E-mail: mchiarelli@co.volusia.fl.us

Office of the Public Defender (Seventh Judicial Circuit)

251 North Ridgewood Avenue, Daytona Beach, FL 32114
Tel: (386) 239-7730 Fax: (386) 239-7731 Internet: www.pd7.org

★Public Defender **James S. Purdy** . . . . (386) 239-7730
Term Expires: January 2, 2017 Fax: (386) 239-7702

Chief Assistant Public Defender **George D.E. Burden** . . . . (386) 239-7730
Fax: (386) 239-7702

Administrative Director **Shannon N. DiBella** . . . . (386) 239-7730
Fax: (386) 239-7702

Office of the Sheriff

P.O. Box 569, DeLand, FL 32721-0569
Fax: (386) 822-5074 Internet: www.volusia.org/sheriff
E-mail: sphillips@vcso.us

★Sheriff **Ben F. Johnson** . . . . (386) 736-5961
Term Expires: December 31, 2016
E-mail: bjohnson@vcso.us
Education: Rollins 1981 BS

Communications Director **John M. Balloni** . . . . (386) 736-5999
Fax: (386) 254-1525

County of Wake, North Carolina

301 South McDowell Street, Raleigh, NC 27601
P.O. Box 550, Raleigh, NC 27602
Tel: (919) 856-6160 Internet: www.wakegov.com

County Seat: Raleigh **Election Type:** Partisan **Population:** 1,024,198 (2015)

Office of the Board of County Commissioners

301 South McDowell Street, Raleigh, NC 27601
Tel: (919) 856-6160 Fax: (919) 856-5699
E-mail: commissioners@wakegov.com
Internet: www.wakegov.com/commissioners

★Chair **Dr. James P. West** (D-District 5) . . . . (919) 856-5573
Term Expires: December 5, 2016
E-mail: james.west@wakegov.com
Education: North Carolina A&T 1964 BS; North Carolina State 1971 MEd, 1981 DEd

★Vice Chair **Sig Hutchinson** (D-District 1) . . . . (919) 856-5575
Term Expires: December 1, 2018

★Commissioner **Matt Calabria** (D-District 2) . . . . (919) 856-5576
Term Expires: December 1, 2018

★Commissioner **Jessica Holmes** (D-District 3) . . . . (919) 856-5579
Term Expires: December 1, 2018

★Commissioner **Caroline Sullivan** (D-District 4) . . . . (919) 856-5574
Term Expires: December 2016
E-mail: caroline.sullivan@wakegov.com

★Commissioner **Betty Lou Ward** (D-District 6) . . . . (919) 856-5566
Term Expires: December 5, 2016
E-mail: bward@wakegov.com

★Commissioner **John Burns** (D-District 7) . . . . (919) 856-5577
Term Expires: December 1, 2018

▶Clerk to the Board **Denise Hogan** . . . . (919) 856-5565

★Elected Official ▲Appointed by Legislature ▼Appointed by Governor ▶Appointed by Board or Commission ●Appointed by Judge
■Appointed by Mayor △Appointed by Freeholders ▽Appointed by Supervisor ▷Appointed by County Executive ○Appointed by Council

Office of the County Attorney

The Justice Center, 301 South McDowell Street, Raleigh, NC 27601
P.O. Box 550, Raleigh, NC 27602
Fax: (919) 856-5504

County Attorney **Scott W. Warren** .... (919) 856-5500
E-mail: swarren@wakegov.com
Education: North Carolina BA; Wake Forest JD
Deputy County Attorney **Roger A. Askew** .... (919) 856-5500
E-mail: roger.askew@wakegov.com
Deputy County Attorney
Mary Elizabeth "Beth" Smerko .... (919) 856-5500
E-mail: beth.smerko@wakegov.com

Office of the County Manager

301 South McDowell Street, Raleigh, NC 27601
Fax: (919) 856-6168

▶ County Manager **James K. "Jim" Hartmann** .... (919) 856-6160
Education: Central Florida BA, 1993 MPA
Deputy County Manager and Chief Financial Officer
Johnna L. Rogers .... (919) 856-5480
E-mail: johnna.rogers@wakegov.com
Deputy County Manager for Operations **David Ellis** ...... (919) 856-5482
Intergovernmental Relations Manager **Chris Dillon** .... (919) 856-6160
Public Relations and Communications Director
Dara Deni .... (919) 856-6160

Budget Department

337 South Salisbury Street, Raleigh, NC 27601
P.O. Box 550, Raleigh, NC 27602
Tel: (919) 856-5480 Fax: (919) 856-6880
Internet: www.wakegov.com/departments/finance.htm

Director **Michelle L. Venditto** .... (919) 856-9374
E-mail: michelle.venditto@wakegov.com
Budget Policy Director **Renee Pascal** .... (919) 857-3909

Community Services Department

P.O. Box 550, Raleigh, NC 27602
Fax: (919) 743-4853

Director **Frank Cope** .... (919) 856-5562
E-mail: fcope@wakegov.com
Planning, Development and Inspections Director
Tim Maloney .... (919) 856-6678

Geographic Information Services

337 South Salisbury Street, Raleigh, NC 27602
PO Box 550, Raleigh, NC 27602
Tel: (919) 856-6360 Fax: (919) 856-6389

Director **Charles Friddle** .... (919) 856-6375
Addressing Supervisor **David Hunt** .... (919) 856-6373

Parks, Recreation and Open Space

Wake County Office Bldg., 10th Fl., 337 S. Salisbury St., Raleigh, NC 27602
PO Box 550, Ste. 1000, Raleigh, NC 27602
Fax: (919) 743-4853

Director **Chris Snow** .... (919) 842-2727

Veterans Services Office

3000 Falstaff Road, Raleigh, NC 27610
Tel: (919) 212-8387 Internet: www.wakegov.com/veterans

Director **Douggy Johnson II** .... (919) 212-8387

Wake County Public Libraries [WCPL]

4001-E Carya Dr., Raleigh, NC 27610-2914
Fax: (919) 250-1097 Internet: www.wakegov.com/libraries

Director **Michael J. "Mike" Wasilick** .... (919) 250-4532
E-mail: mwasilick@wakegov.com Fax: (919) 250-1209

Wake County Public Libraries *continued*

Administrative Secretary **Yvonne Smith** .... (919) 250-1206
E-mail: ysmith@wakegov.com
Computer Operations Manager **Kevin Smith** .... (919) 250-1108
E-mail: kevin.smith@wakegov.com

Department of Emergency Medical Services [EMS]

Public Safety Center, 331 South McDowell Street, Raleigh, NC 27601
Fax: (919) 856-6209

Emergency Medical Services Director (Interim)
Christopher Colangelo .... (919) 856-7135
Medical Director (Interim) **Dr. Jefferson Williams** ...... (919) 856-6020
Education: North Carolina BS, MD, MPH
Deputy Medical Director **Dr. Jefferson Williams** .... (919) 856-6020
Education: North Carolina BS, MD, MPH

Facilities Design and Construction

P.O. Box 550, Raleigh, NC 27602
Fax: (919) 856-6355

Director **Mark Forestieri** .... (919) 856-6353
Project Manager **Patrick T. McHugh** .... (919) 856-6357
E-mail: patrick.mchugh@wakegov.com
Project Manager **John W. Roberson** .... (919) 856-6365
E-mail: john.roberson@wakegov.com

Finance Department

337 South Salisbury Street, Raleigh, NC 27601

Financial Director **Susan S. McCullen** .... (919) 856-6141
Debt and Capital Director **Nicole D. Kreiser** .... (919) 664-5531
Purchasing Director **Thomas G. "Tom" Wester** .... (919) 856-6153
E-mail: twester@wakegov.com

Emergency Management

Public Safety Center, 331 South McDowell Street, Raleigh, NC 27601
Fax: (919) 856-6236 (Fire and Rescue)
Fax: (919) 856-7046 (Emergency Management)
Internet: www.wakegov.com/fire Internet: www.wakegov.com/em

Emergency Management Director
Joshua J. "Josh" Creighton .... (919) 856-6485
E-mail: joshua.creighton@wakegov.com Fax: (919) 856-7046

Fire Services Division

Public Safety Center, 331 South McDowell Street, Raleigh, NC 27601

Fire/Rescue Director and Fire Marshal
Nick Campasano .... (919) 856-6349
E-mail: nicholas.campasano@wakegov.com Fax: (919) 856-6236
Deputy Director/Chief of Operations **Darrell Alford** ...... (919) 856-6487
E-mail: darrell.alford@wakegov.com
Chief Deputy Fire Marshal **Charlie Johnson** .... (919) 856-5519
E-mail: cejohnson@wakegov.com

General Services Administration

401 Capital Blvd., Raleigh, NC 27603
Tel: (919) 856-5777 Fax: (919) 856-6478

Administrator **David L. "Dave" Goodwin** .... (919) 856-5726
E-mail: dgoodwin@wakegov.com
Deputy Administrator **Kelli A. Braunbach** .... (919) 856-5745
E-mail: kbraunbach@wakegov.com

Human Services Department

P.O. Box 46833, Raleigh, NC 27620
Tel: (919) 212-7000 Fax: (919) 212-7309

Director **Regina Petteway** .... (919) 212-7302

COUNTIES

★ Elected Official ▲ Appointed by Legislature ▼ Appointed by Governor ▶ Appointed by Board or Commission ● Appointed by Judge
■ Appointed by Mayor △ Appointed by Freeholders ▽ Appointed by Supervisor ▷ Appointed by County Executive ○ Appointed by Council

Clinical/Medical
Fax: (919) 250-1128
Director **Kimberly McDonald** .... (919) 250-3813

Operations
Fax: (919) 212-7285
Deputy Director **C. Robert Sorrels** .... (919) 212-0494
E-mail: csorrels@wakegov.com

Family Support Services
Fax: (919) 743-4782
Manager **Giang Le** .... (919) 212-1282

Information Services
P.O. Box 550, Raleigh, NC 27601
Tel: (919) 856-5800 Fax: (919) 856-5630
Chief Information Officer **Bill Greeves** .... (919) 856-5800
E-mail: bill.greeves@wakegov.com
Assistant Director, Applications **Angela Strickland** ...... (919) 856-6082
E-mail: angela.strickland@wakegov.com
Assistant Director, Technical Information **John Higgins** .. (919) 856-5800
E-mail: john.higgins@wakegov.com

Human Resources Department
P.O. Box 550, Raleigh, NC 27602
Fax: (919) 856-6256
Director **Angela Crawford** .... (919) 856-6090
E-mail: angela.crawford@wakegov.com

Revenue Department
One Bank of America Plaza, 421 Fayetteville Street, Suite 200, Raleigh, NC 27602
Fax: (919) 856-7128 Internet: www.wakegov.com/tax
▸ Director **Marcus Kinrade** .... (919) 856-5400
E-mail: marcus.kinrade@wakegov.com Fax: (919) 743-4713
Administrative Services Coordinator **Eularia Glenn** .... (919) 856-5400
E-mail: eglenn@wakegov.com Fax: (919) 743-4728
Appraisal/Collection Manager **Ken McArtor** .... (919) 856-5400
E-mail: kmcartor@wakegov.com
Appraisal/Collection Manager **Dan McCarty** .... (919) 856-5400
Fax: (919) 743-4713
Appraisal/Collection Manager **Gwendolyn Nicholson** .... (919) 856-5400
E-mail: gnicholson@wakegov.com Fax: (919) 743-4713
Systems and Training Administrator **Susan Campen** .... (919) 856-5400
E-mail: scampen@wakegov.com Fax: (919) 743-4713

Raleigh/Wake City-County Bureau of Identification [CCBI]
3301 Hamond Road, Raleigh, NC 24603
Fax: (919) 255-7337 Internet: www.wakegov.com/ccbi
Director **Salvatore J. "Sam" Pennica** .... (919) 255-7370
E-mail: sam.pennica@wakegov.com
Deputy Director **Tim Anguish** .... (919) 255-7355
Deputy Director **Kathy Edington** .... (919) 255-7345
Deputy Director **Andy Parker** .... (919) 255-7344
E-mail: andy.parker@wakegov.com
Deputy Director **Tammy Malinowski** .... (919) 255-7327
E-mail: tammy.malinowski@wakegov.com

Office of the Register of Deeds
P.O. Box 1897, Raleigh, NC 27602-1897
300 South Frostburg Street, Suite 700, Raleigh, NC 27602
Fax: (919) 856-5467
★ Register of Deeds **Laura M. Riddick** (R) .... (919) 856-5460
Term Expires: December 31, 2016
E-mail: lriddick@wakegov.com

Office of the Sheriff
330 South Salisbury Street, Raleigh, NC 27601
P.O. Box 550, Raleigh, NC 27602
Fax: (919) 856-6874 Internet: www.wakegov.com/sheriff
★ Sheriff **Donnie E. Harrison** (R) .... (919) 856-6900
Term Expires: December 4, 2018
E-mail: donnie.harrison@wakegov.com

Wake County Board of Elections
337 South Salisbury Street, Raleigh, NC 27601
P.O. Box 695, Raleigh, NC 27602-0695
Fax: (919) 856-5864 Internet: www.wakegov.com/elections
Director **Gary Sims** .... (919) 856-6240

Wake County Public School System [WCPSS]
3600 Wake Forest Road, Raleigh, NC 27609
P.O. Box 28041, Raleigh, NC 27611-8041
Tel: (919) 431-7400 (Customer Service) Fax: (919) 850-1819
Internet: www.wcpss.net

Board of Education
3600 Wake Forest Road, Raleigh, NC 27609
Internet: www.wcpss.net/board
★ Chair **Christine Kushner** (District 6) .... (919) 850-1693
Term Expires: November 30, 2016
3513 Lubbock Drive, Raleigh, NC 27612
★ Vice Chair **Tom Benton** (District 1) .... (919) 431-7400
Term Expires: November 30, 2017
★ Member **Monika Johnson-Hostler** (District 2) .... (919) 431-7325
Term Expires: November 30, 2017
1817 West Academy Street, Fuquay Varina, NC 27526
★ Member **Kevin L. Hill** (District 3) .... (919) 850-8867
Term Expires: November 30, 2016
300 Paprika Court, Raleigh, NC 27614
E-mail: klhill@wcpss.net
★ Member **Keith Sutton** (District 4) .... (919) 431-7327
Term Expires: November 30, 2016
E-mail: ksutton@wcpss.net
★ Member **Jim Martin** (District 5) .... (919) 850-1693
Term Expires: November 30, 2016
324 South Boylan Avenue, Raleigh, NC 27603
★ Member **Zora Felton** (District 7) .... (919) 431-7330
Term Expires: November 30, 2017
8857 Woody Hill Road, Raleigh, NC 27613
★ Member **Susan Evans** (District 8) .... (919) 850-1693
Term Expires: November 30, 2016
7800 Secluded Acres Road, Apex, NC 27523
★ Member **Bill Fletcher** (R-District 9) .... (919) 431-7332
Term Expires: November 30, 2017
5625 Dillard Drive, Cary, NC 27518
E-mail: bfletcher@wcpss.net
Education: North Carolina State 1971 BS

Office of the Superintendent
3600 Wake Forest Road, Raleigh, NC 27609
Internet: www.wcpss.net/superintendent
Superintendent **Dr. Jim Merrill** .... (919) 431-7563

Office of the District Attorney
P.O. Box 31, Raleigh, NC 27602
Tel: (919) 792-5000 Fax: (919) 792-5003
★ District Attorney **Nancy Lorrin Freeman** .... (919) 792-5000
Term Expires: January 2019

★ Elected Official ▲ Appointed by Legislature ▼ Appointed by Governor ▶ Appointed by Board or Commission ● Appointed by Judge
■ Appointed by Mayor △ Appointed by Freeholders ▽ Appointed by Supervisor ▷ Appointed by County Executive ○ Appointed by Council

County of Washoe, Nevada

P.O. Box 11130, Reno, NV 89520
Internet: www.washoecounty.us

County Seat: Reno **Election Type:** Partisan **Year Incorporated:** 1861
Population: 446,903 (2015)

Board of County Commissioners

Building A, 1001 East 9th Street, Reno, NV 89512
P.O. Box 11130, Reno, NV 89520
Tel: (775) 328-2005 Fax: (775) 328-2037

★Chair **Katrina "Kitty" Jung** (D-District 3) . . . . (775) 328-2005
Term Expires: January 2019
E-mail: kjung@washoecounty.us
Education: Humboldt State 1996 BA, 1998 MA

★Vice Chair **Bob Lucey** (R-District 2) . . . . (775) 328-2005
Term Expires: January 2019

★Commissioner **Marsha Berkbigler** (R-District 1) . . . . (775) 328-2005
Term Expires: January 2017

★Commissioner **Vaughn Hartung** (R-District 4) . . . . (775) 328-2005
Term Expires: December 31, 2016

★Commissioner **Jeanne Herman** (R-District 5) . . . . (775) 328-2005
Term Expires: January 2019

Office of the County Manager

1001 East 9th Street, Reno, NV 89512
Tel: (775) 328-2000 Internet: www.washoecounty.us/mgrsoff

►County Manager **John Slaughter** . . . . (775) 328-2000
E-mail: jslaughter@washoecounty.us

Assistant County Manager **Joey Orduna Hastings** . . . . . . (775) 328-2016

Assistant County Manager **Kevin Schiller** . . . . (775) 328-2000
E-mail: kschiller@washoecounty.us

Administrative Secretary **Valerie Wade** . . . . (775) 328-2004
E-mail: vwade@washoecounty.us

Administrative Assistant II **Joanne Watson** . . . . (775) 328-2000
E-mail: jwatson@washoecounty.us

Communications and Engagement

Fax: (775) 328-2037

Communications and Engagement Manager
Nancy Leuenhagen . . . . (775) 328-2069

eGovernment Information Officer **Kelly Mullin** . . . . (775) 328-2068
E-mail: kmullin@washoecounty.us

Community Liaison **Sarah Tone** . . . . (775) 328-2721
E-mail: stone@washoecounty.us

Program Assistant **Andrea Tavener** . . . . (775) 328-2720
E-mail: atavener@washoecounty.us

Internal Audit Division

Internal Auditor **Alison Gordon** . . . . (775) 328-3651

Management Services Division

Director **Al Rogers** . . . . (775) 328-3606
E-mail: arogers@washoecounty.us

Emergency Manager **Aaron R. Kenneston** . . . . (775) 337-5898
E-mail: akenneston@washoecounty.us Fax: (775) 337-5897

Grants Administrator **Gabrielle Enfield** . . . . (775) 328-2009
E-mail: genfield@washoecounty.us

Grants Coordinator **Cathy Ludwig** . . . . (775) 337-5859
Fax: (775) 337-5894

Administrative Assistant II **Alice McQuone** . . . . (775) 328-2699
E-mail: amcquone@washoecounty.us

Office Support Specialist **Debi Gonsalves** . . . . (775) 328-2066
E-mail: dgonsalves@washoecounty.us

Alternate Public Defender's Office

350 South Center Street, 6th Floor, Reno, NV 89501
P.O. Box 11130, Reno, NV 89520-0027
Tel: (775) 328-3955 Fax: (775) 328-3998
Internet: www.washoecounty.us/apd

Alternate Public Defender **Jennifer Lunt** . . . . (775) 328-3955
Education: Nevada (Reno) 1983 BA; McGeorge 1987 JD

Medical Examiner-Coroner's Office

10 Kirman Avenue, Reno, NV 89502
Tel: (775) 785-6114 Fax: (775) 785-6163
Internet: www.washoecounty.us/coroner

Chief Medical Examiner **Ellen G. I. Clark** . . . . (775) 785-6114

Public Defender's Office

350 South Center Street, 5th Floor, Reno, NV 89501
Tel: (775) 337-4800 Fax: (775) 337-4856

Public Defender **Jeremy T. Bosler** . . . . (775) 337-4800
Education: Nevada (Reno) 1988 BA; Cal Western 1993 JD

Public Guardian's Office

P.O. Box 12310, Reno, NV 89510
Tel: (775) 674-8800 Fax: (775) 674-8850
E-mail: guardian@washoecounty.us
Internet: www.washoecounty.us/guardian

Public Guardian **Susan DeBoer** . . . . (775) 674-8800

Registrar of Voters' Office

1001 East 9th Street, Room A-135, Reno, NV 89512
Tel: (775) 328-3670 Fax: (775) 328-3747
E-mail: electionsdepartment@washoecounty.us
Internet: www.washoecounty.us/voters

Registrar **Luanne Cutler** . . . . (775) 328-3670

Department of Community Services

1001 East 9th Street, Reno, NV 89512

Director **David M. Solaro** . . . . (775) 328-3600

Department of Building and Safety

1001 East 9th Street, Reno, NV 89512
Fax: (775) 328-6132 Internet: http://www.washoecounty.us/building/

Building Official **Don C. Jeppson** . . . . (775) 328-2020

Planning and Development Division

1001 East 9th Street, Suite A-275, Reno, NV 89512
Tel: (775) 328-3600 Fax: (775) 328-6133
E-mail: planning@washoecounty.us
Internet: www.washoecounty.us/comdev

Division Director **Bill Whitney** . . . . (775) 328-3617
E-mail: bwhitney@washoecounty.us

Community Planning Services

Senior Planner **Trevor Lloyd** . . . . (775) 328-3620
E-mail: tlloyd@washoecounty.us

Senior Planner **Roger Pelham** . . . . (775) 328-3622
E-mail: rpelham@washoecounty.us

Senior Planner **(Vacant)** . . . . (775) 328-3602

Planner **Eva Krause** . . . . (775) 328-3796
E-mail: ekrause@washoecounty.us

Planner **Grace Sannzzaro** . . . . (775) 328-3771
E-mail: gsannazzaro@washoecounty.us

Planner **(Vacant)** . . . . (775) 328-3621

Planning and Development Division

Manager **Bob Webb** . . . . (775) 328-3623
E-mail: bwebb@washoecounty.us

Senior Planner **Chad Giesinger** . . . . (775) 328-3626
E-mail: cgiesinger@washoecounty.us

(continued on next page)

★Elected Official ▲Appointed by Legislature ▼Appointed by Governor ►Appointed by Board or Commission ●Appointed by Judge
■Appointed by Mayor △Appointed by Freeholders ▽Appointed by Supervisor ▷Appointed by County Executive ○Appointed by Council

Planning and Development Division *continued*

Planner **Eric Young** ....(775) 328-3613
E-mail: eyoung@washoecounty.us
Business License **Karin Kremers** ....(775) 328-3733
Code Enforcement Officer **Lora Barretta** ....(775) 328-3630
E-mail: lbarretta@washoecounty.us
Code Enforcement Officer **Bert Bracy** ....(775) 328-6191
E-mail: bbracy@washoecounty.us
Planning Technician, Code Enforcement
Renee Schebler ....(775) 328-6106
E-mail: rschebler@washoecounty.us

Engineering and Capital Projects Division

1001 East 9th Street, Reno, NV 89512-2845
Tel: (775) 328-2040 Fax: (775) 328-3699
Internet: www.washoecounty.us/pubworks

Engineering and Capital Projects Director
Dwayne Smith ....(775) 328-2040
E-mail: dsmith@washoecounty.us
County Engineer (Acting) **Kimble O. Corbridge** ....(775) 328-2040

Department of Regional Parks and Open Space

1001 East 9th Street, Reno, NV 89512-2845
Tel: (775) 823-6500 Fax: (775) 829-8014
Internet: www.washoecounty.us/parks

Superintendent **Jennifer Budge** ....(775) 328-2181
Volunteer Services Coordinator **Denise Evans** ...(775) 785-4512 ext. 107
Fiscal Compliance Officer **Rosemarie Entsminger** ......(775) 823-6516
E-mail: rentsminger@washoecounty.us
Office Support Specialist **Joanna Schultz** ....(775) 328-2044
E-mail: jschultz@washoecounty.us

Water Utility [WCDWR]

4930 Energy Way, Reno, NV 89502
Fax: (775) 954-4610 Internet: www.washoecounty.us/water

Director **David M. Solaro** ....(775) 954-4666
Senior and Environmental Engineer **John Hulett** ....(775) 954-4612
Water Rights Manager **Vahid Behmaram** ....(775) 954-4647
Central Truckee Meadows Remediation District
(CTMRD) Program Manager **Chris Benedict** ....(775) 954-4642
Northern Nevada Water Planning Commission
(NNWPC) Program Manager **Jim Smitherman** ....(775) 954-4657

Finance and Administration Division

Manager **Ben Hutchins** ....(775) 954-4646

Utilities Division

Manager **Joe Howard** ....(775) 954-4623

Finance Department

Office of the Comptroller

1001 East 9th Street, Room D-120, Reno, NV 89512
Tel: (775) 328-2552
Internet: http://www.washoecounty.us/comptroller/index.php

Comptroller **Cathy Hill** ....(775) 328-2563
Accounting Manager, Operations **Mary Solorzano** ......(775) 328-2659
E-mail: msolorzano@washoecounty.us

Accounting Division

1001 East 9th Street, Room A225, Reno, NV 89512

Senior Accountant **Darlene Delany** ....(775) 328-2653
E-mail: ddelany@washoecounty.us

Purchasing Division

1001 East 9th Street, Room C-200, Reno, NV 89512
Tel: (775) 328-2280 Fax: (775) 328-3696

Purchasing and Contracts Manager **Michael L. Sullens** ...(775) 328-2281
E-mail: msullens@washoecounty.us

Risk Management Division

1001 East 9th Street, Reno, NV 89512
Tel: (775) 328-2665

Risk Manager **Doreen Ertell** ....(775) 328-2665
E-mail: dertell@washoecounty.us

Department of Human Resources and Labor Relations

1001 East 9th Street, Suite A220, Reno, NV 89512
Tel: (775) 328-2081 Fax: (775) 328-6119
Internet: www.washoecounty.us/humanresources

Director **John Listinsky** ....(775) 328-2089
E-mail: jlistinsky@washoecounty.us
Administrative Assistant **Joanne Watson** ....(775) 328-2083
E-mail: jwatson@washoecounty.us
Office Support Specialist **Elaine Anagnostou** ....(775) 328-2083
E-mail: eanagnostou@washoecounty.us

Benefits Administration

Benefits Manager **Ashley Farmer** ....(775) 328-2088
Benefits Specialist **Kristie Harmon** ....(775) 328-2079
Benefits Specialist **Vicki Scott** ....(775) 328-2099

Technical Services Team

Human Resources Administration Manager
Jim German ....(775) 328-2082
E-mail: jgerman@washoecounty.us
Human Resources Senior Analyst **Patricia Knight** ....(775) 328-2087
E-mail: pknight@washoecounty.us
Human Resources Analyst **Cathie Korson** ....(775) 328-2092
E-mail: ckorson@washoecounty.us
Human Resources Analyst **Karen Jeffers** ....(775) 328-2078
Human Resources Analyst **Indu Moore** ....(775) 328-2095

Recruitment and Selection Team

Workforce Development Manager **Kathy Hart** ....(775) 328-2093
Human Resources Analyst **Julie Paholke** ....(775) 328-6383
Human Resources Analyst **Esmeralda Contreras** ....(775) 328-2086
Human Resources Analyst **Carla Arribillaga** ....(775) 328-2096

Workforce Development and Training Team

Workforce Development Manager **Kathy Hart** ....(775) 328-2093
E-mail: khart@washoecounty.us
Training and Development Specialist **Nora Boisselle** .....(775) 328-2091
E-mail: nboisselle@washoecounty.us
Human Resources Specialist **(Vacant)** ....(775) 328-2099

Department of Senior Services

1155 East Ninth Street, Reno, NV 89512
Tel: (775) 328-2575 E-mail: sr_info@washoecounty.us
Internet: www.wahsoecounty.us/seniorsrv

Director **Grady Tarbutton** ....(775) 328-2575
E-mail: gtarbutton@washoecounty.us

Department of Social Services

Building C, 1001 East 9th Street, Reno, NV 89512 (Adult Services)
350 South Center Street, Reno, NV 89501 (Children's Services)
Tel: (775) 785-8600 Fax: (775) 785-5640
E-mail: socialsvs@washoecounty.us
Internet: www.washoecounty.us/socsrv

Director **Ken Retterath** ....(775) 785-8600
E-mail: kretterath@washoecounty.us
Fiscal Manager **Pamela Fine** ....(775) 785-8600
E-mail: pfine@washoecounty.us

Adult Services Division

1001 East 9th Street, Room C-135, Reno, NV 89512
Fax: (775) 328-2739

Director **Ken Retterath** ....(775) 328-2700
E-mail: kretterath@washoecounty.us

★ Elected Official ▲ Appointed by Legislature ▼ Appointed by Governor ▶ Appointed by Board or Commission ● Appointed by Judge
■ Appointed by Mayor △ Appointed by Freeholders ▽ Appointed by Supervisor ▷ Appointed by County Executive ○ Appointed by Council

Children's Services Division
350 South Center Street, Reno, NV 89501

Director **Jeanne C. Marsh** .... (775) 785-8600
E-mail: jmarsh@washoecounty.us
Education: Michigan State BA; Michigan MSW, PhD

Technology Services Department
1001 East 9th Street, Suite C-220, Reno, NV 89512
Tel: (775) 328-2355 Fax: (755) 328-2356
Internet: www.washoecounty.us/technology

Chief Information Management Officer **Craig Betts** ...... (775) 328-2350
E-mail: cbetts@washoecounty.us

Customer and Enterprise Solutions Division
Manager **Carrie Howard** .... (775) 858-5598
E-mail: choward@washoecounty.us

Enterprise Infrastructure Division
Tel: (775) 858-5980

Manager **Tony Kiriluk** .... (775) 858-5985
E-mail: tkiriluk@washoecounty.us

Regional Services Division
Manager **Gary Beekman** .... (775) 328-3619

Business Solutions and Integration Division
Manager **Paul Burr** .... (775) 858-5914
E-mail: pburr@washoecounty.us

Truckee River Flood Management Department
9390 Gateway Drive, Suite 230, Reno, NV 89521
Tel: (775) 850-7460 Internet: www.truckeeflood.us

Director **Jay Aldean** .... (775) 850-7460
E-mail: jaldean@washoecounty.us
Deputy Director **(Vacant)** .... (775) 850-7470
Project Manager **(Vacant)** .... (775) 850-7428
Natural Resource Manager **Danielle Henderson** .... (775) 850-7461
Natural Resource Planner **(Vacant)** .... (775) 850-7430
Senior Hydrogeologist **Ed Evans** .... (775) 850-7465
E-mail: eevans@washoecounty.us
Engineer **Eric Sheetz** .... (775) 850-7423
E-mail: escheetz@washoecounty.us
Administrative and Government Affairs Manager
(Vacant) .... (775) 850-7431
Account Clerk **(Vacant)** .... (775) 850-7454
Public Information Officer **(Vacant)** .... (775) 850-7456
Administrative Assistant **Laura Williams** .... (775) 850-7429
E-mail: lwilliams@washoecounty.us

Washoe County Library System
301 South Center Street, Reno, NV 89501
Tel: (775) 327-8340 Fax: (775) 327-8392
Internet: www.washoecounty.us/library

Director **Arnold "Arnie" Maurins** .... (775) 327-8341
E-mail: amaurins@washoecounty.us Fax: (775) 327-8393
Internet Services Librarian **John Andrews** .... (775) 327-8364
E-mail: jandrews@washoecounty.us
Development and Public Information Officer
Jennifer Oliver .... (775) 327-8360
Fax: (775) 327-8393
Resources Librarian **Deborah Stears** .... (775) 327-8349
Delinquent Accounts **Kathy Atkinson** .... (775) 327-8342
E-mail: katkinson@washoecounty.us
Programs and Community Collaborations
Beate Weinert .... (775) 327-8361
E-mail: bweinert@washoecounty.us

Washoe County District Board of Health
Building B, 1001 East 9th Street, Reno, NV 89512
Internet: www.co.washoe.nv.us/health/dbh/index.php

Chair **Katrina "Kitty" Jung** (D)
Note: Will continue until reappointed or replaced.
Term Expires: December 31, 2015
Education: Humboldt State 1996 BA, 1998 MA
Vice Chair **Julia Ratti**
Term Expires: December 31, 2016
Affiliation: Council Member, Office of the Mayor and City Council, City of Sparks, Nevada
Member **Michael D. Brown** .... (775) 328-2400
Term Expires: December 2018
Member **Oscar Delgado**
Term Expires: December 31, 2019
Member **Dr. George Hess** .... (775) 328-2400
Term Expires: December 31, 2018
Member **John Novak** .... (775) 328-2400
Term Expires: December 2018
Member **David Silverman** .... (775) 328-2400

Washoe County Health District [WCHD]
1001 East 9th Street, Reno, NV 89512
P.O. Box 11130, Reno, NV 89520-0027
Tel: (775) 328-2400 Fax: (775) 328-2279
E-mail: healthweb@washoecounty.us
Internet: www.co.washoe.nv.us/health

Director/Health Officer (Interim) **Kevin Dick** .... (775) 328-2400
Public Information Officer **Phil Ulibarri** .... (775) 328-2483
E-mail: pulibarri@washoecounty.us

Administrative Health Services Division [AHS]
Building B, 1001 East 9th Street, Reno, NV 89512
Tel: (775) 328-2410 Fax: (775) 328-2279
Internet: www.co.washoe.nv.us/health/ahs/index.php

Administrative Health Services Officer **Eileen Stickney** .. (775) 328-2417
EMS Coordinator **Dr. Randall "Randy" Todd** .... (775) 328-2698

Air Quality Management Division [AQM]
Building A, 1001 East 9th Street, Suite 115A, Reno, NV 89512
Tel: (775) 784-7200 Fax: (775) 784-7225
Internet: www.co.washoe.nv.us/health/aqm/home.html

Director **Charlene Albee** .... (775) 784-7200
Branch Chief **Daniel Inouye** .... (775) 784-7200

Community and Clinical Health Services Division [CCHS]
Building B, 1001 East 9th Street, Reno, NV 89512
Tel: (775) 328-2441 Fax: (775) 328-3750
Internet: www.co.washoe.nv.us/health/cchs/index.php

Director **Steve Kutz** .... (775) 328-3645
Public Health Nurse Supervisor **(Vacant)** .... (775) 328-3759
Sexual Health (HIV/STD) Program Manager
Jennifer "Jen" Howell .... (775) 328-3647
Tuberculosis Prevention and Control Program Manager
Diane Freedman .... (775) 785-4787
Women, Infants and Children (WIC) Program Manager
(Vacant) .... (775) 328-2454

Environmental Health Services Division [EHS]
Building B, 1001 East 9th Street, Reno, NV 89512
Tel: (775) 328-2434 Fax: (775) 328-6176
Internet: www.co.washoe.nv.us/health/ehs/index.php

Director **Robert O. "Bob" Sack** .... (775) 784-7200

Epi Center
Building B, 1001 East 9th Street, Reno, NV 89512
Fax: (775) 325-8130 E-mail: epicenter@washoecounty.us
Internet: www.co.washoe.nv.us/health/cdpp/home.html

Director of Epidemiology and Public Health
Preparedness **Dr. Randall "Randy" Todd** .... (775) 328-3736
E-mail: rtodd@washoecounty.us
Senior Epidemiologist **Lei Chen** .... (775) 328-3735

COUNTIES

Assessor's Office

1001 East 9th Street, Reno, NV 89512
Fax: (775) 328-3641 Internet: www.washoecounty.us/assessor

★Assessor **Michael E. Clark** (R) .... (775) 328-2200
Term Expires: January 2019
E-mail: meclark@washoecounty.us
Chief Deputy Assessor **Joshua "Josh" Wilson** (R) ..... (775) 328-2203

Clerk's Office

1001 East 9th Street, Reno, NV 89512-2845
Fax: (775) 328-3122 Internet: www.washoecounty.us/clerks

★County Clerk **Nancy Parent** .... (775) 784-7271
E-mail: nparent@washoecounty.us
Chief Deputy Clerk and Supervisor, Administration
Jan Galassini .... (775) 784-7271
Computer Application Specialist **Jonathan Lujan** .... (775) 784-7271

Board Records and Minutes Division

Supervisor **Catherine Smith** .... (775) 784-7260

Marriage and Business Division

Operations Supervisor **Karen Erickson** .... (775) 784-7260
E-mail: kerickson@washoecounty.us

District Attorney's Office

Mills B. Lane Justice Center, One South Sierra Street, 4th Floor, Reno, NV 89520
Internet: www.co.washoe.nv.us/da

★District Attorney **Chris Hicks** .... (775) 328-3200
Term Expires: January 2019

Public Administrator Office

Fax: (775) 861-4041 Internet: www.washoecounty.us/pubadmin

★Public Administrator **Donald L. Cavallo** (R) .... (775) 861-4000
Term Expires: January 2019
E-mail: dcavallo@washoecounty.us

Recorder's Office

1001 East 9th Street, A-140/A-150, Reno, NV 89512
Tel: (775) 328-3661 (Real Estate) Fax: (775) 325-8010 (Real Estate)
Tel: (775) 328-3660 (Marriages) Fax: (775) 325-8009 (Marriages)
E-mail: recorder@washoecounty.us
Internet: www.washoecounty.us/recorder

★Recorder **Larry Burtness** .... (775) 328-3661
Term Expires: January 2019
E-mail: lburtness@washoecounty.us
Administrative Assistant **Gail Spearman** .... (775) 328-3661
E-mail: gspearman@washoecounty.us
Chief Deputy Recorder **Sandy Gualano** .... (775) 328-3661
Real Estate Supervisor **Veronica Bell** .... (775) 328-3661
Marriage Supervisor **(Vacant)** .... (775) 328-3660

Sheriff's Office

911 Parr Boulevard, Reno, NV 89512
Fax: (775) 328-6308 E-mail: sheriffweb@washoecounty.us
Internet: www.washoesheriff.com

★Sheriff **Chuck Allen** .... (775) 328-3001
Term Expires: January 5, 2019
Undersheriff **John Spencer** .... (775) 328-3001

Detention Bureau

Chief Deputy **Anthony Miranda** .... (775) 328-3001

Operations Bureau

Chief Deputy **Sherman Boxx** .... (775) 328-3001

Administration Bureau

Chief Deputy **Russell Pedersen** .... (775) 328-3001

Treasurer's Office

1001 East 9th Street, Room D140, Reno, NV 89512-2845
Fax: (775) 328-2500 E-mail: tax@washoecounty.us
Internet: www.washoecounty.us/treas

★Treasurer **Tammi Davis** (R) .... (775) 328-2525
Term Expires: January 2019
E-mail: tsdavis@washoecounty.us
Administrative Secretary **Danielle Carlton** .... (775) 328-2525
E-mail: dcarlton@washoecounty.us
Chief Deputy Treasurer **Frances Finch** .... (775) 328-2525

Washoe County School District

Fax: (775) 348-0304

Superintendent **Traci Davis** .... (775) 789-4645
Executive Assistant **Tami Covington** .... (775) 789-4645
E-mail: tcovington@washoeschools.net

Board of Trustees

President **Angela Taylor** (District E) .... (775) 771-1530
Term Expires: December 31, 2016
Vice President **John R. Mayer** (District B) .... (775) 355-0182
Term Expires: 2018
Member **Lisa Ruggerio** (District A) .... (775) 527-0199
Term Expires: December 31, 2016
Member **(Vacant)** (District C) .... (775) 527-2534
Term Expires: 2018
Member **Howard Rosenberg** (District D) .... (775) 825-1399
Term Expires: December 31, 2016
Education: Massachusetts Art 1962 BS; Harvard 1965 EdM, MA
Member **Veronica Frenkel** (District F) .... (775) 351-7448
Term Expires: 2018
Member **Diane Nicolet** (District G) .... (775) 997-9698
Term Expires: December 31, 2016

County of Waukesha, Wisconsin

515 West Moreland Boulevard, Waukesha, WI 53188
Internet: www.waukeshacounty.gov

County Seat: Waukesha **Population:** 396,488 (2015)

Office of the County Executive

515 West Moreland Boulevard, Room 320, Waukesha, WI 53188
E-mail: countyexec@waukeshacounty.gov

★County Executive **Paul F. Farrow** .... (262) 548-7902
Term Expires: April 2019
E-mail: countyexec@waukeshacounty.gov
Education: Carroll Col (WI) 1991 BABA
Chief of Staff **Shawn Lundie** .... (262) 548-7902

Office of the Corporation Counsel

515 West Moreland Boulevard, Room 330, Waukesha, WI 53188
Tel: (262) 548-7432 Fax: (262) 548-7490

Corporation Counsel **Eric Weidig** .... (262) 548-7432
E-mail: eweidig@waukeshacounty.gov

★ Elected Official ▲ Appointed by Legislature ▼ Appointed by Governor ▶ Appointed by Board or Commission ● Appointed by Judge
■ Appointed by Mayor △ Appointed by Freeholders ▽ Appointed by Supervisor ▷ Appointed by County Executive ○ Appointed by Council

Medical Examiner's Office
515 West Moreland Boulevard, Waukesha, WI 53188
Tel: (262) 548-7575 Fax: (262) 896-8079

Medical Examiner **Dr. Lynda Biedrzycki** . . . . (262) 548-7575

Department of Administration
515 West Moreland Boulevard, Waukesha, WI 53188
Tel: (262) 548-7020 Fax: (262) 548-7913

Director **Norm Cummings** . . . . (262) 548-7020
E-mail: ncummings@waukeshacounty.gov
Education: Wisconsin BA; Kentucky MA

Accounting Services Division
515 West Moreland Boulevard, Waukesha, WI 53188
Tel: (262) 548-7020 E-mail: accounting@waukeshacounty.gov

Manager **Lawrence M. Dahl** . . . . (262) 548-7020
E-mail: ldahl@waukeshacounty.gov

Budget Management Division
515 West Moreland Boulevard, Waukesha, WI 53188
Tel: (262) 548-7020 E-mail: budget@waukeshacounty.gov

Manager **Linda Witkowski** . . . . (262) 548-7020

Collections Division
515 West Moreland Boulevard, Waukesha, WI 53188
Tel: (262) 548-7876 Fax: (262) 548-7856
E-mail: collections@waukeshacounty.gov

Manager **Andrew Thelke** . . . . (262) 548-7876

Human Resources Division
515 West Moreland Boulevard, Waukesha, WI 53188
Tel: (262) 548-7044 Fax: (262) 896-8272
E-mail: humanresources@waukeshacounty.gov

Manager **James Richter** . . . . (262) 548-7044
E-mail: jrichter@waukeshacounty.gov

Information Technology Division
515 West Moreland Boulevard, Room CG-53, Waukesha, WI 53188
Tel: (262) 548-7610 Fax: (262) 548-7000
E-mail: informationtechnology@waukeshacounty.gov

Manager **Michael Biagioli** . . . . (262) 548-7610
E-mail: mbiagioli@waukeshacounty.gov

Purchasing Division
515 West Moreland Boulevard, Room 310, Waukesha, WI 53188
Tel: (262) 548-7888 Fax: (262) 548-7668

Manager **Laura Stauffer** . . . . (262) 548-7888
E-mail: lstauffer@waukeshacounty.gov

Department of Emergency Preparedness
1621 Woodburn Road, Waukesha, WI 53188
Tel: (262) 446-5025 Fax: (262) 548-7313

Director **Gary Bell** . . . . (262) 446-5025
E-mail: gbell@waukeshacounty.gov

Department of Health and Human Services [WCDHHS]
500 Riverview Avenue, Waukesha, WI 53188
Tel: (262) 548-7212 Fax: (262) 548-7656
E-mail: hhs@waukeshacounty.gov

Director/Health Officer **Antwayne Robertson** . . . . (262) 548-7212

Department of Parks and Land Use
515 West Moreland Boulevard, Waukesha, WI 53188
Tel: (262) 896-8300 Fax: (262) 896-8298

Director **Dale Shaver** . . . . (262) 896-8300

Planning and Zoning Division
515 West Moreland Boulevard, Room AC 230, Waukesha, WI 53188
Tel: (262) 548-7790 Fax: (262) 896-8071

Manager **Jason Fruth** . . . . (262) 548-7817

Department of Public Works
515 West Moreland Boulevard, Room 210, Waukesha, WI 53188
Tel: (262) 548-7740 Fax: (262) 896-8097

Director **Allison Bussler** . . . . (262) 548-7740

Facility Management Division
515 West Moreland Boulevard, Room AC G1, Waukesha, WI 53188
Tel: (262) 548-7197

Manager **Shane Waeghe** . . . . (262) 548-7197
E-mail: swaeghe@waukeshacounty.gov

Fleet Maintenance Division
515 West Moreland Boulevard, Room AC210, Waukesha, WI 53188
Tel: (262) 548-7724

Manager **Bob Rauchle** . . . . (262) 548-7724

Department of Veterans' Services
500 Riverview Avenue, Waukesha, WI 53188
Tel: (262) 548-7732 Fax: (262) 896-8588
E-mail: vetserve@waukeshacounty.gov

Director **Thomas A. Ludka** . . . . (262) 548-7732

Board of Supervisors
515 West Moreland Boulevard, Room C170, Waukesha, WI 53188
Tel: (262) 548-7002 Fax: (262) 548-7005

★ Chairman **Paul L. Decker** (District 13) . . . . (262) 548-7002
Term Expires: April 2018
E-mail: pdecker@waukeshacounty.gov

★ Second Vice Chair **David W. Swan** (District 10) . . . . (262) 548-7002
Term Expires: April 2018
E-mail: dswan@waukeshacounty.gov

★ Supervisor **Robert L. Kolb** (District 1) . . . . (262) 548-7002
Term Expires: April 2018

★ Supervisor **David D. Zimmermann** (District 2) . . . . (262) 548-7002
Term Expires: April 2018
E-mail: ddzimmermann@waukeshacounty.gov

★ Supervisor **Richard Morris** (District 3) . . . . (262) 548-7002
Term Expires: April 2018

★ Supervisor **Jim Batzko** (District 4) . . . . (262) 548-7006
Term Expires: April 2018

★ Supervisor **Tim Dondlinger** (District 5) . . . . (262) 548-7002
Term Expires: April 2018

★ Supervisor **Jeremy Walz** (District 6) . . . . (262) 548-7002
Term Expires: April 2018

★ Supervisor **Jennifer A. Grant** (District 7) . . . . (262) 548-7002
Term Expires: April 2018

★ Supervisor **Eric Highum** (District 8) . . . . (262) 565-6558
Term Expires: April 2018
E-mail: ehighum@waukeshacounty.gov

★ Supervisor **Michael Starich** (District 9) . . . . (262) 548-7002
Term Expires: April 2018

★ Supervisor **Christine Howard** (District 11) . . . . (414) 745-6421
Term Expires: April 2018
E-mail: choward@waukeshacounty.gov

★ Supervisor **Peter M. Wolff** (District 12) . . . . (262) 548-7002
Term Expires: April 2018
E-mail: peterwolfflaw@yahoo.com

★ Supervisor **Chuck Wood** (District 14) . . . . (262) 548-7002
Term Expires: April 2018

★ Supervisor **William Mitchell** (District 15) . . . . (262) 548-7002
Term Expires: April 2018
E-mail: wmitchell@waukeshacounty.gov

★ Supervisor **Michael Crowley** (District 16) . . . . (262) 548-7002
Term Expires: April 2018
E-mail: mcrowley@waukeshacounty.gov

(continued on next page)

Board of Supervisors *continued*

★Supervisor **Duane E. Paulson** (District 17) . . . . (262) 548-7002
Term Expires: April 19, 2018
E-mail: dpaulson@waukeshacounty.gov

★Supervisor **Larry Nelson** (District 18) . . . . (262) 548-7002
Term Expires: April 2018
E-mail: lsnelson@waukeshacounty.gov

★Supervisor **Kathleen M. Cummings** (District 19) . . . . (262) 548-7002
Term Expires: April 2018
E-mail: kmcummings@att.net

★Supervisor **Thomas J. Schellinger** (District 20) . . . . (262) 548-7002
Term Expires: April 2018
E-mail: tschellinger@waukeshacounty.gov

★Supervisor **William J. Zaborowski** (District 21) . . . . (262) 548-7002
Term Expires: April 2018
E-mail: wzaborowski@waukeshacounty.gov

★Supervisor **Ted Wysocki** (District 22) . . . . (262) 548-7002
Term Expires: April 2018

★Supervisor **Keith Hammitt** (District 23) . . . . (262) 548-7002
Term Expires: April 2018
E-mail: khammitt@waukeshacounty.gov

★Supervisor **Steve Whittow** (District 24) . . . . (262) 548-7002
Term Expires: April 2018
E-mail: ddraeger@waukeshacounty.gov

★Supervisor **Darlene M. Johnson** (District 25) . . . . (262) 548-7002
Term Expires: April 2018

Office of the County Clerk

515 West Moreland Boulevard, Room AC120, Waukesha, WI 53188
Tel: (262) 548-7010 Fax: (262) 548-7722
E-mail: countyclerk@waukeshacounty.gov

★County Clerk **Kathleen Novack** . . . . (262) 548-7010
Term Expires: January 2017
E-mail: knovack@waukeshacounty.gov

Office of the District Attorney

515 West Moreland Boulevard, Room CG72, Waukesha, WI 53188
Tel: (262) 548-7076 E-mail: waukeshacountyda@da.wi.gov

★District Attorney (Acting) **Susan Opper** . . . . (262) 548-7076
Term Expires: January 2017
E-mail: sue.opper@da.wi.gov

Deputy District Attorney **Ted Szczupakiewicz** . . . . (262) 548-7076
Deputy District Attorney **Lesli Boese** . . . . (262) 548-7076
E-mail: lesli.boese@da.wi.gov

Office of the Register of Deeds

515 West Moreland Boulevard, Room AC110, Waukesha, WI 53188
Tel: (262) 548-7583 E-mail: registerofdeeds@waukeshacounty.gov

★Register of Deeds **James Behrend** . . . . (262) 548-7583
Term Expires: January 2017
E-mail: jbehrend@waukeshacounty.gov

Sheriff's Department

515 West Moreland Boulevard, Waukesha, WI 53188
P.O. Box 1488, Waukesha, WI 53187-1488
Tel: (262) 548-7126 Fax: (262) 548-7887

★Sheriff **Eric Severson** . . . . (262) 548-7126
Term Expires: January 2019

Treasurer's Office

515 West Moreland Boulevard, Room AC148, Waukesha, WI 53188
Tel: (262) 548-7029 Fax: (262) 896-8037

★County Treasurer **Pamela Reeves** . . . . (262) 548-7029
Term Expires: January 2017
E-mail: preeves@waukeshacounty.gov

County of Wayne, Michigan

500 Griswold Street, Detroit, MI 48226
Tel: (313) 224-0286 (Information) Internet: www.waynecounty.com

County Seat: Detroit **Election Type:** Partisan **Population:** 1,759,335 (2015)

Office of the County Executive

500 Griswold Street, Detroit, MI 48226
Tel: (313) 224-0286 Fax: (313) 967-6558

★Chief Executive Officer **Warren C. Evans** (D) . . . . (313) 224-0366
Term Expires: December 31, 2018 Fax: (313) 967-6558

Assistant County Executive **June Lee** . . . . (313) 224-0408
Assistant County Executive **Genelle Allen** . . . . (313) 833-3464
640 Temple Street, Fax: (313) 833-3630
5th Floor, Detroit, MI 48201
Executive Assistant/Scheduler **Candice Parker** . . . . (313) 224-0291
E-mail: cparker@co.wayne.mi.us

Deputy County Executive **Richard Kaufman** . . . . (313) 224-0344
Assistant Chief Executive Officer **(Vacant)** . . . . (313) 224-0446
Assistant County Executive Officer **Alan Helmkamp** . . . . . (313) 224-0260
E-mail: ahelmkam@co.wayne.mi.us

Assistant County Executive Officer **(Vacant)** . . . . (313) 224-6673
Press Secretary **Lloyd Jackson** . . . . (313) 967-0041
Inspector General **Mary Rose McMillan** . . . . (313) 224-5406

Department of Corporation Counsel

Wayne County Bldg., 600 Randolph Street, Room 253, Detroit, MI 48226
Fax: (313) 224-4882 Internet: www.waynecounty.com/cc.htm

▷Corporation Counsel **Zenna F. El Hasan** . . . . (313) 224-0055

Department of Health, Veterans, and Community Wellness [HHS]

Guardian Building, 500 Griswold Street, 10th Floor South,
Detroit, MI 48226
Tel: (313) 224-0810 Fax: (313) 224-6187
Internet: www.waynecounty.com/hhs

▷Director **Mouhanad Hammami** . . . . (313) 224-0810
E-mail: mhammami@waynecounty.com
Executive Assistant to Director **Connie Camilleri** . . . . . . (313) 224-0810

Chief Health Officer and Chief of Health Operations
Mouhanad Hammami . . . . (313) 224-0810

Detroit Wayne Mental Health Authority [DWMHA]

640 Temple Street, 8th Floor, Detroit, MI 48201
Tel: (313) 224-7000 (Information Emergency Services)
Tel: (800) 630-1044 (TTY) Fax: (313) 833-2156
Internet: www.waynecounty.com/hhs_mh.htm

Executive Director **Tom Watkins** . . . . (313) 833-2500
Medical Director **Dr. Carmen McIntyre** . . . . (313) 833-2500
Recipient Rights Director **Kip Kliber** . . . . (313) 833-2348
Communications Director **Brooke Blackwell** . . . . (313) 833-2761
E-mail: bblackwell@dwmha.com

Customer Service Director **Michele Vasconcellos** . . . . (313) 833-2392

★Elected Official ▲Appointed by Legislature ▼Appointed by Governor ▶Appointed by Board or Commission ●Appointed by Judge
■Appointed by Mayor △Appointed by Freeholders ▽Appointed by Supervisor ▷Appointed by County Executive ○Appointed by Council

Division of Jail Health Services
Wayne County Jail, Division 1, 570 Clinton, Detroit, MI 48226
Fax: (313) 224-2368

Director **Dr. Keith C. Dlugokinski** .... (313) 224-7901

Medical Examiner's Office
1300 East Warren, Detroit, MI 48207
Tel: (313) 833-2504 Fax: (313) 833-2534 (Administration Fax)
Fax: (313) 833-2571 (Investigation Fax)

Chief Medical Examiner **Dr. Carl J. Schmidt** .... (313) 833-2524
Deputy Chief Medical Examiner **Dr. Leigh Hlavaty** ...... (313) 833-2543
Facility Administrator **Albert Samuels** .... (313) 833-2569
Chief Investigator **Will Kasper** .... (313) 833-2569

Access to Care
640 Temple Street, #370, Detroit, MI 48201
Tel: (313) 833-3450 Fax: (313) 833-7175

▷ Director **Christopher Johnson** .... (313) 833-2142
E-mail: cjohnso3@waynecounty.com

Public Health Department
Health Administration Bldg., 33030 Van Born Rd., Wayne, MI 48184
Tel: (734) 727-7000 Fax: (734) 727-7043

▷ Director/Health Officer **Mouhanad Hammami** .... (734) 727-7006
▷ Medical Director **Dr. Ruta Sharangpani** .... (734) 727-7010

Department of Management and Budget [DMB]
Guardian Building, 500 Griswold Street, 31st Floor, Detroit, MI 48226
Fax: (313) 967-3031

▼ Chief Restructuring Officer **Tony Saunders** .... (313) 224-5063
▷ Deputy Chief Financial Officer **Kevin Haney** .... (313) 224-1329
Chief Payroll Supervisor **Cedric Robinson** .... (313) 224-7691

Division of Assessment and Equalization
Fax: (313) 224-4864

▷ Director **Phillip Mastin** .... (313) 224-2342

Budget and Planning Division
Fax: (313) 224-5541

▷ Director **Kevin Haney** .... (313) 224-5063
E-mail: khaney@co.wayne.mi.us

Division of Cash Management/Accounts Payable
Fax: (313) 237-1138

▷ Manager **Elois Lynch** .... (313) 224-5014
E-mail: elynch@co.wayne.mi.us

Division of Grants Management/Accounts Receivable
Fax: (313) 224-2714

▷ Director **Terry Hasse** .... (313) 224-5114
E-mail: thasse@co.wayne.mi.us

Purchasing Division
500 Griswold Street, Detroit, MI 48226
Tel: (313) 224-5151 Fax: (313) 967-1259

Director **Muddasar Tawakkul** .... (313) 967-8269
Education: Michigan State 1997 BA; Detroit Mercy 2000 JD

Division of Risk Management
Fax: (313) 224-7419

▷ Director **(Vacant)** .... (313) 224-5180

Personnel/Human Resources Department
Guardian Building, 500 Griswold Street, 9th Floor, Detroit, MI 48226
Tel: (313) 224-5901 Fax: (313) 967-1231
Internet: www.waynecounty.com/hr.htm

Director **(Vacant)** .... (313) 224-5907
Deputy Director **Kenneth Wilson** .... (313) 224-0972
E-mail: kwilson@co.wayne.mi.us

Personnel/Human Resources Department *continued*

Director, Benefit and Disability Administration Division
Livia Calderoni .... (313) 224-5901
Director, Labor Relations and Dispute Resolution
Division **Kenneth Wilson** .... (313) 224-0972
Personnel Information Unit Director **(Vacant)** .... (313) 224-5943
Fax: (313) 967-1227
Examinations/Certification Unit Director **(Vacant)** .... (313) 224-5944

Department of Public Services [DPS]
400 Monroe Street, Suite 300, Detroit, MI 48226-2942
Tel: (313) 224-7600 Fax: (313) 224-2609
Internet: www.waynecounty.com/dps

▷ Director (Acting) **June Lee** .... (313) 224-7600
E-mail: jlee@co.wayne.mi.us
Executive Assistant **Joyce Williams** .... (313) 224-7373
Director of Administration **Daisy Tinsley** .... (313) 224-8113

Environmental Services Group
Deputy Director **Kenneth M. Kucel** .... (313) 224-8469

Facilities Management Division [FMD]
400 Monroe Street, 4th Floor, Detroit, MI 48226-2942
Tel: (313) 224-7679 Fax: (313) 224-0045

Director **Elmeka Steele** .... (313) 224-7679
E-mail: eallen@co.wayne.mi.us

Land Resources Management Division [LRMD]
Building E, 3600 Commerce Court, Wayne, MI 48184
Tel: (734) 326-3936 Fax: (734) 326-4421

Director **Patrick Cullen** .... (734) 326-4473

Water Quality Management Division
400 Monroe Street, Suite 400, Detroit, MI 48226-2942
Tel: (313) 224-3620 Fax: (313) 224-0045

Director **Kelly A. Cave** .... (313) 224-8282

Buildings Division
640 Temple St., Suite 300, Detroit, MI 48201
Tel: (313) 833-3390 Fax: (313) 833-3616

Director **Paula Anderson** .... (313) 833-3201

Engineering Division
400 Monroe Street, 3rd Floor, Detroit, MI 48226-2942
Tel: (313) 224-7758 Fax: (313) 224-7773

Director **Ronald Agacinski** .... (313) 224-7775
E-mail: ragacin1@co.wayne.mi.us

Equipment Division
Central Maintenance Office, 29900 Goddard Rd., Detroit, MI 48242
Tel: (313) 734-2190 Fax: (313) 734-3269

Director **David Banka** .... (734) 955-2191
E-mail: dbanka@co.wayne.mi.us

Parks and Recreation Division
Administrative Field Office, 33175 Ann Arbor Trail, Westland, MI 48185
Tel: (734) 261-1990 Fax: (734) 261-0195

Director **Lawrence Hemingway** .... (734) 261-2022

Roads Division
Central Maintenance Yard, 29900 Goddard Road, Detroit, MI 48242
Tel: (734) 955-9920 Fax: (734) 955-2374

Director **Robert Conrad** .... (734) 955-2290

Department of Technology [DoT]
500 Griswold Street, Detroit, MI 48226
Tel: (313) 224-8270 Fax: (313) 237-1130

▷ Chief Information Officer **Ed Winfield** .... (313) 224-8270
Deputy Chief Information Officer **Jeff Small** .... (313) 224-8270
Director, Applications **Nev Malbasic** .... (313) 224-8270

(continued on next page)

★ Elected Official ▲ Appointed by Legislature ▼ Appointed by Governor ▶ Appointed by Board or Commission ● Appointed by Judge
■ Appointed by Mayor △ Appointed by Freeholders ▽ Appointed by Supervisor ▷ Appointed by County Executive ○ Appointed by Council

Department of Technology *continued*

Director, Communication and Hardware **Hector Roman** . . (313) 224-8270
Director, Resource Management **Angela Stevenson** . . . . . (313) 224-8270

Office of the County Commission

Guardian Building, 500 Griswold Street, 7th Floor, Detroit, MI 48226
Tel: (313) 224-2383 Fax: (313) 224-3678
E-mail: commission@waynecounty.com

★Chair **Gary Woronchak** (D-District 13) . . . . (313) 224-0934
Term Expires: December 31, 2016
E-mail: gworonch@waynecounty.com
Education: Michigan (Dearborn) 1978 BA

★Vice Chair **Alisha Bell** (D-District 7) . . . . (313) 224-0936
Term Expires: December 31, 2016
E-mail: abell3@waynecounty.com
Education: Florida A&M BBA; UNLV MEd

★Commissioner **Tim Killeen** (D-District 1) . . . . (313) 224-0920
Term Expires: December 31, 2016
E-mail: tkilleen@waynecounty.com
Education: Michigan State 1992 BS

★Commissioner **Jewel C. Ware** (D-District 2) . . . . (313) 224-0916
Term Expires: December 31, 2016
E-mail: jware@waynecounty.com
Education: Detroit

★Commissioner **Martha G. Scott** (D-District 3) . . . . (313) 224-0878
Term Expires: December 31, 2016
E-mail: mscott2@waynecounty.com

★Commissioner **Ilona Varga** (D-District 4) . . . . (313) 224-0886
Term Expires: December 31, 2016
E-mail: ivarga@waynecounty.com

★Commissioner **Irma Clark-Coleman** (D-District 5) . . . . (313) 224-0942
Term Expires: December 31, 2016
E-mail: iclark@waynecounty.com
Education: Wayne State U 1977 BA, 1981 MA

★Commissioner **Burton Leland** (D-District 6) . . . . (313) 224-0884
Term Expires: December 31, 2016
E-mail: bleland@waynecounty.com
Education: Wayne State U BS; Michigan 1977 MSW

★Commissioner **Diane L. Webb** (D-District 8) . . . . (313) 224-0930
Term Expires: December 31, 2016
E-mail: dwebb1@waynecounty.com
Education: Eastern Michigan

★Commissioner **Terry Marecki** (R-District 9) . . . . (313) 224-0946
Term Expires: December 31, 2016

★Commissioner **Joe Barone** (D-District 10) . . . . (313) 224-0882
Term Expires: December 31, 2016

★Commissioner **Abdul "Al" Haidous** (D-District 11) . . . . . . (313) 224-0944
Term Expires: December 31, 2016

★Commissioner **Glenn S. Anderson** (D-District 12) . . . . . . (313) 224-0907
Term Expires: December 31, 2016
E-mail: district12@waynecounty.com

★Commissioner **Raymond E. Basham** (D-District 14) . . . . . (313) 224-0876
Term Expires: December 31, 2016
E-mail: rbasham@waynecounty.com
Date of Birth: May 24, 1945
Education: Wayne State U (Attended)

★Commissioner **Joseph Palamara** (D-District 15) . . . . (313) 224-0880
Term Expires: December 31, 2016
E-mail: jpalamar@waynecounty.com
Education: Michigan State 1975 BA; Detroit Law 1985 JD

Office of the Clerk of the Commission

600 Randolph Street, Room 462, Detroit, MI 48226
Tel: (313) 224-0903 Fax: (313) 224-3678

►Clerk **Pamela Lane** . . . . (313) 224-0903
E-mail: jpfeiffe@co.wayne.mi.us
Legislative Staff Assistant **Charisse Lewis** . . . . (313) 224-0903
E-mail: clewis@co.wayne.mi.us
Legislative Staff Assistant **Darcel Brown** . . . . (313) 224-0903

Office of the Commission Counsel

500 Griswold Street, Detroit, MI 48226

Commission Counsel **Felicia O. Johnson** . . . . (313) 224-6459
600 Randolph Street, Room 472, Detroit, MI 48226
Education: Eastern Michigan BS; Thomas M Cooley 2003 JD

Office of Fiscal Agency

500 Griswold Street, Detroit, MI 48226

Chief Fiscal Advisor/Budget Director **Dwayne B. Seals** . . (313) 224-0875
E-mail: dseals@co.wayne.mi.us

Office of the Legislative Auditor General

500 Griswold Street, Suite 848, Detroit, MI 48226
Tel: (313) 224-8354 Fax: (313) 224-7974

►Auditor General **Marcella "Marcie" Cora** . . . . (313) 224-0924
E-mail: mcora@co.wayne.mi.us
Deputy Auditor General **(Vacant)** . . . . (313) 224-8354

Department of Administration and Budget

500 Griswold Street, 7th Floor, Detroit, MI 48226
Fax: (313) 224-5822
Internet: www.waynecounty.com/comm_depts_adminbudget.htm

►Director **Tim Johnson** . . . . (313) 224-0948
600 Randolph Street, Room 458, Detroit, MI 48226
E-mail: tjohnson@waynecounty.com

Department of Policy Research and Analysis

600 Randolph Street, Room 406, Detroit, MI 48226
Fax: (313) 967-3557

Director **Pamela Lane** . . . . (313) 224-0909

Department of Public Information

500 Griswold Street, Detroit, MI 48226

Director **Jim Toth** . . . . (313) 224-7263

Office of the County Clerk

Coleman A. Young Municipal Center, Two Woodward Avenue, Detroit, MI 48226
Tel: (313) 224-6262 Fax: (313) 224-5364

★County Clerk **Cathy M. Garrett** (D) Room 211 . . . . (313) 224-0536
Term Expires: December 31, 2016
E-mail: cgarrett@waynecounty.com
Chief Deputy County Clerk **Patricia Ways** . . . . (313) 224-5542
E-mail: pways@waynecounty.com
Personnel Manager **Debra Gibson** Room 211 . . . . (313) 224-0242
E-mail: dgibson@waynecounty.com

Archives Unit

Fax: (313) 567-6011

Department Supervisor **Marcus Hyman** . . . . (313) 224-0725

Court Motions and Appeals Unit

Tel: (313) 224-5510

Chief of Staff **Cheryl Ray** Room 201 . . . . (313) 224-0328

Court Records and Files

Fax: (313) 967-3712

Department Administrator **Tracy Gilbert** Room B-61 . . . . . (313) 224-5530

Elections Division

Two Woodward Avenue, Suite 502, Detroit, MI 48226
Fax: (313) 224-6424

Director **Delphine Oden** . . . . (313) 224-5525
Assistant Director of Elections **Melanie Ryska** . . . . (313) 224-5525
Campaign Finance Manager **Gil Flowers** Room 502 . . . . . (313) 224-5525

Vital Statistics Unit

Chief of Staff **Cheryl Ray** Room 201 . . . . (313) 224-0328

★Elected Official ▲Appointed by Legislature ▼Appointed by Governor ►Appointed by Board or Commission ●Appointed by Judge
■Appointed by Mayor △Appointed by Freeholders ▽Appointed by Supervisor ▷Appointed by County Executive ○Appointed by Council

Office of the County Treasurer

International Center Building, 400 Monroe Street, 5th Floor, Detroit, MI 48226-2942
Fax: (313) 224-2921

★ Treasurer (Interim) **Eric R. Sabree** .... (313) 224-5990
Term Expires: July 1, 2017
E-mail: esabree@co.wayne.mi.us
Education: Detroit Law 1996 JD
Chief Deputy Treasurer **Eric R. Sabree** .... (313) 224-5950
Education: Detroit Law 1996 JD
Deputy Treasurer, Land Management **Kim Homan** .... (313) 224-5950
Deputy Treasurer, Financial Services **Christa McLellan** ... (313) 224-0489
Department Executive **Samia Wilson** .... (313) 224-5952
Department Administrator **Paul J. Zelenak** .... (313) 224-6732
E-mail: pzelena@co.wayne.mi.us
Chief Accountant **Soraya Farver** .... (313) 967-3650
E-mail: sfarver@co.wayne.mi.us

Office of the Prosecuting Attorney

Frank Murphy Hall of Justice, 1441 St. Antoine Street, 12th Floor, Detroit, MI 48226
Fax: (313) 224-0974

★ Prosecuting Attorney **Kym Loren Worthy** (D) .... (313) 224-5777
Term Expires: December 31, 2016
E-mail: kworthy@co.wayne.mi.us
Education: Michigan; Notre Dame 1984 JD
Chief Assistant Prosecuting Attorney **(Vacant)** .... (313) 224-5777

Office of the Register of Deeds

International Center Building, 400 Monroe Street, 7th Floor, Detroit, MI 48226
Fax: (313) 224-5884

★ Register of Deeds **Bernard J. Youngblood** (D) .... (313) 224-5850
Term Expires: December 31, 2016
E-mail: byoungblood@waynecounty.com
Chief Deputy Register **Barbara Johnson** .... (313) 224-5850
Deputy Register **Soumaya Harb** .... (313) 224-5876
Department Executive **Spring Smith** .... (313) 224-5877
Land Records Executive II **(Vacant)** .... (313) 224-8240

Office of the Sheriff

1231 St. Antoine Street, Detroit, MI 48226
Tel: (313) 224-2222 Fax: (313) 224-2367

★ Sheriff **Benny N. Napoleon** .... (313) 224-2233
Term Expires: December 31, 2016 Fax: (313) 224-8728
E-mail: bnapoleo@co.wayne.mi.us
Undersheriff **Daniel P. Pfannes** .... (313) 224-2232
E-mail: dpfannes@co.wayne.mi.us Fax: (313) 224-8535

Wayne County Employees' Retirement System [WCERS]

28 West Adams Street, Suite 1900, Detroit, MI 48226-2920
Fax: (313) 224-1917 Internet: www.wcers.org

Director **Robert J. Grden** .... (313) 224-2822
Administrative Secretary **Wendy Foster** .... (313) 224-2846
E-mail: wfoster@waynecounty.com
Deputy Director **Gerard Grysko** .... (313) 224-2769
Department Supervisor **Felicia Hollis** .... (313) 224-8515
Supervisor of Finance Accounting **Todd Pickett** .... (313) 224-6959
E-mail: tpickett@waynecounty.com

County of Westchester, New York

Michaelian Office Bldg., 148 Martine Ave., White Plains, NY 10601
Tel: (914) 995-2000 (Information) Internet: www.westchestergov.com

County Seat: White Plains **Election Type:** Partisan
Population: 976,396 (2015)

Office of the County Executive

Michaelian Office Building, 148 Martine Avenue, White Plains, NY 10601
Tel: (914) 995-2900 Fax: (914) 995-3113

★ County Executive **Robert P. "Rob" Astorino** (R) .... (914) 995-2900
Term Expires: December 31, 2017
E-mail: ce@westchestergov.com
Date of Birth: May 3, 1967
Education: Fordham 1989 BA
Senior Assistant to the County Executive
Eileen Mildenberger .... (914) 995-2943
▷ Deputy County Executive **Kevin Plunkett** .... (914) 995-2909
E-mail: kjp2@westchestergov.com Fax: (914) 995-3372
Chief of Staff **George Oros** (R) .... (914) 995-2934
E-mail: goo1@westchestergov.com Fax: (914) 995-3372
Education: Pace BBA, JD
Deputy Chief of Staff **Robert Alberty** .... (914) 995-2900
Immigration Services Liaison and Deputy Chief of Staff
Katherine "Katy" Delgado .... (914) 995-2946

Office of Communications

148 Martine Avenue, White Plains, NY 10601-3311
Fax: (914) 995-2939

▷ Chief Advisor to the County Executive/Communications
Director **Ned McCormack** .... (914) 995-2932
E-mail: ejm2@westchestergov.com

Office for the Disabled

148 Martine Avenue, Room 102, White Plains, NY 10601-3311
Tel: (914) 995-2957 TTY: (914) 995-7397 Fax: (914) 995-2799
Internet: http://disabled.westchestergov.com/

▷ Director **Evan H. Latainer** .... (914) 995-2957
E-mail: ehl2@westchestergov.com

Office of Economic Development

148 Martine Avenue, White Plains, NY 10601-3311
Fax: (914) 995-3044

▷ Director **William M. "Bill" Mooney III** .... (914) 995-2900
E-mail: wmm1@westchestergov.com
Education: Villanova BBA; Pace 1992 JD

Office of Tourism

148 Martine Avenue, Suite 104, White Plains, NY 10601-3311
Tel: (914) 995-8500 E-mail: tourism@westchestergov.com

Director **Natasha Caputo** .... (914) 995-8502

Office for Women

112 East Post Road, Room 110B, White Plains, NY 10601
Fax: (914) 995-5054

▷ Senior Manager **Robin "Robi" Schlaff** .... (914) 995-5976

Westchester County Veterans Service Agency

112 East Post Road, 4th Floor, White Plains, NY 10601
Fax: (914) 995-7735

▷ Director **Ronald C. Tocci** (D) .... (914) 995-2146
E-mail: rct1@westchestergov.com

Westchester County Youth Bureau

112 East Post Road, 3rd Floor, White Plains, NY 10601
Fax: (914) 995-3871 Internet: http://youth.westchestergov.com/

▷ Coordinator **Iris Pagan** .... (914) 995-2745

★ Elected Official ▲ Appointed by Legislature ▼ Appointed by Governor ► Appointed by Board or Commission ● Appointed by Judge
■ Appointed by Mayor △ Appointed by Freeholders ▽ Appointed by Supervisor ▷ Appointed by County Executive ○ Appointed by Council

Department of Budget
Michaelian Office Building, 148 Martine Avenue, Room 311, White Plains, NY 10601-3311
Fax: (914) 995-2281 Internet: www.westchestergov.com/budget

▷Director **Lawrence C. Soule** .... (914) 995-2857
E-mail: lcs5@westchestergov.com
Deputy Budget Director **Francesca K. Bossey** .... (914) 995-2866
E-mail: fkb1@westchestergov.com

Department of Consumer Protection
148 Martine Avenue, Room 407, White Plains, NY 10601-3311
Fax: (914) 995-3115 E-mail: conpro@westchestergov.com

▷Director (Acting) **John P. Gaccione** .... (914) 995-2162
E-mail: jpg4@westchestergov.com
Deputy Director/Sealer of Weights and Measures
John P. Gaccione .... (914) 995-2164

Department of Emergency Services
Westchester County Fire Training Center, Four Dana Rd., Valhalla, NY 10595
Fax: (914) 231-1622

▷Commissioner **John M. Cullen** .... (914) 231-1688
E-mail: jmc5@westchestergov.com
Deputy Commissioner **Jennifer Wacha** .... (914) 231-1686
E-mail: jmw3@westchestergov.com

Department of Community Mental Health
112 East Post Road, Suite 219, White Plains, NY 10601-5113
Tel: (914) 995-5220 Fax: (914) 995-6220
Internet: http://mentalhealth.westchestergov.com/

▷Commissioner **Mark Herceg** .... (914) 995-5235
E-mail: msh9@westchestergov.com
Deputy Commissioner **Michael Orth** .... (914) 995-5225
Second Deputy Commissioner **(Vacant)** .... (914) 995-5225

Westchester County Department of Correction [WCDOC]
P.O. Box 389, Valhalla, NY 10595
Tel: (914) 231-1400 Fax: (914) 231-1262

▷Commissioner **Kevin M. Cheverko** .... (914) 231-1054
Director of Administrative Services **William Fallon** .... (914) 231-1435

Department of Environmental Facilities
270 North Avenue, Sixth Floor, New Rochelle, NY 10801
Fax: (914) 813-5460 Internet: http://environment.westchestergov.com/

▷Commissioner **Thomas J. Lauro** .... (914) 813-5450
E-mail: tjl1@westchestergov.com
First Deputy Commissioner **G. Michael Coley** .... (914) 813-5412
Deputy Commissioner **Louis Vetrone** .... (914) 813-5429

Department of Finance
148 Martine Avenue, Room 720, White Plains, NY 10601-3311
Tel: (914) 995-2757 Fax: (914) 995-3230
E-mail: dept-of-finance@westchestergov.com
Internet: http://finance.westchestergov.com/

▷Commissioner **Ann Marie Berg** .... (914) 995-2761
Deputy Commissioner **Dennis C. Kelly** .... (914) 995-8316
Deputy Commissioner **Sergio Sensi** .... (914) 995-2840

Department of Health
145 Huguenot Street, New Rochelle, NY 10801
Tel: (914) 814-5000 Fax: (914) 813-5014
Internet: http://health.westchestergov.com/

▷Commissioner **Dr. Sherlita N. Amler** .... (914) 864-7292
E-mail: samler@westchestergov.com
Education: Texas (Arlington); Arkansas State MS; Arkansas Medical 1996 MD

Department of Health *continued*

Director, Public Affairs **Caren Halbfinger** .... (914) 813-5013
E-mail: cqh4@westchestergov.com

Department of Human Resources
Michaelian Office Bldg., 148 Martine Ave., Suite 100, White Plains, NY 10601
Fax: (914) 995-6304 Internet: http://humanresources.westchestergov.com/

▷Commissioner **(Vacant)** .... (914) 995-2101

Department of Information Technology [DoIT]
Michaelian Office Bldg., 148 Martine Ave., Room 908, White Plains, NY 10601
Fax: (914) 995-2999 Internet: www.westchestergov.com/doit

▷Chief Information Officer **John B. McCaffrey** .... (914) 995-8161
E-mail: JMcCaffrey@westchestergov.com
Telecommunications Director **Lisa A. Losier** .... (914) 995-2976
E-mail: lal1@westchestergov.com Fax: (914) 995-5940

Department of Laboratories and Research
Ten Dana Road, Valhalla, NY 10595
Fax: (914) 231-4458 Internet: http://labs.westchestergov.com/

▷Commissioner/Medical Examiner **Dr. Kunjlata Ashar** .... (914) 231-1715
E-mail: kka4@westchestergov.com
First Deputy Medical Examiner
Dr. Aleksandar Milovanovic .... (914) 231-1600

Department of Law
600 Michaelian Office Bldg., 148 Martine Ave., White Plains, NY 10601
Fax: (914) 995-5858 Internet: www.westchestergov.com/law

▷County Attorney **Robert F. Meehan** .... (914) 995-2660
E-mail: rfm5@westchestergov.com
Education: Fordham 1970 BA; St John's U (NY) 1973 JD
Assistant Chief Deputy County Attorney **Carol Arcuri** .... (914) 995-2660
Chief Deputy County Attorney **James Castro-Blanco** .... (914) 995-2660
Education: SUNY (Albany) 1988; Brooklyn Law 1991 JD
Assistant Chief Deputy County Attorney
Wayne Humphrey .... (914) 995-2660
Assistant Chief Deputy County Attorney
James Robertson .... (914) 995-2660

Department of Parks, Recreation and Conservation [PRC]
450 Saw Mill River Road, Ardsley, NY 10502
Fax: (914) 864-7053 E-mail: parksinfo@westchester.gov
Internet: http://parks.westchestergov.com/

▷Commissioner **Kathleen M. O'Connor** .... (914) 231-4504
Chief of Operations **Neil Squillante** .... (914) 231-4509
Deputy Commissioner **Peter Tartaglia** .... (914) 231-4632

Department of Planning
148 Martine Avenue, Room 428, White Plains, NY 10601-3311
Tel: (914) 995-4400 Fax: (914) 995-9093
Internet: http://planning.westchestergov.com/

Commissioner **Edward Buroughs** .... (914) 995-4402
Education: Rutgers 1975 MCRP
Deputy Commissioner **Norma Drummond** .... (914) 995-2427
Education: Pace 1989 MPA
Land Use Planner **Patrick Natarelli** .... (914) 995-4406

Department of Probation
111 Dr. Martin Luther King, Jr. Boulevard, White Plains, NY 10601
Tel: (914) 995-3529 Fax: (914) 995-6261
Internet: http://probation.westchestergov.com/

▷Commissioner **Rocco A. Pozzi** .... (914) 995-3502
E-mail: rap4@westchestergov.com
Education: Temple 1981 MPA

★Elected Official ▲Appointed by Legislature ▼Appointed by Governor ▶Appointed by Board or Commission ●Appointed by Judge
■Appointed by Mayor △Appointed by Freeholders ▽Appointed by Supervisor ▷Appointed by County Executive ○Appointed by Council

Department of Public Safety
Westchester County Police, 1 Saw Mill River Pkwy., Hawthorne, NY 10532
Fax: (914) 864-7741 Internet: http://publicsafety.westchestergov.com/

Commissioner-Sheriff **George N. Longworth** .... (914) 864-7710
E-mail: GNL1@westchestergov.com
Special Operations Division **CAPT Paul Stasaitis** .... (914) 231-1953
Training **Capt. Mark E. Busche** .... (914) 231-1831
Westchester County Police Academy, 1 Dana Road, Valhalla, NY 10595 Fax: (914) 231-1837

Department of Public Works and Transportation
Michaelian Office Building, 148 Martine Avenue, Room 518, White Plains, NY 10601
Fax: (914) 995-4479

▷ Commissioner **Jay T. Pisco** .... (914) 995-2546

Department of Senior Programs and Services
Nine South First Avenue, 10th Floor, Mount Vernon, NY 10550-3414
Fax: (914) 813-6399

▷ Commissioner **Mae R. Carpenter** .... (914) 813-6431
E-mail: mrc1@westchestergov.com

Department of Social Services
112 East Post Road, 5th Floor, White Plains, NY 10601
Tel: (914) 995-5000 Fax: (914) 995-3285
Internet: http://socialservices.westchestergov.com/

▷ Commissioner **Kevin M. McGuire** .... (914) 995-5501
E-mail: kmm9@westchestergov.com
Assistant to the Commissioner, Constituent Affairs **John Kelly** .... (914) 995-6027
E-mail: jck5@westchestergov.com Fax: (914) 995-3285
Constituent Affairs/Employment Operations/SNAP **Joseph D. Kenner** .... (914) 995-3287
E-mail: jkenner@westchestergov.com
Deputy Commissioner, Children, Family Services, and Child Care **John Befus** .... (914) 995-5686
Deputy Commissioner, Temporary Assistance Field Operations **Rosa W. Boone** .... (914) 995-5520
E-mail: rxb7@westchestergov.com
Education: New Rochelle 1988 BA, 1991 MA
Deputy Commissioner, Finance **Philippe Gille** .... (914) 995-5450
Fax: (914) 995-6021
Children and Family Services Director **Elizabeth Dwyer** .... (914) 995-5300
Human Resources Director **Valerie Raynor** .... (914) 995-7750
Fax: (914) 995-6484
Adult Protective Services Manager **Nancy Sigler** .... (914) 995-5411
Fax: (914) 995-4943
Resource Bureau Program Manager **Hema Pendikatla** ... (914) 995-5631
Fax: (914) 995-5658
Associate Commissioner/Central Program Office **Katherine Waluschka** .... (914) 995-5572
Fax: (914) 995-5535

Office of Workforce Investment
120 Bloomingdale Road, White Plains, NY 10605
Fax: (914) 995-3958

▷ Director **Donovan P. Beckford** .... (914) 995-3707
E-mail: dpb2@westchestergov.com

Westchester Community College [WCC]
75 Grasslands Rd., Valhalla, NY 10595-1698
Tel: (914) 606-6600 (Information) Fax: (914) 606-6780
Internet: www.sunywcc.edu

President **Belinda S. Miles** .... (914) 606-6600

Westchester County Airport
240 Airport Road, Suite 202, White Plains, NY 10604
Fax: (914) 995-3980 E-mail: airportweb@westchestergov.com
Internet: http://airport.westchestergov.com/

Airport Manager **Peter Scherrer** .... (914) 995-4856
Assistant Airport Manager **Stephen Ferguson** .... (914) 995-4855

Westchester County Human Rights Commission
112 East Post Road, 3rd Floor, White Plains, NY 10601
Tel: (914) 995-7710 Fax: (914) 995-7720
E-mail: hrc@westchestergov.com

Executive Director **Mark C. Fang** .... (914) 995-7711
Deputy Director **Jerrice Duckette-Epps** .... (914) 995-7710

Westchester County Tax Commission
110 Dr. Martin Luther King, Jr. Blvd., Room L 221, White Plains, NY 10601-2519
Fax: (914) 995-4333

▷ Executive Director **Mary Beth Murphy** .... (914) 995-4325
E-mail: mbm7@westchestergov.com

Board of Legislators
Michaelian Office Bldg., 148 Martine Ave., Room 800, White Plains, NY 10601
Tel: (914) 995-2800 Fax: (914) 995-3884
Internet: www.westchesterlegislators.com

★ Chairman **Michael B. Kaplowitz** (D-District 4) .... (914) 995-2848
Term Expires: December 31, 2017
E-mail: kaplowitz@westchesterlegislators.com
Education: Hunter BA; SUNY (Buffalo) JD
★ Vice Chairman **James Maisano** (R-District 11) .... (914) 995-2826
Term Expires: December 31, 2017
E-mail: maisano@westchesterlegislators.com
Education: Hunter 1989 BS; SUNY (Buffalo) 1992 JD
★ Majority Leader **Catherine A. Borgia** (D-District 9) ..... (914) 995-2812
Term Expires: December 31, 2017
E-mail: borgia@westchesterlegislators.com
★ Minority Leader **John G. Testa** (R-District 1) .... (914) 995-2828
Term Expires: December 31, 2017
E-mail: testa@westchesterlegislators.com
★ Majority Whip **Lyndon D. Williams** (D-District 13) ..... (914) 995-2837
Term Expires: December 31, 2017
E-mail: williams@westchesterlegislators.com
★ Minority Whip **Gordon A. Burrows** (R-District 15) ..... (914) 995-2830
Term Expires: December 31, 2017
E-mail: burrows@westchesterlegislators.com
Education: Ithaca BA; St John's U (NY) JD
★ Legislator **Francis Corcoran** (R-District 2) .... (914) 995-2800
Term Expires: December 31, 2017
★ Legislator **Margaret Cunzio** (R-District 3) .... (914) 995-2800
Term Expires: December 31, 2017
★ Legislator **Benjamin Boykin II** (I-District 5) .... (914) 995-2827
Term Expires: December 31, 2017
E-mail: boykin@westchesterlegislators.com
★ Legislator **David B. Gelfarb** (R-District 6) .... (914) 995-2834
Term Expires: December 31, 2017
E-mail: gelfarb@westchesterlegislators.com
★ Legislator **Catherine F. Parker** (D-District 7) .... (914) 995-2802
Term Expires: December 31, 2017
E-mail: parker@westchesterlegislators.com
★ Legislator **Alfreda Williams** (D-District 8) .... (914) 995-2833
Term Expires: December 31, 2017
E-mail: awilliams@westchesterlegislators.com
★ Legislator **Sheila Marcotte** (R-District 10) .... (914) 995-2817
Term Expires: December 31, 2017
E-mail: marcotte@westchesterlegislators.com
★ Legislator **MaryJane Shimsky** (D-District 12) .... (914) 995-2821
Term Expires: December 31, 2017
E-mail: shimsky@westchesterlegislators.com
Education: Yale 1982; NYU 1985 JD; CUNY 2007 PhD

(continued on next page)

★ Elected Official ▲ Appointed by Legislature ▼ Appointed by Governor ▶ Appointed by Board or Commission ● Appointed by Judge
■ Appointed by Mayor △ Appointed by Freeholders ▽ Appointed by Supervisor ▷ Appointed by County Executive ○ Appointed by Council

Board of Legislators *continued*

★ Legislator **Bernice Spreckman** (R-District 14) .... (914) 995-2815
Term Expires: December 31, 2017
E-mail: spreckman@westchesterlegislators.com

★ Legislator **Kenneth W. Jenkins** (D-District 16) .... (914) 995-2829
Term Expires: December 31, 2017
E-mail: jenkins@westchesterlegislators.com

★ Legislator **Virginia M. Perez** (D-District 17) .... (914) 995-2846
Term Expires: December 31, 2017
E-mail: perez@westchesterlegislators.com

Clerk and Administrative Officer (Acting)
Sunday Vanderberg .... (914) 995-4604
E-mail: sundayv@westchesterlegislators.com

Office of the County Clerk

110 Dr. Martin Luther King, Jr. Blvd., White Plains, NY 10601
Tel: (914) 995-3081 Fax: (914) 995-4030
Internet: http://www.westchesterclerk.com

★ County Clerk **Timothy C. Idoni** (D) .... (914) 995-3081
Term Expires: December 31, 2017
E-mail: tci2@westchestergov.com
Assistant to the County Clerk
Eileen Songer McCarthy .... (914) 995-4287
E-mail: esm2@westchestergov.com

Executive Deputy County Clerk **Susan Kiernan** .... (914) 995-4499

Office of the District Attorney

County Courthouse, 111 Dr. Martin Luther King, Jr. Boulevard, White Plains, NY 10601
Fax: (914) 995-3779 Internet: www.westchesterda.net

★ District Attorney (Acting) **James McCarty** .... (914) 995-4200
Term Expires: December 31, 2017

First Deputy **John M. George** .... (914) 995-3413
First Deputy **Maryanne Luciano** .... (914) 995-3413
First Deputy **James McCarty** .... (914) 995-3387

Westchester County Board of Elections

25 Quarropas Street, White Plains, NY 10601
Tel: (914) 995-5700 Fax: (914) 995-7753 Fax: (914) 995-3190
Internet: http://citizenparticipation.westchestergov.com/

▲ Democratic Commissioner **Reginald A. LaFayette** .... (914) 995-5705
E-mail: ral4@westchestergov.com

▲ Republican Commissioner **Douglas A. Colety** .... (914) 995-5703
E-mail: dac7@westchestergov.com

County of Will, Illinois

302 North Chicago Street, Joliet, IL 60432
Tel: (815) 722-5515 (Information) Internet: www.willcountyillinois.com

County Seat: Joliet **Election Type:** Partisan **Population:** 687,263 (2015)

Office of the County Executive

302 N. Chicago St., Joliet, IL 60432
Tel: (815) 774-7480 Fax: (815) 740-4600

★ County Executive **Lawrence M. "Larry" Walsh** (D) .... (815) 774-7490
Term Expires: December 3, 2016
E-mail: countyexec@willcountyillinois.com

Chief of Staff **Nick Palmer** .... (815) 774-7488
Deputy Chief of Staff **Dave Tkac** .... (815) 774-7480
Legal Counsel **James Harvey** .... (815) 740-8380

Office of the County Executive *continued*

Manager of Operations **Jennifer Scharf** .... (815) 740-8382
Communications Director **Anastasia Tuskey** .... (815) 740-8376
E-mail: atuskey@willcountyillinois.com
Public Information Officer **Tammy Reiher** .... (815) 774-7485
E-mail: treiher@willcountyillinois.com Fax: (815) 774-3671

Public Defender's Office

58 East Clinton Street, Suite 210, Joliet, IL 60432
Fax: (815) 727-2916 Internet: www.willcountypublicdefender.com

▷ Public Defender **Gerald Kielian** .... (815) 727-8666
E-mail: fastrella@willcountyillinois.com
Education: Valparaiso 1975 JD

Records Management Office

806 Nicholson St., Joliet, IL 60435
Fax: (815) 727-8946

▷ Director **Michael Thompson** .... (815) 727-8456
E-mail: mthompson@willcountyillinois.com

Supervisor of Assessments' Office

302 North Chicago Street, 2nd Floor, Joliet, IL 60432
Fax: (815) 740-4696 Internet: www.willcountysoa.com

▷ Supervisor of Assessments **Rhonda R. Novak** .... (815) 740-4648
E-mail: rnovak@willcountyillinois.com

Animal Control Department

1200 South Cedar Road, Suite 1D, New Lenox, IL 60451
Fax: (815) 462-5630 E-mail: acontrol@willcountyillinois.com

▷ Director **Dr. Leroy P. Schild** .... (815) 724-1520

River Valley Justice Center

57 North Ottawa Street, 3rd Floor West, Joliet, IL 60432
Fax: (815) 730-7150

Director **Michael E. "Mike" Costigan** .... (815) 774-4527
Adult Division Assistant Director **(Vacant)** .... (815) 727-4537
Juvenile Division Assistant Director
Douglas M. Wilson .... (815) 774-4537
River Valley Justice Center, Fax: (815) 727-9326
3206 W. McDonough St., Joliet, IL 60431

Finance Department

302 N. Chicago St., Joliet, IL 60432
Fax: (815) 740-4604

Director of Finance **Karen Hennessy** .... (815) 747-4635
Budget Director **ReShawn Howard** .... (815) 723-1409
E-mail: rhoward@willcountyillinois.com

Department of Highways

16841 W. Laraway Rd., Joliet, IL 60433
Fax: (815) 727-9806 E-mail: highways@willcountyillinois.com

▷ County Engineer **Bruce D. Gould** .... (815) 727-8476
E-mail: bgould@willcountyillinois.com

Human Resources Department

302 North Chicago Street, Joliet, IL 60432
Fax: (815) 774-6355

Director **Bruce Tidwell** .... (815) 740-4634
E-mail: btidwell@willcountyillinois.com

Information Communication and Technology Department

302 North Chicago Street, Joliet, IL 60432
Fax: (815) 740-4706

Director **Michael Shay** .... (815) 740-8361

★ Elected Official ▲ Appointed by Legislature ▼ Appointed by Governor ▶ Appointed by Board or Commission ● Appointed by Judge
■ Appointed by Mayor △ Appointed by Freeholders ▽ Appointed by Supervisor ▷ Appointed by County Executive ○ Appointed by Council

Land Use Department
58 E. Clinton St., Suite 500, Joliet, IL 60432
Fax: (815) 774-7908
Director **Curt Paddock** . . . . . . (815) 774-3321

Building Maintenance
Fax: (815) 740-4330
Director **Michael Miglorini** . . . . . . (815) 740-4715

Waste Services Division
Fax: (815) 722-3410
Director **Dean Olson** . . . . . . (815) 727-8834

Purchasing Department
302 North Chicago Street, Joliet, IL 60432
Fax: (815) 740-4604 E-mail: purchasing@willcountyillinois.com
Director **Rita Weiss** . . . . . . (815) 740-4605
E-mail: rweiss@willcountyillinois.com

Sunny Hill Nursing Home
421 Doris Avenue, Joliet, IL 60433
Tel: (815) 727-8710 Fax: (815) 727-8637
▷ Administrator **Karen Isberg Sorbero** . . . . . . (815) 727-8710 ext. 8650
E-mail: ksorbero@willcountyillinois.com

Will County Board of Health
501 Ella Avenue, Community Room, Joliet, IL 60433
President **John J. Hines** . . . . . . (815) 727-8480

Will County Health Department
501 Ella Avenue, Joliet, IL 60433
Tel: (815) 727-8480 Fax: (815) 727-8484
E-mail: info@willcountyhealth.org Internet: www.willcountyhealth.org
▷ Executive Director **John J. Cicero** . . . . . . (815) 740-8982
E-mail: jcicero@willcountyhealth.org
Education: Southern Illinois BS; Governors State MHA

Will County Emergency Management Agency
302 North Chicago Street, Joliet, IL 60432
Fax: (815) 723-8895 E-mail: ema@willcountyillinois.com
Internet: www.willcountyema.org
▷ Director **Harold Damron** . . . . . . (815) 740-8351
E-mail: hdamron@willcountyillinois.com

Office of the County Board
302 N. Chicago St., Joliet, IL 60432
Fax: (815) 740-8395 E-mail: willcountyboard@willcountyillinois.com
Internet: www.willcountyboard.com

★ Chairman **James G. "Jim" Moustis** (R-District 2) . . . . . . (815) 740-4602
Term Expires: November 30, 2018
E-mail: jmoustis@willcountyillinois.com

★ Board Member **Robert Howard** (D-District 1) . . . . . . (815) 740-4602
Term Expires: November 30, 2016
E-mail: bobhoward.willcountyboard@gmail.com

★ Board Member **Judy Ogalla** (R-District 1) . . . . . . (815) 740-4602
Term Expires: November 30, 2016

★ Board Member **Cory Singer** (R-District 2) . . . . . . (815) 740-4602
Term Expires: December 3, 2018

★ Board Member **Donald A. Moran** (D-District 3) . . . . . . (815) 740-4602
Term Expires: November 30, 2016
E-mail: dmoran@willcountyillinois.com

★ Board Member **Elizabeth J. "Beth" Rice** (D-District 3) . . (815) 740-4602
Term Expires: November 30, 2016
E-mail: brice@willcountyillinois.com

★ Board Member **Kenneth Harris** (D-District 4) . . . . . . (815) 740-4602
Term Expires: November 30, 2016
E-mail: kharris@willcountyillinois.com

Office of the County Board *continued*

★ Board Member **Jacqueline Traynere** (D-District 4) . . . . . . (815) 740-4602
Term Expires: November 30, 2016
E-mail: jtraynere@comcast.net

★ Board Member **Darren Bennefield** (R-District 5) . . . . . . (815) 740-4602
Term Expires: November 30, 2018

★ Board Member **Gretchen Fritz** (R-District 5) . . . . . . (815) 740-4602
Term Expires: December 3, 2018

★ Board Member **Ragan Freitag** (R-District 6) . . . . . . (815) 740-4602
Term Expires: November 30, 2016
E-mail: ragan@raganfreitag.com

★ Board Member **Donald "Don" Gould** (R-District 6) . . . . . . (815) 740-4602
Term Expires: November 30, 2016
E-mail: rocklaw94@aol.com

★ Board Member **Stephen J. Balich** (R-District 7) . . . . . . (815) 740-4602
Term Expires: November 30, 2016

★ Board Member **Mike Fricilone** (R-District 7) . . . . . . (815) 740-4602
Term Expires: November 30, 2016
E-mail: mikefricilone@gmail.com

★ Board Member **Rev. Herbert Brooks, Jr.** (D-District 8) . . (815) 740-4602
Term Expires: November 30, 2016
E-mail: stjohnschurch@comcast.net

★ Board Member **Denise Winfrey** (D-District 8) . . . . . . (815) 740-4602
Term Expires: November 30, 2016
E-mail: dwinfrey13@gmail.com

★ Board Member **Annette Parker** (R-District 9) . . . . . . (815) 740-4602
Term Expires: November 30, 2018

★ Board Member **Lauren Staley-Ferry** (D-District 9) . . . . . . (815) 740-4602
Term Expires: December 3, 2018

★ Board Member **Joseph M. Babich** (D-District 10) . . . . . . (815) 740-4602
Term Expires: November 30, 2016

★ Board Member **Stephen M. Wilhemi** (D-District 10) . . . . . . (815) 740-4602
Term Expires: November 30, 2016
E-mail: wfstax@juno.com

★ Board Member **Suzanne Hart** (R-District 11) . . . . . . (815) 740-4602
Term Expires: November 30, 2018
E-mail: suzannehartwillcounty@yahoo.com

★ Board Member
Charles E. "Chuck" Maher (R-District 11) . . . . . . (815) 740-4602
Term Expires: November 30, 2018
E-mail: chuck.maher@gmail.com

★ Board Member **Ray Tuminello** (D-District 12) . . . . . . (815) 740-4602
Term Expires: November 30, 2016

★ Board Member **Thomas P. Weigel** (R-District 12) . . . . . . (815) 740-4602
Term Expires: November 30, 2016
E-mail: tomweigel@att.net

★ Board Member **Liz Collins** (R-District 13) . . . . . . (815) 740-4602
Term Expires: November 30, 2016
E-mail: etcollins627@yahoo.com

★ Board Member **Mark Ferry** (D-District 13) . . . . . . (815) 740-4602
Term Expires: November 30, 2016
E-mail: mferry@willcountyillinois.com

Chief of Staff to the Board **Bruce Friefeld** . . . . . . (815) 740-8371
Deputy Chief of Staff to the Board **Melissa Johannsen** . . (815) 774-6345

Office of the County Auditor
302 N. Chicago St., Joliet, IL 60432
Fax: (815) 740-4319
★ County Auditor **K. Duffy Blackburn** . . . . . . (815) 740-4609
Term Expires: November 30, 2016
E-mail: dblackburn@willcountyillinois.com

Office of the County Clerk
302 N. Chicago St., Joliet, IL 60432
Fax: (815) 740-4699 E-mail: coclrk@willcountyillinois.com
Internet: http://www.willclrk.com
★ County Clerk **Nancy Schultz Voots** (R) . . . . . . (815) 740-4615
Term Expires: November 30, 2018
E-mail: nvoots@willcountyillinois.com

(continued on next page)

★ Elected Official ▲ Appointed by Legislature ▼ Appointed by Governor ▶ Appointed by Board or Commission ● Appointed by Judge
■ Appointed by Mayor △ Appointed by Freeholders ▽ Appointed by Supervisor ▷ Appointed by County Executive ○ Appointed by Council

Office of the County Clerk *continued*

Chief Deputy County Clerk **Judy Wiedmeyer** . . . . (815) 740-4613
E-mail: jwiedmeyer@willcountyillinois.com

Office of the Circuit Clerk

14 W. Jefferson St., Joliet, IL 60432
Fax: (815) 740-8074

★Circuit Clerk **Pamela McGuire** (D) . . . . (815) 727-8592
Term Expires: November 30, 2016
E-mail: pmcguire@willcountyillinois.com

Office of the Coroner

57 North Ottawa Street, Suite 412, Joliet, IL 60432
Fax: (815) 727-8816

★Coroner **Patrick K. O'Neil** (D) . . . . (815) 727-8455
Term Expires: November 30, 2016
E-mail: po'neil@willcountyillinois.com

Office of the Recorder of Deeds

158 N Scott Street, Joliet, IL 60432
Fax: (815) 740-4638

★Recorder of Deeds **Karen A. Stukel** . . . . (815) 740-4637
Term Expires: November 30, 2016

Office of the Sheriff

14 W. Jefferson St., Joliet, IL 60432
Fax: (815) 727-8565

★Sheriff **Mike Kelley** . . . . (815) 727-8895
Term Expires: December 3, 2018

Office of the State's Attorney

121 North Chicago Street, Joliet, IL 60432
Fax: (815) 727-8405

★State's Attorney **James W. "Jim" Glasgow** (D) . . . . (815) 727-8453
Term Expires: November 30, 2016
E-mail: jglasgow@willcountyillinois.com

Office of the County Treasurer

302 N. Chicago St., Joliet, IL 60432
Fax: (815) 740-4695 E-mail: treasurer@willcountyillinois.com
Internet: www.willcountytreasurer.com

★Treasurer **Stephen P. "Steve" Weber** (R) . . . . (815) 740-4675
Term Expires: November 30, 2018
E-mail: sweber@willcountyillinois.com

Will County Regional Office of Education

702 West Maple Street, New Lenox, IL 60451
Tel: (815) 740-8360 Fax: (815) 740-4788 Internet: www.willroe.org

★Superintendent **Shawn Walsh** . . . . (815) 740-8360
Term Expires: June 30, 2019
E-mail: swalsh@willcountyillinois.com

County of Williamson, Texas

710 Main Street, Suite 101, Georgetown, TX 78262
Tel: (512) 943-1100 Internet: www.wilco.org

County Seat: Georgetown **Election Type:** Nonpartisan
Population: 508,514 (2015)

The Commissioners Court

710 Main Street, Georgetown, TX 78262
Tel: (512) 943-1550 Fax: (512) 943-1662

★County Judge **Dan A. Gattis** . . . . (512) 943-1550
Term Expires: December 31, 2018
E-mail: ctyjudge@wilco.org

★Commissioner **Lisa Birkman** (Precinct 1) . . . . (512) 244-8610
Term Expires: December 31, 2016 Fax: (512) 244-8616
E-mail: lbirkman@wilco.org

★Commissioner **Cynthia P. Long** (Precinct 2) . . . . (512) 260-4280
Term Expires: December 31, 2018 Fax: (512) 260-4284
E-mail: clong@wilco.org

★Commissioner **Valerie Covey** (Precinct 3) . . . . (512) 943-3370
Term Expires: December 31, 2016 Fax: (512) 943-3376
E-mail: comm3@wilco.org

★Commissioner **Ron Morrison** (Precinct 4) . . . . (512) 846-1190
Term Expires: December 31, 2018 Fax: (512) 846-1140
E-mail: rmorrison@wilco.org

Office of the County Auditor

710 Main Street, Georgetown, TX 78262
Tel: (512) 943-1500

County Auditor **David U. Flores** . . . . (512) 943-1500
First Assistant County Auditor **Julie Kiley** . . . . (512) 943-1552
Financial Director **(Vacant)** . . . . (512) 943-1579
Director of Internal Audit **(Vacant)** . . . . (512) 943-1556
Payroll Manager **Karen Knightstep** . . . . (512) 943-1563

Budget Office

710 Main Street, Georgetown, TX 78262
Tel: (512) 943-1551 Fax: (512) 943-1662 E-mail: budget@wilco.org

Budget Officer **Ashlie Koenig** . . . . (512) 943-1551
E-mail: akoenig@wilco.org
Budget Analyst **Jennifer Templeton** . . . . (512) 943-3756
E-mail: jtempleton@wilco.org

Public Information Office

710 Main Street, Suite 101, Georgetown, TX 78262
Tel: (512) 943-1663 Fax: (512) 943-1662

Public Affairs Manager **Connie Watson** . . . . (512) 943-1663
E-mail: cwatson@wilco.org
Communication Coordinator **Kathi Wysong** . . . . (512) 943-3579
E-mail: kwysong@wilco.org

Veterans Service Office

3151 South East Inner Loop, Georgetown, TX 78626
Tel: (512) 943-1900 Fax: (512) 943-1905

Director **Donna Harrell** . . . . (512) 238-2151
Assistant County Service Officer **Will Molidor** . . . . (512) 238-2151
Assistant County Service Officer **(Vacant)** . . . . (512) 238-2151
Assistant County Service Officer **Valerie Zimmerman** . . . (512) 238-2151

Elections Department

301 Southeast Inner Loop, Suite 104, Georgetown, TX 78626
Tel: (512) 943-1630 Fax: (512) 943-1634

Director **Chris Davis** . . . . (512) 943-1630

★Elected Official ▲Appointed by Legislature ▼Appointed by Governor ▶Appointed by Board or Commission ●Appointed by Judge
■Appointed by Mayor △Appointed by Freeholders ▽Appointed by Supervisor ▷Appointed by County Executive ○Appointed by Council

Emergency Communications Department
710 Main Street, Georgetown, TX 78262
Tel: (512) 943-1438 E-mail: 911comm@wilco.org

Director **Scott Parker** . . . . (512) 943-1438

Emergency Management Department
303 Martin Luther King Street, Georgetown, TX 78626
Tel: (512) 943-3747 Fax: (512) 943-1269

Emergency Management Coordinator **Jarred Thomas** . . . . (512) 943-3747
E-mail: jthomas@wilco.org
Emergency Management Deputy Coordinator **(Vacant)** . . . (512) 943-3876

Facilities Maintenance Department
3101 Inner Loop Road, Suite A, Georgetown, TX 78626
Tel: (512) 943-1599 Fax: (512) 943-3301 E-mail: facilities@wilco.org

Director **Gary Wilson** . . . . (512) 943-1599
E-mail: gwilson@wilco.org

Human Resources Department
301 Southeast Inner Loop, Suite 108, Georgetown, TX 78626
Tel: (512) 943-1533 Fax: (512) 943-1535 E-mail: hr@wilco.org

Senior Director **Tara Raymore** . . . . (512) 943-1534
E-mail: traymore@wilco.org

Geographic Information Systems Department [GIS]
301 Southeast Inner Loop, Georgetown, TX 78626
Tel: (512) 943-1489 E-mail: gis@wilco.org

Director **Richard Semple** . . . . (512) 943-1489

Parks and Recreation Department
350 Discovery Boulevard, Suite 207, Cedar Park, TX 78613
Tel: (512) 260-4283 E-mail: parks&rec@wilco.org
Internet: http://parks.wilcogov.org

Director (Interim) **Randy Bell** . . . . (512) 943-1920

Purchasing Department
301 Southeast Inner Loop, Georgetown, TX 78626
Tel: (512) 943-3553 Fax: (512) 943-1575 E-mail: purchase@wilco.org

Director **(Vacant)** . . . . (512) 943-3553

Williamson County and Cities Health District [WCCHD]
100 West Third Street, Georgetown, TX 78626
Tel: (512) 943-3600 E-mail: info@wccdh.org Internet: www.wcchd.org

Executive Director **John Teel** . . . . (512) 943-3600

County Constables

★Constable **Robert Chody** (Precinct 1) . . . . (512) 244-8650
Term Expires: December 31, 2016 Fax: (512) 244-8662
E-mail: rchody@wilco.org
★Constable **Rick Coffman** (Precinct 2) . . . . (512) 260-4270
Term Expires: December 31, 2016 Fax: (512) 260-4275
E-mail: rcoffman@wilco.org
★Constable **Kevin Stofle** (Precinct 3) . . . . (512) 943-1434
Term Expires: December 31, 2016 Fax: (512) 943-1440
E-mail: const3mail@wilco.org
★Constable **Marty Ruble** (Precinct 4) . . . . (512) 532-4181
Term Expires: December 31, 2016 Fax: (512) 352-4186
E-mail: mruble@wilco.org

Office of the County Attorney
405 Martin Luther King Street, Georgetown, TX 78626
Tel: (512) 943-1111 Fax: (512) 943-1120

★County Attorney **Doyle "Dee" Hobbs, Jr.** . . . . (512) 943-1111
Term Expires: December 31, 2016
E-mail: dhobbs@wilco.org
Chief, Civil Division **Henry "Hank" Prejean** . . . . (512) 943-1111
Education: Lamar 1976; South Texas 1983 JD
Chief, Criminal Division **Brian Klas** . . . . (512) 943-1111
Chief, Family Justice Division **Alice Emerson** . . . . (512) 943-1111
Education: Hendrix 1996 BA; Texas 2002 JD
Juvenile Prosecutor **(Vacant)** . . . . (512) 943-1111

Office of the County Clerk
405 Martin Luther King Street, Georgetown, TX 78626
Tel: (512) 943-1515 Fax: (512) 943-1616

★County Clerk **Nancy E. Rister** . . . . (512) 943-1515
Term Expires: December 31, 2018
E-mail: nrister@wilco.org

Office of the District Attorney
405 Martin Luther King Street, Georgetown, TX 78626
Tel: (512) 943-1234 Fax: (512) 943-1255

★District Attorney **Jana Duty** . . . . (512) 943-1234
Term Expires: December 31, 2016
E-mail: jduty@wilco.org
Education: Texas (San Antonio); St Mary's U (TX) JD
First Assistant District Attorney **Mark Brunner** . . . . (512) 943-1234
Appellate Prosecutor **Kristen Elaine Jernigan** . . . . (512) 943-1234
Education: South Texas 1997 JD

Office of the Sheriff
508 South Rock Street, Georgetown, TX 78626
Tel: (512) 943-1300 Fax: (512) 943-1444

★Sheriff **James Wilson** . . . . (512) 943-1300
Term Expires: December 31, 2016

Office of the Tax Assessor/Collector
904 South Main Street, Georgetown, TX 78626
Tel: (512) 943-1603

★Tax Assessor/Collector **Deborah Hunt** . . . . (512) 943-1603
Term Expires: December 31, 2016
E-mail: dhunt@wilco.org

Office of the Treasurer
710 Main Street, Georgetown, TX 78262
Tel: (512) 943-1540 Fax: (512) 943-1590

★County Treasurer **Jerri Jones** . . . . (512) 943-1540
Term Expires: December 31, 2018

COUNTIES

★Elected Official ■Appointed by Mayor ▲Appointed by Legislature △Appointed by Freeholders ▼Appointed by Governor ▽Appointed by Supervisor ▶Appointed by Board or Commission ▷Appointed by County Executive ●Appointed by Judge ○Appointed by Council

County of Yellowstone, Montana

P.O. Box 35000, Billings, MT 59107
Tel: (406) 256-2701 (Information) Internet: www.co.yellowstone.mt.gov

County Seat: Billings **Election Type:** Partisan **Population:** 157,048 (2015)

Office of the Board of County Commissioners

P.O. Box 35000, Billings, MT 59107
Fax: (406) 256-2777

★ Chair **William "Bill" Kennedy** (D-District 3) .... (406) 256-2701
Term Expires: December 31, 2018
E-mail: bkennedy@co.yellowstone.mt.gov
Education: Montana State BE; Eastern Montana MA

★ Commissioner **John V. Ostlund** (R-District 1) .... (406) 256-2701
Term Expires: December 31, 2020
E-mail: jostlund@co.yellowstone.mt.gov

★ Commissioner **James "Jim" Reno** (R-District 2) .... (406) 256-2701
Term Expires: December 31, 2016
E-mail: jreno@co.yellowstone.mt.gov

Office of the Coroner

219 N. 26th St., Billings, MT 59101
Tel: (406) 256-2946

▶ Coroner **Bill Jones** .... (406) 256-2946
E-mail: bjones@co.yellowstone.mt.gov

Disaster and Emergency Services

P.O. Box 35004, Billings, MT 59107
Fax: (406) 256-6947

▶ Director **Duane Winslow** .... (406) 256-2775
E-mail: dwinslow@co.yellowstone.mt.gov

Election Administration

P.O. Box 35002, Billings, MT 59107
Fax: (406) 254-7940

▶ Election Administrator (Interim) **Bret Rutherford** .... (406) 256-2740
E-mail: brutherford@co.yellowstone.mt.gov

Extension Office

P.O. Box 35021, Billings, MT 59107
Fax: (406) 256-2825 E-mail: rbaker@co.yellowstone.mt.gov

Agriculture **Steve Lackman** .... (406) 256-2828
Family and Consumer Science **Jackie Rumph** .... (406) 256-2828
E-mail: jackie.rumph@montana.edu
Horticulture **Amy Grandpre** .... (406) 256-2828
4-H/Youth **Roni Baker** .... (406) 256-2828

Yellowstone City–County Health Department [RiverStone Health]

123 South 27th Street, Billings, MT 59101
Tel: (406) 247-3200 Fax: (406) 247-3202
Internet: www.riverstonehealth.org

▶ Chief Executive Officer and President/Health Officer **John Felton** .... (406) 247-3200 ext. 6474

Human Resources Department

P.O. Box 35041, Billings, MT 59107-5002
Fax: (406) 254-7908

▶ Director **Dwight Vigness** .... (406) 256-2705
E-mail: dvigness@co.yellowstone.mt.gov

Planning Department

2825 Third Avenue N, Billings, MT 59101

▶ Director **Candi Millar** .... (406) 657-8246
E-mail: millarc@ci.billings.mt.us

Probation Office

P.O. Box 35031, Billings, MT 59107

▶ Probation Officer **Tara French** .... (406) 256-2838
E-mail: tfrench@mt.gov

Office of Public Assistance

111 N. 31st St., Billings, MT 59101

▶ Director **Brenda Rush** .... (406) 237-0520

Public Works Department

P.O. Box 35024, Billings, MT 59107

▶ Director **Tim Miller** .... (406) 256-2735
E-mail: tmiller@co.yellowstone.mt.gov

Office of the Auditor

P.O. Box 35014, Billings, MT 59107

★ Auditor **Debby Hernandez** (R) .... (406) 256-2720
Term Expires: December 31, 2018
E-mail: dhernandez@co.yellowstone.mt.gov

Office of the Clerk and Recorder/Surveyor

P.O. Box 35001, Billings, MT 59107
Fax: (406) 256-2736 Internet: www.co.yellowstone.mt.gov/clerk

★ Clerk and Recorder/Surveyor **Jeff Martin** .... (406) 256-2785
Term Expires: December 31, 2018
E-mail: jmartin@co.yellowstone.mt.gov

Office of the County Attorney

P.O. Box 35025, Billings, MT 59107

★ County Attorney **Scott D. Twito** (R) .... (406) 256-2870
Term Expires: December 31, 2018

Office of the Sheriff

Round Bldg, 219 N. 26th St., Billings, MT 59101
Fax: (406) 256-2934

★ Sheriff **Mike Linder** (R) .... (406) 256-2929
Term Expires: December 31, 2018

Office of the Treasurer/Assessor/Superintendent of Schools

217 North 27th Street, 1st Floor, Billings, MT 59101
P.O. Box 35010, Billings, MT 59107
Tel: (406) 246-2802 (Treasurer)
Tel: (406) 246-6933 (Schools) Fax: (406) 256-6930 (Schools)
Internet: www.co.yellowstone.mt.gov/treasurer
Internet: www.co.yellowstone.mt.gov/schools

★ Treasurer/Assessor/Superintendent of Schools **Sherry Long** (R) .... (406) 256-2802
Term Expires: December 31, 2018

★ Elected Official ▲ Appointed by Legislature ▼ Appointed by Governor ▶ Appointed by Board or Commission ● Appointed by Judge
■ Appointed by Mayor △ Appointed by Freeholders ▽ Appointed by Supervisor ▷ Appointed by County Executive ○ Appointed by Council

County of York, Pennsylvania

28 East Market Street, York, PA 17401
Internet: www.yorkcountypa.gov

County Seat: York **Election Type:** Partisan **Year Founded:** 1749
Population: 442,867 (2015)

Board of Commissioners

28 East Market Street, York, PA 17401
Tel: (717) 771-9964 Fax: (717) 771-9804

★ President **Susan Byrnes** (R) .... (717) 771-9301
Term Expires: December 31, 2019

★ Vice President **Doug Hoke** (D) .... (717) 771-9302
Term Expires: December 31, 2019
E-mail: dhoke@yorkcountypa.org

★ Commissioner **Christopher B. Reilly** (R) .... (717) 771-9303
Term Expires: December 31, 2019
E-mail: cbreilly@yorkcountypa.org
Education: Maryland 1985 BA

County Solicitor **Glenn J. Smith** .... (717) 771-9964
Education: Widener JD

Office of the Chief Clerk/Office Manager

28 East Market Street, Room 216, York, PA 17401

Chief Clerk/Office Manager **Sherry L. Baer** .... (717) 771-9656
E-mail: slbaer@yorkcountypa.org

Office of the County Administrator

28 East Market Street, York, PA 17401

County Administrator **Mark Derr** .... (717) 771-9964

Assessment Office

28 East Market Street, Room 105, York, PA 17401
Tel: (717) 771-9232 Fax: (717) 771-4651

Director **E. John Fedor** .... (717) 771-9232

Department of Emergency Services

120 Davies Drive, York, PA 17402
Tel: (717) 840-2990 Fax: (717) 840-7406 E-mail: oem@ycdes.org
Internet: www.ycdes.org

Executive Director **Eric Bistline** .... (717) 840-2990

Department of Human Resources

28 East Market Street, York, PA 17401
Tel: (717) 771-9214 Fax: (717) 771-4669
Internet: www.york-county.org/departments/hr/hr.htm

Director **Kristy Bixler** .... (717) 771-9249
E-mail: kbixler@yorkcountypa.org

Human Services Division

100 West Market Street, Suite 401, York, PA 17401
Tel: (717) 771-9347 Fax: (717) 771-4663
E-mail: humanservices@yorkcountypa.gov Internet: www.ychsd.org

Executive Director **Michelle Hovis** .... (717) 771-9347
Deputy Director - Administration **Jessica E. Mockabee** .. (717) 771-9347
E-mail: JEMockabee@yorkcountypa.gov

Area Agency on Aging

100 West Market Street, Suite 102, York, PA 17401
Tel: (717) 771-9610 Fax: (717) 771-9044
E-mail: aging@yorkcountypa.gov Internet: www.ycaaa.org

Director **Mark Shea** .... (717) 771-9610

Office of Children, Youth and Family

100 West Market Street, Suite 402, York, PA 17401
Tel: (717) 846-8496 Fax: (717) 771-9884 E-mail: cys@yorkcountypa.gov
Internet: www.yccys.org

Executive Director **Terry Clark** .... (717) 771-9868

Department of Veterans Affairs

100 West Market Street, Suite 101, York, PA 17401
Tel: (717) 771-9218 Fax: (717) 771-4617 Internet: www.ycva.org

Director **Philip A. Palandro** .... (717) 771-9218

York/Adams Drug and Alcohol Program [YADAP]

3410-B East Market Street, York, PA 17402
Tel: (717) 840-4207 Fax: (717) 840-4135 Internet: www.ycd-a.org

Administrator **Audrey Gladfelter** .... (717) 771-9222

Department of Information Services

28 East Market Street, Room B021, York, PA 17401
Tel: (717) 771-9762 Fax: (717) 771-9961

Executive Director **Joseph Sassano** .... (717) 771-9321

Elections/Voter Registration Office

28 East Market Street, York, PA 17401
Tel: (717) 771-9604 Internet: www.york-county.org/voters/election.htm

Director **Nikki Suchanic** .... (717) 771-9604

County Archives

150 Pleasant Acres Road, York, PA 17402
Tel: (717) 840-7222 Fax: (717) 840-7224
E-mail: archives@york-county.org Internet: www.yorkcountyarchives.org

Director **Christy Depew** .... (717) 840-7222

Department of Parks and Recreation

400 Mundis Race Road, York, PA 17406-9721
Tel: (717) 840-7440 Fax: (717) 840-7403 E-mail: parks@york-county.org
Internet: www.yorkcountyparks.org

Director **Tammy Klunk** .... (717) 840-7227

Facilities Management

28 East Market Street, York, PA 17401
Fax: (717) 771-4338

Director **Scott Cassel** .... (717) 771-4388
E-mail: sacassel@yorkcountypa.org

Purchasing Department

28 East Market Street, York, PA 17401
Tel: (717) 771-9269 Fax: (717) 771-9226

Coordinator **Tina Blessing** .... (717) 771-9269
E-mail: tlblessing@yorkcountypa.gov

Bureau of Weights and Measures

118 Pleasant Acres Road, York, PA 17402
Tel: (717) 840-7664 Internet: www.york-county.org/misc/WMweb.htm

Director **James S. Crager** .... (717) 840-7664

County Controller's Office

28 East Market Street, Room 232, York, PA 17401
Tel: (717) 771-9616 Fax: (717) 771-4330

★ Controller **Robert P. Green** .... (717) 771-9330
Term Expires: December 31, 2017
E-mail: rpgreen@yorkcountypa.org

Deputy Controller **Deborah K. Myers** .... (717) 771-9308

★ Elected Official ▲ Appointed by Legislature ▼ Appointed by Governor ▶ Appointed by Board or Commission ● Appointed by Judge
■ Appointed by Mayor △ Appointed by Freeholders ▽ Appointed by Supervisor ▷ Appointed by County Executive ○ Appointed by Council

County Sheriff's Department

45 North George Street, York, PA 17401
Tel: (717) 771-9601 Fax: (717) 771-4631 Internet: www.yorksheriff.org

★Sheriff **Richard P. Keuerleber** . . . . (717) 771-9601
Term Expires: December 31, 2019
Chief Deputy - Administration **Richard E. Rice II** . . . . (717) 771-9601
E-mail: rerice@yorkcountypa.org
Chief Deputy - Operations **Michael S. Hose** . . . . (717) 771-9601

County Treasurer's Office

28 East Market Street, Room 126, York, PA 17401
Tel: (717) 771-9603 Fax: (717) 771-4331

★Treasurer **Barbara L. Bair** . . . . (717) 771-9603
Term Expires: December 31, 2019
E-mail: blbair@yorkcountypa.org

District Attorney's Office

45 North George Street, York, PA 17401
Tel: (717) 771-9600 Fax: (717) 771-9738
Internet: www.yorkda.com/index.shtml

★District Attorney **Tom Kearney** (R) . . . . (717) 771-9600
Term Expires: December 31, 2017
Education: Penn State 1973 BS; Dickinson Law 1977 JD

Office of the Prothonotary

45 North George Street, York, PA 17401
Tel: (717) 771-9611

★Prothonotary **Pamela S. Lee** . . . . (717) 771-9611
Term Expires: December 31, 2019
E-mail: pslee@yorkcountypa.gov

Office of the Recorder of Deeds

28 East Market Street, York, PA 17401
Tel: (717) 771-9608 Fax: (717) 771-9582

★Recorder of Deeds **Randi L. Reisinger** . . . . (717) 771-9608
Term Expires: December 31, 2017
E-mail: rlreisinger@yorkcountypa.gov

★Elected Official ▲Appointed by Legislature ▼Appointed by Governor ▶Appointed by Board or Commission ●Appointed by Judge
■Appointed by Mayor △Appointed by Freeholders ▽Appointed by Supervisor ▷Appointed by County Executive ○Appointed by Council

Authorities

Alameda County Water District [ACWD]

43885 South Grimmer Boulevard, Fremont, CA 94538
P.O. Box 5110, Fremont, CA 94537
Tel: (510) 668-4200 Fax: (510) 770-1793 Internet: www.acwd.org

Board of Directors

Fax: (510) 770-1793

★ President **Judy C. Huang** .... (510) 668-4202
Term Expires: December 2018
E-mail: judy.huang@acwd.com
★ Director **James G. "Jim" Gunther** .... (510) 668-4202
Term Expires: December 2016
E-mail: james.gunther@acwd.com
★ Director **Martin L. "Marty" Koller** .... (510) 668-4202
Term Expires: December 2016
E-mail: martin.koller@acwd.com
★ Director **Paul Sethy** .... (510) 668-4202
Term Expires: December 2018
E-mail: paul.sethy@acwd.com
★ Director **John H. Weed** .... (510) 668-4202
Term Expires: December 2016
E-mail: john.weed@acwd.com

Administration

General Manager **Robert Shaver** .... (510) 668-4202
E-mail: robert.shaver@acwd.com
Education: Virginia Tech BSCE
Manager, Project Engineering **Toni Lyons** .... (510) 668-4480
E-mail: toni.lyons@acwd.com
Manager, Finance Department **Shelley Burgett** .... (510) 668-4251

Albany Port District Commission [APDC]

Port Administration Building, 106 Smith Boulevard, Albany, NY 12202
Tel: (518) 463-8763 Fax: (518) 463-8767
Internet: www.portofalbany.com

Office of the Commissioners

Port of Albany, 106 Smith Boulevard, Albany, NY 12202
Fax: (518) 463-8767

▼ Chairman **Georgette Steffens** .... (518) 463-8763
▼ Treasurer **Joseph E. Coffey, Jr.** .... (518) 463-8763
▼ Commissioner **John Bulgaro** .... (518) 463-8763
▼ Commissioner **Dominick M. Tagliento** .... (518) 463-8763
▼ Commissioner **(Vacant)** .... (518) 463-8763

Administration

General Manager **Richard Hendrick** .... (518) 463-8763
E-mail: rhendrick@portofalbany.us
Chief Financial Officer **Terry Hurley** .... (518) 463-8763
General Counsel **Thomas Owens** .... (518) 463-8763
Business Development and Marketing Manager
Anthony "Tony" Vasil .... (518) 463-8763
E-mail: tvasil@portofalbany.us
Human Resources Manager **Annie Fitzgerald** .... (518) 463-8763
E-mail: afitzgerald@portofalbany.us
Real Estate Manager **(Vacant)** .... (518) 463-8763
Security and Threat Assessment Director
David "Dave" Williams .... (518) 463-8763
Information Technology Specialist
Thomas J. McGuinness .... (518) 463-8763
E-mail: tmcguinness@portofalbany.us

Administration *continued*

Procurement Manager **Megan Daly** .... (518) 463-8763
E-mail: mdaly@portofalbany.us

Anne Arundel Economic Development Corporation [AAEDC]

2660 Riva Road, Suite 200, Annapolis, MD 21401
Tel: (410) 222-7410 Fax: (410) 222-7415 E-mail: info@aaedc.org
Internet: www.aaedc.org

Office of the President

President and Chief Executive Officer
Robert L. "Bob" Hannon .... (410) 222-7410
E-mail: rhannon@aaedc.org
Education: Towson State U BS, MA
Executive Vice President **Mary Burkholder** .... (410) 222-7410
Executive Assistant **Christina Holliday** .... (410) 222-7410
E-mail: cholliday@aaedc.org
Administrative Officer **Jill Seamon** .... (410) 222-7410
E-mail: jseamon@aaedc.org
Real Estate Development Vice President **(Vacant)** .... (410) 222-7410
Marketing and Outreach Manager **Theresa Downs** .... (410) 222-7410
E-mail: tdowns@aaedc.org
Manager of Loan Administration **Lisa Grunder** .... (410) 222-7410
Vice President, Financial Services **Steve Primosch** .... (410) 222-7410

Central Contra Costa Sanitary District [CCCSD]

5019 Imhoff Place, Martinez, CA 94553
Fax: (925) 676-7211 Internet: www.centralsan.org

Board of Directors

★ President **Tad Pilecki** .... (925) 229-7303
Term Expires: December 31, 2016
★ President Pro Tem **Paul Causey** .... (925) 229-7303
Term Expires: December 31, 2016
★ Member **Michael R. McGill** .... (925) 229-7303
Term Expires: December 31, 2018
★ Member **James A. Nejedly** .... (925) 229-7303
Term Expires: December 31, 2016
★ Member **David R. Williams** .... (925) 229-7303
Term Expires: December 31, 2018
Education: Purdue BS, MS; UC Berkeley MBA

Administration

General Manager **Roger S. Bailey** .... (925) 229-7300
Deputy General Manager **Ann Sasaki** .... (925) 229-7156
E-mail: asasaki@centralsan.org
Director of Administration **David Heath** .... (925) 229-7305
E-mail: dheath@centralsan.org
Director of Engineering and Technical Services
Jean-Marc Petit .... (925) 229-7112
E-mail: jmpetit@centralsan.org
Collection System Operations Division Manager
Paul Seitz .... (925) 335-7743
E-mail: pseitz@centralsan.org
Capital Projects Division Manager **Edgar Lopez** .... (925) 229-7366
Communication Services and Intergovernmental Affairs
Manager **Emily Barnett** .... (925) 229-7310
E-mail: ebarnett@centralsan.org

(continued on next page)

★ Elected Official ▲ Appointed by Legislature ▼ Appointed by Governor ► Appointed by Board or Commission ● Appointed by Judge
■ Appointed by Mayor △ Appointed by Freeholders ▽ Appointed by Supervisor ▷ Appointed by County Executive ○ Appointed by Council

AUTHORITIES

Administration *continued*

Human Resources Manager **Teji O'Malley** . . . . . (925) 229-7309
E-mail: tomalley@centralsan.org

Planning and Development Services Division Manager **Danea Gemmell** . . . . . (925) 229-7118

Plant Operations Division Manager **Alan Weer** . . . . . (925) 335-7731
E-mail: aweer@centralsan.org

Purchasing and Materials Manager **Stephanie King** . . . . . (925) 229-7307
E-mail: sking@centralsan.org

Secretary of the District **Elaine R. Boehme** . . . . . (925) 229-7303
E-mail: eboehme@centralsan.org

District Counsel **Kenton L. "Kent" Alm** . . . . . (510) 808-2000
Education: UC Santa Barbara 1969 BA, 1970 BA; Hastings 1978 JD

Finance Manager **Thea Vassallo** . . . . . (925) 229-7740
E-mail: tvassallo@centralsan.org

Plant Maintenance Division Manager **Neil Meyer** . . . . . (925) 229-7269
E-mail: nmeyer@centralsan.org

Information Technology Manager **John Huie** . . . . . (925) 229-7335
E-mail: jhuie@centralsan.org

Environmental and Regulatory Compliance Division Manager **Lori Schectel** . . . . . (925) 229-7143

Central Ohio Transit Authority [COTA]

1600 McKinley Avenue, Columbus, OH 43222
Tel: (614) 228-1776 Internet: www.cota.com

Board of Trustees

1600 McKinley Avenue, Columbus, OH 43222

Chair **Dawn Tyler-Lee** . . . . . (614) 275-5800
Note: Will continue to serve until reappointed or replaced.
Term Expires: April 2016

Trustee **William A. Anthony, Jr.** . . . . . (614) 275-5800
Term Expires: April 2018

Trustee **Trudy Bartley** . . . . . (614) 275-5800
Term Expires: April 2017

Trustee **Philip Honsey** . . . . . (614) 275-5800
Term Expires: April 2018

Trustee **Brett Kaufman** . . . . . (614) 275-5800
Term Expires: April 2017

Trustee **Donald B. Leach, Jr.** . . . . . (614) 275-5800
Term Expires: April 2018
Education: Union Col (NY) 1976 BA; Ohio State 1982 JD

Trustee **Gina Ormond** . . . . . (614) 275-5800
Term Expires: April 2017

Trustee **Rev. Harry Wayne Proctor** . . . . . (614) 275-5800
Note: Will continue to serve until reappointed or replaced.
Term Expires: April 2014

Trustee **Jean Carter Ryan** . . . . . (614) 275-5800
Term Expires: April 2017
Education: Smith BA; Ohio State MA

Trustee **Amy Schmittauer** . . . . . (614) 275-5800
Note: Will continue to serve until reappointed or replaced.
Term Expires: April 2016

Trustee **Craig P. Treneff** . . . . . (614) 275-5800
Note: Will continue to serve until reappointed or replaced.
Term Expires: April 2016

Trustee **Richard R. Zitzke** . . . . . (614) 275-5800
Note: Will continue to serve until reappointed or replaced
Term Expires: April 2016

Trustee **(Vacant)** . . . . . (614) 275-5800
Term Expires: April 2016

Administration

President and Chief Executive Officer **W. Curtis Stitt** . . . . (614) 275-5850
Education: Kent State BA; Salmon P Chase 1979 JD — Fax: (614) 275-5894

Administration *continued*

Vice President, Communications, Marketing and Customer Service **Marty Stutz** . . . . . (614) 275-5800
E-mail: stutzr@cota.com

Vice President, Finance and Chief Financial Officer **Jeffrey Vosler** . . . . . (614) 275-5800

Vice President, Human Resources and Labor Relations **Kristen Treadway** . . . . . (614) 275-5800
E-mail: treadwaykm@cota.com

Co-Vice President, Legal Affairs and General Counsel (Interim) **Lindsay Ford Ellis** . . . . . (614) 275-5800

Co-Vice President, Legal Affairs and General Counsel (Interim) **Gary Tober** . . . . . (614) 275-5800

Vice President, Operations (Interim) **Lee Johnson** . . . . . (614) 275-5800

Vice President, Planning **Mike Bradley** . . . . . (614) 275-5800

Corpus Christi Regional Transportation Authority [CCRTA]

5658 Bear Lane, Corpus Christi, TX 78405
Tel: (361) 289-2712 Fax: (361) 289-0605 Internet: www.ccrta.org

Board of Directors

5658 Bear Lane, Corpus Christi, TX 78405
Fax: (361) 289-0605

Chair **Curtis Rock** . . . . . (361) 289-2712
Vice Chair **Mike Reeves** . . . . . (361) 289-2712
Secretary **Mary J. Saenz** . . . . . (361) 289-2712
Director **Vangie Chapa** . . . . . (361) 289-2712
Director **George Clower** . . . . . (361) 289-2712
Director **Thomas Dreyer** . . . . . (361) 289-2712
Director **Tony Elizondo** . . . . . (361) 289-2712
Director **Angie Flores-Granado** . . . . . (361) 289-2712
Director **Ray Hunt** . . . . . (361) 289-2712
Director **Eddie Martinez** . . . . . (361) 289-2712
Director **Lamont Taylor** . . . . . (361) 289-2712
Director **(Vacant)** . . . . . (361) 289-2712

Office of the Chief Executive Officer

5658 Bear Lane, Corpus Christi, TX 78405
Fax: (361) 289-3005

Chief Executive Officer **Jorge Cruz-Aedo** . . . . . (361) 289-2712
Education: Texas State (San Marcos) 1977 BBA

Managing Director of Administration **(Vacant)** . . . . . (361) 289-2712

Managing Director of Program Management **Sharon Montez** . . . . . (361) 289-2712

Dallas Area Rapid Transit Authority [DART]

1401 Pacific Avenue, Dallas, TX 75202
Internet: www.dart.org

Board of Directors

1401 Pacific Avenue, Dallas, TX 75202

Chair **Faye Wilkins** . . . . . (214) 749-3347
Vice Chair **Richard Carrizales** . . . . . (214) 749-3347
Secretary **Gary Slagel** . . . . . (214) 749-3347
Education: Illinois State BS; Amberton U MBA
Director **James F. Adams** . . . . . (214) 749-3347
Director **Sue Bauman** . . . . . (214) 749-3347

★ Elected Official ▲ Appointed by Legislature ▼ Appointed by Governor ▶ Appointed by Board or Commission ● Appointed by Judge
■ Appointed by Mayor △ Appointed by Freeholders ▽ Appointed by Supervisor ▷ Appointed by County Executive ○ Appointed by Council

Board of Directors *continued*

Director **Michael T. Cheney** . . . . . (214) 749-3347
Education: Michigan BA
Director **Jerry Christian** . . . . . (214) 749-3347
Director **Amanda Moreno Cross** . . . . . (214) 749-3347
Director **Mark C. Enoch** . . . . . (214) 749-3347
Director **Pamela Dunlop Gates** . . . . . (214) 749-3347
Director **Tim Hayden** . . . . . (214) 749-3347
Director **Michele Wong Krause** . . . . . (214) 749-3347
Director **Rick Stopfer** . . . . . (214) 749-3347
Director **William M. Velasco II** . . . . . (214) 749-3347
Director **Paul N. Wageman** . . . . . (214) 749-3347
Education: Boston Col 1982 BA; Georgetown 1987 JD

Administration

President and Executive Director **Gary C. Thomas** . . . . . (214) 749-3070
Education: Texas Tech 1980 BS
Deputy Executive Director **Jesse D. Oliver** . . . . . (214) 749-3070
Education: Dallas Baptist BA; Texas JD
Executive Vice President, Operations **Carol E. Wise** . . . . . (214) 749-3013
E-mail: cwise@dart.org
Education: Pittsburgh BA, MPA
Executive Vice President, Growth and Regional Development **Timothy H. "Tim" McKay** . . . . . (214) 749-2926
Education: Michigan Tech BSCE
Senior Vice President and Chief Financial Officer **David Leininger** . . . . . (214) 749-2926
Chief Information Officer **Nicole Fontayne** . . . . . (214) 749-2926
E-mail: nfontayne@dart.org
Education: Nova Southeastern MPA; Roosevelt BA
Vice President, Commuter Rail **Maureen McCole** . . . . . (214) 749-3008
Vice President, Government Relations **Michael Miles** . . . . (214) 749-3269
E-mail: mmiles@dart.org
Vice President, Human Capital **Cheryl D. Orr** . . . . . (214) 749-3345
Education: Rutgers BS, MSW
Vice President, Maintenance **Michael C. Hubbell** . . . . . (214) 828-6780
Vice President, Chief Marketing Officer **Nevin Grinnell** . . (214) 749-2504
Education: Morehouse Col 1986 BA; Kenan-Flagler 1992 MBA
Vice President, Mobility Management **Doug Douglas** . . . . (214) 828-6728
Vice President, Procurement **John Adler** . . . . . (214) 749-2573
E-mail: jadler@dart.org
Vice President, Rail Planning **Stephen "Steve" Salin** . . . (214) 749-3278
E-mail: ssalin@dart.org
Vice President, Transportation **Timothy W. Newby** . . . . . (214) 828-6835
Education: Virginia Tech MURP; Drury Col BA
General Counsel **Scott Carlson** . . . . . (214) 749-3192
Education: Texas Tech 1978 BSCE; Southern Methodist 1983 JD
Internal Audit Director **Albert Bazis** . . . . . (214) 749-3115
Office of Board Support Director **Nancy Johnson** . . . . . (214) 749-3347
E-mail: njohnson@dart.org

Dallas/Fort Worth International Airport [DFW]

P.O. Box 619428, Dallas Fort Worth Airport, TX 75261-9428
Tel: (972) 574-6000 (Information) Fax: (972) 574-5509
Internet: www.dfwairport.com

Board of Directors

P.O. Box 619428, Dallas Fort Worth Airport, TX 75261-9428
Chair **David Samuel "Sam" Coats** . . . . . (972) 574-6000
Vice Chair **William W. Meadows** . . . . . (972) 574-6000
Education: Southwestern
Secretary **Bernice J. Washington** . . . . . (972) 574-6000
Board Member **Lillie M. Biggins** . . . . . (972) 574-6000
Board Member **Henry Borbolla III** . . . . . (972) 574-6000
Board Member **Regina Theresa Coggins** . . . . . (972) 574-6000
Education: Wellesley 1975 BA; Harvard 1978 JD

Board of Directors *continued*

Board Member **Bridget Moreno Lopez** . . . . . (972) 574-6000
Board Member **Betsy Price** . . . . . (972) 574-6000
Education: Texas (Arlington) 1972 BS
Board Member **Curtis E. Ransom** . . . . . (972) 574-6000
Board Member **Michael S. "Mike" Rawlings** . . . . . (972) 574-6000
Education: Boston Col 1976 BA
Board Member **Amir Rupani** . . . . . (972) 574-6000
Board Member (Non Voting) **Linda Martin** . . . . . (972) 574-6000

Office of the Chief Executive Officer

Chief Executive Officer **Sean P. Donohue** . . . . . (972) 574-3200
E-mail: sdonohue@dfwairport.com
General Counsel **Elaine Flud Rodriguez** . . . . . (972) 973-5487
Education: Loyola U (New Orleans) 1978 BA; Tulane 1982 JD
Audit Services Director **Robert R. Darby** . . . . . (972) 973-5525

Administration and Diversity Division

Executive Vice President **Linda Valdez Thompson** . . . . . (972) 973-5215
E-mail: lvthompson@dfwairport.com
Vice President, Business Diversity and Development **Tamela Lee** . . . . . (972) 973-5502
Vice President, Human Resources **Thomas Dallam** . . . . . (972) 973-1100
E-mail: tdallam@dfwairport.com
Vice President, Procurement and Materials Management **Gregory Spoon** . . . . . (972) 973-5610
E-mail: gspoon@dfwairport.com

Airport Operations Division

Executive Vice President **James M. Crites** . . . . . (972) 973-3112
E-mail: jcrites@dfwairport.com
Education: Illinois 1976 BS
Vice President, Environmental Affairs **(Vacant)** . . . . . (972) 973-5563
Vice President, Public Safety **MSgt Alan Black** . . . . . (972) 574-8481
E-mail: ablack@dfwairport.com

Finance and Information Technology Services Division

Executive Vice President and Chief Financial Officer **Christopher A. "Chris" Poinsatte** . . . . . (972) 973-5210
Education: Notre Dame 1979 BBA
Vice President, Information Technology Services and Chief Information Officer **William Flowers** . . . . . (972) 973-5339
E-mail: wflowers@dfwairport.com

Governmental and Stakeholder Affairs Division

Executive Vice President **(Vacant)** . . . . . (972) 973-5752
Vice President, Communications and Public Affairs **Mary Jo Polidore** . . . . . (972) 973-5555
E-mail: mpolidore@dfwairport.com

Revenue Management Division

Executive Vice President **Kenneth "Ken" Buchanan** . . . . (972) 973-5225
Vice President, Customer Service **Byford Treanor** . . . . . (972) 574-8844

Detroit/Wayne County Port Authority [DWCPA]

8109 East Atwater Street, Detroit, MI 48226
Tel: (313) 259-5091 Fax: (313) 259-5093 Internet: www.portdetroit.com

Board of Directors

▶ Chairman **Thomas "Tom" Orzechowski, Jr.** . . . . . (313) 259-5091
Note: Representing Wayne County
Term Expires: September 30, 2016

(continued on next page)

AUTHORITIES

★ Elected Official ▲ Appointed by Legislature ▼ Appointed by Governor ▶ Appointed by Board or Commission ● Appointed by Judge
■ Appointed by Mayor △ Appointed by Freeholders ▽ Appointed by Supervisor ▷ Appointed by County Executive ○ Appointed by Council

Board of Directors *continued*

■ Vice Chairman **Jonathan Cleveland Kinloch** .... (313) 259-5091
■ Member **Alisha Bell** .... (313) 259-5091
Note: Representing the City of Detroit
Education: Florida A&M BBA; UNLV MEd
▼ Member **Frederick W. "Fred" Hoffman IV** .... (313) 259-5091
Note: Will continue to serve until reappointed or replaced. Representing the State of Michigan
Term Expires: September 30, 2014
▶ Member **Lorron James** .... (313) 259-5091
Note: Representing Wayne County

Administration

Executive Director **John Loftus** .... (313) 259-5091 ext. 214
E-mail: jloftus@portdetroit.com
Deputy Director **Kyle Burleson** .... (313) 259-5091 ext. 202
E-mail: kburleson@portdetroit.com
Education: Michigan 2005 BA
Director of Finance **Travis Jackson** .... (313) 259-5091
E-mail: tjackson@portdetroit.com
Chief of Security **(Vacant)** .... (313) 259-5091
Public Dock and Terminal Manager **Vanessa Baker** .... (313) 259-5091
E-mail: vbaker@portdetroit.com

Duluth Seaway Port Authority

1200 Port Terminal Drive, Duluth, MN 55802-2609
Internet: www.duluthport.com

Office of the Commissioners

1200 Port Terminal Drive, Duluth, MN 55802-2609
Tel: (218) 727-8525 Tel: (800) 232-0703 (Toll Free) Fax: (218) 727-6888
E-mail: admin@duluthport.com

○ President **Steve Raukar** .... (218) 262-0201
Note: Appointed by County
214 Courthouse, 1810 12th Ave. East, Hibbing, MN 55746
Education: St Cloud State 1974 BA
○ Vice President **Ray Klosowski** .... (218) 343-2417
1145 Como Avenue, Duluth, MN 55811
○ Secretary **Norm Voorhees** .... (218) 724-5073
3752 Midway Road, Hermantown, MN 55810
Treasurer **Rick Revoir** .... (218) 723-6424
Note: Appointed by County
2631 East Fifth Street, Duluth, MN 55812
Assistant Treasurer **Chris Dahlberg** .... (218) 726-2562
Note: Appointed by County
100 N. Fifth Avenue W, #207, Duluth, MN 55802
Education: Minnesota (Duluth) 1986 BA; Minnesota 2002 MA, 2002 JD
▼ Commissioner **Yvonne Prettner Solon** .... (218) 464-1114
3966 Fountain Gate Drive N., Duluth, MN 55811
Education: Minnesota 1979 BA, 1981 MA
▼ Commissioner **Anthony "Tony" Sertich** .... (218) 723-4040
Term Expires: January 7, 2019
Affiliation: President, Northland Foundation.
600 Sellwood, 202 W Superior Street, Duluth, MN 55802
Date of Birth: January 2, 1976
Education: Hamline 1998 BA

Administration

Executive Director **Vanta E. Coda II** .... (218) 727-8525
E-mail: vcoda@duluthport.com
Chief Financial Officer **Kevin Beardsley** .... (218) 727-8525 ext. 116
Business Development Director **Kate Ferguson** .... (218) 727-8525
E-mail: kferguson@duluthport.com
Trade Development Director **(Vacant)** .... (218) 727-8525 ext. 114
Director of Port Planning and Resiliency
James D. Sharrow .... (218) 727-8525 ext. 110
E-mail: jsharrow@duluthport.com

Administration *continued*

Public Relations Director **Adele Yorde** .... (218) 727-8525 ext. 109
E-mail: ayorde@duluthport.com
Government and Environmental Affairs Director
Deborah DeLuca .... (218) 727-8525
Facilities Manager **Jason Paulson** .... (218) 727-8525
E-mail: jpaulson@duluthport.com

Economic Development Corporation Serving Fresno County [EDC]

906 N Street, Suite 120, Fresno, CA 93721
Fax: (559) 233-2156 Internet: www.fresnoedc.com

Board of Directors

906 N Street, Suite 120, Fresno, CA 93721
Tel: (559) 476-2500 Fax: (559) 233-2156 E-mail: smoua@fresnoedc.com

Chairman **Walt Plachta** .... (559) 233-2564
Vice Chairman **Ed Dunkel** .... (559) 233-2564
Secretary **Tina Sumner** .... (559) 233-2564
Treasurer **Dr. Robert L. Wiebe** .... (559) 233-2564
Education: Missouri BA, MD; UC Berkeley MPH; Stanford MBA

Administration

President and Chief Executive Officer **Lee Ann Eager** .... (559) 476-2513
E-mail: leager@fresnoedc.com
Education: Cal State (Fresno) BA; UC Davis 2005 JD
Vice President, Business Development **Esther Cuevas** .... (559) 476-2507
E-mail: ecuevas@fresnoedc.com
Communications and Investor Relations Director
Karena Riley .... (559) 476-2505
E-mail: kriley@fresnoedc.com
Fiscal and Human Resources Coordinator
Carmen Gonzalez .... (559) 476-2519
E-mail: cgonzalez@fresnoedc.com
Economic Development Analyst **Sergio Hernandez** .... (559) 476-2511
E-mail: shernandez@fresnoedc.com
Economic Development Analyst **Margo Lerwill** .... (559) 476-2510
E-mail: mlerwill@fresnoedc.com

Erie Water Works

340 West Bayfront Parkway, Erie, PA 16507
Internet: www.eriewater.org

Board of Directors

Chairman **John J. McCormick, Jr.** .... (814) 870-8000
Vice Chairman **Shantel D. Hilliard** .... (814) 870-8000
Secretary **Richard S. Wasielewski** .... (814) 870-8000
Treasurer **Thomas M. Kennedy** .... (814) 870-8000
Member **Lou Bizzarro** .... (814) 870-8000
Member **Ann M. DiMarco** .... (814) 870-8000
Member **Bryan D. Fife** .... (814) 870-8000
Member **Paul Gambill** .... (814) 870-8000
Member **(Vacant)** .... (814) 870-8000

Administration

Chief Executive Officer **Paul D. Vojtek** .... (814) 870-8000 ext. 303
Administration Manager **Ronald G. Costantini** .... (814) 870-8000 ext. 306
E-mail: rcostantini@eriewaterworks.org
Customer Service and Meters Manager
Ronald J. Loader .... (814) 870-8000 ext. 119

★ Elected Official ▲ Appointed by Legislature ▼ Appointed by Governor ▶ Appointed by Board or Commission ● Appointed by Judge
■ Appointed by Mayor △ Appointed by Freeholders ▽ Appointed by Supervisor ▷ Appointed by County Executive ○ Appointed by Council

Administration *continued*

Distribution Manager **Peter N. Hirneisen** .... (814) 870-8000 ext. 601
Engineering Services Manager
Craig H. Palmer .... (814) 870-8000 ext. 208
E-mail: cpalmer@eriewaterworks.org
Production and Water Quality Manager
Dave Motherwell .... (814) 870-8000 ext. 406

Erie-Western Pennsylvania Port Authority

1 Holland Street, Erie, PA 16507
Fax: (814) 455-8070 E-mail: info@porterie.org
Internet: www.porterie.org

Board of Directors

208 East Bayfront Parkway, Erie, PA 16507

Chairman **Daniel Harmon** .... (814) 455-7557
Vice-Chairwoman **Sharon L. Knoll** .... (814) 455-7557
Treasurer **Michael Redlawsk** .... (814) 455-7557
Secretary **Jeffrey J. Johnson** .... (814) 455-7557
Assistant Secretary/Treasurer **Brenda Sandberg** .... (814) 455-7557
Member **Jeff Brinling** .... (814) 455-7557
Member **Amos Goodwine, Jr.** .... (814) 455-7557
Member **George Lyons** .... (814) 455-7557
Member **Owen McCormick** .... (814) 455-7557
Member **Eric Mikovch** .... (814) 455-7557
Member **Sean Wiley** .... (814) 455-7557
Education: DeVry U 1993 BS
Member **Dave Zimmer** .... (814) 455-7557

Administration

Executive Director **Brenda Sandberg** .... (814) 455-7557 ext. 223
E-mail: bsandberg@porterie.org
Administrative Assistant **Bonnie Little** .... (814) 455-7557 ext. 221
E-mail: bonniel@porterie.org
Chief Financial Officer **Robin Waldinger** .... (814) 455-7557 ext. 225
General Counsel **Timothy M. Sennett** .... (814) 455-7557
Education: St Bonaventure 1980 BA; Dickinson Law 1983 JD
Director of Operations/Harbormaster
Douglas C. "Doug" Pomorski .... (814) 455-7557 ext. 224
E-mail: dougpomo@porterie.org
Deputy Director of Operations/Dockmaster
John Mulligan .... (814) 456-1931
E-mail: mulligan@porterie.org Fax: (814) 461-8591

Eugene Water and Electric Board [EWEB]

500 East 4th Avenue, Eugene, OR 97401
P.O. Box 10148, Eugene, OR 97440-2148
Fax: (541) 484-3762 Internet: www.eweb.org

Board of Commissioners

★ President **John M. Simpson** (At-Large) .... (541) 685-7000
Term Expires: December 31, 2018
★ Vice President **John H. Brown** (Wards 4 & 5) .... (541) 685-7000
Term Expires: December 31, 2018
★ Commissioner **Dick Helgeson** (Wards 2 & 3) .... (541) 685-7000
Term Expires: December 31, 2016
★ Commissioner **James I. Manning** (Wards 6 & 7) .... (541) 685-7000
Term Expires: December 31, 2016
★ Commissioner **Steve Mital** (Wards 1 & 8) .... (541) 685-7000
Term Expires: December 31, 2016

Administration

General Manager **Roger J. Gray** .... (541) 685-7130

Fairfax County Economic Development Authority [FCEDA]

8300 Boone Blvd., Suite 450, Tysons Corner, VA 22182-2633
Fax: (703) 893-1269 Internet: www.fairfaxcountyeda.org

Commissioners

Chairman **Steven L. Davis** .... (703) 790-0600
Vice Chairman **Michael Lewis** .... (703) 790-0600
Secretary **Ronald C. "Ron" Johnson** .... (703) 790-0600
Treasurer **Arthur E. "Bud" Morrissette IV** .... (703) 790-0600
Commissioner **Catherine Lange** .... (703) 790-0600
Commissioner **Mark C. Lowham** .... (703) 790-0600
Commissioner **Sudhakar V. Shenoy** .... (703) 790-0600

Administration

President and Chief Executive Officer
Gerald L. Gordon .... (703) 790-0600
E-mail: ggordon@fceda.org
Education: Citadel BA; George Washington 1975 MA; Catholic U PhD
Vice President, Communications and Research
Alan A. Fogg .... (703) 790-0600
E-mail: afogg@fceda.org
Vice President, Management **Robin Fenner** .... (703) 790-0600
E-mail: rfenner@fceda.org
Vice President, Marketing **Catherine W. Riley** .... (703) 790-0600
Administration Director **Barbara Cohen** .... (703) 790-0600
E-mail: bcohen@fceda.org
International Marketing Director **Jan Mul** .... (703) 790-0600
National Marketing Director **Rodney Lusk** .... (703) 790-0600
Market Intelligence Director **Donna Hurwitt** .... (703) 790-0600
Business Diversity Director **Karen Smaw** .... (703) 790-0600
E-mail: ksmaw@fceda.org
Real Estate Services Director **Curtis Hoffman** .... (703) 790-0600

Georgia Ports Authority [GPA]

P.O. Box 2406, Savannah, GA 31402
Tel: (800) 342-8012 (Toll Free) Fax: (912) 964-3921
E-mail: info@gaports.com Internet: www.gaports.com

Board of Directors

P.O. Box 2406, Savannah, GA 31402
Tel: (800) 342-8012 E-mail: info@gaports.com

▼ Chairman **James A. "Jim" Walters** .... (912) 964-3811
▼ Vice Chairman **James "Jimmy" Allgood** .... (912) 964-3811
▼ Secretary and Treasurer **Alva Joseph Hopkins III** .... (912) 964-3811
▼ Board Member **H. Kenneth Cronan** .... (912) 964-3811
▼ Board Member **Ben H. Hall, Jr.** .... (912) 964-3811
▼ Board Member **Julie Ewing Hunt** .... (912) 964-3811
Education: Valdosta State U
▼ Board Member **Robert S. "Bob" Jepson, Jr.** .... (912) 964-3811
Education: Richmond 1964 BS, 1975 MS
▼ Board Member **William McKnight** .... (912) 964-3811
▼ Board Member **Alec L. Poitevint II** .... (912) 964-3811
Education: Georgia BA
▼ Board Member **Joseph W. "Joe" Rogers, Jr.** .... (912) 964-3811
▼ Board Member **Charles K. Tarbutton** .... (912) 964-3811

(continued on next page)

AUTHORITIES

★ Elected Official ▲ Appointed by Legislature ▼ Appointed by Governor ▶ Appointed by Board or Commission ● Appointed by Judge
■ Appointed by Mayor △ Appointed by Freeholders ▽ Appointed by Supervisor ▷ Appointed by County Executive ○ Appointed by Council

Board of Directors *continued*

▼Board Member **David Werner** .... (912) 964-3811
Education: Georgia; Emory JD

▼Board Member **Joel O. Wooten, Jr.** .... (912) 964-3811
Education: Georgia 1972 BBA, 1975 JD

Administration

Executive Director **Curtis Jay Foltz** .... (912) 964-3874
Note: Until June 30, 2016 Fax: (912) 966-3615
Education: East Carolina 1982 MBA

Chief Commercial Officer **Clifford R. "Cliff" Pyron** ..... (912) 964-3955
Fax: (912) 966-3615

Chief Operating Officer **Griffith Lynch** .... (912) 964-3955
Education: SUNY Maritime BS Fax: (912) 966-3615

Senior Director of Corporate Communications
Robert C. Morris .... (912) 964-3855
Fax: (912) 964-3921

Senior Director of Finance **J. Russell "Russ" Mincey** ... (912) 964-3893
Education: North Carolina 1983 BS; Fax: (912) 964-3903
Lenoir-Rhyne 2005 MBA

Senior Director of Human Resources **Lise Altman** .... (912) 964-3938
E-mail: laltman@gaports.com Fax: (912) 964-3819

Senior Director of Strategic Operations and Safety
John D. Trent .... (912) 964-3847
E-mail: jtrent@gaports.com Fax: (912) 963-5477

Senior Director of Trade Development - BCO Sales
Chris Logan .... (912) 963-6995
Fax: (912) 964-3869

Senior Director of Trade Development - Carrier and
Non-Container Sales **George H. Hearn** .... (912) 964-3824
Fax: (912) 964-3869

Purchasing Manager **Mike Bray** .... (912) 964-3991
E-mail: mbray@gaports.com

Senior Director of Administration
James C. McCurry, Jr. .... (912) 966-3615
E-mail: jmccurry@gaports.com

Director of Economic Development and State
Government Affairs **Bartholomew "Bart" Gobeil** ...... (912) 965-6213
E-mail: bgobeil@gaports.com
Education: UMass (Amherst) 1994 BA

AUTHORITIES

Greater Augusta Utility District

12 Williams Street, Augusta, ME 04330
Tel: (207) 622-3701 Fax: (207) 622-4539

Board of Trustees

■Chairman **Kenneth "Ken" Knight** .... (207) 622-3701
Term Expires: June 1, 2016

■Vice Chair **David P. Smith** .... (207) 622-3701
Note: Will continue to serve until reappointed or replaced
Term Expires: July 31, 2014

■Treasurer **Charlene Hamiwka** .... (207) 622-3701
Term Expires: July 2, 2016

■Trustee **David "Dave" Bustin** .... (207) 622-3701
Term Expires: April 12, 2016

■Trustee **Kirsten Hebert** .... (207) 622-3701
Term Expires: July 31, 2016
E-mail: khebert@greateraugustautlitydistrict.org

■Trustee **Donald "Don" Roberts** .... (207) 622-3701
Term Expires: July 2, 2016

■Trustee **Sukey Sikora** .... (207) 622-3701
Note: Will continue to serve until reappointed or replaced
Term Expires: February 19, 2014

■Trustee (Non-Voting) **Lesley Jones** .... (207) 622-3701
Note: Will continue to serve until reappointed or replaced.
Term Expires: April 12, 2014

■Trustee (Non-Voting) **Charlotte Warren** .... (207) 622-3701

Administration

General Manager **Brian Tarbuck** .... (207) 622-3701 ext. 108
Assistant General Manager **Andy Begin** .... (207) 622-3701 ext. 131
Plant Manager **(Vacant)** .... (207) 622-3701 ext. 120

Huntsville Utilities

P.O. Box 2048, Huntsville, AL 35804
Tel: (256) 535-1200 Fax: (256) 535-1437 Internet: www.hsvutil.org

Electric Board

Chairman **Ronald W. Boles** .... (256) 535-1200
Vice Chairman **D. Thomas Winstead** .... (256) 535-1200
Secretary **George A. Moore** .... (256) 535-1200
Attorney **E. Cutter Hughes, Jr.** .... (256) 535-1200
Education: Davidson 1965 AB; Virginia 1968 LLB;
U London 1971 LLM

Natural Gas and Water Boards

Chairman **James S. Wall** .... (256) 535-1200
Vice Chairman **Dorothy Huston** .... (256) 535-1200
Secretary **Stanley Statum** .... (256) 535-1200
Attorney **J. Robert Miller** .... (256) 535-1200

Management

President and Chief Executive Officer
Joseph C. "Jay" Stowe .... (256) 535-1200
E-mail: jay.stowe@hsvutil.org

Chief Financial Officer **Ted Phillips** .... (256) 535-1200

Operations Vice President **Tony Owens** .... (256) 535-1200
E-mail: tony.owens@hsvutil.org

Communications Director **Joe Gehrdes** .... (256) 535-1200

Human Resources Director **Janice Capshaw** .... (256) 535-1200
E-mail: janice.capshaw@hsvutil.org

Internal Audit Director **Ron Rizzardi** .... (256) 535-1200

Controller **Keith Moran** .... (256) 535-1200

Management Information Systems Director
David Champigny .... (256) 535-1200

Customer Service Manager **Anna Parvin** .... (256) 535-1200

Electric Manager **Steve Wright** .... (256) 535-1200

Gas and Water Operations Manager **Jimmie Butler** ...... (256) 535-1200

Intermountain Power Agency [IPA]

10653 South River Front Parkway, Suite 120, South Jordan, UT 84095
Fax: (801) 938-1330 Internet: www.ipautah.com

Board of Directors

10653 South River Front Parkway, South Jordan, UT 84095

Chair **Ted L. Olson** .... (801) 938-1333
Vice Chairman **R. Leon Bowler** .... (801) 938-1333
Treasurer **Russell F. Fjeldsted** .... (801) 938-1333
Board Member **Robert Christiansen** .... (801) 938-1333
Board Member **Ed Collins** .... (801) 938-1333
Board Member **Walter M. Meacham** .... (801) 938-1333
Board Member **Fred Moss** .... (801) 938-1333

Office of the General Manager

10653 South River Front Parkway, South Jordan, UT 84095

General Manager **R. Dan Eldredge** .... (801) 938-1333

★Elected Official ▲Appointed by Legislature ▼Appointed by Governor ▶Appointed by Board or Commission ●Appointed by Judge
■Appointed by Mayor △Appointed by Freeholders ▽Appointed by Supervisor ▷Appointed by County Executive ○Appointed by Council

Office of the General Manager *continued*

Assistant General Manager **(Vacant)** .... (801) 521-5800
299 South Main Street, Suite 1800, Salt Lake City, UT 84111
Accounting Manager **Linford E. Jensen** .... (801) 521-5800
Audit Manager **Vance K. Huntley** .... (801) 521-5800
299 South Main Street, Suite 1800, Salt Lake City, UT 84111
Engineering Manager **E. Michael Gaines** .... (801) 521-5800
299 South Main Street, Suite 1800, Salt Lake City, UT 84111
Treasury Manager **Allyn J. Orme** .... (801) 521-5800
299 South Main Street, Suite 1800, Salt Lake City, UT 84111

Jacksonville Port Authority [JAXPORT]

2831 Talleyrand Avenue, Jacksonville, FL 32206-0005
P.O. Box 3005, Jacksonville, FL 32206-3005
Fax: (904) 357-3060 Internet: www.jaxport.com
E-mail: info@jaxport.com

Board of Directors

P.O. Box 3005, Jacksonville, FL 32206-3005
E-mail: info@jaxport.com

Chairman **Dr. John Allen Newman** .... (904) 357-3036
Term Expires: June 1, 2019
Education: Eastern Col BA, MA
Vice Chairman **James P. Citrano** .... (904) 357-3036
Term Expires: June 1, 2017
Treasurer **Edward J. Fleming, Jr.** .... (904) 357-3036
Term Expires: January 2018
Secretary **Joe York** .... (904) 357-3036
Education: Auburn; Troy State
Board Member **John Baker** .... (904) 357-3036
Board Member **John J. Falconetti** .... (904) 357-3036
Note: Will continue to serve until reappointed or replaced
Term Expires: June 30, 2015
Education: Sewanee
Board Member **John Rood** .... (904) 357-3036

Administration

Chief Executive Officer **Brian W. Taylor** .... (904) 357-3036
Senior Executive Assistant to the Chief Executive Officer **Rebecca Dicks** .... (904) 357-3036
Executive Vice President/Chief Commercial Officer **Roy Schleicher** .... (904) 357-3041
Chief Financial Officer **Michael "Mike" Poole** .... (904) 357-3061
Chief Operations Officer **Chris Kauffmann** .... (904) 357-3089
E-mail: chris.kauffmann@jaxport.com
Education: Colorado State 1975 BS; National U 1982 MBA, 1997
Senior Director, Finance **Aaron Kendrick** .... (904) 357-3067
Senior Director, Human Resources **Sheryl Williams** ..... (904) 357-3005
E-mail: sheryl.williams@jaxport.com
Senior Director, Facilities and Development **Joe Miller** ... (904) 357-3001
E-mail: joe.miller@jaxport.com
Senior Director, Government and External Affairs **Eric Green** .... (904) 357-3045
E-mail: eric.green@jaxport.com
Senior Director, Planning and Commercial Development **David Kaufman** .... (904) 357-3043
E-mail: david.kaufman@jaxport.com
General Manager, Business Development **Robert Peek** ... (904) 357-3047
Senior Director, Communications **Nancy Rubin** .... (904) 357-3012
E-mail: nancy.rubin@jaxport.com
Senior Coordinator, Communications **Julie Watson** ...... (904) 357-3084
Controller **Mike McClung** .... (904) 357-3004
Director, Corporate Performance and Contracting **Linda Williams** .... (904) 357-3009
Director, Properties and Environmental Compliance **David Stubbs** .... (904) 357-3082

Administration *continued*

Manager, Risk Management **Chris Crouch** .... (904) 357-3083

Lansing Board of Water and Light [BWL]

1232 Haco, Lansing, MI 48901
Tel: (517) 702-6000 Fax: (517) 702-6855 Internet: www.lbwl.com

Board of Commissioners

Chair **David J. Price** (At-Large) .... (517) 702-6033
Term Expires: June 30, 2018
Commissioner **Dennis M. Louney** (Ward 1) .... (517) 702-6033
Term Expires: June 30, 2017
Education: James Madison; Western Michigan
Commissioner **Mark E. Alley** (Ward 2) .... (517) 702-6033
Term Expires: June 30, 2018
Commissioner **Anthony W. McCloud** (Ward 3) .... (517) 702-6033
Term Expires: June 30, 2019
Commissioner **Sandra Zerkle** (Ward 4) .... (517) 702-6033
Term Expires: June 30, 2016
Commissioner **Anthony M. Mullen** (At-Large) .... (517) 702-6033
Term Expires: June 30, 2017
Commissioner **Tracy Thomas** (At-Large) .... (517) 702-6033
Term Expires: June 30, 2016
Commissioner **Ken Ross** (At-Large) .... (517) 702-6033
Term Expires: June 30, 2019
Education: Michigan BA; Thomas M Cooley JD

Administration

General Manager and Chief Executive Officer (Interim) **Richard R. "Dick" Peffley** .... (517) 702-6312
Assistant General Manager and Chief Financial Officer **Susan C. Devon** .... (517) 702-6256
General Counsel and Executive Director of Employment Affairs **Brandie F. Ekren** .... (517) 702-6725
Executive Director of Water Utility and Special Projects **Richard R. "Dick" Peffley** .... (517) 702-6312
E-mail: rrp@lbwl.com
Executive Director of Strategic Planning and Development **George R. Stojic** .... (517) 702-6347
Director of Electric Delivery **David Bolan** .... (517) 702-7803
E-mail: dcb@lbwl.com
Corporate Secretary **M. Denise Griffin** .... (517) 702-6033
Director of Electric Production **Mark Williams** .... (517) 702-1810

Las Vegas Valley Water District [LVVWD]

1001 South Valley View Boulevard, Las Vegas, NV 89153
Tel: (702) 258-3100 Fax: (702) 870-2011 Internet: www.lvvwd.com

Board of Directors

County Government Center Grand Central Station, 500 Grand Central Parkway, Las Vegas, NV 89155

President **Mary Beth Scow** .... (702) 455-3500
Vice President **Steve Sisolak** .... (702) 455-3500
Date of Birth: December 26, 1953
Education: Wisconsin (Milwaukee) 1974 BS; UNLV 1978 MBA
Member **Susan Brager** .... (702) 455-3500
Member **Lawrence L. "Larry" Brown III** .... (702) 455-3500
Member **Christina R. "Chris" Giunchigliani** .... (702) 455-3500
Education: Avila Col BA; UNLV MEd
Member **Marilyn Kirkpatrick** .... (702) 455-3500

(continued on next page)

★ Elected Official ▲ Appointed by Legislature ▼ Appointed by Governor ▶ Appointed by Board or Commission ● Appointed by Judge
■ Appointed by Mayor △ Appointed by Freeholders ▽ Appointed by Supervisor ▷ Appointed by County Executive ○ Appointed by Council

AUTHORITIES

Board of Directors *continued*

Member **Lawrence Weekly** .... (702) 455-3500
Education: Grambling State BA

Office of the General Manager

General Manager **John Entsminger** .... (702) 258-3104
Education: Northern Colorado BA
Assistant General Manager **(Vacant)** .... (702) 258-3100
Deputy General Manager, Engineering/Operations
David L. Johnson .... (702) 258-3165
Deputy General Manager, Administration
Julie A. Wilcox .... (702) 258-3100
General Counsel **Gregory J. Walch** .... (702) 258-7130
Chief Financial Officer **Gina L. Neilson** .... (702) 258-3105

Los Angeles County Metropolitan Transportation Authority [Metro]

One Gateway Plaza, Los Angeles, CA 90012-2932
P.O. Box 194, Los Angeles, CA 90053
Tel: (213) 922-6000 (Information) Fax: (213) 922-7447
Internet: www.metro.net

Board of Directors

One Gateway Plaza, Los Angeles, CA 90012-2952
Fax: (213) 922-4594 Internet: www.metro.net

Chair **Mark Ridley-Thomas** .... (213) 922-4600
Date of Birth: November 6, 1954
Education: Immaculate Heart; USC 1989 PhD
First Vice Chair **John Fasana** .... (213) 922-4600
Education: Whittier BA
Second Vice Chair **Eric Garcetti** .... (213) 922-4600
Education: Columbia 1992 BA, 1995 MA; London School Econ (UK) PhD
Director **Michael D. "Mike" Antonovich** .... (213) 922-4600
Date of Birth: August 12, 1939
Education: Cal State (Los Angeles) 1963 BA, 1967 MA
Director **Mike Bonin** .... (213) 922-4600
Director **James T. Butts, Jr.** .... (213) 922-4600
Director **Diane DuBois** .... (213) 922-4600
Director **Jacqueline DuPont-Walker** .... (213) 922-4600
Director **Don Knabe** .... (213) 922-4600
Date of Birth: August 15, 1943
Education: Graceland Col 1967 BA
Director **Paul Krekorian** .... (213) 922-4600
Director **Sheila James Kuehl** .... (213) 974-3333
Education: Harvard 1978 JD
Director **Ara James Najarian** .... (213) 922-4600
Education: Occidental 1982 BA; USC 1985 JD
Director **Hilda Lucia Solis** .... (213) 922-4600
Date of Birth: October 20, 1957
Education: Cal Poly (Pomona) 1979 BA; USC 1981 MPA
▼ Director, Non-Voting Member **Carrie Bowen** .... (213) 922-4600
Board Secretary **Michelle Jackson** .... (213) 922-4605
E-mail: jacksonm@metro.net

Administration

Chief Executive Officer **Phillip A. "Phil" Washington** ... (213) 922-6888
Deputy Chief Executive Officer (Interim)
Stephanie Wiggins .... (213) 922-4433
General Manager **Richard Hunt** .... (818) 701-2801
Chief Operating Officer **James T. Gallagher** .... (213) 922-4438
E-mail: gallagherj@metro.net
Deputy Chief Operating Officer **Kimberly Yu** .... (213) 922-3848
E-mail: yuki@metro.net

Administration *continued*

Chief Administrative Services Officer
Michelle Lopes Caldwell .... (213) 922-2452
E-mail: caldwellm@metro.net
Chief Communications Officer **Pauletta Tonilas** .... (213) 922-6340
E-mail: tonilasp@metro.net
Chief of Real Property Management and Development
(Vacant) .... (213) 922-2225
General Counsel **Charles M. Safer** .... (213) 922-2525
Inspector General **Karen Gorman** .... (213) 922-2975
Chief Auditor **Yvette Suarez** .... (213) 922-6800
Chief Planning Officer **Therese W. McMillan** .... (213) 922-7267
Education: UC Davis 1980 BS; UC Berkeley 1983 MCP, 1983 MS
Executive Director, Highway Project Delivery
Douglas Failing .... (213) 922-6840
Executive Director, Maintenance **Alex Di Nuzzo** .... (323) 421-2031
E-mail: dinuzzoa@metro.net
Executive Director and Chief Financial Officer
Nalini Ahuja .... (213) 922-7267
E-mail: ahujan@metro.net
Executive Director, Transit Project Delivery
K.N. Murthy .... (213) 922-3084
Executive Director, Transportation **John Roberts** .... (213) 922-5042
Chief Innovation Officer **Joshua Schank** .... (213) 922-6000
Education: Columbia BA; MIT MCP; Columbia PhD
Manager of Outreach and Strategic Partnerships
Colin Peppard .... (213) 922-6000

Los Angeles Department of Water and Power [LADWP]

111 North Hope Street, Los Angeles, CA 90012
Tel: (213) 481-5411 (Information) Internet: www.ladwp.com

Board of Commissioners

111 North Hope Street, 15th Floor, Los Angeles, CA 90012
Tel: (213) 367-1356 Fax: (213) 367-1423
E-mail: commission@ladwp.com

■ President **Mel E. Levine** .... (213) 367-1356
Term Expires: June 30, 2019
Education: UC Berkeley 1964 BA; Princeton 1966 MPA; Harvard 1969 JD
■ Vice President **William W. Funderburk, Jr.** .... (213) 367-1356
■ Commissioner **Jill Banks Barad** .... (213) 367-1356
Term Expires: May 30, 2018
■ Commissioner **Michael Fleming** .... (213) 367-1356
Term Expires: June 30, 2020
■ Commissioner **Christina E. Noonan** .... (213) 367-1356
Term Expires: June 30, 2016
Secretary to the Board **Barbara E. Moschos** .... (213) 367-1351
E-mail: barbara.moschos@ladwp.com

Office of the General Manager

111 North Hope Street, Room 1550, Los Angeles, CA 90012
Tel: (213) 367-1320 Fax: (213) 367-1455

General Manager **Marcie L. Edwards** .... (213) 367-1320
Chief Administrative Officer **David H. Wiggs, Jr.** .... (213) 367-1320
Chief Sustainability and Economic Development Officer
Nancy Helen Sutley .... (213) 367-1320
Date of Birth: April 20, 1962
Education: Cornell 1984 BA; Harvard 1986 MPP
Assistant General Manager of Customer Services
John X. Chen .... (213) 367-2615

★ Elected Official ▲ Appointed by Legislature ▼ Appointed by Governor ▶ Appointed by Board or Commission ● Appointed by Judge
■ Appointed by Mayor △ Appointed by Freeholders ▽ Appointed by Supervisor ▷ Appointed by County Executive ○ Appointed by Council

Operations Services Organization

111 North Hope Street, Room 1221, Los Angeles, CA 90012
Tel: (213) 367-2160 Fax: (213) 367-1438

Security Services Director **Patrick Findley** . . . . . (213) 367-3153
Supply Chain Management Director **Anselmo Collins** . . . . (213) 367-1096

Employee Relations Organization

111 North Hope Street, Room 1503, Los Angeles, CA 90012

Assistant General Manager **(Vacant)** . . . . . (213) 367-0117
Labor Relations Manager **Rose Garcia** . . . . . (213) 367-1918
Human Resources Director **Shannon Pasquale** . . . . . (213) 367-1988

Financial Services Organization

111 North Hope Street, 4th Floor, Los Angeles, CA 90012
Tel: (213) 367-4300 Fax: (213) 367-4320

Chief Financial Officer **Jeffrey L. Peltola** . . . . . (213) 367-1781
Budget Director **Greg Black** . . . . . (213) 367-4300
Finance Director and Risk Controller **Mario C. Ignacio**
Room 465 . . . . . (213) 367-0690
E-mail: mario.ignacio@ladwp.com
Internal Audit Director **James Tan** . . . . . (213) 367-4436
Controller **Ann M. Santilli** . . . . . (213) 367-3051

Power System

Fax: (213) 367-0313

Senior Assistant General Manager and Chief Operating Officer **David H. Wright** . . . . . (213) 367-4435
E-mail: david.wright@ladwp.com
Transmission and Distribution Maintenance
Andrew C. Kendall . . . . . (213) 367-0772
Integrated Support Services Director **Michael A. Coia** . . . . (213) 367-7573
E-mail: michael.coia@ladwp.com
Construction and Maintenance Director
David B. Thrasher Room 819 . . . . . (213) 367-1716
Power Supply Operations Director **Ken Silver** . . . . . (213) 367-0286
Power and Fuel Purchase Director **Michael Webster**
Room 1255 . . . . . (213) 367-0286
Planning and Development Director **John Dennis**
Room 921 . . . . . (213) 367-0381

Water System

Senior Assistant General Manager and Chief Operating Officer **Martin Adams** . . . . . (213) 367-1022
E-mail: martin.adams@ladwp.com
Water Distribution Director **Joe Castruita** . . . . . (213) 367-1063
Water Engineering and Technical Services Director
Susan Rowghani . . . . . (213) 367-0866
E-mail: susan.rowghani@ladwp.com
Water Operations Director **Richard Harasick**
Room 1449 . . . . . (213) 367-1014
E-mail: richard.harasick@ladwp.com
Water Quality Director **Albert Gastelum** . . . . . (213) 367-1014
Water Resources Director **David Pettijohn** . . . . . (213) 367-0873

Lower Colorado River Authority [LCRA]

3700 Lake Austin Boulevard, Austin, TX 78703
P.O. Box 220, Austin, TX 78767-0220
Tel: (512) 473-3200 (Information) Fax: (512) 397-6732
Internet: www.lcra.org

Board of Directors

3700 Lake Austin Boulevard, Austin, TX 78703

▼Chair **Timothy T. "Tim" Timmerman** . . . . . (512) 473-3244

Board of Directors *continued*

▼Vice Chair **Thomas Michael Martine** . . . . . (512) 473-3244
▼Board Member **Steve K. Balas** . . . . . (512) 473-3244
▼Board Member **Lori A. Berger** . . . . . (512) 473-3244
▼Board Member **Stephen F. "Steve" Cooper** . . . . . (512) 473-3244
▼Board Member **Joe Crane** . . . . . (512) 473-3244
▼Board Member **Pamela Jo "PJ" Ellison** . . . . . (512) 473-3244
▼Board Member **John M. Franklin** . . . . . (512) 473-3244
▼Board Member **Raymond A. "Ray" Gill, Jr.** . . . . . (512) 473-3244
▼Board Member **Bart Johnson** . . . . . (512) 473-3244
▼Board Member **Sandra Wright "Sandy" Kibby** . . . . . (512) 473-3244
▼Board Member **Robert "Bobby" Lewis** . . . . . (512) 473-3244
▼Board Member **George Russell** . . . . . (512) 473-3244
▼Board Member **Franklin "Scott" Spears, Jr.** . . . . . (512) 473-3244
▼Board Member **Martha Leigh Whitten** . . . . . (512) 473-3244

Office of the General Manager

General Manager **Phil Wilson** . . . . . (512) 473-3200
Education: Hardin-Simmons 1990 BA; Southern Methodist 2004 MABA
Chief Financial Officer **Richard Williams** . . . . . (512) 473-3200
Chief Administrative Officer **John Miri** . . . . . (512) 473-3200
Education: Harvard BS
General Counsel **Tom Oney** . . . . . (512) 473-3200
Executive Vice President of Public Affairs
Bill Lauderback . . . . . (512) 473-3200
Executive Vice President of Water **John B. Hofmann** . . . . (512) 473-3200
Education: Texas BA
Chief Commercial Officer **Ken Price** . . . . . (512) 473-3200
Chief Information Security Officer **Larry Whiteside** . . . . . (512) 473-3200

Natural Resource Management

Community Services Manager **Margo Richards** . . . . . (512) 473-3200
E-mail: margo.richards@lcra.org
Chief of Public Safety **Don Brent** . . . . . (512) 473-3200 ext. 3316
E-mail: don.brent@lcra.org

Commercial Operations

Senior Vice President of Generation **(Vacant)** . . . . . (512) 473-3200
Senior Vice President of Wholesale Markets and Supply
Michael McCluskey . . . . . (512) 473-3200

Communication Services

Executive Vice President, Public Affairs
Bill Lauderback . . . . . (512) 473-3200

External Affairs

Supervisor for Strategic Communications **Tobin Harvey** . . (512) 473-3200
E-mail: tobin.harvey@lcra.org
Manager of Communication Services and Media Relations **Stefanie Scott** . . . . . (512) 473-3200
E-mail: stefanie.scott@lcra.org
Manager of Regional Affairs **Heather Richardson** . . . . . (512) 473-3200
E-mail: heather.richardson@lcra.org
Manager of Governmental Affairs **Bill Jerram** . . . . . (512) 473-3200
E-mail: bill.jerram@lcra.org

Financial Services

Senior Vice President of Finance **(Vacant)** . . . . . (512) 473-3200
Controller **Julie Rogers** . . . . . (512) 473-3200

Transmission Services

Executive Vice President **(Vacant)** . . . . . (512) 473-3200
Senior Vice President of Project Services
Stuart Nelson . . . . . (512) 473-3200
Vice President of Transmission Operations **Bill Hatfield** . . (512) 473-3200

AUTHORITIES

★Elected Official ▲Appointed by Legislature ▼Appointed by Governor ►Appointed by Board or Commission ●Appointed by Judge
■Appointed by Mayor △Appointed by Freeholders ▽Appointed by Supervisor ▷Appointed by County Executive ○Appointed by Council

Massachusetts Bay Transportation Authority [MBTA]

10 Park Plaza, Suite 3910, Boston, MA 02116
Tel: (617) 222-3200 (Information) Fax: (617) 222-6180
Internet: www.mbta.com

Board of Directors

10 Park Plaza, Boston, MA 02116

▼Chair **Stephanie Pollack** . . . . . . (617) 222-3799
Education: MIT 1982 BS; Harvard 1985 JD
▼Board Member **Dominic L. Blue** . . . . . . (617) 222-3799
Education: Col Holy Cross BA; Boston Col MBA, JD
▼Board Member **Ruth Bonsignore** . . . . . . (617) 973-8080
Education: UMass (Amherst) BSCE
▼Board Member **Brian Lang** . . . . . . (617) 222-3799
▼Board Member **Robert L. Moylan, Jr.** . . . . . . (617) 222-3799
▼Board Member **Steve Poftak** . . . . . . (617) 222-3799
Education: Middlebury BA; Babson MBA
▼Board Member **Betsy Taylor** . . . . . . (617) 222-3799

Fiscal Management and Control Board

Chair **Joseph Aiello** . . . . . . (617) 222-3200
Member **Lisa Calise** . . . . . . (617) 222-3200
Member **Brian Lang** . . . . . . (617) 222-3200
Member **Steve Poftak** . . . . . . (617) 222-3200
Education: Middlebury BA; Babson MBA
Member **Monica Tibbits-Nutt** . . . . . . (617) 222-3200

Office of the General Manager

Tel: (617) 222-3106 Fax: (617) 222-6180

Chief Administrator **Brian Shortsleeve** . . . . . . (617) 222-3106
Chief of Staff **Mark Fuller** . . . . . . (617) 222-3106
General Manager **Frank DePaola** . . . . . . (617) 222-3106
Note: Retiring June 30, 2016
Education: UMass (Dartmouth) BSCE; Northeastern MSCE
General Manager (Acting) **Brian Shortsleeve** . . . . . . (617) 222-3106
Note: Effective July 1, 2016
Chief of Staff **Adam Hurtubise** . . . . . . (617) 222-3106
Education: Boston Col 1992 AB; New England 1995 JD
Deputy Chief of Staff **Darren McAuliffe** . . . . . . (617) 222-3106
Deputy General Manager and Chief Financial Officer **(Vacant)** . . . . . . (617) 222-4246
Deputy General Manager for Human Resources and Labor Relations **Paul Andruszkiewicz** . . . . . . (617) 222-3200
E-mail: pandruszkiewicz@mbta.com
Deputy General Manager for Development and Real Estate **Mark E. Boyle** . . . . . . (617) 222-3200
Assistant General Manager for Systemwide Accessibility **Laura Brelford** . . . . . . (617) 222-1665
Assistant General Manager for Design and Construction **Ed Hunter** . . . . . . (617) 222-3116
E-mail: ehunter@mbta.com
Assistant General Manager for Diversity and Civil Rights **Julian T. Tynes** . . . . . . (617) 222-6949
Education: UMass (Amherst); Eastern Nazarene; Western New England 1997 JD
Assistant General Manager for Engineering and Maintenance **Erik Stoothoff** . . . . . . (617) 222-3106
Assistant General Manager for Bus Operations **David "Dave" Carney** . . . . . . (617) 222-3368
Chief Operating Officer **Jeffrey Gonneville** . . . . . . (617) 222-3150
Chief Procurement Officer **Jerry Polcari** . . . . . . (617) 222-3290
Chief Safety Officer **Ron Nickle** . . . . . . (617) 222-3200
E-mail: rnickle@mbta.com
Chief Technology Officer **Gary Foster** . . . . . . (617) 222-5731
E-mail: gfoster@mbta.com
General Counsel **(Vacant)** . . . . . . (617) 222-3106

Office of the General Manager *continued*

Treasurer-Controller **Wesley G. Wallace, Jr.** . . . . . . (617) 222-5451
Press Secretary **Joseph "Joe" Pesaturo** . . . . . . (617) 222-5697
E-mail: jpesaturo@mbta.com
Chief of Police **Kenneth Green** . . . . . . (617) 222-1100
240 Southampton Street, Boston, MA 02118
E-mail: kgreen@mbta.com
Deputy Chief Operating Officer, Service Planning Strategy **Charles Planck** . . . . . . (617) 222-3106
Director of Budget **Mary Runkel** . . . . . . (617) 222-3285
E-mail: mrunkel@mbta.com
Director of Environmental Affairs **Andrew Brennan** . . . . . . (617) 222-5731
Director of Marketing and Communications **Rose Yates** . . . . . . (617) 222-5559
E-mail: ryates@mbta.com
Director of Occupational Health Services **Kathy Legrow** . . . . . . (617) 222-5381
Director of Railroad Operations **John Ray** . . . . . . (617) 222-3440
Director of Subway Operations **Dion Stubbs** . . . . . . (617) 222-3433
Executive Director of Transportation Planning **David J. Mohler** . . . . . . (617) 222-3106

Metropolitan Atlanta Rapid Transit Authority [MARTA]

2424 Piedmont Rd., NE, Atlanta, GA 30324-3330
Tel: (404) 848-5000 (Information) Fax: (404) 848-5857
Internet: www.itsmarta.com

Board of Directors

2424 Piedmont Road., NE, Atlanta, GA 30324-3330

Chairman **Robert L. "Robbie" Ashe III** . . . . . . (404) 848-5044
Education: Dartmouth BA; Georgia State JD
Vice Chair **Noni Ellison-Southall** . . . . . . (404) 848-5044
Education: Howard U BA; Chicago MBA, JD
Treasurer **Frederick L. Daniels, Jr.** . . . . . . (404) 848-5044
Secretary **Roderick E. "Rod" Edmond** . . . . . . (404) 848-5044
Education: Morehouse Col 1983 BS; Duke 1987 MD; Georgetown 1993 JD
►Board Member **Roberta Abdul-Salaam** . . . . . . (404) 848-5044
Board Member **Juanita Jones Abernathy** . . . . . . (404) 848-5044
Board Member **Robert F. Dallas** . . . . . . (404) 848-5044
Education: Florida BA, MA; Georgia State 1989 JD
Board Member **James F. "Jim" Durrett III** . . . . . . (404) 848-5044
Education: Virginia; Georgia
►Board Member **Jerry Griffin** . . . . . . (404) 848-5044
Board Member **Freda Hardage** . . . . . . (404) 848-5044
Board Member **Barbara Babbit Kaufman** . . . . . . (404) 848-5044
Board Member **(Vacant)** . . . . . . (404) 848-5044
Ex Officio **Russell McMurry** . . . . . . (404) 848-5044
Ex Officio (Non-Voting) **Christopher "Chris" Tomlinson** . . . . . . (404) 848-5044
Education: Morehouse Col; Georgia State JD

Administration

General Manager/Chief Executive Officer **Keith T. Parker** . . . . . . (404) 848-5065
Education: VCU 1990 BA, 1993 MURP; Richmond MBA
Chief of Staff **Rukiya Thomas** . . . . . . (404) 848-5000
Assistant General Manager, Internal Audit **(Vacant)** . . . . (404) 848-5000
Assistant General Manager, Legal Services and Chief Counsel **Elizabeth O'Neill** . . . . . . (404) 848-5220
Chief Administrative Officer **Edward L. Johnson** . . . . . . (404) 848-5000
E-mail: eljohnson@itsmarta.com
Chief Operating Officer **Rich "Richard" Krisak** . . . . . . (404) 848-5000
E-mail: rkrisak@itsmarta.com
Assistant General Manager, Bus Operations **Joe Earves** . . . . . . (404) 848-5000

★Elected Official ▲Appointed by Legislature ▼Appointed by Governor ►Appointed by Board or Commission ●Appointed by Judge
■Appointed by Mayor △Appointed by Freeholders ▽Appointed by Supervisor ▷Appointed by County Executive ○Appointed by Council

Administration *continued*

Assistant General Manager and Chief, Police Services
Wanda Dunham . . . . (404) 848-4900
E-mail: wdunham@itsmarta.com

Assistant General Manager, Safety and Quality Control
(Vacant) . . . . (404) 848-6220

Assistant General Manager, Communications and External Affairs **Ryland Needom McClendon** . . . . (404) 848-5000
E-mail: rmcclendon@itsmarta.com

Assistant General Manager, Contracts and Procurement
(Vacant) . . . . (404) 848-5000

Assistant General Manager, Finance and Chief Financial Officer **Gordon L. Hutchinson** . . . . (404) 848-5000

Assistant General Manager, Human Resources
Robin E. Henry . . . . (404) 848-5000
E-mail: rehenry@itsmarta.com

Assistant General Manager, Information Technology
Ming Hsi . . . . (404) 848-5000

Assistant General Manager, Planning (Acting)
Donald Williams . . . . (404) 848-5000

Executive Director, Office of Diversity and Equal Opportunity **Ferdinand Risco** . . . . (404) 848-5000

Senior Director, External Affairs
Rhonda Briggins-Ridley . . . . (404) 848-5000
Education: Faulkner 2003 JD

Senior Director, Engineering and Development
David Springstead . . . . (404) 848-5000
E-mail: dspringstead@itsmarta.com

Senior Director, Treasury and Capital Programs and Treasurer **Kevin Hurley** . . . . (404) 848-5000

Director, Configuration Management **Jayant Patel** . . . . (404) 848-5000

Director, Financial Management and Budget
Walter Jones . . . . (404) 848-5000
E-mail: wjones@itsmarta.com

Director, Labor Relations **Louise Jackson Williams** . . . . (404) 848-5000

Director, Marketing **Jennifer Jinadu** . . . . (404) 848-5000

Director, Risk Management **Donna Jennings** . . . . (404) 848-5000
E-mail: djennings@itsmarta.com

Director, Transit Research and Analysis **Carol G. Smith** . . (404) 848-5000

Director, Transit-System Planning **Donald Williams** . . . . (404) 848-5000

Metropolitan Domestic Water Improvement District (Tucson)

6265 North La Canada Drive, Tucson, AZ 85704
P.O. Box 36870, Tucson, AZ 85740
Tel: (520) 575-8100 Fax: (520) 575-8454 E-mail: info@metrowater.com
Internet: www.metrowater.com

Board of Directors

P.O. Box 36870, Tucson, AZ 85740

Chair **Judy Scrivener** . . . . (520) 575-8100
Term Expires: December 31, 2018

Vice Chair **Dan M. Offret** . . . . (520) 575-8100
Term Expires: December 31, 2016
Education: Arizona BA, MA

Member **James O. "Jim" Doyle** . . . . (520) 575-8100
Term Expires: December 31, 2018

Member **Bryan Foulk** . . . . (520) 575-8100
Term Expires: December 31, 2016

Member **Helen Ireland** . . . . (520) 575-8100
Term Expires: December 31, 2018

Administration

General Manager **Joe Olsen** . . . . (520) 575-8100

Assistant General Manager **Warren J. Tenney** . . . . (520) 575-8100
E-mail: wtenney@metrowater.com

Chief Financial Officer **Diane Bracken** . . . . (520) 575-8100

Administration *continued*

District Engineer **Charles A. Maish** . . . . (520) 575-8100
E-mail: cmaish@metrowater.com

Water Resource Manager **Michael W. Block** . . . . (520) 575-8100

Human Resources Specialist **Billie Sue Morelli** . . . . (520) 575-8100
E-mail: bmorelli@metrowater.com

Metropolitan Nashville Airport Authority [MNAA]

One Terminal Drive, Suite 501, Nashville, TN 37214-4114
Tel: (615) 275-1600 (Information) Fax: (615) 275-4575
Internet: www.flynashville.com

Board of Commissioners

One Terminal Drive, Suite 501, Nashville, TN 37214-4114
Fax: (615) 275-4575

■ Chair **Robert "Bobby" Joslin** . . . . (615) 275-1600

■ Vice Chairman **Adrian Dexter Samuels** . . . . (615) 275-1600

■ Secretary **Aubrey B "Trey" Harwell III** . . . . (615) 275-1600

■ Commissioner **Megan Barry** . . . . (615) 275-1600

■ Commissioner **Rod Essig** . . . . (615) 275-1600

■ Commissioner **Amanda C. Farnsworth** . . . . (615) 275-1600
Date of Birth: 1959
Education: Vanderbilt

■ Commissioner **Bill Freeman** . . . . (615) 275-1600

■ Commissioner **Nicole Maynard** . . . . (615) 275-1600

■ Commissioner **Juli H. Mosley** . . . . (615) 275-1600
Note: Retiring 2016

■ Commissioner **Deborah Wright** . . . . (615) 275-1600
Education: Pace

Administration

President and Chief Executive Officer
Robert R. "Rob" Wigington . . . . (615) 275-1600
Education: Pomona 1976 BA; USC 1979 MPA

Senior Vice President and Chief Legal Officer
Robert C. Watson . . . . (615) 275-1600

Senior Vice President and Chief Operating Officer
Col Douglas E. Kreulen . . . . (615) 275-1825
E-mail: doug_kreulen@nashintl.com
Education: Auburn 1980 BS; Troy State 1983 MS; National War Col 2000 MS

Vice President and Chief Information Officer
Vanessa Hickman . . . . (615) 275-1600
E-mail: vanessa_hickman@nashintl.com

Vice President and Chief Financial Officer
Stan Van Ostran . . . . (615) 275-1600
Fax: (615) 275-4004

Senior Vice President and Chief People Officer **(Vacant)** . . (615) 275-1600

Vice President, Strategic Communications and External Affairs **(Vacant)** . . . . (615) 275-1600
Fax: (615) 275-4001

Vice President, Strategic Planning and Sustainability
Christine Vitt . . . . (615) 275-1600
Education: RIT

Assistant Vice President, Continuous Improvement
Walt Matwijec . . . . (615) 275-1747

Chief Engineer and Vice President of Development and Engineering **Robert Ramsey** . . . . (615) 275-1600
E-mail: robert_ramsey@nashintl.com
Education: VMI BSEE; Missouri (Rolla) MS

Assistant Vice President, Properties and Business Development **(Vacant)** . . . . (615) 275-1600

Chief of Public Safety **David Griswold** . . . . (615) 275-2340
E-mail: david_griswold@nashintl.com

AUTHORITIES

★ Elected Official ▲ Appointed by Legislature ▼ Appointed by Governor ► Appointed by Board or Commission ● Appointed by Judge
■ Appointed by Mayor △ Appointed by Freeholders ▽ Appointed by Supervisor ▷ Appointed by County Executive ○ Appointed by Council

Metropolitan St. Louis Sewer District [MSD]

2350 Market Street, St. Louis, MO 63103-2555
Internet: www.stlmsd.com

Board of Trustees

2350 Market Street, St. Louis, MO 63103-2555

▷Chair **Michael Yates** . . . . (314) 768-6224
Note: Will continue to serve until reappointed or replaced.
Term Expires: March 15, 2014
■Vice Chair **James Faul** . . . . (314) 768-6224
Term Expires: March 15, 2017
▷Trustee **Rev. Ronald Bobo** . . . . (314) 768-6224
Note: Will continue to serve until reappointed or replaced
Term Expires: March 15, 2016
■Trustee **Ruby L. Bonner** . . . . (314) 768-6224
Term Expires: March 15, 2018
■Trustee **Annette Mandel** . . . . (314) 768-6224
Term Expires: March 15, 2020
▷Trustee **James I. Singer** . . . . (314) 768-6224
Term Expires: March 15, 2017

Administration

Executive Director **Brian L. Hoelscher** . . . . (314) 768-6245
E-mail: blhoel@stlmsd.com
Secretary to the Executive Director **Tamara Clinton** . . . . (314) 768-6224
General Counsel **Susan Myers** . . . . (314) 768-6202
Education: Missouri Science and Tech; Saint Louis U JD
Secretary-Treasurer **Tim Snoke** . . . . (314) 768-6210
Director of Engineering **Rich Unverferth** . . . . (314) 768-6204
E-mail: rlunve@stlmsd.com
Director of Finance **Marion Gee** . . . . (314) 768-6228
Director of Human Resources **Vicki L. Taylor Edwards** . . (314) 768-6216
E-mail: vitayl@stlmsd.com
Director of Information Systems **Barbara E. Mohn** . . . . (314) 768-2754
E-mail: bmohn@stlmsd.com
Director of Operations **Jonathon Sprague** . . . . (314) 768-6248
E-mail: jsprague@stlmsd.com
Risk Manager **Michael Grace** . . . . (314) 768-6219
E-mail: mgrace@stlmsd.com

Metropolitan Utilities District [M.U.D]

1723 Harney Street, Omaha, NE 68102-1960
Internet: www.mudomaha.com

Board of Directors

1723 Harney Street, Omaha, NE 68102-1960

★Chairperson **Jack Frost** . . . . (402) 504-7147
Term Expires: December 31, 2016
★Member **James Begley** . . . . (402) 504-7147
Term Expires: December 31, 2018
★Member **Timothy W. Cavanaugh** . . . . (402) 504-7147
Term Expires: December 31, 2020
★Member **Thomas F. Dowd** . . . . (402) 504-7147
Term Expires: December 31, 2020
★Member **David J. Friend** . . . . (402) 504-7147
Term Expires: December 31, 2018
E-mail: dfriend847@cox.net
★Member **Gwen Howard** . . . . (402) 504-7147
Term Expires: December 31, 2020
Date of Birth: June 24, 1945
Education: Midland Lutheran 1967 BA; Nebraska 1974 MA

Board of Directors *continued*

★Member **Steve Patterson** . . . . (402) 504-7147
Term Expires: December 31, 2016
Secretary to the Board **Scott Keep** . . . . (402) 504-7147

Office of the President

Tel: (402) 504-7147 Fax: (402) 504-5147
E-mail: customer_service@mudnebr.com

President **Scott Keep** . . . . (402) 504-7106
Senior Vice President and Chief Operations Officer
Ron Reisner . . . . (402) 504-7110

Metropolitan Water District of Southern California [MWD]

700 N. Alameda Street, Los Angeles, CA 90012-2944
P.O. Box 54153, Los Angeles, CA 90054-0153
Tel: (213) 217-6000 (Information) Fax: (213) 217-5704
Internet: www.mwdh2o.com

Board of Directors

700 N. Alameda Street, Los Angeles, CA 90012-2944
P.O. Box 54153, Los Angeles, CA 90054-0153

Chairman **Randy A. Record** (Eastern) . . . . (213) 217-6000
E-mail: rrecord@mwdh2o.com
Vice Chair **Linda Ackerman** (Orange County) . . . . (213) 217-6000
E-mail: lackerman@mwdh2o.com
Education: Colorado
Vice Chair **Gloria D. Gray** (West Basin) . . . . (213) 217-6000
E-mail: ggray@mwdh2o.com
Education: U Redlands
Vice Chair **John W. Murray, Jr.** (Los Angeles) . . . . (213) 217-6000
Vice Chair **Michael Touhey** (Upper San Gabriel Valley) . . (213) 217-6000
Date of Birth: May 13, 1962
Secretary **John T. Morris** (San Marino) . . . . (213) 217-6000
E-mail: jmorris@mwdh2o.com
Education: USC BS
Board Member **Stephen Faessel** (Anaheim) . . . . (213) 217-6000
Board Member **Robert Wunderlich** (Beverly Hills) . . . . (213) 217-6000
Board Member **Marsha Ramos** (Burbank) . . . . (213) 217-6000
Education: Cal State (Northridge) BA
Board Member **Steve Blois** (Calleguas) . . . . (213) 217-6000
Education: Cal Poly San Luis Obispo BSIE
Board Member **Robert Apodaca** (Central Basin) . . . . (213) 217-6000
Board Member **Leticia Vasquez** (Central Basin) . . . . (213) 217-6000
Board Member **Janna Zurita** (Compton) . . . . (213) 217-6000
Board Member **Richard W. Atwater** (Foothill) . . . . (213) 217-6000
Education: Stanford BA; USC MA
Board Member **Peter Beard** (Fullerton) . . . . (213) 217-6000
Board Member **Laura Friedman** (Glendale) . . . . (213) 217-6000
Board Member **Michael Camacho** (Inland Empire) . . . . (213) 217-6000
Board Member **Glen D. Peterson** (Las Virgenes) . . . . (213) 217-6000
E-mail: gpeterson@mwdh2o.com
Board Member **Suja Lowenthal** (Long Beach) . . . . (213) 217-6000
E-mail: slowenthal@mwdh2o.com
Education: UCLA; Cal State (Los Angeles) MBA; USC PhD
Board Member **Glen C Dake** (Los Angeles) . . . . (213) 217-6000
Education: Cornell BLA
Board Member **Paul Koretz** (Los Angeles) . . . . (213) 217-6000
Education: UCLA 1979 BA
Board Member **Jesus E. Quiñonez** (Los Angeles) . . . . (213) 217-6000
E-mail: jquiñonez@mwdh2o.com
Board Member **Lorraine Paskett** (Los Angeles) . . . . (213) 217-6000
Board Member **Brett R. Barbre** (Orange County) . . . . (213) 217-6000
Board Member **Larry D. Dick** (Orange County) . . . . (213) 217-6000
E-mail: ldick@mwdh2o.com
Board Member **Larry McKenney** (Orange County) . . . . (213) 217-6000

★Elected Official ▲Appointed by Legislature ▼Appointed by Governor ►Appointed by Board or Commission ●Appointed by Judge
■Appointed by Mayor △Appointed by Freeholders ▽Appointed by Supervisor ▷Appointed by County Executive ○Appointed by Council

Board of Directors *continued*

Board Member **Cynthia J. Kurtz** (Pasadena) .... (213) 217-6000
Fax: (213) 217-6650

Board Member **Michael T. Hogan** (San Diego County) ... (213) 217-6000

Board Member **Keith Lewinger** (San Diego County) ..... (213) 217-6000
E-mail: klewinger@mwdh2o.com

Board Member **Fern Steiner** (San Diego County) .... (213) 217-6000

Board Member **Yen C. Tu** (San Diego County) .... (213) 217-6000

Board Member **Sylvia Ballin** (San Fernando) .... (213) 217-6000

Board Member **Michele Martinez** (Santa Ana) .... (213) 217-6000

Board Member **Judy Abdo** (Santa Monica) .... (213) 217-6000
E-mail: jabdo@mwdh2o.com Fax: (213) 217-6650
Education: UC Santa Barbara BA

Board Member **David D. De Jesus** (Three Valleys) ...... (213) 217-6000
E-mail: ddejesus@mwdh2o.com
Education: Azusa Pacific

Board Member **Russell J. Lefevre** (Torrance) .... (213) 217-6000

Board Member **Donald Dear** (West Basin) .... (213) 217-6000

Board Member
Donald D. Galleano (Western Riverside County) ...... (213) 217-6000

Administration

General Manager **Jeffrey Kightlinger** .... (213) 217-6211
Education: UC Berkeley 1981 BA; Santa Clara U 1985 JD

Assistant General Manager/Chief Administrative Officer
Gilbert F. Ivey .... (213) 217-6622
E-mail: givey@mwdh2o.com

Group Manager, Business Technology **(Vacant)** .... (213) 217-6241

Group Manager, Real Property Development and Management **John C. Clairday** .... (213) 217-6183

Director of Human Resources and Risk Management
Fidencio M. "Feedy" Mares .... (213) 217-7232
E-mail: fmares@mwdh2o.com

Assistant General Manager/Chief Financial Officer
Gary Breaux .... (213) 217-7121

Assistant General Manager/Chief Operating Officer
Debra C. Man .... (213) 217-6762
E-mail: dman@mwdh2o.com

Group Manager, Water Resources Management
Deven Upadhyay .... (213) 217-6052

Group Manager, Water System Operations
James F. "Jim" Green .... (213) 217-7008
E-mail: jgreen@mwdh2o.com

Assistant General Manager, Strategic Water Initiatives
Roger K. Patterson .... (213) 217-5786

Deputy General Manager, External Affairs **Dee Zinke** .... (213) 217-7747
E-mail: dzinke@mwdh2o.com

General Auditor **Gerald C. Riss** .... (213) 217-6139

Ethics Officer **Deena Ghaly** .... (213) 217-5521
Education: Wellesley BA; Cornell JD

General Counsel **Marcia Scully** .... (213) 217-6000
Education: Michigan BA; Wayne State U MUP; Loyola Marymount JD

Assistant General Counsel **Heather Beatty** .... (213) 217-6517

Metropolitan Water Reclamation District of Greater Chicago [MWRD]

100 East Erie Street, Chicago, IL 60611-2871
Tel: (312) 751-5600 (Information) Internet: www.mwrd.org

Board of Commissioners

100 East Erie Street, Chicago, IL 60611-2871
Tel: (312) 751-5636 Fax: (312) 751-5633

★ Board President **Mariyana T. Spyropoulos** .... (312) 751-5650
Term Expires: December 6, 2016
E-mail: mariyana.spyropoulos@mwrd.org

Board of Commissioners *continued*

★ Finance Chairman **Frank Avila** .... (312) 751-5620
Term Expires: December 2020
E-mail: frank.avila@mwrd.org

★ Commissioner **Michael A. Alvarez** .... (312) 751-5665
Term Expires: December 6, 2016
E-mail: michael.alvarez@mwrd.org
Education: Northwestern

★ Commissioner **Timothy Bradford** .... (312) 751-5646
Term Expires: December 2020

★ Commissioner **Barbara J. McGowan** .... (312) 751-5640
Term Expires: December 6, 2016
E-mail: barbara.mcgowan@mwrd.org

★ Commissioner **Cynthia M. Santos** .... (312) 751-5685
Term Expires: December 2020
E-mail: cynthia.santos@mwrd.org

★ Commissioner **Debra Shore** .... (312) 751-5690
Term Expires: December 4, 2018
E-mail: debra.shore@mwrd.org

★ Commissioner **Kari Steele** .... (312) 751-5700
Term Expires: December 4, 2018
E-mail: kari.steele@mwrd.org

★ Commissioner **David J. Walsh** .... (312) 751-5694
Term Expires: December 4, 2018

Administration

Executive Director **David St. Pierre** .... (312) 751-7900
Education: Eugene Bible; Southern Illinois BS Fax: (312) 751-5681

General Counsel **Ronald Hill** .... (312) 751-6565

Treasurer **Mary Ann Boyle** .... (312) 751-5150

Engineering Director **Catherine O'Connor** .... (312) 751-7905

Finance Director/Clerk **Jacqueline Torres** .... (312) 751-6500

Human Resources Director **Denice E. Korcal** .... (312) 751-5180
E-mail: denice.korcal@mwrd.org

Information Technology Director **John H. Sudduth** ..... (312) 751-5810
E-mail: sudduthj@mwrd.org

Maintenance and Operations Director **Manju Sharma** .... (312) 751-5101
E-mail: manju.sharma@mwrd.org

Monitoring and Research Director **Thomas C. Granato** .. (312) 751-5190

Procurement and Materials Management Director
Darlene A. LoCascio .... (312) 751-6643
E-mail: darlene.locascio@mwrd.org

Milwaukee Metropolitan Sewerage District [MMSD]

260 W. Seeboth St., Milwaukee, WI 53204-1446
Tel: (414) 272-5100 Fax: (414) 277-0318 Internet: www.mmsd.com

Office of the Commissioners

260 W. Seeboth St., Milwaukee, WI 53204-1446

Chair **John Hermes** .... (414) 225-2082

Commissioner **Lyle A. Balistreri** .... (414) 225-2082

Commissioner **James Bohl** .... (414) 225-2082

Commissioner **Milele A. Coggs** .... (414) 225-2082

Commissioner **Kathy Ehley** .... (414) 225-2082

Commissioner **Benjamin Gramling** .... (414) 225-2082

Commissioner **Nikiya Q. Harris Dodd** .... (414) 225-2082
Education: Wisconsin (Milwaukee) 2001 BS, 2007 MS

Commissioner **Carl Krueger** .... (414) 225-2082

Commissioner **Eugene Manzanet** .... (414) 225-2082

Commissioner **Kris Martinsek** .... (414) 225-2082

Commissioner **Michael West** .... (414) 225-2082

Commission Secretary **Anna Kettlewell** .... (414) 225-2088
E-mail: akettlewell@mmsd.com

★ Elected Official ▲ Appointed by Legislature ▼ Appointed by Governor ► Appointed by Board or Commission ● Appointed by Judge
■ Appointed by Mayor △ Appointed by Freeholders ▽ Appointed by Supervisor ▷ Appointed by County Executive ○ Appointed by Council

AUTHORITIES

Office of the Executive Director

Fax: (414) 272-5057

Executive Director **Kevin L. Shafer** .... (414) 225-2088
Education: Illinois 1982 BSCE; Texas 1988 MSCE
Executive Administrator **Anna Kettlewell** .... (414) 225-2088
E-mail: akettlewell@mmsd.com

Finance

Director/Treasurer **Mark Kaminski** .... (414) 225-2050
E-mail: mkaminski@mmsd.com
Deputy Director **Mickie Pearsall** .... (414) 225-2213
Controller **Don Nehmer** .... (414) 225-2190

Community Outreach and Business Engagement

Director **Jeffrey Spence** .... (414) 277-6364
Communications and Public Information Manager
Bill Graffin .... (414) 225-2077
E-mail: bgraffin@mmsd.com

Human Resources

Manager **Candace Richards** .... (414) 225-2068
E-mail: crichards@mmsd.com

Legal Services

Director **Susan B. Anthony** .... (414) 225-2106
Education: Wisconsin 1977 JD
Administrative Assistant **Mary McGivern** .... (414) 225-2095
E-mail: mmcgivern@mmsd.com
Paralegal Administrator **Linda B. Mooney** .... (414) 225-2098
E-mail: lmooney@mmsd.com
Staff Attorney **Tom Nowicki** .... (414) 225-2243
Senior Staff Attorney **Katherine Lazarski** .... (414) 225-2103
Senior Staff Attorney **Joseph T. Ganzer** .... (414) 225-2200
Education: St Norbert 1992 BA; Wisconsin 2000 JD

AUTHORITIES

Management Information Systems

Manager **Greg O'Hearn** .... (414) 225-2186
E-mail: gohearn@mmsd.com

Planning, Research and Sustainability

Director **Tim Bate** .... (414) 225-2156
Manager of Sustainability **Karen Sands** .... (414) 225-2120

Technical Services

Director **Michael Martin** .... (414) 225-2148
Contract Compliance Manager **Pat Obenauf** .... (414) 225-2256
Engineering Design Manager **Kevin Lyons** .... (414) 221-6809
E-mail: klyons@mmsd.com
Capital Program Support Manager **Rick Neiderstadt** ..... (414) 414-2252

Water Quality Protection

Director **Sharon Mertens** .... (414) 227-6384
Lab Manager **Alfredo Sotomayor** .... (414) 277-6369

Nebraska Public Power District [NPPD]

1414 15th St., Columbus, NE 68601
P.O. Box 499, Columbus, NE 68602-0499
Fax: (402) 563-5145 Internet: www.nppd.com

Board of Directors

P.O. Box 499, Columbus, NE 68602-0499

★Chairman **Ken Kunze** (Subdivision 7) .... (402) 362-7438
Term Expires: January 6, 2021
E-mail: krkunze@nppd.com
Date of Birth: April 19, 1949
Education: Nebraska (Kearney) 1972 BABA

Board of Directors *continued*

★First Vice-Chairman **Larry E. Linstrom** (Subdivision 4) .. (308) 534-9182
Term Expires: January 4, 2017
E-mail: lelinst@nppd.com
★Second Vice-Chairman **Thomas J. Hoff** (Subdivision 5) .. (308) 872-3352
Term Expires: January 2, 2019
★Secretary **Jerry L. Chlopek** (Subdivision 9) .... (402) 564-6442
Term Expires: January 6, 2021
E-mail: jlchlop@nppd.com
★Board Member **Mary A. Harding** (Subdivision 1) .... (402) 560-0630
Term Expires: January 6, 2021
E-mail: mary4nppd@gmail.com
★Board Member **Barry DeKay** (Subdivision 2) .... (402) 229-3253
Term Expires: January 6, 2021
E-mail: bddekay@nppd.com
★Board Member **Ron W. Larsen** (Subdivision 3) .... (308) 234-2194
Term Expires: January 4, 2017
E-mail: rwlarse@nppd.com
★Board Member **Edward J. Schrock** (Subdivision 6) ..... (308) 995-4665
Term Expires: January 2, 2019
E-mail: ejschro@nppd.com
★Board Member **Gary G. Thompson** (Subdivision 8) ..... (402) 806-0266
Term Expires: January 4, 2017
E-mail: ggthomp@nppd.com
★Board Member **Virgil L. Froehlich** (Subdivision 10) ..... (402) 379-3452
Term Expires: January 4, 2017
E-mail: vlfroeh@nppd.com
★Board Member **Fred L. Christensen** (Subdivision 11) .... (402) 685-6269
Term Expires: January 2, 2019
E-mail: flchris@nppd.com

Administration

President and Chief Executive Officer
Patrick L. "Pat" Pope .... (402) 563-5029
Education: Nebraska 1979 BSEE, 1995 MBA
Executive Assistant to the President and Chief Executive Officer **Kimberly M. Smith** .... (402) 563-5327
E-mail: kmsmith@nppd.com
Assistant Secretary to Board of Directors
Jan H. Modelski .... (402) 563-5487
E-mail: jhmodel@nppd.com
Vice President and General Counsel **John C. McClure** ... (402) 563-5773
E-mail: jcmcclu@nppd.com
Education: Nebraska JD
Vice President and Chief Financial Officer
Traci L. Bender .... (402) 563-5459
Vice President and Chief Nuclear Officer
Oscar Limpias .... (402) 825-2770
E-mail: oalimpi@nppd.com
Vice President and Chief Operating Officer
Thomas J. "Tom" Kent .... (402) 563-5575
E-mail: tjkent@nppd.com
Education: Nebraska 1985 BSEE, 2005 MBA
Vice President of Customer Services
Kendall B. "Ken" Curry .... (402) 564-5366
Education: Nebraska, MBA
Vice President of HR and Corporate Support (Interim)
Chris Overman .... (402) 563-5810
E-mail: cmoverm@nppd.com
Chief Audit and Ethics Officer **Conrad Saltzgaber** ...... (402) 563-5433
Assistant Treasurer **Donna K. Starzec** .... (402) 563-5126

★Elected Official ▲Appointed by Legislature ▼Appointed by Governor ▶Appointed by Board or Commission ●Appointed by Judge
■Appointed by Mayor △Appointed by Freeholders ▽Appointed by Supervisor ▷Appointed by County Executive ○Appointed by Council

NEW Water

2231 North Quincy Street, Green Bay, WI 54302
Tel: (920) 432-4893 Fax: (920) 432-4302 Internet: www.newwater.us

Office of the Commissioners

2231 North Quincy Street, Green Bay, WI 54302

President **Kathryn Hasselblad** .... (920) 432-4893
Term Expires: December 31, 2016
Secretary **James "Jim" Blumreich** .... (920) 432-4893
Term Expires: December 31, 2019
Vice President **Lee Hoffman** .... (920) 432-4893
Term Expires: December 31, 2017
Vice President **Thomas P. "Tom" Meinz** .... (920) 432-4893
Term Expires: December 31, 2018
Education: Michigan Tech BSChE
Vice President **Mark Tumpach** .... (920) 432-4893
Note: Will continue to serve until reappointed or replaced
Term Expires: December 31, 2015

Administration

Executive Director **Thomas W. Sigmund** .... (920) 432-4893
E-mail: tsigmund@newwater.us
Director of Business Services **Paul Kaster** .... (920) 432-4893
E-mail: pkaster@newwater.us
Director of Operations **Patrick Wescott** .... (920) 432-4893
E-mail: pwescott@newwater.us
Director of Technical Services **Nate Qualls** .... (920) 432-4893
E-mail: nqualls@newwater.us
Communications and Education Coordinator
Tricia Garrison .... (920) 432-4893
E-mail: tgarrison@gbmsd.org
Director of Environmental Programs
William "Bill" Hafs .... (920) 432-4893
E-mail: whafs@newwater.us

New York City Housing Authority [NYCHA]

250 Broadway, New York, NY 10007
Tel: (212) 306-3000 Fax: (212) 306-5189 Internet: www.nyc.gov/nycha

The Board

■ Chair and Chief Executive Officer
Oyeshola "Shola" Olatoye .... (212) 306-3454
E-mail: solatoye@nycha.nyc.gov
Education: Wesleyan U 1996 BA; NYU 2001 MPA
■ Member **Beatrice Byrd** .... (212) 306-3454
■ Member **Derrick D. Cephas** .... (212) 306-3454
Education: Harvard 1975 AB, 1979 JD
■ Member **Zaire Dinzey-Flores** .... (212) 306-3454
■ Member **Victor A. González** .... (212) 306-3454
■ Member **Willie Mae Lewis** .... (212) 306-3454
■ Member **Nnenna J. Lynch** .... (212) 306-3454
Education: Villanova 1993 BA; Oxford (UK) 1996 MS
Secretary to the Board **Vilma Huertas** .... (212) 306-6088
E-mail: vilma.huertas@nycha.nyc.gov

Administration

■ Chief Executive Officer **Oyeshola "Shola" Olatoye** ..... (212) 306-3000
E-mail: solatoye@nycha.nyc.gov
Education: Wesleyan U 1996 BA; NYU 2001 MPA
Chief of Staff **David Pristin** .... (212) 306-3401
General Manager **Michael P. Kelly** .... (212) 306-3000
Education: Princeton 1977 BA; UC Berkeley MArch, MEd

Administration *continued*

Executive Vice President and Chief Administrative
Officer **Natalie Y. Rivers** .... (212) 306-8786
E-mail: natalie.rivers@nycha.nyc.gov
Executive Vice President for Legal Affairs and General
Counsel **David Farber** .... (212) 776-5000
Executive Vice President for Development
William Crawley .... (212) 306-4073
Executive Vice President for Community Programs and
Development **Melanie F. Hart** .... (212) 306-4073
Executive Vice President for Capital Projects
Raymond A. Ribeiro .... (212) 306-8833
Vice President for Capital Projects and Quality
Assurance **Celeste Morgan-Glenn** .... (212) 306-3034
Vice President for Disaster Recovery **Michael Rosen** ... (212) 306-2982
Vice President for Capital Projects **Farhan Syed** ...... (212) 306-3034
Executive Vice President and Chief Information Officer
Robert "Bob" Marano .... (212) 306-8833
E-mail: rmarano@nycha.nyc.gov
Senior Vice President and Chief Supply Officer
Victor Martinez .... (212) 306-3000
Education: Puerto Rico BA, JD
Vice President for Community Operations
Deidra Gilliard .... (212) 306-3450
E-mail: deidre.gilliard@nycha.nyc.gov
Education: Duke
Executive Vice President and Chief Financial Officer
Richard Couch .... (212) 306-3770
Education: Connecticut BSAcc; Fordham MBA
Executive Vice President for Operations
Carlos G. Laboy-Diaz .... (212) 306-8590
E-mail: carlos.laboy@nycha.nyc.gov
Vice President for Operations **Brian Clarke** .... (718) 707-2850
Chief Communications Officer **Jean Weinberg** .... (212) 306-2872
E-mail: jean.weinberg@nycha.nyc.gov
Director of State and City Legislative Affairs
Brian Honan .... (212) 306-8103

New York Metropolitan Transportation Authority [MTA]

2 Broadway, New York, NY 10004
Tel: (212) 878-7000 (Information) Fax: (212) 878-7264
Internet: www.mta.info

Board of Directors

347 Madison Avenue, New York, NY 10017-3706
Fax: (212) 878-7468

▼ Chairman **Thomas F. Prendergast** .... (212) 878-7446
Term Expires: June 30, 2016
▼ Vice Chairman **Fernando J. "Freddy" Ferrer** .... (212) 878-7446
Term Expires: June 30, 2016
Date of Birth: April 30, 1950
Education: NYU BA; Baruch Col MPA
▼ Board Member **Andrew B. Albert** .... (212) 878-7446
Note: Recommended by New York City Transit Riders Council. Will continue to serve until reappointed or replaced.
Term Expires: December 31, 2015
▼ Board Member **Jonathan A. "Jon" Ballan** .... (212) 878-7446
Note: Recommended by Westchester County Executive; Note: Will continue to serve until reappointed or replaced
Term Expires: June 30, 2015
Education: Williams 1979 BA; George Washington 1982 JD
▼ Board Member **John H. Banks III** .... (212) 878-7446
Note: Recommended by New York City Mayor; Note: Will continue to serve until replaced or reappointed
Term Expires: June 30, 2011
Education: Manhattan Col 1985; Baruch Col 1992 MPA

(continued on next page)

★ Elected Official ▲ Appointed by Legislature ▼ Appointed by Governor ▶ Appointed by Board or Commission ● Appointed by Judge
■ Appointed by Mayor △ Appointed by Freeholders ▽ Appointed by Supervisor ▷ Appointed by County Executive ○ Appointed by Council

Board of Directors *continued*

▼Board Member **Robert C. Bickford** .... (212) 878-7446
Note: Will continue to serve until replaced or reappointed; Note: Recommended by Putnam County Executive
Term Expires: June 30, 2010

▼Board Member **Norman E. Brown** .... (212) 878-7446
Note: Will continue to serve until replaced or reappointed; Note: Recommended by Metro-North Railroad unions
Term Expires: December 31, 2006

▼Board Member **Allen P. Cappelli** .... (212) 878-7446
Note: Will continue to serve until reappointed or replaced
Term Expires: June 30, 2015

▼Board Member **Ira Greenberg** .... (212) 878-7446
Note: Recommended by Long Island Rail Road Commuter Council
Term Expires: December 31, 2018

▼Board Member **Jeffrey A. Kay** .... (212) 878-7446
Note: Will continue to serve until reappointed or replaced.; Note: Recommended by New York City Mayor
Term Expires: June 30, 2014
Education: SUNY (Binghamton) BA; SUNY (Albany) MA

▼Board Member **Susan G. Metzger** .... (212) 878-7446
Note: Will continue to serve until replaced or reappointed; Note: Recommended by Orange County Executive
Term Expires: June 30, 2010

▼Board Member **Charles G. Moerdler** .... (212) 878-7446
Term Expires: June 30, 2016
Education: Long Island 1953 BA; Fordham 1956 JD

▼Board Member **John J. Molloy** .... (212) 878-7274
Note: Recommended by Nassau County Executive; Note: Will continue to serve until reappointed or replaced
Term Expires: June 30, 2015

▼Board Member **Mitchell H. Pally** .... (212) 878-7446
Note: Recommended by Suffolk County Executive
Term Expires: June 30, 2016

▼Board Member **Lawrence S. "Larry" Schwartz** .... (212) 878-7446
Term Expires: June 30, 2018
Education: SUNY (Binghamton) BS

▼Board Member **James L. Sedore, Jr.** .... (212) 878-7446
Note: Will continue to serve until replaced or reappointed; Note: Recommended by Dutchess County Executive
Term Expires: June 30, 2010
Education: Siena Col 1965 BBA

▼Board Member **Vincent Tessitore, Jr.** .... (212) 878-7446
Note: Will continue to serve until replaced or reappointed
Term Expires: January 1, 2013

■Board Member **Polly Ellen Trottenberg** .... (212) 878-7446
Term Expires: June 30, 2017
Education: Barnard 1986 BA; Harvard 1992 MPP

▼Board Member **Ed Watt** .... (212) 878-7446
Note: Will continue to serve until replaced or reappointed
Term Expires: January 1, 2006

▼Board Member **Carl V. Wortendyke** .... (212) 878-7446
Note: Will continue to serve until replaced or reappointed
Term Expires: June 30, 2010

▼Board Member **Neal Zuckerman** .... (212) 878-7446
Note: Will continue to serve until reappointed or replaced.
Term Expires: December 31, 2015
Education: West Point BS; Harvard MBA

▼Board Member **(Vacant)** .... (212) 878-7446

■Board Member **(Vacant)** .... (212) 878-7446
Term Expires: June 30, 2020

Board Office Manager **Darlene Slade** .... (212) 878-7448

Board Office Assistant **(Vacant)** .... (212) 878-7235

Officers and Management

▼Chairman and Chief Executive Officer
Thomas F. Prendergast .... (212) 878-7274

Chief of Staff **Donna Evans** .... (212) 878-7224

Chief Operating Officer **(Vacant)** .... (212) 878-7488

Chief Financial Officer **Robert E. Foran** .... (212) 878-7438

Chief Diversity Officer **Michael J. Garner** .... (212) 878-7000

Officers and Management *continued*

Chief Safety Officer **David L. Mayer** .... (212) 878-7000
E-mail: dmayer@mtabt.org
Education: Houston PhD

Senior Director, Business Service Center
Wael Hibri .... (212) 878-7000 ext. 7115
MTA Business Service Center, 333 W. 34th Street, Ninth Floor, New York, NY 10001-2402
E-mail: bscservice@mtabsc.org

Senior Director, Human Resources/Retirement Programs
Margaret M. Connor .... (212) 878-7000
E-mail: mconnor@mtabt.org

Deputy Executive Director and General Counsel
Jerome Page .... (212) 878-7387

Auditor General **Michael J. Fucilli** .... (212) 878-0208

Chief Government Affairs and Community Relations Officer **Justin Bernbach** .... (212) 878-7483
Education: Harvard MPP; Cornell BA

Director, Environmental Sustainability and Compliance
(Vacant) .... (212) 878-7242

Director of Communications **Beth DeFalco** .... (212) 878-7440
Note: Effective June 2016
Education: Colorado

Director, Finance **Patrick J. "Pat" McCoy** .... (212) 878-7183
Education: St Ambrose BA; New School MS

Director, Labor Relations **Anita Miller** .... (212) 878-7438

Director, Security **Raymond Diaz** .... (212) 878-7000

Director, Special Project Development and Planning
William Wheeler .... (212) 878-7274

Director, Strategic Initiatives **(Vacant)** .... (212) 878-7274

Chief of Police **Michael R. Coan** .... (212) 878-1001

Office of the Inspector General

2 Pen Plaza Street, New York, NY 11021
Tel: (212) 878-0000 Fax: (212) 878-0105 Internet: www.mtaig.state.ny.us

Inspector General **Barry L. Kluger** .... (212) 878-0000
Education: CCNY BA; Brooklyn Law JD

Bridges and Tunnels

Robert Moses Building 1, Randall's Island, New York, NY 10035
Tel: (646) 252-7000 Internet: www.mta.info/bandt

President **Don Spero** .... (212) 360-3100

Executive Vice President and Chief of Operations
James Fortunato .... (212) 360-3060
E-mail: jfortunato@mtabt.org

Chief of Staff **(Vacant)** .... (646) 252-7421

General Counsel **Margaret M. Terry** .... (646) 252-7617

Chief Financial Officer **(Vacant)** .... (646) 252-7132

Chief Security Officer **Donald E. Look** .... (212) 360-2812
E-mail: dlook@mtabt.org

Long Island Rail Road [LIRR]

Jamaica Station, Jamaica, NY 11435
Tel: (718) 558-8252 Fax: (718) 558-8212 Internet: www.mta.info/lirr

President **Patrick A. Nowakowski** .... (718) 558-8252

Executive Vice President **Albert Consenza** .... (718) 558-7993

Senior Vice President, Administration (Acting)
Kathleen Meilick .... (718) 558-8252

Senior Vice President/Operations **Dave J. Kubicek** .... (718) 558-8007

Vice President and Chief Financial Officer
Mark D. Young .... (718) 558-7777

Vice President, General Counsel and Secretary
Richard Gans .... (718) 558-8264

Vice President, East Side Access and Special Projects
Lori Katzman .... (212) 643-5480

Vice President, Labor Relations
Michael "Mike" Chirillo .... (718) 558-8284

Vice President, Market Development and Public Affairs
Ed Dumas .... (718) 558-7301

Executive Director, Diversity Management
Michael Fyffe .... (718) 558-7504

★Elected Official ▲Appointed by Legislature ▼Appointed by Governor ►Appointed by Board or Commission ●Appointed by Judge
■Appointed by Mayor △Appointed by Freeholders ▽Appointed by Supervisor ▷Appointed by County Executive ○Appointed by Council

Long Island Rail Road *continued*

Executive Director, Human Resources **Kathy Meilick** .... (718) 558-7332
E-mail: kmeilick@mtabt.org
Senior Vice President, Engineering **Bruce Pohlot** .... (718) 558-7882

Metro-North Railroad

347 Madison Avenue, New York, NY 10017
Fax: (212) 340-3224 Internet: www.mta.info/mnr

President **Joseph J. "Joe" Giulietti** .... (212) 532-4900
Senior Vice President, Operations **John Kesich** .... (212) 499-4300

MTA Bus Company

2 Broadway, 29th Floor, New York, NY 10004
Fax: (212) 878-0205 Internet: www.mta.info/busco

President **Darryl Irick** .... (646) 252-5872
E-mail: dirick@mtabt.org

MTA Capital Construction

2 Broadway, New York, NY 10004
Fax: (646) 252-2266 Internet: http://web.mta.info/capital/

President **Dr. Michael Horodniceanu** .... (646) 252-4274
Vice President and Chief Financial Officer
Anthony D'Amico .... (646) 252-4200

New York City Transit [NYCT]

2 Broadway, New York, NY 10004
Tel: (718) 330-3000 Fax: (718) 243-8501 Internet: www.mta.info/nyct

President **Veronique "Ronnie" Hakim** .... (646) 252-5860
Education: Rochester BA; Pace JD
Executive Vice President **Robert Bergen** .... (646) 252-5888
Education: Brooklyn Law 1973 JD
Senior Vice President, Buses **Darryl Irick** .... (646) 252-5872
Senior Vice President, Capital Program Management
Frederick Smith .... (646) 252-3034
General Counsel and Vice President **Lewis Finkelman** ... (718) 694-3900
Senior Director, Corporate Communications
Paul Fleuranges .... (718) 330-3000
E-mail: pfleuranges@mtabt.org
Senior Director, Capital Projects **William "Bill" Ciaccio** .. (718) 330-3000
Education: NYU; Columbia
Vice President, Human Resources (Acting)
Patricia Lodge .... (347) 643-8320
E-mail: plodge@mtabt.org
Vice President, Office of Systems Safety
Cheryl Kennedy .... (646) 252-5934
E-mail: ckennedy@mtabt.org
Vice President, Security **Owen J. Monaghan** .... (718) 330-3000
Vice President, Subways **Joseph Leader** .... (646) 252-5860

New York Power Authority [NYPA]

123 Main Street, White Plains, NY 10607-3170
Tel: (914) 681-6200 Internet: www.nypa.gov

Board of Trustees

30 South Pearl Street, Albany, NY 12207-3425
Tel: (518) 433-6700 Fax: (518) 433-6780

Chairman **John R. Koelmel** .... (518) 433-6700
Education: Col Holy Cross
Trustee **Terrance P. Flynn** .... (518) 433-6700
Education: Notre Dame 1985 BAcc; Buffalo 1988 JD
Trustee **Dr. Anne M. Kress** .... (518) 433-6700
Education: Florida

Board of Trustees *continued*

Trustee-Designate **Tracy B. McKibben** .... (518) 433-6700
Education: West Virginia State U BA; Harvard 1994 JD
Trustee **Eugene L. Nicandri** .... (518) 433-6700
Education: Rochester BA; Albany Law JD
▼Trustee-Designate **Anthony J. "Tony" Picente, Jr.** .... (518) 433-6700
Education: Utica Col Syracuse 1993 BS
Trustee **(Vacant)** .... (518) 433-6700

Administration

President and Chief Executive Officer **Gil C. Quiniones** .. (914) 681-6200
123 Main Street, White Plains, NY 10607-3170
Education: De La Salle U (Philippines) BS
Chief Operating Officer and Executive Vice President
and Chief Engineer, Power Supply **Edward A. Welz** .... (914) 681-6675
E-mail: edward.welz@nypa.gov
Executive Vice President and General Counsel
Justin E. Driscoll .... (914) 681-6200
123 Main Street, White Plains, NY 10607-3170
Education: American U 1977 BA; New York Law 1981 JD; NYU LLM
Senior Vice President, Corporate Communications
Ethan Riegelhaupt .... (518) 433-6700
E-mail: ethan.riegelhaupt@nypa.gov
Chief Financial Officer and Senior Vice President,
Corporate Planning and Finance **Robert F. Lurie** .... (518) 433-6700
Education: Union Col (NY) BA; SUNY (Albany) MBA
Senior Vice President, Enterprise Shared Services
(Interim) **Rocco Iannarelli** .... (914) 681-6200
Senior Vice President, Energy Resource Management
William J. Nadeau .... (914) 681-6801
Senior Vice President, Human Resources **Kristine Pizzo** .. (518) 433-6700
Senior Vice President, Internal Audit **Jennifer Faulkner** .. (518) 433-6700
Senior Vice President, Power Supply Support Services
(Vacant) .... (518) 433-6700
Senior Vice President, Marketing and Economic
Development **James F. Pasquale** .... (518) 433-6700
E-mail: james.pasquale@nypa.gov
Senior Vice President, Transmission **Philip Toia** .... (518) 433-6700
Senior Vice President of Public and Regulatory Affairs
and Chief of Staff **(Vacant)** .... (518) 433-6700
Director, Energy Services **Paul W. Belnick** .... (914) 287-3828
Vice President and Senior Advisor to the President and
Chief Executive Officer **Rocco Iannarelli** .... (518) 433-6700
Senior Vice President and Chief Risk Officer
Soubhagya Parija .... (518) 433-6700

Norfolk Airport Authority

2200 Norview Avenue, Norfolk, VA 23518-5807
Fax: (757) 857-3265 Internet: www.norfolkairport.com

Board of Commissioners

2200 Norview Avenue, Norfolk, VA 23518-5807

Chairman **Gus J. James II** .... (757) 857-3351
Date of Birth: December 29, 1938
Education: Richmond 1962 BS; William & Mary 1966 JD, 1967 MLT
Vice Chairman **Blythe Ann Scott** .... (757) 857-3351
Treasurer **Malcolm P. Branch** .... (757) 857-3351
Commissioner **Deborah Harris "Deb" Butler** .... (757) 857-3351
Education: Agnes Scott 1975 BA
Commissioner **Dr. Harold J. Cobb, Jr.** .... (757) 857-3351
Commissioner **Peter G. Decker III** .... (757) 857-3351
Commissioner **Mekbib Gemeda** .... (757) 857-3351
Commissioner **William L. Nusbaum** .... (757) 857-3351
Education: Harvard 1976 AB; Virginia 1980 JD
Commissioner **Chris P. Stephanitsis** .... (757) 857-3351

AUTHORITIES

★ Elected Official ▲ Appointed by Legislature ▼ Appointed by Governor ► Appointed by Board or Commission ● Appointed by Judge
■ Appointed by Mayor △ Appointed by Freeholders ▽ Appointed by Supervisor ▷ Appointed by County Executive ○ Appointed by Council

Norfolk International Airport [ORF]

2200 Norview Avenue, Norfolk, VA 23518-5807
Tel: (757) 857-3351 Fax: (757) 857-3265
E-mail: info@norfolkairport.com Internet: www.norkfolkairport.com

Executive Director **Wayne E. Shank** .... (757) 857-3351
Deputy Executive Director **Robert S. Bowen** .... (757) 857-3351
Director of Facilities **Anthony E. Rondeau** .... (757) 857-3351
E-mail: arondeau@norfolkairport.com
Director of Finance **William A. Jones** .... (757) 857-3351
Director of Human Resources **Sheila M. Balli** .... (757) 857-3351
E-mail: sballi@norfolkairport.com
Director of Market Development **Charles W. Braden** .... (757) 857-3351
Director of Operations **Steven C. Sterling** .... (757) 857-3351
E-mail: ssterling@norfolkairport.com

North Carolina State Ports Authority

2202 Burnett Boulevard, Wilmington, NC 28401
P.O. Box 9002, Wilmington, NC 28402
Tel: (910) 763-1621 (Information) Fax: (910) 763-6440
E-mail: busdev@ncports.com Internet: http://www.ncports.com

Board of Directors

2202 Burnett Boulevard, Wilmington, NC 28401
P.O. Box 9002, Wilmington, NC 28402

Chairman **Tom Adams** .... (910) 822-5271
Vice Chairman **Robert A. Sar** .... (919) 606-7302
Education: Wake Forest 1990 BS; Campbell 1995 JD
Board Member **Jerry Cook** .... (910) 576-2881
Board Member **Holly Grange** .... (910) 763-1621
Board Member **Daniel Gurley** .... (910) 576-2881
Board Member **Robert O. Hill, Jr.** .... (252) 939-4111
Board Member **Patrick Joyce** .... (910) 256-9680
Board Member **John Kane** .... (910) 822-5271
Board Member **Bill Keadey** .... (252) 482-1011
Board Member **Bill McMahon** .... (910) 822-5271
Board Member **Nicholas J. "Nick" Tennyson** .... (704) 382-1355
Education: Duke BA; Pepperdine MA

Administration

Executive Director **Paul J. Cozza** .... (910) 763-1621
E-mail: paul.cozza@ncports.com
Deputy Executive Director/Chief Operating Officer
Jeffrey E. "Jeff" Miles .... (910) 763-1621
E-mail: jeff.miles@ncports.com
Education: Col Charleston BA; Duke MBA
Vice President, Administration **Richard B. "Rick" Koch** .. (910) 343-6330
E-mail: rick.koch@ncports.com
Senior Director, External Affairs **Laura Godwin Blair** ... (910) 251-7072
E-mail: laura.godwin@ncports.com
Education: North Carolina; George Washington
Director, Breakbulk and Bulk **Lance Kenworthy** .... (910) 343-6387
E-mail: lance.kenworthy@ncports.com
Director, Community Economic Development
James E. "Jimmy" Yokeley, Jr. .... (910) 763-1621
E-mail: jimmy.yokeley@ncports.com
Director, Engineering and Maintenance **Mark Blake** ...... (910) 763-1621
E-mail: mark.blake@ncports.com
Director, Port Planning and Development
Stephanie Ayers .... (910) 251-7073
E-mail: stephanie.ayers@ncports.com
Director, Purchasing and Materials Management
Wanda Pugh-Trice .... (910) 763-1621
E-mail: wanda.pugh-trice@ncports.com
Director, Real Estate **Edward "Ed" Church** .... (910) 763-1621

Northeast Ohio Regional Sewer District [NEORSD]

3900 Euclid Avenue, Cleveland, OH 44115-2506
Tel: (216) 881-6600 Fax: (216) 881-9709 Internet: www.neorsd.org

Board of Trustees

3900 Euclid Avenue, Cleveland, OH 44115
Fax: (216) 881-7644

President **Darnell Brown** .... (216) 881-6600
Vice President **Ronald D. Sulik** .... (216) 881-6600
Secretary **Walter O'Malley** .... (216) 881-6600
Trustee **Jack M. Bacci** .... (216) 881-6600
Trustee **Timothy J. DeGeeter** .... (216) 881-6600
Trustee **Sharon Dumas** .... (216) 881-6600
Trustee **Robert A. Stefanik** .... (216) 881-6600

Administration

Chief Executive Officer **Julius Ciaccia, Jr.** .... (216) 881-6600
E-mail: ciaccia@neorsd.org
Chief Operating Officer **Kellie Rotunno** .... (216) 881-6600
E-mail: rotunnok@neorsd.org
Administration and External Affairs Director
Constance Haqq .... (216) 881-6600
E-mail: haqqc@neorsd.org
Chief Financial Officer **Jennifer Demmerle** .... (216) 881-6600 ext. 6728
Human Resources Director **Angela Smith** .... (216) 881-6600
Information Technology Director
Chandrasekhar Yadati .... (216) 881-6600
E-mail: yadatic@neorsd.org
Chief Legal Officer and General Counsel **Eric Luckage** ... (216) 881-6600
Operation and Maintenance Director **Ray Weeden** .... (216) 881-6600
E-mail: weedenr@neorsd.org
Watershed Programs Director **Frank Greenland** .... (216) 881-6600

Omaha Public Power District [OPPD]

Energy Plaza, 444 South 16th Street Mall, Omaha, NE 68102-2247
Internet: www.oppd.com

Board of Directors

Energy Plaza, 444 South 16th Street Mall, Omaha, NE 68102-2247

★ Chairman **Michael A. Mines** .... (402) 636-2000
Term Expires: January 2019
★ Vice President **Tim Gay** .... (402) 636-2000
Term Expires: January 2021
★ Board Member **Thomas S. Barrett** .... (402) 636-2000
Term Expires: January 2019
★ Board Member **Michael J. Cavanaugh** .... (402) 636-2000
Term Expires: January 2019
★ Board Member **John K. Green** .... (402) 636-2000
Term Expires: January 2017
★ Board Member **Rich Hurley** .... (402) 636-2000
Term Expires: January 2021
★ Board Member **Anne L. McGuire** .... (402) 636-2000
Term Expires: January 2019
★ Board Member **Frederick J. "Fred" Ulrich** .... (402) 636-2000
Term Expires: January 2017

Administration

President and Chief Executive Officer
Timothy J. Burke .... (402) 636-3200
Vice President and Chief Financial Officer
Edward Easterlin .... (402) 636-2000

★ Elected Official ▲ Appointed by Legislature ▼ Appointed by Governor ▶ Appointed by Board or Commission ● Appointed by Judge
■ Appointed by Mayor △ Appointed by Freeholders ▽ Appointed by Supervisor ▷ Appointed by County Executive ○ Appointed by Council

Administration *continued*

Vice President and Chief Nuclear Officer
Louis Cortopassi . . . . . (402) 636-2000
Fax: (402) 636-3229
Vice President, Information Technology **Kate W. Brown** . . (402) 636-3200
Chief Operating Officer **(Vacant)** . . . . . (402) 636-2000
Vice President, Energy Production and Marketing
Jon T. Hansen . . . . . (402) 636-2000
Vice President and Chief Administrative Officer
(Vacant) . . . . . (402) 636-2000
Vice President and Chief Compliance Officer
Mohamad I. Doghman . . . . . (402) 636-2000
Vice President of Public Affairs **Lisa A. Olson** . . . . . (402) 636-3744
E-mail: lolson@oppd.com
Environmental and Regulatory Affairs Division Manager
Russ Baker . . . . . (402) 636-2316
Facilities Management Division Manager
Ronald Johansen . . . . . (402) 636-3642
E-mail: rjohansen@oppd.com Fax: (402) 636-3660
Production Operations Division Manager
Gregory Alan Krieser . . . . . (402) 636-2603
E-mail: gkrieser@oppd.com
Education: Nebraska BS, MBA
Corporate Marketing and Communications Manager
DJ Clark . . . . . (402) 636-3755
Safeguards and Administration Manager
Rod J. Rogers . . . . . (402) 636-3703
E-mail: rrogers@oppd.com Fax: (402) 636-3660
Information Specialist/Webmaster **Mary Lou Mally** . . . . . (402) 636-3441
E-mail: mmally@oppd.com
Senior Talent Management Specialist **(Vacant)** . . . . . (402) 636-3069
Fax: (402) 636-3912
Corporate Secretary **K. M. Tracy** . . . . . (402) 636-3208
Fax: (402) 636-3229
Vice President of Customer Service **Juli Comstock** . . . . . (402) 636-3200

Orange County Transportation Authority [OCTA]

550 South Main Street, Orange, CA 92868
Tel: (714) 560-6282 Internet: www.octa.net

Board of Directors

550 South Main Street, Orange, CA 92868
Tel: (714) 560-6282

Chairman **Lori Donchak** . . . . . (714) 560-5630
Term Expires: December 2016
Vice Chairman **Michael Hennessey** . . . . . (714) 560-5630
Term Expires: September 2019
Education: UCLA BA
Director **Lisa Bartlett** . . . . . (714) 560-5630
Term Expires: January 2017
Director **Ryan Chamberlain** . . . . . (714) 560-5630
Note: Position filled by a representative of the State Department of Transportation.
Term Expires: 2016
Education: UC Santa Barbara
Director **Andrew Do** . . . . . (714) 560-5630
Term Expires: January 2017
Director **Steve Jones** . . . . . (714) 560-5630
Term Expires: December 2017
Director **Jim Katapodis** . . . . . (714) 560-5630
Term Expires: December 2017
Director **Jeffrey Lalloway** . . . . . (714) 560-5630
Term Expires: December 2016
Education: Rutgers 1986 BA; Villanova 1989 JD
Director **Gary Miller** . . . . . (714) 560-5630
Term Expires: December 2016

Board of Directors *continued*

Director **Al Murray** . . . . . (714) 560-5630
Term Expires: December 2017
Director **Shawn Nelson** . . . . . (714) 560-5630
Term Expires: December 2019
Education: USC BA; Western State U San Diego JD
Director **Miguel A. Pulido** . . . . . (714) 560-5630
Term Expires: December 2016
Education: Cal State (Fullerton) BA
Director **Tim Shaw** . . . . . (714) 560-5630
Term Expires: December 2016
Education: Southern Illinois BS; George Washington MA
Director **Todd Spitzer** . . . . . (714) 560-5630
Term Expires: December 2017
Director **Thomas "Tom" Tait** . . . . . (714) 560-5630
Term Expires: December 2017
Education: Wyoming BS; Vanderbilt MBA, 1985 JD
Director **Frank Ury** . . . . . (714) 560-5630
Term Expires: December 2017
Director **Gregory T. Winterbottom** . . . . . (714) 560-5630
Term Expires: January 1, 2017
Clerk of the Board **Wendy Knowles** . . . . . (714) 560-5676

Administration

Chief Executive Officer **Darrell Johnson** . . . . . (714) 560-5584
Education: UC Riverside
Deputy Chief Executive Officer **Ken Phipps** . . . . . (714) 560-6282
Executive Director, Capital Programs **Jim Beil** . . . . . (714) 560-5646
Executive Director, External Affairs **Ellen S. Burton** . . . . . (714) 560-5923
E-mail: eburton@octa.net
Executive Director, Finance and Administration
Andy Oftelie . . . . . (714) 560-5637
E-mail: aoftelie@octa.net
Executive Director, Government Affairs
Lance M. Larson . . . . . (714) 560-5908
E-mail: llarson@octa.net
Education: USC 1990 BS
Executive Director, Human Resources and Organizational Development **Patrick Gough** . . . . . (714) 560-5824
E-mail: pgough@octa.net
Executive Director, Internal Audit (Acting) **Jane Sutter** . . (714) 560-5591
Executive Director, Planning **Kia Mortazavi** . . . . . (714) 560-5741
General Manager, Transit **Beth McCormick** . . . . . (714) 560-5964

Orange County Water District [OCWD]

18700 Ward Street, Fountain Valley, CA 92708
P.O. Box 8300, Fountain Valley, CA 92728-8300
Tel: (714) 378-3200 Fax: (714) 378-3373 E-mail: info@ocwd.com
Internet: www.ocwd.com

Board of Directors

18700 Ward Street, Fountain Valley, CA 92708
Fax: (714) 378-3365

President **Cathy Green** (Division 6) . . . . . (714) 378-3200
First Vice President **Denis R. Bilodeau** (Division 2) . . . . . (714) 378-3200
Education: UC Irvine BSCE
Second Vice President **Philip L. Anthony** (Division 4) . . . (714) 378-3200
Member **Dina Nguyen** (Division 1) . . . . . (714) 378-3200
Member **Roger C. Yoh** (Division 3) . . . . . (714) 378-3200
Member **Stephen R. Sheldon** (Division 5) . . . . . (714) 378-3200
Member **Shawn Dewane** (Division 7) . . . . . (714) 378-3200
Member **Roman Reyna** (Division 8) . . . . . (714) 378-3200
Member **Harry S. Sidhu** (Division 9) . . . . . (714) 378-3200
Education: Drexel BSME
Member **Jan M. Flory** (Division 10) . . . . . (714) 378-3200
Secretary to the Board **Janice Durant** . . . . . (714) 378-3233

AUTHORITIES

★ Elected Official ▲ Appointed by Legislature ▼ Appointed by Governor ▶ Appointed by Board or Commission ● Appointed by Judge
■ Appointed by Mayor △ Appointed by Freeholders ▽ Appointed by Supervisor ▷ Appointed by County Executive ○ Appointed by Council

Office of the General Manager

General Manager **Michael R. Markus** . . . . . . (714) 378-3200
Assistant General Manager for Water Quality and Technology **Michael Wehner** . . . . . . (714) 378-3297
Public Affairs Director **Eleanor Torres** . . . . . . (714) 378-3268

Philadelphia Regional Port Authority [PRPA]

3460 North Delaware Avenue, 2nd Floor, Philadelphia, PA 19134
Tel: (215) 426-2600 Fax: (215) 426-6800 Internet: www.philaport.com

Board of Directors

3460 North Delaware Avenue, 2nd Floor, Philadelphia, PA 19134
Fax: (215) 426-6800

▼Chairman **Gerard H. "Jerry" Sweeney** . . . . . . (215) 426-2600
Board Member **Robert Bryan** . . . . . . (215) 426-2600
▼Board Member **Robert J. Clark** . . . . . . (215) 426-2600
■Board Member **John Dougherty** . . . . . . (215) 426-2600
▼Board Member **Yassmin Gramian** . . . . . . (215) 426-2600
Board Member **Ward Guilday** . . . . . . (215) 426-2600
Board Member **Vahan H. Gureghian** . . . . . . (215) 426-2600
Board Member **Anthony Mannino** . . . . . . (215) 426-2600
Board Member **Paul D. McNichol** . . . . . . (215) 426-2600
Education: Widener 1988 BA, 1992 JD
▼Board Member **Michael Pearson** . . . . . . (215) 426-2600
▼Board Member **John S. Skoutelas** . . . . . . (215) 426-2600
Education: NYU 1981 BS; Georgetown 1984 JD

Administration

Executive Director **(Vacant)** . . . . . . (215) 426-2600
Senior Deputy Executive Director **(Vacant)** . . . . . . (215) 426-2600
Deputy Executive Director **Jack Dempsey** . . . . . . (215) 426-2600
Chief Counsel **Gregory V. Iannarelli** . . . . . . (215) 426-2600
Communications Director **Joseph P. Menta, Jr.** . . . . . . (215) 426-2600
E-mail: jpmenta@philaport.com
Governmental and Public Affairs Director **Donald Brennan** . . . . . . (215) 426-2600
E-mail: dbrennan@philaport.com
Engineering Director **Lisa Magee** . . . . . . (215) 426-2600
E-mail: mscott@philaport.com
Finance & Capital Funding Director **Edward G. Henderson** . . . . . . (215) 426-2600
Maintenance Director **Mario Dioguardi** . . . . . . (215) 426-2600
E-mail: mdioguardi@philaport.com
Management Information Services Director **Joseph F. Petruzzi** . . . . . . (215) 426-2600
E-mail: jpetruzzi@philaport.com
Marketing Director **Sean E. Mahoney** . . . . . . (215) 426-2600
Procurement Director **Kate Bailey** . . . . . . (215) 426-2600
E-mail: kbailey@philaport.com
Strategic Planning and Development Director **Nicholas Walsh** . . . . . . (215) 426-2600

Port Authority of Allegheny County [PAAC]

345 Sixth Avenue, 3rd Floor, Pittsburgh, PA 15222-2527
Tel: (412) 442-2000 (Customer Service) Fax: (412) 566-5111
Internet: www.portauthority.org

Board of Directors

345 Sixth Avenue, 3rd Floor, Pittsburgh, PA 15222-2527

Chairman **Robert Hurley** . . . . . . (412) 566-5500
Vice Chairman **Thomas E. Donatelli** . . . . . . (412) 566-5500
Secretary **John L. Tague, Jr.** . . . . . . (412) 566-5500
Treasurer **Constance Parker** . . . . . . (412) 566-5500
Director **James R. "Jim" Brewster** . . . . . . (412) 566-5500
Education: California U (PA) BSEd
Director **Dominic "Dom" Costa** . . . . . . (412) 566-5500
Director **Amanda Green Hawkins** . . . . . . (412) 566-5500
Date of Birth: August 7, 1972
Education: Duke 1993 AB; Northeastern 2001 JD
Director **Jeffrey W. Letwin** . . . . . . (412) 566-5500
Education: Pittsburgh 1975 BA; Washington College of Law 1979 JD
Director **D. Raja** . . . . . . (412) 566-5500
Director **Robert Vesico** . . . . . . (412) 566-5500

Administration

Chief Executive Officer **Ellen M. McLean** . . . . . . (412) 566-5311
Chief Financial Officer **(Vacant)** . . . . . . (412) 566-5186
Bus Operations Officer **Bill Miller** . . . . . . (412) 566-5225
E-mail: bmiller@portauthority.org
Rail Operations/Engineering Officer **Keith Wargo** . . . . . . (412) 851-4741
E-mail: kwargo@portauthority.org
Assistant General Manager, Human Resources **(Vacant)** . . (412) 566-5253
Assistant General Manager, Planning and Development **Wendy Stern** . . . . . . (412) 566-5250
Legal Counsel **Michael "Mike" Cetra** . . . . . . (412) 566-5245
Community and Government Relations Representative **Dan Debone** . . . . . . (412) 566-5108
E-mail: ddebone@portauthority.org

The Port Authority of New York and New Jersey [PANYNJ]

4 World Trade Center, 150 Greenwich Street, New York, NY 10007
Tel: (212) 435-7000 Internet: www.panynj.gov
Internet: https://twitter.com/PANYNJ

Board of Commissioners

4 World Trade Center, 150 Greenwich Street, Twenty Third Floor, New York, NY 10007
Tel: (212) 435-7000

▼Chairman **John J. Degnan** . . . . . . (212) 435-4173
Date of Birth: October 6, 1944
Education: St Vincent Col 1966 BA; Harvard 1969 JD
▼Vice Chairman **Scott Howard Rechler** . . . . . . (212) 435-6678
▼Commissioner **Richard H. "Rich" Bagger** . . . . . . (212) 435-6646
Education: Princeton 1982 AB; Rutgers (Newark) 1986 JD
▼Commissioner **Steve M. Cohen** . . . . . . (212) 435-6646
▼Commissioner **Michael D. Fascitelli** . . . . . . (212) 435-6646
Education: Rhode Island 1978 BS; Harvard 1982 MBA
▼Commissioner **Hamilton E. "Tony" James III** . . . . . . (212) 435-6646
Education: Harvard 1973 BA, 1975 MBA
▼Commissioner **George R. Laufenberg** . . . . . . (212) 435-6646
Education: Susquehanna BEc

★ Elected Official ▲ Appointed by Legislature ▼ Appointed by Governor ▶ Appointed by Board or Commission ● Appointed by Judge
■ Appointed by Mayor △ Appointed by Freeholders ▽ Appointed by Supervisor ▷ Appointed by County Executive ○ Appointed by Council

AUTHORITIES

Board of Commissioners *continued*

▼Commissioner **Kenneth Lipper** .... (212) 435-6646
Date of Birth: June 19, 1941
▼Commissioner **Jeffrey Hayden Lynford** .... (212) 435-6646
Date of Birth: 1947
▼Commissioner **Raymond M. Pocino** .... (212) 435-6646
▼Commissioner **William P. "Pat" Schuber** .... (212) 435-6646
Education: Fordham 1969 BA, 1972 JD
▼Commissioner **David S. Steiner** .... (212) 435-6646

Office of the Executive Director

Executive Director **Patrick J. Foye** .... (212) 435-7000
E-mail: pfoye@panynj.gov
Education: Fordham 1978 BA, 1981 JD
Chief of Staff **John Ma** .... (212) 435-4033
Secretary **Karen E. Eastman** .... (212) 435-6528
Deputy Secretary **Linda Handel** .... (212) 435-6684
E-mail: lhandel@panynj.gov
General Counsel (Interim) **Richard J. Holwell** .... (212) 435-3515
Education: Villanova 1967 BA; Columbia 1970 JD; Cambridge 1971
Deputy General Counsel **Phillip H. Kwon** .... (212) 435-3653
Chief Engineer/Director, Engineering Department
Jim Starace .... (212) 435-7449
E-mail: jstarace@panynj.org
Chief, Real Estate and Development
Michael B. Francois .... (212) 435-6482

Office of the Chief Human Capital Officer

Chief, Human Capital and Labor Relations **(Vacant)** ...... (212) 435-8140
Director, Human Resources Department
Mary Lee Hannell .... (212) 435-8148
E-mail: mhannell@panynj.gov
Director, Labor Relations Department **(Vacant)** .... (973) 792-3580
Director, Operations Services Department
Thomas C. "Tom" Lubas .... (201) 216-2800
E-mail: tlubas@panynj.gov
Director, Procurement Department **Lillian D. Valenti** ..... (212) 435-8427
E-mail: lvalenti@panynj.gov

Office of the Chief, Capital Planning

Chief, Capital Planning **Michael G. Massiah** .... (212) 435-6688
E-mail: mmassiah@panynj.org
Director, Office of Business and Job Opportunity
Lash L. Green .... (212) 435-7802
Director, Office of Environmental Policy, Programs and Compliance **Christopher R. Zeppie** .... (212) 435-4415
Director, Office of Strategic Initiatives **Cruz C. Russell** ... (212) 435-4469
Director, Planning and Regional Development Department **Andrew S. Lynn** .... (212) 435-4437
E-mail: alynn@panynj.gov
Director, World Trade Center Construction Department
Steven P. Plate .... (212) 435-5529
Director, World Trade Center Redevelopment Department **Philippe Visser** .... (212) 435-7000
E-mail: pvisser@panynj.gov

Office of the Chief Financial Officer

Chief Financial Officer
Elizabeth M. "Libby" McCarthy .... (212) 435-7738
Education: Saint Louis U BS
Comptroller **Daniel G. "Dan" McCarron** .... (212) 435-6900
Director, Financial Analysis Department **(Vacant)** .... (212) 435-5993
Director, Management and Budget Department
Michael G. Massiah .... (212) 435-2842
E-mail: mmassiah@panynj.gov
Chief Technology Officer **Robert Galvin** .... (212) 435-2711
E-mail: rgalvin@panynj.gov
Director, Treasury Department and Treasurer **(Vacant)** .... (212) 435-7700

Office of the Chief Operating Officer

Chief Operating Officer (Acting) **Stephanie Dawson** ..... (212) 435-7887
E-mail: sdawson@panynj.gov
Director, Aviation Department **Thomas Bosco** .... (212) 435-3703

Office of the Chief Operating Officer *continued*

Director, Capital Security Projects **John J. Drobny** ...... (201) 595-4014
Education: NYU BE; Fordham MBA
Director, Port Commerce Department **Molly Campbell** ... (212) 435-4218
Director, Public Safety Department/Police Superintendent **Michael A. Fedorko** .... (201) 239-3780
E-mail: mfedorko@panynj.gov
Director, Security **Raymond Diaz** .... (201) 239-3780
E-mail: rdiaz@panynj.gov
Director, Rail Transit Department **Stephen Kingsberry** .. (201) 216-6199
Director, Tunnels, Bridges and Terminals Department
Cedrick T. Fulton .... (212) 435-4800

Office of the Inspector General

Inspector General **Michael Nestor** .... (973) 565-4330
Director, Audit Department **Andrew Levine** .... (201) 216-6017
Education: Boalt Hall 2003 JD
Director, Office of Investigations **Steven Pasichow** ...... (973) 565-4302

Office of Public and Government Affairs

Chief of Public and Government Affairs **(Vacant)** .... (212) 435-4174
Director, Government and Community Affairs
Christina M. "Tina" Lado .... (212) 435-6903
E-mail: tlado@panynj.gov
Director, Marketing Department **David McGrath** .... (212) 435-7777
Director, Office of Media Relations **Ron Marsico** .... (212) 435-7777

Port of Beaumont

1225 Main Street, Beaumont, TX 77701
P.O. Drawer 2297, Beaumont, TX 77704-2297
E-mail: info@portofbeaumont.com Internet: www.portofbeaumont.com

Board of Commissioners

P.O. Drawer 2297, Beaumont, TX 77704-2297
Tel: (409) 835-5367 Fax: (409) 835-0512
E-mail: jf@portofbeaumont.com

President **C.A. "Pete" Shelton** .... (409) 835-5367
E-mail: cas@portofbeaumont.com
Vice President **Lee Smith** .... (409) 835-5367
Secretary-Treasurer **Georgine Guillory** .... (409) 835-5367
Education: Lamar BA
Commissioner **Pat Anderson** .... (409) 835-5367
Commissioner **Louis M. Broussard, Jr.** .... (409) 835-5367
Education: Lamar 1983 BBA
Commissioner **Bill C. Darling** .... (409) 835-5367

Administration

Port Director and Chief Executive Officer
David C. "Chris" Fisher .... (409) 835-5367
Education: Lamar 1988 BBA, 1993 MBA
Deputy Port Director **Bill Carpenter** .... (409) 835-5367
E-mail: bc@portofbeaumont.com
Education: Lamar 1974 BBA
Director of Corporate Affairs and Public Information Officer **John R. Roby** .... (409) 835-5367
Operations Director **Kirby L. Dartez** .... (409) 835-5367
E-mail: kld@portofbeaumont.com
Trade Development Director **Ernest L. Bezdek** .... (409) 835-5367
E-mail: elb@portofbeaumont.com
Director of Finance and Administration **Tracy Mills** ...... (409) 835-5367
E-mail: tm@portofbeaumont.com
Human Resources Manager **Janet Floyd** .... (409) 835-5367
E-mail: jf@portofbeaumont.com
Chief of Police **Stephen Davis** .... (409) 835-5367
E-mail: sd@portofbeaumont.com
Dock Superintendent **Al Matulich** .... (409) 835-5367
E-mail: am@portofbeaumont.com

AUTHORITIES

★ Elected Official ▲ Appointed by Legislature ▼ Appointed by Governor ▶ Appointed by Board or Commission ● Appointed by Judge
■ Appointed by Mayor △ Appointed by Freeholders ▽ Appointed by Supervisor ▷ Appointed by County Executive ○ Appointed by Council

Port of Brownsville

1000 Foust Road, Brownsville, TX 78521
Internet: www.portofbrownsville.com

Office of the Commissioners

1000 Foust Rd., Brownsville, TX 78521
Fax: (956) 831-5006

Chairman **John Wood** .... (956) 831-4592
E-mail: jwarealty@aol.com
Vice Chairman **John Reed** .... (956) 343-6415
Fax: (956) 831-5006
Commissioner **Louis Raphael "Ralph" Cowen** .... (956) 755-9855
Commissioner **Sergio Tito Lopez** .... (956) 579-3722
Commissioner **Carlos R. Masso** .... (956) 579-4903
Education: Texas Southmost BMS; Fax: (956) 831-5006
Texas (Brownsville) BA; Southern Illinois 1998 JD

Administration

Accounting Supervisor **Rosie Hinojosa** .... (956) 831-4592
E-mail: rmhinojosa@portofbrownsville.com
Administrative Assistant **Margie S. Recio** .... (956) 831-4592
E-mail: msolis@portofbrownsville.com
Chief of Police and Security **Carlos L. Garcia** .... (956) 831-8256
E-mail: clgarcia@portofbrownsville.com
Deputy Port Director **Donna E. Eymard** .... (956) 831-4592
E-mail: deymard@portofbrownsville.com
Senior Director of Marketing and Business Development
Steve Tyndal .... (956) 831-4592
Director of Cargo Services **Antonio Rodriguez** .... (956) 831-4592
Director of Engineering Services **Ariel Chavez** .... (956) 831-4592
E-mail: achavez@portofbrownsville.com
Tel: (956) 831-6153
Director of Facilities Maintenance **Joe Garza** .... (956) 831-8273
E-mail: jgarza@portofbrownsville.com Fax: (956) 831-5243
Director of Finance and Administration
Steve Fitzgibbons .... (956) 831-4592
E-mail: sbfitzgibbons@portofbrownsville.com
Director of Human Resources **Jaime Martinez** .... (956) 838-7034
E-mail: jamartinez@portofbrownsville.com
Director of Industrial Development
Beatrice Rosenbaum .... (956) 831-4592
E-mail: brosenbaum@portofbrownsville.com
Harbormaster Operations **Michael Davis** .... (956) 831-8256
E-mail: mdavis@portofbrownsville.com Fax: (956) 831-3068
Port Director and Chief Executive Officer
Eduardo A. Campirano .... (956) 831-4592
Fax: (956) 831-5006
Public Information Officer **Patty Gonzalez** .... (956) 838-7004

Port of Greater Baton Rouge

2425 Ernest Wilson Drive, Port Allen, LA 70767
P.O. Box 380, Port Allen, LA 70767-0380
Tel: (225) 342-1660 Fax: (225) 342-1666 Internet: www.portgbr.com

Board of Commissioners

President **Corey Sarullo** .... (225) 342-1660
Vice President **Bobby Watts** .... (225) 342-1660
Secretary **Jimmy Sanchez** .... (225) 342-1660
Treasurer **Brenda Hurst** .... (225) 342-1660
Commissioner **Lee Harang** .... (225) 342-1660
Commissioner **Timothy W. "Tim" Hardy** .... (225) 342-1660
Education: Southern U (Shreveport) 1978 BS, 1981 JD
Commissioner **Jerald Juneau** .... (225) 342-1660
Commissioner **Raymond Loup** .... (225) 342-1660
Commissioner **Travis Medine** .... (225) 342-1660

Board of Commissioners *continued*

Commissioner **Randy Poche** .... (225) 342-1660
Commissioner **Lynn Robertson** .... (225) 342-1660
Commissioner **Clint Seneca** .... (225) 342-1660
Commissioner **Blaine Sheets** .... (225) 342-1660
Commissioner **(Vacant)** .... (225) 342-1660
Commissioner **(Vacant)** .... (225) 342-1660

Administration

Executive Director **Jay G. Hardman** .... (225) 342-1660 ext. 1202
E-mail: hardmanj@portgbr.com
Director of Finance and Administration
Katie LeBlanc .... (225) 342-1660 ext. 1212
E-mail: leblanck@portgbr.com
Director of Business Development
Greg Johnson .... (225) 342-1660 ext. 1209
Director of Corporate and Legal Affairs
Stephen Glusman .... (225) 342-1660 ext. 1203
Director of Engineering and Security
Cortney White .... (225) 342-1660 ext. 1208
E-mail: whitec@portgbr.com
Director of Public Affairs **Karen K. St. Cyr** .... (225) 342-1660 ext. 1206
E-mail: stcyrk@portgbr.com

Port of Houston Authority [POHA]

111 East Loop North, Houston, TX 77029
P.O. Box 2562, Houston, TX 77252-2562
Tel: (713) 670-2400 (Customer Service) Fax: (713) 670-2429
Internet: www.portofhouston.com

Office of the Commissioners

P.O. Box 2562, Houston, TX 77252-2562

Chairman **Janiece M. Longoria** .... (713) 670-2400
E-mail: jlongoria@poha.com
Date of Birth: 1954
Education: Texas 1976 BA, 1979 JD
Commissioner **Theldon Branch III** .... (713) 670-2400
Commissioner **Dean E. Corgey** .... (713) 670-2400
Commissioner **Stephen H. DonCarlos** .... (713) 670-2400
Education: Texas Tech BBA; Texas JD
Commissioner **Clyde Fitzgerald** .... (713) 670-2400
Commissioner **COL John D. Kennedy** .... (713) 670-2400
Commissioner **Roy Mease** .... (713) 670-2400

Office of the Executive Staff

111 East Loop North, Houston, TX 77029
P.O. Box 2562, Houston, TX 77252-2562

Executive Director **Roger D. Guenther** .... (713) 670-2480
Education: Texas A&M BS; Fax: (713) 670-2480
U St Thomas (TX) MBA

Legal

Deputy Executive Director and General Counsel
Erik A. Eriksson .... (713) 670-2614
Associate General Counsel **Linda Henry** .... (713) 670-2663
Associate General Counsel **Thomas Schroeter** .... (713) 670-2423
Education: Vanderbilt; Texas JD
Assistant General Counsel **Margot Campbell** .... (713) 670-2491

Corporate Affairs

Deputy Executive Director, Corporate Affairs
Phyllis Saathoff .... (713) 670-2400

★ Elected Official ▲ Appointed by Legislature ▼ Appointed by Governor ▶ Appointed by Board or Commission ● Appointed by Judge
■ Appointed by Mayor △ Appointed by Freeholders ▽ Appointed by Supervisor ▷ Appointed by County Executive ○ Appointed by Council

Corporate Affairs *continued*

Managing Director, Channel Development and Environmental Affairs and Grant Management
Charlie D. Jenkins .... (713) 670-2592
Education: Texas A&M BS
Director, Organizational Planning and Strategy
Jessica Druce .... (713) 670-2693
Director, Channel Development **Mark Vincent** .... (713) 670-2605
E-mail: mvincent@poha.com
Director, Freight Mobility **(Vacant)** .... (713) 670-2400
Managing Director, Special Projects
Olga Llamas Rodriguez .... (713) 670-1032
E-mail: orodriguez@poha.com
Managing Director, Community Outreach
Gilda Ramirez .... (713) 670-2590
E-mail: gramirez@poha.com
Manager, Community Relations **(Vacant)** .... (713) 670-2579
Senior Captain **Doug Mims** .... (713) 670-2400
E-mail: dmims@poha.com
Manager, Small Business Outreach **Pedro Garcia** .... (713) 670-2588
Manager, Small Business Mentoring Program
Pedro Garcia .... (713) 670-2400
Director, Government Relations **Spencer Chambers** .... (713) 670-2606
E-mail: schambers@poha.com
Director, Communications **Lisa Ashley** .... (713) 670-2644
E-mail: lashley@poha.com
Director, Environmental Affairs **(Vacant)** .... (713) 670-2555

Trade Development

Fax: (713) 670-2564

Managing Director, Trade Development **Ricky W. Kunz** .. (713) 670-2583
E-mail: rkunz@poha.com
Director, Business Development **John A. Moseley** .... (713) 670-2583
E-mail: jmoseley@poha.com
Administrator, Foreign Trade Zone **Shane Williams** .... (713) 670-2604
E-mail: smwilliams@poha.com
Manager, Market Development **Stan Swigart** .... (713) 670-2552

Public Affairs

Fax: (713) 670-2425

Managing Director, Public Affairs **Leslie Herbst** .... (713) 670-2400
E-mail: lherbst@poha.com

Finance and Administration

Deputy Executive Director **Thomas J. Heidt** .... (713) 670-2550
E-mail: theidt@poha.com
Managing Director, Finance and Administration
Ramon Yi .... (713) 670-2555
Controller **Tim Finley** .... (713) 670-2436
E-mail: tfinley@poha.com
Director, Financial Services **Alex Skinner-Klee** .... (713) 670-2415
Director, Information Technology **Brian Bickers** .... (713) 670-2404
E-mail: bbickers@poha.com
Director, Risk Management **Bruce Birdwell** .... (713) 670-2821
E-mail: bbirdwell@poha.com
Director of Procurement **Yvette Camel-Smith** .... (713) 670-2460
E-mail: ysmith@poha.com Fax: (713) 670-2465
Director, Human Resources **Catherine Boutch** .... (713) 670-2478
E-mail: cboutch@poha.com Fax: (713) 670-2479
Managing Director, Internal Audit **Maxine Bucklers** .... (713) 670-2400

Health, Safety, and Security

Managing Director, Health, Safety, and Security
Marcus Woodring .... (713) 670-2555
E-mail: mwoodring@poha.com
Director, Safety **Rich Galle** .... (713) 670-2555
E-mail: rgalle@poha.com
Manager, Emergency Preparedness **Colin Rizzo** .... (713) 670-2555
E-mail: crizzo@poha.com
Chief of Police **Mark Smith** .... (713) 670-3646
E-mail: msmith@poha.com
Fire Chief **William Buck** .... (713) 670-2555
E-mail: wbuck@poha.com

Operations

Managing Director, Operations **Jeff Davis** .... (713) 670-2940
E-mail: jdavis@poha.com Fax: (713) 670-2927
Director, General Cargo **Randy Stiefel** .... (713) 670-2400
E-mail: rstiefel@poha.com
Managing Director, Real Estate **Robert Tanner** .... (713) 670-2400
E-mail: rtanner@poha.com
Managing Director, Operations Support **Paulo Soares** .... (713) 291-5543
E-mail: psoares@poha.com
Director, Project and Construction Management
Roger Hoh .... (713) 670-2400
E-mail: rhoh@poha.com

Port of New Orleans

1350 Port of New Orleans Place, New Orleans, LA 70160
P.O. Box 60046, New Orleans, LA 70160
Tel: (504) 522-2551 Fax: (504) 524-4156 Internet: www.portno.com

Board of Commissioners

P.O. Box 60046, New Orleans, LA 70160

Chair **William T. Bergeron** .... (504) 522-2551
Vice Chair **Michael W. Kearney** .... (504) 522-2551
Commissioner **Arnold Baker** .... (504) 522-2551
Commissioner **Robert Barkerding, Jr.** .... (504) 522-2551
▼Commissioner **Laney J. Chouest** .... (504) 522-2551
Commissioner **Scott Cooper** .... (504) 522-2551
Commissioner **Gregory R. Rusovich** .... (504) 522-2551

Administration

President and Chief Executive Officer **Gary LaGrange** ... (504) 528-3203
Education: Louisiana (Lafayette) BA, 1975 MA
Special Assistant to the President **Stacie Ordoyne** .... (504) 528-3201
E-mail: ordoynes@portno.com
Assistant to the Chief Operating Officer
Andree Fant .... (504) 528-3321
E-mail: fanta@portno.com Fax: (504) 528-3387
Chief Operating Officer **Brandy D. Christian** .... (504) 528-3305
E-mail: christianb@portno.com
Director, Administration **Cynthia Swain** .... (504) 528-3367
E-mail: swainc@portno.com
Director, Business Development **Chris Bonura** .... (504) 528-3222
Education: Loyola U (New Orleans) 1996 BA; Tulane 2009 MBA
Director, Cruise and Tourism **Donald R. Allee** .... (504) 528-3295
Education: Sam Houston State 1973 BA
Director, Finance and Administration **Ronald Wendel** .... (504) 528-3446
E-mail: wendelr@portno.com
Director of Internal Audits **M. Eileen Pansano** .... (504) 528-3249
Director, Legal Services
Gerald O. "Brien" Gussoni, Jr. .... (504) 528-3228
Chief Commercial Officer **Robert M. Landry** .... (504) 528-3262
Director, Port Development **Catherine Dunn** .... (504) 528-3215
E-mail: dunnc@portno.com
Director, Port Operations **Paul Zimmermann** .... (504) 528-3406
E-mail: zimmermannp@portno.com

Port of Oakland

530 Water St., Oakland, CA 94607
Tel: (510) 627-1100 Internet: www.portofoakland.com

Office of the Commissioners

530 Water St., Oakland, CA 94607
E-mail: board@portofoakland.com

■President **Earl S. Hamlin** .... (510) 627-1100

(continued on next page)

AUTHORITIES

★Elected Official ▲Appointed by Legislature ▼Appointed by Governor ▶Appointed by Board or Commission ●Appointed by Judge
■Appointed by Mayor △Appointed by Freeholders ▽Appointed by Supervisor ▷Appointed by County Executive ○Appointed by Council

Office of the Commissioners *continued*

- ■ First Vice President **Alan S. Yee** .... (510) 627-1100
  Education: Princeton 1974 BA; Boalt Hall 1978 JD
- ■ Second Vice President **Michael Colbruno** .... (510) 627-1100
- ■ Commissioner **James W. Head** .... (510) 627-1100
  Education: Georgia 1974 BA, 1977 JD
- ■ Commissioner **Bryan Parker** .... (510) 627-1100
  Education: UC Berkeley BA; NYU 1995 JD
- ■ Commissioner **Joan H. Story** .... (510) 627-1100
  Education: Occidental 1965 BA; UCLA 1967 MA; UC Davis 1977 JD
- ■ Commissioner **Victor Uno** .... (510) 627-1100

Secretary of the Board **John T. Betterton** .... (510) 627-1696

Administration

Executive Director **J. Christopher Lytle** .... (510) 627-1210
E-mail: clytle@portoakland.com

Principal Assistant **Jean Banker** .... (510) 627-1325
E-mail: jbanker@portoakland.com

Chief Audit Officer **Arnel Atienza** .... (510) 627-1257
Education: Cal State (East Bay) MBA

Chief Financial Officer **Sara Lee** .... (510) 627-1668
Education: Wharton 1989 BS; Harvard 1993 MPP

Port Attorney **Danny Wan** .... (510) 627-1340
Education: Yale BA; NYU JD

Director of Aviation **Bryant L. Francis** .... (510) 627-1133

Director of Communications **Mike Zampa** .... (510) 627-1565

Director of Commercial Real Estate **Pamela Kershaw** .... (510) 627-1168
Education: UC Berkeley, MPA

Director of Human Resources **Christopher Boucher** .... (510) 627-1202
E-mail: cboucher@portoakland.com
Education: UC Berkeley BA

Director/Chief Engineer **Chris Chan** .... (510) 627-1331
E-mail: cchan@portoakland.com
Education: UC Berkeley BS, MS

Director of Environmental Programs and Planning
Richard Sinkoff .... (510) 627-1182

Community Relations Representative **Laura Arreola** .... (510) 627-1135

Chief Technology Officer **Ron Puccinelli** .... (510) 627-1391
E-mail: rpuccinelli@portoakland.com

Director of Maritime **John C. Driscoll** .... (510) 627-1243
E-mail: jdriscoll@portoakland.com

Director of Social Responsibility **Amy Tharpe** .... (510) 627-1302
Education: UC Berkeley BA; Harvard MPP

Government Affairs Director **Matthew "Matt" Davis** .... (510) 627-1635
E-mail: mdavis@portofoakland.com

Government Affairs Specialist **Joanne Karchner** .... (510) 627-1384
E-mail: jkarchner@portoakland.com

Media and Public Relations Manager **Robert Bernardo** .... (510) 627-1401

Port of Portland

P.O. Box 3529, Portland, OR 97208-3529
Tel: (503) 415-6000 Fax: (503) 944-7080
Internet: www.portofportland.com

Office of the Commissioners

121 Northwest Everett Street, Portland, OR 97209-4049
P.O. Box 3529, Portland, OR 97208-3529
Tel: (503) 415-6013

- ▼ President **James C. "Jim" Carter** .... (503) 415-6013
  Term Expires: November 30, 2017
  Education: Stanford 1971 AB; Oregon 1976 JD
- ▼ Vice Chair **Tom Chamberlain** .... (503) 415-6013
  Term Expires: May 9, 2019
- ▼ Treasurer **Linda M. Pearce** .... (503) 415-6013
  Term Expires: September 30, 2016
  Education: Portland State BS; Oregon MBA
- ▼ Secretary **Robert L. Levy** .... (503) 415-6013
  Term Expires: April 30, 2017

Office of the Commissioners *continued*

- ▼ Commissioner **Peter J. Bragdon** .... (503) 415-6013
  Note: Will continue to serve until reappointed or replaced.
  Term Expires: September 30, 2015
  Education: Amherst 1984 BA; Yale 1991 MSL; Stanford 1993 JD
- ▼ Commissioner **Alice Cuprill-Comas** .... (503) 415-6013
  Term Expires: September 30, 2019
- ▼ Commissioner **Pat McDonald** .... (503) 415-6013
  Term Expires: February 16, 2020
- ▼ Commissioner **Isao "Tom" Tsuruta** .... (503) 415-6013
  Term Expires: December 12, 2016
- ▼ Commissioner **Gary Young** .... (503) 415-6013
  Term Expires: September 30, 2019

Administration

Executive Director **Bill Wyatt** .... (503) 415-6013
E-mail: bill.wyatt@portofportland.com

Deputy Executive Director **Curtis Robinhold** .... (503) 415-6013
E-mail: curtis.robinhold@portofportland.com

Chief Operating Officer **Vincent "Vince" Granato** .... (503) 415-6059
E-mail: vince.granato@portofportland.com

Chief Financial Officer **Cindy Nichol** .... (503) 415-6051
E-mail: cindy.nichol@portofportland.com
Education: Carleton BA; U London MA; JFK School Govt MPP

Chief Commercial Officer **Keith Leavitt** .... (503) 415-6220
E-mail: keith.leavitt@portofportland.com

General Counsel **Daniel Blaufus** .... (503) 415-6031
Education: Western Oregon U BS

Project and Technical Services Branch Manager
Stan Watters .... (503) 415-6270
E-mail: stan.watters@portofportland.com

Chief Officer of Human Resources and Public Affairs
Bobbi Stedman .... (503) 415-6411
E-mail: bobbi.stedman@portofportland.com

Director, Corporate Communications
Martha Richmond .... (503) 415-6061
E-mail: ContactUs@portofportland.com

Director, Aviation **Vincent "Vince" Granato** .... (503) 415-6164

Port of Seattle

Pier 69, 2711 Alaskan Way, Seattle, WA 98121
P.O. Box 1209, Seattle, WA 98121
Tel: (206) 787-3000 (Information) Fax: (206) 787-3252
Internet: www.portseattle.org

Office of the Commissioners

Pier 69, 2711 Alaskan Way, Seattle, WA 98121
P.O. Box 1209, Seattle, WA 98111
E-mail: commission@portseattle.org

- ★ President **John Creighton** .... (206) 787-3000
  Term Expires: December 31, 2017
  E-mail: john.creighton@portseattle.org
  Education: Johns Hopkins 1980 BA, MA; Columbia JD
- ★ Vice President **Thomas "Tom" Albro** .... (206) 787-3000
  Term Expires: December 31, 2017
  E-mail: albro.thomas@portseattle.org
  Education: U Washington 1985 BS
- ★ Secretary **Stephanie Bowman** .... (206) 787-3000
  Term Expires: December 31, 2017
- ★ Assistant Secretary **Courtney O. Gregoire** .... (206) 787-3000
  Term Expires: December 31, 2019
  Education: Willamette 2001 BA; Harvard 2005 JD
- ★ Commissioner at Large **Fred Felleman** .... (206) 787-3000
  Term Expires: December 31, 2019

★ Elected Official ▲ Appointed by Legislature ▼ Appointed by Governor ▶ Appointed by Board or Commission ● Appointed by Judge
■ Appointed by Mayor △ Appointed by Freeholders ▽ Appointed by Supervisor ▷ Appointed by County Executive ○ Appointed by Council

Executive Office
Pier 69, 2711 Alaskan Way, Seattle, WA 98121

▶Chief Executive Officer **Ted J. Fick** . . . . . . (206) 787-3000
E-mail: fick.t@portseattle.org
Education: U Washington 1982 BA; U Puget Sound 1984 MBA; Stanford 1997 MS

Deputy Chief Executive Officer and Chief of Staff **Kurt Beckett** . . . . . . (206) 787-3000
E-mail: beckett.k@portseattle.org
Education: U Washington 1994

Chief Financial and Administrative Officer **Daniel Reese "Dan" Thomas** . . . . . . (206) 787-3262
E-mail: thomas.d@portseattle.org
Education: Penn State BS; U Washington 1989 MBA

Chief Information Officer **Peter Garlock** . . . . . . (206) 787-3510
E-mail: garlock.p@portseattle.org

Chief Technology Officer **Dave Wilson** . . . . . . (206) 787-3524
E-mail: wilson.d@portseattle.org

General Counsel **Craig Watson** . . . . . . (206) 787-3206
Education: UC Berkeley 1977 AB; Willamette JD

Director of Accounting and Financial Reporting **Rudy Caluza** . . . . . . (206) 787-3057
E-mail: caluza.r@portseattle.org

Director of External Affairs **(Vacant)** . . . . . . (206) 787-3000

Director of Human Resources and Development **Gary Buchanan** . . . . . . (206) 787-3293
E-mail: buchanan.g@portseattle.org

Director of Public Affairs **Julie Collins** . . . . . . (206) 787-3000

Director of Security and Emergency Preparedness **(Vacant)** . . . . . . (206) 787-3117

Director of Social Responsibility **Luis Navarro** . . . . . . (206) 787-3187

Port Fire Chief **Randy Krause** . . . . . . (206) 431-5918
E-mail: krause.r@portseattle.org

Port Police Chief **Colleen Wilson** . . . . . . (206) 431-3490

Sea-Tac Airport
Tel: (206) 433-5388 Fax: (206) 431-5912

Managing Director **Lance Lyttle** . . . . . . (206) 433-5387

Deputy Managing Director **Dave Soike** . . . . . . (206) 439-3000

Director of Airport Operations **Michael Ehl** . . . . . . (206) 248-4833

Director of Airport Security **Wendy Reiter** . . . . . . (206) 835-7554
E-mail: reiter.w@portseattle.org

Aviation Properties Manager **James Jennings** . . . . . . (206) 248-7476
E-mail: jennings.j@portseattle.org

Capital Development Division
Managing Director **Ralph Graves** . . . . . . (206) 787-3000

Real Estate Division
Managing Director **Joe McWilliams** . . . . . . (206) 787-3000

Maritime Division
Fax: (206) 728-3280

Maritime Division Managing Director **Lindsay Pulsifer** . . . (206) 787-3141
E-mail: pulsifer.l@portseattle.org

Deputy Managing Director **(Vacant)** . . . . . . (206) 787-3363

Director, Container Services **Michael Burke** . . . . . . (206) 787-3162
E-mail: burke.m@portseattle.org

Director, Harbor Services **Darlene Robertson** . . . . . . (206) 787-3229
E-mail: robertson.d@portseattle.org

Port of Stockton
2201 W. Washington St., Stockton, CA 95203
P.O. Box 2089, Stockton, CA 95201
Tel: (800) 344-3213 Fax: (209) 466-5986
Internet: www.portofstockton.com

Board of Port Commissioners
2201 West Washington Street, Stockton, CA 95203

Chairman **R. Jay Allen** . . . . . . (209) 946-0246
Term Expires: June 30, 2016

Vice Chair **Elizabeth Blanchard** . . . . . . (209) 946-0246
Note: Will continue to serve until reappointed or replaced
Term Expires: January 26, 2016

Commissioner **Sylvester Aguilar** . . . . . . (209) 946-0246
Term Expires: December 31, 2017

Commissioner **Gary Christopherson** . . . . . . (209) 946-0246
Term Expires: February 20, 2019

Commissioner **Michael Patrick Duffy** . . . . . . (209) 946-0246
Term Expires: June 30, 2017

Commissioner **Stephen Griffen** . . . . . . (209) 946-0246
Term Expires: June 30, 2017

Commissioner **Victor Mow** . . . . . . (209) 946-0246
Term Expires: February 21, 2018

Administration
Port Director **Richard "Rick" Aschieris** . . . . . . (209) 946-0246
E-mail: raschieris@stocktonport.com

Deputy Port Director, Real Estate and Port Development **Steve E. Escobar** . . . . . . (209) 946-0246

Senior Deputy Port Director, Trade and Operations **Jason Katindoy** . . . . . . (209) 946-0246
E-mail: jkatindoy@stocktonport.com

Facilities Maintenance and Construction Superintendent **Steve Cookerly** . . . . . . (209) 946-0246
E-mail: scookerly@stocktonport.com

Facilities Maintenance and Construction Superintendent **Ricardo Navarro** . . . . . . (209) 946-0246
E-mail: rnavarro@stocktonport.com

Director of Operations **(Vacant)** . . . . . . (209) 946-0246

Director of Finance **Dianna L. Baker** . . . . . . (209) 946-0246
E-mail: dbaker@stocktonport.com

Human Resources Manager **Katie Miller** . . . . . . (209) 946-0246
E-mail: kmiller@stocktonport.com

Director of Homeland Security **George Lerner** . . . . . . (209) 946-0246
E-mail: glerner@stocktonport.com

Accounts Manager **Jill McAuliffe** . . . . . . (209) 946-0246
E-mail: jmcauliffe@stocktonport.com

Director, Environmental, Government, and Public Affairs **Jeffrey D. Wingfield** . . . . . . (209) 946-0246

Information Technology Manager **James J. Cooper** . . . . (209) 946-0246
E-mail: jcooper@stocktonport.com

Properties Manager **Debbie Calli** . . . . . . (209) 946-0246
E-mail: dcalli@stocktonport.com

Legal Counsel **Steven A. Herum** . . . . . . (209) 472-7700
Education: Stanford 1975 BA; Hastings 1979 JD

Washington Representative **R.J. Lyerly** . . . . . . (202) 822-8300
1130 Connecticut Avenue, NW, Fax: (202) 822-8315
Suite 650, Washington, DC 20036
E-mail: rlyerly@stocktonport.com

Port of Tacoma

One Sitcum Plaza, Tacoma, WA 98421
P.O. Box 1837, Tacoma, WA 98401
Tel: (253) 383-5841 Internet: www.portoftacoma.com

Office of the Commissioners

The Fabulich Center, 3600 Port of Tacoma Road, Room 104, Tacoma, WA 98424
Fax: (253) 383-9440 Internet: www.portoftacoma.com/commission

★President **Constance T. "Connie" Bacon** .... (253) 383-9402
Term Expires: December 31, 2017
★Vice President **Richard P. "Dick" Marzano** .... (253) 383-9402
Term Expires: December 31, 2017
★Commissioner **Don Johnson** .... (253) 383-9402
Term Expires: December 31, 2019
★Commissioner **Don Meyer** .... (253) 383-9402
Term Expires: December 31, 2017
★Commissioner **Clare Petrich** .... (253) 383-9402
Term Expires: December 31, 2019

Administration

Chief Executive Officer **John G. Wolfe** .... (253) 383-5841
Education: Pacific Lutheran 1987 BA
Chief Operations Officer **Don Esterbrook** .... (253) 383-5841
E-mail: desterbrook@portoftacoma.com
Education: Pacific Lutheran BBA
Chief External Affairs Officer **Sean Eagan** .... (253) 428-8663
Education: U Washington 1994 BA; George Washington 1996 MA
Chief Financial Officer **Erin Galeno** .... (253) 383-5841
Chief Human Resources Officer **Jean Chin West** .... (253) 592-6711
E-mail: jwest@portoftacoma.com
General Counsel **Carolyn Lake** .... (253) 779-4000
Chief Commercial Officer **Tong Zhu** .... (253) 383-5841
Senior Director, Security and Labor Relations **Louis P. Cooper, Jr.** .... (253) 383-5841
Managing Director, Systems and Business Processes **(Vacant)** .... (253) 383-5841

PortMiami

1015 North American Way, Suite 210, Miami, FL 33132
Tel: (305) 347-5515 Fax: (305) 347-4843
E-mail: portmiami@miamidade.gov
Internet: www.miamidade.gov/portmiami/

Administration

Port Director **Juan Kuryla** .... (305) 347-4844
E-mail: juk@miamidade.gov
Senior Executive Assistant **Richard De Villiers** .... (305) 347-4823
E-mail: rdevill@miamidade.gov
Deputy Port Director **Kevin T. Lynskey** .... (305) 347-5503
E-mail: ktl@miamidade.gov
Assistant Port Director, Finance **Miriam Abreu** .... (305) 347-4819
Assistant Port Director, Business Developing and Marketing **Hydi Webb** .... (305) 347-4951
Assistant Port Director, Capital Development/ Engineering **Elizabeth Ogden** .... (305) 347-5524
E-mail: eogden@miamidade.gov
Chief of Safety and Security **Larry Rogers** .... (305) 329-4901
E-mail: rogersl@miamidade.gov
Assistant Port Director, Port Operations **Frederick Wong, Jr.** .... (305) 347-4058
E-mail: fwongjr@miamidade.gov
Senior Manager, Human Resources and Customer Service **Luis Gonzalez** .... (305) 347-4827
E-mail: llg@miamidade.gov

Administration *continued*

Manager, Public Affairs/Marketing **Andria Muniz-Amador** .... (305) 347-4962
E-mail: amuniz@miamidade.gov
Associate Director, Governmental Affairs and International Relations **Debra D. Owens** .... (305) 960-4546
E-mail: dowens@miamidade.gov
Education: Alabama State BS; JFK School Govt 2006
Cargo Development and Foreign Trade Zone 281 **Eric Olafson** .... (305) 577-6427

Regional Transportation Authority (Chicago) [RTA]

175 West Jackson Boulevard, Suite 1650, Chicago, IL 60604
Tel: (312) 913-3200 (Information) Internet: www.rtachicago.com

Board of Directors

175 West Jackson Boulevard, Suite 1650, Chicago, IL 60604
Tel: (312) 913-3219 Fax: (312) 913-3216

Chairman **Kirk W. Dillard** .... (312) 913-3219
Date of Birth: June 1, 1955
Education: Western Illinois 1977 BA; DePaul 1982 JD
Director **Anthony K. "Tony" Anderson** .... (312) 913-3219
Education: Chicago State BS
Director **James Buchanan** .... (312) 913-3219
Director **William R. "Bill" Coulson** .... (312) 913-3219
Director **Donald P. DeWitte** .... (312) 913-3219
Director **Patrick J. Durante** .... (312) 913-3219
Director **John V. Frega** .... (312) 913-3219
Director **Phil Fuentes** .... (312) 913-3219
Director **Blake Hobson** .... (312) 913-3219
Director **Michael W. Lewis** .... (312) 913-3219
Director **Dwight A. Magalis** .... (312) 913-3219
Director **Christopher Melvin** .... (312) 913-3219
Director **Sarah Pang** .... (312) 913-3219
Education: Iowa BA, BS; National Taiwan U
Director **J. D. Ross** .... (312) 913-3219
Director **Donald L. Totten** .... (312) 913-3219
Director **Douglas M. Troiani** .... (312) 913-3219

Office of the Executive Director

Fax: (312) 913-3216

Executive Director **Leanne P. Redden** .... (312) 913-3220
Education: New South Wales; Illinois 1990 MA
Chief of Staff **Jordan D. Matyas** .... (312) 913-3142
Education: George Washington 2001 BA; John Marshall 2004 JD
Senior Deputy Executive Director, Finance and Performance Management and Chief Financial Officer **Bea Reyna-Hickey** .... (312) 913-3283
Executive Director, Capital Programming, Planning, and Performance **Jill Leary** .... (312) 913-3235
Fax: (312) 913-3206
Deputy Executive Director, Governmental Affairs **Jeremy LaMarche** .... (312) 913-3231
E-mail: lamarchej@rtachicago.org
Chief Information Officer **Arnold Crater** .... (312) 913-3219

Office of the General Counsel

Fax: (312) 913-3209

General Counsel **Nadine M. Lacombe** .... (312) 913-3210
E-mail: lacomben@rtachicago.org
Education: Illinois BS; Michigan JD

★Elected Official ▲Appointed by Legislature ▼Appointed by Governor ▶Appointed by Board or Commission ●Appointed by Judge
■Appointed by Mayor △Appointed by Freeholders ▽Appointed by Supervisor ▷Appointed by County Executive ○Appointed by Council

Office of the Secretary of the Authority
Fax: (312) 913-3216

Secretary of the Authority **Audrey Maclennan** .... (312) 913-3219
E-mail: maclennana@rtachicago.org

Sacramento Municipal Utility District [SMUD]

6201 S Street, Sacramento, CA 95817
P.O. Box 15830, Sacramento, CA 95852-0830
Tel: (888) 742-7683 Internet: www.smud.org

Board of Directors
6201 S Street, Sacramento, CA 95817
P.O. Box 15830, Sacramento, CA 95852-0830
Fax: (916) 732-6552

President **Nancy Bui-Thompson** (Ward 2) .... (916) 732-6155
E-mail: nancy.bui@smud.org
Board Member **Renée Taylor** (Ward 1) .... (916) 732-6155
Board Member **Gregg Fishman** (Ward 3) .... (916) 732-6155
Board Member **Genevieve A. Shiroma** (Ward 4) .... (916) 732-6155
Education: UC Davis 1978 BS
Board Member **Rob Kerth** (Ward 5) .... (916) 732-6155
Board Member **Dave Tamayo** (Ward 6) .... (916) 732-6155
Education: UC Berkeley BA
Board Member **Bill Slaton** (Ward 7) .... (916) 732-6155
Education: Texas BBA

Administration
General Manager and Chief Executive Officer
Arlen Orchard .... (916) 732-6201
Chief Grid Strategy and Operations Officer **Paul Lau** ..... (916) 732-6252
Chief Legislative and Regulatory Officer
Michael Gianunzio .... (916) 732-6613
Chief Generation Officer **Frankie McDermott** .... (916) 732-5345
Chief Financial Officer **Jim Tracy** .... (916) 732-6492
Chief Information Officer **Cindy Kelly** .... (888) 742-7683
Chief Workforce and Technology Officer **Gary King** ..... (916) 732-6087
Attorney and General Counsel **Laura Lewis** .... (916) 732-5830
Audit Services Manager **Claire Rogers** .... (916) 732-5680

San Diego Regional Economic Development Corporation

530 B Street, Suite 700, San Diego, CA 92101
Tel: (619) 234-8484 Fax: (619) 234-1935
Internet: www.sandiegobusiness.org

Board of Directors
Chairman **VADM James M. "Jim" Zortman** .... (619) 234-8484
Education: Naval Acad 1973 BS
Vice Chairman **Rob Douglas** .... (619) 234-8484
Vice Chairman **Janice Brown** .... (619) 234-8484
Treasurer **June Komar** .... (619) 234-8484
Education: Ohio State BA

Administration
President and Chief Executive Officer **Mark Cafferty** ..... (619) 234-8484
E-mail: cafferty@sandiegobusiness.org
Education: Assumption Col BA
Executive Assistant to the Chief Executive Officer
Catherine DeYoung .... (619) 234-8484
E-mail: cd@sandiegobusiness.org

Administration *continued*
Chief Operating Officer **Lauree M. Sahba** .... (619) 234-8484
E-mail: ls@sandiegobusiness.org
Senior Vice President, Economic Development
Sean Barr .... (619) 234-8484
E-mail: sb@sandiegobusiness.org
Executive Director, Economic Development Foundation
Jennifer Henry Storm .... (619) 234-8484
E-mail: jh@sandiegobusiness.org
Director, Mega-Region Initiative **(Vacant)** .... (619) 234-8484
Manager, Accounting and Operations **Kathy Lu** .... (619) 234-8484
E-mail: kl@sandiegobusiness.org
Manager, Economic Development **(Vacant)** .... (619) 234-8484
Manager, Events and Investor Relations **(Vacant)** .... (619) 234-8484
Vice President, Marketing and Communications
Sarah Lubeck .... (619) 234-8484
E-mail: sl@sandiegobusiness.org
Investor Relations Coordinator **Raquel Elbachri** .... (619) 234-8484
Project Coordinator **(Vacant)** .... (619) 234-8484

San Diego Unified Port District

3165 Pacific Highway, San Diego, CA 92101
P.O. Box 120488, San Diego, CA 92112-0488
Tel: (619) 686-6200 (Information) Fax: (619) 686-6400
Internet: www.portofsandiego.org

Board of Commissioners
3165 Pacific Highway, San Diego, CA 92101
P.O. Box 120488, San Diego, CA 92112

Chairman **Marshall Merrifield** .... (619) 686-6206
E-mail: mmerrifield@portofsandiego.org
Vice Chairman **Robert "Dukie" Valderrama** .... (619) 686-6206
Commissioner **RADM Garry J. Bonelli** .... (619) 686-6206
Commissioner **Rafael Castellanos** .... (619) 686-6206
Commissioner **L. Daniel "Dan" Malcolm** .... (619) 686-6206
Education: San Diego State 1989 BS; Thomas Jefferson Law 1996 JD
Commissioner **Ann Moore** .... (619) 686-6206
Education: San Diego State BA; San Diego 1984 JD
Commissioner **Bob Nelson** .... (619) 686-6206

Administration
President and Chief Executive Officer **Randa Coniglio** ... (619) 686-7217
Education: UC San Diego 1982 BS
Executive Vice President of Operations **(Vacant)** .... (619) 686-7217
Executive Vice President of Administration
Karen G. Porteous .... (619) 686-6509
E-mail: kporteous@portofsandiego.org
Education: Southern Mississippi
Harbor Police Chief (Acting) **Mark Stainbrook** .... (619) 686-6585
E-mail: mstainbrook@portofsandiego.org
Chief Financial Officer and Treasurer **Bob DeAngelis** .... (619) 686-6476
Chief Policy Advisor **Job Nelson** .... (619) 686-6200
E-mail: jnelson@portofsandiego.org
Vice President, Strategy and Business Development
(Vacant) .... (619) 725-6029
Director, Marketing and Communications
Jenny Windle .... (619) 686-6546
E-mail: jwindle@portofsandiego.org
Director, Business Information and Information Systems
Deborah Finley .... (619) 686-7271
E-mail: dfinley@portofsandiego.org
Director, Engineering **Ernesto Medina** .... (619) 725-6484
E-mail: emedina@portofsandiego.org
Director, Environmental and Land Use Management
Jason Giffen .... (619) 686-6473
Director, Financial Services **Jeanette Sales** .... (619) 686-6267

(continued on next page)

★ Elected Official ▲ Appointed by Legislature ▼ Appointed by Governor ▶ Appointed by Board or Commission ● Appointed by Judge
■ Appointed by Mayor △ Appointed by Freeholders ▽ Appointed by Supervisor ▷ Appointed by County Executive ○ Appointed by Council

Administration *continued*

Director, General Services and Procurement
Garnet D. "Dave" Thompson III .... (619) 686-6437
E-mail: dthompson@portofsandiego.org
Director, Human Resources **Michelle Corbin** .... (619) 686-6431
E-mail: mcorbin@portofsandiego.org
Director, Maritime Operations **Joel Valenzuela** .... (619) 686-6387
E-mail: jvalenzuela@portofsandiego.org
Chief Trade Representative **James "Ron" Popham** ..... (619) 686-6237
General Counsel **Thomas A. Russell** .... (619) 686-6221
District Clerk **Timothy Deuel** .... (619) 686-6203
E-mail: tdeuel@portofsandiego.org
Education: San Diego City
Docket Coordinator **Laura Nicholson** .... (619) 686-6210
Vice President, Public Safety **John Bolduc** .... (619) 686-7266
Education: Bemidji State BA; National U MOL

Snohomish County Public Utility District [PUD]

2320 California Street, Everett, WA 98201
P.O. Box 1107, Everett, WA 98206-1107
Tel: (425) 783-1000 (Information) Fax: (425) 783-8305
Internet: www.snopud.com

Board of Commissioners

2320 California St., Everett, WA 98201

★President **Tanya "Toni" Olson** .... (425) 783-8611
Term Expires: December 31, 2016
E-mail: emailtanyaolson@snopud.com
★Vice President **David "Dave" Aldrich** .... (425) 783-8611
Term Expires: December 31, 2020
E-mail: emaildavidaldrich@snopud.com
Education: UC Berkeley BA
★Secretary **Kathleen "Kathy" Vaughn** .... (425) 783-8611
Term Expires: December 31, 2018
E-mail: emailkathyvaughn@snopud.com

Office of the General Manager

General Manager **Craig Collar** .... (425) 783-8473
E-mail: cwcollar@snopud.com

Office of the General Counsel

General Counsel **Anne Spangler** .... (425) 783-8688
Education: Reed BA; Hastings JD

Communication and Marketing

Corporate Communications and Marketing Director
Julee Cunningham .... (425) 783-1779
E-mail: jacunningham@snopud.com
Government Relations Director **Jessica Matlock** .... (425) 783-8301
E-mail: jdmatlock@snopud.com

Customer and Energy Services

Assistant General Manager **Jim N. West** .... (425) 783-1787
Senior Manager, Energy Services **George Pohndorf** ..... (425) 783-1703
Senior Manager, Customer Service Support
Karen Sparkman .... (425) 783-8552
Senior Manager, Customer Experience **Pam Baley** .... (425) 783-8566
Senior Project Manager **Rich Hazzard** .... (425) 783-8025

Distribution Services

Assistant General Manager **Chris Heimgartner** .... (425) 783-5605
Senior Manager, Distribution Construction Services
Rob McManis .... (425) 783-5454
E-mail: rbmcmanis@snopud.com
Senior Manager, Distribution Engineering Shared
Services **Frank Castro** .... (425) 347-4378
E-mail: fcastro@snopud.com

Distribution Services *continued*

Senior Manager, Planning Engineering Technical
Services **Mark Oens** .... (425) 783-4358
E-mail: maoens@snopud.com
Senior Manager, Regional Design and Construction
Services **Scott Faries** .... (425) 783-5151
Senior Manager, Safety **John "Corky" Carroll** .... (425) 783-5557
E-mail: jwcarroll@snopud.com
Senior Manager, Substation Metering and
Telecommunication Services **Ed Pride** .... (425) 783-4748

Finance

Assistant General Manager, Finance and Treasurer
Glenn McPherson .... (425) 783-8356
E-mail: gsmcpherson@snopud.com
Senior Manager, Controller and Auditor
Julia Anderson .... (425) 783-8027
E-mail: jaanderson@snopud.com
Senior Manager, Treasury Risk Management and Supply
Jim Herrling .... (425) 783-8303
E-mail: jlherrling@snopud.com

Information Technology Services

Chief Information Officer **Benjamin Beberness** .... (425) 783-8783
E-mail: bjbeberness@snopud.com

Power, Rates, and Transmission Management

Assistant General Manager, Power, Rates and
Transmission Management **Joe Fina** .... (425) 783-1825
Senior Manager, Power Scheduling **Kelly Wallace** ...... (425) 783-1602
Senior Manager, Power Supply **Anna Berg** .... (425) 783-1604
Senior Manager, Rates, Economics and Energy Risk
Management **Erin Boyd** .... (425) 783-8286
Senior Manager, Reliability, Compliance and Regulatory
Transmission **John Martinsen** .... (425) 783-8080
Senior Manager, Generation Engineering Operations and
Management **Brad Spangler** .... (425) 783-8151
Senior Manager, Facilities **Serkan Braun** .... (425) 783-8622
E-mail: spbraun@snopud.com

Water

Senior Manager, Water Resources Finance and
Administration **Zeda Williams** .... (425) 397-3001
E-mail: zmwilliams@snopud.com
Senior Manager, Water Resources Operations,
Maintenance and Engineering **Brant Wood** .... (425) 397-3003
E-mail: bewood@snopud.com

South Carolina State Ports Authority [SCSPA]

176 Concord Street, Charleston, SC 29401
P.O. Box 22287, Charleston, SC 29413-2287
Tel: (843) 577-8121 (Information) Fax: (843) 577-8127
Internet: www.port-of-charleston.com E-mail: scspainfo@scspa.com

Board of Directors

176 Concord Street, Charleston, SC 29401

▼Chair **Patrick W. "Pat" McKinney** .... (843) 723-8651
▼Board Member **John F. Hassell III** .... (843) 723-8651
Education: South Carolina BA
▼Board Member **Willie E. Jeffries** .... (843) 723-8651
▼Board Member **Pamela P. Lackey** .... (843) 723-8651
▼Board Member **David J. Posek** .... (843) 723-8651
▼Board Member **Michael Sisk** .... (843) 723-8651
▼Board Member **Whitemarsh S. Smith III** .... (843) 723-8651
Education: Citadel BA
▼Board Member **Bill H. Stern** .... (843) 723-8651
▼Board Member **(Vacant)** .... (843) 723-8651

★Elected Official ▲Appointed by Legislature ▼Appointed by Governor ►Appointed by Board or Commission ●Appointed by Judge
■Appointed by Mayor △Appointed by Freeholders ▽Appointed by Supervisor ▷Appointed by County Executive ○Appointed by Council

Board of Directors *continued*

▼Ex-Officio Board Member **Robert M. "Bobby" Hitt III** . . (843) 723-8651
▼Ex-Officio Board Member **Janet P. Oakley** . . . . (843) 723-8651

Administration

President and Chief Executive Officer
James I. "Jim" Newsome III . . . . (843) 577-8609
Education: Tennessee 1976, 1977 MBA
Executive Secretary **Marsha Read** . . . . (843) 577-8609
E-mail: mread@scspa.com
Senior Vice President and Chief Financial Officer
Peter N. Hughes . . . . (843) 577-8140
Education: Col Charleston 1982 BS
Senior Vice President and Chief Commercial Officer
Paul McClintock . . . . (843) 577-8151
Education: Scranton
Senior Vice President, External Affairs
M. Clint Eisenhauer . . . . (843) 577-8153
Senior Vice President, Operations
William A. "Bill" McLean . . . . (843) 577-8603
E-mail: bmclean@scspa.com
Education: Appalachian State 1979 BS
Senior Vice President, Economic Development and
Projects **Jack Ellenberg** . . . . (803) 726-4572
E-mail: jellenberg@scspa.com
Vice President, Cargo Sales **Art Pruett** . . . . (843) 577-8620
Vice President, Cruise Business and Real Estate
Peter O. Lehman . . . . (843) 577-8601
E-mail: plehman@scspa.com
Education: Stetson 1977 BS; Thunderbird International 1983 MBA; New England 1985 JD
Vice President, Marketing and Sales Support
Byron D. Miller . . . . (843) 577-8197
E-mail: bmiller@scspa.com
Education: Charleston 1993 BA, 1994 BS
Vice President, Security, Risk Management and Human
Resources **Stephen Connor** . . . . (843) 577-8134
E-mail: sconnor@scspa.com
Education: Charleston 1980 BS
Chief Information Officer **Pamela A. Everitt** . . . . (843) 577-8678
E-mail: peveritt@scspa.com
Manager, Government Relations **(Vacant)** . . . . (843) 577-8670
Fax: (843) 577-8121

Marketing and Sales Management

Harbor Master and Supervisor of Container Crane
Operations **William P. "Billy" Lempesis** . . . . (843) 577-8192
E-mail: blempesis@scspa.com
Port Police Chief **Lindy Rinaldi** . . . . (843) 577-8665

Southeastern Pennsylvania Transportation Authority [SEPTA]

1234 Market St., Philadelphia, PA 19107-3780
Tel: (215) 580-7800 (Customer Service) Internet: www.septa.org

Board

1234 Market St., Philadelphia, PA 19107-3780

Chairman **Pasquale T. Deon, Sr.** . . . . (215) 580-7800
Vice Chairman **Thomas E. Babcock** . . . . (215) 580-7800
Board Member **Beverly Coleman** . . . . (215) 580-7800
Board Member **Dwight Evans** . . . . (215) 580-7800
Education: La Salle U 1975 BS
Board Member **Robert D. Fox** . . . . (215) 580-7800
Board Member **Stewart J. Greenleaf** . . . . (215) 580-7800
Education: Pennsylvania 1961 BA; Toledo 1966 JD
Board Member **Kevin L. Johnson** . . . . (215) 580-7800

Board *continued*

Board Member **John I. Kane** . . . . (215) 580-7800
Board Member **Daniel J. Kubik** . . . . (215) 580-7800
Board Member **Kenneth E. Lawrence, Jr.** . . . . (215) 580-7800
Education: Temple; Pennsylvania
Board Member **William J. Leonard** . . . . (215) 580-7800
Board Member **Charles H. Martin** . . . . (215) 580-7800
Education: Lebanon Valley 1964 BA
○Board Member **William M. McSwain** . . . . (215) 580-7800
Board Member **Clarena I. W. Tolson** . . . . (215) 580-7800
Board Member **Michael A. "Mike" Vereb** . . . . (215) 580-7800
Controller to the Board **Stephen A. Jobs** . . . . (215) 580-7800
Secretary to the Board **Carol R. Looby** . . . . (215) 580-7800
E-mail: clooby@septa.org

Office of the General Manager

Fax: (215) 580-3636

General Manager **Jeffrey D. Knueppel** . . . . (215) 580-7070
Deputy General Manager/Treasurer
Richard G. Burnfield . . . . (215) 580-7411
Assistant General Manager, Government and Public
Affairs **Francis E. Kelly** . . . . (215) 580-7442
E-mail: fkelly@septa.org
Assistant General Manager, Operations
Ronald G. Hopkins . . . . (215) 580-8100
E-mail: rhopkins@septa.org
Assistant General Manager, Engineering, Maintenance,
and Construction **Robert L. Lund** . . . . (215) 580-8215
E-mail: rlund@septa.org
Director, Public Affairs **(Vacant)** . . . . (215) 580-7842
Senior Director, Information Services
William J. Zebrowski . . . . (215) 580-7781
E-mail: wzebrowski@septa.org
Director, Legislative Affairs **Pamela Sarne McCormick** . . (215) 580-8047
Assistant General Manager of System Safety
Scott Sauer . . . . (215) 580-7800

Office of the General Counsel

Fax: (215) 580-7078

General Counsel **Gino J. Benedetti** . . . . (215) 580-7445
Education: Temple 1984 BBA; Widener 1990 JD

Tampa Port Authority [TPA]

1101 Channelside Drive, Tampa, FL 33602
P.O. Box 2192, Tampa, FL 33601
Tel: (813) 905-7678 Fax: (813) 905-5109 E-mail: info@tampaport.com
Internet: porttb.com

Board of Commissioners

1101 Channelside Drive, Tampa, FL 33602

▼Chairman **Stephen W. Swindal** . . . . (813) 905-5130
Note: Will continue to serve until reappointed or replaced
Term Expires: February 6, 2016
▼Vice Chairman **Carl Lindell, Jr.** . . . . (813) 905-5130
Term Expires: November 14, 2018
▼Secretary/Treasurer **Patrick H. Allman** . . . . (813) 905-7678
Term Expires: February 6, 2018
Education: Virginia 1983 BS; Tampa 1990 MBA
Commissioner **Bob Buckhorn** . . . . (813) 905-5130
Education: Penn State 1980 BA
▼Commissioner **Gregory Celestan** . . . . (813) 905-5130
Term Expires: November 25, 2017
▼Commissioner **John B. Grandoff III** . . . . (813) 905-5130
Note: Will continue to serve until reappointed or replaced
Term Expires: November 15, 2015
Education: Florida 1980 BA; Stetson 1985 JD

(continued on next page)

★Elected Official ▲Appointed by Legislature ▼Appointed by Governor ▶Appointed by Board or Commission ●Appointed by Judge
■Appointed by Mayor △Appointed by Freeholders ▽Appointed by Supervisor ▷Appointed by County Executive ○Appointed by Council

Board of Commissioners *continued*

Commissioner **Sandra L. Murman** .... (813) 905-5130
Term Expires: November 15, 2016
Date of Birth: August 9, 1950
Education: Indiana 1972 BS

Office of the Chief Executive Officer

President and Chief Executive Officer
A. Paul Anderson .... (813) 905-7678
Education: Florida 1982 BS

Vice President of Operations **Bob Callahan** .... (813) 905-7678
E-mail: bcallahan@tampaport.com

Vice President of Security **Mark Dubina** .... (813) 905-7678
E-mail: mdubina@tampaport.com

Vice President of Engineering **Bruce Laurion** .... (813) 905-7678
E-mail: blaurion@tampaport.com

Facilities Management Director **Norberto Sanchez** ...... (813) 905-7678
E-mail: nsanchez@tampaport.com

Principal Counsel **Charles Klug** .... (813) 905-7678

Vice President of Government Affairs and Board Coordination **John T. Thorington, Jr.** .... (813) 905-7678
E-mail: jtt@tampaport.com Fax: (813) 905-5109

Senior Advisor to the President and Chief Executive Officer **Edward Miyagishima** .... (813) 905-7678

Public Relations Director **Andrew Fobes** .... (813) 905-7678
E-mail: afobes@tampaport.com Fax: (813) 905-5109

Office of the Chief Financial Officer

Chief Financial Officer **Mike Macaluso** .... (813) 905-7678

Chief Information Officer **Ken Washington** .... (813) 905-7678
E-mail: kwashington@tampaport.com

Vice President of Legal Affairs and Deputy Port Counsel **Donna Wysong** .... (813) 905-7678
Fax: (813) 905-5109

Vice President of Human Resources **Joeanne Toledo** .... (813) 905-7678
E-mail: Jtoledo@tampaport.com

Procurement Director **Nancy Marino** .... (813) 905-7678
E-mail: nmarino@tampaport.com

Office of the Executive Vice President and Chief Commercial Officer

Chief Commercial Officer **Raul Alfonso** .... (813) 905-7678

Vice President of Real Estate **Lane Ramsfield** .... (813) 905-7678

Vice President of Planning and Development
Ram Kancharla .... (813) 905-7678
E-mail: rkancharla@tampaport.com

Vice President of Brand Development and Regional Alliances **Karl Strauch** .... (813) 905-7678

Vice President of Marketing and Business Development
Wade Elliot .... (813) 905-7678

Director of Marketing and Business Development, Cargo and Cruise **Greg Lovelace** .... (813) 905-7678

Director of Marketing and Business Development, Latin America **Gonzalo Padron** .... (813) 905-7678

Environmental Affairs Director **Christopher Cooley** ..... (813) 905-7678

Toledo-Lucas County Port Authority [TLCPA]

One Maritime Plaza, 7th Floor, Toledo, OH 43604-1866
Internet: www.toledoportauthority.org

Board of Directors

One Maritime Plaza, 7th Floor, Toledo, OH 43604-1866
Fax: (419) 243-1835

Chairman **James M. Tuschman** .... (419) 243-8251
Education: Miami U (OH) 1963 BB; Ohio State 1966 JD

Member **William J. Carroll** .... (419) 243-8251

Board of Directors *continued*

Member **Jerry Chabler** .... (419) 243-8251
Education: Michigan State; Toledo

Member **Bernard H. "Pete" Culp** .... (419) 243-8251

Member **Dr. Lloyd A. Jacobs** .... (419) 243-8251
Education: Miami U (OH) 1965; Johns Hopkins 1969 MD

Member **Andrea R. Price** .... (419) 243-8251
Education: Michigan BS; Tulane MHA

Member **G. Opie Rollison** .... (419) 243-8251

Member **Nadeem S. Salem** .... (419) 243-8251

Member **Sharon S. Speyer** .... (419) 243-8251
Education: Ohio State 1981; Toledo 1985

Member **A. Bailey Stanbery** .... (419) 243-8251

Member **John S. Szuch** .... (419) 243-8251
Education: Toledo 1970, 1975 MBA

Member **George Tucker** .... (419) 243-8251

Member **Baldemar Velasquez** .... (419) 243-8251
Education: Toledo 1998

Administration

President and Chief Executive Officer **Paul L. Toth, Jr.** ... (419) 243-8251
Education: Toledo BS

Vice President, Administration and Chief Financial Officer **Thomas J. Winston** .... (419) 243-8251
E-mail: twinston@toledoportauthority.org
Education: Ohio Wesleyan 1992 BA; Loyola U (Chicago) 1998 MBA

Director of Facilities and Development Services
Brian Perz .... (419) 243-8251
E-mail: bperz@toledoportauthority.org

Vice President of Business Development
Joseph W. "Joe" Cappel .... (419) 243-1835
E-mail: jcappel@toledoportauthority.org
Education: Ohio State BS

Communications Manager **Holly Kemler** .... (419) 243-8251
E-mail: hkemler@toledoportauthority.org

Washington Metropolitan Area Transit Authority [WMATA]

600 Fifth Street, N.W., Washington, DC 20001
Tel: (202) 962-1234 (Information) Internet: www.wmata.com

Board of Directors

600 Fifth Street, NW, Washington, DC 20001
Fax: (202) 962-1133

Chair **Jack Evans** (District of Columbia) .... (202) 962-2511
Education: Wharton 1975 BA; Pittsburgh 1978 JD

▼First Vice Chair **Keturah Denise Harley** (Maryland) ..... (202) 962-2511
Education: Trinity Col (DC) BA; Howard U JD

Second Vice Chair **Jim Corcoran** (Virginia) .... (202) 962-2511
Education: St Joseph's U; Rider MBA

Principal **Carol Jones Carmody** (District of Columbia) .. (202) 962-2511
Note: Effective June 1, 2016
Education: Oklahoma BA; American U 1982 MPA

Principal **Mortimer Leo "Mort" Downey III** (District of Columbia) .... (202) 962-2511
Note: Until May 31, 2016
Education: Yale 1958; NYU 1966 MPA

Principal **Michael Goldman** (Maryland) .... (202) 962-2511

Principal **Catherine M. Hudgins** (Virginia) .... (202) 962-2511
Education: Arkansas (Pine Bluff) BS; George Mason 1994 MPA

Principal **Corbett A. Price** (District of Columbia) .... (202) 962-2511
Education: Ohio State 1975 MHA

Principal **David L. Strickland** (District of Columbia) ..... (202) 962-2511
Note: Effective June 1, 2016
Education: Northwestern 1990 BS; Harvard 1993 JD

Principal **Harriet Tregoning** (District of Columbia) ...... (202) 962-2511
Note: Until May 31, 2016
Education: Washington U (MO)

★ Elected Official ▲ Appointed by Legislature ▼ Appointed by Governor ▶ Appointed by Board or Commission ● Appointed by Judge
■ Appointed by Mayor △ Appointed by Freeholders ▽ Appointed by Supervisor ▷ Appointed by County Executive ○ Appointed by Council

Board of Directors *continued*

Alternate **Malcolm Augustine** (Virginia) .... (202) 962-2511
Alternate
Thomas J. "Tom" Bulger (District of Columbia)...... (202) 962-2511
Education: West Virginia 1973 MPA
Alternate **Anthony E. "Tony" Costa** .... (202) 962-2511
Education: Bucknell 1982 BA; North Carolina 1984 MRP
Alternate **Leif A. Dormsjo** (District of Columbia) .... (202) 962-2511
Alternate **Christian Dorsey** (Virginia) .... (202) 962-2511
Alternate **Anthony R. Giancola** (District of Columbia) ... (202) 962-2511
Note: Until May 31, 2016
Education: Syracuse BS; Pittsburgh MS, MPW
Alternate **Robert C. Lauby** (District of Columbia) .... (202) 962-2511
Note: Effective June 1, 2016
Alternate **Kathy Porter** (Maryland) .... (202) 962-2511
Alternate **Paul C. Smedberg** (Maryland) .... (202) 962-2511
Education: Allegheny 1983 BA, 1983 BS

Administration

▶ General Manager and Chief Executive Officer
Paul J. Wiedefeld .... (202) 962-1000
Education: Towson U BS; Rutgers MA
Executive Managing Officer **Jack Requa** .... (202) 962-1234
Chief of Staff **Barbara Richardson** .... (202) 962-1740
E-mail: brichardson@wmata.com
Chief of Police, Metro Transit Police Department
Ronald Pavlik .... (202) 962-2162
E-mail: rapavlik@wmata.com
Deputy General Manager, Operations (Acting)
MAJ Andrew Off .... (202) 962-2585
E-mail: aoff@wmata.com
Education: West Point BSCE; Missouri (Rolla) MSEM; Georgia Tech MSCE
Assistant General Manager, Access Services
Christian T. Kent .... (202) 962-2100
Assistant General Manager, Transit Infrastructure and Engineering **MAJ Andrew Off** .... (202) 962-1000
E-mail: aoff@wmata.com
Education: West Point BSCE; Missouri (Rolla) MSEM; Georgia Tech MSCE
Assistant General Manager, Bus Services **(Vacant)** .... (202) 962-2800
Chief Financial Officer **Dennis Anosike** .... (202) 962-1200
E-mail: danosike@wmata.com
Assistant General Manager, Information Technology
Kevin Borek .... (202) 962-2171
E-mail: kborek@wmata.com
Chief Human Resources Officer **Tawnya Moore-McGee** .. (202) 962-1071
E-mail: tmoore-mcgee@wmata.com
Chief Performance Officer **Andrea Burnside** .... (202) 962-2600
E-mail: ahburnside@wmata.com
Chief Safety Officer **Patrick Lavin** .... (202) 962-2150
Education: NYU MA
Special Safety Advisor **Kathryn B. "Katie" Thomson** ... (202) 962-2150
Education: Illinois 1987 BA; Pennsylvania 1990 JD
Real Estate Director (Acting) **Andrew J. Scott** .... (202) 962-2730
General Counsel (Acting) **Mark Pohl** .... (202) 962-2531
Director of Media Relations/Chief Spokesman
Dan Stessel .... (202) 962-1051
E-mail: dstessel@wmata.com
Managing Director of Government Relations
Regina A. Sullivan .... (202) 962-1632
E-mail: rsullivan@wmata.com
Education: Regis U 1978 BS
Inspector General **Helen Lew** .... (202) 962-2515
Education: American U BS
Manager of Media Relations **Sherri Ly** .... (202) 962-1051
Education: Miami
Strategic Executive Adviser (Part-Time) **Kevyn D. Orr** .... (202) 962-1234
Education: Michigan 1979 BA, 1983 JD
Comptroller **La Toya Thomas** .... (202) 962-1602

Washington Suburban Sanitary Commission [WSSC]

14501 Sweitzer Lane, Laurel, MD 20707-5902
Tel: (301) 206-8000 (Information)
Tel: (301) 206-4002 (Emergency Maintenance)
Tel: (800) 828-6439 (Emergency Maintenance)
Tel: (301) 206-4001 (Water Bill Inquiries)
TTY: (301) 206-8232 (Emergency Maintenance) TTY: (301) 206-8345
Internet: www.wsscwater.com

Office of the Commissioners

Chair **(Vacant)** .... (301) 206-8200
Vice Chair **Christopher "Chris" Lawson** .... (301) 206-8200
Education: St Augustine's Col BS
Commissioner **Fausto Bayonet** .... (301) 206-8200
Commissioner **Omar M. Boulware** .... (301) 206-8200
Commissioner **Dr. Alison Bryant** .... (301) 206-8200
Commissioner **Mary Hopkins-Navies** .... (301) 206-8200

Office of the General Manager

Fax: (301) 206-8779 E-mail: communications@wsscwater.com
General Manager **Carla A. Reid** .... (301) 206-8777
Education: Howard U BSCE; Maryland MGA
Chief of Staff **(Vacant)** .... (301) 206-8777
Chief Operations Officer **(Vacant)** .... (301) 206-8000
Chief Financial Officer **Yvette Downs** .... (301) 206-7200
Public Communications Director **Jim Neustadt** .... (301) 206-8100
E-mail: jneusta@wsscwater.com Fax: (301) 206-8186
Corporate Secretary **Sheila Finlayson** .... (301) 206-8200
E-mail: sfinlayson@wsscwater.com

Office of the General Counsel

General Counsel **Jerome K. Blask** .... (301) 206-8400

Utility Services Group

Chief (Acting) **Calvin Farr** .... (301) 206-8600
Customer Care Central Group Leader (Acting)
Rodney Butler .... (301) 206-8600
Customer Care North Group Leader **Nadir Al-Salam** .... (301) 206-8600
Customer Care South Group Leader **Clive Mattis** .... (301) 206-8600
Customer Care West Group Leader **Joe Fulton** .... (301) 206-8600

Information Technology

Chief Information Officer **Mujib Lodhi** .... (301) 206-7950
E-mail: mujib.lodhi@wsscwater.com
Education: Indianapolis
Chief Information Technology Implementation Officer
Minchy Shaw .... (301) 206-7950
E-mail: mshaw@wsscwater.com
Senior Manager, Innovation and Advanced Analytics
Lingyi Zhang .... (301) 206-7950
E-mail: lzhang@wsscwater.com
Information Technology Customer Support Manager (Acting) **Bill Gibson** .... (301) 206-7950
E-mail: bgibson@wsscwater.com
Information Technology Risk and Information Management (Acting) **Julian Caesar** .... (301) 206-7950
E-mail: jcaesar@wsscwater.com
Senior Manager, Network Infrastructure and Data Center Operations **Nick Del Grosso** .... (301) 206-7950
E-mail: ndelgro@wsscwater.com
Quality Assurance (Acting) **Minchy Shaw** .... (301) 206-7950
Systems Support and Operations **(Vacant)** .... (301) 206-7950
Enterprise Architect **(Vacant)** .... (301) 206-7950
Information Technology Contract Administrator
Rosa Wilson .... (301) 206-7950
E-mail: rwilson@wsscwater.com

Wayne County Airports Authority

Detroit Metropolitan Wayne County Airport Authority,
L.C. Smith Buliding, Detroit, MI 48242
Tel: (734) 942-3550 Tel: (734) 485-6666 (Willow Run Airport)
Fax: (734) 942-3765 Fax: (734) 485-6658 (Willow Run Airport)
Internet: www.metroairport.com

Board of Directors

Chairperson **Suzanne K. Hall** .... (734) 942-3550
Term Expires: October 1, 2016

Member **Nabih Ayad** .... (734) 942-3550
Term Expires: October 1, 2020

Member **Irma Clark-Coleman** .... (734) 942-3550
Term Expires: October 1, 2018
Education: Wayne State U 1977 BA, 1981 MA

Member **Michael Garavaglia** .... (734) 942-3550
Term Expires: October 1, 2020

Member **Dr. Curtis L. Ivery** .... (734) 942-3550
Term Expires: October 1, 2019

Member **Michael "Mike" Jackson** .... (734) 942-3550
Term Expires: October 1, 2017

▼Secretary **Ron Hall, Jr.** .... (734) 942-3550
Term Expires: October 1, 2020

Administration

Chief Executive Officer (Interim) **Thomas Naughton** .... (734) 247-7112
E-mail: thomas.naughton@wcaa.us
Education: Michigan State 1979 BA

Executive Vice President and Chief Financial Officer
Terry Teifer .... (734) 247-7907

Senior Vice President of Business Development and Management **Tom McCarthy** .... (734) 247-4923

Senior Vice President of Facilities, Planning, Maintenance/North Terminal Project **Jon Hypnar** ...... (734) 247-7061

Senior Vice President and General Counsel
Emily Neuberger .... (734) 942-3825

Vice President of Human Resources **Gale L. LaRoche** .... (734) 942-3728
E-mail: gale.laroche@wcaa.us

Vice President of Internal Auditing **Istakur Rahman** .... (734) 247-7365

Vice President of Technology Services **Arun Gulati** ..... (734) 247-7379
E-mail: arun.gulati@wcaa.us

Vice President, Public Safety **Mark DeBeau** .... (734) 942-4844
E-mail: mark.debeau@wcaa.us

Director, Airfield Operations **Dianne Walker** .... (734) 942-3571

Director, Aviation **Joseph M. "Joe" Cambron** .... (734) 955-5735

Director, Employee Services **Heather Day** .... (734) 247-7902
E-mail: heather.day@wcaa.us

Director, Human Resources **Rosalind Wallace** .... (734) 247-7111
E-mail: rosalind.wallace@wcaa.us

Director, Labor Relations **Lynda Racey** .... (734) 247-2222
E-mail: lynda.racey@wcaa.us

Director, Landside Services
Matthew "Matt" McGowan .... (734) 955-8776

Director, Maintenance Administration **Angela Frakes** .... (734) 942-6750
E-mail: angela.frakes@wcaa.us

Director, Procurement **Ron Evans** .... (734) 955-3885
E-mail: ron.evans@wcaa.us

Director, Public Affairs **Michael Conway** .... (734) 942-3558
E-mail: michael.conway@wcaa.us

Director, Strategy Management **Peter Gargiulo** .... (734) 955-5705

Director, Willow Run Airport **Chris Mullin** .... (734) 955-6669

Director/Police Chief **Jennifer Williams** .... (734) 942-5376

Director/Fire Chief **Mike Evans** .... (734) 942-3736
E-mail: mike.evans@wcaa.us

Director/Security Chief **Janet Baxter** .... (734) 942-3747
E-mail: janet.baxter@wcaa.us

Controller **Margaret M. Basrai** .... (734) 247-6775
E-mail: marge.basrai@wcaa.us

★ Elected Official ▲ Appointed by Legislature ▼ Appointed by Governor ▶ Appointed by Board or Commission ● Appointed by Judge
■ Appointed by Mayor △ Appointed by Freeholders ▽ Appointed by Supervisor ▷ Appointed by County Executive ○ Appointed by Council

Indexes

Geographical Index

This index lists all municipalities in the directory alphabetically by state.

Name Index

This index lists all individuals in the directory alphabetically by last name.

NAME INDEX

B

NAME INDEX

NAME INDEX

D

NAME INDEX

NAME INDEX

E

NAME INDEX

F

NAME INDEX

NAME INDEX

G

NAME INDEX

NAME INDEX

H

NAME INDEX

K

L

NAME INDEX

M

NAME INDEX

P

Q

R

S

NAME INDEX

NAME INDEX

T

NAME INDEX

NAME INDEX

NAME INDEX

NAME INDEX

Organization Index

This index lists all municipalities in the directory alphabetically.

ORGANIZATION INDEX